PSYCHIATRY TODAY
ACCOMPLISHMENTS AND PROMISES

VIII WORLD CONGRESS OF PSYCHIATRY
ABSTRACTS

EDITORS

C.N. STEFANIS
C.R. SOLDATOS
A.D. RABAVILAS

EXCERPTA MEDICA
INTERNATIONAL CONGRESS SERIES 899
Amsterdam - Oxford - New York

© 1989 Elsevier Science Publishers B.V. (Biomedical Division)

All rights reserved. No part of this publication may be reproduced, stored in a retrieval system or transmitted in any form or by any means, electronic, mechanical, photocopying, recording or otherwise without the prior written permission of the publisher. Elsevier Science Publishers B.V., Biomedical Division, P.O. Box 1527, 100 BM Amsterdam, The Netherlands.

No responsibility is assumed by the Publisher for any injury and/or damage to persons or property as a matter of products liability, negligence or otherwise, or from any use or operation of any methods, products, instructions or ideas contained in the material herein. Because of rapid advances in the medical sciences, the Publisher recommends that independent verification of diagnoses and drug dosages should be made.

Special regulations for readers in the USA – This publication has been registered with the Copyright Clearance Center Inc. (CCC), 27 Congress Street, Salem, MA 01970, USA. Information can be obtained from the CCC about conditions under which photocopies of parts of this publication may be made in the USA. All other copyright questions, including photocopying outside the USA, should be referred to the copyright owner, Elsevier Science Publishers B.V., unless otherwise specified.

International Congress Series No. 899
ISBN 0 444 81188 5

This book is printed on acid-free paper.

Published by:
Elsevier Science Publishers B.V.
(Biomedical Division)
P.O. Box 211
1000 AE Amsterdam
The Netherlands

Sole distributors for the USA and Canada:
Elsevier Science Publishing Company Inc.
655 Avenue of the Americas
New York, NY 10010
USA

Printed in Athens, Greece, by G. Tsiveriotis Ltd.

PREFACE

This book of abstracts is a complete record of the presentations made during the VIII World Congress of Psychiatry, which took place in Athens, Greece, from the 13th through the 19th October 1989. Abstracts corresponding to all forms of presentations have been included in this volume: plenaries, symposia, workshops, special sessions, new research sessions, free communications, posters, films and videos. The contents of the abstracts are the responsibility of their authors. Nonetheless, in many cases retyping was necessary for technical and aesthetic purposes. Further, a few abstracts have been edited, whenever the need arose.

This publication has been made possible through the invaluable contribution of Prof. G. Lyketsos and members of the Scientific and Program Committees. Special mention should be made, however, to the following colleagues who spared no effort in assisting for the publication of this volume: E. Angelopoulos, J.D. Bergiannaki, M. Economou, A. Haidemenos, C. Haralambaki, C. Ioannidis, V. Karydis, A. Kokkevi, V. Kontaxakis, E. Lykouras, A. Maillis, M. Malliori, V. Mavreas, G. Papadimitriou, P. Sakkas, V. Tomaras, G. Vaslamatzis. Secretarial and administrative assistance was skillfully provided by A. Kapsalis, H. Kavadias and M. Marietti.

The Editors

HOW TO USE THIS BOOK

The abstracts bear the same serial number as in the programme of the VIII World Congress of Psychiatry and are listed in the order of their appearance therein.

In keeping with the arrangement of the abstracts by day and session, the table of contents includes the titles of the 494 sessions represented in the Scientific Programme. The page number at the end of the session title marks the beginning of each session.

An alphabetic author's index complements this volume. After each author's or co-author's name the reader will find two numbers. The first number corresponds to the abstract's serial number, while the second, in parenthesis, to the session number where the abstract is presented. When an author has contributed to more than one papers, as author or co-author, the above mentioned sequence of numbers is repeated according to the number of papers.

The subject index concludes the Book of Abstracts. It includes the major topics derived from the session titles. The numbers following each topic apply to the serial numbers of the corresponding sessions.

CONTENTS

Friday, 13th October 1989

	Page
1. Progress in biological research of mood disorders	13
2. International Classification of Mental Disorders	14
3. Results of studies developing instruments for cross-culturally comparative research in psychiatry	15
4. Drug abuse	16
5. Révolution démocratique et naissance de la psychiatrie	18
6. Psychiatry in the Americas today	20
7. Obsessive compulsive disorder: An update	21
8. General aspects of the history of psychiatry	22
9. Psychosocial responses to disasters	24
10. The relevance of psychoanalysis for psychiatry today	25
11. Education in psychiatric rehabilitation	26
12. Psychoimmunology	28
13. Psychosocial factors on development of children and adolescents	31
14. The family of the schizophrenic patient	33
15. Long-term treatment of panic and agoraphobia	35
16. Suicide and schizophrenia	36
17. Schizoaffective disorders: Present status of research	38
18. Sleep disorders medicine: Role of the general psychiatrist	39
19. Experimental pharmacology I	41
20. Epidemiology	43
21. Genetic studies in mental diseases	45
22. Suicidal behavior in psychiatric patients	47
23. Anxiety-phobic disorders	50
24. Schizophrenia: Treatment modalities	52
25. Antidepressants in clinical use I	54
26. Conversion and somatoform disorders	55
27. Psychiatric care policies	58
28. Child and adolescent developmental issues and psychopathology	60
29. Neurochemical variables in depression and mania	62
30. Neuroimaging in psychiatry: An update for clinicians	64
31. Psychoendocrinology	66
32. Issues and challenges with dually diagnosed patients	67
33. Cell communication, brain integrative function and aging	68
34. Cultural psychiatry issues in Africa and South America: Community practice	70
35. New perspectives on the role of serotononergic subsystems in anxious and affective disorders	71
36. Zur Frage der Stigmatisierung durch der Klinikaufenthalt in der Kinder und Jugend Psychiatrie	73
37. Endogenous depression: A valid diagnostic category?	73
38. Topics in general hospital psychiatry	75
39. Psychosomatics in theory and practice	76
40. Schizophrenia: Brain structures and functioning	78
41. Standardized psychiatric interviews	80
42. Eating disorders	82
43. New technologies in psychiatry	84
44. Various aprroaches to brief dynamic psychotherapy	85
45. Cost effective psychiatric screening in large populations	86
46. Photographic imagery in private practice	87
47. Panic disorders: General issues	88
48. Ill-defined psychosocial problems in general health care	89
49. Mental retardation	90
50. Brief psychotherapies	92
51. Involuntary commitment	94
52. History of Psychiatry: Theory and practice over the centuries	95
53. Schizophrenia: Psychophysiologic studies	97
54. Antidepressants in long-term use	99
55. Preventive approaches in child mental health	101
56. Alcohol abuse: Epidemiology	102
57. Affective disorders I	104
58. Suicidology	105
59. Behavioral and other psychotherapies	107
60. Anxiety and adjustment disorders	109
61. Child Psychiatry I	110
62. Pharmacopsychiatry: Antidepressants	112
63. Panic disorders	114
64. Biological psychiatry: Blood cell and HLA studies	117
65. Psychiatric services	119
66. Drug abuse	122
67. Electroconvulsive therapy	124
68. Organic mental disorders	125
69. Exercise, art and folk therapies	128
70. Pharmacopsychiatry: Antipsychotic drugs	129
71. Delusional states and other psychotic disorders	133
72. The dynamics of therapy	135
73. Issues in psychotherapy	136
74. Ancient Greek thought and its contribution to psychiatry	137
75. Today and future of prison psychiatry	139
76. Basic symptoms: Newer results of psychiatric research	140
77. Psychodynamic treatments of children and adolescents	141
78. Experimental pharmacology II	142
79. Side-effects of antipsychotic drugs	144
80. Psychiatry in the resolution of social problems	146
81. Drug abuse trends in Europe and the USA	147

82. Benzodiazepines: Efficacy / side effects and pharmacokinetics / dynamics 148
83. Personality fitness training with patients suffering from bulimia. An intensive psychotherapeutic program 149
84. Panic disorders: Therapeutic approaches . 150
85. Obsessive - compulsive disorders 151
86. Organic mental disorders: Genetic and infectious influences 153
87. Electroencephalography in psychiatry ... 154
88. Migration and mental health I 156
89. Schizophrenia: Course and outcome ... 157
90. Animal studies antidepressants 158
91. Forensic psychiatry in closed institutions 160
92. Pharmacotherapy in child and adolescent psychiatry 162
93. Psychopathological and psychotherapeutic themes I 163
94. Anorexia. Art therapy 165

Saturday, 14th October 1989

95. Schizophrenia: Clinical, epidemiological and psychopharmacological issues 169
96. Psychiatric and mental health services .. 170
97. Ethical and legal aspects of compulsory hospitalization and involuntary treatments 171
98. Chronobiology 172
99. New psychoanalytic approaches to clinical psychiatry 174
100. Insights in the use of trazodone in depressed patients 176
101. Psiquiatria y medios audiovisuales 178
102. Psychiatric aspects of heart transplantation 179
103. Diurnal variations in psychopathology . 180
104. Creativity anxiety and delirium 181
105. Nosology revisited 182
106. Eating disorders: Epidemiological and clinical issues 184
107. Psychiatric inpatient services 186
108. MRI and CT in psychiatry 188
109. Factors influencing the course of affective disorders 190
110. The Composite International Diagnostic Interview: An instrument for cross-culturally comparative epidemiological studies ... 192
111. Current issues on ECT 193
112. Cognitive impairment due to HIV-infection 195
113. Affective disorders: Course and prognosis 196
114. Attitudinal and crosscultural issues ... 198
115. Alzheimer's disease and other psychogeriatric issues 200
116. Alcohol and drug abuse: Clinical issues 203
117. Affective disorders: Psychopathology and psychometrics 205
118. Social psychiatry and psychopathology . 207
119. Psychosomatics and the cardiovascular system 210
120. Lithium treatment 212
121. Psychiatric care in day hospitals and other services 215
122. Family: Effect on psychopathology and family therapy 217
123. Aggressive and self-destructive behaviour in schizophrenia 219
124. Interaction between the immune system and psychic states 221
125. Brain imaging 222
126. Mental illness in the retarded 224
127. Panic attack versus panic disorder: Diagnostic and therapeutic issues 225
128. Tardive dyskinesia and other adverse effects of drugs 226
129. Benzamides and dopamine: Advances in clinical applications 228
130. Psychodynamic understanding in the individual assessment of disturbances in children and adolescents 230
131. Culture-bound syndromes and international disease classifications 230
132. EEG mapping in psychiatry 231
133. Phototherapy and sleep deprivation in depression 233
134. Schizophrenia: Disturbances of thought and affect 235
135. Alzheimer's disease 236
136. Cognitive psychotherapy with difficult patients 238
137. Perspectives in monitoring serum levels of perphenazine. A way to improve quality of life 240
138. Lern und Schulstörungen bei Kindern und Jugendlichen 241
139. On the group and family process 242
140. Issues of global accord 244
141. Sexual dysfunction - Impotence 244
142. Monamines and peptides in mental disorders 246
143. Neurochemical variables in schizophrenia 247
144. Psychotherapy in children with learning difficulties 249
145. Parasuicide and attempted suicide 251
146. Panic disorder: Theoretical and psychopathological issues 253
147. Delusional states 254
148. Epidemiological and clinical studies in child and adolescent psychiatry 256
149. Cross-cultural and trans-cultural studies 257
150. Mental health in youth 259
151. Psychiatric aspects of AIDS 261
152. Consultation-liaison psychiatry 262
153. Psychometrics and psychiatric diagnosis 263
154. Pharmacotherapy of anxiety 265
155. Pharmacotherapy of depression I 267
156. Psychiatric epidemiology 271
157. Psychiatry and old age 274
158. Alcohol abuse I 276
159. Personality disorders 278
160. Psychological reaction to somatic disorders 280
161. Pharmacotherapy of anxiety 281
162. Biological psychiatry: Monoamines and neuropeptides 282
163. Beyond classical antidepressant drug treatment 284
164. Schizophrenia I 286
165. Hyperhypnosis. Psychosis 288
166. Immunological findings in endogenous psychosis 289
167. Therapeutic approaches in schizophrenia 290
168. Psychopathologie de l' expression 292
169. Panic disorders 293
170. Future of scientific publishing 293
171. The development of a programme in psychotherapy in a general children's

	hospital. Introduction to psychodynamic understanding of disturbed children and adolescents	294
172.	Psychopharmacology: Blood cell binding and membrane transport	295
173.	Suicidology: Epidemiological studies	297
174.	Public health psychiatry: An international perspective	298
175.	Child and adolescent psychiatry and mental retardation	300
176.	New strategies in the treatment of aggressive acutely psychotic patients	301
177.	Detecting the patterns of basic emotional structuring	303
178.	The somatotherapies	303
179.	Anxiety states and phobias	303
180.	Alcoholism	305
181.	Psychoneuroendocrinology I	306
182.	Psychopathology and psychosomatics in gynaecology	308
183.	Theory and practice of family and marital therapy	309
184.	Stress and adjustment disorders	311
185.	Psychotherapy in theory and practice	313
186.	Mood stabilizers and antimanic drugs other than lithium	315
187.	Child abuse	316
188.	Non-pharmacological treatment for affective disorders	318
189.	Art therapy. Insomnia	320

Sunday, 15th October 1989

190.	Current biological research in schizophrenia	323
191.	Major international and national diagnostic classification issues	324
192.	Genetic aspects of affective disorders and schizophrenia	325
193.	Phychiatric aspects of HIV infection	326
194.	Computer-analyzed EEG and brain mapping in psychiatry	328
195.	Stress and its effect on the mental and physical well being	329
196.	Brain mechanisms of information processing and psychopathology. The scope	330
197.	Delusional misidentification syndromes	331
198.	Crisis intervention: Clinical management strategies and long-term outcome predictors	333
199.	Update on efficacy and clinical uses of fluoxetine	334
200.	Whom and how to classify in psychiatry	335
201.	Alcohol abuse: Treatment programs and patients follow-up	338
202.	Neuroendocrinology of affective disorders and schizophrenia	340
203.	Next steps that will revolutionize psychiatric education in the 21st century	342
204.	The role of benzodiazepines in the treatment of chronic illness and distress syndromes	343
205.	Biology of alcohol withdrawal psychoses	345
206.	Treatment of negative symptoms in schizophrenia	346
207.	Child and adolescent psychiatry	348
208.	Pharmacotherapy of schizophrenia	350
209.	Obsessive compulsive disorders: Clinical aspects	352
210.	Psychopathology in cancer patients	355
211.	Cognitive functions in schizophrenia	357
212.	MAO inhibitors	359
213.	Classification systems in special patient populations	362
214.	Social and vocational rehabilitation services	364
215.	Personality and psychopathology in children and adolescents	366
216.	Mental health: General issues	369
217.	Rehabilitation in psychiatry	371
218.	Depression in primary care	372
219.	De l'urgence à la Communauté, de l'accompagnement à l'hospitalization	373
220.	Psychiatric education around the world	375
221.	Philosophic perspectives to the development of psychiatric service in a developing country	376
222.	The role of psychiatry in international conflict resolution	378
223.	New and useful psychotropic drugs in child and adolescent psychiatry	379
224.	Phenomenological problems in recent psychopathology	380
225.	Clinical pharmacology of buspirone	382
226.	ECT: Biological correlates	383
227.	Suicidology: Clinical and psychosocial dimensions	384
228.	Mental health policy	386
229.	Serotonergic mechanisms in schizophrenia disorders	387
230.	Aspects of depression in old age	389
231.	Cultural psychiatry issues in the Mid-East and Europe: Social change, immigration and refugee	390
232.	Suicide prevention and antidepressants	391
233.	Chronic pain and antidepressants	392
234.	Psychological and psychopathological issues in medical conditions	394
235.	Clinical neurophysiology	395
236.	Antidepressant treatment outcome and its predictors	397
237.	Psychoneuroendocrinology II	399
238.	Schizophrenia: Disability and related issues	401
239.	Antidepressants in clinical use II	402
240.	Psychoanalysis and the therapeutic relationship	404
241.	Nosological issues in affective disorders	406
242.	Psychotherapies for children, adolescents and their families	408
243.	Diagnostic complexities	409
244.	Schizophrenia II	411
245.	Psychosomatic and somatoform disorders	414
246.	Mood stabilizing drugs	417
247.	Obsessive compulsive disorders	420
248.	Affective disorders II	422
249.	Alcohol abuse II	424
250.	Psychoneuroendocrinology	426
251.	Therapeutic communities and psychosocial services	430
252.	Child psychiatry II	432
253.	Pharmacotherapy of depression III	434
254.	Delusional states and other psychiatric conditions	436
255.	Pharmacotherapy in schizophrenia II	439
256.	Psychological reaction to cancer	442
257.	Anorexia nervosa	442
258.	The psychiatric subspecialty of sleep disorders medicine	442
259.	Classical literature and art expression	443
260.	Digestive / respiratory psychosomatics and	

chronic pain 444
261. Schizophrenia: Rehabilitation programs . 446
262. Military psychiatry 447
263. Application of the psychoanalytic theory . 449
264. Depression in women 451
265. Alcohol abuse: Clinical issues 453
266. Psychiatry and the law 454
267. Mental health. Art therapy 456

Monday, 16th October 1989

268. Major psychotherapeutic approaches .. 459
269. Issues and perspectives in social psychiatry 460
270. Understanding obsessive compulsive disorder 461
271. Assistance and therapies in adolescence . 462
272. The role of psychiatry in mental health policy formulation 463
273. "Why can't they be like us?" Psychiatry and primary care 465
274. The epidemiology of the dementias in community samples 466
275. Psychosocial problems in Psychiatry .. 467
276. Child abuse 468
277. Alcohol: Basic science of clinical importance 470
278. Laterality and pathophysiology in schizophrenia and depression 471
279. Psychiatric epidemiology: Prevalence studies 472
280. Drug abuse: Epidemiology 475
281. Side effects of psychotropic drugs 477
282. Use of reversible inhibitors of MAO-A in major depression and other psychiatric disorders 479
283. Field trials of SCAN 480
284. Serotonin and serotonin uptake inhibitors in depression 481
285. Plasma amino acids: Markers, predictors, therapeutic tools for psychiatric disease 483
286. Psychometrics: Development of instruments 484
287. Issues on classification 486
288. Cellular membranes - receptors and immune system 488
289. Personality disorders 491
290. Community mental health services 493
291. Inpatient services 495
292. Psychopathology in medical patients .. 497
293. AIDS: Psychological implications 500
294. Recent developments in clinical psychopharmacology 502
295. Disability of the elderly and its care .. 504
296. Philosophy and psychiatry 506
297. Etiology of schizophrenia 509
298. Psychosocial and transcultural psychiatric aspects in Latin America 510
299. Relationship between personality disorders and psychosis 511
300. National programs / models of care ... 512
301. Hermeneutics and psychiatry 513
302. The low dose application of neuroleptics in anxiety states 515
303. An elementary pragmatic interactive model: Theory and clinical applications 516
304. The social economic and cultural implications of mental health care in Europe 517
305. Recent advances in the treatment of bulimia 518
306. Community and community oriented services 519
307. Emergency and crisis intervention services 521
308. Psychopharmacology: Pharmacokinetic studies 523
309. Depression and suicide 525
310. Towards a safer treatment of insomnia . 526
311. Psychoanalytic paradigms in clinical practice 528
312. Multi-disciplinary approach in Alzheimer's disease research 530
313. Cognitive approaches to patients suffering from a schizophrenic syndrome 531
314. Psychosomatic and somatoform disorders 531
315. Schizophrenia and related nosological issues 533
316. Schizoaffective disorders 535
317. History of psychiatry: Leading figures . 536
318. Exercise, music and art therapy 538
319. Forensic psychiatry: Clinical issues ... 539
320. Drug abuse: Personality characteristics and psychopathology 541
321. Antidepressants: Their effects in depressed and non-depressed subjects 542
322. Neuroendocrine effects of drugs 544
323. Neuroleptic malignant syndrome 546
324. Affective and schizoaffective disorders . 548
325. Schizophrenic disorders 549
326. Organic mental diseases and various psychiatric conditions 551
327. Biological psychiatry and psychopharmacology 554
328. Experimental psychopharmacology ... 556
329. Brain imaging and EEG studies 558
330. Various psychiatric issues 560
331. Psychiatric history. Hamilton's scale .. 561
332. The psycho-neurobiological contribution to psychiatry 562
333. The role of deception in psychiatric health, illness and treatment 563
334. Islamic views in mental illness and its treatment 564
335. Informal care for the aged. International comparison 566
336. Military psychiatry in a changing world 567
337. Teaching of community based rehabilitation technics in developing countries 569
338. Biological correlates of depression and suicidal behavior 570
339. Theory and practice of "Funktionelle Entspannung" 572
340. Hospital hypnosis 572
341. Drug substitution, cost containment and the psychiatrist's dilemma 572
342. Special classifications 572
343. Delusional disorders, long-term course and outcome 574
344. Family factors in schizophrenia and its management 575
345. Special issues 576
346. Issues on clinical psychiatry 578
347. ECT: Efficacy and technical aspects .. 580
348. General issues in psychiatry 581
349. Panic disorder: Theoretical and psychopathological issues II 583
350. Forensic psychiatry: International perspectives 585
351. Schizophrenia: Diagnostic and nosologic issues 586
352. Antidepressants in clinical use III 588
353. Drugs for the treatment of anxiety disorders and insomnia 591
354. Victimology 592
355. Literature. Music 594

Tuesday, 17th October 1989

356. Clinical and pathogenetic aspects of affective and related disorders ... 597
357. Conceptual and transcultural issues in psychiatry ... 598
358. Quality of life research in psychiatry ... 599
359. Phospholipid metabolism in schizophrenia ... 600
360. Alzheimer's disease: Zinc and other metals in its pathogenesis ... 602
361. Psychophysiology in relation to psychiatry ... 603
362. Sleep regulation in depression ... 604
363. Borderline personality disorder ... 606
364. Specificity of psychoanalysis ... 608
365. Links between psychiatry and general practice: Present trends ... 609
366. Alcohol abuse: Biological correlates ... 610
367. Perspectives in psychiatric education ... 612
368. Positron and photon emission tomography in psychiatry ... 614
369. Eating disorders and transcultural aspects of child and adolescent psychiatry ... 616
370. Methylation, folate, metabolism and S-Adenosyl-methionine in psychiatric disorders ... 617
371. Cross-cultural approaches to the improvement of treatment in psychiatry ... 619
372. Plasma level monitoring of antipsychotic drug therapy - Pros and cons ... 620
373. Issues on international classification ... 621
374. Life events and adjustment disorders ... 624
375. Family psychopathology and family treatment ... 627
376. Psychopathology in restorative medicine ... 629
377. Long-term pharmacotherapy of schizophrenia ... 631
378. Drug abuse: Substitution and other pharmacological treatments ... 633
379. Pharmacotherapy of depression: Current issues ... 636
380. Treatment of drug abuse: Psychosocial approaches ... 638
381. Psychometric studies of psychopathology ... 640
382. Depression in the elderly ... 643
383. Psychiatric management on the primary care level ... 645
384. Psychopathology. Psychosurgery ... 647

Wednesday, 18th October 1989

385. Brain mechanisms in normal and abnormal mental processes ... 651
386. Developmental and age related psychopathological conditions ... 652
387. The emerging interface between psychiatry and medicine ... 653
388. Psychopharmacology of affective disorders ... 654
389. History of the concept of depression ... 657
390. Research on carers of the demented ... 658
391. Defining "dangerousness" in different legal systems ... 659
392. Antipsychotic drugs: Present status and future trends ... 659
393. The interdependence between the mental health care system, the social situation of the mentally ill and the state of human rights with the community ... 661
394. Ethics and mental health policy ... 662
395. Affective disorders in childhood and adolescence ... 664
396. Psycholinguistics ... 666
397. Rehabilitation and care for special groups ... 668
398. Neuro-psychopathology of aging: Clinical and biological aspects ... 670
399. Culture, phenomenology, outcome and therapy of mental disorders ... 672
400. Perceived parental rearing and psychopathology ... 674
401. The use of clozapine in treatment-resistant schizophrenia ... 675
402. Affective disorders: Chronobiology and psychophysiology ... 677
403. Sleep studies ... 679
404. Eating disorders ... 681
405. Beyond classical antidepressant drug treatment ... 683
406. General hospital psychiatry ... 685
407. Effects of drugs on sleep ... 688
408. Pervasive developmental disorders ... 690
409. General issues in mental health ... 692
410. Group psychotherapy, theory and practice ... 694
411. AIDS: Issues related to management ... 696
412. Issues in geriatric psychiatry ... 698
413. Improvement of treatment in psychiatry ... 700
414. Stress and depression: An international symposium on tianeptine ... 702
415. Brain receptor imaging in psychiatry ... 705
416. Clinical disaster psychiatry ... 706
417. Behavioral therapies in schizophrenia disorders ... 707
418. Post-graduate teaching on the prevention and treatment of depression ... 708
419. Institutional care and rehabilitation of the mentally ill ... 708
420. Serotonin reuptake inhibition in the management of depression ... 710
421. Group psychotherapy for adolescents and children ... 712
422. Psychophysiological methods in psychiatry ... 712
423. Short-term dynamic psychotherapy: Videotape demonstration ... 714
424. Critical issues on diagnostic evaluation ... 714
425. Self-mutilation and factitious disorders ... 716
426. Cultural psychiatry issues in Asia and India: Suicidal behavior and sexual problems ... 717
427. New strategies in treatment of schizophrenia ... 718
428. New trends in child psychotherapy: Symbolic play-therapy within the family ... 720
429. On caring and its troubles: Some consequences of "empathic success" ... 720
430. Psychopathological and psychotherapeutic themes II ... 721
431. Studies in transcultural psychiatry II ... 723
432. Issues related to sexual behavior ... 725
433. Psychopathology and neurological disorders ... 726
434. Theoretical and critical issues I ... 728
435. Diagnostic issues in psychogeriatrics ... 729
436. Theoretical and critical issues II ... 731
437. Studies in transcultural psychiatry ... 732
438. Alzheimer's disease and other dementias ... 734
439. Biological psychiatry: Brain structures ... 736
440. Drugs other than antidepressants and antipsychotics ... 738
441. Pharmacotherapy of depression II ... 739
442. Sleep research ... 743
443. Clinical neurophysiology and neuroimaging ... 744

444. Biological psychiatry: Dopaminergic system — 746
445. Adolescent psychiatry — 748
446. Pharmacopsychiatry: Antipsychotics — 749
447. Various topics in psychiatry — 751
448. Pharmacotherapy of depression IV — 756
449. Eating disorders — 758
450. P.R. Films. Self-viewing in the therapy of schizophrenia — 759
451. Drug dependence - Basic science of clinical importance — 760
452. Attention deficit disorder with hyperactivity: Diagnosis, treatment, follow-up — 761
453. New concepts of psychosomatic consultation liaison service — 762
454. The ethics of psychiatric treatments — 763
455. La psiquiatria clinica en un hospital mexicano — 764
456. Key issues and practical proposals for the improvement of institutional care and rehabilitation of mentally ill — 765
457. Outcome of psychotherapies — 766
458. Psychiatric ethics — 767
459. Major depression disorders in anorexia nervosa and bulimia — 769
460. Improvisation therapy — 770
461. Eating disorders: Theoretical issues and psychological correlates — 770
462. Issues in psychophysiology — 772
463. Sexual attitudes and dysfunctions — 774
464. Non-traditional therapies — 775
465. Alcohol and drug abuse: Family-related issues — 777
466. Organic mental disorders: Neurological aspects — 779
467. Sleep disorders — 780
468. Migration and mental health II — 782
469. Famine / hunger. Pilgrimage — 783

Thursday, 19th October 1989

470. Psychiatry: Current state and perspectives — 787
471. Alternative structures of care and promotion of mental health — 788
472. Concept of "Einheitspsychosen": Pro and contra — 789
473. Mental health problems of offenders — 790
474. Diagnosis and treatment of childhood hyperkinetic disorders — 791
475. Personal and professional developmental stages and tasks of medical students — 793
476. Emergency psychiatry — 794
477. Mental health care in Greece — 796
478. Therapeutic community and psychotherapy integration — 798
479. Issues in ethnopsychiatry — 798
480. Panic disorders: Etiopathogenesis and treatment — 800
481. Etiopathogenesis of schizophrenia: Biological correlates — 803
482. Psychopathology and neurobiology: Comprehensive concepts — 805
483. Adopted children and adolescents: Risk for psychiatric pathology? — 806
484. Neuroleptic malignant syndrome — 807
485. Ethical aspects in psychopharmacological treatment — 809
486. Group psychotherapy: Clinical applications — 810
487. Eating disorders: Diagnostic and therapeutic issues — 812
488. Pharmacotherapy of acutely disturbed schizophrenic patients — 814
489. Epidemiological studies on mental patients — 817
490. Behavioral and cognitive therapies — 819
491. Psychiatric training: Themes and variations — 821
492. Integrative approaches to social psychiatry — 824
493. Psychosocial factors in suicidal behavior and self-mutilation — 826
494. Diagnostic tools — 828

ADDENDUM — 831
AUTHOR'S INDEX — 835
SUBJECT INDEX — 865

*Friday
13th October 1989*

Session 1 — Plenary: Progress in biological research of mood disorders

1

PRESENT STATE & PERSPECTIVES IN BIOLOGICAL RES. ON AFFECTIVE DISORDERS
Frederick K. Goodwin, M.D.
Alcohol, Drug Abuse, and Mental Health Admin.
Rockville, Maryland, USA

Given that recent longitudinal studies continue to confirm Kraepelin's observation that the major affective disorders are predominantly recurrent, it is surprising that most contemporary research on the biology of affective illness remains cross sectional. The purpose of this presentation is to highlight three areas of inquiry which may shed light on the biology of recurrence: (1) The "pharmacological bridge", which shaped the amine theories is re-examined from the perspective of the effects of drugs and amine changes on cycle length; (2) Post's kindling-sensitization hypothesis of rapidly cycling bipolar illness and its implications for primary-prevention strategies is considered; (3) Research on biological rhythms suggests that some forms of recurrent affective illness involve a poorly regulated circadian oscillator and/or inadequate "buffering" from periodic events in the natural environment, especially seasonal rhythms.
Theories about the biology of recurrence derive directly from the clinical phenomenology of the illness. With regard to treatment implications, treatment emphasis should be given to pharmacological and psychological strategies aimed at enhancing stability.

2

MOLECULAR GENETICS STUDIES IN AFFECTIVE DISORDERS.

J. Mendlewicz. Erasme Hospital. Free University of Brussels - Brussels - Belgium

Hereditary factors have long been implicated in the etiology of affective illness through family, twin and adoption studies. The identification of the genetic susceptibility to mental illness has recently been stimulated by the application of molecualr neurobiology, and powerful new molecular genetic strategies, such as the linkage studies. In the linkage approach, D.N.A. polymorphisms are investigated in relation to mental illness traits and chromosomal localization can be testd in large kindreds of informative families. Evidence in favor of X chromosomal localization of the locus responsible for an hereditay form of Manic-Depressive Illness has been provided in some families by the establishement of a linkage between this disease and two genetic markers : color blindness and G6PD. The Manic-Depressive phenotype is however heterogenous since X-linked transmission dos not appear in all pedigrees studied, and since a locus on chromosome 11 has also been implicated in one Amish family. This paper provides new evidence of the presence of X-linkage between an X-linked marker and affective illness in a sample of informative families. The genetic chromosomal probes appears to be a powerful and most promising method to investigate hereditary transmission of mental illness at the molecular level. Some of the problems that will have to be considered in future genetic studies in biological psychiatry deal with the well known heterogeneity of depressive illness both from the clinical and genetic point of views.

3

BIOLOGICAL TESTS IN MOOD DISORDERS
Robert T. Rubin, M.D., Ph.D.
Department of Psychiatry, Harbor-UCLA Medical Center, Torrance, California 90509, USA

Mood disorders, notably major depression, have been studied extensively from the neurochemical, neurophysiological and neuroendocrinological standpoints. Attempts have been made to incorporate various findings into tests, for use by clinicians, to aid in differential diagnosis, choice of treatment, and monitoring of treatment response. Unfortunately, reports on most of these tests have been conflicting and their use has been disappointing to many clinicians. Nevertheless, researchers are looking forward to the inclusion of biological criteria in future psychiatric diagnostic systems.
Should current biological tests in mood disorders be simply disregarded, or is there indeed some promise for their use by practitioners? The answer lies both in the informed application of some of the more promising existing tests and in the continued development of new data. The biology of mood disorders, and other psychiatric disorders as well, must be fully elucidated, both from a basic science standpoint and in the application of the biological data to clinical practice. We therefore should continue our cautious optimism, neither accepting these tests uncritically nor rejecting them out of hand. Clinicians need to have a clear understanding of the necessary criteria for a useful biological test.

4

CHRONOBIOLOGY IN PSYCHIATRY

Lennart Wetterberg
Karolinska Institute, Dept. of Psychiatry, St. Gorans Hospital, Box 12500, S-112 81 Stockholm, Sweden

Chronobiology deals with the scientific study of the effects of time and biological rhythms on living systems. An example of life time temporal effect on the genetic regulation is the transition from latent to manifest form in late puberty in affective disorders and schizophrenia. There is an annual periodicity in the increased frequency of births of schizophrenic patients in the first three months of the year in the northern hemisphere. Monthly variation related to the menstrual cycle is seen in several psychiatric diseases. Circadian (about 24 hour) rhythms, day-night variations are probably the most studied, specially in affective disorders where seasonal mood swings occur. Seasonal rhythms are also seen in performance, sleep pattern, metabolic functions, hormonal and neurochemical variables. The phase position in depressed patients is often measured using cortisol and melatonin as markers of rhythm. Chronobiological results emphasize that behaviour is interacting in a periodic dynamic system.

Session 2 — Plenary: International Classification of Mental Disorders

5
REQUIREMENT FOR A CLASSIFICATION OF MENTAL DISORDERS IN THE WORLD TODAY
Dr N.N. Wig
World Health Organization, Alexandria, Egypt

A classification of mental disorders must allow a simple and unequivocal accommodation of the most frequent psychiatric diagnoses and should be suitable for use by those who see the majority of patients with mental disorders. It follows that the classification which the world of today needs must have particularly good provisions for acute psychotic disorders, disorders with predominantly somatic presentations, childhood mental disorders and substance abuse disorders. It also follows that the classification must be suitable for use (or easily adjustable for use) by health workers who are not psychiatrists. Furthermore if a classification is to be used the world over and serve as a means to international communication it must be produced jointly by experts from countries the world over. The draft of the tenth revision of the International Classification of Diseases which the World Health Organization is currently preparing satisfies many of these requirements but not all. Work remains to be done on several parts of the classification which will also have to be produced in several parallel versions - for researchers, practitioners, primary care workers - and in different languages. The establishment of the WHO network of centres and individuals in many countries will make these tasks easier.

6
THE FORM AND CONTENT OF ICD-10 CHAPTER V (F)
Professor J. E. Cooper.
University of Nottingham Medical School,
Department of Psychiatry.

The strategy for the design and presentation of ICD-10 Chapter V (F) - Mental, Behavioural and Developmental Disorders - is described. The new international classification will be presented in different degrees of detail for different purposes, but all versions are basically the same classification. ICD-10 Chapter V (F) contains many more categories than ICD-9, and some space is left to allow future modifications without a major re-design of the whole classification. The version designed for general clinical and educational purposes is called "Clinical Descriptions and Diagnostic Guidelines".

A closely related set of Diagnostic Criteria for Research will be available, and a shorter simpler version for use in primary and general health care settings. A multi-axial system will also be prepared. World-wide contributions from many centres and individuals and equally extensive field trials will ensure the highest possible level of international acceptability.

7
THE WORLD PSYCHIATRIC ASSOCIATION AND THE DEVELOPMENT OF ICD-10
Juan E. Mezzich, M.D., Ph.D., Department of Psychiatry, University of Pittsburgh, Pittsburgh, PA, USA

The need for systematic consultations on classification proposals across cultural and geographical regions is emphasized by the wide international roots of current diagnostic methodology and the centrality of classification models and tools for professional work.
In recent years, the World Health Organization (WHO) and the World Psychiatric Association (WPA) signed an agreement for collaboration on highly significant topics, the first one of which has been the development of ICD-10. Subsequently, the WPA has conducted a consultation with national psychiatric societies on ICD-10 proposals. Thirty-three countries spanning all five continents have participated in this consultation. Substantial support for the proposals was generally accorded and specific recommendations were offered such as the use of multiaxial formulations, the conduction of validation studies and the establishment of bridges with well-known national classifications and previous versions of ICD.
The development of several working groups connected to national societies has been stimulated by the above mentioned consultation. On this basis, the WPA, along with similar professional organizations, should contribute further to the development of the ICD-10 family of classifications.

8
ICD-10 AND CLINICAL PSYCHIATRY
A.V. Jablensky
WHO Collaborating Centre of Mental Health
Sofia, Bulgaria

Having been initiated as a classification of causes of death to aid statistical reporting, successive versions of ICD have increasingly developed provisions for the statistical coverage of morbidity. However only its section on mental disorders (which was the first one to incorporate a glossary in ICD-9) has evolved towards a clinical classification. Drawing on international experience (primarily on DSM-III), WHO has developed the ICD-10 chapter on mental and behavioural disorders (including disorders of psychological development) as a 'clinician-friendly' conceptual scheme and manual. In its design and content, ICD-10 aims to overcome restrictions on clinical thinking which stem from so called operational diagnostic criteria, and to allow, within certain limits, flexibility and adjustment to individual diagnostic styles.

Session 3 — Symposium: Results of studies developing instruments for cross-culturally comparative research in psychiatry

9

SCAN: SCHEDULES FOR CLINICAL ASSESSMENT IN NEUROPSYCHIATRY
Wing, J.K.
Royal College of Psychiatrists, London, UK

SCAN is a set of instruments that systematically covers the phenomena of mental disorders and provides standardized techniques for investigating, recording and classifying them. The core instrument is the tenth edition of the Present State Examination (PSE10), earlier editions of which have been used in clinical, educational and scientific work for twenty-five years. SCAN has been tested in field trials in twenty countries and has proved both practical and reliable in the hands of trained clinicians. Together with associated modules, virtually the whole of ICD-10 is covered by the SCAN computer programmes and most of DSM-III-R. Its chief asset, however, remains its firm basis in clinical phenomenology.

10

THE COMPOSITE INTERNATIONAL DIAGNOSTIC INTERVIEW (CIDI) - RELIABILITY AND APPLICABILITY OF THE CIDI IN DIFFERENT COUNTRIES
Lee Robins, Ph.D.
Washington University School of Medicine, St.Louis USA

A main component of the Joint WHO/ADAMHA Project on Diagnosis and Classification of Mental Disorders, Alcohol- and Drug-Related Problems, is the development of instruments for the assessment of psychiatric problems. One of them is the CIDI, an instrument usable by lay interviewers or clinicians to make psychiatric diagnoses according to a variety of diagnostic systems. Its broad coverage and multiple systems makes it long. However, it can be shortened by selecting diagnoses and systems of special interest. Last year such a reduced "core" was field tested in 19 sites and in 12 languages to assess its reliability and cultural appropriateness in many settings. Respondents were chiefly general medical patients and psychiatric out-patients. Interviewer-observer agreement was excellent. Problems in adapting the CIDI to local conditions inspired many improvements. Since then, questions to cover DSM-III-R and ICD-10 have been added and pretested. The revised core version has been field-tested in patient and community samples. Most earlier problems have been solved. Diagnostic scoring algorithms and training materials have been developed. Its wide application will undoubtedly allow its further improvement.

11

ASSESSMENT OF PERSONALITY DISORDERS IN DIFFERENT CULTURES
A.W. Loranger, Department of Psychiatry, Cornell University Medical College and New York Hospital-Cornell Medical Center, Westchester Division, White Plains, N.Y., USA

The World Health Organization (WHO) and United States Alcohol, Drug Abuse, and Mental Health Administration (ADAMHA) Joint Project on Diagnosis and Classification of Mental Disorders, Alcohol and Drug-Related Problems was established in 1979 to foster a common language and improve the scientific basis of diagnosis and classification in the mental health field. Among other activities the programme includes the development of instruments, which would facilitate comparisons of data about patients living in different cultures. This report describes the early results from a field trial of one of the instruments under development, the International Personality Disorder Examination (IPDE), a semi-structured interview for use by clinicians in the assessment of the phenomenology and life experiences relevant to the diagnosis of the personality disorders in the DSM-III-R and ICD-10 classification systems.

12

ASSESSMENT OF SUBSTANCE ABUSE PROBLEMS IN COMPARATIVE STUDIES
John B. Saunders
Centre for Drug and Alcohol Studies, Royal Prince Alfred Hospital and University of Sydney, Sydney, Australia

The pattern of drug use in society is influenced by traditional practices and the availability of imported and synthetic substances. A drug which is used in a relatively harm-free way in one society may cause major disruption when intruduced into another. When this happens, there is at first a predominance of problems due to acute intoxication, such as trauma and psychosis. Dependence and chronic physical consequences appear later. Assessment of substance abuse should include an estimate of the frequency and quantity of use, the setting in which drug use occurs, behavioural manifestations and physical symptoms of dependence, and the physical, psychological and social sequelae. Several interview schedules have been developed by the World Health Organization to characterise substance abuse in different cultures. In a recent collaborative study, patterns of drinking were found to vary widely. Relationships between the levels of consumption, drinking behaviour, dependence symptoms and psychosocial sequelae showed a much greater degree of similarity. In particular, the concept of dependence appeared a robust one, which seems to be applicable to many different cultures. A series of core questions to assess substance abuse in different cultures appears to be a viable proposition.

13

WORLD HEALTH ORGANIZATION'S WORK ON INSTRUMENTS MEASURING COGNITIVE IMPAIRMENT
C. G. Gottfries
Dept of Psychiatry & Neurochemistry, Gothenburg University, St Jorgen's Hospital, 42203 Hisings Backa, Sweden

The examination of patients with dementia disorders must be adapted to the patient's needs, abilities and limitations. The deficit can be assessed directly when there are normative comparison standards or indirectly when the patient's present performance is compared with an estimation of his original ability level. The most used test battery is the Wechsler Adult Intelligence Scale (WAIS). There are a number of tests that are designed in order to assess verbal, perceptual, visuopractic functions and manual dexterity. The assessment of memory requires examination of its various aspects. As very often there are no normative comparison standards in the testing of elderly demented patients behavioural rating scales must be used. WHO is in the process of presenting a book "Clinical Evaluation of Psychotropic Drugs- Principles and Proposed Guide-Lines" and in this book there is a chapter on "Studies in the Elderly" and in this chapter one part discusses the assessment of cognitive impairment in elderly patients. WHO is also preparing a multi-national study "Collaborative Study on the Development of Evaluation Instruments for the Assessment of Dementia" which is an effort to standarize instruments used when diagnosing & assessing cognitive impairment.

Session 4 — New Research: Drug abuse

14

MEASURING THE PREVALENCE OF DRUG USE AMONG ADOLESCENT STUDENTS : AN INTERNATIONAL STANDARIZED QUESTIONNAIRE
M. Choquet, F.M.H.M. Driessen, L.D. Johnston, A. Kokkevi, S. Ledoux
I.N.S.E.R.M.

To forecast developments in drug abuse and treatment demand, to plan policies regarding drug abuse and to evaluate the effects of preventive measures, policymakers and public health officers need information on the prevalence of drug abuse among the population. Since drug use in adolescence is known to be an important risk factor for problematic use later on developments among the adolescent part of the population are of especially great importance.

In several countries research on drug use among adolescents takes place on a more or less regular basis, but the results of these studies are not comparable because of great differences in methodology and questionnaires. International comparability, would add to the usefullness of such studies.

For this reason the epidemiology expert group of Cooperation Group to Combat Drug abuse (so-called Pompidou group) of the Council of Europe has developed and tested a standarized questionnaire, used in Greece, France, Sweden, The Netherlands, Belgium, Germany, Italy, Portugal, USA, Jamaica and Aruba.

The questionnaire and methodology will be discussed. Beside this some of the results in four countries (France, The Netherlands, Greece and the USA) will be presented.

15

DEPRESSION IN COCAINE ABUSE
C.A. Alfonso, MD; B.E. Bess, MD; M. Daras, MD; J.C. Rodriguez, MD; and P. Singer, MD
New York Medical College, Metropolitan Hospital Center
New York, New York U.S.A

During the last few years the marked increase in cocaine abuse has had an impact on the number of patients brought to psychiatric emergency rooms. The authors hypothesized, from their experience in a New York City municipal hospital, that cocaine induced depression, with or without suicidal ideation and/or attempts, seemed far more common than had been previously reported. Fifty-one cases of patients admitted to Adult In-Patient Psychiatry Units during the year 1988 with a diagnosis of cocaine abuse were reviewed, 23 were considered suitable for the study because they had no concomitant use of other drugs and no premorbid psychotic or affective disorder. All of them tested positive for cocaine metabolites only, in urine toxicology. Route of administration was the smoking of free-base cocaine (crack) in all subjects. Of the 23 patients with cocaine induced psychiatric disorders, 18 (78,3%) manifested serious clinical depression with or without suicidal ideation and/or attempts. Only 3 of the depressed patients manifested psychotic symptoms of hallucinatory voices directing them to suicide. Five patients manifested psychotic symptoms including paranoia with bizarre and disorganized behaviors. The depression associated with cocaine abuse lacked the strong affective component and negatative symptoms seen in primary depression. Unlike recent studies which indicate that the most prevalent symptoms are psychosis, agitatic and assaultiveness, this study suggests that depression is the most common cause for psychiatric admission in cocaine abusers.

16

COCAINE INDUCED NEUROLEPTIC MALIGNANT-LIKE SYNDROME.
M. Daras, A.J. Tuchman, B.S. Koppel, D. Rebischung.
N.Y. Med. Coll. Metropolitan Hosp. New York, N.Y. U.S

Hyperthermia and rhabdomyolysis have been reported in cocaine abuse, but their potential association with a neuroleptic malignant-like syndrome has not been adequately emphasized in the literature.
In the past 6 months while studying neurological complications in cocaine abuse we evaluated 3 male cocaine abusers (24-33 year old), who presented with hyperpyrexia, various degree of confusion and disorientation, muscle pain, tenderness or rigidity rhabdomyolysis and myoglobinuria. There was no evidence of infection nor history of seizures or alcoholism. Urine was positive for cocaine metabolites. Two patients developed disseminated intravascular coagulopathy and one died of renal failure. Chronic depletion of dopamine rather than dopamine receptor block may be responsible for the neuroleptic malignant-like syndrome in cocaine abusers. Use of neuroleptics in agitated, assaultive cocaine abusers may further worsen these symptoms.

17

AN EFFECTIVE PHARMACOLOGIC TREATMENT FOR COCAINE DEPENDENCE
James A. Halikas, M.D., Kenneth Kemp, M.D., Kenneth Kuhn, M.D., Greg Carlson, Fred Crea
University of Minnesota
Minneapolis, MN 55455 U.S.A.

Overwhelming craving for cocaine results in a relapse rate of 80-100 percent for cocaine dependent patients within the first 12 months. At the University of Minnesota, we have developed an experimental pharmacologic treatment for cocaine abusers. In addition to standard rehabilitation efforts, 26 patients to date have been offered carbamazepine. All patients had long histories of substance abuse, cocaine use, unsuccessful treatment attempts, and police problems.

Ten subjects have had clear success, with abstinence ranging from 1-8 months. Ten other subjects have been at least partial successes with progressive periods of cocaine abstinence. Six patients have been judged unsuccessful based on refusal to take medication and continued use of cocaine. There are several theoretical reasons why carbamazepine may be useful in the treatment of cocaine dependent patients. At the conference, these theoretical reasons will be presented, the most up-to-date data on this growing series of patients will be presented, and the treatment protocol will be discussed in depth.

18

TREATMENT OF CRACK COCAINE USE

James A. Halikas, M.D., Kenneth Kemp, M.D., Kenneth Kuhn, M.D., Greg Carlson, Fred Crea
University of Minnesota
Minneapolis, MN 55455 U.S.A.

Crack is a rock crystalline form of cocaine which can be smoked. Once begun, use by this route often pre-dominates as the route of choice. At the University of Minnesota, we have developed an experimental pharmacologic treatment for cocaine abusers. Of 26 patients treated to date, 16 have been crack cocaine users. During the 100 days preceding treatment, the 16 subjects used cocaine by all routes an average of 71 days each. With carbamazepine treatment, 7 highly successful and 6 partially successful patients reduced their use to 0.7 days per 100 days and 26 days per 100 days respectively. Pearson Product Moment Correlation demonstrated a significant association between carbamazepine medication compliance and reduction in days of using cocaine. A full discussion of the treatment program and the results of this open label clinical trial to date will be presented at the conference.

19

DEXTROMETHORPHAN-TREATMENT OF HEROIN ADDICTS: A DOUBLE-BLIND CLINICAL TRIAL

Saydam, M.B.[*] and Koyuncuoğlu H.[**]
[*]Istanbul Medical Faculty, Clinic of Psychiatry
[**]Department of Pharmacology

According to the hypothesis implying that the development of physical dependence on and tolerance to opiates depends on the inhibition by opiates of the brain L-asparaginase/L-glutaminase activity and the blockade by opiates of the aspartatergic/glutamatergic receptors especially NMDA, 29 heroin addicts were taken into a double blind clinical trial. Every one hour 4 mg chlorpromazin (CPZ) and every six hours 10 mg diazepam (DIA) were given to a group consisting of 6 inpatients whereas the remaining received 15 mg dextromethorphan (DM) instead of CPZ. Yawning, lacrimation, rhinorrhoea, perspiration, goose flesh, muscle tremor, anorexia, joint/muscle aches, restlessness, insomnia, mydriasis, emesis, diarrhoea, craving and rejection of smoking as abstinence syndrome signs were observed. Almost all signs were significantly less intense and of shorter duration in the group given DM+DIA than CPZ+DIA. Immediate stop of craving and the early onset of smoking in DM+DIA group were most attractive points. The results were considered as supporting evidence for the hypothesis mentioned above. The blockade of NMDA receptors by non-opioid NMDA-antagonists appears very promising for the treatment of opiate addicts.

20

CLONIDINE IN HEROINE WITHDRAWAL SYNDROME IN INDIAN OUT PATIENTS.
ARUN KUMAR GUPTA, M.D., PSYCHIATRIST.
DR. RAM MANOHAR LOHIA HOSPITAL, NEW DELHI 110001 INDIA.

The study was conducted with an open design to evaluate the efficacy and safety of clonidine for medical treatment of Heroine Withdrawal Syndrome in Indian out patients. Fortyfive males of age range 18 to 45 years were included in the study. They were administered clonidine in dosage range of 0.3 mg to 0.6 mg per day and followed up daily as out patients. Fourteen patients dropped out. Thirtyone could be followed up for three to fourteen days. Only side effect of clonidine observed was giddiness in five patients. All the troublesome Heroine Withdrawal Symptoms were effectively controlled except insomnia and bodyache, which were controlled with chlorodiazepoxide and paracetamol given orally on p.r.n. (as needed) basis. Clonidine appears to be safe and effective for control of Heroine Withdrawal Syndrome in Indian out patients.

21

ELECTROSTIMULATION ANALGESIA OPIATE WITHDRAWAL HUMAN AND ANIMAL VALIDATION

AURIACOMBE M.*, DAULOUEDE J.P.*, STINUS L.**, TIGNOL J.* et LE MOAL M.**
   *Service Universitaire de Psychiatrie Hopital Charles Perrens
    33076 BORDEAUX CEDEX
   **INSERM, Unite 259, 33077 BORDEAUX CEDEX

Transcutaneous electrical stimulation (TES) with Limoge's current (high frequency 100 Kc, 2 usec, pulse trains, 100 Hz, 4 as; 100 mA peak to peak) which is asymptomatic in man has been used in clinical settings for anesthesia and for management of heroin addicts during their withdrawal syndrome. We have valitated the use of TES in man for the opiate withdrawal syndrome in a double blind clinical study (Ellison et al, 1987). TES produced a significant ($p<0,05$) decrease of the abstinence syndrome as measured by Himmels bach's rating scale compared to the control group. We have recently studied TES in animals (rats) to elucidate its biological aspects. We present here results of ongoing research.
1. TES and analgesia : we measured the effect of TES on tail flick latency on naive and morphine treated rats, TES did not modify pain thresholds on naive animals, however analgesic effects of morphine were greatly potentiated. This potentiation of morphine induced analgesia was dose and intensity dependant, TES must start 3 hours before morphine injection (double-blind experiment $p<0,001$), The same results have been obtained with rapifen, fentanyl and palfium (double-blind observation).
2. TES and opiate withdrawal : morphino-dependant rats were obtained by IP injections of increasing doses of morphine twice daily for 10 days. Withdrawal symptoms were induced by interuption of morphine injections and scored on Gellert's scale three times a day for 3 days. TES appeared to reduce the withdrawal symptoms by 50 % $p<0,0001$).
Our results are consistent with clinical observation and give validity to TES. Futher experiments will be performed in order to determine optimal stimulation parameters and to elucidate neurobiological mecanisms of TES.

22

PROGRAMA PREVENTINO PERMANENTE EN DROGA-DEPENDENCIA.
PROF. DR. MIGUEL ANGEL MATERAZZI
HOSPITAL NACIONAL JOSE T. BORDA
CENTRO DE INVESTIGATION MEDICO PSICOLOGICO DE LA COMUNICATION

El Programa Preventino Permanente en Drogadependencia, tiene como primer objetivo generar agentes de Salud Mental Preventivos Multiplicadores, a través de los Talleres Expresivos Creativos, instrumento del Programa por medio del Curso de Agentes Multiplicadores (comprende 10 módulos). El segundo objetivo, consultorios de Orientación y Derivación en 1o Etapa y Atención en Crisis en 2o Etapa.
Instalados los mismos dentro de la Comunidad, independientes de lo Institucional, ejecutando de esta manera una real atención primaria.

Session 5 — Symposium:
Révolution démocratique et naissance de la psychiatrie

23

PINEL AND ENLIGHTMENT

PELICIER Yves - HOPITAL NECKER -
Sce de Psychiatrie- 149 rue de Sèvres
75743 PARIS CEDEX 15
   FACULTE DE MEDECINE   PARIS -

The invention of Psychiatry at time of French Revolution is the result of an extraordinary conjunction :

1 - interest for mind and psychic life following Locke, Condillac and ideologues phylosophy ;

2 - attention to philanthropy, more or less emancipated of religious influence ;

3 - will to consider all human situation as relevant of a rationnal treatment ;

4 - growth of romantic movement with a focus on affective life ;

5 - developping of the meaning and value of observation in medicine and accepting contradiction with tradition

24

UNE REVOLUTION DANS L'HISTOIRE DE LA PSYCHIATRIE ?

Docteur Bernard ODIER

C.H.S. BARTHELEMY-DURAND 91152 - ETAMPES CEDEX - FRANCE -

Stimulées par les thèses critiques de philosophes (M. FOUCAUT) et de sociologues (R. CASTEL), les recherches historiques menées ces vingt dernières années autour de la naissance de la psychiatrie ont donné lieu à un profond renouvellement des idées sur l'articulation entre cette discipline médicale, l'histoire des idées, et celle de la société.

Parallèlement, dans un mouvement qui s'est accéléré à l'approche du bicentenaire, une relance des travaux sur la Révolution Française est observée, en France comme à l'étranger.

L'auteur expose les principaux points sur lesquels porte cet ensemble de réinterprétations : importance relative des transformations sociales et du mouvement des idées, développement de la clinique médicale, impact des idéaux démocratiques sur la place faite à la folie et, a contrario, contribution de la psychiatrie naissante à la révolution anthropologique à l'oeuvre.

25

SUR LA PREMIERE LEGISLATION PSYCHIATRIQUE EN GRECE
ABATZOGLOU GRIGORIS
IPPOKRATION GENERAL HOSPITAL, THESSALONIKI

Nous allons étudier :
- La première législation spécifique pour les malades mentaux (1862) comparativement à son modèle, c'est à dire la loi française du 30.6.1838.
- Le problème de la responsabilité et de l'imputation de l'acte pour les malades mentaux, dans le code pénal.

Ensuite sera examiné le rapport entre ces deux domaines.

Les pratiques cliniques et les pratiques médico-légales, en psychiatrie, seront confrontées aux législations.

26

ENTRE TRAITER ET ASSISTER, UNE AMPHIBOLOGIE PERMANENTE DE LA PSYCHIATRIE ITALIENNE, DE L´AUFKLÄRUNG DE LUCQUES A LA LOI 180.

L. DEL PISTOIA, Via Verdina 28,
55041 CAMAIORE, ITALIE

L´edition lucquoise de l´Encyclopédie (1758) peut être considérée la reference eponime du début de la psychiatrie en Toscane. Mais ses premisses matérialistes n´auront qu´une suite partielle, à cause de la culture locale post-tridentine. Nait ainsi une représentation ambigue du trouble psychique, empathique d´un côté (assister) scientiste de l´autre (organo-mécaniste), se trainant jusqu´à nos jours avec l´antipsychiatrie et la "cure d´âmes" d´un côté, le mécano-pharmacologisme de l´autre.

27

FROM PINEL TO KRAEPELIN IN SPANISH PSYCHIATRY

DESVIAT, Manuel. Servicios Salud Mental-Hospital Psiquiátrico de Leganés. MADRID. ESPAÑA.

Se parte de la revolución francesa, momento constituyente de la psiquiatría como disciplina médica, al necesitar el nuevo orden social una redifinición de los espacios humanos - el lugar del sujeto y la regulación de su responsabilidad civil, ley de 1838- y de otras técnicas de intervención social - paso del encierro y sus absolutistas bastillas al internamiento y al tratamiento moral-, señalando la importancia del concepto de ciudadano y de persona y la influencia epistemológica del empirismo inglés : la observación como método y la clínica como rasgo distintivo de la escuela francesa, para considerar su repercusión en la psiquiatría española. Después se realiza una breve referencia a la psiquiatría y medicina española - las instituciones, la Ley de Beneficencia de 1849, las escuelas de Madrid (ORFILA, MATA, ESQUERDO, VERA, SIMARRO, ACHUCARRO, LAFORA) y de Barcelona (MATA, PESET y VIDAL, GINE y PARTAGAS, MIRA LOPEZ) -, en relación con la ciencia y la sociedad española antes de la guerra civil. Concluye con una reflexión sobre la crisis del paradigma psiquiátrico que se inicia con la Revolución francesa y la obra de Philippe Pinel y Esquirol, las nuevas exigencias sociales - de la intervención en crisis a la atención de los homeless - y las dificultades de encontrar un nuevo consenso teórico en una práctica cada vez más escindida de sus fundamentos doctrinales.

28

LES PRINCIPES CONSTITUTIVES DE LA PSYCHIATRIE EUROPEENNE ET LE DEVELOPPEMENT DE LA PSYCHIATRIE EN GRECE

Ploumbidis Dimitrios, Aeginition Hospital, Athens, Greece

La psychiatrie de notre temps a été fondée sur les principes suivantes:
- La curabilité de la folie, qui ne serait qu'une maladie enracinée dans l'organisme.
- La problematique du sujet, inspirée de la philosophie et le droit.
Dans cette optique les malades mentaux devraient être des citoyens comme les autres et partie prennante de leur guérison.

Une telle attitude thérapeutique n'a pas pu trouver les plus souvent les moyens de son application et nous observons une glissement vers le paternalisme, sans dialogue avec le patient et l'organisation quasi militaire des asiles.

En Grèce, la notion du malade mental-sujet-curable n'a jamais été mise en doute, mais elle est devenue floue sous la règne des théories d'inspiration organiciste (p.e. la dégénérescence) vers la fin du 19 ème siècle.

L' histoire de la psychiatrie grecque a été également marquée par la persistance des formes pré-psychiatriques d' assistance aux malades mentaux, la constitution tardive d'une reseau d'asiles publics et l' apparition précoce du secteur privé.

Session 6 Symposium:
Psychiatry in the Americas today

29
Psychiatric Trends in the United States

Melvin Sabshin, M.D.
American Psychiatric Association

In this paper, the author will speak from his vantage point as the Medical Director of the APA. He will review changes in American psychiatry which occurred after the second World War and then he will discuss the current phase of American psychiatry which began in the early 1970's. Finally, the author will discuss predictions regarding the change in American psychiatry which he anticipates in the early part of the next century.

The current phase of American psychiatry is characterized by the increased use of objectification and empiricism. Biological psychiatry, including recent advances in the neurosciences, tend to dominate psychiatry in the United States at the present time. This contrasts with the domination by various therapeutic ideologies in the phase following World War II. Currently, there is a great interest in nosology, epidemiology, and "re-medicalization" in psychiatry. In predicting changes for the beginning of the 21st Century, the author will emphasize the vitalization of clinical psychiatry, psycho-biological advances in understanding normality and health, and a balancing of the current neuroscience domination with increased scientific developments in the psychosocial aspects of psychiatry.

30
CANADIAN EXPERIENCE WITH PSYCHIATRY, PSYCHIATRY SERVICES, AND TEACHING FOR THESE PURPOSES
Gerald J. Sarwer-Foner, M.D., Director, Lafayette Clinic; Professor, Department of Psychiatry, Wayne State University School of Medicine, Detroit, Michigan, USA

The author will discuss the specific aspects of the Canadian scene; its health insurance plan; its range of psychiatric services; and the training of psychiatric specialists in this context. The author will elaborate and contrast the United States and Canada in these respects as well as compare Canada's one tier system on health care delivery for the entire population with that seen elsewhere in the world where two and three tier systems exist. The influence of United States third party payer attempts at "managed care" and the influence of DRG thinking and planning and its likely effects on the Canadian scheme will be discussed.

31
PSIQUIATRIA Y DESARROLLO EN LATINOAMERICA

ANTONIO PACHECO H.
UNIVERSIDAD CENTRAL DE VENEZUELA

El ejercicio de la Psiquiatria en los paises Latinoamericanos reviste características peculiares, y desborda los limites de la actividad médica, ocupando un espacio que corresponde a las ciencias sociales.
En el presente trabajo, se analizan los diversos factores ambientales que originan una patologia mental compleja y que dificultan la labor profesional de los psiquiatras en Latinoamerica.
Todos estos elementos conforman una situación común a la mayoría de los paises latinoamericanos, que obstaculiza la aplicación de politicas de salud que han resultado exitosos en en otros paises, con un nivel superior de desarrollo.

32
The Role of the Psychiatrist in Medical Education

Rodolfo Fahrer
School of Medicine
University of Buenos Aires

The practical problems of Primary Health Care have brought about a debate on how best to attain the general application of the appropriate technology required to reach successful psychiatric help in PC. One of the most important problems to be solved by the psychiatrist in health planning is the development of the human resources which are needed to manage the health problems of the community, based on the PC subsystem. The unspecialized doctor should not be made responsible for performance tasks in which he has not been adequately trained. These include problems of primary prevention, early basic diagnosis, appropriate therapies, rehabilitation practices etc, as well as the evaluation of psychosocial situations and recognizing the availability of medical tools and specialists where they are needed. The basis of this education and re-education should come from the Psychiatrist to early medical students and should continue to evolve throughout the PCP's working life within the hospital and university milieu.

33

CHANGING STRATEGIES IN PSYCHIATRIC CARE IN URUGUAY
ALTERWAIN,PAULO M.D.,DIRECTOR-NATIONAL PROGRAMME OF MENTAL HEALTH,MONTEVIDEO,URUGUAY

Uruguay has had a National Programme of Mental Health(NPNH)since 1986.This is the effort of a National task force composed by main government and non-government organizations.
NPMH main characteristics are:Integration of MH as a component in all Health activities and its delivery system;Adoption of the Primary Health Care Strategy(in accordance with PAHO/WHO's statements); Effective Community Participation and Public and Private Integration;Descentralization and Accessibility through a broad National and Regional network.At the present time,initial areas of development are being implemented in the Capital City and in one of the provinces.These involve approx. 10% of the country's population.
It is within this context that Psychiatrists must effectively put into practice Integrated Community Mental Health Services,namely through the work of inter-disciplinary teams.
This model implies a substantial need for modification in the curricula and the recycle of most specialists.All of the above will enable the implementation of it through levels of progressive complexity.Some examples will be shown around problems of coordination and integration as well as the strategies used to achieve these goals.The challenge is how to maintain the identity with efficacy and effectiveness in a period of changes and new directions.

Session 7 Symposium:
Obsessive compulsive disorder: An update

34

SEROTONERGIC RESPONSIVITY IN OBSESSIVE-COMPULSIVE DISORDER.

Joseph Zohar*,Thomas R.Insel and Dennis L.Murphy.
*Beer-Sheva Mental Health Center, Beer-Sheva, Israel.

Several lines of evidence indicate that there is a specific role for serotonin in Obsessive-Compulsive Disorder (OCD). The most impressive evidence is that, so far, OCD is the only psychiatric disorder in which only drugs that inhibit synaptic serotonin uptake (i.e. clomipramine, fluvoxamine and fluoxetine) have been reported to be therapeutically effective.
To pursue further the role of the serotonergic system in OCD we compared the behavioral responses to single oral doses of m-chlorophenylpiperazine (mCPP), a novel serotonin agonist, in 12 patients with OCD and 20 healthy controls in a double blind, radomized, placebo-controlled study. Following mCPP, but not following placebo, patients with OCD experienced an acute transient and marked exacerbation of obsessive-compulsive symptoms. Moreover, the obsessive-compulsive patients exhibited incresed behavioral sensitivity to mCPP relative to the controls. These findings are consistent with the hypothesis that increased serotonergic responsiveness is associated with the psychopathologic characteristics of OCD.

35

24 h. URINARY EXCRETION OF PE AND MHPG IN OCD AND ANXIETY DISORDERS.
Ciprian-Ollivier, J.; Stockert, M. et al. Fco. de Vittoria 2324, 1425 Buenos Aires, Argentina.

Obsessive compulsive disorders(OCD) according to DSM 3R is a subtype of anxiety which,is a generic group that contemplate other ones such as Panic Attaks(PA), agora, social and monophobias, general anxiety(GAD) and postraumatic stress disorders. The clinical assessment denotes an overlapping in their psychiatric manifestations. But depression seems a very frequent manifestation; so we studied biological markers for endogenous depression (urinary PE and MHPG) in the following groups of patients according to DSM 3R criteria:
A) 19 O.C.D. (300.30)
B) 14 monophobics (300.29)
C) 34 other anxiety disorders (300.31; 300.01)
D) 20 major depressives (296.3x)
E) 20 other psych.entities(296.4x;295.40;295.70)
F) 33 normal volunteers

The statistical analysis of the data has demonstrated that there was a significant decrease of the excretion of PE between A,B,C and D groups compared with E and F groups, but without differences among them. MHPG had a similar tendency but without significance.

We conclude that these entities have endogenicity features, sharing a biological marker of unipolar depression, with diagnosis and therapeutical implications, making election for antidepressant treatment as a rational and ethiological.

36

FURTHER NEUROPSYCHOLOGICAL STUDIES OF THE OBSESSIVE-COMPULSIVE SYNDROME
Pierre Flor-Henry, M.D., John Lind, Ph.D.
Alberta Hospital Edmonton, Edmonton, Canada.

31 unmedicated patients with primary obsessive-compulsive illness, (18 males; 13 females), were compared to 154 healthy male and 122 female controls in the same age range. (Average age: male obsessionals = 26.3 ±8.9; female obsessionals = 31.5 ±9.8 years). Dynamometric, Finger Tapping, Oral Word Fluency, Speech Sounds, Williams Verbal and Non-verbal Learning, Memory For Designs, Purdue Pegboard and Tactual Performance tests were used to evaluate right and left frontal and temporal functions; frontal functions being also monitored by the Halstead Category test and the Wisconsin Card Sorting test. Hotelling T^2 test showed that the obsessional males had significant deficit on Purdue Pegboard, both hands, Tactual Performance, Preferred, Non-preferred and Both hands ($p<0.02$). The same was true for female obsessionals ($p<0.04$). Obsessional males were also impaired on the Halstead Category test and the Wisconsin Card Sorting test ($p<0.02$) as were the female obsessionals ($p<0.01$). These results indicate that, while temporal functions are intact in obsessionals, in both male and female patients definite and relatively discrete bilateral frontal dysfunction is in evidence. On the full battery a pattern of asymmetric dysfunction emerged: L>R in males and R>L in females, with an excess of non-dextrality in male obsessionals.

37

PSYCHOLOGICAL ASPECTS AND DRUG WITHDRAWAL IN OBSESSIVE COMPULSIVES
B.I. Diamond, W. Albrecht, R.L. Borison, R. Katz*, and J. DeVeaugh-Geiss*. Psychiatry, Medical College of GA, GA and CIBA-GEIGY Corp., NJ, USA

In controlled studies using clomipramine in Obsessive Compulsive Disorder (OCD) we investigated neuropsychological parameters as well as withdrawal reactions. Ten male and eight female patients ranging in age from 23-70 years old comprised our original sample. The average duration of OCD was 11 years. The mean verbal IQ was 101.6 and no patient exhibited severe depression. All patients were administered the symbol digit and complex figure test. Thirty-three percent of the patients showed abnormal performance on the symbol digit test. On the complex figure test the median copy score fell below the 30th% Norm with 27.8% of the sample performing below the 10th percentile. On the recall portion of this test, 2/3rds performed below the 10th percentile for normal adults. Moreover, inefficient organizational strategies were employed by 55.5% of the sample. Three patients on clomipramine had severe withdrawal reactions which consisted of a worsening over baseline OC behavior as well as hospitalization for suicidal ideation (two patients), and homicidal ideation (one patient). These results are consistent with the hypothesis that OCD is an organic brain disorder that involves serotonin.

38

Effect of Behavior Therapy on Serotonin Level In Obsessive-Compulsive Disorder
F.A. Neziroglu, J.A. Yaryura-Tobias, J. Steele, A. Hitri, B. Diamond
Bio-Behavioral Psychiatry, Great Neck, NY, USA.
Psychiatry, Medical College of Georgia, Augusta, Georgia, USA.

Behavior therapy and Clomipramine (CLI) are the treatments of choice for Obsessive-Compulsive Disorder (OCD). Because CLI, a strong serotonin (5-HT) re-uptake blocker modifies 5-HT blood levels, this investigation focused on whether behavior therapy can modify the biochemistry of OCD patients. Eight medication free patients were randomly assigned to either an experimental (Exp.) or waiting list group (C). According to the interrupted time series design of this study the Exp. group had one week of baseline, three weeks of behavioral treatment, and four weeks of follow-up while the C group was on a waiting list for four weeks, after baseline, followed by treatment. Behavior therapy significantly decreased platelet poor plasma 5-HT, and significantly increased Bmax and Kd values. Three of the eight patients improved, and although the biochemical measures varied for these patients, no correlations were found between therapeutic response and the biochemical changes. These findings suggest that behavior therapy modifies biochemical parameters in an OCD population.

39

A Unified Theory of Obsessive-Compulsive Disorder
J. A. Yaryura-Tobias, M.D.
Bio-Behavioral Psychiatry, P.C., Great Neck, N.Y., USA.

Obsessive-Compulsive Disorder is manifested by symptoms reflecting thought, motor, mood, volitional, and perceptual disturbances. Its protean symptoms suggest major pathology of the brain circuitry. Thus, its symptoms may overlap with symptoms of other disorders to configurate subsets. New insights about OCD have been provided by the serotonin (5-HT) hypothesis, and by the therapeutic efficacy of strong 5-HT reuptake blockers. Abnormal neuroimaging of the caudate nucleus, orbital gyrus, left frontal lobe, and a dysfunction of the cerebral glucose metabolism in the same region indicated brain pathology. Further findings included: unspecified EEG abnormalities, QEEG abnormal bifrontal potentials, neurological soft signs, altered evoked potentials and unspecified neuropsychological measurements. The efficacy of behavioral therapy, the cybernetic and the neuropsychiatric model of encephalitis are other aspects to consider in proposing a Unified Theory of OCD.

Session 8   Symposium:
General aspects of the history of psychiatry

40

ALOIS ALZHEIMER
Hippius M, Professor of Psychiatry, Psychiatric University Clinic and Polychinic, Munich, FRG

41

THE ANCIENT GREEK CONCEPT OF THE PSYCHE

Norman Rosenzweig, M.D.
Sinai Hospital of Detroit
Detroit, Michigan USA

The ancient Greeks had no concept of "mind" or "mental", yet they investigated such psychological phenomena as perception, thought, affects, emotional behavior and the relationship of these to the body and its functions, within the scope of their philosophical inquiries into the nature of the "soul". In fact, psychology literally means the "study of the soul" or "psyche". This presentation will examine the enquiries of the Greek philosophers into the psyche, particularly those of the great philosophers of Athens, Socrates, Plato and Aristotle, during the "golden age" of Pericles, to try to identify the relevance of their ideas to those with which we are concerned today.

42

WORLD PSYCHIATRY IN 1881

JOHN HOWELLS
FORMERLY DIRECTOR, INSTITUTE OF FAMILY PSYCHIATRY, UK

In 1881 G A TUCKER left Sydney on a world tour with the intention of visiting as many mental hospitals as possible. From his world perspective, he sought to write a report that would guide the government of New South Wales in setting up services for the mentally ill.

This report of 1564 pages was published by the government of New South Wales in 1887.

This report is comprehensive, perceptive and innovative. It is of continuing interest and some of his recommendations are yet to be implemented today. It is a vehicle that truly brings from the past what is of value to the present.

43

OTTO BINSWANGER (1852-1929) A Biographical Sketch
Charles H. Cahn, M.D.
McGill University, Montreal, Canada

Since the advent of computerized tomography scans of the brain, periventricular hypodensities "consistent with Binswanger's Disease" are being reported more frequently. Who was Binswanger?

This paper presents a biographical sketch of Otto Binswanger, a highly regarded Swiss-German neuropsychiatrist who published numerous papers on a great variety of neuropsychiatric (mostly psychiatric) subjects, including in 1894 the condition of Subcortical Arteriosclerotic Encephalopathy which is often referred to as "Binswanger's Disease".

44

HISTORY OF PSYCHIATRY IN OTTOMAN ERA AND MODERN TURKISH PSYCHIATRY
Ihsan A. Karaagac, M.D., Historian of Psychiatry, Deontologist
Washington, D.C., U.S.A
The author presents, based on authentic manuscripts and original archival documents, the roots of the history of psyhiatry in the Ottoman era and of contemporary Turkish psychiatry with specific emphasis on medical tradition and its institutions related to mental health practice and theoretical understanding. For purpose of historical analysis and evaluation, this presentation is comprised of three sections: 1) Systematic analysis of original documents as primary sources to establish the very archive of Ottoman psychiatry; 2) Descriptive outline of celebrated Ottoman era's achievements to present the legacy of islamic psychiatry vis-a-vis and within the context of clinical, scholastic and administrative objectives of Western classical psychiatry; 3) Critical review of historical records on psychiatric hospitals, mental health foundations and academic institutions to provide specific information on Islamic establishment of State policy and tradition for psychiatric humanism. By attempting a penetrating analysis of its genesis and evolution, the author submits the distinctly significant value of Islamic psychiatry within present day understanding and conceptualization of the history of science and of the medical profession to give hommage to psychiatric humanism in Islam.

Session 9 Symposium:
Psychosocial responses to disasters

45
The Volcanic Explosion in Armero, Colombia

Hernan Santacruz, Julio Lozano
University of Javeriana, Bogota, Colombia

The psychological responses to a major Latin American disaster in Armero, Colombia, 1985, were studied with a standardized screening instrument, the Self-Reporting Questionnaire (SRQ). Seven to twelve months after the Armero disaster, 200 adult victims in camps, and 100 adult patients attending primary health care clinics in the area were screened for the presence of emotional distress. A high prevalence of emotional disaster was identified for these 2 groups (55% and 45% respectively), which indicated a direct association between level of exposure and magnitude of the event. The symptom-profile of victims, the most frequent symptoms and the strongest predictors of emotional distress, however, were essentially the same.

Two and a half years after the Armero disaster, a subsample of the tent victims (40 out of 200) were re-screened with the SRQ. A higher prevalence was found (78%), but the same pattern of symptomatology was noted.

For those victims who were given a semi-structured psychiatric interview to produce DSM-III diagnoses, the most common diagnoses were post-traumatic stress disorder and major depression.

These results indicate a relationship between level of exposure, magnitude of event, and continuing psychosocial stress with prevalence of emotional distress, but the pattern of symptoms was essentially the same. The implications of these findings for the training of health workers in meeting the victims' psychosocial need are discussed.

46
The Puerto Rican Mudslides: A Prospective and Retrospective Study
Milagros Bravo, Maritza Rubio-Stipec, Glorisa Canino
University of Puerto Rico, San Juan, Puerto Rico

Disasters have long been a basic part of life and their psychological sequelae a source of intense study. Past research has produced varied and sometimes contradictory results. Since disaster are unforeseen events, most research and theory is based on cross-sectional and retrospective data, with the inherent limitations involved. In order to clarify these issues, the importance of distinguishing between substantive and methodologically-induced variations have been emphasized. The occurrence of a major disaster in Puerto Rico just a year after an island wide psychiatric epidemiology survey had been completed, enabled the study of this catastrophic event using a combined prospective and retrospective design. Through this integration, the limitations inherent to both types of studies have been accounted for, thus producing an understanding of the studied phenomenon that is greater than that obtained with any one design alone. Even after adjusting for demographic and methodologic factors, a significant disaster effect was observed: persons exposed to the disaster show higher levels of psychiatric symptoms than those not exposed. Since the study is framed in a stress theoretical perspective, its results not only contribute to enhance the understanding of the impact of disasters, but provide some insight into the stress process in general. The implications of the study findings for both disaster and stress research, as well as for methodology in psychiatric epidemiology, are discussed.

47
The Mexican Earthquakes: Acute Emotional Reactions

Jorge Caraveo, Luciana Ramos, Jorge A. Villatoro
Instituto Mexicano de Psiquiatria, Mexico, DF

Following the 1985 earthquakes in Mexico City, a representative sample of 652 victims living in shelters were studied to ascertain the severity and extent of their psychological reactions to the disaster. We used a structured psychiatric interview whose reliability was K=0.86.

The clinical data are presented for symptoms, syndromes and diagnostic categories for three periods: prevalence, incidence in remission and real incidence.

The findings indicate that tension and anxiety are the most frequent symptoms in the immediate post-disaster period; anxious-depressive states were seen about three months following the earthquakes.

The syndromes and diagnostic categories were analysed by selected variables which include sex, age, human and property losses, handling of corpses. They are compared with the DSM-III diagnostic categories of generalized anxiety disorder and major depression.

48
Meeting the Victims' Mental Health Needs

Bruno R. Lima
Johns Hopkins University, Baltimore, U.S.A.

The research conducted on the mental health consequences of three major Latin American disasters has produced important information on the type, extent and severity of psychopathology among victims. The results emphasize the need to design, implement and evaluate appropriate mental health interventions.

Proposed strategies include the involvement of both the specialized mental health sector and the general/primary health care sector. The mutually complementary roles of the specialized mental health workers and the general/primary care workers are described, a trining curriculum is discussed, and relevant policy issues are reviewed.

49

TWO EARTHQUAKES IN GREEK URBAN AREAS: PSYCHOSOCIAL CONSEQUENCES
Bergiannaki, J.D., Soldatos, C.R.
Dept. of Psychiatry, University of Athens, Eginition Hospital, Athens, Greece

The metropolitan area of Athens (more than three million inhabitants) was hit by a 6.9 R earthquake in 1981. Mainly because of the distance from the source of the tremor, damages were not extensive. However, serious biopsychosocial consequences occurred, the most prominent among them being a clear-cut increase of psychosomatic disorders. A major finding from our studies of that event was identification of the syndrome of seismophobia, namely fear of returning to intact houses two months after all tremors ceased.

Five years later, Kalamata (about 60,000 inhabitants) was severely damaged by a 6.5 R earthquake, the source of which lay underneath the city. All inhabitants were ordered to evacuate their houses and dwelled in tents for months. One year later only a few were not housed more permanently. Psychophysiological disturbances, most notably hyperarousal, persisted even one year after the disaster. Various psychobehavioral disorders were present 3-4 weeks after the event but not one year later.

50

PREVALENCE OF MENTAL DISORDERS AMONG SUBJECTS EXPOSED TO SEISMIC PHENOMENA IN NAPLES PROVINCE
F. Veltro, S. Lobrace, F. Starace, M. Maj and D. Kemali, Department of Medical Psychology and Psychiatry, First Medical School, University of Naples (Italy)

A general practice study was carried out in three areas of Naples province: a) Pozzuoli (PZ), a town affected by seismic phenomena in 1983; b) Monte Ruscello (MR), a village built to accommodate the victims of earthquake; c) Monte di Procida (MP), a town near Pozzuoli not significantly affected by seismic events and used as a control. Five GPs were randomly selected from doctors working with NHS in the above areas. Subjects over 18 who contacted these GPs between May 1987 and March 1988 were asked to fill out the General Health Questionnaire (GHQ). Probable cases (GHQ $\geq$ 5) received psychiatric interview. The real prevalence of mental disorders was found to be greater in PZ and MR than in MP. Neurotic depression was the most frequent ICD-9 diagnosis. The relative risk of psychiatric disorders in subjects with social problems (recorded using the Social Problem List by WHO) compared with those without such problems was more than four times greater in PZ and MR than in MP.

Session 10 Symposium:
The relevance of psychoanalysis for psychiatry today

51

BORDERLINE PERSONALITY DISORDERS IN AND BEYOND DSM-III
Hartocollis Peter, M.D., University of Patras, Patras - Greece

The existence of borderline patients was known to psychiatrists before the development of psychoanalysis but the understanding of borderline pathology and its treatment was, developed and adopted as a specific psychiatric entity only after the initiative and research efforts of psychoanalysts. And the angoing debate whether or how to include it as a formal psychiatric entity in either the DSM or the ICD seems to reflect the question about the relevance of psychoanalysis for psychiatry today, the theme of the present Symposium.

52

THE PSYCHODYNAMICS OF ALTERNATING COMPULSIVE AND PSYCHOTIC SYMPTOMATOLOGY
Mentzos Stavros, M.D., University Frankfurt, Frankfurt - West Germany

Obsessive-compulsive symptom formation, which precedes, follows or alternates with psychotic episodes, is not uncommon. This interesting phenomenon has not yet been sufficiently studied and understood, in spite of its probably far-reaching implications for the psychodynamics of psychosis. The investigation of the "microdynamics" of psychosis during intensive long-term psychoanalytically oriented therapy has led to the hypothesis that obsessive-compulsive symptom formation provides a defensive function against psychotic breakdown. Eventhough this hypothesis was confirmed in the course of such therapy by our term in Frankfurt, we believe that it has to be better differentiated and integrated in a comprehensive model, which will take into consideration other psychotic defenses and structural characteristics as well as biological factors. The case of a woman with two schizophrenic episodes followed by severe obsessive-compulsive symptomatology exemplifies the issue.

53

RELEVANCE OF PSYCHOANALYSIS TODAY - TREATMENT OF PERVERSIONS
Berner Wolfgang, M.D., University of Vienna, Vienna - Austria

The usage of the term perversion has changed in the last years, especially in USA. Under the heading of "Paraphilia" in DSM-III-R disturbances of sexuallity are grouped together which have in common that the enacted or phantasied sexual discharge may be against the interest of the sexual partner or may be even dangerous for this partner. This shows an important shift in the direction of bringing object-relatedness more in the scope of consideration than the biological aim of procreation. This of course influenced therapeutical aims too, and by the same token reduced therapeutic pessimism a little.
The Bieber study in 1962 showed principally that sexual behavior and attitude may be influenced by psychoanalysis, even if there are some doubts about the results of this study in the last years. A lot of publications of the last years were also concerned with female paraphilias - a phenomenon thought to be absolutely rare in previous times.

54

TREATMENT OF CHILDREN WITH PERVASIVE DEVELOPMENTAL DISORDERS
Beratis Stavroula, M.D., University of Patras, Patras - Greece

Children with pervasive developmental disorders present great difficulties for the treating therapist because of gross abnormalities in the areas of object relations, language and symbolic play. The developmental model of the psychoanalytic theory helps us on the one hand understand these children diagnostically and on the other hand intervene therapeutically with specific therapeutic plans, which take into consideration the special defects of the individual child and his developmental profile.
The therapist of such children has the feeling of working in a vacuum due to the disturbed relatedness and the poor symbolic communication. Mahler's theory on separation-individuation offers the therapist a working hypothesis, and transitional and fetishistic objects, which energe as symbolic creations in their behavioral repertoire help understand their therapeutic progress. It seems that the better organized the personality of the child the more his transitional object will be similar to those of normal children; the more disturbed the personality of the child, the more deviant the transitional object and closer to fetishistic object.

Session 11 Symposium:
Education in psychiatric rehabilitation

55

INTEGRATING RESEARCH FINDINGS
Robert Cancro, M.D.
NYU Medical Center, New York, U.S.A.
There is a striking paradox between the importance of the problem of psychiatric rehabilitation and the level of professional interest in that problem. This disparity is particularly obvious in the case of young colleagues who show little or no interest in psychiatric rehabilitation. Traditionally, young people are attracted to the important questions in their discipline. Their lack of interest reflects on the scientific naivete of much research in psychiatric rehabilitation. The approach in psychiatric rehabilitation has too often been trial and error, rather than the utilization of cutting edge developments in science. A practical approach to the resolution of this contradiction is initially to divide psychiatric rehabilitation into specific areas such as vocational, social and psychological. Each of these major areas can then be subdivided into the specific behaviors and attitudes necessary for their effective performance. Having identified specific behaviors or attitudes, one can then research the means of influencing those behaviors and attitudes. It is critical to understand that influencing the central system and regulating its activity is at the basis of all rehabilitation. This modification of central nervous system activity can be through experiential, pharmacologic, or other modes of intervention. This paper will present some of the issues involved in the implementation of a coherent program of central nervous system modification that must underlie scientifically sophisticated and, hence, professionally attractive rehabilitation strategies.

56

TEACHING ABOUT COMMUNITY FACILITIES
Wilson O. - UK

57
TEACHING SYSTEMS PLANNING
Gaston P. Harnois, M.D.
Douglas Hospital, Montreal, Canada

Human resources are the main tool of psychosocial rehabilitation. The main actors are: the patient, the family and near relatives, the mental health workers and the community. Each has needs which must be differently met; nonetheless, four goals are aimed at:
- integration of knowledge which favours multidisciplinarity
- transcending the usual areas of practice in favour of the living milieu
- putting all partners to contribution
- openness towards new problems and ideas.

The organization of services, which is most often the responsibility of governments (central, regional, and local), requires a systems approach if it is to have any chance of success.

58
HEALTH PROMOTION AND PSYCHOSOCIAL REHABILITATION
Gittelman M., College of Medicine and Dentistry of New Jersey, USA

59
STAYING CURRENT WITH THE STATE OF THE ART ON REHABILITATION
AMIEL Roger
Professeur de Psychiatrie Sociale - Université de Bruxelles et Paris

Most health and social policies are taking new paths in the field of both prevention and rehabilitation, thus supporting the trend which, epidemiologically speaking (and in terms of efficiency: cost/efficacy ratio) confirms their superiority over current psychiatric therapy. Health education becomes thus foremost amidst an upswing in the number of emotionally vulnerable individuals with a disturbing social and pathological background. In practical terms, this is an attempt to involve people - of any kind - in the efficient management of their daily lives. Further, psychosocial rehabilitation (or tertiary prevention) appears as an operational concept drawn from evidence and daily practice. If secondary prevention consists of reducing prevalence, if primary prevention consists of reducing incidence (liability) of a disease, tertiary prevention is - in a particular manner - an attempt to prevent (or reduce) the incidence of relapses and worsening of the patient's condition by using supportive therapies (ambulatory care or home care), community reinsertion (post-care clubs and halfway houses, sheltered workshops) and reemployment or vocational facilities (rehabilitation workshops). This new approach to understanding psychiatric facts - with the object of socially relocating the mental patient - leads to the concept of rehabilitation, opens out towards a community type pattern for social psychiatry and legitimates a more modern vade-mecum or state of the art

60
EDUCATION IN PSYCHIATRIC REHABILITATION DIVERSITY IN EUROPE
M.G. Madianos, M.D., M.P.H., W.A.P.R., Regional Vice President
Department of Psychiatry, Univ. of Athens, Greece

The Community mental health era and the parallel movement towards the deinstitutionalization of the long-stay mental patients from the asylums in the United States and in many European countries have developed an expansion of the knowledge on psychosocial rehabilitation issues. More than ever before the specialized training of mental health students and professionals in the techniques and methods of psychiatric rehabilitation is required. Recent literature on training programs in psychosocial rehabilitation suggests the three level design, including exposure, experience and expertise. In this respect, we will present an outline of the recent developments in some European states in training professionals to help the mentally disabled persons.
An emphasis is given in the recent psychiatric reforms in some countries and the need for specialized professionals for the community care of the discharged chronic mental patients.

61
AFRICAN PERSPECTIVES
Asuni T., Chairman, Psychiatric Hospitals Board, Federal Ministry of Health, Yaba-Lagos, Nigeria

62
EDUCATION IN PSYCHOSOCIAL REHABILITATION: WHAT IS BEING TAUGHT AND WHAT SHOULD BE
Zebulon Taintor, M.D. (USA)

This presentation proposes a model curriculum for general psychiatry programs on the following aspects that are special to rehabilitation: interviewing chronic patients, assessment of rehabilitation potential, mutability of diagnosis in relation to changes in living situation, employment and socialization, rehabilitation modalities, interaction of psychopharmacolgy and rehabilitation modalities (work, education, housing, skills for activities of daily living), psychiatrist rehabilitation in the context of treatment of team and institutional treatment, matching patients to programs, creating new programs, evaluation of scientific results of rehabilitation studies, rehabilitation research methodologies and selective experience in rehabilitation programs.

Ways of overcoming constraints on time, training requirements, facilities and other system disincentives will be discussed. Ways of getting incentives for teaching rehabilitaion will be described.

The model curriculum's relationships with other medical specialties, goals and objectives for medical students, and continuing education for psychiatrists will be discussed.

Session 12 Special Session: Psychoimmunology

63
IMMUNE FUNCTION AND IMMUNOGENETICS IN ENDOGENOUS PSYCHOSES
N. Müller, E. Hofschuster, M. Ackenheil, R. Eckstein, W. Mempel
Psychiatric Hospital of the University of Munich, Munich, FRG

HLA-Loci of the HLA-A, -B, and -C systems were analyzed in 135 healthy controls. Cluster analysis was performed in this group producing three immunogeneticly different subgroups. In 44 of the 135 controls immune function was investigated by antigen and mitogen stimulation as well as determination of the suppressor cell activity. When comparing the three immunogeneticly different groups, significant differences were found in several lymphocyte stimulation tests, i.e. in the immune function.

Furthermore, in 55 patients suffering from a schizophrenic (n = 48) or schizoaffective (n= 7) psychoses without receiving neuroleptic treatment and 37 patients suffering from an affective psychosis, both the immune functional and the HLA investigations were carried out.

It was shown that, in comparison with healthy controls, a reduced suppressor cell activity and, in some tests, an increased lymphocyte response to mitogens as well as a reduced response to antigens was found in patients with schizophrenic and affective psychoses.

When patients were compared with the three immunogeneticly different groups of healthy controls, more patients with endogenous psychoses were found to be in the group with a higher lymphocyte response to mitogens and a lower lymphocyte response to antigens. Thus, at least part of the divergencies in immune function between healthy controls and psychiatric patients can be explained by immunogenetic differences.

64
PSYCHOIMMUNOLOGIC STUDY ON LYMPHOCYTE SUBPOPULATIONS IN DEPRESSIVE PATIENTS
Wiesbeck G.A.(1), Hiendlmayer G.A.M. (1), Mueller H.A.G. (2), Taeschner K.-L. (1)

(1) Buergerhospital, Stuttgart, Germany
(2) Katharinenhospital, Stuttgart, Germany

The lymphocyte subpopulations of depressive patients were examined using monoclonal antibodies. Contrasted were a group of patients with endogenous depression and a group evincing neurotic depression. Diagnosis was made according to ICD.9.

Lymphocyte surface markers CD 4, CD 8, CD 3, CD 16, Leu-7, CD 19, and CD 45r were used. The count was done with a cytometric analyzer with a fluorescence-activated cell sorter (FAC Star Plus / Becton Dickinson).

Parallel to this, the Hamilton Scale was used to establish a depression score for both groups.

Under the same examination and therapy conditions, some lymphocyte subpopulations in the patient group with endogenous depression statistically differed significantly from those in the comparable patients with neurotic depression.

65

REDUCED CELLULAR IMMUNE FUNCTION IN PRIMARY DEPRESSION AND IN MANIA

Z.Rihmer, J.Barsi, M.Arató and J.Lajos

Natl.Inst.Nerv.Ment.Dis., Budapest 27, Pf. 1. 1281 Hungary

The authors investigated the cellular immunity as reflected in antibody dependent cellular cytotoxicity (ADCC) against red blood cells in 22 consecutively admitted, physically healthy, nonalcoholic inpatients with DSM-III diagnoses of primary major depression (N=11) and mania (N=11), aged between 20 - 60 years (mean: 44,0 years). All patients received low or medium dose of psychotropics.

The mean $\pm$ SD ADCC activity of depressed patients ($36,3 \pm 24,1$) and of manic patients ($46,1 \pm 28,1$) was significantly lower than the same value of the 20 healthy, drug and alcohol free controls of similar age ($68,0 \pm 11,4$, $p < 0,001$ and $p < 0,01$ respectively).

Further analysis showed that this reduced cellular immunity was not the result of the psychotropic medication.

Our findings support earlier results on decreased cellular immune function in primary major depression and in manic phase of bipolar affective disorder.

66

DEPRESSION AND THYROID AUTOIMMUNITY - Experience with Brofaromine.

R. Winand*, A. Gerebtzoff**, M. Eerdekens***

* Institut de Pathologie CHU, Bât. B23, B-4000 Sart-Tilman par Liège 1, Belgium
** Clinical Research and Development, Ciba-Geigy Ltd, Basle, Switzerland
***Ciba-Geigy SA, B - 1720 Groot-Bijgaarden, Belgium

Brofaromine is a new selective and reversible MAOI-A antidepressant. Its safety with regard to human thyroid function has been assessed in-vitro and in-vivo. The compound has no measurable cytotoxic activity in in-vitro experiments. Within the frame of a double-blind clinical trial with brofaromine and phenelzine (a classical MAOI), circulating antithyroid antibodies and thyroid hormone levels were measured in a group of 120 patients before and during treatment. No significant modifications in the thyroid hormone levels were observed either before or after treatment with brofaromine or phenelzine with the exception of one patient with moderate assymptomatic hyperthyroidism at inclusion in the trial. With respect to the thyroid autoimmunity, in an unexpected high proportion of untreated depressed patients (13.3%), pathological antithyroid antibody titers were measured. This titer decreased in some patients treated with brofaromine. Neither brofaromine nor phenelzine induced an increase in antithyroid antibody titers in patients without pathological antibody titers at the start of the trial.

67

The relation between disorders in the immune apparatus and in the HPA-axis during a depressive episode.

M.Maes, E.Bosmans, E.Suy.
Psychiatric Centre, Munsterbilzen, Belgium.

To investigate the relations between the immune apparatus and the hypothalamic-pituitary-adrenal (HPA)-axis function during a depressive period, the authors measured the following : the lymphocyte transformations after stimulation with the mitogens phytohemaglutenin (PHA), pokeweed mitogen (PWM) and concavalin A (CON A), the postdexamethasone cortisol and β-endorphin values, 8 a.m. baseline cortisol values and urinary free cortisol excretion (UFC) in 24 hr urine. We found that the lymphoproliferative capacity to PHA, PWM and CON A was significantly decreased in severely depressed patients. The lymphocyte responses to the three mitogens were significantly inversely related to the 8 a.m. basal cortisol, postdexamethasone cortisol and β-endorphin values. The mitogen-induced lymphocyte blastogenic transformation was positively related to UFC excretion. Up to 45 % of the variance in the immune responses was explained by these HPA-axis variables.

68

PSYCHOIMMUNOLOGICAL RESPONSE TO STRESS AND ANXIETY

G.F. Marchesi, P. Cotani, G. Santone
C. Bartocci*, M. Montroni*

Institute of Pychiatry and *Institute of Internal Medicine, University of Ancona (Italy)

The effect of an academic stressor on lymphocytic and psychological profiles was evaluated in 41 university students. Such an evaluation was done in two phases: on the day of stressor (phase 1) and after a time interval of 5-22 days with no stressor (phase 2). In phase 1, 15 subjects showed a statistically significant reduction of all lymphocytes and of most lymphocytic subsets. Furthermore, these 15 subjects (group 1), using the Anxiety Scale Questionnaire (ASQ-IPAT) and the State-Trait Anxiety Inventory (STAI), presented a higher anxiety mean level with respect to the other students (group 2). On the other hand, all personality tests were within the limits of the norm in all subjects.

In phase 2, the results obtained with ASQ-IPAT and STAI did not show any statistically significant difference between group 1 and 2.

In conclusion, such results permit one to hypothesize the presence of an individual threshold concerning a reversible psychoimmunologic response to the psychic stress, that is in relation to higher levels of anxiety.

69
LYTIC EFFECTOR CELL FUNCTION IN IUVENILE AND ADULT SCHIZOPHRENICS

F. Resch*, E. Pawlik**, Th. Stompe**, G. Schönbeck**, A. Oppolzer*, H. Aschauer**, C. Müller+, C. Zielinsky+

* Department of Child and Adolescent Neuropsychiatry, Vienna, Austria
**Department of Psychiatry, Vienna
+ II.Department of Medicine, Vienna

Natural killer cell activity (NK) and antibody dependant cellmediated cytotoxicity (ADCC) have been examined for detection of lytic effector cell function.
Following the hypothesis that schizophrenics show altered NK activity a comparison of both schizophrenic groups versus matched normal controls will be made. 20 iuvenile and 30 adult schizophrenics have been included. Attention especially was focused on elucidating possible differential influences of psychopathological variables and psychopharmacological drugs on lytic effector cell function with the help of an intraindividual design.
Recent results of this ongoing study will be presented.

70
FACTORS RELATED TO THE PRESENCE OF AUTOANTIBODIES IN MENTAL DISORDERS

Stavroula Yannitsi, MN Manoussakis, AK Mavridis, AG Tzioufas, SB Loukas, GK Plataris, AD Liakos, HM Moutsopoulos. Depts of Psychiatry and Internal Medicine, University of Ioannina, Greece.

Serum samples from 307 hospitalized patients with various mental disorders (DSMIII criteria) were examined for the presence of several autoantibodies. Autoantibody profile included anti-nuclear antibodies (ANA, by indirect immunofluorescence technique, positive titer$\geq$1:80), rheumatoid factor (RF, by latex fixation test, positive titer$\geq$1:40), anti-cardiolipin antibodies (anti-CL, by ELISA method). In addition, isolated cases of antibodies to double-stranded DNA (anti-dsDNA, by ELISA) and Ro(SSA) and La(SSB) ribonucleoproteins (by counterimmunoelectrophoresis) were also evaluated. ANA were found in 39.7%(122/307) of patients, RF in 7.5%(23/307) and anti-CL in 7.6% (23/304, IgM in 12 and IgG in 13 patients).
The analysis of data revealed that the incidence of ANA and RF was closely related with the ageing process ($P<0.0001$ and $P<0.01$ respectively). In addition, the chronic administration of chlorpromazine was associated with the presence of ANA ($P<0.03$) as well as with the presence of IgM and/or IgG anti-CL antibodies ($P<0.003$). Finally, the diagnosis of Schizophrenia correlated with the presence of ANA ($P<0.001$). This study emphasizes the multi-factorial origin of autoantibody response in psychiatric patients.

71
CSF BETA-ENDORPHIN-LIKE IMMUNOREACTIVITY (CSF BLI) IN DELIRIUM

** Koponen H, MD; ** Kajander-Koponen A, MD;
* Riekkinen PJ, MD, prof. Departments of Neurology * and Psychiatry **, Kuopio University Central Hospital, Kuopio, Finland.

Experimental and clinical data provide evidence that dysfunction of the neurons containing beta-endorphin is associated with diseases in which motor, affective, and cognitive functions are disturbed. As these neuropsychiatric disturbances are also seen in delirium, we assayed CSF BLI in elderly patients (mean age $\pm$ S.D. $74,8 \pm 6,4$ years) meeting the DSM-III criteria for delirium (N=69) and in age-equivalent controls (N=19). The triggering factors for delirium were heterogeneous as patients with alcohol delirium were excluded, the most common etiologies were stroke, infections and metabolic disorders.
The CSF BLI was reduced in delirious patients as compared with controls (mean $\pm$ S.D. BLI $12,5 \pm 3,9$ pg/ml versus $15,2 \pm 2,8$ pg/ml; reduction 17 %; $p<0,001$). There was also a decreasing trend in the CSF BLI connected with declining cognitive ability, and a positive correlation was found between CSF BLI and Mini-Mental State Examination score in delirious patients ($r=.29$; $p<0,001$).
Our results suggest a modest disturbance of function or metabolism of the beta-endorphinergic neurons in elderly patients with acute delirium due to various causes, which dysfunction may play a role in the genesis of delirium.

72
PATHWAYS OF BRAIN-IMMUNE INTERACTIONS AND THEIR RELEVANCE IN AGING.
N. Fabris
Immunology Ctr., Gerontol. Res. Dept., INRCA,

Via Birarelli 8, Ancona, Italy.

It is now accepted that physiological interactions link the brain and the immune system and that such interactions involve at least two different levels: one more "central" based on hypothalamus-pituitary-thymus axis with major impact on differentiative processes and one more "peripheral", based on nervous system-lymphocyte interaction, primarely dealing with anti-stress adaptive responses.
Behavioural components may either influence or be influenced by these neuro-immune relationships at both levels of interaction. Experimental findings on social and emotional stressors as well as clinical observation will be reported to support this view. Both thymic hormones and lymphocyte-derived lympokines and cytokines seem to be involved in such complex interrelationship.
Recent data have suggested that disruption of such brain-immune interactions may represent a relevant component of the aging process and may, better than other systemic theories of aging,explain a number of age-related phenomena.

Session 13 Special Session:
Psychosocial factors on development of children and adolescents

73
ADOLESCENTS' RESPONSES TO DAILY STRESSES
Dr. Inge Schamborzki, Vancouver General Hospital, Vancouver, Canada.

This study describes and analyzes within the cognitive-phenomenological theory of psychological stress developed by Lazarus and his colleagues the coping strategies used by 95 9th-grade adolescents in specific stressful events in their daily lives.

Four research instruments were administered three times at five- to six-week intervals: (1) the Semi-Structured Interview Schedule; (2) the Ways of Coping Checklist; (3) the Daily Hassles and Uplifts Scales; and (4) the Hopkins Symptoms Checklist.

Results of the study indicate the most frequently reported hassles and uplifts are consistent with the age and developmental level of this sample. The concerns are primarily frequent, chronic minor events associated with activities of daily living. Hassles and uplifts were positively correlated with each other, as well as with symptomatology and coping strategies. Coping strategies were positively related to symptomatology. Female adolescents reported higher levels of uplifts intensity, more coping strategies, and higher levels of symptomatology than male adolescents. Although significantly fewer coping strategies were reported over time, both problem-solving and emotion-regulating strategies were used in the majority of stressful events. Significant differences in levels of symptomatology appeared as a function of the language-group to which subjects belonged.

74
MENTAL HEALTH, PARENT/CHILD RELATIONSHIPS, SELF-CONCEPT AND COPING
A. Vaz-Serra and Horacio Firmino
Psychiatric Department-University Hospital
3049 COIMBRA CODEX - PORTUGAL

This work considers mental health as the final product of the influence of many variables, among of them are the previous parent/child relationships, the emotional and social developed self-concept and coping strategies. MH=f(p/c,self concept,coping,etc.).
The authors compared (100) patients with emotional disorders with 200 people of the general population, without psychological disturbances.
For the measurement of the variables the following instruments were used:
- SCL90: for mental health.
- QRPE(Bastin and Delrez) for the parent/child relationships.
- CISC (Clinical Inventory of Self-Concept Vaz-Serra,1985), for self-concept.
- PRI (Problems Resolution Inventory,Vaz Serra, 1987)for the measurement of coping strategies.
The obtained results comproved a clear relationship among these variables.Strategies of coping revealed to be the best predictor of mental health.
Comparing the group of patients with "normal" people they had a poor home atmosphere, poor relationships with parents, a worse self-concept and coping strategies and, of course, a worse mental health.

75
LIFE EVENTS AND ACUTE AND CHRONIC CHILD PSYCHIATRIC DISORDERS
Canalda, G., Toro, J., Vallès, A., Mena, A. and Martinez, E.
Department of Psychiatry, School of Medicine, University of Barcelona, Spain

The aim of this study was to assess the role of life events on the onset of children's psychiatric disorders. Using a Children's Life Events Scale (Canalda, 1988) three groups of children were compared: 1)acute psychiatric (N=53), 2)chronic psychiatric (N=112), and 3)healthy children (N=166), all aged 3-12 years.The main groups were compared by three age levels (3-5, 6-9, 10-12yr.) and by four clinical categories (emotional, behavioural, learning, and psychobiological disorder) Results showed that children with acute psychiatric disorders had significantly more life events, in the year prior onset of the disorder,than did the children with chronic psychiatric disorders and the healthy children, during the year before interview. However children with chronic psychiatric disorders differed also from the healthy children. The results were similar in all age levels. When life events were compared among the four clinical categories only small differences emerged. We concluded that life events can contribute to precipitate and/or maintain psychiatric disorders in children. The effects of life events seems to be rather unspecific.

76
EN THEME DE PSYCHOPATHOLOGIE DES ENFANTS DE COUPLE DIVORCEES

GENTILI M.C. STELLA S.
UNIVERSITE' DE FERRARA-CHAIRE DE PSYCHIATRIE-DIR. PROF. RAMELLI E.-FERRARA-ITALIE

Au 1971, lorsque David Cooper publia son travail "The death of the family", un frisson parcourut l'âme de nous tous. Le noyeau constitutif de "n'importe quelle société" avait été attaché de façon clastique et définitive. Ca entraînait l'espoir d'une libération des liens mortifiants et inhibiteurs qui agissent dans toutes les structures sociale reproduisantes le modèle familiale "qui vise à créer normalité et conformisme". L'issue de "la condition familiale" ne pouvait être, depuis lors, que "la folie ou la révolte". L'histoire n'a pas marqué les changements radicaux souhaités par Cooper, au contraire, il y a beaucoup de signaux qui, sous l'aspect sociologique, nous indiquent une découverte en clé positive de l'institution familiale. Toutefois, la famille n'a plus été la strucure intouchable qui c'était auparavant. Après l'introduction en Italie aussi de l'institution du divorce, beaucoup de familles se sont séparées juridiquement. Le but de notre contribution est d'évaluer, avec l'apport d'études personnels, les répercussions d'ordre psychologique et psychopathologique qui se manifestent dans les enfants des couples qui ont conclus par la séparation ou le divorce une condition, souvent assez longue, de crise. Les éléments que nous avons recueillis nous indiquent une prévalence de désordres caracteropathiques et de formes dépressive.

77

SOCIO-PSYCHOLOGICAL CORRELATES OF
JUVENILE DELINQUENT BEHAVIOUR
N.Chakraborty, M.D., D.P.M., Professor &
Head of Psychiatry, N.R.S.Medical College
& Hospital, Calcutta,
M.M.Paik, M.Sc. Ph.D. Psychologist

The present investigation aims at unravelling some of the external socio-cultural variables, early socialising experiences and family relationship of children adjudicated for major or minor transgressions. The demographic features, intellectual level, antecedent events and family background of seventy juvenile delinquent children are compared with those in a control group of seventy matched normal juveniles. Socio-biographical particulars were assessed by using modified Andry's Biographical questionnaire. The delinquent group was found to be significantly associated with lower class families, their homes being marked by parental disharmony and they experienced their 'mother' as the major care-giving and protecting figure; no significant differences were found between the two groups in relation to intellectual level. The delinquent group reported significantly, higher levels of emotional unstability, resentment towards parental punishment and aggresive reactions to stress.
Interaction of many sociological factors thus may be related to a propensity for delinquent behaviour but no particular aspect of intellectual functioning seems to be related to above.

78

TRANSETHNIC ADOPTION AND PERSONALITY TRAITS:
JAPANESE ORPHANS RAISED IN CHINA
Keisuke Ebata (Matsuzawa Hospital, Tokyo),
Wen-Shing Tseng (University of Hawaii), Masahiro
Miguchi (Psychiatric Research Institute of Tokyo)

It was estimated that more than two thousand five hundred children were left as orphans in China at the end of the World War II who were adopted and raised by the Chinese foster parents. Recently, these orphaned Japanese began to return to Japan after more than forty years in China. We interviewed twenty five orphaned Japanese and their Chinese spouses shortly after their return to Japan.
It was found that, despite the fact that all the couple wear Chinese dress, we could distinguish the Japanese partner from the Chinese partner at the level of 80-90 percent, when a simple conversation was carried out as greeting. It was usually found that, in contrast to the Chinese partner, the Japanese partner tended to demonstrate more politeness, orderliness and seriousness in their body expression.
All the Chinese spouses were asked, whether they have noticed any personal characteristic of their Japanese spouses which were different from other Chinese adults of the same gender. Twenty one out of twenty five pairs of spouses (84%) replied positively.

79

ADOLESCENCE AND DELINQUENCY: A PSYCHOSOCIAL STUDY

AGUILAR,R., IGLESIAS,L. & TAPIA,E.
UNIDAD DE PSIQUIATRIA,CONSEJO TUTELAR PARA MENORES
MONTERREY,N,L.,MEXICO

Se informan los resultados preliminares de un estudio prospectivo,transversal y descriptivo desarrollado en una muestra de 200 adolescentes delincuentes detenidos en el Consejo Tutelar para Menores del Estado de Nuevo León,México,durante 1988.Se - destaca la participación interdisciplinaria profesional,que utilizando la técnica de análisis de casos en conjunto,permitió la confrontación de registros y observaciones importantes para la confiabilidad de los datos obtenidos. La evaluación - Psicológica se complementó con la aplicación de exámenes Psicométricos,que incluyeron el Test de Szondi,el Bender,el DAP, y el HIP. Para propósitos de clasificación de los Trastornos de Conducta se utilizaron las categorías diagnósticas del — DSM-III-R (Ejes I y II). Los hallazgos obtenidos revelan un alto índice de antecedentes de Trastornos Neuróticos,Trastornos Escolares,problemas del desarrollo Psicosexual y un curso de evolución en familias con desintegración, promiscuidad,hacinamiento,con baja escolaridad de los padres y de nivel socio-económico marginal bajo. Destaca un estado mental con déficit de inteligencia,trastornos en los contenidos conceptuales del pensamiento,deficiente autocrítica,trastornos - afectivos;predominando rasgos psicopatológicos en sus dinamismos de Personalidad,con alteraciones francas en sus funciones sociales. Los resultados permiten establecer un perfil clínico y psicosocial,imprescindible en la planeación de modelos de - atención integral en adolescentes delincuentes y establecer un marco de referencia para el diseño de investigaciones trans— culturales,en este fenómeno universal y polifacético,propio de nuestras sociedades contemporáneas.

80

Change of Residency: Its Perception by Children
(and their Parents)
Gisela Gerber
Interfakultäres Institut für Sonder- und Heilpädagogik der Universität Wien und Univ.Klinik für Neuropsychiatrie des Kindes- u. Jugendalters Wien

How do young children and adolescents react to re-locations, and which psychological manifestations accompany these experiences? These questions were persued in a study of 361 boys and girls (9-13 years old) from international schools in Vienna and middle- and upperclass-families which are frequently engaged in changes of residence. Almost half of the boys and girls in the sample had been in Vienna for no longer than one or two years. Three-fourth of the children had lived in Vienna for less than five years. There also was a control-group of children which had their permanent residence in Vienna. Both groups were psychologically tested with several items in a questionnaire, drawings, Wartegg tests, a relocation scene etc. The results were ordered in negative experience categories such as "loss", "fear", "uncertainty", and positive categories such as "expectation", "gain","escape to the future", "happiness" etc. The children's compositions yielded almost twice as many arguments against as for a move. Two of three children, almost 64% of the mobile group, were decidedly opposed to a new move. Many of the children who favoured a new move were for a return to the last place of residence where they had felt happy.Of the children permanently resident in Vienna about 75% were opposed to a move. Even a change of residence from one district to another, from one street to another, was viewed as problematic.

81
SYMBOLIC MECHANISMS OF SOCIALIZATION IN THE CHILD

ZERVIS Christos
Hôpital Maison Blanche
8ème section
3, av. Jean jaurès
93330 Neuilly sur Marne, FRANCE

Ce travail établit l'influence de l'entourage sur l'enfant, pour structurer, symboliquement, son idéation et son comportement. L'identité, que l'enfant se forme à travers cette action régulatrice de son monde environnant, que ça soit la mère ou le contexte socio-familial plus large, lui permet d'intégrer son psychisme, qui est, originairement, sans forme En même temps, cette identité est imprégnée par un symbolisme social qui permet à l'enfant de s'inscrire comme membre d'une société.
Cette élaboration, à partir d'un matériel clinique, s'appuie sur les travaux de Freud, Klein, Lacan et Piaget.

Session 14 Special Session:
The family of the schizophrenic patient

82
EXPRESSED EMOTION: CAUSE OR RESULT?

Müller, P.:
Psychiatric clinic, university of Göttingen/Fed.Rep.Germany

Correlations with schizophrenia, bipolar affective disorder and neuroses:
A specific and one-sided causality between the behaviour of relatives and the course of illnes of a patient could not be confirmed. A Camberwell Family Interview was conducted and doubly rated in 42 relatives from schizophrenic patients and 43 relatives from a control group (patients with affective psychoses and neuroses). The EE (expressed emotion) score identified no differences between the two groups. However, high EE did correlate with some negative predictors and symptoms during the previous course of illness.
Therefore, it is apparent, that high EE is rather a result than a cause of unfavourable course of illness with subsequent stress and reaction of relatives.

83
SCHIZOPHRENIA : EE AND FACTORS INFLUENCING FIRST YEAR EVOLUTION.

BARRELET L.F., Szigethy L., Ferrero F., De Saussure N. Institutions Universitaires de Psychiatrie. Genève. Service de Psychiatrie II. Chemin du Petit-Bel-Air 8. Genève. Switzerland.

Factors influencing the short-term follow-up of first hospitalized schizophrenic patients treated in modern psychiatric settings are still difficult to understand. Family Expressed Emotion (EE) has been claimed to be one of the best predictors of evolution.
In a previous paper (BARRELET L. et al. Expressed Emotion and First-admission Schizophrenia : a replication in a Swiss-French cultural environment. British Journal of Psychiatry. 1989), follow-up after a 9 month post-discharge period confirmed results predicted by family EE for a cohort of first-time hospitalized schizophrenic patients in a Swiss-French cultural context. By measuring various follow-up and treatment events, the validity of this relation is reassessed for the one year postinclusion period and compared with various predictive variables.

84
EXPRESSED EMOTION IN FAMILIES OF CHRONIC SCHIZOPHRENICS AND ITS ASSOCIATION WITH CLINICAL MEASURES
V. Mavreas, V. Tomaras, V. Carydi, M. Economou, I. Ioannovich, C. N. Stefanis.
Univ. of Athens, Dept. of Psychiatry Eginition Hospital

A controlled clinical study on the outcome of family intervention in chronic schizophrenics is being carried out in Athens. All subjects reside with their families and attend a rehabilitation unit. Those belonging to high EE households are randomly assigned into either the experimental or the control condition. The former receive family intervention combined with individual treatment the latter receiving individual treatment alone. 75 subjects have entered the study and 121 key-relatives of them were interviewed at baseline with the Camberwell Family Interview. 40 patients (53,3%) were found to belong to high EE families. It was found that the EE status of the family was significantly associated with measures of psychopathology and functioning (BPRS,GAS,DAS, number of residual symptoms). Further analysis revealed that these associations exist only when all key-relatives express high EE. The implications of these findings are discussed.

85

FAMILY ENVIRONMENT AND COURSE OF SCHIZOPHRENIA

N.Manos M.D, A.Karastergiou M.D, G.Garyphallos M.D, G.Liappa M.A, E.Vasilopoulou M.A, A.Papadopoulou R.N, Th.Kapsala R.N, A.Linara R.N.

CMHC - 2nd University Dept of Psychiatry, Thessaloniki, Greece.

The influence of the family environment on the course of schizophrenia is studied on DSM-III-R diagnosed schizophrenic patients at baseline (within a month post discharge) and one year later. A multidimensional assessment battery is used covering the areas of family environment, social adjustment and psychopathology (including FES, MMPI, BPRS, PARS VI, GAF, etc) and a number of parameters are investigated as possible predictors of the course of schizophrenia. Both the family's and the patient's measurements are taken into account. This paper reports on data gathered from the first 25 schizophrenic patients who were evaluated at baseline. Certain family environment variables (such as expressiveness, cohesion and incongruence) proved to predict significantly the patient's clinical status and adjustment at baseline as well as his previous hospitalization record.

86

BOUNDARY DISTURBANCES IN FAMILIES OF A PSYCHOTIC FAMILY MEMBER

Peter Joraschky
Psychiatry Division, University of Erlangen-Nuremberg

The significance of boundary disturbances in regard to schizophrenic psychosis has been pointed out repeatedly in psychoanalytic and psychiatric literature. Our projekt contrasts boundary disturbances within a person with boundary disturbances within a famliy. In order to measure the boundary disturbances we developed a multi-dimensional assessment instrument. We measure them on three levels: individual, interactional (dyadic) and systemic level.

1.) In the validity study we examined 15 nonclinical families, 20 families with a psychotic adolescent member, and 20 families with a neurotic adolescent member. The families were examined on the macroanalytic level with an assessment instrument. The results were subsequently validated on the microanalytic level using the Consensus Rorschach and a sculpture method. There were significant differences between the "normal" and clinical groups on both analytic levels.
2.) In a follow up study we compared families whose adolescents had negative outcomes with those who had less negative outcomes. The magnitude of boundary disturbance proved here to be a significant predictor for the progression of illness. On the one hand we can confirm the results of EE-experimental studies. On the other hand we emphasize the necessity for more differentiated and theoretically based EE-measures.

87

CHANGES OF SOCIAL PERCEPTION DURING FAMILY THERAPY OF YOUNG SCHIZOPHRENICS
M.C.G. Merlo, H. Schwalbach, Psychiatric University Clinic, Bern (Switzerland)

During systemic family therapy of young schizophrenics changes in the perception of relationships and of family environment are investigated in a prospective study. The interpersonal perceptions are assessed with the SYMLOG-method. SYMLOG is an acronym for SYstematic, Multiple Level, Observation of Groups. It was developed by BALES and colleagues as a new field theory for studying relationships in small groups and families. The changes of perception of relevant aspects of family life are rated by a shortened form of FES (Family Environment Scale) of MOOS. Greater convergence of social perception seems to be related to less stressful commitments inside the family and to foster the healing processes in the postacute phase of schizophrenia. The data are analysed statistically between the groups of family members and correlations are computed to psychopathology and social adaptation of the index patient. 9 of 12 families could be rated for the second time after 1 year of therapy.

88

A FAMILY WITH SEVEN SCHIZOPHRENIC OFFSPRING

Mantonakis J.,Liakos A.,Kyriazis D.,Eftichidis L., Stefanis C.
Department of Psychiatry,University of Athens,Eginition Hospital,Athens,Greece.

A family with seven children,all of them suffering from schizophrenia,is described.The mother of these patients was suffering from recurrent major depression and the father has been characterized as a paranoid personality.Four out of eight children of the mother's half sister exhibited psychological symptoms.In addition,a high prevalence of personality disorders and alcoholism in the parental family is noted.The study includes the family tree for two generations with 66 members, 31 male and 35 female.The total phychiatric morbidity in these two generations comes to 24% (16 out of 66).An investigation of the social,environmental and family relationships has also been carried out.
The family belongs to a social class of peasants which has been rated as the lowest in the Greek community.The members of this family exhibit poor social and sexual adjustment.The presence of pathological patterns of communication described in literature as possible causative factors of schizophrenia could not be thoroughly assessed since our approach was mainly clinical. The investigation and follow-up of the family extended 3 years.The exceptionally high prevalence of schizophrenia in the offspring of this family seems to be unique in literature.

89

The relatives of psychiatric patients and their relations to psychiatric care
Margareta Axelsson, BA, County Council of Västmanland, Västerås, Sweden

In connection with a changed psychiatry the situation of the relatives is seldom observed. The great importance that the relatives have to their patients in psychiatry is shown in this study, in which 155 relatives of both committed patients and voluntarily admitted patients have been interviewed at two different occasions.

The mental patients need of care, committed care included, is confirmed by the relatives. The relatives' own situation is greatly influenced by the mental patient. By supporting the patient the relatives have to give up normal activities of their own. In our study we found that a great deal of the relatives had own serious problems of psychological character. A lot of the relatives continously live with an anxiety for the patient committing suicide. On the other hand they are seldom offered to take part in the treatment planning of psychiatry and they do not experience the acceptance of being an important resource to the mental patient. The research clearly points out the importance of giving support to the relatives and of being actively implicated and accepted as important resources in the treatment of the patients.

Session 15 Symposium:
Long-term treatment of panic and agoraphobia

90

The Role of Drug Treatment: Tricyclic Antidepressants
Liebowitz, M. R., Fyer, A. J., Klein, D. F.

Numerous controlled studies testify to the efficacy of TCA's in the treatment of panic disorder (PD) or panic disorder with agoraphobia (PDA). A number of important questions, however, have received less attention, including the following: (1) What is the incidence of relapse following discontinuation of long-term TCA therapy? (2) How long do the beneficial effects of TCA therapy persist after medication discontinuation?

The results of two studies will be reported. In the first, patients with PD or PDA were randomized to either alprazolam or imipramine, treated openly until they were at least six months on medication and four weeks panic free, then discontinued following a fixed schedule. In the second experiment, patients with PD or PDA who panicked to sodium lactate were treated openly with a TCA. Responders were maintained on medication until panic free for at least six months. They were then tapered off TCA and rechallenged with sodium lactate one to six months later while still clinically panic free to examine reemergence of susceptibility to lactate induced panic.

91

BEHAVIORAL AND COGNITIVE TREATMENTS FOR PANIC AND AGORAPHOBIA
Iver Hand, M.D.
Psychiatric University Hospital

The psychological "treatment of choice" for agoraphobics with and without panic attacks is exposure-in-vivo with response management (ERM). For panic without situational avoidance ERM appears to be equally suitable, but Cognitive Behavior Therapy (CBT) has become the more popular treatment. Main conceptual differences between ERM and CBT are outlined.

Results of 10 international follow-up studies with agoraphobics after exposure treatment, and a long term responder/non-responder analysis of some 200 agoraphobics treated in the author's unit, are summarized. Follow-up results of exposure with agoraphobics are compared to those of some 400 other patients with anxiety disorders (simple and social phobia, OCD) with and without panic, also treated in the author's unit.

The relative importance of behavioral, cognitive and pharmacological interventions in agoraphobia and panic is assessed according to the empirical evidence of their effectiveness.

92

PANIC DISORDER AND QUALITY OF LIFE

Myrna M. Weissman, Ph.D.
College of Physicians & Surgeons of Columbia University

Data from the Epidemiologic Catchment Area (ECA), a probability sample of over 18,000 adults living in five U.S. communities, are presented. The data shows that a lifetime DIS/DSM-III diagnosis of panic disorder is associated with pervasive social and health consequences similar to or greater than those associated with major depression. These consequences include subjective feelings of poor physical and emotional health, alcohol and drug abuse, increased likelihood of suicide attempts, impaired marital functioning, financial dependency, increased use of psychoactive medications, health services, and the hospital emergency room for emotional problems.

The social and health consequences of panic disorder will be discussed in light of currently available acute and maintenance treatments.

93

LONG-TERM TREATMENT OF PANIC AND AGORAPHOBIA

Gerald L. Klerman, M.D.
Cornell University Medical College

Much recent research has focused on the treatment of acute symptoms of panic disorder by pharmacologic or psychological means. A number of different drugs and psychological techniques have been demonstrated effective in reducing symptoms and promoting social adjustment over four - ten-week period. The focus of activity now shifts to long-term treatment. In this respect, the field of panic disorder and anxiety disorders is in a similar state to the field of depression 20 years ago when short-term improvement was demonstrated with tricyclics and other drugs. Long-term treatment aimed at preventing relapse and recurrence became a major focus with considerable success. This symposium will explore some of the issues involved in the long-term treatment including the natural history of the disorder and quality of life. The role of pharmacologic treatments with tricyclics and benzodiazepines will be reviewed. The evidence for the long-term efficacy of behavioral treatments will be summarized. Implications for further clinical and research activities will be discussed.

94

THE NATURAL HISTORY OF PANIC AND AGORAPHOBIC DISORDERS

Professor Sir Martin Roth
University of Cambridge

The concept of panic disorder has generated a large volume of fruitful scientific and clinical investigations. It is frequently associated with the agoraphobic syndrome. But recent investigations have shown that patients who fulfill criteria for panic disorder also include a substantial group of subjects with social and other phobias, major and other forms of depression and obsessive compulsive disorder. Personality diagnosis of an Axis 2 disorder can also be made in a high proportion of patients.

A substantial proportion of panic disorder-agoraphobic patients continue to suffer symptoms following all forms of treatment. The lifetime history of the personality setting and the evolution of phobic tendency suggests lines along which the problem of chronicity could be further investigated and improved methods of management that commence at an early phase of disorder instituted.

95

LONG TERM TREATMENT OF PANIC AND AGORAPHOBIA WITH BENZODIAZEPINES

Juan Ramon de la Fuente, M.D.
National Autonomous University of Mexico

The optimal duration of treatment of panic and agoraphobia remains to be established. With benzodiazepines (BZD) when used appropriately, there is a significant reduction in panic attacks and phobic symptoms but a high proportion of patients will experience symptom recurrence if medication is stopped after acute treatment (6-8 weeks). On the other hand, dependence and the development of a withdrawal syndrome upon drug discontinuation have been shown to occur with long-term BZD use. Withdrawal has also been reported after abrupt cessation of low-dose short-term treatment.

To complicate things further, it is not always easy to differentiate clinically between withdrawal symptoms, rebound anxiety and relapse of illness. To clarify some of these issues, evidence from clinical experience, randomized controlled trials and cross-national surveys will be reviewed for its implications for current clinical practice.

Session 16 Symposium:
Suicide and schizophrenia

96

SUICIDE AMONG SCHIZOPHRENICS
A. Roy
National Institutes of Health
Bethesda, M.D., U.S.A.

Suicidal behavior among schizophrenic patients is a major public health problem. For example, it is estimated that up to 10 percent of schizophrenics end their lives by committing suicide. Studies of schizophrenic suicide victims have indicated some risk factors for suicide among schizophrenic patients. These include being male, early onset of schizophrenic illness, depression, treatment for depression, having an admission for depression or suicidal ideation, the post-discharge period, social isolation, frequent admissions, unemployment, hopelessness, and past suicidal behavior. Most suicides occur during the first few years of schizophrenic illness. The data from the relevant studies will be presented. The difficulty of long term prediction will be discussed as well the possible implications for the prevention of suicidal behavior among schizophrenic patients.

97

Depression, Hopelessness & Suicidality in Schizophrenia: The Neglected Impact of Substance Abuse
Stpehn J. Bartes, M.D., & Robert E. Drake, M.D., Ph.D.
Dartmouth Medical School, Hanover, New Hampshire, U.S.A.

Although approximately one half of schizophrenic patients in the community actively abuse substances, studies of depression and suicidality in schizophrenia have generally ignored the potential impact of substance abuse. We will discuss the relationships among substance abuse, depression, hopelessness, and suicidality in three separate samples; an urban sample of 104 inpatient schizophrenics, an urban sample of 115 outpatient schizophrenics, and a rural sample of 79 schizophrenics. Substance abuse was strongly related to dysphoria and depression, and patients reported that alcohol affected these symptoms. Depression and hopelessness were in turn strongly related to suicidal ideation and behavior. However, substance abuse and suicidality were unrelated in two samples and only minimally related in the third. We will discuss the similarities and differences between these two relatively separable subgroups of depressed schizophrenic treatment of sysphoric syndromes in schizophrenia.

98

Phenomenological Analysis of Suicidal & Non-suicidal Schizophrenics
A.J. Prasad* P. Kellner, N. Kumar
*Valley Health Services Association, Dalhousie University & St. Mary's University, Nova Scotia, Nova Scotia

Suicidality is a major problem in the clinical management of schizophrenic population. The problem has been all the more acute as there are few reliable predictors of suicidality in these subjects.

A psychopathological analysis of over 600 R.D.C. Schizophrenics was studied retrospectively over 3 years using the PSE depressive symptoms. A closer look following subcategorization into those who had attempted suicide and those who had not revealed major differences of statistical significance in terms of certain specific depressive symptoms. Replication of these findings can provide us with major phenomenological clues to suicidality in schizophrenics.

99

SUICIDE RISK IN SCHIZOAFFECTIVE DISORDER
Ming T.Tsuang, M.D., Ph.D., D.Sc., Martin Buda, M.D., Jerry Fleming, M.S.
Harvard Medical School, Dept. of Psychiatry at Brockton VA Medical Center, U.S.A.

Over the past decade systematic research has been conducted into the course, outcome, and family history of schizoaffective disorder. Little, however, is known about causes of death, and especially about suicide risk in schizoaffective disorder.
We will present the results of an in depth suicide analysis of a subgroup of the "other psychotics". Forty-six patients, met DSM-III criteria for schizoaffective disorder, of which four had documented suicides based on death certificate information. We are currently analyzing data on these schizoaffectives who have been followed for 30 to 40 years. Information collected at admission in addition to other data is being compared between those schizoaffectives who committed suicide and those that did not. In addition the schizoaffective suicides will be compared to schizophrenic suicides, to determine if differences exist in the profiles of the two groups.

100

An Assessment of the Biochemical Findings in Schizophrenic Patients Who Attempt Suicide.
Michael Stanley, Ph.D., Barbara Stanley, Ph.D., Lil Traskman-Bendz, M.D, Ph.D., Ronald Winchel, M.D., J. Sidney Jones, M.D.
College of Physicians & Surgeons, Columbia University, New York City, New York.

THe suicide rate for individuals with schizophrenia is alarmingly high with estimates indicating that approximately 13% of schizophrenics commit suicide. Despite this high rate of death, suicide in the schizophrenic population is an understudied phenomenon. In part this is the result of the common notion that depression and suicide are inexorably linked. Thus, most research efforts have been focused on studying suicide in major affective disorders. However, in comparing the suicide rates (% of the diagnostic group that commits suicide) they are approximately equal. The few research studies directed at understanding suicidal behavior in schizophrenic demographic and psychosocial risk factors. While a number of these factors have been reported to be associated with suicidal behavior in schizophrenia, these relationships are typically weak and tend to identify more individuals than those who are truly at risk. This approach has, therefore, been shown to be of limited clincial utility.
More recently, studies which have investigated biochemical differences between individuals who have attempted suicide and those who have not suggest that this approach may improve our ability to identify individuals at risk.

101
Attempted Suicide and Depression in Elderly Chronic Schizophrenics

Dr. Navin Savla
Consultant Psychiatrist
Claybury Hospital
Woodford Green, Essex

Dr. T. Sharma
SHO: Claybury Hospital

We are reporting the differences in presentation of six Elderly Schizophrenics who had attempted suicide. The variable data used by Dr. Alec Roy in his paper on "Attempted Suicide in "Schizophrenia" (B.J.P 1984) were used and findings were recorded by studying case notes of patients. We have reviewed literature on Attempted Suicide in Schizophrenia and there is scanty information on Elderly Schizophrenics and attempted suicide. Our findings may show the differences in presentation of symptoms between young schizophrenics and elderly schizophrenics and this may throw light on future management particularly when mental hospitals are planned for closure and patients will be discharged in community.

102
Short & Long-Term Benefits of CLOZARIL/Leponex Therapy

Gilbert Honigfeld, Ph.D.
Senior Associate Director,
Medical Research Department
Sansoz Research Institute
East Hanover, New Jersey 07936

The short-term benefits of CLOZARIL/Leponex (clozapine) therapy of treatment resistant schizophrenia include, in comparison with neuroleptic drugs, rapid, broad-spectrum relief of both negative and positive symptoms of psychosis with little or no extrapyramidal effects liability. These benefits, briefly reviewed, are reasonably well-known. However, the long-term impact of these neuropsychiatric effects are less well-documented. This report assesses the status of patient subgroups treated continuously for two years or longer, demonstrating continued improvement, enhanced quality of life, lower costs of care, and reduced morbidity, including an absence of tardive dyskinesia.

Session 17 — Symposium:
Schizoaffective disorders: Present status of research

103
Strategies for the Assessment of Course and Outcome in Schizoaffective Disorders
Tsuang, Ming T., M.D., Ph.D., Samson, Jacqueline A, Ph.D., Huxley, Nancy A, B.A.
Harvard Medical School, Department of Psychiatry at Brockton VA Medical Center, USA

Previous studies report that schizoaffective patients show long-term outcome that is generally better than schizophrenic patients and worse than affective patients. However, studies of specific outcome domains such as symptomatology, social functioning and occupational functioning indicate that schizoaffective patients show heterogeneity of outcome.

In this presentation we will review the major strategies currently employed in assessment of long-term outcome in schizoaffective disorder and will present preliminary data on course and outcome from our ongoing longitudinal studies at the Harvard Department of Psychiatry, Brockton VA Medical Center. Data will be discussed in terms of the development of new methods for epidemiological studies.

104
LONG-TERM OUTCOME OF SCHIZOAFFECTIVE, AFFECTIVE AND SCHIZOPHRENIC DISORDERS
A. MARNEROS, A. DEISTER, A. ROHDE
Department of Psychiatry, University of Bonn, FRG

The long-term outcome (more than 20 years) of 72 schizoaffective, 97 schizophrenic and 80 affective disorders was investigated. The instruments of evaluation were: the WHO/Disability Assessment Schedule (DAS), the WHO/Psychological Impairment Rating Schedule (PIRS), the Global Assessment Scale (GAS) and psychopathological criteria. We found that schizoaffective disorders had significant differences to schizophrenia but partial similarities with affective disorders. Course and outcome of schizoaffective disorders suggest more similarities with affective than with schizophrenic disorders.

105

PREDICTORS OF OUTCOME DURING A FIVE-YEAR FOLLOW-UP OF SCHIZOAFFECTIVE DISORDERS

W. Coryell, Department of Psychiatry, University of Iowa, Iowa City (USA)

Psychotic features and, more particularly, a diagnosis of schizoaffective disorder, introduces the possibility of a chronically psychotic or schizophrenia-like outcome. Valid predictors of such an outcome would have obvious clinical value. Accordingly, we applied a wide range of potential predictors to a sample of patients who completed a five-year, semi-annual follow-up; at intake thirty had RDC schizoaffective depression, seventy-three had psychotic depression, fourteen had schizoaffective mania and fifty-six had mania with psychotic features. These predictors were considered separately for depressed and manic groups and again for all patients together. With few exceptions, significant predictors of the outcome were derived from historical rather than cross-sectional assessment. Significant and individually independent predictors for the combined sample were, in order of importance, episode duration at intake, a history of psychotic features without prominent affective features, marital status and polarity.

106

MORBIDITY RISK FOR MAJOR PSYCHIATRIC DISORDERS IN FIRST-DEGREE RELATIVES OF TWO SUBGROUPS OF SCHIZO-AFFECTIVE PATIENTS

Mario Maj, Department of Psychiatry, First Medical School, University of Naples (Italy)

A family study was carried out in two groups of patients fulfilling RDC for schizoaffective disorder: in one, a full affective and a full schizophrenic syndrome were simultaneously present, in the other, affective and schizophrenic features occurred within a polymorphic and rapidly changing clinical picture, including depersonalization/derealization and/or confusion. The first-degree relatives of patients of the former group had a higher risk for schizophrenia and a lower risk for major affective disorders as compared with the relatives of bipolars, whereas they did not differ significantly from the relatives of schizophrenics. The first-degree relatives of patients of the latter group had a low risk for both schizophrenia and major affective disorders and a relatively high risk for schizoaffective disorders. These findings confirm the heterogeneity of schizoaffective disorders and suggest that not all schizoaffective syndromes are variants of either schizophrenia or major affective disorders.

107

Response to Lithium-Prophylaxis in Schizoaffective Disorder
G. Lenz, R. Wolf, C. Simhandl, A. Topitz
Psychiatric Clinic, University of Vienna

The importance of polarity in schizoaffective disorder for long-term course has been stressed by many authors in the last years. There are only few studies which focus on the importance of polarity for therapy-response with lithium salts.
In our study we compared 40 patients with ICD-9 Affective Disorder, bipolar type to 40 patients with ICD-9 Schizoaffective Disorder (35 bipolar type, 5 unipolar) in respect to prophylactic response with lithium.
The results confirm the opinion of many authors, that schizoaffective bipolar patients are very similar to bipolar Affective Disorder-patients in respect to course and therapy response. Patients with schizoaffective disorder, bipolar type respond better than those with schizoaffective disorder unipolar type.

Session 18   Symposium:
Sleep disorders medicine: Role of the general psychiatrist

108

INSOMNIA
Kales J.D., Pennsylvania State Univ., College of Medicine, Hershey, Pennsylvania, U.S.A.

Insomnia, the most common sleep disorder, may be secondary to a wide spectrum of psychiatric and medical conditions. Thus a biopsychosocial and behavioral approach is useful. It is more prevalent among women, the elderly and psychosocially disadvantaged persons. Psychiatrists report a much higher percentage of patients who complain of insomnia and are frequently confronted in their office practice with the problem of evaluating and treating insomnia in order to alleviate or prevent its many untoward consequences. Transient sleep difficulty commonly develops in response to stressful events, life changes, or health problems. Chronic insomnia is often the consequence when life-stress factors exist in individuals who are vulnerable because of pre-existing emotional problems, inadequate coping mechanisms and internalization of emotions. In most patients with chronic insomnia, sleep difficulty begins before the age of 40. About 80% of these patients have one or more MMPI scales elevated to the pathologic range. Characteristically, these patients are anxious and ruminative during the day and at bedtime are obsessive about unresolved issues of the day and consequently become emotionally aroused, physiologically activated and hypervigilant. The key to successful treatment requires a multidimensional approach which combines sleep hygiene measures; supportive, insight-oriented and behavioral psychotherapeutic techniques; and the adjunctive use of hypnotic or antidepressant medication where appropriate.

109
PARASOMNIAS
Vela-Bueno A, Autonomous Univ. of Madrid and Sleep Disorders Center, Madrid, Spain

The parasomnias consist of sleepwalking (SW) (somnambulism), night terrors (NT), and nightmares (NM). All three disorders are relatively common in childhood, when developmental factors appear to be responsible, and usually resolve by late adolescence. When they persist into or begin during adulthood, psychiatric factors are usually implicated. Most adults with these disorders have pathological MMPI profiles and a majority have psychiatric diagnoses. About 15% of children sleepwalk, while less than 3% report NT. The two disorders appear to be different manifestations along the same pathophysiologic continuum with NT being the more severe expression. Nightmares, commonly known as "bad dreams," affect about 10% of the general population as a current or past problem. It is important to differentiate between NM and NT: NM occur during REM sleep and thus occur more often later in the night when REM sleep predominates; NT, like SW, occur early in the night when stages 3 and 4 predominate; NM are accompanied by much less anxiety, vocalization, motility, and autonomic discharge than NT; and, NM patients usually have vivid and elaborate recall for the event, whereas NT patients are typically amnesic for their episodes. Management of children with parasomnias includes counseling and reassuring parents that children usually outgrow the condition by late adolescence, or sooner. For adults, psychotherapy is often helpful and treatment for SW/NT may include adjunctive use of benzodiazepines.

110
ENURESIS
Pierce C.M., Harvard Medical School, Boston, Massachusetts, U.S.A.

Enuresis is defined as bedwetting that occurs after bladder control should have been achieved, which is usually around age 4. About 10% to 15% of children continue to wet the bed and the prevalence in young adults is 1% to 3%. This disorder exists in two forms: primary (persistent) and secondary (acquired or regressed) enuresis. Primary enuresis is the more prevalent of the two types, by far, and both forms of the disorder are more prevalent in boys. Enuresis is related more to time of night than to sleep stages. Genetic, maturational, and anatomical factors underlie primary enuresis with the major problem being a smaller functional bladder capacity. In secondary enuresis, the etiology is usually psychological. Nonpharmacologic treatment of enuresis is preferred especially in young children. The first step is to counsel, educate and reassure both the child and parents in order to prevent adverse psychosocial consequences and psychiatric sequelae. Behavioral treatments are widely used, with varying degrees of success. Bladder training exercises to increase capacity and/or provide the child with greater mastery over urinary control may be helpful. Given the psychologic difficulties that typically underlie secondary enuresis psychotherapeutic management is usually indicated. In the pharmacologic management of enuresis, imipramine is the drug of choice. However, its use should be limited to older children and adolescents and then only for short-term special situations.

111
SLEEP IN DEPRESSION: A REVIEW FOR THE PRACTICING PSYCHIATRIST
Reynolds C.F., Univ. of Pittsburgh School of Medicine, Pittsburgh, Pennsylvania, U.S.A

Sleep in acute major depression, particularly in the endogenomorphic subtype, is reliably characterized by: a shortened burst of NREM sleep; a prolonged first REM sleep period with heightened density of rapid eye movements; sleep maintenance difficulties (including early morning awakening); and alterations in slow wave sleep (both a decrease for the night as a whole and a shift of delta power from the first to the second NREM sleep period). The diagnostic and prognostic utility of these physiologic changes will be considered in several contexts: 1) the sensitivity and specificity of these alterations for major depression; 2) the impact of psychotherapeutic and pharmacotherapeutic antidepressant intervention on sleep EEG variables, with respect to treatment response; 3) use of EEG sleep measures to predict relapse and recurrence of major depression; and 4) changes in the sleep EEG associated with mood disturbing events, such as bereavement. In addition, recent information concerning the impact of depression on nocturnal penile tumescence (NPT) will be presented, with respect to the significance of depression in the pathogenesis of erectile dysfunction.

112
NARCOLEPSY AND SLEEP APNEA
Lugaresi E., Univ. of Bologna, Bologna, Italy

The symptomatology, clinical course and medical management of obstructive sleep apnea (OSA) and narcolepsy (both disorders of excessive daytime sleepiness) may result in severe psychosocial consequences that require psychiatric diagnostic skills or psychiatric intervention or both. Thus, it is incumbent upon the general psychiatrist to be familiar with the clinical characteristics, diagnosis and general treatment (including psychosocial management) of these two disorders. Narcolepsy is a disorder of excessive sleepiness characterized by irresistible sleep attacks that may occur in combination with one or more of three auxiliary symptoms: cataplexy, sleep paralysis, and hypnagogic hallucinations. Treatment includes therapeutic naps and stimulant medication for the sleep attacks, and tricyclic antidepressants for cataplexy. The OSA syndrome is basically characterized by two main symptoms: intermittent loud snoring interrupted by nocturnal breath cessation and excessive daytime sleepiness. OSA is more common in men and in those who are obese and/or hypertensive. Treatment may be surgical or medical. Patients with narcolepsy and OSA experience high levels of psychologic distress secondary to their disorders. There is a high incidence of severe psychosocial disruption involving family, social interactions and work situations; in narcoleptics this is usually due to others' misunderstanding of the symptoms of the disorder. Counseling and psychotherapy are often indicated to manage effectively the psychosocial consequences which may result from both disorders.

Session 19 Special Session: Experimental pharmacology I

113
LITHIUM-HYPOTHERMIA: INTERACTIONS AND BEHAVIORALLY CONDITIONING
K.M. Bachmann, U. Dürrenmatt, A. Radvila
Psychiatric University Clinic, Bern, Switzerland

Lithium (as LiCl) given i.p. lowered core body temperature in rats significantly 30-90min after injection in a dose dependent manner. The effect was marked: 60min after injection of 170 mg/kg temperature fell from 38.0 ± 0.3 to 35.9 ± 0.5 °C ($p < 0.001$). Even after 4 days of starvation LiCl shows still a significant effect. LiCl antagonises the temperature rising effect of morphine and enhances the temperature lowering effect of either propranolol (3 mg/kg) or hexamethonium (30 mg/kg) significantly after 30 min.
At a dose of 170 mg/kg the LiCl induced hypothermia could be behaviorally conditioned in the taste aversion model after multiple conditioning sessions.
The possible implications for Li therapy are discussed.

114
LITHIUM, PIGMENT SCREENING AND MELATONIN IN THE FROG RETINA

M. KEMALI, P. MONTELEONE, M. MILICI, C. ORAZZO, M. MAJ and D. KEMALI
Department of Medical Psychology and Psychiatry, 1st Medical School University of Naples, (Italy).

Melatonin, the most known pineal hormone, is synthesized also in the retina where it is believed to modulate pigment screening (PS) by favoring the scleral aggregation of pigment granules during the dark phase. It has been recently suggested that lithium may gain its therapeutic effects in the major affective disorders through the modulation of the eye sensitivity to light. In fact, our previous work demonstrated that lithium can induce a scleral aggregation of the retinal pigment in both light- and dark-adapted frogs. In order to assess whether lithium affects PS directly or via the modulation of retinal melatonin synthesis, we investigated the effects of acute administration of the drug on melatonin levels in the frog retina. For this purpose, 4 light-adapted and 4 dark-adapted frogs were injected intraperitoneally (i.p.) with lithium chloride (1 mg/kg dissolved in 0.1 ml distilled water). Eight more frogs (4 light- and 4 dark-adapted) received i.p. 0.1 ml saline. Two hours later, the animals were killed by decapitation; the retinas with the attached pigment were removed and immediately frozen until processed for melatonin assay. This was carried out by double antibody RIA. Lithium induced a clear-cut decrease of retinal melatonin levels in both light- and dark-adapted frogs. It is possible that this effect was achieved through the inhibition of the calcium-dependent adenylate-cyclase, the enzyme involved in the activation of N-acetyltransferase, the main regulator of melatonin synthesis. These results suggest that the effects of lithium on PS are not a melatonin-mediated phenomenon, at least in the frog retina.

115
LITHIUM EFFECTS ON HYPOTHALAMIC OPIOID PEPTIDE RELEASE: A COMBINED IN VIVO/IN VITRO STUDY
K.E. Nikolarakis, G. Burns and A. Herz
Dept. of Neuropharmacology, Max-Planck-Institut für Psychiatrie, D-8033 Planegg-Martinsried, FRG

Several studies indicate that endogenous opioids are involved in the pathophysiology of affective disorders and possibly mediate the behavioural actions of lithium, however, this opioid/lithium interaction is poorly understood. In the present study the effect of lithium on ß-endorphin (ß-END), dynorphin (DYN) and Met-enkephalin (MET) release from rat hypothalamic slices has been studied in vitro.
Lithium (5 mM) induced a significant increase in the release of ß-END, DYN and MET and this effect was tetrodotoxin (10^{-6}M) resistant. In vitro pretreatment with the opioid receptor antagonist naloxone (10^{-6}M) blocked the stimulatory effects of lithium on ß-END, DYN and MET release. Similarly lithium pretreatment in vitro abolished the known stimulatory effects of naloxone on the release of all three opioid peptides. Additionally chronic in vivo administration of lithium in naive rats resulted in the inability of naloxone to alter DYN and MET (but not ß-END) release in vitro. Finally pertussis toxin pretreatment blocked the lithium effects on DYN and MET (but not ß-END) release. These data indicate that lithium stimulates ß-END, DYN and MET release possibly by interacting with G-proteins associated with presynaptically located opioid receptors (autoreceptors).

116
THE EFFECTS OF CHRONIC LiCl ADMINISTRATION ON MEMORY IN THE RAT
E.Tsaltas,M.M.Schugens,T.Pothitos,S.Kyriakidou,N.Smyrnis and C.Stefanis.
Department of Psychiatry, Athens University Eginition Hospital,Athens,Greece.

Male Wistar rats received daily IP LiCl (2mmol/Kg: n=10) or vehicle injections(n= 11) for 20 days. This injection regime continued throughout behavioral training. Animals were then trained on a T-maze rewarded alteration task. Once all animals achieved criterion,working memory was challenged by introduction of a 45 sec. delay between information and recall trials of the task.There was no difference between the two groups in the acquisition of the alternation.However in the 45 sec. delay phase LiCl-treated animals made significant fewer mistakes than the control group ($t=3.99, p<0.001$).The same LiCl regime also resulted in significant enhancement in the recall of a passive avoidance response in the shuttlebox ($p<0.006$) six hours after a single acquisition trial. Given that successful performance of rewarded alteration has been directly linked to the intactness of the cholinergic innervation of the hippocampus,it is suggested that chronic LiCl administration improves working memory via an effect on the central cholinergic system.

117

NEUROPEPTIDES IN RAT BRAIN: EFFECTS OF MICROWAVE IRRADIATION AND ELECTROCONVULSIVE TREATMENT (ECT)
C. Stenfors, E. Theodorsson and A.A. Mathé
Karolinska Institute, Departments of Psychiatry and Clinical Chemistry, Stockholm, Sweden

Substance P(SP), neurokinin A(NKA), neuropeptide Y (NPY), galanin(GAL) and vasoactive intestinal polypeptide(VIP) were measured by specific radioimmunoassays in rat brain. Concentrations of SP, NKA and NT were about twice as high in animals sacrificed by focused microwave irradiation(MW) as those found in guillotined animals. In contrast, NPY and VIP levels were the same in both groups. Further analysis by reverse-phase HPLC indicated that the higher immunoreactive peptide levels in the MW animals were mainly due to the presence of intact SP, NKA and NT. It is concluded that the MW method leads to rapid enzyme inactivation and should therefore be preferentially used in CNS experiments where HPLC characterization of peptides is not available. One ECT had no detectable effect on the concentrations of SP, NKA, NT, GAL or VIP. However, NPY was elevated. Higher NPY levels were found in all regions except the striatum. The mode of sacrifice, i.e. guillotine or MW did not influence the results. Six ECTs (once daily/6 days) had no effect on SP, NKA, NT, GAL or VIP. In parallel to one ECT, following 6 ECTs, increased NPY was found in all regions, especially hippocampus, the area thought to be of relevance for ECTs action. The results demonstrate specific neuropeptide changes following ECT and raise the possibility that neuropeptides may play a role in ECTs therapeutic mode of action.

118

CHANGE OF MICROTUBULE-ASSOCIATED PROTEIN 2 IN ISCHEMIC GERBIL BRAIN
T. Kudo, K. Tada, M. Takeda, T. Yamashita, S. Hariguchi, J. Shiraishi, T. Nishimura,
Department of Neuropsychiatry, Osaka University Medical School, Osaka, JAPAN

We have previously shown that transient ischemia induces marked decrease in concentration of microtubule-associated protein 2 (MAP2). We have also demonstrated that in Mongolian gerbil with chronic reduction of cerebral blood flow causes impaired learning behavior and the decreased amount of MAP2. In the present study, we examine the mechanism of this change of MAP2 after transient ischemia. Gerbil brain supernatant after 5-15 minutes of bilateral carotid artery occlusion was analyzed by electrophoresis and immunoblotting with anti-MAP2 antibody. In vitro degradation of MAP2 from the normal nonischemic brain extract was also studied to clarify the effect of calcium and protease inhibitors. We obteined the results that:
1. After transient ischemia, MAP2 was degraded into some polypeptides of molecular weight of circa 200-60 kDa. 2. The degradation of MAP2 was most apparent in the hippocampus. 3. The degradation pattern of MAP2 in the ischemic brain was similar to that of in vitro degradation of MAP2 with calcium, which was inhibited by cysteine protease inhibitor. Therefore, we suggest that calcium dependent neutral protease involves the decrease of MAP2 after transient ischemia and that it may be one of the factors which cause the neuropsychiatric dysfunction due to cerebrovascular disorders.

119

IMMUNOLOGICAL STUDY OF EXPERIMENTAL NEUROFIBRILLARY CHANGE
Y. Nakamura, M. Takeda, K. Tada, T. Tanaka, S. Hariguchi and T. Nishimura
Department of Neuropsychiatry, Osaka University Medical School, Fukushima, Osaka, Japan

The constituent of the neurofibrillary change in Alzheimer's disease brain has been extensively studied. Alzheimer's neurofibrillary change is shown to react with phosphorylated tau and phosphorylated 200k neurofilament subunit protein. As a model of Alzheimer's disease, we studied the antigenecity of the experimental neurofibrillary change of the rabbit brain, which was intracerebrally injected with aluminium phosphate. The formaldehyde-fixed and paraffin-embedded tissue slice was immunologically studied with two kinds of anti-200k, anti-160k and anti-68k neurofila ment monoclonal antibodies. The two anti-200k antibodies clearly stained both axons and neurofibrillary changes. The anti-160k antibodies stained neurofibrillary change, while they weakly stained the axons. Neither anti-200k nor anti-160k antibodies stained the perikarya of the neuron without neurofibrillary change. Anti-68K antibodies stained neither axons nor neurofibrillary changes. The results are considered that 200k and 160k neurofilament subunit proteins, heavily phosphorylated, are immunologically constituents of experimental neurofibrillary change, indicating the similarity of the constituents of Alzheimer and experimental neurofibrillary change.

120

Experimental thiamine deficiency

R. Sturlason, dept. of psychiatry, Rigshospitalet
A. Hansen, dept. of physiology, Univ. of Copenhagen
R. Hemmingsen, Dept. of psych., Bispebjerg,
H. Laursen, dept. of pathology, Sundby, Denmark

Thiamine deficiency may result in Wernicke-Korsakoffs disease. Glucose infusion may aggrevate or provoke the symptoms in humans. The reason remain unclear. In this study a model of experimental thiamine deficiency in the male Wistar rat is used. Animals were kept on a thiamine deficient diet and given daily injections of pyrithiamine. Controls were kept on isocaloric diet enriched with thiamine.
At average day 17 the animals developed symptoms of acute organic brain disorder with seizures, opistotonus and nystagmus. At beginning of symptoms four animals were perfusion fixed with buffered paraformaldehyde. Four animals were injected i.p. with glucose and thiamine for five days. Paraffin sections were stained with HE, Luxol Fast Blue or an immmunoperoxidase techique for serum proteins. Circumscribed lesions were seen in the mediodorsal part of thalamus in both groups. The tissue showed neuronal death, frank necrosis, vascular proliferation and infiltration with histiocytic cells. Increased cerebrovascular permeability to serum proteins was always evident in the affected areas, and in the brain stem often together with hemorrhages. It was not possible to distinguish between the two groups. The control group did not show any histological or permeability changes.

Session 20 New Research:
Epidemiology

121
DEPRESSION IN SCHOOL BEGINNERS - A PROSPECTIVE STUDY OF SCHOOL - IMMATURE CHILDREN
Jacek Bomba, Dpt. Child Adol. Psychiatry, Academy of Medicine, Krakow, Poland
Hanna Jaklewicz, Inst. Psychology, University of Gdansk, Poland

This prospective study was aimed to investigate the potential relations between emotional and social immaturity to school adaptation and occurance of depression in school beginners. A representative sample (502) of 6 years old children of a big industrial town was assessed to identify immature to school cases. A year later the same sample was studied with the Krakow Depression Test. School immaturity was found in 10.56% of the total sample expressed more often in withdrawal and then antisocial behavior. Depression was diagnosed in 32,79% of the first year school pupils, significantly more often among those found earlier to be immature to school. Previous child biological development, presence of brain damage symptoms, low IQ - did not explain satisfactory immaturity to school or occurance of depression. Emotional and social school immaturity influence occurance of depression in school-beginners. There is however need for further studies on the role of family and school atmosphere in the pathogenesis of both phenomena.

122
EPIDEMIOLOGY OF ADOLESCENT DEPRESSION : A STUDY ABOUT 744 HIGH SCHOOL STUDENTS.
D. Bailly ; J.Y. Alexandre ; C. Collinet ; Ph. J. Parquet.
Psychopathology and Alcoology Unit , University Hospital of Lille , France.

This study investigates the prevalence and the manifestations and correlates of major depressive disorder in adolescence. The sample for this investigation consists of 744 (438 males and 306 females) high school students aged 14 to 23 (mean age : 17,2 + 1,5 years) attending 15 colleges of the North of France , and represents 97,5 per cent of students invited to participate. Data for the study are obtained by a self-questionnaire investigating sociodemographical , behavioral , medical and environmental factors. Assessment of major depressive disorder is performed by medical doctors using a semi-structured interview. Applying DSM III - R criteria , the prevalence of major depressive episode is 4,4 per cent (16 students refused the clinical interview). Depressed mood , loss of interest or pleasure , psychomotor agitation or retardation, diminished ability to think or concentrate and recurrent thoughts of death are the strongest discriminators in identifying the depressed students. The diagnosis of major depressive episode is significantly associated with some particular features including school difficulties,

123
INCIDENCE OF MENTAL ILLNESS, SUICIDES, COMPULSORY ADMISSIONS OF ASIANS & W/I IN EAST LONDON
A.A. Khan, U.K.
A 96 year survey in a psychiatric hospital in the District, of 4,750 cases records since 1887 was carried out; 20,000 cases referred in Coroners and 30 years of suicides records reveals the origins and the myth of ethnic mental illness. The patient of both non-anglo saxon and anglo saxon names by the country of birth were analysed as to age, Social class, religion, diagnosis, treatment and length of stay. It is concluded that there is an over-representation of ethnic minority patients for certain are groups, and under-representation - if not total absence - of elder age groups, has also implications on admissions legal status, diagnosis and treatment. For the last 10 years no Asians, Muslim, Hindu or Sikh have been admitted to the Department of Psychiatry of Old Age. 24.2% of all the suicides in the Waltham Forest, Redbridge and Newham District are Asians - (34 Hindus & 35 Muslims) 34% of all Asian suicides under the age of 25, 26 over the age of 60 (92% and 80%) of the suicide takes place in Waltham Forest, as compared to 32% suicides in the host community. The total number of murders in Asians 58.69%, 62% under 25, 40% are Hindus and 22% are Muslims. Number of murders under 25, 52% in Waltham Forest and 48% in Redbridge and Newham, between 31st August 1979 and August 1983. 20 suicides in the elderly, 5 in ethnic elders, 3 Muslims and 2 Hindus. So total suicides in ethnic groups all ages in 87 Approx. Accidental deaths in host population 59 for one year, and 1 in ethnic group. There have been 4 cases of child abuse, 1 murder in Muslim.

124
A FIRST ADMISSION INCIDENCE STUDY OF MANIA

Marcus Webb and Ian Daly
Dept. of Psychiatry, Trinity College, University of Dublin. Ireland.

An epidemiological study of the first admission rate for mania in a defined area of Dublin has been carried out, using similar methodology to that of a cross-national study in London (England) and Aarhus (Denmark) reported in 1976. (Leff, Fischer and Bertelsen). A one-year prospective identification of cases and a six-year retrospective case note review were carried out, employing the PSE schedule and symptom check list, with CATEGO diagnosis. Cases also satisfied DSM-III criteria for mania. Thirty cases satisfied the research criteria, giving an annual incidence for first admissions for mania of 5.4 per 100,000. This rate is considerably higher than the rate of 2.6 per 100,000 reported from both London and Aarhus. Possible explanations for the higher incidence rate in Dublin are discussed. Further cross-national studies are recommended to explore the relevance of socio-cultural factors to the incidence of mania.

125

EPIDEMIOLOGICAL INVESTIGATION OF THE PSYCHIATRIC DISEASES IN BULGARIA
Tsoneva-Pentcheva L., K.Milenkov
Institute of Neurology, Psychiatry a.Neurosurgery
Sofia, Bulgaria

All psychiatric diseases included in the Vth Division of the ICD-9 are subject to systematic epidemiological investigation in Bulgaria. The primary information is collected through the official annual reports from all psychiatric services in the country. In the last 30 years much information has been collected concerning both - the activity of the various kinds of psychiatric services and the psychiatric morbidity. Indexes on prevalence and incidence are available according to age and sex. Besides additional investigations are carried out devoted on certain psychiatric diseases in order to reveal the unregistered prevalence.

126

Epidemiological Survey on 150 drug addicts of the drug addiction unit of the P.H.A.

Drug addiction Unit of the P.H.A.

ZACHARIADIS ILIAS

We report the preliminary results of a large scale epidemiological survey on drug addiction.
One hundred and fifty out-patients in the drug addiction unit were given a questionaire which covered questions concerning Social class, first drug used, socio-economic status of the family, legal status ets. All patients participated in the therapeutic programme of the unit.
We investigated variables such as socio - economic status, age, first drug used, social background, legal status, motives, pathological problems, relationships with is the family etc. in relation to treatment.

127

A NATIONWIDE EPIDEMIOLOGICAL SURVEY OF SPOUSAL VIOLENCE IN KOREA
Kwangiel Kim, Youn Gyu Cho, Hanyang University, Korea

This paper presents nationwide epidemiological findings of spousal violence in Korea.
Samples were selected by the 3 stage stratified random sampling. Available samples were 1,326 persons who had lived a married life at least for the last 2 years. By face-to-face interview, respondents were asked to whether they had any experience of being battered by their spouses for the last one year. If they stated to have experience, they were asked to rate the severity according to Straus' Conflict Resolution Technique Scale.
In spite of stereotype, experience rate of spousal violence is definitely high. The overall experience rate of being battered by spouses was 30.9%: 37,5% in women and 23.2% in men. Experience rate of being seriously battered was 22.5%: 12.4% in women and 3.7% in men. The rate was higher in the lower social strata and in the younger couples. The above result was discussed in terms of socio-cultural context.

128

SCREENING FOR PSYCHIATRIC DISORDERS IN PRIMARY CARE SETTINGS

De Marco F., Ascione C., Pizzella A., Venuto G°., Lobrace S°. and Starace F°.

Department of Mental Health, Local Health Unit No. 43, Naples, Italy.
°Department of Medical Psychology and Psychiatry, 1st Medical School, University of Naples, Italy.

A general practice study was carried out in a peripheral district of Naples, in southern Italy.

The 30-item italian version of General Health Questionnaire was completed by 217 consecutive patients aged 18 and above, who contacted their G.P. during the sample days selected for the study.

34.1% of patients were high scores on the GHQ-30 (cut-off point 4/5) and 83.8% of them were found to be "cases" at clinical interview, according to I.C.D.-9 criteria.

Neurotic depression was the most frequent psychiatric diagnosis.

The estimate of the real prevalence of psychiatric disorders according to Diamond & Lilienfeld was found to be 49.3%.

129

STRUCTURE OF MORTALITY OF THE HOSPITALIZED PATIENTS IN 10 YEARS.
F.PRIVOROZKY, E.PHILOSOF, L.KOHEN.
MENTAL HOSPITAL TIRAT HACARMEL HAIFA, ISRAEL

ANALYSIS IS MADE IN A PSYCHIATRIC HOSPITAL for 300 BEDS FROM THE BEGINNING OF ITS FUNCTIONING IN 1978. IN THE RESEARCH THERE ARE DISCUSSED DIFFERENT CASES OF DEATH — NATURAL AND SUICIDE —DUZING TWO PERIODS OF THE HOSPITAL'S FUNCTION:
1. THE 1-ST PERIOD 1978 - 82 WHICH IS NAMED BY US AS A CONSERVATIVE PERIOD.
2. THE 2-ND ONE FROM 1982 UP TODAY WHEN THE PROGRESSIVE TACTICS WERE USED TO SOLVE THE PROBLEM OF HOSPITALIZED PATIENTS.
THIS PERIOD IS LINKED WITH DE-INSTITUALIZATION OF THE PATIENTS, WITH OPENING OF DEPERTMENTS ORGANIZING I.P.C.U. OPENING A DEPAETMENT OF REHABILITATION AND READAPTATION, ORGANIZING A HOSTEL FOR CHRONIC PATIENTS. WHILE OPENING THE DEPERTMENTS WE EXPECTED INCREASE OF LATHELITIES CONNECXED WITH SUICIDE.
BUT ON THE CONTCARY THE DATA IS DIFFERENT, IF IN THE 1-ST PERIOD THE NUMBER OF DEATH WAS 9,8 PER 1000 PATIENTS IN THE 2-ND IT DECREASED TO 6,3 PER 1000, SUIEIDE DECREASED TWICE.
THERE WERE NO CASES OF DEATH LINKED WITH PHARMACOLOGICAL TRETMENT IN THE 2-ND PERIOD MORTALITY.
53,8% AMONG THE MORTALITY SUFFERD FROM SCHIZOPHRENIA. 27,7% SUFFERD FROM ORGANIC PSYCHOSIS.
MOST OF THEM DIED IN JULY — SEPTEMBER. IN THE SUICIDE GROUPS DEATH TOOK PLACE FROM APRIL— TO JUNE.

Session 21 New Research:
Genetic studies in mental diseases

130

MOLECULARBIOLOGICAL STUDIES IN SCHIZOPHRENIA

Aschauer, H.N.*, Aschauer-Treiber, G.*, Isenberg, K.E.**, Todd, R.D.**, Garver, D.L.**, Knesevich, M.**, Cloninger, C.R.**

* University of Vienna, Department of Psychiatry, Vienna, Austria
** Washington University, Department of Psychiatry, St. Louis, USA

Sherrington et al. (Nature 336:164,1988) discovered linkage of schizophrenia with chrom. 5 markers, in contrast Kennedy et al. (Nature 336:167,1988) and St. Clair et al. (Nature 339:305, 1989) found no evidence for linkage on chrom. 5 in families of schizophrenics.
At Washington University in St. Louis, we studied 7 families identified through a schizophrenic proband. Almost 100 family members were personally interviewed using a structured interview. Family history and medical information were also used for consensus diagnosis (A.H., A.G.).
These families have been screened with many Restriction Fragment Length Polymorphism (RFLP)-makers located on different chromosomes.
Two-point and three-point analyses are being performed using the program LINKAGE and different models of affection status.
At this point DNA-probes on chromosome 5 failed to demonstrate linkage to the affection status models.

131

A 26-YEAR FOLLOW UP OF CHILDREN OF SCHIZO-PHRENIC MOTHERS

Bjørn Jacobsen, M.D. & Josef Parnas, M.D.
Psykologisk Institut, Copenhagen, Denmark

The Copenhagen High Risk Study began in 1962 with the examination of 207 children of schizophrenic mothers and 104 controls. The mean age of the children at that time was 15 years, and none of them were psychotic. In 1972, 8.6% of the high risk sample were diagnosed as schizophrenic. The present paper reports diagnostic status at the age of 40 years. Approximately 50% of the sample were diagnosed within the schizophrenia spectrum disorder. Genetic and epidemiological consequences of this finding are discussed. Diagnostic changes from 1972 to 1986 are presented and discussed.

132

PSYCHOSOCIAL FACTORS AND FAMILIAL SUBTYPES OF UNIPOLAR DEPRESSION

AYUSO-GUTIERREZ,J.L.; YAÑEZ,R.; DELGADO,J.; EZQUIAGA,E. and AYUSO-MATEOS,J.L.
Hospital San Carlos, 28040 Madrid, Spain

The aim of this study was to validate Winokur's familial classification of unipolar depression using psychosocial variables.

The study group included 97 patients consecutively admitted to a general hospital with a diagnosis of primary unipolar major depressive disorder according to R.D.C.

The familial subgroups were classifed according to data from a structural familial anamnesis following the criteria of Winokur et al. (1978): Family Pure Depressive Discorder (N=42), Depression Spectrum Disease (N=27) and Sporadic Depressive Disease (N=28). Stressful life events were selected from Paykel's scale.

The results do not show significant differences among the groups, although there is a marked tendency toward less life events in the F.P.D.D. group.

133

PERSONALITY DISORDERS IN RELATIVES OF PSYCHIATRIC INPATIENTS

R. Heun, W. Maier, J. Minges, D. Lichtermann
Department of Psychiatry, University of Mainz, Untere Zahlbacher Str. 8, D-6500 Mainz 31, West-Germany

The spectrum concept was introduced in psychiatry for modelling the cooccurrence of various disorders (especially acute and personality disorders). The schizophrenic spectrum was hypothezised previously in order to match the often replicated finding of an enhanced frequency of odd characters in families of schizophrenic probands. Previous studies and the clinical impression are postulating a link between affective disorders and anxious and acting out personality disorders. An association between schizoid, schizotypal and paranoid personality disorders on one hand and affective disorder on the other hand seems to be unlikely but empirical work in this field is rare and still necessary. Consequently, the aim of the family study we conducted in Mainz (West-Germany) was to examine the morbid risks for personality disorders in the families of patients. 300 (and 50 healthy volunteers) and their living first degree relatives were contacted in order to be personally interviewed by the SADS-LA and the SCID-II as far as they agreed; 75 % of the living first degree relatives participated personally. Healthy volunteers showed the lowest familial loading with personality disorders, bipolar affective disorders the highest. Up to now, no distinct pattern of personality disorders appeared in the family members of probands with affective or schizophrenic disorders. Consequently there is no significant evidence for a specific personality disorder spectrum.

134

Assortative mating of psychiatric inpatients and healthy probands

R. Heun, W. Maier
Department of Psychiatry, University of Mainz, Untere Zahlbacher Str. 8, D-6500 Mainz

Assortative mating has been described for patients with various psychiatric disorders. An augmented prevalence of such disorders in spouses might enhance the risk for psychiatric disorders in the offspring. Such influences have to be taken into consideration when estimates of allel frequencies for genetic analyses have to be done.

In the Mainz family study we compared the prevalence of affective and schizophrenic disorders in spouses of 164 married (out of 300) consecutive inpatients and in spouses of 50 healthy index probands.
Personal interviews according to the SADS-LA (lifetime version) and SCID II were used for diagnoses.

Compared to spouses of healthy volunteers there is a significant increase of affective and schizophrenic disorders in those of index patients. We could not find any clear association between diagnoses in patients and their spouses.

135

THE 3-D syndrome: dysthymia-dysgonosomia-deterioration.
Pascalis J.G., Teyssier J.R. and Havet J.M.
Clinique Universitaire de Psychiatrie.

C.H.U.-H.R.D., rue A. Carrel - 51092 Reims Cedex France

Validated results based on very recent focal study first results reported at the VII Congress in Wien. We studied correlations between Karyotypes and psychiatric histories in 1.100 patients and found evidence supporting the existence of a syndrome that combines mood disorders and mosaic-pattern dysgonosomia. Autosomal chromosome abnormalities may also be present. The mood disorders are reminiscent of manic-depressive psychosis; however, in 3D syndrome, chemotherapy is less effective and dementia ultimately develops. The biologic abnormality underlying this syndrome seems to be chromosome instability.

136

POSSIBLE GENETIC DAMAGE DUE TO LONG-TERM EXPOSURE TO PSYCHOTROPIC DRUGS
Sram R.J., Binkova B., Fojtikova I., Topinka J.
Psychiatric Research Institute, Prague, Czechoslovakia

Unscheduled DNA synthesis (UDS) in lymphocytes and lipid peroxidation (LPO) in some regions of the brain have been studied in rats chronically exposed to meclopin and lithium. Due to a possible free radical mechanism of neuroleptics action, the effect of α-tocopherol on LPO and UDS levels was studied. Both parameters were analysed after 3,6,and 12 months in groups administered with meclopin, lithium, meclopin + α-tocopherol and α-tocopherol. The results indicate that long-term exposure to meclopin and lithium decreased UDS level, induced by MNNG, and increased LPO levels in brain after 3, 6 and 12 month. Simultaneous aplication of meclopin and α-tocopherol eliminated by meclopin induced changes in UDS and LPO. It may be concluded that long-term exposure of rats to meclopin and lithium decreased DNA excision reapair capacity and damaged neuronal membranes. Side effects of meclopin may be effectively supressed by α-tocopherol.

137

LITHIUM RESPONSE AND FAMILY PSYCHOPATHOLOGY IN SCHIZOPHRENIA

S. Kelwala, M. Rovner, A.K. Jain, K. Chapin, V. Ramesh, I. Youssef, M. Bhavsar Wayne-Northville Research Unit & VA Allen Park, Michigan, USA

In an ongoing study on Lithium's efficacy in schizophrenia the presence of psychiatric illnesses in the family of 34 probands [11 schizophrenics (S), 20 schizoaffectives (SA), and 3 schizophreniforms] was evaluated using direct interview or the Family History Method. Li alone was given for 2-6 weeks [$\bar{x}$=29 days] at therapeutic levels 0.8-1.4 mEq/L [$\bar{x}$=0.96]. 4 probands were classified as responders [R], 13 as partial responders [P], and 17 as non-responders [NR] on the basis of our previously published criteria. The table illustrates the frequency distribution of psychopathology in the 1st degree relatives.

	R	P	NR
S/SA/Schizotypal		6(8.7%)	12(10.6%)
Uni. Dep.	5(20%)	9(13.1%)	13(11.5%)
Anx. Dis.	1(4%)	3(4.3%)	9(8%)
Subs. Abuse	3(12%)	10(14.5%)	14(12.4%)
Bipol I&II/Cycloth.		1(1.4%)	8(7%)
Other Dx		1(1.4%)	3(2.7%)
Normal	16(64%)	39(56.5%)	54(47.8%)
TOTAL	25	69	113

Our preliminary data finds a trend towards a higher lifetime rate of mental illnesses, greater risk for developing schizophrenia spectrum disorders and a greater occurrence of multiple psychiatric illnesses in the families of Li non-responsive schizophrenic patients.

138

FRA X SYND RESISTENT TO FOLIC ACID TREATMENT. PSYCHOTROPICS WERE ADDED.

Herman BLEIWEISS, MD; Assit. Prof. in Psychiatry, Buenos Aires University; President of the Argentine Foundation of Genetics Applied to Psychiatry.

We recently added to patients with Fragil X Syndrome resistent to folic acid, psychotropics. After lithium was added there was little improvement. Finally lithium carbonate 50 mg, Haloperidol 0,5 mg. Imipramine 5mg. Folic acid 200 mg was given trice a day Three patients are on treatment. Patient 1, age 17, 105kg,170 cm tall. Testicules 25 ml. Two tests were taken, first in 1982 showed an IQ of 69, and another in 1988 an IQ of 49. Speaks with litany, verbally agressive. Has 14% of Fragil X cells. His mother has 2% of Fragil X cells. Clinically she appears to be in the low normal intelligence range. Treatment began 5 months ago. After 2 weeks, there was a clear improvement. After 3 months medication was changed for placebo and 2 weeks thereafter symptoms worsened. Medication was reinstalled, since then improvement is constant. Patient 2, age 22, 95 kg, 192 cm tall IQ 70. Normally physically. When he speaks gives the impression of being dull, at moments agressive verbally. Has 3% Fragil X cells. Improvement began after 10 days of treatment. Medication was changed for placebo after 2 months. Symptoms worsened after 15 days. Since medication was reinstalled patient is improving. Patient 3, is 19, 80kg, 175 cm tall, IQ75. Physically agressive. Speaks in low tone. Testicules 23ml. Has 5% Fragil X cells. 2weeks after starting treatment there was an improvement. Results obtained until now give us a reasonable expectancy.

Session 22 Free Communications:
Suicidal behavior in pychiatric patients

139

CSF 5-HIAA IN DEPRESSED AND NON-DEPRESSED NON-PSYCHOTIC SUICIDAL PATIENTS

Rajendra Kumar, J.K. Trivedi, P.K. Sinha, R. Mishra, M.P. Dubey*, Department of Psychiatry, K.G's Medical College and C.D.R.I.*, Lucknow, INDIA.

In present study 5-hydroxy indole acetic acid (5-HIAA) has been assessed in Cerbrospinal fluid (CSF) of fourteen patients of MDP-currently depressed with life time history of suicide attempt (Recent or Past) and twenty four patients having neither depression nor psychosis attempting suicide. Ten normal healthy volunteers were also included to have baseline values of CSF 5-HIAA. Selection was made according to predefined stringent criteria. 5-HIAA in lumbar CSF was estimated using high performance liquid chromatography on the same day.

MDP-depressed patients with history of suicide attempt (34.30 ng/ml) and non-depressed non-psychotic suicide attempters (59.50 ng/ml) were observed to have significantly lower CSF 5-HIAA concentrations as compared to normal controls (100.62 ng/ml). When depressed patients were compared with non-depressed non-psychotic group the former were having significantly lower CSF 5-HIAA levels than the latter. Thus, it has been observed that low CSF 5-HIAA levels correlate significantly with suicidal behaviour. The results are discussed in the light of current research.

140

INFANTICIDE-SUICIDE MOTHERS(A REPORT ON SIX CASES)

H.Fotiadis,N.Kokantzis,A.Karavatos,J.Nimatoudis,M. Fotiadou. A´Department of Psychiatry,University of Thessaloniki,Greece.

A number of common characteristics in six married women who during a depressive phase killed,or attempted to,their children and subsequently commited,or attempted to,suicide,are reported.
Mean age 31,8-years(youngest 28,eldest 34-years-old).Five had 2 children,the sixth had one child. Five of these patients had similar psychiatric histories:all of them had a bipolar affective disorder with an early onset.The sixth patient commited her criminal act,at the age of 20,during the first episode of a schizoaffective psychosis.
A common psychopathological trait of all these patients was their numerous ideas of guilt and unworthiness which included other members of the family mainly the husband who was considered by them as being particularly incapable of raising and taking proper care of the children(indeed,two of the husbands were alcoholics).However,none of these acts was characterized by a vindictive tendency against the husband.The three of the patients who survived referred to their deed in a dramatic-heroic manner justifying it as an act aiming to relieve their children from the impending doom.None of the three who survived made a subsequent similar attempt to kill their children,though one of these three did commit suiside six years after event.

141

SCHIZOPHRENIA: POSITIVE SYMPTOMS, NEGATIVE SYMPTOMS AND SUICIDAL BEHAVIOR.

Juan J. Castillón; M.Carmen Tejedor; José M. Pericay. Department of Psychiatry, Hospital Sant Pau. Universitad Autonoma de Barcelona (Spain)

We compare 14 patients diagnosed of schizophrenia (11) or schizophreniform disorder (3) with suicidal symptomatology (9 attempts, 5 ideas), with a control group. Both groups are matched for diagnosis, sex and age. The study of the mental status of the patients is made by the BPRS, SAPS-TP, SANS-TP and HRS-D (18 items). The statystical analysis is made with nonparametric tests (Mann-Whitney).
The most significant results are:
1) HRS-D values differ significantly for both groups.
2) Both SAPS and SANS differ significantly for the two groups.
3) BPRS values do not differ significantly for the two groups.
4) Patients with suicidal attempts (excluding those with only suicidal odeation) differ significantly from the group control in SANS and HDRS value
Conclusions:
1) Almost all schizophrenic and schizophreniform patients with suicidal symptomatology have a superimposed depressive syndrome.
2) Negative symptoms of schizophrenia predispose to the appearance of suicidal behavior.
3) The intensity of positive symptoms is minor in schizophrenia and shizophreniform patients with suicidal symptomatology.

142

SUICIDE DURING TREATMENT IN A PSYCHIATRIC UNIVERSITY CLINIC IN JAPAN

Kaoru SAKAMOTO, Department of Neuro – Psychiatry,Tokyo Women's Medical College, Tokyo, Japan

A total of 45 inpatients were identified and studied who had committed suicide between 1957 and 1986 during inpatient treatment of the psychiatric clinic of Tokyo women's medical college.The distribution of the series by diagnosis was as follows : depression 25,schizophrenia 18,eating disorder 1,organic psychosis 1.
The most common method for suicide was jumping from a high place (40 %),followed by jumping under train (22 %) and hanging (20 %). Suicidal attempts had previously been made by 23 (51 %) of the patients. Our results suggest that patients with previous suicidal attempts were at risk for suicide over a long period of time.As regards the duration of index hospitalization,30 (67 %) had committed suicide during the first 6 months. 11 (24 %) of suicides had taken place between 6 months and 1 year. The latter group was significantly overrepresented when compared with the overall patient population of the clinic.As regards age at time of suicide, it is found that the suicides rate for middle age (35 – 60years) inpatients has significantly increased since 1972.The recent trend of suicides in the general population in Japan might be reflected in this result.
It has been reported in several countries that the suicides rate for psychiatric inpatients has recently signficantly increased. This was, however, not the case in our clinic. Explanations for these differences are discussed with reference to liberal psychiatry, social pressure, rehabilitation activities and early discharge policy etc. The discussion has implications for suicide-preventive measures.

143

HOMICIDE FOLLOWED BY SUICIDE IN SCHIZOPHRENICS

B.J. Havaki-Kontaxaki, V.Kontaxakis, V.A.Protopappa and G.N.Christodoulou

State Psychiatric Hospital of Attica and Department of Psychiatry University of Athens, Greece

In many studies concerning homicide followed by suicide the majority of subjects suffered from depression(Rosenbaum and Bennett 1986).
During the last 29 years(1959-1987) 22 schizophrenic patients committed suicide while receiving inpatient care in the Psychiatric Hospital of Attica in Athens(Kontaxakis et al 1988). Four of them (18%) had committed homicide in the past.In this paper we describe these 4 cases of homicidal-suicidal schizophrenics. All subjects were male, were suffering from paranoid schizophrenia and had previous psychiatric hospitalizations. The age ranged from 31 to 67 years. Three were single and one was widowed. Three had previous depressive episodes and three were suffering from a concurrent neurological illness(cerebrovascular disease or epilepsy). The interval between homicide and suicide ranged from one year to 25 years, while that between date of admission and suicide ranged from three months to 19 years. The victims were:the father,the wife,the erotic rival and a friend of the patient's mother.The methods used for suicide were:hanging(3 patients) and jumping(1 patient).

144

ATTEMPTED SUICIDE BY DROWNING

V.P.Kontaxakis, G.N.Christodoulou, H.A.Ioannidis, B.J.Havaki-Kontaxaki

Department of Psychiatry, Athens University Medical School, Eginition Hospital, 74 Vas.Sophias Avenue, 11528 Athens, Greece

Attempted suicide by drowning, an infrequent method of suicidal attempt, is considered by many authors as a violent way of attempting suicide. During a period of eight years (1978-1985) 33 subjects (15 male and 18 female) with a mean age of $38.9(\pm 18.6)$ years were referred to the Out-patients Department of Eginition Hospital in Athens, as emergency psychiatric cases after they attempted suicide by drowning. These suicidal attempters were compared (on social-demographic and clinical variables) to a random sample of 106 subjects (43 male and 63 female) with a mean age of 30.8 (± 13) years, who in the same period of time, were referred to the same Department after they attempted suicide by drug-overdose (non-violent method of attempting suicide). Attempters by drowning were differentiated from the overdosers in only two variables: age and morbidity. More specifically they were of an older age ($p<0.05$) and were more often suffering from schizophrenia ($p<0.01$). The two groups did not differ in many other variables such as: sex, marital status, employment status, education, living situation, previous suicidal attempts, duration of illness, previous hospitalizations and management.

145
SUICIDAL ATTEMPTS BY SCHIZOPHRENICS

Dr. Denis Morin, Dr. J.Gailledreau
Psychiatre, Chef de Service, C.H.V.Dupouy
d'Argenteuil, France

Suicide in schizophrenics is a longstanding problem which, over time, has interested first moralists, then psychologists and psychiatrists. Suicide by psychotics does not completely fit the model of common suicidal attempts or even the model of melancholic suicide, as none of the affective disorders usually found in such patients is apparent. However, the deliberation and forcefull determination which characterize these attempts are very suggestive of the melancholic patient's deep distress, even though the clinical presentation leaves no doubts as to the true nature of the disorder. These desperate acts pose both a theoretical problem and a practical problem. The theoretical problem is to determine whether two disorders are present, with one (i.e. the dissociative disorder) overshadowing the other (i.e. the melancholic disorder). The practical problem is the question of how suicide can be prevented in such patients. The author reports ten cases of suicidal attempts in true schizophrenics managed for several years at the Argenteuil Hospital.

146
ENFERMEDAD AFECTIVA Y RIESGO DE SUICIDIO

ABRIL GARCIA, A.; ABRIL HERNANDEZ, J.

Spain

En el estado actual de la ciencia médica, donde la aportación de información tanto bibliográfica - como estadística a nivel mundial adquiere dimensiones desorbitadas, es necesario contar con el tiempo suficiente para intentar aunar la información adquirida desde la realidad clínica y la realidad bibliográfico-numérica.

En este Trabajo se realiza una reflexión no solo teórica sino tambien desde la práctica clínica personal del fenómeno depresión-suicidabilidad, en un intento de analizar las aparentes paradojas en que el clínico se suele encontrar a la hora de comprender y explicar la potencialidad suicida de sus enfermos a la luz de los aportes científicos publicados en la literatura.

147
The Increase of Suicides in Psychiatric Hospitals of Southern West-Germany According to Diagnostic Subgroups

Manfred Wolfersdorf, Rüdiger Vogel,
Günter Hole
Department of Psychiatry I and II University of Ulm,
D-7980 Ravensburg-Weissenau, F.R.G.

The increase of hospital suicides in European and North American psychiatric hospitals during the last 15-30 years could be shown by different research groups. In state mental hospitals but also in psychiatric clinic in larger cities we found an increasing number of suicides especially in young male schizophrenic inpatients. There were always high suicide rates in psychiatric inpatients with affective disorders but it seems that the increase of hospital suicides is only significant due to schizophrenic inpatients.
Some data on 55 depressive and 115 schizophrenic inpatients with suicide during hospital treatment compared to inpatients without suicide (matched pairs due to age, sex, diagnostic groups) are shown and discussed.

148
SUICIDAL BEHAVIOUR IN PSYCHIATRIC PATIENTS

R.K.MAHENDRU, MD. AND S. MAHENDRU, MBBS.*
G.S.V.M. Medical College, Kanpur, INDIA.
* Practicing Psychiatrist, Kanpur, INDIA.

Suicide remains one of the most challenging problems for mental health experts. The problem is being further complicated by increasing use of general hospital psychiatric services where patients often feel free to give shape to their ideas and wishes. The present report aims at investigating the prevalence of suicidal behaviour in psychiatric out patients and studying their diagnostic characteristics and socio-demographic variables. Of the 310 psychiatric patients selected for the study, 148 (47.7%) had either attempted, committed, threatened or wished to end their lives. The suicidal behaviour was significantly more frequent in affective disorders as compared to other diagnostic categories. The patients with affective illnesses were mostly the victims of attempted suicide while schizophrenics mainly had suicidal tendencies. One of the interesting and thought provoking observation is that nearly half of the suicidal patients developed the tendencies for this extreme step during the course of treatment. Suicidal behaviour was significantly more frequent in widows, widowers and separated individuals than in married and bachelors. Significantly higher rate of parental deprivation was seen in suicidal patients. The implications of these findings are discussed.

Session 23 Free Communications:
Anxiety-phobic disorders

149
LOCUS OF CONTROL AND DEPERSONALIZATION/DEREALIZATION IN ANXIETY DISORDERS

A.D.Rabavilas and E.Tsaltas,
Athens University Medical School, Department of Psychiatry, Eginition Hospital, Athens, Greece.

The locus of control personality trait (LC) and the depersonalization/derealization clinical state (DD) were hypothesized to phenomenologically share the same characteristics, i.e. the potential dissociation between the "self and the others". In order to test this hypothesis, the probable association between LC and DD was investigated in 243 patients meeting the DSM-III criteria for generalized anxiety (n=82), panic (n=51), phobic (n=48) and obsessive-compulsive (n=62) disorder. Patients were administered a 17-item LC scale, a questionnaire measuring frequency, intensity and duration of DD as well as various questionnaires for direction of hostility, hypochondriasis and obsessionality. The results suggested that LC and DD scores were normally distributed within and across patient groups. External LC was significantly related to frequency ($P<0.001$), intensity ($P<0.05$) and duration ($P<0.01$) of the depersonalization/derealization experiences as well as to introverted hostility ($P<0.005$) and hypochondriasis ($P<0.01$). These findings confirm the hypothsis put forward. Some proposals regarding the psychopathology and the management of the depersonalization/derealization experiences in patients with anxiety disorders are presented and certain suggestions for further research are made.

150
HOME TREATMENT OF HOME-BOUND AGORAPHOBICS

James F. Hooper, M.D.,
Clinical Director, Taylor Hardin Secure Medical Facility,
Tuscaloosa, AL, USA
Assistant Clinical Professor of Psychiatry,
University of Alabama, Tuscaloosa, AL, USA

Based on the numerous studies that have been done on the use of medications to treat panic attacks with agoraphobic symptoms, I decided to evaluate those patients who had such severe symptoms that they could not come to the doctor's office to be seen. In a series of home visits, I established that the vast majority of agoraphobics who were home bound found some coping mechanism to allow themselves limited freedom of movement, and that they responded to treatment with alprazolam equally as well as did patients seen in clinics. Within two weeks, the average agoraphobic patient can comfortably leave their home alone.

I interviewed over a dozen patients in their home, using a complete structured interview designed to be consistant with the multi-center studies published in the Archives of General Psychiatry. These patients gave a very consistant picture of developing panic attacks, then generalizing this to avoidance of specific situations, and finally generalization to being completely homebound. After a period of from six months to five years, they found some system, from alcohol abuse to dependency on a spouse, that allowed them to leave their house.

151
PERCEPTGENETIC SIGNS OF SEPARATION ANXIETY IN AGORAPHOBIA AND ASTHMA

I.A.Rubino,S.Grasso,G.Bersani,N.Ciani
Dept. of Psychiatry,IInd University of Rome,Italy

Perceptgenetic (PG) research allows the experimental assessment of anxiety and defenses by means of the repeated presentation of very brief (tachistoscopic) visual stimuli representing danger situations. In this study a separation stimulus (mother who walks out of a room, leaving a baby on the floor)(Nilsson et al.,1986) was employed to explore PG signs of anxiety in two groups in which the relevance of separation anxiety has been frequently stressed: agoraphobics and asthmatics. The stimulus was administered to 17 agoraphobics (group A), 15 intrinsic asthmatics (group B) and 14 extrinsic asthmatics (group C). Chi-square computations were used throughout. Signs of anxiety bound to the perceptual structure, but not involving awareness of pain were more frequent in group B than in C ($p<.001$) and in A ($p<.05$). Signs of anxiety with awareness of pain were more common in group A than in B ($p<.05$) and in C (trend). These data suggest that: a) the paradigm used is able to differentiate neurotic from psychosomatic anxiety; b) intrinsic asthma is more "psychosomatic" than extrinsic asthma (confirming the 'interaction hypothesis' of Block et al.,1964, which has been challenged by Wistuba, 1986).

152
AIDS PHOBIC SYNDROME IN JAPAN

Tetsuo KUMAKURA
Tokyo Metropolitan Bokutoh General Hospital,
Tokyo, JAPAN

Since the report of the death of a Japanese prostitute due to AIDS in January of 1987, social concern about AIDS has spread rapidly, culminating in widespread fear of AIDS in Japan. Many Japanese have come to worry that they are infected with AIDS. We have named this phenomenon the AIDS Phobic Syndrome. The syndrome can be divided into four categories: the transitory anxiety group, the neurotic group, the depressive group, and the delusional group. In Japan, the number of AIDS in 1988 was 97, and the number of persons infected with HIV was 1,065. Japan thus does not have many AIDS patients, but does have many AIDS phobic patients. The following four points represent the cultural background of the AIDS Phobic Syndrome in Japan. 1) Hypochondriac tendency of the Japanese 2) Scepticism toward doctor's diagnosis of fatal illness 3) Secretive nature of sexuality 4) Concepts of domestic purity and foreign impurity. The last point deserves special attention. From ancient times in Japan, the dominant view has been that pathogenic bacteria usually comes in from the outside. AIDS symbolized the common Japanese fear of imported pathogenetic bacteria in this time of the rapid internationalization, which is one reason for the prevalence of the AIDS Phobic Syndrome in Japan.

153

LA PHOBIE D'IMPULSION : UNE URGENCE PSYCHIATRIQUE A ECOUTER ET A ENTENDRE.
VASSEUR Christian - Annecy (FRANCE)

La phobie d'impulsion pose toujours une question angoissante au psychiatre pris dans l'urgence d'une appréciation pronostique sur l'imminence d'un acte violent.

Or, une observation clinique attentive privilégiant l'approche phénoménologique et l'écoute, permet de rendre à la phobie d'impulsion sa dimension de phobie vraie, dégagée de l'impulsion phobique ou phobie impulsante et de l'obsession impulsion.

Symptôme signal d'une crise de l'identité elle est un appel urgent à ne pas manquer. Comme toute phobie, elle montre, à travers un déplacement métaphoro-métonynique, une histoire en souffrance que le sujet n'arrive pas à entendre. Au psychiatre de comprendre la demande de sens qui lui est adréssée et non d'y faire obstacle en répondant à l'angoisse d'un acte signifiant par un acte qui, se voulant rassurant, sera aliénant condamnant le sujet à rester sourd à lui-même.

Entendue, la phobie d'impulsion, de crise devient moment fécond annonciateur de réaménagement interne et signe de vie psychique.

154

Behavioristic suprastructure in phobias
BENGESSER GERHARD M.D.,M.I.A.E.P.
Wagner-Jauregg-KH , LINZ Austria

A behavioristically seen suprastructure-all conditioned reflexes in Pavlov's sense - is formed in almost all phobic states. The lessening of tension after a ritual is committed ("enhancement") is cementing that suprastructure, so the "sanation" of the depth does not lead to removal of symptoms. Therefore it is necessary for the treatment of phobic states, to "alloy" the gold of analysis with the silver of behavioristic therapy.

155

IS THE PANIC DISORDER EXCLUSIVELY DUE TO THE BIOLOGICAL ANXIETY ?
Slavoljub Djurdjić,M.D.,Ph.D.
DEPT.OF PSYCHIATRY,UNIVERSITY CLINICAL CENTRE,BELGRADE

The panic disorder is considered to be the manifestation of the biological anxiety, without the significant contribution of the situational stimuli in the development of the disorder. While it is true that the situational stimuli that cause the panic attack can not be easily identified, the notion that the panic disorder is of exclusive biological origin represents the oversimplification of the facts.
The author discuss his study in which desenzitizatio n to the anxiety provoking internal stimuli was effective in the treatment of the panic disorder patients. He proposes that the physiological conditioning is significant in the development of the disorder.

156

THE AFFECTIVE NATURE OF ANXIETY NEUROSIS
Prof. Dr. M.Yosry Abdel Mohsen
Prof. of Psychiatry, Faculty of Medicine, Cairo University, Egypt

Anxiety and depression represents diametrically opposed basic ego responses. Anxiety as a reaction to danger indicates the ego desire to survive, while in depression the ego is paralyzed because it finds itself incapable to meet the danger (Zetzel, 1960).
Anxiety disorder occupies an ambiguous position between two different nosological concepts which increased the confusion about its nature being an affective disease or just simple psychoneurotic illness.
68 patients with anxiety and depressive symptoms were the subject of clinical analysis according to their symptom presentation, premorbid personality, precipitating factors, family history and course of the disease.
Results of treatment with maprotiline or bromazepam were evaluated according to predominance of either anxiety or depressive symptoms.

157

MASKED ANXIETY (M.A.)
Adrian Restian, M.D., Uzina "Tractorul"
Brașov; Mircea Lăzărescu, M.D., Clinica
Psihiatrică Timișoara, the S.R. of Romania

It is shown that all diagnostic criteria of anxiety and all anxiety scales include somatic symptoms of anxiety. Literature data and the authors' experience argue for the possibility of introducing the concept of 'masked anxiety' - similar to that of 'masked depression' (Hertrich, Kielholz, and others).
J.Lopez-Ibor's idea of somatic symptoms in anxiety (included in the concept of 'angustia vitalis') is reevaluated. The authors noticed somatic expressions of anxiety in 180 hospitalized patients with anxiety disorders in the interval prior to their admission in the hospital (6 to 24 months). On the other hand, in 300 patients with different somatic diseases, the psychic and somatic signs of anxiety were stronger than depressive signs.
The authors consider that the evaluation of masked anxiety is very important in general practice. It is shown that patients with M.A. had trouble in processing and expressing information.

Session 24 Free Communications:
Schizophrenia: Treatment modalities

158

TEN TO FORTY-TWO YEARS' FOLLOW-UP OF PSYCHOSURGERY IN MENTAL DISORDER
Sadao Hirose
Department of Neuropsychiatry
Nippon Medical School Hospital, Tokyo, Japan.

Concerning my operative series of 523 cases in the past 25 years between 1947 and 1972, I have personally continued follow-up study of these patients from 10 to 42 years up to the present day. Among them more than 50 cases are still working adequately. They have shown the long-term duration of improvement and have mostly made progressively better social adjustment in the later years following the operation. Most of them did not show any undesirable personality deficit. Of course, the excellent results of psychiatric surgery have only been obtained in strictly selected cases. The clinical picture and the premorbid personality of the patients are most important factors in the results to be expected from the surgery. Most satisfactory results have been obtained in protracted depressive states. Outstanding outcome have also been obtained in 'atypical' schizophrenia (schizophreniform psychoses) with well preserved personality, compared with poor results in typical deteriorating schizophrenia of Kraepelin's type, even in the early stages. Most cases with typical schizophrenia covered by Kraepelin's concept show irreversible process to a chronic and general personality dieorganization. In my own experience, any types of psychosurgical operations do not prevent the progressive deterioration caused by the schizophrenic process itself.

159

Intérêt des entretiens d'accueil pour l'élaboration du projet thérapeutique.
GOUGOULIS N., DALLE B. (Centre Hospitalier Spécialisé Sainte-Anne), Paris, France.

Les auteurs souhaitent montrer l'intérêt des entretiens d'accueil en hôpital psychiatrique, effectués en présence du groupe soignant lorsqu'un patient gravement souffrant y est hospitalisé, dans le but d'établir un projet thérapeutique envisageable pour le long cours.
Le cadre du travail portant sur une période de cinq ans est une unité de soins de l'hôpital Sainte-Anne à Paris, dans lequel 20 de nos patients y ont été reçus dans cette visée dès leur admission.
Les entretiens d'accueil ont permis de définir pour eux un quadruple champ de soins : a) psychothérapique b) institutionnel c) familial d) médicamenteux associé, quand nécessaire, selon les modalités qui seront développées. L'expérience présentée met en relief le caractère fondamental de ce type d'accueil ; c'est en effet de l'importance accordée dans des échanges de qualité à des moments privilégiés d'écoute conduisant à des mouvements d'ouverture thérapeutique. Le psychotique peut ainsi nous semble-t-il, poser avec les soignants le cadre transférentiel indispensable dans lequel il devra nécessairement évoluer pour éviter la régression déficitaire.
L'étude des 20 cas présentés permettent de conclure à la possibilité dans ces conditions de maintenir pour le temps nécessaire le cadre thérapeutique hospitalier sans l'exposer à une chronicisation redoutée.

160

Evaluation des psychothérapies au long cours chez les grands psychotiques.

DALLE B., WEILL M, EDEL Y., FERNANDEZ A., ISANRD P., GOUGOULIS N. (Centre Hospitalier Spécialisé SAINTE-ANNE), PARIS, FRANCE.

Les auteurs proposent une réflexion critique sur les résultats qu'ils ont obtenus depuis dix ans en traitant - dès leur admission en unité de soins psychiatriques - des psychotiques gravement souffrants sur un mode fondamentalement psychothérapique et dans un quadruple champ : individuel (par petit groupe soignant désigné), familial, institutionnel, médicamenteux (associé, non systématique). Ils entendent ainsi mettre en relief les éléments d'une dynamique transférentielle psychotique : thérapeutiquement intégrable et apte à modifier - durablement et significativement - le parcours existentiel de certains grands psychotiques.
Attachés à la spécificité des processus individuels, à l'écart des évaluations systématiquement établies en cohortes comparables, les psychiatres-psychanalystes sont-ils capables de proposer des "observations" crédibles ? La revue des travaux antérieurs montre la difficulté pour une telle entreprise d'échapper aux développements classiques de la rémission spontanée ou de la prééminence de la médication associée.
D'où l'établissement d'un programme d'évaluation multiple et longitudinale qui tienne compte à la fois de la problématique spécifique de la psychothérapie des psychotiques et de la nécessité d'une transmission non ésotérique des effets qu'elle est susceptible de produire.

161

PSYCHOTICS IN LONG TERM GROUP ANALYTIC THERAPY
D.Moshonas,M.Tsemperlidou,N.Karapostoli,A.Kakouri
Open Psychotherapeutic Centre. Athens,Greece.

The paper presents clinical and statistical observations on a population of psychotic patients for whom group analytic therapy was the main treatment.
The observations focus on therapeutic results in relation to the demographic features of the population, the type of concurrent therapy, diagnoses,and the phenomena encountered during the group therapeutic procedure.

162

A GENERAL SYSTEMS THERAPY FOR INPATIENT CHRONIC SCHIZOPHRENICS

Paritsis N.
Dromokaiteion Hospital, Athens, and University of Crete, Greece

General Systems Science emphasizes that the relations between the elements of the system significally contribute to the function and behaviour of the systems and sub-systems in which they belong. The advantages of an interdiciplinary approach may be increased through a systems approach, by applying the same principles at all levels of systems organization in a coherent way. The purpose of this work is to apply and test, a systems approach, as a method of treatment by focusing the theraputic intervention on the relations between the elements of the system, at many levels of systems organization.
This approach has been partially applied in a large psychiatric hospital, on a unit with 20 patients, the majority of which were chronic schizophrenics. The results, based on the official documents of the hospital, demonstrate a statistically significant increase in the number of discharges per year, per bed, in this experimental group, as compared to, the group of patients (a) in the same unit the year before, and (b) in another similar unit within the same hospital, the same year this kind of intervention was applied.

163

MENTAL TREATMENT BY NEOMORITAISM FOR CHRONIC SCHIZOPHRENICS
Dr. T. Aritome
Tochigi Pref.Mental Hospital, Japan

We are to make a report about the effective results for the several middle stage schizophrenics through the mental therapy combined with drug therapy. The reporter on the basis of the pour soi genesis theory, schizophrenics get the 無 (nothingness) experience, through the self acceptance pour soi and awake self existence. Actually it is to be done by the universal nature, we are subject to the nature surrounding themselves we are in close contact to the mountain the river the pine tree the cherry tree and somethings, naught to the captured ego, schizophrenics esteem to get the concretly self acceptance pour soi with contradiction and get the 無 (nothingness) experience and deepen the self existence. The therapy base on the theory that schizophrenics stick to the pour soi and to get selfishly thought how to be esteemed by others and how to think others about.

164

GROUP TALKS WITH PARENTS OF YOUNG PSYCHOTIC PERSONS.
Søren Haastrup, Palle Bent Andersen and Anne-Marie Boeck.
Copenhagen County Psychiatric Hospital (Nordvang), Denmark.

Parents of young persons suffering from schizophrenia are emotionally and socially hard strained. Usually they have a vague knowledge of psychiatric diseases and their treatment, for which reason they often feel that their position is not approved and their needs are neglected.
At the Copenhagen County Mental Hospital NORDVANG the obvious needs of the parents have been met by establishing groups of talk for parents of young psychotic persons. Since 1984 8 group courses have been carried through, each course consisting of 7 evenings, where 8 parents and 4 staffmembers have been talking together.
This work has been evaluated by questionnaires and interviews made in 1988. The parents indicated that they had benefited from the talks in the shape of increased understanding of the treatment and the young person's situation, including the increasing ability of putting limits to the young person. The largest benefit formulated was the experience of other people being in the same situation and with whom they could share their own experiences.

Session 25 Free Communications:
Antidepressants in clinical use I

165
FLUOXETINE: REVIEW OF THE LITERATURE AND GUIDELINES FOR CLINICAL USE
Paul Sakkas, M.D., John M. Davis, M.D., Illinois State Psychiatric Inst. Chicago, U.S.A.

Fluoxetine is a new antidepressant drug which has been shown to be a specific serotonin reuptake inhibitor. Over 3,000 patients have been treated with fluoxetine in clinical trials worldwide. Its effectiveness in outpatients with major depression is equal to imipramine, doxepin and amitriptyline. In the long term treatment, fluoxetine showed the same efficacy in prevention of depressive relapses as imipramine and doxepin. Earlier age of onset, chronic course of "atypical" depressive symptomatology and past history of poor response to classical antidepressants are some characteristics of patients who reponded better to fluoxetine. Also, it was effective in the treatment of obsessive compulsive patients. Nausea, nervousness and insomnia were the most frequently reported fluoxetine's side effects. Although these side effects were reported in 20-26% of the patients, they tended to be mild, occurring early in treatment and they resulted in relatively few discontinuations of treatment and they resulted in relatively few weight loss, other adverse experiences were reported more frequently in the comparison group of patients receiving other antidepressants. Fluoxetine decreases heart rate and does not produce any intraventricular conduction delay. The anorexia and weight loss that fluoxetine induces in some patients, may be beneficial in some depressed patients who manifest excessive appetite and weight gain.

166
TRAZODONE R.C. IN MAJOR DEPRESSIVE DISORDER

P. LUIGI SCAPICCHIO, CRISTOS HADJICHRISTOS

S. MARIA IMMACOLATA PSYCHIATRIC HOSPITAL ROME, ITALY

The activity and tolerability of the new controlled release formulation (R.C.) of Trazodone have been evaluated in this open trial.
The study has been carried out on 65 patients (inpatients or outpatients) affected by major depression or depressive neurosis, whose diagnosis is in accordance to the DSM III-R criteria. Patients were both males and females between 18 and 60 years of age. Patients were treated for 6 weeks with dosages of drug varyng from 100 mg/die as the starting dosage to 450 mg/die at the beginning of the 2^ week of treatment. Rating of the psychopatological conditions included the Hamilton Rating Scale for Depression and for Anxiety (HRS-D and HRS-A) administered at the strat of treatment and at days 7, 14. 28 and 42 of therapy. In particular, "insomnia" was studied. The preliminary results are reported.

167
A CONTROLLED TRIAL OF MIANSERIN VS MAPROTILIN IN DEPRESSED OUTPATIENTS
M. de Zwaan, G. Schönbeck, C. Ensgraber, K. Chwatal, L. Pawlik, P. Parzer, R. Macura
Department of Psychiatry, University of Vienna, Austria

The study was conducted to compare the safety and efficacy of mianserin with maprotilin. 42 depressed outpatients (29w, 13m, 21-72yrs), who met DSM III-R criteria for major depressive episode or dysthymia were included. 32 patients completed the study. The trial period was 6 weeks with weekly ratings of clinical state and side effects. Plasma concentrations of drugs were determined weekly. At baseline and the end of study a TRH-test and a physical check up were carried out. Drugs were given in a double-blind, randomised manner. Patients followed a fixed-flexible dosing schedule with a maximum daily dosage of 90mg mianserin or 120mg maprotilin. The only additional psychotropic medication permitted was flunitrazepam. Both drugs proved to be reliable antidepressants. Detailed results with respect to therapeutic efficacy and adverse effects will be presented. 25% of the total sample had a blunted TSH response to TRH before treatment. The relationship of the TRH-test results and of plasma levels with the treatment outcome were also examined.

168
NITROXAZEPINE (SINTAMIL) IN RESISTANT DEPRESSION
R.K. MAHENDRU, MD. AND S. MAHENDRU, MBBS.[*]
G.S.V.M. Medical College, KANPUR, INDIA.
* Practicing Psychiatrist, KANPUR, INDIA.

Nitroxazepine (Sintamil) a new dibenzoxapenine developed by CIBA GEIGY of India has been extensively studied during the last decade for its antidepressant action with fairly good results. 30 adult cases of resistant depression not responding to available antidepressant treatments including ECT were put on switchover trial of Nitroxazepine for a period of six weeks. 3 out of 30 patients dropped out from the trial. 19 out of 27 patients (70.3%) had shown good response (more than 75% reduction in total symptom score), 3 pattients had moderate improvement (50 to 75% reduction in total symptoms score) while 5 (18.5%) failed to show satisfactory response to Nitroxazepine therapy. More than half the cases (54.5%) exhibited positive response at the end of first week, one third patients (31.9%) recovered at the end of 3rd week and the remaining improved after six weeks of treatment. The drug was more or less free from side effects.

169

FLUVOXAMINE THERAPY FOR DEPRESSED PATIENTS
Peter Gaszner
National Institute for Nervous and Mental Diseases, Budapest, Hungary

15 depressed patients (14 endogenous, one none endogenous) had fluvoxamine treatment (dosage between 100-300 mg daily) and were compared to 15 endogenous depressed patients with 100-300 mg maprotiline medication during the 6 weeks single-blind, comparative study. In these patients both drugs showed a good antidepressant effect and there was no significant difference from each other, and were well tolerated. Headache, in the fluvoxamine group, was the only one unwanted effect, but only in a well tolerated level. During the fluvoxamin medication, the patients had lower level of anxiety and sucidal ideation. Because of the good antidepressant effect and the selectivity in the suicidal ideation the fluvoxamine is a good antidepressant compound and the 5TH uptake blocking property should use for treatment of sucidical behaviour. It was used the 50 mg and 100 mg tablets of fluvoxamine, but recommended the use of 100mg tablets for once daily dosing (in the evenings). 15 patients used the fluvoxamine more than 2 months, they were no depressed during this maintenance doses without any side effects.

170

TOLERANCE TO FLUOXETINE TREATMENT

Bruce I. Diamond, Mark Hamner, David Sunde, and Richard Borison - Department of Psychiatry Medical College of Georgia, Augusta, GA 30907 USA

Fluoxetine is a specific serotonin reuptake inhibitor with demonstrated efficacy in the treatment of major depressive disorder. Moreover, it appears to be effective in the treatment of chronic pain and obsessive compulsive disorder. Fluoxetine has an atypical side effect profile for antidepressant reuptake blockers in that it produces insomia and weight loss. We report here four cases of major depressive disorder, two cases of obsessive compulsive disorder, and one case of chronic low back pain in which tolerance developed to the initial theropeutic effects of fluoxetine. In these patients, initial antidepressant, analgesic, and anti-OCD effects were observed following initiation of standard therapeutic doses of fluoxetine. However, each patient required progressive dose increases to maintain these therapeutic effects. Eventually, each patient became refractory to maximum doses of fluoxetine (60 to 80 mg) although remaining tolerant to the drug side effects. The tolerance to therapeutic effects may be secondary to induction of hepatic metabolic enzymes, receptor down-regulatory effects or other possible mechanisms.

171

THE ONSET OF ACTION OF ANTIDEPRESSANTS: a comparison between fluvoxamine and maprotiline
W. F. Gattaz, A. Schmidtke, W. Rost, C. Hübner and K. Bauer
Central Institute of Mental Health Mannheim, F. R. G.

A delayed onset of action of antidepressants (AD) has been suggested by a number of studies, but contradictory findings were also reported in the literature. These inconsistencies might stem from differences a) in the pharmacological mode of action among various AD, b) in the subtypes of depressive illness, and c) in the assessment of the clinical changes.
We investigated the onset of action of a serotonergic (fluvoxamine) and a predominantly noradrenergic AD (maprotiline) in 40 patients fullfilling RDC criteria for "major depressive disorder". To detect subtle changes in psychopathology, patients were assessed over 3 weeks following a tight schedule of subjective and objective ratings.
The improvement in patients on maprotiline began immediately at the start of the trial and continued over the 3 weeks. However this improvement was noticed by the patients (self ratings) with a delay of about 7 days. Patients on fluvoxamine showed less side effects, especially concerning EEG and ECG changes, and a delayed onset of action. The differences between both AD might be due to the sedating effects present in maprotiline and practically absent in fluvoxamine. Nevertheless, our results do not support the hypothesis of a delayed onset of action at least for maprotiline.

Session 26 Free Communications:
Conversion and somatoform disorders

172

CONVERSION DISORDER - ARE THE DSM-III-R CRITERIA ADEQUATE ?

D. Vartzopoulos and F. Krull
Universitäts-Nervenklinik, D-5000 Köln 41, FRG

We questioned, whether DSM-III-R criteria apply to a sample of conversion neurotics diagnosed by traditional methods with neurological examination and psychodynamic interview. The hospital files of patients with psychogenic paresis between 1974-1987 were reevaluated in the light of DSM-III-R requirements. We only included cases with complete remission during hospitalisation: 31 males and 22 females were found. All of them fulfilled the DSM-III-R A,D and E criteria. A temporal relationship between a psychosocial stressor related to a conflict and initiation or exacerbation of symptoms were but in 56% of the cases detectable. In further 5% was mention of the therapist's impression that the patient was consciously aggravating an unconsciously produced symptom. Conclusions: DSM-III-R criterium "B" did not apply to 44% of the sample. In these cases diagnosis was based on the "Gestalt" experience of the patient's attitude and the quality of the doctor-patient relationship. Such a diagnostic procedure is almost impossible to operationalise. Criterium C is equally difficult to evaluate. The concepts of "apparent relation" (crit. B) and of "beeing conscious of his own intentionality" (crit. C) are beset with theoretical presumptions. When DSM-III-R intrudes the field of psychodynamics, operationalisation lives beyond its means.

173
SEX DIFFERENCES IN CONVERSION DISORDER
F. Krull and D. Vartzopoulos
Universitäts-Nervenklinik, D-5000 Köln 41, FRG

There is a time-honoured view that conversion is strongly related to feminity. In this study we set out to determine wether there are any differences between males and females with respect to different conversion symptoms. The hospital files of patients with an hysterical neurosis, conversion type (functional paresis, fits, tremor, aphonia and bladder dysfunction), treated in our clinic between 1974-1987 were evaluated. Diagnosis had been made by neurological examination and psychodynamic interview. The sample comprised 156 females and 83 males. Female patients (mean age: 34.8 years +-14.8) were significantly younger than male patients (42.4 years +-12.6)($p<0.001$). A higher frequency of cases of paresis among males ($p<0.001$) and fits among females ($p<0.001$) were to be found. Conclusions: The theory underlying conceptualisations of conversion is based upon the supposition that the patient´s actual conflict or affect is symbolically converted into a somatic symptom. The symptom conforms to patient´s imageries about disease melded by cultural factors. "Secondary gain" depends on the acceptability of the patient as a sick person by his social milieu. We think, that sex differences in the distribution of conversion symptoms may reflect different social expectencies regarding the "appropriate" illness behavior.

174
L'hystérie en milieu hospitalier algérois

BOUCEBCI M., HAMDANE K., ATTOU A.
CHU de Psychiatrie Drid-Hocine, 16050 Kouba/Alger (Algérie)

L'étude de 123 patients hospitalisés avec le diagnostic d'hystérie a permis de situer la place de cette pathologie et ses expressions actuelles en milieu algérois, société en mutation rapide et profonde.

La fréquence de la dépression et celle des troubles psychotiques est soulignée. Une analyse du groupe "délire hystérique" est faite au plan psychopathologique.

175
DIAPHRAGMATIC MYOCLONUS AND CONVERSION DISORDER

M.P. MARCHAND, N. BATHIEN, J. de RECONDO, P. RONDOT.
Hôpital Sainte Anne, PARIS, FRANCE.

Diaphragmatic myoclonus associated with palatal myoclonus is usually caused by a lesion located in the dentatoolivary system. It has also been stated that some of these disorders could be psychogenic. However, myoclonus of psychogenic origin is an uncommonly reported problem.

We present the case of a woman, 45 years old, with an abdominal myoclonus which had appeared two years before, after a short uncomplicated general anaesthesia. Initially intermittent, these movements soon became permanent and corresponded clinically to focal rythmic myoclonus. Complementary examinations were normal. Electromyographic study confirmed, electrically, diaphragmatic rythmic myoclonus.

This patient had an impressive history of somatization disorder as well as of factitious disorder with physical symptoms. The diaphragmatic myoclonus was considered to be of psychogenic origin. Following transient muscular contractions, the patient elaborated, by a conversive mechanism, a permanent movement disorder.

In 1986, a japanese study reviewed about 50 cases of diaphragmatic myoclonus reported in medical litterature. For most of them, the cause had remained an unsolved question and in over half, hysteria or psychogenic factors were considered a probable etiology.

Understanding the successive links which lead from a psychic disorder to a neurophysiological dysfunction is one of the most stimulating challenges that contemporary neurosciences face.

176
HYPNOTIC CONTROL OF VOCAL CORD SPASM PRESENTING AS ASTHMA OR DYSPHONIA
Wallace LaBaw MD, Kent Christopher MD
& Jeanine LaBaw PsyD
U of Colorado Health Sciences Center,
Denver, Colorado USA

Vocal cord dysfunction presenting as acute asthma is a recently identified syndrome which is very responsive to hypnotic treatment. Patients with this syndrome look, act and feel as though they are suffering from severe bronchospasm. Astute clinicians have been misled. Many patients have been on bronchodilators and other anti-asthma medications for years. Some have been intubated. The etiology of this syndrome is vocal cord spasm. While speech therapy and biofeedback have helped, the greatest success has been achieved through self-hypnosis. It has resulted in rapid and lasting recovery and is now considered to be the treatment of choice. Vocal cord spasm may also result in dysphonia, chronic or acute. Patients with this problem may have only hoarseness or a more severe problem which results in total loss of voice. Some manifest both dysphonia and stridorous respirations. Clinical cases are described and treatment results presented.

177
DIAGNOSTIC CHARACTERISTICS OF CHRONIC AND NON-CHRONIC NON-ORGANIC SOMATIZATION

*Dr Damien Lecompte - Chef de Service Associé
Institut de Psychiatrie
Hôpital Universitaire Brugmann - V.U.B./U.L.B.
Place A. Van Gehuchten 4 - 1020 Bruxelles - BELGIUM*

This study reports DSM-III-R (axis I and axis II) non-exclusive diagnoses of 200 somatizing inpatients without organic disease, consecutively referred to a university hospital consultation-liaison service, compared with a group of 200 consecutive non-somatizing psychiatric inpatients. The data illustrate the heterogeneity of the somatizing disorders, and indicate that fourty percent of the subjects consist of different subgroups of depression; fifteen percent meet the criteria for a dependent personality disorder diagnosis. There are significantly more patients with anxiety and dissociative disorder and histrionic personality disorder in the somatizing group. In accordance with established criteria the somatizing group is divided into chronic and non-chronic somatizers. The findings in the chronic group, compared with the non-chronic group, show significantly more patients with dysthymic disorder and non-affective psychotic disorders. It has been suggested that, in addition to the diagnostic study, an illness behavior pattern investigation in somatization appears useful.

178
SOMATISATION IN PSYCHIATRIC PATIENTS - A STUDY FROM A THIRD WORLD COUNTRY
R.K.Chadda, Lecturer
Dept. of Psychiatry, Univ. College of Medical Scienses and Guru Teg Bahadur Hospital, Delhi, India

Somatisation is a worldwide phenomenon, more commonly reported by patients with lesser psychological sophistication. A wide variety of psychiatric patients present with somatisation ranging from various neurotic disorders to functional psychotic disorders. The phenomenon is more prevalent in developing countries and cultures, where physical symptoms rather than psychological distress are considered as indicative of disease. This cultural belief makes a patient to adopt the somatic symptoms, which he thinks would receive social sanction as an illness and help him in getting a label of sick person. 200 consecutive patients attending a psychiatric outdoor clinic of a general hospital in a developing country were studied. Seventy percent of the patients were found to have different physical symptoms as a part of clinical picture, whereas these were the presenting complaints in about half of the patients. Headache, pain abdomen, pain chest, vague aches and pains, backache, vague somatic sensation in different body parts and fits were the symptoms frequently reported by the sample. Common diagnosis among the somatisers included neurotic depression, anxiety neurosis, hysterical neurosis, endogenous depression and psychogenic pain disorder.

179
FAMILY BASIC ATTITUDES IN SOMATOFORM DISORDERS

M. RUIZ RUIZ, E. SANCHEZ, V. SERRANO, I. MORALES, F. MARTIN y J. ALCALDE
DEPARTMENT OF PSYCHIATRY. UNIVERSITY MALAGA (SPAIN)

En esta investigación fueron seleccionados tres grupos homogéneos (edad, sexo, profesión) para conocer las diferencias de las actitudes básicas familiares entre pacientes con **desórdenes somatoformes, personalidades ansiosas** y personas sin ansiedad manifiesta. El diseño esperimental consideró en cada grupo los núcleos familiares -madre, padre e hijo- siendo distribuidos de la siguiente forma:
Grupo I: Familias en las que el hijo es diagnosticado de **trastorno somatoforme** según los **criterios del DSM-III R.**
Grupo II: Familias donde el hijo presenta una **personalidad ansiosa** detectada por el **16 PF de CATTELL.**
Grupo III: Familias que no cumplen las condiciones anteriores.
Mediante el C.A.B. (**Cuestionario de Actitudes Básicas**, de RUIZ RUIZ y cols.) se valoran los **componentes cognitivos, afectivos y conductuales** hacia la **enfermedad mental, enfermedad crónica, sexualidad, droga, muerte y religiosidad.** Presentamos los resultados obtenidos en las **direcciones y niveles de los acuerdos en la familia**, las diferencias entre los **componentes** y el análisis de las **condiciones** familiares. Asímismo, se conceptualizan los **tipos de familia** según la **consistencia** y **congruencia** de las actitudes.

180
THE INTERPRETATION AND THERAPY OF HYSTERIA : THREE PARADIGMS
Paul L.P. JONCKHEERE
University of Louvain, B-1200 Brussels (Belgium)

Hysteria, though no longer mentioned in the official nosographical manuals, still continues to pose important problems. Three paradigms are raised.
1.A strictly medical model, which often implies useless and expensive examinations. The various treatment lines have only transitory effect. 2.The Freudian model which emphasizes subconscious conflicts. The treatment leads often to a lasting improvement. 3.A third paradigm was developed by Lacan, Israël, e.a. Hysteria is considered as a particular strategy in facing desire.
The role of any paradigm is to bring about a multi-disciplinary confrontation, and to prepare a new paradigm. The phenomenology and the philosophies of existence give rise to three new interpretations. a) Female hysteria results, in part, from a feeling of being-rejected-woman-in the world.
b) Where other pathologies are due to denial or to the "forclusion", Hysteria arises from a contemptuous attitude to the object ("Verachtung"). c) Hysteria is a disease of the "being-with-the-others". It results from the inability of fully realize a bond of love. This new paradigm acknowledges, to the hysteric subject, his status of being sick and preserves, thus, his human dignity. It incites to reformulate the therapy at the phenomenological level.

Session 27 Free Communications:
Psychiatric care policies

182

Deinstitutionalization - Strategies and Human Rights.

Franco Rotelli
Mental Health Services of Trieste, Italy

The progressiv outcome from psychiatry as science to psychiatry as mental health care system - related to the W.H.O.'s goal "Health for everybody in the year 2000 - has changed the subject of human rights.".

Care means not only the protection of the human rights but mainly their production: that is what we mean by being therapeutic.

That is that we have not just to claim anymore the patients' right of a correct therapeutic engagement but that we have to make them able to claim their rights themselves and to make them able to deal with them.

W.H.O. assumes that 50 millions of peopel need psychiatric rehabilitation in the world, therefore we have to perform consequent strategies. Rehabilitation,improving the quality of life, right of beeing fully a subject, are these practical answers to the same matter. In this direction we think it is time to fase some unacceptable realities such as the psychiatric hospital in Leros, the psychiatric hospitals in Japan and also many other countries. However, in the meanwhile it is necessary to inquire into some deinstitutionalization-policies which should have been mistaken as far as they have not determined any concrete rights' production.

The strategies adopted in the deinstitutionalization experiences in Trieste are surveyed in order to review a practical trial of the above-mentioned consepts.

183

THE DIAGNOSIS-RELATED CONTRACT:
ADVANTAGES AND INDICATIONS
Joseph L. Traverso, M.D.
Wayne General Hospital

A new model for time-limited therapeutic contracts is described. Such a contract emerges from the clinical presentation and the diagnoses initially established, and covers both clinical and financial arrangements. This model adequately reflects the current trends of cost containment in mental health, while providing enough flexibility for comprehensive treatments.

The contract requires an accurate estimation of the expected length and intensity of treatment and it mobilizes therapeutic resources according to current standards. Differently from the short-term therapy modalities, the length of treatment is not based on a preconceived number of sessions or the type of focuses at hand; but rather on a procedural concept, similar to the diagnosis-related approach in other medical specialties; indeed the contract is frequently of a long-term nature. When compared to long-term open-ended treatments, this model has shown not to interfere with the development and resolution ot the transference process.

Indications and exclusions are discussed.
Initiation and termination phases are described.
Examples are given.

184

DEVELOPING SERVICES FOR INDIGENOUS PEOPLE OF
NORTHERN ONTARIO (CANADA)
John A. Ward, M. D.
University of Western Ontario
London, Ontario (CANADA)

Psychiatric treatment for indigenous peoples of Canada have often been both inadequate and inappropriate. When the mentally disordered produce problems for their community, they are seized and taken away to a mental hospital several hundred kilometers away to be treated by white professionals who understand neither the language nor the culture. When discharged they go back to an unchanged social situation with little or no possibility of follow-up. Such a process results in repeated admissions and general failure of treatment.

Two approaches may be made to provide a more effective approach to treatment. One of these is in the provision of Native Mental Health Workers with adequate training and backup from the Mental Health System to provide front-line treatment interventions, preventive activities and education. Successful models of this approach have been applied in two areas of Northern Ontario and are now beginning in the Hudson Bay Lowlands. In one area institution of such a programme has been associated with a decrease in mortality rates for both suicide and violent death.

The second approach is in the incorporation of Traditional Indian Spiritual Medicine as part of the treatment plan. A Medicine Man is currently providing treatment for residents of an alcohol treatment centre located on a large Indian Reserve. Such an approach complements regular programmes.

185

ZUSAMMENWIRKEN PSYCHIATRISCHER VERSORGUNGS-
SYSTEME IN DER FRG - EINE EMPIRISCHE STUDIE

R.J. Witkowski, P. Bratenstein, H.J. Ingenleuf, R. Höll,
E. Lungershausen
Psychiatrische Universitätsklinik, Schwabachanlage 6,
D-8520 Erlangen

Nach mehr als einem Jahrzehnt psychiatrischer Modellprojekte und
Förderungsschwerpunkte in der Bundesrepublik findet nun eine
Konsolidierungsphase statt. -

Mit unserem Projekt wurde in einer eng umschriebenen Versorgungs-
region eine Totalerhebung durchgeführt. Die so erhaltenen Daten
wurden einer qualitativen Analyse unterzogen.

In den verschiedenen Einrichtungstypen wurden neben der Leitungs-
ebene auch alle Mitarbeiter befragt. Darüberhinaus befragten wir
niedergelassene Nervenärzte und Psychotherapeuten. Das empirische
Bild wurde durch Patienteninterviews abgerundet.

Die vorliegenden Ergebnisse zeigen den Ist-Zustand einer Versorgungs-
region auf und weisen in manchen Bereichen (z.B. Gerontopsychiatrie,
Kinder- und Jugendpsychiatrie und Versorgung der chronisch kranken
psychiatrischen Patienten) sehr eindrucksvoll auf Defizite in der
Versorgung hin. Auch die Patientenwege in einem Versorgungssystem
lassen sich nicht durch eine administrative Vorgehensweise steuern.
Unsere Ergebnisse zeigen sehr deutlich das Patientenvotum im Bereich
der psychiatrischen Versorgung. Sie stellen eine solide Planungs-
grundlage für die Weiterentwicklung der psychiatrischen Versorgungs-
systeme in einer Region dar.

186

A CASE MANAGEMENT SERVICE FOR THE HOMELESS MENTALLY
ILL
DA Wasylenki, PN Goering.   Clarke Institute of
Psychiatry, Toronto, Canada.
  There are 250 hostel beds for homeless people in
Metropolitan Toronto which serve 12,000 different
persons annually. Estimates of the percentage of
the homeless population which has a psychiatric
diagnosis range as high as 30-40 percent. In 1988
the government of Ontario provided funding for
eight psychiatric case managers to be employed
throughout the hostel system. This paper describes
the case management program and characteristics of
the client population.
  Case managers were trained in psychiatric
rehabilitation and assigned to six hostels.
Clients are screened for psychotic symptoms and
homelessness by staff and then admitted to the
program. This report describes work with 70-80
clients admitted during a six month period. The
process of case management is described as are
relationships between case mangers and clients,
using standardized instruments.
  Client characteristics are also described. Data
include sociodemographic features, history of
housing and homelessness, past and current psychiatric
treatment, substance abuse and criminal activity,
use of services, residential stability, social
isolation, physical and mental health and social
functioning.

187

Homeless mentally ill

M. Nordentoft
Bispebjerg Hospital, Departmenet of
Psychiatry E, Bispebjerg Bakke 23, DK-2400
Copenhagen NV

The Danish survey's of the homeless
mentally ill are reviewed and discussed
in relation to American survey's and with
the chance in organisation of psychiatric
care, development of communication
healthcenters and the chance in attitudes
towards mentally ill.
It is discussed which kind of care would
be the most feasable for the homeless
seriosly mentally ill-

188

A SUICIDE PREVENTION PROGRAM IN A DUTCH MENTAL
HEALTH AREA
J.A. Jenner, M.D., Ph.D.,
Univ. Hospit. Groningen, Holland

For the last ten years a prevention program has
been developed and implemented.   .
Initial problems, basic constituents of the
program and program evaluation will be discussed:
a suicide prevention protocol, prevention program
at secondary schools, training and supervision of
schoolteachers and personnel of the emergency
depts. of regional hospitals and methods to
improve continuity of care.

189

An Evaluation of Psychiatric Care in Two Swedish County Councils

Claes-Göran Westrin, Margareta Axelsson, Inga-Lill Candefjord, Bengt Ekblom, Kerstin Eriksson, Lars Kjellin, Olle Östman

An evaluation of the psychiatric care in two Swedish county councils with differently organized psychiatric services has been carried out in 1986. A representative sample of 100 committed and matched controls of voluntary admitted and their relatives were repeatedly interviewed by independent investigators (psychiatrists and clinical psychologists and psychiatric social workers). Extensive postal questionnaires were answered by about 90 % of the concerned psychiatric personnel and their counterparts in primary care. The results have been analyzed in the light of basic ethical principles. The paper will present the frame of reference and methodology of the study.

The study will allow more specific analyses, for example relating different aspects of outcome to the psychiatric and psychosocial conditions at admission/commitment.

Session 28 Free Communications:
Child and adolescent developmental issues and psychopathology

190

ELECTIVE MUTISM IN TWINS OF PRESCHOOL AGE
Sue Batth, M.D.
The Royal Ottawa Hospital, Ottawa, Canada

The author reviews historical background to and the treatment aspects of elective mutism in preschool age children with a special focus on twins. Clinical case studies will be presented.

191

IS INTELLIGENCE ASSOCIATED WITH BRAIN SIZE?
Nicolaos Rigas
Clinic of Neurology Hessisch Oldendorf
3253 Hessisch-Oldendorf, West Germany

This is a question posed not only by specialists, yet quite frequently by laymen i.e. parents of mentally retarded (MR) patients (P). To throw light upon this subject, 1,105 MR P were studied clinically and genetically in a German institution in Rotenburg, Lower Saxony. The horizontal head circumference (HC) was measured and the IQ calculated with various tests. The frequency of microcephaly ($HC < M-2SD$) was 14,75% of all the P, microcephalics (Mi) with Down Syndrom excluded. Mi had a lower IQ than the rest of the institutionalized P. Therefore, the P with the smallest HC, that means $HC < M-3SD$ had a lower IQ than P with $HC < M-2SD$. Boarderline Mi ($HC = M-2SD$) had a higher IQ than the other Mi. Significant is that male P with macrocephaly ($HC > M+2SD$) often had a slight degree of MR. Some of these P had diagnosed Xqfra-Syndrom. These results show that the HC measurement simplifies the procedure in finding out if a child has the risk of being MR. One useful, clinical application of this observation is that newborns with multifactorial malformations like microcephaly and only among males, macrocephaly, require further comprehensive examinations which would prove if special training from an early phase is needed. Further, parents of these newborns should be aware that if behavioral problems of their children develop, these are most likely linked to their CNS and are very probably connected to their IQ.

192

ON THE ETIOLOGY OF SLEEP DISTURBANCES IN CHILDREN

Lara-Tapia H., Ramirez-Ramirez L.
National University of Mexico, Mexico, DF

Sleep disturbances in children of the variety of parasomnia are frequent, mainly in psychiatric patients, including nocturnal enuresis.
In a sample of 2.660 subjects from more than 500 families, divided into three groups (a normal control, a psychiatric and a neurological group), we observed two principal causes: (1) a strong familial relationship with an obvious genetic influence, in more than 58,66% of cases, (2) a strong correlation of parasomnia with hyperkinesis and other minimal brain disfunction syndromes in the psychiatric group (63% of these children had sleep disturbances).
In all cases these alterations and frequently two or more. One alteration exists only in 56% of the cases.
The order of frequency was: sleep-talking, enuresis, bruxism, night terrors and somnambulism (the most common).
These results suggest the influence of the same neural structures and an evident biological etiology in most, and probably all cases of sleep disturbances in children.

193

LEARNING DISABILITIES AND NEUROLOGICAL SOFT SIGNS.
Roberto MILITERNI, Child Neuropsychiatric Clinic, University of Naples, Italy.

The present study examines the relationship between neurological status and academic school performance in a sample of 152 children in the second grade of a public school. Every child underwent the following test : (a) WISC-R; (b) Bender-Gestalt Test of Visual-Motor Integration; (c) Neurological Examination for Minor Neurological Dysfunction (Touwen); (d) MT Reading Test (Cornoldi). None of the variables considered was significantly correlated. Particularly, the findings suggest that neurological soft signs may not discriminate between learning-disabled children and control. It is difficult to make direct comparisons between the current study and results of other reports because of differences in the method of sample selection, the design of the study and lack of standardization of terminology and tests. Neurological soft signs, learning disabilities and poor cognitive performance are disorders of functions who subtend mechanisms still unknown. In this perspective, rather than bound by a relation "cause-effect", they may be considered to reflect the different aspects of a primary disturbance in the organization of the central nervous system.

194

EMOTIONAL REACTIONS OF NORMAL AND DYSLECTIC CHILDREN TO CLASSIC MUSIC

A.J. Stilianakis, Ch. Bechlivanidis, T. Dardavessis D. Dardavessis, S. Sklavounou-Tsourouktsoglou.

B' Pediatric Clinic, Aristotelian University of Thessaloniki, Greece

The Mozart's "symphony for children" was given to a sample of 112 normal children and to a sample of 18 dyslectic children, aged 7-12 years old, in order to compare the emotional reactions of the two groups to classic music. All the children listened to the music and then descriptions of their fellings, fantacies and colour preference was examined. Results showed the following; a) 65% of normal children responded with feelings of joy and happiness, compared to the 33% of the dyslexics. b) 55% of the dyslexics expressed no emotions, compared to the 23% of the normal children. c) After listening to the music, green was the colour of first choice for normal children and red for the dyslexics. The above findings suggested that dyslexics responded differently to the specific music, when compared to the normal children. This could be an interesting subject for a further study.

195

IMAGES DE PERE CHEZ LES ENFANTS PRESENTANT DES TROUBLES DU COMPORTEMENT.
J. KOUROS, TR. SIDIROPOULOU, J. CHRONOPOULOU.
Société de Psychiatrie Psychologique d'Adulte et d'Enfant. Athènes, GRECE.

Nous avons essayé d'étudier l'image du père chez les enfants qui présentent des troubles du comportement. Nous avons utilisé comme matériel un questionnaire avec 16 doubles questions en modifiant la 4ème partie du test d'adaptation personnelle de C. Rogers. et pour le traitememt statistique leSPSS. Notre population vient de l'Hôpital Pédiatrique Ag. Sophia et consiste à 40 enfants venus pour consulter le Service de Pédopsychiatrie pour troubles du comportement et 40 enfants venus pour consultation aux Services de Pédiatrie et dont l'observation médicale n'a revelée aucune étiologie psychiatrique. Le questionnaire a été rempli par l'enfant, son père et sa mère. Au total nous avons eu 240 réponses. L'âge des enfants a été volontairement choisi de 9 à 13 ans. Nous avons essayé d'avoir le même nombre de garçons et de filles pour chaque groupe. Nous avons utilisé un certain nombre de critères d'exclusion et nos 40 enfants retenus proviennent de 120 cas venus consulter et présentant des troubles de com portement. A noter qu'il s'agit d'enfants habitant Athènes.
Résultats: Les moyennes de notes obtenues pour chaque question de père nous ont permis d'établir une classification par ordre d'importance numérique des caractéristiques pour tous les groupes. La comparaison de ces classifications nous a permis de conclure que dans le groupe pathologique il y a une mésentente conjugale.

196

MORALITY-SPECIFIC HUMAN BRAIN FUNCTION OR SOCIAL CHARACTERISTIC OF HUMAN BEING
Jovan Marić
Department of Psychiatry, University Clinical Center, School of Medicine, Belgrade, Yugoslavia

Morality is the ability of man to make himself the rules of behaviour, to hold these rules permanently and to punish himself by feeling of guilt in case of breaking ones. Superego is an executor of morality and its weapon is feeling of guilt.
According to our concept, morality can be divided into moral judgement /reasoning, thinking/ and moral behaviour /acts/, the former being subdivided into form and content.
The form of moral reasoning is universal-typical for anyone human being. The form of mature morality are: a/ judgement determined by emotions /affective reasoning/ and b/ cognitive orientation determined by internalizade principles.
The form of nonmature morality are: a/ socialy adapted orientation, b/ intuitive-irrational judgement, and c/ egoistic-hedonistic moral reasoning.
The content of moral reasoning is relative dependends of culture,society,religious,individual life history,etc.
In this study the author analyses the form and the content of moral reasoning and moral behaviour in 30 subjects signed as juvenile delinquency using an original test of moral reasoning /TMR 12 moral dilemmas stories and 5 model of reasoning:egoistic,social,emotional,cognitive,intuitive

197

FAMILY RELATIONSHIPS PERCEPTION IN INPATIENT LEUCEMIC CHILDREN
Pierri G., Renna C., Buonsante M., Santoro N.
Institute of Psychiatry University of Bari, Italy

Psychological reaction of children to hospitalization is well known through important studies of many authors.
Relevant importance is given, in this situation, to the attitude of parents towards the illness of their child, according to the severity of its symptoms and its prognosis.
The object of our study is to investigate, in leucemic children, the reaction of the parents, and the perception of the child about his/her parents attitude towards his/her illness, as well as the way this illness modifies family relationships.
For this purpose we employed Family Attitudes Test (L.Jackson), which was also administered in a control group of normal children.
Results are reported in the discussion.

198

EFFECTS OF PARENTAL CHRONIC ILLNESS ON CHILDREN
Nancy Campbell, M.D., Kathleen Franco, M.D.; Monica Proctor; Medical College of Ohio, CAPH, C.S. 10008, Toledo, Ohio 43699-0008

Health value is generally assumed to be universally high, even in children. Much research has therefore, been devoted to studying children's knowledge of health and illness. Studies have typically assessed cognitive understandings of chronically ill children or hospitalized children. Little if any research, however, has explored the child's understanding of illness in relation to the personal experience of having a serious illness in a family member such as a parent. Since it is well known that chronic illnesses can have severe and long lasting effects on all family members, it seems plausible that conditions related to living with a chronically ill parent can effect a child's knowledge of health and illness. It is our hypothesis that children living in a household with a chronically ill parent differ from control children, who did not have a chronically ill parent in their feelings about the stability of their parents, their own health, illness susceptibility, illness prevention, death and family structure. This study will compare the knowledge of health and illness as well as the attitudes or beliefs about illness in children with or without a chronically ill parent.

199

CHILDREN OF AFFECTIVELY ILL AND NORMAL PARENTS
Maria Crigoroiu-Serbănescu
Institute of Neurology and Psychiatry
Bucharest, Romania

AIM of study was to compare psychopathology rate in children aged 10-17 of bipolar (BP) and endogeneous unipolar (UP) parents (C) and to correlate the severity of the psychopathology (SP) in children with factors describing the psychopathological status of both parents, of parents' relatives and familial environment. METHOD: 80 children of BP parents, 70 children of UP parents and two groups of children aged 10-17 of C parents ($C_1 = 80$; $C_2 = 70$) were studied with the procedure described in JAD, 16/1989. RESULTS: Point prevalence of psychic disorders was 61% in children of BP parents, 48% in children of UP parents, 25-26% in the two C groups. The SP in children was related to: severity of the illness of BP/UP parent (in children of BP parents strong relation to the number of manic/mixed episodes), presence of psychopathology in the other parent and in the relatives of both parents, age of onset of BP illness, but not of UP illness in the parent. The sex of the affectively ill parent, parental attitudes, social support were not correlated with the SP in children.

Session 29 Free Communications:
Neurochemical variables in depression and mania

200

IMIPRAMINE BINDING IN PAIN AND DEPRESSION
Erling T. Mellerup and Per Plenge, Psychochemistry Institute, Rigshospitalet Copenhagen, Denmark

Platelet imipramine binding was analysed in patients with psychogenic pain and in depressed patients. In the first group it was found that the patients who in addition to their pain also showed affective symptoms had a decreased imipramine binding. Similarly, in the other group the patients who in addition to their depression also suffered from psychogenic pain had a decreased imipramine binding.
Studies of imipramine binding are now in progress with non-psychiatric patients attending a pain clinic.

201
PLATELET [3H]-KETANSERIN BINDING SITE IN DEPRESSED PATIENTS

Kazuhira Miki, Kazuo Yamada, Hideji Kishimoto and Masaaki Matsushita

Department of Psychiatry, Yokohama City University School of Medicine, Urafune-cho, Minami-ku, Yokohama 232 JAPAN

The authors have made a study of the use of [3H]-ketanserin for the binding site in human platelets in depressed patients. In our studies, human platelet [3H]-ketanserin binding had a pH dependency and optimum pH at about 7.0. This specific binding was linear with pletelet protein. Association and dissociation were rapid. Displacement with cinanserin had two steps, and it seemed this binding had two sites. These facts resemble the studies of saturation which had two binding sites, high and low affinity. Scatchard analysis indicated that this [3H]-ketanserin binding had two sites (high and low affinity sites).
Human platelet [3H]-ketanserin binding in depressed patients also had two binding sites, and the Bmax and Kd of depressed patients were normal as compared to control subjects.

202
THE EFFECT OF ECT ON PLASMA CYCLIC NUCLEOTIDES. A SIMULATED ECT CONTROLLED STUDY.

L. Lykouras, M. Markianos, J. Hatzimanolis, C. Stefanis.

Department of Psychiatry, Athens University, Athens, Greece.

Concentrations of cAMP and cGMP in plasma were measured in 20 drug-free melancholic patients during a simulated ECT (SECT) and a bilateral ECT session. Blood samples were taken every 15 minutes beginning 15 min before and ending 60 min after the SECT or the ECT. Two way ANOVA and paired t-test demonstrated a significant and stronger over time fall in cAMP following SECT. ECT induced a marginal increase ($p<0.05$) at 45 min postictally We postulate that ECT causes an increase in cAMP levels masked by the decrease observed during SECT, caused presumably by the anaesthetic medication. The plasma cGMP levels were increased gradually and significantly after SECT and the same rise was observed during ECT. These effects are discussed in relation to changes in a-adrenergic-cholinergic activities induced by the medication and the electric stimulus.

203
POST PARTUM DEPRESSION: A BIOCHEMICAL PROFILE OF DEPRESSED AND HEALTHY MOTHERS.

P.A.Carney, J. Butler[*], M.P.Fitzgerald.
University Department of Psychiatry, and Pharmacology[*], University College Hospital, Galway, Ireland.

Nine consenting mothers who presented with a depressive illness (I.C.D. 9:296.1) within three months of child birth were compared with eight healthy mothers matched for age; marital status; number of children and time post partum. The mean score of the Hamilton Depression Rating Scale was 18 for the depressed group and one for the controls. The depressed group had significantly raised lymphocyte Beta-adrenoceptor density and reduced platelet 3H-5HT uptake. There was no difference between the patient and control groups in platelet Alpha adreno ceptor density, plasma progesterone, oestrogen and prolactin levels. The abnormal levels in the depressed group returned to control levels following six weeks of treatment with either imipramine or nomifensine. The depressed group had more frequent previous depressive episodes and positive family histories. A trial of nomifensine and imipramine was discontinued when nomifensine was withdrawn for safety reasons.

204
BENZODIAZEPINE BINDING INHIBITORY ACTIVITY IN HUMAN PLASMA

D. Marazziti, S. Michelini, C. Martini[*], G. Giannaccini[*], A. Lucacchini[*], G.C Cassano
Institute of Psychiatric Clinic and "Istituto Policattedra di Discipline Biologiche"[*], University of Pisa, 56100 Pisa, Italy

The theoretical possibility of clarifying some aspects of the biochemistry of anxiety through the identification of endocoids for benzodiazepine (BDZ) receptors has attracted several researchers who have proposed differents compounds as modulators. WE described the presence of a 3H-Flunitrazepam (3H-Flu) binding inhibitor (BBIA) in deproteinized plasma from 14 psychiatric patients. With the present research, we further investigated it in larger samples of anxious (21) and depressed (23) patients, and in 12 healthy volunteers before and after a stressful situation. Our results showed that BBIA was present at significantly higher concentrations in the patients, as compared with the controls in calm situation. The stressed subjects exhibited the intermediate values. These findings are suggestive for the involvement of BBIA in anxiety.

205
BIOCHEMICAL CHANGES ASSOCIATED WITH LITHIUM TREATMENT IN MANIC SUBJECTS
P. Lakshmi Reddy, Sumant Khanna, S.M. Channabasavanna, B.S.S. Rao.

Departments of Neurochemistry and Psychiatry, National Institute of Mental Health and Neurosciences, Bangalore 560029, India.

Although the anti-manic properties of lithium are well established, its mechanism of action remains obscure. In the current investigation 50 manic subjects diagnosed according to Research Diagnostic Criteria were studied. Blood sampling was done at baseline and 3 to 6 months after starting lithium therapy. Biochemical parameters studied included Dopamine Beta Hydroxylase, Mono Amine Oxidase, Na-K ATPase and adenosine deaminase. Cortisol, growth hormone, TSH, prolactin and luteinizing hormones were also assayed. Lithium increased levels of DBH by 14.5 %, MAO by 2 %, Na-K ATPase by 26 %, adenosine aminase by 3 %, cortisol by 22 %, Growth Hormone by 4 %, TSH by 26 % and prolactin by 20 %. There was a 14 % decrease in Luteinizing Hormone.

206
Dopaminergic activity in Late Lutheinic Phase Disphoric Disorder (LLPDD)
P. Castrogiovanni, I. Maremmani, T. Bacci, J.A. Deltito°
Institute of Psychiatry, Pisa University, Italy
°Depression and Anxiety Clinic, New York Hospital, Cornell University, Westchester Division, White Plains, New York, N.Y., U.S.A.

The similarity between LLPDD and Rapid-cycling bipolar affective disorders leads to verify the importance of DA in ethiopathogenesis of this disorder and the possible correlations between this neurotransmitter's activity and the symptomatological picture of each patient.
At the Psichiatric Clinic, Pisa University, patients suffering from LLPDD (according to the diagnostic criteria of DSM III R) were evaluated by means of PAF (Premenstrual Assessment Form) by Endicott and Halbreich on the tenth and on the twentyfifth day of the menstrual cycle.
Dopaminergic activity was investigated by means of the ERG. Each patient recorded her emotional-affective situation and her performance for two months by means of a daily diary.
ERG b wave variations lead to think that the dopaminergic system can have a role of important, even if indirect, modulation on the anxiety experience in LLPDD.

207
NOREPINEPHRINE AND METABOLITES IN CSF, PLASMA, AND URINE IN DEPRESSION

Alec Roy, M.B., David Pickar, M.D., Farouk Karoum, Ph.D., Markku Linnoila, M.D., Ph.D., National Institutes of Health, Bethesda, MD, USA.

Among 140 depressed and control subjects there were significant positive correlations between indices of noradrenergic activity in cerebrospinal fluid (CSF), plasma, and urine. Among the depressed patients, CSF levels of MHPG, plasma levels of NE and MHPG, and urinary outputs of NE and its metabolites NM, MHPG and VMA correlated significantly with postdexamethasone plasma cortisol levels. Also, CSF levels of MHPG, plasma levels of NE and MHPG, and urinary outputs of NE, NM, and VMA were higher among patients who were cortisol nonsuppressors than among either patients who were cortisol suppressors or controls. Depressed patients, who were cortisol suppressors and controls had similar CSF levels of MHPG, plasma levels of NE and MHPG, and urinary outputs of NE, NM, and VMA. These results extend recent observation suggesting that dysregulation of the noradrenergic system and hypothalamic-pituitary-adrenal axis occur together in a subgroup of depressed patients. The possible mechanisms will be discussed.

Session 30 Symposium:
Neuroimaging in psychiatry: An update for clinicians

208
MRI: MORPHOMETRIC STUDIES AND FUNCTIONAL LOCALIZATION.

Nancy C. Andreasen, M.D., Ph.D., University of Iowa College of Medicine, Iowa City, Iowa, U.S.A.

This presentation will review data concerning structural brain abnormalities in schizophrenia and affective disorders, based on total samples of approximately 100 schizophrenic patients, 50 patients suffering from mania, and 100 normal controls. We have confirmed, based on volumetric analyses, prior observations of ventricular enlargement in schizophrenia; we also observe this finding in mania, but to a much less prominent degree. In both illnesses, the finding is contributed almost completely by the male subjects, a finding that may be consistent with perinatal birth injury. In addition, an increased rate of "UBOs" is observed in mania, but not in schizophrenia. We also observe two out of 100 schizophrenic patients to have neurodevelopmental abnormalities of the corpus callosum. We have not reconfirmed frontal, cerebral, or hippocampal atrophy.
The presentation will also review methods for precisely anatomically localizing structural information on structural images.

209

CLINICAL RELEVANCE OF CEREBRAL BLOOD FLOW STUDIES IN PSYCHIATRIC DISORDERS
Roy J. Mathew, M.D., Duke University Medical Center, Durham, North Carolina, USA

A great deal of information is available on factors which influence cerebral blood flow (CBF) in health and disease. In the structurally intact brain, CBF is closely coupled with brain function and can therefore be used as an index of the latter. CBF is influenced by a variety of non-specific factors such as carbon dioxide, age and sex. Under conditions of resting wakefulness, CBF shows an anteroposterior gradient with frontal lobes having highest flow. A number of investigators have reported a reduction in the anteroposterior gradient of CBF in patients with schizophrenia. This finding has also been reported in depression. Several investigators have also reported a reduction in global CBF in depression. Mild degrees of anxiety seem to increase CBF with severe anxiety having an opposite effect. Several studies are available on alcoholism and CBF. According to most, but not all investigators, alcohol withdrawal is associated with sharp CBF decrease which normalizes in a few weeks. Chronic alcoholism with cognitive impairment is accompanied with parallel decrease in CBF. However, with continued abstinence, CBF slowly returns to normal levels. Global and regional CBF reductions characterize different types of dementia and CBF might be useful in differentiating pseudodementia from true dementia. A variety of studies examined the effects of psychotropic drugs and drugs of addiction on CBF.

210

Positron Emission Tomography in Schizophrenia and Affective Illness

Monte S. Buchsbaum, Richard Haier, Erin Hazlett, Chandra Reynolds, Joseph Wu, Steven Guich, Steven Potkin and W. E. Bunney, Jr.

University of California, Irvine, U.S.A.

PET scans were obtained on 48 patients with schizophrenia and 20 patients with affective disorder. Nineteen schizophrenics had never been medicated with neuroleptics. PET scans were obtained following uptake of 18F-deoxyglucose while subjects did the Continuous Performance Test, a visual vigilance task. Patients with schizophrenia showed relatively lower metabolic rates in the frontal lobe and this finding appeared more marked in the right superior frontal gyrus, and among patients who had never received medication. Contrasts with unmedicated affective disorder patients will also be presented.

211

NEUROMETRIC IMAGING IN PSYCHIATRIC ILLNESS
E. Roy John, L. S. Prichep
NYU Med. Ctr. & NKI, NY, NY USA

In Neurometric analysis, quantitative features extracted from the EEG or event related potentials are evaluated statistically relative to normative data. The results yield a matrix with columns representing different regions of the brain and rows representing different aspects of brain electrical activity. A topographic map represents one row from such a data matrix. Psychiatric patients yield neurometric matrices with abnormal findings on several rows. Not only the loci of these abnormal values, but the pattern of relationships among them, are distinctive for different illnesses. Patients with the same illness display similar neurometric profiles. These patterns involve a number of different features. The same features may be abnormal in various pathologies. Thus, diagnosis cannot be reliably inferred from a topographic map alone. We have constructed classification rules for a variety of psychiatric illnesses, including primary degenerative dementia, multiple infarct dementia, unipolar and bipolar major affective disorders, and schizophrenia. Independent replications of these multivariate discriminant functions have shown high sensitivity and specificity. Using cluster analysis, we have identified subtypes of patients with distinctive neurometric profiles within populations of patients with dementia and with schizophrenia. Preliminary data suggest that members of different subgroups display differential responsiveness to drugs.

212

THE CURRENT AND POTENTIAL RELEVANCE OF NEUROIMAGING FOR PSYCHIATRY
David L. Copolov, The Mental Health Research Institute of Victoria, Melbourne and Evian Gordon, The University of Sydney, Australia

The continuing avalanche of new developments in neuroimaging creates a challenge for psychiatric clinicians in their attempts to become selectively familiar with the principles underpinning imaging methods which may eventually find a place in the assessment of their patients. Modern neuroimaging technologies are powerful indeed; positron emission tomography can detect emissions from radioisotopes present in only picomolar concentrations, magnetoencephalography can detect magnetic fields ten billion times weaker than the earth's magnetic field and magnetic resonance imaging (MRI) provides superb spatial resolution. However, despite their power, most modern neuroimaging techniques are likely to remain of primary interest to researchers rather than clinicians for some time to come; the current exceptions being computerised axial tomography and MRI which are useful in screening for gross neuropathology in psychiatric patients suspected of harbouring such pathology from their history or examination.

Session 31 — New Research: Psychoendocrinology

213

THE TRH STIMULATION TEST: A MARKER FOR NON-MELANCHOLIC MAJOR DEPRESSION
Gagiano CA, Fourie J, Müller FGM and Vermaak WJH
Department of Psychiatry, University of the Orange Free State, Republic of South Africa.

Seventy sequential outpatients in a healthy physical state who satisfied DSM III criteria for major depression were selected for further detailed clinical and endocrinological evaluations. Two subgroups emerged, based on phenomenological and neuroendocrinological differences. Changes in the sleeping patterns, body mass and thyrotrophin (TSH) response to thyrotrophin releasing hormone (TRH) constituted the distinguishing features between the two subgroups. Fifty out of the 70 patients had a history of hypersomnia and body mass increase while 20 patients experienced insomnia and weight loss. The Hamilton Depression Rating Scale (HDRS), Basal TSH, Total Triiodothyronine (TT_3); Total Thyroxine (TT_4); Triiodothyronine Resin Uptake (T_3RU); Free Thyroxine Index (FT_4I) levels and Dexamethazone Suppression Tests (DST) were not significantly different between the 2 subgroups. However, the TSH responses to TRH between the 2 groups were significantly different from each other (P = 0,012). This difference became even more prominent when 20 patients with a history of hypersomnia and body mass increase were selected from the original group of 50 patients to serve as an age and sex matched control group for the 20 patients with insomnia and weight loss [TSH response of $x = 14,6$ µ/ℓ (+- 7,5) vs. $x = 8,7$ µ/ℓ (+- 5,5), P = 0,008]. None of these patients had a personal or family history compatible with primary thyroid dysfunction. The above clinical and biochemical data may therefore form the basis for the further refinement of the diagnosis of non-melancholic major depression into two subgroups.

214

CORTISOL RESPONSE TO NALOXONE IN DEPRESSION

Zis, A.P., Grant, B.E.K., Remick, R.A., Clark, C.M.
Department of Psychiatry, University of British Columbia, Vancouver, B.C., Canada

A dysregulation involving the opiodergic system has been implicated in the pathophysiology of depression and the neuroendocrine approach has been utilized to investigate this hypothesis. There are several reports of a decreased prolactin response to opioid agonists in depression, while some studies also suggest that in certain depressed patients, cortisol secretion is resistant to suppression by morphine. Although these findings are suggestive of altered opiate receptor sensitivity, they fail to address the question as to whether there are changes in opioidergic tone in these patients. To investigate this question from a neuroendocrine perspective directly, we examined the effect of the successive administration of three doses of the opiate antagonist naloxone (25, 75 and 225 ug/kg) on afternoon cortisol secretion in eight patients with major depression and eight healthy volunteers. Blood samples were collected at 15 minute intervals. Baseline cortisol levels were higher in the depressed group (T = 3.73, p < 0.006). The integrated one hour cortisol response to each dose of naloxone was calculated as the area beneath the concentration-time curve above the baseline cortisol value. A repeated measures ANOVA revealed that the integrated cortisol response increased with the increase in the dosage of naloxone (F = 19.22, p < 0.0001) but that there was no significant difference between the groups nor any significant group X drug interaction. The implications of these findings for the purported role of the opioidergic system in the pathophysiology of depression will be discussed.

215

ATTENUATION OF PITUITARY-ADRENAL ACTIVATION BY AN OPIATE RECEPTOR AGONIST
G.Tolis, O.Petropoulou, V.Athanasiou
Hippokration Research Unit, Athens, Greece

Pituitary decreased responsiveness to hypophysiotropic peptides imply excess negative feed back from the periphery (i.e. cortisol/ACTH) or enhanced central inhibitory tone (i.e. dopamine/prolactin). Patients with M.A.D. may exhibit such phenomena re: hypothalamic - pituitary - adrenal axis. To assess whether activation of opiate receptors, as it occurs during stress reaction modulates adrenal glucocorticoid output we measured plasma cortisol in 4 healthy non-stressed subjects prior to and after 100γ/kg CRF during a control day and on another occasion 60 min. after fentanyl. CRF in both instances significantly (P<0.005) increased plasma cortisol: CONTROL: BASAL 123.4 ± 19.4 PEAK 123.5 ± 33.5 ng/ml, $\bar{x} \pm$ S.D. EXPERIMENTAL: BASAL 129.3 ± 36.1 PEAK 279.4 ± 42.1 ng/ml, $\bar{x} \pm$ S.D. However, the amount released during the fentanyl experiment was significantly (P<0.005) less than that of the control day.
Above data indicate that activation of µ receptors inhibit ACTH-cortisol output by a suppression of pituitary corticotropes to CRF and may suggest that this mechanism may be operative in chronically stressed patients with M.A.D.

216

DEXAMETHASONE SUPRESSION OF CORTISOL, ACTH, AND B-ENDORPHIN IN RECOVERED DEPRESSIVES AND CONTROLS
A.Barocka*, C.Rupprecht*, M.Rupprecht*, R.Rupprecht**, U.Schrell***, G.Beck*
* Psychiatrische und Universitätsklinik
  8520 Erlangen, FRG
** Psychiatrische Universitätsklinik
  8700 Würzburg, FRG
***Neurochirurgische Universitätsklinik
  8520 Erlangen, FRG

Sixteen in-patients during severe depression and after recovery and twenty-eight healthy controls were studied. The mean HRS-D score of the patients' group was $25\pm 6,8$ during depression and $5\pm 3,9$ after recovery. Blood samples were taken at 7 a.m. and 4 p.m. before and after oral administration of 1 mg dexamethasone at 11 p.m. Plasma cortisol was measured with a standard RIA technique, ACTH with RIA using a specific N-terminal antibody, B-endorphin with a RIA kit using B-endorphin antibodies to Sepharose for extraction. Predexamethasone 7 a.m. ACTH and B-endorphin values were lower in acute patients compared with controls. Dexamethasone had a suppressive effect on cortisol, ACTH and B-endorphin in acute patients, recovered patients and controls. ACTH and B-endorphin were positively correlated. The relative suppression of cortisol, ACTH and B-endorphin was strongest in acute patients, weakest in controls, and intermediate in recovered patients. The degree of suppression was linked with psychopathology.

217

GONADOTROPINS IN SCHIZOPHRENIA OF RECENT ONSET: BASAL LEVELS AND RESPONSE TO GnRH

A.Botsis(1), C.R.Soldatos(2), J.D.Bergiannaki (2), G.Mortzos(1), G.Tolis(3), C.N.Stefanis(2)
(1) Hell.Army Med.Corps,(2) Dept.Psychiat.Univ. Athens,(3) Dept.Int.Med. Univ.of Crete, Greece

Results of previous studies of gonadotropins in schizophrenia have been rather inconsistent, particularly those based on the GnRH test. This is probably due to methodological reasons such as inclusion of patients medicated and non-normal controls. Our patients (N=43, all male aged 22.13 ± 0.5) were naive for psychotropic drugs and their illness duration did not exceed two years. Controls (N=43) were age and sex matched to the patients. In both groups, basal levels of testosterone (T), estradiol (E), sex hormone binding globulin (SHBG), luteinizing hormone (LH), follicle stimulating hormone (FSH) and prolactin (PRL) were assayed. Further, in a subsample of 13 patients and 9 controls, response of LH and FSH to gonadotropin releasing hormone (GnRH) was assessed. Compared with normal controls, schizophrenic patients had significantly higher basal levels of T (5.92 ± 0.32 vs 4.67 ± 0.33 ng/ml, $p<0.01$), SHBG (32.46 ± 1.53 vs 25.15 ± 1.44 nmol/l, $p<0.01$), PRL (183.62 ± 38.41 vs 99.88 ± 12.14 µIU/ml, $p<0.05$), while the basal levels of LH (2.1 ± 0.24 vs 2.55 ± 0.37 ng/ml), FSH (1.35 ± 0.18 vs 1.87 ± 0.27 ng/ml) and E (16.95 ± 3.03 vs 16.05 ± 2.13 pg/ml) did not significantly differ. Patients showed signif. higher response of LH, but not of FSH, to GnRH. Results are discussed in terms of their clinical significance and relevence to etiopathogenetic hypotheses of schizophrenia.

Session 32 Symposium: Issues and challengies with dually diagnosed patients

218

Patterns of Substance Abuse in Borderline Patients
George U. Balis, M.D.

University of Maryland School of Medicine
Baltimore, Maryland USA

Patients with Borderline Personality (BP) are known to show high rates of co-morbidity with substance use disorders. This study compares patterns of substance abuse between 62 BP patients (35 male) and a matched group of 114 other psychiatric (OP) patients (65 male) of various DSM-III diagnoses. Compared to OP patients, both male and female BP patients showed significantly higher rates of substance use disorder, involving both drug and alcohol use. However, alcohol and drug dependence rates were significantly higher only in male borderlines. As to differential substance use patterns, both male and female BP had significantly higher rates in the use of sedative/hypnotic/anxiolytic drugs, and cannabis, in addition to alcohol. There were no significant differences in the use of CNS stimulants, inhalants, and phencyclidine. Male borderlines also showed higher rates in hallucinogen and polysubstance abuse. It appears that BP patients show differential patterns of substance abuse involving primarily CNS depressants. Male borderlines are particularly at high risk in developing polysubstance abuse and substance dependence. These findings will be discussed with a special focus on the self-medication hypothesis.

219

SUBSTANCE ABUSE AND PSYCHOPATHOLOGY AMONG ADOLESCENTS
Monopolis SJ, Brooner, RK, Myhill J.
Francis Scott Key Medical Ctr.,Baltimore, Md., USA

There is increasing appreciation that substance abuse among adolescents may be concomitant to or the result of psychopathology. The traditional views of adolescent substance abuse as "experimentation", "peer pressure phenomenon", "behavior problem", "delinquency", "symptom of family pathology", cannot account fully for all cases and the course of these disorders. Clinical experience supports the notion of a "dual diagnosis" model in some instances. The coexistence of psychiatric disturbance may lead support to the "self-medication" hypothesis of substance abuse (as an attempt to control affect). Disregard of accompanying psychopathology can lead to treatment failures, recurrence of substance abuse and chronicity of psychopathology. Furthermore, this may result in expulsion of "bad students" from school and denial of special education services, as well as management of "delinquents" by the juvenile legal system. It is therefore imperative that adolescent substance abusers receive routinely a comprehensive evaluation in order to detect and treat any underlying psychopathology. Clinical examples, as well as relevant data from an adolescent substance abuse treatment program and a project on the mental health needs of delinquents will be presented. Implications for treatment prevention and research will be discussed.

220

Eating Disorders and Addictive Behavior: Pathophysiologic Considerations
HA Brandt, JA Kassett, MA Demitrack, PW Gold, DC Jimerson. Unit on Eating Disorders, NIMH Bethesda, Maryland, USA

Anorexia nervosa (AN) and bulimia nervosa (BN) share many similarities with the substance use disorders suggesting common pathophysiological defects. Both have a goal-seeking (appetitive) phase and a stereotypic (action) phase. The stereotypic behaviors involved in both illnesses initially relieve emotional discomfort and are pleasurable.

In this presentation, two lines of evidence suggesting the possibility of a common diathesis in eating and addictive disorders will be presented: (1) Utilizing the family interview method, forty bulimic probands and their first degree relatives were studied with systematic interviews, information from relatives and medical records where appropriate. Results indicate significantly higher rates of substance use disorders in the families of bulimics when compared to controls. (2) Utilizing a pharmacologic challenge strategy, we administered naloxone (0.5mg/kg) to patients with AN and BN in a randomized, double-blind design. Eating disorder patients showed hyposensitivity in both neuroendocrine and behavioral effects of naloxone suggesting possible abnormalities in the endogenous opioid system in the eating disorders. Implications of these data will be presented.

221

Substance Use Disorders and Psychiatric Co-Morbidity

Brooner, RK, Bigelow, GE, Schmidt, CW. Jr.
Johns Hopkins University School of Medicine

Opiate dependent, methadone maintained patients with history of intravenous drug use, are known to have high rates of nonopiate drug use and to be a primary risk group for HIV-1 infection and AIDS. In addition, these same patients with concurrent psychiatric disorders have a poor treatment prognosis. Two of our recent studies involving participants (N=66) consecutively enrolled in an HIV-1 Testing and Education Program were given structured psychiatric interviews to determine; (1) the presence of a concurrent (nonsubstance use) psychiatric diagnosis, (2) lifetime rate of abuse of or dependance on nonopiate substances, and (3) number of injections, number and percent times needle sharing, and number of needle share partners for the proceeding twelve months. Sixty percent of the patients were given an additional psychiatric diagnosis. A concurrent psychiatric diagnosis was significantly associated with having a higher number of substance use diagnoses. Patients with a diagnosis of antisocial personality disorder were more likely to abuse multiple substances, reported a significantly greater number and percentage of needle sharing, and reported a greater number of needle sharing partners. These data begin to make clear the complex interaction between IV substance abuse, concurrent psychopathology and at risk behavior for HIV-1 infection.

Session 33 Symposium:
Cell communication, brain integrative function and aging

222

CELL COMMUNICATION AND BRAIN INTEGRATIVE FUNCTION

C. Giurgea
University of Louvain, Louvain-la-Neuve, Belgium
UCB Pharmaceutical Sector, Braine-l'Alleud, Belgium

The problem of communications within the frame of the higher brain integrative functions is discussed in relation with nootropic drugs in particular their prototype Piracetam. It was shown with this drug that while no specific neurotransmitter system is affected, there is nevertheless a general, homestatical-like modulation of most brain neurotransmitters, presumably related to the regulation of the second messengers and other membrane-related mechanisms. As a result, this essentially telencephalic nootropic regulation, leads to brain intra and inter-hemispheric communications facilitation such as seen by cortical sub-threshold intra-hemispheric evoked potentials and/or inter-hemispheric transcallosal evoked responses, as well as of enhanced cortical inhibitory control over subcortical functions. Moreover, the protective nootropic efficiency against brain agressions, facilitates maintenance of higher nervous functions even in pathologic situations, such as for instance hypoxia, drug intoxications, impoverished environmental conditions, etc.
Clinical implications of those fundamental nootropic actions are discussed, particularly in relation to the elderly's autonomy and different learning disabilities.

223

NOOTROPICS IN ALZHEIMER TYPE DEMENTIA (TO WHOM, WHEN AND WHY)

M. Tropper
Geropsychiatric Dept., Geriatric Center Rishon le Zion, Neuropsychiatric Dept. Zamenhof clinic, Tel-Aviv and Bar Ilan University, Israel

Although over 1000 papers related to Nootropics (N) have been published, the topic wether this special class of drugs (with selective action on higher integrative mechanisms of the brain, presumably the telencephalon) represent an indication for treatment (T) in Alzheimer Type Dementia (ATD) has yet not been fully revealed. Our survey is based on available sources of information from 1976-1988. It also includes own experience in long-term T by N published in papers and delivered at international forums, as the main points presented at the last International symposium "Nootropics in Psychogeriatric Medicine" (Chicago, 1987), chaired by us together with Prof. C. Giurgea (University of Louvain, Belgium). Discussed issues : target patients and symptoms ; initial maintaining and supportive dosages ; ways of administration ; treatment periods, efficacy evaluation instruments, among them our based on A. Luria's priciples Geriatric Neuropsychological Assessment & Drug efficacy Evaluation Battery. As ATD represents a multi-stage clinical entity and in its early and middles stages there still exist a constellation of concomitantly impaired and preserved Higher Cortical Functions, we consider target-oriented N therapy as a worthwile interventional strategy in ATD.

224

SPECIFIC VERSUS NON SPECIFIC NEUROMODULATORY ACTIONS OF PIRACETAM ON C.N.S. NEURONS.
A. MAILLIS, E. KOUTSOUKOS, E. ANGELOPOULOS, N. SMYRNIS AND C. STEFANIS.
EXPTL. NEUROPH. & PSYCHOPHARM. LAB., DEPT. OF PSYCHIATRY, EGINITION HOSP., ATHENS UNIVERSITY, ATHENS - GREECE

Piracetam, the prototype of the Nootropics has been shown to improve learning and memory in a variety of animal models and experimental conditions. It was also shown to protect animals from hypoxia and drug intoxications, and to prevent scopolamine-induced amnesia in rats and mice. However, the exact neuronal sites of Piracetam's pharmacological action demand further elucidation. Early experiments with Piracetam have shown an increase of the amplitude of the transcallosal evoked potential, indicative of a rather selective facilitation of interhemispheric communication. Also, despite Piracetam's analogy to GABA, it does not specifically affect cerebral GABAergic function, on the basis of measurements of GABA content, synthesis and receptors. On the contrary, a relatively specific ligant binding effect o² Piracetam was shown for L-glutamate receptor sites. Similarly, central NA activity seems to be increased by repeated Piracetam exposure. as shown by an increased inositolphosphate formation in hippocampal slices. Repeated administration of the substance also increases the density of the muscarinic receptors in the frontal cortex of aged mice, a process which seems uninfluenced by concomittant administration of either choline or scopolamine. Microintophoretic studies with Piracetam on the somatosensory cortex, hippocampus and dentate area of rats have shown that the substance affects neuronal activity by depressing or facilitating the spontaneous firing rate, depending on the area studied. These effects were either additive or counteracting the postsynaptic actions of glutamate, GABA and acetylcholine when administered together on the same neuron. These observations, together with available data including the results reported above, support the assumption that Piracetam may act as a neuromodulator upon specific membrane elements, presumably the synaptic sites.

225

PIRACETAM AS A CELL COMMUNICATION ENHANCER : NEURORECEPTORS
W.E. Müller, L. Stoll, T. Schubert
Department of Psychopharmacology, Central Institute of Mental Health, D-6800 Mannheim

One of the biochemical changes that take place in animal or human brain during the course of normal aging are alterations of density and function of several neurotransmitter receptors. Because of its important role for cognitive function the cholinergic system is especially well investigated in this aspect. We have recently started with the hypothesis that nootropics like piracetam might act in part by restoring such age-related deficits of neuroreceptors. The results obtained so far are strongly in favor of this assumptions since several mechanisms of central m-cholinoceptor function are enhanced by chronic piracetam treatment, e.g. receptor density and receptor response as measured by charbachol induced accumulation of inositol-1-phosphate. Since similar findings have also been reported for other nootropics including phosphatidylserine the data suggest that chronic treatment with nootropics seems to restore age-related deficits of central m-cholinoceptors.

226

INTRACELLULAR COMMUNICATION: ROLE OF SECOND MESSENGERS
A. TOLEDANO
Instituto Cajal. C.S.I.C. Madrid. Spain.

The intracellular step of cellular communication includes all the mechanisms involved in the production of the global cellular response after the external signal has crossed the cellular membrane. It is only in the case of some intracellular receptors that the complex ligand-receptor posseses sufficient "mobility" for permiting its transference to the site that promotes the cellular response. But in most cases, membrane receptor-induced effects occur at a distance from the initial chemical signal, mediated by mobile intracellular molecules that are capable of activating the response mechanisms. These molecules have been called "second messengers". Several types of these molecules have been described: ions (Ca^{2+} K^+); nucleotides (cyclic AMP and GMP); proteins (calmodulin; phosphoproteins); inositols and dacylglycerol; and arachidonic derivatives.
Several second messengers act in a consecutive form to promote a "cascade of cellular events", ending in the final response, which, sometimes, includes a nuclear functional change.
Second messengers represent an important level of integration of external and internal signals, of great interest in the control of neuronal (and brain) function. Several alterations of them have been observed in pathological and aged brains.

227

INTERCELLULAR COMMUNICATION: ROLE OF MEMBRANES
E. CUENCA and O.C. SODERBERG
Department of Physiology and Pharmacology. School of Medicine. University of "Alcalá de Henares". Madrid. Spain, and U.E.R. Pitié-Salpêtrière. University "Pierre et Marie Curie". Paris VI. France.

New concepts about the role of the cell membrane in the communication between cells have emerged in recent years. This has been due to the improved knowledge of the structure and function of constituants of cell membranes.
In this review a brief summary of cell membrane structure and function will be given in order to clarify how the information that reach cells through extracellular messengers, which generally do not penetrate cells, is handle and transformed through mechanisms purely membrane dependent. Emphasis will be given to those central nervous system receptors and other membrane constituents involved in some neuropsychiatric disorders and/or the mechanism of action of certain psychotherapeutic agents.

228

THE EFFECTS OF PIRACETAM ON THE LYSOSOMES AND LIPOFUSCIN OF THE CEREBELLAR AND HIPPOCAMPAL NEURONS OF LONG-TERM ALCOHOL TREATED RATS.
Paula-Barbosa,M.M.,Andrade,J.P.,Pinho,M.C. and Madeira,M.D. Dept. Anatomy, Porto Medical School, Oporto, Portugal.
A precocious and progressive deposition of lipofuscin(Li) was observed in the Purkinje and CA3 pyramids of rats treated with a 20% aqueous ethanol(E) solution. Piracetam (P) belongs to a group of nootropic products which actually might have protective effects in situations of brain anoxia. We decided to test its action using our experimental model to ascertain its interference with the lysosomic (Ly) cell compartment. The following groups of adult rats were studied after treatment during 12 months as follows: a) 20% aqueous E solution; b)pair-fed controls; c)E-treated with 20% E plus P (800 mg/kg body weight); d)pair-fed animals plus P and e)E-fed during 6 months and then switched to water plus P until 14 months. The fraction of primary Ly and Li granules (Vv) was calculated with a MOP-Videoplan. The results obtained in Purkinje and Ca3 pyramidal cells were identical. The amount of Li was reduced in all groups ingesting P. Alternatively, the Vv of Ly was increased in these very same groups. It can be infered that P imped the formation of increased amounts of Li in the neurons of E treated animals. The mechanisms which underly this finding remain to be demonstrated although it is tempting to advance that P might enhance the Ly metabolic machinery including the peroxidative cell capabilities.

229

PIRACETAM INHIBITS CHANGES IN PHOSPHOLIPID MONOLAYERS PRODUCED BY ANAESTHETICS.
A. Fassoulaki, Department of Anaesthetics, St. Savvas Hospital, Athens, Greece.

Anaesthetics (A) might act by altering the ionic permeability and therefore the electrical conductance of cell membranes. We studied the effect of three alcohols, isoflurane and enflurane, alone or preceded by piracetam (P), on the surface potential of the phosphatidylcholine (PC) monolayer. The PC monolayer was formed on 145 mmol KCl in a teflon trough and the surface potential was measured with a Kiethley electrometer. The A produced a negative going change in the surface charge of the PC monolayer. 10 µl (2 mg) of P applied to the monolayer before adding the A partially inhibited the changes produced by them. Since A fluidize the membranes and P opposes this action, P might have an effect on MAC or on recovery time after anaesthesia.

Session 34 Symposium:
Cultural psychiatry issues in Africa and South America: Community practice

230

CASE OF COLLABORATION BETWEEN MODERN AND TRADITIONAL HEALERS IN NIGERIA
Professor O. Morakinyo and Dr. K. Peltzer
Obafemi Awolowo University

One of the key areas in contemporary mental health care in Nigeria is the integration of western type (scientific), and African traditional/religious health care. The Nigerian National Health Policy acknowledges traditional healing. However, western trained practitioners of medicine differ on whether or not traditional healing practices should be integrated or incorporated into the government health care delivery system. Medical students at the Obafemi Awolowo University Teaching hospital, Western Nigeria, were exposed to talks by a competent traditional healer (Babalawo) on traditional healing and mental health care during their psychiatry posting. The teaching and the subsequent discussions were recorded and evaluated, considering (a) course content, (b) teaching method, e.g. the case study, (c) students reactions, and (d) group dynamic process, particularly centering around scientific and supernatural concepts of health practice. Specific recommendations are made regarding curriculum and course development on teaching traditional healing and mental health. In particular it is spelled out which aspects of the traditional illness concept and healing skills should be integrated into psychiatric training and practice in Nigeria.

231

PLACER DES PATIENTS PSYCHIATRIQUES CHRONIQUES CHEZ LES TRADIPRATICIENS
Baba Koumare, J.P. Coudray, E. Miquel-Garcia
Hôpital National du Point G, Bamako, MALI

Se référant aux dispositifs villagecis d'assistance réalisés en Afrique dans la perspective d'une psychiatrie communautaire, les auteurs partent de leur propre expérience de placement des patients psychiatriques chroniques auprès des tradipraticiens pour aborder l'épineux problème de l'intégration des deux systèmes de soins traditionnels et conventionnels ainsi que la collaboration entre psychiatres et tradipraticiens.

Ils insistent sur les aspects fort intéressants et controversés de cette entreprise tout en proposant un cadre de réflexion sur: les critères de choix du tradipraticien, du patient, la place du médicament, les éléments du contrat éventuel à établir pour nouer, entretenir et maintenir la relation de confiance avec le tradipraticien.

232

COMMUNITY PSYCHIATRY IN A PLURALISTIC CONTEXTE (TANZANIA)
Hauli J, Tanzania

233

"Cross-Cultural Psychiatric Issues in Bolivia"
Prof. Dr. Mario Gabriel Hollweg
Universidad Privada Santa Cruz de la Sierra(UPSA). Santa Cruz - BOLIVIA

Bolivia is a country with very heterogeneous population and variable geographically, constituted by white, mestizos (mestees) and indians and a very small group of blacks in the Yungas region in La Paz. The transcultural psychiatric investigation began in 1968 (Gabriel Hollweg) with comparative studies of patiens from the west and from the east of Bolivia. Among these studies it has been analized comparative transcultural aspects of anxiety and depression in the country. The western indians have the tendency of falling in depression. These indians (aymara and quechua) react to their illness with apathy, aboulia, and with an inclination to Psychosomatize.
On the other hand, in the east of Bolivia the ways to react are anxious and exciting. The "coquismo" (chewing cocas leaves) and alcoholism so frequent in the quechuas and aymaras have their origin in their mythical beliefs and the cultivation of the "coca leaf".

234

ETHNOPSYCHIATRIC SYSTEMS IN DIFFERENT CULTURAL AREAS OF PERU
Professor Dr. Roberto LLanos Z.
Universidad Cayetano Heredia

The main nosologic entities in the Andean region are: 1. Malignant possession, 2. Harm, 3. Fright 4. Bad Omen, 5. Evil Eye, 6. Fall into disgrace and 7. Loss of friends. Traditional therapeutic techniques are based on rituals, conjures, and use of plants trying to «clean» the ailing person, or to restore the faith in those who have «lost spirit». The common aim is to attend the paranoid susceptibility, by projecting into third persons the cause of the pathologic state. Some presentations will require the intervention to overcome a superstitious terror of having offended the spirit.
Other cases, especially in children, the belief in a strong or «evil eye» accounts for diverse states that respond to extraction of the bad influence by rubbing an egg on the child.
«Falling from grace» of the spirits is treated by penitence. Each ethnocultural school recognizes and respects the traditional healer, under many denominations (brujo, curandero, shaman, etc).
All these have their doctrinary basis on animistic and demonic beliefs that are culturally defined.

Session 35 Symposium:
New perspectives on the role of serotonergic subsystems in anxious and affective disorders

235

PHARMACOLOGICAL RATIONALE FOR THE ANXIOLYTIC AND ANTIDEPRESSANT ACTIVITY OF 5HT1A AGONISTS
A.J.Puech
Dept. of Pharmacology, Hopital de la Salpetriere
47, Bd de l'Hopital, 75651 Paris, Cedex 13, France

The 5HT1A subclass of serotoninergic receptors is localized as well as on the cellular body and on certain projections of the serotoninergic neurons. Stimulation of the serotoninergic autoreceptors by 5HT1A agonists decreases activity of the neuron and stimulation of the postsynaptic receptors mimics the effect of serotonine. A decrease in activity of serotoninergic neurons has been observed also with benzodiazepines and this seems to be in relation with the anticonflict properties of benzodiazepines when there is a behavioral inhibition due to punishment. This anticonflict effect seen in animal studies predict an anxiolytic activity or more precisely a desinhibitory property in anxious patients.
On the other hand, the rise of the concentration of serotonine in the synaptic cleft (by specific serotonine uptake inhibitors or by non specific antidepressants) produces an antidepressant activity in humans and antihelpless effect in animal studies. The 5HT1A agonists, via postsynaptic serotonine receptors, elicit the same antihelpless effect in rats suggesting that the activation of the 5HT1A receptors may have an important role in the antidepressant properties of serotoninergic drugs.

236

Pharmacology of 5-HT_{1A} receptor related anxiolytics/antidepressants
J. Traber, J. de Vry, T. Schuurman and T. Glaser
Neurobiology Department, Troponwerke, Berliner Str. 156, D-5000 Köln 80, F.R.G.

Research in the 5-HT field has been stimulated by the characterization of 5-HT receptor subtypes. One of them, the 5-HT_{1A} type, is located in the limbic system which is involved in the control of anxiety and affective states. Specific ligands for this subtype have been characterized and found to be active in animal models of anxiety and depression. Among those compounds are the pyrimidinylpiperazines ipsapirone(I), buspirone (B) and gepirone (G). All three drugs inhibit spontaneous raphe cell firing via an agonistic interaction with autoreceptors of the 5-HT_{1A} class. They are partial agonists at the postsynaptic 5-HT_{1A} receptors in the hippocampus (adenylate cyclase inhibition). I, B and G specifically inhibit rat territorial aggressive behavior. They show anticonflict activity in classical conflict tests such as the Vogel- and the Geller-Seifter-test. Fear related ultrasonic vocalisation of rats is reduced. In the rat social interaction test under high light conditions all three compounds stimulated social interaction, whereas under low light only I is active. I,B and G are active in animal models of depression including behavioral despair, the restraint stress and the learned helplessness paradigms. In clinical studies the compounds have been found active in the treatment of anxiety and depression. This underlines the important role of 5-HT in these diseases.

237

$5HT_{1A}$ NEUROENDOCRINE DIAGNOSTIC AND EFFICACY MARKERS

S.M. Stahl, J.L. Rausch, R. Hauger, Veterans Adm. Medical Center, San Diego, CA, and University of California at San Diego, La Jolla, CA, USA.

The hypothalamic-adrenocortical axis can be stimulated in rats through an apparent $5HT_{1A}$ receptor-mediated mechanism. We utilized the $5HT_{1A}$ affinity properties of gepirone to test for neuroendocrine changes in depressed patients, 90 min. after a 10 mg oral dose. Fourteen patients with major depression were tested in a single-blind, within-subjects, placebo design, controlled for time of day. Ten mg of gepirone significantly increased serum cortisol and growth hormone but not prolactin 90 min. post-dose in comparison to placebo. The cortisol response to gepirone was correlated with the Hamilton depression rating scores on acute administration of gepirone ($r=.54$, $p<0.05$), but not placebo ($r=-.19$, n.s.). Consistent with a partial agonist-induced down-regulation of the receptor, the 90 min. serum cortisol response to 10 mg gepirone was attenuated ($12.5 + 1.0$) in comparison to the acute effect of 10 mg gepirone on serum cortisol ($18.5 + 2.0$, $df=2,18$, $F=5.8$, $p<0.02$) in 10 subjects administered gepirone for 3-6 weeks at doses of 30-70 mg per day. The findings suggest that $5HT_{1A}$ agonist stimulation of cortisol may correlate positively with depression severity, and that the same response diminishes after chronic gepirone administration.

238

IPSAPIRONE HYDROCHLORIDE;PHARMACOKINETICS IN MAN
G. Schöllnhammer, B. Kümmel, M. Beneke
Biochemical and Medical Department
Troponwerke 5000 Cologne GFR

Altogether nine phase I clinical pharmacokinetic and tolerance studies in >100 male and female volunteers with Ipsapirone were performed in FRG, USA and J. Dose range was between 1.0 and 10.0mg as single and repeated oral treatment for a maximum period of 28 days. Ipsapirone hydrochloride (INN) was determined in plasma by a radio receptor assay or by HPLC with electrochemical detection, both methods giving identical results.

The pharmacokinetic analysis of these studies showed rapid absorption of the drug. Maximum plasma levels and AUCs are dose dependent after single and repeated treatment. No influence of sex or duration of treatment are found.
Half-life of elimination from plasma as calculated from logarithmic decay over 2-3 periods is in the range of 1.3-2.7 hours and also not influenced by sex or duration of treatment.
Less than 1% of the dose administered is eliminated as unchanged compound into the urine. Ipsapirone hydrochloride is only loosely bound to plasma, the free proportion being in the range of 6-20%.

239

Ipsapirone in the Treatment of Generalized Anxiety Disorder: Results of US phase II-trials

B. Kuemmel, M. Beneke, G. Schoellnhammer, H. Spechtmeyer

Medical Department, Troponwerke, Neurather Ring 1, D-5000 Köln 80, FRG

Ipsapirone a specific $5-HT_{1A}$ receptor agonist is a substance in a new class of anxiolytics/antidepressants representing a possible new therapeutic principle for anxiety and depression.
In a randomized, placebo-controlled, parallel-group study the efficacy and safety of Ipsapirone was investigated in a total number of 267 patients with moderate to severe generalized anxiety (DSM III: 300.02) in dose ranges of 2,5 mg, 5,0 mg and 7,5 mg Ipsapirone t.i.d. over 28 days. The primary efficacy variables in these studies were the Hamilton Anxiety Scale (HAM-A) and the Zung Anxiety Scale, the safety aspects were detected through laboratory routine and listing of adverse reactions. The improvement in HAM-A scores was significantly greater in the 5.0 mg Ipsapirone group than in the placebo group at all visits. The mean HAM-A score was 24.2 at baseline. Improvements in scores of 5.8, 8.2, 9.8 and 10.9 were seen following each consecutive week of treatment. In the 14-item Zung scale a greater improvement relative to placebo was observed over the treatment course with 5.0 mg Ipsapirone with a significance at week 3. The laboratory data were within normal ranges and did not significantly differ from those of the preexamination test. The most frequently reported adverse experiences (% of patients) are: headache (Ipsapirone 20.3%; Placebo 28%); Nausea (Ipsapirone 16%; Placebo 10%); Dizziness (Ipsapirone 45%; Placebo 17%); and Sedation (Ipsapirone 15%; Placebo 6%). With regard to the primary efficacy variables Ipsapirone proved to be an effective treatment of anxiety disorders.

240

THE ROLE OF NON-BENZODIAZEPINE AGENTS IN THE TREATMENT OF ANXIETY AND DEPRESSION

Laux G
Department of Psychiatry
University of Wuerzburg, FRG

Benzodiazepines until recently have been considered as the drugs of choice in the treatment of anxiety. However, several forms of anxiety (phobic, panic disorders) do not respond satisfactory to benzodiazepine treatment as well as major depressive disorders. Moreover, shortcomings are evident regarding potential of abuse, interaction with alcohol, impairment of psychomotor and memory functions, withdrawal and paradoxic reactions. Thus, it is important to develop improved psycho-pharmacological treatments. The following compounds offer a completely different pharmacologic approach, which can be classified as follows:

- Cyclopryrrolone derivatives (e.g. suriclone)
- Low potent neuroleptics (e.g. fluspirilene depot)
- Selective 5-HT uptake inhibitors (e.g. fluoxetine)
- Selective MAO-A inhibitors (e.g. moclobemide, brofaromine)
- Selective $5-HT_{1A}$ receptor agonists (e.g. buspirone, ipsapirone, gepirone)

Clinical data (efficacy, possible advantages, typical side effects) of these agents are critically reviewed and summarized.

241
Benzodiazepine-withdrawal: A Limitation of Therapeutic Use?

I. Hindmarch

Head of Human Psychopharmacology Research Unit, Department of Psychology, University of Leeds, Leeds, LS2 9JT, U.K.

Withdrawal effects following the termination of treatment with benzodiazepines are transitory. Should they persist then it would be assumed that the original anxiety had reappeared. Most well established anti-anxiety agents, including the benzodiazepines, show withdrawal effects after cessation of prolonged therapy, particularly with abrupt discontinuation of treatment.

A review will be made of clinical studies of benzodiazepine withdrawal and the reported effects will be critically analysed to show that there are differences between benzodiazepines in the extent to which they produce withdrawal effects and that many of the withdrawal effects can be mitigated by reducing and tapering the dose at the end of the prolonged therapy.

The importance of dose treatment regimens will be emphasised as determinants in the aetiology of withdrawal effects and ways of avoiding the unwanted effects of this important therapeutic group will be highlighted.

Session 36 Symposium:
Zur Frage der Stigmatisierung durch der Klinikaufenthault in der Kinder und Jugend Psychiatrie

242-248
ZUR FRAGE DER STIGMATISIERUNG VON PATIENTEN UND DEREN FAMILIEN NACH EINEM STATIONAEREN AUFENTHALT IN EINER KJP-KLINIK
Knoelker U. (Chairman), Schulte M., Luecke M. (Med. Universitaet zu Luebeck), Hotamanidis S. (Univ.Kiel), Dieffenbach R., Hoffman D. (Datteln), Ellebracht H., van Husen B. (Bochum)
Klinik fuer Kinder und Jugendpsychiatrie, Luebeck, W.Germany

Das Workshop befasst sich mit der Frage, ob, inwieweit und wodurch Kinder und Jugendliche, die in einer Klinik fuer Kinder- und Jugendpsychiatrie stationaer behandelt wurden, stigmatisiert wurden. In einem Einfuehrungsreferat versucht M.Schulte, (Luebeck) die Problematik von Stigmatisierung im allgemeinen zu eroertern. In einer multizentrischen Studie tragen die Referenten ihre Ergebnisse unter verschieden Gesichtspunkten vor: M.Luecke (Luebeck), A.Hotamanidis (Kiel), R.Dieffenback, D.Hoffmann (Datteln), H.Ellebracht B.van Husen (Bochum). Anhand eines Fragebogens wurden ehemalige Patienten und deren Eltern befragt, (a) ob und inwieweit sie durch den stationaeren Aufenthalt Nachteile in familiaerer bzw. sozialer Hinsicht erlitten haben, (b) ob das soziale Umfeld ueber die Klinikbehandlung informiert waren oder sind, (c) ob, sie mit Vorurteilen bei sich selbst, in der Familie oder im Umfeld konfrontiert waren oder sind u.ae. Des weiteren soll der Frage nachgegangen werden, inwieweit die Anbindung der KJP-Klinik die Einstellung der Patienten und ihrer Familien beeinflusst hat.

Session 37 Symposium:
Endogenous depression: A valid diagnostic category?

249
REVIEW OF TOPICAL EUROPEAN AND AMERICAN CONCEPTS OF ENDOGENOUS DEPRESSION

Berner, P.
Psychiatric Univ.Clinic, Vienna, Austria

After the exposition of the divergencies which separate the representatives of dichotomie and those of a unitarian model of depression, the author discusses the various paradigmatica and operational approaches to this problem.
The theoretical and pragmatical background of the divers approaches is demonstrated and the pros and cons of scales and operational criteria on hand are enlarged upon.
The choice of the systems to be used for different purposes is reviewed and the advantages of a poli-diagnostic approach are emphasized.

250
DESCRIPTIVE AND CLINICAL VALIDITY OF CONCEPTS OF ENDOGENOUS DEPRESSION
Michael Philipp, Wolfgang Maier
Department of Psychiatry, University of Mainz, FRG

Eight competing operational definitions (OD) of endogenous depression were simultaneously applied in 173 psychiatric inpatients presenting with a depressive syndrome of heterogenous phenomenology. These OD were: Research Diagnostic Criteria (RDC); Diagnostic and Statistical Manual of Mental Disorders (DSM-III); Michigan Dicriminatory Index (MDI); Newcastle-Scale I (NC1); Newcastle-Scale II (NC2); Taylor-Abrams-Criteria (TAC); Vienna Research Criteria (VRC); and Hamilton Endogenomorphy Subscale (HES).
Comparing the amount of overlap (Kappa) between all OD the greatest overlap was found for RDC, NC2, and DSM. Using the latent trait model of Rasch six OD prooved to be related to the same latent diagnostic concept (RDC, DSM, NC1, NC2, TAC, and VRC). Using the indepently assesed clinical diagnosis (ICD-9 296.x) as a yardstick six symptoms were identified which were significantly associated with ICD-9 endogenous depression. According to the association with these six symptoms content validity was highest for RDC and NC2 and lowest for MDI and HES. Concurrent validity (association) according to the clinical ICD-9 diagnosis (296.x) was given with RDC, DSM, NC1, NC2, TAC, and VRC; no association was found with MDI and HES. Criterium validity was assesed using the criteria: association with DST-nonsuppression, recurrency, bipolarity; non-association with age, sex and severity of depression). NC2 and VRC met most of the external validity criteria, MDI, HES and DSM met none.

251

THE CONSTRUCT VALIDITY OF THE DIAGNOSTIC MELANCHOLIA SCALE IN THE QUALITATIVE SPECTRUM OF DEPRESSION
P. Bech
Frederiksborg General Hospital, 3400 Hillerød, Denmark

The target syndromes of depression from a psychopharmacological point of view is a quantitative spectrum of symptoms ranging from dysthymia over major depression to delusional depression.
Independently of this quantitative spectrum it is still a controversial problem whether there exists a qualitative spectrum that can predict response to treatment.
We have argued that the quantitative and qualitative spectrum are ontogonial. Hence, within each level of qualitative depression (dysthymia, major and delusional) it is important to describe the qualitative spectrum. The use of latent structure analysis has shown that the diagnostic spectrum is ranging from endogenous over combined endogenous/reactive to pure reactive to neurotic depression. Different response curves have been found within the diagnostic or qualitative spectrum.

252

ARE THERE BIOLOGICAL MARKERS FOR ENDOGENOUS DEPRESSION?

M. Berger, D. Riemann, P. Fleckenstein, W.E. Müller

Central Institute of Mental Health, J 5, 6800 Mannheim, FRG

The clinical distinction between endogenous and nonendogenous/neurotic depression is based on the assumption that the endogenous form is more independent of innerpsychic and psychosocial conflicts, and more determined by biological dysfunctioning of the central nervous system than the neurotic form of the disorder. Therefore a tremendous amount of studies have been performed to elucidate specific biological markers for the endogenous subtype. Main candidates, also of our own investigations, have been the dexamethasone suppression test, the HGH clonidine test, the HGH insulin-hypoglycymia test, and the investigation of REM latency under baseline conditions and after cholinergic stimulation. Different diagnostic subtypes based on RDC, DSM-III, or Newcastle scale have been used as independent variables. Up to now, biological similarities between endogenous and non-endogenous major depressive disorders seem to exceed the differences. Nevertheless at least subgroups of endogenous depression, especially the 48 h rapid cycler, seem to justify the further search for a specific biological marker for the endogenous subtype.

253

THE VALIDITY OF ENDOGENOUS DEPRESSION BASED ON FAMILY-GENETIC STUDY
M.M. Weissman
Dept. of Clinical and Genetic Epidemiology New York State Psychiatric Institute College of Physicians and Surgeons of Columbia University New York, USA

To address the validity of subtype distinctions with a large family study of major depression, probands (n=133) with major depression were classified into several non-mutually exclusive subcategories. Eighty-nine were classified as endogenous depression and subtypes among first-degree relatives were then compared by the proband's depression subtype.
In an previous publication, we showed that the endogenous as compared to non-endogenous depression did not confer a higher risk for major depression in adult relatives once age of onset of conorbid anxiety or alcoholism was controlled. In this paper we extend the findings to include the probands' offspring, ages 6 to 17 years.

254

ENDOGENOUS AND NEUROTIC DEPRESSION: DISTINCT PATTERNS OF FAMILIAL LOADING?
W. Maier, J. Hallmayer, M. Philipp
Department of Psychiatry, University of Mainz, D-6500 Mainz, FRG

Familial patterns of psychiatric disorders in families of psychiatric patients is a crucial criterion for the validity of a diagnostic class. A series of previous family studies (Leckman et al. 1982. Andreasen et al. 1986) have questioned the validity of the endogenous/ non-endogenous and neurotic/non-neurotic distinction in major depression. However. these studies took into account only a minority of the proposed definitions. It remains also an open question if endogenous and neurotic depressions are running true in families.
A family study in 170 inpatients with unipolar major depression and 50 healthy controls will be presented; patients and relatives are classified by a polydiagnostic approach including all diagnostic definitions of endogenous depression available (including DSM-III-R and ICD-10); dimensional classifications will be considered additionally.
The majority of diagnostic subtypes defined this way are not able to discriminate different levels of morbid risks in families. The pattern of affective disorders in families is, however, not clearly against the endogenous/neurotic distinction. Especially the Newcastle Scales are including several items differentiating various patterns of familial loading. The results demonstrate the need for a new approach in defining valid subtypes.

255

THE NATURAL HISTORY OF ENDOGENOUS DEPRESSION
William H. Coryell, M.D.
University of Iowa, Iowa City, U.S.A.

Perhaps the most important features of a valid diagnosis is the prognostic information it conveys. Endogenous subtyping within major depression implies a clearer response to somatic therapy and, perhaps, fewer undesirable life events during follow-up. Neither of these expectations have been well established by studies using contemporary operational definitions of endogenous depression. Moreover, there is very little published data to contrast endogenous and non-endogenous depression by time to recovery, by psychosocial outcome or by the likelihood of relapse, chronicity and psychosis.

The NIMH Clinical Research Branch Collaborative Program on the Psychobiology of Depression - Clinical Studies has collected such data. Specifically, we will describe the course and outcome seen during a 5-year, semi-annual follow-up of 80 patients with RDC nonendogenous, 185 patients with probable endogenous and 467 patients with definite endogenous major depression.

256

SECULAR TRENDS IN ENDOGENOUS DEPRESSION AND COURSE IN AFFECTED RELATIVES
Philip W. Lavori, Ph.D.
Massachusetts General Hospital, Boston, Massachusetts, U.S.A.

Using new data from the National Institute of Mental Health-Clinical Research Branch Collaborative Study of the Psychobiology of Depression, the secular trends in onset of endogenous depression are investigated in the relatives of affected individuals. The subsequent course of illness in relatives is contrasted, over a six year follow-up interval, between endogenous and non-endogenous subsamples. Using survival analysis techniques, the duration of episodes and well-intervals are estimated.

Session 38 Symposium:
Topics in general hospital psychiatry

257

EXPERIENCE IN A PRYCHIATRIC UNIT OF A GENERAL HOSPITAL
Seguin A. - Peru

258

THE CHANGING FACE OF GENERAL HOSPITAL PRYCHIATRY
Rosenzweig R. - USA

259
EVALUATION OF THE QUALITY OF CARE IN GENERAL HOSPITAL PSYCHIATRY
Cervera S., Zarato R., Torres R. - Spain

260
ACUTE PSYCHOSIS IN SEVERELY BURNED PATIENTS
Basse P., Parnas J. - Denmark

261
THE DISEASE BASED MODEL APPROACH IN THE TREATMENT OF HEROIN ADICTION.

Juan J. López-Ibor Jr., J. Pérez de los Cobos, E. Ochoa.

Department of Psychiatry. Ramón y Cajal Hospital. University of Alcalá de Henares (Madrid, Spain).

Biological, psychological and social factors are involved in the ethiology of drugadiction. The epidemics of the last decades and the lack of effective therapy have lead to a situation where social and economic factors have become the leading approach to deal with this huge health care problem. Of course, cultural, economic, and even political conditions favour a market with severe repercussion on individuals and public health. Up to very recently, the only medical treatment available for heroin adiction was the substitution by another opiate methatom which very often become itself part of the drug market. For several years we have been aplying strategy based on methods to cope with enviromental stresses and a naltrexome maintenance treatment. With this approach up to two thirds of heroin adicts are free of their adiction one year after the initiation of the treatment.

Session 39 Special Session:
Psychosomatics in theory and practice

262
LOW DOMINANCE AND PROSTAGLANDINS IN PRIMARY DYSMENORRHEA
Aritzi S., Richardson Cl., Moiras G., Aravantinos D., Creatsas C. and Lyketsos G.C.

A series of studies of seven physical conditions of presumably psychogenic origin revealed the common hostile personality characteristic of low dominance. The present study extends the research to primary dysmenorrhea, to which psychogenic factors have also been attributed. Personality characteristics were investigated in relation to biosynthesis of prostaglandins. The main sample consisted of thirty student nurses suffering from dysmenorrhea and 18 controls. Because these were self-selected, data were also collected from the remaining 88 students of the classes, of whom 19 appeared to suffer from dysmenorrhea. Personality characteristics were measured using Fould's Personality Deviance Scale (PDS) and Scale of Anxiety and Depression (SAD). Wing's Present State Examination (PSE) was administered to 18 cases and 12 controls who gave blood samples at menstruation, when concentrations of PGF_{2a}, PGI_2 and TxA_2 were measured. It was found that scores on the Dominance Scale of the PDS were significantly lower in girls with dysmenorrhea than in controls (p=0.004). All prostaglandins were in much higher concentrations in cases than controls and concentrations of PGF_{2a} and TxA_2 exceeded that of PGI_2 in cases while the reverse was true in controls.

263
BETA-ENDORPHIN'S RELEVANCE IN EVERYDAY PSYCHIATRY PRACTICE
C. Reynaert, P. Janne, A. Collin, M. Vause, S. Goffinet, A. Seghers, P. Decoster, L. Cassiers
University of Louvain, B-5180 YVOIR, Belgium

A growing amount of literature is focused on the "psychiatry-peptides" interface. The aim of the present study is to examine systematic biases present in beta-endorphins (ß-END) dosage and to assess the clinical relevance of such dosages for the everyday practice in psychiatry.
According to this, the importance of variables such as age, weight and sex in ß-END total variance is studied in 87 consecutive in-patients.
Second, co-variations between ß-END and serum cortisol and prolactin (levels and rhythms), thyroid function, as well as several criteria of the immune function (OKT4/T8, IgM, IgG, IgA,...) are examined.
Third, effect of washout, weight loss, use of major and minor tranquilizers, hypnotics, and antidepressants upon ß-END serum levels is examined.
Finally diagnosis (DSM.III-R), self-rating scales (anxiety and depression), pain threshold and tolerance, as well as results at the dexamethazone suppression test are considered in order to understand the remaining ß-END variance.
The results indicate that, when biasing factors are carefully controlled, ß-END dosage remains a useful tool to assess both biological and psychological improvements in the psychiatric patient.

264
OCCURRENCE OF ALEXITHYMIC FEATURES IN A GENERAL POPULATION SAMPLE
Lindholm Tomi, Lehtinen Ville & Veijola Juha
The Rehabilitation Research Center
Turku, Finland

The purpose of this study was to assess the prevalence of alexithymic features in the general population and its associations to sociodemographic factors including sex, age, social order and domicile (rural v. urban).

The material of the study was obtained from the follow-up of a long-term social psychiatric study of a Finnish population cohort. Altogether 747 individuals (349 men and 398 women) aged from 31 to 81 were assessed in relation to alexithymia using the Beth Israel Questionnaire (BIQ).

Alexithymic features (BIQ score 3 to 8) were more frequent in men (34%) than in women (23%) and increased with increasing age. They were also more frequent in lower social strata and in those living in rural areas compared to those living in urban areas.

The findings show a clear association between alexithymic features and sociodemographic factors. Alexithymia should be considered also as a social phenomenon.

265
ALEXITHYMIA AND PSYCHOLOGICAL DISTURBANCE IN CHRONIC PAIN PATIENTS.

M.Joukamaa[1] and T.Nurmikko[2]; Mental Hospital for Prisoners[1], Turku, Finland and Department of Neurology, University Central Hospital[2], Tampere, Finland

Alexithymia has been reported among a wide range of medical and psychiatric disorders. Only a few studies have explored the associations between alexithymia and mental disturbance in different patient groups. The purpose of this study was to determine how alexithymia and mental disturbance are interrelated in chronic pain patients.

The subjects were 61 chronic pain patients in a multimodality out-patient pain service. The controls consisted of 49 patients with chronic non-painful disease (diabetes, myopathies, multiple sclerosis). Alexithymia was measured using the Beth Israel Hospital Questionnaire and mental disturbance by the General Health Questionnaire (GHQ-36).

It was not surprising that alexithymia and mental disturbance were not interrelated. It was, however, interesting that both phenomena were more common in the pain group than in the controls. This finding supports the theory that there are different patterns of psychopathology associated with chronic pain.

266
Problems in the therapeutic management of psychogenic pain
Gerald G. Pope, M.D. - Henry Ford Hospital
Detroit, Michigan - U.S.A.

Chronic pain of obscure etiology is a multi-factorial problem resulting from an interplay of sociocultural, biological and psychological factors. The psychiatric classification of psychogenic pain is unsatisfactory as it does not consider pathogenetic mechanisms. Pain complaints may be also encountered in a variety of other mental disorders.

Treatment approaches are usually along psycho-biologic lines. Extensive clinical experience and research in our psychiatric facility suggests that pain "management", than its eradication, should be considered as a reasonable therapeutic goal.

In addition to issues in diagnostic classification, therapy may be cumbersome or time consuming due to difficulties in coordinating the patient's care through a network of medical and non-medical professionals, multipharmacy, or emphasis in non-medical resolution of "pain and suffering", problems in semantics and communication, and obstacles due to intense transference - countertransference phenomena.

267

PSYCHOLOGICAL PROFILE OF PATIENTS WITH ESSENTIAL HYPERTENSION

G. Voukiklaris, B. Alevizos, G. N. Christodoulou, E. Malama
Piraeus General Hospital and University Eginition Hospital, Athens, Greece

Numerous studies have suggested that suppressed hostility and prolonged emotional disturbances may be involved in the development of essential hypertension, but the psychological development of this disease has not been clarified.
In this study, personality factors such as psychoticism, neuroticism, extraversion and lie scale, hostility (introverted and extroverted), alexithymia, somatization and type A personality pattern as well as anxiety and depressive symptomatology were studied in a group of 38 (34 male, 4 female) hypertensives and 55 (44 male, 11 female) controls, using appropriate psychometric instruments.
Using regression analysis it was found that hypertensive patients scored higher in psychoticism (p=0.04), neuroticism (p=0.05), lie scale (p=0.005), somatization (p=0.007) and state anxiety (p=0.05) in comparison to controls.
The results indicate that anxiety and personality characteristics such as neuroticism and psychoticism as well as somatization may contribute together with other factors (constitutional, hereditary etc) in the pathogenesis of essential hypertension.

268

THE PREVALENCE OF GOITRE IN PSYCHIATRIC OUTPATIENTS SUFFERING FROM AFFECTIVE DISORDER
J. Scherer, P. Buchheim, A. Strauss
Psychiatric Hospital, University of Munich
(Prof. H. Hippius) Nussbaumstr. 7, 8 Munich, FRG
In a prospective observational study the authors evaluated a series of 93 consecutive outpatients with major depressive disorder by ultrasound of thyroid gland. Patients, who at any point of their disease had received lithium therapy, were excluded from the study. The diagnosis of goitre was established by sonographical volume measurement of thyroid gland (vol 21ml). The depression was specified as chronic, if the current episode has lasted two consecutive years without a period of two months or longer during which there were no significant depressive symptoms. The evaluation of the data are leading to the following conclusions: 1) The prevalence rate of goitre in patients with major depression (57/93) was significantly increased as compared to the prevalence known for the total of Bavarian population (some 25%). 2) The prevalence rate of goitre was significantly greater in the group of patients with chronic depression (49/57) (p 0.001). 3) The prevalence rate of goitre was not significantly higher in patients responding to antidepressant treatment (8/36) than in the total of population. 4) 17 patients with chronic depression and goitre were treated with T3 (0.006mg/d) along with antidepressant drugs. 4 patients responded well. 5) 14 patients with chronic depression and goitre were treated with iodine (0.05mg/d) along with antidepressant drugs. 2 patients responded well.

269

THE PSYCHOLOGICAL PROFILE OF PEOPLE SUFFERING FROM NEOPLASTIC DISEASE.
Ioannidis H., Alevizos V., Vaslamatzis G.
Dept. of Psychiatry, Athens University Medical School Athens, Greece.

A sample of 1000 healthy people, randomly selected from the general population of a semi-urban community in the Greater Athens Area was investigated through the use of various personality inventories. Ten years later the same sample was questioned as to their current medical record with special emphasis on the development of neoplasia.
The psychological profile of those who did develop Ca (obtained before the appearance of neoplasia) is examined and analyzed statistically in the context of the general population sample, and the possibilities of formulating a concept of cancer-prone personality are discussed.

Session 40   Special Session:
Schizophrenia: Brain structures and functioning

270

Schizophrenia and Frontal lobe

A. LESUR, M. CANAL, J.D. HURET, F. LEGAULT DE MARE, T. LEMPERIERE - Hôpital Louis MOURIER - 92700 COLOMBES - FRANCE -

The involvement of frontal lobe, especially dorsolateral aera, in the etiopathogeny of schizophrenia proceeds from several arguments (neuroleptic action, cerebral imagery, neuropsychology).
25 DSM III schizophrenics, 18-40 years, in psychotic state and treated, were included in this study. Clinical symptoms were rated with Andreasen's scales (SANS, SAPS). We administred a neuropsychological battery consisting of LURIA's tests, categorisation (WCST) and attentional tests (dichotic listening, stroop-test, cancellation test, trail making test). These patients were compared with 10 normal subjects matched for age and socioculturel level. The analysis of results revealed a neuropsychological pattern independant of the age, the SANS and SAPS's Scores, the duration of illness and treatment. This pattern is different of those, usually, found with the frontal patients. If the schizophrenic and frontal patients exhibit quantitative impairment on tests like block design test, WCST, verbal fluency ; the qualitative analysis of the deficits allow us to discriminate this two populations. In opposition to frontal subjects who show a deficit in ordering or handling of sequential behaviors and an impairment in establishing, maintaining or changing a set, the schizophrenics fail to solve complexe tasks requiring an intermediate and autonomic step of information processing.

271

A STUDY OF FRONTAL LOBE FUNCTIONS IN EARLY STAGE SCHIZOPHRENIC PATIENTS.
Takashi Ishikawa, Hideji Kishimoto, Osamu Takatsu, Haruhiro Fujita and Masaaki Matsushita.
Department of Psychiatry, Yokohama City University School of Medicine, Minami-ku, Yokohama 232, JAPAN.

We studied neurological and neuropsychological frontal functions in patients in whom could be made the exact diagnosis of schizophrenia by examination of psychiatric, neurologic and radiographic evaluations. Our neuropsychological evaluations included general mental status examinations (intelligence, attention and memory); motor functions; sensory, perception and construction functions; language functions; planning function (Wisconsin Card Sorting Test) and so on.

In untreated patients either with positive or negative symptoms, there was no evidence of frontal dysfunction. In treated patients, most of them, even if with negative symptoms, had no frontal dysfunction, but some patients performed poorly on WCST. However, these patients made good improvements after verbal regulated procedure or their poor performance was interpreted as parallel to low-graded intelligence. Therefore, it was not a frontal focal sign but a part of general deterioration.

In conclusion, (1) There was no evidence of frontal dysfunction in many of early stage schizophrenic patients. (2) Psychological mechanism underlying schizophrenic symptoms, even if negative symptoms, had no relation to organic frontal lobe functions (especially planning function).

272

CEREBRAL SPECT IN SCHIZOPHRENIC DISORDERS: A PRELIMINARY STUDY.
Vita A., Dieci M., Garbarini M., Gioibbio G.M., Poggi Longostrevi G., Sacchetti E., Valvassori G., Cazzullo C.L.

Institute of Psychiatry, Milan University
* Nuclear Medicine Laboratory

Regional CBF was evaluated in 11 drug-free schizophrenic patients (DSM-III R diagnosis) and 14 healthy controls. The tracer used in this investigation was Tc 99m-HM-PAO. We demonstrated a diffuse cerebral hypoperfusion in schizophrenic patients as compared with controls. This difference was particularly significant in the left hemisphere: a) in the frontal lobe, both superficial (patients 0.52 ± 0.14; controls 0.63 ± 0.09; t=2.32; $P<0.03$) and deep (patients 0.55 ± 0.10; controls 0.65 ± 0.08; t=2.7; $p<0.01$); b) in the parietal lobe (patients 0.50 ± 0.12; controls 0.66 ± 0.07; t=4.06; $p<0.01$); c) in the temporal lobe (patients 0.53 ± 0.11; controls 0.68 ± 0.06; t=4.03; $p<0.01$). In the right hemisphere the difference of the CBF between patients and controls were not significant. No difference in the antero-posterior gradient of CBF was found between patients and controls. Our results confirm previous observation on the reduction of frontal CBF in drug free schizophrenic patients and are compatible with the hypothesis of frontal hypofrontality at the basis of schizophrenia.

273

REGIONAL BLOOD FLOW IMAGING IN SCHIZOPHRENIA USING 99mTc-HMPAO WITH SINGLE PHOTON EMISSION TOMOGRAPHY (SPECT).
H.Kumbasar, B.Erbaş, G.Ünlüoğlu, A.Aysev, G.Erbengi, C.Bekdik
Ankara/Turkey

^{99m}Tc-HMPAO (hexamethyl propylenamine oxime) has been increasingly used as a new radiopharmaceutical for the scintigraphic evaluation of regional cerebral blood flow. Hypofrontality (hypometabolism and hypoperfusion) has been shown in patients with Schizophrenia using different imaging methods, such as Positron Emission Tomography (PET).
In this study, ^{99m}Tc-HMPAO and SPECT were used to investigate regional blood flow (rCBF) changes in Schizophrenia. We studied 19 acoustic hallucinating patients (11 males and 8 females) aged betwenn 15 and 50 years. The patients had no cerebrovascular disorders, head trauma, and systemic diseases. 15-20mCi ^{99m}Tc-HMPAO was intravenously injected. Using a single-head rotating gamma camera (360^0 for 20 minutes, 60 angular steps each) sagittal, coronal and transaxial slices were performed. The slices were analized quantitatively and qualitatively. Eight regions / hemisphere were drawn on transaxial section and tracer redistribution was calculated for each region. Frontal / occipital ratio (0.916 ± 0.18) and frontal / whole slice ratio (0.975 ± 0.18) were determinated for each patients. The patients had significantly lower frontal / occipital ratio ($p < 0.005$) and lower frontal / whole slice ratio ($p < 0.005$) in comparison to normal group (10 cases). Only two patients had focal decreased activity in the region of basal ganglia. In conclusion, hypofrontality was demonstrated in patients with Schizophrenia using ^{99m}Tc-HMPAO and SPECT.

274

THE LIMBIC COMPLEX IN SCHIZOPHRENIA
A MORPHOMETRIC POST-MORTEM STUDY
Falkai P, Haupts M, Bogerts B, Greve B,
*Machus B, Heinzmann U, Gorny H
Department of Psychiatry, University of Düsseldorf, D-4000 Düsseldorf 12
*C.u.O.Vogt-Institute of Brain Research, University of Düsseldorf, 4000 Düsseldorf
Recent MRI-findings indicate a significant volume reduction of the hippocampus and amygdala, called the limbic complex, in schizophrenics compared to healthy controls. Former research demonstrated a reduced volume of these limbic structures in never treated schizophrenics. Planimetry was performed on post-mortem brains of 10 neuroleptic treated schizophrenics and 14 age-and sex-matched controls. The brains were fixed in formalin, embedded in paraffin, cut in serial whole-brain sections and stained for myelin and nerve cells. Planimetry was done on all sections and computed for volume values for each area of each side separately. The schizophrenic group showed a significant volume reduction of the hippocampus in both hemispheres (left: 30% p=.023, right 35% p=.025), whereas the amygdaloid body was unchanged. The results are discussed in view of developmental anomalies recently found in schizophrenics with hypoplastic hippocampi.

275

NUCLEUS ACCUMBENS IN SCHIZOPHRENIA.
A VOLUMETRIC AND HISTOLOGICAL COMPARISION TO NORMAL CONTROL.
Haupts M, Falkai P, Bogerts B, Greve B,
*Ovary I,
Department of Psychiatry, University of Düsseldorf, D-4000 Düsseldorf 12
*Department of Psychiatry, Semmelweis-Medical-University of Budapest, 1083 Budapest, Hungary

The dopaminergic hypothesis on the pathogenesis of schizophrenic psychoses renders open the question of underlying histological changes in mesolimbic structures. Former research has not demonstrated affection of the nucleus accumbens in untreated schizophrenics. We performed planimetry and histological classification for cellular changes on post-mortem material of 10 neuroleptic treated schizophrenics and 14 healthy controls. Subsequently stained wholebrain sections were inspected microscopically and graded I-III for pathological changes. The results did not show significant differences between the two groups. Although the nucleus accumbens is an important part of the mesolimbic dopaminergic system, it seems to remain histologically unaffected during neuroleptic treatment and exhibit no primary pathology in schizophrenia.

276

Diagnostik und Therapie psychotischer Symptomatik der Läsionen der Limbik
Dr. Jurij Novikov
Allgemeines Krankenhaus Ochsenzoll
Langenhorner Chaussee 560, D-2000 Hamburg

Bei den 21 Patienten mit schizophrener Symptomatik wurden cerebral-computertomographische und kernspintomographische Befunde erhoben. Die Läsionen der Limbik (Dysraphien in regio septalis, Dysplasien im Bereich des vorderen und medialen Temporallappens) führen zu der Herausbildung von psychotischen Symptomenkomplexen, die auf der deskriptiv-phenomenologischen Ebene von schizophrenen nicht zu unterscheiden sind. Die gezielte Überprüfung des Krankengutes unter der Anwendung des polydiagnostischen Ansatzes (ICD-9, DSM-III, Wiener Kriterien nach Berner, Konzept der Basisstörungen nach Huber) zeigte jedoch, daß die korrektere Diagnose "Symptomatische Schizophrenie" lauten soll. Die Studie bestätigt hohe differential-diagnostische Bedeutung der Wiener Kriterien und des Basisstörungs-Konzeptes. Eine sehr hohe EPS-Rate und geringe antipsychotische Effizienz bei der therapeutischen Anwendung von Dopamin-Antagonisten bei diesen Kranken rechtfertigt eine nichtneuroleptische Medikation (z.B.Carbamazepin).

277

THE PARAHIPPOCAMPAL GYRUS IN SCHIZOPHRENICS

Heckers S., Heinsen Y.L., Heinsen H., Beckmann H.

Department of Psychiatry, University of Wuerzburg Fuechsleinstrasse 15, 8700 Wuerzburg, FRG

In recent neuropathological studies of brains of schizophrenics interest was mainly focused on cytoarchitectonic and volumetric abnormalities in the limbic system. We investigated the parahippocampal gyrus, a core region of information processing connecting neocortical and limbic structures, in 20 schizophrenics (11 female, 9 male) and 20 age- and sex-matched controls. Applying stereological methods on Nissl-stained, thick frozen serial sections of complete hemispheres we could find no significant volume reduction of the parahippocampal gyrus in schizophrenics (mean: 3.037 + 0.647 cu mm) compared with the control group (mean: 3.125 + 0.578 cu mm). Methodological problems of delineation and the impact of our findings on a theory of limbic system pathology in schizophrenia will be discussed.

Session 41 Special Session:
Standardized psychiatric interviews

278

VALIDATING THE SCID-II IN CONJUNCTION WITH THE SCID PERSONALITY QUESTIONNAIRE

N.Manos, M.D, S.Hatgisavas, M.D, K.Monas, M.D, S.Donias, M.D, G.Simos, M.D.

CMHC - 2nd University Dept of Psychiatry
Thessaloniki, Greece.

Both the SCID Personality Questionnaire and the Structured Clinical Interview for DSM-III-R Personality Disorders (SCID-II) (which were translated by consensus into Greek by a group of bilingual psychiatrists) were given to 35 patients with Personality Disorders who visited the 2nd University Department of Psychiatry's CMHC. All 35 patients had received a DSM-III-R clinical diagnosis of at least one Personality Disorder. This clinical diagnosis was established by initial clinical consensus diagnosis at the time of intake and review of the diagnosis by the patient's therapist and a senior psychiatrist using the DSM-III-R diagnostic criteria, after a relatively short period of treatment had occured.
The association between the structured interview diagnosis and the reviewed clinical diagnosis is analysed. Overall, SCID-II seemed to confirm the clinical diagnosis, but furthermore it identified additional diagnoses of personality disorders.
The diagnostic-therapeutic implications of the above are discussed.

279

The Psychiatric Interview in Primary Mental Health Care.

Alfons A.M. Crijnen, Dept of Clinical Psychiatry, AMC, Univ. of Amsterdam.
Herro F. Kraan, Dept of Social Psychiatry, Univ. of Limburg, Maastricht.

Attempts to understand the physician-patient communication date to the time of Hippocrates. Freud contributed largely to our understanding of this issue, but it is only recently that empirical studies of the physician-patient communication have been undertaken systematically.

To assess physicians contribution to the quality of the communication in initial medical interviews, we constructed the Maastricht History-taking and Advice Checklist (MAAS-PMHC). The MAAS-PMHC is an 104 item observation instrument consisting of 8 scales measuring discernable dimensions. These dimensions are the exploration of the reasons for encounter, history-taking skills, psychiatric examination, socio-emotional exploration, the presentation of solutions, structuring the interview, interpersonal skills and communication skills. Instrumental utility was extensively studied and generally supported the measurement properties of the pertinent scales.

280

A NEW SYSTEM FOR CLASSIFYING DEPRESSION BY MENTAL STATE SIGNS

Professor Gordon Parker, University of New South Wales, The Prince of Wales Hospital, High Street, Randwick 2031, NSW Australia

Two large samples of depressed patients were studied, using a comprehensive intake assessment of symptoms and signs, the latter assessing retardation and agitation. Multivariate analyses (principal components and latent class strategies) suggested that the signs were far more discriminating than the symptoms. We therefore examined the extent to which a composite "core" sign score differentiated broad depressive types and were able to validate a new system. A comparative analysis of the symptoms and signs confirmed the greater utility of the signs.

281

A COMPARISON OF CATEGO AND DSM III CLASSIFICATION USING THE COMPOSITE INTERNATIONAL DIAGNOSTIC INTERVIEW

Farmer, A.E., Jenkins, P.L., Katz, R., Ryder, L.
University of Wales College of Medicine, Cardiff. United Kingdom.

Diagnostic status of 83 patients interviewed using CIDI are compared using the CATEGO 4 computer program with PSE items drawn from CIDI and DSM III operational criteria.

Diagnostic assignment was shown to be independent of case identity by hierarchical log linear analysis.

There is highly statistically significant agreement for diagnosis. However, DSM III produces a shift away from schizophrenia and anxiety towards affective disorder. DSM III assigns no cases to unspecified psychosis as does CATEGO 4 (N = 5) and disagreement by class of psychosis accounted for 21% of discordancies for current illness and 35% for lifetime diagnosis.

The implications of these findings are discussed.

282

A VALIDITY STUDY OF THE COMPOSITE INTERNATIONAL DIAGNOSTIC INTERVIEW

Jenkins P.L., Farmer, A.E., Martinez G.
University of Wales College of Medicine, Cardiff, United Kingdom.

Validity was assessed in two groups of patients.

Group 1 included 107 General Hospital patients who were interviewed by psychiatric clinicians using the anxiety depression and somatisation modules of CIDI-C. Poor agreement was shown for Generalised Anxiety Disorder where CIDI assigned more diagnoses and Dysthymia where clinicians assigned more diagnoses.

Group 2 included 26 psychiatric patients whose history was summarised and then rated by 5 Psychiatrists unaware of the CIDI assigned diagnoses. Using a case conference format ICD 10 diagnoses were assigned in addition to consensus clinical diagnoses. Good overall agreement was found between CIDI and clinical diagnostic categories.

The implication of these findings for use of CIDI in clinical research are discussed.

283

THE RELIABILITY OF THE NIMH-DIS: LAY INTERVIEWERS TEST-RETEST IN A COMMUNITY SAMPLE

Björnsson, J.K., Lindal, E., Stefánsson, J.G. and Guðmundsdóttir, Á. Department of Psychiatry, National University Hospital, 101 Reykjavik, Iceland.

Most reliability studies of the NIMH-Diagnostic Interview Schedule have compared lay interviewers with psychiatrists, and have in essence been validity studies. A prerequisite for studying the validity of instruments such as the DIS, is adequate reliability.

The basic design of the study was a test-retest administration of the DIS (III-a), where two highly experienced lay interviewers 1) each administered respectively 33 and 32 interviews and, 2) six weeks later readministered the DIS to half of their own and half of each others interviewees. Prior to the second interview, it was ascertained that no major changes which could influence the results, had occurred in the interviewees life since the first administration.

The results indicate that the interview has adequate reliability, but also show that this reliability drops when it is readministered by different interviewers. We therefore conclude that in order to ensure a reliable administration of the DIS, one has to use highly trained and experienced interviewers, that are motivated to do good work. Small mistakes in using this instrument can lead to big mistakes, as e.g. whole sections of the interview can be bypassed.

284

TRANSLATING AND FIELD TESTING THE CIDI: IT'S ALL GREEK TO ME.

C.G.Lyketsos,M.D.(The Johns Hopkins Univ. Dept.of Psychiatry,Baltimore,MD,USA).
G.C.Lyketsos,M.D.(The University of Athens, Dept.of Psychiatry,Athens,Greece).
A.Gerontas,M.D.(Attica Mental Hospital, Greece).
S.Aritzi ,M.D.(Sotiria General Hospital, Greece).

This paper will present a brief account of the field test of the Composite International Diagnostic Interview(CIDI) carried out in Athens. We will focus on two issues. First,the process of translating the CIDI into Greek and the difficulties encountered in this translation will be discussed. Secondly, the results of the Athens field trial will be presented and the agreement between the CIDI generated and clinical diagnoses in the Athens sample will be assessed. Conclusions of the paper will discuss the "Greekness" of the new instrument and its possible applications in national and international research.

Session 42 Symposium:
Eating disorders

285

THE 50-YEAR TREND IN ANOREXIA NERVOSA

A.R. Lucas, C.M. Beard, W.M. O'Fallon, L.T. Kurland, Mayo Clinic, Rochester, Minnesota, U.S.A.

The incidence and prevalence of anorexia nervosa was determined for the population of Rochester, Minnesota during 1935-1984. One-hundred eighty-one (166 female and 15 male) residents fulfilled diagnostic criteria. The incidence rate among female residents fell from 16.6 per 100,000 person-years in the 1935-39 period to a low of 7.0 in 1950-54 and increased to 26.3 in 1980-84. This pattern is due to a quadratic trend in the rates for 10-19 year old girls, while the rates for women age 20 and older remained constant. For females in the 15-24 year age group there was an increasing trend from 13.4 per 100,000 person-years in 1935-39 to 76.1 per 100,000 in 1980-84. The overall age- and sex-adjusted incidence rate was 8.2 per 100,000 (14.6 for females and 1.8 for males). The prevalence rate on Jan. 1, 1985 for Rochester residents was 269.9 per 100,000 for females and 22.5 for males. Among 15-19 year old girls the prevalence was 480.3 per 100,000, making anorexia nervosa the third most frequent chronic illness in adolescent girls.

286

FOOD DIVERSIFICATION IN PATIENTS WITH EATING DISORDERS : A THERAPEUTIC FACTOR ?

Samuel-Lajeunesse B., Simon Y., Criquillion-Doublet S., Hummel P., Divac-Pavlovic S. Clinique des Maladies Mentales et de l'Encéphale, Centre Hospitalier Sainte Anne ; 100, rue de la Santé - 75674 Paris Cédex 14 - FRANCE

The analysis of eating habits among restricting and bulimic subtype of patients with anorexia nervosa has demonstrated that, in addition to quantitative,there are important qualitative disturbances. Techniques aimed at food diversification, applied together with other therapeutic modalities, appear to be useful in maintaining treatment effects

287
Hunger and Satiety Patterns in Eating Disorders

Katherine A. Halmi, M.D. and Suzanne Sunday, Ph.D
Cornell Medical Center, 21 Bloomingdale Road,
White Plains, NY 10605, U.S.A.

Hunger and satiety responses to a liquid test meal were examined in anorectic-restrictors (AN-R), anorectic-bulimic (AN-B), bulimic (B) and controls (C) both pre- and posttreatment. Individual subject's hunger and satiety ratings before, during and after meals were analyzed. These ratings differed between groups across the proportion of meal duration. The pattern of hunger/satiety intersections revealed that most controls showed one intersection during the meal while most AN-R showed no intersections and most AN-B and B showed multiple intersections outside of the meal.

Pretreatment, AN-R and AN-B showed a strong relationship between intersection patterns and amount consumed. This study shows; 1. eating disorder patients perceive hunger and satiety differently from control subjects, 2. eating disorder patients often confuse the perceptions of hunger and satiety.

288
COMPUTERIZED DIAGNOSTIC EVALUATION OF PATIENTS WITH EATING DISORDERS

Simon Y., Criquillion-Doublet S.,
Hummel P., Divac-Pavlovic S.,
Samuel-Lajeunesse B.
Centre Hospitalier Sainte Anne, Clinique
des Maladies Mentales et de l'Encéphale,
100 rue de la Santé, 75014 Paris - FRANCE

The different diagnostic systems for eating disorders which have been proposed on a clinical basis do not clarify patients in a homogenous way.
The rise of a computerized polydiagnostic system including the criteria of DSM IIIR, ICD 10, Feighner and Russell, allows to compare these various classifications.
We present the results of a story including 80 in- and out-patients treated at the Clinique des Maladies Mentales et de l'Encéphale for eating disorders.
The different diagnostic classifications are compared and discussed in the view of their utility for epidemiological, clinical and therapeutic use.

289
SCHIZOPHRENIA AND EATING DISORDERS
C.Foulon, V.Benadon, W.Rein, S.Criquillion Doublet, B.Samuel-Lajeunesse
Clinique des Maladies Mentales et de l'Encephale, Centre Hospitalier Sainte Anne; 100, rue de la Sante-75674 Paris, Cedex 14, France

Results of the Eating Attitudes Test by Garner and Garfinkel in three matched groups of subjects (schizophrenics n=39, patients with eating disorders of the bulimic and restricting subtype n = 23, normal controls n = 125) are presented. Comparison of EAT scores shows that schizophrenic patients also have elevated scores, allowing a detailed description of their pathologic eating habits. Furthermore, schizophrenic patients scored higher on items concerned with body image disturbance and were at that level comparable to anorectics, whereas scores of bulimic patients were higher than those of schizophrenics and anorectics.

290
Disturbances of Reproductive Function in Bulimia Nervosa

Fichter MM & Pirke KM
Psychiatr. Klinik, Universität München & Klinik Roseneck, Prien & Max-Planck-Institut f. Psychiatrie, München (FRG)

We have conducted a series of studies assessing the hypothalamo-pituitary gonadal axis in anorexia and in bulimia nervosa and in healthy controls during fasting. The sensitivity of this hormonal axis with respect to weight loss or reduced caloric intake is reflected in the fact that three of five healthy females with an adult LG secretory pattern developed infantile LH patterns after 8 kg of weight loss. Gonadotropic hormone levels have also been shown to be low in cachectic anorexics and they normalize with weight restoration. In 30 patients with bulimia nervosa we studied gonadotropic and gonadal hormone plasma levels over the total period of a menstrual cycle. Only three out of 30 bulimic patients showed a normal hormone pattern concerning LH, estradiol and progesterone over the total menstrual cycle. 12 out of 30 bulimics (40 %) showed luteal-phase defects. 15 out of 30 bulimics (50 %) in addition showed follicular phase defects indicating impaired follicular development. Data indicate that already a minor weight deficit and minor reductions in caloric intake severely affect the menstrual cycle and fertility in bulimia nervosa.

291
METABOLISM IN ANOREXIA NERVOSA: A MICROCALORIMETRIC STUDY

Sten Theander, Birger Fagher and Mario Monti. Departments of Psychiatry and Internal Medicine. University Hospital, Lund, Sweden.

Basal metabolism as measured by oxygen consumption (BMR) is reduced in anorexia nervosa. As the total cell mass of the body is also reduced, this finding is difficult to interpret. A study of the metabolic activity at cellular level is therefore of interest. By a direct microcalorimetric method the heat production was measured in muscle cells, taken by biopsy, and in platelets. The heat production expressed per unit of tissue mass gives a measure of the overall metabolic activity of the cells. Compared to normal controls cellular thermogenesis in 11 anorexic patients, 6 of restricting and 5 of bulimic subtype, was lowered by about 50 % ($p < 0.001$). Heat production was also lowered in platelets but to a lesser degree ($p < 0.02$). In two normalweight bulimics the heat production was within the normal range. The findings elucidate the metabolic adaptation in anorexic patients and possibly also in other starving organisms.

292
GENETIC VULNERABILITY TO EATING DISORDERS: EVIDENCE FROM A TWIN AND FAMILY STUDY

J. Treasure, A. Holland, Institute of Psychiatry, London

We report on a combined twin and family study of 68 twin pairs in which at least one member had an eating disorder, anorexia nervosa, bulimia nervosa or a mixed diagnosis.

The concordance rate for anorexia nervosa in MZ twins (14/31) was significantly higher compared with DZ twins (2/30)(Fishers p>.001). This was not true for bulimia nervosa where the concordance rate was similar (9/19) MZ twins and (6/19) DZ twins. Excluding the MZ probands' cotwin, anorexia nervosa occurred in 4% of first degree relatives. If a broader group of eating disorders is taken (including anorexia nervosa, bulimia nervosa and obesity) the incidence was 23% in first degree relatives with bulimia nervosa, which is 1.5 times commoner than the incidence in the probands with anorexia nervosa.

Path analysis of this data indicates that approximately 75% of the variance in liability to develop anorexia nervosa is due to genetic factors whereas common life style factors contribute to the familial clustering of bulimia nervosa. The inherited form of eating disorder is restricting anorexia nervosa with young onset without any premorbid obesity. We conclude that the aetiology of anorexia nervosa and bulimia nervosa is different.

The discordant MZ and DZ twin pairs have been compared in an attempt to isolate the transmitted factor which accounts for the genetic vulnerability to anorexia nervosa.

293
THE LONG-TERM OUTCOME OF ANOREXIA NERVOSA

Russell G F M, Ratnasuriya H, Eisler I, Szmukler G. The Institute of Psychiatry and Maudsley Hospital, London, UK.

41 patients with anorexia nervosa were followed up on average 20 years after their admission to the Maudsley Hospital (1959-66). A disconcertingly high number (37%) had a poor outcome including 7 deaths. Among the prognostic indicators, an age of onset of above 18 years was the most reliable indicator of a poor outcome. In comparison with this long follow-up, an earlier shorter follow-up on the same patients had led to several errors in determining clinical outcome. Recovery can occur as long as 15 years after presentation.

The value of any follow-up study of anorexia nervosa is severely limited by selection factors influencing the severity of the illness in the population studied. Nevertheless it permits the identification of prognostic indicators and demonstrates the full range of possible outcomes from full recovery to death.

Session 43 Symposium: New techonologies in psychiatry

294
"SPECT IN PSYCHIATRY"

Srini Govindan, M.D.
Ohio Valley Medical Center
Wheeling, W.V. 26003
Stephen Ward, M.D.
Ohio Valley Medical Center
Wheeling, W.V. 26003

25 patients referred by the Neuroscience Institute-Ohio Valley Medical Center, were studied with (Iofetamine) I-123 brain perfusion/metabolic imaging agent, using multidetector Strichman 810 SPECT unit. The patients were classified based on their diagnosis into depression, schizophrenia, seizure disorder, global amnesia, pseudo dementia, multi infarct dementia, and pre-senile dementia of Alzheimer's type. Findings of I-123 perfusion imaging were compared and correlated with laboratory tests, EEG, CEEG-dynamic brain mapping, CT, and MRI of the brain. SPECT scan was abnormal when CT and or MRI were negative. Beneficial aspects of SPECT imaging in clinical diagnosis and patient management will be discussed. Effect of drugs on SPECT findings and potential benefits of serial SPECT imaging in global amnesia and multi infarct dementia will also be discussed.

295
CT-SCAN IN PRYCHIATRY

Mark V, USA

296
MRI IN PSYCHIATRY

Vargas-Pena E, Paraguay

297
BRAIN FUNCTION MONITORING SYSTEM
IN PSYCHIATRY AND PSYCHOPHARMACOLOGY

Turan M. Itil and Kurt Z. Itil,
New York Medical College and HZI
Research Center, Tarrytown, New York

The Brain Function Monitoring (BFM) unit is a high technology hardware/software system developed and validated in the past five years. It includes four functional components utilizing essentially the same hardware.
1. Clinical Integrated Questionnaire (CIQ) data collection and data management system.
2. Computer-analyzed EEG (CEEG) and Dynamic Brain Mapping.
3. Evoked Potential (EP) and Dynamic Brain Mapping.
4. Neuro-Psychological and cognitive tests (NPT) system.

In addition, sleep analysis, and drug selection and drug monitoring programs were also developed. Identical systems have been installed in more than 50 Beta Site centers around the world and the reliability of the system and the validity of the methods were investigated. Studies of our own and our collaborators are indicative that objective brain function monitoring will be an integral part of every advanced psychiatric practice in the very near future.

Session 44 Symposium:
Various aprroaches to brief dynamic psychotherapy

298
Une démarche psychanalytique en psychothérapie brève

Dr Noël Montgrain, m.d.
Directeur
Département de psychiatrie
Faculté de médecine
Université Laval
Ste-Foy, (QUEBEC)
CANADA

A partir du modèle élaboré par Peter Sifnéos, l'auteur cherchera à présenter sa propre conception de la psychothérapie psychanalytique brève à partir de commentaires en marge de l'évaluation, de l'établissement du focus, du temps et de l'exigence de la brièveté, de même que sur le traitement, sur le silence et de l'activité du thérapeute. Enfin, il montre les avantages d'une telle méthode dans l'enseignement de la psychothérapie.

299
BRIEF ANALYTIC PSYCHOTHERAPY-FOCALITY-INITIAL CHANGE
Edmond Gillieron
Policlinique psychiatrique universitaire
Lausanne - Switzerland

Any psychotherapeutic treatment is composed of two fundamental periods: 1) evaluation, 2) psychotherapy by itself
From a dynamic point of view, each period includes certain specific aspects: Phase1: induce, within the patient, an initial change, that means insight of the intrapsychic nature of the conflict that motivates the consultation. Phase 2: elaborating unconscious phantasies and resistances linked to the conflict. Our research on focality in brief psychotherapy has brought us to pay particular attention to the motivations bringing the patient to the psychotherapist: in the great majority of cases, patients' demand is based on an actual conflict (usually interpersonal), well demarcated; in this, demand is focused. We have been able to experiment the fact that, if one pays attention to this issue, investigation phase can, by itself, have sufficient therapeutic effects for the patient; this as long as the therapist follows some strict rules:
- A precise investigation of the unconscious motivations that have brought the patient to consultation
- Investigation of the chief defences that have been shaken by the actual crisis
- Interpretation connecting the actual crisis to the subject's past.

300
SHORT-TERM INTEGRATIVE PSYCHOTHERAPY FOR BORDERLINES

Miguel A. Leibovich, M.D.
Harvard Medical School, U.S.A.

Borderline patients can benefit from short-term psychotherapeutic approaches. The presentation will focus on the utilization of Short-term Intergrative Psychotherapy for patients exhibiting Borderline Personality Disorders. The type of Borderline patients that can benefit from this technique, indications and contraindications for its use and technical aspects of this kind of brief psychotherapy which is based on the application of concepts of developmental ego psychology will be described. Clinical vignettes will be presented to illustrate the theoretical concepts elaborate upon.

301
SHORT-TERM ANXIETY PROVOKING PSYCHOTHERAPY (STRAPP).

Dr. Peter E. Sifneos, Harvard University, Beth Israel Hospital.

The historical development of Short-Term Anxiety Provoking Psychotherapy with criteria for selection, techniques, and outcome will be presented.

Session 45   Symposium:
Cost effective psychiatric screening in large populations

302
COST EFFECTIVE STRATEGIES AND INSTRUMENTS FOR POPULATION SURVEYS
John E. Helzer
Washington University, St. Louis, MO, USA

In the past twenty years, methodology of population surveys in psychiatric epidemiology has evolved from the use of symptom scales and global assessments of psychological functioning to the use of more specific instruments that can be used to make criteria-based psychiatric diagnoses. This evolution is valuable since the resulting population data are more consistent with and more relevant to psychiatric practice in clinical settings. However, the one drawback of such criteria-based instruments is their length and complexity.

This presentation will discuss a variety of recently developed strategies and instruments that are brief but are still diagnostically based. These include 1) a screening interview for nonclinician examiners based on an analysis of several thousand respondents from the ECA survey in the U.S., 2) a computerized checklist interview for use by clinicians in population or clinical samples, and 3) a computer-based strategy in which the level of clinical detail can be tailored to particular study needs or to individual respondents.

303

The DISSA: An Abridged Self-Administered Version of the DIS Approach by Episode
Vivianne Kovess, M.D. & Louise Fournier, M.A.
Douglas Hospital Research Centre

Many surveys on health-related topics cannot afford the time needed to administer the DIS and train the personnel to use such a complex schedule as the DIS. The DISSA is a self-administered abridged form of the DIS and represents an effort to produce a short and simple instrument for three types of diagnoses: major depressive disorder, all anxiety disorders (generalized anxiety, phobias, panic) and alcohol disorders. DISSA results will be compared with clinicians' judgments, the DIS and a checklist derived from HSC. The DISSA functions in a manner similar to its parent instrument but achieves this in a shorter and less costly mode. Actually, the approach by episode used for assessing depression seems to work better than the DIS. Comparisons with a clinician's checklist interview show a clear superiority of the DISSA for depression, alcohol, and anxiety disorders but not for generalized anxiety. Possibilities to revise this section of the DISSA and to incorporate CIDI questions will be discussed as well.

304

COMPUTERIZED ADMINISTRATION OF THE DIAGNOSTIC INTERVIEW SCHEDULE

Arthur G. Blouin, Edgardo L. Pérez, and Jane H. Blouin, Ottawa Civic Hospital, Ottawa, Canada.

The Diagnostic Interview Schedule (DIS) has proven to be an extremely valuable instrument for assessing symptoms pertaining to DSM-III Axis I diagnosis. The DIS is quite complex however, and requires extensive training to administer. We have therefore developed a fully automated self-administering computerized version of the DIS. In the present study, 100 volunteers consisting of 80 psychiatric patients and 20 normal controls completed the computerized version of the DIS on two occasions. A standardized Computer Attitude Scale (CAS) was administered to each volunteer before the first and after the second computerized DIS (C-DIS). The C-DIS yielded acceptable test-retest reliability. Certain diagnoses were found to yield high test-retest reliability while reliability was lower for others. This general pattern was similar to the results of previous procedural validity studies. Patients found the C-DIS generally easy to use and operate, and after using the C-DIS, felt that their level of expertise in using computers had improved. Generally, the results support the use of computerized administration of the DIS and indicate that most psychiatric patients respond favourably to computerized assessment.

305

SCREENING FOR DEPRESSION IN OUTPATIENT PRACTICES

K. Wells, M.A. Burnam, W. Rogers, M. Potts
The RAND Corporation, Santa Monica, California

We present data from the Medical Outcomes Study, an observational study of adult patients receiving care in one of three types of health delivery systems: health maintenance organizations, large multi-specialty group practices, and solo fee-for-service practices. Each system was studied in three sites - Los Angeles, Boston, and Chicago. We screened 23,000 for depressing disorders using a two-state case-identification procedure. At the first stage, patients completed an 8-item self-administered symptom screener that has high sensitivity and adequate positive predictive power among samples of medical and mental health outpatients. In the second stage, those who exceeded the threshold on the screener were asked to complete an expanded version of the depression section of the Diagnostic Interview Schedule (DIS). In practices of general medical providers, prevalence of current unipolar depression was about 5% and did not significantly differ across sites, or between general practice physicians medical subspecialists. This rate is much higher than that for the Los Angeles household population (2.3%). Thus the medical outpatient setting may be a good point of intervention to increase recognition and treatment of depression. In mental health specialty practices, prevalence of current unipolar depression was about 25%. This did not vary much across systems of care. This finding emphasizes that mental health provides must be prepared to appropriately treat this disorder.

Session 46   Workshop:
Photographic imagery in private practice

306

PHOTOGRAPHIC IMAGERY AS A THERAPEUTIC TOOL IN PRIVATE PRACTICE
Joel Walker

This workshop will acquaint participants with an innovative approach to the use of therapeutic images in private practice.

It will focus upon the use of photographs as a projective method enabling the patient and therapist to more readily explore transferential feelings, penetrate resistance, work through conflicts, and mobilize affect. The photographs are ambiguous and abstract but have a semblance of reality. They are unstructured, which by design permits interpretation.

The Walker Visuals have proven to be a uniquely successful tool in psychotherapy.

Participants will be introduced to the concept and development through an audio-visual presentation, followed by a participatory opportunity for all workshop attendees to utilize the images.

Visuals and instructional guidelines will be available.

Session 47 — New Research:
Panic disorders: General issues

307

THE PREVALENCE OF PANIC DISORDER AND GENERALIZED ANXIETY DISORDER AMONG EMERGENCY ROOM ADMISSIONS.

E. Klein, MD, S. Linn, MD, R. Lang, MD, S. Pollack, MD, R.H.Lenox, MD, Dept. of Psychiatry and Unit of Epidemiology, Rambam Medical Center, Faculty of Medicine, Technion, Haifa, Israel.

Epidemiological studies from the last years have shown that the prevalence of anxiety disorders in the general population (DSM-III criteria) is higher than estimated from psychiatric referrals. It is thus likely that a significant percentage of patients with panic disorder (PD) and generalized anxiety disorder (GAD) are seen in non psychiatric primary care facilities. To further study this issue, we screened patients who were referred to the emergency room of a general hospital (Rambam Medical Center, Haifa, Israel). Four groups were defined: 1) Patients with somatic complaints where no objective finding was evident (N=100). 2) Patients with somatic complaints where objective findings were evident and further treatment indicated (N=109). 3) Consecutive admissions to the emergency room (N=158). 4) Psychiatric referrals to the emergency room (N=150). A stepwise screening procedure which will be described was used. The prevalence of PD and GAD in groups 1 and 4 (6.7% and 4.7% resp.) was higher than in groups 2 and 3 (2% each). Our findings suggest that populations at risk for higher prevalence of anxiety disorders among general hospital emergency room referrals can be defined. The implications of these findings and further aspects of this survey will be discussed.

308

FIELD-DEPENDENCY IN PANIC DISORDER PATIENTS

B. Laverdure, J.C Bisserbe, J.P. Boulenger, E. Zarifian
INSERM U 320 Centre Esquirol CHU 14000 Caen France.

Field dependency- independency (FDI) a dimension used by experimental psychologist as a discriminatory variable of cognitive functioning. was used to study cognitive disturbances in Panic Disorder (PD) patients . The experimental parameters used to define FDI were the classical Embedded Figure Test (EFT) and the Rod and Frame Test (RFT) . EFT gives a measurement of the spatial abilities to separate a target image embedded in a complex background : the subject has to discriminate the target from its context. RFT investigates the relative contribution of the different sensory system involved in the the perception of the verticality. Twenty four anxious patients : 16 PD (13 with agoraphobia , 3 without) and 8 patients with other anxiety disorders were compared to 24 control subjects matched for age and sex. Patients were diagnosed according to DSM III-R criteria; their anxiety was assessed using Spielberger State and Trait Inventory, Hamilton Anxiety Rating Scale and Covi anxiety scale. Preliminary analysis of the results showed a significant positive correlation between field-dependency and anxiety level at the time of testing. The results obtained with the two procedures will be discussed in relationship wih the clinical characteristics of the patients. The possible involvment of the different sensory systems participating to the perception of space in the expression of different type of anxious disorder will be considered.

309

FREQUENCY OF PANIC ATTACKS IN HIGH SCHOOL STUDENTS

J.P. Boulenger, K. Bossey, P. Colace, F. Chastang
INSERM U. 320, Centre Esquirol, C.H.U. Côte de Nacre, 14033 Caen Cedex, France.

Several studies have suggested that sudden episodes of severe anxiety, i.e. panic attacks (PA) occur in non-clinical subjects as well as in patients who fulfill the DSM-III-R criteria for panic disorders. A recent epidemiological survey (NIMH-ECA program) has also shown that in subjects reporting a history of PA, age of onset was found to peak at 15-19 years. In order to assess the frequency of PA, we held a survey in a population of high school students (n=608; mean age: 18.4 ± 1.3) by means of a self-rated structured questionnaire using DSM-III-R criteria. Trait anxiety was also assessed with the Spielberger scale. The results of this survey demonstrate a high frequency of PA in high school students: 30% (n=181) reported sudden episodes of acute anxiety accompanied by at least 4 DSM-III-R PA symptoms in their lifetime. This frequency increased to 43% if only 2 symptoms were required to define a PA. The students reporting a history of PA were characterized by a significantly higher proportion of girls, higher scores of trait anxiety and more frequent anxiety-associated symptoms, e.g. insomnia. In most cases PA were preceded by a period of stressful events. Other characteristics of PA occurring in high school students will also be presented. The relevance of PA in a non-clinical population will be discussed in relation to the psychopathological factors involved in the evolution of panic disorders.

310

A PROSPECTIVE STUDY OF PANIC AND ANXIETY IN AGORAPHOBIA WITH PANIC DISORDER

Metin Basoglu, Isaac Marks, Seda Sengun- Institute of Psychiatry London, U.K.

The phenomenology of anxiety and panic in the natural environment was investigated in 39 patients with chronic agoraphobia and panic disorder by prospective self-monitoring. Most panic and anxiety episodes occurred in agoraphobic situations; a third of episodes occurred at home, cued by both stressful and non-stressful events. Phasic anxiety and panics surged out of a pre-existing plateau of tonic anxiety which lasted most of the day. Panic and anxiety episodes were similar in symptom profile, situational context, time of occurrence, intensity and duration of preceding tonic anxiety, and antecedents. Panics differed from anxiety only in being more intense, shorter and having more and more intense symptoms, but even these features were not reliable discriminators. Spontaneous panics occurred more often at home than did situational panics but were otherwise similar. These findings do not support the DSM IIIR assumption that panic is qualitatively distinct from anxiety and the emphasis on spontaneous panic in classifying anxiety disorders. Catastrophic thoughts of dying and going crazy/losing control accompanied only a minority of panic/anxiety episodes and seemed to be a product of intense panic rather than an aetiological factor.

311

OBSESSIVE-COMPULSIVE SYMPTOMS IN PANIC DISORDER PATIENTS
Susana Alfonso, M.D., Alvaro Rivera, M.D.
Hospital Psiquiatrico Ciempozuelos, Madrid, Spain.

The aim of this study was to measure the incidence of obsessive-compulsive symptoms in a sample of 60 referrals who met DSMIIIR criteria for panic disorder compared with a group of 30 normal controls. We also examine the relationship of obsessive-compulsive features and clinical variables and family history.

Probands with or without obsessive-compulsive symptoms were compared in regard to the existence of affective, personality and alcoholdependence disorders using the SCIP-P interview for DSMIIIR criteria and the FISC for the family study. Severity and clinical variables were assessed by means of age of onset, percentage of remissions, subtype of agoraphobia, Global Phobic and Global Incapacity Scale.

The percentage of panic disorder patients with obsessive-compulsive disorder was 15%, significantly higher than those encountered in the group of normal controls (0%). The existence of obsessive-compulsive disorder does not seem to significantly modify the clinical manifestation, severity or family history.

Session 48 Symposium:
Ill-defined psychosocial problems in general health care

312

PATHWAYS TO CARE: THE WHO STUDY
Goldberg, D., Sartorius, N., Gater, R.

World Health Organization, Geneva & University of Manchester, England

This is a descriptive study of the pathways patients follow while seeking care for psychological problems, and some of the factors associated with delays in reaching mental health care. Surveys were carried out in eleven centres across the world. Most of the delay before seeing a mental health professional occurs between the onset of the problem and first seeking care. The median delay between first seeing a mental health professional is short: four weeks or less in ten of the Centres. Somatic symptoms are the commonest initial problem in six centres and rank second in four. This predominance wanes on the pathway to care giving way to a variety of psychological problems. One group of six centres are shown to have predominantly medical referral pathways; while the other group of five made greater use of native healters and direct referral to the mental health services for the community. The study is the first part of a four year programme of research which will form the basis of the development of new training courses for general and specialised staff, and identify mental health tasks which can be carried out by doctors, nurses, native healers and multi-purpose care workers in order to help the mentally ill and their families.

313

FUNCTIONAL COMPLAINTS IN GENERAL HEALTH CARE IN THE SOUTH EAST ASIAN REGION
Sell, H
World Health Organization

The paper will describe the results of a study which was implemented in six centres in four countries of South-East Asia, coordinated by the Regional Office for South-East Asia of the World Health Organziation between 1981 and 1986.

The aim of the study was the development of a diagnostic tool for the recognition of functional complaints by primary care physicians and the comparison of outcome in such patients following some selected interventions.

Interventions studies were a 2-week course of a benzodiazepine, brief counselling and relaxation, each by a PHC physician.

Surprisingly, the fact of the same intervention being done after referral to a "specialist" made no substantial difference to the outcome. The interventions with the best outcome were the 2-week course of benzodiazepines and instrution into muscular relaxation. There was no significant difference in outcome between the control group and the groups receiving counselling.

314

METHODOLOGICAL CHALLENGES IN THE ASSESSMENT OF MENTAL DISORDERS IN PRIMARY PRACTICE
Prof. Dr. H.-U. Wittchen
Max Planck Institute for Psychiatry, Munich, FRG
currently: World Health Organization, Division of Mental Health

During the last two decades it has become increasingly evident that a large burden of mentally disordered patients present themselves in primary health settings. It is also known however that primary care physicians vary greatly in their ability to detect mental disorders & to treat or refer them appropriately. In general primary care physicians were characterised as prone to be unaware of indications of mental illness.

A number of screening instruments have been developed during the last years which might be useful in helping a physician to identify emotional problems in their patients and to discipline mental disorders. The paper will discuss these instruments, their strengths and weaknesses and will present some recommendations for the future.

315

PATHOPHYSIOLOGY OF NEURASTHENIA
Y. LECRUBIER, A.J. PUECH, P. BOYER

INSERM U 302, Hôpital de la Salpêtrière Pavillon Clérambault, 47 boulevard de l'Hôpital, 75651 PARIS CEDEX 13

Classification and description of mental illnesses are based on different levels:

- syndromic organisation, course of illness including age of onset, family history, existence of psychological traits, response to specific treatments, indentification of biological markers...

When strong links can be shown between two or more of these levels, the probability for the existence of a discrete entity increases.
During recent decades, response to treatment provided important and numerous information at two different levels:

- who are the responders
- what are the symptomatic or psychological changes induced by drugs.

The nosological description of the patients does not appear to be the more appropriate basis upon wich to establish a relation with drug effect or biological results. For this, transnosological dimensions seem to be more accurate, like control of impulse, sedation-stimulation, psychomotor retardation.

An abulic, anhedonic, avolition syndrome has been shown to be modulated by dopaminergic stimulants and blockers in different nosological categories (Schizophrenics with negative symptoms, dysthymic disorders...). A subgroup (half of the sample) of dysthymic patients is hypothesized to present this syndrome as a single pathology. Criteria may be proposed to discriminate them from other dysthymic patients. The significance of the syndrome and its relation to treatment will be discussed.

316

EPIDEMIOLOGY OF ILL-DEFINED PSYCHOLOGICAL PROBLEMS IN GENERAL MEDICAL CARE
G. de Girolamo, Division of Mental Health, WHO, World Health Organization

An extensive series of investigations over the last 25 years clearly demonstrate that psychological problems are very common among patients attending different health facilities and that health workers generally underrecognize these problems. In primary care, mental disorders are present in approximately 25% of patients, ranging, in different countries including developing countries from a low of 11% to a high of 36%. In a WHO study, carried out with a two-stage screening procedure in 4 developing countries, the average caseness rate was about 14%; furthermore, two-thirds of the psychiatric cases were missed by the health workers. With regard to the extent of psychiatric morbidity in the general hospital, research has shown that affective disorders are present from a low of 13% to a high of 61% of general hospital inpatients, and at a rate ranging between 15% and 52% in general hospital outpatients. A high number of psychological problems encountered in primary health care are difficult to diagnose and/or classify. Among them somatic complaints, fatigue and repeated complaints are particularly frequent and represent a major burden for health care services.

Session 49 Free Communications:
Mental retardation

317

PSYCHIATRIC CARE FOR MENTALLY HANDICAPPED IN THE NETHERLANDS

G.J. Zwanikken, Catholic University, Nijmegen, The Netherlands.

The psychiatric care for the mentally handicapped has been neglected for a number of years after the separation of psychiatry and care for the mentally handicapped.
At the moment an appeal for help is made to psychiatry out of the field of the care for mentally handicapped.
Psychiatry and mental handicap are interwoven in many ways.
An account is given of the state of affairs and the desirable developments concerning the consultation of psychiatry in the care for the mentally handicapped.
Areas of attention in the training of psychiatrists are formulated.

318

SERVICES FOR PSYCHIATRICALLY DISORDERED MENTALLY HANDICAPPED ADULTS - A U.K. PERSPECTIVE
Dr. K.A. Day, Consultant Psychiatrist, Northgate Hospital, Morpeth, Northumberland NE61 3BP, England.

Mental handicap is a psychiatric speciality in the U.K. and doctors and nurses working in the field undergo special training. New approaches to care and the planned phasing out of mental handicap hospitals raise questions as to how psychiatrically and behaviourally disturbed mentally handicapped should be catered for in a new service. As yet there is no national policy and the situation is one of conflict and uncertainty. The main areas of debate are: specialised versus generic services, should psychiatry be responsible for the behaviourally disturbed; how should a specialised psychiatric service be provided? The Royal College of Psychiatrists is in favour of a specialised service because of the unique features attending the diagnosis and treatment. (R.C. Psych 1986). Sufficient treatment settings are required to cater for the spectrum of problems presented and the range of intellectual levels. A single campus site enables the provision of a fully comprehensive service, permits the most economic use of specialist staff time and is more cost effective. A working example will be described (Day 1983). Special facilities for rehabilitation and continuing care are also needed together with regional and national provision for those requiring treatment under conditions of security. A model for future service provision will be suggested.
DAY K.A. (1983) A Hospital Based Psychiatric Unit for Mentally Handicapped Adults. Mentally Handicap 11, 137 - 140. Royal College of Psychiatrists (1986) Psychiatric Services for Mentally Handicapped Adults and Young People. Bulletin 10 321 - 322.

319

COMMUNITY PSYCHIATRIC SERVICE FOR PSYCHIATRIC DISORDERS IN MENTAL RETARDATION

N. BOURAS

Division of Psychiatry, Guy's Hospital

This study describes the results of a comprehensive standardised multi-dimensional assessment of 260 referrals to a newly established psychiatric service for people with mental retardation.

The data demonstrates the advantages of using our method and its application, in the diagnosis, therapeutic intervention and planning evaluation of a new service.

320

Continuing care of the Severely Mentally Retarded
ROSS N.J. Frydman D.
Association de VILLEPINTE
5, rue Thimmonier 75009 PARIS   FRANCE

This paper outlines the difficulties encountered by centers caring for the severely mentally retarded (SMR) in France and especially in the Paris region. Spécial attention is paid to the "relay" aspect that must be encouraged between the child centers and the adult centers.

Based on their joint experience in a medico-educative center for SMR children and the relay foyer for SMR adults, the authors develop the inherent problems of successive therapies, therapeutic teams, the various post-institutional orientations as well as the new laws obliging child centers to retain SMR adults.

Special emphasis is placed on the coordination that must exist between these centers in order to deal with the onset of puberty, the SMR families, the occupational and educative approaches when the SMR child reaches adulthood, in order to assure a continuity in the psychotherapeutic and educative processes avoiding regression and familial disinterest.

321

PSYCHIATRIC DISORDERS IN MENTALLY RETARDED CHILDREN - DEVELOPMENTAL APPROACH
ANTON DOSEN, M.D., Ph.D.
CHILD PSYCHIATRIC CLINIC   HOEKSKE, VENLO, HOLLAND

Various developmental factors play the role in the onset of psychiatric disorders in mentally retarded children. The developmental-dynamic approach in the diagnostics and treatment of psychiatric disorders in mentally retarded children focuses on the discovery of the development factors and the fulfillment of developmental needs of the mentally ill, mentally retarded child. By this approach the child, not the handicap, is brought more clearly into focus. Employing a developmental-dynamic model the author describes a number of developmental psychiatric diagnostical categories in mentally retarded children on different developmmental levels.
Clinical experiences in the psychiatric diagnostics and treatment of 730 mentally retarded children are discussed.

322

DOWN'S SYNDROME A COMPARATIVE STUDY ON AETIOLOGICAL VARIABLES.

Dr. Deepali Dutta
Founder- President Monvikash Kendra
Neer, Pub Sarania, Guwahati 781003.

Two groups one consisting of cases of Down's Syndrome and other consisting of rest of the mentally retarded are being compared on various socio-economic and cultural variables with specific reference to IQ , birth order , maternal age , complications during antenatal period and associated abnormalities.

323
INCEST AND MENTAL RETARDATION

Jancar J and Johnston Susan J
Stoke Park Hospital, Stapleton, Bristol BS16 1QU.
England.

The records of 1000 patients admitted to the
Stoke Park Group of Hospitals in Bristol,
previously studied for familial mental
retardation (Jancar, 1983) were re-examined for
the incidence of incest.

The study revealed 12 known incestuous unions
between :

brother and sister	- 5
father and daughter	- 4
uncle and niece	- 2
and grandfather and granddaughter	- 1
Total	12

The number of offspring, their mental and
physical states will be presented. The
consequences of incest, including adoption, will
be discussed and the literature, on incest and
mental retardation, reviewed.

Ref.: Jancar, J. (1983). Familial Mental
Handicap. Bristol Medico-Chirurgical Journal,
98, 23-27.

Session 50 Free Communications:
Brief prychotherapies

324
SHORT-TERM PSYCHODINAMIC INTERVENTION AND BRIEF
THERAPY IN DEPRESSIVE NEUROSIS

M. RUIZ RUIZ
PRESIDENTE DE LA ASOCIACION ESPAÑOLA DE PSICOTERA
PIA ANALITICA. MALAGA (SPAIN)

Exponemos los resultados obtenidos en 34 pacien
tes diagnosticados de neurosis depresivas o depre
siones reactivas que no habían obtenido respuesta
terapéutica con los psicofarmacos ansiolíticos y
antidepresivos. En todos ellos se inició una psi
coterapia analítica a corto plazo (seis meses) o
medio plazo(doce-dieciocho meses) después de ha
ber sido seleccionados y evaluados en su motiva-
ción, estructura yoica y relacion terapeutica. De
los 27 pacientes que obtuvieron resultados satis-
factorios 9 continuaron en una psicoterapia a lar
go plazo (más de 18 meses) y los 16 restantes ter
minanron en el período previsto, produciéndose re
caidas en 3 pacientes que necesitaron de interven
ción psicoterapéutica.
Se discuten las técnicsa psicoanalíticas empleadas
y especialmente en las psicoetrapias breves secon
frontaron los métodos empleados con las escuelas
de MALAN, SIFNEOS y DAVANLOO. Se presta especial
interés en las psicoterapias en las que se necesi
ta más tiempo en la reconstrucción del Yo y el
análisis del "self" partiendo de las concepciones
de KOHUT.

325
PSYCHOTHERAPY OF LIMITED TIME AND DELIMITED
OBJECTIVES
Prof.Dr.Mauricio Knobel
State Univ.of Campinas(UNICAMP),Campinas,Brazil

Based on Psychoanalytic theory a new approach to
short-term psychotherapy is being proposed.Four
items of psychoanalytic technique are reconsidered
1)Transference:known and understood,but not to be
used in interpretations;2)Regression:Practically
avoided.The whole process is kept within the patient's "here and now" reality;3)Working-through
conflicts occurs both in cognitive and affective
levels;4)Internal Objects Mutation leads to substitution of false information for real,objective,
present facts.
There is a search for the most useful personal defense mechanisms."Psychotic-like" structures are
also brought to consciousness.Infantile traumatic
conflicts,made hereby conscious,leave their daily
influence and thus become true personal history.
Concepts such as "Available Setting","Operational
Time" and "Adequate Therapeutic Time" are proposed
and explained.The therapist must be carefully
trained and thoroughly assisted in the process of
overcoming "psychoanalytical biased" resistances.-

326
A SYSTEMIC APPROACH FOR TREATMENT OF CHRONIC
NEUROTIC IN-PATIENTS
R. Saupe, S. Priebe
Department of Psychiatry, Freie Universität
Berlin, Berlin (West), F.R.G.

In treatment of in-patients with chronic neurotic
or personality disorders, who had been continuously suffering from their symptoms for at least
nine months and had already undergone at least one
therapy during this period, we tried both to reduce distress in the therapeutic team (as usually
caused by those patients) and to improve outcome
of treatment. Therefore, three to five guidelines
on how to deal with the patient were given to the
therapeutic team, and illustrated by possible
literal statements to the patient. The guidelines
aimed at a general interactional approach to that
patient and did not determine specific therapeutic
interventions. They were set up following principles of Brief Therapy as developed at the Mental
Research Institute in Palo Alto.
While the therapeutic team rated the guidelines
generally as easy to adopt and helpful, the therapeutic outcome varied greatly, with surprisingly
positive results in some cases. Data about the
effects on the team and on the patients as well as
case examples, are shown. The results from ten
patients are compared with those of a matched pair
control group. Conditions under which our approach
was or was not feasible and helpful, are discussed.

327

PERSONALITY DISORDERS-DEPRESSION:EFFICIENCY OF BRIEF PSYCHOTHERAPY

MARTHA J. de FAHRER et al.
Hospital de Clínicas. Universidad de Buenos Aires

The efficiency of short-term dynamic psychotherapy is more related to the patient's personality structure than to the seriousness of the depression.
The sample of 24 patients between 45/65 years of age fulfills DSM-III-R 309.00 diagnostic criteria-adjustment disorder with depressed mood.(ICD 9 309.1).We diagnose personality disorder according to DSM-III-R Axis 2 and the sample is divided in two groups according to characterologic pathology level; upper level (dependent, obsessive-compulsive) 13 patients, and middle-lower level (schizoid, passive-agressive, borderline, histrionic) 11 patients.
The therapeutic plan consists of 10 sessions distributed as follows:4 weekly;4 fortnightly and 2 monthly sessions.
We consider two focuses since the first session: "depression" and "the ending of treatment".
Results are evaluated according to the modification of the Depressive Symptomatology (codified),Beck Test and additional improvements.
Of the 24 patients 18 ended the treatment and 6 deserted:a)upper level:12 patients ended(92.3%),1 deserted(7.7%);b)middle-lower level:6 ended(54%), 5 deserted(45%). The difference is significance
In both groups the improvement of the patients who ended the treatment was significance and it was not proved any important difference in the degree of improvement between them.

328

Brief Family Therapy and Psychosomatics.

Sakkas Dionyssis
"General Hospital of Athens", Greece

The growing flow of referred psychosomatic patients from other clinics of the general hospital, the great percentage of people who are hospitalized for a short period and live in distant from Athens areas (countryside) and the time limitations, pushed us to try methods for doing psychotherapy briefly.
The difficulties in psychotherapy with psychosomatic patients who have alexithymic charecteristics, are well known (Sifneos and others). We have tried to overcome these difficulties with the combination of Family Therapy and Analogical Communication. So the patient is not the sole focus of theatment, as we include all the family in the theatment sessions doing so prevention for the other members of the family who may have not yet symptoms. Also we have actualized forms of analogical communication based on symbols, metaphors, images, parables e.t.c. that facilitate the flowing of emotions and the following intuitive understanding. (Watzlawick, Vassiliou).
In order to catalyse-regulate therapeutic interventions we invite the family to draw with colors of their choice different things and a joint family drawing, ask each other questions about that and finally to compose a story connecting in some way all the items drawn by them. We see that this process facilitate the expression of emotional themes prevailing in the family, wich could never be expressed through verbal communication. These themes are expressed symbolically and allegorically and can be actualized for morphogenetic development of the family and within this process the improvement of the symptoms of the identifeed patient.

329

METODOLOGIA Y CONSIDERACIONES CLINICAS EN PSICOTE-PIAS BREVES.
Dra.Carmen Pavía, Dra.Lea Kesselman,Dr.Julio Ques Varela, Lic.José Albani y Dr.Luis Albalustri.
Centro de Estudios de Psicol.Médica y Psiquiatría.

Se expone un trabajo realizado en pacientes ambulatorios de un servicio de Psicología Médica y Psiquiatría.Definimos la Psicoterapia Breve como aquella cuya duración no excede el año,con una sesión semanal.Estableciéndose de común acuerdo con el paciente un foco terapéutico y una fecha de finalización.Los tratamientos se realizan en consultorio privado,siguiendo los lineamientos de la teoría y técnica psicoanalítica.Incluimos enfermos de 25 a 55años de edad,de ambos sexos.Se utiliza como elemento diagnóstico el DSMIII,involucrando en el estudio a pacientes del registro neurótico;se excluyen psicopatías,psicosis en general,personalidades borderline y pacientes con enfermedades orgánicas severas y/o terminales. Realizamos con cada paciente los siguientes estudios: a) dos entrevistas clínicas, b)el cuestionario clínico del Serv.de Psiq. del Hosp.Necker de París,cuyo jefe es el Dr.I.Pellicier, c)psicodianóstico inicial y d)otro al año (observamos ítems específicos desarrollados por nosotros en las respuestas al test de Rorschach), e)una evaluación clínica al terminar el tratamiento,y f) follow up hasta 5 años. Se explicitarán los resultados del primer grupo de pacientes.

330

COMPARING TWO DIFFERENT FORMS OF PRYCHOTHERAPY IN CENTRE OF MENDAL HEALTH OF CHANIA
Tzanakaki M.-Tsitsidakis K.-Skalidi M.-Kordosi M. Karabetsos X.-Kotsifaki S.
Centre of Mental Health of Chania Crete

Forty patients with anxiety and personality disorders attend a programme of brief (individual) psychotherapy.

At the same time,twenty of them participate in two Dramatherapy groups.(therapeutic work bases on drama activities using elements of mysic and movements).

The question arises as to whether these people should work through highly process(verbal communication in brief psychotherapy) and/or thriugh a less active not so stressfull one,using verbal and mainly non verbal communication through Drama -therapy.

The results in detail will be describe.

Session 51 Free Communications:
Involuntary Commitment

331

INVOLUNTARY CIVIL COMMITMENT OF MENTAL PATIENTS IN JAPAN AND PATERNALISM.
SHOGO TERASHIMA, M.D.
(FUKUOKA FAMILY COURT, FUKUOKA, JAPAN.)

The Japanese Mental Health Act was revised in 1988 to protect the patient's right more strongly. The Law is composed of two major parts, i.e., (1) the compulsory detainment of the prospective patient by the "danger" standard, and (2) involuntary admission of the patient by the consent of his responsible family member based on the "need-for-treatment" standard. Neither channel requires court review or decision (medical model). Generally speaking either of these two standards or rationales have traditionally have used to justify involuntary civil commitment. In Japan the exercise of "police power" is being discarded (Only 1,947 persons was committed by police power in 1987). On the contrary involuntary admission by the agreement of nearest relative, i.e., paternalistic intervention of the psychiatrists have been accepted very widely and rather loosely and is becoming dominant throughout Japan.
(166,196 persons were committed in 1987 through this channel.)

332

A PSYCHIATRIC STUDY OF COMMITTED PATIENTS AND VOLUNTARILY CONTROLS
Eriksson Kerstin
Psychiatric Clinic, Eastern Sector, Academic Hospital, S- 75017 Uppsala, Sweden

The paper will present psychiatric symptoms and diagnosis or representative samples of committed patients and voluntarily admitted matched controls in a study of psychiatric care in two Swedish county councils as a part in a psychiatric health services research program. More than 90% of the committed patients were diagnosed as psychotics, mostly schizophrenia. None with mania was voluntarily admitted. Measured by BPRS (Brief Psychiatric Rating Scale) anxiety as a symptom was the most common for both types of care. The other symptoms were more often marked for the committed patients, except for depression. At admission, 40% of the committed patients but only 7% of the voluntarily admitted rated themselves "healthy" or "nearly healthy". Assessed by BPRS and GAS patients of both types of care were clearly improved at discharge; committed patients even more than the voluntarily admitted. Suicidal problems were more common among the voluntarily admitted while among the committed patients threats and/or violence were more so.
The staff think it is hard to work in psychiatry and to know what is compulsion or not. 70% of the staff has been exposed to violence by the patients and 9% are still afraid.

333

Patients' Evaluations of Compulsory Psychiatric Care

Inga-Lill Candefjord

A representative sample of committed patients and voluntarily admitted controls were interviewed by independent clinical psychologists after admittance and 3-5 months after a period of in-patient care. The results displayed a mixture of positive and negative experiences, the differences being surprisingly limited between the committed and their controls. The attitudes towards the personnel were on the whole positive but very critical as to the general qualify of the care. There was a general acceptance concerning the need for compulsory care. Decisions of commitment were generally regarded as a clinical question.

334

PSYCHIATRIC EXAMINATION FOR CIVIL COMMITMENT

N.Vaidakis, B.Alevizos, S.Koulis, P.Hatzitaskos, C.Ioannidis, D.Kalyvas, C.N.Stefanis
University Eginition Hospital, Athens, Greece

During 1981 and 1985, a number of 1397 cases were referred for involuntary examination according to civil commitment law, to the University Eginition Hospital, corresponding to the large majority of patients referred for civil commitment decision in the Athens area.
Seventy per cent (N=979) were male and 30 % (N=418) were female. The applicant for examination was frequently a member of the nuclear family (51.7 %), while in 2.7 % was unrelated to family, police, social and other services. From the latter, 7.9 % were found to be free of any psychopathology and this, together with the fact that application does not require medical documents indicative of mental illness, may indicate that individuals can be exposed to legal abuse and deprivation of their personal freedom. In these cases, the applicant was the husband (and rarely the wife) in a proportion of 42 %. In many cases the evaluation carried out several days after application (43 % after the 3rd and 27.4 % after the 10th day), with a possible consequence patients to become in the meantime dangerous as a result of their psychopathology.
The results indicate that civil commitment law in Greece, after a decade of function, should be improved for its implications to civil liberties and for its possible harmful consequenses.

335

INVOLUNTARY HOSPITALIZATION OF PSYCHIATRIC PATIENTS
C.Ioannidis, B.Alevizos, N.Vaidakis, P.Hatzitaskos, S.Koulis, D.Kalyvas, C.N.Stefanis
University Eginition Hospital, Athens, Greece

Dangerousness or "expected improvement or prevention of deterioration" is the standard for involuntary hospitalization by means of mental illness in Greece, since 1978.
During 1981 and 1985, 706 and 691 patients respectively, referred by district attorney through police, were examined at the University Eginition Hospital for commitment decisions. 1036 patients (74.2 %) were committed, 56.6 % for dangerousness to self or others and 43.4 % for "expected improvement or prevention of deterioration" by hospitalization. Fourty nine per cent admitted to private clinics and 38.9 % to the Athens state psychiatric hospital, indicating a preference for private care. 73.1 % of committed patients were suffering from schizophrenia or paranoid disorders, 7.5 % from alcoholism and 2.1 % from drug dependence. One fourth of committed patients were examined more than ten days after the district attorney order. About half of commited had discontinued their drug treatment, while 32 % had never been treated before.
The statutory commitment criteria of medical necessity, in comparison to dangerousness-oriented criteria, permit patients in need of treatment to receive psychiatric care. However, additional requirements regarding diagnosis, minimum time for commitment decision, definite refusal of treatment etc should be established.

336

COMPULSORY ADMISSIONS IN DENMARK 1971-87
Marianne Engberg
Institute of Psychiatric Demography, Denmark

The legislation of compulsory admissions in Denmark has been unchanged since 1938. The legislation is presently going to be revised. The number of commitments to mental institutions in Denmark per year has decreased from 2260 in 1971 to 1245 in 1987. To expose the cause of this decrease in number of commitments a study of age and sex standardized incidence rates of compulsory admissions 1971-1987 with special reference to sex, age, and diagnosis was carried out. The study was based on data from the nationwide Psychiatric Case Register. Age and sex standardization was carried out using ten-years age groups and the Danish population in 1971 as standard population. The results show that age and sex standardized incidence rates of compulsory admissions are decreasing from 47/100.000 inhabitants in 1971 to 22/100.000 inhabitants in 1987 (P<0.0005). The proportion of commitments caused by schizophrenic patients is increasing, whereas the proportion of commitments caused by patients diagnosed non-psychotic during the stay in hospital is decreasing. The results suggest that in the Danish population a reserved attitude to compulsory admission has been taken up generally. The results show that the increased risk of commitment for men compared to women is due to an increased risk in the young age groups, whereas the relative risk for women is increased in the age groups about 45.

Session 52 Free Communications:
History of Psychiatry: Theory and practice over the centuries

337

ANTICIPATORY DEPRESSION-ANCIENT INDIAN IDEAS

A. VENKOBA RAO, MD PhD DSc DPM, Emeritus Professor of Psychiatry and Officer-in-Charge, Centre for Advanced Research on 'Health and Behaviour', Indian Council of Medical Research, Madurai Medical College, Madurai, INDIA.

Depressive Disease has a long ancestry. References to it abound in history, philosophy and the epics of India. The Buddha, Rama (of Ramayana) and Arjuna (of Mahabharatha) stand out as models of Anticipatory Depression or Grief. AD or AG occurs prior to the loss contrary to regular depression which follows it. Buddha experienced AD at the sight of an old man, a sick man and a corpse. The fact that none (including him) could escape these saddened him deeply. The ephemeral nature of the world, illusory nature of pleasures and miseries of men plunged young Rama into a 'dispassion.' Arjuna at the start of the Mahabharatha War (3138-3139 B.C.) sank into anguish at the tragic prospect of killing his kith and kin.

These psychological states reflect preoccupation with existential, spiritual and ethical queries. Buddha sought enlightenment through meditation. Rama was counselled by the Royal Priest Vasishta. Arjuna was imparted 'Gita' by his charioteer Lord Krishna. Kalidasa's poem depicts depression in Rama's dynasty, indicating a genetic predisposition. Psychological explanations for AD are discussed. The principles of therapy are elaborated in the presentation.

338

NEUROPSYCHIATRIC DISORDERS IN THE OLDEST MEDICAL TEXTBOOK IN PERSIAN WRITTEN AROUND 990 A.D.
M.R. Moharreri, M.D.
Department of Psychiatry and Medical Ethics and History of Medicine, A.H.Mehryar, College of Arts and Humanities, Y.Kalafi, M.D., Psychiatric Dept. Medical School, Shiraz University, Iran

Written around 980 A.D., Hidayat-ul Mutaallemin Fil Tibb (Students' Guide in Medicine) is the oldest general medical text known to have been written in modern Persian. Its author is little known but apparently a well experienced practicing physician by the name of Abu Bakr Rabi' bin Ahmad al-Akhawaini from Bukhara who claims to be a second generation student of Razi's. According to one of the manuscripts he was known as the "Physician of the Insane" by his contemporaries. Following the line of other Islamic Medical writers, the author has described the major neuropsychiatric disorders in the chapter dealing with the "Diseases of the Head and Brain". These include melancholia, mania, epilepsy, phrenitis, litharghos and sarsam. Hysteria is, however, described among the diseases of the female reproductive system. Both the terminology used and the authorities quoted betray the author's schooling in and devotion to the Graeco-Roman medical traditions adopted by early Islamic medical writers. He emerges as a hard-headed organic physician firmly committed to the humoral doctrine of mental illness.

339
DREAM SPACE AND THERAPY BY LOGOS IN GREEK ORATOR AELIUS ARISTIDE (117-189 POST J.C.)
Gerard Pirlot-Petroff
Centre Psychotherapeutique, Hopital, Toulouse, France

About 2000 years ago, a Greek orator, Aelius Aristide, born in 117p.J.C., told his dreams in the "Sacred Tales". These complete dream transcriptions of one person during 40 days are a single example in the Antiquity. Freud does not cite this author in his Traumdeutung. Oniropoietic is more important, here,than onirocritic used by example by Artemidore of Daldis (of Ephese). Artemidore and Aristide were contemporary but their relations about dreams were opposed. Artemidore had patients whereas Aristide was himself his patient. His neurosis kept up his oniric activity and helped himself in psychosomatic illness. For the first time in history, the "Sacred Tales", like the Freud's Traumdeutung,showed a live dream experience."The experience of Aristide is subjective"said Dodds,the one of Artemidore was objective. For Aristide the dream is a therapy, but like a psychoanalytic cure his object is possibly not recovery but only help to live.Here the dream exists with the "talking cure" and the dream narration is an evocation of the relation between body and soul. The god Asclepios' intervention, permitted a dream space, a fantasm space irruption, and the dismissal of his person-subject. Asclepios, like alter-ego, is a compromise by which the writer Aristide, draws out of himself by dream, finds again an imaginary representative of his loss,and opens the way to the greek novel.

340
RATIONAL AND IRRATIONAL CONCEPTS OF MENTAL ILLNESS IN EARLY BYZANTIUM
Kotsopoulos, S.
University of Ottawa, Ottawa, Canada

Early Byzantium presents with two contrasting views of the nature of mental illness and its treatment. One was the biological, established by Hippocratic medicine. The other was the demonological, advanced by popular religion. The biological view of mental illness was left to posterity in the writings of the last physicians of Hippocratic medicine, Aetius of Amida, Alexander of Tralles (both of 6th century), and Paul of Aegina (7th century). These authors described the functional psychoses, delirium, senile dementia and other conditions. They attributed them to biological factors. The treatment was also primarily biological. Popular religion on the other hand, explained mental illness as the work of evil spirits intruding into the body. The treatment consisted in chasing the spirits out with the spiritual power of a holy man, a saint, such as St. Daniel the Stylite (5th century), St. Symeon the Salus (6th century), St. Theodore of Sykeon (7th century). In this study the contrasting views on mental illness and its treatment are presented as they appear in the writings of the physicians and the life stories of the saints, referred to above.

341
TWO UNKNOWN DESCRIPTIONS OF AUTOSCOPIC PHENOMENA BY J.KERNER(1786-1862),A DOCTOR-POET OF ROMANTICISM
Hamanaka,T.(Dpt.of Neuropsychiatry,Nagoya City University,Nagoya,Japan.

Only a scanty number of descriptions of autoscopic phenomena are known before 1850, which are cited by modern psychiatric authors treating the topic(Menninger-Lerchenthal 1935/61,Lhermitte 1939/51,Hécaen 1952,Mikorey 1952,Todd/Dewhurst 1957,Leischner 1961 ,Lunn 1970,Damas Mora 1980,Grotstein 1983 etc):Aristotle?,Kraemer-Sprenger/Nider 1604,Lullin/Bonnet 1759,Wagner 1794,Goethe 1811/33,Nasse 1825,Müller 1825,Leuret 1834,Hagen 1835,Wigan 1844 etc. Through the survey of the relevant literature the present author calls attention to further little known documents of the phenomena, among which two are of psychiatric importance, stemming from the writings of Justinus Kerner(1786-1862), a German doctor-poet in the Romantic era. One of them is to find in his autobiography "Das Bilderbuch aus meiner Knabenzeit "(1840), in which he describes his own autoscopic experience, suggesting his psychodynamic conflicts in face of sudden illness of his father, the other in his massive document of a patient-clairvoyante, "Die Seherin of Prevorst"(1829), who exhibited not only the phenomena of external, but also internal autoscopy(Sollier 1903). By the way these two descriptions are not mentioned by Ellenberger(1970) who discussed the work of Kerner, emphasizing the role played by him in the development of the "Discovery of the Unconscious", while he cited examples of "projected dual personality" that are depicted with favour in the literary works of Romanticism.

342
MORAL THERAPY AT THE RETREAT, PAST AND PRESENT
T.M.Reilly
The Retreat, York, United Kingdom

The foundation of The Retreat at York in 1972 heralded a breakthrough in the practical management of the severely mentally ill and a revolution in caring attitudes. Depersonalized, restrictive, often punitive custodial containment was replaced by relative liberty, personal warmth, respect for the individual and a hitherto unique form of social and philosophical re-education. Tuke at The Retreat was joined in spirit by Pinel in France and Chiarugi in Italy in propounding this new "humanitarian gospel" of the treatment of mental illness. The ideological essence of Moral Therapy not only survives but flourishes in The Retreat nearly 200 years later despite inevitable changes – dare we say improvements – in its conceptualization and application. It is now, in addition, married to the best and most modern scientific elements of contemporary biological psychiatry. It exists, too, side by side with high-profile humanistic psychotherapy and, despite, or perhaps even because of, the spiritual framework and distinctive Quaker identify of the former, each of these different philosophies appears not only to compliment but even to augment the efficacy of the other.

343

MEDICATIONS USED AT EGINITION HOSPITAL FROM 1907 FOR AFFECTIVE DISORDERS: RELEVANT CELLULAR EFFECTS
J. Mantonakis[1], M.R. Issidorides[1] and A. Deffner[2]
[1]Psychiatry Dept. Univ. Athens, Eginition Hospital
[2]Quality Control Dept., Squibb AEBE, Athens, Greece

Eginition Hospital was founded in 1904 as the first Neuropsychiatry Clinic of the University of Athens. The hospital records filed in the archives are dated from 1906. Treatments were entered in the records from 1907. The purpose of the present study was to examine to what extent the old medications, persistently used to treat major affective disorders before 1952, held clues for the understanding of the core dysfunction in depression and mania. A random sample of patients' records from 1907 to 1952 was consulted and cases with the symptomatology of major affective disorder (totalling 795) were studied. All compounds appearing in the records as treatments were tabulated according to frequency of use. In a decreasing order the following were used in major depressive disorder: sodium cacodylate, laudanum, chloral hydrate, barbiturates, calcibromine, bromides, etc. In the manic cases the order was: bromides, scopolamine, chloral hydrate, sodium cacodylate, barbiturates, morphine, etc. The cellular effects of some of these drugs on patients' blood cells studied in vitro point to their beneficial actions on the impaired immune function underlying affective disorders. These results will be reported in detail in a separate presentation.

Supported by a grant of the Greek Ministry of Research and Technology (to M.R.I.)

344

THE HISTORY OF PSYCHIATRY IN MODERN GREECE. A CRITICAL REVIEW. (1831-1941)
G.E. Sarantoglou and G.A. Rigatos, Psychiatric Dept. and 1st Dept. of Medical Oncology, Hellenic Anticancer Institute, Athens (GR).

As beginning of the modern Greek Psychiatry could be considered the year 1831, when Dionyssios Pyrros published his "Manual of Physicians" including 11 chapters on mental disorders. The first Psychiatric publication appeared in 1836 in the journal "Asclepios", while at the first medical congress in Greece (1882) 4 among it's 68 communications concerned psychiatry. Although Athens' University Medical School founded in 1837, a chair for Neurology and Psychiatry established in 1893. The first special journal was published in 1902 by S. Vlavianos. A progressive psychiatric legislation has been voted in 1862. The first insane Asylum of Greece was founded in Corfu (Kerkyra) in 1838, while "Dromokaition" in Athens founded in 1886, Eginition University Hospital in 1905 and the State Mental Hospital in 1934.
Personalities who dominated in the above period (Ch. Tsirigotis, M. Katsaras) are mentioned for their scientific and medicosocial activity, while von Economo, a Greek neuropsychiatrist in Vienna, was honoured with Nobel Prize in 1927.-

345

THE HISTORY OF ACETYLCHOLINESTERASE IN SENILE PLAQUES.
P. De Giacomo
Ist. Clinica Psichiatrica, Università degli Studi, Bari (Italy).

The report recalls that senile plaque positivity to histochemical methods capable of demonstrating the presence of acetylcholinesterase in the human brain was first discovered at the Laboratory of Neuropathology, "S. Maria della Pietà" Psychiatric Hospital, Rome, and was first presented at the 4th International Congress of Neuropathology, München, September 1961 (P. De Giacomo, Distribution of Cholinesterase Activity in the Human Central Nervous System. Thema I / Vol.1, page 203. 1962 Thieme Verlag. Stuttgart).

It was discussed later on in a communication presented to the 28th Congress of " Società Italiana di Psichiatria " which met in Naples from the 6th to the 10th of June 1963 (D'Angelo C. and De Giacomo P.: Histoenzymatic Aspects of Alzheimer's Disease).

The finding was quite recently confirmed by Tago and Co-workers (Brain Res. 406, 363, 1987).

In addition to the presence of the enzyme in senile plaques, the communication also indicated a reduced positivity of neuron extensions in the cerebral cortex of subjects who had died from Alzheimers disease vs. the control encephala.

Session 53 Free Communications:
Schizophrenia: Psychophysiologic studies

346

SOMATOSENSORY ERP AND INFORMATION PROCESSING IN YOUNG CHRONIC SCHIZOPHRENICS
J. Böning, F. Drechsler
Department of Psychiatry, University of Wuerzburg
D-8700 Wuerzburg, FRG

In the occurence of neuronal interference phenomene a delayed information processing is regarded as a basis of selective disorders of attention in schizophrenic diseases. In 30 chronic young schizophrenics ($27 \pm 4,5$) and in 15 aged-matched controls, we used in a oddball-paradigm SERP-parameters (latencies, amplitudes and determination of areas of the N1 and P3 component by integration) and reaction-times (RT) to identify the different steps of information processing. Highly significantly reduced areas and prolonged latencies of N1, but not of P3, and significantly prolonged RTs discriminate schizophrenics in remitted state from controls. A significant correlation between decreased N1-areas and prolonged RTs ($r=0,46$, $p<0,01$) respectively high selfrating subscores "disturbance of selective attention" ($r=0,28$, $p<0,05$) can be found only for the left hemisphere. In group-related intraindividual hemisphere comparison, significantly more pronounced N1-areas were found both in controls ($p<0,004$) and in schizophrenics ($p<0,05$) on the left side. This is further proof of the different hemisphere organization of cognitive performance functions. Findings would be in relation with a disturbance of control and maintenance of selective information processing strategy, which constitutes the schizophrenic attention disorder.

347

Saccadic latency prolongation in schizophrenics
M. Flechtner, A. Mackert
Department of Psychiatry (Head: Prof. Dr. H. Helmchen). Free University of Berlin.
Eschenallee 3. D-1000 Berlin 19 (FRG)

Despite the well-known prolongation of manual reaction times in schizophrenics saccadic latencies have been found to be normal. Since schizophrenics seem to display attentional deficits in tasks with high processing demands we used two stimulus programmes with varying demands on processing capacity. Using electrooculography saccadic latencies were determined of 47 schizophrenic patients diagnosed according to RDC-criteria. 28 healthy volunteers served as controls. Stimulus programmes were displayed using light emitting diodes. In the first programme the stimulus duration was chosen at random between 1 - 6 s and the stimulus returned regularly to the center. The second programme was much faster with a stimulus duration of 800 - 1200 ms and it's spatial distribution was completely unpredictable. Reaction times in the first programme (low attentional demands): patients: 219±37 ms, controls: 217±23 ms, n.s. Second programme (high attentional demands): patients: 200±53 ms, controls: 183±16 ms, $p < 0,05$. The results suggest that the controls are able to improve their attentional performance when processing demands are higher. In contrast schizophrenics seem to display an "attentional rigidity", in that they are not able to vary their attentional performance. This effect could be explained by a diminished processing capacity.

348

INFORMATION PROCESSING DEFICITS AND OUTCOME PATTERNS IN SCHIZOPHRENIA
P.W.H. Lee, F. Lieh Mak, K.K. Yu, J.A. Spinks,
University of Hong Kong, Hong Kong

One hundred and fifty seven schizophrenic patients diagnosed with DMS-III-R criteria were studied. Assessment of psychiatric status was done by two psychiatrists. Psychosocial adjustment in interpersonal relationship and at work was assessed by a clinical psychologist. Reaction time, span of apprenhension, dichotic listening, speed of signal detection and susceptibility to masking were measured using automated computer-controlled equipment. Prognostic predictors outlined in the IPSS (WHO) were also collected for all subjects. Factor analyses indicated that five factors, namely quality of life, duration of psychiatric hospitalization, adjustment of medication dosage, daily life heterosexual relationship, and work adjustment, accounted for seventy percent of the outcome variance. The information processing deficits data contributed significantly in explaining the outcome variance independent of those accounted for by the traditional prognostic predictors. The clinical relevance of studying schizophrenic cognitive deficits and their place in mainline research in schizophrenia is discussed.

349

DICHOTIC LISTENING IN SCHIZOPHRENIA AND AFFECTIVE DISORDER: A CONTROLLED STUDY

P.B. Behere, V. Shukla, H.C. Samant, Department of Psychiatry, Institue of Medical Sciences, Banaras Hindu University, Varanasi, India.

The present controlled study was conducted to assess hemispheric dysfunction in schizophrenia and affective disorders with dichotic listening test and compare them with normal controls. The 105 subjects, 35 each having schizophrenia and affective disorders (R.D.C, Criteria) and 35 normal controls with no hearing disorder were selected. The dichotic listening test was repeated in 4-6 and 14-16 weeks interval. Annett's criteria was used to assess handedness. We found that there was left ear superiority in schizophrenia as compared to affective disorders (/ 0.001) and normal controls (/0.001) as assessed by laterality score. The left ear superiority during illness changed to right ear superiority during improvement. The error was more in schizophrenia than normal controls but it did not reach to statistical significant value. Thus on dichotic listening test a noticeable change is seen in patients of schizophrenia and affective disorder from week of illness to week of improvement progressively. It concludes that schizophrenia has left hemispheric dysfunction in right handed person.

350

SOME COGNITIVE AND BRAIN METABOLIC CORRELATES OF SCHIZOPHRENIA

Vesna Medved, Marija Bajc*, Nenad Bohaček, Gordana Vučinić, Darko Ivančević*, Nedeljko Topuzović*

Psychiatric Clinic and *Department of Nuclear Medicine, University Hospital-Rebro, 41000 Zagreb, Yugoslavia

The aim of the present work has been to investigate possible differences in brain hemodynamics and in cognitive function between schizophrenic (SCH) patients with predominantly positive and predominantly negative symptomatology.
Research methodology has included standard psychiatric diagnosis, in terms of positive and negative type of SCH, psychological estimation of cognitive status and SPECT (Single Photon Emission Computer Tomography) brain metabolism imaging method, using Tc 99m-HMPAO. SPECT images have been divided in several regions of interest and quantified by calculating relative perfusion indices for each particular region, with respect to the corresponding brain hemisphere. Data were analyzed using paired t-test, with $p < 0.05$ as the statistical significance level.
The results have shown that:
- brain perfusion ratio of left to right hemisphere on supraventricular level, as well as relative perfusion index of right frontotemporal region on the level of basal ganglia are smaller in negative (N=13) compared to positive (N=13) patients,
- relative brain perfusion index of right occipital region on the level of basal ganglia is greater in negative compared to positive patients.
For the level of basal ganglia these findings could fit into the "hypofrontality" hypothesis in the right brain hemisphere in negative SCH patients.
- Hooper and Waiss tests have resulted with significant differentiation, with positive (N=7) patients performing better than negative (N=7).
Since both of these tests reflect the function of nondominant right hemisphere, these findings can be put in relation with "hypofrontality" in negative patients, found previously. This, in turn, could indicate possible direct connection of cognitive functioning with metabolic basis of brain function in SCH patients.

351
EMOTION-TRIGGERED CHANGES OF HEMISPHERIC PROCESSING ASYMMETRIES IN SCHIZOPHRENIA AND MAJOR DEPRESSION
G. Oepen, M. Fünfgeld, A. Harrington
Dept. of General Psychiatry, University Freiburg, D-7800 Freiburg, West-Germany

The impact of emotional stimulation on two visual half-field tasks was assessed in 50 patients with schizophrenia, 25 patients with Major Depression, and 30 controls. Right visual field advantages for word and left visual field advantages for face decision were found in all 3 groups. Additional emotional stimuli led to a reversed (pathological) asymmetry in the face-test in schizophrenics, and in the word-test in depressive patients. The 3-way MANOVA discriminated significantly between schizophrenic and depressive patients regarding the effect of additional emotional stimuli and visual field asymmetries (p=.002 in the word-test, correctness; p=.006 face-test, reaction time). The results point to an underlying functional pathology of the RH in schizophrenics, and of the LH in depressives. We suggest that the emotional stimulation leads to a breakdown of RH processing capacities in patients with schizophrenia and to a simultaneous increase of LH competence. In depression the capacity of the LH to modulate the function of a morbidly independent RH seems impaired.

352
ALTERED P300 TOPOGRAPHY IN POSITIVE AND NEGATIVE SCHIZOPHRENICS
M.N.Katsanou M.D., K.Alexandropoulos M.D., T.Alexopoulos M.D., V.Avgeri M.D., A.Michalakeas M.R.C. Psych.
Psychiatric Hospital of Attica (2nd Psychiatric Department), Psychiatric Hospital of Corfu, Medical Centre of Athens, Greece

P300 topography has been used in schizophrenia to examine the response to changes in attended stimuli. This study of P300 waveform is important since the main schizophrenic disorder is the inability of the brain to focus on relevant stimuli.
Nine chronic schizophrenics type I and twelve type II were examined during treatment and after four week drug free period. They were compared to twelve normal controls. P300 wave differences were found.
a) Between type I and controls in almost all brain regions (p≤0.01) b) Between type II and controls in posterior-anterior central parietal region (p≤0.01) and medial-posterior right temporal area (p<0.01).
According to our findings there is enough evidence to support the view that schizophrenics show reduced responsiveness to stimuli against normal controls in the following order:
type I < type II < normal control.

Session 54 Free Communications:
Antidepressants in long-term use

353
THE INTEREST OF FLUOXETINE IN PREVENTION OF DEPRESSIVE RECURRENCES

G. FERREY*, J. GAILLEDREAU**, J.N. BEUZEN***

The treatment of depression with thymo-analeptic compounds generally produces partial or global remission within 8 to 28 days. This acute stage is followed by a period of emotional frailty which is generally symptom-free. Nevertheless, it is necessary not to stop the antidepressant treatment too early in order to prevent early relapses. Unfortunately, most trials with thymo-analeptic compounds only assess efficacy during the acute stage and fail to measure the duration of the symptom-free period and the efficacy of these drugs in preventing relapse or recurrence. Furthermore, there has been a general lack of systematic investigation using a sufficiently precise methodology to distinguish between relapse and recurrence.
Several investigations that have claimed to examine prophylactic efficacy in recurrent depression have not specified the need for a minimum symptom-free period before entry, so that they are mere continuation treatment studies rather than true prophylactic studies. Some of these studies will be discussed.
A small number of studies have included defined symptom-free periods before the start of the prophylactic assessment period. The studies of COPPEN et al. (1979), KANE et al. (1982), BJORK et al. (1983) and PRIEN et al. (1984) will also be discussed.
A multicentre study with five French participating centres was performed to test the efficacy of fluoxetine in preventing recurrent depression. The index episode was treated with fluoxetine (40 - 80 mg daily). Responders at 6 weeks (HRSD < 12) were continued on treatment with fluoxetine for a further 18 weeks. Patients who continued to respond with a score on the HRSD of 8 or less at the end of the 6 months were randomly assigned to double-blind treatment with fluoxetine (40 mg daily) or placebo for one year. The difference between fluoxetine and placebo in the prevention of recurrence was significant at 3 months of treatment (p < 0.05), 6 months (p < 0.01), 9 months (p < 0.01) and 12 months (p < 0.001).

  * Centre Hospitalier, 95600 EAUBONNE
 ** Hôpital Richaud, 78100 VERSAILLES
*** Laboratoires Lilly, 92213 SAINT-CLOUD

354
TOLERANCE OF CONTROLLED-RELEASE TRAZODONE IN DEPRESSION. A LARGE MULTICENTRE STUDY.
Moon C A L.,[1] Laws D.,[2] Stott P.C.,[3] Hayes G.[4]
1. Health Centre, Pool, Cornwall, U.K.
2. Herrington House Surgery, Herrington, Tyne and Wear, U.K.
3. Tadworth Farm Surgery, Tadworth, Surrey, U.K.
4. Roussel Laboratories Ltd., Uxbridge, Middlesex, U.K.

Trazodone (Molipaxin) is a highly effective antidepressant available in the UK on NHS prescription, which has the benefit of improving the quality of sleep. The current dosage recommendation for depression and mixed affective disorders, as seen in general practice, is a starting dose of 150mg nocte. To aid compliance, thereby ensuring adequate dosing, whilst maintaining maximum efficacy and useful sedative effects, a 150mg tablet of trazodone can be given as a single evening dose as both starting and maintenance therapy. In clinical practice, the most frequently seen side-effects associated with trazodone usage are drowsiness, dizziness, dry mouth, headache and nausea during the first week of treatment. If it were possible to reduce the incidence and severity of these side-effects, without loss of therapeutic efficacy, an important benefit would be available to patients suffering from depression. Recently, a controlled release formulation of trazodone has been developed. It is hoped that, by avoiding early and relatively high peak plasma drug concentrations, the incidence and severity of side-effects will be reduced or eliminated without losing the benefits of a single nocte dose regimen. The results of the present general practice study, designed to compare the tolerance and efficacy of controlled-release trazodone with standard trazodone 150mg nocte, in 360 depressed patients, will be presented.

355

EFFICACY OF LONG-TERM TREATMENT WITH ANTIDEPRESSANTS

Göran Björling, MD (1), Heimo L Nilsson, PhD (2)

(1) Psychiatric Clinic, NÄL, S-461 85 Trollhättan, Sweden;
(2) CIBA-GEIGY AB, Pharma Division, P O Box 605,
S-421-26 Västra Frölunda, Sweden

An increasing number of patients are given long-term treatment with antidepressants but there are few studies on the efficacy. We have investigated patients with depressive or anxiety syndromes treated with antidepressants for more than one year. The same physician rated 70 patients with two established rating scales for depression (HDRS, CPRS) and CAS as well as visual analogue scales (VAS) for depression, anxiety, panic and obsessive-compulsive symptoms. Daily doses and plasma concentrations of AD were recorded. Global judgement of therapeutic effect was carried out by the physician and by the patient.
Results: 49 females, 21 males, mean age 47±12 years, mean duration of treatment 3.3±2.5 years (mean±SD).
Forty patients had depressive syndromes (mean age 52 years) and 30 had anxiety syndromes (mean age 40 years). The main diagnoses were major depression (33) and panic disorder (23). Global assessments of efficacy by the physician and the patient were similar: 69% scored excellent, 28% moderate and 3% poor. VAS efficacy: 86% clearly improved, 10% no improvement and 4% deteriorated. There was a tendency that the depression group scored worse on VAS compared to the anxiety group. The same tendency was present in the objective rating scales but the scores were low (="healthy").

356

TOLERABLE SIDE EFFECTS ON LONG-TERM TREATMENT WITH ANTIDEPRESSANTS

Heimo L Nilsson, PhD (1), Göran Björling, MD (2)
(1) CIBA-GEIGY AB, Pharma Division, Box 605,
S-421 26, Västra Frölunda, Sweden; (2) Dept Psychiatry,
NÄL, S-461 85 Trollhättan, Sweden

Little is documented of the side effects in patients on long-term treatment with antidepressant drugs (AD). In this study 40 patients with depressive (D) and 30 with anxiety syndromes (A) were investigated with regard to side effects: subjective symptoms (reported and structured interviews), blood picture, liver function and blood pressure. All patients were on prolonged AD medication for more than one year. D: 30 women, 10 men, mean age 52.1 ±12.9 years, mean treatment time 3.5 ±3.2 years; A: 19 women, 11 men, mean age 40.6 ±7.5 years, mean treatment time 3.2 ±3.8 years (mean ±SD). Eight different AD were used and clomipramine was most common (n=42, mean dose 87±63 mg/day).
The most common side effects were: craving for sweets (15%), dryness of the mouth (14%), sweating (10%), weight gain (7%) and memory complaints (7%). No difference was noted between the two diagnostic groups. Only one patient reported a severe side effect (dental problems). Side effects characteristic of acute treatment like tremor, orthostatism, vertigo etc were not reported. The side effects were usually mild and only in isolated cases considered troublesome. In the clomipramine group 40% of the patients reported side effects compared to 29% in the other AD groups. Blood picture and liver function tests were all normal. Thirty-two per cent of the anxiety patients had a blood pressure ≥100 mm Hg (diastolic, supine) compared to 14% in the depressive group (ns).

357

LONGTERM TREATMENT AND PROPHYLAXIS WITH LEVOPROTILINE IN DEPRESSION
Berzewski, H. and Wendt, G.
Psychiatric University Clinic Steglitz, D100 Berlin/BRD; Ciba-Geigy GmbH, Clinical Research, D 6000 Frankfurt/BRD

In the frame-work of a treatment concept for depression, psychopharmacological therapy is especially important to endogenous depression. The therapy within the first 6 months after complete recovery is defined as continuation therapy with the aim of avoiding relapses, medication beyond six months as prophylactic. In our multicenter study, we used the antidepressant levoprotiline, the R (-)-enantiomer of oxaprotiline, a successor of the second-generation antidepressant maprotiline (Ludiomil®). Levoprotiline, without influence upon the noradrenergic system, demonstrated in comparative studies carried out versus the 7 most important antidepressants a reliable efficacy, an earlier onset of action and a distinctly better tolerability. Thus, in levoprotiline we have a suitable antidepressant for longterm treatment of depressive illness.
The aim of this running study is the evaluation of antidepressive effects and tolerability of levoprotiline in acute phases and following continuation and prophylactic treatment for 2 1/2 years. At the time of our presentation the results of about 180 patients (treated 6 months) and about 120 patients (treated 12 months and more) should be evaluated.

358

MAPROTILINE PREVENTIVE EFFECTIVENESS
ON UNIPOLAR DEPRESSION RELAPSES

PHILLIPS R.[*], ROUILLON F.[**], SERRURIER D.[*],
ANSART E.[**], GERARD MJ.[*]

SUMMARY

Although antidepressant treatments have been used for about thirty years, the question of treatments' duration keeps much debated. In fact, among the great number of trials, only some fifteen studies placebo controlled have considered the prophylactic interest of long-term antidepressant treatment. To complete the few products rated to this end (Imipramine, Amitriptyline, Zimélidine, Nomifensine, Fluoxétine), we started a large muticenter (130 psychiatrists) placebo controlled double-blind trial involving 1141 outpatients treated with Maprotiline and including a one year follow-up. The controlled trial was preceded by a pre-involvement period over which 1339 patients were treated in open with 75-150 mg of Maprotiline. Only patients showing clinical improvement (MADRS <10) during this preliminary phase, were included in the prophylactic rating phase, and divided into four groups : Maprotiline 75 mg ; 1/2 tablet of Maprotiline 75 mg ; one placebo tablet ; 1/2 placebo tablet. Relapse was defined by score above 27 on MADRS, or above 25 in two assessments separated by 8 days, or according to experimenter's appraisal. The actuarial rate of relapse after one year was : 16 % with 75 mg of Maprotiline, 23,8 % with 37,5 mg, 31,5 % with a placebo tablet, 37,5 % with 1/2 placebo tablet, the difference being statistically significative between the 4 groups, except for the "placebo" groups between each other. On the other hand, Maprotiline tolerance has proved to be satisfying in long-term treatment.

KEY WORDS : depression, relapses, Maprotiline, prevention.

[*] Laboratoires CIBA-GEIGY - 2 & 4 rue Lionel Terray,
92506 RUEIL MALMAISON
[**] Service de Psychiatrie, Hôpital Louis Mourrier, 178 rue des Renouillers,
92701 COLOMBES CEDEX.

359
BIOLOGICAL MODIFICATIONS IN DEPRESSED PATIENTS THREATED BY AMINEPTINE
Mendonca Lima C.A., Vandel S., Sandoz M., Bechtel P., Allers G., Volmat R.,
Centre Hospitalier Universitaire de Besancon, France

GH, TSH, PROLACTINE response to TRH stimulation were studied in 6 depressed women impatients before and after 21 days of amineptine treatment, and dopaminergic antidepressant.
Urinary elimination of HVA, 5-HIAA and MHPG (total, glucoronide and sulfate) were also studied one day before the two TRH tests and after 5 days of poor tiramine diet.
Any conclusion is possible from the GH and TSH results. PROLACTINE peak after treatment was significantly lower than before treatment as consequence of dopaminergic system stimulation by amineptine.
MHPG, HVA and 5-HIAA were significantly lower after treatment. The reduction of total MHPG levels was caused mainly by the variation of the glucoronide fraction.
This action on the noradrenaline metabolism has a peripheral origin and authors try to verify possible correlations with patient anxiety levels studied by 4 depression scales.
MHPG-glucoronide reduction wasn't verified in another group treated by desipramine. It seems to be an exclusive action of amineptine.

Session 55 Free Communications:
Preventive approaches in child mental health

360
Early Intervention with Infants-At-Risk for Developmental Delay.
Dr. Usha S. Naik - Niloufer Hospital (Hyderabad-India)
Mrs. Gool R. Plumber - APAWMR (Hyderabad-India)

In the field of development delay, the growing emphasis is on early Intervention. However, high centre based drop out rate, prevents regular follow up of infants.

In 1987, the Andhra Pradesh Association for the Welfare of the Mentally Retarded commenced a home based early intervention programme, using 20 Trained Home Visitors, 416 Infants-At-Risk for developmental delay were selected from two Government Hospital Nurseries. The risk factors were -

1. Hypoxic ischaemic encephalopathy 307 cases
2. Very low birth weight - 1.5 kg.
3. Hyperbilirubinemia - 28
4. Neonatal convulsions - 57
5. Meningitis - 4

All these infants come from the lowest socio-economic groups and are therefore at greater risk. Infants are followed up on a weekly basis using the Portage home training programme. Every infant is assessed at the age of 6 months using Gessells and Baley's developmental scales. Children detected to have sensory or motor handicaps have been offered appropriate therapy in addition to the on going intervention programme.
The experiences of the group will be highlighted.

361
The Development of WHO Child Care Facility Schedule: A Pilot Collaborative Study

Tsiantis, J., Lambidi, A., Dragonas, Th., Orley, J.
Department of Psychological Pediatrics, Aghia Sophia; Institute of Child Health; University of Ioannina; Division of Mental Health, WHO, Geneva.

This paper describes the preliminary research work conducted by a WHO collaborative study group for the development of the Child Care Facility Schedule (CCFS) for the assessment of quality in child-care settings. Seven areas of quality child care are covered: Physical Environment, Health and Safety, Nutrition and Food Service, Administration, Staff-Family Interaction, Observable Child Behaviour and Curriculum. An interrater reliability study was undertaken in Greece and Nigeria in 30 and 34 day-care centres respectively; r ranging from .83 to .99 in Greece and .94 in Nigeria. Results suggest that the CCFS is a satisfactory rating scale while modifications were made in the light of refining certain items, altering the scoring system as to grasp nuances and clarifying the instructions of the manual and these of the interviewing technique. The CCFS is a useful tool for the evaluation of quality child care in different cultures.

362
EARLY INTERVENTION FOR CHILDREN OF PSYCHOTIC PARENTS

Gunnar Nirk, M.D. & Pamela C. Rubovits, Ph.D.
The Providence Center for Counseling and Psychiatric Services, Providence, RI USA

With the increase of chronically psychotic patients living in the community the number of psychotic parents caring for their young children has also increased. These children are at risk to develop emotional problems but frequently do not come to the attention of psychiatrists treating their parents. This paper reports on an early intervention program for preschool children of psychotic parents at the Community Mental Health Center in Providence, RI. The program which has been in operation since 1981 has two primary goals: 1) to improve parenting skills, 2) to remediate developmental delays in the children. A variety of therapeutic and educational interventions help parents to increase their reciprocity with these children, learn specific child-care skills, deal with their feelings about children's demands and encourage a sense of separateness.

This paper will report on a follow-up study of 28 children who had at least 50 therapeutic contacts and are now of elementary school age. Data from Child Behavior Checklists (Achenbach) obtained from parents and teachers will be presented. The need for more attention to children living with their psychotic parents will be stressed.

363

Persistent absenteeism and expulsion from school. Cry for help? Preliminary report.
R.Papatheophilou, K.Galanopoulou, T.Kallinikaki, T.Katsantoni.
Adolescent Unit (A.U.), General Hospital of Athens, Greece.

Persistent absenteeism from secondary schools could be due to the adolescents themselves, their families, their schools the community at large. Expulsions from schools follow usually a long history of unacceptable behaviour. On occasions these adolescents discontinue their education and may get in trouble with the police. Research on the above was undertaken by the A.U. with the permission and assistance of the Ministry of Education and the Dept of secondary Education of East Attica. To find the size of the problem members of the staff visited 22 schools catering for 7300 adolescents and filled in a questionnaire about the pupils who had more than 50 unauthorised absences in the school year 1987-88 or had been expelled for 1-3 days tht period. In Greece adolescents are allowed less than 100 hourly absences (1/10 of possible attendances). Half of them must be excused. Otherwise the pupils are not allowed to participate in final examinations and have to repeat the same class next year. Some of them take the opportunity to stop their education. The following parameters were considered. The schools(size, type of school, locality, buildings, staff). The adolescents (age, sex, school class and marks, number of absences and expulsions). Further information re the high risk pupils was acquired by the adolescents themselves and their teachers. The results of this research may give rise to new thoughts re educational policies and planning of health and welfare services.

364

Consultation-Liaison Psychiatry In The Mental Health Of The School

Joji Inomata, M.D.,Kosuke Yamazaki, M.D., Masatsugu Hayashi, M.D., John Alex Mckenzie, M.P.A., TOKAI University School of Medicin, Boseidai Isehara City Kanagawa Pref. 259-11, JAPAN.

Joint school-visiting doctors and teachers committees first emerged in Kanagawa Prefecture (to Tokyo's immediate south) in 1983, and then spread slowly across the nation. These committees assist in helping troubled students to deal with in-school manifested psychiatric problems. We should like to discuss in this report both the prefecture's joint committee and that of Hiratsuka City, both of which through committees of Medical Associations, include secondary school teachers as members.
Both committees have been quite active : in 1989, the Kanagawa Prefectural Committee published a manual on mental health in schools for both visiting doctors and teachers, a manual on illness categories and diagnosis based on patient's drawing-s , and in 1988, a manual on psychiatric interviewing, and finally, in various other ways conveyed psychiatric information to non-psychiatric specialty visiting doctors.
The Hiratsuka Committee, on the other hand, rather then informational publication concentrates on conducting of individual diagnosis and therapy; it has added to Kanagawa's six school refusal special classes, a seventh in Hiratsuka City, and coordinates the referral of cases to individual psychiatrists, psychiatric clinics, and to medical school psychiatrists. In addition, in the past year, the Hiratsuka Committee has actively promoted (through seminars) non- psychiatric specia-lty- liaison with psychiatrists, such that, for examples, pediatrists encounter-ingpossible neurotic complications in students or patients, will refer either's case to a committee-recommended psychiatrist or clinic facility.
The Hiratsuka committee,meeting monthly (through not in January or August), has discussed in great detail 38 cases, at an average of 9 cases per year, and usually 1-2 cases per 3 hour monthly meeting. The majority of these cases (28; 73.8%)are in the school refusal category.
In the nation at large, the number of school refusing students increased rapidly from 1975-1983, but tapered off somewhat, increasing more gradually from 1983 to 1987. In 1987, junior high school refusers numbered 32,725 (an increase of 3,052 over 1986) and primary school refusers numbered 5,286 (an 879 increase over 1986). The Hiratsuka Committee is dealing in the main with a national student trend, that though in degree as to increase is leveling off, is nonetheless a phenomenon showing yearly increase.
Schools in Japan, we feel, are better able to contend with disruptive social chang-e, if they continue to strengthen their active communication and paticipation links with psychiatrists.
Our report is designed to show how this is being done and to indicate the outcome of psychiatric consultations in one such committee.

Session 56 Free Communications:
Alcohol abuse: Epidemiology

365

THE STUDY OF USE AND ABUSE OF ALCOHOL BEVERAGES IN STUDENT MILIEU: A CONTRIBUTION
M.Touhami, M.Bouktib
Psychiatric University Center IBN Rochd
Casablanca, Morocco

The consumption of alcohol beverages seem to be in nett progress in Morocco. We can state actually as the result of it, an increase of morbidity. The assessment of this phenomenon and its medical and social repercussions is difficult in regard of the cultural factors. A contribution to the epidemiological approach is proposed in this paper. A questionnaire based on World Health Organisation's questionnaire concerning drugs abuse was administered to the 1500 students of medicine faculty of Casablanca. The preliminary results of this study show: the consumption of alcohol beverages among medical students is low. The regular users represent less than 1% of the sample. It remains over all occasional and episodic. It reaches much more the males. Nearly the three quarter of students have e pejorative viewpoint to the use and abuse of alcohol beverages and they consider them as a threated transgression. Despite that some regular drinkers regret their act, the majority of these don't think to stop drink. Does this confirm the ambiguous statute; of the use of alcoholic drinks in our context? (prohibition and tolerance). One thing is sure, all the students complain about the poverty of education syllabuses concerning alcoholism in their medical studies. They wish to have integral information concerning silmutaneously tobacco, alcohol and drugs.

366

EPIDEMIOLOGICAL PARAMETERS IN NORTH-WESTERN SPAIN FOR ALCOHOLIC DISEASE
Echarri E., G.Lado I., Diaz del Valle J.C.
Clemente A., Blanco J., Agra S.
Sanatorio Psiquiatrico de Conxo
Santiago de Compostela, Spain

A retrospective study for defining the epidemiological parameters affecting patients suffering from alcoholic disease (303.00 DSM-III) or alcoholic delirium (291.00 DSM-III) is developed over 1988 first-inpatients in a psychiatric hospital in NW Spain.
The alcoholic patient is likely to be a man, about 42 years old, single or married that lives in the country working the land with a primary level of studies. He is hospitalized for 24 days average and is returned to the community with pharmacological treatment and ambulatory periodic control. Its hematic control for CVA and plattelets shows differences of statistical significance.
The assistential support for this kind of patients needs 15-20% of total mediums, and a high rate of rehospitalizations is observed. The discharged patient is treated with 3-4 drugs average, including vitamins, anxiolytics and hypnotics.

367
At Risk Drinking in Primary Care in Brazil

Iacoponi, E., Laranjeira, R.R. & Jorge, M.R.
Escola Paulista de Medicina, S.Paulo, Brazil

This report describes a survey designed to assess the prevalence of at-risk drinking among patients attending the primary health care sector of the largest conurbation in Brazil. Data were collected from 1500 patients consulting 40 randomly chosen health centres. Five percent of the screened population answered positively to two or more questions on the CAGE questionnaire, although this rate was much higher for men than women. Patients socio demographic features were analyzed by means of logistic models. The applications of the results are discussed, as well as suggestions for policy making.

368

Psychiatric Morbidity and Alcohol Use in Women
Dr. Sarah E. Romans-Clarkson
Senior Lecturer
Otago Medical School
Dunedin, New Zealand

A random community survey of psychiatric morbidity in New Zealand women investigated the presence of alcohol problems in urban and rural women. Significantly more rural (9.9%) than urban women (6.5%) saw themselves as currently having a problem with alcohol (p=0.02). Urban women with an alcohol problem were also more likely to show psychiatric morbidity. Although the rural women with alcohol problems were not more likely to show psychiatric disorder, it is clear that alcohol difficulties are a major health problem for rural inhabitants.

369
ALCOHOLISM IN CHINESE AND ABORIGINES:AN ANALYSIS OF RISK FACTORS
Hai-Gwo Hwu[*], Eng-Kung Yeh[+], Yuen-Li Yeh[+]
*Department of Psychiatry, Medical College, National Taiwan University, +Taipei City Psychiatric Center. Taipei, Taiwan R.O.C.

The Taiwan Psychiatric Epidemiological Project(TPEP) was carried out from 1982 to 1986. The Chinese modified Diagnostic Interview Schedule (DIS-CM) was the case identification tool. The samples included a metropolitan city, 2 small towns and 6 rural villages. The total sample size was of 11,000 Chinese, age 18 and over. In 1987, a prevalence study of alcoholism among Taiwan aborigines of 3 ethnic groups was done by using the modified alcoholism section of the DIS-CM to identify the cases. The sample size was 1,500 subjects, age 18 and over. CATMOD of the SAS program was used for logistic regression analyses of the epidemiological risk factors. The independent variables used for analyses were obtained from single variable analyses. There are 9 and 8 variables in the samples of Chinese and aborigines respectively. This paper will present the results and discuss the differentiation of alcohol abuse and dependence defined by DSM-III criteria and the corresponding preventive measures.

370
DETECTING ALCOHOLISM: CORRELATION BETWEEN THE CAGE QUESTIONNAIRE AND SOCIAL BIOLOGICAL INDICATORS
M.A.Ortega, J.Yanguela, J.Somalo, F.Garcia, C.Larrode
Hospital S.S. "San Millan", Logrono, Spain
The objective of our work is the study of the trustworthyness of the four criteria of Cage Questionnaire on alcoholism and their correlation with biological laboratory tests, and psychosocial factors. We have analyzed, a total of 181 patients suffering from different illnesses. They were in different wards of a General Hospital. The diseases which might have changed the biological test results were excluded. The tests which have been used are: 1. The four criteria of the Cage Questionnaire. 2. Psychosocial factors, and Skinner and Holt risk factors of alcoholic dependence, declared consumption of alcohol, and biological indicators. The results show that the relation between the supposed negative cases in the Questionnaire with those that is negative in the biological tests is of a 68%. The relation between the positive ones in the Questionnaire and that of biological tests is almost of a 80%. Final Conclusions: The Cage Questionnaire is trustworthy as a valid instrument for the diagnosis of alcoholism. There is a direct correlation between alcoholic ingestion and unbnormal results of biological tests and positive results in the Cage Questionnaire. The importance of the correlation between risk factors of early alcoholism and parental alcoholism with alcoholism diagnosis, is discussed.

Session 57 Poster Presentation: Affective disorders I

371

PSYCHOTIC DEPRESSION: CLASSIFICATION, DIAGNOSIS AND TREATMENT APPROACHES
Michael B. Sheikman,M.D., Greenville N.C.,U.S.A.

In the last decade a great deal of emphasis has been placed on the value of the distinction between psychotic depression (PD) and nonpsychotic depression (NPD).There is evidence for and against considering PD and NPD as two distinct clinical entities.Some neurochemical findings,family studies,the difference in prognosis and in pharmacological response to tricyclic antidepressants (TCA) support the view that the distinction of these two subtypes is important.Interest in this issue can be explained by the fact that at least 5% of the admissions to the acute care psychiatric hospitals in the U.S. are patients with PD.These patients have twice the hospitalization rate,longer average duration of hospitalization and higher risk of suicide in comparison to patients with NPD.

Criteria for PD relying on cross-sectional psychopathology are based on presence or absence of delusions,hallucinations,thought disorder or grossly inappropriate behavior.PD is usually recurrent, delusions are often mood-congruent and similar from episode to episode.The patients with PD do not respond well to TCA alone or to neuroleptic alone.Clinical observation shows that the combination of these medications is the treatment of choice.ECT was found to be quite effective in patients with PD and should be considered when the patients with major depressive episode with psychotic features do not respond to the pharmacological treatment.

372

AN EPIDEMIOLOGIC SURVEY OF DEPRESSION IN ALGARVE (PORTUGAL)
Seabra, Daniel Psychiatrist
Cruz, Pestana Psychologist
U.O.P. Centro de Saude Mental de Faro
8000 Faro, Portugal

The authors present the results of an epidemiologic survey of Depression in the general population of the Algarve , Portugal.
By an aleatory method, two hundred and seventy nine individuals of both sexes, older than 11 total population of 350.000, formed a representative sample).
Sensitivity of 1% and mean (SD) of 1% were considered.
There were 20 target points and 15 individuals were inquired on each one.
All the individuals in this sample were submitted to the Beck Depression Inventory (BDI).
Factors like, Sex, Age, Profession and Marital Status were studied and correlated with the results of the BDI.
Statistic analysis was applied (descritive statistics and significance tests), and the results will be shown.

373

INCIDENTAL LEARNING VS.FORMAL MEMORY TESTING IN DEPRESSED AND CONTROLS
P.De Bastiani,L.Finotti,P.Arienti,E.Destro et al
Psychiatric Clinic, Neurologic Institute,
University of Ferrara, Italy

Memory problems, commonly reported by depressed patients, have been long investigated in devoted studies failing to support significant differences in memory performance between patients and normals. Incidental learning remains usually untested while most of the patients' complains clearly refer to everyday events where such a memory involvement represents the claimed symptom. Attempting to clarify this particular aspect of memory failure by depressed patients an experimental study is currently run in our laboratory. Subjects and controls (both unaware) are presented with a controlled situation in a standard place (the "inputs room": IP) for a fixed time, then, after a free recall task of a word list (FRW) and a delayed word recall task (DWR) they are invited to report as much information as they can about the IP. Results of the IP protocol are compared to the more canonical testing situation (FRW and DWR).
The experiment, still in progress, methodology, refinements and correlate results shall be discussed.

374

Clinical features of depression linked to social status: study on 867 patients.

Lenzi A., Lazzerini F., Re F., Marazziti D.
Institute of Psychiatry University of Pisa

Social status can result in the virtual imposition of a particular life-style that may in turn predispose towards the development of some forms of illness, the degree and the nature of the illness depending upon individual personality prior to the onset of symptoms. The aim of this report was to investigate whether there exist symptomatological dissimilarities in different social classes in Italy, and whether or not it is possible to identify psychopathological profiles linked to specific socio-economic classes.
In the lower classes, the depressive episode is charaterized by a marked trend towards somatization with polarization on the subject's own body and worries about the subject's own health. In the upper classes, on the other hand, depression is mainly expressed in terms of psychic and cognitive symptoms and it is expressed by a more frequent tendency towards self-accusation of having disappointed people, and towards an excessive fixation with previous experiences and errors as documented by the high score on HAM-D "feelings guilt". Frequent features of depressive illness in this group are paranoid symptoms, together with an increase in suspiciousness or obsessive-compulsive symptoms that sometimes may cover the underlying depression.

375

SOCIAL STUDY OF A GROUP OF DEPRESSED PATIENTS IN A PRIVATE INSTITUTION.
Rachèle M.G.,Burrai C.,Scamonatti L.,Manconi F.
Cattedra di Psichiatria Sociale.Istituto di Neurologia.Università.

Depression is fairly widespread in Sardinia and is prevalently treated in private clinics.
In an attempt to explain this phenomeno,even partially,the Authors carried out a study on all depressed patients admitted to a private clinic in the Sardinian capital over a period of 6 months. Personal and socio-economic data were obtained from each patient during a specific interview and information regarding the illness and therapy already carried out was also obtained.
Moreover, the external health services available in place of residence were studied and the reasons for which the patient had chosen the present services. Furthermore,the reason for admittance to the clinic was investigated and the means by which this was obtained.
Interesting considerations concerning the state of public and private psychiatric services in Sardinia were obtained,also considering the new Psychiatric Health Laws present in Italy.

376

CLINICAL FEATURES AND COURSE OF MOOD DISORDERS: HISTORICAL COMPARISON
Gepponi I., Galli L., Fabiani R., Rinaldi A., San Martino S.G., Lenzi A., Cassano G.B.
Institute of Psychiatry - University of Pisa

The advent of several acute and prophylactic pharmacological strategies for the treatment of affective illness led to change the psycopathological features, the course of ilness and the rate of mortality.
In order to evaluate these differences and the impact of pharmacological treatment on mood disorders, a prospective assessment of affective patients was programmed at the Psychiatric Clinic of University of Pisa. Our sample comprised 65 inpatients affected by a Mood Disorder, according to DSM-III-R criteria.
The "hospitalization" led to selection of the sample, thus resulting a sample similar to that one of the beginning of the century (Pollock 1931).
The preliminary results, after 5 months of observation, as compared with the results reported by Pollock, shows, at admission, a higher prevalence rate of depression (48% in our sample versus 32% in Pollock' survey), and a lower of manic episodes (31% versus 49%), while the percentage of mixed states is similar (14% versus 15%); in Pollock's sample, 4% of the patients were diagnosed as affected by "circular psychosis" and in our sample 17% were diagnosed as schizoaffective.
Furthermore, it seems that the course of disorder is characterized by the presence of a higher number of relapses linked to a briefer lenght of the single episode.

377

DELUSIONAL vs NONDELUSIONAL DEPRESSION: A CASE-CONTROL FAMILY STUDY.

D. Vassilopoulos, L. Lykouras, D. Malliaras, A. Voulgari.
Department of Psychiatry, Athens University, Athens, Greece.

A case-control family study of psychiatric disorders, including unipolar depression, bipolar disorder I, schizophrenia, "nonaffective psychosis", alcoholism and suicide, was carried out in 503 first degree relatives (parents, siblings) of 76 probands with nondelusional depression and 454 first degree relatives of 77 delusional depressed probands. Diagnostic assessment was made mainly by the family history method using multiple informants. There was no significant difference in the morbid risk of the relatives of the two proband groups. The mathematical analysis showed that the multifactorial pattern of inheritance fits best with our data. Heritability estimate based on the threshold model of multifactorial inheritance was found to be 62 for the delusional and 46 for the nondelusional group, while the overall heritability was 50. The present results show the importance of genetic contribution in major depression and that genetic and enviromental factors operate in both delusional and nondelusional depression.

Session 58 Poster Presentation: Suicidology

378

A SUICIDAL FAMILY

M. Kontea, E. Lykouras, G. Papadimitriou
Athens University Medical School,
Dept. of Psychiatry, Eginition Hospital,
Athens, Greece

Psychiatric, social and cultural factors have been implicated and certain hypotheses have been put forward to explain suicidal behaviour. Major depressive disorder is more likely to be associated with suicide although it has been suggested the possibility of a genetically determined transmission of suicidal behaviour by twin and adoption studies. It was thought to be of interest to present a family in which the female proband, aged 61, suffering from bipolar disorder attempted suicide by a nonviolent method. Four other male relatives (two first and two second degree) committed suicide all by violent means. Two of them, by this action, ended a clear depressive episode. It is worthnoting that a male member of the same family committed homicide and another one, male too, was killed in a gunfight. These observations and their implications will be discussed.

379

Neuropeptides and Suicide

Banki,C.M., Kármacsi,L., Bissette,G., Nemeroff, C.B.
(Reg.Neuropsychiatric Institute and Duke University
Med.Ctr., Durham, USA)

Corticotropin-releasing factor (CRF), thyrotropin-releasing factor (TRH), somatostatin (SRIF), and neurotensin (NT) were measured by specific RIA's in subsequent groups of hospitalized psychiatric patients. Immunoreactive peptide levels were compared between patients with and without suicide attempts made shortly before admission. NT and SRIF levels did not discriminate among diagnostic groups, nor did they indicate any alteration in patients having attempted suicide prior to admission. The CRF levels in the CSF were significantly higher in major depression but there was no difference between the suicidal and non-suicidal patients; however, on followup, there were more repeated attempts in those having higher CSF immunoreactive CRF levels. Finally TRH levels is the CSF turned out to be significantly higher in patients with major depression, and within this group there was a tendency for those having attempted suicide by violent means to have the highest TRH values. The results suggest a relatively specific elevation of central TRH and/or CRF production associated with violent suicidal behavior at least in patients suffering from major depression.

380

SUICIDAL BEHAVIOUR IN THE AGED IN THE LIGHT OF AGGRESSION

Janko KOSTNAPFEL, Psychiatric Clinic
of the University, LJUBLJANA, Yugoslavia

In 1982 we compared Slovenia, the republic extending over the north-western part of Yugoslavia, with a population of approx. 1,900.000 (Slovenes), and Kosovo, the autonomous province in the south-eastern part of Yugoslavia, with approx. 1,650.000 inhabitants, mostly Albanians. In Slovenia, which is economically the most advanced region, the incidence of suicide is rather high (suicide rate - SR = 34.2), while the number of homicides is low (homicide rate - HR = 1.5). Just the opposite is true of Kosovo, the least developed part of the country (SR = 2.3, and HR = 4.5). The reasons for this crosslike contrast between the two regions should be submitted to critical examination.
In Slovenia, the incidence of suicide in the age group of 65 years and over is twice as high as in the general population.
The aged must often negate a part of their life. Their previous heteroaggression may thus convert into self-aggression and suicidal behaviour. According to the law of negation of negation (G. W.Fr.Hegel, 1770-1831), it is only re-negation that can result into affirmation ($-a \times -a = a^2$). Yet, an old person has neither time nor energy for re-negation and the resulting affirmation, which can thus be accomplished only in - death.

381

ANALYSIS OF SUICIDES IN THE PSYCHIATRIC HOSPITAL IN WROCLAW (1974-1987)

Sylwia Chladzinska-Kiejna, Andrzej Kiejna,
Dept. of Psychiatry, Wroclaw, Poland

We analysed suicides committed by patients hospitalized in the Psychiatric Hospital in Wroclaw. 26769 case reports of hospitalized patients in the period of 1974-1987 were analyzed.
During these years 40 suicide deaths, and 104 attempted suicides occurred. In the consecutive years the global number of suicides remained stable, while the suicide index was changing.
Among patients who died from suicide 75% were diagnosed schizophrenic. However in several cases one could not exclude drug induced depression, as well depression due to the deprivation.
Most often suicides were commited on the ward, in the morning and by patients hospitalized day and night. Most of the people committed suicide by hanging themselves.
From our analysis we conclude that reforms of the hospital structures during that time had no influence on the intensity of suicidal bahavior.

382

ATTITUDES OF MEDICAL STAFFS TOWARDS SUICIDE PATIENTS
M.J.Hilz, R.Hoell, W.Weidenhammer, T.A.Moesler, E.Lungersbausen
Univ. of Erlangen, Nuremberg, Dept. of Neurology and Psychiatry, FRG
Rather little psychiatric support is given to medical personnel working with patients which just have tried to commit suicide. Little is known about their feelings towards these patients. In order to find out whether there is a difference between medical staffs concerned with self-aggressive patients and those not concerned, 70 statistically almost independent questions were put to 53 physicians and 81 male and female nurses working with these patients, and to 30 physicians and 61 nurses not working with them. 65 items dealt with attitudes and feelings towards suicide and suicide patients, such as ethics, morality, aggression, fear, hostility, empathy, religion, etc. The answers were scaled in 5 categories of acceptance or denial. 5 items concerned sociodemographic aspects of those interviewed. In 26 items, statistical analysis (t-test for independent samples) of the graded answers showed a tendency towards a difference in attitudes ($0.05 < p < 0.10$), or even a significant ($p<0.05$) difference. Interpretation is difficult, as answers certainly depend on what the interviewed believes to be socially desirable and expected. Nevertheless, medical staffs concerned with suicide patients seem to be more aggressive towards these patients; those personnel not confronted are more understanding and less hostile or detached. The results emphasize the necessity of psychotherapeutical help for those working with self-aggressive patients.

383
SUICIDAL RISK AND MODE OF ATTEMPT IN RELATION TO PSYCHOSOCIAL STRESSORS

DR VIMALA RAO, Govt. General Hospital & Madras Medical College, Madras, India.

Two hundred cases of parasuicide attended the Crisis Intervention Clinic of Department of Psychiatry, Government General Hospital, Madras, with history of self poisoning, self immolation, hanging, etc. We have attempted to categorize these people into a high risk and low risk groups in terms of forseeable (conclusive) outcome of virulence, bitterness of the patients act, ie. whether death would have befallen or survival was certain.

This study aims at analysing these risk factors involved with regard to (a) method chosen by the subject; (b) the psychosocial stressors; (c) socio-demographic variable. The psychosocial stress factors most commonly encountered are, marital problems, parental rejection, seperation, financial problems, illness and social isolation. The demographic variables included are age, sex, educational qualification, marital status, family ties, occupational status, etc.

In the study group we find that the intention to kill oneself varied significantly in terms of suicidal behaviour. The commonest method of self-poisoning was by organophosphorus compounds, which was predominant among the younger age group, single, women. The lethality of the intent indicated to quite an extent the seriousness of the intent to die.

The concept of lethality of the act has an important implication for the active management in suicidal behaviour.

384
PAIN, SUICIDE AND SURGERY

Gerhard Bengesser M.D., M.I.A.E.P.
Wagner-Jauregg-KH, A-4020, Linz, Austria

It is astonishing that the percentage of suicides due to (mostly chronic) unbearable pain is so low.
People are more likely to commit suicide because of a damaged car or some other seemingly trivial reason. Certain syndromes very often present with suicidal thoughts, e.g. the Dejerine-Roussy syndrome and the so-called hemianaesthesia dolorase syndrome. In both of these syndromes Professor Ganglberger, an outstanding Austrian surgeon, maintains that stereotactic procedures should be used before other kinds of intervention. In all other cases stereotactic procedures have to be the last resort.

Session 59 Poster Presentation:
Behavioral and other phychotherapies

385
FIRST YEAR CLINICAL EXPERIENCE OF A NEW BEHAVIORAL TREATMENT UNIT. DEMOGRAPHIC AND CLINICAL CHARACTERISTICS OF ATTENDERS.
Yiannis Kasvikis M.D., Dimitra Skaloubaka M. Sc., Spyros Tzeranis M.D., Maria Timoyiannaki M. Sc., and Yiannis Papadatos M.D.
Behavioral Treatment Unit, Center for Mental Health and Research, Zaimi 9 St. Athens 106 82, Greece.
Although the clinical necessity of the behavioral treatment units is well recognised, no outpatient unit working on a walk-in or referral basis existed in Athens, where half the Greek population lives. In October 1988 the Behavioral Treatment Unit was created in Athens, under the auspices of the Center for Mental Heatlh and Research. During the first seven months of its existence 62 patients were refered of which 46 (74%) were found suitable for behavioral treatment, 17 were men. These were sufferers of Agoraphobia(33%), Social phobia(9%), Simple phobia(33%), Obsessive Compulsive Disorder(20%) and Post Traumatic Stress Disorder(2%). Mean age and duration of illness were respectively 42 and 7.5 years for Agoraphobia, 27 and 2.5 years for Social phobia, 28 and 3 years for Simple phobia, 39 and 9 years for Obsessive Compulsive Disorder. Drop-out rate was 15% for all disorders the highest being 26% for Agoraphobia. Of those patients complient with treatment, 90% showed significant reduction or total remission of symptoms by an average of 5.5 weeks in treatment. Psychometric ratings were obtained on the following scales: 1)Main targets of treatment, 2)Fear Questionnaire, 3)Short Beck Depression Inventory, 4)Compulsion Checklist and 5)Work and Social adjustment. Outcome data are presented.

386
REFLECTIONS: A PSYCHOTHERAPY FOR PATIENTS WITH ALEXITHYMIC STRUCTURE
Maria Diallina and Nikos Tzavaras
General Hospital Athens/Gr.University Thrakis/Greece

The concept of alexithymia was introduced to modern psychiatry by Nemiah and Sifneos. The psychosomatic patients are not able adequately to perceive and to express their own feelings ("emotional analphabets"). A special psychotherapeutic technique is advisable. The old relationship between psychosomatosis and psychosis can be better understood on the basis of our finding, which reveal a borderline structure and splitting mechanisms in many psychosomatic patients.
The health of our patient with heavy psychosomatic symptoms after a 10-years psychiatric treatment with high dosis neuroleptics, E.C.T. or Li deteriorated and a acathesia appeared. After 3 years psychotherapy the patient is working, finished his studies, sees again his wife, needs no drug treatment. The therapy is based on: 1. Meditation of emotions. He is encouraged to associate to a dream-image or a fact of reality, we amplify the patient's dreams in order to let the patient relive them with us. 2. The so-called analysis of the superego. 3. Transition from averbal communication toward the verbalisation of transference-feelings(neurotization of the patient) and utilization of classic techniques of individual psychotherapy.

387
THE THERAPEUTIC COMMUNITY: A PRECURSOR TO PSYCHOANALYSIS
BERTOLLI, Roberto & RAVERA, Furio
CREST «LE PORTAGE ITALIA»

The authors pinpoint the utility of the Therapeutic Community in-patients with major psychiatric diseases. They describe two different cases: the first, a complex personality disorder with euphoric crises and drugs abuse; the second, a case of anorexia underlaying hard drug abuse.

Both patients at the end of the sejour in a residential Therapeutic Community showed good features for a successfull psychoanalitic treatment.

388
THE RESULTS OF THE THERAPEUTIC MILIEU PRACTICE

HÜROL,Cem; ÇALAK,Erdoğan; EREN,Nurhan
Psychiatry Dept., Istanbul Faculty of Medicine, Istanbul University

In this study we tried to investigate the relations between the perception of the milieu by the patient and therapeutic outcome, by examining the efficacy of the therapeutic milieu practice established in the Neurosis Inpatient Section of the Psychiatry Dept., Istanbul Faculty of Medicine.
The group was mostly composed of neurotic and character disordered patients while a few stabilized psychotic patients were also present. The study lasted a year with 35 patients, whose length of stay ranged between 2 to 6 months. Therapy team consisted of 2 psychiatrists, 2 psychologists and 3 nurses. Trying to create a milieu encouraging a highest level of interaction from patient to patient and from patient to the team, predominantly group psychotherapy (interaction and psychodrama) was applied.
Moos' Ward Atmosphere Scale and ICD-9 were used in the study.
The results showed that it is not valuable to search for direct and global relations between the perception of milieu and the therapeutic outcome. The factors which might influence the relation between the perception of milieu and the outcome were discussed.

389
SOCIO-PATHOLOGY OF MILIEU THERAPY: A FILICIDE CASE

C. E. LEONE, B. N. LEONE, F. FERRATO

DESPITE IMPORTANT CONTRIBUTIONS FROM BIOLOGICAL RESEARCHES AND PHARMACOLOGIC TREATMENT EACH HAS CURTAILED THE RANGE OF CLINICAL OBSERVATION AND THE CAPACITY FOR INTEGRATION OF TREATMENTS. THE MODELS AND SCIENTIFIC DATA AVAILABLE TO THE CLINICIAN HAVE BEEN LIMITED BY PREVAILING IDEOLOGIES. THE AUTHORS DO NOT IGNORE THE RISKS CONCERNING SUCH REDUCTIONIST SIMPLISM NOT JUST BECAUSE IT INVALIDATES AN EFFECTIVE REHABILITATION TREATMENT BUT ALSO BECAUSE IT EXPOSES TO SEVERE CLINIC RISKS AS IN A FILICIDE CASE. THE AUTHORS DESCRIBE A 36-YEAR-OLD WOMAN WITH A HISTORY OF PREVIOUS SUICIDE ATTEMPS BRUTALLY KILLED HIS FIRST BORN. THIS UNUSUAL HOMICIDE IS, IN FACT, A VARIATION OF EXTENED SUICIDE. THIS CASE IS OF CONSIDERABLE INTEREST BECAUSE IT DEMONSTRATES THAT INTEGRATION OF THERAPIES IS THE FOUNDATION FOR TREATING THE PATIENT POPULATION AT RISK FOR SEVERE DEPRESSION, WHAT EXPRESSES MORE OF LESS COMPLETE HOPELESSNESS.

390
COUPLE THERAPY AND DEVELOPMENTAL PHASE OF COUPLE RELATION WITH STUDENTS
Matti Keinänen, Ilpo Lahti, Anne Kaljonen
Health Care Center for Students, Turku Finland

The aim of this research project has been in the frame of couple evaluation and couple therapy to study structural couplings between the individual development and the epigenesis of couple relation with students. Parameters describing the individual development were diagnosis, studying capacity, the grisp on central life goals and gratifications and the capacity to interpersonal relations. The epigenesis of couple relation was studied according to the model developed by Wynne (1984). The different epigenetic phases following each other are attachment/caregiving, communicating, joint problem-solving, mutuality and intimacy. One can use this model to evaluate couple relation in couple therapy. The phase of attachment/caregiving is crucial for the success of couple therapy. This research, which includes 57 couples, renders possible 1) a new paradigm to understand theoretically the interconnections between the individual development and the development of couple relation 2) valuable information for planning the integrated and need-spesific treatment of couple relation and 3) evaluation of the course and prognosis of couple relation with students.

391
MEDICAL HYPNOSIS IN THE HOSPITAL

Gerard V. Sunnen M.D.
New York University and Bellevue Medical Center
New York, USA

Hypnosis has many applications for relieving distress in hospitalized patients. This paper, through case illustrations, describes the ways in which hypnotic techniques can assist patients undergo medical procedures, surgery, and rehabilitation therapy and cope with life threatening illness.

Session 60 Poster Presentation: Anxiety and adjustment disorders

392
PSYCHIATRIC EMERGENCIES AND SUICIDE ATTEMPTS FOLLOWING AN EARTHQUAKE
Mantonakis, J., Tzemos, J., Monastiriotis, N., Bergiannaki, J.D., Syrengelas, M., Soldatos, C.R., Stefanis, C.N.
Dept. of Psychiatry, University of Athens, Eginition Hospital, Athens, Greece

The greater area of Athens (more than three million inhabitants) was hit by a 6.9 R earthquake in 1981. Mainly because of the 120 km distance from the epicenter, damages were not extensive. However, serious biopsychosocial consequences occurred. One study conducted by our group showed that the flow of emergency cases in the walk-in clinic of our hospital increased during one month following the earthquake. This increase was due to cases of neuroses, whereas cases of psychoses did not show any change; other diagnostic categories, such as alcohol and drug abuse showed a decrease. Another study of ours showed that, although the admission rate in both general and psychiatric hospitals did not change, admissions due to suicide attempts actually declined temporarily following the earthquake. Further, traffic accidents and the use of psychotropic drugs showed an increase. Using multivariate statistics, a number of sociodemographic and other parameters were correlated to the above findings.

393
RELEASE OF ANXIETY AND DEPRESSION FOLLOWING AN EARTHQUAKE

J.D. Bergiannaki, C.R. Soldatos, A. Botsis, M. Syrengelas, P. Hatjitascos, K. Xiromeritis, K. Koundi.
Dept. of Psych., Univ. of Athens, Eginition Hospital, Greece

Two weeks after the earthquake in Kalamata (13 September 1986) which destroyed almost three quarters of the city, we studied the incidence of anxiety and depression in a random sample of 381 persons, who were living in tents. We used the Foulds Self-Assessment Scale for Anxiety and Depression as translated in greek and validated by Lyketsos et al. (1986), as well as a demographic information questionnaire. In our sample 36% showed symptoms of intense anxiety and depression. This percentage is 29% higher than the percentage generally expected to be present in any normally distributed population. Multiple regression analysis was used in which a series of independent variables were related to the reactions of intense anxiety and depression. The regression analysis revealed a difference between male and female population. The anxio-depressive symptomatology was found, in males, to be related to age, while in females it was related to the past physical illnesses and to the present occupational status.

394
AGORAPHOBIA AND COGNITIVE THERAPY: PREDICTORS FOR A GOOD RESPONSE

TUNDO ANTONIO
CENTRO LUCIO BINI - 4, V. CRESCENZIO 00193 ROME - ITALY

The study covered 44 patients, 15 males and 29 females, affected by Panic Disorder with Agoraphobia, sent consecutively for a programme of cognitive therapy. Each subject underwent individual therapy in which the technique of COGNITIVE CONTROL of PANIC ATTACKS (Tundo 1988) was used within a wider strategy of the cognitivist-structuralist type. It didn't use any specific pharmacological support. Some demographic and clinical variables, which might have influenced the response to therapy, where recorded and evaluated for each patient. Statistical checks were carried out on this variables using the chi-square test.
The statistical comparison between Drop-outs (D), Continuers (C), Responders (R), Non-Responders (NR) for the demographic variables did not reveal any difference between groups in sex, educational level or social class. Age at beginning of psychotherapy was important : D were significantly older than C (p .05) and particularly older than R (p .10).
Marital status seemed to be another important variable: fewer C were married compared to D (p .10) and that appears particularly marked in the comparison with NR (p .05). Having an occupation was also important improving response to the therapy (NR vs R p.10).
The comparison of the clinical variables didn't reveal any statistical difference between the various groups in the age of onset of panic attacks, the age of onset of agoraphobia, the presence of relationship conflicts, spontaneous or situational panic attacks, depersonalization and derealization, severity of avoidence, concomitant affective disorders, previous psychological or pharmacological therapy.
Precipitant events were statistically more frequent among R (D+NR vs R p .10), this difference being particularly marked in comparison with NR (p .05). Finally duration of the disorder was significantly longer in the D (D vs C p .05) and this differentiated them most markedly from the R (D vs R p .05).

395
ALCOHOL ABUSE AND DEPENDENCE IN AGORAPHOBIC PATIENTS AND PHOBIAS IN ALCOHOLIC PATIENTS
Lotufo Neto F., Gentil Filho V., Razzouk D.
Hospital das Clinicas - Universidade de Sao Paulo

79 panic disorder with agoraphobia patients were interviewed and 15,2% were abused or had alcohol dependence. Among men 37% used alcohol mainly to control anxiety.
97 alcoholic patients were studied and 37,02% had agoraphobic and social phobic symptoms. Only 3 patients could receive a definite diagnosis of agoraphobia and 9 a definite diagnosis of social phobia.
No consistent order of onset has been found.

396
ELABORATION OF A SELF-ADMINISTERED BEHAVIORAL QUESTIONNAIRE ON ANXIOUS INHIBITION
P.Legeron*, B.Riviere**, J.P.Marboutin**
*Sce Psychiatrie C.H. 94190 Villeneuve St.Georges
**Psychiatrist, Praticien Hospitalier, Service de Psychiatrie Centre Hospitalier, France

35 daily-life situations explore the functioning of anxious patients in physical-motor, cognitive intellectual and socio-relational areas.
In the course of a study involving 4 973 anxious patients, this first questionnaire asked patients to choose the 3 situation in which they experienced the greatest discomfort.
The frequency of choices and the proximity of items as determined by an analysis of the correspondence have allowed the elimination of certain items and the regrouping of others.
The outcome of patients treated with bromazepam for 4 weeks was very favorable, but non-discriminating from one item to another.
At the conclusion of this work a second 20 items questionnaire is proposed, making possible a simplification of the tool while retaining the dimensional behavioral exploration of anxious inhibition.
It should be the object of further validation.

Session 61 Poster Presentation:
Child Psychiatry I

397
MOTHER'S DEPRESSION AND PSYCHOSOCIAL ASPECTS OF BREAST-FEEDING

Tamminen Tuula, MD child psychiatrist
University of Tampere, Department of Public Health, Finland

During the last years there has been a growing clinical and scientific interest in depression in mothers during pregnancy and postpartum. Recent studies have estimated the prevalence of marked depression during postpartum at around 10-15%. There is also increasing evidence that mother's depression has a detrimental effect on mother, mother-infant interaction, child's development and marital relationship.
In the beginning breast-feeding is an improtant part of motherhood and a situation for early mother-infant attachment. The correlation between mother's depression and breast-feeding has been studied mostly by focusing on breast-feeding as a hormonal or psychosocial cause for depression. There is no research data about how mother's depression influences her breast-feeding manners, success, attitudes and experiences.
The material of this longitudinal study is collected from maternity health centers. Mothers are followed up from late pregnancy until about one year after the childbirth. Larger groups of depressed and non-depressed mothers are followed up using questionnaires and smaller subsamples using interviews and a session of videotaped breast-feeding situation. Mother's depression is screened and followed by the Edinburgh Postnatal Depression Scale and confirmed by a clinical interview using the Present State Examination method.
The results will be analysed by focusing childbirth and breast-feeding as marked life-events. Those risk and provoking factors of depression that has been documented elsewhere, as well as possible protective factors, are here studied in combination with breast-feeding. The preliminary results will be presented.

398
QUELQUES PROBLEMES DE L'ADAPTATION DU JEUNE HOMME AU SYSTEME FERME

Chr. Nikolov, E. Kaludiev, O. Djunov, P. Christove

Higher Military Medical Institute
Sogia, Bulgaria

Les auteurs se concentrent sur la notion de système fermé pour les buts de la communication. Après un bref apercu des besoins du jeune homme à l'age 18-20 ans, les auteurs abordent la psychopathologie de l'adaptation et plus précisément celle liée aux conditions d'un système fermé. Le rôle predominant de l'anxiéte et du syndrome végétatif correspondant est relevé. L'expérience des auteurs sur la création et la mise en fonction d'une psychoprophylaxie au niveau du système fermé à personnel renouvelable de jeunes hommes à l'age 18-20 ans est aussi presentée.

399
THE PARTNERSHIP FOR FAMILY PRESERVATION

Ugo Formigoni, M.D., IL Dept. of Mental Health, USA
A network of state and local agencies ensures an array of services to support families with severely emotionally disturbed children and maintain them in their homes and local communities. To overcome established barriers, hampering coordinated treatment, old organizations must be changed and new entities created to produce dynamic and flexible responses.
The Partnership is changing the way caregivers think, fostering respect for the vital contributions of the natural environment, new skills in negotiating across organizations and new technologies in managing information. A free standing screening and case management unit offers a continuous link between families and services.
The goal is to convene a supportive group to surround children at risk and help them cope with crises, overcome difficulties and feel more secure and successful. The staff must display a natural disposition, energy and initiative, and must intervene when and where problems occur: at home, in school and in the neighborhood. The driving principles is the belief in each child potential for growth.

400
EPIDEMIOLOGICAL STUDY ON SCHOOL REFUSAL

Shimizu, M. & Okumura, T.
Department of Psychiatry, Nagoya City University Medical school
Nagoya City, JAPAN

School refusal as a disease is caused by many factors. We are interested in the social influence or sociogenicity within many etiological factors of school refusal. Under such prospect we have studied Japanese junior high school pupils in an urban area (aged from 12 to 14 years old) with questionnaire how their school lives have effects on their mental state. The 117 pupils of latent school refusal were found in 838 sample pupils who attend school every working day. The latent school refusing group showed higher tension in the school, heavier hypochondriacal tendency before exam, social phobic trends and loneliness than the normal pupil group. From these findings we suppose that there would be many latent school refusals in general school attending pupils and we propose that school and administration should pay effort to reduce the tention in school lives in order to prevent the outbreak of school refusal.

401
RESULTS OF A SOCIO-PEDAGOGICAL STUDY CONCERNING 150 DYSLEXIC CHILDREN
PLAISANT ODILE
UNIVERSITY PARIS V

This work is a resume of the results of a socio-pedagogical study which was done in order to analyse the scholastic development of dyslexic children. 547 medical files at the pedo-psychiatry service of the Hopital des Enfants Malades were examined. They all bore the diagnosis: dyslexia/dysorthographia.
150 people agreed to participate in a survey. The socio-pedagogical study took place in Paris region during the winter of 1986 to 1987.
The test group was established according to independent variables: -age (14-24 years old)
-sex (111 males to 39 femelles)
-diagnosis (test Alouette)
The initial hypothesis was as follows: Does dyslexia have more of an effect on one's socio-pedagogical development than other factors such as for example, one's socio-cultural environment?
What conclusions can we draw? That "dyslexic" children obtain diplomas. Several factors influence their acquisition: The family's cultural level, the parental socio-professional level and the seriousness of the dyslexia handicap.
We will not generalize the findings since the ages of our test group are very varied; the constitution of this group is not, perhaps, representative of dyslexic children.

402
ANXIETY & DEPRESSION IN PREADOLESCENT CHILDREN IN THE PUBLIC SCHOOLS.
C. Stavrakaki, M.D.; E. Williams, M.S.W.; N. Roberts, FRCP(C); S. Kotsopoulos, M.D.; S. Walker, M.A.
- Royal Ottawa Hospital, Ottawa, Canada

Grade 5 children (N = 326) were screened in their classrooms using three self-report measures. Those children who met established criteria for anxiety and depression (Revised Children's Manifest Anxiety Scale and Children's Depression Inventory) (RCMAS and CDI) were interviewed by a psychiatrist and further tested on the Diagnostic Interview for Children and Adolescents (DICA) - computer version and Peabody Individual Achievement Test (PIAT). Parents were interviewed by a psychiatrist and research assistant to gather demographic data. A psychiatric diagnosis was given using the Brief Psychiatric Rating Scale for Children (BPRS) and DSM-III-R criteria. School records were also acquired. Psychiatric intervention was given when required. Early detection of anxiety and depression is important due to their relationship to suicide and other problems. The hypotheses we were trying to test were: (1) It is possible to screen school children using standardized self-report measures to identify children who need psychiatric intervention; (2) Self-esteem levels and levels of anxiety and depression are related; (3) Certain demographic variables are related to anxiety and depression. Results indicate that children who met criteria on both anxiety and depression self-report measures require psychiatric intervention, low scores on self-esteem correlated with high scores on anxiety and depression. Brief focused psychotherapy was most helpful with this population.

403
STUDY OF THE DEVELOPMENT OF THE ANALOGICAL PROCESS IN SCHOOLCHILDREN
M. Ohayon, Ankri G., Vernaza P., Soulayrol D, Soulayrol R.
Laboratoire de Traitement des Connaissances, Faculté de Médecine, 27 Boulevard Jean-Moulin, 13385-Marseille, CEDEX 4.

We consider that the analogical process is the basis of many cognitive processes, and is involved in learning, memorization, and general ability to use former experiences to explore, use and understand new objects. Furthermore, we consider anlogy to be the main basis of creative thought, the logical processes being thus used afterwards to validate the analogical inferences. We studied therefore how children of 6-10 years were able to solve simple analogical problems, especially designed so that very little knowledge was necessary, and only analogical abilities were required. The analogies thus include simple (If A becomes B, what about C ?) and chained analogies using geometrical shapes or figurative drawings (as "semantic" analogies). The study included 100 5-10 years school-children. The tests are performed individually; the child is shown as an example how to solve the first problem, and then let free to solve the problems and explain its reasoning. The whole interview is recorded on a video-tape. The average test duration is 20 minutes for 5 problems.

One of the most striking features is that the youngest children are unable to consider more than two criteria at a time, whereas older children are able to use a greater number of criteria. Nevertheless, the analogical process is identical in its stucture regardless to the age, in the ability to see some A->B relation and to transfer it to C. These findings suggest that making analogies is a basic cognitive process, independent from age, even if experiences allow richer and more complex performances.

Session 62 Poster Presentation:
Pharmacophychiatry: Antidepressants

404
KINETICS OF BROFAROMINE IN YOUNG HEALTHY VOLUNTEERS
M. Jedrychowski and P. R. Bieck
Human Pharmacology Institute, Ciba-Geigy GmbH, D-7400 Tübingen, FRG

Pharmacokinetics of brofaromine, a new specific and reversible inhibitor of monoamine oxidase type A, has been studied in 28 young healthy subjects. Administered were single oral doses of 2.5 - 100 mg and repeated weekly increasing doses of 5 - 150 mg/d for 3 - 6 weeks.
Brofaromine is rapidly absorbed and extensively metabolized. Peak plasma concentrations and AUC increase in proportion to the dose. Brofaromine is eliminated from plasma in a dose-independent manner with an elimination half-life of approximately 12 h. Kinetics of brofaromine did not change after prolonged treatment. Above 98% of drug is bound to human serum proteins. Only about 1% of the dose is excreted renally as unchanged drug. No measurable amounts of either brofaromine glucuronide or sulfate were recovered in urine.

405
PHARMACOKINETIC INTERACTION OF H_2-RECEPTOR ANTAGONISTS ON BROFAROMINE•HCl

Degen, P.H., Dieterle, W., Schneider, W. and Czendlik, C.
Research and Development Department, Pharmaceuticals Division, CIBA-GEIGY Ltd., Basle (Switzerland)

The interaction of two H_2-receptor antagonists on the new MAO-A inhibitor brofaromine•HCl was studied in nine healthy volunteers. In a three-way cross over design, a single 75 mg dose of brofaromine•HCl was given alone and after steady-state ranitidine (150 mg b.i.d.) and cimetidine (400 mg b.i.d.).

There was no significant ($p = 0.05$) change in any of the determined pharmacokinetic parameters (C_{max}, T_{max}, $T_{1/2}$, AUC) for brofaromine on ranitidine coadministration. However, after co-administration of cimetidine, Cmax, AUC and $T_{1/2}$ of brofaromine were significantly increased : Cmax (1.22 ± 0.39 nmol•g^{-1}) by 20 %, AUC (20.59 ± 7.58 nmol•g^{-1}•h) by 42 % and $T_{1/2}$ (17.8 ± 9.4 h) by 32 %, on an average.

In conclusion, concomitant administration of brofaromine•HCl and cimetidine does increase the bioavailability of brofaromine, whereas co-administration of ranitidine does not affect the bioavailability of brofaromine•HCl.

406
FLUOXETINE-INDUCED HEAD TREMOR
Sasso E, Calzetti S*, Cirillo R.
Institute of Neurology, Universities of Naples and Parma*, Italy.

A 70 and a 62 year-old women, over a number of 38 depressed outpatients in which fluoxetine were orally administered (20 mg daily), developed a clinically evident head tremor after a 3 weeks therapy.
In both cases a negative familial history for benign essential tremor and/or Parkinson's disease was reported. Liver enzymes and ammoniemia were normal.
Head tremor has been estimated by power spectral analysis of derived accelerometer signal. Frequency values ranged from 3.1Hz (case 2) to 3.8 Hz (case 1), waveform configuration being similar to essential head tremor. In case 2 a mild 6.2 Hz postural hand tremor was also found.
Fluoxetine discontinuation completely abolished tremor in case 2 within four days, whereas movement disorder of case 1 improved more slowly during the next two weeks. Hypersensitization of brain serotonergic neurons and peripheral adrenoceptor involvement could be responsible for this unexpected adverse reaction.
Further studies are invoked in order to probe more closely into efficacy index-side effects rating of fluoxetine.

407

IPSAPIRONE; METABOLISM IN RAT, DOG AND MAN
B. Beckermann, G. Schöllnhammer, W. Opitz, H.D. Dell,
H.M. Siefert, H.J. Ahr, P.R. Seidel
Biochem. Department Troponwerke D-5000 Cologne
Dep. Biokinetics Bayer AG D-5600 Wuppertal FRG

Ipsapirone is extensively metabolized in rats, dog and man, absolute bioavailability being 15% in rat and 4-14% in dog. In the urine <1% of dose is recovered unchanged.
After 14-C-labelled (pyrimidinyl part) Ipsapirone radioactivity is excreted predominantly into feces (rat 2/3, dog 3/4).
Metabolic routes so far identified are hydroxylation and glucuronidation in the 4-position of the pyrimidinyl ring, hydrolysis of the saccharine ring to the carboxylic acid, cleavage to pyrimidinylpiperazine, its hydroxy derivative and saccharinyl butyric acid (GC-MS). The latter represents 18% of dose in male rats and 4% in dogs.

Metabolites in the urine of man are hydroxylated Ipsapirone, saccharinyl butyric acid (12% of dose) and pyrimidinyl piperazine. The latter occurs in approx. 2% of dose after single and repeated administration.

Pyrimidinyl piperazine is also found in plasma in maximum levels of 5ng/ml after 10 mg Ipsapirone. No accumulation occured after repeated treatment.

408

SAFETY AND TOLERANCE OF IPSAPIRONE IN VARIOUS PHASE II TRIALS.

K. Puechler, I.S. Roed, B. Kuemmel
Medical Department, Troponwerke, Berliner Straße 156,
D-5000 Koeln 80, FRG

Ipsapirone is an investigational drug, and current knowledge of the adverse experiences associated with this compound are limited. With regard to phase II trials conducted world-wide, biological tolerance has always been reported as excellent, in particular, no hepato-renal or hematological complications have ever been described. Cardiovascular adverse experiences are uncommon. Potential side effects concern the central nervous system. When administering different doses of ipsapirone, i.e. 0 mg, 5 mg, 7.5 mg and 10 mg t.i.d., the incidence of adverse experiences show dose-dependency. In all treatment groups most frequently reported were: dizziness, headache and nausea. Especially, at 10 mg t.i.d the adverse experiences (prevalently dizziness) associated with ipsapirone initially caused discontinuation from treatment in several cases. Certain habituation to adverse experiences occurred within 3 to 5 days in all dose regimens in the remaining population of patients, treated during a total of 4 weeks. Plasma-level concentrations of ipsapirone correlate with onset (15 minutes) and duration (up to two hours) of adverse experiences. These results provide evidence for the development of a sustained release formulation of the drug which will optimize tolerance with regard to adverse experiences.

409

IPSAPIRONE HYDROCHLORIDE; PHARMACOKINETICS IN MAN
G. Schöllnhammer, B. Kümmel, M. Beneke
Biochemical and Medical Department
Troponwerke 5000 Cologne GFR

Altogether nine phase I clinical pharmacokinetic and tolerance studies in >100 male and female volunteers with Ipsapirone were performed in FRG, USA and J. Dose range was between 1.0 and 10.0mg as single and repeated oral treatment for a maximum period of 28 days. Ipsapirone hydrochloride (INN) was determined in plasma by a radio receptor assay or by HPLC with electrochemical detection, both methods giving identical results.

The pharmacokinetic analysis of these studies showed rapid absorption of the drug. Maximum plasma levels and AUCs are dose dependent after single and repeated treatment. No influence of sex or duration of treatment are found.
Half-life of elimination from plasma as calculated from logarithmic decay over 2-3 periods is in the range of 1.3-2.7 hours and also not influenced by sex or duration of treatment.
Less than 1% of the dose administered is eliminated as unchanged compound into the urine. Ipsapirone hydrochloride is only loosely bound to plasma, the free proportion being in the range of 6-20%.

410

EFFECTS OF VILOXAZINE COMPARED WITH VARIOUS ANTI-DEPRESSANT DRUGS ON LEARNED HELPLESSNESS PARADIGM.
P. MARTIN, J. MASSOL, A.J. PUECH
Dpt de Pharmacologie Pitié-Salpêtrière, 91 Bd de l'Hôpital, 75013 PARIS - FRANCE -
The present study was undertaken to investigate in rats, the effects of viloxazine (4-32 mg/kg/day) compared to tricyclics (clomipramine 12-32, imipramine 2-32 mg/kg/day), monoamine oxidase inhibitors (nialamide 16-32, toloxatone 16-64 mg/kg/day) and atypical antidepressants (clenbuterol 0.5-4, mianserin 1-16 mg/kg/day) in the learned helplessness, an animal model of "depression". Each dose of drug was studied over 5 days. On day 1, groups of experimental rats received inescapable shocks. On days 3, 4 and 5, the number of escape failures of experimental and control rats was recorded in a shuttle-box (S-B) avoidance task. Drugs were injected i.p. each day; i.e. 6h after inescapable shocks on day 1 and then twice a day, in the morning (30 min before each S-B session) and at 18h. This study shows that, like conventional antidepressant drugs, viloxazine induces reversal of helpless behavior during the first S-B session and present an U-shaped dose-effect curve like atypical antidepressants.

411

ACUTE INTOXICATIONS BY VILOXAZINE

M. FALCY, G. RIBOULET-DELMAS, M.L. EFTHYMIOU
Anti-poisons centre of Paris
200, rue du Fg St Denis
75010 PARIS - FRANCE -

From December 1976 to December 1988 inclusive, the anti-poisons centre of Paris was contacted 875 times for Vivalan.

In 752 cases, there were acute intoxications undesigned (75 cases), voluntary (652 cas) or indeterminate (25 cases).

Two kinds of disorders have been specially studied :

1) The central nervous system disorders.
   Apart from disorders of conscience still of a moderate intensity, 10 convulsions and 6 hypertonia have been reported.
2) Cardio-circulatory disorders.
   Some moderate sinusal tachycardia have been notified - 11 ECG anomalies have been noted.

If in 4 cases, convulsions appeared during the ingestion of viloxazine which has been taken irregularly, the other neurological and/or cardio-circulatory symptoms have arisen during polydrug intoxications.

The writers propose to take out the respective imputabilities of all the different drugs (196 intoxications by viloxazine alone, and 566 polydrug intoxications). And finally 3 deaths (0,4 %) will be examined in detail.

Session 63 Poster Presentation:
Panic disorders

412

LIFE EVENTS AND THE ONSET OF PANIC DISORDER

Cathrien De Loof, Eric J.L.Griez, Jan Zandbergen, Henk Pols. Department of Clinical Psychiatry, State University of Limburg, P.O.Box 616, 6200 MD Maastricht ,The Netherlands

In twenty-five panic disorder patients and fifteen obsessive-compulsive disorder patients the number of life events were compared over the last 12 months prior to onset of the disorder. Additionally the number of life events over the total life course up until onset of the disorder were compared. It proved that panic disorder patients do not differ from obsessive-compulsive disorder patients in terms of the number of life events ,they experience during the last year prior to onset of their disorder. However, over the total life course, it seemed panic disorder patients have been exposed to more life events than obsessive-compulsive disorder patients . The findings are discussed in perspective of the existing literature.

413

COMPUTED TOMOGRAPHY IN PANIC DISORDER

Sacchetti E., Vita A.[**], Giobbio G.M., Valvassori G.[*], Massa R.[**], Dieci M., Guarneri L., Garbarini M.
Institute of Psychiatry, Milan University and
[*]Ospedale Maggiore Policlinico or
[**]Ospedale S. Paolo, Milan, Italy

Biochemical, genetic result and the possible neuromorphological linkage between panic disorder and major depression justify the use of the same neuromorphological techniques for the study of anxiety disorders. 29 patients (22 with panic disorder; 7 with generalized anxiety disorder) and 66 controls underwent cerebral computed tomography (CT) scan. Ventricular size was calculated by a manual planimetric method and expressed as ventricular to brain ratio (VBR). Cortical atrophy was evalueted with a subjective method, using a four point visual scale. No significant differences were found in the ventricular size between patients and controls (patients 4.6 ± 3; controls 3.7 ± 2.4; $t=1.23$; $p=N.S.$). However the mean VBR values were significantly different in patients with and without agoraphobia (7 ± 3.7; $3.7 \pm .8$; $t=2.5$; $p=0.02$). Patients with and without co-diagnosis of depression showed no difference in VBR values. Among the 22 patients with a diagnosis of panic disorder we observed a high incidence of cortical atrophy (41%) as compared to controls (16%). Higher atrophy scores were associated with: older age, longer duration of illness and more clinic use of benzodiazepines..

414

EEG Study in Patients with Panic Didorder.

Cordás T.A., Ramos R.T., Navarro J.M., Lotufo Neto F. & Gentil V.
Instituto de Psiquiatria da Faculdade de Medicina da Universidade de São Paulo.

Due to some clinical similarities between Panic Disorder and Temporal Lobe Epilepsy, electroencephalographic changes were systematicaly studied in 27 patients with Panic Disorder and Agoraphobia with Panic Attacks.
The EEG records, obtained with sleep deprivation, photostimulation and hyperventilation showed no abnormalities.

415

DEXAMETHASONE SUPRESSION TEST IN PANIC DISORDER PATIENTS.

C. Díez; J. Vallejo.
Hospital Clínic i Provincial, Barcelona, Spain.

We challenged an oral 1 mg dexamethasone supression test of the cortisol releasing on a group of 25 outpatients who met DSM-III-R criteria for panic disorder with or without agoraphobia. We found a non-supression frequency up to 25 %. Non-supressor patients had more phobic avoidances, higher scores on the Hamilton Depression Scale, and also they were more likely to meet criteria for a major depressive episode. These findings suggest a disturbance of the hypothalamic-pituitary-adrenal axis, even though it would be of less significance than in melancholic patients.

416

DECREASED PLATELET IMI-BINDING IN PANIC DISORDER AND MAJOR DEPRESSION

A.Németh, A.Falus, E.Szádóczky, M.Arató
National Institute for Nervous and Mental Diseases /Hungary/

We studied the platelet 3H-IMI binding parameters in patients with panic disorder /PD n=2o/, in untreated depressed patients /n=2o/ and in neurological patients without concurrent or prior psychiatric illness as control group/n=2o/. We found significantly lower B_{max}/mean +SEM/ in PD /5o1,4+ 52,5 fmol/mg protein/ and major depression /7o9,1+ 37,14/ than in the control group /1o09.1+54.51/. K_d value /mean+SEM/ were similar in the PD /3.19+o,34 nM/ and in the control group /3.28+o,4 nM/. K_d was significantly lower in the depressed patients / 1.96+ o,2 nM/. No significant correlation was found between age and B_{max} or K_d values in either groups. The decreased platelet 3H-IMI binding in panic disorder similar to that observed in affective disorders may further clarify a biological similarity between these two disorders, a dysfunction of serotonergic system in anxiety states.

417

PANIC ATTACKS AND EX ALCOHOLICS

DESPOTOVIC, T. MD, UNIV. PSYCH. CL. BGD.
CVETKOVIC, M. MD, UNIV. PSYCH. CL. BGD.
KOSTIC, V. MD, PHD, UNIV. NEUR. CL. BGD.
YUGOSLAVIA

The relation of neurobiological basis and psychological aspects of ex alcoholic patients with Panic Attacks was assessed.
The authors have followed the group of 15 former alcoholics who developed Panic Attacks after obtaining total abstinence. Neurobiological aspects as well as psychological factors: level of functioning, childhood separation, personality traits were observed.

This research supports the theory of multidimensional nature of Panic Anxiety.

418

PANIC ATTACK
Doctor Henri Amoroso - Neuropsychiatrist
13 rue Massena - 06000 Nice, France

It is the anguish crisis described by Freud with its brutal, spontaneous and unexpected outbreak, very severe in a few minutes, which lasts less than one hour: a feeling of impending danger, of catastrophe, of intense fear; fear of becoming mad, of dying, of depersonalization.
Moreover, tachycardia, dyspnoea, tremor and sweat.
KLEIN considers there is a biological and genetic support. The same crisis can be obtained by perfusing sodium lactate, by taking caffeine, by inhaling carbon dioxide or by subjecting one's organism to hyperventilation.
Panic attack is different from general anxiety for it is accessible to anti-depressant drugs whereas anxiety which is inaccessible to anti-depressant drugs is favourable to benzodiazepin drugs.
For some authors it has direct similarities to spasmophilia. It is necessary to know how to differentiate it from hypoglycaemia, temporal epilepsy, pheochromocytoma, thyroid and parathyroid troubles, rhythm troubles, angor, prolapse of the mitral valve, weaning from alcohol or benzodiazepines.

419

THE CHARACTERISTICS AND THE MEANING OF THE PANIC

MONORCHIO A.**,DE FELICE F.*,QUATTRONE B.**,SERRANO' G.**
*Department of Psychiatry,U.S.L. 28 - LOCRI (Italy)
**Psychiatric Hospital,U.S.L. 31 - REGGIO CALABRIA (Italy)

The concept of panic has entered into the nosographical ambit with the introduction of DSM III.
The authors carry out a study of the history of this term, gathering and unifying in a kind of 'bricolage' the remains of previous conceptual representations.
This is to include the past to the present and to make the concept more comprehensible -in the terms of Aristotle -, starting from the knowledge ot its origin.

420

A NEW COGNITIVE TECHNIQUE FOR PANIC DISORDER WITH AGORAPHOBIA

TUNDO ANTONIO
CENTRO LUCIO BINI - 4, V. CRESCENZIO 00193 ROME - ITALY

The COGNITIVE CONTROL of PANIC ATTACKS (Tundo 1988), a new cognitive technique for Panic Disorder and Agoraphobia, comes from the observation that every Panic Attack (PA) is composed of three elements:
A) Mental images, flash-like whose contents are terrifying for the patient. In the situational attacks, they regard previous crises that have occurred in the same or analogous circumstances.
B) Neurovegetative arousal with the well known somatic symptoms of PA.
C) Thoughts relative to a fear of dying or a fear of doing something uncontrolled.
In the initial phase of therapy the patient first learns to distinguish the PA from the rest of the symptoms. Afterwards he learns to make an effort to recognize at every attack these three different components.
Only when this ability has been achieved can the patient learn to control the attack by a cognitive action on Component A. This consists of confronting the mental image with the actual reality. When this is performed correctly a rapid reduction of somatic symptoms takes place and the attacks gradually becomes less intense and less frequent.
At the same time anticipatory anxiety and agoraphobia are reduced.
This technique has been used, without any specific pharmacological support, in 44 patient, 15 males and 29 females, affected by Panic Disorder with Agoraphobia.
The mean duration of the therapy was 9.5 months (range 2-20 months) with a mean of 38 sessions (range 15-105 sessions).
Of the 44 patients who started this psychotherapy, 13 interrupted treatment at an early stage. Of the remaining 31, 24 responded well to the therapy; while the other 7 failed to respond or responded partially.
The mean follow-up period was 37 months (range 12-63 months).
There was 1 case of relapse during this time.

421

ATTENUATION OF PANIC SYMPTOMS AFTER TREATMENT WITH SEROTONERGIC COMPOUNDS
J.A. den Boer and H.G.M. Westenberg
Department of Biological Psychiatry, State University Utrecht, Nicolaas Beetsstraat 24, 3511 HG Utrecht, The Netherlands

Accumulating evidence indicates that serotonergic neuronal systems may be of critical importance in the pathogenesis of Panic Disorder (PD). Several selective serotonin (5-HT) uptake inhibitors have been shown to possess antipanic properties.
A notable reduction in the number of panic attacks, was however not obtained within 3 weeks, and was preceded by an initial, transient increase in symptom severity. Based upon the hypothesis that this sequence of events might be due to adaptive changes e.g. receptor-downregulation, we investigated the efficacy of ritanserin, a potent and selective $5-HT_2$ antagonist.
In the present study results are presented of a double blind, placebo controlled study with fluvoxamine and ritanserin.
Patients (n=60) suffering from PD (DSM-III-R) with or without phobic avoidance were randomly allocated to one of the three groups and treated for 8 weeks. Fluvoxamine was found to be a potent antipanic agent, followed by a subsequent decrease in avoidance behavior. Ritanserin had no effect on any of the psychometric measurements.
These results suggest, that $5-HT_2$ receptor downregulation is not responsible for the antipanic efficacy of fluvoxamine.

422

CLONAZEPAM IN PANIC DISORDER

Lawrence Annable, Linda Beauclair, Rejean Fontaine, Naomi Holobow, Guy Chouinard

Allan Memorial Institute, Louis-H. Lafontaine Hospital and McGill University, Montreal, Canada

Recent studies have suggested that benzodiazepines, such as clonazepam and alprazolam are effective in the treatment of panic disorder. We carried out a double-blind controlled clinical trial to assess the efficacy of clonazepam against placebo in the treatment of patients with recurrent panic attacks.
Method. Following a 1-week washout period, 22 patients with a DSM-III diagnosis of panic disorder or agoraphobia with panic attacks were randomly assigned to four weeks of treatment with clonazepam or placebo under double-blind conditions. The patients were assessed by the psychiatrist at weekly intervals. Plasma levels of clonazepam were measured weekly.
Results. The endpoint total and factor scores of the rating scales were submitted to analysis of covariance with baseline scores as covariate. Clonazepam was found to be superior ($p<.05$) to placebo on each of the rating scales and there was a significant correlation ($r=.64$) between plasma concentration and reduction in panic attacks.
Discussion. Clonazepam appears to be an effective treatment of panic disorder and could be an alternative to alprazolam and imipramine.

Session 64 Poster Presentation:
Biological psychiatry: Blood cell and HLA studies

423

PLATELET PROSTAGLANDIN E_1 HYPOSENSITIVITY IN SCHIZOPHRENIA: DECREASE IN PGE_1-stimulated CYCLIC AMP FORMATION

Ofuji, M., Kaiya, H., Nisida, A., Uematsu, M., Nozaki, M., Tsurumi, K., Idaka, E[1]., Adachi, S[2]. and Yoshida, H[3]. Gifu University Faculty of Medicine and Industry[1], Gifu/Japan, Gifu City Hospital[2], Inuyama Hospital[3] Aichi/Japan.

<Purpose> To evaluate stimulus-response membranous transduction in mental disorder, cAMP formation via prostaglandin E_1 (PGE_1) or forskolin stimulation were studied in washed intact platelets from 32 schizophrenics and 30 normal controls.
<Methods> Platelet-rich plasma was prepared by centrifuging. Washed platelets were gained using Sepharose 2B gel-filtration and cAMP content determined by radioimmunnoassay.
<Results> No sex- or age effects on cAMP formation were seen in normal controls. No differences in basic levels of cAMP between schizophrenics and normal controls were demonstrated. The increasing rates of cAMP after PGE_1 (10μ M) and forskolin (100μ M) stimulation were both significantly decreased in schizophrenics ($P<0.01$). In conclusion, impaired adenylate cyclase activity as revealed in the present study supports, at least partially, PGE_1 hyposensitivity in platelets of schizophrenics. Involvement in other signal transducing mechanisms leading to a deeper understanding of the pathophyiology of schizophrenia remains to be interpreted.

424

NEUROPSYCHOIMMUNOLOGY OF SCHIZOPHRENIA AND MAJOR DEPRESSION
A.Mihaljević-Peleš, M.Jakovljević, S.Biočina M.Kaštelan, A.Kaštelan and T.Brataljenović Psychiatric Clinic, KBC Rebro, Zagreb, Yugoslavia

An impairment of immune functions has been reported in patients with both schizophrenia and major depression.
We compared mitogen-induced lymphocyte proliferation E, EA, EAC rosetas, T4 and T8 cells and HLA System in male schizophrenic unipolar depressed patients and healthy volunteers.
Lymphocyte stimulation by PHA, Con A and PWM was lower in schizophrenic and depressed patients than in controls. The ratio of T helper to T suppressor cells were higher.
The results of the study suggest the presence of the various immune abnormalities in patients with schizophrenia and uniplar major depression, but which are not specific for any psychiatric diagnoses. The cause of these abnormalities and their possible clinical values are discussed.

425

Reduced monoamine oxidase in blood platelets from schizophrenics and affective patients.
Marco A. Marcolin, M.D., John M. Davis, M.D.
Illinois State Psychiatric Institute
1601 W. Taylor St - Chicago, IL 60612 -USA
and Escola Paulista de Medicina, Depto, Psiquiatr
Rua Botucatu 740 3 andar -Sao Paulo-SP-Brazil 04023

We present a meta-analysis from 304 publications in the international literature. There is consistent data from a number of studies that neuroleptic treatment lowers platelet monoamine oxidase levels. This makes it particularly pertinent to separate studies done after a washout period from studies of patients currently on neuroleptics. We therefore analyze separately drug-free versus currently on drugs. Meta-analysis of schizophrenics currently on drugs indicates a substantial decrease in MAO levels. In drug free patients, almost all studies find little difference between schizophrenics and control. But a few studies found MAO levels lower in schizophrenics. We will also present meta-analysis of platelet MAO levels in affective disorders. The tricyclic antidepressants lower the MAO levels and lithium raises MAO levels, so our meta-analysis was conducted in drug free bipolar and unipolar patients after a washout period versus those currently on drugs.

426

PLATELET MONOAMINE OXIDASE ACTIVITY IN SUBTYPES OF DEPRESSIONS
Ana Luisa Sosa, Gerardo Heinze, Carlos Berlanga, Julia Moreno, Martha Ontiveros, Guadalupe Junco, Enrique Chavez
Instituto Mexicano de Psiquiatria, Mexico

Blood samples were drawn from 99 drug free patients (80 females and 19 males), all of them diagnosed as major depression (DSM-III), 41 with melancholia and 58 without melancholia. Two significant differences were found: first, females registered higher monoamine oxidase (MAO) activity, and second, patients with major depression without melancholia had higher MAO levels. MAO activity and age were not significantly correlated, nor depression severity measured by the Hamilton Depression Rating Scale. These findings are consistent with those previously reported, and confirm the fact that women tend to present a higher platelet monoamine oxidase activity, than males; it also supports the hypothesis that there is a higher MAO activity in non endogenous depression. Studies with a phenomenologic focus and with adequate control of organic and methodological variables that influence MAO activity, need to be conducted in the near future.

427
LYMPHOCYTE DYSFUNCTIONS IN DEPRESSED PATIENTS

D. Marazziti, L. Dell'Osso, W. Mignani, F. Ambrogi*, G.B. Cassano, Institute of Psychiatric Clinic and Dept. of Internal Medicine (sec. Immunology)*, University of Pisa, Pisa Italy.

In these last years, the relationships between the central nervous system and the immune system have become object of increasing interest. Several authors have observed changes of immunoglobulins and lymphocytes (L) in bereavement and in depressive illness. Our study aim was to investigate total L and L subpopulations in a group of 12 depressed patients, as compared with 12 controls. All the patients were suffering from recurrent major depression, and were drug-free for at least one year. The results showed that the patients had a total number of T-L significantly lower than the controls, and also lower T-suppressor L. These findings, although preliminary, are suggestive for a complex involvement of immune system in depressive illness.

428
PSYCHOSES SCHIZOPHRENIQUES ET SYSTEME HLA
Données d'une étude régionale

M. AUDIBERT *, A.V. TRAMONI *, P. MERCIER **, M.A. LARRIEU * R.L. CLAVEL-MORROT *, R.A. JULIEN *
* C.H.S. Valvert Bd des Libérateurs 13011 MARSEILLE (FRANCE)
** C.T.S. 147 Bd Baille - 13005 MARSEILLE

Les auteurs rapportent les résultats d'une étude chez 58 schizophrènes (18 paranoïdes (SP) et 40 hébéphrènes (SH)). Pour l'ensemble SP + SH une augmentation de fréquence de l'antigène (Ag) HLA - A11 et une diminution de l'Ag HLA - A10 sont mises en évidence par rapport à des sujets témoins. Une élévation de fréquence des Ag HLA - B35 et CW4 est observée, sans valeur statistiquement significative. Selon les sous-types cliniques, une augmentation des Ag HLA A11, A33, B35 et CW4 est observée chez les SP. Des associations antigéniques positives fréquentes HLA A11 - B35 et HLA A11 - B35 - CW4 sont mises en évidence chez des SP originaires d'Italie ou de Corse. En excluant de l'analyse ces patients, on observe une élévation de fréquence de l'allèle A11 chez les SP + SH. Chez ces SP, outre cette variation de l'Ag HLA - A11, il existe une augmentation des allèles A33 et B40. L'analyse comparée des patients italiens et corses avec un groupe témoin italien met en évidence une variation significative des fréquences HLA - CW5 et CW7 chez les schizophrènes. Le regroupement des résultats de cette étude avec ceux d'un travail réalisé en 1977 par deux des auteurs dans les mêmes conditions méthodologiques modifie les conclusions antérieures. Dans cet échantillon élargi (N= 119) l'augmentation de fréquence des Ag HLA - Ag, B35, CW4 chez les SP n'est plus retrouvée. Les variations des allèles A33 et B35 est mise en évidence. La comparaison selon la variété clinique différencie les 2 classes : fréquence plus élevée des Ag HLA B35 et plus faible des Ag HLA B8 chez les SP par rapport aux SH.

429
DERMINATION OF AMINO ACIDS IN PLATELETS OF PATIENTS WITH HUNTINGTON'S DISEASE (HD)

L.H.ROLF, K.KÜPPER, H.LANGE*, G.G.Brune
University of Münster, Department of Neurology, 4400 Münster; *University of Düsseldorf, Institute for Brain Research, 4000 Düsseldorf (G.F.R.)

HD is biochemically charaterized by strong disturbances of the amino acid neurotransmitters glutamic acid (GLT), glutamine (GLN), aspartic acid (ASP) and gamma-amino-butryric acid (GABA) in the brain. Human platelets are regarded to be models for amino acid innervated central neurons. It was the aim of this study to compare platelet GLT, GLN, ASP and GABA of patients with HD and healthy controls.

The group of patients (P) consisted of 15 persons who were under medication (8 m; 7 f; mean of age $44,7 \pm 10,4$ years), the control group (C) consisted of 22 persons (12 m; 10 f; mean of age $41,5 \pm 7,3$ years). The platelets were separated from EDTA-blood by method of Weissbach et al. Platelet (pl.) amino acid content was determined fluorimetrically by method of Lenda et al. (HPLC; OPT-derivatization). The results are shown in the table below (amino acid contentrations calculated to $pm/10^8$ pl.; statistics: Student-t-test, s = significant, ns = not significant).

	GLT	GLN	ASP	GABA
P (n = 15)	$31,2 \pm 10,4$	$15,4 \pm 4,4$	$9,8 \pm 3,6$	$1,8 \pm 0,8$
C (n = 22)	$25,9 \pm 5,2$	$12,0 \pm 3,9$	$8,6 \pm 3,4$	$1,6 \pm 0,6$
statistics s/ns	$p < 0,05$ s	$p < 0,01$ s	$p > 0,05$ ns	$p > 0,05$ ns

It was found, that platelet GLT and GLN was elevated significantly in HD while ASP and GABA was not. Our results are in agreement with the hypothesis that an increased activity of GLT-ergic neurons in the central nervous system is a biochemical pathogenetic factor in HD.

Weissbach H, Redfield BG: J.Biol.Chem. 235, 3287-3291 (1962)
Lenda K, Svenneby G: J.chromatogr. 198, 516-519 (1980)

430
Red blood cell membrane transports of L-Tyrosine and L-Tryptophan : clinical relevance in depression.

Ph. BOVIER, J.-M. AZORIN, J. WIDMER, J.-M. GAILLARD, R. TISSOT
Service de la Recherche biologique, IUPG, 10, ch. du Petit-Bel-Air, 1225 Chêne-Bourg, Suisse

The plasma availability and the blood-brain transport of precursors of monoamines, particularly L-Tyrosine and L-Tryptophan have been involved in the biological mechanisms of affective disorders. We have developed a peripheral model, using the red blood cell membrane transports in vitro of these two amino acids. Their concentrations in plasma were also measured.

In depressed patients, the following results were found
1) the abnormalities in these transports differed according to the diagnostic categories (DSM-III);
2) these abnormalities were state dependent i.e. the disappeared with clinical recovery;
3) drug treatment was choosen on the basis of the types of abnormalities in amino acid transports. This led to clinical results that were better than mean results from the literature or from groups of patients for whom red blood cell membrane transports were not measured.

431
WINTER DEPRESSION, LIGHT THERAPY AND PLATELET 3H-IMIPRAMIN BINDING

A. Németh, E. Szádóczky, A. Falus, M. Arató, National Institute for Nervous and Mental Diseases /Hungary/

22 patients /13 females and 9 males/ with winter depression were treated with bright incandescent light /2ooo-25oo lux, for one hour/day for 7 days/. 1o of them were bipolar II. and 12 patients were unipolar depressives. The mean age at the onset of the illness was 25,2 years. The symptoms observed most often were the followings: fatigue and sadness /1oo %/, interpersonal diffculties /91 %/, difficulties at work /77 %/, weight gain and oversleeping /73 %/, increased apetite, carbohydrate craving and diurnal change /68 %/, decreased libido /64 %/. 77% of the patients improved significantly after light therapy /final score on HRSD ≤ 1o or ≤ 5o % of pretreatment HRSD/. We studied the platelet 3H-IMI binding. A significantly lower mean B_{max} value was found in the depressed patients compared to the controls. After light treatment - parallell to a marked clinical improvement - B_{max} increased in each patient and reached the mean values of the controls. These results indicate that the decreased B_{max} in winter depression is state-dependent.

432
3H-SPIPERONE BINDING TO HUMAN PERIPHERAL MONONUCLEAR CELLS: A METHODOLOGICAL APPROACH
N. Wodarz, J. Fritze, J. Kornhuber, P. Riederer
Department of Psychiatry, Clinical Neurochemistry, University of Würzburg

In recent years the search for biological markers of psychiatric disorders gained in importance. For example could a state-independent feature be a useful tool in verifying diagnosis and defining subgroups respectively.
For schizophrenic patients, especially the paranoid-hallucinatory subgroup, a significant and selective increase in binding capacity (B_{max}) of 3H-Spiperone to lymphocytes was described. Although these investigations were based on the "Dopaminehypothesis" of schizophrenia, there is considerable doubt, whether these "3H-Spiperone binding sites" represent the Dopamine-D2-receptor of the CNS.
In view of these problems and the variety of inherent pitfalls in this kind of binding assay, we focussed on the different methodological proceedings. Their importance for the controversial results will be discussed (i.e. stereoselectivity, distribution of 3H-Spip. binding sites on different subtypes of human peripheral mononuclear cells, stereoselectivity)

433
EVIDENCE FOR A RECEPTOR NATURE OF SPIPERONE BINDING SITES OF LYMPHOCYTES FROM HUMAN PERIPHERAL BLOOD
B. Riese & M. Halbach
Psychiatrische Klinik der Universitat Dusseldorf, Bergische Landstrabe 2, D-4000 Dusseldorf, FRG

The nature of specific spiperone binding to lymphocytes from peripheral blood, which has been reported elevated in patients with distinct forms of schizophrenia, has been controversially discussed. Several investigators have found the spiperone binding to lymphocytes nonsaturable and therefore - and for other reasons - have refused to accept the existence of true binding sites on the cell membrane. Others however have reported a discriminable high-affinity binding site compatible with the existence of receptor-like membrane structure. In order to experimentally discriminate between these possibilities we have used the phenomenon of down-regulation of receptors in the presence of agonistic ligands which has been convincingly shown for lymphocyte adrenergic receptors. The incubation of cultured human peripheral lymphocytes with dopaminergic ligands for 48 hours was followed by a characteristic reduction of specific high-affinity spiperone binding. Thus our data argue for the existence of a receptor like binding structure which seems to be regulated similarly to other catecholamine membrane receptors.

Session 65 Poster Presentation: Psychiatric services

434
PSYCHOPATHOLOGY MEASURED BY MMPI IN PSYCHOTIC PATIENTS ATTENDING A PROGRAM OF REHABILITATION
M. COCCOSIS, V. ANTONOPOULOS, M. TYPALDOU, V. KARIDIS
Univ. of Athens, Dept. of Psychiatry
Eginition Hospital

The purpose of this study was to investigate the changes in psychopathology as they are evaluated by MMPI in a group of psychotic patients attending a program of psychosocial rehabilitation.

84 psychotic patients, diagnosed according to DSM III, 56 men and 28 women, with average age 30.9, and average years of education 11.5, were administered the MMPI prior to and after a program of psychosocial rehabilitation.

The results concerning the changes in psychopathology show a statistically significant decrease, in the MMPI clinical scales of Depression (D) Paranoia (Pa) Schizophrenia (Sc) Psychasthenia (Pt) and Social Introversion (Si). These results will be discussed in reference to the patients' social and work adjustment and to the use of MMPI for psychosocial prognosis.

435

Mental health Service: centre of psychiatric treatment.
Nicoletta Goldschmidt, M.D.
Luigi Ferrannini, M.D.

Servizi di Salute Mentale
Regione Liguria - Italia

In the last ten years in Italy the psychiatric reforme law has shifted the centre of psychiatric intervention from the hospital to the community mental health services.
This fact has requested to the operators of the field:
1) to elaborate new ways of organization of the work, much more articulated and complex, able to answer at the needs of different interventions;
2) to re-formulate techniques and cultures which, produced in other fields, had to be integrated (when possible) in a different operative context;
3) to integrate at an operative level various professions and cultural trends using new formative approaches able to hold each member of the staff responsible for the therapeutic project and for a common and shared project of intervention, programmed at a general level.

436

FUNCTIONNING OF A EUROPEAN PROFESSIONAL REHABILITATION CENTRE FOR PHYSICALLY AND MENTALLY HANDICAPED WOMEN
C. Lacombe-Mestas Médecin-Directeur "Le Castel" HYERES (France)
F. Gazano-Jouanon Médecin Chef de Service de la C.P.A.M. du Var

"The Castel" is a professional rehabilitation centre which receives convalescents of nervous and mental illness, but stabilized and with normal understanding ; physic autonomous handicaped are also accepted.
Three formations are given :
- Secretary shorthand typist accountant
- Technician in secretariat
- Accountancy and typist employee

For these three formations there is a common preparatory course more or less long. These three formations are ended by a C.F.P.A. delivered by the Ministry of Labour. This diploma is good for all the E.E.C. States. The average of success is 85,25 %.

The European Parliament has voted on 7th May 1986 the following motion : "...The European Parliament calls the attention to a pilot experiment of professional rehabilitation of handicaped people working out and unique today in the community carried out with the financial assistance of the Social Funds by the French Centre "The Castel" located at Hyères and opened to the handicaped of the E.E.C. States".

The students during their course are payed. In addition, their professional rehabilitation is taken over within the framework of the international collective bargaining by the Service "Tiers payant" of C.P.A.M. The students are coming from E.E.C. with form E 112 mentionning the duration of the apprenticeship. Form F 212 is delivered by CPAM for the duration of the apprenticeship.

437

THE FIRST EPISODES OF PSYCHOSIS IN A HOSPITAL UNIT: METHODOLOGIC PROBLEMS
Ambrosi P., Caverzasi E., Foresti G., Politi P.L.
Institute of Psychiatry, University of Pavia, Pavia, Italy

The suppression of the psychiatric hospital has promoted a radical change in the italian pattern of community care for mental illness; this is now treated in a network of community services, including out-patients and in-patients units located in the general hospitals. The authors discuss the main issues of this decennial experience as regards the problems of an epidemiologic research on the psychotic episodes, analysing the following points:
- what kind of information should be collected to provide an adequate and complete documentation of these conditions?
- which are the effects of the new settings on the process of data collection and clinical observation?
- is it possible to standardize a reliable method of diagnostic judgement?
- what are the requirements for an effective follow-up evaluation?

438

NATURE ET FREQUENCE DES SOINS PSYCHIATRIQUES SELON LE DIAGNOSTIC ET LA GRAVITE
TERRA J. L.[*], HOCHMANN J., DAZORD A., GERIN P., GAUSSET M.F.
[*]Service Pr DALERY, C.H.S. Le Vinatier
95, boulevard Pinel - 69677 BRON CEDEX

Les auteurs ont étudié la nature et la fréquence des actes de soins (consultations, séances de psychothérapie, visites à domicile,...) réalisés par 105 membres du personnel soignant, de 3 équipes de secteur psychiatrique de LYON (FRANCE) à l'occasion de 1024 prises en charge. La comparaison porte sur les soins dispensés à l'Hôpital, dans les centres de consultations et par un service d'hospitalisation psychiatrique à domicile.
Le rythme de production de soins de chaque institution est lié à l'âge du malade sauf pour le service d'hospitalisation à domicile. La fréquence globale des soins est plus dictée par le degré de gravité que le diagnostic. Le nombre de visites à domicile et des entretiens avec la famille du malade est plus faible que celui attendu.
Les soins des infirmières hospitalières sont intenses mais trop irréguliers en raison de l'organisation du travail en équipe.

439
HOW TO DESCRIBE ELABORATE TREATMENTS FOR OUT-PATIENTS
Dr. Bernard Odier, Psychiatrist
C.H.S. B.Durand, 91 152 - Etampes Cedex, France

Normally, treatments of out-patients are looked at from different angles: pharmacological, psychotherapeutic, institutional, and social welfare.
The authors explain why they aim to describe complex interactions between out-patients and a therapeutic team. They record by sample-survey the ties that are established between an out-patient and the therapeutic team as the treatment progresses. Complete statistical analysis is set out. The results surpass the conclusions reached during team meetings.
A typology of the different "encounter quanta" is propounded. The concept of a "diffused institutional milieu" is argued.
The different out-patients patterns of care - utilisation are described. The application of the notion of psycho-analytical transference to what happens between an out-patient and a therapeutic team is studied carefully.
Each psychiatric team extends itself according to its specific style: in our opinion, the analysis of this style is vital.

440
THE "REVOLVING DOOR" PHENOMENA: A STUDY OF PSYCHIATRIC READMISSIONS.
Ll.Jordá; A.Chinchilla; M.Camarero; JL.Carrasco; A.Cebollada and M.Vega.
Ramón y Cajal Hospital. Psychiatry. MADRID

During the period between 1978 and 1986 aproximately 3.600 patients were admitted to the Psychiatric Unit of the Ramón y Cajal Hospital in Madrid. 234 of these (9,8%) were readmitted during the period and 57 (1,6%) were readmitted on two occasions.
In a retrospective study, we found that a high percentage of readmissions were due to a recurrence of the psychopathological disorder. This occurred in patients with severe disorders of a psychotic type and who showed a low level of labour, social and family adaptation in the period between admissions.
The results point to a lack of sufficient outpatient facilities for psychotic patients in our area. There is a need for resources to be directed towards the creation of community based services and which fulfill a transitional rol between primary care and the Hospital, to prevent as far as possible the "Revolving Door" phenomena to which the chronic psychotic patient is susceptible.

441
PSYCHIATRIC EMERGENCY SERVICE IN THE CITY OF COPENHAGEN
Schultz V., Sogaard U., Knop J., Sorensen A.S., Hasselbalch E., Thusholdt F., Jensen E., Hemmingsen R., Jorgensen Aa., Teasdale T.W.
Bispebjerg Hospital, Frederiksberg Hosp., Kommunehospitalet, Rigshospitalet, Copenhagen, Denmark

We present results from a prospective one year random sample investigation of visitors to psychiatric emergency services covering the City of Copenhagen as a whole. Each unit functions as an integrated part of a general psychiatric department placed in the building of a general hospital. The services are free of charge, open 24 hours a day, offer psychiatric evaluation, acute treatment, and necessary somatic evaluation and overnight stay for the population in each of the 4 catchment areas in the city. Every 10th day throughout 1985 all visits were registered. The demographic characteristics of 1969 visits (covering 1595 persons) are: 75% are 20-50 years old, 59% are males, 65% are unmarried/divorced and 37% on disability pension. The predominant diagnoses are: Alcohol dependence (31%) and schizophrenia (20%). Among the repeat visitors these diagnoses are even more frequent. The results demonstrate that emergency services are necessary to prevent admission to psychiatric ward, both for chronic patients and non-psychiatric individuals, who need immediate assistance due to crisis reactions. Coordination between the emergency units in the city and a flexible cooperation with the regional social welfare system is essential for early interventions.

442
MENTAL DISORDERS IN A COMMUNITY-BASED FACILITY IN UNITA' SANITARIA LOCALE 25
Bani A.*, Miniati M.**
* U.S.L. 25, Toscana, Italia
** U.S.L. 13, Toscana, Italia

Italy's National Health Service is actually structured in definite geographical areas: Unita Sanitarie Locali (U.S.L.). Each U.S.L. includes Community-based service. There are 10 services in U.S.L. 25 Val di Cornia (Piombino).
In this study we report the frequency of patients with mental disorders referred in a single service (13056-person area).
Two psychiatrists in two periods of time have used diagnoses according to Diagnostic and Statistical Manual III-R.

Session 66 Poster Presentation:
Drug abuse

443

DRUG ADDICTION AND THE CONSCIOUSNESS
DEVELOPMENT THEORY
Xavier da Silveira Fº, Dartiu
Escola Paulista de Medicina

The abstract outlines an archetypal approach to the addiction phenomena. The author stresses the importance of the two first archetypal cycles, matriarchal and patriarchal, as well the tendency during the adolescence developmental period in determining the arousal of addictive behavior. Foccusing therapeutic problems mainly on addiction related to matriarchal dynamism, he emphasizes the importance of the transferential setting in symbolic psychotherapy. Finally, he distinguishes pathological from non-pathological drug use based on the deep psychological meaning of this behavior within a symbolic perspective of the development of consciousness.

444

CHRONIC CANNABIS-INDUCED PSYCHOSIS.

Dr Denis MORIN - J. GAILLEDREAU

The author reports eight cases of chronic schizophrenia generated by the continued use of hashish. Patients were free of predisposing risk factors and had been taking 50 to 150 mg hashish daily for 7 to 10 years. The author provides evidence that continued use of a so-called soft drug leads to social seclusion, mental weakness and eventually to the development of psychosis that runs its usual chronic course. In view of the fact there is continuing controversy in the literature as to whether cannabis-induced psychosis exists as a separate entity, the author compares the inclusion criteria used in the published works that either disprove or affirm the presence of abnormal psychometric tests in cannabis users.
He explains why the existence of cannabis-induced psychosis should be accepted as a fact.

445

CANNABIS USE IN THE SCHIZOPHRENIC SHIFT
Mario Simoes
Psychiatric University Clinic. Lisbon, Portugal

Two groups of paranoid schizophrenics were compared, one consuming cannabis and the orther not. Does cannabis change symptoms to a "cannabis psychosis" picture? Is there a clinical parameter that differentiate shifts precipitated by cannabis from others?
To answer the questions, scales and questionnaires (BPRS, PANSS, AMDP, IPP 5, APZ, D 2) were applied to in-patients at one week intervals, conclusions:
1. cannabis does not change shift symptoms in the way of a "cannabis psychosis".
2. there is a high probability that cannabis precipitated the shift if a) psychotic symptoms improve significantly after one week of in-patient treatment and b) attention and concentration tests are only slightly affected.

446

THE CLINICAL USE OF PIRACETAM (NOOTROPIL)
IN DETOXIFICATION OF HEROIN DEPENDENTS
H.R. CHAUDHRY, M.D.; K.JAMIL, M.D.; S.CHAUDHRY,M.D.
Z. MOHYUDDIN, M.D.
DRUG ABUSE TREATMENT UNIT, LAHORE BRAIN CENTRE,
LAHORE, PAKISTAN

It has been reported that use of Piracetam (Nootropil) shortens the duration of withdrawal syndrome in heroin dependents. It has been documented that agitation and confusion appearing in delirium tremens disappears with the use of Piracetam.

The present study (sinle blind placebo controlled) was designed to evaluate the effect of Piracetam on the intensity of heroin withdrawal symptoms and on the duration of the withdrawal period. This study included two groups (each of 20 subjects) of heroin dependents. One group received Piracetam in addition to symptomatic treatment and the other group was treated without Piracetam. Both groups were homogeneous as far as age, sex, heroin intake, duration of intake, physical status and social status of patients were concerned.

Evaluation of withdrawal syndroms was performed by means of a rating scale that included 14 parameters. Special attention was given to aches and pains, fatigue, craving for heroin and drowsiness.

In this presentation the results of the study will be discussed.

447

CARBAMAZEPINE MEDIATED INPATIENT METHADONE WITHDRAWAL TREATMENT (MWT).

M. Trenkel, J. Nelles, J. Jakubaschk

Psychiatric University Clinic, Berne, Switzerland

Based on a retrospective study of 54 cases we introduced a combined drug free and drug mediated MWT concept. In MWT neuroleptics and benzodiazepines are of limited use because of their side-effects or addictive potency. Carbamazepine, well documented in alcohol withdrawal treatment, is a well tolerated and easy to handle antiepileptic drug of no addictive potency. Because of its additional stabilizing effects on the limbic system it might be used in MWT too. In a pilot study 24 patients requiring MWT were treated: 12 of them without (group A) and 12 with carbamazepine (group B). 50 % of the patients in group A with an average methadone dose of 45 mg before treatment finished MWT successfully, and 75 % of the patients in group B even in spite of a higher methadone dose (66.3 mg). Number and intensity of the withdrawal symptoms were - compared with drug free MWT - markedly lower in the carbamazepine mediated MWT independent of the methadone dose before treatment. No withdrawal complications or carbamazepine side-effects were observed in any case. From our preliminary results we conclude that carbamazepine may improve outcome of MWT and mitigate withdrawal symptoms.

448

INFLUENCE OF TRIAZOLAM ON THE EXPERIMENTAL MORPHINE ABSTINENCE SYNDROME:
Gibert-Rahola,J; Maldonado,R; Valverde,O; Saavedra, M.C; Leonsegui,I; Micó,J.A. Dept. of Neurosciences. University of Cádiz. Spain.

The use of benzodiazepines (BDZ) by narcotic abusers has been documented in several studies. These drugs have been used as a substitute drugs when the narcotic drugs of primary dependence are not available. There has been no extensive study comparing the relative efficacies of such drugs in alleviating narcotic withdrawal. In the present comparative study, we have investigated the effect of either triazolam (TRZ) or other BZD on the morphine withdrawal syndrome (MWS) experimentally induced in mice.

Opiate dependence was induced in OF1 mice by administration of morphine s.c. twice daily over a period of 5 days and the MWS was induced by i.p injection of naloxone. The number of jumps, wet dog shakes and paw tremor and the presence or ausence of teeth chattering and body tremor were evaluated after naloxone injection. All BDZ were injected i.p 30 min. before naloxone injection.

TRZ is similar to chordiazepoxide (CDP) facilitating the wet dog shake. It differs in a marked way from flunitrazepam (FZP) and from nitrazepam (NZP) wich increase this symptom in a surprising way (FZP more than 1000% and NZP more than 5000%). Of all the BDZ studied only diazepam (DZP) did not modify this sign. TRZ does not differ from the rest of the BZD studied in inhibiting the jumping. In this sense it is more similar to DZP and FZP than to NZP and CDP. TRZ, like CDP, and to a lesser extent DZP, are the BZP wich do not affect the paw tremor in any way. NZP facilitates this sign perceptively while FZP inhibit it. TRZ, like CDP and NZP, does not modify the teeth chattering, while FZP, and to a greater degree DZP, reduce this symptom. TRZ, together with CDP and NZP, does not inhibit the body tremor, FZP only inhibits it at high doses while DZP inhibits it at all doses.

449

AUFNAHMESTATION FÜR SUCHTKRANKE IM LANDESKRANKENHAUS; DIE ERFAHRUNGEN DES ERSTEN JAHRES

S. Skondras, R. Dannhorn, T. Beckmann, T. Bauer, M. Kukla, P. L. Janssen

Westf. Klinik für Psychiatrie Dortmund
-Klinik an der Ruhr-Universität Bochum-
Dortmund, Bundesrepublik Deutschland

Im März 1987 wurde erstmalig im Landeskrankenhaus Dortmund eine Aufnahmestation speziell für Suchtkranke eröffnet. Ziel dieser Differenzierung war die Gewährleistung fachgerechter, auf dieses besondere Patientengut abgestimmter Betreuung, um die Nachteile zu beheben, welche bei der Behandlung dieser Patienten in allgemeinen Aufnahmestationen entstehen. Bereits in der Kürze der Zeit des ersten Jahres wurden die positiven Auswirkungen der Differenzierung für Patienten und teils auch Personal deutlich. Die Ergebnisse, Erfahrungen und Probleme aus der Behandlung von ca. 900 Patienten in dieser Station werden präsentiert und die Auswirkungen dieser Stationsgründung auf das gesamte Wesen der Betreuung von Suchtkranken in dem Versorgungsgebiet des Krankenhauses dargestellt.

450

EFFECT OF PSYCHOTROPIC DRUGS ON FREE RADICALS DAMAGE IN HUMAN LYMPHOCYTES
Binkova B., Topinka J., Sram R.J.
Psychiatric Research Institute, Prague, Czechoslovakia

Side-effects of various psychotropic drugs were proved especially in the schizophrenics. One possible mechanism may be the induction of free radicals, which iniciate the membran lipid peroxidation (LPO) and react also with DNA, causing modification of its structure. We studied an effect of psychotropic drugs (chlorpromazin, haloperidol, meclopin, prochlorperazin, paracetamol) on unscheduled DNA synthesis (UDS) and LPO in the human peripheral lymphocytes from healthy volunteers in vitro. All drugs increased the LPO level in lymphocytes and supress the UDS. These results indicate a possible mechanism of oxidative damage induced by all these drugs during the long-term therapy. Comparing our data in vitro with experiments in vivo as well as in psychiatric patients it may be recommended, that a possible genotoxic activity of these drugs should be thoroughly studied.

451

The narcotic rehabilitation in Italy: A brief report
I. Maremmani[°], M. Cirillo[°°], R. Nardini, O. Zolesi[°°°], A. Tagliamonte[°°°°], P. Castrogiovanni[°].
[°]Institute of Psychiatry, Pisa University, Italy
[°°]Psychiatric Unit USL 4, Regione Toscana, Italy
[°°°]Mental Health Services, USL 20, Regione Liguria, Italy
[°°°°]Pharmacology and Biochemical Pathology Institute, Cagliari University, Italy
Gruppo di Studio e di Intervento sulle Malattie Sociali. (Social Diseases Study and Intervention Association)

Although Methadone therapy is legally applicable in Italy, socio-cultural factors in fact prevent its wide and significant use. This is bad for the health of drug addicts and prevents repression of the intravenous use of heroin, so causing a dangerous spread of AIDS.

Session 67 Poster Presentation:
Electroconvulsive therapy

452

ELECTROCONVULSION: AN ALTERNATIVE FOR SCHIZOPHRENIA RESISTANT TO DRUG THERAPY
F.X.Glocker, R.Maisch, G.Kalfoglou, H.Rether, F.Reimer
Hospital for Psychiatry, Weinsberg, West Germany

In 1988 we treated 36 patients with electroconvulsion at our psychiatric hospital in Weinsberg, West Germany, where more than 3500 patients are admitted per year. In addition to the classical indications (catatonic stupor, depressive stupor, chronic endogenous depression) we treated 16 patients with either hebephrenic or paranoid-hallucinative symptoms with ECT. All of these patients had been on a psychiatric ward for several months in drug therapy including at least two potent neuroleptics as well as clozapine without success. Six (37,5%) of these patients showed marked improvement, four (25%) slight improvement, and six (37,5%) patients showed no response. Our results with the CGIS (clinical global impression scale) are presented with respect to clinical observation of a succession of clonic bodily movements, modus, and number of necessary sessions. The schizophrenic patients' psychopathological findings predicting successful electroconvulsive therapy are discussed.

453

ELECTROCONVULSIVE THERAPY IN GERMAN AND GREEK PSYCHIATRY - A COMPARISON
G.Kalfoglou, R.Maisch, F.X.Glocker, Rether H.,F.Reimer.
Hospital for Psychiatry,Weinsberg, West Germany.

The present study compares German and Greek psychiatric hospitals with respect to differences in indications and frequency of electroconvulsive therapy. For this purpose we created a questionnaire which we sent to 30 Greek and 120 German locals as well as University hospitals for Psychiatry. The obtained results are statistically analyzed and discussed.

454

ANAESTHESIA WITH PROPOFOL IN ECT

Lenzi A.[*], Savino M.[*], San Martino S.G.[*], Venturi L.[**], Sansevero A.[**]
[*] Institute of Psychiatry-University of Pisa
[**] II Department of Anaesthesia and Resuscitation-Chief. Prof. Vagelli A. S. Chiara Hospital, Pisa

After a period of almost complete absence, the use of ECT is again considered an operative therapeutic tool in Italian clinical psychiatry.
Most of the studies devoted to improve ECT efficacy, have been aimed to define the kind of current, the duration of discharge and the advantages of the convulsivant effect, whereas anaesthesia has received little attention. However the anaesthetic drug is frequently of relevance for the patient conditions when he wakes up; in particular the feeling of "traumatic experience" appears to be important toward a good compliance to ECT.
We have found that the characteristics of a new intravenous anaesthetic, Propofol ("Diprivan"), are suitable for such clinical use.
The main properties of Propofol are:
- Anaesthetic power and therapeutic index similar to those of Pentobarbithal
- Short life, with quick reawakening and fast recovery of motor coordination
- Very low incidence of side effects (with very low anxiety rate at reawakening) and absence of immunological and haematochemical complications.
In order to evaluate the efficacy and tolerability of Propofol in ECT anaesthesia, we have compared this drug with Pentobarbithal (a widely employed anaesthetic agent for ECT). In 24 patients, submitted to ECT, we have recorded heart frequency and blood pressure variations before and after anaesthesia, length of sleep period, and elapsed time before recovering full motor coordination; we have also assessed the "quality" of the reawakening.
Our results seem to confirm previous data collected in surgical experiences which suggest that Propofol may be a valid alternative to other drugs currently used in this kind of anaesthesia. The length of action of Propofol was shorter than that of Pentothal as measured by duration of sleep and of time before recovering of full motor coordination. Moreover we did not find blunt feelings nor high levels of anxiety after reawakening, as it is frequently observed in patients anaesthetized with traditional drugs.

Session 68 Poster Presentation:
Organic mental disorders

455

DEPRESSIVE RETARDATION VERSUS AKINESIA IN PARKINSON'S DISEASE.

Baruch P, Jouvent R, Ammar S, Widlöcher D & Agid Y
Hopital de la Salpetriere, Paris, France

Psychomotor retardation has long been considered as a major feature of primary depression. A specific rating scale has been built in our department, specially designed for measuring retardation (Depressive Retardation Rating Scale- ERD). The factorial structure of the scale tested in several samples of depressed patients remains the same. In depressed parkinsonian patients, the presence of extrapyramidal symptoms, in paricular akinesia, makes it difficult to detect depression related retardation. To further examine this point, we evaluated 100 depressed parkinsonian patients (49 women and 51 men aged 61.1 ± 11 years (mean ± sd) meeting DSM III criteria for major depressive episode. These patients received antiparkinsonian treatments but no antidepressant. A neurologist and a psychiatrist independently evaluated parkinsonian (Columbia University Scale - CUS) and depressive (ERD, Hamilton depression rating scale - HDRS) symptomatologies. The main results are as follows : 1) the ERD score is highly correlated to the HDRS score but not to the CUS score, 2) the factorial structure of the ERD computed from our sample is similar to those observed in primary depression. Thus, depressed parkinsonian patients as well as non parkinsonian depressives, exhibit a psychomotor retardation which may be evaluated and distinguished from the extrapyramidal syndrome.

456

CHANGES IN BRAIN LIPID COMPOSITION OF AN ADULT TYPE SSPE

Ohtani,Y.,Takayama,K.,Tamai,Y.,Kojima,H.,Oguchi,T., Ishii,Y.,Mochizuki,Y.,Sugawara,M.and Miura,S.
Department of Psychiatry and Biochemistry,Kitasato University School of Medicine,Sagamihara,Japan.

We had a rare adult-onset case(24 y.o.) of subacute sclerosing panencephalitis(SSPE) who died 3 years and 4 months after the onset of her illness. Lipid composition of the cerebral cortex,cerebral white matter(CWM),putamen and corpus callosum(CC) from the patient's brain was compared with that from normal control brain. In all four resions of the SSPE brain the lipid composition was altered.
Galactolipid(cerebroside and sulfatide) was reduced to 1/3 and 1/4 that of normal levels in the CWM and in the CC,respectively,where the accumulation of cholesterol ester was observed. Ganglioside(GGD) profile,as determined by 2-dimensional thin layer chromatography,revealed a reduced GM1 and GD1a and an elevated GD3 levels in all four resions of the SSPE brain,suggesting that the disturbed GGD metabolism occurred in the SSPE brain. As to the long-chain base composition of GGD,a C20-component was severely decreased in the CC and nearly constant in the other resions.
These alterations in the lipid composition of the SSPE brain are considered to be due to the changes of cellular components and/or lipid metabolism induced by the SSPE pathogen.

457

AMNESIC SYNDROME DUE TO HERPES ENCEPHALITIS: CASE REPORT WITH BILATERAL HIPPOCAMPAL DAMAGE IN MRI.
M.Nakanishi,Dpt. of Neuropsychiatry,Tajimi Hospital; T.Watanabe & T.Hamanaka,Dpt.of Neuropsychiatry,Nagoya City University, Nagoya, Japan.
This report details amnesic syndrome in a righthanded, 49year old patient which manifested itself without any neuropsychiatric deficits in other performances than memory(WAIS IQ=114), following an acute phase of neurologically as well as virologically verified herpes-encephalitis. While the patient exhibited severe disorder of long-termmemory in verbal and non-verbal tasks as well as retrograde amnesia covering 20 years before onset, no marked loss of short-term storage capacity was demonstrated. Sporadic non-productive confabulations in the initial period disappeared in several weeks("temporal amnesia" in contrast to"diencephalic amnesia"). Besides, one remarkable neuro-imaging finding highlights the case, that a MRI-examination, executed one month post-onset, visualized clear high-signality(T2) circumscribed to bilateral hippocampal regions, while no positive findings were obtained in repeated X-ray CT and EEG examinations. These findings are in accordance with the report of Rumbach et al.(1988) who emphasized the diagnostic importance of MRI in cases of herpes encephalitis.

458

TRAUMATIC LESIONS CAUSING PSYCHIATRIC DISEASES

Eva-Maria Feferle, Christina Gollner,
B. Prix, A. Tölk
Psychiatrisches Krankenhaus
Wien/Austria

All the patients admitted for the first time to the acute-cases ward of the Psychiatric Hospital between January 1987 an December 1988 were included in the survey.
The reasons for admission were abnormalities in behaviour considered threatening either by the patient or by his/her social environment.
After they were discharged, the patients were asked in retrospect about the time prior to their admission to the Hospital.
The question was raised whether any single event in the period preceding the exceptional psychological state leading to admission could be found which was directly relatet to that state.
Could a link be established between a traumatic experience and the start of a psychotic episode? An event is defined as traumatic whenever the patient remembers it subjectively as having been traumatic, even if his/her description of the event is not traumatizing but clearly signals the significance of the event.
The survey focuses on personality features and factors of stress prior to the event.
The results are discussed with regard to their therapeutic relevance and explained in terms of theory.

459

DELUSIONS OF PARASITOSIS ASSOCIATED WITH "FOLLIE A DEUX"
D.Agrafiotis-A.Kalogeropoulos-M.Psomiadou
A.Tsoukarela-A.Skyllakos.

We report a case of delusional parasitosis associated with"folie-à-deux".
Delusional parasitosis,initially described by Ekbom in 1938 is an illness in which the patient believes that small animals,maggots,worms or insects thrive inside him or on his skin.
This delusion is not a symptom of an underlying psychotic illness,but occurs on its own and the personality of the patient remains normal.
Delusion parasitosis in 25% of cases is associated with a "Follie-à-deux" situation.

460

CASE REPORT: AN ETHIOPIAN YOUNG WOMAN WITH CAT SCAN ABNORMALITY.
Facincani Orietta Cinzia, Alciati Alessandra
U.S.S.L. No.60 - Vimercate (Milan) Italy

The authors describe the case of a 28-year old Ethiopian woman who developed a full blown psychotic episode during the 24th week of pregnancy. The symptoms - delusion of reference, clouding of consciousness - disappeared two weeks before delivery while the patient was under neuroleptic treatment. A CAT scan showed a lower density area within the right hippocampus. A NMR scan revealed an atrophic zone probably due to a cystic formation. The patient had relapsing episodes that were treated with various neuroleptics without improvement. A lithium salt treatment caused a decrease in the severity of symptoms within three days.

461

PSYCHOTIC EPILEPSY: SCHIZOHRENIA- AND MAJOR DEPRESSION-LIKE EPILEPSY

B.Taneli, S.Taneli, S.Özaskinli, I.Karakilic, F.Karaaslan

Department of Psychiatry, Uludag University, Bursa, Turkey

The dexamethasone supression test (DST) was used to compare major depression (MD) to major depression-like psychotic epilepsy (MDLPE), and also shizophrenic depression (SD) to schizophrenia-like psychotic epilepsy (SLPE).
MD and SD were diagnosed according to DSM-III and ICD-9. MDLPE and SLPE were diagnosed by considering MD and SD synptoms associated with an epileptic activity in EEG, but without any epileptic seizures in medical histories.
Out of the 19 MD patients, 14(73.68%) showed nonsuppression at 16:00, 16(84.21%) at 23:00; out of the 11 patients with MDLPE, 2(18.18%) at 16:00 and 2(18.18%) at 23:00 postdexamethasone samples. Out of the 15 patients with SD, 8 (53.33%) showed nonsuppression at 16:00, 11(73.33%) at 23:00; out of the 17 SLPE patients, 2(11.76%) at 16:00 and 3(17.65%) at 23:00 postdexamethasone samples.
SD and MD patients responded antidepressants and antipsychotics, while MDLPE and SLPE patients were good respondents to antiepileptics.
We concluded, these two groups of patients with the same clinical symptomatology, actually have different aetiologies. Eventhough SD and MD are evaluated as endogenous psychoses, SLPE and MDLPE should be evaluated as epileptic phenomena.

462

MOOD DISORDERS IN EPILEPSY : A SURVEY OF PSYCHIATRIC PATIENTS
DR. SATNAM S. PALIA
MORGANNWG HOSPITAL (GLANRHYD) BRIDGEND, MID GLAM. CF31 4LN U.K.

In Patients and Day Patients with epilepsy in a general psychiatric service were surveyed. Fifty three patients able to co-operate in a detailed assessment were studied using the Hamilton Rating scale and the Beck Depression Inventory. About one-third 932%) of the patients had serious depressive illness, mostly classified as non-endogenous, on the Newcastle Index.
Neurological factors were overshadowed by the psychological and social problems generally found in depressed patients. Almost all of the depressed epileptics gave histories of repeated previous deliberate drug overdose and a past history of depression. The multifactorial nature of depressive states in epilepsy is emphasised.

463

BRIEF CLINICAL EVALUATION OF ORGANIC BRAIN DAMAGE SYMPTOMS
Marek JAREMA, Sławomir KRUSZYNSKI, Grażyna BARANIUK, Janusz WDOWIAK, Janusz KACPERCZYK
Division of Psychopathology, Institute of Neurology and Psychiatry, Medical Academy, Szczecin, Poland

Simple methods for the evaluation of organic brain damage were compared in 30 psychiatric patients aged 20-56 in whom the possibility of organic brain damage appeared during routine psychiatric interview. The evaluation included Mini Mental State (Folstein et al.1975), Organic Brain Damage Rating Scale (Jarema et al.1984), and psychological battery (Benton, Bender, Graham-Kendall).
The correlation was found between all the methods used. The slight differences in the evaluation of organic symptoms reflected rather the **subjectivity of psychiatric evaluation**. The best correlation of all results was proved among patients with serious memory problems. Such correlation, however, did not depend upon the severity of organic symptoms. The study revealed the usefulness of all presented methods for the quick diagnosis of organic brain damage. Both MMS and OBDRS can be used interchangeably for brief clinic evaluation, while psychological tests are more time-consuming.

464

ACUTE AND SUBACUTE ORGANIC MENTAL DISORDERS WITH ALTERED CONSCIOUSNESS
S. Biedert, W. Hewer*, and G. Zech-Uber*
Psych. Landeskrankenhaus, 6908 Wiesloch, and * Zentralinstitut f. Seel. Gesundheit, Mannheim, FRG

We have retrospectively investigated the 71 patients who were treated under the ICD-9 diagnoses 293.0 and 293.1 (acute and subacute "confusional state", respectively) in our institution in 1987 with respect to maximal grade of – qualitatively and/or quantitatively – altered consciousness. On the basis of an available neurological scale describing states of acutely altered consciousness, and by knowing the underlying somatic disease, we have developed prognostic criteria: Accordingly, disorders of heart and circulation associated with acute organic mental disorder (with altered consciousness) carry a fair prognosis for recovery of the mental symptoms in approximately 2/3 of all patients affected, even in advanced age. The same statement is valid with respect to drug-induced acute organic mental disorders, while most patients with cerebrovascular disorders with mental symptoms proceed to chronic types of organic mental disorders. In the patient subsets suffering from neoplasms and brain contusions (closed head injury) with acute organic psychoses, only 30% – 50% of all patients affected exhibited complete recovery of mental functions. Thus, we believe that the clinically descriptive terms "clouding of consciousness", "confusional state", "delirium", "stupor", and "coma" allow easy grading of states of acutely/subacutely altered consciousness. The course of the alteration in consciousness is – in our opinion – a sensitive indicator for the course of disease, the efficacy of treatment, and thereby for the prognosis of the underlying disorder.

465

PSYCHOPATHOLOCIGAL ALTERATIONS IN CASES OF SYMMETRICAL BASAL GANGLIA SCLEROSIS
P.Koenig
Landes-Nervenkrankenhaus Valduna, A-5830 Rankweil - Austria

We present psychopathological and neurological data,EEG and brain-CT scan-results obtained from 62 patients with Fahr's syndrome. In addition the focus on initial symptoms, on possible effects of size and/or localisation of the calcifications are stressed. Additionally members of 2 families with a familial form of the disease are incorporated in this study. Volumetric estimations of the intracerebral hyperdense bodies were calculated by computer-integrated programme,on 31 pt.(conventional)EEGs were performed. Psychiatric manifestations of a group of 35 florid cases were assessed with the HAM-D, BPRS,SCAG, ratingscales, compared to matched controls. Investigations of a possible hormonal etiology of Fahr's syndrome were completed on 15 pt. In the whole group (62pt.) 9 cases of post-thyroidectomy, 7 cases of hypoparathyroidism and 8 cases of pseudohypoparathyroidism were registered. Aetiology was not ascertained in 38 cases. Familial incidence occured in 8 (out of 45) and 2 (out of 2)cases. Out of 62pt.25(40%)revealed initial psychiatric symptoms:(n=25=100%), affective organic syndromes 52%, paranoid hallucinatory organic syndromes 4%, anancasms 4%, dementias 20%, addictions 20% 31 pt. (50%)initially showed neurological symptoms(n=31=100%)seizures 13%, TIA 13%, syncopes 9,7%,EPS19,3%,paresis 19,3%,cephalea 26%

466

QUANTITATIVE INVESTIGATION OF CEREBRAL ATROPHY BY COMPUTED TOMOGRAPHIC CSF-VOLUMETRY
OTT, C.[1], HECHT, M.[1], DEMLING, J.[1], SCHUIERER, G.[2]
1) Department of Psychiatry, University of Erlangen-Nürnberg, D-8520 Erlangen (FRG);
2) Department of Neuroradiology, University of Erlangen-Nürnberg, D-8520 Erlangen (FRG)

In quantifying cerebral atrophy by cranial CT, measurement of cerebrospinal fluid (CSF) volume provides the best results. The method presented here is based on the "pixel-counting" principle, i.e. all pixels with HOUNSFIELD values within a certain range are added up by a special computer program (evaluscope, SIEMENS).
An index section including the anterior horns, third ventricle and quadrigeminal cistern is identified for each scan. The index section and the three sections immediately superior to it are used for data analysis (each section 8 mm thick). A histogram showing the density scores in a defined ventricular region is used to eliminate fluctuations of the scanner. Three irregular "regions of interest" (ROI) are defined in each CT-section:
ROI 1: line drawn along the inner surface of the skull;
ROI 2: line drawn along the cortical brain surface;
ROI 3: line drawn tight around the ventricles.
The difference between ROI 1 and ROI 2 gives the subarachnoidal CSF area, ROI 3 the ventricle-related area in each section. Pixels from -6 to +20 HOUNSFIELD units were defined as representing CSF space. Areas and volumes are computed automatically by the EVA ("evaluscope") program.

467

PERSONALITY AND HEAD INJURIES
Elpido Sanchez Arellano, Neurology of the Atizapan's Gen.Hospital,Mexico

Some months after a head injury a patient may complain of symptoms affecting either physical or mental function or both. These late complications which may follow either mild or severe injuries include epilepsy, intracranial infction, and carotico-cavernous fistula. The basis for the subjetive physical and mental symptoms after mild injuries; post concussional or post-traumatic syndorme remains a matter of controversy.

Sequelae of head injury		
Strongly related to severity of injury.	Loss strongly related.	Unrelated.
Mental: Apathy, Euphoria, Loss of social restraint, Intellectual deficit, Marked memory defect.	"Poor concentration" "Poor memory" "Slowness"	Fastigue Irritability Insomnio. Nervousness Anxiety Depression.
Physical: Dyphasia, Hemianopia, Spasticity, Motor disorder, Ataxia, Tremor, Perceptual disorders.	Anosmia Vertigo Epilepsy	Headache Sensitivity to noise. Dizziness Pain at site of injury.

When an injury produces unconciousness its duration is taken to indicate the severity of the diffuse brain damage and this, can occur without a fracture or any blemish on the scalp. The return of continuous memory marks the end of post-traumatic amnesia and occurs some time after patient has begun to talk and behave normally, and coincides with reorientation and accurate awareness of time and place.

The next are mental sequelae of head injury	
a) General organic dementia – No specific –	Personality Disorders Intellect Memory
b) Local organic syndrome – Specific –	Frontal - Severe behavioural problems. Right hemisphere - Visuo spatial deficit. Left hemisphere - Defective verbal skills – Whitout dysphasia.
c) Post-concussional syndrome – Post-traumatic –	Subjective mental and somatic features.
d) Accident neurosis	Prolongation and exageration of post-traumatic syndrome.
e) Psychosis	Depression. Schizophrenia.

Session 69 Poster Presentation:
Exercise, art and folk therapies

468

BODY-AWARENESS THROUGH RELAXATION, MOVEMENT AND THERAPEUTIC GYMNASTICS
Gyra E., Mantonakis J., Telioni E.
Department of Psychiatry, University of Athens, Eginition Hospital Athens, Grecce.

It is well known that in the process of psychotherapy very little attention has been given to the situation of body experience of psychiatric patients. Nevertheless, the body reflects in a very sensitive and obvious way the state of psychiatric and psychological illness.

Nine years functioning of relaxation, movement and therapeutic gymnastics groups in a Day Hospital is presented with emphasis on the body awareness and the reconstructive experience which is succeded through special exercises and techniques. It is also pointed out that the process of body consciousness regarding the state of the body (inflexibility, wrong respiration, limited movement elimination of free body expression as well as physical contact, fear and stress) encourages a lot and also reflects the process of the whole therapy.

469

SHORT-TERM ART THERAPY IN CRISIS INTERVENTION AND FOCAL PSYCHOTHERAPY: A FIRST REPORT
Fabra, M.[1], Dannecker, K.[2], Brauns, M.-L.[1], Berzewski, H.
1) Psychiatric Outpatient Ward and Crisis Intervention Center of the Klinikum Steglitz, Free University Berlin. 2) Hochschule der Künste Berlin

Part of the treatment of the psychiatric crisis intervention ward was a newly installed art therapy course. Up until six patients participated at each course, which lasted four weeks. The therapeutic staff was formed out of two art therapists; supervision was provided by a psychiatrist and an art therapy teacher from the university following each two sessions. At the beginning and at the end of each four-weeksequence personality inventories were administered and psychiatric ratings were carried out. In addition the subjective evaluation of the treatment by the patients was assessed by use of a semi-structured interview. Psychological testing and interview were received either by control group. For each patient a therapeutic focus was formulated at the beginning of the treatment. Results and processes of therapy will be demonstrated.

470

SHORT TERM ART THERAPY IN PSYCHIATRIC CRISIS INTERVENTION, PART I
Fabra, M., K. Dannecker, H. Berzewski
Psychiatric Outpatient Ward and Crisis Intervention Center of Klinikum Steglitz, Free University Berlin (Head: H. Berzewski, M.D.)

Crisis intervention in inpatient settings is usually terminated after three weeks. It is advisable to define treatment goals and duration right at the beginning, as therapeutic tools and interventions may differ according to when they are used during the treatment - at the beginning, in the middle or at the end. A so-called "therapeutic arch" can be definded, subdivided into four phases: a "warming-up-phase", a "conflict-centered phase", a "phase of integration" and a "phase of separation and discharge". In order to facilitate the discharge, which means "good-bye" to the protective hospital environment, the crisis intervention ward of the Klinikum Steglitz, Free University of Berlin, offers a therapeutic program designed to bridge the gap between hospital and everyday life. It is hypothesized, that this four week program helps to incorporate what was gained in the inpatient treatment into the patient's everyday life. The program usually starts in the second half of the inpatient treatment sequence and takes up the aforeamentioned four phases. Sports therapy, dance therapy and art therapy have been used. In our presentation the advantages of such an art therapy program will be discussed along with the pictures of a depressed patient, which mirror nicely the phases of "the therapeutic arch".

471
AN APPROACH TO ELDERLY INPATIENTS DERIVED FROM GROUP DYNAMICS IN MUSIC THERAPY
M.Kawai, K.Miyamoto, M.Miyamoto
Showa University and Miyamoto Hospital, Ibaragi Japan

There have been comparatively few reports about music therapy for elderly inpatients. Therefore the authors think there is ample room for further study. The authors, applying music therapy, tried to examine the interrelationships of group members in our geriatric ward with an age-group range of 65 to 85, especially dementia inpatients. Our group started a little over four years ago. Each session lasted one and a half hours. Almost all had below-average verbal ability and sub-normal intelligence. Inpatient participation in the session was voluntary. Participants usually were about 30 to 40 of the 60 inpatients of our ward. From the changes in member seat arrangements during sessions, group dynamics were observed which enabled the authors to discern several phases as the changes continued. Another finding was that the group gradually formed into sub-groups. Each sub-group appeared to have an individual character from a diagnostic point of view. Also examined were the ways of approach of new inpatients to the group and the relationship between their change of mental condition and movement into, within or out of the group. In this way, examination of group dynamics such as the manner of concern with the group for each member was regarded to have diagnostic value.

472
THE INFLUENCE OF ZULU MEDICINE ON FAITH HEALING PRACTICES

Wessel H Wessels, University of Natal, PO Box 17039, CONGELLA, 4013, SOUTH AFRICA

The African Independent Churches (AIC) incorporate the traditional concepts of ancestral spirit worship into Christian beliefs. This syncretism has made this the fastest growing African Church. The AIC faith healers enjoy ever greater popularity among the Zulu where many people consult them first when faced with misfortune. They not only employ clearcut faith healing practices but appear to utilize similar methods to those utilized by the traditional healers. The faith healers make use of purification ceremonies in the sea or rivers, enemas, vomiting and purging, holy water and smoke. Herbs and patent medicines are often employed in the above practices in the same way as used by the traditional healers. They furthermore employ the use of ropes and ritual dancing both of which are also well known in traditional Zulu medicine.

Session 70 Poster Presentation:
Pharmacopsychiatry: Antipsychotic drugs

473
HYSTERICAL NEUROSIS-CONVERSION TYPE:A DOPAMINERGIC HYPOTESIS
L. RAMPELLO, F. D'AQUILA AND F. NICOLETTI
ISTITUTO DI CLINICA NEUROLOGICA, V.LE A.DORIA, N°6 CATANIA, ITALY

Although hysterical neurosis has been the subject of extensive investigation, little is known about its pathophysiology, in terms of neurochemical abnormalities.
To reveal a possible alteration of central dopaminergic (DAergic) system, we have studied 33 patients (25 females and 8 males), with diagnosis of hysterical neurosis. Patients were divided into 3 groups and treated with placebo, sulpiride or amineptine. Treatments was performed by placebo-controlled randomized double-blind for 30 days. The large majority of the patients (78 %) responded to sulpiride with a striking improvement in neurotic symptoms. The clinical picture was worsened after treatment with amineptine in 66% of the patients. Hence, we speculate that a hyperactivity of DAergic system may be involved in the development of neurotic symtoms. It cannot be excluded that the increase in prolactin secretion induced by sulpiride may contribute to the therapeutical efficacy of the drug. Accordingly haloperidol, that blocks central dopamine receptors but is less potent than sulpiride in increasing PRL secretion, is not as active in the treatment of hysterical neurosis.

474
DEPOTNEUROLEPTICS: A COMPUTERIZED ADMINISTRATIVE AND RESEARCH SYSTEM

Haffmans P.M.J., Hoencamp E., Ginneken van C., Kamp, J.S., Laar van der M., Siebelink H.J.K.
Psychiatric Centre Bloemendaal, P.O. Box 53002, 2505 AA The Hague, The Netherlands.

A computer assisted data entry program was developed, to register social-demographic data, diagnosis (DSM-III-R), type of medication, dosage, interval, co-medication, side-effects, plasma-levels and laboratory results. Each institute participating in this project has a peripheral PC terminal to enter the data. The data are sent 3-monthly by telephone to a "host-terminal". Review of the own population can be performed at terminal level while on request, a comparison with other populations is made at the "host" level. Furthermore, advanced statistical analysis on **all data** is performed at the "host" level. The system has three main goals:
- administrative support for the participating institutes
- reference base for the participating institutes
- data base system for (furture) indepth research on the use of depotneuroleptics.

As an example of the possibilities of this system we will present analysed data on the use of depot-neuroleptics in two out-patient clinics (n = 150, n = 285). The results include social demographic and diagnostic data, as well as medication regime, co-medication and plasmalevels. Possible correlations between items are discussed.

475

A CASE OF LETHAL CATATONIA: CLINICAL ASPECTS AND PSYCHOENDOCRINOLOGICAL FINDINGS
Janiri L., De Bonis C., Del Carmine R.*, Tempesta E. and Ferro F.M.
Depts. of Psychiatry and *Pharmacology, Catholic University, Rome, Italy

Lethal catatonia is a life-threatening febrile neuropsychiatric disorder, widely reported before the introduction of modern psychopharmacologic treatments, but since then often misdiagnosed.
The present case report is concerned with a young woman showing psychopathologic features and laboratory data which met the criteria for the diagnosis of Stauder's lethal catatonia. The patient, who had never taken neuroleptics, had a positive outcome following 2 months of hospitalization and a normalization of the clinical picture.
Because of the recently emphasized psychopathologic similarity existing between catatonia and affective disorders, we have examined some psychoendocrinological parameters putatively associated with the affective spectrum of psychotic disorders.
Plasma cortisol showed high values with an altered diurnal pattern; dexamethasone suppression test was positive; plasma catecholamines (noradrenaline and adrenaline, but not dopamine) were higher than controls. The same tests were repeated after 24 days, when most symptoms subsided; catecholamines resulted to be normalized.
These findings, pointing to a possible noradrenergic dysfunction, are consistent with the affective hypothesis of catatonia. Additional remarks on the particular case of lethal catatonia are also discussed.

476

RISPRIDONE IN ACUTE EPISODES OF SCHIZOPHRENIA: AN OPEN DOSE-ESCALATING STUDY
S.W.Turner[1], M.R.Lowe[2], G.L.Hammond[3]
[1]Dept. of Psychol. medicine, Basildon Hospital, London, U.K., [2]Dept. of Psychol. Medicine, Basildon Hospital, Essex U.K., [3]Janssen Research Foundation, Wantage, U.K.
Preliminary open studies conducted outside the U.K. in chronic schizophrenic patients suggest that risperidone -a potent mixed dopamine-D_2 and serotonin-S_2 receptor antagonist- has efficacy in the management of both positive and negative symptoms of schizophrenia. These beneficial effects have been accompanied by a lower incidence than expected of extra-pyramidal side effects, suggesting potential advantages for risperidone over conventional neuroleptic antipsychotic drugs.
As an introduction to the U.K. Risperidone Research Programme, an open dose-ranging study has been conducted in which clinical efficacy was assessed using the Positive and Negative Syndrome Scale (PANSS) and the Montgomery Schizophrenia Change Scale. In addition, the effects of this treatment on depressive symptoms were measured using the Montgomery Asberg Depression Rating Scale, whilst extrapyramidal side effects and akathisia were assessed at weekly intervals using the Simpson and Angus, and Barnes/Braude Akathisia Rating Scales respectively. In addition to demographic data, medication and treatment response data for all patients entered into the study will be presented, with particular reference to the level of extrapyramidal side effects.

477

PRELIMINARY U.K. EXPERIENCE WITH RISPERIDONE (R64766) IN ACUTE SCHIZOPHRENIA
T.M.Reilly[1], M.G.Livingston[2], G.L.Hammond[3], D.H.Batchelor[3]
[1]The Retreat, York, U.K., [2]Dept. of Psychol. Medicine, Univ.of Glaskow, U.K., [3]Janssen Research Foundation, Wantage, U.K.
Risperidone (R64766) is a potent mixed serotonin-S_2 and dopamine-D_2 receptor antagonist (Janssen PAJ et al, 1988), which has been selected for clinical research in psychotic disorders. Early open studies have noted a low incidence of extrapyramidal side effects, combined with effects on both positive and negative symptoms of schizophrenia.
Having provided written informed consent, patients who conformed to the DSM-III-R diagnosis of schizophrenia and were Research Diagnostic Criteria positive, were entered into an open dose-ranging study. Assessments using Feighner Criteria were also made. The patients received risperidone suspension (0.5mg/ml) starting at 4mg daily in divided doses and titrated to a maximum of 20mg daily. Treatment response was assessed using the Scale for the Assessment of Negative Symptoms (SANS), the Positive and Negative Syndrome Scale (PANSS) and the Montgomery Schizophrenia Change Scale, the Simpson and Angus Scale for extrapyramidal side effects, and the Abnormal Involuntary Movements Scale. Dosage and efficacy data for all patients entered into the study will be presented, with particular reference to the assessment of treatment effect on negative symptom.

478

A DOUBLE-BLIND COMPALATIVE STUDY OF Y-516, A NEW ANTIPSYCOTIC DRUG ON SCHIZOPHRENIA.
Yoshio Kudo et al., Institute of Clinical Pharmacology, Aino Hospital (Osaka,Japan)

Y-516 is a new antipsycotic drug synthesized and developed by Yoshitomi Pharmaceutical Ind.,Ltd. Chemically, it belongs to the iminodibenzyl group where carpipramine is also included as a drug showing disinhibitory actions,as advocated by Prof. P.Deniker. To determine its efficacy and safety on schizophrenia, a double-blind comparative study was conducted by using haloperidol(HPD) as the reference. Data analysis was made on 96 patients of the Y-516 group and 102 of the HPD group. There was no significant difference in the final grobal judgement or overall safety rating. But, in the rating of usefulness,Y-516 was significantly superior to HPD in the result of "very useful" ($p<0.05$), and there were fewer patients showing the result of "fairly or very useless" in the Y-516 group($p<0.10$). Y-516 also showed greater usefulness in "the cases having lack of spontaneity and apathy plus hallucination and delusion in the foreground". The incidence of extrapyramidal symtoms was 35% for Y-516 and 32% for HPD. No other notable side effects or abnormalities in laboratory tests appeared.
Y-516 was considered to be a useful antipsychotic drug,especially for chronic cases of hallucination, delusion and conceptual disorganization.

479

BEHAVIOURAL EFFECTS OF THE NOVEL PUTATIVELY ANTIPSYCHOTIC AGENT AMPEROZIDE

B. Gustafsson and E. Christensson, Dept. of CNS-Research, Pharmacia LEO Therapeutics AB, P.O.Box 839, S-201 80 Malmö, Sweden.

Amperozide is a novel psychotropic drug with potentially antipsychotic properties. It is characterized by a limbic mode of action. Thus, amperozide significantly blocked conditioned avoidance response in rats and amphetamine-induced locomotion in mice, but did not induce catalepsy or affect amphetamine-induced stereotypies in rats.
Amperozide was found to be a potent inhibitor of spontaneous mouse-killing behaviour and significantly decreased the immobility time in behavioural despair test. Furthermore, amperozide displayed a potent anticonflict effect in Vogel's test. It demonstrated a potent effect on exploratory behaviour without causing sedation which provides additional evidence of an action on the limbic brain areas.
To summarize, amperozide displayed a pronounced effect on emotional behaviours but is devoid of effects in models predicting extrapyramidal side effects. This indicates a limbic profile of action, different from both classical and atypical neuroleptics.

480

AMPEROZIDE - A PUTATIVELY ANTIPSYCHOTIC DRUG: BIOCHEMICAL CHARACTERIZATION IN THE RAT

G. Pettersson, A. Björk, J. Engel*, E. Eriksson and J. Svartengren, Dept. of CNS-Research, Pharmacia LEO Therapeutics AB, P.O.Box 839, S-201 80 Malmö, Sweden, and *Dept. of Pharmacology, University of Göteborg, P.O.Box 33031, S-400 33 Göteborg, Sweden.

Amperozide (a diphenylbutylpiperazinecarboxamide derivative) was selected as a new potentially antipsychotic drug, with effects preferentially on emotional behaviour (see Gustafsson B. et al., this meeting). In this study we have investigated the biochemical properties of amperozide in rat brain.
In vitro amperozide was found to exhibit high affinity for $5-HT_2$ receptors (K_i=16 nM). The drug was weaker in binding to α_1, D_2, $5-HT_{1A}$, α_2 and D_1 receptors with K_i values of 172, 540, 657, 793 and 2900 nM, respectively. Amperozide inhibited the monoamine uptake into chopped striatal or cortical tissue with IC_{50} values in the micromolar range.
In vivo amperozide increased the synthesis of dopamine (measured as accumulation of 3,4-dihydroxyphenylalanine; DOPA) in the mesolimbic brain areas, but not in the striatum. The content of 3,4-dihydroxyphenylacetic acid (DOPAC) was also selectively increased in the limbic brain areas. Furthermore, the synthesis of noradrenaline in the cortex was increased by amperozide, whereas the synthesis of serotonin was unaffected in limbic, striatal and cortical regions.
In conclusion, amperozide has high affinity for $5-HT_2$ receptors and selective dopaminergic action on the mesolimbic system. These properties suggest an antipsychotic activity of amperozide with effects on both negative and positive symptoms and with low risk of producing extrapyramidal side effects.

481

NEUROENDOCRINE EFFECTS OF AMPEROZIDE IN THE RAT

G. Andersson, A. Albinsson, E. Eriksson and G. Pettersson, Dept. of CNS-Research, Pharmacia LEO Therapeutics AB, P.O.Box 839, S-201 80 Malmö, Sweden.

Amperozide is a putatively antipsychotic drug which is characterized by its limbic mode of action and high affinity for the serotonin $5-HT_2$ receptor. In neuroendocrine experiments in the rat it was found that the activity of the pituitary-adrenocortical axis, as judged from the plasma level of corticosterone, was dose-dependently increased after the acute administration of amperozide. In contrast to the $5-HT_2$ receptor antagonists ketanserin and ritanserin, amperozide was found to be a potent stimulator of adrenal corticosterone release. The time-course effect of amperozide on prolactin release was studied in cannulated freely moving rats. Following amperozide treatment (2.5 mg/kg) there was a decrease ($p<0.05$) in plasma prolactin concentration. In accordance with its low affinity for dopamine D_2 receptors there was no effect of amperozide on the basal release of prolactin from isolated and perfused pituitary cells. Compared to some atypical antipsychotics e.g. clozapine, amperozide was found to be a more potent stimulator of the TIDA neurons in the rat. The accumulation of DOPA was increased ($p<0.01$) after the administration of amperozide (1 mg/kg). Hence the decreased plasma level of prolactin following amperozide treatment is probably explained by a stimulatory effect on the TIDA system.

482

Haloperidol decanoate: four year trial in schizophrenic inpatients.
Gaia S., Carnaghi R., Galis A., Nervo D.
Istituto Fatebenefratelli
San Maurizio Canavese Torino (Italy)

In this study lasting 4 years, 41 schizophrenic inpatients, 26 males and 15 females, age range 25-77 years, were treated with haloperidol decanoate (H D) dose range 25-300 mg monthly, so as to verify if, with the introduction of H D in therapy, a reduction of the total neuroleptic dose (evaluated according to the conversion scale by Suy et al. 1982) could be obtained, providing that the clinical state of the patients improved or remained invaried. The extrapyramidal side effects (E.P.S.E rating scale) were also evaluated in 8 cases before and after introduction of H D. RESULTS: in 27% of the cases (11 patients) a reduction of the total neuroleptic dose was possible. In 10% (4 patients) the total dose remained invaried. In 34% (14 patients) it was necessary to increase the total dose. In 29% (12 patients) of the cases, treatment with H D was interrupted due to an increase in psychotic anxiety, hallucinations and delusions. Of the 8 patients evaluated for extrapyramidal side effects, the mean EPSE score before introduction of H D was 23,6 and after 4 years 27,5. In only 2 cases the EPSE total score decreased. CONCLUSION: The patients that appeared to benefit from H D had in common a higher mean age, a longer disease duration and a higher initial neuroleptic total dose therapy.

483
HALOPERDIOL PLASMA-LEVELS IN TREATMENT OF CHRONIC SCHIZOPHRENICS
K. Meszaros, G. Schönbeck, H. Aschauer, G. Koinig, G. Langer, A. Bugnar
*Department of Psychiatry, University of Vienna, Austria

Haloperidol (HAL) is a widely used antipsychotic drug in treatment of chronic schizophrenics. In order to optimize treatment of neuroleptics measurement of HAL plasma-levels might be of great value.
In our study patients received HAL orally and/or in decanoate form. Plasma-levels of HAL were estimated at different intervals during treatment using RIA. In addition, other clinical (BPRS and side-effects) and pharmacological data were collected.
Plasma HAL monitoring indicates a "therapeutic window" for HAL levels (12-27 ng/ml).
Results with regard to plasma-levels and its relationship to change in BPRS and side-effects will be presented.

484
ZUCLOPENTHIXOL ACETATE AS START OF LONGTERM NEUROLEPTIC TREATMENT
A. Wunderink, E.E. Hummel, N.N.A. Dodde (*), G.S.I.M. Jansen and P.M.J. Haffmans.
Psychiatric Centre 'Bloemendaal',
POB 53002, NL-2505 AA The Hague.
(*) Lundbeck b.v., Medical Department,
POB 12021, NL-1100 AA Amsterdam.

Acute psychotic patients needing long-term neuroleptic treatment after recovery from the acute phase, were adjusted to zuclopenthixol (Z)-decanoate according to an adjustment schedule based on available pharmacokinetic data. During the first phase of treatment two doses of 100 mg Z-acetate were administered i.m. with a 3 day interval, and subsequently Z-decanoate was administered i.m. with 2 weeks interval together with oral Z in decreasing dosages during 4 weeks. Aim of the study was to evaluate this schedule in the treatment of psychotic patients during the transition phase to maintenance therapy. The clinical results, as measured by BPRS, CGI, UKU side-effects, degree of sedation, and pharmacokinetic data will be presented.

485
ACUTE PSYCHOTIC PATIENTS TREATED WITH ZUCLOPENTHIXOL ACETATE.
E.E. Hummel, A. Wunderink, N.N.A. Dodde(*), G.S.I.M. Jansen and P.M.J. Haffmans.
Psychiatric Centre 'Bloemendaal'
POB 53002, 2505 AA The Hague
The Netherlands.
(*) Lundbeck b.v., Medical Department,
POB 12021, 1100 AA Amsterdam
The Netherlands.

On the emergency department patients suffering from a first psychotic episode or an acute exacerbation of chronic psychosis were treated with zuclopenthixol acetate (ZA) in an open clinical and pharmacokinetic trial. Symptoms had to be severe enough to justify immediate neuroleptic treatment. Informed consent was obtained, if necessary from close relatives. After administration of 100 mg of ZA i.m. clinical and pharmacokinetic data were collected during seven days. Clinical improvement, as measured by BPRS, CGI, UKU side-effects and clinical degree of sedation are presented in relation to daily blood levels of zuclopenthixol.

486
BROMPERIDOL DECANOATE VS. PLACEBO IN RESIDUAL SCHIZOPHRENIA
Bellini L.*, Smeraldi E.*, Virzì A.**, Aguglia E.***
Clinica Psichiatrica III, Università degli Studi, Milano* - Clinica Psichiatrica, Università degli Studi, Catania**/Trieste***, Italia

A double-blind study in 20 patients (10M, 10F, mean age 42 yrs.) has been performed in order to evaluate the stimulating action on social behavior and the safety of bromperidol decanoate (B) compared to placebo (P) in outpatients affected by schizophrenia (residual phase, residual type) who didn't need any sedative treatment. Patients were randomly treated with a standardized dosage of B 150mg or P i.m. every 4 weeks for 6 months. Five patients on P and 2 on B dropped out for impairment of the symptomatology. The Andreasen scale for positive symptoms, the Herz-Melville Questionnaires for the early symptoms for the family and the patient and the BPRS significantly improved at the end of the therapy, whereas the Andreasen scale for negative symptoms, the Schooler-Hogarty SAS and the Quality of Life Scale showed a trend to the improvement of symptoms and behavior. No variations were observed either in HRSD or in body weight. Extrapyramidal side-effects were transient and mild and improved spontaneously or with an anticolinergic drug. B decanoate showed a good normalizing action on social behavior and good safety.

487

BROMPERIDOL DECANOATE VS. FLUPHENAZINE DECANOATE IN SCHIZOPHRENIA

Casacchia M., Di Michele V., Volontè M.V., Rossi A.
Clinica Psichiatrica, Università degli Studi,
L'Aquila, Italia

A double-blind study in 30 patients (18M, 12F, mean age 29.3 yrs.) has been performed in order to evaluate the effectiveness, the safety and the normalizing action on the social behavior of bromperidol decanoate compared to fluphenazine in schizophrenia. Patients were selected according to DSM-III-R diagnostic criteria (Disorganized Type: 5 pt., Paranoid Type: 10 pt., Undifferentiated Type: 15 pt.) and randomly treated with bromperidol decanoate (B) 85mg (50-100mg min-max) or fluphenazine decanoate (F) 30mg (25-50mg min-max) i.m. every 4 weeks for 6 months. The BPRS and the CBS scores significantly improved at the end of the therapy with both treatments (p$<$0.01 ANOVA difference between times); so the CGI scores did. Side-effects, mainly extrapyramidal ones, were more frequent with fluphenazine (86.7%) than with bromperidol (46.7%). Five patients (3B, 3F) dropped out for lack of efficacy of the therapy; one of them (F) for side-effects too. Bromperidol decanoate vs. fluphenazine decanoate showed a good efficacy on the psychotic symptoms, a good normalizing action on social behavior and a better safety with less extrapyramidal side-effects.

488

THERAPEUTIC INDICATION FOR SULPIRIDE

Dr. Graham Sheppard MB BS MRCPsych
Dr. Anthony McCarthy MRCPsych MRCPI
Ticehurst House Hospital,
Ticehurst, East Sussex TN5 7HU,
Great Britain.

Evidence from controlled studies suggests that sulpiride, a substituted benzamide, is of significant value in the treatment of schizophrenia. There is in addition evidence in the literature that sulpiride may be of value in the treatment of other psychiatric conditions, e.g. depressive illness and anxiety states. The authors will present preliminary work to suggest sulpiride may have a special role in the treatment of two further psychiatric conditions: hypomania and the benzodiazepine withdrawal syndrome.

489

High-potential BD treatment in negative schizophrenic symptoms

Ferenc Martényi, M.D., Judit Harangozó, M.D. and Györgyi Vizkeleti

Department of Psychiatry, Semmelweis Medical University Budapest

Investigating 7 acute and 14 chronic cases

Acute cases: All of our 7 patients, diagnosed as schizophrenic according to DSMIII, displayed vital disorder symptoms, severe inhibited state and some catatonic symptoms, 6 of them without any medication for years and the 7th under neuroleptic treatment for over 3 years.
Similarly to ECT, clonazepam administered intravenously radically diminished inhibition symptoms in minutes for a 4-18-hour-long period.
Chronic cases: 14 of our chronic patients received alprazolam or clonazepam. Pretreatment Andreassen /SANS/-scale scores were over 50 points. During the above period, CT and neuropsychological examinations were carried out. To monitor them during a 6-month follow-up period, we used BPRS, SANS, SCL-90 and the Süllwold-scale for schizophrenic symptoms. We regularly checked drug level in blood.

Session 71 Poster Presentation: Delusional states and other psychotic disorders

490

A PROPOS DE LA FOLIE A DEUX

STELLA S. FERIOLI V.
UNIVERSITE' DE FERRARA-CHAIRE DE PSYCHIATRIE-DIR. PROF. RAMELLI E.-FERRARA-ITALIE

L'expression "folie à deux" fait allusion à une configuration psycopathologique qui implique la transmission d'une certaine pathologie psychique d'un sujet porteur de telle pathologie à un autre sujet qui n'est pas cliniquement malade, après une vie en commun souvent prolongée. Cette expression vient de la terminologie psychiatriche de l'Ecole française, tandis que l'Ecole allemande préfère les termes "folie induite" pour indiquer le même phénomène. Sur le plan clinique, généralement, on met en évidence une symptomatologie caractérisée par des convictions délirantes de persécution ou à thème mystique qui surgit, par exemple, dans un conjoint ou dans l'un des membres d'une famille et s'étende à l'un des autres, d'abitude psychologiquement subalterne. Dans le présent travail nous nous demandons si ce phénomène garde dans le moderne psychiatrie une validité clinique et un correspondent encadrement nosographique. Le DSM III-R parle de "Désordre Paranoïde à Plus Personnes" qui surgit à la suite d'une relation très étroite avec une autre personne qui avait déjà un trouble stabilisé avec un délire de persécution. Dans notre travail on fait allusion à des cas étudiés personnellement; cela nous porte à conclure que cette configuration, même si ce n'est pas si fréquent, est toutefois présente dans les observations d'une clinique actuelle.

491
FOLIE A DEUX: SOME CLINICAL OBSERVATIONS

S. RODIGHIERO, I.G. FRACCON, R. ZILIO
Service of Psychiatry, General Hospital
of Montagnana, Montagnana, Padova, ITALY

In this paper we examined the development and the type of delusions in four cases of folie à deux (8 patients). We observed that appearance of delusions was associated with precipitating life events of loss. In our opinion, delusions show to have a function of "stabilizing norm" in familial environment. We think that the kind of relationship between the members of delusional couple is similar to incest relationship. In the latter, individuals show to be reunified according to model of "caste" because they appear unable to reach individuation process. In our cases of folie à deux delusions seemed "social" defenses because their aims were to reinforce "individual" defenses against paranoid and depressive anxiety provoked by separation.

492
DELIRE A DEUX : UN CONCEPT TOUJOURS D'ACTUALITE.

Docteur Ch. BOYER - Docteur D. BOYER
C. H. S. ALLONNES - 72700 FRANCE

Nous confrontons ici les résultats d'une étude personnelle portant sur 60 cas aux données de la littérature classique et de la nosographie moderne. Notre travail est présenté en trois parties :
1/ Revue des conceptions classiques : définitions de la folie communiquée de Lasègue et Falret, de la folie simultanée de Régis, classification de Gralnick.
2/ Place dans la nosographie moderne : C I M-IX, D. S. M.-III, D. S. M.-III-R
3/ Etude clinique :
a)- Méthodologie : Enquête rétrospective réalisée auprès de 205 Psychiatres hospitaliers de l'Ouest de la France permettant de rapporter les cas rencontrés entre 1985 et 1988.
b)- Résultats : 56 % de réponses, l'étude clinique porte sur 60 cas de délire à deux ou à plusieurs, constituant une population de 133 sujets. Un diagnostic correspondant à une psychose délirante chronique (schizophrénique ou non) a été porté pour 67 % des sujets. L'étude concerne aussi les caractéristiques psychopathologiques classiques des groupes délirants et les cadres nosographiques utilisés.
c)- Conclusions : Le phénomène est peut être moins rare que l'on ne croit. Les conditions classiques de survenue de la folie à deux ne sont pas systématiquement retrouvées. Les critères diagnostiques modernes ne recouvrent pas tous les cas collectés.

493
ANALISIS DE LOS CONCEPTOS DELIRANTES CONTENIDOS EN LOS NEOLOGISMOS.

J.C. Martin; A.V. Moríñigo: I. Mateo; D. Noval; I Guajardo.
Hospital Universitario de Valme. Sevilla. España.

Los neologismos y paralogias esquizofrénicas son signos de intensa gravedad en todas las escalas de evaluación del pensamiento-lenguaje (Andreasen,1986; Solovay,1986). El objetivo de este estudio es investigar los procesos psicolingüísticos que los originan. La muestra está formada por 40 esquizofrénicos dividos en 2 grupos de 20: A)Pacientes con neologismos, B)Pacientes con ideas delirantes, pero sin alteraciones del lenguaje El método es un diseño propio, consistente en dividir y reducir mediante la clínica y entrevistas cada neologismo e idea delirante en los conceptos nucleares que expresan. Se estudia a su vez cómo se asocian éstos en 4 protocolos: Rorschach (Exner,1974); Referencia Personal Simbólica (Ruiz Ogara,1975); Diferencial Semántico (Osgood,1976) y Asociación Libre. Los resultados muestran que hay 5 conceptos nucleares que sintetizan los diferentes neologismos y delirios: Dios, Yo, Los Otros, Cuerpo y Familia. Pero en el primer grupo representan el 60% del total, por el 92% en el segundo (P<0.025). Y tambien es diferente el número de pacientes que presentan asociaciones ambivalentes e el grupo neologismos (n=15), comparado al grupo delirante (n=5; P<0.001). Se concluye que los neologismos son neo-signos lingüísticos que los pacientes han debido generar para expresar su gran pluralidad temática y ambivalente delirante.

494
LES ÉTATS DÉLIRANTS DE DÉBUT TARDIF

DIAS-CORDEIRO, José Carlos
Faculty of Medicine of Lisbon, Portugal

L'involution crée un état de vulnérabilité psychologique particulièrement accrue: l'individu se voit confronté avec des pertes successives, réelles ou craintes — perte de l'activité professionelle, de la santé, du conjoint, de l'activité sexuelle, etc — auxquelles s'associe le sentiment de perte des moyens personnels de faire face aux stress internes et externes.
Sur la base de son expérience clinique, l'auteur analyse les conduites délirantes chez l'âgé, notamment celles survenant après 65 ans, depuis les états transitoires et aigus jusqu'aux états chroniques: délire de préjudice, érotomatique, de négation, délires associés à la privation sensorielle, états paranoides et discute la question de la schizophrénie tardive.

495
PSYCHOGENIC STRESS AND PSYCHOSIS

Nikola Ilanković Ph.D. and Dragana Kastratović M.D.
Psychiatric Clinic of the Clinical Centre of the Belgrade Medical Faculty
Yugoslavia

The authors present modern concepts on the pathogenesis of psychobiological adaptive/maladaptive model in a stressogenic situation, where psychogenic stress is accentuated together with the consequences on mental functioning. The available data for this paper is devided into three psychobiological models: 1. Chronobiological, 2. Psychoneuroendocrinological, and 3. Neurophysiological. These models are interpreted in order to get better insight into pathogenesis of the so called reactive psychosis. Possibilities are being contemplated and recommendations are given for a better goal in the pharmaceutical treatment of reactive psychosis.

496
PSYCHOTIC PHANTASIES IN A "FATHERLESS" SOCIETY.

S.F. Inglese, B. Mottola di Amato.
Service of Mental Health-S.Giovanni in Fiore-Italy.

The Authors point out the connexion between the difficult evolution of the psychic organization of a community in Southern Italy and the strong processes of cultural disgregation existing in this social context. Mass emigration and the consequent concrete and symbolic removal of the paternal figure causes a shift of focus on the sole maternal figure which becomes responsible for all parental functions. In such "fatherless" society, instead of the Oedipus phase, an upsetting drama oc=curs. It should fix the unconscious phantasies to the imago of the phallic-persecutor mother. The individual psychic development is constantly threatened by the corruption of the primal phantasies. In first instance they are represented as psycho=tic phantasies: maternal seduction, preoedipal ca=stration and combined parent-ilago. All this weakens the cohesion of the mental apparatus which is easily put into a critical position by the trauma=tic aggression determined by the individual and collective life events.

497
THE SCHIZOAFFECTIVE PSYCHOSES: ROLE OF THE LIMBIC SYSTEM.

Pedro B. Posligua M.D. Serv. de Psiquiatría Hospital Regional del IESS. Guayaquil-Ecuador.

The endogenous and schizoaffective psychoses, are the reflections of disfunction of the anterior limbic regions, more particulary of the orbital-frontal anterior temporal systems. We think that perturbation of the fronto-temporo limbic regions might be responsible for the perceptual, ideational and mood abnormalities that characterize the funcional psychoses.

The evidence reviewed suggests, therefore, that the schizophrenic syndrome is determined by neuronal disorganization-disfunction of the dominant fronto-temporal limbic regions.

The unipolar depresive psychoses and euphoric disturbance of mood appear to be mediated through non-dominant fronto-temporal limbic systems. The verbal motor disinhibition of manía, in the bipolar depressive, imply contralateral perturbation of the dominant frontal system.

Similarly, the evidence shows that the periodic schizoaffective psychoses, from a primary non-dominant fronto-temporal origin, are associated with contra-lateral disorganization in the dominant temporal regions, thereby inducing the schizophrenic symptoms.

Session 72
The dynamics of therapy
Video:

498
THE DYNAMICS OF THERAPY

Jules H. Masserman, M.D.
Past President
American Psychiatric Association

Compartive animal studies and psychiatric-psychoanalytic principles illustrated and interpreted are as follow:

Biodynamics. All behavior is (1) motivated by emerging physiologic needs, (2) genetically and experientially determined, (3) versatile as to goal and modality, (4) subject to aberrations due to motivational uncertainties or conflicts, following which (5) the "neurotic" or "psychotic" deviations can be alleviated either (a) spontaneously or by (b) need satiation, (c) environmental press, (d) mentored re-exploration, (e) group influences, (f) pharmacotherapy and/or (g) cerebral electro-therapy or specific lesions.

Ultimate (UR) Human Aspirations. These are for I-Physical vitality, II-Social securities and III-Existential faiths.

Basic Parameters of Therapy (Seven R's). (1) the Reputation of the therapist; (2) establishment of Rapport; (3) Relief of symptoms; (4) Review of stresses and vulnerabilities; (5) cognitive Reformulations; (6) behavioral Reorientations; and (7) Recapitulations.

Results. Therapeutic techniques using these modalities are variably successful insofar as they meet one or more of the patient's triune Ur-needs as listed above.

Session 73 New Research:
Issues in psychotherapy

499

THE PATIENT THERAPIST RELATIONSHIP AS RELATED TO PSYCHOTHERAPEUTIC OUTCOME
Gudrun Olsson, PhD, Psychology Department
Göteborg University, Box 141 58,
S-400 20 Göteborg, SWEDEN

The purpose of this study was to investigate the patient-therapist relationship during the course of short-term psychotherapy. Eight therapist-patient couples participated in the study. The therapists were trained psychotherapists with five to ten years of clinical experience. The patients showed a variety of neurotic problems. The sessions were audio-recorded and transcribed. After each session the therapist filled out a questionnaire concerning various aspects of the patient-therapist relationship. The transcripts and the answers in the questionnaire were coded by independent judges according to several aspects.
The outcome of the therapies were related to the occurrence of good and bad feed-back relations. In good outcome therapies (four therapies) trust, cooperation and other positive features of the patient-therapist relationship were mutually induced and dominated over negative features. In therapies with a questionable outcome, (two therapies) negative and positive features created an instable relationship. In therapies with a poor outcome (two therapies) negative interactive patterns dominated, where the patient and the therapist negatively influenced each other. A crucial question is how the therapist may be helped to break a vicious circle.

500

THE PSYCHIATRIC PARADIGM AND ITS INTEGRATION IN THE PSYCHOTHERAPEUTIC PROCESS
Dr.med. Wladlen Rosental, private practice,
Neckargemünd,FRG

We are going to present a psychotherapeutic concept based on the psychiatric paradigm of delusion.In the fields of neurosis psychology and normal psychology this paradigm corresponds to the phenomenon of opinion.In the course of successful therapies it was obvious that the ambivalences did not disappear but the patient was able to get aware of them.The neurotic illness seemed to correlate to the patient`s unability of facing his ambivalence intrepidly. Further explorations led to the following results: any person is confronted with two standpoints: A: to be one`s own self; B: to be the other one towards the others. A life-long syneidological process is beginning existing of the experience, standing and creative solution of ambivalences. The patient is evading the original dualis by means of the one-sided formation of opinions or the deformation of the dualis, e.g. -the person being one`s own self but not himself as the other one (1st element of the dualis); -the person being the other one but not himself as his own self (2nd element of the dualis). Depending on the diagnosed dualis therapy is realized in form of a so-called alienation of conciousness, i.e. an enrichment of type B opinions.If the 2nd element predominates a so-called propriation in form of an interchange of type B opinions and an unexpressed living standpoint of propriation is used.The therapist`s personality should encourage the patient to look unblocked at the exposed dualis.

501

Curative Factors in Group Analytic Psychotherapy
Moroyannis Kostas
Hellenic Association of Group Analytic Psychotherapy.

In this paper, we intend to contribute to the empirical research of the curative Factors in Group Analytic Psychotherapy.
In this attempt,we have given Yalom's questionaire of curative Factors to 46 individuals divided in to two groups the group of the sample and the group of the controls.The group of the sample was consisted of 23 individuals who had succesfully terminated their therapy in several outpatient group analytic groups whereas the group of the controls was consisted of 23 individuals who had succesfully terminated their therapy in several outpatient therapeutic groups of a different therapeutic approach. Data derived from both groups were analysed and compared.
Self - understanding,Catharcis,Cohesiveness,Interprersonal learning(input) and Family reenactment were the most important curative Factors for individuals treated in group analytic groups, whereas Instillation of hope,Altruism,Guidance and Identification were found to be the less important factors.
Further more results seem to indicate that group analytic psychotherapy differs significantly from other types of dynamic group therapy in regard to the therapeutic process.

502

VARIABLES IN DISLIKED MEDICAL PATIENTS
R. White, M.D.
Royal Prince Alfred Hospital, Australia.

Whether a therapist likes or dislikes a particular patient will probably have a significant influence on the outcome of therapy. This is a central postulate of liaison psychiatry. This study examines the attitude of six trained nurses in a plasmapheresis unit towards twelve patients, well known to them, suffering from peripheral nerve disease. The nurses were asked to force rank the patients on four variables. The most liked patient was defined as "the one I most like to spending time with". The nurses completed the Problem Patient Questionnaire of McGaghie and Whitenack (P.P.Q.) and were asked to assign a psychiatric diagnosis. The patients were then evaluated by a consultant psychiatrist using a semi-structured interview and MMSE and were assigned a DSM-III-R diagnosis. Tests were employed to measure variables which might correlate with patient dislike. Preliminary results show that: 1. there is considerable rater agreement (interrater reliability) as regards patient dislike (W=0.551) and Problem Patient status (W=0.429), 2. there is significant correlation between the sum of the raters' ranking on like/dislike and the sum of ratings on the P.P.Q. (rho=o.755), 3. there is an association between dislike of particular patients and (a) nurse identification of psychiatric disorder and (b) psychiatric identification of psychiatric disorder (DSM-III-R). It appears that medical patients who merit a psychiatric diagnosis (DSM-III-R) and who rate highly as Problem Patients will be disliked by therapists.

503

THERAPEUTIC ALLIANCE AS A PREDICTOR OF TREATMENT AND OF OUTCOME IN 89 PATIENTS
N. Aapro, G. Scariati, M.Y. Gognalons, A. Andreoli
Institutions Universitaires de Psychiatrie, Genève, Suisse

Consecutive outpatients have been included in a prospective study to evaluate the processus of treatment assignment and therapeutic outcome. Three main factors have been evaluated: the quality of the first encounter (therapeutic alliance by global indicators); socio- demographic data (age, sex, socio-cultural level); diagnostic elements, according to DSM III (axis I and II). The senior psychiatrist who conducted the first interview was independent of consecutive therapeutic processus. Eighty-nine new outpatients were seen in 10 months at one public consultation facility. Thirty-four patients were not treated here (simple certificate requests, toxicomaniacs, etc.). For the 55 remaining patients, the elements associated with the decision to treat were, initial prediction of improvement (p .000), patient's expectation of help from treatment (p .004) axis I diagnosis (schizophrenic or major affective disorder), sex, nationality. Twenty out of 55 treatments were psychotherapies. Factors predicting psychotherapy assignment were, in order of importance: all the indicators of therapeutic alliance; axis II diagnosis (less psychotherapy assignment to the personality disorders); good educational level, age less than 30. At the 3 month follow-up, a poor initial therapeutic alliance was significantly associated with poor evolution and clearly associated with early drop-outs. We conclude that improvement of outcome and prevention of drop-outs, may be achieved stressing the first therapeutic contact's quality on any psychiatric training programme.

504

TIME AND SELF AFTER CORONARY ARTERY BYPASS SURGERY. Herman C.B. Denber, M.D., Ph.D., Department of Psychiatry, School of Medicine, So.Illinois University, Springfield, Illinois,USA

It is speculated that with cardioplegia during CABG surgery, symbolic death occurs and temporal perception ceases. Following cardiac arrest of varied etiology, clinical death is often followed by a "rebirth" with return of consciousness. After CABG surgery, a 24-48 hour period disappears for which there is no time recall. Healthy postoperative personality changes have been reported as the patient sees the self in a new light, wanting to "do good for others", and speaking of a "profound emotional experience". The preoperative CABG patientmay experience changes in body image, since the clinical symptoms make them feel "different". To some degree, after CABG surgery, they live on "borrowed time".For those who have brushed death, life begins to assume other meanings. In consonance with symbolic death, time stops as biological temporality does, in the here and now death. Time is eternal and death but another form of the eternal existance of which life is but one short phase. The symbolic death is followed by a rebirth with consequent changes in perception, subjective conceptions of the past, review of the present, and more appropriate attitudes to the future. The personal biological clock now slows down

Session 74 Symposium:
Ancient Greek thought and its contribution to psychiatry

505

THE PLATONIC THEORY OF ANAMNESIS: ONTOLOGICAL AND EMISTEMOLOGICAL CONSIDERATIONS

Moutsopoulos E., Greece

506

ANCIENT GREEK CONCEPTS OF MIND AND MADNESS

B. Simon, M.D., Cambridge Hospital, Cambridge, Massachusetts, U.S.A.

Ancient Greek concepts on mind and mental disease are presented here.
The poetic, the philosophical and the medical models of mind and madness are considered in connection with contemporary psychiatric thought.

507

Hesiod inspires S. Freud to describe infantile sexuality
N. Nicolaidis
Société Suisse de Psychanalyse

L'evolution psychosexuelle décrite par S. Freud en comparaison avec l'évolution de la cosmogonie - théogonie d'Hesiode.
De la relation primaire et archaique entre Gaia - Ouranos jusqu'à la domination "oedipienne" de dieux olympiens.
Gaia nomme Ouranos comme père par l'intermediaire de Cronos et elle prepare le regne de Zeus "au nom du Père".

508

ARISTOTLE AND MELANCHOLY

Giuseppe ROCCATAGLIATA
Department of Neurology, Genoa University
Via De Toni, 5 - 16132, GENOA, Italy

Aristotle's theory, according to Hippocrates, states that depressive diseases originate from "black bile". However the physician from Cos admitted the action of the "yellow bile" also. Therefore the aetiology of both melancholy and mania was unified by Aristotle. Depressive symptoms, ranging form melancholy to mania, always originated from variable temperature of black bile.
In Plato's opinion divine influence was needed for human creativeness: talented and ingenous people were needed of divine forces; demon of creativeness, was identified, by Aristotle, in "physis". Habitus melancholicus is specific of creative humans. We can finally think that melancoly, which is depending on the presence of black bile, is to be found in what as the source of creative intelligence.

509

MENTAL ILLNESS IN ANCIENT MEDICINE

Kotsopoulos S., M.D.
University of Ottawa, Ottawa, Canada.

Ancient medicine, a child of the Ionian intellect, understood and treated mental illness along rational and empirical lines. Hippocrates and other physicians of his age observed and described the symptoms of mental illness and the behavior of the mentally ill. They also speculated about the biological substratum of the illness. Over the following few centuries the concepts of mental illness evolved until Soranus and Aretaeus in the 2nd and 3rd century A.D. presented a nosology very similar to each other. The treatment proposed by the ancient physicians was primarily biological. It was consistent with their view that the pathology of mental illness was biological. Compared to biological factors, psychosocial factors were considered not equally important in the pathogenesis of mental illness.

510

PSYCHE AND ITS DISORDERS : THE ANCIENT HELLENIC VIEW

C.N.Ballas, Assoc. Professor, Athens University Medical School, Athens, Greece.

Ancient Greek thinkers, as Alcmaeon of Croton, Plato, Aristotle, the Hipoocratic writers and Aretaeus of Cappadocea, developed a variety of conceptual systems regarding the organization of the psyche and introduced inspiring notions to its deringent. These notions are presented in the context of contemporary schools of thought in Psychiatry. The ideas of ancient Greek thinkers frequently appear modern, vivid and moving for novel developments in our field.

Session 75   Symposium:
Today and future of prison psychiatry

511

TODAY AND FUTURE OF PRISON PSYCHIATRY IN CANADA
A. N. Singh, M.D. Hamilton Psychiatric Hospital
Box 585, Hamilton, Ontario, Canada

Prison psychiatry in Canada is a joint responsibility of federal and provincial governments. Psychiatric management in federal prison services is carried through established prison hospitals of high calibre. The Director General coordinates and guides the multidisciplinary staff of these hospitals. Provincial prison services, in comparison, hires psychiatrist, physician, nurses and psychologist usually on a sessional basis to manage the psychiatric needs of inmates. Every province has a psychiatric service director who coordinates and guides the multidisciplinary staff. Future of prison psychiatry in federal area, at best on paper, is stimulating and exciting but very much under funded. The present day therapy in psychiatric areas are already changing remarkably with the guidance of proliferatory research activities and if prison psychiatry fails to keep pace with either future research activities or future expanding psychiatric therapy then option will be only of warehousing the human being rather than making them rehabilitated and independent persons. Future need of prison psychiatry should be guided on the principle of bringing out the best from mentally ill inmates by controlling their psychiatric disorder and giving them a chance to live an independent, productive and satisfying life.

512

TODAY AND FUTURE OF PRISON PSYCHIATRY IN FRANCE

Dr.Pierre Lamothe, Psychiatrist, Head of "Service medico-phsychologique Regional Prison de Lyon", Lyon, Cedex 2, France

Psychiatry has always had a special place in French prisons with a special status of the practicians who belonged to the Health Administration and not to the Penitentiary Administration with the aim of keeping their independence and the patients' confidence. This status was denied to the general practioners and other specialists. There was no institutional alternative in France to Prison and Psychiatric Hospital and insane inmates were supposed to be cured in Public Psychiatric Hospitals. Some experience however has been developed to solve practical daily problems raising with more and more psychotics in jail like in most countries. A Public Service of Psychiatry in prison has been elaborated and we have since 1986 new laws and organization which offer a good answer to the present needs. Regional Services established on the model of the Public Service of Psychiatry in the free community are in charge of mental health care in prisons with facilities inside the prison itself. Developing these services has led the psychiatrists and the Administration to face some new problems which are exposed in the paper. Right to speach given to the detainees and new standards of care have led some hidden symptoms to develop and appeal for new practices.

513

TODAY AND FUTURE OF PRISON PSYCHIATRY IN JAPAN

Tsutomu Sakuta M.D., Keio University, 35 Shinanomachi, Shinjuku-ku, Tokyo, Japan

The psychiatric treatment performed in prisons in Japan has already reached a certain level. Differences are seen according to the scale of institutions. In general larger scaled prisons are assigned with higher number of medical staff. In order to evaluate psychiatric treatment, it is necessary to discuss the purpose and outline of the prison itself. The purpose and functions of a prison are described below. 1) Retributive punishment to the prisoner himself, 2) Isolation for the public security, 3) Exemplary punishment (for the prevention of other persons to commit a crime), 4) Education and treatment (stimulant drugs, physical diseases, etc), 5) Shelter for those with inability of social adaptation. It may be said that the importance may be and should be changing gradually from 1) to 4) with cultural progression of the mankind. However, the present state is not satisfying. There are many problems remaining to be solved concerning psychiatric treatment such as treatment of those who refuse treatment, following up of prisoners after their release, and effects of New Mental Health Act enacted in July 1988. I will report countermeasures against these problems and make a review of them.

514

TODAY AND FUTURE OF PRISON PSYCHIATRY FOR CHILDREN AND YOUTHS
Joji Inomata, M.D., Kosuke Yamazaki, M.D., TOKAI University School of Medicine, Ryuzo Tsuji, Kokufu Institute for Training and Education of Juvenile Delinquents, Masanori Kobayashi, Fujisawa Central Child Guidance Clinic, Tsutomu Sakuta, Keio University
Boseidai Isehara City Kanagawa Pref. 259-11,JAPAN

The Number of Juvenile Delinquents detaind by police for shoplifting, motor or bicycle theft, and glue sniffing, reached its highest level since the World War II in 1980, while the level has fluctuated up and down between 1981 and 1988,somewhat below the peak level of 1980. Closer examination of statistics showed that the actual number of detainees between 14 and 18 years of age was 187, 172 in 1988. The Juvenile Delinquents currently undergoing treatment and training both in Japan and other countries and in the K Institute in Kanagawa prefecture will be discussed. The institute is located south of Tokyo. The inmates were sent from Japan National Child Guidance Clinics (The K Institute for the training and correction of Juvenile Delinquents, established in 1900, has a holding capacity of male offenders). We have been interviewing and treating psychopharmacologically, since 1975 at the K Institute. Based on statistics in Japan and other countries and those obtained from the K Institute, the current methods of therapy, as well as planned changes in therapy will be discussed.

Session 76 Symposium:
Basic symptoms: Newer results of psychiatric research

515

EARLY RECOGNITION OF IDIOPATHIC PSYCHOSES

J. Klosterkötter, G. Gross, G. Huber, M. Gnad

Psychiatric University Clinic Bonn, FRG

We report on the conception and first results of a new project of research orientated on basic symptoms. Part 1 of this project deals with a subsequent prospective study of 338 patients with personality disorders and neuroses according DSM-III-R-criteria. This sample was chosen from 648 patients examined with the "Bonn Scale for the Assessment of Basic Symptoms" (BSABS), PSE and a battery of psychologic tests in the Bonn Psychiatric Clinic between 1970 and 1988.

Up to now it could be shown in the re-examinations: 1. that patients with basic symptoms have developed psychoses significantly more often than patients without basic symptoms in the index examination, and 2. that the patients having developed psychoses have shown, significantly more often, basic symptoms of the BSABS categories C.1, C.2, C.3 and D in the index examination. This means that basic symptoms relevant for that development are composed of certain cognitive thought, perception, motor disturbances and cenesthesias.

These first results give good reason for supposing that by the analysis of basic symptoms in neuroses and personality disorders a certain group with an increased risk of psychosis can be detected.

516

RELIABILITY OF THE PSYCHOPATHOLOGICAL DOCUMENTATION SCHEME BSABS.

H.H. Stassen*, G. Gross**, G. Huber**, J. Klosterkötter**, M. Linz**

Psychiatric Hospitals *Zurich and **Bonn

Based on the experiences of our investigations into the determinants, the course and the long-term outcome of schizophrenia, we have developed a psychopathological documentation scheme BSABS which has been particularly designed to meet the specific requirements of psychiatric research. This documentation scheme comprises a total of 105 items covering 5 major psychopathological areas plus 1 additional category of items addressing the patient's ability to consciously compensate the illness. In order to test the interrater reliability of the instrument, we have carried out a study with 2 independently assessed groups of n=28 recently hospitalized patients, and a group of r=8 raters who have been specifically trained on the instrument under investigation. All possible pairwise combinations of raters have been made. The statistical method and the results will be demonstrated. All in all, the chosen approach to interrater reliability demonstrated not only the efficiency of the BSABS documentation scheme, but also gave valuable insight into the structural properties of the instrument.

517

Phenomenological aspects and the measurement of basic symptoms in Schizophrenia.
R. SCHÜTTLER
Bezirkskrankenhaus Günzburg, Department of Psychiatrie II, University of Ulm, FRG (Head: Prof.Dr.R. Schüttler)

Basic symptoms in schizophrenia are defined as non-characteristic symptoms, which are experienced and communicated by the patients themselves. These symptoms may be amazingly similar to the symptomatology of certain organic brain syndromes.
Lacking a proper instrument for operational documentation of the basic symptoms we constructed the Günzburg-Self-Rating-Scale for Basic Symptoms (GSBS). Special categories are "dynamic deficiencies", "cognitive disturbances of thought" and "cognitive disturbances of perception".
Construction of the scale included creating the items, selection of items and evaluation of reliability and validity. We demonstrated a good reliability of the new test instrument. A pretest demonstrated also a valid differentiation between schizophrenic and neurotic patients, a further study is done to replicate these preliminary results. The factor analysis showed a good differentiation of the 3 hypothetical categories of basic symptomatology.
Providing a reliable and valid test instrument for rating basic symptoms makes it possible also for other investigators, to replicate results regarding the theoretically and practically important basic symptoms.

518

COGNITIVE BASIC SYMPTOMS IN AFFECTIVE PSYCHOSES

H. Ebel, G. Gross, J. Klosterkötter, G. Huber

Psychiatric University Clinic Bonn, FRG

Basic symptoms are not specific in the sense that they are exclusively noticed in the course of schizophrenic psychoses. They do occur, too, in definable cerebral illnesses, schizoaffective psychoses and endogenous depressions. As to the depressive patients, it was possible to show (GROSS 1986) that basic symptoms originally described in regard to schizophrenias (HUBER 1966, 1983, 1986) can partly also be found, though at a different frequency, among patients in endogenous depressive phases. This led to the following questions: Do the basic symptoms, which play a prominent part in the development of florid psychotic (productive) symptomatology, occur in endogenous depressive phases at a quantitatively lower frequency, and/or are those basic symptoms qualitatively different or not at all represented? The study compares schizophrenic and affective psychoses with regard to basic symptoms. 30 patients in schizophrenic pre-, intra- and postpsychotic basic stages and 30 patients in endogenous depressive phases were examined according to the "Bonn Scale for the Assessment of Basic Symptoms" (BSABS). The most important result is that certain cognitive basic symptoms and cenesthesias which are decisive for the development of florid productive-psychotic phenomena are found more frequently in the group of schizophrenias than in affective psychoses.

519

DISTURBANCES OF BODY SENSE AS A BASIC SYMPTOM OF IDIOPATHIC PSYCHOSES

G. Huber, G. Gross, J. Klosterkötter

Psychiatric University Clinic Bonn, FRG

The disturbances of body sense and equilibrium in idiopathic and especially schizophrenic psychoses were described in context with the delineation of bodily sensations of the cenesthetic type of schizophrenia (HUBER 1957) and in the "Bonn Scale for the Assessment of Basic Symptoms" as type 11 of cenesthesias (GROSS et al. 1987). These pseudo-vestibular sensations are characterized, just as other cenesthesias and cognitive thought and perception disorders, by a peculiar kind of experience. The psychopathological and clinical criteria of these phenomena are described on the basis of self-reports of 200 patients with schizophrenic diseases in prepsychotic (prodromes and outpost syndromes) and postpsychotic basic stages. Psychopathologically identical symptoms in organic brain diseases were found mainly in observations of lesions in the area of limbic system. Based on our findings is shown that these phenomena are psychopathologically different from vestibular and psychogenic dizziness phenomena. The nosological and therapeutic consequences and the meaning of these disturbances of body sense and other cenesthesias and central-vegetative disorders in idiopathic psychoses for the basic symptom concept are discussed.

Session 77 Special Session: Psychodynamic treatments of children and adolescents

520

HOLDING & FACILITATING: FAMILIES & THERAPEUTIC AGENCIES

Stephen Fleck, M.D., Yale University, New Haven, Connecticut 06519 USA

The late Donald Winnicott coined the term "holding environment" to denote one of the important maternal and family tasks. "Holding" can be tangible or intangible. For instance, mother-infant interaction which includes "reading the infant" as to its needs or discomforts, or therapeutic environments where a patient feels helped by being understood regarding his or her needs or moods without overt or explicit communication. "Holding" may be tangible as with a child experiencing a temper tantrum or patients prone to behave destructively, but more important in all human situations is "holding" through relationship power. This involves a need-compliance balance between unequals where it is important for one person to heed direction or needs of another despite the first person's wishes or impulses to the contrary.

"Holding" must be combined with facilitation if growth and development are to occur be that personal growth or advancing group tasks and interests. Growth promotion and caring in the family means learning one's language, making the "reading" explicit and in agencies or treatment services, furthering individual development. In therapeutic agencies facilitation entails patient's restoration to a prior level of functioning or habilitation and rehabilitation designed to recoup illness-induced deficits or stagnation.

521

REFLEXIONS SUR LES INTERACTIONS FAMILIALES DANS L'ANOREXIE MENTALE : A PROPOS DE L'EXPERIENCE D'UN GROUPE DE PARENTS.

M-T MALTESE : HOPITAL ROBERT DEBRE - Service de Psychopathologie de l'Enfant et de l'Adolescent - Pr. DUGAS - Paris. FRANCE

O. HALFON - J. LAGET - Clinique Médico-Psychologique - Fondation Santé des Etudiants de France. Neufmoutiers-en-Brie. FRANCE.

Depuis sa distinction syndromique, l'anorexie mentale a été rattachée à des entités nosographiques multiples.

Sa complexité psychopathologie décrite par les cliniciens, sa survenue à des périodes différentes de la vie, ont orienté la réflexion sur le contexte psychofamilial dans lequel l'anorexie mentale apparait. S'agirait-il d'un trouble lié à des carences précoces de l'environnement ? De l'expression d'un conflit psychique en rapport à des modèles identificatoires sexuels ? D'une interaction pathologique parents/enfants ? Ce phénomène psyché/soma reste difficile à cerner.

Au cours du traitement des jeunes adolescents hospitalisés pour anorexie mentale dans le Service de Psychopathologie de l'enfant et de l'adolescent du Professeur DUGAS, à l'hôpital Hérold, nous avons constaté qu'il fallait nécessairement inclure les parents dans le projet thérapeutique pour qu'une amélioration survienne. Dans cet objectif, nous avons créé un groupe de parents à visée thérapeutique partielle.

Nous définirons d'abord les options prises pour la constitution de ce groupe. Ensuite, nous décrirons ses modalités, son évolution et sa justification. Nous étudierons aussi les mécanismes psychiques qui semblent caractériser ses familles.

522

"La demande de l'enfant en psychanalyse"
"The Demand of a Child in Psycho-Analysis"
Xavier RENDERS
Service de Psychiatrie, Département de Pédopsych.
Université Catholique de Louvain - Belgique

Un enfant souffre-t-il de ses difficultés ? Attend-il quelque chose de la rencontre avec le psychanalyste proposée par ses parents ou par d'autres personnes ? Perçoit-il ce qu'une telle rencontre peut offrir de singulier ?

De quelle manière une cure psychanalytique est-elle présentée à un enfant ? Quelle importance accorde-t-on à son acceptation ou à son refus ? A quels signes peut-on repérer l'engagement d'un enfant dans le travail analytique ?

Voilà quelques unes des questions que la recherche se propose de soulever et d'examiner à travers l'histoire de la psychanalyse d'enfants. Pour l'essentiel, le travail étudie et commente les termes dans lesquels les principaux auteurs praticiens s'interrogent sur "la demande" de l'enfant, et la place qu'ils lui accordent dans leur théorie et dans leur pratique (S. Freud pour "Le Petit Hans"; H. Hug - Hellmuth, A. Freud, M. Klein, D. Winnicott, S. Lebovici et R. Diatkine, F. Dolto).

L'auteur expose aussi sa propre définition du concept de "demande" dans la consultation et la cure d'enfant. Il rassemble brièvement ses convictions actuelles sur la position subjective de l'enfant dans le travail analytique, fondées sur sa pratique personnelle.

523

CRISIS INTERVENTION WITH THE TEAM OF THE INPATIENT PSYCHIATRIC UNIT: A THERAPEUTIC TEAM IN CRISIS
D.Anagnostopoulos, A.Voutsas, I.Tsiantis
Children's Hospital "Aghia Sophia", Department of Child Psychiatry, Athens, Greece

The two years experience of the therapeutic team of the unit for short-term treatment of the Department of Child Psychiatry at the Children's Hospital "Aghia Sophia" is presented.
This experience is discussed in relation to the formation of the identity of the therapeutic team, within its successive crises of the various stages of its development.
The relationship of the team is examined in relation to:
1. The setting, that is towards the triptych Department of Child Psychiatry, the General Hospital, the National Health Care System
2. Its own history
3. Its clinical experience that is the work with the child and the family in crisis
4. The supervision from outside consultants
In this paper we will attempt to discuss the maturity of the therapeutic team as a proccess of the development of identity, common therapeutic language, acceptance of the various roles and finally the common therapeutic position in the setting of milieu therapy which is defined each time by its effectiveness.

524

HOW DO OUR ILLNESSES,SEPARATIONS,LOSSES AND AGING EFFECT OUR PRACTICES?
Belinda C. Straight,M.D.
Faculty,George Washington University,College of Medicine and Children's Hospital National Medical Center,Washington,D.C.,U.S.A.

A psychiatrist and psychoanalyst questions the impact on work with particular patients of her own life experiences with illness,aging, separations and deaths.Calling on memories, dreams,countertransference issues,and patients' observations and critiques,she tries to understand how the therapeutic work was impeded or enhanced and deepened by the handling of these themes.The following are taken up:1)congenital defects,2)loss of limb,3)operations,4)accidents 5)personal illness6)illness of one's child,7) divorce,8)death in the family,9)death of friends 10)aging,and 11)facing one's own mortality.

The autobiographical model is highly recommended as a useful personal guide for the therapist while working with a patient in a crisis of loss or death.

525

INTERACTION PRÉCOCE MÈRE-ENFANT CHEZ L'ADOLESCENTE ET LA FEMME ADULTE
DIAS-CORDEIRO, José ; GONÇALVES, Maria José
Faculty of Medicine of Lisbon, Portugal

Des situations de grossesse et accouchement chez l'adolescente et la femme adulte sont analisées sur la base de l'expérience clinique de l'auteur. La capacité d'investir l'enfant dépend, d'une part, des circonstances et conditions de vie de la femme et, d'autre part, du niveau de son développement psichossexuel. La question de l'importance du contact visuel et cutanée mère-enfant juste après l'accouchement est discutée.
L'expérience de l'auteur prouve que la maturité psychologique de la femme, soit-t-elle adolescente ou adulte, est l'élément le plus important pour l'établissement d'une relation mère-enfant structurante et pour le développement harmonieux de l'enfant.

Session 78 Special Session:
Expreimental pharmacology II

526

REGIONAL DISTRIBUTION OF ^{3}H-PAROXETINE, ^{3}H-CITALOPRAM AND ^{3}H-IMIPRAMINE BINDING IN HUMAN BRAIN.
Per Plenge and Erling T Mellerup.
Psychochemistry Institute. University of Copenhagen. Rigshospitalet. Blegdamsvej 9. 2100 Ø. Copenhagen. Denmark.
Regional distribution of the serotonin transport complex was studied in 12 different brain areas from human brains. The serotonin uptake complex was measured with ^{3}H-paroxetine, ^{3}H-citalopram and ^{3}H-imipramine. The binding site density was highest in the nucleus of raphé, medium in the basal ganglia, and lowest in cortical areas. The specific binding measured with ^{3}H-paroxetine and ^{3}H-citalopram was compared with the high affinity ^{3}H-imipramine binding determined with either 100 µM 5HT or 1 µM imipramine as non specific displacers. ^{3}H-paroxetine and ^{3}H-citalopram allowed a more precise determination of B_{max}, than ^{3}H-imipramine did, but the B_{max}, determined with all three ligands, were within the same range in the individual samples.
Protease digestion of brain membranes showed that the binding site measured with all three ligands disappeared with the same rate as other membrane proteins, and not faster as might be expected from the litterature.
Left/right hemisphere distribution was measured in cortical tissue from 6 brains using ^{3}H-paroxetine. No difference between the two hemispheres was found. In one brain from a lithium treated patient a very low binding was measured, possibly indicating that the lithium treatment had decreased the serotonin uptake mechanism.

527

EFFECTS OF AMPEROZIDE, A PUTATIVE ANTIPSYCHOTIC DRUG, ON RAT MIDBRAIN DOPAMINE NEURONS RECORDED IN VIVO

T.H. Svensson, J. Grenhoff, C.-S. Tung, L. Ugedo
Department of Pharmacology, Karolinska Institutet, S-104 01 Stockholm, Sweden

The effect of the putative antipsychotic compound amperozide on the electrical activity of single identified midbrain dopamine (DA) neurons was investigated in the chloral hydrate anesthetized male rat. While the activity of DA cells in the substantia nigra was unaffected, DA neurons of the ventral tegmental area (VTA), the origin of the mesolimbocortical DA system, were affected in either of two ways: 1) increased firing rate and burst firing, i.e. an excitation, or 2) regularization of the firing pattern. Reversible cold inactivation of the medial prefrontal cortex (PFC) induced a pacemaker-like firing of VTA-DA cells, an effect blocked by amperozide in the cells excited by the drug. Cells responding with a regularization were not protected against the effect of PFC inactivation. These different effects of amperozide, which may in part be mediated by $5-HT_2$ receptor blockade, suggest an antipsychotic activity of amperozide, particularly in schizophrenia with negative symptoms.

528

PHARMACOLOGICAL SENSITIZATION TO INTERMITTENT NEUROLEPTIC TREATMENT
Glenthøj B, Bolwig TG, Hemmingsen R., Depts. Psych. Rigshospitalet & Bispebjerg Hsp., Copenhagen, Denm.

The importance of treatment schedule of neuroleptics in the development of tardive dyskinesia (TD) is of clinical relevance. The kindling phenomenon represents an example of the effect of multiplicity of neuronal plasticity. It bears resemblance to pharmacological sensitization. We have treated 85 rats discontinuously (DIS) or continuously (CON) with haloperidol (HAL) or zuclopenthixol (ZU) for 15 weeks. During and after treatment, we observed vacuous chewing movements (VCM) and tongue protrusions (TP). All HAL-treated animals showed an early rise in VCM. The rise during medication was less pronounced in ZU-treated rats. The change disappeared a few days after termination of CON medication. Remarkably, the significant change in DIS treated rats persisted 11 weeks after withdrawal. Only DIS treated animals developed a rise in the number of TP. After termination of medication HAL-treated rats were electrically kindled in amygdala. The results suggest a cross-sensitivity between DIS HAL-treatment and amygdala-kindling. The reversible increase in VCM seen from the first week of HAL-treatment might result from D1-receptor preponderance according to blockade of D2-receptors; this may be a model of acute dyskinesia. The persisting rise in VCM and TP observed only in DIS treated rats is suggested to be an animal model of TD. This is reconcilable with the hypothesis of a kindling-like sensitization to the dyskinetic side-effects of neuroleptic drugs.

529

THE EFFECTS OF DOPAMINE D-1 AND D-2 RECEPTOR AGONISTS AND ANTAGONISTS UPON MONKEYS.
L. Peacock, H. Lublin, J. Gerlach.
Sct. Hans Hospital, DK-4000 Roskilde, Denmark.

The effects of dopamine D-1 and D-2 receptor agonists and antagonists were studied in 8 Cebus apella monkeys.

SKF 81297 (full D-1 agonist) induced oral hyperkinesia of variable intensity ($P<0.01$), some of the monkeys developing extreme lip smacking, tongue protrusions and licking movements, others only slight lip movements. Combination treatment with LY 171555 (full D-2 agonist) or SCH 23390 (D-1 antagonist) inhibited the oral hyperkinesia induced by SKF 81297 ($P<0.01$, $P<0.02$, respectively).

Racloprid (D-2 antagonist) did not statistically change oral hyperkinesia ($P<0.2$), although 5 monkeys showed increased oral movements, mainly those with pre-existing hyperkinesia.

Treatment with SCH 23390 or racloprid resulted in an identical dystone/cataleptic syndrome. SKF 81297 inhibited the dystonia induced by SCH 23390, while the study was inconclusive in regards to the effect upon racloprid-dystonia.

The investigation indicates that oral dyskinesia may be related to an imbalance in D-1 receptor and D-2 receptor stimulation in favor of D-1. The question is now whether D-1 antagonists, which may have antipsychotic potential, will produce tardive dyskinesia upon long-term use.

530

DOPAMINE UPTAKE SITES IN RAT AND HUMAN BRAIN

Jan Marcusson, Per Allard and Svante Ross*
Dept of Geriatric Medicine, University of Umeå, S-901 87 Umeå and Dept of Pharmacology, Astra Aläb* AB, S-151 85 Södertälje, SWEDEN

Radioligand binding with the dopamine uptake inhibitor (3H)GBR12935 to human and rat brain tissue was characterized. The binding revealed multiple components. Only the binding sensitive to 1 mM dopamine or 0.3 μM mazindol was regarded as specific binding in the human brain. This binding fraction was competitively inhibited by the addition of dopamine or mazindol. The binding was only detected in subcortical areas with apparent affinities of 1-1.5 nM. The binding densities (Bmax, fmol/mg protein) were 1700 in caudate nucleus, 1900 in putamen, 900 in the olfactory tubercle and 300 in pars compacta of the substantia nigra. The (3H)GBR12935 binding was also studied in human putamen with respect to aging: 20 post-mortem samples between 19-100 years. There was a 70% loss of binding sites over this age range, no changes in Kd and no no alterations related to post-mortem storage time. It is suggested that this decrease of (3H)GBR12935 binding sites reflects a loss of dopaminergic neurites in the putamen.
(3H)GBR12935 binding was also studied in rats that had been chronically (3 weeks) treated with dopamine uptake inhibitors, neuroleptics and dopamine agonists. There were no alterations of the binding after these treatments.

531

D-1 DOPAMINE ANTAGONISTS IN SCHIZOPHRENIA
Jes Gerlach, Henrik Lublin and Linda Peacock
Sct. Hans Hospital, Dept. P, 4000 Roskilde, Denmark

Are D-1 antagonists new potential antipsychotics? Unfortunately, no selective D-1 dopamine drugs are available for clinical use. Therefore, the question will be discussed on the basis of studies in Cebus monkeys.

1. In acute administration, the D-1 antagonist SCH 23390 and the D-2 antagonist raclopride induce an identical dystonic-dyskinetic syndrome. In both cases, biperiden (an anticholinergic drug) and LY 171555 (a selective D-2 agonist) counteract the syndrome.

2. A full D-1 agonist (SKF 81297) causes oral dyskinesia, grooming and slight activation, but no anxiety or stereotypies. In contrast, a D-2 agonist induces no oral dyskinesia, but marked arousal and body stereotypies (psychotic-like behavior).

3. During long-term administration of SCH 23390, it was possible to gradually increase the dose 3-4 fold over a 2-month period without increasing the risk of dystonia. In contrast, it was necessary to reduce the dose of raclopride during long-term treatment. Furthermore, it was observed that SCH 23390 induced more sedation than raclopride. Following long-term treatment with SCH 23390, a D-1 behavioral supersensitivity could be observed.

The marked differences between D-1 and D-2 antagonists and the potential clinical implications of these observations will be discussed in relation to the treatment of schizophrenia and extrapyramidal syndromes including tardive dyskinesia.

532

BIOCHEMICAL BASIS FOR A LOADING DOSE THERAPY WITH THE ANTIPSYCHOTIC SAVOXEPINE.
S. Bischoff, J. Krauss, K. Stoecklin and M. Heinrich. CIBA-GEIGY Ltd., CH-4002 Basel, Switzerland.
Savoxepine (SAVOX) is a potent blocker of dopamine (DA) D_2 receptors, with a higher selectivity for those in hippocampus (HIPP) than in striatum (STRI). Another of its properties is a much longer duration of DA receptor occupancy in HIPP than in STRI. By comparison, haloperidol (HAL) (at the same dose) had a shorter duration of action than SAVOX, with no such a difference between HIPP and STRI. With these properties of SAVOX, we hypothesized that a larger dissociation between receptor occupancy in HIPP vs STRI could be achieved using a loading dose therapy. Thus, after a first injection of a high dose of drug (3 mg/kg i.p.) and a wash-out period of 48 h, rats were treated with a maintenance dose of 0.3 mg/kg i.p. for 10 days. We measured DA receptor occupancy by means of the inhibition of (^{3}H)-spiperone binding 2 and 24 h after each treatment. After SAVOX a steady state was rapidly reached with the maintenance treatment leading to a receptor occupancy of 90 and 40 % in HIPP, and 50 and 10 % in STRI respectively 2 and 24 h after treatment. No such dissociation was seen with HAL at any time (80 and 10 % in HIPP; 60 and 0 % in STRI). Therefore, it is expected that such a loading dose treatment would increase the dissociation between antipsychotic efficacy of SAVOX and occurence of extrapyramidal side effects, and reduce the onset of action in schizophrenics.

Session 79 Special Session:
Side-effects of antipsychotic drugs

533

A TEN-YEAR FOLLOW-UP STUDY OF TARDIVE DYSKINESIA

Lawrence Annable, Guy Chouinard, Andree Ross-Chouinard, Naomi Holobow

Allan Memorial Institute, Louis-H. Lafontaine Hospital and McGill University, Montreal, Canada

We report the results of a ten-year follow-up study of tardive dyskinesia (TD) in a cohort of neuroleptic-treated schizophrenic outpatients at the Allan Memorial Institute, Montreal. The patients were treated under carefully standardized conditions during this period and were assessed by the same neurologist and psychiatrist in 1975, 1980 and 1985. Of a total of 256 patients who were surveyed for extrapyramidal symptoms in 1975, 169 patients were reassessed in 1980, and 101 in 1985. In 98 patients who were assessed on each of the three occasions, the prevalence of TD meeting the Schooler and Kane research criteria was 21% in 1975, 38% in 1980 and 56% in 1985. Multiple logistic regression analysis revealed that the principle risk factors for TD were advanced age, poor schizophrenic prognosis and vulnerability to parkinsonism. An association was also found between duration of treatment and severity of the disorder. These findings suggest an annual incidence rate of TD in neuroleptic-treated schizophrenic outpatients of approximately 3%, and that certain subgroups of patients are more at risk for the disorder than others.

534

TWO TYPES OF TARDIVE DYSKINESIA IN NEUROLEPTIC TREATED SCHIZOPHRENICS?
Falkai P, Bogerts B, Tapernon-Franz U,
* Maitenyi K, Klieser E, Tegeler J
Department of Psychiatry, University of Duesseldorf, D-4000 Duesseldorf 12
* Department of Neuropathology, Institute of Mental Health, 1083 Budapest, Hungary

Basal ganglia and the cholinergic and gabaergic system seem to dysfunction in neuroleptic treated patients with tardive dyskinesia. Histological classification of the substantia nigra for neuronal loss and gliosis as well as immunocytochemical staining for Substance P and Methionine-Encephaline were performed on post-mortem material of 8 neuroleptic treated schizophrenic patients with and 12 without tardive dyskinesia. Differing from older patients, schizophrenics with dyskinesia under 40 years of age had a visible Substance P deficit but almost no histological changes in the substantia nigra. These results are discussed in view of recent immunohistochemical findings indicating a Chorea-Huntington-like process underlying the etiology in the under 40 age groupe and a Morbus-Parkinson-like disease process in the older one.

535

ASSESSMENT AND EVALUATION OF EXTRAPYRAMIDAL SYMPTOMS OF REMOXIPRIDE AND HALOPERIDOL IN ACUTE TREATMENT OF SCHIZOPHRENIA
Sven-Erik Westerbergh, Bengt Gustafsson, Mats Blomqvist, Anders Ljungström.
Clinical Research - CNS, Astra Research Centre, Södertälje, Sweden.

Remoxipride is an antipsychotic drug belonging to the benzamide group. In rats, there is a wide separation between doses of remoxipride that inhibit locomotor activity induced by the dopamine agonist apomorphine, and doses that produce catalepsy. This is in contrast to classical neuroleptics, e.g. haloperidol, for which there is virtually no separation. A compound with the pharmacological profile of remoxipride should be less likely than classical neuroleptics to produce extrapyramidal side effects (EPS) in therapeutically equieffective doses in patients.
Nine double-blind studies comparing remoxipride (n=671) to haloperidol (n=440) in acute treatment of schizophrenia comprise the basis for documenting the clinical effects of remoxipride. All studies followed a basic protocol with the main assessments performed according to the same methodology enabling a pooling of data. Different rating scales were used to assess extrapyramidal symptoms during the treatment period. The evaluations of the EPS took into consideration incidences before and during treatment, severity degrees and time course. A substantial difference was seen in advantage of remoxipride in the incidence of EPS despite a significantly more frequent use of concomitant anticholinergic medication in the haloperidol group.

536

SUPERSENSITIVITY PSYCHOSIS INDUCED BY METOCLOPRAMIDE

E.T.ORAL,MD,M.E.CEYLAN,MD,PhD,A.İ.ŞENER,MD, N.B.TOMRUK,MD.
BAKIRKÖY MENTAL HOSPITAL/İSTANBUL/TURKEY

Neuroleptics with different affinities for dopaminergic receptors in different regions of CNS induce supersensitivity psychosis in different prevalences. The half-life of neuroleptics and their active metabolites in brain is important regarding the supersensitivity psychosis. Withdrawal and rebound phenomena or supersensitivity psychosis can be more easily detected if the half-lives of the drug and/or its active metabolites are of short-duration. The effects of neuroleptics such as haloperidol is still active several days after discontinuation of the drug. When, metaclopramide (MCP) a dopamine receptor blocking agent with a shorter half-life was given to schizophrenic patients in high doses sufficient enough to have an antipsychotic effect, it resulted with a clear evidence of supersensitivity upon abrubt withdrawal. In our research, MCP induced supersensitivity psychosis in 10 chronic institutionalised schizophrenic patients is analysed. Patients are followed for 30 days in 3 groups by Brief Psychiatric Rating Scale and by Global Assessment Scale with different doses of drug. The results show that 50 mg MCP per day is not enough for the treatment of psychosis and patients who receive 200 mg per day display the highest sensitivity level. Our study supports the view about the supersensitivity risk of neuroleptics with shorter half-lives though they have an antischizophrenic effect as the others.

537

CARDIOVASCULAR FUNCTIONS DURING LONG-TERM TREATMENT WITH NEUROLEPTIC DRUGS

E.O.Joergensen,Med.Dept.,Sct.Hans Hospital, 4000 Roskilde,Denmark.

Fourtytwo patients who had been treated for more than six months with neuroleptic drugs were studied by conventional measurement of blood pressure(BP)and electrocardiography(ECG) and by exercise electrocardiography and echocardiography. Fourteen patients were treated with clozapine (group I), 14 with perphenazine or zuclopenthixol (group II), and 14 with flupenthixol or haloperidol(group III).
There were no significant differences between groups with respect to mean BP or heart rate(HR) in response to changes in body position. During exercise mean BP and HR changed similarly in the groups. However, a few patients from each group had unchanged or lower BP during exercise.
The ECG in rest showed T-wave changes in half the patients from all three groups.
Echocardiography in rest and during the first five min following exercise showed similar and normal mean values of left ventricular output in all three groups. However, three patients from group I who had normal left ventricular output values in rest had abnormally low values during the first minutes following exercise.

538

NEUROLEPTIC-INDUCED AKATHISIA: TREATMENT WITH TRAMADOL AND AMITRIPTYLINE

C.Botschev, F.Müller-Spahn, A.Straube
Psychiatric Hospital, University of Munich
D-8000 Munich 2, Nussbaumstr.7, West Germany
(Head: H.Hippius)

Akathisia is a frequent and very disturbing side effect of neuroleptic treatment. The pathophysiology and the optimal treatment of the neuroleptic-induced akathisia (NIA) are still not clear. Recent studies suggest that the adrenergic and endorphinergic system may be involved.

Therefore firstly we investigated whether schizophrenic patients with a NIA respond well to single doses of the opioid agonist tramadol and then whether a second group improved after treatment with the tricyclic antidepressant amitriptyline.

40 schizophrenic patients with moderate to severe symptoms of an NIA were enclosed in these studies.

In an open trial 15 patients received a single dose of 50 mg tramadol. 25 patients were treatet open with 50-75 mg amitriptyline up to three weeks.

Tramadol improved symptoms of NIA in some patients within a few hours after application. The preliminary evaluation of results shows a substantial improvement after amitriptyline within the first three days in about 60-70%.

These results suggest that the endorphinergic system may be involved at least partly in the pathophysiology of the NIA. Hypotheses concerning the positive effects of amitriptyline focus primarily on the postsynaptic desensitization of Beta-receptors.

For further evaluation of the role of amitriptyline in NIA a double-blind study is presently carried out comparing amitriptyline with the Beta-receptor blocker propranolol.

539

BROMOCRIPTINE OR LISURIDE IN THE TREATMENT OF NEUROENDOCRINE SIDE EFFECTS OF NEUROLEPTICS
Bizzari D.,Agrimi G.,Lazzerini F., Andreani M.F. Piccini P.
Department of Mental Health, Massa Carrara, Italy

Several of the commonly used psychotropic drugs, particularly neuroleptics, produce hyperprolactinemia and subsequent neuroendocrine side effects that can be unpleasant and may require termination of neuroleptic treatment and increase the risk of psychosis in these patients. Dopamine agonists drugs have been proposed for the therapy of neuroendocrine side-effects. Ten schizophrenic patients (5 females and 5 males, mean age 38.5yr) affected by neuroleptic-induced neuroendocrine syndrome were treated with bromocriptine or lisuride in a double-blind study. Basally and after two months of bromocriptine or lisuride therapy we evaluated complete blood hormonal profile, sexual behavior (SV scale) and psychopathological symptoms (BPR scale). Both bromocriptine and lisuride treatment determined a marked suppression of serum PRL and a significant increase of serum testosterone and total androgens. Clinically we observed a significant reduction in galactorrhea-emenorrhea and extrapyramidal symptoms with both drugs. Lisuride was more effective than bromocriptine in increasing sexual fantasies or activity.

Session 80 Symposium:
Psychiatry in the resolution of social problems

540

ALTRUISM vs. CHAOS

Jules H. Masserman, M.D.
Northwestern University

The author will cite evidence from his own ethologic research, and from anthropology, history, philosophy and psychology (Spencer, Rousseau, Bergson vs. Hobbes, Nietzche, Freud, et al) that biopsychologically innate human altruism makes possible the solution of social problems.

541

FUTURES RESEARCH IN SOCIAL PSYCHIATRY

Stanley Lesse, M.D., Med.Sc.D.
Editor-in-Chief, American Journal of Psychotherapy, U.S.A.

The world is changing at an ever increasing rate sociologically and technologically. The Western nations and Japan are shifting from an industrial to a post-industrial society; many agricultural countries are shifting from a primarily agricultural to an industrial society. The majority of the Third World countries remain agricultural. These shifts and the rates of change make it necessary for all societies to have long-range projections. In other words, there must be futures planning.

Many of our psychological concepts are anachronistic since they are based on concepts and needs for societal and technological forces that were appropriate for past eras. Many patients are therefore inappropriately treated both on an individual and group bases. New concepts and techniques based on futures concepts will be presented.

542

SCIENCE, ECOLOGY & HEALTH CARE
Varma V., India

543

THE COMPREHENSIVE VIEW OF SOCIAL PSYCHIATRY

John L. Carleton, M.D.
World Association of Social Psychiatry,
Santa Barbara, U.S.A.

Solutions to social problems are seldom considered from the comprehensive view of the psychiatrist, more particularly, the social psychiatrist. The author will describe the social psychiatrist approach to the understanding of and solutions for social problems.

Session 81 Symposium:
Drug abuse trends in Europe and the USA

544

DRUG MISUSE IN WESTERN EUROPE : TRENDS AND PRINCIPAL AREAS OF CURRENT CONCERN

Christopher LUCKETT, Council of Europe Co-operation Group to Combat Drug Abuse and Illicit Trafficking in Drugs (Pompidou Group), Strasbourg, France

The paper reviews recent trends in drug misuse in Western Europe based, primarily, on data from treatment and law enforcement agencies. It points out the shortcomings of the available data when used for establishing international comparisons and stresses the need to interpret it in the light of national and local policy and service-provision contexts.

Particular attention is given to the emergence of cocaine misuse, the spread of HIV infection amongst drug misusers and the changes in the structure of the drug misusing population as centres for current concern.

545

DRUG ABUSE TRENDS AMONG YOUTHS IN HUNGARY.
DR. EDIT SANDOR, SOCIAL AND HEALTH MINISTRY, HUNGARY.

I. Until about the 1970's, the drug abuse of school boys and girls in Budapest, because of the low number of instances, was known only to the police, and these few cases were not even brought to the notice of the health authorities./This period is known as the time of obscurity./
II. In 1971, the drug abuse with "Parkan" tablets was most wide-spread among youths/drug abuse in groups and gangs./
III. From 1973 to early 80's drug abuse spread also in the provinces, outside Budapest./Combination of alcohol with psychotropic or psychoactive substances, stimulants, tranquilizers, sleeping pills, etc./
IV. From early 80's to our days, we witness the expansion of drug abuse. The age of those making their first attempt is decreasing. There are more and more "regular abusers". There have been attempts for illegal production of narcotic drugs. "Hard drugs" also appear, although scarcely. More and more deaths occur among young people because of "glue sniffing".
There are no data available in Hungary for drug related AIDS; Hungary belongs to the low infected areas.

546

ILLICIT DRUG USE TRENDS AMONG ADOLESCENTS IN WESTERN EUROPEAN COUNTRIES

A. Kokkevi.

Department of Psychiatry, Athens University Medical School

Existing epidemiologic data from Western European countries reveal different trends in illicit drug use among young people. In the Nordic and Central European countries, with the exception of Ireland, there seems to be a trend towards stabilisation or even towards a decrease of illicit drug use. On the contrary in Southern European countries such as Greece, Portugal, Spain, illicit drug taking by young people is still on increase.

European data however indicate that the spread of illicit drug use in Europe has been more limited compared to North American countries (U.S.A. and Canada), prevalence rates being kept below 20% and ranging in most of the countries between 5%-10% in the age group of 14 to 20 years old.

Differences in trends of illicit drug use among the various European countries are discussed in relation to time-lag differences in the appearance of the epidemic of illicit drugs.

547
DRUG ABUSE IN LATIN AMERICAN POPULATIONS
Madrigal E., USA

548
PATTERNS AND TRENDS IN DRUG ABUSE IN THE UNITED STATES
Nicholas J. Kozel
National Institute on Drug Abuse
Rockville, Maryland
United States of America

Epidemiologic data will be presented describing patterns and trends of drug abuse in the United States. The presentation will include information from major national systems in the United States, as well as local and regional sources and will describe current epidemiologic trends, user characteristics, and consequences of use.

Session 82 Symposium:
Benzodiazepines: Efficacy/side effects and pharmacokinetics/dynamics

549
OVERVIEW OF BENZODIAZEPINE EFFICACY AND SAFETY
Hollister L. E., Univ. of Texas Medical School, Houston, Texas, U.S.A.

Benzodiazepines have been the most widely used class of drugs in medical history. Indications have paralleled those of previous sedative/hypnotics. With proper use, benzodiazepines are highly safe and effective. Effects are essentially limited to the central nervous system; effects on other organ systems are virtually unknown. Although slight pharmacodynamic differences have been proposed for various members, their major effect is mediated by a common receptor linked to gamma-aminobutyric acid. Pharmacokinetic differences are marked, with individual benzodiazepines ranging from ultra-short to very long-acting. Benzodiazepines are perceived as being safer than barbiturates and other earlier sedative/hypnotics; deaths from overdose are rare with benzodiazepines. The ratio between sedation and anxiolytic action is lower and fewer drug-drug interactions are encountered. On the other hand, psychic and physical dependence is a recognized problem, as are disturbances in memory functions.

550
TRIAZOLAM 0.5MG AT NIGHT CAUSES ANXIETY BY DAY
Oswald I, Adam K, Univ. Department of Psychiatry, Royal Edinburgh Hospital, Morningside Park, Edinburgh, United Kingdom

To test further the conclusions of preliminary reports that regular use of triazolam might cause daytime anxiety, 82 women and 38 men, mean age 53, who claimed to be poor sleepers, took a capsule nightly for 45 nights. On 25 consecutive nights the capsule contained triazolam 0.5mg (40 subjects), lormetazepam 2mg (40 subjects) or continued placebo (40 subjects). Both drugs improved sleep, but compared with placebo or lormetazepam-takers, triazolam-takers became more anxious on self-ratings, were judged more often by an observer to have had a bad response, more often wrote down complaints of distress and suffered weight loss. After about 10 days of nightly triazolam administration, they developed panic and depression, felt unreal, and sometimes paranoid. The very short half-life of triazolam, leading to daytime withdrawal symptoms, does not appear to us to be a full explanation.

551

THE WITHDRAWAL SYNDROME WITH BENZODIAZEPINES
Monti J.M., Universidad de Republic, Montevideo, Uruguay

A withdrawal syndrome is known to follow the sudden interruption of benzodiazepine (BZP) administration after treatment with standard therapeutic doses, even when given for a few weeks. A transient increase of symptoms occurring after stopping BZPs, that rapidly returns to normal, can be more properly called a rebound withdrawal. The frequency, intensity and time of appearance of withdrawal symptoms are related, to a large extent, to the BZP's elimination half-life. Thus, BZPs with a short half-life (midazolam, triazolam, alprazolam) have a greater potential for causing withdrawal reactions. Withdrawal symptoms in patients who have used short-acting BZPs occur within 1-3 days and include sleep disturbance (increase in sleep latency, total wake time and number of awakenings), anxiety, dysphoria, tremor, headache, anorexia, hypersensitivity to noise, light, and touch and perceptual changes. Peak decrease of plasma BZP appears concomitantly with the onset of withdrawal. In addition, scores for anxiety (HARS) parallel the rise in the scores for physical withdrawal. Not much is known about the mechanism underlying BZP withdrawal symptoms. It does not appear to be related to changes in BZP receptor number or affinity. However, compensatory changes in other components of the macromolecular GABA/BZP/chloride channel complex cannot be discarded.

552

BENZODIAZEPINE SIDE EFFECTS: COMPARISON OF THREE DRUGS
Bixler E.O., Pennsylvania State Univ. College of Medicine, Hershey, Pennsylvania, U.S.A.

The side effect profiles for flurazepam (FRZ), temazepam (TMZ) and triazolam (TRZ), the three hypnotics currently available in the U.S., have been established through a combination of clinical trials, sleep laboratory studies, daytime performance assessments, Food & Drug Administration (FDA) adverse drug reactions (ADRs) as well as clinical case reports. These three drugs differ considerably according to pharmacokinetics (elimination half-life) and pharmacodynamics (binding affinity). TRZ is the most rapidly eliminated and has the strongest affinity/potency while FRZ is the most slowly eliminated and TMZ has the weakest affinity. CNS side effects can be classified into a number of broad categories: daytime sedation; hyperexcitability; amnesia; other cognitive disturbances and psychotic-like symptoms; affective and other behavioral disturbances; withdrawal and dependency problems; and other CNS side effects. In controlled studies, the frequency/severity of memory impairment, hyperexcitability states and withdrawal difficulties were much greater with TRZ. In the FDA/ADR study, TRZ had the highest rate of CNS adverse effects both at the higher clinical dose (5-10 fold greater) and at the lower clinical dose (3-13 fold greater). Of concern are the results of another controlled study of TRZ 0.25 mg that showed this dose was not significantly effective. Thus, lowering the dose of TRZ decreases the benefit to side effect ratio, as benefits are decreased more than side effects.

553

NOT ALL BENZODIAZEPINES ARE ALIKE
Kales A, Pennsylvania State Univ. College of Medicine, Hershey, Pennsylvania, U.S.A.

Benzodiazepines (BZPs) were first introduced into medical practice in 1960 and continue to be popular therapeutic agents because of their wide range of safety and high degree of efficacy. The 1,4 BZPs initially available were similar in pharmacokinetic and pharmacodynamic characteristics and had few side effects with drowsiness being the most frequent. In the last 2 decades more rapidly eliminated BZPs, often with higher receptor binding affinities and some belonging to the triazolo BZP group, have been introduced. Subsequently, more rapid tolerance, hyperexcitability states such as early morning insomnia and daytime anxiety, more frequent and severe withdrawal difficulties and other "unexpected" side effects such as memory impairment, confusion, disorientation and even delusions and hallucinations have been noted. Elimination half-life and affinity for the BZP receptor differ greatly among BZPs and account for many of these side effects. In addition, some chemical properties of triazolo BZPs are unique. For example, triazolo BZPs activate α_2 adrenoreceptors, inhibit PAF, and do not appear to have total cross tolerance with other BZPs. Also, triazolam's affinity decreases in presence of GABA and increases with higher temperature. It is proposed that the more frequent/severe side effects with the newer triazolo BZPs are related to an interaction of several factors including: rapid elimination; high binding affinity; and unique chemical properties.

Session 83 Workshop:
Personality fitness training with patients suffering from bulimia. An intensive psychotherapeutic program

554

P.F.T.PERSONALITY FITTNESS TRAINING WITH PATIENTS SUFFERING FROM BULIMIA.AN INTENSIVE PSYCHOTHERAPEUTIC PROGRAM.
CRAMER G.P.,M.D.PSYCHIATRIST
FURUHOLMEN D.,M.D.
INSTITUTE FOR FUNCTIONAL PSYCHOTHERAPY IN OSLO.

P.F.T. is an intensive affective and cognitive behavior teaching program provided by seminars lasting 3-4 days over a period of one year.Each seminar is different in depth but related to the others.By using terms from the functional approach to psycotherapy,each member is well oriented in issues such as life areas,personality dynamics,integration and disintegration,etc. Needs,choises,behaviors and images are cen tral issues.
The learning is done by experience and theoretical application as well as group interaction.Goals : Clarifying the eating disorder functions for the personality; Clarifying the E.D.as a form of life; Clarifying the E.D.as a substitute for needs and feelings; Clarify the E.D. as an identity; Expressivity training of feellings; New skills to satisfy adult needs; Changing weakness into strength; Interaction of small and large group settings.
The workshop will be held as a theoretical introduction and self-experience group where the members will be asked to take part in some of the exercise provided in the P.F.T. seminars.

Session 84 New Research:
Panic disorders: Therapeutic approaches

555

DOUBLE BLIND COMPARISON OF CLOMIPRAMINE AND IMIPRAMINE IN PANIC DISORDER
Modigh K., Eriksson E., Lisjo P., Westberg P.
Dept. of Psychiatry and Neurochemistry, St. Jorgen Hospital, Hisings Backa, Sweden

Patients with panic disorder with or without agoraphobia according to DSM-III-R were included in the study. Concomitant episodes of major depressive disorder or dysthymia were considered as exclusion criteria. The patients were, after informed consent randomly administered placebo (n=7), imipramine (I) (n=24) or clomipramine (Cl) (n=21) for three months. Doses were gradually increased depending on therapeutic and side effects (max 250 mg daily). Concomitant medication with diazepam, max 15mg daily, was allowed and supportive psychotherapy was given in addition to the medication. Doses of I and Cl were not significantly different at the end of the study. I and Cl but not placebo reduced anxiety, measured by HARS and as number of panic attacks per week. At the end of the treatment the Cl-group but not the I-group differed significantly from the placebo group with respect to both assessments. The result is interpreted as suggestive evidence that Cl is more potent than I in the treatment of panic disorder.

556

Controlled Trial of Lofepramine and Clomiprimine in Panic Anxiety
Fahy, T.J. MD., F.R.C. Psych. F.R.C.P.I., D.P.M.
O'Rourke, D., Butler, J., and Leonard B.,
University College, Galway, Ireland

Preliminary findings of a recently completed study of 81 DSM-111 R Panic disorder subjects will be presented, including 3 month and 6 month follow up. Biochemical correlates of treatment response will be presented separately.

557

PANIC DISORDER, COGNITIVE THERAPY VERSUS ALPRAZOLAM.

Adnan Takriti M.D. FRCPsych.
Arab Federation of Psychiatrists
Amman-Jordan

Forty patients were divided into two equal groups. Age range was 24 ± 6 for cognitive therapy and 23 ± 5 for Alprazolam patients. Cognitive therapy patients were seen in 12 sessions of 1 hour duration on twice weekly basis. Alprazolam groupan average of 4.5 mg. daily.

Patients were assessed before, in the midst and at the end of treatment by Hamilton anxiety scale, self evaluation questionaire. fear of negative evaluation questionaire and panic symptom questionaire which is based on DSMIII-R. Alprazolam group showed statistically significant improvement in panic symptoms. While cognitive therapy patients showed remarkable improvement in change of self attitude toward panic attacks with moderate diminution of physiological symptoms of panic.

A further 8 weeks of follow up is being carried out. Overall results and final conclusions shall be presented in the original paper.

558

CARBAMAZEPINE (CBZ) IN PANIC DISORDER WITH AGORAPHOBIA

F. Toccafondi, B. Carpiniello, M. Carta & N. Rudas - Istituto di Clinica Psichiatrica - Università di Cagliari - Italy

Several drugs were studied in many studies on agoraphobic anxiety and Panic Disorder (PD). We studied CBZ, a painkiller and anticonvulsive, well known for being a tranquillizer and sedative, and for its application in Affective Disorders. The present study evaluates the possible interference in the short and long term of a concomitant Depressive Disorder on the response to CBZ in PD with Agoraphobia. We selected two groups of outpatients with PD and Agoraphobia (DSM III-R) on the basis of absence (12 p) or presence (18 p) of Major Depression (DSM III-R). After a clinical interview, we used: BPRS, Hamilton Dep., Hamilton Anx., and Hallam and Hafner's Quest. After two weeks wash-out the patients followed the same protocol (50 mg./die in the first 3 days, 150 mg./die in the next 3 days, 300 mg./die from day 7 to day 14, 500 mg./die from day 15 to day 30, 500-800 mg. from the 1st to the 12th month). Blind rating was carried out at 1st, 2nd and 4th week and at 3rd, 6th and 12th month of therapy by the same methods used initially. All patients without Depression presented a fast and marked improvement within the 1st month, that continued in the next months. The patients with Depression showed low responses, which in most cases caused such a progression of the symptoms of depression and anxiety that CBZ had to be interrupted and substituted sucessfully with tricyclic drugs. The results seem to suggest the efficacy of CBZ in PD with Agoraphobia and the negative role of Depression on the response to treatment.

559

SEROTONIN AND ANXIETY: AN OPEN STUDY OF CITALOPRAM IN PANIC DISORDER

Humble, M.; Koczkas, C..; & Wistedt B.

Karolinska Institute, Department of Psychiatry, Danderyd Hospital, S-182 88 Danderyd, SWEDEN

Panic disorder is currently treated with tricyclics, particularly imipramine and clomipramine, or benzodiazepines (e.g. alprazolam). Double-blind studies with the serotonin reuptake inhibitors zimeldine and fluvoxamine have demonstrated that these drugs are at least as effective as the tricyclics but free from anticholinergic side-effects. However, zimeldine and fluvoxamine both exert some noradrenalin reuptake inhibition which, hypothetically, may contribute to their antipanic effect. An open pilot study with the most selective serotonin uptake inhibitor, citalopram, was therefore initiated in order to evaluate the therapeutic efficacy and the dose range in panic disorder patients with or without agoraphobia (DSM-III-R criteria).

20 patients entered the study and were treated with citalopram, 17 completed the 8 week study period. The initial dose was low (5 mg/day) increasing to a maximum dose of 60 mg, if necessary. The dose was flexible in weeks 1, 2, 5 and 6 but fixed in weeks 3, 4, 7 and 8. The patients were assessed by means of the Clinical Anxiety Scale (CAS), the Montgomery-Åsberg Depression Rating Scale (MADRS), and scales of global impression and side effects. Rating results will be presented.

From this pilot study we may conclude that citalopram has antipanic properties, but ameliorates independently also other components of the anxiety syndrome. For instance, in a few cases social phobic symptoms responded better to citalopram than they had earlier responded to tricyclics. The side-effect level was low, although some patients reported initial paradox increase in anxiety, as is commonly reported in tricyclic antipanic treatment. These positive results warrant further investigation and, due to the unique selectivity of citalopram, provide another clue to the pathophysiology of anxiety disorders.

560

RO 16-6028 A PARTIAL BZD RECEPTOR AGONIST ON IMPENDING PANIC ATTACKS

ALTERWAIN P., CHELLE S., PORCIUNCULA H., HOSPITAL PSIQUIATRICO "MUSTO" - MONTEVIDEO - URUGUAY

RO 16-6028 is a partial agonist at the central benzodiazepine receptor and possesses a potent anxiolytic activity. Its action has a rapid onset (first significant activity after 5-10 minutes, $t_{50\%}$ max 20-25 minutes, oral t_{max} 45-60 minutes) and a short duration (effect half-life 3.5h).

An open study was carried out on 20 patients with Panic Attacks (DSM-III$_r$).

The aim was to investigate the efficacy of the intake of a single dose of the drug either prior to a Panic Attack (anticipation symptoms) or at the begining of a Panic Attack, safety and tolerability.

The dosage ranged from 0.5 mg through 1.5 mg.

Results: Much improved 52.9%, very much improved 41.2%.
13 out of 20 patients did not present side-effects, 7 presented minor side-effects, mainly dopiness impaired concentration and amnesia. One patient presented serious side-effects (important behavioural disturbances).
Panic Attacks had a significant decrease in intensity and frequency and there was a decrease of phobic symptoms as well. Two patients had a complete remission of agoraphobia.
Conclusions: RO 16-6028 showed to be effective in this concept of treatment, proving to be safe and with good tolerability at this dosage.

Session 85 New Research:
Obsessive - compulsive disorders

561

OBSESSIVE COMPULSIVE SYMPTOMS IN CHILDREN AND ADOLESCENTS IN BELGRADE

Vida Rakić

Institute for the Mental Health, Belgrade, Yugoslavia

Study's goal was to determine the spread and distribution of neurotic obsessive/compulsive symptoms (OCS) among a general population aged 7-19 in Belgrade. A sample of 332 examinees was formed proportionate to the population's structure as to sex, age and cultural setting in Belgrade. As OCS have the highest continuity and predictive value (Rutter & Hersov 1985, Zeitlin 1986) it is to expect that in time, from the group of neurotic OCS examinees, singled out will be those with a psychopathological development. Thus, this was considered a risk group, suggesting the need for prevention. It was shown that 14.8% of children and adolescents had neurotic OCS; 8.1% in latent age, 12.0% in early and 22.5% in true adolescence. Statistically important is the difference in OCS frequecy between 1st and 3rd (t= 3.27, p<0.01) and between 2nd and 3rd age group (t= 2.05, p<0.05). For female sex the distribution was the same (at the p<0.01 level in both cases); for male - it was uniform in all age groups, as well as between male and female sex. Distribution of individual OCS depended on both sex and age, and most frequently were checking, hand washing, thinking about unpleasant experiences and hesitation.

562

PSYCHOPATHOLOGICAL AND THERAPEUTIC ASPECTS OF OBSESSIVE-COMPULSIVE DISORDER

CASSANO G.B., RAVAGLI S., LENSI P., MAURI M.

Pisa, Italy

Though the boundaries between OCD and schizophrenic and affective disorders are represented by obsession and compulsions, nevertheless since OCD involves affective, behavioural and cognitive levels, it overlaps with other disorders. In fact, anxious and depressive symptoms and different degrees of insight frequently coexist. Considered in the past a rare illness with a poor prognosis, the OCD data on incidence in psychiatric population reported a variable percentage from 0,1 to 4,6% (Judd, 1965, Black 1974, Hollingsworth 1980). More recent studies from NIMH have shown that OCD is about twice as prevalent in the general population (as is panic disorder) (Rasmussen 1986); OCD had a 6 month point prevalence of 1-2% (Myers 1984) and lifetime prevalence of 2-3% (Robins 1984). These results suggested an OCD prevalence in general population higher of that we could imagine on the basis of the real incidence in psychiatric population. Recent advances in behavioural and psycho-pharmacologic approaches to treatment have increased interest for this area of research. The present report on a sample of OCD patients aims to obtain a better knowledge of the clinical characteristics of OCD and its response to treatment with Clomipramine.

563

EFFICACY OF SOME ANTICONVULSANT DRUGS ON RECURRENT INTRUSIVE IDEAS.

Dr Gérard S. COHEN ADAD, CHS de Maison Blanche, Neuilly/Marne, FRANCE.

1. Recurrent intrusive ideas, a clinical variant of PTSD, are commonly part of a symptom constellation where depression (major or minor) is prominent. The intensity of the traumatic event is often less than in typical PTSD and, unlike obsessions (OCD), recurrent intrusive ideas are not experienced as senseless, and no attempt is made to neutralize them. A mechanism involving an epileptiform discharge from temporal lobe foci has been hypothesized, but specific EEG abnormality is not regularly found.
2. In an open study, anticonvulsant drugs were added to the treatment regimen of 7 patients with recurrent intrusive ideas. 5 of 6 patients responded to carbamazepine (1000/1600 mg daily). The CBZ resistant patient subsequently responded to clonazepam (4 mg/day). An other patient did well under valpromide (900 mg/day).
Prior to anticonvulsants, a trial with antidepressants was made (in 6 of 7 patients) without any action on the recurrent intrusive ideas.
A review of the litterature is made and 7 cases vignettes are presented.

Codes #25, #69, #75
Paper in english
Oral free communication
New research session

564

A FIXED DOSE STUDY OF FLUOXETINE 20, 40 AND 60MG VERSUS PLACEBO IN THE TREATMENT OF OBSESSIVE COMPULSIVE DISORDER
A.W. Mcintyre, H.Vosloo, T. Selvan
Department of Psychiatry, Tygerberg Hospital, University of Stellenbosch, South Africa
A few reports on the efficacy of clomipramine (a less specific 5-HT reputake inhibitor) in OCD have been published. Fluoxetine is the most specific 5-HT reputake inhibitor available at present. We participated in a randomised, double-blind, parallel, multicentre Pan European study of 9 weeks duration with an extension of a further 4 months. A group of 16 patients who met the DSM-II-R criteria for obsessive compulsive disorder, moderate degree was selected. Eight weeks of randomly assigned treatment with fluoxetine 20, 40, 60mg or placebo was given double-blind. Patients were assessed weekly during the first month and fornightly during the second month using the following scales:1. Yale Brown Obsessive Compulsive Scale. 2. CPRS-Obsessive Scale. 3. Montgomery Asberg Depression Rating Scale. 4. Hamilton Depression Rating Scale. 5. Covi Anxiety Scale. 6. Patient Global Impression Scale. 7. Clinical Global Impression Scale.
The study is ongoing and still blinded. However, final results will be submitted before 1 August 1989. The authores believe that fluoxetine will prove to be and effective treatment in obserrive compulsive disorders.

565

SERTRALINE IS EFFECTIVE IN OBSESSIVE COMPULSIVE DISORDER
Bick, PA; Hackett, E; Pfizer New York, USA

The results of the first use of sertraline in obsessive compulsive disorder are presented.
Sertraline (1-amino tetrahydronaphthalene) is a non-tricyclic serotonin reuptake inhibitor which is being investigated for use in depression, obesity, and obsessive compulsive disorder (OCD). It demonstrates greater potency and selectivity for the serotonergic System than a number of comparative agents such as fluoxetine, fluvoxamine and chlorimipramine, which have been suggested to be efficacious in OCD due to their serotonin reuptake inhibition. A multicentre doulbe-blind, placebo controlled parallel study was undertaken to evaluate the efficacy of sertraline in OCD. Patients with a DSM III diagnosis of OCD were screened for this study. All patients with a total score of 15 or greater on the Hamilton Depression Scale (24-item) were excluded from entry into the study. After a single-blind placebo washout period lasting one week, patients were randomized to receive either sertraline (50-200 mg) or placebo for 8 weeks. A total of 87 patients were randomized, 44 to placebo, 43 to sertraline. The mean age of the patients was 36-38 years and was comparable between the two groups. Review of the data (2-tailed tests) tests show that sertraline was significantly more effective than placebo on the Yale-Brown Obsessive Compulsive Scale total score ($p=0.05$), the National Institute of Mental Health General Obsessive Compulsive Rating ($p=0.026$), the Clinical Global Impressions severity of illness score ($p=0.047$), and the Clinical Global Impressions improvement score ($p=0.025$). A patient rating instrument, the Maudsley Obsessive-Compulsive Inventory, demonstrated a trend in favor of sertraline but did not reach statistical significance ($p=0.13$).

It is concluded that sertraline is effective in treating obsessive compulsive disorder.

566

IN-PATIENT BEHAVIOURAL PSYCHOTHERAPY FOR OBS-COMPULSIVE DISORDER:OUTCOME

Graham Thornicroft, Isaac Marks, Louise Colson. Bethlem-Maudsley Hospital, London, England.

The Bethlem-Maudsley in-patient behavioural psychotherapy unit uniquely combines 4 aspects of treatment: encouragement of self-treatment, involvement of relatives as cotherapists, minimising medication use, and staff present only from 7.30am to 8.30pm, with considerable cost savings. Over one year of routine clinical practice, 52 neurotic patients were admitted and followed for 6 months post discharge: of these 42 had obsessive compulsive disorder (OCD), 5 were agora- and 2 social phobics. Compared with admission, the OCD group at discharge, and 6 month follow-up were improved for obsessive compulsive severity, time, discomfort and handicap ($p < 0.001$). For the phobics, global and total phobia scores were reduced at the same follow-up points ($p < 0.001$). For all patients anxiety and depression improved ($p < 0.01$), as did work, home management, and social and private leisure ($p < 0.05$). In-patient behavioural treatment is enduringly effective in severe, chronic OCD.

567

TEORIA HISTAMINERGICA DE LAS NEUROSIS OBSESIVAS COMPULSIVAS.

Dr. FERNANDO ALMANSA PASTOR
Neuro-Psiquiatra.
Jefe de S. de Psiquiatría de la Seguridad Social.

Tras el hallazgo fortuito de la espectacular mejora en una paciente con NEUROSIS OBSESIVA de larga evolución, con la utilización de un Antihistamínico (Astemizol) en una afección intercurrente urticuriforme, y recordando la histórica relación entre Antihistamínicos y tranquilizantes, se comenzó a incluir como complemento terapeutico habitual(Clomipramina y Ansiolíticos)el uso de Astemizol en pacientes con Neurosis Obsesiva-Compulsiva,ya que la favorable respuesta en la mayoria de nuestra casuística , que asciende a veintinueve casos desde Febrero del 88´, nos animó a seguirlos.
Asi se estructuró la teoría histaminérgica, como justificación etiopatogénica de nuestra práctica terapeutica, basandonos en la presencia de Histamina como Neurotransmisor en el SNC con receptores específicos del tipo H_1 y H_2, de funcionalismo en muchas facetas antagónicas, que asume la función de Neuromodulador del equilibrio entre los neurotransmisores Acetilcolina y Serotonina, al mismo tiempo que puede incrementar la permeabilidad de la Barrera Hematoencefalica.

Session 86 Free Communications:
Organic mental disorders: Genetic and infectious influences

568

Werner's Syndrome : A CASE REPORT

Brian P. O'Brien, M.A., M.B., F.R.C.P.(C)

Queensway-Carleton Hospital,
Nepean, Ontario
CANADA

Werner's Syndrome, originally described in 1904 by Otto Werner, is an extremely rare autosomal recessive condition in which young adults display clinical features similar to those observed in elderly adults.

The etiology of the condition is not fully elucidated but evidence suggests an enzymatic deficiency resulting in defective protein production.

There have been less than 400 documented cases of Werner's Syndrome in the literature and only one recently described with psychiatric implications.

The author presents a case of Werner's Syndrome in a 40 year old male with symptoms of associated mood disorder and organicity of a diffuse kind.

The clinical course, investigations and treatment of this patient will be described with particular reference to the difficulties encountered in treatment with psychotropic medications.

569

KLEINE-LEVIN SYNDROME : Clinical study, review of etiology, and treatment with Carbamazepine
Dr VALLERY-MASSON, Pr JEZEQUEL
Service Pédiatrie - C.H.U. de Rennes (France)

The authors discribe the Kleine-Levin syndrome, too often unrecognized in adolescent psychiatry : it is characterized by recurrent attacks of hypersomnia, excessive or compulsive eating, striking behavioral and psychiatric symptoms.
Its diagnosis is uniquely clinical, but others sleep, neurological, and psychiatric disorders for differential diagnosis need to be considered.
The authors remind us of the different etiological hypotheses : hypothalamic dysfunction, relation to affective disorders, pertubation of CFS monoamines , and lastly of psychogenic origin.
Finally, the authors underline the interest of a treatment by Carbamazepine from their experience concerning four cases of Kleine-Levin syndrome which was stabilized for more than one year by this treatment.

570

FREQUENCE D'HERPES SIMPLEX CHEZ DES PATIENTS SE PLAIGNANT D'EPISODES DEPRESSIFS OCCURRANTS
M.Spiridione Masaraki, Psychiatre Assistant Hopsitalier Coresponsable, Ospedale Ca Granda
M.Glanlorenzo Masaraki, Psychiatre, Directeur de l'Institute de Rechereche et Therapie Psychosomatique), Milano, Italy

Certains auteurs ont observé la possibilité d'une corrélation entre manifestation herpétique et dépression.
Cette donnée confirmerait, entre autres, l' influence de la symptômatologie psychique sur les réponses immunitaires.
Cette étude effectuée sur 400 cas propose une analyse statistique en matière.

571
BORNA DISEASE - POSSIBLE ETIOLOGY OF PSYCHIATRIC DISORDERS

Karl Bechter MD[1], Sibylle Herzog PhD[2], Reinhold Schüttler MD[1], Rudolf Rott DVM[2]

[1] University of Ulm Department of Psychiatry II and Department of Psychiatry of the Bezirkskrankenhaus Günzburg FRG

[2] Institute of Virology, Justus-Liebig-University Gießen FRG

Borna disease (BD) is a well known encephalomyelitis in Central Europe in equides and sheep, caused by a strongly neurotropic virus, not yet clearly characterized. There is a great variability in symptomatology and course of illness (fatal course or minimal behavioral syndromes), dependent from the virus variant and the host species. 1985 BD-serumantibodies have been reported in psychiatric patients with affective disorders in FRG and USA. We found BD-Serumantibodies in 6,8 % of psychiatric inpatients (n > 2000), but only in 3 % of surgical patients (n > 500). Seropositive patients suffered from the whole range of psychiatric disorders. MR imaging of seropositive patients demonstrated in more than 40 % cerebral lesions. Furthermore we found in about 50 % of seropositive patients an elevated CSF-Serum index of BD specific IgG, indicating cerebral involvement. Etiologic significance of BD for psychiatric disorders is discussed.

572
Psychiatric aspects of Lyme borreliosis

Kohler J*, Heilmeyer H*, Özdaglar A**, Oepen G**

Neurol.* und Psych.** Univ.-Klinik Freiburg/FRG

Die Lyme Borreliose (LB) ist eine häufige, weltweit verbreitete, stadienhaft verlaufende Multisystemerkrankung. An der Diagnosefindung sind üblicherweise verschiedene medizinische Fächer beteiligt. Heute sollte auch der Psychiater die z.T. komplexen Manifestationen der LB kennen, denn in jedem Krankheitsstadium können psychische Auffälligkeiten vorherrschend sein und differentialdiagnostische Probleme bedingen. Das Stadium 1, üblicherweise gekennzeichnet durch dermatologischen Manifestationen (Erythema migrans), kann sich auch allein durch Allgemeinstörungen äußern, die als depressives Syndrom imponieren, Im 2. Stadium dominieren vorallem periphere neurologische Ausfälle (Meningopolyneuritis). Etwa ein Drittel der Patienten weist jedoch auch ein hirnorganisches Psychosyndrom auf, welches im Einzelfall die Klinik bestimmen kann. Chronische Entzündungen des ZNS im 3. Stadium können sich ausschließlich als komplexe psychiatrische Syndrome (paranoid-halluzinatorische Psychosen, Demenz) äußern.

An ausgewählten Einzelfällen werden hierzu klinische Charakteristika und diagnostische Kriterien dargestellt.

573
LYME DISEASE: NEW SPIROCHAETAL CAUSE OF PREVENTABLE PSYCHIATRIC ILLNESS

A. M. Lopker, M.D.; Yale University, New Haven, CT 06520 USA

Lyme disease (LD), once considered an illness of unknown etiology, has been recognized in the past decade as a multisystem infectious disorder caused by the spirochaete, Borrelia burgdorferi. Its pathologic effects have been documented in skin, heart, joints and peripheral nervous system. Prior to this study, scattered reports existed of meningoencephalopathies, but other behavioral disturbances had not been recognized as direct manifestations of LD. Unlike other spirochaetal infections i.e Yaws, Pinta, Endemic Syphilis, the natural history of LD bears a striking resemblance to that of Syphilis; by analogy, behavioral disturbances might be expected late in the natural course of LD. The present study documents a spectrum of behavioral disturbances associated with LD. Fourteen patients with LD confirmed by Rheumatologic and Neurologic evaluations including high IgG antibody titers to B. burgdorferi were studied in a general hospital from Sept. 1985 to Jan. 1987. The presence of psychiatric disorder was confirmed by clinical Psychiatric evaluation including SCL-90. The spectrum of disorders seen can be classified into five groups: psychoses; dementias; chronic mood disorders; personality disturbances; and eating disorders. The most dramatic case yielded clear evidence of historic, serologic, histopathologic and pharmacologic responsiveness consistent with a diagnosis of CNS LD presenting like Neurosyphilis. This patient presented de novo with an insidious psychosis which proved to be associated with encephalitis, serological as well as brain biopsy evidence of infection with the B. burgdorferi spirochaete, and a marked response to penicillin treatment. This case provides a striking example of a behavioural disturbance yielding the initial clue to infection with the LD spirochaete, and offers strong evidence of its neurotropism. The clinician should be aware that LD requiring antibiotic treatment may masquerade as psychiatric illness.

Session 87 Free Communications:
Electroencephalography in psychiatry

574
COMPUTERIZED EEG TOPOGRAPHY ON NON-TREATED SCHIZOPHRENICS.

Toshiro Miyauchi, Kenkichi Tanaka, Hiroshi Hagimoto, Keiko Endo, Hideji Kishimoto, Masaaki Matsushita. Department of Psychiatry, Yokohama City University School of Medicine. Yokohma, Japan.

Recent studies using EEG topography have suggested that schizophrenics showed more slowing in the frontal regions. However, these EEG studies have mostly examined on chronic, medicated patients. We undertook a study of EEGs in thirty non-treated patients(Hebephrenic(H;N=14),Paranoid(P;N=9),Residual(R;N=6),Catatonic(N=1)) fulfilled ICD-9 criteria for schizophrenia, and compared to sex and age-matched controls. The frequency spectrum was collapsed into delta, theta, alpha1, alpha2, beta1 and beta2 bands. These power values were designated as average percentage of total power and t-statistic significance probability maps(SPM) were created. Schizophrenics showed more slowing than controls; high delta activity in the parieto-occipital and theta activity in the right occipito-temporal regions. Alpha2 activity were decreased in the occipital region extending over most of the head. Hs showed the most remarkable slowing in comparison of each subtypes with control. In Hs, delta activity was significantly increased in the occipital region and theta activity in the right occipito-temporal regions on SPM respectively. In Ps, only delta activity was increased in the occipital region. In Rs, alpha2 activity was significantly decreased in the left postero-temporal region. These topographic dissimilarities among patient groups were an useful guideline in separating subtypes of schizophrenics.

575

VALIDITY AND SPECIFICITY OF TOPOGRAPHIC EEG IN SCHIZOPHRENIA

S. Ludwig, Th. Gasser, P. Ziegler, W. F. Gattaz

Central Institute of Mental Health Mannheim, FRG

Topographic EEGs of drug-free schizophrenic patients (RDC) were recorded under standardized conditions. EOG-artefacts were corrected by means of new statistical methods, improving thus the validity of EEG-data, especially in regard to fronto-temporal channels.

The obtained EEG-characteristics in schizophrenics were compared to those of healthy volunteers and to those of patients with other psychiatric disorders, in order to search for any specific pattern for schizophrenia.

Correlations between EEG-data and psychopathological symptoms in schizophrenia were frequently reported in the literature. In our sample the psychopathological state was assessed by means of the Brief Psychiatric Rating Scale and the Negative Symptoms Rating Scale. Data will be presented on the relationships between EEG-characteristics and psychopathological state.

576

EEG MAPPING IN ACUTE AND REMISSION SCHIZOPHRENICS

G.F. Marchesi, B. Nardi, M. De Rosa, G. Paciaroni, S. Borioni, S. Magari, G. Pelotti

Clinical Psychiatry. University of Ancona (Italy)

In recent years many works have pointed out the presence of bioelectrical modifications of EEG Mapping (EEGM) in schizophrenia. The aim of this study was to evaluate EEG activity in acute and remission schizophrenics. Ten right-handed male patients (mean age: 33, range: 25-48 years) with a diagnosis of acute positive schizophrenia were evaluated. The diagnosis was made on the basis of DSM III-R criteria and the Scale for the Assessment of Positive Symptoms (SAPS). Brain computerized tomography (CT) was done to evaluate possible cerebral and/or liquoral space modifications. After admission and before discharge all the patients underwent EEGM during psychosensorial rest (PSR), mental-verbal, and visual-spatial tasks. All patients demonstrated no significant alterations at CT and showed during SAPS a profile indicating a positive syndrome. During remission, with respect to acute stages, EEG patterns showed the following significant differences: (1) EEG activity more stable during RPS, (2) alfa activity more evident, also in anterior regions, and (3) decrease of slow activity during PSR in temporal and occipital regions.

577

NEUROIMAGING AND ELECTROPHYSIOLOGICAL TECHNIQUES IN POSTHYPOGLYCEMIC DEMENTIA

J. Negele-Anetsberger, W.P. Kaschka, Ch. Lang, Departments of Psychiatry and Neurology, University of Erlangen-Nuremberg, Schwabachanlage 6, D-8520 Erlangen, Fed. Rep. of Germany

Insulin and oral antidiabetics of the sulfonylurea group are well known to play a role in chronic factitious disorder and in suicidal attempts. Often, these types of autodestructive behaviour result in irreversible hypoglycemic brain injury which may present clinically as persistent vegetative state or as severe dementia. We had the opportunity to conduct a follow-up study of the clinical course of a patient after attempted suicide with the sulfonylurea derivative glibenclamide over a period of five months and to investigate her repeatedly by means of neuropsychological testing, EEG, CCT, brainstem auditory evoked potentials (AEP), somatosensory evoked potentials (SEP), magnetic resonance imaging (MRI), and single photon emission computed tomography (SPECT). The findings will be discussed with regard to pathophysiological, prognostic, and prophylactic implications.

578

BRAIN SCINTIGRAPHIC STUDIES IN EPILEPSY

Ignatov A. and Kostov K. Department of Nuclear Medicine and Department of Emergency Neurology and Neurosurgery, Bulgarian Medical Academy, Sofia 1527, Bulgaria.

The radionucleide cerebral scintigraphy is applied as a screening tool for the detection of brain lesions associated with increased permeability of the BB barrier which may be the cause of epilepsy. In public health institutions most of the children and youth registered for grand mal fits went trough this examination. A differentiation of the genuine form from the secondary forms due to tumors or other organic lesions was tended. Objects of analysis are the recordings of 150 persons with uncomplicated seizure disorders, with or without focal EEG. Among them positive images with temporal localisation were identified in 5 cases. Focal features were obtained in 4 cases and diffuse lesion in one. The subsequent brain CT-scan revealed one craniopharyngioma and one chronic subdural hematoma - the only case with diffuse lesion pattern. With the aid of cerebral arteriography the remaining 3 cases were identified as benign glioma, meningioma and arterial aneurysm with surrounding hemorrhage. The ensuing operations strengthened the diagnoses from a neuropathological viewpoint. Brain scans have proved to be good first studie in epilepsy.

Session 88 Free Communications:
Migration and mental health I

579
MENTAL HEALTH AND PRIMARY CARE IN ETHNIC GROUPS - GREEK CYPRIOTS IN LONDON
A. Adamapoulou. G. Garyfallos. N. Bouras
Division of Psychiatry, Guy's Hospital

The psychiatric symptoms of 50 consecutive Greek Cypriot patients attending a primary care centre in North London were compared with 50 English attenders.

No difference was found between the two samples. However, the less acultured Greek Cypriots manifested a higher degree of psychological disturbance.

The results indicate possible service needs for ethnic groups on primary care level and specialist psychiatric services.

580
LA REPRESENTATION DE LA SANTE ET DE LA MALADIE MENTALE CHEZ LES MIGRANTS ET REFUGIES EN EUROPE
R. BENNEGADI, FRANCE

La migration est un phénomène où les aménagements de la personnalité sont intenses et où les enjeux de l'acculturation sont souvent énormes. A partir d'une longue expérience clinique, d'une compilation bibliographique, et de comparaisons à travers l'EUROPE, les auteurs tentent de dégager les axes psycho-anthropologiques et psychopathologiques selon que l'entreprise d'acculturation gratifie ou marginalise.

Les exemples concerneront les différentes phases de la trajectoire migratoire, les principales ethnies représentées en FRANCE et dans d'autres pays Européens (PAYS-BAS, R.F.A.), à différents âges des migrants ou des réfugiés.

Cette communication s'appuie essentiellement sur des observations cliniques autant dans les aspects psycho-anthropologiques, médico-juridiques et psychopathologiques.

En conclusion, les auteurs posent le phénomène migratoire comme un aspect en interaction interrogative de la société qui accueille, et, si la santé des migrants peut servir comme indicateur de santé globale d'une société, que ce soit plutôt un "indicateur de santé publique" et non de stigmatisation ambigüe et paralysante.

581
SERVING THE GREEK CANADIANS IN TORONTO - A MULTICULTURAL MODEL
Dr. Hung-Tat Lo
Scarborough Grace General Hospital
Toronto, Canada

A pilot project to provide acute psychiatric care to Greek Canadians is described. Service is delivered by a mobile multidisciplinary team based in a community hospital. Assessment and treatment are provided at home, with significant involvement of community resources. The more severe psychiatric conditions are targeted and a medical model is used.

Some preliminary findings will be presented.

582
PSYCHOPATHOLOGY IN MIGRATORY GROUPS
Dinelli U, Dinelli M, Mascolo M.D. Mottola G, Stefinlongo P. Materazzo M.
Casa di Cura Park-Villa Napoleon-Dipartimento di Psichiatria
Scientific studies by Jaspers, Minkowski and many others, have clearly shown an important link between the eclipse of the "presence" and psychopathology. The pathology (caused) by "deprivation", and "Dasein" disintegration, seem to be the psychodynamic event at the start of the psychotic "graft". Our contribution wants to further prove the existence of such a pathology and is a document tracing the main contributory causes of the psychotic "development" in a migratory population. The study took place following a retrospective method of inquiry, investigating the period 1979-1987. During this time we examined every patient who came to our notice because of psychotic episodes (295-297-298-296-DSMIII).
The sample under examination was homogeneous both according to age and origin (from the Region of Friuli-Venezia-Giulia) and indicative of the way in which a section of the population had turned emigration into a way of life, due to necessity, tradition and culture. the only way to survive. the "azimuth" to be reached, the "ultimate sacrifice", the "expiation on this earth" in order to obtain the material benefits, to the detriment both of one's own image and of the interpersonal relationships. The case-histories consisted of 70 patients (41 males and 29 females) with an average age of 37.6+8.5. The social background of the majority was represented by farm-workers from the plain as well as the mountain districts, the level of education from medium to low. The close study of the family nucleus showed that these patients were an important factor in its fragmentation. The insurgence of the illness calculated on the density of population of the place of origin is more than double compared to that of the population in general. In most cases the first on-set of the illness appears abroad, during migration, with maximum positive pathological symptoms showing over the negative ones. The cure and evolution of the dissociating outline appears more beneficial if operated in Italy, rather than abroad. High in our cases is the sub-acute procedure type of the psycho-pathological lack of compensation with a progressive and recurrent evolution, together with persistence of the defect during the critical periods. The analysis of our results allows us to add our experience to that of the other international studies. These emphasize the "social" element as a possible cause for the derealisation and de-personalition. They often give rise to "false" expectations, from these stems the concept of migratory movement for which the ultimate end is always the "dasein" and in a grotesque way this is torn up during the very attempt (migration) of reaching it.

583
SOCIALPSYCHIATRIC ASPECTS OF FOREIGN WORKERS

Friedl E.J., Pfolz H.
Psychiatrisches Krankenhaus der Stadt Wien
Baumgartner Hoehe, 1145 Vienna, Austria

As usual there exist practical problems with persons coming from socioeconomical less developed countries not only in the public health service but also in psychiatric institutions. Also there are various ways on research methodological problems are concerned with different forms of migrations as well as the interpretations of psychiatric disorders.
In this paper we present a nonselected group of foreign workers. They have been patients of Psychiatric Hospital of Vienna. All of them have been living in a district of Vienna, which can be exactly described by demographic data. We try to explore whether there are connections between the present socioeconomical standard and psychiatric disorders or not.

584
MIGRATION ON STAGE (CROSS-CULTURAL PSYCHIATRY AND THEATRE)

Dr. Jacques A. ARPIN
IUPG, Geneva, Switzerland

Any migration implies a passage from one sociocultural context to another. Whether migration occurs in space or in time, ethnic identities are being challenged. Anxiety appears when cultural defenses are no longer adequate and adjustments cannot be made. In general medical practice, such anxiety often becomes obvious through somatic problems.
A cross-cultural approach of such clinical cases allows for the improvement of the case history and offers prospects for creative therapeutic and preventive strategies.
Migration is the passage from one stage to another. Cultural principles cannot be applied in just any society without creating problems. Society, the audience, evaluates the migrant persons' abilities to adjust and hence judges their deviance in the new environment.
Drama provides a rich material about migration, through authors, actors, designers, a.s.o. who have experienced the rites of such a passage. The cross-cultural approaches of drama and (mental) health are complementary as both have common religious roots and ritual mechanisms,eg. around migration. Such methodology reinforces the information and the understanding in cross-cultural situations, improving the case history and performing primary prevention in both clinical and field areas.

Session 89 Free Communications:
Schizophrenia: Course and outcome

585
GENDER AND OUTCOME IN SCHIZOPHRENIA

Raimo KR Salokangas, Department of Public Health, University of Tampere, Tampere, Finland

According to earlier studies e.g. premorbid psychosocial development, onset of illness and family atmosphere have an effect on the outcome of schizophrenia.
Recently the author has paid attention to the gender of patients as a predictive factor. In two eigth-years' retrospective follow-up studies men remained hospitalized for longer than women and their social outcome was poorer than that of women.
A new sample of 227 new schozophrenic patients defined by DSM III was examined and followed for two years. Five years' follow-up is just ending.
Men showed a poorer premorbid heterosexual development and tended to be more withdrawn than women. Men suffered also from negative symptoms more often than women. At the end of two years follow-up psychosocial outcome of men was in many respect poorer than that of women.
These results will be compared with those of five years' follow-up. Results of the whole study will be discussed in greater detail from the point of view of the male role behavior and damaging effect of schizophrenia on it.

586
CLINICAL FEATURES, COURSE AND OUTCOME OF SCHIZOPHRENIA IN NAGASAKI: RESULTS FROM A 5-YEAR FOLLOW UP-STUDY
K.Araki, S.Michitsuji, Y.Ohta, Y.Nakane
Nagasaki Univ.School of Medicine, Dept. of Neuropsychiatry, Nagasaki, Japan

A follow up study concerning long-term outcome and course of schizophrenia in Nagasaki City was carried out. Sixty-eight patients from the original 107 schizophrenics (ICD-9) who were collected for the WHO Collaborative Study on Determinants of Outcome of Severe Mental Disorders were included in a 5-year follow-up outcome study and assessed by a schedule which included measurements of: (1) "Current Mental State", (2) "Clinical Course" and (3) "Social Adjustment". Our results indicate that for "Current Mental State" 29% of patients showed "complete remission", 40% "incomplete remission" and 24% were still psychotic. For "Clinical Course" 26% of patients displayed only "one psychotic episode", 52% "two or more psychotic episodes" and 13% "continuous psychotic episode". For "Social Adjustment" 50% were found to be "better" and 47% poorer. These results are discussed in this paper.

587

FACTORS INFLUENCING THE COURSE OF SCHIZO-
PHRENIC ILLNESS
Vella G., Pacileo A., Loriedo C., Alliani D.
I Psychiatric Clinic University "La Sapienza"
Rome

Literature on the course of schizophrenia
and its studies is rich and continously up
to date. Researches carried out by many
autors support the hypothesis that the
evolution of schizophrenia might depend
more upon the nature and quality of
enviromental influences than on the
structure of personality. The authors
confront the problem of "natural course"
of schizophrenia with the history of
schizophrenia and with the history of the
ideas on schizophrenia.
The "natural course" is therefore carefully
explored inorder to point out causes and
motivations that are behind the "schizophrenic
story".

588

A TEST OF FOULDS' HIERARCHICAL MODEL OF MENTAL
ILLNESS IN A GROUP OF GREEK SCHIZOPHRENIC PATIENTS

Angelopoulos NV, Economou Marina, Zojes D,
Tzivaridou Despina, Doga Heleni, Pratikakis E.

Department of Psychiatry, University of Ioannina,
Greece.

In order to examine the validity of Foulds' and
Bedford's Hierarchical model of psychopathology,
the Delusions-Symptoms-States Inventory (DSSI)
was administered to 247 patients given the dia-
gnosis of Schizophrenia.
The DSSI consists of twelve subscales: state of
Anxiety, state of Depression, state of Elation,
Conversion symptoms, Dissociative symptoms,
Phobic symptoms, Compulsive symptoms, Ruminative
symptoms, delusions of Grandeur, delusions of
Persecution, delusions of Contrition, delusions
of Disintegration.
These subscales are allocated to the five proposed classes of mental illness: I.Non-personally
ill, II.Dysthymic States, III.Neurotic Symptoms,
IV.Integrated Delusions, V. Delusions of Disintegration.
It was found that a great majority of the cases
(81.5%) produced symptom patterns conforming to
the hierarchy of classes of mental illness model.
More than sixty percent of the patients reported,
apart from Delusions of Disintegration, delusions
of Percecution, states of Anxiety, states of Depression and states of Elation to a lesser degree.

589

A CLINICAL STUDY OF SCHIZOPHRENIA-THE FACTORS
INFLUENCING RELAPSE IN READMITTED PATIENTS
Yasuo Unai, M.D.,Dept.of Neuropsychiatry Showa
University Fujigaoka Hospital, Yokohama, Japan
The factors influencing relapse in schizophrenia
were investigated synthetically-biological,
chronological, situational, family, social and
symptomatological. The purpose of the
investigation was to find means of preventing
relapse and to know the mechanism of relapse. The
data were collected from Nov.15,1971 to Oct.31,
1976. It covered 166 patients at Toyoko Mental
Hospital, who suffered relapses, and of these 74
were readmitted to the hospital. 95 patients who
were used as subjects for this study. They were
divided into two groups. The first group were
patients who had only a few relapses (these were
21 patients-10 male and 11 female). The second
group were patients who had many relapses (these
were 74 patients - 44 male and 30 female). The
patients who had only a few relapses had four
characteristics: 1) there were few negative
symptoms; 2) there were participating factors; 3)
there were children born in the middle-not first-
born or last-born; 4) there was at least 3 years
between admissions. On the other hand, the
patients who had many relapses had the following
characteristics: 1) there were negative symptoms;
2) precipitating factors were unknown or not
clear; 3) they were the eldest or the youngest
child or the only child; 4) they had had relapses
within the past 3 years. A discussion will now be
held on the means of preventing relapses and the
mechanism of relapses in chizophrenia.

Session 90 Free Communications:
Animal studies on antidepressants

590

SIBUTRAMINE HCL AND OTHER ANTIDEPRESSANTS: EFFECTS
ON α_2-ADRENOCEPTORS
D J Heal, M R Prow and W R Buckett, Research Dept,
The Boots Co. PLC, Nottingham NG2 3AA, U.K.
Sibutramine HCl is a novel antidepressant which
inhibits noradrenaline and 5-HT uptake. This drug
produces rapid down-regulation of rat cortical
β-adrenoceptors. The effects of sibutramine HCl
and other antidepressants on pre- and postsynaptic
α_2-adrenoceptors were respectively assessed using
clonidine-induced hypoactivity and mydriasis (Heal
et al, 1988, Br J Pharm 95, 781P). C57/Bl/6 mice
were injected with clonidine (0.1 mg/kg ip) and
hypoactivity was rated 0-3 on 5 parameters at
10 min intervals for 1h. Pupil diameter was
measured at 10 min. Drugs were given daily for
14d at the following doses (mg/kg ip):-
sibutramine HCl (3); clenbuterol (5); desipramine,
zimeldine, amitriptyline, tranylcypromine,
mianserin (10). Behavioural responses were
measured 24h after the first and last dose.
Neither α_2-adrenoceptor response was altered after
a single drug treatment. However, after repeated
administration clonidine-induced hypoactivity and
mydriasis were both attenuated by sibutramine HCl,
amitriptyline, desipramine and tranylcypromine.
Zimeldine, mianserin and clenbuterol were without
effect. Overall, pre- and postsynaptic
α_2-adrenoceptor function was reduced by antidepressants which were inhibitors of either
noradrenaline uptake or MAO. Selective 5-HT
uptake inhibitors and atypical antidepressants did
not affect these responses.

591

THE EFFECTS OF CHRONIC FIPEXIDE TREATMENT IN THE OLFACTORY BULBECTOMIZED RAT MODEL OF DEPRESSION.
B.Earley[1], M.Burke[1], B.E.Leonard[1], C.Gouret[2] and J.L.Junien[2], Pharmacology Department[1], University College, Galway, Ireland and Jouveinal Laboratories[2], 94263, Fresnes, France.

Bi-lateral olfactory bulbectomy produces a series of behavioural changes in the rat, characterized by hyperactivity in the open-field apparatus and deficits in passive avoidance behaviour. This model of depression will selectively detect antidepressant activity only following the chronic administration of the drug. Gouret et al (1989) reported antidepressant properties for fipexide, a potential antidepressant active in the rat learned helplessness test, which induced a down-regulation of both $5HT_2$ and beta receptors in the rat cerebral cortex following chronic treatment. In the present study, male Sprague-Dawley rats were bulbectomized or sham operated and allowed to recover for 14 days before drug treatment commenced. Fipexide was administered for 27 days (32 mg/kg I.P. twice daily) and behaviour in the open-field apparatus measured after the 14th day of treatment. Fipexide reversed the hyperactivity of bulbectomized rats. Fipexide has potential antidepressant activity in this model.

592

ANTI-CHOLINERGIC EFFECTS OF PSYCHOTROPICS CHARACTERIZED IN RAT PAROTID ACINI.
Mogens Undén, Birgitte Nauntofte, and Steen Dissing. Dept. of Psychiatry 2, St. Hans Hospital, DK-4000 Roskilde, Denmark.

Anti-cholinergic effects of the anti-psychotic drug, cis-chlorprothixene, and the antidepressant, amitriptyline, on the secretory events underlying the formation of primary saliva were investigated. Both drugs share the side-effect xerostomia. The inhibitory effects of the drugs upon the cholinergic-induced rise in Ca^{++} as well as on O_2 consumption and Cl^- loss were investigated in isolated rat parotid acini in order to characterize their anti-cholinergic effects quantitatively, using fura-2 as indicator of intracellular free Ca^{++}. Cholinergic-induced rise in cytosolic free Ca^{++} was inhibited by cis-chlorprothixene with half maximal effect at 1.9 μM, and maximal inhibition at 10 μM. For amitriptyline the figures were 0.5 μM and 5 μM, respectively. The same experiments in fetal-calf-serum showed a serum protein binding of 95% in the case of amitriptyline. The findings are consistent with these drugs exerting their effects on the steps leading from agonist-binding to the cholinergic receptor, and to the increase of cytosolic free Ca^{++}. Thus, measurements of stimulation-induced rise in cytosolic free Ca^{++} in the presence of the above-mentioned psychotropics represent a fast and reliable method for detecting inhibitory effects upon autonomic receptor activation.

593

THE ANTI-IMMOBILITY EFFECT OF HIGH BLOOD AND BRAIN LEVELS OF IMIPRAMINE AND DESIPRAMINE IN MICE
I.R. de Oliveira[1,4], B. Diquet[2], V. Van der Meerch[2], J. Gonidec[3] & P.A.S. Prado-Lima[1].
[1]CMME (Paris), [2]Pitié-Salpêtrière (Paris), [3]Delagrange (Chilly-Mazarin) & [4]UFBA (Salvador-Brazil).

We studied the relationship of blood and brain levels of imipramine (IMI) and/or its active metabolite desipramine (DMI) to biological response, in the tail suspension test. Compared to the control group (84.7 ± 11.2* sec., n=21), doses of 3.75, 7.5, 15, 30 and 60mg/kg of IMI given intraperitonially (n=9-10) reduced immobility scores respectively to 30.0 ± 6.8***, 47.6 ± 13.0**, 31.9 ± 7.5***, 10.1 ± 4.9*** and 9.9 ± 4.3*** sec. (Dunnet's test). There were negative correlations ($p < 0.001$, n=70) between doses (r=-.50), brain levels of IMI (r=-.42), DMI (r=-.42), IMI + DMI (r=-.42), blood levels of IMI (r=-.44), DMI (r=-.34), IMI + DMI (r=-.42) and behaviour. Correlation was higher between dose and immobility scores than between the other parameters and immobility. This contrasts with findings in humans. These differences may be explained by different rates of metabolism, which are determined by genetic factors. In mice, doses seem to reflect blood and brain levels, as demonstrated by high correlations between these parameters. Higher levels of IMI, DMI and IMI + DMI in blood and brain did not impair behavioural response. These findings agree with most results found in men treated with IMI, and suggest a linear or sigmoid relationship.
* ± SEM; ** $p < 0.05$; *** $p < 0.01$.

594

PHARMACOLOGY OF SIBUTRAMINE HCL SUPPORTS INCISIVE ANTIDEPRESSANT ACTION

W.R. Buckett, G.P. Luscombe, D.J. Heal. Research Department, The Boots Company PLC. Nottingham NG2 3AA, U.K.

The antidepressant sibutramine hydrochloride has pharmacological properties indicative of a monoamine uptake inhibitor. In vivo it is very potent with oral ED50 values of 0.64 ± 0.20 mg/kg in rat and 1.78 ± 0.68 mg/kg in mouse reserpine antagonism tests. In common with most, but not all, antidepressant treatments sibutramine HCl (1 mg/kg) down-regulates rat cortical β-adrenoceptors and the receptor-linked adenylate cyclase but in only 3 days, which may support the hypothesis of a more rapid onset of clinical action. This effect of sibutramine HCl may be induced in part by the pharmacological activity of its demethylated primary and secondary amine metabolites. In addition the lack of post-synaptic actions (10^{-4}M) at muscarinic, α_1 and β-noradrenergic, dopaminergic (D_1 and D_2) and serotoninergic ($5HT_1$ and $5HT_2$) sites indicated by receptor binding studies and at histaminic (H_1) sites demonstrated in guinea-pig ileum all suggest a selective profile of action. Thus sibutramine HCl may be classified as an antidepressant of novel type, the potency of which predicts an action in severe depression, the rapidity of β-adrenoceptor down-regulation predicts faster action, and the pharmacological profile predicts fewer side-effects.

595

CNS RECEPTOR AUTORADIOGRAPHY IN
RATS TREATED WITH FLUVOXAMINE

D. Vine, M.D., M. Madar, and J.K. Wamsley, Dept. of Psychiatry, Univ. of Utah, SLC, UT U.S.A.

Serotonergic (5-HT) and adrenergic neurotransmitters in the human central nervous system, (CNS) are implicated in the etiology of affective disorders. The clinical efficacy of some antidepressants (AD) appears to correlate with their specificity as a synaptic 5-HT re-uptake inhibitor. The non-tricyclic AD fluvoxamine (FLX) is in this category of drugs. In the present study, ß-adrenergic (ß-A) & 5-HT receptors (5-HTR) in the brains of rats treated chronically with FLX were quantitatively compared with those in control brains by in-vitro autoradiography. Radiolabelled ligands with binding specifity for B_1, B_2, $5-HT_1$ & $5-HT_2$ subtypes were used in labelling experiments. Changes in 5-HTR binding in experimental animals vs controls was subtype specific & limited to discrete areas of cortex & hippocampus. Widespread changes in ß-A binding in treated animal brains were seen when [^{3}H]dihydroalprenolol (^{3}H-DHA) was used as the labelling agent. However, using [^{125}I]Pindolol, a putatively more specific ß label, no change in binding was seen. These findings suggest that ß-A mechanisms at the receptor level may not play a large role in the cellular effects of this type of AD. It also may mean that [^{3}H]DHA is labelling another receptor in addition to ß-A sites, a type which does indeed change with chronic FLX treatment.

596

THE EFFECTS OF IPSAPIRONE, BUSPIRONE, GEPIRONE AND DIAZEPAM IN ANIMAL MODELS OF AGGRESSION, ANXIETY AND DEPRESSION

T. Schuurman, U. Benz, J. De Vry and J. Traber, Neurobiology Department, Troponwerke, Berliner Str. 156, D-5000 Köln 80, F.R.G.

In an ethologically based aggression test, ipsapirone, buspirone and gepirone inhibited territorial aggressive behavior of male resident rats towards male conspecifics intruding their homecages. Other behavioral activities such as exploration and non-aggressive social behaviors were not suppressed by drug treatment. In contrast, diazepam inhibited aggressive behavior only at doses which also suppressed other behaviors. The serotonergic anxiolytics and diazepam desinhibited punished behavior in the shock-suppressed drinking and in the Geller-Seifter conflict test. In a new anxiety model ultrasound vocalisation (22 k Hz) of rats enclosed in a box in which they previously had received footshocks was measured. The four anxiolytics reduced the duration of fear-induced ultrasound significantly. In the social interaction test of anxiety, rats were paired in an unfamiliar observation cage which was strongly illuminated. Under these stressful conditions rats showed a low level of social behaviors. All four test substances stimulated social interactions under these circumstances, which is indicative for anxiolytic activity. Interestingly, ipsapirone was the only substance with prosocial activity under low stress conditions (= low illumination of the observation cage). In animal models of depression, such as the behavioral despair (forced swimming), learned helplessness and restraint-stress test, ipsapirone, buspirone and gepirone showed an antidepressant-like profile, whereas diazepam was inactive. In tests for the assessment of drug effects on sensorimotor functions (balance rod, rotating rod, traction test etc.) diazepam affected performance at much lower doses than the serotonergic anxiolytics.

Session 91 Free Communications:
Forensic psychiatry in closed institutions

597

The medico-legal Psychiatrist of yesterday and today.

Mr. M. TOUARY, Mr. BENGOUJRAH, Mr. B. BENSMAJL

In this study, the authors, from the psychatric reports of the (expertise) in a penal subject, comparl two populations of delinquents subjects mental patients, the first has been expertised during the period of 1970-1975, the second on from 1980 - 1985. After a statistic, desciptive and analytic study of the different variable of the questioning, the authors attempt an approach about the phenomenon of the delinquency of the mental patient by an intermediate of a global approach medico- social psychology. From those results, the authors make suggestions concerning the judicial and psychiatric treatment of those subjects.

598

PSYCHIATRIC TREATMENT ON MENTALLY DISTURBED OFFENDERS IN SWEDEN

Henrik Belfrage and Lars Lidberg
Dept of Social and Forensic Psychiatry
Karolinska institutet, Sweden

The focus of this study are offenders who suffers from a mental disorder that is "equivalent to insanity" according to the Swedish Criminal Code. We have concentrated on the following question: Is psychiatric treatment of the "equivalents" crime preventive? The result is that psychiatric treatment has a positive crime preventive effect on some categories of offenders (especially offenders sentenced for assault), but none of significance on others (especially property offenders). It is therefore erroneous to pose the general question: (a) Does psychiatric treatment have more crime preventive effect than a prison sentence? If individuals who are sentenced for assault are studied, the answer to the question (a) is "yes", but if property offenders are studied the answer is "no". The crude formulation in (a) must therefore be replaced by (b): What crime preventive effect does psychiatric treatment have on different categories of mentally disordered offenders in comparison to that of imprisonment?

599
THE SOCIAL BACKGROUND OF HOMICIDE
Kramp P. Gottlieb P., Denmark

In Denmark the rate of Homicide doubled between 1959 and 1983. The social background of a representative sample of 71 male, non-psychotic defendants charged with homicide is presented and compared with the corresponding data for male prison inmates as a whole and with the general male population. Homicide defendants and prison inmates are very alike, both groups were heavy loaded with broken homes, difficulties in school, unemployment, loneliness etc. Homicide defendants, however, had more often a previous history of attempted suicide and had more often been admitted to psychiatric hospitals than had prison inmates. The major developmental trends in the Danish population during the investigation period were increases in educational level and material wealth. Meanwhile, male homicide defendants and prison inmates were characterized by a constantly low level of education and by a reduction in occupational success. It thus seems that the gap between the general population on the one hand and a social marginal group of homicide suspects and prison inmates of the other has widened. It is concluded, that the increase in the number of socially troubled homicide defendants, as in the criminal population as a whole, seems to reflect some serious consequences of a recent increase i social marginalisation in modern Western societies.

600
A PSYCHO-SOCIAL STUDY OF 28 WOMEN WHO MURDERED THEIR HUSBAND
Kaptanoğlu,C.,M.D.,Seber,G.,Ph.D.,Erkmen,H.,M.D., Dilbaz,N.,M.D.,Tekin,D.,M.D.

Department of Psychiatry, Faculty of Medicine, Anadolu University Eskişehir/Turkey

The study was carried out at Antalya, Afyon, Kütahya, Eskişehir and Sivas city prisons in Turkey. The data for this study were obtained from 28 female prisoners who had been found guilty of murder. A questionnaire was individually applied to each of the subjects, in order to collect data about their psycho-social-cultural characteristics. Also, the W scale which was developed by Frank Costin (1982) for measuring restrictive beliefs about women's social roles, was administered.

About 90% of the subjects were members of lower socio-economic classes. A significantly higher percentage (97%) of the subjects came from the subculture in which there was greater acceptance of social ideology of male dominance over women and of intergroup and interpersonal aggression. 70% of the subjects reported having been physically abused by their husbands. 86% of the subjects indicated that they had economically depended on their victims. W scale scores of the subjects were compared with 30 female undergraduates's scores. There wasn't any statistically significant difference between these two groups's W scale scores. This finding was very interesting because the subjects' beliefs about women's social roles were more liberal than we had expected.

601
MEASURE OF AGRESSIVITY IN A RECLUSE POPULATION
Abril,A.,Nieves,P.,Civeira,J.,Pelayo,A.
Psychiatry Department Complutense University of Madrid (Spain).

Sobre una población penitenciaria de 60 reclusos,representativa del centro penitenciario donde se realiza el presente estudio, se estudian las caracteristicas de la agresividad a traves del test de Mira y Lopez a si como diversas variables psicosociales.

Los reclusos incluidos en este estudio cumplian los criterios de trastorno antisocial de la personalidad segun el DSM III y hbian mantenido conductas hetero y autoagresivas probadas.

El estudio de la conducta agresiva mediante un test proyectivo y sus implicaciones predictivas en el medio penitenciario son analizadas, a si mismo se propone una forma mas abreviada del test de Mira y Lopez para el estudio de la conducta agresiva.

602
COMPARISON BETWEEN GROUPS OF PRISONERS ON SOME PERSONALITY MEASURES
Manuel Riobo
Hospital Son Dureta, Palma de Mallorca, Spain

Sensation Seeking, Extraversion, Neuroticism, Psychoticism, Impulsiveness, Susceptibility to Punishment and Anxiety Scales were administered to a sample of 100 male prisoners in one Spanish prison. This sample was divided into groups according to four variables: Recidivism, Drug-Addiction, Behavior in prison and Type of crime. In the between-groups comparison, the results showed significant correlations for the groups Drug-Addicts and Poor Prison Behavior, on Sensation Seeking, Psychoticism, Impulsiveness, Susceptibility to Punishment and Anxiety. Both Neuroticism and Extraversion scales showed low correlation with all the variables. The results are discussed.

603
PSYCHOLOGICAL FACTORS IN JUVENILE PRISONERS
Mouyas A., C.Asimakopoulos
Psychiatric Hospital for Prisoners
Korydallos, Greece

The study included all admissions to the Kotydallos Reformatory since 15-12-88. There were 90 males under age of 21. On admission a nurse completed a form whitch coveredbiografical data,information about personal and family psychiatric history and substance abuse. The subject also comleted a questionnaire on disthymic symptoms. Two weeks later the nurse filled in a form on the patient's behavioral problems. Finally, the subjects were examined clinically by a psychiatrist

The main results that emerged were as follows:
1. 26 subjects had separated parents, 6 had lost a parent, 5 did not know their fathers.
2. 17 subjects had a parent who abused alcohol.
3. 28 subjects reported substance abuse, in 13 cases heroin.
4. 37 had visited a psychiatrist. Of these 17 were among the 28 subjects who reported substance abuse.
5. Dysthymic symptomatology was present in 60 subjects. 2 subjects were psychotic.
6. 11 subjects injured themselves.

Session 92 Free Communications:
Pharmacotherapy in child and adolescent psychiatry

604
18 YEARS FOLLOW UP OF HYPERKINETIC CHILDREN TREATED WITH LITHIUM
Herman Bleiweiss, MD; Assit.Prof.in Psychiatry, Buenos Aires University; President of the Argentine Foundation of Genetics Applied to Psychiatry.

In 1970 hyperkinetics with agressive behavior were studied from different points of view. Chromosomic abnormalities were found. Probably results were influenced by the fact thay they were chosen for being very hyperkinetic and agressive. From 34 patients, seven (20%) had the following chromosomic composition: one 47,XXY; four 46,XY/47,XXY; one 46,XY/45,XY-C; one 46,XY/47,XYY. One had cryptorchism bilateral, and three unilateral. The EEG was abnormal in 40%. They were treated with lithium carbonate 25 to 100 mg and Thioridazine 30 mg daily. Both drugs were given for about one week. Later lithium alone was given. Improvement began after 2 weeks. There were two different types of curves, one with a peak of 0,60 mEq/l, maintenance of 45 mEq/l. The other's peak was 0,65 mEq/l, maintenance 0,25 mEq/l. There were two cases with a particular curve of 0,98 mEq/l; the other was 1,09 mEq/l. Both had side effects, subsided after suspention of medication. For different personnal reasons, 10 patients withdraw treatment. From the remaining group, six didn't need more lithium. The other 18 needed a maintenance dose because they relapsed when medication was suspended. Even Patient Nº 21 is still improving in his behavior despite he has a very low IQ. So most of them needed medication constantly. Those with chromosomic anomalies responded faster. This study shows the importance of chromosomic studies in these patients. Most benefit from psychotherapy.

605
THERAPEUTIC EFFECT OF TETRAHYDROBIOPTERIN (RTHBP) IN INFANTILE AUTISM

H.Naruse[1], M.Takesada[2], Y.Nakane[3], K.Yamazaki[4], M.Nagahata[5], H.Kazamatsuri[6] :1Kyorin Univ, Tokyo, 2Children Hosp.of Osaka, 3Nagasaki Univ, Nagasaki, 4Tokai Univ, Kanagawa, 5Tsukuba Univ, Ibaragi, 6Teikyo Univ, Tokyo

Based on our new chemical findings in autistic children, we started a study on clinical effect of RTHBP in the disorder. RTHBP was supplied by Suntory Ltd. Clinical symptoms and changes in abnormal behaviors were evaluated by "Rating Scale for Abnormal behavior in Children". A preliminary study with 17 patients suggested effectiveness of RTHBP. Therefore, a double blind trial of RTHBP and inactive placebo was achieved in four institutions (1-4) with 84 patients (62male and 22female). General improvement rating (GIR) of RTHBP group was clearly superior to that of the placebo group at the end of twelfth weeks ($P<0.05$ by Wilcoxon Rank Sum Test). Especially, in the group of children younger than 5 years old, the GIR of the drug group was significantly superior already at the end of 8 weeks. Changes of clinical symptoms were most prominent in a cluster of "autistic behavior" of the rating scale mentioned above. The second trial was an open label clinical test, which was performed in 6 institutions with 99 patients (79 male and 20 female). The clinical changes were observed for more than 24 weeks. Marked and definite improvement was rated in more than half of the subjects. No serious adverse reaction was observed in the both studies.

606
Two Years Followup of Children on Ritalin in Rural and Urban Practice.

Houshang G. Hamadani, M.D.

Review of literature reveals that Ritalin is used to decrease hyperactivity, increase attention span, and improve distrubed behavior. In this study, two groups of children, one in a clinic located in a rural area, the other from a private practice in the city are studied. Ritalin was used for more than two years on both groups. The academic and social as well as psychological adjustments following Ritalin therapy were evaluated regularly. Data reveals that Ritalin is effective in increasing the attention span and improving the school performance regardless of environmental differences. The data also shows that psychological and behavioral disorders of the child, when it is not directly related to attention deficit disorder does not respond to Ritalin. Environmental factors as well as parental attitude seems to be the important factors in improving the behavior of these children. It is also the conculsion of this study that the clinical improvements are not directly related to the dosage of Ritalin.

607

An Open Trial of S-Adenosyl-L-Methionine in ADHD, RS

W. Shekim, R. Asarnow, F. Antun, G. Hanna, J. McCracken

UCLA Neuropsychiatric Institute
Hamad General Hospital, Doha, Qatar

The psychostimulants d-amphetamine and methylphenidate are thought to be the most effective treatment in children, adolescents and adults with attention deficit-hyperactivity disorder (ADHD) because they potentiate both dopamine (DA) and norepinephrine (NE) at the synaptic cleft. These medications are not free from side effects and controversy. Newer effective and safe treatments are needed. S-Adenosyl-L-Methionine (SAM), the active form of methionine acts as a methyl donor and is involved in many metabolic pathways. It has beta adrenergic and dopamine receptor agonist activity. We have been using SAM in a sample of well diagnosed adults with ADHD in a four week open trial to establish its effectiveness and safety. Preliminary data reveal that 75% of patients improve on it and that it is safe. Diagnostic work-up and SAM effects on measures of attention, restlessness, impulsivity and mood, as well as laboratory measures will be discussed.

608

ADMISSIONS TO PSYCHIATRIC HOSPITAL DURING ADOLESCENCE : A SEVEN TO TEN YEARS FOLLOW-UP.

Ferrero F., Giacomini-Biraud V., Tricot L.
Service de Psychiatrie II, IUPG, Geneva (Switz.)

This paper presents preliminary results of a seven to ten years follow-up in a group of 107 adolescents admitted to the Geneva Psychiatric Hospital between 1977 and 1981. This represents all 14 to 18 years old patients hospitalized during this period. Diagnostic stability, particularly in the case of psychoses, justifies the repartition of the patients into two broad categories : psychotic patients (n=36 ; 33.6%), and non-psychotic patients (n=71 ; 66.4%), according to the ICD 9. Among the 50 patients who did not require further treatment, 74% belonged to the non-psychotic group and 26% to the psychotic group. The data provide an analysis of the type of treatment ("channel of care") received by the patients according to the diagnosis as well as to such variables as suicidal attempts and alcohol or drug abuse. The subgroup of deceased patients (n=14 ; 13%) is separately analysed. Specific clues allow an evaluation of the intensity and cost of treatment which appear at least four times larger in the psychotic group than in the non-psychotic group. Furthermore, the results support the usefulness of psychopathological diagnoses in predicting the outcome at seven to ten years in a group of hospitalized adolescent patients.

Session 93 Free Communications:
Psychopathological and psychotherapeutic themes I

609

ASYMPTOMATIC SCHIZOPHRENIA: THE HISTORY OF A MISCONCEPTION

Ion Vianu, Morges, Switzerland

The existence of a hidden form of schizophrenia, a kind of "madness" invisible to the layman, proceeds mainly from three sources: classical German psychopathology, Freudian psychoanalysis, and present-day Soviet psychiatry. A certain relationship may be discovered between these three sources: for instance, Soviet psychiatry was in its beginnings strongly influenced by German psychopathology. Similarly, Bleulerian and Freudian thinking are historically and conceptually interconnected. The aims of the three aproaches remain different however.

610

REVEALING FACTORS IN NEUROSES AND THE SCHIZOPHRENIC PSYCHOSES

P. Hamogeorgakis,
Dromokaetion Mental Hospital, Athens, Greece.

The purpose of this study is to investigate retrospectively some revealing aetiological factors in the development of neurotic and schizophrenic disorders. For this purpose, life events were examined in relation to personality structure and its developmental phases.
Forty-three cases (20 neurotics and 23 schizophrenics) were investigated. Main factors that appeared to coincide with the expression of overt psychopathology were mostly related to early family environment (25%), acute stress in adult life (32%), immigration (14%), marital and occupational discord (15%) and maladjustment to army service (10%).
The role played by environmental versus developmental influences in the evolution of psychopathological conditions is discussed and some suggestions regarding future research are put forward.

611

EMOTIONAL DISORDERS IN CHILDHOOD CREATING MENTAL DISORDERS IN ADOLESCENCE AND ADULTS

P. Hamogeorgakis,
Dromokaetion Mental Hospital, Athens, Greece.

The purpose of this study is to investigate the probable connections between the emotional disturbances in infants, due to parental attitude, and the development of psychopathological conditions (schizophrenic disorders and mixed neurotic states) in the adult life.
Thirty-one cases of schizophrenic disorders, with abnormal psychosexual development, and seven parients suffering from mixed neurotic states were investigated. Parental attitudes were analysed and the conditions most probably related to childhood psychic traumata were described.
The findings of this study are discussed and the main guidelines regarding early modification of unwanted parental attitudes are presented.

612

PSYCHOFUNCIONAL EXAMINATION-PSYCHODIAGNOSIS PSYCHOPATHOLOGIC.
Vitorio Ciupka - Denise Ciupka, Psicologa
Vitorio Ciupka

Semiotécnica psicofuncional objetiva el estudio individual ó colectiva, de síntomas, señales de anormalidades de la vida y fisilogía mental libre, elaborados de las percepciónes y representaciones del mundo exterior y interior, por los estímulos de las imágens y idéas concebidas; mas desde el momento que lo YO desenvolvió las facultades de concientización y de memória. Semiología psicopatológica es el establecimiento del ordenamiento genético-constructiva y remontage hasta los alicerces del distúrbio básico "complejo-nocha-núcleo psicótico, transtorno instintivo-afetivo", por la análisis de los processos psíquicos del patrimonio de las esperiencias anteriores, reveladas y apercebidas. Distinguir neuroses de las psicoses, potencial suicida y homicida, genocida, síndromes psicosomáticas, síntomas de conversion, y otros tipos de afección. Interado responde a quesitos estímulos que incidem sobre la auto-conciencia y hetero-conciencia, és decir, en lo que intenciona, despierta y plasma. Agentes impresionantes se componen de las imágenes, símbolos, idéas y temas universalmente abarcantes; el pensamiento seleciona y se orienta sobre los mismos, correlacionado a las funciones mnemicas, dando formación de juícios y conceptos, sobre la vida dinámica mental - autopsíquica, alopsíquica y emocional, con todos sus aspectos en causas y consecuencias. Actividade psicomotora dibuja sobre objetos de uso personal, animales, figuras humanas y temas abstratos y objetivos.

613

Consideraciones Axiológicas en el discurso psicopatológico

Prof. Dr. Rafael Parada Allende
Hospital Psiquiátrico, Stgo.-Chile.

1. La conceptualización empleada en psiquiatría remite a epistemologías explícitas o implícitas. La historia de esta disciplina muestra la validez de esta enunciación.

2. La terminología empleada en psiquiatría lleva además juicios de valor en distintas esferas, que cambian en el tiempo en acuerdo a la evolución de los contextos socio culturales.

3. Se analizan términos como el de neurosis personalidad limítrofe. Esquizofrenia, Desorden Mental, psicoterapia etc., en la perspectiva axiológica a que han estado sometidos y las bases epistemológicas que las sustentan.

4. Haremos alcances sobre la modificación de las epistemologías, que han de ocurrir necesariamente cuando por razones axiológicas se cambia la terminología psiquiátricas.

5. Proponemos contribuir al estudio de el doble registro que tienen los términos de la conceptualización psicopatológica en acuerdo al técnico y al destinatario.

614

DATA OF MAPPING IN NORMAL ITALIAN PEOPLE

Prof. G. Battista Laurenzi
Dr. Paola Terribile
Roma, Italy

The authors examined a group of 60 normal people. These people were selected by the form where sicknesses before or after birth were excluded. This group had to be free from epilepsy and traumatic events of the brain.
In these registrations the result was medium and the frequency was of 9.2 c/s (between 8.2 and 10.2). In the same group, theta waves were present in 30% and delta waves in 20%.
We also left people with higt percentage of theta and delta waves because this did not make any difference.
Moreover these slow waves were of low voltage and were present for a very short time.
The data are computerised in 2 groups: the first between the age of 20 and 40 years and the second between 41 and 60 years of age.

Session 94
Anorexia. Art therapy

Video:

615
CHANGE IN PATIENT BEHAVIORS AFTER REMOVING CAFFEINE FROM SALE AT A PSYCHIATRIC HOSPITAL.

Marshall O. Zaslove, M.D., Dept. of Professional Education, Napa State Hospital, Napa, CA, USA.

Caffeinated coffee and soft drinks were removed from sale at a state hospital. Incidence of assaults and property destruction resulting in restraint and/or seclusion declined significantly thereafter.

616
PSYCHOTHERAPEUTIC REBIRTH OF PATIENTS WITH PRIMARY DISORDERS
Maria Diallina and Gaetano Benedetti
General Hospital Athens/GR; University Basel/CH

During psychotherapy some patients undergo through certain transference experiences. This may be interpreted as "rebirth experiences". Under this aspect of the rebirth experience we intend to present a case.
The therapist recognized the patient's need to communicate her anxieties by transforming them into artistic expressions. She was creating clay figures. Thus she was experiencing her own personal and existential space, as a newly born existence. Socrates (son of a midwife) in "Symposium" discussed that the truth can be born from our soul to the others. Hence the therapy can be created through the therapist into the soul of the patient:
- the dialectic delivery of the labour by the therapist acting as a midwife and at the same time as a mother-pedagogue, therefore making possible the mental birth of the patient.
- To "therapise" in ancient Greek is also to take care of, to serve. The nursing of the newborn is then the duty of the healer.
- Healing is only possible if empathy between the two partners develops by helping to promote the identification and the counter identification of the patient with the healer, creating human and social integration (Benedetti).

617
BODY-IMAGE CONFRONTATION TECHNIQUE IN THE TREATMENT OF ANOREXIA NERVOSA
Leichner, P., Kasma, J.
Douglas Hospital Centre, Verdun, Québec

This videotape presentation is the description on a videotape body-image confrontation technique which has been used by the author for the past 8 years. Its purpose is to challenge the body-image distortion or dissatisfaction which is typical of anorexic and bulimic patients. The aim of this document is to provide the viewers with the information required to carry out this intervention. A first section presents two clinical cases and their reaction to the confrontation. In general, most anorexics react emotionnaly with surprise at what they see, then sadness and frustation with themselves. The experience is useful to them as a motivator to keep them in treatment. A smaller group continues to deny their emaciation or their feelings about it even when confronted. As other studies have shown, these patients tend to have a higher rate of relapse. The final section of this document will review before and after treatment images of several patients, highlighting the remarkable changes the bodies of these patients undergo in a relatively short period of time. Since most hospitals are equiped with the equipment necessary to carry out this procedure, the author recommends that this therapeutic technique be considered as an adjunct to the treatment of most anorexic and/or bulimic patients. However, this can be a powerful experience and it should always be conducted in the presence of a therapist.

618
ART-THERAPY WITH TEEN-AGERS

Dino Zanetti Junior
Santa Casa de Misericordia de Sao Paulo

This video is about an experience on art-therapy with teen-agers 13 and 17 years old, met in institution and in the ambulatory Psychiatric Clinic by a psychologist.

*Saturday
14th October 1989*

Session 95 Plenary:
Schizophrenia: Clinical, epidemiological and psychopharmacological issues

619

WHY KRAEPELIN WAS WRONG

Robin M. Murray
Institute of Psychiatry, London, U.K.

It is one of the dogmas of psychiatry that schizophrenia is a deteriorating disorder with onset in early adult life. Consequently, when abnormalities on CT and MRI scan, and cognitive deficits were demonstrated, these were thought to be a consequence of progressive deterioration. However, they are present at the onset of the illness, do not deteriorate, and indeed appear to antedate the florid psychosis; indeed neuropathological findings of lighter brains, larger ventricles and cytoarchitectural anomalies imply that the crucial period is during foetal or neonatal life.
Until recently, the favoured aetiological theory was the polygenic multifactorial model. However, now linkage studies suggest the operation in multiply affected families of single major genes, while environmental factors of major affect(e.g. obstetric complications) are operating in other cases. These induce neurodevelopmental deviance and the development of the features of the negative syndrome in childhood and in turn lead to the florid positive syndrome in early adult life. Thus, Kraepelin was correct in suggesting that both heredity and organic brain damage contribute to schizophrenia. However, schizophrenia is more properly considered a congenital disorder rather than an adult onset degenerative disease.

620

CHANGES OF CONSCIOUS FUNCTIONING DURING PSYCHOSES.

Ralf Hemmingsen. Dept. of Psychiatry E. Bispebjerg Hospital. Copenhagen. Denmark.

Karl Jaspers characterized the psychopathological phenomena hallucination and pseudohallucination by reference to the formal aspects of visual sense-perception and ideation in normal individuals. It is questionable whether this dichotomy is applicable in psychotic experiencing. Schneiders first rank symptoms are used to illustrate the question of dichotomy or continuum of psychotic consciousness. The relation between hallucination and perception is discussed: Hallucination may be considered as one of the forms that the stream of (delusional) consciousness may assume. Further aspects of subjective psychotic appraisal are considered ie Wahnstimmung, Anwesenheit, bodily identity, changes of emotion and autism. Finally dissociative reactive states are considered.

621

WHAT IS SCHIZOPHRENIA? -
THE EPIDEMIOLOGICAL PERSPECTIVE

H. HÄFNER
CENTRAL INSTITUTE OF MENTAL HEALTH
D-6800 MANNHEIM 1, F.R.G.

The consistent epidemiological finding of increased rates for prevalence and partly also incidence in the lower class is more likely the consequence than the cause of the disease. When improved epidemiological methods were applied, a transculturally even distribution of annual incidence rates was found - ranging around 0.10 %o for a restricted diagnostic definition of schizophrenia. The lifetime morbid risk also seems to be equal for both sexes. The age-corrected morbid risk seems to remain fairly stable over longer periods of time. This extraordinary epidemiological finding distinguishes schizophrenia from almost all other diseases. It might be explained by a continuous model: The schizophrenic psychosis is understood to be the extreme section of a morbidity dimension extending from spectrum disorder through mild unspecific disturbances to mental health and is evenly distributed in most populations. This assumption is supported by the results from twin, family, adopted and high risk studies. The findings confirm a latent trait of 'vulnerability to schizophrenia' resulting in milder grades of unspecific disturbances. Schizophrenic psyhosis might thus be understood as a neurobiologically homogeneous final pathway, an assumption that later (1920) Kraepelin himself was inclined to share.

622

REDUCING EXPOSURE AND RISK TO NEUROLEPTICS WHEN TREATING SCHIZOPHRENICS.

S.R. Hirsch
Charing Cross & Westminster Medical School,
London, U.K.

There may be stronger clinical benefits in giving neuroleptics only when actual or prodromal symptoms of schizophrenia occur, even though there is an increased frequency of symptoms and relapse. Four studies have been carried out. In ours, 54 stable DSM III schizophrenics randomly and blindly received continuous depot fluphenazine decanoate or placebo. Both groups were given oral haloperidol 10 mgm for 1-2 weeks if prodromal dysphoric symptoms occurred for more than 24 hours. At 2 year follow up, hospitalisation was 4 times more frequent in the intermittent group and there was no difference in other effects to compensate. This is consistent with the findings of Herz et al., (unpublished) but not as good as those of Carpenter et al. (1987) whose patients had regular psychotherapeutic intervention. Low dose treatment topped up by oral medication when prodromal signs appear has had successful results (Marder et al. 1988) and may offer a better strategy. Continuous neuroleptics are still the mainstay medication of maintenance treatment.

Session 96　　　　　　　　Plenary:
Psychiatric and mental health services

623
Dilemmas In Psychiatrically Underserved Areas: Matching Needs With Practice
A. Kales, M.D., Professor and Chairman, Dept. of Psychiatry and Director, Central Pennsylvania Psychiatric Institute (CPPI), Pennsylvania State University College of Medicine, Hershey, Pennsylvania 17033 U.S.A.

Areas may be psychiatrically underserved because of social, economic or geographic factors. Such areas may include sparsely populated and isolated rural areas and urban/ghetto areas both in developed and developing countries. In such areas, it is especially difficult to match the available psychiatric resources with the extensive mental health needs. To illustrate dilemmas incurred, I utilize, as an example, the vast central region of Pennsylvania which is served by the CPPI. One obstacle is third party payer's reimbursement and resultant reinforcement of highly technologic procedures, overspecialization and creation of special interest groups at the expense of the cognitive skills of general psychiatrists. Another problem is the public mental health system's emphasis on utilizing the least expensive, and thus least trained, mental health professional virtually excluding the role of the psychiatrist except as a mass prescriber of psychotropic drugs. This discourages the recruitment and retainment of psychiatric leadership in the care of the seriously and persistently mentally ill. Because of these obstacles, it is more imperative for psychiatrists to be well trained as generalists, skilled in both biologic and dynamic psychiatry as well as in integrating and applying these skills effectively in community mental health consultation, training and care delivery systems.

624
PSYCHIATRIC REHABILITATION IN ASIAN COUNTRIES

Dr. M. Parameshvara Deva
Dept. of Psychological Medicine,
Faculty of Medicine, University of Malaya,
59100 Kuala Lumpur, Malaysia.

If psychiatry is the last priority in the health care programmes of developing countries, then surely psychiatric rehabilitation must be of least importance in that last priority. Most Asian countries that still labour under an institutional past in psychiatric care, and face an enormous task coming to grips with de-institutionalization and decentralising their psychiatric services with acute shortage of trained manpower. Although fairly widespread, family care and support is available in most Asian countries, the concept of institutionalism, half-way houses and hostels have strong influence on the care-givers. Thus, social, psychological and occupational rehabilitative measures remain more the exception than the rule for treated psychiatric patients. Training programmes lag behind in psychiatric rehabilitative skills for all categories of psychiatric workers including doctors. Despite these shortcomings, several countries have embarked on changes by improving teaching, opening new psychiatric rehabilitation programmes and having links with world organizations that deal with rehabilitation. This paper discusses recent moves in this direction and some model programmes.

625
CURRENT STATE OF MENTAL HEALTH SERVICES IN CHINA

Shen Y. - People's Republic of China

626
OUTREACH SERVICES IN PSYCHIATRY
C.S.Ierodiakonou
University of Thessaloniki, Greece

Expansion of welfare-state policies and community-involvement strategies helped psychiatric circles organize Outreach Services. Availability and accessibility of services became possible through sectorization and decentralization of such services. Early diagnosis and continuity of care are two main advantages of Outreach Services, which can only succeed with community and family cooperation.

The structural and functional type of Outreach Services in each country depends on the local conditions and resources. Some such paradigms are described.

The Greek experience of establishing Mental Health Mobile Units through the local Health Centres and by home visits in two rural districts of Northern Greece is presented. Their effectiveness and the population's responsiveness is most encouraging.

Some pertinent issues are raised, like further development of primary or secondary prevention measures, which target-groups should have priority (e.g. children), who should make first contact, the role of Primary Health Care, when is crisis intervention permissible, is cost-effect satisfactory etc.

Session 97 Symposium:
Ethical and legal aspects of compulsory hospitalization and involuntary treatments

627

SOME ETHICAL ASPECTS OF FORCED TREATMENT

Kalle Achté, M.D., Dept. of Psychiatry, Univ. of Helsinki, Finland

For a considerable period of time society has faced the problem of administrating psychiatric treatment against the patient's will. The special nature of mental disturbances has been regarded as sufficient justification for isolating the afflicted from other people and for treating them in closed institutions. Although progress in the development and implementation of psychiatric treatment has proved far slower than in other fields of medicine, the orientation condoning forced psychiatric care still persists. The relatively poor results of forced care have been the principal reason for the marked development of outpatient care in recent decades. Nonetheless, the very nature of mental diseases makes it unrealistic to presume that forced care could be entirely abondoned if psychiatric patients are to be treated efficiently, although it is generally agreed that such treatment could be further reduced. Forced psychiatric treatment poses a persistent dilemma in our society insofar as it encroaches on the individual's liberty and legal security. The ethical problems associated with the implementation of psychiatric treatment are complicated still further by the fact that it is generally not as easy to determine what is best for a psychiatric patient as it is in the case of a patient suffering from a somatic illness.

628

WHEN IS COMPULSORY HOSPITALIZATION JUSTIFIED?

Hans Adserballe, M.D., Psychiatric Hospital, Aarhus, Denmark

No medical intervention may be administered without the informed consent of the patient. However, this generally accepted principle has certain exceptions. A mentally ill person may be deprived of his liberty in accordance with procedure prescribed by law--a fact which has always been the subject of dissent and discussion. Some are included to say that involuntary treatment should be totally abolished as reflecting obsolete medical paternalism. Others think this difficult question should be left to the decision of the responsible doctor in the patient's best interest. The specific character of mental illness--in accordance with medical science--is important in this context. The vast majority of legislations allows deprivation of liberty of mentally ill persons on the indication of danger to self and others. As to nonpsychotic, suicidal persons, the right to terminate one's own life should be kept in mind. Problems are involved in the acceptance of compulsory procedure in the case of nondangerous persons in need of treatment., i.e., some manic and paranoid patients. Most psychiatrists are in favor of this possibility, which also is approved in the Declaration of Hawaii--the ethical constitution of the World Psychiatric Association.

629

COMPULSORY HOSPITALIZATION & TREATMENT: INDIVIDUAL RIGHTS & SOCIETY

Ewald W. Busse, M.D., Duke University Medical Center, Durham, NC, USA

In many societies a precarious, often shifting balance exists between individual human rights and expectations and demands of society. This balance is influenced by social/cultural values, religions, governments, socioeconomic conditions, special interest groups, and advancements in science and technology; thus, current laws may not be consistent with changing accepted behavior; degrees of human rights differ widely among nations and regions. Psychiatry is one of relatively few branches of medical practice that frequently is confronted with decisions regarding compulsory hospitalizations and/or treatment. In many countries, laws affecting involuntary detention and treatment are referred to as civil commitment standards that usually contain two primary features: 1) need for treatment; 2) degree of dangerousness to oneself or to society. England and Wales have the added feature that individuals who demonstrate antisocial behavior cannot be institutionalized unless they are "amenable to treatment." This implies that those whose antisocial behavior cannot be attributed to mental illness must be dealt with in some other manner. Will review variations that appear in some nations and offer explanations regarding selection of individuals for involuntary hospitalization and treatment.

630

INVOLUNTARY CIVIL COMMITMENT OF MENTAL PATIENTS IN JAPAN AND PATERNALISM

Shogo Terashima, M.D., Fukuoka Family Court, Fukuoka, Japan

The Japanese Mental Health Act was revised in 1988 to protect the patient's right more strongly. The Law is composed of two major parts, i.e., (1) the compulsory detainment of the prospective patient by the "danger" standard, and (2) involuntary admission of the patient by the consent of his responsible family member based on the "need-for-treatment" standard. Neither channel requires court review or decision (medical model). Generally speaking either of these two standards or rationales have traditionally been used to justify involuntary civil commitment. In Japan the exercise of "police power" is being discarded (only 1,947 persons were committed by police power in 1987). On the contrary, involuntary admission by the agreement of nearest relative, i.e., paternalistic intervention of the psychiatrists, has been accepted very widely and rather loosely and is becoming dominant throughout Japan (166,196 persons were committed in 1987 through this channel).

631
AN EMPIRICAL STUDY OF COMMITMENT AND INVOLUNTARY TREATMENT IN SWEDEN

Claes-Göran Westrin, M Axelsson, I-L Candefjord, B Ekblom, K Eriksson, L Kjellin, O Östman

Compulsory care is investigated as a health services research problem, considering the actual empirical outcome relative to basic ethical principles. A representative sample of 100 committed and matched controls of voluntarily admitted inpatients and their relatives have repeatedly been interviewed by independent investigators. Extensive postal questionnaires have been answered by about 90% of the concerned psychiatric personnel and their counterparts in primary care.

Prevailing attitudes towards compulsory care among all respondents (patients, their relatives, district doctors and nurses, and social workers) indicate that questions of commitment should be decided by doctors; very few accepted a decisive legal influence.

As to actual outcome of care, the majority of those committed afterwards accepted the justness of the admission and the compulsory care was compatible with considerable improvements in mental status at discharge and 3-5 months later. A majority of primary care personnel believe mentally ill patients also fare badly because of a reluctance to use coercion. At the same time the results indicate different kinds of violation of patient and family autonomy and integrity. Two-thirds of those committed and one-third of voluntarily admitted controls state that they have been subjects of coercive treatment--a result which is confirmed by similar statements from relatives and psychiatric personnel. Few of the patients or relatives felt they had been invited to participate in the planning of care. A substantial proportion of all patients did not know their possibilities for appeal.

The study will allow more specific analyses, for example relating different aspects of outcome to the psychiatric and psychosocial conditions at admission/commitment.

632
LIMITING FREEDOM WHILE PROTECTING CIVIL RIGHTS

Allen R. Dyer, M.D., Ph.D., Albany Medical College, Albany, NY, USA

So-called "free societies" assure the civil rights or liberties of their citizens. Psychiatric patients often, but not necessarily, lack the autonomy to exercise certain of those rights. Such mental illnesses may require treatment against the will of the person. Treatment over objection has traditionally been the prerogative of the treating physician; however, recently it has been recognized that in situations where civil rights may legitimately and necessarily be abrogated, the due process of a judicial review must be assured. The experience of the State of New York (USA), which has instituted strong (but time-consuming) legal safeguards is used as an example.

Session 98 New Research: Chronobiology

633
CHRONOBIOLOGY OF DEPRESSION : EFFECT OF ENVIRONMENT ON HUMAN CIRCADIAN RHYTHMS

E Souetre, E Salvati, JL Belugou, B Krebs, G Darcourt, Clinique de psychiatrie, pav J, Hopital Pasteur, BP 69 06002 Nice Cedex France

Researchers using the chronobiological approach to depression have been thwarted by the knowledge that any measured (overt) circadian rhythm was likely to be an inexact reflexion of the internal "clocks" that drive these rhythms. It is now accepted that overt circadian rhythms consist in two components, an endogenous component related to some form of internal clock and an exogenous component (or masking effect) due to rhythmic changes in the environment. The aim of this study was to explore the effect of making on human circadian rhythms.
The circadian system of 11 normal young vonlonteers were observed under both standard nychtemeral conditions (normal life schedule) and under a constant routine protocol consisting of a 26-h period of constant conditions (constant light, temperature, hourly snacks, continuous bedrest, constant activity). Hormonal circadian rhythms (plasma cortisol, melatonin, thyrotropin (TSH), prlactin (PRL), growth hormone (GH)) were measured using hourly blood samples and RAI. Body temperature was measured using individual rectal probes. The main finding was a drecreased amplitude of the melatonin, PRL, GH and temperature rhythms. In contrast, the nocturnal rise of TSH was higher under constant conditions compared to nychtemeral conditions. The nadir of the plasma cortisol rhythm was slightly advanced under constant conditions. Our finding point out a clear and direct effect of the environment on the human circadian system. In addition, these features of circadian rhythms appear similar to those of depressed patients living in a natural environment.

634
ABNORMAL ENTRAINMENT PROCESS OF CIRCADIAN CLOCKS BY ENVIRONMENT IN DEPRESSIVE ILLNESS

E Souêtre, E Salvati, G Darcourt, Clinique de psychiatrie, pav J, Hopital Pasteur, BP 69 06002 Nice Cedex France

Results of clinical research have consistently pointed out abnormalities of the major circadian rhythms in depression. The majority of investigations indicates that depressed patients have a significant reduction of amplitude (defined as the peak to trough difference) of most of the rhythms. On the other hand results of investigations of a possible phase (clock-time position of the peak of a rhythm) disturbances in circadian rhythms in depression remain inconsistent. Since amplitude of a rhythm has been shown to be an index of the strength of the driven oscillator, depressive illness may be associated to an abnormal entrainment of internal clocks by the natural environment.
In order to test this hypothesis, we performed the comparison of circadian rhythms distorsions (body temperature, plasma cortisol, melatonin, thyrotropin (TSH), prolactin (PRL), growth hormone (GH)) in depressed patients (n=16) living under natural environment and in normal subjects (n=11) living deprived from environmental information (constant conditions). Depressed patients were found to have a decreased amplitude of most of their circadian rhythms whereas phase positions were within normal range. Normal subjects deprived from environmental influences were found to have a decreased amplitude of the rhythms (except for TSH). Our findings point out major similarities between the circadian system of depressed patients living under normal conditions and of normal subjects deprived from environmental influences. This feature supports the hypothesis of an abnormal biological sensitivity of depressed patients to their natural environment

635

CIRCADIAN MHPG LEVELS ARE DISRUPTED IN DEPRESSION

A. Halaris and J. Piletz, Case Western Reserve University, Cleveland, Ohio, U.S.A.

A multitude of studies have indicated that altered noradrenergic function is tantamount to the pathophysiology of affective illness. A noninvasive indicator of noradrenergic activity is the measurement in cerebrospinal fluid, plasma, and urine of 3-methoxy-4-hydroxyphenylglycol (MHPG), the principal CNS metabolite of norepinephrine. Plasma MHPG levels were determined over a 24 hour period in 32 unipolar depressed patients 5 bipolar depressed patients, and 12 healthy control subjects. Following treatment with desipramine, 24 unipolar depressed patients were reanalyzed. Circadian rhythmicity was modeled for each subject to a cosine function, temporal parameters were assigned by linear least squares regression with a fixed 24 hour period, and group differences were compared statistically.
A poorer fit to the cosine model was observed in patients compared to controls, both pre-treatment (F statistic = 5.7 for unipolar depressives vs. controls) as well as post-treatment (F = 8.7 for unipolar depressives vs. controls). These data support the dysregulation theory of depressive illness. Since the disruption in MHPG rhythmicity persisted after treatment, this may be a trait marker for depression.

636

PERIODICITY CHANGES OF BODY TEMPERATURE RHYTHM IN AFFECTIVE DISORDERS.

Bicakova-Rocher A., Gorceix A., Reinberg A., Nouguier J. & Nouguier-Soulé J.
Sce Psychiatrie Hôpital Fernand-Widal & CNRS UA 581 Fondation A. de Rothschild, Paris (France).

Axillary temperature was recorded at least twice during a 48h span at 6 min intervals in 10 hospitalised patients with major affective disorders (DSM III-R). During the clinical occurence of symptoms, 7 out of 10 patients presented a prominent ultradian periodicity (period $\tau < 20$ h) in their temperature time series. Whatever the therapeutic mean (electroconvulsive therapy and/or chemotherapy) the clinical improvement was associated with the "recovery" of a circadian rhytmicity ($20h \leq \tau \leq 28h$). A prominent temperature ultradian rhythm (which occurs only in the newborn) could be the indication of an internal desynchronisation associated with episodes of major affective disorders.

637

CHRONIC NORADRENALINE UPTAKE INHIBITION INCREASES MELATONIN SECRETION IN MAN
E. Palazidou, A. Papadopoulos, D. Skene, J. Arendt, S. Checkley.
The Institute of Psychiatry, London, UK.
Surrey University, Guildford, UK.

There are two opposing theories regarding the mechanism of action of antidepressant drugs on noradrenergic neurotransmission. According to the catecholamine hypothesis antidepressant drugs increase NAergic neurotransmission while the beta receptor downregulation hypothesis claims that they decrease NAergic output after chronic treatment.
We examined this question using melatonin secretion as a marker of net NAergic output. The pineal gland is innervated by NAergic fibres which control melatonin synthesis and secretion. Melatonin secretion in man is increased by acute NA uptake inhibition and alpha2 adrenoceptor blockade and is decreased by beta1 and alpha1 adrenoceptor blockade.
We investigated the chronic effects of NA uptake inhibition using (+)-oxaprotiline as compared to its (-)-enantiomer which is devoid of such properties, in normal subjects and desipramine in depressed patients. In both groups chronic NA uptake inhibition resulted an increase in melatonin secretion. These findings question the hypothesis that beta receptor downregulation is the mechanism of action of antidepressant drugs.

638

AMISULPRIDE: EFFECTS ON NOCTURNAL SECRETION OF MELATONIN AND PROLACTIN AND EEG SLEEP PARAMETERS
H. Wetzel, A. Szegedi, C. Hiemke and O. Benkert
Department of Psychiatry, University of Mainz, D-6500 Mainz, F.R.G.
Amisulpride (ASP), a new substituted benzamide, selectively antagonizes D2-receptors. In low doses, it may improve depressive symptoms and energy loss whereas antipsychotic effects require higher dosages.
In order to explore the effects of low dose ASP on the nocturnal secretion of melatonin (MT) and prolactin (PRL) and on EEG sleep parameters, 3 healthy male subjects were given ASP (50 - 150 mg orally in a single morning dose) in a single-blind placebo-controlled design. Sleep EEG was registered on 21 consecutive nights, and nocturnal hormonal profiles were taken at day 2 (placebo baseline) and 10 (100 mg ASP).
PRL, known to be under inhibitory dopaminergic control, was significantly elevated to the three-fold of baseline levels ($p < 0.005$; two-tailed t-test for paired samples). Moreover, ASP (100 mg) led to a 61%, 67% and 73% decrease, respectively, in AUC nocturnal MT plasma concentrations with large interindividual variations in absolute values. These preliminary data give evidence that, besides by α- and β-adrenergic drugs and some antidepressants, human MT secretion can be modified by D2-dopaminergic antagonists. In EEG sleep, stages III and IV were decreased whereas in 2 of 3 volunteers there was a tendency to increase REM sleep and to advance REM stages to earlier periods in the night.

639

MELATONIN AND SEASONAL PERSONALITY VARIATIONS (16 PF CATTELL TEST). M Freedman, V Di Boscio, R Garcia Novarini and P Wizenberg. Dept. Fisiologia, Facultad de Medicina, Univ. de Buenos Aires, Argentina.

In parallel with a study on seasonal variations in urine melatonin levels (Seasons Around the World Project, directed by Prof. L. Wetterberg, Karolinska Institute, Stockholm) the 16 personality factors of Cattell test (16 PF) was performed in 29 volunteers working at the Univ. of Buenos Aires. Results obtained in october (spring time in southern hemisphere were compared with results obtained in april (fall time in the south). Between the 16 primary factors statistically significant differences were observed in two of them, that were within the media in october and fell out of the expected range in april. The reduction in one factor ($p < 0.05$, t test for paired data) represents a lower super ego and a lower adaptation to the rules of the group. The reduction in the other ($P < .01$, t test for paired data) corresponds to somebody unskillful and clumsy. One factor of second order and profile also changed significantly. Eventual correlations with variations in melatonin levels will be reported during the Congress.

640

SEASONALITY OF BIRTH IN SCHIZOPHRENIA AND AFFECTIVE DISEASE IN MEXICO

Harry Baker I., Jose F. Cortes, Hector Perez-Rincon. Department of Psychiatry and Menthal Health, Universidad Nacional Autonoma de Mexico, Mexico City, Mexico.

Several articles suggest that schizophrenics are born with higher than expected frequency in the winter months, in both the northern and the southern hemispheres. Only one study has been done in a sub-equatorial country (the Philippines).

In affective disease results are still controversial, although there seems to be a seasonality of births in spring in manic-depression, while no such thing has been shown in neurotic depression.

RESULTS

In a sample of 1086 Mexican schizophrenics an excess in the expected number of births was found in autumm, with predominance in the paranoid subgroup, when compared against a control group of neurological patients matched by sex and year of birth (Pike and Morrow's method).

No seasonality was found among other schizophrenic subgroups or among 318 affective disease patients and their controls.

641

SEASONAL DISTRIBUTION PATTERN OF AFFECTIVE PATIENTS' HOSPITALITZATION

Gy. Molnár, Hospital "István" Dept. of Psychiatry, Budapest, Hungary

Selected hospitalization rate and seasonal distribution of PMD and schizoaffective patients were analyzed. (Data processing: 1981-88, ICD-9 and AMDP codes, C-128 computer programs.)
In agreement with earlier references, the depressive patients (bipolar) were hospitalized more frequently in early spring. In our catchment area however, the PMD depressives showed double spring admittance peak in several years of 1981-88.
The schizoaffectives "ordinary" had become in-patients because of their depressive phase in early spring and/or early summer. PMD patients with mania were hospitalized in peak periods of April and mid-summer. The schizoaffectives with manic symptoms showed April, June-July admission increase, with a smaller December peak. In this patient group, the schizoform phases were accumulated in early spring and mid-summer periods.
In 1984-85 the accumulated admission rate of cycloid patients in depressive phase proved to be higher than that of the rest in 8 years periods. (Changes in solar periods?, local and/or escalated problems in population of two large districts of the capital?)

Session 99 Symposium:
New psychoanalytic approaches to clinical psychiatry

642

NEW PSYCHOANALYTIC APPROACHES TO CLINICAL PSYCHIATRY.
RUIZ RUIZ, M., UNIVERSITY OF MALAGA. SPAIN.

The epistemology aspect of clinical psychiatry is revised from the basic paradigmatic wholes: phenomenological, behaviorism and psychoanalysis.

The new psychoanalytical contributions from the self-analysis (KOHUT) and narcissistic patients (KERNBERG) are considered standing out the impotance of group-analysis criticism in the psychoanalitic training on the clinical psychiatry.

643

NEW APPROACHES TO PSYCHOTHERAPY IN PSYCHOTIC DISORDERS.
RUIZ-OGARA, C. UNIVERSITY OF GRANADA. SPAIN.

The new psychoanalytic contributions to self-analysis (H. KOHUT; G.S. KLEIN et al.) and borderline and narcissistic personalities (O. KERNBERG) are review, implanting a new psychoanalytic model.

The self-reconstruction, arising from those theoretical models must be one of the more importants objectives in psychotherapy of psychotic disorders.

644

NEW APPROACHES TO PSYCHOTEHRAPIES IN PSYCHOSOMATIC DISORDERS.
MARTY, P. INSTITUTE OF PSYCHOSOMATIC. PARIS.

We propose a new psychoanalytical theory in psychosomatic disorders emphasizing the first Freud's topic and the life/death individual mouvements.

A psychoanalytical classification of somatic patient was carried out based in that model, consideranting the psychosomatic disorder as a process of desorganization and regression in the evolutive course.

The psychotherapy of psychosomatic disorders must value the importance of phantasy and cathexis in the therapeutic process of those patients.

645

NEW APPROACHES TO BRIEF ANALYTICAL PSYCHOTHERAPY.
TRUJILLO, M. BETH HOSPITAL. NEW YORK.

After a re-examination to the actual theories in brief psychoanalytical psychotherapies concerning to the theoretical development from Sifneos, Malan, and Davanloo and their therapeutic techniques, we propose our research in the field of brief analytical psychotherapy, and we discusse them with the revised literature, stressing the topic about transfer and transfer analysis in order to insight and working through.

646

NEW APPROACHES TO PSYCHOTHERAPY IN CHILDHOOD AND ADOLESCENCE.
KNOBEL, M. UNIVERSITY OF CAMPINA. BRAZIL.

The special psychodynamic characteristics of childrens and teenagers demand a new approache from the psychoanalytical practice.

The more significant psychoanalytical contribution to the development theory are review for discussing one new and integrate model which answers to the theoretical and clinical problems raised by this form of psychotherapy.

647

NEW APPROACHES TO PSYCHOTHERAPIES IN DRUG-DEPENDENCES.
FERNANDEZ, J.M. INST. ADM. MADRID. SPAIN.

Several models have been developed in the therapeutic approache to drug-dependence without good results.

We research the biological, psychological and social factors involved in drug-dependences and we outline a new integrate model at the drug-dependence treatment, including psychoanalytical psychotherapy, that overcome the ineffectiveness from the isolated therapeutic action.

648

NEW APPROACHES TO TRAINING IN PSYCHOANALYSIS.
MARTIN, F. UNIVERSITY OF MALAGA. SPAIN.

The recent theories about the psychoanalysis of narcissistic patient (KOHUT) and the narcissistic problems involved in didactic analysis (KERNBERG) require from the Psychoanalytic Institutions a new outline of training in Psychoanalysis.

The Spanish Association of Analytical Psychotherapy carry out this training including individual analysis, group-analysis and theoretical studies. We considerate the group-analysis a necessary requirement in the training in order to analyse the narcissistic conflicts and to achieve the criticism of psychoanalist during the training process.

Session 100 Symposium:
Insights in the use of trazodone in depressed patients

649

BACKGROUND FOR THE USE OF TRAZODONE IN SPECIAL FORMS OF DEPRESSION.
Bruno Silvestrini, Institute of Pharmacology and Pharmacognosy, University of Rome "La Sapienza", Rome, Italy.

Atypical antidepressants differ from tricyclic antidepressants for their effects on biogenic amines and nervous transmission in the central and autonomic nervous system. Besides it well known theoretical and toxicological implications, this phenomenon is of considerable importance in connection with autonomic changes accompanying depression and requiring specific pharmacological medication. Trazodone displays an alfa-adrenergic blocking action and inhibits the stress-induced sympathetic discharge. Hence, trazodone is indicated in depressive conditions with adrenergic hyperactivity. They include sleep disturbances, male and female functional impotence, opiate withdrawal and others. The above data are also discussed in the light of the dys-stress hypothesis. This hypothesis assumes that, whereas stress normally improves the physical and mental performance, in some instances it impairs such performance by producing paradoxical effects. This phenomenon would be implicated in depression and other pathological conditions, including obesity.

650

Experiences with single daily administration of trazodone
Fabre, Louis F., M.D., Ph.D.
The Fabre Clinic
5503 Crawford
Houston, TX 77004

In order to minimize day-time adverse effects of drug therapy and in particular sedation, trazodone can be given as single doses at night; the resultant sedation can then be put to use to aid sleep, keeping any impairment in alertness the next day to a minimum.

The comparison of the effects on night-time sleep and morning psychomotor performance of the bed-time administration of trazodone, conventional formulation versus controlled-release formulation has been performed. Some results of trials with a conventional formulation and results of trials with controlled-release formulation are reported.

651

DEPRESSION, INSOMNIA AND TRAZODONE

J.F. O'HANLON[1], A.L. VAN BEMMEL[2], E.A.J.M. SCHOENMAKERS[2]

(1) Institute for Drugs, Safety and Behavior, (2) Department of Clinical Psychiatry, State University of Limburg, Postbox 616, 6200 MD Maastricht, The Netherlands

Severe sleep disturbances are often symptoms of clinical depression. This presentation consists of a review of trazodone's therapeutic properties for relieving sleep disturbances in various depressed states. A relationship is drawn between the specific relief of insomnia, as revealed by polysomnographic studies, and general improvement shown by reduction in depression scores on the HAM-D and other scales. Differences are described between the effects of trazodone on sleep and those of tricyclic antidepressants and conventional hypnotics. Finally, an effort is made to relate trazodone's mechanism of action to its effects on sleep in various forms of depression.

652

DO TRAZODONE'S EFFECTS ON REM SLEEP CONTRADICT CURRENT THEORY?

A.L. VAN BEMMEL[1], A.G. HAVERMANS[1], R. VAN DIEST[1], E.A.J.M. SCHOENMAKERS[2], J.F. O'HANLON[2]

(1) Department of Clinical Psychiatry,
(2) Institute for Drugs, Safety and Behavior, State University of Limburg P.C. Box 616 6200 MD Maastricht, The Netherlands

Reported antidepressant effects of both pharmacological and nonpharmacological manipulation of patients' sleep have led to a theory: REM suppression is associated with the remission of depressive symptoms. Certainly many antidepressant drugs suppress REM. However, trazodone's reported effects on sleep fail to conform with this theory. The drug did not suppress REM but instead increased the amount of slow wave sleep and otherwise "normalized" sleep polysomnographic study of trazodone's acute and subchronic effects on sleep in depressed patients. This paper explores its theoretical implications.

653

POLYGRAPHIC PARAMETRES FOR SLEEP QUALITY DETECTION: EFFECTS OF TRAZODONE R.C. ON CYCLIC ALTERNATING PATTERN

Mario Giovanni TERZANO, Liborio PARRINO

Sleep Disorder Center, Dept. of Neurology, University of Parma, Italy

On the basis of the macrostructural variations of sleep, an international consensus has provided the guidelines to identify distinct forms of insomnia.
However, satisfactory sleep quality may be achieved by hypnotic drugs that generally alter the architecture of sleep and, conversely, sleep quality may be unsatisfactory in spite of normal traditional parameters.
Under certain perturbed conditions, the lack of macrostructural changes is accompanied by a significant enhancement of the Cyclic Alternating Pattern (CAP) Rate, a microstructural variable that emerges from the EEG organization of the arousal-dependent phasic events of sleep. CAP Rate, detectable in all NREM stages, is extremely sensitive to environmental conditions and correlates inversely with the subjective appreciation of sleep. The improvement of sleep quality by means of certain drugs without specific hypnotic effects, could be actually due to an inhibitory influence on this microstructural variable. As Trazodone is a non-hypnotic compound that determines an amelioration of poor sleep, the aim of our work is to assess the preservative effects of this drug on a normal sleeping brain actively disturbed by a continuous acoustic perturbation.

654

DEPRESSION AND CEREBRAL STROKE

CATAPANO Francesco
Department of Medical Psychology and Psychitary, First Medical School, University of Naples (Italy)

The correlation between depression and stroke is analyzed in a review of recent literature.
The Author also analyzes the properties of some antidepressant drugs with antiserotoninergic and alpha-adrenolytic activity such as trazodone. This drug may provide an adequate brain protection in high-risk subjects and may be useful in the treatment of post-stroke depression.

Session 101   Symposium:
Psiquiatria y medios audiovisuales

655
AUDIOVISUAL AIDS IN MENTAL HEALTH PROGRAMS
Roger M. Montenegro
APSA - Asociación de Psiquiatras Argentinos

Multiple application possibilities of these elements are described in the different programs for the formation of human resources, be it for professionals, technicians, or community agents.

The usefulness of these means in preventive, therapeutic and rehabilitation programs is also shown, as well as in community working programs.

On the other hand not only the material produced for this specific objectives is appraised but also important material of commercial films and videotapes that achieves an excellent approach to topics related with Mental Health and Illness, which can be reworked in study, discussion, therapy groups.

A summary of the trajectory of the Centro de Investigación Médico-Psicológica de la Comunicación is done.

656
The Use of Videotape Techniques in the Psychiatric Training of PC Physicians
Rodolfo Fahrer
School of Medicine
University of Buenos Aires

To teach the management of psychosocial, psychopathological, psychotherapeutic and psychiatric problems through traditional teaching methods in Medicine is a very difficult task.
The students cannot participate, close to their teachers, as they do in other medical fields, such as clinical and semiological examination of patients. They cannot participate or attend a psychotherapy session either.
This presentation will briefly outline various kinds of video usage which we have found particularly useful in undergraduate, postgraduate, and continuing education training of primary care physicians and psychiatrists.
Several techniques are used in which the students can apply the skills, values and attitudes being learned.
1) Demonstration of a clinical state
2) Teaching interviewing incorporating video-playback
3) Attitude clarification
4) Skill development
5) Recording of Trainee-Patient Encounter

657
IMPLEMENTACION DE LOS MEDIOS AUDIOVISUALES EN LA PSIQUIATRIA
Ruggero P. - USA

658
The Therapeutic Aspects of Family Video Art Therapy

Irene Jakab, M.D., Ph.D.
University of Pittsburgh School of Medicine

The therapeutic aspect of family-video-art-therapy is related to the following factors:
A. During the videotaped art therapy sessions:
1. Collaborative, non-threatening emotional atmosphere fostered by the therapist.
2. The freedom of nonverbal expression of emotions and ideas.
3. Low key interpretations by therapist.
4. Elicited conscious associations of the clients to their art products.
5. Occasional catharctic effect of the free graphic expression.
B. During the viewing (replay) sessions:
1. Observation and interpretation by both the therapist and the clients regarding the family dynamics as revealed on the videotapes.
2. Insights about the interaction patterns and about the individual styles of expressing emotions verbally and nonverbally.
3. Pointers toward corrective measures to decrease the pathology.
Staff education provided by viewing the tapes.

  A 15 minute edited videotape condensed from four hours of family video art therapy sessions will highlight an illustrative case sample.

659
PSICOCINE-PSICOTERAPIA GRUPAL PROGRAMADA
Prof. Dr. Miguel Angel Materazzi
Hospital Nacional Jose T.Borda
Centro de Investigacion Medico Psicologica
de la Comunicacion, Buenos Aires, Argentina

El psicocine es una Psicoterapia Grupal de Corte
Programático que conjuga las siguientes fuentes:
- El Cine
- El Teatro
- La psicopatología
- La sociología
- La filosofía
- La dinámica Grupal

Como método posee un mecanismo de acción e
interacción donde los pacientes psicóticos
pueden externalizar su dramática relacional
interna a través del acto dramático, tenindo
como e je la creación; pibot que permite al
participante en el grupo ad quirir plasticidad
psicológica, movilización de su estereotipia
y trascender su aqui-ahora.
Todo ésto es graficado en un momento de la
historia del grupo a través de un film.

Session 102 Symposium: Psychiatric aspects of heart transplantation

660
PSYCHOLOGICAL ASPECTS BEFORE AND AFTER HEART TRANS-
PLANTATION: 5 YEARS EXPERIENCE
R.A.M. Erdman, Ph.D., Psychologist; R.C. van der
Mast, M.D., Psychiatrist; G.J. Bonsel, M.D.
Cardiology Dept., University Hospital Dijkzigt
Rotterdam, The Nederlands

Fourty eight patients (88% males; mean age 50 years), who underwent heart transplantation (HTRX) in the period from June '84 to March '89, were investigated to evaluate emotional responses, perceived life satisfaction, work resumption and experienced quality of life, before and after HTRX. The first examination was performed during the pre-transplant screening phase, while two follow up investigations were done respectivelly 4 and 13 months after hTRX. Four questionnaires were used measuring anxiety (State-Trait Anxiety Inventory), depression (Zung Selfrating Depression Scale), quality of life (Nottingham Health Profile) and psychological well-being (Heart Patients Psychological Questionnaire). There was a statistically significant decrease in feelings of anxiety and depression; 13 months post HTRX feelings of anxiety decreased even further while feelings of depression stabilized at 4 months. At 4 and 13 months after HTRX all 6 quality of life aspects of the NHP had shown statistically significant improvement when compared to the preoperative phase. The findings on the HPPQ, concerning well-being, feelings of being disabled and displeasure, show the same positive results. Only 40% resumed their original working activities on a full-time basis. Psychiatric and/or psychological assistence was needed in 37% of the cases, due to severe disturbances in emotional adjustment.

661
REHABILITATION & QUALITY OF LIFE AFTER CARDIAC
TRANSPLANTATION
Brett M. Jones
Cardiac Transplant Unit, St. Vincent's Hospital,
Sydney, Australia

Cardiac transplantation is now a viable therapeutic alternative for patients with end stage heart disease. Four year actuarial survival at the above Unit is 80%. However, long term survival is compromised if recipients are not successfully rehabilitated. We have conducted a number of studies to assess recipient adjustment. They have been a prospective study of psychological adjustment for upto 12 months after transplantation; a retrospective study of rehabilitation and quality of life at 12 months after transplantation; a prospective study of the quality of life of recipients on double versus triple therapy and a study of compliance with life-style factors.

Our results showed a significant improvement in mood after transplantration that is maintained upto 12 months after transplantation; a high level of satisfaction with social, family and marital lives and a satisfying rate of rehabilitation. Sixty three per cent of recipients returned to either full-time work, home duties or studies. Double the rapy recipients reported a higher quality of life than triple therapy recipients. Compliance with diet was a problem for male recipients and those patients on double therapy.

662
PSYCHOTHERAPY WITH HEART TRANSPLANTATION RECIPIENTS

Ary Knijnik, M.D., Psychiatrist
Institute of Cardiology/Universitary Foundation of
Cardiology, Porto Alegre, RS - Brasil

The recipient of heart transplantation (HT TX) pass typically to different emotional stages since the indication of the process to follow-up. These stages are describe: evaluation period, waiting period, hospitalization and follow-up period. There are considerations made about the psychotherapy with this patients.

Are discuss questions like denial management and the problems involved with it, the traumatic stress, the mourning for the organ lost, management of the mood disturbance, the emotional relationship with the new organ and the fantasy more frequently found in those patient.

Finally comment the large spectrum of questions that the HT TX programs asks for the psychiatry. In the future, the psychiatrist will be more and more invited to collaborate in the HT TX programs and we have to be prepare for that.

663

QUALITY OF LIFE FOLLOWING HEART TRANSPLANTATION

François M. Mai, F.R.C.Psych.
Dept. of Psychiatry, Ottawa General Hospital
University of Ottawa, Ontario, Canada

Recent developments in surgical and in immunosupressive techniques have resulted in much improved survival rates following Heart Transplantation.

Although there is a strong clinical impression that there is an improvement also in psychosocial adjustment and in quality-of-life after surgery, supportive scientific evidence is lacking.

We have studied 27 subjects before and 24 subjects after heart transplant surgery. Although various parameters show a substantial improvement in psychosocial adjustment and quality-of-life after surgery, our results show that areas of difficulty remain, particulary in employability and in psychosexual adjustment.

664

QUALITY OF LIFE FOLLOWING CARDIAC TRANSPLANTATION

Arthur M. Freeman III, M.D. & Wesley Libb, Ph.D.
Dept. of Psychiatry, University of Alabama at Birmingham, Birmingham, Alabama, USA

As the number of available donor hearts far exceeds the number of potential recipients, careful attention to patient selection criteria is given throughout the world. These criteria include psychiatric status. Qualify of life concerns become increasingly important as survival rates improve. Ideally, we would select those patients who have the most reasonable chance of enjoying a good quality of life. At the University of Alabama at Birmingham we have development the clinical construct of "suitability for transplantation" which we are currently refining. We will report on preoperative and postoperative psychiatric assessments of the first 70 patients undergoing cardiac transplantation at our hospital in terms of our ability to predict outcome. Discussion of broad criteria for relative acceptability and guidelines for future research in this area will be presented. Quality of life includes a number of life domains and functional abilities. Social support, coping style and emotional status prior to surgery may be relevant variables in predicting outcome.

Session 103 Symposium:
Diurnal variations in psychopathology

665

DIURNAL FLUCTUATIONS IN MOOD AND SLEEP DEPRIVATION
Kuhs H., Tölle R.
Dept.of Psychiatry,Münster/FRG
In recent studies the importance of"typical"diurnal variations(TDV)in mood(with morning low and clearing up of the symptomatology in the afternoon/evening) as a diagnostic criterion of endogenous depression has been questioned.
However,from a therapeutic point of view TDV are of considerable interest.They predict a favorable effect of therapeutic sleep deprivation(SD).
Does SD influence diurnal variations in mood? An investigation on 5 consecutive days including 25 endogenous depressive patients revealed: In patients without preexisting diurnal variations SD effected no considerable alteration in the majority of cases, in 18.5% SD effected an alternating daily course(destabilization) and in another 18.5% a TDV. In the case of preexisting inverse diurnal variations a TDV was caused in 6 of 8 patients. In patients without and with inverse diurnal variations the occurence of a TDV can be looked upon as an expression of the therapeutic effectiveness of SD.

666

DIURNAL VARIATION OF MOOD
IMPLICATIONS FOR DEPRESSION RESEARCH

M.C.M. Gordijn, D.G.M. Beersma, E. Reinink, G.E. Gänshirt, A.L. Bouhuys and R.H. van den Hoofdakker

Department of Biological Psychiatry, University of Groningen, The Netherlands.

Diurnal variation (DV) of mood is a frequently observed phenomenon in depressed patients. The purpose of an ongoing study is to assess the occurrence and consistency of DVs, and to see whether DV has any chronobiological background.
As a routine, all depressed patients score their mood three times daily by means of the adjective mood scale, during their entire stay at the closed ward of the psychiatric clinic.
In a group of 12 patients (Major Depression and Bipolar Disorder, Depressed) there were either patients with abundant amounts of DVs (n=7) or patients without DVs (n=5). In the "DV-group" at 51% of 439 days mood improved, whereas the reverse pattern occurred in 6% of the days.
Baseline Hamilton ratings (at 9.00 AM) were not different for the two groups. Also within patients the occurrence of DVs was independent of the severity of depression, as measured in the early morning. The data suggest that diurnal variability is a robust characteristic of a subgroup of depressed patients.
In a longitudinal study we are examining sleep and some other chronobiological rhythms of this subgroup to describe the possible relation between daily changes of mood and other daily rhythms. A detailed analysis is necessary to see whether there is any change in the shape and/or the timing of biological rhythms in patients showing DV.

667

TOTAL SLEEP DEPRIVATION AND DIURNAL VARIATION IN DEPRESSION

E.Reinink, A.L.Bouhuys, M.C.M.Gordijn, R.H.v.d. Hoofdakker and D.G.M.Beersma. Dept. of Biological Psychiatry, University Hospital Groningen, the Netherlands

The relationship was examined between diurnal variation of mood (DV) on the day before total sleep deprivation (TSD) and the effect of TSD on depressed mood.
The first set of data concerns 76 patients (Major Depressed or Bipolar Disorder Depressed) who participated in previous TSD experiments. Depressed mood was measured 3 times daily with a self-rating scale on the day before and after one TSD. Three groups were distinguished: a group with positive DV's (mood better in the evening, n=18), a group without DV's (n=41) and a group with negative DV's (n=17) on the day before TSD. Only the group with positive DV's before TSD improved significantly.
The second set of results concerns an ongoing prospective study. Till now 18 patients (Major Depressed or Bipolar Disorder Depressed) underwent several TSD's dependent on their DV's. They rated their mood 3 times daily during their entire stay in the hospital. Each patient was subjected to TSD's after days without DV's and if they occured, after days with positive and days with negative DV's. Negative DV's occured very infrequently and will therefore not be considered. Some patients (n=10) never showed DV's, the others (n=8) produced them abundantly. The former group did not respond to TSD, while the latter responded positively to TSD regardless of the nature of the prior DV.
The conclusion is that not the actual DV before TSD, but the ability to produce DV's appears to be the important predictor for TSD-response.

668

DIURNAL VARIATIONS OF MOOD IN PSYCHIATRIC PATIENTS

H.-J. Haug
Psychiatrische Klinik und Poliklinik der FUB, Eschenallee 3, 1000 Berlin 19, Germany.

Diurnal variations of mood (DV) with morning lows and evening highs are often considered typical symptoms of endogenously depressed patients and play an important role in various diagnostic classification systems (ICD, RDC, DSM-III). In several studies, we investigated the importance of this symptom. We will present the results of the different studies with the following conclusions: DV are not specific for endogenous depression, we also found them in neurotic depression, schizophrenia, and even in healthy volunteers. There is no correlation between the occurrence of DV and the severity of the depressive syndrome, or the age of the patient. Existence of DV predicts sleep deprivation outcome. One night of total sleep deprivation (SD) eliminates DV for the days after SD. The variable DV creates interesting subgroups of patients (with and without DV) with regard to other psychopathological variables and the course of the antidepressive treatment.

Session 104 Symposium:
Creativity, anxiety and delirium

669

The creative man.

Prof.dr. Vittorino Andreoli
Department of Psychiatry - Verona -

The creative process results from the interaction between brain and environment. It is a mistake any reductionism that limits the study to only one factor. The mental pathology acts in the sense that the relationships with the reality and (possibly) the biological mechanisms (creative brain) are news (altered) compared with the previous normal conditions.
A distinction between "great" and "ordinary" (everyday) creativity is underlined, to include the inventive process among the "survival" mechanisms in the industrial and post-industrial societies.

670

ANGOISSE ET DELIRE DANS L'ENFER DE STRINDBERG

C.R. HOJAIJ

Hosp. Samaritano - Sao Paulo, Brazil

La nouvelle autobiographique "Enfer", de Strindberg, présente un matériel long et profond qui exprime les manifestations délirantes.

Ce travail veut montrer que l'élan créatif de Strindberg est modulé par le phénomène de l'angoisse vitale qui déborde en interprétations et attitudes délirantes sur des évènements de sa vie et du monde autour de lui.

Le travail adopte une méthodologie phénoménologique : les expériences de vie de l'auteur suèdois y sont utilisées et leur signification est recherchée.

671
PSYCHOPATHOLOGY OF EXPRESSION IN THE PLASTIC PRODUCTION OF SCHIZOPHRENICS
M. TYSZKIEWICZ
Department of Health, Gdynia, Poland

The Mental Health Dispensary of Gdynia has for over 20 years been conducting therapy in schizophrenic patients by making them take up plastic activities. The system so formed of patient/his work/therapist was expected to give better insight into the patients mental state, to improve their social standing by admitting them into creative groups in the dispensary (the Club of Amateurs of Art) and introducing them into the world of the healthy by organizing expositions of their production in the dispensary and public ones, and by presenting their creation at psychiatric congresses in this country and abroad. Over 100 patients have so far been submitted to this kind of therapy. Nearly 50 % had attended the Club where during to so-called One Author's Matinees held twice a week the work of one creator is discussed by the group, or the whole of the group work together painting and drawing. Several expositions held every year are preceded by formal inaugurations and invitations sent out to relatives and friends.

672
ANXIETY, CREATION AND PSYCHOSIS
Art creation at the painters-mental patients

D. NEIMAREVIC
Medical Center, Neuro-psychiatric Dept
47000 KARLOVAC, Yougoslavie

Anxiety is an expression of visual arts creation with many psychoses. It is a reflection of their psychic tension (conscious or unconscious) caused by fear. Usually, it is not expressed only in the motif but in the visual arts elements of the graphic or plastic speech. These are lines and colours by which psychosis is expressed. We distinguish three stages of feelings of the mind : anxiety, fear and horror.

With one mental patient we find anxiety present in almost all his paintings because that was his real state of mind. With one woman patient we also notice anxiety in her pictures. She was always coherent, rationally and artistically. She creates a great number of pictures always oppressed by anxiety or even strong fear. Academic woman painter who became ill with psychosis creates some of her pictures in the state of severe unconscious anxiety. She is always rationally and artistically coherent to the highest degree. The third woman painter creates her pictures full of anxiety and even horror only under psychosis as a reflection of her pathological fear. She became an incoherent and deteriorated personality.

Three academic painters who became ill with psychosis create their cool pictures in the state of severe anxiety. In the end they became incoherent and deteriorated personalities. Before mental illness anxiety couldn't be found in their works.

Four painters create pictures without anxiety in the state of psychosis.

673
BIOGRAPHIE PICTURALE DE GERMAINE A TRAVERS LA PSYCHOSE
Ph. COFFINET, Ph. GUYONNET, A. DORNIER, E. CHABOD
C.H.S. SAINT-REMY - 70160 - FRANCE

A travers 9 dessins réalisés récemment par une malade psychotique chronique d'origine vietnamienne, les auteurs analysent le processus dynamique du phénomène psychotique.

Ils expliquent également le télescopage entre le réel et l'imaginaire à travers les productions picturales fantasmées de cette malade.

Présentés sous forme d'une biographie originale, ces dessins, d'apparence énigmatique, révèlent au spectateur une sorte de confidence intime, expression d'une récente ouverture vers l'autre déclenchée grâce à l'atelier de peinture.

Session 105   Symposium:
Nosology revisited

674
PSYCHIATRIC EDUCATION AND COMPOSITE DIAGNOSTIC EVALUATION
Thomas A. Ban
Vanderbilt University, Nashville, TN U.S.A.
The historical development of psychiatric nosology will be outlined with special reference to the shift from "syndrome-based" classifications ("first epoch") through "disease oriented" classifications ("second epoch") to "pattern-based" classifications ("third epoch"). At present it is not known whether classifications from the "first", or from the "second" or from the "third" epoch can provide for valid clinical-diagnostic end-points. Because of this a methodology was developed, which, by allowing for the comparison of conceptually different systems of diagnostic classifications, should make it possible to identify the diagnoses which approximate the most closely naturally occurring mental illness. The methodology is referred to as the Composite Diagnostic Evaluation (CODE) System. It consists of a diagnostic instrument, which by specially devised algorithm, can assign patients to diagnoses in several diagnostic systems simultaneously. In addition to its clinical and research implication, the CODE-System offers an instrument for psychiatric education. This will be discussed with special reference to the CODE for unipolar depressive disorders (CODE-DD). Of the 25 diagnostic systems included in CODE-DD, five are based on the conceptual development in European classifications; 15 are based on classifications in the UK and USA; and five provide links among the different classifications.

675
POLY-DIAGNOSTIC EVALUATION IN
PSYCHIATRIC RESEARCH

Peter Berner
Psychiatric University Clinic, Vienna

Diagnostic attributions in psychiatry can be considered as only preliminary, as long as they are not sufficiently validated.

Up to the present, most classifications focused primarily on reliability rather than on validity. In order to validate diagnostic categories of the comprehensive systems on hand - such as the ICD and the DSM, they should be compared with specific research criteria based on theoretical grounds.

The possibility to refine our diagnostic systems through the application of such a poly-diagnostic approach is illustrated.

676
New tendencies in nosological concepts

P. PICHOT
24 rue des Fossés Saint Jacques
75005 PARIS, France

Modern nosologies claim, in the name of a-theorism, to remain for the most part at a purely descriptive level. But precisely at this level, two basic models of classification exist: the categorical, which implies the existence of discrete classes, and the dimensional, which allows a case to be described by his projections on several dimensions. Although the terminology used (the term syndrome) is traditionally linked with the categorical model, the nosologies refuse explicitly to take a clear position on the subject. The recent tendency as evidenced in the DSM-III-R is to suppress most of the hierarchical rules and to accept multiple diagnoses for the same subject, in fact a step towards the acceptance of a dimensional model. It is suggested that an important progress would be realized if an explicit choice would be made between the two models, each of them being eventually more appropriate in a given group of mental disorders.

677
NOSOLOGY AND BRAIN IMAGING

Musalek, M., Walter, H., Podreka, I., Lesch, O.M./Psych.Univ.Clinic, Vienna.

Previous brain-imaging studies have indicated the presence of characteristic brain function disturbances in patients suffering from endogenous psychoses, but the results have ranged from confirmative to contradictory.

In our symptom-oriented Single-Photon-Emission-Computed Tomography (SPECT) studies, hallucinating patients showed in general - independently from nosological attribution - significantly different r.CBF patterns in comparison to normal controls. In addition, it was also possible to identify r.CBF distribution patterns characteristic in certain hallucinative phenomena.

It appears permissible, therefore, to suggest that contrary to the opinion that regional activity changes measured by brain-imaging methods represent markers for nosological entities, they could be recognized as correlates of certain psychopathological phenomena.

678
Cross-National Utility of the DSM-III Illness Definitions
John E. Helzer, M.D.
Washington University School of Medicine
St. Louis, Missouri, USA

In order to test the cross-national appropriateness and perceived utility of DSM-III illness definitions, we analyzed questionnaire responses from 140 clinicians in 24 countries. Despite the fact that most were required to use some other nomenclature for record keeping and/or clinical work, most preferred the illness definitions provided in DSM-III. An examination by diagnosis showed that 80% or more of all respondents felt that the definitions for the 12 major illnesses were appropriate in their own cultural context.

We next used population survey data obtained using the Diagnostic Interview Schedule (DIS) to examine the relative prevalence of individual psychiatric disorders, the symptomatic expression of illness, and illness risk factors across countries.

We conclude by suggesting that the similarities we find across widely divergent cultures can be interpreted as evidence for the validity of the DSM-III definitions of illness.

Session 106 Special Session: Eating disorders: Epidemiological and clinical issues

679
Anorexia Nervosa: Biopsychobehavioral Correlates

Kales, J.D., Tan, T-L., Kobylski, T.P, Metzger, E., Vgontzas, A., Pennsylvania State University College of Medicine, Hershey, Pennsylvania 17033 U.S.A.

Clinical characteristics, personality patterns and DSM-III diagnoses were studied in 50 anorectics (43 women, 7 men, mean age 20.9 yrs.). Twenty percent of the sample had a concurrent history of bulimia. Onset of disorder was associated with emotional stress, e.g. parental conflict, relocation or first romantic relationship. Fathers were described as hardworking and emotionally distant and mothers, hardworking and controlling. Dieting began on average in mid teens (16.9 yrs.). 28% had a history of being overweight and 26% reported a family history of problems related to food or of an eating disorder. Physical problems included: hypotension (32%); bradycardia (32%); and anemia (42%). Compared to controls, anorectics had significantly higher mean values on all eight MMPI clinical scales, with more than three times as many patients having at least one elevated scale. Elevations of scale 2-D and other clinical scales (4-Pd, 7-Pt) suggested affective and personality abnormalities, with psychopathology being higher in male and older patients. Prevalent diagnoses on Axes I and II were: depressive disorders (N=41) and compulsive (N=18) and borderline (N=13) personality disorders. These data indicate the complex nature of psychopathology in anorexia and the need for an individualized treatment approach. The prominence of minor chronic rather than major depression differs from most previous findings.

680
PSYCHOLOGICAL CHARACTERISTICS OF OBESE PATIENTS: ASSESSMENT WITH THE MMPI

Kokkevi, A., Mailis, A., Katsoyianni, K. Mortoglou, T., Valsamidis, S., Karamanos, B. and Toutouzas P.

Department of Psychiatry, Athens University Medical School
Obesity Medical Institute, Athens

This study aims at assessing the psychological characteristics of obese subjects and their association to obesity related data (weight level, starting age of obesity, previous attempts to loose weight) and hypothalamic-pituitary tests (TRH, DXM supression test). The sample consists of 307 (90 male and 217 female) consecutive admissions to an obesity center.
Assessment with the MMPI showed that the mean MMPI profile for the total sample was within the normal range. However, 28.6% of the obese male and 35.6% of the female subjects had at least two, among the ten basic MMPI scales, elevated above a T score of 70 as compared respectively to the 19.6% and 19.32% in the general population standardization sample. The percent of subjects with elevated Hypochondriasis scale (Hs) above T=70 was significantly greater to that of the general population for both sexes. Psychopathic deviation (Pd) and Schizophrenia (Sc) percent of elevations above T=70 was significantly greater in males compared to their sex in the general population and the same was true for the Hysteria (Hy) and Mania (Ma) scales in females.
A multivariate analysis showed significant associations of six out of the ten scales (Hs, D, Hy, Pa, Pt, Sc) with Body weight on admission. The scales Hs, D, Sc, and Ma, were also significantly associated to morning cortisol levels.
The above findings show that an important proportion of obese subjects present psychological disturbance. Although there is no homogeneity in psychological deviation, obesity seems to be associated with higher somatization in both sexes, more difficulties in controlling impulses and alienation in males and emotional lability and hyperthymia in females. Anxiety, depressive, psychosomatic and paranoid personality features have on the other hand a positive association with increasing weight. The cause-effect association of personality factors to obesity are discussed.

681
Anorexia and Bulimia, a prevalence study

C. Paz Ferreira and M. Helena Azevedo
Department of Psychiatry, University of Coimbra, Portugal

The authors determined the prevalence of anorexia nervosa and bulimia in a large sample of secondary school students, by means of the Diagnostic Interview Children and Adolescents, an instrument constructed to make DSM-III diagnoses. Although the prevalence of bulimic and anorexic behaviors were rather commom, the syndrome of bulimia was found in only 1.6/1000 and the anorexia nervosa in 4.8/1000 of the students. These results, stand in sharp contrast to reports that eating disordres are commom and probably getting more commom.

682
Anorexia Nervosa: an epidemiological-clinical study in an area of North Italy
MANARA F., RAMELLA M., TRIDENTI A.
Chair of Psychosomatics University of Brescia-Italy

The Authors present the results of an epidemiological and clinical study on a group of 37,000 young people aging between 14 and 19, who attended middle school in an area of North Italy (The province of Brescia). Specially modified Morgan-Russell forms were used to study the occurence of Anorexia Nervosa in the subject group in question.
The results are discussed in relation to DSM III-R and the psychopatological characteristics of the subjects suffering from Anorexia Nervosa are pointed out.
The endocrinological and psychopatological characteristics of subjects considered to have a high-risk of developing Anorexia Nervosa are delineated as well.

683
BULIMIA AND WEIGHT VARIATIONS WITHIN A STUDENT POPULATION
Ferrero F., Rouget P.
Service de Psychiatrie II, IUPG, Geneva (Switz.)

This paper analyses some data on the eating habits and weight variations within the student population of the University of Geneva. Of the 11800 questionnaires sent out, 4200 were returned during the following two months. A weight change is wished by 52.1% of women and 37% of men and for 80.9% of them in the sense of losing weight. The men desire to gain weight three times more frequently than the women. 9.8% of men and 22.9% of women are using at least one method to control weight (used in the past : 16.7% of men and 49.2 % of women) ; 9.3% of men and 20.7% of women are dieting ; 0.7% of men and 3.9 % of women are using appetite-reduction medication ; 0.6% of men and 2.4% of women are using laxatives ; 0.3% of men and 2.2% of women are using provoked vomiting. Special emphasis is placed on those aspects describing weight variations from the age of 14 and on as disclosed in the questions concerning : height and ideal weight ratios, as well as actual, maximum, minimum and desired weight. The subjects of the Bulimia Risk Group weighted significantly more than the controls. The averages of the weight fell within the limits of the theoretical ideal weights as measured by the Lorenz formula. However the weight for the majority of the controls were below this value.

684
AN INVESTIGATION OF EATING ATTITUDES IN A POPULATION OF FEMALE STUDENTS
Hale İmre, Alp Üçok, Şahika Yüksel
Department of Psychiatry, Istanbul Faculty of Medicine, Çapa, İstanbul, TURKEY

Eating disorders have been attracting greater attention and popularity in the last decade. Aspects of the western culture have been considered responsible for propogating anorexia, and in part, bulimia, mainly in women. In Turkey, too, where the influence of the western culture exists, and the traditional culture still persists, there are cases of anorexia and bulimia.
This study was designed to investigate the frequency of anorexia and bulimia in Turkey.
A questionnaire based on the items of EAT (Eating Attitude Test) and BITE (Bulimic Investigatory Test, Edinburg) prepared by our team for this purpose was applied to a population of female teenage students.
The results obtained have been compared with the findings in literature.

685
CO-MORBIDITY OF PSYCHIATRIC SYMPTOMS IN EATING DISORDERED PATIENTS
Fornari, Victor, M.D., Lachenmeyer, Juliana R., PhD Sandberg, David, PhD, Matthews, Mike, ACSW, Cohen, Debbie, ACSW, North Shore University Hospital, Manhasset, NY, 11030

Few personality or family variables have consistently been found to be related to bulimia (Koa and Vandereycken, 1985). Recently there has been a focus on the comorbidity of depressive symptoms in patients with eating disorders (Herzog, 1984, Swift, 1986). In the present study, 100 patients referred to an outpatient eating disorder clinic were evaluated using a structured interview-SADS-L. Depressive disorders, anxiety disorders including obsessive compulsive disorder and substance abuse were the most frequently given diagnoses to those eating disordered patients. The prevalence of each of these disorders will be presented and the implications for treatment of comorbidity of other psychiatric symptoms in patients presenting with eating disorders will be discussed.

686
Prevalence of bulimic symptoms (DSM III/DSM III R) among 3300 french adolescents
LEDOUX S., CHOQUET M., FLAMENT M., JEAMMET Ph.
INSERM U169
16 Av Paul Vaillant Couturier
94807 Villejuif Cedex FRANCE

As part of an epidemiological study on health problems in an unselected adolescent population of 3300 students aged 11-20, eating behaviors and eating disorders symptoms were investigated. Responses on a self-report questionnaire showed that 8% of the subjects engaged in binge eating, 2% reported self-induced vomiting, 9% dieting, 7% laxative use.
Symptoms were more frequent among girls, but few youngsters met all the diagnostic criteria for bulimia nervosa.
Prevalence rates, according to DSM III and DSM III R, were compared.

687

EATING DISORDERS: AN EPIDEMIOLOGICAL STUDY ON 5000 STUDENTS IN ITALY.
Luigi Frighi, Massimo Cuzzolaro
Cattedra di Igiene Mentale - I Università Roma - Italy.

The paper presents data of a research on a non-clinical population of 5000 students between the ages of 11 and 25, mean 16,4, of secondary State schools. The aims of the study were to explore the eating disorders in a large sample of students. The students completed the EAT-40 (Eating Attitudes Test of Garner and Garfinkel validated in Italy by M. Cuzzolaro and A. Petrilli) and a questionnaire expressely constructed, forced choice, about age, sex, social class, family, height, weight, etc.
A representative sample of students who scored above the cut-off score on the EAT (30) was retested and interviewed and detailed information relevant to eating disorders was collected. Data are compared with the results of recent epidemiological studies on eating disorders accomplished in other Western countries.

Session 107 Special Session:
Psychiatric inpatient services

688

OPEN IN-PATIENT CARE SUPPORTED BY PATIENTS' RELATIVES PARTICIPATION.
A. Liakos, S. Yannitsi, G. Kosovitsa, G. Plataris.
Ioannina University, Dept. of Psychiatry, Greece.

In the open psychiatric Unit of the Ioannina General teaching Hospital, the in-patients are often accompanied by their relatives, mainly during the first difficult days after admission. The functions of the Unit are based on a Therapeutic Community approach, and the basic criterion for admissions is the patients' agreement. One hundred and twenty patients in need for hospitalization over a six month period were studied. Five per cent of them failed admission. From the admitted patients a 48.2% was accompanied by relatives. Patients' and relatives' attitude towards hospitalization was assessed with a specially constructed questionnaire. The relatives' attitude at the time of admission was more positive than the patients' one (P<0.001). Patients presented a more positive attitude at the end of hospitalization compared to the time of admission (P<0.05). If compared with the patients admitted on their own initiative, the group of patients admitted on others' initiative showed a more negative attitude at the time of admission (P<0.01). This group, if accompanied by relatives, was changing into a more positive attitude at the end of hospitalization (P<0.01).
In conclusion, with the technique of relatives' participation it has been possible to hospitalize in an open psychiatric Unit of a General Hospital the 95% of patients in need of in-patient care.

689

METHODOLOGICAL ADVANCES IN MEASURING DISTURBED BEHAVIOUR IN PSYCHIATRIC WARDS

N. BOURAS - J. P. WATSON
Division of Psychiatry, Guy's Hospital

What happens to a patient in hospital derives from factors in the patient, or from a wide range of environmental factors, or the interaction between them. In day to day clinical practice, inferences about these environmental characteristics are made from the behaviour of patients and/or staff.

The scheme presented here provides a method allowing to measure disturbed behaviour in psychiatric wards over time. Analysis of data from a series of studies in different psychiatric wards supports the influence of environmental factors in patients behaviour.

690

POSSIBILITIES OF SOCIAL REHABILITATION OF PATIENTS IN THE LEROS PSYCHIATRIC HOSPITAL
PAPADATOS,Y.,BOURAS,N.,ZOUNI.M.,LOUKAS,Y.,WATSON,J
-CENTRE FOR MENTAL HEALTH AND RESEARCH
-GUY'S HOSPITAL - LONDON UNIVERSITY

The purpose of this study was to investigate the possibilities of deinstitutionalization for the patients of Leros Psychiatric Hospital, towards which the existing negative attitudes are well known. The questionnaire used measured the personal and social skills of the patients as well as the opinions of both personnel and patients. It was designed in cooperation with the Psychiatric department of Guy's Hospital of the University of London, the National Unit for Psychiatric Research and Development of London and the Centre for Mental Health and Research (Athens). All 1179 patients were interviewed (average age:53.8 years,SD:14.1)821 men (69.6%) and 358 women (30.4%). The opinions of the personnel and the patients were also recorded. A number of patients, were found to prossess enough personal and social skills for social rehabilitation. According to the personnel,15.2% of the patients were able to live "alone" or "with their family", while according to the interviewers, this percentage increased to 24.7%. 81% of all the patients were found to have no communication with relatives or friends. However 30% ask, themselves, for deinstitutionalization and the majority of them (86.6%) would prefer to live with their families. In conclusion, deinstitutionalization is possible for a considerable number of patients, even those of the Leros Hospital. New form of hospital treatment need to be developed for this to be realized.

691

VALID CONSENT OF THE PATIENT FOR ADMISSION

Dontschev P., Shopova E.
Inst.Neurol.&Psychiatry,Sofia,Bulgaria

The court procedure in Bulgaria is the only way of admitting a patient against his will in a psychiatric hospital.This is possible only in case of immediate dangerousness. All of the rest patients who refuse can be admitted only in the case of a mental incompetency with the consent of their legal representative.Proving legal incompetency through the court is a procedure waisting time unsuitable for the purpose of immediate treatment.

Following the study of S.Dabrowsky(1978) from Poland we try to examine the feasibility for replacement the legal and psychological criteria for civil incompetency with some simpler objective criteria for proving specific mental ability for giving valid consent.

In an empirical study involving 365 patients we try to find out to what extent the patient in the moment of entering the hospital is able to recognize <u>where</u> he is proposed to be admitted and <u>why</u>.This study enables us to prove that the vast majority of patients with psychotic symptoms(84%);with non-psychotic syndroms(92%) and with non-organic changed personality(70%) are quite sufficiently oriented in the place and purpose of admission. This expirence gained by the survey gives us a chance to suggest simpler administrative procedure under court control when need of emergency hospital treatment.

692

A SURVEY OF LONG STAY PATIENTS IN A GREEK MENTAL HOSPITAL

A. BOTSIS, V. TOMARAS, S. LYRINTZIS, C. ZAFIRAKOPOULOU, E. KATSOULAKOS
TRIPOLIS PSYCHIATRIC HOSPITAL / GREECE

Tripolis mental hospital is a public institution with 393 inpatients. 73% of them are long-stay patients (their index hospitalisation had been lasting more than 12 months). Assessment included structured measures of symptomatology and functioning, such as BPRS (Brief Psychiatric Rating Scale), DAS (Disability Assessment Schedule), and GAS (Global Assessment Scale). Sociodemographic data were also collected. Diagnoses were made according to ICD-9.

194 out of the 286 long-stay patients were diagnosed as suffering from non organic mental disorders. This group consisted of 106 men and 88 women. Their mean age was 50 ± 12.5 and 54.5 ± 12.7 respectively, the mean length of their illness 21.7 ± 10.3 and 24.7 ± 11.1 years and the mean duration of their present hospitalisation 6.9 ± 5.6, 11.4 ± 10.8 years. Residual schizophrenia was the commoner diagnosis (125 cases). The absence or the mild degree of florid symptomatology characterised the clinical status of most non organic long-stay inmates. On the basis of our findings a target population can be defined, that, after a phase of inpatient rehabilitation, should be provided with extramural services, such as day care, sheltered working environment and hostels.

We hypothesise that the hospital surveyed is a representative Greek mental hospital and that our findings and suggestions could be generalised.

693

Needs Assessments of Long-Stay Hospital Populations: A Comparative Method
Mr P Clifford, Dr N Bouras, Dr M Zouni
Nat. Unit for Psychiatric Research & Development

This paper will outline the development of a methodology for assessing the needs of long-stay patients residing in psychiatric hospitals scheduled to closeor rundown in the move towards community-based care. Results will be presented from assessments of 1500 such patients in 5 UK hospitals. The Analysis focusses on the following issues:
- needs for supported accomodation
- need for 'asylum' or long-term hospital care
- the needs and characteristics of other subpopulations, such as patients with diagnoses of mental retardation or other 'organic' diagnoses
- needs & characteristics of 'new long-stay' pop.
Adefinition of the new long-stay population is proposed that acknowledges the significant proportion of elderly newly-admitted patients. The results suggest that there is little need for the large hospitals to remain open if adequate provision is made. Nevertheless, a small number of patients continue to accumulate for whom community placement is hard to envisage.

The application of the method in non-UK hospitals, such as the Leros asylum will also be presented.

694

ON PREDICTING NEW LONG-STAY PATIENTS

J. Jakubaschk, A. Hug, D. Waldvogel, O. Würmle, C. Zaugg

Psychiatrische Universitätsklinik Bern, Switzerland

At the Psychiatric Clinic of Berne University, a research project on predicting new long-stay patients is at present carried out.
In a retrospective study based upon case histories we investigated the diagnostic and demographic characteristics of new long-stay patients (= length of hospitalization $\geq$ one year; n = 145) as compared with other hospital patients and case-register populations.
In a second project a random sample of patients admitted to hospital (n = 58) was compared with all new long-stay patients of one particular admission year (n = 44). Psychiatric symptoms (BPRS), demographic and illness data, circumstances of admission, inadequate behaviour (modified "Check List of Nonfunctional Behaviors") and level of intelligence (PMT) were recorded. We were able to detect predictors for long hospitalization among the many discriminating items by categorical logistic regression. Even the simplest model comprising only five variables permitted a correct allocation of 84 %.
In a prospective study we checked our variables for their suitability in predicting new long-stay patients. First results show the difference between prediction and reality.

695
RESPITE CARE FOR CHRONIC SCHIZOPHRENIC PATIENTS

Daniel P. van Kammen, M.D., Ph.D.*°, Janice Galanter, M.S.W.*, Welmoet B. van Kammen, Ph.D.*°, Patricia Nealon, M.S.W.*, George Dougherty, M.D.*°, Jeffrey Peters, M.D.*°; *Western Psychiatric Institute and Clinic, Pittsburgh, PA; °VA Medical Center, Pittsburgh, PA, U.S.A.

Respite care for chronic psychiatric patients in a Veterans Administration Hospital is described. The program is called the Community Maintenance Program (CMP). The CMP provides short term scheduled admissions for chronic psychiatric outpatients to diminish the risk of relapse. The CMP is modeled after the respite care for demented patients. The CMP allows the patients to remain outpatients by providing family members with relief from the strain of taking care of a chronically ill family member. Preliminary data indicate that the CMP will reduce acute admissions. Future controlled studies are needed to establish that the crisis free admissions indeed decrease relapse in outpatients, improve the quality of life for our patients and their caretakers, and decrease the costs of hospitalization.

696
SPANISH PSYCHIATRIC REFORM: THE MADRID METROPOLITAN AREA.
DESVIAT, M; FERNANDEZ LIRIA, A; MAS, J.: Servicios de Salud Mental.- Area 9- MADRID - ESPAÑA.

We expose a plan of psychiatric reform that concerns the whole hospitalization services of an urban area of about 1 million of inhabitants and the cohomprensive mental health services of 300.000 inhabitants. In order to that, we have implemented a community-based model and we have obtained prevalence rates of global psychiatric atention, similar to the reported in the developed countries but with hospitalization rates much lower that countries with a long tradition of in-patient care. That includes a very short lenght of stay (15 days) and a no "new long stay" population in a hospital setting. On the other side we have been challenged by the grown of a new out-patient chronicity that have prompted us to develop a cohomprensive network of care and rehabilitation services including housing alternatives and assesment of general practicioners. We try to obtain conclusions about resources and services requirements in our country and to compare it with that of other countries.

Session 108 Special Session:
MRI and CT in psychiatry

697
The significance of magnetic resonance imaging in psychiatry
Wahlund L-O, Agartz, I, Marions O, Sääf J, Wetterberg L.
Karolinska Institute, Department of Psychiatry, St. Göran's Hospital, S-112 81 Stockholm, Sweden

It is a known fact that organic brain lesions can produce mental symptoms. The incidence of focal brain lesions in patients with psychiatric symptoms is not fully established. Noninvasive neuro-imaging techniques such as MRi might be very useful to further elucidate this problem. An ultra low field magnetic resonance imager operating at 0.02 Tesla was installed at the department of psychiatry at St.Göran's Hospital in December 1984. The imager is operating in close relation to be psychiatric emergency ward and patients with acute psychiatric symptoms as well as more chronically ill patients have been investigated. The incidence of various brain lesions such as tumors, cerebrovascular lesions and arachnoidal-cysts among these patients was assessed. Eight percent of the studied patients were found to have pathologies as listed above, whereas the frequence of corresponding pathologies in healthy controls was less than four percent. The majority of the patients did not exhibit any neurological signs. Typical examples of these pathologies will be presented as case reports. The importance of MRI as a part of routine psychiatric investigations and in psychiatric research will be discussed.

698
A CONTROLLED MAGNETIC RESONANCE IMAGING STUDY IN SCHIZOPHRENIA
Tetsuo Abe, Yoshiro Okubo*, Hiroshi Mori, Naoya Miyamoto, Kunihiko Asai and Takuya Kojima*
Asai Hospital, 38 Katoku, Togane-shi, Chiba-ken, * Dept.of Neuropsychiatry, Tokyo Medical and Dental University, Tokyo, JAPAN.

Magnetic resonance imaging(MRI) was used to measure brain size of 39 chronic schizophrenics and 30 normal subjects matched for age and sex. A parasagittal slice and a coronal slice were obtained in each subject. The area measurements were made on seven brain regions: the cerebrums, frontal lobes, parietal lobes and occipital lobes from the parasagital slices, the cerebrums, frontal lobes, temporal lobes, lateral ventricles and the third ventricles from the coronal slices.

The schizophrenics had significantly smaller cerebrums in both slices than the normal subjects. The ventricular enlargements were also significantly shown in the schizophrenics. MRI, which demonstrated much greater detail of brain structure than CT, revealed that the decrease of cerebral size was most pronounced in the frontal lobes for the parasagittal slices and in the temporal lobes for the coronal slices.

Among the subcategories of schizophrenia, a significant difference was shown only in the temporal lobes. The disorganized schizophrenics had smaller temporal lobes than the paranoid schizophrenics.

699
ULTRA LOW FIELD MAGNETIC RESONANCE IMAGING IN FIRST EPISODE PSYCHOSIS.
Agartz I, Sääf J, Wahlund L-O, Wetterberg L.
Karolinska Institute, Department of Psychiatry, St. Göran's Hospital, Stockholm, Sweden.

The brains of 20 individuals (20-45 years) suffering from first episode psychosis were studied with ultra low field (0.02 Tesla) MRI. Morphological characteristics were perceptually rated and demonstrated wider relationship for the prefrontal subarachnoid space, sulci in fronto temporal regions and the basal cisterns for the psychotic subjects compared to the controls. The perception scores were compared to area measurements quantitated with the use of interactive analysis based on tissue classification. Relaxation time constants were calculated in regions of interest and demonstrated significant differences between the groups. Intersexual and interhemispheric differences were investigated as well as the influence of clinical parameters such as duration and character of psychosis medication.

700
SHORTENED T2 OF LEFT CAUDATE IN MRI STUDY OF TD

George Bartzokis, H. Jordan Garber, Stephen R. Marder, William H. Oldendorf. From: UCLA/West Los Angeles V.A.M.C., Los Angeles, CA 90073, USA.

We used Magnetic Resonance Imaging (MRI) to measure spin-spin relaxation times (T2) of the basal ganglia and thus examine if iron accumulation (believed to shorten T2) is involved in the pathophysiology of Tardive Dyskinesia (TD). We studied fourteen male DSM-III diagnosed schizophrenic patients with a minimum cumulative exposure to neuroleptics of one year. Nine of these patients had, and five had not developed TD. Axial images of the head (6 mm slice thickness) were obtained at 1.5 Tesla using inversion-recovery (IR) and multiple spin-echo (MSE) sequences. T2 was calculated by an automated algorithm for each voxel from the MSE signal intensities to produce T2 maps of the brain. We obtained the mean T2 values for a standard 30 voxel (0.3 sq cm) area within the left and right caudate, putamen and globus pallidus. T2 was significantly shorter in the left caudate nucleus of the TD patients (mean=50 msec) when compared to the patients without TD (mean=54 msec), using a two-tailed t-test (t=4.19, p=0.0012). This difference remained significant after making a covariance adjustment for age. Shortening of T2 in the left caudate nucleus of schizophrenic patients with TD may reflect increased iron deposition which could contribute to the risk of developing TD.

701
A CONTROLLED MAGNETIC RESONANCE IMAGING STUDY IN ALCOHOLICS
Hiroshi Mori, Yoshiro Okubo*, Naoya Miyamoto, Tetsuo Abe, Kunihiko Asai and Takuya Kojima*
Asai Hospital, 38 Katoku, Togane-shi, Chiba-ken, *Dep. of Neuropsychiatry, Tokyo Medical and Dental University.   JAPAN

Thirty-four male alcoholics and 15 normal male control subjects underwent magnetic resonance imaging scan. Seven patients of the alcoholics had no history of withdrawal delirium. The other patients had the history of withdrawal delirium and 7 of them showing amnestic syndrome were diagnosed chronic Wernicke's encephalopathy.

The decrease in the cerebral size and the increase in the ventriclar size were significantly shown in the alcoholics in comparison with the contorols. Among the alcoholics, the cerebral atrophy and the ventricular enlargement were most prominent in the patients with chronic Wernicke's encephalopathy. These results were assumed to be consistent with those from the studies with computerized tomographic scan.

As for the mamillary body, the decrease in the diameter was also confirmed in the alcoholics compared with the controls. Furthermore, one way ANOVA indicated that not only the patients with chronic encephalopathy but also the alcoholics with the history of withdrawal delirium showed the atrophy of the mamillary body.

702
COMPUTERISED CEREBRAL TOMOGRAPHY ON 519 PSYCHIATRIC CASES

B.Taneli, T.Pektoylan, I.Karakilic, F.Karaaslan, S.Taneli, S.Özaskinli, H.Tüper, C.Yavascaoglu, M.Bas

Department of Psychiatry, Uludag University, Bursa, Turkey

CT was applied to 519 patients with different psychiatric disorders, in order to investigate organic pathology and correlate clinical findings. 109 cases had various affective disorders. 109 had schizophrenic disorders; 18 had atypical depression; 99, dysthymic disoreders; 31, obsessive-compulsive behavior; 56, various demential syndromes; 37, grand mal epilepsy; 55, complex partial seizures; and 2, hyperkinetic disorders.

263 of the CT's were found to be normal. 256(49.33%) indicated various underlying pathologies. 8 of the CT's indicated hydrocephalus; 69, lateral ventricular (vent.) dilatation (dilat.); 9, 3rd vent. dilat.; 20, 4th vent. dilat.; 24, vent. asymmetry; 17, mega cisterna magna; 67, basal cisterna dilat.; 156, cortical atrophy; 53, cerebellar atrophy; 45, tumor; 11, cyst; 20, cerebral infarction; 6, multiple infarction; 3, intracerebral hematoma; 1, subdural hematoma; 1, aneurysm, 2, encephalomalasia; lenticular nucleus calcification; 1, temporal lobe, anterior part agenesis; and 1, left temporal horn dilatation.

To conclude, 256 out of 519 cases with prominent psychiatric symptomatology, had underlying cerebral abnormalities indicated by their CT's, which proves to be a valuable diagnostic tool.

703

X RAY AND EMISSION, COMPUTED TOMOGRAPHIES IN 20 CHRONIC PSYCHOTICS
J.P.Luaute[1], E.Sanabria[2], B.Bidault[1], R.Dabrowski[1]
[1] Dept. Psychiatry CH Romans 26100 France
[2] Dept. Nuclear Medicine CH Valence 26000 France

Twenty, right-handed psychotic patients (9 females and 11 males) aged from 25 to 67 year, have been selected according to the severity of the negative symptoms and the duration of the illness (that is a mean of 20 years ±11). According to the DSM III R criteria they were classified as having: schizophrenia (n=13), schizoaffective disorder (n=4), affective psychosis (n=2) an adult form of an infantile psychosis (n=1). No one had a history of an organic disease known before the investigations. The results showed 7 X Ray Computer Tomography (X CT) abnormalities: 5 slight cortical atrophies, 1 frontal subcortical bilateral hypodensity and 1 frontal venous angioma, which was confirmed by angiography. They also showed 12 Single Photon Emission Computed Tomography (SPECT) abnormalities: 5 hypoperfusion having a close pattern to that of Dementia of Frontal Lobe Type; 5 hypoperfusion in the left hemispheric cortex (covering the langage zone); 2 had a preferential right frontal or right temporal hypoperfusion. In fact there was a correspondance between X CT and SPECT abnormalities in only 6 patients. Further, in 7 patients both studies (X CT and SPECT) were normal. Therefore, in 13 out of 20 patients both methods employed revealed abnormal results. These results must be discussed according to patterns of cognitive impairment and variables such as age, clinical condition and medications.

704

OBSERVATIONS ON HEAD COMPUTED TOMOGRAPHY OF THE MENTALLY RETARDED
Keiko Endo, Naoji Amano, Kiyoshi Iwabuchi, Yuki Hama, Yoshiteru Yamada, Hirokazu Hosaka
Dept. of Neuropsychiatry, the Kanagawa Rehabilitation Center, Kanagawa, Japan

The present study is to describe the findings of CT scans on mentally retarded (MR) in an institution. The subjects consist of 75 males and 38 females. The age ranges from 17 to 63, and the mean age is 31.9±12.0. They involve 15 cases with congenital or neonatal brain infection, 10 with intoxication, 24 with perinatal physical damages of the brain, 6 with chromosomal abnormality, 1 with psychological problem, 29 of unknown origin and 23 of unknown history. In addition to routine evaluation of CT scan, the morphometrical analysis was done. The ratio of the total area of the bones to the area of the outer circumferential cranial line on settled each CT slice was measured. Fifty nine cases showed the abnormalities of CT scan; Ventricular abnormality was seen in 49 cases. Congenital anomaly was seen in 15 cases. Twenty seven cases showed the parenchymal abnormality. The measurement revealed higher value in MR group than in controls (117 cases) (p<0.001). Its ratio was smaller in the cases with chromosomal abnormality than in other MR groups. The present study showed various abnormalities on CT scans of MR. Ventricular abnormalities were most frequently seen. The cranial bones were very thick in most cases, indicative of maldevelopment or hypoplasia of the brain.

705

COMPUTERISED TOMOGRAPHIC ABNORMALITIES IN OBSESSIVE COMPULSIVE DISORDER
Sumant Khanna, P.N.Jayakumar, Janardhan Reddy Y.C. , B.Y.T. Arya, S.M.Channabasavanna.

Departments of Psychiatry and Neuroradiology, National Institute of Mental Health and Neurosciences, Bangalore 560029, India.

There has been recent evidence to implicate the frontal lobes, the cingulum and the caudate nucleus in OCD. A CT scan study was carried out where 18 subjects with OCD had their planimetric findings on various dimensions compared with 104 normal CT scans. All OCD subjects met DSM-III criteria and had Hamilton Depression Scale scores of less than 17. Qualitative analysis revealed a significantly higher prominence of the frontal interhemispheric fissure in OCD. On discriminant function analysis, the bicaudate and bifrontal diameters were the most discriminating variables between the two groups. Bicaudate diameters were higher even when compared with primary degenerative dementia.

Session 109 Symposium:
Factors influencing the course of affective disorders

706

HOW DO AFFECTIVE DISORDERS RECUR?

PAUL GROF, EVA GROF, MARTIN ALDA, ANNA YAMAMOTOVA
UNIVERSITY OF OTTAWA, ROYAL OTTAWA HOSPITAL
INSTITUTE OF PHYSIOLOGICAL REGULATIONS, PRAGUE

This presentation will focus on the puzzling nature of the recurrent process itself. Many characteristic of the recurrent course have been well described, however its nature still escapes our comprehension. Enormous volume of research has been dedicated to understanding the psychobiology of individual episodes, yet relatively little effort has one into uncovering the mechanisms underlying the persistent return of episodes.
This presentation will reflect the dissatisfaction arising from the attempts to predict future episodes for individual patients from average characteristics of large patient groups.
Some of the hypothesis proposed as an explanation of the nature of recurrence will be briefly reviewed. A theory of recurrences based on several decades of observations of oscillating processes in animals will be outlined: it has been applied to psychiatric disorders by Lat and Yamamotova. The hypothesis assumes that the episodes of acute psychiatric illness take place at the peaks of excitatory oscillations occurring above a specific threshold. Computer techniques make it possible to identify the individual patterns and threshold from clinical data and to extrapolate it into the future. The overall course of illness can be characterized by one class of functions, however with a wide range of parametre values for individual subjects. The data averaging does not improve our understanding of the process, while extrapolation based on the previous course may be useful for successful prediction of future episodes.
This approach offers a promising theoretical basis for understanding the nature of recurrence.

707
EMERGING CONCEPTS OF BIPOLARITY: AN OVERVIEW

HAGOP S. AKISKAL, GIOVANNI B. CASSANO
University of Tennessee, Memphis U.S.A.
University of Pisa, Italy

In reviewing recent findings on affective conditions in the interface of unipolar and bipolar disorders, we find evidence favoring a partial return to Kraepelin's broad concept of manic-depressive illness, which included many recurrent depressives and temperamental variants. This review addresses methodologic, clinical and familial considerations in the definition and characterization of a proposed spectrum of bipolar disorders which subsumes episodic and chronic forms. Episodic bipolar disorders are subclassified into bipolar schizoaffective, and bipolar I and II and bipolar III or pseudo-unipolar forms. Chronic bipolar disorders could be either intermittent or persistent, and are sub-classified into chronic mania, protracted mixed states, and paid-cycling forms, as well as the classical temperaments (cyclothymic, hyperthymic, irritable and dysthymic).
The overview concludes by examining risk factors for bipolarity, especially for the more rapid-cycling and bipolar forms, such as gender, sleep deprivation, transmeridian travel, seasons, borderline hypothyroid indices, temporal lobe dysrhythmia and, finally, exposure to tricyclic antidepressants and other catecholaminergic drugs.

708
SLEEP LOSS: A PREVENTABLE CAUSE OF MANIA

THOMAS A. WEHR
NATIONAL INSTITUTE OF MENTAL HEALTH, BETHESDA, MARYLAND, U.S.A.

Most depressed patients improve rapidly and dramatically when their sleep is interrupted for all or part of one night.
Conversely, patients who improve after sleep deprivation often become depressed again after sleeping, even for as little as two hours. Thus sleep appears to be a depressant, and wakefulness an antidepressants. Like other antidepressant modalities, sleep deprivations also appears to be capable of inducing switchees into mania or hypomania, at least in bipolar patients. My colleagues and I found that the majority of a group of depressed bipolar patients switched into mania or hypomania day after day were deprived of sleep for one night.
In the natural course of bipolar illness a host of factors might trigger mania by disrupting sleep. These factors could be classified as psychological, situation, medical and pharmacological.
The psychiatric literature contains many reports that point to these and other factors as possible causes of manic episodes.
In our investigations of biological mechanisms we have focused on neuroendocrine effects of sleep deprivation.
Neuroendocrine responses to sleep deprivation resemble those to cold-exposure; furthermore, heat attenuates both the neuroendocrine and mood-elevating effects of sleep deprivation.
Therefore, the mania-inducing effects of sleep deprivation might be explained within the context of thermoregulatory physiology.
Attention to the possible role of sleep loss as a triggering factor in the pathogenesis of mania may help clinicians and patients to identify some the factors that influence the natural course of bipolar illness and to device strategies for its preventions and treatment.

709
RAPID CYCLERS

HENRI DUFOUR
Department of Psychiatry, Prilly Lausanne

Rapid cyclers (RC) are probably a sub-type of bipolar affective disorders, defined by at least 4 cyclers/year (Dunner, 1974), lenght cycle of 2 days to 12 weeks (Alarcon, 1985) a mean age at the beginning of about 40 years (koukopoulos, 1983), but with the possibility of very early onset (Jones, 1987). RC are described as having a poor influence on the course of bipolar affective disorders, sometimes of monopolar, in terms of poor treatment response (Lithium) and chronification (Arnold, Koukopoulos). Predisposition factors are sex (female, post-partum and menopausal periods (Alarcon), cyclothymic personality (Akiskal). The more classical inducing agents are antidepressants, particularly tricyclic antidepressants, but their responsability remain controversial.
Concomitant modifications have been recently noticed : hormonal (oestrogens) and a neurohormonal (DST) modifications, hypothyroidism (Joffe, 1988), deficent nocturnal surge of TSH secretion (Sack, 1988), epileptiform paroxysms (Levy, 1988).
The pathogenesis is still unknown, but some treatments have been proposed: combination of Lithium and carbamazepine (Laird, 1987; Post, 1987), clonidine (Alary, 1988), valproate (Mac Elroy, 1988).

710
THE INFLUENCE OF TREATMENTS WITH ANTIDEPRESSANTS.

A.KOUKOPOULOS, A.TUNDO, G.F.FLORIS, D.REGINALDI, G.MINNAI, L.TONDO.
Centro Lucio Bini, Roma - Centro Lucio Bini, Cagliari.

Since the beginning of the use of MAOI and Tricyclic drugs in the treatment of depression several papers have indicated the possibility that they may increase the frequency of recurrences in comparison to the previous course treated with ECT or otherwise, or no treatment at all (Freyhan, Lauber, Arnold and Kryspin-Exner, Hoheisel, Till and Vuckovic). The acceleration of the course of the illness, sometimes up to the point of rapid cyclicity, was related to the precipitation of mania or hypomania in bipolar and unipolar patients (Siris, Wehr, Goodwin, Lerer et al.).
This view has not been accepted by all clinicians and it has been rejected by Lewis and Winocur, Angst et al. Indeed many clinicians use antidepressant drugs as prophylaxis against recurrent depression and several papers indicate their prophylactic efficacy especially in unipolar depression (Seagour and Bird, Imlah et al., Klerman, Paykel, Mindham et al.). The many and difficult methodological problems involved in investigations of this kind make it difficult to perform studies that would yield unequivocal evidence.
The other problem is that of which patients are more at risk in developing mania and eventually increased frequency of recurrences during treatment with antidepressants. Women especially at menopause, young age and hyperthyroidism have been associated with rapid cyclicity while the cyclothymic temperament (Akiskal) was found prone to develop hypomanias.
In an open study we have found that cyclothymic and hyperthymic temperament and patients with a cycle of depression followed by a mania or hypomania are the most prone to undergo an acceleration of the course of the illness during treatment with antidepressants.

711
BIPOLAR AND UNIPOLAR DELUSIONAL DEPRESSIVE SUBTYPES:
A PHARMACOLOGIC DISSECTION
RADWAN F. HAYKAL and HAGOP S. AKISKAL
Mood Disorders Program, Charter Lakeside Hospital - Memphis U.S.A.
University of Tennessee - Memphis U.S.A.

This study examines 50 strictly defined delusional depressions and reports that acute thymoleptic responses are characteristic of patients that, on the basis of pre-established criteria, can be considered pseudo-unipolar, i.e., young probands with acute-onset, psychomotor-retarded, or mixed features, bipolar family history and pharmacologic-hypomania.

By contrast, thymoleptic-nonresponsive patients, who often require neuroleptic or electroconvulsive therapy, are older with insidious onset, tend to pursue a subacute or chronic course, are psychomotor-agitated, lack bipolar family history, and do not develop pharmacologic hypomania.

Session 110 Symposium:
The Composite International Diagnostic Interview: An instrument for cross-culturally comparative epidemiological studies

712
THE RELIABILITY OF THE CIDI IN THE WHO FIELD TRIALS
Professor H.-U. Wittchen
Max-Planck Institute for Psychiatry, Munich, Federal Republic of Germany

The WHO-CIDI field trials are part of WHO's effort to develop a comprehensive diagnostic instrument for ICD-10 and DSM-III-R to be used primarily in epidemiological settings. Nineteen centres from 16 different countries around the world participated in a reliability study that included 575 subjects from different settings. The primary goals of this study were: (a) to determine the acceptability and feasibility of the instrument in different cultures, (b) to identify major gaps in coverage of diagnostic areas, and (c) to test its reliability in different settings and cultures. The results indicate that: (1) although regarded as too long by one third of the centres, acceptance of the CIDI approach in all centres was good to excellent, (2) excellent agreement was reached on the diagnostic coverage of the CIDI (only a few minor additions and revisions needed to be made), and (3) excellent interrater reliability was obtained for all diagnoses covered by the instruments, as well as the additional PSE questions and syndromes. Reasons for discrepancies in CIDI ratings were analyzed in detail and have been taken into account in the most recent revision of the instrument.

713
CORRESPONDENCE BETWEEN CIDI AND CLINICAL EVALUATION IN INDIA
Dr Mohan K. Isaac
National Institute of Mental Health and Neuro Sciences, Bangalore, India

The Composite International Diagnostic Interview (CIDI) was translated into the Southern Indian language, Kannada, spoken in Karnataka State in India. The translated CIDI was used to interview 20 respondents from a rural primary health care clinic and 12 respondents from the out-patient services at the National Institute of Mental Health and Neuro Sciences in Bangalore, by a pair of clinicians and non-clinicians who alternated as interviewer and observer. This paper describes the several problems in translation procedures and the specific difficulties which were encountered in the Probe Flow Chart (P.F.C.) of the instrument. It also discusses the coverage of CIDI in relation to the clinical profile of psychiatric patients in developing countries such as India.

714
PATIENT REACTIONS TO THE CIDI IN BRAZIL
MIRANDA, C.T.; MARI, J.J.; ARRUDA, M.E. RICCIARDI, AA.
DEPARTMENT OF PSIQUIATRY, ESCOLA PAULISTA DE MEDICINA

The CIDI is a psychiatric research instrument which has been developed to be used in different countries to allow for reliable and cross cultural comparative studies. As a part of the Field Trials on the CIDI this instrument was applied to a sample of 29 Brazilian subjects.

The aim of this presentation will be to point out some patient reactions. Regarding the content of the interview it was observed the following points: 1. it tends to cause avoidness in the sections with culturally embarassing items like those of the Alcohol Abuse and Dependence section, mainly for subjects without drinking problems; 2. the subjective evaluation of severity is difficult for subjects with low literacy level; 3. in the Organic Brain Syndrome section subjects with low literacy level tends to give high scores leading to false positive diagnoses.

Regarding the format of the interview the following points were observed: 1. the long lasting interview requiring mainly "yes" or "no" answers, seems to be a difficult task for people with poor schooling; 2. these "low educated" subjects have some difficulty to understand the long phrased questions.

Most of these reactions can be overcome by dividing the interview in two sections; some questions should have to be shortened and rephrased; a small part of the questionnaire (the section of Organic Brain Syndrome for instance) is innapropriate for a fraction of the Brazilian population. In conclusion, the use of almost all the sections of the CIDI in Brazil is feasible, depending on minor modifications on its content, format and method of application.

715

Using the CIDI in the General Population
H.R. Wacker, R. Battegay, C. Schlösser, R. Müllejans
Psychiatric University Outpatient Clinic, Basle, Switzerland

The prevalence rates of Major Depressive Episodes, Generalized Anxiety Disorder, Panic Disorder, and Phobias in the adult general population of the city of Basle, Switzerland, was investigated in spring 1989 by means of the CIDI-R. 300 randomly selected individuals between the age of 18 and 65 years were interviewed by 20 trained university students. The students were trained for their task in groups of 5-10 persons during one week by means of mock-interviews, interviews with psychiatric outpatients and by rating video-taped interviews. The interrater reliability was examined in a test-retest design. Five thoroughly trained editors supervised the students' work and checked each interview for completeness and for possible errors. The results are compared with the corresponding prevalence rates of the aforementioned disorders in the general urban population of the US and of Germany. It is concluded that the CIDI is a reliable instrument to measure prevalence rates of the disorders mentioned above in the general population of a Swiss town.

716

THE RELIABILITY AND ACCEPTABILITY OF CIDI-CORE DRUG AND ALCOHOL QUESTIONS CROSS-CULTURALLY
Cottler, L.B., Robins, L.N., Helzer, J.E. (Washington University School of Medicine, Department of Psychiatry, St Louis, MO, USA), Babor, T. (University of Connecticut, Farmington, USA), Blaine, J. Chiarello, R. (National Institute on Drug Abuse, USA), Grant, B., Towle, L. (National Institute on Alcohol Abuse and Alcoholism, USA)

The CIDI elicits information required to evaluate substance abuse and dependence criteria from the DSM-III, DSM-III-R and ICD-10 classification systems. Data are collected on the abuse of and dependence on alcohol, and psychoactive substances such as marijuana, amphetamines, barbiturates, tranquilizers, cocaine, heroin and other opiates, hallucinogens and inhalants. Onset and recency of each symptom are dated, allowing both historical and cross-sectional diagnoses to be made. Using the International CIDI Field Trial data collected in 1988, reliability estimates of substance use diagnoses in the three classification systems will be presented. Reliabilities will also be provided for common symptoms. Issues of the appropriateness and acceptability of substance abuse questions across cultures will be discussed, and a multivariable analysis will explore whether reliability estimates vary by culture or type of subject (psychiatric, substance abuse, or general medical patient). Modifications made to improve acceptability as a result of the field trials will be addressed.

Session 111 Symposium: Current issues on ECT

717

THE VALUE OF REAL V SIMULATED ECT IN DEPRESSED PATIENTS: A COMBINATION OF THE NORTHWICK PARK AND LEICESTER TRIALS.
Eve C. Johnstone[1], T.J. Crow[1], H. Buchan[2], K. McPherson[2], and S. Brandon[3].
1. Division of Psychiatry, Clinical Research Centre, Harrow. 2. Department of Community Medicine and General Practice, University of Oxford, England. 3. Department of Psychiatry, University of Leicester, England.

The question of the role of electrically induced convulsion in the efficacy of ECT in depressed patients was investigated in 2 randomised controlled trials in England, one at Northwick Park and one at Leicester. Both reported a significantly greater improvement in patients receiving real rather than simulated ECT although their assessment of the magnitude of the benefit and of the effects of subgroups of depressed patients differed. It has been possible to combine the data from the two studies. The combined analysis shows that patients who suffered from depression in which retardation or delusions were features and who received real ECT had a significantly improved outcome at 4 weeks in comparison with those who had simulated ECT. This treatment effect had disappeared at 6 months follow-up. Patients who were neither retarded nor deluded did not gain any significant benefit from real as opposed to simulated ECT.

718

Is ECT still a valid treatment ?
Angelberger-Spitaler H., Conca A., Schneider HJ., König P.
Landes-Nervenkrankenhaus Valduna, A-6830 Rankweil

We report on 120 psychiatric in-patients having undergone ECT during 1980 - 1987. The overall percentage, 0,71% of all admissions, lies within known figures, the indications and diagnoses concur with the well known ones. 44% patients were treated because of drug-resistance, over half of this group after 4 or more weeks of treatment. The drug-dosages applied before ECT are listed and lie in the approved dose-ranges, considering poly-psychopharmacotherapy. In more than 50% bilateral electrode-placement was employed for therpeutical considerations, otherwise the unilateral non-dominal hemisphere placement was adopted, in any case the approved anaesthesiological measures were effected. 62% patients remitted after less than 10 ECTs although in 14% up to 20 or more were needed. The overall remission-rate was 83%.

A comparison of a matched group of ECT/non-ECT treated patients (n=7) was made but yielded no clear results.

Considering strict indications ECT is rated as a valuable treatment-technique for a small group of psychotic in-patients.

719

RECOVERY FROM DEPRESSIVE ILLNESS: AMITRIPTYLINE AND ECT COMPARED.

R. Stocks, A.I.F. Scott, P.A. Shering and L.J. Whalley

University Dept. of Psychiatry, Royal Edinburgh Hospital, Edinburgh EH10 5HF, Scotland, U.K.

The early pattern of recovery from depressive illness may be of clinical value in predicting treatment outcome, and provide clues about the biological process of recovery. Recovery was assessed by improvement in individual items of the Hamilton Rating Scale for Depression and the Montgomery and Asberg Depression Rating Scale. The study was conducted on hospital in-patients meeting DSM III criteria for Major Depressive Episode. Twenty-five patients treated by 150mg amitriptyline and 40 patients treated by an average of 7 ECTs were rated weekly for 4 weeks. Data will be presented on the rate of improvement in individual symptoms and their value in predicting recovery. The patterns of recovery during drug treatment and ECT will be compared and hypotheses concerning their biological basis will be made.

720

ISOFLURANE AND ELECTROCONVULSIVE TREATMENT IN THERAPY OF DEPRESSION

O. Hoffmann, C. Mebius, E. Vinnars, L. Johnson, C. Stenfors, A.A. Mathé

Karolinska Institute - St. Göran's Hospital, Stockholm, Sweden

ECT is considered to be the most effective treatment of major affective disorder, depression. However ca 20-25% of apparently properly diagnosed patients do not derive benefit from ECT. Moreover, its application has at times - for a variety of reasons - been restricted. Thus there is a need to develop alternative methods to treat depression. In view of the hypotheses that deep sleep and general anaesthesia may have antidepressive action, a double-blind study with isoflurane gas was commenced. Patients were randomly assigned to two groups receiving - after induction of anaesthesia with short-acting barbiturate - either isoflurane or ECT. Maximal isoflurane concentration was 4.5% and the gas was applied until a characteristic low voltage EEG pattern was obtained. 6 to 8 treatments, 3 times/week, were given. The clinical assessment - including BPRS, Hamilton scale GAS - was done before, during and after (one day, one week, one month, etc) the treatment. Preliminary results indicate that isoflurane may be approximately as effective as ECT and are thus in agreement with the data reported from Vienna University Hospital.

721

TRH AND MECHANISMS OF ACTION OF ECT
Yiannis G. Papakostas
Athens University Medical School, Dept of Psychiatry, Eginition Hospital

The possibility that some aspects of ECT's action are mediated by TRH will be discussed in this presentation.
The content of TRH in rat brain increases after ECS, but no ECT effect on plasma or CSF TRH could be demonstrated in man. There are several indications that TRH is related to ictal and/or post-ictal activity. For example, there are cases of exacerbation of convulsive disorders after TRH but, on the other hand, TRH can be of therapeutic value in certain forms of childhood epilepsy.
Prolactin increase is considered as a biochemical index of (limbic) seizure activity induced by tonic-clonic seizures, complex partial seizures, and ECT. We will present evidence that this last effect might be a TRH-linked neuroendocrine event.
Finally, the possibility that TRH may be involved in the ECT's antidepressant effect (in support of Fink and Ottosson's neuroendocrine hypothesis) will be discussed.

722

ECT AND MORPHOLOGICAL CHANGES IN THE BRAIN; A MRI STUDY
Hurwitz T.A., Li D.K.B.
Department of Psychiatry, University Hospital Site, B.C. V 6T 2 A1, Vancouver, 2255 Wesbrook Mall, Canada

Electroconvulsive therapy (ECT) may produce a breakdown in the blood-brain barrier which may lead to edema. We used magnetic resonance imaging (MRI) to determine whether ECT causes acute morphological changes in the brain. Eight patients who received a course of ECT were studied prior to and at 3 to 4 hours after the first ECT and at 3 to 4 hours after the last ECT. One patient missed the second set of images because of claustrophobia in the MR imager. ECT was administered using either a right unilateral frontotemporal or bilateral electrode placement. All patients were pre-oxygenated, anesthetized with sodium pentothal and paralyzed with succinylcholine. A T_2 weighted sequence was utilized with a repetition time (TR) of 2100 milliseconds and an echo time (TE) of 40 and 120 milliseconds. This T_2 weighted sequence was selected to be sensitive to detect edema. MR images were coded and rated in random order by visual inspection for the presence or absence of any abnormalities in the gray or white matter. The rater (D.K.B.L.) was blind to the patient and administration of ECT. No changes were noted in any patient in either their second or third set of MR images. We conclude that acute morphological changes as detected by MR imaging does not occur following a course of ECT.

723
ECT ENHANCES PROLACTIN RESPONSE TO FENFLURAMINE CHALLENGE
Baruch Shapira, Seth Kindler, Cornelius Gropp, Pesach Lichtenberg, Bernard Lerer
Jerusalem Mental Health Centre-
Ezrath Nashim Hospital, Jerusalem, Israel

Brain serotonergic mechanisms have been strongly implicated both in the pathogenesis of depressive illness and in the action of antidepressant treatments. Prolactin (PRL) response to fenfluramine (FF) challenge has been extensively used as a measure of central serotonergic responsiveness. We applied this paradigm (plasma PRL response to FF 60 mg orally or placebo) to patients treated with bilateral ECT. Patients were tested drug-free, before and then after a series of 8-12 ECT (N=16). Area under the curve of PRL levels measured over six hours was significantly increased by ECT. The PRL response to placebo was not altered. Fenfluramine blood levels measured prior to and after ECT did not differ significantly. These findings suggest that ECT enhances central serotonergic responsiveness in depressed patients and may alleviate depression by this mechanism. (Supported in part by NIMAH Grant MH40734)

Session 112   Symposium:
Cognitive impairment due to HIV-infection

724
PSYCHIATRIC SYMPTOMS AND NEUROPSYCHOLOGICAL DEFICITS IN HIV-INFECTION
D. Naber, C. Perro, U. Schick, H. Hippius
Psychiatric Hospital, University of Munich,
D-8000 Munich, West-Germany

164 HIV-positive patients, 110 in early stages of infection, underwent psychiatric exploration and neuropsychological testing. 27% of patients showed symptoms of depression, 3% of anxiety and 2% of psychosis. Neuropsychological tests revealed normal functioning in 76% of patients in early stages and in 54% of those in late stages. Clinically relevant was the deficit in 5% and in 19%, respectively. The comparison with HIV-negative controls (n = 100) showed for most tests a significant reduction already in early stages. These neuropsychological deficits correlated highly significantly with the degree of affective symptoms.
This investigation shows in agreement with the sparse literature cognitive deficits already in early and particularly in late stages of HIV-infection. However reduced neuropsychological funktioning does not unequivocally indicate an organic etiology, since the stress of a life-threatening illness with enormous social implications may cause marked psychological reactions.
Repeated measurements of psychopathology and cognitive functioning in 64 patients may help to differentiate somatogenic vs. psychogenic etiology. Moreover, data on neurological examination (incl. CT, EEG, CSF) of 85 patients and their relationships to psychiatric variables will be presented.

725
Neuropsychological deficits in AIDS-patients and HIV-infected persons.
Susanne Lunn, Marianne Skydsbjerg, Hanne Schulsinger, Josef Parnas, Court Pedersen, Lars Mathiesen.
Institute of clinical Psychology,
University of Copenhagen, Denmark.

Since the beginning of the AIDS epidemic, the neuropsychological implications of AIDS/HIV has been discussed. The purpose of this study has been to determine whether, and to what extent, neuropsychological impairment can be seen in AIDS-patients and in asymptomatic HIV-positive subjects.

Methods and Materials: An extensive neuropsychological testbatteri was administered to three groups of danish homosexual men: 20 AIDS patients, 20 asymptomatic HIV-positive and a matched control of 20 HIV-negative subjects.

Results: There was a clear overall tendency in the results. The AIDS-group performed worse than the HIV-positive group, and they in turn performed worse than the control group. The study supported the hypothesis that HIV directly affects the CNS early in the course of the disease.

726
EXAMINATION OF HIV-1 INFECTED PATIENTS WITH NEUROPSYCHOLOGICAL TESTS
Alexius B, Wetterberg L, Saaf J, Wahlund L-O, Sonnerborg A.
Dept. of Psychiatry, Karolinska Institute, Stockholm, Sweden
Objective: To study the natural course of CNS lesions in HIV-1 infected patients, to improve the diagnosis of CNS alterations and to evaluate therapeutic response. Methods: Patients with HIV-1 infection, classified in CDC group II-IVB, have been investigated at one year intervals with a set of 20 neuropsychological tests. Patients with previous neurological or psychiatric diseases, alcohol, drug or narcotic abuse were excluded from the study. Results: The patient group consists to date of 50 homo- or bisexual men - 15 in group II, 15 in group III and 20 in group IVA-B. HIV-1 infection occurred 1-10 years before examination. The control group consists of 20 seronegative homo- or bisexual men. Neuropsychological testing showed impairment in memory function, concentration capacity and fine motor control in patients of CDC group II, III and IVA-B but not in the controls. To date 30 patients have been reexamined one year after the first investigation. Nearly one third of these patients were treated with Zidovudin. In the group without Zidovudin only one test measuring concentration capacity showed significant lower result. The patients treated with Zidovudin showed more impairment in one test measuring fine motor control.
Conclusions: Alterations in the CNS are found at an early state in many of the HIV-1 infected patients. Neuropsychological tests are valuable methods in diagnosing and evaluating such damage.

727
EXAMINATION OF HIV-1 INFECTED PATIENTS WITH MAGNETIC RESONANCE IMAGING (MRI)
Wahlund L-O, Wetterberg L, Saaf J, Alexius B, Sonnerborg A.
Dept. of Psychiatry, Karolinska Institute, Stockholm, Sweden

Objective: To investigate brain white matter lesions in neurologically symptomatic and asymptomatic HIV-1 infected patients in different stages of disease and to be able to follow therapeutic effects of antiviral drugs. Methods: Fifty one homo- or bisexual FV-1 infected men participated in the study. Twenty one patients had clinical significant neurological symptoms. Of the remaining 30 patients, 7 were classified to CDC group II, 13 to group III and 10 to group IVA. Drug addicts or patients with previous or ongoing psychiatric disease were not included. A control group of 20 homo- or bisexual HIV-1 seronegative men were also studied. The patients and controls were examined with an ultra low field MRI and computer assisted classification. Results: A white matter lesion with a significantly decreased T1 value and unchanged or decreased T2 and proton density values was found. The incidence of this lesion was 90% in the group of neurologically symptomatic patients, 53% in neurologically asymptomatic patients and 25% in the control group of seronegative men. The brain lesions were found in the CD groups II, III and IVA. The ratio between the area of pathologically altered brain white matter and the total brain area was also determined. A significant larger ratio was found in the neurologically symptomatic group compared with the neurologically asymptomatic patients and the controls.

728
COGNITIVE FUNCTIONING IN HIV POLYTRANSFUSED PATIENTS
Kokkevi A, Hatzakis A, Arvanitis Y, Maillis A, Zalonis J, Samartzis D, Pittadaki, Mandalaki T, Stefanis C.

A sample of 89 polytransfused patients with blood products was investigated with a battery of computerized tests in order to assess possible cognitive impairment in HIV positive (N=60) as compared to HIV negative (N=29) patients. Patients were also screened for psychopathology and their mood state was assessed by the Beck Depression Scale and POMS. The investigation was blind with regard to the HIV status of the patients.
Preliminary results failed to show any significant differences in cognitive functioning and mood of the HIV positive as compared to HIV negative patients. State comparisons, however, of mean performance between those who were identified as HIV positive for more than five years (N=20) and those identified as HIV positive for less than five years (N=40) revealed significantly higher means in both decision and reaction time in the reaction time test, as well as indication of performance impairment in the tracking test and a tendency for higher depressive mood in the Beck Scale.

Session 113 Special Session:
Affective disorders: Course and prognosis

729
DYSFUNCTIONAL INTIMATE RELATIONSHIPS AS A RISK FACTOR TO DEPRESSIVE DISORDER AND AS A PREDICTOR OF OUTCOME
Professor Gordon Parker and Dr Ian Hickie, School of Psychiatry, The Prince of Wales Hospital, High Street Randwick 2031 NSW Australia

The quality of the principal relationship of 78 non-endogenously depressed subjects was assessed with the Intimate Bond Measure (IBM). The IBM is a self-report measure which generates perceived care and control scores for the partner and which has recently been established as having acceptable reliability and validity. Using a case-control methodology the increased risk of depressive disorder associated with a dysfunctional relationship was quantified. Comparisons were then made with the other known risk factors for depressive disorder in the sample. The sample was then studied longitudinally with interviews at six weeks, six months and eighteen months. Self-report and rater measures of depression, as well as the IBM were repeated on each occasion. We demonstrated that an aberrant IBM score predicted a poor outcome for the depressive disorder if the subject remained in dysfunctional relationship. If, however, the subject separated from their partner, outcome was considerably better and comparable with those who remained in functional relationships. The strength of the IBM as a predictor of outcome was then compared with other personality and demographic variables, and was the strongest predictor.

730
THE GOOD PROGNOSIS OF AFFECTIVE DISORDERS: A MYTH ?
A.Deister, A.Marneros, A.Rohde
Psychiatric Department of the University Bonn, Federal Republic of Germany

Eighty patients diagnosed as having uni- and bipolar affective disorders were investigated longitudinally in regard to long-term course and outcome.
The mean followup period was approx. 25 years, all patients were treated with antidepressive agents, and most bipolar patients have had a prophylaxis with lithium in the last decade.
Psychopathological and social outcome were evaluated using standardized instruments like Present State Examination, Global Assessment Scale, Disability Assessment Schedule and Psychological Impairment Rating Schedule.
One third of the patients showed a residual symptomatology and/or impairments in global functioning.
These results suggest that the prognosis of affective disorders is not always so excellent as often assumed.
Kind and structure of residual symptomatology prove to be different from schizophrenic and also from schizoaffective residual states.

731

The Long-term-course of Affective Components in Endogenous Psychoses.

Kazumasa IWAI, Sakae ISHIHARA
Psychiatric Clinic, Tokyo Women's Medical College

From all patients suffering from endogenous psychoses, who were admitted to the Psychiatric Clinic of Tokyo Women's Medical College between 1965 and 1974 at the first time and were readmitted 5-7 years later, 52 cases with 10 years-observation period were selected. About 60% of patients were observed more than 15 years, and 85% were admitted more than 3 times in the whole course. The sample was divided into two groups, a group of pure affective cases and another group of cases, which showed RDC-schizophrenic symptoms at least once in the whole course. The affective components of clinical picture were continuously estimated through the course according to RDC, in the sense of major depression, mania, minor depression and hypomania. On the other hand schizophrenic symptoms were marked through the course in another dimension.

24 of 52 cases belong to pure affective group, of which 8 were monopolar depressive. 16 had also manic phases. In the longitudinal observation we found a general bias from depressive to manic phases. Namely the "Manic Shift". The Recurrence of mania or hypomania with mitigation of depression was observed in 69% of the late-course of bipolar group. Of 28 cases of another group with schizophrenic symptoms, in 21 cases depression was lacking from the beginning or mitigated in the late-course. Thus 63% showed similar tendency to "manic shift". The direction of affective components in the long-term-course was not influenced by schizophrenic symptoms.

732

COURSE OF ILLNESS IN SUBTYPE OF PRIMARY RECURRENT MOOD DISORDERS

G.F.Placidi, L.Dell'Osso
Institute of Psychiatry, University of Pisa, Italy

In order to delineate clinical features and course of diagnostic categories of affective illness on the basis of prognostic parameters proposed by various authors, a naturalistic study on 200 patients admitted to the Psychiatric Clinic, University of Pisa for a mood episode (DSM-III-R) has been designed.
The comparison among bipolars I, bipolars II, and recurrent major depressives confirmed previous observations such as in bipolar I early onset of illenss, rapid onset and recovery of episodes, that are shorter and with a high risk for suicide; in these patients polarity of onset appears to be predictive of course; the younger age, the shorter latency of hospitalization and the interval from last episode to index one, suggest a more recurrent and sever pattern of illness than other two groups. Bipolars II show intermediate features between bipolars I and recurrent depressives regarding the onset of illness, while in latency and number of hospitalizations and in the risk for suicidal attempts they are more similar to recurrent major depressives. This last group shows a longer duration of hospitalization and a higher percentage of melancholic and psychotic episodes.

733

GENDER AND CLINICAL FEATURES OF MOOD DISORDERS

Perugi G., Musetti L., Simonini E., Savino M., Cassano G.B.
Chair II, Institute of Clinical Psychiatry, University of Pisa, Italy.

In a consecutive clinical series of 538 depressives suffering from primary mood disorders the male-female differences were most skewed (1:4) in recurrent unipolars, 1:2 in single episode and bipolar I subtypes, and about even (1:1) in bipolar II. The two sexes did not differ in age at onset of depression, stressors preceding index episodes, endogenous features, psychotic symptoms, suicide attempts, and rates of chronicity. Females had lower mean number of hypomanic and higher past mean number of depressive episodes. Females also exhibited more anxiety and somatization, and were generally more likely to endorse psychopathologic items on self-report instruments not reflected in objective measures. Finally they were more likely to have been hospitalized psychiatrically. Our data further suggest that these gender differences could in part be explained by the higer prevalence of the depressive temperament in females, and of the hyphertymic temperament in males.

734

SOCIAL SUPPORT, GENDER AND PREDICTING THE OUTCOME OF MAJOR DEPRESSION

Dr T S Brugha
Dept. of Psychiatry, University of Leicester
Clinical Sciences Building, Leicester Royal Infirmary, PO Box 65, Leicester LE2 7LX, England.

130 men and women attending psychiatric hospitals with depressive disorders were interviewed at the time of their initial contact. After a mean four month interval, 119 were reassessed in order to test the hypothesis that initial levels of social support predict clinical improvement, even when other potential risk factors such as age, sex, diagnosis and severity of depression are controlled. Severity and duration of the episode emerged as the only significant background predictors of recovery. The explained variance in recovery from depression due to social support was equal in men and women, and was not diminished by the background clinical predictors. Multiple regression models of outcome favoured a main effect of social support and provided persuasive if inconclusive evidence for a statistical interaction effect with sex. The implications for further research and for theory are discussed.

735

CULTURAL DIFFERENCES IN DEPRESSIVE SYMPTOMATOLOGY IN THREE ASIAN CENTRES - SEOUL, SHANGHAI & NAGASAKI

S. Michitsuji, Y. Nakane, Y. Ohta, H. Yan, X. Wang, S.K. Min, H.Y. Lee

China, Korea and Japan belong to the Asian region and while are geographically close, differ greatly in their language, culture and history. As part of a multiphase study we have been examining the nature of depressive disorders in patients from Shanghai, Seoul and Nagasaki. The first phase of the study examined the assessment of depressive disorder and has been reported elsewhere (Nakane et al., 1988). In the second phase, to be reported here, first contact patients from each centre were screened and 100 cases selected from each centre. Symptoms and total score from the Hamilton Depression Scale of the 300 cases were analyzed and differences between the three centres found. The results are discussed in this paper.

736

Seasonal Affective Disorders: a Retrospective Study

G.L. Faedda,[a,b] G.F. Floris,[b] L. Tondo,[b] A. Kukopulos[c]
Departments of Psychiatry, Harvard Medical School, McLean Hospital,[a] *Belmont, MA, USA; Centro Lucio Bini: Cagliari* [b] *& Rome,*[c] *Italy.*

Patients (N=146) with a DSM-III-R diagnosis of Seasonal Affective Disorder (SAD) were studied retrospectively to evaluate the epidemiology, premorbid characteristics, seasonal pattern, and response to treatment of their disorder. Sex, current age, age of onset, family history, premorbid temperament, and demographic variables were evaluated, as were the month of onset, duration and severity of the episodes. Patients were categorized as manic and depressed (BP-I), depressed with hypomania (BP-II), or depressed without hypomania (UP), according to Dunner et al. Patients also were divided into three subgroups according to the sequence of episodes (mania-depression-interval [M-D-I]; depression-mania-interval [D-M-I]; or continuously cycling [CC]), according to Kukopulos et al. There was an excess of females (71%). The average age of onset was 29y (males = females), current age averaged 40y, and 68% had a family history of affective illness. Diagnostic distribution was: UP, 51%; BP-I, 29%; and BP-II, 20%. Premorbid temperament was: Cyclothymic (64%), Hyperthymic (30%), Dysthymic (3%), or Normothymic (3%). The course distribution was: CC, 75%; M-D-I, 14%; and D-M-I, 11%. Over 90% of patients followed one of two seasonal patterns: *type A*, spring-summer mania & fall-winter depression (BP-I, 63%; BP-II, 57%; UP, 44%) and *type B*, fall-winter mania & spring-summer depression (BP-I, 37%; BP-II, 43%; UP, 56%). BP-I patients who followed the D-M-I course had longer episodes of mania and depression than those with the M-D-I course, as well as an inferior treatment response, confirming previous observations in nonseasonal bipolar patients. None of the BP-II cases followed the M-D-I course. Treatment response of SAD patients may be worse than in randomly selected patients with recurrent major affective disorders, and requires further refinements to optimize treatment for the seasonal course of illness.

Session 114 New Research:
Attitudinal and crosscultural issues

737

ILLNESS BEHAVIOUR IN MENTAL ILL-HEALTH

M. Fakhr El-Islam, FRCP, FRCPsych. and Sanaa Abu-Dagga, B.A.
Faculty of Medicine, Kuwait University.

Two hundred and eight individuals were interviewed in order to study the behaviours and explanations they adopt in relation to the commonest somatic and emotional symptoms of mental ill-health. Illness behaviours included ignoring, brooding, self-help and consultation of others. Subjects' explanations of symptoms were divided into physical, psychosocial and/or supernatural. Somatic symptoms were more likely to have physical explanations and to lead to doctor consultation whereas emotional symptoms were more likely to have psychosocial explanations and to be managed by traditional easing methods. Older individuals tended to resort more frequently to meditation, native healers and doctors and to adopt physical explanations. Males consulted doctors more than females.
Self-help was the most commonly adopted illness behaviour. The symptom of breathlessness was the most likely to have a psychosocial explanation and this confirms its traditional metaphoric use to express distress. No correspondence was detected between symptom explanations and illness behaviour. The results are explained in terms of the social and cultural background of individuals studied which influences their cognitive schemas and illness behaviour.

738

CROSSCULTURAL STUDY ON ATTITUDE TOWARD SUICIDE

Arato, M.,* Abe, K., Hoffmann, O., Knezevic, A., Mitterauer, B., Möller, H-J., Träskman-Bendz, L. and Stefanis, C.
National Institute for Nervous and Mental Diseases, Budapest, Hungary.

The large cross national differences in suicide rates is a puzzling phenomenon for suicide research. We investigated the possible relationship between traditional-cultural influences, assessed by an attitude scale, and the national suicide rates. An international collaborative study on suicide attitude was carried out in seven countries (Austria, Greece, Hungary, Japan, Sweden, W. Germany, Yugoslavia) with different suicide rates, varying from 3 to 45 annual death/100,000 people. One hundred first year medical students were asked to fill out the modified version of the AECOM ST suicide attitude scale of Robert Plutchik. Analyzing the relationships between the individual items, total acceptance or rejection scores and suicide mortality showed a positive association between higher acceptance of justification of suicide and higher national suicide rates. This finding suggests the usefulness of this suicide attitude scale in assessing different populations. It could help us to better understand the role of cultural-traditional factors in suicidal behavior.

739

DEUIL DE MIGRANTS ET DOUBLE CULTUREL
M. Papageorgiou, France

Le double en tant qu'opérateur psychique a pour fonction de délimiter des catégories opposées et d'en inscrire la distinction dans l'appareil psychique (dedans-dehors, morts-vivants, etc...).
Dans le travail du deuil et dans les rites funéraires, culturellement structurés, l'opérateur double permet de gérer la confusion provoquée par la perte de l'objet, la rupture des frontières entre moi et non moi, le même et l'autre.
La rituel constitue un écran sur lequel se projette la problématique des endeuillés, un contenant qui assure le portage - étayage des processus mobilisés.
Les contenus de la réalité externe (représentations, actes, images) sont décodés par le psychisme à partir du cadre culturel interne, contenant transmis d'une génération à l'autre dans une culture donnée.
L'ethnopsychiatrie (consultation d'ethnopsychiatrie, dirigée par T. Nathan, Hôp. Avicenne, Bobigny, Service de Psychopathologie Prof. P. Mazet) méthodologie du double (psychanalytique et anthropologique) permet la compréhension du deuil spécifique des migrants, originaires de cultures non-occidentales, en voie d'acculturation.

Toute rupture, épreuve de deuil est le deuil des contenants psychiques, du cadre culturel interne, tout en essayant d'en préserver les contenus. Les manifestations pathologiques, (syndromes dépressifs, productions délirantes, troubles psychosomatiques, etc ...) sont organisées selon la logique des théories étiologiques traditionnelles telles que la possession et la sorcellerie, opérateurs afin de reconstruire un contenant, un double culturel, vrai cadre thérapeutique pour lutter contre la confusion.
Deux fonctions sont en jeu : la discrimination d'une topographie métaphorique et la réorganisation du déroulement chronologique. Le cadre négocié ainsi dans notre pratique ethnopsychiatrique se situe à l'interaction de deux logiques thérapeutiques : la métapsychologie freudienne et la métapsychologie sorcière.

740

SOCIO-CULTURAL ADAPTATION OF SAUDI STUDENTS AND SPOUSES IN CANADA
VF DiNicola, A Al-Sabaie; Univ. of Ottawa; Canada

We studied the adaptation of Saudi university students and spouses in Canada. We identified key premises about Saudi Moslem culture, culture change and the expression of psychiatric disorders among Saudis. **Hypotheses**: Cultural hypothesis: greater identification with Saudi Moslem culture, through personal expression (eg, religiosity) and socio-cultural context (eg, previous contact with outsiders) correlates with degree of culture-change stress in Canada. Social hypothesis: certain factors lend stability during cultural change. Specific predictions: higher education, marital stability and religious adherence yield better adaptation. **Instruments**: (1) 40-item Saudi-Canada Adaptation Quest. (2) SCL-90-R, a 90-item self-rating scale. **Method**: Each Saudi student was sent two packages (with instruments in English and Arabic) for student and spouse to complete and return independently. We conducted a two-stage survey of 360 Saudi students and spouses in Canada. In the Ottawa pilot study, 51 of 68 packages or 75% were completed. The full survey addressed the remaining 300 Saudis. **Findings**: mixed results in pilot study-some predictions confirmed (eg, respondents who previously visited the West reported better adaptation), others unsupported (eg, women with previous knowledge of English had significantly higher paranoia scores). Sex differences were striking, with significantly higher paranoia scores for women. Preliminary findings of the full study are presented.

741

A CULTURE BOUND DISORDER FROM IRAQ, MUTAWAH
A.K. Al-Sheikhli, Kufa School of Medicine, Iraq

A brief psychotic disorder which occurs specifically in Mid-Euphrates part of Iraq is described, characterised by auditory & visual hallucinations of the ancestors of the prophet of Muslims, Mohammed of whom many are burried within this part of Iraq in special cemetries called the holly shrins, also delusions that they speak through their tongue, they responds well to anti-psychotic drugs & course of Ect & go back to normal within 2-3 weeks, Conditom could be considered as a Culture bound psychiatric disorder occurs specifically in Iraq, review of literature with critical discussion about negligence of DSM & ICD systems.

742

PERSONOLOGICAL AND SOCIAL CORRELATES OF COPING TO CANCER
Grassi L., Stella S., Targa G., Ramelli E.
Cattedra di Clinica Psichiatrica, Università di Ferrara, Italia

It is currently well substantiated that personality characteristics (e.g. locus of control) and social support play a key role in moulding coping mechanisms to cancer. To evaluate such aspects, 76 patients with a diagnosis of primary cancer within 3 months were submitted to the SCL-90-R, the IBQ, the 7-items Locus of Control Scale and the Surtees' Social Support Interview. External locus of control was related with all the dimensions of psychological stress (SCL-90-R) and ineffective coping mechanism (abnormal illness behaviour). Characteristics of close and extended social support had a buffering role on the same parameters, with the exception of hostility and phobic anxiety (SCL-90-R), and hypochondriasis and disease conviction (IBQ). The results confirm the importance of correctly identifying psychological and social variables associated with ineffective coping-to-cancer mechanisms to plan more rational interventions with the treatment of the patients.

Study supported by grant 881203 by IOR-Forli-Italy

743

EFFECT OF FASTING PERIODS(RAMADAN)ON PSY-
CHOMOTOR PERFORMANCE AND MOOD IN MUSLAMS
F. HAKKOU, C. JAOUEN, A. TAZI, L. IRAKI
FACULTY OF MEDECINE, PHARMACOLOGY
CASABLANCA MOROCOO

Ramadan is a compulsory fasting mounth for muslams where the whole life style changes this study was conducted assess the importance of these changes on some psychomotor performance and subjective feelings. 46 Healty volunteers were tested during both the non-ramadan and the ramadan periods, according to a cross-over, randomized method. Critical flicker fusion, choice reaction time and digit symbol substitution were among the objective measures. The visual analogic scale was used by the subjects to evaluate their mood and state changes. The results obstained showed that : - The number of cases filled in the DSST were significantly lowered during the first two weeks (p<0,01). - The thresholds in the CRT test were significantly derreased during the remaining three weeks p<0,01). - The subjects felt significantly more drowsy during the second and the fourth week of ramadan p<0,01). All these data point to an imparing effect of ramadan on psychomotor performances and some subjective feelingss.

744

Salud mental, migración y desarrollo

Alberto PERALES.
Instituto Nacional de Salud Mental
"Honorio Delgado-Hideyo Noguchi"(PERU)

El autor fundamenta la importancia de la salud mental -a la que diferencia conceptualmente de la psiquiatría- para el desarrollo del ser humano y de los pueblos. Bajo esta perspectiva, señala los problemas psiquiátricos y de salud mental más urgentes en el Perú vinculados al proceso migratorio interno que vuelca la población rural hacia las grandes ciudades.

Session 115 New Research:
Alzheimer's disease and other psychogeriatric issues

745

A CASE-CONTROL STUDY OF ALZHEIMER'S DISEASE IN
AUSTRALIA: PRELIMINARY RESULTS
A S Henderson, G A Broe, H Creasey, E McCusker,
A E Korten, A F Jorm, W Longley & J C Anthony.

NH&MRC Social Psychiatry Research Unit, The Australian National University, Canberra & Department of Geriatric Medicine, University of Sydney, Sydney, Australia.

A large case-control study of clinically diagnosed Alzheimer's disease (AD) in elderly persons is reported. Newly diagnosed cases were recruited from 2 dementia clinics in Sydney. Age and sex matched controls were recruited from the same or neighbouring general practices from which the cases had been referred. Risk factor interviews with informants were carried out by trained lay interviewers naive to our hypotheses and to the clinical status of the elderly person. Variables achieving significant odds ratios (OR) were: a history of dementia in a first degree relative (OR=3.6) and a family history of Down's syndrome (OR=9.0). None of the many environmental exposures examined conferred an increased risk of AD. Analysis of this large data set continues.

746

AN ELECTROPHYSIOLOGICAL MODEL FOR ALZHEIMER'S
DISEASE
GEORGE W FENTON
EILEEN SLOAN
KEVIN P STANDAGE
DEPARTMENT OF PSYCHIATRY
UNIVERSITY OF DUNDEE, SCOTLAND

Cognitive testing, computerised EEG and visual (flash and pattern reversal) evoked response recordings were carried out in 10 healthy volunteers before and after subcutaneous injections of hyoscine and methscopolamine each administered during a single recording session. The two sessions were arranged in random order one week apart. The hyoscine induced central cholinergic blockade caused deficits of immediate and delayed recall. A large increase in EEG theta frequencies occurred. The latency of the main positive (P_2) component of the visual evoked potential was significantly delayed while there was no effect on the pattern reversal response. Methscopolamine, a peripheral cholinergic blocker with no central action produced no change in memory performance, EEG or visual evoked potentials. The hyoscine induced electrophysiological changes are similiar to those reported in patients with Alzheimer's Disease and provide the basis for a neurophysiological paradigm to monitor the progress of the disease and assess the effectiveness of new therapeutic agents.

747

Treatment Development Strategies for Alzheimer's Disease
Fünfgeld, E., Med. Faculty of Marburg and Schloßberg-Klinik, 5928 Bad Laasphe, FRG.

Compared to the real (presenile) Alzheimer's disease, clinical signs and symptoms of the senile dementia of Alzheimer's type (SDAT) showed quite a few more varieties and the progression of the disease was usually slower. That is also the case if we compared the neurophysiological findings in the real Alzheimer and the SDAT cases: The latter showed many more differences and varieties in frequencies and the distribution of these frequencies (localization). This led to the opinion that the presenile group is much more homogeneous than the SDAT group. If highly sophisticated and very expensive methods were used (PET, SPECT, NMR) some levels of disturbances were detectable in SDAT patients: Glucose uptake, Oxygen consumption as one of the major parameters, dopamin and others can be marked by tracer substances. But membrane rigidity - one of the theories of aging - special molecular aspects, the influence of free radicals and other primary or secondary or even reactive and reparative changes are not yet detectable. But there is another - indirect - way to observe acute + long-term neurophysiological reactions after the administration of so-called nootropic drugs. From some drugs of this group the most prominent level of action is known: The calcium blocking agent Nicergolin acts in a very specific direction, Phosphatidylserin and the extract of the leafs of the Ginkgo biloba tree acts in a more complex manner. After 3 years of clinical experience Phosphatidylserin and Ginkgo biloba extract showed good results even in double-blind studies. By using the CEEG method, the Dynamic Brain Mapping System (TM) developed by the HZI Research Institute, Tarrytown, N.Y., we objectify the favourable influence on the brain wave activity (faster waves) in short-term and long-term investigations (up to 18 months). In some cases we register a dose-depending influence. Advanced SDAT stages showing a very poor response to one drug we observed additional effects if we combined with other nootropics. The present situation of the treatment of SDAT is the stage of trial and error, if the trial shows a positive reaction, we can help the patient.

748

Computer assisted EEG patterns, a possibility to find drugs for the treatment of incipient disturbances in brain metabolism - prevention of aging?
E. W. Fünfgeld, Med. Faculty of Marburg and Schloßberg-Klinik Wittgenstein, D - 5928 Bad Laasphe FRG.

Dynamic Brain Mapping (TM) and a 20-Frequency band analysis were used since more than two years. Simultaneously a conventional EEG was derived in order to compare these two techniques. We obtained initial recordings from more than 1200 parkinsonian patients, aged between 41 and 90 years. Only 1/3 of the conventional EEG was found absolutely normal or estimated as borderline. From these conventionaly normal records some computerized programs revealed a so-called Theta- or Alpha-Anteriorisation or a focal slowing or asymmetries between the hemispheres. Many of these patients were fully in duty and without any signs and symptoms of psychic alterations as we observed more or less severely disturbed in most of the other cases. The progress given by the use of Dynamic Brain Mapping consisted in:
1. The early and preclinical detection of incipient changes in brain metabolism represented by a slight slowing in some clinical programs of the color mapping and/or of the 20-Frequencyband analysis.
2. The distinction of responders or non-responders following a single test dose of a nootropic drug preferably intraveniously, by infusion, intramuscularly, sometimes after one daily dose orally.
3. Fixed programs and their variety allow the comparison between a different follow-up registration very easily by the use of the colored outprints taken from the monitor.
4. The procedure does not hurt the patient, is easy to handle and inexpensive in comparison to the other imaging techniques. It's a real progress in routine in clinic and practice.

749

COMPETENCY ASSESSMENT OF ELDERLY IN CHICAGO
Benedict L. Gierl, M.D., Illinois State Psychiatric Institute, Chicago, Illinois, U.S.A.

This paper reviews the significant findings from analysis of the data collected from 82 people age 60 and over who were referred for competency assessment. Some form of guardianship was recommended for 67 people who were seen as partially or totally incompetent for personal and/or financial decisions. All of the married elderly were judged to be incompetent. A greater number of errors on the Mental Status Questionnaire (MSQ) was associated with a greater likelihood of being judged incompetent. Elderly with organic mental disorders made more errors on the MSQ and the Global Deterioration Scale (GDS) and were also more likely to be older than functionally disturbed patients. Incompetent elderly had more behavior problems than did the competent. Four of 54 unwilling-to-move were seen as incompetent (chi-square significance .0004).

Older people had a higher MSQ score (r=.40) and GDS score (r=.45). The GDS score correlated strongly with the MSQ score (r=.78). A discriminate function analysis was completed to determine the extent to which competency could be predicted by other variables. Six variables were important: GDS score, number of behavioral problems, age, occupation, race and availability of retirement funds. Competent elderly performed better on the GDS, had fewer behavioral problems, tended to be younger, to have higher status occupations, tended to be white, and to have retirement funds available.

750

LIFE REVIEW GROUPS IN OLDER ADULTHOOD: A COMPARATIVE STUDY
B. Gierl, R. Frankel, W. Borden, A. Ras
Illinois State Psychiatric Institute, Chicago, Illinois, U.S.A. 60612

This study examined the effects of a structured life review group process on psychological well-being and self-esteem in two groups of community-dwelling elderly: 1) persons with chronic mental illness in an out-patient psychiatric clinic, and 2) persons with no history of mental illness in a community center. Participants completed standardized instruments assessing levels of functioning before, during, and after the 7-week group process. They also completed a semi-structured interview at the end of the group. All sessions were audio-taped and videotaped. Results of data analysis show a marked increase in psychological well-being and self-esteem among persons in each group. While the outcomes were similar, the process of each group was different in the ways that members used reminiscence. Persons in the psychiatric group used reminiscence in a therapeutic manner characterized by ventilation, validation and peer support, while members of the community group tended to use the life review process for entertainment, story-telling, and creation of a life story. Findings indicate that the adaptive value of life review processes must be considered in the context of individual differences and situational factors. Developmental, research, and clinical implications are reviewed.

751

"DEMENTIA, DEPRESSION AND PHYSICAL DISABILITY IN A LONDON BOROUGH, A SURVEY OF ELDERLY PEOPLE BOTH IN AND OUT OF RESIDENTIAL CARE AND IMPLICATIONS FOR FUTURE DEVELOPMENTS"
Dr. N. Savla, Mr.R. Harrison, Dr. Kefetz
Claybury Hospital, Social Services Department, Consultant Physician, Whipps Cross Hosp.
We studied 1303 of the 1471 elderly people resident in Part III homes, NHS long stay wards (medical and psychiatric), private and voluntary homes and Local Authority sheltered housing or in receipt of augmented domiciliary services in the London Borough of Waltham Forest. Depression and dementia were studied using the Brief Assessment Schedule and physical functioning by using a modified Barthel index. Residents with high levels of dependency were spread throughout the different forms of residential accommodation. There was little disability outside residential care. There was a high incidence of depression in the study of population. The prevalence of depression in our study was as high as Prof. Mann's study in Part III residential homes. Our study showed equally high prevalence of depression in sheltered housing accommodation and in home care groups who were less physically disabled than those clients in residential care and hospitals. This has not been outlined in any of the studies and ours is the largest sample studied so far and we wish to discuss the future research on this issue as well as the implication on service. (Paper presented at Annual Meeting of Royal College of Psychiatrists on 6.7.89).

752

PSYCHIATRIC SYMPTOMS IN THE ELDERLY ASIAN POPULATION (CMS-AGECAT)

VIMAL K. SHARMA   J. FRANK   J.R.M. COPELAND   K. BHATNAGAR
WALTON HOSPITAL, RICE LANE, LIVERPOOL, U.K.

ASIAN VERSION OF THE GERIATRIC MENTAL STATE SCHEDULE WAS SUCCESSFULLY ADMINISTERED IN A RANDOMLY SELECTED COMMUNITY SAMPLE OF ASIAN POPULATION OVER THE AGE OF 65 IN BRADFORD. THE AGREEMENT BETWEEN THE PSYCHIATRIST'S DIAGNOSIS AND THE AGECAT DIAGNOSIS WAS SATISFACTORY. THE PREVALENCE OF PSYCHIATRIC SYMPTOMS IN THE ASIAN POPULATION WILL BE COMPARED WITH THE ENGLISH POPULATION AND POSSIBLE ROLE OF SOCIO-CULTURAL FACTORS WILL BE DISCUSSED.

753

"DEMENTIA SINE DEMENTIA": PROBLEMS OF SLOWLY PROGRESSIVE APHASIA WITH LATER ONSET OF DEMENTIA.
Hadano,K.,Yamagishi,H.(Dpt of Psychiatry,Kyoto National Hospital),Kato,T.,Tsuji,M.,Hamanaka,T.(Dpt of Neuropsychiatry,Nagoya City University,Japan)

This paper details 4 right-handed patients exhibiting slowly progressive dysphasia with much later onset of generalized dementia caused by primary degenerative cerebral pathology of the praesenium. 3 presented a clinical picture of transcortical sensory aphasia, 1 of them with findings of moderate atrophy dominant in the anterior-inferior portion of the left temporal lobe(X-ray CT) and 2 with definite decrease of cerebral blood flow relatively localized to the same area(SPECT) in the absence of marked atrophic change. In the fourth case exhibiting a non-fluent quasi-global aphasia, severe atrophy was demonstrated in the fronto-temporal cortex with marked dilatation of the sylvian fissure dominant on the left side. In view of these cases described here as well as those reported in the literature(since Pick 1892,Sérieux 1893/97, Franceschi 1908 etc; recently Warrington 1975,Cole 1979,Kirshner 1981/84,Morris 1984,Assal 1985,Hamanaka 1986/87,Poeck 1988,Mehler 1987/89 etc), it is reasonable not to assume in these cases one homogeneous(Mesulam 1982), but rather diverse cerebral pathology that may include Pick's(Wechsler 1982, Holland 1985) and Alzheimer's(Pogacar 1984) disease.

754

EFFECTS, EFFICACY AND THERAPEUTIC RELEVANCE OF NOOTROPICS

W. M. Herrmann, M.D., Professor of Psychophysiology, Dept. of Clinical Psychiatry (Head: H. Helmchen, M.D.), Free University of Berlin, F.R.G.

Fifteen years ago the efficacy of none of the nootropics had been proven to such an extent that there was general acceptance by the scientific community.
In the past five years with a series of different substances, like dopaminergics, cholinergics, serotonergic and norepiphrenine reuptake inhibitors, ATP-enhancers, calcium channel blockers, effects have been proven in prospective, randomized placebo-controlled phase III trials with confirmatory statistical approaches in patients with mild to moderate (GDS 3 and 4) dementia of the Alzheimer type (SDAT) as well as in multi-infarct dementia (MID). New data of several studies will be demonstrated. Therefore, there are no doubts anymore that nootropics can be utilized as supportive instruments within a therapeutic concept for SDAT and MID related mental decline. However, the question of therapeutic relevance of such findings is still not clear. Effects are seen usually not before six weeks of treatment. Only 30-40% of patients can be regarded as responders under active compounds, while 15-20% do respond under placebo. Up to now it could not be clarified why patients become responders or nonresponders, nor could it be demonstrated that compounds work in SDAT but not in MID or vice versa.
In order to make such drug treatment acceptable, better instruments, especially to measure the patient's competence in daily life and to measure the amount of care needed, have to be developed.

Session 116 Free Communications:
Alcohol and drug abuse: Clinical issues

755
DRUG AND ALCOHOL USE IN MEDICAL STUDENTS

Malkah T. Notman, M.D., Harvard Medical School;
Carol C. Nadelson, M.D. & Frederick S. Kanter, M.D.
Tufts University School of Medicine,
Boston, Massachusetts, USA.

Physician impairment compromises the functioning of highly trained professionals, endangers patients, and wastes valuable training resources. The investigators looked at potential predictors of impairment in physicians by surveying medical students (class of 1984) in two Boston medical schools beginning in 1980. Because substance abuse in the most frequent cause of physician impairment, this longitudinal study provides prospective data on drug and alcohol use and abuse in medical students during their four years in medical school. Correlates with other variables including depression, anxiety, somatization, attitudes toward patients, and self-attitudes are reported.

756
THE USE OF PSYCHOACTIVE SUBSTANCES BY MEDICAL STUDENTS
E.Dimitriou, J.Giouzepas, C.Moutzoukis
2nd Psychiatric University Department,
Thessaloniki, Greece

Three hundred and forty six medical students of whom 233 were male (M) and 133 were female (F) completed a specially designed questionnaire. This questionnaire aimed at assessing the use of psychoactive substances, such as coffee, tobacco, alcohol, pain-killers and stronger drugs. The students then completed the BDI, EPQ and the STAI. The aims of the study were: 1) the extent of the use of different substances by medical students, 2) differences between the two sexes, and 3) whether a particular personality is more prone to the use of psychoactive substances. The results showed that 15% of M and 7% of F abuse pain-killers and that 27% of M and 13% of F have at times used stronger drugs. It was further found that M abuse tobacco (42% of M smoked compared to 39% of F), pain-killers, and stronger drugs whereas there were no significant differences in the use of coffee and alcohol between the two sexes. There were no personality differences between those who abuse coffee and tobacco and those who do not. However, individuals who use pain-killers, alcohol and stronger drugs yielded higher scores in the BDI and in scale P of the EPQ and lower scores in scale L of the same questionnaire.

757
LIFE EVENTS AND HEROIN ABUSE

N. Félix da Costa, V. Oliveira, P. Varandas, A. Croca
Drug Abuse Clinic,
Psychiatry Ward of the Hospital de Santa Maria

The discussion concerning the predisposing and causative factors in drug abuse is never ending and inconclusive. One of the main discussion points has always been whether previous critical life events (LE) provokes the addiction or, on the contrary, addicts'LE are consequences of the efforts to obtain heroin.
The study group used a life event scale to study thirty heroin addicts who were voluntary out patients of our Drug Abuse Clinic and a normal sample. The two samples age range between eighteen and thirty five years and they have similar social backgrounds. Heroin addicts have a history of regular drug abuse for more than one year. Both samples answer to LE scale with a perturbation value. Following this they indicated which LE they had experienced and when in their lives. As we already knew the patients onset in drug abuse we could compare their answers before and after addiction with normal sample.
The first conclusion of a simple quantitative analysis was that all heroin addicts had more LE than the other group. We further observe two distinct groups whithin addicts: one has a history of continuous LE and their lives are full of negative LE previously to addiction as parents separation, divorce or death, affective and material deprivation etc whilst the others LE experiences previous to addiction are similar to normals and increase subsequent to drug abuse. A quantitative analysis shows that both samples evaluates higher LE they had experienced. Heroin addicts gave greater values to negative LE probably to their difficulty to tolerate frustation.
Our results identified subgroups amongst the heroin addicts with different pasts and, we think, different prognosis and justifying different psychotherapeutic approaches.

758
ADDICTIONS: "THE BIOPSYCHOSOCIAL ARCHETYPE"
Cesar Fabiani, M.D.   Huntington Hospital
        Willow Grove, Pennsylvania, U.S.A.

Addictions are defined as the archetype of the biopsychosocial paradigm. Self induced (psychological) changes in neurotransmission (biological) which cause or are precipitated by social problems and behaviors (social). The Public Health Model (epidemiologic chain: Agent-Host-Environment) applied to addictions illustrates this approach. Historial evidence corroborates the medical nature of alcoholism and drug dependence. A neuroanatomical hypothesis causes changes in the pleasure centers of the brain, responsible for cocaine craving. Another hypothesis postulates that a deficiency in endorphines plus genetic vulnerability and stress cause ethanol craving. Important sociocultural factors partially explain the current epidemic of "quintessential cocaine" (cocaine smoking disorders: crack in the USA and coca-paste in South America). Above factors are compounded by self-medication of underlying psychopathology the dual diagnosis concept. A misnomer for multiple psychiatric diagnoses. Treatment and prevention of addictions must be biopsychosocial in order to be successful.

759
BENZODIAZEPINE DEPENDENCE: CLINICAL REPORT OF TWELVE CASES

José Nobre Madeira, Hospital de Angra do Heroismo, Angra do Heroismo, Região Autónoma dos Açores, Portugal

In the community we work - Terceira, Azores - we faced an unexpected high prevalence of Benzodiazepine Dependence. In order to study this subject, we decided to examine the cases we had in the last two years. The method we used excluded the benzodiazepine dependence cases that had multiple dependences or major psychiatric disorder. We registered the motive of the initial prescription, the duration of the use, the symptons presented, the medium daily dose and the sort of benzodiazepine. The sample is made up of twelve, mostly middle-aged, women. The reason why they started using benzodiazepines was insomnia and anxiety. The mean duration of the use was four years, and seven of the cases used two or more benzodiazepines. Among the symptoms, the most disturbing ones were anxiety and panic attacks.

760
EARLY OBJECTIVE, LABORATORY AND CLINICAL DIAGNOSIS OF ALCOHOLISM

A. Hećimović, V. Starčević, D. Breitenfeld, B. Lang

Institute for Health Promotion
Health Center "New Zagreb" Zagreb, Yugoslavia
University Department for Neurology, Psychiatry, Alcoholism and other dependences of "Dr. M. Stojanović" University Hospital Zagreb, Yugoslavia

There is a great necessity for the earliest objective diagnostic procedures of alcoholism, especially in factories. The region covered by The New Zagreb Health Center has about 9000 workmen under 5o years old. Research included 15o of them - 5o during the first survey (the certificate for employment), the same number during regularly periodical examination and incidental cases. Moreover, all patients were devided in 3 age groups. Processing of the youngest group (workmen under 3o years old) was recommended. The method was - conducting interview, physical, neurological and mental examinations, also biochemical laboratory tests. Alltogether 76 variables were registered in computer, then crossed among themselves and settle account statistically. Attention was headed at the results of biochemical tests at the most exact findings to the diagnosis.

761
IMPLICATION DES FAMILLES DANS LA PRISE EN CHARGE AMBULATOIRE DES TOXICOMANES
V. GUIEN, R.L. CLAVEL-MORROT, R.A. JULIEN
C.H.S. Valvert, Bd des Libérateurs - 13011 MARSEILLE (FRANCE)

Les changements intervenus dans l'épidémiologie et la signification des toxicomanies depuis une dizaine d'années incitent les thérapeutes à reconsidérer la prise en charge du toxicomane en milieu institutionnel. En matière de thérapeutique, le praticien, en règle générale, n'avait à sa disposition jusqu'ici principalement qu'une possibilité : l'hospitalisation en milieu psychiatrique assortie d'une chimiothérapie et d'une rupture de contacts familiaux et amicaux. En quelque sorte il proposait le plus souvent l'enfermement que le toxicomane acceptait plus ou moins contraint, ce qui expliquait un nombre élevé de rechutes une fois le toxicomane replongé dans son milieu ambiant. C'est dire des possibilités mais également les limites de l'enfermement qui ne sont pas une fin en soi, car la réinsertion du toxicomane doit être d'emblée une priorité. Un suivi de cinq ans nous amène à constater aujourd'hui que sur une centaine de cas, plus de la moitié, est à l'heure actuelle réinsérée. Le projet thérapeutique a consisté à traiter le sujet toxicomane par une prise en charge ambulatoire assortie d'une implication totale de la famille, afin qu'elle puisse prendre conscience du rôle qu'elle joue, et de la responsabilité qu'elle doit assumer pour permettre une circulation des affects et un déblocage des communications affectives qui jusque là, faisaient défaut.

762
VERSUCH DER RISIKOGRUPPENABGRENZUNG BEI BENZODIAZEPINMISSBRAUCH

R. Höll, R.J. Witkowski, A. Barocka, H. Erzigkeit,
G. Beck, T.A. Moesler, E. Lungershausen
Psychiatrische Universitätsklinik, Schwabachanlage 6
D-8520 Erlangen (Direktor: Prof. Dr. E. Lungershausen)

Wir untersuchten im Rahmen einer größeren Studie 137 Männer eines nicht-psychiatrischen Kollektives hinsichtlich ihres Benzodiazepineinnahmeverhaltens und führten ein Benzodiazepinscreening im Urin durch. Drei der 137 Probanden gaben eine gelegentliche Einnahme dieser Substanzen an (2,19 %). Ein Untersuchter nahm regelmäßig Benzodiazepine (0,73 %) ohne die Kriterien einer physischen und psychischen Abhängigkeit zu erfüllen. Im Urinscreening erwies sich keine Probe als sicher positiv, fraglich positiv waren drei Ansätze (2,19 %). Aus unseren Ergebnissen ziehen wir folgende Schlußfolgerungen: Es liegt eine niedrige Inzidenz bei Männern vor, die Neigung zum Mißbrauch ist sehr gering. Die Häufigkeit der Benzodiazepineinnahme und des Nachweises lag noch unter dem erwarteten Verschreibungswert. Im Rahmen der Studie konnten wir nur Männer untersuchen. Deshalb können wir zu Inzidenz und Mißbrauchsgewohnheiten bei Frauen keine Stellung nehmen. Dies schränkt die Aussagekraft unserer Studie ein, da u.a. LADEWIG 1980 die Hausfrauen mittleren Alters mit Schlaflosigkeit und Angst als den "Durchschnittsmißbraucher" charakterisierte. Eine pauschale Betrachtungsweise des Benzodiazepinmißbrauchs bzw. der Benzodiazepinabhängigkeit erscheint nicht gerechtfertigt, eine differenzierte Zielgruppenbetrachtung ist anzustreben. Eine Studie zum Einnahmeverhalten und Screeninguntersuchungen bei Frauen wird sich anschließen.

763

Analgetika-Nephropathien durch analgetisch-psychotrope Kombinationspräparate
Woerz, R., Schmerzzentrum Bad Schönborn
Molzahn, M., Pommer W., Humboldt-Krankenhaus Berlin

Eine Untersuchung von 80 konsekutiven Analgetika-abhängigen Schmerzpatienten ergab, daß alle Patienten von analgetisch-psychotropen Kombinationspräparaten abhängig waren und keiner von einer analgetischen Monosubstanz (Wörz 1979). In nachfolgenden Beobachtungen an über 300 Fällen war dieses Phänomen durchgehend zu bestätigen.
Molzahn, Pommer und Mitarbeiter untersuchten alle Dialyse- und Nierentransplantationspatienten in Berlin-West bezüglich ihres Analgetikakonsums und verglichen sie mit 517 epidemiologisch entsprechenden Probanden.
Der Mittelwert des Mengenverbrauchs analgetischer Substanzen betrug 7,4 kg in der Fallgruppe und 2,0 kg in der Kontrollgruppe. Bei den schmerzmittelabhängigen Nierengeschädigten lag der mittlere Schmerzmittelverbrauch bei 10,0 kg, bei der Kontrollgruppe bei 3,4 kg. Die Schmerzmittel wurden überwiegend als Mischpräparate verwendet. Die Einzelanalyse der Risiken unterschiedlicher analgetischer Präparate ergab, daß nur Kombinationspräparate mit einem erhöhten Risiko verbunden sind (RR 1.76, 95 % C.I. 1.35-2.30). Das erhöhte Risiko für Kombinationspräparate wies eine klare Risikowirkungsbeziehung auf. Die Einnahme von Coffein in Mischpräparaten zeigte eine hohe dosisbezogene Risikosteigerung. Die konsumierten Wirkstoffmengen der coffeinhaltigen Mischpräparate betrugen durchschnittlich das 4,5-fache der chronisch eingenommenen Mengen von coffeinfreien Präparaten.
Aus den Ergebnissen unserer algologisch-psychiatrischen und nephrologischen Studien werden Folgerungen für die Eindämmung von Analgetika-Nephropathien bis zum Jahr 2000 gezogen.

764

DRUG ADDICTION, SOCIAL, BIOCHEMICAL AND ENDOGENOUS ASPECTS. THE IMPORTANCE IN THE DIAGNOSIS AND THERAPY
Dr. Rubens C.Filho, Dr. Persio R.G. Deus
Centro de Estudos e Pesquisas Karl Kleist, Sao Paulo, Brazil

In this work carried out at the Centro de Estudos e Paquisas Karl Kleist we expose our view on treatments of drug addicts. Social, biochemical and endogenous aspects are taken into consideration not only in regard to the patient's potential but mainly to the therapeutic action which must contain elements of these three areas since physical education, leisure and pharmacological treatment affect emotional stabilization.

Session 117 Free Communications:
Affective disorders: Psychopathology and psychometrics

765

DSM-III SUBTYPING OF UNIPOLAR DEPRESSION: AN ETHOLOGICAL ASSESSMENT

Troisi A., Pasini A., Bersani G., Grispini A., Ciani N.
Clinica Psichiatrica, II Università di Roma, Roma, Italy.

The present study was designed to determine whether DSM-III subtypes of unipolar depression could be distinguished on the basis of patients' non-verbal behaviour during psychiatric interview. The subjects were 44 depressed outpatients (11 men and 33 women) with a diagnosis of Major Depression With Melancholia (MDM, N=16), Major Depression Without Melancholia (MDNM, N=13) or Dysthymic Disorder (DD, N=15). The clinical characteristics of the patient population were as follows: age (mean±SD), 48.98±11.95 years; education, 8.18±3.4 years; Hamilton Depression Rating Scale (HDRS) score, 21.32±6.31. Patients' non-verbal behaviour was video-recorded from behind a one-way mirror and scored according to an ethological scoring system including 37 different behaviours. The three DSM-III subtypes differed on severity, as measured by the HDRS (MDM>MDNM>DD), but not on ethological profile. The correlations between HDRS score and behavioural categories were extremely weak. These results could be interpreted as an argument against the validity of our validator rather than that of DSM-III subtyping. However, in a sub-sample of 22 patients, we demonstrated that the ethological profile has predictive validity in that it allowed us to predict amitriptyline response (Troisi et al. J Affective Disord, in press). We suggest that the application of the ethological method to the study of depressive disorders is capable of producing discriminations beyond those achieved by a more traditional clinical approach. Supported in part by FIDIA Farmaceutici.

766

NEUROPSYCHOLOGICAL TASK AND DEPRESSION
Nardini M., Bonelli G., Magnani N., Belardinelli N., Mattafirri R.
Chair of Psychiatry, Siena, Italy

Depressed patients often present a cognitive impairment, (deficit of attention, memory and psychomotor slowing). Cognitive impairment associated to Depression is especially frequent in the elderly, where Affective Disorders should be related to social, physical, material losses, but also, perhaps, to biological+biochemical implications. This condition justifies an increase of disability and dependence in geriatric Depression. The intellectual impairment associated to Affective Disorders implies a particular performance to neuropsychological tasks that we could try to correlate with the severity and the phenomenology of depressive symptoms. Besides, the reversibility of intellectual disorders evidences the emotional implication of cognitive functions, and it could be interesting to observe which type of function is more implicated, considering, for istance, that emotional contents seem to influence more visuo-spatial memory rather than verbal learning or immediate recall, by some authors.
In our study we try to describe a neuropsychological profile among depressive subjects looking for different performance related to various cognitive functions.

767

ALEXITHYMIA IN DEPRESSION: A COMPARATIVE STUDY
Heerlein, A.; Lauer, G.; Richter, P.
Psychiatric Clinic of the University of Heidelberg
Voßstr. 4, 6900 Heidelberg, West-Germany

Clinical observations and psychopathological reports on patients with endogenous depression suggest a high prevalence of alexithymic characteristics in these patients. 21 inpatients with unipolar endogenous depression and 21 with neurotic-reactive depression, classified according to DSM-III and Newcastle criteria, were assessed with the verbal content analysis method of Gottschalk-Gleser and the Beth Israel Alexithymia Questionnaire (BIAQ) as well as other questionnaires at two points of time. The group with unipolar endogenous depression expressed significantly less separation anxiety, diffuse anxiety, total anxiety, hostility directed inward and total hostility in the Gottschalk-Gleser-Scales. This group also showed significantly lower depressivity in the Gottschalk-Hoigaard-Scale and higher scores in the BIAQ than the group with neurotic depression. The psychopathological relevance of these results, the specifity of alexithymia and the significance of this phenomenon in endogenous depression are discussed.

768

OSGOOD'S SEMANTICAL DIFFERENTIAL IN "JOY" OF MANIA AND SCHIZOPHRENIA
Piñas, M., González-Seijo, J.C., Abril, A., Vicente, A.. Psychiatry Department Complutense University of Madrid (SPAIN)

Se realiza un estudio de la cualidad de uno de los polos del mundo afectivo (la alegría) sobre una muestra de cien casos formado por dos submuestras de enfermos mentales diagnósticados siguiendo los criterios DSM-III-R de trastorno maniaco del estado de ánimo y esquizofrenia y un grupo control de personas sin patologia psiquiatrica.

Para ello se ha realizado un análisis del diferencial semántico a través del metodo de Osgood adaptado especialmente para este estudio. Mediante análisis estadístico se evaluan peculiaridades y características del sentimiento alegría, objetivandose diferencias intergrupo en el contenido semántico de este sentimiento.

769

DISTHYMIC DISORDERS - A GENERATIVE APPROACH TO A NOT REFERENTIAL REINFORCEMENT SYSTEM
Isabel Ruiz, M. Purificacao Horta, Jorge Maltez and J. Simoes da Fonseca. Dept. Psychology, Lisbon Medical School, Portugal

Disthymic Disorder (DSM III-R) has been conceptualized by A. Beck mainly under the concepts of cognition and vulnerability. Nevertheless, there is an immediate alternative - it may be the case that there are really no distortions but rather an independent and parallel process, which comes into being, namely there is a normal process of making hypothesis which diverges from reference. Furthermore, the normal process of testable hypothesis formation may be an extreme, near referenciality, of a much wider process of fantasy which serves as an additional dimension in reinforcement. Adding or subtracting a certain quantum which is fancied to referential data may change their value. Under this concept, what becomes apparent in depression is an evolution of the human operator into a state which does not need to produce a defensive value. It may be reasonably supported according to our data that the human system enters a structural change which is dependent on further factors. It plays then the role of a negative goal - exactly the same and symmetrical role as positive reinforcement plays in the usual learning theory. What is purposed is that data available support a double intentionality - one which seeks positive reinforcement by means of submission or assertion of problems and furthermore a trend to a negative value state which stands behind the structure of many human motivations and goes far beyond its utility value in a Pareto or Freudian sense. our multiple choice questionnaire allowed the analysis of phantasy at a syntactic and also at a macro-semantic level. At this macro-semantic level general rules are found.

770

COMPARISON OF ADJUSTMENT DISORDERS WITH PURE MAJOR DEPRESSION

T.Bronisch, H.Hecht
Max-Planck-Institute for Psychiatry

20 inpatients suffering from an adjustment disorder with depressed mood according to the DSM-III criteria were compared with 22 inpatients with a (situationally provoked) major depression without an additional DSM-III/Axis I Diagnosis, with regard to social dysfunctions, personality features as well as social support and number and types of life events and chronic conditions prior to admission. The diagnoses were assessed by a standardized interview, the Diagnostic Interview Schedule, and the socialpsychological variables by semistructured interviews and self-rating questionnaires. Major depressives reported more social dysfunctions, premorbid rigidity and more social stress prior to onset of the depressive episode than adjustment disorders with depressed mood did. There did not exist any differences between these two groups concerning social support prior to admission.

771

COMPARISON OF MAJOR DEPRESSIVES WITH AND WITHOUT COMORBIDITY

T.Bronisch, H.Hecht
Max-Planck-Institute for Psychiatry

According DSM-III criteria 22 inpatients with a pure major depression were compared with 25 inpatients with a major depression with comorbidity. Additional diagnoses concern panic disorder, agoraphobia, simple phobia, obsessive-compulsive disorder and somatization disorder as cross-sectional and life-time diagnoses, using a standardized interview (Diagnostic Interview Schedule). Both patients' groups had an acute onset and no history of a chronic course of their major depression. The following variables were assessed by semistructured interviews of self rating questionnaires: Social dysfunctions, social support, number and types of life events and chronic conditions prior to admission as well as premorbid personality features. Major depressives with comorbidity reported more neuroticism and less close social support prior to onset than the pure major depressives did, whereas pure major depressives reported more not-illness related chronic life conditions than major depressives with comorbidity did.

772

BIPOLAR ILLNESS:MANIC OR DEPRESSIVE PRONE FORMS vs.CLINICAL PARAMETERS.

SAVAS G.TSITOURIDES,MD, MARIA DIAOURTA-TSITOURIDES,MD, ATHANASSIOS BASDRAS,MD, ANDREAS LIAKOURAS,MD,FOTINI NIKOLAKOPOU-LOU-LIONI,MD.

STATE MENTAL HOSPITAL OF ATHENS,GREECE
15th PSYCHIATRIC DEPT.,Director:SAVAS G.TSITOURIDES,M.D.

From the clinical investigation of 121 bipolar patients, diagnosed according to DSM-III Criteria, a preponderance of manic episodes was found in 67(55,37%) of them and a preponderance of depressive episodes in 46(38,02%) of them,whereas in 8 (6,61%) such a differentiation was not observed.

It has been shown that this subtyping into manic or depressive prone forms could be eventually related to the type of index episode and the type of heredity.Namely, in manic-prone subtype, we found a higher incidence of hereditary loading for bi-polar affective disorder and mania as index episode,whereas in depressive - probe subtype, we found a higher incidence of hereditary loading for unipolar

773

SYMPTOM RESOLUTION IN MANIA

JAIN S., CHATTERJI S., JANAKIRAMAIAH N., MURTHY R.S.

National Institute of Mental Health & Neuro Sciences Bangalore, INDIA.
The pattern of disappearance of symptoms in an index episode of mania has not been intensively studied. The influence of illness and psychopathological variation on resolution of symptoms has also not been intensively studied. As part of a larger study on the course and followup of affective disorders, we assessed 45 manic inpatients twice weekly using the comprehensive psychopathological rating scale (CPRS). The frequency and severity of various symptoms in a manic episode were studied. In addition to the classic manic syndrome a number of probands had mixed, and psychotic symptoms. The resolution of individual symptoms, and predefined groups of symptoms was studied till probands had recovered from the episode. The influence of illness variables on recovery was assessed. The findings will be presented with reference to the nosology and description of manic episodes.

Session 118 Free Communications:
Social psychiatry and psychopathology

774

PREDICTION OF RELAPSE WITHIN A PSYCHIATRIC COMMUNITY CARE SYSTEM
I. Steinhart, S. Priebe, G. Bosch
Department of Social Psychiatry, Freie Universität Berlin, Berlin (West), F.R.G.
Since 1974 a comprehensive psychiatric community care system serving a district of 180.000 inhabitants in Berlin (West) has been built up by our department. This model institution includes a day-hospital, a night-clinic, a printing shop for vocational rehabilitation and various out-patient facilities. It provides mainly long term treatment for severely disturbed patients. This study was to identify variables predicting relapse during treatment. Sixty consecutively admitted patients were examined. Frequency and length of partial or total hospitalization during the second to fifth year after admission were taken as indicators of relapse. Patients' age and the duration of their illness was of little predictive value despite statistical significance. Length of in-patient treatment immediately before admission to our department was found to correlate moderately with relapses. Frequency and duration of patients' initial contacts with their therapists and particularly the course of illness during the first year of treatment proved to be the best predictors for relapses within the following four years. The findings suggest that prediction of relapse rates in long term community treatment programmes should be based preferably on initial interactions and experiences within the treatment setting, rather than on sociodemographic or clinical characteristics of the patients.

775

EFFECT OF PSYCHOSOCIAL AND CULTURAL FACTORS UPON CONVERSION REACTIONS
Ebadi G.H., Ozugurlu K., Ozkan S.
Ist Faculty of Med., Dept. of Psychiatry, Turkey

This study aimed to search impact of psychosocial and cultural factors upon the psychopathology of Conversion Reactions by means of clinical evaluation (AMDP), psychometric analysis (Rorschech, Cornell-Index, Intelligence Tests) and psychocultural scales. The study group consisted of 50 women patients manifesting Conversion Reaction and 50 healthy women subjects; matched for educational level, age and marital status.
Overall results implied that psychosocial, cultural factors and value systems dominating interpersonal relations played a determining role in etiopathogenesis of symptom formation and in initiation of symptoms, which appeared to explain the still high prevelance of Conversion Reactions in the Turkish community.

776

SOCIAL STATE AND NEGATIVE SYMPTOMS IN CHRONIC PSYCHIATRIC PATIENTS
Joseph Glaister M.D.
University of Toronto, Toronto, Canada
The gross mental symptoms of chronic psychiatric patients can be largely controlled by use of neuroleptic drugs but the social functions of the patients often limit their capacity to live a satisfying life in the community. The Social Level of Functioning rating scale (SLOF) was administered to 61 stable chronic patients attending a community clinic. Results showed that the population was physically healthy and well tolerated in the community. Work Skills ranged from a few unimpaired patients to the majority who could not work at all. Personal Care Skills and Activities of Community Living gave problems to most patients in varying degrees. Interpersonal Relationships provided difficulty to almost all the patients in varying degrees. These social categories were compared with three items from the Brief Psychiatric Rating Scale (BPRS) which reflect negative symptoms (Emotional Withdrawal, Motor Retardation, Blunted Affect). Results showed that all three negative symptoms correlated with poor performance in Interpersonal Relationships and Activities of Community Living. Only one negative symptom (Emotional Withdrawal) was related to poor Personal Care Skills. None of the three negative symptoms was related to Work Skills. This is an encouraging finding since negative symptoms are generally poorly controlled by medication.

777

THE SITUATION OF FIRST ADMISSION PSYCHIATRIC PATIENTS AFTER DISCHARGE
Stefan Blumenthal, V.Bell, N.-U. Neumann, R.Schuttler, R. Vogel
Bezirkskrankenhaus Gunzburg, Department Psychiatry II of the University Ulm, Ludwig - Heilmeyer - Str. 2, D-8870 Gunzburg, West Germany

The situation of 258 first admitted psychiatric patients was examined in a prospective study after 1 year resp. 5 years.
First, we collected clinical data, for example the psychopathological state, the habit of taking drugs and the compliance.
Second, data of social behaviour were documented, such the utilization of aftercare services and the social activities of the patients.
Third, there were data from the relatives: The main point here was to investigate the burden of the relatives associated with aspects of the illness, such as unemployment, readmission of the patients into hospital and financial problems.
Results of the 1- and 5 year follow-up are compared with one another and suggestions are made how to improve the situation.

778

ETUDE DU SUIVI SUR 2 ANS DE 73 PATIENTS APRES LEUR PREMIERE HOSPITALISATION PSYCHIATRIQUE

F. PEIGNE, I. FERRAND, C. ZEITTER
Hôpital Cochin Paris

L'évolution clinique de 73 patients hospitalisés en 87 dans un service de psychiatrie d'un hôpital général, sans antécédent d'hospitalisation psychiatrique a été étudiée. 18 à 30 mois après leur sortie, un questionnaire leur a été adressé, leur thérapeute a participé à l'évaluation.
Le devenir et le suivi des sujets sont étudiés en fonction de leur pathologie.

779

REHABILITATION OUTCOME IN RELATION TO PSYCHOSOCIAL -PSYCHIATRIC FACTORS IN PSYCHOTIC PATIENTS
V. KARYDIS, M. GEDAKIS, K. KONDILIS, A. ARMENIAKOS G. KARAMOUZIS, M. ZOGRAFOS, M. COCCOSIS, V. ANTONOPOULOS, P. SKALTSIS
Univ. of Athens, Dept. of Psychiatry Eginition Hospital

The purpose of this study was to investigate the relationship of demographic, psychosocial, psychometric and psychiatric factors with psychiatric improvement and work adjustment, in a group of psychotic patients attending programs of rehabilitation at "Eginition" Hospital.

This population consists of 273 psychotics attending the Prevocational Rehabilitation Program. The mean age of our sample was 30.9 years, the educational level of schooling 11.9 years, with very poor the premorbid social and occupational status.

The sample diagnostic categories according to DSM III criteria indicated schizophrenics 59.3%, affective disorders 11.8%, schizoaffective 13.65%, other psychoses 15.4%. The mean age of illness onset was 19.4 years, average hospitalization 3.6 admissions, mean duration in hospital 12.2 months.

The analysis showed a statistically significant improvement in the patients' psychiatric condition, as evaluated by BPRS and GAS.

The findings from a multifactorial analysis applied to all the above mentioned factors will be discussed.

780

GROUP ORGANIZATION AND GROUPANALYSIS IN HEALTH SYSTEM
Sandro Rodighiero - Psychiatric Services
Ulss Nr.22 Este (Padua) Italy

For our professional formation we have organized group activities for Psychiatric Services. We have formed department groups for an early diagnosis and therapy and day psychoanalysis groups cooperating with both socialization and rehabilitation groups. Rehabilitation groups are directed by non-medical staff: social assistants and para-medical psychoanalyst for group therapies. Reflecting on our activities we have analyzed the most active therapeutic factors. The aim was the finding of a theoretic explanation for the obtained results and the future activation of the major factors. We have observed that patients involved in these group activities have developed a better social adaptation and their applications for hospitalization have decreased.

781

INCREASE IN CHRONIC SCHIZOPHRENIA IN-PATIENT CARE DUE TO SOCIAL DISINTEGRATION
H. Geiselhart   C. Brandt-O'Neil   F. Reimer
Psychiatrisches Landeskrankenhaus, Weinsberg, FRG

Weinsberg hospital is exclusively responsible for psychiatric in-patient care of a region with approx. 600000 inhabitants. Since 1968 there are 32 medical-social features of each in-patient treatment being registered allowing an anonymous reconstruction of each treated case. Worldwide we know of 28 such case registers, similar results to our finding have not been published yet. We conducted a retrospective study with those registered data concerning cases from 1972 - 1987 with the diagnosis "Schizophrenia" according to ICD rev. ed. 8 + 9. To illustrate changes during this time three 3-year periods were summarized: 1972-1974, 1978-1980, 1985-1987. The amount of treatments rose in those mentioned periods from 847 to 1465. We observed a percentual decline in admissions for first time diagnosed schizophrenias and an increase for chronic ill patients (5 or more previous admissions) from 239 to 639 (from 28% to 43%). These patients are being described in detail by our medical-social features; the parameters indicating a social and work-related disintegration are rising significantly: e.g. the share of those living alone rose from 18% to 43% the share of still working patients dropped from 48% to 28%. From these data we conclude that from 1972 to 1987 there has been an increasing social disintegration of chronic schizophrenia patients. A decrease in social control seems to cause increased in-patient treatments of these patients.

782

POOR SOCIAL SUPPORT AS A SOURCE OF SOCIAL STRESS

Allan H. McFarlane, Geoffrey R. Norman, Donna L. Lamping*

McMaster University, Hamilton, Ontario Canada
*McGill University, Montreal, Quebec Canada

The conceptualization of stressful events as a characteristic of the environment and relatively independent of the individual may be in error. Rather, it appears that the occurrence of relatively fewer or more stressful events is a differentiating characteristic among individuals. This suggests that research should attempt to identify those characteristics of individuals which predispose to increased risk of stressful events.

In this study the hypothesis was tested that it is the redirection or loss of effective social supports which leads directly to the occurrence of disruptive social events. As a consequence the inadequacy of social support is directly responsible for some of the observed impact of stressful life events on health status.

783
SOCIAL ADJUSTMENT IN MONITORING OF DEPRESSIVE OUTPATIENTS
I.Maremmani, G.Perugi, J.A.Deltito°,
P.Castrogiovanni, G.B.Cassano
Institute of Psychiatry, Pisa University, Italy
°Depression and Anxiety Clinic, New York Hospital, Cornell University, Westchester Division, White Plains, New York, N.Y., U.S.A

The findings of the present short and long term prospective study of depressed outpatients further support previous cross-sectional observations to the affect than the course of depressive illness is often complicated by fluctuating social disturbances manifested by uneasiness in the work area, by disagreements with colleagues, and by difficulty in maintaining conflict-free relationships with significant others.
By contrast, the incapacity to enjoy and use leisure time appeared less related to the symptomatological variation in depression. Although we favor the hypothesis that impairment in leisure activity may represent a trait marker of depression, the hypothesis of it being a residual complication of repeated depressive episodes cannot be ruled out in view of follow up.

Session 119 Free Communications:
Psychosomatics and the cardiovascular system

784
PSYCHOPATHOLOGY AND PERSONALITY FACTORS IN CORONARY ARTERY DISEASE (CAD)

B.Alevizos, G.Voukiklaris, D.Papaioannou
University Eginition Hospital and Piraeus General Hospital, Athens, Greece

The association between behavioral pattern and coronary artery disease has been suggested by the introduction of type A (CAD-prone) personality and hostility, anxiety and depression have been considered as psychological components of this personality.
In this study, the personality dimensions of Eysenck Personality Questionnaire, neuroticism, psychoticism, extraversion and lie scale, the introverted and extroverted hostility, alexithymia, somatization and the type A personality pattern were evaluated in a group of 46 patients with CAD in comparison to 55 controls. Psychopathology was measured by the Spielberger's State-Trait Anxiety Inventory and the Zung anxiety and depression scale.
Patients with CAD scored significantly higher than controls in neuroticism and lie scale, in introverted and extroverted hostility, in somatization, in state and trait anxiety and depressive symptomatogy (U-test). Multiple regression analysis revealed that CAD-dependent variables that differentiated patients from controls were neuroticism ($p=0.001$) and lie scale ($p=0.035$).
The results indicate that patients with CAD are more apt to react with anxiety to stress and provide little evidence that a unique "coronary personality" really exists. The higher level of neuroticism may lead to increased release of catecholamines and other abnormalities associated with CAD.

785
THE RELATIONSHIP BETWEEN A TYPE BEHAVIOR, STRESS AND CORONARY HEART DISEASE
SUPARGO ASIANTO, LEFRANDT REGGY, SALAN RUDY KUSMANA DEDE, SUKAMAN
JAMBI STATE MENTAL HOSPITAL INDONESIA.
CARDIOLOGY DEPT. UNIV.INDONESIA

The Research of 220 subject persons in the stress-test and Rehabilitation unit in cardiology Department of Cipto Mangunkusumo hospital medical faculty of University of Indonesian, Jakarta which consist of 110 persons control group and 110 persons of coronary Disease (CHD) group. In the CHD group, it was found that A type Behavior is 4,5 times bigger than B type Behavior. If it is compared between A type Behavior from CHD and control group, therefore, A type behavior from CHD is 2,2 times begger than the control group.
Where as B type behavior from CHD group is 0,3 times to the control group.
For CHD group type A behavior persons combined with stress in far greater, that is two times. Between CHD and control group, the difference of the responsibility on their work is not prominently.
The difference of the burden of work.
For CHD group is heavier than control group that is 1,75 times bigger. And so does the felling of stress in the work is 2 times bigger in CHD group.

786
PSYCHOLOGICAL PROGNOSIS FACTORS OF CARDIAC OUTCOME ONE YEAR AFTER A MYOCARDIAL INFARCTION
Paolo Antonelli, Silla Consoli, Philippe Sellier, Hôpital Broussais, Paris - FRANCE

A systematic psychological assessment based on a structured interview and on self administred questionnaires was performed on 50 coronary patients (45 males and 5 females, mean age $57,9 \pm 11,6$ years) admitted in a rehabilitation department after a myocardial infarction. The questionnaires filled in by the patients or their physicians one year later revealed that 6 patients were dead, 2 were lost and 42 alive, 7 of them presenting one or more ischaemic heart disease complications (IHDC), and 13 angina pectoris. Age and early ventricular function failure predicted physical outcome over a period of one year. IHDC were related to depression ($p=0.01$) and death to depression ($p=0.006$), emotional impact of infarction ($p<0.03$) and social desirability ($p<0.002$), as assessed in a first time. Nor pattern A neither denial were related to outcome. The links of IHDC and of death with depression persisted when data where adjusted to age and early complications ($p=0.008$ and $p=0.02$, respectively). Angina pectoris during the year of follow up was not related to physical criteria but was more frequent amongst subjects presenting a better emotional control.
These results indicate that depression is an independent predictor of physical outcome after myocardial infarction and should be detected systematically in a preventive aim.

787
TYPE A BEHAVIOUR, LIFE CHANGES AND NEUROTICISM: INTERACTION IN ACUTE M.I. PATIENTS.

S.N.SHARMA, P.N.SOMANI, S.T.BANERJEE, Deptts. of Psychiatry & Medicine, Instt. of Med. Scs., B.H.U., VARANASI, INDIA.

Type A behaviour, level of neuroticism (at the end of first and second week in hospital and first, third and six month after discharge) and life event changes were studied in 53 consecutive patients of acute M.I. and 50 healthy controls meeting fixed inclusion criteria, using JAS (Jenkins et al,1979), PGI Health Questionnaire N_2 (Verma & Wig,1976) and presumptive stressful life events scale (Singh et al,1981) respectively. Mean percentile of type A behaviour and factors S,J & H were significantly higher in patients than controls. Level of neuroticism fell significantly in patients at successive interviews. Life event changes in life time and past one year were significantly higher in patients and majority of the changes were unpleasant. Significant positive correlation were between (a) percentile of type A behaviour and factor S with level of neuroticism and past one year stress scores and (b) life time and past one year stress scores. Age had negative correlation with type A Behavior and factor S.

788
REACTIVITY TO STRESS OF HYPERTENSIVES AND NORMOTENSIVES UNDERGOING A RORSCHACH TEST
Silla CONSOLI, Marianne BAUDIN, Michel SAFAR,
Hôpital Broussais - Paris - FRANCE

Fifty-three subjects including 31 hypertensive patients (HT) not receiving treatement and 22 normotensive subjects (NT) underwent a Rorschach test, with recording of blood pressure (BP) and heart rate in supine position, using a subcontinuous measuring apparatus set to allow one minute intervals between two recorded values. Each experimental phase was preceded and followed by a rest period. BP reactivity, determined by comparing mean values to the first rest period, was higher in HT and in subjects with family history of hypertension. BP variability (standard deviations to mean values of each period ratios) was higher in the NT. By comparison with the NT group, HT subjects undergoing the Rorschach test showed greater repression of aggressiveness, more marked conformity and less expression of anguish. Sequential analysis of the hemodynamic and psychodynamic determinations between plates II, III and IV of the test showed a negative link in both populations between changes in BP values and changes in the expression of aggressiveness (in a given subject, the decrease in BP was correlated with the exteriorization of aggressiveness from one plate to the next).
This study indicates that personality factors and ability to link aggressive drives with mental representations take place in BP reactivity to stress, in both HT and NT subjects.

789
EMOTIONAL STATES AS PRECURSORS OF MIGRAINE AND TENSION HEADACHE ATTACKS

S. Donias M.D., S. Harmoussi-Peioglou M.D.,
G. Georgiadis M.D., N. Manos M.D.

CMHC-2nd University Dept of Psychiatry,
Thessaloniki, Greece.
Headache Clinic, St. Demetrius General Hospital,
Thessaloniki, Greece.
State Mental Hospital, Thessaloniki, Greece

Emotional states have been frequently reported by headache patients as releasing factors of an attack. 90 consecutive tension headache (TH) patients and 50 consecutive migraine (MG) patients of a Headache Clinic matched for age and education were examined with a semi-structured psychiatric interview. There seems to be a differentiation in the profiles of TH and MG groups concerning the emotional precursors of an attack. TH patients reported significantly more frequently negative arousal states (anger, anxiety) as releasing factors of an attack than migraineurs, they reported anxiety more frequently than anger as a precursor, but they cognitively assessed anger as being more strongly connected with their attacks. MG patients did not differentiate between anger and anxiety as more frequent precursors than depression or positive emotional states, and they cognitively assessed positive emotional states (joy, excitement) as being more strongly connected with their attacks. The theoretical and clinical implications of the findings are further discussed.

790
MOOD CHANGES IN ASSOCIATION WITH MIGRAINE HEADACHES - RESULTS FROM A PROSPECTIVE STUDY.
Diana P.Morrison
Karolinska Institute, Dept of Psychiatry & Psychology, Stockholm, Sweden.
A relationship between migraine attacks and emotional changes was first described in the late nineteenth century (1). Recent studies have suggested that fatigue (2) and increased sensitivity/reduced tolerance to stress may precede migraine attacks (3).
In order to determine whether mood changes occurred before, during and after, migraine attacks self report data were collected daily over a 6 week period from 36 female, new referrals to a migraine clinic. The results were compared with patients' retrospective estimates of mood change in relation to migraine attacks.
Retrospective estimates of mood change did not correlate well with changes in mood found in the prospective rating period.
A third of patients had increased anxiety, depression and irritability on days when migraine was present. This was not related to the frequency or duration of attacks. No evidence was found for mood change immediately before or after attacks in the group as a whole, although this was evident occasionally in individual patients.
It is suggested that the patients with mood change may experience more disturbance in cerebral blood flow in the temporal lobe during migraine attacks.

791

PSYCHODYNAMIC FINDINGS IN PATIENTS WITH THROMBANGITIS OBLITERANS

F.Hollatz, H.Heidrich, R.Potthoff
Psychiatrisch-psychotherapeutische und neurologische Praxis Friedrich-Wilhelm-Platz 6,1000 Berlin 41 und Innere Abteilung des Franziskus-Krankenhauses, Burggrafenstr.1, 1000 Berlin 30

20 patients with histologically proved Endangiitis (Winiwarter - Buerger) of the lower extremities were examined by a psychoanalytic orientated interview and psychologic tests (FPI and GT).
The interviews showed in all patients a severe disturbance in relation to the father - who mostly was absent during the development of the child.
Another striking result was the vehement sporting activity of 85% of the patients. Intense smoking of cigarettes(20-40 per day) was another regular finding.
The central psychodynamic theme was the striving for autonomy.
The psychological tests showed a very marked denial of aggression and emotional lability.
The interpretation of these facts brings evidence that the Endangiitis can be regarded as a psychosomatic reaction of a narcistic personality under special circumstances.

792

A BIOPSYCHOSOCIAL APPROACH TO MILD ESSENTIAL HYPERTENSION

N.Chakraborty, M.D., D.P.M., Professor & Head of Psychiatry, N.R.S.Medical College & Hospital, Calcutta,
G.Roy Palodhi, M.D.(Psy) student, University of Calcutta
M.Kar, M.Sc., Bio-Chemist, N.R.S.Medical College & Hospital, Calcutta

Essential Hypertension is increasingly believed to be aetiologically related to social, Psychological and biological factors. This investigation evaluates the personality factors, Psychiatric Symptoms and ascorbic acid status in patients of mild essential hypertension to explore the relationship, if any. 25 patients with mild essential hypertension and 25 matched controls, were compared in terms of personality factors, psychiatric symptoms evaluated clinically, and measurement of plasma ascorbic acid (AA) and plasma dehydroascorbic acid (DHA). Patients of essential hypertension were found to be emotionally less stable, conscentious, suspicious and tense. They also registered a marked decrease in the level of plasma AA and a significant increase of plasma DHA level. The ratio of DHA/AA was also found to be significantly altered. Multifactorial aetiological perspective of mild essential hypertension including psychological, biochemical and sociological factors are thus implicated.

Session 120 Free Communications:
Lithium treatment

793

HALOPERIDOL DECANOATE AND LITHIUM IN MANIC DEPRESSIVE PSYCHOSIS: OUTCOME DATA AFTER 90 MONTHS' EXPERIENCE

.H.Batchelor[1], M.R.Lowe[2]
[1]Janssen Research Foundation, Wantage, U.K.,
[2]Dept.of Psychol.Med. Basildon Hospital,Essex,UK

As noted in a recent review (Lowe and Batchelor, submitted for publication) clinical experience gained in an out-patient lithium clinic has high-lighted the particular problems of three patient groups. Firstly, the manic depressive patient who relapses on prophylactic lithium whilst still treatment compliant;secondly, the patient with schizoaffective disorder who is enadequately controlled on lithium alone; and thirdly, that small group of patients with a rapid-cycling disorder and a history of frequent relapses and chronic disability. With 1sth July 1989 as the index data for duration of treatment, the data presented will describe 15 patients (9 females and 6 males) with an age range of 20-60 years (mean age 48.9), their medication history, treatment response and order. On the basis of up to 90-months' experience, haloperidol decanoate used both alone or in combination with lithium has proved to be an effective prophylactic therapy for some unstable patients.Our observations also suggest that prolonged depot neuroleptic treatment, in combination with lithium, may reduce the severity and frequency of manic episodes. The combined use of lithium and haloperidol would appear to be relatively safe when serum lithium levels are maintained below 1.0 mmol/litre.In addition,no evidence has been found of any lithium/haloperidol interaction: following a detailed examination of the literature (Batchelor and Lowe, submitted for publication) to true interaction between lithium and any neuroleptic can be 256 demonstrated from the published case reports.

794

Lithium, Carbamazépine et Valproate dans les troubles affectifs
Dr B. BLAJEV, Hôpital Psychiatrique Cantonal de Marsens, Suisse. (canton de Fribourg)

L'utilisation des sels de Lithium dans le traitement et la prophylaxie de certains troubles affectifs est largement admise avec connaissance et expérience depuis plusieurs années, sujet de plusieurs publications. Dans certaines conditions cliniques les sels de Lithium ne peuvent pas être utilisés ou ne sont pas efficaces (non-réponse au Lithium, troubles de la glande thyroïde, néphrectomie, insuffisance rénale, troubles électrolytiques, endocriniens, diabète insipide néphrogène etc., utilisation de diurétiques, association avec neuroleptiques et antidépresseurs discutable). Depuis des années une alternative se dégage dans ces conditions avec l'utilisation des antiépileptiques (Carbamazépine et Valproate) avec déjà une certaine expérience et plusieurs publications. Notre expérience consiste à utiliser le Carbamazépine et le Valproate dans ces conditions avec un effet thérapeutique et prophylactique avec les mêmes possibilités de contrôle des taux thérapeutiques et la possibilité de les utiliser en cas d'insuffisance rénale, troubles de la fonction thyroïdienne (hyper, hypo, goitre, exophtalmie), néphrectomie, associés avec des neuroleptiques, antidépresseurs, diurétiques et taux stables, diabète insipide provoqué par le traitement avec sels de Lithium.

795
TREATING RESISTANT OBSESSIVE DISORDERS WITH LITHIUM AND CARBAMAZEPINE.

J. Vallejo; J. Olivares; T. Marcos; A. Porta; C. Díez.
Residencia "Príncpes d'Espanya", Bellvitge, Hospitalet (Barcelona), Spain.

We assessed the lithium (n=6) and carbamazepine (n=6) treatment outcome of 12 outpatients who met DSM-III criteria for obsessive-compulsive disorder. All patients were previously treated with high doses of clomipramine and phenelzine with a poor outcome. We tried to relate the responsiveness with several variables (sociodemographic characteristics, clinical picture, psychometric trends, and biological findings).
Results provided evidence only for a positive relationship between (1) sleep-deprivation EEG disturbances and carbamazepine response, and (2) high scores on an obsessive personality inventory, which had been developed by one of us, and lithium response.

796
LITHIUM SALTS IN ALCOHOL ADDICTION THERAPY

V. Predescu, R. Ionescu, C. Popescu
Institute of Neurology and Psychiatry
Bucharest, Romania

This open clinical psychopharmacological study was intended to assess the therapeutic efficiency of lithium salts in chronic alcoholics, setting out from the hypothesis that mood stabilization may reduce leaving for alcohol. Two groups of alcoholics with moods disturbances were followed up for 12 months. One group was treated with lithium salts, while the other received discontinually disulfiram, vitamins, tranquilizers. The results were evaluated in terms of abstinence/ingestion pattern, subjective state, social, occupational and familial functioning, treatment compliance. We didn't find statistically significant differences between the two groups on these variables. In the alcoholic group treated with lithium salts, the good outcome correlated with the following variables: the patient's strong treatment motivation, a shorter period of heavy alcohol ingestion, anxious-depressive clinical picture and the absence of neurastheniform symptoms.

797
LITHIUM, MEMORY FUNCTIONS AND PHYSOSTIGMINE

R.K. SINGH* B.B. SETHI**, J.K. TRIVEDI**
*LADY HARDINGE MEDICAL COLLEGE, NEW DELHI, INDIA.
**KING GEORGE's MEDICAL COLLEGE, LUCKNOW, INDIA.

Lithium has been implicated to cause memory impairment in patients on prophylactic therapy. There is lack of consensus regarding the cognitive side effects of lithium. This work compares the memory functions in euthymic manic-depressives on lithium therapy with those of normal controls and also euthymic manic-depressives who were on either neuroleptics or antidepressants. Reduction in cholinergic transmission may cause memory impairment and lithium has been shown to impair release of acetylcholine. The acute effects of the cholinesterase inhibitor physostigmine, on memory test performance of patients on lithium were also assessed. The results of this study indicate that lithium does not cause any detectable impairment of memory functioning in the sample assessed. The pre- and post-physostigmine memory test performances were also not significantly different.

798
MORTALITY OF LITHIUM-TREATED PATIENTS WITH AFFECTIVE DISORDERS
B. Ahrens, B. Mueller-Oerlinghausen
Free University of Berlin, Dept. of Psychiatry (Head: Prof. Dr. H. Helmchen), Eschenallee 3, D-1000 Berlin (West) 19, FRG

After a period of clinical experience of the therapeutic effects of about 20 years one important question is unanswered: What is the effect of a long-term lithium treatment on the well-known fact of increased mortality rates in patients with psychiatric illnesses especially with affective disorders? Under the point of view of the discussion of the serotonin agonistic effect of lithium as a factor in prevention of autoaggressive behavior and suicidal attempts and as a factor in the prophylaxis of recurrent affective illnesses, we observed in a retroperspective study since 1967 the mortality of a lithium treated population with affective disorders in the lithium outpatient center at the Free University of Berlin. We found a decreasing cummulative ratio of observed to expected deaths (in comparison with the normal population of the Federal Republic of West Germany). There are differences between the younger and older patients and their causes of death. The younger patients under 45 years have further an excess mortality. Deaths by suicide were substantially increased as were deaths from cardiovascular disease.

799

TEACHING LITHIUM PATIENTS ABOUT THEIR TREATMENT

PEET M & HARVEY N S
Department of Psychiatry
University of Sheffield, Northern General Hospital
Herries Road, Sheffield, South Yorkshire, S5 7AU

Sixty long term lithium treated patients attending a lithium clinic were allocated at random to receive an educational programme or to act as a control group. The educational programme, comprising a short video, written handout, and a follow up home visit, was associated with significant, substantial and sustained improvement in the scores on a Lithium Knowledge Test. Educated patients had greater awareness of factors relating to the safety of lithium treatment, a more favourable attitude towards lithium on a Lithium Attitude Questionnaire, and improved compliance.

800

PROPHYLACTIC LITHIUM TREATMENT GIVEN EVERY SECOND DAY. PRELIMINARY RESULTS.

JENSEN HV*, OLAFSSON K*, BILLE A*, MELLERUP E**, PLENGE P**, ANDERSEN J*.
*DEPARTMENT B, VORDINGBORG PSYCHIATRIC HOSPITAL AND **PSYCHOCHEMISTRY INSTITUTE, RIGSHOSPITALET, DENMARK.

The prophylactic efficacy and side effects of lithium treatment given every second day was evaluated in 10 patients with manic-depressive disorder. The patients had all experienced at least 3 episodes of mania or depression and were lithium-responders. Blind to the patient and to the psychiatrist the lithium intake was changed from one daily dose to intake every second day; placebo tablets were given the intermediate days. The median duration of treatment was 13 months (range:8-19); the median twelve-hour S-lithium concentration in the last month of treatment was 0.7 mmol/litre (range:0.5-1.0). The median total score on the Hamilton Depression Rating Scale, the Bech-Rafaelsen Melancholia Scale and the Bech-Rafaelsen Mania Scale did not change significantly during treatment. Neither did the median total UKU's side effect score change significantly. However, in several patients lithium-induced side effect reduced drastic, when lithium was given every second day e.g. in one patient edema disappeared, in another weight gain decreased. A third patient, an artist who stopped painting during conventional lithium therapy, took up again his work. Two patients reported less frequent nocturnal diuresis. One patient who was well-treated with lithium every second day for 10 months stopped the treatment and relapsed with mania 3 months later. We hypothesize that lithium given every second day preserves its prophylactic efficacy against recurrent episodes of manic-depressive disorders and, at the same time, diminish side effects. The risk of intoxication may also reduce and with it the necessity of frequent control of S-lithium.

801

LITHIUM AND PSYCHOTHERAPY. THE RELEVANCE OF A TWO SIDED APPROACH IN AFFECTIVE DISORDERS.
PAOLO GIRARDI MD, ROSANNA IZZO MD.
Centro "Lucio Bini" Rome

In recent years several approaches hace been tried in the management of Major Mood Disorders. In the past the treatment was generally a pharmacological one. THis way the crisis was cured but the cognitive structure of the patients was not changed. It was taken for granted that psychotherapy was exclusively indicated for neurotic disorders. All those elements that contribute the cognitive structure of the patient were never investigated and evaluated.
One schizoaffective and four bipolar aptients were treated with maintenance lithium therapy and at the same time had cognitive psychotherapy. They responded well and were followed up since 1978 until now.
It is suggested that the therapeutical effect was related both to the mood stabilizing action of lithium and to the better understanding and control of emotional life obtained by the analysis of the cognitive system.

802

PSEUDOTUMOR CEREBRI AS A COMPLICATION OF LITHIUM THERAPY
Lazzerini F.,Bizzari D.,Agrimi G.,Andreani M.F.
Department of Mental Health, Massa Carrara, Italy

The syndrome of Pseudotumor Cerebri is defined by increased intracranial pressure and papilloedema without neuroradiological alterations of ventricles and with normal liquor.
Several authors report cases of intracranial hypertension during treatment with lithium carbonate.
The mechanism by which lithium carbonate causes increased intracranial pressure is not known and the relationship between lithium therapy and development of Pseudotumor Cerebri needs further confirmations. To this purpose we examined 20 patients who have been treated with lithium carbonate for at least two years. At the ophtalmoscopic examination none showed alterations of fundus oculi. Our purpose is to point out the importance of examining recurrently the fundus oculi in subjects in long-term treatment with lithium presenting headache or visual disturbances.

Session 121 Free Communications:
Psychiatric care in day hospitals and other services

803

THE DEVELOPMENTAL PROCESS OF THE FIRST DAY HOSPITAL IN GREECE (1977-1989)
Mantonakis J., Gyra E., Xagorari E.
Department of Psychiatry, University of Athens, Eginition Hospital, Athens, Greece.

The planning and development of the first Day Hospital in Greece is presented in this study through a series of problems, changes and readjustments considered necessary during its 12 year history. The initial obstacles we met with concerning legal, bureaucratic and financial matters as well as the functional and particular characteristics of the Unit, the weekly therapeutic program and the developmental process of the staff on a structural and supervisional basis, are described here.
It should be noted that the function of this Day Hospital is based on the principles of the therapeutic community. Emphasis has been put on the following revisions and readjustments: changes concerning the structural and theoretical orientation of the therapeutic groups, reduction of the patients' paid working hours, enrichment of the program with art therapy and other sociotherapeutic group activities (relaxation, drama improvisation), creation of a follow-up group, procedural changes in professional rehabilitation due to new Rehabilitation Units, rehabilitation programs with additional planning for students (our largest professional group of patients), in order to help them return to their studies.

804

COMPARISON OF DAY AND INPATIENT PSYCHIATRIC TREATMENT

Dawn Black, Francis Creed, University of Manchester, Manchester, England

In order to compare the efficacy of day and in-patient treatment for acute psychiatric illness a random allocation study was performed. It was found that 55% of all admissions could be randomly allocated to day or in-patient treatment.

162 patients were assessed. 89 (55%) were randomly allocated; the numbers treated in the day and in-patient units were 41 and 48 respectively. There was no difference in the severity of illness of the patients allocated to day and in-patient treatment. Patients were reassessed at 3 months and at one year.

63% of in-patients had been discharged at 3 months compared with 41% of day patients ($p < 0.05$). But at one year, 25% of in-patients and 6% of day patients were in hospital ($p < 0.05$). 51% of day patients and 41% of in-patients were at previous level of functioning at one year (NS). The only significant difference at 3 months was greater improvement in in-patients on social role performance, with no significant difference between day and in-patients in psychiatric symptomatology, social performance, burden or behaviour at one year.

In conclusion, a high proportion of patients presenting for admission to an in-patient unit may be treated in a well staffed day hospital and the outcome of treatment is similar to that following in-patient admission.

805

EFFICACY OF REHABILITATION AT A DAY CARE UNIT

Göran Björling MD, Arne Andersson, Day Care Unit SMEDJAN, NÄL, S-461 85 Trollhättan, Sweden

At the day care unit SMEDJAN patients with different diagnosis, neurosis, borderline states and psychosis are treated according to a structured rehabilitation programme. The principles of treatment are continuity, adaptation to specific needs, a common care ideal and structure. The elements of the rehabilitation work are introduction group, contact person, individual care plan and activity groups. Patients who have completed the programme have been investigated regarding their use of hospital care and open care one year after the programme was started, and this has been compared to the situation one year before the rehabilitation programme was initiated.
<u>Result</u>: The number of days in hospital care diminished with 57% after the rehabilitation programme was performed. The cost for these days in our mental hospital was higher than the total budget for the day care unit. There was only a slight increase in the open care contacts with the psychiatric open care team and the primary health nurses after the programme, compared with before treatment at SMEDJAN. The patients also experienced a better life quality after the rehabilitation.

806

THEORETICAL CONSIDERATIONS OF A PSYCHOTHERAPEUTIC COMMUNITY
A.Kokkinidis, I.K. Tsegos, Z.Voyatzaki, N.Karapostoli, Th.Papadakis
Open Psychotherapeutic Centre

The paper focuses on psychotherapy in the context of the Ps.T.C.* and places emphasis on the development and maturation of the healthy part of the patient's ego which, according to a 9 years' experience can be better tackled by:
1) The minimization of the importance of roles in the Community's day life (i.e. the role of the therapist as well as the role of the patient).
2) The alternation of several maturational roles (adult, peer and child) and
3) The alternation between structured and unstructured activities, which is related to the concepts of the Foundation and Dynamic matrices as well as to the concepts of stability and instability ("Controlled Destabilization").

* Ps.T.C. : Psychotherapeutic Community

807

PROFILE OF NON-ATTENDERS OF A PSYCHIATRIC
OUT-PATIENT CLINIC
M.Smythe, P.Vostanis
Highcroft Hospital, Birmingham, England

The aim was to establish the profile of non-attenders (N.A.) to an adult general psychiatric service. All N.A. (excluding first appointments) over a six-month period (1984) were included in the study (n=189). The methodology involved case-note review for a period of 3 years before, and 3 years after the identified N.A. The data collected was demographic, diagnostic (ICD 9), medication, rank of psychiatrist before N.A., and tabulation of admissions, attendance and non-attendance, and lost-to-follow-up over the entire study period. 55% of subjects were still attending 3 years later while 11% were either discharged or transferred. The remaining 34% were lost following the identified N.A. (22%) or, subsequently (12%). The highest overall attendance was in the manic-depressive group. Patients with neuroses and personality disorders were significantly the worst attenders, also accounting for 50% of those lost to follow-up.
There were consistant differences in the attendance profile for each diagnostic category. The results are discussed in terms of the role of out-patient services in the management of different diagnostic populations.

808

Factors influencing dropping out from the Adolescent Unit

K.Dallianis - Th. Kallinikaki - G. Vaslamatzis
Adolescent Unit - General Hospital of Athens - Greece

The aim of this prospective project is to study premature termination of treatment against advice in the Adolescent Unit (A.U.) of the General Hospital of Athens.
Our sample consists of 150 consecutive new cases (aged 13-19 years) which are classified according to the duration of their treatment.
A number of parameters are examined and compared: distance from the Unit, convenience of transportation, length of time on a waiting list, referal source, previous contact with psychiatric services, presenting problem, demographic data and adolescents psychopathology and motivation. Having in mind that in Child and Adolescent Psychiatry parental attitude concerning treatment is fundamental in the acceptance of therapy by the adolescents, we give emphasis in parental personality characteristics, their attitude concerning mental illness in general and about the pressenting problem in particular as well as their expectations from the A.U.
DSM III criteria are used for the diagnosis.
The main findings can be summed up as follows: 10.6% of the adolescents didn't keep their first appointment.
Premature termination was more frequent during the treatment phase compared with the diagnostic one. Remainers had usually the diagnosis of psychosis. All the adolescents who had a specific reason for their attendance (health certificate) completed their collaboration with the A.U.
We finally draw up some conclusions concerning the effectiveness of the A.U.

809

CAN EARLY ASSESSMENT PREDICT SUBSEQUENT SUCCESS
OF DAY HOSPITAL TREATMENT ?

A A VIDALIS BM Neuro Psych MD
G H B BAKER MD FRCPI FRCPsych
Queen Mary's University Hospital
London England

The present study was set up to determine the accuracy of staff prediction to day hospital success of treatment. Measures of depression, self-esteem, loquacity and sociability showed mean clinical improvement in a group of 41 day patients of mixed diagnosis over a period of 6 weeks attendance.
Staff predictions of success made after 2 weeks correlated positively (Spearman's rho=0,53) with an overall assessment of success after 6 weeks, which was positively correlated with improvements in scores on depression (rho=0,58) and sociability (rho=0,66 and 0,60).
The patients for whom staff predicted least success were in 6 cases out of 7 men aged 20-51.

810

PSYCHIATRIC SERVICES IN ITALY: EVALUATION
AS MEASURE OF QUALITY
SCHIASSI A.*, MARTIGNETTI U.°, DI MUNZIO W.˙
*Istitute of Community Medicine, II° Faculty of Medicine, Naples (Italy); °Planning and Quality Control Unit, Campania Region, Naples (Italy); ˙Dept of Psychiatry, National Research Council (CNR), HB 41, Naples (Italy).

In Italy since the coming of National Psychiatric Act (1978) the Psychiatry has been fastly moving from an hospital orientated model to a territorial one: the former characterized by the centrality of care whereas the latter by the need of prevention and health promotion. The new model has implied new specificities such as strong ideological implications, emphasizing values for pilot or experimental experiences, and the distinguish profile attributed to Psychiatry as a regard with Medicine. Nevertheless, as the time goes on, this approach has been quite entirelly accepted by the scientific community as whole, that's why, thanks to the abandonment of paradigmatic experiences and ideological implications as well, it has been facilitated the reintegration of Psychiatry with the other areas of Medicine. As a result what now emerges are new necessities and, because of scarsity, the compulsor of competing in order to obtain human and financial resources. In this paper the Psychiatry as "work in service" in the framework of National Health Service is presented and thus the need of an internal and external accreditation of a systematic and multidisciplinary approach for scientific and not ideological evaluation for Psychiatry has been articulated and stressed.

811

PSYCHIATRIE DE LIAISON DANS UN CENTRE DE BRULES

P.RAVELLA - J.P. PRALLET - S.PARIZOT - P.BOUCHET
HOPITAL SAINT JEAN DE DIEU - SECTEUR XVII
290 ROUTE DE VIENNE - 69008 LYON - FRANCE

La prise en charge des troubles psychiatriques dans un centre de brûlés s'effectue depuis trois ans à l'hôpital ST LUC (LYON) grâce à un groupe de liaison.
Une heure par semaine, plusieurs cas de malades sont abordés dans ce groupe qui rassemble deux psychiatres et l'équipe de soins aux brûlés (médecins, infirmières, A.S., aides soignantes). Chacun précise la nature de la pathologie et des difficultés qu'il rencontre. Ces multiples points de vue composent une image du malade, incluant son trouble psychiatrique actuel, son histoire, son entourage et son registre relationnel. Les psychiatres s'attachent à éclaircir la relation soignant/soigné, à avancer un diagnostic et proposer une stratégie face aux problèmes rencontrés. Le soin psychiatrique est réintégré à la prise en charge somatique, et assuré par ceux qui se trouvent effectivement au contact quotidien du malade.
La communication décrit les avantages de la psychiatrie de liaison par rapport à une intervention directe du psychiatre au chevet du malade. Elle définit les cibles que cette arme thérapeutique peut viser et détaille les résultats obtenus.
En 3 ans, le groupe s'est réuni 104 fois pour 241 "consultations indirectes", à propos de 99 patients différents. On note 50 bons résultats sur place et 5 orientations spécialisées. 10 décès et 11 sorties rapides font échapper 21 patients à l'étude. 17 cas, enfin, sont restés sans suite et 6 sans aucun changement.

Session 122 Free Communications:
Family: Effect on psychopathology and family therapy

812

FAMILY FUNCTIONING AND COPING: DIFFERENTIATION BETWEEN 'NORMAL' AND 'DYSFUNCTIONAL' POPULATION

A. Vaz-Serra, M. Cristina Sousa, C. Ramalheira and H. Firmino
Psychiatric Department – University Hospital
3049 COIMBRA Codex - PORTUGAL

With this paper, the autors have tried to study the interaction at family level and tha relations which are established in the formation of coping strategies, as well as the importance of these two factors in the mental health of the individual.

The authors compared thirty disfunctional families with fifty average families with no psychological problems.

The following instruments were employed to measure the variables:

FACES III (Olson, Partner & Lavee) - which permits the evaluation of the functioning and structure of the family;

PRI (Problem Resolution Inventory, Vaz-Serra, 1985) - to evaluate the coping mechanisms.

The results which were obtained show significant differences between the 'normal' and 'disfunctional' population. The way a family functions revealed itself an important variable in the formation of coping mechanisms.

813

COMPLICATED MAJOR RECURRENT MOOD DISORDERS AND FAMILY THERAPY.
A. Seghers, MD.
St-Luc University Clinic. Psychiatric Department
Catholic University of Louvain
Brussels, Belgium.

89 families with at least one member suffering from bipolar or unipolar recurrent mood disorders were investigated in this study. The influence of the family preferential functioning on the outcome of the identified patient was considered. The most frequent complications before family sessions were 1/3 alcohol or drug problems, 60 % of suicide attempts, with violence in half on this. Family history of depression was + in 44 %. More than half of the patients had taken lithium but only 20 % regularly.
Following family functioning modes were identified : elitism and high standards of conformity, repression of affects and feelings, unhappy tie of the parental couple and an "all-or-nothing" rule without compromising alternative. Therapy work shemes with such families were proposed and discussed.

814

Intrafamilial Issues in Psychiatrically Ill Women

ERDOĞAN B.*, UYGUR N.*, YAMAN M.*, KALELİOĞLU T.**

*Bakırköy State Mental Hospital, İstanbul, Turkey
**Organon - AKZO, Turkey

The authors try to investigate psychiatrically ill women's status in regards to changes in their marital status, marital violence, birth rate and their husbands' attitudes towards their roles as the wife and the mother.

The patients are selected according to the following criteria: at least once hospitalized because of a mental disorder, presently married and having had at least one pregnancy.

A structured questionnaire was given to each patient and her husband succesively. The findings are interpreted for relationships between sociodemographic data, style of family functioning (nuclear vs extended), frequency and duration of hospitalization, marital violence and the mental disorder itself.

815

SYSTEMIC FAMILY THERAPY OF YOUNG ALCOHOLICS - A FOLLOW UP STUDY
DIMITRIJEVIC IVAN M.D.
INSTITUTE FOR MENTAL HEALTH, BELGRADE

This paper presents experience in Systemic Family therapy of young alcoholics which has been carried out since 1980. The following phases are described: First preparatory phase which lasts 2-4-weeks by application of medical methods (detoxication, psychopharmacological, laboratory, EEG, psychological and internal tests, etc.). At the same time the family and social network is being organized. Second phase takes place once a week over a year. Basic method is group meeting during which period 5-10 important persons for each adolescent are involved into therapeutic program. Third phase is club for young alcoholics. Specific therapeutic process and techniques are described as well as specific tasks for subpopulation of young alcoholics. Paper also presents follow up study of 100 young alcoholics 5 years after the beginning of treatment 65% have totally abstained, 25% had occasional relapses and 10% started drinking after one year treatment. Drinking paterns, combination of alcohol and other drugs and tipical relationship between parents and adolescents are being described.

816

STUDY OF JAPANESE FAMILIES OF SCHIZOPHRENICS INFLUENCED BY A DOMINANT AUNT
C. Kondo, T. Iseda, K. Hasegawa, K. Ogawa and K. Watanuki
Department of Neuropsychiatry, Gunma University, School of Medicine, Japan

We have traced the family life histories of schizophrenics over more than three generations in order to understand the reason for their social deviation. We noticed that some schizophrenics lived not only with their parents and siblings but also with their aunts. Most of these aunts had once married but were later divorced or widowed, returning to their family of origin. It was found that these aunts tended to have a domineering influence over the whole family, and also exercised strong leadership in making of important decisions affecting the course of life of schizophrenic patients, especially the choice of school, job and marriage partner. It was often difficult for other family members to lead their own lives without the aunt's help, especially in situations where she had supported the family economically or devoted herself to nursing ill or injured members.

In contrast to these aunts, the mothers of schizophrenics appeared to have little power, and complained that they had been deprived of the role of mother. To make matters worse, the fathers had never supported them against the domineering aunts. Thus it appeared that the overbearing influence of these aunts had led to various distortions in intrafamilial relationships, including poor parental cooperation, ignorance of one of the parents regarding family matters, and mother-aunt confrontation.

Following our attempts to change these distorted relationships, some schizophrenics improved. Therefore we speculate that these familial distortions have a definite influence on the course of schizophrenia.

817

FAMILY AND INTRASOCIAL RELATIONSHIP AMONG SCHIZOPHRENES' RELATIVES

Claudio Mencacci, Maria Cristina, Galeazzi, Enrica Goldfluss, Laura Roberti, Angela Ruggeri
Centro Psico Sociale Psychiatric Department 58
Via Don Gnocchi 2
20064-Gorgonzola (Milan) Italy

The Authors refer to a study about the valuation of the feelings and the relationship in the schizophrenes' families followed by a public psychiatric service.
This research has been realized supplying the following tests: Expressed Emotion, ARS Schedule, BPRS, Knowledge Interview, Andreasen, S.A.S.
This study has the aim of trying to understand and value the modifications of the relationship in the schizophrenes' families after attending an information and support group.

818

CHRONIC MIGRAINE AND THE FAMILY

C.Paar, R.Schmidt, M.Schifferdecker
Universitäts-Nervenklinik Köln, BRD

Important existential fears regularly show up during individual psychotherapy of chronic migraine sufferers. In order to define the interactional impact of attitudes and behaviours correlated with these fears, 30 families of migraine patients were seen for systemic interviews using Milan school techniques.
Two types of families could be differentiated, on the one side those showing features of so called psychosomatic family, on the other side those showing features of so called manic-depressive family.
Even though there were important differences between the families, their value system generally was oriented towards striving for harmony and safety on the basis of a world view characterized by continious threats to the subject.
As psychodynamics of the migraine patient corresponds to the dynamic of his family, family interview offers information about further therapy, prognosis, transference and obstacles.

819
The Family Life Cycle and Mental Health
V e i j o l a Juha & V ä i s ä n e n Erkki
The Rehabilitation Research Center of Social Insurance
Institution, Peltolantie 3. 20720 Turku, Finland

This Family Study is a part of a larger Socialpsychiatric Follow-up Study in Finland. In 1969 1000 persons aged 15-64 years were randomly selected to the main study. In 1969-71 they were interviewed first time. In 1974-76 a 5-years follow-up study took place and in 1985-87 there was a 16-years follow-up.
The Family Study deals with the family life cycles of the families of those 1000 subjects originally selected. Many family therapists emphasis the importance of the stage and the transition from one family life cycle stage to another one. But there are only a few empirical psychiatric studies which deal with the family life cycle.
In this Family Study we used Evelyn Duvall's family life cycle stages. According to the study the prevalence of the psychiatric disorders was highes among those who were "outside" the family life cycle; it is among the unmarried and the divorced. "Inside" the family life cycle the prevalence seems to be higher among couples without children, in falimies where children are leaving home and among single persons in postparental stage. Respectively the prevalence "inside" the family life cycle was lower in childbearing and preschool families, school age families, adolescence families and in postparental stage among couples.

Session 123 Free Communications:
Aggressive and self-destructive behaviour in schizophrenia

820
SCHIZOPHRENIA, HOMICIDE AND ATTEMPTED HOMICIDE: PSYCHIATRIC OBSERVATIONS ON VIOLENT RELAPSE BEHAVIOUR
NIVOLI GC., SANNA MN., PITTALIS A., REPOSSI CL. LORETTU L.
CLINICA PSICHIATRICA - UNIVERSITA' DI SASSARI - ITALY

From a sample of 68 schizophrenic patients who had committed homicide or attempted homicide, the authors found that 36 (52%) had previously committed homicide or attempted homicide. It was possible in particular to isolate specific dynamics in which the repetition of the violent act occurred: 1) context of self defence; 2) criminal subculture; 3) context of suicide (before, after, before and after the crime); 4) sexual context (impotence, hyperactivity, homosexuality, incest); 5) paranoid context (elimination of the aggressor, avenger syndrome, frustrated narcisism, displacement, fusion). The authors formulate that the high percentage of relapses into homicide and attempted homicide by schizophrenic patients is due not only to the specific study sample (patients selected on the basia of gravity of violent behaviour in a high security psychiatric hospital -Philippe Pinel Institute in Montreal-); but also to the modality of the survey carried out by the researchers (objective research into the interview of the patient of "dark number" criminality). The necessity of gathering interview data with the most suitable methodology is stressed and preventative psychiatric measures are shown.

821
CHARACTERISTICS OF HOSPITALIZED SCHIZOPHRENICS WHO COMMITTED HOMICIDE
Yoji Nakatani, Psychiatric Research Institute of Tokyo, Japan
Hideyuki Fujimori, Tokyo Metropolitan Bokutoh General Hospital, Tokyo, Japan

We examined the characteristics of 16 male schizophrenics who had committed acts of homicide before or during hospitalization in a public psychiatric hospital. We found some interesting relationships between psychopathology, motivations for their criminal acts, and response to treatment. Half of the cases committed the crime during the initial stage of psychosis; their crimes were done under the influence of florid symptoms. In many of these cases, they quickly recovered after admission to the hospital and they adapted relatively well to a therapeutic environment. Conversely, of the cases who committed acts of homicide in a chronic stage, or in a recurrence, their previous treatment had been insufficient or easily interrupted. Situational factors are considered to have been an exacebating trigger to their acts of violence. After admission to the hospital, their symptoms tended to persist, they often had poor insight, and they adjusted poorly to the hospital milieu. Based on this study, we emphasise that therapeutic strategy should depend not on standard practice but on the characteristics of each individual patient.

822
SCHIZOPHRENIA AND HOMICIDAL BEHAVIOUR INSIDE GENERAL AND PSYCHIATRIC HOSPITALS
LORETTU L-SANNA MN-PITTALIS A-NIVOLI GC
CLINICA PSICHIATRICA UNIVERSITA'SASSARI-ITALY

The study sample consisted of 15 schizophrenic patients who committed or attempted homicide inside general or psychiatric hospitals. It was possible to isolate specific dynamics on the basis of the single acts of violence:1) structuralisation of delirium caused as a result of internment in hospital;2) displacement of a delirium from outside to inside the hospital; 3) interaction of the delirium of the patient with that of another patient; 4) irritable aggressivity; 5) displacement of non-delirious motivations from outside to inside the hospital. The authors describe the medico-legal and criminological characteristic of the violent act, the characteristic of the victim and the interaction of these with the schizophrenic patient and the latter's clinical psychiatric variables. Preventative psychiatric measures are suggested.

823

PSYCHOPATHOLOGY OF 8 SELF-MUTILATED PATIENTS

H.Fotiadis,N.Kokantzis,A.Karavatos,J.Nimatoudis,T. Didaskalou,M.Fotiadou. A´Department of Psychiatry, University of Thessaloniki,Greece.

This is a report on the psychopathology of 8 male schizophrenic patients who were treated in the Psychiatric Hospital of Thessaloniki in the past 30 years and who had the common characteristic symptom that during one phase of their illness,mutilated themselves by cutting off their genitals.
The first five of them, who were treated between 1958-1975, carried out the mutilation under the influence of ecstatic religious delusions; in fact, three of them maintained that, by this act," got rid of all carnal sins and were sanctified". The other cases, from 1975 to to-day, did not offer any delusional interpretation of their deed.One of them, a chronic autistic schizophrenic, attributed his mutilation to an irresisible impulse, the second of them mutilated himself repeatedly (by cutting off his testicles, the tip of his penis, the nipples of his breasts, the distal phalanx of two of his fingers, ect.) while the third one never offered any explanation of his self-mutilation. These differences are attributed mainly, to the different pharmacological treatment applied to these patients and the way this affected their schizophrenic symptoms.

824

RELATIONSHIP BETWEEN HOSTILITY AND PSYCHIATRIC SYMPTOMS IN A GROUP OF SCHIZOPHRENIC PATIENTS

Economou Marina, Angelopoulos NV, Zojes D, Tzivaridou Despina, Pratikakis E, Doga Heleni.

Department of Psychiatry, University of Ioannina, Greece.

Purpose of this study is to investigate the relationships between hostility structure and psychiatric symptomatology in a group of schizophrenic patients.
The Hostility and Direction of Hostility Questionnaire (HDHQ) and the Delusions Symptoms States Inventory (DSSI) were administered to 172 patients given the diagnosis of schizophrenia.
The HDHQ consists of five subscales: Acting-Out Hostility, Criticism of Others, Projected Hostility, Delusional Guilt and Self-Criticism. The first three subscales reflect extraverted hostility whereas Guilt and Self-Criticism reflect introverted hostility. The DSSI consists of twelve subscales: state of Anxiety, state of Depression, Conversion symptoms, Dissociative symptoms, Phobic symptoms, Compulsive symptoms, Ruminative symptoms delusions of Grandeur, delusions of Persecution, delusions of Contrition, delusions of Disintegration. Significant relationships were found between hostility subscales and psychiatric symptoms, especially between Guilt and Depressive symptoms, Projective Hostility and Delusions of Persecution. It was observed that hostility, although a personality feature, is influenced by psychiatric symptoms.

825

A FILICIDE CASE: PSYCHODYNAMIC HYPOTHESIS ON THE AGGRESSIVENESS

T.Villa, V.Ruggiero, F.Ferrato, C.E.Leone
Servizi Psichiatrici - U.S.S.L.67, Lombardia, Italy

The authors describe a filicide case committed by a 36 years old woman, mother of two cerebropathic children.
The patient since long time depressed, during a serious melancholic episode, killed the older son, while he was sleeping.
The inability of the patient to control her inner aggressiveness is taken into consideration mainly for the psychodynamic aspects.

826

CRIMINALITY OF PSYCOTIC PATIENTS

Mouyas Ath., C.Asimakopoulos
Psychiatric Hospital for prisoners
Korydallos, Greece

The study included all the psychotic patients who were hospitalized from 1/1/89 to 30/6/89 at the 2nd department of the Psychiatric Hospital for prisoners, that is half of the total number of patients, as well as those patients who had remained in the hospital from the previous years. It concerns 55 psychotic patients,18 patients with psychotic symptomatology and an organic disturbance (epilepsy,mental retardation,drug use) and 15 patients with a problem of diagnosis.
    46 patients had received the diagnosis of schizophrenia.In 18 cases the criminal action was either the first manifestation of the illness or was the opportunity for the illness to be officially recognized. The criminal acts comitted included: 13 murders, 10 attempted murders or assaults, 9 thefts or robberies.
    The criminal acts comitted by the patients with psychotic and organic problem included 2 murders, 5 rapes, 2 arsons.
    The acts comitted by the patients with the uncertain diagnosis included 6 murders 3 attempted murders, 2 rapes

827

THE PERCEPTION OF VIOLENT BEHAVIOUR BY THE SCHIZOPHRENIC PATIENT WHO HAS COMMITTED HOMICIDE.
NIVOLI GC., LORETTU L., SANNA MN., CORGIOLU T., PITTALIS A.
CLINICA PSICHIATRICA - UNIVERSITA' DI SASSARI - ITALY

The subject of this study are 62 schizophrenics interned in the maximum security mental hospital "Philippe Pinel" Institute, Montreal. In the course of numerous clinical interviews at regular intervals, the variations in perceception of homicidal behaviour were studied. It was possible to show at least nine psychical mechanisms on the basis of the perception and the variations of perception with the passing of time :1)negation; 2) division of the protagonist; 3)division of the victim; 4)minimization; 5) legitimization; 6)relationization; 7)projection; 8)repetition; 9)suspension of meaning. The importance of perception of the violent act by the schizophrenic patient is stressed, for implications of forensic psychiatry (patients not recognized as mentally ill, patients wrongly interned, etc.) and from the psycho-therapeutic point of view, to better understand the dynamic of violence and individualized treatment to prevent relapse.

Session 124 Symposium:
Interaction between the immune system and psychic states

828

THE IMMUNE SYSTEM SIGNALLING TO THE BRAIN: MHC-SPECIFIC ODORS IN HUMANS
R. Ferstl*, B. Pause*, M. Schüler*, E. Westphal**
*Institute of Psychology, **Dept. of Immunology, University of Kiel, Kiel, FRG

The scent of inbred mice-strains is MHC-related and e.g., changes after a semiallogeneic bone marrow transplantation. To test whether a relation of MHC and bodyscent can be established for humans, two studies were conducted to identify HLA-specific odors in humans:

(1) In an experimental set-up we were able to train rats in a go-no go olfactory discrimination task to identify a group of four persons identical in their MHC-class-I-loci (A_1, B_8). Urine samples were used as odor sources;

(2) 17 women and 2 men, who described themselves as highly sensitive to certain body scents of other persons and 36 index-subjects with aversive body scents as well as 15 index-subjects with attractive bodyscents were tissue typed. Effects of fragrances etc., were ruled out. Data analysis revealed high frequencies of a certain pattern of class-I-loci (especially A_{24} and/or B_{62}) which is highly significant compared to population frequency data.

829

IMMUNOLOGICAL ALTERATIONS FOLLOWING ISOLATION AND OVERCROWDING
Fabris N. - INRCA, Italy

830

PSYCHOIMMUNOLOGY OF ADOLESCENTS AT RISK FOR AIDS: RELATIONSHIP OF STRESS AND DEPRESSION
S. E. Keller, S. J. Schleifer, J. A. Bartlett
University of Medicine and Dentistry of New Jersey, Newark, U.S.A.

AIDS has become the major health threat of the decade and considerable research efforts have been undertaken to find a prevention and cure for this desease. Recently it has become clear that the course of AIDS is not constant with some individuals rapidly progression from sero-conversion to frank AIDS and others showing a much slower course of illness. A major challenge in combatting the current AIDS epidemic is understanding the variable rates of sero-conversion and disease progression in at risk individuals.

Research over the past decade has demonstrated psychimmunologic relationships in both clinical and experimental models. The stressor of bereavement as well as major depressive disorder has been shown to alter immune function. The consequences of increased stress and greater levels of depression will be explored as they impact on the immune system, the natural history of AIDS and risk taking behavior in inner city hetorosexual adolescents. These data support a psychoimmunologic theory of AIDS progression from HIV exposure to frank AIDS.

831
EFFECT OF PSYCHOACTIVE DRUGS ON NEUROPEPTIDES OF THE IMMUNE SYSTEM

Alberto E. Panerai, Dept. Pharmacology, Univ. of Milano, Milano, Italy

Several organs of the immune system synthesize and release neuropeptides such as beta-endorphin (BE), substance P, CCK and others. We investigated whether BE in lymphocytes could be modulated pharmacologically, similarly to what observed in CNS. With this aim, BE concentrations were measured in lymphocytes obtained from rats and human subjects undergoing different pharmacological treatments. In rat acute or chronic treatment with the serotonin receptor antagonist metergoline decreases basal concentrations of BE, and blunts the increase induced by the serotonin precursor 5-hydroxytryptophan and the tricyclic anti-depressant chlorimipramine. The dopamine receptor antagonist haloperidol induces an increase of BE concentrations in lymphocytes that is reversed by the dopamine receptor agonist bromocriptine that, when given alone, decreases the basal concentrations of the peptide. Finally, the GABAergic drug sodium valproate decreases BE concentrations in lymphocytes. In human, haloperidol increases BE both after twenty-four hours, and one month treatment; sodium valproate decreases, and the serotonin precursor 5-hydroxytryptophan increases BE.

Session 125 New Research:
Brain imaging

832
REGIONAL CEREBRAL BLOOD FLOW IN PATIENTS WITH AFFECTIVE DISORDERS

V. Delvenne, F. Delecluse, Ph. Hubain, A. Schoutens V. De Maertelaer, J. Mendlewicz. Free University of Brussels, Erasme Hospital, Dept. of Psychiatry route de Lennik 808 - 1070 Brussels, Belgium

Regional cerebral blood flow at rest was measured by the tomographic 133 xenon inhalation method in 38 patients (17 men and 21 women) with major depressive disorders following the Research Diagnostic Criteria and in 16 controls (8 men and 8 women). All the patients were free of medication and were classified in various clinical subgroups of depression following the same criteria (primary versus secondary, endogenous versus non endogenous, unipolar versus bipolar). The severity of depression was quantified by the Hamilton Rating Scale and the Newcasle Scale for the endogenicity. Finally, we examined biological markers like sleep EEG recordings and Dexamethasone Suppresion Test for all patient groups. The tomographical method used in our study was that developped by Lassen et al 1986. Under these controlled circumstances, global right and left hemispheric blood flow did not differ between major depressed patients and normal subjects. To study the specific cortical blood flow, we have used a method developped in nuclear cardiology to delineate an outer rim on the horizontal third tomographic slice. So, we demonstrated a significant left<right asymmetry in bipolar patients and in patients with an endogenous depression according to the Newcaslte Scale.

833
CEREBRAL BLOOD FLOW IN SITUATIONAL DEPRESSION

L. Schmitt, J.P. Marc-Vergness, P. Celsis, P. Moron Department of psychiatry, Tousouse France

A preliminary study investigating cerebral blood flow in 5 patients was performed using a single photon emission tomograph (TOMOMATIC 64) this was classified according to the following criteria. Situational depression is considered if : 1. first major depressive disorder DSM III, 2. evoked as situational by patients, 3. with stress factors scored above 25 on Holmes Rahe Scale and 4 on axis IV, 4. with positive criteria of neurotic reactive traits described by Winokur. Measures using I.V. Xenon 133 were performed during active treatment by depression (M.A.D.R.S.>21) and after 21 days of treatment by 200 mg/day of Medifoxamine ***. Pre-treatment measure exhibits a decrease in C.B.F. in the temporo parietal areas compared to the entire hemispheric slice between patients and controls. After treatment there is a tendency of decreasing blood flow for all regions of interest. Anterior posterior ratio 1.06 before treatment decreases to 1.02 after treatment and approches value of controls 1.00. Euthymia under treatment goes with homogeneous cerebral blood flow.
*** Medifoxamine is marketed by ANPHAR-ROLLAND (LIPHA Group) as CLEDIAL

834
MRI IN TEMPORAL LOBE IN SCHIZOPHRENIA: VOLUMETRIC FINDINGS AND RELAXATION TIMES

T. Becker, K. Elmer, B. Mechela, F. Schneider, S. Taubert, G. Schroth, W. Grodd, M. Bartels, H. Beckmann

Dept. of Psychiatry, University of Würzburg, F.R.G.

Temporal lobe involvement in schizophrenia is supported by clinical and morphological evidence. MRI is superior to CT in temporal lobe imaging. Relevance of T1 and T2 relaxation time to the pathogenesis of schizophrenia is unclear. Volumetric measurements were obtained from coronal T1-weighted images (1.5 T MR scanner) in 10 young male schizophrenics (DSM-III-R) and 10 age-matched healthy male volunteers. Medial temporal lobe structures were smaller in patients with statistical trend reached for the hippocampus ($p<.07$). Reversed asymmetry (i.e. left>right) was found for the hippocampus in whole sample. T1 and T2 findings reported in the literature are contradictory. We found T1 shortening in parahippocampal gyrus and hippocampus, but no T2 changes. Further considerations regarding our methodology in T1 and T2 calculation in various regions of interest will be presented.

835

TECHNETIUM 99m HMPAO IMAGING IN PRIMARY DEGENERATIVE DEMENTIA CORRELATES WITH SEVERITY
D. PRINGUEY[1]; V.AUBIN[1]; O.MIGNECO[2]; O.RICQ[1]; P.ROBERT[1]; G.BRUNET[1]; J.DARCOURT[2]; G.DARCOURT[1].
1 Department of Psychiatry-University of Nice, C.H.U Pasteur - BP 69 - 06002 NICE-CEDEX FRANCE
2 Nuclear Medecine Center - C.A.L - 06000 NICE

In pilot studies (PET scan and xenon scintigraphy) of primary degenerative dementia of Alzheimer type (PDDA) a paradoxical significant decline in regional cerebral blood flow (rCBF) was shown, mainly located in temporo-parieto-occipital areas. SPECT technique routinely performed with a common gamma camera and Tc 99m HMPAO, can accurately replicate these findings. In order to appreciate the potential use of rCBF imaging as a diagnostic tool for PDDA, we studied a sample of 17 drug free PDDA patients(DSM III R) at various levels of clinical impairment(MMT, Blessed,Reisberg scales). Injection was made a time after venous access, and during the solving of a visual task in dimly light quiet room. Several axial tomographic slices upon the orbito meatal plane were submitted to a semi-quantitative analysis, based on the construct of a step-by-step optimization in detection of pathological features (rCBF reduction and localisation). A positive correlation(r=0,639,p<0006) was found between the degree of typical aspect of rCBF abnormalities and the severity of clinical impairment(MMT). Quantitative measurement of rCBF with SPECT is a new non-invasive technique for the functionnal study of PDDA and a promising tool for pharmacological research and differential diagnosis of pseudementia.

836

IN VIVO AND IN VITRO RECEPTOR AUTORADIOGRAPHY OF THE HUMAN BRAIN USING 11C-LABELLED RO 15-1788
Persson A[1], d'Argy R[2], Gillberg P-G[3], Halldin C[4], Litton J-E[1], Swahn C-G[1] and Sedvall G[1]. Dept of Psychiatry & Psychology[1], Karolinska Institute, Karolinska Pharmacy[4], Stockholm, Dept of Toxicology[2] and Neurology[3], Uppsala Univ, Sweden.

By a combination of new cryosectioning techniques and the use of an 11C-labelled benzodiazepine receptor (BZR) antagonist Ro 15-1788 a study comparing in vivo (PET) and in vitro autoradiography of BZR:s in whole human brain material has been performed. By saturation analysis B_{max} and K_d values were determined. Postmortem human brain tissue of adjacent 100 μm sections was used. Regions deliniated were a cortical region, a cerebellar region and two low BZR density regions, pons and white matter. Five conc 2-75 μm were used for incubation. The obtained autoradiographs were analyzed by computerized densitometry. Optical densities were transformed to pmol/cm^3 for comparison with PET. Regions with high densities of BZR showed saturable binding, whereas low density regions reflect linear nonspecific binding. Data were fitted to hyperbolas using MINUIT. The results show the possibility to perform rapid quantitative in vitro studies with 11C-Ro 15-1788. Compared to PET quantification of BZR, it was found that B_{max} and K_d values were of the same magnitude. The about 50-times better resolution of in vitro autoradiography compared to PET makes the in vitro technique a valuable complement to PET.

837

DOPAMINE D2 RECEPTOR IMAGING WITH SPECT. STUDIES IN DIFFERENT NEUROPSYCHIATRIC DISORDERS.
T. Brücke, I. Podreka, P. Angelberger, M. Steiner, A. Topitz, H. Walter, Ch. Müller and L. Deecke, Neurological University Clinic, Vienna, Austria.

The purpose of the present study is, to visualize and quantitate D2 receptors in the human brain using an [I-123] labeled ligand and the SPECT technique. S(-)-N-[1-ethyl-2-pyrrolidinyl)-methyl]-2-hydroxy-3-iodo-6-methoxy-benzamide (IBZM) has been shown to be a highly selective ligand with high affinity for D2 receptors (Brücke et al. Life Sci. 42, 2097-2104, 1988). 5mCi of [I-123] labeled S(-)-IBZM were administered i.v. to: 8 control subjects, 10 patients under different neuroleptics, 15 parkinsonian patients under L-DOPA therapy, 6 parkinsonian patients without L-DOPA and 5 unmedicated patients with Huntington's disease. Data collection with a rotating double head scintillation camera started 1 hour after injection and lasted for 50 minutes. In a semiquantitative approach ratios were calculated between counts/pixel in the striatum and lateral frontal cortex, and striatum and cerebellum and gave 1.7 ± 0.05 and 1.85 ± 0.04 respectively in the controls. Ratios were reduced by 75 to 80 % under full neuroleptic treatment; under lower doses a good correlation was found between daily dose and receptor blockade. A marked reduction was also found in patients with Huntington's disease, no changes in untreated parkinsonian patients, but a reduction in L-DOPA treated cases. IBZM-binding is reduced significantly with increasing age. Specific binding was markedly reduced when the racemic mixture of IBZM was used, and no specific binding was seen with the R(+)isomere. These results show, that dopamine D2 receptors can be visualized clearly and with high resolution using the SPECT technique and IBZM as a ligand. A semiquantitative approach can give estimates for receptor blockade or receptor density.

838

CEEG PROFILE AND DYNAMIC BRAIN MAPPING OF A NEW DOPAMINERGIC DRUG.

Mucci A., Itil T., Eralp E., Ahmed I., Kunitz A.
N. Y. Institute for Research into Contemporary Medicine, Tarrytown, N. Y.

Quantitative Pharmaco-EEG (QPEEG) and Dynamic Brain Mapping (DBM) have been used to assess the CNS effects and to predict clinical applications of new compounds. SKF 101468 is a DA-D2 agonist with antiparkinson and antidepressant profile in animal pharmacology. In the present investigation, a double-blind, placebo-controlled, crossover study was conducted on four doses of the drug (200, 400, 600 and 800 mcg) and 50 mg of amitriptyline, in 12 healthy volunteers using QPEEG and DBM methodologies. The results indicate that SKF 101468 has systematic CNS effects in man, maximally with the highest dose studied. In comparison with the active control, 50 mg amitriptyline, the experimental drug showed a similar antidepressant CEEG profile, but a weaker discrimination from placebo. Dynamic Brain Mapping demonstrated differences in the onset and duration of CNS effects and in the topography of the drug induced changes. SKF 101468 was also associated with less side effects. Based on previous studies with other antidepressants, the drug can be expected of clinical utility in depressed patients.

Session 126   Symposium:
Mental illness in the retarded

839

Nature of Mental Illness in the Retarded: Prelude to Specific Treatment

Frank J. Menolascino, M.D.
Creighton/Nebraska Department of Psychiatry

This paper will review the behavioral dimensions of mental retardation and how they interact with the specific mental illness noted in the mentally retarded. Frequent symptomatic behaviors syndromes of symptoms, and specific DSM-III-R clinical pictures are reviewed. The latter diagnostic phenomena, which represent the types of mental illnesses noted in the retarded will be specifically assessed as to possible treatment interventions. Current treatment interventions, both primary and adjunctive in type(s), will be presented.

840

DEVELOPMENTAL PSYCHOPATHOLOGY OF THE MENTALLY RETARDED
ANTON DOSEN,M.D.,Ph.D.
CHILD PSYCHIATRIC CLINIC HOEKSKE,NETHERLANDS

The opinion is that the majority of the mentally ill mentally retarded is comprised of individuals with psychiatric disorders rooted in childhood. That is the reason why clinical phenomenological diagnostics often is inadequate when one is dealing with the diversity of clinical aspects involved with respect to the mentally ill,mentally retarded.
In order to achieve insight into the usefulness of the developmental diagnostics,a preliminary investigation was done in a group of 50 behaviorally disturbed and mentally ill mentally retarded adult residents.
The results showed that 70% of probands suffer from behavioral and psychiatric disorders from their preschool or school age.
The finding suggests that the developmental psychopathology often is involved in psychiatric disorders in the mentally retarded adults.Further investigations in this field are necessary because of important implications for the psychiatric diagnostics and classification in this population.

841

A STUDY OF MALE MENTALLY HANDICAPPED SEX OFFENDERS
Dr. K.A.Day, Consultant Psychiatrist,Northgate Hospital,Morpeth,Northumberland NE61 3BP,England

48 pts responsible for 197 sexual incidents during an 18 year period were studied.Heterosexual offences accounted for 52% indecent exposure 25%,homosexual offences 13%,cross dressing and stealing underclothes 9%.One third of the homosexual and one quarter of the heterosexual incidents were rated as serious.Special precipitating factors were present in 10%. 63% of victims were under 17 years,44% under 13 years and 11% under 7 years.48% of the male and 30% of the female victims were well known to the perpetrater.37% of incidents resulted in conviction of the highest frequencies being homosexual 52%,serious incidents(75%), and child victims 58%.The more serious the offence the more likely a psychiatric disposal. The average IQ of the group was 64 and there was a high prevalence of brain damage (42%),child pscyhiatric referral (17%) adult mental illness (31%) psychosocial deprivation (48%),childhood residential placement (48%),and behaviour problems (77%). 85% were involved in more that one and 58% in three or more sexual incidents during a mean period of 10.3 years. 48% had convictions for non-sex offences,they showed a significantly higher prevalence of the above features and were more likely to commit several sex offences.Compared to other mentally handicapped offenders the sex offenders were less likely to be psychopathic, were nearly 10 years older at first conviction, showed fewer adverse psychosocial factors in their backgrounds and had a lower F.H. of criminality. They also displayed a significantly lower frequency of single category sex offences, less specificity for age and sex of victim and a higher frequency of psysical disabilities and brain damage than non-handicap past sex offenders.

842

Mentally retarded criminal offenders in Denmark

Lund, Jens
University of Aarhus, Institute of Psychiatric Demography, Psychiatric Hospital
DK-8240 Risskov, Denmark

Based on data from the Central Criminal Register it is found that the total number of offenders with a valid sentence on a census day has decreased from 290 in 1973 to 91 in 1984. The reduction is caused by shorter sentences and a dramatic decrease in the number of sentenced borderline retarded offenders. The total number of sentences per year is slightly decreasing, but the number of first-time sentences is stable. Crimes of property are decreasing among the sentenced while violence, arson, and sexual offences are increasing, even when stratified for degree of retardation. Behaviour disorder was found in 87.5% of 91 offenders with valid sentence in 1984. Offensive behaviour was significantly predicted by the variables early institutionalization, retarded parents, low socio-economic background, divorced patents, and behaviour disorder of social-aggressive type. By use of multivariate logistic regression the predictors were analyzed, assigning independent significant effect to behaviour disorder and low socio-economic background. All predictors were closely intercorrelated. Biological factors did not have any significant predictive value.

843

GENTLE TEACHING: A NEW
APPROACH FOR COMPLEX RETARDED PERSONS
John J. McGee, Ph.D., Creighton University, Department
of Psychiatry, 2205 S. 10th St., Omaha, NE 68108, USA

An overview will be given of gentle teaching as a prelude to a psychology of human interdependence. This will include: 1) a critical analysis of current practices; 2) the delineation of the major interactional factors that constitute mutual change in caregiver-person dyads; 3) the definition of a new paradigm for helping persons with severe problems of self-injury, aggression, and withdrawal; 4) data-based analyses of the effectiveness of this psychology; and 5) case studies, via videotape demonstration, of the gentle teaching process and its impact on persons with histories of extremely severe behavioral disorders. Gentle Teaching helps caregivers avoid the use of punishment and restraint. It results in mutual change by focusing on decreasing caregivers' dominative interactions and increasing value-giving ones; at the same time, it helps persons with mental retardation and allied behavioral and psychiatric disorders increase their ability to participate with others and concurrently results in significant decreases in aggression, self-injury, and stereotypy.

Session 127 Symposium:
Panic attack versus panic disorder - Diagnostic and therapeutic issues

844

PANIC ATTACKS IN EPIDEMIOLOGICAL AND CROSS-CULTURAL
PERSPECTIVE
H. Katschnig and M. Amering
Psychiatric Clinic, University of Vienna, Austria

Recent epidemiological surveys carried out in the USA, Canada, UK, Germany, Switzerland, Italy and Austria show that panic attacks as such have an extremely high lifetime prevalence, ranging from 10% in the US epidemiological chatchment area study over 17,7% in Vienna, to a high of 34,4% (one year prevalence) in Winnipeg/Canada. In contrast, only about between 1,5% and 2% of the total population are found in these surveys to suffer from formal panic disorder as defined in DSM-III. Research has so far been carried out mainly on this arbitrarily defined disease entity and not on the whole spectrum of the phenomenon, including isolated panic attacks. An example for the possible fruitfulness of studying panic attacks per se comes from cross-cultural research. Comparisons of the symptomatology of panic attacks in clinical populations in different countries and cultures reveal that both similarities and dissimilarities exist. While the "core symptomatology" of palpitations and dizziness/faintness seems to be universal - they feature as prominent symptoms also in some culture-bound syndromes such as Kayak-Angst of the Eskimos in Greenland and Koro of the Chinese in South East Asia - others show specific transcultural differences. E.g., respiratory symptoms such as choking or smothering sensations, together with fear of dying, seem to be much more common in southern than in northern countries. Depersonalization/derealization, together with fear of going crazy, are much more frequently observed in North and Latin America than in Europe. Different recruitment procedures into clinical settings may partly explain these differences in the symptom pattern of single panic attacks. In any case, it is important to be aware of these differences in a time when panic disorder studies are carried out in many different countries and the results are to be pooled to arrive at a coherent body of knowledge. It is concluded that it is worth while to be more specific in describing the individual panic attacks and not to just rely on a global diagnosis of panic disorder when advances are to be made in our scientific knowledge about panic disorder.

845

DIFFERENCES BETWEEN NATURALLY OCCURRING
AND PROVOKED PANIC ATTACKS

Jürgen Margraf, Ph.D., Philipps-University and Christoph-Dornier-Foundation for Clinical Psychology, Marburg, West Germany

Despite much recent research, systematic information about panic attacks is sparse and their possible causes remain obscure. One prominent approach to the study of these issues has been to attempt to induce panic attacks experimentally. Response to challenges with lactate, CO_2, caffeine, or isoproterenol has been proposed as experimental model and possible biological marker for panic attacks. However, the validity of such laboratory models is still dubious. Ambulatory psychophysiological monitoring presents an alternative with greater ecological validity. The results of these studies suggest peripheral physiological changes of moderate intensity during some but not all panic attacks. Self-report measures also generally reveal only moderate severity. In addition, comparisons of concurrent diary and retrospective interview or questionnaire descriptions show a tendency toward retrospective exaggeration in panic patients. "Spontaneous" and situational attacks are surprisingly similar and many "spontaneous" attacks occur in classical phobic situations. Ambulatory monitoring studies provide criteria for the empirical definition of panic attacks as well as the evaluation of treatments and of the validity of laboratory models. It is suggested that the combination of ambulatory monitoring and laboratory strategies will greatly advance our understanding of panic attacks.

846

BIOLOGICAL CORRELATES OF PANIC ATTACKS

Dennis S. Charney, M.D., Chief Psychiatry Service
West Haven VA Medical Center, West Spring Street,
West Haven, CT 06516 U.S.A.

Numerous preclinical and clinical studies suggest a role for specific neuroanatomical substrates as well as neurochemical dysfunction in patients with anxiety disorders. This presentation will review a series of research investigations indicating that panic disorder likely results from abnormalities in more than one neurotransmitter system. There is support that the brain regions, including the amygdala, thalamus, hippocampus, locus coeruleus and the neocortex are all involved in the mediation of fear and anxiety. Abnormal function of brain norepinephrine, serotonin, benzodiazepine and CRF systems have been implicated as causative factors of anxious and fearful behavior. The neurobiological findings emphasize the limitations of current descriptive methods for psychiatric classification designed for etiological purposes and the need for clinically applicable biological tests capable of determining specific neurobiological dysfunctions in anxiety disorder patients.

847

Attack-Related Treatment Strategies I:
The Pharmacological Treatment of Individual Panic Attacks -
A valid Treatment for Panic Disorder as a Diagnosis?

W.A. Merz[1] and H. Katschnig[2]
[1] F.Hoffmann-La Roche & Co Ltd, P.O.Box, CH-4002 Basle, Switzerland;
[2] H. Katschnig, Psychiatr.Universitätsklinik, A-1013 Vienna, Austria

The diagnosis Panic Disorder may be regarded, according to present DSM-IIIR concepts, as a vicious cycle having its onset in endogenously triggered outbursts of anxiety, the panic attacks: Panic attacks lead to anticipatory anxiety, which then may be tied to situations thought to induce panic attacks. These situations are thus avoided; however, due to the conditioning of the patients, they may in fact lead to exogenously triggered panic attacks whenever encountered. This situation in turn increases fear and avoidance behavior - and the vicious cycle is closed.

If this concept is true, an efficient p.r.n. treatment of the panic attacks alone should enable to break the vicious cycle and, thus, to treat Panic Disorder as a whole: Efficient control of the panic attacks by a suitable anxiolytic with rapid onset and short half-life might decrease the anticipatory anxiety, the fear to get a panic attack in a specific situation, which in turn may decrease avoidance behavior and further conditioning, and so on. In this model, a Panic Disorder patient might not longer be under drug than a few hours per week. Moreover, because of the patient's consciousness of protection in case of a panic attack, a combination of p.r.n. treatment with psychotherapeutic exposure techniques may be of special interest.

Ro 16-6028 is a potent partial BZR agonist with a rapid onset of action (5 - 15 min after oral administration) and a short half-life of elimination (mean 2.4 h). Preliminary results in a large open pilot study and in a double-blind placebo-controlled study of limited sample size suggest - on p.r.n. administration - not only suppression or marked alleviation of impending panic attacks, but also a marked reduction of anticipatory anxiety, depressive mood, and avoidance behavior in the untreated interval between successive panic attacks. No withdrawal problems were found after the end of treatment. Side-effects of usually mild intensity occupied less than 1% of the total duration of treatment. This concept of treatment is currently been investigated in a large double-blind placebo-controlled cross-national study.

848

COGNITIVE AND RELAXATION TECHNIQUES FOR THE TREATMENT OF PANIC ATTACKS

D.M. Clark, M.G. Gelder, and P.M. Salkovskis

Department of Psychiatry, University of Oxford, U.K.

In recent years considerable advances have been made in the development of psychological treatments for panic. These treatments are mainly based on the hypothesis that panic attacks result from the catastrophic misinterpretation of certain bodily sensations. One form of treatment (cognitive therapy) uses a range of verbal and behavioural techniques to directly modify patients' misinterpretations of bodily sensations. Another treatment (applied relaxation) teaches patients a special relaxation procedure to use both as a coping technique for managing the physiological changes that occur during attacks and also as a way of reducing the heightened levels of generalized anxiety which make patients vulnerable to attacks. Controlled trials indicate that both treatments are effective, with most patients becoming panic-free. In the controlled trials which have been conducted to date, cognitive therapy and applied relaxation have both been compared with alternative psychological treatments and also, in the case of cognitive therapy, with drug treatment.

Session 128   New Research:
Tardive dyskinesia and other adverse effects of drugs

849

LOW-DOSE CLOMIPRAMINE FOR REFRACTORY ACUTE NEUROLEPTIC-INDUCED AKATHISIA

H. Hermesh, D. Aizenberg, G. Friedberg, Z. Zemishlany, H. Munitz, Geha Psychiatric Hospital, Beilinson Med. Ctr., Petah Tiqva, Sackler School of Med. Tel Aviv Univ. Israel

Four patients with 4 different diagnoses and no significant depression had acute neuroleptic induced akathisia (NIA) which responded favorably to the serotonergic tricyclic clomipramine (CMI) 20-50mg/. The patients' NIA had previously failed to respond to adequate doses of either anticholinergics or to propranolol or clonidine. Our conclusion from the above observations is that CMI has an anti-NIA potential and probably offers a novel addition to the much needed anti-NIA arsenal. The failures of anticholinergics and 2 adrenergic agents to remedy NIA, together with the efficacy of a mainly serotonergic drug suggest a considerable involvement of 5-hydroxy-tryptamine in the patho-physiology of NIA. Other psychopharmacological evidence that support this intriguing hypothesis will be discussed. The relatively low doses of CMI used against NIA as well as the immediate improvement (i.e. within 1-4 days) imply that the anti-NIA influence of CMI is mediated through a neuronal mechanism not identical to the antidepressant one.

850

LOW DOSE BROMOCRIPTINE IN THE TREATMENT OF TARDIVE DYSKINESIA

Marangell,L.B.,Kay,S.R.,and Lindenmayer,J.P.
Albert Einstein College of Medicine-Bronx Psychiatric Center, Bronx, New York, USA

Dopamine (DA) agonists can be used in low doses to preferentially stimulate presynaptic autoreceptors, thereby decreasing DA synthesis and release. The treatment of tardive dyskinesia and psychosis, where DA hyperactivity or supersensitivity may be present, may offer clinical applications of this mechanism.

We conducted a six week single-blind randomized study of adjuvant bromocriptine, 2.5 mg day, in seven neuroleptic-treated chronic schizophrenic patients with tardive dyskinesia. Improvement in tardive dyskinesia, measured by the Abnormal Involuntary Movement Scale, was significantly greater under bromocriptine as compared to the control conditions (paired t - 3.15, p .02). Psychopathology, measured by the Positive and Negative Syndrome Scale, showed trends toward improvement, particularly in thought disorder and activation. The data suggest that bromocriptine in doses of 2.5 mg day ameliorates tardive dyskinesia and possibly psychopathology due to preferential stimulation of presynaptic DA autoreceptors.

851

DILTIAZEM IN TARDIVE DYSKINESIA: PRELIMINARY RESULTS.

Cees H. Doorschot, Hetty A. Verwey, Peter R. Roels, Anton J.M. Loonen.

Psychiatric Hospital Voorburg, P.O. Box 10.150, NL-5260 GB Vught, The Netherlands.

In this double-blind, restrictedly randomized, placebo-controlled, fixed-dosage, cross-over comparison of 4 times daily 60 mg diltiazem vs placebo, we studied 17 neuroleptic-treated, chronic psychiatric inpatients with (tardive) dyskinesias. About 2 weeks before the actual trial began, the patient's clinical condition was assessed. The selected patient sample was randomly allocated by application of the random permuted block technique to either start with diltiazem or placebo for subsequent treatment periods of three weeks. The patient characteristics were assessed about 2 weeks prior to the actual start of the trial. The AIMS score was assessed six times: 2 weeks before the start of the trial, at the start of the trial, and 1, 3, 4 and 6 weeks thereafter. The psychiatric status and general drug tolerability was assessed at the beginning of the trial, and at the end of each three-week treatment period.
The results of this trial, which was terminated at August 2nd, 1989, will be presented.

852

Valproic acid does not affect tardive dyskinesia

Merrill, VanValkenburg, Kluznik
St. Peter Regional Treatment Center

To test the effect of valproic acid on tardive dyskinesia, we reviewed the records of 19 patients who had been treated with valproic acid. We tested for significant correlations between valproic acid dosage and score on the 1290 regularly scheduled evaluations they had with the Dyskinesia Identification System: Condensed User Scale (DISCUS). There was no significant relationship (Multiple R squared = 0.0049, p=0.171).

However valproic acid did have a small but significant effect in increasing scores on the individual item of 'toe movement' ($p<0.001$). It appears that increased toe movement is a minor side effect of valproic acid therapy, accounting for 7% of variance, which is not related to tardive dyskinesia.

853

VALPROIC ACID: PHARMACOKINETICS AND INTERACTIONS WITH OTHER DRUGS

VanValkenburg; Kluznik; Merrill
St. Peter Regional Treatment Center

Valproic acid is increasingly used to treat psychiatric disorders. It is known that carbamazepine decreases serum levels of valproic acid. We reviewed the records of 45 psychiatric inpatients who had been treated with valproic acid in addition to other psychoactive drugs. There was no significant relationship of oral valproate dosage to serum levels. Serum valproate level was significantly lowered by carbamazepine, amitriptyline, protryptyline, chlorpromazine, and thioridazine. Concomitant psychoactive medications accounted for 72% of the variance in serum valproate.

854

Triazolam: Induction of Varying Degrees of Organic Mental Disorder

Bixler, E.O., Kales, A., Manfredi, R.L., Vgontzas, A., Kales, J.D., Pennsylvania State Univ. College of Medicine, Hershey, Pennsylvania 17033 U.S.A.

It is now well documented that triazolam (TRZ) has a narrow margin of safety compared to other benzodiazepine hypnotics. There are numerous clinical reports, controlled studies and surveys reporting a wide spectrum of frequent, severe and largely unexpected CNS adverse effects. These include many symptoms of organic mental disorder (amnesia, confusion, disorientation, delusions and hallucinations) as well as hyperexcitability states, disinhibition and withdrawal difficulties. All of these problems have led to four separate drug regulatory actions in Europe against the drug. In order to assess TRZ's potential for inducing OMD, we evaluated the effects of h.s. drug administration on daytime memory in 3 groups of subjects [TRZ 0.5 mg, temazepam (TMZ) 30 mg and placebo]. On 40% of the days following TRZ intake, subjects experienced episodes of either anterograde memory impairment or amnesia. No such episodes were reported for TMZ or placebo. Further memory assessment in the evening of morning tasks showed significantly more impairment for the TRZ group compared both to the TMZ and placebo groups. These findings emphasize the need for physician/patient education regarding: TRZ's narrow margin of safety, particularly when the current recommended dose (0.25 mg) is one-fourth that originally marketed and promoted worldwide as effective and safe; and the limited efficacy of this reduced dose.

855
EUPHORIC PROPERTIES OF ANTIPARKINSON DRUGS: TWO EXPERIMENTAL STUDIES

Randolf Vågen, *Blue Cross Alcoholism Tretment Center, Trondheim,* and **K.Gunnar Götestam**, *Department of Psychiatry and Behavioural Medicine, University of Trondheim, Norway.*

Two parallel studies were performed to test the euphoric properties of antiparkinson drugs, one on seven psychotic patients, and one on 18 normal healthy subjects. Procyclidin and orphenadrin were compared to placebo in a double blind trial.

A self-rating scale for euphoria (14 items) and the Simpson-Angus rating scale for extrapyramidal side effects, in addition to ratings of some general side effects were used for assessment. Analysis of variance with repeated measures were computed on the results.

In the patients, there was no mood change over time with the active drugs, and no change in extrapyramidal effects were preceived. The patients showed no preference for a special drug, and they could not identify their usual drug. After the study, fewer patients used antiparkinson drugs.

In the healthy subjects, there was a decreased euphoria (dysphoria) over time. There was also a correlation between euphoria and a general drug effect percieved, and between euphoria and side effects, indicating a link between anticholinergic effects and dysphoria.

Session 129 Symposium:
Benzamides and dopamine: Advances in clinical applications

856
THE SUBSTITUTED BENZAMIDE DERIVATIVES AS NOVEL PSYCHOTHERAPEUTIC AGENTS

B. Costall, A.M. Domeney, M.E. Kelly and R.J. Naylor, Postgraduate Studies in Pharmacology, The School of Pharmacy, University of Bradford, Bradford, BD7 1DP, UK

Recent years have seen the development of a series of substituted benzamide derivatives which have a breadth of application in psychiatry. Sultopride has the anti-schizophrenic potential of typical neuroleptic agents, yet with less depressant effects, although it lacks the alerting activity of sulpiride and is indicated more for a classical use in schizophrenia or in mania. A newer generation of modern neuroleptics includes amisulpride which has marked alerting properties at low doses and clear antipsychotic potential at higher doses. Tiapride presents a different profile of preclinical action, lacking antipsychotic potential in reasonable doses, it is anxiolytic and 'calming' in animal studies. This is of particular use in calming agitation, behavioural disorders and anxiety, and to reduce the anxiety and other symptoms associated with withdrawal from drugs of abuse, including alcohol. Thus, as compared with the traditional neuroleptic drugs the newer substituted benzamides present as a group of psychotherapeutic agents having a greater breadth of clinical use in schizophrenia, anxiety and the treatment of drug withdrawal.

857
AMISULPRIDE: EFFECTS ON NEUROHORMONAL SECRETION AND EEG SLEEP PARAMETERS IN HEALTHY VOLUNTEERS
O. Benkert, H. Wetzel and C. Hiemke
Department of Psychiatry, University of Mainz, D-6500 Mainz, F.R.G.

Amisulpride, a new subsituted benzamide, is a selective antagonist at D2-receptors. Animal studies suggest that amisulpride may have a dopamine releasing effect in low doses and antidopaminergic effects in high doses. Moreover, there is evidence for the effectiveness of low dose amisulpride concerning negative symptoms of schizophrenia whereas therapeutic effects upon positive symptoms require higher dosages.
Neuroendocrinological side effects of neuroleptics, e.g. hyperprolactinemia, have attracted attention for a long time and are thought to be responsible for conditions like menstrual irregularities, galactorrhea, gynecomastia and sexual dysfunction.
In order to study its neuroendocrinological profile, amisulpride (20 mg or 100 mg) or saline was administered i.v. to 8 healthy male volunteers in a single-blind design. Prolactin, GH, TSH, LH and cortisol as well as amisulpride plasma levels were determined serially every 15 - 30 min for 7 hours. In another single-blind study, 3 normal male control subjects received amisulpride (50 - 150 mg) or placebo during 21 consecutive days and drug effects on EEG sleep, nocturnal penile tumescence and nocturnal pituitary hormone secretion were examined. The results of these studies will be presented and discussed.

858
OPPOSITE THERAPEUTIC EFFECT OF AMISULPRIDE WITH DIFFERENT DOSAGES
Dr. Patrice Boyer
INSERM, Paris, France

At high dosages (800 to 1200 mg/day) amisulpride has been shown to exhibit a high anti-psychotic activity in productive psychotic disorders ("positive" form of schizophrenia and acute psychotic disorders). Results concerning double blind controlled studies Vs haloperidol will be presented here.
To ascertain if on the contrary low doses of amisulpride were effective in schizophrenics with negative symptoms, 104 patients presenting a pure "negative" form of schizophrenia (mean initial score at the Andreasen's SANS of 97; 77,9% of patients meeting five of the Andreasen's criteria; no positive symptoms present at a significant level) were randomly treated during a 6 week double blind controlled study by either 100 or 300 mg/day of amisulpride or by a placebo. Confirming previous studies (Vs fluphenazine for example), in the mean total SANS score and in each of the subscores showed a significant difference in improvements between the amisulpride and placebo groups. Reduction of scores was about twice as important (40-50% in the amisulpride group compared to placebo 20-25%). The responsivity of positive and negative symptoms to different dosages of amisulpride seems to be an argument in favor of opposite disturbances in dopaminergic activity (decrease Vs increase) in schizophrenia.

859

AMISULPRIDE VS AMITRIPTILINE IN THE TREATMENT OF DISTIMIC DISORDER: A MULTICENTER LONG TERM DOUBLE BLIND TRIAL.

Ravizza L., Torta R., Zanalda E. e A. Agnoli*.
Istituto di Clinica Psichiatrica dell'Università di Torino; 13, via Cherasco 10126 Torino Italia.
*I^a Clinica Neurologica, Dipartimento Scienze Neurologiche Università di Roma "La Sapienza".

Amisulpride is a benzamide derivative with higher activity on D_2 dopamine receptors than sulpiride. Recent studies, suggest that Amisulpride exhibits markedly different potency of action on cerebral dopamine receptors: a high affinity for D_4 limbic and hippocampal receptors and low affinity for striatal receptors. The enhancement of dopamine transmission in the limbic area may be involved in antidepressant activity due to a blockage of dopamine presynaptic receptors. For this reason amisulpride might be used in the treatment of some affective disorders such as Distimic Disorder (DSM-3: 300.4). The present study was designed to evaluate the long-term efficacy and tolerability of amisulpride (50 mg/day) in comparison with amitriptiline (60 mg/day) in 125 Distimic Disorder affected out-patients. The study was planned as a formal multicenter, six centers, double blind, between patients trial. During the trial period (60 days) no significant efficacy differences were found between the two groups of patients. Our results suggest that amisulpride treated group has already improved at the first week. Both treatments were well tolerated therefore side effects were distinctly lower in intensity in the amisulpride treated group.

860

A PLACEBO-CONTROLLED, DOUBLE-BLIND STUDY OF AMILSUPRIDE IN DYSTHYMIC DISORDERS
Ruschel Sandra Ines, Dr.
Costa e Silva, Jorge Alberto, Prof. Dr.
State University of Rio de Janeiro
Rio de Janeiro, Brasil

In the current study, 40 subjects that satisfied the DSM-III-R criteria for Dysthymia (or Depressive Neurosis) 300.40 were treated with amilsupride (a new benzamide substituted derivate) and placebo for 4 weeks, following a period of 2-weeks washout.
Subjects were submitted to physical examination, medical history, laboratory tests, Hamilton Depression Rating Scale, Echelle de Ralentissement de Widlocher, Scale for the Assessment of Negative Symptoms (SANS, Andreasen) and check-list for side-effects.
In the analysis, oral doses of 50 mg/day were statistically significantly superior than placebo. The results are discussed.

861

TIAPRIDE - A DOUBLE-BLIND PLACEBO-CONTROLLED STUDY IN ALCOHOLICS.
GK Shaw, S Waller, SK Majumdar, C Latham, G Dunn
Bexley Hospital, Bexley, Kent UK

In this unit tiapride has been found to compare favourably with chlormethiazole as a primary detoxification agent (Murphy et al, 1983) and to be effective in improving outcome in addictive alcoholics of anxious or depressive temperament (Shaw et al, 1987).
This study reports the effect of tiapride on outcome at 6/12, assessed by multiple measures in 100 chemically dependent alcoholics admitted to a detoxification unit, assessed in double-blind placebo-controlled fashion.
Fifty-four patients took either tiapride or placebo for periods ranging from 1-3/12. At 6/12 54% of patients on active medication were abstinent or drinking in controlled fashion, 42% had improved and 4% were unchanged. In the placebo group 23.3% were abstinent and 76.7% unchanged. The active group achieved similar benefits on all other outcome measures. They spent fewer days in hospital, experienced fewer social complications, scored less on neurotic scales, gained in self-esteem and social stability and expressed higher levels of satisfaction with life circumstances.
Those who complied with medication either active or placebo for 3/12 achieved better results than those who complied for lesser periods but patients on active drug in all instances did best.
Side-effects were minor and rare. Failure to continue to take active medication was related to patient well-being and a belief that further medication was unnecessary.

862

THE ADVANTAGES OF TIAPRIDE IN THE TREATMENT OF SENILE ORGANIC PSYCHOSES
Prof. Kazuo Hasegawa, Department of psychiatry, St.Marianna University School of medicine, Kawasaki, Japan

Because of a rapid acceleration of aging of the population, the number of patients with senile organic psychoses, especially Alzheimer- type dementia or multi-infarct dementia, has been increasing. Therefore the treatment of these disorders has been one of the important clinical issues in the geriatric medicine. Besides the deterioration on the intellectual functions, the demented elderly often manifest a variety of the associated psychiatric symptoms, such as insomnia, hallucination, delusions, delirium and other behavioral disturbances. Appropriate strategy against these disorders is a prerequisite to maintain the residual capacity of the patients as well as to lessen the burden of the caretakers. Phenothiazines or butyrophenones have notorious side effects such as over-sedation and is not necessarily the adequate drugs for the elderly. Therefore, drugs with moderate potency and less side effects are awaited.
Tiapride was demonstrated significantly more effective than sulpiride in improving the disturbed sleep rhythms and delirious state in our controlled study. In our other controlled study, tiapride was proved to be more effective than chlorpromazine especially in the aggressive behaviour, wandering and restlessness with less episodes of a decrease in alertness.

863

THERAPEUTIC EFFECT OF SULTOPRIDE IN MANIA
Atsuyoshi Mori[1], Sadanori Miura[2], Kunitoshi Kamijima[3], Kazuo Hasegawa[4] and Shigeru Kaneno[5]
1) Jikei Univ. Sch. of Med., Tokyo, 2) Kitasato Univ. Sch. of Med., Sagamihara, 3) Kyorin Univ. Sch. of Med., Mitaka, 4) St. Marianna Univ. Sch. of Med., Kawasaki, 5) Tokyo Medical and Dental Univ., Tokyo, Japan

Clinical efficacy and safety of sultopride (ST) for manic patients were studied by a multicenter open trial. Thirty-seven patients were admitted to this trial. A range of a daily dosage was from 150 to 1200 mg and a daily dosage of 300-600 mg was more often employed.
A rate of cases which indicated more than moderate improvement was 48.6% (at 1st week), 70.3% (at 2nd week), 86.5% (at 4th week), 78.4% (at 6th week) and 75.7% (at 8th week). We could find that ST was more effective on manic symptoms such as elevated mood, irritability, psychomotor excitement and flight of ideas and it worked rapidly.
On the side effects, various extrapyramidal symptoms developed with a relatively high incidence. Furthermore, oversedation, drowsiness and conversion into depressed phase were also found more frequently. No significant changes were observed in laboratory examinations.
On utility rating, a rate of patients which showed more than useful was 75.7%, which suggests that an employment value of ST is markedly noticed. It is concluded that ST is as effective in the treatment of mania as lithium carbonte, chlorpromazine or haloperidol.

864

COMPARISON OF THERAPEUTIC EFFECT ON MANIA OF SULTOPRIDE
Yoshio Kudo
Aino Hospital, Ibaragi, JAPAN

The double-blind comparative study was performed using haloperidol(HP) as a reference drug in order to evaluate the anti-manic effect of sultopride (ST) in 77 patients with manic state. The dosage ratio was 1:100(HP:ST). The number of tablets of HP used was significantly more than that of ST in daily maximum, final and mean dose. There was no significant difference in efficacy between the two groups as far as can be determined on an FGIR basis. However, an analysis of individual BPRS items shows that ST was significantly superior with regard to most items relating to psychomotor excitement, while HP was significantly superior with regard to items that express reduction of psychomotor. This is indicative of the characterestics of the two substances.
The ORS results revealed no significant difference between both groups in terms of Safety. However, it should be noted that the incidence of items relating to asthenia and depressive phase was significantly higher in ST. There were few cases of dosage reduction with either substance and there was no cases of discontinuation in ST. These results seem to indicate a high degree of safety.
An U analysis of the GUR indicated that ST was significantly superior to HP.
The résults of these studies seem to indicate that ST is effective as an antimanic drug.

Session 130 Symposium:
Psychodynamic understanding in the individual assessment of disturbances in children and adolescents

865-867

Psychodynamic Understanding in the Individual Assessment of Disturbances in children and Adolescents
Joffe, Ros., Hodges, Jill., Redford P.,
Chid Therapy Section. British Assoc. of Psychotherapists

This symposium will illustrate the contribution which can be made to diagnostic assessment by psychodynamically orrientated individuall interviews with the child or adolescent. Children may living their own conserns and understanding of their situation and problems, which may differ from the views of the adults involved in the referral. A major task of the assesment interviews is to help the child communicate these feelings; this involves techniques of exploration adapted to their developmental level, which facilitates communication via non-verbal means and play where appropriate as well as verbally. Case illustrations will be given of a young child, a child in latency and an adolescent. These will demonstrate some characteristics developmental issues and disturbances some of the techniques of exploration; and some ways of understanding the childs communications within a psychodynamic framework.

Session 131 Symposium:
Culture-bound syndromes and international disease classifications

868

The Place of Culture in Psychiatric Nosology: Taijin Kyofusho and DSM-IIIR.

Laurence J. Kirmayer, M.D.
McGill University

Taijing kyofusho (TKS) is a common Japanese culture-bound syndrome, representing some 7 to 36 percent of psychiatric patient populations. It is characterized by a fear of offending or hurting others through one's awkward social behavior or an imagined physical defect. Although variants of this disorder have been described in other cultures (e.g. dysmorphophobia), the full spectrum appears to be confined to Japan. TKS can be understood as a pathological amplification of culture-specific concerns about the social presentation of self and the impact of improper conduct on the well-being of others. Consideration of the role of social interaction in the cognitive structures that may underlie TKS suggests that the relative importance of culture and biology in psychopathology is not an objective fact but a consequence of a specific clinical perspective. The place of culture in psychiatric nosology differs depending on whether the clinical focus is on disordered biology, individual experience, or the social context of behavior. Thus, any attempt to include cultural variation in psychiatric diagnoses must begin by making explicit the intended use of the classification. Different social contexts and clinical goals demand multiple diagnostic schemes.

869

Descriptively Similar Groups of Culture-Bound Syndromes
Ronald C. Simons, M.D., M.A.
Michigan State University
East Lansing, MI
U.S.A.

It has recently been suggested that the nosological entities usually referred to as culture-bound psychiatric syndromes be included in Western disease classification systems such as DSM and IDC. The occurence of virtually identical syndromes in societies with highly disparate cultures, unrelated historically and widely separated in time and space suggests that descriptions of the constituent behaviors rather than the meanings and values associated with syndromes be used when considering their nosological placements. If culture-bound syndromes are to be included in Western classification systems it is descriptively uniform syndrome groups rather than the individual syndromes themselves that warrant taxonomic placement. Using these syndrome groups has the added advantage of allowing precise placement of isolated single cases of any syndrome which appear in societies lacking marked and named versions of it.

870

SOMATIC COMPLAINT SYNDROMES, DEPRESSION AND DSM-III-R
PRINCE, R. H.
McGILL UNIVERSITY, MONTREAL, CANADA

In many cultures, psychiatric patients do not complain of unpleasant affects such as fear, anger, or sadness, but of bodily complaints such as exhaustion, burning and crawling sensations and variously located pains. A good number of these somatic complaint syndromes have found their way into lists of culture-bound syndromes. This paper describes the examples from Africa and China. Controversy exists both in Africa and China as to whether these syndromes are really depressions in disguise and therefore should be called masked depressions. Regarding their placement in classifications, it is argued that they warrant a distinct somatic complaint category and, when appropriate, additional diagnosis of depression or anxiety should be assigned.

871

ANOREXIA NERVOSA: A CULTURE-BOUND SYNDROME
VF DiNicola; Univ of Ottawa; Canada

The hypothesis that anorexia nervosa (AN) is a culture-bound syndrome (CBS) of developed nations is examined. 5 hypotheses of causation of AN are outlined: 1) biomedical, 2) psychodynamic, 3) family, 4) feminist/social, and 5) CBS/socio-cultural hypotheses. 6 observations comprise the requirements for a comprehensive model and support a CBS approach to AN: 1) female predominance, 2) upper class bias, 3) predominance in developed countries, 4) modern illness with increasing incidence, 5) biological disturbances secondary, and 6) puberty as the key psychobiological trigger event flawed by onset of cases before and after puberty. Problems with the CBS approach are raised: 1) more research required on the ideology of slimness in industrialized nations and its relation to AN; 2) cultural vs. group-genetic differences; and 3) the triggering vs. shaping role of CBS. Implications for classification are discussed, addressing the need to include data on the socio-cultural context of psychiatric illness. "Orphan cases" in atypical contexts challenge the CBS hypothesis and suggest refinements such as the notion of culture-change syndromes.

Session 132 Symposium: EEG mapping in psychiatry

872

COGNITIVE MODE REFLECTED BY MOMENTARY EEG MAP: FUNCTIONAL MICRO-STATES IN THE SUB-SECOND RANGE

D. Lehmann and B.A. Kofmel

Department of Neurology, University Hospital, 8091 Zurich, Switzerland

The momentary functional state of the brain is reflected by the spatial configuration of the scalp-recorded multichannel EEG maps. Different maps indicate different modes or steps of the brain's information processing. Hence, adaptive segmentation of EEG map series into epochs of stable map configuration is expected to yield physiologically defined micro-states, "building blocks of cognition". Adaptive segmentation of spontaneous map series showed mean segment durations of 210 msec, with 50% of the time covered by segments 323 msec or longer. - Different modes of reported thoughts were associated with different segment map configurations, consistant over 20 subjects, examining three dimensions of mentation: Reality-close vs reality-remote thoughts, visual imagery vs. abstract thoughts, emotional vs neutral thoughts. It is to be investigated whether psychotic disturbances of cognition consist of aberrant classes or concatenations or occurrence frequency or durations of these "building blocks" of mentation.

873
EEG TOPOGRAPHIC MAPPING IN SCHIZOPHRENIA AND AFFECTIVE ILLNESS

Monte S. Buchsbaum, Steven Guich, Richard Haier, Erin Hazlett, Chandra Reynolds, Joseph Wu, Steven Potkin and W.E. Bunney, Jr.

Department of Psychiatry and Human Behavior, College of Medicine, University of California, Irvine, CA, USA.

Topographic EEG maps with 32-channel recording were obtained on 40 patients with schizophrenia, 20 patients with affective disorder, and normal controls. Nineteen schizophrenics had never been medicated with neuroleptics. Recordings were made while subjects rested with eyes closed and while subjects did the Continuous Performance Test, a visual vigilance task. Patients with schizophrenia showed relatively higher delta activity in the inferior frontal leads, more marked on the right side. Normals and patients showed a different pattern of delta decrease with task in the frontal lobe. Contrasts with unmedicated affective disorder patients will also be presented.

874
NEUROMETRIC SUBTYPING IN SCHIZOPHRENIA

E. Roy John, L. S. Prichep
NYU Med. Ctr. & NKI, NY NY USA

Neurometric EEG and EP data have been collected from normal subjects and patients with a variety of psychiatric illnesses. Multiple discriminant functions have been constructed which can separate normal from schizophrenic from demented persons. Using cluster analysis methods, it has been possible to identify 5 major subtypes of schizophrenic patients. These subtypes differ with respect to neurometric profile, clinical profile, and response to treatment. Haloperidol responders were restricted to members of 2 of the 5 subtypes. These results raise the perspective of a computerized adjunct to diagnosis and treatment selection in psychiatry.

875
CEEG/DBM, A BIOLOGICAL PREDICTOR FOR OUTCOME OF DRUG TREATMENT

Turan M. Itil, Emin Eralp, and Armida Mucci, New York Medical College, and HZI Research Center, Tarrytown, New York

Based on the findings that all psychotropics produce significant changes in EEG and therapeutically equivalent drugs have similar CEEG profiles, we have established a "Test Dose" procedure to use as biological predictor for outcome. As a first step, the diagnosis of the patient is made and 3-4 drugs as treatment choice are selected. In the second step, in 2-4 day intervals single doses of each of the drugs is administered as the "Test Dose". The CEEG response (profile) of the patient is assessed using CEEG Dynamic Brain Mapping one and three hours after drug administration. The drug which produced the most significant quantitative CNS effects and which according to the data base is most accurately classified is the most bioavailable for this individual patient on the target organ (the brain). The bioavailability is the first requirement for the therapeutic effectiveness of a drug.

876
EEG MAPPING IN DIAGNOSIS AND TREATMENT OF DEMENTIA
B. Saletu, P. Anderer, E. Paulus, J. Grünberger
Department of Psychiatry, University of Vienna
Vienna, Austria

Topographic brain mapping of EEG, CT scans and psychopathometric data were be obtained in 111 mildly to moderately demented patients (77 females, 34 males) with a mean age of 82 years. They were diagnosed according to DSM-III criteria and sub-diagnosed according to CT and Hachinski into 54 SDAT- and 57 MID-patients. SDAT-patients showed slightly to moderately more slow and less alpha-activity as well as a slowing of the dominant frequency (DF) and the centroid (C) than normal controls, while MID-patients exhibited markedly augmented delta/theta and attenuated alpha and beta-activity als well as a slowing of the DF and C. Differences between SDAT and MID patients were found mostly in measures concerning differences between maximum and minimum power and right/left differences in the maps. 67 % of the patients could be correctly classified by such means. Correlation analyses between CT-measures and EEG-variables demonstrated: The greater the anterior horn distance, lateral ventricle distance, and Evans Index and the smaller the anterior horn Index, the more delta/theta activity in the EEG. Moreover, the higher the delta/theta activity, the higher the SCAG score. Common and differential effects of nootropics will be demonstrated.

877
EEG MAPPING and NOOTROPIC DRUG EFFECT in MAN

Walter G Sannita, Guido Rosadini
Institute of Neurophysiopathology, University; Center for Cerebral Neurophysiology, CNR, Genova, Italy; Department of Psychiatry, New York State University, Stony Brook, NY, USA

The quantitative EEG effects of putative nootropic compounds were studied in homogeneous groups of healthy subjects and patients with cognitive impairment due to organic brain pathology. The EEG effects of the compounds which proved active (eg piracetam; phosphatidylserine; l-acetylcarnitine; buflomedil) were comparable, with a significant increase of the alpha activity eventually parallelled by reduction of slow activities. These compounds could however be differenciated by EEG mapping, as the scalp topography of the drug-induced EEG modifications could either match or be independent of the distribution of EEG normal/pathological activities in baseline conditions depending upon the compound administered (eg anterior power increment on alpha frequency range after piracetam). The topography of both EEG activities prior to drug administration and of pathological substrata eventually concurred in defining the distribution of the drug EEG effects. For some compounds these were observed only in peculiar pathological conditions and were not detected upon administration of comparable doses to normal subjects; or were evident only on undamaged or damaged brain areas depending on compound and brain pathology. A correlation between scalp spreading of EEG effects and dose administered was occasionally observed in multidose studies on volunteers. The topographic differences observed in this study question the qualitative similarity of the drug-induced EEG effects and the congruity of these with the "nootropic" hypothesis. Correlations with the pharmacological characteristics or mechanisms of action can be conversely hypothesized.

Session 133 Special Session:
Phototherapy and sleep deprivation in depression

878
PHOTOTHERAPY AND DEPRESSION : CURRENT STATUS OF THE RESEARCH
Salinas, E.O., Hakim-Kreis, C.M.
Centre Hospitalier Sainte-Anne
Clinique des Maladies Mentales et de l'Encéphale
100, rue de la Santé - 75014 PARIS - France

The description of a seasonnal affective discorder (SAD) occurring during the winter and remitting rapidly with bright artificial light has drawn great interest and raised many questions. §-Periodicity of affective disorders. This concept already described in the past on his two-fold (epidemiological and individual) dimensions, founds a greater relevance in SAD (diagnostic criteria of SAD). §-Phototherapy. This new therapeutic approach raises many methodological questions (brightness of light, timing and lenght of light exposure, prevention of relapses). §-Pathophysiology. Three possible mechanisms has been proposed : extension of the photoperiod, phase shifting (phase response curve), total photon's exposure. Many biological variables are discuted : rôle of melatonin, serotonin, hypothalamic - pituitary - adrenal axis, vitamin D, sleep parameters, and other chronobiologic clocks ("zeitgebers"). §Subtype of sensitive patients. Clinical features of SAD and their stability during the course of the illness. This review of the questions raised by the existence of SAD and the hypothetical answers that are herein proposed allows to describe the current understanding of the syndrome and proposes a new frame to formulate further research.

879
LIGHT IN DEPRESSION: DIAGNOSTIC AND THERAPEUTIC STUDIES
B-E Thalén, B F Kjellman, J Beck-Friis, Y Freund-Levi, L Wetterberg
Karolinska Institute, Department of Psychiatry, St. Göran's Hospital, Box 12500,
S-112 81 Stockholm, Sweden

About 40 depressed patients were treated with bright light (350 Candela/m^2) for 10 consecutive days, either between 6-8h in the morning or 18-20h in the evening. Before and after treatment their nightly normal rhythms regarding melatonin, cortisol, prolactin and TSH were examined during one basal night and one night with a "light-test", i.e. one hour light exposure (350 Candela/m^2) between 22 and 23h. Sleep EEG was performed before and after light treatment. The clinical effect of the light therapy was evaluated by two independent raters using the Comprehensive Psychopathological Rating Scale (CPRS) and the Hamilton Rating Scale for depression.
The clinical results of the light therapy will be presented and the clinical effects will be correlated to clinical parameters, the nightly hormonal rhythms before therapy, the changes produced by the light therapy and the result of the "light test" before and after therapy.

880
PHOTOTHERAPY FOR WHICH KIND OF DEPRESSION ?

HAKIM-KREIS, C.M., SALINAS, E.O.
Centre Hospitalier Sainte-Anne
Clinique des Maladies Mentales et de l'Encéphale
100, rue de la Santé - 75014 PARIS - FRANCE -

Sixteen inpatients were treated during three weeks with phototherapy, ten suffered from a seasonal affective disorder (SAD) and six from a recurrent nonseasonal depression (nonSAD). For twelve of them (ten SAD and two nonSAD) depression was associated with hypersomnia, overeating and carbohydrate craving.
The first week, the patients were randomly assigned to two differents kinds of light conditions : (1) white light (3000 lux) and (2) yellow light (300 lux). The second week, the over type of light was administered. The last week one of the two types of light was chosen according to the results of the two previous weeks. Symptoms were regularly quantified using rating scales and eating behaviors daily rated by a dietetician.
After a week or less of 3000 lux treatment, the ten SAD patients showed no longer any sign of depression. Sleep and appetite disorders had also disappeared. For six of them, the improvement remaind after a following week of 300 lux treatment. Among the six nonSAD patients, four showed no sign of improvement. The two who improved under 3000 lux treatment were those who also suffered from hypersomnia and overeating. These last two disorders were also improved by the treatment.
Similar results for SAD patients have already been reported in the litterature but our results also point out the importance of hypersomnia and overeating for the success of phototherapy. This suggest that phototherapy may have a wider range of applicability than previously thought and could for instance be tried in depressions with hypersomnia and overeating.

881

PHOTOTHERAPY IN NON-SEASONAL MAJOR DEPRESSIVE DISORDER
A. Mackert, H.-P. Volz, R.-D. Stieglitz, B. Müller-Oerlinghausen
Department of Psychiatry (Head: Prof. Dr. H. Helmchen), Free University of Berlin, Eschenallee 3, D-1000 Berlin 19 (FRG)

The possible synchronizing effect of bright light exposure in shortened circadian rhythms has found support mainly in reported success of artificial light treatment in patients with seasonal affective disorder. The present study was set up in order to study effects of phototherapy in non-seasonal major depressive disorder. We compared the effects of bright white light (2500 Lux) and dim light (50 Lux) upon 42 patients fulfilling RDC-criteria for major depressive disorder (non-seasonal). During a 7 day period, 21 patients were exposed to bright white light and 21 patients to dim light from 7 to 9 a.m. The severity of depression was assessed with rating scales (Hamilton Depression Scale, CGI, AMDP-System) and through self-rating scales (Complaint-List and Depression Scale by VON ZERSSEN). The data were analysed using a repeated-measurement design (analyses of variance; factor 1: groups, factor 2: day of treatment. No difference was noted between bright light and dim light, though a significant reduction of depressive symptomatology was observed for all patients during the treatment. These results were consistent for both rating and self-rating. The findings are discussed with reference to the phase-advanced theory. Our results do not support the presence of an improved antidepressive effect in bright white light therapy as opposed to dim light in non-seasonal depression.

882

PREDICTION OF SLEEP DEPRIVATION RESPONSE IN DEPRESSED PATIENTS
D. Riemann, M. Wiegand* and M. Berger;
Central Institute of Mental Health, Mannheim and
*Max-Planck Institute of Psychiatry, Munich, FRG

Approximately 60% of endogenously depressed patients show a clear-cut albeit short-lasting improvement of mood following a night of total sleep deprivation (TSD). The present study aimed at evaluating the question whether variables of psychopathology, sleep-EEG parameters and positive diurnal mood variation may predict TSD response.
Methods: 48 depressed inpatients (with major depression; subtype endogenous according to RDC) with a mean age ($\pm$SD) of 46.5 $\pm$ 13.4 yrs. participated in the study. After a wash-out phase of 7 days patients had at least 2 sleep recordings followed by TSD.
Results: 62.5% of the patients reacted favourably to TSD. Response did not correlate with any parameter of psychopathology. Patients with a marked improvement of mood in the evening prior to TSD showed a better response. Patients in the responder group significantly more often exhibited short REM latencies during baseline sleep than non-responders.
Concluding, shortened REM latency and positive diurnal variation of mood are of predictive value for the antidepressive property of TSD.

883

SLEEP DEPRIVATION AS A METHOD OF TREATMENT AND PSYCHOPROPHYLAXIS IN RECURRENT AFFECTIVE ILLNESS
G.N. Papadimitriou, G.N. Christodoulou
Athens University, Dept. of Psychiatry, Eginition Hospital, Athens, Greece

Total (36 hours) sleep deprivation (SD) has been suggested to have a favorable, but transient, mood-elevating effect in affective illness. In order to investigate its therapeutic and possible psychoprophylactic effect, 19 drug-free endogenous depressive patients were totally sleep deprived, twice a week, for four weeks. Sixteen patients terminated the program (five with excellent, three with satisfactory and eight with minimal response) and six of them entered the psychoprophylactic program, once a week (four with excellent response, whilst two terminated the program prematurely). Additionally, five normothymic drug-free patients with affective illness were treated prophylactically with SD, without prior therapeutic treatment with this method. (Three patients showed excellent response, one discontinued his SD sessions and one patient failed to respond). The majority of patients who responded to treatment and prophylaxis were rapid cycler female patients.

884

CNS REGULATION OF NEUROENDOCRINE CHANGES DURING SLEEP DEPRIVATION
A.Baumgartner, A.Campos-Barros, S.Diekmann
Psychiatrische Klinik, FU Berlin, FRG

Depressed patients showed the following changes in hormone secretion during total sleep deprivation (TSD): TSH, thyroid hormones, and cortisol secretion increased, prolactin and testosterone levels fell. The changes in TSH and cortisol were correlated to clinical response. We, therefore, investigated the influence of different receptor antagonist on TSD induced endocrine patterns: TSH and cortisol were measured every 20 minutes during a night of sleep deprivation and 8 nights of TSD in 6 healthy men. During TSD, the following receptor agonists were administered orally at midnight: 1. placebo, 2. prazosin (alpha1), 3. yohimbine (alpha 2), 4. propanolol (ß1/ß2), 5. betaxolol (ß1), 6. methysergid (5HT), 7. biperiden (M1), 8. clonidine.
Results: TSD-induced raises in TSH were prevented by betaxolol, cortisol increases were inhibited by prazosin and by the two betablockers. This suggests that TSD-induced changes in hormone secretion (and possibly also the clinical effect) are -at least in part- due to enhanced beta1 and/or alpha1 adrenergic activity.

Session 134 Special Session:
Schizophrenia: Disturbances of thought and affect

885
THOUGHT DISTURBANCES IN SCHIZOPHRENIA.

BEAUFILS B., MATHIS P., HARDY P., FELINE A.
Hôpital de Bicêtre. Le Kremlin-Bicêtre. FRANCE

We studied different thought disturbances, audible thinking (at), thought echo (te) and thought blockade (tb), among a population of psychiatric patients, diagnosed according to DSM III R, 31 schizophrenic (SP) and 70 non schizophrenic patients (non SP).
We used an open standardised questionnaire to record the presence or absence of these symptoms and to describe their distinctive features. Audible thinking is defined as hearing one's own thoughts in the form of sounds. Thought blockade is the subjective feeling of a sudden and brief interruption in the train of thoughts. Main results were as follows (pat=permanent at, sens and spec denote sensitivity and specificity) :

	SP	non SP	p	sens	spec
at	24/29	14/63	<0,0001	83 %	78 %
pat	14/29	4/63	<0,0001	48 %	94 %
tb	13/27	4/65	<0,0001	48 %	94 %
te	11/28	8/65	<0,01	39 %	88 %

In conclusion, these symptoms are frequent though seldom reported by patients ; they are quite specific for schizophrenia ; besides, audible thinking often seem to be a permanent feature, present long before the clinical onset of the disease and likely to persist. Therefore audible thinking could well be a trait marker.

886
OBJECTIVE BEHAVIORAL ANALYSIS OF NEGATIVE SYMPTOMS IN SCHIZOPHRENIA
Wolfgang Gaebel, Psychiatrische Klinik u. Poliklinik der Freien Universität Berlin, Eschenallee 3, D-1000 Berlin 19 (West)
Negative symptoms are a clinical clue to biological subtyping of schizophrenia. However, their exact definition by objective behavioral measures is still lacking. This prospective study refers to these research questions.
Methods: 100 acute schizophrenics (RDC) either with or without negative symptoms (SANS) are randomly assigned to a 4-weeks-treatment either with haloperidol or perazine. After 4 weeks those patients with persisting or newly developed negative symptoms are switched to clozapine for another 4 weeks. Thereafter half of the patients with persisting negative symptoms are randomly assigned to an additional social skills training for up to another 3 months. This sequential design serves to identify those patients at risk for developing or maintaining negative symptoms in the post-acute treatment phase. 50 depressives (RDC) and 50 normals are included als controls. - For behavioral analysis audio-visual assessment takes place at admission and 4, 8 and 20 weeks thereafter. Facial action, gestures, gaze, speech and voice characteristics are recorded under standardized conditions and subjected to offline analysis.
Results: Design, measurement techniques and preliminary results of this study will be presented at the congress.
Conclusions: The aim of this study is to identify a behavioral risk pattern as an objective correlate of clinically rated negative symptoms. By answering the questions of nosological specificity, time stability and treatment responsivity the study results will contribute to an objective definition of "primary" negative symptoms as rooted in the brain pathology of schizophrenia.

887
Typology of Defect in Schizophrenia

Anatoliy B. Smulevich
Research Institute of Clinical Psychiatry

An integrate model of schizophrenic defect is proposed, which is represented at the psychopathological level by a unity of psychopathy-like and pseudoorganic manifestations; their proportion determines the typological heterogeneity of negative disorders. From the clinical point of view these disorders are ranged in accordance with hypertypical or hypotypical disintegration of personality; it reflects the main tendencies of the pathological process: persistent active character - fading. In the first type defect psychopathy-like changes of "verschrobene" type prevail; they are exhibited by way of pseudoorganic changes (personality decline). In the second type defect pseudoorganic changes of simple deficit type prevail; they affect the structure of psychopathy-like changes (schizoid personality). Clinical and genetic data prove that despite a high level of genotype similarity, the systems of susceptibility to the types of defect mentioned, include heterogenic constitutional genetic factors. The results of research are confirmed by the data of the computerized tomography of probands and their families.

888
SLOWNESS IS NOT A GENERALIZED DEFICIT IN SCHICOPHRENIC PATIENTS WITH NEGATIVE SYMPTOMS
Steinwachs K.C.[1], Lehfeld H.[2], Erzigkeit H.[2]
[1]Bezirkskrankenhaus Erlangen, Am Europakanal 71 und
[2]Psychiatrische Klinik der Universitat Erlangen - Nurnberg, Schwabachanlage 6 und 10, 8520 Erlangen, F.R.G.

Using a dichoptic backward masking procedure intended to measure speed of central information processing of visual stimuli 20 hospitalized schizophrenic patients with negative symptoms were compared to 20 subjects with psychiatric disorders other than schizophrenia and 20 normals. Schizophrenic patients were diagnosed according to ICD-9 and DSM-III criteria of schizophrenia.
Negative symptom ratings were based on SANS. The groups under investigation were paralleled in age, mean age between 25 and 20 years. Speed of input processing was correlated to writing pressure and speed parameters as measures for output performance.
Results show that medicated schizophrenics although not retarded in speed of visual perception clearly demonstrate a reduced rate of motor output. This indicates that slowness may not be considered to be an overall impairment in schizophrenia rather a task-specific deficit.

889

SOCIO-CULTURAL INFLUENCES ON SCHIZOPHRENIC DELUSIONS-COMPARATIVE STUDY
Hideyuki FUJIMORI, Zhan Pei ZHENG
Tokyo Metropolitan Bokutoh General Hospital/Japan
Shanghai Psychiatric Hospital/People's Republic of China

A comparative cross-cultural psychiatric study was performed in order to evaluate the theme of delusions experienced today by schizophrenics in Japan and China, related to their socio-cultural background. The data of this study was derived from the public mental hospitals on a similar scale in Tokyo and Shanghai. The data base was comprised of first-admission schizophrenic cases in each hospital-Tokyo in the period 1981-1983 and Shanghai 1983-(Tokyo: 186 cases=male/female 88/98; Shanghai:200 cases=male/female:112/88), and the analysis was focused on those cases with delusions (male/female: 53/59 in Tokyo; male/female: 70/59 in Shanghai).

The incidence of delusions of physical persecution and of grandeur was relatively high in Tokyo and Shanghai, while the incidence of delusions with hypochondria and guilt was low. The incidence of delusion of poisoning was significantly higher in Shanghai than in Tokyo ($X^2=12.97$, $p<0.001$).

These findings will be discussed from a comparative psychiatric point of view.

890

Depressive syndromes in schizophrenic patients after discharge from the hospital

BANDELOW B[*], MÜLLER P[*], GAEBEL W, KÖPCKE W, LINDEN M, MÜLLER-SPAHN F, PIETZCKER A, TEGELER J - ANI Study Group Berlin, Düsseldorf, Göttingen, Munich

[*]Department of Psychiatry, University of Göttingen, Federal Republic of Germany

314 schizophrenic outpatients who were stabilized for 3 months on continuous neuroleptic therapy after discharge from the hospital were rated according to 3 different scales for depressive syndromes (BPRS anxiety/depression factor, AMDP/depression, and the self-rating PD-S depression scale).
There were low, but significant correlations between social and sexual adjustment scores and depression scores on the self-rating scale, whereas no correlations were found with the psychiatrists' ratings.
High depression scores as rated by the psychiatrists correlated with scales for global psychopathological assessment (CGI, GAS).
Patients who, in spite of neuroleptic treatment, were still suffering from psychotic symptoms in the last 4 weeks prior to evaluation scored higher on all 3 depression scales.
There were significant correlations between extrapyramidal side effects and depression scores which confirm the 'akinetic depression' hypothesis. Concomitant anti-Parkinson medication had no influence on depression scores.
These results will be interpreted on the basis of hypotheses about postpsychotic depression syndromes.

891

POSTSCHIZOPHRENIC DEPRESSION: A CLINICAL STUDY
O. Bastos
Professor of Psychiatry a the Pernambuco Faculty of Medical Sciences of FESP. President and Pro Tempore Rector of FESP. Senior Lecture at the Centre of Health Sciences of the Federal University of Pernambuco - UFPE.

The author presents a study on postschizophrenic depression, considered as a depressive syndrome following the end of a episode of schizophrenic psychosis, integrating its evolutive course. Out of a total of 74 patients, 20 showed depressive epidoses clearly identified as postschizophrenic depression, constituting the standard group (Group A), consisting of 15 males and 5 female patients. A control group (Group B) without postschizophrenic depression, taken from the same source, was matched in relation to age and sex with the standard one. The most expressive results favouring the PSD group appeared in the items depressive mood, feelings of functional incapacity and/or uselessness and late insomia. The others also considered as statistically significant in favour of the depressive group were: psychomotor retardation; slownesse of thought; awareness of their own morbid condition; feeling of helplessness; feeling of ruin and/or hopelessness; ideas of incurability; desire for social isolation; loss of appetite for food, loss of sexual desire; daily oscillation in the sumptomatology and suicidal threats or ideas. Significative differences favouring the PSD group were obtained in relation to the abrupt onset of the psychosis, evolution by episodic attacks, delusional clinical form, presence of manic symptoms in the primitive psychosis, family history of affective disorders and a good prognosis. The presence of

Session 135 Special Session: Alzheimer's disease

892

GENETIC DIFFERENCES BETWEEN PRESENILE AND SENILE ALZHEIMER'S DISEASE
J. Constantinidis
University of Geneva, "Morphological Psychopathology"
Bel-Air, 1225 Geneva, Switzerland

1. Among siblings and parents of 326 proband AD in-cases (Psychiatric University Hospital of Geneva, 97 Presenile : P, and 326 Senile : S) the incidence of AD in-cases is 4 to 10 times higher than in general population. If we take in account also the anamnestic cases, the incidence of AD is 10 to 30 times higher than in general population. For our proband AD cases, in the majority S, the incidence of AD is identical among parents and siblings. For SJOGREN's proband cases (1952), in the majority P, the incidence of AD is higher among parents than among siblings . These findings agree with the hypothesis of a dominant mode for ADP and recessive for ADS.
2. The histological study of 60 elderly brains belonging to 28 families (in one or two generations) and the comparative statistical analysis showed a significant concordance ($P >0.01$) for Neurofibrillary Tangles (NFT), senile plaques (SP) and Dyshoric Angiopathy (DYS) , in sibpairs but not in pairs parent-offspring. These findings agree with the hypothesis of a recessive genetic factor for these lesions in the senium.
3. In one third of families with 2 or more cases of AD (histologically verified) coexist P and S cases. These observations may be explained by the recent findings that the 21 chromosome gene for AD (i.e. a duplication of the areas AM-SOD) may be modulated by facilitatory or inhibitory factors on chromosomes 6 and 16, this modulation being responsible for the dominant (presenile) or recessive (senile) expression.

893

NEUROFIBRILLARY DEGENERATION IN MYELINATED AXONS OF ALZHEIMER'S DISEASE
Tzimos Andreas, Institute of Psychiatry, London, U.K.

Autopsy specimens of ten brains from patients with Alzheimer's disease (AD), have been studied by electron microscopy for 18nm paired helical filaments (PHF) and 15nm straight filaments (SF) in myelinated axons of hippocampus. Brains from ten age-matched controls were also used in the study. Diagnosis of AD was based on clinical history and confirmed histologicaly by light microscopy (numerous tangles and plaques in frontal and temporal cortex). In controls, only the strata radiatum and pyramidale of cornu ammonis presented a small number of myelinated axons with PHF. In AD brains, axons in fibria were free of abnormal fibrilar material. In alveus and stratum lacunosum-moleculare, a moderate number of axons contained PHF, but in strata pyramidale and radiatum a significant portion of myelinated axons contained both, PHF and SF. In addition, in strata pyramidale and radiatum, largely distented myelinated axonal segments have been seen filled with PHF and SF, forming huge intraxonal neurofibrillary tangles (NFT). The presence of PHF and SF in the axons of AD is an indication of possible disruption of axon transport mechanisms, while the presence of axonal NFT suggests a block of this transport. Thus in AD neurons, besides the biochemical shortages, seems to exist a structural lesion, which further reduces neuronal communication.

894

Clinical Heterogeneity of Alzheimer Type

Svetlana I. Gavrilova
All-Union Mental Health Research Center

Variability of clinical manifistations, the course and morphofunctional implications of Alzheimer type dementia have been studied on elderly inpatient cohort. By employing longitudinal clinical psychopathological, neuropsychological and computer tomography methodology it was possible to establish significant variations between the groups of Alzheimer disease (AD) and senile dementia (SDAT) patients in terms of the patient at the onset of the disease, its duration and progressing rate; patients constitutional characteristics as well as psychopathological structure of dementia and its initial symptoms.

The clinical variations in question are in good agreement with the variations of neuropsychological syndrome of higher mental functions disorders in BA and SDAT as well as the differences in the structure and topography of anatomy changes in the brain that were substantiated by computer tomography data. The established differences in clinical and morphofunctional characteristics of BA and SDAT suggest definite clinical subtypes in the framework of Alzheimer type dementia.

895

Single Photon Emission Tomography (SPET) in Alzheimer's Disease (AD)

A. Burns, M. Philpot, D.C. Costa, P. Ell, R. Levy, Institute of Psychiatry and Institute of Nuclear Medicine, London, U.K.

Twenty patients satisfying standard clinical criteria for Alzheimer's disease (AD) and six age-matched normal controls were studied using 99m Tc hexamethyl- propyleneamine oxime and single photon emission tomography. The AD patients had lower regional cerebral blood flow (rCBF) in the temporal and posterior parietal lobes compared to controls. AD patients with apraxia and aphasia had lower rCBF in the lateral temporal and posterior parietal lobes than AD patients without these features. Within the AD group, correlations were found between neuropsychological tests and rCBF: praxis correlated with posterior parietal activity, memory with left temporal lobe activity and language with activity throughout the left hemisphere.

896

ALZHEIMER'S DISEASE AND MULTI-INFARCT DEMENTIA: DIFFERENCES IN TRANSCRANIAL DOPPLER SONOGRAPHY
S. Biedert, J. Förstl[*], and W. Hewer[*]
Psych. Landeskrankenhaus, 6908 Wiesloch, [*] and Zentralinstitut f. Seel. Gesundheit, Mannheim, FRG

We have determined the relative end-diastolic flow velocities (modified Pourcelot indices) of the basal cerebral arteries of 58 individuals aged 60 to 70 years - 27 controls, 17 patients with dementia of Alzheimer type (DAT), and 14 with multi-infarct dementia (MID) - by means of transcranial Doppler sonography (EME TC2-64B). Patients - with a course of the illness of at least two years - were ascribed to DAT and MID subgroups according to NINCDS-ADRDA and DSM-III-R criteria, respectively, and the severity of dementia was estimated through mini-mental state examinations. Hemodynamically efficacious extracranial stenoses of the brain-supplying arteries - as determined by extracranial directional c-w Doppler sonography - served as exclusion criterion. We found statistically significant differences ($2p < 0.005$) in the modified Pourcelot indices of the basilar arteries - 0.47 ± 0.041 (controls), 0.47 ± 0.040 (DAT), and 0.34 ± 0.052 (MID) -, of the middle cerebral arteries - 0.46 ± 0.034 (controls), 0.45 ± 0.049 (DAT), and 0.33 ± 0.029 (MID) -, and, to a lower extent ($2p < 0.01$), of the anterior cerebral arteries. Due to overlapping of the distributions of the data of both patient subsets, we consider a positive diagnosis of MID on the basis of transcranial Doppler findings likely only in the event of a reduction of the corresponding modified Pourcelot index of at least two standard deviations with respect to age-matched controls. We found no correlation between the severity of multi-infarct dementia and the sonographic criteria.

897

EFFECT OF CINEPAZIDE ON INTERHEMISPHERIC
DISCORDANCE IN DEMENTIA
Yasusuke Aoki,M.D*,Naosuke Aoki,M.D*
Hiroshi Miyawaki,B.A*,Masaharu Miyagawa,B.A*
Tetsuo Fukuda,M.D**
*Shiga Institute of Psychiatry,Setagawa Hospital,
 Ohtsu,Japan
**Doshisha University,Kyoto,Japan

Effects of cinepazide,which is supposed to improve
cerebral circulation,on the frequency of EEG power
spectrum and on clinical-behavioral activities
were evaluated in 12 patients with senile dementia
of Alzheimer type. Recording of EEGs was made at
six Specified sites,i.e. F3,F4,C3,C4,O1 and O2
(10-20 method) prior to and one month after
medication of cinepazide (daily dosis of 600 mg
per os). Classification of EEG power spectrum
array of theta and alpha bands into seven
frequency bands enabled to detect with a high
sensitivity the chages in each band power. Total
alpha band powers differed between the hemisphers
and were dominant in the right before medication;
the dominancy then sifted to the left at
occipital area after medication. The sift was
remarkable on slow alpha band. Cinepazide
treatment also reduced significantly the
interhemispheric discordance of total theta band
powers at the frontal area and fast theta band
powers at the central area. Improvement of
behavioral abnormality as objectively evaluated by
means of some scales took place along with such
changes in EEG power spectrum.

898

ALZHEIMER'S DISEASE, AGECAT, INCIDENCE AND SIX
YEAR OUTCOME IN LIVERPOOL

Authors: J R M Copeland, I A Davidson,
            M E Dewey, V Sharma, P Saunders et al

            Dept. of Psychiatry,
            Institute of Human Ageing,
            University of Liverpool, PO Box 147,
            Liverpool L69 3BX.

A random sample of 1070 persons aged over 65
living at home was examined using the Geriatric
Mental State, and psychological tests. Selected
samples were re-examined by psychiatrists and
the AGECAT computer diagnosis applied to the
whole sample. Three years later, 702 survivors
were re-examined by psychiatrists using the
same measures including the History and
Aetiology Schedule. The computerised diagnosis
establishes a consistent standard of diagnosis
which allows the most accurate estimation of
change over time. Prevalence of dementia at
Year 0 was 5.2% and depression of all kinds
11.3%. At Year 3, overall mortality was 5.6%
per year, greater amongst those with dementia
and male depressives. Less than half mild
depressives had recovered. A year incidence
rate of 0.96% was found for dementia as a
whole. The computer method has identified one-
third of the new cases as sub-cases at Year 0.
Four, five and six year follow-up will be
reported.

Session 136   Symposium:
Cognitive psychotherapy with difficult patients

899

Treatment of Cognitive Disorders in Schizophrenia: Approaches and
Results

Brenner H.D., Hodel B.
Psychiatrische Universitätsklinik Bern/Switzerland

In rehabilitation of schizophrenic patients cognitive treatment,
in the sense of therapeutic interventions on disordered atten-
tional/perceptual and cognitive processes has been noticed only
recently.
Actual treatment approaches tackling such disorders of information processing, concern either direct or indirect interventions
on cognitive disorders. Direct interventions - like dichotic
listening - aim at attentional/perceptual disorders. Indirect
interventions - like training of self-instruction or of molar
interpersonal skills - reduce cognitive disorders by improving
social skills.
We developed an Integrated Psychological Therapy Program (IPT)
for schizophrenic patients which includes both direct and
indirect interventions, carried out with "reality-related"
materials. It is based on the assumption that improvements on
attentional/perceptual and cognitive disorders have positive
pervasive effects on more complex behavioral deficits. IPT
consists of five subprograms (Cognitive Differentiation, Social
Perception, Verbal Communication, Social Skills, Interpersonal
Problem Solving) in which patients first work on improving
attentional/perceptual and cognitive processes. Finally, patients
are trained in skills to overcome social dilemmas preventing goal
attainment.

Results of the main studies concerned with these different
approaches are discussed for the importance and limitations of
cognitive treatment procedures in schizophrenia.

900

BEHAVIOR AND PROBLEM ANALYSIS IN THE
THERAPEUTICAL PROCESS WITH PSYCHIATRIC
PATIENTS
Roder V. - Psychiatrische Universitätsklinik, Bern,
Switzerland

901

STUDY ON COGNITIVE VS SOCIAL SKILLS TRAINING IN CHRONIC SCHIZOPHRENICS.

Möller, H.-J., Krämer, S., Zinner, H.J.

Psychiatric Department of the Technical University Munich and Psychiatric Department of the University Bonn

Behaviour therapy in schizophrenic patients seems to be successful, especially social skills training combined with cognitive training. The question of differential and specific effects of these two approaches is not answered yet. - 43 chronic schizophrenic patients of a psychosocial rehabilitation centre were randomized allocated to two groups. The patients of the cognitive therapy group underwent a training with different cognitive materials (verbal, non-verbal), a training in discrimination of social situations and a problem-solving program. The patients of the social skills training performed exercises of different social situations. This behaviour therapy approach, lasting about 4 months, was integrated in a complex rehabilitation program. The therapeutic result was measured by a large battery of standardized ratings and test procedures. - According to the preliminary result, the expected differential effects could not be demonstrated. There was, in general, a tendency to better results in the cognitive training group. But a final conclusion can only be drawn after a more sophisticated data evaluation.

902

COGNITIVE THERAPY OF PERSONALITY DISORDERS
Arthur Freeman
University of Medicine and Dentistry of New Jersey
Department of Psychiatry, School of Osteopathic Medicine

The personality disorder is probably one of the most striking examples of Beck's idea of schema. These schema may be personal, cultural, religious, or gender related schema and develop through the interactive processes of assimilation and accomodation. Some schema do not mature and are maintained at an earlier level of development and continue to be inappropriately applied during later, more demanding times.

Schema are reinforced or modeled by parents, or are reinforced by the society. Therapy with Axis II patients is difficult because the treatment will evoke high levels of anxiety. The individual is being asked to step out of the well established pattern and to therefore become vulnerable.

The therapist has several options of what might be done to work with the schema and may be viewed as part of a continuum of change. 1)schematic restructuring, i.e. deciding to tear down the old structure and build a new structure in its place; 2) schematic modification, i.e. smaller changes to the basic manner of responding to the world; 3) schematic re-interpretation, i.e. helping the patient to understand and reinterpret their lifestyle in more functional ways; and 4) Schematic camouflage, i.e. helping the patient to gain skills at covering the basic affective or instrumental propensity to appear more functional. The most reasonable goal when working with an Axis II patient is to either modify or reinterpret the schema. By schematic modification or reinterpretation the therapist can find ways of the patient dealing with their schema in more adaptive and functional ways.

903

COGNITIVE, DELUSIONAL AND EMOTIONAL ASPECTS OF COMMUNICATION WITH THE PSYCHOTIC
G.De Luca, M.C.Gislon, G.C.Zapparoli

With this present study we intend to emphasize above all that the pathologic psychotic shows a "resistance to change" peculiar for its intensity and tenacious respect to that found in other psycho-pathologic forms and which refers to certain of its aspects both structural and dynamic. Secondly, we intend to present the hypothesis that the psychotic subject expresses his characteristics and specific needs through such resistance to change. Thirdly, we intend to underline how little are these needs and characteristics taken into consideration by people working in the psychiatric field, in so far as this would mean becoming participants of the emotional world of the subject; an experience highly disturbing, which renders the task of identification somewhat difficult. Finally, this study aims to demonstrate how the task of people working in the psychiatric field could be facilitated by considering separately three distinct ways of communicating with a psychotic subject: a) the cognitive level, b) the delusional level and c) the emotional level and the process of integration that they establish within these levels.

904

INTEGRATING COMPONENTS IN A COMPREHENSIVE COGNITIVE TREATMENT PROGRAM FOR PATIENTS WITH A SCHIZOPHRENIC DISORDER
Perris C, Thoresson P, Skagerlind L, Warburton E, Gustavsson H, Johansson T
Department of Psychiatry, Umeå University, Sweden.

From a cognitive therapeutic perspective, schizophrenic disorders are conceived as a heterogeneous group of multidetermined morbid conditions which share some common features but also show marked interindividual differences. In addition, a wide range of social handicaps greatly contribute to the global disability of patients labelled as 'schizophrenic'. Hence, both a treatment exclusively based on biological assumptions and a treatment with an exclusive emphasis on intrapsychic processes are to be regarded as unnecessarily reductionistic.
Since 1986 a comprehensive treatment program for young patients with a schizophrenic disorder has been developed at Umeå. The program, carried out at three small, community-based treatment centres, comprises milieutherapy, grouptherapy-sessions, individual therapy, interventions with the families, and appropriate medication whenever required and is based on cognitive-behavioural therapy principles. The focus is on the identification and eventually correction of basic dysfunctional assumptions about the self in the patients participating in the program. Within such a framework, each therapeutic intervention has an interrelated effect with the aim of achieving a successively higher level of integrating in the patients.

905

COGNITIVE PSYCHOTHERAPY WITH MANIC PATIENTS. PRELIMINARY EXPERIENCES.
Linge E
Department of Psychiatry, Umeå University, Sweden.

Patients suffering from a bipolar, manic depressive disorder and especially those presenting with mainly manic episodes, are less frequently considered for intensive psychotherapy, even though notable exceptions do obviously occur. Among the reasons for such a neglect, there is the evidence for a marked biological component in the occurrence of manic disorders, the fact that manic episodes, as a rule do respond well to pharmacological treatment without leaving any appreciable impairment, and the fact that most manic patients seem to be less motivated to psychotherapeutic work when the morbid episode is over. It is also still largely unknown to what extent psychotherapeutic interventions add to the overall improvement obtainable with drugs and which therapeutic strategy is the most appropriate to achieve a further improvement. Against this background, studies of the use of psychotherapy with manic patients are still badly needed.
In this paper a cognitive psychotherapeutic approach to a small series of patients suffering from a manic disorder will be reported. Although the findings cannot be regarded but as very preliminary, the results of the uncontrolled study to be reported seem to be encouraging. A mapping of the patients' dysfunctional cognitions and a first attempt at a reconstruction of their possible development, suggest avenues for further research.

Session 137 Symposium:
Perspectives in monitoring serum levels of perphenazine. A way to improve quality of life

906

SCHIZOPHRENIA: TREATING THE DISABILITY, NOT THE PERSON
Per Bech
Hillerød General Hospital, DK 3400 Hillerød

The concept of quality of life (discomfort) in psychosomatic research has focused on items like function in daily life, productivity and performance of social roles rather than on the biomedical approach to disability (Bech, 1987). In anxiety disorders and in mood disorders it has been shown (Bech, 1988) that disability and discomfort reflect different aspects of outcome of treatment.
In schizophrenia, however, the dynamic structure of psychotic disability must be considered as the most important dimension (e.g. as defined by BPRS) by which progress or lack of it in response to treatment is measured (Andersen et al., 1988). The subdivision of the psychotic disability into positive and negative symptoms might be useful. However, it is of greater interest to define schizothymia which is considered as the dimension of schizophrenia without psychotic disability. Since this dimension includes anhedonia as its most important item it is difficult to apply the traditional quality of life scales in schizothymia. The structure of depression is different from the structure of schizothymia. Treating schizophrenia is the art of treating psychotic and non-psychotic disability without side effects. The halo effect of quality of life is the capacity of the patient to live alone.

907

OPTIMAL SERUM CONCENTRATION RANGE FOR PERPHENAZINE (TRILAFON).
LARSEN, NIELS-ERIK AND HANSEN, LARS B.
Clinical Pharmacological Laboratory, Glostrup University Hospital, DK-2600 Glostrup (Denmark).

Clinical studies including 385 psychotic patients treated with perphenazine or perphenazine decanoate have revealed excellent therapeutic outcome associated with serum concentrations of perphenazine above 2 nmol/l concomitant with a low risk of provoking extrapyramidal side effects with serum concentrations below 6 nmol/l.

In another study including 52 psychotic patients treated with perphenazine decanoate it was shown that the sum of two measurements of the perphenazine concentration early during treatment at day 14 and 21 correlates nicely (r=0.96) to the steady state serum level obtained after 3 months. Consequently, a nomogram has been constructed to read out the dose and the lenght of the dose interval to ensure a serum concentration of perphenazine about 4 nmol/l, i.e. in the middle of the therapeutic range, after 3 months of treatment.

908

CONSUMPTION OF ANTIPSYCHOTIC MEDICINE IN A HOSPITAL DEPARTMENT
P. Kragh-Sørensen, E. Andersen, K. Brøsen, F. Gerholt, P. Glue, M. Hørder, C.S. Kjeldsen, N.A. Klitgaard, G. Krarup, N.-E. Larsen, P. Rask.
Odense University Hospital, DK 5000 Odense C

In controlled clinical investigations a good antipsychotic effect has been found with serum perphenazine concentrations over 1.5 nmol/l, while the risk of neurological side effects is slight with serum concentrations $\leq$ 6 nmol/l. Clinical, financial and organizational aspects of these findings have been sought evaluated in a cost-effectiveness investigation. The investigation has been carried out in an ordinary psychiatric department (112 beds, 2000 admissions yearly, catchment area 250.000 people).
The patient material consisted of 594 patients undergoing neuroleptic treatment (peroral/parenteral) According to the research protocol, 185 persons entered the investigation. The dosage was adjusted after 10-14 days' treatment. All patients were sought placed within a serum concentration range of 2-6 nmol/l perphenazine. 75% of the patients showed good to moderate therapeutic effect. In the period consumption of neuroleptics and anticolinergics (DDD/1000 ptt.) was reduced by about 50% and total expenses for medicines was reduced by 20%.

909

CLINICAL AMELIORATION FOLLOWING PERPHENAZINE SERUM CONCENTRATION MONITORING

F. Haffner M.D. Lab. Neurochemistry and Pharmacology Dept. Psych. Buskerud County Hospital, Lier, Norway

53 hospitals submitted 431 sera from 292 patients. 151 (52%) of all serum values were above the recommended (2-6 nmol/l). Thirteen revealed massive doses or interfering substances. 108 patients (36%) were within the terapeutic range recommended. 34 (12%) were below, of these six were suspected for non complience.
We received new samples from 83 patients. Fortyone patients had lower perphenazine concentration in the second serum sample. Twelve of these improved clinically; four had less adverse effects and ten had better antipsychotic effect. Twentyfour were unchanged. Three got worse, and we lacked information on two.
The mean serum concentrations before and after improvement in the twelve patients were 23 and 7 nmol/l respactively. Those who got worse had 5 and 2 nmol/l. One responded immediately upon increased dosage.
Neuroleptic drugs used in our hospital fell from about 200 daily doses in 1984 to 157 in 1987. Only three out of 41 patients became worse and twelve improved. This indicates that the chance of amelioration may be good upon reduction of high perphenazine doses.

Session 138 Symposium:
Lern und Schulstörungen bei Kindern und Jugendlichen

910

Lern - und Schulstörungen bei Kindern und Jugendlichen

Introduction

Gerhardt Nissen
Kinder- u. Jugendpsychiatrie Univ. Würzburg

Among the problems parents have with their children, disturbances of learning and difficulties at school take the first place. Since the entrance into professions, not only into technical schools and universities, only depends on success at school, the number of children presenting with learning difficulties has risen sharply. In the past, when exclusively genetic factors seemed to be responsible for certain talents resignation and therapeutic nihilism dominated. Today, as emotional disturbances and social deficits have been recognized as severe impairments for motivation of learning, this often results in an unjustified therapeutic optimism displayed by parents and teachers. Psychiatric diagnostics has to consider etiological and descriptive phenomena equally in order to arrive at a promising - often complex psychodynamic, behaviourally and pharmakologically oriented scheme of therapy.

911

Overtaxing structures among school failures

H.-J. Friese, G.-E. Trott, G. Nissen
Kinder- und Jugendpsychiatrie der Univ. Würzburg

The desire for a good school education leads with increasing frequency to overtaxing syndromes among children. Symptoms, structure dynamics and psychopathological peculiarities of cognitively overtaxed children will be discussed with examples of short-term and chronically progressing overtaxing. The peculiarities of psychic and biological effects of findings such as differentiation of stimuli, memory, vigilance and motorics are presented. Besides the depressive, aggressive and anancastic school failure child, the "pseudo-debile child" is characterized in an empiric examination with learning test methods.

912

Emotional disturbances during school time

D. Bürgin/ D. Biebricher
Kinder- und Jugendpsychiatrischer Dienst der Universtät Basel

Emotional disturbances during the period of primary and secondary school are quite frequent. Preexisting, latent intrapsychic conflicts may become manifest through the normative forces on the schoolsystem. Besides this, school as an institution may create certain emotional troubles in children, which tend to remain stable through many years, as e.g. the feeling of not being accepted. Group dynamics and the skills of the teaching staff play thereby an eminent role. The expectations of the parents and their attitudes toward the school have partially a protective partially a damaging effect. School as an institution in the sense of a possibility for living/learning experiences and for the limitation of disturbing factors has also a preventive task, expecially in the field of narcissistic and depressive illnesses of children.

913

Hyperacktive children at school.

Götz-Erik Trott, H.-J. Friese

Hyperactive children are very disturbing in school and they are a great burden for the teacher. On the other hand these children are very impaired by their motoric restlessness. Secondary neuroticisms and social maladjustment often result.

Teachers, parents and in some cases children themselves urge the doctor to take remedial measures. In some countries psychostimulant drugs are prescribed very liberally - in others very restrictively. In both cases it can be assumed that a thorough child and adolescent psychiatric examination was not done.
Motoric restlessness in school does not automatically permit the diagnose of an ADDH to be made. Other causes must be considered in differential diagnostics. In the case of ADDH the administration of psychostimulant durgs has proved its worth. But a dramatic succes cannot be achieved in al cases. Numerous pedagogic measures have to be taken also which in addition to medication prove to be effective.

914

The conduct disordered child in school

M.H. Schmidt
Central Insitute of Mental Health,
Mannheim, FRG

Learning disorders can be as well the cause as the results of conduct disorders. Learning disorders promote the development of dissocial behavior and in return dissocial disorders are associated with factors promoting learning disorders (e.g., specific developmental delays, low parental educational levels, chronic fights, family size, dissocial behavior of sibling). Models regarding learning disorders as cause and as result for conduct disorders are discussed with reference to empirical results of a cohort study with 8 to 13-year-old children. Dissocial behavior is known to be rather stable, hence it calls for long-term therapeutical efforts. The same applies to learning disorders. In view of the bad prognosis of conduct disorders we are in dire need of more efficient therapeutical methods. The prognosis of learning disorders is rather good as far as it is possible to clear away the underlying conduct disorders. Inclusion of the family or change of the social environment seem indispensable for successful treatment. Most probably therapy outcome can be improved by early intervention and by developing more specific behavior therapy approaches.

Session 139 Symposium:
On the group and family process

915

HOLDING & FACILITATING: FAMILIES & THERAPEUTIC AGENCIES
Stephen Fleck, M.D., Yale University, New Haven, Connecticut 06519 USA

The late Donald Winnicott coined the term "holding environment" to denote one of the important maternal and family tasks. "Holding" can be tangible or intangible. For instance, mother-infant interaction which includes "reading the infant" as to its needs or discomforts, or therapeutic environments where a patient feels helped by being understood regarding his or her needs or moods without overt or explicit communication. "Holding" may be tangible as with a child experiencing a temper tantrum or patients prone to behave destructively, but more important in all human situations is "holding" through relationship power. This involves a need-compliance balance between unequals where it is important for one person to heed direction or needs of another despite the first person's wishes or impulses to the contrary.

"Holding" must be combined with facilitation if growth and development are to occur be that personal growth or advancing group tasks and interests. Growth promotion and caring in the family means learning one's language, making the "reading" explicit and in agencies or treatment services, furthering individual development. In therapeutic agencies facilitation entails patient's restoration to a prior level of functioning or habilitation and rehabilitation designed to recoup illness-induced deficits or stagnation.

916

TRANSGENERATIONAL FAMILY PSYCHOTHERAPY (AS PREVENTION AND FACILITATION)

David Mendell, MD, University of Texas Medical School, USA

The study, evaluation and psychotherapy of successive generations as a unified system over time demonstrates the transmission of therapeutic effect increasingly in successive generations. Communication, conflict resolution and marital selection demonstrate results. The flow thru the longitudinal family is accompanied by the transverse spread of therapeutic effect from individuals to families and outward.

917

SOCIAL FUNCTIONING AS A BASE OF THE PSYCHIATRIC HEALTH.
Stanislav Nikic
Clinic of Psychiatry Military Medical Academy, Belgrade, Yugoslavia

The comprehension of the functioning of Anthropos requires the conceptualisation of him/her as a bio-psycho-social System the out come of the transaction of biological, psychosocial, sociocultural and economicosocial processes.
Entropic developments along the lines of the above processes generate increasing malfunctioning. Consequently, Yugoslav psychiatry is focusing on sociopsychiatric approaches for therapy. We are currently attempting to develop activities which will enable us to continue participating in the WHO programes up to the year 2000. The most important though, is that we proceed preventively educating people how to live in a balanced way, integrating their self as they develop from kindergarten to school and they join agricultural communes factories, the army or as they pursue professional careers.

918

GROUP, FAMILY AND SOCIETY

Janos Furedi
Medical University of Postgraduate Education, Budapest, Hungary

Several researches are investigating the families in different societies when they are in a distressing situation. However, there is very little knowledge about families living in Eastern European countries.
The author is the leader of psychiatric department working mainly on the basis of systematic family orientation. He has observed that, in his everyday work, he can hardly rely on the self reestablishing efforts of the family.
In his presentation the author tries to analyze this phenomenon. The basic assumption is developed according to a socio-ecological view. It is supposed that during the stalinist period, all ideology was based on such groups as the party, the working team, the Trade Union while the role of the family, community, religion was completely neglected.
Because of this reason, in our preventive work we should put more emphasis to reestablish new views about strengthening these later groups. In the meantime in our clinical work the family is the reachable group format where we can realize our treatment and rehabilitation goals.

919

The Criterion of Adaptation

Toma Tomov, M.D.
Dept. of Psychiatry, Sofia..

The advent of change in psychotherapy has often been evidenced by the emergence of more adaptive styles. The adaptation/maladaptation dimension, though, is meaningful from the point of view of the observer only. The quality of being adapted is not an intrinsic characteristic of any one act or behavior. A therapist involved in a process of transaction with a patient is little helped by the above notion of adaptation. Adaptation though, conceptualised as behavior generated by the transaction of therapist ⇌ patient is an _emergent_ in every effort preventive or therapeutic with individuals families or groups. This point will be briefly illustrated.

920

Brief Family and Group Psychotherapy with the Synallactic Collective Image Technique.
George Vassiliou, M.D., Director.
The Athenian Institute of Anthropos.

Within the Dialectic-Systemic approach of the Athenian Institute of Anthropos we have developed and actualised the Synallactic Collective Image Technique for Brief Family and Group Psychotherapy. The Therapist and the Collective Image are the two Catalytic-Regulatory subsystems guiding and enhancing transactions of members for brief psychotherapy. A common theme emerges. Members transacting around it are helped to become conscious and modify malfunctional behavior.

921
DISCUSSING THE ACTUALISATION OF GROUP AND FAMILY PROCESS IN PREVENTION, THERAPY AND REHABILITATION
Visotsky H. - Dept. of Psychiatry, Northwestern University of Chicago, USA

923
International Promise for Research in Space

Pierce, C.M., Harvard Medical School, Boston, Massachusetts, 02138 U.S.A.

The promise of lunar colonization and extra-terrestrial travel within the lifetime of current medical students offers psychiatry the opportunity to participate in one of history's great scientific movements. At present, all countries involved in space research emphasize the impossibility of reaching this promise without sustained and intense international collaboration. This paper focuses on the issue of "heterogeneity," especially of nationality, race and gender, and how this relates to stress in space missions. Simulation experiments are in progress or are being designed to evaluate the impact of social attributes which can influence the groups' performance and efficiency in a space mission. Examples include: educational background; occupational status; and command structure and its interaction with sociocultural factors. A review of several international initiatives will be presented, e.g. Scientific Committee on Antarctic Research, and U.S. National Research Council Group. Finally, the World Psychiatric Association should be aware of the opportunities to plan, develop and facilitate relevant cross-national studies within this important new area of research.

Session 140 Special Session: Issues of global accord

922
THE DYNAMICS OF WORLD CONCORDANCE
Jules H. Masserman, M.D.
Honorary Life President
World Association for Social Psychiatry, USA

Universal empathy and collaboration among nations, as well as individuals, is attainable on the following bases:

1. All mankind is a single species, homo habilis -- the user and misuser of tools, still evolving toward the status of homo sapiens -- man the wise.
2. All human beings are similarly actuated by three fundamental (Ur) conations: Ur I, for physical vitality and longevity; Ur II, for interpersonal securities; and Ur III, for existential serenities.
3. All languages are derived from common Chomskyan roots and express a need for social communications, rendering possible meaningful transcultural messages for friendly collaboration toward mutual Ur-attainments.

This Congress presents wondrous opportunities for further discussion on how, through mutual understandings, mankind's health, cultural progress and creative equanimity could be achieved.

Session 141 New Research: Sexual dysfunction - Impotence

924
SEXUAL DESIRE, ORGASM AND SEXUAL FANTASIES - A STUDY OF 625 DANISH WOMEN BORN 1910, 1936 AND 1958.
Inge Lunde, Gunvor Kramshøj Larsen, Eva Fog and Karin Garde.
ETICA Treatment Center, Borgergade 40, Copenhagen.
Institute of General Practice, University of Copenhagen.

The study presented is a part of a more extended study of female sexuality in three generations: Women born in 1910, 1936 and 1958: Female sexual behaviour, experience, knowledge and attitude. The participants were selected at random in the Copenhagen county, from the central person register and invited to an interview by one of the authors, supplied by a medical examination. The method was a standard interviewschedule with 300 precoded questions in all sexual areas, about social conditions and general health. At the time of interview the women were 70, 40 and 22 years old respectively.
72%, 67% and 95% had experienced spontaneous sexual desire and 88%, 96% and 91% had experienced orgasm. 38%, 47% and 81% respectively had masturbated at least once, and fantasies during masturbation were used by 50%, 48% and 68%. Women born 1910 and 1958 were asked about sexual fantasies in general and during sexual intercourse: 7%(1910) and 44%(1958) had general sexual fantasies, while 14% and 39% had fantasies during intercourse. The fantasies could be placed in some main groups: sex with a stranger/anonymous, forced sex, rape, new forms of sex, sex with perverse men, old men, with several men at the same session and sex-fantasies developed from pictures in sex-magazines. The importance of the sexual fantasies for sexual desire, ability to obtain orgasm and quality of orgasm will be discussed

925

SEX AS THERAPY FOR CHRONIC RESISTANT NEUROTIC DISORDERS.
Dr. M. Maher Hussian, M.B.B.S., D.P.M.,
Govt. N.P. Petral, P.H.C., Gingee T.K. S.A.Dt., Tamil Nadu, India.

A case study was made of Chronic Neurotic disorders with unsatisfactory response to Medicines and psychotherapy mainly Dysthymic disorders, Chronic hysteria and somatisation. They were found to have sexual frustrations and unsatisfactory sex life. They were treated as group and were encouraged friendly, social and psyical sexual relationships without any pressure on anyone at any stage. They were encouraged to talk about their life, occupation, sexual experiences, fantasies, expectation, frustrations etc. The group consisted of 54 persons - 30 females and 24 males and met twice a month. During sex therapy also individual psychotherapy and Medicines were continued. Good results were obtained within 2 or 3 months. Out of total 54 cases - 41 out of 44 dusthymic disorders, 7 out of 9 cases of chronic hysteria and one lone case of somatisation disorder all showed good results. On the whole results were encouraging and further research work is needed in this area.

926

CAVERNOUSAL INSTITUTED MUSCLE RELAXANT INJECTIONS (CUMRI) AS A MAINTENANCE TREATMENT FOR ERECTILE IMPOTENCE: REPORT OF 41 CASES
M.J.H.Qureshi, M.J.Crowe
New Cross Hospital, Wolvehampton, West Midlands, U.K.

There is good evidence that in most cases of erectile impotence, erection can be obtained by intracavernousal injections of either a-adrenergic blocking agents or smooth muscle relaxants. Double blind placebo controlled trials of the treatment have shown that a combination of Papaverine and Phentolamine produced erection in impotence patients. Most centers now use Papaverine (a smooth muscle relaxant) either alone or in combination with Phentolamine (an a-adrenergic blocker) as the drug of choice. The advantages and disadvantages of this form of treatment have not been widely discussed and the enthusiasm for intracavernousal injections has sometimes run ahead of the evidence on acceptibility and patient response. The purpose of this article is to present both the positive and the negative aspects of CUMRI in 41 cases.

927

DRUG TREATMENT OF IMPOTENCE: IDAZOXAN

Michael T Haslam. Medical Director,
The Harrogate Clinic, Harrogate, Yorkshire
United Kingdom.

A number of drugs within the general area of alpha 2 adronergic uptake inhibitors have been used in the treatment of male erectile dysfunction, the model of Yohimbine guiding the early research.

A new drug CR85/041 Idazoxan from Reckitt and Colman has been tested in a double blind cross over placebo trial on forty patients suffering from secondary erectile incompetence.

Results show an improvement in performance and sexual desire over placebo by the active product at one week. A significantly greater number of side-effects was seen in the active preparation. The details of this and the data on treatment results will be detailed.

Those patients who had not responded to the new product were subsequently treated non-blind by Yohimbine and a further proportion showed improvement.

928

EFFECT OF APOMORPHINE ON PENILE TUMESCENCE

R.T.Segraves, M.D.; M.Bari, M.D.; K.Segraves, Ph.D.
Case Western Reserve University, Cleveland, Ohio, U.S.A.

In a double blind study utilizing physiological recording of penile tumescence, brachial subcutaneous apomorphine HCl injections elicited penile erections in men with idiopathic erectile dysfunction. Erectile response to .50 mg, .75 mg and 1 mg apomorphine were significantly greater than placebo beginning 20-25 minutes after injection ($p < .01$). The maximum erection recorded ranged from .3 to 3 cm. Significant side effects including nausea and hypotension were associated with the 1 mg dose level. This observation is compatible with the hypothesis of central dopaminergic involvement in human penile erection.

929
SEXUAL DYSFUNCTION IN MULTIPLE SCLEROSIS PATIENTS

E. Stenager, E. Stenager, J. Boldsen, Ph.D., K. Jensen, Clinical Neuropsychiatric Research Unit, Odense University Hospital, DK 5000 Odense C

Multiple sclerosis is a disease, which gives rise to sexual problems in a majority of affected patients. All former investigations are made on patients with variable mean disablement, and because of this they are not comparable.
Our investigation covers 117 patients, representatively chosen among all patients having MS, admitted to The Department of Neurology, Odense University Hospital, Denmark, in the period 1.1.1973 to 31.12.1985.
The patients were asked, whether they experienced changes in their sexual function after onset of disease. All patients had a neurological examination, and their physical disablement was evaluated using Kurtzke's disability status scale.
The sexual dysfunction was evaluated in relation to age, sex and the physical disablement.
The results were statistically evaluated, and the pattern of covariation was analysed using a log-linear model for contingency table analysis.
65 patients (55%) had experienced changes in their sexual function after onset of disease.
No statistically significant correlation between sex, age, disablement and sexual dysfunction has been found.
A trend toward greater sexual problems among young men < 45 years and elder women > 45 uears was seen.

Session 142   New Research:
Monamines and peptides in mental disorders

930
CSF NEUROPEPTIDE Y IN SCHIZOPHRENIA

Daniel P. van Kammen, M.D., Ph.D.*°, Jeffrey Peters, M.D.*°, Joel Gelernter, M.D.+, David Shaw, Ph.D.*, Thomas Neylan, M.D.*°; Western Psychiatric Institute & Clinic, Pittsburgh, PA; °VA Medical Center, Pittsburgh, PA, +VA Medical Center, West Haven, CT, U.S.A.

Neuropeptide Y (NPY) is a 36-aminopeptide has recently been discovered in the CNS. NPY is co-released with norepinephrine from some monoadrenergic neurons as well as with somatostatin. We measured NPY with a NPY specific antibody radioimmunoassay in the CSF of 35 male schizophrenic patients (DSMIII) with a mean age of 34 ± 7.8 years and 10.5 ± 6.83 years of illness. They had been drug-free for at least 2 weeks. Thirty one patients were withdrawn from chronic haloperidol treatment (12 ± 8.9 mg/day). Eleven patients relapsed and 19 did not within 6 weeks of placebo replacement. They received an LP within days of relapse or after having been drug-free for 6 weeks. CT scans of the brain were obtained.
Results. CSF NPY correlated negatively with age and duration of illness. Haloperidol withdrawal was associated with a significant increase in CSF NPY ($p = 0.002$). CSF NPY was not significantly different between relapsers and nonrelapsers. Positive correlations with schizophrenic symptomatology were only observed in the nonrelapsers. CT scan measures such as VBR, cerebellar atrophy and sulcal widening correlated negatively with CSF NPY. The implications of these findings for a potential role of NPY in schizophrenia will be discussed.

931
CSF MONOAMINE METABOLITES AND SUICIDAL BEHAVIOUR IN DEPRESSED PATIENTS: A FIVE YEAR FOLLOW UP STUDY

Alec Roy, M.B., Judith DeJong, Ph.D., Markku Linnoila, M.D., Ph.D., Laboratory of Clinical Studies, DICBR, National Institute on Alcohol Abuse and Alcoholism, Bethesda, MD

We carried out a 5 year follow-up study of suicidal behaviour among depressed patients who earlier had determinations of cerebrospinal fluid levels of monoamine metabolites. Patients who reattempted suicide during the follow-up had significantly lower cerebrospinal fluid levels of both the serotonin metabolite 5-hydroxyindoleacetic acid and the dopamine metabolite homovanillic acid. Melancholics who re-attempted suicide during the follow up had a mean CSF 5-HIAA level of 57.2 ± 14.4 pmol/ml compared with a mean of 92.4 ± 3.01 for patients who did not re-attempt suicide and 115.2 ± 34.8 for patients who never attempted suicide. Melancholic reattempters had a mean CSF HVA level of 65.2 ± 21.4 pmol/ml compared with a mean of 121.5 ± 48.0 for patients who did not re-attempt and a mean of 194.2 ± 89.1 pmol/ml for patients who never attempted suicide. These follow-up results suggest that reduced central turnover of serotonin and dopamine may be associated with further suicidal behaviour among depressed patients who have previously attempted suicide.

932
Catecholamine measures in patients treated with Phenelzine.
SHARMA,R;JANICAK,P;JAVAID,J;PANDEY,G;GIERL.B;DAVIS J: Illinois State Psychiatric Institute, CHICAGO.

We examined the relationship between peripheral catecholamine measures and behavioral response in 27 depressed patients treated with phenelzine. The following measures were obtained after a washout period (mean=15.3 days), and then repeated during the 4th week of treatment; 24 hour urinary MHPG excretion (including volume and creatinine measurements), platelet MAO inhibition levels, leukocyte adenylate cyclase activity and the Hamilton depression rating scale (HAMD). Phenelzine was titrated to a mean daily dose at week 4 of 46.7 mg. Urinary MHPG was analyzed both as an absolute value, as well as in relationship to the 24 hr excretion of creatinine (MHPG/CREAT). Baseline analyses revealed increased absolute MHPG excretion in depressed patients with psychotic features ($p=0.05$). Phenelzine induced a significant decrease in both absolute MHPG as well as MHPG/CREAT during the 4th week of treatment (MHPG: $p=0.004$; MHPG/CREAT: $p=0.003$). We found no correlation in the total sample between decreases in MHPG excretion and improvement on the HAMD. However, when we separately analyzed those patient's that had a definite clinical response to phenelzine, we observed a significant correlation between decreases in HAMD scores, and decreases in both the absolute MHPG levels ($r=0.67$, $n=11$, $p=0.02$), as well as the MHPG/CREAT ratio ($r=0.68$; $n=11$; $p=0.02$).

933

DIET & DIALYSIS IN PATIENTS WITH SCHIZOPHRENIA.
R. Cade, H. Wagemaker, M. Privette, R. Howard.
Univ. of Florida Med. School, Gainesville, FL. USA

Eleven patients with Research Diagnostic Criteria Schizophrenia were treated with dialysis, a gluten or casein free diet, or both. In addition to the psychiatric exam, each patient was serially evaluated with an MMPI, Brief Psychiatric Rating Scale (BPRS), Assay of Urinary Polypeptide Excretion(UPE) & plasma IgA antibody to gliadin & casein. If IgA antibody was strongly positive an appropriate diet was recommended. Two patients were treated with diet alone, 3 with diet and dialysis and 6 with dialysis alone. UPE showed 3 abnormal patterns; Type 1, excess peptides eluting from a G-25 Sephadex column at 4.2 x void vol.(v.v.);Type 2, excess polypeptides eluting at 2.4 x v.v.;Type 3 excess polypeptides eluting at both 4.2 & 2.4 x v.v. Patients with Type 1 responded well and rapidly to dialysis, the peak eluting at 4.2 x v.v. becoming normal in size within 3 mos. & BPRS & MMPI even more rapidly than that. Patients with a Type 2 pattern improved slowly requiring 9-12 mos. for urinary peaks, MMPI & BPRS to reach normal values. Patients with a Type 3 pattern responded poorly to dialysis. Patients in this group have, thusfar in our experience, had either gliadin or casein sensitivity. When they were put on an appropriate diet improvement was rapid. Two patients treated with diet alone improved slowly over a 9-12 mo. period. In all patients there was a good correlation between polypeptide peak size & BPRS & MMPI scores.

934

CHRONIC LITHIUM TREATMENT INCREASES PLASMA 5-HT BUT NOT PLATELET 5-HT.

F. Artigas, M.J. Sarrias, P. Celada, E. Martínez, E. Alvarez (*) and C. Udina (*). Departments of Neurochemistry, C.S.I.C. and (*)Psychiatry, Hospital de Sant Pau, Barcelona, 08034, SPAIN.

The effect of lithium salts administered chronically to bipolar patients on peripheral measures of the serotoninergic system has been studied. Plasma free serotonin (5-HT), plasma 5-hydroxyindoleacetic acid (5-HIAA), platelet 5-HT and plasma tryptophan have been analyzed in 22 bipolar patients treated with lithium carbonate (mean daily dose 1280 mg) and compared to healthy controls. Mean duration of lithium treatment was 24 months. Lithium salts induce significant increases on plasma 5-HT (+159% with respect to controls, $p<0.01$) and on plasma 5-HIAA (+39%, $p<0.02$) but not in platelet 5-HT. Plasma tryptophan was also unaffected. These results suggest that lithium salts increase the synthesis and/or release of 5-HT from intracellular stores. On the other hand, since platelet 5-HT is not affected (platelets take up 5-HT from the plasma) an inhibitory action on the platelet 5-HT uptake system is also suggested. The effect of short term lithium given to naïve patients seems to confirm these results, with increases of plasma 5-HT, plasma 5-HIAA and lack of change of platelet 5-HT.

935

"IN VIVO" INCREASE OF PLASMA AND PLATELET 5-HT AFTER MAO INHIBITORS

F. Artigas, P. Celada, E. Martínez, E. Alvarez (*) and C. Udina (*). Departments of Neurochemistry, C.S.I.C. and (*)Psychiatry, Hospital de Sant Pau, Barcelona, 08034, SPAIN.

Results from this laboratory show the existence of a marked decrease of plasma 5-HT, platelet 5-HT and plasma 5-HIAA -the main metabolite of 5-HT- in the blood of untreated melancholic patients (1). Such peripheral measures provide an excellent model to study the effects of antidepressant treatments on the 5-HT system. Therefore, we have examined the effects of two different MAO inhibitors (brofaromine and phenelzine) on plasma 5-HT, plasma 5-HIAA and platelet 5-HT in the blood of patients treated with such drugs (N=13). After 6 weeks of treatment, plasma 5-HT and platelet 5-HT increase significantly (+150% and +73% respectively). We propose the use of the ratio plasma 5-HIAA/plasma 5-HT to study the effect of MAOI treatments on the serotoninergic system. Unlike platelet MAO -which is of the B-type-, such index is indicative of the "in vivo" activity against 5-HT (deaminated primarily by MAO-A). A dramatic decrease of this ratio has been observed after treatment during 6 weeks with such MAO inhibitors (9.9 before , 2.6 after treatment, $p<0.005$).

(1) Sarrias et al. Biol. Psychiatry 22:1429-1438 (1987).

Session 143 Free Communications:
Neurochemical variables in schizophrenia

936

SERUM IMMUNOGLOBULINS AND PSYCHOPATHOLOGY IN SCHIZOPHRENIA.

S.N.SHARMA, R.M.GUPTA, A.P.S.SANDHU, Deptts. of Psychiatry & Pathology, Instt. of Medi.Scs.,B.H.U., VARANASI, INDIA.

Forty one schizophrenics, 30 non-schizophrenic psychiatric patients and 30 healthy age and sex matched individuals were studied for serum immunoglubulins G, A & M. Patients in both groups were diagnosed according to R.D.C.(Spitzer et al,1978). All the subjects studied met fixed inclusion criteria, were physically normal and routine urine, stool, blood, LFT and serum proteins were within normal range. Total proteins, Al, Gl, Hb did not differ significantly in three groups. Statistically significant observations were: IgG & IgA were higher in schizophrenics than controls and in paranoid schizophrenics than other phenomenological subtypes of schizophrenia. Hostility and agitation were associated with higher IgG & IgA. IgG was lower in patients with lack of appropriate emotions,blank spells, incoherent speech, mannerisms and postures and labile emotional responses. Raised IgA was seen with inner tension, blank spells and incoherent speech. Withdrawal was associated with low IgA levels.

937
PLATELET MAO IN SUBGROUPS OF SCHIZOPHRENIA

I.Sharma, A.Kumar, J.P.N.Chansouria
Institute of Medical Sciences, B.H.U. Varanasi, India

The present study was undertaken to study and compare platelet monoamine oxidase (MAO) activity in schizophrenia mania and healthy control. Platelet MAO activity was estimated by Radio Isotopic Technique using 14 C tryptamine bisuccinate as the substrate in 60 drug free male schizophrenics, 33 drug free male manics and 36 male controls. There was no significant difference in the enzyme between the schizophrenics, manics and healthy controls. Platelet MAO activity in the disorganised, catatonic and paranoid schizophrenics was significantly lower as compare to the enzyme activity in the manic and healthy control group. Platelet MAO activity appears to be related to subgroups of schizophrenia disorganized, catatonic and paranoid. Limitations and scope for future research have been out lined.

938
DECREASED IN VITRO TYROSINE TRANSPORT IN SCHIZOPHRENIC PATIENTS.
Bjerkenstedt,L. Hagenfeldt,L. Wiesel,F-A. Wenizelos,N.
Dept.Psychtr & Psych,Dept.Clin.Chem.Karolinska Inst.
S-10401,Stockholm,Sweden.
Thirty-seven unmedicated schizophrenic patients(21 men,16 women)compared to healthy controls (50 men,15 women) had significantly higher postabsorbtive plasma concentrations of taurine, methionine,valine,isoleucine,leucine,phenylalanine and lysine. Except for taurine,these amino acids share the L-transport system for neutral amino acids.In the patient group,the plasma levels of the amino acids competing with tyrosine and tryptophan for transport into brain,were all significantly and negatively correlated to the CSF concentrations of HVA and 5-HIAA. The HVA level in CSF was decreased in the patients.
On this basis we have proposed that schizophrenic patients may have a defect in the transport of tyrosine.Amino acid transport in fibroblasts from schizophrenic patients was measured by the cluster tray technique.Initial rate of transport was measured during 60 sec at different amino acids concentrations and data were analyzed graphically.
Skin biopsies were obtained from 7 male schizophrenic patients. Five of the patients were drug free at the time of biopsy,one of them had never received neuroleptics.Control cell lines were from healthy subjects without first degree relatives with psychiatric disease.A significant lower V_{max} was observed for tyrosine transport in cell from the patients while the K_m remained the same as in control cells.
These findings motivate the study of tyrosine transport across the blood brain barrier in vivo.The results have also implications for the study of genetics of schizophrenia and for designing new therapeutic approaches.

939
Abnormal regulation of spiperone binding to lymphocytes from schizophrenic patients under the influence of glucocorticoids.
M.Halbach & U.Henning
Psychiatrische Klinik der Universität Düsseldorf, Bergische Landstraße 2, D-4000 Düsseldorf, FRG
The binding of spiperone, antagonized by butaclamol, to peripheral blood lymphocytes has been reported elevated in patients with certain forms of schizophrenia.
We have studied the spiperone binding of peripheral lymphocytes in tissue culture under the influence of glucocorticoids. While spiperone binding to healthy persons was only slightly elevated the glucocorticoid induced increase in spiperone binding was far more expressed with lymphocytes from patients with distinct forms of schizophrenia. All patients of this study had never been treated with neuroleptic drugs before or were free of psychotropic medication for at least 6 months. We have experimentally excluded the possibility of unspecific or cytotoxic glucocorticoid effects on lymphocytes as a hypothetical cause of differential spiperone binding. From our data we have to assume an abnormal sensitivity of lymphocyte spiperone binding structures to glucocorticoid regulation. This effect could easily be correlated with well known clinical features of psychosis like therapeutic glucocorticoid induction or induction by severe chronic stress.

940
CPK activity in newly admitted psychiatric patients
C. Touloumis, P. Vachtsevanos
Psychiatric Hospital of Attica
ATHENS - GREECE

We have studied the alterations of CPK activity in psychiatric patients admitted to the short-stay therapy department of the Psychiatric Hospital of Attica (Athens). More than half (56,4%) of the 110 admitted patients (67 men, 43 women) had shown high levels of CPK activity. The summation of the values of CPK activity in men had been estimated to be four times higher than that of women. Although the clinically estimated patient's hyperactivity had been significantly correlated with CPK elevation, this cannot be considered as the cause for CPK elevations. A higher percentage of "psychotic" patients had shown levels of CPK activity above normal values (max.179U/Lit) compared with the percentage of "non psychotic" patients ones. Very high levels of CPK activity (CPK > 300 U/Lit) were observed only in "psychotic" patients.

941

PLATELET MAO ACTIVITY AS MARKER OF DEGENERATIVE PROCESS IN CENTRAL NERVOUS SYSTEM
P. Bongioanni, Scuola Superiore di Studi Universitari e di Perfezionamento-S. Anna, Pisa, Italy.

Human blood platelet monoamine oxidase(pMAO) activity has been studied in several neuropsychiatric diseases, such as schizophrenia(Bongioanni,1988), affective disorder(Fieve et al.,1980), Huntington's chorea(Mann and Chiu,1978), Parkinson's disease(PD)(Mann et al.,1983), dementia of Alzheimer type(DAT)(Alexopoulos et al., 1984). In this study pMAO activity values of PD and DAT patients are compared to those of healthy controls.
Both PD and DAT patient pMAO activity(39.48 ± 15.22(mean$\pm$SD) and 44.37 ± 9.36 nmols/mg prot./h, respectively) is significantly ($p<0.001$) higher than that of control subjects(26.84 ± 4.26 nmols/mg prot./h).
Such findings are discussed in terms of use of pMAO activity as a marker of biochemical derangements occurring in neurological degenerative processes.
REFERENCES.
Alexopoulos G.S. et al.(1984)Am.J.Psychiatry,141:97; Bongioanni P.(1988)N.P.S.,8:191; Fieve R.R. et al.(1980)Biol.Psychiatry,15:473; Mann J. and Chiu E.(1978)J.Neurol.Neurosurg.Psychiatry,41:809; Mann J. et al.(1983)J.Neurol.Neurosurg.Psychiatry,46:905.

942

Behavioural items related to variability of MAO platelet activity
P. Castrogiovanni, D. Marazziti, I. Maremmani, J.A. Deltito°
Institute of Psychiatry, Pisa University, Italy
°Depression and Anxiety Clinic, New York Hospital, Cornell University, Westchester Division, White Plains, New York, N.Y., U.S.A.

Healthy volunteers were evaluated in relation to MAO platelet activity and by means of MMPI, in order to verify the nature of the correlations between this activity and personality traits. The results show that relatively high MAO activity values correspond to behaviours characterized by emotional lability, insecurity and sensitivity, rigidity, strength of Super-Ego and lack of sociability.

943

Cytoarchitectonic abnormalities in rostral entorhinal fields of schizophrenics

Heckers S., Heinsen Y.L., Heinsen H., Beckmann H.

Department of Psychiatry, University of Wuerzburg, Fuechsleinstrasse 15, 8700 Wuerzburg, FRG

The entorhinal region is composed of a variety of fields. The size and the extension of the latter are a matter of dispute. In extension of our previous findings (Jakob & Beckmann 1986; Heinsen & Beckmann 1989) we can demonstrate circumscribed abnormalities of the most rostrally located entorhinal fields of the lateral entorhinal area comprising disturbances of either the pre-alpha layer, the pre-beta layer or combined abnormalities by means of a modified Nissl technique. Quantitatively, these defects have only little impact on the composition of the total lateral entorhinal area. Generally, glial cell number is enhanced in schizophrenics. But in our opinion the described cytoarchitectonic abnormalities are not the consequence of degenerative processes.

Jakob H, Beckmann H (1986) J Neural Transm 65: 303-326
Heinsen H, Beckmann H (1989) Psychopharmacology (in press)

Session 144 Free Communications:
Psychotherapy in children with learning difficulties

944

CHILDREN WITH LEARNING PROBLEMS: ASSESSMENT AND TREATMENT.
HADJI H, KOUROS J.
Society for Psychological Psychiatry of Adult and Child(E.PS.PS.E.P)ATHENS-GREECE
Children from the whole spectrum of psychopathology can exhibit learning problems.
In certain cases the learning problem is primarily psychogenic(anxiety problems and/or positive motivation not to learn), in others educational or socio-cultural factors predominate, while in some cases minimal brain dysfunction or genetic predisposition are implicated.
Thus, evaluation of a child who presents a learning problem as one of the chief complaints should be encompassing and integrating both psychodynamic and neuropsychological perspectives, the aim being, the specification of the habilitation techniques, best suited for the individual child.
We are presenting some cases of neurotic children. The evaluation process, as well as the treatment strategies employed(individual, psychoanalytically-oriented psychotherapy, educational tutoring, marital therapy for the parents)are presented and the different treatment phases are analysed.

945
DEPISTAGE PRECOCE DES TROUBLES D'APPRENTISSAGE EN MATERNELLE
SIDIROPOULOU TR, KOUROS JEAN
SOCIETE DE PSYCHIATRIE PSYCHOLOGIQUE(E.PS.PS.E.P) ATHENES

Nous decrivons ici comment se fait et comment doit se faire le depistage précoce en maternelle des troubles de l'apprentissage scolaire et de l'arrieration de toute origine et comment un traitement adapté peut commencer aussitôt.
Nous expliquons les particularités de la "réalité" Athenienne et nous insistons sur les difficultés de la "tache";
Nous présentons aussi les possibilités de placement dès cet âge en institution spécialisée ainsi que les autres possibilités d'aide en externat ou avec de cours d'éducatio spécialisée dans de centres comme EPSEP (institutions "légères") voir même de cours à domicile comme ca se fait pour les enfants normaux.
Nous présentons quelques cas qui demontrent bien l'importance du sujet.

946
TROUBLES DE L'APPRENTISSAGE SCOLAIRE CHEZ L'ENFANT ET L'ADOLESCENT.
DIMOU D, KOUROS J.
PIKPA, EPSPSEP.

Determination du terme "troubles de l'apprentissage scolaire" du point de vue clinique et pedagogique. Categorisation et analyse des difficultés d'apprentissage dès la classe maternelle jusqu'à la 3ème, suivant les exigences et difficultês grammatologiques à chaque classe et à toute matière dans le système d'éducation nationale. Classification des troubles: dyslexie, dysorthographie, d'autres troubles et expressions des difficultés d'apprentissage chez les enfants normaux et "arriérés".
Determinants explicatifs: Motifs organiques ou personnels, arieration mentale, symptomes sentimentaux, psychomoteurs, troubles de la parole; motifs ou determinants pédagogiques, composition scolaire, rélation apprentis-instituteurs, programes et exigences scolaires relations parents-apprentis.
Methodes d'approche: diagnostique clinique, pédagogique; Methodes de résolution pédagogique, clinique, therapeutique. Modèles proposées de résolution des difficultés d'apprentissage scolaire; exposition de quelques cas.

947
DIFFICULTES DE L'APPRENTISSAGE CHEZ LE JEUNE ADULTE

ANTONOPOULOU FAL, KOUROS JEAN
ORGANISME DE PROTECTION DES ENFANTS INADAPTES(OPEPEA)

Nous decrivons le mode de fonctionnement de l'unité d'apprentissage préproffessionnel pour jeunes adultes avec arriration mentale légère de l' OPEPEA.
Le programme de l' unité est financé par la Communauté Européenne dans le cadre de la réforme psychiatrique en Grèce.
Nous expliquons le fonctionnement des divers ateliers existants(certains sont uniques en Grèce)
Nous insistons tout particulierement au fonctionnement de l'equipe d'accueil(pedopsychiatre, psychologue, assistante sociale, orthophoniste, psychomotricienne, ergotherapeute).
Nous présentons aussi quelques cas qui demontrent bien le rôle du psychologue et même du psychotherapeute étant donné qu'on retoue toujours des problèmes("complexes")psychologiques sécondaires à l'arrieration ou même primaires(qui sont responsables de l'arrieration)

948
TRAITEMENT PSYCHOPEDAGOGIQUE DES ENFANTS PRESENTANT DES TROUBLES DE L'APPRENTISSAGE
SIDIROPOULOU TR, KOUROS J.
SOCIETE DE PSYCHIATRIE PSYCHOLOGIQUE(E.PS.PS.E.P) ATHENES

Nous decrivons ici notre technique de traitement des troubles d'apprentissage scolaire des enfants qui souffrent des problèmes psychologiques divers.
Les séances d'éducation spécialisée ont lieu en groupe de 3-4 enfants du même âge et du même Q.I. environ et durent une heure scolaire.
Nous essayons de combiner un cour adapté aux besoins scolaires des enfants avec une approche psychologique voir psychotherapique.

Nous faisons les changements néssaires, surtout au début de l'année scolaire afin que les groupes deviennent vraiment homogènes et fonctionnels(problèmes de rivalité, ajustement du rythme d'apprentissage e.t.c.)
Le materiel utilisé est d'une qualité superieure à celle offerte par les parents habituellement en Grèce(jeux Nathan, e.t.c.)ce qui facilite nos résultats pédagogiques, mais notre personnel(psychologues, psychopedagogues, éduquatrices spécialisées e.t.c.) travaille avec enthousiasme et c'est surtout grâce à celà que nos résultats sont très satisfaisants.
L'originalité de notre travail consiste au fait que nous travaillons dans une institution privé à but non lucratif et nous parvenons avec des revenus très minimes d'offrir une qualité de services exceptionnelle pour notre domaine en Grèce.

949

L'EQUIPE SOIGNANTE FACE AUX PARENTS DE L'HANDICAPE MENTAL
ANTONOPOULOU FAL, KOUROS JEAN
ORGANISME DE PROTECTION DES ENFANTS INADAPTES(OPEPEA)

Nous decrivons ici le mode de fonctionnement des réunions des parents des enfants handicapés mentaux de l'unité d'éducation preprofessionnele de l' OPEPEA. ainsi que les divers problèmes posés par les parents séparement à l' équipe medicopsychologique(équipe d'accueil et"de soutien"de l'unité).
Nous insistons particulierement à la nessessité des réunions de synthèse hebdomadaires de toutes les équipes qui permettent la résolution des conflits entre les membres des équipes et les enfants et surtout avec les parents qui souvent à cause de leurs sentiments de culpabilité et leurfatigue et angoisse ont tendance à mal interpreter les évenements(sans pour autant être paranoiaques et malades comme on a "trop"souvent tendance à dire en psychiatrie)et il faut être toujours vigilants pour discuter les problèmes dès leur apparition.
Nous présentons quelques cas à titre d'exemple.

Session 145 Free Communications:
Parasuicide and attempted suicide

950

Interview survey of hundred patients admitted after attempted suicide.
P.Rubin, M.Nordentoft.
Psychiatric department, Bispebjerg Hospital, Copenhagen, Denmark.

100 patients referred to psychiatric consultation at Københavns Amtssygehus,Gentofte 1986-1987 after suicide attempt were interviewed by the authors.Results:Two thirds of the patients were women, average age 41,2 years. 86% had poisened themselves while 14 have used violent methods. 13% were psycotic, 64% had only mild or no mental illness. 42% were out of work.72% had had previous psychiatric treatment, 42% had alcohol abuse and 15% drug abuse. The level of social integration was lower than in the normal population. Problems with significant others were the main reason for suicide attempt for 45% of the patients. 44% of the patients considered loneliness and 46% depression as a problem.A scale was developed in order to measure the suicidal intention. Two thirds had a high suicidal intention. 62% of the patients wished to die at the time of the suicide attempt while only 28% still had a wish to die at interview.Conclusion:The group of patients is strained with regard to social parameters, alcohol abuse, loneliness and problems with significant others. The suicidal intention is high in two thirds but temporary.

951

ATTEMPTED SUICIDE IN GREEK AND DANISH WOMEN: A CROSS-CULTURAL STUDY
Tata-Arcel L.[1], Mantonakis J., Jemos J., Kaliteraki E., Petersson B.[1] and Stefanis C.
[1]Institute of Clinical Psychology, Univ. Copenhagen
Department of Psychiatry, University of Athens

This study was based on the observation that Greece has the lowest incidence of suicide in Europe in contrast to Denmark where high incidence is observed. Thirty five Greek and 35 Danish non-psychotic women, aged 15-45 years (random sample) were interviewed according to an extensive questionnaire, covering a wide spectrum of women's psychosocial life. Some similarities between the two groups were: a) feelings of humiliation and shame in connection with the provoking episode, b) desire for greater autonomy, c) opposition to tasks involving caring for others. Differences between the two groups - as illustrated by the Greek women - were:1) attempted suicide at a younger age, 2) spoke more often about their intention, 3) presented a greater desire to die, 4) exhibited better planning of the suicide, 5) had more previous attempts, 6) had been exposed to more violence by their husbands, 7) showed better awareness of oppression in their marriage/family, 8) attempted suicide in order to express anger and protest, 9) had a vaguer knowledge of the drugs used, 10) had less often a psychiatric history and 11) had lower incidence of suicides or attempts in their families. Finally, Greek women stated that one of the worst things they experienced was to be oppressed and unloved, whereas the worst thing stated by Danish women was that nobody needed them.

952

ATTEMPTED SUICIDE:A STUDY OF 100 CASES IN TEHRAN

L. Davidian M.D. MRCPsych.
D. Poormand M.A. Clinical Psychologist
Taleghany Hospital, Evin, Tehran, Iran

100 consecutively admitted cases to Loghman Adham Hospital for attempted suicide were studied.
69 patients were females and 31 males, mostly from middle and lower middle classes. The incidence was more frequent between the ages of 10-20 in women and 21-30 in men. 35(51%) of females and 15(48%) of males were married,17(37%) were illiterate, 6 males were unemployed and 34 females were housewives. The main reasons for attempting suicide in females were 23(33%) marital problems,12(17%) husbands' long-standing unemployment and 10(14%) frustration. In males the reasons were 16(51%) psychiatric problems, 7(23%) unemployment and 6(19%) marital problems. In psychiatric examination, 11(47%) had epilepsy, 7(30%) depression, 2(8%) obsessive-compulsive disorder and 2(8%) undifferentiated psychoses. Methods used were 75 by pills, 12 insecticides, 6 opium, 6 detergents and 1 wristslashing. 51 regretted their survival and 31 stated they were determined to attempt again. 24 patients had history of attempted suicide, 16 within the past 12 months.
The sex-ratio, age distribution and commonest methods of attempt are comparable with those described in other cultures. Taking pills as the commonest method once more emphasises the hazards of easy availability of medications.

953
PARASUICIDE IN LONG-TERM COURSE OF FUNCTIONAL PSYCHOSES
A. ROHDE, A. MARNEROS, A. DEISTER
Department of Psychiatry, University of Bonn, FRG

As part of the Cologne study we investigated the suicidal behaviour of 97 schizophrenic, 72 schizoaffective and 80 uni- und bipolar affective patients during long-term course (more than 20 years on average). Parasuicide was frequent in all three groups, most frequent in female patients with unipolar schizoaffective disorder.
Investigating also suicidal behaviour in any episode and interval of illness (up to 20 episodes per patient) we found several factors influencing suicidal behaviour, i.e. familial, socioeconomic, psychological and psychopathological variables. The clinical relevance of these findings will be discussed.

954
COMPARISON OF PARASUICIDES WITH DEPRESSIVES WITH LOW SUICIDAL IDEATION
Daja F., Rivero G., Martinez S.
Dept.of Psychopharmacology,Psychiatric Clinic and Neurochemistry Div., IIBCE, Montevideo, Uruguay

30 women that had attempted suicide (WAS) (36.9 ± 13.8 years old)and 21 depressed with low suicidal ideation patients(44±6 years old) were studied at the Psychiatric Hospital in Montevideo.Only10% of WAS had a diagnosis of major depressive episode with melancholia,in comparison with 54.5% of depressives.Similarly,76% of WAS received a diagnosis on DSM III axis II (mainly Histrionic-46.1%) compared with 13.7.% of the depressives. CPRS global scores were 30.7±10.6 while the subscale for depression (CPRS-D) showed a median of 13.1±4.3.
5 hydroxyindolacetic acid, homovanillic acid and noradrenaline cerebrospinal fluid levels for WAS did not differ from the values obtained from depressives neither from those of a sample of psychotic women in their first episode.
Apparently therefore, and in spite of the clinical differences,both groups would be similarly depressed. This would imply,e.g. a risk of suicide in the non-WAS group. This work was partially supported by the Swedish Agency for Research Cooperation with Developing Countries.

955
SUICIDE IN MIDDLE AGE

H. Kanamura and M. Kurihara
Toranomon Hospital, Tokyo, Japan

Suicide in middle age is becoming more and more important in our society. Here, we present three men who commited suicide by jumping. Their self-destruction were related to "desperate defence" for self-esteem.
Case A,aged 40,was in fear of loss of his job, because of his manic-depressive illness. Case B, aged 52, was in fear of loss of his success for which he had worked hard suppressing emotional pleasures of private life. He was suffering from agitated depression. Case C,aged 60 was in fear of loss of his health and happy remainder of life. He was suffering from depression with hypothyroidism.
These cases had respectively their own troubles to be surmounted. They had to adjust themselves to situation, but they could not accept any change of their attitude. They struggled more and more agressively against the enemy which had threatened their self-esteem.
They could not survive over their impaired self-esteem, as if they were soldiers of the Emperor of Japan.
This traditional self-esteem in our society will be discussed.

956
SUICIDE ATTEMPTS: MODE, SERIOUSNESS OF INTENTION AND PRECIPITATING FACTORS. DIFFERENCES BETWEEN MEN AND WOMEN.
J. Tripodianakis, S. Theodoropoulou, D. Saranditis M. Priami, E. Pachi, A. Yalouris.

We studied the suicide attempts admitted to medical wards of Evagelismos General Hospital over the past 3 years. The total sample consisted of 838 persons, of whom 201 (24%) were men and 637 (76%)women. The mean age of the total sample was 33. Mean age of men was 37 years of age and of women 32 years of age.
The study was concerned with possible differences between men and women in relation to the mode of the attempt, the seriousness of the intention and the precipitating factors.
We found that men employ more violent methods compared to women (p<0.0001), their attempts are more seriously intented (p<0.0001) and the precipitating factor is less likely to be troubled interpersonal relations (p<0.0001).

Our findings are discussed and compared to main research in the field.

Session 146 Free Communications:
Panic disorder: Theoretical and psychopathological issues

957
AVOIDANCE AND INTERNAL STRUCTURE OF PSYCHOPATHOLOGICAL VARIABLES IN PANIC DISORDERS - A CLASSIFICATORY MODEL
M.Luisa Figueira, A.Batista, H.Bacelar Nicolau
Dept. Med.Psychol.Fac.Medicine,Lisbon, Portugal

In order to analyse the internal structure of psychopatological variables in relation to the degree of avoidance in Panic disorder, an hierarchical clustering model was used based on affinity coefficients. An exploratory analysis was performed in 58 patients diagnosed as Panic Disorder with Agoraphobia (DSMIII-R). The patients were divided in three sub-groups according to the degree of avoidance (mild, medium and extensive avoidance). The variables under analysis were: (1) measures of general psychopathology: anxiety, depression, obsessions and compulsions, interpersonal sensitivity; (2) measures of panic-anxiety: panic frequency and panic intensity, agoraphobic thoughts, cognitive anxiety, somatization and body sensasions; (3) measures of phobia and phobic anxiety; (4) measures of trait anxiety. Patients were assessed with the Anxiety Disorders Interview Schedule; Hopkins Symptom Checklist; Fear Questionnaire; Mobility Inventory, Agoraphobic Cognitions Questionnaire, Body Sensations Questionnaire; Cognitive Somatic Anxiety Questionnaire and State-Trait Anxiety Inventory
In each group of avoidance different clustering results were obtained defining diferent structures of psychopathological characteristics of panic disorder.

958
PHENOMENOLOGY OF PANIC DISORDER AND PANIC ATTACKS.

C. Díez; A. Corominas; J. Vallejo; A.Otero
Hospital Clínic i Provincial, Barcelona, Spain.

We studied 61 outpatients who met DSM-III-R criteria for panic disorder with or without agoraphobia. We assessed the frequency and intensity of several panic attack symptoms, the level of free-floating anxiety, the presence of major depression, and the phobic avoidance behaviors.
Results suggested different panic attack symptoms relationships. Free-floating anxiety, depression, and phobic avoidance seemed to cluster around a group of patients who had a more severe panic syndrome. Depressive patients were one third of the total sample. Agoraphobic patients had a prior onset than patients with panic disorder without agoraphobia or with limited phobic avoidance.

959
MODELE PSYCHANALYTIQUE ET PHENOMENOLOGIQUE DE L'ATTAQUE DE PANIQUE
Docteur Pierre Meyer, 7 rue de Lon 74200 THONON-LES-BAINS/FRANCE

A partir d'exemples cliniques, l'auteur met en évidence des aspects sémiologiques nouveaux, chez les patients atteints d'attaque de panique. Il montre que ces patients présentent deux modalités perceptivo-cognitives, l'une de type adulte dominée par les mécanismes de la pensée conceptuelle et logique, auxquels correspondent des capacités de réponses comportementales élaborées, adaptées à la réalité, l'autre équivalente à ce qui se passe chez un nourrisson avant l'âge de un an, dominée par des mécanismes proto-mentaux de nature prélogique, préconceptuelle et présymbolique, auxquels correspondent des capacités de réponses comportementales très peu spécifiques, de nature exclusivement biologique et motrice. En dehors des crises aiguës d'angoisse, les deux modalités perceptivo-cognitives sont fonctionnelles simultanément, tandis que durant les attaques de panique, seule la seconde reste fonctionnelle et le patient se comporte alors comme un nourrisson en situation d'agression violente. L'auteur poursuit en utilisant des théories élaborées par d'autres chercheurs et propose un modèle théorique général applicable à l'attaque de panique. Ce modèle est psychanalytique principalement par le fait qu'il autorise une prise de connaissance thérapeutique par le sujet, de la signification singulière que peut revêtir sa conduite "attaque de panique". Par ailleurs, il est en accord avec les thèses fondamentales de la pensée phénoménologique. L'auteur montre comment ce modèle autorise une synthèse harmonieuse des théories existantes concernant l'attaque de panique; il termine sur des pespectives nouvelles pour la compréhension du phénomème anxieux et d'autres manifestations psychopathologiques.

960
ATTENUATION OF PANIC SYMPTOMS AFTER TREATMENT WITH SEROTONERGIC COMPOUNDS
J.A. den Boer and H.G.M. Westenberg
Department of Biological Psychiatry, State University Utrecht, Nicolaas Beetsstraat 24, 3511 HG Utrecht, The Netherlands

Accumulating evidence indicates that serotonergic neuronal systems may be of critical importance in the pathogenesis of Panic Disorder (PD). Several selective serotonin (5-HT) uptake inhibitors have been shown to possess antipanic properties.
A notable reduction in the number of panic attacks, was however not obtained within 3 weeks, and was preceded by an initial, transient increase in symptom severity. Based upon the hypothesis that this sequence of events might be due to adaptive changes e.g. receptor-downregulation, we investigated the efficacy of ritanserin, a potent and selective $5-HT_2$ antagonist.
In the present study results are presented of a double blind, placebo controlled study with fluvoxamine and ritanserin.
Patients (n=60) suffering from PD (DSM-III-R) with or without phobic avoidance were randomly allocated to one of the three groups and treated for 8 weeks. Fluvoxamine was found to be a potent antipanic agent, followed by a subsequent decrease in avoidance behavior. Ritanserin had no effect on any of the psychometric measurements.
These results suggest, that $5-HT_2$ receptor downregulation is not responsible for the antipanic efficacy of fluvoxamine.

961

CHILDHOOD AND FAMILY CHARACTERISTICS IN PANIC DISORDER

Kaptanoğlu, C.,M.D., Seber,G.,Ph.D. Erkmen,H.,M.D. Dilbaz,N.,M.D., Tekin,D.,M.D.

Department of Psychiatry, Faculty of Medicine, Anadolu University Eskişehir/Turkey

One of the more important new diagnoses in DSM-III is panic disorder. In this study 40 patients who met the DSM-III-R criteria for panic disorder and agoraphobia with panic attacks were examined and also compared with 30 patients who met the DSM-III-R criteria for dysthymia (or Depressive Neurosis).

This study shows that patients with panic disorder or agoraphobia with panic attacks more often had lost or separated from their fathers and/or mothers before the age of 15 years (55% of the subjects), furthermore, they had more often experienced chronic anxiety in childhood than patients who had dysthymia. There was a considerable degree of violence in the homes of the subjects. 58% of them reported having been physically abused by their parents. Also, 62% of their fathers displayed violence toward their mothers and other children in the household as well.

In conclusion, the present study indicates that childhood enviromental factors are important in the development of panic disorder.

962

THE RELATIONSHIP BETWEEN DEPRESSION AND PANIC DISORDER

Cassano G.B, Musetti L., Perugi G., Petracca A., Nisita C.

Chair II, Institute of Clinical Psychiatry, University of Pisa, Italy.

The relationship between anxiety and depressive states has been widely documented at the level of familial, clinical and pharmacotherapeutic findings. Nevertheless, the precise nature of the relationship between the two groups of disorders remains uncertain.

Major depression is not infrequently associated with panic disorder; in the present study the percentage of patients with major depression concomitant with panic disorder was similar to that observed by others Our data along with the literature review we have undertaken suggest that depression seen in the course of panic disorder most commonly represents symptomatic elaboration or complication of panic disorder; less often an associated independent entity; or, more hypothetically, alternative clinical expression of a shared underlying diathesis for both conditions. Future prospective research efforts, especially along familial-genetic lines, are needed to clarify the precise nature of the cross-sectional and logitudinal overlap of anxiety and depressive states.

Session 147 Free Communications: Delusional states

963

PARANOIA - NOSOLOGICAL CONCEPTS FROM KRAEPELIN TO DSM III-R

P. Hoff
Psychiatric Hospital of the
University of Munich
(Head: Prof. Dr. H. Hippius)
Munich, FRG

Most authors agree that paranoia should be conceptualized as delusional disorder with a chronic course. But points of view differ widely as far as nosological status of paranoia, the differentiation from schizophrenic and affective disorders and the problem of etiology are concerned. Therefore paranoia has often been standing in the center of basic psychopathological discussions.
Using the historical development of the term and concept of paranoia as a guideline, we want to show the relevance and problems of the nosological question in psychiatry in general. Furthermore, psychopathological data of about 50 in-patients of our hospital are presented; these patients are suffering from a chronic delusional disorder and their symptomatology has been assessed over a period of at least 5 years. These data will be interpreted on the basis of the above mentioned theoretical considerations.

964

NEUROPHYSIOLOGICAL ASPECTS OF DELUSIONAL PARASITOSIS

M.Musalek, I.Podreka, B.Saletu, O.M.Lesch, H.Walter, M.Bach, V.Passweg, R.Strobl
Department of Psychiatry, University of Vienna, AUSTRIA

In a Tc-99m-HMPAO-SPECT-study we investigated 11 drugfree patients with delusions of parasitosis. The results showed significant differences between relative regional cerebral blood flow (rCBF) of patients with delusional parasitosis and normal controls: a frontal hypoperfusion coupled with a hyperperfusion in basal ganglia. Apart from that a reduction of relative rCBF in inferior temporal regions could be estimated. In a following study we did quantitative topographic EEG-analyses (EEG-Brain-Mapping) in 19 drugfree patients with delusional parasitosis. The prominent result of this study was a significant increase of Delta-activity both in frontal and temporal regions. The corresponding EEG- and SPECT-findings in delusional parasitosis patients support the hypothesis, that delusional parasitosis may primarily occur when the normally inhibitive influence of the upper cortical centers over the basal structures diminishes, resulting in relative hyperactivity in basal regions.

965

DELUSIONAL PARASITOSIS VERSUS CHRONIC ITCHING - A COMPARATIVE STUDY

M.Musalek, M.Bach, H.Walter, O.M.Lesch
Department of Psychiatry, University of Vienna, AUSTRIA

The most important question of psychopathological research in delusional parasitosis (D.P.) is: which are the specific conditions leading from tactile sensations to delusional ideas of being infested by parasites ? To gain deeper insight in this problemacy we compared in a clinical prospective study social, psychic and physical factors - which are considered as important in etiology and pathogenesis of delusions - found in 34 personally examined patients with D.P. with those found in 34 patients suffering only from chronic itching. We found significant differences between the two groups in educational level, social isolation, cleanliness, in some aspects of quality and localization of tactile sensations, former skin diseases, former psychiatric disorders and psychiatrc disorders in blood relations. So we can assume that these factors are of great importance in the development of D.P. No differences could be found in sex, age, occupational level, financial status migration, childhood and animal phobias.

966

DISCUSSION ON THE NOSOLOGY OF CIRCUMSCRIPT STATES OF DELUSION-PRESENTED BY MEANS OF ILLUSTRATION OF THE PERSONAL ODOUR DELUSION

T.A.Moesler, T.Frontzek, E.Lungershausen
Psychiatry Div.,Univ.of Erlangen-Nuremberg, FRG

5 patients demonstrating so-called auto-smell delusion a their primary symptom were treated at the psychiatric clinic of the University of Erlangen. Organic brain diseases or other physical diseases were be ruled out as causes in all cases in light of current medical knowledge. The patients underwent thorough psychiatric and psychological testing; their individual development of symptoms was observed by applying various methods of therapy. Clear indications of endogenous psychosis could not be ascertained in any of the patients.In particular, no patient experienced hallucinations. As to the prerequisites and development of their personal odour experiences,the 5 cases showed a number of relevant similarities which have also characterized other circumscribed delusion states: all patients were subjected to continuing psychosocial stresses which caused insecurity. Their background showed numerous psychogenic and psychosomatic symptoms. A situation of conflict could be detected in all 5 cases as a hypothetical cause which was evidenced by the personal odour delusion.The symptom of personal odour delusion was related to the specific biographic development in each case. The results of our examinations will be discussed in light of the relevant literature. Based on the results, the personal odour delusions of our 5 patients will be classified within the group of delusion-like psychogenous disturbances.

967

DYSMORPHESTHESIES (DYSMORPHOPHOBIA) ET DEMANDE DE CHIRURGIE ESTHETIQUE

M. FERRERI, M. GODEFROY, M. BOSSARD-LEGRAND, J.M. ALBY
Département de Psychiatrie et de Psychologie Médicale

L'étude de 100 demandes de chirurgie esthétique pour mammoplasties comparée à un groupe témoin précise davantage d'antécédents d'anxiété, de ruptures dépressives et un évènement de vie marquant récent et souligne la dimension narcissique de la personnalité et surtout retrouve toujours une distorsion du sentiment esthétique de l'image de soi qui nous fait nommer ces troubles : dysmorphesthésies, vocable plus adéquate que dysmorphophobies.
Si on refuse l'intervention chez 8 % des patients "suspects" ou "insatiables" de chirurgie, dans la majorité des cas l'intervention apporte un réinvestissement narcissique du corps qui peut permettre de débloquer des situations de conflit, de réparer un manque narcissique, de restaurer l'estime de soi à condition que le sujet admette qu'il peut être aimé tel quel et que l'intervention n'apporte qu'une satisfaction de surcroit.
Les complications sont rares avec cependant une fréquente anxiété voire un épisode dépressif transitoire.

968

PROGNOSIS IN DELUSIONAL PSYCHOSES

Jørgensen, P.
Psychiatric Hospital in Aarhus, Denmark

The prognostic value of psychopathological and socio-vocational variables in psychotic patients are highly disputed because of disagreement.
The results of a prospective follow-up study of first-admitted patients with delusional psychoses i.e. functional psychoses with delusions are presented.
It is concluded that good prognosis is exceptional and from a nosological approach attached to patients with reactive psychoses. However, socio-vocational variables at index admission are predictors of higher statistical information than any clinical variable.

969

DIFFICULTE DE TRAITEMENT DU PARANOIAQUE OU
TROUBLE DELIRANT PARANOIDE
Dr. Noel Garneau
Institute Philippe Pinel de Montreal
Montreal, Quebec, Canada

The author discusses the difficulties to identify and treat such patients.
After an analysis of ten cases which responds to the Diagnostic of Delusional (Paranoid) Disorder DSM-III-R code 297.01, the author gives the issue observed after many years of treatment.

Session 148 Free Communications:
Epidemiological and clinical studies in child and adolescent psychiatry

970

CHILDREN'S EMOTIONAL AND BEHAVIOURAL PROBLEMS IN JAPAN, CHINA AND KOREA
Yoshiro Okubo, Masato Matsuura, Takuya Kojima
Ryo Takahashi, Kunihiko Asai*, Yu-feng Wang**
Yu-cun Shen** and Chung-Kyoon Lee***
Dept. of Neuropsychiatry, Tokyo Medical and Dental University, 1-5-45 Yushima Bunkyo-ku, Tokyo, *Asai Hospital, Chiba-ken, JAPAN, **Beijing Medical University, CHINA, ***Seoul National University, KOREA

An epidemiological investigation of emotional and behavioural problems in primary school children, aged 6 to 14 years, was carried out in Japan, China and Korea with the support of WPRO, WHO. A large sample of children (n=7045) was rated by their teachers and parents using the questionnaires developed by Rutter.
The prevalences of children with deviant scores on the Rutter scales were 12.9% at home and 3.9% at school in Japan, 8.3% at school in China, and 19.1% at home and 14.1% at school in Korea. Antisocial behaviours were more frequent than neurotic problems in Japan and Korea. Somatic complaints were commoner in the three countries compared with previous reports using the same scales from other countries. Furthermore, there were major effects of area, sex, school achievement and family background on emotinal and behavioural problems in children, and limited effects of grade, sibship size and birth order.

971

CHILD PSYCHIATRIC CONSULTATION
E.A.F. van Weel
Child psychiatrist from the Amsterdam Academic
Hospital, Holland

The results of two years ('87 and '88) of child psychiatric referral (0-18 years) in the Amsterdam Academic Hospital will be presented. Data have been gathered on reason of referral, symptoms and complaints, family history, psychiatric diagnosis (DSM-III-R) and recommendations of the consultant. Affective disorders, anxiety disorders and somatoform disorders are most frequently seen.
Data from the family history suggest that in affective and anxiety disorders there is often a psychiatric illness in one of the parents; in somatoform disorders the medical history of the (extended) family shows more somatic complaints and/or illness.
The population seen in a child psychiatric consultation service is significantly different from the population seen in the outpatient clinic.
These are strong arguments for the existence of a separate consultation-liaison service: and for more and specific research.

972

SCHOOL MENTAL HEALTH CLINIC

DR.(MRS.)DHAVALE H.S./ DR. PATKAR A.P.
T.N.M. College & B.Y.L.Nair Hospital, Bombay, India.

Childhood Psychiatric Disorders are relatively difficult to recognize. This would result in these disorders being missed by Parents, Teachers or even Doctors. Any school forms a major part of the child's environment and is more structured and uniform than the home. Hence, a child posing problems in the school could be reflecting psychiatric disorders. These prompted us to initiate a Child Preventive Psychiatric Project in the schools of Bombay.

We are running this Clinic for last 9 years and here we are presenting a analysis of last 4 years' visits.

Total number of children seen in last 4 years are 1374, and the diagnostic break up is as follows:-

Diagnosis	1985	1986	1987	1988
1. Neurotic	25	65	114	47
2. Conduct Disorders	7	5	30	30
3. Hyperkinesis	8	12	10	14
4. Psychosis	1	13	2	5
5. Scholastic Backwardness	129	181	370	252
6. Enuresis	28	33	50	75
7. Speech Disorders	24	21	38	50
8. Epilepsy	7	32	10	55
9. Physical Defects	7	19	78	25
10. Others	20	4	10	15

973
MULTICENTRIC STUDY ON THE JUVENILE DISTRESS
De Marco F.,De Leo V.,Perozziello F, Chelucci C.
Department of Mental Health U.S.L.57 Polla (Sa)Italy

The authors wanted to study the problem of the distress in young students in various social and cultural areas.In fact the selected cases,in considerable number(about 2.000),belong to very different environment conditions.
The geographic areas examined are:a rural environment lacking in industrial requisis (Vallo di Diano),a metropolitan environment,full of discrepancies(Napoli) and, like a control case,an islander reality, touristic but still intact(Isola d'Elba). As material,they have used a questionnaire (J.D.E.Q.)enquiring about the different areas of the juvenile distress:drug addiction,school,working future,psychic unfitness,sex.
The authors have come to very interesting data which are now in gradual processing and will be introduced in the congressional seat.

974
A CROSS-CULTURAL COMPARISON OF CHILD PSYCHIATRY OUT-PATIENTS
Dr. S.V. Moodley, M.B.B.S., M.Med (PSYCHIATRY)
Midlands Hospital Complex, Pietermaritzburg, South Africa.

A two-year retrospective study was undertaken of a random selection of 200 patients seen by the Child Psychiatric out-patient clinic at Durban's Addington Hospital which serves the mental health needs of the white and coloured communities. The hospital ward and out-patients department were the most common sources of referral. The coloured population group was referred by outside agencies to a much lesser extent than the white. Most patients belonged to social class five. Parental status revealed an over-representation of divorce, separation or desertion. An even stronger correlate was separation experiences. The study found that 59% of the patients had experienced a significant period of separation from their parents, with most patients being separated from either the father and/or both parents. The majority of the sample revealed major depression and adjustment disorder. The study indicated

1) an urgent need for improvement of delivery or services to children
2) the need for greater social work services for single-parent families.

975
Personality Characteristics of Diabetic Adolescents

M.Liakopoulou M.D., M. Korvesi, C. Dakou M.D.
"AGIA SOFIA" Children's Hospital, Athens Greece

In order to examine anxiety, locus of control, and self competence, 40 diabetic adolescents and preadolescents ages 11-18 and 40 matched controls were given the following scales: The Manifest Anxiety Scale, the Nowicki-Strickland locus of control scale and the Harter Self-Competence Scale. The Mann-Whitney test was performed for the locus of Control Scale, and the MANOVA tests for the Manifest Anxiety and the Harter Scale.

The results show no significant difference in the locus of control ($P > 0.10$) between diabetics and controls, as well as in the self-competence scale. The scores of only one subscale of the Harter Scale, that of Scholastic Competence for children showed statistically significant difference ($P=0010$). There was slight difference in Anxiety between the two groups ($P=0.056$).

Session 149 Free Communications:
Cross-cultural and trans-cultural studies

976
CROSS CULTURAL DIFFERENCES IN PUBLIC OPINION TOWARDS ELDERLY AND ELDERLY WITH DEMENTIA.
Ingvad, B., Hagberg, B. Gerontology Research Centre, Lund, Sweden and Ferrey, G. Hospital E. Roux, Eaubonne, France.

One of the major concerns of aging research today is the public opinion on the elderly. The elderly meet with quite different reactions ranging from being looked upon as someone obsolete, alienated and beside the main stream of societal activity. Or in the other extreme a resource of wisdom that is of great value to society, especially as a keeper of traditional values. An accentuation of these attitudes towards the elderly can be expected when major diseases such as dementia is present and especially if treatment and rehabilitation of the demented patient take place integrated in the community at large.In order to analyse cross-cultural differences in these respects a co-operative research project was set up in France and Sweden. The results show clear differences in attitudes with regard to aging and to the care of patients with dementia. While the French material show a more positive attitude in questions concerning neighbour interactions and exchange of services among the elderly, in the Swedish responses were found a better orientation about the disease, more contact with patients, and a more positive attitude to integration of dementia care in society. The results seem to reflect basic value differences in the two communities which have to be considered in future planning.

977

CROSS-CULTURAL RESEARCH: THE IRANIAN EXPERIENCE
Iradj Siassi M.D., Prof.of Psych.UCLA. L.A.,CA,U.S.A.;
Bahman Eozouni,Ph.D.,Director F.and W.Associates,
Pgh, PA,U.S.A.; Shahrzad F. Siassi Ph.D.,Private
Practice,L.A.,CA.U.S.A.

The controversy over the scientific merit of psychometric instruments developed in the U.S.(West) for use in a non-western culture for research is a major issue among psychiatrists interested in cross-cultural studies. The conventional wisdom has viewed psychopathology as culture specific and idiosyncratic to a host of cultural parameters including child rearing patterns, communal organizations and institutionalized coping resources. Those who subscribe to this view are naturally skeptical about the pertinence of western diagnostic criteria and the usefulness of the associated psychometric instruments. On the other hand, the thrust of modern psychiatric epidemiology increasingly points to a universal (culture-independent) conception of psychiatric disorders. From this perspective diagnostic criteria can be universally applied and the psychometric instruments derived from these criteria can be validly used in cross-cultural research. This presentation will address some of the key issues in this controversy, by discussing their findings from two decades of research with Iranian populations. The studies reported here have relied on both converted western psychometric batteries as well as indigenous and ad-hoc instruments. They range from large scale surveys in Iran to small studies of immigrants.

978

MENTAL DISORDERS: A CROSS-NATIONAL POPULATION COMPARISON. Ali-Asghar Kashfi, M.D., Medical Director, West Lake Hospital, Altomont Spring, Florida, U.S.A.; Shahrzad F. Siassi, Ph.D, Private Practice, L.A., Ca, U.S.A.; and Iradj Siassi M.D., Prof. of Psychiatry, U.C.L.A Med. Sch. L.A., Ca., U.S.A.

Cross national and cross cultural comparison in the field of psychiatric epidemiology can present interesting insights into the factors that influence the manifestations of psychiatric symptoms. In this presentation we compare one-month prevalence of mental disorders in Iranian and U.S. populations. The Iranian prevalence results are determined from 11,984 persons interviewed between 1976 and 1979 for the National Epidemiological Study of Mental Illness, Addictions and Mental Retardation in Iran. They constituted a representative sample of the entire nation. U.S. population estimates are based on the combined site data of the first-wave community samples (18,571 persons) of all five sites that constituted the National Institute of Mental Health Epidemiologic Catchment Area Program. Higher prevalence rates of all mental disorders were found in the U.S. population with the exception of somatization disorders. Procedures for drawing the comparisons are discussed and the evidence for their validity reviewed.

979

THE EFFECT OF CULTURAL CHANGE ON THE MENTAL HEALTH OF IMMIGRANTS
Mavreas V., Bebbington P.
Athens University Medical School
Institute of Psychiatry, London

The study was carried out in a random sample of 291 Greek Cypriots living in SE London. The subjects were interviewed with a battery of instruments including the PSE for the assessment of psychopathology and the Greek immigrant Acculturation Scale for assessing the degree of acculturation into the host culture. The sample was divided into three categories: high, moderate and low acculturation, one third falling into each category. Prevalence rates of cases (ID5+) were 8.8% for males and 19.4% for females. Rates for males were 13.7%, 8.3% and 4.2% and for females 10.9%, 18.4% and 28.6% for the high, moderate and low acculturation categories respectively. Log-linear analysis revealed a statistically significant interaction effect between acculturation and gender indicating a convergence of prevalence rates between sexes with increasing acculturation. The results are discussed in the light of the changes cultural change implies in the roles of sexes.

980

MEXICAN AMERICAN: HOW HIS CULTURE AFFECTS HIS MENTAL HEALTH
Earl M. Stenger, M.D.
Pain Clinic, San Antonio, Texas   USA

The study to determine to what extent the culture of the Mexican-American affects his mental health. Fifty-five Mexican-American psychiatric outpatients were interviewed with special emphasis on culture, background and environment as related to symptomatology.

Cultural areas addressed included: 1. Family structures; 2. Religious beliefs; 3. Witchcraft and curanderismo; 4. Attitude towards mental health; 5. Cultural barriers; 6. Generation level of Mexican-American.

Study confirms the hypothesis that mental abnormality found in the Mexican-American is often attributable to different aspects of the Mexican-American culture and/or to the conflict between the culture and that of the dominant culture within the United States.

It was also determined that ignorance of the Mexican-American culture by a therapist is a significant barrier to successful treatment.

981

SEX DIFFERENCE IN NEUROSIS AMONG THREE ETHNIC MINORITIES IN TAIWAN
Tai Ann Cheng, M.D., Ph.D.(London) Department of Psychiatry, National Taiwan University, Taipei, Taiwan, R.O.C.

The female excess in neurosis, evident in most previous work in Western societies, was examined in one patrilineal (the Bunon), one matrilineal (the Amis) and one bilineal (the Atayal) aboriginal ethnic groups in Taiwan.

Three random samples aged 15 and above, each from four tribes of one ethnic group, were drawn in nearly equal size (n=242 in Atayal, 251 in Amis, and 247 in Bunon). The field work consisted of an ethnographic observation and a detailed sample interview with inventories concerning physical health, psychosocial problems and the extent of acculturation. Psychiatric assessment was carried out using a modified Clinical Interview Schedule.

Results have shown a female excess of neurosis in women in the Bunon, which was not observed in the Atayal. For the Amis, the female excess in neurosis was evident among respondents < 65. A conversely higher rate in men was however found among respondents $\geq$ 65. Findings have lent support to a proposed hypothesis that although the female excess in neurosis will be found in patrilineal society (Bunon), there will be no such difference in the bilineal society (Atayal), and a male excess will be found in the matrilineal society (Amis). Implications of the findings were discussed in a crosscultural context.

982

ALCOHOLISM AMONG FOREIGNERS IN A LARGE CITY IN WEST-GERMANY
Dieter H. Friessem

Psychiatrische Klinik des Bürgerhospitals
Stuttgart, Fed. Rep. of Germany

Stuttgart, a city with 558 000 inhabitants and 19% foreigners, has already been the scene of reports made by the author on epidemiological and clinical-psychiatric observations. In the clinic where the author is employed, more than 2 200 patients are treated for mental disorders. This represents the majority of patients with psychiatric disorders who need to be cared for as in-patients.

The number of alcoholics is particularly large among the German patients. In the present report, the author compares the frequency of alcoholism among Turks, Yugoslavians, Greeks, Italians, Spaniards and other nationalities. Turks and members of Islamic nations who, as expected, are less often found to be dependent on alcohol, are given a particularly thorough analysis. Finally, in connection with the latter, some comparative and transcultural psychiatric considerations are put forward.

Session 150 Free Communications:
Mental health in youth

983

FONDATION SANTE DES ETUDIANTS DE FRANCE - PSYCHIATRIE ET PEDAGOGIE
O. HALFON - J. LAGET - M. FAVIEZ -
Fondation Santé des Etudiants de France
Neufmoutiers-en-Brie (France)

L'originalité de la FSEF est d'accueillir des adolescents qui présentent des troubles psychiatriques graves et qui sont capables de suivre une scolarité. Le Clinique Médico-Psychologique reçoit 30 adolescent(es) qui sont scolarisés sur place.
Nous admettons des patients présentant des troubles de l'humeur, des névroses graves, des troubles du comportement, des états limites. Une pathologie familiale importante coexiste presque toujours. Les durées de séjour sont variables, représentant en moyenne une année scolaire.
Compte-tenu de la longueur des durées de séjour et de la sévérité de la pathologie psychiatrique et de l'échec scolaire, nous avons voulu mettre en place une évaluation : 1°) des soins - 2°) de l'aide pédagogique que nous pouvions apporter à ces adolescents. Pour tenter de répondre à ces questions, nous faisons passer systématiquement à tous les patients un entretien clinique semi-structuré (KSADS et SADS) se référant à la classification DSM III R. Les patients ont la même évaluation à la sortie, avec, en plus, l'échelle d'évènements vitaux de Rutter.
Sur le plan pédagogique, nous essayons de correler le niveau scolaire au moyen d'éléments standardisés (WRATT), au Quotient Intellectuel et à la pathologie psychiatrique. Dans cette communication, nous comparons les résultats de ces évaluations concernant 40 patients.

984

COMMUNITY CHILD PSYCHIATRY:
CHALLENGES AND OPPORTUNITIES
S. Monopolis, M. Stein, M. Cohen, C.W. Schmidt, Jr.
Francis Scott Key Med. Ctr., Baltimore, Md., USA

This paper presents our experiences at a Community Adolescent Psychiatry Service. We provide comprehensive diagnostic, treatment and preventive interventions in order to maintain children in the least restrictive treatment and social environments consistent with their welfare. This is achieved through an outpatient clinic, an after school program, a home intervention/community outreach program. Emphasis is given to multimodality treatment, multidisciplinary approaches, and consultation/liaison with schools, social services, pediatrics, juvenile services, adult psychiatry. Current challenges are: delayed treatment, negative attitudes toward mental illness, lack of parental involvement in treatment, poor compliance, chaotic families, inadequate cooperation by school and social agencies, reaching those who "fall between the cracks," evaluation of treatment effectiveness. Demographic, diagnostic, treatment process, and follow-up data are presented. Future directions include: enhance early interventions, promote parental involvement in treatment, improve compliance establish collaborative programs with schools and social agencies, foster parental treatment, promote primary prevention, enhance training of mental health professionals, institute on-going research.

985

EPIDEMIOLOGICAL STUDY OF UNIVERSITY STUDENTS' MENTAL HEALTH
ALEXANDRIS,V., HATZICHRISTOU,C., STOYIANNIDOU,A. PAPADATOS,Y.
CENTER FOR MENTAL HEALTH AND RESEARCH

This study examined the incidence and prevalence of general health and mental health problems in university students coming from semi-urban and rural areas of the country and dealing with the frustration of going away and the development of their autonomy and independence. The sample was random and representative and consisted of 253 students staying in the university's dormitories in Athens and Thessaloniki. Their ages ranged from 18 to 24 years. The following questionnaire were administered to the students: a demographic questionnaire with additional questions regarding drug and alcohol use, the General Health Questionnaire (GHQ 28 - Goldberg), the Beck Depression Inventory and the State-trait Anxiety Inventory (Spielberger). The incidence and prevalence of somatic symptoms,depression, anxiety, social dysfunction, drug and alcohol use were explored and related to various demographic variables.
A high percentage of cases of psychiatric risk was identified. The profiles of these students consists of a combination of high scores on depression, somatic symptoms and anxiety. Drug and alcohol abuse was minimal.

The findings are discussed in relation to stages of ego development and their impact on university mental health services.

986

100 ETUDIANTS EN MEDECINE VUS EN PSYCHIATRIE ET LEUR EVOLUTION APRES 15 ANS.
DROUIN, Jacques, Université de Sherbrooke, Canada

Cent étudiants ont été évalués et traités par le même psychiatre sur une période de 15 ans dans une clinique de service aux étudiants. Soixante-dix d'entre eux sont venus d'eux-même et trente ont été dirigés pour traitement. La pression et les difficultés à s'organiser ont été les principales raisons. A ce jour, 61 ont complété leur traitement, 39 l'ont abandonné, 15 ont quitté l'école de médecine. 85 ont gradué. Les principaux moyens thérapeutiqes furent la psychothérapie à court ou moyen terme et toujours dans chaque cas d'orientation analytique. Nous avons l'impression que 18 d'entre eux n'ont pas changé, 30 sont légèrement améliorés et 30 modérément améliorés tandis que 22 sont très améliorés. Plusieurs observations sont faites sur la maturité que les patients ont développé et sur le stress qu'ils ont dû subir durant leurs études. Nous étudierons leurs évolutions, la population du Québec étant peu mobile, il est relativement facile de pouvoir retracer ceux qui nous ont consulté même si notre cohorte fut établie il y a plus de 15 ans. Leur devenir est très variable, si deux sont devenus directeurs d'hôpitaux, deux vivent sans emploi, d'allocations gouvernementales.

987

EPIDEMIOLOGY OF PSYCHOLOGICAL PROBLEMS OF SCHOOL AGE GREEK CHILDREN
F. Motti-Stefanidi, J. Tsiantis, K. Richardson.
Department of Psychological Pediatrics, "A. Sophia" Children's Hospital, Athens, Greece.

The behavioral and emotional problems and the competencies of non-referred children from Athens were studied. Additionally, Greek norms for the scales of Achenbach's Child Behavior Checklist were developed. This checklist was administered to the parents of 466 children aged 6-11 years and scores were calculated on its subscales as defined by Achenbach. Low ($r=-0.3$) but significant ($p<0.01$) negative correlations were found between social competence and total behavior problem scores.
Relatively high scores were found on the internalizing (means: 15.1 for boys and 13.3 for girls) and externalizing scales (16.4 and 18.6) to the extent that the cut-offs for the indication of high-risk suggested from U.S. data were exceeded by 36% of boys and 39% of girls. Appropriate cut-offs (90th percentile) of the scales were computed from our sample.Similar results were obtained for narrow-band behavior scales.These data permit the use of this checklist as a screening instrument with Greek children of this age range. Further research is needed to elucidate the clinical relevance of these scales.

988

PSYCHOLOGICAL PROBLEMS OF SCHOOL-AGE GERMAN AND GREEK CHILDREN:A CROSS-CULTURAL STUDY
J. Tsiantis, F. Motti-Stefanidi, K. Richardson
H. Schmeck, F. Pustka.
Dept. of Psych. Pediatrics."A.Sophia"Children's Hosp Athens,Greece; Zentrum der Psychiatrie der J.W. Goethe Universität,Frankfurt,Germany

The behavioral and emotional problems and the competencies of non-referred children from Athens,Greece and Westphalia,Germany were examined in a cross-cultural study. Achenbach's Child Behavior Checklist was administered to the parents of 466 Greek and 799 German children, aged 6-11 years.Statistical analyses revealed that Greek children received overall higher scores on the behavior problem scales and lower scores on the social competence scale The Greek parents reported on the average 24 of the 118 behavior problems as present whereas the German parents reported only 16.Greek children were rated higher than German children ($p<0.001$) on the total behavior problem scale (means for Greeks:35,8 for boys and 36,3 for girls;and for Germans 20,7 and 16,6, respectively). A significant interaction effect between sex and culture is present.This can be explained by the finding that on the externalizing scale German boys scored higher than girls and Greek girls higher than boys.On the internalizing scale boys scored higher than girls in both countries.The findings reveal the influence of culture on the behavioral and emotional problems of childhood.

989

Indicators of Mental Health in Young Women.
Sharma, S.D. and Nagpal, R.
Directorate General of Health Services,
New Delhi. INDIA

The study aimed at developing indicators of mental health in young women using Subjective Wellbeing Inventory and Fordyce Ladder. The sample consisted of the cohort of children born in 1970 who have been extensively studied for growth pattern and healthy psychosocial development. The results show that young women, compared with young men, reported significantly higher on Transcendence factor - belongingness with mankind and belief in a common force, but manifested significantly less confidence in managing unexpected or crises situations, and in coping with future. In Perceived ill health factor of the test, young women reported significantly more frequent pains in various parts of body, palpitations, giddiness, disturbed sleep and getting tired easily. They scored relatively lower on expectation-achievement congruence, and perceived their social contacts as deficient. No significant differences were observed on family group support, social support and overall general well-being status.

The study has heuristic implications for planning intervention programmes.

Session 151   Poster Presentation:
Psychiatric aspects of AIDS

990

BEHAVIOURAL STYLES IN PATIENTS WITH AIDS
Bauco A.R., Piccione M., Castellet y Ballarà F., Valitutti R., Sbona I.
Istituto di Psichiatria, Università "La Sapienza", Roma, Italy.

Terminal illnesses bring very severe psychological problems well known since long, even more if the brain or also the brain is affected.
In-patients with AIDS of the Infectious Diseases Department have been studied. Some of them completed MMPI.
Our results show that modifications of behaviour and life style appear to be in relation to the onset of clinical symptoms, not to the notice of detection of HIV antibodies.

991

L'IMPACT EMOTIF DU SIDA SUR LES SUJETS SERONEGATIVES SANS FACTEUR DE RISQUE: ASPECTS PSYCHIATRIQUES.
Zamperetti Marco, Goldwurm G.F.
Servizio Psichiatrico "Origgi I°" e Centro di Medicina Comportamentale - Ospedale Cà Granda Niguarda - Milano - ITALY -

Parmi des sujets seronegatives sans facteurs de risque nous avons observé et classé selon le DSM III-R, trois cas de ce qu'en litterature on a appelé Pseudo-SIDA et deux cas d'un délire très particulier induit d'une patiente atteinte du SIDA. Donc on presentera les cas suivantes: F.C., boucher de 42 a., marié, a développé un délire de culpabilité et de ruine centré sur le SIDA au cours d'une Depression Majeur avec Manifestations Psychotiques concordantes avec l'Humeur (296.34); L.C., pharmacien de 26 a., mariée, a presenté un Trouble Obsessionel Compulsif (300.30) avec des idées et des images sur le SIDA qui s'imposaient malgré elle et avec comportements rituels afin d'éviter l'infection; M.Z., employé de 38 a., marié, a montré une Hypocondrie (300.70) centrée sur la crainte que chaque petit symptôme physique pût être une manifestation du SIDA; enfin il y a les cas de G.R., maîtresse d'école de 56 a., divorcée, et de sa mère G.E., pensionnée de 77 a., veuve, qui ont presenté un délire dermatozoique qu'on peut classer comme un Trouble Psychotique Induit (297.30): en effet ce syndrome délirant et hallucinatoire a été induit en elles à cause de l'excessive participation émotive et affective pour M.P., leur fille et petite-fille, atteinte du SIDA et d'une cirrhose hépatique, qui, au cours des ces graves pathologies, avait manifesté sur le plan psychique un typique Délire Dermatozoique d'Ekbom.

992

POSSIBLES CORRELATIONS ENTRE SIDA ET TROUBLES PSYCHIATRIQUES.
Zamperetti Marco, Vergani D., Fernandez I., Cusini M*, Zerboni R*
Servizio Psichiatrico "Origgi I°"-Ospedale Cà Granda Niguarda-
*Clinica Dermosifilopatica-Università degli Studi-Milano-ITALY-
Nous voulons proposer une synthèse des observations cliniques que nous avons effectué dans deux année à l'Hôpital de Niguarda et à la Clinique Dermosyphilopathique de l'Université de Milan sur les différents corrélations entre SIDA et troubles psychiatriques. Les complications psychiatriques en cours de SIDA ont été présentes dans le 37,6% (47/125) des patients dont les troubles mentaux organiques étaient le 42,6% (20/47), donnée qui confirme ceux de la litterature. En effet une évaluation effectuée avec le Cognitive Behavioural Assessment 2.0 sur 43 sujets séro positives a mis en évidence que le 40% des sujets a des problemes psychologiques dont les plus significatifs sont la depression, 23% des cas avec un risque suicidaire très élevé, et le psychoticisme, 39% des cas comme trait de personnalité le plus commun parmi les toxicomanes. Nous croyons aussi que la présence des troubles psychiques induise une telle réduction des capacités de jugement d'entraîner plus fréquemment que dans la population générale les typiques conduites à risque pour l'infection de HIV: cette hypothèse, du SIDA comme complication des troubles mentaux, a été confirmé en observant la prevalence des séropositives hospitalisés dans notre service psychiatrique qui a été, à la fin du premier année, du 6,1%, quinze fois celle (0,4%) trouvée en même temps dans le group de contrôle des donneurs de sang. Il faut enfin considérer une troisième corrélation: celle due à l'impact émotif du SIDA sur les séronegatives, en distinguant les sujets selon qui aient ou non des facteurs de risque.

Session 152 Poster Presentation:
Consultation-liaison psychiatry

993
FIRST YEARS OF EXPERIENCE IN CONSULTATION-LIAISON PSYCHIATRY IN GREECE
PAPAMICHAEL E., PERTESSI E., SPIROPOULOS J
LIOSSI A., STATHIS P.
GENERAL HOSPITAL OF NIKEA, PIRAEUS, GREECE
The purpose of this report is the investigation of the parameters in the area of Consultation-Liaison Psychiatry in Greece. A retrospective study of rates, which have been given by the psychiatric departments of Greek Hospitals, during the first years of their function (until 1987) has been compiled. The Consultation-rate among Hospitals is between 0.43%-3.01%. Special Hospitals (Cancer-treatment departments) reach a rate up to 9.80%. The mean of the age for the referrals is 39.89 to 51.40 years old. In all Hospitals, the internal medicine departments have an increased rate (52%-81.50%) followed by surgical departments (15%-48%). The largest categories by referrals are: the affective disorders (22.63%-64.74%) followed by suicidal attempts (16.10%-43.10%), anxiety disorders, somatoform disorders and dissociative disorders (9.11%-28.40%). If someone estimates the existance of depression at the suicidal attempts, it will be clear that depression is the basic reason for referrals. Finally, the adoption of a common medical terminology by psychiatrists working at General Hospitals is a requisite for a satisfactory data investigation.

994
LIAISON PSYCHIATRY
LORETTU L-SANNA MN-PITTALIS A-REPOSSI C
CORGIOLU T-NIVOLI GC
CLINICA PSICHIATRICA UNIVERSITA' DI SASSARI - ITALY.
In this study the authors examine, through experiences gained from the application in Italy in 1978 of the law 180 to the present time, the evolution of the activity of psychiatric liaison defined as "consultation psychiatry", carried out in non-psychiatric wards and institutes in the University sphere (Sassari University, Italy). The authors show the psychiatric pathologies concomitant to organic illnesses (independent or associated pathologies), psychogenous reactions to oncological illnesses (in initial, intermediate and terminal phases), fictitious disturbances, etc. Variables are considered such as modalities, symptomology, time and type of ward asking for liaison psychiatry, and diagnoses of admission and discharge are also compared.

* LIAISON PSYCHIATRY (CONSULTATION PSYCHIATRY)

995
USE OF A STANDARDIZED DATABASE FORM IN A CONSULTATION-LIAISON SERVICE: CONSIDERATIONS AND CRITICS

Castellet y Ballarà F., Valitutti R., Sbona I., Bauco A.R., Piccione M.
Istituto di Psichiatria, Università "la Sapienza", Roma, Italy.

The availability of a standardized database form in a Consultation-Liaison Psychiatry Service, on one hand allows the focusing, the gathering and the statistical analysis of many data, on the other limits and coerces the possibility of recording the patient's emotional word.
From this considerations a database form has been elaborated which scans several mental functions in as widest and descriptive way as possible to limit at maximum the loss of life experiences never adequately registrable.

996
LEVELS OF ANXIETY AND DEPRESSION IN GENERAL HOSPITAL PATIENTS: SELF ASSESSMENT AND PHYCISIANS EVALUATION
Sakkas P., Soldatos C.R., Bergiannaki J.D., Economou M., Theodorou K., Syrengelas M.
Dept. of Psych., Univ. of Athens, Eginition Hospital, Greece
The present study assesses the frequency of anxiety and depression met in patients of a general hospital. The patients were interviewed by means of the Foulds Self-Assessment Scale for Anxiety and Depression and the doctors by a special questionnaire aimed to examine their views concerning the existence of anxiety and depression in their patients. The results were the following: 32.6% of the patients interviewed reported intense symptoms of both anxiety and depression, while their respective doctors reported these symptoms in only 19.5% of their patients. It is important to note that only 8.7% of the patients' answers corresponded with those of their doctors. It appears also that the doctors found it especially difficult to diagnose cases of depression as in such cases the answers corresponded with only a 5.8% of the patients, while in anxiety cases the corresponding answers were 10.9%. Data analysis showed that only the sex of the patients had a statistical significance in relation to the intensity of his/her anxiety or depression. Thus, our results indicate that many of the patients reporting symptoms of anxiety/depression had been failed to be diagnosed by their doctors (general physicians and surgeons).

997
LIAISON PSYCHIATRY IN AN INSULAR COMMUNITY

José Nobre Madeira, Hospital de Angra do Heroismo, Angra do Heroismo, Região Autónoma dos Açores, Portugal

The present paper reflects our experience during an year's work in a Psychiatric Ambulatory Unit (P.A.U.) in an Azorean Island. The Unit serves over 75 thousand people, mainly rural working class, living in three islands: Terceira, S. Jorge and Graciosa. Our goal in writing this paper is to examine the work done in 1987 in order to provide a better liaison with community doctors. With this purpose we discuss the clinical characteristics of the sample - 264 patients, commenting who referred them and the reason why they were sent, the clinical diagnosis and the follow-up. One of the main conclusions we came to is that the majority of the patients referred to the P.A.U. could have been treated or followed by family doctors with benefits for the patients and the community.

998
ORGANIZATION AND IMPORTANCE OF THE CONSULTATION-LIAISON PSYCHIATRY IN THE GENERAL HOSPITAL
Piccione M.,Bauco A.R.,Sbona I.,Valitutti R.,Castellet y Ballarà F.
Istituto di Psichiatria, Università "la Sapienza", Roma, Italy.

In the last years the Consultation-liaison Psychiatry became more and more important in Italy not only in patient-care, diagnosis and therapy but even in education and research.
The Authors, on the ground of their clinical experiences, emphasize that close collaboration between experts in different but not separated fields supports, on one side the exportation of Psychiatry, setting it free from a perverse ideology of segregation, on the other side gives the chance of intervention in the main interest of the suffering man otherwise ignored and neglected.

Session 153 Poster Presentation:
Psychometrics and psychiatric diagnosis

999
PSYCHOMETRIC TESTS AS PREDICTIVE FACTORS OF THERAPEUTIC EFFICACY IN DEPRESSIVE PATIENTS
Fischer,U., Strauss, W., Klieser, E.
University Clinic of Psychiatry, D'dorf

There are hints in the literature that in depressive patients the cognitive disorders caused by depression normalize prior to the reduction of affective symptoms and thus might be used as an indicator for the response to antidepressive pharmacotherapy. At the University Clinic of Psychiatry in Duesseldorf we conducted a study in 48 patients with the diagnosis of depression according to the DSM III classification of a "Major Depressive Disorder" subtype Melancholia who received a standard medication of 150 mg Amitryptiline for 8 weeks, in order to determine whether the extent of cognitive disorders measured pretreatment by psychological tests (multiple vocabulary choice test, coloured-word-interference-test, attention-distraction-test, Leeds-Motor-Test), could be an indicator for the therapy efficacy in those patients who respond to treatment. The response to treatment was measured by a reduction of minimal 15 points in the HAMD and BDI. Results revealed that some subtests of the psychometric tests could be used as indicators for therapy response.

1000
A NEW LIFE EVENTS SCALE : EVE (FERRERI, VACHER)

M. FERRERI, J. VACHER, S. TAWIL, J.M. ALBY

Department of psychiatry and medical psychology (Pr J.M. ALBY) - Hopital Saint-Antoine 75012 - PARIS (FRANCE)

Most of the studies on life events - depression relationships make a clear-cut separation between predisposing and precipitating factors i.e. events appearing during childhood or later on in adult life. Based on a self-estimation of a life events scale (EVE, Ferreri, Vacher) our new approach take into account the all biography of individuals in order to determine their vulnerability and a depressive risk in a more preventive prospective.

1001

VALIDATION OF THE COMPREHENSIVE PSYCHOPATHOLOGICAL RATING SCALE (CPRS)
H. Sauer, P. Richter, Ch. Hornstein, H. Saß
Psychiatric Dept., Heidelberg University, FRG

The CPRS has been translated into German (KUNY et al.) and subscales have been constructed (MAURER et al.). However, the validity of the CPRS has not yet been examined on the basis of longitudinal data. For this purpose, the four week treatment course of 60 RDC schizoaffectives (31 schizo-depressives, 29 schizomanics) was investigated using the CPRS and other rating scales. Our first aim was to investigate construct validity, i.e. the question whether the Depressive, the Manic and the Schizophrenic CPRS subscales measure the psychopathological constructs that it is intended to measure. This could be confirmed by our cross-sectional and longitudinal findings. Furthermore, the convergent validity was examined by multitrait-multimethod matrices. It is shown that the Depressive, the Manic and the Schizophrenic CPRS-subscales correlate with a minimum level of $r > 0.75$ with the Hamilton Depression, Young Mania Rating scale and the BPRS, respectively. The discriminant validity is also discussed. It is concluded that the CPRS is a useful rating scale when investigating treatment course.

1002

EVOLUTIONARY ANALYSIS OF DEPRESSIVE SINDROME BY THE TEQ-DE
Vicente, A.; Abril, A.; Badía, M.A.; Fonseca, V.. Psychiatry Department Complutense University of Madrid (SPAIN)

Depressing symptoms are analyzed for one hundred cases, diagnosed as depressive sindrome by the TEQ-DE method after six months of measuring (four dimension structural questionnaire for the depression), developed by prof. Alonso-Fernández.

The four clinical schemas described by the TEQ-DE (for 4,3,2 and 1 dimension) were evaluated at the beginning of the study, and one, three and six months after, evaluating the different dimensional profiles as well as their reaction to the standarized anti-depressing treatment.

1003

THE FACTORIAL STRUCTURE OF TEQ-DE
Martín, M., Civeira, J.M., Sanchez, L., Dominguez, C.. Psychiatry Department Complutense University of Madrid (Spain).

The Tetradimensional Structural Questionnaire for Depression (TEQ-DE) is based in a new clinical model of depression obtained through an examination of patients using a phenomenological structural method. The TEQ-DE is made up of 63 items distributed into the four dimensions of the model. And each items is evaluated on a scale of 0 to 4 points.

This study have been done in an acute unit and 434 psychiatric in-patient have completed the questionnaire. 48.2% were depressive patients. To obtain the factorial structure a principal component analysis (PCA) was performed.

15 factors were found explaining 58% of total varianza. The items are distributed into the factors in the following manner: 19 items (over 21) of dimension I (Humor depressive) in _four_ factors, 8 items (over 14) of dimension II (Anergy) in _three_ factors, 8 items (over 14) of dimension III (Communication disorder) in _two_ factors and 10 items (over 14) in _five_ factors. The other items not count here are part of a factor which principal agrupation belongs to a different model's dimension. The items present in the factors made possible to name each one easily.

1004

CBS-R, A NEW SCALE FOR BURDEN ON RELATIVES OF SCHIZOPHRENIC PATIENTS, EFFECTS OF EDUCATION
Bergmark Tord, Wistedt Börje, Karolinska Institute Psychiatric Clinic, Danderyd Hospital, Stockholm, Sweden.

The burden on the families of schizophrenic patients has increased during deinstitutionalisation. Faulty information, lingering mistreatment of the families and lack of rehabilitation in the community are partly responsible. Apart from antipsychotic medication, the emotional climate in the families has a great impact for prognosis. Education about the nature of schizophrenia is believed to influence the family climate. A new scale, Care Burden Scale for Relatives, CBS-R, is developed and under validation. The scale focuses on the psychic and physical burden; on effects on health and work; on the situation of siblings; and on attitudes to medication and psychiatry (90 items). 18 relatives were measured before and after 7 educational sessions regarding schizophrenia. A control group received no education. Preliminary results indicate both a reduction of the psychic burden, and a favourable change in the attitude to antipsychotic medication and psychiatry.

1005

DSM-III-R AXIS V; EFFECT OF SYMPTOMS ON ASSESSMENT OF SOCIAL FUNCTIONNING
P.Robert, V.Aubin, M.Dumarcet, T.Braccini, G. Darcourt
Hopital Pasteur - CHU Nice 06002, France

The aim of this study was to investigate relationship and differences between two scales assessing subject's adaptative functionning. On one hand axis V in DSMIII-R (G.A.F.) include specific symptoms for each level of functioninning described. On the other hand Psychosocial attitude rating scale (PARS), (ROBERT 1988) does not include clinical symptoms. A total of 78 psychiatric inpatients were rated independently in the same interview by two trained psychiatric residents. The first rater used GAF and the second rater PARS. Diagnosies according to DSMII - R axis I were checked independently during the hospitalisation.
Results: The tow ratings were correlated for the whole sample and for each diagnostic catergory. Diagnosis (axis I) explained 63,9 % of the variance in axis V and only 23,8 % in PARS. Axis V is then redundant with axis I which is opposite to the aim of a multiaxial system.
PARS describe aspects of the disorder that are distinct of clinical symptoms. These occupational and social aspects may be of great interest for a best evaluation of severity in mental disorders.

Session 154 Poster Presentation:
Pharmacotherapy of anxiety

1006

ANXIOLYTIC EFFECT OF BETA-BLOCKERS
Einwaechter Hans-Martin
Bad Neuenahr-Ahrweiler, FRG

In the last 25 years beta-adrenergic blockers were found to be effective in the treatment of anxiety. Pitts and Allen (1979) gave a review about the numerous reports. Since then a great number of newer beta-blockers was developed. This study is to test and compare some new agents in their efficiency.
In a 6 week trial 24 patients were treated with oxyprenolol, metoprolol, atenolol or penbutolol. From a number of neurotic anxiety patients persons with predominantly somatic symptoms favouring those with panic heart attacks were selected. 4 of the patients were continuously ECG-recorded using a 24 h tape recorder. Rating of anxiety was made using the heart rate and the Hamilton Anxiety scale by averaging each group rating. The ECG monitored patients were selected suffering from mainly nocturnal panic heart attacks, and had to record a sleep protocol. This proved the theory of James (1890) that the physical symptoms of anxiety elicited the mental changes. The patients reported to be awaken due to palpitation and the ECG record showed an earlier start of tachycardia. Especially this group took most advantage of the beta blockers. All tested beta blockers were consistently noted to be significant effective in relieving somatic anxiety syndroms as palpitation and tachycardia in the sequence: oxyprenolol>penbutolol>metoprolol>atenolol.

1007

A PLACEBO-CONTROLLED, DOUBLE-BLIND STUDY OF AMILSUPRIDE IN DYSTHYMIC DISORDERS

Costa e Silva, Jorge Alberto, Prof. Dr.
State University of Rio de Janeiro - Rio de Janeiro - Brazil.

In the current study, 40 subjects that satisfied the DSM-III-R criteria for Dysthymia (or Depressive Neurosis) 300.40 were treated with amilsupride (a new benzamide substituted derivate) and placebo for 4 weeks, following a period of 2-weeks washout.

Subjects were submitted to physical examination, medical history, laboratory tests, Hamilton Depression Rating Scale, Échelle de Ralentissement de Widlocher, Scale for the Assessment of Negative Symptoms (SANS, Andreasen) and check-list for side-effects.

In the analysis, oral doses of 100mg/day were statistically significantly superior than placebo. The results are discussed.

1008

Suriclone, an new anxiolytic, in the treatment of GAD.
B. Musch, Ph. Guillet
CNS Clinical Research Dept. Rhône-Poulenc-Santé. Antony. FRANCE.

In this multicenter, double-blind placebo-controlled study, the efficacy and safety of suriclone (0.2 mg tid), a new anxiolytic of the cyclopyrrolone series, were compared with those of lorazepam (1 mg tid) in 150 outpatients with Generalized Anxiety Disorder, treated by their general practitioner.

Treatment duration was four weeks.

Patients returned at weekly intervals for evaluation of efficacy parameters and adverse experiences; laboratory safety variables were measured pre- and post-treatment.

Primary efficacy variables consisted of the Hamilton anxiety Scale (HAM-A) and the Physicians' Clinical Global Impression (CGI) .

In the Suriclone group, CGI showed significant improvement from baseline over the placebo group on Day 28.

The incidence and severity of side-effects were significantly lower with suriclone than with lorazepam.

In the setting of general practice, Suriclone appears to be more efficacious and better tolerated than lorazepam in patients suffering from Generalised Anxiety Disorder.

1009

LORAZEPAM VERSUS DIAZEPAM AND PLACEBO:
A SINGLE-BLIND CLINICAL TRIAL
BARTILOTTI R. ALLIANI D.
PSYCHIATRIC CL. "PARCO DELLE ROSE"ROME
ITALY.

The AA. report, in this work clinical data
from a single-blind trial of Lorazepam,
Diazepam and placebo in the treatmen of 63
in-and out-patients with anxious symptoma
tology. The characteristics of the examined patients for trial admission were reported. The mean daily doses used were 3
mg. of Lorazepam versus 6 mg. of Diazepam
during the first week and 6 mg. of Loraze
pam versus 12 mg. of Diazepam during the
next five weeks. Hamilton Rating Scale for
Anxiety and tests aimed at expectations
from the drug and at effects achieved with
the drug were given weekly. The trial data
suggest that expectations from the drug
change according to effects given.
Results show that, although Lorazepam grea
ter than placebo, Lorazepam seems to have
a greater concordance with the changing
expectations.

1010

LOR AND BRO COMPARED DOUBLE-BLIND FOR SAFETY &
WITHDRAWAL IN GAD
D.J.McClure, C.F.Mayes, H.Mesic
University of British Columbia, Vancouver, Canada

Lorazepam (LOR) and bromazepam (BRO) are
intermediate-acting benzodiazepines with similar
halflives. No studies comparing therapeutically
equivalent doses have been completed to date.
Sixty outpatients (22 55 yr) received
therapeutically equivalent doses of LOR 1 mgm
t.i.d. and BRO 4.5 mgm t.i.d. for 3 weeks
following a 1 week placebo wash-out period. The
drugs were then abruptly withdrawn by substituting
placebo, for 2 weeks. HARS, CGL and SCL 90 were
conducted weekly and the withdrawal symptom
checklist was added during the final 2 weeks. A
consent form was signed by each participant. A
physical examination and routine laboratory tests
were performed at baseline and at study
completion. The treatment groups differed (p<0.05)
in sex (LOR: 25 M, 9 F; BRO: 11M, 15 F), but age
range was similar. LOR and BRO were equally
effective in relieving anxiety. Both treatment
groups experienced a progressive reduction in HARS
scores over the 3 week treatment period.
Approximately 41 different side effects were
recorded with the BRO group reporting twice as
many complaints as the LOR group. Those most
frequently mentioned were drowsiness, dry mouth,
fatigue and decreased libido for LOR, and
drowsiness, drugged/intoxicated feeling, decreased
concentration, fatigue, irritability and dry mouth
for BRO. Analysis of HARS and SCL 90 data showed
that the withdrawal effects were similar for the
two groups. Their frequency, severity and duration
will be discussed.

1011

BUSPIRONE VS. DIAZEPAM IN TREATMENT OF ANXIETY IN
GENERAL PRACTICE
Moring J, Alarotu P, Haukijärvi A, Ilvonen T, Kerä-
nen P, Kukkonen P, Ollinen M, Rasmussen M, Tamminen
P, Lehto H. Dept. of Psychiatry, University of Oulu
and Research Center, Farmos Group Ltd,Turku,Finland

87 patients with generalized anxiety disorder were
treated for six weeks in a double blind trial with
buspirone (B) or diazepam (D). Patients had no
prior treatment with anxiolytics for 12 weeks or
for 2 weeks. HAM-A score was at least 18 at entry,
and no concomitant psychotropic medication was allowed. Initial dose of B and D was 5 mg t.i.d. 57
patients completed the whole 8 week study period.
In this group the Initial score of HAM-A was 22.8
in B group and 22.1 in D group. The scores at the
end of the treatment period were 7.5 and 8.9 respectively. The patients were re-evaluated two weeks
after the withdrawal of therapy. HAM-A was 8.1 in
the B group and 11.9 in the D group, which indicates withdrawal symptoms in D group. There were 7
drop-outs in B group and 8 in D group during the
drug treatment. The reasons were unwillingness to
continue the trial (B and D), fatigue (mostly D)
subjective feeling of ineffectiveness of the drug
(B). Spontaneous side-effects reported during the
trial were fatigue (8 B, 19 D), dizziness (6 B,5D),
headache (2 B, 3 D) and paresthesia (2 B). In conclusion, buspirone and diatzepam appear to be equally effective in the treatment of generalized anxiety in general practice. The advantages of buspirone seem to be: less fatique and lack of withdrawal symptoms.

1012

BUSPIRONE VERSUS OXAZEPAM IN TREATMENT OF
GENERALIZED ANXIETY IN GENERAL PRACTICE
Hetta J, Strand M, Rosén A, Sörensen S, Malmström R, Fabian C,
Marits K, Vetterskog K, Liljestrand A-G and Hegen C.
Dept of Psychiatry, University Hospital, 751 85 Uppsala, Sweden

230 patients with generalized anxiety and a Hamilton Anxiety
Rating Score (Ham A) ≥ 18 were in a double blind design randomized
to buspirone (B) 5-10 mg TID or oxazepam (Ox) 10 mg - 20 TID
oral treatment for 6 weeks. Prior to entrance no anxiolytic treatment
was allowed for three months. 20 patients (12 B, 8 ox) were excluded
from efficacy analysis due to drug treatment < 7 days, and 4 were
excluded due to concomitant psychotropic medication (1 B, 3 Ox).

In the 206 efficacy patients (100 B, 106 Ox) there was a decrease of
Ham A (mean ± S.D.) from 23.9 ± 4.1 to 10.6 ± 7.7 in the B group
and from 23.9 ± 4.2 to 11.5 ± 8.0 in the Ox group. The slope of the
fall in HAM A was similar for the two groups. The two treatment
groups behaved practically identical also in the other ratings (Ham
Depression, Raskin, Covi, and HSCL-56). In none of the efficacy
variables was oxazepam superior. In 127 of 230 patients (64 B, 63
Ox) spontaneous adverse events were reported. They included
drowsiness, dizziness, headache, nausea and nervousness and were
relatively similar in the two groups in both pattern and frequency.
The events causing treatment withdrawal included drowsiness (mostly
Ox) dizziness and nausea (mostly B), and depression.

In conclusion, buspirone and oxazepam appear to be equally
effective in the treatment of generalized anxiety. This outcome in
combination with previously documented abscense of dependency
liability makes Buspirone a clinically important anxiolytic drug.

1013
DOTHIEPIN (DOSULEPIN) IN ANXIETY ASSOCIATED WITH DEPRESSION. AN OVERVIEW

N.P. Cartwright, S. Donovan, Research Department, The Boots Company PLC, Nottingham, UK.

Most patients presenting with depression in General Practice have accompanying symptoms of anxiety. Symptomatic treatment with a minor tranquiliser alone relieves anxiety but not depression. We review the evidence of the anxiolytic effect of dothiepin (Dp) in mixed anxiety and depression.

Four controlled trials to evaluate the anti-depressant effect of Dp on patients with mixed anxiety and depression have demonstrated the useful anxiolytic properties of Dp (1,2,3,4).

Dp has also been shown to have anxiolytic effects comparable to chlordiazepoxide over one(5) and three(6) weeks and to alprazolam over four weeks(7).

Dp can thus provide effective anxiolytic benefit in depressed patients without the risk of dependency associated with benzodiazepines.

1. Lipsedge MS et al, Psychopharm. 1971;19:153
2. Pierce D, Neuropharmacol. 1980;19:1219
3. Sharma SD, J. Assoc. Phys. Ind. 1981;29:725
4. Takahashi R et al. Clin. Eval. 1983;11:201
5. Zapletalek M et al. Act. Nerv. Sup. 1973;15:119
6. Johnson F et al. Practitioner. 1973;211:362
7. Cropper A et al. Pharmatherap. 1987;5:76

1014
OPEN STUDY OF PRAZEPAM : TYPOLOGY OF 2420 ANXIOUS PATIENTS BY THE F.A.R.D.
R. von Frenckell, M. Ferreri, D. Bonnet, J.P. Girre Neuropsychiatric Dept., University of Liege, C.H.U. (B35), B-4000 LIEGE SART TILMAN BELGIUM

An open trial (prazepam 30 mg per day) was planed:
- *to confirm a prevalidation (R. von Frenckell et al., 1989) of the FAR Diagram;*
- *to study the specific efficacy of the drug on the four factors of the diagram.*

Factor analyses (multiple correspondences and principal components) have shown :
- *that each item, scored from 0 to 6, has a good range of gravity and that each degree of them is correctly ordered;*
- *that the sum of the scale is possible in terms of the participation of each item at the same latent measure;*
- *that the prevalidated structure is correctly pointed out with the classical four factors (somatic, relational, cognitive and vigilance).*

By the way of a cluster analysis, four profiles of patients were extracted : two clusters were characterized by the global level of their profiles (low and high), the third cluster was characterized by the high level of the somatic factor and the last cluster was characterized by the high level of the cognitive factor.
Each cluster was studied in terms of response to prazepam and in terms of dosage. The FAR Diagram was very useful to point out the evolution of these specific groups of patients.

1015
THE EFFICACY OF D,L-KAVAIN IN THE TREATMENT OF ANXIETY - A SURVEY

A.Klimke, E.Klieser, E.Lehmann, W.H.Strauss
Department of Psychiatry Duesseldorf, FRG

The psychopharmacological treatment of anxiety for example by benzodiazepines can be a problem because of addiction and other side-effects.
D,L-Kavain ($\pm$ 5,6 Dihydro-4-methoxy-6-styryl-pyron), which corresponds to one of the psychoactice components of the Kawa bush (Piper methysticum), seems to be effective in the treatment of non-psychotic anxiety without these undesired effects.
In spite of methodological objections referring to some earlier studies which proved the clinical efficacy of D,L-Kavain (Kryspin-Exner 1974, Scholing and Clausen 1977) some recent studies (Krach 1986, Klimke et al. 1988, Möller et al. 1988) suggest a placebo-superior efficacy in the treatment of anxiety, psychovegetative and psychoreactive disorders. A survey of the history of development of D,L-Kavain will be given and any available information from clinical trials will be presented and discussed.

Session 155 Poster Presentation
Pharmacotherapy of depression I

1016
TRAZODONE C.R.(CONTROLLED RELEASE) IN DEPRESSIVE SYNDROMES.
Claudio Albano, Giuseppe Roccagliata, Gabriella Besio, Paolo Mainardi, Angelo Patrone, Paola Tognetti, Carlo Pandolfi. Department of Neurology, Genoa University, Via De Toni 5, 16132, GENOA, ITALY.
Trazodone C.R. has been administered to 18 out-patients, grouped according to DSM III-R diagnostic criteria: 6 cases of Dysthymia, 6 Major Depression - Single Episode and 6 Major Depression - Recurrent. Daily dosage was from 100 to 250 mg. (bid) in Dysthymia and from 150 to 300 mg. (bid) in Major Depression. Inclusion criteria were the following: informed consent, age ranging from 18 to 60. Weekly follow up procedures were: Hamilton Rating Scale for Depression (HRSD); Hamilton Rating Scale for Anxiety (HRSA); Clinical Global Impression (CGI); blood tension, and pulse rate recordings. Laboratory tests were performed on admission and at the end of the study: -hematology (including blood count, platelets and reticulocytes count) and -blood chemistry (including bilirubin, alk. phosphatase, SGPT, Creatine); -EKG. Significant improvement was shown in all the patients after one week of treatment with only one 150 mg. evening administration. A significant correlation was found between therapeutic power and those HRSD items usually higher in Major Depression. No adverse reactions have been shown, nor dangerous or troublesome effects were shown respectively by clinical examination and biological recordings.

1017
TRAZODONE AS ADJUNCTIVE THERAPY IN NON-RESPONDING DEPRESSED PATIENTS
Giuseppe Roccatagliata, Gabriella Besio, Paolo Mainardi, Angelo Patrone, Paola Tognetti, Claudio Albano
Department of Neurology, University of Genoa, Genoa Italy

A lot of studies shown "non-responders" depressed patients to be a frequent problem, leading to many trials with any adjunctive treatment. 18 non-responders depressed patients on tricyclic treatment agreed to be studied on Trazodone, as adjunctive drug.
After 15 days of Trazodone i.v. at a daily dosage of 150 mg. we saw a significant clinical improvement and a tricyclic plasma level increase.

1018
FLUVOXAMINE VS AMITRIPTYLINE IN THE TREATMENT OF DEPRESSED PATIENTS.
*Szulecka TK, **Whitehead AM
* Bassetlaw District General Hospital, Worksop, UK
** Duphar Laboratories Limited, Southampton, UK

Fluvoxamine vs amitriptyline in the treatment of hospital out-patients suffering with depression according to the DSM III diagnosis of "Major Depressive Episode". This was a double-blind, randomised, multicentre, parallel group study. Patients between the ages of 18 and 65 years, scoring at least 17 on the 17-item Hamilton Depression Scale (HAMD), after a one week placebo washout period, were eligible. Data from 69 patients were analysed.
Active treatment consisted of a one week fixed dose of 100mg/daily of fluvoxamine or amitriptyline and in the following five weeks, treatment was 50-150mg/daily of drug.
Both treatments significantly improved ratings of depression over the six week active treatment period. The HAMD and the Global Impression/Improvement Scales showed statistical significance in favour of amitriptyline at weeks 2 and 4. However at the end of the study this difference was not significant.
Amitriptyline produced significantly more anticholinergic effects, particularly dry mouth and constipation while fluvoxamine produced significantly more reports of nausea.

1019
FLUVOXAMINE VERSUS MIANSERIN; A DOUBLE-BLIND STUDY.
*Twomey MPK, ** Whitehead AM
*Garlands Hospital, Carlisle, United Kingdom
**Duphar Laboratories Limited, Southampton UK

The efficacy and sedative effects of fluvoxamine were compared with mianserin in hospital outpatients. Patients met DSMIII criteria for Major Depressive Episode and scored 30+ on the Montgomery Asberg Depression Rating Scale (MADRS) after a 1 week placebo baseline. Active treatment was for 6 weeks starting with 100mg fluvoxamine or 60mg mianserin; and could be increased to 300mg or 180mg respectively. Data from 63 patients (30 received fluvoxamine) were analysed. The groups were comparable. MADRS scores were improved by 63.2% with fluvoxamine and 63.0% with mianserin; there were no significant differences between treatments at any assessment. Sedative effects were assessed using the Leeds Sleep Evaluation Questionnaire and the digit symbol substitution test (DSST). Mianserin caused a shift in the first week in all scales towards sedation ie getting to sleep and sleep quality were improved but waking was more difficult and there was more hangover. Similarly, the mianserin group performed worse on the DSST. The study confirmed that both drugs were effective treatments for depressive illness but that mianserin gave rise to sedation during the first week.

1020
MULTICENTER, OPEN, RANDOMIZED STUDY FLUVOXAMINE(F) VERSUS CLOMIPRAMINE (C) IN DEPRESSION.
JD Guelfi*, JC Evreux, H Maisonneuve, R Douge.
CMME - CHS STE ANNE - 100, rue de la Santé 75674 PARIS CEDEX

528 out-patients with a minimum MADRS score of 21, after randomization, received for 90 days in an open study, 100 to 300 mg of fluvoxamine (363 cases) or 50 to 150 mg of clomipramine (163 cases). Clinical assessments were performed on Day 14, 28, 42, 56 and 90, biological values on Day 0, 42 and 90. Adverse event analysis was conducted by 4 experts with the method used to assess unexpected or toxic drug reactions by the French Regional Drug Monitoring Centers. On baseline, the two groups of patients were not statistically different. 120 drop-outs were observed : 85 out of 363 in the F group and 35 out of 163 in the C group. Efficacy analysis did not show any statistically significant difference between groups. Mean MADRS score decreased from 32.77 ± 6.20 to 11.97 ± 9.33 in the F group and from 32.42 ± 5.67 to 10.57 ± 7.97 in the C group. Efficacy was maintained during 3 months for both drugs. Tolerance analysis showed : in the F group, 37 notifications of adverse events widely dominated by digestive troubles ; in the C group, 21 notifications of adverse events widely dominated by anticholinergic effects. The global tolerance was good with more constipation, dry mouth, dizziness and tremor spontaneously expressed by patients with C and more nausea and stomach pain with F. No serious biological variations were observed in both groups.

1021

ANALGESIC EFFECTS OF THE ANTIDEPRESSANTS FLUVOXAMINE AND CLOVOXAMINE

Gibert-Rahola J., Elorza J., Casas J., Gomez-Cama M., Casais L., Mico J.A.
Dept.Neurosc.and Toxicology,Univ.of Cadiz, Spain

Antidepressants (ADs) are widely used as analgesics in chronic pain. The side effects of ADs -mainly anticholinergic- limit their prescription because ADs may be taken by patients suffering from other severe pathological syndromes (e.g. complications of cancer). The aim of the present study was to investigate whether two new ADs, devoid of anticholinergic properties,possess analgetic effects in experimental pain.The hot plate, acetic acid and tail flick methods were used. The doses used were: 2.5,5,10,20 and 40 mg/kg injected i.p 30 min. before test to OF1 male and female mice. Both fluvoxamine (FVX) and clovoxamine (CVX) show a clear and dose-dependent effect in the hot plate and acetic acid test, and middle analgesic effect in the tail flick test. FVX was more effective in female mice in the hot plate (from 2.5mg/kg U=16 p<0.05) while CVX exhibit a more pronounced effect in male mice in the same test (from 2.5mg/kg U=16 p<0.05). In the acetic acid test the degree of analgesia was equipotent for both ADs at the same dose (2.5mg/kg) in female and in male mice (U=0 p<0.01). In conclusion, FVX and CVX are two ADs with analgesic effects. The different pharmacological properties of these compounds (FVX, 5HT reuptake inhibitor; CVX NA reuptake inhibitor) could influence the degree of analgesia in some tests. Additionally,sex differences were observed.

1022

A multicenter double-blind study of the efficacy and safety of rolipram in three doses for four weeks in inpatients with major depressive disorders.
M. Sastre-y-Hernández, H. Schmeding-Wiegel, K. Fichte
Department Clinical Psychiatry and Department General Biometrics, Research Laboratories of Schering AG, Berlin/ Bergkamen F.R.G. The study was conducted on 58 hopitalized patients (40 women and 18 men; age 18 - 74 years) with major depressive disorders (DSM III 296.23, 296.22, 296.33, 296.32, 296.53 und 296.52) for testing the dose-effect relationship of different doses of the new cAMP-phosphodiesterase inhibitor rolipram.
Methods: After a wash-out period of at least three days, each patient received 0.25 mg Rolipram, 0.50 mg Rolipram or 1.00 mg Rolipram 3 x daily for four weeks. The efficacy was assessed by HAMD (Hamilton Depression Scale), CGI (Clinical Global Impression Scale) and SDS (Self-Rating Depression Scale). In addition, patients completed visual analogue scales (VAMS) every day. Tolerance was monitored by DOTES/TWIS, laboratory parameters were determined and clinical examination and ECG were recorded. Case history was recorded on day 00 and again on day 28 using PTR. Interrater training was given before the start of the study.
Results: The assessment of the therapeutic efficacy on the basis of the total HAMD-score, the response rates according to the Hamilton definition of clinically relevant improvement, the total SDS score and the findings from VAMS showed differences between the three treatments in favour of the 3 x 0.50 mg dosage of Rolipram. On the other hand, no significant differences between the groups were demonstrable on the basis of the CGI items. All three dosages displayed very good tolerance. There were no additional findings that might cast doubt on the safety of the dosages tested.
Conclusions: As regards the desired effect, the 3 x 0.50 mg dosage stands out from the other dosages in all relevant parameters with the exception of the CGI items. As regards the response rate, the efficacy of the 3 x 0.25 mg dosage is at about the same level as that reported in the literature for placebo. The inferior performance of the 3 x 1.00 mg dosage compared to the 3 x 0.50 mg dosage might indicate both incipient interference between effects and side effects and a reverse U-shaped dose-effect relationship.
Acknowledgements: We thank the trialists listed below for their cooperation without which this study would not have been possible: Prof. Dr. med. P. Berner, Psychiatric University Clinic, Vienna, Austria; Dr. med. W. Gerlach, Canton Psychiatric Clinic, Solothurn, Switzerland; Prof. Dr. med. H. Hinterhuber, Psychiatric University Clinic, Innsbruck, Austria; Primarius Dr. med. H. Jaklitsch, Psychiatric Clinic, Graz-Eggenberg, Austria; Prof. Dr. med. B. Pflug, Psychiatric University Clinic, Frankfurt/M, West-Germany; Primarius Univ. Doz. Dr. med. H. Schubert, State Psychiatric Hospital, Hall, Austria

1023

INPATIENT DEPRESSION: IS ROLIPRAM AS EFFECTIVE AS AMITRIPTYLINE?
A.I.F. Scott, P.A. Shering, A.F. Perini and L.J. Whalley, University Department of Psychiatry, Royal Edinburgh Hospital, Edinburgh EH10 5HF, Scotland.

Rolipram (a dialkoxyphenyl-2-pyrrolidone)increases availability of noradrenaline and inhibits cAMP phosphodiesterase. Its antidepressant efficacy and side-effects were compared to amitriptyline in the treatment of depressive illness necessitating hospital admission. 50 patients meeting DSM III criteria for Major Depressive Episode whose scores on the Hamilton Rating Scale for Depression(HRSD) were above 17 after 5-7 days on placebo were randomly allocated to either treatment. By 4 weeks 12 out of 25 rolipram-treated patients and 6 out of 25 amitriptyline-treated patients had been withdrawn because of lack of efficacy. Scores on HRSD and the Montgomery and Asberg Depression Rating Scale were consistently higher in the rolipram-treated group during 6-week follow-up. Rolipram produced less sedation, dizziness and anticholinergic effects, but more nausea and headache. We conclude that rolipram is not as effective as amitriptyline in the treatment of depressed hospital inpatients.

1024

PAROXETINE VS IMIPRAMINE IN DEPRESSIVE PATIENTS.
A clinical study in psychiatric practice.

S.Oehrberg, P.E.Christiansen, B.Severin, B.Nilakantan, A.Borup, J.Soegaard, S.B.Larsen, D. Loldrup**, B. Bahr, N.Siebuhr, B.Gregersen, F.Jacobsen, M. Liljeström*, P.Bech**

Specialist practice, Denmark, *Novo-Nordisk Danmark, **Dept.Psychiat. Frederiksborg General Hospital DK

While the majority of patients with major depression are treated in a setting of GP or specialist practice outside hospitals, most clinical trials in Scandinavia performed to evaluate the efficacy of new antidepressants, describe results of inpatients. Both the severity of symptoms as well as tolerance differ between in- and outpatients, hence the true clinical efficacy is difficult to evaluate.

In Denmark the psychiatric specialist practitioner covers patients independent of social status in contrast to many other countries where private psychiatrists treat only a narrow range of the social dimension. The Danish health care system covers 15 consultations annually for each patient, which makes it possible to treat depression both short and medium term.

Thirteen practising psychiatrists participated in a controlled study comparing the new antidepressant paroxetine (5-HT uptake inhibitor) with imipramine. From October 1988 to June 1989 150 patients were included, which covers both short term (6 weeks) as well as medium term treatment (<6 months).

This patient material and the primary results (HAMD) from the short term study will be presented.

1025

A DOUBLE-BLIND PLACEBO-CONTROLLED STUDY OF PAROXETINE AND IMIPRAMINE IN DEPRESSION
Ram Shrivastava MD Saraswati Shrivastava
Park Lexington Regional Research Center
U.S.A.

A double-blind placebo controlled randomized trial was carried out to compare the efficacy and safety of Paroxetine and Imipramine in out patients with moderate to moderately severe major depression with out mania.
Following 4 to 14 days placebo washout period one hundred and twenty adult patients suffering from major depression (DSM-III) were randomly assigned to Paroxetine Imipramine or Placebo for 6 weeks. Paroxetine produced significantly superior ($p \leq 0.05$) improvement over Placebo in all observer-rated.

1026

DOUBLE BLIND STUDY ON EFFICACY AND TOLERANCE OF FLUOXETINE VERSUS AMITRIPTYLINE IN DEPRESSIVE IN- AND OUTPATIENTS

D. Blaschke, G. Laakmann, B. Kriszio
Psychiatric Clinic of the University of Munich, FRG
Director: Professor Dr. H. Hippius

With fluoxetine, a selective reuptake inhibitor, two double blind studies were carried through in order to compare its efficacy and tolerance with that of amitriptyline. 130 outpatients and 201 inpatients were included in the studies.
The patients, suffering from endogenous depression, got either fluoxetine 40 mg/day or amitrityline 100 mg/day for five weeks. For the documentation of tolerance the physicians' rating scales HAMD and CGI and the patients' self-rating scales SDS and EWL were used. Efficacy was judged by the CGI, item 4, side effects, the shortened AMP-4 sheet, laboratory data and vital symptoms.
Results: Outpatients showed distinct improvement under both drugs in all the rating scales with no differences at any time of treatment. After having classified the patients according to their depressive syndrome (inhibited, vitally disturbed, agitated), amitriptyline proved to be more effective in inhibited depressive patients.
Inpatients also improved comparably distinctly with both medications. When they were classified according to their depressive syndrome, severity of illness, duration of illness or previous illnesses, no differences could be seen.
Under both drugs the level of improvement is higher in outpatients than in inpatients with comparable values at the beginning of treatment.
The frequency of side effects is distincly greater under amitriptyline, mainly after the beginning of treatment (70 % vs. 40 % for outpatients, 80 % vs. 60 % for inpatients).
Dryness in the mouth and daytime fatigue were significantly more frequent after amitriptyline. Dizziness, perspiration and trembling were more frequent, yet not significantly.
After fluoxetine, the inpatients mentioned more nausea, pressure in the head, restlessness and sleep disturbances. On the whole, the frequency of side effects reported after fluoxetin is distinctly less then that mentioned after amitriptyline.

1027

AMOXAPINE'S THERAPEUTIC EFFECT IN ALL TYPES OF DEPRESSION
Uriarte V., M.D. (Cols.)
UNAM, Mexico City

This is an open and multicentric study of the rapid therapeutic response, efficacy and security of the amoxapine in adult patients who suffered different types of depression, which was based upon DSM: neurotic depression 50%, recurring major depression 25%, and a first episode of major depression 10%. The study was performed during 8 weeks evaluating the patient in 6 occassions the days 0,7,14,28,42 and 56. Evaluations included: Clinical history, psychiatric diagnostic, physical examination, Hamilton, Zung and Side Effects Depression Scales. The dosage was initiated with 100mg/day and it was increased up to 400mg/day in necessary cases. The side effects which were more frequent were the ones related to the muscarinic/anticholinergical effect such as: xerostomy 47%, constipation 30%, tremor 9% and blurred vision 7% In none of the cases, the patient drops out of the study because of severity or inconvenience to side effects. The first and second week of treatment, the modifications in the clinical conditions evaluating exclusively the depressive symptoms – were statistically significant – the effect continued up to the third and fourth weeks. This group of findings points out amoxapine as a secure antidepressant.

1028

IPSAPIRONE: LONGTERM MULTIPLE ORAL DOSE TOLERANCE STUDY.

I.S. Roed, K. Puechler, B. Kuemmel
Medical Department, Troponwerke, Berliner Straße 156, D-5000 Koeln 80, FRG

24 male volunteers (4 parallel groups, informed consent obtained) from the Quincy Research Center, Kansas, USA, were administered different doses of ipsapirone tablets (0, 2.5, 5.0 and 10 mg) during 28 successive days. Dose regimen consisted of single application during day 1, t.i.d doses during days 2 - 27, and one additional single application on day 28.
All doses were well tolerated. Besides dizziness (duration about 15 to 30 minutes), headache was the most commonly reported transient adverse experience. Dizziness occurred predominantly in the 10 mg-dosage group. Vestibular involvement could be excluded. Headaches exhibited no distinct pattern and no dose-relationship.
During safety assessments none of the physical and physiological parameters escaped normal ranges. Pharmacokinetics were assesssed as additional token of drug safety. No changes in kinetic parameters between day one and 28 could be detected. Thus, cumulation of the drug under investigation can be excluded.

Session 156 Poster Presentation:
Psychiatric epidemiology

1029

EPIDEMIOLOGICAL STUDY OF PREMENSTRUAL SYNDROME IN THE FLORENTINE AREA
Giardinelli L., Donati D., Tanini N., Balenzano T., Cabras P.L.
Department of Neurology and Psychiatry
University of Florence - Italy

The Premenstrual Syndrome (PMS) today is at the centre of numerous studies which concentrate above all on investigating its possible causes and symptomatological expression. In the litterature there are disagreements about the prevalence of the PMS, and this phenomenon is mostly attributable to methodological problems which invalidate many papers. Our study makes use of an structured interview and of a questionnaire which investigates premenstrual symptomatology. The interview which we have worked out collect data concerning the subjects familiar, social and sexual substratum, with the evident aim of investigating the possible risk factors and vulnerability of the syndrome. For the study of the prevalence of the PMS we have used the Premenstrual Assessment Form, a self-evalueting questionnaire with 95 items. The group of women considered was randomly extrapolated from the patients of some general practitioners. Considering that under the current Italian National Health System each citizen is assigned to personal doctor, this group is there fore rapresentative of the population at large.

1030

THE EPIDEMIOLOGY AND TYPOLOGY OF ENDOGENOUS PSYCHOSES
Mircea Lăzărescu, M.D.; Doina Schrepler, M.D., Clinica Psihiatrică Timişoara, the S.R. of Romania

Using the Case Register (covering a county with 700,000 inhabitants) between 1985 and 1988, all new cases of endogenous psychoses involving people over 15 years old were recorded. Endogenous psychoses represent 8% of all new cases (as defined by hospital admission). The authors analyze the structure and incidence of these psychoses. The frequency of schizophrenia was approximately 70 cases per year.
The authors deal separately with affective psychoses (with congruent and incongruent delusion), short-term and long-standing delusional psychoses (whose onset occurs before and after the age of 45), as well as other, more or less typical psychoses. The clarifications and modifications of the diagnosis were examined in relation to the clinical evolution of the patients.
The findings are commented upon in terms of ICD-9 and ICD-10.

1031

EPIDEMIOLOGICAL RESEARCH CONCERNING OUT-PATIENTS' IN A PSYCHIATRIC CENTRE DEPARTMENT
G. BIFFI - C. ZAPPALAGLIO - G.L. TOMASELLI - G. ANDREINI
Psycosocial Centre (CPS) - Social and sanitary local unit (U.S.S.L.) n. 28 - Ponte San Pietro - Bergamo, Italy

The authors describe the reason, methodos, diagnostic principles and result of an epidemiological research about the socio-demographic characteristics of 721 patients and the services given by the CPS in the period from 1983 to 1987.
The research, concerning the 120.000 people belonging to the U.S.S.L. n. 28, has been carried out in order to analyse the situation and the modifications wich are taking place, thanks to the law 180/78, and the changes in the relationship with healthy people, family doctor, organizations and institutions.

Hipothesis: Are today the CPS ways of intervention qualitatively and quantitatively different from those it used in the past year? For each patient of the CPS a file has been drawn up including the details about patient, family, number and type of therapies per year, number of hospitalizations, diagnoses. Until now the research has considered for each year, the following points:

A) the first visit data considered: sex, age, people, sending the patients to the CPS, diagnoses.

B) Pharmacological therapy, according to the diagnose by mouth, depot, combined. Analysing the different variables, the first hypothesis is confirmed: the CPS, while evolving, tends to have patients with different psychopatological situatiions and to give diversified and integrated therapies (Pharmacological, psychotherapeutical, rehabilitative).

1032

A PUTATIVE SINGLE PACEMAKER REGULATES WINTER BIRTHS OF PATIENTS WITH MAJOR PSYCHIATRIC DISORDERS

Vito MARTINO, M.D.; Sandro ROMEO, M.D.; Maria Antonietta PIEMONTESE, M.D.; Antonello BELLOMO, M.D.; Anna MAGGIO, M.D. and Roberto VALENTE, M.D.

Department of Psychiatry - University of Bari (Italy)

The whole population of inpatients, years 1968-87, (Department of Psychiatry, University of Bari-Italy), has been studied to determine whether the season-of-birth effect occurs in the following DSM III-R categories: Schizophrenia, Delusional (Paranoid) Disorder, Psychotic Disorders Not Elsewhere Classified, Mood Disorders, Organic Mental Disorders, Anxiety and Somatoform Disorders, Personality Disorders, Additional Codes, Axis III and other DSM III-R diagnostic categories. The Walter and Elwood test for the seasonality of events has been used on each category to assess the statistical significance of the season-of-birth phenomenon and its parameters (acrophase and amplitude). The schizophrenics were split into two subgroups: age<23, age>23, to remove the "age-incidence" and "age-prevalence" effects. Our data seem to confirm the existence of the season-of-birth effect, probably regulated by a single pacemaker with an acrophase in February, in all patients with major psychiatric disorders: Schizophrenia, Delusional (Paranoid) Disorder, Major Mood Disorders and Organic Mental Disorders.

1033

MORBIDITY OF MENTAL DISORDERS IN SPANISH IMMIGRANT POPULATION
Casais L.*, Failde I.**, Elorza J.*,
Chevalier J.,***, Zafra J.A.**
*Ment. Health Center (IASAM), Dept. Neurosc. and Toxic. **Dept.of Public Health, Univ.of Cadiz, Spain, ***Service of Epidem."Assistance Publique Hopitaux de Paris", France

The aim of this study has been to compare the psychiatric morbidity between hospitalized Spanish population resident in France and autochthonous French population. The study was conducted in the "Assistance Publique" centers in Paris during 1985. The diagnoses were codified according to OTARIE system using DSM-III-R. They were grouped according to the etiology as follows: intoxications, defined psychiatric disorders and diverse symptoms. Proportional morbidity rate, sex and age-specific rates and standardized rates were calculated. The results showed significant differences only in the morbidity rates at the level of the psychiatric symptoms (paranoid disorder, psychotic disorder NOS, symptoms and syndromes and depressive disorders NOS, corresponding to the 297 298,307 and 311 DSM-III-R codes). The proportional morbidity rate in Spanish males was 2,30% and 0,69% in the French males($p<0.001$) and 0.82 versus 1,45% in females respectively ($p<0.02$). The distribution of cases was 76% and 24% in male and female immigrant respectively and 30% and 70% in the French population. Age-specific male rates were different in the 15-24 ($p<0.001$) and 35-44 ($p<0.0001$) years age-groups. In conclusion, the psychiatric symptomatology was more frequent in the 15-24 years age-male Spanish population.

1034

PSYCHISCHE VERÄNDERUNGEN BEI REEMIGRIERTEN GRIECHISCHEN STUDENTEN
K.Bikos, N.Tzavaras
Psychopathological Laboratory, Medical School, University of Thrace, Alexandroupolis, Greece.

Es geht um die psychopathologischen Folgen der Rückkehr griechischer Studenten in ihre Heimat nach Absolvierung ihrer schulischen und gymnasialen Ausbildung in einem westeuropäischen Land.
Vorherige Erfahrungen des genannten Personenkreises bezüglich Griechenlands waren lediglich auf die Ferien beschränkt. Ihre Integration in die griechischen Hochschulen entsprach allerdings ihrem eigenen Entschluss oder dem Wunsch ihrer Familien.

Aus der erfassten Klientel werden drei Fälle mit der Initialsymptomatik "Akuter Angstzustände" dargestellt. Die Besonderheiten die sich anschliessernden Krankheitsverlaufs sowie die konsekutiven therapeutischen Massnahmen werden diskutiert.

1035

PSYCHISCHE STÖRUNGEN EHEMALIGER MITGLIEDER NEUERER GLAUBENSBEWEGUNGEN
(SECTS, CULTS AND MENTAL DISORDERS)
Ulrich Müller

FORSCHUNGSSTELLE FÜR
PSYCHIATRISCHE SOZIOLOGIE

Psychiatrische Klinik der Universität
-Rheinische Landesklinik-
4 Düsseldorf 12, Bergische Landstr. 2 FRG

Eine Studie zur Erfassung von psychisch kranken ehemaligen Mitgliedern Neuerer Glaubensbewegungen im Land Nordrhein-Westfalen, BRD, ergab, dass in untersuchten Fällen (N=35) stets eine psychisch auffällige prämorbide Persönlichkeitsstruktur vorlag. Den Einflüssen der Mitgliedschaft Neuerer Glaubensbewegungen muss dekompensatorische Wirkung zugeschrieben verden

1036

Comparative study of psychiatric activities between Japan and Philippins
U.UEMOTO, H.IDE, T.ASANO, M. MASUI*, P.LEE, B.V.REYEZ**
*Department of Psychiatry, School of Medicine, Kobe University
**Department of Psychiatry, Faculty of Medicine, University of Philippines

This is a baseline comparative study of two Asian countries, the Philippines and Japan. Both of which have similarities and differences in terms of their social, political, economic and cultural orientation. In this regards, psychiatry involves itself with relationships of a person's illness and his sociocultural values and attitudes, correlational data between two separate countries could enhance a better understanding of mental illnesses inherent in each country.

The comparative study on the mental health in the Phil. and Japan was conducted by Japanese and Filipino psychiatrists from Kobe University, Japan and the University of the Phil., Phil. In the Phil. a survey questionaire was distributed to 80 psychiatrists while in Japan (Kobe) the same standardized questionaire was distributed to 99 institutes. These questionaires were separately collated and discussed by psychiatrists of both universities.

This comparative research study showed differencies on data concerning sources of referral, employment status of patients, attitudes of families of patients, recovery criteria, treatment and effects of social factors like religion and native healers.

1037

CATAMNESTIC STUDY OF PSYCHIC DISORDERS IN YOUNG MEN IN RESTRICTED CIRCUMSTANCES
Penka Christova
Higher Military Medical Institute-Sofia
Bulgaria

The survey includes 762 male patients in 18-20 age group, who underwent treatment during 1978-1982. All nosological units except oligophrenia are included in the survey. A methodology of catamnestic study has been evolved including 4 different inquiry cards.
Results: About 70% of the persons are not in the statistical registration lists of dispensaries-they are qualified cured. Neurotic symptoms combined with varied vegetative disfunctions are more frequently met with in persons with higher education. Psychiatric symptoms persisted in the remaining persons. Their dynamics and patomorphosis have been followed up. The diagnosis of schizophrenia has the comparatevely ewakest prognostic validity. An analysis of the prerequisites for psychic disorders in the barracks is also made as well as of the sources of diagnostic errors.
The paper is a retrospective study of the dynamics in clinical picture and diagnosis in soldiers with psychic disorders during their military service.

1038

DEMOGRAPHIC DATA AND TREATMENT METHODS IN THE LEROS PSYCHIATRIC HOSPITAL
PAPADATOS,Y.,TYHOPOULOS, G.,PAPAGEORGIOU, G., CRAIG,T., CLIFFORD,P.
- CENTRE FOR MENTAL HEALTH AND RESEARCH
- N.U.P.R.D., LEWISHAM - LONDON

The purpose of this research is to investigate the demographic characteristics of the patients of the Leros Psychiatric Hospital, in relation to the way of admission, the duration of stay in a Psychiatric Hospital, the reported diagnosis (according to the ICD-9) and the drug treatment provided. All the patients who were being treated during the period October-December 1988 were interviewed on the basis of special questionnaires. The population consisted of 1179 individuals (average age 53.8 years, SD=14.1), 821 men and 358 women. The majority (92%) were single and 84.1% had come from other Psychiatric Hospitals, while 12.6% were admitted straight to Leros. In 4.9% the way of admission was not reported. The average period of stay was 20.5 years (SD=5.9). More than half (54.5%) are referred to as schizophrenic psychosis and 32.8% as mentally retarded. 55.6% were under drug treatment (66.3% men and 33.7% women), while 44,4% were under no drug treatment. It is note-worthy that the vast majority of the patients come from other Psychiatric Hospitals and are chronic patients. It is also remarkable that a great percentage were under no specific medical or drug treatment. There is an obvious need for identification of those patients who would benefit from a rehabilitation programme.

1039

DEPRESSIVE SYNDROMES IN OUTPATIENT PSYCHIATRIC FACILITIES
Villasana Cunchillos,A.(*);Recondo Garcia,M (•); Bobes Garcia,J.(*); Bousoño Garcia,M(*); Rubio Larrosa,V(*);
(•)Ph D;(*)M.D.Associated Prof Psychitry.E.U.E. Universidad del Pais Vasco.Spain

A random sample of 100 persons attending during a twelve months period, out-patients psychiatric facilities is analized. Statistiscal analysis has been made according to age, sex, marital status, previous and present treatment, previous and present hospitalitation etc. Conclusions: Dysthymia, major depressive states (MDS), and schizo-affective psychosis (SAP) constitute more than half of the sample, 59%; while dysthymia alone accounts for 47% of all cases. The general features of dysthymia being: early age onset than other types of depression, female sex, often married, previously treated as out-patient, scarcely hospitalized. In the present study, 97% receive psychopharmacological drugs, 36% group psychotheray, 2% family therapy, having a low level of hospitalization of 2%. The pictures of MDS, SAP, and the remaining diagnoses, each one show different socio-demograhic characteristcs and consumes different treatment kinds, either psychopharmachological or psychological. They also differs at hospitalitation rates, showing high rates SAP patients 66%.

1040

A NOSOLOGICAL STUDY OF A COMMUNITY MENTAL HEALTH CENTER IN CADIZ.

Casais,L; Elorza,J; Failde,I; Ezcurra,J. Mental Health Center (IASAM). Dept. of Neurosciences and Toxicology. University of Cádiz. Spain.

It has been analized the first 1000 patients studied in our Mental Health Center with an ascribed population of 137.838 habitants. The mean age was 36.1, 45.6% males and 54.4% females. They were applied the DSM-III-R diagnostic criteria, detailling over the axes I and II and the results obtained were: Anxiety disorders of childhood or adolescence 8.2%; Organic mental disorders 5.3%; Psychoactive substance-induced organic mental disorders 2.4%; schizophrenia 9.7%; Delusional (paranoid) disorder 0.6%; Psychotic disorders not elsewhere classified 1.6%; Mood disorders 17.9%; Anxiety disorders 6.6%; Somatoform disorders 6.8%; Dissociative disorders 1%; Sexual disorders 0.4%; Sleep disorders 1.5%; Factitious disorders 0%; Impulse control disorders not elsewhere classified 0.1%; Adjustment disorder 14.8%; Psychological factors affecting physical condition 0.1%; Personality disorders 3.9%; V Codes for conditions not attributable to a mental disorder 4.8% and Additional codes 14.3%.
These criteria were correlated with other variables as age and sex distribution, status, geographical area and origin. Moreover it has been made a criticisme of the difficulties presented by DSM-III-R criteria for some diagnostics. Additionally, the primary care quality was evaluated relating the geographical area with the variables quoted.

1041

CLASSIFICATION AND OUTCOME OF MENTAL PATIENTS DIFFICULT FOR MANAGEMENT

Horita N., Kaneko T., Yamada H., Takei M. Mashiko S.
Tokyo Metropolitan Matsuzawa Hospital Tokyo Japan

Our hospital is a public mental hospital for adults (1300 beds) founded by Tokyo Metropolis. We are frequently asked to accept and treat patients difficult for management from private mental hospitals, public mental health agencies, public prosecutor's offices, etc. in Metropolitan District (population 13 million). For 2 years, we treated 52 those patients (male 38, female 14) in highly restrained wards. Twenty-one were schizophrenics including 10 homicides, 5 aggressive and assaultive patients, etc. Patients repeating manslaughters and/or attempted murders were difficult for us to manage and could not be managed in open door system and/or discharged. Twelve were drug psychoses and dependences (methamphetamine, glue sniffing, analgesics, etc.), and/or personality disorders. Most of them were juvenile delinquents during adolescent period (13-8 y.o.), and trouble-makers in mental hospitals. Eleven (female 7) were mentally retarded, having many problems in behaviors from childhood. Except for patients frequently committing manslaughters and/or attempted murders and mental deficients, they were almost managed in more open door system or discharged within a few years. It is, therefore, thought that we should do our best to sufficiently treat even very difficult patients for management.

1042

MORTALITY AMONG PSYCHOTIC INPATIENTS IN POLAND

Andrzej Kiejna, Dept. of Psychiatry, Wroclaw, Poland

On the basis of making up computer statistical sheets (MZ)Szp-11b), death cases with different psychotic disturbances in all psychiatric hospitals in Poland from 1978 to 1985 have been analysed.
During the above period, in psychiatric institutions 1 317 389 cases were hospitalized (schizophrenia amount to 33.2%, affective psychoses 5.8%, senile and presenile psychoses 4.3%, alcoholic psychoses 4.2%). In the course of 8 years 26283 deaths were noted (schizophrenia amounts to 37.8%, affective psychoses 3.1%, senile and presenile psychoses 37.8%, alcoholic psychoses 3.3%).
Mortality ratio in every diagnostic group was evaluated for both sexes in each year separately and compared with total patient populations.
A considerable differentiation of mortality ratio was noted in diagnostic and age groups. A large fraction of deaths occurred during the first month of hospitalization. The cause of death were varied, depending on psychiatric diagnoses. The most commonly recognized reason of death were diseases of circulatory system.

Session 157 Poster Presentation
Psychiatry and old age

1043

EPIDEMIOLOGICAL ASPECTS OF GERONTOPSYCHIATRY

Gliemann,R., Milch,W., Schneemann,N., Ernst,R., Wegener,H.

A report was presented on a spot check carried out on 100 patients of a gerontopsychiatric ward at the time of their admission to hospital; the statistical survey employed standardized medical, neurological, psychopathological and socioanamnestic procedures.
A markedly high proportion of the patients surveyed (some 75%) were female.
Male admissions were, on the average, older than the female patients.
Possible explanations for these findings were discussed.
Considerable attention was paid to the multiple morbidity of the patients surveyd; the implications of this for the development of integrative program of treatment were discussed, as were the associated demographic aspects.

1044

INTERINSTITUTIONELLE WEITERVERMITTLUNG ALTER MENSCHEN MIT PSYCHISCHEN STÖRUNGEN IM NETZ PSYCHIATRISCHER VERSORGUNG. PATIENTENWEGE AM BEISPIEL EINES VERSORGUNGSGEBIETS IN DER FRG.

H.P. Bratenstein, H.J. Ingenleuf, R.J. Witkowski, E. Lungershausen
Psychiatrische Universitätsklinik, Schwabachanlage 6, D-8520 Erlangen

Seit Beginn unseres Jahrhunderts kann in ganz Europa und in den Vereinigten Staaten ein Anstieg der Lebenserwartung und des Durchschnittsalters der Bevölkerung verzeichnet werden. Dabei ist allerdings auch eine Zunahme der Zahl psychiatrischer Alterspatienten, die professioneller Betreuung bedürfen, zu beobachten.

Mit unserem Projekt wurden in einem abgegrenzten Versorgungsgebiet verschiedene Institutionen, die mit der Betreuung und Behandlung gerontopsychiatrischer Patienten betraut sind, aufgesucht und deren Leitungen sowie Mitarbeiter befragt. Einbezogen waren ambulante, komplementäre und stationäre Einrichtungen.

Aus unseren Ergebnissen in diesem Bereich werden Defizite deutlich, die durchaus als "gerontopsychiatrischer Notstand" zu bezeichnen sind, der sich nach epidemiologischen Schätzungen ohne gezielte Gegensteuerung in der Zukunft noch verschärfen dürfte. Die Ergebnisse sind im Versorgungsgebiet als Grundlage zur Verbesserung der gerontopsychiatrischen Versorgung nutzbar und können mit Einschränkungen auch auf andere Regionen übertragen werden.

1045

THE EFFECT OF A PSYCHOGERIATRIC UNIT ON HOSPITAL STAY AND REVOLVING DOOR PHENOMENON.
D De Leo, A Baiocchi, A Stella, L Serraiotto, L Pavan, R Talamo, Rossi.
Psychogeriatric Unit, Padua Geriatric Hospital, Padua, I

This paper describes a six-year experience of psychiatric consultation in Padua Geriatric Hospital (Italy). Motivation for the request for psychiatric treatment, diagnosis, recommended treatment and compliance with it by the geriatric medical staff are reported. The authors stress the radical change in the activities of the consultants since the establishment in 1986 of a new psychogeriatric unit, probably still the only such unit in formal existence in Italy. The service offered by the team thus underwent considerable innovation, leading to substantial modifications in treatment and, especially, to a reduction in the duration of hospital stay of patients admitted to the psychogeriatric unit.

1046

COGNITIVE IMPAIRMENT IN AGED SUBJECTS AND DEFANYL®
M. Caulet, M. Ohayon, N. Hugon, Serratrice G., Y. Millet.
Laboratoire de Traitement des Connaissances, Faculté de Médecine, 27 Boulevard Jean-Moulin, 13385-Marseille, CEDEX 4.

The aim of this work is to study the effects of Amoxapine (Defanyl® 50-150 mg/day) on the cognitive performances in aged patients with mild dementia.
We studied three groups of 60-80 years old patients: 1) Controls, without clinical symptoms either of depression or dementia; 2) a "Depressive" group (MADRS≥25, ERD≥20, DSM-III criteria of a major depressive episode); 3) a "Dementia" group without the former depressive symptoms and mild dementia (MMS ≤ 23).
The valuations were performed at days 0, 7 and 21. They included the MADRS and ERD, the analogical tests, MMS, EEG night recording.
The effects of Amoxapine on these variables are analyzed in the three groups. The evolution of the cognitive disorders in depressive or demetia groups under treatment are compared.

1047

A STUDY OF INTELLIGENCE FUNCTION OF THE AGED PATIENTS WITH CHRONIC SCHIZOPHRENIA-USING THE OKABE'S BRIEF MENTAL SCALE
S.Okabe*, T.Nakagawa**, I.Fukunishi, N.Kashima***
E.Baba**, K.Hosokawa
Dept. of Neuropsychiatry, Kagawa Medical School, Kagawa, Japan, *Dept. of Psychology, Tokyo Psychiatric Institute, Tokyo, Japan,**Baba Mental Hospital, Kagawa, Japan, ***Tokyo Metropolitan Matsuzawa Hospital,Tokyo,Japan

A study of intelligence function in aged patients with chronic schizophrenia has been hardly carried out so far. Therefore, in the present study an assessment of intelligence function of aged schizophrenic patients was performed using the brief mental scale developed by S.Okabe (1983). The subjects consisted of 75 patients with chronic schizophrenia hospitalized for more than 15 years (the average age, 68.6). For the control group, 75 healthy aged persons, matched to the subjects for sex and age, were selected. The main results obtained were as follows: 1) In the total intelligence, almost half of the subjects were within either normal or sub-normal range, whereas 80% of the controls were within either normal or sub-normal range. 2) In the digit span sub-scale, however, no significant difference was observed between the two groups. Although these results were obtained by means of psychometry, these may suggest that it should be necessary to reconsider the long term inpatients with schizophrenia as far as intelligence functions are concerned.

1048

SPECTRAL ANALYSIS OF EEG IN DELIRIUM.

** Koponen H, MD; ** Kajander-Koponen A, MD;
* Riekkinen PJ, MD, prof. Departments of Neurology
* and Psychiatry **, Kuopio University Central Hospital, Kuopio, Finland

As information concerning possible correlations between clinical symptoms in delirium and EEG changes is still limited, we conducted routine and spectral analysis of EEG for 51 elderly delirious patients (mean age $\pm$ S.D. 74,3 $\pm$ 6,6 years) meeting the DSM-III criteria and for 19 age-equivalent controls. The triggering factors for delirium were heterogeneous as patients with alcohol delirium were excluded, the most common etiologies were stroke, infections, and metabolic encephalopathies.
As a whole group, and also when subdivided according to the type of delirium, severity of cognitive decline, or the type of central nervous system disease, delirious patients showed significant reductions of alpha %, increased theta and delta activity and slowing of the peak and mean frequencies, and these changes were also obvious in individual recordings. The alpha % and various ratio parameters correlated significantly with Mini-Mental State score, and delta % and mean Frequency with the lengths of delirium and hospitalization.
Our results indicate an association between spectral EEG changes and severity of cognitive decline in delirium.

1049

A study of fluvoxamine versus mianserin in elderly depressed patients

Phanjoo A, *Wonnacott S, *Hodgson A, *Whitehead AM.
Royal Edinburgh Hospital, Scotland, U.K.
* Medical Department, Duphar Laboratories Ltd., Gaters Hill, West End, Southampton, U.K.

Fluvoxamine is a new class of antidepressant which is both chemically and pharmacologically distinct from the tricyclic antidepressants. It is a potent inhibitor of serotonin re-uptake in both platelets and brain synaptosomes whilst having negligible effects on noradrenaline re-uptake. In this multicentre, double-blind, randomised parallel group study the antidepressant effects of fluvoxamine and mianserin were compared in 57 elderly depressed hospital patients. Following a one week wash-out period on placebo, patients initially received either 50 mg fluvoxamine or 20 mg mianserin. Dosage was titrated according to response during the six week active treatment period. Both drugs demonstrated statistically significant improvement in symptoms of depression as assessed by the Montgomery Asberg Depression Rating Scale and Clinical Global Improvement/Impression Scales. However there was no significant difference between the two drugs.

Tolerance was good; interestingly, no nausea was reported in the fluvoxamine group. No statistical differences were seen in cardiovascular parameters or in haematological/biochemical data.

1050

A gerontopsychiatric double-blind dose-finding study of Rolipram in patients with major, "minor" and atypical depression

M.Sastre-y-Hernández, D. Crippa, M. Schratzer, K. Fichte
Research Laboratories of Schering AG Berlin/Bergkamen F.R.G.

The aim of this study was to test the dose-effect relationship of three different doses of the new cAMP-phosphodiesterase inhibitor rolipram on gerontopsychiatric depressed patients. The study was carried out as a multicentre, interindividual double-blind study on patients with major, "minor", or atypical depressive disorders (DSM-III 296.23, 296.22, 296.33, 296.32, 296.53, 296.52, 301.13, 300.40, 296.82). A total of 43 women and 21 men participated in the study. The patients' age was 65 to 90 years.

Methods: After a wash-out period of at least three days, each patient received 0.25 mg Rolipram, 0.50 mg Rolipram or 0.75 mg Rolipram 3 x daily for four weeks. The efficacy was assessed on study days 00, 03, 07, 14, 21 and 28, by HAMD (Hamilton Depression Scale) and CGI (Clinical Global Impression Scale). Tolerance was monitored by DOTES/TWIS on days 00, 03, 07, 14, 21 and 28, laboratory parameters were determined on days 00, 07 and 28, and clinical examination and ECG were recorded on days 00 and 28. Case histories were recorded on day 00 using APDI and again on day 28 using PTR.

Results: A reduction of the mean values over time was demonstrated in the three groups with respect to the pre/post value comparison of the HAMD total scores. Between groups the results of univariate tests showed no relevant differences.
The response rates according to Hamilton's definition of "responder" (50 % reduction of the initial HAMD score at the end of the treatment compared to baseline) were only 20 % for patients under 3 x 0.25 mg Rolipram/day compared to 40 % and 47 %, respectively, for those under 3 x 0.50 mg and 3 x 0.75 mg Rolipram/day. No significant differences between the three treatments were found on the basis of the CGI items.All three dosages tested displayed very good tolerance. None of the laboratory tests, clinical examinations or ECG recordings performed revealed any medically relevant findings that might cast doubt on the safety of the Rolipram dosages tested.

Conclusions: The study demonstrated the antidepressant efficacy of 3 x 0.50 mg Rolipram/day and 3 x 0.75 mg Rolipram/day in the treated gerontopsychiatric patients with major, "minor" or atypical depression. However, the results available for the dosage of 3 x 0.25 mg Rolipram/day indicate that this dosage is inferior to the two other dosages. The reason why no difference was demonstrable between the 3 x 0.50 mg dosage and the 3 x 0.75 mg dosage may on the one hand be that the sample size was not big enough for such a difference to be found from the start and, on the other, that the dose interval chosen was possibly too narrow.

Aknowledgements:

Prof. Baroni, INRCA-Ospedale le Fraticini, Firenze, Italy
Prof. Canal, Osp. S. Raffaele, Universita di Milano, Italy
Prof. Cucinotta, Divisione di Geriatria, Ferrara, Italy
Dr. Galetti, Osp. S. Ferardo Dei Tintori, Monza, Italy
Dr. Inzoli, Osp. le Fatebenefratelli, Brescia, Italy
Prof. Vecchi, Cattedra di Geriatria e Gerontologia Univ. di Modena, Italy

1051

PHARMACOKINETICS OF THE MAO-A INHIBITOR BROFAROMINE•HCl IN ELDERLY

Degen, P.H., Dieterle, W., Schneider, W. and Theobald, W.
Research and Development Department, Pharmaceuticals Division, CIBA-GEIGY Ltd., Basle (Switzerland)

The influence of age on the pharmacokinetics of the new MAO-A inhibitor brofaromine•HCl was studied in six elderly (62-79 years) healthy volunteers and compared to those in younger (24-31 years) healthy volunteers.

Both age groups were treated with single peroral doses of 50 mg of brofaromine•HCl as filmcoated tablets. Plasma concentrations of brofaromine were measured by gas chromatography up to 48 hours after administration.

In the elderly volunteers, the mean area under the plasma concentration-time curve (14.59 ± 3.76 $nmol \cdot g^{-1} \cdot h$), the mean peak plasma level (1.04 ± 0.4 $nmol \cdot g^{-1}$) and the mean apparent elimination half-life (14.1 ± 2.9 h) were about 30% higher as compared to younger volunteers. However, the differences were statistically not significant.

In conclusion, old age does only slightly affect the pharmacokinetics of brofaromine•HCl.

Session 158 Poster Presentation:
Alcohol abuse I

1052

CHRONIC ALCOHOLISM - THE PROBLEM OF DIAGNOSIS

Lesch, O.M.
PSYCHIATRIC UNIVERSITY CLINIC, VIENNA

05

Generations of researchers until nowadays have discussed the problem of differentiation between alcohol abuse and addiction. Diagnostic instruments like ICD-9, DSM-III and DSM-III-R, mainly influenced by the American point of view, clearly show this diagnostic uncertainties. Especially from therapeutic studies it is well known, that psychopathological as well as somatic-biological differences represent important predictors for further illness course.

Heterogenity of this group of patients is demonstrated by means of a prospective long term follow up study. Out of this study 4 therapy=-relevant subgroups of chronic alcoholic patients were developed. These homogeneous subgroups help to differentiate better the therapeutic strategies necessary as well as to differentiate better the basic data gained in scientific research - better than the simple diagnosis "chronic alcoholism" could ever do.

1053

PSYCHOMOTOR RETARDATION IN ALCOHOLIC IN-PATIENTS

J.HAUSER The Clinic of Psychiatry University School of Medicine, Szpitalna 27/33 POZNAŃ, POLAND

The aim of the research undertaken was to compare the profile of psychomotor retardation in alcoholics with symptoms of depression with a group of patients with endogenous depression. The investigations were carried out on 1/ 85 in-patient alcoholics on the first day of hospitalization following a period of alcohol consumption, 2/ 50 in-patients with endogenous depression. In 60% of alcoholic, depressive symptoms were observed /Hamilton Rating Scale for Depression 24,8 points/, which did not last more than 10 days. In alcoholics psychomotor retardation /estimated by means of Widlöcher's ERD scale/ affected the psychic sphere, whereas no conspicuous motor retardation was observed. The results that have been obtained show that similary as in endogenous depression also in depressive states in alcoholics there exists a correlation between a general severity of depression and the disturbances of psychomotor activity.

1054

AGGRESSION AND ALCOHOLISM IN MALE ALCOHOLIC PATIENTS.

M.Suárez Richards, A.Ilarregui, A.Barros, J.Beccia, N.Zelaschi. Hosp.A.Korn, Psychiatry Dpt. La Plata Medical College. 60 y 120 (1900). La Plata. Argentina

Relationship between alcohol and human aggression is a fact well documented in human beings. Light doses of alcohol can increase aggresive behaviour. Morover it has been suggested that pharmacological mechanisms have a minor role that the psychologicals one; alcohol itself do no seems to raise aggression per se but it would help the situation that finally lead to aggression. We selected a sample of 98 male alcoholic patients (mean age: 42.7) with heavy antecedents of alcohol abuse and at least 10 years of evolution. 56% of them were law offenders. Mean amount of beverage was 3.33 l/day specially red wine. They had started to drink heavylly at the mean of 20 and had continued for the following 20 years without interruptions. O.A.S.(Overt Aggression Scale) was used to evaluate aggression. One "degrees by cases" special index was calculated in order to compare the four kinds of scores provided by the scale. Aggression was not correlated with the extension of the period of addiction nor to the amount of alcohol drinked. Complex psychopathological factors but not the pure pharmacological drug related alcohol' action should be taken into account.

1055

IN THEME OF ALCOHOLISM AND DEPRESSION
Mura F., Erba S., Pintore P., Salis P.G., Nivoli G.C.
Department of Psychiatry, Sassari University, Italy

The potential association between depression (D) and alcoholism (A) rises not only from psychopathologic and nosographic considerations, but also from clinical and preventive ones.
In this view a preliminary and clinical survey on a group of patients affected by D and A was carried out at the Department of Psychiatry, University of Sassari.
With the help of D Autoevaluation Scale by CASSANO and CASTROGIOVANNI and the evaluation test for alcohol misuse and alcohol risks (VARA test) by CASSANO, CONTI, GARONNA, 35 patients of both sexes, aged between 24 and 71, with diagnosis of A and D were surveyed. The obtained data allowed a first global evaluation, a second one for each item, and a third one by means of factor analysis.
Results are in accordance with the existence of close relationships between D and A. The indicate that the combination of these two conditions makes the clinical picture more serious. They correlation between both pathologies appears to be significant only within some levels of seriousness; beyond such levels it becomes less significant.
Moreover in the A associated with D the risk of committing suicide increases considerably.

1056

CULTURAL STUDY OF DRİNKİNG PATTERNS İN ALCOHOLİCS

Can Tuncer,MD Assoc.Prof.of Psychiatry, Mansur Beyazyürek,MD Assoc.Prof.of Psychiatry,Çetin Ersül MD.,Oğuz Karamustafalıoğlu,MD.
Dept.of Psychiatry,Cerrahpaşa Faculty of Medicine,İstanbul University,İstanbul Turkey,Bakırköy Mental Hospital,İstanbul Turkey.

In most cultures,types of alcoholic beverages consumed depend on the traditional ones.However,in Turkey beer seems to be on the increase comparing with the traditional spirit 'rakı'. Onset of drinking and the places, environment at where they prefer and the developed patterns new to culture are emphasized.The alcoholics' beliefs on drinking patterns,their attitudes towards withdrawal from alcohol are investigated.The demographic features were revealed and discussed on the basis of cultural background.

1057

DRINKING PATTERNS AND DRUG ABUSE IN PRE-REVOLUTIONARY IRAN. Iradj Siassi,M.D.,U.C.L.A. Med.Sch.,L.A. CA,U.S.A.; Shahrzad Siassi Ph.D.,Private Practice. L.A.,CA, U.S.A.;and Bahman Fozouni,Ph.D.,Dir.F.and W. Associates,Pgh,PA,U.S.A.

The authors report on a nationwide survey of the prevalence of alcohol use and drug abuse in the pre-revolutionary Iran. The study was a part of the National Epidemiological Survey of Mental Illness, Addiction and Mental Retardation which was conducted between 1976 and 1979 in Iran. The prevalence (life-time and point),the age first used, the quantity and frequency of use were assessed by a grid-like format. In addition,a translated and adapted version of Michigan Alcoholism Screening Test (MAST) was administered to all alcohol users; and urine samples of all respondents were collected and tested for drugs by both paper chromatography and immunoassay techniques.The study was of representative sample of all those 15 years or older in the general population. The findings of the survey are compared with those from similar studies in the United States. The complex role of social and religious variables , differentiating a developing Moslem country and an advanced non-Moslem country are discussed.

1058

RESEARCH ON THE USE OF ALCOHOLIC DRINKS IN THE POPULATION LIVING IN FERRARA
GUIDI E., STELLA S., ARIENTI P., FERIOLI V., PINOTTI A., RIGHI R., SANGIORGI R.
PSYCHIATRIC CLINIC, UNIVERSITY OF FERRARA, ITALY.

The prevalence of the adeguate e/o inadeguate use of alcoholic drinks in the population from 18 to 75 years old living in Ferrara has been investigated by our group of study. The research has been led in two different areas from the economic and social point of view: middle class the former, agricultural the latter. After the selection of a significant sample in each area, a questionnaire including Cage's and Mast's questions has been given to the interviewed at home with our help. The family doctor, the interviewed always refers to, collaborated to the inquiry, writing down a list of questions about the health state of the same interviewed. The obtained data have been analysed in every area and then comparated. The final results are discussed.

1059

COMPARED RESULTS BETWEEN GROUPS OF WOMEN AND MEN - FOR DISTURBANCIES CAUSED BY ALCOHOL

A. Hećimović, D. Breitenfeld, V. Starčević, J. Cvrk - Bikčević

Institute for Health Promotion
Health Center "New Zagreb", Zagreb, Yugoslavia
University Department for Neurology, Psychiatry, Alcoholism and other dependences of "Dr. M. Stojanovi" University Hospital, Zagreb, Yugoslavia

Blue collar female workers from various industrial enterprises from the region of New Zagreb were screened. A 5 % random sample of the examinees aged up to 5o years was processed and compared to the matched sample of workers. 76 variables were studied plus general data. A directed interview was applied and the examinees were checked up (somatic, neurologic and psychiatric examinations as well as to following laboratory tests: gamma GT, MCV, SGOT/PT, bilirubin). Results were obtained by comparison of these two groups indicate the existance of severe alcohologic problems in workers especially in the middle aged ones (from 31 to 4o) and in drivers and psychosomatic problems in female workers.

Session 159 Poster Presentation:
Personality disorders

1060

THE PLEONECTIC PERSONALITY: A TENTATIVE DIAGNOSTIC CLASSIFICATION.

Arthur G. Nikelly, Ph.D., University of Illinois Health Center, Urbana, Illinois U.S.A. 61801.

Dysfunctional behavior cannot be understood apart from the society in which it occurs. Current economic and political conditions foster the values of wealth and acquisitiveness. Based on these prevailing economic values a provisional pleonectic (pleon, more, and ktisis, possession) personality disorder is described, a term that epitomizes the acquisitive motive. The criteria that describe this personality trait depend on the outcome of acquisitiveness on self and others. The desire to have more than one's share and to deprive others of their basic needs spawns pathological behavior in the pleonectic person and destroys the natural condition of societal harmony and balance. The objective of assessment is to identify and treat the individual whose behavior creates environments that are harmful to others.

1061

STRATEGIC SELF-THERAPY FOR
REGRESSIVE PERSONALITY DISORDERS

John O. Beahrs, M.D. & Claudette H. Beahrs, M.S.S.W.
Oregon Health Sciences University, Portland, OR, USA

Strategic Self-Therapy (SST) is a treatment method utilizing limited intensity, rigorous therapeutic boundaries, and contextual reframing as the vehicle for change -- developed as a safe, effective and cost-efficient alternative to exploratory psychotherapy (EPT) for regressive personality disorders. Theory follows systems and hypnosis research showing intrapsychic structure to vary with its psychosocial context, which is strategically manipulable by assigning different meanings to otherwise invariant entities and events. Regressive dependency is minimized by explicitly differentiating the roles of patient, therapist, and social system. Patients do the "work" of defining and redefining their identity and direction, agreeing to refrain from destructive behavior; therapists as "consultant" prescribe self-therapy projects enabling patients to reframe/redirect discordant aspects of themselves; and independent social systems serve as crisis resource. 33 personality disordered SST patients were compared with 32 in EPT along several clinical parameters (composite therapist estimates rated 0-4+, mean inter-rater $r_{tt} = + 0.80$). Therapeutic progress was satisfactory for both SST and EPT (TPRS = 2.26 & 2.49, ns). SST patients had a higher dropout rate, but lower regressive dependency levels (RDL = 1.00 v 1.41, $p = 0.05$). RDL correlated with patients' regressive potential strongly within EPT ($r = + 0.74$, $p < 0.001$), less so within SST ($r = + 0.45$, $p < 0.01$). TPRS correlated strongly with patients' self-therapeutic activity level within both SST and EPT ($r = + 0.75, + 0.78$; p's < 0.001). To enhance patients' self-therapeutic activity is validated as an important target for psychotherapeutic intervention.

1062

COMPUTER-AIDED DIAGNOSIS OF PERSONALITY DISORDERS

Petrov Raiko
Sofioter University "Climent Ochridski", Sofia, Bulgaria

Code No.49

Still limited is the usage of computer techniques for "diagnosis" in psychiatry. It is due mainly to the difficulty to formalize the psychiatry terms system by means of cybernetic language. Dilutedness and ambiguity of the psychiatry symtomatics exaggerate the quantitative changes to the detriment of the qualitative ones. Despite those and many other restrains computer-aided techniques have a certain place in psychiatry.

We made use of a computerized model for "diagnosis" of personality disorders connected with socially averse and antisocial features of behavior. Included were algorithms for processing of information gathered from tests. These tests supplied us with data separated for memory, attention, emotions, thinking and other mental processes, conditions and reactions.

We compiled a computer program comprising several blocks - one for test data input, one for information processing and interpretation and outgoing data block with subprograms for determining the profile of examined person, the mental condition and sorting into "norm"/"pathology" class. Auxiliary programs were used for registering and filing, information storage, results integration with possibility for statistic processing.

The concrete results received from computer-aided examination of socially averse and antisocial persons formed the basis for the compilation of personality profile and "picture" of the condition featuring the respective mental process and reaction.

1063

MAGISTROGENY AND GONEUSOGENY

Moutafov Stefan
Sofioter University "Climent Ochridski", Sofia, Bulgaria

The Author describes for the first time (1986) two kinds of sociogenies formed as a result of erroneous interpersonal relations in the school system "teacher-parent". Sometimes a bad attitude of the parents to their child's teacher causes the illness "goneusogeny"(goneogeny). Incorrect relation of a teacher to the parents of his pupil may cause "magistrogeny" in the parents. Bad interrelations among teachers themselves lead to "heteromagistrogeny", which is the pedagogic version of the general collegogeny.

Magistrogeny and goneogeny show most often a clinic picture of the respective "anxiety neurosis" with the typical "magistrophoby", respectively -"goneusophoby". Observed are also several cases of "magistromania" and "goneusomania".

For the prophylaxis of magistrogeny and goneusogeny most helpful will be following the principles of the pedagogic deontology, the docimology and the general ethics.

1064

A PRELIMINARY REPORT ON TREATMENT OF
PATHOLOGICAL GAMBLERS
S.Aksoy, MD, M.Ziyalan, MD, A.N.Babaoğlu MD, A. Tolgay,Bakırköy Mental Hospital, Istanbul,TURKEY

In 1988 patients meeting the DSM-III-R criteria for pathological gambling were hospitalized(n:10). All were males with a mean age of 39. 5 patients had instable familial conditions in childhood. 4 patients were confronted with gambling before or during their adolescence.Mean age of beginning to gamble is 27. 4 patients were facing divorce. 4 patients were problem drinkers. 1 patient had posttraumatic stress disorder prior to gambling, 3 patients suffered from severe depression, 5 patients displayed antisocial features at the time of admission, all indicating possible causality relations.Mean duration of hospitalization is 76 days.At least 6 patients returned home and/or to work.At least 1 patient has stayed for 1 year, at least 4 patients have stayed for 6 months free of gambling.The general personality profile derived from individual Minnesota Multiphasic Personality Inventory results shows a personality structure reluctant to change with predominant features concerning psychopathy and distrustfulness. Spielberger Anxiety Inventory results show high general and situational anxiety levels,the latter indicating an anxiety reaction.These gamblers came before exhausting their resources and exibited an impressing endurance.The extended family structure seems to be vital in the course of these cases.

Session 160 Poster Presentation:
Psychological reaction to somatic disorders

1065

THE PREVALENT SYMPTOMS IN ONCOLOGISTS' REFERRALS TO THE PSYCHIATRIC DEPARTMENT
G.E.SARANTOGLOU* and G.A.RIGATOS**
Psychiatric Dept.* and 1st Dept.of Medical Oncology**,Hellenic Anticancer Institute, Athens (GR)

In a two years period (Jan.1987-Dec.1988) 328 cancer patients (187 women and 141 men) have been referred by oncologists to the Psychiatric Department (P.D) of the "Hellenic Anticancer Institute". Of them 227 patients (69%) have been admitted to P.D.by medical and 101 (31%) by surgical wards. Among them 78 patients (24%) were suffering from a previous psychiatric disorder and they were excluded of this research, as well as 14 (4%) urgent requests for just one psychiatric crisis intervention. The remaining sample of 236 referrals concerned 134 women (mean age 43,8) and 102 men (mean age 45,4) who have been admitted to P.D.for the following, according to their oncologists, main reasons: I.Depression with or without anxiety: 128 patients (54%) II.Anxiety manifestations: 54 p.(23%) III.Non-compliance,refusal of treatment:22p.(9%) IV.Unjustified physically pain:12p.(5%) etc. This work attempts to interpret the prevalence of depressive symtomatology among the sample's cancer patients and suggests that the agreement of oncologic wards referrals' symptoms with D.S.M.-III P.D.'s diagnoses depended on the degree of collaboration-liaison between them.

1066

Psychological aspects of cancer pain perception
G.C.M. Orsolini, I. Maremmani, M.S. Damiani, J.A. Deltito°, P. Castrogiovanni
Institute of Psychiatry, Pisa University, Italy
°Depression and Anxiety Clinic, New York Hospital, Cornell University, Westchester Division, White Plains, New York, N.Y., U.S.A.

In order to investigate the relationships between psychopathology and aggressive behaviour on one hand and cancer pain perception on the other, patients who suffered from neoplasm where investigated by means of SCL-90 by Derogatis, Q.T.A. by Buss-Durkee, S.A.D. by Cassano & Castrogiovanni and M.P.Q. by Melzack.. The results show that when psychopathologic symptoms are present, they lead the patient to feel pain as unbearable and he could become violently homicidal. Features of aggressivity once experienced, lead to an almost personified and extremely active image of pain.

1067

Depression and somatic pathologies

Celani T., Pellegrino F., Sposati P.
Department of Medical Psychology and Psychiatry, I Medical School, University of Naples, Italy

The setting up of clinics for psychiatric consultancy to which "those patients whose pathology presents important psychological implications" can turn is certainly the first step in establishing a relationship of collaboration between general practitioners and consultants conforming with recent orientation in "consultation-liaison-psychiatry". In fact in hospital and university structures anxiety and depression are elements frequently found in various forms: abnormal reactions to the illness, a strictly psychopathological event, but also primary depression which is only expressed on the somatic side (masked depression).
The aim of our work has been to evaluate the depression symptom in patients seen for consultancy in the Psychiatric Clinic of the First Medical School, University of Naples, using a clinical psycho-diagnostical approach which involves the use of scale (Hamilton, MHQ, Zung).

1068

EFFECTS OF AGE AND TIME OF AMPUTATION ON DEPRESSION AND PSYCHOPATHOLOGY

Dilbaz,N.,M.D., Erkmen,H.,M.D., Seber,G.,Ph.D., Kaptanoğlu,C.,M.D., Tekin,D.,M.D.

Department of Psychiatry, Faculty of Medicine, Anadolu University Eskişehir/Turkey

In order to investigate the effects of age and time of amputation on psychiatric symptoms, 30 amputees were interviewed during the post amputation period; using a questionnaire, Symptom Checklist-90 (SCL-90) and Hamilton Depression Scale.
The interviews were based on a prearranged schedule encompassing socio-demographic aspects, the cause and site of the amputation and psychiatric features following the procedure.
On assessment of depression using the Hamilton Depression scale, 11 of the 30 patients scored 0, 6 scored 1-7, 14 scored 7-14 and 5 scored over 14; that means nearly half had depressive features ranging from depressive neurosis (14 patients) to reaction severe enough to be labelled as major depression (5 patients). Over all adjustment and psychopathology were assessed by SCL-90 and the results were 0.74 for Somatization, 0.79 for Obsessive-Compulsive, 0.99 for Interpersonal sensitivity 0.84 for Depression, 0.71 for Anxiety, 0.76 for Hostility, 0.52 for Phobic anxiety, 0.58 for Paranoid ideation and 0.43 for Psychotism.
We compared the SCL-90 profiles of acute amputees with those of chronic amputees and of the entire sample. All data were analyzed using biostatistical methods and the results were discussed.

1069

SEXUALITE IMAGE DU CORPS MAMMECTOMIE

N.GRAFEILLE, R.ROUSSILHES, P.CONSTANTOPOULOS, G.BRUN

Nous avons fait une enquête auprès des patientes mammectomisées dans le Service de Gynécologie de l' Hôpital Saint-André à Bordeaux (de 1981 à 1988).

Il existe de nombreuses enquêtes sur le mode de vie et l'évolution psychologique de ces patientes après leur traitement ; c'est pourquoi nous n'avons pas questionné nos patientes à ce niveau.

Il nous a semblé intéressant d'apporter un éclaircissement sur la vie sexuelle de ces femmes et sur leur vécu de l'image du corps. Chaque questionnaire est rempli par le médecin qui a reçu les patientes. Nous avons sélectionné les femmes de 29 à 60 ans parce qu'au delà de cet âge, les questions sur la sexualité étaient mal vécues ou la réponse était systématiquement :"aucune sexualité".

1070

PRELIMINARY RESULT OF "AUTOGENE TRAINING" IN TREATMENT OF IDIOPATHIC PROCTOCOLITIS. L. Sorribes, N. Conti, M. Hagelsteen, P. Possoz, P. Bories. Groupe de Recherche en thérapeutique comportementale et Clinique des Maladies de l'Appareil Digestif, Hôpital St-Eloi, Montpellier, France.
Au cours de la rectocolite hémorragique (RCH), aucune des nombreuses évaluations de profil de personnalité n'a montré de déviance significative par rapport à une population standard. Cependant, l'expérience dans une consultation hospitalière révèle de manière générale l'incapacité des malades atteints de RCH à parvenir à toute sensation de détente. Un essai préliminaire de thérapie de relaxation par training autogène de Schultz a été entrepris chez des malades atteints de RCH basse.
L'indication de training autogène a été retenue chez 20 malades ambulatoires atteints de formes basses de RCH résistantes aux traitements habituels (sulfasalazine, lavements de corticoïdes ou de 5 ASA). Parmi ces 20 malades parfaitement informés des modalités thérapeutiques, 6 seulement ont accepté le traitement comportemental, les 14 autres ayant refusé le principe de sa réalisation en milieu psychiatrique.
Parmi ces 6 malades, 4 ont poursuivi le protocole complet (13 séances), 2 malades sont en cours de traitement. L'amélioration jugée sur des critères fonctionnels et morphologiques (rectoscopie-biopsie) a été spectaculaire chez les 4 malades parvenus au terme des 13 séances avec un recul d'au moins 9 mois.
Conclusion : cet essai préliminaire de training autogène au cours des formes basses de RCH montre 1) la réticence des malades à se confier à des médecins psychiatres même pour une thérapeutique strictement comportementale; 2) l'efficacité décisive de la méthode chez des malades compliants.

Session 161 Poster Presentation:
Pharmacotherapy of anxiety

1071

MAPROTILINE DROPS:PILOT STUDY IN ANXIETY ADAPTATIVE DISORDERS
J.P.LHUILLIER,J.B.GARRE,R.PHILLIPS,J.B.ORLER, J.L.KAZAKEVICIUS.

For several years, the use of antidepressant drugs in the therapeutics of anxiety states has been justified by a certain number of studies. In our own pratice, Maprotiline which has known effects on anxiety, seemed appropriate in this specific treatment.

Thirty patients of both sexes presenting adaptative disorders according to DSM III criteria and not fulfilling the diagnosis criteria of a major depressive episode were included in an open, non-comparative study. The patients were followed for a maximum period of 45 days using evaluation scales at the outset, then on the 7th, 28 th and 45 th days.

This pilot study indicates that the anxiolytic activity of Maprotiline appears to develop independently of the antidepressive action, an improvement of the anxiety possibly occurring as early as the first week of treatment.

1072

LONG TERM COMPATIBILITY OF FLUSPIRILENE IN ANXIETY AND ADJUSTMENT DISORDERS

Osterheimer M, Reifschneider G, Beckmann H, FRG

Fluspirilene is a Diphenylbutylpiperidin, which releases slowly from the intramuscular injection depot and which has been described as a potent, specific and safe drug. With a view on the problem of extrapyramidal side effects we carried out a study on the long term compatibility of Fluspirilene with a special aspect on tardive dyskinesia and on pharmacological induced depression. The study was performed in private practices. Several rating scales for side effects had been used, also psychopathometric evaluation had been done. All data show an extraordinary long during treatment and an unusual large number of injections with Fluspirilene. In 4 of 5 scales the Fluspirilene group ranges higher according to the mean total scores of the side effect ratings, but there was no significant difference at all. In the AIMS score we had a trend on differences. It has also to be discussed wether the rating scales are useful for a correct evaluation of side effects. Our clinical findings will be reported too. Individual analysis showed some advise for the occurence of Fluspirilene-induced depression in a subgroup of patients. Benefit and risks of low dose neuroleptics will be discussed according to the different aspects of the results.

1073

EFFICACY ON ANXIETY OF FLUVOXAMINE VERSUS PRAZEPAM, DIAZEPAM WITH ANXIODEPRESSED PATIENTS.
JP Chabannes*, R Douge
Clinique du Nivolet CHS BASSENS 73011 CHAMBERY.

60 out-patients, treated by a psychiatrist for somatic complaints with a low mood and anxiety, received fluvoxamine (F) (n=30), or diazepam (D) (n=30) for 42 days. 4 patients dropped out in the F group, 1 in the D group. Initial depression level was 23.4 (HDRS) for the 60 patients. Mean Hamilton anxiety scale global score decreased from 26.00 ± 2.33 to 13.59 ± 6.60 in the F group and from 26.43 ± 3.37 to 13.62 ± 5.13 in the D group. Percentages of improvement were equal (48 %).

130 out-patients, treated for a major depressive syndrom with somatic complaints and anxiety, received fluvoxamine (F) (n=44), fluvoxamine + prazepam (F+P) (n=44), or prazepam (P) (n=42) for 42 days. 19 patients dropped out in the F group, 18 in the F+P group, 13 in the P group. Initial depression level was 31.8 (MADRS) for the 130 patients. Mean Hamilton anxiety scale global score decreased from 30.2 ± 6.4 to 13.1 ± 11.3 (F group), from 27.9 ± 5.2 to 11.7 ± 8.6 (F+P group), from 28.3 ± 5.2 to 15.0 ± 12.8 (P group). Percentages of improvement were 57 % (F), 58 % (F+P) and 47 % (P).

In both trials, a significant difference was observed within each group since D7 but not between groups. A new serotoninergic compound had a strong effect on anxiety. This effect was comparable to two references anxiolytic drugs.

1074

LOW DOSE NEUROLEPTICS FOR ANXIOUS DEPRESSIVE DISORDERS - EFFICACY AND RISK.
Sieberns, S., Budde, G.,
Troponwerke GmbH & Co. KG, 5000 Köln 80, FRG

Today low dose neuroleptics - especially the long acting depot formulations are wide spread for therapy of anxious, depressive and psychosomatic disorders.

Devoid of influence of activity and performance low dose neuroleptics improve depression, anxiety and agitation. However, their wider applicability was limited by extrapyramidal side effects. A time limited prescription of the low dose depot formulation for just 3 months like e.g. 10 mg flupenthixoldecanoat per 2 ws may reduce the aforementioned risk. The depot form guarantees a good bioavailability and improves compliance. It prevents from uncontrolled selfmedication; a disadvantage which may occur e.g. under benzodiazepine treatment. However, the indication of a low dose neuroleptic therapy should be stated with caution. The results of a multicentre trial of 4.355 patients with depressive, anxious, psychosomatic, and psychoreactive disorders who were allocated to low dose treatment with flupenthixoldecanoat will be presented. Main issues of the trial were (a) prescription habits in general practice like concomitant medication, (b) patient criteria, but also (c) onset of action and (d) efficacy depending on the concomitant therapy, and (e) tolerability of low dose neuroleptics.

1075

DOSULEPIN VS LORAZEPAM AND PLACEBO IN MENOPAUSAL ANXIETY AND DEPRESSION

R.C. Winning, T. Clarke, P.F. Boston, D.P. Rhinds, S. Kimber and D. Prudham

Dosulepin (dothiepin) (D) Lorazepam (L) and placebo (P) were compared in a 4 week, single blind, parallel group study involving 74 patients with perimenopausal emotional symptoms, with or without vasomotor symptoms. Dosage of D was 75mg/day and of L was 2mg/day, this was increased to 150mg/day or 3mg/day respectively if considered appropriate.

Assessment of depression was made using the Hamilton rating scale (HRS) at 0, 2 and 4 weeks. Global condition and adverse reactions were also monitored at weeks 2 and 4. Patient self assessments were also recorded on diary cards.

HRS score decreased in all groups at weeks 2 and 4. Mean decreases in the D treated group were higher than in the other two groups. By week 4 all patients in the D treated group were rated as "improved" or "much improved" compared with 75% on L and 71% on P. Similarly, patients self assessments at 4 weeks rated 94% of patients on D, 81% on L and 47% on P as "improved".

The incidence of side effects was recorded as 32% in the D treated group, 45% in the L treated group and 25% in those treated with P. Drowsiness was reported in all groups and dry mouth in the D and L groups.

Although the numbers studied in this trial were too small to produce statistically significant results further studies of dothiepin may be warranted in menopausal anxiety and depression.

Session 162   Poster Presentation:
Biological psychiatry: Monoamines and neuropeptides

1076

DISCRIMINATION OF AMINE PROFILES IN OCD, GAD, MAD, AND NORMAL CONTROLS

J.A. Yaryura-Tobias, W. Essman, S. Kaplan, F. Neziroglu, E. Essman, and C. Taylor.
Bio-Behavioral Psychiatry, Great Neck, NY

Blood serotonin, dopamine, epinephrine, norepinephrine, and 5-hydroxyindoleacetic acid levels were measured in nonmedicated subjects (55 obsessive-compulsives, 21 depressed, 31 anxiety disordered, and 28 normals). No significant differences in mean amine concentrations were found between the obsessive group and the other diagnostic groups. Discriminant analysis did not differentiate among groups on the basis of amine profile. Within each diagnostic group, Pearson correlations were computed between pairs of amines. Three sets of correlations differentiated the control group from the obsessive group and two sets of correlations differentiated the depressed group from the obsessive group. Amine correlations did not distinguish the anxious group from the obsessive group. Results suggest that hypothesized monoamine disturbances in obsessive-compulsive disorder, generalized anxiety disorder, and major depression are more complex than has been previously believed.

1077

EFFECTS ON INCREASED 5HT ACTIVITY ON PLASMA HVA IN PSYCHOTIC PATIENTS
Lesieur Ph., Foulot M., Varoquaux O., Morin D., Dollfus S., Petit M.
Centre Hospitalier Specialise du Rouvray, France

Among the evidence supporting the DA hypothesis of schizophrenia, plasma HVA has been shown in man as a usefull index of DA activity in psychotic disorders and their treatment. However, the role of 5HT systems remains more hypothetical since clinical and preclinical data provide strong evidence for a functional relationship between the two systems.
In order to investigate the clinical meaning of such a relationship, nine clinically improved psychotic patients, treated with a stable dosage of haloperidol were involved in this study. The diurnal plasma HVA variations over a 3 hours period (9am to 12:00) after the morning dosage of haloperidol (day 1) were compared (day 2) to those observed after an acute increase of 5HT activity induced by a bolus of clomipramine- 15mg over a 10 min. infusion - (Laakman et al., 1983). On day 1st, the expected morning fall from baseline was found for the 9 patients starting to reach a significant level at the 90 min of the study (m±sd: 9.0 ± 3.0 vs 7.0 ± 1.9 ng/ml respectively $p<.01$) whereas on day 2nd the I.V. clomipramine bolus induced a fairly stable plasma HVA level over the same 3 hours period. The biological data will be discussed with the individual clinical characteristics of the patients.

1078

BIOCHEMICAL CHARACTERIZATION OF 5-HT_{1A} RECEPTOR RELATED ANXIOLYTICS

T. Glaser, J. Greuel, E. Horvàth and J. Traber
Neurobiology Department, Troponwerke, Berliner Str. 156, D-5000 Köln 80, F.R.G.

The pyrimidinylpiperazine derivatives buspirone, gepirone and ipsapirone have been shown to possess anxiolytic and antidepressive properties in several animal models as well as in clinical studies. Radioligand binding studies revealed as a common feature of these compounds a high affinity for serotonin (5-HT)$_{1A}$ receptors. Their overall receptor profile is somewhat different insofar as buspirone had a higher affinity for dopamine D2 receptors than the two others, while ipsapirone interacted more potently in an antagonistic and agonistic manner with α_1- and α_2-adrenergic receptors, respectively. On presynaptic (somatodendritic) 5-HT_{1A} autoreceptors buspirone, gepirone and ipsapirone acted like the reference 5-HT_{1A} receptor agonist 8-OH-DPAT as full agonists by inhibiting raphe neurone firing. On postsynaptic receptors in rat hippocampus, the pyrimidinylpiperazine derivatives are partial agonists while 8-OH-DPAT is a full agonist as measured by inhibition of forskolin-stimulated adenylate cyclase activity. The effects of 8-OH-DPAT and ipsapirone on local cerebral glucose utilization (LCGU) were studied by means of the ^{14}C-2-deoxyglucose technique. Both compounds reduced the LCGU in most of the brain regions studied with the 8-OH-DPAT effects being more pronounced than those of ipsapirone. The LCGU data suggest a suppression by 8-OH-DPAT and ipsapirone of neuronal activity, especially in structures of the limbic system.
The present results support the hypothesis of an involvement of 5-HT_{1A} receptors in the anxiolytic and antidepressive actions of buspirone, gepirone and ipsapirone.

1079

ANIMAL MODELS OF 5-HT_{1A} RECEPTOR FUNCTION

J. Traber, J. De Vry, R. Schreiber and E. Horvàth, Neurobiology Department, Troponwerke, Berliner Str. 156, D-5000 Köln 80, F.R.G.

Attempts have been made to study the functional role of the 5-HT_{1A} receptors and to characterize selective ligands on biochemical and behavioral levels. In vitro, 5-HT_{1A} receptor ligands can be characterized as full or partial agonists, depending on the extent to which they cause an inhibition of the forskolin-stimulated adenylate cyclase in the rat hippocampus. In rats, 5-HT_{1A} receptor agonists induce particular elements of the so-called 5-HT syndrome, such as reciprocal forepaw treading, increased locomotor activity and Straub's tail. Furthermore these compounds induce contralateral circling in rats with a unilateral lesion of the dorsal raphe nucleus and induce drug stimulus generalization in rats trained to discriminate the selective 5-HT_{1A} agonist 8-hydroxy-2-(di-n-propylamino)tetralin (8-OH-DPAT) from vehicle. Results obtained in the 5-HT syndrome model and the circling model are relatively similar: only selctive 5-HT_{1A} receptor agonists, e.g., 8-OH-DPAT and BAY R 1531 (6-methoxy-4-(di-n-propylamino)tetralin), induce full activity in both animal models, whereas 5-HT_{1A} receptor partial agonists, e.g., buspirone, gepirone and ipsapirone, as well as 5-HT_2 receptor agonists, e.g. 5-OMe-DMT, DOI and quipazine, only show moderate or no activity in both models. 5-HT receptor ligands, not selective to the 5-HT_{1A} receptor subtype, e.g., TFMPP, ICS 205-930, ketanserin and ritanserin, fail to induce activity. Selective 5-HT_{1A} receptor partial agonists and non-selective 5-HT_{1A} receptor antagonists (methiothepine, spiroperidol and (-)-pindolol) partially or completely antagonize the effects of 8-OH-DPAT in both models. Rats trained to discriminate 8-OH-DPAT from vehicle completely generalize to other 5-HT_{1A} full agonists, as well as to 5-HT_{1A} partial receptor agonists; no generalization or only partial generalization is obtained with non-selective 5-HT_{1A} receptor ligands or 5-HT ligands without high affinity to the 5-HT_{1A} receptor.

1080

SOMATIC SYMPTOMS AND NEUROTRANSMITTER ENZYMES IN MAJOR AFFECTIVE DISORDERS.
Wahlund B, Sääf J and Wetterberg L.
Karolinska Institute, Department of Psychiatry, St. Göran's Hospital, Box 12500, S-11281 Stockholm, Sweden

Platelet monoamine oxidase (MAO), erythrocyte catechol-O-methyl transferase (COMT) and plasma dopamine- -hydroxylase (DBH) play important roles in the transformation of biogenic neurotransmitter amines. In the present study the activities of all three enzymes were determined in 77 individuals. Forty-four were patients with major affective disorders and 33 apparently healthy controls. Both patients and controls were rated according to the Comprehensive Psychopathological Rating Scale (CPRS). Analysis of principal components for the enzyme data discriminated with statistical significance two subgroups of patients. One of the subgroups was characterized by a high incidence of low activities of MAO and DBH, together with a high activity of COMT. This group of patients also exhibited a high prevalence (67 %) of somatic symptoms (e.g. muscular tension, ache and pain) which was not found in the other subgroup (11 %). The subgroups did not differ in other CPRS items or in any other clinical parameter e.g. sex, age, and medication.

1081

CHARACTERIZATION OF SIGMA AND PHENCYCLIDINE BINDING SITES ON NEURAL CELL LINES

T. Glaser and A. Friedl, Neurobiology Department, Troponwerke, Berliner Str. 156, D-5000 Köln 80, F.R.G.

Benzomorphane opiates and phencyclidine (PCP) produce psychotomimetic effects in man which are believed to be mediated by both haloperidol sensitive sigma and PCP receptors. In the present study several cell lines (NCB-20 hybrid neurotumor, rat pheochromocytoma PC-12, neuroblastoma x glioma hybrid NG108-15, rat glioma C6-BU-1) were investigated for the presence of these receptors by means of radioligand binding studies and compared with rat brain material. For quantitative receptor binding assays the specific radioligand [^{3}H]-DTG radioligands [^{3}H]-DTG (di-o-tolylguanedine), [^{3}H]-(+)-3-PPP (3-(3-hydroxyphenyl)-N-(1-propyl)piperidine), [^{3}H]-(+)-SKF 10047 (N-allylnormetazocine) and [^{3}H]-TCP (n-[1-(2-thienyl)-cyclohexyl]) were used. Binding sites for the specific sigma ligands [^{3}H]-DTG, [^{3}H]-(+)-3-PPP and the sigma/PCP-ligand SKF 10047 were found on membranes of all neural cell lines. Binding sites for the PCP-ligand TCP were present in membranes of the NCB-20 and NG108-15 cells. The various cell lines expressed both common as well as ligand specific binding sites for the different sigma and PCP ligands as revealed by saturation and competition analyses. Furthermore, the pharmacological profile of these sites seems to be different from that of corresponding brain receptors. The present data suggest in cell lines the existence of several types of sigma and PCP receptors. Besides the already in mammalian brain described receptors novel types possibly exist in cultured cell lines. The cell lines used in this study may prove useful tools in further pharmacologically characterizing these sites and investigating their functional role.

1082

PLASMA NEUROPEPTIDE PATTERN IN MENTAL DISORDERS

J. Saiz-Ruiz, J.L. Carrasco, C. Grande & A. Hernanz
Hospital Ramón y Cajal (S. de Psiquiatría) & Hospital La Paz (S. de Bioquímica). Madrid Spain.

Recent studies have shown the important role that neuropeptides play in the regulation of behavior. Moreover, the actions of these peptides over brain functions have led to several etiologic postulates in mental disorders. In spite of studies performed on CSF samples, plasma levels of neuropeptides have been rarely investigated. We have studied a population of 22 schizophrenic patients, 23 connate oligophrenics (both groups treated with neuroleptic drugs) and a miscellaneous group (untreated) of affective and anxiety disorders (25 patients). A control sample matched in age and sex (11m, 9f; range 21-42y.) of healthy subjects were used. Determinations of Somatostatin, Bombesin, Neurotensin, VIP and β-Endorphin were carried out by RIA methods. The results show significant differences between groups and neurochemical data. These findings must be discussed considering the lack of knowledge about of peripheric neuropeptides.

1083

NEUROLEPTIC EFFECTS ON SUBSTANCE P NEURONS IN THE NIGROSTRIATAL AND MESOLIMBIC SYSTEMS
J. Constantinidis and C. Bouras
University of Geneva, "Morphological Psychopathology" Bel-Air, 1225 Geneva, Switzerland

Substance P (SP)-activating and Dopamine (DA)-inhibiting pathways are related in the nigrostriatal and mesolimbic systems. Neuroleptics are considered as postsynaptic DA blockers and decrease DA activity in the nigrostriatal and mesolimbic systems. The question arises whether neuroleptics also induce changes of SP in these systems. In the present study, the neuroleptic haloperidol was administrated to rats, acutely and chronically (on a daily basis of 10 mg/kg s.c.). SP content in various areas of the brain was evaluated by microscopical observation of SP-like specific immunoreactivity visualized by Coon's immunohisto-fluorescence. Globally, haloperidol induces a decrease of SP content in the nigrostriatal system, that means SP-hyperactivity (excess of synaptic release and decrease of presynaptic storage) and an increase in the mesolimbic habenulo-interpeduncular system, that means SP-hypoactivity. But, DA is inhibitor in nigrostriatal and mesolimbic systems and the haloperidol-DA-blockage should induce SP-hyperactivity in both. This asymetry may be explained : 1) by the existence of an inhibitor interneuron between DA and SP in the mesolimbic system (probably from the N.Accumbens to the Habenula Medialis via the Stria Medullaris or a GABA neuron in the Habenula Medialis) or 2) by a direct primary inhibitory action of the neuroleptic on the mesolimbic SP-neuron, and therefore, secondary inactivation of the DA mesolimbic neuron. In this case, an inhibitor interneuron between DA and SP may act in the nigrostriatal system (probably a GABA neuron in the Striatum or a Glycine neuron in the S. Nigra).

Session 163   Poster Presentation:
Beyond classical antidepressant drug treatment

1084

Evaluation of the efficacy of Thymopentin associated with Imipramine in the therapy of M.Depression
Aguglia E.,Azzarelli O.,Biondi M.R.,Cardillo A.
Clinica Psichiatrica,Trieste and Clinica Psichiatrica,Catania, Italy

With the aim of studying interrelations between C.N.S.,immune system and endocrine system,the A.A. carried out a study to evaluate the efficacy of the association of a thymic hormone,Thymopentin (TP5),and Imipramine in the treatment of subjects affected with Major Depression.20 male patients aged between 18 and 55 with diagnosis of M.D. according to DSMIII R and ICD-9 were divided at random in 2 groups and,after a 5 days wash-out period,were treated for 4 weeks in the following way:group A took TP5(Sintomodulina^R),50 mg s.c. 3 times a week and Imipramine 50 mg daily;group B took Imipramine 50 mg daily and placebo for 4 wks. Subjects with prostatic adenoma, glaucoma, autoimmune, allergic and infective diseases were excluded. The patients underwent the following tests:HDRS,Zung SAS,M.A.scale,at baseline and then after 8,15,29 days of treatment: only patients with HDRS values ≥17 were considered.At baseline and after 29 days routine hematochemical, neuroendocrine(ACTH, cortisol) and immune parameters(total T-lymphocyte count,T-subsets,lymphocyte function assessed by proliferative response to PHA and IL-2 production)were evaluated.Our results show that TP5 added to Imipramine has a synergistic effect, inducing a more rapid improvement.A trend toward normalization of immune parameters was also observed.

1085

EFFECTS OF THE BETA-MIMETIC DRUG
CLENBUTEROL IN CHRONIC DEPRESSIVES
M. Bach, C. Alf, G. Schönbeck, G. Pinter
Department of Psychiatry, University of
Vienna, Austria

According to the noradrenalin hypothesis
of depression an antidepressant activity
was proposed for beta-mimetic substances.
In previous studies the antidepressant
activity of salbutamol - usually used as
a bronchodilatating compound - was shown
to be comparable to tricyclic antidepressants. In addition to this findings
an antidepressant activity is also discussed for other bronchodilatating compounds. In this open study we investigated the effects of the beta-mimetic
drug clenbuterol in thirteen therapy-
resistant (chronic) depressives classified by DSM-III. Each patient received
increasing oral doses of clenbuterol
(range 0.04-0.20mg/day) over four weeks.
Significant clinical improvement was
observed. The results concerning efficacy
tolerance and clinical profile are
demonstrated and discussed.

1086

BENTAZEPAM, A BENZODIAZEPINE, ASSOCIATED
TO TRICYCLIC ANTIDEPRESSANT IN DEPRESSION
TREATMENT.
Calcedo, A.(1); Fdez. Benitez,J.(2); Otero,
FJ.(3); Rodríguez, A. (4); Garrido, J. (5).
(1) Hosp. Gregorio Marañón; (2) Hosp. Gómez
Ulla, (3) C.S.M.Villalba; (4) C.S.M. San
Blas; (5) Lab. Knoll-Made, S.A.

Tricyclic antidepressant (TCA)/ benzodiazepine
(BZ) association is usual in psychiatric
practice, both in hospitals and out-patients.
However, few controlled trials have studied
this topic.

Our study has been conducted in two populations:
in-patients (n = 40) and out-patients (n = 40)
from two hospitals and two Mental Health Centers.
In any case, patients were major depression
diagnosed (DSM-III-R criterium) and randomized
to clomipramine 100-150 mg/day or clomipramine
100-150 mg/day plus bentazepam 75 mg/day during 6
weeks. Hamilton Anxiety Scale (HAS) and Hamilton
Depression Scale (HAD) were performed at the
end of weeks 1st, 2nd, 4th and 6th. Results
were analysed in function of time to obtain
improvement in HAS and HAD comparing results
among two conditions: in-patients vs. outpatients. Clinic use of association TCA/BZ is
discussed in function of risk/benefit rate of
both treatment schedules.

1087

BENZODIAZEPINE DRUGS IN DEPRESSIVE DISOR-
DERS:A COMPLEMENTARY TREATMENT
A. Chinchilla;M. Vega;M. Camarero and L. Jorda
Ramon and Cajal Hospital.Psychiatric Service.MADRID.

Treatment with solely antidepressant drugs(AD) could
be insufficient for some patients with depression because
of the delayed effect of the AD.During this period the
risk of suicide and non-compliance are high,above all
when symptoms of anxiety and agitation are predominant.
We studied the complementary use of BZD in a sample of
190 inpatients diagnosed with depressive disorders as
set out in ICD-9 and who received AD as a principle
treatment.
 BZD was used in 73,6 % of the patients as follows:
Depressive Neurosis,83%;Depressive Psychoses,71,7%
AND other depressions 58,8%.A hypnotic was also used
in 20,3% of cases.Of the BZDs used the most frequent
were Clorazepate (CLZ) (60,7%) and Loracepam (LZ)
(27,8%).Other BZDs were scarcely used.
 There is a need to adjust the dose of BZD according
to the clinical state and the predominance of symptoms to
prevent the risk of suicide,to aid anxiolysis and psychotherapy and above all to rapidly velieve the patient's
suffering.

1088

CHROMOTHERAPY FOR DEPRESSION
A.Cavallaro, A. Nigro, L. Nuzzolo, F. Polito
Cattedra di Psicologia - Magistero - Messina
Italy

A model of chromatic prevention for depression
was planned in the context of Cybernetic
Psychiatry (Pisani, Nigro).
An important moment for depression is the
disconnection between two persons: normal
connection is defined as "psychosynapsis".
Within the spychosynapsis chromatic communication
exercises a function of modulation, which can
result in determining the order of maintenence of
mental balance. The modulation speeds up or
delays the "ultradian".
The look is the most important datum in the
chromatic communication and is feeded by the
chromatic enviropment.
The blue component of such chromaticity results
in favour of the mental balance.

Session 164 Poster Presentation:
Schizophrenia I

1089

Coping Behavior of Schizophrenics: First
results of a longitudinal study.
R. Saupe, R. Gebhardt, R.Stieglitz,
H. Helmchen   Dept. of Psychiatry, Freie
Universität Berlin, Berlin (West) F.R.G.

Under the conditions of a sufficient drug-
therapy the course of schizophrenia may
be influenced by life events and living
conditions outside hospital. Although
effort is done to understand cognitive and
functioning deficits of schizophrenics,
little is known about the influence of
positive coping capacities of the patients
and wether a certain coping behavior is
more favorable than a different one. Here
first cross sectional data and data of a
6 months follow up are presented analyzing
coping behavior (including moderator
variables) of schizophrenics regarding
their illness and their every day life.
Theses data are part of a longitudinal
study, which is set up for 5 years.

1090

INTERACTIVE PATTERNS AND FAMILY BINDS IN
SCHIZOPHRENIA
Vella G., Loriedo C., Alliani D., Bartolomei S.,
Pacileo A., Piro A., Preziosa P.
Psychiatric Clinic University of Rome, Italy

Coherently with the systemic view, the authors
consider the family interaction patterns in
schizophrenia.
Some typical redundant behaviors in the family
system appear to be typical of schizophrenic
family.
The authors investigate the family system through
the family stories.
Special emphasis in this work is placed upon the
modalities of weaning from the parental figures,
the conjugal bind of the parents and the
interactive patterns with grandparents.
In order to study these binds, family stories are
confronted with the different phases and critical
events in the family life cycle.

1091

EXPRESSED EMOTION (EE) OF SCHIZOPHRENICS' RELATIVES:
ONE YEAR FOLLOW UP.
FAVRE S.,FERRERO F.,GONZALEZ C.,LENDAIS G., de
SAUSSURE N., SZIGETHY L.
INSTITUTIONS UNIVERSITAIRES DE PSYCHIATRIE
GENEVA SWITZERLAND
EE of relatives living with schizophrenic patients
tends to be stable.High EE relatives maintain a
high rate of critical comments and of emotional
over-involvement over time.Low EE relatives are
less critical and overinvolved.However ,it is hypothesized that some Low EE families may become more
critical and therefore High during a period of
symptomatic relapse or exacerbation of psychotic
symptoms.22 patients with schizophrenic or paranoid
symptoms on the Present State Examination (CATEGO
Classes S+,S?,P+,P?,O+) were included in the study
and reevaluated after one year.In parallel their
relatives were categorized as High or Low EE. At
one year,50% of the patients changed to non-schizophrenic or -paranoid symptoms; 18 of 22 relatives
remained stable while 4 changed categories.In this
latter group, all 4 patients at one year showed no
or less florid schizophrenic or paranoid symptoms
while the EE of their relatives changed either from
High to Low (two cases) or from Low to High(two
cases).In the latter two,crisis factors unrelated
to the patients status were evidenced. These preliminary results suggest that although the families'
EE tends to remain stable over time, other factors
than the patients symtomatic picture may influence
eventual changes.

1092

DEPRESSION IN CHRONIC SCHIZOPHRENIA
(STUDY OF SOME OF THE PREDISPOSING AND
PRECIPITATING FACTORS)

H.R.CHAUDHRY,M.D.; A. BASHIR,M.D.; M.R.
CHAUDHRY,M.D. FOUNTAIN HOUSE LAHORE,
PAKISTAN

Depressive syndromes that occur during
the course of Schizophrenia are not
clearly understood but have important
implications for the treatment of the
Schizophrenic patient.
Present study was designed to look for
various predisposing and precipitating
factors for depression in chronic Schizophrenics.
Twenty two chronic schizophrenic patients,
known to have depressive illness were
matched with twenty two non-depressed
chronic schizophrenics, all of them residing at Fountain House,Lahore,Pakistan.
They were matched for age, sex and social
class. There should be absence of depressive episodes in previous six months
among the control group.
DSM III was used to diagnose both group
of patients. The severity of depression
had to rate a minimum of 15 on the Hamilton Rating Scale for depression.
In this presentation, results of the
study will be discussed.

1093

A TEN YEARS LONGITUDINAL RORSCHACH STUDY IN SCHIZO= PHRENIC INPATIENTS

Virginio NAVA, Gabriella CILLI, Elisabetta RIVA e Salvatore ZIZOLFI

Department of Mental Health, COMO, Italy

40 male unmarried inpatients, 20-65 years old, under going a long-lasting continous hospitalization (at least 5 years), satisfying DSM-III-R criteria for chronic schizophrenia, were administered the Rors= chach test, according to the Scuola Italiana Rors= chach (RIZZO et al., 1980). After ten years of per= manent hospitalization, the same 40 inpatients were retested by the same psychiatrist, in order to verify the test-retest reliability of the Rorschach test in such a group of subjects after a long test-retest period. The data were statistically analysed by means of Pearson product-moment correlation coeffi= cient ('r'), and by means of Student two tailed 't' test. Rorschach data from total number of subjects and from clinical subgroups (paranoid vs. disorgani zed type; 'negative symptoms' vs.'positive symptoms' type; clinically unchanged vs. worsed) were conside red. An highly statistically significant test-retest correlation was found for the majority of Rorschach formal variables, very few statistically significant variations in Rorschach variables were observed bet ween test and re-test, in all the groups considered.

1094

LIFE EVENT AND THE RELAPSE OF CHRONIC SCHIZOPHRENIA
Yoshioka,H., Sugamata,J. and Nanko,S.*
Hatsuishi Mental Hospital, Chiba, *Dept. of Psychiat. Univ. of Teikyo Sch. of Med. Tokyo JAPAN

The possible role of environmental stress in precipitating schizophrenia was reported by many authors, but limited to acute type. The present study investigated the relapse of chronic schizophrenia in terms of life events.
Subjects and Method: Subjects were 53 inpatients of 8th and 10th wards of Hatsuishi Mental Hospital who were suffering from schizophrenia more than ten years and readmitted during this two years. All met criteria of schizophrenia chronic type, according to the RDC. Control subjects were 75 hospital staffs. The life-event schedule by Paykel et al.(1969) was used. Patients were interviewed personally and the case notes were examined for the presence of events during six months preceding admission. Controls were asked to fill out the questionnaire concerning events during six months.
Results: Of the 53 schizophrenics, 30 were found to have experienced life events, while 36 out of 75 controls reported an event. There is a tendency that females have higher frequency of events than males, in both patients and controls. The differ- ence is significant in patients(x^2=3.98, P<0.05), but not in controls.
Discussion: This result might indicate the possibility that female chronic schizophrenics were more sensitive than males, even if affect blunted.

1095

SCOTTISH FIRST EPISODE SCHIZOPHRENIA STUDY: 2 YEAR FOLLOW-UP
Scottish Schizophrenia Research Group, N.A.TODD

Crichton Royal Hospital, Dumfries. Gartloch Hospital, Glasgow. Gartnavel Royal Hospital, Glasgow. Leverndale Hospital, Glasgow. Royal Edinburgh Hospital, Edinburgh.

Of 49 schizophrenic patients followed-up two years after their first admission to hospital, only 37% had no readmissions to hospital nor schizophrenic symptoms. A poor outcome was associated with male sex, poor outcome after the first five weeks of the first admission, negative schizophrenic symptoms on first ad- mission, and a diagnosis of Feighner 'definite' or 'probable' schizophrenia. Only 23% were in employment. A small double-blind discontinu- ation study of maintenance antipsychotic medi- cation during the second year found more relapses in those switched to placebo medication. Repeat psychometric assessment at two years confirmed modest improvements found at 12 months; that is, there was no evidence of intellectual decline. Relatives showed no more psychosocial distress than that found in a normal community sample; what distress there was correlated with patients' schizophrenic symptoms.

1096

CHARACTERISTICS OF THE NON-COMPLIANT OUT-PATIENT SCHIZOPHRENIC
Mantonakis J., Markidis M., Kontaxakis V., Chri- stodoudou G.
Department of Psychiatry, University of Athens, Eginition Hospital, Athens, Greece.

In view of the positive correlation between discontinuation of medication and relapse in schi- zophrenia, it is of great interest to identify the profile of the non-compliant schizophrenic patient.

A series of studies carried out at the Athens University Psychiatric Department revealed that the characteristics of the out-patient schizophre- nics most likely to discontinue maintenance medi- cation are the following:
1. Young age (about 25 years of age)
2. Single status
3. A single psychiatric hospitalization
4. Inadequate insight
5. Complaints about side-effects of medication
6. Living with parental family
7. Low academic level of family members.

1097
GENDER DIFFERENCES IN SCHIZOPHRENIA

ERMENTINI A.,LANZINI L.,GOZIO C.,FAZZARI G.,
PISCHEDDA P.L.
DEPARTMENT OF PSYCHIATRY,BRESCIA STATE UNIVERSITY
ITALY

Lewine has proposed sex differences in schizophrenics in age at first psychiatric hospitalization, age at first reported symptoms and premorbid social competence. Other studies do not provide unequivocal support for Lewine's hypothesis,however.
To evaluate Lewine's hypothesis we collected clinical and social data on all 545 schizophrenics and 1644 non schizophrenic patients at their first hospital admission to Brescia Psychiatric Department (Italy) during the last twelve years.
We also followed 30 young schizophrenics for an average of 5-6 years after first hospitalization. When we controlled for differences in the age,sex and marriage rates of the diagnostic group,we found that more young male than young female were diagnosed as schizophrenics and that the marriage rates is higher for female than male schizophrenic patients. This report provides support for Lewine'hypothesis.

1098
SCHIZOPHRENIA AND MUSIC, RESEARCH INTO NONVERBAL COMMUNICATION.
Lund Grethe, Graamejsevej 24, 88oo Viborg,Denmark
Viborg Sygehus

Music therapy. Active music therapy is a form of treatment which provides schizophrenics with the chance to communicate without the use of words.
The supposition that a specific schizophrenic language will manifest itself under the musical improvisations/communications and that the schizophrenic will make use of other musical elements and instruments than non-schizophrenics seems not to be so.
Research indicates that the most important factor in the musical communication with schizophrenics (and others) is the therapist's respect for the patient's musical sound-range. It appears that one condition for a positive interaction and improved therapeutic treatment is, that the patient and the therapist have the same sound-range.
This research is inspired by the book "The Language of Psychosis" by Bent Rosenbaum & Harly Sonne (1979).
The lecture will be supplemented with tape-recordings from music therapy sessions in the Psychiatric Hospital, Viborg.

1099
MAIN CAUSES FOR THE READMISSION OF SCHIZOPHRENIC PATIENTS

J.Nimatoudis,H.Fotiadis,N.Kokantzis,A.Karavatos,M. Fotiadou. A´Department of Psychiatry,University of Thessaloniki,Greece.

During the period between 1970-1985, 200 patients with confirmed diagnosis of schizophrenic psychosis were treated with psychotropic drugs and group psychotherapy.After each treatment they were discharged with considerable improvement of their clinical condition. 612 readmissions took place because of a relapse due,mainly,to the discontinuation of their drug treatment,despite their doctors´orders,and failure,on the patients´part,to continue to visit their doctors.Life events and other factors were the cause of the relapse in only a small percentage of the cases.Average time of the discontinuation of the drug treatment was sometime during the first 12 months from their discharge. Average time of the reappearance of their psychotic symptomatology was 3 months from the time they stopped taking their drugs.A small number of patients were readmitted not because of a relapse but due to purely socio-economic reasons.

Session 165   Video:
Hyperhypnosis. Psychosis

1100
HYPERHYPNOSIS
LEVELS OF UNCONSCIOUSNESS DEPTH
by Gabriel J. Castellá and Herminio Castellá - Buenos Aires - Argentina

The levels, that will briefly be described as follows have outcome from the clinical and research work with adequate hypnosis techniques.

The first 3 levels of hyperhypnosis were found in about 200 people (they were the whole that were hypnotically induced). The first works began 25 years ago. The latest 3 levels were discovered in March, October and November 1988 respectively, and searched in a ten people group.

Level 1: wakefulness state. It is the consciousness level.
Level 2: somnambulic hypnotic state. Focused consciousness level and hypersuggestibility level. It is the level in which classical hypnosis develops.

The levels that will be described from now on are as follows:
Level 3: it is the rector and coordinator level of personality, performer of actions. It is the one that classifies and distributes what flows between consciousness and unconsciousness.
Level 4: It is the level of phobias, fears, faults (negative emotions). It plans defensive and personal protection strategies.
Level 5: It is the level of comprehension and love to oneself and to the others. It is the internal harmony level.
Level 6: level of positive wisdom. It stores the human-being treasure. The great creations or every-day life wisdom: knowing how to enjoy what life gives us, depend on this level.
Level 7: the great fears of mankind (in a social sense) are concentrated here. It files the data of great violences, of great tragedies, epidemics, starvations, and so on.

The 4th, 5th, 6th and 7th levels file the personal experiences and the ones inherited from ancestors.
Level 8: this level integrates, coordinates and harmonizes the other levels, specifically the negative ones (4th and 7th).

In each level exists sublevels of depth, which will be enlarged in the original work.
A videocassette will be presented showing each level.

1101

TALLER EXPRESIVO CREATIVO PREVENTIVO CON
PACIENTES PSICOTICOS
PROF. DR. MIGUEL ANGEL MATERAZZI
HOSPITAL NACIONAL JOSE T. BORDA
CENTRO DE INVESTIGACION MEDICO PSICOLOGICA
DE LA COMUNICACION

El Video muestra la dinámica con un grupo
de pacientes Psicóticos, ante la propuesta de que se transformen en agentes preventivos, de la misma emerge un acto creativo configurado en una historia creada
espontáneamente por los integrantes y posteriormente analizada.
La técnica implementada es una de las variantes de la propuesta del Psicocine
(Terapia Grupal Programada).

Session 166 Symposium:
Immunological findings in endogenous psychosis

1102

IMMUNOLOGICAL FINDINGS IN SCHIZOPHRENIA

M. H. Rapaport
NIMH, Clinical Neuroscince Branch, Bethesda, MD., U.S.A.

There have been a large number of conflicting reports of immunological changes associated with schizophrenia. However, recent advances in immunology such as flow cytometry and the discovery and characterization of cytokines, and the development of more precise phenomenological definitions of schizophrenia have stimulated our laboratory to begin studies of immunological variables in schizophrenia. Our laboratory has been investigating the autoimmune hypothesis of schizophrenia for several years and preliminary evidence of differences in both the humoral and cellular components of the immune system have been noted. In particular, data demonstrating differences in lymphocyte phenotypic markers, the effect of typical and atypical antipsychotic agents on these markers, the effects of typical and atypical antipsychotic medication on mitogen stimulated T lymphocyte responses, and data demonstrating differences in levels of soluble interleukin-2 receptors will be presented.

1103

IMMUNOLOGICAL ASPECTS IN DRUG FREE SCHIZOPHRENICS

ST. THEODOROPOULOU-VAIDAKI, C. ALEXOPOULOS, C. STEFANIS.

A number of interesting immunological abnormalities have been observed in schizophrenic patients, in a study using several in vivo and in vitro immunological parameters.
More specifically the majority of schizophrenic patients were anergic to most common recall antigens despite the fact that the absolute number of circulating T-cells was found to be not statistically different from the normal. Conversly the absolute number of B-cells was found significantly higher in the peripheral blood of schizophrenic patients.
More over previous findings that an unusually high proportion of atypical or transformed lymphocytes are circulating in the peripheral blood of those patients were confirmed.
The most intriguing finding however was an increased spontaneous transformation of peripheral lymphocytes of schizophrenics. This finding accounted for diminished blastic transformation or total transformation indices and pathological spontaneous production or migration inhibition factor of lymphocytes of schizophrenic patients.
On the basis of our findings we propose that the presence of atypical lymphocytes, increased spontaneous transformation and spontaneous production of migration inhibition factor have a common denominator.

1104

CELLULAR IMMUNITY IN SCHIZOPRHRENIC PATIENTS: IS THE ELEVATION OF T-CELLS RELATED TO THE LONG-TERM-COURSE?
N. Müller, E. Hofschuster, M. Ackenheil
Psychiatric Hospital, University of Munich, Munich, FRG

Cellular immunological parameters of 55 patients suffering from schizophrenia (ICD 295.0 - 295.6) or schizoaffective psychosis (ICD 295.7) were studied before neuroleptic treatment, 24 of these patients were reinvestigated after clinical improvement. The results were compared with these of 51 healthy controls

An enhanced lymphocyte response to PHA, PWM and an antigen-cocktail, a lower response to stimulation with vaccinia-tuberkuline-, rubella-antigen and reduced suppressor-cell-activity point to a defect in cellular immunity in schizophrenic patients. $CD4^+$ and $CD3^+$-cells were found to be elevated.

Immunological alterations in schizophrenic patients were described by several authors and discussed under pathogenetic aspects, but no relationship to the schizophrenic symptomatology or the course of the disease was described until now.

It will be discussed if the positive correlations of the BPRS-scores and the numbers of $CD4^+$ and CD3-cells ($r = .36 - .73$; $p = .053 - .000$) found at the reinvestigation after clinical improvement reflect a connection between cellular parameters and the long-term-course of schizophrenia.

Furthermore a cluster-analysis of the results of HLA-A, -B and -C-typing was performed. The cluster-analysis shows that the reduced suppressor cell activity and the altered lymphocyte response to certain antigenes in schizophrenic patients may be determined immunogenetically.

1105

IMMUNOLOGICAL STUDIES IN ENDOGENOUS PSYCHOSES

G.Kolyaskina, T. Sekirina, T. Voronkova, T. Micheeva, S. Kushner, A. Ivanushkin, T. Tsutsulkovskaya
All-Union Mental Health Research Center, Academy of Medical Sciences of USSR, Moscow, USSR

The cause of endogenous psychoses remains unknown. Laboratory and clinical observation suggest an autoimmune process, a viral infection, or a combination of two. Evidence favoring an immunopathological process in schizophrenia is indirect but has, in our view, become increasingly compelling in recent years.

As it becomes apparent, regulator T-cell function and number may be abnormal in schizophrenia: schizophrenic patients with chronically progressive disease show low T-suppressor cell number and function an average with wide variations between individuals. IL-2 production is decreased in some forms of schizophrenia. The reason of why T-suppressors and IL-2 production fall in schizophrenia is not known. B-cell overstimulation is observed in schizophrenia as well.

The use of immunomodulator in combined therapy of schizophrenic patients leads to the improvement of both the immune function and clinical condition. It allows us to suggest that the immune abnormalities are the component of pathogenesis of schizophrenia.

Session 167 New Research:
Therapeutic approaches in schizophrenia

1106

PATTERNS OF LITHIUM RESPONSE IN SCHIZOPHRENIA

S. Kelwala, MD; A. Jain, MD; K. Chapin, PhD; S. Yerasi; I. Youssef, MD; H. Baruch; S. Gershon, MD
Wayne-Northville Research Unit, Michigan, USA

Traditionally psychotropic medications have been viewed as effective or ineffective for specific psychiatric conditions. Such conceptualization may have led psychiatrists to prematurely reject many psychotropic medications as not useful for conditions where they could play a partial therapeutic role. Lithium (Li) for schizophrenic illnesses appears to be a good example of this phenomena. As part of a study to evaluate Li efficacy in schizophrenia, 58 inpatients were treated with Li alone from 2-6 weeks at levels 0.8-1.4 mEq/L. Li showed a significant therapeutic response as measured by BPRS, NHSI and CGI (repeated ANOVA on BPRS, $F=14.956$, $p<000$). However, Li response was far more complex than simple effectiveness. While 22% (N=13) showed a good therapeutic response ($>40\%$ decrease on the BPRS or NHSI) enabling them to be discharged from the hospital on Li alone, almost 41% (N=24) showed a partial response ($>20\%$ decrease on the NHSI/BPRS). The partial response itself was of two types. Those (N=10) who showed early partial response then relapsed after 2-3 weeks of Li treatment and those (N=14) who sustained their partial response over 4-6 weeks of treatment. About 23% were non-responders to Li ($<20\%$ decrease on NHSI/BPRS). With further research these complex patterns of Li response can be usefully integrated in the pharmacotherapeutic management of schizophrenia.

1107

Therapeutic response of psychoses to valproic acid
Kluznik, VanValkenburg, Merrill
St. Peter Regional Treatment Center

Valproic acid was added to the treatment regimens of 42 patients whose response to previous medications had been unsatisfactory. Clinical Global Improvement scores were recorded. Contrary to expectations, patients with unipolar or bipolar affective disorder were not more likely to improve than those with schizophrenia. Presence of mental retardation, organic brain disorder, and convulsive disorder also did not predict response. The one clinical variable did correlate with response to valproic acid was the initial severity of the patients' illness ($p=.0104$). This suggests that valproic acid's beneficial effects in the treatment of psychoses are not limited to cases of affective disorder.

1108

SELEGILINE, A B-TYPE MAO INHIBITOR AND CHRONIC SCHIZOPHRENIA

Liggio,F. Bucci,L;,Buono,A.
S. Maria della Pietà Hosp.Rome,Italy.

It has been postulated that two different types of schizophrenic syndromes may be differentiated according to their symptoms-complex:type 1 and type II.The former,characterized mainly by the positive symptoms,i.e. delusions and hallucinations,probably due to the dopamine metabolism derangement responding favorably to neuroleptics,and considered reversible.The latter characterized by the predominance of negative symptoms, e.g. affect flattening,withdrawal and poverty of speech,equivalent to a"defect state" probably due to brain structural changes.
Such classification based only on therapeutic response is questionable.
24 chronic schizophrenic patients (16 females and 8 males) suffering from the so-called type II schizophrenia were treated with neuroleptics and selegiline combination for several months.
The promising results obtained and the safety of the latter drug are reported.

1109

POSTPARTUM PSYCHOSIS AND NEUROLEPTIC DOSAGE

John A. Baker III, M.D., Dale A. D'Mello, M.D.
Melpomeni G. Kavadella, M.D.
Michigan State University, Dept. of Psychiatry
St. Lawrence Hospital, 1210 W. Saginaw St.
Lansing, Michigan 48915   USA

The postpartum period is one of particular vulnerability for women with coexistent psychiatric disorders. Hormonal and neuroreceptor changes are compounded by complex psychodynamic conflicts, particularly in unmarried women who anticipate losing custody of their newborn infants.
A preliminary retrospective review was completed on all patients who were treated for postpartum psychosis on a 30 bed inpatient psychiatric unit between 1981 and 1988. Eight patients were identified, ranging in age from 19 to 35 years, with a mean age of 25 years. The mean duration of postpartum admission (70.6 ± 49.0 days) was longer than the antepartum admission (45.5 ± 47.9 days), ($z=2.5$, $p<0.05$). The mean discharge neuroleptic dosage for the postpartum admission (1256 chlorpromazine equivalents) was significantly greater than that of the antepartum one (587 cpz equiv.), ($z=3.2$, $p<0.005$). If longer duration of hospitalization and greater neuroleptic requirement can be interpreted as paralleling more severe psychopathology, then women prone to psychosis are likely to suffer a more severe disturbance postpartum than at other periods of the life cycle.

1110

BUSPIRONE AS A TOOL TO BETTER UNDERSTAND AND MODIFY COGNITIVE PROCESSES.
V. Andreoli*, G. Carbognin**, G. Guerani***, M.P. Carrieri****, A. Abati**, C.A. Righetti**, D. Berto*, G. Vantini*
*Ospedale S. Giovanni Battista (Verona, Italy), **Ospedale Sacro Cuore (Negrar, Verona, Italy), ***Bristol Italiana (Sud) SpA, ****Statistician (Rome, Italy)

Buspirone is a psycotropic compound with a well-demonstrated anxiolityc action.
In this study our purpose was to evaluate the action of Buspirone on the cognitive functions (attention and memory) with a double blind cross-over study. 5 mg of Buspirone or Placebo were administered for 4 weeks followed by 1 week wash out and 4 weeks cross-over treatment. Two groups of 20 patients, 65 to 75 years old hospitalized with or without anxiety were studied. The parameters measured were the following: memory index (from RANDT test), association memory and the attention test of Zazzo. Assessments were made before and after drug administration. The t-test for matched pairs was performed separately for the patients with or without anxiety and for the two treatments. Efficacy of treatment was evaluated by analysis of covariance

Results
The anxiolytic effect of Buspirone was confirmed ($p \leq 0.0001$).
T-test analysis of the memory index ($p \leq 0.0001$) and associacion memory ($p < 0.01$) showed significant improvement in the Buspirone treated patients with or without anxiety. Positive modification of memory index in the analysis of covariance was demonstrated for the non-anxious group only ($P=0.0016$). These data suggested improvement in memory function as measured by the above tests in non-anxious patients treated with Buspirone. This leads us to reconsider the hypothesis that the improvement of memory processes during treatment with Buspirone is related only to the decrease of anxiety. This effect is particolarly evident after the resolution or in the absence of anxiety and may represent a particular effect of Buspirone on cognitive parameters.

1111

NEGATIVE EFFECTS OF PSYCHOPHARMACOTHERAPY AND THEIR MANAGEMENT
G. Avrutsky
Moscow Research Institute of Psychiatry, Moscow, USSR

Negative medicamentous pathomorphosis develops in long-term and clinically unfounded use of neuroleptics. In attack-like schizophrenia it results in protracted and incomplete psychotic episodes, their higher frequency, diminishing distinctions between the attack and the remission, continuous though slow-progressive course, fixation of insufficiently reduced symptomatology and abrupt rise of specific not clearly defined depressions. These and other psychopathological phenomenae are characterized by pronounced persistent symptoms and resistance to psychopharmacological drugs.
Measures restricting use of neuroleptics, and methods of alternative intensive therapy are considered: drug withdrawal, intensive insulin-coma therapy and ECT

1112

EFFECT OF UNMADBHANJANRASA AN AYURVEDIC COMPOUND ON SCHIZOPHRENIA AND MANIA
Dr. Ajay Kumar Sahu
S.K. Gautam, R.P. Swamy, P.S. Gehlot, D.C. Satiga, B.L. Suwalk, Jaipur, India

A Clinical Scientific Research Trial of an Ayurvedic Compound of Unmadbhanjanrasa was done on 50 patients at a Psychiatric centre, under the S.M.S. Medical College Jaipur, India, in collaboration with National Institute of Ayurvedic Jaipur, India from 1980-1981 by the author. For the first time not only in India but also all over the world. 22 schizophrenic patients were divided in two groups, 11 were put on a Placebo and 11 on UBR an Ayurvedic Compound. 8 patients of UBR group have shown good response, fully cured (72,7%) and 3 patients (27,2%) who have chronic schizophrenia no response, compared with 11 patients Placebo group. There was no response in Placebo group. 28 manic patients were divided in two groups, 19 in UBR group and 9 in a Placebo group. Out of 19 UBR group, good response fully cured 19 (100%) compared with 9 patients in Placebo group 3 patients in Placebo group have responded in 45 days research trial without electro convulsion therapy and modern drugs. UBR has no side effects. Details will be discussed.

Session 168 Symposium:
Psychopathologie de l' expression

1113
HANDWRITING AND DEPRESSION

R. VOLMAT, Cl. J. BELIN, B. BONIN
Clinique neurologique et psychiatrique, Centre Hospitalier Universitaire, 25030 Besançon Cedex, France

Patients complaining being in bad health are often deprimed and in conclusion are coming to consult a psychiatrist.

Those patients without background in psychiatry after complete check up were prouved to have good reactions to on antidepressif treatment.

The handwriting from those patients was analysed and showed evidence of depression.

1114
Socio Cultural Influences on Children's Drawings

Irene Jakab, M.D., Ph.D.
University of Pittsburgh School of Medicine

Children are influenced during their developmental years by the visual impact of their environment. These influences are manifested both in spontaneous products and in what they learn. The environmental influences are manifested in the style and the content of their drawings and paintings. In psychopathological cases, however, both the style and the content acquires specific traits above and beyond the cultural influences of the environment. Examples of normal and of psychotic children's drawings will be presented to illustrate the enviornmental influence on their art work.

1115
REPRESENTATION DU TEMPS DANS LE DESASTRE

E. MOUSSONG-KOVACS, M. NABOULSI
Université p. Formation Continue Médicale, Budapest, Hongrie

Centre d'Etudes Psychiques, Tripoli, Liban

Nous analysons l'expression graphique de l'horizon temporel dans les états psychologiques particulièrement désastreux :

    a) La menace vient de l'extérieur, massive, brusque, inévitable et affecte l'intégrité psychosomatique. Effets des catastrophes et des évènements de guerre ;

    b) La menace vient de l'intérieur, furtive et lente comme le cancer qui vise la destruction du corps ;

    c) La crise réside au niveau des relations interpersonnelles, danger d'autodestruction ;

    d) La menace consiste dans l'effondrement de l'intégrité mentale. Qu'il soit réel chez les psychotiques, ou imaginaire, angoisses hypocondriaques, ce danger se manifeste dans une réaction de catastrophe psychologique.

La représentation graphique du temps rend visibles à part des signes destructifs de la détresse aussi bien les manifestations autoprotectives et d'adaptation. Le message de ces dessins et leurs caractères formels seront mis en rapport.

1116
DYNAMIC EXAMINATION OF ANIMAL-DRAWING

Istvan HARDI M.D., Ph.D.
Pest County Semmelweis Hospital - Psychiatric Out-Patient Center, Budapest, Hungary

After having dealt with the serial-comparative drawing of man the author reports the application of the same method with the drawings of animals. The serial animal pictures of psychiatric patients show the same formal and content changes as those of man. With the delineation of man the subject of the examination is given. There is a free choice when the drawing of an animal is asked. Theoretical and interpretative aspects differ from the well-known projective ones. Two main groups could be differentiated : figures of domestic and non-domestic animals. The pictures of domestic animals are analogous to the conventional, "vulgar"
Rorschach-responses. Among the non-domestic animals we find the wild ones, mainly the products of patients with personality disorders /e.g. tiger of aggressive psychopaths, wild-hog of some alcoholics/ or sometimes with schizophrenics. Regression is expressed -- beside the formal traits -- through depicting baby animals, pets, Teddy-Bear etc. Of course mythic and prehistoric beings are also of special interest. The serial-comparative follow-up of animal-drawings is a very good completion and reinforcement for the dynamic examination of the drawing of man to help our understanding and pratice in psychiatry.

1117

IMAGES PHOTOGRAPHIQUES D'UNE MATERNITE
(L'album de Yoyo)

G. ROUX
Pau, France

L'observation d'un état dépressif névrotique passe par la connaissance d'un album de photographies que la malade concernée transporte avec elle, et qui révèle la puissance de fantasmes constitués autour de la maternité ; tout comme il permet de mesurer l'ampleur des perturbations de l'existence de la patiente.

Session 169   Film:
Panic disorders

1118

THE PANIC PRISON

Blamphin J.M., Director, Div. of Publ-Affairs, American Psychiatric Association

"The Panic Prison" is an emotionally involving true-life film that captures the experiences of panic disorder patients and the doctor who treats them, psychiatrist Jack M. Gorman, M.D. of Columbia Presbyterian Medical Center in New York City. There is no "acting" in the film. The doctor and patients are real. Through Dr. Gorman's medical interviews and vivid flashbacks to the patients' experiences, the viewer sees the terror of panic disorder and the frustration patients experience in obtaining an accurate diagnosis and effective treatment. The viewer learns about research to uncover the causes of the disorder, and learns about effective treatment using behavioral therapy, psychotherapy and medications.

Session 170   Symposium
Future of scientific publishing

1119

THE FUTURE OF SCIENTIFIC PUBLISHING
Dr. Thomas Thiekotter
Springer-Verlag, Heidelberg, Federal Republic of Germany

The future of scientific publishing is a topic of some speculation. It will depend to a very considerable extent on further developments in the field of information technology. In the future we will see the emergence of a multilevel information system, in which the traditional forms of publication such as books and journals will coexist alongside newer forms such as data bases, information networks, microfilms and CC-rom. In certain areas, "publishing on demand" will become the rule. The extent to which modern technology can be implemented in the distribution of information in the future will, however, depend very much on the availability of compatible user-friendly information systems offering the required flexibility.

1120

COMPUTER WORD PROCESSING AND PUBLICATION
Monte S. Buchsbaum, Professor of Psychiatry
University of California, Irvine, U.S.A.
With the appearance of small personal computers in scientists' laboratories and computerized photo-composition in publishers' and editors' offices, the process of preparation of scientific manuscripts for publication has a potential for undergoing rapid change. Scientific publications involve complex vocabulary, extensive numerical tables, special symbols, and a requirement for high accuracy; logic suggests that this information could move directly form the scientist's entry to the printed page. The technical problems of converting manuscript text from a variety of word processing formats to standard ASCII and the subsequent addition of codes controlling the typesetting are relatively easily solved. Optical scanning of most typewriter copy allows researches without word processing to enter the data flow. More difficult is the conversion of special symbols and tabular data which differ widely among word processing programs and may be deleted in the ASCII conversion. But the solution of these relatively mechanical problems should not allow the manuscript to bypass copy editing. Automatic spelling dictionaries fail to detect homonym errors and false cognates; grammar, clarity of style and conciseness still require skilled human attention. Used wisely, computer manuscript preparation should assist the scientist in presenting the most accurate and detailed presentation of his findings to the world, focusing on expression, clarity and rapid exchange.

1121

SCIENTIFIC PUBLISHING - THE ACADEMIC VIEW

H. Katschnig, Prof. of Psychiatry,
Psychiatric Clinic, University of Vienna,
Austria

Psychiatric Clinic, University of Vienna, Austria
It is becoming increasingly unclear how the role
of academic psychiatry is to be understood today.
The pursuit of academic ideals, the unity of
university practice teaching and research is
obviously lost in vigour, not only due to
specialization of psychiatry into different
branches. Also many of those who teach do not do
research and vice versa and members of both
groups may have lost a firm clinical basis. Not
without justification practitioners tend to
regard academic psychiatry as ivory tower
psychiatry and, mainly due to financial reasons,
the focus of research is moving away from medical
faculties to non academic groups or is at least
coming under heavy non academic influence. In
this situation of dwindling academic
identification, scientific publishing has a
crucial role to play in shaping the future of
academic study. Issues to be discussed in this
paper will include both the need for a multitude
of scientific journals and publications - to
prove academicians free access to make their
ideas and research results public - and the need
for books, journals and articles integrating
knowledge and being digestable and interesting
for those who practice psychiatry, those teaching
it and those doing research on it. Examples of
such publications already exist and are quite
successful. It is hoped that they will contribute
to re-establish the endangered academic identity
of clinical practice, teaching and research.

1122

AN APPROACH TO THE EVALUATION OF MEDICAL RESEARCH
Katherine Levy
Medical Research Council
London, England

The Medical Research Council (MRC) is the largest
publicly funded body supporting biomedical
research in the UK. Research evaluation which is
itself crucially dependent on peer review, is at
the heart of its activities. A brief description
is given of the Council's role in relation to
other bodies (e.g. Government Departments,
Charities) and the external factors which it has
to take into consideration both in evaluating
research and in taking decisions about funding.
Particular consideration is given to the reasons
for the establishment of the newly formed
Committee of Council, the Strategy Committee, and
to the strengthening of the traditional peer
review process, by for example the systematic
reviews of scientific fields, the use of
assessment criteria, and the MRC's position
regarding the use of bibliometrics and other
performance indicators.
Although the paper concentrates on the MRC
experience, it is suggested that the pressures,
challenges and opportunities it faces are not
dissimilar from those confronting other
comparable bodies.

1123

THE CONSUMER'S VIEW - DEVELOPING COUNTRIES
Rahim S. - Saudi Arabia

Session 171   Workshop:
The development of a programme in psychotherapy in a general children's hospital. Introduction to psychodynamic understanding of disturbed children and adolescents

1124

The development of a Programme in Psychotherapy in a
General Childrens Hospital.Introduction to psychodynamic understanding of distrurbed children and adolescent
J. Tsiantis Associate Professor
Department of Psychological Pediatrics Childrens Hospital " AGIA SOFIA "

In this workshop the experiences and observations
from the attempt to develop an in-service training
programme in psychoanalytic psychotherapy for children and adolescents within a General Children's
Hospital will be presented.
The programme is directed at N.H.S child psychiatrists and clinical psychologists and includes baby
observation and work study seminars as well as
theoretical semirars on child development and is
partly funded by the European Social Fund.
For the development of the programme there is
advisory assistance from members of the training
comittee of the Child Therapy Section of the British Association of psychotherapists members of
which are panelists at the workshop.
On the other hand the discussion relating to the
symposium " Psychodynamic Understanding in Individual Assesment of Disturbances in Children and
Adolescents " will continue as a theme so important
for the introduction of a programme of psychoanalytic psychotherapy for children and adolescents.

1125

The Development of an Infant Observation Seminar in Athens
D. Anastasopoulos
Dept. of Psychological Paediatrics, "Aghia Sophia" Children's Hospital, Athens

Since 1948, when the observation of babies was first introduced in the training of child Psychotherapists in Tavistock by E. Bick, it spread to various countries as an integral part in the training of psychotherapists and analysts.
With the encouragement and help of the Child Psychotherapy Training Committee of BAP, an infant observation seminar has begun on 1988 in Athens. Many difficulties had to be faced by the trainers and the trainees, concerning the anxiety for involvement, fears of intrusion into the families and questions about professional roles.
The process of this group is discussed, in relation with the difficulties and gains from the training on the following issues: learning from experience about human growth and development, distinguishing normality from pathology, concepts of time and timing, ability to observe, self control, recognising the child in the adult, giving and taking, keeping the professional boundaries.

1126

Introduction to Psychodynamic Understanding of Children Through a Work Seminar
Sotiris Manolopoulos
Dept. of Psychological Paediatrics, "AGHIA SOPHIA" Children's Hospital

A work study seminar has been held for the last two years introducing Child Psychiatrists and Psychologists to psychoanalytic psychotherapy of children.

The following issues will be examined

1. How learning through experience takes place
2. Resistances. How they manifest themselves
3. The effect of the seminar process of the different levels of experience
4. How the dynamics of Hospital hierarchy affect the seminar's work.

Teaching psychotherapy of children is a complex process. We need to appoach it in an atmosphere of working alliance. As we deepen our understanding of our patients'unconscious we need the support of the group to experience this understanding convincingly inside us and learn from it.

Session 172 Special Session:
Psychopharmacology: Blood cell binding and membrane transport

1127

EFFECT OF KETANSERIN ON UPTAKE, STORAGE, AND EFFLUX OF SEROTONIN IN HUMAN PLATELETS

O. Lingjaerde, Gaustad Hospital, Oslo, Norway

Ketanserin (KAS) also has other effects than being a potent $5HT_2$ receptor blocker. Thus, studies by the present author with the human platelet model (performed in 1982 but so far unpublished) have shown the following:
1) KAS inhibits 5HT uptake already at 10^{-8}M, but with a less steep inhibition curve than usually found with TCA. The inhibition is mixed competitive/noncompetitive.
2) KAS has the following effects on storage/efflux, as measured in platelets preloaded with ^{14}C-5HT: (a) When present during the efflux (but not the preloading) stage, KAS increases the rate of efflux from the "deep", granular compartment, from about 10^{-7}M (TCA have this effect only at 10^{-4}M or above). (b) When present during the preloading phase, KAS reduces the relative size of the granular compartment (like reserpine/tetrabenazine). The rate of efflux is increased from the cytoplasmatic and reduced from the granular compartment (unlike the effect of reserpine).
These effects of KAS either represents a new type of effect on platelet handling of 5HT, or a peculiar combination of effects. Interestingly, tetrabenazine-displaceable KAS binding sites have recently been described in brain and platelets (J Leysen et al, J Pharmacol Expt Therap 1988, 244,310-321).

1128

L-TYROSINE AND L-TRYPTOPHAN MEMBRANE TRANSPORT IN ERYTHROCYTES AND ANTIDEPRESSANT DRUG CHOICE
R. TISSOT[1,2,3], J.M. AZORIN[1], Ph. BOVIER[2], J. WIDMER[2], R. JEANNINGROS[3]

1) Clin. Psychiat. et de Psychol. Méd. CHU Timone, r. Saint-Pierre, F 13385 Marseille Cedex 5
2) Serv. recherche biol. IUPG, 10, ch. du Petit-Bel-Air, CH 1225 Chêne-Bourg
3) Unité de Psychiat. Biol. CNRS, Fac.Méd., 27, bd Jean-Moulin, F 13385 Marseille Cedex 5

In the treatment of depression, when antidepressant drug choice is made according to the individual patient alterations of erythrocyte membrane transport of L-tyrosine and L-tryptophan, the clinical results are superior to those obtained when drugs are prescribed following the physician's experience. This is demonstrated by comparing 3 experimental groups : I, 100 patients treated in relation to their L-tyrosine and L-tryptophan transport; II, 30 patients treated according to the clinician's experience; III, 38 subjects treated against the L-tyrosine and L-tryptophan transport indications. In these groups, the frequency of patients improved by more than 70 % is 77 %, 47 % and 16 %, respectively.

1129

Characteristic features of spiperone binding to different white blood cells.
U. Henning & M. Halbach
Psychiatrische Klinik der Universität Düsseldorf, Bergische Landstraße 2, D-4000 Düsseldorf, FRG

Spiperone has been shown to selectively bind to D2 dopamine receptors in the brain. Several authors in recent years have presented controversial data on spiperone binding to lymphocytes from human peripheral blood. Following the "dopamine hypothesis" of schizophrenia lymphocyte spiperone binding has been discussed as an easily accessible peripheral marker system possibly reflecting the status of the dopaminergic receptors in the CNS.
We have studied the characteristics of the specific binding of spiperone, antagonized by (+) butaclamol, to several types of highly purified white blood cells including subtypes of lymphocytes and report on the specific differences and similarities of spiperone binding characteristics of different cell types. Our findings of a considerable variability between different cells prove the importance of highly purified cell preparations in pharmacological studies of spiperone binding to blood cells.

1130

Glucocorticoid-induced increase of spiperone binding to lymphocytes: Clinical implications of a dynamic peripheral marker system in schizophrenia.
G. Scheidt & M. Halbach
Psychiatrische Klinik der Universität Düsseldorf, Bergische Landstraße 2, D-4000 Düsseldorf, FRG

Spiperone binding to peripheral lymphocytes from patients with distinct forms of schizophrenia has been shown abnormally elevated under the influence of glucocorticoids in vitro.
In order to study the importance of this dynamic marker system for clinical purposes in schizophrenia we have investigated the extent of glucocorticoid induced increase of spiperone binding to lymphocytes from patients suffering from a variety of different subgroups of schizophrenia. Furthermore we have studied the influence of clinical factors in schizophrenic psychosis on this dynamic marker system like the specific course of illness (acute relapsing or chronic, age of onset, duration of illness), the pattern and duration of neuroleptic treatment, and the success of pharmacological treatment.
Our data, which will be discussed in detail, seem to indicate the usefulness of this marker system for practical clinical requirements as the verification of the diagnosis and estimation of pharmacological response in schizophrenia.

1131

Increased spiperone binding to peripheral blood granulocytes from schizophrenic patients.
P. Kern, U. Henning, M. Halbach
Psychiatrische Klinik der Universität Düsseldorf, Bergische Landstraße 2, D-4000 Düsseldorf, FRG

The binding of spiperone, a D2 receptor specific ligand in the CNS, to lymphocytes from human peripheral blood has been reported to be elevated in patients with certain forms of schizophrenia. These binding data, however, are controversially discussed by different investigators arguing from theoretical and experimental considerations.
In the course of a systematic investigation of the spiperone binding properties of various white blood cells we have found specific spiperone binding to granulocytes exhibiting similar binding characteristics as reported for lymphocytes. Analogous to the studies on human peripheral lymphocytes reported so far we have investigated the spiperone binding to granulocytes from patients with and without neuroleptic treatment suffering from different forms of schizophrenia. As granulocytes (and other cells) in routinely performed cell separation procedures may contaminate lymphocyte populations to a variable extent, a hypothetical contribution of spiperone binding to granulocytes to the findings of elevated spiperone binding to lymphocyte preparations has to be taken into consideration.

1132

^{3}H-SPIPERONE BINDING SITES IN LYMPHOCYTES.

Benítez, G., Heinze, G., Ortega, H., Huerto Delgadillo L., Raull, J.
Instituto Mexicano de Psiquiatría. Calz. México-Xochimilco 101, 14370 México, D.F.

Recently, Bondy et al reported an increased density of putative D_2 dopaminergic receptors in lymphocytes of schizophrenic patients. This evidence suggest that dopaminergic sites could be a vulnerability marker inherited together with the tendency to suffer this illness.

However the existence of these binding sites in lymphocytes is controverted since ^{3}H spiperone binding to these cells had not been reproduced by other authors. In our findings we included 30 schizophrenic patients, 34 patients-first degree relatives, and in 20 healthy volunteers.

^{3}H-spiperone uptake was discarded by cell sonication after incubation with the radioactive ligand.

Our preliminary results suggest that patients with schizophrenia were different when compared to the healthy volunteers, but similar to the group of family members. This difference was present only in the variability but not in the mean value.

Session 173 Special Session:
Suicidology: Epidemiological studies

1133

DEPRESSION AND SUICIDE IN MEXICO
Lara-Tapia H., Faculty of Psychology, National University of Mexico, Mexico, DF

We present a review of clinical research in the Mexican Republic in a period of 20 recent years, including epidemiological, clinical, geographic and psychiatric records of a sample of more than 20.000 cases of suicide. The rates of suicide in Mexico are of the lowest in the world (2,1 per 100.000 hbs). Nevertheless is higher in the states of mexican border with USA (8,5/100.000 hbs) and in mexican immigrants to USA(7,9/100.000 hbs) On the other hand, suicide in psychiatric populations increases to 34,2 commited suicide and 83,5 in suicidal attempts. We observe in these patients mainly depressive disorders, in more than 80% of cases of suicide. In neurotic cases, principally - in depressive and hysterical women, the depressive syndrome is related to premenstrual tension. Comparison of more than 110 depressive patients through Hamilton Depression Scale show that the mean of psychotics is higher to other types, but the mean of depression in suicidal patients is similar to major depressive disorders. Sociocultural and historical factors have been also taken into consideration to account for these findings.

1134

SUICIDES AMONG ADOLESCENTS AND YOUNG ADULTS IN FINLAND

Hillevi Aro and Jouko Lönnqvist
National Public Health Institute, Helsinki, Finland

First, changes in suicide rates of adolescents and young adults in Finland were examined during the time period 1921-87, using official suicide data. Second, suicides of adolescents and young adults were analyzed from the nationwide psychological autopsy data of all suicides in Finland during one year 1987-88.

Suicides in children under 15 years of age were extremely rare, and the rates remained at a low level 1921-87.

In 15 to 19 year old boys, there was a peak in suicide rates around 1930, the rates then declining till the 1960's. Since late 1960's there was a marked increase in suicide rates among boys until the mid-1970's, since when the rates have stayed at a high level. In girls of this age group there was some increase in suicide rates around 1930, the rates then declined till the 1940's, and have remained at a fairly steady level thereafter. The suicide rate per 100 000 inhabitants in 1987 in this age group was 25.3 among boys and 4.4 among girls. The figures demonstrate a high male-female ratio which in the 1980's has averaged 5:1.

In 20-24 year olds, a roughly similar pattern as in 15 to 19 year olds has occurred. The absolute suicide rates for 20-24 year olds have usually been about double those among 15-19 year olds, in 1987 the rate was 49.0 among boys and 10.4 among girls.

The results will be discussed from developmental and social perspective. Possible explanations for the especially high suicide mortality of young men in Finland will be searched for from preliminary results of the psychological autopsy study.

1135

THE TRUTH ABOUT SUICIDE IN PORTUGAL
Elsa Ferreira de Castro, F. Pimenta, I. Martins
Miguel Bombarda Hospital, Lisbon, Portugal

It seems odd that male suicide rates decreased in Portugal for the last few years whereas the opposite happens in most countries. In order to investigate the reasons for such a decrease, suicide rates were compared with controversial cases (WHO category E 980-989) and with homicide victims rates. Statistical treatment of the data included Student's t-test for the difference of means of two independent samples, and correlation analysis between variables. The results showed that since 1980 and coinciding with the use of ICD-9, controversial cases increased 12 and 21 times among males and females respectively, becoming their profile similar to that of suicide, namely by sex, age groups, marital status and seasons. Rates for homicide victims remain steady and have a distinct profile. It is concluded that in Portugal since 1980 there is an important under-report of suicides which are registered as controversial cases. The difficulty of suicide investigation and prevention with such statistical data is stressed, and an improvement in suicide reporting and registering is demanded.

1136

The methodologic problem of suicide in the Spanish State.
Rodríguez Pulido, F. Gracia Marcos, R. Sierra López, A; Frugoni Perdomo, A; Rivera, J.L.G.

El registro oficial (I.N.E.) de la mortalidad por suicidio no permite obtener información fiable dado que tiene grandes deficiencias desde un punto de vista cuantitativo, al registrar una cifra de suicidios consumados muy inferior a las cifras reales, y desde un punto de vista cualitativo, al tener grandes oscilaciones en su registro temporal, no permitiendo ni siquiera valorar las tendencias. En el período de estudio (1977-1983) en el Archipiélago Canario el número de suicidios consumados registrados por el I.N.E. es el 50% de los recogidos por nosotros.

1137

Suicide in Singapore

Dr Chia Boon Hock
Singapore Medical Centre

The republic of Singapore lies just 85 miles north of the equator. It is an island 26 miles long and 14 miles wide. It is strategically located in South East Asia.

Singapore became fully independant in 1965 after 146 years of British colonial rule. Today Singapore is a modern city. The population of Singapore is 2,600,000 and is an immigrant society comprising mainly of Chinese, Malay and Indian. Singapore has the 4th highest urban area population density in the world, pure and abundant supply of water, an excellent system of public health and hygiene and civic cleanliness unmatched anywhere in the East. There is modern transport, comunication and electric power network. The standard of living is high and there is education opportunities and good jobs and good housing for all.

Singapore has a suicide rate of 9 - 12 per 100,000 population per annum. Compare to other countries the official suicide rate is reliable.

In this paper the unique features of suicide pattern in Singapore are highlighted. Where possible a comparison is also made between the pattern of suicide in Singapore and that found in the West.

1138

SUICIDE RATE IN AN ITALIAN AREA BETWEEN 1975 AND 1984
DESTRO E., SANGIORGI R., STELLA S., GRASSI L., FINOTTI L., BOZZA C.
CHAIR OF CLINICAL PSYCHIATRY, UNIVERSITY OF FERRARA (Italy)

The suicide rate and the concomitants and determinants of suicide behaviours during a period of ten years (1975-1984) were examined for the area of Rovigo (North Italy). Several aspects of suicide behaviour were analyzed, evaluating and relating the more significant elements gathered by using a proper survey instrument, which is presented.

The results emerged from the study are discussed.

1139

THE DIFFICULT DETECTION OF SUICIDAL DRIVE. OBSERVATIONS FROM PADUA.
D De Leo, A Caneva, M Predieri, D Banon, M Cadamuro, L Pavan.
Dept. of Psychiatry, University of Padua, Italy.

In Italy the official data on Suicidal behaviour, especially those concerning parasuicide are not reliable. The incidence of parasuicide is officially estimated to about 5-10 cases/year/100.000 inhab. In a previous report (1983) based only on a survey of the Emergency Dept. of Padua General Hospital was showed that the incidence was of about 80 cases/year/100.000 inhab. In 1986 we have formed a monitoring which extended its scope to others health units services (Intensive Care Units, General Practitionners, etc.). It was observed that the incidence was estimated to be about 100 cases/year/100.000 inhab., and evidencing how in this way it was possible to identify a number of suicides not officially reported. Since September 1988 we have extended further our field of study to include other institutions (Army Personal, Old People's nursing rest homes, etc.). We can now estimate the incidence of parasuicide to be about 120-130 cases/year/100.000 inhab.. Furthermore the extention of the scope of our study allowed to evidence a considerable number of "hidden" cases of suicidal behaviour, confirming the increasing trend shown in the previous years.

Session 174   Special Session:
Public health psychiatry: An international perspective

1140

NATIONAL PROGRAMMES OF MENTAL HEALTH - A SIGNIFICANT DEVELOPMENT IN PUBLIC HEALTH PSYCHIATRY
N.N. Wig,
World Health Organization, Alexandria, Egypt

In many countries of Asia and Africa, where the number of psychiatrists and other mental health professionals is still very small, the private sector psychiatry is covering the needs of only a small part of the population mostly in big cities. A large number of people in these countries particularly in the rural areas do not receive adequate psychiatric care. Furthermore, the private sector psychiatry is largely concerned with curative aspects, paying relatively little attention to prevention of diseases and promotion of mental health.

With the help of the World Health Organization a large number of countries in Asia and Africa have now developed specific national policies and programmes of mental health. The main objective of these national programmes is the provision of essential mental health services, curative, preventive and promotive, for all sections of population, particularly for those who are currently unserved and underserved. The main strategies of these programmes are multisectoral approach, the integration of mental health into general health services and provision of psychiatric care through the existing infrastructure of health at primary health care. The success of these programmes is likely to set a trend for future of psychiatry in developing countries.

1141

Quelle psychiatrie pour un pays en voie de développement?

KACHA F.
Centre Psycho Social Universitaire, Cheraga/Alger (Algérie)

Confrontés à des taux de natalité importants, à une inflation des urgences en matière de développement sanitaire et une insuffisance des moyens humains et matériels, les pays en voie de développement doivent trouver un modèle d'organisation adapté évitant de détruire la tolérance familiale et sociale pour les maladies mentales.

1142

DEVELOPING PSYCHIATRIC CARE IN NICARAGUA - NATIONAL AND INTERNATIONAL PERSPECTIVES

Trinidad Caldera, Psychiatric Institution, University of León, Nicaragua.

Psychiatric care in Nicaragua has been very traditionally organized until 1979. There was one mental hospital in Managua erected in 1932 with about 500 beds at most. After the revolution the government has tried to follow the WHO-concept of building a decentralized psychiatric care utilizing the primary health care as the main care level. There is great emphasis on the integration of the mental health care in the local community.

Another goal in the national mental health plan is to avoid admissions of patients to the only psychiatric hospital in Managua by offering care through Centro de Atencion Psicosocial (CAPS) that are placed in the local community. The country is divided into regions and the plan is to have several CAPS in each region.

The Ministry of Health is trying to base the national mental health plans on scientific data on the morbidity in the country. Different aspects of the epidemiology of mental disorders in Nicaragua are studied in collaboration with Swedish and Italian scientific groups. Another important element in the development of the psychiatric care in Nicaragua is the cooperation with foreign institutions like Mexican Family- and Group Psychotherapy Associations and Italian and Swedish psychiatric institutions.

1143

On the Present Situation of Mental Care in Japan

Imamura Kyuetsu
Imamura Internal & Mental Hospital

Japan has long had a bad reputation for its mental care for the following reasons; 1) much care has not been taken to the patients' personal problems; 2) freedom has not sufficiently been given to the patients. In view of the situation, the author has visited quite a few countries around the world to see if these problems are actually speicfic to Japan. Besides, he has made best efforts to improve our systems for mental cares, employing those of other counties'. The present paper is an attempt to show the result of such a practical study on mental cares with the purpose described above. From the study, it could be found that it is very rewarding to give best possible freedom to the patients; especially, 1) giving a room without locks allowing the patients to go and come to the hospital freely, 2) freedom of correspondence through the telephone and the letter to the outside of the hospital, and 3) freedom of patients to chose to stay at hospital or at home for the day-care purpose. All the changes have been found to be greatly improving the healing of the patients. As a conclusion, the author proposes an ideal figure of a society as well as a hospital where the patients, especially the aged patients, can live up to the best parts of their lives.

1144

TEN YEARS OF COMMUNITY MENTAL HEALTH PRACTICE IN TWO AREAS OF ATHENS
M.G. MADIANOS, A. PAPAGEORGIOU, A. KAPSALI, M. ECONOMOU, E. VAPORIDOU
Department of Psychiatry Community Mental Health Center, University of Athens

In the late seventies there was the begining of criticism and reconsideration of the effectiveness of the mental health care delivery system in Greece. As a result of the revealed need fro the development of sectorized community mental health services, a Community Mental Health Center (C.M.H.C.) the first of its kind, was developed in two middle lower, and lower class areas of Athens. The C.M.H.C. serves a total population of 100.000 and it has started opperating since October 1979. In this paper we present the ideological and the methodological issues related to the organizational structure of the Center, the selection of prevention strategies and the developmental stages. The basic scheme of C.M.H.C. functioning was the assessment of mental health needs⟶ results⟶ delivery of care⟶ evaluation

Evaluation results on social and clinical characteristics of the clients served for ten years and indicators of the community mental health intervention programmes effectiveness will be also presented.

1145
SYSTEMS TRANSFORMATIONS IN ITALY AND U.S.

Ugo Formigoni, M.D.
IL Dept. Mental Health U.S.A.--Fatebenefratelli, Italy

Mental Health delivery changes demonstrate specific characteristics:
° the phasing down of the Psychiatric Hospital in Italy was gradual but definite, preventing new admissions in 1979 and readmissions in 1981. In the U.S. deinstitutionalization was drastic between 1965 and '75, but admission and readmissions have increased dramatically;
° territorial services were intended as alternative in Italy, while in the U.S. are complementary with public hospitalization continuing at a high rate.
° acute inpatient treatment in psychiatric units of general hospitals is closely connected with community care in Italy, but generally is quite separate and independent in the U.S.:
° the same team provides outpatient, inpatient and domiciliary care in Italy; while greater and more varied resources lead to fragmentation in the U.S.
In conclusion, following major reforms the shortcomings are often more evident than the accomplishments. An examination of approaches and outcomes provides a broader perspective and suggests corrective interventions.

Session 175 Symposium:
Child and adolescent psychiatry and mental retardation

1146
DEVELOPMENTAL ASPECTS OF ADULT DISABILITY
Prof. J.A.Corbett
Birmingham University, England

Longitudinal Studies of children identified as developmentally disabled will be reviewed. Specific impairment in social interaction and communication may be identified in childhood which predict for adult personality vulnerability in people with mental retardation. These continuities in development will be considered in relation to the proposed glossary for mental disorders of the 10th revision of the international Classification of Diseases ICD 10.

1147
THE MEASURE OF THE ANXIETY IN MENTALLY RETARDED CHILDREN
J.R.Sacristan, Chairman
Dept. Psychiatry, Child Psychiatry Clinic, Univ. of Sevilla, Spain

The anxiety is a relevant component in the personality structure of children with M.R. (M.R.=Mental Retardation). The way of expression of the features, states and disorders of anxiety in children with M.R. are difficult to diagnose and to evaluate. In the present research, with a sample of children with M.R. (N=454), we have proceed in three ways: a)Through the application of the diagnostic criteria used by International Classifications (DSM-III-R). b)Using Evaluation Technics of anxiety (STAIC, GASC, CMAS, TASC, COVI); General Scales for psychopathological behaviours and desadaptative behaviours scales (Reiss's Screen for Maladaptative Behaviour, ABS). c)Putting in order those phenomena, obtained from the application of the previous criteria. Results report us about: 1) The own and genuine identity of mental health problems in children with M.R. 2) The psychological, clinical and epidemiological differences of the anxious phenomena between those children affected with M.R. and those without M.R. 3) Information and experience around the anxiety evaluation's technics or Scales in M.R. to the difficulties of using traditional diagnostic criteria and the "put in order" of clinical phenomena.4) Frequency of the inhibition, escape, avoidant mechanisms and the derivated behaviours.

1148
DRUG THERAPY IN CHILDREN SELF-ABUSE BEHAVIOUR

Renato COCCHI, MD, PhD
Gruppo Italiano per lo Studio Scientifico e Terapia dell'Insufficienza Mentale, Mongolismo e Autismo Infantili - via Liberta' 21, I-61030 San Costanzo (Italy)

Self-abuse could be better interpreted as compensatory mechanism working for coping with physical depression and blood hypotension, as the reactions to any kind of stress in children with genetic or acquired easiness to parasympathetic outcome. Stress reduces type A GABAergic inhibition, with, in some cases, increased type B GABAergic inhibition; in its turn this latter inhibits brain ACH, DA, 5-HT and NA, increases the outflow of endogenous opiates and produces parasympathetic stimulation via hypothalamic pathways. Outside of CNS hypotension is one of the symptoms derived. Self-abuse, as aggressive bahaviour, determines a temporary outflow of peripheral AD and NA which short-time relieve hypotension, and of corticosteroids able to increase the synthesys of brain 5-HT, DA and NA. This short-lived compensatory mechanism seem working at low efficiency, which fact could explain the need of its reiteration. An anti-stress drug therapy with B6, DZP, CBZ all drugs mainly acting on type A and type B GABAergic receptors, + 5-HTP, can also relieve this symptom, as reported for naltrexone. Results in non-psychotic and psychotic Down children and in psychotic non-Down children are presented.

1149
PSYCHIATRIC DISORDERS IN MENTALLY RETARDED
CHILDREN - DEVELOPMENTAL APPROACH
ANTON DOSEN,M.D.,Ph.D.
CHILD PSYCHIATRIC CLINIC HOEKSKE,VENLO,HOLLAND

Various developmental factors play the role in the onset of psychiatric disorders in mentally retarded children.The developmental-dynamic approach in the diagnostics and treatment of psychiatric disorders in mentally retarded children focuses on the discovery of the developmental factors and the fulfillment of developmental needs of the mentally ill, mentally retarded child.By this approach the child, not the handicap,is brought more clearly into focus.Employing a developmental-dynamic model the author describes a number of developmental psychiatric diagnostical categories in mentally retarded children on different developmental levels.
Clinical experiences in the psychiatric diagnostics and treatment of 730 mentally retarded children are discussed.

1150
SPEECH THERAPY OF THE MENTALLY AND VERBALLY
RETARDED CHILDREN
Tsutomu Sakuta M.D., Keio University, 35 Shinano-machi, Shinjuku-ku, Tokyo, Japan
One can never lead a social life without linguistic ability, so that speech therapy should have a pivotal position in the treatment of the mentally and verbally retarded children. The therapeutic techniques used to date are, in historical order, psychoanalytic play therapy, non-directive play therapy, sensorimotor stimulative play therapy and therapeutic educational method, and finally behaiour therapy. The former two have tended to lose favour whilst the latter two are now more often used. The therapy for the mentally and verbally retarded children which the author proposes can be summarised as follows. 1) Symbolic function is the prerequisite to the acquisition of spoken language. 2) Play therapy in which both sensori-motor stimuli and behavioural approach are applied, is used to facilitate the appearance of symbolic function as well as to stimulate the development of inter-personal relationship.
3) Once Symbolic function has been observed, the treatment will be focused on the acquistition of language. If the children have difficulty in mastering spoken language, operant conditioning is the preffered method of language training at this stage and onwards. 4) The therapeutic effect can be maximized by maintaining the treatment at home.

1151
APPROCHE GLOBALE DU HANDICAPE MENTAL
ET DE SA FAMILLE
Prof. W. BETTSCHART, Service Universitaire de Psychiatrie de l'Enfant et de l'Adolescent Avenue de la Chablière 5, 1004 Lausanne (Switzerland)

L'établissement de l'étiopathogenèse par un bilan somato-psychique est indispensable dans chaque cas d'arriération mentale, en vue du traitement, des soins adaptés et de l'intégration sociale, scolaire et plus tard professionnelle. Néanmoins le relevé du seul aspect déficitaire est insuffisant. Pour être efficace sur le plan clinique et dans une équipe pluridisciplinaire avec des éducateurs et des enseignants il faut s'appuyer sur les potentialités évolutives et les ressources qui sont souvent négligées. Ceci permet de donner au handicapé un sentiment de réussite et d'augmenter son estime de soi. Chaque succès, aussi minime soit-il, doit être valorisé et souligné. Il est parfois nécessaire d'apporter une aide thérapeutique sur les plans individuel et familial qui permette de lever des obstacles et empêche l'accentuation d'une évolution déficitaire. Une supervision régulière de l'équipe éducative peut également apporter des éléments nouveaux et dynamiques, permettant un meilleur travail avec les handicapés mentaux.

Session 176 Symposium:
New strategies in the treatment of aggressive acutely psychotic patients

1152
SURVEY OF TREATMENT STRATEGIES IN ACUTELY PSYCHOTIC PATIENTS

Taylor, Pamela Jane
Institute of Psychiatry/Bethlem Royal & Maudsley Hospitals,
London, England

Strategy is the key word. Aggressive, psychotic behaviour is the product of illness and environment, and can only be treated satisfactorily in the light of assessment procedures which take full account of this.

Environmental manipulation is commonly the necessary, but not sufficient means of containing the aggression. Psychoses restrict normal perception and cognition, such that violence may be the only method of coping with his surroundings left to the patient. Furthermore those surroundings may in reality be insensitive, even provocative. Seperation from potential victims, physical security and specialist nursing skills are among needs for consideration.

Medication is usually the necessary, but often insufficient means of containing the psychosis, which may not only restrict coping, but also directly drive serious violence. Treatments must be as specific as possible. The risks of escalating doses of medication polypharmacy and releasing of other pathologies are real, although each, on occasion, may be turned to advantage.

An optimal balance between the ordering of environment and prescription of medication is the ultimate goal for most patients. Rarely, legal compulsion may be required. Given such powers, it is essential that treatment strategies can be presented for each patient in terms that can be submitted to continuing scientific evaluation.

1153

Development of the Staff Observation Aggression Scale and Example of Application

Palmstierna T,
Clinics of Psychiatry, Västerås Central Hospital, Sweden

Some of the controversies between different studies of violent inpatient behaviour has probably been the lack of reliable methods for assessment. Traditional rating scales are not useful since the episodic nature of violent behaviour is not taken into account.

The Staff Observation Aggression Scale (SOAS) is constructed as a report scale for assessing degree, frequency and some other aspects of aggressive acts performed by psychiatric inpatients. It is based on a simplified and systematized reporting procedure where the staff is asked to report five consecutive aspects of aggressive behaviour, namely kind of immediate provocation, means, aim, result of aggressive behaviour and immediate action taken by staff to prevent further aggressive behaviour. The items means, aim and result of aggression are possible to score on an ordinal scale permitting ranking of different aggressive acts for comparative analyses.

The SOAS is found to have high reliability. It has been used to characterize and reveal factors determinating aggressive behaviour in both long-term psychogeriatric inpatients and in acutely, involuntarily admitted patients. It is expected to be useful in evaluating effects of treatment programs in order to prevent violent inpatient behaviour.

1154

Aggressive incidents against staff and emotional reactions of the staff

Omerov M.
Psychiatric Unit, Karolinska Institute, Danderyd Hospital, 182 88 Danderyd, Sweden

Since 1984 all injury reports have been continuously recorded at the psychiatric unit of Danderyd Hospital. The result showed that aggressive incidents were increasing.

In order better to evaluate emotional reactions of the staff, when faced with threat or violence, a systematic research was started on two wards for involuntarily admitted patients.

The two research periods did not include summertime-holidays in order to ensure that the ordinary staff was working. In both research years (1987 and 1988) SOAS (Staff Observation Aggression Scale) was used.

During the first period (1987) every person who reported an aggressive incident according to the scale was interviewed using a semistructured questionnaire, many of the questions concerned emotional reactions after violence or threat of violence. Most of the members of the staff reported feelings of being insulted and many have had difficulties in coming back to work again. Seventysix aggressive incidents were reported in 1987.

In the second period (1988) the same procedure were used, but this time the staff was interviewed with an anonymous questionnaire instead of an open interview. Otherwise there were no changes in administrative routines or treatment strategies except one important change. A new formulation of antipsychotic medicine zuclopentixol acetate, newly registered, was available in Sweden and this drug is now used for treatment of aggression.

Thirtysix aggressive incidents were recorded in 1988. Details of the study will be presented at the symposium.

1155

Clinical Experience with Zuclopenthixol Acetate and Co-injection of Zuclopenthixol Acetate and Zuclopenthixol Decanoate.
Hebenstreit, Gert F.
II. Psych. Dept. of the lower Austrian hospital for Psychiatry and Neurology, A-3362 Amstetten/Mauer, Austria

176 patients with the diagnosis paranoid schizophrenia or manic episode in the course of affective disorders were treated with zuclopenthixol acetate in an open multicentre study. The aim of the study was to investigate the antipsychotic effect, the sedative effect and the side effects of zuclopenthixol acetate. The dose of the first injection of the drug ranged from 50 to 200 mg. If necessary the injection could be repeated twice. 71% of the patients had a moderate to marked effect of the treatment. Most of the patients were transferred to different neuroleptics after treatment with zuclopenthixol acetate. The experience gained from the study suggests that zuclopenthixol acetate offers advantages over the neuroleptic preparations conventionally used.

The results of a co-injection study of zuclopenthixol acetate and zuclopenthixol decanoate in patients with exacerbations of chronic psychoses will be presented. The results of this study indicate that it is possible to mix zuclopenthixol acetate and zuclopenthixol decanoate in the same syringe and to give this as the first injection.

1156

Zuclopenthixol Acetate and Haloperidol in Acute Psychotic Patients - A Randomized Multicentre Study

D. Bobon, E. De Bleeker
"Notre-Dame des Anges" Psychiatric Hospital, University of Liège, Glain-Liège, Belgium.
Psychiatric Hospital, St. Lucia, St. Niklaas, Belgium.

Zuclopenthixol acetate (CPT-A) is a new type of formulation for use in the initial treatment of acute, psychotic patients. Its clinical effect has been compared with that of haloperidol (HAL). The patients were stratified into three groups, acute psychoses, exacerbation of chronic psychoses and mania, and they were randomly allocated to open treatment over 6 days with CPT-A i.m. or HAL i.m. followed by oral administration.

Of 103 patients 92 were included in the analyses. Most patients received 2 doses of 50-150 mg CPT-A during the 6-day period. HAL was administered much more frequently.

Ratings on the CGI and BPRS showed that CPT-A and HAL were equally effective in acute, non-manic patients and chronic patients. CPT-A caused a more rapid remission of symptoms in manic patients than HAL. CPT-A caused a somewhat stronger initial sedation than HAL. HAL induced significantly more extrapyramidal symptoms (EPSE) than CPT-A.

It is concluded that CPT-A is very useful in the treatment of acute psychotic patients because of its rapid onset of effect, its prolonged duration of action and a relatively low risk of EPSE.

Session 177 Workshop:
Detecting the patterns of basic emotional structuring

1157

DETECTING THE PATTERNS OF BASIC EMOTIONAL STRUCTURING
Calehr H - FRG

Session 178 Workshop:
The somatotherapies

1158

SOMATOTHERAPY: the new frame for body therapies and the body in therapy
MEYER Richard, Psychiatrist, Ph. D.
Editor of "Somatothérapies"

While "somatotherapy" is a new term, its meaning is clear as it designates not only all "body therapies" but also the whole dimension of "body work" in therapy. It creates a new class alongside psycho- and socio-therapies, grouping together a range of otherwise disparate and minor practices in what has finally become a major category. It specifies a common approach focused on the body and demands a strict methodology and its own particularly "somatological" theorization. In harmony with the different body functions, somatotherapies are themselves varied in form, some fitting into extremely precise frameworks, others being open to all potential situations, taking into consideration not just the body, but the entire, individual person in question. For the body is no more than a place destined for therapeutic work and its analysis including both psycho- and sociological dimensions. Nevertheless, this form of privileged access via the body constitutes one of the specificities of the "somatotherapist".

Session 179 New Research:
Anxiety states and phobias

1159

GENERALIZED ANXIETY DISORDER: CLINICAL DELIMITATION AND THERAPEUTIC APPROACH.
G.B. Cassano*, G. Guerani**, D. McNair***, G.B. Melis****, C. Nisita*, A. Petracca*
*II Cattedra Clinica Psichiatrica Università di Pisa, **Bristol Italiana (sud) SpA, ***Clinical Psychopharmacology Laboratory, Department of Psychology, Boston University, ****Clinica Ostetrica Ginecologica Università di Pisa

Generalized Anxiety Disorder has been conceptualized as a chronic disorder with moderate symptoms, often considered as a stable personality trait, little influenced by drug treatment.
Definition and relationship with anxiety and mood category has been debated.
Comparing demographic and clinical features of 40 patients with Generalized Anxiety Disorder (GAD), 152 with Panic Disorder (PD) and 241 with Major Depressive Disorders (MDD) we found some support for clearly differentiating GAD from panic-phobic and depressive disorder.
We further reported data about double-blind comparison between buspirone and lorazepam in GAD, showing efficacy of both drugs with different improvement rates. Relapse symptoms after abrupt treatment discontinuation were not observed in buspirone treated patients.
Our data suggest that new and more specific anxiolytics, with limited side effects and long term risk of dependence, are becoming available to treat mild and long lasting anxiety forms.

1160

Anxiety disorders in cardiologic outpatients
J-M. CHIGNON, J-P. LEPINE
Clinique Anxiété, Hopital Bichat-PARIS

The relationship of anxiety to cardiovascular function and symptoms has been of long history interest, culminating in the recent emphasis given to the modulation of cardiovascular response in panic patients.
Cognitive approaches to panic postulate an interaction of physiological and psychological factors in the maintenance of panic disorder. Parmacological approaches postulate a dysfunction of central alpha-adrenoceptors in panic and also in some cardio-vascular diseases.
Ambulatory heart rate recordings confirm the presence of major cardiovascular changes during panic attacks and in several studies.
We have carried out an ongoing study in an unselected population being explored in an outpatient cardiology unit with 24 hours Ambulatory heart rate recordings.
All patients were assessed with a dimensional anxiety scale and have been interviewed with the S.A.D.S.-L.A. Preliminary results in 30 patients show, 74% of Panic disorders, 30% of Obsessive-Compulsive disorders, 23% of Social Phobias, 18% of Major Depressive Disorders (These diagnoses are not exclusive) with an high comorbidity.
Further results will be presented and discussed

1161

CONCURRENT USAGE STUDY FOR SWITCHING FROM BENZODIAZEPINES TO BUSPIRONE

Udelman H.D., Udelman D.L.
Biomedical Stress Research Foundation Phoenix, Arizona, USA

We conducted a study of thirty-three (33) subjects between the age of 24 and 63 with the diagnosis of generalized anxiety disorder. They had taken benzodiazepines-Xanax, Ativan, and Valium-for at least 3 months and were tapered from their benzodiazepine anxiolytic medication in a double blind study with either buspirone or placebo. Physical examinations, laboratory studies and cardiograms were performed prior to entry into the study. Psychological tests, including Ham-A, Ham-D, and SCL-90, were done at the onset, weekly and at termination. Results of the study were analyzed and will be presented. Safety and efficacy of buspirone was clearly demonstrated. Hypotheses arising from these data will be discussed.

1162

THE ABSENCE OF WITHDRAWAL EFFECTS OF RITANSERIN AFTER CHRONIC DOSING
F. Kamali, S. Stansfield*, C.H. Ashton,
J. Hammond* and M.D. Rawlins
Department of Pharmacological Sciences, University of Newcastle Upon Tyne, Newcastle Upon Tyne and Janssen Pharmaceutical Ltd*, Grove, Wantage, Oxon, England

Ritanserin (R) is a new potent centrally acting 5HT2 antagonist. Whilst R has been shown to have anxiolytic properties it has no direct action on GABA receptors. The objective of this study was to assess the effects of abrupt withdrawal on clinical ratings of anxiety and sleep following chronic R administration to healthy volunteers. Thirty five volunteers (19 males), aged between 18-39 years took part in the study. After a placebo run-in period of 2 weeks subjects received R (10 mg once daily) for eight weeks under single blind conditions. This was followed by double-blind randomisation to either placebo or continued R for a further four weeks. Assessment of potential withdrawal symptoms, and anxiety and depression (HAD) was made on 11 occasions (at weekly intervals during the double-blind phase) and anxiety, concentration, quality of sleep and morning vigilance were measured by visual analogue scales daily. No change was detected in any parameter following abrupt cessation of R treatment, suggesting that under the conditions of this study R does not appear to be associated with withdrawal symptoms.

1163

PLACEBO-CONTROLLED EVALUATION OF RITANSERIN IN SIXTY NEUROTIC OUT-PATIENTS.
M.Wang, F. Guimaraes, K.Ashcroft & J.F.W.Deakin, University Hospital of South Manchester, West Didsbury, Manchester, M20 8LR. U.K.

Deakin (1988 Pharmacol.Biochem.Behav. 29;819) suggested that 5HT2 receptor down-regulation might be a common mechanism of anxiolytic effect of antidepressants and of 5HT1A agonists. To test this theory, the 5HT2 receptor antagonist ritanserin (10mg od) and placebo were compared in patients stratified by symptoms of anxiety, depression or both, excluding major depressives. On computerized self-ratings of anxiety and depression (STAI;SCL;Beck), ritanserin (n=29) was superior to placebo (n=27) in males and in mixed anxiety-depression (ANCOVA). However, as in most trials in this patient group, treatment effects were small.

Skin conductance (SC) and heart-rate (HR) responses to tones were measured in a one-trial aversive classical conditioning paradigm. Enhanced (conditioned) SC responses to tones following a tone - loud noise pairing were significantly reduced by ritanserin but not placebo after one week of treatment in the most anxious patients. No additional effects on SC or HR measures emerged after 4 weeks treatment.

Ritanserin reduces symptoms of anxiety and depression in minor affective disorder. Interactions with 5HT mechanisms in classical aversive conditioning may contribute to efficacy.

1164

LONG TERM RESULTS AFTER BEHAVIOR THERAPY WITH DENTAL PHOBIA

K.Gunnar Götestam, Dagfinn Berntzen, Rolf Gråwe, Trond Haug & Geir Lyngstad, *Department of Psychiatry and Behavioural Medicine, University of Trondheim, Norway.*

Seventeen dental phobic patients (DSM-III criteria) were after three (1.5 x 2) hours of information randomly assigned to either an exposure, or an applied relaxation treatment package for eight hours. A behavioral contract was signed, and the patients paid $600 at the before treatment, and received $400 back at the end of treatment ($200 serving as a quite low fee for the treatment). A behavioral test (including sitting in a dentists chair) assessing anxiety and heart rate, as well as questionnaires (Temple Fear Schedule, Dental Fear Scedule, cognitions related to dentist, probability of going to the dentist) were completed pre and post to treatment. The exposure included explanation of rationale, exposure by video, exposure to sounds in dentist chair, and was completed with filling in a small hole. The applied relaxation included explanation of rationale, relaxation training down to a short and conditioned version, and using the relaxation in the dentist's chair. The results showed significant effects of both treatments, with a clear tendency to superiority of the exposure treatment. The treatment results, including 6-and 12-months results will be presented.

Session 180 New Research: Alcoholism

1165

ALCOHOLISM: A CONCEPT OF DUAL DISORDER, DISEASE OR MANIFESTATION?
Srivastava Amresh Kumar.
Stress Clinic, Thane-Bombay, India.

In clinical practice patients presenting with alcohol problem exhibit complex interaction of alcoholism, other psychiatric diseases, physical morbidity and various psychosocial aspects. There have been constant efforts in conceptualising alcohol problem & developing treatment programmes accordingly. By & large the recognised concept is that alcoholism is a disease per se. Reviewing the literature it is observed that relationship of alco-holism & other psychiatric disorders needs to be looked at from a different angle. While conducting trials on other psychiatric disorders, alcoholism has been used as the stringent exclusion criteria whereas while researching alcoholism presence of other psychiatric disorders has been used as major exclusion criteria for selecting patient population Application of these exclusion criterias has isolated large number of patients suffering from alcoholism as well as other psychiatric disorders. This study has been undertaken to delineate the complex interaction existing with these disorders & to find out whether alcoholism is a DUAL DISORDER Initial findings of 100 patients coming for treatment is presented here. Preliminary findings indicate that approximately 80% patients have 2 diagnosis on DSM III Axis I, about 50% are found to have alcoholism with schizophrenic disroder, & 30% with other disorders in lower & middle class socio-economic Indian cultural group population.

1166

ANXIETY, DEPRESSION & PSYCHOLOGICAL DISTRESS IN ALCOHOLIC PATIENTS
Rizzardo R, Chiarparin O, Forza G, Borgherini G.
Inst. of Clinical Psychiatry, Univ. of Padua, Italy
In this study 42 patients were assessed at their first contact with an Alcoholic Unit whilst staying on a medical ward of the Palmanova General Hospital, Udine and compared with 44 subjects attending regional clubs for alcoholics on treatment (CAT) for at least one year. None of the patients had any previous history of psychiatric disorders. The scope of this study was to assess the psychiatric symptoms at first contact and that following a 6 month period of treatment. The following self-rating scales were used: GHQ to assess the general mental & physical health, BSI to rate the symptoms in various psychopathological areas, STAI to assess state and trait anxiety, ZUNG scale to rate depression. Factorial analysis of the scores obtained from the various tests on the whole sample evidenced the presence of 2 underlying factors which accounted for 73% of the variance. The first consists of the ZUNG, STAI and GHQ scales, whilst the second consists of the hostility, psychoticism, paranoia and personal sensitivity scales of the BSI. This could suggest that in alcoholic patients, psychopathological aspects are partly due to anxiety & depression and partly due to psychotic features. Moreover, the results of the inpatients group were compared with those obtained from the outpatient subjects. The patients do not differ in their socio-demographic characteristics. The inpatients obtain significantly higher scores on GHQ, ZUNG, STAI for trait anxiety and on the obsession, depression, anxiety, psychoticism scales and the total number of symptoms of BSI. So it seems that following a period of treatment, an improvement into psychiatric symptoms was noted. An alternative hypothesis could be that discontinuing the drinking behavior could disclose psychopathological symptoms which were hitherto masked by alcoholism.

1167

COEXISTING ANXIETY DISORDERS AND ALCOHOLISM

D. SERVANT, C. NAVARRE, D. BAILLY, Ph. J. PARQUET
Psychopathology and Alcoology Unit, Hôpital de la Charité, University Hospital of Lille, France

There has been recently interest in the coexistence of anxiety disorders and alcoholism. Few epidemiologic and clinical investigations have found an increase prevalence of panic disorder, phobias, generalized anxiety disorder, obsessive-compulsive disorder in alcoholics compared with that reported in the general population. In this study, 152 consecutively admitted patients to a alcohol rehabilitation program were screened over a 1 year period for anxiety disorders. Thirty nine percent of the patients met D.S.M.-III-R criteria for anxiety disorder.
We then compared the group of subjects with anxiety disorder (N = 60) with the group without anxiety disorder (N = 92). We found that the subgroup where coexist alcoholism and anxiety disorder had more personal history of depression and more psychotropic medication. These results give an account of the interest to identify patients with these two disorders and to determine the appropriate treatment.

1168

SOCIOCULTURAL ASPECTS IN CHANGING PATTERNS OF ALCOHOL USE IN GREECE
Dimitra Madianou, Ph.D., Assistant Professor of Anthropology
Pantion University of Social & Political Sciences and Athens University, Dept. of Psychiatry, Athens, Greece

Patterns of alcohol consumption were significantly differentiated among three generations, as well as among rural/urban areas from a nation-wide, general population survey. Younger populations, especially in urban centres, exhibit a higher percentage of alcohol related problems, compared to drinkers of rural areas or of an older age group.
Questions generated from these results led to an ongoing medico-anthropological study in two communities, a rural wine-producing and an urban one, on the sociocultural factors that may be assumed to influence the patterns and regulation of alcohol use.
The study which is part of the WHO "Community Response to Alcohol Related Problems" one, aims first at identifying culturally transferred drinking norms, values and rituals which function as a protective mechanism to a community and thus leading to "cultural immunity" of alcohol related problems, and second, at the early identification of alcohol related problems at the community level.
The data collected so far, highlight a number of theoretical and conceptual issues concerning alcohol use/abuse that require further study.

1169

"In vivo" STUDY ON THE EFFECTS OF ETHANOL ON RAT BRAIN MONOAMINE OXIDASE
P.Bongioanni¥P.Pietrini,S.Marchi°,F.Loprieno, M.Guazzelli,GM.Pacifici§
Clinica Psichiatrica I,*Scuola Superiore-S. Anna,°Clinica Medica I,§Patologia Generale Università di PISA, I T A L Y

Monoamine oxidase(MAO) has attracted considerable interest in biological psychiatry, because of its possible role as biochemical marker of several psychiatric disorders. Many studies have been carried out on MAO activity in brain and in blood platelets. As far as alcoholism is concerned the results obtained are contradictory. In the present work we have evaluated "in vivo" ethanol effects on rat brain MAO activity, using benzylamine as enzyme substrate. We have found that rats fed with 10% ethanol solution have a very significantly($p<0.001$) higher MAO activity than control animals(32.60 ± 3.36 vs 25.36 ± 2.58 nmols/mg prot./h). Another group fed with 20% ethanol solution has still higher activity values(mean:37.76 nmols/mg prot./h). These findings are discussed in relation with a possible biological pathogenesis of alcoholism.

1170

PSYCHIATRIC EPIDEMIOLOGICAL RESEARCH IN TWO STAGES ON ZARAGOZA CITY
A. Seva, R. Magallon, A. Sarasola and J.A. ME
University of Zaragoza. Zaragoza. Spain.

We study a representative sample of 1.200 p. Was interviewed in their homes using a adaptation of the "Enquete Santé Quebec" and also the G.H.Q.-28 of Goldberg, the Clinical Interview Schedule(C/I/S) and the CAGE for the screening of alcohol-abuse problems.

For the statistical analys was used the S.P.S.S package.

The general prevalence was 11.79 %(8.8%for males and 14.03 % for females).

Distimic and anxiety disorders was more detected on women, and personality disorders and alcoholism problems on men.

Social problems was more common on the group of psychological and psychiatrical affected.

The prevalence of phisical illness is also significantly associated with psychological and social disturbs.

This epidemiological research was officially supported for the Regional Government of Aragon(Spain) with the name SAMAR-Project on Mental Health.

Session 181 Free Communications:
Psychoneuroendocrinology I

1171

Influence of releasing hormones on the pituitary hormone secretion in healthy male and female subjects

HINZ A, LAAKMANN G, WINKELMANN M, DAFFNER C

Psychiatric Hospital of the University of Munich
Nußbaumstraße 7, D-8000 München 2

Desipramine(DMI)-induced growth hormone(GH) stimulation is age- and sex-dependent, as has been shown in our pharmacoendocrinological investigations. In healthy male subjects DMI induced a significantly greater GH stimulation than in healthy female subjects which, however, decreased with increasing age in both groups.

We examined the secretion of GH, cortisol and TSH in 29 healthy male and 39 healthy female subjects after combined administration of growth hormone releasing hormone (GHRH), corticotropin releasing hormone (CRH), gonadotropin releasing hormone (GnRH) and thyrotropin releasing hormone (TRH).

The results showed that GHRH-induced GH stimulation is, like the DMI-induced GH stimulation, age-dependent. Healthy female subjects had a significantly greater GHRH-induced GH stimulation than healthy male subjects. CRH-induced cortisol stimulation and TRH-induced TSH stimulation seemed to be neither age- nor sex-dependent.

These investigations should be a basis for further neuroendocrinological studies on releasing hormone-induced GH, cortisol and TSH stimulation in endogenous depressive patients.

1172

Growth hormone secretion over 24 hours and after stimulation with releasing hormones in healthy male subjects

VODERHOLZER, U.; LAAKMANN, G.; HINZ, A.; HOFMANN, H.-P.

Psychiatric Hospital of the University of Munich, F.R.G., Nußbaumstraße 7, D-8000 München 2

Within the last years disturbances of growth hormone (GH) secretion have been described in patients with endogenous depression. Schilkrut et al. (Neuropsychobiol, 1, 70-79, 1975) found a diminished GH secretion during the night whereas Mendlewicz et al. (J Clin Endocrinol Metab, 60, 505-512, 1985) reported a GH hypersecretion by day in depressive patients. The GH response to various stimuli including GHRH (Laakmann et al., Pharmacopsychiatry, 19, 235-236, 1986) was reported to be blunted in endogenous depressive patients. The direct cause for this finding is yet unknown. The aim of this study was to determine whether the GH response to combined application of four releasing hormones (GHRH, CRH, GnRH, TRH) depends on the GH and cortisol secretion within 24 hours before stimulation.
Methods: 13 male (age: 21-59 a) subjects participated in this study. GH and cortisol secretion were determined in 15-min intervals beginning at $8.^{30}$ h (day 1) until $10.^{30}$ h (day 2). At $8.^{30}$ h (day 2) four releasing hormones (GHRH 100 g, CRH 100 g, GnRH 100 g, and TRH 200 g) were given i.v. over 5 min.
Results: Between the AUCs of GH secretion over 24 hours and the GH secretion within 2 hours after releasing hormone stimulation a positive correlation was found (r = 0.58; p < 0.05). No relationship was found between GH stimulation and cortisol stimulation (r = 0.29) as well as the total 24-hour cortisol secretion (r = 0.15).
Conclusion: It therefore seems unlikely that the blunted GH stimulation of depressive patients is caused by a feedback inhibition due to a GH hypersecretion.

1173

NOCTURNAL PROLACTIN SECRETION DEPENDS ON THE FIRST REM PERIOD EVIDENCE IN NORMAL SUBJECTS AND DEPRESSED PATIENTS
J.D. Bergiannaki, C.R. Soldatos, P.N. Sakkas, M. Syrengelas, C.N.Stefanis, University of Athens, Department of Psychiatry

The claim has been previously made, that in both normal subjects and depressed patients there is no consistent relationship between sleep stages and prolactin (PRL) secretion. Purpose of this study was to investigate the relationship, if any, between the occurrence of the highest increment in nocturnal PRL secretion and the first REM period (REMP1). Subjects, all males, included eight patients with major depression (age 40.5 ± 16.3), and ten normal individuals (age 36.7 ± 14.2). Blood samples were hourly (8.00p.m. to 8.00a.m.) collected through a continuous withdrawal pump. Sleep was recorded for an 8-hour period (11.00p.m. to 7.00a.m.). Our results show that, in both normal individuals and depressed patients, the first REM period occurs either during the hour of the highest increment of nocturnal PRL secretion or the preceding hour. Further analysis showed that the time lapsed between termination of REMP1 and the highest PRL increment was quite similar between normals and depressives. The findings of this study support the hypothesis that the neurophysiological substrate of the occurrence of the first REM period may be involved also in the occurrence of the highest increase of nocturnal PRL secretion.

1174

AN ABNORMALITY OF NOCTURNAL PROLACTIN SECRETION IN SCHIZOPHRENIA: PRELIMINARY OBSERVATIONS
C.R.Soldatos, P.N.Sakkas, J.D.Bergiannaki, M.Syrengelas, P.Hadjitaskos, C.N.Stefanis
Univ. of Athens, Dept. of Psychiatry

The possibility of an abnormality in the tuberoinfundibular dopaminergic neurons and/or pituitary dopamine (DA) receptors has been researched in schizophrenic patients through daytime hormonal studies. Purpose of this study was to investigate any aberration in nocturnal secretory patterns of PRL in schizophrenia. Blood samples were hourly (8.00p.m to 8.00a.m.) collected through a continuous withdrawal pump from seven male chronic schizophrenic patients (age 27.6 ± 8.6) and ten normal individuals (age 36.7 ± 14.2). Our results showed that in average, nocturnal PRL levels were higher in the group of schizophrenic patients as compared to the normal subjects (0.41 ± 0.03 vs 0.23 ± 0.02 mIU/ml, $p<0.01$). The assessment of the highest increment of nocturnal PRL secretion showed that in schizophrenic patients it occurs independently of the time of occurrence of the first REM period (REMP1). Further analysis showed that the time lapsed between termination of REMP and the highest PRL increment differed between schizophrenic and normal individuals (mean rank 11.43 vs 5.00, $p<0.01$). Our findings suggest that in schizophrenic patients with a presumed dysfunction of the DA system there may be a dysregulation of PRL's nocturnal secretion.

1175

PROLACTIN CIRCADIAN RHYTHM IN MENTAL PATIENTS.

M.G. Minervini, M. Balducci, S. Papagni, A. Giovine, B. Brancasi*
Psychiatric Hospital "Opera Don Uva" - Bisceglie
*2nd Neurological Clinic - University of Bari

With the increasing knowledge of neurotransmitter involvement in neuroendocrine function, measurement of pituitary hormones secretion have been used to assess central neurotransmitters pathophysiology. Particularly, dopamine containing neurons in the hypothalamic tubero-infundibular tract inhibit prolactin secretion, so that the blockade of the dopamine receptors by the neuroleptics determines an increase in the plasmatic levels of the hormone. In this view, prolactin has been proposed as a marker of neuroleptic drugs and of their side--effects, but the data are controversial.
In the attempt to demonstrate a correlation between prolactin plasma levels and therapeutic response to neuroleptics, we evaluated prolactin circadian rhythm in mental patients on chronic neuroleptic therapy.
Our results demonstrate that there is no correlations between hormonal levels, therapeutic response to neuroleptics and the side-effects they induce.

1176

SERUM TESTOSTERONE IN PSYCHOTIC DISORDERS

E.Frangos, G.Athanasenas, P.Alexandrakou, N.Manusis, D.Filokyprou, and N.Thalasinos
Private psychiatric clinic (GALINI) and Endocrinological Department of University of Athens.

Serum testosterone levels (mg/ml) were measured upon the admission in a mental hospital in male drug-free patients in the diagnostic groups: schizophrenic mainly paranoid and major depressive disorder endogenous).
The ($\pm$ S.E.) testosterone levels were found significantly higher ($P \simeq 0.02$) in the schizophrenic group (637 ± 48) than in patients with major depressive disorder (469 ± 42).
The differences were not due to age, weight and height or overall severity of illness.
These findings suggest that testosterone system displays a quite different functional pattern in those major psychotic disorders.

1177

Use of Saliva Steroid Hormone Assays in Psychiatric Studies.
Harris B., Walker R., Cook N., Read G and Riad Fahmy D.
University of Wales College of Medicine, Cardiff. U.K.

Steroid hormones including progesterone, cortisol and testosterone, can be accurately measured in saliva, the values reflecting free plasma levels. This important stress free technique of salivary sampling together with monitoring of psychiatric parameters is useful for investigation of various conditions both intensively and over relatively long periods of time. 3 examples are given -
Studies of puerperal mood, both in terms of 'blues' and major depression have implicated an association of progesterone, levels being lower in depressed breast feeders and higher in depressed bottle feeders.
The Dexamethasone Suppression test has also been carried out using saliva in 300 routine psychiatric admissions, results being equal to those with plasma. A study of the effect of anxiety on the results of the 'saliva' DST showed little effect of anxiety.
Saliva cortisol and testosterone have been studied in male marathon runners together with psychological parameters, in the 3 days prior to a marathon race, as well as during the race. There was no significant association between hostility, depression and anxiety with cortisol or testosterone levels.

Session 182 Free Communications:
Psychopathology and psychosomatics in gynaecology

1178

A PSYCHO-ANAMNESTIC STUDY OF THE PRE-MENSTRUAL SYNDROME
Tridenti A. - Manara F. - Tonelli F. - Clinica Psichiatrica - Università - Parma - Italy

The writers have studied the psycho-anamnestic characteristics of 100 women, by giving a questionnaire to members of a family planning clinic. The women were divided into 2 groups, those who complained of suffering from pre-menstrual tension, and those who did not have any indisposition whatsoever. For each group, 26 conditions related to each subjects personal and medical history were considered as was the psychological state of each individual: the conclusion reached for the 2 groups have been compared, in order to identify what main characteristics it is probable that women affected by pre-menstrual tension have.

1179

Prostagrandins and premenstrual syndrome

N.Koshikawa[1], T.Tatsunuma[1], M.Doi[1], N.Ichinowatari[1], K.Somemura[1], T.Kono[2], K.Furuya[2], K.Seki[2], I.Nagata[2]
1) Department of psychiatry, National Defense Medical College (NDMC), 2) Department of gynecology and obstetrics, NDMC. (Japan)

Although the etiology of the premenstrual syndrome (PS) is not fully understood, the involvement of factors of prostaglandins (PG) is probable. We measured the plasma concentrations of $PGF2\alpha$, PGE, PGE2, TXB2 and 6-keto $PGF1\alpha$ sequentially throughout three menstrual cycles in 12 patients with PS, comparing with 13 control subjects without PS. The aim of this study was to confirm the attribution of prostagrandin activity to the symptoms of PS.
In patients with PS, the concentration of $PGF2\alpha$ in the follicular phase was lower and that of TXB2 in the luteal phase tended to be higher compared with normal women. Furthermore, detailed examination of each patient suggested that the patients with PS could be classified into 3 groups: 1) the cases in which the change of PG had profound effect on occurrence of symptoms of PS, 2) those in which ovarian hormones were considered to be the probable main etiological factor of PS, 3) those in which other factors were considered as the cause of PS. Therefore, precise clinical classification of PS is necessary to clarify the etiology of PS.

1180

PSYCHODYNAMIC CHARACTERISTICS IN NORMAL AND ABNORMAL PREGNANCY COURSES
Tzavaras N., Malagaris E.G., Anastasiadis P
Psychopathological Laboratory, University of Thrace Medical School, Alexandroupolis. 88,77.
Pregnant women with normal and abnormal pregnancy courses, were examined psychiatrically, using psychoanalytically orientated interviews. We noticed the complexity of psychodynamics which emerge during adolescence -and become distinctive in later developmental stages because of prevailing psychopathological relations-from the conflictual character, that is imposed both on the level of instinctual impulses and the level of Narcissism. Our direct clinical observations confirm the views of contemporary analysts, who attribute particular importance in the most archaic forms of relating of daughter to the mother, for the psychosexual development and maturation of the first.

1181

Premenstrual Symptoms and Response to Progesterone Suppositories
Ellen W. Freeman, Ph.D., Karl Rickels, M.D., Steven Sondheimer, M.D.
Department of Obstetrics/Gynecology and Psychiatry
University of Pennsylvania, Philadelphia, PA 19104

Although several small studies of progesterone suppository treatment showed that total symptoms of PMS were not reduced by progesterone more than placebo, progesterone continues to be the most widely recommended treatment for PMS. One hundred forty women completed a double-blind, placebo-controlled study of progesterone suppository treatment in a 2-period crossover design. Progesterone dosages were 400 mg in the first cycle and 800 mg in the second cycle for the last 12 days of the menstrual cycle. The primary outcome measure was the daily symptom record (DSR), a list of 17 common premenstrual symptoms, scored daily from 0 (none) to 4 (incapacitating) by the subject.

Results showed significant decrease from washout but no significant difference between progesterone and placebo treatments in reduction of total symptoms, emotional or cognitive symptom clusters. Physical symptoms did not decrease significantly from baseline with progesterone treatment and showed more improvement with placebo than with progesterone (p .005). The sample size and method had at least a 90% chance of detecting a drug-placebo difference at the 2-tailed 5% significance level. Conclusions are that vaginally-administered progesterone is not clinically useful for PMS treatment.

1182

THE COGNITIVE BEHAVIOURAL ASSESSMENT: MENOPAUSE DISORDERS

M.C.Turola, m.R.Folegatti, G.Targa, S.Stella
Psychiatric Clinic, University of Ferrara, Italy

The Cognitive Behavioural Assessment (C.B.A.) was administered to a group of 136 women aged from 36 to 62 years (mean age 51.1±5.4), who spontaneously applied to a menopause center. C.B.A. is a recent psychometric battery, self-reported and computerized, composed of a psychological and clinical survey and by tests which inquire into different areas such as anxiety, depression, somatization, fears etc. The group was divided into two subgroups: 82 women with physiological menopause and 54 women with sugical menopause (not neoplastic disease). A second subgroup was formed by 61 women aged from 36 to 51 year (mean age 42.±3.3) who had undergone only hysterectomy without oophorectomy. The most frequent troubles regard sexuality, affective life, fears and somatizations in general. The surgical menopause group is not very different from the physiological one, except for the intensity of the disorders and for the tendency to somatization. In the women who had only hysterectomy, the symptomatology is less frequent.

Session 183 Free Communications:
Theory and practice of family and marital therapy

1183

FAMILY THERAPY:
EXISTENCE ENDANGERED
L. van Dijk, M.D. Psychiatrist
Head Dpt Family Therapy, Licht en Kracht, Assen, The Netherlands

Family therapists have to question what is constitutive of family therapy and what is the position of family therapy in psychotherapy in general.
How can family therapy exist as a useful adjunct to psychotherapy and psychiatry?
We have to make a distinction between the different levels of abstraction in which we think and in which we act. We have to use the words we want to use in a plain, unequivocal sense.
In this way we have to search the essentials of family therapy, even if we would come to the conclusion that family therapy were much less of a seperate and exclusive form of psychotherapy then we expected it to be.
The author will try to show how systems theory and systems thinking influences psychotherapy. He will try to define the meaning and the use of frequently used words in het theory of family therapy.
He will state in which sense in his opinion family therapy does exist and is different from other branches of psychotherapy, and in which sense family therapy is just another therapeutical technique within the broad field of psychotherapy.

1184

THE FIVE STEP STRATEGY OF POSITIVE FAMILY THERAPY

Nossrat PESESCHKIAN, M.D.
Daily Clinic, Wiesbaden, West Germany

The principles and techniques of Positive Psychotherapy can be applied within the framework of family therapy:
1. We try to describe general concepts of medicine, psychiatry and psychotherapy in terms of Positive Family Therapy, to make new ways of thinking accessible to the patient, and to provide the stimulus for a new orientation within therapy and self-help. The patient gives up his old role as the patient and becomes aware of the possibilities available to him for self-help (the patient/the family as therapist).
2. People generally tend to ask about HOW something happens (conflict process). We ask WHAT happens and look for the contents that determine the conflict (conflict contents; four forms of dealing with conflict). This process of looking at the game rules enables us to identify the family's existing capacity for self-help and at the same time work through the conflicts in the family.
3. The five step strategy is a conflict-centered therapy. It is divided into observation/distancing, inventory, situational encouragement, verbalization and broadening of goals. Within this model different psychotherapeutic directions can work together.

1185

DILEMMAS POSED IN TREATING DISTURBED MARRIAGES OF JAPANESE WOMEN AND WESTERN MEN.

Dr. Steve Fochios
Private practice; New York City, USA

The treatment of disturbances in the marital relationship between Japanese women and American men demands special skills of the therapist. In addition to being well trained in family and couple therapy, the clinician has to be very well experienced in the psychology and culture of the Japanese woman. Ordinarily, couple counseling includes the delicate handling of each member's individual psychological make-up plus the accurate determination of each individual's contribution to the malfunction. In the instance of a bi-cultural marriage, the therapist has to also be a skilled 'culture interpreter'. That is, he has to be fluent in both "cultural languages". The purpose of this communication is to show how the interface of two culture systems containing many crucial opposites produces confusion and frustration not only between the married couples, but between the therapist, in this case an Occidental, and the Japano-American system. The clinical material is gathered from a private practice in New York City where the presenting problems of the Japanese women were marital, depressions, phobias, and children's school adjustment. These observations reflect approximately 400 interview sessions. The mix of Western men were: Greek American, Jewish American, Black American, Hungarian American. All the women were born in Japan and most had difficulty with English.

1186

PROCESSUAL SELF-REFERENCE, TIME: MYTHS AND RITUALS IN FAMILY THERAPY

Serge Goffinet
Dept. of Psychiatry, St. Luc Hospital, Catholic Univ. of Louvain, 1200 Brussels, Belgium.

Confusing logical levels, the familial system can't operate change without psychiatric symptom production of the assigned patient. Comrehensive models of familial self-reference are phenomenological (behaviours and rules of behaviours) and mythical (interdiscursive indicatory of context of contexts). Belonging and inclusion rituals indicate two forms of relationship from the individuals to collectivity. An analysis of rituals dynamic is purposed. Self-reference relations are explained at discriminant epistemological levels: biological, individual, familial and social.
Processual self-reference and homeostasis are maintained.
1. by repetitive alienation loop (familial rules determined by roles), 2. by a ritual time (related to life-events of familial members; 3. by a mythical time which has no relations with individuals histories.
This time analysis helps to the diagnosis of system fluctuation threshold.
In therapy, this search for familial differentiation defines familial specificity against cultural imaginary on the family.
Metacommunication on roles, familial identity influences mythical change, which confirms homeostatic change.

1187

Family Therapy in General Hospital
"Making Contract"
Sakkas Dionyssis
"General Hospital of Athens", Greece

This paper presents some special aspects of the activities of the Therapeutic Team's work with families, in the context of a newly formed (3 year-old) Psychiatric Department of a general hospital.
The problems emerging during the introduction of a new epistemology. We follow the Autonomy Paradigme in the context of a Systemic Dialectic approach (Durkin-Vassiliou) are being discussed.
Those circumstances present a special interest: Family Therapy is addressed not to a sophisticated population ready to accept Family Therapy, but mainly to a population which seeks help from a general hospital and its Outpatient Clinic-given that there are no Centers of Mental Health in the area.
During this phase of development the Process of establishing a Contract with colleagues within the Department, with trainees (residents in Psychiatry and other professionals) and with colleagues in the other departments of the general hospital who are referral sources, we find to be of paramount importance.
By means of this Contract-Making procedure, on the one hand we achieve a sensitization undispensable for reaching our therapeutic, research, and training goals. On the other hand, an other equally major goal is achieved: We avoid the wasting of our own resources.

1188

OVERCOMING DEFENSE AGAINST CLOSENESS

Yukio Ishizuka M.D.
Clinical Assistant Professor of Psychiatry
New York University Medical Center

Defense against closeness is the central challenge of successful couple therapy:
1. Five defenses--anxiety, anger, physical-symptoms, depression, and psychosis-- block closeness.
2. Defense is there to "protect" the individuals against the very closeness they need to be "happy".

Overcoming the defenses to achieve and maintain closeness is the objective of successful couple therapy:
1. Acute distress in couples present opportunity.
2. Breakthroughs require setbacks.
3. Therapeutic resources mobilized determine outcome.

The therapist should be an active advocate:
1. "Closeness" vs. "Defense"
2. Structural model of intimacy is essential.
3. Four key steps to overcome defense.
4. Daily tracking of intimacy in therapy is vital.

"See-saw" phenomenon characterize breakthroughs:
1. See-saw between partners.
2. See-saw among three spheres of personality.
3. See-saw among dimensions of intimacy.
4. See-saw among elements within dimensions.

Session 184 Free Communications:
Stress and adjustment disorders

1189

Mental Health Aspects of Long Stay in Antarctica-
An Indian Experience.

Sharma, S.D. and Deshpande, S.N.
Safdarjang Hospital, New Delhi INDIA.

The Antarctica Expedition teams have to face extreme climatic conditions, prolonged isolation, deprivation in a monotonous milieu, and absence of accustomed sources of emotional gratification. A study of Indian teams was undertaken with a view to studying the medical and psychological problems including group dynamics, and the positive or negative effects on their psyche and health. Structured personality tests, including Cattell's 16-PF, Subjective Wellbeing Inventory and a specially designed Indian Antarctica Questionnaire were used. Boredom, feeling irritated, and loneliness were the major psychological problems commonly reported in the members of the two Indian Wintering teams. Sleeplessness, loss of taste for food and feeling easily tired were the most frequently reported somatic problems. Compared with findings of researchers in other countries, the Indian teams did not show signs of 'staring' or 'drifting' phenomena.

The results have applicative value for screening of team members and their effective functioning.

1190

PSYCHOSOCIAL EFFECTS OF A DISASTER: THE EARLY AND LATER POST-IMPACT PERIODS
C.Soldatos,J.Bergiannaki,M.Syrengelas,M.Economou, A.Botsis,K.Sofia,A.Koumoula,C.Theodorou,
Dept.of Psychiatry,Univ.of Athens,Greece
Kalamata, a middle-size Greek city, was severely damaged by a 6.5 R earthquake in September 1986. About one third of the population moved to other cities, while the rest stayed in tents for months. One year later all of them were housed. At about 3 weeks following the disaster we interviewed a random sample of 115 tent dwellers (47 males & 68 females) in Kalamata and of 97 inhabitants (38 males & 59 females) of Tripolis, a nearby city where the tremor was felt but no damages occurred. A semi-structured questionnaire was used and scales such as the SCL-90 & the Spielberger Anxiety Inventory. The Kalamata sample was followed up one year later. T-test, x2 and multiple linear regression were utilized.
During the earthquake: (1) inactivity was the least prevalent behavior; (2) those with physical illness were more likely to be inappropriately mobilized; (3) there were intense emotional and psychophysiological reactions, particularly in women and anxious individuals. During the early post-impact period: (1) there was considerable psychopathology and continued psychophysiological hyperactivity; (2) depression was more likely in those who remained inactive during the disaster; (3) there was a need for verbalizing emotions. During the later post-impact period: (1) psychopathology indexes subsided to pre-disaster levels; (2) a degree of psychophysiological hyperactivity persisted; (3) protracted exposure to the consequences of the disaster and old age are risk factors for the continuation of psychobehavioral disturbances.

1191

BURN-OUT: PERSONAL ORGANIZATIONAL OR CULTURAL DISEASE?
Hubert A. Wallot, MD, Ph.D., psychiatrist, professor, Université du Québec à Chicoutimi.
Pierre Dorion, M.R. Psychiatrist, Robert Giffard Hospital, Beauport (Québec), Canada.
Brunot T. Laplante, MD, psychiatrist, Robert Giffard Hospital, Beauport (Québec), Canada.

Burn-out resembles several different diagnoses without being totally comparable to any of them, because, among other reasons, it does not have systematic criteria for including and excluding symptoms. The level of burn-out, as measured by the scales, is related to several organizational characteristics: the worker's age, role conflict, role ambiguity, work satisfaction and leadership style. Finally, the increasing importance of burn-out in our societies seems related to a cultural phenomenon about the meaning of work. A diagnostic decision tree is proposed for clinicians. According to the authors, burn-out is a kind of adjustment disorder, implying some personnality traits and some organizational stressors, but it is not a disease.

1192

A BASIC TENDENCY OF PATTERN OF DAILY LIFE STRESS

Shunichiro Hayashi/Department of Mental Health, School of Hygienic Sciences,Kitasato University/ Sagamihara-City,Japan

Concerning psycho-social stress,two major research directions are known, Major Life Event Stress of T.H.Holms,R.H.Rahe et al. and Daily Life Stress of R.S.Lazarus et al. which has been intended by rather low correlation of the former to health condition. We conducted surveys of Daily stress of the population around Tokyo with modified scales of 125 and 120 items, first of 597 subjects and second of ca. 700, both including University hospital's out-patients. Apart from analyses of contents which gave reasonable results, we tried to see the pattern of the stress according to the life conditions, by examining the average intensity and frequency of respective groups, also some statistical tests as Hotelling's T^2 test or internal consistency test by deleting the items. We obtained the result that the standard life condition shows a higher frequency and smaller intensity comparing with the antagonistic condition; e.g. healthy vs. patient, salaried vs. other type worker, lower administrator vs. upper or general personnel in company, male vs. female, etc. When this pattern is shown, T^2 test and consistency test are proved in parallel. The second survey also results the same. We imagine this phenomenon might be a basic tendency of the Daily stress.

1193

TECHNOLOGICAL-ORGANIZATIONAL CHANGES: STRESS-STRAIN EFFECTS IN MANAGERIAL WORK
Fulcheri M, Muttini C, Novara F, Camerone E, Maina G, Ravizza L.
Dept. of Psychiatry - University of Turin, Turin, Italy

The impact of technological and organizational changes on strategies, structures, criteria of success, leadership styles, work relations and role interactions, have complex and contradictory consequences on managerial work.

In order to understand and explain the multifactorial pathogenesis of mental stress and its many-sided effects, our study intends: a) to consider all the potential and interacting stressors in the working life and personal conditions of living, within the frame of the biographical background and relevant experiences of the subjects; b) to pursue this integrate consideration by an interdisciplinary approach, involving psychiatry and mental hygiene, organizational psychology, occupational medicine.

The research is carried out:
-on a sample of about 300 male managers, defined according to: a) the field of activity (industry, services, public administration); b) the age level (under 45, over 45 years, retired);
-on two comparison groups: a) about 50 women managers; b) about 60 highly skilled employees.

The basic frame is an epidemiological approach both descriptive (study of distribution) and analytical (study of determinants), using medical anamnesis, biographical questionnaire, psychiatric interview, psychodiagnostic tests.

1194

DEPRESSIVE AND ANXIOUS CONSEQUENCES OF CHRONIC STRESS

GC Davis and N Breslau, Henry Ford Hospital; Detroit, Michigan, U.S.A.

Six month and lifetime rates of DSM-III Major Depression (MD) and Generalized Anxiety Disorder (GAD) and depressive symptoms were compared in mothers of children with severe disabilities (chronic stress, n=310) and a probability sample (controls, n=357). MD and GAD were ascertained by the NIMH-DIS and current depressive symptoms were measured by the CES-D. Mothers in the chronic stress sample had significantly higher rates of GAD and depressive symptoms. Six months and lifetime GAD in the chronic stress sample were 17.5% and 56% respectively, and in the controls, 11.5% and 45% respectively. The rate of depressive symptoms (CES-D score >16) was 30.2 in the chronic stress vs. 16.1% in controls. Rates of MD were not significantly different in the two groups: six months and lifetime MD were in the chronic stress sample 8.4% and 18.4% respectively and in the controls, 6.8% and 16.6%. The data indicate that chronic stress increases the risk for depressive and anxious symptoms but not for major depression.

1195

PLENTY IN THE MIDST OF STARVATION: LOSS OF SELF-SUFFICIENCY AND ITS IMPACT ON CAMBODIAN REFUGEES IN THAILAND.
Maurice Eisenbruch, M.D., M.Phil.
Dept. of Child and Family Psychiatry, Royal Children's Hospital, Flemington Road, Parkville, Victoria 3052

Refugees need food, yet are helplessly dependent on food distribution by international agencies such as World Food Program. This paper reports the psychological and cultural effects of a lack of the capacity of people to get their own food for themselves, and to use this food as part of their normative ritual lives. The case of Cambodian refugees in UNHCR camps and displaced persons in UNBRO camps in Thailand is considered. The people at Site 2 have to rely on food and water and Western medicine being trucked to them. This is a people who for thousands of years have subsisted as rice farmers in what was the richest rice bowl in Southeast Asia. The World Health Organization states that if a person takes in 1,750 kilocalories of food each day, the body will just function at a basal metabolic rate. The ration of food in some camps was 1,750 kilocalories per day per adult. According to the Basic Ration Information of the UNBRO Nutrtion Unit, during 1986, the number of children per family affected the number of calories per person. If there were no children, then there was 1.2666 mean rations per person (mrp); with one child, it goes down to 0.876 mrp; two children, 0.601 mrp, three children 0.592 mrp, and four children, 0.508 mrp. The development of refugee children demands careful attention. Physically the child may have insufficient food to grow. Intellectually they may be so nutritionally deprived as to have impaired brain development, and they may suffer a poverty of cognitive stimulation. The paper describes the food themes in the drawings made by a number of children. The lack of food, energy and power leads to a disruption of the religious rituals available to people at the very time when they need to assuage their guilt through that ritual. They are unable to make offerings in the war if they have no food. In delivering aid, whether in UNHCR or UNBRO camps, there is a reduction in explicitly Cambodian behaviour and, more importantly, Cambodian solutions for the daily problems of body and mind.

1196

Perceived stress in psychiatric nursing.

*G. Pieters, L. Lefèvre & V. Vercruyssen
School voor Maatschappelijke Gezondheidszorg,
Dienst voor Geestelijke Gezondheidszorg,
Katholieke Universiteit Leuven,
Leuven, Belgium.*

*A scale, designed to measure occupational stress as perceived by psychiatric nurses, was presented to a large sample of Flemish psychiatric nurses, working in psychiatric wards of general hospitals and in psychiatric hospitals. The scale represents different aspects of the job situation: administrative organizational issues, staff conflict, limited resources, scheduling issues, negative patient characteristics and staff performance.
The results are discussed, and the data are linked to theoretical considerations of job-stress and burnout in psychiatric nursing.
Possible implications for the prevention of stress and burnout are shortly mentioned.*

1197
EFFECT OF STRESS ON OPIOID LEVELS IN POST-TRAUMATIC STRESS DISORDER (PTSD)
Ana Hitri and Mark B. Hamner
Department of Psychiatry, Medical College of GA.
Augusta, GA. 30912 USA

In view of PTSD as a form of conditioning response with the implicated endogeneous opioids, we have studied the stress response in animals and humans in relation to Beta endorphin (BE) plasma levels. Rats (38) were trained in a two-way shuttle avoidance paradigm and after the last training session they were subjected to restraint stress, along with the untrained rats (16). After the stress test they were decapitated and their blood collected for BE assay. In the human study 7 male combat veterans with PTSD and 8 control subjects were exposed to maximal excercise (ME) in a treadmill test. Blood was collected at rest and following ME. In the conditioned avoiding rats the baseline BE levels were 2.5 fold lower than in the controls. In humans, the resting BE levels were comparable between groups. In animals exposure to stress elevated BE levels by 360% in the avoiding and by 73% in the controls. In humans, the PTSD patients had a 492% and the controls 292% elevation in BE following ME. The data indicates that both the conditioned animals and the PTSD patients exhibited a higher magnitude of increase in plasma BE levels secondary to acute stress than the controls.

Session 185 Free Communications:
Psychotherapy in theory and practice

1198
A PSYCHOANALYTICAL APPROACH TO THE SYMPTOM IN FACTICIOUS ORGANIC DISORDERS
Christian PY, Marianne BAUDIN, Silla CONSOLI
Hôpital BROUSSAIS - Paris - FRANCE

The detailed case-report of four subjects presenting facticious organic disorders, completed by the results of personality projective tests (Rorschach and T.A.T.) allows the proposal of a psychodynamic conception of symptom formation. These cases concerned a facticious dermatitis, a lymphoedema of a finger due to the use of a tourniquet, and covert ingestion of anti-vitamine K, in one patient, and of anti-hypertensive in another. The four subjects presented severe personality disorders, dominated by difficulties in mental elaboration and by dynamics of relationship underlined by aggressive sado-masochistic drives. In these subjects, an oral complex of the cannibalistic type, close to the melancholic incorporation process, could occur within the body space, the lost object being embodied in the facticious physical disorder. The symptom formation could respond to a simple figuration (Darstellung), as described by Freud in the hysterical attack, rather than to a representation activity (Vorstellung).
The facticious physical symptom could thus be considered as an acted equivalent of a hysterical conversion, conveying a subject's inability to represent conflicts with traumatic value in a merely imginary mode, on the bodily scene.

1199
A NEW FORMULATION OF PSYCHOSIS AS OBSERVED IN JUNGIAN ANALYSIS

Dr. Murat KEMALOĞLU
Private practice in jungian analysis.

Jungian analysis reveals three major states during prepsychotic period that have marked differences from each other. I. The State of Anhedonia 2. The State of Pananxiety 3. The State of Apocalypse.

It is through overpowering anxiety that a person succumbs to psychosis. Anxiety has not an object. It is free floating. In the world of dreams there is no anxiety, but there is fear. The fear in dream is felt as anxiety in consciousness. The dream world is an underworld for the survival of the fittest. If the dream ego can not survive in his world, it escapes into consciousness. Psychosis is the hernia of the dream ego. Dream ego and conscious ego are the symbiotic identical twins of the psyche whose relationship resemble mythological divine twins. They normally have symbiotic vertical existence. However they exist horizontally in the consciousness during psychosis, in this case dream ego instead of being the autonomous soul image of man in the unconscious world becomes an antagonistic spiritual double in the conscious world.

A peculiar onset of psychosis is depicted after a dream in which the conscious ego of the dreamer enters into the dream world during dreaming. The dreamer loses his identity with the dream ego by falling into a state of participation mystique with the whole dream world.

Ending of a psychotic episode requires the restoration of the vertical symbiosis between dream ego and conscious ego, and dream ego's strength in the dream world.

1200
PERSPECTIVES FOR PSYCHIATRY IN XXI CENTURY - PSYCHODYNAMIC PSYCHOTHERAPY
Thome JT., Tarelli E., Ferreira V., Grimberg S., Cury B.
Instituto Sedis Sapientiae - Sao Paulo, Brazil

The XXth Century has accompanied the excessive importance given to specialization ended by breaking up the complete being who is our patient. Psychodynamic Psychotherapy proposes for work to be executed in the area of mental health in the XXI Century. Psychodynamics consider the man as a bio-psychosocial entity who lives in relation with other beings.
In such a context, self-knowledge and a knowledge of Psychoanalytic Theory are basic tools for the work of the practitioner in mental health area. Therefore, if the disease is the individual's last attempt to maintain a link with reality and the transference is the perception of this relation, Psychodynamic Psychotherapy proposes to, through the therapeutic relationship understand this "link-disease", establishing, for this purpose, a psychodynamic diagnostic, and after this is done, plot an appropriate treatment.

1201
SCHIZOPHRENIC EXPERIENCES-UNDERSTANDING THROUGH PSYCHODYNAMIC APPROACH
G.S.Gekas, K.Papaioannou, N.A.Kokantzis
1st Psychiatric Clinic, Aristotelion University, Thessaloniki, Greece.

We present the case of the patient I.M., male, 33 years old, who is under treatment in our clinic. He was admitted for the fifth time in 1985 under the diagnosis of "Mixed schizophrenic and affective psychosis". According to our view, the collected material from the detailed protocols during the consecutive sessions with the patient in the framework of the supporting psychotherapy, reassures the theory of the Developing Model, which is based on the principles of Edith Jacobson and Margaret Mahler about the first months of the individual's life.
Our intention, by presenting this case, is to promote the understanding and the therapeutic approach of the schizophrenic experiences.-

1202
Empirical evaluation of psychological defense mechanisms in a clinical population
H. Schauenburg, E. Leibing, G. Schüssler;
Abteilung für Psychosomatik und Psychotherapie der Universität D-3400 Göttingen, FRG

There is a long tradition in the clinical assessment of conscious derivates of psychological defense mechanisms. Severe methodological problems had to be overcome and are – however – still inherent. Vaillant et al. (1986) stated a hierarchy of certain patterns of "defensive styles", labeled as "mature" ("coping mechanisms"), "intermediate" and "immature". Bond et al. (1983, 1986) previously were able to show a relationship between psychological deense mechanisms and ego-development. Among other instruments they used a selfadministered "Defense Style Questionnaire". They could not find a correlation between DSM III-diagnosis and defense styles. Larger empirical confirmations of these findings in clinical populations do not exist. We studied a sample of 180 patients of an psychosomatic-psychotherapeutic out-patient clinic and consultation-liaison service and a non-patient sample of 100 medical students. A reduced version of the Bond Questionnaire was applied. The study aimed at the investigation of the taxonomy by Vaillant et al. and the research by Bond et al.
Results are presented and discussed on methodological and clinical implications. Furthermore relationships between multi-axial diagnosis, proposed therapeutic intervention and defense styles found by factor analysis are presented.

1203
PSYCHOANALYTIC PSYCHOTHERAPY IN ADULTS
HADJI H, KOUROS J.

Society for Psychological Psychiatry of Adult and Child(E.PS.PS.E.P)ATHENS-GREECE
Adults with psychological problems are consulting usually in Greece when their problems become very urgent and they interrupt the therapy as soon as they feel better.They also interrupt the treatment if this takes more time than they judge enough for thir ilness.
We are trying to explain this phenomenon on the basis of socio-cultural particularities of life's "reality"in Greece;and demonstrate the fact that an abnormal behaviour for some country's "civilisation" may be absolutely normal in the context of a different "civilisation".
We believe that personnality's defensive mechanisms are used in a very different percentage according to the socio-cultural standards of the environment to which someone has to be adapted.
We are presenting some cases to elucidate our point of view.

1204
ADLERIAN THEORY AND PRACTICE WITH THE PSYCHOTIC PATIENT
Anglesio A., Farina S.
Private psychotherapists, Torino, Italy

Adlerian and neo-adlerians theories, such as those of Shulman and Parenti supply us with a conception of the mind which is not so well known as the Freudian one.
Subjectifying, mind as a field, teleology, fictionalism, compensation, life style as the creative power which answers to the environment are some of the conceptions of adlerian theory. The authors will show how they may help us to deal with the psychotic patient in a larger setting both in individual psychotherapy and in managing rehabilitation programs in public mental health service.
Some examples will be used for a short demonstration of the adlerian therapist's style of working with the patient both in private practice and in managing rehabilitation programs for chronic patients in a Psychiatric Hospital.

Session 186 Free Communications: Mood stabilizers and antimanic drugs other than lithium

1205

CARBAMAZEPINE VS LITHIUM IN BIPOLAR DISORDER

Trevor Silverstone, Neil Coxhead, John Cookson
St Bartholomews and The London Hospitals, London
England

Of 31 patients with a DSM-III-R diagnosis of bipolar disorder, aged 23-66 in good physical health, who had been taking lithium (Li) 15 were randomly allocated to receive carbamazepine (CBZ) and 16 to continue on Li under double-blind conditions. No other psychotropic medication was allowed. At monthly intervals the Bech-Rafaelson Mania Scale and the Hamilton Depression Scale were completed and side-effects noted. Thyroid function and renal function were measured at 0, 6 and 12 months.
14 completed 1 year (7 CBZ, 7 Li). 13 (6CBZ,7 Li) required additional treatment or hospitalisation: for mania - 5 CBZ, 5 Li; depression - 1 CBZ; mixed affective state - 2 Li. 1 Li patient was non-compliant. 2 on CBZ were withdrawn following a rash, 1 on Li because of diarrhoea. All 7 CBZ completers remained virtually symptom-free; of the 7 Li completers, 1 became mildly depressed and 1 mildly manic during the year. On CBZ there were initial complaints of drowsiness (6) dizziness (6) nausea (5); 1 patient showed a mild elevation of alkaline phosphatase at 6 months, 1 a transient drop in WBC and 1 slight hyponatremia. 4 on Li complained of thirst and polyuria.
CBZ appears comparable in efficacy and tolerability to Li in the prophylaxis of bipolar disorder.

1206

CLONAZEPAM IN ACUTE MANIA AND MANIC SPECTRUM DISEASES
Guy Chouinard, Luc Turnier, Linda Beauclair, Lawrence Annable, Naomi Holobow

Allan Memorial Institute, Louis-H. Lafontaine Hospital and McGill University, Montreal, Canada

Clonazepam (CZM) has been considered as an alternative to neuroleptic medications in the treatment of acute mania. We report the results of three studies of its use in acute mania.
In the first study, twelve acutely manic patients were randomly assigned in a double-blind crossover design to CZM and lithium carbonate. CZM proved more effective than lithium in controlling the symptoms of mania and necessitated less use of haloperidol prn.
In the second study, CZM was compared on a double-blind basis to haloperidol in the first week of treatment. During the second week, all patients were given lithium and during the following three weeks, CZM or haloperidol was decreased. In this study (still ongoing), only one patient terminated the trial prematurely.
In the third study, I.M. CZM was compared on a double-blind basis to I.M. haloperidol in a 2-hour rapid tranquilization treatment of agitated patients with manic spectrum disease. All patients completed the study, and there were no significant differences between the drugs in terms of therapeutic efficacy.

1207

A STUDY OF ANTIMANIC EFFECTS OF VERAPAMIL AND NIFEDIPINE
A.K.Vohra, A.K.Gupta, D.K.Puri, Deptt. of Psychiatry, Medical College, Rohtak,India.

Manic episodes are associated with transient increase in serum calcium. Lithium shares cationic properties with calcium and it alters its absorption and metabolism. Similarities are found between actions of lithium,verapamil and Nifedipine in several ways in decreasing spontaneous sinoatrial depolarization,inhibiting release of TSH and anti diuretic hormone and blocking adenyl cyclase activity. Because of these relationships it was hypothesized that verapamil and nifedipine would exert antimanic effects and the present study was undertaken.

A double blind study to see the efficacy of verapamil and nifedipine in cases meeting DSM-III criteria for manic episodes were randomly distributed in four groups of 15 patients each. All these patients were admitted and put on verapamil 80mg, Nifedipine 20mg and lithium carbonate 375mg q.i.d.each and on placebo. Young Rating Scale for mania to assess the severity of illness was administered on 0,7,14 & 21 days. Regular serum lithium levels were estimated. There were significant differences in relieving symptoms with all three drugs between day 0 and day 21. (P/ 0.01)showing their significant antimanic activities. No major side effects observed during the study.

1208

THE THERAPEUTICAL VALUE OF CARBAMAZEPINE IN NONRESPONSIVE PSYCHOSES
Penka Christova, Christo Nicolov, Nicola Karakanev, Georgi Mitev
Higher Military Medical Institute, Sofia, Bulgaria

21 patients with affective disorder (noninfluenced by neuroleptic and antidepressant therapy) were treated with carbamazepine (600 mg) in the acute phase of the disease or as prophylaxis.
The catamnestic period of following is 4 years. We found a good therapeutical and prophylactic effect in 3/4 of the patients. The manic and mixed psychoses are influenced better.

1209

Carbamazepine (CBZ) in Brief Reactive Psychoses (BRP).
R.Quartesan,P.Moretti,L.Natalicchi,P.Borri
Psychiatric Clinic University of Perugia
Our experience concerns the use of CBZ in out patients (pt) departement.We used CBZ in BRP meaning the historical relationship between psychoses and temporal epilepsy (Trimble 1984) Over the last 2 years we treated for a minimum of 2 months and a maximumof 12 months with CBZ 8 pt with BRP. There were 2 drop out (hospitalization). For 5 pt there was a complete remission of simptomatology and 1 slight improvement.E-EG and CT scans result normal in all pt. In particular we noted an improvement rela ted to hostility,dyscontrol, instability and interpersonal agitation in agreement with Sramek et Al. (1988).Among the side effects we had only 1 case of leukopenia and 1 case of cutaneus allergy.2 pt after withdrawl of CBZ continue to have weekly supportive talks with psychiatrist.In conclusion it sometimes seem possible to improve the pharmacological prognosis to a psychotherapeutic prognosis.
REFERENCES
Sramek J. et Al.: Am.J.Psychiat.145,748, 1988
Trimble M.R.:Act.Psych.Scand.313,9,Suppl. 1984

1210

AN EFFICACY STUDY COMPARING CARBAMAZEPINE AND CHLORPROMAZINE IN MANIC PATIENTS.
VERİMLİ MD,ARKONAÇ MD,BEYAZYÜREK MD,KOÇAK MD.
BAKIRKÖY STATE MENTAL HOSPITAL ISTANBUL TURKEY.
To compare efficacy and safety of carbamazepine with chlorpromazine in moderately and severe manic pa tients a 6week randomized,double-blind crossover study was performed.Subjects(24women,38men)between ages of 18-65yrs who met DSM-III criteria and requi red to have total score of at least 21 on 9 item of IMPS were included.Those with history of serious in ternal disease,substance use,allergic to drugs who received ECT,antimanic drugs within the previous 3 weeks and pregnant women were excluded.Side effects vital signs,drug compliance,sleep were evaulated da ily.IMPS(manic items),ECG,routine blood tests were performed at the begining and once a week there af ter.Dose ranges were 525-1750mg/day and 600-2200mg/ day for chlorpromazine and carbamazepine respective ly.Patients were cross over at the 3rd week.Because of severe side effects 3,uncontrollable manic exci tation 8,uncompliance 14,total 25 patients termina ted the study prematurely.Significant differences (p .001)favouring Chlorpromazine at the end of 3rd week disappeared at the end of study.Other than 1 coma,1 severe ataxia(carbamazepine) and 1 case of high fever(40C chlorpromazine)no side effects was considered to be serious.Carbamazepine exerts an an timanic effect in moderately severe manic cases. It's antimanic efficacy appears to be equal to Chlorpromazine at the end of a 6weeks trial in 600-2200mg/day dose range with favourably comparable side effects.

1211

DROGAS GABAERGICAS EN LA TERAPIA Y PROFILAXIS DE LA MANIA

A. Moríñigo, J. Martin, I. Mateo, D. Noval.

S. Psiquiatría. H. Univ. Valme. Sevilla. España.

En las útimas décadas se han investigado los efectos psicotrópicos de las sustancias anticonvulsivantes. La búsqueda de alternativas terapéuticas en los pacientes afectivos que no responden al tratamiento con sales de litio constituye un campo de gran interés. La neurotransmisión GABA se ha implicado en la patogenia de los trastornos afectivos (Emrich, 1980). Ciertos anticonvulsivos, agonistas GABA, como la carbamacepina (CBZ) y el valproato sódico (VAL), se han empleado con éxito en el tratamiento de la manía y depresión, y en la profilaxis de los trastornos afectivos bipolares (Emrich, 1983 y 1985; Post, 1986; Moríñigo, 1989).
Se presentan 17 casos de pacientes diagnosticados de Episodio Maníaco, segun los RDC (Spitzer, 1977), tratados 9 con CBZ y 8 con VAL. Se analiza la evolución clínica durante 18 días, de modo doble ciego, con la ENM (Beigel, 1971). Se monitorizan los niveles plasmaticos de ambas sustancias, y el perfil de cortisol plasmático (8 a.m. y 16 p.m.) de los casos tratados con VAL. Un 80% de pacientes presentó una mejoría clínica tras la primera semana del tratamiento, mantenida al final del estudio. Los pacientes respondedores son seguidos durante 2 años, observándose una recaída que requiere hospitalización, y otro caso con una fase hipomaníaca y un episodio depresivo leve que remiten con tratamiento ambulatorio.
Se analizan las variables clínicas que influyen en la mejoría. Los pacientes tratados con VAL presentan una secreción de cortisol normal.

Session 187 Free Communications:
Child abuse

1212

EFFECTS OF SEXUAL ABUSE ON CHILDREN

Irena Haughton, M.D. and Ruth P. Zager, M.D., Jefferson Medical College of Thomas Jefferson University Hospital, Philadelphia, Pennsylvania, U.S.A.

This paper reports on 290 children and adolescents who were seen in a special follow-up clinic for sexually abused children. Children from chaotic and disrupted families were more likely to become victims, as they searched for the attention and affection they had not received from their parents. These families, which usually consisted of multiple generations all living together without stable paternal figures, often produced children who were impulsive, overactive, and had poor judgment. Mothers who themselves had been sexually abused, generally had poor parenting skills, at times abused their own children, and often did not protect them adequately from abusers. Ninety percent of the abusers were family members or were persons known to the children prior to the abuse.

1213
THE ABANDONING IMPULSE IN HUMAN PARENTS

James B. Hoyme, M.D., Pennsylvania Hospital
Philadelphia, U.S.A.

The hostility of parents toward children is an insufficiently recognized force in family life and personality development. An "abandoning impulse" in parents is postulated.

Two psychiatric case vignettes illustrate the theme. The childhood experiences of these women are reminiscent of familiar folktales, i.e., Hansel and Gretel and Snow White.

Parental hostility toward children abounds in folktales. However, in The Uses of Enchantment, Bettelheim asserts that these stories were made by benevolent adults for the psychological benefit of children. An alternative view is that these stories give disguised expression to adult impulses toward injuring or abandoning children, impulses also in abundant evidence in the work of Aeschylus and Sophocles.

Certain similarities exist between folktales and dreams. If one assumes that a folktale is a dream of family life, can the meanings in the dream be illuminated by discerning the identity of the dreamer? The heuristic merit of this line of inquiry is shown with examples which highlight parental hostility toward children.

Thus, psychotherapy, Greek drama, and a reading of folktales as dreams of family life point toward an insufficiently recognized reservoir of adult hostility toward children.

1214
CHILD PHYSICAL ABUSE IN KOREA

Kwang-iel Kim, M.D., Ph.D., Hanyang University, Seoul, Korea.

Current status and problem of child physical abuse(CPA) were reviewed for clinical and social arousal. Incidence of CPA is high: 97-98% of children were battered at least once in their life; 66% per year; 46% a month; 18% a week. The severely battered is 7-8%. And 5.8% was sexually abused; 1.9% being pressed to exposure sexual organs, 0.8% being caressed, 1.7% being kissed and 1.4% being raped. CPA is more serious and prevalent in the lower social strata, in the broken family and in families of large sibling size. CPA occurs with multiple family violences. Family's cohesion and excessive attachment to the blood-relatedness, vertical relation between parent and child, early parental overprotection and later excessive demanding, authoritative and meddling attitude of parent over child, toleration of violence in the family and society, a lack of public educational program regarding CPA, and poor community support system could be attributed to the higher rate of CPA. Public education for full under standing of CPA and for the change of attitude, and establishment of community support system would be an urgent issue.

1215
CHILD SEXUAL ABUSE: EFFECTS & TREATMENT

C. Stavrakaki, M.D., E. Williams, M.S.W.
Royal Ottawa Hospital, Ottawa, Canada

Sexual victimization of children is a relatively new area of investigation, although the problem has historical roots in ancient times. Initial studies have been directed towards identification and etiology. One reason for this delayed interest in treatment may be the controversy regarding the effects of child sexual abuse. It is only recently that treatment issues of victims of sexual abuse are becoming a matter of concern. In many communities the importance of reporting child abuse cases has been well publicized and has resulted in a greater number of abuse cases being identified. However, once identified, treatment programs are found lacking.

This presentation will review the effects of child abuse for the victim, and outline the targets for intervention. A review of selected treatment methods and programs that address these issues, as well as some case studies, will be presented.

1216
PHYSICAL ABUSE OF CHILDREN IN FAMILY
S. Boyadjieva, D. Terziev, M. Shoylecova
Medical Academy, Child Psychiatric Clinic
Sofia, Bulgaria

The hospital records of 162 consecutivelly admitted children with DSM-III-R defined emotional and/or behaviour disorders were investigated, out of which 17 cases of physical abuse were found.

In all cases the perpetrator was only one of the parents, and only in one case the batterer was the mother. Physical abuse was associated with the sex of child/male/, with the presence of psychological child maltreatment and parental alcoholism, but not with "anomalous parenting situation" in ICD-X' terms. The family pathology and some maladaptive parental personality traits or disorders may "convert" culturally accepted forms of punishment into physical child abuse.

1217

EL SINDROME DEL NIÑO MALTRATADO EN LA EDAD DE LA ADOLESCENCIA

VOGE HARMS, DONALD O.
EJERCICIO PRIVADO, MERIDA, YUCATAN, MEXICO

Este trabajo no describe una entidad noeologica nueva. Describe lo que ocurre en el Sindrome del Niño Maltratado al llegar a la edad de la adolescencia. Esto es un tiempo de cambios fisicos y emocionales cuando el adolescente cuestiona las condiciones de vida a que ha estado sujeto hasta este momento. Describe la etiologia y dinamica del sindrome en la inversion de papeles que ocurre en este momento con las secuelas probables para cada individuo. A la vez, discute las probabilidades de exito del tratamiento psicoterapeutico y su posible importancia para cada individuo. Este trabajo sugiere que es en la adolescencia el periodo mas critico para inhibir nuevos casos del Sindrome del Niño Maltratado.

1218

PSYCHOPATHOLOGY AMONGST THE ADOLESCENT VICTIMS OF FATHER-SON INCESTS.

Syed Arshad Husain, M.D., FRCP(C), FRC Psych.
University of Missouri-Columbia

History of father-daughter incest is very commonly encountered amongst the girls hospitalized in a psychiatric facility and not all of them report being adversely effected emotionally to such an experience. The father-son incest is however very rare but the associated psychopathology is very severe. In this paper the author reports the findings of a study of homosexual incest. Of one thousand consecutive admissions to an adolescent psychiatric hospital over five year period one hundred of 417 (23.9%) girls reported being the victim of incest, while only 11 of 583 (1.88%) boys reported being homosexually victimized by their fathers. The most astounding findings are that all adolescent victims had strong homicidal fantasies towards their fathers. Six (56%) of them actually were successful in killing the perpetrators of incest. All subjects were severely depressed and expressed strong suicidal tendencies particularly those who could not carry out their desire to kill their abuser. One adolescent made a serious suicide attempt by shooting himself in the chest. The author discusses the dynamics underlying these findings and makes some suggestions for intervention.

1219

The Borderline Diagnosis in Adolescence

Ana Lucia G. Maciel, M.D., Liliana Goibelman, M.D., Matilde Dorfman, M.D.
Universidade Federal do Rio Grande do Sul - Department of Psychiatry

The authors present two clinical cases of borderline adolescents, describing their symptoms, and clinical presentation. They also discuss the impact of child abuse (physical and/or sexual and/or negligence) in the pathogenesis of their clinical entity.

Issues about preventive measures applicable in other cases and/or populations are discussed.

Session 188 New Research:
Non-pharmacological treatment for affective disorders

1220

BRIGHT LIGHT BENEFITS NONSEASONAL DEPRESSION

Daniel F. Kripke, M.D., Daniel J., Mullaney, M.S.,
J. Christian Gillin, M.D.
Department of Psychiatry, M-003 UCSD
La Jolla, CA 92093 USA

We have now completed four placebo-controlled studies which show that bright light treatments benefit major depressive disorders which are not seasonal. The patients have been veterans (almost all male) hospitalized on a research ward in a Veterans Administration Medical Center. In the most recent study, 25 patients completed one week of treatment with bright cool-white fluorescent light $\geq$1500 lux, given mainly from 2000-3000 in the evening. In parallel, 26 patients were randomly assigned to control placebo treatment with dim red light < 50 lux. The bright light treatment produced a drop in Hamilton and Beck depression scores from baseline; further, some relapse occurred within 2 days of discontinuation. The reduction of depression ratings was 17.8% better with bright white light than with the dim red light placebo ($p<0.023$). Bright light appeared to produce a much greater benefit than can be achieved with antidepressant drugs in a similar time frame. The long-term benefits and risks of bright light for nonseasonal depressives have not yet been studied. Futher controlled comparisons are needed before bright light treatment can be recommended for nonseasonal patients outside research settings.

1221

THE EFFECTS OF LIGHT THERAPY IN MAJOR DEPRESSION

Praško,J., Seifertová,D., Prašková,H., Filip,V., Höschl,C. and Karen,P.

Psychiatric Research Institute, Prague, Czechoslovakia

Forty inpatients with major depression were treated with early morning light therapy applied for 3 subsequent days during a placebo period. Thereafter they were treated with either maprotiline or levoprotiline for 21 days.
The therapeutic response to phototherapy as well as to antidepressants was evaluated on the MADRS and HAM-D rating scales. Furthermore, 24 hour profile of body temperature was measured before and after the light therapy and on the 21-st day of the treatment with maprotiline or levoprotiline.
The results based on evaluation of 40 patients will be presented at the Congress.

1222

LIGHT THERAPY AS A MAINTENANCE TREATMENT SEASONAL AFFECTIVE DISORDER
P. Sakkas, M.D., H.Lahmeyer, M.D., C. Eastman*
Univ. of Illinois at Chicago,
*Rush-Presbyterian-St.Luke's Medical Center
It is known that the effect of light therapy in seasonal affective disorder (SAD) are short lasting. We report our results of continuous bright light treatment throughout the winter and spring. After completion of two weeks phototherapy and two weeks of placebo, patients were evaluated. Eight patients who responded favorable to bright lights (a 50% or more decrease in Hamilton Depression Scale(HDS), entered the study. Five of them received every day light therapy and three were used as controls. After the two weeks "washout" period, a unique tendency toward rebound of symptomatology was noticed. The mean score of the modified HDS reached the 21.6±6.3. However, after two weeks reinstitution of the light therapy the score was decreased to the same level as before (16±6.2) and following another two weeks of light treatment the symptomatology was practically absent(8±4.6). The score remained at the same low levels till the discontinuation of the treatment in mid April. Thereafter, only one patient complained for symptom relapse. On the other hand, 2 out of 3 controls did complain of reoccurrence of SAD symptoms. Our preliminary results indicate that light therapy should be continued until the end of spring.

1223

IS COGNITIVE THERAPY SPECIFIC FOR DEPRESSION?
George E. Murphy, M.D. & Richard D. Wetzel, Ph.D.
Washington University School of Medicine
St. Louis, Missouri, U.S.A.

The close agreement in outcome of seven studies comparing Cognitive Behavioral Therapy (CBT) to antidepressant medication (TCA) suggests the question of specificity versus nonspecificity in time limited treatment. We chose Relaxation Training (RT) as a non-cognitive, non-pharmacologic control for this comparison, since it lacked credentials as a treatment for depression. Thirty-seven outpatients with mild to moderate uncomplicated major depressive disorder were randomly assigned to CBT, RT, or TCA for 16 weeks treatment. Three patients dropped out of RT, five from TCA. At termination, nine of 11 CBT patients scored $\leq$ 9 on the BDI, as did eight of 11 in RT and only one of seven in TCA treatment.
The near parity in outcome between CBT and RT fails to support the specificity hypothesis of CBT. A nonspecific mode of action, such as the patient's expectation of being well at the end of a specified term of treatment, is not rejected. It is, of course, possible that RT is a powerful treatment in its own right. The poor showing by TCA is consistent with the claim of Stewart, et al.* (1983) that depressed patients scoring below 14 on the HRSD respond poorly to antidepressant medications, but may to placebo.

*Arch. Gen. Psychiatry 40:202-207;1983.

1224

TECHNIQUE DE RELACHEMENT PAR BIOFEEDBACK DES MALADES AVEUGLES

Fernandes da Fonseca, Antonio - Portugal

Resumé: L'expérience clinique nous a démontré que les techniques psychothérapeutiques les plus connues trouvent des dificultés à obtenir un succès raisonable dans des situations psychiatriques associées à des phénomènes de privation sensoriel.

En réalité, la structure et l'intégrité du corps ("self corporel") jouent un rôle très important dans l'organisation de ce qu'on appelle "self mental" et quelque défaut au niveau des fonctions corporel peut exercer une influence negative dans la compréhension et tentative de reorganization de quelques fonctions psychiques.

Telles difficultés ont été prouvées par toutes les techniques psycothérapeutiques utilisées dans des déficients sensoriels, y compris les aveugles, même avec les techniques de ce qu'on appele "immagerie mental".

Dans le sens de surmonter ces difficultés, nous sommes en train d'utiliser dans notre Departement de Santé Mental la technique du "biofeedback" dans des malades aveugles ayant des problèmes psychiatriques et dont les résultats nous voulons présenter.

Session 189   Video:
Art therapy. Insomnia

1225

ART THERAPY & PSYCHIATRY
DR N D MINTON
DEPARTMENT OF PSYCHIATRY, ST PETER'S HOSPITAL,
GUILDFORD ROAD, CHERTSEY, SURREY. KT16 OPZ

The University of London Audio-Visual Centre has collaborated with the department of Psychological Medicine at St Peter's Hospital, Chertsey, Surrey, and the Art Psychotherapy Unit at Goldsmiths' College to produce a new educational videotape. The video demonstrates how a holistic approach to visual Art Therapy is effective in the rehabilitation of patients in a General Hospital.

Several patients talk about their work, and there are many examples shown of their paintings, drawings and sculptures. The discussion emphasises the importance of the relationship between the Psychiatrist and Art Therapist for effective therapy, in the context of modern General Psychiatry and Psychotherapy.

The programme is based on a paper on Art Therapy by Dr N D Minton, who gives an introduction. Professor Christopher Cornford, emeritus Professor of the Royal College of Art, chairs the final discussion between Dr N D Minton, Consultant Psychiatrist and Tutor at St Peter's Hospital, Diane Waller, who is the head of the Art Psychotherapy Unit at the University of London Goldsmiths' College and Joanne Weller, an Art Therapist at St Peter's Hospital. The programme was directed for the University of London Audio-Visual Centre by Trevor A Scott.

Copies of this VHS are obtainable from ULAVC, North Wing Studios, Senate House, Malet St, LONDON, WC1E 7JZ.

1226

TRAINING TAPE FOR THE MANAGEMENT OF INSOMNIA IN GENERAL PRACTICE
Waldvogel, F.A., Hovaguimian, Th., Dubuis, J., Naville, P.A., Raetzo, M.A., and Riba, F.J.
Departments of Internal Medicine and Psychiatry, University of Geneva, Switzerland.
This is a two part video-tape accompanied by a manual, suitable for use in tutored seminars or in a self-teaching setting.
Part 1 (18') presents an interviewing scheme that elicits the criteria to diagnose the presence of insomnia, v/s other sleep disorders, and to assess its cause, (physical, drug, psychiatric, behavioral or multifactorial aetiology). This scheme, designed to meet the non-specialist competence and the general practice consultation constraints, is illustrated with live interviews.
Part 2 (17') teaches a set of intervention methods for the various types of insomnia, including patient education, appropriate use of psychotropic drugs, management of cases addicted to hypnotics, non-pharmacological treatments of behavioral insomnias and demonstration of general doctor-patient interpersonal skills.
The manual provides complementary details, which interact with the tape, including mnemothecnic outlines, screening and monitoring tools, and a glossary of terms.

Sunday
15th October 1989

Session 190 — Plenary:
Current biological research in schizophrenia

1227
CENTRAL NERVOUS SYSTEM ASSESSMENT IN SCHIZOPHRENIA

Robert Cancro, M.D.
NYU Medical Center, N.Y.C.

Independent of the etiology of the schizophrenic disorders - be they experiential or genetically preprogrammed - the pathogenesis must involve the central nervous system. All of the behavioral manifestations of these disorders are expressed through the central nervous system. The study of the nervous system, therefore, becomes etiologically neutral and can allow the study of pathogenesis without the emotionally overcharged issue of etiology.

Historically, the study of the nervous system could not be done adequately particularly during the lifetime of the individual. More recently a number of techniques, including brain imaging modalities, have emerged. These techniques allow the study of the nervous system in the living, functioning organism. They allow not only vertical snapshots but sustained motion pictures of normal brain activity.

This presentation will review some of the recent developments in CNS assessment including their contributions and methodologic limitations. New directions for future research will also be discussed.

1228
A CONCEPT OF THE FUNCTION AND LOCUS OF THE PSYCHOSIS GENE

T. J. Crow, Clinical Research Centre, Northwick Park Hospital, Harrow, HA1 3UJ, U.K.

A recent post mortem study has shown that lateral ventricular enlargement in schizophrenia (by contrast with Alzheimer's disease) is selective to the temporal horn, and left side of the brain. This indicates that the disease process directly involves the determinants of cerebral asymmetry; the gene could be the "cerebral dominance gene".
A gene locus in the pseudo-autosomal (exchange) region of the sex chromosomes was proposed to account for (i) the excess of sex chromosome aneuploidies in psychotic populations (ii) concordance by sex in siblings with psychosis. The predictions that sibling pairs with psychosis (i) will be concordant for sex with paternal inheritance, and (ii) will share alleles above expectation at the telomeric DXYS14 locus have been confirmed.
It is concluded that psychosis may be due to an anomaly of the cerebral dominance gene located in the pseudo-autosomal region.
Crow TJ (1988) Brit.J.Psychiat. 153:675-683.
Crow TJ, Colter N, Brown R, Bruton CJ, Johnstone EC (1988) Schiz. Res. 1:155-156.
Crow TJ, DeLisi LE, Johnstone EC (1989) Brit. J. Psychiat. (in press).
Collinge J et al. (1989) Human Gene Mapping 10, (in press).

1229
CURRENT STATUS OF PET-IMAGING IN SCHIZOPHRENIA
Goran Sedvall
Dept. of Psychiatry and Psychology, Karolinska Institute, Stockholm, Sweden

PET-scanning is an indirect imaging technique that allows the analysis by time of the distribution of labelled molecules within the living human brain. In studies in schizophrenic patients this technique has been used to evaluate regional metabolic rates and characteristics of D2-dopamine receptors. PET-determinations of regional glucose metabolism in schizophrenic patients have given highly variable results, but several studies indicate reduced metabolic rates in a number of brain regions. On the basis of previous studies that have several methodological limitations four hypotheses have emerged: 1) hypofrontality, 2) left-right asymmetry, 3) left temporal lobe hypometabolism, 4) general reduction of metabolism. Quantitative PET-measurements of D2-dopamine receptor characteristics have also given discrepant results. Either elevated D2-dopamine receptors or no change in the number of such receptors have been reported. This plenary lecture will deal with possible methodological limitations of previous PET-scan studies and also give an outline of the recent technical developments of this methodology, that may further increase its potential for analyzing functional brain alterations in schizophrenia.

1230
SCHIZOPHRENIA - NEW HYPOTHESES AND TREATMENTS

William E. Bunney, Jr., M.D.
University of California, Irvine

New treatment approaches to schizophrenia will be presented along with research concerning the mechanisms of actions of atypical neuroleptics. Hypotheses will be reviewed concerning the interaction of dopamine, excitatory amino acids and GABA neurons. The possible role of the thalamus in schizophrenia will be discussed along with the description of relevant neuronal circuitry systems and their implications for understanding the psychotic process. Contributions of brain imaging and restriction fragment length polymorphism technology as they relate to our present and future understanding of schizophrenia will be briefly reviewed.

Session 191 — Plenary:
Major international and national diagnostic classification issues

1231
CLASSIFICATION OF MENTAL DISORDERS IN THE ICD – AN HISTORICAL PERSPECTIVE
Erik Stromgren
Institute of Psychiatric Demography,
Aarhus Psychiatric Hospital, Risskov, Denmark

The ICD had its origin in the "International Classification of Causes of Death (adopted by the International Statistical Institute in 1893) which later was expanded to include diseases and injuries. Between World Wars I and II the Office of Hygiene of the League of Nations participated in the development of the classification, and in 1948 WHO became responsible. In the first post-war editions psychiatry had an unsatisfactory position, as illustrated by Stengel's classic review (1959) of existing classifications, which became the starting point for the ICD 8 and ICD 9. The psychiatric sections of these were unique among the sections, being accompanied by detailed "glossaries". The preparations for the ICD 10 have been greatly influenced by the occurrence of the DSM III, which, although being a national classification, has gained wide international attention and application, thus making compatibility between the two classifications desirable. One basic feature of ICD should be its applicability in all cultures and by all kinds of mental health workers.

1232
DSM-IV: Work in Progress

Frances, A., Pincus, H., Widiger, T., Davis, W. Cornell University Medical College

The authors present an overview of the on-going work in progress on DSM-IV. After a brief historical review, we discuss the principles and multiple purposes of the DSM-IV effort and outline the three stages of its empirical documentation: systematic literature reviews, analysis of unpublished data sets, and field trials. Next, we discuss several of the basic conceptual issues that are implicit in revising a nomenclature. These include the definition of mental disorder, the epistemology of psychiatric diagnosis, the balance between multiple diagnosis and differential diagnosis, the use of categorical and dimensional models of classification, and issues involved in the construction of criteria sets. Finally, we summarize the most important specific questions being reviewed by each of the DSM-IV Work Groups.

1233
CURRENT TRENDS IN FRENCH DIAGNOSTIC PATTERNS

PULL C.B., Centre Hospitalier de Luxembourg, 4 Rue Barblé, 1210 Luxembourg - LUXEMBOURG, et Université Louis Pasteur, Strasbourg, FRANCE

In 1983, at the World Congress of Psychiatry in Vienna, the present author presented a number of papers comparing French and International Classification Schemes. The general conclusion of those comparisons was that French diagnostic patterns did differ substantially from other classification schemes in several major areas, concerning in particular non-affective psychoses and mood disorders.

The situation has changed considerably during the last six years, owing to a renewed interest in psychiatric nosology and a tendency of French psychiatrists to adopt internationally accepted diagnostic patterns. In research settings, French clinicians now almost systematically refer to DSM-III or DSM-III-R. In addition, the successive drafts of ICD-10 have stirred considerable interest in the French psychiatric communitty.

On the whole, it seems highly probable that French psychiatrists will progressively abandon their national classification scheme and align with one or the other internationally recognized classification system.

1234
DIAGNOSTIC PATTERNS AND CLASSIFICATION PRACTICES IN PSYCHIATRY IN THE USSR

Tiganov A. S.
Institute of Clinical Psychiatry of the All Union Research Center of Mental Health Academy of Medical Sciences, Moscow, USSR

The presentation will discuss the basics of the national classification of psychiatric disorders which is traditionally based on nosological principles. The reasons for the conventions concerning certain rubrics of classification related to the extension of knowledge about the etiology and pathogenesis of some psychiatric disorders will be included. The main focus will be given to the problem of the classification of endogenous disorders and borderline states which has been the subject of much discussion. A commentary on certain chapters of ICD-10 will be given, particularly so far as they can be adapted to the Soviet national classification.

Session 192 Symposium:
Genetic aspects of affective disorders and schizophrenia

1235
GENE MAP IN PSYCHIATRY
Jan Wahlström
Department of Clinical Genetics
East Hospital
S-416 85 Göteborg, Sweden

There are 139 psychiatric diseases known with a possible genetic etiology. Out of these the location to chromosome is known in 36 cases. Examples of disorders with a known gene locations are Alzheimers disease 21q21-q221, Huntingtons disease 4p22-pter, Wilsons disease 13q14-q22, Depressive disorder 11p155, Manic depressive psychosis Xq27-q28, susceptibility for Schizophrenia 5q112-q133. A gene map of psychiatric disorders can be used for linkage analysis and identification of so called candidate genes. With knowledge of the gene sequence it is possible to find the responsible protein disturbed in the disorder and furthermore it is possible to find a suitable pharmacological agent to treatment of the actual disorder.

1236
GENETIC LINKAGE STUDIES IN AFFECTIVE DISORDERS AND SCHIZOPHRENIA
Kenneth K Kidd
Department of Human Genetics, Yale University School of Medicine, New Haven, Ct 06510, USA

Lingake studies are powerful tools for identifying segregating loci underlying the trait in psychiatric disorders. With informative markers most of the human genome will soon be covered. Large families suitable for studying linkage in affective disorders and schizophrenia are now available. The evidence for an X-linked and a chromosome 11 form of manic-depressive disorder is strong, but not yet proof.

In schizophrenia Sherrington et al. have recently identified linkage of markers on chromosome 5 in Icelandic and British families. Using a Swedish kindred segregating schizophrenia showed strong evidence of exclusion of linkage between schizophrenia and the same region of the proximal long arm of chromosome 5. Experiments testing linkage strategies to detect gentic heterogeneity within the phenotypes of affective disorders and schizophrenia are ongoing and hopefully more answers will be forthcoming in the near future.

1237
DIAGNOSTICS OF SCHIZOPHRENIA AND AFFECTIVE DISORDERS: A SWEDISH EXAMPLE
Lennart Wetterberg
Karolinska Institute, Department of Psychiatry, St. Göran's Hospital, Box 12500, S-112 81 Stockholm, Sweden

The studies indicate that an important genetic contribution is an aetiological fact both in affective disorders and schizophrenia. Reliable and valid diagnoses are essential for genetic linkage studies to have a successful result. Informative families suitable for studying linkage are also needed. The clinical data such as signs and symptoms, age of onset, pheotypic expression, penetrance and environmental factors and others are relevant and several sets of criteria will enable subtyping of affective disorder and schizophrenia according to different diagnostic systems. A polydiagnostic computerized programme based on case records, personal interviews and follow-up data, and an example from a large Swedish kindred with schizophrenia will be given. Clinical findings including cerebro-spinal fluid examination and magnetic resonance brain imaging in schizophrenia will also be presented.

1238
ICELANDIC FAMILIES SELECTED FOR LINKAGE STUDIES IN SCHIZOPHRENIA.
PÉTURSSON, H.[*], BRYNJÓLFSSON, J.[*], GURLING, H.[**] & SIGMUNDSSON, Th.[*].
[*]Department of Psychiatry, Borgarspitalinn, 108 Reykjavik, Iceland. [**]Molecular Psychiatry Laboratory, Academic Department of Psychiatry, University & Middlesex School of Medicine, London, U.K.

During the last few years a substantial number of families with high incidence of schizophrenia have been studied in Iceland. The pedigrees were selected specifically for linkage studies which have been a part of a collaborative U.K./Iceland research project into the genetics of mental illness.

The paper describes the population background characteristics in Iceland as well as methods of selection, diagnostic assessment, interview schedules and clinical aspects. The study chose to select high density pedigrees with shcizophrenia in at least 3 generations. Extensive pedigree tracing work aimed at selecting families without manic depression (bipolar disorder) present, as well as obtaining families in which there was only 1 possible source of shcizphrenia allele segregating into the kindred.

Linkage analysis of the first 5 families has identified a locus on chromosome 5 that confers susceptibility to the development of schizophrenia. The present state of the project will be discussed briefly.

Session 193 New Research:
Phychiatric aspects of HIV infection

1239

ANXIETY AND DEPRESSION IN HIV-INFECTED PATIENTS
C.L.Cazzullo,C.Gala,T.Tavola,E.Pellegrini,F.Durbano
Dept. of Psychiatry,University of Milan,Italy
Objective: To collect data on the prevalence of clinical anxiety(A) and depression(D) among HIV infected patients.
Methods: 100 HIV infected subjects (II,III,IV CDC), 100 subjects at risk for HIV infection, 100 healthy controls were examined with Zung Self-rating Anxiety and Depression Scales.
Results: HIV+ subjects showed a significantly higher prevalence of A(30%) and D(31%) as compared to control subjects (6% for both A and D),but not in comparison to HIV- subjects(respectively 25% and 29%).HIV+ drug-addicts showed a significantly higher prevalence of A(31%) and D(35%) as compared to gay men(A=27%;D=18%).Such higher prevalence of A and D is observed more frequently in subjects reporting actual use of opiates as compared to subjects who interrupted it.Finally,a decrease of A and D,even not significant,is observed in relation to worsening of disease.
Conclusions:A and D responses of HIV+ gay men and drug-addicts are not related to HIV diagnosis,but they are more likely related to psychological characteristics of patients before infection.

1240

ATTEMPTED SUICIDE AND HIV INFECTION
C.L.Cazzullo,C. Gala,A.Pergami,R.Russo,M.Rossini
Dept. of Psychiatry,University of Milan, Italy

Objective: To evaluate suicidal behavior among HIV infected subjects after Knowledge of infection.
Methods: 225 HIV infected subjects were assessed in order to investigate the occurrence of attempted suicides(AS) preceeding and following the developement of the disease. They were also assessed for their past medical and psychiatric history.
Results: 12 patients(5%) reported an AS after the diagnosis of HIV infection:8 within 6 months and 4 within 3 years.Out of them,7 reported an AS before diagnosis.Log-rank analysis showed:an increase of relative risk of AS(RR) for the patients reporting a previous AS(RR=5.3),a psychiatric history (RR=7.7)and external copings(RR=4.6).Multivariated analysis confirmed the strict association of AS after diagnosis and previous AS,psychiatric history and externality.
Conclusions:A psychological and psychiatric assessment at the time of diagnosis of HIV infection can anticipate psychopathological responses such as an AS.

1241

Psychosocial disorders displayed by HIV positive Haemophiliac and Thalassaemic children and their parents.
J.Tsiantis,D.Anastasopoulos,M.Piperia,H.Assimopoulos, D.Panits,M.Meyer,E.Platokouki,V.Ladis,S.Aroni, Ch.Katamis.
Dept.Psychological Pediatrics,1stUniv.Dept.Pediatrics, Haemophilia Unit at "AGIA SOFIA"Childr.Hospital,Greece

In this paper the psychosocial disorders of serum positive HIV Haemophilia and Thalassaemia children and of their parents will be described and discussed. The study was done in a group of 30 positive HIV (20 Haemophilia and 10 Thalassaemia) with the use of semistructured interviews as well as questionnaires and projective tests.A control group of 20 HIV negative was also used. Some of the findings are:All parents reacted with anxiety and depression to the disclosure of seropositivity. In the Rutter and Graham semistructed interview about the child, the HIV positive families recorded significantly more frequently pathological score p=0.047 than the control group. In Piers-Harris scale the factor of Anxiety only is statistically significant higher in HIV positive in comparison to the control group.
In the TAT the serum positive children had significantly higher scores than controls in the following: Preoccupation with Death p=0.050, Loneliness p:0.003, Death Anxiety p:0.049,Separation Anxiety p:0.011, in comparison to the control group.
Our intervention programme will also be briefly described.

1242

PSYCHODIAGNOSTICAL EVALUATION OF ANXIETY, DEPRESSION & PSYCHOSIS IN A SAMPLE OF 33 AIDS INPATIENTS
Di Giannantonio M, Mattioni T, Persico A, Janiri L, Lestingi L, Zeppetelli E and Tempesta E.
Dept.of Psychiatry, Catholic University, Rome
This work reports the evaluation of psychiatric symptomatology in a sample of 33 AIDS inpatients - 23 Intravenous drug abusers (IVDA) and 10 homosexuals (homo). 82% patients belong to IV group of CDC-AIDS criteria. Mean age 30.6 in IVDA and 32 homo. Cultural level is lower among IVDA (65.2% minimal school degree versus 10%) than in homo. The patients were all tested by a set of psychodiagnostic tools: a)clinical interview, b)Hamilton RS Anxiety (HRSA), c)Hamilton RS Depression (HRSD), Brief Psychiatric Rating Scale (BPRS). Anxiety area: Both groups were affected by high prevalence and incidence of generalized anxiety (300.02) (80% homo versus 87% IVDA), with greater intensity in IVDA than in homo (score:23 versus 19.1). Important to note is that IVDA HRSA high scores are mainly related to somatic items. Affective area: Both groups were affected by high prevalence of depression (311.00) but either a major incidence (90% homo versus 74% IVDA) than intensity (score:26.1 vs 20.9) regard homo patients. Schizoaffective area: Both groups were affected by schizoaffective troubles with depression (295.70). According to our point of view, the high levels of anxiety are linked with the consciousness of the lethal progressive ilness' doom. The IVDAs seem more involved (specially in somatic areas) because of their psychopathology, which, so often, has sociopathic and characteriological aspects. Depressive problems are more present in homo patients because they seem to use "stronger" and "more adult" defense mechanisms. Homos in fact are people who are not usually affected by specific psychiatric disturbances and are able to have more "realistic" insight. Schizoaffective troubles affect both groups but their incidence is highest within the first 7 days of hospitalization.

1243

THE PSYCHOPHARMACOTHERAPY OF AIDS PATIENTS: A RETROSPECTIVE STUDY.
Di Giannantonio M., Persico A.M., Zeppetelli E., Lestingi L., Mattioni T., Weisert A., Janiri L., Tempesta E.
Dept. of Psychiatry, Catholic University of S.Heart, Rome

The clinical management of AIDS patients often requires that psychiatrists administer psychoactive drugs of relief anxiety, depression, cognitive impairment, psychotic or behavioral disturbances. These patients have been reported to be particularly sensitive to psychotropic drugs and to their side effects. This may be due to several causes. There may be significant variations in parameters that influence the pharmacokinetics of drugs, such as body weight and serum proteins content. At the same time, the CNS of these patients suffers from both HIV neurotropism and frequent opportunistic infections. Finally pharmacological interactions may occur with non-psychotropic drugs.
The aim of our study is to draw some guidelines in order to define a correct approach to the psychopharmacotherapy of AIDS patients. Particular attention will be devoted to drug addicts who are predominant in our sample.

1244

ELECTRICAL BRAIN MAPPING FOR DEMENTIA IN HIV POSITIVE PATIENTS
L.D. Young, M.D. Goldstein, Ph.D., E.L. Liberakis, M.D.,Ph.D., The Medical College of Wisconsin, Milwaukee, WI., USA

The AIDS epidemic is well established in the U.S. The HIV which causes AIDS has a tropism for the central nervous system. Various cognitive and emotional disorders of interest to psychiatrists occur in the course of HIV infection. Those with an organic bases are generally referred to as AIDS Dementia Complex (ADC). It would be helpful for psychiatrists and other physicians to differentiate ADC associated behavioral disturbances from social and emotional reactions.

Many tests are available which may be useful to differentiate ADC from other disturbances. These include MRI, CSF analysis, SPECT or PET scanning. Electrical brain mapping by Brain Atlas has not been extensively employed in HIV positive patients. We have had the opportunity to examine several HIV positive patients using this technique. We have focussed on the usefulness of P300 in early detection of ADC. Early findings will be reviewed. Our technique will be presented, and preliminary findings will be discussed.

1245

CORRELATED DRUG ADDICTION AND HIV PATHOLOGY: EMOTIONAL FAMILY PROFILES
CLERICI M., BERTRANDO P., BRESSI C., CAFISO E., GARAVAGLIA R., FERRARINI F., CAZZULLO C.L.
Department of Psychiatry, University of Milan, Milan, Italy

Everyone knows the importance of family factors in the genesis and maintenance of the toxicomanic symptoms. The father is often absent-minded, detached, whereas the mother keeps up an indulgent and overprotective relationship with her son. Both parents are barely able to acknowledge their son's autonomy, and they often have an adhesive-symbiotic relationship with him/her. As regards the functional structure, those families can be defined either "enmeshed" or "disengaged". the former reveal a greater sense of belonging and a lesser personal autonomy; the latter lack loyalty and mutual support.
The present study reports on family Expressed Emotion factors, particularly those empirically related with a higher relapse rate in psychiatric disturbed patients. Outcomes revealed a high EE in all families of our sample (with equal emotional profile and high relapse rate): 90% of high EE relatives showed a widespread high Criticism, associated (in 50% of the cases) with Hostility. Overinvolment was present too. However, we must underline that fairly high levels of Warmth were observed as well. We highlightened a family emotional profile which differs from all other EE profiles (schizophrenia and psychosomatic diseases) so far assessed. Family emotional profiles in each scale are carefully analyzed in order to evaluate its virtual influence upon the drug addict's behaviour and relapse.

1246

SOROCABA AMBULATORY EXTERNAL SERVICE RELATED TO AIDS AND ACCOMPANIED WITH USERS OF INJECTABLE DRUGS
Ramos,T.F., Dos Anjos,R.M.P., Goncalves,V.L.C., Gomez,M.C.O.
Amb.de Ref.p/AIDS do Conj.Hospitalar de Sorocaba,Brazil

In the period from August to October 31,1988 after an epidemiological investigation, 1382 analyses were performed to detect anti HIV antibodies (through ELISA recombined methods) on individuals considered of Risk Behaviour. From 309 (22,35%) users of injectable drugs that were tested, 182 (58,89%) positive results were obtained. This group was composed of drug addicted individuals using injectable drugs periodically. From 182 cases we verified: a) age varied from 14 to 38 years (mean age 22,21 years); b) males were the predominant sex, totalling 138 (75,82%) cases; c) 08 cases (4,39%) corresponded to CDC diagnostic criteria (Atlanta,USA); d) in 14 months maximum attendance period, 10 (5,49%) individuals were evolved to death; e) 126 (69,23%) persons were frequenting the External Service during this period regularly with medical, psychiatric and psychological attendance and continuous educational work on AIDS. Following evaluation of the ones that desired to use injectable drug after knowing the results of the analysis and educational work of the multiprofessional team, we obtained the following results: a) 66 (52,38%) desired to use injectable drugs; b) 31 (24,60%) did not desire to use injectable drugs; c) 29 (23,01%) were considered doubtful.

Session 194 Symposium: Computer-analyzed EEG and brain mapping in psychiatry

1247

CEEG/DYNAMIC BRAIN MAPPING IN CLINICAL PSYCHIATRY

Turan M. Itil and Constantin R. Soldatos, New York Medical College, Tarrytown, New York; and University of Athens, Greece

The successful applications of computer-analyzed EEG, even recorded from a limited area of the brain, has been demonstrated in psychiatry, and particularly in psychopharmacology. With the advancement of computer technology, it is now possible to obtain information on brain function not only from "real" recorded areas, but also from thousands of mathematically interpolated points. This technique, which enhances the information on brain function, is called "brain mapping". We could further enhance the value of the information obtained from the brain by increasing the conventional four frequency bands up to 22 and by recording and analyzing electrical activities up to 50 Hz and above.
Thanks to reliable multilead and on-line/real time quantification of EEG, the information on brain function of different diagnostic groups with or without drug effects were collected and stored in data bases now being used for both conventional EEG diagnosis and classification of patients and drug selection and monitoring.

1248

THE USE OF DYNAMIC BRAIN MAPPING IN PSYCHIATRIC PRACTICE

Songar A. - Turkey

1249

DYNAMIC BRAIN MAPPING AND TREATMENT OF SCHIZOPHRENICS
S. Galderisi, A. Mucci, M. Di Gregorio, P. Bucci, M. Maj and D. Kemali, Department of Medical Psychology and Psychiatry, First Medical School, University of Naples, Italy.

The Dynamic EEG Brain Mapping was used to investigate: 1) resting C-EEG differences between drug-free schizophrenics and healthy controls; 2) C-EEG changes induced by both acute and chronic haloperidol treatment in the patient group.
Drug-free patients, in comparison with controls, had increased delta relative activity (RA) in most of the explored leads and slower alpha frequency.
After acute haloperidol treatment a reduction of delta RA, an increase of alpha and beta RA were observed in schizophrenics.
Chronic haloperidol treatment induced a decrease of both delta and beta RA and an increase of alpha RA.
C-EEG changes were similar in responsive and non responsive-patients, although more marked in responders.

1250

E. W. Fünfgeld, Med. Faculties of the Universities Saarbrücken/Homburg and Marburg and Schloßberg-Klinik Wittgenstein, D-5928 Bad Laasphe, FRG.
Dementive processes have multiple causes and the different levels of disturbances (glucose uptake, membrane rigidity, deficits in different neurotransmitters, calcium overloading, stress and genetic factors, exitotoxines, free radicals) are not yet detectable in an individual case. Compaired to the variety to the disorder possibilities the clinical pictures and changes obtained by different technical equipment are much more uniform: multiple causes and defects are reduced to a few clinical syndromes. Concerning the different drugs influencing the cerebral tissue we have to distinct drugs having a selecting action (e.g. Calciumblocking agents as Nicergolin), agents influencing mainly the glucose or the RNA uptake in the nerve cells (Pyritinol, Piracetam), agents influencing the membrane stability, enhancing the Dopamin turnover with some noradrenergic effect (the Amantadin derivative Memantine). Besides of these *chemical* drugs two *natural* compounds are available: The phospholipid fraction Phosphatidylserine - a preparation coming from cow's brain (FIDIA, Abano Terme, Italy) - is able to produce more fluidity of cell membranes and have some influences on transmitters, the extract of the leafs of the Ginkgo biloba tree has an effect on multiple levels (capillary permeability, metabolism - ATP and glucose - thrombocytes aggregation, acethylcholinergic receptors). Until now the only way in humans is to observe the clinical result of a given drug by using standardised tests or questionairies after a given time (weeks or months). Since we use the computerized EEG method, the Dynamic Brain Mapping System (HZI Research Center, Tarrytown, New York) in clinical routine with follow-up studies we are able to test the cerebral reaction in dementive patients. It is even possible to find in elderly healthy persons the so-called Theta- or Alpha-Anteriorisation which seems to be the first sign of an incipient metabolic change; these signs are reversible by a nootropic therapy preclinically. By the diagnostic aid of Dynamic Brain Mapping system we are appearently able to retard the cerebral aging.

1251

DYNAMIC BRAIN MAPPING IN DEPRESSION
A. El Azayem, M.D., A. Dosoky, A. Abdeen
Psychiatric Institute, Nasr City, Cairo, Egypt

Introduction: Dynamic brain mapping in depressive disorders revealed significantly lower relative activity in alpha band in central leads and reduced L/R ratio of amplitude. These findings have been found to be correlated with the clinical profile of depressive symptoms of the patient and not to the diagnostic subgroup to which he is assigned.
The problem: is to study the pattern of correlation between these two types of variables: The quantitative EEG findings and the profile of depressive symptoms within two major diagnostic subgroups: the group of psychotic depressives and the group of non psychotic depressives. The aim is to find out the possible utility of quantitative EEG measures in the differential diagnosis between these two groups.
The sample: has been drawn out from a private hospital inpatient and outpatient. The subjects are all drug free.
The method patients have first been assigned to the psychotic or the non-psychotic group, based on their score on the Hamilton depressive scale. Then, dynamic brain mapping has been done for each patient.
Statistical analysis: Discriminate function analysis applied to the quantitative EEG data in order to discriminate between these two diagnostic subgroups.

1252

DYNAMIC BRAIN MAPPING IN DRUG ABUSE

Reese T. Jones, Department of Psychiatry, University of California, San Francisco

Illicit drug use is associated with behavior harmful to both the user and to others. Behavioral disturbances are generally considered to have something to do with brain function, though clear linkages between measures of brain function, behavior, and drug effects, particularly longer lasting effects associated with drug abuse, remain elusive when measured by conventional evoked potential or EEG techniques. Brain mapping techniques appear to be sensitive measures of psychoactive drug-induced changes. Acute and chronic effects of cocaine will be illustrated using Brain Function Monitoring (BFM) and Computerized EEG (CEEG) procedures applied to normal volunteers administered oral, nasal, intravenous, and smoked cocaine under controlled laboratory conditions. The increases in beta activity confirm nicely what Berger reported after some of his first experiments with cocaine in the mid-1930's. The utility of the brain mapping technology will be illustrated by contrasts with less clear evidence of cocaine effects apparent in more traditional paper EEG records. Examples will be offered showing both close relationships between brain mapping indices of cocaine, subjective and behavioral effects, and other examples (e.g., during chronic cocaine administration) where dissociation between brain electrical changes and behavior occurs.

Session 195 Symposium:
Stress and its effect on the mental and physical well being

1253
STRESS AND CULTURE SHOCK OF USSR
Vizner T. - USA

1254
STRESS AND PSYCHOSIS
Milovanovic D. - Professor, Belgrad University, Jugoslavia

1255
STRESS AND ALCOHOLISM
Poleksic J. - Professor, Belgrad University, Jugoslavia

1256
STRESS AND DISCHARGE OF PSYCHOTIC PATIENTS
Maric J., Kunovac J. - Belgrad University, Jugoslavia

1257
STRESS AND POLITICS
Strikovic J. - Hospital St. Sava, Belgrade, Jugoslavia

1258
STRESS AND CHILDREN
Mandic B. - Albert Einstein Medical School N.Y., USA

1259
STRESS WITH KOREAN ADOLESCENTS
Min B. - Chung-Ang University, Seoul, Republic of Korea

Session 196 Symposium
Brain mechanisms of information processing and psychopathology.

1260

Shift of Attention and Schizophrenic Symptoms

Bonnie Spring, Ph.D.
UHS/The Chicago Medical School
North Chicago, Illinois, USA

Disability in shifting attention was once proposed to be a marker of vulnerability to schizophrenia, but initial findings yielding negative results. When shift of attention was measured by crossmodal reaction time, relatives of schizophrenics showed no impairment. More recently, though, Wisconsin card sort findings demonstrate impaired ability to shift set among individuals vulnerable to schizophrenia. This suggests that disability in shift of attention may indeed be a component of vulnerability to schizophrenia and perhaps related to the pathogenesis of important symptoms. This presentation will review the association between psychopathologic symptoms and shift of attention as measured by three procedures: (1) crossmodal reaction time; (2) the Wisconsin card sort task; and (3) a new paradigm, reorientation of attention after a period of selective listening. Preliminary data from a sample of relatives of schizophrenics will also be presented for the latter procedure.

1261

P300 AS AN INDEX OF TREATMENT RESPONSE IN SEASONAL AFFECTIVE DISORDER
Connie C. Duncan
National Institute of Mental Health, Bethesda, MD, USA

The winter depressive symptoms of seasonal affective disorder (SAD) can be treated by exposure of the eyes to bright artificial light ("phototherapy"). This sensitivity to light suggests the importance of studying visual information processing in these patients. We used the P300 component of the event-related potential (ERP) to investigate whether clinical improvement following phototherapy is associated with increased visual attention. Auditory ERPs were also recorded to assess the specificity of changes in attention.

Subjects were 17 SAD patients and 11 matched normal controls. The subjects were tested twice, once following at least nine days of phototherapy and once either prior to or nine or more days after the termination of phototherapy. Depression in the patients decreased significantly following phototherapy ($p < .0001$). In the visual modality, SAD patients who exhibited the most clinical improvement following phototherapy showed the greatest increase in P300 amplitude ($r = -.71$, $p < .005$). In contrast, clinical response was uncorrelated with changes in P300 to auditory stimuli ($r = -.18$). No changes were seen in the normal controls. The results indicate that a positive clinical response to phototherapy in SAD patients is associated with a significant increase in the attentional resources that are mobilized to process visually-guided information.

1262

CEREBRAL MECHANISMS OF INITIATION OF EEG REACTIVITY AND SCHIZOPHRENIC SYMPTOMS

M. Koukkou, M.D., E. Tremel, M.D.
Research Department, University Hospital of Psychiatry, CH-8029 Zürich, Switzerland

Schizophrenic positive symptoms are unspecific and modifiable "spontaneously", by environmental information and drugs.
We present a model of their pathogenesis based on research on brain mechanisms of EEG-reactivity to information and on the concept of EEG-defined functional states of the brain (FS) with state-dependent information processing and their role for the organization of behavior.
The FS are multifactorially determined and continuously readjusted in answer to the demands made by received information as evaluated by the pre-attentive processes (cerebral mechanisms of information processing). The evaluation relies on the contents of the momentarily accessible memory storages. The FS defines which storages are accessible at each moment to these processes.
In normals differences in cognitive-emotional-behavioral style are paralleled by differences in FS (EEG activity and reactivity). Schizophrenics with positive symptoms show deviant EEG reactivities. The symptoms are explained as "inadequate" evaluation of internally and/or externally received information due to the accessibility of "inadequate" storages via the deviant FS. The pathogenesis of this deviant FS will be discussed.

1263

PSYCHOSES, SECOND-ORDER REPRESENTATIONS AND THE BRAIN
Christopher D. Frith
Division of Psychiatry, Clinical Research Centre, Harrow, U.K.

There are striking similarities between the negative symptoms of schizophrenia and impairments in childhood autism. There is a lack of normal two-way social interactions ('autism'), verbal and non-verbal communication is impaired, and spontaneous behaviour is reduced and replaced by stereotyped activity. These impairments can be explained by a failure to form second-order representations. This prevents the formation of a 'theory of mind'.

Positive symptoms can also be explained within this framework. Here second-order representations are formed, but erroneously. Thus delusions of reference occur when an intention to communicate is incorrectly inferred. Thought broadcasting and delusions of control occur when second-order representations are confused with actual states of the world.

In monkeys second-order representation is required to learn conditional tasks of the form 'if there is a carrot the reward is under the white counter'. The frontal lobes and the hippocampus are involved in the learning and retention of such tasks. The same structures are implicated in in-vivo imaging and post-mortem studies of schizophrenia.

1264

BILATERALLY ASYMMETRICAL CEREBRAL DYSFUNCTION IN THE ENDOGENOUS PSYCHOSES

Pierre Flor-Henry,
Alberta Hospital Edmonton, Edmonton, Canada.

PET studies in schizophrenia have shown frontal hypometabolic activity, maximal in the left frontal regions (left>right) in chronic negative symptomatology syndromes and hypermetabolic activity (left>right), in acute schizophrenia. Neurochemical (dopamine, GABA & glutamate) and microstructural abnormalities in the left hemisphere of schizophrenics have been reported. Convergent lines of evidence suggest that the cerebral mood systems are asymmetrical: bilateral frontal and nondominant frontotemporal; but the mood controlling systems depend on dominant hemispheric mechanisms. Different emotions have different lateralization: euphoria and anger related to dominant, dysphoria and depressive to the nondominant systems. The reciprocal transcallosal neural inhibition responsible for mood stability is disrupted in the transition from depression to mania (deepening nondominant disorganization), thus releasing the euphoric-irritability and verbal-motor disinhibition of mania, all derivative of dominant hemispheric neural structures. "Acute schizophrenia" - in contrast to dementia praecox forms - appears to be an extension of this process. In dementia praecox the basic deficit in the dominant hemisphere leads secondarily to functional changes in the nondominant hemisphere.

1265

Information Processing in Schizophrenia: Clinical Approaches

Hans D.Brenner,M.D.,Ph.D., Professor of Psychiatry
Bettina Hodel, M.A., Research-Psychologist
Abteilung für Theoretische und Evaluative Psychiatrie / Psychiatrische Universitätsklinik Bern / Bolligenstrasse 111 / CH-3072 Bern/Switzerland

It is assumed that in schizophrenia improvements on elementary attentional/perceptual and cognitive dysfunctions exert positive, pervasive effects on more complex disorders of overt behavior - as well as vice versa. This assumption has led to the conceptualization and implementation of an Integrated Psychological Therapy Program (IPT). It consists of various cognitive and social treatment interventions. This therapy program for schizophrenic patients should help to break two vicious circles: On the one hand connections between impaired attentional/perceptual and conceptual, cognitive processes and their integrating organizations, and on the other hand the positive feedbacks between cognitive dysfunctions and psycho-social stressors. The present results of several evaluation studies concerning this therapy program show its effectiveness for schizophrenic patients with different degrees of chronicity. But they also show that the interaction between cognitive and social treatment interventions cannot be fully explained by the assumption of pervasive effects over the different levels of functioning. Emotional factors as well as influences from the activating system seem to be of equal importance for a better comprehension of the manner in which therapy effects will be achieved and thus for our understanding of schizophrenia.
As a heuristic frame of reference, a model of the interactions between cognitive, emotional and neural control processes is being developed, starting from recent models of behavior control in psychology. It is discussed, how the pathogenetic role of cognitive disorders in schizophrenia could be understood within this model. Finally, implications for improved treatment strategies for patients suffering from schizophrenic syndroms are derived.

Session 197 Symposium:
Delusional misidentification syndromes

1266

DELUSIONAL MISIDENTIFICATION SYNDROMES: PATHOGENETIC HYPOTHESES
G.N. Christodoulou
Athens University, Department of Psychiatry, Athens, Greece

Attempts to explain the delusional misidentification syndromes (Syndrome of Capgras, syndrome of Fregoli, Syndrome of Intermetamorphosis syndrome of subjective doubles) and particularly the first sub - type are centered around the following hypotheses:
1. The syndrome is an agnosia of identification produced by a conflict between affective accompaniments of sensory and mnemonic images (Capgras and Reboul - Lachaux, 1923).
2. The syndrome is produced by personality disintegration to primitive modes of thought (Todd, 1957).
3. The syndrome is a mechanism by which the love - hate conflict is resolved by directing hate to an imagined double (Enoch and Trethowan, 1963).
4. The syndrome is caused by delusional evolution of experiences produced by cerebral dysfunction (Christodoulou, 1975-1983).
5. The syndrome is produced by interhemispheric disconnection between the areas of the two hemispheres that decode afferent sensory information (Joseph, 1987).
6. The syndrome may, in some cases, be considered as a manifestation of a broadly speaking "epileptic" psychosis (Christodoulou, 1975).

1267

THE MISIDENTIFIED IN CAPGRAS' SYNDROME

Dr Geoffrey Wallis
Fulford Grange Hospital Leeds England

The patient in Capgras' syndrome often imagines the replacing double to be an inferior impersonator or impostor. The patient then conceives the original as faultless. A grandiose patient, on the other hand, may attribute superiority to the substitute.
Thus a favoured explanation in the psychogenesis is that the misidentification resolves painful ambivalence of the patient towards the original. Often, however, there is no evidence of such ambivalence.
In a study of 96 Capgras patients culled from the literature plus eight personally seen, the attitude of the patient towards the first original was found to be ambivalent in only 20. It was significantly more often ambivalent or hostile in schizophrenics than in the affectively or organically disordered, so that it may have been determined principally by the underlying diagnostic category.
Another finding was that when the patient and the original were parent and child the sexes of the two were usually the same but there was not an apparent excess of ambivalence even in this same-sex parent/child relationship.
This study suggests that fear or hope of losing a loved one may play a part in the genesis of the syndrome.

1268

A PSYCHOPATHOLOGICAL CONCEPTION OF THE SUBJECTIVE DOUBLES SYNDROME.

M.Markidis, R.Markidis, G.N.Christodoulou
Eginition Hospital, Athens - Greece

This study represents an attempt to conceptualize the relation of the human subject to the subjective Double, starting from the suggestions of the Hegelian Phenomenology of the spirit and the Lacanian Mirror stage.
The construction of the Ego is considered as a narcissistic alienation to the image of the self reflected by the mirror, that is to an ideal "other". The potential exit from this alienation lies in the Symbolic Order of society, inhabited by the structure of the language. The patient suffering from a Delusional Subjective Misidentification Syndrome gets into this Order already trapped by the reflective image, in psychoanalytical terms by his own "projection". The patient cannot grasp the inner meaning of this projection. He is haunted by a Double, by an exact copy of himself, that, however, he regards as "another".
This theoretical conception is applied to F.Dostoyevsky's early novel "The Double".

1269

MYSELF AND MY OTHER SELF

A.C.P. Sims, Dept. of Psychiatry Univ. of Leeds

Disorders of self in Jaspers Psychopathology include disorders of activity, of singleness, of identity, and of the boundaries of self.
Delusional misidentification syndromes are usually not obviously evidenced in disturbance of self image. However, Christodoulos variant, the syndrome of subjective doubles, is essentially a disturbance of self-image. Disorders of the awareness of unity, or of singleness, include multiple personality, mortoscopy, and lability in the awareness of personality. The Doppelganger phenomenon may be both psychotic and either or neurotic. This paper explores some descriptions of neurotic disturbance of self image in which the patient made a distinction between "myself", "my other self", "my ideal self" and my "rejected self". The technique of the repertory grid is used to explore the associations between these different aspects of the self. Some conclusions are drawn on the phenomenology of self-image in neurotic disorders.

1270

POSSIBLE SIGNIFICANCE OF NEURO-PSYCHOLOGICAL TESTING APPLIED TO PATIENTS WITH DMS.

ATHANASE TZAVARAS
NURSING SCHOOL, ATHENS UNIVERSITY.

This paper deals with the methodological and epistemological issues raised by the application of a neuropsychological testing in order to investigate the possible mechanisms underlying a psycho-pathological condition. The discussion is based on the neuropsychological studies of cases presenting Delusional Misidentification Syndromes. These studies present paradigmatic value because they permit:
a/ Comparisons between two clinical homologous phenomena but in any case two rare clinical states, namely prosopagnosia and DMS and b/ Exploration of the labile functions of face recognition and persons identification and their dysfunction during organic damage of CNS and psycho-pathological states. The real meaning of actual data on the neuropsychological testing of patients presenting various face recognition and person identification dysfunction is evaluated and a general discussion tends to generalize some principles concerning neuropsychological testing of psychopathological states.

1271

CAPGRAS' SYNDROME AND DEMENTIA OF ALZHEIMER TYPE

J.P.Luaute, E.Bidault
Dept. of Psychiatry C.H. Romans 26100, FRANCE

Capgras' syndrome is one of the most frequent delusions of dementia of Alzheimer type.
Two new cases were investigated by neurosychological tests which revealed perceptual and above all memory impairments.
It was concluded that Capgras' synndrome only occurs during the first stages of dementia and when fabulation is associated.
The syndrome can be paralleled with the degree of misidentification of the demented patients vis a vis their own mirror-images.
These cases provide arguments for the anatomical basis of the syndrome.

Session 198 Symposium:
Crisis intervention: Clinical management strategies and long-term outcome predictors

1272

WORKING ALLIANCE AS A PREDICTOR OF CRISIS INTERVENTION LONG TERM OUTCOME
A. ANDREOLI, M.D.; M. GOGNALONS-NICOLET, Ph.D.; J. ABENSUR, M.D.; P. GERIN, M.D.; B. REITH, M.D.; A. DAZORD, M.D.; Department of Psychiatry, University of Geneva.

This paper reports a major result of a 2 years follow-up study investigating long term clinical outcome of the overall patients asking for acute psychiatric hospitalisation in a Geneva (CH) catchment area within 2 months. The whole sample of 53 patients adressed to a crisis intervention special program were carefully and reliably assessed for DSM III-R diagnosis and rated on a number of clinical instruments (BPRS, Montgomery, HSRS) social functioning measures at the entry, crisis intervention completion, 1 and 2 years follow-up. Therapeutic and working alliance measures were also obtained at crisis intervention start and completion. Working alliance measures were observed to be related to better clinical outcome, treatment compliance 1 and 2 years later and to better treatment goals attainment prediction ($p < .05$ to $< .001$). Association was stronger in the DSM III-R major depressive episodes/anxiety adjustment disorders subsample. In DSM III-R PD patients alliance measures only predicted less worse 1 and 2 years clinical outcome. Therapeutic and working alliance measures are suggested to be a valuable tool to investigate clinical effectiveness of multimodal treatments adressing institutional management of large populations and/or selected diagnostic groups of psychiatric patients.

1273

ASSESSMENT OF PSYCHOTHERAPEUTICAL CRISIS INTERVENTIONS IN THE EMERGENCY WARD OF A GENERAL HOSPITAL, AFTER TWO YEARS
Dr. Michel de Clercq
Psychiatrist Responsable for the crisis psychiatric team at St.Luc Clinics, Belgium, Bruxelles

The number of psychiatric emergencies arriving in emergency wards of general hospitals is increasing. The crisis psychiatric team St.Luc Clinics in Brussels (Catholic University of Louvain) has developed a specific programme to deal with such psychiatric emergencies. In a first step, the team staff perform a crisis interaction and analyse the urgency of the demand - talk with individual and/or family, provisional admission for 24 hours, when necessary.
A second step leads to a crisis intervention of the crisis team right on the spot or of a mental health centre team further to a first interview in the emergency ward.
And finally, other patients (less than 15%) will be admitted to a psychiatric dept. or directed to specialised medical advice.
The sample will be assessed two years later for evaluation of follow-up development and compliance with treatment.

1274

PSYCHOSOMATIC VULNERABILITY AND ACUTE PSYCHIATRIC EPISODES; A NEW ASSESSMENT STRATEGY
Nicolaidis N. - Institutions Universitaires de Psychiatrie, Switzerland

1275

LONG-TERM OUTCOME OF CRISIS INTERVENTION IN DSM III-R MAJOR DEPRESSIVE EPISODES
Dr. Nicolas de Coulon / Dr. Thomas Giger
Secteur psychiatrique de l'Est Vaudois
1820 Montreux Suisse

Our study focuses on a population carrying the diagnosis of major depressive episodes. The patients of the choosen cluster out of a total of 78 persons were treated during 2 months with a follow-up of 2 years after the crisis intervention (Andreoli: Geneva Follow-up study). They all showed severe symptoms for psychiatric hospital admittance. Instead of that measure, they were referred to the crisis management outfit.

The appraisal of different studies points benefits of a specialised therapeutic intervention without too much delay. We are looking for the forerunner indicators that could foretell these patients' evolution. The current litterature shows that sociodemographic factors are put in the background as well as personal and clinical history. Nevertheless, we stress the diagnostic variables (maximisation with co-morbidity as alcoholism, personality disorders...)

1276

"LES CENTRES D'ACCUEIL ET DE CRISE EN FRANCE FACE A L'URGENCE"

BAILLON
CHS de Ville-Evrard 93330 NEUILLY sur MARNE / FRANCE

Les Centres d'Accueil et de Crise sont une des modalités fraçaises originales de réponse institutionnelle à ce qu'il est habituel de désigner en termes d'urgence psychiatrique.

Nous avons lancé en 1988 une enquête nationale pour évaluer l'importance de cette modalité de réponse.

Le double intérêt de cette enquête est d'être la première à l'échelle nationale et de permettre la comparaison avec la totalité de l'équipement français en psychiatrie de Service Public ; en effet après les textes législatifs de 1985 et 1986 les 1070 équipes de secteur sont créées et organisent la totalité de la Psychiatrie de Service Public selon une grande variété d'Unité de soin distinctes (plus de 12) - Ceci est résumé chaque année dans un rapport annuel du Ministère.

Cette enquête montre donc les grandes tendances actuelles, et permet de distinguer les centres organisés par une seule équipe et les centres organisés par plusieurs équipes - Cette distinction reflète des orientations thérapeutiques nettement différentes.

L'enquête montre aussi la diversité des réponses, l'importance du choix de la disponibilité des soignants 24 heures sur 24 à l'intérieur même du périmètre du secteur et à distance d'un hôpital comme donnée essentielle de ce soin.

1277 *

★ Number left open for technical reasons not corresponding to any abstract

Session 199 Symposium:
Update on efficacy and clinical uses of fluoxetine

1278

THE ROLE OF 5-HT IN AFFECTIVE DYSFUNCTION
Eckart Rüther, Psychiatric Hospital, University Göttingen, FRG

In a critical review on the role of 5 HT in affective dysfunction the following hypotheses are discussed:
1) Serotonergic neuronal systems influence affective functions in connection with other neuronal transmitter systems. It is to be expected, that multiple affective functions are modulated by 5 HT.
2) The pharmacological influence on affective functions by 5 HT is unspecific concerning diagnoses and may be used therapeutically in many psychiatric diseases.
3) The pharmacological interventions with serotonergic drugs induce changes of 5 HT-receptor modulation, which improves affective dysfunction during time as a psychic reaction.
4) During treatment with serotonergic drugs the empiricaly defined profile of clinical effects is important for the therapeutic use. The individual reaction of the patient to the drug may be predicted by neuroendocrinological and metabolic investigations after tryptophan challenge.

1279

THE EFFECTIVENESS OF FLUOXETINE IN ACUTE STUDIES AND LONG-TERM TREATMENT
J.M.Danion, Dept. of Psychiatry, Centre Hospitalier Universitaire, 67091 Strasbourg CEDEX

The effectiveness of fluoxetine, a new antidepressant drug which selectively inhibits the reuptake of serotonine has been demonstrated in short-term as well as in long-term clinical trials. 834 patients were treated in short-term placebo-controlled studies. The efficacy of fluoxetine was clearly better than placebo in 6 out of 7 placebo-controlled studies: in the 2 placebo-and reference-controlled studies, fluoxetine was no different from imipramine and better than placebo. Five dose studies revealed a dose response relationship with best efficacy associated with the 20 and 40 mg doses. The prophylactic efficacy of fluoxetine has been investigated in a one year placebo-controlled study involving patients suffering from recurrent depression. Fluoxetine was found to have a highly significant prophylactic efficacy, which was demonstrated in the reduction of new episodes of depression (26%), compared with placebo (57%). This study provides the strongest evidence so far available for the true prophylactic effect of an antidepressant.

1280

FLUOXETINE IN THE TREATMENT OF ANXIETY, AGITATION AND SUICIDAL THOUGHTS
Stuart Montgomery
St Mary's Hospital Medical School, London UK

The use of sedative tricyclic antidepressants (TCAs) to treat the anxiety associated with depression is based on convention rather than evidence of increased efficacy. A selective advantage in reducing the anxiety symptoms have been reported with several non-sedative 5HT uptake inhibitors compared with TCAs. 17.5% of all patients treated with fluoxetine in placebo and reference controlled studies had moderate or severe degrees of agitation in entry to the studies. A metanalysis showed there was a significant ($p<0.05$) advantage for fluoxetine (n=786) compared with reference TCAs (n=321), and with placebo ($p<0.001$) (n=176). This advantage in treating agitated depression is surprising in view of the increased nervousness reported early in treatment in some patients. Fluoxetine appears to be comparatively safe in overdose and in post marketing surveillance in the USA there have been no deaths from the drug alone in one million patients. A selective advantage in the reduction of suicidal thoughts, reported with several 5HT uptake inhibitors, suggests they have a dimensional selectivity for suicide, agitation and anxiety.

1281

SEROTONIN AND OBSESSIONAL SYMPTOMS
Juan J. Lopez-Ibor Jr.
Dept. of Psychiatry, Ramon y Cajel Hospital, Univ. of Alcala de Henares (Madrid, Spain)

Obsessive Compulsive disorder is a highly therapy resistant and chronic condition. In such cases the study of positive responses may give clues to basic neurochemical mechanisms involved in it. CMI was the first drug which has been accepted both on grounds of controlled studies and clinical experience as standard anti-obsessional drug. Being CMI a potent 5-HT reuptake blocker, a deficit in the serotonin function has been suggested as basic in OCD. Experience with fluoxetine and other 5-HT selective reuptake blockers coincide with this hypothesis. The basic underlying neurochemical disturbance is still not clear and the timing of the clinical response to this drug is most important to analyse this problem. Nevertheless, selective 5-HT reuptake blockers are becoming both useful tools for the research and more and more standard treatments for OCD.

1282

THE EFFICACY AND SAFETY OF 20MG ONCE DAILY FLUOXETINE
J.F.Wernicke, Ph.D, M.D.

Lilly Research Laboratories, Eli Lilly and Company, Indianapolis, Indiana, U.S.A.

Fluoxetine, a selective serotonin uptake inhibitor has been shown to be a safe and effective antidepressant, using both escalating and fixed dose regimens. In two large multicenter trials 20 mg of fluoxetine given as a once daily dose was found to be effective in the treatment of depression. Only nausea, anxiety, and insomnia were reported significantly more often by patients taking 20 mg/per day of fluoxetine than by those taking placebo.
In a third fixed dose study it was shown that after three weeks at 20 mg/day, patients continued to improve equally well whether they were given 20 mg/day or 60 mg/day of fluoxetine for an additional five weeks. Thus, 20 mg/day of fluoxetine is the proper starting and maintenance dose.

Session 200   Special Session: Whom and how to classify in psychiatry

1283

THE RELIABILITY OF CHECKLIST-GUIDED DIAGNOSES FOR DSM-III-R

Wolfgang Hiller, Michael Zaudig, Werner Mombour
Max-Planck-Institute of Psychiatry, Munich, F.R.G.

Standardized and quantified psychopathological findings are required by the new psychiatric classification systems DSM-III-R and ICD-10 for clinical as well as for scientific purposes. A set of criteria-related checklists has been developed for these systems to serve as a guideline during the process of exploration and data collection. Operationalized diagnoses, based on clearly defined diagnostic algorithms, can be derived directly by the diagnostician as soon as the exploration is finished. This instrument, the "Munich Diagnostic Checklists" (MDCL), is available for the most prevalent psychiatric disorders (covering categories for affective, anxiety, schizophrenic, organic, and substance-use disorders). The reliability of the MDCL for DSM-III-R diagnoses was evaluated in a controlled test-retest study under psychiatric outpatient conditions. Satisfactory reliability coefficients, throughout similar to results obtained in fully or semi-structured diagnostic interviews, were found for most categories. Checklists can enhance the diagnostic process for several reasons: (1) all relevant criteria can be screened systematically and comprehensively; (2) third-party and observed information can easily be included; (3) clinical application is possible in acute psychiatry where patients often cannot be explored in a systematic manner (e.g., intoxication).

1284

Modern Problems of Psycopathology

Alexander S. Tiganov, Director
Research Institute of Clinical Psychiatry

Research in general psychopathology at the present stage of development of psychiatry enables to distinguish between general and particular psychopathological laws of syndromes development. The analysis of the psychopathological syndromes dynamics showed that it is closely associated with progredient and regredient syndromes and with the study of nosology and pathogenesis problems.

The problems of the specific nosological character of syndromes is important: the analysis of psychopathological states of various degrees demonstrates their different specific nosological character.

Lack of knowledge in the correlation of positive and negative disorders in the syndromes structure is a very topical problem: the analysis of a wide range of conditions demonstrated a definite interdependency between positive and negative disorders in the condition clinical picture.

The study of psychopathological syndromes in the age aspect is extremely important; It concerns the determination of a number of age-specific conditions and also the specific features of the same syndromes observed in various age categories.

1285

A NORMALITY MODEL IN MENTAL HEALTH AND MULTIAXIAL DIAGNOSIS
PERALES.Alberto; LEON.R; MEZZICH J.E.
INSTITUTO NACIONAL DE SALUD MENTAL "HONORIO D.-HIDEYO NOGUCHI"

The authors propose a simple theoretical model of normality useful for the mental health teams's work. Such a model allows:

1º To conceptualize normality and abnormality as the final result of the dynamic balance established between healthy and unhealthy areas of the human being. In this sense, absolute normality or abnormality would be clinical utopias.
2º To make the diagnosis of such a balance by systematic evaluation of as much of the subject's psychopathology as of his healthy resources.
3º To emphasize that in Mental Health a healthy dynamic balance can be obtained either by the reduction of what constitutes the unhealthy area or by the growing and maturation of its counterpart, the healthy one.
4º To design the therapeutic strategy facilitating not only the integration of different therapeutic techniques but also the coordinated participation of the mental health team members and even of the patient's family members allowing the correct delegation of therapeutic tasks.
5º To estimate a comprehensive prognosis of the case.

Finally, the authors propose to systematically include the evaluation of the patient's biopsychosocial potentials in the multiaxial diagnosis claiming for the urgent need to develop better clinical tools and techniques for that purpose.

1286

WHO NEEDS TREATMENT? A CASE IDENTIFICATION DILEMMA AND METHOD
M.G. MADIANOS, J. VLACHONIKOLIS, C. STEFANIS
Department of Psychiatry University of Athens Faculty of Medicine

"Case" identification has been considered a major issue in cross-sectional psychiatric epidemiologic surveys. The question is what is a "case" and how reliable and valid criteria can be selected? This paper deals with this issue with respect to our experience obtained from a cross-sectional home survey on psychosocial issues and mental health carried out with a nation-wide probability sample of 4292 respondents aged 12-17, 18-24 and 25-64 and included respondents from Greater Athens, Thessaloniki rest of urban, semi and rural areas of Grecce.

Mental health status was assessed by use of the CES-D and the Langner Scales. A high proportion (29%) of respondents was characterized by a degree of mental impairment scoring above the cut off points in both scales. In order to identify the true psychiatric "cases" and consequently those were in need for treatment, a total of nine clinical and help seeking criteria were selected after examining their descriminant power.

Finally a much lower proportion of the sample was identified as probable (7.2%) and definite (8.0%) psychiatric cases in need of care.

1287

Peculiarities of the Formation of Basic Diagnosis Classification Systems in Psychiatry
Peter V. Morozov
All-Union Mental Health Research Centre

The aim of the present investigation is to study the peculiarities of the formation of basic diagnosis classification systems in psychiatry. The main stages of formation and development of various mental diseases classifications in France, U.K., Germany, U.S.A. & some developing countries were studied in their dynamics.

The data obtained in this study are the result of the literature analysis, interviews with directors of leading psychiatric clinics of the world, as well as of the analysis of the answers to the questionnaire that we worked out especially for this purpose.

Analysed in the presentation are the factors influencing the formation of classification systems in different psychiatric schools, as well as correlations revealed between the peculiarities of the social and economic advance of the society at the present stage of the historical development, the structure of psychiatric services in this or that country & the diagnosis classification concept of a psychiatric school.

1288

CATEGORICAL VS DIMENSIONAL APPROACHES TO DSM-III PERSONALITY DISORDERS

Wim van den Brink, M.D. State University of Groningen, Dept. Social Psychiatry, Groningen, The Netherlands.

Using a semi-structured interview (SIDP) and a self-report questionnaire reliability and some validity aspects of DSM-III PD's were assessed in a sample of 73 psychiatric outpatients.

RELIABILITY: Interrater reliability was excellent for almost all criteria, dimensions and diagnostic categories. Test-retest Kappa's for diagnostic categories ranged from .14 (STP) to .77 (BPD) and Intraclass Correlation Coefficients for dimensions ranged from .46 to .82 (mean .61).
CONCURRENT VALIDITY: Correlations between comparable scales of the SIDP and the PDQ were substantial (mean .55) and their factor structure was nearly identical (Tucker's Phi .85 - .96). Correlation between the SIDP and the ICL were in the hypothesized direction but lower than expected.
CONTENT VALIDITY: There was extensive overlap between pathology and "normality" (also Kass et. al, 1985) and between the different PD's (also Pfohl et. al, 1986). In a factor analytic approach of the interrelationship between the different personality four factors were extracted. The first two were concordant with DSM-III clusters A and B. DSM-III cluster C was represented by two factors; one with DEP and AVD, the other with COM and PAG (also Kass et. al, 1985; Tyrer & Alexander, 1979).
CONSTRUCT/PREDICTIVE VALIDITY: Of all patients with a PD 65% had an Axis I disorder with a chronic course, whereas among patients without a PD "only" 36% had a chronic Axis I disorder. In addition patients with a PD had more psychosocial problems and reported more "life-long complaints and social disabilities".

CONCLUSIONS: (1) reliability acceptable, (2) concurrent validity present, (2) categorical approach invalid, (3) DSM-III clustering of PD's valid (stable over time, instruments and populations), (4) construct/predictive validity present.

1289

LECTICS AND SEMANTICS IN CURRENT DIAGNOSTIC AND CLASSIFICATION SYSTEMS OF MENTAL DISORDERS.
C.N. Stefanis, C.N. Ballas
Univ. of Athens, Medical School.

At the present state of knowledge, psychiatry has to rely almost entirely on clinical judgement for the diagnosis and classification of mental disorders. This is reflected in the criteria, rules and guidelines adopted by both the ICD-10 and the DSM-III (R). Selection of terms is thus of paramount importance for achieving universal comprehension and acceptance of the meaning embodied into the names (lectics) that are chosen to describe or categorize mental states.

In order to promote lectic consistency and conceptual clarity in currently used psychiatric terminology, the present study was undertaken which evolved in three successive stages:
 a) Identification, tracing the linguistic roots and categorization of the major terms employed in the ICD-10 and DSM-III (R).
 b) Assessment of Greek origin words included in ICD-10 and DSM-III (R) terminology as regards their linguistic accuracy and relevance to their original meaning.
 c) Construction of a tree-like system of classification consisting entirely of Greek root words and their derivatives adaptable to both DSM-III and ICD-10.
 The results of this study are presented.

1290

Personality Disorders : comparison of clinical judgements and diagnosis according to DSM III criteria

J. D. GUELFI, C. RODIERE-REIN and M. SIMON, Clinique des Maladies Mentales et de l'Encéphale 100, rue de la santé 75674 PARIS Cédex 14 - FRANCE

French clinical diagnoses and DSM III criteria of personality disorders were compared in 791 outpatients. Ninety-seven french psychiatrists were provided with a check list of the 11 personality disorders and the corresponding 92 DSM III criteria presented in a random order. 441 of these patients have a single clinical diagnosis of personality disorder according to the diagnostic criteria. The most frequent clinical diagnosis were histrionic (N = 82) compulsive (N = 67), paranoid (N = 54) and antisocial (N = 50) disorders. The rate of agreement between clinical and DSM III evaluation was highly variable, the lowest one being found for borderline (45 %), passive-aggressive (21 %), narcissistic (15,4 %) and schizoid (5 %). If one considers only the diagnosis based upon criteria, we can assume that DSM III is over-inclusive for several personality disorders such as schizotypal, borderline, histrionic, passive-aggressive, paranoid and dependent. A principal component analysis with a subsequent varimax rotation has been performed on the criteria. A four factor solution assigns 75 criteria in one sole factor. F1 : aggressiveness-impulsivity, F2 : suspiciousness-social isolation and restricted ability to express emotions, F3 : overly dramatic and reactive behavior with affective instability, F4 : dependence.

1291

Further investigations with AMDP in multiaxial classification

R.-D. Stieglitz, H. Helmchen
Department of Psychiatry
Free University of Berlin, FRG

In accordance with existing multiaxial systems Stieglitz, Fähndrich and Helmchen (1988) proposed that AMDP-variables could be grouped into the axes "symptomatology" "etiology" and "time". The descriptive validity of these axes was shown using three diagnostic groups (ICD-9: schizophrenic psychosis paranoid type, endogenous and neurotic depression) by comparison of frequencies as well as uni- and multivariate analyses. The predictive validity was examined in relation to the following criteria: "length of hospital stay", "positive change in psychopathology", and "assessment of success". The results were replicated in two studies using patients from different nosological groups (ICD-9: schizoaffective disorder, obsessive-compulsive disorder). Problems of the course of the illness and the establishing of subgroups based on a multiaxial description were also investigated.

Session 201   Special Session:
Alcohol abuse: Treatment programs and patients follow-up

1292
ALCOHOLIC WOMEN. A CONTROLLED FOLLOW-UP STUDY FROM A SPECIALIZED UNIT (EWA).
Lena Dahlgren MD. Associate professor
Department of Clinical Alcohol and Drug Research (EWA Unit), Karolinska Hospital
Stockholm
Sweden

Women with alcohol problems constitute an increasing number of the patients in medical service. Do they need a special care? How should the treatment program be designed?
The specialized female EWA-unit at the Karolinska Hospital in Stockholm, Sweden was opened in 1981. The aim of the project is to reach women in an early stage of alcohol dependence behaviour and to develop treatment programs specific to the needs of females alone.
In order to investigate the value of such a specialized female unit a controlled two years follow-up study was carried out including 200 women. The probands were treated in the female only EWA-unit, whereas the controls were placed in the care of traditional mixed sex alcoholism treatment centres.
The two year follow-up study showed a more successful rehabilitation regarding alcohol consumption and social adjustment for the women treated in the specialized female unit (EWA). Improvement was noted also for the controls but to a lesser extent. Probably one of the most important achievements of a specialized female unit, such as EWA is, to attract women to come for help earlier?

1293
CLINICAL CONDITIONS DURING LONG-TERM ABSTINENCE AND CIRCUMSTANCES IN RELATION TO RELAPSE IN ALCOHOL DEPENDENT PATIENTS.
Voltaire A, M.D., Borg, S., M.D., Ph.D.
Karolinska Institute, Department of Psychiatry, St. Göran´s Hospital, Stockholm, Sweden.

A treatment program has been developed in order to study alcohol dependent male patients during long-term abstinence and the circumstances in relation to relapse and to correlate clinical symptoms to biochemical findings. The patients had no previous or current psychiatric disease and no medication. After one week in the hospital for evaluation and treatment of acute withdrawal they were followed for 6-12 months as outpatients 3 times a week. A rating scale was developed from CPRS which is a Scandinavian psychopathological rating scale. Items of special interest for alcoholism and a special check-list for signs prior to relapse were added. Urine was sampled every day and blood once a week for analyses of 5-hydroxytryptophol (5-HTOL) and carbohydrate deficient transferrin (CDT). This treatment model with prospective longitudinal design with observations and clinical ratings related to biochemical findings, gives an opportunity to study the natural cause of the alcohol dependency syndrome and detect early signs prior to relapse.

1294
Alcoholic Follow-up: Death, Abstinence and Recidivism
Demmie Mayfield, M.D.
U. of Texas Health Science Center at San Antonio
L. Rubin, J. Campbell and B. Powell
Kansas City VA Medical Center

Over a 7 year period, 2215 patients were admitted to the 28 day Alcoholic Rehabilitation Program. Most (1617) were treated on only one occasion and a sample (360 pts.) of these systematically studied at index and again (89%) one year following discharge showed a substantial incidence of complete abstinence (24%) or much improvement (48%).

Approximately one-half (184) of these subjects were located for telephone re-survey at 3-6 yrs. post-discharge. A striking rate (17%) of death was noted but an impressive rate of abstinence (mean of 87 weeks abstinence) was observed as was a strong correlation between antabuse use and abstinence. Though a high rate of participation (65%) in Alcoholic Anonymous was observed, this did not correlate with abstinence.

Repeat treatment was not associated with improved outcome; 420 (19%) were admitted a second time, 109 (26%) of these were treated a third time and 69 (62%) of these were admitted four or more times. Most patients (80%) completing three courses of treatment had well documented relapse to excessive drinking while only one patient was definitely improved.

1295
PHARMACODYNAMICS OF DISULFIRAM (D) IN ALCOHOLICS WITH LIVER CIRRHOSIS
J. Nelles*, H.U. Fisch*, Ch. Beyeler, R. Preisig
Departments of Psychiatry* and Clinical Pharmacology, University of Berne, 3010 Berne, Switzerland.

D irreversibly inhibits hepatic acetaldehyde dehydrogenase. After ethanol ingestion, acetaldehyde levels in plasma (AA) increase with consecutive AA dependent drop in blood pressure (BP). Severe liver dysfunction is considered to be a contraindication for D treatment, but this has not been evaluated so far. A standardized disulfiram alcohol reaction (DAR) was performed in 24 alcoholics, 10 with documented alcoholic liver cirrhosis and 14 with normal liver function, serving as controls. Liver function, assessed by galactose elimination capacity and aminopyrine breath test, was markedly decreased in cirrhotics. Contrasting with controls, AA and ensuing BP drop were significantly less pronounced in cirrhotics (peak AA 1.5 ± 1.1 μg/ml versus 5.6 ± 2.3 in controls; BP systolic/diastolic $14 \pm 13/17 \pm 15$ mmHg versus $29 \pm 13/43 \pm 14$ in controls, all $p<0.01$), whereas ethanol concentrations in plasma were similar in the two groups (0.3 ± 0.1 mg/ml versus $0.31 \pm 0,1$ in controls). Conclusions: In patients with severely impaired liver function, cardiovascular effects during the DAR are minimized due to low AA levels in plasma. Thus, lack of pharmacodynamic effect (rather than safety reasons) may be the rationale for withholding D in alcoholics with liver cirrhosis.

1296

FIRST ADMISSIONS FOR ALCOHOLISM IN A BRAZILIAN PSYCHIATRIC HOSPITAL
Dias de Moraes E.,Ribeiro J.,Motta M.,Franco A.
Federal University of Bahia, Brazil

A survey is made of all first admissions for alcohol-related diagnoses(291,303,305 ICD/9) during a ten-years period,representing 10,58% of the total number of first admissions, for the same interval,to the Ana Nery Hospital,in the city of Salvador,capital of the state of Bahia,Brazil.Data were collected from patients' histories. The population is dominantly male,white, married, blue-collared,aged 31-40,not born in Salvador but residing there for more than a decade. Admissions were mainly social security-sponsored. The majority of patients had been previously admitted to other psychiatric hospitals. They showed up mostly sober, having worked up to the day before, accompanied by relatives, and agreeable to hospitatal treatment.Discharge took place after a medium stay of 57 days. Most patients presented uncomplicated alcoholism, the majority corresponding to the alcoholic psychosis. Epilepsy was the most commonly associated diagnosis.A majority of patients showed family histories of psychiatric interest;in 25% of cases,there were antecedents both of alcoholism and of mental illness. In the majority of cases, it was possible to identify personality traits previous to the onset of alcoholism,of which the most frequent were those described as nervousness-explosiveness.Most common single symptoms were: agression-insomnia-irritability-auditory and visual hallucinations.

1297

CARBAMAZEPINE IN THE TREATMENT OF ALCOHOL WITHDRAWAL
Ch.Stuppäck, Ch.Barnas, A.Whitworth, K.Hackenberg, W.W.Fleischhacker
Dept. of Psychiatry, Innsbruck University Clinics, A-6020 Innsbruck, Austria

Since the beginning of the seventies anticonvulsants, especially carbamazepine(CBZ), are discussed for the treatment of alcohol withdrawal. Various studies report favorable results of CBZ, usually combined with sedative agents, in the treatment of alcohol withdrawal. 18 out- and 19 inpatients suffering from alcohol dependence were treated with CBZ for 7 days at our department. The trial design was open and the "objective clinical scale in assessment and measurement of alcohol withdrawal" was used for treatment evaluation. CBZ monotherapy was attempted, the dose was adjusted individually and ranged from a mean dose of 761 mg on day 1 to 388 mg on day 7. Statistical analysis showed a significant improvement for out- as well inpatients. 4 inpatients needed a concommitant medication of 30 mg oxazepam daily during 2 days. 1 patients developed a delirium tremens after the first dose of CBZ.In 2 cases CBZ had to be discontinued because of side-effects (nausea, pruritus).

1298

EVALUATION OF THE RESULTS OF AN ALCOHOLOGIC PROGRAM: A CATAMNESTIC STUDY.
Piani Francesco, Pettoello Gianni.
Alcohologic Service of the U.S.L. n.6, San Daniele del Friuli, Udine, Italy.

The alcohologic Department of the U.S.L. n.6 was set up in November 1980 and it was formed by an internist doctor, a psychiatrist, a psycologist, a social worker, nursing staff, and followed prof. V. Hudolin's school for alcoholic treatment. In The area of the U.S.L. (about 47.0000 inhabitants) there are 25 Clubs (club for treated alcoholics): they are the basis for the methodology, organize the weekly follow up of the alcoholics for a period of 5 years. We examined all the 124 subjects treated during 1980-81-82 by the alcohologic service. At the date of this research we had the following results: 18 people were dead (14.5 %), 6 people were not found (6.4 %), 2 people didn't accept the interview.
We interviewed 93.6 % of the people treated in the considered period. We gave all the subjects a complete questionnaire to be filled, divided by life functioning areas with interview and clinical examinations made by a phisician just in their own homes in order to check the answers. The results concerning abstinence and treatment continuation are surely good: actually 78 % of the subjects is still abstinent. There is also a meaningful correlation among attendance to the club, use of Disulfiram medicine and abstinence.

1299

EXPECTATIONS AND PERSONAL BELIEVES ABOUT ALCOHOL AND TREATMENT OF ALCOHOLICS
J. Pinto Gouveia (1)
Conceição Fernandes (2)
Constantino Ferrão (2)
Fátima Lopes (2)
F. Santos Costa (2)

The literature concerning alcoholism problems suggest that personal believes and expectations about alcohol effects may have an important role on the development and maintaince of a alcchoism.
In the present research using the Personal Believes and Alcohol Expectations Inventory(P.B.A. E.I.) in a population of alcoholics in treatment, the authors investigated the personal believes and expectations about alcohol and its connection with the drinking habit and treatment evolution.
The subjects completed the P.B.A.E.I. and filled in a questionnaire of patterns of drinking habits, before the beginning, at the of the treatment and after a three-month follow-up.
The results obtained showed that the personal believes and expectations about alcohol are an important factor in alcoholism and should deserve a special attention on the alcoholics treatment programs.

---
(1) Psychiatrist Hospital Universidade Coimbra
(2) Residents of psychiatry Hospital Psiquiátrico do Lorvão

Session 202 Special Session:
Neuroendocrinology of affective disorders and schizophrenia

1300

Pituitary hormone stimulation test in endogenous depressive patients and healthy subjects

LAAKMANN G, HINZ A, VODERHOLZER U, NEUHAUSER H, WINKELMANN M, DAFFNER C

Psychiatric Hospital of the University of Munich
Nußbaumstraße 7, D-8000 München 2

Previous pharmacoendocrinological studies demonstrated that in various stimulation tests (insulin hypoglycemia, apomorphin, L-Dopa and clonidine tests) and in our investigations with the Desipramine(DMI) test (Laakmann, 1980; 1987) endogenous depressive patients show a blunted GH response compared to healthy subjects.

In further investigations we made efforts to explore whether the dysfunction of the pituitary hormone secretion is cause of hypothalamic or pituitary failure.

We examined the secretion of growth hormone (GH), cortisol and thyrotropin (TSH) in seven endogenous depressive female patients (21 - 61 years) and seven age-matched healthy female subjects after combined administration of growth hormone releasing hormone (GHRH), corticotropin releasing hormone (CRH), gonadotropin releasing hormone (GnRH) and thyrotropin releasing hormone (TRH).

The endogenous depressive female patients showed a significantly lower GH stimulation ($p < 0.05$) and a lower TSH stimulation compared to age-matched controls, whereas the cortisol response was similar in both groups.

These results indicate that the impaired GH secretion in endogenous depressive patients is responsible for the dysfunction of the GH production or a failing responsiveness of the somatotrope. However, other mechanisms are to be discussed.

1301

THE DEXAMETHASONE SUPPRESSION TEST IN DEPRESSION: W.H.O. COLLABORATIVE STUDY

M.T. Abou-Saleh, Senior Lecturer in Psychiatry, University of Liverpool, Royal Liverpool Hospital, P.O. Box. 147, Liverpool. England. M. Gastpar, Director of the Department of Psychiatry, Essen-Holsterhausen, Virchowstraße 174, Hufelandstraße 55, 4300 Essen 1, Vermittlung (0201) 723 - 1, West Germany.

The response to the Dexamethasone Suppression Test (DST) was examined in 543 patients suffering from major depressive illness and 246 healthy controls, from 13 research centres, representing 12 different countries, in a World Health Organisation Collaborative Study. The overall sensitivity of the test (non-suppression > 50 ng/ml) for RDC major depression was 49.2% and specificity of 89.1% in normal controls. The most significant source of variation in DST results was the centre. Non-suppression was associated with increased severity of illness and increased age, but there was no association with diagnostic category. Detailed analysis of the clinical characteristics of non-suppressors on the WHO Standardized Schedule for Assessment of Depressive Disorders, showed an assocation with excessive anxiety, fitful sleep, psychomotor restlessness, aggression and change in body weight, findings that support a stress - activation model to explain DST non-suppression.

1302

HYPOTHALAMIC PITUITARY CHALLENGE AND PSYCHOPATHOLOGICAL DISTINCTION OF DEPRESSION AND SCHIZOPHRENIA

G.Wieselmann[1], B.Gallhofer[1], B.Malle[2], S.Kunz[1], G.Fueger[3],
[1]University Departments of Psychiatry and Neurology, Institutes of [2]Psychology and [3]Nuclear Medicine, Graz Austria

There is evidence of a context between biological modulation of states of the mind and collusive functioning of various brain pathways. In this presentation a study of 10 schizophrenic (SCH) and 10 unipolar depressive (D) patients - of whom 50% had been drug naive before being admitted to the study - demonstrates the factors of discriminance of neuroendocrine changes between both groups.
A battery of mainly neuropsychological tests was applied to all patients to assess cognitive brain functioning. Beck`s Inventory HAM-D, Visual Analogue Scales, FPI parameters, BPRS, SANS and DSM III-R-criteria were used to assess quality and quantity of symptoms.
A challenge cocktail, consisting of TSH, Metoclopramide, Insuline and Dexametasone was injected after the extraction of two baseline values and Responses of TRH, PRL, HGH, Plasma Cortisol and a new complex plasma compound of 5 HT and metabolites were screened 30 (3), 60 (4), 90 (5) and 120 (6) minutes after the application.
SPSS stepwise discriminant analysis shows first PRL increase (PD23) as most explanative for the difference of psychopathology between SCH and D (Wilks Lambda 'WL'=.6, p.05) while TRH increase (TD34) ranks second (WL=.275,p.01).
Nonresponders to the challenge were significantly more frequent in the depressive group.

1303

CLONIDINE TEST IN SCHIZOPHRENICS

P. Rinieris, J. Hatzimanolis, M. Markianos, C. Stefanis.
Department of Psychiatry, Athens University Medical School, Eginition Hospital, Athens 11528, Greece

Clonidine (0.15 mg), an alpha-2 adrenergic receptor agonist, and placebo (10 ml saline) were administered intravenously in 12 male patients with paranoid type of schizophrenia, 13 male patients with disorganized (hebephrenic) type of schizophrenia, and 13 healthy male subjects. The growth hormone (GH) responses to clonidine or to placebo in the group of patients with paranoid type of schizophrenia did not differ significantly from those of the group of healthy subjects. The group of patients with disorganized type of schizophrenia presented significantly greater GH responses to clonidine, as well as to placebo, than those of both the groups of patients with paranoid type of schizophrenia and healthy subjects. These findings are compatible with an alteration in the neuroendocrine mechanisms which regulate GH secretion in a subgroup of patients with disorganized type of schizophrenia.

1304

PLASMA MELATONIN AND CORTISOL LEVELS IN SCHIZOPHRENIC PATIENTS

FANGET F., DALERY J., CLAUSTRAT B., BRUN J., TERRA J.L.
Centre Hospitalier Spécialisé Le Vinatier
95, boulevard Pinel - 69677 BRON CEDEX

Low nocturnal levels of melatonin with high cortisol levels have been reported in depressive patients. In the present study, plasma melatonin and cortisol levels of a group of schizophrenic inpatients under medication were measured.
The 23 patients with DSM III criteria of "schizophrenic disorders" were evaluated with Brief Psychiatric Rating Scale. This patient group was compared with a control group of 26 healthy subjects who had the similar mean age and sex ratio. All the biological studies were conducted at the same season. Ten milliliters of blood were drawn into heparinized plastic tubes at midnight in darkness and at midday the following day. Concentration of plasma cortisol, melatonin was determined by radioimmunoassay. RESULTS show that midnight melatonin levels were lower in the schizophrenic group than in the control group ($p<0.01$). Plasma cortisol ratios did not yield statistically differences between the schizophrenic and control groups. Methodological aspects and results will be discussed with personal and other authors' data.

1305

GRF TEST: A POTENTIAL DIAGNOSTIC MARKER IN PSYCHIATRIC DISORDERS.

M.A. Albarrán, A. Pérez, M. Fernández, F. Otero, J.A. Alvarez, C. Borrás, A. Rodríguez, R. Cacabelos. Department of Psychiatry. Santiago University Medical School. Spain.

The GH response to GRF has been studied in: (a) young schizophrenic patients (YSchP) (N=7) (Age=32.85$\pm$9.28 years); (b) elderly depressed patients (EDP) (N=6) (Age=62.00$\pm$ 9.14 years); (c) young healthy subjects (YHS) (N=6) (Age=32.00$\pm$8.48 years); and (d) elderly healthy subjects (EHS) (N=10) (Age=67.00$\pm$ 3.76 years). GRF(1-29)NH2 (150 ug) was injected as an intravenous bolus, and plasma GH levels were measured by RIA. YSchP showed similar basal plasma GH levels to YHS (YSchP=0.34$\pm$0.42 ng/ml; YHS=0.53$\pm$0.47 ng/ml); however the GH response to GRF was significantly lower in YSchP than in YHS with a maximum peak at 45 min. (YSchP=6.93$\pm$4.32 ng/ml; YHS=29.72$\pm$6.81 ng/ml, $p<0.005$). EDP and EHS exhibited similar basal plasma GH levels (EDP=0.30$\pm$0.15 ng/ml; EHS=1.00$\pm$0.45 ng/ml). A blunted response of GH to GRF was observed in EDP (maximum peak=3.93$\pm$1.22 ng/ml). These data seem to indicate that the GRF test may be of utility as a neurobiological marker in schizophrenia, and in some psychogeriatric disorders.

1306

TSH DURING ECT: A SIMULATED ECT CONTROLLED STUDY

Y. Papakostas, G. Papadimitriou, M. Markianos, C. Stefanis
Athens University Medical School, Dept. Psychiatry, Eginition Hospital

The immediate effect of electroconvulsive therapy (ECT) on serum thyrotropin (TSH) is not clear as some studies report a TSH increase and others don't. Still, a third intermediate position holds that if a TSH response is going to occur, a seizure activity of certain duration is necessary.
To clarify this issue, we studied serum TSH in 10 female, drug-free patients suffering from major depressive disorder (DSM-III) undergoing treatment with ECT. Blood samples were drawn at -10, 0, 5, 15, 30 and 60 min after ECT during the first two ECT sessions. The duration of seizure activity was estimated by clinical observation ("cuff method") and by electroencephalogram (EEG). During the first session all procedures regarding ECT administration were followed except that current did not pass ("Simulated" ECT or SECT). During the second session a real ECT was administered.
The effect of ECT on TSH was negligible as opposed to prolactin and cortisol which were both increased after ECT as it was expected. The ECT effect on growth hormone varied. In conclusion, no systematic ECT effect on serum TSH could be demonstrated.

1307

CHANGES IN NOCTURNAL SECRETION OF ANTERIOR PITUITARY HORMONES FOLLOWING A SERIES OF ECTs
C.R. Soldatos, J.D. Bergiannaki, P.N. Sakkas, C. Christodoulou, A. Botsis, C.N. Stefanis.

We studied the effects of ECT on nocturnal plasma concentrations of prolactin (PRL), growth hormone (GH), thyroid stimulating hormone (TSH) and cortisol (F). In six male drug free schizophrenics blood samples were hourly (8.00 p.m. to 8.00 a.m.) collected through a continuous withdrawal pump, the night before the first and the night after the first and the sixth of a series of ECTs. Levels were determined using radioimmunoassay methods. Our results show that nocturnal PRL secretion did not significantly change following the first ECT (NS), while there was a trend towards a decrease following the sixth ($p<0.1$). Total amount of GH secretion was not markedly affected by either the first or the sixth ECT (both NS), although the latter caused a 2-hour phase advance of GH peak. TSH secretion increased after the first ECT and even more after the sixth (both $p<0.001$), whereas T3 and T4 secretion was not significantly affected. Finally, secretion of F did not show any statistically significant change either after the first or the sixth ECT (both NS). The finding regarding the effects of ECT on pituitary-thyroid axis suggests that ECT may cause a degree of hyporesponsiveness of the thyroid gland.

1308

HPA AXIS ASSESSMENT IN DEPRESSED AND PARANOID-HALLUCINATORY PATIENTS
W. Baischer, G. Koinig, G. Schönbeck, P. Parzer
Department of Psychiatry, Vienna

The study investigates the relationship between HPA axis and recovery process in functional psychoses. 87 depressive and 17 paranoid-hallucinatory patients were examined before therapy.
The patients underwent a dexamethasone suppression test (DST). Subsequently they received daily infusions of clomipramine or haloperidol respectively. Weekly psychometric measurements were conducted till recovery.
The comparison with a group of healthy subjects showed a four fold higher rate of hypercortisolism in the depressives and a two fold higher rate in the paranoid-hallucinatory group. There was no significant relationship between DST results and the time required for recovery. Sex and cortisol base-line also did not influence the same. The depressives recovered earlier than the paranoid-hallucinatory patients.

Session 203 Symposium:
Next steps that will revolutionize psychiatric education in the 21st century

1309

THE PLACE OF MENTAL HEALTH IN PUBLIC HEALTH EDUCATION
Henderson, John H.
St. Andrew's Hospital, Northampton, England

Public health today is a modern and broad interpretation applied to concepts of public health by many disciplines and organisations, which is essentially different from the inheritance of the past.

Public Health medicine requires the leadership of medical practittioners though many disciplines, professions, institutions, agencies and organisation are involved. Multi-disciplinary training is essential in the new Public Health.

Mental Health as an essential component of Public Health education conveys the necessary emphasis also on behavioural sciences, demography and epidemiology. The paper will address in particular the Mental Health function of the Public Health worker; the curriculum content for students in Public Health and career functions and prospects for Mental Health in Public Health.

1310

THE FUTURE OF PSYCHIATRIC EDUCATION IN THE WESTERN PACIFIC REGION
F. Lieh Mak
University of Hong Kong

The Western Pacific Region is characterized by diversity in size of countries, ethnicity, political systems, cultures, economic development and religion. The countries in this region are also in different developmental stages in the provision of psychiatric services and the training of professionals to meet these needs.

the WHO and WPA held a meeting in Fukuoka to deal with the issues relevant to the future of psychiatric education in this region. As a result of this meeting a Declaration of Fukuoka was formulated.

This paper will discuss the conclusions and the recommendations of this meeting in the areas of undergraduate and postgraduate psychiatric education, psychiatric education for non-psychiatric medical practitioners and the humanization of medicine.

1311

THE FUTURE OF PSYCHIATRIC EDUCATION IN NORTH AFRICA
D.MOUSSAOUI
CENTRE PSYCHIATRIQUE UNIVERSITAIRE IBN ROCHD CASABLANCA MOROCCO.

Psychiatry is well established in developed countries. On the contrary, psychiatry in developing countries is considered by many policy makers as a luxury, far behind in interest infectious diseases and malnutrition for example.Epidemiology is the only way to convince policy makers and medical students on the interest of psychiatry in developing countries.

The international WHO study on schizophrenia is a good model, showing that the prevalence of this disease is approximately the same in developed and developing countries.

The experience of Casablanca, Morocco will be presented. Three kind of epidemiologic studies have been conducted among hospitalised patients, among patients consulting G.P.s and in general population.

The results show the same figures than those found in developed countries. They allow us to focus education on relevant objectives.

1312
THE FUTURE OF PSYCHIATRIC EDUCATION IN THE WESTERN PASIFIC REGION
Bousnello E. - Centro Medico Social Sao Jose Murialdo, Brazil

1313
THE DECLARATION OF FUKUOKA ON PSYCHIATRIC EDUCATION FOR THE 21ST CENTURY

Nishizono, M., M. D.
Dept. of psychiatry
Fukuoka University, School of Medicine, Japan

The first WHO/WPA Joint Meeting on Psychiatric Education for the 21st Century was held in Fukuoka, Japan in March, 1989. As the result of the Meeting, we adopted the Declaration of Fukuoka and four Recommendaions on psychiatric education (undergraduate, postgraduate, for non-psychiatrists and humanization of medical education).
 In advance of the Meeting, I distributed a questionnaire on psychiatric education to each participant of the Meeting. And we used the results of the questionnaire as data to discuss the problems and the strategies on psychiatric education at the Meeting.

Session 204 Symposium:
The role of benzodiazepines in the treatment of chronic illness and distress syndromes

1314
BENZODIAZEPINES IN STRESS AND ADAPTATION REACTIONS TO CHRONIC ILLNESS.
David Wheatley, M.D., F.R.C.Psych.
The Stress Clinic, Maudsley Hospital, London, UK.

The effects of stress are mainly manifested through the cardiovascular system and anxiety accompanying coronary heart disease and hypertension can be controlled with benzodiazepine (BZD) anxiolytics. Other illnesses with an anxiety component are: sexual disorders, menstrual disorders, asthma, gastro-intestinal conditions, dermatological conditions and chronic illnesses such as arthritis, malignancy and AIDS. Lack of sleep is a subtle form of stress exerting an adverse effect in almost every illness known to man and BZD hypnotics are effective in relieving this. Depending on the nature of the insomnia, ultra-short acting and short-acting BZD are particularly convenient with minimal disadvantages. Anxiety, as either cause or effect, accompanies many medical illnesses and the use of BZD as concomitant therapy can both reduce morbidity and improve prognosis. The results of a number of trials of BZD anxiolytics and hypnotics undertaken by the Psychopharmacology Research Group will be presented.

1315
HEALTH STATUS AND BENZODIAZEPINE LONG-TERM TREATMENT
B.Geiselmann, M.Linden
Dept.of Psychiatry, Free University of Berlin, W-Germany

Benzodiazepine (BDZ) long-term treatment has been seriously criticized because of possible side-effects, such as tolerance, dependence, and cognitive and psychomotor impairment. Nevertheless, BDZ are widely used. General physicians and internists in private practice account for the majority of BDZ prescriptions. However, there is little knowledge about illness characteristics of those patients receiving BDZ treatment, especially on a long-term basis. This information is a prerequisite to discuss alternative treatment options.
In a study in general and internist private practices, we examined 200 patients, who had been using BDZ for 6 months or longer. The patients' health status was evaluated as well as patients' own reports of health complaints, present medications, the doctors' diagnoses, and the research psychiatrist's scientific diagnoses. Results show that polymorbidity and multiple complaints in the context of chronic illness are important factors related to BDZ long-term treatment. This has important consequences for any cost/benefit analysis, especially as the patients themselves play an important role in treatment decisions.

1316
EUTHYMOTROPIC EFFECTS OF BENZODIAZEPINES AND ILLNESS TOLERANCE

Günter Debus
Institut für Psychologie
Jägerstr. 17-19, 5100 Aachen

As the rule the emotional therapeutical effects of benzodiazepines have been restricted to anxiety reduction. The "anxiolytic" effect as measured by ratings in clinical studies is probably a simplification. Subjective-emotional drug profiles do not show drug effects only selectively in the "anxiety" category but also in categories such as "general well-being", "self-confidence" and "elation". Furthermore also behavioral effects have been shown in human subjects: behavioral responses, which are depressed by response-contingent punishment or conditioned fear, increase. These subjective and behavioral effects may be explained by a system-theoretically guided approach of emotion. They might reflect a pharmacological influence upon a single emotional system which plays an important role in stress and illness tolerance.
The contribution reviews the empirical evidence for the view outlined above and discusses the stress-prophylactic role of drug administration.

1317
THE PATIENT'S PERSPECTIVE IN LONG-TERM BENZODIAZEPINE TREATMENT

Clare A. - Professor, Eire St. Patrick's Hospital Dublin

1318
A SOCIOLOGICAL PERSPECTIVE ON TRANQUILLISER PRESCRIBING

Jonathan Gabe
General Practice Research Unit, Institute of Psychiatry, DeCrespigny Park, Denmark Hill, GB-London SE5 8AF

This paper outlines a sociological approach to benzodiazepine tranquilliser prescribing. The analysis focuses on both the micro level of the doctor-patient relationship and the macro level of those political, economic and cultural factors which structure the prescribing process. This makes it possible to account for both the overall decline in benzodiazepine prescriptions in the 1980s and the fact that they are still being prescribed on a long-term to a significant number of people.

1319
FEASIBILITY AND LIMITS OF BENZODIAZEPINE LONG-TERM TREATMENT
Karl Rickels, M.D., University of Pennsylvania, Philadelphia, Pennsylvania, U.S.A.
Many anxiety and panic conditions are rather chronic in nature, frequently necessitating more than a 3 to 6 week course of anxiolytic therapy. Similarly, benzodiazepines are quite rightfully prescribed for prolonged periods of time for many patients suffering from chronic medical illnesses. Since prolonged benzodiazepine therapy does entail the danger of physical dependence, many authors suggest to use benzodiazepines only intermittently. While tolerance to the sedative effects clearly does develop, this is not necessarily true for their anxiolytic effect. Yet, many chronic users, after years of therapy, may well treat only their underlying physical dependence rather than their underlying illness. We found that chronic users of benzodiazepines for over 10 years clearly felt better and had significantly lower rating scale scores for anxiety and depression after they had been off their benzodiazepines for at least 5 weeks. Benefits and risks need to be discussed with the patient prior to therapy onset, and alternative or additional therapies such as various psychotherapies or behavioral therapies and counseling need also to be discussed

1320
MEDICATION ALTERNATIVES FOR BENZODIAZEPINES

M.Linden
Dept.of Psychiatry, Free University of Berlin, W-Germany

Any treatment has to be evaluated under consideration of therapeutic alternatives. Benzodiazepines (BDZ) have for example been substitutes for bromides or barbiturates. It is, therefore, important to know the pharmacological alternatives for BDZ at hand for the physician in day-to-day practice.
From a pharmacological perspective, a long list of substances can have tranquilizing properties. Some of these are interesting alternatives for BDZ in special indications, others must be seen as therapeutically obsolete. From the practitioner's point of view, who is asking how to cope with certain illness states, a quite different list of medications emerges as alternatives for BDZ. Results of an inquiry under practitioners on possible alternatives for BDZ show that they are used in the treatment of many illness states, other than anxiety disorders, and that changes in BDZ prescriptions may lead to substitution by quite different medication classes, which go beyond the group of "tranquilizers". The interpretation of any BDZ prescription data, which only focuses on anxiety states, can therefore not be adequate, and will overlook important therapeutic areas as well as explanations for the prescription of BDZ.

Session 205   Symposium:
Biology of alcohol withdrawal psychoses

1321
TREATMENT OF THE ACUTE ALCOHOL WITHDRAWAL SYNDROME (A-ADRENERGIC AGONISTS, B-BLOCKERS, BENZODIAZEPINS, PEPTIDE ANTAGONISTS)

Gallant D. - Professor, Tulana Medical School New Orleans, Luisiana USA

1322
INTERRELATION OF CLINICAL SYMPTOMATOLOGY WITH CHANGES OF CATECHOLAMINE LEVELS IN ACUTE ALCOHOL PSYCHOSES

Anochina I., Kogan D. - Professor, All-Union Research Institute for Narcol, Soviet Union

1323
DIAGNOSTIC AND TREATMENT STUDIES OF DELIRIUM TREMENS
B. NICKEL, J. NEUMANN, R. SCHMICKALY
Central Clinic for Psychiatry and Neurology "W. Griesinger", Berlin/GDR

Diagnostic observations (EP,ERP,CT,MRT) and treatment studies overviewing 700 patients with severe delirium tremens will be reported, including remarks to mortality.

The 10-year review of a fully equipped intensive care unit reports preclinical, clinical, psychopathological, psychometrical findings, refers to rare cases e.g. Wernicke Encephalopathy, Central Pontine myelinolysis and deals with the results of different prospective treatment studies including Physostigmine, Benzodiazepines, Etomidate, Dehydrobenzperidol, Magnesium, Calcium-channel-blockers.

1324
CHRONIC ALCOHOLISM - THE PROBLEM OF DIAGNOSIS
Lesch, O.M.
Psychiatric University Clinic, Vienna

Up to the very present, generations of researchers have discussed the problem of differentiation between alcohol abuse and addiction. Diagnostic instruments such as ICD-9, DSM III, and DSM III R - mainly influenced by the American point of view - clearly show these diagnostic uncertainties. Especially from therapeutic studies, it is well known that psychopathological as well as somatic-biological differences represent important predictors for further illness course.

The heterogenity of this group of patients is demonstrated by means of a prospective long-term follow-up study. Out of this study, 4 therapy-relevant sub-groups of chronic alcoholic patients were developed. These homogenous sub-groups help to more adequately differentiate the therapeutic strategies necessary, as well as to better evaluate the basid data gained in scientific research, in order to improve upon the simple diagnosis of "chronic alcoholism.

1325
The pharmalogical treatment of alcohol relapse

D. Ladewig and W. Pöldinger

The pharmalogical treatment of alcoholism concerns mostly the acute withdrawal symptoms. The pathophysiology of late withdrawal symptoms, craving for alcohol or so called relapse to drinking is unknown yet. Some possible mechanism have been discovered.

A wide spectrum of drugs have been evaluated; like benzodiazepines, carbamazepine or antidepressants. Calciumacomprosat (AOTA-CA) is a homotaurine derivate which has a stimulating effect of the GABA ergic system. A protective effect on membranes is additionally known.

In animal experiments as well as in clinical studies, AOTA-CA showed an effect on drinking behaviour. The relapse rate of alcoholics was reduced significantly.

1326
CONSTRUCT VALIDITY OF THE WITHDRAWAL SYNDROME SCALE FOR ALCOHOL AND RELATED PSYCHOACTIVE DRUGS
P. Bech, S. Rasmussen, A. Dahl, B. Lauritsen and K. Lund
Frederiksborg General Hospital, 3400 Hillerød, Denmark

The Withdrawal Syndrome Scale (WSA) consists of seven items observed by the nursing staff. A weighted total score of these items has since 1983 been used in the daily routine in our department as guidelines for anti-abstinence treatment with phenobarbital. This procedure has during the years been found valid and safe.
By use of latent structure analysis (Rasch) the items of pulse, tremor, motor restlessness constituted the lower rank (mild degree) of the target syndrome, the items of temperature and sweating constituted the moderate degree, while desorientation and hallucination constituted the severe degree.
This hierarchical construct seemed, thus, to show that one underlying dimension is sufficient to quantify the clinical target syndrome of withdrawal. It involves in its mild degrees an autonomic hyperactivity and in its moderate to severe dgrees a dopaminergic hyperactivity. In cases with high total scores of the WSA in spite of phenobarbital treatment, antidopaminergic drugs like haloperidol are very effective in combination with the phenobarbital treatment.

Session 206 Symposium:
Treatment of negative symptoms in schizophrenia

1327
PYRAMIDICAL MODEL OF SYNDROMES IN SCHIZOPHRENIA
Stanley R. Kay, Ph.D.
Albert Einstein College of Medicine, Bronx, NY, USA
Efforts to better understand and treat schizophrenia have been complicated by its heterogeneity and the lack of well operationalized, standardized assessment methods. We developed and validated a 30-symptom Positive and Negative Syndrome Scale (PANSS) to meet this need and delineate positive and negative features. With this method we sought to study the validity and sufficiency of the positive-negative distinction for a model of schizophrenia. We obtained PANSS data on 240 schizophrenic inpatients and subjected these to principal component analysis to identify the emergent factors. The results suggested a pyramidlike triangular model of independent but nonexlcusive syndromes that encompassed all 30 symptoms. Negative, positive, and depressed components emerged as divergent points of a triangular base, and excitement as a separate vertical axis. The interaction of paired syndromes could account for symptoms of paranoid (positive-depressed), disorganized (positive-negative), and catatonic (negative-depressed) diagnostic subtypes. The transversal positions in this model suggested polarized dimensions, including a prognostic axis (depression - cognitive dysfunction). The findings imply that: (a) negative and positive syndromes show factorial validity, mutual distinctiveness, and distinction from depression but, alone, do not accommodate the full diversity of symptoms; (b) schizophrenia subtypes derive from co-occurring but independent syndromes that may explain the heterogeneity of schizophrenia and suggest syndrome-specific treatments.

1328
NEGATIVE SYMPTOMS AND BIOCHEMICAL CORRELATES

Johnstone, E.C., Owens, D.G.C., Crow, T.J., Frith, C.D. and Roberts, G.W.
Division of Psychiatry, Clinical Research Centre, Watford Road, Harrow, HA1 3UJ. U.K.

There is ample evidence to suggest a relationship between positive symptoms in schizophrenia and neurotransmission particularly dopaminergic transmission. Such evidence regarding negative symptoms is much more fragmented but data concerning dopaminergic symptoms drawn from clinical trials of dopamine agonists (apomorphine and L-dopa) dopamine blockers (pimozide and chlorpromazine) and anticholinergics (procyclidine), neuroendocrine studies and post-mortem work will be presented. Similarly studies concerning the relevance of serotonin and neuropeptides for negative symptoms will be reviewed. The difficulties in the clinical assessment of negative symptoms and the problem of their separation from extrapyramidal side effects will be discussed and the limitations that these problems may have placed upon the investigation of the basis of negative symptoms considered.

1329
BPRS SYMPTOM FACTORS AND SLEEP VARIABLES IN SCHIZOPHRENIA
K. L. Benson, J. G. Csernansky & V. P. Zarcone, Jr.
Stanford University School of Medicine
Palo Alto, CA, USA

The relationship of positive and negative symptoms to sleep variables has been the subject of several reports. Sleep measures as well as the methods of assessing negative symptoms have varied. We have analyzed a larger sample (n=20) using the BPRS higher-order factors.

We studied 15 schizophrenics and 5 schizoaffectives, mainly schizophrenic. Diagnoses were made using RDC; their mean age was 34.4 years. All patients were neuroleptic free for at least 2 weeks before the 3 night sleep study. To enhance overall reliability, the average of 2 rating sessions was analyzed: one within 7 days of the sleep study, and a second within 14 days. We analyzed 2 higher-order factors: thinking disturbance and withdrawal-retardation. These factors correlate with positive and negative symptoms respectively.

In this sample, we found no correlation between the withdrawal-retardation factor and measures of slow wave sleep minutes (mean = 45.9) or stage 4% (mean = 1.2%), a more conservative measure correcting for variation in total sleep time. As in other studies, sleep latency in the schizophrenics was prolonged: mean = 78.9 min. Sleep latency was significantly correlated (r = +0.60, p < .005) with the thinking disturbance factor.

1330
DRUG TREATMENT AND THE NEGATIVE SYMPTOMS OF SCHIZOPHRENIA
J.C. Cookson, The London Hospital, England.

Although the 'deficit syndrome' is unresponsive to conventional antipsychotic medication, negative symptoms occurring in the acute phase of schizophrenia do improve. Negative symptoms may also improve through treatment of depression or extra-pyramidal side effects.
Antipsychotic drugs with selectivity for blockade of dopamine receptors such as pimozide, bromperidol and benzamide derivatives have less sedative properties. In low doses they may also cause activation, which is not specific to schizophrenia.
Drugs that have been investigated for effects upon negative symptoms include propranolol, alprazolam, fenfluramine, procyclidine, verapamil, amphetamine and L-DOPA.
Clozapine may improve patients who are resistant to other anti-psychotic drugs. Particular interest has focussed upon its ability to block 5HT-2 receptors. Selective 5HT-2 antagonists such as ritanserin allow the role of 5HT in schizophrenia and in the action of drugs to be investigated further. Ritanserin appears to improve negative symptoms when used as an adjunct to anti-psychotic medication.

1331
RISPERIDONE: A NEW APPROACH IN THE TREATMENT OF SCHIZOPHRENIA
Peuskens J., Claus A., De Cuyper H., Bollen J., Eneman M., Wilms G.
University Psychiatric Centers, Leuven, Belgium.

Risperidone (R 64 766) is a potent combined serotonin-5HT$_2$ and dopamine-D$_2$ antagonist. In previous open studies in chronic psychotic patients it was demonstrated that this substance combines an effective antipsychotic action with an important improvement of negative and affective symptoms, and a significant reduction of existing extrapyramidal symptoms (EPS).
To confirm these results, 42 treatment-unresponsive chronic schizophrenic patients were selected for a 12 week double-blind comparative study versus haloperidol. Patients were evaluated by means of the SADS-C, PANSS, NOSIE-30, CGI, and ESRS. Their ventricle-to-brain ratio (VBR) was compared with the mean VBR of a matched normal population, and in the group of schizophrenic patients, possible correlations were evaluated between the VBR and psychopathology.
CONCLUSIONS
- Risperidone has a rapid onset of action; it improves positive symptoms, negative symptoms and general psychopathology more than haloperidol, while it has a safer EPS profile: consumption of antiparkinson medication is 10 times less with risperidone.
- Chronic schizophrenic patients have a significantly larger VBR than normal controls; only the schizophrenics have a significant correlation with the age in the range of 20-65 years. No correlation was found between the VBR and Positive symptoms, Negative symptoms, General Psychopathology or EPS.

Session 207 New research:
Child and adolescent psychiatry

1332

RELATION BETWEEN FAMILY FEATURES AND OBSESSIONS IN CHILDREN
Vida Rakić
Institute for the Mental Health, Belgrade, Yugoslavia

As the dynamics of family relations is crutial for emotional and social development of child, in order to determine the relation between the obsessiveness/compulsiveness (OC) in children and adolescents and their family features, we have identified, from among 332 examinees of the general population aged 7-19, an experimental group of 49 latent aged children and adolescents with OC and, by matching, a control group. A statistically significant relation has shown to exist between the examinee from experimental group and the following family features: unsatisfactory family atmosphere ($C=0.33$, $p=0.01$); family discord, most frequently (28.6%) due to alchoholism ($C=0.46$, $p=0.000$); behavior during discord ($C=0.39$, $p=2.898^{-3}$); mothr's way of bringing up ($C=0.37$, $p=0.009$); mother over 36 at the birth of examinee ($C=0.25$, $p=0.04$); divorced mother ($C=0.28$, $p=0.04$); chronic disease of mother ($C=0.22$, $p=0.02$). Detailed analysis of individual variables is given, including those which are statistically insignificant. Findings point to the possibility of and the need for prevention in children and adolescents.

1333

THE NECESSITY OF EXTENSIVE DYNAMIC DIAGNOSIS REGARDING CHILDREN AFFECTED BY DIVORCE
Gertrude BOGYI,Ph.D.& Georg SPIEL,M.D.
Univ.Klinik f.Neuropsychiatrie Ki.u.Jugendl.Wien
Abt.f.Psychiatrie u.Neurol.Ki.u.Jugendl,FU Berlin
The fact of divorce,accompanied by change of life circumstances means an important stress to children'and adolescent's well-being.It happens not only during different stages in personality configuration,but possibly affects them showing personality disorders of various degrees.The experience of divorce cannot be dealt with without considering life-history and object relationships The interpendence between chronic familiar con - flicts and child personality development is to be taken into account.Not to forget new objects to transference.
For nosological description and differentiation of these processes,a classification scheme by W.& G.SPIEL(1989) was used,which esp. focuses on the developmental psychopathological aspects. In the mean time an unselected sample (Jan.-June 1989)of 90 case histories of outpatient children, aging from 2,5 till 18, with various symptoms,but with a divorce in their past history,was analysed Various types of dysfunctional processes of personality development can be differentiated, whereby the discrimination between external,internal and deep inner conflicts (A.FREUD) plays an important role. The used form of classification leads immeadiately to a differential indication of therapeutic means.

1334

TODAY THERAPEUTIC MEASURES FOR CHILDREN WITH AUTISTIC SYNDROME.

Dr G. S. COHEN ADAD, Dr R. BEROUTI, CHS de Maison Blanche, Neuilly/Marne; Dr M. SMADJA, Hop. de Gonesse; FRANCE.

1. The goals and objectives of psychotherapy and special educationnal procedures for children with autistic syndrome are generally limited. These 2 approaches should be associated rather than considered as separate measures.
2. Infantile autism is now viewed as a syndrome of many different etiologies. Psychogenic and organic hypotheses on the etiology of autistic syndrome should not be perceived as mutually exclusive. Recent preliminary results of empirical studies (Cohen Adad et al., Bursztejn et al.) show that psychogenic and organic etiological factors may coexist in a certain number of patients.
3. Some authors (Berouti et al.) affirm that early psychoanalytic therapy (in the 1st and 2nd year of life) is of help for children with autistic syndrome or with autistic features.
In some cases, these children have a better clinical outcome (dysharmonie évolutive (Mises)). They are able to acquire language and develop satisfactory object relationships.

Codes #07, #77
Paper in french
Oral free communication
New research session

1335

Child rearing practices - An Indian Scene.

Dr. Shail Verma,
Psychiatryunit Bhilai Hospital & Research Center.
Bhilai, India.

Keeping in view, the concept of cultural relativism, this study was conducted, as a preventive step to Mental disorders of children as well as adults. In India in every 60 miles, there is a change of culture, language, and dress. Child rearing practices in ten different cultures of India had been studied and compared in its psychopathological and psychopathoplastic effects. In the same culture different socioeconomic group were also compared with a focus of children reared in poverty and slum areas. An attempt has been made to come forward with an ideal child rearing model free from cultural effect. The attempt is not to apply a diagnostic lebel to the child but to study and understand the child rearing effects so that appropriate educational procedures or interventions could be undertaken. Results and detailed analysis will be discussed during presentation as it is a new research findings.

1336
A THIRTY CASES STUDY OF THE FIRST DAY-HOSPITAL FOR ADOLESCENTS CREATED IN ZARAGOZA
Civeira J.M.,Garcia M.P., Abril, A.

Psychiatry Department Complutense University of Madrid (Spain)

Desde que en 1.933 surge el primer centro de hospitalización diurna en Moscú, el concepto de HOSPITAL O UNIDAD DE DIA se ha ido haciendo más complejo si bien, las funciones límites y actividades que desarrollan los Hospitales (o Unidades) de Dia de niños y adultos han sido bastante estudiados, como se ha comprobado en una revisión bibliográfica de los últimos diez años, queda un vacio para la atención del adolescente.

Una vez elaborado todo el material bibliográfico, se ha puesto en marcha en Zaragoza (España) la primera U.D. solo para a dolescentes.

A traves del seguimiento de los treinta primeros casos ingresados en esta unidad desde el 1/1/89 hasta el 30/6/89 valoramos las hipótesis de partida analizando los medios y métodos utilizados en este primer programa piloto de atención extrahospitalaria, concluyéndose que la creación de la U.D. para la atención especifica del adolescente, está justificada tanto por los resultados clínicos obtenidos, como por la repercusión económica y social.

1337
ADOLESCENTS WITH EMOTIONAL AND CONDUCT DISORDERS: A FOLLOW UP STUDY
Dr. Peter Wells, FRC.Psych, FRANZCP,DPM,DCH,DRCOG.
Young People's Unit, Macclesfield, England.

E. Brian Farragher, M.Sc., FSS.
Head of Medical Statistics,
University Hospital, South Manchester, England.

A two year follow-up study of 135 teenage in-patients treated for emotional and/or conduct disorders is described and the preliminary findings discussed.

The young person, their parents and the professional referrer are given forms listing the young person's presenting problems. The three respondents are asked to place a cross on a rating scale for each presenting problem to show how satisfactorily or otherwise the teenager has managed each one up to admission, and at one month, one year and two years after discharge. Comparison of the mean score per problem before admission and at follow-up shows a sustained improvement for at least two years, although respondents differ significantly as to the degree. The most optimistic respondendent is the young person, the least is the professional referrer or other care giver still involved.

This method avoids the bias derived from therapeutic staff rating their own results.

1338
CONDUCT DISORDER, DEPRESSION AND SUICIDALITY IN HOSPITALIZED ADOLESCENTS
S. Tyano, A. Apter, Geha Psychiatric Hospital, Beilinson Medical Center, Petah Tiqva, Sackler School of Medicine, Tel Aviv University, Israel

One-hundred-and-sixty-three consecutive admissions to an adolescent unit were examined, using a semi-structured psychiatric interview. In addition to a DSM III diagnosis, quantitative scores for 12 symptom clusters included three types of depression, conduct disorder and suicidality. The results showed the following: Depression and suicide are highly correlated; conduct disorder symptoms and suicide are highly correlated; depression and conduct disorder symptoms are not correlated.Thus it is possible that two different types of suicidal behavior exist in adolescence. Among the diagnostic group, the anorexia nervosa patients were highly depressed and suicidal (type 1 suicidality) while the conduct disorder patients were not depressed but were highly suicidal (type 1 suicidality) while the conduct disorder patients were not depressed but were highly suicidal (type 2 suicidality). The implications are discussed in the paper.

1339
SOCIAL COMPETENCE AND BEHAVIORAL PROFILE OF TLE IN ADOLESCENCE
A. Apter, S. Tyano, Geha Psychiatric Hospital, Beilinson Medical Center, Petah Tiqva, Sackler School of Medicine, Tel Aviv University, Israel

A group of 26 adolescents with temporal lobe epilepsy, was compared to a matched control group of 26 adolescents with chronic bronchial asthma and with a group of 90 healthy adolescents, using the social competence measure and the behavior profile of the Child Behavior Checklist. Both chronically ill groups had more social and behavioral problems than the healthy adolescents, but were similar to each other on the social and behavioral profiles. The one area in which the TLE and asthmatic groups differed from one another was that of "schizoid" psychopathology, although this difference was confined to males. Since some of the items subsumed under this label are similar to those described in the literature as being characteristic of TLE in adults, this difference may be a real one and not merely a statistical artifact. Thus, while many of the emotional and social difficulties of adolescents with temporal lobe epilepsy are probably a non-specific result of chronic illness and social stigma, some may be due to a selective, specific neurobehavioral dysfunction.

1340
AN ERP ASSESSMENT OF ATTENTION DEFICIT HYPERACTIVITY DISORDER IN 6 TO 8 YEARS OLD CHILDREN.

P. ROBAEY, M. DUGAS and B. RENAULT.

URA 654 CNRS, LENA, Hôpital de La Salpêtrière, Paris, France and Service de Psychopathologie de l'Enfant et de l'Adolescent, Hôpital Robert Debré, Paris, France.

Event-related potentials (ERPs) were recorded from two groups of twelve children (attention deficit hyperactivity disorder - ADHD - and normal controls). Subjects were submitted to four different tasks implying categorization of words, digits, pictures or figures. Amplitudes and latencies of a fronto-central N150-P250 complex and of a parieto-occipital N250-P350 complex were measured. In the parieto-occipital regions, ERP amplitudes and latencies vary differently in both groups according to whether the task implied reading or not; in contrast, no such differences were observed in fronto-central regions. In addition, ADHD children produced P250 of higher amplitude and P350 of shorter latencies, whatever the stimulus type. These results are discussed in terms of relations between orienting reaction and cognitive processing.

Session 208 New Research:
Pharmacotherapy of Schizophrenia

1341
HALOPERIDOL BLOOD LEVELS AND CLINICAL EFFECTS IN SCHIZOPHRENIA
I. Bitter, J. Volavka, T.B. Cooper, J. Scheurer, L. Camus, R. Bakall, New York University and N.S. Kline Institute for Psychiatric Research, Orangeburg, NY USA

Clinical improvement in schizophrenia has been reported to depend on the plasma level of haloperidol; this relationship assumed the inverted U-shape("therapeutic window").

To test the hypothesis of therapeutic window, we have randomly assigned acutely exacerbating schizophrenic and schizoaffective patients to one of three plasma levels of haloperidol:2-13, 13.1-24, or 24.1-35 ng/ml. Patients who did not improve after six weeks of this treatment were randomly re-assigned to one of the three HAL levels for another six weeks. The improvement was defined as at least 50% reduction of BPRS total score. The study is in progress. The results obtained in 111 patients do not support the hypothesis of therapeutic window. No consistent relationship between plasma level of haloperidol and clinical improvement has been detected. Patients in the low haloperidol range tended to have less side effects and improved just as rapidly as the other patients. Switching the patients from one haloperidol range to another one had no consistent effect on the outcome.

These results suggest that acutely decompensated schizophrenic patients in the USA are receiving more haloperidol than they need. If confirmed, these findings may have a major impact on public health policy.

1342
S McLaren - J C Cookson - J T Silverstone

+Academic Unit of Human Psychopharmacology, St. Bartholomew's Hospital, London.
++Department of Psychiatry, The London Hospital (St. Clement's), London.

This one year double-blind trial compared the efficacy and side-effects of bromperidol decanoate and fluphenazine decanoate in the maintenance therapy of 47 outpatients with an ICD-9 diagnosis of schizophrenia. The 2 groups were well matched on entry for age, sex, duration of illness and previous medication.

No statistically significant differences were found between the two groups regarding total efficacy or side effect scale scores, with both groups remaining well controlled.

Patient weight measures showed no significant differences but with a tendency to reduced weight when receiving bromperidol decanoate, and increased weight when receiving fluphenazine decanoate.

Details of the efficacy, side effect and dose equivalence data will be presented and discussed.

1343
PERPHENAZINE ENANTHATE IN MAINTENANCE TREATMENT OF SCHIZOPHRENIC SUBGROUPS

Marek JAREMA
Division of Psychopathology, Institute of Neurology and Psychiatry, Medical Academy, Szczecin, Poland

The effect of maintenance treatment with perphenazine enanthate (Trilafon enanthate /TE/ in amp. 100mg/ml) in 10 out-patients who met the DSM-III-R criteria for schizophrenia is discussed in the preliminary report. TE was administered intramuscular every 2-3 weeks for at least 6 months. Seven patients improved during TE treatment; in 2 od them, 6 and 12 months lasting TE therapy allowed to complete the trial because of very good clinical improvement. Remaining 5 patients showed satisfactory clinical improvement. In 2 cases TE was discontinued after 1 or 2 injections because of extrapyramidal effects One patient did not improve during TE treatment and the drug was replaced by another neuroleptic. Patients with systematic hebephrenia showed best clinical improvement, but at the same time, one patient who did not respond to TE maintenence treatment was diagnosed as having systematic hebephrenia as well. The diagnosis of positive/negative schizophrenia did not predict clinical improvement, however one patient with negative schizophrenia improved very well. Younger patients improved better.

1344
LOW DOSE FLUPHENAZINE DECANOATE IN SCHIZOPHRENIA.
Andrea Salteri. S.P.D.C. U.S.S.L. 65. Sesto San Giovanni. Milano. Italia.
Although the value of neuroleptic drugs in the prevention of psychotic relapses has been well demonstrated, there is now a trend to establish lower, but effective, antipsychotic doses, in order to improve the benefit/risk ratio. In this study, I am reporting the preliminary findings about efficacy of low dose fluphenazine decanoate (FD) in a population of schizo phrenic patients.
METHODS. The sample consisted of 60 patients of our Psychiatric Operative Unit, affected by DSM-III schizophrenia. They were divided into two homogeneous groups receiving a low dose (6,25 mg./3 wk.) or a standard dose (25 mg./3 wk.) FD, and followed with regular ratings for six months.
FINDINGS. 6 patients of low dose group and 8 patients of standard regimen were considered relapsed.
CONCLUSIONS. Compliance, absence of side effects and effectiveness of low dose FD are remarkable in this study that will be replicated with a longer follow-up.

1345
COMPARATIVE STUDY OF AMISULPRIDE AND FLUPHENAZINE IN NEGATIVE SCHIZOPHRENIA
B. Küfferle, A. Topitz, P. Földes, B. Saletu, J. Grünberger, P. Berner
Psychiatric University Clinic of Vienna

42 hopitalised patients with residual schizophrenia and predominant negative symptoms were included in a double blind study comparing the benzamide amisulpride with fluphenazine. The study design called for treatment for 8 weeks with either 50 mg/daily amisulpride or 2 mg/daily fluphenazine in the first 2 weeks and 100 mg amisulpride or 4 mg fluphenazine thereafter. Since 2 patients discontinued treatment within the first 3 days for non-drug related reasons, the amisulpride group consisted of 19 patients and the fluphenazine group of 21. Evaluation of psychopathology included CGI, SANS scale and AMDP scale. Psychometric and psychophysiologic tests were carried out before and 4 hrs after the first single dose (acute effect), at hour 0 of day 14 (subacute effect), at hour 0 of day 42 (chronic effect) and 4 hrs after one additional dose on day 42 (superimposed effect). While global assessment showed a similar course of improvement in both groups, certain differential treatment effects could be detected utilising the detailed psychopathological/psychometric evaluation. Dropouts after a minimum of 2 weeks treatment included 4 amisulpride patients and 5 fluphenazine patients. Reasons for early discontinuation of amisulpride were emergence of productive symptoms (3 patients) and marked depression (1 patient), while for fluphenazine it was marked depression (2 patients), productive symptoms (2 patients) and severe EPS (1 patient). Problems of the pathogenesis of negative symptoms and the respective relevance for treatment evaluation will be discussed.

1346
INTERACTION BETWEEN ALCOHOL AND FLUPHENAZINE DECANOATE IN CHRONIC SCHIZOPHRENICS
Som D. Soni, J. S. Bamrah, M. Brownlee, and Janet Krska
Psychiatric Research Unit, Salford Health authority, Hope and Prestwich Hospitals, Salford, M6 8HD, UK

Seven chronic schizophrenic patients, stable for over 12 months on maintenance fluphenazine decanoate, were administered 40 gms of alcohol orally 2 hours after their regular injection. Blood samples for estimation of serum neuroleptic and prolactin levels were collected at various intervals over a 12 hour period. The procedure was repeated at their next regular injection but without alcohol. It was found that alcohol ingestion produced a significant drop in both serum neuroleptic and prolactin levels which persisted during the study period.

1347
A DOUBLE-BLIND COMPARATIVE MULTICENTRE STUDY OF REMOXIPRIDE B.I.D. AND T.I.D. IN COMPARISON WITH HALOPERIDOL T.I.D. IN SCHIZOPHRENIA
Beckmann H[1], Laux G[1], Klieser E[2]
Departments of Psychiatry, University of Wuerzburg[1], University of Düsseldorf[2], FRG

Remoxipride (R) is a novel substituted benzamide derivative with selective D_2-receptor blocking properties and preferential action on the mesolimbic dopamine system.
A double blind multicentre study was set up to compare R 150-600 mg/day with haloperidol (H) 7,5-30 mg/day in floridly ill schizophrenic patients according to DSM III. N=160 inpatients entered the study, the median age was 36 years, paranoid type predominated in 58% of the cases. No statistically significant differences were seen between the treatment groups in CGI and BPRS total score, the negative items and the anergia factor were in favour of R b.i.d.. The proportion of premature termination was 27% in total. Sedatives/hypnotics were used somewhat more in the R groups. As concerns the EPS symptoms, there was significantly less hypo-/akinesia, rigidity and tremor in the R groups. So, the therapeutic efficacy of R seems to be of the same order of magnitude as that of H with predominant effect on negative symptoms and clear advantage for R in relation to H concerning extrapyramidal symptoms. R appears to be as clinically effective and well tolerated when given b.i.d. as when given t.i.d..

1348

REMOXIPRIDE, A NEW D2-SPECIFIC RECEPTOR ANTAGONIST - RESULTS FROM A DOUBLE-BLIND TRIAL PROGRAMME IN SCHIZOPHRENIA

D. Morrison, B. Gustafsson, T. Lewander, S. Ögenstad, S-E Westerbergh

ASTRA RESEARCH CENTRE SÖDERTÄLJE
S-151 85 SÖDERTÄLJE, SWEDEN

The first clinical trials with remoxipride began in 1982. It is rapidly absorbed, has high bioavailability and peak plasma levels appear within 2 hours. No active metabolites have been detected and plasma levels increase proportionally with dose.

Promising results from open, non-comparative studies were presented in 1985. New data from a double-blind, comparative trial programme conducted in 9 countries consistently demonstrate that remoxipride is as effective as haloperidol in both acute and long term treatment of schizophrenia. The clinical relevance of the specificity for D2 receptors is apparent in the improved side effect profile; in particular the decrease in exptrapyramidal symptoms. As a consequence of the latter the need for concomitant anticholinergic medication is substantially reduced. The drug is well-tolerated and, based on the information available, appears to offer a high degree of safety.

The combination of equivalent antipsychotic efficacy, reduced side effects and good pharmacokinetic properties make remoxipride a significant advance in the treatment of schizophrenia and other psychotic conditions.

1349

PRELIMINARY CLINICAL AND BEAM FINDINGS ON THE NEW NEUROLEPTIC RISPERIDONE

H.J. Möller*, M. Jansen**, W. Kissling**, E. PELZER*

*Psychiatric Department of the University Bonn and **Psychiatric Department of the Technical University Munich

Risperidone is a new chemical compound (a benzisoxazole derivative) exhibiting potent serotonin-S-2 and dopamine-D-2-receptor blocking properties in pharmacological experiments. Because of this specific pharmacological profile and based on experiences with ritanserine, a drug with similar anti-serotonergic activity, it was suggested that this new compound is a potent neuroleptic probably with two important advantages with respect to the treatment of negative symptoms and to the reduction of extrapyramidal symptoms. - The preliminary results of an open clinical pilot study on 10 acutely schizophrenic patients leads to the conclusion that risperidone demonstrates a typical antipsychotic profile. The tolerability was remarkable: no extrapyramidal or other significant side-effects occurred. Changes in electrical activity were not particularly different during haloperidol or risperidone treatment. Power in summary maps of the alpha-range was unchanged but there was a slight shift of amplitude maximum to lower frequencies in the alpha-band.

1350

RISPERIDONE: TREATMENT OF SCHIZOPHRENIC PATIENTS WITH NEGATIVE SYMPTOMS
Monfort*, Manus*, Bourguignon*, Bouhours**
* Service de psychiatrie, 94010 Créteil, France
** Laboratoires Janssen, 92513 Boulogne, France

. The patients included in this open study met DSM III criteria for chronic schizophrenia (DSM III 295.1.2) with a SANS rating > 50. After a one week wash-out, they were treated with Risperidone (Ri) 1 to 2 mg b.i.d during six weeks. SANS, BPRS, ESRS and CGI were performed on days-7 (selection), 0 (baseline), 14, 28 and 42.
. 12 patients were included, their mean age was 32.6±11.01 years. Mean±SD duration of the disease was 7.6±3.35 years. In 6 subjects the dose was increased from 1 mg to 2 mg b.i.d. The clinical condition of one patient worsened (agitation) and after 5 weeks, Ri was discontinued.
. Their mean±SEM SANS total clusters scores at baseline (71.75±3.34) dropped significantly at the end of the six weeks period (52.17±4.75 ; p ≤ 0.01 ; % change : -27.3). BPRS total score % change was: -12.7 (p ≤ 0.01). Following BPRS clusters improved : anxiety-depression (p ≤ 0.01), anergia (p ≤ 0.05), and negative symptoms (p ≤ 0.05). Although the patients had a rather low score on the ESRS at baseline, a further moderate decrease of EPS was observed during the 6 weeks trial.
. Global evaluation rated therapeutic activity as excellent, good or moderate in 8 patients ; tolerance was excellent or good in 8 patients. No clinical adverse experience and no safety parameters abnormalities (blood pressure, ECG, laboratory analysis) were reported.
. In 6 of these patients, with predominant negative symptoms, Ri was continued beyond the end of the study and was able to replace a "classical" neuroleptic therapy (one year follow-up).

Session 209 Free Communications:
Obsessive compulsive disorders: Clinical aspects

1351

CLINICAL AND PSYCHOPHYSIOLOGICAL EVIDENCES OF TWO KINDS OF THE OBSESSIVE-COMPULSIVE DISORDER.
BOGETTO FILIPPO, MAINA GIUSEPPE, TORTA RICCARDO, LUIGI RAVIZZA
University of Turin, Dept. of Psychiatry

In the last few years new attentions has been paid to obsessive-compulsive disorder. So many studies on biological, clinical and psychodynamic aspects of the O.C.D. have appeared in this field.
We report the results of one of our studies which evidenced two groups of obsessive-compulsive patients (n = 70). The first group presents ciclic course, symptomatology with obsessions and without compulsions, generally preceded depression, feelings of guilt, middle insomnia and good responsiveness to the antidepressants. The second group presents continuous course, symptomatology with compulsions with or without obsessions, reactive depression, phobias and somatoform disorders, early insomnia and poor responsiveness to antidepressants.
We also have studied some psychophysiological aspects of these patients related to their anxiety trait: EMG, galvanic skin response, heart rate and skin temperature.
We think that those advances in the nosography of obsessive disorders are very important, above all

1352
CHARACTERISTICS OF OBSESSIVE-COMPULSIVE DISORDER IN AN OUT-PATIENT SAMPLE

Gr. Simos M.D., N. Manos M.D., E. Dimitriou M.D.

CMHC-2nd University Dept of Psychiatry, Thessaloniki, Greece

In recent years there seems to be a growing interest in the study of the Obsessive-Compulsive Disorder. Out of 1308 adult out-patients who visited the CMHC of the 2nd Univ. Dept. of Psychiatry during the period 1980-1988, fifty five patients (4,2%) received a clinical consensus diagnosis of Obsessive-Compulsive Disorder according to DSM-III/DSM-III-R criteria. The demographic and clinical characteristics of this sample are discussed and compared with the existing literature.

1353
EXPLORATION OF OBSESSIVE COMPULSIVE PHENOMENA

Sumant Khanna, V.G.Kaliaperumal, S.M. Channabasavanna

Departments of Psychiatry and Biostatistics, National Institute of Mental Neuro Sciences, Bangalore 560029, INDIA

The issue of what is an obsession has dogged clinical investigators for quite some time. While Lewis and Kanner focussed on senselessness and resistance, Jaspers regarded irrationality as being more important. Different dimensions of obsessions and compulsions were explored in 103 obsessions and 60 compulsions recorded from 32 subjects diagnosed as OCD according to DSM-III. Intrusiveness and repetitiveness formed relatively discrete dimensions, while resistance, distress, irrationality, interference and ease of dismissal tended to be associated with themselves on both factor and cluster analysis.

1354
ETIOPATHOLOGY AND TREATMENT OF OBSESSIVE COMPULSIVE DISORDERS

Ali Razavi
Razi Psychiatric Centre Tehran Iran
(Amin Abad Shahr Rey)

The probable association of the obsessive-compulsive symptomatology with certain CNS functional areas is critically reviewed. Since 1987 experiments have been performed on patients suffering from obsessive compulsive disorders with satisfying results by using Ludiomil (Maprotilinbydrochloric) a tetracyclic antidepressant. These results confirmed the hypothesis of a connection between CNS functioning and obsessive-compulsive symptomatology.

1355
FLUVOXAMINE AND EXPOSURE IN OBSESSIVE-COMPULSIVE PATIENTS. A CONTROLLED STUDY
J. COTTRAUX, E. MOLLARD, M. BOUVARD, I. MARKS, A.M. NURY, R. DOUGE

Sixty DSM-3 obsessive-compulsive out-patients were randomly assigned to three groups : Antiexposure + Fluvoxamine, Exposure+Fluvoxamine, and Exposure + Placebo. After 8 weeks of treatment between group comparison of the changes showed that the two groups receiving Fluvoxamine presented a stronger decrease in rituals duration per day, but not in depression. After 24 weeks of treatment between-group comparisons of the changes (n=44) found that the two groups receiving Fluvoxamine showed a stronger decrease in depression measured by Hamilton Rating Scale of Depression, but not in rituals. Six months after the end of the treatments, follow-up (n=37) found not between group differences in rituals and depression changes. Antiexposure+Fluvoxamine showed a robust correlation (.88) between decrease in rituals duration and decrease in depression. The baseline level of the behavioral avoidance test was the best single predictor of improvement at post-test for Exposure and Fluvoxamine. Habituation mechanisms as explanation of Exposure and Fluvoxamine effectiveness in obsessive compulsive disorder are discussed.

1356

CLOMIPRAMINE VS. PHENELZINE DOUBLE-BLIND TRIAL IN OBSESSIVE DISORDERS.

J. Vallejo; J. Olivares; T. Marcos; A. Bulbena; A. Otero.
Residencia "Prínceps d'Espanya", Bellvitge, Hospitalet (Barcelona), Spain.

We conducted a double-blind, random assignment, 12-week comparison of clomipramine (n=14), and phenelzine (n=12) treatments for obsessive-compulsive disorder. Subjects were 30 outpatients who met DSM-III criteria for obsessive-compulsive disorder. Four patients dropped out during the trial. Results provided no evidence for a better response in one of the two treatment groups. The anti-obsessive efficacy of both clomipramine and phenelzine had no relationship with the presence or absence of depression by the beginning of treatment challenge.

1357

TREATMENT OF SEVERE TOC. WITH INTRAV. CLI.

DR. Adolfo CALLE. H. CRUZ ROJA. VALENCIA. SPAIN. Alboraya nº18 St. 46010.

Los TOC. han sido siempre una enfermedad difícil de tratar por la "PSIQUIATRIA" se le ha llamado la cruz del psiquiatra. Las respuestas al tratamiento bien con quimioterapia ó psicoterapia, han sido bajos. Una revisión de distintos tratamientos clásicos y un breve resumen de los tratamientos conCLI por vía intravenosa publicados en la literatura mundial se exponen diez casos clínicos de pacientes con TOC. que no habían respondido previamente a tratamiento son explicados. Estos diez casos fueron tratados en Hospital con unas series de goteros con CLI. La medicación y su administración fue bien tolerada con resultados muy buenos desapareciendo sintomatología obsesiva, mejoría de la depresión. Se discute el porque la vía intravenosa de la CLI. es más eficaz que la vía oral.
*Key words! TOC. Trastorno obsesivo compulsivo.
CLI: Clorimipramina.

1358

AN EXPERT SYSTEM FOR DIAGNOSIS OF OBSESSIVE COMPULSIVE DISORDERS

A. Garcia Mas, M. Roca Bennasar.-Dpt Psychology. Universitat Illes Balears. Palma. Spain.

The developement of Artificial Intelligence(AI) has brought about remarkable improvements in various fields:natural language, automatic learning, robotics and expert systems(ES). ES are computer programs that encode some of the knowledge used by experts in a particular field and apply an inference-making procedure to this knowledge.
We present an ES made up of un knowledge base and a probabilistic inference engine, written in LISP, for the diagnosis of obsessive-compulsive disorders. The structure studies previous personality, symptomatology and diferential diagnosis. We use mono and multivaluated variables. It has 98rules of inference and 38 questions in natural language to the user. ES such as this one, seem to be serious attempt to standardize diagnoses, being highly reliable, allowing for the study of predictive factors, the easy inclusion of new diagnosis criteria and wide application teaching.

1359

OBSESSIVE-COMPULSIVE DISORDERS - AN EXISTENTIAL APPROACH

Molly D. Niv, M.D. New York Medical College

A genetic link with familial clustering has been recently found among patients with multiple tics (MT), Gilles de la Tourette Syndrome (TS) and obsessive-compulsive disorders (OCD). An evolution of OCD into a catatonic psychoses may occur in some cases. Existential analysis of the subjects given to such apparently diverse disorders finds a common denominator as the source of their psychopathology. A wide array of hostilities hide behind tics which betray the hateful thoughts/feelins; these may also be shouted out as is the case with TS patients. The obsessed with hate may resort to compulsive rituals which serve to placate guilt. But malicious intentions may burst also into action - converting then, the neurosis into a catatonic psychosis. Instead of targeting the symptoms of these disorders, Existential psychotherapy directs the patient to neutralize his hate by acts of benevolence. Tics, compulsions and rituals disappear when the patient is able to humble himself and engage in some service to group, community, church. Fear breeds superstitions; faith engenders hope. A case will be presented as illustration.

Session 210 Free Communications:
Psychopathology in cancer patients

1360
SOCIO PSYCHIATRIC RESEARRCH ON SECONDARY DEPRESSION TO CANCER

La Raja Maria Cristina
La Sapienza I Clinica Chirurgica - Centro Tumori - Palazzo Baleani - Corso Vittorio Emanuele 244 - Roma - Italia

Tale studio pilota e' durato un anno,ed e' avvenuto col patrocinio della Lega Italiana per la lotta contro i tumori.
Sono stati trattati con cure psicoterapiche e, in minor misura psicofarmacologiche,15 pazienti di entrambi i sessi che avevano subito intervento per cancro alla mammella,al grosso intestino allo stomaco e all'esofago,negli anni 83.84,85 e inizio 86.Tali pazienti sono stati messi a confronto con altri 15 pazienti randomizzati,che avevano subito gli stessi interventi negli stessi anni,ma non erano seguiti con psicoterapia.Alcuni pazienti di entrambi i gruppi erano anche trattati con chemioterapia o radioterapia.Inoltre i pazienti in psicoterapia erano stati sotoposti a monitoraggio immunologico. I dati sono stati sottoposti a elaborazione elettronica.
Il gruppo studiato e quello di controllo sono risultati del tutto omogenei circa i parametri psico-sociali(eccetto ovviamente la psicoterapia) e medico chirurgici(gli stadi del tumore erano gli stessi nei due gruppi e non c'erano recidive ne' metastasi).
Circa la'evoluzione della depressione e della malattia tumorale, il gruppo trattato con psicoterapia,nell'arco dell'anno,aveva avuto un notevole miglioramento della depressione e non aveva avuto ne' recidive ne' metastasi;invece il gruppo di controllo presentava 2 casi di metastasi.
Inoltre il monitoraggio immunologico mostrava,che alla fine dell'anno di studio,dei 15 pazienti trattati con psicoterapia,4 avevano un'immunita' cellulare migliorata e 11 un'immunita' cellulare normalizzata.

1361
PSYCHOSOCIAL ADJUSTMENT TO BREAST CANCER AND ITS TREATMENT
Miroslava Jašović-Gašić, Marina Bogdanović, Sanja Totić, V.Diligenski
Department of Psychiatry,University Clinical Center,Medical School of Belgrade,Yugoslavia

A substantial minority of women who are treated for early breast cancer develop psychosocial and sexual difficulties (Maguire,G.P.1978;Hughes,J. 1981;Dean,C.1987).Similar data for Eastern European women is not yet available.
This paper is a preliminary report of data collected by the Yugoslav team,in the joint research project between London and Belgrade.The aim of the study is to determine the psychosocial adjustment of Yugoslav women with early breast cancer to different aspects of treatment.It is a prospective study lasting 3 years,on a randomised sample of women hospitalized at the Department of Oncology, Belgrade,that are:under 70 years of age;Dg:carcinoma mammae;TNM staging:stage I and II;no evidence of metastatic spread;no previous or concomitant malignancy.Patients are interviewed preoperatively,3 and 12 months postoperatively,using the following instruments:SD-sociodemographic and biographical data;PSE-Present State Examination (Wing et al., 1974);HADS-Hospital Anxiety and Depression Scale (Zigmond,A.S.1983);TTP-Treatment Toxicity and Pain Data-semistructured interview;PAD-Practical Abilities Data-brief self-rating scale;CSS-Social Status Assessment-adjustment to breast surgery,social support assessment,assessment of coping responses (O'Connor and Brown,1984;Morris et al,1985).

1362
PSYCHOLOGIC STRESS BEFORE HYSTERECTOMY AND MASTECTOMY
A. Kourkoubas, G. Iatrakis, L. Giannikos, G. Sakellaropoulos and G. Kourounis.
Depts of Obstetrics and Gynecology, Red Cross Hospital,Laiko Gen Hospital, Athens, Greece.

Major surgical procedures such as hysterectomy and mastectomy that produce a change of body image often undermine the patient's self-esteem and sense of personal worth and have a dramatic psychological impact for the patient. In an attempt to clarify the issue further, we investigated the psychological stress in 93 female patients prior to a major operation for hysterectomy or mastectomy. The patients were divided into two groups according to the operation planned. The first group (candidates for hysterectomy) comprised 51 patients (ages 34-57, $x \pm SD$ 40.1 $\pm$ 12.3) and the second group (candidates for mastectomy) comprised 42 patients (ages 31-49, $x \pm SD$ 36.2 $\pm$11.9). Both groups were interviewed during the two weeks preceding the operetion using the C.G.I scale. Hysterectomy candidates exhibited anxiety-depression up to 47% of the sample (24 out of 51). In the second group (mastectomy) psychologic stress was diagnosed in 37 women (88.1%). The difference between the two groups is statistically highly significant ($p < 0.01$, Student's t-test). We conclude that the psychologic trauma before mastectomy is significantly greater than that before hysterectomy.

1363
PSYCHOLOGICAL IMPACT OF HYSTERECTOMY
Nancy Campbell, M.D.; Kathleen Franco, M.D.; Stephen G. Jurs, Ph.D.; Regina Fondren, Jann Stripling; Medical College of Ohio, CAPH, C.S. 10008, Toledo, Ohio 43699-0008

Women, who had undergone hysterectomy, were asked to complete the Millon Clinical Multiaxial Inventory, the Beck Depression Inventory, and a demographic questionnaire. Irritability, insomnia, and lower energy levels were reported by more than half. Reduced sexual interest was the forth most commonly noted concern. Single women scored significantly higher on depression scales, while higher educational levels of women and their spouses were protective against this symptom. Many desired more support from their spouses and physicians but were frequently unable to communicate this. Conflicted feelings about marital, sexual and emotional issues were often left unexplored despite the patients' desires that it be otherwise. Increased irritability with and discipline of their children in the post-hysterectomy period was reported as worrisome by a sizable number. Fifty percent of those whose hysterectomy was more than a year earlier reported anniversary reactions of a physical or psychological nature on the date of their prior surgery. Recommendations are made regarding the psychiatrist's role in conjunction with the gynecologist to facilitate optimal care of the patient and her family.

1364
A PSYCHOANALYTIC APPROACH IN PSYCHOSOMATIC: THE SYMBOLISM OF THE AFFECTED ORGAN

SYNODINOU Claire
34, rue Pierre Larousse
75014 Paris, FRANCE

Ce travail portera sur notre expérience clinique de certaines cures analytiques des maladies psychosomatiques et plus spécialement du cancer. Au cours de ces cures, nous avons constaté que l'organe atteint est inscrit dans l'histoire du patient bien avant la manifestation de la maladie, comme lieu des conflits intrapsychiques. Le sens de cet ancien traumatisme explicité, la structuration progressive du sujet qui advient, permet une amélioration clinique.

1365
TEACHING CANCER PATIENTS TO ACCESS THEIR UNCONSCIOUS MIND
Jordan P. Weiss, M.D.
University of California, Irvine
Irvine, California
U.S.A.

Recent interest in the use of positive mental approaches to cancer patients--including imagery--have been used with often mixed or equivocal results. It has been assumed that all patients have an equal investment in getting well and that their conscious responses to questions about "positivity" in fighting their cancer, as well as various life issues, were accurately reflected in their conscious responses.

By contrast, most therapists accept the unconscious mind and believe that this part of the mind may be much more accurate in reflecting the patient's true thoughts and feelings. A series of related techniques will be described that demonstrate to the patient and therapist a more accurate reflection of these deep feelings. Since the images are self-generated, there is little or no resistance or much need for interpretation, and therapeutic work can proceed much more rapidly.

The techniques, in addition, will lead to clearer data when studying these patients to determine more precisely the value of positive mental techniques on cancer and related illnesses.

1366
Psychological Problems in Mastectomized Women

Meyer, Lennart

Department of Social and Forensic Psychiatry, StLars Hospital, Box 646
S-220 06 Lund Sweden

Two issues may cause distress in mastectomized women, the reaction to a potential fatal illness and the adjustment to the breast mutilation. The following issues are discussed: Does breast cancer surgery more often result in a psychopathology than cancer surgery of some other organ.- Is breast conservation or reconstruction a possible way of diminishing the burden of cancer treatment. -Can intervention programs support the cancer patients. -Is it possible to identify patients at risk for psychopathological reactions preoperatively. Some conclusions to be drawn are: There is no clear indication that breast conserving treatment will protect from mental disturbances, but it seems to preserve the woman's female identity. Patients satisfaction with the surgical result is mainly not related to eventual surgical complications but with certain personality traits. Patients with a previous history of psychoneurosis seem to aggravate their problems after surgery. Surgical personnel should form the initial contact for supporting the operated woman.

1367
EVENEMENTS DE VIE ET CANCER DU SEIN : ETUDE CAS-TEMOINS ET FOLLOW-UP A 4 ANS
GUILLAUD-BATAILLE J. M[*], TERRA J. L[*], BERNARD G., GAUSSET M. F., GUYOTAT J.
[*]Service Professeur J. DALERY, C.H.S. Le vinatier 95, boulevard Pinel - 69677 BRON CEDEX

Les auteurs présentent les résultats d'une étude cas/témoins portant sur les événements de la vie survenus dans les 5 années précédant l'apparition d'un cancer du sein chez 83 femmes. La comparaison avec les témoins n'indique pas un surnombre d'événements dans le groupe des cas mais un impact affectif supérieur probablement lié à la note dépressive.
Dans le groupe cancer, 46 femmes ont pu être interviewées 4 ans plus tard et 15 sont décédées. Le pronostic semble indépendant du nombre d'événements avant le diagnostic du cancer.
Les événements de vie explorés sur une période de 9 ans sont plus concentrés autour de la phase initiale de diagnostic et du traitement.
Les aspects méthodologiques du recueil des événements de vie sont discutés à la lumière de ces résultats.

1368
STUDIES ON DEPRESSION SECONDARY TO TUMORS
Maria Cristina La Raja
University of Rome "La Sapienza"-Tumors Center
I Surgical Clinic-Palazzo Baleani-Corso Vittorio 244

This pilot study which lasted one year was supported by a grant received from the "Lega italiana per la lotta contro i tumori". A study group of 15 patients of both sexes who underwent surgical treatment for cancer of breast, large intestine, stomach and the esophagus, from 1983 through the first part of 1986, were treated with psychotherapy and in a minor respect psycho-farmacologically. These 15 patients that were compared with another randomly chosen control group of 15 patients that were only surgically treated for the same tumor pathology, during this same study period, but without psychotherapy. A few patients from both groups were subsequently treated with chemotherapy or radiotherapy. Immunological monitoring was carried out on only those patients who underwent psycotherapy. Statistical analysis was done on both the control group and the study group.
Both groups demonstrated no statistical differences regarding psycho-social parameters nor medical-surgical parameters at the beginning of the study. The tumor staging was equivalent in both groups and neither group showed tumor recurrence nor metastatic diffusion. The study group undergoing psychotherapy demonstrated at the end of the study period, a notable improvement from depression and no tumor recurrence or metastasis. The control group however had 2 cases of metastatic complications. In addition, with immunological monitoring of the 15 patients undergoing psychotherapy, 4 patients showed an improvement in their cellular immunity and 11 patients showed normalization of their cellular immunity state at the end of the study period.

Session 211 Free Communications:
Cognitive functions in schizophrenia

1369
COGNITIVE DEFICITS AMONG AGING SCHIZOPHRENIC PATIENTS.

G. Angelides, Th. Aivazian, K. Fotiadou.
Psychiatric Hospital Petra Olympus, Greece.

Schizophrenia does not resemble a typical organic illness, but evidence suggests that it has an organic component. The aim of the study reported here was to provide preliminary answers to questions about cognitive impairment in aging schizophrenic patients residing in the community, such as: do elderly schizophrenic patients manifest more cognitive dysfunction than their age peers hospitalized in a general hospital suffering from vascular diseases? The Mini Mental State (MMS) and the Brief Cognitive Rating Scale (BCRS) were administered to 30 randomly selected elderly schizophrenic outpatients in a public aftercare facility in Katerini, Greece, and also to 30 patients with no history of serious psychiatric illness, hospitalized in a general hospital. There were no significant differences between them with respect to age or education. T tests were used to contrast the MMS and the BCRS scores of the two samples. The findings indicate that older schizophrenic patients living in the community exhibit more cognitive impairment than their age peers hospitalized in a general hospital, suffering from vascular diseases. Future studies must explore the nature and evolution of cognitive deficits as well as identify the clinical subgroups that may be especially prone to cognitive decline

1370
ON THE USE OF NOT REFERENTIAL DATA BY PARANOID SCHIZOPHRENIC PATIENTS.
Jorge Maltez, Isabel Barahona da Fonseca, Fátima Ferreira and J.Simões da Fonseca.
Depart.of Medical Psychology and Psychopathology, Fac.of Medicine of Lisbon.

The evaluation of the role played by Life Events in Mental Disturbance has been under discussion for many years since the initial proposals of Holmes and the subsequent theoretical reavaluation connected with the consideration of the meaning that Events may have to individual subjects. It has not been suficiently discussed the vulnerability concept concerning Life Events. A multiple choice objective method to evaluate the "preparedness" of individuals belonging to different diagnostic groups has been under study, using thirteen scales which dealed with phantasy strategies "used to evaluate the use of not referential data " or else on the contrary the role of reference of reality to produce an artificial change in a predicted unfavourable outcome of Events proposed as if they were really occurring. A definite pattern separated Normal Volunteers from Paranoid Schizophrenics - outside of the Conventional Psychopathological symptom and syndromatic domain has been found. Initial scores were obtained couting the numbers of responses in each scale. Afterwards Multivariate Stepwise Discriminant Analysis was performed. We also compared differences which appeared concerning five distinct proposed Life Events: (a) Disease of a close relative ; (b) Unemployment situation; (c) Deep Afective loss; (d) Legal situation involving injustice; (e) Sucessful love involvement; (f) Personal reference not implying any of the preceeding five situations. Finally it is made a discussion of a grid based on evaluations concerning the self or the others based on an admitted transformation by phantasy of Referential data.

1371
THE EFFECTS OF EMOTIONAL AROUSAL ON COGNITIVE PERFORMANCE IN SCHIZOPHRENIC PATIENTS
Strauss,W.H., Klieser,E., Falkai,P.
Department of Psychiatry Duesseldorf, FRG
Both CT studies as well as post mortem studies show that in one fourth of all schizophrenic disturbances there is an evidence of an atrophy of cerebral matter in the paralimbic and limbic parts of the temporal lobe or the parasagittal frontal cortex. Since this part is supposed to distinctly influence the emotional sphere, we investigated the cognition and recognition of emotional stimuli in so far 35 schizophrenic patients (DSM III) with or without atrophy of cerebral matter. Furthermore studies have been executed showing that schizophrenics can be disturbed in their perception of mimic and gestic expressions and their cognitive performance by emotional arousal. Thus patients of both groups were showed randomly either a section of a film with high or low emotional expression. Before and after the film the patients performed achievement tests and graded their feelings by means of the Adjective Check List. In addition the cognitive and recognitive performances on emotional irritation were investigated by means of an Emotion-Recognition-Test layed out by our team.

1372
COGNITIVE FUNCTIONS IN SCHIZOPHRENIA AND MANIA

E.ABAY,MD,S.H.SAYITA,MD,M.E.CEYLAN,MD PhD,A.İ.ŞENER, MD,E.T.ORAL,MD.
BAKIRKÖY MENTAL HOSPITAL/İSTANBUL/TURKEY

In recent years there have been some advances in the field of cognitive functions in schizophrenic and manic patients.Clinical and nueropsychological investigations have indicated that these deficits can be as severe as deficits observed following brain damage.Researchers are interested in functional deterioration of cognition and its relation with the diagnosis and prognosis.Schizophrenic patients have been examined for general intellectual functioning attention,memory,language and abstract reasoning.Examination of cognitive function in bepolar mood disorders is not yet sufficient enough as the former.In this study schizophrane (30) and manic (30) patients were examined for cognitive functions.Brief cognitive examination scale,Benton visual retention test,Wechster Adult Intelligence scale for schizophrenics and Beck's mania scale for manic patients were also applied to the groups.Cognitive deterioration both in schizophrenic and manic patient,and a positive correlation between clinical recovery and cognitive development has been found.Thus,the results were significant ($p<0,001$) for schizophrenic and manic patients and no differences between male and female patients were found in both groups.Age and duration of illness also showed no relation with cognitive impairment as the sex of the patients.

1373
COMPREHENSION IN SCHIZOPHRENIC

Hojaij, C.R.
Hospital Samaritano (Sao Paulo - Brazil)

The Author carries out a research concerning Comprehension (as the empiric behavior that allows the intuitive knowledge and close companionship) in schizophrenics, having abated the delusions manifestations under the influence of antipsychotics.

Making use of psychopathological criteria from Bleuler, Schneider and Ey, five patients are selected from those who had a weekly follow up for a long time (3 to 11 years). The basic medication used is butirofenon (1mg to 45mg; maintenance doses: 1mg to 5 mg). The patients's experiences are the basic material of the study.

The idea of Psychic Process (Jaspers) meets its realization in Schizophrenia, believing that this disease is a chronic and irreversible transformation of the personality. In this sense the Process shall resist the effects of antipsychotics. The Author questions how the Comprehension process in schizophrenics is presented, abated the symptomatology that usually takes the patient to treatment: the delusions manifestations. He admits that Schizophrenia appears more clearly after the elimination of classic symptoms, obtaining through that procedure the fundamental structure of the disease, wich can be mixed with the Psychic Process. The research intends to bring out indicative elements of diagnosis of Schizophrenia through peculiar alterations in the Comprehension of schizophrenics.

The Phenomenology and the Comprehension (Dilthey) appear as the methoda utilized.

1374
Über die schizophrene Ich-Störungen
(On the schizophrenic disturbebce of ego)
SHINICHI HIRASAWA
Tokyo Women's Medical College, JAPAN

Über die schizophrene Ich-Störungen hat K.Schneider bemerkt,daß sie auch als Störungen der Meinhaftigkeit des Erlebens bezeichnet werden können.Mit dieser Bemerkung hat er die Definition von Jaspers modifiziert,während er das Tätigkeitsgefühl,das Aktivitätsbewußtsein von Jaspers umwandelt in das Erlebnis der Meinhaftigkeit hat.Nämelich können wir die Ich-Störungen nicht ganz auf die gestörte Tätigkeit des Ichs reduzieren.Aber diese Unabhängigkeit des Ichs von seiner Tätigkeit ist noch nicht gründlich geschätzt,z.B. sei es von der Psychologie,die das Ich an Dynamik seiner eigenen Tätigkeit anknüpft,sei es von der Phänomenologie,die als Wesen des Bewußtseins,einschließlich des Ichbewußtseins,seine Intentionalität bestimmt.Deswegen z.B.kann es nicht ausreichend klar machen,worin der psychopathologischen Unterschied zwischen schizophrener Störungen der Aktivität und depressiver Störungen besteht,usw.
Um die solche Probleme aufzuhellen,wie die Ich-Störungen zustande kommen und sie mit weitere anderer Störungen sowohl Denkens wie Willens zusammenhängen,müssen wir den Vorgang der Entstehung des Ichs anthropologisch begreifen.Wir versuchen uns mittels des Begriffs der personalen Emanzipation(HERMANN SCHMITZ) an der Psychopathologie der Ich-Störungen.

1375
REVERSIBLE AMUSIC DISTURBANCES IN DIFFERENT MENTAL STATES
Reinhard Steinberg, Lydia Raith, Wilfried Günther

Pfalzklinik Landeck and Psychiatric University Hospital Munich, FRG

Experiments are described, in which 78 psychiatric inpatients, suffering from schizophrenia, bipolar affective disorder or neurotic depression, as well as 20 controls were repeatedly examined concerning their musical abilities. With growing remission musical test performance normalized and was not at all different from matched controls. This intraindividual design allows for an assumption, that the cognitive and motor disturbances of mental diseases can be regarded as an amusic disturbance, which is reversible as the mental state. EEG-mapping data give some indication, that in the disturbed state schizophrenics during musical stimuli show a quite different cerebral activity from matched controls. This effect also vanishes with remission.

1376
FAILURE TO DIFFERENTIATE BIPOLAR DISORDER FROM SCHIZOPHRENIA ON MEASURES OF NEUROPSYCHOLOGICAL FUNCTION
A.L.Hoff, Ph.D., S.Shukla, M.D., T.Aronson M.D., B.Cook, D.O., C.Ollo, Ph.D., S.Baruch, B.A., L.Jandorf, M.A., J.Schwartz, Ph.D.

Thirty inpatients diagnosed with schizophrenia were compared to 35 inpatients with bipolar affective disorder, manic type, on a large group of neuropsychological measures, including measures of intellectual, memory, visual-perceptual, and motor function. Factor analyses yielded significant loadings on Verbal, Spatial and Speed factors. Controlling for the effects of age, education, sex, duration of illness, number of pervious hospitalizations, and medications at time of testing, there were no significant differences between diagnostic groups on factors or on individual test variables. Patients on medication performed more poorly on Speed variables than those off medication. These findings call into question the notion of differential patterns of cognitive deficit among psychotic diagnoses. The failure to discriminate schizophrenic patients from bipolar patients may be due to recent suggestions that bipolar patients like schizophrenics also have abnormalities in brain morphology (reviewed by Nasrallah et al., 1989). That these groups do not differ on cognitive measures may also support the unitary concept of psychosis, in which bipolar illness and schizophrenia are on the same continuum of illness (Crow, 1986; 1987).

1377
Functional Behavioral Evaluation in Schizophrenic Patients
Adlestein, J., Bixler, E.O., Coronado R., Noori, S.S., Kettl, P.A., Pennsylvania State University College of Medicine, Hershey, Pennsylvania 17033 U.S.A.

As part of an ongoing cognitive rehabilitation program for schizophrenic patients being implemented by the Central Pennsylvania Psychiatric Institute, a systematic functional behavioral instrument was used. It consists of 36 7-point items clustered into 5 scales. It was applied to three different schizophrenic populations: a sample residing on an inpatient unit (N=41); a sample of outpatients requiring intense supervision (N=27); and a sample of outpatients requiring only minimal supervision (N=18). Three scales demonstrated increasing level of functioning, progressing from the inpatients to the minimally supervised outpatients. These scales were: behavior, independent living and social functioning. Inpatients scored highest on the communication scale, perhaps because they have more frequent contact with staff and are better adapted to their evaluation environment than either of the two outpatient groups. In terms of cognitive impairment the mean values indicated no differences among the groups. Finally, in terms of items related to negative symptoms, no group differences were found. In contrast, the inpatient group had significantly more hallucinations and delusions. Thus, with this instrument, outpatients differ from inpatients primarily by demonstrating less impaired reality testing and in their ability to function independently and not in terms of global cognitive impairment.

1378
INVESTIGACION DE LAS ALTERACIONES SEMANTICAS EN ESQUIZOFRENIA
J.C.Martín y A.V. Moríñigo
Hospital Universitario de Valme. Sevilla. España.

Esta investigación estudia la configuración semántica en la esquizofrenia, y sus posibles alteraciones, que han despertado un renovado interés recientemente (Andreasen,1979; Holzman, 1986). La muestra está compuesta por 60 pacientes esquizofrénicos (criterios RDC; Spitzer,1977), divididos en 3 grupos de 20: A) Pacientes con trastornos en la significación del lenguaje, B) Pacientes con ideas delirantes, C) Pacientes con remisión psicopatológica. Existe un grupo control de 20 enfermos hospitalizados sin enfermedad mental. A todos ellos se les realiza el Diferencial Semántico (Osgood,1976) con los siguientes 14 conceptos: Trabajo, Hogar, Médico, Amistad, Vida, Yo mismo, Enfermedad, Madre, Dios, Amor,Padre, Sexo, Muerte. Mediante este instrumento de investigación semántica, pretendíamos conocer el significado de estos conceptos claves y universales para el esquizofrénico (Martín,1987). Los resultados muestran una intensa alteración del significado de conceptos tan básicos como Madre. Este se separa significativamente en los esquizofrénicos productivos(comparado con el grupo en remisión y el control),de categorías como Hogar y Vida. Otro concepto tan importante como Padre, se separa a su vez de Madre y Amistad. Esto confirma que en la esquizofrenia se produce una profunda alteración e incluso inversión de los significados convencionales.

Session 212 Free Communications: MAO inhibitors

1379
CLINICAL AND NEUROCHEMICAL EFFECTS OF MOCLOBEMIDE IN DEPRESSED PATIENTS

B.Alevizos, J.Hatzimanolis, M.Markianos, C.Stefanis
Athens University, Eginition Hospital, Athens

The effects of MAO-A inhibitor moclobemide on clinical and neuroendocrine variables and amine metabolites were studied in 26 depressed patients in an open, 4-week clinical trial.
Fourteen patients (54 %) responded to moclobemide (50 % or more reduction of Hamilton scale score). 51.5 % of responders and none of nonresponders had abnormal DST (χ^2=10.15; p<0.002), while 50 % of responders and 72.7 % of nonresponders had blunted TSH response to TRH. Responders had significantly higher than nonresponders pre-dexamethasone (11 pm) cortisol (p<0.04, U-test) and TSH (8 am) levels (p<0.04) and showed greater prolactin response to dexamethasone. Platelet MAO activity did not correlated with treatment response.
Plasma MHPG decreased significantly by moclobemide treatment (p<0.001), but pre-treatment mean values did not differentiate responders from nonresponders. Urine MHPG (μg/24 h) also decreased significantly by moclobemide (p<0.001). Pre-treatment values were significantly lower in responders than in nonresponders (p<0.04). Urine HVA decreased significantly by treatment (p<0.01), especially after 2 weeks of treatment.
These findings indicate that abnormal DST together with the lower MHPG excretion may predict outcome to moclobemide treatment and suggest that this drug may primarily affects the noradrenergic system.

1380
POTENTIATION OF TYRAMINE EFFECTS BY MOCLOBEMIDE IN DEPRESSED PATIENTS
[1]Dajas F.,[1]River G.,[2]Vranesic D.,[2]Allen S., [2]Stabl M.
[1]Psychopharmacology Dept., Psychiatric Clinic, Faculty of Medicine and Neurochem.Div., IIBCE, Montevideo, Uruguay and [2]Dept.of Clinical Research and Development, F.Hoffman-La Roche & Co.Ltd. Company, Basle, Switzerland

The first generation of irreversible and nonspecific MAO inhibitors(MAOI) increased the sensitivity of the noradrenergic neurons to tyramine. Quite recently, Moclobemide, a new MAOI with good antidepressant properties specific for MAO-A, reversible and short-acting has been developed. This study was undertaken to confirm in depressed patients the low potentiation of tyramine shown after Moclobemide intake in healthy subjects. The tyramine pressor test (TPT) (the minimum amount of tyramine necessary to increase the systolic blood pressure (SBP) by 30mm Hg), was performed before and after 3 weeks of treatment with two different doses of Moclobemide (150 and 300mg/day) in a population of depressed patients(major depression). In the 150mg group, the expected 30mmHg-SPB increase occurred with a dose of 8.0mg tyramine at baseline and 2.5mg after three weeks of treatment. The potentiation was 3.20 and 3.35 times with 150 and 300mg respectively. These data are showing the weak potentiation of TPT provoked by Moclobemide.

1381
MAPROTILINE OR MOCLOBEMIDE: DOUBLE BLIND THERAPY OF MAJOR DEPRESSION
H.R. Wacker, C. Schlösser, R. Battegay
Psychiatric University Outpatient Clinic, Basle, Switzerland

Moclobemide, a benzamide derivative, is a reversible MAO inhibitor with predominant inhibition of the A-form of the MAO. This study compares effects and side-effects of moclobemide with maprotiline in 21 outpatients (12 females, 9 males) with a Major Depressive Episode who received either drug in a double blind controlled trial lasting 4 weeks. The dose range for moclobemide was 300 mg to 450 mg daily, the one for maprotiline 75 mg to 150 mg per day. By means of Hamilton's Depression scale and of the CGI the changes of the depressive symptomatology were measured on day 3,7,14,21 and 28. At each visit blood pressure and pulse rate were monitored and suspicious side effects were evaluated in a semi-structured interview. The patients received no specific diet during treatment.
Altogether the results confirm an antidepressive effect of both drugs. They are discussed on the background of a possible differential effect on symptoms of anxiety within the frame of depressive disorders.

1382
BROFAROMINE - A SELECTIVE AND REVERSIBLE MAO-INHIBITOR IN COMPARISON TO IMIPRAMINE
Kissling, W., Uebelhack, R. and Wendt G.
Psychiatric Hospital of the Technical University, D 8000 München/BRD, Clinic of Neurologie and Psychiatry, Humboldt University, DDR 1040 Berlin/GDR Ciba-Geigy GmbH, Clinical Research, D 6000 Frankfurt/BRD

Brofaromine is a new selective and reversible MAO-inhibitor Typ A as demonstrated in animal and human pharmacological studies. In comparison to tranylcypromine it showed a much (about 6 times) smaller tyramine potentiating effect and a much shorter pharmacodynamic halflife (1,5 days versus 2 - 3 weeks). Therefore it is expected to be better tolerated than the classical MAO-inhibitors especially regarding hypertensive crises ("cheese effect").
The aim of our multicenter double-blind study carried out vs. imipramine without strict diet was to evaluate the efficacy and tolerability of brofaromine in dosages of 100-150 mg in hospitalized patients with major depressive disorders (DSM III). The results in a total of 124 patients showed a comparable antidepressant efficacy in both groups. The most distinct differences in favour of brofaromine were obtained in the median of onset of action (day 9, $p<0.10$). Although the tolerability of both drugs was good, fewer patients experienced undesired effects under the treatment with brofaromine.

1383
THE SELECTIVE AND REVERSIBLE MAO-INHIBITOR BROFAROMINE IN COMPARISON TO TRANYLCYPROMINE IN DEPRESSED INPATIENTS
Möller, H.J., Faltus, F., Zapletalek, M. and Wendt, G.
Psychiatric University Clinic, D-5300 Bonn
Psychiatric Clin., Karls-University, CS 12821 Praha

Brofaromine is a new selective and reversible MAO-inhibitor type A as demonstrated in animal and human pharmacological studies. The aim of this study was to investigate the efficacy and tolerability in comparison to tranylcypromine in patients with therapyresistent depression (major depressive disorders, DSM III).
Duration of treatment was 6 weeks. Daily doses are 2 x 50 mg brofaromine and 2 x 10 mg tranylcypromine resp. Responders received maintenance therapy with unchanged daily dosages, non-responders received increased doses (150 mg and 30 mg b.i.d. resp.). The results in a total of 92 patients showed a comparable antidepressant efficacy and the tolerability was good in both groups. Further results will be demonstrated.

1384
A MULTICENTRE STUDY IN MORE THAN 300 DEPRESSED OUTPATIENTS TREATED WITH THE SELECTIVE AND REVERSIBLE MAO-INHIBITOR BROFAROMINE

Wendt G. and Binz U.
Ciba-Geigy GmbH, Clinical Research, D 6000 Frankfurt/BRD

During recent years the MAO-inhibitors reached a progressive importance in clinical practice. It was attempted to solve problems of tolerability by a new generation of MAO-inhibitors. Brofaromine is a MAO-inhibitor of the second generation, a selective, reversible and short acting MAO-A-inhibitor, promising that the dangerous "cheese effect" will occur only under extreme conditions. The clinical trials performed till now, among other doubleblind tests versus tranylcypromine and imipramine, demonstrate a good antidepressive efficacy and a good tolerability.
The results in more than 300 depressed outpatients indicated that the treatment with doses of 75 mg - 150 mg of brofaromine daily administered for 6 - 8 weeks without dietary restrictions is well tolerated. Brofaromine did not have any statistically or clinically significant effects on blood pressure or pulse rate. Remarkable undesired effects were disturbed sleep and nausea in few patients. Pathological changes in the chemogram (including liver enzymes), hemogram or urine of the patients were not seen. The antidepressant efficacy (evaluated with HAMD and Bf-S) were very good and good in more than 75%. Brofaromine was shown to exert a definitive antidepressant effect and to be well tolerated.

1385
MAO INHIBITORS IN OTHER PSYCHIATRIC DISORDERS

Dr. Frank Schneir, Dr. Raphael Campeas,
Dr. Michael Liebowitz

Columbia University, New York, NY 10032 - USA

MAO Inhibitors (MAOIs) have demonstrated effectiveness in a variety of psychiatric disorders in addition to depression. For example, controlled studies have demonstrated MAOI efficacy in panic disorder with agoraphobia, social phobia, and bulimia. For panic disorders with agoraphobia, there is some suggestion that MAOIs are more effective than other medication treatments in helping patients overcome phobic avoidance. In social phobia, the standard MAOI phenelzine, has been found significantly more effective than both placebo and beta blockers. Also, the reversible MAOA Inhibitor moclobemide, has been found superior to placebo and similar in efficacy to phenelzine. Although no MAOI-tricyclic comparison exists in social phobia, MAOIs are helpful for many patients who do not respond to tricyclics. Overall, MAOIs appear extremely helpful in reducing phobic avoidance and exaggerated interpersonnal hypersensitivity.

1386
CLINICAL AND BIOCHEMICAL FINDINGS WITH NEW MAO-A-INHIBITORS IN MAJOR DEPRESSIVE DISORDER

G. Laux, T. Becker, W. Classen, K.-P. Lesch, E. Sofic, G. Carl, M. Struck, P. Riederer, H. Beckmann
Department of Psychiatry, University of Wuerzburg D-8700 Würzburg, FRG

Renewed therapeutic interest in MAOIs has followed the advent of a new generation of reversible, selective MAO-A-inhibitors. Inhibition of MAO-A is likely to be the decisive factor in antidepressant action of MAOIs. Lack of hepatotoxicity and reduced risk of hypertensive crisis ("cheese effect") facilitate clinical use (no diet restrictions), they are likely to be due to reversibility of MAO inhibition. Data from 4 clinical studies are presented comprising
* a double-blind study with Moclobemide (Mo) vs. Maprotiline (n=42)
* a long-term study with Mo (up to 2 years) (n=13)
* an open study with Brofaromine (Br, n=13)
* a controlled study with Br (n=30)

Clinically, antidepressant efficacy of Mo and Br could be confirmed, no case of hypertensive crisis was observed in spite of normal diet. Restlessness and insomnia were the most common adverse effects. Biochemistry showed an increase of Noradrenaline in CSF and plasma. Psychometric tests revealed some activating profile. Loss of clinical effect was observed in Mo long-term treatment in spite of increasing dose and control of plasma levels.

1387
DOSE, BLOODLEVELS AND SLEEPDISTURBANCES OF MAO-INHIBITORS IN DEPRESSION

P.M.J. Haffmans and G.S.I.M. Jansen.
Psychiatric Centre Bloemendaal, P.O. Box 53002, 2505 AA The Hague, The Netherlands.

Patients suffering from a major depression and resistant to cyclic antidepressants were, after a 1 week wash-out period, blindly treated with tranylcypromine (irreversible MAO-A-B inhibitor, max dose 100 mg/day) or brofaromine (reversible MAO-A inhibitor, max dose 250 mg/day) for 4 weeks. Blood samples were taken weekly. Sleep EEG recordings were performed before and after 4 weeks of treatment.
Brofaromine (n=12): No clear correlation was found between dosage and bloodlevel of brofaromine. However, plasmalevels were correlated with number and duration of intermittent awakenings. Brofaromine did not cause problems with falling a sleep no matter what plasmalevel was reached. Furthermore, REM density, was decreased, REM sleep was severely interrupted and efficiency of sleep was reduced significantly.
Tranylcypromine (n=8): A possible correlation between dosage and bloodlevel of tranylcypromine was found. Furthermore, disturbances of falling a sleep as well as number and duration of intermittent awakenings were plasmalevel dependent. With exception of low doses (20 mg daily), REM sleep was completely abolished while delta sleep was of bad quality and occurred hardly. Separate sleep cycles could hardly be distinguished.

Session 213 Free Communications:
Classification systems in special patient populations

1388

The use of DSM-III multiaxial classification in analyses of length of stay.
M. Kastrup, T. Vilmar, S. Hjortsø, P. Bech.
Dept. Psychiatry, Frederiksborg General Hospital.

A comprehensive registration including a diagnostic evaluation of all patients entering psychiatric service from a geographical defined area was carried out. 880 consequtively admitted patients were evaluated using ICD-8 and a DSM-III multiaxial classification at the time of entry and dischange from services. The median length of stay was calculated for each diagnostic group, and its value used for a dichotomy of each group. The socio-demographic background, living arrangements and economic conditions were analysed in relation to diagnostic group. These parameters as well as psychiatric history and severity of symptomatology were related to the length of stay.

1389

COMPARATIVE USE OF DSM III-R AND DESCRIPTIVE-PHENOMENOLOGICAL DIAGNOSIS IN CONSULTATION-LIAISON PSYCHIATRY
Piccione M., Castellet y Ballarà F., Valitutti R., Bauco A.R..
Istituto di Psichiatria, Università "La Sapienza", Roma, Italy.

Descriptive-phenomenological diagnosis and DSM III-R have been comparatively used for a classificatory purpose in a sample of 800 referrals to the Consultation-liaison Psychiatry Service of Polyclinic Umberto I of Rome. In this paper the advantages and biases deriving fron the use of these two diagnostic systems in this peculiar area of Psychiatry, are carefully analized.
In the Authors' experience utilization of DSM III-R in Consultation-Liaison Psychiatry meets with difficulties arising from the time limited contact with the patient, the prevalent need for "status" diagnosis instead of "global" diagnosis and the common overlapping with somatic diseases, psychosocial and forensic medicine problems. On the other side Descriptive-phenomenological Diagnosis even though allowing larger freedom and closer relation to the clinical ground, exposes itself to censures regarding liability, accuracy and communicability of results.

1390

PROBLEMS OF DIAGNOSIS OF NON-WESTERN PATIENTS WITH THE DSM-III-R.
Arthur G. Nikelly, Ph.D. University of Illinois Health Center, Urbana, Illinois 61801, U. S. A.

Non-Western patients may manifest emotional dysfunction that is not consistent with DSM-III-R criteria of psychopathology because these criteria reflect Western ethnopsychology. Non-Western patients tend to focus on somatic problems and expect their treatment to be somatotherapy. They are less apt to use the "psychologizing" idiom of expression or to invoke personal dynamics. The pathogenetic aspect of their condition is biological, while the pathoplastic is cultural. Patients from non-Western societies may be misdiagnosed or overdiagnosed, and either complicates treatment. Therapists treating non-Western patients should apply Western criteria of pathology with caution, and must be aware of the values and belief systems underlying their problems.

1391

CAN REFERENCE AND MEANING BE UNIFIED BY A GENERALIZED LEARNING THEORY?
J.Simões da Fonseca, Isabel Barahona da Fonseca, J.Serro and Paula Sargaço.
Depart. of Medical Psychology and Psychopathology, Fac. of Medicine of Lisbon.

The problem which was under study concerned a "free system of value attribution to referential data" when they were contextualized by meaning.
Defense mechanisms appear in this approac as normal strategies of hypotheses formation and prediction of the value of reinforcement. Their rank is the same which is attributed to referential data.
In the hypothetical - deductive construction of reality, free systems of reinforcement appear in information prossessing regularities which allow the formation of equivalence classes concerning the value of distinct strategies.
The concept of reinforcement acquires a new signification - related to a system semantic - referential aggregation distinct from the conventional hedonically biased viewpoint.
It is shown using experimental measures that this approach allows the retrievel of most of the relevant diagnostic groups of psychopathology providing cross-validation to symptom based taxinomy and acquiring the status of a new explanotory system for symptom formation.

1392

Psychodynamic diagnosis, descriptive diagnosis and psychotherapy.
Lingiardi V., Madeddu F., Da Ponte C., Vanzulli L., Maffei C.
Institute of Medical Psychology, University of Milan-H.S.Raffaele V.Turro Milan Italy

The interest in diagnostic and evaluation "dynamic" instruments seems to be growing. They exceed the presence/absence symptoms area, typical of Rating Scales, moving to an area more difficult to quantify, that is the personality deep structure, in other words the "psychodynamic categories". The Authors face the problem of indication to psychotherapy, in the light of the clinical usefulness of diagnostic instruments for the development of a psychodynamic profile of the patient. Clinical and theoretical foundations of "psychodynamic", or "structural", diagnosis are finally related to those of the "descriptive" diagnosis (with a particular attention to the Personality Disorders spectrum according to DSM III-R) as well as to some indications suggested by findings from psychodiagnostic projective tests.

1393

DIAGNOSTIC CRITERIA FOR J. GUYOTAT's CLASSIFICATION OF CHRONIC PSYCHOSIS
O. CHAMBON, J. GUYOTAT, J. PELLET, M. MARIE-CARDINE
Laboratoire de Psychologie Médicale

The aim of our study was to provide the classification of chronic psychosis of J. GUYOTAT with semiological diagnostic criteria. According to this classification, every chronic psychotic can receive the diagnosis of type I or type II, taking into account variables from very various areas : therapeutic responance, psychodynamic structure, family organisation, genetic spectrum, clinical pictures. In this study we try to supply this classification with diagnostic criteria. So, firstly, we searched to extract semiological diagnostic criteria for each of the two types, then, secondly, we studied the face validity, the sensibility and the discriminant validity of these clinical pictures. In that aim, a first group of physicians evaluated the semiology of 51 chronic psychotics using a scale, the LICET-S (liste intégrée de critères d'évaluation taxinomique). Another groupe of physicians, experts, made the diagnosis of type I or II. By comparing diagnosis and semiology, clinical pictures have been elaborated for the both types. The study showns very good results for the face validity, the sensibility and the discriminant validity of our lists of diagnosis criteria. In conclusion, the GUYOTAT's classification of chronic psychosis which interest is to integrate the biopsychosocial points of view of mental illness, benefit now valid diagnostic criteria.

1394

Familiality of DSMIII Self Defeating Personality Disorder
Reich, James H., M.D., M.P.H.
Harvard Medical School

In order to determine the familiality of DSMIII self defeating personality disorder 22 relatives of self defeating personality disorder (SDPD) were compared to 51 relatives of screened controls. (SDPD used to be called masochistic personality disorder) Only first degree relatives were used. A standardized measure of personality disorders was utilized. All raters of relatives were blind to the diagnoses of the probands. Significantly more relatives of SDPD probands than relatives of controls were diagnosed as having SDPD (p .025). The possible contributions of genetics and social learning to this finding are discussed.

1395

A CLINICAL FOLLOW-UP STUDY OF DSM III R DEFINED PERSONALITY DISORDERS.
VISINTINI R.*, VITA A.*, SACCHETTI E.**

*Inst. of Psychiatry-Schizophrenia Research Center University of Milan-v.F.Sforza,35-Milan- Italy.
**Dept. of Psychiatry-S.Paolo Hospital-v.di Rudini n.8 - Milan, Italy.

In a long-term follow-up study of personality disorders we have found that the diagnosis of a personality disorder according to the DSM III criteria is not stable over time in a proportion of cases. In fact, we observed significant changes in the symptomatological profile, quality of life and social and relational functioning of 13 on 23 patients between the first and follow-up evaluation after a period of 1 to 3 years.
This suggests that the DSM III diagnoses of personality disorders may individuate more a psychopatological status than a stable personality "structure".
Characteristics of the premorbid phase had relevance for the outcome of the single patients' psychopathology, especially for the remission of "break-down states".
We observed the following: a) in most cases the diagnosis of personality disorders was multiple; b) diagnostic variability was higher in patients with schizotypal personality disorder; c) the diagnostic variability seems to depend both on the initial diagnosis and on the quality of premorbid adjustment.

1396

Personality disorders (DSM-III-R) and MMPI : an interrelation study

COSYNS P., SCHOTTE C., MAES M.

Department of Psychiatry,
University Hospital Antwerp (U.Z.A.)
Antwerp, Belgium

MMPI and SCID-II (Struct. Clin. Interview for DSM-III-R Axis II) are widely used instruments for the diagnosis of personality disorders. The aim of the present study is to explore the interrelations of these two instruments in the diagnosis of personality disorders. Seventy inpatients with a personality disorder, diagnosed by SCID-II according to the DSM-III-R criteria, completed the MMPI. The results of the SCID-II interviews and the MMPI validity and clinical scales are correlated for these seventy inpatients.
The correlations between the MMPI variables and the specific DSM-III-R personality disorders and also the three Axis II clusters are congruent with the theoretical expectations of the DSM-III-R.

Session 214 Free Communications:
Social and vocational rehabilitation services

1397

WORKING ABILITIES OF THE MENTALLY ILL IN TIMES OF SOCIAL CRISIS
Kecmanović,D. Psychiatric Clinic,Sarajevo Yugoslavia
In Yugoslavia a special Commision evaluates the working abilities of insured ill people. In the last fourteen years there has been an increase of the number of those referred to the Commision.
Investigation of all individual requests (N=1563), made in the course of 1982 in Bosna and Herzegovina, for retirement of partial or full pension on the basis of mental disorder, has been carried out. A follow-up of those who were awarded pensions has also been made.
The results obtained indicate that the willingness to retire is widespread among insured persons, quite often regardless of the actual impairment of their working abilities. Data are interpreted in the light of the severe socio-economic crisis Yugoslavia has been going through in the last decade.

1398

REHABILITATION CARE FOR CHRONIC PSYCHIATRIC PATIENTS
Tzethaki M, Kondylis K, Armeniakou S, Christidou Th, Karydi V.
Department of Psychiatry, Athens University, Athens, Greece

There is a general agreement that individuals with long term mental illness require a wide range of basic rehabilitation services and support. The purpose of this presentation is: a) to describe a system of three rehabilitation units aiming at psychosocial and vocational adjustment; the programme includes prevocational, vocational and rehabilitation training as well as co-operative units and b) to present some sociodemographic factors related to social isolation in 273 psychotic patients who participated in these programs. Depressive symptoms according to DSM-III criteria are related to sociodemographic factors such as age, sex, social class, educational level, work experience, social withdrawal, as well as a number of non-specific factors.
A multifactorial statistical analysis was performed. Its relevant findings are discussed.

1399

Follow up of young persons who completed or interrupted their training in a vocational workshop.
R.Papatheophilou - Ch.Karadimou
Workshops - A.U. - G.H.A. - OAED. Athens, Greece.

The vocational workshops of the Adolescent Unit (A.U.) of the General Hospital of Athens (G.H.A.) started functioning in Jan. 1987 with the financial assistance of Man Power Employment Organisation (OAED). 24 young persons (y.p.), 11 boys, 13 girls aged 15-25 y. had graduated or interrupted their training by December 1988. Length of training 3-24 m. Most of them are followed up weekly at the "Graduates Club". Information about the remaining y.p. was acquired by telephone. The following parameters were studied one and six months after discharge. Residential Arrangements (At home with family, alone or with frends, in an institution). Occupation (work in the free market, subsidised by Oaed, related or not to their training, sheltered workshops of some kind, further Education, at home helping a little in the house). Relapses. The above were examined in relation to the socioeconomic status of the family and its pathology, the age, sex, education of the y.p., the diagnosis, the duration of training. Outcome 1 month after discharge: 20 of the y.p. lived at home with their families. 50% of them had some sort of work. 12.5% continued training elsewhere. Frequent changes of work as well as relapses occured later on with occasional short stay in-patient treatment. The danger of relapses and eventual institutionalisation is strssed, if further forms of occupation such as sheltered workshops, production centers, or subsidisid workshops are delayed.

1400

A THREE YEARS EXPERIENCE IN A COUNTRY "HALF WAY HOUSE" NEAR MADRID
Fresnillo and Torrecano
C.E.T.E.V.A., Madrid, Spain

The trial experience of three years work carried out in a therapeutic "half-way-house", allows us to confirm the value of this type of centre as an alternative to a conventional psychiatric hospital and/or other "out patient" therapy programmes, in the context of the present-day public Mental Health Services.
The work was carried out with seventy patients of both sexes with ages ranging from 20 to 70 years.
Most of them were psychotic cases and they were resident in the Institution during their treatment.
Their psychosocial evolution throughout their stay was measured within the framework of the therapeutic programmes offered at the Centre. Whereas the technical results obtained in these Centres are good, they would prove a material impossibility without the financial backing of Public or State funds or a Foundation.

1401

Management of crisis in a substitutionproject for chronic psychiatric patients.

A.Kaasenbrood, J.A.C. Bleeker

Provinciaal Ziekenhuis Santpoort, Santpoort-Zuid
The Netherlands

38 Longstay hospital patients (70% DSM Schizophrenics, average length of stay 13 years) were housed in regular appartments in the city of Amsterdam december 1986. The patients' housing does not differ from the other 600 appartments of the building. They do not live in groups. 24Hour supervision is provided by a nursing staff, housed in the same building. Provisions have been made for medication control, meals, skillstraining, social work etc. The patients are however stimulated to use community services rather than those supplied by the hospital-organisation.
21 Patients are still there and doing well after $2\frac{1}{2}$ years. The majority of those who returned to the hospital went back in the first four months. For these patients, and for those who managed to cope, the management of crisis appeared to be a critical skill that had to be learnt by the staff.
The method of management of crisis will be presented and analysed in terms of social psychiatric treatment and crisisintervention theory (Lindeman, Tyhurst, Caplan).

1402

APPARTEMENTS THERAPEUTIQUES ET DECHRONICISATION

M.A. LARRIEU, M. PAULIN, A.V. TRAMONI, R.L. CLAVEL-MORROT
R.A. JULIEN
C.H.S. Valvert Bd des Libérateurs - 13011 MARSEILLE (FRANCE)

Parmi les alternatives à l'hospitalisation temps plein, l'appartement thérapeutique s'est révélé être un instrument de soins et de réinsertion sociale particulièrement intéressant. Trois appartements de ce type mis en place par le sixième secteur de Psychiatrie Générale à Marseille, ont permis à des patients, hospitalisés au long cours, de tendre, voire d'accéder à une réelle autonomie. La dynamisation des processus de communication entre soignants et patients, la mobilisation des capacités adaptatives, la responsabilisation sont quelques uns des principaux avantages de cette formule de soins. Il ressort de notre expérience qu'un travail spécifique et préliminaire à l'accueil en appartement thérapeutique, prenant en compte les difficultés propres à chaque patient, diminue les risques d'échec.
De même, une réflexion en matière d'indications et d'organisation du séjour doit être poursuivie. Nous voudrions enfin insister sur la souplesse, le caractère modulable du fonctionnement de ces structures permettant d'articuler au mieux les exigences d'ordre sécuritaire et thérapeutique.

1403

EINFLUßFAKTOREN DER VERLEGUNG PSYCHIATRISCHER PATIENTEN IN DAUERWOHNHEIME.
(REFERRING PSYCHIATRIC PATIENTS TO BOARDING HOMES)

Anne M. Leimkühler, Ulrich Müller
Forschungsstelle für
Psychiatrische Soziologie
Psychiatrische Klinik der Universität
- Rheinische Landesklinik -
4 Düsseldorf 12, Bergische Landstr. 2 FRG

Angesichts der zunehmenden Bedeutung von Heimverlegungen stellt sich die Frage, nach welchen Kriterien welche Patienten in welche Heime verlegt werden.
Wir untersuchten anhand eines halbstandardisierten Fragebogens alle Verlegungen von Patienten, die innerhalb eines Jahres aus unserer Klinik in Dauerwohnheime verlegt wurden.

Unsere Daten belegen eine signifikant höhere Verlegungswahrscheinlichkeit für gerontopsychiatrische Patienten im Vergleich zu jüngeren chronisch Kranken, einen Einfluß von Parametern der Klinikstruktur auf die Verlegung insbesondere der über 65jährigen sowie geschlechtsspezifische Unterschiede zuungunsten der Frauen.

1404

WORK PERFORMANCE AND ADJUSMENT IN PSYCHOTIC PATIENTS ATTENDING A REHABILITATION PROGRAM
M. ZOGRAFOU, P. SKALTSI, G. KARAMOUZI, V. ANTONOPOULOS, M. COCCOSIS, V. KARIDIS
Univ. of Athens, Dept. of Psychiatry
Eginition Hospital

The purpose of this study was to investigate the relation of skills and characteristics related to work performance, with work experience, education, mental functioning -assessed by WAIS- and work adjustment in a group of psychotic patients attending a program of prevocational training at Eginition Hospital.

193 psychotics diagnosed according to the DSM III criteria, 136 men, 57 women, with a mean age of 30.9 years, mean years of education 11.9 years and 61% of patients with working experience, were evaluated with a work skills rating scale while being in a pre-vocational training program.

This scale was specifically constructed by the staff for the assessment of the patients' skills and other characteristics related to work performance and adjustment, for the specific prevocational training context.

The findings from a multifactorial analysis concerning all the above mentioned factors will be discussed in reference to the use of this rating scale for work adjustment prognosis.

1405

THE PROVISION OF SUPPORT IN VOCATIONAL REHABILITATION

M.Y. Ekdawi
Netherne Hospital

One of the important measures of outcome is the employment status of rehabilitees on follow up. It is recognised that job tenure and vocational adjustment are dependent on a combination of satisfaction and satisfactoriness (Watts, 1983); there is a dearth of literature, however, on techniques to achieve them in the long term. A follow up study is reported from an English National Demonstration Service for Rehabilitation showing the importance of on-going support in this field.

1406

A REHABILITATION SERVICE IN A GENERAL HOSPITAL DISTRICT
Dr. F.Oliver, MB.ChB., MRC.Psych., DPM
Tameside General Hospital, Ashton-under-Lyne
Lancashire, OL6 9RW, England

The first 5 years of a service are described consisting of a rehabilitation ward, community team and committee to plan for the social, educational, housing and employment needs of long term patients. The service works flexibly with any agency in the community, i.e. State, voluntary or private. Most referrals from acute psychiatric wards and most patients have developed their handicaps secondary to psychoses in the community. Patients' assets and deficits in attitude, daily living skills and socialisation are assessed and an individual programme assigned. Patient is kept fully aware and paid for his progress. Team work with family to reduce over-protective response is applied. Patients are encouraged to use community facilities. Team also resettled 12 longstay patients from mental hospitals in staffed group homes. In 1989 ward moved to community unit and an assessment workshop opened on industrial site. During last 5 years for population of 250,000 only 5 longstay patients under 65 years remained as inpatients. Essential for consultant in every district to lead and give continuity to service, e.g. all other staff in this service changed within 3 years.

Session 215 Free Communications:
Personality and psychopathology in children and adolescents

1407

CHILDHOOD FEAR; NORMAL DEVELOPMENT AND CHILDHOOD PANIC DISORDER
Prof.Dr.Mauricio Knobel
State Univ.of Campinas(UNICAMP),Campinas,SP,Brazil

"Fear" is an affective personality component not quite clarifyied up till now. It is different from anxiety and from phobia and has normal aspects very necessary for normal psychoaffective development. Some very brief and focal panic crises in childhood (beginning of school,transient parental separation, travelling)are _normal_ reactions which turn to be useful for a normal psychoaffective development. When fear reactions are persistent and/or repetitive,or they appear abruptly and unexpected,without clear possible external motivation,it is necessary to think on "Childhood Panic Disorder",with concomitant suffering and also hampering normal psychoaffective development.It is possible to detect a basic anxious-depressive personality structure,with parental figures in severe conflicts.This is being postulated for understanding this special childhood psychopathology and its possible treatment. Psychotherapy is always necessary,but its association with antidepressive and anxiolytic medication demonstrated to be more effective.
A study of twenty two children with this kind of disorder proved that the association of amineptine and benzodiazepine was more effective.

1408
PANIC DISORDER IN PREPUBERTAL CHILDREN
B. Vitiello, MD, D. Behar, MD, S. Wolfson, MD, S. V. McLeer, MD, Medical College of Pennsylvania, Dept. of Psychiatry, Philadelphia, PA, USA.

Few reports on panic disorder in children are available, despite the retrospectively documented onset in childhood of about 20% of the cases of adult panic disorder. We report on 6 prepubertal children, aged 8-13 years, who met DSM-III-R criteria for panic disorder. Hyperthyroidism, cardiologic and respiratory problems were excluded, as well as abuse of caffeine or drugs. The first attack occurred at 5-11 years of age, with an average interval of 3 years between onset of the disorder and diagnosis. Although the first attack never occurred in school, 3 children developed school phobia a few months after. Given the association between panic disorder and mitral valve prolapse in adults, echocardigrams were obtaine in these children. Mitral valve prolapse was documented in 2 children. Family history was invariabily positive for panic disorder, whose presence was always detected in one side only of the family, either paternal or maternal. This is consistent with an autosomic dominant transmission.

Panic disorder can be diagnosed in prepubertal children using adult-type criteria. Although not common, its presence should be considered in children with school phobia and positive family history. As in adults, mitral valve prolapse should be suspected in this children.

1409
HYPERACTIVITY SYNDROME IN CHILDREN : CLINICAL-DYNAMIC AND PATHOGENETIC ASPECTS
V.Kovalev, V.Krasov, G.Mendes, M.Uzbekov
Moscow Research Institute of Psychiatry, Moscow, USSR

The hyperactivity syndrome (HS) in children and adolescents attracts attention of investigators due to its prevalence (3-10% of junior children) and insufficient existing knowledge of its dynamics, outcome and pathogenetic mechanisms. By means of clinical-dynamic, neuropsychological and clinico-biochemical investigations of 150 children with HS two unfavourable prognostic variants of the syndrome have been found: /1/ in 2/4 of patients, characterized by gradual transformation into deviant behavior of the affective-excitable type, and /2/ in 1/4 of patients, characterized by school maladjustment caused by borderline mental deficiency (IQ 70-75). Biochemical data on catecholamine and indolamine excretion levels have revealed the role of impaired serotonin metabolism in the pathogenesis of HS. The latter should be accounted for while choosing an adequate therapy.

1410
TYPOLOGY OF THE PATHOLOGICALLY AGGRESSIVE BEHAVIOUR IN CHILDREN AND ADOLESCENTS
C.Oancea, M.Safer, I.Dobrescu.Gh.Marinescu Hospital, Bucharest, Romania

A study was carried out in 46 children aged 8 to 16 years, hospitalized with manifestations of aggressivity as one of their main psychopathologic disturbances.Although the psychotics, the epileptics IQ below 60 had been excluded, still the nosologic context of aggressivity was very diverse. Near the aggressivity as a conduct disorder,transient or stable trait of ADDH,adjustment disorder, there were identified that associated with neurotic disorder and "pure" aggressivity.
The small number of associated features, the situational character and the absence of causating factors created difficulties in categorisation of some cases. The episodic forms seemed to have significant psychogenic reasons. Though narrowly defined in DSM-III, aggressivity can have multiple etiologies:incompletely recognised personality trait,genetic or lesional;acquired trait as a coping style learned after a coercitive model, by assimilating the aggressive behaviour of adults and other mechanisms.
Still some clinical forms remain unclarified by the modern theories.

1411
FUNCTION OF BEHAVIORAL DISORDERS IN CHILDREN AND ADOLESCENTS.

J.B. ORLER, J.B. GARRE, J.P. LHUILLIER, R. WARTEL.
Centre Hospitalo-Universitaire d'ANGERS.
Département de Psychiatrie du Pr. R. WARTEL.
17 X 49040 - ANGERS Cedex. FRANCE.

At an age where acting prevails over saying, behavioral disorders in children and adolescents are very common and their function.

They are to be seen and looked at and therefore their initial function is to challenge the family environment in order to modify its dynamics.

Behavioral disorders are a sign of dis-ease and their recognition allows the diagnosis and the therapeutic orientation to be specified.

Beyond the family and the doctor, behavioral disorders represent a message that the child or the adolescent addresses to himself : he is both the transmitter and the receiver of the signal thus acted out.

The decipherment of behavioral disorders offers the chance of an encounter for the child whereas its avoidance leads to their repetition.

1412
JUVENILE DELINQUENCY : THE IMPORTANCE OF PARENTAL REARING PATTERNS
HATZICHRISTOU,C., Ph.D., PAPADATOS, Y., M.D.
CENTER FOR MENTAL HEALTH AND RESEARCH

This study examined the implications of parental rearing behavior in juvenile delinquency. The sample consisted of the total population of juvenile delinquents during 1986-1987 in the institutions and prisons for delinquents in Greece (Athens,Thessaloniki,Patra,Larissa,Volos),thus of 287 individuals, 260 males (91.2%) and 25 females (8.8%). Their ages ranged from 11 to 21 years. All the individuals were interviewed by professionals and questionnaires regarding demographic information, family background, childhood problems, delinquent behavior were completed. Perceived parental rearing behavior was assessed with the EMBU questionnaire.

Based on the mean values of the four main factors of the EMBU (Rejection, Emotional Warmth, Overprotection, Favouring (Subject) two groups were formed for each factor and for perceived paternal and maternal behavior independently. The intergroup differences were assessed in relation to social and family variables. Various social and family characteristics of juvenile delinquents were found to be associated with rejective, emotionally responsive and overprotective paternal and maternal rearing patterns. The findings underscore the importance of parental psychological neglect in delinquent behavior.

1413
THE CORMAN TEST APPLIED TO CHILDREN WITH COOLEY'S ANAEMIA
Antoaneta Bugner, Cornelia Siara, C. Predescu
The Centre of Haematology and Blood Transfusion, Bucharest, Romania

In this paper we shall present the preliminary observations from the application of the Corman test "of drawing a family" on eight children-aged between 6-14 years - with Cooley's anaemia.
Aspects of the personality development of the children including defense mechanisms, object relationships, affective responses, etc as they are depicted in the drawings of the children will be presented and discussed in the light of the possible impact the chronic desease has on the personality development of the child.
Further follow-up studies are needed in an attempt to establish a possible relationship between the evolution of the disease and the possible impact on personality development.

1414
ADOLESCENTS AND HOMICIDE: A PSYCHOLOGICAL STUDY

Aguirre,R & Iglesias ,L.
Unidad de Psiquiatría,Consejo Tutelar para Menores
Monterrey,N.L.,México
En este estudio piloto se describen los principales hallazgos obtenidos en un grupo de adolescentes homicidas que fueron valorados en la Unidad de Psiquiatría del Consejo Tutelar para Menores del Estado de Nuevo León ,México, durante los años de 1986 a 1988.
Se hace especial énfasis en la Batería de Pruebas Psicológicas que se utilizó para la valoración y en los indicadores de personalidad relevantes en el adolescente.
Se destacan aspectos importantes de algunas variables relacionadas como lo son: el estatus socio-económico,el nivel de escolaridad y la edad.
Se describen las pruebas psicológicas utilizadas,las razones por las que se escogieron, y se señalan al mismo tiempo las dificultades y limitaciones que se presentan en nuestro medio a la hora de intentar estudiar al adolescente.
Se discuten los resultados al final y se proponen líneas de investigación.

1415
CONTRIBUTION A LA COMPREHENSION DES MANIFESTATIONS AUTISTIQUES DANS LE SYNDROME DE RETT.
Urwand S.
I.M.P. Marie Auxilliatrice
2 avenue Henri Barbusse
91210 Draveil FRANCE
 Contribution to the comprehension of autistic disorders in the Rett syndrome.

Les essais de prise en charge en internat de quelques enfants présentant un syndrome de Rett , nous ont amené à nous interroger sur la symptomatologie appartenant à la série autistique observée dans les tableaux cliniques.
La double prise en charge psychothérapique et psychopédagogique nous permet de constater la rencontre de l'aspect neurologique avec les angoisses archaiques de type autistique.
Nous décrirons quelques aspects du traitement d'une petite fille actuellement placée dans notre institution , en focalisant notre reflexion sur la jonction neuro-psychologique.

Session 216 Free Communications:
Mental health: General issues

1416
INCIDENCE AND SPONTANEOUS RECOVERY OF STUTTERING IN YOUNG ADULTS
A.Botsis, N.Vaidakis and A.D.Rabavilas,
Athens University Medical School, Department of Psychiatry, Eginition Hospital, Athens, Greece.

The total number of young men (n=12.436) who were enlisted in the army between the years 1986-1989 in a military training center were examined by means of a 31-item structured interview regarding the incidence, clinical signs, recovery rate and main factors related to onset, evolution and recovery rate of stuttering. 239 individuals (1.9%) reported as having had some form of stuttering during their early childhood. Most of them (n=201, 84%) were symptomless on examination, while the remaining (n=38, ratio 1:5) were still suffering from stuttering. Mean age of onset ranged from 3-10 yrs and mean age of spontaneous recovery ranged from 15-18 yrs. Prolongation of syllables followed by word repetitions constituted the commonest form of stuttering at onset in total subjects affected. Recovered stutterers demonstrated significantly higher incidence of sinistrality, poorer family relationships, attributed their condition to intrinsic, mostly, factors and had more interruptions than the combination of repetitions and interruptions as compared with the active stutterers (P range from <0.05 to <0.005). These findings are discussed and some suggestions regarding further exploration of the probable factors related to spontaneous recovery from stuttering are put forward.

1417
The Psychiatric Case Register in a Mental Health Center in Northern Tuscany
Andreani M.F., Raimondi R., Agrimi G., Lazzerini F., Bizzarri D.- Departement of Mental Health of Massa Carrara, Italy.

The epidemiologic studies smooth the way to programmation of sanitary resources and to preventive, assistential and reabilitating intervention. After the transition from asylum psychiatry to a chiefly extramural psychiatry emerged the need to monitor the new hospital and extra-hospital activities, that is to say the need to weigh the new services, their performance, their efficacy and efficiency besides the necessity to control the gradual elimination of old psychiatric institutions. Our first goal is to get to a quantitative and qualitative evaluation of services and of the relation between patients and services in a perspective of possible reorganization and replanning of models of psychiatric assistance. A mean for a correct evaluation seems to be the Psichiatric Case Register together with a specific evaluation of internal and external departmental activities and together with the planning of intervention methodologies of Quality Assurance.

1418
MODERNIZATION, INDUSTRIALIZATION AND THE MENTAL HEALTH. Shahrzad F.Siassi Ph.D., Private Practice, L.A.,CA, U.S.A.; Iradj Siassi M.D., Prof. of Psychiatry, U.C.L.A. Med. Sch.,L.A.,CA,U.S.A.;and Bahman Fozouni Ph.D., Director F.and W. Associates,Pgh,PA,U.S.A.

What are the impacts of rapid socio-economic changes on the mental health in the developing nations? Different investigators have reported conflicting results concerning the effects of industrialization and modernization on the mental health of the affected populations. This paper presents epidemiological data on the prevalence and incidence of mental disorders in an Iranian village at two points in time, twelve years apart, which had experienced rapid changes and industrialization, soon after the initial study. The same investigators (Professors K.Bash and Bash-Liechte of Berne, Switzerland), employing the same screening instruments and exactly the same clinical evaluations of the suspected cases, conducted the second wave of the study : The results indicate a far more complex relationship between modernization and mental health than a unilinear one suggested by some investigators. The incidence and point prevalence of mental disorder were not significantly different despite the major environmental and occupational changes. It is suggested that the structure of the family which had not undergone appreciable changes throughout the modernization experience may be a highly significant moderator variable.

1419
STUDY OF THE PSYCHOPATHOLOGY CAUSED BY UNEMPLOYMENT
Dinelli U. Dinelli M. Mascolo MD, Mottola G, Stefinlongo P, Materazzo M. Collot G.
Casa di Cura-Park Villa Napoleon-Dipartmento di Psichiatria, Treviso

Specialized studies have demonstrated in an unequivocal way that the number of unemployed persons are overrepresented among those who commit parasuicides compared to the population in general (10:1). Moreover the unemployed who have been out of work for more than a year have a higher psychopathological risk than those who have been out of work for a shorter time. Having taken into account the scientific data, we undertook a study among industrial institutions, with the aim of demonstrating a possible relationship between the Unemployment Supplement Fund Benefit (Cassa Integrazione Guadagni -CIG) and psychopathology and between the different forms of CIG and personality changes leading to suicide. 150 workers were chosen, selected after two preliminary talks directed at the appraisal of the social background, the critical position towards the CIG and the motivation of their cooperation. From this initial grouping, 3 separate groups emerged: a) ex-CIG workers, having worked for at least one year; b) workers under the CIG scheme for more than 5 years, permanently out of work; c) workers under the CIG scheme from one to three years with uncertain prospectives of employment. They all took the MMPI test, with algebraical signs and histograms. The statistical analysis of the results has shown that in Group A signs of conformity, submission, dependency and apathy are constantly present; in Group B compulsive tendencies, depressive syptoms, opposition to the environment and a degree of indifference; in Group C were negative radical neurosis, strong opposition to the environment, hypothism, lack of confidence, lack of adaptability and a very high level of stress. The results showed that it is really in this last group, where the projected security of the return to work is lacking, that more frequently self-destructing thematics are developed. The CIG should not be seen as a measure interpreted in a punitive sense, because it acts suddenly on workers chosen by the employer for an indefinite time, but rather as a random technical mean, for short periods of time, which acts on successive groups of workers in an alternating and cyclical way.

1420
ATTITUDE TOWARDS MENTAL ILLNESS IN THREE POPULATION SAMPLES
D.Sarantidis, G.Frantzios, N.Zachariadis
Evangelismos Gen. Hosp. & Attiki Psych. Hosp.
Athens, Greece

3 groups of population were studied in order to examine how certain variables can affect their attitude towards mental illness. These variables were unique for each group. The 1st group consisted of 262 policemen and we examined the variable of escorting mental patients to ps. hospitals. The 2nd group consisted of 188 students of nursing school and we examined the variable of their year of education. The 3rd group consisted of population samples and we examined the variable of proximity to mental health units. The tool used was the O.M.I. questionnaire (Standardization in Greece by M.Madianos). Statistical analysis (ANOVA) showed: 1. No significant results found in the sample of policemen. 2. Significant differences were found in the sample of students. The 3rd year students scored higher in factor A. 3. In population, were compared samples of inhabitants living in Tripolis (provincial town with psychiatric hospital), Agrinion (provincial town with no psych. facility at all), Exarchia (neighborhood of Athens with M.H.C only) Haidari (neighborhood of Athens with psychiatric hospital) and Ilioupolis (neighborhood of Athens with no psychiatric facility at all). In factor A Agrinion scored higher than Tripolis. In factor B Agrinion scored higher than Tripolis. Both Exarchia & Haidari scored higher than Ilioupolis. In factor C Tripolis scored higher than Agrinion, Ilioupolis scored higher than Exarchia and Haidari. In factor D Exarchia scored higher than Ilioupolis. (All compar. p<0.05)

1421
MEASUREMENT OF PSYCHOTROPIC DRUGS UTILISATION IN BALEARIC ISLANDS (1987-88): CLINICAL IMPLICATIONS
M.Roca Bennasar, A.Garcia Mas, P.Ventayol
Dept. Psychology. Univ Illes Balears. Spain

The Balearic Islands is a group of 3 islands with approximately 700,000 inhabitants. The utilisation of psychotropic drugs is analyzed for the years 1988-89, according to OMS indications, from the following data sources: a) Total consumption; b) Social Security c) General Hospital, d) Psychiatric Hospital.
In the study, all drugs are converted into Defined Daily Doses(DDD), The DDD is the average maintenance dose of the drug recommended on its major indication and should be considered as a technical unit of measurement. Our data are analyzed and compared with available data for northern countries which are those best studied. Under ideal circumstances the number of DDDs per population ought to agree with morbidity data. The pitfalls with this unit of measurement (DDD) include major discrepances between recommended and prescribed doses in the case of drugs used on diferent indications, like the psychotropics. We discuss this results, especially in the fields of primary health care in Spain.

1422
Obsessive Compulsive Disorder: A Demographic Study
Jose A. Yaryura-Tobias, Ricardo A. Yaryura, Fugen Neziroglu, Christina J. Taylor
Bio-Behavioral Psychiatry, Great Neck, N.Y.

Epidemiological and clinical data were analyzed in 307 outpatients diagnosed as Primary Obsessive Compulsive Disorder. Data were gathered for age, sex, marital and socioeconomic status, religion, birth complications, age of onset, age of first consultation, secondary diagnosis, marital disturbance, drug and alcohol abuse, family psychiatric history, and treatment. Chi square statistics were used to analyze the data. Where applicable, control groups from the general or a psychiatric population were utilized. Compared to the general population there were significantly fewer married males in the OCD group. Significant gender differences were also found for marital status and age of onset. Mean age of onset was 17.9 years, mean age for first consultation was 22.8 years, and mean interval between onset of illness and first consultation was 7.4 years. Marital disturbances were present in 58%, illegal drug use in 31%, and an alcohol dependence in 9.3%. Psychiatric family history

1423
FREQUENCY OF VARIOUS DIAGNOSIS IN PSYCHIATRIC OFFICE PRACTICE OF URBAN TURKEY
ZELIHA TUNCA, M.D.
DOKUZ EYLUL UNIVERSITY, SCH. OF MEDICINE
DEPARTMENT OF PSYCHIATRY

In this research, the file documents of 658 patients seen in 5 years of urban office practice of Turkey were retrospectively analyzed in accordance with DSM III criteria, and the frequency of diagnosis were grouped with respect to age and sex. Major depression was the leading diagnosis (17%), followed by somatization (12%). When major depression, dysthymic disorders, unipolar and bipolar depression were taken as a group, the rate of affective disorders reached a value of 40%.

According to age group (16-30, 31-55, above 55) depression among patients above the age of 55 was 30%, somatization and dysthymic disorder were mainly the disease of young and middle aged patients, panic disorder was most frequent among the middle aged patients and this disturbance was less prevalent as the age escalated, meanwhile fobic disorders were equally frequent in all age groups. Other diagnostic groups were also investigated according to age and sex of the patient population.

1424
PREVALENCE OF DEPRESSION IN HEALTH AND INDUSTRY SECTORS
Reyes Moreno and Martinez Carreras
Lascasiana, S.A. de C.V., San Luis Potosi, S.L.P. Mexico

Due to the curriculum, social and economic class of physicians it might be expected a low frequency of depression among them.
To know the truth about this fact the Zung test was applied to 70 professionals of health. 6 depressed persons were found out, which means the 8,5%. The percentage among general population goes from 3% to 10%. To compare the results the same test was applied to 76 workers of an industry with a high level of technology. One depressed person was found out (1.3%).
Although the test does not examine the environment, the interviews revealed that the tested industry workers are more optimistic and biophilic. This fact may be due to better working conditions, payment, incentives and better relationships among the personnel within that industry. On the other hand, the interviews revealed that physicians had not achieved their life expectancies, their working conditions cause more stress and the relationships among the personnel were worse.

Session 217 Symposium:
Rehabilitation in psychiatry

1425
REHABILITATION OF CHRONIC SCHIZOPHRENICS IN A DEVELOPING COUNTRY LIKE PAKISTAN
PROF. MOHAMMAD RASHID CHAUDHRY
FOUNTAIN HOUSE LAHORE, PAKISTAN

MENTAL HEALTH SERVICES IN PAKISTAN AS IN MOST DEVELOPING COUNTRIES HAVE NOT ADVANCED BEYOND ELEMENTARY LEVEL. CONSIDERING THE POPULATION SIZE, THERE ARE FEW BEDS IN PSYCHIATRIC WARDS OR HOSPITALS FOR THOSE IN NEED, AND LITTLE IF ANY, OPPORTUNITY FOR MENTALLY ILL INDIVIDUALS TO RECEIVE AID AND ASSISTANCE IN THE COMMUNITY. ONE MODEL WHICH PROVIDES A COMPREHENSIVE ARRAY OF SERVICES FOR CHRONIC MENTAL PATIENTS IN THE COMMUNITY IS KNOWN AS THE 'CLUBHOUSE' SINCE 1971 FOUNTAIN HOUSE HAS PROVIDED SOCIAL, VOCATIONAL AND RESIDENTIAL SERVICES TO CHRONIC SCHIZOPHRENICS IN LAHORE BASED ON THE CONCEPT OF MENTAL PATIENTS AS MEMBERS OF A CLUB RECEIVING SELF HELP THROUGH MUTUAL COOPERATION. EQUALLY BASIC TO THE MODEL IS THE CONCEPT OF FAMILY STRUCTURE. BASED ON 14 YEARS OF EXPERIENCE, IT HAS BEEN FOUND THAT THE CLUBHOUSE MODEL CAN BE INITIATED, GROW, AND THRIVE IN A DEVELOPING COUNTRY. ESSENTIAL TO THIS PROCESS HAS BEEN FULL INVOLVEMENT OF THE COMMUNITY. THE MODEL CAN BE FULLY INCORPORATED WITH ADAPTATION REFLECTING LOCAL CONDITIONS AND CIRCUMSTANCES IN OTHER DEVELOPING COUNTRIES.

1426
ETHICAL ASPECTS IN REHABILITATION OF THE MENTALLY ILL

Kabanov M., Bekhterev Inst., Leningrad, USSR
Since rehabilitation of mental patients is their resocialization, the most complete restoration (conservation) of the individual and social value, their personal and public status, the essence of a rehabilitational approach to a patient is in the unity of step-wise biological and psychosocial efforts aimed at various sides of his living and mediated through his personality. The patient's relations with therapist (psychologist), family, friends, co-patients and community is a central point in this approach. Studies at the Bekhterev revealed prevalence of moral qualities over professional skills in the personnel as evaluated by patients. Rehabilitation efficacy depends on the patient attitude to applied measures: patients (schizophrenics, endogenic depressives) exclusively aimed at medication and denying psychosocial measures have much worse prognoses. The research has also demonstrated the significance of patient value orientations for rehabilitation efficacy and prognosis. Patients with protracted depressions and high-level social maturity, high health values and open for rehabilitative efforts showed remissions of better quality.

1427
COGNITIVE THERAPY OF SCHIZOPHRENICS IN THE REHABILITATION
G.-E. Kühne, K. Peter, A. Schlichter
Dept. of Psychiatry of the Friedrich-Schiller-Univ., Jena DDR-6900, G.D.R.

Cognitive disorders were used as disorders in thought, speech and perception as important clinical symptoms in the historical development of the diagnostics of schizophrenics. Cognitive disorder patterns can be recorded experimentally and lay claim to their place in a multiple factorial manner of view of schizophrenia. Starting from the base disorder conception, clinicians have taken up these phenomena again frequently and therefore they were able to develop first therapeutical influence possibilities of cognitive disorders. Within a complex therapy of schizophrenic psychoses we developed a therapy programme to the training of cognitive, communicative and social impairments. Now we can report on the therapeutical progresses of 66 patients and deduce conclusions for further investigations.

Within to framework of our investigations we could also obtain some more differentiated statements to the applicability of the "Frankfurt's Complaint Questionnaire" (Frankfurter Beschwerdenfragebogen) - FBF).

1428
PSYCHIATRIC REHABILITATION IN MALAYSIA

Dr. M. Parameshvara Deva
Department of Psychological Medicine
Faculty of Medicine, University of Malaya
59100 Kuala Lumpur, Malaysia.

Psychosocial rehabilitation of the mentally ill is not as easily available as is needed in developing countries. Limited resources of trained manpower and funds make rehabilitation a luxury in many parts of the developing countries. The emphasis on acute treatment and secondary prevention of mental illnesses are at the expense of rehabilitation and causes relapses and promote chronicity and dependence.

A programme involving a network of 17 treatment centres that have started rehabilitation units for the mentally ill who have been treated in Malaysia shows that both for the chronic and the acutely ill mental patients, rehabilitation is not a luxury but a necessity. This paper describes these innovations at low or no cost to the patient.

1429
PSYCHIATRIC REHABILITATION IN CHINA

Weng yongzhen, Huilongguan Hospital, Beijing
There are more than one millon chronic schizophrenics in China. Part of them have to be in the psychiatric hospital for a long time.
In order to improve the life quality of life of the patients, Shanghai took the lead in establishing a research group on psychiatric rehabilitation in 1985.
In 1988, Chinese Psychiatric Rehabilitation Sociaty was founded. Decades of papers were presented.
The National Conference of Psychiatric Rehabilitation was held in Mianyang City, Sichuan Province in October, 1988. The papers sent to the conference added up to more than 80 copies. One of the reports was given by Dr. Weng Yongzhen, the main idea of the report was about the four-step rehabilitation programme for the handicapped caused by chronic schizophrenia. 1) Increasing initiative; 2) Social skill training; 3) Vocational training and 4) Preparing to came back to the community. The programme was taking place in Huilongguan Hospital. The experts attending the conference were very interested in this programme and saticefied with the curative effect of it.
In this conference a new plan of the work for the future was formed.

1430
THE REHABILITATION OF PSYCHOTIC DISORDERS AROUND THE WORLD
Ulf Malm, MD, Psychiatric Department Centrum, Göteborgs Sjukvård, Box 31108, S-400 32 Göteborg, Sweden.

During recent years rehabilitation programmes for psychotic disorders have been established independently in many countries, in the research setting as well as in international joint ventures, and in clinical practice.

Worldwide features are discussed under four headings:

- the role of the psychiatrist,
- treatment methods,
- goals, and
- entry into the community.

To summarize the state of the art, the psychiatrist should lead a rehabilitation team that combines and coordinates diagnostic skills, new psychobiological knowledge about brain function in psychosis, individual alliances, group therapy, social skills training and other psychosocial therapies, and psychotic medication. Talk and interaction are the hallmarks of the treatment.

The goals are concerned with citizen identity of the patient and standard of living and quality of life issues. Entry into the community should comprise regular activities together with other people.

Session 218 Symposium:
Depression in primary care

1431
DEPRESSION IN THE PHYSICALLY ILL

Alfred M. Freedman, M.D., U.S.A.

A significant number of patients with physical illness are depressed according to ICD-9 or DSM III-R criteria. Among the hospitalized medically ill, estimates range up to 25 percent. Regrettably, these depressed individuals are often not diagnosed and if diagnosed are not adequately treated. Reasons for failures of diagnosis and lack of appropriate treatment will be presented. The importance of proper diagnoses and treatment is critical for the general practitioner, medical specialists other than psychiatrists and consultation-liaison psychiatrists.

1432
DEPRESSION IN THE ELDERLY
Ballus C. - Professor, University of Barcelona, Spain

1433
ANXIETY AND DEPRESSION: DIFFERENTIAL DIAGNOSIS

Costa e Silva, Jorge Alberto, Prof. Dr.
State University of Rio de Janeiro, Rio de Janeiro, Brazil

The relations between anxiety and depression must be well explained. Both anxiety and depression are two different clinical realities frequently associated.

The comprehension of these phenomena is very important, not only for a better distinction of them, but for a better therapeutic handling.

The author makes a revision of these two concepts by a physiopathological, biochemical, nosological, clinical and therapeutic points of view. On the conclusion, the author presents a clinical model to a better comprehension of these two phenomena isolated or associated in a same mental disorder.

1434
The Primary Care Physician: Managing Depression

Rodolfo Fahrer
School of Medicine
University of Buenos Aires

The notion of Primary Health Care, where the PCP is the one who must recognize early depressive disorders and eventually take the decision to handle the patient himself or transfer him to a more specialized level, has helped considerably to bridge the gap between the detection of early symptoms and primary prevention. The PCP thus becomes the principal supplier of treatment for the patient and his family, in view of his availability, accessibility and continuity. There is a program of planned and sequential suggestions which he can follow regarding diagnoses, possible referral, prescribing and available therapeutic tools. The PCP is the first contact level for the patient, his family and the community with the health system and ideally, his role should develop through a national and continuous program of aggiornamento.

PCP= Primary Care Physician

Session 219 Symposium:
De l'urgence à la Communauté, de l'accompagnement à l'hospitalization

1435
REPÈRES HISTORIQUES

Pierre BAILLY-SALIN
Centre de Consultation Spécialisé du 7ème Arrondissement

Repères historiques: modifications dynamiques de la société, interactions avec l'évolution de la psychiatrie.

1436

HÔPITAL: TEMPS SPÉCIFIQUE ET PARTICULIER
DE L' ÉVOLUTION DU MALADE.
PAPANIKOLAOU GEORGES
**SOCIETY OF PSYCHIATRY AND MENTAL
HEALTH**

À l' Association de Santé Mentale du 13ème
arrondissement de Paris, les soins offerts
aux patients psychotiques graves se font
en grande partie dans la communauté, en
ambulatoire et dans des institutions in-
termédiaires. Néanmoins nous possédons
un hôpital psychiatrique dans la banlieue
parisienne. Nous concevons l' hospitalisation comme une résistance dynamique du
projet familial et donc communautaire
d' exclure, par une hospitalisation psychiatrique, le sujet présentant des troubles psychiques insupportables pour
autrui.
Résister dynamiquement c' est accepter
l' hospitalisation tout en la rendant,
dès la première minute, conflictuelle,
problématique et critique, visant à une
réinsertion rapide du sujet dans son milieu naturel. Ces notions seront étayées
par des cas cliniques.

1437

ACCUEIL, CRISE, URGENCE, MOMENTS ÉVOLUTIFS
DES OBJECTIFS D' UNE ÉQUIPE.
Guy BAILLON
CHS Ville Evrard 93330 NEUILLY SUR MARNE
FRANCE

Les étapes évolutives d' une unité de soin
ouverte 24h sur 24 créée en ville par une
équipe de secteur qui a reconverti de façon variée son patrimoine asilaire.

La différenciation des stratégies
d' Accueil, de Crise et d' Urgence est de-
venu un objectif actuel de cette unité;
elles constituent un temps introductif
essentiel précédant la continuité des
soins; elles semblent influencer profondément aussi bien l' observation clinique
des soignants que le parcours des patients
dans les soins et dans la vie.

1438

HOSPITALISATION À DOMICILE COMME ALTERNA-
TIVE AUX SOINS À L' HÔPITAL
VASSILIS KAPSAMBELIS
INSTITUT NATIONAL MARCEL RIVIÈRE

Il s' agit de la description d' une expérience
des soins intensifs à domicile chez des
patients psychotiques chroniques en
phase aigue. Les rapports avec les autres
membres de la famille sont décrits, ainsi
que les relations avec la communauté.

L' hospitalisation à domicile est assurée
par des soignants de specialités différentes sous contrôle psycho-dynamique.
Les soins ne se limitent pas à la période
aigue, mais prennent la forme d' un accompagnement à long terme.

1439

TRAVAIL AVEC LA COMMUNAUTÉ ET DANS LA
COMMUNAUTÉ.
PANAYIOTIS SAKELLAROPOULOS
Section of Social Medicine and Mental
Health Dimokrition University of Thrace

L' offre multidisciplinaire des soins psychiatriques à la communauté. La sensibi-
lisation et la participation du public
concerné dans tout le parcours de la pré-
vention à l' hospitalisation à domicile.
Modification de l' attitude de la population envers la maladie mentale, la dangerosité et l' internement.

Session 220 Symposium:
Psychiatric education around the world

1440

PSYCHIATRIC EDUCATION IN MALAYSIA - THE CASE FOR BROADER PERSPECTIVES

Dr. M. Parameshvara Deva
Department of Psychological Medicine
Faculty of Medicine, University of Malaya
59100 Kuala Lumpur, Malaysia.

Malaysia is a developing country that has its own medical school only 25 years ago. Since 1964, the three (3) medical schools in the country have all had foundation departments of psychiatry with healthy undergraduate curricula in psychiatry including 8 to 10 weeks of clinical clerkships. In a country with only 48 psychiatrists for 17 million people, the undergraduate psychiatric curricula have assumed a crucial role in spreading psychiatric knowledge. Despite this, there remains a large void in psychiatric knowledge among primary care workers, general practitioners and health workers. The challenge in a developing country is to spread as much basic psychiatric knowledge as possible to as wide an area as possible among health care workers. This paper describes some wider perspectives in the teaching of psychiatry involving innovations in teaching.

1441

TRAINING POSSIBILITIES IN LIAISON PSYCHIATRY

Ballus C. - Professor, University of Barcelona, Spain

1442

FUTURE DEVELOPMENTS IN PSYCHIATRIC EDUCATION IN LATIN AMERICA

Costa e Silva - Professor, Universidade do estado do Rio de Janeiro, Brazil

1443

TRAINING THE GLOBAL PSYCHIATRISTS

Gerald J. Sarwer-Foner, M.D., Professor of Psychiatry, Wayne State University Medical School, Director, Lafayette Clinic, Detroit, Michigan, USA

The psychiatrist of the future must be trained as a solid physician. He should be exposed to an adequate training in psychiatry in his undergraduate years (for all physicians). He then should do a comprehensive rotational 12-month internship which would establish good familiarity with the patterns of disease, seen in all organ systems and thus solidify his knowledge of pathophysiology and his sense of identity as a physician. In his formal psychiatric training that follows all appropriate aspects of psychiatry should be taught; the biological, genetic aspects, the influences of culture and society, and above all the psychodynamic understanding of human beings, their development, their needs and motivations and their defenses. Not teaching any of these components would produce poorly-trained psychiatrists.

The author will elaborate in his presentation.

1444
Teaching CB Techniques in Developing Countries

Martin Gittelman, Alfred Freedman N.Y. Med. Coll.
Tolani Asuni-U. Lagos, Nigeria
Vijay Nagaswami S.C.A.R.F., Madras, India
J Dubuis, Villeurbanne, Sector France

In most developing areas, the mentally ill are cared for by their families without access to psychiatric treatment, rehabilitation or information. To cope with this problem, the W.H.O. has promoted emphasis away from the mental hospital model towards the adoption of Community Based Rehabilitation (CBR) programs within the context of national planning.

This paper describes the methods and content of some CBR training programs. It discusses the strategy used in developing countries to provide the families of the mentally ill with information on etiology, characteristics and course of mental illness as well as the three modes of relapse and disability prevention: medication, stress and conflict reduction and social and vocational rehabilitation. Examples of CB in developing countries and recommendations for psychiatric education curriculum will be given. Data on relapse rates will be presented.

Session 221 Symposium:
Philosophic perspectives to the development of psychiatric service in a developing country

1445
PHILOSOPHICAL OUTLOOK TO DEVELOPMENT OF PSYCHIATRY SERVICES IN A DEVELOPING COUNTRY.

Prof. W. Bodemer, Pretoria, S.Africa.

Developing countries have to cope with limited financial and professional resources. Experts in the field of psychiatric services in developing countries will address us during this symposium on the planning of a psychiatric service for:
  I. A developing country.
  II. A community service in a predominantly rural region.
  III. An urban and per-urban community.
  IV. The comparative for forensic psychiatric services in two countries on different levels of development.
  V. Perspectives from the view of another progressive developing country.
This symposium is intended to stimulate discussion and generate new ideas on this extremely relevant subject.

1446
DEVELOPING COMMUNITY ORIENTATED SERVICES IN A DEVELOPING COUNTRY.
A.LEVIN, S.AFRICA.

The development of community orientated psychiatric services in developing countries presents one of the greatest challenges to psychiatric administrators. Shortages and maldistribution of professional manpower, facilities, limited funds and negative attitudes towards psychiatric care need to be overcome. South Africa has an extensive existing institutionally orientated psychiatric service with hospital-centric community services. In the past these services have tended to be monodisciplinary nursing services. Attempts are now being made to shift services away from institutions towards community clinics and to reemphasise multi-professional service delivery. A model network of clinics is being created which utilizes multiprofessional team members more appropriately. Pharmacists instead of nurses dispense medication. Psychologists provide councilling and short-time therapy. Social workers deal with family matters and community resources. Nurses act as case managers and primary therapists. Psychiatrists and medical practitioners diagnose, refer, treat, and co-ordinate. Due to improved community care, patients are being re-admitted with less gross morbidity and spend less time in hospital. The major challenges are to spread care to "have-not's" in keeping with ethnic/cultural needs and to train and retain sufficient personnel to ensure the viability of the service.

1447
SOUTH AFRICAN PSYCHIATRIC SERVICES.
A.LEVIN, SOUTH AFRICA.

South African psychiatric services represent one of the most cost-effective services in Africa provided under difficult circumstances. Due mainly to selective emigration there are 200 psychiatrists for 30 million people. There are 24 000 long term psychiatric beds of which 11 000 are provided by private entrepreneurs at the expense of the State. There are another 2 000 beds in community halfway houses and hostels for the mentally handicapped or psychiatrically disabled. There are 1 200 acute general hospital psychiatric beds of which 700 are in private hospitals. Delivery is in a state of transition. There is a growth of community services, primary care, private facilities, and an increase in general hospital facilities. The greatest challenges are to increase the number of psychiatrists, increase medical student exposure to relevant psychiatry and to fill the gap between the "haves" and the "have not's". Multi-disciplinary teams predominate with nurses and a growing number of clinical psychologists, social workers and occupational therapists. More than 20 000 medical practitioners play a supportive role. Voluntary organisations, crisis intervention services and self-help groups have become increasingly active. Voluntary treatment is replacing involuntary commitment. The D.S.M.(R) provides a diagnostic framework. Treatment tends to be eclectic. Crosscultural and ideological issues dominate discussion.

1448

DEVELOPMENT OF A PSYCHIATRIC COMMUNITY SERVICE IN THE ORANGE FREE STATE.
Prof. C.A.Gagiano, Bloemfontein, S.Africa.

Up to 1984 the following problems in the total psychiatric service were experienced: Neuroclinics were overcrowded, there was an unacceptably high re-admission rate and physically violent psychotic patients were detained in police cells. Because of large numbers of patients acute psychiatric disorders little primary intervention was done. From June 1985 a model based on the following principles was developed: Orange Hospital, the specialized psychiatric hospital would handle only serious, complicated or therapy-resistant patients. Three large general hospitals would be developed to serve as regional psychiatric hospitals for uncomplicated conditions, admit patients for detoxification, treat delirium and provide rehabilitation on an outpatient basis. Primary care teams at 58 clinic points would identify and treat patients with uncomplicated conditions and refer complicated and therapy-resistant. The service should be curative as well as for primary intervention with training and educational programmes for the primary health team as well as the general public. After four years there has been a dramatic drop in bed occupation, re-admission rate and number of patients detained in police cells. Improved patient compliance and the development of unique social support systems for schizophrenia, substance abuse, depression and anxiety has occurred. The number of patients treated in the community has increased from just over 20 thousand to over 50 thousand per annum during the past four years.

1449

MODEL FOR DEVELOPING OF PSYCHIATRIC SERVICES IN A MAINLY URBAN AND PERI-URBAN AREA

H. Olivier, Weskoppies Hospital, South Africa

The general model of a central psychiatric hospital linked to the facilities of a general hospital as well as to a University, complemented by peripheral hospitals and psychiatric clinics are outlined. The importance of community psychiatry is emphasized, especially to supply information and education, evaluation, referral, outpatient treatment and follow up.

Special problem areas, such as increasing number of patients, socio-economically bound psychiatric conditions and transcultural psychiatry, are discussed.

1450

COMPARING FORENSIC PSYCHIATRY IN THE ORANGE FREE STATE AND NAMIBIA
Dr. P.H.J.J. van Rensburg

The Department of Psychiatry at the University of the Orange Free State provides forensic psychiatric services for Namibia as well as the central region of South Africa. A highly specialized multi-professional team is responsible for the evaluation and treatment of these patients. The Orange Free State has a very well developed community psychiatric service. This service plays an important role in providing adequate information in the evaluation process. The community service also cares for discharged and conditionally discharged patients. Therapeutic patient groups even in the most remote area of the Orange Free State provide a unique support system and improve patient compliance. This is very important for patients in need of constant maintenance therapy such as epilepsy and schizophrenia. The groups also serve as an early detection system for relapse. On the other hand, the evaluation of Namibian patients is difficult because of vast cultural and language differences. Due to distance from a home there is often a lack of family support. The situation is complicated by a virtual lack of psychiatric community service. Discharging Namibian patients on probation, especially patients from more remote areas, is usually impossible because of the lack of follow-up care for the patients. The main difference in forensic psychiatric service between the two areas is the existence of a well developed community psychiatric service in the one area. With the pending independence of Namibia, it is highly recommended that the development of a comprehensive psychiatric service including forensic phychiatric service be given priority.

1451

AN OVERVIEW OF THE DEVELOPMENT OF PSYCHIATRIC SERVICES IN A PROGRESSIVE AFRICAN COUNTRY

Detei D. - Kenya

1452

PSYCHIATRIC SERVICES IN A THIRD WORLD SETTING.
Professor G.A.D. Hart, S.Africa.

The structure of community psychiatric services will obviously vary from situation to situation depending on local conditions.The shortage of psychiatrically trained nurses and the extreme shortage of psychiatrists are two critical factors in the structuring of psychiatric community services in the third world setting.Integration of psychiatric services with the general health services is necessary.The primary health nurse should be trained to deal with common and urgent psychiatric situations.The psychiatric nurse should act as a consultant and educator to the primary health care nurse.The mental state examination needs to be vigorously taught.In addition the psychiatric nurse of necessity will need to be able to prescribe certain psychotropic agents.Nomadic consultant psychiatrists' function should be broad but mainly as consultants and educators to the psychiatric nurses.Their teaching should take the form mainly of clinical workshops.Input into the structure of the services would of course be part of the wider function of the psychiatrist.For a cost effective,efficient service,psychiatry must come back into the main stream of medicine and not be treated like an infectious disease.New patients should be seen by the psychiatric nurse.Occupational therapists have an extensive contribution to make in a consultative role and in training assistants to carry out prgrammes.Again shortage of occupational therapists is a grave problem.Psychologists need to be oriented toward a much wider function within the psychiatric setting of the third world.

Session 222 Symposium:
The role of psychiatry in international conflict resolution

1453

The Role of Psychiatry in International Conflict Resolutions
John Woodall, M.D. (USA), Muhammed Said Kamal (West Bank via Israel), Raphael Moses (Israel), Muhammed Shaalam (Egypt).

Each theoretical school of psychiatry has offered it's version of the human social experience. The refinement of psychiatric social theory is essential if our field is to remain relevant to the needs of our times. An overview of the theoretical contributions of psychiatry to international conflict will be given. Specifically, the core role of the formation of group identity in "Collective Centers" will be introduced as a unifying concept of intrapsychic and social cognition. The role of Collective Centers in the negotiation process will also be explored. Special emphasis will be placed on the Arab-Israeli conflict.

1454

COLLECTIVE CENTERS OF IDENTITY AND CONFLICT RESOLUTION.
John Woodall, M.D.
University of California-Irvine

Each Theoretical School of Psychiatry has offered it's version of the human social experience. The refinement of psychiatric social theory is essential if our field is to remain relevant to the needs of our times. An overview of the theoretical contributions of psychiatry to international conflict will be given. Specifically, the core role of the formation of group identity in "Collective Centers" will be introduced as a unifying concept of intrapsychic and social cognition. The organization of standards of ethics around Collective Centers of Identity will be outlined. The role of Collective Centers in the negotiation process will also be explored. Special emphasis will be placed on the Arab-Israeli situation.

1455

PSYCHIATRIC CONTRIBUTIONS TO THE RESOLUTION OF THE ARAB-ISRAELI CONFLICT.
Mohammed Said Kamal, M.D.

A deeper level of analysis is required to find solutions to social conflict. The Middle-East offers unique opportunities to investigate the nature of the interaction between intrapsychic processes, powerful socializing forces like religion and ethnicity, and the creation of political policies that attempt to balance these forces. Psychiatry, as a discipline, has unique tools for this analysis and can help in the process of creating new contexts in which these conflicts can be viewed. This presentation will attempt to extend fundamental insights derived from clinical work to what can be observed in the beliefs and aspirations held by participants in the Arab-Israeli situation.

1456
PSYCHIATRIC INSIGHTS INTO THE ARAB-ISRAELI CONFLICT
Raphael Moses, M.D.

This presentation will explore the psychodynamic factors involved in social and political processes in international conflict. Special attention will be given to issues raised in protracted conflict. The Arab-Israeli situation lends itself to study in particular due to the deeply held convictions rooted in social and religious tradition that influence political policy and color interpretation of events. Areas of interest include: the nature of escalation and the factors that exacerbate a crisis in the Middle-East, and psychological factors that hinder the negotiation process.

1457
THE PSYCHODYNAMICS OF ETHNICITY IN THE ARAB-ISRAELI CONFLICT.
Mohammed Shaalam, M.D.

Ethnic identification plays a key role in the identity of an individual and in the manner in which that individual sets ethical standards for themselves and the society in which they live. The way in which ethnic identity can either strengthen or weaken when faced with perceived threat is a central issue when considering the factors involved in the Arab-Israeli conflict. The value and meaning of Arab identity will be explored in the context of expectations of the future of the Middle-East. An understanding of defense mechanisms in relation to preserving an individual identity can be applied in viewing ethnic identities in the Middle-East.

Session 223 Symposium:
New and useful psychotropic drugs in child and adolescent psychiatry

1458
Introduction

G. Nissen
Klinik und Poliklinik für Kinder- und Jugendpsychiatrie der Universität Würzburg

In certain cases psychotropic substances are by far no substitute for psychotherapeutic treatment which, only for practical reasons, cannot be applied in childhood and adolescence. In other indications psychopharmacological substances lead to unrivaled improvement rates, especially when combined with psychotherapeutically oriented intervention and intensive parent consult.

The opinion of some doctors that one should not prescribe psychopharmacological drugs to children is only true in so far as children should never be treated unnecessarily. The therapy should always be based on an exact knowledge of effects, dosage and side effects of the drugs and a preceding thorough physical, neurological and psychopathological examination.

1459
Treatment of Insomnia in Childhood and Adolescence with L-Tryptophan
Elliger, Tilman, Götz-Erik Trott
Klinik und Poliklinik für Kinder- und Jugendpsychiatrie der Univ. Würzburg

Since 1967 numerous studies on the psychopharmacology of L-Tryptophan (L-TRP) have confirmed the hypnogenic effects of this amino acid, but the status of L-TRP as a hypnogenic agent is still in question.

In view of these observations, the effect of L-TRP was studied in twenty unselected insomniac children and adolescents, aged 8 to 16 years. Patients suffering from a sleeping disorder classified as "psychophysiological, persistent" were included in an open pilot study. The washout period was 4 weeks, the maximal doses were 50 mg/kg body weight per die. At the doses used, L-TRP was well tolerated. Self-rating protocols and the assessment of sleep behaviour revealed that the subjects' sleep improved significantly between the 7th and 14th day after starting treatment.

The result suggest that L-TRP has hypnogenic properties with a high benefit-risk ratio in children and adolescents. The findings warrant further studies in controlled trials.

1460
MOCLOBEMID - FIRST EXPERIENCES IN CHILDREN AND ADOLESCENTS
G.E.Trott, T.Elliger, G.Nissen
Klinik und Poliklinik fuer Kinder und
Jugendpsych. der Universitaet Werzburg

Moclobemid-a selective MAO-A-blocker has been shown to be an effective antidepressive substance in adults. In comparison to therapy with tricyclic antidepressants a better tolerance along with less side effects was noted.
Due to special development of neurobiological features it is not possible to simply transfer results found in adults to childhood and adolescence. In an open clinical study efficacy and tolerance of moclobemid were investigated in depressive adolescent patients. The rating scales used were HAMD, PP, NOSIE, DOTES and CEI.
Moclobemid was also administered to children and adolescents with compulsive obsessive syndromes. PP,HZI,NOSIE and CEI were used as rating scales. EEG and blood biochemistry were controlled.
Possible cognitive impairments were checked on in a computerized test psychological investigation.
In a few cases moclobemid was also administered to children with ADDH. First results of this study are presented.

1461
CLOZAPIN IN JUVENILE PSYCHOSES
M.H.Schmidt, J.Niemeyer, G.E.Trott, G.Nissen
University Heidelberg, Mannheim, W.Germany

Some years ago child and adolescent psychiatrists started to use Clozapin in treating adolescent schizophrenics. Like in adults, this was only done after having used other drugs - sufficient in dosage and duration - without success.
40 patients (mostly inpatients) from two departments are examined retrospectively regarding diagnosis, course of disorder, former kinds of treatment, subsequent Clozapin-treatment and its outcome.
Attention is given to possible side-effects on blood, electroencephalogram and other parameters.
As Clozapin proved to be a helpful enrichment of therapy of juvenile psychoses, the identification of appropriate cases should be improved. Up to now there only exist some scattered data on medium-term outcome of Clozapin treatment in adolescent schizophrenics.

1462
MILNACIPRAN AND USE OF ANTIDEPRESSANTS IN CHILD AND ADOLESCENT PSYCHIATRY
Sacristan J. - Professor, Universidad de Sevila, Spain

Session 224 — Symposium
Phenomenological problems in recent psychopathology

1463
Handeln und Sehen in der existenzphänomenologischen Psychiatrie
Bin Kimura
Dep. Psychiatry, Kyoto Univ.Hospital, Kyoto, Japan

Diskutiert wird über die Objektivität von Erkenntnissen der existenzphänomenologischen Psychiatrie (EPP). Es handelt sich hier nicht um ein gegenständliches Erkennen zeitlos vorgestellter Einzelphänomene. In der EPP ist ein wesentlich anderer kognitiver Akt in Spiel: Jedes mitmenschlich-therapeutische Handeln fungiert als solches i.S.eines Sensoriums für das ganze dort vorgehende Geschehen, eines Sensoriums, das K.Nishida "handelndes Sehen" nannte. Von diesem Sehen im Handeln werden keine objektiven Dinge (im Jap. "Mono") gesehen, die mit Substantiva darstellen lassen, sondern etwas, was im Zwischenraum und in der Zwischenzeit zwischen Therapeuten und Patienten sich zeigt und zeitigt, was stets mit Zeitwörtern auszusagen ist, also etwas, was im Japanischen "Koto" heißt. Insofern die EPP sich mit der Erörterung von Koto beschäftigt, kann und darf sie nicht nach der Objektivität in der Ebene des Mono suchen. Die Verifizierung und Falsifizierung ihrer Aussage ist nur möglich, wenn man sich eigens ins therapeutische Handeln hieinsetzt und sie durch eigenes handelndes Sehen nachvollzieht. Von hier aus versteht sich auch das Verhältnis der EPP zur Praxis. Heilsame therapeutische Beziehungen mit den Patienten sind Voraussetzung und Folge zugleich eines gut fundierten Sehens in der EPP. Von einer direkten Anwendung der EPP auf die Praxis kann keine Rede sein.

1464
PHENOMENOLOGICAL VERSUS SYMPTOMATOLOGICAL
DIAGNOSIS IN PSYCHIATRY
A. Kraus
Psychiatric Clinic, Heidelberg University, FR Germany

When making diagnoses in psychiatry the practitioner in general proceeds in two different ways: 1) as proposed by the diagnostic manuals he determines alongside strict operationally defined criteria the symptoms of the disease suggested (morbus-oriented), 2) he tries to get a deeper understanding of the problems and alterations of the patient as a person in his world (person-oriented). Methodologically, the diagnostic process in the first case is based more on a natural scientific nomothetic methodology summing up isolated facts, whereas in the second case it is based more on a human science idiographic and holistic methodology oriented in the singularity and wholeness of a person. The latter is often considered to be subjective, impressionistic, not scientific and is therefore repressed. The serious, rarely noticed consequences of this change in diagnostic practice makes it necessary to work out, as we intend to do, more clearly the difference between both ways of diagnosing, the symptomatological-criteriological and the hermeneutic-phenomenological one and to show possibilities of a scientific foundation of the latter.

1465
METHODOLOGISCHE PROBLEME IN PSYCHOPATHOLOGIE:CAPGRAS-SYNDROM=PSYCHOPATHOLOGICAL PROBLEMS OF CAPGRAS.
T.Hamanaka & Y.Suzuki,Dpt. of Neuropsychiatry,Nagoya City University,Nagoya,Japan.

Das Capgras-Syndrom(CS) steht heute erneut im Brennpunkt der psychiatrischen Debatte, zumal,einer psychodynamischen Interpretation(Berson 1983 etc) gegenüber, seit Gluckman(1968),Weston(1971) etc eine hirnorganisch erklärende Hypothese von verschiedenen Seiten(Wilcox 1983/86 etc) vertreten wird, die öfters so weit geht, das CS eher als Misidentifikation wie als Wahnbildung aufzufassen und es u.U.als dasselbe Phänomen wie reduplizierende Paramnesie(Alexander 1979) zu betrachten oder dem rechtshirnig verursachten Symptom der Prosopagnosie(Hayman 1979, Schraberg 1979 etc) eine bedeutende pathogenetische Rolle zuzumessen. Im vorliegenden Beitrag werden in psychopathologisch-methodologischer Sicht grundlegende Probleme besprochen wie folgen:1)die begriffliche Vieldeutigkeit des CS(einfache Personennegation/isolierter Doppelgängerwahn/im umfassenderen Wahnsystem eingebetteter Doppelgängerwahn), 2)die Fragwürdigkeit einer atomistischen Betrachtungsweise(CS=Prosopagnosie+Frontallappensymtom+etc), bei der eine holistische Sicht auf das Gesamtbild verloren geht, 3)die Frage nach der (Un-)Möglichkeit einer thematisch spezifischen Wahnbildung bei organischen/funktionellen Psychosen(ätiologische Aspefizität jeder Wahnbildung!), 4)das Problem um den Begriff vom "organic" mental syndrome, der im DSM-3(-R) vieldeutig gebraucht wird(z.B. "organic delusional syndrome" gegenüber "amnesic syndrome").

1466
SPECIAL USE OF THE PHENOMENOLOGICAL
APPROACH IN PSYCHIATRY
W. Blankenburg
Klinik für Psychiatrie, Universität Marburg (FRG)

The phenomenological approach is a methodologically founded procedure that does not tend immediately to "explain" but beforehand to "understand" and more previously to participate. Step-wise conversions of "view" into "insight" take the place of primary objectivating as the method for verification or falsification of hypotheses. Awaring precedes observing. The relationship to empathy is obvious.
A primary objectivating procedure and a phenomenological approach are different but complementary methods, and so the indications for the use of them. Three indications for the latter are significant:
1) Disorders close to the patient's relatively autonomous selfstructurizing of his life, i.e. close to his person, disorders of such sort as we find among DSM-III categories 297., 295.5, 298., 301.81/3, 309., V62.82 etc.).
2) The existential phenomenological approach is important in all fields where removing-strategies (Beseitigungsstrategien) are failing and the doctor often means there would be "nothing" to do. but coping behavior is necessary, and
3) in those - increasing - cases in which more is feasible by medic(in)al strategies than is healthy for the patient.

1467
Schizophrenie bei Zwillingen : Non-Standardmodell als ein Postulat

Sei-ichi Hanamura, Jichi Medizinische Hochschule, Tochigi, Japan

Studien über schizophrene Zwillingsgeschwister tragen sehr heuristisch nicht nur zur Festsellung des erbbiologischen Morbusfaktors, sondern auch zur Untersuchung der psychopathologischen Problemen bei. Der Referent hat sich 17 Jahre lang an einem Fall von eineiigen Zwillingsschwestern (A und B) beteiligt und beobachtet, was nach der Erkrankung der einen (B) aus der Zwillingsgemeinschaft wird. Heute wird Schwester B immer noch psychotherapeutisch sehr sorgfältig behandelt. Schwester A stand, nachdem ihre Ehe in eine Sackgasse geraten war, in ständiger Unruhe und nahm sich schließlich das Leben, aber befand sich doch bis zum Ende ihres Lebens in einem "Borderline"-Zustand. Beim Rezidiv machte Schwester B der Schwester A und dem Therapeuten gegenüber Capgrassche Personenverkennung. Danach spitzten sich gleichzeitig und pararell ihre Zwillingsgemeinschaft mit Schwester A und ihre therpeutische Gemeinschaft mit dem Referenten krisenhaft zu. Schwester B soll mit etwa 10 Jahren dazu geneigt haben, absichtlich sich selbst zu übertreiben oder typische Merkmale eines anderen Menschen nachzuahmen. Diese Neigung kann man eben bei den Zwillingsgeschwistern als Ausdruck des "Spiegelzeichens" betrachten, das als Anfangsymptom der Schizophrenie bekannt ist. Ob es die Übertreibung des Selbst oder die Nachahmung des Anderen ist, handelt es sich dabei um nichts als die Realisierung der Mimikry durch Wellenbewegung der Intensität. Schwester B setzt ihr ganzes Leben nicht auf den Sinn, sondern auf die Intensität: nicht aufs Original, sondern auf die Ikonizität. Dabei kann man alle Symptome als semiologische Verwandlung ihres Daseins verstehen. Nach dem Tod der Schwester A haben sich therapeutische Beziehungen mit Schwester B verändert. An dieser Veränderung kann man Brücke zwischen diesem Fall und üblichen Fällen bauen. Aus dieser Erfahrung bringt der Referent statt des gewöhnlichen Standardmodells ein Non-Standardmodell der Schizophrenie vor, das ein wenig mathematisch formuliert ist.

1468 *

*Number left open for technical reasons not corresponding to any abstract

Session 225 Symposium:
Clinical pharmacology of buspirone

1469

THE CLINICAL PHARMACOLOGY OF BUSPIRONE
Jean-Philippe BOULENGER, M.D. & Edouard ZARIFIAN, M.D.
INSERM U. 320, Clinical Psychopharmacology Group,
Centre Esquirol, C.H.U. Côte de Nacre, 14033 Caen Cedex, France
Abstract for the Bristol-Myers symposium at the VIII World Congress of Psychiatry, Athens, October 15, 1989.

Buspirone is the first molecule of a new chemical family of anxiolytic drugs which do not interact with benzodiazepine (BZD) receptors: the azaspiro-decanediones. Clinical trials have demonstrated that the efficacy of buspirone is similar to BZDs in the treatment of anxiety disorders. However, contrary to BZDs, buspirone appears to be devoid of sedative side effects, does not impair psychomotor performances and does not potentialize alcohol-induced impairment.

We undertook a cross-over study involving 12 healthy volunteers in order to compare the central effects of buspirone (10 mg p.o.), diazepam (10 mg p.o.) and placebo using standardized testing procedures. Although buspirone induced significant subjective effects 1 hour after administration in some subjects, it did not impair memory, attention or concentration abilities; on the other hand, diazepam induced sedative effects in most subjects as well as a decrease in delayed memory scores and an impairment of psychomotor skills as reflected in DSST scores. In other studies, experimental or real-life paradigms measuring driving skills in healthy volunteers have also demonstrated that acute therapeutic doses of BZDs may induce impairment of driving abilities, whereas doses of buspirone (5-10 mg) do not show any significant difference to placebo effects.

In another study the influence of repeated buspirone administration (5 mg t.i.d. for 7 days) on cognitive performance was studied in 10 healthy volunteers in a cross-over double-blind placebo-controlled study. At the end of the week's treatment there was no significant difference between buspirone and placebo on various performance tests measuring cognitive and psychomotor abilities. We also administered triazolam (0,25 mg p.o.) to the subjects on the 7th day of buspirone or placebo treatment in order to determine possible pharmacokinetic and pharmacodynamic interactions between the two drugs. However, the repeated administration of buspirone for 7 days did not modify the central effects nor the plasma concentration curve of triazolam, thus demonstrating the safety of such an association in clinical practice.

Since buspirone interacts selectively with the 5HT-1A subtype of central serotonergic receptors without affecting the GABA-BZD-Cl- channel supramolecular complex, it would be interesting to determine whether the differential effects of buspirone and BZDs on psychomotor and cognitive performances are related to the differences in their neurobiological profiles.

1470

MANAGEMENT OF DEPRESSIVE DISORDERS WITH 5-HT 1A AGONISTS
Karl Rickels, Stuart & Emily B.H. Mudd
University of Pennsylvania, U.S.A.

Buspirone, a 5-HT 1A agonist of the azaspirodecanediones, is the first non-benzodiazepine anxiolytic introduced into medicine. Recently buspirone has been demonstrated also to possess antidepressive properties.

Three independent, placebo-controlled, trials were conducted in the U.S. with patients diagnosed as suffering from Major Depressive Disorder (MDD) with secondary anxiety. In this subgroup of depressed patients, which is estimated to encompass at least 70% of all MDD patients, these three studies demonstrated significantly more antidepressant effects produced by buspirone than placebo. For example, the authors' group found in an 8 week placebo controlled study carried out with 143 patients a decrease in the Hamilton Depression Scale (HAM-D) score of 11.2 for buspirone and 5.8 for placebo ($p < .01$) at treatment endpoint.

Similar significant buspirone-placebo differences were observed in several HAM-D core depression factors, global ratings, and the patient completed Hopkins Symptom Checklist.

Gepirone, another 5-HT 1A agonist and a close cousin to buspirone, is presently under study in patients suffering from GAD or MDD. Preliminary results of placebo controlled studies demonstrate anxiolytic as well as antidepressive properties. An update of the clinical studies presently underway with gepirone in depression will be given.

1471

STRESS, FEAR AND ANXIETY: AN UPDATE
Richard I. Shader, M.D.
Professor and Chairman, Department of Psychiatry, Tufts University School of Medicine and Psychiatrist-in-Chief, New England Medical Center Hospitals

Stress, fear and anxiety are clinically distinct concepts and yet their meanings are not delineated in most clinical discussions. In man, these concepts, while separable, also are interactive. These concepts and their interactions will be discussed. The implications of these differences for treatment will also be reviewed. Anxiety *per se* also needs further differentiation. Panic attacks have received considerable attention in the last decade, while the companion concept, generalized anxiety disorder (GAD), remains understudied and obscure. At the core of GAD is worry. Worry itself is a poorly defined concept. How do event- or stimulus-based worry about the past or future or worry without an apparent stimulus differ? What are the treatment implications? A hypothesis is evolving which suggests a utility to beginning the classification of worry into subconcepts. Stimulus-based worry (particularly about the future) may be more amenable to reassurance than worry rooted in guilt or shame or low self-esteem. Varying distributions of these subtypes of worry could account for the variability of placebo effect seen among studies of GAD patients. Similarly, these subtypes could differentially respond to psychopharmacological agents with different putative mechanisms of action (e.g., $5HT_{1A}$ or GABA-benzodiazepine). Preliminary efforts to examine these working hypotheses will be discussed.

1472
ANXIETY AND DEPRESSION: A COMMON BIOLOGICAL SUBSTITUTE?

D.L.Temple,Jr.,M.S.Eison,A.S.Eison
CNS Research
Bristol-Myers Company, Pharmaceutical Research and Development Division,
5 Research Parkway, Wallingford,
CT 06492

It has long been debated as to whether anxiety and depression are separate disorders or are disorders that lie on a continuum related to graded neurotransmitter activity. Similarly, the roles of various neurotransmitter systems have been questioned, and attempts have been made to determine if any single neurotransmitter system is fundamental to both anxiety and depression. Existing anxiolytic and antidepressant drugs affect long noradrenergic (NE) and serotonergic (5-HT) pathways which project from the brain stem and innervate hippocampal and cortical targets. Although it is clear that NE neurons play a major role in certain conditions such as panic attacks and benzodiazepine withdrawal, recent studies with newer drugs which selectively interact with 5-HT receptors suggest that the "state" of the 5-HT system is fundamental to the etiology of both anxiety and depression. In particular, the new 5-HT$_{1A}$ agonist drugs buspirone and gepirone are effective in the treatment of both disorders as evidenced by well-controlled clinical trials. Preclinical evidence indicates that these 5-HT$_{1A}$ partial agonists bind to both presynaptic (dorsal raphe) and postsynaptic (hippocampus, cortex) 5-HT$_{1A}$ binding sites. The acute and chronic consequences of these receptor interactions are dependent on the functional state of the 5-HT system. The 5-HT$_{1A}$ partial agonist class of drugs are then able to reduce 5-HT tone in 5-HT excess disease (anxiety) and to increase the tone in 5-HT deficiency disease (depression). These observations suggest an important role for selective, new drugs, that can act to maintain homeostasis within the 5-HT system.

Session 226 Special Session:
ECT: Biological correlates

1473
SEROTONIN AND ELECTROCONVULSIVE THERAPY-INDUCED PROLACTIN RELEASE
Y.Papakostas,M.Markianos,G.Papadimitriou,C. Stefanis
Athens University Medical School,Department of Psychiatry,Eginition Hospital

Data from preclinical and clinical studies suggest that some of the electroconvulsive therapy (ECT)actions,including its antidepressant effect, might be mediated by central serotonergic mechanisms.This notion has been supported,among others, by the finding that methysergide,a serotonin(5-HT) receptor blocker,was able to reduce the ECT-induced prolactin(PRL)increase.However,methyseride is not a selective serotonin blocker but in addition to its 5-HT$_1$ and 5-HT$_2$ receptor blocker effect it has dopaminergic properties as well.
In order to differentiate between 5-HT$_1$ and 5-HT$_2$ mechanisms,the PRL response to ECT was investigated after pre-treatment with ritanserin,a potent and selective 5-HT$_2$ receptor antagonist.Seven female patients suffering from major depressive disorder were studied.They were given either ECT alone or ECT after pretreatment with ritanserin 10 and 20 mg p.o.PRL was estimated in blood samples taken before and after ECT administration. The PRL response to ECT was not modified after pretreatment with ritanserin.We concluded that if serotonergic mechanisms are involved in the ECT--induced PRL increase,this neuroendocrine response may be a 5-HT$_1$ rather than a 5-HT$_2$ mediated event.

1474
BIOGENIC AMINE TURNOVER DURING ELECTROCONVULSIVE TREATMENT OF MELANCHOLIC PATIENTS.

L. Lykouras, M. Markianos, J. Hatzimanolis, D. Malliaras, C. Stefanis.
Department of Psychiatry, Athens University, Athens, Greece.

Although electroconvulsive treatment (ECT) has proved to be an effective treatment in major depression, information concerning the mechanisms related to its therapeutic efficacy remains so far limited. In the present study we measured the urinary monoamine metabolites 3-methoxy-4-hydroxyphenylglycol (MHPG), homovanillic acid (HVA) and 5-hydroxyindoleacetic acid (5-HIAA) in 14 unmedicated unipolar depressed patients prior to and during a course of 10 ECT sessions. MHPG and HVA excretions increased significantly after the fourth (only HVA) seventh and tenth ECT treatment. In 5-HIAA excretion no significant change was found. Seven depressed patients who responded favorably to ECT (reduction in HDRS 50% or more), but not the 7 nonresponders, had significantly higher MHPG excretion after the final ECT compared to baseline levels. A significant relationship was found between low pre-treatment MHPG excretion and therapeutic response.

1475
TRH-Test and ECT-Treatment, TSH-Response

Hofmann, P., Schönbeck, G., Koinig, G., Gangadhar, B.N., Hatzinger, R.
Psychiatrische Universitätsklinik Wien
Währinger Gürtel 18-20, 1090 Wien
Austria

Drugs and ECT are the important biological treatments for psychoses. Their mechanisms of action are incompletely explained. The TRH-Test has emerged as a potent endocrinological tool for monitoring the therapeutic process.

33 female inpatients (20 DSM III-major depressive disorder, 13 other functional psychoses), who were referred for modified bilateral ECT were studied. TRH-Test and clinical-state assessment were performed before the first and after the last ECT.

40% of patients had blunted TSH-response (5 mcU/ml). TSH-response did not change after ECT. Over 50% of patients recovered, but had no change in TSH-response. Pre ECT TRH-Test did not predict therapeutic response nor the number of ECTs to be administered.

1476

TRH-Test and ECT-Treatment: PRL-Response

Gangadhar, B.N., Koinig, G., Schönbeck, G., Hofmann, P., Hatzinger, R.
Psychiatrische Universitätsklinik Wien
Währinger Gürtel 18-20, A-1090 Wien
Austria

Drugs and ECT are the important biological treatments for psychoses. Their mechanisms of action are incompletely explained. ECT has marked influence on prolactin (PRL). TRH stimulates the release of PRL. This PRL response in TRH-Test was used to reveal the therapeutic mechanisms of ECT.

12 female depressed inpatients referred for modified bilateral ECT were studied. TRH-Test and clinical state assessment were conducted before the first and after the last ECT.

PRL response was blunted (60 ng/ml) in 40% of pateints and did not change after ECT. 50% of patients recovered, but had no change in PRL-response. The therapeutic response or the number of ECTs to be administered could not be predicted by pre-ECT TRH-Test results.

1477

NEUROELEKTRISCHE THERAPIE BEI AKUTEN PHARMAKOTHERAPIERESISTENTEN SCHIZOPHRENIEN

A.Klimke, E.Klieser, U.Fischer, Psychiatrische Klinik der Universität Düsseldorf

An der Psychiatrischen Klinik der Heinrich Heine Universität wurden 30 Patienten, die an einer akuten Exacerbation einer länger bestehenden Schizophrenie litten und von einer Psychopharmakotherapie nicht profitierten, mit Neuroelektrischer Therapie (NET) behandelt. Der Erfolg der Behandlung wurde mit dem CGI und der BPRS bewertet. Erstaunlicherweise sprachen 60 % der Patienten günstig auf die Behandlung an. Deutliche Nebenwirkungen waren nur bei 1 Patientin in Form eines deutlichen psychoorganischen Syndroms, das innerhalb von 4 Wochen abklang, nachzuweisen.
Die Patienten, die auf die Behandlung ansprachen, zeigten bereits nach 2 - 3 Behandlungen eine deutliche Besserung der psychopathologischen Symptomatik.

Session 227 Special Session:
Suicidology: Clinical and psychosocial dimensions

1478

SUICIDE IN ALCOHOLICS: THE TERMINAL PHASE
George E. Murphy, M.D.
Washington University School of Medicine
St. Louis, Missouri, U.S.A.

It has been shown[1] and replicated[2,3] that loss of a close interpersonal relationship is predictive of increased suicidal risk in alcoholics. The latest study extends this finding to other substance abusers. Interpersonal disruptions are common in alcoholics. Why does this type of event act as a precipitant at one time, but not at another? Half of the subjects had experienced rejection in the marital realm in their lives, but in only one-fifth of cases was the last rejection the victim's first experience with it. Particularly striking was the recent decline or long continued absence of ancillary social support among the suicides. This was true of two-thirds of the sample. A major depressive syndrome was found in two-thirds as well, although it is unusual in alcoholics entering treatment programs. Depression and/or loss of social support are even more characteristic of alcoholic suicides than is interpersonal loss.

1. Murphy, G.E. and Robins, E. JAMA 199:303-308;1967.
2. Murphy, G.E., et al. Arch. Gen. Psychiatry 36:65-69;1979.
3. Rich, C.L., et al. Arch. Gen. Psychiatry 45:589-592;1988.

1479

FACTORS ASSOCIATED WITH ADOLESCENT SUICIDAL ATTEMPTS IN GREECE
Beratis Stavroula, M.D.
Department of Psychiatry, Medical School, University of Patras, Patras, Greece

The cultural characteristics of a population may affect the relevant importance of the various factors involved in suicidal attempts. This study investigated the factors which led Greek adolescents to such attempts. During the four-year-period from September 1984 to September 1988 all youngsters up to the age of 16 years, who were brought, because of a suicidal attempt, to the emergency room of the Department of Pediatrics of the University of Patras Medical School, at the "Aghios Andreas" General Hospital, were included in the study. Family disruption was significantly greater in the group of the attempters than in the control subjects. However, parental restriction of the youngsters' personal freedom emerged as the major factor resulting in suicidal attempts. It was reported by 55% of the attempters and only by 17% of the control subjects. In 48% of the attempters, restriction of freedom was the reason of the quarrels and strained relationship between the youngsters and their parents. Psychiatric disorders were significantly more frequent in the attempters (52%) than in the control subjects (3%). The findings indicate that several factors make adolescents attempt suicide, but suppression of personal freedom by the parents is a major risk factor for suicidal attempts in Greek adolescent girls.

1480
SEASONAL, CLIMATIC AND OTHER FACTORS RELATED WITH SUICIDE IN ASTURIAS (SPAIN).

García-Prieto, Angel
Bobes García, Julio
Bousoño García, Manuel
Suarez-Noriega, Luis Antonio.
SOCIEDAD ASTURIANA DE PSIQUIATRIA(SPAIN).

Based on epidemiologic methodology, different factors related to suicide consummated in Asturias (Spain), during 1983-1987 were analysed.
The following factors were studied: age, sex, procedure of suicide, climate variables (atmosferic pressure, frequency of south-winds), seasons of the year and moon phases in wich suicides were consummated.
The incidence was 11,13/100.000. In respect to several factors, significant differences were found (X 2 test): age, sex and suicide procedure depending on sex in relation to other factors , although some diferences were observed in relation to sex, no significant differences were present.

Cases: 638 (1983-1987)
Cases/year: 123
Rate: 11.13/100.000
Sex Ratio (m/f): 1/2.7

1481
Clinico-Socio-demographic correlates of attempted suicide -a study in Assam, India.
1. Dr. Deepali Dutta.
2. Dr. Suresh Chakravorty
   Department of Psychiatry,Gauhati Medical College, Assam.

Suicide and attempted suicide have always been considered as behaviour specific to mankind by philosophers, priests, writers,poets and theologians. Emil Durkheim's famous monograph on the subject(1857) generated lot of interest amongst the psychiatrists all over the world.
In Indian Hindu Community common belief is that there is a god of suicide who with his hanging noose lures the adolescents and young-men to this act. Hence often we hear of suicide prevailing in micro-epidemic form in some villages.

Here in this cross-sectional study of 100 cases of attempted suicide collected during one year period in Department of Psychiatry, Gauhati Medical College an attempt has been made to study the various clinical and socio-demographic variables with an objective to find out the high risk group from the low risk group. The authors feel that this human tragedy is a preventable problem if timely intervention is undertaken.

1482
EMPIRICAL DIFFERENCES BETWEEN PATIENTS THINKING ABOUT SUICIDE AND THOSE ATTEMPTING IT
Dr. Roland Kalb and Dr. Dieter Ebert
Dept of Psychiatry, University Erlangen,
W.Germany

To learn something about suicidal acts we examined 150 patients with suicidal thoughts, 71 of whom had made a suicidal attempt some days ago.
Discriminant analysis predicted 74% correctly, while an empirical knowledge base consisting of 26 rules derived from this study, predicted 81%
In a controlling study with 80 patients having suicidal thoughts, 44 of whom had made a suicidal attempt, discriminant analysis predicted 70% correctly and the empirical knowledge base 77%

1483
PSYCHOSOCIAL PARAMETERS IN ATTEMPTED SUICIDE

Mantonakis J.,Jemos J., Kaliteraki E., Tata-Arcel L.[1]
Department of Psychiatry, University of Athens.
[1]Inst.of Clinical Psychology,Univ. of Copenhagen.

Two hundred and eighty-four suicide attempters (229 women and 55 men, f:m ratio= 4.2:1) admitted to a General Hospital were studied. The investigation was based on personal interview as well as a specifically designed questionnaire.
The comparison of male and female groups revealed the following significant differences: The men are of an older age, live more often alone, more often have a phychiatric history, hospitalization in a psychiatric clinic and previous attempts.
As to the mode of the attempt, women more often used drugs (tranquilizers or analgesics),toxic or caustic substances, while men more often used jumping or hanging.
The days more often prefered for attempted suicide were Monday and Tuesday for women, Monday and Friday for men.
As to the persons or facts related to the attempts, women, more often than men, mention the husband, the lover, their parents and their studies. Men, however, more often than women, mention the difficulties in their job or their attempt is related to psychiatric illness.

1484
THE PSYCHOPATHOLOGY OF SUICIDE IN NORTH WESTERN PELOPONNESE
Gabriel I, M.D., Paschalis Ch, M.D.
Department of Psychiatry, Medical School, University of Patras, Patras, GREECE

Previous studies concerning suicide have shown that people who commit suicide do not consist of a united psychological and social entity. Therefore division into various subgroups should give a better insight of the syndrom and its prevention.

A post-mortem inquiry of one hundred five legal documents concerning suicide deaths obtained from the Office of the District Attorney covering the province of Achaia were carefully studied for the fifteen year period 1970-1984. The suicides were classified into two groups, group A consisting of 59 suicides (with history of chronic psychiatric illness) and group B consisting of 46 suicides (with no history of chronic psychiatric disturbance). The findings suggest that suicides with history of chronic psychiatric illness are people disorganized in their personal and social life, who had more frequently previous suicidal attempts and used mainly violent methods for committing suicide, where as the suicidal behavior of people without history of chronic psychiatric illness seems connected to some exogenous traumatic event which dislocated proggressively or abruptly their life. They also used violent methods of suicide.

Session 228 Special Session:
Mental health policy

1485
BUILDING INTEGRATED SERVICE DELIVERY SYSTEMS
DA Wasylenki, PN Goering.   Clarke Institute of Psychiatry, Toronto, Canada.

In order to provide effective mental health services, the range of components must be organized into an integrated system with a shared vision and with a focal point of responsibility. In building such systems, a number of key issues must be resolved. This paper uses a major planning exercise to provide an integrated mental health service to a population of 1.8 million to illustrate key issues.

The first issue involves identification of the chronically mentally ill as the target population. The second issue is the role of the general hospital psychiatric unit in providing short-term treatment. The third issue is the role of the mental hospital in tertiary care. The fourth issue involves community support services, and the fifth issue is continuity of care to overcome fragmentation. The sixth issue is comorbidity as several subgroups of patients suffer from more than one disorder. Finally, the importance of establishing integrating mechanisms in a given jurisdiction to ensure that an organized network is created and monitored is discussed.

Data from the planning process demonstrate approaches to the key issues. The challenge presented is to mobilize political, administrative and financial resources to create this more progressive approach to care.

1486
CAN COMPREHENSIVE PSYCHIATRY CHANGE THE MENTAL STATUS IN A SOCIETY?
H.C.Knudsen, M.Nordentoft, B. Jessen-Petersen, A. Krasnik, H. Sælan
Institute of Social Medicine, University of Copenhagen, Denmark.

In December 1987, the Copenhagen Municipal Council agreed to a proposal for the development of the mental health care system in the city of Copenhagen for the period of 1988 - 2000. The main purpose of the proposal is to improve the mental health care system and to increase the mental health status in the city, by establishing a proper mental health community service.

To evaluate the effects of the changes in the mental health care system a research project has been established. The fundamental design of the evaluation is the so-called quasi-experimental design, in which the selected districts each have to be compared with a comperable control district before, during and after the evaluation period

The mental health status in the community has been looked upon as a result of the interaction between:

1) the social system and the health care system

2) the patients and the clients in direct contact with the social system and/or the health care system, and

3) structure and population characteristics describing the districts involved.

The project and the preliminary results from the first part of the data collection will be presented.

1487
INNOVATIONS IN THE FIELD OF PSYCHIATRY
B.AUBIN, P.REBOUL CMP STE-MARIE CLERMONT-FD (FR)

For fifteen years, the organization of Public Psychiatry in France has been completely changed by the application of the "sector" policy, the opening and division of hospitals into small diversified units, together with the distribution of "financial allowance" allowing chronic mentally sick persons to become almost socially self-sufficient. Among the varied structures which can now be found in our sectors, we would like to set out the original solution of two very specific "day-centers" : - The first one is destined, through psychotherapy, to take charge of neurotic patients who are not scared anymore by the image of illness which psychotic patients reflected. The refusal to answer requests for any modification of the course of treatments avoid manipulation and opposition. We propose the Rogerian psychotherapy, Gestalt and psychodrama.   - The second one aims at restoring the patient's occupational abilities and at preparing him of his reinsertion in the world of work. The improvement of his school level and the organization in work-groups (cooking, sewing, printing, plumbing and gardening) as well as the work outside for private customers allow the patient to undergo a period of training in a firm, to find a job or to be accepted to a training centre or a centre of protected work.

1488

THE AMERICAN DISILLUSIONMENT WITH COMMUNITY PSYCHIATRY IS PREMATURE
Andreas Laddis, M.D. & Alberto Lopez-Loucel, M.D.
Massachusetts Mental Health Center, Boston, U.S.A.

The movement for deinstitutionalization can be reborn effectively heeding criticism that it exposed the patients to deprivations and indignities and their families and neighborhoods to consum-ing neediness. In three steps, we argue that community psychiatry is exhausted from costly vascillation between rehabilitative and custodial care:
1) Rehabilitation envisions mental patients as enjoyable and useful in the social mainstream. It eluded realization because of inattention to the fundamental social attribute of productivity, the critical performance to which patients should be rehabilitated. Productivity singularly rules all human associations before it may include gainful employment. It entails commitment of one's powers to satisfaction of his own and other's needs. Rehabilitation must plan that mental patients, too, make commitments, despite even chronic handicaps and use of other's mental strengths as crutches.
2) Only rehabilitation to productivity is sustainable as a community modality; custodial care in "the least restrictive setting" hides a contradiction and the seed of reinstitutionalization.
3) Rehabilitative psychiatry requires a novel mode of clinical administration pursued in the concept we name "progressive clinical consensus."

1489

Economic cycles and mental health policy in Greece
Yfantopoulos J. and Gatzonis S.
University of Athens

In economic analysis the concept of a "cycle" was frequently used to describe both prosperity and recession periods. According to the "cyclical" economic movements certain diseases of the mental health system alternate between high programme activity and stagnation. This article examines the cyclical aspects of the economic system (see fig. 1) in conjuction with the mental health policy making activity. We develop static, progressive, discontinuous and differential equation models in an attempt to investigate the interplay between the dynamics of public economic policy and mental health. Furthemore we make use of advanced econometric techniques in order to investigate in a conceptually colerent way the cyclical framework of the Greek mental health system.

Fig. 1

1490

PORTUGAL: MENTAL HEALTH POLITICS IN QUESTION
Antonio Albuquerque, Jose Jara, Luis Gamito, Ricardo Jardim, Suzana Teiga
Hospital Julio de Matos, Lisbon, Portugal

Mental Health Services in Portugal are heavily underdeveloped.
The authors make a survey of human and material resources, namely technical staff in mental health, hospitals and hospital beds, outpatient services, day hospitals, sheltered workshops, communitarian residences and its distribution over the country. Portuguese law in Mental Health will be shortly analysed.
Budget minded politics of last years is criticized with a main reference to the danger of a destruction of Mental Hospitals without any consistent alternatives.

Session 229 Symposium:
Serotonergic mechanisms in schizophrenia disorders

1491

Serotonergic/Dopaminergic Interaction in Schizophrenia
Herbert Y. Meltzer, M.D.
Case Western Reserve University School of Medicine, 2040 Abington Road, Cleveland, Ohio 44106, U.S.A.

There is abundant evidence from preclinical and clinical studies that brain serotonergic and dopaminergic neurons exert important regulatory influences on each other. Recent studies suggest that atypical antipsychotic drugs such as clozapine, melperone, amperozide, risperidone, etc. exert part of their action via their ability to influence both serotonergic and dopaminergic neurotransmission on the basis of their antagonism of serotonin$_2$ and dopamine-2 receptor subtypes. Direct effects on dopamine-1 and 5-HT$_1$ or 5-HT$_3$ receptors seem of lesser importance to their actions but this does not rule out the possible importance of indirect effects of these receptors. Evidence from spinal fluid metabolite and neuroendocrine challenge studies for an abnormal interaction of these two neurotransmitters in schizophrenia will be discussed.

1492
5-HT$_3$ RECEPTOR ANTAGONISTS AS POSSIBLE ANTIPSYCHOTICS

J.M. Barnes, N.M. Barnes, B. Costall, A.J. Cox, A.M. Domeney and R.J. Naylor, Postgraduate Studies in Pharmacology, University of Bradford, Bradford, BD7 1DP, UK

Rat and primate models of mesolimbic dopamine excess, sensitive to the actions of known antischizophrenic agents, have included acute injections of amphetamine or infusions of dopamine into the rat nucleus accumbens, infusions of dopamine into rat amygdala or primate ventral striatum, injections of a neurokinin agonist DiMe-C7 into the mesolimbic cell body area in the ventral tegmentum (for which biochemical correlates can be determined e.g. the DA/DOPAC ratio in limbic terminal areas). In each test situation locomotor hyperactivity could also be inhibited by selective 5-HT$_3$ receptor antagonists, ondansetron, zacopride, ICS205-930, granisetron. These compounds were more potent than presently available antischizophrenic agents, lacked sedation, influence on the extrapyramidal system, or on prolactin levels. The 5-HT$_3$ receptor antagonists therefore appear to have potential to modulate a mesolimbic dopamine excess without the side effect potential of neuroleptic agents. Their antipsychotic potential may relate to action on recognition sites in limbic and cortical regions as defined using radioligands such as ^{3}H.zacopride.

1493
PHARMACOLOGY OF 5-HT$_2$-RECEPTOR ANTAGONISTS

C.J.E. Niemegeers, Janssen Research Foundation, Beerse, Belgium

The broad clinical exploration of ketanserin (R 41 468) showed that peripheral 5-HT$_2$-antagonism is a useful and sound therapeutic principle in maintaining a functional microcirculation. With ritanserin (R 55 667) and risperidone (R 64 766), the potential of central 5-HT$_2$-antagonism was approached. Pharmacologically 5-HT$_2$-receptor antagonists were found to inhibit at low doses the serotonergic syndrome induced by tryptamine, mescaline, 5-HTP and DOM but to be devoid of LSD-like internal stimulus properties. 5-HT$_2$-antagonists produced over a wide dose range a disinhibitory effect in rats with subnormal tendency to explore the surroundings. In conventional conflict tests, however, in which electric shock is used, they were almost devoid of activity, thus they did not induce indifference to punishment. Selective 5-HT$_2$-antagonists were further found to increase markedly the total amount of deep SWS, while not affecting sleep induction.
In contrast to virtually all classes of centrally acting drugs, the administration of potent central 5-HT$_2$-antagonists did not result in overt behavioral changes and is apparently devoid of direct neurological consequences.

1494
SEROTONERGIC DISTURBANCES IN SCHIZOPHRENIA

Bleich A; Brown S-L; Kahn R; van Praag HM
Albert Einstein College of Medicine/Montefiore Medical Center, Bronx, N.Y., USA

Though one of the first hypotheses in modern biological psychiatry proposed a relationship between serotonin (5-hydroxytryptamine; 5-HT) dysfunction in the brain and schizophrenia, work in this field was kept simmering once the neuroleptics with their strong impact on dopaminergic functioning were introduced. Recently, however, evidence has been found that blockade of certain populations of 5-HT receptors may result in antipsychotic effects. Ritanserin, a 5-HT$_2$ receptor blocker and risperidone, a combined 5-HT$_2$ and dopamine (DA)$_2$ receptor blocker were, in a preliminary way, studied in human subjects. The antipsychotic potential of 5-HT$_3$ receptor antagonists was inferred from animal experiments and no human data are as yet available. These findings justify the question whether in schizophrenic patients 5-HT disturbances do occur. The relevant literature will be critically discussed, based on which the following conclusions will be reached.
1. The available data are contradictory, but:
   a, scarce; b, collected without attempts of symptomatological differentiation of patients, while; c, up-to-date functional 5-HT measures have not yet been used.
2. The exciting findings with selective 5-HT receptor blockers should re-kindle the study of 5-HT in schizophrenia.

1495
SEROTONIN 5-HT$_2$ RECEPTOR ANTAGONISM IN THE TREATMENT OF SCHIZOPHRENIA

Y.Gelders, S.Heylen, G.Vanden Bussche, A.Reyntjens, P.Janssen
Janssen Research Foundation, Belgium

Because of the evidence that some serotonergic abnormalities may exist in schizophrenia, it has been hypothesized that selective serotonergic agents may prove efficatious in the treatment of schizophrenia. After preliminary studies with various mixed serotonergic compounds, great progress in the study of central serotonin antagonism was made by the discovery of ritanserin, the first specific central serotonin 5-HT$_2$ antagonist. Ritanserin, which is characterized by particular sleep-wakefulness regulatory and thymosthenic properties, found several applications in the treatment of chronic schizophrenic patients, mainly suffering from negative symptomatology. The results obtained following open and double-blind administration of ritanserin in this indication show significant improvement on negative and affective symptoms, whilst reducing extrapyramidal symptoms (EPS) of conventional neuroleptic drugs. As the advantages of a monotherapy in the treatment of schizophrenia are undeniable, in a next step, new compounds combining pharmacological 5-HT$_2$ and D$_2$ antagonism in the same substance were searched for. Risperidone, a new benzisoxazole derivative, meets these criteria. The first open and double-blind studies in chronic schizophrenia demonstrate that risperidone combines potent antipsychotic efficacy, with strong resocializing properties by improvement of negative symptoms, and a very low potential of inducing EPS.

Session 230 Symposium:
Aspects of depression in old age

1496
OUTCOME OF DEPRESSION IN THE ELDERLY
- Results of a 12 months Follow-up Study -
STUHLMANN, W., Chr.Kretschmar, C. Wurthmann
Rheinische Landesklinik/
Psychiatrische Klinik der Heinrich-Heine-Universität Düsseldorf

This study continues a research project aiming at finding predictors for the success of treatment in depressed psychogeriatric patients we tried to find out which of the predictors that showed after an eight week treatment period still remained relevant 12 months after the first treatment report. From the origin sample of 61 patients only 34 (5 males and 29 females) could be checked 12 months later. The medium age rate was 70,6 years.
The ratings were performed with the Hamilton-Depression-Scale, the AMDP-system, the Plutchik-Geriatric-Rating-Scale and a semistructured interview. The Hamilton-total-score-difference was taken as the criterium for therapeutical success. The predictors were determined by finding out correlations between the initial findings of the scales and subcales of Hamilton, AMDP and Plutchik and the Hamilton-total-score-difference after 8 weeks and after one year.
There were significant differences in the Hamilton-total-scores which proved a clear improvement of the depressive syndrome within 8 weeks as well as after one year.
The subscale "anxiety" of the AMDP proved to be a valid predictor for a good outcome. Patients with high anxiety scores at the beginning of treatment showed best improvement after 8 weeks as well as after one year.
Further results of the Hamilton subcales and the other scales are reported.

1497
CEREBRAL CHANGES IN ELDERLY DEPRESSIVES
George S. Alexopoulos, M.D.
Cornell University Medical College,
White Plains, New York, U.S.A.

A complex clinical and biological relationship exists between geriatric depression and neurological brain disorders. Reversible cognitive dysfunction as well as transient localizing neurological and neuropsychological findings have been reported in depression. Conversely, depression is part of the symptomatology of neurological dementing disorders. Finally, common abnormalities in brain structure and function have been found in both depression and in dementia syndromes. These include dilatation of lateral brain ventricles, reduction in cerebral blood flow and oxidative metabolism, reduction in sleep and sedation thresholds to barbiturates, dysfunction in brain monoamine neurotransmitters. Late-onset depressives have less family history of affective disorders than early-onset depressives. Late-onset depression is more often associated with cognitive dysfunction or dementia and with morphological brain abnormalities than early-onset depression of geriatric patients. The hypothesis has been advanced that late-onset depression is a heterogeneous disorder which includes a large subgroup of patients who develop depression as part of a neurological disorder that may or may not be clinically evident when the depression first appears. The implications for clinical studies and research will be discussed.

1498
Antidepressant use in the elderly, special considerations.
Jennifer S. Wakelin, G.H.Besselaar Associates, Brussels, Belgium.

When compared to younger populations of patients, depression in the elderly tends to be more chronic, often more severe and can be refractory to treatment. These findings are very important as it is estimated that at least 11% of the population over 65 years have a clinical depression, with the increasing elderly population this problem will increase.
It has been shown that associated with the normal ageing process are reductions in central NA, DA and 5HT. These changes are important as they are similar to those seen in depression, to which there maybe a greater susceptibility with age. The tricyclic antidepressants (TCAs) which generally effect their activity via the inhibition of NA and/or 5HT neuronal reuptake are associated with approximately a 60% improvement rate. However, their associated anticholinergic (ACH) activity increases the risk of (pseudo-)dementia and confusion in the elderly (in whom the acetylcholine is decreased). Additionally, adverse cardiovascular effects can limit their use. Recently, it has been confirmed that long-term maintenance therapy with antidepressants can reduce the rate of relapse by $\pm$ 40% compared to placebo. This, and the general need for a more prolonged treatment period in the elderly, means that the choice of treatment is therefore often defined by the side-effect profile of antidepressants (ADs). The new generation of ADs, which have less ACH and adverse cardiovascular effects than the TCAs appear to be potentially useful in the short and long-term treatment of the elderly.

1499
PHYCHIATRIC MORBIDITY AND BED OCCUPANCY IN GERIATRIC IN-PATIENTS
Katona C.L.E., Ramsay R., Wright P., Katz A. and Bielawski C.
University College and Middlesex School of Medicine and Whittington Hospital.

The results of a survey of consecutive acute geriatric in-patients will be presented. Subject assessments include the Mini Mental State, the Geriatric Depression Score, and the General Health Questionnaire; and the short CARE interview administered by a separate investigator.

The prevalence of depression as well as of delirium, and dementia will be estimated, and the sensitivity, specificity and predictive power of the rating scales measured. The influence of depression and other psychiatric illness on bed occupancy will be assessed, allowing for type and severity of physical illness.

Session 231 Symposium: Cultural psychiatry issues in the Mid-East and Europe: Social change, immigration and refugee

1500

THE COMPLAINT OF "TIGHTNESS" IN THE SAUDI POPULATION
Dr. Ahmed El-Assra, Consultant Psychiatrist
Riyad Armed Forces Hospital, Saudi Arabia

322 new patients were clinically examined by the author over a period of 3 years at the Psychiatric Out-Patient Clinic at Riyad Armed Forces Hospital. 61 patients complained of "tightness in chest" (Deega), "feeling uptight", "oppresion" (Katma), "dizziness" (Dokha), with or without other psychiatric symptoms. The subgroup of patients with "tightness" were further investigated in detail in terms of socio-demographic data, contributing social factors, diagnoses, psychiatric treatment and prognosis. The study showed that the complaint of "tightness" is more frequently made by middle-aged married housewives in relation to men (2:1), by illiterate or low educated patients, and that the main social precipitating factor encountered is predominantly a marital problem. The most frequent diagnoses were those of depressive illness, anxiety neurosis or the absence of any psychiatric illness. Consequently antidepressants and anxiolytics were the commonly prescribed psychotropic medication, in addition to supportive psychotherapy and social intervention in the form of counselling and marital therapy. The prognosis was favourable when adequate psychiatric intervention was applied. The results of the study are discussed in the light of the recent social changes in the Saudi society and the development of psychiatric care over the past 20 years with its implication on the Saudi psychiatric population.

1501

THE FIRST WIFE SYNDROME OBSERVED IN SAUDI

A. Darwish, M.D.
Armed Forces Hospital for Southern Region
Khamis Mushaye, Saudi, Arabia

With the great "boom" in Saudi of the late seventies and early eighties, the people could afford more pleasure and have more exposure to the world at large. In rural Saudi one of the pleasure men can afford more easily with the increase in wealth is acquiring a second wife. Women are now more exposed to media which do not take for granted that a woman shares her husband. This conflict in attitude is sounded in what the author calls "First Wife Syndrome".

The author describes nine cases in which women are presented to psychiatric clinics with multiple somatic symptoms that do not respond to any treatment. Psychiatric symptoms are those of anxiety and depression, these symptoms are characterized by their intensification with the husbands becoming involved with his new wife. The line of treatment that works best for the author is to get the couple to "fight it out" in sessions.

Outcome depends on the couple's success to acknowledge the problem for what it is and work through to a settlement in which the wife feels appreciated and the husband is released from feeling guilty.

1502

SUICIDAL ATTEMPTS AND RELIGION

M.CARUSO, D.MOUSSAOUI : CENTRE PSYCHIATRIQUE UNIVERSITAIRE IBN ROCHD-CASABLANCA-MOROCCO.

INTRODUCTION : Eventhough the incidence of suicides et suicidal attempts is steadily growing, many people still believe that islamic religion protects against suicide. Our hypothesis is that religion per se does not protect against suicide, but strong community links do.
METHOD : A group of 65 individuals who have committed an attempt of suicide have been compared to a control group of 65 individuals, matched by sex, age, educational level, socio-economic status, and psychiatric diagnosis when present. The semi-structured interview searched especially for the religious faith, belief and practice, as well as social links with the nuclear and the enlarged families and the professional insertion.
RESULTS : All the patients and the individuals from the control group stressed their religious faith ; those who committed suicidal attempts had significantly less religious practice than the control group ($p<.05$). On the other hand, suicidal attempts group had very significantly less nuclear and enlarged family integration ($p<.001$) as well as lower professional integration ($p<.001$).
Theses results will be discussed.

1503

Mental health problems of "Aussiedler" from Eastern Europe
(Dr. Maria Stöckl-Hinke)

The relationship between migration and mental health problems has been examined for a long time. Migration can mean emigration by one's own decision, refuge or return to the homeland of oneself or of one's family.
This study examines psychiatric disorders of German "Aussiedler" from Eastern Europe, who return to West-Germany.
The term "Aussiedler" means people of German origin, who have lived with other peoples and in other political systems for one or more generations and return to West-Germany after the year 1950. They come from the Soviet Union, Poland, Czechoslovakia, Rumania, Hungary and Yugoslavia.
Out of all admitted patients to the Psychiatric Hospital of Kaufbeuren in the year 1987, 31 patients were found, who could be identified als "Aussiedler": 14 patients came from Rumania, 9 from Czechoslovakia, 7 from Poland and 1 patient from the Soviet Union. The commonest diagnostic categories were alcoholism (11 cases) and depressive disorders (12 cases), whereas the depressive disorders included in many cases paranoid symptoms.
The main cause of the mental health problems of these re-immigrants seams to be acculturation problems. Many "Aussiedler" have a wrong image of Germany and deny the existing cultural and political differences between them and the German people, which leads to maladjustment. Especially young people, taken by their parents to Germany, who have little or no knowledge of the German language and who have grown up in a socialist system have identity problems and problems in coping with the totally foreign system and society of West-Germany. Some of them get criminal or lead marginal existences.
As long as these acculturation problems, which can lead to severe mental health problems are undervalued by politicians and our whole society, no prevention and no real help is possible.

1504

COMMUNICATION PROBLEMS IN THE TREATMENT OF IMMIGRANTS

Günsel Koptagel-Ilal
Istanbul, Turkey

Communication is one of the major problems in the treatment of immigrants from different sociocultural backgrounds. The difficulty in establishing a satisfactory therapeutic relation with them lies not only in the insufficiency of verbal expression but also in the reciprocal emotional attitudes which have an impact upon the therapeutic process. Nonverbal expression forms, behaviour patterns and the metaphoric use of the native language which are closely connected with sociocultural backgrounds and characteristics play an important part in the communication. They must therefore be correctly understood and evaluated during the conversation.

Attempts to overcome the language barrier with the help of translators will remain unsuccessful if the qualities of the translator are not suitable for this function and his/her role in the therapeutic setting is not clearly defined. This kind of a therapeutic process demands an alteration in the therapeutic setting in which the role of the translator is changed from merely a transmitter of words into a co-therapist with an intermediary function. To fulfill this function adequately, the translator should have the necessary professional qualifications of a co-therapist besides a perfect command of both languages including their semantic contents and metaphoric uses and must be well acquainted with the sociocultural characteristics of the patients.

1505

CULTURE, MENTAL HEALTH AND TRADITIONAL MEDICINE IN INDOCHINESE REFUGEE CAMPS
Wolfgang G. JILEK & Louise JILEK-AALL
Department of Psychiatry, University of British Columbia, Vancouver, Canada

Based on experiences in Thailand where the presenting author was UNHCR Refugee Mental Health Coordinator, mental health problems in refugee camps are briefly reviewed with special focus on the Laotian hilltribes refugees, paradigmatic of a displaced tradition - directed tribal population exposed to rapid sociocultural change and confronted with existential decisions. Psychosocial sequelae include exacerbated conflicts between the generations and sexes with an increase of suicidal behaviour among the younger people. With UNHCR support, voluntary agencies are mobilizing indigenous resources for treatment and prevention, and also integrate traditional medicine and shamanic ritual in comprehensive primary mental health care.

Session 232 Symposium:
Suicide prevention and antidepressants

1506

WHY DO FATAL OVERDOSE RATES VARY BETWEEN ANTIDEPRESSANTS?
Farmer R.D.T., Prof. of Community Medicine, Charing Cross and Westminster Medical School (University of London)

Age specific death rates for different antidepressant drugs, based on the numbers of prescriptions dispensed, were calculated for England and Wales for 1981-1985. There are marked variations in mortality associated with different drugs; the highest rates are found with amitriptyline and dothiepin whereas the lowest were associated with mianserin and clomipramine. For all drugs the recorded mortality rates for the over 65 year olds was lower than patients under 65 years of age. A high proportion of the amitriptyline and dothiepin fatal overdose involved more than one substance.

The implications of these findings are discussed. It is concluded that the variations in rates are in part due to variations in the inherent toxicity of the drugs (particularly the anticholinergic effects) and in part due to possible differences in compliance. It is suggested that the risk of death from overdose should be taken into account when assessing the overall safety of antidepressant drugs in overdose.

1507

TOXICITY OF ANTIDEPRESSANT DRUGS IN OVERDOSE IN AUSTRALIA

Graham Burrows, Professor of Psychiatry, Department of Psychiatry, University of Melbourne, Australia

Introduction
Depression is an illness with an inherent risk for suicidal ideation. These patients will frequently use medicaments in overdose as a means for attempting suicide. In most cases antidepressants will be amongst the ingested compounds. It has been published that the toxicity of specific antidepressant drugs in overdose varies considerably, if examined by using mortality statistics in the U.K.

Objectives
The objectives of this study are to compare antidepressant drugs frequently prescribed in Australia in terms of toxicity in overdose, examining clinical data from hospital records in a sequence of two years, 1987/1988. All major hospitals in 5 major Australian states will be involved encompassing 70% of the Australian population. The records provide patient data as well as drug data and the seriousness of the event can be indicated: fatal/non fatal, type of treatment (intensive care), recovery status.

Project programme
Phase I:
Covering a period of two years, the distribution of hospitals per state admitting the majority of suicide attempts on antidepressants can be examined. Coded (ICD9 Code: 969.0) hospital discharge data from the various central State Health Authority databases are used.

Phase II:
These hospitals selected from Phase I will now be visited and their specific records studied. This will provide anonymous patient details, drug details and treatment details together with the discharge status of the patient.

Phase III:
Analysis of data, eventually comparing the antidepressants widely used in Australia in terms of the fatality ratio (fatalities per million prescriptions) and the seriousness of intoxication of the survivors (intensive care treatment, discharge status).

1508

ANTIDEPRESSANTS AND THE NATIONAL SUICIDE
PREVENTION PROJECT IN FINLAND
Jouko Lönnqvist
National Public Health Institute, Helsinki,
Finland

The research project "Suicides in Finland 1987"
is a first phase of the National Suicide
Prevention Project in Finland, the target of
which is to reduce the suicide mortality rate by
20% from 1987 to 1995. The aim of research is to
collect information, on the basis of which
conclusions can be drawn about how the decrease
of high suicide rate in Finland can be achieved.
Data was collected concerning all deaths (N=1400)
which occurred between 1.4.87-31.3.88 in Finland
and were classified by the medicolegal expert as
suicides or undetermined deaths in which the
possibility of suicide existed. The clinical
diagnosis was assessed by a group of independent
psychiatrists using criteria of the DSM-III-R.
Special attention was paid to depressive disorders
and their treatment. Preventive conclusions will
be discussed.

1509

DEATH DUE TO OVERDOSE OF ANTIDEPRESSANTS, DATA FROM NORWAY

Retterstøl, N. Prof., University of Oslo, Gaustad
Hospital, Gaustad 0320 Oslo 5, Norway

The number of suicides in Norway has doubled during
the last two decades, as has also the number of
suicides by intoxication. Poisoning is now the
preferred method by 40% of the female and 23% of the
male suicides. Barbiturates were the main intoxicating
drugs in nearly 20% of all suicides by intoxication in
1970 as against only 3% in 1987. Antidepressants on
the contrary have increased its percentage from about
10% in 1970 to nearly 40% in 1987, and are today the
drugs of choice in suicide. This applies especially to
the older tricyclic antidepressants. As to the
treatment of neuroses anxiety and insomnia,
barbiturates were for deaths the dominating drugs.
Their drawback was their tendency to make a
development of dependency possible, and not least
their toxicity, which made them so dangerous, as they
were present in the drug boxes in most homes. It has
been a great advantage that benzodiazepines have taken
over their place, because their tendency to give
development of dependency is less, and they are much
less toxic and are seldom the main drug in
"successful" suicides.

In depressions suicide is the most important risk-
factor. Antidepressants are to be found in the drug
boxes in many homes, and accordingly prescription of
antidepressants with low toxicity ought to have much
attention from the side of clinician. It is strongly
to be hoped that the effective antidepressants in the
future also will be less toxic than they are today and
that new generations of antidepressants will be
ineffective as drugs for producing suicide.

1510

SUICIDE AND PARASUICIDE: THE INTERNATIONAL PICTURE

Diekstra R.F.W., Prof. Dr.
Professor and Chairman Dept. of Clinical & Health Psychology
University of Leiden, The Netherlands

In many countries of the world the number of persons
that commit or attempt suicide has risen considerably
over the past two decades. Particularly among young
people suicide rates have increased dramatically,
suicide now rating as the second of third cause of
death among them.
On the base of the results of a study carried out
under the auspices of WHO in 18 European countries, it
appears that the rise in suicide and attempted suicide
is related to a complex of eight social variables,
comprising both demographic, socio-cultural, familiar
and behavioural changes in the populations of the
countries studied. Evidence from studies in seven
countries suggests that these eight social variables
are related to an increase in affective disorders,
especially in certain age groups, although the
specific nature of the relationship remains obscure.
As far as affective disorders can be considered to be
a risk condition for suicidal behaviour, the
relationship between social developments and suicidal
behaviour might be explained by a model in which
affective disorders serve as a moderator-variable.

As will be outlined, depressive disturbances, showing
an increase in prevalence in the same period and
populations in which suicides and suicide attempts
have risen, presumably play an important moderator
role between social factors and suicidal behaviour.

Session 233 Workshop:
Chronic pain and antidepressants

1511

CHRONIC PAIN AND ANTIDEPRESSANTS
HISTORICAL REMARKS

PD Dr. R. Wörz, Schmerzzentrum Bad Schönborn
Waldparkstr. 20, D-7525 Bad Schönborn

In 1960, it was published simultaneously by several workers that imipramine was effective in the
treatment of neuralgia, myalgia and cancer pain.
In open clinical trials, amitriptyline has proved effective in chronic tension headache, psychogenic and neuralgic facial pain and, in double blind studies, a prophylactic efficacy in migraine was shown.
In patients with predominantly psychogenic headache, trigeminal tic douloureux and chronic neck
and back pain, doxepin has been found to be effective. The remaining tricyclic and the tetracyclic antidepressants have not been sufficiently well evaluated.
During the 1960s, it was observed that the MAO
inhibitors nialamide and phenelzine decreased migraine attacks. In respect of potentially serious side effects, these substances should only
be given in problematic cases resistant to conventional therapy.
In spite of 30 yrs of clinical experience and an
increasing number of double blind studies, our
knowledge regarding the usefulness, indications
and adverse effects of antidepressants in treating chronic pain syndromes is incomplete in many
areas.

1512
COMMON PATHOGENETIC MECHANISMS IN CHRONIC PAIN AND DEPRESSIVE DISORDERS.

Lars von Knorring, M.D., Department of Psychiatry, Umeå University, S-901 85 Umeå, Sweden.

Depressive symptoms are common in chronic pain syndromes in the same way as pain is a common symptom in affective disorders. In fact, the two syndromes have so pronounced clinical similarities that it has been suggested that they share a common pathogenetic mechanism, that chronic pain is a masked depression, that chronic pain is one disorder in depression spectrum disease or that chronic pain is a variant of depressive disease. In both chronic pain syndromes and in affective disorders the results indicate a high frequency of first degree relatives with affective disorders, specific personality traits, shortened REM latency in sleep EEG, hypercortisolemi and pathological DST, low platelet MAO activity, low concentrations of 5-HIAA in CSF, low ^{3}H-imipramine-receptor binding, low concentrations of melatonin in serum and urine and normal or high endorphins, Fraction 1, in CSF.
The results indicate that the two syndromes at least share a common pathogenetic mechanism. In both disorders, the results indicate disturbances in the serotonergic systems and in both conditions, treatment with tryptophan, ECT or antidepressants has been successful. Furthermore, serotonin reuptake inhibitors are more effective than noradrenaline reuptake inhibitors.

1513
HEADACHES HELPED BY ANTIDEPRESSANTS

S. Diamond, M.D., Diamond Headache Clinic ltd. 5252 North Western Av., Chicago, Ill. 60625, USA

The use of antidepressants in the prophylactic treatment of headache was first reported in 1964. Antidepressants have also been recognized for analgesic properties, independent of their antidepressant effects. All types of antidepressants are potentially effective analgesics as they influence the concentrations of norepinephrine and serotonin, and thus affect both the etiology and regulation of pain.
Several studies have demonstrated the effective use of the tricyclic antidepressants, amitriptyline and doxepin, in the treatment of migraine headaches and the mixed headache syndrome. Clinical results have confirmed the outcome of these studies. The monoamine oxidase inhibitors (MAOI) have been successfully used for many years in the prophylaxis of tension hedaches and migraine Careful patient selection is essential in the use of singular MAOI therapy, or in concomitant therapy with MAOIs and the tricyclics.
The patient most commonly seen in pain and headache clinics is probably the patient with mixed headaches, that is a combination of migraine and muscle contraction (tension) headaches. This patient presents a complex therapeutic problem, that ist often further complicated by habituation to analgesics or ergots.

1514
Antidepressants as analgesics in facial pain.

Dr Charlotte Feinmann. Eastman Dental Hospital London England.

In a double-blind controlled trial of dothiepin (Prothiaden) 71% of patients were relieved of pain after 9 weeks, compared to 46% on placebo. This action appeared to be independant of any antidepressant effect, as 55% of cases were psychiatrically normal, only 33% were depressed and this was probably secondary to the pain in many cases. Tricyclics are known to relieve pain in psychiatrically normal individuals and are used in the management of tension headache, migraine, back, pelvic and cancer pain.

In our clinical practise tricyclics antidepressants are not used is isolation. A pragmatic treatment approach is adopted in which the diagnosis is first established by a careful history which identifies other psychosomatic pains and seeks out stressful life events. The patient is reassured that no serious illness is present and medication is prescribed in slowly, increasing doses until therapeutic levels are achieved.

1515
BEHANDLUNG DES TIC DOULOUREUX MIT DOXEPIN

Thomalske G. - Zentrum für Neurochirurgie der Johann Wolfgang von Goethe Universität, FRG

Session 234 — New Research:
Psychological and psychopathological issues in medical conditions

1516

PERSONALITY DISORDERS IN PEPTIC ULCER DISEASE

Borgherini G., Bernasconi G., Di Mario F., Magni G.
Department of Psychiatry and Gastroenterology,
Univ. of Padua (Italy).

Twenty-five patients with an active peptic ulcer disease admitted to medical and gastroenterology units of the Padua General Hospital were studied. Patients with less than 18 years and more than 70 years, those with other significant intestinal diseases (cyrrhosis, cancer etc.) and those with a peptic ulcer disease in a remission phase were excluded from the study. The structured interview for DSM-III personality disorder (STOP) was administered by two psychiatrists to all the patients and one of their close relatives. Results showed one or more personality disorders (PD) in about half of the sample with peptic ulcer disease; there was not a specific PD that was particulary prevalent and in about half of the patients in whom PD were found multiple diagnosis were performed. Dependet PD was no particularly frequent in the studied experimental population. These data will be compared to those gathered from a control group matched for age and sex with experimental population, suffering from other non-gastrointestinal organic pathologies like for example hypertension and hospitalized because of that in the same hospital. These results if confirmed by further studies will be of help in better understanding the psychosocial aspects of peptic ulcer disease.

1517

EVOLUTION OF ANXIETY IN ONCOLOGICAL PATIENTS. PSYCHOPHARMACOLOGY.

PRIETO AGUIRRE, J.F.; LLORCA, G.; MONTEJO, A.L.; BLANCO, A.L.; PRIETO MESTRE, P.

UNIVERSITY CLINICAL HOSPITAL OF SALAMANCA.

533 patients with neoplasia and the anxiety disorders incidence in these patients are studied. Three well delimited anxiety periods have been described: suspicion anxiety in relation with prediagnostic period (A); expectancy anxiety, that appear during the medical treatment period (B) and lastly, the anxiety of abandonment during the cancer terminal period (C). The need of specific treatment in each of these A, B, and C periods has been supported with the combination of anxiolytics substances, antidepressants and neuroleptics. An adequate psicoterapeutic support with different nuances is suggested: contention psychotherapy (period A), antidepressant psychotherapy (period B) and attendance psychotherapy (period C).

1518

PSYCHOMETRIC ASPECTS OF PSYCHIATRIC DISTURBANCES IN CANCER PATIENTS

Grassi L., Stella S., Targa G., Ramelli E.
Cattedra di Clinica Psichiatrica, Università di Ferrara, Italia

In recent years, evaluation of psychiatric symptoms through reliable and specific criteria (e.g. DSM III) indicated that 30% to 40% of cancer patients had depressive symptoms, mainly adjustment disorders and, in a lower percentage, mood disorders (major depressive episode or dysthimia). To investigate the relationship between different nosological categories of depression and specific psychological problems, 42 cancer patients with a DSM III-R depressive syndrome within 3 months from the diagnosis (14 adjustment disorder with depression and 13 with mixed emotional features, 11 major depression, and 4 dysthimia) completed the SCL-90-R and the IBQ. Patients with a diagnosis of major depression reported higher scores on SCL-90-R Anxiety, Phobic anxiety, Paranoia and Psychoticism Scales ($p = 0.01$) than patients with other disorders. No difference between the groups was shown on the dimension of illness behaviour (IBQ). The study indicates the need of evaluating a large spectrum of psychological symptoms in cancer patients.

Study supported by grant 881203 by IOR-Forli-Italy

1519

A COMPARATIVE STUDY MIANSERIN-PLACEBO IN DEPRESSED CANCER PATIENTS

VAN HEERINGEN, C.; VAN MOFFAERT, M.; DE CUYPERE, G.
Dept of Psychiatry, University Hospital
Ghent, Belgium

The aim of this study was to evaluate in a seven week randomized double blind study the comparative efficacy of a single daily dose of 30 mg mianserinhydrochloride, which was raised to a single daily dose of 60 mg after 1 week of trial medication and placebo in the treatment of depressive female patients with breast cancer.
A total of 55 patients participated.
After two weeks of treatment the total score on the Hamilton Rating Scale for Depression for the mianserin-treated females was significantly ($p < 0.05$) lower than this score for the placebo-treated patients. The same holds for the sub-scores Retardation Depression Factor Score and the Melancholia Factor Score.
No statistical analysis was performed for differences between the two groups after four resp. six weeks of medication due to the large number of females who stopped the trial medication before the end of the study. This number was significantly ($p < 0.01$) higher in the placebo-treated group than in the mianserin-treated females.

1520
THALASSAEMIA MINOR AND AFFECTIVE DISORDERS

A.Bocchetta, M.Pedditzi, F.Bernardi, R.Corona*, M.Del Zompo

Department of Neuroscience, University of Cagliari, and * Central Laboratory, "S.Giovanni di Dio" Hospital, USL 20, Cagliari, Italy.

A possible association between thalassaemia minor and psychiatric illness, particularly affective illness, was suggested by a preliminary report by Joffe et al (1986). We have performed haemoglobin electrophoresis in 180 consecutive outpatients of the Service of Clinical Pharmacology, Univ.of Cagliari to study the prevalence of heterozygous beta-thalassaemia in patients with psychiatric disorders. Diagnoses were made according to the Research Diagnostic Criteria. The prevalence of the hematological disorder in our overall population (17.8%) was similar to that known for the general population in Southern Sardinia. However, there was a trend for an increased prevalence in patients with bipolar disorders (including schizoaffective) (22.4%) compared with unipolar disorders (9.1%). Moreover, the proportion of heterozygous beta-thalassaemia was significantly higher ($p < 0.01$) in patients with bipolar schizoaffective disorder (14/45 = 31.1%) compared with those with other affective disorders (17/126 = 13.5%). The relevance of our findings to the current knowledge on the genetic transmission of affective illness will be discussed.

1521
HEALTH ATTITUDES IN CHRONIC LOW BACK PATIENTS AND THEIR SPOUSES

S.P. Saarijärvi
The Rehabilitation Research Centre of the Social Insurance Institution, Turku, Finland

Health attitudes were studied with the Attitude Scale and compared between 64 chronic low back pain (CLBP) patients and their spouses. The CLBP patients, and especially men experienced significantly more feelings of guilt at having pain than their spouses ($p = 0.0001$). The male patients also experienced more than female patients that pain is dependent on chance ($p=0.03$). In the health locus of control the CLBP patients were significantly more internally orientated than their spouses ($p=0.0001$). The spouses were more externally orientated than the patients ($p=0.0001$). In other health attitudes; faith in the future, confidence in health care authorities, contentment with information concerning the health problem, and acceptance of psychological factors influencing the pain problem no significant differences were observed. Conclusion is that guilt is associated with CLBP, especially in men. The more external health locus of control in spouses may reflect their caretaking attitudes.

1522
THE CORMAN TEST APPLIED TO CHILDREN WITH COOLEY'S ANAEMIA

Antoaneta Bugner, Cornelia Siara, and C. Predescu
The Centre of Haematology and Blood Transfusion, 2, C-tin Caracas str., Bucharest, S-1, Romania

The Corman Test (a test which requires to make a drawing of a patient's family) was applied to children with Cooley's an-aemia with a view to evaluate the psychoaffective status and to assess the role of the illness in inducing changes in the behaviour of the young patients. A group of 34 children were investigated, and results of 8 suggestive tests have been selected for presentation. Patients' ages ranged between 6 and 14 years. All had received therapy (blood transfusions and Desferal) in the same medical unit for periods of 2-5 years. All the tests disclosed a certain degree of change in the pattern of psycho-affective reactions, considered to be normal for patients of this age, although the changes did not correlate linearly with the severity of the disease, or the condition of the patients at the time of the test.

Session 235 New Research
Clinical neurophysiology

1523
CEREBRAL MAPPING IN PSCHIATRIC DIAGNOSIS – KEY WORD: PSCHIATRIC MAPPING

Prof. G.Battista Laurenzi
Dr. Paola Terribile, Roma, Italy

The authors used the mapping system of the ATLAS Biologic machine to see the difference between a control group and psychiatric syndromes. The control group was composed of 60 normal people: 30 between the ages of 20 and 40 years and 30 between 41 ad 60 years of age.
This comparison between maps of the normal group and maps of depressed patients or schizophrenic or involutive and anxiious patients evidenced different increases of theta and delta waves in various places of the brain. 150 patients were examined with different diagnoses: anxious, depressed, schizophrenic, involutive.
The authors found significant differences.

1524

B.E.A.M. MEASURED LATERALISATION OF BRAIN FUNCTION IN SCHIZOPHRENIC AND DEPRESSED PATIENTS

B.Gallhofer, B.Malle[1], G.Wieselmann, E.Körner, S.Kunz

University Departments of Psychiatry and Neurolgoy and University Institute of Neuropsychology[1], Graz, Austria

40 patients suffering from either schizophrenia (SCH, N=20) or unipolar depression (D, N=20) and 10 healthy volunteers were subjected to a study into their regional spectral brain power textures by means of (B.E.A.M.). Both groups with positive psychopathology consisted of patients who were either on psychoactive drugs (ON DRUGS) or they were drug naive or medication had been withdrawn for longer than at least 14 days (OFF DRUGS; N=10 respectively).
One important aspect was to look into laterality effects depending upon different wavebands and brain regions. MANOVA with polynomial contrasts for the factor 'region' revealed significantly distinct laterality patterns in the theta band for the two ON DRUGS groups. SCH patients showed a linear regional function in the right hemisphere (decreasing from frontal to occipital leads) and a quartic function in the left hemisphere (with a peak in the temporal leads), whereas the reverse pattern was found for D patients, showing a quartic function in the right hemisphere and a linear regional decrease in their left hemispheric activity. Healthy controls as well as SCH and D patients of activity in both hemispheres.
It is concluded that lateral differences in psychiatric patients may not always indicate dysfunctional activity but could also represent a self-regulating or drug-induced mechanism of "natural" hemispheric asymmetries. Further methodological improvements are proposed in order to discriminate between drug effects and dispositional neuropsychological imbalances.

1525

A Coherence - Estimation of Hemispheric Activation in Schizophrenics
J. Micheloyannis, N. Paritsis, P. Trikas, A. Yannopoulos, N. Marketos, E. Prokopakis

Medical Division of University of Crete

Previous researchers have found significant neurophysiological differences between groups of schizophrenic and normal persons but the results are controversial and they are without diagnostic value. We examined 28 schizophrenics using a motor activation task EEG recording and measuring the hemispheric activation by the estimation of the coherence after calculating the power spectrum using our software. After a resting EEG of each hemisphere we recorded the EEG during movements of the contrallateral hand. We analysed 12 artifact-free EEG´s. We also examined 12 normal adults as controls with the same method. In the control study of 12, the 8 coherences we examined in each hemisphere, showed an increase of the coherence of the alpha band during the task. In contrast, in 8 cases with schizophrenia, we found not increased and in 4 cases decreased coherence. These differences were statistical significant. These findings are suggesting brain dysfunction which we can identify at least in some categories of the disease.

1526

CONTINGENT NEGATIVE VARIATION AND SEVERITY OF DEPRESSION

P.Papart, M.Ansseau, J.M.Devoitille, H.Mantanus, M.Timsit-Berthier, CHU, Liège, Belgium.

Contingent negative variation (CNV) is a slow potential shift that develops during a simple experimental situation in which stimuli and responses are serially organized. CNV studies in depressive patients have shown abnormalities in both amplitude and duration. The purpose of the present study was to assess the relationship between CNV amplitude and severity of depressive symptoms. Fifty-nine major depressive inpatients, drug-free for at least 2 weeks, were assessed using Montgomery and Asberg depression scale (MADS) and Hamilton depression scale. CNV was recorded according to a procedure previously described (Timsit-Berthier et al., Ann N Y Acad Sci, 425, 629-637, 1984). CNV amplitude exhibited a very significant relationship with the severity of depressive symptomatology: $r=0.54$ ($p=0.001$) with MADS scores and $r=0.43$ ($p=0.001$) with Hamilton depression scores. These results indicate that low CNV amplitude is associated with a particular severity of depression.

1527

ELECTRORETINOGRAPHIC FINDINGS IN PSYCHIATRIC INPATIENTS
Fornaro P., Fioretto M*, Berti A.
Clin.Psich Universita di Genova, Centro per le distimie, Dir.Prof. F.Giberti
*Clin.Oculistica Universita di Genova
Dir. Prof.Zingirian
Italy

The same putative neurotransmitter present in the Central Nervous System (C.N.S.) have been detected at level of the retina.
According to this, and to some electrophysiological findings indicating a relationship between the b wave amplitude of Electroretinogram (ERG) and the level of dopaminergic activity in the retina, which is a part of the C.N.S., an investigation on a sample of psychiatric inpatients suffering from different mental disorders and treated with psychoactive drugs has been performed.
The results obtained, showing ERG changes mainly concerning the b Wave amplitude in most patients, suggest that also in the retina, as in the C.N.S., neurobiological changes which may be related to the psychiatric disorder and/or to the psychopharmacological treatment occur.

1528

THE EFFECTS OF HEPATIC ENCEPHALOPATHY ON THE CHEMICALLY INDUCED CONVULSIONS
A.B.Turkoglu,M.K.Arikan,S.Bulut,G.Baydas,A.Songar
The University of Firat & the University of Istanbul, Turkey

The possible effects of hepatic encephalopathy on the threshold of pentylenetetrazol induced convulsions (PTZ-IC) were researched. The goal of this study was to make a contribution to the explanation of pathogenesis of hepatic encephalopathy. The ammonia is tamponed by glutamate in the brain. There is a Yin-Yang relationship between glutamate and GABA (gamma amino butyric acid). This relationship suggests that hyperammoniemia, inhibiting glutamatergic neurotransmission, may also potentiate GABAergic neurotransmission. So the PTZ-IC levels might be raised. On this hypothetical base, we planned a preliminary study. Three cross-bred healthy dogs were used. First dog is selected for control. We started the injection ammonia to the second dog. On the third dog, end-to-side portacaval shunt was constructed by the method of Eck-Pavlov. Throughout this study we measured PTZ-IC levels. We pursued the levels of zinc, ammonia, sugar, urea, activity of arginase in the venous blood samples. The levels of parameters did not change in the first dog. In the second dog the zinc levels were decreasing while the ammonia and PTZ-IC levels increased. In the portacaval shunted animal PTZ-IC levels were parallel to the second animal. In the beginning only were the levels of ammonia increasing in spite of the decrement of PTZ-IC levels. Later both values increased in parallel. Finally, these results are analysed under the hypothetical bases mentioned above.

1529

NADPH-D POSITIVE NEURONS IN QUIN-INDUCED HUNTINGTON'S DISEASE RAT MODEL
G.O. Peker, P.J.Roberts, B. Arvin, E. Demirtas
Ege University School of Medicine, Departments of Physiology and Pathology, Bornova, Izmir, Turkey
University of Southampton, Department of Physiology and Pharmacology, Southampton, UK.
The endogenous excitatory amino acid, QUIN has recently been proposed as a convenient lesioning tool in animal models for Huntington's disease (HD). In this study, the local (cortical)and the distant (striatal) excitotoxic effects of various doses (2, 5, and 10 mg.s) of QUIN were investigated by light-microscopic evaluation of thionine and NADPH-D-stained rat brain coronal sections, prepared on the 20th day following lesioning of the right parieto-occipito-temporal dural surface. Prominent aggressive behavior and manifest motor characteristics implying chorea were observed in the QUIN-administered animals in repect to dose. All doses of QUIN caused local neuronal death and consequent gliosis. 10 mg QUIN had a very strong lesion-inducing effect on the contralateral cortical area and the ipsilateral corpus striatum, implying diffusion and excitotoxicity via the corticostriatal glutamatergic pathway respectively. NADPH-D positive neurons were spared regardless of dose in all regions. Our results are in accordance with similar studies on Huntington patients'postmortem brain material and animal models, thus supporting the excitotoxic hypothesis in neurodegeneration with emphasis on the possible involvement of the endogenous excitotoxin, QUIN, in HD.

Session 236 Free Communications:
Antidepressant treatment outcome and its predictors

1530

CLINICAL PREDICTORS FOR THE SEVERITY OF THE DEPRESSION AND FOR THE EFFICACY OF ANTIDEPRESSIVE THERAPY
M. Paes de Sousa
Dept. of Psychiatry. Faculty of Medicine of Lisbon. Hospital Stª Maria. Av. Prof. Egas Moniz. P-1600 Lisbon. Portugal.

424 depressive patients treated with several antidepressant drugs were described and assessed before and after 1-2 months of treatment with the AMDP system. A principal components analysis made before and after the treatment enabled us to isolate in both cases two factors (Depression/Inhibition and Anxiety/Agitation). Taking into consideration each one of these factors obtained before and after treatment, an analysis of variance was performed among some psycho-social and pathological variables which showed some significant differences. Whenever there was more than two possibilities for one single variable, the Bonferroni t test was applied to discriminate the sense of the significance. We think that the significant variables obtained before treatment could be predictors of the depression severity and of the therapeutic indication and after treatment could be predictors of the therapeutic response.

1231

THERAPY RESISTANT DEPRESSION: A CLINICAL INTEGRATED APPROACH
Siracusano A., Brogna P., Fiorentini A., Niolu C., Vella G.
Iˆ Psych.Clinic, University of Rome (Prof. G.Vella), Italy
The concept of "resistant depression" ("R.D."), today is essentially centered on the clinical course in relation to the ineffectiveness of the treatment (Kielholz, 86). This condition, needs to be studied in depth with an integrated approach, considering the problems relative to serious personality disorders often present in resistant subjects. Among the different pharmacological therapies proposed for "R.D." we have utilized with success, in our clinical practice, a combined treatment with the addition of lithium carbonate to a therapy with antidepressants carried out without effectiveness for at least 3 weeks: treatment proposed by De Montigny and Coll. (1981,83,85) and many others (Craig-Nelson 86, Price 86). In this report the data relative to the cases in which we tried this pharmacological combination (in an open study) will be exposed. The personality disorder patients, during the period of the therapy, underwent frequent clinical interviews: a sort of supportive therapy as suggested by Akiskal ('85). The AA. put in light the seductivity of the concept of "R.D." when founded exclusively on the lack of response with antidepressant therapies. The hypothesis about the relation between the lack of response to the therapy and personality disorders in the resistant cases, will be critically discussed.

1532

Can the clinical efficiency of maprotiline in depressed patients be predicted by early REM sleep changes ?

LEMOINE P., FERBER C., TAILLARD J., PHILLIPS R*., MOURET J.,
UCPB, Hôpital du Vinatier, 95, boulevard Pinel, 69677 Bron cedex
*CIBA-GEIGY FRANCE

Ten major depressive patients were sleep recorded during three nights before treatment and on nights following days 8 to 10 of maprotiline treatment. Evaluations (MADRS, HARS) were performed weekly until day 28 of treatment.
Sleep changes, at the time when the study was performed, were limited to an increase in Stage II sleep and an increase in the number of intra-sleep awakenings, a decrease in REM sleep time occured which did not reach statistically significant level.
The analysis of individual REM sleep changes shown that maprotiline treatment was followed by a regulatory process leading to a decrease of REM sleep in those patients with high control REM sleep amounts and an increase in those with low control amounts. Clinical efficiency was excellent or good when REM sleep amounts were low or medium in control conditions whereas no improvement was observed in those patients who had high REM sleep amounts in control conditions and a decrease in this sleep stage during the studied treatment period.

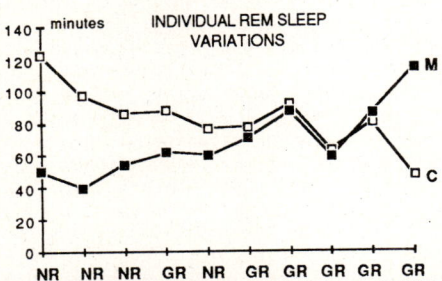

C = (opened squares) Control REM amounts, M = (filled squares) REM amounts under maprotiline for the ten patients, C and M REM amounts for a given patient are on the same abscissae.
NR : Non-responder , GR = Good clinical response

1533

CAN PLACEBO-EFFECT PREDICT OUTCOME OF ANTIDEPRESSIVE MEDICATION?
S. Priebe, M. Bröker, J. Bohlken
Department of Psychiatry, Freie Universität Berlin, Berlin (West), F.R.G.

Early clinical improvement has repeatedly been found to predict outcome of neuroleptic treatment. In this study we investigated whether clinical improvement within the first two days of antidepressive medication could predict the eventual outcome, and we tested whether an initial improvement under placebo could also be of predictive value for the treatment with the antidepressive drug.

Forty-two patients with depressive syndromes who were to be treated with maprotiline, clomipramine and tranylcypromine received genuine medication or placebo in a double-blind situation within the first two days of treatment. From the third day all patients received the regular antidepressive medication. In both groups, reduction of depressive symptoms within the first two days as rated on the Hamilton Depression Scale was significantly correlated with outcome at the end of treatment (a maximum of four weeks). So initial placebo-effects can predict outcome of antidepressive medication. Implications for theoretical concepts of interaction of biological and psychological processes in antidepressive treatment are discussed.

1534

RITANSERIN IN ASTHENO-ANXIOUS AND ASTHENO-DEPRESSIVE PATIENTS.

L. CROCQ, J. HOFFMANN et Ph. BOUHOURS -
Université René Descartes, Paris, France.

Ritanserin is a selective centrally acting serotonin-S_2 antagonist and was studied in astheno-anxious and astheno-depressive patients (anxiety and disthymic disorders in DSM III) in a double-blind placebo control multi-centric general practice trial.
138 patients were included in the study : 46 placebo, 46 R. 2,5 mg (b.i.d.) and 46 R. 5 mg (b.i.d.) during 28 days, followed by 14 days without treatment.
Evaluations were made at D0, D14, D28 and D42 by using 6 V.A.S. (general wellbeing, fatigue, asthenia, sleep disorders) and the Asthenia Scale of Crocq and Bugard (15 clinical items iventoring main somatic and psychic aspects of asthenia, anxiety and depression) which also allows to establish clinical profile of each patient.
The statistical analysis of the results shows a comparative clinical efficacy of ritanserin 2,5 mg (b.i.d.) and 5 mg (b.i.d.) better than placebo, on 6 V.A.S. and on several items of Asthenia Scale. Best responses are found on "psychosomatic" symptoms and on "sleep-wakefulness" parameters and for ritanserin 5 mg (b.i.d.) at day 14.
No withdrawal signs or rebound phenomena were reported following stop of therapy. Adverse experience profile of ritanserin is not different from placebo.

1535

FLUOXETINE EFFICACY IN DEPRESSIVES WITH IMPULSIVITY VS BLUNTED AFFECT

JOUVENT R*, BARUCH P*, AMMAR S*, MONTREUIL M*
BEUZEN JN** & WIDLÖCHER D*
(*) INSERM U 302, LA SALPETRIERE, PARIS, FRANCE
(**) LILLY FRANCE, PARIS

This pilot study with fluoxetine was designed to compare its respective efficacy in depressives with anxious impulsivity or with blunted affect. Two such groups were formed from 16 patients fulfilling DSM III criteria for major depressive episode. After a 4-day wash-out period, all patients received 20 mg per day of fluoxetine from D 0 to D 14, then 20 to 40 mg per day until D 28. Ratings were made by two independent raters blind towards the aim of the study, using Hamilton depression rating scale (HDRS) and Tyrer anxiety rating scale, Abrams-Taylor blunted affect scale and Echelle d'Humeur Dépressive, a polydimensional depressive mood scale (EHD).
Tolerance was good and similar in both groups. Results show : 1) a significant improvement on HDRS for the 16 patients (ANOVA, $p < 0.01$). 2) a significant superiority of fluoxetine in anxious impulsive compared to "blunted" patients (two factors ANOVA on HDRS, $p < 0.01$). 3) On mood factors of EHD, a significant improvement limited to Emotional blunting and Sadness factors in blunted patients as opposed to an effect on a greater number of dimensions, Irritability, Affective lability, Emotional incontinence and Sadness factors in anxious impulsive patients. These results are discussed in the light of biological and pharmacological hypothesis concerning impulsivity and blunted affect.

1536
A DOUBLE BLIND COMPARATIVE STUDY : AMINEPTINE VERSUS IMIPRAMINE
Mendis N.
University of Colombo

The aim of the study was to compare the antidepressant effects of amineptine with imipramine in depressive illness.

According to the DSM III criteria 33 patients diagnosed as having depressive illnesses were either given imipramine or amineptine, 50 mg - 100 mg and 100 mg - 200 mg respectively per day on a double blind basis over a period of two months. Both groups presented steady improvement of the symptoms of depression during treatment, as scored on the Hamilton and Montgomery and Asberg Depression Rating Scales and Clinical Global Impression Scale. Amineptine produced fewer anticholinergic effects than Imipramine.

The results obtained show that amineptine, as well as imipramine, is well suited for treating depressed patients.

Session 237 Free Communications: Psychoneuroendocrinology II

1537
MULTIPLE HORMONAL RESPONSE TO TRH IN DEPRESSIVE PATIENTS

J.Hatzimanolis, B.Alevizos
Department of Psychiatry, University of Athens, Eginition Hospital, Athens, Greece

In fifty patients with endogenous depression, the TSH, cortisol, prolactin and growth hormone response to TRH was studied.
Fifty per cent (N=25) of the patients were found to have blunted TSH response to TRH. Patients with blunted TSH response showed significantly lower prolactin response, especially at 20 minutes ($p<0.05$) in comparison to those with normal TSH response. Growth hormone response to TRH was also lower, but not at significant degree, in patients with blunted TSH response.
When patients with recent or past suicide attempt (N=15) were compared with nonattempters, the TSH response to TRH was significantly lower in suicide attempters, especially at 90 minutes ($p<0.05$). Prolactin response to TRH was also lower in suicide attempters, but this difference was not statistically significant.
These findings may indicate that the blunted TSH response to TRH is connected with blunted response of other hormones i.e. prolactin and growth hormone and that the blunted response of TSH and possibly prolactin may be associated with suicidal behavior.

1538
MULTIPLE HORMONAL RESPONSES IN SUICIDE ATTEMPTERS

B.Alevizos, J.Hatzimanolis
Department of Psychiatry, University of Athens, Eginition Hospital, Athens, Greece

Cortisol, TSH, prolactin and growth hormone (GH) responses to DST and TRH were studied in 15 depressed patients with suicide attempts and 38 patients without a recent or past suicide attempt. In 11 attempters and 18 nonattempters the hormonal responses to clonidine were further studied.
Abnormal DST was found in 53.5 % of attempters and 50.0 % of nonattempters, blunted TSH response to TRH in 53.3 % and 36.4 % and blunted GH response to clonidine in 45.5 % and 77.8 % respectively.
Suicide attempters had a significantly higher than nonattempters retardation score of the Hamilton scale ($p<0.01$). Post-dexamethasone prolactin levels (11 p.m.) tended to be significantly lower in attempters as well as the prolactin response to TRH at 40 minutes ($p<0.1$). The cortisol response to clonidine was significantly higher in suicide attempters, especially at 45 minutes ($p<0.05$). Recent attempters had a significantly lower cortisol response to clonidine at 90 minutes ($p<0.05$).
The results of this study failed to provide convincing evidence that hormonal responses in depressive patients may identify suicidal patients and predict suicidal behaviour.

1539
RELATIONSHIP BETWEEN DEPRESSION AND THYROID FUNCTION IN RURAL KENYA
John J. Haggerty, Jr., M.D., Mark Marquardt, M.D., George Mason, Ph.D., Charlotte Newman, M.D., Arthur J. Prange, Jr., M.D., University of North Carolina, Departments of Psychiatry and Family Medicine, Chapel Hill, NC, and UCLA, School of Public Health, Los Angeles, CA, U.S.A.

While thyroid dysfunction is known to be a predisposing factor to the development of affective disorders, the interaction between thyroid function and affective disorder has not been well studied in non-clinical populations. Therefore, we measured total thyroxin (T_4), free thyroxin (FT_4), and thyroid stimulating hormone (TSH) concentrations in serum of 443 adult rural Kenyan subjects who had also completed the Standardized Report Questionnaire for depression as part of a community wide nutritional and morbidity survey. Thirteen percent of females and four percent of males met criteria for major depression. Serum FT_4 was relatively low for the entire sample. Male depressed subjects had a significantly reduced mean FT_4 and increased T_4 compared with non-depressed counterparts. Female depressed and non-depressed subjects did not differ significantly on any thyroid measure. However when males and females were combined there was a trend toward a higher sex adjusted TSH ($p = .14$) and T_4 ($p = .15$) and lower FT_4 ($p = .12$) in depressed subjects. Expected sex related differences in TSH and FT_4 occurred in non-depressed subjects, but were abolished in the depressed group. Our findings may be due in part to iodine deficiency, which may have a previously unappreciated influence on the development of affective disorders in predisposed populations.

1540

Neuroendocrine tests in anxiety disorders

G. Koinig, D. Nutzinger, C. Alf, P. Parzer
G. Schönbeck.
University of Vienna, Department of Psychiatry

Psychobiological indicators predicting therapeutic effect of psychopharmacological drugs have not been adequately investigated. Using neuroendocrinological investigation we have demonstrated one such indicator to predict therapy response. Blunted TSH-response in TRH-test identified patients with psychoses responsive to psychopharmacological treatment.
The applicability of this test to predict treatment response in nonpsychotic patients was investigated. 24 in patients (males and females) with a diagnosis of anxiety disorders (DSM-III) were examined. TRH-test and DST were done before starting the treatment. Patients received 4-5 weeks psychopharmacological treatment and psychotherapy. The clinical state was assessed periodicalyy using appropriate rating scales by clinicians blind to results of endocrine tests.

1541

CLOZAPINE AND NON-DOPAMINERGIC TRANSMISSION: TRH TEST IN SCHIZOPHRENIA

V.R. Paunović, I. Timotijević and D. Marinković

Departments of Psychiatry, University Clinical Center and Clinical Center Dedinje, Belgrade, Yugoslavia

Two groups of in-patients treated for productive form of schizophrenia (Crow type I) were submitted to haloperidol (30 mg p.d.) and clozapine (150 mg p.d.), respectively. Thyrotropin (TSH) response to thyrotropin-releasing hormone (TRH) was monitored prior to the onset of neuroleptic therapy and 20 days later. In the haloperidol group, TSH response remained unchanged or slightly elevated, whereas in the clozapine group this response was attenuated. These results confirm the thesis that neuroleptic-induced dopaminergic blockade weakens inhibitory action of dopamine at hypothalamic site. This is the case with haloperidol, a typical antipsychotic drug acting predominantly on dopamine receptors. The obtained data suggest a non-dopaminergic action of clozapine on the hypothalamo-pituitary axis. We hypothesize that this atypical neuroleptic inhibits noradrenergic transmission in hypothalamic structures. This inhibition abolishes facilitatory noradrenergic action on TSH. Thus, blunted response to TRH may be expected when noradrenergic transmission is disturbed and this, in fact, was registered in our clozapine treated patients.

1542

THE CORTICOTROPIN-RELEASING FACTOR STIMULATION TEST IN ANXIETY DISORDERS.
D. Bailly ; D. Servant ; D. Dewailly ; Ph.J. PARQUET
Psychopathology and Alcoology Unit , Endocrinology and Diabetology Department , University Hospital of Lille , France.

Recent studies showed that the corticotropin-releasing factor (CRF) system may play a role in anxiety disorders and more particularly in panic disorder. In order to check this hypothesis , a 100 µg bolus of synthetic o-CRF (UCB, France) was administered at 12.00 hrs intravenously to ten non - depressed patients (aged 31 - 43 yrs) with panic disorder and to five non - depressed patients (aged 34 - 47 yrs) with obsessive compulsive disorder according to the DSM III - R criteria. No patient took medication at least fifteen days before the test. Plasma ACTH was determined by a commercial radioimmunoassay (ACTH K - PR CIS , France) and plasma cortisol by a fluorimetric method. Results were compared with those obtained in seven normal control subjects (aged 22 - 25 yrs). No significant difference in plasma cortisol response was found by variance analysis between the three groups. The plasma ACTH response was significantly higher in patients with panic disorder and in patients with obsessive compulsive disorder respectively than in controls ($p < 0,05$ by variance analysis in both cases). No significant difference in ACTH response was found between the two groups of patients with anxiety disorders.

1543

EFFECTS OF SHORT-TERM ADMINISTRATION OF PHOSPHATIDYLSERINE ON THE NEUROENDOCRINE RESPONSE TO PHYSICAL STRESS IN HUMANS.

P. Monteleone[1], M. Maj[1], L. Beinat[2] and D. Kemali[1]
[1]Institute of Medical Psychology and Psychiatry, 1st Medical School, University of Naples, Italy and [2]Fidia Research Laboratories, Abano Terme (PD), Italy

(3-sn-phosphatidyl)-L-serine (PS), a natural component of cell membranes, is involved in many aspects of transmembrane signalling essential to the function of neurons in the central nervous system. Experimental evidence indicate that prolonged treatment with bovine brain cortex-derived PS (BC-PS) restores membrane functionality in aged rats, modulates neurohormonal balance and results in an improvement of higher cerebral activity such as learning processes, memory, mood and stress response. These data prompted us to investigate the short-term effects of BC-PS on the neuroendocrine response to a physical stress paradigm in humans. For this purpose, 8 healthy male subjects (aged 26-48 yrs) underwent three experiments with a bicycle ergometer, between 8.00 and 11.00 a.m., one week apart. The physical exercise was performed with the following load: 6 min - 1.5 W Kg, one min rest; then 6 min - 2 W Kg, one min rest and, finally, 6 min - 2.5 W Kg. According to a double blind design, 10 min before starting the exercise, each subject received intravenously 50 or 75 mg of BC-PS or a volume-matched saline in random order. Before and after the physical performance, blood samples were collected for plasma hormonal and catecholamine determinations; heart rate, systolic and diastolic blood pressure were also registered. A significant increase in plasma epinephrine (E), norepinephrine (NE), ACTH and cortisol was observed following exercise in placebo treated subjects. Short-term BC-PS administration (either 50 and 75 mg) resulted in a significantly blunted response of E, NE, ACTH and cortisol to the acute physical stress. No significant changes in plasma levels of GH, PRL and dopamine were observed after exercise either in placebo- and in BC-PS treated volunteers. Hearth rate, systolic and diastolic blood pressure were affected similarly by physical stress after both placebo and BC-PS administration. These results show, for the first time, that acute administration of BC-PS is able to blunt the activation of hypothalamic-pituitary-adrenal system by a physical stress paradigm in humans. Both central and peripheral mechanisms may be invoked for this effect.

Session 238 Free Communications:
Schizophrenia: Disability and related issues

1544

RESIDUUM AND DISABILITY IN FUNCTIONAL
PSYCHOSES - METHODOLOGICAL SHORTCOMINGS
A. MARNEROS
Department of Psychiatry, University
of Bonn, FRG

On the grounds of our own investigations
we tried to identify some important
methodological shortcomings which can
influence the comparability of studies.

The most important problems are concerning:
(a) Brod definitions of disorders,
(b) Generalization of the term "outcome",
(c) Partialization of the term "prognosis",
(d) Egualization of the terms "course" and "outcome",
(e) Ignoring the polymorphism and inhomogeneity of disorders,
(f) Global evaluation of outcome, and
(g) Short observation time.

Corrections of the above mentioned shortcomings will be suggested.

1545

THE EVOLUTION OF THE WORKING CAPACITY IN
SCHIZOPHRENICS
Mircea Lăzărescu, M.D.; Monica Ienciu, M.
D., Clinica Psihiatrică Timişoara, Spitalul Psihiatrie Gătaia, the S.R. of Romania

A long term study was carried out on 503
schizophrenics (ICD-9)(cathamnesis average - 17 years) concerning their socio-professional capabilities.
The onset of working incapacity is important in the first 5 years after the onset of the disease in 60% of the cases, and in the first 2 years after the onset of the disease in 40% of the cases. Afterwards, the rate of pensioning off decreases.
The patients who did not reach retirement within 10 years after the onset of the disease were characterized by a later onset of the disease, higher learning and professional levels, and higher marital insertion than the patients who lost their working capacity irremediably. A complete recovery may occur after retirement, and is maintained in about 10% of the cases. Other clinical characteristics of the groups with favourable and unfavourable socio-professional evolution are stressed.

1546

A CLINICAL STUDY OF SCHIZOPHRENIA--FACTORS INFLUENCING
CHRONICIFICATION IN SCHIZOPHRENIA---

Yasuo UNAI, M.D., Department of Neuropsychiatry,
Showa University Fujigaoka Hospital, Yokohama, Japan.

We define chronicification as a process having two factors that are associated with the onset of chronicity. These are: a state that has an unfavorable prognosis, and negative symptoms. Some factors influencing chronicification in schizophrenia were investigated systemtically.
These data were collected from Nov.1971 to Oct. 31,1976. They covered 166 patient at Toyoko Mental Hospital, who had suffered relapses. Of these 166 patients, there were 107 patients for whom the disease persisted for 5 years or more. These subjects were devided into two groups. The first group were 61 patients who conformed to our definition of chronicification. The second group were 46 patients who had no indication of chronicification. The following factors were significantly different in the two groups:sex difference,age of first onset, precipitating factors, marital state, initial symptoms(these correlate to 0.1% level of significance). At the 1% level of significance were family history of schizophrenia, duration of hospitalization, the duration of regular medication and regular ambulation, acceptance of family, age difference between mother and patient. At 2% level of significance were the manner of occurrence of initial somatic symptoms and pulse. At 5% level of significance were duration from onset of manifestation to admission, time since cessation of pharmacotherapy and ambulation, blood pressure at the time of admission. There was no correlation with other factors.
The conclusion are: It is thus important to have early treatment for schizophrenia to prevent chronicification. The mechanism of chronicification will be discussed.

1547

The discharged schizophrenic patient: assessment and outcome of occupational disability over five years.

Rüdiger Vogel, V. Bell, St. Blumenthal, N.-U. Neumann, R. Schüttler

Bezirkskrankenhaus Günzburg, Department Psychiatry II of the University Ulm, Ludwig-Heilmeyer-Str. 2, D-8870 Günzburg, West Germany

Reviewing psychiatric follow-up studies there is some evidence that only a few theoretical and methodological progress has been made in identifying the degree of unsuccessful occupational adjustment and factors that are impeding the adjustment process. Our study applies new approaches, such as using valid and sensitive measures of adjustment, a longitudinal strategy and homegeneous samples. Moreover there was an attempt to study the adjustment in different stages of the illness (first and fifth year) and to compare the outcome patterns with those of different other psychiatric disorders.
Results indicate that 1. the mean extent of disbility does increase over time 2. patients with extreme scores show no or only little change over time, whereas patients with an initially intermediate disability score tend to change 3. the patterns of disability of schizophrenic patients do not significantly differ from the other diagnostic subgroups, except patients with alcohol dependency.

1548

SOCIAL PROGRAMS AND DEPOT NEUROLEPTICS IN SCHIZOPHRENICS TREATMENT

Virginio NAVA, Gabriella CILLI, Elisabetta RIVA e Salvatore ZIZOLFI

Department of Mental Health, COMO, Italy

40 male inpatients, 40-65 years old, satisfying DSM-III-R criteria for chronic schizophrenia, undergoing a long-lasting continous hospitalization (more than 20 years), previously treated with oral neuroleptics in an hospital ward without any social support, were maintained on a long-acting depot neuroleptic (haloperidol decanoate, I.M., once monthly) during the last three years, and received, in addiction, various forms of social supports during the last two years. Once monthly each patient was administered the Brief Psychiatric Rating Scale (BPRS), the Clinical Global Impression (CGI) and a Side Effects Rating Scale, in order to identify, on clinical grounds, according to a single blind design, the lowest neuroleptic dosage more able to obtain the best results in terms of maintenance treatment. At the end of 3-years study, clinical data were retrospectively analysed: no statistically significant variations in BPRS ratings was observed at various times of the observation period; a statistically significant reduction of neuroleptic mean dosage was seen during the last 2 years (up to 70% of the initial dose), in relation to social support

1549

PREDICTORS OF RESISTANCE OF TREATMENT IN SCHIZOPHRENIA

Müller, P.*, B.Bandelow*, W.Gaebel, W.Köpcke, M.Linden, F.Müller-Spahn, A.Pietzcker, J.Tegeler - ANI-study-group Berlin, Düsseldorf, Göttingen, München
*Psychiatric clinic, university of Göttingen/Fed.Rep.Germany

Of 346 schizophrenic patients who were discharged after treatment and received ambulant aftercare, 51 % were unable to be brought into complete remission. Predictors of resistance of treatment are: (1) male sex, (2) early onset of illness, (3) lack of social, sexual and personal contact prior to illness, (4) at present, the administration of highly dosed neuroleptics with subsequent development of extrapyramidal side effects. A possible conclusion: even an increased administration of neuroleptics over a short or average period of time is unable to bring a patient into remission, if early negative predictors are present and were not considered or treated effectively during the onset of the illness. Consequences of future treatment strategies and course studies are to be discussed.

1550

THE DOCTOR AS A PATIENT WITH SCHIZOPHRENIC DISORDERS.
Tamburro G.A.; Brunetti N.A.; Di Sciascio G.; De Giglio F.
Cattedra di Psicologia Medica
Università di Bari (Italy)

In a sample of 50 doctors that have requested a psychiatric intervention, n. 16 cases, bearers of schizophrenic or schizoaffective disorders, have been singled out. It has been examined: the average age, the specialization, the professional activity and the seniority into the same. Furthermore it was studied the report between psychosis and medical practice, the eventual risk for patients, the quantity and the quality of psychiatric taking over.
The results of the study bear evidence of a patient/doctor who is unacknowledged and slighted in his needs, and of a therapist's emotional order that is problematical because of the importance of counter-transferal movements.

Session 239 Free Communications:
Antidepressants in clinical use II

1251

INTEREST OF AMINEPTINE (SURVECTOR 100MG) IN DEPRESSIVE ILLNESS THERAPY AND PREVENTION OF RELAPSES

M. FERRERI

Department of psychiatry and medical psychology (Pr J.M. ALBY) - Hôpital Saint-Antoine
75012 PARIS (FRANCE)

The efficiency of continuation therapy with antidepressants on prevention of relapses is now well established.

The aim of this double blind versus placebo study is to illustrate the very special benefit of amineptine in that indication and to corroborate its efficiency and long term (1 year) acceptability.

We divided our study in 2 stages :

- Stage 1 : open trial over 3 months (Amineptine 200mg) a day)

- Stage 2 : double blind versus placebo for patients cured.

460 depressed patients fulfilling DSM III criteria were included in stage I. This first phase confirmed the efficiency of amineptine : after 3 months, 81 % of good results were observed. This work pointed out the good clinical acceptability of amineptine and the low incidence of side effects with only 4.3 % of patients dropping out.

62 % of stage I patients were treated in stage II. The rate of relapses will be discussed in both groups and the amineptine efficiency and acceptability will be reassessed.

1552

A DOUBLE-BLIND STUDY OF TRAZODONE AND AMITRIPTYLINE IN THE TREATMENT OF MOOD DISORDERS.
BEYAZYÜREK MD, ARKONAÇ MD, VERİMLİ MD, TUNCEL MD, ERSÜL MD, KALYONCU MD, TOKER MD,
BAKIRKÖY STATE MENTAL HOSPITAL. ISTANBUL TURKEY

To compare the antidepressant and anxiolytic efficacy of Trazodone with that of a standart antidepressant Amitriptyline in patients suffering from moderately severe to severe depressive disorders with some anxiety a double-blind non-cross over study was performed. Efficacy was evaulated by using HAM-D and HAM-A scales in 53 patients (12 female and 41 male) age between 18 and 65yrs and fulfilling the DSM-III-R criteria for mood disorders. Patients with risk of coneption, psychotic, organic, substance use, seizure disorders, mental deficiency, ECT in the preceeding 6months, antidepressant medication within the previous 28 days, depression severe enough to warrant ECT were excluded. At the end of 4week trial no significant differences were evidenced as to the antidepressant and anxiolytic efficacies of both drugs at 300-600mg/day and 150-250mg/day doses for trazodone and amitriptyline respectively. The over all incidence of side effects was similar between groups. No side effect was considered to be signifi cantly interferring with the patient's daily acti vities and no case of priapism was seen. Overall the therapeutic efficacy in relation to the insidence of clinically significant side effects, favoured both drugs for the treatment of depressive disorders with some anxiety.

1553

ZWEI KLINISCH-EXPERIMENTELLE STUDIEN ZUR WIRKSAMKEIT UND VERTRÄGLICHKEIT VON TRAZODON
E. Klieser, E. Lehmann, H.L. Jüntgen
Psychiatrische Klinik d. Universität
D4000 Düsseldorf 12, Bergische Landstr. 2

An der Psychiatrischen Klinik der Heinrich Heine Universität Düsseldorf wurde unter strikten experi mentellen Bedingungen die Wirksamkeit und Verträglichkeit von Trazodon bei der Behandlung von vitalisierten Depressionen getestet.
In einer ersten Doppelblindstudie wurde die gute Wirksamkeit von Trazodon, das dem Vergleichspräparat Amitriptylin ebenbürtig war, an 60 ambulanten depressiven Patienten nachgewiesen. Der antidepressive Effekt von Trazodon wurde dann in einer weiteren Doppelblindstudie bei 45 stationären Patienten einer geschlossenen Aufnahmestation, die an sehr schweren Depressionen litten, im Vergleich zu Amitriptylin und Placebo bestätigt.
Auch wegen seiner in beiden Studien gezeigten ausgezeichneten Verträglichkeit, ist Trazodon eine wirkungsvolle Alternative zu den klassischen Trizyklika und sollte daher zu den Mitteln der 1. Wahl in der Depressionbehandlung gezählt werden.

1554

Efficacy and Safety of Fluoxetine vs. Clomipramine in the Treatment of Outpatients with Major Depression
G. Pakesch
Department of Psychiatry, University of Vienna, Austria

In order to evaluate the results of fluoxetine treatment in outpatients with major depressive disorder in terms of safety and efficacy, 15 general practicioners, psychiatrists and neurologists participated in this study. They were familiarized with the 14 items of the modified HAM-D Rating Scale and had the opportunity to practice rating by means of video tapes, so that inter-rater variability was verified to be insignificant before the beginning of the study and homogeneity in rating practice was guaranteed. The study was designed as a multicenter, randomised double-blind parallel study that compared 20 mg of fluoxetine, 40 mg of fluoxetine and 50 mg of clomipramine. A total of 139 patients participated in the study, 125 of whom completed the four-week study (five visits). 45 patients were treated with 20-mg doses of fluoxetine, 46 with 40-mg doses of fluoxetine and 48 with 50-mg doses of clomipramine.

Comparisons of overall efficacy ratings and the majority of the modified (14-item) Hamilton Psychiatric Rating scores indicated no statistically significant differences in the results of treatment. On day 14 of the study (visit 4), patients receiving 20 mg of fluoxetine and 40 mg of fluoxetine showed better global improvement than patients treated with 50 mg of clomipramine.
Treatment was well tolerated by all patients. Statistically significant differences in the frequency or severity of adverse events under fluoxetine or clomipramine therapy were not observed.

1555

Placebo-Controlled Trial of Venlafexine for the Treatment of Major Depression

E Schweizer, C Weise, C Clary, K Rickels - University of Pennsylvania, Philadelphia, USA.

Venlafexine is a novel antidepressant belonging to the phenethylamine class of compounds. It exhibits reuptake blockade of serotonin, norepinephrine, and dopamine, in descending order, but has no significant affinity for cholinergic, histaminergic or noradrenergic receptors. A previous pilot study by us suggested antidepressant efficacy in doses ranging from 75-450 mg. per day. We report here on the first double-blind placebo-controlled comparison of 3 fixed daily doses of Venlafexine in the treatment of major depression in outpatients with a HAM-D $\geq$ 20. Seventeen patients (base HAM-D = 24.9) were randomized to receive 6 weeks of active treatment on Venlafexine at the low dose (75 mg/day), 16 patients (base HAM-D = 26.0) at the intermediate dose (225 mg/day), 16 patients (base HAM-D = 25.4) at the high dose (375 mg/day), and 16 patients (base HAM-D = 24.4) received placebo. The mean age of the total sample was 46 years, with 58 % males. There were no significant between-group differences in any baseline demographic or clinical variables. By week 6, mean HAM-D total scores on available patients had **improved by 16.1 for the low dose group, by 15.3 for the intermediate dose group, by 19.3 for the high dose group, but only by 8.8 for the placebo group. Each active treatment group was significantly more improved than placebo ($p < .05$ for each dose). Parallel improvements were observed in other clinical measures. Overall the medication was well-tolerated, though less so at the high dose, where nausea was a prominent side effect (63 % of patients). Venlafexine appears to be a promising new medication with antidepressant effects across a wide dosage range.

1556
COMPARATIVE EFFICACY OF ORG 3770 AND AMITRIPTYLINE IN MAJOR DEPRESSION.
Prof. D. Petrovic, Institute of Mental Health, Belgrade, Yugoslavia.

Two hundred and fifty-one male and female patients with a diagnosis of major depression (DSM-III) were randomly assigned to double-blind oral treatment with amitriptyline (75-225 mg/day) or Org 3770 (20-60 mg/day) for 6 weeks. Efficacy was determined by use of the Hamilton Depression Rating Scale (HAMD) at baseline and every week during the trial. General psychopathology was assessed using the Brief Psychiatric Rating Scale and functioning by use of the Global Assessment Scale. Emergent symptoms were monitored weekly with a Record of Symptoms Emerging form. Laboratory parameters and vital signs were measured at baseline and every two weeks.
Equal improvement of depressive symptoms and degree of functioning was seen in both groups. There were no statistically significant differences between the two treatments. The side-effect profile of Org 3770 was very mild while the side-effects associated with amitriptyline (particularly dry mouth and sweating) were more troublesome. Neither compound produced severe adverse drug reactions nor adverse clinical laboratory experiences. The response rate (>50% reduction in HAMD baseline scores at end point) was approximately 70% in both groups.

1557
COMPARATIVE EFFICACY OF ORG 3770 AND CLOMIPRAMINE IN MAJOR DEPRESSION.
Prof. M. Patris, Strasbourg University Hospital, Strasbourg, France.

One hundred and seventy-four male and female patients with a diagnosis of major depression (DSM-III) were randomly assigned to double-blind oral treatment with clomipramine (50-200 mg/day) or Org 3770 (20-80 mg/day) for 6 weeks. Efficacy was determined by use of the Hamilton Depression Rating Scale and the Montgomery Asberg Depression Rating Scale at baseline and every 2 weeks. General psychopathology was assessed using the Brief Psychiatric Rating Scale and functioning by use of the Global Assessment Scale. Emergent symptoms were monitored weekly with a Record of Symptoms Emerging form. Laboratory parameters and vital signs were measured at baseline and every two weeks.
Equal improvement of depressive symptoms and degree of functioning was seen in both groups. There were no statistically significant differences between the two treatments. The side-effect profile of Org 3770 was qualitatively similar to that of clomipramine but the symptoms associated with Org 3770 were milder and less frequent while the side-effects of clomipramine (particularly tremor, dry mouth and sweating) were more troublesome. Neither compound produced severe adverse clinical laboratory experiences.

Session 240 Free Communications:
Psychoanalysis and the therapeutic relationship

1558
SUDDEN DEATH OF A THERAPIST: EFFECT ON A PATIENT
Irena C. Haughton, M.D.
Thomas Jefferson University Medical School, Philadelphia, PA USA

This paper is about the sudden death of a therapist by suicide; and the effect on one patient treated by a colleague and friend of the deceased. The paper particularly examines the effects of countertransference issues for the second therapist, and further discusses the expectation that this therapist will frequently serve as a transitional object for the patient, which can eventually be replaced.
Given the nature of the therapeutic relationship and its effect on the patient, the sudden death of a therapist has significant and potentially devastating pscyological consequences for this patient and raises important issues; ethical, practical and emotional for the profession and especially for the substitute therapist.

1559
PARENTIFICATION AND PATERNALISM.

J. Pols
P.C. "Licht en Kracht", Assen, The Netherlands.
F.M.H. Schenkelaars
P.C. "Coudewater", Rosmalen, The Netherlands.

Paternalism in the doctor-patient relationship is resembling the attitude of a parent towards his or her child in so far as the parent is intending to benefit independently of the child's consent.
The concept of parentification tends to clarify the phenomenon of a child enacting the role of a parent towards his or her parents in one or more important respects. In this way a caring, paternalistic attitude is being learned. If this attitude would be carried on in adult life, and if a career as a doctor or therapist would be chosen, this could lead to problems in professional functioning. The different ways in which this attitude could lead to manifest problems and dysfunctioning are described.

1560
IDENTIFICATION AND EMPATHY
Dr. Eugenio Cornide Cheda
Asociacion Argentina de Psiquiatras, Buenos Aires
Argentina

This piece of work deals with the identification and empathy by means of the existant relationship between both concepts. If both concepts are dealt with separately, it's possible to see in each of them, aspects of the other one. Through these individual processes it's possible to get to a more general process, in which we can experience somebody's self. During the growing process we go from the identification to the empathy. In this dynamic development it's possible by means of identification, to be in somebody else's place. Moreover, we can think about ourselves in somebody else's situation through introspection. During the therapy it is possible to realize the empathic activity where the process of identification is implicit. But whereas in the latter we can see only one aspect of the person, in the empathy we can observe a bigger number of identifications by means of an imaginative activity. This process is only possible when the own personality is definitely consolidated and it is possible to do away with the own partial identification. It's necessary to modulate the cathexis of the self image to be able to do is in the best possible way.

1261
"THE TRAGIC MOMENT AS ADVENT OF THE SUBJECT"
Pr Michel Patris, Dr Constantopoulos Michel
Clinique Psychiatrique - Centre Hospitalier
Universitaire - 1 place de l' Hopital -
67091 Strasbourg Cedex - France

Starting from a clinical case whose passage in our unit coincided with an essential life choise, we shall approach the "mourning's work" as a necessary stage in the individual's life.
This is what we proposed to call the Tragic moment of advent of the subject within the space liberated by withdrawl of a mythical discourse hitherto serving as and obligated reference.

1562
PSYCHOTHERAPY OF A SCHIZOPHRENIC IN EVROS

L.Liakopoulos,N. Stambolidou,P.Sakellaropoulos
Department of Psychiatry, Demokritos University of Thrace, Alexnadroupolis,Greece.

This study is about the psychotherapy of a 25 year old graduating University student and the psychotherapeutic approach that has been used by two psychiatrists.
The psychotherapy takes place in the State Mental Health Center of Alexandroupolis and is carried out by a couple of psycho-therapists once a week.
In this anouncement we shall describe the process of the case and the improvement of the patient . Special importance will be given to the part of the two psycho-therapists as regards the transference to them and the countertransference to the patient.

1563
DYNAMIC CONFLICTS, PERSONALITY AND DEFENSES IN PSYCHIATRIC PATIENTS.
V.K. VARMA, A. AVASTHI, ANJU SARUP & D.K. ARYA
Postgraduate Medical Institute, Chandigarh, [INDIA]

Research into the psychodynamics of well-being and ill-health present significant methodological problems and has suffered from lack of clear conceptualization and objective methods of assessment.

The present paper is a part of an on-going study, to study the psychodynamic conflicts (PC), Defense Mechanisms (DM) and personality types (PT) of mentally well and ill populations. The present paper pertains to 10 patients each of Anxiety Neurosis, Depressive Neurosis, Schizophrenia and Affective psychosis.

A standard format was evolved and tested for conducting psychodynamically oriented interviews. The methodology to study the personality variables was tested for reliability.

The results of the study reveal that the two study groups of neurosis and psychosis showed some differences in the personality variables. The defenses mostly present in the neurotic group were rationalization, hypochondriasis and reaction formation, while those in the psychotic group were acting out, splitting of others image and mood incongruent denial. The personality types commonly represented in the psychotics were schizoid, paranoid and avoidant while those in neurotics were dependent, passive-aggressive and masochistic.

The study also suggests some relationship between personality types, defense mechanisms and emotional conflicts.

1564

LA FORCE PERSPECTIVE
N.Nicolaidis, M.D., Université de Genève,Switzerl.

Le comment et le pourqoi de la transformation des premières perceptions-sensations(internes-externes) en représentant psychique de la pulsion demeurent la question de la psychan.à toute époque.Cela permet d'émettre l'hypothèse que pendant les lères relations mère enfant il y a un résidu d'excitation qui reste immétalisable par les premières repèsentations psychiques de la pulsion.Ce résidu(perceptions-sensations)se manifeste par une"force"perceptive, présente"physiologique ment"en début de vie,qui exerce une sorte d'aimantati réciproque dans la relation mère-enfant.Il s'agit pourait-ondire d'une rencontre quasi symétrique par contguité non encore métaphorisée.Nous pouvons émettre l'hypothèse que cette force naturelle perceptivo-sensorielle réapparait dans toute sa fraîcheur au cours de certains points culminants de vécu psychotique,c'est-dire pendant les mouvements où le sujet fonctionne dan le registre des défences les plus primaires(voire archaïques). L'expression psychopathologiquede ces défenses emploie le mécanisme que nous avons appelé imageant.Le méchanisme"imgeant"consiste au fait que ces manifestations se ressourcent par la partie la plu primaire de la représentation,la partie perceptive dont l' image est le premier élément:les premières figurations du bébé,celles du sein, al figuration oniriques, etc.   Imageant et perceptif est doncle méchanisme et non forcément le contenu, dans le sens que ce méchanisme,par sa force,s'impose et saisit le sujet.

Session 241 Free Communications:
Nosological issues in affective disorders

1565

SEASONAL AFFECTIVE DISORDERS.

G.F. FLORIS, G.L. FAEDDA, A. KOUKOPOULOS, L. TONDO
CENTRO LUCIO BINI, CAGLIARI ITALY
DEPT. OF PSYCHIATRY, HARVARD MEDICAL SCHOOL BELMONT U.S.A

1043 patients suffering of recurrent affective disorders that were treated as out patients at the Centro Lucio Bini of Cagliari were examined as regard the seasonality of their recurrences.
This population consisted of 557 unipolar depressives, 262 BP II, 129 BP I, 13 suffering of cyclothymia and 82 bipolar schizo-affective patients.
According to DSM-III-R diagnostic criteria 146 of them suffered of Seasonal Affective Disorder. 104 were women and 42 men. The age at onset was the same for both sexes, 29 years.
74 were UP, 43 were BP I and 29 BP II.
44 out of 72 bipolar patients and 33 out of 74 unipolar patients followed the seasonal pattern of mania-hypomania in spring-summer and depression in fall-winter, while 28 out of 72 bipolars and 41 out of 74 unipolars followed the pattern of mania-hypomania in fall-winter and depression in spring-summer.
The course of the disorder and the response to treatment were also studied.

1566

DRIVE(ANTRIEB) AND THE SEASONAL DISTRIBUTION OF PHASES IN ENDOGENOUS PSYCHOSIS
YOSHINORI HOSHINO & SHIN-ICHI HIRASAWA
Tokyo Women's Medical College, Tokyo, JAPAN

We investigated the seasonal distribution of phases in 101 endogenous psychotics(totally 599 phases). At first those phases were retrospectively and cross-sectionally diagnosed by means of RDC, and then respectively evaluated according to the variance in the drive(Antrieb). Total number of the patients having phases during each of the third part of a month(TNPP) were summed up. The results were as follows: The distribution of TNPP of Major Depressive Disorder showed the annual curve with the top in the last ten days of April, and the bottom in the middle and the last ten days of Septmber. The annual curve of Manic Disorder, on the contrary, had the top in the last ten days of October, and the bottom in the last ten days of April. The shape of the curve of Schizophrenia was similar to that of Manic Disorder with some differences. On the other hand, when all patients were reevaluated in view of drive change, the annual curves of TNPP were more smooth, and the reciprocal relationship between the increasing and the decreasing phases of the drive was more distinct than those of Major Depressive Disorder and Manic Disorder mentioned above. We thus suppose that the seasonal variation in endogenous psychosis would be based on the fluctuation of drive. In other words, the seasonal variation would be one of the circumstantial evidence for our hypothesis that the drive is the most fundamental element in endogenous psychosis.

1567

FREQUENCY OF SYMPTOMS IN DEPRESSIVE DISORDERS
Ozcan Koknel, Guler Bahadir
Dept. of Psychiatry, Istanbul Faculty of
Medicine, Istanbul, Turkey

In this study, the clinical picture and the frequency of symptoms in depressive disorders have been established by Beck Depression Inventory and Hamilton Depression Scale with reference to cases diagnosed within the frame work of DSM-III as bipolar, unipolar and dystimic depressions.
On the basis of the listed frequency of symptoms of depression obtained from Beck and Hamilton scales, we grouped the clinical symptoms as follows: physical, vegetative, affective, cognitive.
The physical and vegetative symptoms occur independently from the actual or probable etiological factors. They are free of the cultural, economic and social structure of the patient.
Affective symptoms are common symptoms of depressive disorders. Cognitive symptoms are considered as ego defence mechanisms against affective change, particularly anxiety. Affective and cognitive symptoms depend on the cultural, economic and social structure of the patient.

1568
DEPRESSION AS AN AGENT IN NATURAL SELECTION

Dr Geoffrey Wallis
Fulford Grange Hospital   Leeds   England

Hibernation has much in common with retardation and agarophobia in human depression and makes a patient "stay put" when moving or otherwise changing the environment would be disadvantageous.

Migration similarly has properties akin to agitation and encourages an agitatedly depressed human to change his or her circumstances.

Depression caused by personal failure owing to defect or weakness may act to the benefit of the group by removing that member from the group.

Low self-esteem in depression could help an organism to adjust to reduced status in an hierarchy.

After the loss of a mate depressive searching behaviour and reduced libido tend to preserve the pair bond if the missing partner has actually survived.

Premenstrual depression, often occurring as a sequel to coitus at the best time for conception and perhaps representing "after the party blues" could prevent dislodgement of the embryo by more coitus.

These theories, although speculative and apparently untestable, draw attention to the depressive way of life and may have an important bearing on treatment.

1569
PATTERNS OF MANIC DEPRESSIVE CYCLE TEN YEARS LATER

KOUKOPOULOS A., REGINALDI D., TUNDO A., FLORIS G., MINNAI G. and TONDO L.
CENTRO LUCIO BINI 4, V. CRESCENZIO 00193 ROME ITALY

In 1979 the course of 434 bipolar patients (256 woman, 178 men) was studied longitudinally. The prevailing patterns of the manic depressive cycles at the end of the observation time were: mania followed by depression (MDI) 28%; depression followed by mania (DMI) (usually hypomania), 25% and continuous circular course, with long cycles, 19%, or with short (rapid) cycles, 20%. The cycles followed an irregular pattern in 8% of the patients.
As the intensity of the episodes, 52% of the patients had severe depressions and hypomanias; 26% had severe manias and mild depressions and 22% had severe depressions and severe manias. No significant sex difference was found regarding the patterns of the cycles or the intensity of the episodes except among the rapid cyclers, where women (61) outnumbered men (26). Ten years later the course of the disease, the sequence of the manic depressive phases and the intensity of the episodes in the same patients were examined again and were comapred with the previous course.

1570
DIFERENCIAS SOCIODEMOGRAFICAS ENTRE DEPRESIONES NEUROTICAS Y PSICOTICAS.(SOCIODEMOGRAFIC DIFERENCES BETWEEN NEUROTIC AND PSYCHOTIC DEPRESSIONS).
ALVAREZ LOBATO,P(**), MEGIA LOPEZ,P(**),MARTINEZ RODRIGUEZ,J.(*), LUCAS MANGAS,S.(*) y LEAL HERRERO,F.(**). (*) Servicio de Salud Mental de la Junta de Castilla y León, Valladolid; (**) H. Psiquiátrico "Dr. Villacián", Valladolid. España.

En este estudio se analizan las diferencias sociodemográficas y asistenciales existentes entre depresiones psicóticas y neuróticas de 1185 pacientes depresivos en 24 Servicios Asistenciales de la Comunidad Autónoma de Castilla y León, durante el año 1986. En el conjunto de las depresiones, un 71,1% son depresiones neuróticas. Los pacientes son atendidos en Centros de Salud Mental o Consultas Ambulatorias, en el 73,8% de los casos. Se observa una asociación significativa entre el diagnóstico y el sexo (p 0,13). Predomina el mejor nivel de instrucción en las depresiones psicóticas (p 0,01), de las cuales un 43% recibe una pensión pública; un 32,9% de los depresivos neuróticos trabajan (p 0,05), frente a un 44,5 de depresivos neuróticos que nunca han trabajado. Se observa que el 21% de los depresivos psicóticos tienen familiares con la misma patología y el 61,3% de los depresivos neuróticos carece de antecedentes familiares (p 0,59).
La brevedad del espacio obliga a omitir otros datos de interés.

1571
SPECIFITY AND TYPIFICATION OF PRECIPITATED FACTORS IN DEPRESSIVE SYNDROME
Diez A., Civeira J., Sanchez L, Martin M.
Psychiatry Department Complutense of Madrid, Spain

We present a new concept: "Depressive situation". It is a precipitating factor of depressive disorders. We point out the difference between "depressive situation" and "life events". There are four types of situations, each one of these have different operative mechanisms and the relationship with the semiological tetradimensional structure of depressive syndrome is also different.
We confirmed the specifity and the typification of these situations in a study of 178 patients, 99 inpatients and 79 outpatients, in San Carlos Hospital of Madrid. The samples are composed of 67 "cases" and 111 "controls". A depressive case is defined by the scoring in "TEQ-DE" (Alonso-Fernandez, 1986).
A "Situational Questionnaire", which has been elaborated by us, was applied. We identified 27 situations whose results were discriminatory between "cases" and "controls" in frequency and severity, with the statistic contrast "x^2" and "T-student".

Session 242 Free Communications:
Psychotherapies for children, adolescents and their families

1572
COMPLIANCE IN PSYCHOTHERAPY OF CHILDREN AND JUVENILES
G.Gerber, W.Leixnering. T.Reinelt
Interfakultares Institut fur Sonder-und Heilpadagogik der Universitat Wien und Univ.Klinik fur Neuropsychiatrie des Kindes-u.Jugendalters Wien, Austria

We tried to pursue the questions of what variables were important for accepting or neglecting an offer to the patients for psychotherapy at our hospital. 1. Some of the intra-personal variables we tried to interprete hermeneutically as there were those of:Pressure of suffering and ability of suffering. These were reflected in its ontogenesis and their meaning for the initial contact with the therapist and the further compliance of the patient-therapist relationship. 2. Other variables could be pursued empirically for this study of a group of patients to which was offered a psychotherapy within one year after their initial contact to the hospital(106 children and juveniles-62 males,40 females).Some of the results were: No statistic significant influence on the acceptance or refuse of the offer for therapy showed the variables of sex or age of the patients,the distance from the living area to the hospital,the employance of the mother,the qualifications of the father in his job, or psychiatric diseases of relatives.Statistically significant influence on the other hand showed the variables of the time to wait for a therapy to begin, a therapy with drugs and also the necessity of a depth-psychologically orientated single-therapy.

1573
A CRITERION OF FAMILY APPROACH IN DRUG-RESISTANT EPILEPSY
M.G.Atza-Infant Neuropsychiatrist at the children's epilepsy
Center of U.S.S.L., 75/1-Milano, Italy

When epilepsy is diagnosed to be drug-resistant, a change in therapeutic approach is necessarily required.To the specialist,this means that he has to help the patient and his/her family to coexist with the disease trying to restore the equilibrium the illness caused them to lose. Under these circumstances the referral on a large scale to family therapy isn't applicable. The kind of support referred to above must be therefore "administered"without delay,generally soon after the onset of the seizures,when the family is anxious to talk about the event and to receive instructions. First of all,one has to identify rapidly the member of the family who could best play the role of the interlocutor.According to the General Theory of the system there are three interacting sub-systems,namely: Operator Subsystem (concerned with management of the disease); Controller Subsystem(responsible for attainment of family's goals); Regulator Subsystem (concerned with establishment of behaviour rules) The specialists should compare the reality of the family,which he should approach,with the general pattern previously described,recognizing the member belonging to Regulator Subsystem and helping to establish new rules of family life.

1574
FAMILY SYSTEM THERAPY IN GILLES DE LA TOURETTE SYNDROME.
M. Paci, M.G. Petroni
Istituto per l'Infanzia, Trieste, Italy.

Despite disagreement in literature on the etiopathology and proper nosographic collocation of the G.d.T. Syndrome, authors concord on the severity of the illness from a prognostic viewpoint, due to its' psychopathological and social implications. Various therapeutic approaches have been proposed.
The Authors report 3 cases followed respectively for 7, 5 and 4 years after recovery through Family System Therapy. They discuss the usefulness of this approach in breaking the vicious circle of symptom priming within the family and social environment.

1575
PSYCHIATRIC CARE FOR IMMIGRANT IRANIAN ADOLESCENTS
Shahrzad F.Siassi Ph.D., Private Practice, L.A., CA, USA and Iradj Siassi M.D., Prof. of Psychiatry, U.C.L.A. Med. Sch., L.A., CA, USA

An estimated one million Iranians have found their way to U.S. since the 1979 Iranian revolution. The transition from a tradition rich and stable society to an amorphous, sex, violence and drug oriented environment has had its most adverse effects on the adolescents in this population. The incongnuity between their parental values and those of host peer culture severely interferes with the consolidation of inner standards - a major task of adolescence. Primary prevention of serious psychological disorganization and drug and alcohol abuse in many of these adolescents, can often be achieved by minimal help from culturally sensitive therapists who can appreciate relevant stressors in various stages of these adolescents' life cycle. Secondary prevention requires accurate differential diagnosis between major psychiatric disorders and the aforementioned adjustment struggles. This paper will focus on the pertinent issues of ethnically based differential diagnosis, and with the aid of several case histories it will show the critical importance for the therapist to ally himself with and reinforce the values and standards of the original culture. The paper will also discuss why psychodynamic psychotherapy is the treatment of choice for the majority of these patients.

1576
PSYCHOANALYTIC THERAPY OF CHILDREN WITH SOCIAL BEHAVIOUR DISORDERS.
KOUROS J, SIDIROPOULOU TR, CHRONOPOULOU J.
SOCIETY FOR PSYCHOLOGICAL PSYCHIATRY OF ADULT&CHILD (E.PS.PS.E.P) ATHENS-GREECE.

We are describing here our experience from psychoanalytic psychotherapy of children with social behaviour disorders and our method: 1. In the beginning their feelings about their father were absolutely negative(desire of death), so for several months we have been very "maternal"(love,concern,forgiveness) and progressively we became "paternal"(rules,limits, punishments) but we were all the time giving friendly exrlanations and keeping the role of an adult facing a child(Empathy). 2. The activities, during the meetings, were chosen always by the children(painting talk,toys). The therapy's room was simly decorated so as not to be obliged to stop destructive activities. 3. All parents were seen every week or month by another therapist to discus arising problems, during the period of their child's therapy(2-4 years)and we were informed this way about disappearance of symtoms. 4. The therapeutic "double-bind" had to be very well organised, because both parents and children tried often to put the therapists in a "scapegoat"position and interrupt the therapy. We present especially one case of a child with the diagnosis of "border-line" because of his very well done paintings wich demonstrate clearly the evolution of his feelings, his superior I.Q., the defensive mechanisms of "self"and how they"arise" when someone has to solve his problems and finally how Emmanuel"left" the world of creatures of outer-space(his fantaisies)to live as a normal person the"routine" of every day's life!

1577
HOMICIDIAL BEHOVIOUR, IN ADOLESCENTS

IGLESIAS L, TAPIA E., AGUILAR R.
UNIDAD DE PSIQUIATRIA, CONSEJO TUTELAR PARA MENORES
MONTERREY, N.L., MEXICO

Se presentan los resultados de un estudio clínico y psicosocial de cáracter descriptivo y retrospectivo de una muestra de 33 adolescentes homicidas, detenidos por el Consejo Tutelar para Menores en Nuevo León, México de 1986-88; que fueron sujetos a evaluación psiquiátrica y psicosocial. En los hallazgos obtenidos es notable la baja frecuencia de antecedentes de trastornos del desarrollo psicomotor, contrastando con altos índices de trastornos escolares. En el perfil de personalidad sobresalen rasgos estructurales y dinámicos que afectan la orientación en la realidad, la tolerancia a la frustación, control impulsivo y la adaptación sociopersonal. El estudio familiar muestra grupos prolíficos, nucleares, estructurados, con indicadores de hacinamiento y promiscuidad y conflictos graves de autoridad, dirección e integración. En la valoración psiquiátrica destaca el bajo índice de trastornos de las funciones corticales con trastornos de la esfera afectiva, juicio y funciones sociales. El análisis de la conducta homicida mostró una estrecha relación entre condiciones ambientales que favorecen la dilución del control social de la agresión y estados físicos y emotivos alteradores de la conciencia. Los resultados obtenidos intentan contribuir en la construcción de modelos de atención de adolescentes con graves deficiencias en el control de la agresión.

1578
Termination in Psychotherapy: Reactions in a child, an adolescent and an adult.
Ana L. G. Maciel, M.D.
The Johns Hopkins University

The author describes and discusses fully the termination phase of the dynamic psychotherapy of three patients of different age groups. This termination of treatment was due to a study trip of the therapist. A short-term follow-up of the child and of the adolescent that continued psychotherapy with another therapist is given.

There is an association in these cases between the clinical and dynamic diagnoses, the life history and the clinical material of the sessions, which are thoroughly exemplified and discussed. The author also discusses larger possible applications of the findings to other settings.

Session 243 Free Communications:
Diagnostic complexities

1579
DIAGNOSTIC COMPLEXITIES: FROM STIGMATA TO MUENCHAUSEN SYNDROME
NICHOLAS DUNKAS M.D., F.A.P.A.
NORTHWESTERN UNIV. MED. SCHOOL CHICAGO IL. U.S.A.

This paper refers to the limitations of currently available official diagnostic classification systems in terms of meaningfully correlating deviant human behaviours with relevant cognitive, affective and psychophysiologic-somatic phenomena and manifestations, their psychodynamic origins, predispositions and other involved biological and sociocultural factors. It emphasizes the need of the clnician to conceptualize the individual characteristics to each patient and his illness, rather than thinking strickly in terms of fitting the patient to specific "fixed" diagnostic categories. The so called Muechausen syndrome along with other "unusual" "exotic" or "atypical" psychiatric disorders are presented as cases in point. The various other proposed names for the Muenchausen syndrome such as " hospital hoboism" and the more currently in use "chronic factitious disorder" likewise lack objectivity and add to the confusion. Two cases both with aspects of "peripatetic illness" are sited. The first is a case of stigmata: spontaneous episodic bleeding from the eyes and ears in a hysterical personality documented by impressive photographic slides. The second, a case of apparently suicidal behaviour, resulting in self inflicted mutilation of the neck and trachea, under conditions of dissociation in a paranoid personality.

1580

HYPOCHONDRIASIS REVISITED : PERCEPTUAL INFORMATION PROCESSING IN HYPOCHONDRIACS, NORMAL CONTROLS, PAINFUL AND PAINLESS PATIENTS.

P. Janne, A. Collin, M. Vause, C. Reynaert, J. Costermans, L. Cassiers
University of Louvain, B-5180 Yvoir, Belgium

It remains unclear wether hypochondriasis and somatoform disorders are resulting from a cognitive mislabeling of truly existing perceptual dysfunctions or, on the contrary, from psychic convictions only. Signal Detection Theory (S.D.T.) provides information on both sensory and attitudinal dimensions of perceptual processes. Such an approach is of value to understand the basic mechanisms underlying somatoform disorders, and more specifically the decision processes leading to such an "overcomplaining" behaviour in hypochondriac patients. We included 10 patients meeting hypochondriasis criteria according to the DSM III (300.70) as well as having high scores at the M.M.P.I. Hypochondriasis subscale. 10 matched controls, 10 patients having painful (angina) myocardial ischemia and 10 patients having painless myocardial ischemia were also included in the SDT study. The SDT tasks are performed by the subjects on a personal-computer by means of a self-rating scale decision procedure. Both electrical and visual stimulations are randomly submitted to the subject by means of a software giving a complete and automated analysis of the subject's perceptual abilities and decision strategies.

The results pinpoint a general overcomplaining behaviour in hypochondriacs as well as a higher rate of false positive answers. These findings are not present in normal controls and coronary patients. On the contrary, painless (silent) myocardial ischemia is characterized by a general undercomplaining behaviour pattern. Perceptual information processing thus appears to be a powerful tool for the psychiatrist attempting to differenciate between hypochondriac, normal, painful and painless illness behaviours.

1281

OCULAR MUNCHHAUSEN'S SYNDROME

Wolfgang P. Kaschka and Peter Joraschky, Department of Psychiatry, University of Erlangen-Nuremberg, Schwabachanlage 6, D-8520 Erlangen, Fed. Rep. of Germany

Patients with Munchhausen's syndrome do not represent a homogenous nosologic entity, but confront us with a variety of differential diagnostic and therapeutic difficulties. Typical personality traits of a patient with ocular Munchhausen's syndrome will be demonstrated in a case report. A 26-year-old female medical student had furtively induced disturbances of wound-healing after a knee-joint operation A few years later, she injured her left eye deliberately, which led to corneal ulceration and transplantation. After that she destroyed the transplant, and enucleation of the left eye became inevitable. Psychiatric advice was first sought, when she had injured the cornea of her right eye and the necessity of another corneal transplantation was evident. We discuss the typical mimicry phenomenon, the perfect deception tactics, which appear to possess unconscious significance and represent a phenomenon of interaction. Finally, we report on aspects we have dealt with during six months of psycho-analytic therapy.

1582

A STUDY OF "HALLUCINATION PSYCHOMOTORICE VERBALE" (J. SÉGLAS)

Y. Kogita, E. Saito, S. Abe, Y. Mukouse, I. Kanamori, T. Ban, H. Suzuki and T. Mita, Iwate Medical University, Morioka, Japan.

"Hallucination psychomotorice verbale" denoted by J. Séglas is the motor hallucination deriving from vocal organs.
 We investigated the relationship between this and other symptoms in four cases: disturbance of self-awareness, monologue and other types of hallucination.
 All cases showed depersonalization, experience of influence, broadcasting of thought and thought resonance as disturbance of self-awareness. The vocal organs involved in Séglas' symptom were larynx and lips. Monologue was observed subjectively in all cases.
 We discuss "hallucination psychomotorice verbale" from the viewpoint of "Strukturanalyse".

1583

ORIGIN AND ESSENCE OF THE HALLUCINATION

M. Milev, Department of Psychiatry, Sofia, Bulgaria

In the course of many years the author is writing on some problems of the verbal hallucination. He studies their origin, essence and psychopathology. It is confirmed that in their story there can be found all schizophrenic disturbances of thinking and others. A special place is devoted to their provocation, as well as to the translating of common thoughts into hallucination and the reverse. The important role of the attention for the genesis and the extra projection of hallucinator's imaginations is well motivated. New phenomena are described: "dublicating hallucinations", "echo of the picture", "functional optic hallucinations".

1584

NEITHER NEUROSIS NOR PSYCHOSIS
Venga E., Clinical Neuropsichiatrica,Napoli,Italy

As far as our research is concerned we aim at investigating the meaning of both neurotic and psychotic functions of a neural organization. For this purpose we have assumed to be absurd the dicotomy between neurosis and psychosis as our research regards the structural organization and not the representation of the function itself. Eventhough we maintain that the above mentioned dicotomy has no reason to exist, we have to admit how widely it has conditioned us in the process of identification and classification of those symptoms which need even more to be placed sometimes within the neurotic sphere and sometimes within the psychotic one. We do not know the precise meaning of both terms neurosis and psychosis.Anyway we are accustomed to considering a symptom to be neurotic or psychotic only according to a diagnostic differentiation which,in the most of cases,is provided by parameters which make te skilful operator doubtful as far as the psychic representation is concerned.
There can be no doubt at all in maintaining that both neurosis and psychosis have no reason to exist as they have been pointed out because of a functional interpretation exclusively. In this prospect there can be no neural differentiation because only later it will be possible to determine a neuropsychotic representation in those terms we have commonly meant it. Accordingly those functions which will
  allow us to determine the neural-organization, must not be considered according to neurotic or psychotic terms because that is a pure matter of energy-neuroenergy.

1585

PSYCHOSIS AS COMPULSIVE SELF-KNOWLEDGE
AND COMPULSIVE GIFT
Dr Timen Borilov Timev
Psychiatric Hospital, Karloukovo, Bulgaria

Classical psychiatry defended society from the attacks of the individual. It termed illness everything in which the individual was superior to society. Modern psychiatry defends the individual from the attacks of society. It terms illness everything in which society is superior to the individual. In classical psychiatry doctors treat society from the traumas which the individual inflicts upon it. Modern psychiatry treats the individual for the traumas which society inflicts upon him: the imperative to be logical the major policemen of which are the Language, the Logic and Morality. The traumas which the individual inflicts upon society are: paralogic as a logical rebellion against logic parathmia as an emotional rebellion against obligatory euthymia, paraboulia as a volitional rebellion against behaviour, megal manis as a restoration of the truth about humans being godlike and having omnipotent brains, etc. As paralogic, psychosis is compulsive poetry. As paraphrenia, psychosis is compulsive metaphysics and compulsive theology. As schizophasia, the psychosis is actualizing of the omniintersignum in Corpus Callosum. The psychosis as derealization and disruption of the sensory synthesis actualizes the subject of quantum mechanics. Psychosis is the return of the brain crust to the brain centre, the return of Cortex Cerebri to Corpus Callosum, from a monosemanticism of consciousness towards omnisemanticism of the unconscious. Psychosis is logic's fear of the illogical, the planetary's fear of the cosmic, the psychosis as the obligatory distance between paradigms, as an obligatory chasm of unknowableness which accompanies the replacement of one paradigm by another.

1586

Aspectos psicopatológicos y terapéuticos de las Psicosis Reactivas.

Psychopathological and Therapeutic Aspects of Reactive Psychoses

Bello, Marco Antonio
Puente, Maria Clemencia
Navarro, Cecilia

Instituto de Psiquiatría. Universidad Austral. Chile, Clinica de Psiquiatría. Universidad Marburg, R.F.A.

Introducción: Estudio de 23 casos de Psicosis reactiva o psicógena, correspondiente al Código 298.de la C.I.E. de la O.MS. que fueron tratados en el Hospital de Valdivia, Chile. Estudio abarca 3 años
Método: fenomenológico-hermenéutico.
Resultados: Entre los datos generales destaca promedio de edad de 38 años, predominio de mujeres (74%) sobre hombres (26%) y baja escolaridad. En lo psicopatológico se encontró: alteración de conciencia en el 91%. Alucinaciones en el 57%. Delirio en el 52% y alteraciones conductuales severas en el 48%.
Conclusiones: Se corrobora la importancia del diagnóstico de Psicosis reactiva con un perfil determinado dentro de las Psicosis. Se entregan nuevos elementos en cuanto a la presentación clinica y terapia de estos cuadros.

Session 244 Poster Presentation:
Schizophrenia II

1587

Outcome of positive and negative schizophrenic symptoms: relationship with cerebral ventricular size.
Boato P., Vita A., Cazzullo C.L.
Institute of Psychiatry, Milan University-Ospedale Maggiore Policlinico

In recent years, the positive-negative distinction of schizophrenic symptoms has stimulated new hypotheses on the etiopathogenesis of schizophrenia.To validate such distinction,long-term follow-up studies that allow to evaluate the symptoms outcome over time, their response to pharmacological treatment and factors associated to such response,are requested. We have analyzed the clinical outcome on a 1 year follow-up of 18 outpatients(10 M, 8 F, mean age 30.5$\pm$11.6 years) diagnosed as schizophrenic according to the DSM IIIR criteria(9 disorganized,5 paranoid,4 undifferentiated)and treted with long-acting neuroleptic drugs.All patients had CTscan of the brain and the ventricular-brain-ratio(VBR) was calculated.The percentage of patients who shared significantly improvement were:hallucinations 60%, delusions 50%, bizarre behaviour 54,5%, formal thought disorder 50%, affective flattening 16,7%, alogia 28,6%, apathy 29,4%, anhedonia 11,8%. Ventricular size predicted outcome of the symptoms: delusions (patients with improvement:3.9$\pm$2.4 vs 7.57$\pm$4.9,t= 1.75, p .05), positive formal thought disorder(improved 3$\pm$2.2 vs 7.35$\pm$4.5, t=1.95, p .05).

1588
STUDY OF POSITIVE SYMPTOM AND NEGATIVE SYMPTOM SCHIZOPHRENIA

Dr.R.L.Narang & Dr. Satish Verma M.D.
Dayanand Medical College & Hospital,
Ludhiana Punjab, India

This being one of the most recent and throbing areas and there are only a few studies, especially in Indian set up, depicting the difference on various socio-demographic and clinical variables. The present work was intended to explore the evaluation of Negative & Positive Symptoms in relation to an exhaustive list of variables like - age, sex and duration of illness, marital adjustment, type of family and community, religious activity, number of episodes in past, number of hospitalisations in past, occurence of life events, neuroleptic treatment, family history of psychiatric illness, associated drug abuse, suicidal attempts, Rees Eysenck body index, androgyny score, subtypes based on present period of illness etc.
60 Schizophrenics were studied. The negative & positive schizophrenias differed on variables like age, education, premorbid adjustment, Rees Eysenck body index, subtypes based on present period of illness as per Research Diagnostic Criteria. Though the distinction between negative and positive subtypes of schizophrenia phenomenogically is well documented in the literature it is difficult to differentiate the two subtypes of schizophrenia on many of the sociodemographic and clinical variables except the above.

1589
PRIMITIVE REFLEXES IN SCIZOPHRENIA

H.R. CHAUDHRY,M.D; M.S.KESHAVAN, M.D.;
JASPREET BRAR,M.D.; A.BASHIR, M.D.;
M.R. CHAUDHRY, M.D.

FOUNTAIN HOUSE LAHORE-PAKISTAN

WESTERN PSYCHIATRIC INSTITUTE
PITTSBURGH, P.A. U.S.A.

Primitive reflexes include Grasp,Palmomental, Snout, Corneomandibular and Glabellar reflexes. Primitive reflexes have been reported to occur more frequently in Schizophrenics as compared to normal Subjects.
In the present study Primitive Reflexes were examined in Schizophrenics (100 Schizophrenics were on Neuroleptic Medications and remaining 30 were free of Neuroleptic Medication).
The severity of psychosis was rated by the Brief Psychiatric Rating Scale. The Negative symptoms were rated using the Wing Negative Symptom Scale. Cognitive function was assessed by the Minimental State Exam.
In this presentation results of the study will be discussed.

1590
RED SOCIAL Y APOYO SOCIAL COMO PREDICTORES DE EVOLUCION EN ESQUIZOFRENIA:
A. Moríñigo, J. Martin, D. Noval, I. Mateo, A. Vázquez.
S. Psiquiatría. Hosp. Universitario Valme. Sevilla. España.

Diversos factores clínicos, psicológicos y biológicos han sido tenidos en cuenta como factores pronósticos de las esquizofrenias. Ultimamente la investigación familiar, los factores emocionales y acontecimientos vitales, y la Red Social (RS) y Apoyo Social (AS), ha adquirido una gran relevancia.
Cuarenta pacientes con diagnóstico de esquizofrenia, según los RDC (Spitzer, 1977), son investigados con la MISU (Veiel, 1987) para objetivar la RS/AS, y evaluados clínica y psicopatológicamente con la BPRS (Overall, 1962), al final de una estancia hospitalaria breve, motivada por sintomatología productiva de primer rango y/o graves trastornos de conducta. Se estudia además la EE familiar con la Entrevista Familiar de Camberwell abreviada (Vaughn y Leff, 1976).
La muestra recogida será reevaluada a los 3, 6 y 12 meses, con los mismos instrumentos.
En los pacientes estudiados se comprueba la hipótesis de la existencia de una RS de pequeño tamaño, restringiéndose las funciones de apoyo al medio familiar. Se señala la hipótesis de que cuánto más reducida es la RS mayor es el riesgo de hospitalización.

1591
PERICOLLICULAR MYELINOLYSIS AND SCHIZOPHRENIA WITH "KLEINIAN" SYMPTOMS

Midori Endo, M.D.
Department of Neuropsychiatry, Shimane Medical University, Izumo, Japan

A small MRI anomaly was detected in central brainstem of a young schizophrenic girl with typical paranoid onset and cannibalistic visual hallucinations concerning the mother's breast. This 20 yearold patient had experienced an episode of dehydration at 4 months after birth because her mother had withdrawn her milk to stop diarrhea. She developed almost normally after the accident until 12y of age except for somewhat delayed initial gait. Then she began to have delusions of reference, thought broadcasting and auditory hallucinations. Ambivalent thought insertion, delusions of poisoning and Capgras syndrome followed a few years later. Bloody, aggressive visual hallucinations mentioned above then took place gradually and persisted as the almost only residual symptom after medication. The main theme was cutting up her mother's breast and sometimes eating it in "sashimi". Her attitude was infantile; her verbal IQ was 74 and performance IQ was too low to be scaled at 19y of age. MRI examination revealed T_2 enhancement in mesencephalic tegmentum around corpora quadrigemina. It suggested central brain-stem myelinolysis possibly caused by some electrolyte imbalance. The relationship between this lesion and her mental symptoms which remind us of Melanie Klein's theory will be discussed.

1592

PROBLEMS AND POSSIBILITIES OF CHRONIC
SCHIZOPHRENIC'S REHABILITATION
Judit Farkas, Teaching-hospital Jahn Ferenc,
Budapest, Hungary

61 chronic schizophrenic patients were treated in our general psychiatric department during the period between 1984-1988. As one of our basic functions was planned to admit chronic psychotic patients too and to try to rehabilitate them, so an integrated day hospital was organized. The patients investigated now lost their working ability, got disability pension, usually were hospitalized for many years (3-17) before coming to us. The therapeutic strategy was complex: psychopharmaca, long-acting deriv., therapeutic community, non-verbal therapies, occupational therapy, psychotherapies, extrahospital programs, etc. During 5 years from 61 patients 18 are working now, 16 go to day hospital, 18 can live at home active, in 10 cases the rehabilitative efforts were unsuccessfull. There were taken different factors into account from the point of view of the difficulties in the rehabilitation as the social background, the life and oppositions in the family, etc. The patients' common psychic symptoms originated from their previous long hospitalization and illness career are discussed.

1593

WORKING DISABILITY IN SCHIZOPHRENIA:
A FIVE YEAR FOLLOW UP STUDY
Antti Pakaslahti
Research Institute for Social Security
Social Insurance Institution
Helsinki, Finland

Subjects comprise schizophrenic patients (DSM-III-R) in a cohort of all consecutive first life-time admissions to the psychiatric hospitals of Helsinki (N=297) during one calendar year (1981). At the time of the index hospitalization patients were interviewed with the PSE, psycho-social and past history data was obtained.

Data on the outcome was collected during a follow-up period of 5 years (1982-86) from several sources: working disability data from the National Health Insurance Institution, causes of death from the National Mortality Statistics, and psychiatric data from the psychiatric hospitals and mental health centers of Helsinki.

Results showed that about 25% of the schizophrenics became permanently disabled already at the index hospitalization. The rest showed a variable outcome: 25% were disabled for less than 6 months, 15% for 2-4 years and 35% for intermediate periods. The results and risk factors of working disability are discussed.

1594

THE PROGNOSIS OF SCHIZOPHRENIA:RESEARCH
AND CLINICAL PRACTICE INSSUES
Alexandrescu LC, Predescu I, Predescu O,
Sima D, Opprescu I, Predescu V.
Institute of Neurology and Psychiatry -
Bucharest,Romania

After concluding a retrospective study of the medical records of 350 patients with various forms of schizophrenia, the authors amphasize the fact that most of the assessed clinical therapeutical, and psychological variables had no univocally good or poor prognosis signifiance.
Function of other patients characteristics one and the same prognostic indicator can point toward a favorable outcome in one case, be indifferent in another, or spell failure in a third one. Moreover the prognosis as a single general cathegory reflects insufficiently the differential post-morbid adaptation (or beck of it) selectivelly realized by the patient in a distinct areas of his or her life. The statistical approach of prognosis studies should perforce be a very complex one. Even thus, there would remain many patients whose outcome can be understood or even predicted on holistic, descriptive individual terms, although statistically their prognosis can not be determined with the present assessing instruments, or in the opposite of the real one.

1595

PROCESS SCHIZOPHRENIA: OUTCOME.
ESQUIZOFRENIA PROCESAL: PRONOSTICO.
Villasana Cunchillos,A(*);Recondo Garcia,M(•);
Rubio Larrosa,V.(*); Bousoño Garcia,M.(*);
Bobes Garcia,J.(*).
(•)Ph D; (*) M.D. Associated Prof. Psychiatry.
E.U.E.Universidad del País Vasco. España.

Durante un periodo de doce meses ,679 pacientes fueron diagnosticados de esquizofrenia nuclear e internados , al menos por 24 h. en los Servicios psiquiatricos de Bizcaia (1.200.000 hab.). Siendo distribuidos en dos grupos: A) grupo experimental (GE) 244 pacientes cuyo ingreso fuera superior a tres años. B) grupo control (GC). 129 pacientes con estancias inferiores a 180 días.
Métodos :Se realizó una comparación de las frecuencias que presentaba cada uno de los grupos en cada variable, mediante X^2 y CC de Pawlick, detectándose un total de 20 variables estadísticamente significativas; algunas de ellas intrínsecas al proceso esquizofrenico y otras extrínsecas a él. Con objeto de clarificar sus posibles interrelaciones se procedió a un análisis factorial de correspondencias múltiples .
Resultados dichas variables no conforman un sistema unitario, sino que comprenden tres subsistemas interrelacionados: a) subsistema socio-demográfico b) subsistema de variables clínicas c) subsistema de variables inherentes a la red psiquiátrica asistencial.

1596

THE COURSE OF SCHIZOPHRENIA: THE EXPERIENCE OF A COMMUNITY MENTAL HEALTH CENTER
Biancosino B., Masina L., Merini A.
Department of Psychiatry - University of Bologna
Italy

The authors investigated the total schizophrenic patients of a Community Mental Health Center in Bologna (Department of Psychiatry - University of Bologna Italy) in 1979-1980.
These patients have been followed up until 1988. Clinical, social and behavioural parameters were evaluated and the results are presented.

1597

RELAPSES IN A GROUP OF PSYCHOTIC PATIENTS DURING REHABILITATION (PILOT STUDY)
V. Alexandris, D. Petridou, P. Sakellaropoulos
Society of Social Psychiatry & Mental Health

In this study we analyze the quantity & quality data refering to the relapses which have been observed in a group of psychotic patients during a project of social & vocational rehabilitation. The study concerns 17 patients-members of a Foyer in a rural area for the years 87-88. The variables which have been used refer to demographic data, to the characteristics of the illness & to elements of: a) psychiatric care (number of therapists, individual sessions, medication) b) relapses (number, duration, date, causes, medication & hospitalization) c) subjective & clinical symptoms during the relapses (B.P.R.S.) d) causative factors (from the patients & their families sessions) & e) the period of social & family readaptation. The following points will be discussed: Relation of the relapses with the confrontation (in & out-patient care, increase of therapeutic hours, of supervisions & of medication) Relation of the relapses with the causative factors (for the patient himself, the socialization-rehabilitation & interruption of the medication). Relation of the clinical data of the relapses with the causative factors. The drawn conclusion is: the number, the duration, the frequency, the gravity of the relapses during the desinstitutionalization & the re-education of the patients is minor than during the equal participation of the patients in the community. The continuation of this follow-up study is essential.

1598

PROTECTION FROM SCHIZOPHRENIA AND CYCLOPHRENIA BY THE SYSTEM OF YOGA.
D-r Ruska Dimitrova Kirova
Psychiatric hospital in the town of New Iskar, Sofia, Bulgaria.

The frequency of the good motive activity has been investigated in 75 patients with schizophrenia and in 25 patients with cyclophrenia, a total of 100 from the available ones in the psychiatric hospital in the town of New Iskar, Sofia. They all had been vulnerable children. The interview of the patients and of his relatives and also the patients' history of the illness have been used. Our control group consisted from 76 psychic healthy persons who had been vulnerable children as well. The average age of the investigated and of the control group was almost the same. Good motive activity was found in 40% from the investigated and in 86,84% from the control group. The system of yoga has been studied. The following conclusions have been drown: 1. The motive activity plays a role for preventing the coming of schizophrenia and cyclophrenia in persons, who had been vulnerable children 2. The system of yoga is the best system for physical upbringing, is able to change the reactivity of the organism and must be applied for prophylaxis of schizophrenia and cyclophrenia in vulnerable child.

Session 245 Poster Presentation:
Psychosomatic and somatoform disorders

1599

USE OF FANTASY IN THE EVALUATION OF LIFE EVENTS BY PSYCHOSOMATIC PATIENTS.
Silvia Ouakinin, M.Purificação Horta, Madalena Fenha and J. Simões da Fonseca. Depart. of Medical Psychology and Psychopathology, Fac. of Medicine of Lisbon.

The use of a method of evaluation of fanthasy to change referential data or else the relevance of reference to modify phantasy has been studied in psychossomatic patients as compared with Normal Volunteers. The lack of phantasy in working through problems posed by reality confirms significantly the diminution of use of phantasy by psychosomatic patients only for a sub-group of them. Furthermore using indicator variables belonging to thirteen dimensional evaluation scales in Multivariate Discriminant Analysis subjects of this diagnostic group appear closer, along the First Discriminant Function to Disthimic Disorder and Neurotic Obsessive patients and more distant on one side from Normal Volunteers and on the other hand from Acute Paranoid Schizophrenic Patients. Those differences were found in data elicited by references to a possible disease of a close relative, unemployment, and the phantasy of a successful love relationship. Concerning the situation of unemployment results were not so relevant in the Multivariate Discriminant Analysis.

The X^2 test of the selected indicator variates was significant with $p \leq .005$.

A discussion of the meaning of those results as far as the comparison between the vulnerability of these subjects and, on the other hand, Normal Volunteers and other distinct diagnostic groups was interpreted within the frame of reference of an enlarged concept of reinforcement.

1600

THE IMPACT OF BEREAVEMENT OF PSYCHIC AND
PSYCHOSOMATIC WELL-BEING
Hale Imre, Bilgin Saydam
Istanbul Medical Faculty Psychiatric Department
Turkey

This study was an attempt at investigating the
symtomatology of bereaved persons who have
consulted the Outpatient Department of our
clinic. The cases had been psychiatrically
symptom-free prior to bereavement and had
consulted psychiatric help for the first time
within the first year of bereavement. STAI, ZUNG
Depression Scale, SCL-90-R and questionnaire to
assess grief prepared by our team was given to
each case.
Depressive finding were more common and acute in
the first month, especially in cases of sudden
unexpected bereavement. In cases of death due to
a chronic illness, PSDI (positive symptom
distress index) scores were lower compared to the
former, in whom earlier referral for psychiatric
help with a higher PSDI score was observed.
We have also observed that somatization is a
common component of the symptomatology of
bereavement, and in earlier referrals, depression
and anxiety is accompanied by
obsessive-compulsive symptoms more frequent.

1601

A PSYCHOSOMATIC APPROACH TO RAYNAUD'S PHENOMENON
O.Bayle, S.Consoli, M.Baudin
Hospital Broussais - Paris - France

Thirty subjects presenting Raynaud's phenomenon
were examined on the occasion of hospitalization
to determine etiology. As a function of physical
criteria,14 subjects were subsequently classified
as idiopathic Raynaud's disease (RI), and 13 as
Raynaud's secondary phenomenon (RII), most often
of sclerodermal origin. Mean age in the RII group
was higher. The psychodynamic investigation,based
on assessment scales and on projective tests, was
carried out without knowledge of the etiological
diagnosis by either the patients (except in 2
cases) or the investigators. The results demonstrated that whereas the RI subjects were
distinguished by the relative frequency of manifestations of hysterical personality and by
evasive behavior when confronted with their own
aggressivity, RII were more distant and more
conformist, suppressing their emotions but more
readily exposing themselves to social aggressions
disabled in mental elaboration of their conflicts
and in verbal expression of their affects and
being little able to request help when confronted
with a difficult situation. Several scores,
designed for quantifitation of the efficiency of
mental functioning, differentiated RI and RII
subjects and were not age-correlated. These
results are taken together with studies on type C
profile. The latter have been described as
associated to proliferative or dysimmune
disorders.

1602

PSYCHOSOCIAL FACTORS AND DUODENAL ULCER

BARBOSA, A. and GUERREIRO, A.S.
HOSPITAL PULIDO VALENTE,CONSULTA UP,LISBOA,PORTUGAL
The aim of this prospective study was to define the effect on
duodenal ulcer course (estimated by initial healing and
recurrent relapse rate) of environmental and psychosocial
factors. 154 duodenal ulcer outpatients were assessed at 1/6/
12 months after the endoscopic demonstration of DU, in order
to study smoking habits, coffee and alcohol consumption,
analgesic intake, peptic ulcer family history,serum pepsinogen
concentration, parental style (PBI),psychopathology in general
(SCL 90),personality (MMPI,Bonfils profile),defense mechanisms
and coping abilities(DMI), life events exposure (Paykel) and
social adjustment and funcioning (SPG).
The results indicate little effects of the various factors
on the initial healing process (1st month): the most relevant
finding was the more minimizing way the non-cicatrized ulcer
patients had to deal with the severity of the perceived threats
or conflicts and fail to acknowledge the existence of obvious
danger. In the relapsers we noticed a significantly higher
frequence of early separations from father and mother,in
their personal history. It was also elicited a personality
trait of introversion and a defensive style in which intra-
punitive manoeuvres were deployed to falsify reality for the
purpose of reducing perceived threats to one's self-esteem.
We conclude for the relevance of personal psychological
features in the healing process and relapse career of the
duodenal ulcer patients in the context of a multifactorial
comprehensive model of pathogenetic factors in UD.

1603

PREMENSTRUAL SYNDROME IN TURKISH WOMEN:
SELF-ESTEEM AND FEMININITY ROLE
Dilbaz, N., Erkmen,H., Kaptanoglu,C.,
Tekin,D.,M.D.
Department of Psychiatry, Faculty of Medicine,
Anadolu University Eskisehir/Turkey
The relationship of women's self-esteem and their
traditional feminine role with Premenstrual
Syndrome (PMS) were investigated. Women who
visited a gynecological clinic with premenstrual
symptoms were interviewed using the Moos Menstrual
Questionnaire (MDQ), Rosenberg self-esteem
inventory, Minnesota Multiphasic Personal
Inventory's M-F scale (MMPI,M-F). A good deal of
attention has been given to the possibility that
the majority of people demonstrating premenstrual
symptoms have an underlying neurosis and reject
the feminine role. The MMPI,M-F scale, Rosenberg
self-esteem inventory were administered during the
follicular and luteal phases of the menstrual
cycle to women with PMS and without PMS. Each
participant completed the MDQ on days 7 and 25 of
the menstrual cycle. Women whose scores on the MDQ
were > 80 on day 7 or < 95 on day 25 were excluded
from PMS. Those with MDQ scores > 80 on day 7 or >
94 on day 25 were not accepted as control
subjects. The degree of self-esteem and femininity
role of the Turkish women with PMS and without PMS
will be compared. Results will also be compared
with the results of other countries. A general
discussion will follow.

1604

AGGRESSION, ALEXITHYMIA AND SEPARATION-
-INDIVIDUATION IN A PSYCHOSOMATIC SAMPLE
I.A.Rubino,B.Pezzarossa,S.Grasso,A.Sonnino,N.Ciani
Dept. of Psychiatry, IInd University of Rome,Italy

The aim of the present research was to test the following hypotheses about psychosomatic patients,compared to normal controls: a)greater potential for spontaneous aggression, as measured by the FAF (Matussek et al.,1985);b)higher scores for alexithymic functioning, as measured by the Toronto Alexithymia Scale (Taylor et al.,1985);c)stronger evidence of separation-individuation disorders, as quantified by the Separation-Individuation Process Inventory (Christenson & Wilson,1985).The three scales were administered to 70 psychosomatic patients (asthma, psoriasis,dermatitis)(group A) and to 89 normal controls (group B). All hypotheses were supported. One-way ANOVAs showed that group A was higher on the measures of spontaneous aggression (p=.037),aggressive excitability (p=.001),alexithymia (p=.016) and separation-individuation disorders (p<.001).The present data lend support for a psychological heterogeneity between psychosomatic and normal subjects. The particular strength of SIPI results points decidedly toward a new field of psychosomatic research. The aggression profile here outlined is not to be contrasted but complemented to the low dominance found among asthmatics by Lyketsos et al.,1984.

1605

ALEXITHYMIA IN CONVERSION DISORDER
Bremner A., Hurwitz T.A.
Department of Rehabilitation Medicine, University
UBC Hospital Site, Vancouver, Canada

Depression is the most common underlying psychiatric disorder in patients with conversion symptoms. Why patients somatize their psychological distress is unclear but may be due to an inability to use words to express feelings. We have used art as an adjunctive uncovering technique in patients with conversion symptoms on the hypothesis that non-verbal communication might provide better access to underlying feelings. 2 patients with conversion symptoms are described who received weekly art sessions in conjunction with interviews and narcoanalysis. Paintings typically summarized their core experiences and revealed feelings and themes that were both apparent and inapparent and could precede,parallel or follow material that emerged during other uncovering techniques. Both patients were severely depressed, 1 of whom was psychotic. Both patients eventually required ECT. Our work with conversion patients using art suggests that an individual's nonverbal experience reflects a separate but parallel domain of conscious experience that can operate in the absence of a conscious verbal counterpart. This occurs presumably because of powerfull denial mechanisms that operate at a verbal level and are responsible for the alexithymic state.

1606

MANAGEMENT OF PSYCHOSOMATIC DISORDERS

Dr.Nicolae Enăşescu   Dr.Ovidiu Nicoară
Psychiatric Hospital Jebel
Romania

In this paper the authors emphasize some practical aspects of their own experience in the field of the Psychosomatic Medicine.Even this term was excluded from the ICD-lo Draft,the authors are strongly agree with the concept of Psychosomatic. In the introduction it is briefly presented some alternative therapeutic concepts (including the Traditional Extreme-Oriental Medicine) and their correlations with the classical psychosomatic theories,from the hollistic point of vue.In the second part of the paper the authors present 586 patients with psychosomatic disorders(digestive disorders,functional heart disorders,respiratory disorders,skin disorders, endocrinological disorders,headaches)and their complexe management: from the classical drug-therapy,to psychotherapy(emphasizing on the empathic relationship patient-psychiatrist),acupuncture and the original Romanian therapy with "Boicil". The results were the following: 4ol patients(68.4 per cent) had a very good recovery,lo5 patients(18.2 per cent) a good and satisfactory recovery and failure in the case of 8o patients(13.4 per cent).

1607

RHEUMATIC DISEASES: A PSYCHO-SOMATIC APPROACH

Prof.A.Pacheco Palha; Prof.A.Lopes Vaz; Luisa
   Ramos; Mário Lourenço

Faculty of Medicine, Hospital de S. João
                 Oporto, Portugal

   The authors make a psycho-somatic approach of the rheumatic diseases through a study that took place in the Rheumatology Service of S.João Hospital of Oporto.
   A comparative study was done in a group of patients with rheumatic diseases (2 sub groups: one of rheumatoid arthritis and another with fibrositis) and another group with diabetes mellitus studying clinical, psychometric (anxiety, depression, coping mechanims and self image), and social parameters.
   The results are commented by the authors in a rheumathological and psychological point of view.

1608

DOTHIEPIN TREATMENT OF ANXIETY AND DEPRESSION IN RHEUMATOID ARTHRITIS

Swannell AJ[1], Chuck AJ[1], House AO[2], Pownall R[3], Dept of Rheumatology[1], The City Hospital, Nottingham, Dept of Clinical Neurology[2], Radcliffe Infirmary, Oxford, Research Dept[3], The Boots Company PLC, Nottingham, UK.

The Hospital Anxiety and Depression rating questionnaire (HAD) was used to select patients for entry into a double-blind, placebo-controlled study of the efficacy and tolerability of dothiepin 75mg daily therapy for anxiety and depression associated with rheumatoid arthritis. Ninety one patients (44%) of 184 screened reached 8 or more on the A or D sections, or 12 on the combined HAD score, and 58 of these were recruited.

The mean HAD score of the dothiepin-treated group fell from 20.4 to 15.5 at two weeks and was 13.8 at the end of the six week study. In the same sequence the mean HAD scores of the placebo-treated group were 17.5, 15.2 and 14.0. Within-treatment changes were all highly significant ($p<0.01$). Between-group differences were not statistically significant. Mood and sleep improvements, together with pain and grip strength measurements, suggest that dothiepin treatment produced beneficial changes more rapidly than placebo. The dothiepin group were considered to be receiving the more effective treatment by the investigators at two weeks ($p=0.002$). Incidences of adverse drug reactions were identical showing the good tolerability of dothiepin when given with other drugs in rheumatoid disease to assist pain relief and reduce anxiety and depression.

1609

Defanyl® AND SOMATOFORM DISORDERS IN GENERAL MEDICINE

M. Ohayon, N. Hugon, M. Caulet.
Laboratoire de Traitement des Connaissances, Faculté de Médecine, 27 Boulevard Jean-Moulin, 13385-Marseille, CEDEX 4.

The somatoform disorders are often thought of as mere symptoms of anxio-depressive disorders. Thus an antidepressive treatment should be useful in many cases. The study uses a computerized clinical observation, including: 1) the clinical diagnosis and main symptoms, according to the clinician, 2) the DSM-III automatic diagnosis, performed by our Expert System Adinfer, 3) a 36 items somatic sysmptoms schedule, 4) The relational Depression Rating scale and MADRS scores for the depressive symptoms, 5) Covi's Anxiety rating scale, 6) analogical visual scales for anxiety and depression. The valuations were performed at days 0, 7, 21 and 30.
The Expert system was especially modified for this study: the system scanned successively the decision trees of affective disorders, anxiety disorders and somatoform disorders. Thus the criteria present in the three syndroms were stored. The clinical effects of Defanyl are studied globally and in the "depressive", "anxioux", and "somatoform" groups, according to the expert systems answers and depression and anxiety scores at day 0. The criteria studied are 1) the lessening of somatic complaints, 2) the Depression scores, and 3) the anxiety scores.

1610

Adinfer SOMATOFORM DISORDERS: USE OF AN EXPERT SYSTEM FOR AUTOMATIC DIAGNOSIS IN GÉNÉRAL MEDICINE.

N. Hugon, M. Ohayon, M. Caulet.
Laboratoire de Traitement des Connaissances, Faculté de Médecine, 27 Boulevard Jean-Moulin, 13385-Marseille, CEDEX 4.

Somatoform disorders are one of the most frequent complaints. They are often considered as anxiety or depressive symptoms. Their nosography is by no means clear, and includes many diagnoses from "hysteria" to "hypchondria" or "psychosomatic", "somatisation" and so on. In this study, we compare the symptoms collected by general practicioners, and their clinical diagnoses to the results of an automatic DSM-III diagnostic program, Adinfer. The Expert System Adinfer was used in previous studies in depressive and unselected psychiatric disorders. In the present paper, Adinfer was modified so that three DSM-III decision trees were systematically scanned: depressive, anxiety and somatoform disorders. This study allows an epidemiological study of the somatic complaints, and their relations with depression and anxiety. We discuss the signification of the DSM-III classes compared to the nosography used by french clinicians. The scores of Anxiety and depression rating scales are compared to the diagnoses of the clinicians and the expert systems.

Session 246 Poster Presentation:
Mood stabilizing drugs

1611

EFFECTS OF STABILIZING-MOOD DRUGS ON THE SEROTONIN TRANSPORTER COMPLEX
Marazziti D., Lenzi A., Cassano G.B.
Department of Psychiatry, University of Pisa, Pisa, Italy

Lithium salts (L), carbamazepine (C), valproic acid (VA), and calcium blockers, have been reported to be useful in the prophylaxis of bipolar disorders. Serotonin system seems to be involved in mood disorders. Blood platelets represent a reliable peripheral model of serotonergic neurons. We thus studied the effects of L, C, VA and 2 calcium blockers, nifedipine (N) and verapamil (VP), on the binding of ^{3}H-imipramine (IMI) and the uptake of ^{14}C-serotonin in platelet membranes, as compared to tricyclics (imipramine and desipramine). VA, NF and VP exerted a concentration-dependent inhibition of the IMI binding, although tricyclics were stronger. The same effect was observed on serotonin uptake. L or C showed no effect. These results suggest that the stabilizing-mood effects of different drugs are likely related to different mechanisms.

1612

NEUROENDOCRINE EFFECTS OF LITHIUM

A. Baumgartner, B. Müller-Oerlinghausen, A. Campos-Barros
Psychiatrische Klinik, FU Berlin, FRG

Study 1: Lithium was administered to 12 healthy males over a 12-days period. TSH, T4, T3, rT3, LH, FSH, testosterone, estradiol, cortisol, and prolactin were measured before and after treatment. TSH increased, and T4 and rT3 decreased significantly. As rT3 is merely a metabolization product of T4, the results suggest an interaction of lithium with intracellular T4 metabolization.
Study 2: T4, T3, and TSH were measured in 17 currently euthymic patients with MDD, who had been on Li^+ continuously for at least 5 years. We found a significant positive correlation between prophylactic response and T3 levels (lower T3 values in responders).
Study 3: The influence of Li^+ on the 3 thyroid hormone dejodinating enzymes were investigated in rat brains in vivo. We found different effects of Li^+ on central T4 metabolization: An inhibition of 5'I dejodinase and complex interactions with 5III dejodinase activity. The results show that Li^+ influences brain T3 levels and favour the hypothesis that a central Li^+/T4 interaction may be somehow involved in the antimanic or prophylactic action of the drug.

1613

THYROID PATHOLOGY IN CHRONIC TREATMENT WITH LITHIUM SALTS
Nardini M., Belardinelli N., Dore F., Franchi G., D'Errico I., Bonellig G.
Chair of Psychiatry, Siena, Italy.

The elaboration of the nosological concept of "bipolar spectrum" has allowed for the "rationale" in use of lithium salts in different areas of those usually indicated.
As already verified in many medical reports, it is certain that their onference on the thyroid function allows for clear pathological induction of the organ.
Different biological mechanism of interaction has been hypothesized. The aim of this study is to verify the incidence of thyroid disfunction and its association with auto-antibody presence in long term treatment subjects.
In fact data from present medical reports hipothesise that lithium could indirectly influence thyroid function exacerbating an underlying autoimmune pathology.
We studied 30 subjects undergoing a chronic treatment with lithium, selected for the absence of anamnestic clinical and biological thyroid disfunction signs. The patients were divided in two groups according to initial therapy criteria and the following tests were performed: haematic levels of T3-FT4-TSH before and after TRH stiumlus; haematic levels of antimicrosome and antithyroglobulin antibodies; thyroid ecography and scintiscans. Control were performed at predetermined times. Our results indicate a thyroid disfunction with various levels a structural alteration correlated to the duration of the treatment.

1614

LITHIUM AND ANTIDEPRESSANTS IN LONG TERM THERAPY OF AFFECTIVE DISORDERS
W.König, T.Heinrich, F.Reimer
Psychiatric Hospital Weinsberg, FRG
Head: Prof. Dr. F. Reimer

In the treatment of affective disorders the use of a combined psychopharmacotherapy is nowadays common among physicians both in practice as well as in clinics. Analyses of prescriptions have shown that polypharmacy sometimes is used even more often than monotherapy. The aim of the study was to analyse prescription habits of the psychiatrists in a large hospital. Using the archives of the Psychiatric Hospital Weinsberg, all patients hospitalized in 1978, 1983 and 1988 and diagnosed as affective disorder have been selected. Medication at the day of discharge has been recorded. The number of patients was N = 245 in 78, N = 189 in 83 and N = 177 in 88. Mostly two or three different psychotropic drugs were administered as maintenance therapy (55 - 90 %). Monotherapy with antidepressants was rarely used, only 15 % of all patients. The number of lithium prescriptions decreased, on the other hand in 1988 carbamazepine was administered in appr. 12 %.
Detailed information will be given.

1615

CARBAMAZEPINE VS. LITHIUM IN PROPHYLAXIS OF BIPOLAR AFFECTIVE DISORDERS
Denk E., Ch.Simhandl, K.Thau, A.Lovrek, A.Topitz
Department of Psychiatry, University of Vienna, Austria

As recent studies had shown Carbamazepine (CBZ) plays an important role in prophylactic treatment of affective and schizoaffective disorders. Our study has been conformed to investigate prophylactic efficacy of CBZ versus Lithium carbonate (LI) according to blood levels. 75 patients (diagnosed by DSM III) are randomly treated with LI (25 patients: blood level range 0,6-0,8 µMol/l) or CBZ (25 patients on "high blood level": 28-35 µMol/l and 15 patients on "low blood level": 15-25 µMol/l). For clinical evaluation CGI, BPRS and MSBR are used.
Additional medication, duration of illness, age of onset, number and duration of episodes and symptom free intervals are recorded.
Preliminary results of a comparison between dropped out patients and those who continue prophylactic medication will be presented.

1616

LONG TERM TREATMENT WITH LITHIUM: CORRELATION OF BODY WEIGHT CHANGES, LITHIUM PLASMA CONCENTRATIONS AND AFFECTIVE STATE
Timotijevic I., Paunovic VR.
Clinical Hospital CTR "Dr Dragisa Misovic" Clinic of Psychiatry, Yugoslavia

The change and increase of body weight in the course of long term therapy with lithium is a phenomenon the patients often complain about and is considered to be the most frequent side effect. The change of body weight has been researched with 53 patients on maintenance therapy of lithium, both sexes, aged of 18-65, diagnosed according to ICD-9 and DSM-III as bipolar affective disorders.
All examined patients belonged to the group of manic-depressive psychosis (40) and schizoaffective (13).
The change of body weight of examined patients was followed in correlation with lithium plasma level and depression intensity (determined Hamilton score), the period of therapy with lithium and psychiatric entity.
The results showed that lithium plasma concentration and affective state don't influence the change of body weight, but there is a positive correlation with the period of treatment with lithium and psychiatric entity.

1617

EARLY MARKERS OF RENAL DAMAGE DURING CHRONIC LITHIUM THERAPY.
A. Rasi, F. Campari*, A. Mutti, R. Alinovi, B. Saccardi*, I. Franchini, C. De Risio*.
Laboratory of Industrial Toxicology, Institute of Clinical Medicine and Nephrology, and *Institute of Clinical Psychiatry, University of Parma, Parma, Italy.

The urinary excretion of tissue (brush border) and plasmaproteins was studied in patients on lithium therapy for more than six months. Thirty patients aged 50.9 (SD 14.7) were compared with two sex- and age-matched ($\pm$ 3 years) control groups composed respectively of 30 healthy subjects and 30 psychiatric patients assuming drugs other than lithium carbonate. Additional admission criteria were: (i) no signs or history of kidney disease; (ii) no intake of potentially nephrotoxic drugs other than those under investigation; (iii) no leukocyturia or bacteriuria. The mean duration of the treatment was 9.4 years (SD 5.1) and Li levels in serum averaged 0.72 mEq/L (SD 0.14).
ANOVA and Duncan's multiple range test showed much higher levels of albuminuria (GM 20.6 mg/g creatinine, GSD 5.1) in patients on Li treatment as compared to both healthy (GM 4.7, GSD 1.7) and psychiatric controls (GM 6.7, GSD 1.6). The urinary excretion of beta$_2$-microglobulin and brush border antigens revealed by monoclonal antibodies also showed a significant increase in patients on Li, thus suggesting that the glomerulopathy indicated by abnormally high albuminuria was associated with either functional or structural damage to the proximal tubuli. Interestingly, all such markers were intercorrelated and showed a negative relationship with urinary osmolality, wich is known to be lowered by Li therapy. Whereas no relationship was found between the dose and any of the above markers, the occurrence of renal damage and/or dysfunction was dependent on the duration of treatment. At the individual level, clearly pathological values were found only in patients treated for more than six years. These results suggest that Li-induced renal lesions are not confined to the distal part of the nephron, and that in addition to tubular atrophy and interstitial fibrosis, glomerulosclerosis leading to abnormally high albuminuria may also develop as a consequence of long-term Li administration. Although they may not be an indication that therapy be stopped, such changes require a close monitoring of renal function.

1618

18-YEAR EXPERIENCE WITH LITHIUM-THERAPY

Scheuchenstein, A., Berzewski, H.

Psychiatric Outpatient Ward and Crisis Intervention Center of the Klinikum Steglitz, Free University Berlin

Since 1970 our Psychiatric Department has had a special lithium consultation-hour during which 120 patients (mean age: 46.7 yrs) with unipolar, bipolar and schizoaffective psychoses were prescribed lithium treatment as of 1988. This retrospective follow-up study provides an overview of initial and late side-effects and of the course of these illnesses. Long-term ingestion of lithium produced quantitative and qualitative improvement of the psychoses. A high incidence of hypothyroidism, but also cases of hyperthyroidism, were observed in conjunction with lithium therapy. One-third of the bipolar and schizoaffective cases were insufficiently suppressed by dexamethasone. Social and psychological changes are described according to the Global Assessment Scale (GAS).

1619

A CASE OF ACUTE LITHIUM INTOXICATION SECONDARY TO ACUTE GOUT ATTACK
ZELIHA TUNCA, M.D. AND MEHMET TUNCA, M.D.
DOKUZ EYLUL UNIVERSITY, SCH. OF MEDICINE
DEPT. OF PSYCHIATRY

We saw a 51 years old male patient with bipolar affective disorder, depressed, using lithium at prophylactic dosages for 10 months who developed acute lithium intoxication 24 hours after the beginning of acute gouty arthritis. The previous renal status of the patient was normal, all his biochemical analyses (BUN, serum creatinin, serum uric acid levels) and his regular serum lithium determinations were repeatedly normal. His serum lithium value on the first day of acute gouty arthritis was 0.8 mEq/Lt, and an acute delirium rapidly developed during the next 24 hours. On the second day of the crisis his serum lithium level had risen to 2.1 mEq/Lt, and his serum creatinin (1.8 mg/dl) and serum uric acid (6.8 mg/dl) values were slightly raised.
The patient was treated with i.v. fluids and colchicine, lithium was discontinued and he normalized in three days.
Renal effects of lithium are not very well known. Lithium's interference with uric acid metabolism is even less clear. To our knowledge this is the first case of acute lithium intoxication secondary to acute gout crisis.

1620
LORAZEPAM IN TREATMENT OF A MANIC-DEPRESSIVE ILLNESS'S CASE WITH COUNTERINDICATION OF NEUROLEPTICS. (MULTI-LOCULAR SCLEROSIS)
D. Bernard, H. Fossat
(Pedo)-Psychiatrist - Praticien Hospitalier
S.T.P., Marseille, France

Utilisation de doses élevées de Lorazepam à visée essentiellement sédative chez une patiente souffrant de graves troubles dysphoriques à prédominance maniaque et présentant dans ses antécédents une sclérose en plaque peu évolutive justifiant une corticothérapie et contreindiquan l'utilisation de neuroleptiques.

Session 247 Poster Presentation:
Obsessive compulsive disorders

1621
OBSESSIVE-COMPULSIVE DISORDER: A CLINICAL, NEUROPSYCHOLOGICAL AND PET STUDY.
J.L.Martinot,J.F.Allilaire, B.Mazoyer, A.G.DesLauriers,P.Hardy,F.Legaut,J.D.Huret, S.Pappatta,J.C.Baron,A.Syrota.
Service Hospitalier F.Joliot, C.E.A. 91406, ORSAY, FRANCE.

Non-depressed obsessive-compulsive patients (OCD) (n=16), were compared to 8 normal controls (NC) of similar age for resting-state regional cerebral glucose metabolic rates (rCmrGlu) using positron emission tomography with the Fluorodeoxyglucose method. OCD were rated for clinical data and a neuropsychological battery was administered to 14 patients the day of the scan. Absolute rCMRglu for whole cortex was significantly lower ($P<0.0001$) in OCD than in NC, and prefronto-lateral metabolic ratio (i.e. latero-prefrontal divided by whole cortex values) was significantly lower ($P<0.02$) than in NC. No significant difference between treated (n=10), drug-free since 15 days (n=3), drug-free since 4months (n=3) OCD was found for those variables. Although no relationship between rCmrGlu and clinical data was found, OCD were significantly impaired in the neuropsychological tasks assessing memory and attention.Also, latero-prefrontal metabolic ratio in OCD was negatively correlated to Stroop-test subscores, a "frontal-oriented" task assessing the ability to inhibit immediate but inappropriate responses tendancies. These results suggest a relationship between the latero-prefrontal cortex rCMRglu decrease and a selective attention deficit in OCD

1622
SEX AND AGE OF ONSET IN OBSESSIVE COMPULSIVE DISORDER

Sumant Khanna

Department of Psychiatry, National Institute of Mental Health and Neurosciences, Bangalore 560029, India.

Obsessive compulsive disorder normally has an age of onset in the second or third decade. A differential effect of age of onset has been reported earlier (Khanna et al. 1986) with men having a peak age of onset before 20 years and women having a prolonged period of age of onset extending into the fourth decade. A subsequent prospective sample of 127 OCD probands were added to the initial sample of 410 retrospectively studied cases with regards to age of onset. There were no statistically significant differences between the prospective and retrospective samples. Females continued to display a later age of onset with a prolonged peak covering two decades. Possibilities for this include the importance of marital factors and the later development of the serotonergic system in females.

1623
PREDICTORS OF THERAPEUTIC EFFICACY IN OBSESSIVE-COMPULSIVE DISORDER.
J.L.Carrasco;A.Chinchilla;A.Cebollada; R.Viñas;I.Moreno;P.Sánchez;L.Jordá;M.Vega and M.Camarero.
Hospital Ramón y Cajal.Psych.Dept. MADRID

A study was made of 46 patients (28 women and 18 men)with a diagnosis of Obsessive-Compulsive Disorder(ICD-9 criteria). All of them were inpatients in our Psychiatric Unit. The aim of this clinical, therapeutic and evolutional study was to find predictors of therapeutic efficacy. 59% of the patients exhibited an obsessive previous personality which resulted in a worse evolution; improvement was obtained in 100% of the cases where no personality disorder existed either in the patient or the parents. Sudden onset was found in 24% and insidious in 76% . The most frequent symptomatic form was the ideatory one; the predominantly motoric forms of the disorder had a worse evolution in time.
The various previous treatments are stated as are those used during the hospital stay. The most frequently used drugs were: 1) Clomipramine associated with 5-OH Tryptophan and/or Maprotiline. 2) Fluvoxamine. Similar efficacy was obtained with both of them.

1624
GROWTH HORMONE RESPONSE TO CLONIDINE IN OBSESSIVE COMPULSIVE DISORDER
Sumant Khanna, P. Lakshmi Reddy, M.N. Subhash, B.S.S.R. Rao, S.M. Channabasavanna.

Departments of Psychiatry and Neurochemistry, National Institute of Mental Health and Neurosciences, Bangalore 560029, India.

There have been reports of a blunted, normal and accentuated response of growth hormone to clonidine in obsessive compulsive disorder. There have also been reports of the clinical efficacy of clonidine in OCD and related Gilles de la Tourette syndrome. A recent report focussed on clinical improvement after intravenous clonidine. Eighty subjects who met DSM-III criteria for OCD and who had Hamilton Depression Scale scores less than 17 were studied. On qualitative analysis the three possible responses of growth horome were obtained : accentuation, normal and attenuation. Clinical correlates of these parameters will be discussed.

1625
CLOMIPRAMINE-INDUCED MANIA IN OBSESSIVE--COMPULSIVE DISORDER
E. Vieta, M. Bernardo
Subdivisión de Psiquiatría y Psicología Médica, Hospital Clínic i Provincial, Barcelona.

The authors describe one case of manic episode in a patient with obsessive-compulsive disorder treated with clomipramine. A computerized literature search yielded two prior case reports, both indicating a reciprocal relationship between both clinical phenomena. Possible physiopathological links between manic--depressive illness and obsessive-compulsive disorder are examined.

1626
Obsessive Compulsive Symptoms in Panic Disorder with Agoraphobia patients.
Lotufo Neto F., Bernik M., Gentil Filho V., Andrade L.S.G., Cordas T. & Ito L.M.
Hospital das Clínicas - Universidade de São Paulo.

34 Panic Disorder with Agoraphobia patients were studied with the Present State Examination and the Maudsley Obsession Compulsion Inventory 13 patients had the presence of the ON Syndrome in the PSE.
Comparisons were made among the ON positive group with the ON negative group showing that the obsessive compulsive symptoms were present mainly in patients with depressive symptoms.

1627
Habituation Patterns of Anxiety Within Sessions During Exposure in Imagery
Fugen A. Neziroglu, J. Shaffer, Christina J. Taylor
Bio-Behavioral Psychiatry, Great Neck, NY
Sacred Heart University, Fairfield, CT

The habituation process during behavioral treatment was studied in fourteen outpatients diagnosed as obsessive-compulsive disorder (OCD). Patients were randomly assigned to one of two treatment groups. In the fast presentation style group, imagined phobic stimuli were presented quickly and with great detail. In slow presentation group, imagined scenes were presented very gradually. During 8 flooding sessions, anxiety levels were measured. Results revealed a curvilinear pattern of anxiety reduction for the slow presentation style as compared to a linear decrement for the fast presentation group. The results of latter were similar to in-vivo exposure which has been found to yield a better treatment outcome than exposure in imagery. This study's findings suggest that using a fast presentation style in imagery may be more therapeutically efficacious.

1628

OBSESSIVE NEUROSIS - AN ANALYSIS OF A STRATEGY OF ACTING OUT OF REFERENCE.

Paula Sargaço, J.Serro, M.Fátima Ferreira and J.Simões da Fonseca.
Depart. of Medical Psychology and Psychopathology, Fac. of Medicine of Lisbon.

A multiple choice card sorting questionary has been constructed in a way such that semantic disturbances are included in equivalence classes. This approach is the analogue at the level of meaning to what has been tried at the formal syntactical level in phenomenological psychopathology.

If we consider obsessive symptoms formation it appears a clear shift into a not referential domain of data which at that level of thematization become not controlable according to a referential profit-cost matrix.

This deviation from referente is nevertheless denied by means of the substitution of environmental data by the self representation of the environment taken as of it was referential.

Data rendered available through the conceptual network implied in the evaluation instrument constructed by the Lisbon group show that obsessive patients stay at an intermediary state between Normal Volunteers and Paranoid Schizophrenic patients in one dimension as well as they also stay at an intermediate position concerning semantic expression of affective and or else psychosomatic disturbances.

1629

TIAPRIDE EFFECTIVNESS IN BEHAVIORAL DISORDERS OF ELDERLY PATIENTS

De Marco F., D'Ambra L., Ulisse T., Ascione C., Di Pietro E.
Mental Health Service - USL 43 Naples (Italy)

Authors study effectivness of Tiapride in behavioral disorders of elderly patients. Study is performed on 200 subjects aged 65 and over, selected according to the following criteria: a) diagnosis of cerebral decay caused by vascular or functional diseases; b) behavioral disorders, absence of any other serious diseases. Subjects treated with major tranquillizers, psychostimulating and antidepressing drugs are kept out of the research.
Standard dosage of Tiapride is of 300 mg daily for three months.
Authors use special form for anamnesis, four scales for evalutation of results (behavioral, psychopathological, etc.) and one form for monitoring side effects.

1630

COGNITIVE BEHAVIORAL TREATMENT OF OBSESSIVE COMPULSIVE DISORDER
Juliana R. Lachenmeyer, Ph.D.
North Shore Univ. Hospital, Manhasset, NY

A functional analysis of obsessive-compulsive disorder suggests that some symptoms are anxiety arousing and some are anxiety reducing. Two cases of successfully treated child and adolescent obsessive disordered patients will be presented. In the child case, the OCS symptoms were anxiety arousing and included fears of being poisoned. Treatment involved family intervention and reinforcement of incompatible behaviors. In the adolescent case, exposure and response prevention was used to eliminate hoarding behavior. In both cases, the patient was on medication which was seen as necessary but not sufficient for successful treatment. Clinical implications of cognitive behavioral treatment of Obsessive Compulsive Disorder as well as issues specific to child and adolescent treatment of Obsessive Compulsive Disorder will be discussed.

Session 248 Poster Presentation:
Affective disorders II

1631

ASSERTIVENESS AND DEPRESSION

Véra L., Sarron C.
Centre Hospitalier Sainte Anne, Clinique des Maladies Mentales et de l'Encéphale, 100 rue de la Santé, 75014 Paris, France.

Assertion training has been used with a broad range of presenting concerns and associated interpersonal problems, including depression and other troubles. A lack of assertive behavior may be related to deficits in social skills or interfering emotional reactions and thoughts.
The aim of this work is to assess in psychiatric in-patients (depression) the interpersonal anxiety. We used the Hamilton Depression Scale, the Fear Survey Schedule (FSS III, Wolpe), the Assertiveness Schedule of Rathus and we observed the in-patients in social situations.
The assessment has been repeated since the patients were identified like no depressives by the psychiatrist and the score of Hamilton Depression Scale. A comparison of results between the evaluations is made. The discussion refers to relationships of assertiveness and depression.

1632
Influence of "natural delivery room" in postpartum mood changes
P. Castrogiovanni, I. Maremmani, Buffi C°, P.M. Martellucci°, Grandi B°.,
Institute of Psychiatry, Pisa University, Italy
°Obstetrical and Gynaecological Division " P. Burresi Hospital", Poggibonsi, SI, Italy

Women who were in the "natural delivery room" of a gynaecologic division were compared with a control sample, to test the impact of this kind of approach in the manifestation of Maternity Blues.
The women in childbirth were evaluated by means of SCL 90 and Mood Changes Rating Scale on the eighth month of the pregnancy and on the fourth day after the delivery.
The results bring a further contribution to the understanding of psychosocial factors' role in the origin of Maternity Blues.

1633
LIFE EVENTS AND PERSONALITY IN AFFECTIVE PSICHOSES
M.Vega;A.Chinchilla;J.L.Carrasco;A.Cebollada;M.Camarero;P.Sanchez;R.Viñas;I.Moreno and L.Jordá.

60 bipolar patients and 30 patients with recurrent major depression, both fulfilling DSM-III criteria, were studied in terms of sociodemographic profiles, personal and family antecedents, clinical psychopathology,personality type and triggers of the first episodes. We found a greater frecuency in the bipolar group of personality disorders of the hypomanic, cyclothymic and sociopathic type;the melancholic-anancastic being more associated with unipolar depression. The bipolar patients in our study had a higher socioeconomical and cultural level compared with the unipolar patients. More than 50% of the depressive episodes of each group had unfavourable life-events triggers; 45% of the manic episodes also had previous unfavourable life-events; 44% of the patients of this later group exhibited a previous hypomanic, sociopathic or cyclothymic personality.

1634
TROUBLES OF THE HUMOR TONE IN THE POSTPARTUM: POSSIBLE PREDISPOSED FACTORS
De Gregori P., M.D., Foglietta D., M.D., Siracusano A., M.D., Vella G., M.D.
I Psychiatric Clinic University, "La Sapienza", Roma, Italy

Aim of this study was to find out the possible "risk situations" which may contribute to the development of a depressing symptomatology in the postpartum. Another aim was to describe the various predisposing factors (conugal factors, life events, personality characteristics, perinatal compliations, social support, economic conditions etc.). Further we wish to point out the little relative attention, that this pathology, still difficult to frame has.

1635
AFFECTIVE DISORDERS: "DESCRIPTIVE" AND "EXPLICATIVE" HYPOTHESIS OF DIAGNOSIS
Laddomada A., Martis G., Pirino F., Reda M.A.
Instituto di Clinica Psichiatrica Universita' di Cagliari, Italy

The aim of this work is the analysis of the approach followed by the DSM-III-R about mood disorders.
We want to evaluate the difference between desriptive and empirical methods, utilized by the DSM-III-R and other diagnostic systems, and explicative methods utilized in Cognitive Psychotherapy, that considers the development processes of mental organization, in the structural approach to psychopathology.

1636
EXTRAPYRAMIDAL SYMPTOMS IN DEPRESSED PATIENTS.

BARUCH P, AMMAR S, DE BILLY A & JOUVENT R
INSERM U 302, LA SALPETRIERE, PARIS, FRANCE

This study aims to assess extrapyramidal symptoms in 72 inpatients (46 women and 26 men, aged 20 to 81- mean : 47.1), meeting DSM III criteria for a major depressive episode and 60 controls (30 women and 30 men aged 18 to 89 - mean : 41.4) free of any psychiatric or neurological disturbance. No subject in either group had received any neuroleptic treatment for the 8 previous weeks. The neurological evaluation included an extrapyramidal symptoms rating scale (ESRS) derived from the Columbia University scale and chronometered tasks. Psychopathological evaluation (Hamilton Depression & Depressive Retardation Rating Scales, Echelle d'Humeur Dépressive) was performed by an independant investigator. In both groups, the distribution of subjects according to the ESRS score followed a half Gauss curve, with the median at point 0. Among the 60 controls, only 17 subjects were rated more than 0 on the ESRS and the maximum is 7 (mean ± sd : 1,02 ± 1,94). In the depression group, 26 patients exhibited a score ≥ 10 points (mean ± sd : 8,63 ± 8,88, range : 0-32) with symptoms essentially related to akinesia and hypertony. Tremor was rare. The existence or severity of extrapyramidal symptoms was not correlated to age or psychopathological scores. These soft neurological signs do not appear related to depressive psychomotor retardation. Their nature - depressive related extrapyramidal syndrome or incipient Parkinson's disease - should be discussed.

1637
DISTINCT MOOD QUALITY IN MAJOR AFFECTIVE DISORDERS AND ALEXITHYMIA

C. Ponce-de-Leon*, J. Ramos**, L. Montejo*, P. Del-Valle*, A.Cordero**.
*Psychiatric Service. Hospital Clinico S. Carlos. Madrid.Spain.   **Mental Health Service. Madrid Community. Madrid.Spain.

The distinct quality of depressed mood was part of the diagnostic criterium in the melancholic depressions until its recent removal as such from the revised D.S.M. III.

The way that sadness is experienced is a difficult sign for the psychiatrists to evaluate and the "distinct quality" is a symptom which does not always appear in depressed subjects.

The authors examine - using a previously designed objective device - the prevalence of the "distinct quality" as well as its relations to alexithymia (measured with the Sifneos questionnaire) in a randomly selected group of depressed patients.

The results are compared to the hypothesis that those patients who do not report a subjective experience of "distinct quality of mood" suffer alexithymia.

The effect the verification of such a hypothesis would cause is discussed.

1638
COMPORTEMENTS D'ATTENTION ET DEPRESSION : ETUDE LONGITUDINALE*
Guillemin J., Kilcher H., Weber B. & Lalive J.
Institutions Universitaires de Psychiatrie, Genève, Suisse

Selon nos hypothèses les manifestations dépressives dans un système incluant un patient avec un état dépressif majeur (DSM III) influenceraient les interactions, notamment au niveau de l'attention que s'accordent les participants. L'attention se manifesterait sous des formes et avec une intensité particulières, et elle se modifierait au cours du temps avec l'évolution de l'état dépressif.
Pour tester ces hypothèses nous étudions huit couples (dont un conjoint présente un état dépressif majeur), qui interagissent avec un thérapeute. Les séances des six premiers mois de la prise en charge sont enregistrées en vidéo; l'analyse porte sur les interactions non verbales (orientation et proxémique) et verbales (répartition des échanges et analyse de contenu).
Les premiers résultats montrent plusieurs configurations d'attention, avec des évolutions différentes en fonction des contributions spécifiques des trois participants. L'étude devrait permettre de décrire à terme une sémiologie interactionnelle de la dépression.

*Etude subventionnée par le Fonds National de la Recherche Scientifique (Suisse), subside No 3.895-0.88

Session 249 Poster Presentation:
Alcohol abuse II

1639
BIOCHEMISCHE UND KLINISCHE ASPEKTE DES METHANOLSTOFFWECHSELS BEI CHRONISCHEM ALKOHOLISMUS

Dr. M. Soyka: Psychiatric Hospital of the University of Munich, FRG, 8000 München 2, Nussbaumstr. 7

Endogen offenbar kontinuierlich gebildetes Methanol läßt sich im Serum Gesunder in einer Konzentration von 0,5 - 1 mg/l nachweisen. Methanol wird fast ausschließlich durch die Alkoholdehydrogenase metabolisiert und kumuliert bei gleichzeitiger Äthanolbelastung wegen der höheren Affinität des Äthanols zur ADH. Wiederholt wurden erhöhte Methanolspiegel als "biologischer Marker" für Alkoholismus postuliert. In einer Studie an 78 zur Entzugsbehandlung aufgenommenen Alkoholikern (42 Männer, 36 Frauen) wurden über einen 5tägigen Zeitraum Methanol sowie andere Begleitstoffe (Iso-Propanol, n-Propanol, Butanol-2 etc.) bestimmt. Die mittlere Serummethanolkonzentration (SMK) betrug 29,4 (0,5-78,2) mg/l, in 75% der Fälle über 10 mg/l. Eine Korrelation zwischen der Höhe der SMK und dem Ausprägungsgrad des Alkoholentzugssyndroms konnte nicht nachgewiesen werden. Weitere biochemische, klinische und forensische Aspekte des Methanolstoffwechsels werden diskutiert.

1640

Examens nephrographiques isotopiques de la fonction renale des malades a toxicemanie non causee par l'alcool
Ignatov,A.,F.Lazarov,A.Anguelov.Académie médicale,Laboratoire des radioisotopes-2,Chaire de Psychiatrie,Sofia,Bg.

Des examens nephrographiques isotopiques ont été effectués sur des malades présentant des toxicomanies non dues à l'alcool dans le but d'étudier l'état de la fonction rénale.Bienqu'effectués par screening les examens permettent d'obtenir une idée rapide et distincte de l'état fonctionnel des reins.Les malades faisant l'objet de l'étude sont divisée en trois groupes:1/phase d'intoxication chr. 2/phase d'abstinence 3/Phase où l'organisme ne sent pas le besoin.Les malades analysés n'ont pas d'anamnese d'une maladie rénale.Ils sont agés de 20 à 35 ans. Le grope témoin est composé de sujets sains(33 personnes) qui n'emploient pas de drogues.Les criteres utilisés pour juger de la fonction des reins sont les indicateurs qualitatifs et semiquantitatifs tirés de la courbe de la fonction.Les déviations pathologiques observées dans la fonction rénale sont unilatérales et bilatérales et touchent la phase de secrétion et la phase d'excrétion.Les déviations unilatérales de la norme ne sauraient etre expliquées par un effet pharmacologique.Les déviations bilaterales sont dues probablement à l'effet antidiurétique.

1641

CLOMETHIAZOL VERSUS CLORAZEPATE IN THE THERAPY OF DELIRIUM TREMENS
Dieter Caspari and Wolfgang Bellaire
Universitats-Nervenklinik-Psychiatrie-
(Head: Prof. Dr.med. K.Wanke), Oskar-Orth-Str.,
D-6650 Hamburg, Fed.Rep. of Germany

Different drugs and drug combinations have been described for the treatment of alcohol withdrawal. Since November 1987 we have compared clomethiazol and clorazepate in the therapy of delirium tremens Until now we treated eighteen men with full-developed symptomatology, nine by clomethiazol infusion, nine by clorazepate injections. They were twenty-eight to seventy-six years old. Patients with pulmonary diseases always received clorazepate.
The results of our study indicate that both drugs are effective in controlling delirium tremens. In both groups intravenous therapy lasted seven days. We found no relevant side effects in patients treated by clorazepate, but serious complications in three patients of the clomethiazol group, one even died by a cardiac standstill. As fas as we can conclude from the small number of patients, we recommend clorazepate for the treatment of delirium tremens, because it is safe and effective For the final presentation of our paper data will be actualized including patients treated in the meantime.

1642

INTEREST OF DOSULEPINE IN THE TREATMENT OF DEPRESSION AND SLEEP TROUBLES DURING ALCOHOL WITHDRAWAL
Docteur GUJADHUR - C.H.S.P. SAINT-EGREVE 38521
BP 100 FRANCE

La dosulépine est un antidépresseur tricyclique dont l'activité clinique est caractérisée outre l'action sur l'humeur par une régularisation du sommeil. L'étude a été menée chez 30 patients éthyliques (8 femmes et 22 hommes) moyenne d'âge 40 ans tous alcoolo-dépendants selon le critère DSM III et ayant un score MADRS ≧ 22 et des troubles du sommeil appréciés par l'échelle de Spiegel et un carnet d'auto évaluation. En règle générale seul le méprobamate fut autorisé en traitement associé durant les 15 premiers jours du sevrage.
Les malades ont été contrôlés à J0 J14 et J28, 4 patients sont sortis d'essai pour inefficacité et rechute éthylique. Les troubles du l'humeur furent améliorés les premiers dans environ la moitié de cas dans une moyenne de 10 jours et les troubles du sommeil d'une manière concomittante dans les 50 % restants.
Cette étude montre l'intérêt de la dosulépine à la posologie moyenne de 150 mg/jour dans le traitement de ces troubles chez des patients éthyliques et de sa très bonne tolérance.

1643

Metadoxina in the Treatment of Alcohol Abuse
M. Cirillo°, I. Maremmani, M. Marchioro°°, P. Castrogiovanni
Institute of Psychiatry, Pisa University, Italy
°Psychiatric Unit USL 4, Regione Toscana, Italy
°°Medical Division " 'S. Croce' Hospital", Castelnuovo Garfagnana, LU, Italy

Alcoholic patients, according to DSM III inclusion criteria, were included in a double-blind trial, metadoxina vs. placebo. After the check of inclusion criteria, patients, in total abstinence from alcohol and before the three days wash-out period, were evaluated by means of personality and behaviour tests (Q.T.A., PFS, VARA-Test); in the meantime socioanagraphical and clinical-internistical data were recorded. At the random inclusion of patients in the two groups, each patient was evaluated by means of SCL-90 and SAD, in autoevaluation.
SCL-90 , SAD and a clinical form were administered again on the 1st, 3rd, 6th and 12th month , verifying the abstinence by means of family news and of alcoholism evaluation. Possible drop-out were evaluated at the trial discharge. At the end of the trial Q.T.A. and PFS were again administered to each patient. Preliminary results allow to verify the effect of alcohol detoxification by means of Metadoxil (per os, intermuscular and intravenous) compared with placebo. Moreover they allow to seek for possible variations of clinical, neurological, psychological and behavioral aspects during the treatment and the individuation of socio-environmental, clinical, personological and behavioral factors which can predict the treatment outcome.

1644

Assessment of time-bounded effect of Antidepressive Drug Regiment (A study with Maprotiline in Alcoholic Population)
DOĞAN,Y.B.; SÖZER,Y.; DEMİRBAŞ,H.
Medical School of Ankara Univ.Dept.of psych. Ankara, TURKEY

To investigate the most effectfull phase of antidepressive regiment has been the main interest of this study. Seven alcohol inpatients who were given Maprotiline in divided doses for eleven weeks form the sample. Hamilton-D scale has been chosen in order to evaluate both the existence and intensity of depression.

All patients were given the scale on admission and this was followed by consecutive applications on a weekly basis. The week where an obvious symptomatic relief occured was accepted the most effectfull phase of antidepressive drug regiment.

Tentatively precising such a spot of time therefore is believed to have some clinical implications in the treatment of alcoholic depressed inpatients.

1645

PSYCHOTROPIC ACTIONS OF IPSAPIRONE AND ALCOHOL IN NORMAL VOLUNTEERS

Dr. Beneke, M., Lieser, A., Wildt, P., Lüdtke, W.
Troponwerke Cologne, F.R.G.

36 healthy volunteers received either 5mg ipsapirone, 5mg diazepam or placebo (t.i.d) for 3 days under double blind conditions. Subjects were tested under three conditions: baseline (week 1), drug (week 2), and drug + 0.5g/kg bodyw. alcohol (week 3). Testing procedures included self-assessments, spatial imagination tasks, simple and choice reaction times, finger tapping, and long term attention. Blood pressure, heartfrequency, and side-effects were additionally registered. With regard to psychological performance variables there were only significant differences between placebo and drugs in choice reaction times indicating pronounced deteriorating effects under diazepam treatment. There were no significant profile differences between drugs or placebo in the mood scales. Additional alcohol had no modifying effect and did not interact with drug treatment. Side-effect indicate that the predominant symptom under ipsapirone is dizziness.

1646

PREVENTION AND REHABILITATION OF ALCOHOLISM IN FACTORIES

A. Hećimović, D. Breitenfeld, V. Starčević, B.Lang

Institute for Health Promotion
Health Center "New Zagreb",Zagreb, Yugoslavia
University Department for Neurology, Psychiatry, Alcoholism and other dependences of "Dr. M. Stojanović" University Hospital, Zagreb, Yugoslavia

The latest achievements in prevention, diagnosis, therapy and rehabilitation of disturbancies caused by alcohol in the New Zagreb region are presented particularly in various working organizations.Difficulties in organizing prevention of drinking problems during working hours are described. Possibilities of district hospital treatment are also described (pointing out treatment without sick leave) including an alcoholic's family and working enviroment. The wide range of alcoholic rehabilitation groups in working organization of New Zagreb is considered, with a willing assistance of specially trained staff in out - patients services. They were almost the only ones who took over completely professional work in clubs in Zagreb within their original coordination committee together with supervisional meetings.

Session 250 Poster Presentation:
Psychoneuroendocrinology

1647

The use of a single basal TSH value for confirming the diagnosis of major depression.

M.Maes, M.Vandewoude, C.Schotte, P.Blockx, P.Cosyns.
University Hospital,Antwerp, Belgium.

A blunted thyrotropin secreting hormone (TSH) response to thyrotropin releasing hormone (TRH) is one of the most consistently reported abnormal findings in major depressed patients. We have shown - using ultrasensitive TSH assays - that the blunted TSH responses are attributable to decrements in basal TSH secretion. The basal TSH values performed well as clinical tool separating major from minor depression : at a threshold value $\leq 1 \mu IU/mL$ the sensitivity was 50 % and the specificity 96 %. The Δ max TSH values (i.e. peak TSH response minus basal TSH) performed not as well. It is suggested that to carry out the TRH-test is useless since a single determination of basal TSH - measured with an ultrasensitive TSH assay - contains all information as regards major depression.

1648
VASOPRESSIN BASELINE - PREDICTOR OF TSH BLUNTING IN DEPRESSIVES

F.Resch*, E.Pawlik**, G.Schönbeck**, G.Koinig**, G.Langer**, Th.Stompe**, P.Parzer**, J.J.Legros+

* Department of Child and Adolescent Neuropsychiatry, Vienna, Austria
** Department of Psychiatry, Vienna
+ Unité de Psychoneuroendocrinologie Université de Liège, Belgium

40 patients who met the criteria for major depression in DSM-III-R have been subjected to a neuroendocrinological test battery (TRH-test and baseline of cortisol, glucose, prolactin, somatotropin (HGH), neurophysin I (hNp I; reflecting vasopressin plasma levels) and neurophysin II (hNp II; reflecting oxytocin plasma levels). Likelyhood-ratio-tests between regression models for explanation of TSH blunting revealed that the chance to show a blunted THS response increases with higher levels of hNp I and low levels of cortisol and basal prolactin.
These intriguing findings will be discussed in the light of established psychoneuroendocrinological hypotheses.

1649
TOTAL SLEEP DEPRIVATION AND THYROID FUNCTION IN DEPRESSION

W.P. Kaschka, D. Flügel, J. Negele--Anetsberger, A. Schlecht, J. Marienhagen, P. Bratenstein, University of Erlangen--Nuremberg, Department of Psychiatry, Schwabachanlage 6, D-8520 Erlangen, FRG

We conducted a whole night's sleep deprivation (SD) in 22 inpatients, 15 women and 7 men, suffering from a major depressive episode, melancholic subtype (DSM III-R). Thyroid stimulating hormone (TSH), T_4, free T_4 (fT_4), T_3, and free T_3 (fT_3) were determined on three consecutive days, SD being performed between days 2 and 3. Psychopathological symptoms were rated each morning using von Zerssen's BfS and BfS' scales and the Hamilton Depression Scale (HAMD). The criterion for SD response was an improvement of 30% or more in the HAMD score. The results showed marked increases of TSH, T_3, fT_3, T_4, and fT_4 upon SD. Responders (n=9) differed from non-responders (n=13) in that SD effects on hormone concentrations were more distinct and longer lasting in the former group than in the latter. In accordance with data published by others, we could not demonstrate a statistically significant correlation between ΔTSH and ΔHAMD scores.

1650
EFFECTS OF THYROTROPIN-RELEASING+HORMONE-TARTRATE (TRH-T) ON PARKINSONISM
S.Fasullo, A.Galofaro, F.Scoppa, G.G.Vinci*
Institute of Neuropsychiatry, Division of Neurology Ospedale Civico*, Palermo, Italy

The authors present five cases of psychotic depression (in accord with DSM-III-R), with 55 mean age (2 male and 3 female) that had been treated with haloperiodol and clorimipramine. Since the utilization of anticholinergic drugs the five patients have exhibited an akinetic-hypertonic syndrome (drugs Parkinsonism). On the base of literature of TRH pharmacology (dopaminergic pre and post-synaptic activity) the AA was administered to these five patients a 2mg/die i.m. bolus of TRH-T in a period of ten days. In all five cases the AA have observed a fast and notable reduction of extrapyramidal disorders. On the base of this evidence the AA propose TRH as a new form of therapy for neuroleptic Parkinsonism.

1651
Pre and postdexamethasone β-endorphin, ACTH and cortisol values in depression.
E.Suy, C.Christiaens, M.Maes.
Psychiatric Centre, Munsterbilzen, Belgium.
Pre and postdexamethasone β-endorphin, adrenocorticotrophic hormone (ACTH) and cortisol values were determined in normal controls and depressed patients. The postdexamethasone β-endorphin, ACTH and cortisol values were significantly intercorrelated. It is suggested that the 8 a.m. postdexamethasone β-endorphin values could prove to be the most sensitive (80%) and specific (100%) criteria in order (1) to reflect the disorder in the negative feedback on the HPA-axis during depression and (2) to confirm the diagnosis of major depression. The pathophysiological processes underlying cortisol escape to 1 mg dexamethasone are (1) an augmented ACTH escape linked to the severity of illness and (2) other background effects not linked to depression, i.e. decrements in the bioavailability of the test substance, increasing age and an increased spontaneous secretion of cortisol.

1652

BLUNTED ACTH BUT NORMAL β-ENDORPHIN RELEASE FOLLOWING CRH ADMINISTRATION IN DEPRESSION
R. Rupprecht, K.P. Lesch, U. Müller, G. Beck, H.M. Schulte
Department of Psychiatry, University Wuerzburg, FRG

Several investigators reported abnormalities of the hypothalamic-pituitary-adrenal (HPA) system in response to direct stimulation of the corticotroph cells in patients with psychiatric disorders. To further explore the HPA system integrity in major depressive disorder, 13 drug-free patients and normal subjects matched for age, sex, ovarian status and body weight received 100 μg synthetic human CRH as an iv bolus dose. As compared to the normal subjects, in the depressed patients a significant attentuation of the net ACTH release following CRH administration could be observed, while β-endorphin and cortisol responses did not differ significantly between the groups. The magnitude of ACTH and cortisol release were negatively correlated in the patient group only. The blunted ACTH response to CRH in depression might be related to hypercortisolemia, while the implications of the apparent dissociation of ACTH and β-endorphin after CRH administration remain still unclear.

1653

INTERRELATIONS BETWEEN THE HYPOTHALAMIC-PITUITARY-ADRENAL AND -SOMATOTROPIC SYSTEM IN DEPRESSION
R. Rupprecht, K.P. Lesch, C. Rupprecht, M. Rupprecht, M. Noder, J. Mössner
Department of Psychiatry, University of Wuerzburg, FRG

In order to evaluate the possible effect of glucocorticoids as neuromodulators of the hypothalamic-pituitary-somatotropic system in depression cortisol, GH, and IGF-I concentrations of 16 patients during depression after recovery, and of 28 healthy controls were studied before and after oral administration of 1 mg dexamethasone at 11 pm. While there were no significant differences in GH and IGF-I levels between depressed, recovered or control subjects, GH and IGF-I concentrations of cortisol non-suppressors were significantly elevated when compared with suppressors. Moreover, postdexamethasone cortisol, GH, and IGF-I levels were positively correlated. Dexamethasone had a stimulating effect on GH and IGF-I values in patients during depression and in cortisol non-suppressors only, which did appear neither in recovered nor control subjects nor in cortisol suppressors. Thus, hypercortisolemia may be of great importance for the dysregulation of the hypothalamic-pituitary-somatotropic system reported in depression.

1654

CLINICAL AND DST EVOLUTION OF DEPRESSIVES DURING FIVE YEARS.

BOBES GARCIA JULIO (*). BOUSOÑO GARCIA MANUEL (*). VILLASANA CUNCHILLOS ANTONIO (**). GARCIA PRIETO ANGEL (*). MARTINEZ LOPEZ AURELIO (*).

(*) UNIVERSIDAD OVIEDO. SPAIN.
(**) UNIVERSIDAD PAIS VASCO. SPAIN.

The authors studied a group of unipolar depressive outpatients, with A.M.D.P. clinical protocol, D.S.M. III standard method for diagnosis, and D.S.T. (Neuroendocrine marker); and followed this group for 5 years, during which they were treated with standard clinical procedures. To be admitted in the study, any physical or psychical condition different from depression, were ruled out.
During the 5 years of the study, the authors took account of recoveries, relapses, refractory cases, patients with need for continued medication, or any type of prophylaxis, deaths or suicides. The results, were analysed in search of prognostic markers, clinical, socioeconomic, or neuroendocrine.

1655

NEUROLEPTIC WITHDRAWAL AND DEXAMETHASONE SUPPRESSION TEST IN SCHIZOPHRENIA

P. MONTELEONE[1,2], M.G. ARIANO[1], F. FRANZA[1], P.M. FIUMANI[1], M. MAJ[1] and D. KEMALI[1]
[1]Department of Medical Psychology and Psychiatry, 1st Medical School University of Naples, and [2]Mental Health Service, U.S.L. 41, Naples (Italy).

A number of intervening factors have been invoked to explain the variability in the sensitivity of the dexamethasone suppression test (DST) in psychiatric patients. Among them, attention has been recently paid to withdrawal of medications with anticholinergic activity, that could produce a transient disinhibition of hypothalamic-pituitary-adrenal axis. Although the abrupt discontinuation of phenotiazines and butyrophenones has been proposed as potential source of DST variability, so far no study has been done to investigate the effects of neuroleptic withdrawal on DST. For this purpose, 32 chronic schizophrenic patients treated with conventional or depot haloperidol, underwent DST either before and after abrupt discontinuation of treatment. DST results were analyzed also with regard the occurrence of negative and positive symptoms, the presence of dyskinetic movements and other clinical and demographic variables.

1656

PLASMATIC VASOPRESSIN NEUROPHYSIN IN DEPRESSION.

M. LARUELLE, A. SEGHERS, S. GOFFINET, S. BOUCHEZ and J.J. LEGROS

St-Luc University Clinic. Psychiatric Department Catholic University of Louvain - Bruxxels, Belgium.

26 inpatients meeting DSM III criteria for major depressive episode (7 bipolar and 19 unipolar) versus 16 normal controls, matched for age, sex, menopausal status, estrogens administration and smoking, were investigated as follows : Plasmatic Vasopressin Neurophysin (hNpI) and Cortisol levels were determined by radioimmunoassay at 8 a.m. and 8 p.m during 4 consecutive days. On days 2 and 3, 0,5 mg dexamethasone (DXM) was given orally. Patients showed higher evening cortisol levels, higher cortisol values during the 2-day DXM administration period and an earlier cortisol escape. hNpI values were significantly lower in patients than in controls. Multiple regression analysis between the mean hNpI value for each subject (as independent variable) and : age, sex, menopausal status, estrogens and nicotine intake, did not show any difference. No significant contribution of polarity, escapers versus non-escapers, HDRS score, HRSA score, and lormetazepam administration to hNpI values was fund in patients. Results were discussed and further studies considered.

1657

EFFECTS OF REMOXIPRIDE CR AND IR ON PLASMA PROLACTIN IN SCHIZOPHRENICS

S Soni, D Tench, T Ashwood and G Movin

Prestwich Hospital, UK, Astra UK and Sweden

Remoxipride is a selective D_2 dopamine receptor antagonist and an antipsychotic which produces a low incidence of extrapyramidal side effects. A controlled release formulation (CR) of remoxipride was developed to see if it can be given once a day and to examine whether adverse events that may be related to high peak plasma concentrations can be reduced. We have previously described the single dose and steady state pharmacokinetics of remoxipride immediate release (IR) and CR. Here we report the effects on plasma prolactin and the clinical tolerability of the two formulations. Twenty four stable chronic schizophrenic inpatients were entered into a double blind cross-over study of 14 days remoxipride CR 400 mg once daily and 14 days remoxipride IR 200 mg BID. Each treatment period was preceded by a 7 day washout. Repeated plasma samples were taken on Day 1 and Day 14 of each treatment period to follow single dose and steady state pharmacckinetics. Prolactin concentrations increased in all patients after remoxipride from both IR and CR capsules. Although the dose of remoxipride CR was twice as large as that of the IR there was a tendency for a lower prolactin C max for CR compared to IR both after single and repeated doses. The peak prolactin concentrations were reached earlier after IR compared to CR administration and they were also reached faster after single doses compared to steady state. C max for prolactin was reached faster than C max for remoxipride especially after CR. Both formulations were equally well tolerated. There was little or no change in the severity of the patients illness when treated with either formulation, probably because of the chronicity of the illness.

1658

TRIPARTITE DST-TRH-GNRH TEST IN PATIENTS WITH SCHIZOPHRENIA AND MAJOR DEPRESSION
M. Jakovljević, V. Plavšić, N. Bohaček, M. Lanović and V. Jukić
Psychiatric Clinic, KBC Rebro, Zagreb, Yugoslavia

Theoretically multiple hormonal analyses may provide objective and confident markers for more precise identifying some forms of mental disorders, better predicting and monitoring response to treatment and more rational choice of drugs. While the most studies have examined responses in a single neuroendocrine axes, we used series of neuroendocrine parameters to examine hypothalamic-pituitary, hypothalamic-pituitary-adrenal, hypothalamic-pituitary-thyroid and hypothalamic-pituitary-gonadal axes. 12 male patients with schizophrenia, 12 male patients with unipolar major depression and 12 male healthy volunteers were included in the study. Plasma T3, T4, TSH, LH, PRL, FSH, testosterone, oestradiol, cortisol as well as the responses of TSH, PRL, GH, LH, FSH to TRH-GnRH stimulation and dexamethasone suppression test were determined. After the 4 weeks drug therapy in schizophrenic and depressed patients all these parameters were measured again. The findings of this study indicated that patients with unipolar major depression and schizophrenic patients show abnormalities from various neuroendocrine axes, but not specific for any psychiatric diagnoses. Some appear to be state dependant and indicators of therapeutic response to different drugs.

1659

TREATMENT OF SEXUAL OFFENDERS WITH A GONADOTROPHIN-RELEASING HORMONE AGONIST.
B. CORDIER, V. CAILLARD, J.M. KUHN
Departments of Psychiatry and of Endocrinology
CHU Rouen and Caen - France.
In order to help 2 sexual offenders asking for a medical aid, in whom cyproterone Acetate (CA) 150-300mg daily was uneffective on clinical and hormonal basis, a treatment using a gonadotrophin-releasing hormone agonist (GnRH-A) has been started after informed consents were obtained. A long-acting GnRH-A (Decapeptyl^R, Ipsen-Biotek laboratories, France) was administred (3.75mg IM) monthly. Clinical, psychometric and hormonal parameters (testosterone (T) and gonadotrophin plasma levels) were evaluated before therapy and then monthly for six months. During treatment, sexual fantasies and sexual activity were dramatically reduced and the quality of life improved. By contrast to that measured during the treatment with CA (6.40 and 4.10 ng/ml respectively) plasma T levels dropped from 11.00 and 14.60ng/ml (before any treatment) to 0.18 and 0.28ng/ml respectively. No side effect was observed. These preliminary results show that : i/ the treatment of male sexual offenders with GnRH-A is effective and appears more powerful than CA in the 2 cases studied ; ii/ intramuscular way avoids uncontrolled withdrawals of the therapy ; iii/ although cautions are needed for long-term treatment, the well tolerated and reversible castration induced by GnRH-A appears to be an interesting alternative for treating informed and self willed sexual offenders.

Session 251 Poster Presentation: Therapeutic communities and psychosocial services

1660
THE USE OF THERAPEUTIC COMMUNITY PRINCIPLES IN THREE TRAINING SCHEMES
I.K.Tsegos, Z.Voyatzaki, E.Morarou, B.Tsilimigaki
Institute of Group Analysis. Athens, Greece.

The paper describes the structure of three Training Communities: that of the Athens Institute of Group Analysis (duration 5 years), the Training Community for Therapeutic Community staff, of the Open Psychotherapeutic Centre (O.P.C.) (duration 4 years) and the Training Community in Psychological Testing also of the O.P.C. (duration 4 years).
These Training Communities are based on the use of T.C. and group analytic principles, and were developed after an 8 years experience. They include a variety of activities (therapy, theory, supervision, sensitivity and policy meetings etc.) which give a unique opportunity for observations in relation to learning and to issues such as Selection, Suitability, Insight, Knowledge, Creativity and Skill.

1661
STRUCTURAL INNOVATIONS IN A PSYCHOTHERAPEUTIC COMMUNITY
P.Papageorgiou, Ch.Terlidou, M.Athitakis, I.K. Tsegos
Open Psychotherapeutic Centre. Athens, Greece.

An outline of the main structural innovations which have emerged from a 9 years' experience in a Psychotherapeutic Community (Ps.T.C.), which has adopted the theory and practice of Group Analysis as its main therapeutic approach. The Ps.T.C.'s basic aim is to provide effective treatment for the severe psychiatric cases in a day centre context and to affect therapeutically both the patients and the therapists.
The focus is on the following:
1) integration of Sociotherapy and Psychotherapy 2) free choice of the therapeutic activities by the patients themselves 3) underlining of the Sociotherapist's status in the multiproffesional team of the Ps.T.C.'s staff 4) admission and incorporation procedure in the Ps.T.C. 5) the mode of payment and 7) the regular change of Leadership in the Ps.T.C.

1662
STAFF CRISIS IN A T.C. : REACTIONS FROM THE PATIENTS' SIDE
M.Athitakis, V.Apostologlou, M.Manthouli, Ch.Terlidou, E.Yiomela, I.K.Tsegos
Open Psychotherapeutic Centre. Athens, Greece.

Material from T.C. groups as well as from experiential groups has been collected in order to study the repercussions that destructive behaviour, on the part of the conductors or the co-conductors, had on the members of the groups. A comparison was made between material from the T.C. groups and the experiential groups, in connection to the reactions of the group members and to the percentage of drop outs.
Attempts are made to interpret the findings, in relation to group cohesion and the wider matrix of the network (T.C. and Seminar).

1663
OUTPATIENTS OF A PSYCHOSOCIAL CENTER: A 12-MONTH PROSPECTIVE STUDY.
Facincani Orietta Cinzia
U.S.S.L. No.61 - Carate Brianza (Milan) Italy

From January 1st to December 31st 1984 we analysed the clinical files of 142 outpatients - 57 males and 85 females - who attended one of the 20 CPS - Psychosocial Centers - in Milan. We collected the data by means of a questionnaire divided into three main sections. 1st Section: Patient's socio demographic data and psychopathologic history. 2nd Section: Sender, companion, patient's motivations and requests. 3rd Section: Efficacy of the service and development of the service-patient relationship. After analysing all the information in the clinical files we made a codified diagnosis according to the criteria of DSM III. As a result we defined a profile of the patients who attended our Psychosocial Center, their psychopathology, and the therapeutic strategies carried out by the medical staff. Our data analysis shows that most of the patients (69.7%) are non psychotic subjects and that 27% of the female patients and 15.7% of the male patients present a diagnosis classifiable within the psychotic disorders. The high percentage of drop-outs (28% males and 44.7% females), suggests the need of a better approach.

1664
SOZIOSTRUKTURELLE BEDINGUNGSFAKTOREN
IN DER PSYCHIATRISCH-PSYCHOSOZIALEN VERSORGUNG
IN DER FRG - EIN STÄDTEVERGLEICH
H.J. Ingenleuf, H.P. Bratenstein, R.J. Witkowski,
E. Lungershausen
Psychiatrische Universitätsklinik, Schwabachanlage 6,
D-8520 Erlangen

Bei strukturellen Betrachtungen der psychiatrisch-psychosozialen Versorgung stand bislang meist der Stadt-Land-Vergleich im Vordergrund. Mit diesem Beitrag soll versucht werden, das Augenmerk auf sozialstrukturelle Spezifika von Städten zu richten im Hinblick auf daraus resultierende differierende Versorgungslagen und deren Implikationen.

Die beiden in der Untersuchungsregion liegenden Städte scheinen aufgrund ihrer heterogenen Sozialstrukturen in besonderem Maße geeignet für einen Städtevergleich. Die Bildungs- und Erwerbsstruktur zeigt sich dahingehend divergent, daß im einen Falle eine Universität und ein großer Betrieb der Hochtechnologie das Bild der Stadt entscheidend bestimmen und ihr das Gepräge einer Akademikerstadt verleiht, während im anderen Falle eine Vielzahl von Produktions- und Gewerbebetrieben das Bild einer Arbeiterstadt entstehen läßt.

Die soziodemographischen Daten zur Bevölkerungsstruktur erhärten diesen Eindruck und ergaben ein solides Fundament für die Resultate der Studie, die auf die Deskription und Analyse differierender Versorgungsniveaus und unterschiedlicher Klientel in den Einrichtungen abzielt.

Interessante Aufschlüsse ergeben sich bei der Ausstattung der Einrichtungen und bei der interinstitutionellen Kooperation, die einen Schwerpunkt der Arbeit bildet.

Von Interesse sind auch die Patientenstrukturdaten wie etwa Altersaufbau, Geschlecht, Ausländeranteil und Aufnahmediagnose der Klientel in Abhängigkeit von der Wohnregion.

1665
THE ORGANIZATION OF THE PSYCHIATRIC CARE IN THE
DEPARTMENT OF EVROS
M. Livaditis T. Tadalaki L. Kariolou S. Pliatskidi
P. Sakellaropoulos
University of Thraki

In the department of Evros, the University Psychiatric Clinic in the General Hospital of Alexandroupolis makes an effort to apply a social oriented model of psychiatric care.
There is given emphasis in the sensitization of the community, in the development of the role of a nurse-therapist and in the avoidance of the institutionalization. We have created intermediate structures such as: a crisis intervention centre in the General Hospital, a Mobile Psychiatric Unit, a day hospital, a Foyer and cooperative groups.

In our poster we present the whole of our activities and some statistical data of our work in all these fields.

1666
GROUP FAMILY CARE OF SCHIZOPHRENIC PATIENTS:
NEW ZAGREB EXPERIENCE

V. Starčević

Institute for Health Promotion
Health Center "New Zagreb", Zagreb, Yugoslavia

New Zagreb Health Center is taking care of 1o.ooo inhabitans including about 1ooo schizophrenics of which approximately 9o % has been in their homes/families. The existing mental - health facilities could hardly cover their needs of their families. Recognizing this fact only some new techniques may change the unfavorable situation in this rapidly growing part of the city. One decided therefore to concent rate on the family members of schizophrenics. We are developing new techniques of home care. Our previous investigations pointed to a strong relatiship between quality of home care and the lenght and number of hospitalization of schizophrenic patients, so we decided to develop appropriate techniques to teach key - members of the patients families to control over - or under - protection of patients, as well as instrucing them for certain monitoring and/or behaviour modification techniques. Objective evaluation programms of these community efforts are right underway. Similar approaches are used for post-cardiac -infarcts patients too.

1667
IN DER KLINIK VORBEREITETE NACHSORGE UND
WIEDERAUFNAHME.
(REHOSPITALIZATION AND PREPARED CARE AFTER
DISCHARGE.)

Anne M. Leimkühler
FORSCHUNGSSTELLE FÜR
PSYCHIATRISCHE SOZIOLOGIE
Psychiatrische Klinik der Universität
- Rheinische Landesklinik -
4 Düsseldorf 12, Bergische Landstr. 2 FRG

Der Beitrag erörtert die Frage nach dem Zusammenhang von Wiederaufnahme und vorbereiteter Nachbetreuung in Abhängigkeit von soziodemographischen, diagnostischen und strukturellen Parametern (z.B. Wiederaufnahmefrist). Die empirische Grundlage bilden Daten der Psychiatrischen Basisdokumentation des Landschaftsverbandes Rheinland (BRD) aus den Jahren 1986 und 1987.
Die Ergebnisse werden im Hinblick auf Konsequenzen für das klinische Handeln und die Funktionalität der Psychiatrischen Basisdokumentation als Instrument zur Versorgungsplanung diskutiert.

1668
PATIENTS' VIEWS OF TREATMENT IN A PSYCHIATRIC COMMUNITY CARE SYSTEM
U. Polzer, S. Priebe, T. Janssen, W. Reichwaldt
Department of Social Psychiatry, Freie Universität Berlin, Berlin (West), F.R.G.

In a district of 180.000 inhabitants in Berlin (West) a comprehensive psychiatric community care system has been built up by our department. This social psychiatric model institution includes a day-hospital, a night-clinic, a printing shop for vocational rehabilitation and various out-patient facilities.
This study was to investigate patients' views of treatment within this system. In 100 patients with different diagnoses, undergoing treatment in different units of our department, views of and experience with treatments and therapeutic relationships were studied. Patients' wishes regarding their treatment and their concepts of illness were also examined. In order to reflect adequately the often vague and holistic views of the patients, simple questions and visual analogue scales were used.
Patients' views are shown as well as how these views are related to the patients' clinical characteristics and to their psychopathological symptoms. Additionally, results are compared with those of patients in a psychiatric state hospital and those of out-patients outside our department, who were examined using the same methods.

Session 252 Poster Presentation:
Child psychiatry II

1669
CLINICAL VALIDATION OF A NEW CHILDREN'S LIFE EVENTS SCALE
Canalda, G., Toro, J., Vallès, A., Martinez, E. and Mena, A.
Department of Psychiatry, School of Medicine, University of Barcelona, Spain.

The development of a Life Events Scale for children 3 to 12 years of age is presented. The scale consist of a list of 84 negative or neutral life events with some spaces for including events not specifically listed. The impact of life events (life change units) were obtained for three age groups (3-5, 6-9, 10-12 years) using a similar method to Coddington's American Scale (1972) and Monaghan et al. British Inventory (1979), which consisted on professional ratings. Several comparisons with the assigned values to each life event were done between:1)subgroups of professional raters, 2)the professional raters (N=160) and a sample of parents (N=26), 3)the american scale, the british inventory, and our scale (common items). High agreement about the values of each event was found between subgroups of professional raters and between the professional raters and the parents sample. Small cultural differences were observed between the values of the three compared scales. The reliability test-retest, 3 months interval, was r=0.797 ($P<0.0001$)and percentage agreement for specific events was 73.21%. The scale allows to differenciate between clinic and nonclinic groups of children.

1670
CYSTIC FIBROSIS: PSYCHIATRIC CONSEQUENCES IN PATIENTS AND THEIR PARENTS
E. Lara, M.E. Duarte Silva, A.P. Folques and L. Marques Pinto
Department of Psychiatry, Faculty of Medicine of Lisbon, Hosp.Santa Maria, Lisbon, Portugal

The psychological and psychiatric aspects of cystic fibrosis (CF) were analysed in a comparative study with normal controls. Normal subjects (n=22) and CF children (n=22), aged between 6 and 12 yrs, were evaluated using the "Personality Inventory for Children"(PIC), the "Children Psychiatric Rating Scale" (CPRS) and "Rutter Inventories"; DSM III-R was used for psychiatric diagnosis. Parents were submitted to a psychiatric interview as well as to rating scales for anxiety and depression. The two groups of children were matched for age, sex, intelligence and social background. A full reevaluation of some CF subjects (n=7) was performed at the end of a 3 yrs follow-up period. Model II ANOVA and a chi-square analysis were used for statistical comparisons.
The results show that CF patients have increased scores in measures of hyperactivity, impulsive behaviour and somatic concern. Psychiatric diagnoses are more frequent in CF patients, including "disruptive behavioural disorders" and to a less extent "adjustment disorders" (DSM III-R). The parents of CF children have higher scores of anxiety and depression, and psychiatric diagnoses are more frequent than in controls. In CF children the 3 years follow-up showed some deterioration of cognitive functions and more important emotional disturbances.
One would expect that these indications contribute for a better definition of the role of both psychologists and psychiatrists in health care programs to CF patients and their families.

1671
LITHIUM CARBONATE IN THE TREATMENT OF INFANTILE AUTISM
St. Milea
Institute of Medicine and Pharmacy-Buch

Lithium carbonate in doses determining a 0.60-0.80 mEq/L plasma concentration was administered in a group of 16 children aged 4-9 years who fulfilled the DSM-III-R criteria for infantile autism.
The response was compared before (with and without other therapeutic methods), during and after experimental dropping-out lithium therapy. Its far better performance and promptitude entitled the long-term administration of lithium carbonate in 4 cases. In other 5 cases, the fair performance had to be supplemented by neuroleptic treatment. Six cases with poor beneficial effect and one with severe symptomatology were withdrawn from lithium therapy.

1672

PHARMACOCLINICAL INVESTIGATION OF THE DA HYPOTHESIS IN CHILD AUTISM
DOLLFUS S., PETIT M., LESIEUR Ph.
CHSR - Rouen - 76301 - FRANCE

An alteration of dopaminergic (DA) function, more complex than a simple overactivity, has been hypothesized in child autism. Therefore we have tested in a double blind cross-over study the clinical effects of two DA drugs with claimed opposit mechanism of action : Amisulpride (Ami) a DA antagonist and bromocriptine (Bro) a DA agonist.

Nine autistic children, according to the DSM III criteria, received either drug in a random order for 4 weeks with an in-between placebo period of 6 weeks. The treatments effects were assessed with the "Evaluation Résumé du Comportement" (ERC) scale for autism (Barthelemy and coll. 1986) and with the the abbreviated Conners scale for hyperactivity. Five out of 9 children showed a global improvement as assessed by a more than 20 % decrease on the ERC scale : 3 with Ami and 2 with Bro. Ami appears significantly effective ($p < 0.05$) on the ERC subscale for specific symptomatology as Bro does on the Conners scale and on the non specific symptomatology ERC subscale.

These data show that eitheir Ami (1,5 mg/kg/d) or Bro (0,15 to 0,20 mg/kg/d) could be effective treatment for child autism depending on the symptomatology concerned and quite interestingly without apparent opposit clinical action (i.e no apparent overlapping and/or worsening effects during the cross-over).

1673

THERAPEUTIC AND ADVERSE EFFECTS OF HALOPERIDOL IN INFANTILE AUTISM
Ilona Herczeg, Sára Nagy, György Bartkó
National Institute for Nervous and Mental Diseases, Budapest, Hungary

The outcome of a 28-day haloperidol treatment at conservative doses level of 1,5 - 6mg/day was investigated in 15 autistic children /DSM-III criteria/ ages 4 - 10 years. In the second part of the study the long-term /10-15 months/ effects of haloperidol on the abnormal involuntary movements was evaluated in 10 children who responded well to this drug during the short-term trial. The Brief Psychiatric Rating Scale for Children /BPRS-C/, Clinical Global Impressions /CGI/ and Abnormal Involuntary Movement Scale /AIMS/ were used.
The administration of haloperidol resulted in significant decreases in behavioral symptoms, emotional withdrawal, attention disturbance and in global clinical improvement. However, there was no change in autistic thinking disturbance, blunted affects and speech deviance. Three of the 10 patients studied prospectively, haloperidol yields worsening of preexisting abnormal involuntary movements. The results were evaluated for the indication of the treatment.

1674

PSYCHOPHARMACOTHERAPY IN MENTAL RETARDATION
Dr E. BERMEJO, Lavigny/SMP Valaisan - CH
Dr Prof. W. BETTSCHART, Université Lausanne - CH
Dr J. VOEGELI, Institution de Lavigny - CH

It has been stated by various authors that 39 to 55% of psychopharmaceutical treatments prescribed for the management of psychiatric problems in mentally retarded subjects are inadequate. We have investigated, in Switzerland, a population of mentally retarded patients aged less than 20 who were receiving psychopharmaceutical treatment. We worked out a questionnaire concerning psychological problems, mental level, drugs administered, therapeutical results, side effects, i.e. 51 variables, whereof 32 where concerned with psychic disorders and therapeutical results. We performed various crossings and evidenced a series of target symptoms such as heteroagressiveness, anxiety, agitation, sleep disturbances, and auto-agressiveness. These symptoms were rated mild, severe or very severe. Drugs given included neuroleptics (82%), minor tranquilizers (9%), antidepressants (7%) and hypnotics (2%).
The best results were seen in patients where treatment was limited to one single neuroleptic. Chlorprothixene and thioridazine accounted for 57% of all neuroleptic drugs. This study shows a very low prescription rate for minor tranquilizers, antidepressant drugs and hypnotics, preference being given to sedating neuroleptics.

1675

MENTAL ACTIVITY AND ALTERATION IN THE VEGETATIVE NERVOUS SYSTEM OF METALLY DEFICIENT CHILDREN
Em.Marinov, Sofia University, Department of Defectology, Bulgaria

The activities related to the educative work often act as a stressing factor upon the vegetative nervous system and cause numerous alterations in it. The alterations in the sympaticoadrenal activity depend to a great extent on the variety of emotional experience of the individual, on his subjective perceptive particulates, as well as on the individual stereotype of reaction.
The actual statement analyses the alterations performed in the vegetative nervous system of students with incosiderable mental deficiency, when resolving tests for a fixed time.
The mentally deficient students were divided into two groups: erectile/excitable/and torpid/tranquil/.
Routine methods of research work on vegetative nervous system have been used and the following items have been reported on:
alteration in blood pressure, alterations in pulse frequency, alterations in respiratory movements frequency, alterations in skin termperature, alterations in the electrical resistance of the skin.

Session 253 Poster Presentation:
Pharmacotherapy of depression III

1676
LONG-TERM TREATMENT OF DEPRESSIONS WITH MOCLOBEMIDE AND CLOMIPRAMINE:
Jens Knud Larsen(1), Per Holm(2)
1. Department of Psychiatry, Frederiksberg Hospital
2. International Clinical Research (Nordic Region) Roche A/S, Copenhagen (Denmark)

Moclobemide (Ro 11-1163), a benzamide derivate, is a MAO-inhibitor which selectively and reversibly inhibits monoamine oxidase type A.
Material: Onehundred and sixty depressed patients participated in three randomized trials (1, 2, 3) lasting 42 days. The trials compared moclobemide with clomipramine. Ten patients on moclobemide and 12 on clomipramine who all responded well to treatment entered into long-term treatment. The median duration was 196 days, range 56 to 364 days.
Results: The antidepressant effect was maintained in all but one patient. Two patients on clomipramine dropped out: one owing to relapse and the other one because of a suicidal attempt. Two patients on moclobemide dropped out owing to bad taste and insomnia. Only mild side-effects were noticed, but anticholinergic side-effects were more common on clomipramine. No laboratory abnormalities were recorded.
1. Larsen J K, Holm P, Mikkelsen P L. Acta Psychiatr Scand 1984:70:254-260.
2. Koczkas C, Holm P, Karlsson A, Nagy A, Ose E, Pétursson H, Ulverås L, Wenedikter O. Acta Psychiatr Scand (in press).
3. Larsen J K, Holm P, Høyer E, Mejlhede A, Mikkelsen P L, Olesen A, Schaumburg E. Acta Psychiatr Scand (in press).

1677
GLC ANALYSIS OF BROFAROMINE - ITS APPLICATION IN PHARMACOKINETIC STUDIES
G.S.I.M. Jansen, J.J.M. Bommelé and P.M.J. Haffmans
Psychiatric Centre 'Bloemendaal', Dept. Clin. Pharm., The Hague, The Netherlands

Brofaromine (B;CGP11305A;4-(5-methoxy-7-bromo-benzofuranyl-2)-piperidine HCl) is a new short-acting, reversible and selective inhibitor of MAO-A. Until now very few data have been published on the determination of B and on its pharmacokinetic proporties. B seems to be effective as an antidepressant. However, various side effects are seen, especially sleep disturbances. So far there exist no reliable guidelines for effective dosages. As a start of a series of clinical studies of B a GLC method was developed to measure blood levels of B and its main metabolite, desmethyl-B. Results will be presented of a pharmacokinetic study in geriatric depressed patients (both single dose and repeated single dose). Data on steady state levels at different dosages will be presented in both geriatric and non-geriatric depressed patients. Comparison of blood levels with dosages and clinical (side)effects might help to define the right strategy for an effective treatment of depressed patients with B.

1678
BROFAROMINE AND TRANYLCYPROMINE IN RESISTANT MAJOR DEPRESSION

Willem A. Nolen, Judith Haffmans
Department of Biological Psychiatry, Psychiatric Centre Bloemendaal, The Hague, The Netherlands

In a still ongoing double-blind study the efficacy of brofaromine, a new selective and reversible MAO-A-inhibitor (max 250 mg daily) and tranylcypromine, a classical MAO-inhibitor (max 100 mg daily), both given during 4 weeks, are compared. Until now 20 patients with major depression according to DSM-III, who had not responded to earlier treatment with at least one cyclic antidepressant given during 4 weeks in an adequate dose and with therapeutic plasmalevels, completed the study. Respons is defined a decrease of $\geq 50\%$ on the Hamilton Rating Scale for Depression. Eight patients received tranylcypromine. Three of them responded, while another patient, after a partial response during the study, recovered during follow-up. Of the twelve patients who received brofaromine, five responded during the course of the study, while one patient recovered during further treatment.
Differences in side-effects favoured brofaromine: seven patients receiving brofaromine showed mild transient orthostatic hypotension (decrease of bloodpressure after standing ≥ 20 mm), not leading to further problems or complaints. In contrast, five of the patients who received tranylcypromine developed severe orthostatic hypotension, while two other patients suffered from hypotension, both when standing and lying. Sleep disturbances were found during both treatments. Other serious side-effects were not be observed.

1679
DOUBLE-BLIND COMPARISON OF INTRAVENOUS VERSUS ORAL DOXEPIN IN ENDOGENOUS DEPRESSION.
ANTIDEPRESSANT EFFICACY, ONSET OF ACTION, PLASMA LEVELS
Laux G[1], König W[2], Lesch KP[1], Stein A[2]
[1]Department of Psychiatry, University of Wuerzburg
[2]Psychiatric State Hospital, Weinsberg, FRG

Infusion therapy with antidepressants (ADI) has been established in recent years as one of the standard treatments of so-called therapy-resistant depressions ('oral non-responders'). Possible advantages of ADI comprise pharmacokinetic factors (bioavailability), assured compliance, rapid onset of action and clinical efficacy as well as psychological factors ('infusion setting'). Remarkably few controlled studies comparing drip infusion with controlled oral antidepressive medication have been published. Most of these studies did not reveal any therapeutic superiority of ADI, there were no pharmakokinetic advantages either. Small patients samples, patients selection and other methodological shortcommings, however have restricted the impact of these results. A double blind study was conducted involving n=45 "therapy-resistant" endogenous depressive inpatients who were treated with doxepin intravenously or orally. After a period of three weeks there was no significant difference in the clinical ratings (HRSD, SDS). In the parenteral treatment group however was there a statistically significant quicker onset of action (day 3). Compared to oral application higher doxepin plasma concentrations during day 1-6 could be obtained by drip-infusion in spite of lower dosage.

1680

ETUDE CONTROLEE DE L'EFFICACITE ET DE LA TOLERANCE
A LONG TERME DE LA CLOVOXAMINE DANS LA DEPRESSION
Dr A. Kasas, Dr H. Van
Clinique psychiatrique
Directeur Dr H. Van
2713 BELLELAY

RESUME

La Clovoxamine est un antidépresseur majeur, ce dont témoigne l'étude clinique à long terme (52 semaines) menée en ouvert.

Son profil est celui d'un antidépresseur qui est proche de la Clomipramine, agissant efficacement sur l'humeur, l'anxiété psychique et le ralentissement psychomoteur. Le mode d'action biochimique de la Clovoxamine est son agissement sur la recapture de la noradrénaline (NA) et de la sérotonie (5-HT).

Dans cette étude, 38 patients dépressifs ont été traités (25 femmes et 13 hommes). 5 patients ont arrêté le traitement à cause d'intolérance (excitation psychomotrice, état maniforme, nausées, vomissements et anorexie. Sur 38 patients, 23 ont terminé 52 semaines avec un score moyen de Hamilton de 2,6.

Dans cette étude ouverte, nous avons pu constater que la Clovoxamine est un antidépresseur efficace, bien toléré dans le traitement d'état dépressif aigu et à long terme.

1681

DOUBLE-BLIND STUDY OF MINAPRINE VS AMITRIPTYLINE IN MAJOR DEPRESSION
M. Del Zompo, F. Bernardi, M. Pedditzi, S.M. Chierichetti*, S. Sommacal*
Department of Neurosciences, University of Cagliari, Italy
*Medical Department, Midy S.p.A. Sanofi, Milan, Italy

Minaprine is an original psychotropic drug showing a particular profile as antidepressive. In fact, minaprine appears to produce an activation of both serotoninergic and dopaminergic neuro transmissions, by as yet not clarified mechanism of action. In this randomized controlled double-blind study, the therapeutic effect and tolerance of minaprine was evaluated in comparison to amitriptyline in 60 patients (mean age 47 years; range 19-69; 43 females - 17 females) suffering from major depressive episode (DSM III).
After a week placebo run-in period, during which placebo responders were excluded, 28 patients received minaprine 200-300 mg daily and 30 patients received amitriptyline 50 - 75 mg for 6 weeks. To assess the symptomatology the Hamilton Depression Rating Scale, the Zung self-Rating Scale and the Covi Anxiety Rating Scale were used. Patients were also evaluated by a final clinical global impression (CGI). Possible adverse reactions were evaluated with a special symtpoms scale. Both groups showed a significant reduction in the Hamilton R.S. and in the other scales used without statistical difference between the 2 groups of patients. It is of interest that the side-effect showed by the patients treated with minaprine were less and of lower intensity compared to the patients of the other group. This study confirms the efficacy and the good tolerance of minaprine in the treatment of depressive disorder.

1682

ASSOCIATING VILOXAZINE AND IMIPRAMINE: A NEW WAY FOR THE TREATMENT OF RESISTANT DEPRESSIONS?
S.Brion, J.Plas, J.F.Chevalier, J.Gailledreau, J.Lavoisy
Versailles, Cedex, France

Treating depressions with imipramine or viloxazine alone usually leads to a rate of success of about 60 to 70% So 30 to 40% of the patients remain insufficiently treated of their depressive symptomatology. A few number of studies have been conducted in order to determine which treatment could be useful to this category of patients. A retrospective study including 8 of them, ranged from 32 to 81 years of age (mean 58) has been conducted in Versailles. The diagnosis criteria for inclusion referred to the French INSERM classification and evolution was assessed by a systematic clinical examination led by one of us. 75% of the patients have presented a good or a very good response after 3 weeks of treatment associating 30 to 150 mg of imipramine, and 100 to 300 mg of viloxazine. One of them has presented slight gastralgia.
We will discuss the clinical way of assessment used in this study, and the results observed in each of these 8 patients.
The good results observed in this study suggest the need for development of further studies to confirm the good efficacy of associating viloxazine and imipramine.

1683

MIANSERIN: WIRKPROFIL BEI DEPRESSIVEN PATIENTEN IN DER NERVENARZTPRAXIS
Chwatal K., Macura R., Schönbeck G.:
Psychiatrische Universitätsklinik Wien, Österreich

Ziel des vorliegenden Untersuchungsprogrammes war es, Erfahrungen über die Anwendung von Mianserin und seines speziellen Wirkprofils zu sammeln. Die Diagnose erfolgte nach DSM III und ICD 9. Der Ausprägungsgrad des depressiven Syndroms wurde in dem 42 Tage dauernden Programm zu definierten Zeitpunkten mittels Selbst- und Fremdbeurteilungsskalen beurteilt. Die Dosierung des Medikamentes wurde mit 60mg bzw. 90mg/die empfohlen. Von den 121 Patienten (39 männlich, 82 weiblich) beendeten 75 das gesamte Programm regulär. Bei 46 Depressiven wurde als Abbruchgrund non compliance (12x), kein Ansprechen auf Tolvon (12x), oder unerwünschte Nebenwirkungen (7x) angegeben. Bei 3 Patienten wurde die Medikation wegen rascher Besserung abgesetzt. Mianserin erwies sich in der Anwendung beim niedergelassenen Facharzt als gut einsetzbar und zeigte eine rasche und verlässliche antidepressive Wirkung. Differenzierte Ergebnisse werden vorgestellt.

1684

THERAPEUTIC FAILURE AND HIGH BLOOD LEVELS OF TRICYCLIC ANTIDEPRESSANTS.

AE Balant-Gorgia, LP Balant, G Garrone, Department of Psychiatry, University of Geneva, 1211 Geneva 4, Switzerland

Seven patients are described who displayed excessive concentrations of imipramine (IMI) or clomipramine (CLO) and their demethylated metabolites (DESI, DECLO) on routine blood level monitoring. Under these conditions, the patients did not respond to the treatment and suffered from side effects. Three patients were characterized as poor hydroxylators of debrisoquine: Mrs B, 75 mg IMI/day (125 ng/ml IMI + 1730 ng/ml DESI); Mr F, 150 mg CLO/day (235 ng/ml CLO + 980 ng/ml DECLO); Mr G, 225 mg CLO/day (160 ng/ml + 960 ng/ml DECLO). Three patients had concomitant treatment with a phenothiazine and were thus rendered poor metabolizers of IMI or CLO: Mrs C, 150 mg IMI/day (IMI 55 ng/ml + DESI 755 ng/ml); Mrs D, 150 mg IMI/day (IMI 35 ng/ml + DESI 490 ng/ml); Mrs E, 175 mg IMI/day (IMI 45 ng/ml + DESI 335 ng/ml). One elderly patient (Mrs H, 75 mg CLO/day) suffered from antidepressant intoxication (CLO 410 ng/ml + DECLO 1010 ng/ml). All patients were markedly improved when daily dosage of the drug was reduced with a simultaneous decrease in blood levels.

1685

TOTAL TCA SERUM LEVELS IN DEPRESSED OUTPATIENTS.

A. Kourkoubas, B. Haviaras, E. Anagnostou, M. Vranakis, C. Zervos, S. Karvounis, K. Karetsou G. Sakalis.
Evangelismos General Hospital Athens, Greece.

Twenty depressed outpatients, both men and women mean age 52.3 years (S.D ± 15.1) fulfiling DSM-III criteria for Major Depression were treated openly with Amitriptyline or Nortriptyline. The effect of these drugs on the myocardium, particularly in the aged, are well known therefore it is desirable to keep dosage as low as possible. Equally well known is the "paradox of research" with fixed doses; we therefore used the floating dose.
Assays were carried out before initiation of treatment and at steady state employing the method of Fluor Polarization Immunoassay. This method gives us a total TCA level thus obviating the need to make separate measurements of the active Hydroxy-derivatives of the drugs. Accordingly we obtained high serum levels and kept dosages low, i.e 75-150mg/diem with favorable response as recorded on the HDS. There was also a correlation between dose and serum level. The method employed, is relatively easy and accurate and although much more work is needed in this field, it seems to us, that for the time being it would be suitable for routine use.

Session 254 Poster Presentation: Delusional states and other psychiatric conditions

1686

TWO CASES OF KORO SYNDROME IN ITALY.

Massimo Rabboni
SPDC Vergani, Ospedale Niguarda, Milano, Italia

The Koro syndrome is characterized by recurring fits of intense anxiety, lasting from a few hours to several days, due to the patient's conviction that the penis is withdrawing under the skin until it disappears. The crisis is coupled with a sensation of imminent death and, almost always, with loss of identity and troubles of the consciousness. This syndrome is comparatively spread in China and Malaysia, most uncommon in Western countries.
The A. report two cases of Koro syndrome, not associated with other psychic pathologies, observed in male subjects of low cultural level; both subjects were born and reside in a restricted area of Lombardy; one of them evolving towards recovery, the other instead toward a deficitary psychosis.
Starting from the discussion of the two cases, for which the cultural element seams to be of scarce importance in the genesis of the disease, the A. suggest some considerations of the psychopathology and psychodynamics of the syndrome, considered also as the typical pathology of adults (adult identity) and of aggressive pulsion.
The Koro syndrome, therefore, might represent a form of defence - and selfpunishment - with regard to feelings of jealousy and primary envy, felt in a scissional way.

1687

KORO GRAFTED UPON AN UNDERLYING PSYCHIATRIC ILLNESS

E.Frangos, S.Frangou and P.Alexandrakou
Athens, Greece

The concurrent appearance of the Koro syndrome either with typical psychiatric illness or pathology of the central nervous system is rather rare.
A case of a patient with a diagnosis of schizophrenia according to the D.S.M.III criteria who displayed for a long period the typical symptoms of Koro syndrome is presented.
After a series of electroconvulsive shock treatment the Koro symptoms resolved while florid schizophrenic symptoms still remain predominating in the clinical picture of the patient.

1688
DELUSION OF JEALOUSY IN THE ELDERLY MAN

Masashi Yamaguchi & Tomoko Yamaguchi
Minami-Yachimata Hospital & Tokyo Women's Medical College, Japan

People of Japan are living to older age, the prevalence of age-related psychiatric problems is increasing. One of the frequent abnormal changes in the elderly man who has retired from the active social life, include jealous delusion and accusatory behavior to the spouse. The domestic violence based on the jealous delusion has been recognized as a social problem for which divorce or hospitalization is considered, and the elderly violent or aggressive patients are among the most difficult to manage.
4 cases were evaluated for presentation; 2 in-patients and 2 out-patients. Generally the physical violence was not severe; verbal threats were common, accompanied by phenomena such as tail and watch. Usually women were innocent except a questionable case. Chronic illnesses such as hemiplegia, arthritis and diabetes played a role to develop the symptoms. The personality patterns were dualism for the man; avoidance for the woman. Manic-depressive disorder or transient delirium with mild dementia were observed. Furthermore most suspiciousness was related to the alcoholism.

1689

DELUSIONAL (PARANOID) DISORDER
D.H.Batchelor*, T.M.Reilly**
*Janssen Research Foundation, Wantage, United Kingdom, **The Retreat, York, United Kingdom

The term "Delusional (Paranoid) Disorder" appears for the first time in DSM-III-R, replacing the term "Paranoia" previously preferred in DSM-III. The historical evolution of this diagnostic concept is outlined and its current descriptive and nosological status is reviewed.
The differential diagnoses are described and especial reference is made to the somatic subtype, emphasizing recent advances in management, particularly with the diphenylbutylpiperidine neuroleptic pimozide.

1690

MUNCHAUSEN'S SYNDROME: DIAGNOSTIC DIFFICULTIES
LORETTU L-NIVOLI GC-SANNA MN-PITTALIS A CORGIOLU T
CLINICA PSICHIATRICA UNIVERSITA'SASSARI ITALY.

The authors, after a bibliographic review of the diagnostic difficulties involved with Munchausen's syndrome, describe a clinical case. The case concerns a 38 year old patient who underwent numerous surgical operations and frequent, repeated anti-dolorific therapy which brought no relief or reduction in the patient's alleged symptoms. At a diagnostic level, the authors illustrate the various admissions of the patient in internistic, anaesthesiological and surgical wards, which show the difficulties linked to a correct psychiatric diagnosis. The difficulty is emphasised of understanding the etiology and dynamics of this disease, and of the adoption of valid therapeutic projects.

* MUNCHAUSEN'S SYNDROME=acute fictitius disturbance with physical symptoms (after the classification of the DSM III - R)

1691

SOCIAL-PSYCHIATRIC CHARACTERISTICS OF REACTIVE PSYCHOSIS

Ass. Prof. Marko Munjiza, M.D. Ph.D., Institute for Mental Health. Belgrade, Palmotićeva 37, Yugoslavia

Acute psychotic disturbances, which are mostly caused reactively, present a very significant field of research in clinical and social psychiatry. This paper is to do with a longitudinal analysis of these illnesses in the period between 1971 and 1987 in Belgrade. During this research records from the Registry of Psychosis in Belgrade was used, which enabled the testing of the hypothesis of a psychiatric morbidity in our enviroment.

Analysis has shown us that reactive psychosis is one of the most frequent psychiatric disturbances, where the index prevelention and incidencie are rather high (40%) in the group of all psyvhosis. This is confirmed by the rather high morbidity risk for this group of illness — which amounts to around 2%. The distribution of clinical entities of these disturbances confirm the allegations in literature that there is a greater frequency of acute paranoic and depressive disturbances.

A large number of acute confused states are characteristic for our enviroment. Due to the extencity of the research it was not possible to define more precisely the cause of these illnesses of the personality structure, egzogene and endogamic factors. Researching for this paper a frequent recediv a very different development of the illness was noticed, as opposed to the allegations of the literature that was at our disposal.

A large risk of becoming ill was noticed in almost all age groups, especially in the period of late adolescence and pre-seniie period. No significant differences were noticed regarding professional status, immigational and family characteristics, nor in urban and rural enviroments. The vulnerability of the personality was stressed more so in the age group and structure according to sexes, than in any other sociodemographic characteristics of the interviewed population with a big risk of having reactive psychosis.

This paper confirms the hypothesis that a large number of frequencies of these disturbances are among psychotic patients, even up to 40% in the early involutional period, with bimodal features of the incidencle age line and the risk of becoming ill.

1692

HYSTERICAL PSYCHOSES
A.Cebollada, A.Chinchilla, J.L.Carrasco, M.Vega, I.Moreno, R.Vinas, P.Sanchez, Jorda y M.Camarero
Psych.Dept., Hosp. Ramon y Cajal, Madrid, Spain

30 patients admitted to our psychiatric service with the initial diagnosis of psychogenic psychosis, dissociative psychosis or hysterical pseudo-psychosis are studied anamnestically and in their catamnesis (average follow up 5.1 years).
In this study we found a greater percentage of women (3/1), with a previous hysterical personality in more than 50%; many of the patients were hospitalized in order to clarify the diagnosis; in 70% we found psychogenic triggers. There was a greater predominance of an abrupt onset of the disorder; 60% had fluctuating symptoms. In almost 100% there was a complete remission during the hospitalization on period (average 22.7 days), which would bring them closer to the present concept of brief reactive psychosis.
We think that these disorders are well delimited, both clinically and nosologically, not having received an exact placing in modern classification systems (DSM-III, ICD-10, etc.).

1693

PSYCHOPATHOLOGICAL OUTCOME OF PUERPERAL PSYCHOSES
B. Guerrini degl'Innocenti, R. Frassine, G. Marchetti, S. Rosseti, P. Benvenuti, P.L. Cabras
Department of Neurological and Psychiatric Sciences
University of Florence - ITALY

The study of puerperal psychopathology seems to be a very interesting subject because of the controversial nosographical category, the psychological and physical binding with pregnancy and delivery, and the possible effects on the quality of the mother-baby relationship. For this reason thirty cases with diagnosis of puerperal psychoses were examined. All these cases were referred to the Florence Psychiatric Services as inpatients in the period from January 1973 to December 1988. The psychopathological state at the first hospital admission was assessed retrospectively by means of a structured interview designed to detected social and demographic data, family history, social adjustment and psychiatric symptoms, according to RDC and DSM-III-R criteria. In a second stage the present psychopathological state of the same patients, was assessed with the same interview. Moreover the present nosological set up was compared with the onset diagnosis. The changes in terms of social adaptation, interpersonal relationship and personality variables related to the illness was also investigated. At the same time, by means of a contact with the patients' close relatives and their own doctor, some informations were collected to reconstruct the natural history of the puerperal psychoses in terms of the outcomeof the puerperal crisis, the presence of such relapses and if thesewere or not related to following motherhood.

1694

ACTION OF ANTIDEPRESSANT DRUG (TRIMIPRAMINE) ON DELUSIONAL DISORDERS
P. Robert, T. Braccini, V. Aubin, G. Darcourt, F. Raffaitin
Hopital Pasteur - CHU - Nice 06002 - France
Laboratoire Specia - France

Since Laseque in 1852 chronic delusional disorders were the subjects of many descriptions in French psychiatric litterature. Several studies suggest that delusional disorders without discordant symptoms (incoherence, marked loosening of association) are unrelated with schizophrenia. The aim of this study is to investigate links between delusional disorders without dissociative syndrome and affective disorders. 10 patients diagnosed according to French empirical criteria of delusional disorders, (furthermore MADRS total score must be lower than 25), received during 28 days 100 mg to 300 mg of Trimipramine alone. Patients were, evaluated each week with the scale for the assement of positive symptoms (SAPS - N. ANDREASEN), BPRS and MADRS. In after 28 days of treatment SAPS total score was equal or lower than the initial score patients received Trimipramine and chlorpromazine. Results indicate:
-Relationships between French empirical criteria and DSMIII-R axis 1.
-Evaluation of therapeutic response with antidepressant (trimipramine) alone or in association with neuroleptic.
-Evaluation of therapeutic response of each delusional symptoms.

1695

"LE SYNDROME DES CAMBRIOLES-VANDALISES"
C. Lacombe-Mestas, Médecin-Directeur "Le Castel" HYERES (Var)

The number of house robberies is increasing dangerously from day to day. Paradoxicaly, it does't seem that the Authorities are taking any action against these persons who are often considered as heroes by media (particularly when they reached the murder).
We have pointed out some common symptoms to ransacked persons. This survey has been done over 250 cases.
The first important point is the following : all the persons are placing into the background the financial prejudice even the poorest ; on the other hand what is revolting them is: IT IS THE ROBBERY, OR RATHER THE RAPE OF THEIR MEMORIES. An old woman of 80 years told me "they have killed my past".
Generally, three types of symptoms are observed :
1° Cardio-vascular symptoms : state of shock - hypotension syncope - bout of blood pressure in hypersensitive patients - heart attack - angine pectoris.
2° Digestive troubles : nauseas - vomiting - diarrhoeas - loss of appetite.
3° Neuropsychiatric troubles : severe anxiety (digestive cardiac - pharyngeal) anxiety - depressive disorders (from tear crises to suicide envy) sleep disorders with mares.
This syndrom reduced gradualy at the end of 2 years, but sequelaes are always remaining.
The therapeutic is only symptomatic but it would be prophylactic with elimination of these parasits of humanity by exemplar penalties.

1696
THE TIME ARRANGEMENT IN FAMILIES OF NEUROTIC PATIENTS
Mirko Pejović, M.D., Ph.D
Department of psychiatry, University Clinical Centre, Belgrade, Yugoslavia

As part of family interactions psychoneuroses are frequently contagious diseases if they are manifest for a long time. A neurotic person is characterised by contradictory motivations, conflict relations, anxiety in face of demands.

In the families of neurotic patients we usually find the conflicts because of lack of agreement about the schedule of duties and limitations. Each family has its own lifetime as well as its mechanisms of time use and distribution. Neurotics are inconsistent and confused in the distribution of their time. Frequently they neither know how to choose adequate principles of time arrangement of their own nor they accept the family's common time arrangement.

In our poster we are going to present detailed time arrangement in such families as well as the importance of therapeutic intervention for solution to the discord among family members.

Session 255 Poster Presentation:
Pharmacotherapy in schizophrenia II

1697
Treatment of Schizophrenic Patients With Leucocyte Interferon /IFN/
Jerzy Leszek., A.D.Inglot., K.Cantell, A.Wasik
Psych.Clin.Univ.Med.School, Wrocław, Inst.Immunol.and Exp.Ther.Pol.Acad.Sci., Wrocław, Poland and Central Publ. Health Lab., Helsinki, Finland.

We studied the effects of the IFN treatment on the course of chronic schizophrenia. IFN was administered s.c. daily in the dose of 3×10^6 U/ml, for 6 wks. Eight pts improved. In 4 pts the remission was complete. Nine of the pts did not improve. In 4 pts the pejoration of the psychotic symptoms was observed. Ten of 17 pts who completed the 6-wks IFN course were subsequently treated with chlorpromazine. All of the patients were found to be oversensitive to the drug. Fifteen control pts /8F,7M/ after 2 wks wash out period received placebo treatment only /daily injection of saline/. No change in their overall psychic condition or pejoration /except one/ was observed during 2-6 wks observation period. In conclusion we suggest that the administration of IFN-α may induce remission in schizophrenia pts.

1698
LONG-TERM TREATMENT OF FEMALE CHRONIC PATIENTS WITH NEUROLEPTIC DRUGS
Echarri-Arrieta Eduardo, Agra-Romero, Santiago
Sanatorio Psiquiatrico de Conxo
Santiago de Compostela, Spain

With the aim of investigating the hematic and hepatic effects of long-term therapy with neuroleptic drugs in terms of measurable laboratory parameters, 32 female chronic patients who had been treated uninterruptedly with oral and long-acting neuroleptic drugs for 5 to 36 years were examined through laboratory tests in the last two years.
Hemograms, WBC counts, glucose, urea, uric acid, cholesterol, total proteins, total and direct bilirrubine, GOT, GPT, GGT enzymes, were studied and adverse drug reactions, somatic diseases and body weight changes were evaluated.
The results are discussed under the security use of long-term neuroleptic therapy point of view. We have obtained a very little rate of hematic parameters variation, with interesting modifications of body weight and appearance of somatic and neurological diseases.

1699
THE DOMPERIDONE TEST IN SCHIZOPHRENIA

D. Nerozzi*, A. Magnani, E. Scaramucci, V. Sforza, M. Cerilli, C. Moretti, G. Bersani, A. Pasini
*Dept. Medicina Sperimentale, and Istituto di Clinica Medica V, University of Rome "La Sapienza"

Growth Hormone (GH) and Prolactin (PRL) responses to 20 mg of Domperidone, a peripheral dopamine blocking agent, were evaluated in a group of 16 young (20 ± 1.3), acute, drug-free male schizophrenics and in a group of 10 sex and age-matched normal controls in order to investigate the dopamine receptor function, which has been repeatedly found altered in schizophrenia. After an overnight fast at 8 o'clock a catheter was inserted into a forearm vein and baseline samples were drawn before the administration of Domperidone per os, further samples were collected at +60, +90, +105, +120. Results showed a blunted PRL response in approximately 70% of our schizophrenic subjects when compared to controls (ANOVA $p=0.000$).
Our data seem to point out an abnormal receptor sensitivity and consequently an abnormal dopaminergic function in our patients, while any attempt to correlate the biological data with psychopathological features (such as clinical diagnoses, according to DSM-III and RDC, positive and negative symptoms, according to Andreasen) were unfruitful.

1700

NEUROLEPTIC-INDUCED CATATONIA OR A MILD FORM OF NEUROLEPTIC MALIGNANT SYNDROME ?

H.Valergaki, V.Kontaxakis, N.Vaidakis and G.N.Christodoulou
Department of Psychiatry, Eginition Hospital, 74 Vas.Sophias Ave., 11528 Athens, Greece

Neuroleptic-induced catatonia(NIC) and Neuroleptic malignant syndrome(NMS) have been described in patients receiving antipsychotic agents.These two conditions share parkinsonian features,catatonic symptoms and mild fever.We describe a case of a patient who can be diagnosed either as NIC or as a mild form of NMS and who has been treated successfully with a combination of amantadine and diazepam.The patient,a 20-year old man with a schizophreniform disorder and a mild mental retardation had received haloperidol 40 mg,thioridazine 600 mg, and biperiden 6 mg per day,without favorable response.Ten days after receiving an intramuscular injection of 300 mg haloperidol decanoate he developed marked rigidity,tremor,dysphagia,sialorrhea, diaphoresis,tachycardia,tachypnea,mild hypertention catatonic symptoms and mild fever(37.5°C).CPK was 65 U/l and WBC reached 14600/mm³.The neuroleptics were discontinued and diazepam 30 mg/day and amantadine 600 mg/day were instituted.A few days later the patient's symptoms subsided markedly.
The differential diagnosis between NIC and mild NMS cases is very difficult and might lead to an overestimation of the incidence of NMS.The overlaping between NIC and mild NMS cases reinforces the possibility of the existence of a "neuroleptic toxicity spectrum".

1701

COMPUTERISED MONITORING OF DEPOT NEUROLEPTICS REDUCES POLYPHARMACY

Dr P Jauhar & Dr M Stewart, Parkhead Hospital, 81 Salamanca Street, Glasgow G31 5ES, United Kingdom

The computerised monitoring of all patients in the Eastern District of Glasgow, was initiated 3 years ago, to improve compliance by closer monitoring; increase awareness of dose adjustment to minimal maintenance dosage and possibly reduce readmission by improving compliance.

This computerised monitoring is one of two modules designed to monitor clinical care of chronic psychotic patients. The system ensures all patients in the community are monitored by psychiatrists and community psychiatric nurses, with computerised monthly reports to consultant psychiatrists of all their patients on depot neuroleptics.

A study was undertaken of patients registered on the computer who received depot neuroleptics during a two year period (October 85 - October 87). An analysis of a random sample of 110 patients who were registered on the computer in October 1985 was undertaken to evaluate if closer monitoring was effective in reducing polypharmacy, reducing default from medication and readmission to hospital.

An analysis of their computerised monitoring shows that polypharmacy was reduced - 66% were maintained on a single neuroleptic, with no concomitant medication, including antiparkinsonian medication; comparable studies in Britain have identified only 39% on a single drug.

Improved monitoring was associated with dose adjustment in nearly 50% of patients, reflecting psychiatrists awareness of side effect profiles and lower maintenance dosage; as well as lower readmission rates (21%).

1702

NEUROLEPTICS AND COPING BEHAVIORS IN THE RECOVERY FROM SCHIZOPHRENIA

G.Yagi, F.Kinoshita A.Kikuchi and T.Inada, Dept. Neuropsychiat., Keio Univ. School of Med. Tokyo, Japan.

It has been recently suggested that patient's coping behavior(CPB) and subjective responses to neuroleptics(NLP) may have some influence on the outcome of schizophrenia. The present study attempted to elucidate an interaction between NLP and CPB in the recovery from acute schizophrenic psychosis.

Thirteen schizophrenics(SZ) under NLP and sixteen depressives(DP) under antidepressants (control group) were interviewed at the time of their recovery. They were asked how they have coped with their illness and their perceptions about the effectiveness of prescription drugs.

Various CPBs were reported by 12 patients(92%) in the SZ group and by 15 patients(96%) in DP. Concerning coping strategies, the changes (mainly an increase) in physical activity were more frequently reported by the SZ(62%) group than by the DP(25%) group. The desirable drug effects were less frequently and less clearly perceived by the SZ(31%) than by the DP(69%). In particular, a desirable hypnotic effect (0% in SZ, 50% in DP).

These findings indicate that the interaction between NLP and "antipsychotic behavior" in the recovery process of SZ might be quite different from that between antidepressant drug and "antidepressive behavior" in DP.

1703

SERUM NEUROLEPTIC ACTIVITY IN THE RECOVERY FROM SCHIZOPHRENIA

S.Kanba,H.Kohno,F.Kinoshita,A.Nakamura,K.Suzuki and G.Yagi, Dept. of Neuropsychiatry, Keio Univ. School of Med., Tokyo, Japan.

It is widely accepted that therapeutic effect of neuroleptics(NLP) for schizophrenia may be based on blockade of central dopaminergic transmission. However, there is no clear clinical evidence for this hypothesis. In this study, we attempted to clarify relationship between clinical improvement of psychotic symptoms and serum neuroleptic activities(SNA) for neurotransmitter receptors.

The subjects consisted of 7 newly admitted schizophrenics(ICD-9); 6 men and 1 woman. They were aged 25 to 45 (a mean of 36.4 years). All patients were treated without any structure in a usual clinical setting. SNA for dopamine-D1,-D2 and muscarinic acetylcholine(M-Ach) receptor were measured by radioreceptor assay. Blood samples were obtained on the day 0, 7 and 28.

During this period, 4 patients showed marked response to NLP, but the remaining 3 did not. In the responders, a rapid rise of SNA for both D2 and M-Ach receptor was found as a common change, while in the non-responders only SNA for M-Ach receptor increased. No consistent change was found in SNA for D1 receptor in either group.

Our data suggest that the rapid and marked rise of SNA for D2 receptor plays an important role in the recovery from acute schizophrenic episodes under the NLP treatment.

1704

CARDIOVASCULAR ACTIVITY AS A POSSIBLE PREDICTOR OF NEURO-
LEPTIC RESPONSE IN ACUTE SCHIZOPHRENICS
VOLZ H-P, MACKERT A, FRIEDRICH A, GAEBEL W, STOCK G*
Psychiatrische Klinik der Freien Universität Berlin,
Eschenallee 3, D-1000 Berlin 19 (FRG)
* Schering AG, Müllerstr. 165, D-1000 Berlin 65

Autonomic psychophysiologic measures have shown a high base line of electrodermal and cardiovascular acitivty and slow rate of adaptation to new stimuli (ZAHN 1988). These patterns predicted a poor outcome on a 3-month follow-up.
To test cardiovascular activity and reactivity of 20 acute schizophrenics without and then with neuroleptic treatment for 4 weeks (perazine or haloperidol) we used an orthostatic challenge test and a single test-dose-design (oral application of 150mg perazine in the morning).
Patients with higher variability of cardiovascular parameters (heart rate and blood pressure) and a "physiological" reaction during the orthostatic challenge showed good response (according to BPRS) to neuroleptic treatment. The data are compared with other function of cardiovascular regulation, like plasma-concentration of vasopressin, renine, angiotensine 2 and aldosterone.
Results are discussed - beside the autonomic aspect - with regard to a disturbed dopaminergic modulation of central cardiovascular regulation.

Literature: ZAHN TP: Studies of autonomic psychophysiology and attention in schizophrenia. Schiz. Bull. 14: 205-208 (1988)

1705

OBSERVANCE DU TRAITEMENT NEUROLEPTIQUE PAR LES PATIENTS
PSYCHOTIQUES CHRONIQUES
K. RADDAOUI, M. PAES, J.E.KTIOUET,S.KETTANI,OULD AMMAR,MEKNASSI
CLINIQUE UNIVERSITAIRE DE PSYCHIATRIE - RABAT MAROC

L'arrêt du traitement neuroleptique ou son observation partielle voire anarchique est un phénomène de constatation quotidienne chez les patients psychotiques chroniques. Ceux-ci font souvent l'objet d'hospitalisations itératives et présentent de nombreuses rechutes gênant leur réinsertion socio-professionnelle.
Les auteurs tentent, à travers une étude prospective effectuée sur un large échantillon de patients hospitalisés, d'évaluer l'importance et les raisons de ce problème.

1706

RELATIONS BETWEEN BOYD WEIGHT; HEIGHT AND FEMALE
SEX and TARDIVE DYSKINESIA
Steinwachs K.C.[1], Bartonek R.[2], Sandmann R.[2], Fisher V.[2].
1) Bezirkskrankrankenhaus Erlangen, Am Europakanal 71, 8520 Erlangen. F.R.G.
2) Psychiatrische Universitätsklinik Erlangen, Schwabachanlage 6, 8500 Erlangen. F.R.G.

In the present study we examined the role of multiple variables in the frequency of tardive diskinesia (TD) with the purpose of delineating a spectrum of factors to TD. Our study included 383 psychiatric patients of the Bezirkskrankenhaus Erlangen. 47,5 % of these patients (N=182) hat TD. Mean ages and total neuroleptic dose were 61,5 and 1,5 kg CPZEq for the patients with TD and 45,7 and 1,3 kg CPZEq for the subjects without TD. Drug history and other neuroleptic side-effects were documented. All patients were rated on SKAUB(AIMS) and on BPRS-score Motor behavior was measured by the registration of handwriting pressure parameters.
In our study age was the dominant factor for TD and many significant intercorrelations at other variables were found. For that reason experimental effects were tested by the analysis of covariance. Independant from age we found significant (P o.o1) interaction effects between small weight, little height female sex and lower writing pressure and TD. There was no significant effects between TD and neuroleptic dose, BPRS-scores and additional organic brain disorder. Our results suggested a constitutional disposition for TD.

1707

A PROSPECTIVE STUDY OF TARDIVE DYSKINESIA
T. Inada, K. Ohnishi, M. Kamisada, G. Matsuda,
O. Tajima, Y. Yanagisawa, K. Hashiguchi, S. Shima,
Y. Oh-e, Y. Masuda, T. Chiba, K. Kamijima,
S. Kanba and G. Yagi, Dept. Neuropsychiatry,
Keio Univ. Med. School, Tokyo, Japan.

Many psychiatrists are more aware of tardive dyskinesia(TD) since it has become a serious clinical problem in mental hospitals. In 1987 we examined prevalence of TD in 1595 patients who received psychiatric therapy for at least 6 months at one of our psychiatric facilities.
Of the 1595 patients, 1140 had a diagnosis of schizophrenia, 118 of mental retardation, 94 of manic-depressive illness and 243 of other illness such as epilepsy, alcohol related psychoses, personality disorders, neuroses and so forth. The severity of TD was assessed with the Abnormal Involuntary Movement Scale (AIMS) and we regarded a patient as having TD when the total AIMS score was higher than 2. Past history of somatic therapy, complication of parkinsonism, duration of neuroleptic treatment and current daily doses of neuroleptics were also recorded. The prevalence of TD in 1987 was 7.6 % for all patients. TD variants were recognized such as tardive dystonia, tardive akathisia and so forth. In 1988 we reexamined the same group except 490 dropouts. The 1 year's TD incidence from 1987 to 1988 was 1.0 %.
Subclassification of TD by a multivariate analysis and by clinical features, risk factors of TD and relationship between TD and neuroleptics will be discussed.

Session 256 — Video:
Psychological reaction to cancer

1708
PSYCHOSOCIAL ADAPTATION IN BREAST CANCER

Achté, Kalle, Clinic of Psychiatry,
Helsinki University Central Hospital,
Helsinki, Finland;
Vauhkonen, Maija-Liisa, Hesperia Hospital,
Helsinki, Finland;
Lindfors, Olavi, Jorvi Hospital, Espoo;
Salokari, Markku, Jorvi Hospital, Espoo,
Finland

Psychosocial adaptation in breast cancer –video presentation is aimed to be used in the education of medical students and in the training of other medical staff. The video outlines the psychosocial coping and defence mechansims which most often can be seen in breast cancer patients. The adaptation is decribed as a highly individual process, although some categories of adaptation styles can be named.
Case examples - interviews of breast cancer patients in their fourth post-mastectomy year - are shown which highlight three basic coping mechanisms: future-oriented optimism and fighting spirit; minimization or denial of illness; capitulation and depression. The case examples which are based on authentic clinical cases show how psychosocial support and succesfull psychiatric counseling can influence the course of adaptation.

1709
THERE IS NOTHING TO WORRY ABOUT

ALAN LYALL, M.D., Univ. of Toronto, Toronto Can.

PURPOSE: This is a multi-purpose teaching video made to demonstrate the psycho-social dynamics of an illness and to illustrate an expanded role for Psychiatry in medical education. It allows an examination of the havoc created in a well adjusted patient by the investigation of a breast lump, and of the efficacy of the roles played by various doctors.
FORMAT: The video centers on the narrative of an individual patient as she explains to a psychiatrist her thoughts and feelings from the moment she first noticed a lump in her breast through the various professional and personal interactions from those who said, "there is nothing to worry about." to the moment when she finally heard the phrase "it was just a benign lump." A minimum of diagrams and voice-overs are used to set context, highlight key points, raise discussion questions and pull together a summary conclusion.
USES: To heighten awareness of the impact of illness on the psycho-social system of a patient. To illustrate the psycho dynamics of loss. To stimulate the examination and discussion of the role of the Doctor in the total care of the person who becomes a patient. To illustrate an area of medical education where psychiatry can and must play a greater role. To facilitate interdisciplinary co-operation in the care of the person who suffers an illness.

Session 257 — Film:
Anorexia Nervosa

1710
Anorexia Nervosa: Eine Dokumentation

Gerlinghoff, M. und Backmund, H.
Max-Planck-Institut für Psychiatrie
Kraepelinstraße 10
8000 München 40   FRG

In einem Film der zusammen mit dem "Institut für den Wissenschaftlichen Film", Göttingen, produziert wurde, wird die Entwicklung und Behandlung der Anorexia nervosa und Bulimie dokumentiert. Die Darstellung typischer Szenen durch Patienten, Eltern und Therapeuten ermöglicht eine hohe Authentizität. Der Film wurde für die Ausbildung von Therapeuten konzipiert und kann auch bei gruppentherapeutischen Sitzungen als Diskussionsgrundlage eingesetzt werden.

Session 258 — Workshop:
The psychiatric subspecialty of sleep disorders medicine

1711
THE PSYCHIATRIC SUBSPECIALTY of SLEEP DISORDERS MEDICINE
Soldatos CR,[1] Manfredi RL,[2] Vela-Bueno A,[3] Bergiannaki JD,[1] Sakkas PN,[1] Julius D[4]; [1]Univ. of Athens, Greece; [2]Penn State Univ., U.S.A.; [3]Autonomous Univ., Spain; [4]Med. Coll. Virginia, U.S.A.

This workshop is intended to develop and sharpen the skills of the psychiatrist interested in the psychiatric subspecialty of Sleep Disorders Medicine (SDM). Subspecialists in SDM have three major goals: to educate general psychiatrists and other physicians about SDM; to provide backup consultation to physicians for the severe and intractable cases of sleep disorders; and to develop and implement clinical/research programs and activities in SDM. The workshop will focus on three general diagnostic categories: developmental sleep disorders in children (sleepwalking, night terrors, nightmares, primary enuresis); sleep disorders in which psychiatric factors are prominent (insomnia, secondary enuresis and the parasomnias in adults); and organic sleep disorders (narcolepsy/cataplexy and sleep apnea) where psychosocial consequences are often pronounced. A multidimensional evaluation and treatment approach, with emphasis on biopsychosocial and behavioral approaches is emphasized. Participants are instructed on: 1) how to maximize the use of a comprehensive sleep history; 2) recent developments in the classification of sleep disorders (ICD-10 and DSM-III-R); and 3) scoring of sleep records. The workshop concludes with a discussion on how to integrate the office/clinic findings and laboratory results utilized within the psychiatric subspecialty of SDM.

Session 259 Free Communications:
Classical literature and art expression

1712

SHAKESPEARE AND THE GENETICS OF BEING

Robert H. Burgoyne, M.D., Clinical Associate Professor, Dept of Psych, Marianne Harding Burgoyne, Ph.D, candidate, Dept of English, Univ of Utah, Salt Lake City, Utah, U.S.A.

"Is there any cause in nature that make these hard hearts?" asks Lear about his daughters, who have treated him despicably. "How hard it is to hide the sparks of nature!" says Belarius about King Cymbeline's sons who unknowingly demonstrate their princely blood. "A devil, a born devil, on whose nature Nurture can never stick!" exclaims Prospero whose humane teachings are quite lost on Caliban. Shakespeare, particularly in his later plays, raises the psychiatric nature-nurture question about man's genetic inheritance and to what degree can it be shaped by environment?

Although the works of Shakespeare are complex and defy reduction, evidence within the texts themselves supports the theory that Shakespeare believed that genetic composition plays a role in man's behavior. His later character studies reveal that man is trapped to some degree by the 'womb' which bore him. Kail's The Medical Mind of Shakespeare and Edgar's Shakespeare, Medicine and Psychiatry, help conjecture Shakespeare's medical ideas.

After a hundred years of assigning Freudian causal relationships to human foibles, science has rediscovered heredity as a factor in some psychiatric illnesses. There may be hope for Caliban yet. Reading Shakespeare today proves as relevant as during the apex of analytic Shakesperean criticism.

1713

POEMS AS SUICIDE NOTES: CLUES TO SELF DESTRUCTION

Owen E. Heninger, M.D., University of Southern California, Los Angeles, U.S.A.

A local newspaper reports, "Since his suicide the dominant question among those who knew him is, "Why?" There always seems to be an intense search for clues as to why a person commits suicide.

This paper maintains and gives evidence that in the context of their lives, poems some people write shortly before they commit suicide, give additional and often special information on their motivation to suicide.

Life context will be given for four people (including Sylvia Plath and Kóstas Kariotákis) who wrote poems and then committed suicide. Their last and/or significant poems will be read and discussed. A comparison is made between these poems and suicide notes, including: indications of unendurable pain, hopelessness, helplessness, loss, rejection, ambivalence and unhappiness; demonstrating the writer's thinking and/or thought content; showing the desire for egression and the goal of cessation.

There will be a summary and suggestions for further research and study.

There will be no attempt to evaluate these poems on their literary merit. It is acknowledged that suiciding poets may not be representative of all suicides and there is no arguement given that poems can predict their author's suicide.

1714

FROM INTERPRETING LITERATURE TO INTERPRETING THE WORLD

PLAISANT ODILE, ASSANTE MICHELE, RAVEAU FRANCOIS UNIVERSITE PARIS V, ECOLE HAUTES ETUDES EN SCIENCES SOCIALES, CREDA.

La lecture littéraire n'est pas acte de soumission pour le lecteur. Sans doute, le livre offre-t-il une réalité matérielle et le texte un réseau fortement tissé de significations déterminées, mais sa lecture suppose une implication du lecteur façonné par un vécu, une mémoire, un imaginaire, des attentes, un savoir.

Les discours gravitant autour d'un roman "l'étranger d'Albert CAMUS nous semblent bien illustrer l'espace ouvert entre le lecteur et le texte. Les uns (sociologiques, culturels, politiques) privilégient le fond, la société algéroise dans les années 40, les autres (métaphysiques, psychanalytiques, psychiatriques) le personnage de MEURSAULT en prise à une fatalité ou ou un mal-être existensiel. Ce faisceau de lectures converge-t-il vers un seul lieu pour mieux l'éclairer ou dissocie-t-il ses rayons en des trajectoires isolées? Autrement dit, une articulation entre ces discours ne s'avère-t-elle pas nécessaire pour enrichir notre réflexion sans pour autant prétendre à l'exhaustivité? Plus particulièrement, le regard médical isolé du contexte environnemental acquiert-il toute son acuité? Cette approche de l'écrit nous renvoie à la position du thérapeute face au patient. Le sujet ne lui offre-t-il pas à lire un récit enraciné dans son univers social, culturel, pathologique.

1715

CARTOGRAPHY, PLANS, MAPS OF THE WORLD, CADASTRAL SURVEYS.

Docteur Guy ROUX - PAU - FRANCE

The presence of imaginary maps in the drawings of psychotic patients, the making of plans and representation of globes and cadastral surveys crop up in a set of observations. Yet, it is not possible to relate this style of drawings to schizophrenia in any exclusive way.

1716
THE INFLUENCE OF PSYCHOANALYSIS ON S. DALI's WORK AND LIFE
G.E. SARANTOGLOU
Psychiatric Dept., Hellenic Anticancer Institute, Athens (GR).

Salvador Dali's relationship with psychoanalysis has begun in 1922 when he was a student in Madrid and red Freud's "Interpretation of Dreams". In his autobiography Dali considered this reading as "one of the capital discoveries" in his life. A few years later, he has met Jacques Lacan in Paris, in 1933, and Freud in London, in July of 1938 and he had the chance to exchange ideas with them. This paper describes the details of theese two meetings which had crucial formative influences on Dali's work: It supports that Dali's theory and practice of "paranoic-critical method" has been based on Lacan's Thesis "On Paranoiac Psychosis and its Relation with the Personality" (1932). This paper attempts also to demonstrate that Dali's early painting (1925 -1950) consisted of images springing directly from the unconscious and especially from dreams; therefore, Dali could be considered as the iconographist of freudian theories. Furthermore this paper suggests that Dali's histrionic and exhibitionist behaviour, as well as his constant obsession for sublimation, constituted mechanisms of defense against his own self-destructive instincts.

Session 260 Free Communications:
Digestive/respiratory psychosomatics and chronic pain

1717
Psychiatric Disturbances in Ulcerative Colitis : A case-control study
G. MAGNI [1,2], G. BERNASCONI [2], P. MAURO [2], A. D'ODORICO [3], G. CANTON [4], G.C. STURNIOLO [3], S. MARTIN [3].
[1] WYETH-AYERST European Clinical Research and Development, Paris, France, Departments of [2] Psychiatry and [3] Gastroenterology, University of Padua, and [4] Department of Psychiatry, Vicenza General Hospital, Italy.

The possible association between psychiatric disturbances and ulcerative colitis (UC) is a topic still open to debate. To date, there are in fact few controlled studies on this subject that used operational psychiatric diagnostic criteria derived with a standardized interview.
We have assessed the prevalence of psychiatric disturbances in 50 consecutive patients suffering from UC and in 50 matched controls afflicted mainly by urolithiasis. The experimental sample is made up of 27 males and 23 females with a mean age of 36 years (SD14,1). The great majority of the experimental sample (N=49) at the moment of the study was in a remission phase of the disease or during a period of mild activity of the UC. Patients and controls were interviewed with the Schedule for Affective Disorders and Schizophrenia, Life time version (SADS - L) that allows the formulation of psychiatric diagnoses according to the Research Diagnostic Criteria. Moreover patients and controls fulfilled the Symptom Check-list-90 (SCL-90), a widely used self-rating scale to evaluate psychological distress. It is designed to measure nine different symptomatological areas : somatization, obsessiveness - compulsiveness, interpersonal sensitivity, depression, anxiety, hostility, phobic anxiety, paranoid ideation and psychoticism. In the two groups the prevalence of psychiatric diagnoses was evaluated for the period preceding the onset of the physical disease (UC and urolithiasis) and at the moment of the interview.
A psychiatric disturbance was present in the anamnesis of 11 UC patients (22 %) and of 8 controls (16 %) (N.S.) ; affective disorders and alcoholism were the most frequent diagnoses in the UC group (N=8) and in the control group (N=3) respectively. At the moment of the interview a psychiatric disturbance was present in 31 UC patients (62%) and 4 controls (8 %) (p < 0.01). The most frequent diagnoses in the experimental group were minor depression (N=18 ; 36 %) and generalized anxiety disorder (GAD) (N=11 ; 22 %). Patients with UC scored significantly higher than the controls in all the different SCL-90 subscales.
The results of this study suggest that minor depression and GAD are very frequent in UC ; the affective disorders are however mild in their nature since no one case of major depression was found. The fact that psychiatric disturbances are more frequent in the experimental group only at the moment of the interview, but not before the onset of the physical disease, seems to indicate that the psychological suffering is secondary to the physical disease. A traditional "psychosomatic process" in the onset of UC is therefore not supported by these data ; they however point to the need of an integrated bio-psycho-social approach to the treatment of UC patients.

1718
STRESS PROFILE: A METHOD FOR ASSESSMENT IN PSYCHOSOMATIC GASTROENTEROLOGY
M.C. Turola, G. Targa, S. Gullini, E. Ramelli
Psychiatric Clinic, University of Ferrara, Italy

The stress profile is the registration, in a controlled environment, of psychophysiological peripheral parameters: frontal muscle electromyography (EMG), peripheral temperature (THP), skin conductance level (SCL), peripheral pulse rate (PPR), both in base-line conditions and under stress conditions such as mathematical calculations, Sack's test of incomplete sentences, white noise and cold pressor test. The registration has been taken on 100 consecutive patients who were affected with ulcerative colitis, Crohn's disease, duodenal ulcer and irritable bowel syndrome.
The analysis made for all the subjects permitted to evaluate the importance of the component bound to stress and consequently to prepare a therapeutic aimed treatment (relaxation, biofeedback, or stress management training).
Even though in the great variability of each individual reaction to stress, the statistical testing in groups reveals some peculiarities of the answers and suggests hints for further researches.

1719
FROM HEMORRHOIDS TO ULCERATIVE COLITIS: THE STORY OF A SYMBIOSIS
La Torre D., Biondi R.L., Mottola P.
Cattedra di Psicologia Medica Istituto di Scienze Mentali - Universita' di Messina - Italy

The authors, first, carry out a review of the starting from general theories about psychology and psychopathology of Psychosomatic Syndromes detailed in the works of Alexander, Marty, D'Uzan, Balint, etc. They, then, describe the latest experimental work, related to patients affected by Ulcerative Colitis.
The authors describe a case of ulcerative colitis examined by a combined methodology (clinical studies, interviews, questionnaires, personality tests), which permit a pathogenetic and dynamic elaboration. The singularity of the case consists of the existence of symbiotic relationship with the mother which is rooted and organized in the anal region. This acquires an erotic function with a sado-masochistic feature which establishes a pathological continuity between childhood experience and the present structure of the personality.

1720
PSYCHOLOGICAL TREATMENT OF PATIENTS WITH REFRACTORY IRRITABLE BOWEL SYNDROME

Elspeth Guthrie, Francis Creed, David Dawson, Department of Psychiatry, Manchester Royal Infirmary, Manchester, England

102 patients with refractory irritable bowel syndrome were entered into a randomly controlled trial of psychological treatment. The treatment group received three months of individual psychodynamic psychotherapy plus relaxation training, in addition to conventional antispasmodic medication and a bulking agent. The control group continued with conventional drug treatment alone. Blind psychiatric and gastroenterological assessments were carried out, and in addition patients filled in self-report questionnaires.

After 3 months the treatment group, compared to controls, significantly improved on the gastroenterologist's ratings and patients ratings of diarrhoea and abdominal pain.

The improvement in bowel symptoms were correlated with improvement in psychiatric status indicating that reduction of anxiety and depression was a mediating factor in treatment.

This is the first study to have shown that irritable bowel syndrome patients with DSM III anxiety and depression make a good response to psychotherapy. Those with intermittent pain exacerbated by stress also did well whereas those with constant abdominal pain were little helped by this treatment.

This study demonstrated that two thirds of patients with refractory irritable bowel syndrome can be effectively treated by psychological intervention.

1721
PSYCHOPATHOLOGY AND BRONCHIAL ASTHMA

D.Papaioannou, E.Malama, K.Kontou-Phili, B.Alevizos
Department of Allergiology, Laikon General Hospital and University Eginition Hospital, Athens, Greece.

Psychopathology, as evaluated by the Langner's 22-item questionnaire (anxiety and depressive symptoms), the Spielberger's State-Trait Anxiety Inventory and the Zung Depression Scale and the recent stressful life events were studied in 50 patients with bronchial asthma in comparison with 93 controls.
Mann-Whitney (U-test), discriminant analysis and multiple regression were used for statistical analysis.
Asthmatic patients scored significantly higher than controls in general psychopathology (22-items) (p 0.002) in state (p 0.03) and in trait anxiety (p 0.006) (U-test). Women exhibited significantly higher than men anxiety and depressive symptomatology scores. A possitive significant correlation was found between life events and Langner's (p 0.04) as well as trait anxiety (p 0.04) scores.
The results indicate that psychopathology, especially anxiety, may be associated with bronchial hyperactivity, but a causal relationship between psychopathology and the inception of bronchial asthma can not be supported.

1722
PSYCHOTROPIC DRUG THERAPY IN CHRONIC PAINFUL DISEASE
Budde, G., Sieberns, S.,
Troponwerke GmbH & Co. KG, 5000 Köln 80, FRG

A chronic painful disease with physical disability like e.g. rheumatoid arthritis shows a high prevalence in developing depression and anxiety. Different clinical studies show a prevalence of 22 to 60 % of clinical relevant depression (Zaphiropoulos, Krüskamper, Robinson, Walsh, Rimon, Raspe). Anxiety and depression lower the threshold of pain. It appears that major depression and chronic pain are separate entities with some overlap (Pilowsky). Depression and chronic pain alter the central serotonin level (Sternbach, Lindsay). Many clinical studies show a significant pain relief with psychotropic drugs (Johannsson, Turkington, Ward, Carette, Lindsay, Getto). The benefits observed included improved pain, stiffness and grip strength, increased pain threshold and decreased daily doses of standard analgesics (Zorumski).

Conclusion:
Despite partially inconsistent result it seems appropriate to prescribe tentatively psychotropic drugs to patients suffering from chronic painful diseases. Among the benefits to be expected are reduction in pain reports and a decrease of standard analgesic doses.

1723
PSYCHOTHERAPY AND CHRONIC BACK PAIN MANAGEMENT

Earl M. Stenger, M.D.
Pain Clinic, San Antonio, Texas USA

A control study was done to determine the efficacy of psychotherapy in the management of chronic back pain. Sixty-one patients suffering from chronic back pain were divided into two groups. The first group received physical therapy and medication. The second group received psychotherapy in addition to physical therapy and medication. Psychotherapy was open ended, supportive in nature and included pain counseling and behavioral management at home.

The patients were followed for 13 months. The group receiving psychotherapy showed a statistically significant improvement over the group without psychotherapy. The group receiving psychotherapy also significantly decreased all medication.

Psychotherapy can be a vital factor in the management of chronic back pain. Chronic pain management requires psychotherapy in order to address depression, negativity, and abuse of medication.

Session 261 Free Communications:
Schizophrenia: Rehabilitation programs

1724

PUBLIC CONTROL HELPS THE CONSENSUS ON EARLY TREATMENT AND FREEDOM OF PSYCHOTICS
Kappéter István MD.PhB. Bp. Határőr u.24. "Balassa"Hosp.-Policl.-s,Budapest,HUNGARY

In 1924 in Budapest Oláh and Fabinyi began to organize a station for discharged psychotics and their families. Independent psychiatric out-patient centres have worked since 1931 in Budapest and since the 1950's in the whole country. Since 1945 in Hungary there have been only 3 large mental hospitals. The acute psychotics are treated mainly in psychiatric departments of general hospitals. In 1950 there were only 7 beds for 10 000 inhabitants in Hungary when there were 32 in the U.K. Hollós in 1931, Benedek in 1957 and Bakonyi in 1983 published popular books about psychiatry. According to a 1966 act patients who have been treated in hospital against their will for more than 4 weeks have to be shown to a committee controlled by a judge. They or their relatives can immediately apply for such a control.
I learned, just as Achté, and Csiky and Csiky did, that many schizophrenics have a worse career today than those ones had whose intensive treatment began in earlier stages of the disease. If we can work under a strict but well informed public control as we can do it in Hungary,we can convince our patients and their families that sometimes early treatment is needed.

1725

PUBLIC HOUSING AND SOCIAL LIFE OF SCHIZOPHRENIC PATIENT IN TOKYO

Shunichiro Hayashi/Department of Mental Health, School of Hygienic Sciences,Kitasato University/ Sagamihara-City,Japan

In order to study our clinical experiences that shizophrenic out-patients living in The Tokyo Metropolitan Public Housing give a milder impression than the others, we sampled 167 (77 in own house,45 private apartments,23 Public Housing,22 other) patients by using a newly developed checklist containing 147 items of prognostic course and objective as well as subjective life condition items. The direct statistics tell that the overall life traits (objective indices as income, family member size, etc.) of the Public Housing group lie generally between the own house group and the apartments group, but the subjective indices are more complicated. For the purpose to understand comprehensively, we made Principal Component Analysis producing two axes and which allow the interpretation that there are two clear types among the Public Housing group, i.g. good life condition with poor dynamic trait or poor life with more dynamic whereas the apartments group has the traits of good life with dynamic or poor life with good dynamic, and the own house group has every combination of these characteristics. We conclude that the Public Housing provides a peaceful life for patients who could not live in society without them.

1726

STRATEGY AND THERAPEUTIC ALLIANCE IN THE TREATMENT OF SCHIZOPHRENIC DISORDERS
Claudio Mencacci, Enrica Goldfluss
Day Hospital of Cernusco Sul Naviglio(Milan)of the Psychiatric Department USSL 58
Piazza Martiri Libertà
20063-Cernusco Sul Naviglio(Milan) Italy

In the course of the years our day hospital's experience showed us that the psychosis' treatment must include a series of different services.
Our therapeutic program is based on an integrated method which includes pharmacotherapy, psychotherapy and assistance. Consequently, our work is developped through four channels:
-the community channel, which consists in creating an emotional residence for our patients;
-the individual channel which consists in the therapeutic program that is obviously specific and different for each patient;
-the third is the family channel which consists in realizing a therapeutic alliance with the families of our patients and their family doctors;
-the fourth is the social channel which consists in a series of social events in order to give our patients the chance to experience some positive social situations, such as going to cultural exhibitions, theatre, etc.; for some of them the introduction in handicraft workshops. Another very important experience is the period of Summer holidays during which four operators take the patients' group to a sea-side locality for a week. For us it important to create alliance with the community associations, parishes and voluntary assistants.

1727

PROGNOSTIC PARAMETERS IN OCCUPATIONAL REHABILITATION OF SCHIZOPHRENIC PATIENTS
Mantonakis J., Jemos J., Lykouras E., Christodoulou G.
Department of Psychiatry,University of Athens,Eginition Hospital, Athens, Greece.

Three studies carried out at the Athens University Department of Psychiatry (Aspects of Preventive Psychiatry, Bibliotheca Psychiatrica no 160, Karger, 1979—Acta Psychiat. Scand. 66, 306, 1982— Book of Abstracts,Regional Symposium of the W.P.A. for Psychiatric Rehabilitation, Rome, 1984, p.136) point to the following parameters most likely to positively influence occupational rehabilitation of schizophrenic patients: 1) precipitation of illness by stressful life events, 2) advanced age at illness onset, 3) absence of a long history of unemployment, 4) involuntary hospitalization, 5) avoidance of early discharge from hospital, 6) living apart from spouse or parents after discharge, 7) consistent maintenance pharmacotherapy, 8) female sex, 9) lack of chronicity of illness 10)lack of long-term prior unemployment.
Reasons for discontinuation of work reported by the patients are, in order of frequency,the following: a) poor performance and easy fatigue,b) loss of satisfaction from work, c) re-appearance of psychopathology.

1728

A FOLLOW-UP STUDY. CLINICAL EVALUATION IN RELATION TO PSYCHOSOCIAL FACTORS
Karidi V.,Tzedaki M.,Kondylis K.,Armeniakou S.,Skeltsi P.

The field of rehabilitation in psychiatry is developing rapidly. The purpose of this study is to investigate the clinical changes in 147 chronic schizophrenics, all controlled by use of neuroleptics after undergoing a psychosocial treatment in relation to their present social status, as well as their long term follow up. The measuring of the psychopathology and functioning (B.P.R.S, G.A.S, residual symptoms) was statistically significant as compared between the two measurings. Clinical data such as signs and symptoms, age at onset, environment factors, attitudes to the illness and to the neuroleptics and the follow-up data will be given. Different categories of social status were compared with the three items from the Brief Psychiatric Rating Scale (B.P.R.S.) which reflect negative symptoms (Emotional Withdrawal, Motor Retardation, Blunted Affect). Discriminal analysis was carried out. Results of all the above findings will be discussed.

1729

ANHEDONIA AND PSYCHOPATHOLOGY IN SCHIZOPHRENICS ATTENDING A REHABILITATION PROGRAM
M. COCCOSIS, G. TRIKKAS, V. ANTONOPOULOS, V. KARYDIS, G.N. CHRISTODOULOU

ATHENS UNIVERSITY, DEPT. OF PSYCHIATRY, EGINITION HOSPITAL

Anhedonia has been studied mainly with reference to the schizophrenic syndrome. Schizophrenics are considered to be anhedonic, i.e. they get little pleasure out of anything, including work.

The purpose of this preliminary study was to investigate the changes of schizophrenic patients in measures of anhedonia and general psychopathology, while being in a short-term rehabilitation program.

Thirty-four psychotic patients diagnosed according to DSM III criteria, were given the following psychometric teste, prior to and following a period of 3 months; 1. Chapman's Physical and Social Anhedonia Scales, 2. The Symptom Distress Checklist (SCL-90), 3. The Watson-Klett-Lorei Anhedonia Scale (from MMPI) and 4. The MMPI Social Introversion Scale.

The results concerning anhedonia and general psychopathology did not show differences between the first and the second evaluation.

Our findings indicate that a short-term rehabilitation program has not been effective with respect to anhedonia and general psychopathology measured by the above scales. Anhedonia may be considered to be a more stable personality characteristic.

1730

SETTING AND EQUIPE: essential elements in the project of an integrated theraphy for schizophrenic patients.
TAMBURINI R., CAPODIECI S., SBRACCIA F..
CENTRO DI IGIENE MENTALE - OSPEDALE CIVILE - MIRANO (VENEZIA)

This work is included in the discussion upon the search of models, which deal with the problem of schizophrenes' therapy.
In Italy the need of a deeper search was also determined by the trasformation of the mental service after the reform's law.
If the abrogation of Mental Hospital, considered as absolute institutions, allowed todiscuss the problem of mental disease also over the logic of isolation and containment, especially as far as the schizophrenes concerned, it was necessary to create space and time, that applied much more to the management than to the therapy.
This experience, which was developed by our group, results from a consideration and an analysis about place and time, that are necessary to relize a therapeutical change into the patients.
From the examination of the setting and of the equipe's concept, it stars a project of intervention into chronical schizophrenes according to a psychodinamical trend, that during its developement has made use of integrated and multifocal approach.

Session 262 Free Communications:
Military psychiatry

1731

DISTURBANCE OF CONSCIOUSNESS IN COMBATANTS

H. Davidian, MD, FRCPsych, DPM
M. Sanati, MD, MRCPsych
Rouzbeh Hosp. Kargar Ave. Teheran, Iran

Headache and clouded consciousness accompanied frequently with disturbed behaviour were among the most striking symptoms presented by warriors of Iran-Iraque war referred as acute psychiatric cases.

The most peculiar type of headache in terms of its recurring attacks of immense intensity, short duration and unusual topography together with clouding of consciousness prevail the clinical picture.

50 consecutively referred warriors diagnosed as acute post traumatic stress disorder were studied systematically for disturbance of consciousness. 37 (group A) had disturbed and 13 (group B) had clear consciousness. The two groups were investigated physically, were compared with each other with respect to cognitive functions and a number of psychosocial factors including the premorbid personality. The findings point to a general transitional organic disorder most probably induced by blast shock of explosion in an unusually intense stressful situation on predisposed persons, which can not appropriatelly be classified under post traumatic stress disorder.

1732
PSYCHOSES AND DEMENTIA FOLLOWING WAR BRAIN DAMAGE. Preliminary report.

K. Achté, L. Jarho[1] and T. Kyykkä[1], Department of Psychiatry, University of Helsinki, Helsinki, and [1]Kauniala Hospital for Disabled War Veterans, Kauniainen, Finland

The material comprises roughly 10,000 Finnish war veterans who sustained brain injuries in the 1939-1945 War. This material is unique. In Finland, the treatment and rehabilitation of war invalids has been both medically and socially monitored centrally. Those with moderate or severe brain injuries who have or have had psychotic disturbances, or who are demented (current estimated to amount to 500 individuals) will be selected as subjects. Psychological, neurological, neuroradiological, neuropsychological and social data will be collected for those to be included: cause, nature, location, primary symptoms and early complications of the injury, neurological and neuropsychological disturbances, main symptoms, treatment and medication during follow-up, special examinations (PEG, EEG, CT and psychological tests), social background data from childhood to social and professional status before injury, and development during rehabilitation, family and working life following the injury. Psychological disturbances resulting from organic changes are an important issue in the problematics of brain injury. At their severest, they can alter the patient's personality and attitudes toward the environment. The study investigates the relation between brain injuries, and psychotic disturbances and senile dementia. How does the severity and location of injury affect the development and nature of psychoses? Do psychotic symptoms become worse with time or are they connected with senile dementia? How do individual and social factors affect the genesis of psychoses? What is the prognosis of treatment and social and professional coping, and what are the factors affecting the prognosis? What is the incidence and significance of suicide and alcoholism in the patient material?

1733
PSYCHOLOGICAL TRAUMA OF CAPTIVITY AND PSYCHIATRIC MORBIDITY
DR. K. KHAN, B.Sc., M.B.B.S., D.P.M., F.R.C.Psych, Ph.D.
DEPARTMENT OF PSYCHIATRY, CLATTERBRIDGE HOSPITAL, CLATTERBRIDGE ROAD, BEBINGTON, WIRRAL, MERSEYSIDE. L63 4JY.

In modern British military history the plight of British prisoners of war held by the Japanese during the Second World War was uniquely traumatic.

A group of randomly selected former prisoners of war were investigated and the results compared with a matched control group.

The investigation consisted of I) a specially written structured interview, II) examination of mental state including Wing's Present State Examination Schedule (IXth) Edition, III) and Hamilton's Anxiety Rating Scale, IV) followed by two self administered rating scales i.e. Beck's Depressive Rating Scale and Goldberg's 60-Item General Health Questionnaire.

The former prisoners of war were found to be psychologically more maladjusted with high psychiatric morbidity. In most cases their psychiatric illness have some distinct features and are mostly chronic in nature with consequent profound effect on the quality of their social, domestic and working lives.

1734
54 CASES OF POST TRAUMATIC STRESS DISORDER (P.T.S.D)
S.Ahmad Jalili M.D.
Tehran University of Medical Sciences, Tehran, Iran

54 cases of P.T.S.D. have been interviewed on the basis of Davidian's psychiatric inventory and I.C.D.9 criteria used for diagnosis. Statistical analysis was performed for marital status, military rank, battle related responsibility and the presence of mental illness in patients and their family members. No significant difference between patient and control group was found.
The most common diagnosis was depressive reaction. The more the duration of staying in the war front, the less became the degree of depressive reaction and the more intense the anxiety reaction.
Based on the above findings we can conclude that heridity and predisposing factors, marital status, responsibility in the battle front have no significant influence in the emerging of these reactions. It also could be concluded that fatigue among patients and a decrease of depressive reactions after staying in the war front for a while suggest the necessity of paying attention to a person's physical readiness before dispatching him to the front, so as to prevent these reactions.

1735
PHENOMENOLOGICAL AND PSYCHOMETRIC ASSESSMENT OF POSTTRAUMATIC STRESS DISORDER

G.MITEV, V.RAINOV, R.MOSKOV
MILITARY MEDICAL ACADEMY, SOFIA, BULGARIA

THE AUTHORS INVESTIGATE TWO GROUPS: I/26 PERSONS/, WITH ENDURED HEAD INJURIES /FROM 6 MONTHS' UP TO 2 YEARS/ AND II/ 20 HEALTHY PERSONS/ CORRESPONDING IN AGE, PERSONAL CHARACTERIZATION/ EYSENCK' TEST/ AND TO A LESSER EXTENT IN EDUCATION. THE PERSONS FROM THE TWO GROUPS WERE PLACED AT THE SAME STRESSOGENIC CONDITIONS. USING THE FOLLOWING TESTS: SIGNAL DETECT, VIGILANCE, CONTINUANCE OF ATENTION, COORDINATION ACHIEVED BY A COMPUTER - PSYCHOLOGICAL SYSTEM "WINER TEST SYSTEM", THE AUTHORS FOUND CHANGES IN THE SPEED OF MOVEMENTS, THE VIGILANCE OF STTENTION, THE COORDINATION ETC. IN THE FIRST GROUP. THE PERSONS WITH ENDURED HEAD INJURIES ARE MORE SUSCEPTIBLE TO DESDAPTATION IN STRESSOGENIC ENVIRONMENT.

1736
HEAD INJURIES IN IRAQUI-IRANIAN WAR 1980-1988

Dr. Mudheffer Z.Al-Qassim, Dr. Qassim Al-Awadi
Iraqi Society of Neurologists and Psychiat., Iraq

A study of 1045 cases of head injuries and their complications and sequelles before and during the Iraqui-Iranian War 1980-1988.
There were 844 cases of closed injuries and 201 cases with penetrating injuries. The cases were divided into 3 groups:
1. - Cases seen during a year time just before the onset of the war. i.e. Sept. 1979 - Aug. 1980
2. - Cases seen during the 1st year of the war. i.e. Sep. 1980 - Aug. 1981
3. - Cases seen during the 4th year of war. i.e. Sep. 1984 - Aug. 1985
Comparison of the groups were made and incidence of complications and sequelles were discussed and ended with conclusions.

1737
ETUDE PSYCHOPATHOLOGIQUE DE JEUNES FRANÇAIS REFUSANT LE SERVICE NATIONAL.
B.SAMUEL-LAJEUNESSE,L.SVARNA.
CENTRE HOSPITALIER STE-ANNE,PARIS.

Etude clinique de 92 sujets consultant en vue de constituer undossier médical propre à entraîner leur reforme du Service National dans le but de préciser les structures psychopathologiques sous-jacentes. Une enquête sur les motivations a mis en évidence diverses raisons d'ordre idéologique,psychologique (en majorité),ou matériel. La symptômatologie spontanément alléguée concerne l'anxiété,les difficultés relationnelles,les sentiments dépressifs. L'examen clinique fait ressortir l'isolement,des troubles du cours de la pensée, des troubles du caractère,des conduites toxicomaniaques. Seuls 8 cas sont exempts de tout symptôme psychopathologique.
Au total la symptômatologie globale peut être résumée en deuxtableaux: un tableau dominé par les difficultés de contact et le retrait social évocateur de schizophrénie et un tableau évocant un état névrotique peu ou mal structuré,ou bien des traits de personnalité pathologique.
Les données détaillées du bilan psychométrique de ces sujets feront l'objet d'une publication ultérieure.

1738
PREDICCION DE TRASTORNOS DE CONDUCTA
FACTORES PERSONALES DE VULNERABILIDAD
ABRIL,J.;LLAQUET,l.;QUIROGA,M.;ROBLES,JI.;
Clínica Psiquiatrica Militar-Ciempozuelos
MADRID-ESPAÑA

Conscientes los autores de lo ambicioso de sus fines comienzan con una reflexion previa haciendo destacar en primer lugar como de una larga experiencia clinico-pericial van a surgir iniciales hipotesis de trabajo tales como la probable relacion significativa entre trastornos de personalidad que giran en torno al eje inestabilidad-impulsividad-explosividad y las declaraciones de No Aptitud para una profesion que implica el manejo de armas. Por otra parte algunas concepciones actuales de caracter operativo como las referidas a los Factores de Vulnerabilidad Ambiental, y publicaciones ya algo mas antiguas sobre "Reconocimientos periodicos seriados" incitaron y obligaron a la vez a los autores a una continuada autocritica de su intento de trasladar al campo de la Prevencion Psiquica lo que se venia realizando en el mundo de la patologia somatica.
Este trabajo se orienta a resaltar el valor de un diagnostico psiquiatrico prospectivo que intente predecir la adaptacion-inadaptacion del individuo a su medio y ello fijandose particularmente en aquellos factores psicologico-psicopatologicos de vulnerabilidad personal, entre los que sobresaldrian la hiperestesia-sensitividad, la hipertimia-expansividad, la impulsividad-inestabilidad y la inseguridad-dependencia.
Termina la comunicación con la exposición y crítica de Cuestionarios-Test adoptados y adaptados por nosotros y que a nuestro juicio pueden ser utiles en el estudio y deteccion de la potencial conflictividad intra e interpersonal.

Session 263 Free Communications:
Application of the psychoanalytic theory

1739
ANALYSE DE LA PRODUCTION ONIRIQUE DE SUJETS SCHIZOPHRENES

E. Torre - E. Borla - E. Roveyaz et M. Ancona - "Clinica Psichiatrica Università di Torino" Turin - Italie.

Il s'agit d'une étude ayant pour objet les rêves de seize patients atteints de troubles schizophrènes, diagnostiqués selon la méthode DSM III, comparés à ceux de seize autres individus, tous homogènes du point de vue sexe, âge et niveau d'instruction et sans précédents psychiatriques. L'analyse de la production onirique a été effectuée selon deux méthodes standardisées: d'une part l'évaluation des pulsions et de la force du "moi" et d'autre part l'analyse des contenus manifestes du rêve. En résumé, l'analyse statistique a mis en évidence des différences significatives: (a) Le "moi" du schizophrène est plus faible par rapport à celui des sujets normaux, tandis que ses pulsions sont plus éloignées et considérées par le sujet comme inacceptables. Les pulsions exprimées par les rêves du groupe de contrôle apparaissent au contraire de manière plus distincte, elles sont en outre mieux acceptées et reconnues comme appartenant au "moi". (b) En ce qui concerne les contenus manifestes, les rêves des schizophrènes se caractérisent par un nombre limité de personnages, souvent inconnus, et par des interactions peu nombreuses qui sont surtout agressives. Par ailleurs, les événements oniriques sont vécus de manière fortement menaçante et sont à l'origine d'une profonde angoisse. En effectuant une nouvelle distinction à l'intérieur du groupe des schizophrènes entre le type "paranoiaque" et celui "indifférencié" (DSM III), il a été mis en évidence que les rêves appartenant au premier sous-groupe sont plus riches du point de vue thématique. Enfin, les auteurs analysent les aspects symboliques de ces rêves et leurs implications psycho-dynamique.

1740
UNE FOLLE PASSION DE CONSTRUIRE

Patrick DE NEUTER
Unité PSCL - Université Catholique de Louvain
Clos Chapelle-aux-Champs 30 Bte 3049 -
1200 Brussels - BELGIUM.

Louis II de Bavière fut pris d'une passion extrême pour la construction de châteaux aussi fastueux qu'inutiles. Cette passion le protégea durant de nombreuses années des tendances destructrices et auto-destructrices inhérentes à sa psychose. Lorsque ses financiers et son gouvernement ne lui permirent plus de construire de nouveaux châteaux, il s'enfonça dans sa psychose et finit par se suicider.

1741
STUDYING EFFECTS OF PSYCHOANALYTIC PSYCHOTHERAPY BY THE DMT- ONE CASE ILLUSTRATION.
D. Kyriazis, G. Balsamatzis, B.Tserpe
Psych. Depart. of Hellenic Air Forces General Hospital, Psych. Depart. of Athens University, Aiginition Hospital,Athens, Greece.
Summary: Studied by the Defence Mechanism Test(DMT) one case of Narcissistic Personality Disorder before and after one year treatment with Psychoanal./Psychotherapy. In the first DMT,defences such as:projective identification,splitting,introaggression,reaction formation, isolation of affect and a lack of stimulus recognition showed up. In PG I the identification of hero and in PG II the identification of PP, with the opposite sex prevailed. The distribution and the quality of the defences suggested a hypothesis that a psychological "trauma" took place when the patient was 8-11 years old. In the second DMT the changes were: disappearance of archaic defences and reaction formation, an over all increase of isolation of affect,disappearance (for hero) or reduction (for PP) of the identification with the opposite sex and an infantile PP.The changes of the defensive structure were followed by clinical changes as well, which were depicted by MMPI (Pd and Schiz scales showed reduction) and by clinical material,which also verified the "trauma hypothesis" as was predicted. The structural implications of findings are discussed in relation to psychotherapy.

1742
THE USE OF DREAM SERIES IN ANALYTICAL GROUPS: MANIFEST ASSOCIATED ELEMENTS
H.Sausgruber
Sozialpsychiatrie Bregenz, Austria

Long dream series permit the elaboration of manifest associated elements, MAE, avoiding the use of latent material.
The dream protocols can be transformed into predictive structures/lists using a descriptive language like PROLOG.
Procedures to extract focal conflicts from hallucinotic material and possible modes of introduction in an analytical group are discussed.
JUNGian concepts like "hallucinotic context" or "serial amplification" and HALL and Van de CASTLES dream content analysis are methodologically compared to the FREUDian procedure based on free association.
Concepts of the use of dreams in group psychotherapy from WENDER, SCHILDER, WOLF AND SCHWARTZ, BATTEGAY are presented.

1743
PSYCHOTHERAPIES BREVES D'INSPIRATION ANALYTIQUE
DIMOU D, KOUROS J.

PIKPA-E.PS.PS.E.P.

Determination de psychotherapie et psychotherapies brèves.But:double intention,psychanalytique(se connaître)et therapeutique.
Categorisation suivant le mode de la therapie individuelle,avec parents,avec instituteur;l'âge du psychanalysé;la composition de sa personnalité;du problème à résoudre.
Durée du travail:de 6à 100 séances suivant la gravité du problème et de la sociabilité du sujet.
Types de psychotherapies brèves:infantine,adolescente,adulte;scolaire,psychologique,psychosomatique, mixte(psychanalyse+scolaire+orthophonie),familiale, d'institution.
Méthodes:libre, dirigée,interventive,consultative, de support,"methode d'élargissement d'interêts"(surtout chez les arrierés),psychanalyse du symbolisme.
Analyse et exposition de quelques cas.

Session 264 Free Communications:
Depression in women

1744

SITUATIONS IN THE DEVELOPMENT OF THE WOMEN'S DEPRESSION
FONSECA, V.L.; PELAYO,A. NIEVES,P.
UNIV. COMPLUTENSE OF MADRID, SPAIN

The concept of situation have to be understood as dialectic relation between the subject and his enviroment; from this point of view we have an important conceptual instrument for the comprehension of depression disorders. This study have been done in the Hospital Clinico San Carlos of Madrid. This objective was to find the more frequent situational's profiles in the grow-up (0-16 years old) in the depressed women. 84 women with unipolar depression were evaluated in their depressive features with TEQ-DE (Alonso-Fernandez, 1986) and HDRS, and in their situational features with an own questionaire which has been development by our team. We have found that the more current features of the situational's profiles are: early parent's lost, father's inflexible behavior and a depreciated and easily afraid mother with whom the daughter make an identification.

1745

Reactive Depression Among Young Yemeni Women

Dr. Abdel Magid S. Al-Khulaidi
Health & Medical Research Unit, Sana'a University, Ministry of Health,
P.O. Box 1224, Sana'a, Yemen Arab Republic.

Reactive depression is a common phenomena among all ages in Yemen, but it is a more dominant feature among young Yemeni women.

Reactive depression is considered as the first psychiatric diseases in the country during the last 25 years as a result of social conflicts, rapid socio-economic change, migration and cultural differences among generations.

Young women in Yemen are the target group of reactive depression, because of the effect of many causes, such as early marriages, enforcement of marriage to some one older or non-loved partner, etc.

1746

PUERPUERAL DEPRESSION: VULNERABILITY AND RISK FACTORS
Benvenuti P., Donati D., Giardinelli L., Greco L., Meloni A., Pallanti S., Rivelli S.A., Tanini N.
Department of Neurological and Psychiatric Sciences
University of Florence - Italy
This research is conducted on the pregnant women who present themselves at the Obstetric and Gynaecological Clinic of the University of Florence.
The research, now underway, aims at the quantification of the frequency of puerpueral depressive disorders, but also the identification of any factors of vulnerability and of risk, and is carried out in 3 different phases:
1) administration a semistructured interview model adapted from the one proposed by Brown and Harris, to women from the 28th to 32nd weeks of pregnancy. In the same session Eysenk Personality Inventory is distributed, together with the Life Events and Difficulties Schedule, the Brief Psychiatric Rating Scale, the Hamilton Rating Scale for Depression, and the Beck Depression Inventory.
2) In the week following the birth, we have used the Edinburgh Post-Natal Depression Scale, a specific scale for the evaluation of puerpueral depression.
3) In the 12th week after the birth, the diagnostic investigation is repeated and the previously distribuited questionnaire are given out again.

1747

Depressive Features in Menopausal Syndrome
M.F. Andreani[°], I. Maremmani, O. Zolesi[°], J.A. Deltito[°°], P. Castrogiovanni,
Institute of Psychiatry, Pisa University, Italy
[°]Mental Health Services, USL 20, Regione Liguria, Italy
[°°]Depression and Anxiety Clinic, New York Hospital, Cornell University, Westchester Division, White Plains, New York, N.Y., U.S.A.

Studies concerning depressive experience, often following the end of the reproductive period in women, have been directed to biological, psychological, social and cultural sectors. They tried to clarify the possible relations between depressive-anxious experience, biohumoral variations and psychosocial factors.
The biologic event has assumed the role of a necessary condition but is not sufficient to justify the presence of a depressive-anxious symptomatology during the menopause, whereas particular personal problems, put in a well defined socio-cultural structure, hold a prominent position.

1748
EPIDEMIOLOGY AND CLINICAL STUDY OF DEPRESSIVE SYNDROME IN THE CLIMATERIUM
Sanchez L., Civeira J., Martin M., Diez A.
Psychiatry Department Complutense University of Madrid, Spain

Depression study is one of the current issues in occidental psychopathology, and shows a higher emphasis in women.
The climacteric woman is in a phase of life where depression is particularly intense, with clinical characteristics being well defined.
In our study of 6.039 inpatients, in a General Hospital psychiatric unit, over a period of six years (1982-1988), we established a depression rate of 3:1 in women and men. Therefore, we found that 40% of those institutionalized women were diagnosed as depressive, and almost 36% were classified in the climacteric state, which was found to have a higher significant index of reoccurence.
The depressive symptomatology in these women were characterized by a higher degree of symptomatology (established by TEQ-DE and HDRS). These characteristics are established mostly from a higher discommunication and energetic downfall. The explanation should be based on biological vulnerability and psychosocial characteristics of climacterium.

1749
Descriptive approach for a reconceptualization of Maternity Blues
I. Maremmani, L. Daini, A. Di Muro, J.A. Deltito°, P .Castrogiovanni
Institute of Psychiatry, Pisa University, Italy
°Depression and Anxiety Clinic, New York Hospital, Cornell University, Westchester Division, White Plains, New York, N.Y., U.S.A.

In order to show the degree and the quality of symptomatological manifestations of Maternity Blues and its incidence in the Italian population, over one hundred women in childbirth were evaluated by means of standardized instrument on the eighth month of pregnancy and four days after the delivery.
The psychopathological symptomatology was investigated by means of SCL-90 by Derogatis, whereas a special symptomatological scale: MCRS (Mood Changes Rating Scale) was made to study mood modifications.
The results lead to consider Maternity Blues not like a mood disorder, but like an emotional reaction to a physiological event of change.

1750
AMBIVALENCE IN THREATENING PREMATURE LABOUR
Malagaris E.G., Tzavaras N., Anastasiadis P.
University clinic of Obstetrics and Gynaecology and Psychopathological Laboratory. University of Thrace Medical School. Alexandroupolis Greece.
17,77,88,.
Increased anxiety levels have been held responsible for the initiation of premature uterine contractions, in pregnant women with a diagnosis of Premature Labour. In our clinical psychiatric study of a mixed cultural speciment of Premature Labour cases, ambivalence towards pregnancy prevailed and was connected to two inter-related categories: a) Woman's Autonomy vs. Dependence upon man, b) Desire to have a child vs. Emotional immaturity/uncertainty about mother's (woman's) role. We noticed also that the exposure of pregnant women to stressful life events -especially if they were non-manual professionals- was more likely to affect pregnancy course rather, than in manually working pregnant women. The conflictual character of changes in the social status and the re-determination of women's role, which in accelerating rhythms has occured in the relatively underdeveloped area of rural Thrace, characterized by heterogeneous population synthesis, should also be emphasized.

1751
PSYCHIC TROUBLES OF THE POST-PARTUM:
A CRITICAL ANALYSIS.

De Gregori P.,M.D.;Foglietta D.,M.D.;
Sira Cusano A.,M.D.; Vella G.,M.D.
I Psychiatric Clinic, University "La Sapienza", Roma, Italy.

The authors, on the ground of an analysis of the existent medical literature about partum, point out the difficulties to frame them nosographically.
The results of this investigation are that the unsolved problem, since the times of Kraepelin, is still open.

Session 265 Free Communications:
Alcohol abuse: Clinical issues

1752
CLINICAL FORMS OF ALCOHOLISM
N.N.Ivanets
All-Union Research Center of
Narcology,Moscow, USSR

Clinical data indicate that under similar conditions subjects of the same sex and age develop different forms of alcoholism. It has been shown that constitutionally determined premorbid personality traits are responsible for not only some symptoms and syndromes of alcoholism but also for general clinical regularities of the development of alcohol dependence, and the rate of its progress in the first place. The rate of progress of alcoholism is one of the most adequate criterion for determining different clinical forms of alcoholism that display high, median and low rate of progress. The rate of progress of the disease is influenced by peculiarities of the pathogenesis of alcoholism. The data obtained indicate that there are significant clinico-biological correlations between premorbid personality traits, dopamine-beta-hydroxylase activity, rate of development of alcoholism, severity of its clinical forms, and pattern of alcoholabuse. Social consequences of alcoholism and somato-neurological disturbances related to alcohol should be taken into account in distinguishing clinical forms of alcoholism.

1753
ALCOHOL CONSUMPTION AND PSYCHIATRIC MORBIDITY IN ELDERLY MALES
P A Saunders, J R M Copeland, M E Dewey, I A Davidson, V Sharma, C McWilliam and C Sullivan
Department of Psychiatry and the Institute of Human Ageing, University of Liverpool, Liverpool, England.

A random community sample of the elderly was re-interviewed after three years by psychiatrists using the Geriatric Mental State Examination and History and Aetiology Schedule. Men who admitted to having been heavy drinkers for a period of five years or more at some time in their lives, are found to have a greater than five-fold risk of suffering from a psychiatric disorder at the time of follow-up. Among subjects with a history of heavy drinking, past alcohol consumption is significantly greater for subjects with a current psychiatric diagnosis compared to those who are well. However, this association between heavy alcohol consumption in earlier years and psychiatric morbidity in later life is not explained by differences in current drinking habits.

1754
NEURO PSYCHOLOGICAL EVALUATION OF ALCOHOLICS - A CONTROLLED STUDY
Dr.R.L.Narang M.D. & Dr. Dinesh Garg MBBS
Dayanand Medical College & Hospital,
Ludhiana Punjab, India

This study was carried out with the aim to find out the degree of cognitive impairment in Indian alcoholics (DSM-III Criteria). The cognitive impairment was measured by a standardized, Battery of Brain dysfunction on Indian patients. A group of 30 alcoholic patients were taken from outpatient Dept. of Psychiatry, Dayanand Medical College and Hospital, Ludhiana. The alcoholics were diagnosed as suffering from alcohol abuse or alcohol dependence by DSM-III criteria. These patients were matched with 30 healthy, non - alcoholic controls on socio-demographic variables and cognitive functions. The cognitive functions were assessed by P.G.I. Battery of Brain dysfunction. This battery consists of tests for intelligence, memory and perceptomotor acquity. There was significant relationship between cognitive impairment and duration of alcohol use. The cognitive impairment increases with the duration of alcohol use. There was significant difference on cognitive functions in alcoholics as compared to controls.
This work is first of this kind in Indian patients. Further work of correlation of these cognitive impairment with C.T.Scan findings and other social factors is going on. The present work is a part of a larger on going study.

1755
PIERCING ALCOHOL AMNESIAS
Dr. George D.Scott
Inst.of Psychotherapy, Kingston, Ontario, Canada
Alcohol induced amnesias (black outs) occur in heavy drinkers and in persons who literally drink large amounts of alcohol in a four to six hour period. The amnesia may be complete or may be interspersed with small islands of recall. During the amnesic period the subject functions more through his emotional reactivity than his cerebral system. His physical activities through the amnesic period may entail implicated physical acts which reflect perceptual and motor ability that is immediately forgotten. This paper outlines a successful approach to this type of amnesia through the intravenous use of Pentobarbital, a short acting barbituate, a hypnotic, and Methylphenidate HCL, a mild CNS stimulant (Ritalin-CIBA). The procedure requires back up equipment for emergency situations with O_2, cardiac resuscitation unit, blood pressure monitoring and careful physical evaluation. The treatment period (60 minutes)is recorded for the patient's own use in later associative memory recall. The technique is of monumental importance in disclosing to the patient his reactions during his so called alcohol black out periods. Four to six sessions are usually required for a full recall with the dissociated repressions slowly moving into the associative consciousness. In criminal cases, such evidence is not admissable in reference to the Doctor's testimony, but is admissable in the patient's evidence as his memory recall has been activated.

1756

Forensic psychiatric issues related to alcoholism.

Gerald G. Pope, M.D.
Henry Ford Hospital, Detroit, MI 48202, U.S.A.

Whether alcoholism is caused by metabolites of tetrahydroisoquinoline or B-Carboline category or genetic predisposition and deficiency in the cerebral opioid system, its effects on psychological and social functioning, may lead to conflict with the prevailing socio-legal milieu.

Social and legal remedies and controls provided may vary, but as to alcohol related deprivation of reason and aberrant behaviour, the insanity defense cannot be employed to exculpate the offender, unless a "status of being ill" is proven. Definition of alcoholism by W.H.O. and A.M.A., the former defining alcoholism as "chronic behavioural disorder" and the latter as: "illness characterized by significant impairment, also reflect this dichotomy.

National data and statistics from the Detroit tri-county area, show a significant correlation between alcoholism and intentional or unintentional injuries and crimes, but contradictions in the law stemming from conflicting alcohol ideologies (moral blame vs. disease excuse) tend to jeopardize law enforcement and undermine accountability of one's actions associated with alcohol abuse.

1757

ALCOHOLISM AND INCEST
A Three-Stage Psychotherapeutic Treatment
Geerhard E. Schaap, M.D. General Psychiatric Hospital "Wolfheze", Holland

Alcohol and incest problems quite often occur together in the same families. I would like to illustrate the consequences of growing up in an alcohol-incest family. Incest problems require prolonged and intensive psychotherapy. The three-stage psychotherapeutic treatment of incest victims is composed of the basic treatment in a therapeutic community, the psychotherapy with a therapist couple in the clinical setting and the outpatient continuation of the psychotherapy with the male therapist.

Session 266 Free Communications:
Psychiatry and the law

1758

MENTAL HEALTH LEGISLATION OF ONTARIO, CANADA: A CRITIQUE
Dr. Ranjith Chandrasena
University of Ottawa and Royal Ottawa Hospital, Ottawa, Ontario, Canada.

The Mental Health Act of Ontario was substantially revised in 1987. The present legislation favours a civil libertarian approach to the patients and is opposed to the "best interests" approach of the medical model. The presentation will review each aspect of the legislation, viz., involuntary detention, involuntary treatment, competency to consent to treatment, release clinical records, appoint substitute consent, manage financial affairs, and a review of childrens psychiatric hospitalization. Clinical case histories are provided to discuss the advantages and the disadvantages of each aspect of the legislation. The Act, which was modified based on the Canadian Charter of Rights and the Civil Commitment Legislation, experience of several States in the U.S., has now caused considerable concern among Ontario Psychiatrists. The presentation discusses why Psychiatrists need to be involved at every stage, from an early stage prior to drafting new Mental Health Legislation, need for protecting the right to care and treatment of patients, and also the rights of families. Any Country revising its' Mental Health Legislation has much to gain by reviewing the Ontario experience.

1759

Legal Psychiatry in Algéria - Past - Present and - the futur

Mr. M. Touary - Mr. B. Bensmayl

After the recall of the Charia (Moslem legislation) concerning the penal responsibility of mental patients the outhors evoke the french penal code of 1810 and particularly its article 64. This penal code has been applied in Algéria till the independence, where ist has been supressed in order to be replaced by the Algerian penal code Algeria till the independence, which, globaly is inspired from (Code Penal French) but in fact it differs for what is much about the penal procedure concerning the psychiatric expertise on this subject that the level of the Algerian penal code where its article 47 is much more clear concerning the imputation and the responsibility of the offender mental patient. However, those two codes don't study the case of the anormal mental offenders it is for this subjects category that the authors make juridical suggestions.

1760

SCIENCE AND UTOPIA:THE ITALIAN PSYCHIATRIC LEGISLATION
DE FELICE F.*,MONORCHIO A.**,QUATTRONE B.**,CONDEMI F.**
*Department of Psychiatry,U.S.L. 28 - LOCRI (Italy)
**Psychiatric Hospital,U.S.L. 31 - REGGIO CALABRIA(Italy)

The law 180 which in Italy has ordained the dismantling of Psychiatric Hospital seems to be,after a thorough study,the result of an irremediable conflict between science and politics.
The policy,which according to Aristotle,is an art if it loses its contact with reality,loses sight of the human dimension.
The Authors give as an example the event of the Italian Psychiatric Hospital (that of Reggio Calabria).

1761

Decision-making in compulsory admission

A.Kaasenbrood, M. Janssen, M.Donker
The Netherlands Institute of Mental Health (NcGv)

Between 1985 and 1988 the NcGv studied decision-making in compulsory admission to a psychiatric hospital. In the Netherlands danger resulting from mental illness is lawfully required in these cases. The investigators were present in 31 situations in which a psychiatrist considered compulsory admission. Afterwards they interviewed all parties concerned (i.e. the patient, his family, neighbours, the police etc). The process by which the decision was reached appeared unbalanced. In most cases the criterion of danger was not met. The diagnostic process proved unreliable and alternatives for compulsory admission were seldom considered. In the most cases the patients experienced this as an injusticeand, even after several months, did not agree with the admission.
A proposal for new laws and regulations governing compulsory admission has been under discussion for the past 18 years.The results of the present research will probably not affect the new law. The disconcordance between law and practice will in all probability continue.
This disconcordance is mainly due to the pressures of the hectic situation on site and the conflicting interests of its participants. These circumstatial factors severely impair the quality of the decision. Recommendations for improvement are discussed.

1762

CONCLUSION ON THE DEFINITION BY LAW OF CRITERIA FOR EXPERTISE ON ADDICTS
Mouyas Ath.
Psychiatric Hospital for Prisoners
Korydallos, Greece

The work concerns my experience based on 480 medical expertises which I carried out after criteria were induced by ministerial decision 3982/87 to define the addicted persons. Any scepticism on regards the establishment by law of psychiatric diagnostic criteria, is beyond the scope of this work.
Given that in no case was article 1a of the ministerial decision implemented (5day admission,laboratory examination) since the infrastructure is lacking;only article 1b (clinical examinasion) and article 2 includes 9 criteria on the presence of withdrawal s mptoms,tolerance, soc'al and rofessional adjustment were implemented.
The main conclu ions are as follows:
1.Intravenous use and the obvious presence of marks on veins remain the main criteria
2.Subjects with antisocial personality disorder are "favoured" in that they are covered by the criteria.
3.In effect, the criteria which strictly concern drug use (withdrawal symptoms, tolerance, relief) are oriented towards opioid users only.

1763

VOLUNTARY AND INVOLUNTARY MENTAL HOSPITALIZATION:
A COMPARATIVE STUDY
Almenta Hernandez E., Calcedo Ordonez A.,
Gregorio Maranon Hospital, Madrid, Spain

Recently, legislation about involuntary hospitalization of the mentally ill has been revised in our country. We attempt to evaluate the impact of these changes and to identify differences between committed patients and those who enter to hospital voluntary. All 784 patients admitted over a 1-year period to the psychiatric clinic of Gregorio Maranon Hospital from Madrid were investigated and followed until discharge. Two study groups were established according to the legal type of hospitalization: voluntary (91,2%) and involuntary (8,8%). Clinical, sociodemographic and circumstantial factors were analyzed in both groups comparing the results with well known statistical criteria. We found some differences on the basis of several variables. The commitments usually were related with disturbed social behavior, police involvement and more severe impaired mental status. The committed patients were often young, male, unemployed and reported a higher proportion of hospital admissions and history of prior arrests than the voluntary population.

1764

Aspectos legales del ingreso psiquiàtrico en España.

Cabrera Forneiro Josè y Cañas Francisco

Hospital Psiquiatrico San Josè, Ciempozuelos, Madrid, ESPAÑA.

En ESPAÑA desde 1983 existe una particular legislación por la cual y a grandes rasgos todos los ingresos psiquiàtricos salvo los VOLUNTARIOS, deben someterse al control estricto de la Justicia por medio de los Jueces y Fiscales.

Esta Ley, 13/1983, ha modificado algunos aspectos administrativos, mèdicos y sociales de forma significativa y por ello en el momento actual aùn se plantean importantes problemas con ella.

UN problema especial es el de los pacientes psìquicos crònicos ingresados desde hace largo tiempo, y a los cuales se debe "legalizar" igualmente. Nosotros estàmos llevando a cabo por primera vez en España, dicha "legalizaciòn" en nuestro Hospital con màs de 500 pacientes, implicando para ello a los propios pacientes, a sus familias, a la Justicia local y a la propia Instituciòn Sanitaria.

LOs pasos seguidos para este objetivo fueron:
1º)Que las familias notificaran a la Justicia su deseo de aco9modaciòn de sus pacientes a la Ley 13/83. 2º)La visita del Juez con la emisiòn de la Autorizaciòn Judicial de Internamiento v 3º)El inicio de los tràmites de incapacitaciòn.

Session 267   Video:
Mental health. Art therapy

1765

The Homeless Mentally Ill: A Challenge to Mental Health Professionals
Derrell Tidwell, ACSW, LCSW
St. JOhn's Hospital & Health Center

The St. John's Hospital (Santa Monica, Ca.) Homeless Outreach Project will be presented. The presentation will cover the following areas. (1) Program description. This portion of the presentation will describe the Santa Monica and Venice community as well as the various outreach community sites where project staff perform psychiatric evaluations, refer and treat the homeless mentally ill. The project's unique funding sources will also be described. (2) program findings. This portion of the presentation will discuss the findings of the past two years. Typologies, demographics, psychiatric diagnosis, Causes of homelessness, and disposition will be covered. (3) Problems and recommendations will address obstacles in the hospitalization laws, and the resistance inherent in major psychiatric disorders. In addition, the presentation by a 14 minute video tape documentary describing the program.

1766
MY NAME IS ON THE DOOR

Dr. Stelios Philadetakis
Kant.Psych. Klinik Solothurn, Switzerland

A report about the flat-sharing-communities in Solothurn/Switzerland.
Since spring 1973 there are 23 flat-sharing-communities for psychical ill persons in the canton of Solothurn/Switzerland. The communities are taken care of by the staff (two psychiatric nurses per unity) of the cantonal psychiatric hospital of Solothurn during their off-duty time. The costs for their attendance are settled by the Association for the Care of Psychical Ill Persons, which is a private institution. The lodgings are situated in Solothurn and the surrounding municipalities in ordinary multi-family houses.
The flat-sharing-communities are proven alternatives for longterm hospitalized patients to live in and contribute essentially to their social re-integration.
The video which was made in 1988 tries to give an insight into the way of life and dynamics of those communities with sketches of four individual fates and two interviews and also informs about the infrastructure of the "Solothurn model".

1767
PAINT THERAPY ?

N. ROSS ; J.C- DAVID
FOYER DE VIE "SAINT-LOUIS"
35, rue de l'Eglise
93 420   VILLEPINTE   France

Video presentation (V.H.S) depicting the use of painting as a therapeutic approach with the institutionalised mentally retarded.

*Monday
16th October 1989*

Session 268 — Plenary: Major psychotherapeutic approaches

1768

COGNITIVE PSYCHOTHERAPY. CURRENT APPRAISAL AND FUTURE DIRECTIONS.
PERRIS C. Dept of Psychiatry, Umeå University, S-901 85 UMEÅ, Sweden.

Cognitive psychotherapy (CPT) has initially been used mostly in the treatment of depression. In this field, the efficacy of CPT as compared with antidepressant medication has been validated by a large number of controlled trials and is now well established. Further, CPT has proved to be an effective treatment method also for several other morbid conditions e.g., anxiety and phobias eating disorders, behavioural disorders in children and adolescents, adjustment problems of the elderly, substance abuse, and a sizable number of psychosomatic disorders. Its most recent and challenging application concerns patients with a personality disorder or suffering from a schizophrenic syndrome.
CPT is flexible and can easily be integrated with other treatment approaches. It is also economical in terms of time, it is comprehensible to the patients, and it is easily teachable to several othe categories of mental health workers, who in addition to (or in the lack of) doctors and psychologists are directly involved in the support and treatment of mentally ill people. It is in particular those last mentioned characteristics together with its emerging effectiveness in most severe disorders which make of CPT a viable treatment alternative.

1769

THE ROLE OF BRIEF PSYCHOTHERAPIES IN THE PSYCHIATRIST'S ARMAMENTARIUM
Sifneos P., M.D.
Harvard University

The paper will present a brief account of the development of Brief Psychotherapies and their role in the Psychiatrist's Armamentarium.
The evaluation process of appropriate candidates, the techniques utilized and outcomes obtained will be presented.
Several types of Brief psychotherapeutic interventions will be listed.

1770

"BRIEF REFLECTIONS ON FREUD'S IMPACT ON TODAY'S PSYCHIATRY"
Chasseguet-Smirgel Janine
Vice-President of the International Psychoanalytical Association.

L'auteur tente une réflexion sur les développements de certains courants de la psychiatrie actuelle qui semblent la pousser à s'écarter de la découverte freudienne de l'Inconscient et propose au patient une thérapie avant tout médicamenteuse. En cette année où l'on commémore le cinquantenaire de la mort de Freud, il est frappant de constater que, si la psychanalyse continue à se développer dans plusieurs parties du monde, elle n'en connaît pas moins une certaine désaffection de la part de la psychiatrie. Les motifs en sont-ils uniquement dus aux découvertes qui tendent à conférer aux troubles mentaux une origine organique, voire génétique? Ne faut-il pas, également, incriminer la démographie psychanalytique qui s'est révélée galopante autour des années 1970? Mais, au delà de ces raisons apparemment évidentes, n'y en a-t-il pas de plus profondes, liées, à notre insu, à l'état-même de notre civilisation? C'est là une hypothèse que l'auteur se propose de développer dans le temps qui lui est imparti.

1771

PSYCHOEDUCATIONAL FAMILY MANAGEMENT FOR SCHIZOPHRENIA
Samuel J. Keith M.D. and Susan M. Matthews, B.A.
National Institute of Mental Health, Rockville, Maryland, U.S.A.

There has been a growing interest over the past decade in developing treatments which are environmentally oriented, in part because of the assumed importance of environmental factors, and in part because perhaps a more thorough, and comprehensive treatment strategy could be given. We are particularly interested in one such environmentally delivered treatment, psychoeducational family management, for the following reasons:
1. Over 65% of schizophrenic patients discharged from the hospital return to their families.
2. Families are the natural support system.
3. Research has indicated that families identify potential relapse better and earlier than do patients.

There are currently five controlled studies of family treatment of schizophrenia. Four from the expressed emotion era (Hogarty, Lett, Kottgen and Faloon) and one from the 1970's (Goldstein). Although the specifics of family management strategies varied, common among them are the following:
1. The enlistment of the family in a positive clinical alliance.
2. The provision of psychoeducational material.
3. The provision to the family of principles of management skills in the areas of problem solving and communication.
4. Encouragement to families to expand their social networks particularly through mutual interest groups.

This paper will present the results of these studies and review implications of their implementation.

Session 269 — Plenary: Issues and perspectives in social psychiatry

1772
SOCIAL PSYCHIATRY, 2000
J.K.Wing, MRC Social Psychiatry Unit, Institute of Psychiatry, London, U.K.

By "social psychiatry", I mean the knowledge we have derived, by experience and experiment, about the environmental distribution, causes, treatments and effects of psychiatric disorders. "Schizophrenia" (whether singular or plural) illustrates the progress we have made and the distance we have yet to travel. The biological impairments underlying a substantial part of the manifestations make people who are afflicted highly sensitive to environmental influences. "Understimulation" makes the "negative" symptoms and signs worse; "overstimulation" exacerbates the "positive" symptoms. The puzzles raised by current knowledge about the distribution are intelectually as intriguing as any in medicine. Was it rare before 1800? Is it now declining and its severity decreasing? Why is there an "epidemic" among some second generation "immigrants" to the U.K? Can the incidence really be the same all over the world? Is the course really more benign in third world countries? Just as important, because the manifestations will still be plaguing us in the year 2000, what can we learn from the experience of different societies about how to help those afflicted and their families with maximum effectiveness and economy?

1773
THE STIGMA OF MENTAL ILLNESS
Fink P.J., M.D.
Albert Einstein Medical Center

Stigma is a worldwide problem for psychiatry and for mentally ill patients. The ramifications of the problem run very deeply and create a series of difficulties that have to be understood, addressed, and resolved. These include, but are not limited to, problems of housing, jobs, the law, insurance reimbursement, adequate systems for caring for the mentally ill, recognition of the individual's personhood and problems in the media which continues to present negative stereotypes. This stereotyping infringes upon the mentally ill person's ability to enter the every day world as an equal citizen. In the paper the author will expound not only on the nature of stigma, but what has occurred over the past five years to turn the tide.

1774
ATTITUDES TOWARDS THE MENTALLY DISABLED
G. Lyketsos, M.D.
Univ. of Athens, Dept. of Psychiatry, Eginition Hospital, Athens, Greece

Attitudes towards the mentally disabled is the other face of the coin which determines their fate. Several studies have shown that people's attitudes vary according to their cultural and social context, traditions, education, type of occupation and age. Negative attitudes attribute negative qualities to the mentally disabled, such as incompetence, unpredictability, dangerousness and incurability: Interaction between society and mentally disabled is avoided. The mentally disabled are not without a part to play in this process. By definition they are socially disabled and incompetent: A long term burden on the traditional families or the closed networks which is gradually displaced on to the society.
Public opinion changes over time. It is exposed to educational and mass media influences: sophisticated fiction, political, religious and ethical issues, new and special features. Negative attitudes are specific to place and resistant to time. Those who hold negative attitudes may conform verbally with the prevalent public opinion but they do not necessarily act accordingly when personal values are involved, to the detriment of the mentally disabled.

1775
THE PSYCHIATRIST AND SOCIAL ISSUES IN THIRD WORLD

VIJOY K. VARMA
Postgraduate Medical Institute, Chandigarh, [India].

Psychiatrists and mental health professionals can and should make a significant contribution to the elucidation and resolution of a number of social problems - problems concerning the entire human race. The present paper draws attention to two such problems and underscores its relevance to the developing third world.

One major problem is that of world peace - nuclear holocaust, in particular, which threatens to cataclysmically annihilate all life on this planet. Contrary to popular misconception, this matter is of as much, if not greater, concern to the developing countries on account of certain special factors which will be discussed.

The other issue is ecological - the plunder and waste of earth's resources and pollution of its environment. The rapid technological change in the developing world is giving rise to new and unanticipated problems. There is a great need to look at these so as to evolve novel solutions appropriate to the developing world, rather than following the example of the developed world. This may require enforcement of reasonable controls over technology and consumerism to obviate the undesirable consequences of development.

Session 270 Symposium:
Understanding obsessive compulsive disorder

1776

Epidemiology and Clinical Features of Obsessive Compulsive Disorder
Steven A. Rasmussen, M.D., Butler Hospital, Providence, RI, USA

Recent epidemiologic studies have suggested that OCD is one of the more common major neuropsychiatric disorders, with a lifetime prevalence of 1-2% in the general population. However, as it remains unclear how many of these probands suffer from clinically defined illness, the significance of these findings remains in doubt. We have systematically collected data on the clinical features of 300 probands meeting DSM-III-R criteria for OCD over the past 6 years. The phenomenologic subtypes and core features of this group will be discussed with regard to the heterogeneity of the disorder. In addition, data related to the coexistence of other Axis I and Axis II disorders with OCD will be presented. These findings will be discussed with regard to their significance for nosologic classification, treatment prediction, and outcome. Finally, a preliminary two site family genetic study of 100 probands meeting DSM-III-R criteria for OCD that has utilized structured interviews for all probands and family members has been recently completed. Findings supporting familial and genetic transmission of the disorder will be presented.

1777

"SOCIAL ASPECTS OF OBSESSIVE COMPULSIVE DISORDER"

G.D. Burrows, T.R. Nonman, J. Cornwell, K. Moore, J. Tiller
Department of Psychiatry, University of Melbourne, Austin Hospital, Heidelberg, Victoria, Australia, 3084

Obsessive compulsive disorder affects not only the individual, it also affects his or her family, and their total social relationships. Areas involved include difficulties in interpersonal relationships, employment problems, and the type of work the person may be able to undertake. Certain occupations are found to attract or predispose those who have particular rituals eg. nursing for people who suffer with hand washing rituals. This paper will discuss these areas in greater detail, and will elaborate on the development of obsessive compulsive disorder support groups, in the voluntary mental health sector and the importance of such groups for the on-going support, and general assistance to the well-being of these sufferers and their families.

1778

CHILDHOOD OBSESSIVE COMPULSIVE DISORDER: NEW ADVANCES
Judith L. Rapoport, M.D., Susan Swedo, M.D., Henrietta Leonard, M.D., Marge Lenane, M.S.W., NIMH, Bethesda, MD USA

A prospective ongoing study of childhood onset obsessive compulsive disorder (OCD) has yielded powerful evidence for a biological basis of this disorder. Twenty-five percent have a first degree relative with OCD suggesting a genetic basis. Clomipramine (CMI) has a selective antiobsessional effect, while desmethylimipramine (DMI) does not differ from placebo.
Neuropsychological test data, Brain imaging studies, and a study of patients with Sydenham's chorea all implicate dysfunction of the Basal Ganglia and their interaction with the frontal lobes as etiologic.
The selective efficacy of clomipramine in other childhood onset disorders, including nail biting and hair pulling (trichotilomania) suggests that OCD is part of a spectrum of disorders in which grooming behaviors are released inappropriately.

1779

CLINICAL MANAGEMENT OF OCD

John H. Greist
University of Wisconsin, Madison, WI 53792

As with all psychiatric disorders, treatments for obsessive-compulsive disorder (OCD) are based on theories of psychopathology and results of empirical clinical work and controlled research. While elegant and intriguing theories underly psychodynamic therapies, evidence for their efficacy, despite decades of use, is meager. Electroconvulsive therapy is also ineffective for OCD unless patients suffer severe depression. Antipsychotics are only rarely and unpredictably helpful and have substantial liabilities in long-term use. Crude early psychosurgery, too widely employed in desperate situations when no other effective treatments were available, has now been refined and has a small role to play in the treatment of otherwise unresponsive OCD.

The cornerstones of OCD treatment are serotonin reuptake blocking medications (clomipramine and fluvoxamine proven; fluoxetine and sertroline probable) and behavior therapy (exposure in vivo and imagination plus response prevention). Either alone or in combination upwards of 90 percent of patients with OCD are helped by these treatments.

This presentation will review evidence regarding the efficacy and safety of serotonin reuptake blocking medications and behavior therapy for both acute and maintenance treatment of obsessive-compulsive disorder.

1780

MULTI-CENTER TRIALS OF ANAFRANIL IN ADULTS AND ADOLESCENTS WITH OCD
J. DeVeaugh-Geiss, G. Moroz, P. Landau, R. Katz
CIBA-GEIGY Corporation, Summit New Jersey, USA

Two adult and one adolescent multi-center trials compared Anafranil (up to 250 mg daily in adults and 3 mg/kg in adolescents) with placebo during ten weeks (for adults) or eight weeks (for adolescents) of double-blind randomized treatment. Patients were seen weekly for efficacy and safety assessments. Efficacy measures included the Yale-Brown Obsessive Compulsive Scale (Y-BOCS), the NIMH Global OC Scale, a Physician's Global Scale, and a Patient Global Self-Rating Scale. Placebo patients showed a minimal improvement, no more than 5-10% reduction in mean scores at any time during treatment. Anafranil patients showed a monotonic decrease in group mean Y-BOCS and NIMH Global scores throughout the trial. By the end of the trial the group mean scores had declined by 30-45%. Corresponding reductions in Physician and patient Global scores were seen for the Anafanil group, while the placebo group did not improve on these measures. Between-treatment group differences were statistically significant beginning at week two of treatment. Side effects observed during these trials were those typical of tricyclic antidepressants, including dry mouth, blurred vision, sedation, and sexual dysfunction. Patients responding to treatment in the adult studies were permitted to continue for one year. Results from this follow up will also be presented.

1781

PET scan findings in patients with severe OCD undergoing psychosurgery
Mindus P. (1,2), Nyman H. (1), Mogard J. (3), Meyerson B.A. (2), Ericson K. (3).
From the departments of Psychiatry and Psychology (1) Neurosurgery (2), and Neuroradiology (3), T he Karolinska University Hospital, S-10401, Stockholm, Sweden.

Increased cerebral metabolic rate of glucose has been observed with PET in the nc caudatus and in the gyrus orbitalis in subjects suffering from OCD. Disordered functions have been postulated in these regions in OCD.

We examined, with PET and 11-C glucose as tracer, five consecutive right-handed, patients suffering from OCD (DSM III) so chronic, intractable, and incapacitating that psychosurgery was recommended. PET scans were made before, and two and twelve months after capsulotomy, an established form of limbic system surgery. Our preliminary data confirm previous reports of a disordered metabolism in the above mentioned brain regions. Moreover, in patients benefitting from surgery, the metabolic rate of 11-C glucose was significantly reduced post-operatively. However, pre-operative PET scans indicated a lower metabolic rate in the above regions, as compared to healthy controls examined with the same PET system. A number of methodological and clinical factors may account for the discrepancy between these and previously published data, including the fact that our cases had ceased to respond to conventional treatment. It may be assumed that the PET scan findings in our cases reflect the particularly malignant forms of OCD from which they had suffered.

Session 271 — Symposium: Assistance and therapies in adolescence

1782

INTRODUCTION TO THE PROBLEM OF ASSISTANCE AND THERAPIES IN ADOLESCENCE
Mauricio Knobel,UNICAMP,Campinas,SP,Brasil

Adolescents are generally brought to a special service seeking "assistance"for the problems they present to their adult environment.Thus it becomes necessary to discriminate "normal adolescent behaviour" from psychpathology or adjustment difficulties or mere cultural and generational conflicts.THAT ONES CAN BE HANDLED THROUGH ASSISTANCE,in several well differentiated levels and techniques.
The true PSYCHOPATHOLOGICAL problems will deserve specialized treatment(which shall be differentiated from COUNSELLING).
TREATMENT implies use of structured techniques within proven theoretical lines of psychiatric or psychological theories.It also becomes necessary to establish if treatment shall begivento the adolescent, to the parents,to both of them or to the significative network of the adolescent. Sometimes a combinationof assistance and therapies seems to be the most adequate procedure.All of this demand spetialization inthe field of adolescents' mental health and discriminative capacities.

1783

REHABILITATION OF ADOLESCENTS AFTER PSYCHIATRIC REHABILITATION.
DR.E.CHIGIER, M.B.B.Ch., M.R.C.P.Ed., D.C.H.
Director Medical Services, Youth Aliyah
12 Kaplan St. Tel Aviv, Israel

The use of chemotherapy and active psychotherapeutic intervention has resulted in a shorter period of hospitalisation for adolescents and young adults with severe psychiatric illnesses. However, the question is what happens after discharge from hospital. Due to inadequacies or psychopathology in the family, the competitive envirarment of high-school or college and the stigmatising attitudes and behaviour of the community, adequate treatment or rehabilitation may become impossible on return to home and thus the result may be repeated hospitalisation.

1784

MISSING PARENTS
Carlos R.Collazo, M.D; Marta Gerpe PhD.
Universidad del Salvador, Bs.As.
Pueyrredon 1625, Argentina

The literature about the troubles in the development of the identity in adopted adolescents is very rich. The lacunae identity that springs up from the filiation breakdown is stressed by all the authors.
This situation becomes more intricate when the adoptee's biological parents are missing on account of a subversive war and the adoptive parent are committed in such missing.
This paper deals with the difficulties in the mourning process, the identifications and de-identifications, the phantasies and defenses both in the adolescent and the adoptive parents.
The paper discuss the role of the psychotherapist coping with this special situation considering that he is also a member of the same society and therefore, he is trapped in the same signification net, fact that puts under risk his therapeutic and scientific objectivity.

1785

Depressive Disorders in University Students

Rodolfo Fahrer. Alfredo Ortiz Frágola
School of Medicine
University of Buenos Aires

In the Unit of Late Adolescence, Mental Health Division, Hospital de Clínicas, University of Buenos Aires, students with emotional problems are treated.
Last year 30 patients were treated, 76% of them present some kind of depressive symptomatology. University studies usually determine a socially accepted psychological prolonging of adolescence. But this partial delay in a certain phase of the life cycle, which sometimes involves migration and separation from his family, causes an effort of adaptation and mental pain. This can be followed by depressive symptoms.
This report deals with the difficulties to differentiate depressive disorders from normal or "normative" process of adaptation to specific demand of their situation.
Wrong diagnosis of these mood disorders can be dangerous:1) False positive:unnecessary prescription of drugs or psychotherapy when just a psychological assessment is enough.2) False negative: depressions can be overlooked, and they are important at this age for at least two reasons, a)suicide (increasing rate in adolescence in many countries); b) academic failure.

Session 272 Symposium:
The role of psychiatry in mental health policy formulation

1786

THE ROLE OF PSYCHIATRY IN MENTAL HEALTH POLICY FORMULATION
Allan Beigel, M.D.
University of Arizona

The development of public mental health policy is an important influence on the direction of mental health services programming in all countries. As the principal mental health profession, psychiatry should play an active role in guiding that development and in determining the content of policy. However, the actual role of psychiatrists varies in different countries of the world. In some countries, policy development is influenced by only those psychiatrists who are employees of the government. In other countries, both governmental and non-governmental psychiatrists play an important role. There are also differences among various countries in the relative influence of psychiatrists in contrast to other medical and non-medical government officials and in contrast to other mental health disciplines. Members of the Section will describe the specific role of psychiatry in their different countries and discuss some of the strategies that can be used to increase the relative influence of psychiatry on mental health policy development.

1787

AUSTRALASIAN PSYCHIATRISTS AND MENTAL HEALTH POLICY FORMULATION
Dr. John Grigor, Health Department of Victoria, Melbourne, Australia.

The 1980s saw the introduction of new mental health legislation in Australasia.

The legislation had an emphasis on patients' rights, more stringent admission criteria and the establishment of Review Boards or justification in Courts of Law for the continued detention of patients.

Psychiatrists often played only a minor role in the drafting of the new legislation and this led to an ambivalence and distrust in publicly employed psychiatrists. Common reactions have been to discharge patients prior to formal review, failing to admit sick patients because of an overly legalistic concern with the criteria for involuntary hospitalisation and a continuing drift of psychiatrists to private practice.

Australia and New Zealand continue to be heavily reliant on overseas psychiatrists.

This paper identifies strategies to re-engage public psychiatrists and their associations in the task of refining legislation so that a fresh balance is achieved between the needs of the patient and a workable environment for the public psychiatrist.

1788

THE ROLE OF PSYCHIATRY IN MENTAL HEALTH POLICY FORMULATION IN CANADA
Harnois, Gaston P., M.D.
W.A.P.R., Montreal, Canada

Most countries of the world have legislation dealing with compulsory admissions of the mentally ill to hospitals. More recently, a number of countries have drafted mental health policies outlining the philosophy and functioning of mental health programs.
This usually includes an assessment of the scope of mental illness in a given society, a description of programs available, including prevention as well as promotion of mental health. Mention is also made of the desirability of having rehabilitation programs which may start in the hospital and extend in the community, often as a part of the deinstitutionalization process. The ultimate objective of maintaining the chronic mentally ill in the community is emphasized.
The main actors are the individual, the family, the mental health workers and professionals, and the community, all acting in a spirit of partnership. The role of psychiatry as a key component in both treatment and rehabilitation will be outlined.

1789

THE ROLE OF PSYCHIATRY IN MENTAL HEALTH POLICY DEVELOPMENT IN LATIN AMERICA
Costa e Silva, Jorge Alberto, Prof. Dr.
State University of Rio de Janeiro - Rio de Janeiro - Brazil

Mental health in Latin America has not been regarded by authorities in Public Health as it should be. The same thing happens with Psychiatry among the other medical specialities - there is no recognition of its importance.
We can divide the role of Psychiatry in the development of Mental Health Policy in three levels: patients care, education and research. We try to identify and analyse the contributions of the Psychiatry in each of these levels taking into consideration the integration among them. Special emphasis is given to socioeconomic difficulties that exist in Latin America that no doubt act as obstacle to reach many of the objectives proposed.

1790

THE ROLE OF PSYCHIATRY IN MENTAL HEALTH POLICY FORMULATION IN INDIA
Narendra N. Wig
World Health Organization, Alexandria, Egypt

At the time of independence in 1947, India, with a population then estimated to be around 500 million, had only a handful of qualified psychiatrists, working in about 20 mental hospitals scattered over vast geographical areas. The population is now 800 million and psychiatry has made rapid progress since 1947. The first major development which started in the 1950s, was the provision of local training facilities for psychiatrists. There are now over 30 university postgraduate training centres where over 120 new psychiatrists qualify every year. The second major development was the opening of a large number of general hospital psychiatric units. The third development was the extension of mental health services to the district level: in many states now, a specialist in psychiatry is available at almost every district government hospital. However, the most significant development has been the adoption of a comprehensive national policy and programme of mental health based on the primary health care approach and integrated within general health care. The programme was prepared, discussed and approved by leading psychiatrists and other mental health professionals of the country in 1982, and subsequently adopted by the Government of India. Through this programme, mental health services are now being extended to far off rural areas through hundreds of primary care doctors, health workers and their supervisors, all of whom have been provided with basic training in mental health.

1791

THE ROLE OF PSYCHIATRY IN MENTAL HEALTH POLICY FORMULATION - AN EGYPTIAN PERSPECTIVE
Prof. A.Okasha
Ain Shams University, Cairo, Egypt

The studies on psychiatric morbidity can influence the planning of mental health policy. Recent studies on incidence, prognosis, open door policy in schizophrenia, depression in urban and rural Egypt, absence of work and lack of production in relation to psychosomatic and psychoneurotic disorders had an impact on the total health policy in Egypt. The uprise of heroin abuse in Egypt forced the country to pass new legislation, to erect new centres, to implement mass media propaganda and to change the attitude towards mental health policy.
Health priorities were restricted to bilharsiasis, birth control, infant mortality and cerebro-cardiac disorders but with the new mental health policy, psychiatry is at the top of the agenda.

Session 273 Symposium:
"Why can't they be like us?" Psychiatry and primary care

"WHY CAN'T THEY BE LIKE US?"
PSYCHIATRY AND PRIMARY CARE

János Füredi, M.D.
Medical University of Postgraduate Education, Budapest-Hungary

For many decates there had been a deep gap between the fields of psychiatry and general practice without any hope of communication.
In our workshop we would try to find out what do these specialities expect from each other. We can collect a library in which, psychiatrists want to cram the colleagues' head with their science.
On the other hand I could recognize three types of attitude in the approach of the GPs. They have been wanting to keep some of their patients in their own hands even if they have had mental problems or they have just wanted to learn the vocabulary of psychiatry to be able to pass on their unbearable patients or they have been wanting to assimilate to the psychiatrists psychotherapists even on the prize of modification of their career.
The main aim of the workshop is to find the right solution for this steadily increasing problem.

1792

MENTAL HEALTH IN THE MAINSTREAM OF PRIMARY HEALTH CARE IN THE EUROPEAN REGION OF WHO

Dr J.G. Sampaio Faria, World Health Organization Regional Office for Europe, Copenhagen, Denmark

For the last 10 years increasing attention is being given by Member States of the European Region of WHO to the need for developing comprehensive primary health care systems. The implications of this development for the care of persons affected by mental disorders as well as for the prevention of disease and the promotion of mental health are reviewed. The paper also focuss its attention on the role of psychiatry in meeting the needs for mental health care in community settings.

1793

THE ORGANIZATION, PRACTICE OF PSYCHIATRIC CARE AND PERSPECTIVE OF THEIR DEVELOPMENT IN THE USSR.

Dr. N.M.Zharicov
Moscow Medical School, Moscow, USSR

Already during the first of the Soviet power a new approach to the organization of psychiatric care and principles of the mental patients treatment were developed and put into practice: special emphasis was laid on creation of various forms of out-patient aid, on social and vocational adaptation as well as rehabilitation of patients under conditions of specialized and general industrial establishments.
An analysis of statistical data concerning incidence and morbidity dynamics, also results of epidemiological studies helped to determine some geographical distribution characteristics of mental diseases, the importance of various factors and resources of psychiatric care for social and vocational rehabilitation of mental patients and for prevention of mental diseases.
Social and political reorganization taking place in the Soviet Union has created conditions for further development of optimal forms of psychiatric care.

1794

FAMILY, SOCIETY AND THERAPY
J.Füredi
Medical University Postgraduate ED, Budapest, Hungary

Several researches are investigating the families in different societies when they are in a distressing situation. However, there is very little knowledge about families living in Eastern European countries.
The author is the leader of psychiatric department working mainly on the basis of systematic family orientation. He has observed that in his, everyday work therapy, he can hardly rely on the self reestablishing efforts of the family.
In this presentation the author tries to analyze this phenomenon. The basic assumption is developed according to a socio-ecological view. It is supposed that during the stalinis period all ideology was based on such groups as the part, the working team, the Trade Union while the role of the family community religion was completely neglected.
Because of this reason, in our preventive work we should give more emphasis to re-establish new views about strengthening these later groups. In the meantime in our clinical work the family is the reachable group format where we can realize our treatment and rehabilitation goals. For this reason the process should be much more based on educational form as on exploratory methods.

Session 274 Symposium:
The epidemiology of the dementias in Community samples

1795

THE EPIDEMIOLOGICAL STUDY OF DEMENTIA IN ZARAGOZA, SPAIN
Antonio LOBO, Pedro SAZ, José-Luis DIA-SAHUN, Buillermo MARCOS, Francisco MORALES, Maria-Jesús PEREZ-ECHEVERRIA, Luis-Fernando PASCUAL MILLAN, Tirso VENTURA, Eva GRACIA
Hospital Clinico Universitario, Zaragoza, Spain

An epidemiological study was designed to document the psychiatric moribidity in the geriatric population in the city of Zaragoza, Spain. A two-phase screening was programmed; standardized lay interviewers administered the Geriatric Mental State (GMS) and the "Mini-Examen Cognoscitivo" in the first phase; standardized psychiatrists administered the same instruments and the History and Aetiology Schedule (HAS) to "probable cases" and controls, in the second phase. A neurological evaluation was programmed for a third phase. Preliminary data suggest prevalence rates concordant with those reported in modern international studies. The computerized programme AGECAT permits the comparison with a similar study in a British community (study "Zaragoza-Liverpool"); the prevalence of global morbidity is similar in both cities but statistically significant differences have been documented in the prevalence of several psychopathological symptoms in the "neurosis" sections.

1796

INTERNATIONAL COMPARATIVE STUDIES OF DEMENTIA: THE NEW COLLABORATIVE EPIDEMIOLOGICAL STUDY IN LIVERPOOL U.K. P A Saunders*, J R M Copeland, A Scott, M E Dewey, B Larkin. Department of Psychiatry and the Institute of Human Ageing, University of Liverpool, England.

The results of Comparative Studies so far are briefly outlined.
The design and methodology of the new collaborative Longitudinal Study examining dementia in random sample of 6000 elderly community subjects is described and the application of computer technology to methods of data collection and case identification discussed. The GMS-HAS-AGECAT package provides a flexible, modular, epidemiological tool which allows comparison between Studies of differing design as well as providing the user with a choice of diagnostic criteria. AGECAT is a computerised diagnostic program which can be applied to data gathered using versions of the Geriatric Mental State examination (GMS) and History and Aetiology Schedule (HAS).
The performance of a system developed for field administration of the GMS-HAS-AGECAT package by portable copmputer is reviewed. This technique solves many of the logistical and quality control problems associated with large scale epidemiological Studies and facilitates the use of complex survey instruments.

1797

Epidemiological Study of Dementia in Iceland.

Helgason, T. and Magnússon, H.
National University Hospital, Department of Psychiatry, 101 Reykjavík, Iceland.

A birth cohort of 5395 Icelanders alive at the age of 13-15 years in 1910 has been followed until the age of 86-88 years. Information has been collected on every member of the cohort until this age or until the probands' disappearance from the study, most often by death.

At the last follow-up 83,5% of the 1049 members of the cohort alive at that time were interviewed using the Geriatric Mental State Schedule. The information collected has been sufficient to assign psychiatric diagnoses to the probands.

The results will be presented as prevalence rates at the average age of 61, 75, 81, and 87 years, as well as expectancy rates for developing dementia before the probands reach the specified age levels according to various demographic variables.

1798

The Epidemiological Study of Dementia in Bordeaux, France.

PERE Jean-Jacques and Paquid Study Group

Paquid Study Group, Université de Bordeaux II, 33076 Bordeaux cedex.

Paquid is a five year prospective study carried on a representative sample of 4000 subjects aged 65 years and older who are living independently in two districts in the South Western region of France (area of Bordeaux). The major goal of Paquid is to determine incidence, risk factors and preclinical signs of Senile Dementia of Alzheimer Type. Paquid was designed to test three major hypotheses : (1) slight changes in cognitive functionning could be preclinical signs of SDAT ; (2) depressive symptomatology could play a role in the ulterior development of SDAT ; (3) familial antecedents of dementia could increase the probability of SDAT.
Methodology and preliminary results will be presented.

1799

CROSS CULTURAL STUDIES OF ALZHEIMER'S DISEASE: THE NIA WHO/SPRA PROGRAM
T.S. Radebaugh[1], Z. Khachaturian[1], J. Litvak[2]
[1]National Institute on Aging, Bethesda, Maryland
[2]WHO/SPRA, Bethesda, Maryland

The most important problem in the epidemiology of Alzheimer's disease is the identification of risk factors which will point to testable hypotheses regarding etiology. While theories regarding the etiology and pathogenesis at the molecular level abound, robust risk factors other than age and familial aggregation do not exist. The examination of many countries, cultures, ethnic and population groups, with different exposures and habits may offer important clues to the etiology of the disease.

A major limitation is lack of adequate instrumentation, especially for detecting early cases. This should be relatively free from socio-cultural bias. Several efforts are underway to address this problem, including the Alzheimer's Disease Research Centers, the Consortium to Establish a Registry for Alzheimer's Disease (CERAD), the work on the development of CAMDEX, and the WHO/SPRA multi-center study of the epidemiology of dementias. The NIA and the WHO/SPRA are encouraging the development of multinational field studies of the dementias which incorporate internal comparative studies of two or more instruments and their respective yields against a standardized clinical examination.

Session 275 Symposium:
Psychosocial problems in Psychiatry

1800

PSYCHOSOCIAL PROBLEMS AND/OR PSYCHO-SOCIAL FACTORS
C.S.Ierodiakonou,Prof.of Psychiatry, University of Thessaloniki, Greece.

Psychosocial problems is an ill-defined term,but an existing and everyday reality in clinical practice.Situational conditions and social maladjustments of previous psychiatric classifications,or more recent entities like adjustment disordres and V Codes are part of those "problems",and all exlude mental disorder in their definition.Psychosocial factors may be causal,contributing or precipitating of many conditions,-emotional, somatic or psychosomatic,and may influence the course or treatment.
In Greek society close ties of relatives,family pride,a "social superego" etc play significant roles in eliciting a disorder.In a study of children of immigrants we found a somatic "failure to thrive" in 61-96%, in 48% psychosomatic problems (due to grandmother's anxiety) and an emotional "radar's gaze"in 87%. Depressive reactions we found to be (1/3) adjustment disorders due to psychosocial problems(with in-laws etc).Strict cultural rules(e.g.against remarrying) contribute to psychosocial manifestations etc.
Ps/social problems remain often untraced and GPs should be guided accordingly.

1801

PRIMARY, SECONDARY AND TERTIARY PREVENTION OF SUICIDE
Walter Pöldinger, M.D.
Psychiatric University Clinic
CH - 4025 Basel/Switzerland

Of these three forms of suicide prevention, the most useful and most frequently practised one is the tertiary prevention. That means every form of prophylaxis to prevent a relapse of suicidal activities.

Secondary prevention which intends to prevent suicidal activities as well as suicidal ideas is common practice of medical doctors in support of in- and outpatients. In this field there are again a variety of private organizations involved.

Very bad is the situation in primary prevention. Primary prevention pertains to activities trying to change the suicidal climate to a non-suicidal climate in the population at large. This should start e.g. very early in families and in schools. Unfortunately there are so many taboos and misunderstandings that more activity in primary prevention is necessary.

1802

SEXUAL RELATIONSHIPS AND MARITAL PROBLEMS
Dimitriou,E.C.,Aristotelian University of Thessaloniki Medical School, Thessaloniki,Greece.

Marital problems are alarmingly on the increase.Couples seek divorce more frequently, although divorce is not always the best solution.
While disturbed communication is certainly one of the main reasons of marital discord,sexual relationships appear to be second on the list.
Based on 86 cases of couples that sought professional help for their marital disharmony we found that more than 50% of husbands and 30% of wives were complaining of sexual problems encountered on their spouse. The main complaint of husbands about their wives was the lack of "co-operation" and diminished interest in sexual activities, while wives were mainly complaining about the "hastiness" of their husbands.Impotence was also a frequent complaint.
We conclude that people nowadays talk more freely about their sexual relationships, marital or extramarital,pay more attention to their personal satisfaction, feel more secure and thus seek divorce more easily.
Our findings are discussed in relation to other relevant studies and to the Greek socio-economic and cultural reality.

1803
SOCIAL PROBLEMS IN DEPRESSION

HEBENSTREIT G.F.
II. Psychiatric Department of the Lower Austrian hospital for Psychiatric and Neurology, A-3362 Amstetten/Mauer, Austria

Discussing social problems in depression one can see several approaches to this theme. Firstley factors of early environment, chronic stress-situations and specific stages of lability as puberty, adolescence, marriage, involutioniary-states and senile demenita with their increased stress on the neurotransmitter-system may be the social problems for depression.
Secondly clinical symptoms of depression as depressive mood, psychomotoric inhibition, vegetative symptoms, depressive paranoid ideas or inhibition of intellectual fluidy may induce psychosocial problems concerning school- and studying-ability, family life, employment situation, financial problems and increase the tendency to commit a suicide tremendously.
There is a strong interaction of social problems between depression inducing factors and problems caused by depression.
The clinical link of improvement properly will be the balance of neurotransmitters acting on psychic as well as on somatic problem and this way neutralising the old controversy between two originally opposite positions.

1804
PSYCHOSOCIAL FACTORS IN PSYCHOSOMATICS
G.N.Christodoulou
Athens University, Dept.of Psychiatry, Athens-Greece

Modern psychosomatic theory is based on two approaches developed in ancient Greece by physicians and philosophers (e.g. Socrates in Plato's "Charmidis"). Both approaches regard psychosocial factors as essential prerequisites for the production of illness and for the maintenance of health.
The importance of psychological factors, however, in not of equal degree in all psychosomatic illnesses. Research carried out at Athens University Department of Psychiatry (Christodoulou et al., Psychother. Psychosom. 39,55, 1983 and 32,297, 1979) has shown that life events are of paramount importance in peptic ulcer and consequently this illness can with justification be regarded as psychosomatic. In irritable bowel syndrome, however, life events have not been found to be of particular importance contrary to depression which was very prominent in these patients (Christodoulou and Alevizos, Psychosomatic Medicine: Past and Future, G.N.Christodoulou, editor, p.233, Plenum, N.Y.1987).
On the basis of these findings the "psychosomatic" nature of irritable bowel syndrome is challenged and George Orwell's "Animal Farm" is paraphrased as follows: "All illnesses are psychosomatic but some illnesses are more psychosomatic than others".

1805
PSYCHOSOCIAL PROBLEMS IN EPILEPSY
Kugler J. - University of Munich, FRG

Session 276 Symposium:
Child abuse

1806
CHILD SEXUAL ABUSE-ABUSIVE PROFESSIONAL RESPONSES

Ingrid K. Cooper
McGill University, Montréal, Québec Canada

The recent «discovery» of child sexual abuse, particularly incestuous abuse, has resulted in a great increase in the number of families investigated by child protection services. Often professionals' zealous search for the facts and a guilty party causes them to overlook the needs of the victims, traumatizing them further. Several factors including lack of knowledge, inadequate training and the taboo nature of the behaviour can lead professionals to intervene in an inappropriate, coercive way, damaging to both victim and family. Sources of trauma for the victim include multiple interviews (with intense psychological pressure to disclose everything), medical examinations, temporary or permanent separation from the family and testifying in court against a family member. Removal of non-abused children and incarceration of a family perpetrator can have severe consequences for the family such as marital separation, family disbandonment, financial hardship and public humiliation. The events in Cleveland, England in 1987, when 123 children were removed from their homes for suspicion of sexual abuse on the basis of an unproven medical test, the anal dilation test, well illustrates the abusive nature of professional responses to child sexual abuse.

1807

OBTAINING REPRESENTATIVE SAMPLES IN TRANSGENERATIONAL SEXUALITY

Richard Green, M.D., J.D. University of Calif., Los Angeles. L.A., Calif., United States

U.S. laws mandate that physicians notify the state when sexual interaction between a child and an adult is suspected. The adults face lengthy prison sentences. The state has concluded that transgenerational sexual interaction per se is abusive to the child. Clinical samples of adults (usually women labelled "survivors") recalling childhood sexual experiences with adults underline its negative impact. However, population studies have not adequately filled in the picture for women who may not be troubled. Evaluations of children occur in the context of forensic investigations to gather evidence with which to convict. Because of mandatory reporting laws, population studies of children are impossible. Furthermore, many evaluated children are not re-evaluated as adults.

Representative retrospective and prospective data will impact on the current view that all adult-child sexual interaction is traumatic and scarring and must be countered by mandatory disclosure and lengthy imprisonment.

1808

PREVENTING CHILD ABUSE AND NEGLECT DEATHS

Cyril Greenland, Toronto, CANADA

Homicide is one of the leading causes of infant mortality in the U.S.A. A majority of the victims, usually children of poor families, were under school age. A substantial proportion of them had been previously hospitalized for physical abuse or severe neglect.

The perpetrators, male and female, tended to be young, poor and socially isolated. But the male perpetrators, in many cases, were not biologically related to the victims.

Based on an international study of child abuse and neglect deaths in the U.K., U.S.A., and Canada, the author concludes that Forensic Psychiatrists should play a more prominent role in preventing or at least reducing the incidence of C.A.N. deaths in their communities. This would involve a much closer partnership between Forensic Psychiatrists, Child Protection Agencies, the Police and the Judicial System.

1809

PROSTITUTION AMONG SEX ABUSED BOYS

D.J. West

Surveys of both male and female prostitutes have found a high prevalence of histories of sex abuse in childhood. Ongoing research into young male street prostitutes catering to homosexuals in London confirms this finding.

Further analysis shows that the association may not be one of direct cause and effect. These youths have often grown up in unhappy or broken homes or institutions and their exposure to sexual molestation has been but one feature of a conglomeration of adverse influences. Running away from unhappy homes may have little to do with sexual experiences, but doing so without money or accommodation encourages resort to crime and prostitution.

Other research into the histories of homosexual males reveals a high prevalence of early sexual contacts with men. Molestation in boyhood may sometimes be an effect rather than a cause of anomalous sexual development. Finally, there may be a tendency to retrospective bias or exaggeration by individuals anxious to justify a disapproved lifestyle.

1810

MODE OF PRESENTATION AND MANAGEMENT OF CHILD SEXUAL ABUSE

Dr. A. N. Singh, Hamilton Psychiatric Hospital, Hamilton, Ontario, Canada

The sexual abuse of children is becoming a major challenge of forensic psychiatry. Presentation usually occurs in six ways; a) an account by the child b) behavioural disturbances and psychiatric features c) physical signs or symptoms d) allegation by parents, relatives and other adults e) with combination of other forms of maltreatment and, f) deterioration of school academic progress. Management on the other hand needs multidisciplinary team effort which not only includes health professionals but also the investigative agencies. The treatment regime is based on meeting the need of the individual child and family. These needs vary according to the age of the child, structure of the family and kind of abuse. The mother's attitude in most cases becomes the key to the prognosis. Effort should be made to correct the underlying disturbances of the family which either precipitated or created the child abuse. In some cases pharmacotherapy of patients and some members of the family are also indicated. Multiple forms of therapy and an individualized plan works to bring out the best prognosis.

Session 277 Symposium:
Alcohol: Basic science of clinical importance

1811
GENETIC HIGH RISK RESEARCH IN ALCOHOLISM

Joachim Knop, Donald W. Goodwin, Fini Schulsinger and Sarnoff A. Mednick.

Psykologisk Institut, Department of Psychiatry, Kommunehospitalet, DK-1399 Copenhagen K, Denmark

Both family, twin and adoption studies have demonstrated that genetic factors play a significant role in alcoholism. An outline of the results from these basic studies is presented.
The paper also focuses on main results from research on biological markers and other vulnerability factors.
The longitudinal high risk methodology is presented as a promising research strategy to test both biological and environmental hypotheses in the development of alcoholism.
Design and premorbid results from a Danish prospective study on young men at high risk for alcoholism is presented.

1812
NEUROENDOCRINE CONCOMITANTS OF ALCOHOL AND COCAINE ABUSE
Mendelson, Jack H., Mello, Nancy K.
Harvard Medical School-McLean Hospital, Belmont U.S.A.

Ethanol, cocaine and heroin abuse may cause adverse effects on the hypothalamic-pituitary-gonadal and hypothalamic-pituitary-adrenal axis in men. However, acute alcohol intake by healthy men may either induce a fall or an increase in plasma testosterone levels depending upon the degree of antecedent gonadotropin stimulation. Similarly acute alcohol intake by healthy women during periods of the menstrual cycle when gonadotropin levels are elevated may result in a significant increase in plasma estradiol levels.

Cocaine abuse may cause persistent hyperprolactinemia as a consequence of cocaine's adverse effects on neural dopaminergic systems. Alterations in prolactin secretion due to cocaine abuse and dependence may enhance risk for infectious disease including AIDS, but paradoxically, cocaine may be administered acutely in order to perturbate pituitary, gonadal and adrenal hormones with attendant reinforcing effects. The significance of alcohol and cocaine induced perturbations of neuroendocrine function for the reinforcing properties of these abused substances will be discussed.

This research was supported, in part, by grants DA00064, DA00101 and DA04059 from the National Institute on Drug Abuse and AA06252 from the National Institute on Alcohol Abuse and Alcoholism.

1813
ANTAGONISM BY CALCIUM CHANNEL ANTAGONISTS ON ETHANOL-INDUCED STIMULATION ON BEHAVIOR AND DOPAMINERGIC ACTIVITY.
J. A. Engel, C. Fahlke, P. Hulthe, E. Hård, K. Johannessen, B. Snape, and L. Svensson.
Department of Pharmacology, University of Göteborg, S-400 33 Göteborg, Sweden.

In the present series of experiments we have studied the effects of the dihydropyridine calcium channel antagonist nifedipine on ethanol-induced changes in behavior and dopamine (DA) release and metabolism. The locomotor-stimulatory effect of low doses of ethanol (2.5 g/kg) was antagonized by nifedipine, whereas ethanol-induced sedation observed after higher doses (4.5 g/kg) was potentiated. Biochemical studies indicated that ethanol enhanced the metabolism and release of DA in the striatum and the DA-rich limbic regions measured by post mortem analyses of DA-metabolites by HPLC with electrochemical detection and by in vivo voltammetry in anaesthetized rats, respectively. Pretreatment with nifedipine antagonized the stimulatory effects of ethanol on the DA-system. Nifedipine reduced the preference for ethanol, estimated by the relative intake of ethanol (6% v/v) and water in a free-choice situation, suggesting an influence of nifedipine not only on the stimulatory but also on the positive reinforcing effects of ethanol. The present results indicate that the locomotor-stimulatory and positive reinforcing effects of ethanol as well as its enhancing effects on dopaminergic activity may involve an enhancement of calcium mediated mechanisms. It is proposed that calcium channel antagonists of the dihydropyridine type could provide a new approach for moderating ethanol intake in problem drinkers.

1814
ALCOHOLIC WOMEN. A CONTROLLED FOLLOW-UP STUDY FROM A SPECIALIZED UNIT (EWA).
Lena Dahlgren MD. Associate professor
Department of Clinical Alcohol and Drug Research (EWA Unit), Karolinska Hospital
Stockholm
Sweden

Women with alcohol problems constitute an increasing number of the patients in medical service. Do they need a special care? How should the treatment program be designed?
The specialized female EWA-unit at the Karolinska Hospital in Stockholm, Sweden was opened in 1981. The aim of the project is to reach women in an early stage of alcohol dependence behaviour and to develop treatment programs specific to the needs of females alone.
In order to investigate the value of such a specialized female unit a controlled two years follow-up study was carried out including 200 women. The probands were treated in the female only EWA-unit, whereas the controls were placed in the care of traditional mixed sex alcoholism treatment centres.
The two year follow-up study showed a more successful rehabilitation regarding alcohol consumption and social adjustment for the women treated in the specialized female unit (EWA). Improvement was noted also for the controls but to a lesser extent. Probably one of the most important achievements of a specialized female unit, such as EWA is, to attract women to come for help earlier?

1815

ALCOHOL AND THE FETUS: WHERE ARE WE IN 1989?

Ann Pytkowicz Streissguth, Ph.D., Professor,
Department of Psychiatry and Behavioral Sciences,
University of Washington,
Seattle, Washington, 98195, USA

Psychopathology attributable to teratogenic exposure is only recently being recognized. Alcohol is the most frequently used teratogen in the Western World. While prenatal alcohol exposure is now recognized as the leading known cause of mental retardation, other types of psychopathology are also caused by prenatal alcohol exposure. This paper wil review recent research on alcohol-related psychopathology associated with exposure at both ends of the alcohol-use continuum.

The first study involves children of alcoholic mothers. Findings from a long term follow-up study of 91 adolescents and adults with Fetal Alcohol Syndrome and Fetal Alcohol Effects will be presented. Changes in morphology associated with the onset of puberty, recognition of FAS/FAE in the adult, and the characteristic behavioral phenotype and psychopathology will all be discussed.

The second study involves children of social drinking mothers. Findings from a population-based study involving a cohort of approximately 500 children who have received standardized examinations between birth and 7 years of age will be presented. The contributions of prenatal alcohol exposure to attention deficits, learning disabilities, and problem behaviors will be discussed within the framework of statistical analyses that permit adjustment for some of the other pre and postnatal experiences that could also compromise development and behavior in the young child.

Implications of this body of research for the field of psychiatry will be discussed. Funding by USPHS (NIAAA & IHS)

Session 278   Symposium:
Laterality and pathophysiology in schizophrenia and depression

1816

SCHIZOPHRENIA AS AN ANOMALY OF DEVELOPMENT OF CEREBRAL ASYMMETRY

Crow, TJ, Ball J*, Bloom SR*, Brown R, Bruton CJ, Colter N, Frith CD, Johnstone EC, Owens DGC, Roberts GW. Northwick Park Hospital, Harrow, *Hammersmith Hospital, U.K.

Schizophrenia is associated with structural changes (eg. a mild degree of ventricular enlargement) in the brain, although whether these precede onset of or progress with episodes is not established. Here in a post mortem study of 56 brains of patients with schizophrenia and 56 controls we find that ventricular enlargement affects the posterior and particularly the temporal horn of the lateral cerebral ventricle. By comparison with controls and with patients (30 patients with dementia with age-matched controls) suffering from Alzheimer-type dementia (in which there is also temporal horn enlargement) the change is highly significantly ($p < 0.001$) selective to the left hemisphere. This deviation was not accompanied by an increase in glial cell numbers (examined chemically by assay of diazepam-binding inhibitor peptide and microscopically by density of staining with the Holzer technique). The findings are consistent with the view that schizophrenia is a disorder of the genetic mechanisms that control the development of cerebral asymmetry.

1817

AMINO-ACID NEUROTRANSMITTERS AND THE PATHOLOGY OF SCHIZOPHRENIA

DEAKIN,J.F.W., SLATER,P., SIMPSON,M.P., ROYSTON,M.C. Dept. Psychiatry, Withington Hospital, Manchester University, M20 8LR, UK.

Glutamatergic pyramidal cells and GABA neurones could be involved in the pathology of schizophrenia. In-vitro ligand binding of 3H-D-aspartate (DASP) to glutamate uptake sites and 3H-nipecotic acid (NIP) binding to GABA uptake sites in brain membranes from 14 schizophrenics and 14 age/sex matched controls were used to assess the integrity of presynaptic neurones. 3H-kainate and 3H-TCP binding were the ligands for post-synaptic neuronal glutamate receptors. Bilateral increases in DASP, kainate and TCP binding were found in orbital frontal cortex (OFC) from schizophrenics including 6 drug-free (> 5 mths) patients. Arrested callosal development could result in an excessive glutamatergic innervation of OFC in schizophrenia and the increase in glutamatergic markers (Deakin et al, 1989, J.Neurochem. in press).
NIP and DASP binding were significantly reduced in left polar temporal cortex (PTC). There was also evidence of a generalised loss of NIP binding sites in OFC, PTC, hippocampus and amygdala. The pathology of schizophrenia appears to be neurochemically and anatomically specific and to be assymetric.

1818

LEFT STRIATO-PALLIDAL HYPERACTIVITY MODEL OF SCHIZOPHRENIA Early TS, Posner MI, Reiman EM, Washington University Sch.Medicine, St. Louis MO 63110 USA

Previous work in our laboratory has demonstrated abnormally increased relative cerebral blood flow in a group of 10 neuroleptic-naive schizophrenic patients compared to 20 controls ($p<0.0002$) overall by ANOVA). (1) We have also recently observed that schizophrenic patients have difficulty shifting attention to the right visual field, a very subtle form of hemineglect ($p<0.0002$).(2) Attempts to relate these two findings have resulted in a theory of relating many of the manifestations of schizophrenia to impaired function of a loop in the left hemisphere that includes anterior cingulate gyrus, ventral striatum, ventral pallidum, and the medio-dorsal nucleus of the thalamus.(3) Striato-pallidal hyperactivity and hemineglect are seen following lesions such as unilateral dopaminergic denervation (4) or frontal ablations. This model can potentially account for other findings of hemineglect in schizophrenia, the association between left-sided temporal lobe epilepsy and psychosis, eye tracking abnormalities, and the beneficial effects of direct dopaminergic agonists on the positive symptoms of psychosis. Findings of left hemispheric dysfunctions may represent a "hemineglect of higher cognitive functions." Finally, the model suggests reasons for some of the phenomenological symptoms experienced by some schizophrenic patients and suggests further testable approaches to understanding this disorder.
1. Early et al. Proc.Natl.Acad.Sci. 1987;84:561.
2. Posner et al. Arch.Gen.Psychiatry 1988;45:814.
3. Alexander et al. Neurosci. 1986;9:357.
4. Schallert et al. Behav.Brain Res. 1988;30:15.
5. Hosokawa et al. Brain Res. 1985;343:8.

1819
EMOTION AND HEMISPHERE DYNAMICS IN SCHIZOPHRENIA AND MAJOR DEPRESSION
Oepen G, Harrington A, Fünfgeld M.
Dept. of Psychiatry, Freiburg, West-Germany

Regarding neuropsychological baseline performance only, a predominant left hemisphere (LH) dysfunction may be linked with schizophrenia, and right hemisphere (RH) dysfunction with depression. In the present study, the dynamic reactivity of hemisphere asymmetries to emotional stimulation allowed the discrimination of primary and secondary dysfunction in the dual hemispheric system. In a tachistoscopic study, right visual field (RVF) advantages for words and left visual field (LVF) advantages for faces, on different levels, were found in 50 patients with schizophrenia, 25 patients with Major Depression and 30 controls. Additional emotional stimulation revealed a deterioration in RH (LVF) performance and a marked improvement in LH (RVF) performance in schizophrenic patients. In contrast, patients with Major Depression showed an overshooting improvement in RH (LVF) performance but no remarkable change in LH (RVF) performance in the emotional test runs. We suggest that the emotional stimulation leads to a breakdown of RH-processing capacities and to a subsequent release of LH competence in schizophrenia; in depression, the capacity of the LH to modulate the processes of a morbidly independent RH seems attenuated. This is supported by the effect of neuroleptic treatment and neurometabolic findings in Mescaline-induced schizophreniform psychosis.

1820
AFFECTIVE DISORDERS FOLLOWING STROKE
Robinson, Robert G., Starkstein, Sergio E., Parikh, Rajesh M. The Johns Hopkins University School of Medicine, Baltimore, MD U.S.A.

Using structured psychiatric interviews and DSM-III diagnostic criteria, 30-50% of acute stroke patients have major or minor depressions which usually last more than one year without treatment. The frequency of these mood disorders is not strongly associated with severity of impairment, demographic characteristics, social supports or prior personal history. Major depression, however, is often strongly associated with left frontal cortical or left basal ganglia lesions as well as pre-existing subcortical atrophy as evidenced by increased ventricular-to-brain ratios. While the aetiology of these mood disorders remains unknown, they are responsive to treatment with the tricyclic antidepressant nortriptyline and serotonergic or noradrenergic dysfunction may play a role. Mania is a rare complication of stroke, although the clinical presentation and response to treatment are usually the same as mania without brain injury. Post-stroke mania is strongly associated with both a specific right hemisphere lesion location and a second predisposing factor, such as either a genetic loading for affective d-sorder, pre-existing subcortical atrophy or a seizure disorder. Mania may be mediated through frontal lobe dysfunction and does not appear to be a mirror image of the mechanisms involved in depression. Thus, the lesion method represents a potentially fruitful technique for investigating the pathophysiology of mood disorders.

Session 279 Special Session:
Psychiatric epidemiology: Prevalence studies

1821
MENTAL HEALTH OVER TIME IN DIFFERENT BIRTH COHORTS

Lehtinen V, Lindholm T, Veijola J, Väisänen E, The Rehabilitation Research Centre, Turku, and the Universities of Turku and Oulu, Finland

Results are presented from a Finnish epidemiological 16-year follow-up study of a population sample (born in 1905 to 1945) representing the normal population. Previously, the same sample has undergone a five-year follow-up. There were altogether 723 individuals of the original sample of 1000 persons who were evaluated in the original study and in the both follow-up studies. The total prevalence of mental disorders in the original study was 21.4 % in males and 34.0 % in females, in the five-year follow-up 23.2 % in males and 31.2 % in females, and in the 16-year follow-up 25.9 % in males and 33.0 % in females. The increase of the prevalence has occurred in males in the youngest birth cohort (15-34 years of age in the original study), and in both sexes in the middle-aged cohorts (35-44 years). On the other hand, the prevalence has decreased in females in the youngest cohort (15-24 years) and in the older cohorts (45-64 years of age in the original study).

1822
EPIDEMIOLOGY OF MENTAL DISORDERS IN RURAL AREAS. A COMMUNITY STUDY

B.CARPINIELLO*,M.CARTA*,P.L.MOROSINI** & N.RUDAS
*Institute of Psychiatry,University of Cagliari
** National Health Institute,Rome-ITALY

Community studies can be considered reliable methods to assest true prevalence of mental disorders,to identify risk factors,to give information about services utilization and therapeutical approaches by general practitioners and so on.Given these premises,the Authors present here the preliminary results of a community study on urban and rural populations of Sardinia,one of the two major islands of Italy. Only data concerning rural areas,represented by two small villages of the southern part of the isle are shown.About 5,000 inhabitants were resident in the catchment area.A randomized sample,stratified for sex and residence was drawn from Registry Office Lists (431 subjects).374 of them (86.8%) were effectively inteviewed by means of PSE (IX ed),Short Version for community studies,and submitted to an anamnestic interview (APDI).Interviews were conducted by trained psychiatrists.Before starting inter rater reliability by means of Cohen's "kappa" coefficient was calculated.Cases and diagnostic labels were identified according Catego procedures.57 (15.2%) cases were found.**Prevalence rates by sex,age and diagnosis are then presented.**

1823
THE LIFETIME PREVALENCE OF MENTAL DISORDERS IN ICELAND AS ESTIMATED WITH THE NIMH DIS.

Stefánsson, J. G., Lindal, E., Björnsson, J.K. and Gudmundsdóttir, Á. Department of Psychiatry, National University Hospital, 101 Reykjavik, Iceland.

This is a prevalence study of mental disorder in Iceland. The cohort consisted of one half of those born in the year 1931. The survey instrument was a Icelandic translation of the NIMH Diagnostic Interview Schedule. Lay interviewers conducted 862 interviews and received a participation percentage of 79.5 % of the cohort.
Results. The lifetime prevalence of generalized anxiety was 18 %, psychosexual disorders 16.3 %, alcohol abuse and dependence 16.2 %, dysthymia 6.4 % and major depression 5.4 %. The results will be compared to previous Icelandic findings and results from the NIMH-ECA study.

1824
THE LIFETIME PREVALENCE OF PHOBIA IN ICELAND AS ESTIMATED BY THE NIMH-DIS.

Lindal, E., Stefánsson, J.G., Björnsson, J.K. and Gudmundsdóttir, Á. Department of Psychiatry, National University Hospital, 101 Reykjavik, Iceland.

The lifetime prevalence of phobia was estimated in a study of the prevalence of mental disorders in Iceland. The survey instrument was a Icelandic translation of the NIMH Diagnostic Interview Schedule. The cohort consisted of one half of those born in the year 1931. The participation rate was 79.5 %.
Results. The overall rate of phobia was 14.7 %, the most common one being simple phobia (8.2 %), followed by agoraphobia (3.8 %) and social phobia (2.7 %). The subjects with phobia were women in 58 % and men in 42 %. Of those with simple phobia the most common items were a fear of heights (41 %); claustrophobia (34 %); being on public transportation (31 %);the fear of being in crowds and speaking in front of others (28 %); of being alone (24 %); of insects,flies spiders etc. (22 %); of bad weather (21 %); and of being in water (20 %). In addition to the above mentioned items, 17 % mentioned phobias not mentioned in the DSM-III.

1825
The Course of Depression, Anxiety Disorders and Psychosomatic Illness in a Community Sample (Upper Bavarian Study)
Fichter MM & Rehm J
Psychiatr. Klinik, Universität München & Klinik Roseneck, Prien (FRG)

A representative community sample of adults was assessed in the "Upper Bavarian Study". On the basis of a 5-year longitudinal design. The subjects were interviewed by physicians in their home in the 1970s and in the 1980s. The prevalence and course of mental illness was assessed. In the present paper data on the course of depression, anxiety syndromes and psychosomatic illnesses is presented. An increase of depression as has been reported by others was not confirmed in our study. We found a clear decrease of depressive symptoms and diagnoses over the 5-year time-period. Persons with depressive syndromes showed more impairment and disability while anxiety syndromes showed a more chronic course of illness. Psychosomatic illnesses differed from depressive and anxiety syndromes with respect to sociodemographic characteristics (sex, age, social class). Using multivariate linear statistics (LISREL) we tested causal models concerning the course of illness and factors influencing the course. The impact of the following variables on the course of illness was analyzed: 'childhood factors', 'social support', 'severity of mental illness' at first cross section, 'number of threatening life events' (assessed in an interview described by Brown & Harris 1978), 'number of chronic difficulties' and 'score of PERI-demoralization-scale'. The main model derived from this linear causal analysis showed a very high goodness of fit (0.90). The variable 'demoralization' (based on concepts of Frank and Dohrenwend), which contains cognitive but not behavioral symptoms of depression, was shown to be of central importance as a mediating variable.

1826
LA SANTE MENTALE DES ENSEIGNANTS : UNE ENQUETE DE POPULATION
CHANOIT P.F., DAMBASSINA L., KOVESS V.
Institut Marcel Rivière - Paris (France)

Une enquête postale auprès de 4000 mutualistes enseignants et non enseignants tirés au sort sur les listings de la Mutuelle Générale de l'Education Nationale (M.G.E.N.) de la région Midi-Pyrénées a été entreprise en 1987-88.
Cette recherche prospective, sur une durée d'un an et 4 mois comprend un questionnaire d'évaluation initiale et 4 suivis ; le taux de réponse a été d'environ 60 %.
L'objectif est d'évaluer les liens respectifs entre les éléments de la vie professionnelle et ceux de la vie personnelle (famille, couple, vie sociale, loisirs) et leur vécu avec :
- la santé physique (questionnaire de santé, Hopkins Symptom Checklist)
- les patterns d'utilisation des soins.
L'originalité dans notre approche de "l'évènement" est sa mise en parallèle avec les "préoccupations" rapportées par les sujets.
Nous nous proposons ici d'exposer notre méthodologie de recueil des "évènements de la vie" et des "préoccupations", d'en exposer les différences et les similitudes et enfin, d'exposer ces différences et similitudes selon les professions afin de saisir les particularités de la profession ciblée par notre recherche, c'est à dire les enseignants.

1827
PREVALENCE AND COMORBIDITY OF DYSTHYMIA IN 500 PSYCHIATRIC INPATIENTS

Joachim Krause, Michael Philipp, Wolfgang Maier

Department of Psychiatry, University of Mainz (Head: Prof.Benkert), 65 Mainz, FRG

The prevalence of dysthymia and intermittent depression was investigated in an inpatient sample of 500 patients suffering primarily from affective, schizoaffective and schizophrenic disorders. Patients were interviewed by means of a polydiagnostic interview (PODI) by trained research assistants who were blind to the patients` clinical diagnosis. A syndrome of intermittent depression was diagnosed more frequently than a dysthymic syndrome according DSM-III and DSM-IIIR (23% vs. 17% vs. 16%). The majority of mild depressive patients suffered from additional psychiatric diagnoses. The overlap between intermittent depression and dysthymia according to DSM-III and DSM-IIIR is moderate (kappa.67) suggesting that the concepts tap related but not identical phenomena. The overlap between DSM-III and DSM-IIIR dysthymia is surprisingly high (kappa .98) considering the major changes in the inclusion and exclusion criteria and their algorithm when DSM-IIIR dysthymia was operationalized.

1828
EPIDEMIOLOGY AND PSYCHIATRIC EMERGENCIES IN MOROCCO
M.Paes, K.Raddaoui, O.Sall, D.Lahlou, J.E.Ktiouet, Sekkat
Clinique Universitaire de Psychiatrie Rabat, Maroc

L'urgence psychiatrique est un concept complexe et fuyant, car à facettes multiples où les facteurs culturels ne sont pas étrangers.
Les auteurs, à propos d'une enquête effectuée auprès de cinq cents patients vus en urgence à la Clinique Universitaire de Psychiatrie de Rabat-Salè, rapportent leurs caractéristiques sociales et cliniques, leur mode d'accès à la psychiatrie et le rôle et l'attidute de la famille. Ils analysent également la génèse de l'urgence psychiatrique.

1829
MENTAL DISORDERS IN NUEVO LEON, MEXICO

IGLESIAS L., AGUILAR R. MENDOZA A.
CENTRO DE ESTUDIOS E INVESTIGACIONES MEDICOSOCIALES A.C.
MONTERREY, N.L., MEXICO

Los autores han realizado una investigación epidemiológica de tipo descriptivo y transversal para detectar la prevalencia de trastornos mentales. El estudio incluye los diversos estratos socioeconómicos, en los ámbitos urbano, rural y marginal. Fue encuestada una población de 3,374 personas detectandose un 7.1% de enfermos en la población total de acuerdo a criterios de la OMS en su novena revisión. Los datos son semejantes a los encontrados en otros países en vías de desarrollo, - - apreciándose una tendencia a afectar a grupos m-as jóvenes.

1830
AN EPIDEMIOLOGIC SURVEY OF DEPRESSION IN ALGARVE (PORTUGAL)
Seabra Daniel, Psychiatrist, Cruz Pestana Psychologist
U.O.P. Centro de Saude Mental de Faro
8000 Faro, Portugal

The authors present the results of an epidemiologic survey of depression in the general population of the Algarve, Portugal.
By an aleatory method, two hundred and seventy nine individuals of both sexes, older than 11 were investigated (total population of 350.000, representative sample).
Sensitivity of 1% and mean (S D) of 1% were considered.
There were 20 target points and 15 individuals were inquired on each one.
All the individuals in this sample were administered the Beck Depression Inventory (BDI).
Factors like, sex, age, profession and marital status were studied and correlated with the results of the BDI.
Statistic analysis was applied (descriptive statistics and significance tests) and the results are presented and discussed.

Session 280   Special Session:
Drug abuse: Epidemiology

1831

A STUDY OF SUBSTANCE ABUSE PATTERN IN JAPAN

Suwaki,H., Akita,I., Kubouchi,H. and Horii,S.
Kagawa Medical School, Department of Psychology, Kagawa, Japan

Substances of abuse are quite different according to the availability and the social and cultural backgrounds of the country. Besides, people do not necessarily continue to depend on a single substance but often shift from one substance to another or depend on multiple substances concurrently. In 1988 we conducted a survey of the pattern of substance abuse including alcohol, tobacco, soft drinks and gambling in patients with the diagnoses of substance abuse and alcoholism who visited psychiatric hospitals in Japan. We got the detailed data from 188 patients and classified their pattern of abuse into four types with seven subcategories. Type I is a group of relatively steady abusers of alcohol for a long period and some of them combined hypnotics and analgesics with alcohol in later life. Type II is the multiple abusers usually beginning with organic solvents in adolescence. Type III is the amphetamine abusers often with the combined use of alcohol and other drugs, and Type IV is the drug abusers other than alcohol, organic solvents or amphetamine. The number of female patients was 15 (8%), of whom 13 were classified into Type I.

1832

DRUG ABUSE IN INDONESIA

Dadang Hawari,MD;Dept of Psychiatry, Faculty of Medicine University of Indonesia Jakarta, Indonesia.

In Indonesia it was since 1969 that the first drug addict came to the attention of the psychiatrist profession in Jakarta and since that the early date an increasing number of adolescents and young adults; their estimated now amounting 10.000 persons are "hooked" on a variety of drugs (official number).
Observations since 1969, the drug abuse is not only a medical problems, but mainly a psychosocial. The personality disorders of the abusers are the major factor from the point ofpsychiatric examination. In our experience, in dealing with the drug abuse, parents/community should be involved. The approaches should be balanced between "security approaches" in one hand and "welfare approaches" on the other. For Indonesia, problems encountered in dealing with drug abuse are lack of supporting funds and facilities. The mechanism and guides for inter-departmental coordination and cooperation both at the local and national levels have not been established sufficiently.

1833

Epidemiological Survey on 150 drug addicts of the drug addiction unit of the P.H.A.

Drug addiction Unit of the P.H.A.

Zachariadis Ilias, Matsa Katerina

We report the preliminary results of a large scale epidemiological survey on drug addiction.
One hundred and fifty out-patients in the drug addiction unit were given a questionnaire which covered questions concerning Social class, first drug used, socio-economic status of the family, legal status etc. All patients participated in the therapeutic programme of the unit.
We investigated variables such as socio - economic status, age, first drug used, social background, legal status, motives, pathological problems, relationships with is the family etc. in relation to treatment.

1834

THE PREVALENCE OF SUBSTANCEUSE DISORDERS IN ICELAND AS ESTIMATED WITH THE NIMH DIS

Guðmundsdóttir, Á., Lindal, E., Stefánsson, J.G. and Björnsson, J.K. Department of Psychiatry, National University Hospital, 101 Reykjavik, Iceland.

The cohort under study consisted of one half of the population born in the year 1931. The instrument used in the survey was an Icelandic translation of the NIMH Diagnostic Interview Study. By submitting the questionnaire it is possible to obtain DSM-III diagnosis. Interviews conducted 862 interviews and received a cohort participation rate of 79.5%.

The results are analyzed according to life time prevalence of alcohol abuse and alcohol dependence, according to sex. The mean age for the earliest and the last positive symptoms for alcohol abuse and dependence is calculated. Rates for other substance abuse and dependence are also calculated.

1835

PATTERN OF SUBSTANCE ABUSE IN INDIA

DHAVALE HEMANGEE DR.(MRS.)
T.N.M. College & B.Y.L. Nair Hospital, Bombay, India.

India is a vast nation characterised by heterogenous population and drug abuse patterns are quite widely different in different areas. In the last 10 years there is a rapid growth in the drug abuse and in the introduction of newer drugs. The probability is that this will further grow into much larger proportions.

We are presenting the comparative data of number of indoor addicts in 1984 and 1987 in one of the Municipal Hospitals in Bombay. Total number of drug addicts admitted in 1984 was 155 which increased to 315 in 1987. Alcohol and brown sugar are the commonest drugs used in Bombay. In 1984, alcoholics were 99 in number which has marginally increased to 113. Brown sugar consumption has tremendeously increased from 37 to 165. The use of only charas was found in only 4.51% in 1984 and still gone down to 1.26% in 1987. But number of multiple addiction has increased from 7.74% to 10-47%. Majority of the multiple addicts were combining charas with alcohol or charas with brown sugar. First drug use was charas in 50% of cases and brown sugar in 40.8% cases. Brown sugar addiction was more common in younger age group and alcohol in middle age group. The data is compared with percentage of whole Bombay city and 8 major cities in India.

1836

SUBSTANCE USE AMONG GREEK IMMIGRANT STUDENTS IN MUNICH

Malliori Meni, Psychiatrist, Eginition Hospital

The descriptive results of this study show to what extend the use of tobacco, alcohol, pharmaceuticals, as well as the use of illicit drugs prevail among the Greek immigrant students in Munich.
The aim of this study, is to compare this outcome with that of a corresponding study in Greece, as well as other equivalent international studies. This study included all the Greek students 15 to 18 years old, attending the last four classes of Greek high-school in Munich. They were given questionnaires which they had to fill in themselves. The reliability, validity and cooperation of the students were checked, and the results proved very satisfactory.
It is evident, from the findings that the Greek students in Munich smoke, drink and take pills in percentages much smaller in comparison with the international findings and also lower, in comparison with the corresponding figures, emanated from a related study in Athens.
As far as illicit drugs are concerned the findings show a uniformity among other countries, Greece excepted where students try or take drugs in smaller percentages.
Contradictory to the insufficient bibliographical data the enforcement of the traditional values, beliefs and habits, as well as the goals of the immigrant Greek students in Munich, act against their developing patterns of high risk behaviour.

1837

PSYCHOSOCIAL FACTORS INFLUENCING DRUG ADDICTION

Oğuz Karamustafalıoğlu, MD, Can Tuncer, MD Assoc.Prof.of Psychiatry., Mansur Beyazyürek, MD Assoc.Prof.of Psychiatry. Bakırköy Mental Hospital, İstanbul, Dept.of Psychiatry, Cerrahpaşa Faculty of Medicine, İstanbul University, İstanbul Turkey.

When we studied the case histories of the drug addicts, it was found that many of the patients were faced to the drug addiction for the first time during their stay in foreign countries, especially in western countries. Some of the patients were born in western countries or left home at an early age with their families to foreign countries. Some of them were belonging to the 'second generation' group. The age group, cultural shock, types of drugs they encountered and their consequences were analyzed and discussed.

1838

MORTALITY OF SOCIOMEDICALLY TREATED ALCOHOLICS.

A. Fiore and F. Poldrugo, Alcohol Research Group, Dept. of Psychiatry, University of Trieste/School of Medicine, 34126 Trieste, Italy

The results of a ten year experience with alcoholics followed-up by a prolonged psycho-social intervention involving collaterals and community factors are reported.
A sample of more than 1,000 alcoholics (males and females) was investigated. Positive results were found (in terms of social integration and mortality rates) when compared to the traditional medical intervention. They were related to the creation of an extensive network of "treated alcoholics" organized in the voluntary sector collaborating with the health service delivery system. A higher involvement of significant others was especially evident for females. The ratio between observed and expected deaths in alcoholics treated according to the new modalities was 0.61 (0.51 for females).

References:
Poldrugo F (1979) Alcoholism 15:63-78;
Poldrugo F, Fiore A (1987) Anali Klinicke bolnice "Dr M. Stojanovic" 26:231-237

Session 281 Special Session: Side effects of psychotropic drugs

1839
DIAZEPAM INDUCES A DISSOCIATION BETWEEN EXPLICIT AND IMPLICIT MEMORY

J.M. Danion, M.A. Zimmermann, D. Willard-Schroeder, L. Singer
Clinique Psychiatrique, Centre Hospitalier Universitaire, 67091 STRASBOURG Cedex, France

The effects of 0.2 mg/kg orally-administered diazepam on explicit memory, implicit priming and knowledge memory were studied using a free recall test, a word-completion test, and a category generation test respectively. 24 healthy volunteers were randomly assigned to a diazepam or a placebo group, and a double-blind procedure was followed. Diazepam induced a dissociation between explicit and implicit memory. Diazepam significantly impaired free recall ; in contrast there was no impairment of implicit memory. The drug also spared knowledge memory. Diazepam-induced sedation, as measured by visual analogue scales, was inversely correlated to free recall, but not to word completion. The results support the distinction between explicit and implicit memory. The observed pattern of memory disruption caused by diazepam is similar to that of organic amnesia such as Korsakoff's disease and may provide a pharmacological model of this disorder.

1840
An overview of the side-effect profile of Lofepramine

J.C. KERIHUEL
MERCK-CLEVENOT Laboratories / Nogent-sur-Marne / France

Up to now, about 820 patients have been randomized to Lofepramine (L) in 24 comparative studies versus tricyclic agents (Imipramine; Desipramine; Clomipramine; Amitryptiline). Taken separately, none of these studies was potent enough to allow a clear analysis of the clinical interest of L in the treatment of depression when a tricyclic is indicated. To help to get an opinion a systematic overview of all randomized trials was made with an intention-to-treat method using a modified Mantel-Haenszel technique.
Globally the percentage of patients presenting clinical side-effects was significantly lower with L (2 p < 0,0001) with a relative odds ratio for L of 0,54 (95% confidence interval : 0,44-0,66). Concerning efficacy judged on global scores, the percentage of patients who improved is also significantly in favor of L (2 p < 0,02). These results confirm the favorable tolerability of L which appears to have reduced anticholinergic side-effects in comparison to available tricyclics.

1841
Impairment Of Cognitive Functions And Psychomotoric Disturbances During Carbamazepine (CZ)-Therapy
M.OSTERHEIDER, B.UNSORG, U.MILECH

CZ plays an important part in neurological pharmakotherapy.
In the last years different authors could verify the efficacy of CZ in prophylactic treatment of affective psychosis.
In relation to the side effects of CZ, there are many experiences with neurological patients.
In prophylactic treatment the CZ-induced impairment of cognitive functions and psychomotoric disturbances have got a special significance. Referring to this there are only a few examinations in psychiatric patients.
Different authors found cognitive and psychomotoric disturbances in patients during anticonvulsive therapy with CZ.
They saw especially psychomotoric disturbances. We present a study in outpatients with affective disorders (ICD 295.7, 296.X), in which we examine the frequency of these side effects. The reference group are Lithium-treated patients (matched in age, sex, ICD-diagnosis).

The outcome of Lithium versus CZ outpatients in a pre-post study design will be presented and discussed.

1842
Frequency and Severity of Tardive Dyskinesia in Long-Term Psychiatric Inpatients

K.v.Oefele, E.Erice-Keppler, R.Grohmann, E.Rüther

Psychiatric Hospital of the University of Munich (Head:Prof. Dr. H. Hippius), Nussbaumstr.7, D-8000 München 2
Fed. Rep. of Germany

Frequency and severity of Tardive Dyskinesia (TD) have been investigated in 228 long-term psychiatric inpatients. TD were assessed in each region of the body by using the AIM-scale of Simpson and Angus and a special rating scale developed in our hospital.
When patients with minimal symptoms are included, 51,8% showed signs of TD, clear symptoms were seen in 27,2%.
Mainly affected regions were the tongue and the upper extremities.
We could not find links between TD and age, sex, duration of treatment or risk factors like smoking.
In relation to previous epidemiological studies we can demonstrate that frequency and severity of TD are not fluctuating or increasing.

1843

ESSENTIAL FATTY ACID SUPPLEMENTATION IN TARDIVE DYSKINESIA AND SCHIZOPHRENIA

DR K S VADDADI   CRAWLEY HOSPITAL   CRAWLEY UK
DR D F HORROBIN   SCOTIA PHARMACEUTICALS LTD
                                 GUILDFORD SURREY UK
DR C J GILLEARD   SPRINGFIELD HOSPITAL LONDON UK

Abnormal Involuntary Movements such as tardive dyskinesia (T.D.) are a major complication of neuroleptic treatment.

This study reports the results of a double blind placebo controlled trial of Essential Fatty Acids (EFA) in a group of psychiatric patients mainly schizophrenics with tardive dyskinesia. Lipid analysis of Red Blood Cell Membrane data showed EFA deficiency state. Patients with more severe TD had the lowest EFA levels. The antidyskinetic effect of EFA was marginally significant: however, there was significant reduction in schizophrenic psychopathology scores and memory scores. In the second phase of the trial when co-factors involved in EFA metabolism were added, there were significant elevations in R.B.C. membrane EFA fractions. The therapeutic implications of these results will be discussed.

1844

OXIDATIVE POLYMORPHISM: CLINICAL EFFICACY / SIDE-EFFECTS OF IMIPRAMINE
J.W. Meyer, B. Woggon, A. Küpfer
Psychiatric University Hospital, CH-8029 Zurich

Two genetically controlled hydroxylation defects have been described: sparteine/ debrisoquine (DEB) and mephenytoin (MEPH) polymorphism. Swiss population studies showed an incidence of 10% for the first and of 6% for the second. - Imipramine (IMI) is metabolized largely to desipramine and by 2-hydroxylation of IMI and desipramine to their hydroxy-metabolites. 2-hydroxylation depends almost exclusively on sparteine oxygenase. Deficient hydroxylation correlates with considerably altered steady-state concentrations of IMI and its metabolites. - To examine possible correlations between these oxydative polymorphisms and clinical efficacy as well as side-effects of IMI treatment, we performed a retrospective study: 42 patients who had been treated in double-blind trials with IMI could be reexamined 5 to 15 years later. Four (9,5%) could be classified as poor metabolizers for DEB (PM-D) and five (11,9%) as poor metabolizers for MEPH (PM-M). No correlation was found between hydroxylation deficiency and side-effects during treatment with IMI (!) - Based on the global judgment of therapeutic outcome four of the five PM-M were responders whereas all four PM-D were non-responders, suggesting that PM-D - indicating a low capacity for hydroxylation - need and tolerate higher IMI-doses than 150 mg daily.

1845

PROPRANOLOL AND BIPERIDEN TO PREVENT EPS IN NEUROLEPTIC TREATMENT.

ARKONAÇ MD,ERKOÇ MD,ALPKAN MD,ÖZMEN MD,ALGÜR MD
BAKIRKÖY STATE MENTAL HOSPITAL.ISTANBUL TURKEY

As there is no study comparing beta blocker and anticholinergic drugs in preventing EPS in neuroleptic treatment,this double-blind,plecebo controlled cross over study was performed.30patients(16male,14 female)ranging in age from 18 to 57yrs,23sch,1sch. aff,6NOS(DSM-III-R)were psychotic,not receiving neuroleptics for 7days.Cases with organicity,substance use,profound retardation,epilepsy,EPS,contraindication for either drug were excluded.Every patient was given Chouinard EPS,HAM-A scales at the beginingand once a week thereafter.All received Haldol(5-75mg/day)for 6weeks,and biperiden(2-8mg/day),propranolol (20-120mg/day),plecebo(2-8tabl/day)and crossedover at 15th,29th day.At the end 1st and 2nd week of a crossover period:1)In HAM-A scores in all groups , all drugs were equal in preventing akathisia.2)Biperiden,propranolol were better than plecebo(sig.)and biperiden was superior to all(sig.)in preventing parkinsonism.3)In dystonia biperiden and propranolol were equal and better than plecebo(sig.)4)Globally, while biperiden was better than others(sig.),plecebo and propranolol were equal.In parkinsonism,patients felt that propranolol was better only than plecebo and only for the 1.week(sig.)(student t-test). It can be concluded that propranolol did not appear significantly better than biperiden in preventing EPS in haldol treatment of 2 weeks duration at these doses.

1846

LITHIUM SALTS PREVENT EXTRAPYRAMIDAL SIDE EFFECTS

Schony Werner, Schwarzback Heinz
Wagner-Jauregg Krankenhaus Linz, Austria

Lithium seems to prevent supersensitivity of Dopaminreceptors developed after administration of neuroleptics.
Patients with high risk for acute extrapyramidal side effects after neuroleptic treatment were pretreated with Lithium salts. We call this Lithium impregnation. After the Lithium pretreatment, neuroleptic drugs were given and there we had no essential problems with extrapyramidal side effects any more. We report about data obtained from a pilot study on this subject.

1847

TARDIVE DYSKINESIA AND COGNITIVE FUNCTIONS IN SCHIZOPHRENIA
David Neill & Som D Soni
Prestwich Hospital, Manchester. M25 7BL. U.K.

The treatment of schizophrenia is at present limited to a single class of drugs known as neuroleptics. These drugs have a high incidence of seriously disabling side effects some of which, like tardive dyskinesia, may be irreversible.

Patients with TD may sometimes show evidence of cognitive dysfunction but the nature of these has not been investigated in any detail. This study was undertaken to investigate the specific issues of focal cerebral dysfunction in patients with TD.

Methods and Results. Twenty two patients with clinical evidence of TD were matched with 22 patients without TD for age, sex, diagnosis and neuroleptic treatment. Both groups were assessed on various clinical rating scales for schizophrenia and neuroleptic side effects including TD and subjected to a neuropsychological battery to assess regional cortical dysfunction. Preliminary analysis suggests that there are no differences in the two groups with respects to regional cortical functions. Details of the findings will be discussed at the meeting.

Session 282 Symposium:
Use of reversible inhibitors of MAO-A in major depression and other psychiatric disorders

1848

REVERSIBLE MAO-A INHIBITORS: BASIC NEUROCHEMICAL ASPECTS

M. Da Prada, Pharmaceutical Research Department,
F. Hoffmann-La Roche & Co., Ltd., CH-4002 Basle

The demonstration that monoamine oxidase (MAO) exists in two catalytically different forms (type-A and -B) and the clinical evidence that the antidepressant effect of MAO inhibitors is due to inhibition of the A form (as is the case with the irreversible inhibitor clorgyline), stimulated the search for reversible and selective MAO-A inhibitors with novel chemical structure. Moclobemide (MOCLO, p-chloro-N-[2-morpholinoethyl]benzamide, Ro 11-1163, Aurorix^R) is a non-hydrazine, reversible and selective MAO-A inhibitor (RIMA). In vitro MOCLO behaves as en enzyme-activated inhibitor since its intrinsic activity is increased when the compound is incubated with tissue homogenates. In the rat in vivo, in contrast to the long-lasting irreversible inhibitors phenelzine and tranylcypromine, MOCLO induces short-lasting effects, increasing the level of brain biogenic amines and decreasing that of their main metabolites for 16 hours only. MAO inhibition induced by MOCLO p.o. is reversed in rat brain homogenates by dialysis or simple incubation, indicating rapid metabolic inactivation. Rat experiments and all the clinical data available show that MOCLO is completely devoid of hepatotoxic effects. In contrast to the irreversible inhibitors phenelzine and tranylcypromine, MOCLO has a very low liability to potentiate tyramine pressor effects. In conclusion, due to its well-documented safety and to its lack of anticholinergic effects, MOCLO provides an innovative therapy of depressive disorders.

1849

ANTIDEPRESSANTS, ALCOHOL AND PSYCHOMOTOR PERFORMANCE

Dr. J.W.G. Tiller
University of Melbourne, Australia

Antidepressants impair psychomotor function and potentiate the performance impairing effects of alcohol. The effects of moclobemide in animal and human models of induced cognitive deterioration indicate that it may not only reduce these deficits but may actually enhance performance. The interaction of moclobemide (100, 300, 3x200 mg), alcohol and psychomotor function has been evaluated in young and elderly subjects and compared to clomipramine (2x25 mg) and trazodone (100 mg). The data from these studies reveal that in contrast to the comparative drugs which reduced cognitive efficiency, moclobemide improved performance on tasks assessing information processing, reaction time, memory scanning and signal detection sensitivity. The concomitant administration of alcohol (0.5 g/l, 0.6 g/l) further worsened psychomotor performance in subjects receiving clomipramine or trazodone. The administration of alcohol to moclobemide treated subjects was associated with significantly reduced cognitive deterioration compared to the other antidepressants. While the combination of alcohol and the comparative drugs caused increased number of adverse events, combining moclobemide with alcohol actually reduced the complaints associated with alcohol. These data indicate that moclobmide potentiate the effects of alcohol far less than do other antidepressants and more interestingly may actually reduce the alcohol induced impairment of psychomotor performance. Additional results of a recent study on the psychomotor effects of moclobemide (100, 300 mg) as compared to those of amitriptyline (25, 75 mg) will be presented.

1850

EFFICACY OF REVERSIBLE MAO-A INHIBITORS IN VARIOUS FORMS OF DEPRESSION
Prof. Y. Lecrubier
Hôpital de la Pitié - Salpetrière
Paris

The reversible MAO-A inhibitor moclobemide is an effective antidepressant drug, as shown in placebo-controlled studies.
The antidepressant efficacy of moclobemide has been demonstrated for endogenous and for non-endogenous forms of depression. Approximately two out of three patients with endogenous-type depression respond well to moclobemide, as judged by global (CGI) and standard symptom records of efficacy (Hamilton, Montgomery-Asberg).

This is noteworthy having regard to the widely prevalent tendency to discount the value of monoamine oxidase inhibitors in endogenous depression since about 1965, the date of publication of the large Medical Research Council of the U.K. controlled therapeutic trial of antidepressive drugs, which found imipramine to be effective and the irreversible MAO inhibitor phenelzine to be without therapeutic value.

1851

MOCLOBEMIDE IN COMPARISON WITH OTHER ANTIDEPRESSANTS
Prof. M. Versiani
Institute of Psychiatry,
Federal University of Rio de Janeiro

The reversible MAO-A inhibitor moclobemide has been shown to be more effective than placebo and equieffective to standard comparator drugs for the treatment of depression in comparative trials.

These studies have also shown that moclobemide is better tolerated than standard tricyclic antidepressants (imipramine, clomipramine, desimipramine, amitriptyline), as judged by a global assessment of tolerance and by observed and reported adverse events.

Anticholinergic side effects such as dry mouth, tremor, sweating, constipation, blurred vision occurred to a greater extent with these preparations than with moclobemide and cardiovascular tolerability also tended to be better with moclobemide.

1852

REVERSIBLE AND IRREVERSIBLE MAO INHIBITORS IN OTHER PSYCHIATRIC DISORDERS
Dr. M. Liebowitz, Dr. F. Schneir, Dr. R. Campeas
Columbia University, New York, N.Y. 10032 - USA

Irreversible MAO inhibitors (MAOIs) and reversible MAO-A-inhibitors have demonstrated effectiveness in a variety of psychiatric disorders in addition to depression. For example, controlled studies have demonstrated MAOI efficacy in panic disorder with agoraphobia, social phobia, and bulimia. For panic disorders with agoraphobia, there is some suggestion that MAOIs are more effective than other medication treatments in helping patients overcome phobic avoidance. In social phobia, the standard irreversible MAOI phenelzine, has been found significantly more effective than both placebo and beta blockers. Also, the reversible inhibitor MAO-A (RIMA) moclobemide, has been found superior to placebo and similar in efficacy to phenelzine. Although no MAOI- or RIMA-tricyclic comparison exists in social phobia, MAOIs are helpful for many patients who do not respond to tricyclics. Overall, reversible and irreversible MAOIs appear extremely helpful in reducing phobic avoidance and exaggerated interpersonnal hypersensitivity.

Session 283 Symposium:
Field trials of SCAN

1853

Continuity of development: PSE9 and PSE10

Bebbington, Paul E.
Institute of Psychiatry

This paper introduces a new instrument for the assessment and classification of mental disorders, Schedules for Assessment in Neuropsychiatry (SCAN), developed under the auspices of the WHO/ADAMHA Joint Project on Diagnosis and Classification of Mental Disorders. The main core element of SCAN is the 10th edition of the Present State Examination. This new edition shares its philosophy and many features with the well-known 9th Edition of the PSE. The rationale underlying the development of the 10th edition is described, and the new edition compared with its predecessor in order to emphasize the major changes. Data collected in SCAN schedules are processed by a new edition of the CATEGO programme, CATEGO5, which embodies algorithms for generating ICD10 and DSMIIIR categories. PSE9 items and ratings can be derived from PSE10 by a conversion programme, and then processed by CATEGO4. Data from the field trials have been converted in this way and illustrate the progression from PSE9 to PSE10.

1854

ICD-10 AND DSM-III-R DIAGNOSES

Dr T.B. Üstün
Hacettepe University, Ankara, Turkey

The International Classification of Diseases, Tenth Revision (ICD-10), Chapter V, and the Diagnostic and Statistical Manual of Mental Disorders, Third Revision (DSM-III-R) are both state-of-the-art reifying our contemporary view on the mental disorders. Creating, defining and confirming categories displays the hidden logical structure of our theory of knowledge. Whatever the algorithms beyond these classification systems are, it is crucial that they should be translatable to each other in one-to-one correspondence as long as they address the same material reality.

This paper deals with the similarities and dissimilarities of both systems, together with the diagnostic tools of each classification system (namely SCAN and DIS). Although there is some divergence between the diagnostic categories, possible mechanisms to maintain compatibility are discussed briefly having the confirmatory epidemiologic evidence for the "fitness of categories" as a reference point.

1855
SCAN IN BANGALORE: THE NEED FOR A THIRD WORLD MODULE
DR MOHAN K ISAAC et al
National Institute of Mental Health and Neuro-Sciences, Bangalore, India

Schedule for clinical assessment in neuropsychiatry (SCAN) was translated into Kannada - a language spoken in the Southern Indian State of Karnataka by more than 21 million people. The translated version was used to assess a group of 30 respondents (predominantly psychotic) who were either inpatients or outpatients at the National Institute of Mental Health and Neurosciences in Bangalore by a pair of interviewer and observer. The field trial raised several linguistic and cultural problems in translation of the instrument as well as the need for certain culture appropriate questions and probes to assess specific phenomena prevalent in third world countries like India. These include particular patterns of somatic complaints, possession states and complaints related to reproductive system. Based on these observations, the need for a 'Third World module' for SCAN is highlighted.

1856
Reliability of SCAN Categories and Scores
Results of the field trials

T. Tomov, V. Nikolov

Symposium on "Field Trials of the Schedules of Clinical Assessment in Neuropsychiatry"

The SCAN system is intended to provide instruments for the recovery of clinical information, which can be applied in a variety of settings across cultures. Unlike its predecessor, the PSE, the development of SCAN is being concerned not only with the reliable collection of primary data such as psychiatric signs and symptoms, but with the provision of reliable algorithms for higher order constructs as well, such as syndromes and diagnoses. To this end field trials have attempted to measure agreement between pairs of raters not only on presence of symptoms but also on computer generated classes and categories arrived at from these symptoms by applying the operational diagnostic criteria specified in ICD 10 and DSM-IIIR. Agreement rates have been shown to be high in the case of such clinically meaningful entities as CATEGO SZ(core schizophrenia), MNBP(bipolar affective disorder) and DP(depression) classes and low in the case of PNGA(panic and anxiety disorders) and DL(delusional psychosis, nonschizophrenic type) classes. Operational criteria and/or hierarchical arrangements on which decision making is based used further refinement.

1857
DIAGNOSING DEMENTIA WITH THE SCAN
V. Mavreas, V. Kontaxakis, D. Ploumbidis
University of Athens, Medical School, Department of Psychiatry, Eginition Hospital

Section 13 of the SCAN deals specifically with cognitive impairment. In the present study this section has been applied on a number of patients suffering from dementia at different levels of severity. The preliminary results show that section 13 of the SCAN is able to diagnose dementia and detect from mild to very severe degrees of impairment in memory and intellect, and deterioration in self-care. SCAN is not intended specifically for diagnosing dementias and associated modules will be recommended when indicated by the computer programme. Section 13 is also used to measure cognitive impairment in other psychiatric disorders.

Session 284 Symposium:
Serotonin and serotonin uptake inhibitors in depression

1858
POSSIBLE SELECTIVE INDICATIONS FOR 5HT UPTAKE INHIBITORS
D.B. Montgomery, S.A. Montgomery
St Mary's Hospital Medical School, London UK

5HT uptake inhibitors were initially developed for the treatment of depression where evidence of their efficacy is now overwhelming. They appear to be as effective as reference tricyclic antidepressants but to have some extra selective effect in treating the anxiety associated with depression including panic. This has led to their investigation in disorders that are sometimes separate from depression. There is now convincing evidence of a selective effect in obsessive compulsive disorder where other antidepressants are ineffective. Likewise, there is evidence of an advantage in treating bulimia where other drugs are relatively ineffective. Some of the 5HT uptake inhibitors appear to have effects on weight reduction particularly in high doses. There are some suggestions of a role for 5HT uptake inhibitors in treating recurrent brief depression, addiction behaviour including alcoholism, dementia, aggression and migraine. The evidence of efficacy at different dose levels in different indications suggests a possible effect at different receptors which requires investigation.

1859

Serotonin and serotonin uptake inhibitors in depression

William F. Boyer, M.D., John Feighner, M.D.
Feighner Research Institute, Encinitas, CA, USA

Despite significant advances in the pharmacological treatment of depression there are still four substantial problem areas with current technology. These are side effects, toxicity in overdose, delay in therapeutic onset, and non-response.

The selective serotonin reuptake inhibitors (SSRIs) are a new class of psychotropic medication. They include fluoxetine, fluvoxamine, sertrline, paroxetine and citalopram. The SSRIs have demonstrated antidepressant efficacy and have shown promise in the treatment of obsessive-compulsive disorder, panic atttacks and obesity. Several studies indicate they are effective for maintenance treatment and are well tolerated by the elderly.

The evidence suggests that the SSRIs are an improvement in three of the four problem areas. They are devoid of the troubling anticholinergic, cardiovascular, and weight gain side effects of tricyclic antidepressants. Limited data suggests they may be safer if taken in overdose. Although systematic data is lacking, our experience and that of others suggests that many patients who do not respond to, or cannot tolerate, conventional antidepressants will respond to one of the SSRIs. There is currently no data to suggest that SSRIs are more rapid in onset of therapeutic effect.

The SSRIs are also interesting from a theoretical standpoint. At clinically relevant doses their only pharmacologic action is inhibition of serotonin reuptake. This raises the possibility of being able to pharmacologically dissect CNS function and challenges some theories of antidepressant action.

1860

EFFECTS OF CITALOPRAM AND ETHANOL IN NORMAL SUBJECTS
Malcolm Lader
Institute of Psychiatry, University of London, London, England.

In study 1, citalopram, 20mg and 40mg, amitriptyline 50mg and placebo were given in single dose. Citalopram decreased slow-wave EEG activity whereas amitriptyline increased power. Citalopram increased tapping rate and symbol copying whereas amitriptyline impaired these and other psychomotor tasks. Subjectively, amitriptyline was much more sedative than citalopram.

In study 2 citalopram 40mg, amitriptyline 75mg, and placebo were given for 9 nights. Subjectively, citalopram was associated with feelings of shaking, nausea, loss of appetite and physical tiredness; amitriptyline produced feelings of shaking, nausea, loss of appetite, dryness of mouth, irritability, dizziness and indigestion. Plasma metabolites were in the expected range.

In the third study, similar courses of citalopram, amitriptyline and placebo were given and on the 8th day, ethanol was given. Amitriptyline increased the 7.5-13.5 Hz wave-band, and impaired critical flicker fusion frequency, tapping, DSST and reaction time; citalopram affected DSST and immediate memory recall. Ethanol impaired performance and produced sedation but did not potentiate drug effects.

1861

Studies of the Efficacy and Side-Effect Profile of Citalopram
David M. Shaw
Depart. of Psychological Medicine, University of Wales College of Medicine, Cardiff, CF4 7XB, Britain

Citalopram is a highly specific 5-HT-reuptake blocker with antidepressant properties. Its relative efficacy and pattern of side-effects have been compared with amitriptyline, maprotiline, mianserin, and clomipramine in fixed and flexible-dose regimes.

The results of these individual trials and of the overall patterns of efficacy which these data suggest will be evaluated.

1862

Citalopram vs Mianserin - A Double-Blind Trial in Depressed Patients
Mertens, Claudine
Psychiatrische Centra V.Z.W., Evergem, Sleidinge, Belgium

Citalopram, a selective re-uptake inhibitor of 5-HT is compared with mianserin, a generally accepted antidepressant drug, in 60 patients suffering from endogenous depression.

Citalopram revealed to be as effective as mianserin with a tendency in favour of citalopram although the difference was not statistically significant.

Both drugs had few side effects and may be considered as rather safe antidepressant agents.

1863

Side Effects of Citalopram and Reference Antidepressants including Side Effects in Elderly Patients

C.G. Gottfries, P. Bech
University of Göteborg, Dept. of Psychiatry and Neurochemistry, St. Jörgen's Hospital, Hisings Backa, Sweden. Centralsygehuset, Hillerød, Denmark.

The side effect profile of citalopram in short term and long term treatment is presented. Citalopram treated patients showed nausea, increased sweating and headache. In most patients these side effects were mild and transient. Side effects registered in short term are compared with side effects of tricyclic antidepressants. Citalopram shows fewer anticholinergic side effects than tricyclic antidepressants and has not been demonstrated to influence the cardiovascular system. ECG's from 500 patients have been investigated - and there was no significant changes. Citalopram is safe when taken in overdose.

This side effect profile makes citalopram very advantagous when treating elderly patients and other patients who cannot be treated with tricyclic antidepressants in optimum doses.

The experience of treatment with citalopram in elderly patients, several with concomitant somatic disorders, is reported. Very few side effects are seen in this patient category when treated with 10-30 mg of citalopram daily.

Session 285 Symposium:
Plasma amino acids: Markers, predictors, therapeutic tools for psychiatric disease

1864

ACUTE INFLUENCES OF BREAKFAST ON AMINO ACIDS AND BEHAVIOR IN NORMALS
Bonnie Spring[1], Michael Bourgeois[2], Deborah K. Atnip[2], Robert D. Garvin[2], and Kenneth Kessler[1]
[1]UHS/The Chicago Medical School, North Chicago, IL, USA; [2]Texas Tech University, Lubbock, TX, USA

We previously reported that a noon-time meal high in carbohydrate and relatively lacking in protein causes fatigue in parallel with an elevation of the ratio of plasma tryptophan to other large neutral amino acids. Fatigue after eating carbohydrate could not be explained by reactive hypoglycemia and was prevented by the addition of protein to the meal. We now present data from a study of 21 normal males and females who fasted or ate breakfasts varying in their proportions of carbohydrate, protein and fiber. Eating breakfast, versus skipping breakfast, usually enhanced mood and sometimes enhanced performance, but results depended upon the nutrient composition of the meal. Compared with more balanced meals, a breakfast high in carbohydrate but lacking protein or fiber impaired Digit Symbol Substitution performance. Moreover, late-morning fatigue was as great after such a breakfast as after fasting. Associations between behavior and plasma glucose, insulin and amino acids will be reported and discussed.

1865

DEPRESSION: TREATMENT RESPONSE ASSOCIATED WITH PLASMA AMINO ACIDS
Svend Erik Møller, Clinical Research Laboratory, St. Hans Hospital, DK-4000 Roskilde, Denmark.

The response in depressed patients to antidepressive therapy varies greatly and is influenced by diagnostic classification, pharmacokinetic factors and biologic variation. This paper elucidates the latter item. In a series of controlled trials including a total of 167 inpatients with major depressive disorder, the relationship between the pretreatment plasma ratios of tryptophan (Trp) to other large neutral amino acids (LNAA) and tyrosine (Tyr) to other LNAA and the therapeutic response to 8 different antidepressant treatments has been studied. (Ratios Trp/LNAA and Tyr/LNAA are thought to reflect brain serotonin and noradrenaline formation, resp.) Statistically significant relationships have been shown between the plasma amino acid ratios, on the one side, and the final Hamilton depression rating scale (HDRS) score, and/or percent reduction of HDRS score, on the other side. When the 3 major treatment groups comprising 86 depressives treated for 4 weeks with either amitriptyline, nortriptyline or imipramine were separated, retrospectively, in halfparts by the mean values of the plasma amino acid ratios, the one halfpart showed significantly greater clinical improvement whereas the other halfpart showed significantly smaller improvement than the total patient sample. The data suggest that treatment efficacy can be improved by prior selection of the patients by means of amino acid ratios.

1866

PHENYLALANINE MARKER FOR TD/AFFECTIVE COMPONENT IN SCHIZOPHRENIA
Mary Ann Richardson
Nathan S. Kline Institute for Psychiatric Research
Orangeburg, NY USA

Data defining PKU as a risk factor for tardive dyskinesia (TD) development in the mentally retarded and manic-like affective symptoms as associated with TD in schizophrenics, led to a hypothesis of phenylalanine metabolism being implicated in TD. To test this theory, male schizophrenics (N=53) were studied for group differences on measures of phenylalanine metabolism based on the presence or absence of TD, a history of suicide attempts and a family history of depression.

The plasma phenylalanine/large neutral amino acid ratio (higher levels) was found to be a significant risk factor for TD with substantial predictive power. This ratio was also found to be significantly different (higher) for those patients with a history of suicide attempts and a family history of depression.

Based on these data it is thus proposed based on a PKU model of catecholamine function that higher phenylalanine/large neutral amino acid ratios mark a hypodominergic subgroup of schizophrenics who are vulnerable to TD and affective symptomatology.

1867

INCREASED CSF AMINO ACIDS AND VENTRICULAR ENLARGEMENT IN SCHIZOPHRENIA
Michael A. Reveley
The London Hospital Medical College, Dept. of Psychiatry

In a study of eleven schizophrenics, and age and sex matched controls, significantly higher levels of cerebrospinal fluid alanine, glycine, leucine, and phenylalanine, were found in schizophrenic patients compared to healthy controls. Ventricular enlargement was present in four of the eleven schizophrenics and elevated CSF alanine was highly correlated with ventricular enlargement. The implications of these findings in light of the relevant literature will be discussed.

1868

BEHAVIORAL AND ENDOCRINE EFFECTS OF TYROSINE AND TRYPTOPHAN IN HUMANS
Hendrik Lehnert, Dept. of Endocrinology and Metabolism, III. Medical Hospital, University of Mainz

Brain noradrenaline and serotonin neurons participate in a number of relevant physiological functions such as cardiovascular regulation, secretion of anterior pituitary hormone secretion and certain aspects of behavior such as mood, sleep or cognitive performance. In a number of animal studies we have demonstrated profound effects of the precursor amino acids tyrosine and tryptophan on autonomic tone (e.g. reduction of preganglionic sympathetic activity and blood pressure), stress-induced ACTH secretion (attenuation following administration of tyrosine) and locomotor behavior.
We now report on chronic and acute effects of tyrosine and tryptophan on various endocrine and behavioral parameters in both control persons and those suffering from borderline hypertension. In general, the chronic administration of l-tryptophan tended to increase sleep duration and to decrease sleep latency even in not sleep-disordered persons, while performance in a concentration task was markedly enhanced. Oral intake of tryptophan (5 g) only led to an increase in growth hormone levels, no changes were noted for prolactin or TSH. The administration of tyrosine on the other hand was found to attenuate the TSH- and metoclopramide rise in prolactin secretion, while TSH levels were augmented, thus confirming the relevance of prior neuronal activation.

Session 286 Special Session:
Psychometrics: Development of instruments

1869

THE NORRIS VAS AND THE ADA INVENTORY : A FACTOR ANALYSIS IN OUTPATIENTS
J. D. Guelfi, R. Von Frenckell and Ph. Caillé, Clinique des maladies mentales et de l'encéphale 100, rue de la santé 75674 PARIS Cédex 14 - FRANCE

The ADA Inventory and the sixteen 100 mm VAS scales were administred to 632 asthenic outpatients (without manifest anxiety or mood disorder) in General practice. The scales were scored before treatment in a controlled trial of Toloxatone (MAOI) versus placebo and Amineptine. Factor analysis using a principal component solution and an orthogonal rotation of the factor matrix were computed. Two factors were selected on the VAS (53 per cent of the total variation). Each of the 16 scales seems to load clearly on one of these factors. The first factor (8 scales) : asthenia is quite identical to the alertness factor of Bond and Lader (Muzzy, dreamy, feeble, lethargic, drowsy, mentally slow, incompetent and clumsy). The other scales correspond to a second affective factor. Three factors were identified on the ADA inventory (46 % of the total variation), quite identical to those of Pichot and Brun. A factor analysis was also performed on the differences : baseline from post-treatment scores. The same three factors were then identified, but only in the toloxatone group. These results can be helpful for evaluating the profile of action of drug treatment on asthenia, anxiety and depression.

1870

A factor Analysis of the ADA (Anxiety-Depression-Asthenia) inventory in General Practice.
J. D. GUELFI, R. Von FRENCKELL and Ph. CAILLE, Clinique des Maladies Mentales et de l'Encéphale 100, rue de la santé 75674 PARIS Cédex 14 - FRANCE

The ADA inventory can be used to select for specific therapeutic trials sub-groups of patients characterized, for example, by asthenic symptoms with a low level of anxiety and depression. This inventory was administered to 632 outpatients seen by general practitioners for an asthenic state (without manifest anxiety or mood disorder). The inventory was scored before treatment in a randomized controlled trial of Toloxatone (Humoryl*), a MAOI compound, versus placebo and Amineptine, a tricyclic stimulant antidepressant.
The baseline scores of this sample were quite different in the three dimensions isolated in one prior study (8 items × 3 scored from 0 to 4) : Anxiety : 3.3 (+ 0.15), Depression 3.5 (+ 0.15) and Asthenia 13.8 (+ 0.22). Factor analysis using a principal component solution and an orthogonal rotation of the factor matrix was computed. Using the Kaiser criterion, three factors were selected which accounted for 46 per cent of the total variation. Twenty one items (7 × 3) seem to load clearly on one sole factor. These three subscales are quite identical to those of PICHOT and BRUN. A new principal component analysis was also performed on the differences : baseline from post-treatment scores. The same three factors are identified in the Toloxatone group but not in the placebo or in the Amineptine group. These results can be helpful for evaluating the profile of action of drug treatment.

1871

AN ORIGINAL SCALE FOR THE ASSESSMENT OF ANXIETY IN PSYCHOTICS: THE "PSYCHOTIC ANXIETY SCALE".

O. Blin, J.M. Azorin, Y. Lecrubier, A. Souche, J. Fondarai
Clinique des Maladies du Système Nerveux et de l'Appareil Locomoteur, C.H.U. Timone, 13385 Marseille Cedex 5, FRANCE

We propose the first scale for evaluating anxiety in psychotics: the "Psychotic Anxiety Scale" (P.A.S.).
A list of items underlying the evaluation of anxiety in psychotics was tested in 45 psychotic patients. A principal components analysis revealed that 4 factors account for respectively 32%, 14.7%, 14%, and 7% of the variance. The first factor may be considered as representative of general anxiety, the second factor assesses patient inhibition. The third factor may characterize the patient's dimension of self-aggressiveness, and the fourth is interpreted as representing the changes of anxiety in time. This scale thus evaluates anxiety along 4 axes: severity of the symptomatology, inhibition, self-aggressiveness, and evolution in time.
The multiple correspondence factorial analysis revealed that 4 factors account for respectively 50%, 18%, 17% and 7% of the variance. The lack of valid, currently existing, reference scale allowed to show the validity of the P.A.S. by calculating the correlation between the total P.A.S. score and the clinician's overall assessment of anxiety ($R=0.663$, $p<0.001$), and by determining the correlation of each separated item with the clinician's assessment of anxiety ($p<0.001$ for 4 items, and $p<0.05$ for 7 items). The P.A.S. is an homogeneous scale ($p<0.05$ for 15 items). The inter-rater reliability was assessed by a method which compared a rater with the others along 2 axes: the severity, and the profile of the assessment. The inter-rater reliability was unsatisfactory for only three items. They have been now modified.
The analysis of the P.A.S. support the hypothesis of the lack of specificity for the anxiety in psychotics and provide informations on the various modalities, and meaning of anxiety in psychotics. Further studies with levomepromazine (a sedative neuroleptic), haloperidol (an incisif neuroleptic), and risperidone are now underwent to precisely determine the P.A.S sensitivity to change, and to better define the notion of psychotic anxiety itself, not to mention the importance of distinguishing this factor both clinically and therapeutically.

1872

A new factor analysis of the CHESS (chek list for the evaluation of somatic symptoms)
J. D. GUELFI, C. DULCIRE, S. AUDRAIN, Clinique des Maladies Mentales et de l'Encéphale 100, rue de la santé 75674 PARIS Cédex 14 - FRANCE

The 71 items of the CHESS were scored before treatment on 347 depressed outpatients with major depressive episode or dysthymic disorder according to DSM III criteria in a multicentric open trial of Tianeptine in general practice.
A principal component analysis with a subsequent varimax rotation has been performed on 63 items (excluding 8 items with an overall frequency under 5 per cent). With the Kaiser criterion, 18 factors were obtained (61.4 per cent of the variation). The optimal saturation threshold inclusion of an item in a factor was 0.40. It assigns 52 items in one sole factor and three items in two different factors. Sixteen factors seem to have a clear clinical significance and are compared to those found in prior studies. The main factors correspond to : Digestive Aches (5 items), Other (Muscular) Aches (5 items), Insomnia (3 different factors : 10 items), Digestive and General Somatic complaints (3 items) and Neurological Signs (3 different factors : 9 items).
According to these results a 55 items new version of the check list, CHESS-R is proposed. The utility of standardized somatic symptom assessment in depressed patients before and during treatment will be discussed.

1873

DEVELOPMENT OF A SCALE FOR RATING DEPRESSION IN SCHIZOPHRENIA
ADDINGTON D, ADDINGTON J, SCHISSEL B.
University of Calgary, Calgary Alberta Canada

Scales for assessing depression are well developed for non psychotic populations but have been criticized for being inappropriate for psychotic populations. As a result we have developed a new rating scale for the measurement of depression in schizophrenia based on items selected from the Hamilton Depression Rating Scale and the Present State Examination. The selection was based on Factor and Reliability Analyses of the depression scale items rated on 50 acutely ill schizophrenics meeting DSM III criteria for schizophrenia assessed at two points in time. Our results indicate that several items from both scales form a superior instrument for measuring depression in schizophrenia. The fourteen items generated a reliability coefficient of 0.83.

1874

A SHORT FORM OF THE ORGANIC-DEPRESSION INDEX OF THE GMS

M.E. Dewey, Lecturer in Psychological Statistics, University Department of Psychiatry, Royal Liverpool Hospital, P.O. Box. 147, Liverpool. L69 3BX. England.

Studies of dementia in the community need a simple method of detecting cases of cognitive impairment for further assessment. Cognitive tests have been widely used, but have the disadvantage that depression may also cause moderate levels of cognitive impairment.

The Geriatric Mental State (GMS) has been widely used, in combination with the diagnostic system AGECAT, in community studies. The short form of the Organic-Depression Index (ODI) presented here adds a subset of the ratings from the GMS to produce organic and depressive scores. Cut-offs lead to a three way decision: well, depressed, dementia. A suitable set of cut-offs on the ODI gives a sensitivity for organic cases of 1.00 and a specificity of 0.80 and simultaneously a sensitivity of 0.80 for depression and a specificity of 0.94. These cut-offs are appropriate for a study concentrating on dementia; other cut-offs may be used for studies of depression.

1875
CLASSIFICATION OF NATURAL AND SUPERNATURAL CAUSES OF MENTAL DISTRESS: DEVELOPMENT OF A MENTAL DISTRESS EXPLANATORY MODEL QUESTIONNAIRE
Maurice Eisenbruch, M.D.
Dept. of Child & Family Psychiatry, Royal Children's Hospital, Victoria, Australia

This paper describes the background and development of a Mental Distress Explanatory Model Questionnaire to explore how people from different cultural backgrounds explain mental distress. A 45 item questionnaire was developed with items derived from the Murdoct categories, together with additional items covering Western notions of physiological causation and stress. The questionnaire was administered to a sample of 261 people, mostly college students. Multidimensional scaling analysis shows four clusters: a)stress; b)Western physiological; c)non-Western physiological; and d)supernatural. These clusters form two dimensions: Western physiological vs. supernatural, and impersonal vs. personalistic explanations. There is a clear separation of natural and stress items from supernatural and non-western physiological items along the first dimension. Brain damage, physical illness, and genetic defects have the greatest separation along the first dimension. Being hot, the body out of balance, and wind currents passing through the body most strongly represent the non-western physiological category. The partial overlap between so-called natural and non-natural causes is indicative of the conceptual problems with this commonly used western dichotomy. The questionnaire has the potential to be used for community screening and for monitoring clinical populations, with students in the health sciences, and with health practitioners.

1876
INTERPRETATIVE CONSISTENCY OF SCL-90-R AND THE MMPI

G. Liappa, M.A, E. Vasilopoulou M.A,
S. Donias, M.D, N. Manos, M.D.

CMHC - 2nd University Dept of Psychiatry,
Thessaloniki, Greece.

The present study was intended to examine the relationship between the nine clinical scales of the SCL-90-R and a considerable number of clinical scales of the MMPI (all the basic scales and many research scales), particularly the ones included in the automated scoring and interpretative report, the Minnesota Report.
Both the SCL-90-R and the MMPI were administered to a sample of 250 consecutive out-patients who visited the CMHC of the B' Department of Psychiatry. All patients also received a DSM-III-R diagnosis. Comparisons of the SCL-90-R constructs and like constructs of the MMPI showed significant correlations and high interpretative consistency.

Session 287 New Research:
Issues on classification

1877
A comparison between DSM-III and DSM-III R axis 2: Reliability, predictive validity.

Vaglum S, Vaglum P, Friis S, Larsen F.

Dep of Baehavioural Sciences in Medicine, Oslo, Norway. Psychiatric dep.B, Ullevål hospital, Oslo, Norway

94 non psychotic consecutive day-patients were diagnosed by the axis 1 and 2 in the DSM-III and DSM-III-R system, and their treatment response during their stay was measured by the Health Sickness Rating Scale (HSRS). The interrater reliability was equally good for both diagnostic systems. On axis 1, there were only minor differences between DSM-III and DSM-III-R. On axis 2, the frequency of schizotypal disorder was reduced by forty percent and the frequency of histrionic disorder by two thirds. The number of schizoid disorders increased from zero to five. Of the DSM-III-schizotypals who lost this diagnosis in DSM-III-R (n=8), four got a new diagnosis of schizoid personality disorder and four maintained their borderline diagnoses. In DSM-III-R there was a sharper demarcation between patients with severe and non severe personality disorder with regard to treatment outcome, indicating an increased validity of these categories. There was also a sharper demarcation between borderline versus histrionic and schizotypal, and between schizotypal and schizoid diagnoses.

1878
DSM-III-R: A DIMENSIONAL AND CATEGORICAL INSTRUMENT IN THE STUDY OF DEPRESSIVE DISORDERS
O.Chambon, P.Cialdella
Laboratoire de Psychologie Medicale, Lyon, France

The nine items which constitute the part A of the DSM-III-R Major Depressive Episode definition are supported to represent an homogeneous diagnostic category. We have wanted to verify this homogeneity by studying whether the nine items describe a unidimensional phenomenon. So, on these items, we have carried out a principal component analysis (A.C.P.) with varimax rotation and a Rasch logistic model from a sample of 461 depressive patients (RCD criteria and MADRS score superior to 20). The A.C.P. gives results not easily interpretable mainly by the fact of the items distributional asymmetry which conduct us to principally use the RASCH Model as a test of the unidimensionality. Parameters of three items among the nine have not been estimated because of the presence of these items in almost the totality of patients. On the other hand, the remaining six items entirely fulfill the conditions of RASCH Model and therefore seem to provide a unidimensional measurement of depression. In drug trials these items could then be used at once for the categorical diagnosis and for a dimensional measurement of depression. This would amplify and standardize the evaluations.

1879

DIAGNOSTIC COMPARISON OF SCHIZOPHRENIA AND MOOD DISORDERS BETWEEN FRENCH CLASSIFICATIONS (F.C.) AND DSM-III-R
LAZARTIGUES A., MURGUI E., MORALES H., BARUA U.
Clinique DUPRE, FSEF, 30 av F. Roosevelt,
92331 SCEAUX CEDEX FRANCE

OBJECTIVES : To compare diagnostics obtained with F.C. (Mises et al) and DSM-III-R for chizophrenia and mood disorders with 40 patients of age 16-19 years.
METHODOLOGY : Sample constitution : from a cross section of hospitalised patients for whom a clinical diagnosis of schizophrenia and mood disorder given. Data collected by rating standardized interview (videotyped) constructed with items of SADS, PSE, SANS and emperical wich allowed to explore entire criteria of studied 2 diagnostic systems. DSM-III-R diagnosis made from rating index. F.C. diagnosis made by one research worker from video typed standardized interview. Inter-rater reliability of given ratings controlled regulary from interview drawned (1:8) and rated independently by 4 clinicans. The same procedures done for diagnostic reliability.
RESULTS : Every patients given diagnosis of 2 classifications. By classifications given the percentage of class and non-class dividing up between catagory and subcatagories, concordance et non-concordance, inter-rater reliability by catagories.
CONCLUSION : the reason of non concordances are analysed.

1880

DIAGNOSTIC COMPARISON OF SCHIZOPHRENIA AND MOOD DISORDERS BETWEEN DSM-III-R AND ICD-10
MORALES H., BARUA U., LAZARTIGUES A., MURGUI E.
Clinique DUPRE, FSEF, 30 av F. Roosevelt,
92331 SCEAUX CEDEX FRANCE

OBJECTIVES : To compare diagnostics obtained with DSM-III-R and ICD-10 for schizophrenia and mood disorders with 40 patients of age 16-19 years.
METHODOLOGY : Sample constitution : From a cross section of hospitalised patients for whom a clinical diagnosis of schizophrenia and mood disorder given. Data collected by rating standardized interview (videotyped) constructed with items of SADS, PSE, SANS and emperical which allowed to explore entire criteria of studied 2 diagnostic systems. DSM-III-R and ICD-10 diagnosis made from rating index. Inter-rater reliability of given ratings controlled regularly from interview drawned (1:8) and rated independently by 4 clinicans. The same procedure done fordiagnostic reliability.
RESULTS : Every patients given diagnosis of 2 classifications. By classifications given the percentage of class and non-class dividing up between catagory and subcatagories, concordance et non-concordance, inter-rater reliability by catagories.
CONCLUSIONS : the reason of non concordances are analysed

1881

DIAGNOSTIC COMPARISON OF SCHIZOPHRENIA AND MOOD DISORDERS BETWEEN FRENCH CLASSIFICATIONS (F.C.) AND ICD-10
MURGUI E., MORALES H., BARUA U., LAZARTIGUES A.
Clinique DUPRE, FSEF, 30 av F. Roosevelt,
92331 SCEAUX CEDEX FRANCE

OBJECTIVES : To compare diagnostics obtained with F.C. (Mises et al) and ICD-10 for schizophrenia and mood disorders with 40 patients of age 16-19 years.
METHODOLOGY : Sample constitution : from a cross section of hospitalised patients for whom a clinical diagnosis of schizophrenia and mood disorder given. Data collected by rating standardized interview (videotyped) constructed with items of SADS, PSE, SANS and emperical which allowed to explore entire criteria of studied 2 diagnostic systems. ICD-10 diagnosis made from rating index. F.C. diagnosis made by one research worker from video typed standardized interview. Inter-rater reliability of given ratings controlled regularly from inter interview drawned (I:8) and rated independently by 4 clinicans. The same procedures done for diagnostic reliability.
RESULTS : Every patients given diagnosis of 2 classifications. By classifications given the percentage of class and non-class dividing up between catagory and subcatagories, concordance et non-concordance, inter-rater reliability by catagories.
CONCLUSION : the reason of non concordances are analysed.

1882

ICD-10 Field Trial - Analysis of Agreement at Center 228/POA/Brazil
BUSNELLO, E. , ABREU,P. OSÓRIO, C.
Department of Psychiatry - School of Medicine - Federal University/RS
The data obtained from phase 2 and 3 of WHO ICD-10 Field Trial at Center 228(Porto Alegre, Brazil) is analyzed, with calculation of Kappa coefficients based on intraclass correlation coefficients for independent scores of 11 raters based on

written case-summaries following the general rules of the WHO study. The overall Kappa for major diagnostic categories was 0,490 for phase 2 and 0.668 for phase 3.It meant fair to good agreement, very similar to the results of Mezzich in US. The scores were lower for especific subcategories (0.294), corresponding to a poor agreement: Personality, Physiological Dysfunctions and Schizophrenic Disorders had the highest Kappas, and Neurotic and Somatoform, Developmental and Organic Mental Disorders the lowest. The system displayed good reability and applicability to latin-american cultures, with some of its categories and subcategories still requiring additional refinement.

1883
DIAGNOSING PSYCHIATRIC IN-PATIENTS WITH THE CIDI.

G. TACCHINI, R.M.W. SMEETS, A.C.ALTAMURA
Institute of Psychiatry-University of Milan, Via F. Sforza 35, 20122 Milano-ITALY

Among the W.H.O. CIDI Field Trials partecipating centres, Amsterdam and Milan resulted having similar patient samples, though the former comprised psychiatric in-patients and the latter out-patients seen one month at least after dismission from the ward.
CIDI was really meant for use in epidemiological settings, but the choice of the two centres was intented to meet local needs.
In such clinical settings CIDI proved valuable and appropriate all the same, and this work analyses the feasibililty of CIDI in psychotic patients samples in terms of duration and length of the interview, acceptability and appropriateness, together with some problems peculiar of these particular samples.

1884
THE MEASUREMENT OF CLINICAL VARIABILITY IN PSYCHIATRIC PATIENTS.

A.C.ALTAMURA, B. CESANA, G. TACCHINI, M.T. COPPOLA, A. MUSAZZI

Institute of Psychiatry-University of Milan, Via F. Sforza 35, 20122 Milano, Italy

Measures of variability are a central topic in all in all medical disciplines: this is particularly true in psychiatry where the same clinical phenomenon may retain different names, or viceversa, beyond the knowledge of the clinician.
The most widespread way to bypass this empasseis to establish common definitions and to measure agreement by means of Cohen's Kappa in its various forms (weighted, overall etc.).
Other measures of clinical agreement are known (Fleiss Kappa, Pi, alfa, Maxwell Random Error, Yule's ij...), each one with its particular traits and limits.
Since anyway Kappa remains the most widely used, our work focusses on the influence of specificity, sensitivity and prevalence Cohen's Kappa and attempts some further developments supported by mathematical models and a general applicability.

Session 288 New Research:
Cellular membranes - receptors and immune system

1885
ANTIPSYCHOTICS AND RECEPTOR REGULATION

P. Rogue, A. Malviya, J. Zwiller & G. Vincendon
Centre de Neurochimie du C.N.R.S.
5, rue Blaise Pascal, 67084 STRASBOURG FRANCE

Neuroleptics induce a delayed dopaminergic D2 receptor upregulation. The antipsychotic effect of these drugs follows a similar time course. The D2 receptor may be upregulated in the CNS of schizophrenics independently of treatment. Thus understanding how receptors are regulated may tell us more about the mode of action of neuroleptics and the pathogenesis of schizophrenia.
  Receptors are subjected to various forms of regulation, ranging from feed-back phosphorylation by protein kinase activated during signal transduction to change in gene expression. We studied the effect on the binding parameters of the D2 receptor of phosphorylation by protein kinase A and protein kinase C. The results will be discussed with respect to the pleiotropic role of phosphorylation in the regulation of signal transduction. And particular emphasis will be laid on the significance of these modifications for the receptor adaptations involved in the mechanism of action of neuroleptics and possibly in the pathogenesis of schizophrenia.

1886
BRAIN OXYGEN COMSUMPTION AND SCHIZOPHRENIA

Alessio DALLA LIBERA, M.D.
Psychiatric Department, Vicenza ITALY

Brain blood flow increased in schizophrenic patients; the cerebral metabolic rate of oxygen also increased. This hyper-availability of O2 may produce free radicals in excess; free radicals produce cellular membrane damage and lipid peroxidation. Studies on frontal lobe of schizophrenics showed ultrastructural damages and intracytoplasmatic accumulation of lipofuscine, a pigment made by per-oxidized unsaturated fatty acids. Malondialdheyde reckoning in the serum of schizophrenics before and after treatment with chlorpromazine showed, after the therapy, significantly lower values.
Therefore neuroleptic effectiveness of chlorpromazine may be correlated to its antioxidative properties.

1887

DOPAMINE D-1 RECEPTOR DEVELOPMENT DEPENDS ON ENDOGENOUS DOPAMINE STIMULATION
H.A.Gelbarrd MD PhD, M.H.Telcher MD PhD, A.Gallitano, J.Zorc, G.Faedda MD, E.Marsh and R.J. Baldessarini MD. The Depts. of Psychiatry and Neurology, Mc Lean Hospital, the Children's Hospital, and Harvard Medical School, Boston, MA., USA

An important principle in dopamine (DA) receptor pharmacology states that excess DA stimulation leads to receptor down-regulation, and understimulation leads to receptor up-regulation. A contrary dictum in developmental neurobiology states that disuse leads to atrophy. We thus sought to determine the role of endogenous DA in the development of rat striatal DA D-1 receptors in order to see which principles apply. We observed that profound neonatal DA depletions (98-100% DA depletion in nucleus accumbens-olfactory tubercle[NA/OT], produced by intracisternal 6-hydroxydopamine, were associated with a linear loss of binding sites for the selective D-1 antagonist 3H-SCH 23390 (r=0.84, p<0.005). Receptor density fell to a terminal value of about 500 fmol/mg protein at 100% depletion, which represents a 77% loss of receptor sites relative to control littermates. Thus, loss of endogenous DA in early development leads to underdevelopment of D-1 receptors. This process was reversed by daily administration of the selective D-1 agonist SKF-38393 (3 mg/kg/d ages 6-18d), which preserved DA receptor number even in 100% depletion. In developing control animals, however, there was a striking inverse association between levels of DA in the NA/OT, and density of D-1 binding sites in the striatum (r=0.79, p<0.01). Striatal D-1 receptor density was estimated at 3203 fmol/mg protein when limbic DA content was 3 ng/mg tissue, but was 1944 fmol/mg protein when limbic DA content was 5ng/mg tissue. Thus receptor up- and down-regulatory processes may match receptor density to DA levels during the course of normal development. However, in pathological states where the DA system is severely damaged, disuse may lead to receptor atrophy, and compensation through other mechanisms.

1888

USE OF PCR FOR THE AMPLIFICATION OF THE HUMAN DOPAMINE-2 RECEPTOR GENE

MIHAEL H. POLYMEROPOULOS, LLOYD G. MITCHELL, CARL R. MERRIL
NIMH LBG, Washington D.C., USA

There are two types of Dopamine receptors, Dopamine-1 and Dopamine-2. The Dopamine-2 receptor has been implicated in the pathophysiology of several disease states, including schizophrenia. In order to further study the role of D2 receptor in schizophrenia, we designed strategies for the isolation of the human D2 gene, utilizing the polymerase chain reaction. Based on the published nucleotide sequence of the rat D2 cDNA, we synthesized sets of mixed oligonucleotides, representing all the possible codons for two seven amino acid residues, which were used in PCR amplification experiments. We used several DNA templates including human genomic DNA, genomic and cDNA libraries. To facilitate subsequent cloning of the PCR amplified products, we included in the 5' end of the primers recognition sequences for restriction enzymes.
We are currently sequencing PCR amplified products either after cloning in plasmid vectors or by using one biotinylated primer during PCR, and subsequently separating the strands using a Sephadex column.

1889

THREE DIMENSIONAL STRUCTURE OF THE DOPAMINE D2 RECEPTOR

S.G. Dahl, Ø. Edvardsen, E. Heimstad and I. Sylte
Department of Pharmacology, Institute of Medical Biology
University of Tromsø, N-9001 Tromsø, Norway

Specific binding of ligands to macromolecules usually involves enclosure of most of the ligand molecule by a binding pocket in the macromolecule. Electrostatic interactions may contribute to the stabilization of such complexes, and molecular electrostatic potentials provide useful information about the mechanisms of ligand receptor interactions. The AMBER (Assisted Model Building with Energy Refinement) programs were used to calculate three dimensional molecular structures, electrostatic potentials and molecular dynamics of dopamine and a series of neuroleptics. The MIDAS (Molecular Interactive Display and Simulation) programs were used for molecular graphics with an Evans and Sutherland PS390 computer graphics system. Molecular structures of agonists and antagonists, together with the amino acid sequence of the rat dopamine D2 receptor (1), where used to construct a three dimensional model of the receptor. Postulated agonist and antagonist binding sites are located in the transmembrane parts. Molecular dynamics simulations demonstrated that unlike the static structures in a crystal, both dopamine, neuroleptic drugs and the receptor molecule must be considered as flexible entities which have considerable freedom to move in the biophase. This demonstrates the importance of the dynamic aspect for understanding mechanisms of drug-receptor interactions at the molecular level.

(1) Bunzow J.R. & al.: *Nature* 336, 783-787 (1988)

1890

DESENSITIZATION TO DOPAMINE D1 AND D2 ANTAGONIST-INDUCED DYSTONIA
Daniel E. Casey, M.D.
V.A. Medical Center and Oregon Health Sciences University, Portland, Oregon, U.S.A.

Drug naive monkeys develop increasing dystonia (sensitization) during the initial phases of repeated treatment with typical neuroleptic drugs (D2 or mixed D1/D2 antagonists). However the long-term course of this acquired sensitization is insufficiently studied.

Fourteen cebus monkeys that had received prior neuroleptic treatment and had stable, sensitized drug-induced dystonic responses, received 10 doses (once every 3-4 days) over 31 days with the test drugs and a saline challenge test. Group 1 (n = 7) received the D2 antagonist haloperidol .025 mg/kg i.m. and Group 2 (n = 7) received the D1 antagonist Schering 23390 .025 mg/kg i.m. Dystonia was scored by a rater blind to drug dosage.

Both groups showed similar significant (p < .01) gradual decreases in dystonia over the 31 days (45% for haloperidol; 55% for Schering 23390).

These results suggest similar rather than different processes mediating the decrease (desensitization) in either D1- or D2-induced dystonia. Perhaps these findings model the well recognized clinical phenomenon of tolerance to acute extrapyramidal syndromes produced by repeated neuroleptic treatment.

1891

Comparative effects of amisulpride and P 40 on the immune systems in mental disease

GEKIERE F.*, BIZZINI B.°, KRAMARZ P., SAILHAN M. FATTAL-GERMAN M. and BORENSTEIN P.

*Centre Hospitalier Spécialisé VILLEJUIF (FRANCE)
°Institut Pasteur Unité d'immunochimie des protéines (PARIS)

In a previous study concerning more than 300 psychiatric patients, selected according to the semiologic criteria of the french nosographia and those of the DSM III, we have shown a clear difference of responses to tetanus vaccination and skin tests with tuberculin and candidin between the patients with dementia (low responses) and schizophrenic patients (strong responses). On the basis of these results, we are studying 3 groups of psychiatric patients : schizophrenic, demented patients and mental arrieration states (with organic disease, with or without epilepsia). The effects of a neuroleptic, amisulpride and of an immunomodulator, P 40 are observed on : 1) the responsiveness to tetanus vaccination and to skin tests with tuberculin and candidin. 2) The plasmatic levels of prolactine, interleukin 2, INF gamma, INF alpha, reactive protein C (CRP) and prealbumin. 3) Psychiatric neurologic examinations and psychometric tests. From these preliminary results we conclude that interrelationships exist between the nervous and immune systems.

1892

IMMUNE INTERFERON MODULATES PERIPHERAL-TYPE BENZODIAZEPINE RECEPTORS.
F.Dadone and P.Bongioanni
Scuola Superiore di Studi Universitari e di Perfezionamento-S.Anna, Pisa ITALY

Two types of benzodiazepine receptors have been demonstrated in CNS (1), pharmacologically and biochemically distinct from each other. While the so-called "central-type" receptors mediate benzodiazepine central effects, the physiological role of "peripheral-type" binding sites is still unclear. It seems, however, that benzodiazepines may influence cell growth and differentiation via "peripheral-type" receptors (2). In the present study we have evaluated immune interferon effects on both "central-type" and "peripheral-type" receptors in mouse brain. We have found that low concentrations of interferon significantly ($p<0.01$) inhibit Ro-5-4864 binding to mouse cerebral membranes, while have a scant, if any, effect on Ro 15-1788. Such results are discussed in terms of relationships between CNS and Immune System, with special regard to benzodiazepine psychopharmacology.
REFERENCES:1) Moehler H. and Okada T.C., Sci. 198,849('77); 2) Wang J. et al. PNAS 81,753('84)

1893

IMMUNE ACTIVITY IN ANXIOUS AND DEPRESSED PATIENTS.

G.Somenzini,"L.Dezza, "R.D'Uva,C.Francesconi, E.Di Paolo, P.Tosca,F.Zerbi, F.Savoldi.
Neurological Clinic-"Medical Clinic II University of Pavia -Italy.

Immune functions were studied in 20 patients with anxious and depressive disorders, classified according to DSM-III-R criteria and submitted to Hamilton Rating Scale for Depression (HAMD) and State-Trait Anxiety Inventory (S.T.A.I. X-1-2). In particular, T lymphocytes, obtained by rosetting with sheep red blood cells (SRBC) AET treated from peripheral blood samples, were stimulated to proliferate with mitogens (PHA phytohemagglutinin). Blastogenesis was evaluated after 3Htdn incorporation.
Our preliminary results showed that T lymphocytes proliferation is significantly reduced in anxious and depressed patients with respect to normal controls.The mechanisms underlying to these immunological modifications are not well understood. It is likely that, as recently suggested, the interactions between neuroendocrine system and immune activities may be mediated by increased steroid release.

1894

H L A ANTIGENS AND SCHIZOPHRENIA:A FAMILY STUDY
*G.BERSANI,+M.VALERI,*A.FIGA'-TALAMANCA,+A.PIAZZA
+D.ADORNO,+C.U.CASCIANI,*A.GRISPINI,*N.CIANI
* Department of Psychiatry- II University of Rome
+ Department of Surgery - II University of Rome(I)

Aim of the study was to investigate HLA segregation in families with at least 2 subjects with schizophrenia. 9 families with 45 individuals were studied; 20 of them affected by RDC schizophrenia, with no subtyping in clinical form.
All patients were typed for HLA A,B,C,DR antigens. LOD score, recombination fraction and sib-pair test were used for linkage analysis. The preliminary results didn't show a linkage between single HLA antigens and schizophrenia. No HLA haplotypes was found increased. HLA data were available for 9 schizophrenic sib-pair (Sc SP) and 7 normal sib-pair (N SP). The number of haplotypes shared (2,1 or 0) is expected to be 25/50/25% if normal segregation occurs. The observed number were respectively 0/5/4 (0/56/44%) in Sc SP and 1/4/2 (14/57/29%) in N SP. These data seen to be consistent with a segregation of HLA antigens and disease within families, thus supporting the hypothesis of a genetic contribution to schizophrenia.

Session 289 Free Communications:
Personality disorders

1895

Cultural bereavement of refugees in the United States and Australia

Maurice Eisenbruch, M.D.
N.H. & M.R.C. Research Fellow,
Royal Children's Hospital Research Foundation, Parkville, Victoria 3052.

This paper aims to demonstrate that the reactions of uprooted refugees can be defined in terms of *cultural bereavement*; that these reactions are strongly coloured by the policies of the host country; and that cultural bereavement is an important factor in the health transition of refugees. The paper reports a study which developed a means of measuring cultural bereavement, which can be used to provide an indication of a community's state of health transition.

Cambodian refugees living in Australia and the USA have been studied in order to assess the impact of traumatic loss of society and culture (or cultural bereavement), the problems of adaptation to a new and very different society, the associated mental health problems and the importance of culture in shaping health problems. Significant differences were found between unaccompanied minors placed in (1) American foster homes and (2) Cambodian foster homes in America and those in Cambodian group care in Australia. Those placed in a culturally alien environment were somewhat better acculturated but suffered more cultural bereavement, while their counterparts placed in Khmer cultural setting were more poorly acculturated but suffered less cultural bereavement. Adjustment problems seemed worsened by failure to allow traditional and culturally familiar practices such as religious ritual. The well-being of the refugees was improved when they were allowed to validate their cultural beliefs through appropriate rituals and behaviour. Lack of access to culturally familiar medical care

The long-term aim of this study is to influence the development of better informed health and social policies relating to refugees and other immigrants, leading to reduction of cultural bereavement and associated psychiatric morbidity, culturally appropriate detection of resettlement problems, and better clinical engagement of immigrant patients with improved compliance and, therefore, better health.

1896

THE PROBLEM OF CLASSIFICATION OF PERSONALITY DISORDER AND THAT OF DELIMINATION TO THE NORMAL POPULATION.

LESCH, O.M.

Definition as well as classification of personality disorder is still a challange in psychiatric research. Typologies on a nosological basis have not yet been developed. One of the main reasons for that situation, as we think, can be found in the influence of selection criteria. Therefore we did not define our patient groups according to diagnosis, but formed instead of this 3 groups of psychotic patients according to treatment form. One group consisted of patients admitted to a psychotherapeutic ward, one of those admitted to a general psychiatric ward and the third group consisted of patients who remained after dismission in an ambulatory outpatient treatment. They were examined with psychometry as well as with the SKID and DIB scales. SKID as well as DIB showed little correspondance, whereby DIB exhibited a rather low sensitivity as a screening instrument for borderline disturbance. Psychometric investigation resulted in a clear demonstration of the heterogenity of these patients.
Therefore we underline the necessity

1897

AN ATTEMPT OF DIMENSIONAL EVALUATION OF PERSONALITY DISORDERS(PD)
Katsumi Yoshimasu,Department of Psychiatry, Tokyo Women's Medical College,Tokyo,Japan.

We have two types of evaluation system of PD: one categorial and the other dimensional. Most classifications of PD for psychiatric use are categorial.However,we also evidently need to evaluate PD dimensionally when we evaluate chronological developments or changes of personality.
We present here our dimensional evaluation system of PD.It is a part of our system of pure symptomatology of psychiatry which intends to evaluate patient's mental state itself from the holistic point of view.
Our system consists 4 axes:
I.The negative aspect of ego function disturbance,indicated with subjective ego-weakness and objective disturbance of sequence of behavior etc.
II. The positive aspect of ego function disturbance,indicated with ego-weak or ego-strong reactions and prevalence of "egoistic"interests.
III. The negative aspect of emotion-drive disturbance,indicated with lack of "releasing" interests and disturbance of emotional reality orientation.
IV.The positive aspect of emotion-drive disturbance,indicated with prevalence of "binding" interests.
The relation of this system to categorial ones is not contradictory but complementary.

1898

NARCISSISTIC PERSONALITY DISORDER: THE DSM III-R DESCRIPTION EXPANDED AND CLARIFIED.

V. Siomopoulos, M.D.
University of Illinois College of Medicine at Chicago

Narcissistic personality disorder is a new and still not adequately described clinical entity. This paper discusses certain features of this disorder often mentioned in the literature but not included in DSM-III-R (e.g., self-effacement, mortification, deficient social conscience, cognitive and language peculiarities). The author emphasizes the dynamic nature of the clinical features of this disorder. Thus certain DSM-III-R features (e.g., grandiosity) may be covered up by the patient's defenses, and other DSM-III-R features (e.g., lack of empathy, rage) may or may not be present depending on the patient's current life circumstances, i.e., the presence or absence of a close relationship with a person whom the patient experiences as a potential source of need gratification. This may obscure the clinical presentation of this disorder. This paper attempts to enlarge and clarify the DSM-III-R description of narcissistic personality disorder and thus enhance the clinician's ability to detect hidden narcissistic pathology.

1899

L'INSTITUTION INTERROGEE ET MISE AU DEFI PAR LE PERVERS

Docteur M. PEYRON et Docteur M. REY-CAMET
(C.H. EAUBONNE - FRANCE)

L'institution est défiée par le pervers. Plus que par la perplexité qu'elle induit, la perversion met les soignants au pied du mur de leur impuissance par la menace qu'elle représente :
- menace du plaisir de soigner, qui nous est "volé" par le pervers
- menace de l'"ordre" soignant, mise en relief par l'analogie non fortuite entre perversion et suicide L'institution, dans sa démarche obsessionnelle et son désir de maîtrise, risque de s'organiser sur une pente déviant l'ordre de la Loi vers une Loi de l'Ordre, s'essayant à "désarmer" le patient.
- menace de l'identité du soignant, par la nature de l'angoisse provoquée, par la dangereuse fascination qu'exerce le pervers en réveillant en nous nos fantasmes de violation d'interdit.
- menace enfin du soignant dans son rapport au savoir ; ce type de pathologie, situé à la frange de nos catégories nosographiques, nous plonge dans une grande incertitude et remet en cause la pertinence de notre savoir.

C'est donc dans le doute et l'inquiétude, dans l'indécision, que le soignant peut trouver une résonance à la souffrance du patient, s'imposant ainsi une extrême souplesse et la capacité de soutenir ce travail longtemps. Le temps est alors notre essentiel instrument de travail afin de pouvoir trouver un lieu de rencontre et de soin.

1900

SEARCHING COGNITIVE CORRELATES OF ANTI-SOCIAL PERSONALITY BY TESTS AND CEEG
Tarhan N.*, Guven S., Ozkan S., Burkovik Y., Yavuz D.
* GATA Haydarpasa Teaching Hospital, Dept. of Psychiatry, Istanbul, Turkey

In this study, we have aimed to search into the role of cognitive correlates in the etiopathogenesis of antisocial personality disorder. Neuropsychological tests (Bender, Fraisse Benton), clinical scales (STAI Forms) and Dynamic Brain Mapping (CEEG) were applied to each subject at the same time intervals and correlated.
The subjects consisted of those patients who, after clinical and psychometric analysis, were diagnosed according to DSM-III-R. Those with medical problems or any other psychiatric disorder were excluded.
Of the 31 subjects, 47 percent disclosed statistically significant borderline-abnormal CEEG findings; mainly dominance of theta waves with occasional spike waves. Those with aggressive characteristics displayed both meaningful CEEG abnormalities and history of head traumas.
The results of CEEG and neuropsychological tests were correlated with past psychosocial history and with clinical features.

1901

PERSONALITY IN PRIMARY HABITUAL ABORTION SYNDROME

S. Daini, B. Cinque, B. Longo, S. Dell'Acqua
Università Cattolica del S. Cuore, Rome, Italy

Because of the recognized importance of psychic factors in high risk pregnancies, particularly subsequent to abortions of unkown origin (Fischer 1973; Stray-Pedersen, 1984), Authors studied 20 consecutive cases of women with a prior history of habitual abortion (age 22-41 yrs).
Belonging to unkown etiology group was checked by diagnostic screening of both husband and wife, excluding genetic, immunogenetic factors and the presence of uterine anomalies of pathology. Ss were compared with a control group of 20 normal women, matched for age, education and socio-economic status. Both groups had psychiatric interview and the following tests: Rorschach, HFDT (Human Figure Drawing Test) and IPAT. Parametric measures were statistically elaborated by analysis of variance, while nonparametric data were compared by chi square method.
On DSM-III-R criteria, 13 Ss showed Personality Disorders (6 Borderline, 4 Schizotypal and 3 Obsessional-Compulsive) whose onset preceded abortions.
The whole experimental group showed, compared to Controls, significantly reduced productivity, lack of adequate impulse control and marked introversion, as well as higher anxiety scores, particularly of paranoid and guilt type.
Authors discuss possible interactions between personality patterns and abortions, as stressful life events, in conditioning che course and outcome of subsequent pregnancies.

1902

A COMPARATIVE STUDY OF PATIENTS WITH SCHIZOTYPAL PERSONALITY DISORDER AND CHRONIC SCHIZOPHRENIA
Alv A. Dahl, M.D.
Department of Psychiatry, University of Oslo, Norway

Matched samples of 21 male patients with schizotypal personality disorder (SPD) and with chronic schizophrenia (CS) were compared. Since SPD has been seen as a diathesis for CS, the study investigated protective and provocative factors of psychosis.
No differences between the groups were found concerning perinatal complications and MBD. The patients with SPD had significantly more mothers with neuroses and fathers with alcoholism, while no differences were registered concerning psychosis among first-degree relatives. Patietns with SPD had a more turbulent family life during their childhood tha patients with CS. The SPD patients therefore had to deal with more emotional problems at an early age. The patients with CS had more problems during adolescence with failure in school and more dependence on their parents. When reaching the problems of adolescence, the patients with CS had less experience with emotional conflicts, and they coped less well with the stresses of that life phase. However, the symptoms of patients with SPD had an earlier onset, and they sought help at an earlier age.

The patients with SPD seem to havemore problems during childhood and cope better with adolescence, while the opposite seems to be true for patients with CS, This is of importance for psychosis later

1903
"WRIST-SCRATCHING" SYNDROME
Koldobsky Nestor M.S., Astorga Claudia
Hospital A.Korn M.Romero, Unidad 10, Argentina

This work is based in an attempt to classify "wrist-scratching" syndrome. Within the different aspects, a clinic psychopathologic analysis of this autoagressive behaviours was chosen in this study.
Clinic cases obtained from Neuropsychiatric Hospital ward and from a Neuropsychiatric Institute were analyzed.

Session 290 Free Communications:
Community mental health services

1904
Development of Community Care in a Sectorised population in the U.K. and it's effects on acute Hospital admission profile of the mentally ill population.
Dr.Abdo.A.ALI, M.B.,Bch. SHO. Runwell Psychiatrict Hospital.
Dr.C.S.Mukherji M.B.,B.S., MRCPsych. DHMSA, Dip. N.B. Consultant Psychiatrist for the Castlepoint Sector, Runwell Hospital, Wickford, Essex SS11 7QE.

The Sydervelt Health Community Centre is a fully operational multidisciplinary resource centre with an open referral system for the mentally ill. It opened in Oct.84. It lies in the heart of Castlepoint Sector in Southend District and it serves approximately 80,000 persons.
This paper seeks to detail the growth of Community Services in Castlepoint Sector and examine whether it has had any effect on hospital admission profile.
The acute admissions to psychiatric wards between Nov.- March 84-85 (72 pts) and Nov.-March 88-89 (54 pts. up to now) were studied and compared retrospectively and prospectively. Significant differences have emerged. They have included significant shifts between diagnostic groups of patients, source of referral and other factors, i.e. physical illness.
The authors have failed to relate the impact of developing Community Services to this changing picture.
With the imminent closure of the large psychiatric hospitals, the authors have focused on current developmental needs in the Sector to minimise the need for hospital admission.
The recommendations are likely to be put into practice and will be the source of continuing study and research

1905
EFFECT OF CRISIS INTERVENTION ON HOSPITAL ADMISSIONS AND COSTS
Dr. N. Rao Punukollu
National Institute of Crisis Intervention Therapy & Research   Huddersfield   England

During the research period 54 psychiatric referrals to one Community Mental Health Team were identified as being crisis and were offered crisis intervention as the primary form of management. First fifteen cases were studied in detail with therapeutic outcome,cost effectiveness and burden on carers being evaluated. Results suggest that severely emotionally disturbed individuals can be maintained and treated successfully at home, that such a service could be cheaper than hospital admission and that a reduction in hospital admission figures, particularly of first admissions can be achieved. These fifteen patients were followed up over a two year period and their history compared with those of two groups of controls over the same period.Crisis intervention significantly reduced the time patients needed to spend in hospital, if they are admitted at all. The cost of the experimental group is significantly less compared with the two control groups.

1906
THE COMMUNITY MENTAL HEALTH CENTER IN PAGRATI ATHENS :FACTS AND REMARKS
George Giannios,Theoni Triantafillou,Nikos Soldatos,Hariklia Tsarmakli.

Community Mental Health Center, Adults Department, Pagrati,Athens

A comprehensive range of services providing mental health care, including CMHCs, is in the process of development, in this country.
In the context of this reform, this report outlines the development of the Pagrati Center with emphasis on its present operating condition as a full-scale CMHC, and presents the last year's evaluative work of the Adults Dept.
Social, demographic and psychiatric characteristics of the people attended the Center during the year,are described.
Obtained data are analysed,are compared with corresponding data of previous years and some findings on prevailing trends are discussed.

1907

A PROGRAM FOR THE INCREASE OF UTILIZATION OF A CMHC BY THE COMMUNITY

George Giannios, Gerassimos Frantzios, Christina Eprem, Maria Marathoniti

Community Mental Health Center (Adults Department) in Pagrati, Athens

The Community Mental Health Center (CMHC) in Pagrati, Athens, renders its services to a community of about 250.000 people. This catchment area coincides with the second municipal district of the city of Athens.

However the CMHC has, for the time being, to serve people from outside the catchment area, owing to the present shortage of community services. So of the 182 new attendants of one year, at the Adults Dept., 40% came from the catchment area. Meanwhile both figures, namely the total number of attendants and the percentage coming from the catchment area show a steady annual increase.

In order to intensify this increase and augment the utilization of our services by the community, the Adults Dept., launched an appropriate program that is now in progress.

This report deals mainly with this program, its targets and prospects, the employed techniques for the task, the given limitations of the effort, and the various difficulties we are confronted with, as well.

1908

COMMUNITY MENTAL HEALTH DEVELOPMENT BOARD OF JAKARTA, INDONESIA

Dadang Hawari, MD; Dept of Psychiatry Faculty of Medicine University of Indonesia, Jakarta, Indonesia.

Community Mental Health Development Board (CMHDB) of Jakarta was established in 1981. This Board is a forum of consultation and coordination in developing and facilitating mental health programmes in the community. In developing mental health programmes and activities, it should need a unification and comprehensive approaches through multi disciplines and sectors and also by social involvement and participation.
Indonesia is a country undergoing rapid social change and its big cities (especially Jakarta the capital city) passing through an almost uncontrollable that it also facing tremendous mental health problems.
Funds, personnels and the mechanism in implementing the programmes have not been established sufficiently.

1909

A district psychiatry : a response to psychotic deficient patient
Alain BRACONNIER ; Georges PAPANIKOLAOU
Association de Santé Mentale du 13ème arrondissement de Paris

The Mental Health Association of the 13th "arrondissement" of Paris was the first in France to apply the concept of "sectorisation" with the aim of emphasizing outpatient psychiatric follow-up so that the patient is not cut off from his natural surroundings. This concept is now widely accepted. Within this framework, the problems of severely disturbed children with different forms of child psychosis, involving mental retardation and affective dysfunction, which is always characterised by massive stress in the face of any type of change, has led to the development of a therapeutic unit with two aims. First to focus on outpatient follow-up and, second, to ensure the existence of a common approach to healthcare between institutions taking care of these people during childhood and institutions responsible for them during adulthood. A day hospital is therefore available for children under 16 years of age, a separate day hospital for young people aged between 16 and 25, and a Day Center working in close contact with a small specialised hospital unit takes care of severely retarded adults. Work in different day hospitals is based on the theoretical concepts of "holding" and "object presenting". These are complemented, as regards the hospital unit, with the concepts of intense nursing and "handling".

1910

A "BUSINESS" ORGANIZATION IN A COMMUNITY MENTAL HEALTH
Dr. Giovanni Giusto
S.S.M. VI^ U.S.L. - Liguria - Italy

We will consider the work of one the Mental health centre equipes which operates on a territory that includes little municipalities prevalently characterized by a rural culture. The work group is programmed so to consider the productiveness, i.e. the capability to answer to the needs expressed as disease of the single citizen. The needs are resolved with the more convenient tools avoiding, as far as possible, the hospitalization. The work is realized in an integrated and interdependent way, central points being the three per week equipe meetings where the work is planned and verified. The tools of work are two kind of cards:
- one is for the reception of new cases
- the other for the collection of familiar environment anamnestic data, and for the formulation at short, medium and long time of the therapeutic programmes.
The verification of trend of the cases is sone dusing the weekly reunions and in six monthy terms to verify the work hypotheses and the data coming from the reality.

1911

A STUDY OF DEMANDS A MENTAL HEALTH CENTRE, IN THE DISTRICT OF HORTALEZA (MADRID).
VICENTE,N. , JUAREZ,E. , ESTEVEZ,L.
C.S.M. DE HORTALEZA.

Se trata de analizar las condiciones en las que se establece el primer contacto entre el Centro de Salud Mental y el cliente.
Para ello se realiza un estudio prospectivo de las demandas presentadas en el Centro de Salud Mental de Hortaleza, durante el periodo comprendido entre el 1 de Diciembre de 1988 y el 31 de Mayo de 1989.
Se recogen datos sobre el agente de la demanda, via de derivacion al Centro, motivo y caracteristicas de la solicitud de intervención, factores vitales mediatos e inmediatos que pudieran haber influido en el desencadenamiento de la misma, asi como datos socio-demograficos del sujeto y existencia de antecedentes psiquiátricos previos. Se estudia también la respuesta ofrecida por los profesionales del Centro a cada demanda en concreto y la aceptación de esta respuesta por parte del paciente.
Los datos obtenidos se analizan a través de un programa estadistico, aplicando las pruebas bioestadisticas correspondientes.
Se comunicarán los resultados.

1912

DEMANDA ASISTENCIAL EN UNA RED DE SERVICIOS DE SALUD MENTAL. (PATIENT UTILIZATION OF A MENTAL HEALTH SERVICES NETWORK).
LUCAS MANGAS, S.(*), MARTINEZ RODRIGUEZ, J.M.(*), ALVAREZ LOBATO, P. (**), MEGIA LOPEZ, P. (**) y LEAL HERRERO, F. (**). (*) Servicio de Salud Mental de la Junta de Castilla y León, Valladolid; (**) H. Psiquiátrico "Dr. Villacián", Valladolid. España.

En el presente estudio se realiza una evaluación de los patrones de demanda asistencial que ha recibido durante 1.988 la red de servicios de salud mental comunitaria perteneciente a la Diputación Provincial de Valladolid (España), que está organizada en cinco sectores de asistencia psiquiátrica.

Las tasas de utilización de servicios varían entre los diferentes sectores asistenciales, oscilando desde 309/10.000 habitantes en el 2º sector a 593/10.000 habitantes en el 4º. También se observan diferencias notables entre las tasas de utilización urbanas (407/10.000 habitantes) y rurales (1.107/10.000 habitantes). Esta distribución diferencial se asocia a factores demográficos, geográficos, culturales así como a la oferta de servicios psiquiátricos por parte de otras instituciones asistenciales públicos y privados.

La demanda de servicios ha aumentado entre 1.985 y 1.987 en un 62,76%, principalmente a expensas de la población más joven. Actualmente un 50,6% de las primeras consultas son menores de 24 años.

Session 291 Free Communications:
Inpatient services

1913

A CONVENTIONALIZED PSYCHIATRIC CLINIC: COMMUNITARY REHABILITATIVE ORGANIZATION
Dr. Giovanni Giusto
Clinic Villa Ridente - Albissola Mare - Italy

We will consider a private conventionalized psychiatric clinic and its organization model, and how it's insered in a more global rehabilitative project for psychiatric patients, in collaboration with the competent public Mental health services.

1914

PSYCHODYNAMICS OF THE CHIEF PHYSICIAN WARD ROUND IN PSYCHIATRIC HOSPITAL
Kohler G.K., Professor of Medicine, Senior Physician of the Psychiatric Hospital of the Evangelische and Johanniter Krankenanstalten Duisburg-Nord/Oberhausen (public utility company) Steinbrinkstr. 96a, D-4200 Oberhausen 11, West Germany
Rosin U., MD, PhD, Senior Physician of the Psychotherapy and Psychosomatic Hospital University of Dusseldorf

In the experience of the patients, of the chief physician and his/her staff (senior physicians, ward doctors, nursing staff, etc) the ward round is of great importance. Descriptions, conceptions or indeed empirical investigations of the ward round have been presented neither for somatic medical nor for psychiatric hospitals. We have recorded on tape ward round conversations led by the chief physician of a psychiatric hospital. There followed workups of a formal schematic and content-analytical character to describe the operational sequences. The objective was to determine from practice what behaviors are helpful from a therapeutic point of view. Afterwards, a concept of "ward round psychotherapy" for psychiatric wards is outlined.

1915

Quality measurement in mental health care.

J.H. Werner, Mental Health Inspectorate in the Netherlands, Rijswijk

First a general framework is described which provides a base for quality measurement. By publishing so called "Guidelines to Quality" in different areas of mental health care the Inspectorate has started a process of information exchange with professionals and patients. Their remarks and suggestions on quality were incorporated in successive editions of these "Guidelines". Thus, continuous improvement of the concept of quality is ensured. Instances of items from the "Guidelines" will be given.
Next, several methods will be discussed which have been used to measure the quality of mental health care in various institutions. Special attention was given to the adequate respresentation of distinct dimensions of care. Results were obtained in psychiatric wards and in psychogeriatric nursing homes. Recently, investigations have started into the possibility to assess the quality of care by a specially designed questionnaire. The basic idea is to build a quality information system useful to health workers and external authorities as well. Some preliminary results will be presented of an experiment which was aimed at the evaluation of the application of coercive measures such as seclusion and restraint to psychiatric patients.

1916

Special Depression Treatment Wards in the Federal Republic of Germany - an overview

G. Hole, M. Wolfersdorf, W. Kopittke
Psychiatric Hospital Weissenau, Department of Psychiatry I University of Ulm, D-7980 Ravensburg-Weissenau, F.R.G.

In the last 15 years there is a rising tendency to develop new therapy concepts due to groups of psychiatric inpatients homogenous in symptoms, behavior, nosology or treatment strategies.
One of the essential therapeutic developments in recent years is an increasing number of socalled depression treatment wards for psychiatric inpatients. Uptonow there exist 7 "depression treatment wards" in Germany-West, mostly in large state mental hospitals. "Helpful therapeutic interaction between staff and patients" and "activation" are important parts to create a warm and understanding ward-atmosphere for individual and group psychotherapy, antidepressant medication, occupational therapy etc.. Since September 1976 the opening of the Weissenau Depression Ward more than 2200 inpatients (admissions or about 1800 first inpatients) were treated with this program. This paper reports some experiences and data due to 7 depression treatment wards in the Federal Republic of Germany.

1917

OUTCOME OF INVOLUNTARY HOSPITALIZATION

Erik Simonsen, M.D., University of Copenhagen, 9 Blegdamsvej, DK-2100 Copenhagen Ø, Denmark.

In Denmark 3% of all psychiatric admissions are involuntary hospitalizations.
All 58 patients from the non-dangerous group (1/3 of all) committed for treatment in Copenhagen County in 1985, a representative sample of the total number in Denmark (N=445), participated in a study of outcome. The mean age was 42.9 (range 17-70; SD 16.2), 28 (48%) were women and 30 (52%) men. 30 (57%) had schizophrenia, 12 (23%) paranoia, 5 (9%) manic depression, 3 (6%) "psychogenic psychosis" and 3 (6%) dementia. The mean length of hospitalization was 73 days (range 2-330). - According to the psychiatrists responsible for the treatment, half of the patients did considerably better after treatment, 1/3 had some improvement and 1/5 were unchanged. Half of the patients found that they had improved because of the treatment, 1/4 were unchanged and 1/4 felt that the treatment had worsened their mental health. Manio-depressive and patients with psychogenic psychoses had a better outcome than did the schizophrenic and paranoia group of patients. The BPRS-subscale for schizophrenia showed that 2/3 of the schizophrenic had improved. - At the presentation the author will outline positive and negative predicting variables (socio-demographic, first admission/numerous earlier admissions/committed before, length of treatment, the kind of compulsory treatment used and so on) for a good outcome.

1918

Self concept, stage of development and ego identity in young adult psychiatric inpatients
H.P. Kapfhammer, R. Neumeier
Psychiatric Hospital of the University of Munich (Director: Prof. Dr. H. Hippius)
Psychological problems and/or psychiatricly relevant symptoms in young adults quite often occur in the context of attempts to find personal solutions of normative developmental tasks during the time of transition from adolescence to young adulthood. Without intending to establish causal relationships between patterns of psychosocial adaptation and psychiatric syndromes 120 young adults (17 - 25 years) admitted to an acute psychiatric hospital, diagnosed according to DSM III and ICD 9th r. were investigated by Offer's Self-image questionnaire, Loevinger's Sentence completion test for measuring ego development, Adam's § Grotevant's Extended version of the objective measure of ego identity. A detailed developmental and psychosocial history was taken.
Results will be presented regarding the patterns of psychosocial adaptation (dominance and consistency of the stage of ego development, dimensions of self-image, structures of identity formation), their relationship to psychiatric syndromes, to previous psychosocial development. It will be reported of the stability vs. variability of these test parameters during the time of hospital treatment. A comparison to test results in a control-group of medical and nurse students will be tried.

1919

THE PLACE OF PARTIAL HOSPITALIZATION PROGRAMS IN THIRD WORLD NATIONS.
Marie-Claude Rigaud, MD MPH, Assistant Professor
University of Illinois at Chicago.

The paper is a comprehensive discussion of large scale utilization of Partial Hospitalization Programs in the delivery of Mental Health Services in Third World Countries.

First, the author briefly reviews Mental Health Services within the goals and objectives of the World Health Organization. This is followed by a presentation of statistics depicting actual or expected incidence and prevalence of mental disorders, as well as a critique of the condition of mental health services in many of the Third World Nations. The hard socioeconomic realities and choices facing most of these nations are discussed with particular emphasis placed on the interface between those realities and the achievement of WHO's goals of "(Mental) Health for All in the year 2000".

The author then gives an overview of the clinical and administrative aspects of Partial Hospitalization Services and Programs, lists the various types of programs and discusses the potential applications, utilization and benefits of such programs as part of an array of mental health services in Third World Countries.

In conclusion, the author demonstrates the implementation and benefits of Partial Hospitalization as alternative to hospitalization in one particular Third World country which is now facing severe socieconomic problems, resulting in low priority for all health programs.

1920

LA PSYCHOTHERAPIE INSTITUTIONNELLE A L'EPREUVE DU SECTEUR

LE CORRE J.J. ; PUEL J. ; SANCHEZ F. ; STEPHANATOS G.
CENTRE HOSPITALIER SPECIALISE MAISON BLANCHE
35° Secteur de Psychiatrie Générale de Paris

En France, depuis plus de 40 ans, un courant de pensée s'inspirant de la sociologie et de la psychanalyse et connu sous le nom de Psychothérapie Institutionnelle nous transmet son savoir et son expérience. Plus récent est le système actuel d'organisation du service public de soins psychiatriques : le Secteur.
Il serait inadéquat de ne voir là qu'une évolution linéaire, un système remplaçant l'autre et le rendant obsolète.
Hors les murs comme dans les murs les notions de transfert multiréférentiel, de médiation, de dialectique entre soins et théorisation, d'analyse permanente du sens de "ce qu'il-y-a-là" demeurent des instruments indispensables pour notre pratique quotidienne de soins au Sujet psychotique.
Nous verrons donc comment Psychothérapie Institutionnelle et Politique de Secteur peuvent se rejoindre et se nourrir mutuellement et comment le concept d'Institution demeure d'actualité.

1921

PSYCHIATRIC SERVICES FOR DEAF IN NORWAY
Anne Regine Foreland, M.D.
Deaf persons represent a communication problem to the medical and psychiatric staff. Deaf persons need, therefore, to have psychiatric services in their own language. Every country should have a specialized Deaf-Unit, where the staff is trained in sign-language and lip-reading. Very few countries in the world have such units. So far there are only 8 in existence in the entire world. I started Norway's first and only Deaf-Unit in 1978 at Gaustad Hospital in Oslo (head: Prof. Nils Retterstøl, M.D.). Our aim is to give a broad psychiatric service to all prelingually deaf (deafened before the age of 3 years) in Norway. This group represents about 1% of the country's total population. Not all the patients need to be admitted in our unit in Oslo to be treated; we can do much on our consultations around the country, and by giving information and supervision to local health workers. Besides our unit, we also act as a flying squad. We work in a multi-professional team (psychiatrist, psychologist, nurses, social worker, art therapist, occupational therapist and physiotherapist). Rehabilitation is a very important part of the treatment, and we have teachers for deaf connected to our unit. Rates of specific psychiatric disturbances are presented for a five year period of functioning of the Unit. A 3 year duration follow-up study of 214 patients, using DSM-III-R diagnostic criteria along with rating-scales for assessment of social functioning, global assessment and so on has recently started in the Unit.

Session 292 Free Communications:
Psychopathology in medical patients

1922

MITRAL VALVE PROLAPSE IN BIPOLAR MOOD DISORDER.
ARKONAÇ MD,TOKER MD,ÖZER MD,GÜLTEKİN MD,ÜNER MD.
BAKIRKÖY STATE MENTAL HOSPITAL. ISTANBUL TURKEY
42(DSM-III-R)bipolar patients(17women,25men;age 19-66yrs)were selected at random from psychiatric outpatients,matched by sex,age with 32 control subjects(10 women,22men;age 24-59yrs)consisting of doctors,nurses,employees.Groups did not differ in demographic variables significantly.After the manic phase subjects were evaluated by SCID and M-Mode and two dimentional echography.All recordings were reviewed by two readers who arrived at a consensus diagnosis.10(4women,6men)of bipolars were diagnosed as MVP(%23.8),only 4(3women,1men)of controls were MVP (%12.5).Bipolars with and without MVP were not different on demographic and clinical variables. No subject had any sceletal deformities.It was concluded that prevelance of MVP in women was not significantly different from men neither in all subjects(7/27.%25.9 and 7/47.%14.8 respectively.$\bar{x}^2$=0.736. df=1.p$>$0.7)nor in bipolars(4/14.%23.5 and 6/25.%24. $\bar{x}^2$=0.163.df=1 p$>$0.05).There was no significant difference between MVP prevalences in controls and bipolars either($\bar{x}^2$=2.3414.df=1 p$>$0.1).
It was hypothesized that the relation between MVP and bipolar mood disorder is either a trait which may be considered in terms of genetic linkage or alternatively an exacerbation of MVP mimics the bipolar mood disorder.

1923
PSYCHIATRIC DISORDERS IN THE MEDICALLY ILL: PREVALENCE & RISK FACTORS
Ming-Been Lee, M.D., Yue-Yoe Lee, M.D. National Taiwan University, Taipei, Taiwan

In order to understand the psychiatric disorders in the inpatients of non-psychiatric departments, 759 adult patients were selected randomly for study. Each patient was assessed via a psychiatric interview and self-rating scales for measuring psychopathology, personality and family functions. The results indicated that 22.8% of the patients received a DSM III diagnosis. Approximately 44% of the diagnoses consisted of adjustment disorders, with 16.8% representing organic brain syndromes (OBS). As to the central symptoms, 30.6% of the diagnoses were depression; 22.0%, anxiety; and 17.3% mixed depression and anxiety. The patients with older age and longer hospital stay were prone to OBS. The risk factors for non-organic mental disorders were lower educational level, lower social status, being widowed, more numbers of past hospitalization, poorer family functions and personality traits with prominent neuroticism and introversion. In total, 6.9% of the total subjects received psychiatric consultation during the index admission. The patients of OBS, and non-organic mental disorders with severe psychopathology were more frequently referred.

1924
STRESS REACTIVITY AND SOMATIC ILLNESS

J.L. González de Rivera, C. de las Cuevas, L. Fernández, y A.L. Monterrey, R.Pulido, R. Gracia. Cátedra de Psiquiatría. Universidad de La Laguna. Facultad de Medicina. Tenerife.

The stress reactivity index (SRI) was administered to 400 newly admitted medical patients in a General Teaching Hospital and to 530 normal healthy controls. The mean SRI was 10.46 ($\pm$4.8) for the inpatients group and 9.68 ($\pm$5.4) for the control group (p<0.01). Age, socioeconomic and cultural levels and type of pathology do not relate to SRI differences. There are, however, significant sex differences in both groups, with a mean SRI of 9.6 ($\pm$4.8) for men and 11.36 ($\pm$4.7) for women (p<0.001) in the patient sample and 8.59 ($\pm$5.4) for men and 10.65 ($\pm$5.37) for women in the control population (p<0.001).
In view of previous research that shows no change of SRI under transitory stress situations, the higher SRI in medical patients supports SRI as a new marker for stress-related increased susceptibility to somatic illness.

1925
HOSTILITY IN THALASSEMIA

G.TRIKKAS, C.POLITIS, A.TZONOU, A.VOULGARI, H.VRETOU, G.N. CHRISTODOULOU

ATHENS UNIVERSITY, DEPT. OF PSYCHIATRY, EGINITION HOSPITAL

The aim of this study was to provide further information concerning the personality characteristics and the incidence of psychiatric symptoms in thalassemic patients.
131 patients suffering from thalassemia and 65 normal controls sharing the same demographic and sociocultural characteristics were given the following psychometric tests; 1.Zung's Self-Rating Scale for Depression (SRSD), 2.Spielberger's State-Trait Anxiety Inventory (STAI), 3.The Eysenck Personality Questionnaire (EPQ), and 4.Foulds' Hostility and Direction of Hostility Questionnaire.
Clinical and laboratory parameters (age of splenectomy, iron chelation therapy, frequency of transfusions, mean values of ferritine and hemoglobin) were also estimated in the patients' group.
Patients were differentiated from controls with respect to personality characteristics and psychopathology. More specifically patients had more hostility but less anxiety than controls and scored higher in the L factor of EPQ.
Regression analysis did not reveal any association between clinical and laboratory parameters on the one hand and personality characteristics and psychopathology on the other.
Our findings indicate that hostility is an important component of the psychological profile of thalassemic patients, a finding in keeping with the well-known difficulties in the psychological management of these patients.

1926
BOULIMIE ET DIABETE INSULINO-DEPENDANT
BULIMIA AND INSULIN DEPENDANT DIABETES MELLITUS (IDDM)
P. MATHIEU
HOTEL - DIEU DE PARIS

Il s'agit d'une étude sur une population de 29 diabétiques insulino-dépendants d'âge moyen, 25,3 ans, présentant des troubles du comportement alimentaire

- soit anorectiques boulimiques
- soit boulimiques vomisseuses

selon les critères du DSM III r.
Sont étudiées les méthodes particulières utilisées afin de ne pas grossir,
la non compliance à l'insulino-traitement,
l'importance des complications neurologiques dans une brève période d'évolution de la maladie métabolique :

- présence de neuropathie périphérique, 72 %
- présence de neuropathie végétative, 38 %
- présence de complications ophtalmologiques, 62 %.

L'étude permet de s'interroger sur la place de la boulimie comme facteur de risque des complications dégénératives chez la diabétique insulino-dépendante.

1927

SYSTEMIC LUPUS ERYTHEMATOSUS AND PSYCHIATRIC DISORDERS

A. Piro, C. Loriedo, C. Valitutti, G. Valesini, S. Bartolomei, D. Bomprezzi, P. Martini di Nenna, G. Vella.

Iª Clinica Psichiatrica dell' Universita "La Sapienza" Viale dell' Universita 30 Roma, Italy

Neuropsychiatric manifestations in Systemic Lupus Erythematosus can be expressed in different ways: depression, organic psychosis, schizophenic psychosis, personality disorders. In this essay the authors attempt to reply to some questions as concerns the manifest correlation between SLE and psychopathology for instance, the research for a "Model Outline Personality" in the suffering patients from SLE, the occurence of life stress events during a previous time to SLE pathology croping up. The patients are considered in hospital environment by pointing out parallelly biological and psychiatric data. Psychiatric data are pointed out by using:
- MMPI, in order to consider normal and pathological personality's features and, thus, to have a possible diagnostic trend.
- PAYKEL SCALE for life stress events in order to consider probably stress events before SLE's occurence.
- PSYCHIATRIC INTERVIEW

1928

SPECIAL CHARACTERISTICS IN ANXIETY MANIFE-STATIONS OF HYPERTHYROIDISM.

A.Iacovides, I.Papavasiliou, F.Grammatikos, K.Goutsiou, C.Ierodiakonou.

C´Dep.of Psychiatry and Dep.of Nuclear Medicine, Aristotelian University of Thessaloniki, General Hospital AHEPA, Greece.

The aim of this study has been the investigation of patients with hyperthyroidism regarding a qualitative and quantitative evaluation of anxiety symptoms. An attempt has been made to find out special characteristics which might help in the differential diagnosis of the clinical manifestations of hyperthyroidism from anxiety manifestations of other patients which frequently seem similar.
  Twenty five hyperthyroid patients and twenty five anxiety neurotic euthyroid were investigated. Differentiation of hyperthyroidism and euthyroidism was based on the levels of serum T3,T4,TSH and a clinical index of hyperthyroidism. The Hamilton--Anxiety Scale was used and a more detailed comparison of subitems of each of the 15 items of the scale was carried out.
  In the group of hyperthyroidism a significantly higher level of the scores referring to somatic symptoms and complaints was found and a lower level of the scores referring to psychic anxiety, mainly in the form of irritability; on the contrary, in anxiety neurotics the predominant items were those of anxiety expectation of a vaque, imminent danger, fear of loneliness etc. The findings indicate the possibility of an early clinical differentiation.

1929

PATIENTS WITH SCLERODERMA: HOSTILITY FEATURES AND PSYCHIATRIC SYMPTOMS

Angelopoulos NV, Drosos A, Tzivaridou Despina, Liakos A, Moutsopoulos H.

Department of Psychiatry, University of Ioannina, Greece.

Twenty-nine patients with scleroderma were investigated for Hostility structure and psychiatric symptomatology. Thirty-three healthy women were used as controls. The utilized psychometric instruments were: the Hostility and Direction of Hostility Questionnaire (HDHQ), the Delusions Symptoms States Inventory/states of Anxiety and Depression (DSSI/sAD) and the Symptom Check List 90-R. The scleroderma patients were significantly increased over normal controls in Depression and Anxiety and to a lesser degree in psychotic symptoms, obsessive-compulsiveness, interpersonal sensitivity and somatization. No significant differences were detected regarding hostility.
The scleroderma patients are also compared with groups of patients suffering from primary Sjogren's Syndrome (N=41), Systemic Lupus Erythematosus (N=51) and Rheumatoid Arthritis (N=65). The differences and similarities among the patients with the connective tissue diseases on hostility structure and psychiatric symptomatology are presented and discussed.

1930

Verbal exression vs emotional experience in greek infertile couples.
I. Tarlatzis, J. Diakoyannis, B. Tarlatzis, J. Bondis, C. Phocas, A. Pitsavas, G. Kaprinis.
A´Dep. of Psychiatry & A´Dep. of Ob & Gyn Aristotelian University of Thessaloniki, Greece.

  The psychological cost of infertility in the greek milieu has been the focus of this study.
  It has been hypothesized that the infertile couples undergoing different treatment procedures use repression as the major defense mechanism in order to adapt, verbally denying their emotional state and namely stress, anxiety and depression.
  Sixty nine females and 18 male spouses coming to the infertility clinic were given semi-structured and structured interviews, the life Events Scale, The Side-Effect Checklist and the Marlow-Crown/ Taylor Scale. Women´s results indicate the presence of defensive anxiety while men showed a repressed anxiety greatly connected to psychosomatic illness.
  Infertility is firstly faced with denial and surprise and then guilt and anger. The sharing of feelings is restricted to the immediate family while their marriage seems to be greatly threatened and their sexual live mostly changed.
  Women report the presence of anxiety and depression while the opposite stands for males, though the presense of repression is supported by their psychological investigation.
  Our findings differ from an American population studied where males as well as females showed a great extent of repression.
  This difference should be attributed to male - female roles in the two societies and medical treatment procedures used.

Session 293 Free Communications:
AIDS: Psychological implications

1931

HIV-ANTIBODY PREVALENCE AND DRUG MISUSE 1985-1989 - THE VIENNESE EXPERIENCE
Loimer N., Presslich O., Hollerer E., Pfersmann D., Pakesch G.
University of Vienna, Dept. of Psychiatry, Austria

This study presents the epidemiology of HIV infection among intravenous drug users in Vienna during the years 1985-1989. Our data show an increase of HIV seroprevalence from 8,5% in 1985 to 25,6% in 1988 (data 1989 are in progress).
Two factors linked with seropositivity:
Frequency of drug injection and sharing of drug injection equipment are discussed in respect of the low frequency of HIV antibodies among viennese drug addicts. Furthermore possible local conditions that prevent rapid spread are described.

1932

ASESSMENT OF THE MENTAL STATE OF PATIENTS WITH HIV INFECTION.
G. Pakesch, D. Pfersmann, J. Grünberger, L. Linzmayer.
Department of Psychiatry, University of Vienna, AUSTRIA

It has been reported that the AIDS can present neurpsychiatric symptoms like major depressive disorder, adjustment disorder with depressed mood and organic brain syndrome with affective, delusional and demented features.

In the study 60 patients, age 18-45 years, have been included. 30 patients showed HIV infection group II and III, 30 group IV (CDC). 30 patients belonged to risk group 1, 30 risk group 2. Noopsychic performance has been measured by PMT-Raven (fluid intelligence) and MWT (cristallized intelligence), visual retention and organic brain syndrom by Benton-Test, and specifical memory by the Numerical Memory Test. Attention and concentration was objectivated by Alphabetic Reaction test. Personality was assessed by MMPI, state and trait anxiety by STAI 1 and 2. By means of a clinical psychiatric exploration psychopathological features were documented using AMDP and BPRS, depressed mood was rated by HAMD.

First results showed impairment of noopsychic performance (Benton-Test, Numerical Memory Test) and a tendency of impaired, attention and concentration, which reach in risk group 2 statistical significance. Depressive Symptoms mainly were found in risk group 2. Impairment of noopsychic performance are not frequent and reach seldom the clinical feature of dementia. They rather show the picture of "lowered noopsychic level" and are significant more frequent found in risk group 2.

1933

COGNITIVE IMPAIRMENT IN HIV INFECTED HEMOPHILIACS

Horesh N.*, Sancovici S., Varon D.**, Floro S.*, & Martinowitz U.**
The Department of Psychiatry* & The National Hemophilia Center**, Tel-Hashomer, Israel.

The cognitive functioning of 20 hemophiliacs with human immunodeficiency virus (HIV) infection and of HIV seronegative matched controls was assessed. Neuropsychological testing indicated that HIV infected patients showed a significant decline in the performance subtests of the Wechsler Intelligence Scale and in the Bender Gestalt Test. HIV positive patients exhibited prominently a significant slowing of visual-motor as well as of verbal cognitive functioning; memory, concentration and learning disturbances, and difficulties in visual-motor tasks and in fine motor coordination. Magnetic resonance imaging had abnormal findings in most of them, and validated the results of neuropsychological tests. The findings show that cognitive disturbances are detected even in the early stages of HIV infection, before the development of the clinical picture of AIDS-related disease and suggest an early central nervous system involvement. Neuropsychological investigation is shown as a sensitive method in documenting early brain involvement in HIV infection.

1934

THE IMPACT OF AIDS EDUCATION AMONG ELEMENTARY SCHOOL STUDENTS
P. C. Chandarana, P. Conlon, S. Noh, V. Field
University of Western Ontario, London, Canada

As the AIDS epidemic continues to progress, it has become evident that preventive health education is key to curbing its further spread. Consistent with this, a curriculum on AIDS was recently introduced in Ontario, Canada elementary schools. The objective of this study was to assess the impact of this curriculum on students' knowledge, attitudes and beliefs. 1626 students were examined, of whom 848 formed the experimental group and 778 students, not exposed to AIDS education, formed the control group. All students in the experimental group completed a self-report questionnaire prior to the AIDS education program and then at two intervals after classes on AIDS. The control group, similarly completed the questionnaire at the same intervals. The results show a significant increase in knowledge in the experimental group following their exposure to AIDS classes. Generally, students in the experimental group also reported greater communication with their parents on the topic of AIDS and demonstrated a positive attitude toward the curriculum. The authors conclude that education on AIDS needs to be an ongoing process integrated to match the level of the development of students. Finally, they suggest that this process should be assessed at a variety of educational levels in an effort to devise an overall cohesive program in AIDS education for the future.

1935
PSYCHO-SOCIAL AND IMMUNOLOGICAL ASPECTS OF AIDS

Nicholas Destounis, M.D., Ph.D.,
Professor of Psychiatry & Mental Health Sciences
Medical College of Wisconsin
Chief, Psychiatry Service
Zablocki VAMC, Milwaukee, Wisconsin

Stavros D. Kottaridis, Ph.D., Director of Virology Dept.
Cancer Institute, Athens-Greece

The diagnosis of this catastrophic illness has not only medical implications for the patient but it will also affect family, friends, and fellow workers. In our research study, evidence will present to suggest that they have contracted a dreadful disease that could well result in a rapid change of life.

The psychological treatment will force the patients to develop an *Adaptation Syndrome* due to the realization that they have a terminal illness. Our study will prove that the HIV virus directly affects the CNS and it may cause less psychiatric manifestations before signs of immunodeficiencies appear. Socio-cultural data will furnish evidence that in two minority groups a massive *preventive model* is necessary to stop the *unparalleled* catastrophic consequences on these population groups (Black-Hispanic).

The virulence of the human immunodeficiency virus (HIV) lies in its ability to cripple the system that protects the body against invasive pathogens. T4 lymphocytes, the key elements for generations and regulating the immune response, are impaired and cannot perform their functions. In vitro studies have provided evidence for persistent infection of monocytes by HIV. The development of full blast AIDS is due to the failure of the immune system to control the dissemination of HIV. Why the disease is chronic, how the virus is disseminated, the mechanism of T-cell depletion, and why the immune system is rendered ineffective are questions which will be discussed.

1936
TOXICOMANES ET PARTAGE DES SERINGUES

F. FACY;* E. LE HUEDE**
*Inserm, Le Vesinet, **Centre L'Envol - Rennes, FRANCE.

Le partage des seringues constitue le mode privilegie de contamination du virus HIV dans la population des heroinomanes. L'etude presente vise a apprecier l'impact des mesures prises en France sur le comportement des toxicomanes utilisateurs de seringues, notamment la liberalisation de la vente des seringues en pharmacie. L'echantillon etudie est constitue de 479 sujets pour la plupart heroinomanes traites en centres specialises. Deux tendances essentielles surgissent de l'enquete: 1. Un group de toxicomanes traites qui ne sont pas concernes par la loi sur la liberalisation de la vente des seringues: leur estimation se situe autour de 20%; 2. Un group largement majoritaire de toxicomanes traites, utilisateurs de seringues (ou l'ayant ete), pour lesquels il est interessant de noter l'evolution en matiere de modes d'usage depuis la loi. C'est ce groupe de 385 sujets qui va etre analyse par la suite. Les toxicomanes qui ne partageaient pas leurs seringues (19% du total) avant les mesures de prevention paraissent avoir persiste dans leur attitude. Les sujets ayant arrete les injections intra-veineuses representent 39% de ceux qui auparavant partageaient leurs seringues. Pour ce groupe, il est difficile d'attribuer le changement d'attitude aux seules mesures reglementaires ou a la decou- verte de la seropositivite ou encore a une pathologie associee. Les sujets ayant arrete le partage des seringues constituent le groupe le moins important puisqu'il ne represente que 22% des sujets qui partageaient leurs seringues avant les mesures. Les sujets continuant a partager leurs seringues representent 39% des sujets qui partageaient leurs seringues avant les mesures. Ce sont les toxicomanes qui continuent a emprunter et/ou a donner leurs seringues. Comme dans toute mesure de prevention dans le domaine de la Sante Publique, on assiste la a la presence d'un "noyau irreductible" qui continue ses comportements d'habitude avec, parfois, renforcement pour certains.

1937
NEUROPSYCHOLOGICAL ASSESSMENT IN AIDS PATIENTS

E.Aguglia, P.Zolli, M.DeVanna, G.Nasca
Clinica Psichiatrica di Trieste, Italy

The peculiar tropism of the HIV virus as regards the nervous and lymphatic system determines an early disease in the Central Nervous System. The neurological symptoms mark the outbreak of the disease in 10-30% of patients. The presence of the HIVAg in the cerebrospinal fluid, indicating a recent or advanced infection, besides reflecting a presymptomatic stage of the cerebral infection may represent a factor of an unfavourable prognosis.
15 patients affected by AIDS, whose age ranged from 20 to 40, have undergone a neurological examination as well as an EEG and a Cerebral TAC. The dosage of the Ac specific viruses and the identification of the HIVAg, the dosage of the Beta 2 microglobulin and of the cells in the cerebrospinal fluid have also been assessed.
The Luria-Nebraska Neuropsychological Battery has been employed to outline the neuropsychological, cognitive functions.
The obtained data outline the opportunity of a thorough neuropsychological exam for evaluating the degree of the encephalopathy in AIDS and of the disease itself.

1938
Beyond Morality: The Need for Psychodynamic Understanding and Treatment of Responses to the AIDS Crisis.

Rita R. Rogers, M.D., Clinical Professor of Psychiatry, University of California in Los Angeles

The purpose of this paper is to identify a broad range of issues that both impact, and are impacted by, psychiatric intervention in AIDS and AIDS-related cases, with a special concern toward emphasizing the need for application of a psychodynamic perspective in the understanding and treatment of pathological responses to the AIDS crisis. As a cornerstone of the psychiatric model, psychodynamic evaluation and treatment can provide a breadth of focus and depth of understanding crucial to a resolution of some of the deeper psychosocial aspects involved in the reaction to the spread of the AIDS virus. A case example is used to illustrate psychodynamic factors which precluded the patient's ability to choose monogamy, and which contributed to the "transmisstion" of a cyclic pattern of psychodynamic pathology.

1939
COPING OF HEMOPHILIACS WITH/WITHOUT HIV-INFECTION

M.M.Schneider*, O.Seidl*, M.Ermann*, W.Schramm**
*Abt.f.Psychother.u.Psychosom.,Psychiatrische Klinik
**Abt.f.Hämostaseologie,Medizinische Klinik Innenstadt, der Universität München, FRG

The information about a positive HIV-Ab-test result is a highly traumatic event for hemophiliacs. We tried to find out whether the coping strategies, in respect of hemophilia and of HIV-infection, are stable and whether there are any differences in coping strategies between HIV-Ab-positive and negative hemophiliacs regarding the hemophilia.
We examined 20 HIV-infected asymptomatic hemophiliacs and 10 HIV-negative ones with same severe state of hemophilia A by depthpsychological interview technique. The interviews were rated according to a coping-manual(Heim,1986)relating to hemophilia and, in the respective cases to HIV-infection also.
HIV-infected hemophiliacs describe their dealing with HIV-infection as being similar to coping with hemophilia. There is a predominance of nonacceptance, denial and minimizing of illness, social isolation and lack of love. In contrast to this group the HIV-AB-negative ones try to cope with hemophilia mainly by acceptance of illness, emotional relief, extraversion and social care.
Our results show that coping strategies of HIV-infected hemophiliacs seem to be an invariable reaction towards hemophilia and HIV-infection. The fact that the coping strategies regarding infected and noninfected hemophiliacs are different might inpoint to some psychical cofactors of the disease which should be considered within psychosocial care.

Session 294 Free Communications:
Recent developments in clinical psychopharmacology

1940
CLINICAL TRIALS OF AMPEROZIDE IN SCHIZOPHRENIA

MERTENS C.*, DE WILDE J.,DIERICK M.**, BERGMAN I., GUSTAVSSON G.*** *Psych. Centra, Sleidinge, Belgium **St.Camillus, St Denys Westram, Belgium ***Pharmacia LEO Therapeutics AB, Helsingborg, Sweden

AMPEROZIDE is a novel substituted diphenylbutylpiperazinecarboxamide derivative with a high affinity for $5HT_2$ receptors but almost no affinity to neither D_1 nor D_2 binding sites in brain. Besides modulating dopaminergic nerve transmission in vivo in limbic pathways it has a unique limbic functional selectivity in both electrophysiological, biochemical and behavioural tests.
A total of 33 male patients with schizophrenia according to DSM III were treated with **AMPEROZIDE**. Ten of the patients were treated according to a dose escalation schedule from 2.5 mg b.i.d. to 10.0 mg b.i.d. and 23 patients were treated with either 2.5 mg b.i.d. or 5.0 mg b.i.d. in a double blind manner. Treatment period was four weeks.
The Brief Psychiatric Rating Scale (BPRS), the Comprehensive Psychopatological Rating Scale (CPRS) and the Clinical Global Impressions Scale (CGI) were used for analysis of therapeutic efficacy. Assessments for safety were made on a rating scale for extrapyramidal adverse symptoms (Simpson and Angus) and on a questionnaire for other adverse events. Laboratory investigations, ECG, pulse rate, blood pressure and body weight recordings were performed weekly during the study.
According to CGI 24 patients responded to the treatment. Two patients were unchanged and 7 nonresponders. The responders decreased their mean BPRS score with 52 % and mean CPRS score with 51 %. No differences in response could be noted between the dosage groups. Positive as well as negative symptoms of schizophrenia were reduced. Global tolerance was generally good with few and mild adverse events. Most frequent symptoms were nausea, anxiety and inner tension. These events were dose related. Mean score of the Simpson and Angus rating scale decreased from 1,1 to 0 during the treatment period. Laboratory investigations showed no clinical relevant deviations. No changes in plasma prolactin levels or body weight were recorded.
IN CONCLUSION the results of the present studies indicate that **AMPEROZIDE** is a nonsedative antipsychotic drug with effect on positive as well as negative symptoms, without extrapyramidal symptoms and with few and mild adverse symptoms.

1941
AMPEROZIDE - A NEW PUTATIVELY ANTIPSYCHOTIC DRUG WITH LIMBIC SELECTIVITY

E. Christensson, Dept. of CNS-Research, Pharmacia LEO Therapeutics AB, P.O.Box 839, S-201 80 Malmö, Sweden.

Amperozide, a diphenylbutylpiperazinecarboxamide derivative, was selected as a new potentially antipsychotic drug with effects exclusively on limbic system influenced behaviour in the animal screening. This agent is characterized by a high potency to block amphetamine-induced locomotion and a strong influence on emotional behaviour: it inhibits spontaneous mouse-killing, blocks social aggression, decreases immobility time in the behavioural despair test and displays potent anticonflict properties. Furthermore, amperozide blocks conditioned avoidance and spontaneous exploratory behaviour without causing sedation or ataxia of any kind. However, in contrast to classical neuroleptics amperozide does not induce catalepsy and does not block amphetamine-induced stereotypies. The selective limbic mode of action was further underlined by both biochemical and electrophysiological experiments.
In contrast to classical neuroleptics amperozide shows almost no affinity for D_2 receptors in the brain. Besides a rather high affinity for $5-HT_2$ receptors amperozide in tested systems exhibits an affinity only for the α_1 receptors. The almost total lack of dopamine receptor blocking potency may explain why amperozide does not cause evident extrapyramidal side effects in monkeys and does not increase prolactin levels, neither in rats nor in man.
Taken together, the activity profile of amperozide points towards the possibility that this agent could ameliorate both positive and negative symptoms in schizophrenic patients. Results from preliminary clinical trials have been promising and fit in very well with these predictions.

1942
EFFECT OF MELPERONE IN TREATMENT-RESISTANT SCHIZOPHRENIA

H.Y. Meltzer, L.D. Alphs, B. Bastani and L. Ramirez, Case Western Reserve University, Cleveland, Ohio, U.S.A.

Melperone is a butyrophenone antipsychotic drug (APD) with properties similar to clozapine: e.g. weak catalepsy and transient plasma prolactin (PRL) increases in rodents as well as low extrapyramidal symptoms (EPS) in man. Both drugs are potent serotonin$_2$ antagonists relative to their D-2 dopamine receptor antagonism.
Results of an open study in which melperone and clozapine were each given to 20 treatment resistant schizophrenic patients will be presented. Preliminary results indicate melperone in doses up to 500 mg/day produced slight-moderate reductions in positive and negative symptoms in approximately one-third of the patients but had no apparent effect by 6 weeks in the others. Clozapine was somewhat more effective in 60-70% of the patients. Side effects with both drugs were minimal. Melperone did not block tardive dyskinesia, whereas clozapine did. The results of biological studies comparing melperone to clozapine and typical neuroleptic drugs will also be presented. The similarities and differences between melperone and clozapine will be discussed.

1943

VINPOCETINE IN THE TREATMENT OF DEMENTIA

H.-H. Fuchs*, H. Erzigkeit**
Department of Neurology and Clinical Neurophysiology, Städt. Krankenhaus München-Bogenhausen, ** Department of Psychiatry, University of Erlangen-Nürnberg, Fed.Rep.of Germany

A placebo controlled, randomised double-blind multicenter study to determine the efficacy and tolerance of orally administered vinpocetine was performed on 165 patients suffering from a mild to moderately severe dementia. The treatment groups were uniformly distributed in a 30 mg/die and a 60 mg/die vinpocetine and a placebo group. The Clinical Global Impression (CGI) and the cognitiv performance test SKT were employed as aim parameters.
The CGI of the treating physician indicated in the degree of sverity a significant improvement compared with placebo, also in the change in the condition. In the SKT, a statistically significant difference was found after eight weeks of treatment in the 30 mg/die group, at the end of the study in both verum groups. Therapeutic effectivness received a significantlybetter evaluation for 30mg/die vinpocetine, atrend existed for this respect for the 60mg/die dosage. The tolerance of the drug tested was designated both by the physicians and the the patients almost without exception in their final evaluation as good or satisfactory.
A more than incidental improvement has been determined in the symptoms of dementia.

1944

The Clinical Efficacy of Citalopram in Treatment of Emotional Disturbances in Dementia Disorders.

A L. Nyth, C-G. Gottfries, K. Elgen, K. Engedal, A. Harenko, P. Juhela, I. Karlsson, T. Koskinen, H. Nygaard, V. Pedersen, S.M. Samuelsson, A. Yli-Kerttula.

The clinical efficacy of a selective 5-HT reuptake inhibitor, citalopram, was investigated in 98 patients with moderate AD/SDAT or vascular dementia (VD). The investigation was conducted as a Nordic multicentre study with a combined double-blind and open technique with placebo and citalopram. Analyses were made for each diagnosis after four weeks of double-blind treatment. In addition to the cognitive impairment most patients also showed a great deal of emotional disturbances. Patients with AD/SDAT treated with citalopram showed a significant improvement in emotional bluntness, confusion, irritability, anxiety, fear-panic, depressed mood and restlessness. Those improvements were not found after treatment with placebo. There were no significant improvements in patients with VD. No improvements were recorded in motor or cognitive impairment. Citalopram was found to provoke few and comparatively mild side effects. None of the changes observed during the double-blind withdrawal period could be identified as withdrawal symptoms or rebound phenomena.

1945

SCREENING OF THE ANTIDEPRESSANT MINAPRINE ON ENCEPHALOTROPIC EFFECTS VS PIRACETAM AND PLACEBO AFTER ACUTE AND SUBCHRONIC ADMINISTRATION IN HUMANS - USING HYPOXIA-MODEL

K. Schaffler[1], G. Kauert[2], M. Gierend[3]

Minaprine - an amino-phenylpyridazine derivative - used as an antidepressant especially in inhibitory states - is devoid of anticholinergic effects, but facilitates (pre- and postsynaptic) dopaminergic, serotonergic and cholinergic transmission. Studies on depression in demented patients showed positive results vs placebo. In senile dementia - especially of Alzheimer type (AT) - there exists a lack of dopaminergic and cholinergic mechanisms with or without concomitant depressive states. Due to its pharmacological profile the drug seems to be useful in AT and NAT senile dementias.

Animal and human models of hypoxia have demonstrated to be an adequate approach for partial simulation of dementia with respective influences on cerebral metabolism and blood supply and a down-regulation of CNS-related information processing.

To approach the respective potency of minaprine as an encephalotropic an experimental set-up was designed in healthy subjects to avoid statistically inhomogeneous samples of dementia patients with different pathophysiological states. It was a randomized, placebo-controlled, double-blind 3-way crossover study in 9 healthy male subjects with acute and subchronical administration (1 week) of minaprine and piracetam as reference (dosages ac/sc: 200 and 400 mg, 2400 and 2400 mg respectively). Psycho- and electrophysiological methods used were: Oculodynamic Test (ODT = Electrooculography and choice reaction), Resting- and Vigilance-controlled EEG, each under normobaric administration of 10.5 % oxygen. After normoxic and hypoxic prevalues further p.a.-assessments were done at hrs 1, 2 and 4 (at day 1 and 8 of each medication period with a one week washout-period in between).

Main variables of ODT (latency, reaction time, correct responses), which have a tight relation to everyday life (and its resulting socio-economic consequences), were positively influenced under hypoxia in the direction of a return to normoxia (improvement) by minaprine in acute and even more accentuated in the subchronic phase. Piracetam demonstrated positive influences too, but was less consistent in its pattern and decreasing in its efficacy from acute to subchronic drug administration. Time-efficacy pattern seems to be attributed more to the p-OH-metabolite of minaprine than to the mother drug or the lactam-derivative - as seen in correlation of pharmacodynamics[1] and qualitative kinetics[2] in this study. Drug effects on EEG were mainly seen in V-EEG. Hypoxia itself raised total power and absolute power of single frequency bands. Again minaprine demonstrated a more stimulating pattern (decrease in lower and increase in higher frequency bands in relative EEG-power), more consistent and longer-lasting effects than piracetam - thus fitting the same EEG-pattern as seen in gerontopsychiatric patients treated with encephalotropics.

---

[1] Institute for Pharmacodynamic Research, Kronstadterstr. 9, D-8000 Munich 80, FRG

[2] Institute for Forensic Medicine, University of Munich, (Head: Prof. Dr. Spann), Frauenlobstraße 7a, D-8000 Munich 2, FRG

[3] Sanofi-Midy, Augustenstraße 10, D-8000 Munich 2, FRG

1946

DIFFERENTIAL EFFECTS OF BROFAROMINE AND MOCLOBEMIDE ON MELATONIN SECRETION
Bieck, P. R., Mühlbauer, B., Antonin, K. H.
Human Pharmacology Institute Ciba-Geigy GmbH, D-7400 Tübingen, F.R.G.
Alterations in melatonin synthesis and release may be relevant to the mode of action of MAO-inhibiting drugs. We compared the effect of acute administration of the two new selective reversible MAO-A inhibitors brofaromine and moclobemide on daytime plasma melatonin measured by RIA. The drugs were given p.o. in clinically used doses to 8 healthy subjects at 9.00 a.m. with an interval of 1 week.

RESULTS:

Treatment	Dose <mg>	AUC (0-7h) <(ng/ml)*h>	Change <(ng/ml)*h>	
Placebo		101 ± 56		
Brofaromine	150	522 ± 267	+ 421	p< 0.002
Moclobemide	300	145 ± 52	+ 44	n.s.

CONCLUSION: Contrary to brofaromine, moclobemide does not influence daytime melatonin secretion. This might be due to weaker MAO-inhibition or to additional nonspecific effects.

1947
A DOUBLE BLIND COMPARATIVE TRIAL OF MELPERONE AND LORAZEPAM IN GENERALIZED ANXIETY DISORDER.

Ernst Rainer, Psychiatric clinic, Salzburg, Austria

Study objectives: To compare efficacy and safety between an atypical neuroleptic, melperone (Buronil[R], Eunerpan[R]) dosed 10 mg t.i.d. or 20 mg t.i.d. and a benzodiazepine, lorazepam dosed 1 mg t.i.d.

Material and methods: A randomized parallel group design was used. The study started with a single-blind placebo wash-out/run-in week, follow by four weeks of double-blind active treatment. Main inclusion criteria were Generalized Anxiety Disorder (DSM III) and a total score of at least 18 on HAMA after the wash-out week. 32 patients were included in the melperone low-dose group, 38 in the high-dose group and 34 in the lorazepam group. 103 of the 104 patients completed the study. Efficacy evaluations consisting of HAMA, CGI and a self rating scale for satisfaction level of medication were performed at admission, after the wash-out week and after 1, 2 and 4 weeks of active treatment. Adverse reaction evaluations and vital sign measurements were performed on the same occasions.

Results: Both melperone doses were as effective as lorazepam in improving anxiety symptomatology measured by HAMA and CGI. The patients were as satisfied with neuroleptic as with benzodiazepine therapy. The only adverse reaction arising was tiredness, experienced by single patients in each group. No orthostatic reactions, no influence on mean blood pressures and no body weight changes were registered.

Conclusions: The atypical neuroleptic, melperone, was as effective and safe as a benzodiazepine, lorazepam in reducing anxiety symptomatology. The high dose of melperone had no advantage over the low dose. These results agree with those of two studies by W.J. Pöldinger. In these, both melperone 10 and 25 mg t.i.d. were superior to placebo in anxiety patients. Also here the two doses were equally efficacious.

1948
DEPRESSION; LITHIUM AUGMENTATION VERSUS THE MAO-1 BROFAROMINE
Hoencamp E., Haffmans J., Dietrich R., Schipper J.
Psychiatric Centre Bloemendaal, P.O.Box 53002, 2505 AA The Hague, The Netherlands

An open controlled (pilot) study was performed to compare the addition of lithium to maprotiline (MaLi) with the reversible MAO-A-I brofaromine (B) in depressed out-patients. Patients were elegible for this study if they met the following criteria; refractory to cyclic antidepressant (maprotiline for at least 4 weeks with adequate dose and plasmalevel); major affective disorder (DSM-III-R); HRSD-score of at least 14. After a pretreatment assessment patients were radomly assigned to one of the treatment groups. Patients were seen for 7 consecutive weeks. On every visit the HRSD was rated by an independant blind rater and the standerdized Side Effect Scale by the therapist. The results of 11 patients will be presented as well as the results of 5 patients who were treated with B after MaLi combination, which did not lead to remission of the depressive symptoms (HRSD>14). Brofaromine seems to be at least as effective as MaLi using a 50% drop of the HRSD score as a positive response. B showed clear activation of the patients also of patients with longstanding depression and anxiety. On the neurosensory and neuroautonomic subscales of the side effect scale B showed less symptoms. The affective behavioral subscale scored higher for B because of sleep disturbances.

Session 295 Free Communications:
Disability of the elderly and its care

1949
THE FACTORS THAT INFLUENCE DISABILITY IN THE AGED

Dr.R.Sathianathan, Asst. Professor
Dr.V. Ramachandran, Addl. Professor
Department of Psychiatry
Madras Medical College, Madras, India.

This study is an offshoot of the project "Psychiatric Morbidity and Disability among the aged" sponsored by the Sandoz Foundation for Gerontological research, conducted in Madras, India. In this cross sectional community survey of a probability sample of aged people disability was assessed.

In India, the status of the aged is high and they are well integrated in the society. The various factors such as occupation, income, housing, family system, bereavement, recreation, social isolation, capacity for self care, health status, and disability were studied. A multiple regression analysis is carried out to estimate the extent of influence of these factors on disability. This paper will focus on the issues that emerged from this study.

1950
BECOMING DEPENDENT: MENTAL HEALTH WORKER'S FEARS OF ELDERLY PEOPLE.
Dr. Brian V. Martindale
Paddington Centre for Psychotherapy and St. Charles Hospital, London, UK.

My paper stems from clinical experience in psychotherapeutic work with the elderly and supervision of mental health professionals. The latter are often at a very different phase in their life cycle from their elderly patients.

I intend to talk about a group of elderly patients who have a range of symptoms with the same underlying, often unconscious, anxieties and fears of actually becoming dependent with accompanying fear of dependency needs not being met.

Younger mental health workers are at life phases where they are consolidating their individuation from their parents and building their own careers and families. They are often fearful that their parents will become severely dependent in a way that will seriously compromise their own developments. A professional relationship with a disturbed elderly person can elicit major transference anxieties for both partners in the psychotherapeutic encounter.

I will give brief clinical vignettes to show how failures to disentangle the two transferences leads to breakdowns in the provision of appropriate mental health care and mistaken attempts to provide brief interventions exacerbating the underlying fears of the elderly persons.

1951
DEVELOPMENT OF GERIATRIC PSYCHIATRY: THE NEXT STAGE
Martin G. Cole, St. Mary's Hospital, Montreal, Canada

The dramatic rise of geriatric psychiatry around the world may be viewed as an evangelical movement to improve the mental health care of the elderly. Inspired by values and fueled by rhetoric the geriatric psychiatry movement has focussed attention on the mental health needs of the elderly and has successfully lobbied educational institutions and governments to improve training and services in geriatric psychiatry. In the next stage of development, geriatric psychiatry must commit itself to expansion of the geriatric psychiatry knowledge base: rhetoric and superficial generalities must be replaced by sophisticated indepth knowledge needed for effective management of mental disorders common to old people. To this end, geriatric psychiatry research must focus first on four areas: diagnosis and treatment of depression, cost-benefit of neurological investigation of dementia, effectiveness and efficiency of geriatric psychiatry services, and finally, development of instruments to assess mental competence.

1952
A STUDY OF MULTIHANDICAPPED PATIENTS IN AMSTERDAM.
R.De Reus, W.R.A. Duurkoop, J.A.C. Bleeker.
Provincial Hospital Santpoort
Box 50, 2080 AB Santpoort
The Netherlands.

Multihandicapped patients (MHP) are patients with combined psychiatric and physical illness or handicaps. These patients appear to be difficult to plan for in the large scale modernization of mental health care in Amsterdam.
 The aim of this study is to define the psychiatric, physical and behavioral disturbances of MHP in the Amsterdam area.
 At the moment MHP are admitted by negative selection to a specialized (140 beds) ward of the Santpoort psychiatric hospital. There is a waiting list. Patients usually are old or very old. Aging of the dutch population as a whole makes it important to plan and prepare facilities for these patients.
 All 140 patients present were scored on a validated set of scales for psychiatric in-patient observation.
 The test battery was shown to discriminate for physical functioning and activities of daily living. Profiles of MHP differed from other in-patients. Several subgroups of MHP have been identified.

1953
DAY CARE OF THE ELDERLY MENTALLY ILL BY VOLUNTARY WORKERS

DR. F. OLIVER
Tameside General Hospital
Ashton-under-Lyne
Lancashire, OL6 9RW, England.

A joint Health Service project with the charity "Age Concern". Patients referred from Day Hospital for social support and rehabilitation with aim of full integration in general community.

Diagnoses - psychoses 45%, neuroses 40%, mild dementia 15%, living alone 50%, age over 75 years 45%.

Advantages:-

(1) Relieves Day Hospital at low cost to Health Service.

(2) Non hospital atmosphere reduces sickness behaviour.

(3) Personal attention of enthusiastic volunteers and members choice of activity, e.g. craft, games, conversation, cookery, trips.

(4) Access to consultant, community psychiatric nurse or social worker if necessary.

(5) Community psychiatric nurse supports meetings to share information of members and volunteers about social facilities in general community, resulting in 30% of members moving on.

(6) Volunteers trained, some moved on to paid work with elderly.

1954
INTENSIVE TREATMENT IN A PSYCHOGERIATRIC UNIT
F.Privorozky
Mental Hospital Tirat Hacarmel, Haifa, Israel

In this research we represent the experience at an acute closed psychogeriatric department (24 beds) which serves a 1/2 mil, population between September 1983 and March 1989.
During this period we hospitalized 504 patients with various diagnoses. Due to our new treatment strategies 88,8% from those who were hospitalized returned home and only 11,2% were transferred to other institutions to continue treatment.
Meanwhile mortality in our department was only 0,16 per 1000 among hospitalized patients.
Our method is based on five principles.
1. Urgent and deep physical and psychiatric check up of the patients.
2. Intensive pharmacological treatment from the first minute of the patients' hospitalization.
3. A high professional level in choosing the biological treatment used for each patient individually according to his age, physical status, the duration of his illness, diagnosis and the previous treatment.
4. Knowledge of the contemporary approach of using psycholeptic medicines in old age.
5. Different combinations of pharmacological treatment with ECT therapy and OT psychotherapy. Including sports and art therapy.
A condition for multifaceted treatment is a continued observation of the formerly hospitalized patient in psychogeriatric out patient clinic.

1955

SOCIAL CARE WORKER PROJECT FOR THE ELDERLY MENTALLY INFIRM
Satnam Singh Palia
Glanrhyd/Penyfai Hospitals, Bridgend, Mid Glam.
CF31 4LN South Wales, U.K.

On jointly financed basis between social services and health services, social care worker project team was established in OGWR (Bridgend) South Wales, in February 1988. It consists of a community psychiatric nurse, a social worker, a secretary and numbers of social care workers appointed on hourly basis to relieve the stress of carers in looking after their elderly mentally infirm (EMI) relatives. They are to perform a wide variety of domestic duties and to arrange for day care/relief admissions, day/night sitters etc. The full description would be given.
The data collected over a year (which would be described in detail) reveals that this team was involved with 45 clients and was successful in their primary goals of
(a) Releiving the stress of carers (lowering of general health questionnaire score)
(b) Lowering the need for long term residential care (old peoples home/hospitals) of the EMI and
(c) Improving the quality of life of such patients
Certainly this has become another novel way of looking after the elderly in their own home improvement.

1956

REHABILITATION OF DEMENTIA PATIENTS
Friedl E.J., Pfolz H.
Psychiatrisches Krankenhaus der Stadt Wien
Baumgartner Hohe, 1145 Vienna, Austria

The population-stastistics of the most industrial countries show an increase of the elderly people, which means also an increase of dementia patients and demand for gerontopsychiatric hospitals, ambulances and specialised social services.
In this paper we will describe a gerontopsychiatric treatment-model of the Psychiatric Hospital of Vienna. It offers extensive diagnostic, therapeutic and rehabilitative services. Also home treatment is organized by the hospital. The diagnostic and therapeutic acting will be shown, a special documentation system will be presented.
Based on current data we discuss, whether it is possible to make prognostic statements about the rehabilitation of dementia patients or not.

Session 296 Free Communications:
Philosophy and psychiatry

1957

MELANCHOLIA : THE CONCEPTUAL DIFFERENTIATION OF THE TERM IN ANCIENT HELLENIC LITERATURE.
C.N.Ballas
As a term medical, philosophical, as well as of the everyday language, "Melancholia" (Melancholy) has a very long history. Beginning in Hellenic antiquity is found with a very different at times content. In this work is made a comparative study of the conceptual differentiation of the term in the various medical and philosophical texts of ancient Hellenic literature, especially in Corpus Hippocraticum, Plato, Aristotle and Aretaeus of Cappadocia.
Greeks not only first put forward the question of depression, but they also gave its first answers. And these answers are of the foremost importance even for the present day Psychiatry, although their interpretation remaine inadequate. Hellenic thought made a unique course without its parallel, so that an interpretative approach of the Hellenic concepts on depression to be not a simple gesture of reverence - a vain historical occupation - but an effort to understand a difficult problem which harasses and will harass humanity maybe for ever.

1958

PROBLEMS RELATED IN AESTHETICS IN PSYCHIATRY
Christo Christozov, Liudmila Marinova
Medical Academy, Sofia, Bulgaria

The personality of man as a subject of medicine, and more particularly psychiatry, represents a unique individuality, and what's more, in it the biological and social aspects merge in a unity. The same holds true for the relationship of the beauty and health concepts. Consequently, the struggle against pathological conditions is a strive for beauty. The daily round of physician "abound ng of misfortunes" is a stimulus for a still more energetic search for aesthetic supporting points. Here the role played by the psychiatrist is of paramount importance, since he is called upon not only to accomplish the therapeutic goals in handling a concrete patient, but also to create a psychological climate of harmony and confidence which is absolutely indispensable for any human being, especially in the event of a mental disease.

1959

A PHILOSOPHIC APPROACH TO INTEGRATIVE MEDICINE AND PSYCHIATRY

VOGE HARMS, DONALD O.
PRIVATE PRACTICE, MERIDA, YUCATAN, MEXICO

The fields of Integrative Psychiatry and Integrative Medicine hold a great interest for the medical profession as a whole and especially for the future of Psychiatry. Both fields are discussed and it is made clear that there is no real separation between them but a gradual merger in areas common to both, with each specialist accepting the colaboration of other specialists in benefit of the patient, who is our real reason for being.

1960

MULTIPLE PERSONALITY AND KANT'S PARALOGISMS

Walter Massing, Tagesklinik der Nervenklinik Langenhagen, Königstraße 6 A, 3000 Hannover 1, West-Germany

One unproven assumption in our living together is, that I, you, we, each human person is a indivisible individual, continuous in "substance". The psychiatric phenomenon "multiple personality" reveals a change of paradigma in such a way, that the - philosophically formulated- commonplace: "as a soul I am simple substance and therefore I must be one - and not more than one - person" is not valid any longer. This situation draws the view to the remarkable parallel between the actually lived existences of "Multiple Personality" and the opinion of some philosophers (Hume, Kant..), that it is impossible to prove, that a person is one and the same across time. In a brilliant manner Kant shows, that the "proofs", giving evidence for "Personal Identity", are paralogisms - shamproofs.

1961

CRITICA A JASPERS

CARLOS ROBERTO ARICO
NEPP; SAO PAULO, BRASIL

The author criticizes Jasper's study on the "Comprehendible connections of Psychic Life", which until today influences psychiatric care. Jaspers attempts to show in this study the limitations existing on interpretations, which always assume a theoretical structure. It is worthy of noting that Jaspers uses on several occasions the "hermenetic" method which he himself questions.
The author stresses the fact that many events are incomprehensible, if we do not consider the theory and practice of the unconscious.
At the end of the presentation, analogies between Lacan and Szasz are presented, citing the real, imaginary and symbolic planes, unknown to Jaspers.

1962

CONTEMPORARY PSYCHIATRY AND POST-MODERNITY

R.Rogue, G.Vincendon, Centre du Neurochimie du C.N.R.S., Strasburg, France

A renewed interest for taxonomy is manifest in contemporary psychiatry. Current classifications emphasize description and reliability, and pretend to be atheoretical with regards to aetiology. This itself is theoretical as underlying this approach are pragmaticism and logical empiricism, a particular philosophy of science which considers causes as general predictive laws derived from observation. The social impact of diagnosing is another underrecognized aspect of nosography. According to M. FOUCAULT clinical psychiatry originated when insanity ceased to be seen as determined by a mistaken apprehension of reality, and began to be thought of in terms of behaviours deviating from a norm. Psychiatrist became thus invested with a normative power. In this perspective diagnosis is not simply a classificatory step but also has strength of judgment. This raises the question of the necessary emancipation of the patient from this form of power embodied in knowledge ("pouvoir-savoir"). From a similar perspective critical theory, in the writtings of T. ADORNO or J. HABERMAS, also sets out to unveil such ideological deviations. This analysis of psychiatric thought is an application of the more general critique of modernity. The issues raised by the post-modernist critique will be discussed with respect to their potential importance for contemporary psychiatry.

1963

MIND AND MATTER, BODY AND BEHAVIOR, A GLOBAL PERSPECTIVE
Magno J. Ortega, M.D., Assoc. Clin. Prof., UC, S.Francisco

The concept of "psyche" as spirit is unchanged, but as "mind" it changed after "logos" as "intelligence" produced such absolutes as "truth" and "beauty" with the predictable circularity of "logic".

"Mind" as "consciousness" was separated from matter by the Greeks, from the body by theologians, from spirit by Descartes, from "reason" by Freud, and then from logic by Piaget.

Piaget lists (A) sensori-motor development in infants, (B) pre-operational or pre-conceptual intuition and con-cretistic trial-and-error search for solutions among toddlers, and ends with (C) "rational" thought or formal abstractions and logical reductionism.

In fact, after our brain is squeezed during delivery, we start with (A) "feeling" or "wishing" or "believing" and then regain (B) "animal intuition" with leaps of insight or visceral knowledge without intellectualization. Some doubts generate cogitation which get recognition as (C) "thoughts" or "theories" or "reasons" to (D) probe, test or prove, or enable us to (E) connect, invent, or create.

Our doubts can take us beyond Piaget and psychoanalysts and away from their separate goals of liberating or leading the mind or consciousness from or out of irrational, if not illogical, oppression or arrested development.

We can get far with (D) comparative rationalysis to sort out ratios in exploring correlations, and further with (E) creativity in discovering non-random connections to (1) restore "spirit" to mythology and mysticism, (2) reunite the "mind" with the body, and the brain with behavior as matter in motion, and (3) get past "reason" and "logic" to homology in biology for a post-logical, post-industrial civilization.

1964

THE MAJOR DYSCHRONIES
Agrimi G., Andreani F., Arena A., Bizzari D., Dazzini E., Lazzerini F., Piccini P., Raimondi R.
Department of Mental Health, Massa Carrara, Italy

Being in synchrony with the world is not very difficult for a mineral, for a vegetable and also for an animal. Things are different for human beings. Especially being in synchrony with the world, for the more civilized populations, becomes more complex and, therefore, difficult. The time experience is the resultant of three contemporary temporalities. When this resultant permits one to live in synchrony, timewise, with other human beings, it determines a psycho-condition which is then called "Eucronia". The three temporalities derive from different functions. The first one is functional to the necessity of living in synchrony with the world, the second one to the necessity of being in the world diachronicly, the third-one to the need to decrease the pain and overcome the difficulties produced by the experience of the diachronical flowing of the time. The predominance or the absence, for primary or secondary causes, of one of temporality functions, relatively to the two others, determines an abnormal psycho-condition reconductable, in different forms, to the main psychiatric disturbances.
Such abnormal psychical conditions are gathered into the group of Dyschronies.

1965

DALLA FILOSOFIA DEL BISOGNO ALLA FILOSOFIA DELLE PROGETTUALITA'. NECESSITA' DI UNA SCELTA TEORICA NELL'INDIVIDUAZIONE DI UNA STRATEGIA GESTIONALE PER UN DAY HOSPITAL PSICHIATRICO.
E.Lazzarin, M.Mondino, T.Chirco, 1o Centro di Salute Mentale, Vicenza, Italy

Gli autori riesaminano criticamente le difficoltà teoriche e pratiche da loro incontrate nel progettare, organizzare ed attivare un D.H.P.. In particolare si soffermano sulla necessità di individuare una strategia gestionale e sul perchè, tra varie possibili caratterizzazioni di essa siano stati portati a previlegiare quelle terapeutiche e sul come ciò comporti l'inevitabilità di scegliere tra posizioni teoriche diverse. Organizzare un'esperienza che permetta di cogliere e potenziare le capacità residue di uno psicotico di progettarsi nella realtà riconquistando una sua dimensione storica è stato preferito al creare uno spazio di comprensione e di espressione del bisogno psicotico, pur non negandolo da una parte nè dall'altra sforzandosi per un suo inutile contenimento o presuntuosa repressione.

1966

CONFLICT ANALYSIS: THE FORMAL THEORY OF BEHAVIOR
Albert J.Levis, U.S.A.

This presentation reviews the contribution of two recent publications: **Conflict Analysis - The Formal Theory of Behavior**, which introduces an historical conceptual breakthrough, and **Conflict Analysis Testing and Training**, applying the theory into psychometrics and psychoeducation. The Formal conceptual breakthrough transforms behavior into a pure natural science which reconciles traditional schools of thought and integrates the humanities, the social science disciplines, into an orderly, conceptual continuum. Individual psychopathology, cultural phenomena, religions, political theories and value systems are clarified as part aspects of the totality. The formal conceptualization and technology lead to the accurate evaluation of individuals and systems and facilitate reaching personal insights of universal validity.

Methodologically, the theory analyzes behavioral phenomena in terms of Conflict Resolution Process (CRP) units. The CRP unit is physics' Simple Harmonic Motion (SHM) applied to behavior. CRP is a cyclic phenomenon entailing a mental oscillation described by the constructs and the formulas of the oscillation of the pendulum. CRP processes lower forms of energy, stress-conflict, into higher forms, order, insights, and growth. The CRP is a pump for the upgrading of energy.

The implications of the formal organization of mental and behavioral experience are profound but finite, i.e., the Conflict Resolution Process as a typical syndromal entity. Four alternative power structurings of relations, each lead to different resolutions, personality profiles, and constellations of outcomes. The Formal Theory is relevant to the development of psychoeducation programs, including the integration of knowledge, attainment of personal insights through the creation and formal analysis of sample personal processes to educate the individual in the factors leading him to the creation of conflict and facilitation of its resolution.

Session 297 Symposium:
Etiology of schizophrenia

1967
ETIOLOGY OF SCHIZOPHRENIA: AN OVERVIEW

Einar Kringlen

Department of psychiatry, University of Oslo.

Schizophrenic disorder involves the interaction of biological and environmental factors. Epidemiological and family research, in particular twin and adoption studies, has shown the significance of both genetic and environmental factors. However, neither genetically nor environmentally oriented research has yet been able to identify the etiological factors that are necessary and/or sufficient for the disorder.

Today there is a hectic activity in the field of linkage studies and molecular biology in order to identify the genetic basis of the disorder. However, for several reasons the task ahead will be extremely difficult.

The schizophrenic symptoms and functioning are evidently not inherited, but acquired by social learning and human interaction. However, we do not know how this learning takes place. Some blame early interaction between child and mother, others emphasize the family as a whole, and still others point to personality factors and life events.

In this general review, I shall draw attention to the many puzzles that confront us in this field, and emphasize previous research data, that nowadays often tend to be forgotten.

1968
THE NEURODEVELOPMENTAL MODEL OF SCHIZOPHRENIA

ROBIN MURRAY, SHON LEWIS, ALICE FOERSTER
GENETICS SECTION, INSTITUTE OF PSYCHIATRY, DE CRESPIGNY PARK SE5

Pre- and perinatal hazards (henceforth termed obstetric complications or OCs) are well known to increase the risk of later schizophrenia. Our research shows that OCs are associated with enlarged ventricles and widening of the cortical sulci; furthermore, schizophrenics with a history of OCs have an earlier onset, fewer affected relatives, and more premorbid abnormalities of personality and intellectual function.

We consider that damage (particularly hypoxic-ischaemic) during the pre- or perinatal period, induces abnormalities of neural development in such cases; damage can act additively with, or even substitute for, genetic predisposition. The hippocampus is particularly vulnerable to such damage, and cytoarchitectural abnormalities consistent with abnormal neuronal migration to the hippocampus have been reported in several recent studies of the brains of schizophrenic patients.

Data will be presented to show that such a model can explain what have hitherto been regarded as curious epiphenomena of schizophrenia - abnormal laterality, soft neurological signs, and the earlier onset of schizophrenia in males. A collaborative study is now examining the relationship between genetic risk, OC's, childhood abnormality and adverse life events in schizophrenics and a comparison group of affective psychotics

1969
THE RELEVANCE OF HIGH-RISK RESEARCH

Fini Schulsinger

University of Copenhagen, Copenhagen, Denmark

High-Risk studies in schizophrenia were for the first time implemented by Mednick and Schulsinger in Copenhagen 1962. They used the longitudinal prospective research design on a sample of 207 children of severely schizophrenic mothers and 104 matched low-risk controls. They were 10-20 years old at the beginning of the study.
Repeated follow-up examinations have resulted in the identification of risk-factors: Perinatal complications, cerebral ventricular enlargement, early institutional rearing. These risk factors resulted in schizophrenia spectrum diseases only in interaction with genetic risk for schizophrenia. The implications of these results will be discussed in relation to ongoing new research on the etiology of schizophrenia.

1970
Life events and Expressed Emotion in Schizophrenia.

P.Bebbington

Evidence over a long period suggests that psychosocial stress influences the timing and course of schizophrenic disorders. Most attention has been devoted to life events and family stresses. I will review the evidence about life events, which remains thin. Extensive studies of family stress have used the Expressed Emotion (EE) measure. They are of particular interest because they have implications at once theoretical and clinical. I will give an account of the development of the EE measure over the last thirty years and of the early studies using it carried out in the MRC Social Psychiatry Unit, London. There have now been a considerable number of studies from around the world demonstrating the predictive value of EE, although two recent investigations reported negative findings. These results will be placed in context. Good evidence of the value of EE comes from intervention studies, and these will be reviewed. Investigations of the construct validity of EE will be described. Finally, the clinical implications of the EE research will be identified.

1971
CULTURAL FACTORS IN THE ETIOLOGY OF SCHIZOPHRENIA

Dr Norman SARTORIUS, World Health Organization, Geneva

The findings of WHO studies on schizophrenia throw new light on its etiology. The fact that incidence of schizophrenia in different countries is so similar could be interpreted as indicating that the syndrome of schizophrenia is a common form of presentation for a variety of diseases whose frequency varies in different countries. The variance in the course and outcome of schizophrenia, confirmed in cross-cultural studies carried out by WHO, would offer support for this interpretation.

The results of several recent studies indicating a decrease in the proportion of cases of schizophrenia with dramatic features and a decrease in admissions for schizophrenia to hospitals in countries with well developed services as well as the appearance of the disease slightly later in years according to observations made in recent years are possibly also indications of a change in the nature of the disease parallel to changes of the environment in time.

1972
* Number left open for technical reasons not corresponding to any abstract

Session 298 Symposium:
Psychosocial and transcultural psychiatric aspects in Latin America

1973
TRANSCULTURAL ASPECTS IN THE OCTAGONAL CLASSIFICATION IN PSYCHIATRY

Ramirez E. - Puerto Rico

1974
MANIFESTACIONES DEL PROCESO TRANSCULTURAL DEL PERU

Dr. Manuel Ponce (Dr. Roberto Llanos Zuloaga)
Instotuto Nacional de Salud Mental "Victor Larco Nerrera"

El A. señgla que la imibricación de culturas en el Perú no sólo ha producido el mestizaje o criollo racial sino que ha dado lugar a conductas y comportamientos "sui generis" que por momentos sparecen caóticos y en otros aspectos surgen como conductas adaptativas de la mayor especificidad. Las orientaciones cultural y conductuales en el Perú se debaten en una disyuntiva multirectorial pero que se pueden resumir entre regresar a modos de comportamiento tradicionales de épocas anteriores, hasta remontarse a las organizaciones sociales del Imperio Incaico, por un lado o de avanzar en procesos de aculturacjon promovidos por la cienca y la technología actuales pero que suponen una ruptura casi total con la Historia y la tradición. Tal disyuntiva tiene como resultado conductas contradictorias, no confluentes y a vaces absurdas. El A. también analiza una variedad de aspectos de la vida de los individuos y del grupo tales como el uso de la vía pública, las actividades comerciales, las actividades sociales, actividades deportivas y ce recreación, actividades laborales y actividades politicas, etc. Se señala la urgencia de una toma de decisiones que definan la orientación cultural y conductual del grupo a fín de concluir y alguna vez integrarse como nación.

1975
TRANSCULTURAL ASPECTS OF ALCOHOLISM IN ARGENTINA

Lluesma O. - Universidad de Salvador, Buenos Aires, Argentina

1976
PSYCHIATRIC AND TRANSCULTURAL ASPECTS OF THE SYMBIOTIC MIGRATING MARRIAGES

Roberto Llanos, M.D.
Universidad Cayetano Heredia; Lima 27, Peru

1. En las parejas de países europeos desarrollados (ej. Alemania), la proximidad simbiótica puede producirse como necesidad de defensa del capital reunido (capital económico e intelectual), o para asumir, funciones en una sociedad de consumo.
2. En les países en desarrollo, el matrimonio simbiótico puedo tomar una de las tres formas siguientes:
PADRE SALVADOR -- Niño adaptado sumiso:
(genio o lastima) Tristeze o culpa.
PADRE CRITICO -- Niño adaptado sumiso:
miedo y remerdimiento.
PADRE CRITICO -- Niño adaptado rebelde:
Culpa y resentimiento.
3. Les parejas matrimoniales peruanes, pueden reunirse en cuatro grupos significatives.

1977
SALUD MENTAL, MIGRACION Y DESARROLLO

Alberto Perales, M.D.
Instituto Nacional de Salud Mental "Honorio Delgado-Hideyo Noguchi" (PERU)

El autor fundamenta la importancia de la salud mental - a la que diferencia conceptualmente de la psiquiatría - para el desarrollo del ser humano y de los pueblos. Bajo esta perspectiva, señala los problemas psiquiátricos y de salud mental más urgentes en el Perú vinculados al proceso migratorio interno que vuelca la poblacion rural hacia las grandes ciudades.

Session 299 Symposium:
Relationship between personality disorders and psychosis

1978
CLASSIFICATION OF PERSONALITY DISORDERS AND DEMARCATION TO NORMALS
Lesch, O.M.
Psychiatric Univ.Clinic, Vienna, Austria

Definition and classification of personality disorder still represents a challenge. Typologies on a nosological basis have not yet been developed. One of the main reasons for this could lie in the influence of selection criteria.
We refrained,therefore,from defining our case groups according to diagnosis, but formed instead 3 groups of psychotic patients in regard to treatment: Group 1/ patients admitted to a psychotherapeutic ward;- Group 2/those admitted to a general psychiatric ward;- and Group 3/former hospital patients, subsequently under out-patient care. All cases were examined under application of psychometry, as well as SKID and DIB. SKID as well as DIB showed little correspondence. DIB exhibited a rather low sensitivity as a screening instrument for borderline disturbance.Psychometric investigation resulted in a clear demonstration of the heterogenity of these patients. Therefore, we recommend a polydiagnostic approach with special emphasis on personal vulnerability and attribution styles, mode of treatment, sociological lifestyle, and life-events.

1979
Personality traits and schizophrenia

Henning SASS, MD.
Psychiatric Clinic, University of Munich

Three main questions are contained in this topic: Firstly, are there abnormal personality traits in the relatives of schizophrenics, i.e. the concepts of inherited vulnerability and schizophrenic spectrum disorder. Secondly, do persons manifesting schizophrenic symptoms later in life, show special personality traits beforehand, i.e. the concept of a specific premorbid personality. Thirdly, which are the abnormal personality traits of schizophrenic or formerly schizophrenic patients, i.e. the concepts of interaction or comorbidity between schizophrenic and personality disorders. The conceptual issues of these possible relationships are discussed. Empirical data on the second and third points are presented gathered during the personality assessment of patients with schizophrenic disorders according to DSM-III criteria. The personality traits were registered with an integrated checklist for personality disorders according to DSM-III and ICD-10. In addition four "subaffective" personality disorders were investigated according to the typologies of Kretschmer and K. Schneider (asthenic, cyclothymic, dysthymic and depressive form). The results show a marked overlap between the personality disorder within axis 2, but there are also close relationships between the registered abnormal personality traits and different types of schizophrenic disorder on axis 1.

1980
PARANOIA AND PARANOID PERSONALITY DISORDER

G.Darcourt, Ph.Robert
Clinique de Psych.et de Psychol.Médicale
Hopital Pasteur, 06002 Nice, France

Paranoia and paranoid personality disorder can be compared from four viewpoints:

1.- Feelings of persecution or jealousy... are delusions in paranoia while these feelings are,in the paranoid personality disoder, suspiciousness or even conviction. The limit cannot be clearly defined.

2.- Hypersensitivity as, for example the tendency to be easily slighted and quick to take offence is not a symptom of paranoia. It was a major aspect of the Paranoid Personality Disorder in the DSM III and it is a minor aspect in the DSM III R.

3.- Restricted affectiviy,also, is not a symptom of paranoia. It was a major aspect of the Paranoid Personality Disorder in the DSM III and it is a minor aspect in the DSM III R.

4.- Rigidity of the Personality is not considered in the DSM III and DSM III R,neither for Paranoia nor for the Paranoid Personality Disorder. However, it is an important symptom in the French psychiatric classifications.

1981
Personality and personality disorders in mood disorders.

S. Torgersen, R. Alnaes,
Department of Psychology,
Department of Psychiatry,
University of Oslo, Norway.

Recent results from a study of consecutive psychiatric outpatients in Norway are presented. One-hundred-and-eighty-nine patients with mood disorders are compared to 84 other patients as to personality and personality disorders. It turns out that a specific pattern of personality and personality traits are typical for each of the mood disorders, the bipolar disorder, major depression, cyclothymic and dysthymic disorder. The personality of socalled double depressions and mixed anxiety-depression cases are also discussed.

1982
PROBLEMS OF PREMORBID PERSONALITY IN THE ATYPICAL PSYCHOSES

Tetsuo FUKUDA, M.D., D.Med.Sci., Osaka Institute of Clinical Psychiatry, Osaka-Takatsuki 569, and Doshisha University, Kyoto 602, Japan.

Atypical Psychoses are identified with various designations, i.e. acute schizo-affective psychosis(Kasanin), schizophreniform psychosis(Langfeldt), Cycloid psychosis(Leonhard), to name only a few. As the proponent of the cycloid psychoses, Leonhard and von Trostorff find the prepsychotic temperaments to be "Überschwenglich"(accentuated or exuberant) prone to strong affect-excitability in Angst-Glücks-psychose, and "abschweifend"(deviating) or "langsam"(slow-tempoed) in Verwirrtheitspsychose, respectively; a "Bewegungstemperament" associated with rich expressive movement belongs to Motilitätspsychose. In our Atypical Psychoses, prepsychotic personality has been recognized to be either cyclothymic or epileptoid, exhibiting enthusiasm, immaturity, lack of self-control in many and the ixothym(sticky-prolix:Strömgren) in some. These are on the whole pretty much similar to what Leonhard's school has found as in the above if the 3 clinical types are looked upon as interchangeable as they are in reality. Important dissimilarity, however, lies in the fact that Leonhard does not seem to deal with an involvement of the epileptoid coloring in prepsychotic personality.

Session 300 Symposium:
National programs/models of care

1983
CARE OF MENTAL HEALTH IN SPAIN AND SPANISH SPEAKING COUNTRIES
Sacristan J.R., Chairman Dept. of Psychiatry
Child Psychiatric Clinic, Univ. of Sevilla, Spain

The problems arising from the mental health disorders in people with mental retardation in the spanish-speaking cultural area are analysed. These are: 1) Degree of awareness of the problems, 2) Professional changes of attitude, 3) The relationship between the practical application of the principle of normalization and integration in each country and the psychopathologic disorders presented, 4) The organization of the attending services, 5) The influence of economic and social factors, 6) Topics and technical problems that are more interesting: Epidemiology; the ways of evaluation; professional training. We have gathered comparative data from several countries, especially referred to Spain.

1984
SERVICES FOR PSYCHIATRICALLY DISORDERED MENTALLY HANDICAPPED ADULTS - A U.K. PERSPECTIVE
Dr. K. A. Day, Consultant Psychiatrist
Northgate Hospital, Morpeth, Northumberland, England.
Mental handicap is a psychiatric speciality in the U.K. and doctors and nurses working in the field undergo special training. New approaches to care and the planned phasing out of mental handicap hospitals raise questions as to how psychiatrically and behaviourally disturbed mentally handicapped should be catered for in a new service. As yet there is no national policy and the situation is one of conflict and uncertainty. The main areas of debate are: specialised versus generic sevices, should psychiatry be responsible for the behaviourally disturbed; how should a specialised psychiatric service be provided? The Royal College of Psychiatrists is in favour of a specialised service because of the unique features attending the diagnosis and treatment (R.C. Psych.1986). Sufficient treatment settings are required to cater for the spectrum of problems presented and the range of intellectual levels. A single campus site enables the provision of a fully comprehensive service, permits the most economic use of specialist staff time and is more cost effective. A working example will be described (Day 1983). Special facilities for rehabilitation and continuing care are also needed together with regional and national provision for those requiring treatment under conditions of security. A model for future service provision will be suggested. DAY K.A. (1983) A Hospital Based Psychiatric Unit for Mentally Handicapped Adults. Mentally Handicap 11, 137-140. Royal College of Psychiatrists (1986) Psychiatric Services for Mentally Handicapped Adults and Young People. Bulletin 10 321-322.

1985
CURRENT MODELS OF CARE IN JAPAN
Akihiko Takahashi; Kisen Center for Development; Disabilities. Tokyo, Japan.
Our recent survey study revealed that facilities for developmentally disabled children of Japan are using many methods and techniques for treatment of behavior disorders seen in mental retardation such as psychotherapy, PT, OT, behavior modification, Montessori method, holding method, and others. Among their most preferred ones as the basis for their treatment were Ayers' sensory integration method and pedagogical method for preschool children. Although there are such a wide variety of methods and techniques under use, it has become obvious that most therapists took the following two as their fundamental aims of treatment in common, that is, to compensate disordered function(s) in sensori-motor area and to stabilize emotional states of children. Those findings show that, regardless of difference of method, critical issues in clinical situation of treatment is to integrate remedial approach to particular function and stabilizing approach to emotional condition. Key issue in doing this is to create a relationship of reliance between the client and therapist at the initial contact of session. Desirable relationship can be achieved through either acceptance or directive intercourse. The essential cue is not in the procedure of handling of children but the attitude of sympathy and the will to understand the child on the side of the therapist.

1986

PSYCHIATRIC CARE FOR MENTALLY HANDICAPPED IN THE NETHERLANDS

G.J. Zwanikken, Catholic University,
Nijmegen, The Netherlands

The psychiatric care for the mentally handicapped has been neglected for a number of years after the separation of psychiatry and care for the mentally handicapped.
At the moment an appeal for help is made to psychiatry out of the field of the care for mentally handicapped.
Psychiatry and mental handicap are interwoven in many ways.
An account is given of the state of affairs and the desirable developments concerning the consultation of psychiatry in the care for the mentally handicapped.
Areas of attention in the training of psychiatrists are formulated.

1987

THE SYSTEM OF SERVICES FOR MENTALLY RETARDED PERSONS IN BELGIUM
Jaak Geutjens, M.D.
St.-Oda Institute, Overpelt, Belgium
Till fifteen years ago the care of the mentally retarded persons in Belgium was often restricted to big institutions for mentally retarded children with overcrowded wards. The adult retarded persons either stayed at home without adequate help or occupations, or were placed in large psychiatric hospitals. Yet thousands of adult mentally retarded persons remain in densely populated wards with a mixed population of chronical psychiatric patients and mentally retarded persons. In the last few years more and more small adapted homes and day-treatment services were founded. The big institutions for children grew to services with various possibilities: day-treatment, residentual services, community-settings, e.t.c. Services for home-assistance were established a few years ago, with a well trained staff (pedagogue, social worker, various therapeutists), providing home-care for the parents and mentally retarded persons, who prefer to stay at home. The care of the mentally retarded persons in Belgium is, as for other matters, separately organised in the Dutch-speaking part (Flanders) and the French-speaking part (Wallonia) of the country. In Flanders "The Medical, Social and Pedagogical Fund for handicapped Persons" subsidises the complete local working (buildings, staff, e.t.c.), but takes by itself no initiatives to create facilities or services. Due to the recent evolution to smaller facilities the problems of mentally retarded persons with conduct disorders or psychiatric problems are strongly recognized. On governmental level there are plans to create in every province ($\pm$ 1.000.000 people) a special unit for observation and treatment of mentally retarded persons with psychiatric symptomatology and conduct disorders.

1988

PSYCHIATRIC SERVICES FOR THE MENTALLY RETARDED/ MENTALLY ILL IN THE UNITED STATES

Frank Menolascino, M.D.
Univ. of Nebraska Medical Center, Omaha,NE.,U.S.A

In the United States, psychiatric services for mentally retarded citizens tend to be provided: A) In institutions for the mentally retarded (e.g. by visiting consultants rather than full-time professionals); B) As active parts of an outpatient clinic (e.g., Program of Dr. Steve Reiss in Chicago IL); C) As part of a University Affiliated Program (e.g., usually via a multi-disciplinary team), and D) Special inpatient – outpatient service systems for these complex citizens (e.g., like the St. Joseph Center for Mental Health in Omaha, NE).
An increasing number of private practitioners (i.e., psychiatrists, social workers, and clinical psychologists) are presently entering this special field of mental health services in the United States.
The overall pattern of services, and how they differ in different regions of the United States will be discussed. Lastly, recent national guidelines for the provision of these services will be provided.

Session 301   Symposium:
Hermeneutics and psychiatry

1989

HERMENEUTICS, DIALECTICS AND PSYCHIATRY

Otto Doerr-Zegers
University of Chile in Santiago, Dept. of Psychiatry

Hermeneutics -understood as the art of interpretation- reveals itself as essential for understanding psychopathological phenomena insofar these surpass the possibilities of natural sciences. An hermeneutic attitude is important both in the pre-verbal as well as in the verbal encounter with psychiatric patients. Examples of the role of hermeneutics in the first stage of encounter are Rümke's description of "Praecox-Gefühl" (feeling of what is schizophrenic) and our description of "Melancholie-Gefühl" (feeling of what is melancholia). Apart from the obvious importance of hermeneutics in psychotherapy we focus our analysis of the verbal encounter describing its role in the comprehension of thought and/or language disorders.
After a brief description of the transcendence of dialectics in the history of western thinking, we try to demonstrate the advantages of such perspective in psychiatry: to see the positivity of the negative; to question the rigidity of concepts normal-abnormal, healthy-ill, etc.; to look at the different psychopathological conditions as displayed in polarities, being one side the positivity respecting the other one and viceversa, and to consider the healing process as a way in the opposite direction till getting the balance in the right proportion or greek measure. Finally, we attempt to show how hermeneutics and dialectics are essentially linked, because the opening characterizing hermeneutics is materialized in the question, whose inherent negativity is isomorph with the one of dialectic experience. In turn, psychiatry praxis demands the capacity of knowing how to question, how to fail and how to dialectically rescue the knowledge just from this failure.

1990
INDICATIONS FOR HERMENEUTICS IN PSYCHIATRY

Prof. Wolfgang Blankenburg
Klinik für Psychiatrie, Marburg

In this context, a methodological procedure that does not wish to "explain" but to "understand" is designated as hermeneutic. As step-wise conversion of "view" into "insight" takes the place of the verification or falsification of hypotheses. The relation between participating and objectivating acts which is fundamental to all cognition is shifted in favor of the former, although the postulate of objectivation does not have to be abandoned. This means that empathy is accorded greater significance for cognition. With regard to objectivating research, hermeneutics can assume a hypothesis-generating function.

Indications for primary operationalizing and hermeneutic procedures (with their advantages and disadvantages) are compared and contrasted. Two applications of hermeneutic approach is given priority:

1. Disorders relatively close to the ego as we find among the DSM-III categories: 297., 295.40, 298.80, 309., 301. (e.g. 301.81 and 301.83).

2. The hermeneutic access has a complementary function in those cases in which more is "feasible" by theory than is healthy for the patient.

Interactions between philosophical hermeneutics (cf. Gadamer) and psychiatry may become fruitful.

1991
HERMENEUTICS AND PSYCHOTHERAPY

Hermann Lang, M.D.
University of Heidelberg, Psychosomatic Clinic

In principle, hermeneutics is a technique for the interpretation of difficult texts. The technique was especially valuable for incomprehensible texts passed on in history. From the perspective of Gadamer's philosophical concept of hermeneutics, however, this is only a limited definition. According to his view, hermeneutics has a universal purpose, that is, to make understandable what is encountered as incomprehensible in human life. Hermeneutics in this sense -"the art of understanding and making understandable"-, is demanded when the communication between human beings is disturbed. A disturbance of this kind is present in neurosis, psychosis and psychosomatic disorder, as disease means an impairment of communication. With regard to psychoanalysis this will mean "hermeneutics of the unconscious", because the unconscious with its inherent conflicts can only be disclosed by interpretation.

In addition, the role of hermeneutics is discussed with regard to a) client-centered therapy (Rogers) with special emphasis on the verbalization of emotional experiences, b) the systemic approach, as far as a "reinterpretation" of the present "deleterious" concepts of reality is concerned, and c) the cognitive model of behavioral therapy, as far as a change of cognitions underlying negative feelings is the central aim.

1992
HERMENEUTIC AND MENTAL DISORDERS

Rafael Parada-Allende
Hospital Psiquiátrico, Santiago, Chile

1. We expose the central ideas forming an hermeneutical thinking, as well as the opposite ideas that make it relative.
2. We confirm the theoretical consideration in the psychotherapeutic practice, where man shows himself and asks for help to understand or live better his existence.
3. Language and gesture will be the ones that propose ordering systems to evaluate an hermeneutical historicism and structuralism, although this represents in appearance opposite visions.
4. We propose an epistemological conception that orders, arranges hierarchically, opposes or complements the human phenomena in their psychopathological manifestations.
5. Considerations about the three spheres in which Gadamer distributes the hermeneutical experience are made: the aesthetic sphere, the historical sphere, and the sphere of language.
6. Guidelines to analyze better the concepts of prejudgement (Gadamer), previous understanding (Heidegger) and interest (conceptions of the critical social sciences) are given.
7. Finally it is asked: Is it possible to find, and in what conditions, the theoretical bases for a psychiatric hermeneutics?

1993
DIAGNOSING IN PSYCHIATRY AS A HERMENEUTIC PROCESS

Alfred Kraus, M.D.
Psych. Clinic, Univ. of Heidelberg

When making diagnoses in psychiatry the practitioner in general proceeds in two different ways. On the one side, as proposed by diagnostic manuals, he determines alongside strict, operationally defined criteria the symptoms of the disease suggested. On the other side he tries to get a deeper understanding of the problems and alterations of the patient as a person in his world. The first way is morbus-oriented, the second person-oriented. Methodologically, the diagnostic process in the first case is based more on a natural scientific nomothetic methodology summing up isolated facts, whereas in the second case it is based more on a human science idiographic and holistic methodology oriented in the singularity and wholeness of a person. The latter is often considered as being subjective, impressionistic, not scientific and is therefore repressed. The serious, too little noticed consequences of this change in the diagnostic practice make it necessary to work out, as we intend to do, more clearly the difference between both ways of diagnosing, the symptomatological-criteriological and the hermeneutic-phenomenological one and to show possibilities of a scientific foundation of the latter. We want to do this in the light of the philosophical endeavors of H.G. Gadamer for an understanding of the essence and the structure of hermeneutic processes. With respect to the significance of language in herm. processes we want especially to investigate the processes of semanticization of the patient verbalizing his, e.g., psychotic experiences and of the diagnostician giving psychopathological etiquettes to these.

Session 302 Symposium:
The low dose application of neuroleptics in anxiety states

1994

IS THERE A PHARMACOLOGICAL AND BIOCHEMICAL BASIS FOR LOW-DOSE APPLICATION OF SOME NEUROLEPTICS IN ANXIETY-STATES
Dr. Sc. Carlos Niemegeers
Janssen Research Council, Belgium

Specific interaction with central dopamine-D_2 receptors results in dose-dependent biphasic changes in the behaviour of animals. Low doses of dopamine antagonists induce slight activation, which disappears at higher doses and reverses to progressively increasing inhibition. With agonists the opposite is seen. The low dose activation phase following specific neuroleptics is considered to be the result of a low level of D_2 receptor occupation. Biochemical mechanisms support a subsequent disinhibition of the dopaminergic system. A corresponding clinically valuable, low dose activation appears to require a sustained low level of D_2 receptor occupation, which is most easily reached with diphenylbutylpiperidine neuroleptics.

1995

FUNDAMENTALS AND RESULTS OF CONTROLLED STUDIES IN NEUROLEPTANXIOLYSIS
K. HEINRICH, E. LEHMANN, J. TEGELER
Psychiatric Clinic, University of Duesseldorf

Patients suffering from abnormal anxiety, psychosomatic complaints or psychoreactive disorder are difficult partners, and the combination of the two large groups of procedures psychotherapy and psychopharmacological therapy is necessary for the treatment of such patients.

In the conflict with problems in benzodiazepine therapy our group conducted 4 systematic studies with neuroleptics in low dosages, especially Fluspirilene as an alternative.

We found:
1. Fluspirilene is particularly advantageous in patients with a high degree of somatic anxiety.
2. The tolerance is good and if side-effects occur, they have an adverse effect on therapeutic results.
3. There exists a clear dose-effect relationship.
4. We have no proof that a long-term Fluspirilene application bears the risk of abnormal movements. We think that neuroleptanxiolysis is useful in psychosomatic patients.

1996

Low dose neuroleptic treatment in general practice
Rüther, E., Department of Psychiatry, University of Göttingen, FRG.

In general practices (N=2.282) 13540 psychosomatic outpatients were treated with low dose Fluspirilene (1,5 ml/week) for 6 weeks. Special ratings were applied weekly. Functional heart and body complaints improved in 80 % (self ratings) or 83 % (objectiv ratings) of patients. 50 % of the patients were treated before study with benzodiazepines or antidepressives which were withdrawn during study. 51 % were treated additionally with internal drugs before and during study. Adverse drug reactions occured in 9 % of patients with sedation in 2.4 %, increase of appetite in 1.9 %, dry mouth in 0.6 % and extrapyramidal symptoms in 0.3 % without any tardive dyskinesia. A body weight increase more than 3 kg/6 weeks was observed in 2.6 % of patients. Overall low dose Fluspirilene was judged as effective and well tolerated in patients with psychosomatic complaints. Supported by Janssen, FRG.

1997

NEUROLEPTICS USED AS ANTIDEPRESSANTS

MARY M ROBERTSON, CLE KATONA
ACADEMIC DEPARTMENT OF PSYCHIATRY
UCMSM
MIDDLESEX HOSPITAL
MORTIMER STREET LONDON W1N 8AA

The use of major tranquillisers as antidepressants will be reviewed. Double-blind studies suggest that some neuroleptics have antidepressant properties, although the majority of investigations were conducted on mixed anxiety-depressive states. Possible advantages over the tricyclic antidepressant compounds are the early onset of action and the relative lack of side effects. "Post psychotic depression" following neuroleptic therapy is considered, and it is concluded that it is likely to be part of the underlying illness and not a drug-induced effect. Mechanisms of action of these agents and implications for the pathophysiology of depression will be discussed.

1998

Tardive Dyskinesia And Low-Dose-Neuroleptics In Non-Schizophrenic Patients

M.OSTERHEIDER, REIFSCHNEIDER,G., SCHMIDTKE, A., BECKMANN,H.

In several countries so called low-dose neuroleptics seem to become an alternative to benzodiazepines for example in non-psychotic disorders.
According to a review of the relevant literature, data will be presented of a long term compatibility (risks of EPS/TD) study with Fluspirilene (FLU), in which we investigated 70 patients with minimum 26 injections of FLU 1,5 mg/weekly in the past 3 years. Patients had been treated in private practices. For comparison we also examined 56 patients under Benzodiazepine (B-) treatment in the same range of indications. Different side effect rating scales were used /AIMS,EPS,WEBSTER,UKU,Akathisia-Scale). Also psychopathometric evaluation had been done. Results showed no significant differences in the side effect ratings.
The risk for development of TD under low dose neuroleptic treatment seems not to be increased in comparison to spontanous occurance.
At last a critical evaluation of the benefit of rating scales in this topic and an individual analysis (case report) on TD will be given.

Session 303 Symposium:
An elementary pragmatic interactive model: Theory and clinical applications

1999

THE THEORETICAL BASES

Pereira O.G., Ferreira C.P.and Mich L.
Università di Lisbona (Portugal) -
Università di Trento (Italy)

As from 1976 a group of psychiatrists and informatics began to work at a model of human interactions defined Elementary Pragmatic Model.
This model derives from its being based on communication pragmatic (according to C. Morris) and is defined elementary since it reduces interactions between two subjects to single BIT of information, according to Shannon and Ashby. Information is then expressed as triplets, including the proposal of the first subject, that of the other, and finally the result of the interaction.
In the unit of time an observer, by observing a long series of interactions, notices certain redundancies, certain repetition, certain regularities. These regularities correspond to 4 COORDINATES of human relationship.
-- accepting the other´s world
 (Acceptance Coordinate),
 corrisponding to the bit 0 1 1
-- maintaining one´s own world
 (Maintenance Coordinate),
 corrisponding to the bit 1 0 1

2000

THE TESTS BASED ON THE ELEMENTARY PRAGMATIC MODEL
Pierri G. and Corfiati L.
Ist.Clinica Psichiatrica,Università di Bari, (Italy)

On the basis of the Elementary Pragmatic Model, SISCI-1 and SISCI-3 tests have been developed for testing the interactional style of a subject or a group (like family). They are based on the subject´s original opinion on a set of facts and on his/her later opinion following a perturbation. In practice a set of 90 Holtzman tables is used as the set of objects in which to choice, so that the choice is rescricted as little as possible by subjective, cultural, emotional, or other factors. The impact-perturbation is achieved following a fixed modality in SISCI-1, and a computerized modality in SISCI-3. Among others, initial data of the experimentation, are statistically significant, showing that schizophrenics maintain their initial choices less than normal subjects in the control group. The pre-established impact-perturbation obtained mainly SISCI-3 shows that the relational style of "going towards the patient´s world (F5)" make the patient more capable to maintain his/her own "world" towards the experimenter.

2001

SHORT TERM PSYCHOTHERAPY OF NEVROSES AND PSYCHOSOMATOSES
Margari F., De Nigris S. and Arvizzigno C.
Clinica Psichiatrica,Università di Bari, (Italy)

Our approach to the nevroses and psychosomates treatment may be defined "short term interactional psychoterapy". Our intervention modalities are oriented mainly towards "processes", that is, all symptomatic behaviours are inscribed in highly repetitive interactive sequences. Therefore therapeutic moves attempt to modify repetitive relational patterns, the family "rules". Our approach stems from the theoretical framework of the Elementary Pragmatic Model (De Giacomo and Silvestri) as a mere classification of interactions and changes, and from time evaluation (in relation to the number of elementary interactions). In other terms it is possible to distinguish in our interventions a interactional style prescription and a temporal map (when, how long, how often and according to which sequence: Zerubavel,1981) prescription. At last we consider the involvement of the patient and his/her whole family (in cases of obsessive disorders) or the involvement of the patient and one family members (in cases of anorexia nervosa).

2002

PSYCHOTHERAPY OF PSYCHOSES

Buonsante M. and Catucci S.
Ist.Clinica Psichiatrica,Università di Bari, (Italy)

In family therapy field many models exist: some, like those of Maturana and Varela, refer to the complexity and have a centrifugal tendency, that is to try more and more to find from the "outside" the key to understand and treat. There are other models, like those of De Giacomo and Silvestri, that have a centripetal tendency and aim at a central knot, at a focus to be reach and modify. The second way permits a more rapid and incisive procedures in the psychoses pyschoterapy. This is not the case to consider all the interventions that can be used either separately or in sequency. We present some prescriptions which are moves that belong to an always longer and harder work. An example is our prescription named "to appear unit body and soul". This intervention, mainly used by us in schizophrenia family therapy, consists in a cognitive construction. It aims at making the parents, with a sort of mutual, implicit or explicit, opposition between them, appear united in the eyes of their children.

2003

THE RELATIONAL PSYCHOTHERAPY AND THE AUTISTIC CHILD: RESULTS
Santoni Rugiu A.
Ist.Clinica Psichiatrica,Università di Bari, (Italy)

The follow-up of 30 autistic children with whom the systemic communication approach has been used during these last 10 years is reported. Of the various models applicable in the area of communication the Elementary Pragmatic Model developed by De Giacomo and Silvestri was essentially used. Our samples include cases of child autism (whether or not on an organic basis), that were diagnosed by specialist psychiatrists and neurologists not belonging to our Family Therapy Team, according to DSM III criteria. Data for processing were obtained from a questionnaire developed by our group in such a way that the most characteristic items in the autistic child's behaviour: Language, Stereotypes, Avoidance, Aggressiveness, Closing-up and Achievements at school. The questionnaire was used on three occasions: at the beginning and at the end of the sessions and one year later. The most conspicous changes are observed in the autistic behaviours.

Session 304 — Symposium: The social, economic and cultural implications of mental health care in Europe

2004

A SOCIAL - PHILOSOPHICAL REFLECTION ON THE HISTORY OF PSYCHIATRY BETWEEN EXPULSION AND SOCIAL INTEGRATION OF THE MENTALLY ILL

Prof. dr. M. Richartz, State University Limburg, the Netherlands

Psychiatry, as a medical specialty and social institution, originated from the movement of thought and social changes reflected by the philosophical concepts of the eighteenth century - the era of the Enlightenment. From these roots psychiatry and mental health care derive their two contradictory sides that have persisted to this very day. On the one hand, psychiatry has shown a recurring tendency to promote a social and political system exacting predictable, self-controlled and 'reasonable' behaviour: those who prove 'unpredictable', disturb 'public order' or interfere with 'productivity', are isolated in 'panoptic institutions', soon to be categorized into establishments ministering to the treatable and custodial wards for the untreatable.
On the other, there are the human rights, exponent of humanistic values and respect for the individual, first claimed during the enlightenment and integrated in psychiatry praxis to free the mentally ill from physical restraint and social compulsion.
The history of European psychiatry is outlined tracing this dialectic of the enlightenment, which culminates in a strained relationship between the 'reasonable' sensus communis and the 'unreasonable' sensus privatis, i.e. between social control and emancipation.

2005

HUMAN RIGHTS IN MENTAL HOSPITALS IN THE EUROPEAN COMMUNITY
Prof.dr. M. Richartz / State University Limburg / The Netherlands
Whether scientific progress in psychiatry leads to a more human care-system, depends upon the cultural, the socio-economical and sociopolitical development. This development influences the availability of sufficient funds and the attitude and tolerance of the population towards its most vulnerable members. These factors will determine whether psychiatrically ill people will be integrated or excluded from society. The split between psychiatry as science and psychiatry as system of care has also contributed to relatively too high expectations or an over-estimation of short term therapeutic interventions possibilities versus guidance and rehabilitation possibilities. In spite of many efforts to improve the situation, especially the living conditions of chronic patients in psychiatric institutions in our countries are still, to some extent, insufficient specifically in regard to humane and material standards. The Eight World Congress 1989 will be held in Athens. We acquainted ourselves with the 1984 report of an expert team on behalf of the EC-commission regarding the state of mental health care in Greece and the proposals for improvement. We also know that the European Community has provided 60 million ECU for the improvement of the short term and intermediate situation as well as for the future development of a care system, which will meet the needs of the population as to regional and rehabilitation requirements. To bring about reforms by financial means and the willingness of interested laymen and psychiatric professionals will not succeed unless penetrating measures are used to influence public opinion and the economic infrastructure in areas, like Leros, where the population economically leans heavily on the presence of psychiatric patients in large institutions. The Symposium does aim at engaging in a constructive dialogue, based on historical knowledge and actual facts as well as on selfcriticism. Finally and most important we would hope to analyse the existing conditions and formulate realistic plans for change with due consideration of the possibilities to bring about change.

2006

POVERTY AND PSYCHIATRY IN THE LIGHT OF THE REFORM OF MENTAL HEALTH CARE IN TRIEST, ITALY

Rotelli F. - Direzione Servici di Salute Mentalle, Italy

2007

BACKGROUNDS AND RESULTS OF THE REPORT OF THE STUDYGROUP OF THE EUROPEAN COMMISSION CONCERNING THE MENTAL HEALTH REFORM IN GREECE

Browne I. - reland

2008

LEROS: FIRST YEAR OF WORK

A. BOUSOULEGAS, P. ZOGRAPHOS, J. LOUKAS, G.M. PAPAGEORGIOU
STATE MENTAL HOSPITAL, LEROS, GREECE

The overall situation in Leros by August 1988 was in a stagnate state. Hence, establishing foundations in a four-fold program which consist of:

A. Commiting to a rehabilitational campaign to achieve maximum operational efficiency of the hospital. This can be attained by redefining the relations between nursing personnel and patients, nursing personnel and hospital and finally between the hospital and the community.

B. Daily intervention by the hospital trying to ameliorate the quality of patients' living standards as well as effective daily-care services through training or experienced nursing personnel.

C. Informing all personnel and the community in general about the contents of newly-applied rehabilitation-deinstitutionalization programs applicable at the present and in the future. Seeking collaboration and cooperation between greek and european mental-health specialists.

D. A program in the future in diminishing patient population which will resolve to an active short-term patient mental hospital in the 9th Health District in Greece.

Session 305 Symposium:
Recent advances in the treatment of bulimia

2009

THE EPIDEMIOLOGY OF BULIMIA NERVOSA

Christopher G. Fairburn.
Department of Psychiatry, University of Oxford, Warneford Hospital, Oxford, OX3 7LS, England.

Since the emergence of bulimia nervosa in the 1970s there has been much research on its epidemiology. It is the aim of this paper to consider what has been learnt from this large body of work. First, the initial media-based studies will be described. There will follow an examination of the prevalence studies, the studies being classified on the basis of their research design. Then three special types of study will be considered: the studies of particular subgroups, the longitudinal studies, and the ones designed to investigate secular changes. Finally, new directions for future research will be proposed.

2010
BIOCHEMICAL ASPECTS OF BULIMIA NERVOSA
P.E.Garfinkel, MD, FRCP(C)
The Toronto Hospital, Toronto, Canada

Over the past decade there has been great interest in understanding the etiology of bulimia nervosa(BN); most clinicians and researchers now embrace a multidetermined model of pathogenesis of BN that includes biological factors which may predispose to, perpetuate for exacerbate the disorder. At the same time there has been a great increase in knowledge concerning the neurotransmitters involved in the regulation of food ingestion; serotonin (5-HT), dopamine (DA), norepinephrine (NE), neuropeptides and the gastrointestinal hormones such as cholecystokinin (CCK), have all been found to play a role in the control of food intake. However, knowledge of their specific involvements in BN is limited by some methodological considerations, which will be reviewed. Recent attention has focused on the role of brain 5-HT for 3 reasons: 1.Central 5-HT dysfunction has been implicated in depression, suicide, alcoholism, impulsivity, aggression and anxiety, all of which commonly occur in BN, 2. 5-HT has been found to play a role in both satiety and macronutrient selection. 3. Dieting, which regularly precedes bulimia, has been shown to alter a variety of parameters of 5-HT functions, especially in women. There is indirect evidence of altered 5-HT function in BN such as findings of lowered 5 HIAA levels in the CSF of weight recovered anorexics with bulimia; stimulation studies with L-tryptophen and m-chlorophenyl-piperazine have suggested decreased 5-HT activity, as does recent evidence of increased platelet 5-HT uptake. Low doses of DA and DA agonists stimulate eating whereas higher doses are inhibitory. An increase in appetite and weight occur when patients are administered dopamine blocking agents, such as neuroleptics. In animals, injections of NE increase meal size. Leibowitz has demonstrated that application of alpha 2 agents to the PVN produce hyperphagia. While data in humans with AN and BN suggest decreased catecholaminergic function, as evidenced by plasma and urinary end product measures, and by reduced NE response to an orthostatic challenge, the effect of low weight could account for these findings. Similarly abnormalities in the opiate system and CCK have been described in BN and could be due to some of the behaviors or the bulimics, but also give rise to further features seen in BN. These will be discussed in terms of their implications for understanding how the neurochemical changes brought on by the disorder help to perpetuate it.

2011
CURRENT TREATMENTS OF BULIMIA
J.E.Mitchell, M.D., E.D.Eckert, M.D., R.L.Pyle, M.D.
University of Minnesota Medical School, Minneapolis, Minnesota, U.S.A.

Over the last decade a large body of research has been generated on the treatment of bulimia nervosa. While many reports have been descriptive or anecdotal, several controlled trials have also been completed. These controlled trials have focused on two sorts of interventions: medication therapy, typically using antidepressant drugs, and psychotherapy, in particular therapies employing cognitive behavioral techniques in both group and individual formats. This paper will review the controlled trials in bulimia nervosa, with particular attention to the forms of treatment, patient characteristics in each trial, non-completion and completion rates, and improvement in symptoms. As will be seen, both antidepressants and certain forms of psychotherapy appear to be quite effective in suppressing target symptoms in patients with active bulimia nervosa.

2012
REVIEW OF CLINICAL STUDIES OF FLUOXETINE IN BULIMIA

B. Timothy Walsh, M.D.

Department of Psychiatry, College of Physicians and Surgeons, Columbia University, 722 West 168th St., New York, N.Y. 10032

In the last decade, there has been great interest in the utility of antidepressant medication for the treatment of bulimia nervosa. Over a dozen double-blind trials have now been reported documenting the superiority of antidepressant medication over placebo. The potential efficacy of the novel antidepressant fluoxetine is of interest for both practical and theoretical reasons. The low frequency of side effects associated with fluoxetine makes it potentially attractive from a clinical perspective. In addition, its efficacy is of theoretical interest as fluoxetine selectively blocks the reuptake of serotonin, a neurotransmitter known to be involved in the control of eating behavior.

This paper will review the studies conducted to date of fluoxetine in bulimia nervosa, including a large (382 patients) double-blind, placebo-controlled trial which found that fluoxetine, in a dose of 60 mg/day, was superior to placebo.

Session 306 Special Session:
Community and community oriented services

2013
COMMUNITY RESOURCES: TOOLS OF CHOICE IN SOCIAL RE-INTEGRATION
Manuel Galiana, m.d., Ara Dakessian, m.d., psychiatres, Hôpital Rivière-des-Prairies, Montréal, Canada

H.R.D.P. offers a complete range of child psychiatric services. Eight years ago special out-patient resources were developed for severely handicapped psychiatric patients not requiring hospitalization but unable to live at home or in traditional foster homes. These resources proved so effective that they now total 13, further expansion limited only by financial restraints. Each resource or "residence", usually a home rented in a residential district, houses 4-5 patients depending on their psychopathology and the physical limitations of the house. A team of hospital-employed professionals, usually "special educators", provide all services and supervision. Community recreational facilities are utilized and during the day children attend school and young adults go to protected workshops. Any specific individual therapeutic interventions are provided by a multidisciplinary team headed by a psychiatrist. Thus, the residence serves as a therapeutic tool in learning tasks of daily living as well as a means toward social re-integration. The principles of normalization are easier to attain in small group settings where peer and adult relationships are closer to the ideal. These residences are grouped into 2 programs: one for children and adolescents with predominant psychiatric profiles and one for young adults with chronic psychoses usually associated with mental retardation and histories of long-term hospitalization.

2014

THE EFFICACY OF OUTPATIENT COMMITMENT IN THE UNITED STATES
Roger Peele, M.D.; Guido Zanni, Ph.D.; Leslie deVeau, MSW. District of Columbia Commission on Mental Health Services, Washington, D.C., USA.

Outpatient commitment is a recent form of mental health treatment in the United States that has grown out of the dramatic shift in the clinical setting from inpatient to outpatient care. Outpatient commitment provides for an additional choice apart from inpatient hospitalization.

With the development of community treatment, the problem of the "revolving door" patients has surfaced. This type of patient recovers rapidly with appropriate hospital treatment but once released fails to follow prescribed treatments and quickly deteriorates to the point of needing rehospitalization. An outpatient commitment order breaks this cycle. The patient is mandated to follow an outpatient regime. Failure to do so usually results in the patient being re-hospitalized. The real benefit is that outpatient commitment provides the opportunity for early intervention should the patient stop medication or treatment, thus preventing serious deterioration.

Currently, 26 states and the District of Columbia have provisions for outpatient commitment. We review the growing body of literature on its use, especially our studies which demonstrate that utilization of outpatient commitment reduces hospitalization. Also discussed are the complex and controversial legal, philosophical, political, and economic issues surrounding its use.

2015

A FOLLOW-UP STUDY OF THE FORMER RESIDENTS OF A HALFWAY HOUSE
G.Vaslamatzis[1], K.Katsouyanni[2], A.Lymberopoulou[1]
[1]Department of Psychiatry, [2]Department of Hygiene and Epidemiology, Athens University

Contact with the former residents of the Halfway House of the Athens University Psychiatric Clinic was made during the 5th year from the establishment of this new transitional facility. 18 of the 59 former residents were not found or refused to have a contact with us. The remaining 41 subjects included 13 females (32%) and 28 males (68%). The follow-up period ranged from 8 to 52 months (mean 32 months) and the rehabilitation outcome was estimated alternatively by hospital recidivism (19 patients -46% of the sample- did not report rehospitalization) and by a more complex index based on rehospitalization, employment and living independently (in the latter case, the patients were divided into four outcome groups). The role of the following variables on the outcome was evaluated: months of follow-up, sex, age, years of education, diagnosis, previous hospitalizations, duration of residency and reasons for admission, compliance to medication, score in "Behavior in Halfway House Scale"(BHS), participation in prevocational program and in group psychotherapy. Chi square tests, analysis of variance and discriminant analysis were used for the statistical evaluation. Compliance to drug therapy, duration of residency and score in B.H.S. are found to be associated with rehabilitation outcome.

2016

FACTORS AFFECTING EMPLOYMENT OF THE MENTALLY DISABLED
Kuokkanen M.I., Puumalainen J.
University of Tampere, Rehabilitation Foundation, Helsinki, Finland

The aim of rehabilitation examination is to assess client's working capacity and her potential to benefit from rehabilitation. At the rehabilitation Foundation more than 800 clients are examined yearly. A third of them are mentally disabled. The Foundation has started a follow-up study on the rehabilitation process of clients with mental problems. A questionnaire has been mailed to 779 former clients with mental disability who were examined in 1981-83. The follow-up period lasted approximately two years. 78% of former clients responded. Altogether 19% of respondents were employed or in education. In this paper some preliminary results of logistic regression analysis of factors affecting employment of 606 former clients will be presented.

2017

ACHIEVING CONTINUITY OF CARE
D.A.Wasylenki
Clarke Institute of Psychiatry, Toronto, Canada

Continuity of care is essential to effective treatment of the chronically mentally ill. This requires a single person responsible for the well-being of each patient and a service system where in components are linked to provide integrated programs. The Continuing Care Division of the Clarke Institute of Psychiatry provides continuity of care to severely disabled patients by utilizing those principles. This paper describes the development and operation of the Division.
The Division provides treatment for 300-400 patients with a staff of 50. Key therapeutic modalities are case management and skills training. The Division operates four Continuing Care Teams, each of which is responsible for the treatment of approximately 100 patients. The Division also operates two inpatient services, i.e. an intensive care service and an intermediate care service, as well as a day centre which focuses on skills teaching. Responsibility for the care of individual patients resides with team-based case managers and psychiatrists, regardless of the treatment environment. Patients are not transferred to other professionals when their treatment needs change. In addition, all components of the Division are closely linked with staff working in more than one setting. Data suggest that this is a higly successful approach.

2018

CONTINUITY OF CARE: CHALLENGES AND LIMITATIONS.
Ioannidis H., Mitrossilis S., Panayotopoulou I., EGINITION HOSPITAL, ATHENS GREECE.

Continuity of care is a basic notion of current outpatient services. It provides a frame in which a person can live and outlive a life-crisis situation not ruptured from or incomprehensible in the sequence of his life. It gives special emphasis on the therapeutic situation by respecting the potentials and limitations of the transaction of the people involved (therapist-client). Continuity of care means that the person asks help for his life, a part of which (and only that) comprises the crisis.
The danger involved in this new form of care delivery, is a subtle institutionalization-stagnation, which instead of promoting individuation and autonomy, could maintain a state of dependency or inertness, which in turn, almost like a new revolving door may hinder the termination of the need for such a network.
The greek experience with this notion is discussed.

2019

THE RHETORIC AND THE REALITY OF THE
COMMUNITY MENTAL HEALTH MOVEMENT
Thomas T. Tourlentes, M.D.,
Associate Clinical Professor of Psychiatry
University of Illinois College of Medicine
Peoria, Illinois USA

Few knowledgeable and experienced psychiatrists would argue seriously that the major objectives of the American community mental health movement have been substantially met as originally envisioned. Furthermore, opportunistic forces, external and internal, have taken advantage of this idealistic rhetoric to pursue more self-serving realities. Greater understanding of these shortcomings will be necessary if we are to cope more effectively with this complex psycho-political problem in the future.

Issues to be addressed include: 1. the vested interests of the public and private practice interface; 2. funding competition of other human service providers; 3. blurring of professional roles and vying for power and prestige; 4. the forced marriage of adversarial and clinical processes and purposes; 5. lingering political reliance on historic institutional remedies; 6. the intrusions and distortions of managed care brokers; and 7. the shortage and maldistribution of skilled psychiatric administrators.

Session 307 Special Session:
Emergency and crisis intervention services

2020

ACUTE PSYCHOTIC CASES. HOSPITALIZATION IN THE PATIENT'S HOME.
P. Sakellaropoulos, P. Panagoutsos, D. Katsoulas
University of Thraki

A 15 years study analyzing quantity & quality data, refers to the home hospitalization of acute psychotic cases by a specialized psychiatric group. 240 acute psychiatric cases have been studied (1/3 urban area & 2/3 rural): psychiatric group composition, confrontation of the patient & his family with a moderated psychoanalytic technique, accompanied medication, hospitalization's duration & frequency, continuation of follow-up & evolution of the cases after the crisis. A blind control procedure of the 240 cases is presented in order to find out the needs of in & out-patient care.

The following are discussed: a) The therapeutic validity of this kind of crisis intervention, b) the "evolution" of the emergency cases into better forms of treatment & follow-up.

Conclusion: a) With the presence at home, the pathologic interaction with the family is decreased, b) The patient's projective persecutive mechanisms towards family & therapeutic system are suspended. The essential transference is imposed for the patient's therapeutic future, c) The number of the patients which are hospitalized in asylums is decreased & d) Therapists of a higher specialization are trained for the crisis intervention.

2021

SERVICES FOR PSYCHIATRIC EMERGENCY IN ITALY
R. Rizzardo, G. Colombo, M. Florian, G. Forza
Department of Psychiatry - University of Padua - Italy

After the psychiatric reform of 1978 the organization of the response to psychiatric emergency in Italy is of particular interest. We carried out a survey of all the hospitals in the chief town of the provinces of Italy. We sent out a questionnaire to the Health Directors and Heads of Psychiatric Services with the request to supply information on the characteristics of the structures and on the type of response given to psychiatric emergency. Almost all the hospitals contacted replied. Not all have psychiatric beds available yet (Servizio Psichiatrico di Diagnosi e Cura - SPDC); a minority have an autonomous service for psychiatric emergency that in few cases intervenes in the community. More than half the hospitals mention the existence of a psychiatric team operating in the community without SPDC. In more than 10% of the hospitals only the General Emergency doctor attends psychiatric emergency; in some hospitals a neurologist still intervenes as consultant, but in most, a psychiatrist is called who, in more than half the cases, is on call outside the hospital. In emergencies in the community the psychiatric area team intervenes in three quarters of the cases, the general practitioner is called in 62% of cases. A large part of the proposal for compulsory treatment are made by the general practitioner and more often are only endorsed by the psychiatrist. In one third of the hospitals the transport of committed patients takes place without the Mayor's authorization as required by law. In three quarters of cases forces of public order intervene and in two thirds of cases psychiatric service personnel are called. Some differences between North and South Italy emerge.

2022
ASSESSMENT OF CRISIS INTERVENTIONS IN THE EMERGENCY WARD OF A GENERAL HOSPITAL, AFTER TWO YEARS.
Michel DE CLERCQ
Responsable for the crisis psychiatric team at St-Luc Clinics.

The number of psychiatric emergencies arriving in emergency wards of general hospitals is encreasing. The crisis psychiatric team of St-Luc Clinics in Brussels (Catholic University of Louvain) has developed a specific programme to deal with such psychiatric emergencies.

In a first step, the team staff perform a crisis interaction and analyse the urgency of the demand-talk with individual and/or family, provisional admission for 24 hours, when necessary.

A second step leads to a crisis intervention of the crisis team right on the spot or of a mental health centre team further to a first interview in the emergency ward.

And finally, other patients (less than 15%) will be admitted to a psychiatric dept. or directed to specialised medical advice.

The sample will be assessed two years later for evaluation of follow-up development and compliance with treatment.

2023
Does outreaching emergency psychiatry really prevents hospitalization?

P. Schnabel, H. Oosterbaan; Netherlands Institute of mental health (NcGv), Utrecht, The Netherlands.

Introduced by A. Querido in the thirties, the Amsterdam Municipal Health Authority has now a longstanding experience in providing a 24-hours service in emergency psychiatry (crisisintervention at home). This internationally acclaimed facility has never been evaluated for its effectiveness in the prevention of hospitalization. A two-year follow-up study of 382 patients who were seen by a psychiatrist of the facility in 1982, showed that 1) the majority of the patients eventually were admitted to a hospital, and 2) approximately half of them were to be considered as chronic psychiatric patients at the time of the screening. In the long term prevention of (re-)admission appeared to be almost impossible.

2024
The use of self report (SCL-90) for investigating a sample of psychiatric emergency patients.

D. CREMNITER(1), A. MEIDINGER(1), C. PAYANT(2) P. STOESSEL(1), J. FERMANIAN(2).

(1) Serv. Pr. BOURGUIGNON, Hop. Henri Mondor, Créteil.
(2) Lab. Biostatistique, Hop. Necker, Paris.

In order to investigate more precisely the clinical features of patients attending to a psychiatric emergency department in a general hospital, 457 patients were asked to fill up a self report, the SCL-90. Among them, 293 patients accepted to do so. The factorial analysis which was performed on the data collected from this sample of patients after varimax rotation showed 5 factors which explained 40% of total variance. The first factor (25% of total variance) is composed of 12 items of depressive symptomatology. The second factor (5%) is composed of 9 items of somatization expressing anxiety. The third factor (4%) is formed of 6 items which reflect an interpersonal sensitivity. The two last factors (3% each) are represented by impulsivity and psychotic syndrome. These results are compared to the data from the litterature. Besides, the stability of the factorial structure of the SCL-90 is discussed according to the nature of the sample.

2025
THE ORGANIZATION OF EMERGENCY PSYCHIATRIC SERVICES A COMPARISON OF SEVERAL MODELS
Marianne Donker, Paul Schnabel
Netherlands Institute of Mental Health
Utrecht, The Netherlands

All over the (western) world emergency psychiatric services are differently organized. Some are hospital based, others community based. Some have a high threshhold for patients, others can be characterized as walk-in centres. In some services the psychiatrist has a dominant role, in others the service relies strongly on social workers. Differences exist in many other areas.
At the core of these differences lies a difference of opinion about the true nature of a psychiatric emergency: is the emergency predominantly a result of the disease of the individual patient, or is it essentially of a social nature? Different views result in different solutions and a different organization of emergency psychiatric services.
A comparison of several models for emergency psychiatry will be presented on the basis of a literature review and Dutch research findings. The pros and cons of the models will be discussed in the light of the essential functions an emergency service must perform.

2026

ETUDE DU SUIVI A 6 MOIS ET A 2 ANS DE 457 URGENCES PSYCHIATRIQUES VUES EN HOPITAL GENERAL

D. CREMNITER (1), C. PAYANT (2), M. THENAULT (1)
I. FERRAND (2), S. JAMAIN (1), B. LE MOUEL (1), J. FERMANIAN (2)

(1) Service de Psychiatrie du Pr BOURGUIGNON
HOPITAL HENRI MONDOR - CRETEIL
(2) Laboratoire de biostatistique
HOPITAL NECKER - PARIS
(3) Service de Psychiatrie du Dr PEIGNE
HOPITAL COCHIN - PARIS

457 patients vus aux urgences d'un hôpital général pour un problème psychiatrique ont été inclus dans une étude comprenant un ensemble de procédures d'évaluation : entretien à visée diagnostique, recueil de données quantitatives au moyen d'échelles d'évaluation (BPTS, PBHF), questionnaire d'auto-évaluation (SCL - 90) rempli par les patients.

Les patients ont été recontactés à 15 jours, 6 mois et à 2 ans de façon à préciser l'évolution clinique par rapport au tableau initial et le suivi thérapeutique à distance.

Nous connaissons ces paramètres chez 80 % des patients à 2 ans. On constate :
- une amélioration très nette et sans suivi des troubles de l'adaptation
- une stabilité évolutive chez les psychotiques avec un suivi psychiatrique
- une tendance à la rechute chez les déprimés.

Session 308 Special Session:
Psychopharmacology: Pharmacokinetic studies

2027

PHARMACODYNAMICS AND KINETICS IN RITANSERIN-TREATED DYSTHYMIC PATIENTS - RELATIONSHIP TO CLINICAL EVALUATION
M.Larsson, A.Stokland, A.Manhem, A.Forsman
Dept. of Psychiatry III, Lillhagen Hospital,
Univ. of Goetebertg, 422 03 Hisings Backa, Sweden
The 5-HT_2 receptor-blocking agent ritanserin was given to 18 dysthymic patients in daily doses of 20mg during 6 weeks. The pharmacokinetics were investigated after single doses of the drug as well as after multidose administration. Serum steady-state concentrations, C_{max}, T_{max}, biological half-life, V_D, bioavailability, free fraction and ritanserin levels in CSF were determined. In connection with psychiatric ratings with HDRS and CPRS on days 0,21 and 42 of treatment, blood samples were collected for assays of 5-HT, its precursor tryptophan, and ritanserin. CSF samples were collected from 12 patients on days 1 and 42 for assays of the monoamine metabolites MHPG, HVA, 5-HIAA and of tryptophan. 10 of the 18 patients had improved their total HDRS and CPRS scores with more than 60%, i.e.there were 10 responders and 8 non-responders. The blood 5-HT level was slightly increased, but no significant change occurred in the precursor tryptophan. No significant differences were observed between responders and nonresponders in CSF concentrations of 5-HIAA before the start of the study, but highly significant differences between groups were seen in the CSF levels of 5-HIAA after ritanserin treatment (p<0.01). The CSF 5-HIAA level was unchanged or slightly decreased in the responders, while an increase of, in mean, 28% was seen in the nonresponders (p<0.05).These findings probably reflect both pre-and postsynaptic events

2028

Plasma Monitoring of Perphenazine Treatment in Paranoid Conditions.-Clinical and economic aspects.
C.S. Kjeldsen, P. Kragh-Sørensen, E. Andersen, F. Gerholt, P. Glue, M. Hørder, N-A. Klitgaard, G. Krarup, N-E. Larsen, P. Rask.
Department of Psychiatry, Odense University Hospital.
The investigation contains a cost/benefit analysis of low dose perphenazine treatment of paranoid psychoses. The aim has been to evaluate perphenazine plasma monitoring as a supplement to clinical assessment of effect of treatment on the basis of:
1. adjustment of dosage so that plasma concentrations fall within a defined therapeutic interval (2-6 nM/l). 2. Reduction in risk of side effects and thereby noncompliance, 3. reduction in extent of polypharmacia. 4. Reduction in spectrum of neuroleptics and amount of anticholinergics with a view to reducing total drug expenses. The material covers 594 patients in neuroleptic treatment, admitted to the department in the course of one year. 185 patients satisfied the inclusion criteria, of these 141 completed treatment/monitoring program (peroral or parenteral). The results show good or moderate effect for 75% of the perorally treated group (mean plasma concentration 3.9 nM) and for 85% in the parenterally treated group (mean plasma concentration 5.4 nM). Noncompliance was possibly the reason for low treatment effect for 41% of the non-responders in the group perorally treated. Side effects were observed in 21% of the total patient group. The investigation showed a reduction in use of anticholinergics and neuroleptics (DDD/1000 pt.) amounting to 50%, and total expenses for drugs

2029

PLASMA LEVELS AND CLINICAL COMPARISONS BETWEEN IV AND ORAL CLOMIPRAMINE
O.Varoquaux, A.Grégoire, M.Blondet, J.Gailledreau, N. Brion, J.Plas, J.F Chevalier, S.Brion, C.Advenier, M.Pays. Laboratoire de Pharmacologie, Centre Hospitalier de Versailles, 78157 Le Chesnay Cedex France

The monitoring of clomipramine (CMI) and 4 of its metabolites was performed in a double blind parallel study in patients receiving a 75 mg slow IV infusion (n=35) or an oral 150 mg administration (n=35) during 14 days, then a 150 mg of oral CMI per day for each patient. A double oral dose was choosen according to the bioavailability factor of CMI in order to obtain a closest equivalence of the drug exposure in the 2 groups. Plasma CMI and its 8-hydroxy (8-OHCMI), demethyl (DMC), 8-hydroxydemethyl (8 OHDMC) and didemethyl (DDMC) metabolites were determined by HPLC with coulometric detection on days 1, 4, 7,14 and 28 before and after infusions. A simultaneous clinical evaluation of efficiency and tolerance was made (S.Brion et al, presented in this meeting).
The results showed similar plasma levels for CMI before infusion at day 7 (76.7±4.6 vs 99.4±10.8 ng/ml, NS), day 14 (98±3 vs 110.6 ng/ml, NS) and day 28 (99.9±16.5 vs 100.1±53.4 ng/ml NS) for the IV and oral groups respectively, eventhough the oral dose was double. The steady state plasma level was reached earlier for the oral route. DMC and 8 OHCMI levels were significantly higher for the orally treated group at day 4,7 and 14 as for the 8 OHDMC especially at day 14. No difference was shown for DDMC levels in the 2 groups. The CMI/DMC ratios were significantly higher for the IV group at every measure.
Clinical MADRS scores showed an equal antidepressant activity in the 2 groups. The absence of efficiency difference between the 2 groups may be elucidated by similar CMI levels achieved. Metabolites, notably DMC, could partly intervene, on the one hand in the activity especially in patients showing a baseline MADRS score > 34, faster improved with the oral route, on the other hand in side effects concerning adrenergic and anticholinergic properties, or the excitation factor, being significantly higher in oral group.
Interindividual variations and individual correlations of plasma levels clinical parameters will be also presented.

2030
PLASMATIC MONITORING OF ANTIDEPRESSANTS: STATE OF THE ART.
SIRACUSANO A., BROGNA P., CORTESE D., FIORENTINI A., NIOLU C., VELLA G.
I^ PSYCH. CLIN. UNIVERSITY OF ROME (PROF. G.VELLA)

The AA. evaluate the more recent contributions of the literature relevant to the routinary use of the plasmatic monitoring of the antidepressants (antidpr.), with a particular relevance to the tricyclic drugs. Starting from a basal evaluation on the actual clinical utility of the antidpr. dosage, relevant to the possibility of establishing for each patient the proper dose with a terapeutic effect for an acute or a chronic treatment (mantenance, prophylactic, problem of "non responders"), the definition of the following main aspects of the problem are reached by the personal experience of the authors: 1) relation between the diagnosis (unipolar or bipolar depression) plasmatic level and therapeutic response; 2) difference of the various types of antidpr. their plasma levels and their therapeutical effects; 3) relation between peronality structure antidpr. plasma levels and collateral effects.

2031
IMPROVED RESULTS OF ANTIDEPRESSANTS AFTER MEASURING PLASMA-LEVELS.
de Blécourt, dr. C.V. and Gudde, drs. H.
psychiatric and pharmacologic dept, Streekziekenhuis Koningin Beatrix, Winterswijk, The Netherlands.

Measurement of plasma-levels of antidepressants was prompted by observation of patients with therapy-resistant major depression, who were treated with maximal doses. They appeared to have low or sub-therapeutical plasma-levels(A and B).
Later on another(greater) subgroup of patients was identified, showing signs of intoxication at normal doses(C). In one and the same patient various results could be obtained for different drugs(D).

Patient (sex/age)	Drug (gener.name)	Dose (mg/day)	Level (ng/l)	Ther.range (ng/l)
A(f,70)	doxepin	300	60	100- 200
	mianserin	90	40	35- 125
B(m,39)	mianserin	90	40	35- 125
		120	135	
C(m,52)	imipramin	100	760	100- 300
		50	290	
		25	110	
D(m,62)	fluvoxamin	200	70	50- 200
	thioridazin	200	5345	750-1500
		60	1470	

Discussion: results of treatment were improved in a substantial number of such patients after appropriate correction of the dose, such as in B,C and also D; explanation of these findings to patients throughout treatment favours the development of the doctor-patient relationship.

2032
A METHOD FOR ASSESSING THE QUALITY OF CLINICAL PHARMACOKINETIC STUDIES ABOUT ANTIDEPRESSANTS
I.R. de Oliveira[1,4], R. Dardennes[1], G. Galbaud du Fort[2] and J. Fermanian[3].
[1]CMME (Paris), [2]CESAM (Villejuif), [3]Hôp. Necker (Paris) and [4]Universidade Federal da Bahia (Brazil).

Three classes of relationship may be found between plasma levels of antidepressants and antidepressant efficacy: 1. Linear or sigmoid. 2. Curvilinear with an optimum intermediate range or "therapeutic window". 3. Absence of any relationship. There are now at least 120 studies which have examined this subject. Imipramine, nortriptyline, amitriptyline, clomipramine and desipramine are the most studied antidepressants, permitting some conclusions. Some authors suggest that the striking lack of agreement between different studies result from heterogeneity of their quality.
Here, we have developed a method for assessing the quality of these studies. It is based on Chalmers et al.'s study (1980) concerning controlled clinical trials. Its 30 items are presented in 4 parts: 1. Identification of the study. 2. Protocol. 3. Statistical analysis. 4. Presentation of data and discussion. Only parts 2, 3 and 4 are scored. Blinding concerning the study is preffered so that the examiner is not influenced by the reputation of the author or the journal. Total score ranges from 0.00 to 1.00. This method is at present being validated.

2033
PHARMACOKINETICS OF THE NEW ANTIDEPRESSANT LEVOPROTILINE IN MAN

Dieterle, W., Ackermann, R., Kaiser, G.
*Reimann, I.W. and *Schwabe, S.
Pharmaceuticals Division, CIBA-GEIGY Ltd., Basle (Switzerland) *Humanpharmakologisches Institut CIBA-GEIGY GmbH, Tübingen (F.R.G.)

The new antidepressant levoprotiline•HCl is chemically the R-enantiomer of racemic oxaprotiline•HCl. Its pharmacokinetics were evaluated after single i.v. and p.o. as well as after multiple p.o. dosing in healthy volunteers. Levoprotiline was determined in blood by gas-chromatography-mass spectrometry.
 In a pilot study, 4 subjects were dosed with 15 mg i.v. and 75 mg p.o.. Judged from the dose corrected AUC-values, the absolute bioavailability of levoprotiline was 44%. After i.v., blood concentrations of levoprotiline declined in a polyphasic manner with a very fast distribution. The mean terminal elimination half-life was 21h, independent of the dosing route. The systemic clearance of levoprotiline was 15.8 ml/min/kg.
 After repeated peroral daily dosing with 75 mg (N=6) for 15 days, the kinetics of levoprotiline did not change. The accumulation ratio for the blood levels of levoprotiline was 1.9. Experimental trough levels as well as the concentration profile after the last dose corresponded very well with predicted concentrations obtained by simulation based on the concentrations after the first peroral dose.

Session 309 Symposium:
Depression and suicide

2034

THE TIME FACTOR IN THE ESTIMATION OF SUICIDE RISK

Jerome A. Motto, M.D. and Alan Bostrom, Ph.D.
University of California, San Francisco, U.S.A.

Empirical approaches to the estimation of suicide risk have not been widely accepted, though assessing risk remains a critical task. Empirical instruments developed for this purpose have usually considered a risk period of two years following the assessment, though clinical needs require a measure of risk over a much shorter time. Indicators of high risk over the near term (within 60 days) may have limited long-term value, and long-term (over one year) indicators of high risk may be of little help in the immediate clinical situation.

To clarify this question we are examining 101 variables in a prospective study of 3005 persons hospitalized for a depressive or suicidal state. The characteristics of those who suicided within 60 days, 60 days to 1 year, 1-2 years, 2-5 years, 5-10 years, and 10-15 years will be identified and compared. The short-term risk indicators can be helpful clinically, while the long-term risk indicators can provide epidemiological clues to improving suicide prevention on a societal level. Inherent limitations of empirical methods and the potential advantages of this approach for clinicians will be emphasized.

2035

PROSPECTS FOR SUICIDE PREVENTION
Kalle Achté, M.D., Dept. of Psychiatry, Univ. of Helsinki, Finland

Although increasing efforts are being made to reduce the number of suicides, the results are discouraging, especially in countries where the number has increased among young people. Why is the situation being aggravated rather than improved? Are social or psychological factors to blame? Suicide prevention does, however, bring results in individual cases. What I want to discuss is the increasing number of suicides among youth, the role of treatment organizations, risk evaluation, ethical aspects, the need for research, modern biological implications for suicide prevention and future prevention programs which could reduce the suicide rate. Since therapeutic care alone is often sufficient to prevent suicide, the first approach would be to refer anyone at risk without delay. Then the risk of each patient should be evaluated correctly, and, thirdly everyone who needs help should get it. The effectiveness of suicide prevention cannot be demonstrated simply from studies in the literature which evaluate suicide prevention institutions and programs. There are many individual factors which govern suicide prevention, such as appeal for help, the level and quality of care offered, and amenability to influences. These must be analyzed in further studies if suicide prevention programs are to be improved. More training is needed in the methodology of suicide research, and more international cooperation.

2036

PSYCHOTHERAPEUTIC AND PSYCHOPHARMACOLOGICAL TREATMENT OF SUICIDAL DEPRESSED INPATIENTS

Manfred Wolfersdorf, Dr. med.
Depression Treatment Ward, Psychiatric Hospital Weissenau
Department of Psychiatric I University of Ulm, D-7980 Ravensburg F.R.G.

Depressive patients are one of high-risk-groups due to suicidal behavior and death by suicide. Suicide rates are counted high between 500 and 900 due to 100000 depressives, in literature suicide mortality is found reaching 15 % of all primary depressive patient. Of our own depressive inpatients 20 % admissions are because of suicide attempts, about 29 % depressive inpatients of our depression treatment ward have suicide attempts in former history. Among suicides during psychiatric hospital treatment there are significantly more inpatients with depression than in the whole hospital clientele and inpatients with affective psychoses especially with delusional depression are overrepresented. Hopelessness, higher scores in depression scales, feelings of guilt and worthlessness, delusions seem to differentiate depressives with and without suicidale behavior. Treatment of these patients means psychotherapeutic measures which can be described in terms of crisis intervention, brief psychotherapy, and antidepressive medication as a treatment of the underlying depression sometimes in combination with neuroleptics.

2037

Suicide in patients with delusional psychoses.
Nils Retterstøl
University of Oslo, Gaustad Hospital
P.O. Box 24, Gaustad
N-0320 Oslo3, Norway

A sample of 334 first-admitted patients with delusional disorders was selected by the author. Included were patients where delusions were a prominent feature, while bipolars and patients with confusional states were excluded. The living patients were followed by personal re-examinations by the author 5-18 years after index admission, later by Dr. Opjordsmoen after 22-39 years. During the first observation period 28 had died, 5 by suicide, during the next observation 90 patients, 8 by suicide. The diagnoses at index admission were: reactive psychosis 6, schizophrenia 3, schizophreniform psychosis 3, organic psychosis 1. In addition, 3 patients died by accident where a possible suicide can not be excluded. Most suicides took place outside hospitals when the patients were apparently of sound mind. The risk of suicide decreases as years pass after index admission, but there still is an overmortality of suicide.

2038
SUICIDALITY AND PSYCHOPHARMACOLOGY
Walter Poeldinger
Psychiatric University Clinic, Basel

Whereas psychological and psychosocial aspects dominated the field of suicide research for a long period of time, there are numerous signs now - fitting into the biopsychosocial concept of diseases - that biological aspects gain increasing significance also for suicidology. This has three reasons:
1) There is evidence that genetic factors are not merely responsible for suicidality via the path of the manic-depressive illness but that within certain families there are genetic aspects influencing aggression, self-aggression, impulse-control directly and hereby suicidality.
2) Within the frame of biochemical research there is increasing evidence that a lack of serotin is correlated with a heightened suicidality risk.
Aside from these research results the possibility has been available since the discovery of modern psychoactive agents to treat acute states of movement, outbursts of affect and depression pharmacologicly. This is relevant for crisis-intervention as well as for secondary and tertiary prevention.
In addition the studies encouraged by MONTGOMERY have shown that neuroleptic or antidepressant medication can have a prophylactic effect with respect to suicidality which is independent of the disturbances or diseases underlying the suicidal action.

2039
DIFFERENT TOXICITY OF PSYCHOTROPIC DRUGS IN CASES OF SUICIDAL INTOXICATION.

Möller, H.-J.

Psychiatric Department of the University Bonn, FRG

An overview of the literature on this topic will be presented, focusing on suicidal intoxications with neuroleptics, antidepressants and benzodiazepines. Among other, a clear result is that intoxications with benzodiazepines are much less dangerous than intoxications with neuroleptics and antidepressants. But also within these groups are interesting differences with respect to lethal toxicity. This point will be demonstrated using the antidepressants as paradigma. The knowledge of these differences can be helpful when prescribing drugs for depressive patients with suicidal thoughts.

Session 310 Symposium:
Towards a safer treatment of insomnia

2040
SAFETY OF HYPNOTICS : WHERE WE STAND.

C. GUILLEMINAULT.
Sleep Disorders Center, Stanford, University, School of Medicine, Stanford, CA, USA.

Before approval, hypnotic drugs must meet rigorous criteria for safety, and adverse drug reactions have demonstrated the risk associated with certain drug familles or specific chemical radicals. New concerns related to untested effects of sedative-hypnotics now accompany the better understanding of the changes in physiology linked to age, circadian rhytm, and states of alertness (wake, NREM and REM sleep). The elderly, often multi-drug users, are the most common consumers of hypnotics, often with erratic intake and little attention to drug interactions. Shift workers, and professionals in high-risk jobs with rotating shifts, are increasingly using sleeping pills. To avoid iatrogenic symptoms, sedative-hypnotics must be evaluated frequently during the 24h cycle. Evaluation of performance is commonly made, but not of residual sleepiness during wake. Effects on vital functions must also be considered. Will a CNS depressant drug modify chemo- or barosensitivity during sleep, affect muscle coordination of the upper airway, further decrease bronchociliary movement and cough reflex, affect cognition and the normal circadian variation of many functions, from hormone secretions to core temperature control, or place patients with coronary heart disease or stroke at risk ?

2141
THE SAFETY ISSUE FOR A NEW HYPNOTIC :
A METHODOLOGICAL CHALLENGE
B. MUSCH and F. MAILLARD
RHONE-POULENC SANTE, ANTONY, FRANCE

Hypnotics are widely used drugs which demand a highly favourable risk/benefit ratio.
In developing a new hypnotic such as zopiclone (an original molecule unrelated to any existing drugs) further to the usual assessment of safety, specific issued have to be adequately investigated. The necessary studies involved different solved and unsolved problems. It is particularly relevant for a hypnotic not to interfere with daily mental functionning. Studies to assess residual effects after night administration, especially with respect to memory, are crucial and demand objective and methodologically adequate measurements.
Interaction with alcohol is also important to be assessed according to specific study designs.
The assessment of abuse and dependence potential is one of the major challenge for a new hypnotic. Studies related to the factors involved in the genesis of this potential are mandatory and they have been performed with zopiclone. Post marketing surveillance (PMS) implements knowledge about safety, but it should not be restricted to self reporting, especially in the case of a completely new drug. An extensive PMS program has been initiated with zopiclone, including open follow-up studies up to one year treatment and cross-tolerance studies after benzodiazepine discontinuation.

2042

HYPNOTICS AND THE CONTROL OF BREATHING DURING SLEEP
J. MOURET
Hôpital Le Vinatier, 95 bd. Pinel 69677 BRON Cedex FRANCE

Sleep leads to a number of physiological changes which should be taken into account when prescribing an hypnotic drug. This is especially true when considering breathing patterns due to the fact that on the one hand hypnotics are mainly prescribed to elderly patients and that, on the second hand, sleep-related respiratory disorders become increasingly common with age.
Whether of central or peripheral (obstructive) origin, sleep apnea and hypoventilation syndromes may also greatly worsen an already compromised ventilation and trigger severe drops in oxygen saturation.
Sleep apnea are virtually absent during stages III and IV sleep which can thus be considered as providing a protection against such disorders.
Benzodiazepine hypnotics are known to interact with the sleep-related control of breathing, while their well-known inhibitory effect on stages III and IV sleep increases the probability for sleep apneas to occur.
New hypnotics, suc as zopiclone, not only have much less respiratory depressant effects but they also tend to increase stages III and IV sleep, which provides a supplementary protection against sleep-related breathing disorders.
The importance of these differences will be discussed.

2043

RESIDUAL EFFECTS OF HYPNOTICS ON MEMORY, COGNITIVE FUNCTION AND INFORMATION PROCESSING.
I. HINDMARCH
Human Psychopharmacology Research Unit, University of Leeds, LEEDS, UK.

It has long been known that many hypnotics have a residual sedative activity which impairs psycho-motor functions and sensori-motor coordination. Less attention has been paid to the mnestic sequelae of night time sedatives.
Many benzodiazepines hypnotics (nitrazepam, flurazepam, triazolam, temazepam) have been shown to impair telephone number recall tasks the morning following nocturnal use. Such deficits could well be due directly to residual sedative activity and/or the type and nature of the psychometric test. There do exist important differences between drugs in their propensity for impairing psychological aspects of information processing. A series of studies have demonstrated the relative lack of disruptive activity of the cyclopyrrolone zopiclone with respect to conventional benzodiazepine like nitrazepam, flunitrazepam and flurazepam.

2044

EFFECTS OF ZOPICLONE ON NOCTURNAL SLEEP AND DAYTIME VIGILANCE.
H. ITOH, T. TAKAHASHI, T. KABASHIMA, M. SASAKI and A. MORI.
Department of Psychiatry, Jikei University, School of Medicine, Tokyo, Japan.

The purpose of the study was to assess the effects of three hypnotics : zopiclone (10mg/ZPC) flunitrazepam (2mg/FNZ) triazolam (0.25mg/TRZ) on nocturnal sleep and daytime vigilance.
Methodology :
. Cross-over study with 3 sequences of 7 days with a 21-day wash-out period between each sequence.
. Healthy volunteers.
. Assessments : polymonography, Multiple Sleep Latency Test (MSLT), Stanford Sleepiness Scale (SSS).
Results : zopiclone did not impair stages 3 + 4, REM stage, MSLT and Stanford Sleepiness Scale. With FNZ and TRZ, there was either a significant decrease of stages 3 + 4 or an impairment of daytime vigilance.
This study confirms the lack of decrease of stages 3 + 4 and REM sleep with zopiclone, at variance with benzodiazepines.
MSLT shows that zopiclone is free of residual effects during the following day.
The clinical meaning of these results will be discussed.

2045

POST-MARKETING SURVEILLANCE STUDY OF ZOPICLONE IN 21.974 INSOMNIACS.
H.ALLAIN*, C. DELAHAYE**. B. FERRAND**, C. PIEDELOUP**.
*Laboratoire pharmacologie expérimentale et clinique —Centre Hos. Rég. RENNES/FRANCE
**Théraplix-Groupe Rhône-Poulenc PARIS/FRANCE

In 1987, Théraplix initiated a clinical trial covering 26.600 insomniacs patients treated by general practitioners in France. 5.320 GPs took part in the open, non-comparative, multicenter study of 3 week duration.
Patients of either sex, aged over 18 years and presenting with current sleep disorders with a minimum duration of 2 weeks, whether or not treated with a hypnotic, were included. Zopiclone was prescribed at a daily dose of 3.75 or 7.5mg for 21 days. No procedure for the switch-over from the previous hypnotic was stipulated. At inclusion, the following sleep disorder parameters were evaluated : history, type, frequency, previous hypnotic treatment and Spiegel sleep questionnaire. Data input covered all cases completed by end August 1988, yielding 21.974 cases. At present the preliminary analysis on 10.000 patients confirm the safety profile of zopiclone observed in phase II and III studies. A crucial problem appears to be the interpretation of ADRs in patients who switched from BZD to zopiclone. The final results and their interpretation will be discussed at the Symposium.

2046

REBOUND INSOMNIA AND WITHDRAWAL SYNDROMES : THE CRITICAL ISSUE.
VELA-BUENO Antonio
Universidad Autonoma de Madrid / Spain.

Two different withdrawal phenomena have been described with hypnotic benzodiazepines. One occurring after an abrupt withdrawal (rebound insomnia) and another which occurs during administration (early morning insomnia).

A significant or noticeable increase in wakefulness above baseline levels, after a sudden drug withdrawal is what is known as rebound insomnia. The withdrawal state can generally vary depending on the type of drugs; it can be infrequent,delayed and moderate in intensity with long elimination half-life drugs; frequent, slightly delayed and of moderate intensity with intermediate half-life drugs; and immediate and of severe intensity after withdrawal of short half-life drugs.

Early morning insomnia is a significant increase in wakefulness above baseline levels which occurs during the final hours of the night when a hypnotic drug has been administered at bedtime. Two ultra short half-life hypnotic drugs have shown to cause this phenomena, these are triazolam and midazolam. The incidence of early morning insomnia and associated daytime anxiety are two potential sources of drug taking behavior and eventually lead to dependence.

2047

DOUBLE-BLIND STUDY OF ZOPICLONE AND TRIAZOLAM IN INSOMNIACS : HYPNOTIC AND WITHDRAWAL EFFECTS.
D.J. Mc LURE, J.E.A. FLEMING, C.F. MAYES.
Sleep Disorders Clinic - Shaughnessy Hosp.
VANCOUVER - Canada.

A double-blind study comparing zopiclone and triazolam, in 48 healthy, chronic insomniacs, was undertaken in two centres to compare the hypnotic and withdrawal effects of both compounds.
Comparable doses of 7.5mg zopiclone and 0.25mg triazolam were given at bedtime for 21 nights after a 3 day wash out period, followed by 4 placebo nights of withdrawal monitoring.
During the investigation, a 17 item post-sleep questionnaire was completed daily, the Clinical Global Impression (CGI) scale weekly, the Hamilton Anxiety Scale (HAM-A) at baseline and at the end of the study. Withdrawal effects were evaluated with a withdrawal symptom checklist and CGI (withdrawal).
Results indicated that both compounds improved sleep and were equally effective. However, a larger number of triazolam subjects withdrew from the study because of ineffectiveness or adverse side effects. A greater number of zopiclone subjects experienced taste perversion. Significant deterioration in nearly all sleep parameters were noted after the first withdrawal night of triazolam; much fewer modifications of sleep parameters were observed following the discontinuation of zopiclone.

2048

CROSS-TOLERANCE STUDY OF TRIAZOLAM 0.25mg AND ZOPICLONE 7.5mg.
P. LEMOINE*, C. DELAHAYE**.
* Hôpital Le Vinatier,95 bd. Pinel 69677 BRON Cedex
**Théraplix,Groupe Rhône-Poulenc,PARIS/FRANCE

The aim of this randomised, multicenter, parralel groups study in insomniacs treated for at least 3 months with triazolam, was to evaluate the appearence of possible withdrawal phenomena when patients switch from triazolam 0.25mg (TRZ), a benzodiazepine, to zopiclone 7.5mg (ZPC) a cyclopyrrolone.
Two substitution schedules were compared :
a) abrupt switch
b) gradual switch: reduction of TRZ to 0.125mg add on of ZPC at 3.75mg for the first week, then TRZ discontinuation and monotherapy with ZPC at 7.5mg for another week.
104 insomniacs previously on TRZ 0.25mg for at least 3 months were included in the study by general practitioners.
Non concomittant medications were allowed.
This study deals with the crucial practical problem that a new hypnotic, unrelated to any previous drug, has to face when it becomes available to doctors and can be substituted to previous drugs, known to cause withdrawal symptoms on discontinuation.
Analysis of data is ongoing and final results will be discussed at the Symposium.

Session 311 Symposium:
Psychoanalytic paradigms in clinical practice

2049

COPING AND DEFENSE
Raymond Battegay, M.D., Psychiatric University Outpatient Department, Kantonsspital, Petersgraben 4, CH-4031 Basel, Switzerland

Defense and coping may act complementary in the sense of a better integration of the individual into the social system. Whereas the defense mechanisms of the ego have the aim to diminish the stimuli, the coping has the aim to develop patterns of actions or reactions facilitating the accommodation in respect to a given situation. Defense mechanisms, if they set back unconscious desires may have for the ego in that sense a liberating effect, that it becomes now free to cope with stressful life-events. If the defense, however, becomes too rigid and/or when it consists in projective identifications, then the coping with the outside world is hindered. In individuals with a genetic predisposition the defense mechanisms, released often by stressful life-events, may go so far that they attack in autoimmune-processes the own body. In terminal diseases there is a marked interaction between defense and coping. It seems that the extremes of defense, i.e. a total denial of or a totally passive-permissive attitude towards the illness, show bad results in respect to the time of survival or the duration of the interval-free relapses. Coping with chronic pains and defense against them seems to be the best possible if anxiety which is only little related to objects is turned to an object-related fear.

2050
INVESTIGATION PSYCHOSOMATIQUE DE PATIENTS EN CRISE

N.Nicolaidis
UNIVERSITE DE GENEVE

Etude de patients de "tout venant" dans un centre de crise (Institutions universitaires psychiatriques genevoises : I.U.P.G.)

On a visé à déceler la dépression essentielle, franche ou déguisée en dépression, proche de celle des décompensations névrotiques graves.
La recherche que nous avons entreprise, a stimulé notre réflexion sur les points suivants :
- La crise constitue-t-elle une "solution" alternative à la désorganisation somatique ou au contraire une étape vers celle-ci ?
- Les patients réagissant à des états de crise, ont-ils des caractéristiques communes avec les patients psychosomatiques et lesquels ?
- Peut-on établir un profil psychosomatique du patient en crise par rapport au patient psychosomatique et évaluer le risque d'évolution psychosomatique de l'un par rapport à l'autre ?

2051
LE PSYCHIATRE, LE MEDICAMENT ET LA PSYCHOTHERAPIE

Professeur G. GARRONE et Mme A.E. BALANT - GORGIA
Département de Psychiatrie - Faculté de Médecine de Genève (Suisse)
Institutions Universitaires de Psychiatrie / GE

Les auteurs font état de la constatation quotidienne de la discordance qui existe généralement entre la qualité et la quantité de médicaments prescrits par le psychiatre et l'opinion qu'il semble avoir, intimement de ceux-ci. Cette opinion s'exprime généralement dans des conditions inconscientes : p.ex. l'oubli d'en tenir compte dans une évaluation de trajectoire, la dévalorisation de l'apport médicamenteux par rapport à la psychothérapie dans des traitements combinés. La majorité des psychiatres cliniciens prescrivent beaucoup, mais avec beaucoup de culpabilité. Les auteurs essayent de mesurer à la fois la portée et les origines de cette conduite particulière à travers une enquête menée avec la collaboration d'un groupe de psychiatres travaillant les uns en milieu institutionnel, les autres en privé.

2052
SOME THOUGHTS ON INSIGHT AND ITS RELATION TO COUNTERTRANSFERENCE
A.Alexandri, M.D., Gr. Vaslamatzis, M.D.
Department of Psychiatry, Athens University.

A lot has been written and discussed about insight on the narrow and wide sense of the term. Patient's and therapist's insight has also been dealt as well as insight in relation to psychoanalytic situation, interpretation, working through, goals of therapy, transference-countertransference and patient's individuality. However in the literature clinical examples supporting the theories are rather few.
In this paper clinical material from several cases of psychoanalytic therapy will be presented, attempting to demonstrate how countertransference is related to the patient's and therapist's insight and, mainly, how countertransference affects the kind of insight which the therapist choses to offer to his patient.
The clinical material is taken from personal cases of co-authors as well as from supervised cases by them.

2053
Suicidal Patient's "Selfobject Transference Attacks".

Dr. W. E. Milch
Psychiatrisches Krankenhaus Gießen, Akademisches Lehrkrankenhaus der Universität Gießen, Licher Str. 106, D-6300 Gießen

This paper is a clinical study on the meaning of aggression in the therapy of suicidal borderline patients. In the literature on the subject various authors show that suicidal patients provoke rejection. Furthermore, during the course of therapy, the therapist often is used as a "selfobject", an object that regulates narcissistic equilibrium. To demonstrate this idea, I shall present case histories of patients who created a "selfobject transference" by means of attacks on the therapist similar to those they themselves had experienced in their childhoods. In this manner the patients were able to preserve their self-integrity: They mobilized their aggression instead of relinquishing themselves to the total control of the selfobject. The massive, hidden attacks were also very troublesome to the therapist's own feeling of self-worth. By becoming more aware of these complicated processes, the therapist can prevent dangerous transference and countertransference patterns.
The object-relations of such patients are demonstrated with the Grid-technique (Kelly).

Session 312 Symposium: Multi-disciplinary approach in Alzheimer's disease research

2054
AN OVERVIEW OF ALZHEIMER'S DISEASE RESEARCH
Zaven S. Khachaturian, Ph.D.
National Institute on Aging, National Institutes of Health, Bethesda, MD, USA

Research on Alzheimer's disease (AD) in the United States covers a broad spectrum of topics and scientific disciplines, attempting to solve problems concerning: diagnosis, etiology, treatment, patient management, epidemiology and psycho-social issues concerning patients and family care providers. During the last 10 years, the number of investigators interested in AD, the quality of research and the prospects of funding research have been improving. The presentation will provide a brief overview of the important unresolved scientific issues that need more attention and a discussion of recent leads concerning the etiology of AD. One of the crucial questions in the etiology of AD concerns the problem of selection vulnerability of neurons. Recent evidence provides strong support for the hypothesis that mechanisms regulating cytosol calcium concentrations are critical links or provide the final common pathway for neuronal death in AD.

2054 A
Clinical Heterogeneity of Alzheimer Type Dementia
S. I. Gavrilova, S. B. Vavilov, N. K. Korsakov
All-Union Mental Health Research Centre, Moscow

A variability of clinical manifestations, course & morphofunctional implications of Alzheimer type dementia has been studied on the elderly inpatients cohorts. By employing longitudinal clinico-psychopathological, neuropsychological & computer-tomography methodology, it was possible to establish significant variations between the groups of Alzheimer disease and senile dementia patients in terms of some clinical parameters including the age of the onset and duration of the disease; its progressive rate, constitutional characteristics of the patients, frequency of exogenous-external impacts of life status prior to illness & directly before the onset, as well as psychopathological structure of dementia & its initial symptoms. The clinical variations in question are the variations of neuropsychological syndrome of higher mental functions disorders, AD & SD & differences in the structure & topography of anatomic brain changes substantiated by the data of computer tomography. The established findings of clinical & morphofunctional characteristics of AD & SD suggest definite clinical subtypes in the framework of Alzheimer type dementia.

2055
GENETIC EPIDEMIOLOGICAL AND MOLECULAR GENETIC APPROACHES IN FAMILIAL ALZHEIMER'S DISEASE: EVIDENCE FOR HETEROGENEITY
LA Farrer(1),PH St.George-Hyslop(2),RH Myers(1,2), JL Haines(2),LA Cupples(1),R.Tanzi(2),TD Bird(3), J.Hardy(4),AM Goate(4),R.Polinsky(5),L. Heston(6), C Van Broedkhoven (7), D.Crapper-McLachlan(8),J.F. Guzella(2) and JH Growdon(2).
1.Boston Univ.,MA; 2.Massachusetts General Hospital and Harvard Univ.,Boston; 3. Univ. of Washington & VA Med. Center, Seattle, 4.St. Mary's Hospital,London,UK; 5.NINCDS, Bethesda,MD; 6. Univ of Minnesota,MN, 7.Univ.of Antwerp, Belgium; 8.Univ of Toronto, Ontario, Canada.

Age at onset and life time risk for Alzheimer's disease (AD) were evaluated in 70 kindreds with familial AD (designated FAD) using survival analysis techniques. Risk of AD was assessed in 541 affected and 1,066 unaffected offspring of demented parents who were identified retrospectively. Using a method which takes into account affected persons with unknown onset ages and unaffected persons with unknown censoring ages, life time risk of AD among at-risk offspring by age 87 was 64%. Analysis of age at onset among kindreds showed evidence for a bimodal distribution: in this sample early-onset families have a mean onset age of less than 58 years and late-onset families have a mean onset age greater than 58 years. At-risk offspring in early-onset families had an estimated life time risk for dementia of 53% which is significantly less than the risk of 86% that was estimated for offspring in late-onset families. Male & female offspring in early-onset families have equivalent risk of dementia. In late-onset families the risk to female offspring is significantly higher than to male offspring but this difference is marginally significant. Life time risk of dementia in early-onset FAD kindreds is consistent with an autosomal dominant inheritance model. Our results also suggest that late-onset FAD has at least two etiologies; AD in some families may be transmitted as a dominant trait whereas, a proportion of cases in these and other late-onset families may be caused by other genetic or shared environmental factors. This hypothesis may explain why genetic linkage studies of these families suggest that a predisposing gene for early-onset FAD is located on chromosome 21, whereas linkage to the same group of markers is not detected in the late-onset families. The results of a multicenter collaborative linkage study using DNA markers on chromosome 21 will be presented.

2056
HIGH-RISK GROUP STUDY ON ALZHEIMER'S DISEASE
Amaducci - Italy

2057

NEUROCHEMICAL CHANGES IN BRAINS FROM PATIENTS WITH DEMENTIA DISORDERS

C.G. Gottfries
Dept. of Psychiatry and Neurochemistry, Gothenburg Univ., St.Jorgen's Hospital, Wisings Backa, Sweden

Postmortem human brain investigations from patients with Alzheimer's disease (AD/SDAT) have shown cholinergic deficit as marked by reduced activity in choline acetyl transferase (CAT) and acetylcholine esterase (AChE). Also nicotine receptors seem to be reduced while the data about muscarinic receptors differentiate. Also monoaminergic neurotransmitters and their metabolites are reduced in brains from patients with AD/SDAT. Imipramine binding of brain tissue is a marker for the presynaptic 5- hydroxytryptamine (5-HT) neuron. Also this marker indicates a rather severe disturbance of the 5-HT system. The activity of monoamine oxidase-B is increased by aging and still further increased in brains from patients with AD/SDAT. The increase in brain tissue seems to be due to a gliosis. The same enzyme is, however, also increased in platelets. According to data from our institute this increase seems to be related to a vitamin B-12-deficiency in a subgroup of SDAT-patients. Also amino acids, that function as neurotransmitters, and neuropeptides seem to be disturbed in brains from patients with AD/SDAT. To this should be added that some reports indicate white matter disturbances in this dementia disorder. The multiple changes foud in grey as well as in white matter of brains from AD/SDAT-patients indicate that the changes may be of secondary nature and caused by a more fundamental disturbance of the brain, the nature of which we still do not know.

2058

CLINICAL ASSESSMENT OF ALZHEIMER'S DISEASE

Copeland J. - Professor, University of Liverpool, UK

Session 313 Workshop:
Cognitive approaches to patients suffering from a schizophrenic syndrome

2059

COGNITIVE APPROACHES TO PATIENTS SUFFERING FROM A SCHIZOPHRENIC SYNDROME

Carlo Perris M.D., Umea, Sweden.

This workshop will present an integrated therapeutic approach to working with patients suffering from a schizophrenic syndrome. Specifically, ways of eliciting and dealing with the dysfunctional cognitions of those patients will be addressed. A particular emphasis is put on the importance of the kind of therapeutic relationship necessary from working with those type of patients. Strategies for engaging the schizophrenic patient in therapy will be discussed and a variety of cognitive-behavioural techniques feasible with severely disturbed patients will be presented. A short videotape will show how an integrating and comprehensive tratment programme is currently carried out at three small community-based treatment centres at Umea.

Session 314 New Research:
Psychosomatic and somatoform disorders

2060

Chronic pain and depressive symptoms in the general population : an analysis of the NHANES I. data

G. MAGNI[1], C. CALDIRON[2], S. RIGATTI-LUCHINI[2].
1- WYETH-AYERST European Clinical Research & Development, Paris, France
2- Department of Statistics, University of Padua, Padova, Italy

Several studies have suggested the existence of a relationship between chronic pain and depression ; however the vast majority have been carried out on selected samples gathered in hospitals or pain clinics, while data on general population are almost completely lacking.
The National Health and Nutrition Examination Survey I (NHANES I) is a survey of the nutritional and general health status of the civilian non-institutionalized population of the United States; data on chronic pain and depressive symptoms are available for a representative subsample known as the Augmentation Survey.
The measure of depression is the Center for Epidemiologic Studies Depression Scale (CES-D); chronic pain cases were subjects suffering from pain on neck, back, hip, knee or having significant swelling and pain of joints on most days for at least one month in the 12 months preceding the interview.
The sample is made up of 3023 subjects, 25-74 years of age, 1319 males and 1704 females : 416 suffered from chronic pain, 2388 had no chronic pain and the last 219 were "uncertain cases" in the sense that they had pain on most days for at least one month, but it was not possible to determine if they suffered from it in the last 12 months.
Chronic pain subjects scored significantly higher than normals at the CES-D (10.68 +/- SEM 0.76 vs 8.05 +/- 0.23, p<0.01) with uncertain cases scoring similar to the pain population (11.13 +/- 0.76). Prevalences of depression in the three groups were 23.6%, 15.4% and 24.9% using a cut-off of 16 at the CES-D and 18.3%, 8.8% and 14.5% using a more conservative cut-off of 20 at the CES-D.
Considering various sociodemographic variables able to influence the depressive symptoms it was found that the chronic pain group was characterized by an older age, a greater percentage of females and a lower income than the normal group. There was no difference between the two samples for education, civil status and race. Logistic regression was used to estimate the likelihood of becoming depressed adjusted for possible confounding variables. Female sex, low income and chronic pain in a decreasing order of potency were the most significant predictors of depression.
These findings show that chronic pain is significantly associated with depressive symptoms in the general population; if this association is specific of the chronic pain condition or is shared by other chronic non painful diseases is not possible to say from these data.

2061

HYSTERICAL PSYCHOSIS: NEED FOR SPECIFIC AND DESCRIPTIVE CRITERIA.

Dr L. R. FENOY, CHS Esquirol, St Maurice; Dr G. S. COHEN ADAD, CHS de Maison Blanche, Neuilly/Marne; FRANCE.

Hysterical psychosis seems to have a place as a third psychosis separate from schizophrenia and the affective psychoses.
The concept of hysterical psychosis, as defined by Follin (1961), has not received full acceptance in the scientific community. Many explanations may be provided: 1. the failure by the authors to reach concensus on the criteria, 2. the difficulty of interreliability of the diagnosis of hysterical personality.
The clinical usefulness of the concept of hysterical psychosis has not been fully supported by data because cases reported in the litterature are scarce.
Specific and descriptive diagnostic criteria in the style of the DSM 3s reflecting a concensus of current formulations of different authors are suggested. Tested on cases reported in the litterature, the validity of these proposed criteria seems to be good.
A case of hysterical psychosis will be presented.

2062

THE COMPARISON OF SUBJECTIVE PSYCHOSOMATIC RESPONSES IN TURKISH UNIVERSITY STUDENTS.
BİRSÖZ,S.,BÜYÜKBERKER,Ç.,GÜCER,M.,KARAMAN,T.
AKDENİZ UNIVERSITY,DEPARTMENT OF PSYCHIATRY.
ANTALYA(07050)/TURKEY.

Akdeniz University Medical college student's subjective psychosomatic responses have been studied by General Health Questionnaire of Goldberg (G.H.Q) in 949 subject during the years of 1983-1988 prospectively.It has been found that the negative responses were increasingly higher during the years and mostly in male students.
The same test was given to 708 medical and 160 agricultural college students at the same time and the responses were compared according to sociodemographic variables.A high correlation was found between the GHQ scores and education,sex, accomodation and income levels. The medical college students showed more psychopathology and negative responses than the agricultural college students. The results were also compared with the Ankara University's medical college students.(n=698). These findings were discussed according to psychosocial stresses related to medical education.

2063

HOSTILE PERSONALITY CHARACTERISTICS AND PROSTAGLANDINS IN ESSENTIAL HYPERTENSION.
Aritzi S, Demakis J, Demakis G, Fareed J, Reid R, Duncas N, Richardson C, Lyketsos G.
A series of studies in Greece has shown the hostile personality characteristic of low dominance to be a common feature of eight physical conditions of presumably psychogenic origin. In two, primary dysmenorrhea and essential hypertension, biosynthesis of prostaglandins is considered to be involved in the pathogenesis of the organ's physical dysfunction. A recent study correlated two further hostile personality characteristics, extrapunitiveness and intropunitiveness, with prostaglandins in primary dysmenorrhea. The present study in the USA examines the relation of prostaglandins to personality characteristics in essential hypertension. A sample of 33 hypertensives and 18 controls was obtained from consecutive outpatient appointments at Hines VA Hospital. Personality characteristics were assessed by Foulds' Scales of Anxiety and Depression (SAD) and Personality Deviance (PDS), and neurotic symptoms by Wing's Present State Examination (PSE) and the Anxiety and Depression section of the CIDI. Laboratory measurements included PGI2 and TxA2 concentrations in blood samples. Preliminary results show significantly lower dominance in the hypertensives and a correlation between PGI2 and dominance in the controls. Full analysis of the relations between these and other clinical and laboratory variables will be reported.

2064

CLOMIPRAMINE IN THE PREMENSTRUAL SYNDROME: A PILOT STUDY
Elias Eriksson, Björn Andersch, Kerstin Andersson, Pia Lisjö, and Kjell Modigh. Department of Pharmacology, University of Göteborg, Sweden.
The premenstrual syndrome (PMS) is characterized by decreased impulse control, increased irritability and dysphoria. A decreased serotonergic neurotransmission has been attributed importance for all these symptoms; moreover, the activity in brain serotonin synapses is influenced by changes in blood concentrations of estradiol and progesterone. Hence, it is tempting to suggest that PMS may be due to a sex steroid induced alteration in central serotonergic function. To evaluate the possible benefit of a serotonin reuptake inhibitor in the treatment of PMS, we have, in a pilot study, administered clomipramine (10-50 mg/day) for at least five consecutive menstrual cycles to five non-depressed women suffering from servere premenstrual irritability and dysphoria. Usually the placebo response is marked in PMS patients; however, the participants in the present study were known from a previous double-blind placebo-controlled trial (comprising placebo, ritanserin and clonidine) not to respond to placebo. During treatment with clomipramine all patients reported an almost total relief in premenstrual complaints, also reflected in a dramatic and statistically significant reduction in self-rated irritability and dysphoria in the days preceeding the menses. The reduction in PMS symptoms persisted throughout the study; in contrast, the effect of placebo in PMS ususally fades after a few cycles of treatment. Our preliminary findings thus indicate that clomipramine, at considerably lower doses than is usually recommended for the treatment of depression, may be very effective in reducing premenstrual irritability and dysphoria.

2065

SOMATIZATION DISORDER: SOCIO-CULTURAL STATUS, SYMPTOMATOLOGY, DEPRESSION
Telaferli B, Kayaalp L, Emik C, Songar A.
Cerrahpaşa Medicine Fac. Department of Psychiatry
University of Istanbul

55 out-patients, who are according to DSM III-R criteria diagnosed as having a somatization disorder, are assessed in relation to their socio-cultural status, symptoms and depression scales. Compared to the control group which has different psychiatric diagnoses, it was seen that among our group, the incidences of being a female, being married and belonging to a low education level, are observed to be significantly high. However between the two groups there was no significant difference in their family types, where they come from (urban/rural) or the way they're grown up. A story of a functional enuresis, a surgical operation, and similar psychiatric disorders in the family were observed to be of a very high incidence in the somatization group. Assessing the symptoms it was seen that some symptoms such as palpitation, shortness of breath, sexual indifference were very frequent, while others like pain in sexual indifference were very frequent, while others like pain in sexual organs, deafness, blindness were very rare. Besides these, some symptoms which are not included in the criteria, but that can be accepted as a somatization symptom (paresthesia, astasia, abasia) had a high frequency in our population. Above all in some patients certain uncommon symptoms which are not originated from an organic or psychiatric disorder, but are thought to be originated from one's culture and the way he expresses himself, were observed. In more than half of the patients moderate or severe depression (12 mild, 23 moderate, 16 severe) was indicated, and it was observed that where is a positive relation between the number of somatic symptoms and the degree of the depression.

2066

Psychiatry in intensive care units (I.C.U.)

DALAKAKI Xanthoula, Psychiatre
Institutions Universitaires de Psychiatrie
1225 Chêne-Bourg / Genève-Suisse

Intensive cares play a dynamic role in modern medecine. Psychiatric contribution to the comprehension and the adjusting of the patients' affects, could influence the illness evolution.

The real somato-socio-psychological crises, which the individual goes through, provokes varying levels of regression. The feeling of vital threat, such as patients experienced during the accident, heart-attack or any other acute disturbances justifying his stay in I.C.U. and the sensory-deprivation, defined by the type of care in these units, interferes in this momentary dynamics with the patients' structure of personality and the environment capacity to "holding" (according to Winniccot.)

A psychotherapeutic relationship has been carried out on patients in the different levels of consciousness up to coma stage III as an example of investigation.

Lastly, a catamnestic study which has been carried out through a semi-directive interview from 5 to 7 years after a long stay in I.C.U., confirms hypothesis of regression that can go up to cognitive desorganisation, breach of contact with the external reality and appearing of delirious ideas.

Psychic restructuration and "how" exterior aide (resurection-care-contacts) was used by ex-patients in the search for a way out are analysed.

Several interrogations on the psycho-affective development appear.

Session 315   New Research:
Schizophrenia and related nosological issues

2067

LANGFELDT'S SCHIZOPHRENIFORM PSYCHOSES FIFTY YEARS LATER
Mina Bergem, MD, Alv A. Dahl, MD, Cato Guldberg, MD, Helge Hansen, MD.
Department of Psychiatry, University of Oslo, P.O.Box 85, Vinderen,
0319 Oslo 3, Norway.

Due to follow-up studies published in 1937 and 1939 Langfeldt divided schizophrenia into two groups. Typical schizophrenia had a poor outcome. The schizophreniform psychoses had a less typical clinical picture and a good outcome. Langfeldt's cases of schizophreniform psychoses have been reclassified according to the ICD-9 and DSM-III-R diagnostic systems. Most of the schizophreniform psychoses did not appear "schizophrenia-like" at all, but turned out to be mainly affective disorders by modern standards. Langfeldt's schizophreniform psychoses were found too heterogenous to be valid clinical syndrome.

2068

CHARACTERISATION OF RELAPSES IN SCHIZOPHRENIA
Reed Paul
Psychiatric Research Unit, Hope and Prestwich Hospitals, Salford, UK
A review of the literature on relapse rates of schizophrenia shows that authors use different criteria for defining a 'relapse'. The chief objective of this investigation was to study all consecutive patients with schizophrenia who were reported as 'relapsing' during a period of 12 months with a view to determining specific criteria used by the reporting agency for 'relapse' and comparing them with objective assessments on various clinical rating scales. A follow-up at 3 months after the initial relapse ensured that the evolution of that relapse was taken into account and therefore gave a more accurate description of that episode. All cases were interviewed immediately (within 24 hours) on a semistructured interview followed by rating on various clinical scales for positive and negative symptoms of schizophrenia as well as for depression, neuroleptic side effects and life events. The data obtained was subjected to a detailed statistical analysis. The results showed that, after admissions due to side effects of drugs and respite for families were excluded, four distinct syndromes of relapses could be identified on factor analysis. These four accounted for a cumulative variance of 77.4%. Details of these syndromes will be discussed in the paper.

2069
AUTOMATIC ANALYSIS OF FACIAL ACTION IN
SCHIZOPHRENIC AND DEPRESSED PATIENTS

Frank Schneider, Hans Heimann, Waldemar Himer
Psychiatric Hospital, Univ. of Tübingen, FRG

With a newly developed automatic analysis the
space coordinates of light reflecting points,
glued onto the face of subjects, are filmed for a
specific length of time, thereby quantifying
facial actions reliably and validly.
20 schizophrenics, 20 depressives, and 20 controls
participated in this pilot study. Four small
pieces of adhesive tape were placed on the subjects's face (next to the beginning of each
eyebrow and at each corner of the mouth). Positive
as well as negative emotions were induced in a
verbal and non-verbal situation, respectively.
In each of the four experimental conditions the
subjects's mimic was analysed for 2.5 minutes.
Findings indicate that depressive and schizophrenic subjects exhibit a reduction of mimical
movements in the upper part of the face. Schizophrenic subjects show a "unified mimical style"
across different situations and emotions, i.e. an
indifference in mimical response ability.
The following seems to apply to schizophrenics: a
patient expresses all the more facial action the
more seriously ill he becomes and all the less the
more negative symtoms he exhibits. By comparison
the facial actions of depressives tend to be
reduced during symptom exacerbations.

2070
EPILEPTIC SCHIZOPHRENIA: PATHOGENESIS AND COMPLICATIONS
Dr Femi Oyebode MB BS MRCPsych and Dr Kenneth Davison MB
FRCP(Ed) FRCP FRCPsych DPM Department of Psychological
Medicine Newcastle General Hospital Newcastle United Kingdom

This study examined the pathogenesis and complications of
schizophrenia in epileptic patients. Twenty-seven (27)
patients with clinical diagnoses of partial seizures and in
addition Research Diagnostic Criteria (RDC) diagnoses of
schizophrenia were identified and compared to nineteen (19)
control subjects drawn from a neurological clinic with
diagnoses of partial seizures without history of psychiatric
illness. There was no statistical difference in the mean ages,
sex distribution, marital status, premorbid sociability and
mean ages of onset of epilepsy between the groups. There was
a history of formal psychiatric illness in the relatives of
13 (50%) of the index group but only in 1 (5.3%) of the
control group. This difference was highly significant
($p = 0.004$). There was a trend for the frequency of partial
seizures to be lower in the index group. There was no
demonstrable association between laterality of electrical
focus and schizophrenia in the index sample. This negative
finding held even when handedness was controlled for. The
mean scores on the Folstein Mini-mental state were not
different between the groups. Twenty (20) of the index sample
had been unemployed for five (5) years or more compared with
six (6) of the control group. This difference was
significant ($p = 0.0104$). This study suggests that family
history of psychiatric disorder in individuals with partial
seizures is a vulnerability factor for schizophrenia. Lower
frequency of seizures may have pathogenic consequence. The
high levels of unemployment in the index group demonstrate
the adverse social sequelae of the combination of
schizophrenia and epilepsy.

2071
DRUG DEPENDENCE VERSUS DIFFERENT PSYCHOTIC CHRONIC
DISEASE: AN INTEGRATIVE MODEL OF TREATMENT
I. Carta, M.Clerici, G.C.Galvano, R.Garavaglia
G.Landoni, G.Maggio
Department of Psychiatry - University of Milan

We compare two populations composed of subjects
with different nosographic tables(DSM III R),
homogeneous as regards the clinical condition of
treatment by multiple associated therapies and all
the other foreseen clinical variants, with the
exception of the drug dependance variant in the
second population characterized besides by the
presence of an undrpopulation of probationers for
whom the only disease caused by the use of psychoactive substances has been diagnosed.
The obtained results concern:
1) Individualization of specific outlines of integration which are defined by therapeutic courses
in the different areas of association.
2) Individualization of correlation between such
outlines and the different nosographic tables.
3) Incidence evaluation of the drug dependence
variant in the occurred clinical change.

2072
NEUROPSYCHOPATHOLOGICAL HETEROGENEITY OF REDUPLI-
CATIVE PHENOMENA.
Ohigashi,Y.(Sect.of Student Health, Kyoto Univer-
sity), Hamanaka,T.(Dpt of Neuropsychiatry, Nagoya
City University, Nagoya, Japan)

Expanding the concept of reduplicative paramnesia
(RP: Pick 1901/03), Weinstein(1952/69) introduced
the notion of "phenomenon of reduplication"(PR),
which covered, besides of the paramnesic aberration
in the original sense of Pick, a series of such diverse neuropsychopathological states as follow,
partially in the terminology of other authors who
described the corresponding phenomena earlier or
later: 1)déjà-vécu, identifying or associative paramnesia, 2)geographical mislocation, 3)delusion
of a double, 4)misidentification of mirror image,
5)autoscopic phenomenon, 6)pseudo-polymelia, 7)re-
duplication of objects, 8)non-aphasic misnaming.
Other authors reported under the rubric of RP such
varied conditions, which deviate more or less from
the original descriptions of Pick, as "topographical delusion"(Rosenberg 1912,Levine 1984)="délire
topographique"(Vighetto 1981/85), double orienta-
tion(Cummings 1985), simple negation of persons or
Capgras's syndrome(Alexander 1979,Staton 1982). Our
paper, clarifying once more the notion of PR, tries
to bring in order its neuropsychiatric interpretation that has been mislead by the deviated concept-
formations. 3 illustrating cases are reported.

2073
LANGUAGE DISORDERS IN PARANOID SCHIZOPHRENIA

Andrzej Czernikiewicz, Department of Psychiatry, Lublin, Poland
Schizophrenics appear to have difficulty with coherent discourse processing. This hypothesis was tested by assesing verbal behavior of 30 subchronic and 30 chronic patients that fulfilled DSM III Criteria for paranoid schizophrenia. The samples of spontaneous speech were analysed by Scale for the Assesment of Thought, Language, and Communication /TLC/. Every subject was examined in acute phase of psychosis and in remission. Mental state of Ss was scored by BPRS. In acute phase of psychosis were observed marked verbal disorders in the speech of Ss. During the remission language disturbances diminished but majority of utterances revealed mild pathology of speech. The language pathology among studied schizophrenics was mainly caused by "lack of structural coherence" of the discourse. The higher results of positive disorders and loose associations were found in the group of chronic patients. Language "negative disorders" did not differ significantly in the subchronic and chronic paranoid schizophrenics.

Session 316 Free Communications:
Schizoaffective disorders

2074
COMPARISON OF PREMORBID AND SOCIAL FEATURES IN FUNCTIONAL PSYCHOSES

A. Deister, A. Marneros, A. Rohde, B. Staab
Psychiatric Department of the University Bonn, Federal Republic of Germany

As a part of a long-term followup study (Cologne Study) we investigated premorbid and social features of 249 patients with functional psychoses. 97 patients were diagnosed as having schizophrenia, 72 pat. as schizoaffective disorder, and 80 pat. as affective disorder.
We compared sex distribution, age at onset, educational and occupational level, marital status, social class, premorbid personality and premorbid social interactions.
The results supported the assumption, that schizoaffective psychoses have a position between both other diagnostic groups, but they have much more in common with affective than with schizophrenic disorders.

2075
A FAMILY STUDY OF SCHIZOAFFECTIVE DISORDER IN SARDINIA

A. Bocchetta, L. Garau, M. Migoni, S. Mulas, M. Del Zompo; Dept. of Neurosciences, Service of Clinical Pharmacology, Univ. of Cagliari, Cagliari, Italy.

First-degree relatives (n=1311) of 178 probands were studied with interviews, information from relatives, and review of medical records. Diagnoses were made according to the Research Diagnostic Criteria. The probands included 55 schizoaffective bipolar (SA-B), 30 schizoaffective depressive (SA-D), 37 bipolar 1 (BP-1), 27 bipolar 2 (BP-2), and 29 unipolar (UP) patients. The proportion of risk passed by each relative was computed according to the $\log_e$ age at onset in probands and ill relatives with UP, BP, and SA illness. The age at onset for SA illness (median age, 24 years) was found to be significantly lower than for BP (29 years) and UP (men, 38; women, 31) illness. Lifetime prevalences of major affective disorder were 10%, 5%, 12%, 14%, and 6% in relatives of probands with SA-B, SA-D, BP-1, BP-2, and UP illness. The most frequent disorder in relatives of all types of probands was UP illness. The probands with SA-B illness had the highest frequency of SA-B illness in relatives. The probands with SA illness had more schizophrenic first-degree relatives than did other probands. The overall morbid risk of bipolar disorder (SA-B, BP-1, or BP-2) was similar in relatives of bipolar probands (4-5%), but significantly lower in relatives of SA-D or UP probands (1-2%).

2076
THE CASE FOR INDEPENDENCE OF SCHIZOAFFECTIVE PSYCHOSIS
Prof. S.S. Raju, M.D., Head of Psychiatry
Kasturba Medical College, Manipal, Karnataka, India

Schizoaffective psychosis, has been variously regarded as a subtype of schizophrenia, a subtype of affective disorder, or as a separate clinical entity, and its nosological status remains controversial. 45 consecutive cases of schizoaffective psychosis admitted to a general hospital psychiatric inpatient unit over a 3-year period, from 1983 to 1985, have been compared with 45 cases of schizophrenia and 45 cases of manic-depressive psychosis, admitted over the same period, across the following dimensions: Clinical symptomatology; Response to drug treatment; Outcome; and family history studies. RCD criteria were used for diagnostic purposes and FH-RDC for family history diagnoses. The results show that schizoaffective psychosis is a definite clinical entity with its characteristic phenomenology, treatment response and outcome, and high genetic loading of psychoses. The study suggests that schizoaffective psychosis is not a subtype of schizophrenia of affective disorder, but an independent illness with 2 subtypes, schizomanic disorder, and schizodepressive disorder, which can be further characterised as unipolar or bipolar. It is advocated, with due reasons, that schizoaffective psychosis should be classified as an independent clinical entity in ICD-10 and DSM-IV.

2077

TREATMENT AND PREVENTION OF SCHIZOAFFECTIVE DISORDERS.

Pedro B. Posligua M.D. Serv. de Psiquiatría Hospital Regional del IESS. Guayaquil-Ecuador.

To our knowledge, a total of 86 patients treated, and prophylatic effects with Carbamazepina-Tioridazina or Clonazepan-Haloperidol, during the lasts seven years.
Ower reports demonstrate, pharmacokinetic interactions between anticonvulsants and other psichotropic drugs for treating severe psychotic espectrum behavioral disorders, in three categories of schizoaffective syndrome: Manic, Depressive and Paranoid patients.
Dosage can then be adjusted to achieve maximum therapeutic effect and is especially effective in preventing mood swings.

2078

THE PERSONALITY OF RDC SCHIZOAFFECTIVES

H. Sauer, P. Richter, Ch. Hornstein, H. Saß
Psychiatric Dept., University of Heidelberg, FRG

In 60 patients suffering from an RDC schizoaffective psychosis (29 of the manic, 29 of the depressive type) the personality was investigated after remission of the acute illness, using the Rorschach-test and the MMPI.- In the Rorschach-test no significant differences were found between the schizoaffectives and a RDC depressive control group (n=21, 20 % bipolar); according to the MMPI, however, the schizoaffectives appeared to be more schizoid and autistic. On dividing the schizoaffectives into the schizodepressive and schizomanic subtypes a large number of significant differences were found, mainly concerning the schizodepressives. These were characterized by low adaptive affects (FC), a poor affective report (C) and increased stereotyped thinking (A %) in the Rorschach-test and by a MMPI profile indicating social introversion and paranoid behavior. The schizomanics, on the other hand, hardly differed from the affective control group.- Thus the personality profile of the schizoaffectives seems to be heterogeneous. The finding that the schizomanics are more similar to the affectives, whereas the schizodepressives probably more resemble schizophrenics is in accord with results from recent outcome and hereditary studies.

2079

LONG-TERM COURSE OF AFFECTIVE AND SCHIZOAFFECTIVE DISORDERS
A. ROHDE, A. MARNEROS, A. DEISTER, B. STAAB
Department of Psychiatry, University of Bonn, FRG

80 affective, 72 schizoaffective and 97 schizophrenic disorders were investigated regarding their long-term course (more than 20 years on average, min. 10, max. 59 years).

Important elements of course were evaluated, i.e. number and length of episodes, intervals and cycles, type of episodes, syndrome shift, precipitating factors, inactivity of the illness etc.
Important differences were found suggesting several differences between schizoaffective and schizophrenic disorders and similarities between affective and schizoaffective disorders.
Comparing unipolar and bipolar forms of affective and schizoaffective disorders, we found some differences in both disorders which support the necessity to separate unipolar and bipolar forms of illnesses.

Session 317 Free Communications:
History of psychiatry: Leading figures

2080

THE WELFARE OF OUT PATIENTS IN FRANCE DURING THE NINETEENTH CENTURY
Dr. Bernard Odier, Psychiatrist
C.H.S. B.Durand, 91 152 - Etampes Cedex, France
1838 is well-known for the introduction of a french law concerning mental institutions and internment.
Less renouned are the foundation of several charitable institutions four years later, dedicated to patients leaving the asylums. In 1842, a parisien alienist of Salpetrier, Docteur Jean-Paul Fabret organised a welfare system, with the help of clergy, a central organisation of parisian hospitals, and of several prominent philanthropists.
In each parisian district, a small team mostly composed of nuns were informed about the convalescents departure from Salpetriere. They could receive visits, financial aids, and if necessary, they could be welcomed in special refuge city centers, where they would find meals and work.
To what extent is that sort of philanthropie institution a relic of centuries of charity, and in what way is it an ancestor of social psychiatric statements.
The institutions which pursue projects specifically aimed at short-term assistance encounter the same resistance as those past and present, when they have to care for chronic patients.

2081

DIE AKTUALITÄT DER WECHSELWIRKUNG
ZWISCHEN K.JASPERS UND M.WEBER
N.Tzavaras, Psychopathological Laboratory
University of Thrace, Alexandroupolis,
Greece.

M.Weber hat wie wenige Gesellschaftswissenschaftler die Methodologie der Psychopathologie beeinflusst. In dieser Arbeit wird erneut der Versuch unternommen, die konvergenten Denkrichtungen zwischen ihm und seinem Schüler K.Jaspers hinsichtlich ihrer wissenschaftstheoretischen Konzeptionen hervorzuheben. Insbesondere wird Wert auf die aktuelle Forderung nach strigenteren Deskriptionskategorien gelegt, um die beide Denker in ihrem Werk bemüht blieben.

2082

Benjamin Rush, Father of American Psychiatry:
A dream finally realized
Richard A. Shadoan,M.D., Melvin Sabshin, M.D.
California Psychiatric Association
American Psychiatric Association

The United States Institute of Peace was established in 1984 and was one of Benjamin Rush's most cherished dreams. His public affairs activities, besides an active abhorrence of war, included: Publishing articles protesting the treatment of the colonies by England, and advocacy for the right to equal education for all people, the abolition of slavery and the reform of jails.
His peace plan was published in 1793. Rush had the belief that wars could be avoided by conscientious study and teaching.The concept of having a Department of War was so far ahead of its time that it was left fallow for almost two hundred years. In 1981 a national commission recommended that the President and the Congress should establish a United States Academy of Peace. Congress acted, and on October 19, 1984 President Reagan signed into law the United States Institute of Peace Act. Benjamin Rush's dream had finally become a reality.
His belief-that wars do not work and nations must be taught non-violent conflict resolution-though first articulated in the 18th century, certainly belongs to the last half of the 20th century.

2083

PSYCHOLOGICAL BASIS IN BOOKS OF MARTYR MOTAHHARI
Vaezi S.Ahmad, M.D.
University of Medical Scienses of Iran, Tehran,
Iran

In heavenly cultures specifically in Islam there are detailed positive and negative commands for accomplishment or keep away of individual social ethical policies. Obeying them will obtain suitable area of psychical health. The mentioned area will solve the majority of the difficulties and disorders which we have in our daily living in society.
Martyr Motahhary who is one of the greatest thinkers of Islam in new years has explained these social Islamic orders and their positive traces on psychical health.

2084

THE HENRI EY'S ORGANO-DYNAMIST THEORY

GARRABE J. and KAPSAMBELIS V.
Institut National Marcel Rivière

Herni Ey (1900-1977),one of the founders of W.P.A., has been a significant personnality of contemporary french psychiatry.His extensive work is based on organo-dynamism,a theory which permitted him to elaborate a coherent conception of mental illness. This theory constitutes a response to two major problems : the specificity of psychiatry's field and the dilemma between organogenesis or psychogenesis of mental disorders. Organo-dynamism is opposed to both mechanistic organicism, in which mental disorders are conceived as direct expressions of C.N.S.' diseases, and theories of pure psychic causality, as psychoanalysis. H. Ey revisited and developped the ideas of the English neurologist Hughlings Jackson (1834-1911) : a)mental functions are "hierarchical" (graded), every level integrating inferior levels; b)pathological states correspond to functions' dissolutions with regression to inferior functionning levels; therefore disorders have always a double aspect : negative (deficient), i.e. the expression of direct effects of pathological process, and positive, i.e. the expression of subsistent levels' liberation; c)dissolutions may be partial (neurologic disorders) or global (psychiatric disorders); d)psychiatric disorders are not "anatomical/clinical entities" but syndroms of various etiologies (every dissolution corresponds to a typic clinical feature, but many organic or psychic causes may induce the same dissolution). The organo-dynamist model has two components : 1)organicist, because psychopathological facts are inconceivable without any disorganization of mental structures; 2)dynamist, because disorganization is a normal energetic system's instabilization (reference to P.Janet's theories). This conception leads H.Ey to place in the center of his psychopathology not the unconscious, but the conscious (the most achieved form of mental hierarchy), then to create, at the end of his work, the concept of psychic body.Using this approch, he modified the theorization of both some psychophysiological phenomena, e.g. the dream, and of the pathology of acute and chronic psychoses. Organo-dynamism is an important phase in the evolution of psychiatric ideas of the 20th century.

Session 318 Free Communications:
Exercise, music and art therapy

2085

ART-THERAPY GROUPS:"FROM THE PART TO THE WHOLE", "FROM THE EXTRACT TO SYNTHESIS"
Gyra E.,Mantonakis J.,Denegri Z.,Telioni E.
Department of Psychiatry,University of Athens,Eginition Hospital,Athens, Greece.

Nine years constant functioning of Art-therapy groups,which are part of a broader therapeutic program in a Day Hospital,is presented with emphasis on the modifications and the evolution regarding the structure and the content of these groups.Specifically,the Art-therapy group techniques that are analyzed are those which encourage analogic expression through the emancipation of suppresed feelings and unconcious material as well as the comprehension of all this material through analytic digital expression.Basic presupposition is the creation and maintenance of the group and the main tool for the elaboration of the dynamics and the transpersonal relationships in the group is the expression and communication through free drawing.Through the developmental process of the group and the representations of drawings we can observe the function of the opposites:verbal - non-verbal,illness-health, delusion-reality,child-adult,etc.as well as the reconstructive experience which is expressed step by step in the transition of the part to the whole and the extract to synthesis.Art-therapy because of being a non-verbal therapeutic technique can speed up this transition and eliminate the defenses and the resistances which more often appear in verbal communication.Some characteristic drawings are presented and an attempt to relate them with the patients' current psychopathology is tried.

2086

SHORT TERM ART THERAPY IN PSYCHIATRIC CRISIS INTERVENTION, PART II
Fabra, M., Hesse, C., Berzewski, H.
Psychiatric Outpatient Ward and Crisis Intervention Center of the Klinikum Steglitz, Free University Berlin (Head: H. Berzewski, M.D.)

The goals of crisis intervention in an inpatient setting are as follows: the so-called environment-centered intervention includes the therapist's help by coping with the event precipitating the crisis and by getting social support. The so-called person-centered intervention facilitates the reduction of innerpersonal tension, deals with the crisis' focal conflict according to a psychoanalytical point of view and is mentioned to strengthen the self's healthy aspects. A four week art therapy program was established at our above mentioned crisis intervention ward. This program offered a chance to up to six patients at a time to work with their creative and artistic potentials during crisis in a group therapy setting. There were five four-week-sequences attended by 19 patients alltogether; 8 more patients dropped out during the course of the therapy. Before and after the therapy sequence psychological data were collected from the patients, using a number of psychological tests and a semi-structured interview. The answers in this interview were categorized by several raters, the categories representing the technics of crisis intervention mentioned above. A control group of 30 patients, not attending art therapy underwent the same procedure. 12-18 months later there was a follow-up study. The results will be discussed in our presentation.

2087

TWO THERAPEUTIC TECHNIQUES BASED ON PATIENT-ATTITUDE CHANGE TO THERAPISTS.
Daniel Kahans, Wingrove Cottage Community Clinic, Eltham, Victoria, Australia.

TECHNIQUE 1 - "Therapy Through Patient-Evaluation of Therapist": This study was undertaken to establish that, in an audience situation, music may facilitate an immediate attitude change toward a therapist by patients. To determine the characteristics of such a change, recorded (popular and classical) and live (cello) music was employed. A semantic differential was used to measure attitude change by psychiatric inpatients and control subjects (medical students and student nurses). Results are discussed in terms of therapist preferences, diagnostic categories, cognitive consistency theories and therapeutic gains. Maximal attitude change towards a therapist occurs under conditions in which the therapist presents new aspects of behaviour (in terms of previous exposure) to the patients.
TECHNIQUE 2 - "Improvisation Therapy": Musically-proficient-performing-therapists performing patients' ideas for patients' musical improvisation through therapists' immediate response to patients' ideas via patients' simple hand and other non-verbal/verbal direction. Variables discussed: therapist-patient personality; diagnostic categories; patients' previous musical knowledge; dyadic role-reversal of usual therapist-patient relationship; creative modes other than music; use in group therapy, psychodrama and dyadic interactions; facilitation of both spontaneity and rehearsal modes.

2088

GROUP MUSIC THERAPY AMONG COLLEAGUES IN A PSYCHIATRIC UNIT
PAPAMICHAEL E., LIOSSI A., SPIROPOULOS J., PERTESSI E., STATHIS P.
GENERAL HOSPITAL OF NIKEA, PIRAEUS, GREECE

The purpose of this paper is to present a case of a group music therapy among colleagues in a new Psychiatric Unit at a General Hospital. Group size: 13 permanent participants. Therapy duration: 4 months, 75´ per session. Frequency: 1 session/week. The technical order of the group was circular directed by two coordinators. The method used was Guided Imagery in Music (GIM) by Helen Bonny, extended to the group in order to let imageries, symbols and most inner feelings come out. The first quarter of each session included listening to music selected by group members or coordinators. Music listening functioned as an acceptable element between the members in order to express transference and anti-transference. It was noted that individuals who did not take an active role in the group never brought a selection for musical listening. Old songs brought interesting memories and revival feelings. Someone who expressed aggressiveness and leadership tendencies during the 4 months sessions could also express them afterwards. After the end of the last session 5 group members started receiving Dynamic Psychotherapy. It seems that GIM groups help colleagues develop easily a strong familiarity between them: 1)Music helps them express feelings safely, 2)It functions as a catalyst accelerating the procedures of self-knowledge, 3)It may constitute an introductory stage towards Dynamic Psychotherapy of those engaged in Psychiatry.

2089
AEROBIC EXERCISE IN SECONDARY DEPRESSION

Selami Aksoy, MD, Mustafa Ziyalan, MD.
Bakırköy Mental Hospital, Istanbul, TURKEY

Aerobic exercise will be a part of a treatment program for depression we want to introduce in Turkey. In a pilot-study we tried to evaluate it in the treatment of secondary depression. 60 inpatients, meeting the DSM-III-R criteria for alcohol dependence and for depression one week after the withdrawal period, had no counterindication for exercise or antidepressant medication, were from the age group 20-50 and adequately motivated, were randomly divided into two groups. First group underwent a "running therapy" program getting no psychopharmacological treatment. Second group was given adequate antidepressant medication. Depression of patients was evaluated by a "blind" clinician using Zung and Hamilton Scales prior to treatment and after the fourth and eighth weeks of treatment. Their vital capacities were also measured before and after the treatment. There was statistically a more signif2icant decrease in depression scores (25 %) and a more significant increase in vital capacities (35 %) in the first group compared with the second group (15 %, 10 %; t=5,52; p<0.001) and no sideeffects in the second group. We concluded that our conventional depression treatment should be rewieved and that aerobic exercise is therapeutically as much effective as psychopharmacological antidepressive agents.

2090
SPORTTHERAPIE IN PSYCHIATRIE, PSYCHOSOMATIK UND SUCHTBEHANDLUNG

R. Höll, R.J. Witkowski, T.A. Mösler, P. GEYER
Psychiatrische Universitätsklinik, Schwabachanlage 6,
D-8520 Erlangen (Direktor: Prof. Dr. E. Lungershausen)

Die Sporttherapie nimmt heute in der Behandlung psychisch Kranker einen festen Platz im Gesamttherapiekonzept ein. Bislang wurde diese Therapieform von einer sehr heterogenen Therapeutengruppe (Sportlehrer, Beschäftigungstherapeuten, Pflegepersonal, Ärzte), die sich selbst in Körper- und Sporttherapie fort- und ausgebildet hatte, ausgeübt. Ab 1990 soll ein Hochschulaufbaustudium die Ausbildung zum Sporttherapeuten in Psychiatrie, Psychosomatik und Suchtbehandlung vereinheitlichen. In diesem Beitrag soll der heutige Stellenwert, die Ausbildungssituation und die Ziele der Sporttherapie diskutiert werden. Die Sporttherapie bedient sich dabei der Möglichkeiten der Behandlung von Krankheiten mit Elementen des Sports, der Bewegungslehre und den körperorientierten (Psychotherapie-) Verfahren. Dabei kann - was heute noch wenig verbreitet ist - die Sporttherapie alleinige Therapieform sein oder ihren Platz als ergänzende Behandlungsmethode neben Beschäftigungstherapie, Musiktherapie, Psychotherapie und medikamentöser Therapie einnehmen.

Das Ziel unserer therapeutischen Bemühungen ist es, den in seinen Freiheitsgraden eingeschränkten Patienten alte und/oder neue Entfaltungsmöglichkeiten zu geben, ihn herauszuführen aus seiner Isolation und ihm Möglichkeiten der Nutzung seiner Energien aufzuzeigen oder erleben zu lassen.

2191
EMOTIONS AND PHYSICAL ACTIVITY IN HEALTHY WOMEN

Thomas Flynn, B.S.; Grant Miller, M.D.; Lisa Hill, B.S., R.D.; Barbara Scott, M.P.H.; Sachiko St. Jeor, Ph.D., R.D., University of Nevada School of Medicine, Reno, Nevada 89557, U.S.A.

Positive relationships have been reported between psychological well-being and physical activity. However, measures of physical activity have been problematic. The purpose of this study was to examine the relationship between selected emotional states as measured by anxiety, depression, and general severity index scores of the Symptom Check List-90R and improved measures of physical activity estimated by an accelerometer. Subjects were 26 normal weight and 20 obese women (mean weight = 132.5 vs 181.4, and %IBW = 102.3 vs 134.8, respectively) ages 40-49 (mean = 44.5) participating in the Reno Diet-Heart Study. Total energy expenditure was estimated in kcal/day using 7-day mean accelerometer readings. Resting energy expenditure was estimated by the accelerometer using height, weight, age and sex. An activity factor was derived using the ratio of resting energy expenditure to express different levels of physical activity. Using analysis of variance, no significant differences were found between normal and obese for activity factor, anxiety, depression, and general severity index. No significant correlations were found either. This study does not support the popular notion of a positive relationship between psychological well-being and physical activity in healthy women.

Session 319 Free Communications:
Forensic psychiatry: Clinical issues

2092
FORENSIC ASPECTS OF PARANOIA QUERULATORIA

Pfolz H., Friedl E.J.
Psychiatrisches Krankenhaus der Stadt Wien
Baumgartner Hoehe, 1145 Vienna, Austria

There is no doubt, that paranoid syndroms make necessary multidimensional interpretations to assign them to psychiatric disorders. This way is essential for practical work. To assess the criminal responsibility the forensic psychiatrist has to follow more the density of paranoid syndroms than the constellations. This paper tries to discuss this problem.

2093
CRIMES COMMITTED DURING EPILEPTIC AUTOMATISM: CHARACTERISTICS
Van Rensburg PHJJ, Gagiano CA, Meyer CJ, Verschoor T.
Department of Psychiatry, University of the Orange Free State, Republic of South Africa

Because opposing views are held by researchers, a prospective study was done over a six year period (1980-1986). Fifty-six epileptics who allegedly committed crimes and who were referred to Orange Hospital (R.S.A.) for observation in terms of sections 77 (triability) and 78 (criminal responsibility) of the Criminal Procedure Act (51 of 1977) were included. Patients were subjected to a multi-professional team clinical evaluation as well as an EEG and CT scan. Calculated at a prevalence of 6 per 1000 there are ± 20.000 epileptics in the catchment area of Orange Hospital. In our assessment, criteria mainly advocated by Fenton (1972) were used. Eleven cases were identified where crimes were committed during an episode of epileptic automatism. Our results proved that these crimes, though rare, do exist. The finding is supported inter alia by the research of Asuni (1969) and Odejide (1981). A careful analysis of the characteristics of the crimes concerned, a personality evaluation of the identified cases, as well as their EEG and CT scan results was made. Characteristics will be proposed for assessing whether there is a causal relation between epileptic automatism and crime.

2094
SUR LE PASSAGE A L'ACTE HOMICIDE (P.A.H) CHEZ LES MALADES MENTAUX DANGEREUX
OULIS PANAYOTIS
EGINITION HOSPITAL, ATHENS

La fréquence relative du p.a.h eu égard à la categorie diagnostique (c.d) de la nosographie française qui leur avait été appliquée a été evaluée chez 1281 malades mentaux de sexe masculin admis en service de Sûreté (S.S.) pendant la periode 1954 - 1984.

La comparaison des c.d de schizophrenie (336 patients dont 89 avec p.a.h) et de délires chroniques non-schizophreniques (170 patients dont 80 avec p.a.h) a fait apparaître la plus grande dangerosité des patients de la seconde c.d eu égard au p.a.h. Par ailleurs la prise en compte de l´appartenance eventuelle des victimes a l´entourage familial, du type de leur lien familial avec les patients (parents ou conjoints), de l'age moyen des patients au moment du p.a.h ainsi que de la durée moyenne de leur sejour en S.S ont permis de différencier davantage les patients de ces deux c.d

Enfin un commentaire des resultats obtenus est proposé.

2095
HANDEDNESS AND CRIMINALITY
Katsuya Maehara, Natsumi Negishi, Atsushi Tsai, Takahito Momose*
Juntendo University School of Medicine, Department of Neuro-psychiatry
Kawagoe Juvenile Prison*, Tokyo, Japan

There are only a few studies of the cerebral lateralization in criminals and these results are controversial. We have conducted this research into handedness of criminals from the developmental point of view. Subjects and Methods: Participants were 1,059 male and 965 female prisoners aged from 20 to 69 years. The questionnaire was a partially corrected Edinburgh Inventory which contained ten items for measuring handedness. The right-hander was defined as a person who manipulated all ten items with his/her right hand. Results: In prisoners, the frequency of right handedness was significantly lower than in controls in any age groups. From 20 to 29 years old, for example, it was 60% in male and 57% in female prisoners, and 80% and 81% in the control groups respectively. We could see the aging effects on the right-handedness percentages as the "S-shaped" curve showed in the diagram. When compared, the controls' is and criminals' curve were similar in shape though different in location; the criminal's curve was below and to the right of the controls' curve. Discussion: Because of this "S-shaped" curve indicating the process of the cerebral lateralization, we considered that criminals could have some developmental abnormalities in cerebral organization.

2096
PERSONALITY-DISORDERS IN A FORENSIC TREATMENT
W.Berner, K.Berger, P.Berger, K.Gutieres, G.Willinger

A WHO-ADAMAHA multi-center-study is testing reliability and comparability of personality disorders diagnoses according to ICD-10, DSM-III-R respectively with a new developed half-standardized interview - IPDE (LORANGER et al.)
In a connected pilot-study the diagnoses of 10 screened cases of Vienna University-Outpatient-Clinic are compared with 10 consecutively admitted cases in a special prison institution for treatment of 'psychopaths' (as they are diagnosed by court-experts).
The cases will be compared regarding
-distribution of diagnoses
-security of judgment
-differences in diagnostic procedure.
Study objective is to introduce modern personality diagnosis in forensic psychiatry and to break down the blurred old 'sociopathy' of 'psychopathy'-diagnoses in better defined ICD-10 and DSM-III-R diagnostic entities.
The pilot study will give some hints at differences in diagnosing inside and outside a forensic institution.

Session 320 Free Communications:
Drug abuse: Personality characteristics and psychopathology

2097

PSYCHIATRIC DISORDER IN ILLICIT DRUG ABUSERS

A. Kokkevi, V. Alevizou, M. Malliori, K. Cheropoulou, J. Liappas, C. Stefanis
Department of Psychiatry, Athens University Medical School

Comparative data on the prevalence of psychiatric disorders of two samples of illicit drug abusing males are presented. The samples consist of: a. 88 incarcerated abusers (IA) and b. 66 abusers attending health services (HSA).

Findings from the DIS showed that 92% of the IA and 89% HSA met criteria for a life-time prevalence of some DSM-III psychiatric disorder apart from substance abuse and dependence disorders.

The IA as compared to HSA had higher prevalence rates of antisocial personality (75% vs 58%) and psychosexual dysfunction disorders (57% vs 27%), while the HSA sample had higher prevalence rates for anxiety disorders (44% vs 7%) and dysthymic disorders (11% vs 6%). Life-time prevalence for major depression was for both groups around 12%. The HSA sample presented higher prevalence of alcohol dependence than the incarcerated sample (65% vs 49%).

The predominance of antisocial personality disorder in the IA sample is associated with higher incidence of law breaking behaviour as compared to the HSA sample. On the other hand the observed higher rates of anxiety and mood - dysthymic type - disorders prevalent in the HSA sample is further supported by higher scores in CESD and MMPI depression scales.

Prevalence of psychiatric disorder found in greek drug abusing subjects is discussed in comparison to findings from similar studies in other countries.

2098

SUBSTANCE ABUSE AND MENTAL ILLNESS: THE DUAL DISORDERS CLINIC
N. el-Guebaly, MD, J. Gottschalk, RN
The University of Calgary, Canada

The relationship between substance abuse and other mental disorders is a complex one. One group of patients suffer from both a major substance abuse disorder and another major psychiatric illness. Another group uses alcohol and/or other drugs in ways that affect the course and treatment of mental illness. The prevalence of this dual problem ranges between 20-60% of psychiatric patients depending on the criteria, the location, the patient's age and sex and the diagnosis involved. The clinical impact is significant resulting in misdiagnosis, a stormy management and poor prognosis. The last 2 years a program has evolved in a teaching hospital to address a number of clinical issues: 1) Assessment: amidst a number of screening measures, the Addiction Severity Index (ASI) is the major evaluative tool; 2) Prevention: a drug education program is part of the stress reduction and coping skills training targeted at the young adult psychiatric population; 3) Treatment: a two-track group process, open and closed is available. The essential features of our groups in terms of expectations, the issue of primary and secondary diagnoses, the "good drug bad drug" dilemma, the education and involvement of self-help groups, the optimal pharmacotherapy required and the appropriate community support will be discussed. ASI assessment and follow-up records (n=65) across diagnostic groupings will be presented.

2099

Investigation of Psychopathology and Differential diagnosis of Cannabis-induced Psychoses.
Taeschner, Karl-Ludwig, Psychiatrische Klinik des Buergerhospitals der Stadt Stuttgart, Tunzhofer Straße 14-16, D-7000 Stuttgart 1, Bundesrepublik Deutschland

Investigations of Psychopathology and Differential diagnosis of Cannabis-induced Psychoses
* triggered schizophrenias.

From 237 patients with drug-induced psychoses, 50 cannabis psychoses were examined according to the criterion "main of addiction" and 107 according to the criterion "consumption during the last three month before hospitalization". The cannabis psychoses were compared to the other drug-induced psychoses as well as to control group consisting of 219 schizophrenic patients without drug consumption. General agreement was found with the other drug induced psychoses as well as with the group of schizophrenic patients. Judging by the results of our investigations, it must be concluded that there is no disease "cannabis psychosis" in its own right, just as the disease "drug-induced psychosis" also does not exist in its own right. The psychopathological cross section does not permit a differentiation in the individual psychoses/groups mentioned, although this has often been attempted in the literature. That there are no relevant psychopathological differences between cannabis psychoses and endogenous schizophrenia could, for one, be based on the fact that we are observing the final stage of one and the same underlying pathological process. In this case both syndromes would in practice be exogenous psychoses, with the cause not being known in one case. The psychopathologic similarity of these two psychoses forms could,however, also be based on the assumption that cannabis psychoses are*

2100

COMPARATIVE PERSONALITY AND PSYCHOPATHOLOGY ASSESSMENT BY THE MMPI OF IMPRISONED AND TREATMENT SEEKING DRUG ABUSERS

V. Alevizou, A. Kokkevi, E. Anastasopoulou, Y. Arvanitis, V. Boukouvala, D. Ifantis

Department of Psychiatry, Athens University Medical School

The MMPI was administered to two samples of drug abusing male subjects: a. 88 incarcerated (IA) and b. 66 attending health services (HSA).

In both samples the MMPI profile configuration was similar and characterised by having the Psychopathic deviation scale as the highest one (T score between 70 and 80). Paranoia, Schizophrenia, Hypomania and Psychasthenia scales presented similar for both samples T score elevations (between 60 and 70). Depression scale had a higher mean score in the HSA as compared to the IA.

Imprisoned abusers had higher percentage of scores above T=70 than HSA for Paranoia (42.8% vs 33.3%) and Mania (37.5% vs 29.4%) scales, while higher percentage of scores above T=70 was found in HSA for Depression (29.9% vs 10.9%), Schizophrenia (52.9% vs 35.7%), Psychopathic deviation (68.6% vs 48.2%) and Psychasthenia (37.3% vs 14.3%) scales.

The above findings are discussed in conjunction with findings deriving from the DIS and the CESD scale administered to the subjects as well as in relation to their criminal record.

2101
PERSONALITY TRAIT IN COCAINE ADDICTION

Frederick Lemere, M.D., Schick Shadel Hospital
Seattle, Wa., USA

The relationship of cocaine abuse to affective disorders, such as depression and cyclothymia, is unclear. An analysis of 292 patients treated for cocaine addiction formed the basis for the following impressions. A history of premorbid psychiatric disorder was rare. Psychopathology at the time of treatment was more the result of than the cause for addiction. Factors contributing to cocaine abuse included environmental forces acting on an addictive personality. In certain individuals, an additional determinant in the choice of and abuse of cocaine was an underlying nonpathologic unipolar hypomanic trait. This manifested itself more as a characteristic of temperament than as a disorder. These individuals had been by nature out-going, sociable, fun-loving and action and goal oriented extroverts before their addiction. Cocaine was used initially to enhance euphoria rather than to escape dysphoria. The rush and life-style of cocaine fit the imperatives of their personality. In a significant number of cocaine users, an underlying hypomanic personality trait appeared to be an important ingredient of the fascination for and addiction to cocaine.

2102
CATHA EDULIS ABUSE; INTRODUCTION AND REPORT OF A CASE WITH PSYCHOSIS
H.E.Soufi, M.D., (USA), Acting Chairman,
Psychiatric Dept., College of Medicine, King Saud University, Abha Branch, Abha, Saudi Arabia,
Mahasen M. Afifi, MB, Bch, M.S. (Psych)
Psychiatrist, Mufareh R.Gh. Alshehry,
Psychologist, Abha Psychiatric Hospital, Saudi Arabia

The purpose of this paper is to report a case of repeated acute psychosis with a final diagnosis of "Mixed Personality Disorder" which stood out during a one-year review. First admission diagnosed as "Paranoid Schizophrenia", on readmission "Mania" and found having used Khat prior to each admission.
Catha Edulis is present in the leaves of Khat trees with its use endemic and traditional on location. Recently taken Western psychiatric literature continues to be thin on the subject.
Method used: Clinical review and review of Western literature of similar cases.
Summary of findings: Khat on location is used in groups that try to direct behavior. Unwanted effects seem more prevalent when used far from tradition; acute psychosis may be misdiagnosed.
Conclusion: Further clinical works needed to determine roles of socio-traditional and behavioral factors that may influence the clinical picture and course.

2103
SUBSTANCE ABUSE AND VIOLENT BEHAVIOR

Spyros Monopolis, M.D. and George U. Balis, M.D.
Department of Psychiatry, University of Maryland
Baltimore, Maryland, USA

This paper presents data correlating adult aggressive/violent behavior with psychoactive substance use disorders. The subjects (426 psychiatric patients) were classified into 5 groups: I. non-aggression, II. verbal aggression, III. object-directed aggression, IV. person-directed aggression without serious body harm, V. person-directed aggression with serious body harm/murder. Data were collected via a self-reported neuropsychiatric inventory. Statistical analysis (ANOVA, Tukey HSD) showed that severity of recidivist violent behavior correlates proportionally with co-morbidity rates of psychoactive substance use disorders. More specifically, assaultive patients (groups IV and V), when compared with non-violent or non-assaultive patients (groups I and II), showed statistically significantly higher frequencies of substance abuse and dependence, especially with regard to: alcohol (p. 0001), hallucinogens (p.005), cannabis (p. 017), and polysubstance abuse (p.002). There were no statistically significant intergroup differences for stimulants, asedatives/hypnotics anxiolytics, opioids and phencyclidine. The findings and their implications are discussed.

Session 321 Free Communications:
Antidepressants: Their effects in depressed and non-depressed subjects

2104
PAROXETINE EFFECTS ON PSYCHOMOTOR PERFORMANCE AND ACTUAL DRIVING
H.W.J. Robbe, E.A.J.M. Schoenmakers, J.F. O'Hanlon
Institute for Drugs, Safety and Behaviour, Federal University of Limburg, Maastricht, the Netherlands

Paroxetine, a selective 5-HT re-uptake blocker, is recommended in a dose-range of 20-50 mg for the treatment of depression. Sixteen healthy male volunteers were treated with paroxetine 20 and 40 mg, amitriptyline and placebo in separate 8-day series according to a 4-way, double-blind, cross-over design. The subjects' laboratory test and driving performance were assessed twice on the 1st and 8th days of each series. The test battery included: critical flicker fusion (CFF), critical instability tracking, continuous recall, divided attention, memory search and reaction time, tapping and sustained attention or vigilance. The driving test involved uninterrupted operation of a specially instrumented vehicle. The subjects attempted to maintain a constant speed and steady lateral position. Speed, steering wheel movements and lateral position were continuously recorded and later analysed. The most important is the standard deviation of lateral position. Subjects completed questionnaries to describe their sleep quality, the occurrence and severity of several side effects, perceived driving quality and effort invested in performing the tasks as well as mental activation.
Performance in nearly all tests, including driving, was significantly impaired by amitriptyline on the 1st but not on the 8th day. The higher paroxetine dose caused less but still significant performance impairment in some laboratory tests. Both amitriptyline and paroxetine 40 mg had significant subjective effects of an unpleasant nature and the latter also impaired subjective sleep quality. The lower paroxetine dose had no significant effect on any performance or subjective parameter.

2105

DEPRESSED PATIENTS' SLEEP AND PERFORMANCE DURING TRAZODONE THERAPY

E. A. J. M. SCHOENMAKERS[1], A. L. VAN BEMMEL[2], R. VAN DIEST[2], J. F. O'HANLON[1]

1) Institute for Drugs, Safety and Behaviour
2) Department of Clinical Psychiatry, State University of Limburg.

The study's main purpose was to verify the reputed beneficial effects of trazodone (in a new controlled release formulation) on sleep as measured by polysomnographic recording.

A further purpose was to correlate, if possible, sleep improvement and changes in daytime performance capabilities as revealed by psychometric examination. Ten depressed patients with sleep disturbances were tested repeatedly in sleep and performance laboratories over the course of a 5-week period of trazodone medication and during pre and post placebo control periods (single blind). Changes in their clinical condition were monitored by serial application of the HAM-D scale. Preliminary results of this study are reported.

2106

INFLUENCE OF DOTHIEPIN (DOSULEPIN) ON PSYCHOMOTOR PERFORMANCE

S. Donovan, Research Department, The Boots Company PLC, Nottingham, UK

Many psychoactive drugs can affect psychomotor performance. Dothiepin (Dp) is a tricyclic antidepressant with sedative properties. The implications of this property on psychomotor performance has been the subject of a number of investigations which are reviewed here.

Vigilance is less impaired by Dp than amitriptyline(1) and there is no impairment of morning psychomotor performance after an evening dose of Dp(2). There are no significant differences between Dp and placebo in measures of driving performance other than a slight decrease in concentration(3) and subjective feelings of sedation which disappear by 4 hours post-dose.(4)

Whilst care should be taken in prescribing any medication which has the potential to impair psychomotor performance in patients who routinely drive or operate machinery, the administration of Dp at bedtime will minimise the effects on psychomotor performance the following morning.

1. Ogura C, Neuropsychobiol. 1983;10:103
2. Moon C, Proc. Rec. Adv. Psych. Tr; Berlin, 1987
3. Stille G, Herberg K-W. Forschr. Med. 107;(2):1989
4. Hindmarch I, Human Psychopharm. 1987;2:177

2107

COGNITIVE AND PSYCHOMOTOR PATTERNS IN DEPRESSED PATIENTS UNDER THERAPY

M.Paes de Sousa, C.R. Vieira, L.C. Pestana, M.Feio
Dept. of Psychiatry. Faculty of Medicine of Lisbon. Hospital Stª. Maria. Av. Prof. Egas Moniz. P-1600 Lisbon. Portugal

Since Previous studies showed that activating antidepressive therapy improves cognitive and psychomotor performances of depressive patients, the question remained if the same effect was achieved with sedative antidepressive drugs.

In matched samples of depressive patients submitted to activating (Amineptine) and sedative (Dothiepine and Trazodone) antidepressive treatments, tests of central nervous arousal (CFF), attention, short-term and iconic visual and verbal memory and choice reaction time (CRT), were performed before and after four weeks of treatment. The data obtained were statistically (means, standard deviations and ANOVA) compared among themselves and also with the data obtained with the same battery of tests in a sample of normal subjects. The results were analysed and discussed.

2108

Fluvoxamine versus mianserin; psychomotor performance in depressed patients.

*Moon CAL, **Jesinger DK
* Pool Health Centre, Redruth, Cornwall
** Duphar Laboratories Ltd., Gaters Hill, West end, Southampton, SO3 3JD

A single centre double-blind randomised study in general practice compared the effects of fluvoxamine and mianserin on psychomotor performance measured using Critical Flicker Fusion Threshold (CFFT) and Digit Symbol Substitution (DSST) in conjunction with the Leeds Sleep Evaluation Questionnaire (SEQ). Sixty-two patients meeting the DSM III criteria for Major Depressive Episode and achieving a score of at least 25 on the Montgomery Asberg Depression Rating Scale (MADRS) after a 1 week placebo baseline baseline period were recruited. Treatment was for 6 weeks with an initial dose of either 100 mg fluvoxamine or 60 mg mianserin; after one week the dosage could be increased to 300 mg fluvoxamine or 180 mg mianserin.

Mianserin significantly decreased CFFT at day 1 compared to placebo, which coincided with sedation seen on the SEQ. Fluvoxamine did not affect CFFT threshold and caused less sedation on SEQ. No differences were seen on DSST or efficacy variables.

Weight increase on mianserin was significant compared to baseline, whereas fluvoxamine had no effect on weight.

2109

ADVANTAGES AND LIMITATIONS OF USING ANTI-DEPRESSANTS IN THE THERAPY OF BULIMIC PATIENTS
J.L. VENISSE, M. SANCHEZ, et Y. SARANTOGLOU
S.H.U.P. Hôpital St Jacques 44035 NANTES CEDEX (F)

Prescription of antidepressants for bulimic patients is based on an assumed association of bulimia with depression. Various arguments have been advanced for this relationship, and most experiments with antidepressants have shown symptomatic improvement. However, these results cannot presently be considered as definitive and adequate. For example, the following problems remain : type of classification and inclusion criteria differ from study to study ; follow-up data are often inadequate since given only for a short period, even of several weeks ; and the method of patient recruitment is sometimes questionable and groups too small and lacking in homogeneity. In addition to these considerations, the authors question, in terms of their own experience, whether early, systematic recourse to chemotherapy in these patients might not risk reinforcement of a dependence state. This could be detrimental to the resumption of their development which, in the scope of the adolescence process, often involves the psychical working out of a depressive phase.

2110

CLINICAL EXPERIENCE WITH TRAZODONE IN THE ACUTE PHASE OF STROKE.
Luigi Allori and P. Di Tono, Ospedale Coniugi Bernardini Palestrina, 00036 Palestrina, Italy

The idea for the use of trazodone in the acute phase of stroke dates back to 1973 and was based on two orders of considerations: first, the severity of stroke is not only related to its etiology and to the site and extent of the area directly involved by vascular damage, but also to phenomena of altered vascular motility and permeability produced by an essentially serotoninergic mediation; second, trazodone is a strong inhibitor of the peripheral effects of serotonin, reduces CSF pressure and prevents the formation of edema.
Based on the above considerations, a non randomized study has been performed in patients with focal ischemic cerebral lesions. Trazodone was given at the dose of 10 mg i.v. twice daily for 3 days. Results obtained show a significant reduction in the overall neurological deficit and duration of hospitalization. No significant effect was noted on the death rate.

Session 322 Free Communications:
Neuroendocrine effects of drugs

2111

TRICYCLIC ANTIDEPRESSANTS: THERAPEUTIC AND NEUROENDOCRINOLOGICAL RESPONSES
KARAZMAN R., LANGER G., KOINIG M., SCHÖNBECK G.
Tricyclics are an important biological treatment for major depressive disorders. Their mechanisms are not completely explained. The TRH-Test, the Dexamethason-Suppression-Test and the Insuline-Tolerance-Test have emerged as potentendocrinological tools for biological classification and monitoring of the therapeutic process.
31 patients(male/female) with DSMIII-major depressive disorders have been treated with Clomipramine for more than 1 year. TRH-Test,T_3,T_4 and clinical assessment with HRSD were performed during the whole period, DST and ITT during in-patient-period of 5 weeks. LH-RH-Test was performed at the end of inpatient-period.
70% of patients with a blunted TSH-response ad admission ($<$5mcU/ml). During inpatient the TSH-response normalised in general to 25% blunted responses and staid stable during outpatient-period. Abrnormal Cortisol-responses in DST decreased from 40% to 12%. No significant alteration had been shown in HGH-, Prolactine- and Cortisol-Responses to ITT. The LH-RH-Test was at normal values at all male patients. The therapeutic response increased in patients with disblunting TSH-responses and the risk of relapse increased in relation to blunted TSH-responses during outpatient-period(HRSD-Score on 16 items$\leq$9).

2112

ENDOCRINE RESPONSES TO 5-HT_{1A} RECEPTOR ACTIVATION IN PSYCHIATRIC DISORDERS
K.P. Lesch, R. Rupprecht, J. von Disselkamp-Tietze, H.M. Schulte, M. Osterheider
Dept. of Psychiatry, 8700 Würzburg, FRG
Multiple recognition sites for 5-HT_1 have been classified as 5-HT_{1A-D}. To assess the role of 5-HT receptor subtypes in hypothalamic-pituitary-adrenal (HPA) axis activation in humans, various doses of ipsapirone (IPS), a centrally acting pyrimidinylpiperazine derivative with high affinity and selectivity for 5-HT_{1A} recognition sites, were administered to 6 healthy men aged 24.3 ± 3.1 (± SD) years. Each subject was tested on 4 separate occasions and studies were separate by a minimum of 7 days. The test agent consisted of one of three doses (0.1, 0.2 or 0.3 mg/kg) of IPS or identical placebo tablets, and was administered orally at 17:30 in a randomized double-blind fashion. Plasma corticotropin (ACTH) and cortisol were measured at -30, 0, 15, 30 - 180 min, analyses employed standard RIA techniques, and the hormonal responses were calculated as the maximum increase corrected for baseline. IPS dose-dependently increased plasma ACTH concentrations from a baseline value of 0.5 ± 0.8 pmol/L to a maximum of 8.6 ± 6.6 pmol/L ($p < 0.01$, Friedman's two-way ANOVA) and plasma cortisol concentrations from 8.3 ± 20.3 nmol/L to 223.5 ± 127.0 nmol/L ($p < 0.01$) at a dose of 0.3 mg/kg. In conclusion, investigation of HPA responses to direct-acting 5-HT_{1A} ligands, such as IPS, should facilitate the selective assessment of 5-HT receptor sensitivity in depression, obsessive-compulsive and panic disorder.

2113

Results of 'serotonergic' probes during depression.
M. Maes, C. Schotte, E. Suy, M. Vandewoude.
University of Antwerp, Psychiatric Centre, Munsterbilzen, Belgium.

To examine the serotonin hypothesis of major depression, the authors investigated the cortisol, prolactin (PRL) and adrenocorticotrophic hormone (ACTH) responses to 5-hydroxytryptophan (5-HPT), L-tryptophan (L-TRP), fenfluramine (FEN), dex-fenfluramine (DEXFEN) and metachlorophenylpiperazine (m-CPP) in minor and major depressed patients. The latter were characterized by (1) an increased plasma cortisol and PRL secretion after 5-HTP, (2) an increased urinary free cortisol excretion after L-TRP and (3) an increased PRL secretion after FEN. It is suggested that these findings corroborate the hypothesis of a central serotonergic hyperfunction during major depression. Our latest results on DEXFEN and m-CPP probes will be presented.

2114

HORMONAL RESPONSES TO FENFLURAMINE IN DEPRESSED AND CONTROL SUBJECTS
P. B. Mitchell and G. A. Smythe
School of Psychiatry, University of New South Wales, and Garvan Institute of Medical Research, St. Vincent's Hospital (Sydney, Australia)

Abnormal endocrine hormone responses to drugs which perturb the activity of brain monoamines have long been proposed as indices of neurotransmitter disturbances in mental diseases such as depression. We examined whether the responses of serum cortisol and prolactin to fenfluramine (FEN), a putative serotonin agonist drug, differ between normal and depressed patients and if the responses could be disease predictors. A total of 27 depressed patients and 14 normal subjects were administered FEN (60 mg, oral) and blood sampled at hourly intervals for 5 h. Compared with control subjects, the population of depressed patients demonstrated a reduced prolactin response ($p<0.05$ using repeated measures ANCOVA). Measures of the prolactin and cortisol responses intercorrelated significantly ($p<0.01$) in control subjects, but not in the depressed group. The data indicate that the responses of both prolactin and cortisol to FEN in depressed patients differ from those of controls and that there is significant dissociation of mechanisms regulating hormonal release in depression. While the modest differences are unlikely to be of clinical diagnostic utility, they point to disturbances in brain function in depression being revealed by FEN.

2115

NEUROENDOCRINE EFFECTS OF ALPRAZOLAM
Bizzarri D., Lazzerini F., Agrimi G., Andreani M.F., Arena A., Piccini P.
Department of Mental Health, Massa Carrara, Italy

Alprazolam, a triazolobenzodiazepine with anxiolytic action, has been shown to be an effective anti-depressive drug. However, recent data have pointed out that prolonged treatment with this compound gives rise to extrapyramidal signs and symptoms. In addition some experimental studies have reported that alprazolam inhibits the activity of dopaminergic (DA) neurons. In this study prolactin (PRL) secretion was chosen as a parameter for functional exploration of central DA systems in women with anxiety-neurosis, before and after alprazolam treatment. Ten normomenstruate women with anxiety-neurosis, underwent TRH stimulation test before and after a 30-day alprazolam therapy (1.5mg/die per os). Basal PRL levels were not modified by the treatment, but the TRH stimulated PRL values were significantly enhanced after alprazolam therapy. These results seem to confirm the hypothesis that alprazolam may interfere with central Daergic activity.

2116

INCREASED SENSITIVITY OF DST WITH DISULFIRAM

Per Bergsholm and Dag Oulie
Sandviken hospital, Bergen, Norway

This is an extension of a report (Abstract No 203, XXII Nordiske psykiater-kongres,Reykjavik,Aug 1988) on increasing the sensitivity of DST giving 800 mg disulfiram on the dexamethasone and postdexamethasone day(DSTd). DST and DSTd were done with an interval of one week.Thirty individuals,14 men and 16 women aged 18-57(median 35)years,were included.Eight patients with stable non-psychotic symptoms included four in whom it was sought to differensiate between primary depression and adjustment disorder, three with chronic atypical depression,and one with intermittent explosive disorder.Mean cortisol(nM/l) in DSTd,143(34-281), was threefold that in DST, 45 (32-66)($p=0.02$). In two patients with stationary incomplete remission and DST-cortisol of 76 or 61, DSTd-cortisol-levels were 242 and 129,respectively. The former had persistent impotence,the latter soon relapsed in bipolar depression. One dysphoric woman with severe fibromyalgia feared relapse of psychotic depression.However,cortisol in DST was only 26 and in DSTd 20,and no relapse has occurred for a year without prophylaxis. Five patients were tested during ongoing improvement.Cortisol was normal and nearly the same in DST and DSTd, 58(20-110) and 48 (20-95), and improvement was followed by longlasting remission. Likewise,DST and DSTd were normal and not significantly different, 32(22-43) and 40(24-56) in in four women after complete remission for years. In 10 unscreened controls DSTd-cortisol was significantly higher than DST-cortisol: 83(23-176) vs 51 (20-123) ($p=0.03$).However,after exclusion of controls with possible causes of false positive test,the residual five screened controls had nearly equal values for DST and DSTd,36(20-71) and 40(23-67), respectively. - CONCLUSION: DSTd may markedly increase the sensitivity of DST without decreasing the specificity,as long as the exclusion criteria for the test are respected. A normalized DSTd may indicate a complete remission from HPA-axis dysfunction.

2117
EXTENDED DEXAMETHASONE SUPPRESSION TEST: INFLUENCE OF L-TRYPTOPHAN

U. Witt, D. Glaubitt, M. Teimoorian. FU Norddeutschland, Federal Republic of Germany

The dexamethasone suppression test (DST) with an additional profile of serum growth hormone and prolactin was reported to show no significant difference of results between a group of 10 patients with endogenous depression and a group of 30 patients with non-endogenous depression (Witt et al., 1988).
More recently in a psychiatric ambulance 10 patients with endogenous depression (DSM III), 10 patients with other types of depression and 20 patients with non-depressive neurologic diseases (e. g. epilepsy, trigeminal neuralgia) underwent a DST. Among these 40 patients, 15 each were treated with L-tryptophan or carbamazepine; 10 received a therapy with carbamazepine and L-tryptophan. Serum cortisol, growth hormone and prolactin were determined by radioimmunoassay.
Under the influence of L-tryptophan all 10 patients with endogenous depression responded to dexamethasone with a statistically significant suppression of serum cortisol and growth hormone. Neither a treatment with carbamazepine nor with a combination of L-tryptophan and carbamazepine produced such an effect.
In summary, in 10 of 40 psychiatric or neurologic patients the response to dexamethasone was significantly modified by a therapy with L-tryptophan.

Session 323 Free Communications:
Neuroleptic malignant syndrome

2118
NEUROLEPTIC MALIGNANT SYNDROME: THE FIRST FIVE HUNDRED CASES.
Paul Sakkas, M.D., John M. Davis, M.D., Jin Hua, M.D., Illinois State Psychiatric Inst. Chicago
We present our data after a review of 541 cases reported in 275 publications in the international literature. We analyzed data of 55 parameters which may influence the occurrence, the clinical and the laboratory findings, the treatment and the outcome of NMS. Men (59%) and elderly patients are more likely to reveal NMS. 40% of the NMS cases had an affective component in their clinical picture. The common practice of use high dose in neuroleptic treatment (in 42% the dose was $>1000mg$ of CPZ/day), the rapid increase in dose, and the concomitant use of lithium (in 11%) are some of the factors that facilitate NMS. 58% of the NMS cases reveal their symptomatology within only the first two days after the induction of neuroleptic treatment. The severity of NMS was correlated with the rise in body temperature, the drop in blood pressure, the cloudiness of the sensorium or the presence of agitation ($p<.01$). Fever was correlated with leukocyte count, CPK and hepatic enzymes values ($p<.01$). Overall mentally retarded patients have the most unfavorable outcome (40%). Treatment with dantrolene and bromocriptine was effective in half of the cases used. ECT was used with controversial results. Patients who took oral medication recovered more quickly from NMS than did those who took depot ($p<.05$). The reinstitution of neuroleptics in a patient after an NMS episode was related with the symptoms relapse in 40% of the cases.

2119
NORADRENERGIC FUNCTION IN THE PATHOGENESIS OF NEUROLEPTIC MALIGNANT SYNDROME
Y. Inoue, H. Takeshita, S. Ishiguro, H. Hazama
Department of Neuropsychiatry, Tottori University School of Medicine, Yonago, Japan
We made a retrospective study on the symptom and the clinical course of neuroleptic malignant syndrome (NMS) and speculated that noradrenergic hyperfunction may contribute to the pathogenesis of NMS. Five delayed full blown NMS cases and ten milder cases which lacked one or more symptoms of the major NMS criteria (Levenson, 1986) were examined. Symptoms of milder cases and prodromes of full blown cases seemed to be quite similar to each other. The coefficient of variation of ECG R-R interval as a marker of sympathetic tonus showed extremely low level in both milder and severe cases regardless of their severity of autonomic symptoms. The urinary levels of noradrenaline and adrenaline were extremely high and were not related to the severity of autonomic symptoms. After administration of metoprolol tartrate, a β-adrenergic blocking agent, autonomic symptoms were improved and extrapyramidal symptoms decreased. These results suggest that NMS is a continuous spectrum of physiologic reaction to neuroleptics in which some patients take severe form and other patients take milder imcomplete form. Extrapyramidal symptoms and autonomic symptoms are in a series of continuous symptoms of NMS and both may share underlying biochemical abnormality. Also our results may provide a physiological basis of β-adrenergic blocking agents for treatment of NMS.

2120
TREATMENT AND AFTERCARE OF THE NEUROLEPTIC MALIGNANT SYNDROME (NMS)
J. Schröder, B. Sczesni
Dept. of Psychiatry, Heidelberg, FRG
Dept. of Neurology, Bochum, FRG

A group of 11 NMS patients (age 19-64 ys.) with various psychiatric prediagnoses such as schizophrenia or major depressive disorder are presented. Basically, our treatment consisted in parenteral fluid supply and low dosage heparine. All neuroleptics were stopped. Diazepam or dantrolene alone resolved NMS in two cases respectively. One was referred to ECT, another recovered under bromocriptine. Three patients received a combination of dantrolene with either bromocriptine, amantadine or biperiden. Four cases received lisuride, a new dopaminergic agent; two of them had previously not responded to other substances.
To four patients neuroleptics were reintroduced after the NMS. These patients tolerated neuroleptics well, even if they received the same drug which had initially provoked the NMS. There were no hints for an increased susceptibility to malignat hyperthermia.
In conclusion, treatment of NMS should start with a single substance after stopping all neuroleptics. Severe cases require a combination with dantrolene. In four cases, lisuride proved ist ability to resolve NMS. Reintroduction of neuroleptics was tolerated well after the patient's full recovery from NMS.

2121
TREATMENT OF PSYCHOSIS AND NEUROLEPTIC MALIGNANT SYNDROME

James F. Hooper, M.D.
Clinical Director
Taylor Hardin Secure Medical Facility, Tuscaloosa, AL, USA
Clinical Assistant Professor of Psychiatry
University of Alabama, Tuscaloosa, AL, USA

In cases which we have reported previously, in the *American Family Physician* (November, 1988) and *The British Journal of Psychiatry* (January, 1989), a colleague and I found that many cases of Neuroleptic Malignant Syndrome are not diagnosed. We looked at the dilemma of working with patients who develop this dangerous complication of therapy, necessitating removal of anti-psychotic medications, and the treatment of their thought disorder which can be not only life threatening but also pose severe complications to behavioral management.

Ultimately, we went on to treat two patients concomitantly with bromocriptine and thioridazine and were able to control both the psychotic symptoms and those of the Neuroleptic Malignant Syndrome. We feel that our data show that careful monitoring of serum Creatine Phosphokinase levels is the most accurate method to safely monitor patients in this situation, and indeed the most accurate method to monitor such patients over all.

In the United States, lawsuits are beginning to be filed against psychiatrists who fail to watch for possible Neuroleptic Malignant Syndrome. Criteria are urgently needed to predict which patients are at risk at a given time. Further exploration of possible ways to manage Neuroleptic Malignant Syndrome are discussed.

2122

Two cases of "Neuroleptic malignant syndrome" (N.M.S)

A.KALOGEROPOULOS-S.BAKOURAS-D.AGRAFIOTIS-
S.GHIANNAKODIMOS-A.SKYLLAKOS.
GENERAL HOSPITAL OF LARISSA-GREECE

We report two psychotic patients who developed the so-called "neuroleptic malignant syndrome"(N.M.S.) The N.M.S.is a potentially fatal complication of treatment with neuroleptic drugs,and is characterised by increased muscular tone,hyperpyrexia and coma.Tachycardia and hypertension also occur.The first patient developed the syndrome after receiving neuroleptics orally and intramuscularly,while at the same time he consumed large amounts of alcohol. This patients made a complete recovery.
The second patient 7 days after starting neuroleptics for agitation due to organic brain syndrome he developed N.M.S. and despite intensive treatment he died.
We discuss the probable aetiology of the syndrome, we describe the clinical picture and we stress the importance of early diagnosis and of differentiating this syndrome from other extrapyramidal sydromes due to neuroleptics.

2123

NEUROLEPTIC MALIGNANT SYNDROME: SUCCESSFUL TREATMENT WITH DIAZEPAM AND AMANTADINE
Zoymadaki A.- Tzanakaki M.- Markoulaki S.- Albanopoulou I.
Psychiatric Hospital of Chania

We present a case of a woman 18 years old with schizophreniform disorder by D.S.M. III-R who was treated with Haloperidol and Biperiden.
On the 9th day of treatment she presented: high fever, tremor,dysarthria,canatonic -like symptoms, enuresis, encopresis, dysphagia, tashykardia, taghypneea, perspiration and interchangeable levels of conscience.
A brain C.T. scan and E.E.G. were normal.
An N.M.S. diagnosis according to S.Levenson (1985) was made. Neuroleptic were stopped and a new treatment was given,with 30mg Diazepam and 100mg Amantadine (Symmetrel) orally per day.
The clinical manifestations regressed progressively and after 7 days the patient returned to her previous levels of functioning.
In conclusion: an alternative treatment in some cases (forms) of N.M.S. can be achieved with diazepam and amantadine.

2124

NMS: A CLINICAL SURVEY AND AN ANIMAL EXPERIMENTAL MODEL
Chen Cheng-Chung, Yang Ming-Jen
Ko Wei-Kung, Chen Shun-Sheng*
Departments of Psychiatry and neurology*
Kaohsiung Medical College, Kaohsiung, Taiwan, R.O.C.

A clinical follow-up of neuroleptic malignant syndrome (NMS) and the study of possible animal model of NMS were conducted. Twelve admission cases were followed-up, half of whom were males. The mean age was 33.2 ± 12.3 year-old. During the follow-up period, eleven cases survived and lived in the community. They were evaluated by the Brief Psychiatric Rating Scale and the Community Psychiatric Rating Scale. One case died of pneumonia. The mean follow-up period was 14.1 ± 5.7 months. In groups with neuroleptic treatment, no more NMS was occured. Rat model was designed in two parts, including the study of neuroleptic and hyperthermic (up to 42°C) effect on rat muscles. The rats received haloperidol of fluphenazine decanoate continuously for six months. Direct open biopsies were performed and muscle specimens were prepared for routine histochemical stains and light microscopic examinations. The possible peripheral pathogenesis of NMS will be discussed in detail.

Session 324 Poster Presentation:
Affective and schizoaffective sidorders

2125

INSULIN RECEPTORS AND GLUCOSE INTOLERANCE IN ENDOGENOUS DEPRESSION.

G. Michel[+], K. Diebold[*], U. Pfeifle[*], Th. Lenz[++], B. Seifert[+]

[+] Abbott Laboratories, European Research and Development, Wiesbaden, FRG. [*] Psychiatric Clinic, University of Heidelberg, FRG. [++] Institute of Physiology II, University of Heidelberg, FRG.

Impaired glucose tolerance (IGT) is frequently observed in endogenous depression (ED). The underlying pathomechanism has not been identified so far. We have tested the hypothesis that changes in cellular insulin receptors may cause this phenomenon. Insulin receptor binding (competitive binding assay using human 125 I (Tyr A14) Insulin as tracer) to monocytes was measured in patients with ED (n = 30) and compared to groups of schizophrenics (S, n = 22) and healthy controls (C, n = 9). Assays were done at admittance to the clinic and after successful treatment (discharge). An oral glucose tolerance test (OGTT) was performed to verify IGT in the ED group. OGTT was normal in S and C. In addition to glucose, insulin and C-peptide, insulin-antagonistic hormones and metabolites were measured. Specific insulin binding ($I/10^7$ monocytes) comprised to 4.3 ± 0.3 (ED), 4.2 ± 0.2 (S), and 4.4 ± 0.5 (C), showing no statistically significant differences between the groups. Although IGT returned to normal after treatment in ED, insulin binding did not change significantly (4.6 ± 0.3). Normalization of IGT was paralleled by significant decreases in plasma cortisol (150 µg/l vs. 120 µg/l; $p < 0.001$) and free fatty acids (496 µM vs. 342 µM; $p < 0.001$). As insulin secretion was normal in all patients (shown by C-peptide levels in OGTT) and insulin receptor binding was not affected, we suggest that IGT found in ED may be attributed to a postreceptor defect in cellular insulin action, which is restored to normal after improvement of disease.

2126

Preventive Therapy of Relapse in Affective & Schizoaffective Psychoses
E. Kostyukova, T. Kudryakova
All-Union Mental Health Research Centre

The prevention of relapse in affective & schizoaffective psychoses is one of the most important problems of contemporary psychopharmacotherapy. The research is devoted to the investigation of preventive characteristics of carbamazepine & the comparison of these with the preventive effect of lithium carbonate. 118 patients with affective & schizoaffective psychoses having both monopolar & bipolar course, were examined using the clinical & pharmacokinetic methods. The research demonstrated a high efficiency of the preventive therapy of carbamazepine as compared to lithium carbonate. Differentiated indications to the use of both drugs were formulated, optimum methods of carbamazepine preventive therapy were elaborated, as well as methods of its use to eliminate the faults of lithium preventive therapy (resistance, side effects, complications).

2127

Preventive Therapy of Affective & Schizoaffective Psychoses : Economic Aspects
Y. Ushakov, E. Kostyukova, L. Kalugina, M. Mirzoyan
All-Union Mental Health Research Centre

The paper features the results of the comparative study of various medication methods' efficiency in the prevention of affective & schizoaffective psychoses relapse. The study was based on the multifactor investigation of various economic & socio-economic indicators, characterizing costs & benefits of the use of carbamazepine & lithium carbonate. The comparative analysis demonstrated a high normothymic activity of carbamazepine & lithium carbonate in the patients under examination; the clinical & economic evaluation testified to a more marked preventive effect of carbamazepine.

2128

CLONAZEPAM IN THE PROPHYLAXIS OF BIPOLAR DISORDERS

Altamura AC, Mauri MC, Invernizzi G.
Institute of Clinical Psychiatry, University of Milan, Italy

Alternative drugs to lithium in the prophylaxis of Bipolar Disorders are of interest both for the treatment of non responders and in case of side effects and toxicity problems.
Clonazepam (CLN), seems to exert a stimulant effect on 5-HT synthesis and its efficacy in different psychiatric disorders including panic attacks, mood disorders and schizophrenia has been recently shown.
We report six cases (3M, 3F; mean age 48.16 ± 2.92 yrs SD) affected by bipolar disorders according to DSM III-R, treated prophylactically for 19-34 months (mean 28.3 ± 5.26 SD) with CLN mean daily dosage 1.25 mg ± 0.41 SD p.o.
During the follow-up low doses of neuroleptics (4 pt) or tricyclic antidepressants (1 pt) were combined. One case was treated with CLN alone.
All cases remained free from relapses and side-effects except for transient complaints of moderate dose-related sedation.

2129

Avortement et dépression à Athènes.

L. MOURADIAN, UER PARIS XIII, FRANCE.
Malgré les progrès en matière de contraception, des femmes deviennent enceintes sans l'avoir désiré et recourrent à l'avortement. A Athènes, 30 femmes de 18 à 35 ans, interrompant leur grossesse ont été étudiées, lors d'un entretien semi-dirigé le jour de l'intervention. Une dépression a été recherchée avec l'échelle de Hamilton; 20% présentaient une dépression correspondant à un score minimum de 18 pour l'échelle : pour 5 d'entre elles, il s'agit d'une dépression réactionnelle, pour une, c'est la décompensation d'un état dépressif préexistant. Parmi les interrogées, un tiers des femmes subissait un 2e avortement et un quart, un troisième. Les facteurs associés à la dépression sont : nombre plus élevé d'avortements antérieurs, délai plus court entre les avortements, célibat et concubinage, décès d'un parent. La vive réticence envers la pilule explique le taux important de récidive(58%). Ces résultats montrent que l'avortement, bien que très fréquent, reste un évènement dont la répétition et les conséquences psychologiques peuvent être dépressiogènes. Une écoute spécialisée et un effort d'information pourraient peut-être prévenir ces complications

Session 325 Poster Presentation:
Schizophrenic disorders

2130

NEUROLOGICAL SOFT-SIGNS IN ACUTE AND CHRONIC SCHIZOPHRENIA

J. Schröder, H. Sauer, H. Betz, R. Niethammer, F.J. Geider, M. Binkert, C. Reitz
Dept. of Psychiatry, Heidelberg, FRG
Dept. of Neuroradiology, Heidelberg, FRG

To study the reversibility of Neurological Soft-Signs (NSS) 26 patients with DSM III-schizophrenia and schizophreniform disorder were investigated on admission, one week and two months later. A comprehensive 18 items NSS-scale was applied, the clinical status was assessed by various other scales (BPRS, CPRS, RSESE, InSka) and a CT performed. 14 healthy volunteers served as controls.
Both diagnostic groups showed significantly more NSS than the controls. When contrasting patients with a remitting or chronic disorder, there was no difference in NSS at admission. However, in the clinical course the remitting conditions were associated with a rapid and significant decrease of the NSS, whereas in the chronics, who also presented with a significantly higher degree of cerebral atrophy in CT, the NSS remained almost constant. These results were confirmed by a discriminant analysis. NSS were not associated with extrapyramidal side-effects. The data presented suggest a correlation between NSS and the clinical course.

2131

SCHIZOPHRENIA PSYCHOSIS AND FOLLOWING GENETICAL MARKERS
Petrovic D. Dukič S.
Faculty of Medicine CHC "Kragujevac"
Clinic of Psychiatry Kragujevac YU

Our abstract presents the importance of association of hapto-globeshaped phenotypes, as well as some characteristics of schizophrenic illness. The most attention was paid to the statistical important association of the positive family anamnesis and hapto-globeshaped type Hp 1-1 (p less 0,05). The statistical important association of schizoaffective phenomenology and hapto-globeshaped type 1-1 is also interesting. By following the concentration of hapto-globes (as the biological constancy of the organism) we assumed that the same correlates, through the clinical deteriorations of the chronic schizophrenic psychosis among all the schizophrenic patients. Summarizing the results of the work in the biological-clinical study we are quite certain that such investigations must be completed by a great number of genetical markers in correlation with schizophrenia and in this way the biological indicators should be determined.

2132

PSYCHOPATHOLOGY OF EXPRESSION IN THE PLASTIC PRODUCTION OF SCHIZOPHRENICS

Dr. hab. Magdalena Tyszkiewicz
Department of Health, Gdynia, Poland

The Mental Health Dispensary of Gdynia has for over 20 years been conducting therapy in schizophrenic patients by making them take up plastic activities. The system so formed of patient/his work/therapist was expected to give better insight into the patients' mental state, to improve their social standing by admitting them into creative groups in the dispensary (the Club of Amateurs of Art) and introducing them into the world of the healthy by organizing expositions of their production in the dispensary and public ones, and by presenting their creation at psychiatric congresses in this country and abroad. Over 100 patients have so far been submitted to this kind of therapy. Nearly 50% had attended the Club where during the so-called One Author's Matinées held twice a week the work of one creator is discussed by the group, or the whole of the group work together painting and drawing. Several expositions held every year are preceded by formal inaugurations and invitations sent out to relatives and friends.

2133

Expressed Emotion and Communication Style in Schizophrenics' Families
A Guiding Light in Family Education
Akio Takano, M.D., Kosei Kido, M.D.,
Takashi Yamaguchi, M.D., Hiroshi Usui, M.D.,
Masanori Nagashima, M.D., Akihisa Takanashi, M.D.,
Takeshi Sukegawa, M.D.
Department of Neuropsychiatry, Nihon
University School of Medicine Tokyo, Japan.

Effective family psychoeducation has reduced the relapse rate in scizophrenia. But it is necessary to clarify the style of communication between schizophrenics and their relatives in order to intervene. To date, however, concrete communication styles have not been established using the expressed emotion (EE) ratings for relatives of schizophrenics.
This study was performed to evaluate the style of communication used between schizophrenics and their relatives. About thirty schizophrenics and fifty parents were evaluated using a communication style checklist consisting of fifty-five questions. Comparisons were made between the results of the patients' and relatives' communication style checklist, and those of the parents' knowledge of schizophrenics, and their EE level (The Five Minute Speech Sample).

2134

Relapse and Parents' Knowledge about Schizophrenia:
A Japanese Study
Akihisa Takahashi, M.D., Kosei Kido, M.D., Takashi Yamaguchi, M.D., Hiroshi Usui, M.D., Masanori Nagashima, M.D., Akio Takano, M.D. and Takeshi Sukegawa, M.D.
Department of Neuropsychiatry, Nihon University School of Medicine Tokyo, Japan

Although the relationship between the patients' relatives' level of expressed emotion (EE) and relapse in schizophrenics has been studied extensively, there has been no comparable inquiry made into the relatives' knowledge about schizophrenia.
Accordingly, 44 parents of 26 schizophrenic inpatients were interviewed by means of the Knowledge Interview (KI), after which, the EE among 37 of the interviewed parents was assessed by the brief method (The Five Minute Speech Sample).
The results of the KI showed that the parents of schizophrenics were divided into two groups, according to the following: (1) understanding of schizophrenia, (2) recognition of symptoms, (3) expectations concerning the patients' future, and (4) recognition of the need for medication.
These results were compared with the symptomatic relapse rate of patients', who remained on antipsychotic medication, within the nine month period following discharge from the hospital.

2135

COGNITIVE DEFICIT IN SCHIZOPHRENIA : A SUB-CORTICAL MECHANISM ?
Ph.GALLOIS[1], M.SMETS[2], P.HAUTECOEUR[2],
G.FORZY[2], J.F.DEREUX[2], Ph.J.PARQUET[3]
(1) C.H.S. de SAINT-VENANT (France)
(2) C.H. St-Philibert. LOMME (France)
(3) C.H.R. de LILLE (France)

Auditory event-related potentials (ERP_s) were recorded in 17 schizophrenic patients ($DSM\ III_R$) and in 30 control subjects matched for sex and age. A "Oddball" paradigm was used.
13 patients (76,47 %) showed abnormal responses : the increase in the latency of N_2 ($P<0,003$), P_3 ($P<0,00005$) and N_3 ($P<0,002$) peaks and the decrease in the amplitude of P_3 ($P<0,00005$) are in favor of a cognitive deficit involving especially decision making and short memory processes.
A significant increased latency of the N_1 peak ($P<0,05$) was also observed.
This lengthening of N_1 latency has already been reported in the sub-cortical dementia of Parkinson's disease. Therefore a sub-cortical disorder might account for cognitive deficit in some schizophrenic patients (such as those with ventricular enlargement in CT scan ?)

2136

MULTIMODALITY EVOKED POTENTIALS IN SCHIZOPHRENIC PATIENTS
M. SMETS[1], Ph.GALLOIS[2], J.F.DEREUX[2],
Ph.J.PARQUET[3]
(1) C.H.S. de SAINT-VENANT (France)
(2) C.H.St-Philibert. LOMME (France)
(3) C.H.R. de LILLE (France)

Auditory brain-stem (ABS), somatosensory (SEP_s) and visual (flash and pattern-VEP_s) evoked potentials were recorded in 18 schizophrenic patients ($DSM\ III_R$) and in 20 control subjects matched for sex and age.
- 3 patients (17,64 %) exhibited abnormal ABS responses : lengthening of I-V inter-peak interval.
- 8 patients (44,44 %) showed abnormal SEP_s : there was a significant decrease in the amplitude of N_{20} ($P<0,07$) and a significant increase in the latency of P_{45} following left median nerve stimulation ($P<0,007$).
- Concerning VEP_s (flash), 6 patients (35,29 %) exhibited an increase in the latency of peak III and/or peak VII especially in the left occipital cortex ($P<0,008$).
- For VEP_s (pattern), 9 patients (56,25 %) had a decrease in the amplitude of P100 for 4 different spatial frequencies and an increase in the latency of P100 only for the highest spatial frequencies ($P<0,006$).
These results do not provide support for the localisation of lesions in the brain-stem but they suggest a disorder at the cortical hemispheric level, especially in the left occipital and right parietal cortex.

2137

REMOXIPRIDE AND HALOPERIDOL IN SCHIZOPHRENIA: A DOUBLE-BLIND MC-STUDY

U-G Ahlfors[1], R Rimon[2], B Appelberg[2], U Hagert[3], H Katila[2], A Mahlanen[7], O-P Mehtonen[4], H Naukkarinen[2], J Outakoski[5], H Rantanen[1], A Sorri[6], T Tamminen[2], E Tolvanen[3]

[1]Hesperia Hospital, Helsinki; [2]Psychiatric Clinic, Helsinki University; [3]Nikkilä Hospital, Nikkilä; [4]Pitkäniemi Hospital, Pitkäniemi; [5]Oulunsuu Hospital, Oulu; [6]Psychiatric clinic OUCH, Oulu; [7]Moisio Hospital, Mikkeli; Finland

Ninety-two patients with schizophrenia were included in a double-blind multicenter parallel group trial comparing remoxipride and haloperidol. The mean daily dose was 271 mg (range 150-600 mg) in the remoxipride group and 8.3 mg (range 5-20 mg) in the haloperidol group.

The study period was six weeks with at least one day of wash-out. For 12 patients the treatment was discontinued before day 12 of the study. The patients were evaluated using the Clinical Global Impression Scale (CGI) and the 18-item Brief Psychiatric Rating Scale (BPRS) at baseline and at weekly intervals thereafter.

CGI ratings as well as total BPRS scores had declined at the end of the trial compared with pretreatment values in both patient groups investigated. No significant differences were found between the remoxipride and haloperidol groups with regard to treatment outcome. According to the CGI, 45 percent of the patients improved clearly or markedly in both patient groups studied.

Treatment-emergent extrapyramidal symptoms such as akathisia, hypokinesia, rigidity, tremor, and dyskinesia were statistically more frequent and more severe during haloperidol than during remoxipride treatment. Harmful and severe extrapyramidal side effects were the most frequent reason for premature treatment termination in the haloperidol group, whereas ineffectiveness was the main reason for early withdrawal in the remoxipride group.

In conclusion, remoxipride seems to be as effective as haloperidol. With regard to adverse events/symptoms, there is a clear advantage for remoxipride in relation to haloperidol.

2138

Risperidone in the treatment of chronic psychosis

Jansen A.A.I.[1] and Boom A.J.[2]
[1] Janssen Pharmaceutica B.V., Tilburg, The Netherlands
[2] St. Streekziekenhuis Walcheren, Vlissingen, The Netherlands

In an open label study 24 chronic psychotic patients, admitted to the psychiatric ward of the Hospital of Vlissingen were treated with risperidone after a placebo wash-out period of one week. Therapy started with 1 mg b.i.d. The maximally allowed dose was 10 mg b.i.d.

The PANSS and ESRS were used as main evaluation methods. During the study period of 3 months, risperidone was confirmed to be an effective antipsychotic with effects on both positive and negative symptoms. The average daily dose was 5 mg.
Extrapyramidal symptoms due to previous neuroleptic therapy almost completely disappeared. Sleep quality parameters improved while a transient daytime sleepiness was reported during the dose-adaptation period.

2139

COGNITIVE EFFECT OF BROMOCRIPTINE IN SCHIZOPHRENIA

R. de Beaurepaire, C. Simon-Soret, M. Cleau and P. Borenstein. CHS du Bon-Sauveur, 14012, Caen, and CHS de Villejuif, 94400, Villejuif.

Several trials of treatment of schizophrenia with bromocriptine have been published, and the results are conflicting, depending on the dose used, the length of treatment and the schizophrenia subtype. In those trials the BPRS was always used for evaluation and never were neuropsychological variables assessed in patients. Nevertheless cognitive defects are common and major features in chronic schizophrenia. We therefore explored the effects of a long term treatment (4 months) of schizophrenia with bromocriptine (10 mg/day) on 10 neuropsychological items. Nine hospitalized chronic schizophrenics (mean age 51) were included in the study. All patients had a neuroleptic treatment unchanged throughout the study. Four testing sessions were performed: the first the day before treatment initiation, the second and the third after 2 and 4 months of treatment, and the fourth 2 months after treatment withdrawal. The results show significant improvements for the WAIS performance scale and for the Benton test, and not for the WAIS verbal scale and the Porteus test. The improvements remained unchanged 2 months after treatment withdrawal. Therefore long term bromocriptine treatment improves intellectual (WAIS performance) and visuo-constructive (Benton) functions in chronic schizophrenia, but not anticipation (Porteus) and not verbal and memory capacities (WAIS verbal). Several different mechanisms of action of bromocriptine can be proposed: action on the dopaminergic systems and particularly an agonist action on the meso-cortico-frontal dopamine system, action on the cerebral blood flow, and the possibility of a neurotrophic effect may be raised to explain the long-term improvement.

Session 326 Poster Presentation:
Organic mental diseases and various psychiatric conditions

2140

Psychological Response to an Earthquake

V.M.Garnov

First Moscow Medical College

The paper presents the results of structural-dynamic analysis of mental state in a selected part of the population surviving in an earthquake. Here is given a description of the types of the psychological reaction and some regularity in the organization of psychopathology. The above-mentioned results were the basis for creating a conceptual model of psychological response to an earthquake.

2141
MENTAL DEPRESSION ANTEDATING THE ONSET OF PARKINSON'S DISEASE

I.Fukunishi, T.Hayabara and K.Hosokawa
Department of Neuropsychiatry, Kagawa Medical School, Kagawa, Japan

Although many studies have shown the relationship between Parkinson's disease (PD) and mental depression (MD), the nature of the relationship is not clear at present. Recently, the existence of PD with MD antedating the onset of PD has been recognized. The present study was undertaken to examine MD antedating the onset of PD.

The subjects consisted of PD patients with MD: MD antedating the onset of PD (A group, N=9), MD postdating the onsetof PD (B group, N=10). For the control groups, PD patients without MD (C group, N=10) and MD patients (D group, N=10) were selected. The severity of PD and MD was assessed by the Yahr's classification and the General Health Questionnaire (GHQ) developed by D.P.Goldberg (1970), respectively.

The results obtained were as follows.
1) Although there were no significant differences statistically, the A group had milder PD symptoms than B and C groups
2) The A group had more severe MD symptoms than B and D groups.
3) The effects of antidepressants in the A group were poor, compared with B and D groups.

Judging from these findings, PD with MD antedating PD was different from PD with MD postdating PD and PD without MD. This PD may be one of specific sub-types.

2142
Comparative Age-Specific Features of Alzheimer Disease Clinical Picture & Course
N.Seleznyova
All-Union Mental Health Research Centre

The comparative analysis of age-specific features of AD clinical picture & course was based on non-selective longitudinal examination of 89 patients with the onset between the age of 37 & 78. Disease progression proved to be faster in case of late onset (after 60) than early manifestation (before 60). The psychopathological structure of AD initial manifestations shows a marked variability, determined by higher cortical & mnestico-intellectual functional disorders & personality changes at the initial stage. Three basic clinical types of the disease initial stage were singled out that correlate with progression rates & age at the onset. The type of initial stage determines the dementia structure at the subsequent stages of the disease. It is expressed in the correlation between the high cortical & mnestico-intellectual functional disorders. The early onset proved to correlate with higher frequency of premorbid personality accentuation, of constitutional deficiency in cortical functions & with the frequency of the exogenous exposure both during the premorbid life period & the stage prior to or concurrent with the onset.

2143
EFFECTS OF ILOPROST ON MOTOR AND SEIZURE ACTIVITY*
Akarsu,E.S. and Ayhan,I.H. M.D., Ph.D.
Dept.Pharmacol., Med.Sch.Ankara Univ., Turkey

The effects of intracerebroventricular (icv) injected iloprost,a new chemically stable analogue of prostacyclin, on locomotor activity (LMA) and pentylenetetrazol (PTZ)-induced seizures were studied in rats. Depression on LMA was observed after 500 ng/icv dose whereas anticonvulsive property could be obtained at 20 ng/icv dose. At this dose, the intensity of clonic convulsions and the incidence of deaths were reduced. At higher doses all seizure parameters improved.Thus, the time until onset of clonic convulsions was prolonged and the number of animals which were protected from the clonic convulsions was increased,mortality,incidence of tonic convulsions and intensity of seizures were decreased.Regarding other prostanoids, iloprost seems to have potent anticonvulsive activity against PTZ - induced convulsions without marked LMA depressive action. This is suggested that,the anticonvulsive activity of iloprost might involve a specific mechanism.

*This work constitutes a part of PhD thesis of ESA
This study was supported by Eczacıbaşı Sci. Res. Award Fund (1989) and Ankara Univ.Res.Fund (89.09. 00.02). The authors are grateful to Dr.Schillinger (Schering AG) for his gift of iloprost.

2144
PSYCHOMOTOR RETARDATION AND NEUROPSYCHOLOGY IN PSYCHIATRIC DISEASES
C. Herrmann, S. Schlegel, C. Schmalzbrot, D. Nieber
Dept. Psychiatry, University of Mainz, 65 Mainz, FRG

Psychomotor retardation - assessed by the Bech-Rafaelsen-Melancholia-Scale (BRMS)- was found to be associated with baseline plasma cortisol and ventricle size in depressed patients (Schlegel et al, 1988, 1989). Therefore the present study investigated the question whether the rated motor retardation - independent of the diagnosis - is correlated with objective neuropsychological measurements. 29 inpatients (mean age:42) with a major depressive episode and 31 (mean age:33) with a schizophrenic or schizophreniform disorder (DSM III) were investigated, all were drugfree. We assessed blindly the BRMS. Reaction time measurements were examined on the computerized Viennese determinaton device (VVD), motor performances on the motor performance series (MPS) developed by Schoppe. The neuropsychological data were correlated with the sum scores of BRMS and the sum of the retardation items (motor, verbal, intellectual, emotional) (BRMS-R) of BRMS. In schizophrenia the number of correct reactions was negatively and the number of delayed reactions positively correlated with BRMS-R. In depression no such relationship could be detected. The analysis of the MPS revealed correlations of BRMS-R with the number and duration of failures on the "steadiness"-subtest in depressed patients.
The value of reaction time measurements and motor performances test regarding their association with various psychopathological aspects will be discussed in detail.

2145

BUSPIRONE IN THE SYMPTOMATIC TREATMENT OF ACUTE ALCOHOL WITHDRAWAL Louis Fabre, M.D.,Ph.D., Julie Vettraino MSN, Allison Stephens RN and David McLendon, Ph.D., The Fabre Clinic, Houston, TX USA
This one week open study was conducted in 12 inpatients admitted for alcohol detoxification with impending delirium tremens within 36 hours of quitting alcohol. The objective was to assess buspirone treatment in acute alcohol detoxification. Assessments included investigator-rated and patient-rated psychometric scales including the Alcohol Withdrawal Symptom Scale. Significant improvement was observed as early as two hours after initiating buspirone treatment with excellent recovery by study day 3. Good agreement exists between Investigator's (11 of 12) and patients (9 of 12) global evaluation of effect. (moderate improvement or better) While this was an open uncontrolled study, the results were compared with 28 alcohol withdrawal patients receiving placebo in a similar concurrent blind study. Placebo patients also had good recovery by study day 3. However, on study day 2, the Buspar patients were significantly improved (p .01) when compared on the Alcohol Withdrawal Symptom Scale. Ten Buspar treated patients terminated before day 7: seven improved, one not-improved, and two uncooperative. The mean total daily Buspar dose during the first three days was 80mg; administered 20mg q.i.d. No patients experienced seizures. Side effects attributable to Buspar were mild and similar to those seen in anxiety studies. In conclusion, buspirone appears to be markedly effective and well-tolerated in the treatment of acute alcohol withdrawal.

2146

CRISIS INTERVENTION IN PATIENTS WITH A HISTORY OF DELINQUENCY
N. Konrad
Krankenhaus Moabit, Berlin, FRG
In a population of 301 patients who had been treated between May 1985 and May 1986 in a crisis intervention inpatient department for an average of about 5 days, 38 patients with a history of delinquency were studied with regard to some sociodemographic and clinical variables at the time of treatment and 2-3 years after. This sample was contrasted with the other 263 patients without a history of delinquency. The criminal sample consisted mainly of men with the primary diagnosis of personality disorders, substances dependencies (according to ICD 9). In about half of the cases the crisis was brought about by conflicts in partnership relations of by social problems. Of all patients treated there was a higher rate of attempted suicide in patients with a criminal history (50%) than in those without (35%).
2-3 years after discharge 85% of the delinquent sample considered the treatment as helpful and especially 60%, the group therapy treatment. In comparison with the other patients the delinquent sample stressed significantly the importance of the therapeutic team. 75% of the delinquent sample assessed an improvement of their case history. The investigators had the same rating in regard to psychiatric symptoms, substances abuse and social situation. It could be useful to discuss, where and to what extent a treatment based on the model of inpatient crisis intervention might be practised in Forensic Psychiatry.

2147

A CALCIUM ANTAGONIST, NIMODIPINE, IN THE TREATMENT OF ALCOHOL WITHDRAWAL SYNDROME

Altamura AC, Cavallaro R, Regazzetti MG, *Porta M.

Institute of Clinical Psychiatry, University of Milan, Italy.

Recent data show that central nervous system (CNS) dihydropyridine-sensitive Ca^{++} channels may be involved in rats' chronic ethanol toxicity and withdrawal phenomena. Moreover calcium channel antagonists, including dihydropyridines, were found to reduce or prevent withdrawal symptoms in rats. Aim of the study was to evaluate the efficacy and tolerability of the Ca^{++} antagonist nimodipine in human alcohol withdrawal syndrome (AWS). 10 hospitalized alcoholics of both sexes suffering from AWS according to DSM III criteria were treated for 3 weeks in monotherapy with nimodipine p.o.. Evaluation of AWS symptoms was performed at baseline and after 3,5,7,10,14 and 21 days. A significant global improvement of AWS symptoms was early observed (particularly in neurovegetative and psychopatological symptoms) and lasted up to the end of the study without noticeable side-effects.
From these findings nimodipine seems to be effective in the treatment of mild-moderate AWS.

2148

OCCUPATIONAL EXPOSURE TO MANGANESE AND MENTAL DISORDER
Gabriel Cizinsky[1], Göran Struwe[1], Maud Hagman[2], Anders Iregren[2], Lotta Johansson[2], Arne Wennberg[2].
[1]Dept. Psychiatry, Huddinge University Hospital, Huddinge, Sweden. [2]National Institute of Occupational Health, Solna, Sweden.

It is well known that strong exposure to Manganese (Mn) causes neurological and psychiatric disorders (parkinsonism, psychosis). However, the effects of low-graded but sustained exposures in current occupational settings have not been studied earlier.

A group of 30 steel-workers exposed to Mn well below present threshold limit values were therefore examined in a comprehensive health survey, comprising neurophysiological, neurological, psychometrical and psychiatric investigations, and compared with 60 age-matched non-exposed blue-collar workers. Though no exposed subjects were found to suffer from illness, the results do indicate an effect of the low-graded Mn exposure on the CNS.

The psychiatric ratings thus indicated a tendency for the exposed subjects to suffer from symptoms of inexactitude, vertigo and fatiguability, and these results showed a significant correlation with impairments of relevant neurological and psychometrical parameters for motor coordination.

The implication is that presently allowed occupational exposures may cause subclinical forms of parkinsonism and neurasthenia.

2149
EFFECT OF MALKANGINI OIL (HERBAL DRUG) ON MENTAL RETARDATION
Dr. Ajay Kumar Sahu, Member/International Epilepsy Congress, Indo US Child Mental Health, Indian Psychiatry Society, Orissa, India
S.K.Gautam, R.P.Swamy, P.S.Gehlot, D.C.Satija, B.L.Suwalk, Mrs. Verma, Psychologist, Jaipur, India

So far for the first time in the world, one herbal drug "Malkangini" Oil was researched on 13 Mental Retardation patients at Psychiatric centre under S.M.S. Medical College, Jaipur, India in collaboration with National Institute of Ayurved Jaipur, India from 1980-1981 by the author.
13 patients, out of them sever 1, sever subnormal 9, subnormal 1, moderate 1, moderate sub-normal 1, were diagnosed by author, psychiatrist and psychologist at OPD psychiatric centre, Jaipur, India. Medicine Malkangini Oil was administered by author, for one month to each patient, 3 drops twice daily, with milk. IQ was examined before giving the medicine to each patient by psychologist.
In 11 patients 2-40 IQ in 2 patients 41-50 IQ were observed.
Malkangini Oil was very effective on Mental Retardation. In 13 patients IQs had been increasing after one month trial.

Session 327 Poster Presentation:
Biological psychiatry and psychopharmacology

2150
Dopamine Receptors and Diagnosis of Mental Illness

T. Lenz[+] and G. Michel[*]

[+] 2nd Department of Physiology, University of Heidelberg, FRG.
[*] Abbott Laboratories, European Research and Development, Wiesbaden, FRG.

It is assumed that physiological and pathological changes in alpha$_2$- and beta$_2$-adrenoceptors of human blood cells reflect alterations of the same receptor type in other target tissues. To look for a suitable model of D$_2$-dopaminergic receptors, we have used the radioligand ^{3}H-spiperone, known to bind to central D$_2$-dopaminergic receptors, to identify dopamine receptors in human mononuclear leukocytes (MNL). In none of our binding experiments performed using ^{3}H-spiperone (0.1-5nM, 60min; 37°C; n=12) did we find evidence for displacement by specific D$_2$-dopaminergic antagonists, e.g. butaclamol, haloperidol, or sulpiride (10^{-6}M). This was also true of experiments performed with different cell isolation procedures and binding buffer systems. These conditions, however, in parallel allowed us to demonstrate insulin receptor and ß-adrenoceptor binding. Also after 72h mitogen-stimulation, no dopaminergic spiperone binding sites were detectable. Chloroquin (1µM), a lysosomal uptake inhibitor, reduces spiperone binding by 30-40% indicating that a large portion of the radioligand is trapped inside the cells. It is concluded that there is no functional role for dopamine receptors in human MNL. Our findings are in strong contrast to those of other authors (Bondy et al., Biol. Psychiat. 1984; 19: 1377). This discrepancy remains to be explained. The absence of dopaminergic receptors in MNL is further confirmed by our observation that the stimulation of adenylate cyclase by dopamine is mediated via beta$_2$-adrenoceptor because the effect is inhibited by the beta blocker propranolol but not by D$_1$- or D$_2$-dopaminergic antagonists.

2151
A NON-INVASIVE VISUAL TECHNIQUE FOR ASSESSING FUNCTION OF CORTICAL DOPAMINE SYSTEMS IN SCHIZOPHRENICS

F.K. Skinner, A.I.M. Glen, E.M.T. Glen,*D.M. Parker

Highland Psychiatric Research Group, Inverness, Scotland.
*Dept. of Psychology, Aberdeen University, Scotland.

Until now, positron emission tomography has been the only technique available for measuring central dopaminergic activity (DA). A technique using a visual illusion of orientation (the tilt after-effect - TAE) has been shown by a group in Bristol to reflect functioning cortical DA. An initial study of schizophrenic patients receiving depot neuroleptics with dopaminergic-blocking activity showed down-regulation in the expected direction. The group also showed that in normal volunteers the system was sensitive to up-regulation by L-dopa and down-regulation by dopaminergic antagonists. In a preliminary study we have examined schizophrenic patients receiving depot neuroleptics and shown a reproducible, cyclical fluctuation of DA, depending on the time interval before and after the injection. The changes seemed to be more sensitively measured by TAE than by clinical ratings. The technique could be used to develop depots with more uniform release. We are also examining patients with an early diagnosis of schizophrenia, who are drug-free, to assess baseline levels of dopamine function.

2152
NEUROENDOCRINE RESPONSES TO mCPP IN ENDOGENOUS DEPRESSION
P. Lakshmi Reddy, S. Khanna, M.N. Subhash, S.M. Channabasavanna, B.S.S. Rao

Departments of Neurochemistry and Psychiatry, National Institute of Metal Health and Neurosciences Bangalore 560029, India
Serotonergic hypofunctioning or down-regulation of serotonin receptors has been documented earlier in endogenous depression. In the current investigation oral mCPP (0,5mg/kg. body weight) which is a relatively specific 5-HT1B agonist was used to study this receptor function in depression. Ten patients who met DSMIII criteria for Major Depression with Melancholia without psychotic features received oral mCPP. Blood was sampled baseline and after 120, 180 and 240 minutes. Patients were also rated on Hamilton Depression Scale, and compared to matched controls. There was significant reduction in suicidal ideation after mCPP. The cortisol, growth hormone and prolactin responses were accentuated. These findings are discussed in the context of the neurochemistry of endogenous depression and suicide.

2153
ORAL mCPP CHALLENGE IN OBSESSIVE COMPULSIVE DISORDER : FAILURE OF REPLICATION

Sumant Khanna, P.L. Reddy, M.N. Subhash, B.S.S.R. Rao, S.M. Channabasavanna

Departments of Psychiatry and Neurochemistry, National Institute of Mental Health and Neurosciences, Bangalore 560029, India

Earlier studies have implicated 5HT1B receptor hypersensitivity in OCD based on exacerbation of obsessive-compulsive symptoms following oral mCPP although the same effect has not been observed after parentral administration. In the current investigation 14 subjects who met DSM-III criteria for OCD received 0.5 mg/Kg. body weight oral mCPP in a fasting state. Blood was sampled baseline, at 120, 180 and 240 minutes. The patients samples were compared with normal controls. Although there was a blunted neuroendocrine response to mCPP there was no significant behavioural change noticed by the subjects. The implications of this finding and the reasons for failure of replication will be discussed.

2154
A LONGITUDINAL STUDY OF THE FORM AND CONTENT OF OBSESSIVE COMPULSIVE PHENOMENA

Sumant Khanna

Department of Psychiatry, National Institute of Mental Health and Neuro Sciences, Bangalore 560029, India

It is recognised that obsessions and compulsions can change over time. However most longitudinal follow-up studies have focussed on overall clinical state rather than on specific symptoms. In the current investigation, 24 subjects who met DSM-III criteria for OCD were recruited for monthly follow-ups. They were rated on the NIMHANS Obsessive Compulsive Symptom Check List (Khanna & Channabasavanna, 1989) on each visit. Patients were undergoing therapy, either drug or behavioral, during the process of this study. Preliminary analysis reveals that most patients continue to have obsessive-compulsive phenomena, inspite of therapy. Form appears to be consistent across time, wheras content shows variability. The implications of bio-psychosocial interactions in such a model are discussed.

2155
INCREASE OF RAT PLASMA 5-HT AFTER 5-HT UPTAKE INHIBITORS.

E. Martínez, J. Ortiz, F. Artigas. Department of Neurochemistry, C.S.I.C. Barcelona, 08034, SPAIN.

We have recently characterized the existence of a free pool of serotonin (5-HT) in rat and human plasma. Such a pool is affected by drugs in a different way than the more concentrated (>100 times) pool of 5-HT in platelets (1). Platelets and endothelial remove free 5-HT from the plasma by high affinity uptake. Thus, we have examined the effects of clomipramine, paroxetine and citalopram on the plasma and platelet pools of 5-HT, in rats. Animals have been treated with 10 mg/kg of each drug and their effects examined 30 min later. All three compounds induce a dramatic increase of plasma 5-HT (CIM, +200%; PAR, +400%; CIT, +300%) without affecting platelet 5-HT. Such effect is consistent with a rapid "in vivo" blockade of the uptake mechanism for 5-HT, and shows that actual increases of free 5-HT are produced after administration of these drugs. This effect is similar to that produced on extracellular 5-HT in rat brain by 5-HT uptake inhibitors (Adell and Artigas, in preparation) and suggests that plasma 5-HT and brain free 5-HT respond similarly to these treatments.

(1) J. Ortiz, F. Artigas, E. Gelpí. Life Sciences 43:983-990 (1988)

2156
RISPERIDONE IN THE TREATMENT OF BEHAVIORAL SYMPTOMS IN MENTAL RETARDATION: A DOUBLE-BLIND PLACEBO-CONTROLLED CROSS-OVER STUDY.

Geutjens J.*, Gelders Y. and Heylen S.

St. Oda Institute, B-3583 Overpelt, Belgium

Behavioral symptoms in mental retardation is an often recognised therapeutical problem. The ideal pharmacothera-peutical tool to deal with this problem should focus on 3 criteria: acting only on the behavioral symptoms, without reducing the general level of functioning, and without inducing disturbing side effects. Risperidone, a combined central serotonin 5-HT$_2$ and dopamine D$_2$ receptor antagonist, was found to have thymosthenic properties in the treatment of chronic schizophrenia, improving negative, affective and hostility symptoms, and reducing pre-existing extrapyramidal symptoms. Therefore it was postulated that this substance could be of value in the treatment of behavioral symptoms associated with mental retardation. The present study was initiated to test this hypothesis. Thirty patients with a diagnosis of mental retardation (DSM-III-R: mild, moderate, severe, profound), presenting behavioral disturbances insufficiently responding to conventional treatment entered the trial. The evaluation was based on the Aberrant Behavior Checklist, the Clinical Global Impresion and the Extrapyramidal Symptom Rating Scale. An individual target symptom was assessed by means of a Visual Analogue Scale. During the trial, the previous medication was kept unchanged. The first week was a run-in week, to obtain a stable baseline. Then risperidone and placebo were added to the previous medication in a double-blind cross-over design for 2 periods of 3 weeks, separated by a placebo wash-out period of 1 week. At the end of each cross-over period, a safety assessment was performed, including hematology, blood biochemistry and ECG. The results will be presented and briefly discussed.

2157

PLASMA METANEPHRINE FOR DIAGNOSIS AND THERAPY CONTROL IN PSYCHIATRIC DISORDERS.

G. Michel[+], K. Diebold[*], B. Seifert[+], K. Iinuma[++]

[+] Abbott Laboratories, European Research and Development, Wiesbaden, FRG. [*] Psychiatric Clinic, University of Heidelberg, FRG.
[++] Dainabot Co., Tokyo, Japan.

The biogenic amine hypothesis focuses on CNS neurotransmitters specifically attributing depression and mania to concentration changes of these substances in the brain. Though a large number of studies related to measurement of catecholamines and their metabolites have been published, few data are available on blood levels of methylated catecholamines in mental disease. We have used a commercial radioimmunoassay (Dainabot Co., Japan) to systematically determine metanephrine (MN) and normetanephrine (NMN) in plasma of patients with endogenous depression (ED), neurotic depression (ND), schizophrenia (S), schizoaffective disorders (SA), organic psychosis (OP), and personality disorders (PD) at admittance to the clinic. Wheras no statistically significant differences were found in NMN concentrations, mean MN (pg/ml $\pm$ 1 SD) was elevated to 143 $\pm$ 126 (SA, n = 12), 138 $\pm$ 173 (S, n = 41), 129 $\pm$ 126 (ED, n = 46), 100 $\pm$ 114 (ND, n = 13), 76 $\pm$ 102 (PD, n = 15), and 60 $\pm$ 68 (OP, n = 22) as compared to 26 $\pm$ 8 for a healthy control group (n = 53). Multiple range testing showed high significance for MN increases found in S, SA, ED, and ND ($p < 0.001$) but no significant differences between these 4 groups. Most interestingly, in S and SA, plasma MN returned to normal range upon improvement and discharge from the clinic. Our data provide direct evidence of the potential usefulness of easy to perform MN-RIA in psychiatric diagnostics and therapy control.

2158

Rehability treatment of psychotic disorders in a psychiatric Day Hospital: Methods and Results
Galvano G.C, Beltz J, Bianconi G., Lucchin A, La Greca P., Landoni G, Pazzaglia P.
Department of Psychiatry - University of Milan

We examine the results that are derived from the study of new clinical methodologies for the rehability treatment of the mental pathology in the ambit of communities and the significance of the clinical variations that are determined by their application to a population of psychotic chronic patients who stay in a psychiatric Day Hospital.
The authors propose to verify the rehability functions of the interventions that are employed and the clinical effectiveness of their association in the same therapeutic area, coherently with an operative model which provides a specific relational order of the clinical seat for the treatment.
We compare, for the validation of the clinical significance of the occurred modifications, values of longitudinal observations that are carried out by periodical scanning on the same sample and on an external group of control.
Psychosocial and psychopathologic indicators will be used.

Session 328 Poster Presentation:
Experimental psychopharmacology

2159

GABA-MONOAMINE INTERACTIONS FOLLOWING ANTIDEPRESSANT (AD) TREATMENT.

Z. Papadopoulou-Daifotis, A. Sakellariou, C. Spyraki
Departments of Pharmacology, Medical School, University of Athens and Crete.

The involvement of brain monoaminergic transmission in depression and in the action of antidepressant (AD) drugs is well established. Recently, a role of GABA in the pharmacodynamics of AD therapies has been suggested on the basis of experimental studies revealing alterations in GABA receptors following chronic AD treatment. The extent to which the AD-induced changes in GABAergic transmission influence brain monoaminergic function has not as yet been examined. We tried to give some insights to that issue with the present experimental approach.

We investigate the effect of acute (2 day) and chronic (21 day) imipramine (IMI 10mg/Kg/day, ip) on cortical striatal, hippocampal, hypothalamic NE, 5HT, 5HIAA, DA DOPAC and HVA levels of male wistar rats challenged 48 hrs after the last IMI injection with saline diazepam (0,5mg/Kg, ip) progabite (150mg/Kg, ip), gabalinoleamide (50 and 150 mg/Kg, ip).

The results showed that imipramine treatment induces plastic changes of the GABA receptor which do not concern the BZ site of the GABA-BZ complex. The induced changes influence cortical, hippocampal 5-HT transmission and cortical and striatal DA transmission but do not affect NE transmission at the brain areas tested. The results give evidence for GABA-5HT and/or DA interactions following AD treatment which may be of importance to the AD therapeutic effect.

2160

MICROIONTOPHORETIC STUDY ON THE MODE OF ACTION OF R- OXAPROTILINE AND ITS INACTIVE ENANTIOMER (LEVOPROTILINE) ON HIPPOCAMPAL NEURONS.
N. Smyrnis, A. Maillis D. Avramopoulos and C. Stefanis.
Dept. of Psychiatry, Athens Univ., Eginition Hospital. Athens Greece.

Current hypotheses on the mode of action of the antidepressants link their clinical effects with their ability to block the uptake of Noradrenaline on central neurons. However a number of new antidepressants does not seem to act always via the above mechanism neither it is possible to confirm or reject experimentally the implied causal connectivity between the effects of the antidepressants on the biochemistry of biogenic amines and their clinical effects on mood.
We have thus been tempted to test more directly the effects of a biochemically active and an inactive compound, namely the R and L-enantiomers of Oxaprotiline on hippocampal neurons by local microiontophoretic applications of the substances through multibarrel micropippetes in order to circumvent the temporal, chemical and structural restrictions met in other experimental procedures.
Our observations have shown the existence of sensitive and non-sensitive neurons. All sensitive units responded promptly with depression of their spontaneous firing rate to the administration of either of the above substances in a dose dependent way without any appreciable alteration on the spike configuration. The R-enantiomer however, exhibited quantitatively stronger responses. Following discontinuation of drugs application, neurons showed a rather fast recovery frequently followed by a higher level of spontaneous activity. When these substances were compared with the depressant effects of Noradrenaline on the same neurons, no clear synergy was seen, though cummulative depressant effects were often observed. These results together with the observations that during depression neurons were recovering promptly under the coadministration of Glutamate suggest that they are able to act upon rather specific synaptic elements but not nessesserily upon the NA-receptors.

2161

DIRECT ACTIONS AND POSTSYNAPTIC INTERACTIONS
OF NEUROLEPTICS ON SINGLE C.N.S. NEURONES

Anthony Maillis and Costas Stefanis

Dept. of Psychiatry, Athens Univ., Eginition Hospital. Athens Greece.

Current hypotheses link the anipsychotic effects of Neuroleptics with the functioning of central catecholamines. However, no consistent changes in catecholamine metabolism has been detected so far in schizophrenia, nor is there a constant pattern of catecholamine-responsive neurons in central synapses.
Also, certain neuroleptic effects cannot be fully interpreted on the basis of the catecholamine interactions alone. Moreover, many neuroleptics have complex metabolism with several metabolites which differ in their activities, thus complicating the matter considerably. In an effort to elucidate the problem, we have undertaken an extensive microiontophoretic study of Chlorpromazine (CPZ) alone and/or in combination with a variety of neurotransmitter substances i.e. Acetylcholine, DA, NA, 5-HT,
GABA, Glyc., Glut., Aspart.and Homocyst. acid, on single central neurons on cats. The results from more than 1000 neurons studied shows that CPZ alone was able to exert strong effects on the spontaneous firing neurons. Predominant excitatory responses were seen in the Hippocampus and Vermis, while Cerebellar and Cerebral Cortical neurons responded mostly with depression. When the action of CPZ was compared with that of each of the neurotransmitter substances used in this study, either synergy or antagonism was seen, depending mainly on the direction of the postsynaptic responses of the two substances, which varied in different brain areas. It is suggested that the curent hypothesis on the specificity of the neuroleptics in modifying catecholamine actions needs to be reevaluated on the basis of the more direct data presented above.

2162

DIFFERENTIAL POSTSYNAPTIC EFFECTS OF NEUROLEPTICS
ON CENTRAL CATECHOLAMINERGIC SYNAPSES.
Anthony Maillis and Costas Stefanis
Dept. of Psychiatry, Athens Univ., Eginition Hospital. Athens Greece.

Current hypotheses link the antipsychotic effects of the Neuroleptics with the functioning of central catecholamine (CA) synapsess. However, CA-ergic activities are practically present in almost all brain areas showing remarkable differences in their postsynaptic effects. Direct observations from microiontophoretic studies have shown that depression of the postsynaptic neurons is the dominant responce to CA though excitatory actions are not so rare and in a few areas are even prevailing. Moreover, certain neuroleptic effects cannot be explained on the basis of catecholamine hypotheses alone,and the specificity of Chlorpromazine (CPZ) towards certain postsynaptic actions of CA was questioned (Maillis and Stefanis 1973). The following table summarizes some more recent results from microiontophoresis of CPZ,NA and DA, in four brain areas on cats.

T A B L E

	HIPPOCAMPUS				SENSIMOT.CORT.				CEREBELL.COTR.				VERMIS			
	E	D	N	Nb	E	D	N	Nb	E	D	N	Nb	E	D	N	Nb
NA	6	84	10	129	16	58	26	82	7	76	17	42	76	8	16	38
DA	3	70	27	101	5	49	46	96	4	77	19	27	69	23	8	35
CPZ	86	6	8	230	7	85	8	274	0	98	2	105	96	4	0	116

(E=Excitation,D=Depression,N =No Effect,Nb=Numb.of Neurons stud.) When the action of CPZ was compared with those of catecholamines at least four different interactions was seen, varying from synergistic excitations or depressions to antagonisms of their excitatory or inhibitory postsynaptic effects.The data presented above, suggest that current hypotheses that link the antipsychotic effects of the neuroleptics with catecholaminergic dysfunction has to be looked under more close scrutiny.

2163

DIRECT OBSERVATIONS ON THE FUNCTIONAL ROLE OF
α-CASEIN EXORPHINS ON SINGLE C.N.S. NEURONS
A.Maillis,E.Koutsoukos,E.Angelopoulos,N.Smyrnis and C.Stefanis(*)
S.Loukas, and C.Zioudrou (**)
Dept. of Psychiatry, Athens Univ., Eginition Hospital. Athens Greece.
(**)NRC "Democritos", Agia Paraskevi, Athens - GREECE.

Syntheticaly derived peptides, coresponding to the sequence 90-95 Arg-Tyr-Leu-Gly-Tyr-Leu (P6) and 90-96 Arg-Tyr-Leu-Gly-Tyr-Leu-Glu (P7) of α-casein, have been shown to displace opioid radioligants such as DALAMID and dihydromorphine from rat brain membranes and to inhibit the contractions of the electrically stimulated mouse vas deferens. Moreover these inhibitory effects were reversed by Naloxone. Also,in preliminary studies from our laboratory we have reported that these substances strongly affect the spontaneous activity of CNS neurons following local microapplications. Here we are reporting the results from a more extensive microiontophoretic study on cortical and hippocampal neurons on rats, which are shown in the following table.

T A B L E

	SOMATOSENSORY CORTEX					HIPPOCAMPUS				
	E	D	ME	NE	Nb	E	D	ME	NE	Nb
P6	0	28	5	33	66	7	109	5	42	163
P7	7	57	5	19	88	6	99	10	25	140

(E=Excitation,D=Depression,ME=Mixed Effect,NE=No Effect,Nb=No,Neurons) Sensitive and non sensitive units were found in both areas studied. Responsive units reacted mostly with depression of their spontaneous firing rate. Facilitatory responces were more rare as it is the case for some mixed responses. The above results together with the observations that responsive units did not show any appreciable alteration of their spike configuration and that depressed units were promptly recovering by Glutamate's administration, strongly suggest that α-casein exorphins are able to modify central neuronal activity acting upon rather specific membrane elements pressumably the synaptic sites.

2164

MODIFICATION OF THE EVOKED HIPPOCAMPAL FIELD POTENTIALS BY THE
LOCAL MICROAPPLICATION OF α-CASEIN EXORPHINS

E.Angelopoulos, A.Maillis, A.Andreou, E.Koutsoukos and C.Stefanis(*).
S.Loukas and C.Zioudrou(**).

Dept. of Psychiatry, Athens Univ., Eginition Hospital. Athens Greece.
(**)NRC-"Democritos", Agia Paraskevi, Athens - GREECE.

α-Casein exorphins have beeen shown to exert peripheral and central opioid-like activities (Zioudrou et al.,1979; Loukas et al.,1983).
Also, preliminary results (Maillis et al.,1985) and ongoing studies of our Laboratory have shown that these substances strongly affect the spontaneous activity of CNS neurons following local microapplications. We are now reporting the results obtained on the commissurally stimulated CA-1 area of the hippocampus during local microiontophoresis of α-casein exorphin (Arg-Tyr-Leu-Gly-Tyr-Leu), morphine, naloxone, and DSLET {D-Ser2}-Leu-Enkephalin-Thr, a specific δ-agonist. All the above substances except naloxone, increased the amplitude of the evoked population spike, 30-60 sec after the onset of drugs application in a dose dependent way. This effect was overlasting for 20-70 min following discontinuation of α-casein and DSLET administration, while morhine's similar actions were much shorter 3-10 min. All the above actions were antagonised by the previous administration of naloxone. The data presented above supports further the opioid action of α-casein exorphins on central neurons.

2165
BUSPIRONE-INDUCED BEHAVIORAL SYNDROME IN RATS

Gürdal,H., Palaoğlu,Ö. and Ayhan,İ.H.

Dept.Pharmacol., Med.Sch.Ankara Univ., TURKEY

Buspirone, an anxiolitic drug, has been shown to bind with high affinity to both $5HT1_A$ and D_2 receptors. Moreover, a stereotyped behavioral syndrome induced by drugs increasing synaptic serotonin and dopamine has been described. Such a behavioral syndrome is controversial for buspirone. In the present study, buspirone (1.25-10 mg/kg ; i.p) has been shown to produce a dose-dependent back-muscle contraction and head weaving flat body posture, hind limb abduction which may all be considered as a 5HT like behavioral syndrome. Male albino rats (200-280g) were continuously observed for 60 minutes and observations were recorded for every 10 minutes interval. It was demonstrated that head weaving induced by buspirone was significantly attenuated by haloperidol (0.50 mg/kg ; s.c) and potentiated by amphetamine (0.25 mg/kg;s.c). While metisergide (5 mg/kg ; s.c) was found to antagonize buspirone induced back-muscle contraction, it was not effective against head weaving. Thus, the mechanism of action of buspirone induced behaviour seems to involve not only serotonin but dopamine as well.

2166
5-HT RECEPTOR AGONISTS 1-(2,5-DIMETHOXY-4-IODOPHENYL)-2-AMINOPROPANE (DOI) AND 8-OH-DPAT INCREASE WAKEFULNESS IN THE RAT

J.M. Monti, G. Piñeyro, C. Orellana, M. Boussard, H. Jantos, P. Labraga, S. Olivera and F. Alvariño

Dept. of Pharmacology and Therapeutics. Clinics Hospital. Montevideo, Uruguay

The effects of 5-HT2 agonist DOI and 5-HT1A agonist 8-OH-DPAT were compared with those of 5-HT2 antagonist ritanserin in rats implanted for chronic sleep recordings. DOI (250 µg/kg) and 8-OH-DPAT (250-500 µg/kg) significantly increased wakefulness (W) and decreased slow wave sleep (SWS) and REM sleep (REMS). At 500 µg/kg ritanserin increased SWS and depressed REMS but did not alter W. Pretreatment with ritanserin (250 µg/kg) reversed the effect of DOI (250 µg/kg) on W and SWS. However, ritanserin did not prevent the increase of W EEG induced by 8-OH-DPAT. Thus, selective activation of 5-HT2 or 5-HT1A receptors increased W and decreased sleep. In addition, pharmacological insomnia induced by DOI was prevented by pretreatment with 5-HT2 antagonist ritanserin.

Session 329 Poster Presentation:
Brain imaging and EEG studies

2167
SHAM MAGNETIC RESONANCE IMAGING BY MEANS OF A SEWER PIPE

Hans van Berkestijn, Jaap Korf

Department of Psychiatry, University of Groningen, The Netherlands

Magnetic Resonance Imaging (MRI) of the brain is difficult to achieve in some patients, including patients with movement disorders, claustrophobic patients and patients with dementia.
We developed a simple method in order to accustom patients to the narrow head coil and the unpleasant noise of the equipment. Using this procedure interruption of the MRI scanning, which is rather expensive, may be prevented.

2168
IMAGING BASAL AND ACTIVATED BRAIN FUNCTION IN PSYCHIATRIC ILLNESS

R. Hunter*, G. Goodwin*, D. Wyper+, K. Shedlack* and G. Fink

*MRC Brain Metabolism Unit, Edinburgh, Scotland
+Institute of Neurological Sciences, Glasgow, Scotland

Single photon emission tomography (SPET) permits investigation of functional brain anatomy and offers opportunities for understanding the biology of psychiatric illness. The use of the radioligand ^{99m}Tc-hexamethyl propyleneamine oxime (^{99m}Tc-HMPAO) to measure basal rCBF and its relation to neuropsychological function in presenile Alzheimer's disease and Korsakoff's psychosis will be described. This technique has been adapted for use in the investigation of neuropharmacological and neuropsychological interventions. The potential of this approach will be illustrated by the use of intravenous physostigmine in Alzheimer patients to activate cortex and thalamus. This approach provides a way of investigating specific neurotransmitter systems in other psychiatric illnesses. The change in regional brain function during neuropsychological tests was also investigated using this technique. We describe a novel method for sequentially obtaining both basal and activated SPET images of the same brain regions using the verbal fluency test in healthy subjects.

2169
SLEEP PATTERNS IN MAN: A TWIN STUDY
Linkowski P., Kerkhofs M., Hauspie R., Susanne C. Mendlewicz J.

Hopital Erasme, University of Brussels, Belgium

All night EEG sleep recordings were performed for three consucutive nights in 26 pairs of normal male twins (14 monozygotic and 12 dizygotic) in order to investigate genetic components of sleep. The analysis was based on average values of repeated sleep measures and controlled for the effect of cohabitation. Our results indicate that a significant proportion of variance in stages 2, 4 and delta sleep as well as in REM density is genetically determined in man. Genetic influences on stage 1 and REM are strongly confounded by a synchronising effect of the cohabitational status.

2170
PSYCHOMOTOR RETARDATION AND COMPUTERIZED EEG/P300 IN MAJOR DEPRESSION
D.Nieber, C.Herrmann, J.Fried, C.Hain, S.Schlegel
Department of Psychiatry, University of Mainz, F.R.G.

Previous studies demonstrated associations between psychomotor retardation -assessed by the Bech-Rafaelsen-Melancholia-Scale(BRMS)- with increased ventricle size (Schlegel et al.,1988) and elevated plasma cortisol (Schlegel et al.,1989).Therefore the present study was planned in order to investigate a possible relationship between psychomotor retardation and neurophysiological examinations.
Patients and methods:
In 29 patients (age:20-60) with a major depressive episode(DSM III) psychomotor retardation -assessed by BRMS- and event related potentials (acoustic P300) were investigated. The single BRMS-items of motor,verbal,intellectual and emotional retardation resp. the sum of these four items (RET-BRMS) were correlated with the power spectra of the theta/delta-,alpha-,beta-band,the amplitude and latency of P300 (channels:F3,F4,T3,C3,Cz,C4,T4,P3,P4,O1,O2)
Results:
Positive correlations (p 0.05) were found between the RET-BRMS and the theta/delta-band resp. the P300 latency.RET-BRMS correlated negatively with the beta-band over frontal electrodes and the amplitude of the P300.RET-BRMS was not associated with the alpha range.
The meaning of these findings with regard to information processing and neurophysiological disturbances will be discussed in detail.

2171
A POLYSOMNOGRAPHIC STUDY IN CHRONIC SCHIZOPHRENIC PATIENTS TREATED WITH RISPERIDONE.
De Buck R., Hoffmann G. and De Smet S.
Brugman Hospital, Brussels, Belgium.

Risperidone (R 64 766) is a potent combined serotonin-$5HT_2$ and dopamine-D_2 antagonist. In previous open studies in chronic psychotic patients it was demonstrated that this substance combines an effective antipsychotic action with an important improvement of negative and affective symptoms, and a significant reduction of existing extrapyramidal symptoms (EPS).
It has been reported that in chronic schizophrenic patients the duration of slow wave sleep (SWS) is inversely correlated with the severity of negative symptoms. On the other hand it was shown that ritanserin, a potent and selective $5HT_2$-antagonist, improves negative symptoms and increases the amount of SWS.
To evaluate possible correlations between the effects of risperidone on clinical psychopathology, objective and subjective sleep parameters, 10 chronic schizophrenic patients (age range 18-45 years) were selected for this open trial. After a wash-out period of 1 week, patients were treated for 2 weeks with 5 mg, and for another 2 weeks with 10 mg risperidone daily. They were evaluated by means of the PANSS, CGI, and ESRS. A polysomnographic recording, together with assessment of subjective sleep parameters was performed at baseline, after 1 day, and at the end of each 2-week drug period. The results will be presented and discussed.

2172
Neurometric Subtyping of Obsessive Compulsive Disorders
L.S. Prichep[1,2], E.R. John[1,2], F. Mas[1] & R. Levine[1]
1.NYU Med. Ctr., 2.Nathan S. Kline Inst. Psych. Res

The normal development of EEG features of absolute power, relative power, coherence, symmetry and mean frequency from age 6 to 90 have been described by a set of polynomial equations. Using factor analysis, factor waveshapes have been identified which permit reconstruction of visual and auditory evoked potentials as linear combinations of factors, each weighted by the appropriate factor score. The significance of the deviations of individual EEG or EP data from the normal domain are quantified by Z-transformation against these normative data. Abnormal findings in normal individuals occur at the random level. Distinctive profiles of abnormal values characterize groups of patients with different psychiatric disorders. Discriminant functions using these features have been shown to classify patients with high accuracy. Using cluster analysis, different subtypes of patients have been identified within samples of schizophrenic patients and in samples of dementia patients. In both cases, responders to particular drugs seem to belong to particular subtypes. In this study a group of patients (n=33) with DSMIII diagnosed Obsessive Compulsive Disorder were Neurometrically evaluated. Clear subgroups with different pathophysiology were found. The profiles of these subtypes and the relationship between subtype and treatment response will be presented.

2173
IMAGING OF ELECTRIC CHARGE DISTRIBUTION INSIDE HUMAN BRAIN RELATED TO EVOKED POTENTIALS BY USING AN ALGEBRAIC RECONSTRUCTION TECHNIQUE

E.Ventouras*, N.K.Uzunoglu*, C.Papageorgiou**, A.D.Rabavilas** and C.N.Stefanis**
* Department of Electrical Engineering, National Technical University of Athens, Greece.
**Department of Psychiatry, Athens University Medical School, Eginition Hospital, Athens, Greece.

An imaging technique concerning the electric charge distribution inside human brain associated with the ERP has been developed. A three layered concentric spherical human head electric model is adopted to express the relation between the measured potential values on the head surface and the spatial charge distribution inside the brain. In this context, new analytic methods have been developed by using an integral equation technique. Assuming that the electric potential values are known from measurements on the head surface at 16 or 32 points, the charge distribution patterns within the human head are computed by inverting the measured data. To this end, an Algebraic Reconstruction Technique is applied. This inversion technique is widely known in X-Ray tomography systems. The accuracy of this technique is examined thoroughly by using computer simulation and by comparing the self consistency, of the proposed algorithm. The presented imaging technique is considered to be of importance in the field of psychopathology research.

2174
DEVELOPMENT OF QUANTITATIVE INDICATORS EXTRACTED FROM THE MEASUREMENT OF EVENT RELATED POTENTIALS

N.K.Uzunoglou*, S.Papadakis*, Ch.Papageorgiou**, A.D.Rabavilas** and C.Stefanis**
* Department of Electrical Engineering, National Technical University of Athens, Greece,
**Department of Psychiatry, Athens University Medical School, Eginition Hospital, Athens, Greece.

Measurements of event related potentials (ERP) in patients and healthy individuals indicate that it is possible to define quantitative indicators based based on the comparison of the measured waveforms. In the present report, two specific indicators are defined, i.e. :
(a) N100 waveform associated with the "attention" variable and
(b) P300 waveform associated with the "short duration memory" variable.
Concerning (a), a gated integral weighted with a delay term is employed to quantify the delayed reaction in patients. With regards to (b), the findings indicate that in healthy individuals there are two p-pulses, while in patients a single pulse is observed. In comparing these two different waveforms, the Fourier transformation of the gated ERP is computed. Processing of already gathered waveforms shows that these two indicators are presenting significant differences between healthy individuals and patients.

Session 330 Poster Presentation:
Various psychiatric issues

2175
Pre- and perinatal stress and psychopathology: fact or fiction?
Wolpert, E. M.
Psychiatric Dep., Elisabethenstift Hospital, Darmstadt, FRG

A quasi experimental stress situation for unborn babies is furnished by treatment of abortion risk with betasympaticomimethics. As severe stressors work as well the side effects of these drugs (palpitation, severe sweating, nervousness, vomiting, headache etc.) as different specific fears (of birth complications, handicapt children, pain, narcosis, dead, loss of self control etc.).
The hypothesis currently held by a large number of authors contends that prenatal stress mith eventually result in psychological and behavioral dysfunction later in life. This was not supported by data comparing 50 healthy pregnancies with 50 pregnancies whith undervent a stressful hospital admission and antabortion drug treatment. Children of these otherwise matched groups did not reveal any psychopathologically relevant differences at the age of three to five years.
the study suggests the need for revising current concepts on the effects of prenatal and perinatal stress on psychological development.

2176
DSM-III-R AXIS-I-DIAGNOSES IN PRIMARY CARE

P. Winter, M. Philipp, R. Buller, C. Delmo, J. Krause, O. Benkert
Department of Psychiatry, University of Mainz, Untere Zahlbacher Str. 8, FRG

This poster presents the distribution of non-organic DSM-III-R axis-I-diagnoses in a randomly selected sample of 500 primary care patients suffering from functional complaints. Computerized diagnoses were established after conducting a two-hour-structured interview using the POLYDIAGNOSTIC INTERVIEW "PODI".

A preliminary evaluation of the first 250 patients revealed a predominance of affective (27.2%) and anxiety related (18.0%) disorders. NOS-disorders were diagnosed surprisingly often (depressive disorder NOS: 40.0%; anxiety disorder NOS:44.0%). These results are in contrast to a psychiatric inpatient sample (n=500), which showed very few NOS-diagnoses. We discuss the applicability of the structured interview and of DSM-III-R criteria to patients seeking help in non-psychiatric primary care settings. There might be a need for subclassification of these psychiatric disorders not otherwise specified.

2177

PSYCHOTHERAPY TECHNIQUE CHOICE IN BURNS
Kachalov Pavel V., Serbsky Institute of Psychiatry, Moscow, USSR

Psychiatrist interviewed 64 randomly selected burn victims who met PTSD criteria. They were randomized for therapy: 18 for hypnotherapy(HT), 16 for narcosynthesis(NS), 22 for cognitive therapy(CT), 8 comprised the control group(CG). For two weeks seven 15 min. sessions were provided. Symptoms were assessed using the Serbsky Institute Standard System and 3 psycometric scales. HT technique was adapted from M.H.Erikson and concerned pain problems only. CT technique was adapted from AT Beck. NS was original and was performed by intravenous injection of hydroxybate sodium and caffein up to euphoria with concomitant self-suggestion education. All patients in therapy improved not alike CG. CT had the strongest psychodynamic effect. Beck depression(BD), state(SA) and trait(TA) anxiety dropped($p<0,01$). NS showed SA($p<0,01$), BD($p\ 0,05$) and TA($p<0,1$) drops. HT decreased SA only a bit ($p<0,1$). HT was the most powerful tool in pain management($p<0,01$), while for NS it was $p<0,05$ only and CT failed. (10 self-rate pain scale were used).

2178

Difficulties in Social Rehabilitation of the Mentally Ill in Siberia
Siomin Igor R.
Tomsk Medical Institute

Forty hundred urban and rural citizens of the Tomsk region have been polled to study their attitude to the mentally ill. The research was carried out with the help of the special "social distance" scale. The negative attitude towards mental patients was pointed out. No direct correlation between the level of "psychiatric literacy" and tolerance of the population has been found. The data obtained are used for optimization of complex rehabilitational programmes for the mentally ill.

2179

Express Diagnosis of Human Functional States on the Basis of Oral Speech Parameters
Yudin Y.
Public Health Ministry of Ukraine

Human oral speech correlates with changes in the functional state, which can be of natural or artificial origin (alcohol, narcotic drugs). The measurement & calculation complex & method of assessment that was elaborated enables to carry out the analysis of physical speech characteristics & to produce their graphical expression with subsequent comparison with standard samples. The complex & method of assessment can be competitive with other techniques of measuring human functional states.

Session 331 Video:
Psychiatric history: Hamilton's scale

2180

EMOTIONAL DEVELOPMENT TO PSYCHIATRIC HISTORY OF LONG DURATION
P.C.A.M.den BOER
R.I.A.G.G.-Breda, The Netherlands

Studies of Modern Psychoanalysis for the Borderline and Narcissistic PD and the Schizophrenic Disorders, lighten the problems of overwhelming transference and countertransference reactions. They also illustrate the need to develop on the level of self-object differentiation for a better integrative, emotional and adaptive functioning. To cope with that an outpatient treatment model has been developed of: 1- a well-defined structured organization of patient care that guarantees continuity and facilitates an undifferentiated positive transference; 2- a strictly structured peer-counselling method that explores the childhood and brings into awareness distinctions between that experience and adulthood; 3- an individual therapeutic relationship with attention for ego-functioning that guards psychiatric and emotional crisis and resistance patterns. Many case reports have been shown that the model gives good results for those severely suffering patients who have a complicated psychiatric history of long duration. Video-presentation will be shown.

2181
VIDEO TAPE DEMONSTRATION OF THE USE OF ORIGINAL HAMILTON RATING SCALE FOR DEPRESSION.

Presented by: Dr. M.S. Alexander -Consultant Psychiatrist, St. James's Hospital, Leeds.

The Hamilton Rating Scale to assess the severity of depression has been in existence since 1960 and it is used all over the world to measure depression. The scale is translated into many languages. There have been many attempts, by many people, to modify the scale to improve its efficiency and many people attempted to make their own rating scale to measure depression, with the intention of doing better than the original Hamilton Rating Scale. In spite of all these attempts, during the past 30 years, the original Hamilton Rating Scale continues to remain as The Rating Scale to measure depression.

In this video tape, we can see Professor Hamilton himself interviewing patients using his world famous rating scale and then in the second part, giving his own score for each individual item in the scale for the patient interviewed, and in the third part, discussing the correct use of the Rating Scale.

Professor Hamilton died in 1988 and this video tape has become a very important historic and authentic document. I intend to present this tape to the world Psychiatry Association as a memory to the great contribution to the Science of Psychiatry by Professor Hamilton and also to inform the Members of the Conference, the correct way of using this Rating Scale.

Session 332 Symposium:
The psycho-neurobiological contribution to psychiatry

2182
NEUROPSYCHOPSYSIOLOGY AND SCHIZOPHRENIA: SYNDROMES AND X CHROMOSOMES

John Gruzelier
Dept. Psychiatry, Charing Cross & Westminster Med. School, University of London

Psychophysiological studies of schizophrenia have shown that patients differ in the direction of imbalances in hemispheric functional activation (Gruzelier & Manchanda, 1982). Patients with delusions and increased levels of arousal (Active Syndrome) showed higher left hemispheric activity, while classical negative symptoms (Withdrawn Syndrome) were associated with higher right hemispheric activity. Auditory halucinations were nondiscriminatory. Neuropsychological tests have shown double dissociation between left and right hemispheric functions in schizophrenia with losses of function occurring in the less activated hemisphere, i.e. the right in the Active Syndrome and either the left or bilateral in the Withdrawn Syndrome. X chromosome abnormalities are also associated with patterned neuropsychological deficits involving lateralisation, in particular the right hemisphere in XO and the left hemisphere in XXY. X chromosome abnormalities have been implicated in a neurodevelopmental theory of schizophrenia (Crow, 1988).

2183
CEREBRAL BLOOD FLOW (CBF) IN CHILDREN WITH AUTISTIC BEHAVIOR.
GARREAU, B., BRUNEAU, N., RAYNAUD, C., POURCELOT, L. and LELORD, G.
INSERM U316 - CHRU Bretonneau,
2, Bd Tonnellé - 37044 TOURS CEDEX - FRANCE.
Among the different neurophysiological dysfunctionings proposed as underlying the autistic syndrome, the possibility of an impairment in cerebral hemisphere specialization has been proposed. The CBF approach is possible with SPECT and transcranial doppler method. We report two studies using these techniques:
1) Twenty autistic children (age 4 to 12) were studied using SPECT. Two regional CBF measurements were performed using 133 Xe : at rest and during a simple binaural auditory stimulation (80 dB, 750 Hz, 200 msec). During the stimulation CBF was significantly decreased in the posterior part of the left superior temporal area.
2) Eight autistic children (age 3 to 8) were studied using transcranial doppler. The blood flow (BF) measurements were made in the same conditions like SPECT, on the left and right middle cerebral arteries (MCA). The left MCA BF was lower in autistic during the stimulation. The abnormal left BF on auditory stimulations in patients confirms the possibility of a left hemisphere dysfunctioning and may be related to clinical features as language disabilities and paradoxical reactivity to auditory stimuli.

2184
EVALUATION OF DEPRESSIVE PATIENTS: INTEREST OF AN INTEGRATED APPROACH OF CNS (EEG, CNV, NEUROENDOCRINE TESTS)
M. Timsit-Berthier, H. Mantanus, D. Marchot, M. Ansseau, P. Papart, M. Timsit.
CHU - University of Liege - Belgium.
This paper gives an overview of studies led since 1984 at the CHU of Liege on depressive episodes (as screened by DSM III Criteria). In a psychoneurobiological approach, we combined neuroendocrine tests (Apomorphine, Clonidine, Dexamethasone Suppression Test), neurophysiological recordings (computerized analysis of EEG, CNV and Sleep Analysis), and clinical inventory with respect to psychiatric background (Axis 4 of the DSM III), category of depression (PSE), severity of depression (HAM-D, MADS), and psychological features (Rorschach test).
This integrated perspective allowed us to identify aspects common to all forms of depression: slowering of Reaction Time, post-imperative activity following CNV, and blunted response to Clonidine test. Besides those generalized aspects of depression, two "poles" could be defined: the one was characterized by low CNV amplitude, blunted response to Apomorphine test and "rigid" Rorschach protocols; the other gathered subjects with high CNV amplitude and overresponsiveness (with aggressive pattern) to the Rorschach test. The interest of such analysis lies in an improved understanding of the complexity of each individual case, which in turn helps the psychiatrist's therapeutical decision.

2185
THE CORTICAL-SUBCORTICAL INTERPLAY IN TIC DISORDERS

Aribert Rothenberger
Clinic for Child and Adolescent Psychiatry at the
Central Institute of Mental Health,
D-6800 Mannheim 1, FRG

Neurophysiological research in tic disorders showed that (1) there seems to be no preparing cortical electric brain activity (readiness potential) before the execution of an unvoluntary simple motor tic. (2) During the preparation of a simple voluntary movement (flexion of the index finger) tic children, in contrast to normals, develop high electric brain activity over fronto-cortical areas before movement onset. Finally, (3) when tic children are successfully treated with dopamine receptor blocking agents like tiapride they tend to normalize the topography of their movement-related electric brain activity (i. e. shift of amplitude maximum from frontal to central areas). On the basis of these results the interplay between basalganglia and frontal cortex will be explained to better understand pathophysiology and treatment of tic disorders.

2186
BRAIN ELECTRICAL POTENTIALS DURING GOAL-DIRECTED PERFORMANCE IN PARKINSON'S DISEASE

D. Papakostopoulos*, N.K. Banerji**, P.V. Pocock*

*Burden Neurological Institute, Bristol, England
**Musgrove Park Hospital, Taunton, England

Brain macropotentials of 20 untreated Parkinson patients aged 61.1 ± 7.3 years were compared with those of 10 normal adults aged 22.8 ± 3.5 years and another 20 aged 60.1 ± 7.4 years. All subjects performed a self-paced goal-directed task. Knowledge of results was provided on-line.

An automated method for quantification and analysis was used.

A precentrally developing negative potential, associated with reafferent activity, was absent in the old group and patients. A positivity following action and related with knowledge of results was slightly delayed in the old group and more in patients. The Bereitschaftspotential (BP) of the young and old groups were similar. The BP amplitude discriminated three groups of patients:

(1) Low BP, dominated by rigidity and responding
    well to treatment.
(2) Normal BP, dominated by tremor and responding
    poorly to treatment.
(3) High BP, dominated by akinesia and responding
    to treatment very well.

These results offer neurophysiological evidence of impaired preparation in the early stage of certain groups of Parkinson patients.

2187
The Bereitschaftspotential in early schizophrenics
G.A. Chiarenza* and C.L. Cazzullo**
*Ist.Neuropsich. Inf. Univ. Milano (I)
**Clin. Psichiatria. Univ. Milano (I).

The state of uncertainty of schizophrenics during thinking and acting reveals the absence of purposive behaviour. This uncertainty comes out in verbal and behavioural expression as lack of logicality and fluidity and it has been attributed to some interference which interrupts the organization of a preparatory set. It has been proposed that the Bereitschafts-potential (BP) is an electrophysiological manifestation of the preparatory processes to movement. In an earlier work, Chiarenza et al. have demonstrated that the BP of chronic schizophrenics is absent in all cerebral areas, during a skilled motor task. 7 early schizophrenics drug free and 13 normal subjects matched for age, sex and IQ were studied. The schizophrenics were less accurate in performing the task and the BP was of significantly lower amplitude in the frontal areas in comparison to the controls.
It seems that for this group of subjects the psychological functions, linked to the BP are early deteriorated.

Session 333 Symposium:
The role of deception in psychiatric health, illness and treatment

2188
DECEPTION IN MENTAL HEALTH, ILLNESS, AND NATURAL EVOLUTION

Claudette H. Beahrs, M.S.S.W. & John O. Beahrs, M.D.
Oregon Health Sciences University, Portland, OR, USA

Deception of others occurs throughout the animal kingdom; both predator and prey gain a critical advantage by knowing their counterparts' actions and intentions, while preventing others from gaining comparable knowledge about themselves. The complexity of human mentation probably evolved partly from escalating competition between organisms to more skillfully deceive others while better detecting deceptions by others. Deception occurs throughout all human living, along a continuum. At one end are the healthy deceptions known as "tact," "diplomacy," and "timing" that are so essential for success in courtship, occupational advancement, and other social relationships. At the other end are forms of willful dissimulation known as malingering and perjury, and "factitious disorders" where the motive is simply to gain the patient role. Neuroses and personality disorders lie in between. These are characterized by self-deceptions that are equally as purposeful, but experienced as if beyond voluntary awareness or control; i.e., as symptoms. The emerging science of evolutionary biology is grappling with the dilemma of how behaviors as maladaptive as neurotic symptoms could have survived natural selection. A promising hypothesis (Trivers, Alexander, Nesse) is that a weaker organism can better survive by skillfully deceiving its stronger competitors; and that such deception better avoids detection when carried out congruently, by likewise deceiving oneself. An additional question is how social cooperation and altruism evolved within a competitive milieu. Current thinking favors reciprocity and unity in the face of a common threat.

2189
SELF-DECEPTION IN FORMING AND MAINTAINING PSYCHOLOGICAL STRUCTURES

John O. Beahrs, M.D.
Oregon Health Sciences University, Portland, OR, USA

Hypnotic phenomena provide a research paradigm for the study of involuntary action and unconscious awareness, and how these can become concretized into psychological structures. In a hand levitation, a subject's hand "just lifts" while a "part" of the subject purposefully made it lift; in hypnotic anesthesia, the subject can painlessly undergo major surgery, while a "hidden observer" fully experiences the associated pain and suffering. Three lines of research clarify the parameters of these phenomena: (1) "Neodissociation:" hypnosis is real and dissociative in essence; when created and rigidified by trauma, hypnotic-like dissociated elements may persist as enduring psychological structures resistant to change. (2) "Non-state:" hypnosis is inseparable from the waking continuum, validating complex consciousness and its structures within this wider context. (3) "Social-psychological:" subjective nonvolition can occur only by a subject purposefully doing something, knowingly suppressing awareness, at the same time denying either awareness or voluntary control to his or her overall self. This is self-deception in relatively pure form. In addition, the form of dissociated structures varies inextricably with the psychosocial context in which elicited. This finding is anomalous for theories that postulate fixed structures, but is compatible with the evolutionary view that deception of self and others is at the core of human mentation. This may help us to better understand mechanisms of proximate causation of psychological structures, that can bridge psychodynamic, systems, and evolutionary points of view.

2190
DECEPTION IN SOMATIZING DISORDERS

Alfonso Troisi, M.D. & Michael T. McGuire, M.D.
Clinica Psichiatrica, II Universita di Roma, Roma, Italy, and Neuropsychiatric Institute, U.C.L.A., Los Angeles, California, USA

Deception of self and/or others plays a major role in the clinical phenomenology of several psychiatric disorders consisting of physical symptoms for which no organic cause can be found or which are intentionally produced. DSM-III-R classifies these disorders under the rubrics of Somatoform Disorders, Factitious Disorders, and Malingering. We think that, irrespective of the specific diagnostic type, these syndromes may involve the dysfunctional use of behavioral mechanisms which have a phylogenetic basis. The following evidence is relevant to our evolutionary hypothesis for somatizing disorders: (1) deception is a common strategy used by animals to manipulate the behavior of conspecifics; (2) disease simulation is just a specific type of deception which has been observed in nonhuman species as well; (3) care of the sick is not limited to human beings; (4) selection for deception is expected to generate self-deception because self-deception improves the deception of others by hiding from other individuals the subtle signs of self-knowledge that may give away the deception being practiced. In somatizing disorders, deception of self and others, in various mixtures, would allow the patient to simulate a disease and evoke predictable reactions from his or her interpersonal environment.

2191
DECEPTION IN PSYCHOTHERAPY

Michael T. McGuire, M.D.
University of California at Los Angeles,
Los Angeles, California, USA

An implication of evolutionary theory is that homo sapiens has evolved to engage in deceptive communication in preference to "honest" communication. Talking therapies are conducted in this context, and both patient and therapist engage in deception. The focus of this paper will be on therapist deception. Examples of therapist deception include: not revealing thoughts or feelings about patients, implied or stated optimism about the process of treatment, the outcome of treatment, patients' capacities, the importance of the patient to the therapist, and therapists' capacities; and, implied or stated importance of patients minimizing deceptive behavior. The positive therapeutic effects of these forms of deception are examined by contrasting them to therapies in which therapists attempt to minimize their deceptive behavior. Also addressed, is the difficulty distinguishing deceptive from nondeceptive communications.

Session 334 Symposium:
Islamic views in mental illness and its treatment

2192
ROLE OF ISLAMIC FAITH IN MENTAL HEALTH, PREVENTION AND TREATMENT.
GAMAL ABOU EL AZAYEM. M.D.
SECRETARY GENERAL WORLD ISLAMIC ASSOCIATION FOR MENTAL HEALTH.
CHAIRMAN
ABOU EL AZAYEM RESEARCH CENTER - CAIRO EGYPT.

* The meaning of divine Faith.
* Faith as a dynamic factor.
* The preventive role of Faith.
* Faith and increasing terrors.
* The enforcement of Faith.
* Faith activates insight.
* Universality of Faith.
* Faith and morals.
* Faith and experimentation.
* Benefits of Faith.
* Why Faith is getting weak.
* How to regain the power of Faith.
* Practical application.
* The community Psych-religious center
* Faith as treatment in substance abuse.

2193
ROLE OF MOSQUE IN MENTAL HEALTH

PROF. MOHAMMAD RASHID CHAUDHRY
FOUNTAIN HOUSE LAHORE, PAKISTAN

MOSQUE, BEING A SYMBOL OF ISLAMIC IDEOLOGY, IS NOT JUST A PLACE TO OFFER PRAYERS FIVE TIMES A DAY BUT IT IS ALSO A COMMUNITY CENTRE WHERE COMMON PROBLEMS CAN BE DISCUSSED AND SOLVED. THE MOSQUE CAN ALSO CONTRIBUTE TO THE ALLEVIATION OF INDIVIDUAL PROBLEMS OF MENTAL HEALTH. APART FROM CONVENTIONAL MODE OF TREATMENT RELIGIOUS THERAPY INTRODUCED IN THE FOUNTAIN HOUSE LAHORE HAVE PLAYED A MAJOR ROLE IN IMPROVING MENTAL HEALTH OF THE MEMBERS WHO ARE ENCOURAGED TO OFFER PRAYERS FIVE TIMES A DAY IN THE FOUNTAIN HOUSE MOSQUE IN ADDITION TO THE RECITATION OF HOLY QURAN IN THE MORNING ASSEMBLY. PHYSICAL EXERCISE AND PRAYERS HAVE BEEN FOUND TO BE EFFECTIVE PRESCRIPTION ALONGWITH MEDICATION. IN A WORLD FULL OF STRESSES AND STRAINS PEOPLE ARE LOOKING FOR PEACE OF MIND AND ARE RESORTING TO MEDITATION, TRANSCENDENTAL MEDITATION AND YOGA EXERCISES AND WHAT NOT BUT THE HOLY QURAN EMPHASIS AS CONTEMPLATION WITH GOD ALMIGHTY WHICH IS A SOURCE OF REAL CONTENTMENT. OFFERING PRAYERS FIVE TIMES A DAY HELP TO GET RID OF TENSION,

2194
ISLAMIC VIEWS OF MENTAL HEALTH AND ITS TREATMENT

Mohammed Farouk El Sendiony, PhD
Riverina-Murray Institute of Higher Education,
Wagga Wagga NSW 2650 Australia

In Muslim culture religion holds supreme sway over behaviour, thinking, and feeling (Patai, 1962). The impact of religion upon daily life is spectacular. The calls to prayer from the mosques in Muslim nations are as different from church bells in Christian countries as night is from day. This may seem puzzling to a Westerner. But Islam is not a mere Friday-go-to Mosque kind of religion. It is a way of life - a code of honour and a system of law that permeates the lives of its adherents through and through. This fact has transcultural psychiatric implications. If we accept the World Health Organisation's definition of health as "a state of complete, physical, mental and social well being and not merely the absence of disease" then in a society that defines self (and hence mental health) in religious rather than secular Western psychiatric terms, serious consideration has to be given to the forces which lend unfailing spiritual sustenance to believers. Conversely, in a society that defines self in scientific terms, the secular psychotherapeutic experience may be the meaningful and acceptable way of achieving "a state of well being". Therefore to simply reduce the experiences of Muslim patients to Western psychiatric taxonomies and systems of treatment is a denial of the reality of another mode of human experience.

2195
HISTORICAL COURSE OF PSYCHIATRIC HUMANISM AND MENTAL ILLNESS IN ISLAM
Ihsan A. Karaagac, M.D.
Historian of psychiatry, Deontologist Washington, D.C., U.S.A.

In this presentation the historical course of psychiatric humanism in Islam is outlined. To trace the origin of psychological and psychopathological tradition the "Temple Medicine" and practices of "Incubation" in the sanctuaries of Imhotep and Asclepios are reviewed; undissociated nature of physiology and psychology in Hippocratic treatise on "Sacred Disease" is conceptually analysed. By so exposing the historical archive of medicine, the distinct and specific realm on the nature of man's becoming mentally ill in Islam is juxtaposed for a comparative study. A hypothesis, based on history of science, is presented to show that in the pattern of Islamic culture, its early characteristics of deeply unified and astonishing regularity of common faith, devotion to moral ideals and discovery of truth are the spiritual leitmotives for Islamic civilization. Therefore, despite scientific exclusion of faith and soul from psychopathology, Islam by principle, and Islamic medicine, views soul and faith as most profound and indispensable ingredients of the human mind and to be applied for mental wellbeing and for a sane society.

2196
An Islamic prospective to psychopathology and psychotherapy

Ass. Prof. Al-Atrouny, Mohammad Hafez.
Dept. of Psychiotry, College of Medicene,
Mansoura Univ., Mansoura, EGYPT.

Various contemporary schools of psychology had discussed some pathological aspects as being responsible for mental troubles, and suggested the goal for psychotherapy. Each of these schools start from an objective and logic idea, reaching a subjective stage due to biase to their specific view. In this paper, we illustrate that all the objective primary ideas are accepted by the Islamic prospective. While the subjective views are avoided by this Islamic prospective.

2197
Group Therapy An Islamic Approach

Dr. Osama M. Al Radi, M.D., Pres. World Islamic Mental Health Association.
Dr. Mohammad A. Al-Mahdy, Member World Islamic Mental Health Association.

The history of humanity reveals a number of events in which a group functions for the welfare of its individual members. In Islamic religion group is emphasized in most muslem's activities and worships e.g muslem must attend the mosque for praying in a group five times a day (praying in group is said to be twenty seven times closer to the giving of God than praying alone), more larger group is held weekly in big mosques at Friday, more and more larger group in festival praying twice yearly (Eed Al-Fitres and Eed Al-Adha) and Al-Haj in Macca is the largest human group which is held yearly and includes millions of people coming from allover the world.

Since six years we have tried group therapy inside the mosque after prayers for treatment of fourty addicts admitted to Shahar Hospital (Taif-Saudi ARabia) and the results were stimulating where 75% of those addicts remained abstinent for more than two eyars of follow up. This good result encouraged us to continue the trial in my private polyclinic in Taif-Saudi ARabia for patients with various diagnoses. An eclectic orientation derived from Islamic worships practices, Holy Quran and Prophet's Hadith was arranged. We also applied the accepted techniques of the contemporary schools which proved to be effective to conduct the objectives of the program. The preliminary results of twenty sessions of this approach were also encouraging to continue.

2198
MOTIVATION OF ABSTINENCE VERSUS RATE OF RELAPSE IN SUBSTANCE USE DISORDERS
Al-Atrouny M. - Egypt-Arab Rep.

Session 335   Symposium:
Informal care for the aged. International comparison

2199
CROSS CULTURAL DIFFERENCES IN PUBLIC OPINION TOWARDS ELDERLY AND ELDERLY WITH DEMENTIA.
Ingvad, B., Hagberg, B. Gerontology Research Centre, Lund, Sweden, and Ferrey, G., Hospital E. Roux, Eubonne, France.
One of the major concerns of aging research today is the public opinion on the elderly. The elderly meet with quite different reactions ranging from being looked upon as someone obsolete, alienated and beside the main stream of societal activity. Or in the other extreme a resource of wisdom that is of great value to society, especially as a keeper of traditional values. An accentuation of these attitudes towards the elderly can be expected when major diseases such as dementia is present and especially if treatment and rehabilitation of the demented patient take place integrated in the community at large. In order to analyse cross-cultural differences in these respects a co-operative project was set up in France and Sweden. The results show clear differences in attitudes with regard to aging and to the care of patients with dementia. While the French material show a more positive attitude in questions concerning neighbour interactions and exchange of services among the elderly, in the Swedish responses were found a better orientation about the disease, more contact with patients, and a more positive attitude to integration of dementia care in society. The results seem to reflect basic value differences in the two communities which have to be considered in future planning.

2200
UN VILLAGE DE VIEUX EN GRECE

C. ZERVIS - C. SYNODINOU - G. FERREY
Université d'ATHENES - Centre Hospitalier Emile Roux - 95602 EAUBONNE - FRANCE

Ce travail témoigne d'une enquête réalisée dans un village rural grec, situé au centre d'une île montagneuse de la mer ionienne.
Il avait comme but de décrire la situation psychologique et sociologique des personnes âgées dans un village traditionnel, à l'écart des mutations socio-économiques des villes.
Il est courant d'affirmer la préservation de la prise en charge des personnes âgées par les jeune générations, dans un milieu traditionnel.
Les résultats de l'enquête ne confirment pas la persistance d'une prise en charge par la famille patriarcale, mais une solidarité limitée au sein d'une communauté néoformée tout à fait originale et constituée exclusivement de personnes âgées relativement autonomes. Une telle communauté ne semble pas permettre la prise en charge permanente d'une pathologie somatique ou psychique lourde au cas où elle surviendrait.
A l'inverse, pour la plupart de ses membres en assez bonne santé, le groupe social, que représente le village, assure une sécurité affective, à l'aide d'échanges relativement limités, permettant d'assumer, avec une certaine sérénité, le vieillissement et l'ineluctabilité de la mort.

2201
LE MAINTIEN A DOMICILE DES PERSONNES AGEES ATTEINTES DE DEMENCE
FERREY G.
Centre Hospitalier Emile Roux - 95602 EAUBONNE
FRANCE

Le maintien à domicile des personnes âgées en FRANCE comme dans la plupart des pays occidentaux industrialisés, interesse plus de 90 % d'entres elles.

Ceci entraîne le fait qu'un bon nombre de personnes âgées sont atteintes de démence et de troubles psychiques à leur domicile. Malgré les diverses aides proposées, il existe une forte surcharge des soins nécessités, qui incombe à l'entourage de ces malades, souvent composé de personnes âgées elles-mêmes malades ou ayant des difficultés relationnelles avec le patient du fait de sa maladie. Ces diverses circonstances expliquent les limites du maintien à domicile qui cède brutalement par une hospitalisation en urgence ou un placement brutal en institution.

Il serait très important de savoir reconnaître le moment où doit se terminer le maintien à domicile du fait de trop fortes charges soignantes et affectives qu'il représente. En ce cas on pourrait éviter la médicalisation ou la psychiatrisation parfois artificielle de la décision.

2202
LES SOINS AUX PERSONNES AGEES EN MILIEU RURAL MAROCAIN
A. MAMOU, M. TOUHAMI, D. MOUSSAOUI
Service Universitaire de Psychiatrie - CASABLANCA

Un ensemble de "3 douars" (village du Moyen-Atlas) a été étudié. Chaque douar comprend environ 30 adultes dont 7 au-dessus de 65 ans. L'enquête a porté sur 19 familles.
9 femmes pour 10 hommes (moyenne : 77,5 ans). 9 veuves pour 2 veufs ; 8 hommes s'étaient remariés de façon systématique. Le nombre d'enfants varie de 0 à 9 (moyenne 3,5).
Le niveau socio-économique est généralement bas ; il explique le faible recours à la médecine. On a retrouvé 6 malades âgés mais sans atteinte psychique.
Nous avons trouvé trois types de prise en charge :
1) Un homme âgé qui est aisé, est pris en charge dans la majorité des cas par sa femme toujours beaucoup plus jeune ;
2) Quand le niveau socio-économique est bas aussi bien pour l'homme que pour la femme, cette prise en charge est assumée par la famille surtout les enfants qui sont proches ou vivent sous le même toit ;
3) La femme aisée vit seule, ou avec ses enfants qui la soutiennent ; mais en tout état de cause sa condition reste meilleure que pour la femme pauvre.
Nous avons noté, à chaque fois, qu'il y a une famille, une bonne prise en charge de la personne âgée qui reste le sage qui donne son avis avant toute décision.
Nous n'avons pas dépisté d'affection mentale ou psychiatrique.

2203
LES SOINS AUX PERSONNES AGEES EN MILIEU RURAL ET URBAIN
GARRABE
INSTITUT MARCEL RIVIERE

L'expérience d'un secteur de psychiatrie générale desservant une zone rurale en voie d'urbanisation par la création d'une ville nouvelle dans la région de Paris, montre que l'assistance aux personnes âgées doit être envisagée de façon différente même si l'on dispose des mêmes moyens techniques en milieu rural et en milieu récemment urbanisé.

Session 336   Symposium:
Military psychiatry in a changing world

2204
MILITARY PSYCHIATRY IN A CHANGING WORLD

L. Crocq, MD, F.D. Jones, MD, O. ADELAJA, MD.
Committe of the Section of Military Psychiatry W.P.A.

<u>Scope and aims of the symposium</u> :

The technical and social evolution of the world and the military guides the future trends of military psychiatry.
In peace time, the complexity of weapons and equipments, the transplantation from the civil life in the military lead to a greater psychological adjustment on the part of the soldier. The increase of pathosocial behaviours in general society can also concern the military. Indeed, military psychiatry must elaborate new mental health plans adapted to the new pathology and to the social conjoncture.
The participation of the military to the rescue operations in mass disasters makes it necessary to reformulate the "immediate psychological assistance organisation" and the control of stress in rescuers.
In war time, the eventuality of intensive and continuous combat can provoke the reappearance of numerous combat-exhaustion cases. The eventuality of N.B.C. war or threat adds other factors of stress, such as psychological isolation and specific archaïc fears, with possibility of collective panic or collective inhibition. New forms of war, such war in urban environment, civil war, subversive war, terrorism and captivity in inhuman conditions, create new forms of P.T.S.D.
Training of personels must be adapted to these new trends.

2205
ACTUAL TENDENCIES OF MILITARY PSYCHIATRY IN PEACETIME AND IN THE NEW FORMS OF WAR

G. Belenky (USA), C. Collazo (Argentina), C. Doutheau (France), O. Adelaja (Nigeria), L. Crocq (France), & F. Jones (USA). Walter Reed Army Institute of Research, Washington, D.C. 20307-5100, USA.

Military psychiatry began with the introduction of mass armies and total national mobilization in the late 19th and early 20th centuries, and evolved in response to changes and developments in war and advances in the understanding of human behavior and human behavioral neurobiology. The destructiveness of war has increased dramatically over the last 200 years. Modern massive conventional war is disastrous, and, when accompanied by the use of chemical and nuclear weapons, catastrophic. Partly in response to this, quasi-military activities have become more common - terrorism, hostage taking, and guerilla war. Acute stress reactions and post-traumatic stress disorder (PTSD) are frequent sequelae of the entire span of violent action. The military psychiatrist strives to prevent and, in the event, to treat reactions to trauma. Treatment for acute stress reactions consisting of a short period of rest, physical replenishment, and opportunity to tell one's story has been in use beginning in the Russo-Japanese War, and studies confirm its effectiveness. Treatment for the chronic sequelae of traumatic stress is less well worked out.

2206
P.T.S.D. IN SOLDIERS AND CIVILIANS IN LEBANON

J. Assaf, MD, C. Baddoura, MD, Y. Pélicier, MD, Prof.
Hôpital La Croix, Beyrouth, Liban.
Centre Hospitalo-Universitaire Necker, Paris, France

The authors have examined 50 soldiers and 50 civilians who have suffered of a war psychotraumatism in Lebanon. They have proceeded by clinical interviews and application of a standardized P.T.S.D. questionnaire of 350 items distributed on 50 questions, inventoring biography, personality, psychotraumatism and symptoms of P.T.S.D. and classical war neurosis.
Statistical results have showed that 10% of the subjects did not present any mental disorder, 11% presented psychotic disorders, 5% common neurotic disorders and 74% war neuroses. However, only 30% had a complete war neurosis (with the regression of personality) and only 46% responded strictly to the criteria of PTSD in DSM III R. The repetition syndrom (recurrent memory, flash-back, nightmare and startle reaction) was present in 68% of the cases. War neuroses or P.T.S.D. were more frequent in civilians (84%) than in soldiers (64%).
In comparing these results to the clinical profiles observed in other conflicts (Belenky, Solomon, Crocq), the "lebanese profile" appears to be near the W.W.II profile (anxiety, somatisation), with elements of the law intensity combat profile of Algeria or Vietnam (social withdrawal and agressivity).

2207
PTSD IN ISRAELI SOLDIERS IN THE LEBANON WAR

Lt. Col. Dr. Zahava Solomon

Research Branch, Department of Mental Health,
Medical Corps, Israel Defense Forces

In the Lebanon War, Israel's longest and most controversial war, the IDF had several hundred combat stress reaction casualties. As part of its concern for the well being of these casualties the IDF Department of Mental Health initiated a multi-cohort, longitudinal study.
In this lecture some of the major findings of this study will be presented:
1. The long term sequlae of CSR in the form of PTSD, somatic complaints, and social functioning.
2. The effect of repeated exposure to combat. We shall present data pertaining to the question whether combat experience "immunizes" or weakens soldiers' resilience.
3. Rates, types, and course of reactivated CSR.
4. Rates and types of delayed onset of PTSD in the Lebanon War.
5. The transgenerational deterimental effect of the Holocaust on PTSD in the Israeli soldiers in the Lebanon War.
The epidemiological and clinical implications of these findings will be discussed.

2208
PTSD OF LONG DURATION 40 YEARS AFTER WW II CAPTIVITY

M.A.CROCQ, F.BEHR, F.DUVAL, S.ROSENBERG, J.P.MACHER
Centre Hospitalier Spécialisé, -68250, Rouffach, FRANCE

We studied the prevalence of symptoms of Post-traumatic Stress Disorder (PTSD) by collecting questionnaire responses of about 1400 survivors of the forcible draft into the German Armed Forces (Wehrmacht) in World War II and the subsequent captivity as Prisoners of War (POW) in the Soviet Union. All persons were from Alsace-Lorraine (disputed borderland between France and Germany). We analyzed responses of a random sample of 520 completed questionnaires.
The majority crossed the lines to surrender (37.4%) or let themselves be captured (19.6%). The following PTSD symptoms were observed: 84% still experience recurrent nightmares with themes of war or captivity, 83% intrusive memories or war related intrusive thoughts, 84% anxiety in situations reminiscent of war or captivity and about 60% dissociative symptoms. These symptoms were found to be associated with the duration of POW captivity. Additional interviews and materials indicated the presence of guilt feelings and personality changes.

2209
AIDS IN THE U.S. ARMY: AN UPDATE

John M. Plewes, M.D., Major, M.C.
Chief, Inpatient Psychiatry Service
Walter Reed Army Medical Center
Washington, D.C. USA 20307-5001

The United States Army has been a leader in the detection and treatment of many infectious diseases, one of the most recent of which is infection by the Human Immunodeficiency Virus (HIV), felt to be the causative agent in the Acquired Immunodeficiency Syndrome (AIDS). The paper examines the history, epidemiology, and social and economic impact of AIDS worldwide, in the United States as a whole, and in the United States military in particular. It describes current approaches to diagnosis, evaluation, treatment, and disposition of afflicted service members and their dependents, and discusses potential biological and psychiatric research initiatives aimed at assisting this special population. (This is an update and expansion of a paper given at the Regional WPA Symposium in Buenos Aires in 1987.)

Session 337 Symposium:
Teaching of community based rehabilitation technics in developing counties

2210
PSYCHOSOCIAL REHABILITATION OF THE MENTALLY ILL IN DEVELOPING COUNTRIES

M.Gittelman, A.Freedman, N.Y. Medical College,USA,
Tolani Asuni-U., Lagos, Nigeria,
Vijay Nagaswani, S.C.A.R.F., Mandras, India,
J. Dubuis, Villeurbanne, France.

This presentation will descrice the techniques and the policy underlying community based rehabilitation of the mentally ill in developing countries. Utilizing a six-point method it has been possible to disseminate information on community based rehabilitation in developing countries. The method employed encompasses the following points :
(a) Organization and policy changes.
(b) Cognitive understanding of mental illness.
(c) Utilization of psychotropic medication.
(d) Reduction of stress and conflict.
(e) Vocational and social rehabilitation.
(f) Evaluation.
This method will be described and discussed and some preliminary data will be presented.

2211
PSYCHOSOCIAL REHABILITATION: THE AFRICAN EXPERIENCE

Asuni T. - Nigeria

2212
Psychosocial Rehabilitation in India - the way ahead.

Dr Vijay Nagaswami, Asst Director,
Schizophrenia Research Foundation, Madras, INDIA.

Psychosocial rehabilitation programmes for persons with chronic mental illnesses are few and far between in India. This is not surprising as a total of about 3000 mental health professionals in the country, with 25,000 hospital beds at their disposal are trying to cater to the needs of about 20 million service seekers of whom about 5 million suffer from chronic mental illnesses. The National Mental Health Program for India attempts to offer decentralised mental health services to the consumer by integrating mental health in the primary care infrastructure. Unfortunately, no clear strategies or working models for the rehabilitation of such patients have been elucidated. The Schizophrenia Research Foundation (India), a voluntary n g o, has been working towards the formulation of rehabilitation models for use in urban and rural India. One such is the Community based rehabilitation (CBR) programme in a defined rural catchment area of 100,000 population. This paper discusses the state of the art of psychosocial rehabilitation programmes in India, and describes in detail the logistics involved in setting up a CBR program, the scope of CBR, the elements of the program, a few critical issues involved, and the feasibility of integrating a mental health component within the framework of ongoing CBR programs for the physically handicapped. The conclusion reached by the author is that CBR represents an effective compromise between needs and resources in the 3rd World.

2213

A PERSPECTIVE FROM CHINA ---mental health in primary health care

Shen Yucum, M.D.
Institute of Mental Health
Beijing Medical Univesity

Mental health care in China is at a time of transition. With a well-developed primary health care system emerging in 70,s, Chinese psychiatrists extended their service from hospitals to communities by integration of mental health service with primary health care in urban, suburban and rural areas. For example, an urban model of community mental health care was developed in Shangai on the basis of clinics affiliated to neighbourhood bodies or factories, while a suburban model of mental health home care was initiated in Beijing with support from existing primary health care system in countryside. Its successful experience was then introduced to the whole rural district of Yental Prefecture, Shandong Province. Key points in the promotion of mental health in primary health care may include: (1) properly professional training for primary medical workers; (2) widely spreading knowledge of mental health among lay people and (3) well mobilizing the sources of and co-operation among various social bodies, the administration authorities concerned in community in particular. Also inestimable aid are the Chinese cultural traditions relating to family cohesion and the country's public health policy and organization.

2214

PSYCHIATRIC REHABILITATION - PRIORITIES FOR DEVELOPING COUNTRIES

M. Parameshrava Deva, Dept.of Psychological Medicine, Faculty of Medicine, University of Malaya, 59100 Kuala Lumpur, Malaysia

Psychiatric rehabilitation has only recently been recognised as very necessary for those mentally ill which are under control but whose lives are still not normal. The re-integration of a life affected by seriours mental illness involves methods and needs that vary considerably from country to country. Concepts such as recreational therapy and occupational therapy in a developing country often mean a method of making the mentally ill person productive. Shortages of trained manpower make necessary complex courses for mental health workers in simple sets of processes. Fewer industries lead to training for home productivity and farming. Absence of social security means also fewer social workers. A strong family network may mean revision of concepts such as half-way houses and hostels or boarding houses for the mentally ill. This paper discusses a re-orientation of psychiatric rehabilitation for the priorities and needs of developing countries.

Session 338 Symposium:
Biological correlates of depression and suicidal behavior

2215

SUICIDE AND SEROTONIN - TOWARDS AN INTERPRETATION OF THEIR RELATIONSHIP

Marie Åsberg Department of Psychiatry Karolinska hospital 10401 Stockholm Sweden

One of the more surprising developments in biological psychiatry is the recent finding of a strong and consistent relationship between certain biological variables and an increased risk of suicide in depressed patients. For many decades, it has been taken more or less for granted that the important determinants of suicide were social and psychological. The finding, in 1976, of an association between low concentrations of the serotonin metabolite, 5-hydroxyindoleacetic acid (5-HIAA) and suicide attempts of a violent, active type suggested, however, that biological factors might also be of importance. The present paper will review these findings and subsequent studies of serotonin markers in suicidal patients. The possible predictive value of CSF 5-HIAA as a risk factor for subsequent suicide will be discussed, as based on recent follow up studies of suicide attempters.

It is proposed that personality traits, in particular impulsiveness and aggressiveness, may be important mediators between serotoninergic functions and suicidal behaviour. Preliminary data from studies of healthy volunteers, but also of subjects with known problems in controlling aggression (such as homicide offenders, and young men known to be aggressive during their early teens) will be presented in support of this contention. A tentative model for suicidal behaviour, intended to integrate available biological, psychological and psychodynamic knowledge will be presented.

2216

SEROTONERGIC DISTURBANCES IN SUICIDAL BEHAVIOR

H.M. van Praag, M.D., Ph.D.
Dept. of Psychiatry, Albert Einstein College of Medicine/ Montefiore Medical Center, Bronx, New York U.S.A.

In a majority of studies, disturbances in central 5-HT have been found in (violent) suicide attempters, irrespective of diagnosis. Negative studies have also been reported. In this presentation, we will discuss possible explanations for negative results.
The following conclusions are reached:
1. The hypothesis relating 5-HT dysfunction and suicidal tendencies seems well founded.
2. The negative studies can be explained if one takes into account that:
   a. the relation 5-HIAA/ suicidality is most pronounced in recent SA
   b. in depressed SA
   c. in those with strong suicidal intent; that the
   d. depression tends to clear after the SA and that the
   e. strength of the suicidal impulse correlates poorly with the severity of the attempt
3. It has not been excluded that the aggression/ 5-HT relationship is an indirect one and that the proper relationship is with either lack of impulse control or with heightened activity.

2217

EVOLUTIONARY MODIFICATION FOR COPING: EXPANDED STORAGE OF NORADRENALINE IN HUMAN LOCUS COERULEUS AND ITS DEPLETION IN DEPRESSION AND SUICIDE
*M.R.Issidorides,**V.Kriho and ** G.D.Pappas
*Dept. of Psychiatry, Athens University, Greece and **Dept. of Anatomy and Cell Biology, Univ. of IL at Chicago

A large fall in noradrenaline (NA) concentration in the locus coeruleus (LC) region is critically involved in mediating behavioral depression (Weiss & Simson, 1986). With methods designed for the localization of NA by electron microscopy (EM) we have shown that a large number of huge dense core vesicles is present in human LC perikarya in contrast to animals where few small dense core vesicles are present in these cell bodies. We view this NA accumulation in man as a back-up storage compartment, necessary for meeting the increased demands to cope with unpredictable stresses inherant in man's own ecological (social) environment. In postmortem tissue of suicides depressed subjects we found that in the LC the dense core vesicles or globules were as numerous as in the controls, but their EM density, reflecting NA concentration, was greatly reduced indicating depletion of the local neuro-transmitter. Abnormalities of the fine structure of the membranes surrounding the dense core vesicles suggest that the NA depletion may be secondary to leakage from the vesicles due to defective membrane function. This local loss of NA stores has repercussions on the firing pattern of the lC neurons and justifies the behavioral deviations described in depression (Weiss & Simson, 1986).
Supported by grants of the Ministry of Research & Technology (to M.R.I)

2218

NEUROENDOCRINE FUNCTION AND SUICIDAL BEHAVIOUR

B. Alevizos, G. Papadimitriou, J. Hatzimanolis, K. Katsouyianni, C. Stefanis.
Dept. of Psychiatry, Athens Univ.,Eginition Hosp. Athens, Greece

Clinical studies have suggested a higher rate of cortisol nonsuppression and TSH blunted response to TRH in suicidal attempter than in nonattempter depressed patients. These,however,findings have not been confirmed by other researchers.
The present study was undertaken in order to investigate multiple hormonal responses (cortisol,TSH prolactin and growth hormone) to DST and TRH test in 37 attempter and 214 nonattempter depressed patients.

The two groups did not differ significantly in cortisol nonsuppression and TSH blunted response to TRH as well as in prolactin and growth hormone response to dexamethasone and TRH. Patients with higher suicide item score of the HDRS had significantly higher basal ($p<0.03$) and significantly lower ($p<0.05$) TSH level at 20´as well as significantly higher ($p<0.03$) post-dexamethasone cortisol level at 8 p.m.

These results indicate that hormonal responses to DST and TRH test failed to differentiate suicidal attempter from nonattempter depressed patients.

2219

IMPULSIVITY, SUICIDAL BEHAVIOUR AND THE SEROTONERGIC SYSTEM

Juan J. López-Ibor Jr, J. Saiz, F. Lana, I. Moreno and R. Viñas

Department of Psychiatry. Ramón y Cajal Hospital. University of Alcalá de Henares (Madrid, Spain).

The association of 5-HT abnormalities as measured by low concentration in CSF of its metabolite 5-HIAA with suicidal, specially impulsive, behaviour is one of the most established findings in biological psychiatry. Other patterns of behaviour, not all of them pathological, characterized by a deficit in the control of impulses, fit well with these biological findings. CSF studies have some drawbacks, among them, the fact that they can not be carried in samples numerous enough, therefore other alternatives have been tried. Serotonergic challenges with substances able to induce changes in the secretion of hormones controlled by hypothalamic factors are most usefull tools despite that it has been claimed that none of them is specific or clean enough. Nevertheless, the fenfluramine and the clomipramine (CMI) test show that impulsive behaviour correlates with the same abnormal response.

2220

GENETIC ASPECTS OF SUICIDAL BEHAVIOR

*G. Papadimitriou, **P. Linkowski, **J. Mendlewicz
*Dept. of Psychiatry, Athens Univ., Athens, Greece
**Dept. of Psychiatry, Brussels Univ., Brussels, Belgium

The important role of genetic factors in suicidal behavior was supported by family, twin and adoption studies.
In order to investigate the family history of suicide as predictor of suicidal risk in depressed patients we studied 713 depressives (260 males and 423 females, unipolar and bipolar type). Out of them 77 (11%) attempted suicide using violent and 162 (22%) non violent means, while 123 probands (17%) has a history of completed suicide in first or second degree relatives. A family history of suicide is associated with a greater frequency of violent suicidal behavior in women (more often bipolar type) and also in men without polarity differences.
The possible mode of transmission of suicidal behavior was also investigated using Slater's computational model based on the analysis of ancestral secondary cases on the paternal and maternal sides of the probands. Our results are compatible with polygenic inheritance of suicidal behavior. In probands using violent means a significantly greater number of secondary cases were from the maternal side, while in non violent probands from the paternal side.

Session 339 — Workshop:
Theory and practice of "Funktionelle Entspannung"

2221

THEORY AND PRACTICE OF "FUNKTIONELLE ENTSPANNUNG" (FUNCTIONAL RELAXATION)
T. Reinelt, G. Gerber
Interfakultäres Institut für Sonder- und Heilpädagogik, Vienna, Austria

"Funktionelle Entspannung" (functional relaxation), developed by Marianne FUCHS, is a body-oriented method of therapy, well-grounded in depth psychology. This therapeutical approach has it's special importance for individuals (as for instance handicapped persons, or persons, suffering from psychosomatic complaints) who are impaired or disturbed in their (breathing) rhythm and differenciated physical self-perception. By practising playing and rhythm-controlled movements, they realize bodily differences and experience how physical bracings can be relaxed by "tolerated action". This is deepening and stabilizing the autonomous individual rhythm and strengthening the dialectic of tension and relaxation, of giving and receiving. That, in itself, has an effect on the soul. Mental changes caused by bodily "work" can be experienced by physically and psychically handicapped individuals and this is corresponding to the holistic view of man in "functional relaxation". An initiating introduction into theory and application of "Functional Relaxation" is intended to be given in this workshop by means of the following activities: 1. a short lecture with the theoretical basis and practical application of "Funktionelle Entspannung". 2. A video tape illustrating exampels of the most important aspects of this therapy method. 3. Self-perception and self-experience by utilizing models (examples) of "Funktionelle Entspannung".

Session 340 — Workshop:
Hospital hypnosis

2222

HOSPITAL HYPNOSIS

Gerard Sunnen, M.D.

Hospitalization is a difficult experience for many patients. Procedures, operations and rehabilitation are usually anticipated with apprehension. In an alien milieu, the stress of discomforts, treatment outcome may be greatly enhanced.

Hypnotic, meditational and imaginal techniques can assist patients in coping successfuly with their hospitalization. Centering on multi-level relaxation and making use of the beneficial influence of positive imagery, several dimensions of patient comfort may be attended to: physical symptoms may be assuaged, anxiety alleviated and optimism kindled.

This workshop examines the indications and patient selection for appropriate utilization of medical hypnosis. Methods including variants specifically geared to the hospital setting are described and demonstrated. Workshop participants will derive an appreciation for the potential of hospital hypnosis to enhance the quality of patient care.

Session 341 — Workshop:
Drug substitution, cost containment and the psychiatrist's dilemma

DRUG SUBSTITUTION, COST CONTAINMENT AND THE PSYCHIATRIST'S DILEMMA
L. Schwartz, P. Lavinson - USA

Session 342 — Symposium:
Special classifications

2223

SPECIAL NATIONAL CLASSIFICATIONS: DSM IV

A. Frances
Cornell University, New York, NY.

Although DSM-III was developed by a national psychiatric society, it has had considerable international impact. Some of its innovative features encompassed the use of operational or specific diagnostic criteria, a phenomenologically based reorganization of the catalogue of mental disorders, and the employment of a multiaxial schema. The experience gained over the past several years with the application of DSM-III and DSM-III-R is now being systematically assessed and this process constitutes a crucial basis for the development of DSM-IV.

2224

CLASSIFICATION IN CHILD PSYCHIATRY
Helmut Remschmidt and Beate Heprertz-Dahlmann
Clinic for Child & Adolescent Psychiatry,
Philipps-University, Marburg (FRG)

Classification systems in child psychiatry may be subdivided into three groups: unidimensional systems, multiaxial systems of clinical origin, and statistically derived multidimensional classification systems.
During the last years, the latter ones have been widely introduced into clinical practice and research. This development implies a great progress for training and mutual understanding of child psychiatrists in different countries. It promotes general knowledge about psychiatric disorders in children and adolescents and facilitates transcultural multicenter studies. But there are differences between findings based on clinically derived multiaxial systems and those based upon multivariate statistical approaches. Results are presented from two German studies on ICD-9 and of special aspects of ICD-10, both using a multiaxial framework.

2225

Special Classificaiton of Chronic and Psycho-
  geriatric conditions
Michael von Cranach
Ltd Azrte Direktor, Bezirkskrankenhaus Kaufbeuren
FRG

As general classifications like ICD-10 and DSM-3-R cover the whole field of psychiatric diagnoses, they must be designed in a uniform way and be as comprehensive as possible to find general acceptance. This means that htey cannot include special classifications for subgroups, especially if these overlap with the standard diagnostic categories or represent special problems. A review will be presented of different proposals to describe the course aspect of psychiatric disorders as well as multiaxial descriptions of chronic populations and psychogeriatric patients.
The idea that one classification cannot fulfil all purposes will be discussed.

2226

Classifications of Disability

H. Katschnig M.D.
Psychiatric University Clinic, Vienna

In the "International Classification of Impairments, Disabilities and Handicaps" published by the World Health Organization in 1980 "disability" is defined as "any restriction or lack (resulting from an impairment) or ability to perform an activity in the manner or within the range considered normal for a human being". Classificaitons of disabilities are both beset by terminological problems - boundaries to terms like impairment, handicap, social adjustment and others are not clear and by the fact that most types of disabilities are only well understood if life stage social and cultural contexts are taken into consideration. Existing classifications of disabilities will be critically reviewed under this perspective.

2227

MULTIAXIAL CLASSIFICATIONS

Juan E. Mezzich
University of Pittsburgh, Pittsburgh PA, USA

The multiaxial approach involves the formulation of the patients condition in terms of separate aspects or axes, which are presumed to be highly informatice and are systematically appraised and recorded. The primary purpose of specific schemas reflecting this approach is to understand better the complexity of the patient's condition and to prepare a comprehensive treatment plan. Accessory goals include the enhancement of professional training, research on the causes, course and treatment of illness, and development of clinical services and public health policies.

Types of axes frequently considered encompass clinical diagnoses (i.e., mental disorders, personality conditions and general medical problems), environmental or psychosocial factors and dysfunction or disabilities. Some multiaxial schemas attempt to characterize clinical syndromes further by specifying their severity, course and etiology. The need for the empirical evaluation of multiaxial schemas and their potential generalizability to general health care will be discussed.

Session 343 Symposium: Delusional disorders, long-term course and outcome

2228

DELUSIONAL DISORDERS. LONG-TERM OUTCOME (22-39 YEARS) WITH SPECIAL REFERENCE TO PARANOIAC PSYCHOSES AND SCHIZOPHRENIFORM PSYCHOSES.
Nils Retterstøl & Stein Opjordsmoen
University of Oslo, Gaustad Hospital, Oslo, Norway

A sample of 301 first-admitted patients with delusional disorders was selected by Retterstøl. Included were patients where delusions were a prominent feature, while bipolars and patients with confusional states were excluded. The long-term group (n=132) had been hospitalized in 1946-48, and the short-term group (n=169) in 1958-61. Retterstøl carried out a personal follow-up of all patients 2-18 years after first hospitalization, a new follow-up of the short-term group 3 years later, and Opjordsmoen has examined the patients still alive, extending the observation period to 22-39 years. At all 3 follow-ups, the group of patients with the discharge diagnosis of reactive psychosis did best, patients with Langfeldt's nuclear schizophrenia worst, and with patients diagnosed as having schizophreniform psychosis according to Langfeldt inbetween, but closer to the reactive psychosis group. Out of the sample, 26 suffered from a paranoiac psychosis with systematized delusional ideas, most (18) of the jealousy type. At follow-up the diagnostic distribution according to ICD-9 in these patients were: paranoia 50%, schizophrenia 8%, personality disorder 4%, remitted 38%. Only 4 patients (15%) had a GAS-score below 50 at follow-up. The postulate "once paranoia - always paranoia" does not hold.

2229

DELUSIONAL DISORDERS. A COMPARATIVE 22-39 YEAR FOLLOW-UP STUDY OF MAJOR PSYCHOSES ACCORDING TO DSM-III
Stein Opjordsmoen
University of Oslo, Gaustad Hospital
P.O.Box 24, Gaustad, N-0320 Oslo 3, Norway

Delusions are characteristic symptoms in delusional disorder (paranoid psychosis), but are also frequently a main feature in other psychoses. In order to study the long-term course and outcome in delusional disorders, a sample of 301 consecutively hospitalized patients were selected and followed for 5-18 years by Retterstøl, and later followed up after 22-39 years by the author. At index hospitalization 94 patients met DSM-III criteria of schizophrenia (S), 53 paranoid disorder (PD), 47 schizophreniform disorder (SFD), 35 schizoaffective disorder (SAD), 54 major affective disorder (AD), and 18 other disorders (O). At last follow-up S patients did poorest, O patients slightly better. AD patients had favourable outcome, while PD, SFD and SAD patients showed an intermediate position between S and AD, but closer to AD. Factors important for prognosis will be discussed.

2230

DELUSIONAL DISORDERS, THE VIENNA EXPERIENCE AS TO COURSE AND OUTCOME
P.Berner, H.Schanda
Psych.Univ.Clinic, Vienna, Austria

Since onset of the 20th Century, course and outcome of paranoid disturbances have been divergently commented upon, thus reflecting the still existing diagnostic dilemma and the unclear formulations in regard to outcome.
90 patients showing mood-incongruent delusional symptoms, classified in reference to the Viennese syndromatological aspects, were assembled for a follow-up study (mean observation period 7,3 years). It was possible to ascertain that apart from the relatively high suicidal rate (4,4%), the social prognosis appears in fact more hopeful that the somewhat unreflected pessimism with which it has heretofore been regarded, seemed to permit.
Within the scope of the syndrome diagnostic derived from Kraepelin, as well as under application of modern operationalized diagnostic criteria, it is possible, by means of precise psychopathological description, to define sub-groups presenting a relatively homogenous illness course. In reversal of Jaspers' hierarchical rule, it is obviously the affective symptoms that carry decisive prognostic weight.

2231

PROGNOSIS IN DELUSIONAL PSYCHOSES

Jørgensen P.
Psychiatric Hospital in Aarhus, Denmark

The prognostic value of psychopathological and socio-vocational variables in psychotic patients are highly disputed bacause of disagreement.
The results of a prospective follow-up study of first-admitted patients with delusional psychoses i.e. functional psychoses with delusions are presented.
It is concluded that good prognosis is exceptional and from a nosological approach attached to patients with reactive psychoses. However, socio-vocational variables at index admission are predictors of higher statistical information than any clinical variable.

Session 344 Symposium: Family factors in schizophrenia and its management

2232

"Behavioral Family Management of Schizophrenia"

Robert Paul Liberman, M.D.
UCLA School of Medicine

Family intervention programs for schizophrenia, when combined with neuroleptic medication, have demonstrated improvements in social and role functioning of patients as well as significant decreases in relapse rates. These family treatment programs share a number of common features, including their being based in practical, educational and behavioral approaches (rather than analytic or interpretative). In addition, education about schizophrenia is undertaken in straightforward manner and family members and patients are treated with respect and helped to develop coping strategies. The growing success of these behavioral management approaches are bringing psychiatrists, patients and relatives into a partnership in sharing the responsibilities for managing the schizophrenic illness.

2233

EXPRESSED EMOTION: RISK AND PROTECTIVE FACTORS IN SCHIZOPHRENIA RELAPSE IN GREECE

V.Tomaras, V.Karydi, V.Mavreas, M.Economou

EE is a new area for research in Greece. A controlled intervention study is being carried out to test: a) whether family intervention combined with individual psychosocial treatment in the context of medication is more effective in improving the clinical and social prognosis of schizophrenic patients belonging to high EE families than the mere individual psychosocial treatment in the context of medication is, and b) whether family intervention exerts its possible beneficial effect through the modification of the emotional interactions, i.e. the reduction of EE.
Treatment in the control and the experimental condition is described. Results of the ongoing trial, which are presented and discussed concern: the distribution of EE scores among key relatives at baseline assessment; the association of households' EE status with the patients' psychopathology and functioning at intake, as well as with their pre-admission hospitalization rates and employment record; the family intervention consisting of group sessions with key relatives along the lines of the psychoeducational model; post-intervention reversals of EE status both in the experimental and the control groups.

2234

"Economical Methods for Predicting Relapse in Schizophrenia"

Stephen R. Marder, M.D., Malca B. Lebell, Ph.D. and Jim Mintz, Ph.D./UCLA School of Medicine

Three brief and economical scales were administered to relatives of patients with schizophrenia to ascertain their family emotional environments as predictors of relapse. The scales were the Kreisman Rejection Scale, the Hogarty Global Judgment Criticism Scale, and the Gottschalk-Gleser Hostility/Anxiety Scales for rating five minute speech samples. Subjects were 42 patients with DSM III criteria for schizophrenia who were followed for 2 years on fluphenazine decanoate maintenance therapy. All three scales for rating the family environment significantly predicted relapse. Four demographic factors (age, education, ethnicity, duration of illness) also significantly predicted relapse. When these variables were controlled in a survival analysis, the Gottschalk-Gleser Hostility Scale remained in a significant predictor of outcome ($p = 0.004$).

2235

"Role of Family in Ensuring Success of Intermittent Drug Therapies"

Marvin I. Herz, M.D.
State University of New York @Buffalo Sch of Med

Schizophrenic patients who could tolerate intermittent, targeted neuroleptic maintenance therapy were followed for two years in a prospective study of course of illness. While significantly more patients on the intermittent-targeted dose therapy relapsed over a 2 year period, a substantial number of patients were able to survive without clinically intrusive exacerbations or relapses, or rehospitalizations. Family members were engaged in the treatment trial as "enablers" and "helpers" in facilitating patients' adherence to the therapy. Methods for engaging relatives in a help-giver role will be described in this presentation.

Session 345 New Research:
Special issues

2236
CIRCUMSTANCES OF ALTERED STATES OF CONSCIOUSNESS OCCURRENCE

Andrzej Kokoszka, Copernicus School of Medicine, Department of Psychiatry, Krakow, Poland.

The questionnaire survey of relatively representative group of 295 Polish People was done. An experience of slight Altered States of Consciousness (ASC) was reported by approximately 75% of subjects and half of them have it often, whereas deep ASC by about 50% and as a rare phenomenon for 2/3 of them.

Deep ASC were experienced statistically more often in religious situations and during contact with people and accompanied by feelings: being inspired by divine power; unity with everything; devotion to God; light that fills mind, whereas slight ASC during cognitive processes; aesthetic experiences; resting and everyday life situations and were accompanied by feelings: of lack of any thought; slightening of thinking; constriction of perception; loss of reality feeling; being sunk in pleasant, positive feelings; identification with someone else.

The results are discussed in terms of psychopathology and anthropology with emphasis on lack of subjective experiences of cognitive disturbances in deep ASC whereas they are reported in slightly ASC.

2237
Primary experimental results of a sonorous projective method for personality assessment
Galvano G.C, Davalli C., Lazzari M, Maggio G.
Masserini C, Colmegna F, Pazzaglia P.
Department of Psychiatry - University of Milan

We present, in this study, the first experimental evidences relevant to the validness of an instrument of projective sonorous survey of personality: " sonorous diagnostic reactive for personality assessment".
The authors propose
1) the description of the formal characteristics of a technique of psychometric survey, whose perceptive determinants that are built up in comparison with the Rorschach Test, are constitued of sonorous lines and not of visual spots.
2) the presentation of the clinical methodologies used for its standardization.
3) the analysis of the results that are derived from the observation of the clinical "sensitivity" of the reactive, that's verified in this phase of the research, applaying the principle of the concurrent or correlation validity with an external criterion that is represented by the diagnosis of different forms of schizophrenic disease.

2238
MEMORY RECORDING : A MEDICAL HYPOTHESIS
Bangos George, Ph.D., M.D. Ierapetra, 72200 Crete
Frangakis Haralabos, Professor
Faculty of Technology, University of Thessaloniki
54006 Thessaloniki, Greece

Until today all efforts have failed to trace the special biological substratum on which the memory is recorded. This failure has as a result our inability to understand the function of the mind. The main causes must be found in the persistence of researchers who guide their efforts only towards the study of the material part of the cell. In this paper, for the first time, the cellular energy magnetic fields of the central nervous system are proposed, as the biological substratum on which the memory is recorded.
The arguments which will support this view are many and such that we cannot ignore them.
It is well known that the electromagnetic fields are recording information and that all the biochemichal activities and the variations of biological parameters which are observed at cell level are intermidiate functions with which the electromagnetic fields are transformed from one form to another.
Based on the existing international bibliography this hypothesis is modelled and tested using computer simulation models. A further research is proposed.

2239
A POSSIBILITY TO KEEP THE INDIVIDUAL EXPERIENCE OF THE PSYCHIATRIST.
Dimitrov Iv. Michov V., Rouskov R., Trifonova E.
A small popular possibility on the basis of the English Schell is proposed from the authors.
During his practical action the psychiatrist accumulates individual experiments which are unic because of their complexity and specification of the deseases. The conservation of this experience may be done through several methodes: By verbal descriptions; by the usage of audiovisual systems; by publications. By this moment, investigations dealing with the possibilities of computers for accumulation of the individual experiments of the psychiat are still unsufficient. The group of authors propose an original method for the creation of expert systems with the help of a magnetic record for the registration of the individual profetional experience. The created basis of knowledge may be used for didactic scientific purposes.

2240

MAGICAL THINKING AND ABNORMAL BEHAVIOUR

Dr Gérard S. COHEN ADAD, CHS de Maison Blanche, Neuilly/Marne, FRANCE.

A few cases of abnormal behaviour like cannibalism, vampirism or human bone necrophagia are reported in the scientific litterature.

When such abnormal behaviour is observed in an individual, a psychiatric diagnosis is not always easily made. And even when a diagnosis is made, it does not really explain the occurrence of abnormal behaviour in a given individual.

Unusual fantasies and beliefs linked to magic, sorcery or ancient pagan cults may, in some instances, underlie this abnormal and rare behaviour.

2 case reports will be presented:
a case of clinical vampirism and a case of human bone necrophagia.

2241

Anxiety as a realistic fear reaction in torture survivors.

Søren Bøjholm
Chief of Psychiatry
RCT
Juliane Maries Vej 34
DK-2100 Copenhagen Ø

Many studies of torture survivors revealed symptoms associated with the diagnoses of posttraumatic stress disorder, major affected disorder as well as sequelae compatible with head trauma. There is some confusion regarding the concepts of signs and symptoms in the field of organized violence reresearch. The psykological methods of torture and coping strategies are described as well as the most common symptoms, e.g. anxiety. The similarities and differences of anxiety and fear reactions are discussed.

2242

INFLUENCE OF GREEK MYTHOLOGY VS. THE BIBLE (BOOK OF GENESIS) ON PSYCHOANALYTIC CONCEPTS.

Dr J. KRAMKIMEL, Dr G. S. COHEN ADAD, CHS de Maison Blanche, Neuilly/Marne, FRANCE.

1. Relations between parents and children have long been the focus of psychoanalytical litterature and have been explained by references to Greek mythology (Oedipus and Electra's stories).
2. Reference to the Bible (book of Genesis) seems to be relevant to describe some basic features of rivalry between siblings (as illustrated by the stories of Cain and Abel, Jacob and Esau, Joseph and his brothers).
3. S. Freud's biography could be of interest in order to try to understand his negligence of the biblical material.
4. S. Freud shares with the biblical figure Joseph a common involvment in the explanation of dreams. A possible subsequent identification process with Joseph has been hypothesized, but S. Freud has not been able to explain Joseph's dreams with his theories.
5. S. Freud mentionned (in a letter to Fliess) the death of a young brother and his subsequent guilt; however, he did not write additional papers on this subject.

2243

Psychopathology and Fiction The Golden Pot Reconsidered
Robert Kristof, Ferenc Martényi dr., Judit Harangozó dr.

University of Economic Sciences Budapest
Medical University Semmelweis Budapest

The authors focus on E.T.A. Hoffmann's The Golden Pot, i.e. on its protagonist. The short story the authors argue, is about a young man's journey into madness, a brilliantly presented deterioration, a desperate attempt to constitute the Self that finally is precisely what tears the Self apart.
From ontological insecurity through the lesion of personal autonomy and the oscillation between the polarities of total isolation and total merging of identity to the cultivation of death-in-life as a defence against the pain of life leads the path of the protagonist. The ultimate desire of Anselmus is to reach Atlantis, a symbol of self-cancellation with a series of marked schizophrenic episodes. Anselmus/ a telling name itself/is a prey of his'desiring imagination', and his story is related by the persona dramatis, who, the authors suggest, is the hyperreflexive fragment of the protagonist's self. And what Anselmus, the unembodied self does and realize in his mind is the very dream of the persona, the embodied self, who gives an account of a trema-apophenia-apocalypsis process.

Session 346 New Research:
Issues on clinical psychiatry

2244

TOWARD A NEURODEVELOPMENTAL ETIOLOGY OF KRAEPELIN'S ENDOGENOUS PSYCHOSES:IMPLICATIONS FOR CLASSIFICATION: Letten F Saugstad,National Case Register,Oslo,Norway.

The hypothesis of a neurodevelopmental etiology of manic-depressive psychosis(MDP) and schizophrenia (S) is based on the relation between onset of puberty and the final regressive events in the CNS, and the discrepancy in body build in the two disoreders which is similar to that between early and late maturing individuals.
The marked rise in MDP and decline in S,particularly the more malignant hebefrenia,catatonia and dementia simplex,accompanying the decline in pubertal age by some 4years,have been taken as evidence suggesting that MDP affects early maturers and S very late maturers.The gender differences and social differentials accord with a localization of the two disorders at each extreme of maturational rate. Maturational irregularities are most likely to occur at the extremes.Incomplete adjustment with persistent redundancy of neuronal synapses characterizes MDP and reduced synaptic density S,whereas "normality" with optimal density is in between.A continuum of psychosis from MDP to S,therefore unlikely. However,classical S is unique whereas S is also a brain reaction to adverse factors pre-,peri-and post-natally affecting 1st & 2nd regressive events in the CNS.A variety of psychopathological conditions is observed,which might give the impression of a "continuum of psychosis"

2245

BEHAVIOR AND EXPERIENCE IN THE NEGATIVE SYNDROME OF SCHIZOPHRENIA
Istvan Bitter, Judith Jaeger, Jan Volavka,
Pal Czobor New York University and N.S. Kline Institute for Psychiatric Research, Orangeburg, New York, USA

Current research on the negative syndrome(NS) in schizophrenia emphasizes behavior. Little is known about the subjective experience of the patients and its relationship to behavior.

We examined this relationship using Andreasen's Scale for the Assessment of Negative Symptoms (SANS) which measures the behavioral signs of the NS, and the Subjective Deficit Syndrome Scale (SDSS), which measures the subjective experiences of the patients. The SDSS was developed on the basis of Huber's pure defect concept. 93 acute and 26 chronic patients with schizophrenia (DSM-III) were included in the study. BPRS, Hamilton Rating Scale for Depression (HAM-D), SANS, SDSS and the Neurological Rating Scale (NRS) were administered at baseline and after 6 weeks of haloperidol treatment in acute patients, and once in the chronic group.

The main findings are: 1.No significant correlations were found between the behavioral and experiential aspects of the NS. 2.The subjective deficit symptoms reflect depression in the acute, but not in the chronic phase. 3. There is an increasing discrepancy between behavior and experience in the course of schizophrenia as reflected by the SDSS and HAM-D correlations. 4.The neurological side effects are related to neither the behavioral nor the experiential items of the NS.

2246

NEGATIVE SYMPTOMS, BASIC PHENOMENA AND EGO FUNCTIONS IN SCHIZOPHRENIA
Maier, Ch.,
Socialpsychiatric University Clinic, CH-Berne (Director Prof. L. Ciompi)

Schizophrenic patients frequently display non-productive symptoms and uncharacteristic phenomena after the active phase of the psychosis. The author examined 26 non-chronic schizophrenics after easing off the productive symptoms. The investigation was centred on the negative symptoms and the so-called basic symptoms or phenomena. Another focal point of the research was the psychoanalytic conception of various ego functions. In addition to the clinical examination the negative symptoms (SANS), the basic phenomena (BSABS, FBF) and the ego functions (Bellak) were recorded instrumentally. Communities and correlations of the mentioned phenomena were represented statistically. Special interest was paid to the representation and classification of prominent groups of symptoms and phenomena.

2247

FINE MOTOR ACTIVITY IN DEPRESSION
J.J.M. van Hoof [1], W. Hulstijn [2], H. van Mier [2] & M. Pagen [2].
1) Department of Psychiatry, University of Nijmegen The Netherlands
2) NICI (Nijmegen Institute for Cognition Research and Information Technology), University of Nijmegen, The Netherlands.

Psychomotor retardation is one of the central features of depression. Its research focuses on motor behaviour in naturalistic situations, speech, facial expressions and gross motor activities. As an alternative the study of the psychomotor aspects of handwriting and drawing will be proposed.
With the help of a digitiser and a small computer it is possible to record pen movements easily and accurately, allowing measurements of a number of movement parameters. The figure copying tasks that have been developed allow the separate manipulation of cognitive and motor variables. They can easily and repeatedly be administered in rather naturalistic settings. A preliminary study on nine depressive patients showed very promising results. The patients needed much more time to complete the tasks than control subjects and performed them in a different way. Differences in motor activity between a first and second testing correlated highly with improvements assessed by clinical observation. It is concluded that the study of fine motor activity in writing and drawing may help in disentangling the more cognitive influences from the pure motor aspects in psychomotor retardation. In addition it provides objective parameters to measure progress in therapy.

2248

TREATMENT RESPONSE OF SEVERE AND NON SEVERE PERSONALITY DISORDERS

Vaglum P, Friis S, Irion T, Johns S, Karterud S, Larsen F, Vaglum S.
Dep of Behavioural Sciences in Medicine, Oslo, Norway. Psychiatric depB, Ullevål hospital, Oslo Norway.

In a consecutive sample of 94 day patients from a therapeutic community ward, 50 patients with borderline, schizotypal or paranoid personality disorders (severe personality disorder, SEVPD) were compared with 22 patients with other personality disorders (OPD) and 22 with no personality disorder (only axis 1 disorder) (NOPD). The personality disorder variable had a significant impact on the treatment response measured by SCL-90 and Health Sickness Rating Scale also when axis 1 disorders, sex and age were controlled for. The SEVPD-group was often discharged in an irregular way and perceived the ward atmosphere less favorable than the other groups. The NOPD and OPD-groups had the same level of nervous symptoms at admittance, while at discharge the symptom level was significantly lower in the NOPD group. The results validate the discrimination between axis 1 and axis 2 disorders and are more in favor of a dimensional model of personality disorders.

2249

Different parental bonding of borderline and histrionic patients.

S. Torgersen, R. Alnaes,
Department of Psychology, Department of Psychiatry, University of Oslo, Norway

Forty-one out-patients with DSM-III borderline personality disorder are compared to 23 out-patients with histrionic personality disorder without additional borderline personality disorder, 155 out-patients with other personality disorders and 52 out-patients with no personality disorders on the Parental Bonding Instrument scores. The results showed that patients with borderline personality disorder described their parents as more cold and controlling compared to patients with histrionic as well as other and no personality disorders. Patients with both borderline and histrionic personality disorder appeared similar to patients with borderline personality disorder without coexisting histrionic personality disorder. Details about the reported childhood experiences contrasting patients with borderline and histrionic personality disorder will be reported.

2250

DIFFERENT PSYCHICAL DISORDERS INTO THE SAME INTEGRATIVE MODEL OF TREATMENT
I. Carta, G. Bianconi, G.C. Calvano, A. Lucchin, G. Maggio
Department of Psychiatry, University of Milan, Italy

The results of the clinical application of a model of integrative treatment which provides the approach of different clinical intervention and their association in specific therapeutic areas about a psychiatric population composed of subjects with a different diagnosis (DSM III R) are analysed.
The a a propose:
1) To determine specific outlines of integration by the relief of the frequency indexes of the temporal trend of the moving in the different areas of therapeutic association.
2) the verification of the hyphotheses which under the same occured change in the clinical conditions of the analysed subjects the determing variant is constitued by interested association areas, by the moving in the different areas and the specification of the outlines for every nospgraphic table.
3)the individualization of the specific problematical aspects of the model of integrative treatment characterized by the centrality of the figure of the supervisor.

2250 A

DIFFERENCES IN ANGER EXPRESSION BETWEEN BORDERLINES AND DEPRESSIVES
Valerie DeLain, Ph.D., Helene Lycaki, Ph.D., Jesse Bell, Ph.D., Karen Chapin, Ph.D., Gerald Sarwer-Foner, M.D.
Lafayette Clinic, Detroit, Michigan, U.S.A.

To differentiate between borderline personality disorder and affective disorder, this study compared 18 depressed borderline with 16 depressed patients and 17 non-psychiatric controls along variables of anger. The DSM-III and DSM-III-R, Gunderson's Diagnostic Interview for Borderlines, and the Schedule for Affective Disorders and Schizophrenia identified participants. The three groups were then compared on the 16 Personality Factor Questionnaire and Minnesota Multiphasic Personality Inventory, utilizing MANOVA'S. Borderlines and depressives revealed similar levels of depression, personality variables, emotional distress and pathology, and were significantly different from normals. To test the main hypothesis, a MANOVA and discriminant function analysis of the Buss-Durkee Inventory scores were performed. The results indicated that borderlines expressed anger outwardly and maintained it inwardly significantly more than depressives and normals. Depressives experienced anger inwardly significantly more than normals. Furthermore, results revealed an affective continuum, ranging from normals to depressives to borderlines with significantly increasing levels of anger. Depressed borderlines were distinguishable from depressives and normals by their level of agressive acting-out and passively harbored anger. Depressives were more angry than normals.

Session 347 Free Communications:
ECT: Efficacy and technical aspects

2251

Electrode placement in electroconvulsive therapy (ECT). A review.
Dorte Sestoft, Kirsten Behnke
Bispebjerg Hospital, Psychiatric Ward
Bispebjerg Bakke 23, DK-2400 Copenhagen

Electroconvulsive therapy (ECT) is an efficacious but controversial treatment in the state of depression. One of the impairment seen after a cours of treatments, several studies have indicated that the use of unilateral electrical stimulation on the non-dominant hemisphere in contrast to bilateral electrical stimulation could minimize the cognitive side effects without affecting the therapeutic effect of the treatment. (d'Elia and Raotma 75, Weiner 78, Fink 79, Strömgren 84). However, during the last decade, the constant current, brief pulse and EEG recording during and after the seizures, has made a revision of the clinical practice regarding efficacy, side effect and electrode placement, relevant. Especially EEG recording has madeit possible to evaluate the seizure, and several variables such as seizure threshold, seizure duration and the degree of symmetrica generalization of seizure throughout the brain, has been shown to influence the degree of side effects and efficiency (Daniel 84, Staton 85, Saccheim 87). This confirm that it is the interaction between electrode placement and different variables mentioned above that is responsible for differences in side effect and not brain damage caused by the electrical energy as previously thought (Weiner 84). The therapeutic consequences will be discussed.

2252

UNILATERAL OR BILATERAL ECT IN MAJOR DEPRESSION

E.T.ORAL,MD,M.E.CEYLAN,MD,PhD,A.İ.ŞENER,MD, N.TOMRUK,MD.
BAKIRKÖY MENTAL HOSPITAL/İSTANBUL/TURKEY

ECT is one of the most effective treatments for major depressive episodes,available to psychiatry still in our time.However,uni or bilateral electrode placement in ECT has varying effects on concentration orientation,memory and on perception of light sensation.In major depression both types of applications can be eligible for treatment, though it differs in response to treatment.In this study,28 right-handed male patients with major depression received right unilateral (10),left unilateral (10) and bilateral (8) ECT.Ratings of psychopatology by Hamilton Depression Scale (HDS), of concentration and memory by Benton-F,Fraise tests and orientation examination were assessed. In all patients our data indicated that ratings in HDS improved more in patients who received bilateral ECT than unilateral groups.However,no differences were found between the groups by means of concentration and memory.On the other hand, disorientation for time was greater in bilateral ECT,than dominant unilateral ECT and disorientation for time had recovered later than the other components of disorientation.There was also a correlation between unilateral ECT and counterlateral hypoaesthesia,and between bilateral ECT and bilateral hypoaesthesia.

2253

ULTRABRIEF PULSES IN ELECTROCONVULSIVE THERAPY. A PILOT CLINICAL TRIAL.

Hyrman,V., Patrick,L.L and Weldon,K.L., Royal Columbian Hospital, B.C., Canada.

Animal experiments suggested that therapeutic seizures may be induced with a fraction of the energy and power required by conventional brief pulse ECT. A theory that this could be accomplished by using ultrabrief pulses was tested using an experimental ECT device. The stimuli consisted of pulses of 0.06-0.07ms duration repeated at 200 p/s. With the device, 473 stimulations were given to 60 patients in 70 courses of ECT. Generalized tonic-clonic seizures of adequate duration were induced in majority of stimulations. The dose of electrical energy required to produce seizures was generally smaller than with conventional brief pulse ECT.

A retrospective chart review compared these 60 patients with 28 matched controls treated with MECTA brief pulse device. The therapeutic effect of the ultrabrief pulse ECT seems to be equivalent to that of brief pulse ECT, while confusion and memory loss after the treatment appear significantly reduced.

2254

Measurements of impedance during ECT

B.N. Gangadhar, G. Laxmanna and C. Andrade
National Institute of Mental Health and Neurosciences (NIMHANS),
Bangalore 560 029, INDIA

The contention that electrical stimulus used in ECT is a mere means to produce a fit and only this is therapeutic, has been questioned. We have demonstrated that sinewave ECT, which carries higher st ulus energy, is therapeutically more potent than brief pulse ECT, even when comparable seizure parameters are achieved. These and other results from contemporary studies reviewed, indicate the importance of stimulus parameters during ECT. One of the problems in quantifying the electrical dose is the unpredictable quantum of interelectrode impedance. In an initial attempt to face this problem, we designed a sinewave ECT instrument to permit electrial dosimetry. Our results confirm earlier observations. The impedance values very markedly across patients and within patients across sessions.

We discuss these results in the light of 'second generation' ECT devices and issues related to electrical dosimetry.

2255
REVIEW OF CONTROLLED REAL V SHAM ECT STUDIES IN DEPRESSIVE ILLNESS
Dr. Graham Sheppard MB BS MRCPsych
Ticehurst House Hospital,
Ticehurst, East Sussex TN5 7HU.
Great Britain.
Dr. Saad Ahmed MB ChB DPM MRCPsych
Hellingly Hospital,
Hailsham, East Sussex BN27 4ER,
Great Britain.

The thirteen published controlled real v sham ECT studies in depressive illness will be critically reviewed. The criticisms of the studies are analysed along a wide range of parameters. The authors conclude that all of the studies can be criticised on both numerous parameters and important parameters. Moreover, irrespective of any criticisms, the reported data at the end of the controlled phase of the studies and subsequent follow-up data, as a body of evidence, does not in the opinion of the authors significantly indicate that real ECT is more effective than sham ECT in treating depressive illness.

2256
PATIENTS' EXPERIENCES WITH ELECTROCONVULSIVE THERAPY IN THE NETHERLANDS
A.M. Koster,
Chief Inspectorate on Mental Health,
Rijswijk, Holland

In this contribution prospective data will be reported from 98 ECT-patients, and their relatives and psychiatrists. Interviews took place at four different times: just before and just after termination of ECT and at 3 and 12 months after the last application of ECT. Data refer to pre and post-treatment information. Topics relate to patients' and doctors' expectations of ECT, diagnosis and the way patients and their relatives verbalize patients' problems, doctors' reasons for terminating ECT-treatment, and the relationships between these variables. Finally some preliminary findings about patients' conditions at 3 months follow-up are presented.
Results indicate that before starting ECT patients' expectations are rather ambiguous. Persons who have received ECT previously are more hopeful. Doctors' expectations are mixed but in most cases they express hope for quick relief from serious complaints. Most patients are geriatric patients with medication resistance. After ECT many patients show a substantial reduction of their psychiatric complaints as far as vital depressive syndroms are concerned. Other patients however show a substantial increase of neurotic problems. It is hypothesized that this is because they have been confronted with the reality of their situation.

Session 348 Free Communications:
General issues in psychiatry

2257
QUALITATIVE MATHEMATICAL MODELS OF NEUROPSYCHIATRIC PHENOMENA
Jon Heiser, M.D., James Hearne, Ph.D., Christopher Reist, M.D.
University of California Irvine, Irvine, California, U.S.A.

Our group has been working simultaneously on a top down and bottom up approach to qualitative mathematical modeling of psychiatric phenomena. Qualitative reasoning has always been a prominent, albeit frequently unnoticed element of mathematical analysis and has formed an increasingly important factor, permeating most areas of modern mathematical thought. Qualitative models are confined to a higher than usual level of abstraction and are restricted to a narrower range of relations between crucial variables and their derivatives. Mathematical properties of greatest interest include the presence of maxima, minima, inflection points and stable regulative states, as well as singularities, bifurcations and catastrophes. Mathematical modeling is perceived as obscure and impractical to research in neuropsychiatric phenomena because quantitative information and precise functional relationships between crucial variables are not known. However both the nature of psychiatric disorders at a descriptive level and the mechanics of the neuronal synapse constitute systems amenable to qualitative mathematical modeling. Our top down program is a topological analysis of psychiatric diagnosis. Our bottom up research models neural behaviors at the synaptic level which are accessible to computer simulation. Our primary goal is to account for some well known or paradoxical diagnostic phenomena and neuropharmacological effects. For example, the observation that some patients worsen when placed on appropriate medication treatment suggests the existence, perhaps at the synaptic level, of feedback-oriented, regulative mechanisms with hidden stable states. We predict that the rigor imposed by the qualitative mathematical modeling will lead to more precise hypotheses about psychiatric diagnosis and the effects of drugs on the nervous system.

2258
A SYSTEM' THEORETICAL APPROACH TO THE EXPLANATION OF SYMPTOM FORMATION.
J.Barahona da Fonseca, J.Simões da Fonseca, J.Mira and Roberto Moreno Diaz.
Depart. of Medical.Psychology and Psychopathology, Lisbon Medical School.

An algorithimically defined set of relationships involving (a) decision-making rules and self and others evaluation; (b)transient or else structured approaches to adaptation in the referential domain; (c) Self concept and its transformation and finally (d) a dual system involving not referential phantasy data which nevertheless are expressed in a regular set of relational analytic rules is used to implement a model of interaction with the environment.
The self reflexive level of analysis is also considered and an ensemble of restrictions results from the test of the model.
Decision-making theory is used to built modelsin an abductive approach and to test them within a construct validation.
Hypothesis concerning psycho-physical relationships, involving the syntactical and the semantic levels of analysis are considered, using psychopathological data in a system's epistemic approach.

2259

AN EXAMPLE OF THE INFORMATICS METHODS AND
MICROCOMPUTERS APPLIANCE IN DEPENDENCY DISEASE
RESEARCHING
V.Cuk, V.Starcevic, A.Hecimovic
Institute for Health Promotion, Health Center "New
Zagreb", Zagreb, Yugoslavia

Classical methods of analysis do not satisfy the
needs of large sample analysis with a great number
of variables in the research field of dependency
diseases. It becomes, therefore, inevitable to
introduce modern statistical and informatics
methods and microcomputers. In this work, the
suggested informatics model has been presented
using the IBM PC-XT compatible personal computer
Olivetti M24 PC, with 640 Kb RAM memory and a
fixed disk of 20 Mb capacity. Three phases of
analysis are presented: 1. the forming of the
database of patients and other persons under
research, 2. the data transfer and conversion from
the database to the statistical macro program and
3. the detailed multivariate analysis. This
program has been examined and tested on the data
collected in order to estimate the possibilities
of the early and objective diagnosis of the
dependency diseases. The research included three
groups of subjects assessed through 76 variables
grouped in 5 subgroups. Applying the above
mentioned methods the variable groups have been
significantly reduced, to get the minimal optimal
and practically appliable variable set,
significant for the early and objective diagnosis.
The use of personal computer has significantly
accelerated the whole procedure of the data
analysis.

2260

La Psicofarmacología, Clínica. Análisis
y Evaluación Clínica en la Actualidad.
Prof.Dr.C. Márquez y Prof.Dr.R.Ucha Udabe.
Instituto Privado de Psicopatología.

La revolución de Charpentier en la complejidad del Laboratorio de Investigación cam-
bió totalmente la historia de la Psiquiatría El Hombre y la Sociedad con la desa-
parición del Htal. Psiquiátrico Clásico
y la integración de la Especialidad en el
Hospital General. La Psicofarmacología
permitió la investigación bioquímica apli-
cada y la obtención de psicosis experimentales en el hombre y los animales. Se con-
troló la exitación, la agresividad, la angustia, la depresión, la confusión y el
delirio, permitiendo la aplicación de --
técnicas psicoterapéuticas grupales e individuales. La aparición en "diluvio"
en los años 60/70 de distintos grupos quí-
micos activos impidió que muchos de ellos
fueran valorados adecuadamente en su momento. La complejidad de lo expuesto invi-
ta a un replanteo general tanto en la investigación psicofarmacológica, clínica -
como experimental en vistas a un futuro
de constante desarrollo.-

2261

JULIO DE MATOS HOSPITAL:THE BEST IN LISBON
INSANELY PUT TO DEATH
António Albuquerque, José Jara, Ricardo Jardim,
Suzana Teiga, Luis Gamito.
Hospital Julio de Matos- LISBON-PORTUGAL

Mental Health services in Portugal are among
the more underdevelloped und understaffed in Europe. Julio de Matos Hospital is the best reknown
portuguese psychiatrist institution since first
World Congress of Psychiatry(1950)and its name is
associated with the last Nobel Prize attributed
to psychiatry(Egas Moniz-1949).
 Today, less than half a century after its foundation, Julio de Matos Hospital remains the best
equipped in Portugal. Nevertheless, governnmental
authorities have decided to sell it in order to
build luxurious residences in its area.
 WHO principles and rules for Mental Health Services transformation have not been considered,
and the so called alternatives to the dying Hospital in 1991 are not even planned until now.
 The demolition of the best hospital in Lisbon is
a clear expression of a budget minded politics,
disguised with a false mental health modernism.

2262

Utilisation des Psychotropes de Base dans un pays en
développement
BOUCEBCI M.
CHU de Psychiatrie Drid-Hocine, 16050 Kouba/Alger (Algérie)

Dans un contexte de sous-développement socio-économique
le psychiatre est confronté au dilemme de la nécessité
d'une gamme suffisante de psychotropes et des limites
de son travail quotidien liées à un certain nombre de
paramètres.

Trois aspects ont fait l'objet d'une étude découlant
des aléas économicopolitiques survenus en Algérie:

- les ruptures de stock
- les changements de fournisseurs avec la question du
  contrôle des médicaments fournis
- les toxicomanies médicamenteuses qui connaissent une
  augmentation très importante notamment chez les jeunes

Des mesures sont envisagées à partir de l'analyse de ces
points.

2263
NON-VERBAL BEHAVIOR: A PSYCHOPATHOLOGICAL INTERPRETATION.
Bonelli G., Nardini M., Magnani N., Belardinell N., Maio A.
Chair of Psychiatry, Siena, Italy

Ethological elements, facial expression and gestures could be useful, in association with other clinical data, to diagnose and cure psychiatric disorders.
In fact, we could consider non-verbal behavior common to all people, normal and pathological subjects, so that we could try to identify emotional contents also by this mean.
This is important especially for such psychiatric disorder where clinical pattern is not so evident than that described in literature, for istance in geriatric Depression, where diagnosis is made basically on somatic sympotms. Facial expression and gestures imply biological aspects and factors related to psychological elements, and by them, perhaps, it could be possible to undertake a correct treatment (decoding of expressed emotion).
In our study, we try to differentiate, among normal subjects, patients with Organic mental Disorder, and psychiatric patients (especially in the elderly), a pattern of facial expressions and gestures that could describe (we purpose to verify its existence) a peculiar expresiveness of emotions in these pathologies, and, if possible, also the different attention to environmental stimuli.

2264
HYPERGLYCEMIA - EITHER A RESULT OF NEUROLEPTIC THERAPY OR A BELATED GENERICAL PHENOMENON
N.Ilankovic, P.Djordjevic, B.Radosavac, D.Jevdic and D.Kastratovic
Psychiatric University Clinic, Belgrade,Yugoslavia

An increase of frequency was noticed in the disregularity of glycemia on the population of chronic psychotic patients with long-lasting neuroleptic treatments. This paper contemplates the endocrine aspect of secondary reactions and the effect of neuroleptics on the systems that regulate glycose in the blood.
It is inferred that neuroleptics disturb the metabolism of glycose by effecting the hypothalamus-hypophysis axis (central effect) and also their effect on peripheral tissue (damaged insulin receptors and post-receptor damage) which leads to diabetes mellitus type II - an indifferency to insulin. Also hypercortisism as a generical or a consecutive phenomenon with mental illnesses. The functioning of the liver is also being researched for the possible participation of the hepatitis "puffer" in the regulation of glycemia. Unselective neuroleptics as are phenothiazines (chlorpromazines, thioridazines, fluphenazines) and benzamides (partial to dopamines of periphery receptors) increase the risk of hyperglycemia appearing in patients who are on long-lasting neuroleptic therapy. Female patients are more partial to the development of diabetes mellitus.

2265
BRIGHT GIRLS BECOMING CLEVER WOMEN
Dr P Sepping MB BS BSc(Med) DPM MRCPsych
Department of Child & Adolescent Psychiatry, Child Development Centre, Poole General Hospital, ENGLAND.

Adolescent depression in high achieving females presents the psychiatrist with several diagnostic and therapeutic problems. The depression is usually rationalised as being simply nervousness due to educational pressure. Frequently the girl suffers conflict between conforming to the traditional female role of future wife/mother versus an intellectually demanding career. The therapy often uncovers a denial of the more female character of sexual identity; a difficulty incorporating the mother as an adequate role model; a relatively greater attachment to the father; or failing that, an alternative attachment figure, often with inappropriate sexual content in the relationship. The importance of this group lies not in their high frequency of presentation. By definition they include only high IQ female adolescents with depression. However, failure adequately to diagnose and treat this group will result in the significant loss of future productivity as this is a potentially high achieving group of adolescents. Over a three year period seven such referrals were made. Six of the adolescents maintained a commitment to individual therapy for an average of 1.6 years (SD 0.9) which represented a staff input of average 59 hours (SD 25), well in excess of the clinic average of 6 hours per patient, although this difference to some extent represented a particular need for these adolescents to receive individual therapy rather than a more rapid family therapy approach. Previous sexual abuse and current eating disorder were frequent, though sometimes late disclosures. The prognosis must be guarded. Three of the six adolescents are not symptom-free despite the above intensive and prolonged treatment.

Session 349 Free Communications:
Panic disorder: Theoretical and psychopathological issues II

2266
The role of sense of control and predictability in the pharmacological provocation of panic.
G. PIETERS, O. VAN DEN BERGH, P.EELEN, F. VANDENDRIESSCHE and K. VAN DE WOESTIJNE

School voor Maatschappelijke Gezondheidszorg, Dienst voor Geestelijke Gezondheidszorg, Katholieke Universiteit Leuven,
Leuven,Belgium.

The effects of breathing a 5% CO_2-solution on the subjective experience of physical symptoms was studied in a group of normal high and low fear (as selected by the STAI-trait) volunteers, using air as a placebo in the same subjects. Subjects were differently instructed as for the symptoms they could expect and for the possibility to control the CO2- or placebo-delivery. The results seem to indicate that the level of habitual fear is an important modulator of the effect of predictability and sense of control on the subjective experience of physical symptoms. A number of conflicting findings in the experimental literature on the pharmalogical provocation of panic could be explained by taking these variables into account.

2267
PANIC ATTACKS AND TWO DIFFERENT QUALITIES OF ANXIETY
Jaime Smolovich, M.D.
Asociacion Argentina de Psicofarmacologia
Buenos Aires, Argentina

The singular position of the panic attack inside the frame of anxiety disorders needs a reevaluation considering the relevance of the treatment with antidepressants and the practical no influence of anxiolytics like the classical benzodiazepines.
For a better understanding it is useful to consider not a single anxiety but two different qualities of it: a) Depressive anxiety and b) Paranoid anxiety. The first one includes all fears of any kind of object loss. The second, all fears of any aggression (from outside or from the self).
Both kinds of anxiety are in a continuous interrelationship and when one of them gives the most important symptoms, the other may be latent or subclinical, but anyway each one paves the way for the other's appearance.
The recurrent panic attacks may be a good example of this alternative continuum between both kinds of anxiety (with the concomitant neurovegetative responses).
But the core of the panic attack is the depressive situation and from this it is possible to supply a psychodynamic explanation of the specific effect of antidepressants and alprazolam on panic attack.

2268
UNRECOGNIZED DIAGNOSIS OF PANIC ATTACK IN GENERAL MEDICAL PRACTICE AND INA GENERAL HOSPITAL
D'AMBROSIO Antonio MD;MORRONE Giuseppina MD;LANERI Roberto;QUARTUCCI Sara
Mental Health Dept.U.S.L.N°38 NAPLES ITALY

The syndrome of panic disorders is becoming delineated from a myriad of medical,cardiologic and psychiatric diagnoses.This syndrome is characterized by the sudden onset of episodes of panic and terror, accompanied by extreme physiologic symptoms including:tachycardia,chest pain,shortness of breeth, trembling,faintness etc.These patients become quite anxious and hypochondrial and begin to avoid certain situations in which they feel a recurrence of a panic attack would be dangerous or embarassing. From data collected within the frame of a longitudinal epidemiologic study,the prevalence rate in the general population of panic attacks was found to be about 3% or more!Evidence suggests that many of these patients are currently unrecognized in primary care,internal medicine and cardiology practices. This research examines the capacity of 250 general practitioners,and physicians in a general hospital in Naples city District(about 200.000 inhabitants), to make a correct diagnosis and therapy of such attacks,by means of structured interview.The relative prevalence of the above disorders among the patients population is analyzed.

2269
PANIC SYNDROM: SOME PRELIMINARY FINDINGS IN COPING BEHAVIOUR
R.Beck, E.Trenkamp
University of Oldenburg, Germany

Panic attacks with a prevalence between 10 and 14% are considered increasingly important for the differentation and treatment of anxiety disorders. Method: from Oct. 1986 until May 1988, 80 Patients with anxiety disorders contacted my neurologic-psychiatric ambulance; 20 Patients could be selected - psychiatric exploration, DSM III-R, Hamilton-anxiety scale, socio-demographic data - as patients with panic disorders. Each patient had to write down his personal records focused on emotionally remembered interactions.Data-analysis, and qualitative analysis describe the net-work of emotional, cognitive and behavioural dimensions to get to an understanding of the interactions leading to panic disorders.
Results: The preliminary findings of our small sample demonstrate, that typical coping strategies are involved in panic attack progression: emphasizing rigid rational life concepts, overemphasize proprioceptive self-percetion concepts, cognitive disconnection of emotional and somatic body-stimulus, anxiety induced self-denial etc. Panic-disorder-discriminating-test is finally formulated.

2270
Interactions patterns in partnerships of panic patients

Stefan Arnold
Psychiatry Division, University of Erlangen-Nuremberg

Vorgestellt werden vorläufige Ergebnisse einer Studie, in der Partnerschaften mit einem Angstpatienten untersucht werden.
Im Mittelpunkt steht die Frage, welche Kompensations- und Bewältigungspotentiale von Angstkrankheiten in Partnerschaften zur Verfügung stehen, die auch als Verlaufsdeterminanten betrachtet werden.

Session 350 Free Communications:

Forensic psychiatry: International perspectives

2271

Neuropsychiatric Correlates of Violence

George U. Balis, M.D.
University of Maryland School of Medicine

This study purports to demonstrate correlations between a scaled continuum of aggressive/violent behavior and various clinical parameters of neuropsychiatric symptoms, psychopathology, and EEG findings, in 426 adult psychiatric patients evaluated for aggressive dyscontrol. These patients were classified, on the basis of an aggression scale, into 5 groups that ranged from non-aggression to severe assault/murder. The data strongly suggest that the degree of aggression and especially severity of assaultive behavior, correlates with (1) severity of a cross-sectional psychopathology, (2) paroxysmal epileptoid symptoms (3) findings suggestive of organicity, (4) degree of impulsivity and emotional instability, and (5) with specific DSM-III diagnoses, and most prominently, borderline personality and antisocial personality. On the other hand, schizophrenia and other psychotic disorders, bipolar disorder, major depression, schizoaffective disorder, as well as partial complex seizures and EEG abnormalities, showed no significant intergroup differences.

2272

A STUDY OF MALE MENTALLY HANDICAPPED SEX OFFENDERS

Dr. K.A. Day, Consultant Psychiatrist, Northgate Hospital, Morpeth, Northumberland NE61 3BP, England.

48 pts responsible for 197 sexual incidents during an 18 year period were studied. Heterosexual offences accounted for 52% indecent exposure 25%, homosexual offences 13%, cross dressing and stealing underclothes 9%. One third of the homosexual and one quarter of the heterosexual incidents were rated as serious. Special precipitating factors were present in 10%. 63% of victims were under 17 years, 44% under 13 years and 11% under 7 years. 48% of the male and 30% of the female victims were well known to the perpetrator. 37% of incidents resulted in conviction with the highest frequencies being homosexual 52%, serious incidents (75%), and child victims 58%. The more serious the offence the more likely a psychiatric disposal. The average IQ of the group was 64 and there was a high prevalence of brain damage (42%), child psychiatric referral (17%) adult mental illness (31%) psychosocial deprivation (48%), childhood residential placement (48%), and behaviour problems (77%). 85% were involved in more than one and 58% in three or more sexual incidents during a mean period of 10.3 years. 48% had convictions for non-sex offences, they showed a significantly higher prevalence of the above features and were more likely to commit several sex offences. Compared to other mentally handicapped offenders the sex offenders were less likely to be psychopathic, were nearly 10 years older at first conviction, showed fewer adverse psychosocial factors in their backgrounds and had a lower F.H. of criminality. They also displayed a significantly lower frequency of single category sex offences, less specificity for age and sex of victim and a higher frequency of physical disabilities and brain damage than non-handicap past sex offenders.

2273

STATUS OF FORENSIC PSYCHIATRY IN INDIA

J.K. Trivedi, Department of Psychiatry, K.G's Medical College, Lucknow, INDIA.

Forensic Psychiatry in India is still governed by rules which were formulated at the time when understanding of psychiatry was in its infancy and this sub-speciality was not properly demarcated and legally identified. The present paper will discuss in detail the existing status of law in relation to detention of mentally ill and their civil and human rights in India.

Criminal responsibility of the mentally ill is an area of intense debate all over the world. McNaughton rule is generally applicable in this country but it has been shown time and again that this is neither adequate nor sufficient. Unfortunately psychiatry and law did not have the kind of interaction which would have helped both these specialities.

2274

PSYCHIATRIC EVALUATION OF A SERIES MURDERER IN INDONESIA
Wahjono Soemarto M.D.
Health Department of Indonesian National Police H.Q. Jakarta Indonesia

Series murders committed by a man is a rare case. There are 4 cases of series murders in Indonesia during the last 30 years. The last case happened between Oct 88-Febr 89 in a small town in East Java, in which 6 women were killed. The victims were widowers 30-40 years old, low socio-economic status. The murderer, a divorced man 35 years old, low socio-economic status, killed the victims with popular food made of cassava mixed with poison, without force or threatened. After each victim died, he put off their clothes, touched heir breasts and their external genitalia without penetrating the vagina or doing masturbation. He stated the feelings of calm and pleasure after the acts without pity or guilty feelings. On the other hand he could not exactly explain the real motive of his acts. Based on the clinical diagnosis finding, assumption of the real motive could be made by understanding the psychodynamic explanation. Psychiatric evaluation revealed the clinical diagnosis of Inhibited Sexual Excitement(Axes I) and Antisocial Personality Disorder(Axes II). To make a firm diagnosis of Atypical Paraphilia(Necrophilia) as another possibility(Axes I) is still a problem.

2275

PSYCHIATRIE ET DROIT PENAL PORTUGAIS
DEVELOPPEMENTS RECENTS
Francisco Santos Costa - Mª.Helena Pinto de Azevedo
FACULTÉ DE MÉDECINE
COIMBRA - PORTUGAL

    Les auteurs analysent et commentent les modifications introduites par les récents articles de loi, conditionnant une pratique psychiatrique médico-légale différente.

    Ils dressent quelques considérations sur la Psychiatrie dans son rapport avec le Droit, dans le contexte portugais, mettant en perspective une façon d'agir qui rende possible, de fait, une meilleure contribution à l'application du Droit Pénal et à l'administration de la Justice.

    Ils attirent l'attention sur la matière réellement innovatrice que constitue l'"*expertise portant sur la personnalité*" (art. 160º du Code de Procédure Pénale, 1988), et désignent les lignes d'orientation qui doivent guider sa réalisation.

2276

SCHIZOPHRENIA AND OTHER PSYCHIATRIC DISORDERS IN MENTALLY ILL DELINQUENTS.
SOLER VIÑOLO, M. and SOLER ARREBOLA, P.
Dept. Psychiatry. University of Granada. Spain.

    The relationship between schizophrenia and delinquency was analyzed and compared in mentally ill patients with similar disorders (alcoholic, drug addict, epileptic, psychopathic, mental retardation, etc.).

    The study population consisted of 518 subjects admitted by court order to the Granada Provincial Psychiatric Hospital over a period of 27 years. Of this group, 82 (15.83%) were schizophrenics. A series of clinical, social, criminal and legal variables were studied in the schizophrenics and the rest of the mentally ill population, and statistical correlations sought.

    These findings suggest among other conclusions, that schizophrenia and alcoholism are associated with similar types of crimes (against persons as opposed to property). No significant differences were found between the subtype of schizophrenia and type of crime, but violent behavior was found to be related with paranoid schizophrenia. A statistically significant correlation was also noted between schizophrenia (and other mental illnesses) and variables such as socioeconomic status, urban background, sociofamilial conflictivity, experts testimony and court measures taken.

Session 351 Free Communications:
Schizophrenia: Diagnostic and nosologic issues

2277

METHODOLOGY FOR INVESTIGATING THE CLINICAL PROGRESS OF PATIENTS IN BEGINNING PHASES OF SCHIZOPHRENIA.
G. Borsetti, P. Cotani, E. Alfonsi, V. Volterra*
Psych. Institut - University of Ancona (Italy)
*Psych. Dept. - University of Bologna (Italy)

As part of a project sponsored by the C.N.R. (National Research Council), a comparative evaluation was made of the results of two different treatment procedures (pharmacological and psychotherapeutic) in patients in beginning phases of schizophrenia. In an effort to solve the many conceptual difficulties of setting up the research (from diagnostic criteria to criteria selected for therapeutic programmes), we considered it particularly interesting, because of the broad implications, ranging from the sociopsychological significance of the concept of clinically improving and healing the psychotic patients to the scientific nature and necessary reproducibility of the methodology used, to make a contribution to the definition of the methodology for evaluating the therapeutic results.
While for one group of 15 patients standard-procedure psychopharmacotherapy was used, the order 15 were treated with analytically oriented psychotherapy (individual for 7 subjects, group for the other 8). A psychotherapeutic group was also set up involving the patients' parental ties in group analysis. This too was conducted according to Foulkesian methods with twice-monthly 2-hours sessions of 18 participating parental figures.

2278

COMPUTER AIDED DIAGNOSIS IN SCHIZOPHRENIA
R.Rouskov,Hospital of Psychiatry, Kardjali,Bulgaria
30,49

    In this article is described the created from the author system for computing differentiation of schizophrenia and the similar to its states.It is shown on original approach in the decision of this difficult for the psychiatrical practice problem.There,one can find information about the running of the system and its results.A comparision is made with other systems with the same functions.Some conclusions are made for the possibilities of application of electronic computers which can help with the diagnosis,prognosis and the treatement of psychiatric deseases.

2279
Sex Differences in Age of Onset of Schizophrenia and Phenomenological Subtypes
G. Lenz, H. Katschnig
Psychiatric Clinic, University of Vienna

The consistent epidemiological finding that age of onset in female schizophrenic patients is higher than age of onset in male patients has not yet been conclusively explained. We explore the possibility that age of onset is not only related to sex but also to specific symptom patterns, i.e., to specific phenomenological subtypes of schizophrenia, and that the lower age of onset in male schizophrenics is due to a higher proportion of a phenomenological "early onset subtype" among male patients.

A series of 200 first ever admissions of patients with functional psychotic disorders to two mental hospitals in Vienna was carefully documented by means of an extended version of the Present State Examination developed for polydiagnostic assessment, and by a number of other schedules, including an evaluation of the onset of the disorder.

2280
ON THE CURRENT NOSOLOGICAL STATUS OF SIMPLE SCHIZOPHRENIA
Predescu V., Predescu I., Predescu O., Georgescu MJ. Alexandrescu LC.
Institute of Medicine and Pharmacy - Bucharest, Romania

The logic of nosological classification implies that a clinical picture of schizotypal personality disorder might exist in which a clear-cut onset, post-dating adolescence, can be established. Such a disorder may be viewed as an equivalent of the ICD-9 "latent" or "borderline" schizophrenia (code 295.5), while the ICD-9 simple form of schizophrenia (code 295.0) remains with no correspondence in DSM-III and DSM-III.R. The current amphasis on the negative and positive syndromes of schizophrenia suggests that the validity of the diagnosis of simple schizophrenia as a nosological entity might increase and thus the present confusion in this area could diminish by considering the possibility of them being two variants of this disorder, with either the positive (but mitigated) or the negative syndrome over being present.
The authors attempt to test this hypothesis based on findings from a retrospective study of the medical records of 25 patients with relevant diagnoses.

2281
B.E.A.M: A COMPARISON OF POSITIVE WITH NEGATIVE SCHIZOPHRENIC PATIENTS
K.Alexandropoulos, MD, T.Alexopoulos, MD, M.N. Katsanou, MD, V.Avgeri, MD, E.Boubioti, Ch. Michalaki, MD, and A. Michalakeas, M.R.C. Psych.
Psychiatric Hospital of Attica (2nd Psychiatric Department)-Psychiatric Hopsital of Corfu - Medical Centre of Athens - Greece.

In our study we compared Brain electrical activity of type I and type II Schizophrenics with normal controls. We also compared B.E.A.M between type I and type II Schizophrenics. The purpose was (1) to confirm or not the findings of previous work which showed disfunctioning in frontal and temporal lobe in Schizophrenics and (2) to investigate whether there is a significant difference as far as B.E.A.M is concerned between type I and type II Schizophrenia. Twenty one (9 type I and 12 type II) chronic Schizophrenics were examined during treatment and after a four week drug free period. Those groups were compared with 12 normal controls. We found statistically significant differences between: a) type I and type II schizophrenics in temporal beta waves ($p<0.05$) b) type I and controlls in temporal delta waves ($p<0.01$) c) type II and controls in delta waves of the central and precentral regions billaterally ($p<0.01$). Our findings suggest that there are differences in electrical activity between type I and type II as well as between those two groups and controls.

2282
ACUTE "BOUFFEE DELIRANTE" AND SCHIZOPHRENIC EVOLUTION: PROGNOSTIC VALUE DSM III
H. Lazaratou, Centre Hospitalier Spécialisé de Maison-Blanche, Paris, France

The relationship between acute "bouffee delirante" and the DSM III classification is examined. DSM III criteria were applied at the beginning of a 5 years follow-up period in 55 patients admitted in a psychiatric hospital between 1975 and 1980 with the diagnosis of acute "bouffee delirante". According to these criteria, 15 patients presented a schizophrenic disorder, 18 patients a schizophreniform disorder, 9 patients an atypical pshychosis, 5 patients a brief reactive psychosis and 8 patients an affective disorder. Five years later, the French diagnosis, based on the evolution, was schizophrenia for 20 patients, bipolar affective disorder for 9 patients, recurrence of similar non schizophrenic disorder for 10 patients and no recurrence of psychiatric disorders for 16 patients. In a second step, the relationships between this evolution and the initial DSM III clasification were examined. The schizophrenic evolution was observed in 60% of the patients initially presenting a schizophrenic disorder according to the DSM III, and a bipolar disorder evolution in 50% of those initially presenting an affective disorder. In a third step, the most predictive initial symptoms with regard to the schizophrenic evolution were identified using a logistic regression. It appears that the DSM III criteria show some prognostic interest.

2283

SCHIZOPHRENIA AND EATING DISORDERS

Foulon C., Benadon V., Rein W., Criquillion-Doublet S., Samuel-Lajeunessse B.
Clinique des Maladies Mentales et de l'Encéphale, Centre Hospitalier Sainte Anne ; 100, rue de la Santé - 75674 Paris Cédex 14 - FRANCE

Results of the Eating Attitudes Test by Garner and Garfinkel in three matched groups of subjects (schizophrenics n = 39, patients with eating disorders of the bulimic and restricting subtype n = 23, normal controls n =125) are presented. Comparison of EAT scores shows that schizophrenic patients also have elevated scores, allowing a detailed description of their pathologic eating habits. Furthermore, schizophrenic patients scored higher on items concerned with body image disturbance and were at that level comparable to anorectics, whereas scores of bulimic patients were higher than these of schizophrenics and anorectics.

2284

SEXUAL PROBLEMS IN SCHIZOPHRENICS

DR. G.C. KAR, M.D., F.I.P.S., S. C. B. MEDICAL COLLEGE, CUTTACK, INDIA.
DR. T. PATI, M.D.,F.I.P.S., S. C. B. MEDICAL COLLEGE, CUTTACK, INDIA.
DR. L.P. VARMA, M.D.,D.P.M.,F.R.C.Psych,RANCHI, INDIA.

Impairment of sexual activity is oftenencountered among schizophrenics, be it a feature or consequence of the illness or side effect of treatment. The present study has been undertaken with the objective of exploring the sexual behaviour and problems of the schizophrenics.

The study sample comprised of 100 recovered, communicative male schizophrenics diagnosed as per the guidelines of ICD-9. The patients and their families were interviewed to assess and collect relevant information about their sexual behaviour during the illness as well as before. One hundred apparently normal persons adjusted with respect to age, sex, education, social status and domicile, formed the control group and were similarly analysed for comparison. Both the groups belonged to the same cultural background.

The schizophrenics had an earlier acquisition of knowledge about sex but with a higher rate of unpleasant reaction. They also had a greater rate of masturbation associated with guilt feeling and that of sexually unpleasant marital life. Analysis of premarital and extramarital sexual life revealed that they had a greater affinity for prostitutes and the nonmarital sex was more often associated with guilt feeling.

The present study, being one of the rare such in the Indian setting, is expected to throw more light on the sexual behaviour of schizophrenics especially against the typical culturalbackground.

2285

TOLERANCE OF AMBIGUITY IN AFFECTIVE AND SCHIZOPHRENIC DISORDERS
A. Heerlein, P. Richter, T. Niedermeier
Psychiatric Clinic, Heidelberg University, FR Germany

In a study to determine the relationship between tolerance of ambiguity and different psychiatric disorders classified according to DSM-III criteria, 108 consecutively admitted inpatients at the Psychiatric Clinic of the University of Heidelberg and 53 normal subjects completed the Kischkel Tolerance of Ambiguity Scale as well as other psychometric instruments in the 5th week of treatment. The group of unipolar depressives (n=37) showed significantly lower scores than the control group and the schizophrenic group (n=22). Bipolar depressives (n=8), schizophrenics and a mixed group of patients with anxiety or dysthymic disorder (n=41) did not differ from the control group who showed the highest scores. The clinical and psychopathological meaning of this 'Intolerance of Ambiguity' among depressive patients and its relevance in psychosocial research are discussed.

Session 352 Free Communications:
Antidepressants in clinical use III

2286

MULTICENTER COMPARISON OF LOFEPRAMINE AND AMITRIPTYLINE IN DEPRESSION
Prof. Dr.DR. DOONGAJI, Med.College BOMBAY, Ass. Prof.Dr. S.BAL Med. College, CALCUTTA, Ass. Prof. Dr.S. RAJKUMAR, Dept. Gyt. Gen. Hospital, MADRAS.

In this double-blind comparison 126 outpatients with Major Depressive Disorder (DSM-III) have been treated with either Lofepramine (n=63) or Amitriptyline (n=63). The assessmentperiod covered 6 week's treatment.
Main topics of this study were to compare the therapeutic efficacy and side-effect frequency of Lofepramine (L), an antidepressant of the new generation of tricyclics, and Amitriptyline (A), a classic antidepressant.
As expected no major differences in therapeutic efficacy could be detected. Clinical Global Impression (CGI), Severity Scores for patients on L were 4.42 ± 0.07 before and 1.58 ± 0.18 after 6 weeks' treatment. Corresponding figures for patients on A were 4.57 ± 0.09 and 1.71 ± 0.17 respectively. The CGI Efficacy Index for L was 2.1 ± 0.13 and that for A was 1.7 ± 0.09.
Thirty percent of L patients reported no side effects (SE), 46% reported one SE and 24% two or more. Corresponding figures for patients on A were 18,28 and 54% respectively. The difference in SE frequency was highly significant (p<0.01 Mann Whitney). Other important points to be discussed;
1. Are there any differences in therapeutically effective dosages neede for optimal treatment of moderate to severe depression in patients of Western and Asian origin?
2. Are there any social or other factors, which explain the differences in drop-out rates seen in the 3 centres involved in this multicenter study?

2287

FLUOXETINE VS. MAPROTILINE - EFFICACY AND DOSAGE

S. Kuha, M.D. Ass.prof., A. Henttonen, M.D. (Kuopio University Central Hospital, Psychiatric Clinic), M. Naarala, M.D. (Oulu University Central Hospital, Psychiatric Clinic), O-P Mehtonen, M.D. (Tampere University, Department of Pharmacology, and Pitkäniemi Hospital), Finland.

Fluoxetine, an interesting new selective serotonin re-uptake inhibitor is compared with maprotiline in a five week double-blind parallel study in patients with unipolar major depressive disorders. Maprotiline is also an example of a more selective noradrenalin uptake inhibitor which differentiates it from tricyclic antidepressants. Several studies have been published supporting the efficacy of 20 mg of fluoxetine. After a washout period of 3-7 days patients were treated with fluoxetine 20 mg/day during the first 3 weeks and thereafter with a maintenance dose of 20-60 mg/day for five weeks. The maprotiline dose was 50-150 mg/day. On a weekly basis Hamilton psychiatric rating scale for depression (at least 17 on the first 17 questions in the beginning), Raskin depression scale, Covi anxiety scale, clinical and patient global impressions, adverse events, concomitant medication, body weight, BP, pulse rate and temperature were monitored. Haematology, blood chemistry and urine analysis were analyzed at three occasions during the study.
The results of the first 80 out/in-patients will be presented and discussed.

2288

AMOXAPINE VERSUS TRIMIPRAMINE IN THE MANAGEMENT OF PSYCHOTIC DEPRESSION

Dr. A. N. Singh, Hamilton Psychiatric Hospital, Hamilton, Ontario, Canada

The objective of this double blind comparative study was to identify a suitable monotherapeutic agent for psychotic depression along with comparing the pharmacological and therapeutic profiles of amoxapine in a comparison to trimipramine.
This study was of 8 weeks duration and 40 patients with psychotic diagnosis were included.
Therapeutic responses were measured in 6 cluster groups. Both drugs showed statistically significant improvement in patient's psychopathologies but in paranoid symptoms and depersonalization trimipramine initially showed deterioration and rate of overall response was half of amoxapine in the end study. Besides cognitive factors and retardation showed superior response in amoxapine groups of patients than in trimipramine group. The onset of a therapeutic action in amoxapine was 12.5 days in comparison to 18.6 days in the trimipramine group. The study confirmed the early reports of therapeutic superiority of amoxapine in the management of psychotic depression over trimipramine.

2289

ACTION OF TRIMIPRAMINE ON RETARDATION AND KEEP DISORDERS IN 19 INPATIENTS WITH MAJOR DEPRESSIVE DISORDERS

J.F. ALLILAIRE[*], R. CALVEZ[**], V. DANTCHEV[*], F. RAFFAITIN[***], D. WIDLOCHER[*]

[*] Hôpital Pitié-Salpétrière, Sce du Pr WIDLOCHER,47 Bd de L'HOPITAL
[**] Laboratoires SPECIA.16 rue CLISSON 75013 PARIS .
[***] 17 rue des Marronniers ,75016 PARIS .

N = 19 Inpatients (11 males, 8 females, mean age 41 years) with major depressive disorders according to DSM 3 R criterais and MADRS > 25 were included in an open study to confirm the efficacy of Trimipramine particularly on depressive retardation and on sleep disorders by SPIEGEL.

The treatment was a monotherapy with daily doses of trimipramine of 100 to 150 mg during 4 weeks after 8 days of wash out.

An evaluation was done with MADRS, HDRS, ERD and Spiegel ratin scale at J0, J7, J14, J21, J28 to compare the evolution global scores and the evolution of retardation and sleep disorders.

Trimipramine showed or very effective antidepressant effect on this population, with a therapeutic index at between J28 and J0.

The mean score from J0 to J28 was

- for MADRS from 35 to 7 (80 % improvement)
- for HDRS from 30 to 7 (80 %) improvement)
- for ERD from 28 to 8 (80 % improvement)
- and SPIEGEL from 28 to 8 (80 % improvement)

* the comparison beetween scales showed a very good correlation during the evolution beetween HDRS and ERD

* Similary a good correlation beetween MADRS and ERD especially with items 7 of MADRS

*The comparison beetween HDRS and ERD showed a very good correlation as well at beetween MADRS and ERD and beetween Spiegel and ERD.

Similary a good correlation beetween ERD and items 7 tiredners of MADRS was found wich shows the importance of retardation as specific dimension to measure the evolution of depressive episode an under treatment.

In conclusion : trimipramine appear to be a very efficient on sleep disorders wich improve very quickly and retardation wich appears to be a very good index and may a more specific dimension of depressive disorder.

2290

USE OF PLACEBO IN CONTROLLED TRIALS OF ANTI-DEPRESSANT DRUGS.

BRION S., PLAS J., GLUCK N., and GAILLEDREAU J.

Placebo is now widely used in controlled trials of antidepressant drugs. The main interest of placebo is the opportunity of significant differences obtained versus an active compound with a relatively restricted number of patients. However, it has been demonstrated (PAYKEL, 1988) that the placebo-response of depressed patients tends to increase as the Hamilton Depression (HDRS) score at inclusion tends to decrease. Furthermore, serious ethical considerations such as the suicidal risk with patients not treated with the best compound for depression, lead to the necessity to include in placebo-controlled trials only Major Depressive Disorders with moderate intensity and quite low initial HDRS score. Because of the higher rate of placebo-response of this population, this may lead to the necessity of including a larger number of patients. Depression realizes a stroke in the patient's mood, and the damage occured by this phenomenon cannot be repaired only with placebo. Some criteria will be proposed in order to differentiate placebo and non placebo responders. Since not depressed patients should not be included in clinical trials of anti-depressant drugs, placebo ought to be excluded as a reference medication, not only for ethical reasons, but for methodological reasons too.

2291
TREATMENT OF POST-PSYCHOTIC DEPRESSION

Salteri A. Unità Operativa Psichiatrica
Sesto San Giovanni (Milano)

In the course of schizophrenic psychoses it may happen to patients to experience periods of serious depressive simptomatology, unresponsive to neuroleptic treatment alone. Moreover, such timic deflections are often underrated, in despite of the fact that they can become dangerous clinical conditions with global personal impairment and high suicidal risk. We have identified a group of 20 patients of our Psichiatric Operative Unit with a depression superimposed to a chronic schizophrenic disorder, in accordance with DSM-III criteria. Depression was rated by the Hamilton Depression Rating Scale (HAM-D). Treatment consisted in addition of Trazodone, a new generation antidepressant, to the current neuroleptic therapy; daily dose was mantained between 100 and 400 mg. Patients were followed with weekly ratings using the Schedule for Affective Disorders and Schizophrenia (SADS), the Global Clinical Index (CGI), the HAM-D. Results showed a marked improvement of mean HAM-D score, with only one case of psychotic simptomatology getting worse.

2292
PERSONALITY VARIABLES AND PREDICTION OF ANTIDEPRESSANT RESPONSE
Arthur M. Freeman III, M.D.[1], Srdjan R. Stankovic, M.D.[2], J. Wesley Libb, Ph.D.[1], and Roberta Silver Sokol, M.A.[1]
Department of Psychiatry, University of Alabama at Birmingham, USA[1]
Department of Psychiatry, Belgrade University Clinical Center, YU[2]

Borderline, dependent, and passive-aggressive personality disorders (P.D.) are frequently reported among psychiatric patients with major depressive disorders (M.D.D.). Research also suggests poor treatment response in the M.D.D. patient with concomitant P.D.
M.D.D. patients in a prospective clinical trial with a new antidepressant, mepirzepine, were administered the Millon Clinical Multiaxial Inventory (MCMI) and the Hamilton Rating Scale for Depression (HAM-D) at the beginning of the study. The HAM-D was readministered after 8 and 12 weeks of treatment. Eighty-five percent of the 73 patients administered the MCMI at the beginning of treatment had test scores highly suggestive of a P.D. Over half reported passive-aggressive (56%) and/or dependent (51%) features; 37% presented borderline, and 29%, avoidant characteristics. Ten participants were first-week placebo responders. These patients were significantly more histrionic and tended to be more dependent and less schizoid than other participants in the study.
Nineteen of the 40 patients re-evaluated at week 12 were rated improved based on a 50% or greater decrease in HAM-D scores. The MCMI profiles of those who improved were significantly higher on the histrionic scale (t = -3.296, p = 0.002) and significantly lower on the avoidant scale (t = 2.569, p = 0.014). The schizoid scale also tended to be lower in improved patients (t = 1.943, p = 0.059). In addition, lower scores were found on the borderline scale for patients who met the 50% improved criteria on the HAM-D at week 8. These findings were not present at week 12.
Our results suggest that depressed patients with avoidant, schizoid and borderline personalities respond less well to antidepressant therapy than those with histrionic or less prominent personality characteristics. Questions of the reliability of the existing instruments and methods for personality assessment remain open and necessitate further study. More comprehensive evaluation with several different instruments, sources of information (including the family) and biological markers for depression may refine prediction of antidepressant response.

2293
RAPID AND VALID PREDICTION OF RESPONSE OF ANTIDEPRESSANT TREATMENT BY MEANS OF HAMDS AND MADRS

N.-U. Neumann, R.-M. Schulte
Departement II of Psychiatry/University Ulm

Using MADRS and HAMDS the improvements seen in depressed patients after 14 days on Dosulepin can enable clinicians to accurately predict response/non-response at day 28. In 272 patients, suffering from depression of different origin and severity, the efficacy of Dosulepin was assessed during a 28-day period by two independent observers using HAMDS and MADRS. The number of responders (HAMDS/MADRS) at the end of the study was n= 163/173 (59,9%/63,6%). The number of non-responders respectively n = 109/99 (40,1%/34,4%).

Response was defined as HAMDS sumscores $\leq$ =16 (sum of two raters) or a decrease of either scale sumscore by more than 50 % from baseline. Mean decrease of sumscore at day 14 in patients eventually meeting response criteria at day 28 was 33,3% (HAMDS) 34,3% (MADRS) whereas sumscores of 20,4% and 21,9% or less at 14 days correlated significantly with non-response at study end. MADRS and HAMDS correlated well with each other. As the MADRS only has 10 items, it could be utilised in clinical practice to modify treatment strategies at an early stage.

2294
EEG-CHARACTERISTICS BEFORE AND AFTER FIRST INFUSION OF AN ANTIDEPRESSANT AS PREDICTORS OF THERAPY OUTCOME

H.-J.Haug, E.Fähndrich, G.Ulrich, W.M.Herrmann

Psychiatrische Klinik und Poliklinik der Freien Universität Berlin - Eschenallee 3, 1000 Berlin 19, West Germany

108 in-patients (RDC-diagnosis "Major Depressive Disorder") received antidepressant drug-treatment for three weeks following a drug-washout period of at least 4 days. One daily infusion of clomipramine or maprotiline respectively was administered at fixed doses (75 mg for the first 3 days, then 100 mg).
On the day prior to beginning therapy comprehensive psychopathology-ratings were conducted. For an assessment of response patients were again judged on day 21 of intravenous therapy using the same psychopathology-rating method. Additionally, global judgements by the patient as well as his physician on the success of therapy were registered. Before and after the first infusion the EEG was recorded over a 15-minute rest period.
The clinical data were compared with the Spectral Difference Index (SDI) as a global measure of changes and vigilance-indicating variables of the spontaneous EEG and differences before and after infusion were investigated.
The results are discussed considering (1) prediction of therapy outcome by EEG-variables before and after first infusion, (2) changes of EEG attributable to the infusion, and (3) prediction of response to therapy by the pattern of changes of EEG after first infusion.

2295
TREATMENT OF DYSTHYMIC DISORDER WITH RITANSERIN

Ann Stokland M.D., Margareta Larsson ass.prof., Anders Manhem M.D., Anders Forsman ass.prof. UNIVERSITY OF GÖTEBORG, Department III of Psychiatry, SWEDEN

Clinical effects were studied in 19 dysthymic patients (DSM III, 300,40) treated with a daily dose of 20 mg Ritanserin, a new postsynaptic serotonin-2 receptor blocker. Initial total score was at least 15 in the Hamilton Depression Rating Scale (HDRS), the 17 item issue. The study period was 8 weeks with an initial 2 weeks' placebo treatment followed by 6 weeks of active drug treatment. The patients were analyzed on day -14, 0, + 21, and + 42 for change in "severity of depression" (HDRS and a subscale of the Comprehensive Psychopatholocical Rating Scale), and clinical global and patients' global impression. Side effects were registered.
18 patients completed the study. Only a minor and not significant reduction was observed during the placebo period. During 3 weeks with Ritanserin there was a significant reduction in HDRS from 20.2 ± 2.6 points to 13.2 ± 5.5 ($p<0.001$) followed by a further improvment after 6 weeks, mean score 8.2 ± 5.1 ($p<0.001$). A mild obstipation was noted in some patients and a moderate weight gain was observed, mean 1.2 kg ($p<0.05$). There were no significant changes in heart and blood pressure, but a prolonged QT and QTc time in the ECG recordings were observed ($p<0.001$). No severe adverse reactions were encountered. Sleep pattern changes were recorded in 12 patients by means of a 9 channel Medilog 9000 system. The amount of REM sleep following Ritanserin treatment was unchanged but the delta sleep time increased from a mean of 111 to 149 minutes ($p<0.05$) at the expence of stage 1 and 2 sleep. The number of awakenings was reduced.

Our results indicate that serotonin-2 receptor blockade by Ritanserin might alleviate symptoms of dysthymia already after 3 weeks of treatment. This is accompanied by a higher quality of sleep as reflected by a sustained increase in deep sleep and a reduced number of awakenings. Side effects were judged to be negligible.

Session 353 Free Communications:
Drugs for the treatment of anxiety disorders and insomnia

2296
LEVOPROTILINE - NEW PERSPECTIVES IN ANXIOLYSIS
G.-E. Kühne, G. Wendt, T. Kiszka, U. Binz, H. Kluge and W. Zahlten
Dept. of Psychiatry of the Friedrich-Schiller-Univ., Jena, DDR-6900, G.D.R.

Levoprotiline is the R(-)-enantiomer of oxaprotiline, the hydroxylated derivative of the antidepressant maprotiline. In contrast to oxaprotiline and maprotiline, it is completely devoid of NE reuptake inhibiting properties. The clinical profile is characterized by a reliable antidepressive effect, by distinct anxiolytic properties and by an earlier onset of action compared with hitherto existing antidepressants. We have been testing levoprotiline in patients with anxiety states for about two years. In this report some rating scales were compared to find out that scale which is most qualified to describe anxiolytic effects of the drug. On the other hand, using DSM III categories, patients with generalized anxiety were slightly more improved than those with panic syndromes. Furthermore, first results on platelet serotonin contents of levoprotiline treatment are presented. On the molecular level, erythrocytic calmodulin-stimulated Ca-ATPase was not affected by levoprotiline in vitro.

2297
PANIC DISORDER

ABD EL AZIM, SAID, M.D.
CAIRO UNIVERSITY

The study includes :

1-Demographic and Epidemiological aspects of anxiety disorders including panics in Saudi Arabia.
2- Clinical and psychometric evaluation of panic disorder in comparison with other types of anxiety.
3- Experience of treatment of panic disorder with Alprazolam and other psychopharmacological agents.

The study revealed that Anxiety Disorders are among the frequent psychological diseases in Saudi Arabia. Panic attacks and phobic disorders are more frequent in Saudi Arabians than among Egyptians.

Experience with Alprazolam proved its superiority in treatment of panic attacks in comparison with other benzodiazepines or antidepressant.

2298
RITANSERIN VERSUS LORAZEPAM: A STUDY OF REACTION TIMES IN HEALTHY VOLUNTEERS
ALTAMURA AC, COLACURCIO F, MORO AR, MARINI S
Laboratory of Neuropsychopharmacology, Department of Psychiatry, University of Milan, Italy.

Ritanserin, a benzydrilen-piperidine derivative, with a potent, selective and long-lasting antagonist activity on serotonin type 2 receptors, has shown anxyolitic properties and a lesser sedative profile than benzodiazepines. Ritanserin and lorazepam at therapeutical doses, were compared in eight healthy volunteers in a double-blind, cross-over study in order to detect possible different impairments of performances. Before and during the treatment, all subjects were daily submitted to a test of rapidity and regularity of response to acoustic and visual stimuli by means of an electronic device. A visual analogue scale for the self-assessment of the drowsiness was also administered. Ritanserin did not modify reaction times, while lorazepam significantly prolonged them. The analogical scale for concentration showed a significant reduction with lorazepam whereas for drowsiness no alteration occurred with either drug.
In conclusion ritanserin seems preferable to lorazepam in anxiety disorders, for its higher neurochemical specificity and reduced impairment of performances.

2299

LONGITUDINAL STUDY ON PHARMACODYNAMICS AND PHARMACOKINETICS OF ACUT-STEADY-STATE, AND WITHDRAWN QUAZEPAM

K. Schaffler[1], G. Kauert[2], C.H. Wauschkuhn[1], W. Klausnitzer[1]

1. Institute for Pharmacodynamic Research, Kronstadter Straße 9, D-8000 Munich 80, FRG
2. Institute for Forensic Medicine (Head: Prof. Dr. Spann), University of Munich, Frauenlobstraße 7a, D-8000 Munich 2, FRG

To assess pharmacodynamic and pharmacokinetic properties of acute, subchronic and withdrawn quazepam, a single-blind, longitudinal study was run in eight male, healthy young volunteers. The design covered a one week placebo run-in period, a period with daily oral night-time administration of 15 mg quazepam until a pharmacokinetic steady-state was reached (three weeks) and a two-week placebo withdrawal period.

Oculodynamic Test (ODT) (EOG-registration with simultaneous choice reaction task) and Adaptive Pursuit Tracking Test (APTT) were used for assessment of intradiurnal and long-term profiles of attention, perception, cognition, objective sedation, psychomotor and muscular (force-related) parameters and cardiorespiratory measures under workload. Visual analogue scales (VAS) of sedation, excitation and state anxiety were applied additionally.
Plasma levels of quazepam and its metabolites (oxoquazepam and desalkyl-oxoquazepam) were intermittendly analyzed by GC, within 24 hours after actual blood sampling in the morning of assessment days, to check the attainment of the intended criterion for termination of medication (steady-state, "on-line kinetic procedure"). Adverse effects were recorded by subjects' written free recall and a symptom-checklist.

Although a *pharmacokinetic steady-state* could be reached in sequence for the mother-drug quazepam and its metabolites within three weeks, there was *no pharmacodynamic steady-state* at the end of this period, but a continuous impairment in oculomotor variables. Performance in the choice reaction task and the APTT showed a similar tendency, which was masked to a certain extend by learning effects. There were no signs for rebound effects within the two weeks after withdrawal. Carry-over phenomena declined after three days of withdrawal. Oculomotor parameters however showed, that an impairment - due to quazepam might persist about two weeks after withdrawal, but only on the low and clinically non-relevant level of sedation as with acute quazepam. Intradiurnal profiles showed that impairments were most accentuated in the late morning hours (10 a.m.) and decreased during daytime to a neglectable level. In general the objective level of sedation after subchronic administration of quazepam was lower than after acute or long-term administration of other well-known benzodiazepines (midazolam, bromazepam, lorazepam, diazepam, oxazepam).

Pharmacokinetic steady-state was reached for quazepam and oxoquazepam after 7 days, for desalkyl-oxoquazepam after 14 days. Two days after withdrawal plasma-concentrations of quazepam and oxoquazepam were already below respectively on the level of acute administration. At the end of the two-week withdrawal period the plasma concentration of desalkyl-oxoquazepam was on a level corresponding to that observed between acute and one week administration.

2300

Suriclone, a new anxiolytic, in the treatment of GAD.

B. Musch, Ph. Guillet

CNS Clinical Research Dept. Rhône-Poulenc-Santé. Antony. FRANCE.

In this multicenter, double-blind placebo-controlled study, the efficacy and safety of suriclone (0.2 mg tid), a new anxiolytic of the cyclopyrrolone series, were compared with those of lorazepam (1 mg tid) in 150 outpatients with Generalized Anxiety Disorder, treated by their general practitioner.

Treatment duration was four weeks.

Patients returned at weekly intervals for evaluation of efficacy parameters and adverse experiences; laboratory safety variables were measured pre- and post-treatment.

Primary efficacy variables consisted of the Hamilton anxiety Scale (HAM-A) and the Physicians' Clinical Global Impression (CGI).

In the Suriclone group, CGI showed significant improvement from baseline over the placebo group on Day 28.

The incidence and severity of side-effects were significantly lower with suriclone than with lorazepam.

In the setting of general practice, Suriclone appears to be more efficacious and better tolerated than lorazepam in patients suffering from Generalised Anxiety Disorder.

Session 354 Free Communications: Victimology

2301

Etica y Psiquiatría - Ethics and Psychiatry

Darío M. Lagos-Equipo de Asistencia Psicológica Madres de Plaza de Mayo. Argentina.

Durante los últimos años se han producido en la Argentina diversas situaciones que han conmovido el cuerpo social y algunas más particularmente a la comunidad profesional psicoterapeútica. Entre 1976 y 1983 se implantó una dictadura que ejerció una feroz represión contra el pueblo.
Durante el gobierno constitucional posterior a la misma sólo fueron condenados los miembros de las tres primeras juntas militares, quedando impunes la inmensa mayoría de los crímenes cometidos.
Las gravísimas violaciones a los derechos humanos, así como la impunidad actual han producido efectos psicosociales a corto y largo plazo, con implicancias ético-políticas y ético-profesionales.
Me interesa analizar problemas relacionados con hechos tales como el proceso de restitución a sus familias de hijos de detenidos-desaparecidos, a la posibilidad del ejercicio legal de la profesión médica por parte de profesionales de reconocida participación en la represión, en la tortura y en el secuestro de niños nacidos en cautiverio bajo el regimen militar o a la demanda de asistencia psicológica en centros asistenciales públicos y privados de personas vinculadas de una u otra manera a la represión.
Las situaciones esbozadas no son meras abstracciones, sino que nos ubican a los psicoterapeutas ante problemas concretos que nos demandan respuestas también concretas. Planteando una problemática de índole ética que afecta de manera directa la práctica clínica, problemática sobre la cual me propongo reflexionar.

2302

TORTURE ON PRISONERS AND PTSD

Şahika Yüksel, M.D., Psychiatry, Assis.Prof.
Faculty of Medicine, University of Istanbul
Murat Paker, M.D., Prison of Tekirdağ
Özgün Paker, M.D., State Hospital of Tekirdağ

Nowadays the risk of development of PTSD after torture is being discussed. Our aim was to investigate the relationship between torture experiences of prisoners and their psychological consequences. We did this research in the Prison of Tekirdağ. Our research group was set up of 250 non-political prisoners (230 male, 20 female). The range of age was 18 to 60. We took the prisoners who had lived in a prison at least six months to the research group.
We used a specific and semi-structured interview form which consists of the following sub-sections:
1. Sociological characteristics, 2. Crime and punishment characteristics, 3. Characteristics of prison life, 4. Medical examination.
In addition, each prisoner filled in the form of SCL-90. Finally, we interviewed with prisoners in order to evaluate PTSD using the diagnostic criteria of DSM-111-R.
We tried to examine the following variables:
1. Torture, 2. Solidary confinement, 3. Duration of prison life, 4. Interaction effects of variables mentioned above, 5. Gender differences, 6. Types of crimes.
We discuss both PTSD in traumatized prisoners and general psychological profile of prisoners directly, and the prison as an establishment indirectly.

2303

SEXUAL TORTURE AND INFLICTED HEAD - INJURY - RELATION TO MENTAL AFTER-EFFECTS
Jiørgen Ortmann and Inge Lunde
ETICA, Treatment Center Borgergade 40,
Copenhagen, Denmark

The study comprises 148 torture victims and is a part of a more embracing study. The aim was to clarify a possible relation between 2 selected methods of torture and the mental after-effects. Sexual torture was selected, because this method was suggested to be deeply destructive, and the inflicted head-injury too: provoking fear of loss of sexual ability, fertility and intelligence. The sample was examined physically and mentally. All fullfilled the criteria of posttraumatic stress disorder, DSM III-R. The most frequent mental symptoms were sleep-distrubances, nightmares, impaired memory, inability to concentrate, anxiety, depression, changed identity, low self-esteem and sexual disturbances. 68% had been exposed to sexual torture, 62% to head-injury. Anxiety and sexual disturbances were significantly more frequent in victims, exposed to sexual torture($p=0,006$ and $0,012$ respectively) The victims exposed to inflicted head-injury suffered significantly more frequent of impaired memory, inability to concentrate and low self-esteem ($p=0,02$, $0,016$ and $0,014$ respectively). The possible pathogenesis is discussed. From treatment results so far, the mental disturbances appear reversible through psychotherapy, but follow-up studies are necessary to certify the preliminary results.

2304

TRANSEXUALITY AND VIOLENT BEHAVIOUR IN CLOSED INSTITUTIONS: VICTIMOLOGICAL OBSERVATIONS.
PITTALIS A., LORETTU L., SANNA MN., NIVOLI GC.
CLINICA PSICHIATRICA - UNIVERISITA' DI SASSARI - ITALY

The authors describe 126 acts of physical violence on the self and on others suffered by 47 transexuals held in prisons in Sardinia (Italy). After a bibliographic review of the psychiatric and victimilogical aspects of primary transexualism ("empty depression", schizoid or obsessive behaviour, symbiotic interpersonal relations, relatioships of dependancy, frequent "acting out",etc.) and of secondary transexualism ("passive effeminate" and "drag queen" roles, paranoid personalities, etc.), the authors show specific psychical dynamics which can take place between transexuals and prison officiers and between transexuals and other male prisoners. In particular the behaviour of prison officers is emphasized; this is based on the role of exploitation of the transexual as prostitute, or on the rigid and authoritarian imposition on the transexual as prostitute, or on the rigid and authoritarian imposition on the transexual of a male role, or on the exploitation of the transexual as a mysterious sexual object. The behaviour of prisoners towards the transexual, most often linked to violent acts, is described in the relations of "lover-lover","son-mother", "prostitute-client","man-maid", etc. On the basis of the typologies discussed, the authors show the dynamics of violence (anticonservative acts, autolesionism, attempted homicides, bodily harm, etc.) and illustrate preventative aspects.

2305

VICTIMILOGY OF THE MENTALLY DEFICIENT INMATE IN CLOSED INSTITUTIONS.
SANNA MN., LORETTU L., PITTALIS A., CORGIOLU T., NIVOLI GC.
CLINICA PSICHIATRICA UNIVERSITA' DI SASSARI - ITALY

The authors have made a clinical study of the victimological behaviour of 85 inmates suffering from varying degrees of mental deficiency in prison mental hospital and jails. It is emphasised that victimilogical behaviour is influenced not only by psychical characteristics of the subject(incapacity to judge, incapacity to evaluate the consequence of one's own actions, tendency to obtain immediate pleasures, suggestibility, etc.), but also by the type of psychiatric institution in which the study was made (Psychiatric Hospital, Prison Mental Hospital, maximum, medium or minimum security prisons). The authors propose, by means of an exemplification with clinical cases, a typology of the roles which may be taken on by the mentally deficient inmate within closed institutions:1)the "scapegoat" for the aggressive tension of others; 2)as a means of discharging others' sexual anxieties; 3)object of abuse; 4)involuntary role of delator; 5)symbol of the worst aspect of mental illness; 6)complementary role to other psychopathologies. The authors suggest preventative measures which can lead to a reduction of victimological damage to the mentally deficient inmate in closed institutions.

2306

HOMOSEXUALITY AND VIOLENT BEHAVIOUR IN CLOSED INSTITUTIONS
Sanna M.N., Naitana M.L., Lorettu L., Pittalis A. Nivoli G.C.
Clinica Psichiatrica Universita' Sassari, Italy

The authors describe 420 cases of physical violence (self-injury attempted homicide, personal lesions, assault), the victims of which were homosexual prisoners. Numerous dynamics are emphasized regarding violent behaviour linked to the problem of homosexuality amongst male prisoners in closed institutions. In particular, the authors show: 1) various forms of homosexual panic; 2) violent reaction to homosexuality; 3) physical conquest of the sexual relationship; 4) conflicts within homosexual couples; 5) abuse of the passive homosexual and his reaction; 6) the function of "scapegoat" of homosexuality; 7) symbolic and dangerous roles linked to the figure of the passive and active homosexual. The authors relate the above dynamics to the type violent acts, stressing the psychological and psychiatric effects and illustrating preventive and therapeutic aspects.

2307

The long term impact of sexual and physical abuse on mental health

P.E. Mullen, S.E. Romans-Clarkson, V.A. Walton, G.P. Herbison

University of Otago Medical School

The level of psychiatric symptomatology was assessed using the General Health Questionnaire and the Present State Examination in a random community sample of women. Subsequently it was ascertained which of the women had been the victims of sexual or physical abuse either during childhood or adult life. Those with a history of previous abuse were significantly more likely to have raised scores on both measures of psychopathology and to be identified as psychiatric cases. For example, 20% of women exposed to sexual abuse during childhood were identified as having psychiatric disorders, predominantly depressive in type, as compared with 6.3% of the non-abused population. Significant increases in psychopathology were also found in those sexually abused in adult life. These findings demonstrate that the deleterious effects of abuse on mental health can continue to contribute to psychiatric morbidity for many years.

2308

VIOLACION A LOS DERECHOS FUNDAMENTALES, REPARACION PSICOLOGICA INDIVIDUAL Y SOCIAL.

Dr. Consuelo Macchiavello, Dr. Angelica Monreal, Dr. Elisa Neuman. Programa Medico Psiquiatrico.

Reflexion a partir de nuestra práctica terapéutica con personas vulneradas en sue Derechos Humanos, donde hamos acogido procesos de aflicción y sufrimiento ligados a experiencias de destruccion, pérdidas y duelos.
Estas experiencias limites muestran en toda su dimensión la estrecha articulatión entre padecimiento subjectivo y daho social, y en las actuales condiciones las dificultades para la elaboración de un duelo normal, los mecanismos de defensa utilizados en estas situaciones y sus consécuencias perturbadoras tanto en lo subjectivo individual como en la sociedad toda.
Por último planteamos en una aproximación al tema de la reparación psicológica, ciertas tareas futuras ineludibles: el esclarecimiento de los hechos represivos, la discriminación de las responsabilidades en estos hechos, la resignificatión de êstos en un contexto social amplio, la busqueda de la justicia como función doblemente reparatoria, tanto para los afectados como para la sociedad y sus instituciones, en la reconstrucción de la identidad colectiva.

Session 355
Literature. Music

Video:

2309

"EL PAQUETE"

PROF.DR.MIGUEL ANGEL MATERAZZI
HOSPITAL NACIONAL JOSE T.BORDA
CENTRO DE INVESTIGACION MEDICO PSICOLOGICA DE LA COMUNICACION.

En base a experiencias vividas por el autor a nivel institucional y social del "Metie" Psiquiátrico, se visualiza a través del Corte Transversal en un momento de la historia de un ser humano, mecanismos que los conducen a un replanteo profundo de su existencia.
El relato está planteado en términos de Literatura de anticipo a través de una forma de expresión subrealista.

2310

MUSIC AND HUMAN DYNAMICS

Jules H. Masserman, M.D.

Co-Chairman Emeritus, Psychiatry and Neurology
Northwestern University, Chicago, USA

In this 40 minute color and sound videotape Dr. Masserman illustrates verbally and by passages on a violin how human beings react empathetically and therapeutically to musical themes ranging from a lullaby through a child's play ditty, a school song, a dance tune, a love song, a patriotic air, a military march, a funeral dirge, or finally to a religious threnody promising peace and immortality -- all with therapeutic implications.

**Tuesday
17th October 1989**

Session 356 — Plenary: Clinical and pathogenetic aspects of affective and related disorders

2311
INTERFACE OF PERSONALITY AND AFFECTIVE ILLNESS

Hagop S. Akiskal, M. D., University of Tennessee, Memphis, U.S.A.

In recurrent affective illness, symptoms and traits are not easily distinguished, and the impracticality of prospective studies further complicates matters. Psychodynamic theory has long traced the personality of the affectively ill to developmental vicissitudes and has assigned them a predisposing role in the origin of affective episodes; other theories have emphasized cognitive factors involving negative evaluation of the self and the world. The emerging data from systematic studies is more in favor of the reverse position, namely that personality disturbances, initially of a short term nature - but in a third of cases more enduring- arise as post-morbid sequelae of disabling affective episodes; such sequelae include the controversial category of "borderline." Other considerations suggest that traits might pathoplastically color the clinical form of the illness (e.g., neurotic vs endogenous). Finally, new data have partly upheld the classical position that derives recurrent - especially bipolar - disorders from subaffective temperaments such as the depressive, the hyperthymic and the cyclothymic. Reviewing current research conducted in Memphis, Oregon, at NIMH, Zurich and Pisa, the author attempts to integrate these seemingly contradictory positions in a multifactorial conceptualization of mood disorders.

2312
OBJECT LOSS IN DEPRESSION

Daniel WIDLÖCHER
Department of Psychiatry
Hôpital de la Salpêtrière
Paris (France)

The role of actual loss of love objects in the genesis of depression has largely been supported by epidemiological studies of life events. However, this approach leaves several questions unanswered, such as the distinction between normal mourning and depressive reactions, the existence of psychomotor retardation, which is the target of antidepressive pharmacotherapy, and finally the pertinence of the learned helplessness model. This paper suggests that the main role played by the subjective of loss, whatever its origin, is an inability to actualize plan of action concerning the lost object (either person or situation) or to experience reward or incentive for thinking about that object. This hypothesis takes into account the above-mentioned objections, in particular that concerning psychomotor retardation, and has implications for treatment management, especially psychotherapy.

2313
CHILDREN OF ALCOHOLICS

Ann Pytkowicz Streissguth, Ph.D., Professor Department of Psychiatry & Behavioral Sciences, University of Washington, Seattle, Washington, U.S.A.

Children of alcoholics are at risk for several types of psychopathology. These include alcohol abuse, conduct disorders, attentional deficits, depression and fetal alcohol effects in the case of women abusing alcohol during pregnancy. The roots of these psychopathologies are genetic, cultural, and/or teratogenic.

The implications of these psychopathologies for psychiatryu will be discussed.

2314
COMORBIDITY BETWEEN ANXIETY AND MOOD DISORDERS

Cassano G.B., Perugi G., Musetti L., Savino M.
Second Chair of Psychiatric Clinic, University of Pisa. Pisa, ITALY
The comorbidity between anxiety and mood disorders has been widely documented at the level of family, clinical and pharmacotherapeutic findings. The presence of concomitant disorders poses nosological, psychopathological and theoretical dilemmas. Most diagnostic systems make use of exclusion criteria which specify that certain diagnoses are not permitted in the presence of another disorder or class of disorders, but at present there is no definitive evidence for a hierarchical priority for most disorders.
We evaluated a group patients with Panic Disorder. In selecting this group, enlarged DSM-III-R criteria were used without the restraints of any hierarchical diagnostic schema.
When evaluated without such a hierarchical schema, more than 70% of patients with panic disorder tend to have additional concomitant diagnoses including generalized anxiety disorder, depression, hypochondria, social phobia, depersonalization-derealization and obsessive-compulsive disorder.
The study of co-morbidity phenomena in this area of psychopathology has brought the panic-derealization-phobic syndrome into a central position linking mood and neurotic disorders with the temporal lobe syndrome.
Diagnostic criteria which exclude the possibility of an anxiety disorder in the presence of mood or other disorders lead to a loss of information which could be important in understanding the relationships between various syndromal entities. On the other hand, approaches that encourage the adoption of multiple diagnoses give rise to justified criticism. Nevertheless, in the light of theoretical and practical considerations the use of discrete multiple diagnostic categories appears to offer the best solution.

2315
THE INTERFACE BETWEEN ANXIETY & DEPRESSIVE DISORDERS & ORGANIC STATES
Sir Martin Roth
University of Cambridge Clinical School

The lecture is not intended to discuss the many recent advances made in attempts to define the biological origins of anxiety and affective disorders. Considerable progress has been made in these endeavours but no conclusive theories regarding causation of either group of conditions has emerged; the single gene that causes bi-polar disorder in some rare families and its tentative mapping to specific loci is an important advance. But pathophysiology in both these groups of conditions remains obscure in most respects. It is intended to focus instead on that group of syndromes in the borderlands of these disorders in which the anxiety and affective disorders respectively are associated with cerebral or extra-cerebral disease. The syndromes associated with definite lesions in the temporal lobes overlap with phenomena of the more severe anxiety disorders as for example the panic-agoraphobic states. And affective disorders in every part of the life span have been found to be associated with physical disease at a frequency beyond chance expectation. The complex implications of these phenomena for aetiology of conditions that were only recently called "functional" will be discussed.

Session 357 Plenary:
Conceptual and transcultural issues in psychiatry

2316
NECESSITY OF ETHNOPSYCHIATRIC STUDY IN GENERAL PSYCHIATRY PRACTICE

PELICIER Yves - HOPITAL NECKER -
Sce de Psychiatrie - 149 rue de
Sèvres - 75743 PARIS CEDEX 15
Faculté de Médecine - Paris -

Ethnopsychiatry is not a simple formulation of psychiatry valuable in specific areas. Migrations, changing work, age, sex, etc. induce deep modifications both in healthy or altered psychism. Ethnopsychiatric training is a method to assume the difference and the alterity without restricting the quality of interpersonnal relation. It is mainly an other approach of identity problem for patient and psychiatrist also.

2317
The concept of mental illness from pharaonic times to present day Islam
Professor A. Okasha

Department of Psychiatry-Ain Shams University
Cairo, Egypt

No known physician's title in the pharaonic times suggests specialization in mental illness although psychic and mental symptoms are mentioned in many clinical observations. The heart and mind were synonymous and the aetiology of mental illness was attributed to cardiovascular and uterine causes long before Hippocrates, only in few conditions spiritual aetiology was alleged. The therapeutic approach was physical rather than mystical. The concept of mental illness in Islam is nonspecific. The word Mad is only mentioned in the Koran to ascribe what people felt about prophets. The psyche (ALNAFS) was mentioned 185 times in the Koran as a broad meaning to the human existence as a body, behavior, affect,e.g. the accusing, secure, inspired, fulfilled and fulfilling and temting sin Nafs. If we take the meaning concretely, mental illness can be attributed to posession by Djenne or evil spirits, magic or envy but if we explain it abstractly,it means alienation or disharmony because of an aborted Sofi experience or foreign body existence with extreme solitude and detachment from the wholeness (painful atheism).
Evaluation of these concepts and its present relevance will be discussed.

2318
PSYCHOANALYTIC THEORY AND PRACTICE IN THE ORIENTAL CULTURAL CONTEXT

Nishizono, M., M. D.
Department of Psychiatry
Fukuoka University, School of Medicine, Japan

Psychoanalysis, which was established at the end of the 19th century in Vienna, had a great impact on many countries not only as a treatment method but also as a way to understand mental disorders. However, psychoanlysis as a treatment had developed only in some limited culture. It seems to be related to the aim of psychoanalytic therapy to attempt a formation of individual self by promoting self-understanding through remembering the past.

Before the World War II in Oriental countries, psychoanalysis was practiced only as an exception because each culture insisted on its own self formation pattern.

After the World War II, however, Japan, Korea, and Hong Kong became interested in psychoanalytic therapy and started to practice it. It was deeply related to economic, social, and cultural change in each country. When remembering the past is taken in a treatment in such countries, here and now is emphasized more than there and then. Though it is a common trend in modern psychoanalysis, it is more remarkable in Oriental countires. I guess it is because of influence of characteristics of each culture.

2319

NORMALITY AND THE BOUNDARIES OF PSYCHIATRY
Sabshin Melvin, American Psychiatric Association
In this paper the author explores the reasons for the relative neglect of empirical studies on normal behavior by psychiatrists. Deleterious consequences of this neglect have become more obvious in recent years in the context advances in psychiatric nosology and also in the context of social and economic pressures exerted upon psychiatrists to define the boundaries between mental illness and mental health more precisely. In previous papers, the author has proposed the use of multi-axial studies in the process of elucidating the boundaries between normal behavior and mental illness. These proposals will be reviewed briefly in this presentation along with examples of other empirically based methods to deal with the complexity of boundary problems. It is recognized that much careful work is required but the need to address the conceptual, epistemological, and clinical aspects of the boundaries between mental illness and health is so great that the efforts must be made. In the United States, these issues have become accentuated because of questions of reimbursement for psychiatric treatment and some of these questions will also be discussed in the paper. Psychiatrists have special skills in adding to an understanding of normal behavior. While empirical studies of normality are indeed a multidisciplinary effort, the special knowledge of psychopathology by psychiatrists can provide a necessary perspective to the multidisciplinary studies. The author looks forward to a time when future nosological systems can include the best available empirical basis for drawing the boundaries between illness and health. This paper is a contribution to that process.

Session 358 Symposium:
Quality-of-life research in psychiatry

2320

DIAGNOSTIC IMPLICATIONS OF QUALITY OF LIFE MEASUREMENTS IN CLINICAL PSYCHIATRY
Per Bech
Hillerød General Hospital, DK 3400 Hillerød
The activities in assessing psychiatric disability and discomfort have mainly been concerned with the dynamic structure of clinical syndromes (disability) by which progress or lack of it in response to treatment is measured. However, as a by-product of these activities the correspondence between such clinical syndromes (disability) and the halo effect of discomfort (quality of life) on the part of the patient have been analysed. The patient's quality of life, as it relates to his or her mental health, can be seen as the distance between the patient and his/her ideal position, i.e. before any manifestations of the illness (disability).
Results from a cross-national collaborative panic study have shown that patients with anxiety states have a basic quality of life disorder.
From a psychometric point of view patients with schizothymia have by their narcissistic anhedonia ontological uncertainties about the existence of goodness in life. This basic personality (ego) pathology in schizothymia might be masked by structured clinical interviews. The cognitive disorganization requires an unstructured interview to be identified and measured.

2321

DESCRIPTION OF THE QUALITY OF LIFE

Professor John E. Cooper
University of Nottingham, U.K.

In many psychiatric patients, even when symptoms, diagnosis, social disability and problems have been described, the total effect upon their life and personal experience is not completely described. It is suggested that much of what is missing can be subsumed under the concept of "Quality of Life", and approaches to the description of this will be discussed. A new 3-part framework of ideas is suggested as a simple but comprehensive way of organising its description; the three parts refer to continuity with the past, satisfaction with the present, and planning for the future.

2322

The Impact of Burden of Care on Judgements of Function and Disability in Schizophrenia
Professor Gordon Parker, School of Psychiatry, The University of New South Wales, Prince of Wales Hospital, Randwick 2031, NSW Australia.

The development of the Life Skills Profile, a measure of function and disability in those with schizophrenia, will be briefly reviewed. We demonstrate its high reliability when completed by professional staff or by residential care managers. Its lower reliability when completed by family members is demonstrated to reflect a burden of care bias. A number of validity studies will be reviewed. Its impressive properties suggest its utility in profiling services and patients and in assessing key variables effecting quality of life in those with schizophrenia.

2323
Sucidial Behavior and Panic Disorder

Myrna M. Weissman, Ph.D.
Columbia University, College of Physicians & Surgeons; New York State Psychiatric Institute
722 West 168th Street, New York, NY 10032, U.S.A.

This paper will present data on suicidal ideation and attempts associated with panic disorder drawn from an epidemiologic study of over 18,000 adults living in the U.S. The major finding is that panic disorder as compared to other psychiatric disorders is associated with an increased risk of suicidal thought and attempts. These findings are consistent with independent reports of follow up clinic samples showing increased mortality in patients with panic disorder due to suicide.

2324
A QUALITY OF LIFE STUDY IN SOUTH MANCHESTER COMMUNITY FACILITIES

C.E.Hyde, Withington Hospital, Manchester, England
C.J.Simpson, Friarage Hospital, Northallerton
E.B.Faragher, Withington Hospital

The quality of life of chronic mentally ill persons in District General Hospital acute wards, a community based hostel ward and group homes was compared. Within this spectrum of care those with the most disabilities and impairments were on the DGH wards while those with least were in the group homes. There was an overall tendency for QOL to be better in group homes with higher levels of global well being, subjective satisfaction with the living situation, total social contacts, better finances and comfort. For the chronically mentally ill on DGH wards the situation was less impressive, with the highest levels of victimisation, although there were higher levels of social cohesion, objective leisure, subjective satisfaction with the living situation and mental care. The hostel ward residents seemed to occupy an intermediate position, their environment is socially cohesive, comfortable, has a high level of total social contacts and appears to be the safest yet they are disadvantaged financially as they remain officially hospital patients. Controlling for levels of psychopathology has some effects on the initial QOL scores in that apparently significant differences favouring the group home sample for subjective health, social relations and social contacts outside the facility were lost.

2325
MULTIAXIAL CLASSIFICATION IN MENTAL HANDICAP

B Sacks et al. Charing Cross Hospital, London, England.

A system of classification for use in mental handicap should be multiaxial in structure for several reasons i.a. 1. The high incidence of multiple handicaps. 2. Biological, psychiatric, functional and psycho-social factors may all play equally important parts.

Seven axes would cover the items needed for a comprehensive system. Individual axes could be used in various combinations.

1. Life context and service contact.
2. Cognitive Level.
3. Developmental Disorders. Impairments of language, neuromuscular function etc.
4. Physical Illness - as in the general I.C.D.
5. Psychiatric/Behavioural Disorders. Including the diagnoses that appear in the I.C.D. category F.
6. Psycho-social Factors - family structure, vocation, living conditions and other environmental factors.
7. Functional/Adaptation - self-help and social skills and functioning.

The suggested axes are largely based on existing sections in the proposed I.C.D.10 and on existing measuring instruments of function with suitable modification for use in the handicapped.

Session 359 Symposium:
Phospholipid metabolism in schizophrenia

2326
ESSENTIAL FATTY ACIDS (EFAS), PROSTAGLANDINS (PGS) AND SCHIZOPHRENIA (SP)

David F. Horrobin, Efamol Research Institute, POB 818, Kentville, NS B4N 4H8, Canada

EFAs make up 20% of brain dry wt. They are required for membrane structure and modulate membrane-bound enzymes and receptors. EFAs are precursors of PGS which influence nerve conduction and transmitter function. The EFA/PG system is involved in pain & inflammation which may be relevant to pain resistance and rarity of rh arthritis in SP. Blood samples were collected from SP patients and controls in five countries including Japan. In every centre SPs showed abnormalities of plasma phospholipid (PL) EFAs, the most consistent being a lowering of linoleic acid. Samples of frontal and cerebellar cortex were also obtained from SPs and controls post mortem. There were no abnormalities in SP cerebellum, ruling out a general effect of anti-SP drugs. However, in frontal cortex P-ethanolamine, the PL fraction richest in EFAs, SPs had significantly low 18 and 20 carbon EFAs, with elevated 22 carbon EFAs. This suggests abnormal EFA metabolism in SP cerebral cortex.
A double-blind, placebo-controlled, 8 month cross-over trial was performed in 39 SPs with tardive dyskinesia (TD). EFAs produced minor but clinically unimportant improvement in TD. EFA-treated patients improved sig more than placebo patients on the overall and schizophrenia sub-scale of the CPRS, and also improved sig on Wechsler memory scores. EFAs offer a new safe approach to SP therapy.

2327
PHOSPHATIDYLCHOLINE CONTENT IN BLOOD CELLS OF SCHIZOPHRENICS

R. Hitzemann, J. Hirschowitz, F. Henn, J. Rotrosen, B. Angrist, A. Wolkin
Dept. Psychiatry, SUNY at Stony Brook, NY; Psychiatry Service, VAMC, NY; Dept. Psychiatry, NY University, USA

There is now a significant body of evidence to support the view that the underlying pathology of the psychoses results, at least in part, from abnormalities in membrane dynamics. Psychotic patients have functional membrane abnormalities in such diverse activities as ion transport, phospholipid metilation, hormone stimulated adenyl cyclase and drug and neurotransmitter receptor binding. We argue that such abnormalities result from deficits in membrane dynamics and are sufficiently generalized to be detected in a wide variety of tissues, including the formed blood elements. Our interest has focused on the membrane phospholipids, particularly the erythrocyte membrane phospholipids and on the dynamic properties (order) of such membranes. Twelve studies from seven different laboratories, including our own, have examined the phospholipid content in a total of 334 schizophrenics and 242 normal controls. The most commonly observed abnormality (8 of 12 studies) has been a decrement of membrane phosphatidylcholine (PC) content. In 7 of 12 studies, a significant increase in phosphatidylserine was observed. The decrement in PC appears to be associated with a significant decrease in membrane phospholipid methylation. It has also been shown that there is a significant and strong correlation between the decrement in PC content and a increase in membrane order. These data will be discussed in light of current studies and recent advances in this area.

2328
ARACHIDONIC ACID AND PHOSPHOLIPIDS IN PSYCHIATRIC PATIENTS

Lothar Demisch, Dept. of Psychiatry, Hospital of the University, D-6000 Frankfurt FRG.

These studies were designed in order to elucidate alterations in membranal functions with respect to lipid regulators such as arachidonic acid (AA) by using blood platelets as cellular model systems. AA and the oxygenated metabolits of this unsatu- rated fatty acid are involved in membrane function and transmembranal receptor-effector signal transductions. The study sample consisted of unmedicated (>6months) patients (N=41) diagnosed according to DSM III and healthy controls (N=32). The total amount of different phospholipids (PL) and the distribution of ^{14}C-AA incorporated into PL was measured. Platelets from patients with a schizophreniform or schizoaffective disorder contained twice as much phosphatidylinositol (PI) compared to the controls. A significantly reduced amount (40-80% decrease) of ^{14}C-AA incorporated into PLs (PI>PS,PC,PE) was measured in platelets from these patients and patients with a major depression. No significant effects were measured with respect to patients with an schizophrenic disorder. The results point to an altered AA-PI and, to a lesser degree, of AA-PC metabolism in patients with phasic psychosis or a first manifestation of a psychotic episode.

2329
EVIDENCE FOR PROSTAGLANDIN E_1 HYPOTHESIS OF SCHIZOPHRENIA

Kaiya, H.

Department of Neurology and Psychiatry, Gifu University School of Medicine, Gifu/Japan.

We are of opinion that prostaglandin E_1 (PGE_1) is deficient in schizophrenia, and PGE_1 deficiency causes PGE_1 hyposensitivity. Platelet is a good probe for studying neurochemical abnormalities in psychiatric disorders, because it has biochemical characteristics resembling those of neurons. Platelet PGE_1 receptor is coupled to the cAMP generating system, i.e., PGE_1 receptor = GTP-binding proteins = adenylate cyclase linkage. Activation of the receptor on platelet by PGE_1 results in increased formation of cAMP, that causes inhibition of platelet aggregation response(PAR). We demonstrate PGE_1 hyposensitivity in schizophrenia by showing significantly decreased PGE_1- and forskolin-stimulated cAMP formation in platelet and lowered inhibitory effects of PGE_1 on PAR in schizophrenics.

2330
INCREASED PHOSPHOLIPASE A2 ACTIVITY IN SCHIZOPHRENIA

W. F. Gattaz, T. J. Nevalainen, P. K. J. Kinnunen
Central Institute of Mental Health Mannheim, F R G

Phospholipase A2 (PLA2) is a key enzyme in the metabolism of phospholipids. Because a disordered phospholipid metabolism has frequently been reported in schizophrenia we investigated the PLA2 activity in serum from 14 drug-free paranoid schizophrenics, 20 healthy controls and 8 nonschizophrenic psychiatric patients. Schizophrenics showed significantly higher PLA2 activity than controls and nonschizophrenics ($p < 0.001$). The increment in schizophrenics was not due to increased concentration of pancreatic secretory PLA2, as concerning the latter no differences were found between the 3 proband groups. The present findings confirm the results of our previous study and suggest that increased serum PLA2 activity might reflect an increment of the intracellular enzyme activity in schizophrenia. In the brain the activation of intracellular PLA2 results in changes in neuronal activity due to alterations in receptor sensitivity and in neurotransmitter metabolism. The possibility that such PLA2-induced mechanisms are involved in the etiopathogeny of schizophrenia warrants further experimental clarification.

2331
ACCELERATED BREAKDOWN OF MEMBRANE PHOSPHOLIPIDS IN THE FRONTAL LOBE OF SCHIZOPHRENICS: A IN VIVO 31P NMR SPECTROSCOPY STUDY

M. Keshavan, J. Pettegrew, K. Panchalingam, D. Kaplan, J. Brar, K. Kambhampti

Western Psychiatric Institute and Clinic, Pittsburgh, USA

31P NMR spectroscopy provides an in vivo noninvasive measure of the phosphomonoester (PME) and phosphodiester (PDE) resonances which arise mainly from the precursors and breakdown products of membrane phospholipids.

Eight neuroleptic naive patients with a first episode of DSM III schizophrenia or schizophreniform disorder and 8 age-matched normal volunteers were studied with 31P NMR spectroscopy of the prefrontal cortex. The schizophrenic patients were also studied after 3-4 weeks of neuroleptic treatment. The following alterations were observed: 1.Decreased levels of PME at entry (p=0.02) which were further decreased after 4 weeks of neuroleptics (p=0.05); 2.Increased levels of PDE at entry (p=0.01) and after treatment with neuroleptics (n.s.). These findings suggest that schizophrenia may be associated with accelerated breakdown of membrane phospholipids that could lead to alterations in membrane bound receptors, channels and second messenger mediated events.

Session 360 Symposium:
Alzheimer's disease: Zinc and other metals in its pathogenesis

2332
ALZHEIMER'S DISEASE : PRIMITIVE CORTICAL DEGENERATION PRODUCING SECONDARILY SUBCORTICAL DISTURBANCES
R. Guntern, C. Bouras & J. Constantinidis
University of Geneva, "Morphological Psychopathology"
Bel-Air, 1225 Geneva, Switzerland

The "Primum Movens" in AD is Amyloid (AM) formation in the cortex inducing neighbouring peri-AM neuritic alterations (Paired Helical Filaments) and distant neuronal body lesions (Neurofibrillary Tangles), for ex. in the Acetylcholine (ACh) neurons of the Basal Nucleus (BN) and in the Noradrenalin-neurons of the Locus Coeruleus.

In an early stage, the AM induces zinc deficiency (observed in the hippocampus) and therefore a deficiency of the zinc enzyme Glutamate - Dehydrogenase results in an excess of GLU, excitotoxicity and neuronal death . So in advanced stages cortical GLU decreases and there is deficiency of the excitatory cortico-subcortical GLU pathways, leading to hypo-activity of the substance P (SP) striato-palllido nigral pathway and of the Somatostatine (SOM) in the BN.

These SP and SOM hypoactivities are morphologically observed in these nuclei as quantitative increase of SP and SOM because of the low synaptic release and the resulting excess of presynaptic storage.

The hypoactivity of the excitatory SP in the S. Nigra may induce a nigro striatal Dopamine hypoactivity (slight extra pyramidal symptoms).

SOM is excitatory of the BN ACh neurons ; its hypoactivity may contribute to the ACh baso-cortical deficiency.

2333
ALZHEIMER'S DISEASE : THE TIMING FROM AMYLOID TO TANGLE
J. Richard, P. Bovier & J. Constantinidis
University of Geneva,"Morphological Psychopathology"
Bel-Air, 1225 Geneva, Switzerland

Primitive cortical Amyloid (AM) inducing secondarily Neurofibrillary Tangles (NFT).
The timing between :
1) Amyloid (AM)-Senile Plaque (SP) formation,
2) peri-AM Paired-Hellical Filaments (PHF) induction and
3) distant neuronal body Neurofribrillary Tangle (NFT) production may be appreciated by the study we realized in Geneva concerning the **length of survival after the onset of Amnesia**,

	Group A SP without neuronal body NFT	Group B SP with NFT only in the hippocampus	Significance
Number of cases	79	83	
Incidence of Amnesia (%)	73,33	97,43	p< 0,001
Survival after the onset of Amnesia (months)	14,69 ±12,30	51,46 ±15,11	p< 0,001

In the group A, 1/4 of cases do not present Amnesia, probably those with **Asymptomatic AM, without neuritic alterations**, and 3/4 are Amnesic, probably those in which the cortical AM induced **neighbouring neuritic alterations** (PHF). An average survival of **14 months** should be necessary for the production of peri-AM-PHF.
Practically, all cases of group B with NFT in the hippocampus are Amnesic. An average survival of **51 months** should be necessary for the AM induction of distant neuronal body NFT.
Prevent AM of producing PHF-NFT should mean prevention of clinical symptoms.

2334
ALZHEIMER'S DISEASE : THE ZINC HYPOTHESIS
J. Constantinidis
University of Geneva, "Morphological Psychopathology"
Bel-Air, 1225 Geneva, Switzerland

In Alzheimer's dementia (AD), the Primum Movens is **Amyloid** (AM) production on precapillaries: Dyshoric Angiopathy, and capillaries : Senile Plaques (SP).
Cerebral AM alone may be **asymptomatic**. Clinical symptoms (Amnesia, Instrumental Disorders) appear when AM induces neighbouring neuritic alterations : Paired Hellical Filaments (PHF) and Distant neuronal body lesions : Neurofibrillary Tangles (NFT).
The Amyloid induces zinc deficiency which produces the tangles.
In AD cerebral **zinc decreases** particularly in the hippocampus.Without AM, NFT are produced by **metalotoxicity** and therefore brain **zinc displacement**
- by **lead** : Encephalopatia **saturnica**
- by **calcium** deficiency - **Guam** Encephalopathy
- by **aluminium**
- by Blood-Brain-Barrier (BBB) disturbances leading probably to an abnormal entry of metals in the brain (Dementia **Pugilistica, viral** encephalitides). NFT may be produced by deficiency of the following zinc enzymes:
1) those of DNA metabolism inducing abnormal DNA and therefore **abnormal protein synthesis** : PHF-NFT
2) those of neuronal detoxication : SOD, Carbonic Anhydrase, Lactate-Dehydrogenase leading to neuronal toxicity particularly in the hippocampus normally rich in SOD,
3) of Glutamate-Dehydrogenase resulting in an **excitotoxic** increase of Glutamate.
Therapeutic implication : a comestible zinc complex crossing the BBB should be useful.

2335

ZINC DEFICIENCY AND ALZHEIMER'S DISEASE - A NEW APPROACH
Ch. Nachev [1], P. Bonchev [2], G. Kirov [3], K. Kissiova [4], A. Goudev [1]
[1] Clinic of Cardiology, Medical Academy, Sofia, Bulgaria
[2] Faculty of Chemistry, University of Sofia, Bulgaria
[3] Worlingahm Park Hospital, Surrey, Great Britain
[4] Clinic of Psychiatry, Medical Academy, Sofia, Bulgaria

Zinc deficiency in regions of the brain which are damaged in Alzheimer's Disease, seems proven. The reason for this deficiency and the consequence of the morphological changes are still under discussion.
According to Nachev's hypothesis about the critical role of apometallothioneins in zinc homoeostasis and their role in the pathogenesis of various diseases, it is possible to conjecture the same mecanism in the earlier stages of Alzheimer's disease.
The high level of corticoid receptors in the hippocampal neurons could allow a moderate hypersecretion of cortisol (as inconditions of chronic stress), to lead to high levels of apometallothioneins and sequestation of operative zinc in neurons of this part of the brain. The local deficiency of zinc, either by impending the NGF, or by inhibiting zinc-dependent enzymes, could lead to neuronal death and morphological chages, typical of this disease.
Our therapeutic trial with zinc suplementation on 6 patients with an early onset Alzheimer's disease for 4 weeks showed a good improvement in two of them which reversed after discontinuation of treatment. Further experience with such trials is needed in order to establish the best drug and dosage of treatment.

Session 361 Symposium:
Psychophysiology in relation to psychiatry

2336

AN INFORMATION PROCESSING PERSPECTIVE ON PSYCHOPHYSIOLOGICAL MEASUREMENTS AND THEIR DEVIATIONS IN PSYCHOPATHOLOGY

M. Koukkou, Research Dept., University of Zürich, Switzerland.

Psychophysiological measurements have long been used in psychopathology. However, there is no consensus among psychophysiologists on the mechanisms which underlie these measurements, their intra- and inter-individual fluctuations and differences as well as their deviations in psychopathology.
We present a comprehensive model of these mechanisms. The model draws on an integration of well established principles of psychophysiology and is expressed in cognitive, information-processing terms. It illuminates the role of the factors which define the brain's functional states in the organization of human behaviour and of its psychophysiological measurements.
It suggests that the brain's functional states at each moment in time is multifactorially defined, can be measured with the brain's electrical activity and is continuously readjusted (functional adaptation) to the momentary significance of incoming events as estimated by the brain's information processes. The different psychophysiological measurements reflect similar functional adaptations of the organism.
This model is used to discuss some of the ways in which the factors defining the brain's functional states interact in psychopathology and lead to the deviations of the psychophysiological measurements.

2337

BRAIN MACROPOTENTIALS ASSOCIATED WITH GOAL DIRECTED PERFORMANCE IN PSYCHIATRY
Papakostopoulos D.
Burden Neurological Institute, Bristol, England

The Skilled Performance Task is a self paced, autoregulated and goal directed behaviour which allows simultaneous quantification of the subject's performance and strategy together with the related brain, autonomic and myographic activities. Planning, execution, evaluation and modification of performance are associated with specific neurophysiological signals. The Bereitschaftspotential and heart rate deceleration precede the action. The motor cortex potential and GSR activity are action linked. Finally the skilled performance positivity, late positivity and heart rate acceleration are reflecting activities related with knowledge and evaluation of the performance. Multichannel recordings and automated computer controlled collection, analysis and presentation of the results leads to the development of the subject's psychophysiological profile. Aging, Parkinson's disease, Downs syndrome, Schizophrenia and other psychiatric conditions have characteristically different profiles which are relevant both in the understanding and treatment of those conditions.

2338

EEG MAPPING AND NEUROPSYCHOLOGICAL TESTS IN SCHIZOPHRENIC SYNDROMES.
John Gruzelier, David Liddiard, Peter Dennis, Leigh James and Lillian Pusavat, Dept. Psychiatry, Charing Cross and Westminster Medical School, University of London, W6 8RF, UK.

Acute schizophrenic patients show lateral imbalances in hemispheric activity. The direction of imbalance has delineated Active and Withdrawn syndromes. Neuropsychological testing has shown a predominance of losses in the less activated hemisphere, namely the right in the Active syndrome (delusional, positive and labile affect, raised activity and hallucinations) and the left in the Withdrawn syndrome (social and emotional withdrawal, blunted affect, poverty of speech, motor retardation and hallucinations). In a preliminary study with new procedures of EEG topographical mapping (28 electrodes) ten Active syndrome patients were compared with ten normal controls during resting EEG (eyes open and closed) the Warrington recognition memory test for words and faces, and Luria's finger-thumb apposition test. Patients as predicted showed specific losses in the right hemispheric memory for faces test. This was accompanied by differences in topographical region in 18-30 Hz activity. Patients also differed in the left hand Luria task and in eyes open EEG. A replication study will be presented which included Active and Withdrawn syndromes and patients in remission. EEG during the Wisconsin Card Sort was also examined.

2339

COGNITIVE AND NEUROPHYSIOLOGICAL STUDIES IN SCHIZOPHRENIA

Tonny Andersen, Univ. of Umea, Sweden

Cognitive disturbances have been recognized as important elements of schizophrenic symptomatology ever since the first clinical definitions of the condition by Kraepelin and Bleuer. During the last two decades there has been a growing interest in cognitive functions within the behavioural sciences generally, which also has been obvious in psychiatry and in schizophrenia research. A large number of studies on cognitive dysfunction have been published and - perhaps most interesting - several comprehensive models of schizophrenia, based on cognitive theory, are presently being developed and evaluated. This study adopts a general information processing paradigm attempting to describe various important aspects of schizophrenic cognitive dysfunction and some possible neurobiological correlates. The heterogenicity of schizophrenic syndromes and the assumption that different types of cognitive dysfunction may dominate during different phases of the disease led us to focus on patients with stable residual schizophrenic conditions. We compare 22 patients with 22 matched normal controls and will present preliminary results on certain cognitive functions and some preliminary results within the neurophysiological area of cognitive ERP. Clinical implications of cognitive dysfunction and neurophysiological correlates in this patient group will be discussed.

2340

SPECT WITH [^{123}I] IMP IN THE DIFFERENTIAL DIAGNOSIS OF PSYCHIATRIC DISORDERS

R.O'Connell, R.Van Heertum, S.Billick, St.Vincent's Hospital and Medical Center of New York, New York City, USA.

Single photon emission computed tomography (SPECT) with [^{123}I] N-isopropyl iodoamphetamine-[^{123}I] IMP- was used to study regional cerebral blood flow (rCBF) in 94 psychiatric patients and six controls. Patients with dementias had distinct brain-image patterns, consistent with the expected neuropathology. Major depressives had decreased cortical and subcortical rCBF. Increased caudate rCBF was observed in schizophrenics and other psychoses with positive symptoms. SPECT is a practical method of functional brain imaging with potential in the differential diagnosis of neuropsychiatric disorders. Further studies are needed to assess the effect of other variables on brain-image patterns.

2341

EDR HABITUATION : NOSOLOGICAL, PERSONALITY AND SUBJECTIVE CORRELATES

A.D.Rabavilas, Athens University Medical School, Psychiatric Dept.,Psychophysiological Laboratory, Eginition Hospital, Athens, Greece.

This study examines the relations of EDR habituation on three different levels, (a) to disease entity,(b) to symptoms and traits and (c) to subjective (cognitive) evaluation, in patients with generalized anxiety, phobic, panic, obsessive-compulsive, dysthymic and somatoform disorders (DSM-III) and a group of normal controls. The results show that (a) patients demonstrate significantly slower habituation than controls. Within patient groups, dysthymic patients show the slowest habituation in conparison to other groups (P range from <0.05 to <0.01). The remaining groups can only be marginally differentiated. (b) Habituation is primarily dependent on the phasic component of the EDR and secondarily on state anxiety and some personality traits in both patients and normal controls. However, the contribution of habituation to the total anxiety variance clearly differentiates patients from controls.(c) 25% of the patients investigated and 35% of the controls can reliably evaluate habituation speed on visual analogue scales. High phasic EDR to normal and novel stimuli, delayed habituation, depression, trait anxiety, neuroricism and externality of locus of control appear to confound the ability to subjectively evaluate habituation. The implications of these findings to psychiatric research and practice are discussed.

Session 362 Symposium:
Sleep regulation in depression

2342

Sleep in Depression from Infancy to Old Age: A Developmental Perspective

C.F. Reynolds III, P.A. Coble, D.J. Kupfer
University of Pittsburgh

EEG sleep abnormalities in depression, such as shortened first NREM sleep period, increased early REM sleep and phasic activity, diminished slowwave sleep, and increased arousal after sleep onset, all appear to represent both illness effects per se and effects of advancing age. Thus, in comparison to healthy controls, depressed patients show an accelerated age-dependent REM sleep disinhibition, perhaps the secondary expression of an accelerated age-dependent decay in slowwave sleep and sleep continuity. The reversibility of these changes appears to be only partial (in response to sleep deprivation) and is an important unresolved issue, particularly in late life, because failure of sleep changes to become age-appropriate may signal higher risk for recurrent illness.

At the other end of the life cycle, in newborn, preliminary data suggest an increase in phasic REM activity counts in the offspring of depressive mothers. Thus, subtle sleep abnormalities may occur from early on in those at risk for depression, become more marked with advancing age (particularly after puberty), and remain abnormal in those who have been clinically ill and who remain at highest risk for recurrence.

2343

REM SLEEP ABNORMALITIES IN PRIMARY AND SECONDARY MAJOR DEPRESSIVE DISORDERS

M. Berger, D. Riemann, P. Fleckenstein, F. Hohagen
Central Institute of Mental Health, Mannheim

REM sleep desinhibition at the beginning of the night is a characteristic biological abnormality of primary depressive disorders as well of the endogenous as of the nonendogenous subtype. The occurrence of very short REM latencies (sleep onset REM periods) can be strongly increased by a cholinergic stimulus - like the orally acting agonist RS 86 - directly given before sleep onset.
Extensive own studies focused on the question whether these abnormalities are specific for primary depression, or whether they occur also in secondary depression, or even in patients with nondepressive psychiatric disorders. It could be shown that as well under baseline conditions as after cholinergic stimulation REM sleep abnormalities do not take place in patients with anxiety disorders, eating disorders, or personality disorders independent of concomitant that means secondary depression. Surprisingly, however, this was not true for patients with chronic schizophrenic spectrum disorders. They exhibited short REM latencies under baseline conditions and a strongly increased reactivity to the cholinergic stimulus. This rises some interesting questions about neurochemical similarities between primary depression and chronic psychotic/schizophrenic disorders.

2344

SLEEP, SLEEP DEPRIVATION AND DEPRESSION

R.H. Van den Hoofdakker, Department of Biological Psychiatry, University of Groningen, The Netherlands

There is increasing evidence that the presence or absence of sleep can be of crucial importance for the course of depressive mood. Timing and intensity of sleep are presently considered to be regulated by a circadian and a homeostatic process respectively. Consequently, the question may be raised whether the importance of the presence or absence of sleep in depression can be explained by disturbances in one of these processes.
In this presentation the evidence will be reviewed with respect to both possibilities. The first part will be dedicated to baseline data which might shed light on the integrity of the circadian and the homeostatic regulation of sleep in depression. Are there substantial indications of dysregulations in these areas? The second part deals with the relevant experimental data. What inferences can be made from the antidepressant or depressogenic effects of manipulations of circadian and homeostatic parameters, s.a. phase and amplitude on the one hand and intensity on the other with respect to possible disturbances in depression? The third issue deals with the link between baseline and experimental findings. Do baseline characteristics predict the results of experimental manipulations?
It is concluded that disturbances in circadian or homeostatic regulatory processes in depression are not firmly established. Data on experimental interventions suggest that both processes might be affected.

2345

ABNORMALITIES OF NAPS IN DEPRESSION
C.R.Soldatos, J.D.Bergiannaki, P.N.Sakkas, C.N.Stefanis
Dept. of Psychiatry, Athens University, Athens, Greece

Information stemming from research of napping in depression is rather limited. Two studies have shown that abnormalities detected in nocturnal sleep of depressed patients, including a short REM latency (REML), are also present during daytime naps. In our study of habitual early afternoon nappers (depressed patients vs normal controls), an impressive value of short REML as a diagnostic index for depression was obtained; for the early afternoon naps at the cut-off of 45 minutes the diagnostic sensitivity reached 67% and the specificity 91%. Most patients with a positive DST had also a short REML in naps, while patients with positive TRH test were evenly distributed among those with a short and those with a normal REML in naps. In a study of the influence of daytime naps on the therapeutic effect of sleep deprivation, a depressogenic effect of these naps was demonstrated. However, in our study, both depressed patients and normal controls reported a significantly improved mood following naps without previous sleep deprivation. Further investigations are needed to clarify the diagnostic validity and the influence on mood of naps in depression.

2346

SLEEP AND HORMONAL RHYTHMS IN AFFECTIVE DISORDERS.

J. Mendlewicz

Free University of Brussels, Erasme Hospital, Dept. of Psychiatry, route de Lennik 808 - 1070 Brussels Belgium

Sleep EEG and hormonal disturbances have been described in the acute phase of affective illnesses. The question arises as to wheter these biological marker disturbances are state or trait related. This important issue can be adressed by evaluating changes in sleep EEG and hormonal parameters from a chronobiological approach before and after antidepressant treatment. Among the circadian variables explored in affectively ill patients are REM sleep and slow wave sleep, as well as circadian secretion of plasma GH, cortisol, ACTH and prolactin.

Session 363　　Special Session:
Borderline personality disorder

2347
BORDERLINE STATES AND CHAOS
Peter L. Giovacchini, M.D.
Dept. of Psychiatry, Univ. of Illinois, College of Medicine, Chicago, Illinois, U.S.A.

Borderline patients have defects in the ego executive system and, therefore, can function in the external world only at a marginal level. The inability to relate to the external world heightens feelings of inadequacy and intensifies their already existing lack of self-esteem which, in turn, will be reflected in the identity sense. Borderline patients have poorly defined identities.
I will present a brief vignette of a college student who illustrates the above phenomena. In addition to difficulties in coping with the exigencies of their milieu, borderlines have difficulty in maintaining inner psychic regulation. They are unable to soothe themselves and frequently have to face a state of chronic agitation and this is often clearly discernible in their behavior. In other instances, these patients are able to construct subtle defenses in which they can get others to absorb their chaos. Thus, we have a situation in which the patient is calm but the therapist or other significant persons feel that they are on the verge of madness. I will again present a clinical situation in which the therapist's countertransference difficulties are characterized by his absorption of the patient's disruptive agitation.

2348
Borderline personality organization - a five year prospective follow-up
Gunnar Kullgren M.D.
Department of Psychiatry Umeå Sweden

Objective: To examine descriptive, concurrent and follow-up validity of the concept of borderline personality organization (BPO).
Patients/design: Forty-six inpatients were diagnosed according to Diagnostic Interview for borderline, DSM-III and the structural interview according to Kernberg.
Results: 55% of the patients fulfilled criteria for BPO. Various concomitant axis I and axis II disorders were identified among BPO-patients. The different levels of personality organizations were highly predictive for social functioning and hospitalization during follow-up. Diagnostic instability was, however, high and closely linked to an index diagnosis of major affective disorder
Conclusions: Despite some predictive power the findings did not support the validity of the concept of personality organization. The concept of BPO is too inclusive and unstable. The diagnosis is highly influenced by a concomitant axis I disorder and does not seem to represent a stable personality structure. It is suggested that a diagnosis of personality organization should not be made in the presence of a significant axis I disorder.

2349
LONELINESS FEELINGS BY BORDERLINE PERSONALITY

Dr Hugues SCHARBACH - CENTRE HOSPITALIER REGIONAL ET UNIVERSITAIRE - 9, rue de Gigant - 44100 NANTES - FRANCE -

Borderline patients have difficulties in establishing syntonic relation and usually complain about living with boredom, weariness and loneliness feelings.
No guilt feeling is noted, but fears concerning the loss of the sense of life and of internal coherence.
The efforts made by the patient to offset this state, are generally unsuccessful and take factitious connotations. That leads to a re-enforcement of feelings of loneliness and/or emptiness. Acting out may represent a way to discharge tensions temporarily.
A double polarity emerges :
- subjects who have devotional object relationship, dependent relationship, who are addicted to a human object or to a drug, close to self-objects of H. KOHUT. They treat and consider the other as part of themselves in the same way as the infant considers its mother's breast.

- other personalities are closer to the narcissistic structure, who do not endure to be very near to the other, which brings about an intrusive dimension ; so, they keep a position of proud withdrawal and tend to empty exchanges of their affective contents. The feelings of loneliness are different from those described in the other configuration ; it is rather a more or less freely accepted solitude.

Features and symptoms during chilhood and the different aspects of dysharmonic development are evoked and discussed.

2350
BORDERLINE PERSONALITY DISORDER: A PSYCHOPATHOLOGICAL EVALUATION
Gr. Vaslamatzis, V. Kontaxakis, N. Adamou M. Markidis
Department of Psychiatry, Athens University

The purpose of this study is to clarify the psychological characteristics of patients with Borderline Personality Disorder (BPD), diagnosed according to DSM-III criteria. A psychometric comparison has been attempted between BPD patients (N=13) and patients with a diagnosis of Major Depression (N=13) and Schizophrenia (N=13). All patients were males and have been hospitalized in the Psychiatric Clinic of Athens University Medical School during the years 1982 to 1987. Patients with a BPD diagnosis on axis II of DSM-III who also met the criteria for Major Depression (or other disorders) were excluded.
The Diagnostic Interview for Borderlines (DIB), the Brief Psychiatric Rating Scale (BPRS), the Hamilton Depression Rating Scale and the MMPI were used in order to evaluate the psychopathological condition of the patients.
Results: Borderline patients were differentiated sharply from the other two groups by the DIB. Other significant differences were found between Borderlines and Depressives in Hamilton scores, and between Borderlines and Schizophrenics in BPRS scores. As to the profiles in the MMPI, Borderlines were more close to the Depressives than to the Schizophrenics.

2351

DST-RESPONSES AND NEUROTRANSMITTER PARAMETERS IN BORDERLINE PERSONALITY DISORDER
V.Kontaxakis, M.Markianos, G.Vaslamatzis, M.Markidis, E.Evripidou and C.Stefanis
Department of Psychiatry, Eginition Hospital, 74 Vas. Sophias Avenue, 11528 Athens, Greece

The DST-response, the levels of the metabolites of noradrenaline(MHPG), dopamine(HVA) and serotonin (5-HIAA), and the activity of the enzyme DbH were estimated in a group of Borderline personality disorder patients(BPD,n=14) and compared to the values of a group of patients with Major depression (MD,n=15) and a group of patients with Schizophrenia(SCH,n=16). The diagnoses of patients were based on DSM-III criteria. Psychopathology was rated in all patients using BPRS and HDRS. Analyses of variance revealed significant differences regarding BPRS(H=10.8, p<0.005), HDRS scores(H=17.3, p<0.001), mean plasma cortisol level at 8 a.m. (F=5.73, p=0.05), at 4 p.m.(F=8.81, p=0.01) and mean urinary level of HVA(F=4.34, p=0.02). The comparison by pairs of the three groups of patients showed that both BPD and MD patients were differentiated from the SCH patients with respect to the frequency of abnormal DST-responses(non-suppressors, 57% and 53% vs 13% respectively, p=0.01),the plasma cortisol levels at 8 a.m.(p<0.05) or at 4 p.m.(p<0.02) and the urinary levels of HVA (p<0.03).

2352

THE OPERATIONALIZATION OF PSYCHOTHERAPY WITH THE BORDERLINE PATIENT.
R. Forssmann-Falck, Private Practice
Richmond, VA. USA
M. Katherin Hudgins, University of
Wisconsin, Madison, WI. USA

This paper presents the Stage Process Model as a vaiable option to operationalize long-term psychotherapy with the borderline patient. It holds that the internalization of the therapeutic relationship is a major curative factor of the treatment with the borderline patient. It also provides the structure necessary for such treatment by identifying five successive stages. The components of the therapeutic relationship serve to differentiate the stages:
Stage I: The narcissistic alliance (Bonding);
Stage II: The therapeutic alliance (Trust);
Stage III: The transference (Change); Stage IV: The real relationship (Integration) and finally Stage V: Termination (Mourning). The stages will be described from a clinical vantage point emphasizing therapist behavior and predicted patient behavior change. Then we will discuss the ramification for teaching and research of such a model.

2353

L'INTERVENTION DE CRISE COMME PREMICES
A LA PSYCHOTHERAPIE DU PATIENT BORDERLINE
Dr. Nicolas de Coulon
Secteur Psychiatrique de l'Est Vaudoise
1820 Montreux Suisse

Le patient borderline présente un trouble relationnel qui l'empêche très souvent de demander clairement l'aide psychothérapeutique dont il a besoin. Il est, par contre, prédisposé à des réactions que nous qualifions de crises psychologiques et qui l'amènent à nouer contact avec une équipe psychiatrique. Dans ce contexte, une prise en charge intensive s'avère souvent nécessaire.

Le psychiatre est alors exposé à un arsenal d'angoisses diffuses et de mécanismes primitifs de défenses qui se manifestent avec une violence particulière et s'opposent justement à l'instauration d'une alliance de travail. Le patient provoque habituellement deux attitudes contradictoires, soit une acceptation sans conditions ni possibilités de négociation, soit un rejet pur et simple. L'intervention de crise permet à l'équipe thérapeutique de se situer au coeur de ce paradoxe, dans un registre qui fait place à la fois au "holding" et à une confrontation plus conflictuelle.

2354

THE BORDERLINE PERSONALITY DISORDER AND THE FORENSIC PSYCHIATRY
Ermentini A. Benzoni O. Fazzari G. Galliani I. Gozio C. Gradante G.
Dept. of Psychiatry University of Brescia, Italy

The concept of borderline personality disorder is a very interesting one in Forensic Psychiatry. Since, acting outs behaviour in these patients are very frequent phenomena.
The clinical picture is polymorphic, and the authors found significant divergences in definition of this syndrome.
In this study we compared the M.M.P.I. profiles of a group of borderlines patients diagnosed after a follow-up of three years with 20 borderlines, who have been admitted in the Criminal Asylum of Castiglione delle Stiviere (Mn) for severe injuries against the person. The findings are discussed.

2355

BORDERLINE PATIENTS IN LONG TERM GROUP-ANALYTIC PSYCHOTHERAPY
A.Kakouri, I.Piperyia, E.Kouneli, M.Karaolidou
Open Psychotherapeutic Centre, Athens, Greece.

The therapeutic process of a large population of borderline patients, where group analytic therapy was applied as the main type of treatment, is presented.
The study correlates variables such as age, sex, duration of treatment, concurrent therapies, etc. with the therapeutic outcome.

Session 364 Symposium:
Specificity of psychoanalysis

2356 *

2357

VALIDITY AND JUSTIFICATION OF PSYCHOANALYTIC THINKING
Telemaque Maratos

My participation in the Symposium aims at raising some points on the justification validity and effectiveness of Psychoanalysis as seen from a layman's point of view.

Doubts have been expressed as to whether Psychoanalysis is in fact scientific as it seems to exclude doubt and work in a logically closed system.

What is the 'cost' of psychoanalysis to society in general and to the individual?

Whereas the influence of psychoanalytic theory in the modern world is widespread and beyond doubt, the effect of psychoanalytic treatment on the individual is less well known.
I would like to pose these questions to the panel.

2358

COMMENT ON PEUT AIDER AUTREMENT EN PSYCHANALYSE

NICOLAIDIS NICOS
SOCIETE SUISSE DE PSYCHANALYSE

La visée du processus psychanalytique : changement ou équilibre ? Normalité ou pas ? un faux problème. La dynamique de la régulation entre plaisir-déplaisir est la préoccupation majeure de la cure analytique. Offrir au patient de nouvelles défenses "moins coûteuses en déplaisir".
L'apparente antinomie des réflexions de Freud : A sa lettre au pasteur Pfister il souligne que la cure a comme but d'analyser; c'est au patient à faire la propre synthèse de ses défenses. Cependant analyser jusqu'où ? En 1938 dans "Analyse terminée et analyse interminable" Freud se demande si nous devons "réveiller le chat qui dort" autrement dit éviter à viser d'autres changements et se contenter de l'équilibre, même conscient, du patient.
L'interprétation dans la cure : outil majeur de l'analyste... mais à double tranchant.
L'interprétation ne doit provoquer que des vagues, disait J. Lacan.

---

* Number left open for technical reasons not corresponding to any abstract

2359

SPECIFICITY OF THE ANALYTIC OBJECT AND KNOWLEGDE

Potamianou Anna
Hellenic Psychoanalytic Study Group

In the context of the Symposium on "the specificity of Psychoanalysis" I propose to examine some specific aspects of the psychoanalytic object and of psychoanalytic thinking as a theory and praxis that simultaneously tackles the work of negativity and the work of existing traces in the psychic apparatus. I will also endeavour to answer questions pertaining to the place of psychoanalysis among other sciences and to the specificity of psychnalytic knowledge.

2360

Specificity of Psychoanalysis

Daniel P. Schwartz, M.D.
Austen Riggs Center, Inc.
Stockbridge, MA
U.S.A.

"Psychoanalytic specificity" arises from a technique which allows and demands a projective and interactive examination of human inner life, its forces and structures, from an historic developmental understanding of inner views of self and inner views of others, all influenced by concurrent psychoanalytic interpersonal interaction. As a consequence of this projective interaction, new organizations of the self and its relations to the world evolve. As these new organizations emerge, men and women find they have within themselves the possibility and potentiality--as a product of that "specific psychoanalytic work"-- to live their life rather than be lived by it, to understand and create their own history rather than merely to be subject to it, and to vitally and clearly perceive themselves and their loved ones rather than be seen partially and without dimension. Clinical examples of this will be presented.

Session 365 Symposium:
Links between psychiatry and general practice: Present trends

2361

LIAISON PSYCHIATRY: A PARTNERSHIP WITH PATIENTS AND GENERAL PRACTITIONERS
Parquet J. - France

2362

WHEN THE PATIENT IS BACK HOME AFTER HOSPITALISATION: WHO TAKES CARE OF HIM?
Berner P. - Psychiatric University Clinic, Vienna, Austria

2363

THE CHRONIC PSYCHOSIS AND GENERAL PRACTICE
Paes de Souza M. - Hôpital de Sta Maria, Dept. of Psychiatry, Lisbon, Portugal

2364

GENERAL PRACTITIONERS, PSYCHIATRISTS AND DEPRESSION: HOW SHOULD THEY COLLABORATE?
Ferreri M. - Hôpital St. Antoin, Paris, France

2365

GENERAL PRACTITIONERS PSYCHIATRISTS AND ANXIETY DISORDERS
Parmentier G. - France

2366

GENERAL PRACTITIONERS PSYCHIATRISTS AND SLEEP DISORDERS
Faludi G. - Canada

2367

IS IT REALLY POSSIBLE FOR GENERAL PRACTITIONNERS TO UNDERSTAND PSYCHIATRIST'S POINT OF VIEW?
Aslanian P. - France

Session 366 Special Session:
Alcohol abuse: Biological correlates

2368
RELATIONSHIP BETWEEN THE DEVELOPMENT OF ACUTE ALCOHOL PSYCHOSES AND CHANGES IN THE CATECHOLAMINE SYSTEM FUNCTIONS
I.P.Anokhina and B.M.Kogan
All-Union Research Center of Narcology,
All-Union Institute of General and
Forensic Pscyhiatry, Moscow, USSR

Our previous studies showed that a major role in the pathogenesis of alcohol dependence is played by the disturbances of the catecholamine (CA), particularly dopamine (DA), system functions. The objective of this work was to study correlations between the clinical status of patients with alcohol psychoses of various severity, patients with severe alcohol-abstinence syndrome, and CA system functions. The results show a pronounced correlation between disturbances of DA and cAMP content of the blood, MAO and CA activity, the affinity of alpha-and amount of beta-adrenoreceptors and the severity of the clinical picture. The application of the therapeutic schemes aimed at normalizing the biochemical disturbances leads to a rapid arresting of major clinical symptoms of the alcohol abstinence syndrome and delirium tremens. This indicates the pathogenetic role of functional disturbances of the CA neuromediation in the development of extreme states in alcoholism.

2369
ENDOCRINOLOGICAL STATUS OF ALCOHOLICS DURING WITHDRAWAL AND ABSTINENCE
WP Pienaar, RA Emsley, MC Roberts, JJF Taljaard, C Aalbers from the Medical Research Council Unit for the Neurochemistry of Mental Diseases, University of Stellenbosch, South Africa.

Although it is recognised that alcohol has profound effects on the hypothalamic-pituitary axis, the exact nature of these changes in patients with alcohol dependence remains unclear. Previous studies have yielded conflicting results - at least in part due to the fact that patient groups were poorly defined and did not take into account the possibility that different stages of alcohol dependence may reflect different states of disordered physiology. To further investigate these changes we applied a dexamethasone-suppression test (DST) and thyroid releasing hormone (TRH) stimulation test tot 16 patients with symptoms of alcohol withdrawal and 13 abstinent alcoholics. Reference data were obtained from 13 healthy volunteers with sober habits. Significantly more alcoholics with withdrawal symptoms had abnormal DST results when compared with abstinent alcoholics and healthy volunteers ($p<0.05$). Alcoholics with withdrawal showed a severly blunted TSH response to TRH stimulation when compared with abstinent alcoholics ($p<0.05$) and healthy volunteers ($p<0.0005$). Severity of withdrawal symptoms correlated significantly with elevated basal serum cortisol ($p<0.05$) and a blunted delta TSH ($p<0.05$). DST abnormalities tend to normalise more rapidly than TRH stimulation test abnormalities after withdrawal.

2370
DELIRIUM TREMENS AND POTASSIUM IN BLOOD SERUM AND CEREBROSPINAL FLUID
E. Holzbach
Psychiatrische Abteilung
St. Josef-Hospital Oberhausen
W.-Germany

Nach neueren Untersuchungen tritt beim D.t. die Erniedrigung des Kaliumspiegels im Blutserum erst während des Krankheitsverlaufs auf. Dies führte zur Frage, ob die Delir-Symptomatik vom Kaliumspiegel abhängig ist. Eine Untersuchung an 95 Delir-Patienten zeigte, daß der Kaliumspiegel im Blutserum mit verschiedenen Delir-Symptomen korreliert, während diese Korrelationen bezüglich des Liquor cerebrospinalis nicht nachgewiesen werden konnten. Auch war die Erniedrigung des Kaliumspiegels im Liquor cerebrospinalis weit weniger ausgeprägt als im Blutserum.
Die Veränderung des Kaliumspiegels während des Delirverlaufs scheint also im wesentlichen peripher zu verlaufen ohne gravierende Folgen auf das ZNS. Dieses Ergebnis unterstützt die Hypothese der Blut-Alkalose durch Hyperventilation während des D.t.

2371
WATER EXCRETION AND VASOPRESSIN IN ALCOHOL WITH= DRAWAL AND ABSTINENCE
RA Emsley, JJF Taljaard, G Joubert
From the Medical Research Council Unit for the Neurochemistry of Mental Diseases, University of Stellenbosch, South Africa.

Reports describing the fluid balance status of al= coholics are varied and conflicting. We further examined this question by administering a standard water load test to a group of alcoholics with symptoms of withdrawal (n=17) and a group of ab= stinent alcoholics (n=14), and recording resultant changes in a number of relevant parameters, inclu= ding levels of plasma vasopressin. Reference date were obtained from a group of age and sex matched healthy volunteers (n=14). Compared to healthy volunteers, alcoholics with withdrawal symptoms excreted a significantly smaller ($p=0.0001$) and abstinent alcoholics a significantly greater ($p=0.0004$) volume. Alcoholics with withdrawal symptoms also had higher minimum urine osmolali= ties ($p=0.0001$) and elevated basal plasma vasopres= sin levels ($p=0.0045$). We believe that these findings are best explained by a resetting of osmoreceptors, a supposition in keeping with con= temporary views on the pathogenesis of alcohol dependence and withdrawal. This would imply that chronic ingestion of alcohol leads to an enduring suppression of vasopressin secretion, while the alcohol withdrawal state is associated with a transient rebound hypersecretion of vasopressin.

2372

ETHANOL-RELATED ORGAN IMPAIRMENT: PSYCHOMETRIC AND APPARATIVE FINDINGS IN ALCOHOLIC PATIENTS.
OTT, C.[1], DEMLING, J.[1], HUK, W.H.[2], OTT, G.[1], MUGELE, B.[3], HEYDER, N.[4], CLAUS, D.[5]
Departments of 1) Psychiatry, 2) Neuroradiology, 4) Medicine, 5) Neurology, University of Erlangen-Nürnberg; 3) Bezirkskrankenhaus Erlangen, D-8520 Erlangen (FRG)

In chronic alcoholic (20-45 years) inpatients, we are examining the organic and psychopathological effects of chronic alcoholism. The study includes diagnostic and psychometric rating scales, CCT, liver sonography, and visual evoked potentials. CT and psychological testings are repeated after 5 weeks of detoxification.
Preliminary results are:
1. CT scans revealed cortical and inner atrophy of variable degree in almost every case. Cerebellar atrophy was found in a high percentage. - Comparison of individual CT scans (first week of detoxification vs. 5 weeks of abstinence) showed a significant reversal of brain shrinkage in most subjects.
2. Psychological tests showed a variety of disorders. Depression and anxiety scores and suicidal tendencies are characterized by great individual variation. Mental information processing velocity improved significantly with abstinence.
3. Liver sonography yielded pathological findings in 80 %.
Correlations of organ findings with psychological test results are being drawn and will be presented in detail.

2373

Sleep pattern in alcoholics

W. Jernajczyk, L. Cyganik, M. Kobusiak
Institute of Psychiatry and Neurology
Warsaw and Psychiatric Hospital Wrocław

Acute withdrawal from alcohol in the chronic alcoholic is characterized by a prolongation of sleep latency, reduction in deep sleep NREM and an increase of REM stage. This report explores differences between sleep parameters of alcoholics and sound subjects. Ten hospitalized physically healthy alcoholic males 31-43 years old were studied. They took no psychotropic drugs. Their drinking bout lated at least 7 days and the period of sobering up before investigation was 1 day. The control grup constituted 10 healthy males. Each subject was examined during two consecutive nights.
THe results were analyzed with the t-test and Wilcoxon test.
Results: incease of sleep latency /0.002/
 decrease of total sleep time /0.01/
 decrease of stage 4 NREM /0.005/.

2374

A TWO-COMPONENT HYPOTHESIS FOR THE DEVELOPMENT OF PHYSICAL AND MENTAL SIGNS OF ALCOHOL WITHDRAWAL.

R. Hemmingsen & P. Kramp.

Dept. of Psychiatry, Bispebjerg Hospital, University of Copenhagen, Denmark.

In a material of 12 patients experiencing withdrawal psychoses we measured CBF by SPECT-technique. Greater CBF was significantly correlated with visual hallucinations and agitation. The physical withdrawal signs in patients are not increased in proportion to the severity of psychosis. In a rat-model multiple episodes of alcohol intoxication and withdrawal were studied. The non-convulsive withdrawal signs (eg. tremor, rigidity, irritability) were not increased during repeated episodes. However, spontaneous seizures developed in 25% of the animals (n=49) during 10-17 episodes; the development of seizures could be attenated by barbital treatment during the first 9 episodes of withdrawal. CNS hyperexcitability prevails after multiple intoxication-withdrawal episodes both in man and animals. We hypothesize that the mechanisms causing cumulated CNS hyperexcitability is different from the mechanism of simple physical dependence.

2375

PSYCHOIMMUNOLOGICAL ASPECTS IN CHRONIC ALCOHOLISM

E. Aguglia, P. Zolli, P. Mora, M. DeVanna
Clinica psichiatrica di Trieste, Italy

In a statistical sample of diagnosed chronic alcoholic (according to the DSM-III-R criteria) the authors study the cell-mediated factor and its correlations with the neuroendocrinal parameters.
Furthermore the possible impairment of the cognitive functions is evaluated through a set of psychological tests.
The study comprises 15 subjects of both sexes with an age ranging from 40 to 60.
For being admitted to the trial, the diagnosis of the patients was to be that of chronic alcoholism according to the DSM-III-R criteria. The patients were not to be carriers of immunological and neoplastic diseases.
The morphological and functional aspects of the immunitary cells of all the subjects is evaluated of the T-lymphomonocitary subpopulations.
The data, analyzed by statistical instruments, indicate a meaningful alteration of the parameters taken into account and suggest the opportunity of employing them for a more correct prognostic evaluation of alcohol addiction.

2376

COGNITIVE IMPAIRMENT IN THIAMINE DEFICIENT ALCOHOL INTOXICATED RATS WITH INTACT BRAIN STRUCTURE.

R. Hemmingsen, J. Ulrichsen, H. Lauersen, J. Mogensen, D.E. Barry.
Dept. of Psychiatry, Bispebjerg Hospital, University of Copenhagen, Denmark.

The purpose of the study was to investigate whether behavioral abnormalities during thiamine deficiency and previous long-term alcohol intoxication are detectable before the appearance of structural brain lesions Four groups of 12 rats were studied by foot shock avoidance test after a 5 weeks diet regimen comprising 1) normal diet, 2) thiamine deficient diet, 3) thiamine deficient diet plus ethanol (50g/l) and 4) normal diet plus ethanol. Escape avoidances and escape latency was studied. Both the thiamine deficient groups differed statistically significantly from controls and on several variables these groups were also significantly impaired as compared with the ethanol intoxicated group. No structural brain lesions prevailed in any of the groups. In conclusion thiamine deficiency but not alcohol alone was accompanied by impaired cognitive function at a time when no structural brain lesion prevailed. The findings may be of relevance for treatment during the early phase of thiamine deficiency in alcoholics (Wernickes encephalopathy)

Session 367 Special Session:
Perspectives in psychiatric education

2377

TIME LIMITED CERTIFICATION, A NEW AMERICAN STANDARD

Layton McCurdy, M.D.
American Board of Psychiatry and Neurology

In the near future the American Board of Psychiatry and Neurology will issue a <u>time limited</u> specialty certificate in psychiatry. This will lead to reexaminations during the psychiatrist's professional lifetime. This step is in keeping with a growing public concern in the U.S.A. for monitoring physicians' knowledge and skill. Several American medical specialty boards are already recertifying their members. The paper will focus on the professional and public factors that contribute to this important change and will comment on the problems of reexamination and recertification of practicing psychiatrists, many of whom have become subspecialists in the field.

2378

PSYCHIATRIC EDUCATION—GLOBAL CONSIDERATIONS

Christine McGuire Masserman
Department of Medical Education
University of Illinois at Chicago, USA

Emerging health needs ranging from the world-wide scourge of substance abuse to global anxiety stemming from inability to cope with our burgeoning technology, changing demands of the profession, and evolving concerns of trainees and practitioners are examined. Their implications for revisions in the content, organization, instructional methodology and assessment practices of psychiatric training and continuing education programs are explored. Illustrative innovations in each of these aspects of psychiatric education are described and discussed.

2379

TRAINING PSYCHIATRISTS FOR THE FUTURE IN AFRICA

Prof. Ayo Binitie
University of Benin, Benin City, Nigeria

The future psychiatrist must capture the spirit of 2 worlds. An increasingly improvised and numerous African population and a technologically advanced western world. It is clearly necessary that this gap be gridged; also a situation where the psychiatrists from third world cannot communicate with their counterpart in the western world would develop in Africa; up to 20% of the patients seen formal psychiatric setting have organic psychiatric problems. In non-formal psychiatric setting, the psychiatrist has to double up as family doctor and general practioner.

The ideal doctor for the future should be able to take cognisance of all factors in the management of his case. His training should encompass a strong medical background in order to funcion efficiently as a common doctor for ordinary physical ailments; strong training in neurology to deal with the problem of organic psychoses. Adequate knowledge of sociology and anthropology in addition to the usual ones involved in the training of psychiatrists. In training of such experts, there is need for international exposure. It is our hope that the collaboration of western countries to meet this need will be forthcoming in the future years.

2380
A COURSE OF DIAGNOSTICS FOR PSYCHIATRIC RESIDENTS

J. Pols
P.C. "Licht en Kracht", Assen, The Netherlands.

As a complement to the daily diagnostic activities of psychiatric residents, a course has been organised aiming at a reflection on the meaning, values and limits of the diagnostic process. This process is being described and interpreted as a process of step-by-step increasing reduction and interpretation, as a hermeneutic translation of the experiences and behavior of the patient in the scientific language of psychiatry.
This translation could be viewed in three connected levels of abstraction. First, the practical level of skills in interviewing and examining the patient. Second, the theoretical level, i.e. the many different frames of reference giving rise to and expressing different meanings to the first level. Third, the metatheoretical level clarifying the scientific status of concepts and theories.

2381
TRACKING THE CLINICAL PSYCHIATRIC LITERATURE: WHAT IS OUT THERE?

M. Chisolm, A. Hanson, C. Lyketsos, M. McGuire, N. Ranen, A. Stoline;
The Johns Hopkins University, Baltimore, U.S.A.

The goal of this paper is twofold. First we will review the various conventional and computerized means available to clinical psychiatrists for keeping up with and for researching the large and growing volumes of literature relevant to contemporary psychiatry. This section will cover library resources (regional, national and international), computerized databases, professional advisors, key journals and review schemes available by subscription. The second part of the paper will report the results of a survey of clinical and academic psychiatrists and of psychiatric residents designed to assess how they track the clinical psychiatric literature. The surveyees' knowledge of available resources, their usual searching practices and their thoughts and suggestions about deficiencies in the resource network will be described in a comparative fashion. Conclusions will be drawn about the most efficient means of tracking the literature for various purposes and suggestions will be made about improving resources.

2382
IMPLICATIONS OF THE WOUNDED-HEALER PARADIGM FOR PSYCHIATRIC EDUCATION

Grant D. Miller, M.D., University of Nevada School of Medicine, Reno, Nevada 89557, U.S.A.

The wounded-healer paradigm, having its orgins in classical Greek mythology, holds that deep within every healer lies an inner wound which plays an important role in vocational choice, clinical behavior, and may constitute the most significant factor contributing to healing in patients. This paper will outline how psychiatric educators may emphasize and teach humanitarian clinical behaviors through increasing awareness of existential and literal wounds. The paper will also show how non-humanitarian factors including arrogance, entitlement, and lack of empathy, warmth, and acceptance are minimized by awareness of inner wounds. A diagrammatic model will be presented analyzing the interactional dynamics in the healer-patient encounter. A related model will be presented to help psychiatric educators be more effective in teaching medical students and psychiatric residents.

2383
SOCIAL SKILLS TRAINING IN PSYCHIATRIC STAFF
S.Maggioni, S.Masaraki
Niguarda Hospital, Milan, Italy

This work is based on the consideration that psychiatric nurses have high level of stress, due to the emotional over involvement which is typical of people who deal with psychiatric patients.
We thought that a six months training (for a total number of 40 hours) would have reduced the overinvolvement of the staff and the related burnout; moreover improved the abilities of interpersonal relationship among nurses and patients. To test the outcome of experience we used the Maslach Burnout Inventory both before and after the training.
The results have been compared in order to assess the validity of the present method.

2384
PSYCHIATRY CLERKSHIPS IN PRIMARY CARE AMBULATORY SETTINGS
Cyril Worby, M.D. and Marsha Worby, Ph.D.
Dept. of Psychiatry and Behavioral Sciences; Dept. of Family and Community Medicine, University of Nevada School of Medicine, Reno, Nevada 89557 USA

Psychiatry clerkships in North America are 6-8 weeks in duration, usually in the third year and take place in psychiatric inpatient units for the most part. Yet most persons with non-psychotic DSM-III-R diagnoses are treated by primary care physicians in primary care ambulatory settings. In a pilot study we compared two groups of students over two consecutive eight week clerkships. One group trained in traditional psychiatric inpatient settings, the other in a family practice ambulatory setting. Both groups attended the same didactic seminar series. There were no significant differences in knowledge or performance between the two groups. Clerks trained in the family practice center appeared to have greater knowledge of effects of illness on families and had more experience in counseling couples and families. These findings suggest that outcome research comparing these two training contexts is worthy of pursuit.

Session 368 Special Session:
Positron and photon emission tomography in psychiatry

2385
DECREASED IN VIVO INFLUX RATE OF TYROSINE ACROSS THE BLOOD BRAIN BARRIER IN SCHIZOPHRENIC PATIENTS AS MEASURED BY PET.
F-A Wiesel, C Halldin, G Blomqvist, I Sjögren, S Stone-Elander, L Bjerkenstedt, L Hagenfeldt, N Venizelos
Department of Psychiatry and Psychology, Karolinska Hospital, S-104 01 STOCKHOLM, Sweden.

The brain is the only organ to which the transport of tyrosine is limited. In vitro studies have shown a lower transport of tyrosine across the fibroblast membrane in schizophrenic patients. In vivo studies with PET were therefore performed to study the influx of tyrosine from the blood into the brain.

Healthy volunteers (n=5, men) and drugfree schizophrenic patients (DSM-III-R, n=5, men) fasted in 12 hours before L-(1-^{11}C)-tyrosine (200 MBq) was injected i.v. as a bolus. Tyrosine concentrations were determined in plasma. PET-scans were made every 10 second in 4 min and the radioactivity in blood was measured every second. The radioactive data were analyzed with a compartment model for the determination of k_1 (the intransport constant) and k_2 (the outtransport constant). The influx of tyrosine into the brain was computed from k_1 and the tyrosine concentration in plasma.

The influx rate was significantly lower in the patients (1.94+0.49 SD nanomole/gram x min) than in the controls (2.89+0.53 SD nanomole/gram x min) (t = 2.898 p<0.05). The in vitro and the in vivo findings may indicate that schizophrenic patients suffer from a general membrane dysfunction more than a disturbance in a specific neuronal system.

2386
BRAIN UTILIZATION OF [^{11}C]L-DOPA AND [^{11}C]5-HYDROXY-TRYPTOPHAN STUDIED BY PET IN HEALTHY VOLUNTEERS AND DEPRESSED PATIENTS.
H. Ågren, L. Reibring, J. Hetta, P. Hartvig, P. Bjurling, J. Ulin, B. Långström. Dept. of Psychiatry and University Hospital Pharmacy, Dept. of Organic Chemistry, Uppsala University, S-751 85 Uppsala, Sweden

The monoamine hypothesis for the etiology of affective disorders was formulated more than 20 years ago on the basis of pharmacological observations on the inhibition of reuptake of serotonin and norepinephrine by tricyclic antidepressant drugs. However, no relation between affective disorders and impaired monoamine turnover has been definitely proven.

We have studied utilization of and [^{11}C]L-dopa with PET as a means to assess serotonin and dopamine topographical metabolism in both healthy volunteers and in patients with DSM-III diagnoses of melancholic and non-melancholic depressions. The radioactive doses varied at 75–200 MBq corresponding to 20–50 µg of 5-HTP and L-dopa—distinctly subpharmacological levels. In [^{11}C]5-HTP experiments, reexaminations after pretreatments with PCPA, benserazide, tryptophan, and i.v. 'cold' 5-HTP revealed selective changes of uptake. A similar selectivity was noted in [^{11}C]L-dopa experiments before and after pretreatments with benserazide and p.o. and i.v. 'cold' 5-HTP. Depressed patients were investigated with [^{11}C]methionine, [^{11}C]L-dopa and [^{11}C]5-HTP and reinvestigated after antidepressant treatment regimens. The rate constant for brain utilization, k_3, was calculated using the Patlak-Gjedde plot using cerebellum as reference. Differences between k_3 values were tested for significant differences by means of analysis of covariance allowing specific tests for slope and intercept deviations.

The utilization of [^{11}C]5-HTP ran parallel to that of [^{11}C]L-dopa and was most intense in striatal areas and the frontal lobes. We report a specific decrease of [^{11}C]5-HTP utilization in the frontal lobes during the sick phase of melancholia, normalizing following recovery. No similar change was found for [^{11}C]L-dopa. • *We conclude that 5-HTP and L-dopa visualized in the brain with PET quantitate selective processes in the* in vivo *synthesis of serotonin and dopamine of possible pathophysiological meaning.*

2387
THE CBF, $CMRO_2$ AND GLUCOSE UTILIZATION IN AFFECTIVE DISORDERS USING POSITRON EMISSION TOMOGRAPHY.
Tadashi Tokairin, Hideji Kishimoto, Osamu Takatsu, Haruhiro Hujita, Shiro Ohno and Masaaki Matsushita. Department of Psychiatry, Yokohama City University School of Medicine, Minami-ku, Yokohama 232 Japan.

Brain CBF, $CMRO_2$ and glucose utilization of depressed patients were studied by positron CT and $C^{15}O_2$, $^{15}O_2$ and ^{11}C labeled glucose. Diagnosis of the patients was based on DSM-III R. The main findings of these studies were as follows ; the ^{11}C brain counts in the depressed patients were significantly (p<0.025) lower, in the global area of the brain cortex, after the oral administration of ^{11}C-glucose as compared to controls. The percentages of reduction were around 30 in the brain of depressed patients applying this method of ^{11}C-glucose utilization. On the other hand, the CBF and $CMRO_2$ were normal as compared to control subjects. These global glucose utilization changes of the brain cortex characterize the affective disorders significantly compared to other mental disorders. These studies indicate that the PET is a significant new method for understanding of metabolic and functional activity of the brain of the patients of affective disorders.

2388

SINGLE PHOTON EMISSION TOMOGRAPHY IN DEMENTIA AND DEPRESSION IN ELDERLY

A.K. Upadhyaya, M.T. Abou-Saleh, M. Critchley*, K. Wilson and J.S. Grime*.
Department of Psychiatry and Department of Nuclear Medicine*, Royal Liverpool Hospital, Liverpool, U.K.

Single Photon Emission Tomography (SPET) using Tc - 99m HMPAO was carried out in three groups of age matched subjects: Dementia (no. 12). Major depressive Disorder(no. 12) and healthy controls (no. 6). They were evaluated with Geriatric Mental State, History and Aetiology Schedule, CAMCOG, Hachinski Scale and Montgomery Asberg scale for depression. All patients with dementia of Alzheimer type (no. 14) showed hypoperfusion in Frontal/Parietal Temporal/Occipital areas. A small subgroup (no. 2) of patients with vascular dementia showed no perfusion defect, although they were demented to an advanced degree. The healthy control group showed normal perfusion pattern. A small subgroup of dementia patients with marked aphasia showed clear hypoperfusion in the dominant frontal area. All the patients of Major Depressive Disorder showed normal perfusion pattern, except two, who had hypoperfusion in the frontal/parietal/temporal area, similar to that seen in Alzheimer type dementia patients. The relevance of perfusion abnormalities, in the differential diagnosis of dementia will be discussed.

2389

BENZODIAZEPINE RECEPTOR OCCUPANCY IN VIVO DETERMINED BY POSITRON EMISSION TOMOGRAPHY (PET)
S. Pauli, G. Blomqvist, A. Persson, L. Farde, C.Halldin, G. Sedvall.
Dept. of Psychiatry, Karolinska Hospital, Stockholm, Sweden.

Benzodiazepines (BZ) excert their pharmacological action by binding to receptors in the brain. Animal studies have demonstrated a high correlation between pharmacological action of BZ and the degree of receptor occupancy. In the present study BZ-receptor occupancy of diazepam was determined using compartment analysis of regional time-activity data from PET-measurements.
Method: Four male volounteers were selected. The positioning in the PET-camera was made according to CT-scans in which the Foramen Monroi was localized. The benzodiazepine antagonist 11C-Ro 15-1788 was injected i.v. as a bolus. The specific activity was > 200 Ci/mmol. Two PET-experiments were performed during 1 hour each. The second PET-experiment started 2 hours after 30 mg diazepam had been administered orally. Venous blood samples were analysed (radioactivity and diazepam-concentration).
Calculations: To establish a reduction in receptor binding after diazepam intake, the quotient (total uptake in one PET-slice)/(total plasma-uptake) was determined. By calculating the 'binding potential' using the expression Bmax/Kd (Bmax is the receptor density, Kd is the equilibrium dissociation constant) before and after oral administration of diazepam, the receptor occupancy (relative change in Bmax/Kd) was determined. A fast, linear, noniterativ least square method (1) was used to estimate Bmax/Kd, 1/koff, Bmax*kon (kon and koff are association and dissociation rate constants).
Results: Using the quotient between PET-slice and plasma the reduction in upptake due to diazepam was 16±3% (sem). Using the kinetic analysis we found that the mean receptor occupancy in a frontal neocortical region was 20±6%. The Bmax/Kd-values were in the range 4.0 to 7.4 which is in agreement with our equilibrium method investigation..
Comments: This method demonstrates the posibility to measure receptor occupancy of diazepam in the human brain using kinetic analysis and an internal reference region, pons.
References:
1. Blomqvist, G., Pauli, S, et al.: Determination of receptor density, association- and dissociation rate constants for radioligands with PET; a comparison between the equilibrium and the kinetic approaches. In Europ Nucl Med Congr., Aug 20 – Sept 2,1988, Milano, Italy.
2. Persson, A., Pauli S., et al: Saturation analysis of specific 11C-Ro 15-1788 binding to the human neocortex using positron emission tomography. Human psychopharmacology, vol 4, 21-31 1989.

2390

SCHIZOPHRENIAS: DISEASES IN THE ASSOCIATION AREA OF THE CORTEX? -A STUDY USING PET-

Hideji Kishimoto, Osamu Takatsu, Haruhiro Fujita, Takashi Ishikawa, Taiko Hashimoto, Masaaki Matsushita, Masaaki Iio* and Miwako Saito*.
Department of Psychiatry, Yokohama City University School of Medicine, Minami-ku, Yokohama 232 and Nakano National Hospital*, Tokyo 160, JAPAN

In this report the authors want to describe new findings of disturbances in association areas of the cortex in never treated chronic schizophrenia which were diagnosed with DSM-III criteria by using the method of 11C-glucose, C15O2 and 15O2 PET. The authors could get the PET image of amino acid pools especially of glutamic acid by using a 11C-glucose tracer, also the image of cerebral blood flow (CBF) and the cerebral metabolic rate of oxygen (CMRO2) by using C15O2 and 15O2 respectively, and of the oxygen extraction ratio (OER) by using both C15O2 and 15O2.

The most important findings of this study are the disturbances in the association areas of the cortex in chronic schizophrenia found using 11C-glucose and C15O2 PET. The most impaired areas were Brodmann's areas 10, 38 and 40 which are called the association areas and are new gyri which are only seen in human beings among the primates and in those areas where human beings are creative: language, concept, culture and society. Bleuler stated that schizophrenia is a group of diseases of association which is confirmed in this study of PET.

2391

D2 DOPAMINE RECEPTOR PET SCANS IN SCHIZOPHRENIA
L.Tune, D.F.Wong, J.Pearlson, H.N.Wagner
Johns Hopkins School of Medicine
Baltimore, Maryland 21205, U.S.A.

In a study of twenty patients with chronic schizophrenia, D2 dopamine receptor density (BMAX) was estimated using a four compartment kinetic model to evaluate data from two pet scans using C-11 N-Methylspiperone as a Ligand. D2 BMAX in drug naive schizophrenics was 33.1±20.5. This was significantly different when compared with 14 normal controls (BMAX=14.4±8.6). Age, sex, duration of illness, nutritional status were all evaluated: All patients were assessed using the present state examination, the brief psychiatric ration scale, and the cannon spoor premorbid adjustment scale. Multiple regression analysis demonstrated a trend for sex and psychosis scores to be important when compared to age, onset, duration of illness. When regression analysis required age, there was a similar trend for dependence on the regression model for psychosis scores. Educational level (r=-.46, p=.05) and premorbid adjustment (r=.45, p=.05) were significantly correlated with BMAX, suggently a relationship with BMAX and chronicity of disease. These findings are compatible with those found in bipolar illness where the range of psychosis scores is greater because of the presence of non-psychotic patients in pet scan studies.

2392

SPECT STUDIES OF ALCOHOL DEPENDENCE USING IODINE-123 IMP

T.Gyobu[1], H.Matsuda[3], H.Nagata[2], M.Ii[1], M.Miyasaka[2], and K.Hisada[3].

Departments of Psychiatry[1] and Radiology[2], Koseiren Namerikawa General Hospital, Namerikawa, Toyama 936 and the Department of Nuclear Medicine[3], Kanazawa University School of Medicine, Kanazawa, Ishikawa 920, Japan.

Atraumatic three-dimensional imaging, using N-isopropyl-(I-123)p-iodoamphetamine (IMP), was performed with single photon emission computed tomography (SPECT) in a group of sixteen neurologically unaffected alcohol dependent patients (DSM III).
  Early (30-62 min p.i.) IMP images, reflecting regional cerebral blood flow, showed selectively and significantly decreased uptake in the medio-frontal area including the anterior cingulate gyrus. Estimation of flow values using IMP (Matsuda's method) demonstrated a similar trend in that area, resulting in chronically decreased perfusion. The medio-frontal decrease was also observed in late (180-212 min p.i.) IMP images, suggesting poor retentivity. However, the latero-frontal decrease was not obtained in both images. This characteristic pattern of IMP uptake is probably specific to alcohol dependence versus those associated with other disorders, including schizophrenia or Alzheimer-type dementia, which display widespread hypoactivity throughout the frontal lobe. In addition, it appears that this selective hypoactivity cannot be reversible despite cerebral shrinkage recovery with long-term abstinence, implying that medio-frontal changes may not be readily explained by so-called "alcoholic atrophy". Furthermore, the results revealed an age-related hypoactivity in the medio-frontal area. Interestingly, a high concordance of hypoactivity in that area between aged controls and alcohol dependent patients was also observed. The findings hence lend credence to the hypothesis of accelerated aging processes in alcoholics (Tarter. Int J Addict 10:327-68, 1975).
  In conclusion, our results from alcohol dependent patients may suggest a selective constant alteration of neuronal function, and perhaps even structure, in the medio-frontal area, supporting a previous positron tomographic study (Samson et al. J Neurol Neurosurg Psychiatry 49: 1165-70, 1986).

2393

MESCALINE-INDUCED PSYCHOSIS, SCHIZOTYPY AND RIGHT HEMISPHERE FUNCTION
G. Oepen, M. Fünfgeld, A. Harrington, L. Hermle
Dept. of General Psychiatry, University Freiburg
D-7800 Freiburg, West-Germany

Following experimental induction of a schizophrenic-like psychosis, caused by intake of .5 g Mescaline-Sulfate, 12 healthy male volunteers were studied neurometabolically (SPECT) and neuropsychologically (tachistoscopic visual half-field tests). The 99m-Tc-HMPAO SPECT, undertaken at the peak of the psychosis, revealed a marked right-sided striato-limbic increase of 99m-Tc-HMPAO uptake under Mescaline in comparison with that found earlier under control conditions ($p=.013$ MANOVA). This was significantly more pronounced in high schizotypy subjects than in low schizotypy ones, using a schizotypic questionnaire ($p=.023$). In parallel with the metabolic changes, repeatedly monitored RH capacity to recognize tachistoscopically-presented face stimuli was reduced, possibly because of competition or interference between the RH demands of the testing material and RH demands on the subjects imposed by the drug-induced visual hallucinations. The role of a primary striato-limbic hyperactivity of the RH in acute (beginning) schizophrenic-like psychosis is discussed.

Session 369   Symposium:
Eating disorders and transcultural aspects of child and adolescent psychiatry

2394

The Changing Spectrum of Eating Disorders
    Winston S. Rickards, M.D.
    Honorary Consultant Psychiatrist
Royal Children's Hospital, Parkville, Vic. Australia
Since the 1950's, children and adolescents with severe eating disorders presenting to the Royal Children's Hospital, Melbourne, Australia, have been treated through collaboration with the Department of Psychiatry and Behavioural Studies. Follow-up studies of these children are continuing, and a series of over 200 cases has been gathered. A sub-sample of female children fulfilling the criteria for anorexia nervosa, admitted first between 1977-83, were reviewed after a follow up interval of over four years. The review indicated inter alia that the weight of subjects at follow-up was consistent with the normal population. Menstrual outcome was less satisfactory in nearly half the group despite normalisation of weight in most instances. Eating behaviour was difficult to assess reliably. Distorted appetite or hunger, or satiation patterns, changed over time, in some cases reflecting both the changing norms of the adolescent peer group and the spectrum of psychopathological states. Approximately one-sixth of the group developed bulimia nervosa.
Bulimia nervosa has become a major focus of clinical concern and research, and intensive ongoing work with some patients can indicate the relationship of anorexia nervosa to bulimia nervosa. Knowledge has been extended to community based programs including support group networks and community education, instituted by the Anorexia and Bulimia Nervosa Foundation of Victoria

2395

The Clinical Treatment of Patients with Anorexia nervosa

Schmidt, Martin, Prof. Dr. med. Dr. rer. nat.
Niemeyer, Joachim, Dr. med.

Central Institute of Mental Health, J 5,
D-6800 Mannheim (FRG)

The paper describes a stepwise clinical inpatient treatment program for patients with anorexia nervosa on the basis of cognitive behaviour therapy. Four phases of the therapeutic measurements are distinguished:
(1) Interventions with respect to stabilization of vital functions
(2) Weightgain by eating according to an individual eating plan
(3) Cognitive modification of eating behaviour including insight therapy
(4) Including the family in order to modify causal or maintaining mechanisms of the disorder.
Treatment results are presented.

2396
Anorexia Nervosa and Drepression
Remschmidt, Helmut, Prof. Dr. med. Dr. phil.
Herpertz-Dahlmann, Beate, Dr. med.
WPA Section Child Psychiatry
Clinic f. Child µ Adolescent Psychiatry,
Hans-Sachs-Straße 6, D-3550 Marburg (FRG)

Summary
To investigate the relationship between weight deficit and depressive symptoms 48 adolescent patients (41 females, 7 males) fullfilling DSM III R criteria for anorexia nervosa were also assessed for DSM III diagnosis of Major depressive disorder (MDD). Patients who met diagnostic criteria for MDD had a significant lower body weight than patients without a current episode of MDD. In turn patients with high weight loss lad higher mean depression scores (HAMD, SDS) than patients with less weight deficit. With increase of body weight we found a highly significant decrease of depressive symptoms.
The authors hypothesize that DSM III criteria for MDD might not specifically distinguish between starvation-related psychopathology in anorexia nervosa and primary affective disorder.

2397
A Long-Term Follow-Up Study in 103 patients with Anorexia Nervosa
Remschmidt, Helmut, Prof. Dr. med. Dr. phil
WPA Section Child Psychiatry
Clinic f. Child & Adolescent Psychiatry,
Hans-Sachs-Str. 6, D-3550 Marburg (FRG)

Follow-up studies using the same prognostic criteria have shown that about 48% of the patients had recovered at follow-up, while 28% revealed further difficulties with eating, weight and figure, and 24% remained anorectic. Our own study on 103 patients who underwent inpatient treatment revealed unexpectedly good results: according to the Morgan & Russell criteria, 72% (n=58) showed a good prognosis, 11% (n=9) a fair, and 17% (n=14) an unfavourable prognosis. 3 patients had died during the follow-up interval. It was possible to predict the long-term outcome from weight recovery during inpatient treatment, more successfully in patients with favourable than unfavourable outcome. The long-term outcome was better in those patients who revealed no premorbid eating difficulties.

2398
Course of Bulimia nervosa: Two Year Follow-up of 273 Inpatients
Fichter MM & Quadflieg N
Klinik Roseneck, Prien & Psychiatrische Universitätsklinik, München (FRG)

First results of a large scale follow-up study of 635 consecutive admissions for inpatient treatment of an eating disorder will be presented. 273 patients suffered from a bulimic syndrom. Using questionaires and expert ratings, detailed information of the status was obtained on hospital admission, discharge from inpatient therapie and at a two year follow-up. The battery of instruments for assessment contained the Anorexia Nervosa Inventory for Self-Rating (ANIS), the Eating Disorder Inventory (EDI), the Structured Interview for Anorexia and Bulimia Nervosa (SIAB), the Beschwerdenliste by von Zerssen, the Beck-Depression Inventory, the Hopkins Symptom Checklist (SCL 90R), personality inventories and the Parental Bonding Instrument (PBI) by Parker. Follow-up data was obtained with these questionaires and in a personal interview (SIAB). For comparison with bulimic inpatients a second sample of 100 bulimic women, who had responded to a press survey and who had not received in- or outpatient therapy was also assessed longitudinally. The few studies in the literature concerning the course of bulimia point to high rates of chronicity and rapidity of relapse (Keller et al. 1989). Our study addresses itself 1. to the effects of inpatient therapy, 2. the nosology of bulimic syndroms and their relationship to affective illness, 3. the identification of predictors for relapse (risk factors) and 4. the application of linear causal models for the effects of personality factors, sociodemographic variables, chronic difficulties, the severity of an eating disorder, the severity of other mental syndroms and treatment on the two year outcome. Inpatient treatment had clinically and statistically siginfcant effects on eating behaviour and other psychiatric symptoms. Preliminary results of this on-going study on the course of bulimic syndroms will be reported.

Session 370 Symposium:
Methylation, folate, metabolism and S-Adenodyl-methionine in psychiatric disorders

2399
ANTIDPRESSIVE ACTION OF SAME, CLINICAL EVIDENCE FROM ITALY
Diego de Leo, M.D.
Dept. of Psychiatry, University of Padua,
Via Guistiniani, 2 Padua, Italy

Data from numerous international studies, both open and double blind controlled, indicated that SAMe, given parenterally or orally to depressed subjects, produces significant clinical improvement. SAMe is reported to act more rapidly than traditional antidepressant (4-6 days) and appears to be free of side effects, save for the possible induction of mania and increased agitation. The mechanism of its pharmacological action is not yet known: it may be related to increased turnover of serotonin and noradrenaline, or to some change of membrane linked biological signal transmission due to the phospholipid methylation induced by SAMe. The compound was initially studied in Italy, and its antidepressive action was clinically observed in the early seventies. After these preliminary but significant indications, numerous other studies gave confirmatory results. In the eighties more diagnostically defined studies furnished the definitive conviction that SAMe has a clinically relevant action in depressive syndromes, especially in major mood disorders. Today the clinical use of SAMe is well established in Italy and its properties against depression widely recognized.

2400

ORAL S-ADENOSYL-METHIONINE IN THE TREATMENT OF DEPRESSION.
B.L. Kagan, D.L. Sultzer, N. Rosenlicht, H. Gerner
West Los Angeles V.A. Medical Center, Dept. of Psychiatry, UCLA School of Medicine and UCLA Neuropsychiatric Institute, Los Angeles, CA 90024.

Methylation has long been implicated in the etiology of psychiatric illness. Parenterally administered S-adenosyl-methionine (SAM, a biologically important methyl group donor, has previously been shown to be an effective antidepressant. We studied the antidepressant effect of oral SAM in a double-blind, placebo controlled trial in 15 inpatients with major depression. Our results demonstrate that oral SAM, like parenteral SAM, appears to be a safe and effective antidepressant with virtually no side effects and a rapid onset of action. We also found that SAM induced mania in a patient with no previous history of bipolar illness. We suggest that SAM may have potential for use in a broad spectrum of patients who cannot tolerate tricyclic antidepressants. These findings support the hypothesis that methylation may play a role in the pathophysiology of affective disorders.

2401

SHORTENING OF LATENCY PERIOD IN DEPRESSION TREATED WITH SAM
E. Alvarez, C. Udina, R. Guillamat
Dept. of Psychiatry, School of Medicine, U.A.B. Hospital Sant Pau, Avda. Sant Antoni Maria Claret, 167 / 08025 Barcelona, Spain

S-Adenosylmethionine (SAM) is the main physiological donor or methyl groups in the brain. It plays an important role in most transmethylation reactions. Clinical studies have given evidence of its beneficial effects on mood. We carried out a trial with the aim of studying the possible shortening of therapeutic latency in the conventional pharmacological treatment of depression. We included 22 out-patients. All were diagnosed as having major depressive disorder according to DSM III criteria. The patients had to score 20 or more on the 18-item Hamilton rating scale of depression (HRSD). The day improvement began was detected by means of the above mentioned analogical scale, evaluating the patient according to HRSD and the Beck self-rating scale. Improvement was considered to have begun on the day on which there was a score reduction of at least 60% compared with day 0 values. With respect to this clinical parameter, there is a significant difference in favor of the group treated with SAM, who showed improvement before those given placebo (SAM 10.7, placebo 25.8, p. less than 0.05) U-test.

2402

An Open Trial of S-Adenosyl-L-Methionine in ADHD, RS.
W. Shekim, R. Asarnow, R. Antun[*], G. Hanna, J. McCracken

UCLA Neuropsychiatric Institute
[*]Hamad General Hospital, Doha, Qatar

The psychostimulants d-amphetamine and methylphenidate are thought to be the most effective treatment in children, adolescents, and adults with attention deficit-hyperactivity disorder (ADHD) because they potentiate both dopamine (DA) and norepinephrine (NE) at the synaptic cleft. These medications are not free from side effects and controversy. Newer effective and safe treatments are needed. S-Adenosyl-L-Methionine (SAM), the active form of methionine acts as a methyl donor and is involved in many metabolic pathways. It has beta adrenergic and dopamine receptor agonist activity. We have been using SAM in a sample of well diagnosed adults with ADHD in a four week open trial to establish its effectiveness and safety. Preliminary data reveal that 75% of patients improve on it and that it is safe. Diagnostic work-up and SAM effectiveness on measures of attention, restlessness, impulsivity and mood, as well as laboratory measure will be discussed.

2403

ORAL S-ADENOSYL-L-METHIONINE: ITS ANTIDEPRESSANT POTENTIAL AND ITS EFFECT ON THYROTROPIN AND PROLACTIN RESPONSES TO THYROTROPIN-RELEASING HORMONE STIMULATION.

Jerrold F. Rosenbaum, M.D., Maurizio Fava, M.D., Robert MacLaughlin, M.S., William E. Falk, M.D., Mark H. Pollack, M.D., Lee S. Cohen, M.D.

Clinical Psychopharmacology Unit, Massachusetts General Hospital ACC 715, Boston, MA 02114, USA

S-adenosyl-l-methionine (SAMe) is a naturally occurring substance that has been found to be effective and well-tolerated in parenteral form as a treatment of major depression. Although its mechanism of action is still a matter of speculation, it has been postulated that SAMe may increase the dopaminergic tone in depressed patients. To explore the antidepressant potential of oral SAMe, we conducted a six-week open trial in 20 outpatients (10 males and 10 females) with major depression, including those with (N=9) and without (N=11) prior history of antidepressant non-response. The group as a whole significantly improved with oral SAMe with 7 of 11 non-treatment resistant and 2 of 9 treatment resistant patients experiencing full antidepressant response. Side-effects appeared to be mild and transient. Since dopamine inhibits both thyrotropin (TSH) and prolactin secretion, we also investigated the effects of treatment with SAMe on the TSH and prolactin response to thyrotropin-releasing hormone (TRH) stimulation in 17 of the same 20 depressed patients (10 males and 7 females). At the end of the six weeks of treatment with SAMe, there was a significant reduction in the response of both prolactin and TSH to TRH stimulation in the group of 10 depressed male patients compared to pre-treatment values, while there were no significant changes in prolactin and TSH responses to TRH in the female group. Our results seem to suggest an antidepressant effect of oral SAMe and to support, at least in males, the hypothesis of a stimulating effect of SAMe on brain dopaminergic pathways.

Session 371   Symposium:
Cross-cultural approaches to the improvement of treatment in psychiatry

2404
Cross-cultural aspects of WHO collaborative studies: advantages and problems
Prilipko, L. L.
World Health Organization

WHO is in a unique position in the field of health, representing a neutral platform which can bring about international collaboration in research. WHO research is carried out within a worldwide network of institutions, scientific groups and individuals in member countries of WHO. This approach can lead to the creation of studies aimed at investigating problems which would be difficult or even impossible to solve at a national level in individual countries. For example, cross-cultural studies in such areas as the development of a common language; specific clinical, biological and social characteristics of widespread mental, neurological and psychosocial problems etc; the development of methods of treatment and prevention of these problems etc. At the same time, there are certain requirements identified on the basis of long-standing WHO experience which can be satisfied only in cross-cultural collaborative research because such studies otherwise would lead to undesirable consequences. The advantages of cross-cultural approaches as well as problems and possible solutions would be discussed.

2405
WHO Multicentre Research Programme of the Prophylactic Effect of Lithium
Marat E. Vartanian
All-Union Mental Health Research Centre

The WHO has created a multicentre programme studying the prophylactic effect of lithium in affective psychoses and the possible prediction of individual sensitivity of patients to this drug.
This program involves research workers of the WHO centres working in the field of biological psychiatry & psychopharmacology in Belgium, Italy, India, West Germany, USSR, Czechoslovakia, Japan, etc. The main goal of the programme is to determine the clinical, hereditary and pharmacokinetical parameters, correlating with the positive prophylactic effect of lithium therapy. The report discusses clinical features of patients-responders and non-responders, as well as their pharmacokinetical characteristics. The most informative parameters were used for the calculation of the so called integrative quantitative index, which may be used for the individual prediction of the preventive effect of lithium in affective psychoses. The methodology of multicentre studies of the preventive action of lithium is being discussed. Perspectives of transcultural studies of the effect of lithium therapy are also reviewed.

2406
COMPARATIVE STUDIES OF THE EFFECTS OF ANTIDEPRESSANT MEDICATION IN DIFFERENT POPULATIONS
B B SETHI, SANJAY GANDHI POST GRADUATE INSTITUTE OF MEDICAL SCIENCES, LUCKNOW, INDIA.

Antidepressants have been extensively investigated, since, only about 70% of the depressed patients are helped by these drugs and the remaining mainfest a poor response. A number of cross cultural studies employing different populations have confirmed the variable nature of the phenomenon of variation in dose requirements. A multicentric WHO Collaborative Study carried out at 7 centres in 5 countries has conclusively demonstrated that 75 mg/day of antidepressant drugs produce similar therapeutic results as 150 mg/day of these drugs in socio-culturally and ethinically different populations. Based on these observations it is hypothesised that there exists constitutional, acquired and environmental differences in antidepressant dose response. The author in this communication have critically compared the data from a number of comparative studies of antidepressant drugs in different populations and have also summarized the WHO multicentric study. Guidelines for future research in this area have been outlined.

2407
TREATMENT OF THERAPY RESISTANT DEPRESSION
Gastpar M.
Rheinische Landes und Hochschulklinik, Essen, W. Germany

The presentation includes first a discusssion of the various definitions of the term "therapy resistance depression", then gives an example based on a WHO collaborative study on treatment of depressed patients. The results show the influence of various degrees of therapy resistance on treatment outcome and the characteristics of the patients in terms of present symptoms and previous course of the illness. Conclusions for the treatment strategies and for the planning of further studies are drawn.

2408
NEW TREATMENT OF ANXIETY STATES
Garranza J. - Mexico

Session 372   Symposium:
Plasma level monitoring of antipsychotic drug therapy - Pros and cons

2409
CONDITIONS FOR MEANINGFUL PLASMA LEVEL MONITORING OF NEUROLEPTICS

Svein G. Dahl

Institute of Medical Biology, University of Tromsø
N-9001 Tromsø, Norway

The rationale behind plasma level monitoring of neuroleptics is that lack of response to antipsychotic drug treatment might be due to inappropriate drug concentrations in the brain. Besides guiding drug concentrations into a range optimal for therapeutic response, further goals of therapeutic monitoring of neuroleptics are to reduce concentration-dependent side effects in patients who obtain high drug levels on normal doses due to pharmacokinetic variations, and to control and increase compliance. In order to obtain clinically useful results from such monitoring, the following conditions must be fulfilled: (1) A therapeutic and/or toxic plasma level range has been established in studies using randomly allocated, fixed doses of the drug, (2) no other neuroleptics are concomitantly administered, (3) blood samples are collected at steady state and at least 8 hr after drug intake, and (4) the assay method is sufficiently specific, accurate and sensitive. If these conditions are not fulfilled, such blood level monitoring may be misleading. Up to now therapeutic plasma level ranges have been reported from studies with chlorpromazine, fluphenazine, haloperidol, perphenazine, sulpiride, thioridazine and thiothixene, while other studies have found no such relationship. The present status concerning plasma level response relationships for neuroleptics will be briefly reviewed.

2410
A THERAPEUTIC WINDOW FOR HALOPERIDOL

Theodore Van Putten, M.D., Veterans Administration Medical Center, Los Angeles, USA

Sixty-seven (67) newly (re)admitted drug free schizophrenic men were randomly assigned to receive haloperidol either 5, 10 or 20 mg daily for four weeks. Clinical response was measured at the end of the fixed dose period, and haloperidol was assayed by a radioimmunoassay. We found a powerful curvilinear, but not linear, relationship between clinical response and plasma haloperidol during fixed dose treatment. The therapeutic window appeared to be between 2 and 12 ng/ml. The "acid test," however, is whether patients with plasma levels greater than 12 ng/ml improve as their plasma levels are lowered. When plasma levels above 12 ng/ml were lowered into the therapeutic window, all cases improved to varying degrees, and no patient deteriorated. When nonresponders within the therapeutic window had their plasma levels raised above 12 ng/ml (as in routine practice) they, on balance, deteriorated in that these patients became more dysphoric. Patients with plasma levels below 2 ng/ml improved as their plasma levels were raised into the therapeutic window. On the 20 mg dose, half the patients had plasma levels above 12 ng/ml.

2411
CLINICAL EXPERIENCE WITH THERAPEUTIC PLASMA LEVEL MONITORING OF HALOPERIDOL
LP Balant, AE Balant-Gorgia, G Garrone, Department of Psychiatry, University of Geneva, 1211 Geneva 4, Switzerland

"Incisive" neuroleptics such as haloperidol are necessary drugs, but are difficult to use: they have a narrow therapeutic margin and their steady-state plasma concentrations show large inter-patient variability, both after i.m. and p.o. administration. This variability results from the pharmacokinetic properties of the drug or from poor compliance of the patient. Therapeutic monitoring is thus a valuable help for the clinician in the individualization of posology. In Geneva, about 250 plasma samples of neuroleptics are analyzed each year. This had a number of consequences such as: a) Improved dosage adaptation when changing from i.m. to p.o. and depot administration; b) Use of low dosages; c) Lower incidence of severe side-effects; d) Case reports for teaching pharmacotherapy to medical and nursing staff; e) Improved confidence in the potential of neuroleptics and better understanding of their limitations. However, more work is necessary in order to further improve the risk to benefit ratio of these drugs in individual patients.

2412

PLASMA LEVEL EFFECT RELATIONSHIPS OF ORAL BENZAMIDES AND PHENOTHIAZINES
Wiesel, F-A. and Farde, L.
Department of Psychiatry and Psychology
Karolinska Institute and Hospital
104 01 STOCKHOLM, Sweden

In the early phase of drug treatment of schizophrenic patients it is possible to deomostrate a positive correlation between chlorpromazine concentrations in serum and clinical improvement. This relationship is lost at the same period of time as tolerance for the drug effect on dopamine metabolism was developed. The development of tolerance may explain the loss of the correlation between drug concentrations and clinical effects.

The benzamide sulpiride has less complicated metabolism than chlorpromazine and should therefore be more optimal in the study of relationships between drug concentrations and clinical effects. In a first study it was possible to demonstrate a therapeutic window for sulpiride concentrations in the treatment of patients with schizophrenia. In a later study it was only possible to demonstrate the lower point of an optimal concentration interval.

The lack of unequivocal linear correlations between clinical effects and drug concentrations may be explained by the fact that D2-dopamine receptor blockade is following a hyperbolic function. Since receptor occupancy in the treatment with conventional doses of neuroleptics are at a high level 65-85%, a several fold difference in drug concentrations between patients will only result in minor differences in receptor occupancy.

2413

THERAPEUTIC PLASMA LEVELS OF DEPOT NEUROLEPTICS
S.R. Marder, Brentwood V.A. Medical Center and UCLA, Los Angeles, U.S.A.

The author will review the current state of knowledge of the usefulness of plasma level measurement for monitoring patients on depot neuroleptics, and will present new data from ongoing studies. The first study compares metabolism of fluphenazine (FLU) in patients who received oral and depot FLU. Samples were analyzed using radioimmunoassays for fluphenazine (FLU), fluphenazine sulfoxide (FS), 7-hydroxy fluphenazine (7OHFLU), and fluphenazine N-oxide (FNO). For oral FLU the levels of FS and 7OHFLU were significantly higher than levels of FLU. For fluphenazine decanoate (FD), the levels of metabolites were not significantly different than FLU levels, indicating that drug metabolism is more important for patients treated with an oral as opposed to a depot phenothiazine. In another study, FLU levels were analyzed in patients in a comparison of 5 vs 25 mg of FD. We studied the relationship between FLU at 6 and 9 months and rate of psychotic exacerbations with logistic regression during the subsequent year. Both analyses were statistically significant (at 6 mo, $p=.04$; at 9 mo, $p=.01$); suggesting that measuring FLU plasma levels in patients treated with FD may be clinically useful.

2414

SERUM LEVELS AT LOWEST EFFECTIVE NEUROLEPTIC DOSAGE

Jes Gerlach & Kristen Kistrup

Sct. Hans Hospital, Dept. P, 4000 Roskilde, Denmark

Two groups of schizophrenic outpatients were treated with perphenazine decanoate (N=20) and cis(z)-flupenthixol decanoate (N=24). Every 3 months the dose was gradually reduced until symptoms appeared that were suggestive of a prodromal phase of a psychotic episode. A slightly higher dose was then promptly reinstituted (the lowest effective dose). At each dose level, 2 blood samples were drawn for determination of serum concentration.

The mean effective dose of perphenazine decanoate was 99.3 mg/2 weeks (range 21.5-270.5), while the lowest effective dose of cis(z)-flupenthixol decanoate was 60 mg/2 weeks (range 20-250). The corresponding mean serum levels of perphenazine decanoate was 7.3 nmol/l (range 2.0-18.1), of cis(z)-flupenthixol decanoate 8.5 nmol/l (range 1.3-40.0).

There was a significant correlation between the administered doses and the corresponding serum levels ($r=0.87$, $P<0.01$). A weak positive correlation was found between serum levels at the lowest effective dose and BPRS scores ($r=0.53$, $P<0.02$) for perphenazine, but not cis(z)-flupenthixol ($r=0.11$). No correlation was found between serum levels and side effects, diagnoses or length of neuroleptic treatment. The results do not support the existence of a therapeutic window when using perphenazine decanoate and cis(z)-flupenthixol decanoate in the maintenance phase of schizophrenic outpatients.

Session 373   Special Session:
Issues on international classification

2415

The ICD-10 Criteria List - A New Diagnostic Instrument
V.Dittmann*, H.J. Freyberger* & R.-D. Stieglitz**
* Department of Psychiatry, Medical University Lübeck
** Department of Psychiatry, Free University Berlin

In addition to the WHO field trial on ICD-10 the Diagnostic Comission of the German Psychiatric Association (DGPN) carries out an empirical study with an own design. Fields on special interests are: comparison of ICD-9, ICD-10 and DSM-III R diagnoses, evaluation of frequency, relevance, sensivity and specifity of the diagnostic criteria, relation between the diagnostic categories, influences of interviewer variables and last not least, a development of a computer expert system. During the preparation of this study it was obvious, that a diagnostic instrument was necessary, which should contain all criteria and be practicable under clinical circumstances as well. Therefore the ICD-10 Criteria List was developed. About 750 diagnostic criteria were grouped under aspects of psychopathology, behaviour, environment and somatic disorders. First empirical results of a multicentric study are demonstrated.

2416

Reception of ICD-10 in German-speaking Countries

H.J. Freyberger*, H. Dilling*, V. Dittmann* &
R.-D. Stieglitz**
* Department of Psychiatry, Medical University
  Lübeck
** Department of Psychiatry, Free University Berlin

Based on the data evaluated during the multicentric field trial for assessing the ease of understanding and use of the "Clinical Descriptions and Diagnostic Guidelines" of ICD-10, chapter V, 1987 draft, the reception of ICD-10 in German-speaking countries will be discussed. With respect to the structure of ICD-10, goodness of fit of the different diagnostic categories, interrater-reliability of diagnostic categories and between participating centres and differences between diagnoses in ICD-9 and ICD-10 are presented.

2417

An Approach to an Expert System for ICD-10

P. Gugel*, R.R. Engel* & V. Dittmann**

* Department of Psychiatry, Ludwig-Maximilians-
  University Munich
** Department of Psychiatry, Medical University
  Lübeck

The present paper describes the current state of the work in progress of an expert system. The purpose of that system should be to give support to psychiatrists concerned with diagnoses of mental disorders in terms of ICD-10 categories. The frame-based system will incorporate all diagnostic categories of ICD-10 and should be able to deduce all possible ICD-10 diagnoses from symptoms, signs and characteristics mentioned by the "ICD-10 Criteria List" developed by DITTMANN et al. (1988). Data are acquired in dialogue with the user or by managing queries to a database system. Several difficulties in designing the structure of the knowledgebase, translating ICD-10 rules to a machine acceptable form and concerning necessary and usefull fill-up`s for the ICD-10 rule system are discussed. Furthermore the eventual fields of application of the system will be discussed.

2418

Schizophrenic and Affective Disorders in ICD-10

M. Albus* & M. Zaudig**
* Department of Psychiatry, Ludwig-Maximilians-
  University Munich
** Max-Planck-Institute for Psychiatry, Munich

Focussing at the diagnostic approach to schizophrenic and affective disorders, the most important innovations comparing ICD-9 and ICD-10 were discussed. Concerning the results of the multicentric field trial in German-speaking countries, reliability coefficients obtained for schizophrenic and affective disorders and goodness of fit of these diagnostic categories are presented.

2419

Dementias according to ICD 10 and DSM-III-R

M. Zaudig, J. Mittelhammer, W. Hiller
Psychiatric Outpatient Department
Max-Planck-Institute for Psychiatry, Munich

There are still no diagnostic screening instruments which include DSM-III-R and ICD 10 algorithms for detecting dementia syndroms. The authors describe a structured interview (SIDAM) for the standardized assessment of dementia syndroms according to DSM-III-R and ICD 10. The instrument can be easily used by physicians and clinicians. The average time for the interview is 28 minutes. Scores for the Mini Mental State (Folstein et al., 1980) are included within the instrument as well as the Hachinski Score (Hachinski et al., 1975). Our results indicate a good to excellent reliability and validity (e.g. concordance rates on the diagnostic level with kappa values between 0.85 and 0.95); test-retest reliability on diagnostic, criterion and item level have generally been found to be good with kappa values between 0.4 and 1.0. Results of the test-retest-study and other data are discussed in detail. The SIDAM was found to distinguish between diagnostic categories among older subjects with a wide range of cognitive deficits. These advances have immediate relevance with respect to the choice of therapy and pharmacological treatment trials.

2420

CRITERIA OF ICD-8, 9 TO 10 IN NATIONAL STATISTICS OF MENTAL DISORDERS FROM 1971 TO 84.

Masaaki Kato, Tokyo Medical College, Japan.

Based on national Statistics of Mental Disorders in Japan, some criteria on ICD-8, 9 to 10 were pointed out. The statistics was depended on one day survey on every third Wednesday of July. Although total number of patients increased, outpatient 80%, inpatient 7%, remarkable increase was shown in senile psychosis, depression, neurotic depression, drug dependence etc. Along with these results, some criteria will be pointed out on the application of ICD-9 and 10 in Japan.

2421

STRUCTURAL ANALYSIS OF DEPRESSION WITH A HIERARCHICAL CLUSTERING MODEL

M. Paes de Sousa and M.H. Bacelar Nicolau
Dept. of Psychiatry. Faculty of Medicine of Lisbon Hospital Stª. Maria. Av. Prof. Egas Moniz. P-1600 Lisbon. Portugal

The symptomatology of 424 patients (220 hospitalized and 204 ambulatory) suffering from different nosologic types of depression (endogenous bipolar and unipolar, neurotic, reactive, endo-reactive and involutional) was assessed by the AMDP system. A correspondance analysis performed on the matrix of the scores of each symptom gives us a clear distinction between the endogenous and exogenous types of depression; the endo-reactive and involutional types of depression remained in an intermediate position. Later we used a hierarchical clustering model based on the validity of link under general statistical hypothesis. The clustering tree branches we obtained clear define a general depression structure and also a set of symptom patterns of the different depressive nosologies.

2422

DATA ON A TAXONOMY OF AFFECTIVE DISORDERS BASED ON POLARITY

G. Ionescu
"Dr. Gh. Marinescu" Clinical Hospital,
Bucharest, Romania

Out, of 860 patients hospitalized for nonbipolar and bipolar affective disorders, the author selects eight apariate groups, of 30 patients each, corresponding to the four categories of polarity: unipolar I, II, III, IV and bipolar, I, II, III, IV, respectively.

The taxonomy was based on the study of the in-patients, who were investigated under the aspect of :
— personal psychiatric antecedents ;
— disorder history in patient's family ;
— "present" clinical examination by structured interview, as well as by non-directive (non-conducted) examination ;
— personality features, examined during remission periods ;
— therapeutic responsiveness.

The importance of the paper consists in the fact that the belonging to one polarity group offers predicting elements as regards :
— therapeutic (psycho-pharmacological) responsiveness ;
— disorder course and prognostic.

2423

PREMIERE NOSOGRAPHIE ENSEMBLISTE

MARCHAIS Pierre, Hôpital Foch, 40 rue Worth, 92151 - SURESNES, FRANCE.

Les maladies mentales ne sont pas réductibles à des phénomènes naturels. Elles résultent aussi de conventions entre psychiatres. En outre, les recherches actuelles témoignent que le trouble mental se développe dans un espace pluridimensionnel. Il convient donc d'envisager une refonte de la nosographie.

Cette nosographie doit être cohérente en elle-même et en étroite correspondance avec les réalités cliniques observées.

Le recours à une logique d'ensembles permet de proposer une première nosographie ensembliste fondée sur des processus psychopathologiques.

2424

A COMPARATIVE STUDY OF SCHIZOPHRENIA AND MOOD DISORDERS AMONG FRENCH CLASSIFICATIONS (F.C.), DSM-III-R AND ICD-10.
BARUA U., LAZARTIGUES A., MURGUI E., MORALES H., Clinique DUPRE- FSEF, 30 Avenue F. Roosevelt, 92331 SCEAUX CEDEX-FRANCE

OBJECTS : To compare diagnostics obtained with F.C. (MISES et al), DSM-III R and ICD-10 for schizophrenia and mood disorders with 40 patients 16-19 years.

METHODOLOGY: sample constitution: from a cross section of hospitalised patients for whom a clinical diagnosis of schizophrenia and mood disorders given. Data collected by rating the standardized interview (videotyped) constructed with items of SADS, PSE, SANS, and empérical which allowed to explore the entire critéria of studied 3 diagnostic systems. DSM-III-R and ICD-10 diagnosis are made from the rating index. French classification diagnosis made by one research worker from the videotyped recorded standardized interview. Interrater reliability of the given ratings controlled regularly from interview drawned (I : 8) and rated independently by 4 clinicians. The same procedures done for the diagnostic reliability.

RESULTS : Every patients given diagnosis of three classifications. By classifications given the percentage of class and non-class dividing up between catagory and sub-categories, concordance and non concordance, inter-rater reliability by categories.

CONCLUSIONS : The reason of non-concordances are analysed.

2425

VALIDITY ISSUES OF THE CIDI IN THE DIAGNOSIS OF PSYCHIATRIC IN-PATIENTS.

G.TACCHINI, A.C.ALTAMURA, M.T.COPPOLA, A.MUSAZZI

Institute of Psychiatry - University of Milan
Via F. Sforza 35, 20122 Milano - ITALY

Our Institute has taken part to the W.H.O. CIDI Field Trials with a sample of chronic psychiatric patients.

Since procedure validity of CIDI has already been assessed in the Field Trial Study, our work focusses on content or internal validity: in fact among the pre-requisites for eligibility of a patient in our sample a minimum of 3' hospital in-stays with 3 concordant clinical diagnoses.

Since clinical diagnosis is generally regarded as the standmark, our study correlates the clinical diagnosis of each patient with his CIDI diagnosis, and attempts sensibility and specificity assessment.

Main sources of discordant diagnostic assessment are identified and briefly analyzed.

Session 374 New Research:
Life events and adjustment disorders

2426

SANTE ET RESEAU DE SUPPORT DE SOIGNANTES NATURELLES DU MALADE MENTAL.
RICARD N., COUSINEAU H.
L'UNIVERSITE DE MONTREAL

Cet exposé présente les résultats d'une étude récente qui avait but de vérifier l'existence de relations entre l'état de santé de soignantes naturelles de malades mentaux chroniques et leur réseau de soutien social et professionnel. La problématique de cette recherche porte sur les conséquences iatrogéniques de la désinstitutionnalisation des malades mentaux, sur la santé des femmes qui doivent assurer la responsabilité de la prise en charge de ces malades. Un échantillon de convenance de 61 femmes vivant avec un malade suivi en psychiatrie, a été utilisée. Des instruments standardisés ont évalué la santé physique, mentale et sociale des répondantes, leur réseau de soutien social et professionnel et les exigences des soins au malade. Sommairement, il ressort que 50% des répondantes rapportent un niveau élevé de détresse psychologique. Elles rapportent plus de problèmes de santé physique et consomment plus de tranquillisants et de sédatifs, que des femmes de mêmes groupes d'âge. Les analyses en régression n'indiquent pas de liens entre le soutien social et professionnel et l'état de santé des soignantes. Les exigences des soins sont en corrélation significative modérée avec la santé mentale et physique des répondantes. Les recherches futures devraient faire une meilleure évaluation du fardeau de soins, ce que nous réalisons actuellement dans le cadre d'une nouvelle recherche dont nous présenterons le devis.

2427

DEPRESSIVE AND ANXIOUS CONSEQUENCES OF CHRONIC STRESS

GC Davis and N Breslau, Henry Ford Hospital; Detroit, Michigan, U.S.A.

Six month and lifetime rates of DSM-III Major Depression (MD) and Generalized Anxiety Disorder (GAD) and depressive symptoms were compared in mothers of children with severe disabilities (chronic stress, n=310) and a probability sample (controls, n=357). MD and GAD were ascertained by the NIMH-DIS and current depressive symptoms were measured by the CES-D. Mothers in the chronic stress sample had significantly higher rates of GAD and depressive symptoms. Six months and lifetime GAD in the chronic stress sample were 17.5% and 56% respectively, and in the controls, 11.5% and 45% respectively. The rate of depressive symptoms (CES-D score >16) was 30.2 in the chronic stress vs. 16.1% in controls. Rates of MD were not significantly different in the two groups: six months and lifetime MD were in the chronic stress sample 8.4% and 18.4% respectively and in the controls, 6.8% and 16.6%. The data indicate that chronic stress increases the risk for depressive and anxious symptoms but not for major depression.

2428

LIFE-EVENTS AND BIOLOGICAL MARKERS OF DEPRESSION

M.Ansseau, C.Lamberty, R.von Frenckell, P.Papart, M.A.Gérard, J.Wauthy, G.Franck, CHU, Liège, Belgium.

Over the last decade, the so-called "biological markers" of depression have attracted increasing interest. However the influence of external events on such biological parameters has been little studied. The purpose of the present study was therefore to analyze the relationship between the life-events preceding hospitalization and abnormalities in the dexamethasone suppression test (DST) and the growth hormone (GH) to clonidine and apomorphine neuroendocrine challenges in 41 major depressive inpatients. Neuroendocrine procedures have been previously described (Ansseau et al., Psychiatry Res, 12, 261-272, 1984); the collection of life-events was performed according to the method of Paykel and Mangen. Results showed significantly more total negative impact of life-events among patients exhibiting DST nonsuppression or blunted GH response to apomorphine. In contrast, blunted GH response to clonidine was not associated with higher level of life-events. These findings suggest that DST and apomorphine test may represent state-markers of depression whereas clonidine test may represent a trait-marker.

2429

PSYCHOLOGICAL DISTURBANCE AFTER DISASTER AT SEA

Dr. Peter Storey
The Priory Hospital
London
England

34 crew members (excluding officers) survived a ferry disaster (Herald of Free Enterprise) in March 1987. All but one were seen seven months later. Ages 17-58 (mean 33); 31 men, 3 women; spouse or other relative in 33:34; general practitioner medical record seen for each.

Results include: tension 34:34 (severe 13); anxiety 33:34 (severe 16); depression 25:34 (severe 4); aggression/irritability 31:34 (severe 5).

Post Traumatic Stress Disorder (more than minor)

Re-experiencing type   19:34
Numbing type   26:34
Arousal type   20:34

Considerable family effects   27:34

Two year follow up data on 19 will be available by October 1989.

2430

SEVERE PATERNAL INCEST DURING CHILDHOOD AND SYSTEMATIC AGRESSION AGAINST THE FAMILY AND INSTITUTION
Leichner, P. Bigras, J. Perreault, M. Lavoie, R. Douglas Hospital

In the course of supervising nursing staff on a general adult psychiatric unit, 11 chronic psychotic patients with severe behavior problems were identified. In the study of these patients: 5 males and 6 females revealed that all had been abused by their father during their childhood. The abuse appeared early, 9 patients being abused for the first time at the age of 5 or earlier. The abuse were of long duration approximately 7 years. Eventually, 11 victims became chronic psychotics and developed a severe behavioral disorder which became the systematic agression against the family and the institution. In each of these cases worsening of the symptoms was precipitated when they were rejected totally by their family and/or the institution. The social-demographic and clinical characteristics of this group will be presented and compared with those of other studies. This suggest that the severity of the psychiatric symptoms is associated with the severity and the precocity of the incest. The purpose of this presentation is to draw attention of health care professionals to the presence of a history of precocious and violent incests in these most difficult patients. Early identification may allow for specific interventions that may prevent the tragic outcome in these patients.

2431

HOPELESSNESS IN MILITARY DRAFTEES: THE FIRST 50 DAYS IN SERVICE
A.Botsis*,C.R.Soldatos**,S.Liritzis*,A.Kokkevi**
*Hell.Army Med.Corps,**Dept.Psychiat.Univ.Athens, Greece

As part of a large project aiming at identifying risk factors for suicide attempts in military draftees, the present study focused on the prevalence of feelings of hopelessness and their correlates. The representative sample of 600 young (19-29 years of age) draftees were examined immediately following recruitment (time point A). Of them, 528 were re-examined at about 50 days later (time point B), the remaining 72 being unavailable. In addition to an inventory of basic sociodemographic parameters, a battery of self-administered psychometric instruments was utilized: Beck's Hopelessness (BHS) and Depression (BDS) scales, Fould's Hostility and Direction of Hostility scale, MMPI, Codington's Life Event scale (SRRS). Because of restrictive reliability criteria, the sample subjected to analysis was limited to N=412.
In 14% of the sample (N=57), BHS scored high (>5) at either time point A or B. Of them, 8 scored equally high at both time points, 26 scored higher at time point A and 23 higher at time point B. Statistical analysis showed that psychopathology, particularly that of the depressive type, as well as self-destructive ideation were more pronounced in the subsample which manifested an increase of hopelessness 50 days following recruitment. Data were subjected to multivariate analysis and the relative contribution of various factors to the development of hopelessness was identified.

2432

Grief in endogenous and neurotic depression
and in depressive reaction in advanced age.

Prof. Dr. Dr. Bernhard Bron
Klinik für Psychiatrie der Universität Göttingen

This study is based on the investigation of pathological grief reactions in 339 patients older than 45 years. All subjects underwent psychiatric treatment for endogenous or neurotic depression or for depressive reaction. Grief reactions mostly were preceded by loss of father, mother, partner, child, sibling or other relative, or by loss of friends and acquaintances - the loss occuring some years ago or just before the start of the actual treatment. Pathological grief reactions show a lot of different manifestations. Their frequency in endogenous and neurotic depression as well as in depressive reactions in advanced age and intersexual differences are discussed. Pathological grief reactions are distinctly more frequent in women; for endogenous depression this finding even reaches statistical significance. Factors complicating the work of mourning are specially described.

2433

Life events and social network as
independent factors in depression.
C.M.Cornelis, M.D.; Prof.Dr.F.de Jonghe;
E.H.Ameling, Ph.D.
Psychiatric Clinic of the University of
Amsterdam, Amsterdam, The Netherlands

This paper reports the results of a study concerning the role and mutual independency of social network and life events as factors in depression. The study population (N=48) consisted of 24 new outpatients with as DSM III diagnosis Major Depression or Dysthymic Disorder, and 24 healthy matched controls. Measurements were made by means of the semistructured interview for Recent Life Events(Paykel), a social network inventory using objective and subjective criteria, and the Zung Depression Rating Scale. If both life events and social network independently influence the degree of the depressed state, these variables would be correlated with a measure for depression and not with each other. In our sample the correlations between social network parameters appear to be almost zero, while their separate correlations with the criterium variable for depression, the ZDRS, were statistically significant. The results show that life events and social network act as independent factors in depression, together accounting for 29,8% of the total variance.

2434

Does Our Emperor's Death Provoke
Mental Disorder?

NANKO,S.

Dept. of Psychiat. Univ. of Teikyo
Sch. of Med.   Tokyo   JAPAN

Our Emperor died on 7th of January, 1989. It was a great shock for the most of Japanese people, because He was regarded as a god before the World War II. Immediately after His death, at least four Japanese committed a suicide following Him.
He was reported to be seriously ill on September the last year. We were very much concerned about His illness. Thus we studied whether this event influenced on mental condition of the psychiatric patients or not.
Subjects and Method: 89 patients with schizophrenia, affective disorder or neurotic disorder who visited the Outpatient Clinic, Dept of Psychiat, Teikyo Univ Hosp. from 20th to 28th of December, 1988, were asked to fulfill the questionnaire.
Result: 22 patients admitted that their mental condition got worse since Sept. last year. Of them, four thought it was due to our Emperor's illness.

2435

AMITRIPTYLINE IN THE TREATMENT OF PTSD IN TORTURE SURVIVORS:
A CASE STUDY
Metin Basoglu, Isaac Marks, Seda Sengun- Institute of Psychiatry
London, U.K.

So far there are no systematic treatment studies of post-traumatic stress disorder (PTSD) in torture survivors. Single case studies have shown that antidepressants can be useful in treating PTSD related to other types of trauma but these studies have used global measures of outcome without a detailed analysis of drug effect on different PTSD symptoms. The present study investigated the effect of amitriptyline on PTSD symptoms in a torture survivor 7 years after the trauma. After a pre-treatment assessment period of one month, amitriptyline 150 mg nocte was started and regular follow-up assessments were carried out up to 6 months. Assessments included patient- and assessor-ratings of depression, anxiety, PTSD symptoms, and social and work adjustment. Patient's symptoms showed no change during the pre-treatment assessment period. An overall improvement of 70% was noted 8 weeks after the start of treatment. Improvement was most marked in depression (90%), anxiety (80%), and in social and work adjustment (80%) but less so in PTSD symptoms (40%). Residual symptoms included nightmares, constricted affect, aggressive urges, startle response, and phobic avoidance. The results are suggestive of a general, patholytic drug action and are thus consistent with the findings of other drug studies in anxiety disorders. The limitations of drug treatment and the implications of these findings for psychotherapy of torture survivors will be discussed.

Session 375   New Research:
Family psychopathology and family treatment

2436
THE NIMH BEHAVIOR FAMILY THERAPY SKILL MEASURE (BFTSM): RELIABILITY AND VALIDITY
Laporta M; Falloon IRH; Shanahan W; Hole V; Mental Health Service, Buckingham, England.

Behavioral Family Therapy (BFT) has been shown to be significantly effective in reducing the clinical, social and family morbidity in schizophrenia. We have developed a measure to quantify therapist BFT skills which we will relate to outcome in multicenter NIMH study of treatment strategies in schizophrenia. In this way, we hope to detail how the approach conveys its therapeutic effects. The BFTSM will also serve in standardizing BFT training. The measure consists of eight scales of basic BFT technique clusters used in each BFT session, and a Global Impression of Skills, all rated on a 5-point meter. Eleven BFT audio tapes were rated by three independent raters for the psychometric studies. The average difference in skill ratings were less than 0.5 ($p < 0.05$) for any two raters. Preliminary validity measures show a significant linear relationship.

2437
PSYCHO-SOCIAL PROFILE OF FAMILIES WITH SCHIZOPHRENIC MEMBERS
BELTZ J., GARAVAGLIA R., BERTRANDO P., BRESSI C., CLERICI M., MALAGOLI M., INVERNIZZI G.
Department of Psychiatry, University of Milan, Milan, Italy

The Association for the Research on Schizophrenia (ARS) is working with families of schizophrenic patients in an area between public and private health service. We investigated a sample of 182 subjects who belonged to 140 households with a schizophrenic member, focusing on their psycho-social profile and their needs and requirements as well as our effectiveness in planning and performing such interventions. Findings revealed that:
1) as to the duration of the illness, patients are grouped into subpopulations: the first one has about two-year peak, the second one about seven-year peak; 2) among patients of families attending ARS, 45% were receiving a public service treatment, 28% a private assistence and 25% none at all; 3) public service mostly offers long-acting drug therapy, whereas psychotherapy is more common in private centers; 4) families' average school level seems to be higher than local mean population one; 5) relatives' demands concern most of all coping with the patients (46%), general aid (37%), diagnosis and treatment (26%), although a great deal of families already experienced a psychiatric service; 6) relatives' demands are anyhow similar, either their ill relative is under cure or not; 7) patients tend to stay a long time with their parental families.

2438
EXPRESSED EMOTION AND TREATMENT OF SCHIZOPHRENIA: ONE YEAR FOLLOW-UP
CAZZULLO C.L., BERTRANDO P., BRESSI C., CAMBIAGHI P., CLERICI M., DONATINI L., MERATI O.
Department of Psychiatry, University Of Milan, Milan, Italy

Family intervention with relatives of schizophrenic patients run at the Association for the Research on Schizophrenia (ARS) falls into two sequential series of group sessions: information and interpersonal relation groups. During step one relatives are offered a wide range of information about schizophrenia and discuss them; during step two, on the contrary, they are led to think upon and compare their own family interactions.
We selected a sample of 24 relatives for assessing the impact of their emotional styles on their response to group intervention. Before starting the group, each family member was reated according to the Expressed Emotion (EE) scales and, at the same time, his/her level of information was measured by means of the Knowledge Interview (KI). The early EE evaluation showed that 86% of relatives had "high EE" patterns (associated with a patient's high relapse rate), compared to an average 31% with relatives of schizophrenic patients. An additional KI, at the end of the information group, revealed, however, that information was actually received, aside from single relative's EE pattern.

2439
PSYCHOEDUCATIONAL GROUPS FOR RELATIVES OF SCHIZOPHRENIC PATIENTS
J. Bäuml, B. Bals, W. Kissling, H. Lauter

Psychiatrische Klinik rechts der Isar der TU München, W-Germany

Relapse rates of schizophrenic patients under standard therapy during the first year after discharge amount to about 50 to 60 %. The main reason is probably the fact that only 40 to 50 % receive maintenance therapy with neuroleptics. In order to influence the patients' therapy motivation beneficially, relatives were trained with a psychoeducational program for six months. According to comparisons before and after relatives felt more competent in managing the problems of the illness and showed improvement in their knowledge about schizophrenic disorders. At the end of ten sessions 80 to 90 % of the relatives accepted and emphatically supported neuroleptic maintenance therapy. During a 1-year follow-up about 85 % of the participants showed a very similar attitude with a positive effect on patients' compliance. One year relapse rate was about 15 %. In order to prove whether this good outcome is a specific effect of training the relatives, we are presently investigating a control group.

2440

FAMILY SYSTEMS TREATMENT IN ALCOHOLISM AND OTHER CHRONIC ILLNESSES

B. Gaccić, Center for family Therapy of Alcoholism, Belgrade, Yugoslavia.

In short introduction the author presents his point of view, based on 15 years experience, that alcoholism is the chronic human dysfunction, problem of the whole family context.
Similarities between alcoholism and other chronic illnesses are emphasized: development, maintenence, disabilites, adaptation coping strategies, treatment programs,etc. Family dysfunction and low quality of life style are pointed out among chronic disorders commonalities. Living with chronic illness, as well as, the need for better understanding and solving human problems are discussed. The change of attitudes for both professionals and family contexts in this era of deinstitutilization is important.
In conclusion the goal of the treatment is to improve the quality of life of all members of family. In author´s believe family therapies have become the treatment of choice: systemic, as well as, psychoeducational interventions. In fact, a conbination of interactive professional and non-professional (self-help) procedures is the best approach to both chronic psysical and mental illnesses.

2441

EXPRESSED EMOTION IN FAMILIES OF DISTURBED AND NORMAL CHILDREN

Hibbs ED, Hamburger SD, Lenane M, Rapoport JL, Kruesi MJP, Keysor CS. National Institute of Mental Health, Bethesda, MD, U.S.A.

Expressed Emotion (EE), which has been related to poor outcome in adult psychiatric groups, was measured in the parents of 124 children and adolescents with conduct disorder (CD) N=34, obsessive compulsive disorder (OCD) N=49, and normal controls (NC) N=41, to examine some of the determinants that influence parental EE.
Parental psychiatric diagnosis (using the SADS-L and DSM-III criteria), was significantly related to High-EE for both patient groups and for mothers and fathers, separately. While the EE of the patient groups did not differ from each other, each was significantly higher than that of the control group.
Low-EE was significantly related to absence of psychiatric diagnosis in both mothers and fathers of the control children. Fathers were five times more likely to be of High-EE status when they had any psychiatric diagnosis, and mothers were five times more likely to be of High-EE status when they had an affective disorder.
Hostility (using the Buss-Durkee hostility Inventory), was related to maternal EE; no such relationship obtained for the fathers. SES, age, and severity of the illness in the child, as tested with a logistic regression, did not seem to be a determinant for High-EE in the father.

2442

FAMILY EXPRESSED EMOTION IN CHRONIC RENAL PATHOLOGIES

BRESSI C., BERTRANDO P., CHIESA S., HEIG E., PIVA A., INVERNIZZI G.
Department of Psychiatry, University of Milan

Chronic nephropathy requires at first dialysis and often a kidney transplant. The patient's family system is fully involved in the illness as its management and adjustment to it are influenced by family members' reactions. Relatives, in fact, are the immediate mirror in which one can see the social ability of accepting a "chronically ill" person. People on dialytic treatment experience for a long time a clear-cut reduction in their psychophysical well-being and social life. Moreover, they go through a change of roles within the family, which will readjust its own transactions.
The present study aims at finding out whether relatives' Expressed Emotion (EE) rates may influence patient's adjustment to the therapy (dialysis) or to the surgical operation (kidney transplant). Our early sample is composed of 20 patients with complete six-months follow-up. Those families show an average EE rate quite high. Generally high Emotional Overinvolvement is related to high Warmth: This means that in this group family relationships were very good before the onset of the illness. Conversely low rates of Emotional Overinvolvement and Warmth characterize a high score of Hostility-related Criticism. A detailed analysis of each scale enabled us to detect family emotional factors which chiefly influence the patient's adjustment to the disease.

2443

CAMBERWELL FAMILY INTERVIEW: A STUDY OF ITS LINGUISTIC PARAMETERS

BERTRANDO P., BRESSI C., CLERICI M., CUNTERI L., ALBERTINI E., CAZZULLO C.L.
Department of Psychiatry, University of Milan, Milan, Italy.

Family Expressed Emotion (EE) assessment is obtained by means of the Camberwell Family Interview (CFI), which is the instrument for measuring the emotional asset of families with a psychic pathology. Starting from relatives' communication pattern during the interview, we centred our investigation on the form and content of the communication during the interview, in order to outline its relation with EE asset. The present paper aims at making some quantitative evaluation preliminary to the more complex study of communication patterns run with the Camberwell Family Interview. We therefore examined 16 CFI following these parameters:"time latency" (latency interval between the end of the question and the beginning of the answer) and "amount of speech" (amount of words uttered), together with some semantic criteria, such as thematization of the talk, redudancy, effects of disconfirmation. The outcomes showed that high EE relatives tend to give answers characterized by a reduced latency time and by a greater amount of speech. Under the semantic point of view, high EE group's answers are marked by the elusion of the task and tendency to collusion with the interlocutor.

Session 376
Free Communications:
Psychopathology in restorative medicine

2444

INFLUENCE OF PERSONALITY PROFILE AND FAMILY SOCIAL ENVIRONMENTAL CHARACTERISTICS IN THE ADJUSTMENT TO CHRONIC HEMODIALYSIS
J.E.Garcia-Camba,G.Barril,J.A.Traver,C.Bernis,V.Alvarez,J.Hz.Jaras,V.Paraiso,C.G.Canton,J.Ayala
Servicios Psiquiatría y Nefrología.Universidad Autónoma. Hospital de La Princesa. Madrid. Spain.

Patients with chronic renal failure receiving Hemodialysis (HD) treatment are in a stressful condition not only themselves but also their families.In our study we have analyzed the influence of patient psychological profile and their family enviroment on adjustment to the HD as well as in their attitude towards kidney transplantation.

The study included 57 patients(34M,23F) mean age 58.2 ± 1.8 y. and an average 34.5 months on HD.We got information about sociolaboral situation,adaptation and behavior in the care unit,degree of impairment of personal freedom because of HD,attitude and motivation towards renal transplantation.Biochemical variables were used to register disruption of medical compliance or dietetic transgression (K,PRC,BUN, weight gain).The personality was assesed along the 16 PF(Cattell) and the mesure of family climate by use of the Family Enviroment Scale(Moos and Moos).

The results showed significant diferences in the Cattell's source traits depending on they adjustment to the HD.The most positive attitudes to transplantation were found in patients with high scores in affectothyme pole and in those who came from families with the highest degree of cohesion and expresiveness.Agressivity and non compliance during HD sessions were associated with high family confict and low independence in family members.

2445

ADAPTABILITY TO DIALYSIS

A. Vaz-Serra, H.Firmino, F. Pocinho, M.João Costa, M.João Galvão and A. Marques
Psychiatric Department - University Hospital
3049   COIMBRA Codex - PORTUGAL

The autors tried to find psychological variables which could predict one's adaptability conditions to dialysis conditions to dialysis, as well as the incidence of depressive behaviour in this kind of patients.

To that purpose, the following measuring instruments were utilised:

PRI (Problem Resolution Inventory) - in order to evaluate the coping mechanisms;

Clinical Inventory of Self-concept - in order to evaluate self-concept;

A purpose-built Inventory to evaluate the adaptability to dialysis.

The results which were obtained demonstrate that a good level of sel-concept and good coping strategies facilitate a good adaptability to dialysis.

Furthermore, depression is frequent in dialysed patients and is directly related to bad coping strategies and a poor level of self-concept.

2446

A PSYCHIATRIC PROFILE OF DIALYSIS PATIENTS - A CLINICAL STUDY

Dr.R. RAJARAM MOHAN, B.Sc.,M.D.,(Psy) D.P.M.,
Dr.P.JONES RONALD, B.Sc.,M.D.,D.M.,(NEPH).
GOVERNMENT HEAD QUARTERS HOSPITAL, SALEM-636 007
TAMIL NADU - INDIA.

25 patients of chronic renal failure on haemo dialysis at Salem were studied over a period of one year for their psychiatric manifestations. The profile of psychiatric symptoms observed in these patients were categorised according to I.C.D.9 (WHO 1975). The different observations were correlated to patient's age and sex, socioeconomic status, martial status, duration and frequency of dialysis, and the future plan of therapy. The significance of their correlation was assessed by chi Square (X^2) test. The study revealed depression to be the commonest symptom, the others being suicidal behaviour, insomnia, disturbed interpersonal relationship and deviant illness behaviour. There was no significant correlation with regard to age and sex, martial status and duration of dialysis to the severity of psychiatric symptoms. However, the severity of psychiatric symptoms are found to be significantly related to the socioeconomic status, frequency of dialysis and future plan of therapy. The possible pathogenetic factors explaining this correlation are elucidated.

2447

PSYCHIATRIC ASPECTS OF HEART TRANSPLANTATION
Ary Knijnik - Institute of Cardiology,RS Brazil

Much has been written about the psychiatric aspects of heart transplantation, from biological to psychodynamic point of view.

Many complications have been reported such as anxiety, depression, organic mental disorder and alterations induced by immunosuppressive therapy. Another problem refers to patient's compliance with the treatment.

Examining 4 patients submitted to such procedure, the author observed psychological phenomena similar to those found in literature.Besides, it was noted that all patients revealed a primary preoccupation with the type of relation they had developed towards the new heart.Exploring their fantasies and its psychodynamic meaning, it was concluded that difficulties in management observed in the post - transplantation period and the use of ego's mechanism of defence so regressive as denial have close relation with fantasies connected to the trans - planted organ.

This presentation discusses fantasies founded and how they interfere in the clinical course of the procedure, determining, in some cases, even death by noncompliance or suicidal equivalents.

Finally the author suggests managements and shows that the situation of transplantation asks of the psychiatrist a total understanding of processes and interactions of several factors involved in emotional disease and, more than ever, in the situation of heart transplantation.

2448

EMOTIONAL ASPECTS OF CARDIAC TRANSPLANTATION

J. Boman Bastani, M.D. and Nilufer Vajarund
Bryan Memorial Hospital, Lincoln, Nebraska, U.S.A.

Cardiac Transplantation is not only a physical ordeal, it has strong psychological and financial implications. This paper describes the process of cardiac transplantation in which psychological complications may occur. The transplantation is perceived as an on-going process from the time of diagnosis of end stage heart disease when the psychiatrist is called on to play a significant role with his medical peers in determining the eligibility of the candidate. The psychiatric symptoms (depression, anxiety) associated with the stress of the illness and arising from the decompensating cardiac status (delirium, organic hallucinosis) play a significant role, but are not the sole criteria for exclusion from identifying them as transplant candidates. Psychiatric manifestations after surgery are seen from immediate post operative to several months after the transplant and the candidate being asymptomatic. Changes brought about by the medications and its side effects, distortions in self-image (real and imagined), upheaval in interpersonal relationships, threat of superimposed infection with changes in lifestyle are significant stresses seen in referrals to the psychiatrist by the Heart Team. The common psychiatric manifestation seen by the Heart Transplant Team and the treatment approach adopted will be discussed with appropriate examples.

2449

PSYCHIATRIC ASPECTS OF THE FIRST 68 HEART TRANSPLANTS AT THE ROYAL VICTORIA HOSPITAL, MONTREAL
Leon L. Phipps, B.Sc., M.D., F.R.C.P.(C)
Allan Memorial Institute, Royal Victoria Hospital.

The cardiac transplant team has comprised a psychiatrist since its inception in 1984. This operation has become increasingly popular due to selection of healthier patients and donor organs, and improvement in immunosuppressive therapy. The purpose of this exposé is to highlight the important contribution the psychiatrist can make in patient selection and treatment. The task is to assess the patients' past and present psychological functioning and identify candidates with significant psychopathology for whom compliance may be a problem in the post-operative period. He/ she also educates patients regarding emotional aspects of transplantation and assesses their support systems. 125 patients have been evaluated pre-operatively, 107 males (mean age 49.9) and 18 females (mean age 51.25). Method: Using a semi-structured interview, all patients undergo psychiatric evaluation with mental status examination. Using DSM III, 12% of patients have been diagnosed with adjustment disorder and depression; 16% with anxiety; and 44% with no apparent psychiatric diagnosis. Post-operative: 60 men (mean age 54.8) and 8 women (mean age 54) received operations; 15% have died. Following transplant 18% developed delirium, 6% mania, 26% depression. Discussion: Suitability for transplant depended mainly on clinical prediction of post-operative compliance with medical and surgical treatment, good social and family support systems. Heart recipients with questionable psychiatric suitability, history of mood or personality disorders, or without pre-operative evaluation generally did poorly in the post-operative period. Conclusions: Proper patient selection will indicate a greater role for psychiatry.

2450

AUTOMATIC CARDIOVERTER DEFIBRILLATOR IMPLANTATION : PSYCHIATRIC ASPECTS

M. Van Moffaert, L. Jordaens, G. Van Damme, D. Clement

Dept. of Psychiatry & Dept. of Cardiology, University Hospital, Ghent, Belgium

The association between psychosocial stress and sudden cardiac death is supported by scientific data from animal experiments, human experimental pathophysiological observations and epidemiological studies which link emotional stress to cardiac morbidity, including fatal arrhythmias.
Successfully resuscitated patients who continu to have electrical instability and who are therefore equipped with a A.I.C.D. (Automatic Internal Cardioverter Defibrillator Implantation) have been available for psychiatric investigation. From the psychiatrist's viewpoint research in this field differentiates insufficiently the emotional links with sudden death in its different components : personality factors (trait) , psychiatric co-morbidity (state), history of psychiatric disorder, life events, coping style and acute psychosocial stress. This investigation indicates that sudden death may not be as instantaneous as it would appear, and that the fatal attack is often the last link in a chain of stressful events with mounting tension, dejection, depression and disappointment. The risk of sudden death is strongly associated with anxiety, depression, sleep disturbances, fatigue and emotional strain.

2451

Body schema disturbances in dreams of amputees with phantom limbs
B. Frank, E. Lorenzoni
Neurologische Klinik mit Klinischer Neurophysiologie - Medizinische Hochschule Hannover
Konstanty-Gutschow-Str.8,D-3000 Hannover 61, FRG

A phantom limb does not only occur in the waking-state but also in dreams. The purpose of the study was to draw more attention to the phenomenon of body schema disturbances of patients with phantom limb sensations in dreams.

One hundred eighty-one limb-amputated patients with phantom limb sensations and a more or less phantom pain were examined. Eighty-fore patients are able to give informations of presence or abscence of the phantom limb in dreams; 65 of them had the upper and 15 the lower extremities amputated. At the time of the examination 77 patients out of 84 had a phantom limb in the waking-state and 7 had none. The lätter however, had had a phantom limb at times in the past.

The phantom limb was divided into complete,reduced or shortenend and intermittent. The same type of phantom in the waking-state and in dreams were found in 40 patients, 44 had a different type. There was no relationship between in intensity of phantom pain and the occurence of a phantom limb in dreams. The mechanism which lead to different phantom limb sensation in the waking-state and in dreams were discussed.

2452

Personality and Social Circumstances as Predictors for Organic Psychoses after Open Heart Surgery?
G. Ott
Psychiatrische Universitätsklinik, Schwabachanlage 6-10, D-8520 Erlangen

Our contribution deals with the appearance of '"psychic disturbances" in patients undergoing an artery coronary bypass operation with extracorporal circulation. Differentiation and classification of "psychic disturbances" seemed to us specially important. For the psychiatrist the last term may be as unspecific as the diagnosis "disease of heart" for the cardiologic collegue or the heart surgeon. These terminological difficulties may be the cause of differences in frequency of incidence from 23 to 90 % in earlier studies.
The aim of our investigation was asking for predictors of psychopathologic disturbances in a group of patients after open heart sugery. Therefore from February to May 1988 we explored about 100 inpatients undergoing an artery coronary bypass operation with open heart conditions in the Department of Heart Sugery (Chief Prof.Dr.J.von der Emde, Chirurgische Universitätsklinik Erlangen). Valvular or other cardiac diseases were not considered in this study. We only evaluated pre- and postoperative psychopathologic findings including primary personality as well as psychosocial conditions. Furthermore we induced self-reports on axiety defence, denial tendeniecies, type-A-coronary-prone-behavior pattern (JENKINS, 1965) and coping mechanisms in coronary patients. We used a partitially standardized interview including a global inquiry of anamnestic data. The AMDP-system (Arbeitsgemeinschaft für Methodik und Dokumentation in der Psychiatrie) as well as HAMA and HAMD (Hamilton Rating Scale for Anxiety/Depression), DSI and ASI (Depression/Anxiety Status Inventory, ZUNG 1965) were used for documentation.

2453

PREDICTING REHABILITATION IN HEART TRANSPLANTATION
R. Meyendorf, M. Dassing, J. Scherer, W. Klinner, B. Kemkes, B. Reichart

Professor of Psychopathology (R. Meyendorf) and Cardiac Surgery (W. Klinner), University of Munich/Germany

27 patients who underwent heart transplantation (HTP) 1 to 5 years ago, were evaluated concerning psychological and social adjustment after HTP. Predictors before HTP for good rehabilitation are: 1. Absence of psychopathology, 2. Compliance, 3. Good social support, 4. Reentry into occupation, 5. Absence of history of alcoholism. Age is not a predictor.

Criteria for good rehabilitation (CRH) correlate positively with the predictors and with each other: 1. Psychopathology with PP 1,2,3 and with all CRH except 7; 2. Compliance with PP 2,3,5 and CRH 1 and 4; 3. Social rehabilitation with P 3 and CRH 1; 4. Reentry into occupation with P 2 and CRH 1 and 2; 5. Physical well-being with none of PP and with CRH 1,3, and 4; 6. Life satisfaction with none of PP and with CRH 1 and 5; 7. Physical fitness with none of PP and with CRH 5.

Session 377 Free Communications:
Long-term pharmacotherapy of schizophrenia

2454

STAGES OF LONG TERM TREATMENT OF SCHIZOPHRENIA
Pfolz H., Friedl E.J.
Psychiatrisches Krankenhaus der Stadt Wien
Baumgartner Hoehe, 1145 Vienna, Austria

Based on the experience of neuroleptic treatment, which enables to influence not only the basic but also secondary symptoms of schizophrenia, long-acting neuroleptics doubtless are of great importance. Nevertheless the combined social-psychiatric setting and drug-treatment produce special problems, which overlap the simple drug reactions.
Based on the practical experience of twenty years in the Psychiatric Hospital of Vienna we developed a three stage model for neuroleptic long term treatment. We divide an adjustment- reduction- and maintenance-stage.
A temporal delimination of these stages is possible. The different therapeutic aspects of these stages will be discussed.

2455

BRIEF INTERMITTENT NEUROLEPTIC PROPHYLAXIS FOR STABLE SCHIZOPHRENIC OUTPATIENTS: TWO YEAR OUTCOME.

A.G.Jolly, S.R.Hirsch, E.Morrison, A.McRink, L.Wilson
Department of Psychiatry Charing Cross & Westminster Medical School, Fulham Palace Rd., London W6, U.K.

We investigated a novel approach to the prophylaxis of schizophrenic relapse characterised by the administration of brief intermittent courses of neuroleptic medication for early non-psychotic signs of relapse. 54 stable, remitted DSM-III positive schizophrenics were randomised double-blind to receive brief intermittent treatment alone or in combination with continuous depot neuroleptic prophylaxis. Some 19 relapses were recorded, of which 10 (53%) were preceded by non-psychotic prodromal signs. At two year follow-up, relapse was significantly more frequent amongst patients receiving intermittent treatment when compared with those receiving continuous neuroleptic prophylaxis. Hospitalisation for relapse was four times more frequent with intermittent treatment and 8 of these patients and only 1 of the continuous treatment controls were withdrawn from double-blind status because of prolonged or frequent relapse. Dysphoric and neurotic symptoms also occured more frequently with intermittent treatment. Less extrapyramidal side effects were recorded with intermittent treatment, but periodic assessments of social function (SAS-II) failed to reveal any social advantages accrueing from this.

2456
THE EFFECT OF NEUROLETICS AND DEPOT NEUROLECTICS IN THE COURSE OF SCHIZOPHRENIA
Biancosino B., Masina L., Merini A., Nolet M.
Department of Psychiatry - University of Bologna
Italy

The authors studied 83 schizophrenics, the total schizophrenic patients of a Community Mental Health Center in Bologna (Department of Psychiatry - University of Bologna - Italy). They studied the effects of regular half-life neurolectics and depot neurolectics in the course of schizophrenia, observing the number of relapses (admissions to hospital). The authors also studied the importance of compliance of patients; they described the regularity of consumption and interviewed the patients.

2457
DEPOT NEUROLEPTIC POTENCY OF NEW PHENOTHIAZINE ESTERS IN PRECLINICAL TRIALS

Király I., J. Borsy, M. Tapfer, L. Toldy and I. Tóth Institute for Drug Research, Budapest, Hungary

For the long-acting antipsychotic therapy of schizophrenic patients several depot neuroleptic drugs are developed among the phenothiazine derivatives.
Several esters of fluphenazine have been described in the literature /i.e. esters with long-chain fatty acids, trimethoxybenzoic acid and 1-adamantanecarboxylic acid/.
Practically no data can be found in the literature about the biological effect of other esters. Among the fluphenazine esters only heptanoic and decanoic esters /Fluphenazine enanthate and decanoate/ have been used in the clinical practice.

In our chemical work the new 2-trifluoromethyl-phenothiazine esters were synthetized by using sterically hindered acids of lipophyllic character. The biologically most active esters were formed with carboxyllic,- related carboxyllic-and propionic acids. Because of technological advantage, compound GYKI-22441 /4-chlorophenoxy-isobutyric ester/ was selected for further examination. The preclinical studies /pharmacolgical,-pharmacokinetical, all of toxicological safety studies/ have been just finished, and this compound seemed to be equiactive with Fluphenazine decanoate.
The clinical studies were started this year.

2458
I.M. CLOPIXOL V/S MODECATE IN CHRONIC SCHIZOPHRENIA - A DOUBLE-BLIND STUDY, B. Saxena, D. MacCrimmon, E. Busse, P. Turner, L. Fagan, J. Kenny, J. Reeves, Dept. of Psychiatry, McMaster University, Hamilton, Ontario, Canada

A total of 50 chronic schizophrenic out-patients were selected according to pre-defined research criteria. Following the stabilization period on Modecate, patients were randomly assigned to one of the two treatment regimes and were followed in a double-blind fashion for a period of one year. In the present study Clopixol was available at 200 mg./ml., and Modecate at 25 mg./ml. For the purpose of dosage adjustment 1 ml. of each drug was considered equipotent. During the first twelve weeks of the study period drug dosage and treatment intervals were adjusted according to clinical response of individual patients. Evaluation of therapeutic efficacy included: BPRS, CGI, AMDP subscale for schizophrenia, Steven's social rating scale, AIMS, and Side-Effects Inventory. Safety evaluations were based on physical and laboratory investigations including EKG and ophthalmic examination. Assessments were completed prior to the commencement of the double-blind phase and at regular intervals thereafter. An overall significant clinical improvement was noted in assessment scales only in Clopixol group and was associated with minimal side-effects over the course of the study. The present results show that Clopixol is a highly effective and safe agent which may provide therapeutic advantages over other existing I.M. neuroleptics.

2459
DEPOT ANTIPSYCHOTIC MEDICATION AND WEIGHT CHANGE IN CHRONIC SCHIZOPHRENIC PATIENTS

J.C. Cookson (on behalf of The Depot Antipsychotic Weight Change Study Group) The London Hospital, (St. Clements), London, United Kingdom.

Surveys of patients attending out-patient clinics for long-term treatment with depot antipsychotic medication have consistently confirmed marked weight gain in many patients (D.A.W. Johnson and M. Breen, Acta Psychiat. Scand. 1979, 59, 525-528; T. Silverstone et al, Brit. J. Psychiat. 1988, 153, 214-217).

Following a pilot study which noted a non-significant trend towards less weight gain with haloperidol decanoate when compared with fluphenazine decanoate (J.C. Cookson et al, Int. Clin. Psychopharm. 1986, 1, 1, 41-52), The Depot Antipsychotic Weight Change Study Group have conducted a double-blind study on 188 patients entered at 15 centres throughout the United Kingdom.

Having provided written informed consent, patients were randomly assigned to either haloperidol decanoate or fluphenazine decanoate. Dosages were adjusted according to individual patients' requirements and their clinical status was assessed on entry and after 12, 24, 36 and 52 weeks' treatment.

To date, 52-week assessments have been completed on 109 patients, with a further 49 patients still in the study. Thirty patients have dropped out of the study, including two patients whose deaths were unrelated to treatment, 15 with a clinical relapse, and 13 patients who were non-compliant or who withdrew consent to further treatment.

A description of the study methodology together with a detailed follow-up of the withdrawn/relapsed group will be presented.

2460

PERPHENAZINE DECANOATE IN SCHIZOPHRENIA-
-RELATION TO SERUM NEUROLEPTIC LEVELS
S. Teiga, S. Caldas, A. Albuquerque, J.M. Jara,
R. Galvão Videira, A. Daskalos, M. Gaio,
A.Dinis, R. Bartlett,V. Claúdio, M. L.Figueira.
Hosp.Júlio de Matos, Lisbon, Portugal

In an open prospective study 45 schizophrenic patients (DSMIII-R) were treated with Perphenazine Decanoate, with a fixed depot interval and an individual dose, guided by clinical evaluation combined with plasma concentration monitoring. Degree of illness was rated using the Clinical Global Impression Scale with additional social adaptation items. Patients were also evaluated with the BPRS scale, The Scales for Assessment of Negative and Positive symptoms (N.Andreasen) and a list of side effects. A modified version of Stroop Test was used to evaluate attention and selective processing of information in two experimental conditions (neutral and threath stimulus). Recent memory was also assessed with conventional psychometric measures.
Differences in clinical efficacy and reduction of side effects (extrapiramidal and cognitive) were observed after two months of treatment. The results are discussed in the perspective of social adaptation and long-term treatment of schizophrenia.

2461

The emotional meaning of long acting therapy among psychotic patients.
G. Panico°, I. Maremmani, J.A. Deltito°°, P. Castrogiovanni
Institute of Psychiatry, Pisa University, Italy
°Mental Health Services, USL 19, Regione Liguria, Italy
°°Depression and Anxiety Clinic, New York Hospital, Cornell University, Westchester Division, White Plains, New York, N.Y., U.S.A.

The clinical use of long-acting drugs showed its utility in maintenance treatments, during the remission phase, of schizophrenic disorders, especially in relation to patients with poor compliance. However, such a use could lead to disregard some variables, such as the patient's, the physician's and the family's experience, which have a sure importance in transferal relations between psychiatrist and psychotic patient.
The experience of the pharmacological treatment, according to the administration modality (short acting or long acting) was, therefore, evaluated in two groups of psychotic patients (diagnosed according to DSM III criteria).
For the evaluation of clinical-anamnestic components rating scales were used, while the experience of the pharmacological treatment was investigated by means of Osgood's Semantic Differential Test in its classic version of ten couples of opposite adjectives.
The results allow interpretative hypotheses either on the possible activation of transferal dynamics from the drug, or on the meaning that it can assume inside them.

2462

LONG ACTING NEUROLEPTICS AND TARDIVE DYSKINESIA

D.MOUSSAOUI,A.SEMCHAOUI,B.BENTOUNSI,N.KADRI
Centre Psychiatrique Universitaire Ibn Rochd,
Casablanca, Morocco.

It has been shown in a non controlled study (D.MOUSSAOUI,S.DOUKI,et al, 1988) a higher prevalence of tardive dyskinesia (T.D) with fluphenazine oenanthate Vs Pipotiazine palmitate, two long acting neuroleptics (LAN). A controlled double blind study has been designed to clarify this issue.

METHOD AND PATIENTS : Two groups of 57 patients each were studied. They were matched by sex, age and diagnosis. They were assessed by two psychiatrists, blind to the diagnosis and to the treatment,with the AIMS. There was no difference between the two groups in taking anticholinergic medication when combined with LAN. There was no difference also in neuroleptics combined with LAN.

RESULTS : There was a strong difference between the two groups : 42% had TD in the fluphenazine group and 22.80% in the pipotiazine one (p<025). There was no difference in the location of the TD between the two groups.
These results will be discussed,regarding the preventive aspect of LAN prescription.

Session 378 Free Communications:
Drug abuse: Substitution and other pharmacological treatments

2463

INPATIENT METHADONE WITHDRAWAL TREATMENT (MWT).
M. Trenkel, J. Nelles, J. Jakubaschk
Psychiatric University Clinic, Berne, Switzerland

Liberalisation of methadone treatment programs were followed by an increase of patients requiring MWT. Since no MWT concepts were described in the literature, we investigated 54 cases - unsystematicly treated as inpatients in a ward specialized in opiate addicts - in a retrospective study to evaluate the efficacy of drug free treatment vs. drug mediated on therapy outcome and to develop a MWT concept. Methadone was completely withdrawn on admission; 39 patients were treated without (group A) and 16 with different drugs, e.g. neuroleptics and benzodiazepines (group B). In group A 52 % of the patients finished MWT successfully, in group B 75 %. In group A the methadone dose before treatment was on average 38.8 mg (therapy finished) and 65.8 mg (therapy ceased), in group B 65.6 and 72.5 mg respectively. Patients with 80 mg of methadone or more finished MWT only when drug mediated. The outcome of patients with 40 mg or less was independent of drug treatment. Drug treatment slightly improved the outcome of patients with methadone doses between 40 mg and 80 mg. On the basis of these findings we introduced a combined drug free and drug mediated MWT in order to confirm our retrospective data in a prospective study.

2464

HABITUATION IN A METHADONE POPULATION
Loimer N., Jagsch R., Linzmayer L., Groenberger J. Presslich O.
University of Vienna, Department of Psychiatry, Vienna - Austria

50 subjects maintained on methadone in the drug dependence treatment ambulance of the psychiatric University Clinic of Vienna participated in this study. During the MMP patients are tested every two weeks by means of EMITR in Urine samples in order to determine relapse to opiate, barbiturate cocaine, amphetamine or methaqualone. Habituation was measured by means of a computer assisted procedure. 15 acustic stimuli were presented (500 Hz tone of 70 db intensity lasting for five hundred msec) to the patient. Habituation criteria was reached when there were no reactions to three consecutive stimuli. Emotional reflexion and the mean amplitudes were calculated too. A relation between habituation, methadone dosages and urine samples could be observed.
The first aim of the present study was to objectify habituation among the methadone population, the second was an attempt to specify relapse during a MMP.

2465

A DOUBLE-BLIND STUDY ON DETOXIFICATION TREATMENTS IN METHADONE ADDICTS
Tempesta E., Janiri L., Persico A.M., Ciaramella A., Agnes M., Di Giannantonio M.
Dept. of Psychiatry, Catholic University, Rome, Italy

Among opiate addicts, patients receiving methadone on a long-term basis present peculiar problems while detoxification treatments are undertaken. In this study we addressed the issue of methadone detoxification, comparing the effects of different treatments on withdrawal symptoms. Thirty-three patients who applied for detoxification after a methadone maintenance program of at least 1 year, were hospitalized. Methadone dosage was decreased over a period of 4-12 days, by 5 mg every 2 days up to a standard daily dose of 10 mg. Patients were then randomly assigned to 3 groups receiving the following 1 week (T_0-T_7) treatments: 1) clonidine (T_1-T_7) + methadone (T_1-T_3); 2) lefetamine (T_1-T_7)+ methadone (T_1-T_3); 3) buprenorphine (T_1-T_7). Withdrawal objective and subjective symptoms were assessed in double-blind with the CANAS rating scale. All drugs were discontinued on T_8. Groups did not significantly differ as to mean withdrawal scores on T_0. During detoxification, the lefetamine sample reported the highest levels of discomfort; clonidine resulted in better scores, during the first half of the week; every day, buprenorphine tended to be the most effective treatment (statistically significant differences on T_3 and T_5). It is concluded that a buprenorphine substitution may be the most suitable treatment for long-term methadone dependent patients, at least with respect to conventional (clonidine) or symptomatic (lefetamine) therapies.

2466

Clinical experience with Naltrexone in Opiate Drug-Addict inpatients.
Gaia S., Carnaghi R., Galis A., Nervo D.
Istituto Fatebenefratelli
San Maurizio Canavese, Torino (Italy)

Study objective. To assess the efficiency and manageability of Naltrexone in disintoxication from opiates and also in the induction of opiate receptor saturation (insensibility to opiates). Thirty opiate drug addict inpatients, divided into two groups of 15 each were treated according to two different protocols. In the first protocol Clonidine was given orally and Naloxone by intramuscular injecton in the disintoxication phase so as to obtain a drug-free state and only then Naltrexone was administered orally to induce receptor saturation. In the second protocol Naloxone was not used, but only Clonidine and Naltrexone both orally so as to induce simultaneously a drug-free state and receptor saturation. Comparisons were made between the two protocols to evaluate tolerability, side effects, manageability, compliance, efficiency, security and duration of treatment. Conclusions. The protocol with only Clonidine and Naltrexone resulted more valid especially regarding the better compliance due to the shorter duration of treatment and the exclusive use of oral administration. This last point, i.e. not having to use intramuscular injectons, reduces significantly for the sanitary staff the risk of contracting contagious diseases (HTLV III, HBsAg, Treponema Pallidum, etc.).

2467

Naltrexone in prevention of recurrent relapses of heroine drug addicts
I. Maremmani, L. Daini, G.C.M. Orsolini, P. Castrogiovanni.
Institute of Psychiatry, Pisa University, Italy

At the Psychiatric Clinic, Pisa University, an Antagonist Unit treats subjects in voluntary or forced abstinance by means of opioid antagonist drug for prevent recurrent relapses.
The intervention is articulted in three weeks: in the first week, in Day Hospital, the opioid detoxification is treated by administration of an intravenous diazepan and tiapride; in the second, after Narco-test, the antagonist induction is realized. From the third week and for a period of twelve months, the patients are given three administrations a week, and followed like outpatients.
Psychopathological and abstinential symptomatology are monitored by means of SCL 90, SASA and SESSB; behavioral traits are recorded by means of Q.T.A..
Preliminary results are reported.

2468

CORTISOL SECRETION AFTER ADMINISTRATION OF FENFLURAMINE DURING NALTREXONE MAINTENANCE TREATMENT
J.J. López-Ibor Jr., J. Pérez de los Cobos and F. Lana
Ramón y Cajal Hospital, Madrid, Spain

The consequences of prolonged Naltrexone maintenance treatment on cerebral metabolism are not very well known. The role of those related to the serotonergic function may be important because 5-HT is closely related with control of impulses and regulation of affects, which are psychological factors to achieve abstinence. In order to evaluate these aspects 13 patients with the diagnosis of opiate dependence disorder (DSM III) under Naltrexone maintenance treatment (350 mg/weekly) were tested with the fenfluramine challenge. A single dose of 60 mg of fenfluramine was administered and samples of serum before and after (-30, 0, 60, 120, 180 and 240 min) the administration of the serotonergic agent were taken in order to measure cortisol concentration (mg/dl). An identical procedure was followed with a control group matched for sociodemographic characteristics (N=11).

The cortisol concentrations of the patients were greater in all the samples. The differences reached statistical significance (Student's t) in the samples corresponding to basal values (19.3 vs 13.8 p<.0014), 60 min (14.5 vs 8.9 p<.0019) and 240 min (15.2 vs 11.7 p<.034). But when the difference between maximum and minimum concentrations was considered, the increases were greater in the control group. So the average increase in the patients was 5.3 (44.3%) while in the control group the increase was 7.7 (112.2%). Therefore the subjects under Naltrexone treatment tend to present higher cortisol concentrations. But the magnitude of the response after the stimulation of the serotonergic system measured by the cortisol reaction is reduced in those that receive the opiate antagonistic. The results should be taken into account in order to evaluate all kinds of consequences that appear in the treatment and maintenance with Naltrexone.

2469

CLONIDINE IN OPIATE WITHDRAWAL

Dr. D.M. Dhavale, Dr. V.M. Abhyankar
Hospital for Nervous Diseases, Revenue Colony, Shivajinagar, Pune - 411 005
(INDIA)

Clonidine (ARKAMIN) has been reported to be useful in treatment of Opiate withdrawal symptoms.

Mostly it has been used in conjunction with Methadone, where Methadone still remains the treatment of choice for Opiate withdrawal. In this country, due to non-availability of Methadone, the conventional treatment of Opiate withdrawal in most centres has been with tranquillisers (major and minor) and hypnotic drugs.

The authors treated 5 cases of Brown Sugar (Heroin) addiction successfully using high dose Clonidine regime. The patients, who were their own controls, found this treatment superior to conventional treatment.

2470

A TREATMENT PROGRAM FOR BENZODIAZEPINE DEPENDENT PATIENTS - ONE YEAR FOLLOW-UP RESULTS
B.Vikander, H.Bergman, I.Bergman, K.Engelbrektsson, I.Lindgren, P.Sandberg, U.Toenne, S.Borg
Karolinska Institute, Department of Psychiatry, St.Goeran's Hospital, Stockholm, Sweden

A treatment program for primary benzodiazepine dependent patients has been developed. A slow gradual reduction of drugs with 10% for 2-3 times a week on an inpatient basis was followed by an outpatient period for about one year with councelling. Withdrawal symptoms were registered 3-5 times a week. Cognitive functioning was followed by psychometric testing. Patients were receiving councelling throughout the treatment period. Matched controls were referred to ordinary psychiatric treatment. One year follow-up showed significantly better results in the treatment group compared to the controls. A majority of the patients showed psychometric impairment before treatment and normalization after one year of abstinence.

2471

NALTREXONA vs PLACEBO EN ADICTOS A HEROINA
San L, Pomarol G, Peri JM, Olle JM.
Sección de Toxicomanías.Hospital del Mar. Barcelona. Spain.

En un ensayo doble ciego se evaluó la eficacia de la naltrexona frente al placebo en el tratamiento de pacientes adictos a opiáceos (heroína) durante un año.
La muestra estaba constituida por 50 pacientes, de ambos sexos con un rango de edad de 18 a 30 años diagnósticados de dependencia de opiáceos (DSM-III). Los pacientes siguieron tratamiento de desintoxicación con clonidina en régimen hospitalario durante dos semanas. Posteriormente y de forma ambulatoria todos los pacientes fueron tratados con naltrexona durante un mes (350 mg/semana/vía oral) y a partir del 2º mes se realizó la asignación aleatoria al grupo naltrexona (n= 28) o al grupo placebo (n= 22) hasta completar 6 meses de tratamiento farmacológico. Todos ellos siguieron el mismo programa de tratamiento (visitas médicas, apoyo psicológico, control de constantes, determinación de drogas en orina, etc) durante el periodo de estudio hasta completar un año.
Ambos grupos fueron comparables en las características sociodemográficas e historia toxicológica. La eficacia del tratamiento farmacológico (acceptabilidad, tipo de alta médica, tasa de retención y uso de opiáceos) fue similar en los dos grupos. No se observaron diferencias estadísticamente significativas en la tolerancia a la medicación (efectos indeseables) ni en el cumplimiento de la misma.

Session 379 Free Communications:
Pharmacotherapy of depression: Current issues

2472
ELEVATED PLATELET ADRENOCEPTOR BINDING IN DEPRESSION

A. Halaris and J. Piletz, Case Western Reserve University, Cleveland, Ohio, U.S.A.

Numerous investigators have measured radioligand binding to alpha$_2$ adrenoceptors from platelets of depressed patients in search of evidence for the alpha$_2$ hypersensitivity theory of depression. Using purified plasma membranes from platelets of healthy subjects, we demonstrated the presence of both super-high (K_D=11pM) and high affinity (K_D=1.5nM) binding sites for ^{3}H-para-amino-clonidine (^{3}H-PAC), an alpha$_2$ adrenoceptor partial agonist. In the present study, purified platelet plasma membranes were used to compare ^{3}H-PAC binding in 18 depressed patients and 24 sex- and age-matched controls. Two site-selective concentrations of the radioligand were used (0.06nM and 1.5nM) to investigate two high affinity ^{3}H-PAC binding sites. Radioligand binding was significantly elevated in platelets of depressed patients at both concentrations of ^{3}H-PAC, whether expressed per milligram protein, per platelet, or per micron^2 of platelet surface area (overall p 0.02). These data suggest that a sub-set of platelet alpha$_2$ adrenoceptors, recognized by clonidine and its derivative PAC, is upregulated in depressed patients. These findings provide further support for the alpha$_2$ adrenoceptor hypersensitivity theory of depression.

2473
INTENSIVE DESIGN IN TESTING EFFECTS OF ANTIDEPRESSANT DRUGS

V. Gabrovska
Medical Academy, Institute of Neurology, Psychiatry & Neurosurgery, Sofia, Bulgaria

Because of the controversies in the literature concerning the biochemical changes in depression as well as those produced by antidepressants during and because of the clinical vs. research paradox in psychopharmacological research, an investigation using a different approach - the so called intensive design was undertaken. This study is based upon within-patient averages and various relevant hypotheses are tested using the data for each patient separately. Thus it overcomes one of the major difficulties of the Extensive, or patient-group averaging approach, in which the degree of heterogeneity of patient-characteristics generally makes it very difficult to clearly identify particular patient-variables associated with a significant effect of the drug used.
We believe such an approach is helpful in overcoming the above-mentioned controversies in literature and in defining more precisely the indications for treatment with a given antidepressant.

2474
CURRENT ISSUES IN PHARMACOTHERAPY OF DEPRESSION

Atsuyoshi MORI and Hiroshi ITO
Department of Psychiatry
The Jikei University School of Medicine
Tokyo, Japan

Since the first introduction of imipramine into the market of Japan, the various tricyclic antidepressants have been widely used in the therapy of depression.
Recently, so-called second and third generation antidepressants are registered for clinical use in our country and became the first choice drugs for especially mild depressed patients because of the advantages of their slight anticholinergic and cardiovascular side effects. These drugs are evaluated as effective as the classical drugs by the several double blind controlled trials of our country. The results showed the average efficacies of the drugs were 70-80% in slight to marked improvement of depressive symptoms.
On the other hand, one of the important problems in today's clinical practice is the increase of intractable or therapy-resistant depression. By our data, the intractable cases are seen in 16% of the total inpatients. For these cases, besides the antidepressants, lithium carbonate, carbamazepine and some kinds of benzodiazepines are tried in combination with psychotherapy. Based upon the results of our recent survey on in and outpatients, the present status of pharmacotherapy of depression will be discussed.

2475
A DOUBLE BLIND COMPARISON BETWEEN IV AND ORAL ADMINISTRATION OF CLOMIPRAMINE
S. BRION, J. PLAS, J.F. CHEVALIER, J. GAILLEDREAU, J.M. GAUTHIER, B. VANIER, N. BRION, O. VAROQUAUX, C. ADVENIER, C. DUSSAUT.
75 inpatients aged between 18 and 65 years old and suffering from Major Depressive Disorders (D,S,M, III) were enrolled randomly in a double blind parallel study comparing IV and oral administration of clomipramine (CMI), 38 (16 males and 22 females) received placebo tablets and IV administration of 75 mg of CMI daily, and 37 (9 males and 28 females) received IV placebo and 150 mg of oral CMI per day. After 14 days, every patient was given 150 mg of oral CMI daily during 2 further weeks. The aim of the study was to compare efficacy and tolerance during the 14 first days and after 28 days of treatment in each group. Efficacy was assessed with MADRS, CGI scale, and a visual analogic rating scale. Somatic tolerance was assessed with a systematic inventory of somatic symptoms. General tolerance was assessed by measurement of cardiac frequency and blood pressure in both standard and supine positions. The two groups (IV Vs oral) appeared to be similar (t-tests) according to age (47±10 Vs 44±11 years of age), weight (65±14 Vs 61±12 Kg), size (167±8 Vs 163±5 cm) and MADRS score (30±7 Vs 31±6) at the beginning of the trial. Analysis of Variance (ANOVA) with MADRS scores was performed between baseline and Day 14. A significant decrease was observed through the first 14 days (p<0.0001), but no difference appeared between the two groups. However, a global difference appeared in the factor "excitation" of the visual scale, with a upper level for patients treated with oral CMI, ANOVA was performed between baseline and Day 28 for each somatic symptom. The oral administration of CMI seems to have a worse tolerance than the IV one ; a significant difference (p<0.001) appeared for dry mouth, irritability, urinary disturbances, blood pressure, heart rate, sweat, weight variation, palpitations, orthostatic hypotension. The interest of IV administration of CMI in opposition with giving a double posology through the oral way will be discussed.

2476

LEVOPROTILINE - AN ANTIDEPRESSANT WITHOUT NORADRENALINE UPTAKE INHIBITION
I.W. Reimann, L. Firkusny, G. Wendt, U. Binz and P.R. Bieck
Human Pharmacology Institute, Ciba-Geigy GmbH, D-7400 Tübingen, FRG

The noradrenaline (NA) uptake concept of antidepressant action is challenged by differential effects of the S(+)-enantiomer CGP 12 104 and the R(-)-enantiomer CGP 12 103 (levoprotiline, LP) of oxaprotiline. In a double-blind multicenter study vs. amitriptyline (AMI, 150 mg/d, LP 150 mg/d, n = 2 x 45 patients) LP showed stronger and faster antidepressant effects than AMI:

Treatment	Hamilton score (median)				
	pre	1.	2.	3.	4. week
LP	26	19	15	14	10
AMI	26	23	20	16	13

I.v. NA and tyramine (TYR) pressor tests in 6 normal subjects support animal data that NA uptake inhibition is caused only by CGP 12 104. I.v. NA doses causing a syst. BP increase of 30 mm Hg decreased from 9.5 ± 2.2 (placebo) or 11.5 ± 3.1 ug/min (LP) to 2.2 ± 0.8 ug/min after CGP 12 104. The respective TYR doses rose from 4.0 ± 1.2 and 4.3 ± 1.5 to 18.4 ± 7.4 mg. The antidepressant levoprotiline thus does not inhibit NA-uptake in man. Our data do not support the "amine hypothesis" of antidepressant action.

2477

DOUBLE BLIND STUDY OF MINAPRINE, AMITRIPTYLINE AND PLACEBO IN DYSTHYMIC DISORDER
E. Torre, L. Ancona*, E. Tempesta*, M. Ancona, S.M. Chierichetti**, S. Sommacal**
Ist. Clinica Psichiatrica, Università di Torino, Italy, * Ist. di Psichiatria e Psicologia, Università "Sacro Cuore", Roma, Italy, **Direzione Medica Midy S.p.A. Sanofi, Milano, Italy

Minaprine (M), is an original psychotropic drug which exhibits an atypical profile of antidepressant.
It facilitates serotoninergic and dopaminergic transmission and in addition it acts as a muscarinic cholinergic agonist.
The antidepressive efficacy and tolerance of M, amitriptyline (A) and placebo (P) were compared in a controlled double blind randomized trial in 102 out-patients (mean age 42.2+9.5 years; range 18-65; 34 males - 68 females) with a diagnosis of dysthymic disorder (DSM III).
After a week P run-in period, during which P responders were excluded 32 patients were randomly assigned to received M 200-300 mg daily, 35 patients received A 50-75 mg and 35 patients received P for 6 weeks.
Efficacy was assessed after 7, 14, 21, 28, 42 days of therapy by means Hamilton DRS (HDRS), BECK DI (BDI), Covi ARS, moreover adverse effects were reported. Patients were also evaluated by a clinical global impression (CGI).
M and A groups showed a significant reduction in the HDRS and in the BDI as compared to P group, whereas M and A exhibited no statistical difference between them.
At the end of the study 81%, 66% and 60% of patients in the M, A and P group showed an improvement according to investigator CGI.
In conclusion M has shown efficacy as an antidepressant agent in patients suffering from dysthymic disorder.

2478

LOW DOSE BUPROPRION IN DEPRESSED OUTPATIENTS

N.E. Harto and R.J. Branconnier, Institute for Psychopharmacologic Research, Danvers, MA USA

Buproprion (BUP) at doses of 450 mg/day or greater is a safe and effective treatment for hospitalized depressed patients. However, the minimum effective dose for depressed outpatients is not established. Therefore, the present placebo-controlled study was designed to evaluate the efficacy and safety of low dose BUP in the treatment of depressed outpatients.

Twenty-nine patients who met DSM-III-R criteria for Major Depressive Episode were entered into this study. After an initial week of placebo (PBO), patients were randomized to treatment with either 300 mg/day BUP or PBO for 6 weeks.

Major outcome assessments were made with the Hamilton Depression Scale (HAMD), and Montgomery-Asberg Depression Scale (MADRS). ANOVA revealed a significant difference in favor of BUP for both the HAMD, $F(1,20)=7.97$, $p<0.01$ and MADRS, $F(1,20)=4.10$, $p<0.05$. Adverse reactions were mild and well tolerated in both groups. The only adverse reaction where the incidence was significantly higher for BUP was headache.

The results suggest that low dose (300 mg/day) BUP is a safe and effective treatment for major depression in outpatients.

2479

LEVOPROTILINE, AN ATYPICAL ANTIDEPRESSANT IN SEARCH OF ITS MECHANISM: ELECTROPHYSIOLOGICAL FINDINGS:
H.-R. Olpe*, H.-L. Haas** and A. Dresse***,
*Res. and Dev. Dept. CIBA-GEIGY Ltd., CH-4002 Basel, **Dept. of Physiology, Univ. of Mainz, GDR, ***Univ. de Liège, Pathol. Institute, Liège, Belgium.

Levoprotiline is the (-)-enantiomer of oxaprotiline and was shown to be therapeutically active as an antidepressant although it is devoid of noradrenaline uptake blocking properties, and does not down-regulate beta-receptors. The drug shares certain features with classical antidepressants and differs from them in other respects. In contrast to classical antidepressants, acutely administered levoprotiline has no effect on spontaneous neuronal activity of locus coeruleus in vivo. However, levoprotiline, similar to maprotiline and desipramine affects the limbic system resulting in an increased hippocampal cell excitability. Intracellular recordings from these neurons in hippocampal slices revealed a moderate depolarizing effect on the membrane potential. In rats chronically treated with levoprotiline, the basal firing rate of dopaminergic neurons in the ventral tegmental area was reduced and the sensitivity of hippocampal neurons to locally applied dopamine was attenuated. In chronically treated rats, the sensitivity of cingulate neurons to substance P was increased similar to other antidepressants.

2480
ASSESSMENT OF EFFICACY AND TOLERABILITY OF IPSAPIRONE IN THE TREATMENT OF NEUROTIC DEPRESSION.

K. Puechler, I.S. Roed, B. Kuemmel
Medical Department, Troponwerke, Berliner Straße 156, D-5000 Koeln 80, FRG

Having received informed consent, a randomized double-blind, placebo-controlled trial was conducted on in-patients (psychosomatic hospital, FRG) suffering either from neurotic depression (30 subjects) or anxiety neurosis (29 subjects). Patients were diagnosed on the Hamilton Anxiety Scale (HAM-A, minimum score: 18) and on the Hamilton Depression Scale (score: no less than 20) and assigned to either of the aforementioned syndroms. Following random allocation to either ipsapirone (7.5 mg t.i.d.) or placebo treatment, psychiatric assessments were conducted twice a week during 4 successive weeks and after termination of the trial. Decreases (statistically significant) in the scores of efficacy variables, i.e. HAM-D, HAM-A, D-S, STAI-X1/X2 were recorded in the following types of analyses: visit-wise, carry-forward, intent-to-treat and final outcome. Both populations improved under ipsapirone treatment. The physicians judged ipsapirone to be as safe as placebo (clinical global impression). 77 % of all patients treated with ipsapirone were recommended to continue this therapy, compared to only 24 % in the placebo group.
As to adverse experiences, most commonly dizziness and dazedness were reported in both, the ipsapirone (74%) and placebo (38%) treatment group.

Session 380 Free Communications:
Treatment of drug abuse: Psychosocial approaches

2481
AN INTEGRATED PROJECT FOR TREATMENT OF DRUG-ADDICTS.
Nuno Silva Miguel + Luís Duarte Patrício
CENTRO DAS TAIPAS
Rua das Taipas, 20
1200 Lisboa

The treatment of drug-addicts involves a project with various answers and adjusted to the sick person, the drug-addict. The therapeutic investment to be made should be adapted to the familiar and social problems of the sick person. The psycopharmacologic, psycotherapeutic and sociotherapeutical intervention must be conjugated along with a long and adjusted treatment process. As from the experience of the Centro das Taipas(CT), the authors broach the therapeutic course of an urban population who apply freely to this Institution. This Institution, CT,disposes of a consultation without waiting list which take place on weekdays (from Monday to Friday) 9am to 9pm. An Internment Service, a Day Centre with occupational and professional purposes. An Emergency Service working 24 h a day, a Night Centre. All these services coordinated with therapeutic communities.We think very significant the statistic elements of this CT with 21st months of activity: 1st consultation - 4.835
Sequence consultation: 26.492 Total: 31.327
Internments: 521 persons Emergency: 5.207 persons
Day Centre: 426 persons

2482
DRUG ADDICTION AND THE THERAPEUTIC COMMUNITY:
A CONTINUUM OF CARE MODEL
GARNEAU, Dr. Noël & VAMOS, Peter
THE PORTAGE PROGRAM

The authors discuss the therapeutic community approach as an effective primary response for the treatment of drug addicted.

They discuss the theoritical underpinning of the modern therapeutic community and locate it on a continuum of care model. Some strengths and weaknesses of the paradigm are discussed and future trends and developments predicted.

2483
A THERAPEUTIC RESEARCH ON PSYCHOACTIVE SUBSTANCE USE DISORDERS
M.Ruiz Ruiz, J.M.Fernandez, F.Martin, V.Serrano, I.Morales
Dept. Psychiatry, Univ. Malaga, Spain

Psychosocial factors and therapeutic resources for drug-dependence are reviewed in order to outline a therapeutic research involving 40 drug-addicts with different treatments. Results support a new model for the drug-dependence treatment that overcome the ineffectiveness of the isolated therapeutic actions.

2484

NEW MODEL OF HEROIN ADDICTION TREATMENT
Francisco Vilhena
Faculty of Psychology - University of Lisbon
Portugal

The several factors responsible for genesis and maintenance of addiction must be handled in the process of treatment/rehabilitation, namely bio-psychosocial aspects, in systemic inter-action. Medical detoxication carried out at home with the cooperation of the family, in a systemic family therapy, followed by psycho-social approaches aimed at obtaining a job and enlarging friendship relationships, frequently demanding a psychotherapeutic approach, carried out by professionals and/or self-help groups. This model of integrative treatment is different from punctual approaches giving priority either to medical treatment, or psychotherapy, or family therapy, or therapeutic community alone. The A. integrates these different aspects into a continuous chain of interventions, by phases, in order to maximize the therapeutic resources, which are applied only in cases with best chances to succeed therapeutically.
The A. analyzes the results of this method of treatment in 30 cases, with follow-up.

2485

"ONE EAR COUNSELING AT A PARENTS AGAINST DRUG ABUSE (PADA) ASSOCIATION "

DEGLERIS NICK
CENTRE FOR MENTAL HEALTH,PIRAEUS,GREECE

A hundred of families with member(s) involved on drug abuse(great area of Athens) established an association of public benefit to fight against on a tri-axial basis:prevention-repression-treatment.A year before the PADA counseling section started functionning with the following activities:
a) Informative seminars about the different substances,the personnality problems and the psychopathology concerning the individuals,the possibilities of various detoxification programs,the frustration and the confrontation of the social stigma.
b) Sensibilization of the people through mass-media with the collaboration of the Hellenic Society Against Drug Abuse(NGO).
c) Attempts of modification in family intra-communication based on a systemic-multiaxial schedule reconstructing the psychopathological balance of the members.
d) Application of an alternative treatment strategy offering to the addicts behavioural substitutes for coping mainly major depression and life crises associated with heroin use.

2486

Motivation of abstinence versus rate of relapse in substance use disorders.

Ass. Prof. Al-Atrouny, Mohammad Hafez.
Dept. of Psychiotry, College of Medicene,
Mansoura Univ., Mansoura, EGYPT.

This work shows the significance of the type of motivation in maintaining successful treatment for substance use disorders. 100 cases of this disorder attending for treatment in a special centre, were investigated and subjected to management.
Management was based on an Islamic programme.
Motivations of abstinence were divided into three categories :
1- Due to physical complications.
2- Due to psychosocial problems.
3- Due to inner religious considerations related to faith and repentence to Allah.
Minimum relapse rate was observed in cases with the third category.
While the other two groups show very high relapse rate after solving their motivating problems.

2487

COMPREHENSIVE CARE ABOUT ADDICTED TO DRUGS
IN THE COMMUNITY OF NEW ZAGREB
A.Hečimović, S.Sakoman, V.Starčević, B.Lang

Institute for Health Promotion
Health Center "New Zagreb", Zagreb Yugoslavia
University Department for Neurology, Psychiatry,
Alcoholism and other Dependences of
"Dr. M.Stojanović" University Hospital
Zagreb, Yugoslavia

Although the drug addicts have been present in our national morbidity for over 20 years now, the primary health care has not defined its place and role in their comprehensive care. For most of the doctors in Primary Health care those rare, accidental cases in individual area is not known, and every estimate of the number is arbitrary, and is not based on epidemiologycal research.
These are some of the reasons to undergo an investigation on the teritory of New Zagreb - with the aim to find out characteristics of at least that part of the population which has been recorded in some form by Primary of secondary (psychiatric) Health care, Social service or Drug Department the City Police.
The data from these sources are united in such a way a Register of these cases has been formed at one place. After that each team of the Primary Health care has a list with addresses on the teritory covered by them. So as to carry out patronage visit inside of school institutions, factories and similar.
On this occasion the fundamental data of each addict have been collected by means of a special questionnare. After the data processing an insight into general characteristics of this population has been obtained. Former attempts of the Health and other care and their treatment have been obtained as well. After the end of investigation they got down to work on the Programme of the universal protection of the addicts on the teritory of individual community.
By this investigation and formation of the Register - the Model of comprehensive care of drug dependences of one area has been given.

2488
"STANDARDS FOR EVALUATION OF DRUG ABUSE SERVICES: A PROJECT FOR EUROPEAN COOPERATION"

TERESA DI FIANDRA
National Health System SAT - Via dei Riari 48 00165 Rome, Italy.

Moving from an overview of existing health care centers for drug abusers in Europe, the need has been underlined for a common standard reference in order to analyse and assess the activities of such services.
The availability of European standards could mean, for professionals working in the field as well as for administrators and politicians, the possibility of comparing results of activities and studies conducted in different Countries, so to use at its best any successful experience, to improve services' performances, to design future intervention.
Those premises led me to prepare a proposal for a Concerted Action which should be promoted and granted by the Commission of the European Communities inside the Research and Development Coordination Programme "Medical and Health Research".
The preparatory phase, a European Workshop, has already been approved and has taken place.
This paper will present the first agreement on the general design for the Concerted Action.
We will also analyse and discuss a proposed model for a common evaluation methodology, keeping in mind that in the field of drug abuse it is difficult to directly utilize methods and techniques generally applicable to other health services.
The proposed model aims to allow for flexibility and comparability so to facilitate the input of existing data collection systems and to promote implementation and immediate utilization in the field.

2489
EVALUATION OF ACTIVITIES IN THE FIELD OF ILLICIT DRUGS SERVICES IN ITALY

MARIANI F.[1], BIANCHI F.[1], PROTTI M.A.[1], PELLEGRINO L.[1], BASSO A.[2], BURGIO F.[2], CANZIAN G.[2], CERNIGOJ D.[2], COROSSEZ L.[2], DEL DEGAN T.[2], DIODATO S.[2], FABBRO T.[2], FAGNOL A.C.[2], FRANCESCUTTI C.[2], LUCCHITTA G.[2], MALAGARNE D.[2], MIRAGLIA S.[2], MOZZON L.[2], PAULON S.[2], PUNTIN M.[2], RIOSA G.[2], SILAN M.[2].

[1] Epidemiologic and Biostatistic Department of Clinical Physiology Institute, National Research Council Pisa Italy.
[2] Health Services of Local Sanitary Units, Region Friuli Venezia Giulia Italy.

Monitoring the health and social services, in the field of illicit drugs addictions, should be a continuous process of assessing the results of services so that adjustments can be made to make them more effective, adequate, efficient and with technical scientific quality appropriate to the intervention. Monitoring should include all forms of output or input measurement of system and these should be analysed in a standardized way in time and space.
In Friuli Venezia Giulia, one of 20 administrative Regions of Italy with 402000 people aged by 15-39 years (defined as "risk population") and with a estimated prevalence rate of 2.9X1000 of I.V. heroin addicts, the introduction of monitoring systems have been carefully investigated in a combined research project by the National Research Council and Regional Sanitary Administration. The preliminary results for the six months of application have shown that such a system would be practicable.
The project has been articulated in two principal activities: the monitoring of routine statistics referred to the clients of 12 services participant and the monitoring of activities (in term of time employed for each activities, for each subject in charge) developed in the different programmes (pharmacological, psychological, sociassistential, etc.) of drug abusers services.
The major findings of assessment of this preliminary data are: feedback and discussion with local bodies, and staff agencies; a handbook of regional resources and guidelines for responding to drug problems; some local news and information sheet; the identification of priority areas for actions; a continued monitoring of trends (in terms of improvement of data gathering, definition of routine monitoring key indicators, developing a local care reporting system).

2490
TREATMENT ALTERNATIVES TO PRISON FOR DEPENDENT SUBJECTS IN ITALY.

A. Fiore, C. Tamburlini and F. Poldrugo
Alcohol Research Group, University of Trieste, 34126 Trieste, Italy

Legislative measures allowing the active participation of treatment programs for dependencies instead of imprisonment have been introduced in Italy since 1985.
The research has examined the results of the first 3 years of application of these measures in the district of Udine and Pordenone (North-East Italy).
A minority of subjects (34 out of 2,500), benefited from treatment. Among them 4 were alcohol-dependent, and 30 drug-dependent. Treatment outcome was positive in all except for 2 having concomitant personality disorders.
These results demonstrate that treatment as an alternative to imprisonment has been requested and granted only to a minority of subjects. The responsibility for the scarce implementation of these innovative measures falls on the process of selection used (refusal of subjects without a strong motivation/clear clinical picture, or with personality disorders); the distrust toward the Therapeutic Communities which, in Italy, are private in nature; the irrelevant cultural perception of a need for treatment by alcohol-dependent subjects, and, finally, the existence of other benefits with an easier access.

Session 381 Free Communications:
Psychometric studies of psychopathology

2491
DYNAMICS OF INTERPERSONAL AND INTRAPERSONAL PERCEPTION.

Daniel Kahans and Naomi Crafti, Wingrove Cottage Community Clinic, Eltham, Victoria, Australia.

The hypothesis that people assess both others and themselves in terms of an 'ideal' image, has lent a new dimension to theories of inter-and intra-personal perception. Investigation of these theories has led to the development, at Wingrove Cottage Community Clinic, of a test aimed at elucidating the role of the 'ideal,' both for greater theoretical understanding of this concept and for its obvious utility in clinical application. Using standard personality questionnaires, (Cattell's 16 Personality Factors Test (16PF) and Edward's Personal Preferences Questionnaire (EPPQ), both patients and nonpatients were presented with an eleven points scale between the standard descriptions of these factors. They were asked to rate:- (i) themselves, (ii) their ideal self, and either (iii) (a) Wingrove Receptionist, or (b) their spouse. In addition, each subject completed the full-form of these scales, in order to establish an 'actual' personality profile. The results of these studies, comparing the four profiles obtained, provide strong evidence for the existence of an internalised socially constructed and cognitively-prejudicing 'ideal' personality profile which significantly influences both the interpersonal relationships and self-esteem of patients. The findings obtained, afforded a powerful basis for subsequent psychotherapy, i.e., discussion and analysis between patient, therapist and spouse, through which prejudices were revealed and cognitively/affectively unlearned.

2492

THE USE OF ONSET AND RECENCY PROBES IN A COMMUNITY SAMPLE: RESULTS OF A PROSPECTIVE STUDY WITH THE ALCOHOL SECTION OF THE SPANISH VERSION OF THE 1987 CIDI
Rubio-Stipec, M., Canino, G. and Bravo, M.
University of P.R., Med. Sc. Campus, Dept Psyc., San Juan, PR

The CIDI has included Onset and Recency probes throughout all Alcohol questions. This decision has several potential advantages: it can be less confusing because a single format is used; parallel DSMIII and PSE diagnoses can be made in the same research; and makes it possible to calculate the age at which a respondent first fully met diagnostic criteria (Robins 1988).

For the onset and recency probes to be useful, they must be able to ascertain accurate recollection of the first time and last time that each symptom was experienced. In Puerto Rico, an earlier version of the CIDI (1987) was used on a community sample of 912 persons. Some of these persons (375) had been previously interviewed with a version of the DIS which does not request the onset and recency of each symptom (Canino et al, 1987).

In this paper, using those persons previously interviewed, we analyze the "accuracy" of the recollection. Each positive lifetime symptom coded in 1984 is compared with the onset of that symptom as retrospectively reported in 1987. An "accurate" recollection would be one in which both reports agree. Furthermore, the factors associated to the level of recollection is assessed. Is recollection affected by sex, age education or other demographic variables? Is severity of the symptom associated with recollection?

Since the accuracy of the recollection can be affected by a tendency of those previously interviewed to report less symptomatology in a second interview (report effect); we have studied the presence of a report effect in this sample. Our findings indicate that there is no evidence of a report effect when using the DIS alcohol section in this sample. When analyzed jointly, those previously interviewed and those interviewed for the first time, no significant differences in their report of alcohol symptoms between both groups was identified. These result were maintained even after accounting for differences in sample composition.

2493

CIDI AS A PART OF A PSYCHOSOCIAL GENERAL HEALTH STUDY-THE NORWEGIAN COMMUNITY DIAGNOSIS PROJECT
I.Sandanger, G.Ingebrigtsen, T.Sørensen, O.S.Dalgard
Research Institute, Oslo, Norway

The data to be reported in this paper are collected in a survey of a representative sample of the adult general population in two communities in Norway: 1000 people from a suburban part of Oslo and 1000 people from the island of Lofoten.
The aim of the study is to estimate riskfactors and resources in the communities regarding health in general, with emphasis on mental health. During a two hour long personal interview, the respondents are screened also by Hopkins Symptom Checklist, 25-items. Caseness, 1.55 or more on the HSCL-25, are interviewed with the Composite International Diagnostic Interview, CIDI. In addition a random sample of the respondents are also CIDI-interviewed.
We will report on the feasability of using the CIDI in a general population study. We will also give some preliminary results of the CIDI-diagnoses and the correlation with the HSCL-25 score.

2494

MMPI limitation in detecting schizophrenia in Greek late adolescents.
G. Kaprinis, I. Tarlatzis, C. Phocas, A. Tousina, J. Diakoyannis.
A'Dep. of Psychiatry, Aristotelian University of Thessaloniki, Greece.

Seventeen subjects (6 females and 11 males) with a mean age of 18,4 years and clinically diagnosed as active schizophrenics, were given the MMPI. Their psychological personality profiles were found to be in normal limits reflecting "normal" personality characteristics.

These profiles did not lead to a defensive basis or lying.

The mean female profile shows a difference in validity scales where the F scale is greater (6 T scores) in male profile than in female. Moreover, in the Male mean profile the highest score is Pt where in the Female the Si is the highest.

Our results show the limitation of the MMPI to give reliable profiles for this age group, clinically diagnosed as schizophrenics. Our results are discussed in terms of maturation process, high educational level of the sample.

Moreover, the special age group characteristics may need to be reevaluated in the standardization of the MMPI.

2495

PSYCHOANALYTICAL RORSCHACH DIAGNOSTICS:
BORDERLINE VS SCHIZOPHRENIA
1. Stephanie Loeben-Sprengel, Dipl.Psych.
2. Rudolf Pfitzner, Dipl.Psych.
3. Helga Rehm, Dipl. Psych.
Psychiatrische Klinik, Universität München
Dir.: Prof.Dr.H. Hippius, Abt.-Vor.:Prof.Dr.Ermann

In our department are often presented inpatients to clarify the diagnosis either schizophrenic psychosis or borderlinepathology. Apart from usual psychoanalytic diagnostics Rorschachtest turns out to be essential to this question. 15 patients with first clinical diagnosis of both these groups were tested by it. Blinddiagnostic in regard to clinical classification the gained material is signed and evaluated according to formal criteria (Bohm 1985; Beizmann 1975) by one investigator independently from a group of experts who interprete it according to content and process.
It is our aim to obtain differentialdiagnostic relevant configurations. We are guided by the hypothesis that borderlinepatients have at their disposal a higher organized level of personality and reality-control, which renders it possible for them to get rid of impulsive and effective stress outwardly and not to regulate in an autoplastic way as the psychotics do. Our further expectation is, that it is possible to disclose specific dynamics inferred from content and process of Rorschachprotocol and that this will be a decisive step toward significant diagnostic criteria.
- Some typical illustrations of our proceeding will be given.

2496

REY-OSTERREITH COMPLEX FIGURE TEST IN PSYCHIATRIC POPULATION
Galindo C., Cortes J., Salvador J. & Colin R.
Instituto Mexicano de Psiquiatria. Mexico

In the psychiatric setting the most frequent task for the neuropsychologist is the differentiation from organic vs. functional disturbance. Until now many of the instruments we have, have not been sufficiently studied as to offer the necessary orientation to provide this kind of diferentation That is why the purpose in this study is to look for characteristic performance patterns in a psychiatric population. Rey-Osterreith Figure Test (R.F.) is a widely used stimulus in neuropsychological set being basically applied to neurological patients. However very little is known about this test in relation to psychiatric patients. In this study results have been obtained from 40 mood disorder patients. The results have been analyzed from a quantitative and qualitative point of view. Quantitative analysis has been done considering total scores of execution, this comparison was made by ANOVA. Qualitative analysis was made considering the attributes of each unit of the stimulus. Although there is no significant differences between groups there are some performance patterns that do differentiate groups demonstrated by frequency analysis (Fisher's exact test). The data obtained are strongly related to neuropsychological framework but we need still other studies in different types of psychiatric populations for better conclusions.

2497

EVALUATION OF A SELF-ADMINISTERED BEHAVIORAL QUESTIONNAIRE ON ANXIOUS INHIBITION
P. Legeron
Sce Psychiatrie C.H.94190 Villeneuve St.Georges
France

35 daily life situation explore the functioning of anxious patients in physical-motor, cognitive intellectual and socio-relational areas.
In the course of a study inolving 4973 anxious patients, this first questionnaire asked patients to choose the 3 situations in which they experienced the greatest discomfort.
The frequency of choices and the proximity of items as determined by an analysis of correspondance have allowed the elimination of certain items and the regrouping of others.
The outcome of patients treated with bromazepam for 4 weeks was very favorable, but non-discriminating from one item to another.
At the conclusion of this work a second 20 items questionnaire is proposed, making possible a simplification of the tool while retaining the 3 dimensional behavioral exploration of anxious inhibition.

2498

ANHEDONIA AND PSYCHOPATHOLOGICAL CONDITIONS

G. TRIKKAS, N. MOROS, G.N. CHRISTODOULOU

ATHENS UNIVERSITY, DEPT. OF PSYCHIATRY,
EGINITION HOSPITAL AND STATE PSYCHIATRIC HOSPITAL, CORFOU

Anhedonia is regarded by some as a symptom (usually within the schizophrenic spectrum) and by others as a genetically transmitted characteristic.
The aim of this paper was to delineate the concept of anhedonia and provide more information concerning its incidence in psychopathological conditions.
Eighty psychotic patients (65 schizophrenics and 15 manic-depressives) and 43 neurotics were given Chapman's Physical (P.A.) and Social (S.A.) Anhedonia Scales. Fifty-six medical students were also given the same scales in a test - retest reliability assessment.
Schizophrenics were differentiated with reference to P.A. from neurotics ($p < 0.001$) and manic-depressives ($p < 0.05$) and from neurotics concerning S.A. ($p < 0.001$). Manic-depressives were also differentiated from neurotics concerning S.A. ($p < 0.05$). Schizophrenics with more than ten years hospitalization were differentiated from schizophrenics with less than ten years hospitilization (P.A. $p < 0.05 < 0.1$, S.A. $p < 0.05$). Both scales showed considerable correlation in the test-retest reliability assessment (P.A. $r = 0.893$, $p < 0.001$, S.A. $r = 0.920$, $p < 0.001$). The anhedonia scores were significantly lower in the students' group compared to those of the patients' groups.
Our findings indicate that anhedonia, as measured by Chapman's Scales, is present in schizophrenic, manic-depressive and probably neurotic patients.

2499

THE USE OF PSYCHOLOGICAL TESTS IN THE EVALUATION OF GROUP ANALYTIC PSYCHOTHERAPY
A.Kakouri, M.Manthouli, V.Papadopoulou, K.Oikonomou, A.Kokkinidis
Open Psychotherapeutic Centre. Athens, Greece.

The paper presents a pilot study of a sample of over 20 individuals treated by group analytic psychotherapy who belong to a wide range of diagnostic categories. The average duration of participation in the group analytic group was four years.
The evaluation of changes in personality structure, focuses on an estimation of the quantitative and qualitative parameters of the MMPI, Rorschach and Rotter tests which were administered before and after treatment by the same tester. The study identifies significant changes in the parameters of the tests, which seem to reflect the profound changes to the personality which come about after group analytic treatment.

2500
USEFULNESS OF M.M.P.I.IN CLINICAL DIAGNOSIS

Tzanakaki M.-Skalidi M.-Papadaki A.-Tsakiri M.-Zoumadaki A.-Kandidaki S.
Psyshiatric Hospital of Chania,Centre of Mental Health of Chania,Crete.

One hundred and twenty psychiatric patients under treatment (prychotherapy) alone or in some cases with psychopharmace at the Hania Centre for Mental Health were assessed with M.M.P.I as standarised for Greece by N.Manos (1982).

The diagnosis derived from M.M.P.I. was compared to that of D.S.M.-III -R for the same patients. Sex,age and educative status were also used comparatively,the latter above the required standards.

85% of the derived M.M.P.I. profils agree with the D.S.M.III-R diagnosis.

After the therapy was over,1/3 of the cases were assessed again with M.M.P.I,with at heast 8 months interval between initial and second assessement.The two profiles were compared to obtain any differentiation in M.M.P.I scales before and after therapy.

Session 382 Free Communications:
Depression in the elderly

2501
DEPRESSION AND AGE

Musetti L., Perugi G., Soriani A., Mignani V., Cassano G.B.

Chair II, Institute of Clinical Psychiatry, University of Pisa, Italy.

Systematic and detailed psychopathological examination of 538 consecutive primary major depressives failed to confirm common clinical stereotypes which ascribe greater somatization, hypochondriasis, agitation, psychotic tendencies and chronicity to old age. In the present study neither chronicity, nor interepisodic residuals, were related to old age. It is also noteworthy that melancholic and psychotic features did not distinguish the elderly depressives from their younger contemporaries; if anything, younger depressives had a trend for greater mood incongruence. Furthermore, our elderly depressives, rather than being agitated, displayed greater motor retardation. The major differences emerging from this study are represented by diagnostic subtypes of primary mood disorder and their familial distribution at different ages at onset. Thus, Bipolar I, Bipolar II and Recurrent (Unipolar) Depressive Disorders typically arise before age 65 and show high familial prevalence of mood disorders; this is particularly true for the Bipolar I subtype characterized by mania. Single Episode Depressions, by contrast, were significantly more common after age 65; environmental factors such as stressors identified within 6 months of the onset of depression, were more common in this subtype. These data tend to support a spectrum model of primary mood disorders where differences in genetic risk favor the appearance of less precipitated and high episode frequency, especially bipolar disorders with heavy constitutional load manifesting in temperamental pathology earlier in life and, genetically less penetrant and environmentally precipitated single episode varieties, later in life.

2502
CEREBRAL CHANGES IN ELDERLY DEPRESSIVES
George S. Alexopoulos, M.D.
Cornell University Medical College,
White Plains, New York, U.S.A.

A complex clinical and biological relationship exists between geriatric depression and neurological brain disorders. Reversible cognitive dysfunction as well as transient localizing neurological and neuropsychological findings have been reported in depression. Conversely, depression is part of the symptomatology of neurological dementing disorders. Finally, common abnormalities in brain structure and function have been found in both depression and in dementia syndromes. These include dilatation of lateral brain ventricles, reduction in cerebral blood flow and oxidative metabolism, reduction in sleep and sedation thresholds to barbiturates, dysfunction in brain monoamine neurotransmitters. Late-onset depressives have less family history of affective disorders than early-onset depressives. Late-onset depression is more often associated with cognitive dysfunction or dementia and with morphological brain abnormalities than early-onset depression of geriatric patients. The hypothesis has been advanced that late-onset depression is a heterogeneous disorder which includes a large subgroup of patients who develop depression as part of a neurological disorder that may or may not be clinically evident when the depression first appears. The implications for clinical studies and research will be discussed.

2503
Psychopathology and Diagnosis of Late Functional Psychoses
Victor Kontsevoy
All-Union Mental Health Research Centre
USSR Academy of Medical Sciences

Late functional psychoses represent a group of nosologically heterogeneous psychoses that appear in the involution and old age periods and are not accompanied by organic dementia.It includes both endogenous psychoses manifested in the old age and a small group of age psychoses associated with the ageing process.
Irrespective of nosology, clinical and psychopathological manifestations of functional psychoses are characterised by 3 basic tendencies:narrower range of syndromes as compared with previous ontogenesis periods,syndromes reduction and the appearance of syndromes prevailent in the old age. A close interrelation between the formation and dynamics of psychopathological syndromes and situational factors is revealed.
The difficulties in distinguishing between functional psychoses only on the basis of their psychopathological manifestations make it necessary to take into account in the diagnosis such parameters as constitutional and genetic factors, periods of disease prior to its manifestation and basic features of its course.

2504

A RASCH ANALYSIS OF THE GERIATRIC DEPRESSION
SCALE IN A FRENCH SAMPLE
Cialdella Ph., M.D.,M.Sc., Guillaud-Bataille J.M.
Gausset M.F., M.D.
Research Dept., C.H.S. Saint-Jean-de-Dieu,
290 route de Vienne, 69008 Lyon, France

The Geriatric Depression Scale (GDS) is a recent
30-items autoquestionnaire designed by Yesavage
and Brink (1983) for the assessment of depression
in old people. We have asked 120 elderly women
who either lived in old people' homes or attended
a geriatric day-hospital to fill the GDS. In this
sample 53 women were found to suffer from an
affective disorder according to DSM-III. With a
Principal component analysis, 3 factors extracted
more than 5% of the total variance, but these
factors were highly correlated. No clear
interpretation emerged from this analysis. Thus,
we performed a Rasch analysis, which is a
statistical tool aimed at modelling the
probability of a correct answer as a logistic
function of the difference between the person and
the item parameter. The goodness-of-fit for each
item allows the detection of gross departures
from unidimensionality. A satisfactory model was
found with the deletion of only 4 items. The
Rasch model seems to be a very useful tool for
assessing unidimensionality, especially when
factor analysis gives no clear result. The GDS
with few items deleted appears to be a good,
quasi-unidimentional scale, and constitutes a
promising instrument.

2505

LA DEPRESSION ET LES EVENEMENTS AUX PERSONNES AGEES

Georges Kleftaras, Docteur en Psychologie Expérimental
Laboratoire de Psy. Exp. de Univ. Paris X, France

Le but de la présente recherche est de contribuer à mieux
comprendre la dépression chez les personnes âgées et plus
précisément à étudier les relations entre la dépression et
certains facteurs de nature comportementale (activité et
événements agréables et désagréables) et socio-culturelle.
310 personnes âgées françaises valides, d'un âge moyen de
78.75 ans vivant dans des foyers-logements pour personnes
âgées ont participé à cette étude. Elles ont répondu au
Questionnaire de la Symptomatologie Dépressive de Pichot
et al. et aux deux Questionnaires des Evénements Agréables
et Désagréables. Les structures factorielles de ces
instruments telles qu'elles ont été établiees à partir
des réponses de notre échantillon sont satisfaisantes.
Les résultats de cette recherche sont positifs et confirment
nos hypothèses. Ainsi, plus une personne est déprimée:
a) plus la fréquence, le degré d'agrément subjectif et le
renforcement positif reçu des événements agréables diminuent,
b) plus la fréquence, le degré de désagrément subjectif et
l'aversion ressentie des événements désagréables augmentent.
Par ailleurs, selon nos résultats plus une personne âgée
est déprimée plus elle est âgée, plus son niveau d'instruction
est bas et plus la fréquence des visites qu'elle reçoit
diminue. De même, la mauvaise santé et les mauvaises relations qu'une personne âgée entretient avec ses enfants
augmentent significativement les risques de dépression.

2506

METAMEMORY AND DEPRESSION IN GERIATRIC PSYCHIATRY

M. Tropper
Neuropsychiatric Dept.Zamenhof central multi-disciplinary Out-patient Clinic,Tel-Aviv,Bar Ilan University, Israel
Memory and Cognitive(MC Disorders represent an
underestimated topic in the early evaluation of
Depression in the elderly.115 patients (PT) aged
67-78(mean71+1,2)characterized at the onset of
their disease as suffering from forgetfullness
for names,placement of objects,"tip of the tongue"
phenomenon,amnesiophobia etc.as well as a control
group were assessed and followed-up putting the
emphasis on their affective state.Among the applied techniques were:Hamilton,Zung,Yesavage,Folstein
Reisberg's and the Geriatric Neuropsychological
Assessment Battery.Our main goal was the elucidation of the relationship between MC complaints,MC
performance and PT's affective state in the absence of symptoms pathognomonic for Alzheimer Type
Dementia(D),Multi-Infarct D,Subcortical D PT's
(in their early stages) and PT's Metamemory (MM).
MC and MM findings were processed and their relationship analyzed in the light of Cognitive Psy-
chology(P),Behavior P,Geriatric Neuropsychology
and current concepts concerning Depression.Corre-
lations were made between MM findings and the severity of Depression,by applying different treatment approaches.In 42% MM data were helpful in
the early differential diagnosis.Results point to
the necessity to carry out concomitantly MC and
MM assessments for effective intervention.

2507

IMIPRAMINE PLUS MIANSERIN VERSUS IMIPRAMINE
ALONE IN ELDERLY DEPRESSED PATIENTS
L. Lauritzen, R. Klysner, L. Clemmesen, D. Loldrup,
M. Lunde, E. Schaumburg, S. Waarst, A. Geisler and
P. Bech
Frederiksborg General Hospital, 3400 Hillerød,
Denmark

This is the first controlled clinical trial in which a
combination of mianserin and imipramine has been
evaluated in depressed patients. In total 40 patients
aged 35 to 75 years (mean 65) were treated with either
imipramine plus mianserin or imipramine plus placebo.
The imipramine dosage was flexible in order to
maintain a plasma level of 200 nmol/l, while mianserin
was given in a fixed dosage of 30 mg daily. In both
groups of patients 73% completed the planned trial of
six weeks. The post-treatment Hamilton Depression
score was 14.2 in patients treated with imipramine
alone, whereas the imipramine plus mianserin group
scored 6.0. This difference was statistical significant
($P \leq 0.01$). The pharmacokinetic and pharmacodynamic
aspects of these findings will be discussed.

2508
PLASMA TRAZODONE CONCENTRATIONS IN ELDERLY DEPRESSED PATIENTS.

Monteleone P., Gnocchi G.
Department of Psychiatry, U.S.L. 41, Naples, Italy.

Plasma monitoring of antidepressant drugs may be a useful means of maximizing clinical response and avoiding potentially serious adverse effects. This is particularly suitable in elderly patients in which antidepressants achieve steady-state plasma concentrations significantly higher because of alterations in pharmacokinetics. For this reason, we assessed the relationships among plasma trazodone levels, clinical outcome and side effects in the elderly depressive disorder. Steady-state plasma trazodone concentrations were determined by HPLC in 11 depressed subjects (age range 60-74 yrs) who underwent a 5-week treatment with 150 mg/die trazodone. Clinical antidepressant response was significantly correlated with steady-state plasma trazodone concentrations ($r = 0.80$, $p < 0.0008$; Pearson's correlation test). Moreover, the plasma trazodone level of 650 ng/ml was identified as threshold value for a good antidepressant response. No correlation was found between the occurrence of side effects and plasma levels of trazodone indicating that higher the level of the drug, the higher is the probability of obtaining a good clinical response with no higher occurrence of side effects.

2509
OUTCOME OF DEPRESSIVE ILLNESS IN A RANDOM COMMUNITY SAMPLE OF PERSONS OVER 65 LIVING IN LIVERPOOL (GMS-AGECAT).
V.K.Sharma, J.R.M. Copeland, M.E.Dewey, I.A.Davidson P.A. Saunders, Christopher McWilliam, Carolinge Sullivan, L.N.P. Voruganti.
INSTITUE OF HUMAN AGEING, UNIVERSITY OF LIVERPOOL, LIVERPOOL, U.K.

A random sample of 1070 subjects aged 65 years and over was interviewed using a semistructured mental examination, the Geriatric Mental State (community version) to which can be applied a computerised psychiatric diagnosis - AGECAT. The sample was followed up 3 years later by psychiatrists using the Geriatric Mental State, the History and Aetiology Schedule, the Social Status Schedule, Mini-Mental State and a Self Rating Depressive Scale for the elderly. The overall prevalence for depression in the original sample was 11.3%. At the time of follow up 19% of the depressed subjects were dead; 27.3% were still depressed, 32.2% were no longer ill. Only 3.3% had dementia and 4% had neurotic disorders. Overall prevalence of depression at follow up was 8.2%. Only around 4% of the depressed patients were receiving antidepressants at the initial as well as at follow up assessment, although one third of them were receiving hypnotics and sedatives. Further data will be presented on outcome by age, sex, social support and physical disability, type of diagnosis and symptoms profile.

2510
DEPRESSION AMONG ELDERLY MEDICAL IN-PATIENTS
Fred R. Fenton, Martin G. Cole, Frank Engelsmann, Iradj Mansouri, St. Mary's Hospital, Montreal, Canada.

The aim of this cross-sectional-longitudinal survey was to estimate the frequency of major depressive episode (MDE, DSM-III criteria) among medical in-patients aged 65 and older. Information was obtained systematically from 362 patients, at the time of admission to a medical ward of a general hospital and 1,3 and 12 months later. Two thirds of these patients were aged 75 or older. The point prevalence rates of MDE on admission were relatively high: 28% among patients aged between 65 and 74; 31% among patients aged between 75 and 84, and 25% among patients aged 85 or older. The total point prevalence rate of MDE at each of the four time points was also relatively high: 29%, 29%, 24% and 33% respectively. 49% of patients experienced episodes of MDE lasting at least 3 months and 65% had one or more episodes during the year. There are at least two applications of this work. First, knowledge of the influence of social, medical and psychiatric variables on the course of MDEs will provide a rationale for more effective treatment. Second, knowledge of who becomes "newly depressed" during the year is the first step towards identifying interventions which would decrease the risk of serious depression occurring in this setting.

Session 383 Free Communications:
Psychiatric management on the primary care level

2511
WHO SHOULD TREAT A MENTAL PATIENT - A SPECIALIST OR A G.P.? - A SURVEY IN RURAL INDIA
HIRANMAY SAHA - Consultant Psychiatrist, G.S. Clinic, Calcutta,India; GOURANGA BANERJEE - Associate Prof., N.R.S.Medical College,Calcutta,India and D. N. NANDI Consultant Psychiatrist, G.S. Clinic, Calcutta, India.

The National Mental Health Programme of India aims at integration of mental health care with general health care. For this programme people's ability to detect mental illness and their choice of mode of treatment are important. To study this aspect of public awareness and behaviour we designed a field Survey in a rural area. A questionnaire with 20 case reports dealing with both physical and mental illness was given to a random sample of 50 school teachers (viewed by the villagers as their guide in health matters) of that area. They were asked to give their opinion about the types of illness and their choice of healers for the treatment of those disorders.

The most striking features of the findings are (a) Psycotics are most often correctly detected and help from specialists of modern medicine is sought for them (b) Neurotics are less often detected and a large number of respondents preferred help from indigenous healers and (c) Except for some physical conditions (gastroenterits,Snake bite, fever) very few respondents wanted the help of a G.P.

In conclusion it may be said that rural people prefer the help of either the indigenous healers or the specialist for mental illness. The programme of integration of mental health care with general health care through the Primary care Physician (G.P.) needs re-evaluation in the light of this findings.

2512

Detection of Emotional Disorders by Primary Care Physicians in Brazil
Iacoponi,E.
Escola Paulista de Medicina, S.Paulo, Brazil

Factors related to doctors, patients and settings are known to influence the detection of emotional disorders in the primary care sector. These factors have been studied separately in the past, but in the present investigation they were observed in interaction, by means of logistic regression. Standardized instruments were used to collect data from 1460 patients attending consultation with 67 doctors in 38 primary care clinics in the city of S.Paulo, Brazil. Although factors related to doctors and clinics had significant effects on the detection of emotional disorders, the single strongest effect was the patients level of psychiatric morbidity, showing that detection increases with higher levels of morbidity. The implication of these results are discussed in the light of the delivery of health services.

2513

THERAPY MOTIVATION OF JAPANESE STUDENTS
(LEIDENSQUELLEN DER JAPANISCHEN STUDENTEN)

Masato Uno, Psychiatric Research Institute of Tokyo, Japan
Emiko Ando, Department of Psychiatry in Health Service Center of Tokyo University, Japan

The present paper is an investigation concerning the motivation of 88 students who spontaneously visited the Health Service Center of the Tokyo University for the first time during the year from April 1987 till March 1988 and requested consultation. They represent 0.60% of the entire student enrollment. Phenomenologically, their sufferings can be divided into two areas. The first area comprises the individual life of the student and may relate either to the somatic or psychic disorders. In the second area fall the social (intersubjective) conflicts related either to other people in general or to special groups or persons. The conclusion is that, apart from the 16 students enrolled in the first semester where the distribution is fairly equal, the individual suffering prevails as motivation for seeking a treatment (53 students) as compared with the intersubjective conflicts (19 students).

2514

ILLNESS BEHAVIOR AND ANXIETY IN DENTAL PATIENTS
Renzo Rizzardo, Luigi Cappelletti, Giuseppe Borgherini
Department of Psychiatry - University of Padua - Italy

One problem posed by oral cavity pathology is that of patients' delay in seeking dental treatment. The aim of this work is to evaluate the influence of illness behavior on this problem and the relationship with state and trait anxiety and with some social-demographic and clinical data. 100 patients aged between 16 and 65 were studied; they were chosen at random from people who presented themselves for dental treatment after at least 6 months had elapsed since their previous visit. The instruments used are: a medical history form, and the self-assessment scales IBQ (Illness Behavior Questionnaire) and STAI (State-Trait Anxiety Inventory); furthermore one researcher compiled a clinical form for the evaluation of the dental pathology on account of which the patient had come to surgery (caries or parodonthal pathology). On the basis of the degree of lesion the patients were divided into those who came early and those who came late for treatment. The patients who come late present significantly higher scores for negation factor and also tend to show greater conviction of illness and affective inhibition on the IBQ scales. There is no relation between anxiety and early or late requests for treatment. On the contrary the state anxiety is significantly higher in those patients with a family habit of only going to the dentist when there is a real need, with having experienced discomfort in previous dental visits, with unwillingness to go to the dentist and with the presence of pain. There is also a relationship between better education and more frequent dental visits, less affective inhibition and greater psychological perception of the illness.

2515

PREVENTIVE TECHNIQUES FOR THE OVERSENSITIVE STRESS BEARERS (OSB) MISMANAGEMENT.
NAISBERG YACOV
RAMBAM MEDICAL CENTER, HAIFA, ISRAEL.

OSB is a term to define an inherited or acquired sensitized susceptability to social and environmental stressors, regardless of their intensity and duration. In this respect preventive measures are cristalized:
1. Screening for OSB detection amongst children and adolescents;
2. Incorporating an awareness about the nature of OSB vulnerability and a need for remedy;
3. Exercizing a lifelong medication for organisms homeostasis restoration;
4. Indoctrinating training programmes for acquiring accommodative basic survival and achievemental skills;
5. Enhancing and maintaining lifelong cooperative behavior process, which minimizes the stress exposure;
6. Introducing a systematic educational Mental Health programme in schools (grades I to I2) on drug and alcohol addictions, suicide attempts, anti-social behavior and other significant topics in prevention.
  All the above measurements are implemented under standardized training and assessment and will reduce and eliminate the adult psychiatric impairment.

2516

Evaluations of psychiatric care by primary care personnel
Lars Kjellin, BA
County Council of Västmanland, Västerås Sweden

The aim of this study is to investigate attitudes in social services and primary health care towards the psychiatric care and the mentally ill.

In two Swedish counties (C and U) with differently organized psychiatric services, a postal questionnaire was sent to 733 district doctors/nurses and social workers. 86% answered. Nearly all have regularly a professional contact with psychiatry. The majority expresses humanistic rather than custodial attitudes towards mental illness. Both social workers and primary health care personnel express strong critical views regarding psychiatry. Less than half of the answering persons states good confidence in psychiatry. Approximately one third says that the psychiatric organization takes its responsibility for the mentally ill in the catchment area. 50% finds psychiatry a bad partner in co-operation. The critical attitudes are especially strong in U county with relatively small psychiatric resources and emphasis on out-patient care and somewhat stronger from social workers than from primary health care personnel.

156 persons (87%) in a district (A) in another part of Sweden answered the same questionnaire. A is relatively well provided with psychiatric resources and has long experience of a sectorized psychiatric organization. The social and primary health care personnel were more satisfied with the psychiatric care in A district than in C and U counties.

2517

MENTAL DISORDERS IN MEDICAL SETTINGS (GENERAL HOSPITAL AND PRIMARY CARE)
A.PEZZOLI G.BERTI CERONI F.BERTI CERONI R.BIVI A.CORSINO
P.DE MARCO S.GHERARDI G.MINENNA C.NERI
Psychiatric Service U.S.L. 27 and U.S.L. 22, Bologna, Italy.

Clinical and extraclinical features and course of mental disorders identified in medical non-psychiatric settings have been evaluated in a multicentric research in Emilia-Romagna, Italy. A group of more than 900 subjects has been examined in medical wards (casualty departments and G.P.s. surgeries) with a self-report test, the Symptom Questionnaire (SQ) by Kellner and Fava, and by a clinical interview - About 20% of the subjects suffered from a diagnosable disorder following the DSM-III, frequently with chronic course. In 80% of the cases, such a disorder was unknown and untreated. Women were more frequently affected, while there was quite homogeneous age distribution.

The clinical and extraclinical features of these patients, have been compared with those of a patient group attending to the Psychiatric Services for the first time, and with a control group of "healthy" patients randomly choosen in medical settings.
A clinical course evaluation for these three groups (patients attending to psychiatric services, for the first time, patients with mental disorders in medical settings, "healthy" patients) has been planned, with a three month, one-year and two year follow-up (the last one is not yet finished and complete data are still unavailable).
Moreover the subjects with disorders identified in medical settings have been randomly sent either to local psychiatric services or to a "naturalistic" course, in order to study and compare possible differences of course, treatment and outcome.

2518

LES SOINS PRIMAIRES EN SANTE MENTALE AU MAROC

M. PAES, M.J. JULIAN, K. RADDAOUI, J.E. KTIOUET
CLINIQUE UNIVERSITAIRE DE PSYCHIATRIE - RABAT-MAROC

Différents travaux et études sur l'organisation des soins psychiatriques au Maroc ont montré les besoins importants de la population en matière de santé mentale d'une part et l'insuffisance de l'infrastructure psychiatrique à leur égard, ainsi que les ressources et les moyens dont elle dispose d'autre part.
Parmi les différentes alternatives susceptibles d'améliorer cette situation, l'intégration des soins psychiatriques dans les structures sanitaires de base apparait plus particulièrement adéquate et susceptible de répondre aux besoins.

Ce travail, se basant sur une enquête auprès du personnel médical et paramédical en fonction dans les structures sanitaires de base et dans l'analyse de leurs programme d'enseignement,effectue une approche globale de cette alternative et suggère les mesures pour la réalisation de celle-ci.

Session 384   Video:
Psychopathology. Psychosurgery

2519

"EL" (Historia de un Esquizofrénico)

PROF. DR. MIGUEL ANGEL MATERAZZI
HOSPITAL NACIONAL JOSE T. BORDA
CENTRO DE INVESTIGACION MEDICO PSICOLOGICA DE LA COMUNICACION

El Video presenta un corte transversal en la vida de un paciente esquizofrénico, señalando en particular el proceso de despersonalización y la dicotomía mente-cuerpo, además de análisis institucional. Por otro lado, la representación está efectuada por un equipo mixto de profesionales del Centro y Pacientes Psicóticos de la Colonia Cabred - Open Door - Provincia de Buenos Aires.

2520

FRIDA KAHLO'S PAINT: "NATURAL HISTORY OF DEPRESSION OR THE SUBLIMATION OF A CHRO-- NIC SADNESS?

DRA. ARACELY GRANADOS DIAZ.
MEDICO PSIQUIATRA PSICOTERAPEUTA.

Frida Kahlo fue una mujer pintora mexicana que nace en 1907, a lo largo de sus 47 años de vida; 18 años como pintora representa en sus obras cada época de su vida como autobiografiada en dolor, la tristeza, del amor a la muerte y su necesidad de vivir. Después de un accidente automovilístico que además de destrozarle la columna vertebral, le destruye también la realización de sus metas como Médico. En 1954 muere después de diez fallidos intentos de suicidio, y su último cuadro: "NATURALEZA MUERTA" que irónicamente titula: "VIVA LA VIDA". Entre alcoholismo y tranquilizantes ella anota en su diario que su muerte es voluntaria. A través de su historia y de la observación de sus pinturas, aparece el cuestionamiento: ¿Fue su obra una constante solicitud de ayuda? ¿Es la pintura la mejor expresión no verbal del estado afectivo?.

El dibujo, como expresión gráfica de la comunicación humana aparece con la historia de la humanidad desde sus orígenes, a la vez que escultura y pintura como productos geniales mágicos de aquel antepasa

2521

MODERN PSYCHOSURGERY IS AN INDISPENSABLE TREATMENT

Paul Bridges, Geoffrey Knight Unit for Affective Disorders.
Guy's Hospital Medical School, London, SE1 9RT U.K.
Psychosurgery is no longer controversial. Although it is used much less round the world, it has become established and quite widely accepted in Britain. This national unit uses the operation of sterotactic subcaudate tractotomy(SST), first performed in 1961 and since then about 1,200 operations have been carried out. The lesion is produced by small radio-active yttrium rods. There have been one death, 19 patients (1.6%) with one or more post-operative epileptic fits, one post-operative haemorrhage successfully treated by an emergency operation and no significant infections. There have been no adverse personality changes. The indications include intractable affective disorders unipolar and bipolar, anxiety and phobic anxiety, tension states and obsessional disorders. The clinical results can be dramatic, with severe and frequently long-standing illnesses often recovering completely. We now insist that a combination of a tricyclic in a high dose, with L-tryptophan and lithium, must have been tried and failed before acceptance for surgery. Thus, when a patient is severely incapacitated by an appropriate illness but does not respond to determined treatments, failing to consider SST should be now regarded as clinical negligence.

THE TALK WILL BE FOLLOWED BY AN AWARD WINNING VIDEO - presentation (12 minutes)

*Wednesday
18th October 1989*

Session 385 — Plenary: Brain mechanisms in normal and abnormal mental processes

2522

BRAIN AND THINKING
Bechtereva NP Medvedev SV Abdullaev YG
Institute of Experimental Medicine, Leningrad, 197022, USSR

In neurophysiology of thinking, 60s and 70s can be regarded as time when value of neuronal correlates of thinking was evidenced and basic data were obtained on principles of cerebral organisation of mental processes. Cerebral activity was shown to be maintained by cortical-subcortical system with rigid and flexible links and that subcortical structures are not only energy sources for cortex. The foundation was laid due to achieves in clinical applying implanted electrodes, computer stereotaxis, polyelectroneurography and computer data processing. This has created basis for developing major trends in neurophysiology of thinking and assisted in working out the strategy for further research. These are: (1) Structural functional organization of brain including micromapping; (2) system functioning mechanisms; (3) neurolinguistics; (4) neuroinformatics. Recently developed micromapping of cortex has already presented quite new data on neuronal mechanisms of thinking. The most promising perspective of brain research is joint one with using both neurophysiological and imaging techniques as positron emission and photon tomography, magnitoencephalography.

2523

BRAIN AND THE IMMUNE SYSTEM IN MENTAL DISORDERS

C.L. Cazzullo

Dept. of Psychiatry-University of Milan-Italy

The connections between the CNS and the immune system are frequently grouped under the heading of 'Psychoneuroimmunology' or 'Psyconeuroendocrinoimmunology'. The two definitions indicate the bidirectional activity of the two systems capables of reciprocally influence each other. In any case such connections are accompanied by psychologcal or psychopathological manifestations. a) It will be considered the interaction between emotions and immunity particularly evident under stress conditios. b) Special kinds of infections affecting the CNS like HIV are always accompanied by psychopathological phenomena as ansiety and depression which are also observed in some autimmune diseases like multiple sclerosis. c) In certain group of patients with affective disorders as well with schizophrenia many researchers have shown abnormality in some immunological parameters. d) In this light immunogenetic studies are very important. Starting from a previous study in 1974 an association between HLA antigens and schizophrenia was demonstred. It was observed the significant increase of DR3 antigenic system in schizophrenic patients and their parents where a morbidity risk is doubled vs normal population.

2524

ARE INFLAMMATORY AND AUTO-IMMUNE DISEASES MANIFESTATIONS OF PRIMARY DEFECTS IN THE CENTRAL NERVOUS SYSTEM: RHEUMATOID ARTHRITIS AS A MODEL SYSTEM
E.M. Sternberg, M.D.
National Institutes of Mental Health and National Institute of Arthritis and Musculoskeletal and Skin Diseases, Bethesda, Maryland

Although psychological stress and depression have long been thought to be associated with the initial onset and exacerbations of inflammatory and autoimmune diseases, such as rheumatoid arthritis, strong scientific proof of this thesis has remained elusive. In part, the lack of an apparent biological basis for such a relationship has made testing of the hypothesis difficult. The elucidation of a counter-regulatory feedback loop between the immune system and the central nervous system (CNS), however, now provides a biochemical and molecular framework for hypothesizing that a relationship between depression and rheumatoid arthritis may be rooted in a common neuroendocrine defect. Both inflammatory and behavioral stresses, through stimulation of the corticotropin releasing hormone (CRH) neuron, activate a final common neuroendocrine pathway: the hypothalamic-pituitary-adrenal axis. The association between psychological stress and development of inflammatory disease may therefore be related to alterations of this common pathway, or to defects in the intricate feedback loops that exist between the immune system - CNS loop to susceptibility to arthritis, as well as our recent findings of imbalances of this loop in depressive disorders, provide models for a common neuroendocrine defect underlying both susceptibility to inflammatory diseases and depression.

2525

STRESS-RESPONSIVE NEUROTRANSMITTERS: A BRIDGE BETWEEN PSYCHODYNAMIC AND BIOLOGICAL PSYCHIATRY
Philip W. Gold, M.D.
National Institute of Mental Health, Bethesda, Maryland

For many of us, the decision to enter psychiatry reflected a sense that psychiatry involved the utilization of humanistic concepts as a principal mode of treating disease, a kind of applied literature in which one's knowledge about the world could influence the course of an illness. With the advancement of tenable hypotheses regarding biological factors in major psychiatric disorders coupled with the clear efficacy of psychotropic agents, the pendulum seemed to shift away from sychodynamic psychiatry, which many came to see as unscientific.
Although the successes of biological psychiatry lured some away from the intellectual attractions of the unconscious, these same successes now make an integration of psychodynamic and biological psychiatry more feasible. Hence, recent work which has further delineated both the biological landscapes of responses ordinarily called into play during stressful situations and pathophysiologic mechanisms in illnesses such as major depression and anorexia nervosa tells us that these terrains share many features. Such work supports the notion that even subtle, constitutionally-mediated alterations in mechanisms controlling the activation or inactivation of stress-responsive neuromodulators could interact with great burdens of internal conflict or external adversity to influence the natural history of these illnesses. Accordingly, whereas psychopharmacologic intervention of illnesses such as major depression may be required to resolve an active episode or to prevent recurrences, psychotherapy may be equally important to lessen the burdens imposed by unconscious factors and counterproductive defenses. In the present lecture, I would like to develop this theme further by showing that the cardinal clinical and biochemical manifestations of melancholic and atypical depression seem associated with dysregulation of the two major effectors of the generalized stress response, namely the corticotropin releasing hormone and norepinephrine-locus ceruleus systems.

Session 386
Developmental and age related psychopathological conditions

Plenary:

2526

ISSUES IN THE DIAGNOSIS AND CLASSIFICATION OF CHILDHOOD DEPRESSION - THE NEWCASTLE CHILD DEPRESSION PROJECT
Kolvin, I., Barrett, L., Bhate, S.R., Berney, T.P., Famiyuwa, O.O., Fundudis, T. and Tyrer, S.

A fundamental issue in the current debate about depression in childhood concerns the validity of diagnostic criteria, and how best the classification of depression in children should proceed. Some consider it possible to diagnose major depression in childhood using criteria identical to those used in adults (Spitzer et al., 1978; Puig-Antich, 1980); others feel that different considerations should apply where children are concerned. This is reflected in alternative diagnostic schemas, three of which are those devised by Puig-Antich and Chambers (1978), by Weinberg et al (1973) in the USA and by Kolvin et al. (1984) in Newcastle. How valid are each of these in the diagnosis of depression and to what extent do these schemes agree or disagree with each other?

Another issue of major importance is how depression in childhood should be classified. In adult psychiatry this is a notoriously complex area, and even if childhood depression were similar, classification problems would be compounded by issues of child development. For these reasons, and particularly for clinical purposes, many consider it better to describe disorders in a systematic way rather than to attempt any sophisticated sub-classification. this can be done by giving an account, first, of the severity of depression and secondly, by documenting any specific disorders associated with depression. The wisdom of this approach is underlined by the fact that it is not yet certain whether depression in children is a homogeneous or a heterogeneous condition. If the latter, is depression missed because of concealment by other symptoms and, if so, what is the extent and nature of the association?

2527

THE PLACE OF DEVELOPMENTAL PSYCHOPATHOLOGY IN CHILD AND ADOLESCENT PSYCHIATRY

Remschmidt, Helmut

Philipps-University Marburg (FRG)

The developmental perspective can be looked upon as a kind of bridge between different disciplines and a unifying concept for the understanding of psychopathological disorders in children and adolescents. There exist important research fields and strategies in developmental psychopathology: sex differences and individual differences, continuity and change of behavior, risk research, research on protective factors, research on prediction, research on the nature of the developmental process itself, and, of course, classification of disorders under the developmental perspective. In the paper, several of these issues are discussed, ending at the conclusion that the integrative character of developmental psychopathology requires a close collaboration of researchers and clinicians of different disciplines.

2528

Epidemiology of Dementia and Cognitive Decline: an incidence study
E S Paykel C Brayne F A Huppert C Barkley C Gill

University of Cambridge
School of Clinical Medicine
Cambridge CB2 2QQ UK

Epidemiological studies of dementia have mainly concerned prevalence. This paper reports an incidence study of dementia and rates of cognitive decline in a general population sample aged over 75 studied twice at a two year interval A two stage procedure was used. All subjects were screened using the Mini Mental State Examination (MMSE). Failures, and additional subsamples, received a detailed standardised interview from psychiatrists, the Cambridge Examination for Mental Disorders in the Elderly (CAMDEX). Age specific rates of decline on MMSE scores, and incidence of new cases of dementia on CAMDEX will be reported.

2529

Antisocial Personality and Criminal Career

D.J. West.
Institute of Criminology, Cambridge, England

A cohort of 400 boys have been followed from age 8 to age 32 and their social adjustment and delinquent behaviour recorded. Over a third have acquired a criminal conviction record.

Coming from large sized, low income families having criminal parents, being troublesome at school and displaying aggressive attitudes and behaviour were important predictors of later criminality. It proved possible to identify at age 8 a vulnerable minority destined for a high incidence of social problems in adult life, including criminal convictions and unstable family relationships.

Deviant life style and attitude was typical of the worst offenders, both when interviewed at 18 and when seen at age 32. The findings are congruent with the concept of delinquent character formation and with the inter-generational transmission of social problems.

Although adverse background factors were highly predictive of adult problems, some individuals who had been severely deprived in their early years achieved a reasonable adjustment by age 32.

Session 387 Symposium:
The emerging interface between psychiatry and medicine

2530

TUBERO INFUNDIBULAR AND HIGHER BRAIN FUNCTION IN TRANSEXUALS: MODULATION BY SEX STEROIDS
G. Tolis, M.D., F.R.C.P., Canada
Prof. Med. Univ. of Crete, Director Endocrine Division, Hippokration Hospital, Athens, Greece

Assessment of the hypothalamic pituitary gonadal axis was performed in nine karyotypically male (46xy) to female and one female (46xx) to male transexuals seeking hormonal manipulation of their phenotype and/or ablative plastic surgery. Of them 1 male was a professional organ player and the female was a painter and music composer, student of renowned Canadian artist.

All males had "upsetting" nocturnal erections and the female had a monthly vaginal bleeding. Plasma testosterone and serum prolactin were normal in all males; in 2 out of 2 pituitary gonadotropin release (GnRH tested) was normal. Nocturnal tumescence studies were normal as far as frequency and amplitude of erectile episodes. Serum estradiol, progesterone and prolactin levels were within normal luteal range in the female tested.

Suppression of gonadal function with D, TRP6 GnRH analogue led to remarkable changes concerning the artistic performances which were further accentuated or attenuated according to the treatment used.

Above data document that the hypothalamic pituitary gonadal axis functions properly despite altered gender identity and demonstrate a plasticity of adult brain function in transexualism as manifested by the steroidal effect on "behavior".

2531

PATHOPSYSIOLOGICAL MECHANISMS IN MAJOR DEPRESSION AND CUSHING'S DISEASE
P.W.Gold,M.D., M.A.Kling,M.D., H.J.Whitfield,M.D., G.P.Chrousos,M.D., National Institute of Health,Bethesda,MD, USA.

We have advanced several lines of evidence showing that the pituietry corticotroph cell in patients with melancolic depression responds appropriately to glucocorticoid negative feedback,and that hypercortisolism in these patients reflects a defect at or above the hypothalamus resulting in the hyersecretion of corticotropin releasing hormone(CRH).In contrast,our data show that the pituitary corticotroph cell in patients with Cushing's disease is grossly unresponsive to glycocorticoid negative feedback,while the CRH neuron is appropriately suppressed by long standing hypercortisolism.On the basis of this differential pathophysiology,patients with major depression and Cushing's disease show antithetical plasma ACTH responses to CRH which can help in the differential diagnosis of these two disorders.Moreover,in the light of the pronounced CNS effects of CRH, differences in the CRH systems in could account for the defferential presentation of depressive symptomatology in these disorders.

2532

SUSCEPTIBILITY TO ARTHRITIS IN THE LEWIS RAT IS MEDIATED BY DEFICIENT RESPONSIVENESS OF THE CRH NEURON
E.M.Sternberg,M.D.,G.P.Chrousos,M.D.,P.W.Gold,M.D., R.L.Wilder. National Institutes of Health,Bethesda, MD, USA.

A negative feedback loop exists between the immune and central nervous systems,in which immune-proinflammatory mediators signal the hypothalamic CRH neuron to promote pituitary-adrenal activation and, hence, glucocorticoid mediated restraint of the immune responce.We have recently shown that the increased susceptibility to streptococcal cell wall (SCW)-induced arthritis in the Lewis rat is the result of a defect in the central component of this negative feedback loop,resulting in deficient CRH responses to challenge with a variety of inflammatory mediators,including SCW,interleukin-1a,and the serotonin agonist quipazine.In contrast to LEW/N rats,histocompatible Fischer(F344/N)rats show enhanced resistance to SCW-induced arthritis in association with significantly greater increases in the synthesis and release of CRH following stimulation by the same inflammatory mediators.These data indicate that susceptibility to SCW-induced arthritis in LEW/N rats is mediated by the central nervous system via the hypothalamic CRH neuron, a finding which may be relevant to susceptibility to a wide variety of other inflammatory diseases.

2533

BIOCHEMICAL AND BEHAVIORAL ALTERATIONS IN NON-SYMPTOMATIC OFFSPRING OF PATIENTS WITH ESSENTIAL HYPERTENSION.
David Goldstein,M.D.,
National Institutes of Health,Bethesda, MD, USA.

To explore whether asymptomatic first-degree relatives of patients with essential hypertension showed enhanced vulnerability in the responsiveness of catecholaminergic systems which could predispose to the development of hypertension or behavioral disorders,norepinephrine spillover into arterial plasma was assessed during a baseline period,during challenge with phychological stress(e.g.video game),and during pharmacologic challenge with the alpha-2 blocker yohimbine.Compared to controls,non-symptomatic offspring of a parent with essential hypertension showed exaggerated norepinephrine spillover during video game challenge and,preliminarily,a greater subjective anxiety during challenge with yohmbine.These data suggest that an intrinsic hyper-responsiveness of the sympathetic system may confer enhanced vulnerability to the subsequent development of hypertension. Speculatively, such a vulnerability could also predispose to hyperarousal and anxiety.

2534

IS THE LUTEAL PHASE NECESSARY FOR THE LATE-LUTEAL (PRE-MENSTRUAL) SYNDROME ?
David Rubinow, M.D.
National Institutes of Health, Bethesda, MD, USA.

In studies utilizing the progesterone antagonist RU 486, we have shown that pharmacological termination of the luteal phase with this agent to initiate the next follicular phase does not abolish or alter the timing of the expected cyclic affective episode, which still occurs on schedule despite RU 486-induced luteolysis. This finding in association with data that all tested indices of luteal phase neuroendocrine regulation are normal in patients with the late luteal phase mood disorder indicate that hormonal changes in the late luteal phase are not crucial to the development and maintenance of the pre-menstrual syndrome. Indeed, the most striking hormonal abnormalities in patients with the pre-menstrual syndrome were found in the follicular phase, suggesting that the fundamental biological nature of this disorder requires redefinition.

2535

PATHOPHYSIOLOGICAL MECHANISMS IN THE HYPERCORTISOLISM OF ANOREXIA NERVOSA
G.P.Chrousos, M.D., H.Gwirtsman, M.D., P.W.Gold, M.D.
National Institutes of Health, Bethesda, MD, USA.

To study the pathophysiology of hypercortisolism in patients with anorexia nervosa, we examined plasma ACTH and cortisol responces to ovine corticotropin releasing hormone (CRH) before and after correction of the weight loss. Before their weight loss was corrected, anorexic patients had marked hypercortisolism but normal basal plasma ACTH. The hypercortisolism was associated with a marked reduction in the plasma ACTH response to CRH. When these patients were restudied three to four weeks after their body weight had been restored to normal, the hypercortisolism had resolved but the abnormal responses to CRH remained unchanged. In a parallel study, we showed that CSF CRH levels were elevated in underweight anorexics and correlated with the degree of depression, and fell towards normal with resolution of hypercortisolism after correction of the weight loss. We conclude that in underweight anorexics, the pituitary is normally restrained by glucocorticoid negative feedback, and that hypercortisolism in these patients reflects hypersecretion of endogenous CRH. The return to eucortisolism soon after correction of the weight loss indicates resolution of this central defect despite persistence of abnormalities in adrenal function.

Session 388 New Research:
Psychopharmacology of affective disorders

2536

A DOUBLE BLIND COMPARATIVE STUDY: AMINEPTINE VERSUS IMIPRAMINE

Mendis N.
University of Colombo

The aim of the study was to compare the antidepressant effects of amineptine with imipramine in depressive illness.

According to the DSM III criteria 33 patients diagnosed as having depressive illness were either given imipramine or, amineptine, 50 mg - 100 mg and 100 mg - 200 mg respectively per day on a double blind basis over a period of two months. Both groups presented steady improvement of the symptoms of depression during treatment, as scored on the Hamilton and Montgomery and Asberg Depression Rating Scales and clinical Global Impression Scale. Amineptine produced fewer anticholinergic effects than Imipramine.

The results obtained show that amineptine as well as imipramine, is well suited for treating depressed patients.

2537

PAROXETINE IN THE TREATMENT OF MAJOR DEPRESSION
Ari Kiev, M.D., Social Psychiatry Research,
150 East 69th Street, New York, NY 10021 - U.S.A.

This study compared the efficacy and safety of paroxetine versus placebo in the treatment of outpatients with major depressive disorder. Following placebo washout, patients were randomized into treatment groups. Those on active medication were dosed according to a fixed/flexible schedule and could receive 10 to 50 mg paroxetine per day as a single morning dose. The efficacy analyses clearly showed the superiority of paroxetine over placebo, with significant ($p \leq 0.05$) therapeutic differences noted at week 6 in a variety of observer and patient-rated measures of depression: HAMD Total; the Cognitive Disturbance, Retardation, and Sleep Disturbance factors of the HAMD; SCL Total; the Obsessive-Compulsive, Interpersonal Sensitivity, Depression, Anxiety factors, and the Anger Hostility subcluster of the SCL-56; the MADRS; Raskin scale; the Severity of Illness and Global Improvement portions of the Clinical Global Impressions; and the Patient's Global Evaluation. The only adverse experiences that occurred significantly ($p \leq 0.05$) more often in the paroxetine group were asthenia (18% vs. 3%) and dry mouth (18% vs. 3%). Additional safety data-- physical examinations, ECGs, laboratory evaluations, and vital signs--showed no serious drug-related abnormalities. The data from this study indicate that paroxetine is a safe, well-tolerated, effective treatment for major depressive disorder.

2538

ADINAZOLAM IN OUTPATIENT DEPRESSION

Abuzzahab, F. S., Sr., MD, Ph.D., Minneapolis, Minnesota, University of Minnesota, USA

Since alprazolam (Xanax) has proven effective in anxious depression, a double blind study of adinazolam, a triazolobenzodiazepine derivative, versus imipramine was undertaken in outpatients suffering from major depressive disorder. Twenty-five patients suffering from major depression were treated with adinazolam (n=12) or imipramine (n=13) for up to 12 months at average usual doses of 64.5 mg adinazolam or 179.5 mg imipramine. Patients were assessed on the following Scales: Hamilton Depression, Global Assessment, Raskin Depression, Covi Anxiety, Carroll Rating Scale for Depression and patient Self Rating Symptom Scale. Three adinazolam and one imipramine patient completed the 48 week study; five adinazolam and four imipramine patients completed at least 24 weeks. Analysis of the Hamilton showed adinazolam better than imipramine: in depressed mood at week 28 (p 0.004), in anxiety at week 8 (0 0.008), in insomnia at week 8 (p 0.008), and on the total score at week 28 (p 0.007). Imipramine was better than adinazolam in depersonalization/derealization at weeks 4 (p 0.016) and 12 (p p.024). Two adinazolam patients reported seizures. More of the imipramine patients reported dry mouth/decreased salivation (p 0.05). (Supported in part by Psychopharmacology Fund, Minneapolis, MN)

2539

COMPARISON OF ADINAZOLAM, AMITRIPTYLINE AND DIAZEPAM IN ENDOGENOUS DEPRESSION

M.Ansseau, J.M.Devoitille, P.Papart, E.Van Brabant, H.Mantanus, M.Timsit-Berthier, CHU, Liège, Belgium.

Adinazolam is a new triazolobenzodiazepine which appears more potent than alprazolam in several pharmacologial tests predictive of antidepressant efficacy. The purpose of the present study was to confirm possible true antidepressant activity of adinazolam among carefully selected melancholic inpatients. The diagnosis should be confirmed by at least one biological abnormality: dexamethasone suppression test (DST) nonsuppression and/or pathological contingent negative variation. Three parallel groups of 22 patients received in double-blind conditions either adinazolam (90 mg/d), amitriptyline (225 mg/d), or diazepam (45 mg/d) over a 4-week period, with weely assessment by the Hamilton depression scale. Results showed significant superiority of amitriptyline over diazepam on total Hamilton depression scores. On the subscale of Thase, adinazolam induced significantly better improvement than both diazepam and adinazolam whereas both amitriptyline and adinazolam exhibited significantly better antidepressant efficacy on the core symptoms of depression. These findings suggest that adinazolam possesses an antidepressant efficacy intermediate between amitriptyline and diazepam.

2540

CONTROLLED STUDY OF MILNACIPRAN 200 MG IN ENDOGENOUS DEPRESSION

J.M.Devoitille, M.Ansseau, R.von Frenckell, C.Serre, Hôpital du Petit Bourgogne and CHU, Liège, Belgium, and CRPF,Castres, France.

Milnacipran is a new potential antidepressant selected for its equipotent inhibition of noradrenaline and serotonin uptake and its lack of effect at any postsynaptic receptor. In a multicenter study, we compared the antidepressant efficacy and the tolerance of milnacipran (200 mg/d) and amitriptyline (150 mg/d) in 2 parallel groups of 43 major depressive inpatients, endogenous subtype, as defined by Research Diagnostic Criteria. The duration of the study was 4 weeks, with weekly assessments by means of the Montgomery and Asberg depression scale, the Hamilton depression scale, the Clinical Global Impression (CGI) and the Target Emergent Signs and Symptoms. Results showed similar improvement in both groups but better tolerance with milnacipran (less drowsiness and anticholinergic side-effects), reflected in the better scores on the therapeutic index of the CGI. The clinical profile of the two drugs was somewhat different with more sedation and appetite stimulant activity with amitriptyline and more improvement in concentration difficulties, inability to feel, retardation, and helplessness with milnacipran.

2541

TREATMENT OF MANIC EPISODES BY NIMODIPINE : AN OPEN PILOT STUDY.
G.BRUNET, P.ROBERT, B.CERLICH, G.DARCOURT
Clinique de Psychiatrie, Pavillon J, Hôpital Pasteur, B.P. 69, 06002 NICE CEDEX

This is a controlled open study of Nimodipine in manic episodes, following previous works showing an action of others v.o.c. calcium blockers in this application. We choosed Nimodipine for it crosses the blood-brain barrier and has a specific action on brain.

We treated 6 inpatients with severe manic episodes. The total daily dose was 360 mg (6 x 60 mg) and we controlled the study during 7 days. We used the BPRS scale, the Beck manic scale. We also controlled E.E.G., E.C.G. and biologic items, specially blood calcium and leaver parameters. Results are very good as there is an highly significant response after 7 days comparing to day-0 ($p < 0,001$) in manic scales.

We did not notice any side effect nor biological modification but a sligh increase of calcemia on D7. Of course, further studies are needed but Nimodipine could be a possible alternative treatment besides the usual neuroleptic treatment of manic episodes.

2542

RS 86 IN MANIA

Hans van Berkestijn, Liesbeth Mulder, Frans Flentge, Louise Dols, Rudi van den Hoofdakker

Department of Psychiatry, University of Groningen, The Netherlands

Eight patients fulfilling DSM-III criteria for manic disorder were treated with the cholinergic agent RS 86 in a placebo-drug-placebo-drug design. Four patients completed the study. They did not show convincing benefit of the drug.
The results do not confirm earlier studies on the effects of centrally active cholinomimetic compounds in mania.

2543

MAGNESIOCARD® AS A MOOD STABILIZER FOR RAPID CYCLERS

G. Chouinard, L. Beauclair, R. Geiser*, and P. Etienne*
Allan Memorial Institute, and Hôpital Louis H. Lafontaine, Montreal, Canada; *Research Department, CIBA-GEIGY Corp., Summit, N.J.

In an open labeled 8-week study a magnesium salt preparation was found to be equivalent to lithium in a small group of severe manic-depressive patients, and perhaps superior to lithium in about one third of these patients. Starting after withdrawal of all prior medications, including lithium, nine patients suffering from bipolar illness (DSM-III criteria) were given magnesium aspartate hydrochloride (Magnesiocard®), and were seen at weekly intervals. All patients were classified as rapid cyclers, having had at least four cycles in the previous year, and were considered by the treating physician to be refractory to conventional therapy. Because seven of the patients appeared to benefit from their 8-week treatment with Magnesiocard®, a 24-week prolongation study was added with evaluations at week 10, 12, 16, 20, 24, 28, and 32. In the CNS magnesium plays an important role in the control of excitatory aminoacid neurotransmission through its interaction with NMDA (N-methyl-D-aspartate) receptors which are regulated by voltage-dependent binding of magnesium ions inside the channel. While it is not possible at the present time to relate precisely the behavioral effects of lithium on its many biochemical changes, magnesium and calcium may be involved in lithium effects, as lithium can result in an increase in plasma magnesium and a positive whole-body magnesium balance.

2544

Le sélénium et certains troubles de l'affectivité

Victoria Irimia, I. Popescu=CSM=Pitești=Roumanie

Les auteurs ont déterminé la concentration sérique de sélénium, par spectrophotométrie d'absorbtion atomique, dans certains états dépressifs.
On a étudié deux groupes de malades psychiques: le premier étant formé de 114 malades présentant des dépressions de différents degrés (névrotiques, psychotiques, états psychopathoïdes, chez les toxicophyles éthanoliques); le second, aleatoire, constitué par 59 malades psychiques, suivant une cure d'entretien avec Lithium carbonique.
On a constaté une relation constante entre la diminution de la disposition et l'augmentation de la séléniémie, pour trois semaines au minimum. Chez les malades traités avec du Lithium carbonique, proportionnellement avec l'accroissement de la lithémie survient spontanément une augmentation de la séléniémie.
Les auteurs concluent que la séléniémie pourrait être un indicateur séro=diagnostique psychiatrique pour objectiver les troubles de l'affectivité.

Séléniémie
Séro=diagnostique psychiatrique

2545

The combination of lithium and carbamazepine in the treatment of bipolar affective disorders
Otto Dörr-Zegers, Jorge Cabrera and Pedro Retamal
University of Chile in Santiago and Psychiatric State Hospital of Santiago

The effectivity of lithium in the prophylaxis of bipolar affective disorders is known since more than 20 years. The prophylactic action of carbamazepine for the same disease was described in the middle of the 70s. Since then carbamazepine is used as alternative to lithium in the treatment of non responder cases or in cases with intolerance to lithium. In this paper we describe the excellent results obtained in 12 cases of severe forms of bipolar affective disorders with the combination of lithium carbonate and carbamazepine. It deals with cases where lithium was given during a long time without obtaining complete relief of symptomatology and/or of the frequency of manic or depressive episodes. When doses oscilating between 400 and 800 mgrs of carbamazepine were added, the phases began to disappear till reaching the patient's complete normality. The observation period without relapse since the beginning of the combined treatment varies between one and five years and the evolution of the disease before adding carbamazepine fluctuated between two and fifteen years. Interesting relationships between clinical form, course and previous personality traits were reported.
It is concluded that the combination lithium/carbamazepine represents a very good treatment as well as prophylaxis in severe forms of bipolar afeective disorders, all the more because carbamazepine clearly diminishes known side effects of lithium like hand shaking.

Session 389 Symposium: History of the concept of depression

2546

ARISTOTLE AND MELANCHOLY

Giuseppe ROCCATAGLIATA
Department of Neurology, Genoa University
Via De Toni, 5 - 16132, GENOA, Italy

Aristotle's theory, according to Hippocrates, states that depressive diseases originate from "black bile". However the physician from Cos admitted the action of the "yellow bile" also. Therefore the aetiology of both melancholy and mania was unified by Aristotle. Depressive symptoms, ranging form melancholy to mania, always originated from variable temperature of black bile.
In Plato's opinion divine influence was needed for human creativeness: talented and ingenous people were needed of divine forces; demon of creativeness, was identified, by Aristotle, in "physis". Habitus melancholicus is specific of creative humans. We can finally think that melancholy, which is depending on the presence of black bile, is to be found in what as the source of creative intelligence.

2547

ANTICIPATORY DEPRESSION-ANCIENT INDIAN IDEAS

A.VENKOBA RAO, MD PhD DSc DPM, Emeritus Professor of Psychiatry and Officer-in-Charge, Centre for Advanced Research on 'Health and Behaviour', Indian Council of Medical Research, Madurai Medical College, Madurai, INDIA.

Depressive Disease has a long ancestry. References to it abound in history, philosophy and the epics of India. The Buddha, Rama (of Ramayana) and Arjuna (of Mahabharatha) stand out as models of Anticipatory Depression or Grief. AD or AG occurs prior to the loss contrary to regular depression which follows it. Buddha experienced AD at the sight of an old man, a sick man and a corpse. The fact that none (including him) could escape these saddened him deeply. The ephemeral nature of the world, illusory nature of pleasures and miseries of men plunged young Rama into a 'dispassion.' Arjuna at the start of the Mahabharatha War (3138-3139 B.C.) sank into anguish at the tragic prospect of killing his kith and kin.

These psychological states reflect preoccupation with existential, spiritual and ethical queries. Buddha sought enlightenment through meditation. Rama was counselled by the Royal Priest Vasishta. Arjuna was imparted 'Gita' by his charioteer Lord Krishna. Kalidasa's poem depicts depression in Rama's dynasty, indicating a genetic predisposition. Psychological explanations for AD are discussed. The principles of therapy are elaborated in the presentation.

2548

HISTORY OF MELANCHOLIC STUPOR/ G.E. Berrios/ University of Cambridge/ United Kingdom.
Stupor names an involuntary reduction or absence of relational functions.Spontaneous and/or reactive behaviour may be involved.The inaccessibility of the stuporous patient has strained the explanatory power of postcartesian psychology.For example, a distinction was made during the 19th century between stupor (related to the bodily machine) and stupidity (affecting its resident ghost). The former state was explained in terms of motion-related concepts such as akinesia, catalepsy and aboulia; the latter in terms of an inhibition of mental contents. The history of melancholic stupor between 1840 and 1890 illustrates how these views affected the analysis of the insanities. Melancholia attonita, acute dementia, stupemania, and confusion mentale primitive, did all have stupor as a common referent. Melancholic stupor also played a role in the development of the unitary psychosis concept for it provided a bridge between depressed states and terminal dementia. Of the 26 cases included in Kahlbaum's monograph on Catatonia, 11 had suffered from depression before developing 'melancholia attonita'. Melancholic stupor was also relevant to the concept of depressive pseudodementia. The high rate of recovery reported in this condition led to the belief that it consisted in an inhibition of function. Psychodynamic theory encouraged the eventual transformation of inhibition into emotional repression. This explains the neglect that has since befallen the neurobiological study of depressive stupor.

2549

TIMOTHIE BRIGHT'S TREATISE OF MELANCHOLY

JOHN HOWELLS
FORMERLY DIRECTOR, INSTITUTE OF FAMILY PSYCHIATRY, UK

Timothy Bright was the author of the first major text in English on the subject of mental illness. A graduate in medicine from the University of Cambridge, he published his Treatise in 1586. He had an unusual career becoming a physician at the Royal Hospital of St Bartholomew in London, losing his post, founding shorthand, founding a spa and ending his days as a clergyman.

On the title page is found the scope of the book "to set forth the causes of melancholy, describe its psychological and somatic symptoms, with a differential diagnosis between melancholy and "afflicted conscience', and offer spiritual advice as well as physical prescriptions, the whole interspersed with philosophical discourses for the entertainment of the reader." He had a powerful influence on Shakespeare and on Richard Burton's 'Anatomy of Melancholy'.

2550

André Dulaurens et la mélancolie à la fin de la Renaissance.
Jacques POSTEL, Médecin-Chef
Centre Hospitalier Sainte-Anne
1, rue Cabanis 75674 PARIS CEDEX 14

André Dulaurens qui fut professeur de médecine, puis grand chancelier, de l'Université de Montpellier, a publié en 1597 un "discours des maladies mélancoliques" qui est ici commenté et discuté. Son originalité tient surtout à ce qu'il inaugure la conception d'une mélancolie qui serait surtout un trouble de l'entendement, un délire. Cette conception de la mélancolie comme délire partiel ou sur un seul objet, prévaudra durant les deux siècles suivants. Elle permettra l'abandon progressif de la vieille pathogénie humorale héritée d'Hippocrate et de Galien.

Session 390   Symposium:
Research on carers of the demented

2551

STUDIES OF CARERS: INTRODUCTION

Tom Arie
Department of Health Care of the Elderly,
University of Nottingham, England.

Research on carers of the demented is now becoming more rigorous and specific. Earlier studies were concerned with measurement of burden, but more recent studies are directed towards establishing with greater precision those aspects of care which are most likely to be burdensome for different individuals and families. Family style is important, as are gender, family relationship, quality of past relationship, and social class. Studies of quality of care and nature of burden in relation to gender are of particular interest.

How can inputs by professional services most effectively enhance the coping capacity of informal carers? Standard "packages" of support are not enough - they have to be matched carefully to the profile of individual need. A prime objective must be to enhance the coping capacity of carers, rather than necessarily to replace this by professional care systems.

Special problems are posed by the demented person who lives alone. The widespread tendency in many countries to increase private institutional care for the elderly in place of rehabilitative and supportive community services also raises difficulties. There are important implications for patterns of services.

2552

PREDICTORS OF DECISION TO INSTITUTIONALIZE INDIVIDUALS WITH DEMENTIA
Carole A. Cohen, Dolores P. Gold, K.I. Shulman
Sunnybrook Medical Centre, Toronto, Ont., Canada

This study examined the factors that determined whether caregivers were able to maintain individuals with dementia in the community or decided to institutionalize them. 200 subjects suffering from a variety of dementia syndromes and still living at home were examined by a psychiatrist who documented their mental status including a rating of the severity of the dementia. Their caregivers were interviewed at length and completed standardized measures concerning their reactions to caregiving, their social support system, their own health, and their decision regarding institutionalization. These subjects were subsequently followed for up to two years and reinterviewed at 6-month intervals. Discriminant functional analysis was used to determine the important caregiver and dependent variables which determined decision to institutionalize. Results are interpreted with regard to the use of appropriate interventions that may ease the task of caregiving and allow individuals with dementia to remain in the community for longer periods of time.

2553

5 YEARS AFTER - A RETROSPECTIVE STUDY OF CARE-TAKING FAMILIES.
Jens BRUDER, Ärztl.Beratungsstelle für ältere Bürger und ihre Angehörigen, Norderstedt, FRG

During 1977 - 1979 140 families with a frail elderly relative were studied longitudinally with respect to a number of features (somatic and mental health, social and economic features, burden, coping-styles, biographic and personality factors).Correlations between health of the old person and that one of the caretaking relative were of major interest.- 5 - 7 years later 120 of these families could be studied again with a modified questionnaire.Apart from information about the further course (continuation, institutionalisation, death) information was obtained about retrospective appraisal of the efforts performed.Furthermore several attitude scales were presented refering to the old relative and the perspective of the caretaker of her own age (fear of health problems, especially mental deterioration, dependency, neglect).Special emphasis is put on correlations between certain characteristics of care (duration,degree of burden, death at home or following institutionalisation) and anxious or confident connotations of the caretakers age expectation.

2554

POUR UNE GESTION FAMILIALE DE LA CRISE DE DEMENTIFICATION

JM Leger, ER Lombertie, MD Mouty
C.H.S. Esquirol, Limoges, France

Les auteurs, au travers de leur propre expérience psychogériatrique essaient de faire le point sur les éléments de diagnostic précoce du trouble démentiel de l'âge. Ils notent la fréquence importante de l'anxiété et de l'inquiétude des familles parfois de la sollicitude autour du dément, qui viennent masquer et compenser une symptomatologie cognitive déficitaire frustre. Ils remarquent qu'en fonction de l'aptitude des professionnels médicaux à prendre en compte le message de la famille, des incitations diagnostiques et thérapeutiques seront impliquées.

Décripter et redéfinir l'inquiétude permet de mieux situer les niveaux cliniques de l'atteinte, mais aussi de reconnaître toute la valeur thérapeutique des compensations mises en place.

A partir de là, les auteurs ont pu travailler à l'accompagnement de la prise en charge à domicile des déments par leur famille en étant sensible à toutes les initiatives positives des membres aidés, et des progrès ou du ralentissement des pertes et des diminutions du nombre de symptômes du patient.

Cette façon de procéder leur paraît être un moyen de favoriser les adaptations naturelles d'une famille à une tâche difficile à laquelle elle s'astreint volontairement et spontanément dans un pourcentage élevé de cas. Gérer la crise de démentification de l'aïeul est un bon moyen d'éviter l'institutionnalisation et ses répercussions sur l'économie qu'elle soit individuelle, familiale voire sociale.

2555

RESEARCH ON CARER ABUSE.

C.J. Gilleard and A.C. Horner, St. George's Hospital Medical School, Tooting, London, SW17., ENGLAND.

The present paper reviews some of the principal research issues concerning abuse by and abuse of caregivers to the frail elderly. Attention is drawn to the interacting framework between the carer and cared for relationship and the structural support systems in which the relationship is embedded. The problems are viewed as ones involving opening out a private relationship into a public space which may or may not be itself abusive of such relationships.

Data from an empirical study of elder abuse amongst the recipients of local respite care services will be drawn upon to illustrate the problems of elucidating what we mean by abuse, and in particular the relative influence of caregiver stress and caregiver support in determining who seems to be abused and who abuses.

Finally the relevance of this subject to the central issue concerning family vs. state provision of support and care to the elderly will be emphasised and parallels drawn with the political distinction between state vs. individual terrorism. The distinctions between child and elder abuse will therefore be emphasised and the rôle of "family" pathology questioned.

Session 391 Workshop: Defining "dangerousness" in different legal systems

2556

DEFINING "DANGEROUSNESS" IN DIFFERENT LEGAL SYSTEMS

James F. Hooper, M.D., University of Alabama, USA, *Roger Peele, M.D.,* APA, USA, *Elissa Benedek, M.D.,* APA, USA, *C. Roy, M.D.,* Forensic Section, WPA, CANADA, *Prof. Jaque Berheim,* Institute for Legal Medicine, SWITZERLAND, *Prof. H.E. Ehrhardt,* University Institute of Forensic & Social Psychiatry, FR GERMANY

The structure and format of this workshop is to be a round-table discussion among the panelists and the audience. Each panelist (as listed above) will be asked to briefly present an overview of the forensic system in their respective countries, or states in the US, and define how they make the determination that a patient is no longer dangerous and may be released from custody. Open discussion with the audience, and of any differences between the systems will follow. No differences in the basic format of panelists are expected.

The scope of the workshop will be limited to the methods and systems used to determine dangerousness. We will not digress into discussions of capital punishment, types of treatment, etc. We will listen to data presented by any participant showing follow-up studies to justify their methods.

Our aims will simply be an increased understanding of various viewpoints on this issue. Resolution is not expected.

No Audio-visual aids are expected to be needed at this time.

Session 392 Special Session: Antipsychotic drugs: Present status and future trends

2557

ANTIPSYCHOTIC TREATMENT RESPONSE PREDICTION IN SCHIZOPHRENIA

Daniel P. van Kammen, M.D., Ph.D.*°, *Western Psychiatric Institute and Clinic, Pittsburgh, PA; °Veterans Administration Medical Center, Pittsburgh, PA, U.S.A.

With an increased understanding of antipsychotic drug treatment, the emphasis in research and clinical practice is shifting towards the patients who do not respond or who respond only in part. At present the clinician can only determine after the fact whether a schizophrenic patient will respond. Antipsychotic drug response is seen as state dependent and may be determined by the biochemical condition of the patient. The authors reviewed studies of biochemical measures and antipsychotic drug response. It appears that psychotic patients with elevated catecholamine release are likely to respond rapidly to neuroleptic treatment, while psychotic patients with lower CSF or plasma catecholamine levels are most likely to be treatment nonresponders. A dysregulation of the locus coeruleus may affect the dopamine systems responsivity to pharmacological interventions.

2558

THE EFFECT OF NEUROLEPTICS IN VARIOUS SUBGROUPS OF SCHIZOPHRENIA
Marek JAREMA, Janusz KACPERCZYK, Sławomir KRUSZYNSKI, Janusz WDOWIAK
Division of Psychopathology, Institute of Neurology and Psychiatry, Medical Academy, Szczecin, Poland

The group of 44 patients aged 19-49 who met the DSM-III-R criteria for schizophrenia was studied. All patients were diagnosed as having systematic or nonsystematic schizophrenia, or cycloid psychosis, and positive, negative, or mixed schizophrenia. Patients were randomly selected for the treatment with 4 groups of neuroleptics: phenothiazines, butyrophenones, thioxanthenes, and clozapine.
The best effect of neuroleptic therapy was found among patients with cycloid psychoses. The therapy was more effective among patients with systematic than nonsystematic schizophrenia. Phenothiazines appeared to be more effective in nonsystematic schizophrenia while these patients failed to improve after butyrophenones. Better clinical improvement showed patients with positive or mixed schizophrenia after treatment with phenothiazines than butyrophenones. Treatment with phenothiazines and clozapine was not effective in patients with negative schizophrenia.

2559

HIGH- VS. LOW-DOSE HALOPERIDOL (HL) IN THE TREATMENT OF ACUTE SCHIZOPHRENICS.
M.R.Louzã*, F.Müller-Spahn, E.Rüther, J.Scherer. Psychiatrische Klinik, Nussbaumstr. 7, 8000 München 2, FRG.

In a double-blind, fixed-dose study, 20 acute, florid schizophrenics (RDC) were randomized to receive 0.4 mg/kg/day (high dose) or 0.15 mg/kg/day (low dose) HL during 42 days. Patients were evaluated with BPRS on days 0,8,15,29 and 42. HL plasma level (RIA) was measured on days 2,5,8,15,29 and 42. Considering the whole period of treatment there was no difference in the clinical response of both groups even though the high-dose group had a faster initial improvement. HL steady state plasma level was significant higher for the high-dose group than for the low-dose group (41 ± 11 ng/ml vs. 13 ± 4 ng/ml, $p<.001$) and showed large interindividual variation although daily dose was expressed in mg/ml. No relationship between HL plasma levels and clinical response was observed. The lack of direct relationship between plasma levels and clinical response indicates disparity between measurable variables and effects at specific receptor sites.

*DAAD-Fellow. Institut of Psychiatry, University of São Paulo, C.P. 8091, 05403 São Paulo S.P., BRAZIL.

2560

INTERNATIONAL STUDY OF NEUROLEPTIC DOSE IN PATIENTS WITH SCHIZOPHRENIA
Bhatia, SC; Hsieh, HH; Theesen, KA; Kulhara, P; Chadda, R; and Hu, WH. Creighton University, Omaha, Nebraska USA

This study was conducted to evaluate the differences in neuroleptic dose needed to treat 150 first admission schizophrenic patients, i.e. 50 each from India, (Asian Indians) Taiwan (Orientals) and the USA (Caucasians). All three racial groups had age-sex matched patients which included 19 females (mean age of 30.2 years) and 31 males (mean age 26.8 years). Chlorpromazine (CPZ) equivalent daily dose per Kg body weight were calculated from the neuroleptic dose needed to achieve optimal outcome at discharge. The mean $\pm$ standard deviation of CPZ equivalent doses were Kg for males and females respectively were 15.71 ± 15.15 and 12.97 ± 8.64 for Asian Indians, 9.75 ± 6.53 and 10.92 ± 13.42 for Orientals, and 13.69 ± 15.08 and 13.98 ± 14.73 for Caucasians. A raceXsex (3x2) ANOVA was performed. There was no statistically significant difference in CPZ equivalent dosages in three racial groups. The correlation of body weight and dose was .1388 ($p<0.05$). This data is discussed in the light of current controversies surrounding this important subject.

2561

MEASUREMENT OF HALOPERIDOL PLASMA-LEVELS: A TRANSCULTURAL STUDY
H.R. Chaudhry+, K. Meszaros*, G. Schönbeck*, A.Bugnar*, M.R. Chaudhry+
*Department of Psychiatry, University of Vienna, Austria
+Fountain House Lahore, Pakistan

Monitoring of Haloperidol plasma-levels (HPLs) might be of value for several reasons. A therapeutic window for Haldol may exist but the evidence for it is inconsistent. There are suggestions that Asian patients may require lower dosages of psychotropic drugs than their western counterparts. Ethnic, genetic and nutritional factors may influence response to psychotropic drugs in different populations. HPLs of 31 Pakistanian schizophrenic patients were compared with 31 Austrian schizophrenics. HPLs were estimated by RIA-technique. Patients were diagnosed by DSM-III and Viennese Research Criteria. The patient's data on age, sex, height, weight, BMI were gathered. Also duration of illness, pharmacological data, neuroleptic side-effects and BPRS were recorded. Change of BPRS total score in relation to HPL was studied. Results of the transcultural study will be presented.

2562

SAVOXEPINE, A NOVEL NEUROLEPTIC, BLOCKS DA-D2-REC. IN THE HIPPOCAMPUS
F.A. Gnirss, R. Thomann, P. Buess
Psychiatric Clinic Koenigsfelden, Switzerland

Savoxepine (CGP 19486) is a new tetracyclic compound with a neuroleptic profile. Preclinical studies have demonstrated promising characteristics: 1. a potent and selective anti dopaminergic effect with a highly preferential blockade of dopamine (DA)-D2-receptors in the hippocampus, 2. a long duration of action and 3. possibly no DA-supersensitivity after long-term treatment. In consequence Savoxepine - when compared to classical neuroleptics - is expected to reveal a strong antipsychotic effect as well as good tolerability with regard to extrapyramidal symptoms.
In an open clinical trial over 28 days 17 patients suffering from an acute episode of schizophrenia were treated with Savoxepine in a "low dose regime" - maximum daily doses progressively increasing from 0.1 mg to 1.0 mg. As a result of the study a strong antipsychotic effect, particularly on thought disturbances, hallucinations and delusions and an overall tolerability of the drug but no complete dissociation between therapeutic and extrapyramidal effects were demonstrated. The hypothesized dissociation of therapeutical and extrapyramidal effects was then checked in a further open clinical trial with "a loading dose regime". The rationale and the results of this study will be discussed in details.

2563

ANTIPSYCHOTICS OF THE FUTURE: MEDICAL NEEDS AND RESEARCH STRATEGIES
T. Lewander
Astra Research Centre AB, S- 151 85 Södertälje,
and Psychiatric Research Center, University of Uppsala,
S-750 17 Uppsala, Sweden.

Classical neuroleptics share antipsychotic, specific calming and unspecific sedative actions, although in various proportions. Tolerability is hampered by extrapyramidal, autonomous, endocrinological symptoms. Unwanted effects on cognitive, affective and conative functions interfere with compliance and thereby therapeutic usefulness during maintenance treatment. However, some of these effects are utilized for controlling specific symptoms (e.g. excitation, agitation) in the acute phase of schizophrenia. Current hypotheses on mechanisms of the above actions will be reviewed. There is a medical need in the treatment of schizophrenia for drugs with better efficacy (higher response rate, completeness of response, faster onset of action) and less side-effects (particularly extrapyramidal, endocrine and psychic). Since both efficacy and tolerability of available antipsychotics seem to be related to their common antidopaminergic actions, one research strategy in seeking to avoid side effects has been to develop drugs with an action on subtypes of post-synaptic dopamine, e.g. D_2, receptors. Some characteristics of selective D_2-antagonists, vz antipsychotic benzamides (i.a. remoxipride, raclopride), will be presented. Drugs interfering with other receptors (e.g. presynaptic DA, 5HT2, 5HT3, σ-opioid) are under development. Clinical data are as yet limited, however. It is anticipated that antipsychotics with mechanisms of action other than blockade of postsynaptic DA-receptors will have clinicopharmacological profiles quite different from available neuroleptics. Problems with the clinical evaluation of such compounds and with their reception within the psychiatric community will be discussed.

2564

BIPOLAR EFFECT OF PIPOTIAZINE ACCORDING TO DOSAGE IN NEGATIVE AND POSITIVE FORMS OF SCHIZOPHRENIA

M.F. POIRIER-LITTRE*, A. GALINOWSKI*, P. PERON-MAGNAN*, J.M. VANELLE*, F. RAFFAITIN*, J.J. PIRON**, M. PIKETTI*, H. LOO*

* Service du Pr. LOO, Hôpital Ste-Anne, 1 rue Cabanis, 75014 PARIS
** Laboratoire Spécia - 16 rue Clisson, 75016 PARIS

Pipotiazine in a neuroleptic of the phenothiazine Piperidine group.

It would possess a neuroleptic affinity for D2 DA receptors in low dosage and a marked affinity for D1 DA post-synaptic receptors in high dosage. In order to validate this bipolar activity we compared the efficacy of the 0.1 mg/kg of pipotiazine in schizophrenic patients with predominantly negative symptoms (SANS 3 > 75, SAPS < 60), to the efficacy of 0,6 mg/kng) of the drug in productive schizophrenic patients (SAPS > 75, SANS < 60).

All 25 patients were diagnosed according to DSM III R criteria. The evolutions of plasma prolactin, drug levels and scores on rating scales were compared at days 7, 21, 42 and 90.

Pipotiazine was used as the single drug except for biperiden in case of extra pyramidal side effects, which were assessed regurlaly with Simpson and Colombia rating scales.

Authors discuss the evolution of clinical data and biological parameters in both types of schizophrenia.

Session 393 Symposium:
The interdependence between the mental health care system, the social situation of the mentally ill and the state of human rights with the community

2565

THE ESSENTIALS OF A COMPREHENSIVE MENTAL HEALTH CARE SYSTEM
M. Bauer, Municipal Hospital Offenbach, Federal Republic of Germany
(1) Mental health care should be community oriented. This calls among others for abandonment of facilities remote from the community in favour of service in closer proximity. Also the function of big mental hospitals featuring a centralized organization must certainly be transferred to community oriented comprehensive mental health care systems. (2) Mental health care should cater to consumer needs and be extensive, to the benefit of all groups of mentally ill and disabled people. In this respect, provision of appropriate care for those suffering from a chronical mental illness merits special attention. Their professional, possibly lifelong, guidance in the community requires a differentiated and functionally harmonized system of qualified services and facilities organized to suit the following axes: "Cure/Care/Rehabilitation", "Housing", "Work", "Day-structuring options", and "Participation in social and cultural activities". (3) Existing regional services of this adequacy should yet be subjected to patient oriented coordination. Any essential operations and facilities lacking should be provided for. The community oriented care principle-though still assigning a central position to the hospital for the moment - is thereby transformed into one advocating community integrated care, which no longer gives the hospital a dominant place but rather the community itself, with its range of general and special facilities for both healthy and handicapped citizens. Mental health schemes thus become inherent in municipalities' public health and social planning. (4) Finally, putting the mentally ill on a par with perons having a somatic disorder is an absolute must to any comprehensive mental health care system. In terms of in-patient treatment this means an integration of mental health care in general medicine and a close-down of the mental hospital, e.g. by adjoining mental health departments to general hospitals, the latter taking over the regional obligation to offer clinical care for the mentally ill.

2566

ASYLUMS, PSYCHIATRIC REFORM AND THE NECESSITY OF THE OUT-PATIENT CARE.
P. Sakellaropoulos
Sector of Social Medicine and Mental Health, University of Thraki, Greece.

Presentation of the psychiatric situation in Greece, especially in the department of Attica (asylums, out-patient care services). Reference to the psychiatric hospital of Leros.
For the department of Evros: presentation of a greek psychiatric care model which covers the different sectors of needs: education of the community-Mobile Psychiatric Unit-Mental Health Centre for children and adults-Clinic in the General Hospital-Foyer of chronic desinstitutionalized patients.
A characteristic of the greek recent psychiatric care is the inexistence of out-patient care services, sectorized or not. This inexistence makes impossible any organization related to the desinstitutionalization and even any psychiatric reform.

2567

THE OPPOSITIONAL PATIENT-MOVEMENT IN THE NETHERLANDS; FROM DEPENDENCY TO PARTICIPATION IN THE LOCAL AND NATIONAL DECISIONS ABOUT MENTAL HEALTH CARE AND MENTAL HEALTH POLITICS.

Egbert van der Poel / scientific member, dept. Social Psychiatry, State University Limburg / The Netherlands

An effort is being made to describe the position of the patient-opposition movement with respect to the Insanity Law and with respect to the organization of mental health care. In conclusion, three stages were found to be crucial in the development of Dutch opposition movement.
(1) In the 1970s, the opposition movement appeared to operate within the borders of a closed system in which the medical profession had a high degree of autonomy.
(2) By the end of the 1970s, a shift could be detected in the opposition movement from the old desire to work within the system to a new desire to alter the system as such.
(3) Since 1980, it has been possible to detect a third development. The existence of the mental health care system as a social institution has been critically appraised to propagate the de-institutionalization of the existing system of clinical psychiatry.

2568

POSSIBILITIES AND LIMITATIONS OF INTERNATIONAL COLLABORATION IN MENTAL HEALTH REFORM.

A.J.W. Vrijlandt, psychiatrist, PMS Vijverdal, The Netherlands

Mental Health reform aims at improvement of the physical and economic situation of (chronic) psychiatric patients, but most of all it tries to establish an enriched social environment for them, an optimal integration in their local society.
The different therapeutic, organizational and educational political levels on which changes should occur in order to realize this objective, are described. With reference to psychological and sociological change-theory the powerfull possibilities of introducing practical international collaboration on the spot, in order to act on the different levels as change agent, will be discussed in relation to a recent example in Europe. The advantages on the local as well as the international level, the support in political discussions, the training possibilities and the challenge for basic -transcultural- research will be mentioned. Also the limitations, the costs and the pitfalls of an international approach to local Mental Health reform will be presented.
Amongst others, the overall importance of strong local-culture bound leadership and support from the highest political level will be stressed, but also the information and relation to all professionals involved and to the local general public.
The presentation will be closed with a discussion on the importance of these international psychiatric collaboration projects with respect to the unification of Europe.

Session 394 Symposium:
Ethics and mental health policy

2569

AUSTRALASIAN PSYCHIATRISTS AND MENTAL HEALTH POLICY FORMULATION
Dr. John Grigor, Health Department of Victoria, Melbourne, Australia.

The 1980s saw the introduction of new mental health legislation in Australasia.

The legislation had an emphasis on patients' rights, more stringent admission criteria and the establishment of Review Boards or justification in Courts of Law for the continued detention of patients.

Psychiatrists often played only a minor role in the drafting of the new legislation and this led to an ambivalence and distrust in publicly employed psychiatrists. Common reactions have been to discharge patients prior to formal review, failing to admit sick patients because of an overly legalistic concern with the criteria for involuntary hospitalisation and a continuing drift of psychiatrists to private practice.

Australia and New Zealand continue to be heavily reliant on overseas psychiatrists.

This paper identifies strategies to re-engage public psychiatrists and their associations in the task of refining legislation so that a fresh balance is achieved between the needs of the patient and a workable environment for the public psychiatrist.

2570
MÖGLICHKEITEN UND GRENZEN PSYCHIATRISCHEN WIRKENS FÜR MENSCH UND GESELLSCHAFT

Friedrich Weinberger, Starnberg, FRG

Ungeachtet der großen Dienste, die die Psychiatrie den Menschen und seiner Gesellschaft geleistet hat und leistet, zeigte sie von ihren Anfängen an auch fragwürdige, vereinzelt gar verhängnisvolle Seiten. Beispiele auch aus jüngerer Zeit und Gründe dafür werden aufgezeigt. Mit ihren erweiterten Möglichkeiten der Hilfeleistung könnte die Psychiatrie der Zukunft auch erhöhte Gefahren in sich bergen. Um sie hintanzuhalten, ist nötig, auch über die Grenzen psychiatrischen Wirkens zu sprechen.

2571
Therapeutic Decision-making in Public Psychiatry

Dr. Ion Vianu

The therapeutic decision is influenced mainly by two categories of factors benefits and opinions. It may benefit the patient but also the patient's family (macrogroup) and the psychiatric institution itself. On the other hand it is influenced by the current knowledge in the field and by the prevalent scientific and political ideologies. The mutual relationships of these factors and the choices they imply are discussed.

2572
RESPONSIBILITY OF PSYCHIATRY FOR THE DEHUMANISATION OF MEDICINE.

Anatoly I. Koryagin
Switzerland.

Paradoxically, it is urgently necessary to cure the profession that itself is meant to cure. Medical abuse is in itself a kind of AIDS, effecting Twentieth Century medicine. The pathogen agent destroys the immunity system of our profession, the medical ethics that defend our medicine from moral decline. The features more and more take the character of an epidemic, being spread by transmitting the infection in the process of intimate contact between the healthy part of medicine and the sick part, as a consequence of neglecting prophylactic measures. All cures put to effect sofar have not had a positive effect. Psychiatry nowadays remains the most dangerous and entirely open focus of this infection. Therefore, particularly psychiatrists are responsible for this.

2573
REFLECTIONS ABOUT VIRTUES, SCIENTIFIC FACTS AND LAW.

Seymon Gluzman
Kiev. U.S.S.R.

The very essence of virtue in medicine is, according to M. Vartovsky, a certain constant, outliving both the doctor himself and his patient. The basis of this constant is the ethical Hippocratic Oath (don't harm). Psychiatry is a science only conditionally, as the presentation of so-called scientific psychiatric facts includes in itself a significant compilation of conventional culture. Therefore psychiatry, more than other medical disciplines, needs in the conscience of its personal unflinching, trans-historical ethical norms. Observing the presumption of the defencelessness of mentally ill is the basis, that regulates the moral state of psychiatric practice in any state.

2574
ETHICS AND THIRD PARTY PAYMENTS
Beigel A. - University of Arizona, USA

Session 395 Special Session:
Affective disorders in childhood and adolescence

2575
Incidence and Prevalence of Depression Among High School Students
R.E. Roberts, P. Lewinsohn, H. Hops
Oregon Research Institute, Eugene, Oregon, U.S.A.

The focus is on the epidemiology of adolescent depression: prevalence, incidence, and associated risk factors. Data are from a prospective community study of DSMIIIR depression in a sample of 1,800 high school students in Oregon assessed twice over a 12-month period. Diagnoses were made using the Schedule for Affective Disorders and Schizophrenia for School-Age Children; data also were collected using the Beck Depression Inventory, Center for Epidemiologic Studies Depression Scale, and a suicide scale. Lifetime prevalence of major depression was 17.6%; current prevalence was 2.2%. Lifetime prevalence of all disorders was 36.5%; current prevalence was 9.8%. Over 40% of the subjects reported significant numbers of depressive symptoms. Depressed adolescents are more worried, experience more suicidal ideation, oppositional and antisocial behavior, lack self-confidence, are more critical of their social skills, are lonely and sensitive to rejection, in need of approval from others, more pessimistic and blaming the self for failures, and had poorer coping skills, but were more likely to be in conflicted environments.

2576
Adolescent Bipolar Illness and Personality Disorder

S. Kutcher, P. Marton, M. Korenblum; Sunnybrook Medical Centre, University of Toronto, Toronto, Canada.

The relationship between adolescent bipolar illness and personality disorder has not been explored. Studies of adult bipolars suggest a bipolar illness/ borderline personality disorder (BPD) association. Twenty euthymic bipolar teens were assessed using the Personality Disorders Examination. 35% met DSM-III-R criteria for at least one personality disorder. Three of the twenty (15%) had a borderline personality disorder diagnosis. The bipolar illness with personality disorder group differed significantly from the bipolar illness without personality disorder group in terms of increased lithium unresponsiveness ($p < 0.05$) and neuroleptic treatment at time of personality assessment ($p < 0.01$) but not in terms of age, sex, age of illness onset, serum lithium level, rapid cycling, substance abuse history, alcohol abuse history or number of suicide attempts. Issues regarding the study of personality disorder in adolescent bipolars are discussed.

2577
BEHAVIOUR PROBLEMS AS KEY SYMPTOM IN ADOLESCENT MAJOR DEPRESSION
Gagiano CA and Le Roux JF
Department of Psychiatry, University of the Orange Free State, Republic of South Africa.

Forty-eight adolescents (18 male/30 female) eighteen years or younger, fulfilling DSM III-R criteria for major depression were included in this prospective study. They were physically healthy, had no other psychiatric disorder and were free from substance use or abuse. Phenomenological and biochemical variables were studied and a family history for depressive disorders taken. Presenting complaint as well as prominent behaviour problems were noted. Cortisol serum levels after 1 mg dexamethasone overnight suppression and TSH levels before and after TRH stimulation were noted.

Using Winokur's classification 23 percent belonged to the pure depression group, 46 percent to the depressive spectrum group while 31 percent did not have a positive family history of depression. The mean serum cortisol levels were elevated at 23h00 while the mean basal TSH and the mean delta max TSH were within normal limits. 48 Percent of patients presented with behaviour problems, fifteen percent presented with suicidal behaviour, while 26 percent actually complained of depression.

Because behaviour problems are often the presenting symptom, major depression is missed in adolescents by primary care physicians. Awareness of the high incidence of major depression among adolescents, a sound knowledge of diagnostic criteria for major depression and the ability to effectively apply it, could make the diagnoses relatively easy. Biological markers in this study could only serve to support the clinical diagnoses.

2578

ETUDE PROSPECTIVE D'ADOLESCENTS DELIRANTS :
CLINIQUE, EVOLUTION ET TRAITEMENT.

O. HALFON - Fondation Santé des Etudiants de France
NEUFMOUTIERS-EN-BRIE (77)

M. DUGAS - Hôpital Robert Debré - PARIS (75)

La présence d'idées délirantes au cours d'un épisode
thymique entraîne-t-elle une aggravation ?
Qu'en serait-il alors de ses rapports avec la Maladie Maniaco-Dépressive, la schizophrénie et la schizo-affective.
Jusque vers les années 80, les adolescents délirants sont considérés la plupart du temps comme des schizophrènes. Avec l'introduction du DSM III, ils sont plutôt considérés comme des Maniaco-dépressifs. La catégorie schizo-affective devient résiduelle.
Nous avons constitué une cohorte d'adolescents délirants présentant ou non des troubles de l'humeur qui vont être suivis 5 ans. Nous décrivons les antécédents familiaux, personnels, la sémiologie délirante de l'épisode index, l'évolution et le traitement de la cohorte. Il s'agit d'adolescents hospitalisés en 84,85,86, de 13 à 20 ans, des deux sexes. L'âge du début des troubles est à peu près équivalent quel que soit le diagnostic.
Dans les antécédents familiaux, on constate une nette prédominance des troubles de l'humeur.
Dans les antécédents personnels, il y a une majorité d'épisodes thymiques chez les patients maniaco-dépressifs et schizo-affectifs, et une majorité de troubles schizophréniformes chez les patients schizophrènes.

2579

L'OPTIMISATION DES STRATEGIES ANTI-DEPRESSIVES
A L'ADOLESCENCE
Loubeyre J-B, Lachal C, Giron N, Coudert A-J.
Centre Rochefeuille, C H R U, Clermont-Fd, France.

Une revue de la littérature consacrée aux traitements anti-dépresseurs à l'adolescence, fournit surtout des vérifications en double aveugle de l'efficacité des T C A. Ces études soulignent l'importance de l'effet placebo. Toutefois, la vérification d'hypothèses élémentaires, quantifiables, ne peut fonder totalement les décisions thérapeutiques.
Une étude rétrospective systématique a porté sur une population de 110 adolescents, hospitalisés sur 2 ans, dans un centre spécialisé. L'étude a analysé la succession des décisions et la rationalité des choix thérapeutiques, face à un syndrome dépressif majeur. Les patients étaient évalués selon le D S M III par 2 psychiatres entraînés. La clomipramine était le T C A de première intention et les taux plasmatiques étaient monitorés. Un délai sans chimiothérapie d'une semaine était respecté.
L'étude a démontré l'existence de stratégies thérapeutiques différenciées, construites par progression dont les principes organisateurs définissent une expertise rationnelle.
La nécessité d'autres approches thérapeutiques était systématiquement évaluée : la séparation familiale ; les supports éducatifs et cognitifs ;

2580

UNRESOLVED GRIEF & IMMUNOLOGIC IMPAIRMENT AFTER AN
ADOLESCENT'S SUICIDE
Harry Lesch, M.D. Private practice, Los Gatos, CA
Clinical Associate Professor, Stanford Univ. (USA)

The clinical work consists of parallel treatment
of the parents and sister of the young man who
suicided. Because of the patterns in this family,
they were not seen together - contrary to usual
practice. Each of them brought in a series of
dreams, which showed the evolution of their
reactions to the suicide. In their struggle with
guilt and blame, fear and shame, they redefined
their sense of self and their relation to others.
A psychobiological issue - depression of the
immune system during bereavement - emerged during
the father's treatment (probable cause of a post-
operative infection four months after son's
death). Recent immunological studies, which
provide insight into this phenomenon, will be
discussed.

2581

EPIDEMIOLOGY AND CLINICAL STUDY ON
DEPRESSION IN SCHOOL POPULATION
Badía, M.A.; Vicente, A.; Sánchez, L.;
Fonseca, V.. Psychiatry Department
Complutense University of Madrid (SPAIN)

En este estudio se investiga la presencia y sintomatología de la depresión en niños y adolescentes cuyas edades están comprendidas entre los 8 y 18 años.
En dos colegios de Madrid, uno público y otro privado, se ha realizado una entrevista a un total de 225 niños y a sus padres, aplicándoles los criterios del DSM-III para trastornos afectivos, otros trastornos afectivos específicos, trastornos afectivos atípicos y trastorno adaptativo con disminución del estado de ánimo; así como un cuestionario elaborado con 54 síntomas depresivos.
La frecuencia de cuadros depresivos hallada es de 2.6 % en trastorno afectivo mayor, 1.3 % en trastorno distímico, 0.8 % en trastorno adaptativo con estado de ánimo deprimido, y un 2.6 % en depresión atípica. La sintomatología depresiva se distribuye entre síntomas comunes con los adultos y otros propios de estas edades.
La depresión infanto-juvenil se puede diagnosticar en población escolarizada con los criterios diagnósticos del DSM-III, pero existen síntomas propios de estas edades que deberán ser considerados para el diagnóstico de la depresión.

Session 396 Special Session: Psycholinguistics

2582

INVESTIGATION OF THE LANGUAGE : CONSTRUCTION OF A QUESTIONNAIRE OF AMBIGUOUS SENTENCES.
M.Markidis, M.Markianos, V.Kontaxakis, Gr.Vaslamatzis, Chr.Ioannidis, R.Markidis.
Eginition Hospital, Athens - Greece

Recent linguistic theory refers to "linguistic competence" as a mean of creative use of the language. Besides, a number of psychopathological disorders, mainly schizophrenia, have been associated with distortions of the language.
This study is an attempt to construct a questionnaire in order to evaluate linguistic competence on the basis of ambiguity as a syntactic characteristic of the sentences. We checked the validity of 34 items in a mixed population of 134 people (70 normals and 64 schizophrenics) using the four contingency tables test. The evaluation procedure (with a limit of statistical significance $p<0.10$) established the validity of 18 items in normal people, as well as in schizophrenics. The items of structural ambiguity had the highest statistical significance (E.g. "His father was sorry because he made a mistake").

2583

PAUSES AS ORGANIZING UNITS IN PARANOID SCHIZOPHRENIC 'DISORDERED SPEECH'
Hub Faria, I., Figueira, M.L.
Dept.Linguistics;Lab.Med.Psych.Univ.Lisbon,Portugal
Following the pioneer work by F. Goldman-Eisler on the temporal organization of speech with reference to pausing and speech planning, our study is concerned with the analysis of both the content and the words chosen, after short, medium and long pauses in paranoid schizophrenic discourse.We are comparing speech samples of five minutes each, produced by the patients during two semi-structured clinical interviews that took place within one month interval. During this period, the patients, who were rated for psychopatology using the Brief Psychiatric Rating Scale (BPRS), had cloxazolam added to their previous neuroleptic medication. In a previous study by Figueira, Faria and als, 1989, of the same population, it was observed that: a) the speech rate and the articulation rate, although high, decreased after cloxazolam treatment; b) the duration of sequences, before and after pauses,was identical for both interview sets. However, duration of pauses significantly augmented during second interviews and longer non-breath pauses appeared in a larger scale, pointing to higher degrees of planning and greater control of speech and articulation rates. The grid of analysis now presented aims to a more elaborated description of content and lexical choice after pauses, therefore to a better understanding of each patient degrees of cognitive complexity, before and after cloxazolam treatment.

2584

COMPREHENSION OF THE LANGUAGE STATEMENTS IN SCHIZOPHRENICS.
M.Markidis, V.Kontaxakis, Gr.Vaslamatzis, Cl.Katsouyanni, R.Markidis.
Eginition Hospital , Athens - Greece

This study examines the linguistic competence of 33 paranoid (21 males, 12 females) and 31 disorganized schizophrenics (21males, 10 females) on the basis of a validated instrument of ambiguous sentences (Markidis et al. 1989). The control group consists of a random sample of 70 people (38 males and 32 females) from the general population. Comparisons between the above groups were made using the questionnaire score as a dependent variable, and as independent variables age, sex, schooling, attention (Weis), psychotisism (Eisenck) and psychopathology (BPRS).
Statistical evaluation was made by mustiple linear regression and Pearson's correlation coefficient. Results showed that schizophrenic patients differ sharply from normal people as to the questionnaire score. Moreover, the groups of patients differ significantly between them as to the overall psychopathology (BPRS) and the questionnaire score, with a poorer performance on the part of the disorganized schizophrenics.

2585

LANGUAGE EVALUATION IN SCHIZOPHRENIC AND BIPOLAR PATIENTS
J.Obiols,E.Nieto,E.Vieta and J.Guarch
Subdivisión de Psiquiatría, y Psicología Médica
Hospital Clínic i Provincial,Barcelona,Spain

The language of 60 patients (30 schizophrenic, 14 manic and 16 depressed) diagnosed through RDC criteria was evaluated using the Andreasen´s TLC scale.
A first evaluation was conducted during the patients admission and a re-evaluation was made after a minimum of three months.
Schizophrenic patients were classified through the SANS and SAPS (Scale for Assessment of Negative and Positive Symptoms)
Bipolar patients showed a tendency to a complete remission in their linguistic pathological characteristics.This tendency was also evident,but to a lesser degree in "positive" schizophrenics,while "negative" schizophrenics tended to show language disturbances in a more persistent way.

2586

Computerised Linguistic Analysis in Mental Illness and Mental Handicap
Fraser W., Thomas P., King K.
Universities of Wales, Manchester and Scotland

The computer assisted linguistic analysis technique of Morice and Ingram has been conclusively shown to have diagnostic value in psychotic illness. The utility of this method in the diagnosis of abnormal mental states in borderline mentally handicapped people has now been investigated. Prompted monologues from Aspberger's and mentally ill handicapped females were analysed using this procedure and repeated after several years. Recent studies have shown that the language of schizophrenics of normal intellect deteriorates markedly with the passage of years. The linguistic profiles and changes over time in the mentally ill mentally handicapped females mirrored that in people of normal intelligence. The Aspberger's syndrome showed a distinctive unchanged profile.

2587

THE LANGUAGE OF THE SCHIZOPHRENIC PATIENT
Loriedo C., Alliani D., De Angelis C., Vella G.
Psychiatric Clinic University of Rome, Italy

Sometimes, facing with schizophrenics we grasp something that draws attention and induces as to make a diagnostic evaluation through our feelings. Later on, in a subsequent phase we will center, on another factor for, diagnosis: verbal communication. Verbal communication may be altered in the form, content, or both.
Communication studies of the schizophrenic language imply two different problems: the apparent "incommunicability" and the psychotic language's comprehension. To solve these problems is the prerequisite to have access to the "schizophrenic drama". In the present work the authors make an analysis of the schizophrenic patient language, on the basis of recorded verbal material. The theoretical support of this study is derived from the work of Arieti, Matte-Blanco, Wynne-Singer, Piro.
The role played by some peculiar alterations in the schizophrenic language (such as: looseness of associations, clang associations, derailment, tangentiality, some structural alteration of speech, and so on) is exsplored.

2588

SCHIZOPHRENIA : A SUBGROUP WITH SPEECH PECULIARITIES.

BARRELET L.F., Corradini S., Piguet D., Pelizzer G.
Institutions Universitaires de Psychiatrie. Genève. Service de Psychiatrie II. Chemin du Petit-Bel-Air 8. Genève. Switzerland

Previous workers, who studied speech and utterances of schizophrenic patients, postulated that these patients were not following the pragmatic rules of verbal communication. To observe such specific peculiarities and perturbations, we used the verbal communication test of Glücksberg et al. Subjects describe an abstract picture in such a way that a listener can choose the corresponding image in a set of seven. 45 subjects were observed. Out of the 25 schizophrenic patients, 7 subjects showed speech perturbations such as vagueness in the use of pronoms and ignorance of the listeners' feedback. 6 of these patients had a diagnosis of Schizophrenia, Disorganized Type. In contrast, patients with Schizophrenia, Paranoïd Type were similar to the non-schizophrenic patients. The hypothesis that speech peculiarities are present only in a subgroup of schizophrenic patients is confirmed. The changes of these perturbations in time will be studied further.

2589

LECTURE ET RECIT CHEZ LE PSYCHOTIQUE

Docteur M. PEYRON (C.H. EAUBONNE - FRANCE)

La lecture est un phénomène indissociablement lié à notre civilisation et à notre culture. Elle a été l'objet de nombreuses recherches soit expérimentales, soit psycho-pédagogiques, qui enrichissent nos connaissances sur l'acquisition, les mécanismes et les défaillances de la lecture. Notre étude se situe à un niveau différent, dans une double perspective, au point d'intersection de la lecture et du langage.
En effet, travaillant avec une population de sujets psychotiques en hôpital de jour, nous nous interrogeons sur le contenu du livre que le psychotique choisit de lire, sur le récit qu'il peut en faire, sur la façon dont il fait ce récit. Lorsqu'un psychotique choisit une oeuvre littéraire, la choisit-il de façon arbitraire ? Sinon, y-a-t-il un lien entre le choix et son histoire personnelle ? S'il propose un résumé, quels en sont les items ? Sont-ils de purs produits imaginaires ou se réfèrent-ils au texte lu ? S'il y a conflit dans l'histoire, dans la mesure où le psychotique l'aurait perçu, comment l'aborde-t-il ?
On conçoit que cette approche soit d'une forte complexité, d'où notre souci de nous limiter à un champ théorique restreint.
Après une présentation méthodologique, nous présenterons 3 vignettes cliniques et tenterons d'analyser les résultats.

2590

LANGUAGE DISORDERS IN PARANOID SCHIZOPHRENIA
Andrzej Czernikiewicz, Department of Psychiatry, Lublin, Poland

Schizophrenics appear to have difficulty with coherent discourse processing. This hypothesis was tested by assesing verbal behavior of 30 subchronic and 30 chronic patients that fulfilled DSM III Criteria for paranoid schizophrenia. The samples of spontaneous speech were analysed by Scale for the Assesment of Thought, Language, and Communication /TLC/. Every subject was examined in acute phase of psychosis and in remission. Mental state of Ss was scored by BPRS. In acute phase of psychosis were observed marked verbal disorders in the speech of Ss. During the remission language disturbances diminished but majority of utterances revealed mild pathology of speech. The language pathology among studied schizophrenics was mainly caused by "lack of structural coherence" of the discourse. The higher results of positive disorders and loose associations were found in the group of chronic patients. Language "negative disorders" did not differ significantly in the subchronic and chronic paranoid schizophrenics.

Session 397 New Research:
Rehabilitation and care for special groups

2591

TEACHING SELF-CARE SKILLS TO CHRONIC SCHIZOPHRENIC PATIENTS
Joanna Meder, Maryla Sawicka, Andrzej Axer
Department of Psychiatric Rehabilitation
Institute of Psychiatry and Neurology
Warsaw, Poland

Community adaptation of the chronically mentally ill is hindered by deficiencies in independent living skills. There is also some evidence showing that highly structured intervention based on social learning principles may increase the level of instrumental functioning in this population. Such a program has been recently developed at the Rehabilitation Day Center of the Institute of Psychiatry and Neurology in Warsaw, Poland.
This paper presents the structure and content of three training modules focused on such daily activities as budget planning, personal hygiene and food preparation. Preliminary results of the study aimed at evaluation of of short-term outcome of the training modules are also described. The data collected so far suggest that at least some chronic schizophrenics improve their self-care skills through the behavioral intervention including specific instructions, repeated practice, in vivo exercises and homework assignments.

2592

THE OUTCOME OF REHABILITATION ON SCHIZOPHRENICS LIVING IN THE COMMUNITY: A FOLLOW-UP STUDY
V. Tomaras, I. Ioannovich, A. Kapsali, M. Madianos, C.N. Stefanis.
University of Athens, Dept. of Psychiatry

65 schizophrenic patients, diagnosed according to DSM-III criteria have attended a community based rehabilitation programme lasting for one year and consisting of vocational training and social therapy in the context of medication. Those 58, who were not terminated, were followed-up for two years after discharge and their social and clinical course was assessed. Results indicate that the patients have been significantly improved in terms of hospitalization rates and work functioning within the follow-up period as compared to the 2-year pre-intake period. The length of hospitalizations during the follow-up is associated with the number and length of pre-intake hospitalizations and educational level. The stronger predictor of rehospitalization is the number of hospitalizations prior to intake. Postdischarge employment status is associated with the number of jobs prior to intake, the age of disease onset, the level of social and work functioning at discharge, as well as the presence of florid symptoms and the number of residual symptoms at discharge. The social functioning level at discharge and the pre-intake employment record appear to be the best predictors of reemployment. The relationship between the two measures of treatment outcome (i.e., work functioning and duration of hospitalization) used in this study is discussed.

2593

CONTROLLED STUDY OF HEALTH VISITOR INTERVENTION IN THE TREATMENT OF POSTNATAL DEPRESSION: IMPLICATIONS FOR CLINICAL SERVICES
Cox J.L., Holden J., Sagovsky R., Cookson D.,
Departments of Psychiatry, Universities of Keele & Edinburgh

A study designed to determine whether counselling by a Health Visitor was helpful in the management of postnatal depression has recently been reported. This was a controlled random order trial and took place in Health Centres in Scotland. 60 women were identified as being depressed by screening at six weeks postpartum and by a psychiatric interview carried out at about thirteen weeks after delivery.

The intervention consisted of eight weekly counselling visits by Health Visitors who had been given a short training in non-directive counselling. The standardised psychiatric interview devised by Goldberg et al and the ten item Edinburgh Postnatal Depression Scale were used to identify depression before and after the intervention. The research psychiatrist was not told to which group the women had been allocated. After 3 months, eighteen (69%) of the 26 women in the treatment group had fully recovered compared with 9 (38%) of the 24 in the control group. The changes in the total symptom scores and the self report scales were all significant at 0.01.

The results of this study together with the clinical experiences of the author indicated that a day hospital staffed by mental health professionals skilled in such counselling techniques, would be an optimal clinical facility. The development of the Parent and Baby Day Unit will be described and the preliminary results of a survey presented. 103 women discharged from the day hospital completed a patient satisfaction questionnaire. The paper will draw attention to the frequency of depression following childbirth, to the need to educate health professionals and provide more optimum treatment facilities.

2594

Group therapy and sonorous space: experimental reliefs of a new clinical methodology for rehability treatment of psychotic disease
Davalli C.,Galvano G.C, Landoni G.,Maggio G. Masserini C. Lucchin A, and I. Carta
Department of Psychiatry, University of Milan

The a.a propose the analysis of the data that are derived from the clinical application of a new method for the rehability treatment of the psychotic disease employing the musical sonorous objects as an indirect vector for the communication within the group.
The use of sonorous material as an intermediate object and non verbal mean of therapeutic relation in a setting that's oriented analytically differentiates the proposed clinical experience from those analogous ones that tend to employ the sound as a medicine(iatromusic).
We will point out, by the analysis of the psychopathologic modifications that are occurred and made objective by a periodical giving to the examided population:
1) the character of projective support and of protective container that is carried out by the sonorous space
2) the peculiar connection that exists between the Psychological modifications that are impelled by the psychosensorial acustic evebt and specific aspect of the psychotic experience.

2595

INSTITUTIONAL REVOLUTION IN PSYCHIATRIC CARE IN THE FRG: TEN YEARS EXPERIENCE

Wolpert E.M.
Psychiatric Dep.,Elisabethenstift Hospital, Darmstadt, FRG
According to the so-called "Psychiatrie-Enquete" of 1973, wherever possible, psychiatric units at general hospitals should replace distant state mental hospitals. In 1979/80 most of the roughly 100 units with 80-120 beds now in existence had been established and were supported by the so-called "Model-Programm der Bundesregierung" between 1981 and 1986, including the development of community support. Data from most units studied are compared to those from state hospitals. The evaluation by now shows the following:
1. Units at general hospitals can be efficient in caring for all psychiatric patients provided that community support is available.
2. As a consequence, psychiatric beds can be reduced to less than 0.5 per 1000 inhabitants.
3. Stay in hospital can be reduced to less than half the time required in state mental hospitals.
4. Costs per case are apparently not higher than in the state hospital model, although the costs per day are much higher in the units.

2596

Why patients leave mental health services?
Mastroeni A., Colombo G., Colombo M.G., Travasso B., Faggioli L.
U.S.S.L. 70 - Legnano (Milano) - ITALY
In Legnano area,where a Psychiatric Case Register is running since 1.10.1983, a cohort of patients included in the "Year Prevalence" count of 1984 ,were followed-up for four years.For the purposes of the current study we analysed in terms of outcome and social functioning the patients who were not "in-care" at the end of the observation period.We considered both patients who left the therapeutic setting against the opinion of the therapists and those who were lost for death,emigration or other;furthermore we verified what happened to those patients who were "discharged" as "non-case" after a consultation visit as well as patients who were supposed to be "cured". The study was carried on by interviewing the General Practitioners and -when possible- the same patients.It was intended as a contribution to the analysis of the "selection processes" which operate on psychologically disordered individuals -beyond severity of psychopathology -to make them abitual users of the mental health services.

2597

ASISTENCIA TERAPEUTICA A PRESOS POLITICOS EN PENALES

MACCHIAVELLO CONSUELO,NEUMAN ELISA,ERAZO RODRIGO

F.A.S.I.C.

SANTIAGO,CHILE

FASIC,en el contexto de su tarea de ayuda solidaria a los p perseguidos políticos del régimen militar chileno,ofrece a p partir de 1987,asistencia terapéutica a presos políticos(pp) al interior de los penales en un número aproximado de 256,a fines de septiembre de 1988.
Esta modalidad de trabajo terapéutico ha sido planteada como complemento del efectuado previamente con presos político en libertad y con otros afectados por la represión.

En el trabajo presentado se describen: 1) CARACTERISTICAS DE LOS RECINTOS PARA PRESOS POLITICOS 2)CARACTERISTICAS DE LA POBLACION ATENDIDA, 3)FORMAS DE INTERVENCION TERAPEUTICA Y CONDICIONES EN QUE ESTA SE VERIFICA, 4)EVALUACION PARCIAL DE RESULTADOS, Y 5)ALGUNAS CONSIDERACIONES TEORICAS SOBRE LA VA LIDEZ Y PROYECCION DE ESTE MODO DE INTERVENCION.

2598

NATURAL LEADERS - MARIA ANTONIETA SILVA DE CASTRO

CENTER OF INFORMATION AND EDUCATION FOR THE PREVENTION OF DRUG ABUSE
(CEDRO)

For the third consecutive year, CEDRO will apply its preventive program called "Natural Leaders". Through this program high school students are trained so that they will be able to help school mates in different problems and serve between their peers as preventive agents.

This program was applied in 1987 only in one school, being extender in 1988 to four. Due to ots successful aplication, it will be applied in 5 schools simultaneously in 1989. Progressively more school throughout the country will be involved in this preventive program.

This paper shows the program's procedures in the various schools where it was applied; difficulties found in its development - and an evaluation of the results obtained during the two years it was carried out.

2599

PATTERNS OF PSYCHIATRIC CARE IN ITALY BEFORE AND AFTER PSYCHIATRY REFORM ACT.

C.L.CAZZULLO, G.TACCHINI, A.MORONI

Institute of Psychiatry - University of Milan
Via F. Sforza 35, 20122 Milano - Italy

In 1978 a Reform Act abolished in Italy mental hospitals, restricted in-patient care to general hospital psychiatric wards, and demanded out-patients care to community based services.
The law was and is applied in very different forms in the various parts of our Country, but a shift in clinical practice and in psychiatric population is generally oriented towards psychotic patients.
Our work takes into account the various local patterns of care and outlines the differences introduced by the law in large samples of both inpatients and outpatients, drawn from the spontaneous "before" and "after" the law psychiatric populations.

Session 398 — Symposium:
Neuro-psychopathology of aging: Clinical and biological aspects

2600

NEURO-PSYCHOPATHOLOGY OF AGING: CLINICAL AND BIOLOGICAL ASPECTS.
LUIGI RAVIZZA
UNIVERSITY OF TURIN, DEPT. OF PSYCHIATRY
Via Cherasco 15 - 10126 TURIN (ITALY)

Aging involves a large number of psychopathological disorders related to the major biological vulnerability and to the many life events experienced in late life.
Depression is certainly one of the most frequent disorders of aging. Psychogenic depressive states, related to the many experiences of losing of aging, are prevalent.
There are no epidemiology changes of endogenous or major depressions. Typical depressive disorders of aging are depressive pseudodementias and organic depression that develops from a degenerative process of the brain (Alzheimer's disease and multi-infarct dementia).
Anxiety disorders are comparable, from a clinical and epidemiological point of view, to those of adult age with slight differences in symptomatology.
There are then the different kinds of dementia which represent a dramatic estate of aging (AD, SDAT, MID). AD and MID account for roughly 65-70% of dementing illnesses and AD is more frequent than MID.

2601

NEUROPHYSIOLOGICAL ASPECTS OF AGING

Turan M. Itil and Kurt Z. Itil,
New York Medical College, and HZI Research Center, Tarrytown, New York

Neuropathological changes in brain structures due to aging have already been observed more than a century ago. The neurophysiological and neurochemical changes which may be responsible for the anatomical changes in aging, particularly in pathological aging, were established in this century. The improvement of diagnostic technology in recent years has provided new information regarding physiological changes in pathological aging such as dementia. These findings, if confirmed, have significant clinical implications.
Using the latest electrophysiological technology, computer-analyzed EEG (CEEG) and Dynamic Brain Mapping, we established that the elderly healthy male population has significantly less alpha activity in all brain areas than that of a group of healthy young males. The patients with pathological aging, such as dementia, have even less alpha activity than healthy elderly. Patients with severe dementia, such as Alzheimer's, show further decline of alpha activity than less severe demtnia patients. Thus the decline of alpha activity and increase of slow waves from young healthy to elderly healthy, light to severe dementia, appears to be an important finding.
The other interesting findings are:
1) All anticholinergic substances, particularly those that produce confusional pictures with marked short term memory impairment, decrease alpha activity; 2) All drugs, including nootropics, cerebrovascular compounds and even the plant extracts, such as from Ginko-Biloba, which are claimed to be "effective" in dementia or memory problems, produce an alpha activity increase and decrease in slow waves. Also, cholinesterase inhibitors, such as tetry hydro-aminoacrin (THA), reverse the acute clinical confusional states induced by anticholinergic compounds and increase alpha activity and decrease slow waves in EEG.
Based on these facts, we have outlined a working model to: a) develop new "antidementia" compounds"; b) prevent pathological aging; c) tailor a treatment program for each individual patient.

2602

DEPRESSIVE DISORDERS, BIOLOGICAL ASPECTS
C.G.Gottfries
Department of Psychiatry and Neurochemistry,
Gothenburg University, St.Joergen's Hospital,
Sweden

Epidemiological investigations indicate that the frequency of depression varies between 8 and 30% after the age of 65. Dysthymic disorders maintain a relatively consistent prevalence throughtout the life cycle.
Reifler et al. (1986) found that 30% of patients with dementia of the Alzheimer type meet the criteria for having a major affective disorder. The suicide rate is still high among the elderly. The etiology of primary affective disorders is unknown. Genetic factors are of importance. In the pathogenesis of the disorder it is obvious that reduced metabolism in the noradrenaline and/or the 5-hydroxytryptamine system is of importance. In some investigations a relationship between infractions, especially on the left side, and depressive disorders has been proven.
It is obvious that the normal aging process, idiopathic dementias, parkinsonism and also some forms of vascular dementia are accompanied by reduced activity in the monoamine metabolism. Some similarities between dementia disorders and depression are obvious. Both types of disorders go with a hypothalamic disturbance.
Neuroendocrine studies in the two disorders have revealed a hypothalamic dysfunction both in demented and depressed patients.

2603

EEG MAPPING IN SDAT AND IN NON-ALZHEIMER DEMENTIAS

Cazzullo C.L., Pugnetti L., Mangoni A., Altamura A.C., Gianetti S., Caputo D., Morselli R., Masserini C., Motta A., Mendozzi L., Cattaneo A.M.
Centro Sclerosi Multipla "Don Gnocchi"
University of Milan, ITALY

In an attempt to better define the usefullness of the electrophysiological monitoring of the senile and pre-senile dementias,in 1988 we have undertaken a collaborative study which is still in progress.
A large number of patients with primary degenerative dementia of the Alzheimer type,vascular or mixed vascular-degenerative type, secondary to neurological disorders (mainly multiple sclerosis), and Down Syndrome are being investigated.Diagnoses are established by means of clinical,laboratory,and neuroradiological examinations,and formulated according to the DSM III-R criteria.EEG investigations are being carried out at least once during the diagnostic period in a drug-free condition and then every two months for those patients who are willing to collaborate in the follow-up.
This presentation will deal with the results of the EEG studies carried out so far at baseline on a group of more than 50 patients, and on the preliminary analysis of some follow-up studies already completed.

2604

NEUROMORPHOLOGICAL AND BIOLOGICAL PATTERNS OF ALZHEIMER DISEASE
A.C. Altamura, C. Masserini, L. Pugnetti, B. Panetta, T. Girardi
Department of Psychiatry, University of Milan, Italy

Alzheimer's Disease (AD) is the major cause of dementia in the elderly. The data on the possible relationship between clinical aspects or specific symptoms and some biological patterns are lacking. Aim of this study was to relate cognitive impairments and other clinical symptoms of AD to neurophysiological, neuromorphological, biological variables.The study was performed on 20 patients, age ranging from 48 to 84 years, all diagnosed as AD according to DSM III-R. Clinical evaluation consisted of the Mini Mental State Examination , Wechsler Memory Scale , Gottfries Rating Scale, and Buscke Test. Neuromorphological and neurophysiological evaluations included CAT,SPECT, Cognitive Evoked Potentials (P300) and computerized EEG. Finally plasma levels of lipidoperoxides were measured and results were compared with age-matched healthy control group.
Preliminary results seem to indicate that the degree of cognitive impairment is related to the alterations of the neurophysiological and biological patterns.

2605

ANXIOUS DEPRESSIVE SYMPTOMS IN ELDERLY

GIORDANO Pierluigi - LA BARBERA Daniele
PSYCHIATRIC DEPT. UNIVERSITY OF PALERMO
Via G. La Loggia 1 - 90129 PALERMO (Italy)

Mental illness in the elderly may be considered as a pattern of a psychiatric disorder in which biological, psychological and social aspects are close connected.
Anxiety and depression represent the two basic way to respond to these discomforts in the elderly, anxiety being linked to the fear of danger; depression to experience of loss.
Clinical relationship between anxiety and depression as well as their psychodynamic value are investigated with special regard to the coexistence of somatic disorder.
The Authors also draw some guidelines of psychological and pharmacological treatment of anxious-depressive syndromes in elderly.

2606

PHARMACOTHERAPY OF ANXIETY AND DEPRESSION IN THE ELDERLY
S.A. Montgomery, D. Baldwin, M. Green, N. Fineberg
St Mary's Hospital, London Uk

There are special problems in treating depression in the elderly. The elderly appear more vulnerable to the cardiotoxic effects of antidepressants both as a direct effect on the myocardium and postural hypotension. The direct cardiotoxicity in overdosage contributes to the high lethality in overdosage of TCAs. The elderly are a difficult group to treat because of a higher proportion of concomitant physical illness, leading to the use of multiple drugs. It is important therefore to avoid antidepressants with multiple unnecessary pharmacological actions. The possible links of cholinergic receptors in dementia makes the use of drugs with marked anticholinergic side effects potentially dangerous. The elderly show altered pharmacokinetics with both increased and more variable plasma levels which has led to the practice of using lower doses. The anxiety component of depression in the elderly responds well to antidepressants and the concomitant use of benzodiazepines may lead to dependence and increased confusion.

Session 399 Symposium:
Culture, phenomenology, outcome and therapy of mental disorders

2607

CULTURE, PHENOMENOLOGY, OUTCOME AND THERAPY : AN INTRODUCTION

VIJOY K. VARMA
Postgraduate Medical Institute Chandigarh, [INDIA].

Transcultural researh in mental illness can help separate the differences across cultures representing the pathoplastic influence of the culture from the commonalities, thus elucidating the core nature of the illness. The symposium will review transcultural research in mental illness - its incidence, typology, manifestation, course and outcome.

The relationship between culture, personality and mental illness can be understood in terms of a number of socio-cultural variables. The social inter-relationship can be epitomized on a dependence-autonomy continnum which may influence coping mechanisms and illness. The health-sustaining aspects of traditions, customs and rituals as also social institutions and values need to be underscored. Other variables like social support, expressed emotions, psychological sophistication, cognitive style and linguistic competence may influence vulnerability and illness.

Treatment in general and psychotherapy in particular can not ignore the cultural background in which it is taking place and must take into account relevant socio-cultural factors to adapt psychotherapy to a particular socio-cultural setting.

Cultural factors are being increasingly recognized for its role in both health and illness. The present symposium addresses itself to many facets of this interaction.

2608

AN OVERVIEW OF GLOBAL, CROSS-CULTURAL RESEARCH IN MENTAL ILLNESS
Sartorius N. - World Health Organisation, Switzerland

2609

ROLE OF EXPRESSED EMOTIONS AND RELATED VARIABLES IN MENTAL ILLNESS
Strömgren E. - Institute of Psychiatric Demography, Risskov, Denmark

2610
SOCIAL AND FAMILY FACTORS IN MENTAL ILLNESS
Wynne L. - USA

2611
OUTCOME VARIABLES IN SEVERE MENTAL DISORDERS

Assen Veniaminov Jablensky
WHO Collaborating Centre of Mental Health, Sofia, Bulgaria

Comparative studies of mental disorders in different cultures, and in particular WHO-coordinated research into schizophrenia and allied conditions, has demonstrated that: (a) the basic nosological forms of the severe psychiatric disorders can be identified in all areas studied up to date, and their symptomatological "cross-sections" are similar across cultures; (b) the patterns of course and outcome vary significantly within and across cultures; and (c) there are consistent trends in the variation across cultures, setting apart patients in developing countries and patients in developed countries. No single major factor has yet been established to account for such differences. As measures of different faces of course and outcome become more refined, the net result appears to be explicable in terms of synergistic effects of multiple variables operating at consecutive stages of the disease process.

2612
A REVIEW OF REPORTED RESEARCH IN CROSS-CULTURAL ASPECTS OF MENTAL ILLNESS
Favazza A. - Dpt. of Psychiatry, Three Hospital Drive, Columbia, Missouri, USA

2613
CULTURE, SELF AND MENTAL ILLNESS
Marsella A. - NIMH/WHO Schizophrenic Program, The Queen's Medical Centre, Honolulu, Hawai, USA

Session 400 Symposium: Perceived parental rearing and psychopathology

2614

A CROSS-CULTURAL STUDY OF THE RELATIONSHIP BETWEEN PARENTAL REARING, DYSFUNTIONAL ATTITUDES AND PSYCHOPATHOLOGY
C.Perris, M.Eisemann, S.Lindgren, J.Richter, R.Vrasti
Dept. Psychiatry of WHO Collaborating Centre Umea University, Sweden

Within a framework for linking the experience of parental rearing attitudes with manifest psychopathology the occurrence of basic dysfuntional attitudes was studied in series of psychiatric patients from different countries (Sweden, Hungary, GDR and Romania).
The results show that there are statistically significant correlations between perceived parental rearing and dysfunctional attitudes across cultures. The mechanisms through which negative rearing practices impact on the development of psychopathological conditions are also discussed.

2615

FACTORS ASSOCIATED TO PERCEIVED PARENTAL REARING PATTERNS IN DRUG ABUSE

Kokkevi, A., Stefanis, C.

Department of Psychiatry, Athens University Medical School

Our previous work showed that imprisoned drug dependent males perceived their parents as less rejective, their mother as warmer, more overprotective and permissive than a control group from the general population. However no substantial differences were found when imprisoned drug dependents were compared to imprisoned non dependent subjects. Similarities between drug abusing and non abusing subjects lead us to the need of exploring a possible contribution of sociopathy, characterising both groups, in the perceived parental rearing patterns by drug abusing subjects.
The interaction between perceived parental rearing patterns and sociopathy in male imprisoned (IA) and attending health services (HSA) drug abusers was therefore studied using a multivariate regression analysis. In addition to psychopathic personality, demographic, familial, user's, mood related and legal status while interviewing were introduced as independent variables.
Findings showed that rejection by both parents and maternal overprotection are significantly associated to the psychopathic personality of subjects. They also showed that parental rejection is more pronounced in IA than HSA. HSA emerged as being more overprotected by both parents while the mother of IA is perceived as being more warm towards them than the mother of HSA. Finally rejection by mother is significantly associated with depressive mood.

2616

PERCEIVED PARENTAL REARING STYLE IN SPANISH ADOLESCENTS AND PARENTS: VALIDATION OF TWO NEW FORMS OF THE EMBU
J.Castro, J.Toro, W.Arrindell, J.van der Ende, J.Puig
Hospital Clinic i Provincial, Barcelona, Spain

The EMBU, a Swedish self-report questionnaire, was originally designed to assess adults' memories about their parents' rearing behaviour. The present paper deals with the development of two further versions of the EMBU; one for adolescents and one for parents opinion about their rearing of children. The structural constancy of these new versions as compared with the original, was studied in a sample of 124 normal adolescents and of 227 parents respectively. The dimensions obtained for the new versions were almost identical to the original EMBU with high inveriance coefficients for the scales of "Rejection", "Emotional Warmth" and "Overprotection". The scale reliabilities and their internal consistency proved to be satisfactory, as well. It appears from these results, that the new adolescents and parents versions of the EMBU are as reliable as their original proving dimensional identity for the three main scale.

2617

PARENTAL REARING AND DEPRESSIVE SYMPTOMS IN ADOLESCENTS
P.Baron, L.Prud'homme, N.Joubert
University of Ottawa, Ottawa, Canada

The present paper intends to report on two recent studies using the EMBU with Canadian adolescent samples. The purpose of the first study was to examine the relationship between parental rearing and dysfunctional attitudes. One hundred and eightly English speaking adolescents, whose ages varied from 13 to 15 years, participated in the study. All subjects completed the EMBU and the DAS in the context of regular classes. With regard to the second study its purpose was to examine the relationship between parental rearing and depressive symptoms. One hundred and fifty two French-speaking adolescents, ranging in age from 15 to 19 years, were involved in the study: they all completed the EMBU and the BDI. The EMBU factor structure obtained with adults. Results are also discussed in light of the literature on adolescent depression.

2618
REPORTED PARENTAL REARING AND DEPRESSION: FURTHER EXPERIENCES WITH THE EMBU IN DIFFERENT COUNTRIES
M.Eisemann, P.Gaszner, M.Maj, C.Perris, J.Richter, R.Vrasti
Dept. of Psychiatry, Umea University, Sweden

The present paper deals with further studies on the relationship between parental rearing experiences assessed by the EMBU and depression. In addition to the three factors used previously, i.e. "Rejection", "Emotional Warmth", "Overprotection" the original 14 subscales have been studied to cover a wider range of rearing practices. The results show that the differences reported on earlier, between depressives and normals become more pronounced by this approach. These differences could be established in all the samples included, irrespective of cultural background. The importance of childhood experiences as a risk factor in the background of depression is discussed.

2619
FINDING UNIVERSAL DIMENSIONS OF INDIVIDUAL VARIATION IN MULTICULTURAL STUDIES OF PARENTAL REARING STYLES: THE EMBU SURVEYS
W.A.Arrindell, W.Hageman (Vrije Universiteit, Amsterdam) and J. van der Ende (Erasmus Universiteit, Rotterdam), The Netherlands

For the purpose of testing the cross-national generality of associations between child-rearing methods and psychopathology, a large ongoing project is being carried out in over 25 countries, world-wide. The first stage of the project entails the examination of the suitability of a measuring device (EMBU) originally devised in Sweden and tested for dimensionality in the Netherlands for use in several different national settings. The study describes findings on the dimensional equivalence of the major dimensions of parental rearing behaviour that were obtained from comparisons involving the following countries: Sweden, Greece, Spain, Italy, the Netherlands, Australia, Denmark, Japan, GDR, Venezuela, Singapore, Brazil, Rumania, Canada and China. The study also contrasts results obtained at the individual level using intra-cultural analysis with those yielded at the level of culture using non-metric multidimensional scaling methods for clustering cultures.

2620
Parental rearing practices and personality in alcoholics classified according to family history.
Vrasti R.*, Eisemann M.**, Podea D.*, Olteanu I.*
Psychiatric Hospital, Jebel, Romania*
Dept of Psychiatry, Umeå University, Sweden**

Within a framework of a multifactorial model of alcoholism perceived parental rearing has been studied in male alcoholics with positive(+) or negative(-) family history(FH). Furthermore it was investigated whether the influence of dysfunctional parental rearing was mediated by personality traits of the probands.
As compared with healthy controls the male alcoholics with FH+ scored higher on overprotection and rejection scales of the EMBU parental rearing questionnaire. As concerns personality the latter group showed high scores on somatic anxiety, muscular tension, impulsivity, detachment, psychasthenia and low scores on socialization and social desirability of the KSP inventory, indicating a high degree of neuroticism and a weak ego. Correlations between EMBU factors and KSP scales point to a significant covariation of parental overprotection with soamtic anxiety, muscular tension and irritability in alcoholics with FH+.
These results suggest underlying mechanisms between hereditary factors and perceived parental rearing in shaping a vulnerability for alcoholism.

Session 401 Symposium:
The use of clozapine in treatment-resistant schizophrenia

2621
SOURCES OF DETERIORATION AND IMPROVEMENT IN SCHIZOPHRENIA
John S. Strauss, M.D.; Department of Psychiatry; Yale University School of Medicine

In the last 20 years it has become increasingly clear that schizophrenia does not always have a bad outcome. Rather, the course and outcome of this group of disorders is extremely diverse. Numerous determinants of this diversity have been identified including such prognostic factors as previous levels of social relations and work functioning and prior duration of illness. During the illness itself, medication and intervention with the patient's family are important. In all probability the role of patients' actions on their own behalf and of stressful life events are crucial to the course of disorder as well. The characteristics and number of these factors suggest that influencing the course of schizophrenia involves dealing both with the person and the disorder. When, for example, medications are found that reduce symptoms, that is important indeed; but even then, evidence suggests that the patient needs help in finding a way to live and to find a sense of self without the symptoms that have been so painful. Based on these concepts, a way for evaluating and treating a person suffering from schizophrenia will be suggested.

2622

LONG-TERM TREATMENT WITH CLOZAPINE
EFFICACY, SIDE-EFFECTS AND TOLERABILITY

D. Naber, M. Leppig, H. Hippius
Psychiatric Hospital, University of Munich
D-8000 Munich, West-Germany

Retrospectively, effects of clozapine therapy were evaluated in 87 out-patients, treated for 5-11 years in a daily dosage of 145 $\pm$ 110 mg. 54 patients were schizophrenic, others had diagnoses such as tardive dyskinesia, schizo-affective psychosis, endogenous depression, mania or movement disorders.
78% of schizophrenic patients considerably improved, re-hospitalization occured significantly less under clozapine than under previous neuroleptic treatment. Most of the positive and also some negative symptoms declined (e.g. 40% of chronic schizophrenics had marked improvement of anergia and 25% of previously unemployed patients were able to work again.
In 6% of patients, severe side-effects led to discontinuation of clozapine treatment. Most often were sedation/hypotension, EEG-alterations, fever, increase of liver enzymes and weight gain. No case of leucopenia occured, no extrapyramidal symptoms were observed.
Most patients tolerated the drug well and were compliant. The benefit/risk ratio of long-term clozapine treatment is high.

2623

A Prospective Trial of Clozapine in Treatment-Resistant Schizophrenia
Meltzer, H.Y., Bastani, B., Ramirez, L.F., Lee, M., Alphs, L., and Kwon, K.
Case Western Reserve University and Cleveland Veterans Administration Medical Center

An open trial of clozapine at a mean dose of 500 mg/day in schizophrenic patients who had persistant moderate-severe positive symptoms despite multiple trials with available neuroleptic drugs demonstrated significant improvement in symptomatology and social functioning in 40-50% of patients. Some very regressed patients were able to obtain full time jobs or return to college. Initial improvement occurs within the first few weeks of treatment in some patients but others require 6-12 months of treatment. Improvement occurs in both positive and negative symptoms, even in some patients with a severe deficit state. Improvement in negative symptoms may be independent of improvement in positive symptoms. Psychosocial treatments should accompany clozapine to achieve optimal results. Rehospitalization rate was significantly decreased. The results from 25 patients treated for 12 months will be presented at the Congress.

2624

GRANULOCYTOPENIA IN ASSOCIATION WITH CLOZAPINE
P. Krupp, M.D. and P. Barnes, MBBS
Drug Monitoring Centre, Clinical Research, Sandoz Ltd. Basle, Switzerland

The major risk associated with the use of Clozapine is that of granulocytopenia. The incidence of this potentially fatal adverse reaction is not known with certainty, but appears to be at least ten times greater than that reported for classical neuroleptics. Analysis of the cases reported has revealed that the early detection of the white blood cell depression by the means of regular white blood cell count monitoring is the most important factor in avoiding morbidity and mortality resulting from granulocytopenia. In an effort to elucidate the pathogenesis of this adverse reaction, research along several lines is being conducted in an effort to decrease this risk inherent to the treatment with this drug.

2625

CARDIOVASCULAR AND EXTRAPYRAMIDAL SIDE EFFECTS OF CLOZAPINE.
J. Gerlach, E.O. Jørgensen & L. Peacock.
Sct. Hans Hospital, 4000 Roskilde, Denmark.
As other antipsychotics, clozapine may induce different side effects, most frequently hypersalivation, sedation, constipation and weight gain. Clozapine may also influence cardiovascular functions, while extrapyramidal side effects are rarely seen.

Clozapine may cause fall in orthostatic blood pressure and sinus tachycardia. Collapse has been seen during the first day of treatment with clozapine, 100 mg b.i.d., and cardiac frequency may increase by more than 20 beats per minute. ECG may show a flattening or an inversion of the T-waves, changes which diminish slightly over time and disappear following discontinuation. In a few case reports, more serious heart affections have been described. New data from a prospective study of exercise electrocardiography and echocardiography before and during clozapine treatment will be presented.

At recommended dose levels (up to 600 mg/day), clozapine does not appear to induce extrapyramidal side effects, although some slowing of movements and reduced facial expression may be seen. Clozapine may even counteract tremor (12.5-75 mg/day). Available evidence indicates that clozapine in low doses (50-250 mg/day) has minimal dyskinesia-suppressing effect but may allow a spontaneous recovery of the syndrome without aggravating the primary pathophysiological process. In higher doses (400-900 mg/day), clozapine can moderately dampen TD, but due to the cardiovascular side effects, such a high dose treatment can only be recommended for younger TD patients.

2626

BENEFITS AND RISKS OF CLOZAPINE TREATMENT IN SCHIZOPHRENIC PATIENTS RESISTANT TO OTHER NEUROLEPTICS

H. Hippius
Psychiatric Hospital, University of Munich
D-8000 Munich, West-Germany

Over the last 15 years, 352 schizophrenic patients were treated with clozapine. The following conclusions can be drawn:
1) Patients resistant to at least two previous neuroleptics, showed slight improvement in 38% and markedly improved in 45%.
2) Adverse effects occured in 56% and led to discontinuation in 6%. Most often were sedation, EEG-alteration, hypersalivation, fever and tachycardia.
3) No case of agranulocytosis occured, extrapyramidal symptoms were not observed.
4) At dismissal, clozapine was the only neuroleptic in 61%.
5) Evaluation of benefits vs risks is satisfactory in most of the negatively selected patients. Nevertheless, careful control of hematological and other variables is highly recommended.
6) With regard to the risk of tardive dyskinesia, low or non-existing for clozapine, is it justified to treat only those patients with clozapine who are resistant to other neuroleptics?

2627

BENEFITS AND RISKS OF CLOZAPINE TREATMENT IN SCHIZOPHRENIC PATIENTS RESISTANT TO OTHER NEUROLEPTICS

H.Y. Meltzer
Case Western Reserve University, Hanna Pavilion, University Hospitals of Cleveland, 2040 Abington Road, Room B-68, Cleveland, Ohio 44106-5000

Schizophrenia is a syndromatic disease process with heavy morbidity and increased mortality from suicide, the effects of institutionalization, poor self care, etc. The quality of life of schizophrenic patients is greatly diminshed compared to their premorbid level of function or to non-affected identical or fraternal twins. These deleterious effects of schizophrenia are most apparent in those resistant to standard neuroleptic drugs. Clozapine can produce improvement in psychopathology, social and work function and a lessened need for rehospitalization in about 40-60% of treatment-resistant patients. In a fortunate few, the degree of improvement is extraordinary. The risk of usually reversible agranulocytosis in closely monitored patients seems well worth this potential benefit. New long term outcome data which demonstrates the full extent of this benefit will be presented.

Session 402 Special Session:
Affective disorders: Chronobiology and psychophysiology

2628

SKIN CONDUCTANCE LEVEL AND DEPRESSIVE SYMPTOMATOLOGY
A.D.Rabavilas, Psychophysiological Laboratory, Dept. of Psychiatry, Athens University Medical School, Eginition Hospital, Athens, Greece.

This study investigated the relation of depressive symptomatology to SCL in 100 patients (45 females and 55 males) selected according to DSM-III criteria for generalized anxiety, panic, phobic and obsessive-compulsive disorders. Depressive symptoms were assessed by means of the Zung's Depression Scale (ZDS), while SCL was measured bilaterally through a 15 min. testing period. In overall patients, SCL was negatively and significantly related to depressive symptoms (L hand r=-0.363, P<0.0001 R hand r=-0.366, P<0.0001). Furthermore, a sensitivity-specificity cutoff point was searched for between patients who scored below 50 on the ZDS (n=19 mean 45.2+4.2) and an equal number of top scorers on the same scale (mean 76+5.5). A cutoff point of 2.6 µmhos with a sensitivity of 73.7% and specificity of 89.4% appeared to clearly differentiate these groups. These results suggested that: a) low SCL could predict quite reliably the presence of depressive symptoms in anxiety disorders and b) the value of low SCL as a marker of a circumscribed depressive illness is questionable. However, the possible validity of this measure as an auxiliary diagnostic tool in addressing the anxiety/depression issue in clinical populations is discussed.

2629

Psychoendocrine, polysomnographic and PET investigations in a 48 h-rapid cycler

P.Fleckenstein, D.Riemann, J.Kammerer, W.E.Müller, M.Berger
Central Institute of Mental Health, Mannheim, FRG

48h-rapid cycling is one of the most fascinating clinical features of an affective disorder.
We conducted psychoendocrine and polysomnographic investigations in a 64 years old male, up to that time untreated patient displaying a 48h-cycling of depression and hypomania:
1. There was no hGH(human growth hormone) response to clonidine neither on a depressive day nor on a hypomanic day. 48h hormone profiles(30 min. intervals) showed a blunted hGH secretion pattern.-The cortisol profile was enhanced on the depressive day in contrast to the hypomanic day.-TSH secretion was decreased on both days.-Polysomnographic measurements revealed nearly always short REM latencies on depressive days and only slight changes on hypomanic days.
2. TSD(total sleep deprivation) as well as carbamazepine therapy led to an impressive improvement and a strong tendency toward normalisation of neuroendocrine and sleep EEG variables.
PET studies on a depressive and a hypomanic day did not reveal a significant difference.

2630

Heart rate circadian rhythm as a biological marker of desynchronization in depression.

TAILLARD J., SANCHEZ P., LEMOINE P. and MOURET J.
UCPB, Hôpital du Vinatier, 95, boulevard Pinel, 69677 Bron cedex

Heart rate (HR) was countinously monitored during successive 24 hour-periods together with performing sleep recordings in 13 healthy subjects and 30 endogenous depressives according to DSM III criteria and MADRS scores. Recordings were performed after a two-week wash-out period and the morningness-eveningness questionnaire of HORNE as well as self assement were used in order to determine the typology of each subject.
The acrophase, amplitude, mesor and rhythm probability (PR) were calculated by the single cosinor method from the smoothed HR curves of each subject.
In normal subjects, HR follows a circadian rhythm (PR>69%) with the lowest values at night. Morning type subjects have an earlier peak time (14:00) than evening type subjects (17:30) while acrophase is related with sleep habits and synchronized by the usual wake time.
In endogenous depressive patients this analysis allowed their splitting into two groups : In the first one a circadian rhythm of HR persists (PR>50%) with a strong decrease in amplitude (41%) while, in the second one, no circadian rhythm of HR exists (PR<30%, decrease in amplitude >56%) in relation with the absence of through during the night. In the group of patients with persisting HR circadian rhythm no phase advance was observed.
Our results suggest that heart rate circadian rhythm, is likely to represent a chronobiomarker and a depression indicator. Chronobiological studies, especially in relationship with clinical changes after treatment are presently under progress. Of importance is the necessity of taking into account morningness and eveningness typologies in any chronobiological study.

2631

AROUSAL IN RELATION TO EFFECTS OF TOTAL SLEEP DEPRIVATION IN DEPRESSION

A.L. Bouhuys, F. Flentge and R.H. van den Hooffdakker
Dept of Biological Psychiatry, University Clinic, Groningen, The Netherlands.

The possibility that the clinical response to total sleep deprivation (TSD) is mediated by dimensions of arousal was investigated in depressed patients. Various arousal-related parameters were assessed before, during and after TSD, i.e., urinary cortisol, voice pitch, observed behaviour during an interview and self report of activation and stress. TSD increased the cortisol excretion and shifted the maximum excretion of cortisol and the maximum of the voice pitch to an earlier moment. These effects of TSD were not related with the mood response or with the subjective arousal responses to TSD. Some relationships might support the presumption that mood response is related with dimensions of arousal: the significant relationships between mood response on the one hand and responses of subjective stress and activation to TSD and some arousal-related observed behaviours during baseline on the other.
Patients with relatively high levels of behavioural arousal during baseline, responded with more cortisol excretion. The peakshift of the pitch was positively correlated with the cortisol excretion response to TSD. The findings indicate that TSD effects are clearly related with various arousal-related parameters and justify further exploration of the role of changes in arousal in the antidepressant effects of TSD. It is suggested that mood change after TSD could be ascribed to different cognitive labeling of the biochemical and physiological changes induced by TSD.

2632

MOOD(M) AND DRIVE(D) CHRONOPSYCHOMETRY IN AFFECTIVE DISORDERS(AD).
A.Sciolla, L.Risco, L.Firinguetti, R.Rees, F.Lolas. Psychophysiology Unit, Faculty of Medicine, University of Chile, Santiago, Chile.
Disruptions of physiological rhythmic phenomena are thought to underlie the pathogenesis of AD. We want to find out whether such disruptions have a psychological counterpart. The segmented visual scale for self-assessment ESTA-III yields scores for the variables M and D. Two bipolar items, "Anxiety/Easiness"(A/E) and "Drowsiness/Alertness"(D/A) were added as further indicators of AS. Six subjects were diagnosed with an ad-hoc instrument, which includes DSM-III/RDC criteria among others, as having Bipolar Disorder(2), Major Depression(2), Adjustment Disorder(1), and No Mental Disorder(1). AS assessments were made every 8 hours for about a month. Time series analysis of data found periodicities ranging from 1 to 20 days in the four variables, and they did not coincide within in each subject. Period coincidences were found between: M and D (four patients and one control); A/E and D/A (one patient); M and A/E (one patient); D and D/A (one patient and two controls). A comparison with results from others and a discussion of theoretical implications and shortcomings of our findings will be provided.

2633

DEPRESSIVE MOOD AND THE ULTRADIAN RHYTHM OF REM AND NON-REM SLEEP.

D.G.M. Beersma[1], D.J. Dijk[2], R.H. Van den Hoofdakker[1]
[1]Dept. Biological Psychiatry, University of Groningen, The Netherlands
[2]Pharmacological Institute, University of Zürich, Switserland

The temporal organisation of the alternation between sleep states in humans is very complex. Homeostatic and circadian processes contribute to this regulation. The interaction between REM sleep and non-REM sleep has been the subject of a recent study in our institute.
Nine healthy subjects have been deprived from REM sleep during the first five hours after sleep onset. Afterwards recovery sleep was undisturbed. During the deprivation interval the nonREM EEG power spectrum was reduced when compared to baseline for the frequencies up to 8 Hz, though nonREM sleep was not experimentally disturbed. During recovery a significant rebound of REM sleep was observed, whitout a significant increase in nonREM EEG powers. A control study in which the same subjects were deprived of nonREM sleep learned that these changes were not a direct consequence of the increased amount of wakefulness.
Apparently, an increased pressure for REM sleep results in a reduced intensity of nonREM sleep. Vogel and coworkers (Arch. Gen. Psychiatry, 1975) showed that the elevation of REM pressure could be a common factor in most kinds of antidepressive treatments. On the basis of our REM deprivation experiment in healthy subjects, the opposite hypothesis seems justified: The suppression of nonREM sleep may cause the reported antidepressive effects of REM deprivation, total sleep deprivation and antidepressant drugs.

2634

EEG SLEEP IN DYSTHYMIC AND ANXIOUS PATIENTS
F. Arriaga, P. Rosado and T. Paiva
Laboratory of EEG, Centro de Estudos Egas Moniz, Hosp. Santa Maria, Lisbon, Portugal

EEG sleep gave support to the subdivision of "dysthymic disorder" proposed by Akiskal, but little is known about sleep of non-affective forms of dysthymia. Also the nosographic status of these conditions is controversial. Are these "neurotic" and "characterologic" types closer to affective illness or to anxiety disorders?
All night EEG sleep recordings were compared in normals (n=22) and patients with "generalized anxiety disorder" (n=13) and "dysthymic disorder" (n=23). Selection was made according to DSM III; only dysthymics with syndromatic neurotic features and no evidence of underlying personality disorder were included. Visual scoring was made according to Rechstschaffen and Kales criteria and visual EEG classification was performed in order to detect certain sleep microevents.
As compared to normals, both dysthymic and anxious patients show a fragmented and superficial sleep; there is a predominance of wake and stage 1 NREM and a decrease of slow wave sleep (SWS); REM sleep features are unchanged. Using a full set of conventional sleep parameters, no clear separation between the two pathological groups arises. The occurrence of some microevents was different in the two groups.
Our results indicate that non-affective dysthymics and anxious patients have similar disturbances of sleep continuity and architecture, but it should be further investigated whether microstructural changes of sleep EEG can provide a discrimination between the two clinical conditions.

2635

DEPRESSION, COGNITIVE DISORDER AND MELATONIN

Prof. A. VENKOBA RAO & Prof. S. PARVATHI DEVI
Centre for Advanced Research on 'Health and Behaviour,' Indian Council of Medical Research, Madurai Medical College, Madurai 625 020, India.

This presentation discusses observations on 45 cases of Major depression (DSM III) on the role of cognitive disorder in its causation and occurrence of relapses. Following antidepressant therapy, 41 subjects struck remission. Of these, 27 were free from cognitive disorder while in 14 cognitive disorder persisted. Its absence was statistically significant. Follow-up revealed eight relapses of which six were from the group of 14 with cognitive disorder and two from the 27 without cognitive disorder. Follow-up at 30 months indicated that subjects who had cognitive disorder in remission were significantly more susceptible to early relapses in contrast to those without cognitive disorder.

Melatonin estimations (HPLC) during index, remission and relapse stages showed that variations in melatonin levels have a close bearing on cognitive disturbances. In almost all cases of depression there was a fall in 24-hour melatonin with reversal of the daynight rhythm. The failure of melatonin to return to normal during remission is indicative of possible recurrence and this runs parallel with the persistence of cognitive disorder in states of remission. These observations will be discussed.

Session 403 New Research:
Sleep studies

2636

EPIDEMIOLOGY OF INSOMNIA IN CASABLANCA

H. KHERRATI, D. MOUSSAOUI
Centre Psychiatrique Universitaire Ibn Rochd
Casablanca, Morocco.

Insomnia is a frequent symptom in occidental countries. No epidemiologic study has been conducted in maghrebian countries (Algeria, Tunisia, Morocco) on the prevalence of insomnia in the general population.

Material and methods : the study has been done during the winter of 1988 ; a representative sample of the adult population (from 20 to 45 years old) in Casablanca has been determined, based on the last national census.
The sample of 900 persons has been classified by gender, age, profession and housing. All the pesons interviewed with a questionnaire were living in Casablanca for at least one year.

Results : Among the interviewed persons, 12.7% were dissatisfied with their sleep, qualifying it as bad or very bad. 11% presented an insomnia with defined criteria : 14.6% of males and 7% of females. The most frequent insomnia is of the beginning of the night (50%). On the other hand, 8.5% declared having taken hypnotics during the past year.

These results and others from this study will be discussed.

2637

Neuropsychological Assessment of Patients with Severe Sleep Apnea
Vgontzas, A., Cadieux, R.J., Lehman, R.A.W., Bixler, E.O., Ingram, D.H., Kales, A.,
Pennsylvania State University College of Medicine, Hershey, Pennsylvania 17033 U.S.A.
This study, which linked severe obstructive sleep apnea with dementia, examined the degree of mental impairment and possible associated brain damage in 25 patients who had obstructive sleep apnea of sufficient severity to warrant recommendation for tracheostomy. Measurements included the WAIS-R and Halstead-Reitan immediately before and 6 months after tracheostomy. Patients' premorbid intelligence was estimated with a demographical index for the WAIS-R. The group was divided into mild, moderate and severe subgroups based on the severity of clinical symptoms, sleep apnea index and minimum oxygen desaturation. Comparisons (premorbid, pretreatment, and 6 months after treatment) were made both within and among subgroups. The severe subgroup performed significantly worse than the mild subgroup on a number of items such as Vocabulary, VIQ, and Category test. Further, six months after tracheostomy, the severe subgroup had some indices of higher-level cognitive function such as verbal I.Q., Block Design and Wisconsin Card Sorting that showed no improvement. In addition, their verbal I.Q. as measured with the WAIS-R both presurgically and six months after was significantly lower than their estimated premorbid verbal I.Q. The deficits found correlate with brain damage primarily in the left temporal, parietal and frontal areas, suggesting permanent irreversible impairment of higher-level cognitive functions associated with severe sleep apnea.

2638

SLEEP ARCHITECTURE AND DREAM REMEMBERANCE
M.M.Schneider*, S.Loeben-Sprengel*, R.Lund**,
H.Pohl*, Y.Winkelmann*, M.Ermann*
Abt.f.Psychotherapie u. Psychosomatik*,Psychiatrische Klinik u.Poliklinik**,Universität München,FRG

Intro: We examined 23 patients with psychogenic sleep disorders to find out wether the frequent spontaneous awakening during the night is tight to NREM or REM (with its high psychic activity) and wether the awakening in its physiological context as a symptom of psychogenic sleep disorders correlates with a psychic state in which dreams can be remembered.
Methods: After 2 adaptation nights in our sleeping lab, the patients were questioned during the third night four times about dreams: After spontaneous awakening from REM and NREM as well as after being awakened in REM and NREM. The evaluated sleep parameters were related to the achieved dream reports.
Results: 1.Spontaneous awakening is as frequent in REM as in NREM; it is thus independent from the two states of sleep. 2.Dream rememberance after spontaneous awakening is independent from REM or NREM. In about 50% of all questionings after spont.awakening dreams are being reported. 3.Dream rememberance after being awakened is dependent from REM and NREM. In about 70% of questioning after REM-awakening, but only in 20% after NREM-awakening dreams are remembered. Our findings will be discussed based on the psychophysiological model of Lehmann/Koukkou about dream rememberance and different functional states of brain during sleep. Consequences for psychotherapy will be pointed out.

2639

ISOLATED SLEEP PARALYSIS IN PANIC DISORDER PATIENTS

Susana Alfonso, M.D., Alvaro Rivera, M.D.
Hospital Psiquiatrico Ciempozuelos, Madrid, Spain

The aim of this study was to measure the incidence of isolated sleep paralysis in a sample of 60 referrals who met DSMIIIR criteria for panic disorder compared with a group of 30 normal controls. We also examine the relationship of the sleep disorder and clinical variables and family history.
Probands with or without sleep paralysis were compared in regard to the existence of affective, personality and alcohol dependence disorders using the SCIP-P interview for DSMIIR criteria and the FISC for the family study. Severity and clinical variables were assessed by means of age of onset, percentage of remissions, subtipe of agoraphobia, Global Phobic and Global Incapacity Scale.
The percentage of panic disorder patients with isolated sleep paralysis was 40%- significantly higher than those encountered in the group of normal controls (20%). The existence of sleep paralysis does not seem to significantly modify the clinical manifestation, severity or family history in the patients.

2640

ONEIRIC ACTIVITY AND BENZODIAZEPINES

SIRACUSANO A., FIORENTINI A., VELLA G.
I^ PSYCH. CLIN. UNIVERSITY OF ROME (PROF.G. VELLA)

The Authors besides to consider the classical effects of the BDZ about the sleep, point out, by a personal experience with patients suffering from GAD (DSM III-R), the action to oneiric activity. The analysis of the results permitted through a critical comparison with the international literature to formulate a proposal of classification of the oneiric activity of the patients with the diseases of anxiety using BDZ that is so divided:

1) Nightmares
2) Anguish dreams
3) Representation of the anguish during the dream

Especially the third point represents a group of the experimental psychodynamics and psychopathological observations of this work.

2641

ETUDE POLYSOMNOGRAPHIQUE SUR LES CAS DE DEMENCE
POLYSOMNOGRAPHIC STUDY IN CASES OF DEMENTIA
E.Gözükırmızı*, E.Eker**, H.Kaynak*,
S.Madazlıoğlu**
* Dept.Neurology, Cerrahpaşa Med.School Univ.
  Istanbul, TURKEY
** Dept.Psychiatry, Cerrahpaşa Med.School Univ.
  Istanbul, TURKEY

15 sujets agés plus de 80 ans ayant une démence ont été étudiés au cours de 2 nuits successives pendant leur sommeil spontané de nuit. Nous avons enregistré l'EEG., les mouvements oculaires, l'EMG. des muscles du menton et de la jambe, la respiration nasale et orale. On a constaté que l'organisation du sommeil est beaucoup plus perturbé par rapport aux sujets sans démence. Nous avons corrélé les frequents réveils avec les apnées et les mouvements périodiques de jambe. L'EEG. de veille étant normal, on n'a pu différencier les stades du sommeil (veille, non-REM, REM) que par les paramètres d'EOG. et d'EMG. à cause de l'activité monotone du sommeil et on a corrélé cette détérioration avec la sévérité de la démence.

2642

COMPARISON OF ZOPICLONE AND FLURAZEPAM
TREATMENTS IN INSOMNIA
SINGH, Dr. A. N. Hamilton Psychiatric
Hospital, Hamilton, Ontario, Canada

Zopiclone, a cyclopyrrolone derivative is a new sedative agent which is chemically unrelated to either benzodiazepines or barbiturates. In this double-blind study, two doses (7.5 and 11.25 mg) of zopiclone were compared to one dose (30 mg) of flurazepam. Efficacy of treatment were assessed using a validated sleep questionnaire thrice a week on the first week and twice a week for the following 3 weeks. Patients were seen weekly by the principal investigator to assess compliance of drug intake, collect the sleep questionnaire and record spontaneously reported side effects. No significant difference was shown between the two zopiclone dosages at any time during the study for sleep efficacy and psychomotor performance and the most frequently reported side effect was taste perversion at the higher dose. Compared to flurazepam, zopiclone was slightly less effective for sleep induction and sleep soundness variables specifically on the third week of the study. However, flurazepam was constantly worse than zopiclone for the daytime psychomotor performance. This finding was also confirmed by the incidence of side effects related to hypnotic residual effects. From this study, both zopiclone dosages are shown active and safe in the treatment of insomnia and exhibit a true advantage over flurazepam by its low incidence of residual effects.

Session 404 New Research:
Eating disorders

2643

Eating behaviour in adolescent males and females: a longitudinal study

Nils Johan Lavik, professor

Department of Psychiatry, University of Oslo, Norway

1968 adolescent males and females in junior and senior high school (age 13-18) answered a shortened version of EAT-26 in April 86 (response rate 95.4%). The questionnaire comprehended at the same time information about psychopathology, personality, family relations and socio-demographic background. Two cohorts at age 13-14 and 16-17 were followed with a new questionnaire in April 89.

The study will give information about:

- the prevalence of deviant eating behaviour in a "normal" population of males and females

- the factor structure of the shortened version of EAT-26 test in males and females

- the stability versus changes in eating behaviour over time

- the relationship between eating behaviour and other psychopathology, personality, family relationship and socio-demographic background.

2644

EATING DISTURBANCES AND ASSOCIATED RISK FACTORS IN A HIGH-SCHOOL POPULATION.
H. Steiger, Ph.D., G. Puentes-Newman, M.A., N. Gotheil, B.A., P. Leichner, M.D., Eating Disorders Program, Douglas Hospital, Montreal, Canada.

We developed the Risk for Eating-Disorder Development Scales (REDDS) to assess risk factors for anorexia and bulimia nervosa derived from biopsychosocial models of etiology. We surveyed 999 high-school girls using the REDDS and the Eating Attitudes Test (EAT-26), repeating our assessment on a subgroup after 7 months. In the first assessment, a 12% prevalence of eating disturbance was identified (15% in girls over 14). Symptomatic girls differed on the REDDS from Asymptomatic ones in theoretically important ways: The former group showed elevations on measures of Unstable Mood, Body-Image Concerns, Impulsivity, Interpersonal Anxiety and Achievement Needs. Symptomatic girls rated themselves and family members (especially mothers) as being prone to weight, mood and other disturbances. Of greatest interest, the REDDS scores of the most symptomatic students compared closely with those of chronic patients, meeting full DSM-III-R criteria. The follow-up yielded comparable prevalences, replicated findings on risk factors and suggested that eating disturbances are stable over a year in most cases. These findings urge that subclinical eating pathology identified in students be regarded seriously, since such disorders appear etiologically comparable to those of the patient group.

2645

ROLE OF DOPAMINE IN ANOREXIA NERVOSA

AYUSO-GUTIERREZ, J.L.; PONCE DE LEON, C.; RUBIO, M.E. BARABASH, A.; MAESTRO, M.; DEL VALLE, P.; CAÑAMARES, V. and CABRANES, J.A.
Hospital San Carlos, 28040, Madrid, Spain

In order to asses the role of dopamine system in ANOREXIA NERVOSA we studied six patients with severe symptomatology. We compared baseline and TRH-induced PRL and GH levels -by radioinmunoassay- before and after oral administration of a selective D2 dopamine receptor antagonist during a week. We have found two endocrine profiles:

A) Normal basal PRL with normal response to TRH and lack of response of GH to TRH.

B) Mean basal PRL significantly lower with normal PRL response to TRH and "paradoxical" response of GH to TRH.

Following administration of sulpiride there were in both groups higher levels of PRL with a blunted response to TRH and in the group B the paradoxical response of GH to TRH was not found.

These data support the hypothesis of dopamine hyperactivity in a subgroup (B) of patients with anorexia nervosa and suggest the dopamine implication in the PRL response to TRH.

2646

MENTAL HEALTH IN MALNOURISHED CHILDREN'S MOTHERS

Miranda, C.T;Mari, J.J.; Andreoli, S.B.. Marcolin, M.A.; Goihman, S.; Puccini, R.
DEPARTMENT OF PSYCHIATRY, ESCOLA PAULISTA DE MEDICINA, SP,BRAZIL

The aim of this study is to investigate the mental health status of low income mothers of malnourished children. Few studies have been conducted about the role of the mental health of the parents in the nutritional status of their children, although many socioeconomic and cultural variables are considered to be associated.

The study was conducted in a primary medical care setting in a low income housing area. Seventy nine mothers of moderate and severe malnourished children were compared with sixty mothers of eutrophic children in a case control design. Nutritional status of the children were evaluated by comparing height and weight measurements with a growt curve and the criterion of malnourishment was that proposed by Gomez (1946). The mental health status of the mothers was assessed by the Adult Psychiatric Morbidity Questionnaire (QMPA), a Brazilian screening instrument.

Mothers of malnourished children showed a higher probability of being probable cases (OR = 2.23, MH = 5.26, $p < 0.03$).

Lower income (OR=4.07, MH= 4.27, $p < 0.050$), lower schooling (OR=3.37, MH= 8.25, $p < 0.01$); and older mothers (OR= 8.23, MH= 10.36, $p < 0.001$); and those mothers with a higher number of siblings (OR= 6.84, MH= 6.99, $p < 0.01$) were also in a higher risk of being cases. When controlling, in a single way, for the above mentioned risk factors, the probability of a malnourished child of having a mother probable mental disturbance was still statistically significant. It is suggested therefore, that regardless of other sociodemographic variables, in this setting, there is an association between the 2 studied variables. Logistic Regression Analysis will be presented.

2647

BODY IMAGE DISTURBANCES IN OBESITY: MEASUREMENT, THEORY AND CLINICAL SIGNIFICANCE

T.Slunecko, D.O.Nutzinger, G. Schönbeck, M. de Zwaan, I. Mendler, E. Pawlik
Department of Psychiatry, University of Vienna, Austria

In several studies it has been shown that anorectic as well as obese patients overestimate their body size. It has been suggested that there is a relationship between the degree of distored body image and the prognosis of these eating disorders.
In this study we used two different video distortion techniques and a paper-pencil-procedure to measure body image disturbances in a total group of 62 overweight and 25 normal weight woman. Obese women overestimate their own body width but not the dimensions of a neutral object. The accuracy of body size estimation was not correlated with emotional attitudes toward the own body, measured by a questionaire. The emotional body attitudes, however, proved to be the variable with most predictive value for successful weight loss and showed significant correlations with depression and other psychological variables. Both the perceptive and emotional aspects of the body image were investigated during 3 months of weight reducing treatment and 12 months of follow-up.

2648

Estudio de los aspectos psicopatológicos y endocrinológicos en un grupo de pacientes obesos y respuesta al tratamiento con fluoxetina.
M. D. Crespo;D. Huertas;LL. Jordà;E. Ochoa;P. Zurita;L. Cuellar;J. Balsa;J. López.
Hospital Ramón y Cajal. (Madrid).

Presentamos un estudio prospectivo en un grupo de 40 pacientes afectos de obesidad exógena realizado por los Servicios de Psiquiatría y Endocrinología de nuestro Hospital. Se pretenden conocer las características sociodemográficas, las pautas alimentarias y el perfil de la muestra a través de pruebas psicológicas (l6PF, test de Zuckerman, test de Bortner, BITE, HARS; HDRS y GHQ), cuestionario psicosocial y de pautas de alimentación y pruebas endocrinológicas (T3, T4, PRL, GH, Cortisol, TSH Glucemia e Insulina y Ac. Antitiroideos. Niveles urinarios de Catecolaminas, 5-HIAA y Creatinina. Test de Fluoxetina.).
El grupo, de edades comprendidas entre 15 y 55 años, distribuido de forma randomizada en 2 subgrupos, se sigue durante 6 meses mediante un diseño cruzado (3 meses reciben tratamiento con fluoxetina –40 mg/día– y dieta; 3 meses sólo dieta).
Se presentan para su discusión los resultados obtenidos hasta el momento actual.

2649

Food intake in major depression: Effect of trimipramine ± chronobiological interventions

R. Stohler, K. Kräuchi, E. Holsboer-Trachsler, M. Hatzinger, L. Sand, and A. Wirz-Justice.
Psychiatric University Clinic, CH-4025 Basel, Switzerland

Affective disorders and antidepressant medication are often accompanied by changes of weight and appetite. Nothing is known about the influence of sleep deprivation on food intake. Light therapy selectively suppresses carbohydrate intake in seasonal affective disorder (SAD). In an ongoing study, we therefore analysed food intake in depressive inpatients by means of a daily questionnaire specially developed to assess food amount, preferences, and taste during main meals and snacks. Body weight was measured weekly. Patients with a major depressive episode were randomly assigned to either treatment with trimipramine (200 mg/d) alone, trimipramine and late sleep deprivation, or trimipramine with light therapy (6-8 p.m., bright white light, 5000 lux) for 6 weeks.

Preliminary results: Patients (N=11, 5m, 6f; mean age 50.5 years, range 40-63) improved significantly by the end of 6 weeks (Hamilton 17-item Rating Scale, mean±SD: 22.0±4.7 to 12.8±7.8; $p<0.001$, one-way ANOVA). They preferred carbohydrate-rich foods (CHO) to protein-rich foods in main meals and snacks. In the course of treatment CHO preference in the evening meal and in morning snacks decreased. Those patients who gained weight during treatment were those who tended to eat more snacks. Thus not only SAD but also depressed inpatients show a selective preference for CHO intake which tends to decrease during recovery.

2650

ELECTRODERMAL ACTIVITY AND PERSONALITY TRAITS IN ANOREXIA NERVOSA PATIENTS

Rivera, M.L., Casas, N. and Lázaro, M.D.
Department of Psychiatry, University of Seville Medical School, Seville, Spain.

In a previous study (Rivera at al., Anal Psiquiat 3:41-44, 1987) we elucidated electrodermal activity changes in patients with anorexia nervosa diagnosed according to the DSM-III criteria. In the present investigation we assessed the relationship between electrodermal activity and some psychodiagnostic variables. Skin conductance level, skin conductance response and habituation to acoustic stimuli were evaluated and related to personality traits estimated by psychological testing. Psychodiagnostic tests administered included the Minnesota Multiphasic Personality Inventory and some other tests chosen to establish a more complete psychological profile of the patients with anorexia nervosa (Machover Test, Beck Depression Inventory, Wolpe Fear Questionaire, STAI, etc). Present study results show the subtle but reliable relationship between observed changes in electrodermal activity and personality traits in anorexia nervosa patients.

Session 405 Free Communications:
Beyond classical antidepressant drug treatment

2651

USE OF TRYPTOPHAN IN THE TREATMENT OF DEPRESSION

Earl M. Stenger, M.D.
Pain Clinic, San Antonio, Texas   USA

Control study was done to determine the effectiveness of Tryptophan as an antidepressant. The patient sample consisted of 83 patients diagnosed with generalized dysthymic disorder (DSM III). The patients were seen on a weekly outpatient basis for seven months.

The patients received insight-oriented psychotherapy and medication. The patient sample was divided into three groups. The first group received Amitriptyline, the second group received Tryptophan and the third group received placebo. Other parameters were equal among patient groups.

Groups receiving Amitriptyline or Tryptophan plus psychotherapy did significantly better than the group receiving psychotherapy plus placebo. There was no statistical difference in the results of the group receiving Amitriptyline and the group receiving Tryptophan.

This study demonstrates that Tryptophan can be as effective as Amitriptyline in the treatment of generalized dysthymic disorder.

2652

THE EFFECT OF SAM IN REDUCING THE ONSET OF ACTION OF IMIPRAMINE

Berlanga Carlos M.D., Heinze, Gerhard M.D., Ortega, Héctor, M.D.
Instituto Mexicano de Psiquiatría. Mexico, D.F. Mexico

One of the main disadvantages of almost all antidepressants is the initial delay in their onset of action. In the last several years, S-adenosyl-methionine (SAM) has prove to have antidepressant properties when administered in its exogenous form. In contrast to other antidepressants it has no notorious side effects and a notable rapid onset of action. One question not yet answered is if given simultaneously with other antidepressant may help reduce the onset of action of the later. To answer this questions the present study was carried with 40 depressed out-patients. All patients were given oral imipramine (150 mg/d) for 8 weeks, and at the same time randomly assigned in a double blind fashion to receive IM either placebo (n=20) or SAM 200 mg. (n=20) daily during the first 14 days. Evaluations were performed every 2 days during the first 2 weeks and then weekly. Improvement was measured with the Hamilton Scale and side effects with a standarized scale. In preliminary results a statistical difference with regard to the onset of the antidepressant effect is found in the SAM group. No differences are found with respect of the side effects. The final results when completing the total sample will be further discussed.

2653

ANTIDEPRESSANT PROPERTIES OF S-ADENOSYL METHIONINE

Lara MC, Leon C, Ortega H and De La Fuente JR.
Instituto Mexicano de Psiquiatria, Mexico, D.F.

The endogenous methyl donor S-adenosyl-methionine (SAMe) has been suggested to have antidepressant properties. In a double-blind clinical trial conducted in 12 patients with DSM-III diagnosis of major depression over a 2-week period we compared the effects of 200 mg/day of intramuscular SAMe vs. those of 75 mg/day of intramuscular chlorimipramine (CIP).

Blind evaluations according to HDRS were conducted at days 3, 6, 9 and 14. At the end of the 2nd week of treatment SAMe patients had reduced their HDRS by 45% whereas CIP patients had reduced it by 59%.

It was concluded that the acute effects of both drugs were similar. Interestingly, two patients in the SAMe group that improved the most had pretreatment low folate levels. It may be that depressed patients with low folate conform the group for which SAMe is the drug to use.

2654

EFFECTIVENESS OF RUBIDIUM IN DEPRESSION THERAPY

Rachele M.G., Scamonatti L., Burrai C.
Cattedra di Psichiatria Sociale, Istituto di
Neurologia, Universita - Cagliari, Italy

Rubidium is an alkaline metal belonging to the same periodic sequence as potassium, sodium and lithium; its physiological properties are very similar to potassium. Rubidium salts are characterised by a long biologic half-life and, in the past, were used in the management of some neuropsychiatric diseases. It has recently been hypothesized that rubidium has a specific antidepressant activity based on its neurochemical, neurophysical and behavioral characteristics, which are contrary to the properties of lithium. A good number of studies, both blind and open, confirm rubidium's efficacy in the treatment of depression. In our open study we worked to test rubidium's effectiveness in depression and also to check its therapeutic effects after a specific period of time after suspension. Thirty female inpatients, aged from 20 to 57 suffering from non-organic depressive disorders according to DSM-III were administered 540mg/die of rubidium chloride for four weeks, and if necessary, benzodiazepine at night. Each was assessed with clinical interview and with HRSD at the beginning, at the end, and one month after suspension.

2655

REPEATED TOTAL SLEEP DEPRIVATIONS DURING AMITRIPTYLINE TREATMENT OF DEPRESSIVE PATIENTS

Werner Ettmeier, M.D., Wolfgang Schreiber, M.D.,
Michael Wiegand, M.D., Dip.-Psychol.

Max-Planck-Institute of Psychiatry,
Kraepelinstr. 10, D-8000 Muenchen, F.R.G.

Total sleep deprivation (TSD) has not become a routine approach in treating depression because its beneficial effects are only short-lasting. In single cases it has been observed that the effect of TSD is less transitory when patients are continuously treated with antidepressants. To examine the clinical effects of this combination, 15 patients with major depressive disorder (DSM-III-R) were treated with amitriptyline 150 mg/d and subjected to TSDs twice weekly for three weeks. Psychopathology, sleep-EEG and several neuroendocrine parameters were repeatedly measured.
Preliminary data indicate a beneficial clinical effect for the combination of drug treatment with repeated TSDs. Intraindividual responses to repeated TSDs varied considerably. Shorter REM latencies in the night preceding TSD seem to predict a response. Our data do not presently point to a predictive value of other neurophysiological or neuroendocrine parameters.

2656

A PLACEBO-CONTROLLED TRIAL OF ROLIPRAME IN SEVERE DEPRESSION: 5-HT MARKERS

M.T. Abou-Saleh, Senior Lecturer in Psychiatry, J. Collins, Senior Registrar in Psychiatry, A. George, Lecturer in Pharmacology and E. Ryan, Research Technician, University Department of Psychiatry, Royal Liverpool Hospital, P.O. Box. 147, Liverpool. England.

The efficacy and safety of Rolipram a cyclic-AMP phosphodiesterase inhibitor was investigated in comparison with placebo in the treatment of severe depression. 39 patients with major depressive disorder (DSM-III) were studied. Following a week's washout period, patients received Rolipram or placebo under double-blind conditions for weeks. The Hamilton Rating Scale for Depression and the Montgomery Asberg Depression Rating Scale were administered at baseline and at weeks 1,2,3 and 4 weeks on the trial.

$5-HT_2$ receptors and 5-HT uptake into platelets were measured at baseline and at days 7, 17 and 28 on the trial. These results will be presented and discussed.

2657

FROM POLYSOMNOGRAPHY TO DOPAMINE:TREATMENT OF DOPAMINE DEPENDENT DEPRESSIONS(DDD) WITH L-TYROSINE.

MOURET J., LEMOINE P., SEBERT P and ROBELIN N.
UCPB , Hôpital du Vinatier, 95, boulevard Pinel, 69677 Bron cedex

Parkinson's disease is one of the best models offered by pathology when trying to relate some specific sleep-polygraphic changes to dopaminergic dysfunction. Of interest is that although depression often represents the earliest symptom of parkinson's disease no clear relationships between dopamine and depression had been developped until recently.(1-2)
Given the occurence on the sleep records of drug-free major depressive patients of qualitative (blepharospasms) and quantitative (reduced average duration of REM episodes) features similar to those described in parkinsonian patients, the possible dopaminergic origin of their depression was tested using a dopamine agonist (piribedil) which administration was followed by a rapid (24 hours) improvement of mood and sleep patterns.After a negative search for clinical symptoms of parkinsonism, we coined the term dopamine-dependent-depression.
We then hypothesized that, as well known from both human and experimental neurochemical data, tyrosine hydroxylase in anatomically or functionnally intact DA neurones was,due to compensatory hyperactivity, likely to be no longer saturated by endogenous tyrosine.
Administration of l-tyrosine to DDD patients who gave their informed consent induced a rapid (less than one day) and long-lasting (more than 3 years) improvement of mood and sleep patterns. Such a treatment is ineffective in other types of depression except those associated with narcolepsy, a genetically determined disease the symptoms of which are controlled by l-tyrosine administration.
Some associated clinical characteristics allow the diagnosis of DDD : inextinguishible glabelar reflex, agitated sleep, a stressfull life, reduced or absent red meat intake, anhedonia, and major depression without loss of self-esteem.

1- MOURET, J., LEMOINE, P., MINUIT, M-P.Sleep polygraphic, clinical and therapeutic markers of dopamine dependent depressions. C.R.Acad. Sci. Paris, t.305,III, 301-306, 1987
2- MOURET, J., LEMOINE, P., MINUIT, M-P., and ROBELIN,N. Immediate and long-lasting treatment of dopamine dependent depressions by L-tyrosine. Aclinical and polygraphic study. C.R.Acad. Sci. Paris, t.306,III, 93-98, 1988
3- MOURET, J., LEMOINE, P.,SANCHEZ,P., ROBELIN,N., TAILLARD,J and CANINI,F., Treatment of narcolepsy with L-tyrosine. The Lancet, Dec 1988, 1458-1459.

2658

NEUROENDOCRINE EFFECT OF TRYPTOPHAN: RELATIONSHIP TO CLINICAL FEATURES & OUTCOME IN DEPRESSION

A.K. Upadhyaya, J.F.W. Deakin, I. Pennell, Department of Psychiatry, Withington Hospital, Manchester, U.K.

Prolactin (PRL) and Growth Hormone (GH) response to L-Tryptophan infusion was studied in 31 patients of Major Depressive Disorder and 22 controls. The peak rise of GH (ΔGH) was blunted only in the patients with endogenous depression according to Newcastle criteria. The blunted ΔGH was also associated with better response to antidepressant. The peak rise of PRL (ΔPRL) was heavily influenced by weight loss and bore little relationship with clinical features or outcome. There was no difference in the basal or the peak rise in plasma tryptophan (TRP or ΔTRP) level between the depressed and the control group. In the depressed group the basal TRP level was lower in the patients with better response to antidepressant. However the ΔTRP was poorly correlated with ΔGH.
In conclusion, the study shows evidence for a presynaptic deficit of 5-HT function in depression, which allows antidepressants to exert a therapeutic effect. Independent of the presynaptic deficit, the blunted ΔGH may be a marker for endogenous depression, indicating either a disturbance at the level of 5-HT receptors or beyond in the hypothalamus.

2659

5-HT$_{1A}$ RECEPTOR FUNCTION IN DEPRESSION (DP), PANIC (PD) AND OBSESSIVE-COMPULSIVE DISORDER (OCD)
K.P. Lesch, S. Mayer, J. Disselkamp-Tietze, A. Hoh, A. Schmidtke, M. Osterheider
Dept. of Psychiatry, Füchsleinstr. 15, 8700 Würzburg, FRG
To assess the role of the 5-HT$_{1A}$ receptor subtype in thermoregulation, various doses of ipsapirone (IPS), a centrally acting compound with high affinity and selectivity for 5-HT$_{1A}$ receptors, were administered to normal subjects. The specificity of the action of IPS was evaluated using 5-HT receptor antagonists. In 6 men IPS dose-dependently decreased oral body temperature from 4.7 ± 6.3 to -53.6 ± 9.3 °C min ($p < 0.001$) at a dose of 0.3 mg/kg. In 6 women and 3 men the nonselective 5-HT receptor antagonist metergoline partially blocked the hypothermic ($p < 0.05$) to IPS. The nonselective ß-adrenergic and stereoselective 5-HT$_{1A}$ receptor antagonist (±)-pindolol completely antagonized IPS-induced hypothermia ($p < 0.001$). The selective ß$_1$-adrenoceptor antagonist betaxolol did not alter the hypothermic to IPS. The results establish that IPS produces a dose-related hypothermic response indicating agonist properties at the presynaptic (somato-dentritic) 5-HT$_{1A}$ receptor, while (±)-pindolol completely antagonized hypothermic responses following IPS, indicating antagonist properties at this receptor subtype. Presynaptic 5-HT$_{1A}$ receptor function was assessed in DP, PD and OCD using this thermoregulation paradigm. Compared with controls (57.2 ± 8.3 °C min), hypothermic responses to IPS were attenuated in drug-free patients with DP (20.8 ± 3.6 °C min; $p < 0.01$) and PD (15.4 ± 4.4 °C min; $p < 0.01$), while no difference was found in patients with OCD (48.5 ± 14.3 °C min; ns). These preliminary findings suggest an impaired 5-HT$_{1A}$ receptor function in DP and PD, but close to normal function of this 5-HT receptor subtype in OCD.

2660

EPIDEMIOLOGY OF SEASONAL AFFECTIVE DISORDERS

Siegfried Kasper, Thomas A. Wehr, Norman E Rosenthal. Psychiatric Department of the University of Bonn, FRG National Institute of Mental Health, Bethesda, USA

Depressions that recur on an annual basis in winter and summer have been termed seasonal affective disorders (SAD) and been described in several studies. In an effort to use a standardized approach for obtaining information on behavioral seasonal variations in humans we conducted a series of epidemiological studies in random samples in Montgomery County/USA as well as in different latitudes. For the center in Washington D.C. we found that 92 % of the population noticed seasonal changes of mood and behavior to varying degrees. For 27 % of the population seasonal changes were a problem, and 5 to 10 % of the general population - depending on the case finding definition - rated a degree of impairment equivalent to that of patients with SAD. The seasonal pattern of "feeling worst" exhibited a bimodal distribution with a greater winter and a substantially lower summer peak (ratio 4.5:1). Multivariate statistical analyses demonstrated that younger females who have a problem with the changes with the seasons and who feel worse on short days tended to exhibit the highest seasonality scores. The results of the multicenter study carried out at different latitudes in USA revealed that significantly higher rates of winter SAD and its subsyndromal form were found in more northern latitudes. It is apparent from our studies that SAD represents the extreme end of the spectrum of seasonality that affects a large percentage of the general population.

Session 406 Free Communications:
General hospital psychiatry

2661

ANXIETY AND DEPRESSION IN A PSYCHOLOGICAL CLINIC OF GENERAL HOSPITAL

Xu Jun Mian, M.D. Department of psychiatry Shanghai Medical University, Shanghai, China

The paper reports an epidemiological observation on anxiety disorders and depressions in a psychological clinic of general hospital in Shanghai during the past two years. Of 1013 patients, 298 patients were diagnosed as anxiety disorders (29.42%) and 190 patients were with depression (18.76%). In 275 cases with anxiety disorder, phobic disorder (26.18%), other anxiety disorder (41.82%), obsessive compulsive disorder (30.91%) and posttramatic stress disorder (1.09%) were included. In 181 cases with depression, most cases were in mild form and 8.84% of them were bipolar. This report suggests that the anxiety disorders and depressions in China are not uncommon as the past reports showed. Since all these patients are nonpsychotic, they would not like to go to a psychiatric hospital for seeking help. Developing the service as a psychological clinic in general hospital will provide an opportunity for such patients to get the help.

2662

RESULTS OF ONE YEAR ACTIVITY OF A CONSULTATION-LIAISON PSYCHIATRY SERVICE IN THE GENERAL HOSPITAL
Castellet y Ballarà F.,Valitutti R.,Sbona I.,Bauco A.R.,Piccione M.
Istituto di Psichiatria, Università "La Sapienza" Roma, Italy.

After one year activity of the Consultation-Liaison Psychiatry Service of the Polyclinic Umberto I of Rome, data have been collected by means of a standardized database form elaborated for computer based statistical analysis.
From the studied sample, coveringthe period 1/1/88 -12/31/88, consisting in a unselected consecutive series of 800 patients, symptoms regarding the various mental functions through a duplicated diagnostic interpretations (DSM III-R and Descriptive-phenomenological) have been taken into consideration. Besides the demographic features, the social-economical status, the medical diagnosis and the consultant psychiatrist 's disposals have been studied.
In conclusion it is noted that, thanks to the efficiency and continuity of such a service, many admissions can be avoided in psychiatric, medicine and surgery wards, and that a relationship of positive collaboration between colleagues helps the understanding of the patient from a certainly more correct point of view.

2663

MENTAL ILLNESS IN A HOSPITAL'S GENERAL PRACTICE CLINIC IN TAIWAN.
Tai Ann Cheng, M.D., Ph.D.(London) Department of Psychiatry, National Taiwan University, Taipei, Taiwan, R.O.C.
   Aims of the present study were to investigate the psychiatric morbidity, characteristics of attendants with such morbidity, and the psychiatric case finding practice of physicians in a hospital's general practice clinic in Taiwan.
   A random sample (n=180), aged 15 and above, was drawn from consecutive attendants of the clinic. They first received a general health enquiry including their chief problems and previous illness behavior. Following the medical service given by physicians, all of them were separately interviewed by a psychiatrist using the Chinese version of the Clinical Interview Schedule.
   96.1% of the total sample were found to have entirely physical chief complaint(s). The total prevalence of mental disorders was 61.1% (s.e. 3.6%) with no sex difference. The most prevalent diagnostic entity was neurotic disorder (56.1%). 24.4% of the sample were identified by the physicians as having certain psychiatric illness. The rather low validity of physicians' case finding against the psychiatrist's diagnosis was mainly attributable to a very low sensitivity figure (30.9%). Various possibilities related to the low case finding rate of physicians were enquired and discussed. The need to improve psychiatric case finding and preventive measures in general practice settings were stressed.

2664

TREATMENT OF PSYCHIATRIC IN-PATIENTS IN GENERAL HOSPITALS
Adnan A.Fadhli
Mental Health Care - University of Baghdad Centre
Iraq

For the first time psychiatric patients were admitted to a general hospital in Baghdad. Some beds were allocated for this purpose without the other necessary facilities of a comprehensive psychiatric unit. With these limitations 218 patients were admitted within two years and only 14 were referred to mental hospitals. Sixty patients were admitted with attempted suicide. It is felt that more effort should be made to establish a comprehensive psychiatric unit within Medical City Teaching Hospital.
In the past few decades the treatment of psychiatric illnesses and emotional disturbances have made impressive strides forward. The advances in various physical and psychological methods of treatment, the increasingly impartial attitude of people to psychiatric illness, as well as the improvement in the setting and environment where treatment is taking place, all contributed to this progress.

2665

ORGAN TRANSPLANTATION: PSYCHIATRIC ASPECTS

Owen S. Surman, M.D.
Massachusetts General Hospital, Boston, MA, USA

   Organ transplantation is a growing surgical subspeciality with challenging clinical and ethical considerations for psychiatric consultants.

   Through recognition and treatment of perioperative psychological impairment the transplantation psychiatrist facilitates access to surgical care and promotes rehabilitation.

   In formulating selection criteria it is essential for psychiatrists to acknowledge the limit of their predictive skills.

2666

STAFF PERCEPTIONS IN THE CARE OF COLOSTOMISED PATIENTS

S. Daini, B. Galimberti, M.F. Coletti, M. Pescatori

Università Cattolica del S. Cuore, Rome, Italy

Rehabilitation and counseling of colostomised patients have been extensively studied from psychological and psychiatric points of view (Morrow, 1976; Sandei, 1983). However, there is less experimentation on patient's image and identification processes of medical and nursing staff caring them.
So, we studied groups of doctors and nurses, on the hypothesis that patients' image could be different according to their basic pathology (cancer vs inflammatory bowel diseases) and to professional role of staff.
111 Ss (63% surgeons, mean age 37 yrs and 37% nurses, mean age 33,7 yrs) were studied by Semantic Differential, measuring affective meaning of a series of concepts concerning Self, image of stomised Patients, and clinical work. Results were analysed by analysis of variance, comparing medical and nursing staff.
Both groups described Self concept as significantly distant from stomised patients and from rehabilitation and follow-up activities, that were devalued and involved in difficulty to hold powerlessness feelings. Surgeons appeared more sensitive than nurses to cancer patients' depression.
Problems in emotional relation with colostomised patients are discussed as expression of defense mechanisms affecting professional performance, and their possible solution as a guideline for consulting Psychiatrist.

2667

TEACHING, LEARNING AND CONSULTING

Luca Alverno, M.D.
Associate Clinical Professor of Psychiatry
Medical College of Wisconsin
Chief, Psychosomatic Liaison Consultation Service
Zablocki VAMC, Milwaukee, Wisconsin

What is the hallmark of *Consultation-Liaison* Psychiatry? A dialogue is entertained with an imaginary resident in psychiatry over the peculiarities of this subspecialty. An example is that patients seen by consultation psychiatrists do not necessarily present with (diagnosable) psychiatric disturbances.

The steps of the *consultation process* are elucidated, paying attention to usually overlooked, but very important clues such as signs of visitors, meal trays (used or untouched) and observing patients at meal times.

Semi-humorous advice is offered, with emphasis on not being in the way of other hospital workers, avoiding irritating remarks when writing the consultation notes, or, put differently, trying to *facilitate*, rather than hamper, the function of that complex organism called *General Hospital*.

Consultation-Liaison is a wonderful *exercise* for students and young doctors of all medical specialties where the psychiatrist is in direct contact with medicine and with his non-psychiatric colleagues. The primary scopes of consultation liaison are clinical care, education and research. *Education* has its special characteristics within the liaison programme, since it includes the teaching of psychiatric methods, psychosocial, cultural, *ecological* influences, and clinical comprehensiveness in health and disease in general to *non-psychiatric staff* as well as to psychiatric trainees and members of the psychiatric profession and related disciplines (Destounis, N. 1971, 1978, 1986).

2668

THERAPEUTIC ENVIRONMENT IN ICU: BASIC OR DIFFERENTIATED INTERVENTION MODELS IN CLP
BARBOSA, A. and CARDOSO, G.
HOSPITAL DE SANTA MARIA, LISBOA, PORTUGAL

The authors investigate the most relevant environment and psychopathological problems in two Intensive Care Units-Coronary (CCU) and Burnt Patients (BCU)- trying to establish a theoretical model of intervention. They analyse the results of 116 crisis situations they were called to attend, during one year, as Psychiatric Liaison Consultants. Data were collected by means of clinical semi-structured interview, staff attitudinal scale (SAS) and Moos questionnaire (WAS). They found as the most frequent environmental problems: the isolation with little contact with the family, the technological environment and the lack of personal objects in CCU; isolation strict protective measures against infection and permanent therapeutic manipulations in BCU. The most frequent psychopathological situations in both units were adjustment disorders with anxious and depressed mood and with disturbance of conduct. The most common attitudes of the staff faced with psychiatric disturbance were: anxious therapeutic hyperactivity and low tolerance level to non compliant patient behaviour, with hostility, rejection or passivity, in both units. They found a high agreement (mainly in CCU) between the patients and the staff satisfaction with a higher score in the following sub-dimensions: involvement, practical problems orientation and order. Their theoretical intervention model is basically centred in the creation of a psychological therapeutic environment facilitating the verbalization of phantasies related to the clinical situation. Due to different traumatic situations, personality types and mean time of permanence in the units their psychotherapeutic intervention differed: in CCU it was more centred on tranquilization here and now and in BCU more directed to clarification of previous organizing phantasies.

2669

EMOTIONAL ASPECTS OF CARDIAC TRANSPLANTATION

J. Boman Bastani, M.D. and Nilufer Vajarund
Bryan Memorial Hospital, Lincoln, Nebraska - USA

Cardiac Transplantation is not only a physical ordeal, it has strong psychological and financial implications. This paper describes the process of cardiac transplantation in which psychological complications may occur.

The transplantation is perceived as an on-going process from the time of diagnosis of end stage heart disease when the psychiatrist is called on to play a significant role with his medical peers in determining the eligibility of the candidate. The psychiatric symptoms (depression, anxiety) associated with the stress of the illness and arising from the decompensating cardiac status (delirium, organic hallucinosis) play a significant role, but are not the sole criteria for exclusion from identifying them as transplant candidates.

Psychiatric manifestations after surgery are seen from immediate post operative to several months after the transplant and the candidate being assymptomatic. Changes brought about by the medications and its side effects, distortions in self-image (real and imagined), upheaval in inter-personal relationships, threat of superimposed infection with changes in lifestyle are significant stresses seen in referrals to the psychiatrist by the Heart Team. The common psychiatric manifestation seen by the Heart Transplant Team and the treatment approach adopted will be discussed with appropriate examples.

2670
TESTING A SPECIAL NURSING ASSESSMENT FORM FOR MENTAL PATIENTS
Raya A, Priami M, Andrea S, Kalokerinou A, Androulaki O, Brokalaki H, Halkiadaki H, Matziou V, Agtzidou A, Galactopoulou S, Korkou P, Zervou A, UNIVERSITY OF ATHENS DEPT OF NURSING, ATHENS, GREECE.

Object of the study: To test a form of nursing assessment of mental patients for use as a means to assess their nursing needs and as a basis for planning, implementation and evaluation of their personalized holistic nursing care.

Methodology: Nursing assessment of 548 mental patients in mental hospitals and psychiatric departments of general hospitals, by observation, interviewing and completing a questionnaire followed by a concluding statement about the nursing needs of each patient.

Results: This is an on-going research in the stage of statistical analysis of the data, expected to be completed by next October. The indentified patients'nursing needs will be classified and studied in two categories: somatic and psychological, each having nine subcategories. Mental patients will be divided and studied in two groups: the general hospital group and the mental hospital group, to facilitate comparisons. It is hoped that the nursing conclusions drawn from this research study, being the first in Greece, will be used for the promotion of psychiatric nursing education, practice, and further research.

Session 407 Free Communications:
Effects of drugs on sleep

2671
CLINICAL AND SLEEP POLYGRAPHIC EFFECTS OF TRIMIPRAMINE IN DEPRESSED PATIENTS

Jacques MOURET, Patrick LEMOINE, Marie-Paule MINUIT, Patrick SANCHEZ and Jacques TAILLARD.

Clinical Unit of Biological Psychiatry, Hôpital du Vinatier, BRON and Physiology Department Université Claude-Bernard LYON France

The subjective sleep improvement of depressed patients treated with trimipramine, as assessed by a multicenter trial, prompted us to perform this sleep polygraphic study on 10 inboard major depressed patients in order to compare objective sleep measurements to their subjective counterparts. Ten patients diagnosed as major depressive according to global clinical impression and classical criteria (DSM III, MADRS) gave they informed consent to participate in this study. After a drug withdrawal period of at least 3 weeks, sleep recordings were performed, after an habituation night, during the last three nights without any treatment (C), and those following days 1 to 3 (I) and 12 to 14 (T) of treatment.

As soon as during the initial treatment period an increase in Total Sleep Time (TST), TST minus Stage I sleep, Stage II sleep, and Sleep Efficiency, together with a decrease in all intra-sleep wake items, took place that persisted at the end of the study. During the T period some additional changes were observed, namely an increase duration of REM sleep and Delta sleep. As opposed to the effects of classical antidepressant, REM related measurements remained unaffected by treatment except for a slight decrease in REM% to TST in I.

Mood changes occured early in the treatment period and improvement at the end of the study was correlated with a Total Sleep Time of less than 420 minutes in the control period.

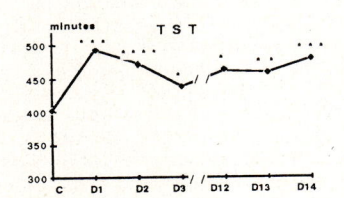

2672
POLYGRAPHIC PARAMETRES FOR SLEEP QUALITY DETECTION: EFFECTS OF TRAZODONE R.C. ON CYCLIC ALTERNATING PATTERN
Mario Giovanni TERZANO, Liborio PARRINO
Sleep Disorder Center, Dept. of Neurology, University of Parma, Italy

On the basis of the macrostructural variations of sleep, an international consensus has provided the guidelines to identify distinct forms of insomnia.
However, satisfactory sleep quality may be achieved by hypnotic drugs that generally alter the architecture of sleep and, conversely, sleep quality may be unsatisfactory in spite of normal traditional parameters.
Under certain perturbed conditions, the lack of macrostructural changes is accompanied by a significant enhancement of the Cyclic Alternating Pattern (CAP) Rate, a microstructural variable that emerges from the EEG organization of the arousal-dependent phasic events of sleep. CAP Rate, detectable in all NREM stages, is extremely sensitive to environmental conditions and correlates inversely with the subjective appreciation of sleep. The improvement of sleep quality by means of certain drugs without specific hypnotic effects, could be actually due to an inhibitory influence on this microstructural variable. As Trazodone is a non-hypnotic compound that determines an amelioration of poor sleep, the aim of our work is to assess the preservative effects of this drug on a normal sleeping brain actively disturbed by a continuous acoustic perturbation.

2673
EFFECT OF THE ANTIDEPRESSANTS LEVOPROTILINE, OPIPRAMOL AND CGP 12.104 A ON SLEEP EEG VARIABLES IN MAJOR DEPRESSION
Möller, H.J., Pelzer, E., Unverzagt C. and Koppetz, R.
Psychiatric Hospital of the University,
D 5300 Bonn/BRD

REM-sleep suppression has been proposed to be the key mechanism underlying treatment response of antidepressant agents. However, trimipramine, an efficacious tricyclic antidepressant with an atypical pharmacological profile, does not suppress REM-sleep. The aim of this study was to investigate the effect of three agents with antidepressive activity but different pharmacological profiles (Levoprotiline, Opipramol, CGP 12.104 A) on sleep EEG parameters (REM-sleep, slow wave sleep, sleep efficiency, sleep continuity, sleep organization).
In 24 major depressive inpatients (aged 18 to 65) seven polygraphic sleep recordings each (two baseline nights after wash-out, three drug treatment nights, two withdrawal nights) and regular ratings (HAMD, KUSTA, Bf-S von Zerssen, subjective sleep questionnaire) were performed.
Our results suggest a relationship between REM-sleep suppression and pharmacological profiles. They do not confirm an association of REM-sleep suppression with clinical response. Further results are in process and will be demonstrated referring to actual concepts of the pathophysiology of depression.

2674

SLEEP LABORATORY STUDIES ON SINGLE DOSE EFFECTS OF SURICLONE

Saletu B., Frey R., Grünberger J., Kurpka M., Anderer P. and Musch B.
Section of Pharmacopsychiatry and Sleep Laboratory Department of Psychiatry, University of Vienna, Austria.

Suriclone (SUR) is a new anxiolytic of non-benzodiazepine structure. Single dose effects on sleep and awakening were investigated in a double-blind, placebo-controlled sleep laboratory study. 16 healthy young volunteers spent ten nights in the sleep laboratory: 1 adaptation night, 1 baseline night and 4 drug nights (placebo; 0,2 mg, 0,4 mg SUR; 2 mg lorazepam (LOR) as reference drug) and 4 subsequent wash out nights (drug-interval:one week). Somnopolygraphic investigations (10:30 PM to 6:00 AM) were commenced half an hour after drug-intake. A self-rating scale for sleep and awakening quality as well as psychometric tests were completed in the morning. Number of awakenings decreased significantly after 0,4 mg SUR and LOR as compared to placebo, which was reflected also in a significantly improved subjective sleep quality. Generally hypnotic effects were most pronounced after LOR, especially in regard to total sleep time and sleep efficiency. Subjective awakening quality, well-being, affectivity, drowsiness, attention and concentration in the morning were significantly better after 0,2 mg and 0,4 mg SUR than after LOR. CFF and muscle strength decreased after LOR only.

2675

MOCLOBEMIDE IMPROVES MOOD IN DEPRESSED PATIENTS WITHOUT SUPPRESSING REM SLEEP

Jaime M. Monti, Paulo Alterwain and Daniel Monti
Dept. Pharmacology and Therapeutics. Clinics Hospital. Montevideo, Uruguay

The effect of moclobemide, a short-acting, reversible, preferential type-A MAO inhibitor (300 mg daily in 3 divided doses) in a 4 week therapeutic trial on the sleep of 10 depressed patients was assessed by polysomnographic recordings.

Compared to placebo, patients receiving moclobemide showed improved sleep continuity as judged by the decrease of wake time after sleep onset and total wake time, particularly during the intermediate and late stages of drug administration. Total sleep time increase was comprised of larger amounts of stage 2 NREM sleep and REM sleep. Withdrawal of moclobemide was followed by a further increase of REM sleep although values did not surpass these observed in adults with normal sleep.

Clinical efficacy of moclobemide was confirmed by the results from the Hamilton depression rating scale, Beck scale and self-evaluation rating scale all of which showed significant improvements in symptoms of depression. There were no significant changes in vital signs including blood pressure and heart rate.

2676

Effects of Lipophilic vs Nonlipophilic Drugs on Nightime Sleep

Kales, A., Bixler, E.O., Manfredi, R.L., Vela-Bueno, A., Vgontzas, A., Pennsylvania State University College of Medicine, Hershey, Pennsylvania, U.S.A.

Several commonly used classes of drugs such as beta-blockers and HMG-CoA reductase inhibitors have been reported to cause disturbed sleep. Sleep disturbances appear to be in part related to a drug's capacity to enter the CNS, which in turn, is highly dependent on its degree of lipid solubility. We assessed in the sleep laboratory the effects on sleep of two drugs with low lipophilicity, nadolol and pravastatin, and a highly lipophilic drug, lovastatin. Nadolol was administered for 4 weeks in a 32-night experimental protocol in 6 patients with mild hypertension. Lovastatin and pravastatin were administered for 2 weeks in a 22-night protocol in groups of 6 subjects each. Neither dose (20 and 80 mg) of nadolol had a disrupting effect on sleep, whereas the 80 mg dose improved sleep efficiency and also had a REM sleep-enhancing effect. The administration of pravastatin was not associated with sleep disturbance. In contrast, significant disturbance of sleep occurred during the administration of lovastatin [significant increase of wake time after sleep onset and also a significant increase of stage 1 (light) sleep]. This potential for lovastatin to produce sleep disturbances needs to be assessed further in clinical populations.

2677

Effects on Dreaming of Two Beta-Blockers (Nadolol vs Propranolol)

Kales, A., Bixler, E.O., Vela-Bueno, A., Manfredi, R.L., Soldatos, C.R., Pennsylvania State University College of Medicine, Hershey, Pennsylvania 17033 U.S.A.

The potential of beta-blockers to induce CNS side effects appears to be related to their degree of lipophilicity. Among the most common side effects are sleep disturbances, with nightmares among the most frequently reported. To assess the effects on dreams of beta-blockers with various degrees of lipid solubility, we compared propranolol (high lipophilicity) with nadolol (low). Both drugs were studied at a dose of 40 mg in the sleep laboratory according to an 18-night protocol to evaluate the initial and short-term (nights 5-11) and intermediate-term (nights 12-18) effects as compared to baseline (nights 1-4). With short-term administration propranolol induced significant increases in dream vividness, violence and dream color and a significant decrease in dream pleasantness. In contrast, nadolol resulted in significant reduction in dream emotionality, pleasantness, color, violence and physical activity. Thus, our results point to a decrease of the emotional, sensory and motor characteristics of dreams with nadolol, probably as a result of the general decrease in autonomic arousal and possible resultant mild sedation. In contrast, propranolol resulted in an increase in dream vividness, violence and color, which is consistent with clinical reports of nightmares, which perhaps relate to partial agonist effects of the drug.

2678
SLEEP LABORATORY STUDY OF THE EFFECTS OF ZOLPIDEM IN INSOMNIAC PATIENTS

Jaime M. Monti and Daniel Monti

Dept. of Pharmacology and Therapeutics. Clinics Hospital. Montevideo, Uruguay

Zolpidem is an imidazopyridine which interacts with the GABA receptor-benzodiazepine receptor complex, having biochemical characteristics and regional distribution of the W1 subtype. The effect of zolpidem (10 mg) on the sleep of patients with persistent psychophysiological insomnia was assessed by polysomnographic recordings. An improvement in sleep with no rebound insomnia was observed during a two week period of drug administration. Wake time after sleep onset was reduced after one week and increased after two weeks, whereas sleep latency remained reduced.

Zolpidem markedly increased the duration of stage 2 sleep without affecting either slow wave sleep or REM sleep. Subjective evaluations of sleep improvement correlated well with sleep laboratory findings. Zolpidem did not impair patient's immediate memory or psychomotor performance the morning after its administration. Side-effects during the period of drug administration included drowsiness, fatigue and headache. They were mild or moderate and wore off soon after awakening.

2679
Trazodone: its effects on sleep and penile erections during sleep in healthy young adults.

J. Catesby Ware, Ph. D., A.C.P.

Eastern Virginia Medical School, Norfolk, VA

Trazodone (TRZ) because of its unique pharmacological activity, may potentiate sleep and penile erections.

Method: Six young normal volunteers participated in a double-blind, active drug and placebo-controlled, crossover study. Subjects completed three five-night evaluation periods. Trimipramine (TRI) was used as the active-control AD.

Results: TRZ increased the amount of deep sleep (stage 4) (TRZ-24%; TRI=18%; PLA=17%). TRZ subjects also had less fragmented sleep. There was no significant suppression of REM sleep (TRZ=21%; TRI=20%; PLA=24%). TRZ increased erectile activity as indicated by more minutes of total tumescence time (TRZ=223; TRI=145%;PLA=112) and delayed detumescence. A significant drug-by-night interaction indicated a dose response to TRZ.

Discussion: The increase in deep sleep and the lack of distortion of normal sleep patterns, e.g., no suppression of REM sleep, suggest that TRZ has the potential to be used as a hypnotic. However, follow-up with insomnia patients is necessary. In addition, TRZ dramatically increased penile erection time during sleep. The alpha adrenergic blocking activity of TRZ and the lack of anticholinergic activity, which when present may suppress REM sleep from which erections normally occur, are hypothesized to be important factors. The potential for use as an anti-impotency agent needs to be further investigated.

Session 408 Free Communications:
Pervasive developmental disorders

2680
INTERPERSONAL PERCEPTION IN AUTISTIC CHILDREN

Ladisich, W., Hollmann, S., Oppolzer, A.

Universitätsklinik f. Neuropsychiatrie d. Kindes-und Jugendalters, Vienna, Austria

24 autistic, 23 retarded, 30 normal children and available parents were investigated. They had to undergo tests for recognition of facial emotional expression and for tachistoscopic perception (TP). The normal children were superior to retardates and autists in both emotion recognition (ER) and TP whereas there was no difference between the two latter groups. When matched according to age, sex and intelligence, however, autists were significantly inferior to nonautistic children in both tasks. The mothers of normal children showed more ability in ER than mothers of retardates. In TP the mothers of normal children were superior to the mothers of autists. The lower performance of autists in TP appears of particular interest. TP showed a highly significant correlation with ER in children but not in adults. Thus TP can be hypothesized to be responsible for an impaired development of ER in autists.

2681
SEROTONIN AND AMINO ACID CONTENT IN PLATELETS OF AUTISTIC CHILDREN

L.H.ROLF, F.Y.HAARMANN, G.G.BRUNE, H.KEHRER[*]
University of Münster, Department of Neurology, [*]Department of Psychiatry, 4400 Münster (G.F.R.)

Human platelets are established models for monoamine and amino acid containing neurons. The hitherto existing results concerning serotonin (5-HT) in platelets from autistic children (A) are contradictory. As well elevated as decreased platetet 5-HT was reported. This might depend on relatively small investigated groups of patients. Until today no amino acid researches in autistic children have been performed. The aim of this study was to investigate platetet 5-HT of a greater number of age limited patients and furthermore to investigate possible alterations of amino acid turnover of glutamic acid (GLT), glutamine (GLN), aspartic acid (ASP) and gamma-aminobutyric acid (GABA).

Group A consisted of 29 children (22 m; 7 f; mean of age 10,5 ± 2,9 SD years), the control group (C) consisted of 14 children (8 m; 6 f; mean of age 11,5 ± 2,0 SD years). Platelet separation and determination of platelet 5-HT was performed by method of Weissbach et al. and platelet amino acid was analyzed according to Lenda et al..The results are presented in the table below (calculation of 5-HT and amino acids in pm/10^8 pl.; statistics: Student-t-test, s = significant, ns = not significant).

	5-HT	GLT	GLN	ASP	GABA
A(n=29)	45,0 ± 15,7	24,7 ± 6,6	10,7 ± 8,7	6,0 ± 2,4	1,5 ± 1,1
C(n=14)	31,4 ± 9,1	31,8 ± 6,9	13,8 ± 2,9	7,5 ± 2,3	1,8 ± 0,6
stat. s/ns	p < 0,0025 s	p < 0 0025 s	p < 0,005 s	p < 0,05 s	p < 0,20 ns

Platelet 5-HT was significantly increased and amino acids were significantly decreased (excepted GABA) in autistic children as compared to controls. The data from platelets may be an index of elevated 5-HT and of reduced amino acid brain turnover in autism.

Weissbach H, Redfield BG: J.Biol.Chem. 235, 3287-3291 (1962)
Lenda K, Svenneby G: J.Chromatogr. 198, 516-519 (1980)

2682

SPECT AND AEP STUDIES IN CHILDHOOD AUTISM

M. ZILBOVICIUS, B. GARREAU, B.M. MAZOYER,
C. RAYNAUD, N. TZOURIO, G. LELORD, A. SYROTA.
SHFJ Orsay, H. BRETONNEAU Tours, France.

Modifications of auditory evoked potentials (AEP) have already been shown to correlate with clinical symptoms (Bruneau.N. and al. Electroenceph. Clin. Neurophysiol. 1987: 584-589). To investigate cortical response of cerebral blood flow (rCBF) to auditory stimuli, 2 groups of autistic children, whose AEP showed a normal (6 cases) and abnormal (5 cases) modulation, were studied with single photon emission computerized tomography (SPECT) and 133-Xenon following a light premedication. Three rCBF measurements were made - at rest during simple tonal 80db binaural auditory stimulation and while listening to music. During the 80db stimulation rCBF was significantly decreased in all patients in the left postero-superior temporal cortex; on these patients only children with abnormal AEP showed a significant rCBF increase in the right latero-frontal and infero-temporal cortex; music stimulation induced a significant rCBF decrease in the left superior temporal cortex in all patients.
Correlations observed between AEP and rCBF changes during auditive stimulation provides additional data to the physio-pathology of autism.

2683

PROGNOSIS OF INFANTILE AUTISM IN JAPAN:
THE OUTCOME IN ADOLESCENCE AND ADULTHOOD

Kosuke Yamazaki, Masatugu Hayashi, Issei Takamura, Johji Inomata and Humio Matuda
Dept. of Psychiatry, Tokai Univ. School of Medicine, Kanagawa, Japan.

In recent years, with the accelerated development of the biological studies on infantile autism, concrete methods for its therapy and guidance have been outlined, and emphasis has shifted to the importance of skill training in everyday life, in school, on job, and in society.
At our clinics, 614 cases of infantile autism have been diagnosed since going into operation in 1975, with 199 cases being above age 15 as of April 1, 1988. Cases having reached adolescence and early adulthood vary largely from low-functioning to high-functioning groups.
For elucidating the relationship between long-term prognosis of infantile autism and the content of therapy and guidance, serial guidance was given and observation made, and for the 61 cases in whom evaluation was possible for when they were 18 years old:1)present circumstances and degree of adaptation, 2)course of therapy and its content, and 3)course of education, guidance and its content were surveyed, which will be reported.

2684

HYPERACTIVITY SYNDROME IN CHILDREN : CLINICAL-DYNAMIC AND PATHOGENETIC ASPECTS
V.Kovalev,V.Krasov,G.Mendes,M.Uzbekov
Moscow Research Institute of Psychiatry, Moscow, USSR

The hyperactivity syndrome (HS) in children and adolescents attracts attention of investigators due to its prevalence (3-10% of junior children) and insufficient existing knowledge of its dynamics, outcome and pathogenetic mechanisms. By means of clinical-dynamic, neuropsychological and clinico-biochemical investigations of 150 children with HS two unfavourable prognostic variants of the syndrome have been found: /1/ in 2/4 of patients, characterized by gradual transformation into deviant behavior of the affective-excitable type, and /2/ in 1/4 of patients, characterized by school maladjustment caused by borderline mental deficiency (IQ 70-75). Biochemical data on catecholamine and indolamine excretion levels have revealed the role of impaired serotonin metabolism in the pathogenesis of HS. The latter should be accounted for while choosing an adequate therapy.

2685

THE SHIFTER FUNCTION OF ANGUISH IN CHILDHOOD
J.B.Orler, J.B.Garre, J.P.Lhuillier, N.S.Thomas, R.Wartel
Centre Hospitalo-Universitaire d'Angers,
Departement de Psychiatrie du Pr. R.Wartel, 49040
Angers Cedex, France

Anguish plays a fundamental role throughout the structural phases in childhood, as underlined by Freud, Klein, Spitz, Glover, Lacan and others. Anguish brings about a shift, a suspension in ideal and imaginary identifications leaving the child in a fading state.
The instant of anguish signifies to the child that he can, in no way assimilate himself to his world of representations and that his being is incongruous with these attributes, with his "havings".
In this ontological experience of anguish, the possibility of a new state is made available and provides the chance of choosing to inscribe a beginning, of exploiting this opening in relation to the discourse into which he is born.
In anguish, the child seizes the vertigo of liberty and faces the undetermined, the unexpected with a free-floating disposition making the emergence of an encounter possible.
Not all is played at birth, nor following the Oedipal period: the child can mark a turning point and at this fertile point of anguish where shifters such as acts, encounters and chance have their origin.

2686
ETHOLOGISCHE UND BIOLOGISCHE ASPEKTE DER KINDER- UND JUGENDPSYCHIATRIE
F.Held
Stuttgart, BRD

Die ethologische und biologische Interpretaton der Symptome des Kindes- und Jugendalters ist Haeufig sowohl diagnostisch als therapeutisch fruchtbarer als ihre tiefenpsychologische Interpretation, die zu Fehldiagnosen und Fehlbehandlungen fuehrt. Zur Diagnostik: Ethologische Betrachtungen zu Depression, Angst, Zwang, Mutismus, Enuresis, Naegelbeissen, Anorexie. - Die larvierten Depressionen. - Die "biogenen" Depressionen. - Die verschiedenen Teilretardierungen und Reifungsdissoziationen des Kindes- und Jugendalters als Ursachen von Verhaltens- und Leistungsstoerungen. Zur Therapie: Die medikamentoes unterstuetzte Reifungs- und Nachreifungstherapie. - Die Verhaltenstherapie als Alternative zur Verhaltenstherapie mit psycholigischen Mitteln. Fazit: dieselbe Symptomatik im Kindes- und Jugendalter kann ebenso aus biologischen Ursachen, die im Kind selbest liegen, als aus biographischen Ursachen, die im Milieu liegen, als aus einem Zusammenwirken beider Ursachenbereiche entstehen.

2687
HERODOLOGY AND SCHOOL PERFORMANCE

Campos, R. F^a. - Deus, G.P. - Perez, C. - Tomasi
Centro de Estudos e Pesquisas Karl Kleist - São Paulo - Brazil.

In the present work done in the "Centro de Estudos e Pesquisas Karl Kleist" we will try to show the relatonship between low school performance and herodology antecedents related to the big group of epilepsy.
For that purpose, it was used a casuistry of a hundred children at school age who were said to present school difficulties, irritability, agitation and socialization difficulty. Children who were attended by a multidisciplinal team received a montly medical - psychiatric attendance the weekly psycological attendance concerning to social assistance, including the leading to other professionals, whonever it is necessary (Occupational Therapy, Phonoaudiology etc..).
The date related to the social-economic rank, as well as the dinamics at home obtained though a field research were considered intervinient variables, since they could increase or decrease a certain characteristic in the child psychological development, but never cause it.
The parents, on their turn.

Session 409 Free Communications:
General issues in Mental Health

2688
SOCIAL CHANGES AND MENTAL DISORDERS IN AN AREA OF SOUTH-ITALY.
S.F. Inglese,B. Mottola di Amato,R.M. Mirarchi.
Service of Mental Health-S.Giovanni in Fiore-Italy.

The Authors point out,in such a geo-cultural area, the relationships existing among mass emigration,the processes of acculturation and the diffusion of psychotic disorders.The processes of social change should cause the dispersion of the cultural heritage,the loss of the defensive function of the old magic-ritual devices as well as the intergenerational anomia within families.In such a "social cradle" the harmonic development of a cohesive cultural identity is not assured any more.On the contrary the processes of change should have a strong traumatic effect on these people weakening their capacity of adaptation to new experiential realities.This situation causes the detaching of a "psychopathological drift" which,in its turn,succeeds in loose= ning the links of social and family solidarity.
All this gives an explanation for the persistence in such a community of a widespread,depressive and persecutor feeling of exstraneousness which can become a factor leading to a psychopathological crise.

2689
AN INVESTIGATION OF THE ATTITUDES TOWARDS THE MENTALLY ILL
Sedat Özkan,Güler Bahadır,Hale İmre
Department of Psychiatry,İstanbul Faculty of Medicine,İstanbul University,İstanbul,TURKEY.

The aim of this study was to investigate the effects of education,socio-cultural level in the attitudes toward the mentally ill and to search into the determinants pertaining to the conception of mentally handicapped in a sample of Turkish community.For this reason,our subjects consisted of two groups:The families of those mental patients who are being treated at the Department of Psychiatry,Istanbul Faculty of Medicine and the students of Istanbul Faculty of Medicine.
The research instrument consisted of a demographic questionnaire referring to place of residence, gender,education,etc.and a questionnaire for measuring attitudes towards the mentally ill and the conception of occupational potential of mentally ill,acceptance of the former patient into the community.
Within this context,the impact of prejudices and superstition-based prejudices on the mental patient were especially researched to understand how information and experiences about mental illness correlated attitude to the mentally ill. The results are discussed within the changing socio-cultural and psycho-social values in Turkey.

2690

"ANALYSIS ABOUT POLITICS AND PSYCHIATRY"

Roger M. Montenegro

APSA - ASOCIACION DE PSIQUIATRAS ARGENTINOS
(ASSOCIATION OF ARGENTINE PSYCHIATRISTS)
Buenos Aires, ARGENTINA

Code N° 90-74-64

Close interdependency between state political decisions and the psychiatric practices and ideologies is described. Some examples through the historical experience of different countries are given.

The author proposes a greater international fluidness among the professionals of mental health care (which would be better assured in the wide discussion spaces outlined by the professional associations), improving the relationships with public powers and with the community(which is better granted in countries and societies with a democratic organization).

Difficulties in operating the necessary reforms in the psychiatric practices are analyzed; they derive from multiple factors, as well as from advances and retrocessions of every process, less dangerous than the rigid iatrogenic institutionalization.

It is concluded that the ethic consideration of every analysis and action is prioritary.

2691

INSTITUTE FOR HEALTH PROMOTION IN THE COMMUNITY OF NEW ZAGREB

V. Starčević, Ž. Kulčar

Institute for Health Promotion
Health Center "New Zagreb", Zagreb, Yugoslavia

The community New Zagreb has 159,000 residents. Age index is 0,319 which means that getting old of the residents has not started. This community is one of 14 communities of the city of Zagreb, capital of SR Croatia. The main principle of the work of the Institute is socialization of the medicine, active participation of the patients in taking care of their health, intersector co - operation and international co - operation. The Institute is engaged in the prevention and fighting hypertension, cardiac diseases, dental carieses, getting out of smoking and a special care is kept of the mental health. There are Clubs of treated alcoholics, being active in each local community and factories and Clubs of schizophrenic patients. We also carry out a program for early detection of charge in behaviour of the youth. All these activities are carried out by the teams and then are centralized in the Institute, which monitors are evaluates the results of these programs.

2692

ABOUT DEISTITUTIONALIZATION IN ITALY
Prof. Bartilotti R., Dott. Alliani D.
Psychiatric Clinic "Parco delle Rose" Rome, Italy

During 1978 in Italy has been promulgated the law number 180 which ratifies the deistitutionalization of psychiatric inpatients. The theory on basis of the law was: mental hospitals have influence on course and chronicization of psychiatric disease. The law 180 do not mention istitutions to build or to maintain for chronic psychiatric inpatients. The AA. after examining the condition and the situation of chronic psychiatric patients in Italy, particularly at Rome, suggest some alternative environment solutions not necessarily in hospital and not necessarily for life, where laid special stress on occupational therapy aimed at getting and allowing a free expression of personality even if a perfect reinstatement in the society cannot be attained.

2693

COMPLIANCE TO TREATMENT PER TYPE OF INSURANCE:
Demetrius A. Trakas, M.D.
Swedish Covenant Hospital, Chicago, IL USA

In a private practice setting - providing outpatient psychiatric services to (1) persons paying individually or by private commercial insurance; (2) members of a Health Maintenance Organization; and (3) persons under the state of Illinois welfare system - 2807 visits were scheduled in 1988. 1947 visits for self-pay patients, 519 visits for welfare recipients and 341 visits for HMO members.
The overall rate of missed visits was 6.9%: 6% for self-pay patients, 7.12% for welfare recipients and 13.28% for HMO members. The demographic data and diagnosis distribution were the same for all three groups.
The private patients as well as the welfare recipients had been referred by their primary care physician, other agencies, clergy, friends that had received our services or had found our offices through the telephone book. All HMO members had no choice but to be seen at our offices according to their policy.
It is concluded that the reason why the HMO patients had the highest rate of attrition was the fact they had no right to choose their own psychiatrist but had to see the psychiatrist assigned by the HMO.

2694
OUTCOME OF SEVERE OBESITY IN FINLAND

Marja Koski M.D.
Hesperia Hospital Helsinki, Finland

The study investigates the epidemiology of obesity in Finland from data collected by the Social Insurance Institution. In 1979 1,047 persons received pension primarily due to obesity, or 2,674 if obesity is included as the first additional illness. Obesity was the second additional illness in 1,696 cases. At the end of 1979 5,390 pensions had been granted at least partly on the basis of obesity.

Anyone aged over 16 having lived in Finland for at least 5 years is insured under the Social Insurance Act and is entitled to a national pension irrespective of nationality.

On 31 December 1979, 834,198 persons received national pension. Most pensions are granted due to mental problems and cardiovascular diseases.

Obesity is studied from the social psychiatric and psychosomatic point of view using epidemiological and psychiatric methods. The number of persons receiving pension due to obesity, and age structure, domicile, social structure, onset of disease, severity, family history of obesity and other concomitant diseases are also investigated. The aim is to determine whether obesity is prevalent in certain areas and to identify common denominators among those retiring because of it.

2695
PROFESSIONALS AND SELF-HELP ORGANIZATIONS

Leichner, P., Hetherington, K.
Douglas Hospital Center, Verdun, Quebec

Self-help organizations (SHO) have been increasing in numbers and gaining an importance over the past two decades. This has largely been due to budgetary restrictions to services, the growing acceptance of systemic interventions such as group, family therapy, and psychoeducation and the biopsychosocial model. Health care professionals seem uncertain as to their roles within these organizations. The purpose of this presentation is to encourage interested professionals to get involved in self-help organization. Self-help groups can provide valuable adjunctive therapy in the treatment of the psychosocial aspects of psychiatric disorders. While giving examples of his personal experience in working within the Anorexia Nervosa an Bulimia Foundation of Canada, the authors will present the obstacles that may face the professional from patients, families and from him or herself. These center around frustrations from the families and patients with the health care system, lack of information leading to inappropriate expectations of what medicine can offer and finally impatience. The professional may him/herself be inadequately trained as a consultant and feel threatened by the members of a SHO, he/she must be able to be willing to share his knowledge and skills as an equal member of a SHO rather than as a professional. Knowing these possible problems can help those interested in making a meaningful contribution within self-help organizations.

2696
PSYCHOLOGICAL DISORDERS IN YOUNG METAL WORKERS: A COMPARATIVE STUDY

Grassi Aldrigo - Falzoni Maria Cristina
Unità sanitaria locale n. 30 -Cento- Italy

The aim of this study is the investigation of the relationship between workers considered to be exposed to mental health risks and psychological disorders.
The subjects chosen are all young males, aged between twenty and twenty nine, resident in the same geographical area for at least ten years and still living with their original family.
From a random process of selection four groups have been formed:
-first group: metal workers exposed to occupational mental health risks (30 persons);
-second group: metal workers not exposed to occupational mental health risks (57 persons);
-third group: full time students (30 persons);
-fourth group: persons unemployed (for at least six months) or seeking their first job (40 persons).
The subjects from each group completed the questionnaire to determine the index of psychological disorders (IDP).
The average IDP-score and the frequency of psychological disorders in the different groups were then calculated and tested statistically.
Significantly higher frequencies and averages have been found in the group of metal workers exposed to mental health risks, while no statistically significant results have been noted in the other groups, including the group of unemployed.

Session 410 Free Communications:
Group psychotherapy: Theory and practice

2697
GROUP PSYCHOTHERAPY WITH INPATIENT PSYCHOTICS

HÜROL,Cem; ÇALAK,Erdoğan; EREN,Nurhan
Psychiatry Dept., Istanbul Faculty of Medicine, Istanbul University

This study was carried out to investigate the effects of group psychotherapy on a group of patients with the diagnoses of schizophrenia and schizophreniform psychosis, who were hospitalized in the Psychiatry Clinic of Istanbul Faculty of Medicine.

The prominent aim of this group approach proposed by Yalom is to improve the problem creating behaviour of the patient and thus enable better social functioning. Each group session is structured so the patients do not experience any confusion and insecurity about what can happen during the session. The aim is to orient the attention, enable communication and improve social skills.

The patients were selected randomly and divided into two groups. Yalom's "Inpatient Group Psychotherapy" was applied to the first group. The second was kept without group therapy as a control group. All the patients were in acute psychotic state and had medication likewise.

The difference of recovery rate between the two groups was assessed blind, using Macc behaviour Scale and Nurse's Assesment Scale. Demographic aspects and the length of stay were also considered.

It was found that the outcome of the patients who were in the therapy group was significantly better than the control group. All the patients showed improvement in their symptoms and behaviour patterns being in the therapy or control group, but this improvement was higher in the former.

2698

THERAPEUTIC FACTORS IN GROUP THERAPY

P. Vostanis, D. O'Sullivan
Uffculme Clinic, Birmingham, England.

This study is intended to evaluate therapists' and patients' perceptions of therapeutic factors operative in analytically orientated group therapy. Two different settings of small groups were assessed: the first one based on daily intensive group sessions (on a day-patient or in-patient basis up to a maximum of a year). The second one an out-patient programme, with groups meeting on a weekly basis. 23 patients and 17 therapists of the intensive programme, and 25 patients and 16 therapists of the out-patient programme took part in the study. The median number of small group sessions was 130 (8-240) for the intensive, and 40 (10-90) for the out-patient sample. Patients and staff members completed Yalom's Therapeutic Factor Questionnaire. The results were statistically analysed. The ranking of the factors was similar in all four samples: catharsis, self-understanding, cohesiveness and interpersonal learning were valued as the most helpful factors. Guidance, family re-enactment and identification emerged as the least helpful ones. There were significant differences in the rating of the 12 factors between the samples. Patients in intensive therapy rated higher six of the factors. Patients valued guidance significantly higher than the therapists, while therapists valued family re-enactment and identification as more helpful.

2699

MEMBERS OF PSYCHOTHERAPEUTIC SELF-HELP-GROUPS

W.D. Braunwarth, R.J. Witkowski, E. Lungershausen
Psychiatrische Universitätsklinik, Schwabachanlage 6
D-8520 Erlangen

In the course of an explorative study we investigated members of psychotherapeutic self-help-groups in the greater Nuremberg area. The data obtained showed that the enormous range of mental disorders and psychic problems represented in these groups included a considerable number of individuals who had a history of endogenic psychoses besides those with neuroses and rather temporary problems.

A great majority had made intensive use of the existing professional psychotherapeutic services before they decided to join a self-help-group. They also turned out to be well informed about psychological/psychiatric issues. Together with the social data these findings demonstrate that members of these groups do not belong to a class of people who have no access to professional psychotherapy.
The expectations related to the group predominantly referred to a process of continual psychosocial learning within a group of equally committed people as well as to the constitution of new interindividual relations.

The main conclusion is that psychotherapeutic self-help-groups may gain even more weight in the future with the stress put on aftercare rather than on primary psychosocial care.

2700

ASSESSMENT OF GROUP ASSERTIVENESS TRAINING IN PSYCHIATRIC PATIENTS

Degleris N., Agathon M., Samuel Lajeunesse B. *

WOLPE defined assertive behavior as the appropriate expression of any emotion excluding anxiety toward subject to better express his opinions toward others, to recognize and to accept the opinions of other people and to express his feelings without aggressivity.
The present study has been carried on an heteregeneous group of patients. It shows, in submary,
- that RATHUS's "30 item Schedule for Assessing Assertive Behavior" which has been translated in French and analyzed is a usefull instrument for assessing assertiveness in psychiatric patients,
- that assertive training, when practiced in a group of patients whatever is the motivation or the degree of assertiveness, appear to be useful in a reasonnable delay, independently of the associated pathology.
Nevertheless, it is necessary to carry out further studies in order to precise the nature of the assertive dimensions which can be treated and the duration of the improvement obtained.

* Clinique des Maladies mentales et de l'Encéphale 100, rue de la santé 75674 PARIS

2701

THE EFFECT OF THE GROUP THERAPISTS'S EMOTIONAL STATE ON THE INITIAL STAGES OF TREATMENT
M. Tsilimigaki, M. Karaolidou, P. Papageorgiou, I.K. Tsegos
Open Psychotherapeutic Centre. Athens, Greece.

A correlation has been attempted between the psychological state of the therapist and the beginning and continuation of psychotherapeutic relationships with patients (in preparation for entering in a group). The emotional state of the group psychotherapists of the Open Psychotherapeutic Centre in Athens has been examined retrospectively for a specified period of time, through the use of a questionnaire based on the Life Events Scale of Holmes and Rahe.
The results were then compared with the number of psychotherapeutic relationships initiated and continued by each therapist during the same period. The first results have shown a positive correlation; that is, the unfavourable emotional state of the therapists, due to significant life events, is directly related to the patient's refusal to start or to continue therapy.

2702

PSYCHOTHERAPY "ON FIELD" IN CRISIS SITUATIONS AMONG MILITARY PERSONNEL
Muscara M.*, Pastena L.**, Stracca M.***
* Difesan, Roma, Italy, **Dept. of Neurological Sciences-University "La Sapienza", Roma, Italy ***Psychology Section of Medical Service of the Italian Navy, Roma, Italy

All hierarchical organizations, like the military, try to find a remedy in adverse situations within their proper system, i.e. increase of authoritative interventions, poor inclination in discussing problems, potentiations of the hierarchical chain. The consequences are often unfavourable for the group. The individuals may react with some automatisms which arise from each personality and eventually became a group behaviour. An alternative could come from a psychological assistance available for "on field" interventions which enable individuals to face different crisis situations. Such interventions aim at making those who have command responsibilities aware of their own difficulties and the conflicts related with their role. This paper shows two examples of our interventions with a team of specialists in two different crisis situations: at the two Navy Recruitment Centers and in a Special unit. The methodology used was the Balint group approach.

2703

COMPOSITE TECHNIQUES IN GROUP PSYCHOTHERAPY WITH CHRONIC PSYCHOTICS. M Freedman, L Aguilar, M Baranda, M Carreiro, G Cosula, S Dimaio, M. Escribano, A Garcia, E Guimarey, S Juarez, L Kuper, N Madariaga, R G Novarini, R Rollan A Zheidan and N Dilorenzo. Hosp Nac T Borda, Bs Aires, Argentina

Group psychotherapy with composite techniques was applied, during three months, to 43 psychotic chronic patients. Each of 10 parameters was scored 0, 1, 2 or 3 according to a specific code prepared by us. Five groups (n= 7,10,9,8,9) were evaluated:

	G 1	G 2	G 3	G 4	G 5	Tot
1) Outward appearance	NS	<0.1%	NS	NS	NS	<0.1%
2) Social integration	<1%	<0.1%	<1%	<2%	NS	<0.1%
3) Works	NS	NS	NS	NS	NS	NS
4) Reality contact	NS	<2%	<0.1%	NS	<0.1%	<0.1%
5) Delir.	NS	NS	<5%	NS	<5%	NS
6) Hallucin.	NS	NS	NS	NS	NS	NS
7) Family integration	<5%	<0.1%	<1%	NS	NS	<1%
8) Attendan.	NS	NS	NS	NS	NS	NS
9) Authorized walks	<0.1%	<0.1%	<0.1%	NS	NS	<0.1%
10) Hospital depart	<0.1%	<0.1%	NS	NS	NS	<0.1%

Chi square test (NS > 5%). Significance level was obtained from the differences between first and last group reunion. These results will be discussed at the Congress.

2704

DROP-OUTS IN GROUP ANALYTIC PSYCHOTHERAPY

Th.Papadakis, V.Apostologlou,Z.Denegri,E.Morarou
Open Psychotherapeutic Centre. Athens, Greece.

A nine year study of early termination in group analytic psychotherapy in relation to several variables(sex, age, diagnostic category, length of stay in the group, age of the group, timing of termination and concurrent therapies), is presented.
Our results, which seem to be in accordance with those of other similar studies, relate early termination to the patient´s psychopathology, to the experience of the therapist, to the age of the group, as well as to the season of the year.

Session 411 Free Communications:
AIDS: Issues related to management

2705

PROBLEMS IN COUNSELLING AND CARE OF HIV-INFECTED HOMOSEXUALS AND HEMOPHILIACS
O.Seidl, M.M.Schneider, M.Ermann
Abt.f.Psychotherapie und Psychosomatik, Psychiatrische Klinik der Universität München, FRG

Counselling and care of HIV-infected persons cause a lot of special problems of transference and countertransference as a result of the precondition of the infection: homosexuality or hemophilia.

The interaction behavior of the infected persons is descriptively analysed, resulting from records of more than 500 contacts of counselling and medical treatment over a period of several years. A BALINT-group with 10 nurses caring especially for AIDS-patients was evaluated with the Core Conflictual Relationship Method.

The main problems of counselling, medical care and nursing are more of a psychological than technical nature. Unconscious mechanismes play an important role. Unfulfilled expectations of one's own competence, feeling of insufficiency and hostility against the patients, problems with one's own sexual identity, overidentification with the patients, and the defense of phantasies in respect of a possible guiltiness as to what caused the disease, will handicap an empathic understanding as a base for psychosocial care.

A supervision which does not neglect the unconscious mechanismes of interaction is necessary for all those who care for patients with AIDS.

2706

COPING MECHANISMS AND SUFFERING IN AIDS PATIENTS
Nuno Felix Costa, Silvia Ouakinin, Maria Luisa Figueira
Dept. of Medical Psychology, Lisbon Medical Sch.
Portugal

The diagnosis of human immunodeficiency virus infection (HIV) is a dramatic event no matter what the clinical stage of the disease. May be the analysis of the predominant coping mechanisms in this situation is relevant to patient's approach.
The aim of our study is to establish correlations between certain coping mechanisms and the degree of suffering assessed by the intensity of the symptoms. We studied one hundred AIDS and HIV + patients from all the risk groups, in and out patients refered by I.D. Department of our general hospital (Hospital Santa Maria, Lisbon). Assessment included besides a clinical evaluation, a psychopathological evaluation using the AMDP IV and V, the Beck's Depression Scale and a inventory of coping strategies specifically developed by ourselves. Our results show a positive correlation between certain degree of denial and a low score in Beck's Depression Scale. Other mechanisms like guilt, suspiciousness, hostility or drug abuse correlate highly with the intensity of symptoms in the AMDP and Beck's Scale. We concluded that psychotherapeutic approach should be cautious and flexible in order to avoid failure of some protective defenses that in another existential context would be maladaptive.

2707

LIFE EVENTS AND SOCIAL SUPPORT IN THE PATIENTS WITH THE AIDS
M.De Vanna, P.Zolli
Clinica Psichiatrica di Trieste, Italia

In those subjects affected by AIDS the coping mechanisms of the disease are heavily conditioned by serious psychological and social implications as well as by some personality traits and by the presence or absence of an adequeate social support. The personal history of the disease is characterized by a whole range of events contributing to the individual and collective anguish of the patients.
The authors have analysed some personality characteristics in a statistical sample of 30 patients with an age ranging from 20 to 40, made up by drug addicts resorting to the EPI, the intensity of the community life of the subject according to the Surtees's Social Support and their life events.
The diagnosis of the anxiety has been made according to the DSM-III-R criteria.
The data, which have been statistically elaborated, have outlined, in the 76% of the subjects, the role of the life events and the difficulties of the patients. The diagnosis results in conditioning the anxious pathology, compromising the patients' ability of coping and favouring their psychoemotional isolation.

2708

DETRESSE PSYCHIQUE AIGUE ET MODIFICATION BIO-CLINIQUE DE L'INFECTION V.I.H.
Dr H. DAOUD - S. KINDYNIS
Service de Psychiatrie Adultes - Hôpital Fernand VIDAL - PARIS

Cette communication relate le suivi psychiatrique en relation individuelle ou lors de thérapeutie familiale de patients toxicomanes ou homosexuels séropositifs ou atteints du SIDA adressés à la consultation ou admis en urgence dans le service.

Nous avons centré notre travail sur l'étude des épisodes aigüs annonçant et précédant une modification de l'équilibre clinique liée au V.I.H. ; chez des patients jeunes, hyper-informés, en fait très à l'écoute de leurs corps, exprimant par ce désarroi psychologique une modification non encore consciente de leur état somatique.

La reconnaissance de ce syndrome et de son étiologie permet d'éviter à ces patients des passages à l'acte suicidaire graves, conséquence d'un "raté" dans la relation psychothérapeutique Celà nécessite bien entendu que les psychiatres prenant en charge ce type de patients soit tout à fait informés de la clinique et de la biologie du SIDA.

2709

AIDS: PROPOSAL OF PSYCHOSOCIAL TREATMENT IN DRUG ABUSERS
R. FAHRER et al.
HOSPITAL DE CLINICAS.UNIVERSIDAD DE BUENOS AIRES
40 drug abuse patients were examined, 20 HIV positives and 20 with somatic disorders not related with AIDS and with a different degree of severity.
It was used: semistructure interviews, GAIS Scale, Karnofsky's Scale, and DSM-III-R diagnostic criteria for the use of psychoactive substance use disorders. In both groups the GAIS average showed a global adaptation to the illness of an ambivalent type. The average of Karnofsky's Scale was 70. Although the whole of the patients reject all kind of psychiatric treatment, 60% of them accepted and fulfilled the clinical treatment adequately.
The psychosocial reaction of drug abuse patients after the HIV positive is similar to the psychosocial one of the drug abusers with another type of somatic disorders. This is more related to the patient's personality structure than to the nature of the somatic illness. This result show us the Internist as the best to treat psychiatric aspects of these patients. Psychiatrists will act as support and trainer of the Internist.
Moreover it would have to be promoted at the General Hospital the organization of high complexity centers which include substance abuse services and AIDS Units for the conduction of special AIDS intravenous drug abuse programs.

2710

NEUROPSYCHIATRIC DISORDERS IN THE ADQUIRED IMMUNEDEFICIENCY SYNDROME (AIDS).
M.D.Crespo, N.Vicente, E.Ochoa, J. Pérez de los Cobos.
Servicio Psiquiatría.Hosp. Ramón y Cajal.

Se realiza un estudio de los pacientes afectados por SIDA ingresados en el Servicio de Enfermedades Infecciosas y vistos por la Unidad de Psiquiatría de enlace del Hospital Ramón y Cajal durante los últimos años.

Del total de 107 pacientes, 84 varones (78%) y 23 mujeres (22%) se estudían las características sociodemográficas, estado de la infección, patología psiquiátrica y tratamiento psiquiátrico.

El 95% de los pacientes eran adictos a heroina vía intravenosa, presentando problemas psicopatológicos un 53%, distribuidos 56% síndrome ansioso, 18% confusión mental, 14% depresión y 41 síndrome de abstinencia y un 6% no psicopatología.

La evolución de los pacientes dos años después de haber sido vistos se ha valorado con los siguientes datos, patología médica y psiquiátrica, número de ingresos, estadío del SIDA, y su situación respecto a la adicción.

2711

THE PSYCHOPHARMACOTHERAPY OF AIDS PATIENTS: A RETROSPECTIVE STUDY.

Di Giannantonio M., Persico A.M., Zeppetelli E., Lestingi L., Mattioni T., Weisert A., Tempesta E.

Dept.of Psychiatry, Catholic University of S.Heart, Rome

The clinical management of AIDS patients often requires that psychiatrists administer psychoactive drugs to relief anxiety, depression, cognitive impairment, psychotic or behavioral disturbances. These patients have been reported to be particularly sensitive to psychotropic drugs and to their side effects. This may be due to several causes. There may be significant variations in parameters that influence the pharmacokinetics of drugs, such as body weight and serum proteins content. At the same time, the CNS of these patients suffers from both HIV neurotropism and frequent opportunistic infections. Finally pharmacological interactions may occur with non-psychotropic drugs.
The aim of our study is to draw some guidelines in order to define a correct approach to the psychopharmacotherapy of AIDS patients. Particular attention will be devoted to drug addicts who are predominant in our sample.

2712

ADJUNCTIVE HYPNOSIS WITH HEMOPHILIC AIDS PATIENTS
Jeanine LaBaw, PsyD & Wallace LaBaw, MD
University of Colorado Health Sciences Center, Denver, Colorado USA

Clinicians have long observed the advantage that calmer patients seem to have over more agitated ones in terms of clinical outcome. The mechanism by which ataraxia contributes to clinical results is getting attention as it is documented in patients with AIDS. Patients seem to thrive better when taught relaxation techniques. This is likely because anxiety exerts a biochemical influence which compromises the immune system. By utilizing hypnosis, which is anxiolytic, patients help their immune system to function at a more optimal level. Hemophiliacs were early recognized as being at high risk for AIDS and it is now known that many are HIV positive. However, many with hemophilia also have an important tool to help resist the illness. Hemophiliacs have been trained to use self-hypnosis in a program begun by the authors and promulgated by the University of Colorado (1968-88). These bleeders are expert in its use and may use their hypnotic skills to modify the seemingly immutable advance of this devastating virus. Cases are presented.

Session 412 Free Communications:
Issues in geriatric psychiatry

2713

Presenile Dementia - Alzheimer's Disease

Fredman, Ralph
Department of Psychiatry
Veterans Administration Medical Center
Beckley, West Virginia, USA 25801

It is a progressive cerebral degeneration with a pathological picture of senility occurring in middle age. It is not inherited. The essential lesion is a diffuse degenerative change of the cerebral cortex involving all its layers. It is most marked in the frontal lobes. There are argentophilic masses. Neurofibrillary tangles are most numerous in various basal nuclei, the thalamus, and the hippocampus.

The onset is insidious. The symptoms are a progressive dementia with apraxia and speech disturbance. Duration of the disease is from one to fifteen years.

The etiology of Alzheimer's Disease is still unknown. Treatment, at present, remains supportive.

2714

"HOMICIDE BEHAVIOUR IN THE ELDERLY"

Dr. Navin Savla,
Claybury Hospital,
Woodford Bridge,
Woodford Green,
Essex. IG8 8BY
UK.

Dr. Andy Souter,
Registrar - UCH
Middlesex,
UK.

Three cases with dangerous homicidal act against their spouse were admitted to psychogeriatric unit. The patients had made a suicidal as well as homicidal attempts. There have been very few studies reported when violence is considered. We have looked at the statistical date of criminal offences in England and Wales and the elderly group comprises about 1% of all violent crimes. The papers by Martin and Roth, Milton Rosenbaum, West, Gibson and Klein, Hunder Gillies, John Lanzkron were reviewed, we were able to compare the crime rates in U.S.A, Scotland and England and there were some international differences. Overall in the over 60 age group homicide is a rare occurrence. The incidence of suicide particularly in men rises with age. It is from this group of patients that 20% of murders suicides arise. It is important for the clinician to consider the possibility of homicide as well as suicide in the elderly. Further research in this area is required.
Poster presentation at International Conference on Affective Disorder - Israel 1987.

2715

PROBLEMS IN AGING INSOMNIA IN GENERAL HOSPITALS INPATIENTS
Bani A.*, Miniati M.**
* U.S.L. 25, Toscana, Italia
** U.S.L. 13, Toscana, Italia

Benzodiazepines (BDZ) are the first choice drugs in the treatment of insomnia. However, during psychiatric liaisons onwards, we can observe an inappropriate large use of these compounds.
The Authors review some problems in clinical management of insomnia.
Distinguishing primary and secondary insomnia they find two wrong attitudes in treatment: first the abrupt discontinuation of hypnotics and second the continuation in prescribing BDZ for long time after discharge with dependence instauration.
Management of withdrawal is suggested.

2716

Dementia (DSM-III-R) After Chronic Solvent Exposure
von Bose, M.J., Zaudig, M.
Psychiatric Outpatient Department
Max-Planck-Institute for Psychiatry, Munich

Since the early seventies numerous reports, especially from the Scandinavian countries, have indicated a growing incidence of dementias after chronic exposure to mixtures of organic solvents. Symptomatology varies widely, but from a psychiatric point of view can best be summarized as: dementias with cognitive and neurological deficits, neurasthenic and neurotic syndromes. By means of a single case study typical features of clinical symptomatology and course are described with an emphasis on psychometric assessment and difficulties in diagnostic classification according to the new classification system DSM-III-R. In a review the need for appropriate preventive measures and a high index of suspicior is pointed out.

2717

EFFECT OF ANTIOXIDANTS THERAPY IN ELDERLY POPULATION AND IN CHRONIC ALCOHOLICS
Sram R.J., Binkova B., Topinka J., Kotesovec F., Hanel I., Klaschka J.
Psychiatric Research Institute, Prague, Czechoslovakia

The aging process may affect the effectiveness of DNA damage and the process of lipid peroxidation (LPO). UDS and LPO were studied as characteristics informing about a possible injury by free radicals. The longitudinal study on elderly population was carried out in order to determine UDS and LPO level in relation to the age and sex. As a significant decrease of UDS and an increase in LPO were observed, 120 subjects were daily vitaminized by 1000mg of ascorbic acid and 300 mg of a-tocopherol. The effect of antioxidants therapy was followed for a period of 3, 6 and 12 months, simultaneously with 120 untreated controls. These subjects were examined using psychological tests. The same approach was used for the evaluation of antioxidants therapy in groups of chronics alcoholics. Comparing the observed results for alcoholics, control groups and elderly male population it may be speculated, that chronic alcohol consumption speeds up the process of agin in males approximately for 15 years. The antioxidants therapy seems to protect against the free radicals damage.

2718

PSYCHOACTIVE DRUG USE IN ELDERLY OUTPATIENTS: AN ITALIAN SURVEY.
Lucilla Frattura and Alberto Spagnoli
"Mario Negri" Institute for Pharmacological Research, Milan, Italy.

A random sample of 46 general practitioners (GPs) in Turin recruited 802 elderly outpatients and collected information about compliance and current drug treatment. Then, each patients received a home interview and details were collected on drug compliance and use of drugs other than those reported by the GPs. An average, each patients was taking 3.6 drugs, of which 2.9 were correctly reported by the GPs and 0.7 were unreported. Cardiovascular drugs, diuretics and psychoactive agents were the most prescribed therapeutic groups. 26% of the sample were taking "cerebroactive" agents (mostly prescribed by the GPs), 22,4% were on benzodiazepines, 4% on antidepressants, and 3 % on neuroleptics. Benzodiapezines were the most common unreported drugs (48% of the overall benzodiazepine prescriptions were not detected by the GPs). The frequent long-term use of benzodiazepines and the widespread prescription of "cerebroactive" agents (whose efficacy is not documented and whose risks and costs are widely recognized) will be discussed.

2719

DEPRESSION ET RESOLUTION DES PROBLEMES AUX AGES

Georges Kleftaras, Docteur en Psychologie Expérimental
Laboratoire de Psy. Exp. de Univ. Paris X, France

Les personnes âgées constituent une population particuliére, confrontée à de nombreaux problèmes. Parmi ces problèmes la dépression semble être non seulement le plus fréquent, mais aussi le plus grave. Le but de cette recherche est d'etudier une des dimensions cognitives de la dépression et plus précisément l'aptitude cognitive à résoudre des problèmes interpersonnels. En fait, celle-ci comprend la genèse des solutions alternatives efficaces mais également les stratégies qui permettent d'organiser et de structurer un programme étape par étape et en phases successives, afin de mettre en pratique la meilleure solution choisie pour atteindre le but souhaité dans une situation interpersonnelle problèmatique. 310 personnes âgées françaises valides, d'un âge moyen de 78.75 ans vivant dans des foyers-logements pour personnes âgées ont participé à cette étude. Elles ont répondu au Questionnaire de la Symptomatologie Dépressive de Pichot et al. et à la procédure de la résolution de problèmes interpersonnels. La structure factorielle de ces instruments telle qu'elle a été établie à partir de réponses de notre échantillon est satisfaisante et conforme aux résultats antérieurs. Les résultats confirment notre hypothèse. Ainsi, plus une personne âgée est déprimée plus l'aptitude cognitive à résoudre des problèmes interpersonnels est inefficace et deficitaire. Ceci montre l'importance qu'il faut accorder à l'étude de la capacité à rèsoudre des problèmes interpersonnels pour comprendre la dépression chez les personnes âgées.

2720

Psychosocial Stress and Coping Mechanism of Families of Dementia Patients
S.K.Khandelwal, S.Gupta, G.K.Ahuja
All India Institute of Medical Sciences,New Delhi

Majority of the dementias seen in the old age are irreversible and progressive. With advances in the investigative skills, a number of cases are diagnosed to be secondary in nature and thus afford a better prognosis. But in primary dementias the outlook still remains gloomy notwithstanding the fact that with better understanding of their nature, course and outcome, a number of psychosocial measures can be employed at individual, family and community level for providing relief. In India, family remains the most important unit to look after a patient suffering from dementia. Community awakening and resources are still highly inadequate. Because of the very nature and prognosis of the problems dementia brings about a significant psycho--social stress to the members of the family who react to these stresses variously. Such stresses and reactions of the family members of 30 patients of dementia were studied in a descriptive study. Patient's deteriorating clinical state, inability to look after oneself, various psychiatric symptoms, necessity of constant care and regular medical supervision and social embarrasment of such a person in the family were the usual stresses. Inability to explain the disorder or to guess its course and outcome or inevitability of downhill course added to the problem.

Session 413 Symposium:
Improvement of treatment in psychiatry

2721

OPTIMAL DOSES OF HALOPERIDOL: WHO COLLABORATIVE STUDY

S. Potkin, D. Kirch, W. Bunney (USA), H. Hippius (FRG), D. Moussaoui (Morroco), B. Sethi (India), M. Vartanian (USSR) & I. Yamashita (Japan)

A WHO cross-national study was undertaken to evaluate the relationship between blood concentrations of haloperidol and therapeutic response. Patients meeting ICD-9 and DSM-III criteria for schizophrenia were included providing they had active hallucinations and delusions. Patients were excluded if they had history of drug abuse, alcoholism, or severe medical illness. Patients were drug free for at least one week before being randomly assigned to either a fixed low dose (0.15 mg/kg) or a fixed moderate dose (0.24 mg/kg) of haloperidol. Patients were treated for a 6-week period during which weekly BPRS and CGI ratings were obtained. End-point analysis demonstrated significant improvement for both groups. The two groups did not differ from each other in percentage improvement as measured by BPRS. There were no significant blood concentration differences among the WHO collaborating centres, suggesting that patients with similar haloperidol blood concentrations respond equally well to haloperidol regardless of culture. Subsequent data analysis examining whether a therapeutic window for haloperidol is present and whether the boundaries of this window differ by centre will be presented.

2722

Pharmacological therapy of depression, achievement and prospect

A. Delini-Stula

Research and Development Department, CIBA-GEIGY Ltd. Basel, Switzerland

Pharmacological therapy of depressive disorder is incontestably essential for a substantial population of moderately and severely ill patients. It is known today that the claim of large placebo response and spontaneous recovery primarly applies to mild depressions and to "non-endogenous" depressive states.
The research on antidepressants during the last decades was guided by the classical monoamine-concept of depression and oriented towards development of more selective and specific acting drugs. In this respect particular emphasis was placed on selective 5-HT uptake inhibitors and selective and reversible MAOI-inhibitors.
Comparative biochemical and pharmacological studies of a large serie of clasical and these new antidepressants have led to a great gain in the basic knowledge of the cns functions and provide a retrospective and prospective pharmacological rationale for their clinical use also in other psychiatric indications. An important achievement is the better safety of new drugs: a clear-cut differentiation between the classical and new antidepressants, such as selective 5-HT-uptake inhibitors and selective and reversible MAOI, could be demonstrated. A rational drug-design in respect to the side-effect profiles appears therefore possible. However, presently identified pharmacological or biochemical properties of antidepressants do not yet permit the understanding of their mode of action. Some new drugs, emerging from the research and not fitting into the present concepts are perhaps offering a new perspective in this field of research.

2723

HISTORY AND NEW DEVELOPMENTS IN NEUROLEPTIC TREATMENTS

Pierre DENIKER

Sainte-Anne Hospital- PARIS (FRANCE)

From 1952 to 1963, chlorpromazine, reserpin and haloperidol are introduced into Psychiatry, and common pharmaco-clinical definition was established before the discovery of the anti-dopaminergic mode of action. Long-acting compounds are usefull in non-compliants patients. In 1965, benzamides are also introduced and new drugs are now coming from this group.

Since 1955, the efficacy of neuroleptic chemotherapy in chronic psychoses was confirmed. But following the concept of "CPZ-equivalent", opposed to the differenciation between sedative and "desinhibitory" drugs, the problem of tardive dyskinesias appears very serious. With the consequence that neuroleptics are put in a "Warming list" in U.S.A.

The "antipsychotic" activities in schizophrenias have induced the dopaminergic theories which are open to discussion. It would be underlined that the specific "anti-manic" action, which is part of the early definition, was to soon neglected. In fact mania is the contrary of depression and the antidepressants are anti-neuroleptics.

2724

CHRONOBIOLOGY OF AFFECTIVE ILLNESS :
A WHO COLLABORATIVE STUDY ON SLEEP EEG
J. Mendlewicz, M. Kerkhofs. Free University of Brussels, Erasme Hospital, Dept. of Psychiatry, route de Lennik 808, 1070 Brussels Belgium

The aim of this cross-cultural collaborative study was to investigate the consistensy of sleep EEG disturbances in affective disorder. The following WHO centers were involved in the study : Athens, Brussels, Mexico, Munich, Naples, Sapporo, Tokyo, Zagreb. Each center was asked to perform sleep polygraphic recordings in 10 depressed patients aged from 20 to 65 years, presenting a Major Depressive Disorder and in 10 age and gender matched controls. All patients were studied after a drug washout period of 10 days and were classified according to the RDC (I.C.D. and DSM III optionnaly) and the Newcastle Scale. Severity of depressive episode was assessed by the Hamilton Rating Scale for depression and by the Bech Rafaelsen Melancholia Scale. To be included in the study the score at these two scales need to be at least 17 an 15 respectively. 67 patients (28 males and 39 females) and 66 controls (30 males and 36 females) were included in the study. Comparison of sleep polygraphic variables in patients and in controls showed significant sleep continuity disturbances and Rem sleep measures abnormalities in depressed patients. Further comparison taking into account the effect of the center showed the persistance of an effect of the diagnosis for sleep onset latency and for Rem latency. The effects of endogenicity, age, severity of the illness were also investigated and will be discussed.

2725

LITHIUM PROPHYLAXIS OF MAJOR AFFECTIVE DISORDERS: LONG-TERM OUTCOME IN PATIENTS INITIALLY CLASSIFIED AS COMPLETE RESPONDERS

M. Maj, R. Pirozzi and D. Kemali

Department of Medical Psychology and Psychiatry, First Medical School, University of Naples (Italy)

43 bipolar and 36 unipolar patients who had been classified as complete responders to lithium after the first two years of prophylactic treatment were followed up prospectively for a further period of five years (treatment period II), during which their psychopathological state was assessed monthly or bi-monthly. 49 patients completed the treatment period II, two died during this period, 7 did not attend the unit anymore and could not be traced, and 21 definitively interrupted lithium before the end of the period. 25 patients relapsed during treatment period II. Four relapsers had three or more episodes concentrated during the last two years of treatment, in spite of an apparent good compliance.

These results suggest that the predictive value of an initial favourable response to lithium should not be overrated, and that the impact of the drug on the long-term course of major affective disorders in ordinary clinical conditions might be less dramatic than currently believed.

2726 *

* Number left open for technical reasons not corresponding to any abstract

---

Session 414   **Symposium:**
Stress and depression: An international symposium on tianeptine

2727

NEURONAL VULNERABILITY IN AGING, ALCOHOLISM AND STRESS
Mc Ewen BS, Westlind-Danielsson A, Gannon M, Gould E, Ronchi E, Spencer R, Laboratory of Neuroendocrinology, Rockefeller University, 1230 York Avenue, New York N.Y. 10021 USA

Neuronal damage and death occur during the aging process and as a result of transient ischaemia, as in stroke, and chronic alcohol treatment. Neurons of the hippocampal formation are among the most vulnerable to these insults, and they are also affected in degenerative neurological diseases such as senile dementia of the Alzheimer type. Among the causal factors in such damage, glucocorticoids (GC) produced by the adrenal cortex have been implicated along with excitatory amino acids, calcium ions and free radicals. At the same time, GC's are essential for long-term survival of the organism, especially under conditions of stress. Two receptor types exist in the brain. Type I receptors, concentrated in the hippocampus, septum and amygdala, respond to the lower, diurnally varying level of GC's, whereas Type II receptors, found in hippocampus and also in all other parts of the brain and in glial cells as well as neurons, respond to the higher, stress-induced levels of GC's. Type I receptors therefore mediate the cyclic activation of the waking state and hunger for food, whereas Type II receptors mediate the adaptive response to stress, as exemplified by the cyclic AMP system, and also the tonic maintenance of glial cell properties, especially myelin lipid deposition and certain key structural proteins and enzymes. Type II receptors are associated with cholinergic and nerve-growth factor containing neurons of the basal forebrain. Functioning of Type I and possibly also the Type II receptors in hippocampus is linked via the hypothalamus to negative control of ACTH secretion from the pituitary, and either the presence of constant level of GC's or deficiencies of Type I and Type II receptors lead to failed shut-off the stress response. It is the failure to shut off the stress response that is most likely to lead to damage and neuronal loss, as opposed to the beneficial effects which GC's have.

2728

EFFECTS OF TIANEPTINE* AND OTHER ANTIDEPRESSANTS ON A RAT MODEL OF DEPRESSION
Curzon G, Kennett GA, Sarna GS, Whitton P, Department of Neurochemistry, Institute of Neurology, London, WC1N 3BG, UK

Restraint stress (2h) increased rat plasma corticosterone, decreased locomotion 24h later in open field and caused hypophagia. Behavioural adaptation occured on daily restraint (x5).

Failure to adapt is a relevant depression model as (1) it is associated with corticosterone elevation, a characteristic of the illness : (2) female rats show defective adaptation which parallels the higher incidence of the illness in women : (3) adaptation occurs together with increased postsynaptic 5-HT function as revealed by the behavioural response to 5-MeODMT. We have therefore investigated the effects of tianeptine and other antidepressants on the model. Chronic pretreatment with two antidepressant 5-HT reuptake inhibitors (desipramine, sertraline) significantly normalised open field activity measured on the day after a single restraint. Tianeptine (10 mg/kg i.p.) or 5-HT$_{1A}$ agonists (8-OHDPAT, gepirone etc) given as one dose 2h after the end of restraint significantly normalised the subsequently measured open field activity. Both 8-OHDPAT and tianeptine acutely decreased brain extracellular 5-HT (in vivo dialysis method). The possible involvement of this property in their antidepressant effects will be discussed.

2729

GLUCOCORTICOIDS AND STRESS
Vaudry H[1], Delbende C[1], Szafarczyk A[2], Mocaër E[3], Kamoun A[3]
1. Lab. Molecul. Endocrinol., CNRS URA 650, Univ. Rouen, 76134 Mt St Aignan, France
2. Lab. Neuroendocrinol. CNRS URA 1197, Univ. Montpellier, France
3. IRIS, 27, rue du Pont, 92202 Neuilly sur Seine, France

Almost any kind of stress will cause stimulation of two important neuroendocrine systems, i.e. catecholamine and glucocorticoid secretion. Stress-induced stimulation of CRF-containing neurons appears to be mediated at least by serotoninergic and noradrenergic neuronal pathways. CRF triggers secretion of the pituitary hormones ACTH and β-endorphin and this effect is potentiated by vasopressin and oxytocin. CRF also induces stimulation of the sympathetic system leading to elevated adrenal catecholamine secretion. Although adrenocortical cells are clearly under the control of multiple factors, there is no doubt that ACTH plays a pivotal role in the regulation of corticosteroid secretion. Various signals released by adrenal chromaffin cells (e.g. adrenaline, serotonin and(or) enkephalins) may also participate in the physiological regulation of glucocorticoid secretion. Glucocorticoids exert a negative feedback control both on CRF-producing neurons and pituitary corticotrophs. There is also some evidence that glucocorticoids inhibit their own secretion by acting directly on adrenocortical cells. Finally, a negative feedback suppression likely occurs in the brain, particularly on serotonergic neurotransmission. Chronic treatment of rats with the antidepressant agent tianeptine* (10 mg/kg : 2 weeks, twice a day) causes a significant decrease of hypothalamic CRF and pituitary ACTH levels, suggesting that tianeptine may attenuate stress-induced stimulation of the hypothalamo-pituitary-adrenal axis.

Supported by INSERM (CRE 84-6020 and 88-6016), DRET (87-135) and MRT (88C595)

* Stablon®

2730

TIANEPTINE : FIRST DRUG INDUCING PRESYNAPTIC SEROTONIN UPTAKE WITH ORIGINAL BEHAVIOURAL EFFECTS
Labrid C, Mocaër E
Institut de Recherches Internationales Servier, 27, rue du Pont, 92200 Neuilly sur Seine, France

Tianeptine is an antidepressant with original biochemical effects : it has been already shown that after ex vivo acute and chronic treatment, it increases serotonin uptake in rat brain cortex and hippocampus and in rat and human platelets. Recent studies showed tianeptine also increases serotonin uptake in vivo : it decreases rat brain extracellular 5-HT levels measured by in vivo microdialysis technique, potentiates the decrease in rat brain 5-HT levels induced by H75/12 contrary to 5-HT uptake inhibitors and increases rat hippocampus 5-HIAA levels measured by in vivo voltammetry technique contrary to fluoxetine. Furthermore, tianeptine has indirect effects on dopamine and acetylcholine neurotransmission. With respect to electrophysiological effects, tianeptine increases the firing rate of hippocampus pyramidal cells and their recovery velocity after iontophoretic 5-HT or GABA administration. This peculiar biochemical and electrophysiological profile is in agreement with original behavioural effects : tianeptine is devoid of sedative effects ; it increases focalized attention in the cat and improved learning and memory in the mouse ; it antagonizes stress-induced behavioural deficits in rats (immobilization stress, learned helplessness situation). Finally, recent experiments showed effects of tianeptine on rat hypothalamo-pituitary axis, suggesting a role of tianeptine in the regulation of the emotional response to stress.

2731

DYNAMIC ELECTROPHYSIOLOGICAL STUDIES IN THE EVALUATION OF PSYCHOTROPIC DRUGS
De Montigny C, Blier P, Chaput Y, Godbout R, Bouthillier A, Curet O, Neurobiological Psychiatry Unit, McGill University, Department of Psychiatry, Montreal, Quebec, CANADA H3A 1A1

A hallmark of the clinical effect of antidepressant treatments in major depression is the delay of their therapeutic action. Therefore, any neurobiological investigation bearing on the substratum of their clinical effect must integrate this time constant.

Several electrophysiological single-cell recording studies have demonstrated that long-term, but not acute, administration of diverse types of antidepressant treatments results in an enhanced central serotoninergic (5-HT) neurotransmission. Interestingly, the mechanisms whereby this potentiation is achieved differ from one class of treatments to the others. Tricyclic antidepressant drugs and electroconvulsive shocks augment the responsiveness of postsynaptic neurons to 5-HT. Monoamine oxidase inhibitors, which increase the availability of the neurotransmitter, induce a desensitization of somatodendritic 5-HT autoreceptors, allowing 5-HT neurons to regain a normal firing activity following an initial period of marked reduction of their firing rate. A similar temporal pattern in the firing activity of 5-HT neurons, also resulting from a desensitization of their somatodendritic 5-HT autoreceptors, has been observed with long-term treatment with 5-HT reuptake blockers as well as with selective $5-HT_{1A}$ agonists.

The conclusion from these dynamic electrophysiological studies that an enhancement of 5-HT neurotransmission might be a common pivotal substratum for the therapeutic effect of antidepressant treatments is consistent with the potentiation of these treatments by lithium in resistant depression, since lithium increases 5-HT neuron function, as well as with the recent demonstration that a low tryptophan diet can reverse the therapeutic effect of these treatments.

2732

CONTRIBUTION OF BEHAVIORAL STUDIES IN THE EVALUATION OF ANTIDEPRESSANTS
Thiebot MH, Martin P, Puech AJ
Service de Pharmacologie, C.H.U. Pitié-Salpêtrière, 91, bld de l'Hôpital, 75013 Paris, France

Designing models of psychiatric disorders in animals, in order to predict the therapeutic effect of drugs such as antidepressants is quite unrealistic. However it is possible to evaluate, in an experimental situation, the changes in behavior induced by drugs and to make hypothesis on the functions of the CNS implicated.

This can lead to a more heuristic classification of psychotropic drugs than "antidepressants", "anxiolytics" and "antipsychotics", and to better define the best indications of psychotropic drugs.

In the field of the so called "antidepressants", the results in the forced swimming test and in the learned helplessness paradigm, suggest an "antihelpless" effect of antidepressants. Antidepressants seem to increase in rats the drive toward a strategy of searching for a solution rather than to give up. This behavioral effect in animals suggests a primary effect of antidepressants in man on psychomotor retardation rather than on mood itself.

On the other hand, drugs which increase NE or 5HT transmission ("antidepressants") are able in a waiting model (T-maze) and the DRL 72 s. paradigm, to help animals to wait and/or to postpone an active response. This effect in animals could be in relation with the therapeutic effect of these drugs on impulsiveness in humans.

The relationship that may exist between these 2 behavioral effects remains to be precisely delineated.

2733

CLINICAL RESEARCH IN PSYCHOPHARMACOLOGY : NEW STANDARDS FOR DRUGS DEVELOPMENT
Guelfi JD
Clinique des maladies mentales et de l'encéphale, 100, rue de la Santé, 75674 Paris, France

This paper will compare the report of the first consensus conference on the methodology of clinical trials of antidepressants in Europe (Zurich, 1988) with the new guidelines for the clinical investigation of antidepressant drugs (WHO).

Antidepressants are drugs that have been shown, "in comparison with placebo, to improve all symptoms characteristic of the depressive syndrome".. Placebo-controlled studies are judged to be the design of choice to test the efficacy of a new drug in some of the pilot therapeutic studies. The main therapeutic trials compare the new drug with well-known antidepressants. The following problems will be discussed : type of patients to include and to exclude (diagnosis), advantages and disadvantages of various rating scales (for assessing the severity of depression, the unwanted effects, or the measurement of change), concomitant medications, recommended lenght of trials, sample size and criteria for the degree of response. It is important to obtain evidence that antidepressants are sufficiently effective and well-tolerated over a long period of time to justify their continued use. At least 100 patients treated for one year should be available. During these trials self-rating scales for quality of treatment, quality of life and life events are useful as well as reports of any severe drug reactions occuring to the National adverse drug reaction monitoring system.

2734

LONG TERM ANTIDEPRESSANT ACTIVITY OF TIANEPTINE* IN DEPRESSED PATIENTS
Lôo H[1], Ganry H[2]
1. Service Hospitalo-Universitaire de Santé Mentale et de Thérapeutique, Hôpital Sainte Anne, Paris
2. Institut de Recherches Internationales Servier, Neuilly sur Seine

The antidepressant action of tianeptine has been evaluated in several controlled trials. Tianeptine occupies an intermediate position between sedative and stimulant antidepressants. A multicenter open trial, included depressed patients with major depression, single or recurrent episode, without melancholia or psychotic features, or with dysthymic disorder (DSM III). This first european study, aiming at treating during a one year period more than 300 depressed patients, allows to evaluate the maintenance of therapeutic efficacy as well as clinical and paraclinical acceptability in long term prescription of tianeptine.

This work presents results of 356 depressed patients treated for a one year period with tianeptine as well as the results of the total sample of depressed patients included in the trial.

After one month of treatment the antidepressant activity of tianeptine is confirmed by a reduction of 51 % of the mean score of the Montgomery and Asberg Depression Rating Scale (MADRS). A similar amelioration has been found with the Hamilton Anxiety (HARS) and the H.S.C.L., a self-evaluation scale.

Our results, showing that the improvement observed after 3 months is maintained until the 12th month of treatment, confirm that tianeptine prevents depressive relapses. Only 13 % of patients relapsed on treatment ; this result is similar to that observed with classical tricyclic antidepressants.

The therapeutic index (C.G.I.- item 3) estimated at 2.4, after one month, proves its excellent safety, confirmed by multivariate and item by item analysis of the C.H.E.S.S. 84, a rating scale assessing somatic complaints. We can also confirm an improvement of the somatic complaints reported at the beginning of the trial, and a lack of notable side effects,particularly anticholinergic effects.

In long term treatment tianeptine entails neither orthostatic hypotension, nor weight variations ; it does not alter, hematological, hepatic, biochemical and cardiovascular parameters studied.

* Stablon®

2735

SLEEP LABORATORY STUDIES IN THE EVALUATION OF ANTIDEPRESSANTS: METHODOLOGICAL ISSUES
C.R.Soldatos,P.N.Sakkas,J.D.Bergiannaki, C.N.Stefanis,Dept. of Psychiatry,Athens University, Athens, Greece

In conducting sleep laboratory studies of antidepressants a number of methodological issues arise.Drug related issues include among others the following:a)antidepressants are not a chemically homogeneous drug class and,therefore,they should not be expected to share the same effects on sleep;b)physiologic effects following long term use of a certain drug are often different than those following short term use; c)the drugs'effects on sleep of depressed patients may be different than those on sleep of normal volunteers.Subject related issues include:a)inferences regarding antidepressant efficacy can be made only when utilizing depressed patients;b)similarly,hypnotic, efficacy should be evaluated in depressed patients complaining of insomnia;c)different diagnostic subtypes of depressed patients should be identified within the total study sample; d)normal volunteers can be utilized as controls.In the design several issues need to be addressed such as:a)duration of drug administration;b)use of placebo within each subject group to evaluate adequate baseline and withdrawal periods; c)use of a parallel group to allow for comparisons between drugs.

2736

ALCOHOL ABUSE AND DEPENDENCE : ROLE OF TIANEPTINE*
Malka R, Centre Gilbert Raby, Thun, Meulan

It has been found that alcoholism and depression are often met in medical practice. Alcohol interfering with central serotonin metabolism, the prescription of antidepressants, like tianeptine with neurochemical serotonin properties, is particularly suitable for depressed patients after withdrawal.

A multicenter open trial included alcoholic depressed patients after withdrawal from alcohol abuse or alcohol dependence and presenting either with major depression, single or recurrent episode, without melancholia or psychotic features, or with dysthymic disorder (DSM III). This study allows to evaluate the maintenance therapeutic efficacy as well as clinical and paraclinical acceptability during long term prescription of tianeptine.

This work is, in our knowledge, the first clinical trial presenting the evolution of 119 depressed patients with alcoholism after withdrawal, treated for a one year with an antidepressant. Furthermore, the results of the total sample of alcoholic depressed patients included in the trial are detailed.

Antidepressant activity of tianeptine is confirmed after a month of treatment, by a 52 % reduction of the mean score of the Montgomery and Asberg Depression Rating Scale (MADRS) together with a concomitant improvement of the mean scores of the Hamilton Anxiety Rating Scale (HARS) and of the Hopkins Self report inventory (HSCL).

Furthermore, our results confirm the maintenance of therapeutic efficacy during long term treatment with tianeptine and its action on preventing depressive relapses.

We can also confirm the lack of notable adverse effects particularly anticholinergic effects and an improvement of somatic complaints noted at the beginning of the trial using a check list for the evaluation of somatic symptoms (CHESS 84). Tianeptine, in long term treatment, entails neither orthostatic hypotension, nor weight variations. It also does not alter the biological parameters studied, confirming its excellent safety.

Tianeptine has been found to be an effective and safe antidepressant of particular interest in this population with somatic alterations.

* Stablon®

2737 *

---

* Number left open for technical reasons not corresponding to any abstract

Session 415 Symposium:
Brain receptor imaging in psychiatry

2738

THE NEW BIOLOGICAL TOOL FOR DIAGNOSIS AND TREATMENT IN MENTAL ILLNESS : PET

Hideji Kishimoto, Masaaki Matsushita and Masaaki Iio* Department of Psychiatry Yokohama University School of Medicine, Yokohama 232 and Nakano National Hospital*, Tokyo 160, JAPAN

Positron emission tomography is a significant new technique for understanding the function of the living human brain. It is hoped that PET studies will provide clues about mental illnesses, disorders that have long eluded understanding.
Recently, a large number of positron emitting ligands for labelling human brain receptors are in clinical use. These include the following ligands: SCH23390(D_1), methylspiperon, raclopride, bromspiperone(D_2), methyl-LSD, ketanserin(5-HT$_2$), Ro15-1788, flunitazepam(benzodiazepine), carfentanil(opiate), QNB(cholinergic).

PET is now providing valuable quantitative and qualitative information on the mechanism of receptors in the brain in mental illnesses. For example, which receptor is increased in schizophrenia- D1 or D2 or other receptors. Can we diagnose mental illness by PET today?

We will get these answers in this symposium on " Brain Receptor Imaging in Psychiatry ".

2739

D_1- AND D_2-DOPAMINE RECEPTOR BINDING EXAMINED BY PET IN SCHIZOPHRENIC PATIENTS
Farde L, Wiesel F-A, Nordström A-L, Sedvall G.
Dept of Psychiatry and Psychology, Karolinska Institute, S-104 01 STOCKHOLM, Sweden.
The binding of 11C-SCH23390 and 11C-raclopride, selective D_1- and D_2-dopamine receptor antagonists, respectively, was examined in vivo by PET. For both ligands, saturable and stereoselective binding was demonstrated in the basal ganglia. Saturable 11C-SCH23390 binding was found in the neocortex whereas no specific 11C-raclopride binding was found in any neocortical region.
In 20 schizophrenic patients treated with any of 11 chemically distinct classical antipsychotics there was a more than 70% reduction in 11C-raclopride binding (D_2-dopamine receptor occupancy). In 3 patients treated with the atypical neuroleptic clozapine the D_2-occupancy was 65, 42 and 40% whereas the D_1-occupancy was higher than for classical neuroleptics.
Several groups have reported increased densities of D_2-dopamine receptors in the basal ganglia of postmortem brain tissue from patients with schizophrenia. We have used (11C)raclopride and a saturation procedure in vivo for quantitative determination of D_2-dopamine receptor density (B_{max}) and affinity (K_d) in 20 healthy controls and 18 drug-naive schizophrenics. When the two groups were compared no significant difference in B_{max} or K_d-values were found in the putamen or in the caudate nucleus. In patients, but not in healthy controls, significantly higher densities were found in the left than in the right putamen.

2740

IMAGING RECEPTORS AND THEIR INTERACTIONS: IMPLICATIONS FOR PSYCHIATRY

JD Brodie*, JS Fowler, AP Wolf, SL Dewey, A Wolkin*, F Barouche*, ND Volkow, MR Smith^, J Rotrosen*, B Angrist*, R MacGregor, and D Schlyer

NYU Med. Ctr.*, SUNY SB^ and Brookhaven Nat. Labs. New York, USA

The dopamine (DA) receptor has been imaged in the human striatum using 18-F-methyl spiperone (NMS). Neuroleptics block the striatal binding of labeled NMS but after five days of washout there is virtually complete freeing of striatal DA receptors. Data from these images has shown that haloperidol blockade reaches a maximum at relatively low plasma concentrations (10-15ng/ml). Plasma haloperidol measurements can be used to predict the degree of blockade but not response to treatment. Furthermore, schizophrenic drug responders and non-responders showed equivalent blockade in the striatum, which is evidence for at least two biological sub-types of schizophrenia. This result also suggests that failure to respond to neuroleptic treatment is probably not due to failure of drug delivery.
The cholinergic (ACh) receptor in human and primate brain has also been successfully visualized in vivo using 11-C-benztropine (Bz) and positron emission tomography (PET). The distribution and some of the properties of the ACh receptor will be shown. The effects of Bz on images of neuroleptic binding and the relationship between neuroleptic binding and the relief of extrapyramidal symptoms (EPS) with anticholinergics will be interpreted. There is high reproducibility of Bz uptake within a given brain but a several fold difference in uptake in different animals. It has been suggested that Bz may be binding to the DA transporter. However, the failure of nomifensine to diminish uptake of Bz would suggest that this process is not of pharmacologic significance in the relief of EPS in vivo.
The use of PET to image neuroreceptors will be discussed in terms of present and future application to psychiatric practice.

Supported in part by NIH grant NS-15638 and the Dept of Energy

2741

A variation in the binding-potential of benzodiazepine-receptor and C-11 Ro15-1788 in the same healthy volunteer

TOSHIRO YAMASAKI , National Institute of Radiological Sciences, Chiba, Japan

In-vivo binding potentials of the central type benzodiazepine receptor and C-11 Ro15-1788 were measured in normal volunteers using PET.
The distribution and concentration of the ligand was the highest in the cerebral cortex ; the concentration in brain stem and white matter was low. And there was much difference in the time course of the frontal lobe radioactivity, depending on individuals.
The most important and interesting finding in this study is the significant different time courses of cerebral activity observed in some of the same individuals. But in other cases, any difference in the time course of cerebral activity was not recognized.
From these data, it will be concluded there are several types of the time activity curve in the frontal cortex. And some of them may be changeable according to psychological conditions such as mental stress. So there may be a possibility to show either a high trait anxious individual or low trait one.

Session 416   Symposium:
Clinical disaster psychiatry

2742
Etiology of post-traumatic anxiety and depressive disorders.

Ulrik Fr. Malt, MD
University of Oslo, Department of Psychiatry

Post-traumatic anxiety and depressive disorders are related to the experience of death-anxiety when injured, degree of helplessness, and lack of control over the traumatic experience. Recent Norwegian retrospective and prospective, longitudinal studies including more than thousand victims do point to the role of other important factors, however. Effective treatment of post-traumatic mental disorders calls for an exploration of these other sources of psychic trauma and stressful secondary events. In this presentation, the 12 most important areas of distress in relation to the development of post-traumatic mental disorders are elucidated by means of clinical key-words and European artists expression of appraisals of threat, loss and conflict.

2743
Individual and Organizational Responses to Disaster

LARS WEISÆTH Professor Division of Disaster Psychiatry, University of Oslo/The Joint Norwegian Armed Forces Medical Services.

Based on experiences in Norway ranging from severe technological disasters causing more than a hundred deaths to lesser accidents with few deaths, an intervention model is described for the prevention of psychosocial problems in the wake of the disaster.

A total disaster brings primary disaster stress, namely those stressors that are part of the acute disaster trauma, while secondary stressors, such as dislocation, unemployment, economic problems etc. may follow in its wake. The obvious disaster victims are (1) the dead, (2) the bereaved families and (3) the survivors with their physical and mental injuries. But also other groups of persons are affected and may have an increased risk of post-disaster psychiatric morbidity: (4) Rescue and health personnel, (5) on-lookers, (6) workmates in occupational disasters, (7) persons with responsibility roles, (8) evacuees, and (9) the body handlers.

Examples are given of the particular stress reactions during and after the disaster and some preventive psychiatric support services for these groups are described. The main findings from our research projects are presented.

2744
The Nature of a Traumatic Stressor: Handling Dead Bodies

Robert J Ursano, MD & James E McCarroll, PhD
Department of Psychiatry, Uniformed Services University of the Health Sciences, Bethesda, Maryland &
Department of Military Psychiatry, Walter Reed Army Institute of Research, Washington DC.

Exposure to death and dead bodies has been repeatedly identified as a major stressor following disasters, combat, and international terrorism. We examined exposure to dead bodies of over 400 volunteer body handlers who participated in the body identification process following a plane crash which killed 248 soldiers. In addition, we conducted interviews and observations with approximately 50 civilian and military personnel with extensive experience with and exposure to handling bodies in rescue, recovery, identification and transport.

Case vignettes illustrate the role of magical thinking, identification, and symbol formation. In addition, the unique traumas of viewing, smelling, and touching the grotesque and the experience of the unusual, novel, and untimely are unique elements of the stressor of exposure to death. Children's bodies were most toxic of exposures. Intense exposure to massive death and dead bodies increases feelings of danger, loss of control, and the expectation that "something" dangerous may happen. Such exposures can be both individual and community-wide events.

2745
Traumatic bereavement

Tom Lundin, MD
University of Uppsala, Akademiska sjukhuset, Uppsala, Sweden.

Sudden and unexpected and untimely bereavement might cause increased morbidity and mortality. Different conditions affecting the grief, the mourning process and the outcome have been reported.

When the major disaster strikes, many people will be traumatically bereaved at the same time and as an effect of the same event, usually under very dramatic circumstances. The psychological effects of personal losses will not only be an addition of individual reactions.

Based on recent studies on sudden bereavement following different disasters some aspects on theoretical and clinical-practical issues will be presented.

2746
Psychosocial support services for bereaved families after disaster.

Pål Herlofsen, MD
Division of Disaster Psychiatry, University of Oslo/The Joint Norwegian Armed Forces Medical Services.

In the last three years Norway have experienced three large disasters causing up to 36 deaths. In every disaster a psychosocial support service system were constructed within the already existing health service.

The importance of having a structured organization, good training and crisis management will be focused upon along with discussion on selection of professions and personalities for those who are to meet the bereaved families.

The place of local authorities in memorial services and the attitude towards the press both from the bereaved families and the helpers will be discussed. The need for psychological debriefing of the helpers and their leaders will also be mentioned.

Session 417   Symposium:
Behavioral therapies in schizophrenia disorders

2747
COGNITIVE THERAPY VS. SOCIAL-SKILLS-TRAINING IN CHRONIC SCHIZOPHRENIC PATIENTS
S. Kraemer, H.-J. Zimmer, H.-J. Möller
Psychiatric Clinic of the Technical University Munich, FRG

In this study two therapeutic approaches for schizophrenic patients are compared. The first treatment is a cognitive one with components of cognitive rehearsal, social perception and problem-solving-training.
The other treatment consists of social-skills-training with role-playing-techniques with special emphasis on high-expressed-emotion-situations such as critique, social pressure or overinvolvement. The design includes cognitive, social and psychopathological measures as well as pre-, post- and process-oriented measurements.
First evaluations seem to indicate that the cognitive treatment obtained the better overall effect for most of the variables, especially for the enhancement of negative symptoms. Further results are discussed with respect to special basic disorders and their relationships to outcome-measures.

2748
COGNITIVE AND SOCIAL TREATMENT FOR CHRONIC SCHIZOPHRENIC PATIENTS
Hodel, B., Regli, D., Brenner, H. D.
Dept. of Theoretical and Evaluative Psychiatry, Psychiatric Clinic of the University Bern
Bolligenstrasse 111, CH-3072 Bern/Switzerland

The Integrated Psychological Therapy Program (IPT) is one approach of cognitive and social treatment in schizophrenia. It is based on the assumption, that improvements on cognitive dysfunctions exert positive pervasive effects on disordered social functions and vice versa. However, several single cases with chronic schizophrenics showed that improvements on cognitive dysfunctions exert only moderated pervasive effects to levels of social functioning.
For an analysis of the variables moderating the pervasiveness of improvements on cognitive functions, a study with 20 chronic schizophrenic patients was carried out. The study followed a mirror-design in which cognitive and social interventions of the IPT were repeated twice. Each of the interventions lasted two weeks.
The patients were divided into two groups. One group started with cognitive, the other with social interventions. The control measures were cognitive tests (D2), rating-scales for subjective disorders (FCQ), for the self-concept (SIS) as well as social adjustment (NOSIE). The results indicate that the pervasiveness of cognitive as well as social improvements may probably be inhibited by moderating variables like emotional blickades or unstable self-concepts.

2749
COGNITIVE AND PSYCHOEDUCATIONAL THERAPY APPROACH IN SCHIZOPHRENIC PATIENTS

G.Buchkremer, U.Bruns, B.Schmitz-Niehues
Department of Psychiatry, University of Münster, Münster, FRG
Based on new results about the efficacy of cognitive therapies in schizophrenics (BRENNER et al., 1988) a cognitive and psychoeducational strategy to reduce rates of relapses will be presented. The cognitive therapy aims to increase the competence of patients to cope with emotional intra- and interpersonal problems. By means of exercising problem-solving-strategies patients should be able to protect themselves against overcharging stress, to cope with initial symptoms and to increase their psychological and social functioning. Besides patients should be able to influence their pharmacological therapy in a certain frame. By means of information and a specific pharmacological training the knowledge and self-responsive attitude towards neuroleptics shall be increased. This training, conducted in groups, will be presented and problems in the procedure will be discussed.

2750
METHODOLOGICAL EVOLUTION OF SOCIAL SKILLS
TRAINING WITH YOUNG SCHIZOPHRENICS
I. Fernandez, F. Mastrangelo
Corso Plebisciti 6, Milan - Italy

This study reflects the experience matured in 6 years of rehabilitation work with young schizophrenic patients in a Psycho Social Center in Milan.
The methodological evolution, in relation to the results attained, regards: engagement and selection of patients, instruments of individual and family assessment, group formation, conduction modalities, the cognitive-behavioural techniques employed, training length.
For each one of these aspects, we present the data that have supported the methodological choices taken, as well as the moments and ways (assessment, homeworks, problem solving meetings at home) of the intervention in extrafamilial social environments.

2751
BEHAVIOUR ORIENTATED TRAINING OF EARLY ASSESSMENT OF SYMPTOMS IN SCHIZOPHRENICS
W.H.Strauss, E.Klieser, H.Luthcke
Department of Psychiatry, University of Duesseldorf, F.R.Germany

Inpatients suffering from schizophrenia, we have investigated whether the frequency and duration of hospitalization of recidives could be influenced by a psychological training program in early assessment of the schizophrenic symptoms. The study includes 30 patients with the DSM-III diagnosis of schizophrenia with at least two manifestations of the illness. The patients were assigned at random either to the training group or to a Progressive Relaxation group. The therapy was conducted in 10 weekly one hour sessions. The following variables were assessed pre and post treatment: BPRS, AMDP, MMPI, PD-S, SKT, BENTON, MWT, frequency and duration of hospitalization and the psychopathological state at time of hospitalization. All patients received neuroleptic medication mostly in depot - neuroleptic form. The results show that such training with an intensive analysis of the psychotic symptoms does not lead to decompensation and exacerbation. Two years catamnestic results will be presented.

Session 418 Symposium:
Post-graduate teaching on the prevention and treatment of depression

2752-2758
POSTGRADUATE TEACHING ON DEPRESSIVE DISORDERS
THE WORK OF THE SWEDISH PTD-COMMITTEE
Göran Eberhard, Gunnar Holmberg, Anne-Liis von Knorring, Wolfgang Rutz, Börje Wistedt, Jan Wålinder, Anna Åberg-Wistedt, Sweden.

The International Committee for Prevention and Treatment of Depression (The PTD-Committee) comprises groups of psychiatrists with the aim of launching postgraduate teaching programs on the epidemiology, causes, diagnostics, treatment and prevention of depressive disorders to doctors in primary care as well as to psychiatric teams. The Swedish PTD-committee was founded in 1977 and works according to the guidelines laid down by the International organization. This symposium deals with the program used by the Swedish PTD-group including a scientific evaluation of a teaching program offered to general practitioners in a restricted area in Sweden, the island of Gotland. Attention will also be paid to depressive disorders in children and adolescents.

Session 419 Symposium:
Institutional care and rehabilitation of the mentally ill

2759
INSTITUTIONAL CARE AND REHABILITATION OF THE MENTALLY ILL
G. Lyketsos, M.D.
Univ. of Athens, Dept. of Psychiatry, Eginition Hospital, Athens, Greece

Humanization of the asylum and improvement of the quality of life of the extremely mentally disabled is a presumption for their deinstitutionalization. It includes the parallel improvement of both living conditions and psychosocial interventions of their environment.
Such an improvement developed in Greece in the 1950's and can serve as a model providing lessons for practical application.
It concerns a section of the Dromokaition Mental Hospital with 230 extremely disabled patients. In 1947 the leadership of a psychiatrist with the support of the administration proved sufficient to improve the quality of life of these patients. The psychiatrist educated the attendants to teach social skills to the mentally disabled. In the 1950's psychosocial interventions completed what was, then, called psychotherapeutic community.

2760
ADDING LIFE TO YEARS OF THE MENTALLY DISABLED

Dr J.G. Sampaio Faria, World Health Organization Regional Office for Europe, Copenhagen, Denmark

The WHO Strategy for Attaining Health for All states that by the year 2000 the average number of years that people live free from major disease and disability should be increased by at least 10%. It also states that disabled people should have the basic opportunity to develop and use their health potential as well as have access to the physical, social and economic opportunities that allow at least for a socially and economically fulfilling and mentally creative life. It is in this context that the European Office of the World Health Organization has been collaborating with Member States either in developing alternative or complementary forms of community based care to the more traditional psychiatric institutions as well as in fostering the quality of life of those affected by mentally disabling disorders.

The paper describes the situation regarding the desinstitutionalization process in the European Region and gives a summary account of the action being taken by the European Office of WHO in this field.

2761
Institutional Care and Rehabilitation of the Mentally Ill: A Prospectus from Britain.
J.P. Watson,
United Medical and Dental Schools of Guy's and St Thomas's Hospitals, London.

This presentation is an exposition of several propositions

1. Rehabilitation must be distinguished from resettlement on the one hand and long-term care on the other.

2. Rehabilitation applies potentially to all patients with serious psychiatric illness, not only to long-term residents of psychiatric hospitals.

3. For people with a severe psychiatric illness an inpatient phase may be an essential beginning of the rehabilitation process after a phase of acute illness is passed.

4. The potential for rehabilitation of many long-term residents of psychiatric hospitals may be considerable and can be measured using valid and reliable methods.

5. Psychiatric health service and wider political ideologies may retard or facilitate processes of rehabilitation and resettlement as well as community care generally. Indeed such ideological forces are inevitably of importance in this this context.

2762
INSTITUTIONAL CARE AND REHABILITATION IN GREECE

MICHAEL G. MADIANOS, MARINA ECONOMOU
Department of Psychiatry Community Mental Health Center University of Athens

The mental health care delivery system until recently was characterized by centralization of services, mainly based on four large mental hospitals, unequal regional distribution of psychiatrists and lack of community mental health services. However several changes have started occuring during the last decade, including the development of community mental health centers and psychosocial rehabilitation services.
Institutional care, despite all these developments, is still considered the major issue in the Greek psychiatry. An estimated number of 3900 inpatients stay longer than 12 months in the eight state mental hospitals including the striking case of the Leros state hospital, of whom a total of 1900 patients are exhibiting minor psychopathology and remain in the hospitals because of lack of alternative placements in the community. This paper presents the regional distribution of these long stay mental patients and the available places of their rehabilitation. There will be also a focus on the issue of Leros mental hospital, a description of the recent status and the developments in improving the quality of care and living conditions. Finally we will discuss the various constraints and the possible action needed for deinstitutionalization.

2763
INSTITUTIONAL CARE AND REHABILITATION OF THE MENTALLY ILL:NORTHERN GREECE-THESSALONIKI PSYCHIATRIC HOSPITAL

DIMITRIOU E.C.,
UNIVERSITY OF THESSALONIKI MEDICAL SCHOOL

Institutional care in Northern Greece started in the twenties with the establishment of the Psychiatric Hospital of Thessaloniki. The population of this Hospital expanded progressively to that of 1500 patients and its function soon acquired all the characteristics of an asylum. With the invention of neuroleptics and the slow but steady increasing of funds for the mentally ill a slow process of rehabilitation and de-istitutionalization started, which accelerated in the 80's. In this paper we describe briefly the "natural history" of the Psychiatric Hospital of Thessaloniki and the rehabilitation efforts made by some innovative members of its staff up to the end of the 70's. We also describe more extensively the Hospital rehabilitation programmes in the 80's. We follow closely for 5 years all those in-patients who were classified as chronic schizophrenics and report some results regarding the impact the various rehabilitation programmes had had on them.

2764

Institutional care and rehabilitation for children in Greece
J. Tsiantis, O. Maratos
Department of Psychological Peadiatrics, "Aghia Sophia" Children's Hospital
Centre for Pre-school Children "Perivolaki"

In this paper some findings, facts and trends regarding the institutional care and rehabilitation of children in Greece are presented. It is estimated that the total number of institutionalised children are 16.500. Out of these 2.200 are handicapped. Of the latter 45 are in the State Hospital "Child Psychiatric Unit" and 181 in the PIKPA foundation unit, both located in Leros. Most of the individuals in these two units are older than 18 years, are severely pysically and/or mentally handicapped whereas a small percentage are mentally retarded. The care of these individuals is poor, institution orientated and custodial. The environment does not facilitate their personal development and/or socialization and the contact with their families and the outside world is minimal or non existent. The last few years some attempts have been made to develop community care for children and to improve the living conditions in Institutions. These attempts have been paralleled with some developments in the Child Mental Helth Services. The constraints for the development of community care for children as well as the upgrading of the living conditions in Institutions are discussed. The need for a policy and a plan is stressed together with recommendations for implementation.

Session 420 Symposium:
Serotonin reuptake inhibition in the management of depression

2765

SEROTONIN IN DEPRESSION: RECENT FINDINGS
G.R.Heninger, M.D., Dept. of Psychiatry, Yale Univ. Medical School, New Haven, CT, U.S.A.
There is considerable evidence pointing to abnormalities in the function of the serotonergic (5HT) system in depression. A number of studies have found reduced imipramine binding to the 5HT transporter in the platelets of depressed patients. Recently, the prolactin and growth hormone response to infused tryptophan has been found to be blunted in depressed patients, and some patients have a blunted prolactin response to the 5HT-releasing drug fenfluramine. In order to study the effects of a direct 5HT agonist on neuroendocrine effects in patients, preliminary studies were conducted in monkeys. M-chlorophenylpiperazine (MCPP) is a metabolite of trazodone and has equal effects on both 5HT1 and 5HT2 systems. The tryptophan infusion affects the 5HT1 system. Depressed patients have a blunted prolactin and growth hormone response to tryptophan, but a normal prolactin and cortisol response to MCPP, although there is a slight blunting to growth hormone. The 5HT uptake inhibitor fluvoxamine and other drugs including desipramine, tranilcypromine and lithium, but not trazodone. Produced an increase in the prolactin response to tryptophan in depressed patients on treatment. A most interesting new finding is that when a tryptophan deficient diet and amino acid drink produces a 90% reduction in plasma tryptophan, 66% of remitted patients have a return of symptoms. The above data support the role of the serotonin system in depression and the mechanism of action of antidepressant treatments. It indicates that adequate function of the 5HT system is necessary but not sufficient for an effective antidepressant response.

2766

ALTERATION OF 5-HT NEURON PROPERTIES BY 5-HT REUPTAKE BLOCKERS
Pierre Blier, Claude de Montigny and Yves Chaput
Neurobiological Psychiatry Unit, Department of Psychiatry, McGill University, Montreal, Quebec, Canada H3A 1A1

The therapeutic efficacy of selective 5-HT reuptake blockers (RB) in major depression has been well established by numerous double-blind controlled studies. A salient feature of the antidepressant effect of all 5-HT RB studied thus far is their delayed onset of action, which contrasts with their immediate effect on the reuptake process. In an attempt to unravel this apparent discrepancy, we undertook electrophysiological studies in the rat.

The acute and short-term administration of 5-HT RB results in a marked reduction of the firing activity of dorsal raphe 5-HT neurons, through the activation of their somatodendritic autoreceptors (SD-AR) by endogenous 5-HT. With the repeated administration of the drugs, this is followed by a progressive recovery, which is complete after 14 days of treatment. This recovery was shown to be due to the desensitization of somatodendritic 5-HT autoreceptors.

The acute intravenous administration of 5-HT RB fails to modify the effectiveness of the stimulation of the ascending 5-HT pathway in suppressing the firing activity of postsynaptic neurons in the dorsal hippocampus. However, the long-term administration of these drugs markedly enhances the effectiveness of the stimulation. Evidence was provided that this is attributable to a desensitization of terminal 5-HT autoreceptors which control the release of 5-HT.

It is concluded that long-term administration of 5-HT RB enhances 5-HT neurotransmission through the desensitization of both the somatodentritic and the terminal 5-HT autoreceptors. It is proposed that this might be the substratum for the delayed therapeutic efficacy of 5-HT RB in major depression.

2767

CLINICAL OVERVIEW OF 5HT REUPTAKE BLOCKERS

E. Schweizer, Karl Rickels, U.S.A

5HT reuptake blockers, representatives of the third generation of antidepressants, show great promise in psychiatry. This paper summarizes the clinical pharmacology, adverse event profiles and clinical efficacy for several 5HT reuptake blockers, namely zimelidine, fluoxetine, fluvoxamine, sertraline, paroxetine and the broader MAO reuptake blocker venlafexine. Buspirone and gepirone, not 5HT reuptake blockers but post-synaptic 5HT-1A agonists, will also be shortly mentioned.

This third generation of antidepressants will be compared to the classic tricyclic antidepressants in terms of efficacy, speed of onset and adverse event profile.

2768
PHARMACOLOGY OF SERTRALINE, A POTENT AND SELECTIVE INHIBITOR OF SEROTONIN UPTAKE

B.K. Koe

Pfizer Research, Eastern Point Road, Groton CT

The mechanism of action of several new classes of therapeutic drugs is based on modulation of central serotonergic funtion. These include antidepressant drugs based on selective blockade of serotonin (5-HT) reuptake into nerve terminals (fluoxetine), non-benzodiazepine anxiolytics based on agonist activity at $5-HT_{1A}$ receptors on 5-HT neurons (buspirone) and an anorectic/antiobesity agent based on enhanced release of 5-HT from nerve terminals (fenfluramine). Sertraline (1S, 4S-N-methyl-4-(3, 4-dichlorophenyl)-1, 2,3,4-tetrahydro-1-naphthalenamine) is a potent and selective 5-HT inhibitor uptake of novel structure, which is found to exert antidepressant effects in humans. In animal studies, the selective inhibition of 5-HT uptake (versus dopamine or norepinephrine uptake) observed in vitro is accompanied by the effective blockade, ex vivo and in vivo, of 5-HT uptake in brain following administration of sertraline. Accordingly, several acute actions of the latter are consistent with increased synaptic concentrations of 5-HT resulting from inhibition of 5-HT reuptake, such as potentiation of the behavioral effects of 5-hydroxytryptophan (5-HT precursor) and inhibition of firing of 5-HT neurons.

In laboratory studies simulating the time course of clinical efficacy, several effects of repeated administration of sertraline are observed in rats, which may have relevance for its antidepressant action. These are induction of subsensitivity of the ß-adrenoceptor system and desensitization of the $5-HT_2$ receptor transmembrane signaling system (phosphoinositide hydrolysis) in rat brain. In both instances, the increased serotonergic transmission induced by 5-HT uptake blockers may be responsible for these delayed effects on second messenger effector systems. The preclinical pharmacology of sertraline indicates antidepressant activity without accompanying anticholinergic or cardiovascular side effects. The implication of 5-HT as an important modulator or regulator in many physiological and behavioral systems suggests that a selective 5-HT uptake blocker, such as sertraline, may have broad use as a psychotherapeutic drug in psychiatric and behavioral disorders (e.g., depression, obesity).

2769
SERTRALINE IN COMPARISON WITH AMITRIPTYLINE AND PLACEBO IN THE TREATMENT OF OUTPATIENTS WITH MAJOR DEPRESSION

Joseph Mendels

Philadelphia Medical Institute, 1015 Chestnut Street, Suite 1303, Philadelphia, PA 19107

A double-blind placebo-controlled parallel-group multicenter study was conducted in approximately 450 outpatients with major depression. Patients received either Sertraline (S) (50, 100, or 200 mgs), Amitriptyline (AMI) (50-150 mgs), or Placebo (P) for 8 weeks.

Efficacy evaluation at the last visit showed tht S was superior to P and at least equal to AmI in terms of antidepressant effect. Improvement on S (vs. placebo) was demonstrated by changes in total score on HAMD; percentage change in total HAMD; item 1 of HAMD; mean CGI improvement score; and mean change in the SCL-56 depression factor score. For example:

Hamilton Rating Scale for Depression	Sertraline	Amitriptyline	Placebo
Mean change from baseline	-12.43*	-14.06*	-8.71
Mean % change from baseline	-53.59*	-60.87*	-37.24

Clinical Global Scale

Mean change from baseline in severity:	-1.73*	-1.98*	-1.13

*$P \leq 0.001$ compared with placebo

Side Effects: S patients had a significantly higher incidence of GI upset, dry mouth, tremor and male sexual dysfunction than P patients. Of these effects nausea, diarrhea and male sexual dysfunction were more frequent in S than in the AMI patients. In contrast, AMI patients had significantly more sedation dry mouth, constipation, problems with urination, tremor and dizziness, than P patients. AMI patients also had significantly more sedation, dizziness, dry mouth, constipation and problems with urination than S patients.

A more detailed decription of the patient population, efficacy findings and side effects will be provided.

This study clearly indicates that Sertraline, is an effective antidepressant and constitutes a potentially important addition to that class of antidepressants which block the re-uptake of serotonin at the synaptic cleft. Future studies examining other aspects of S's effectiveness, as well as its comparative effects with other drugs within its class (e.g. Fluoxetine) are in progress.

2770
SERTRALINE TREATMENT OF GERIATRIC MAJOR DEPRESSION COMPARED WITH AMITRIPTYLINE

Louis Fabre

The Fabre Clinic, 5503 Crawford, Houston, TX 77076

This 8-week double-blind study was conducted in 241 depressed patients aged 65 years and older. One hundred sixty-one patients received sertraline and 80 received amitriptyline. Doses for sertraline were 50, 100, or 200 mg per day, and for amitriptyline were 50, 100, or 150 mg per day. Assessments included investigator-rated and patient-rated psychometric scales including HAMD, CGI and SCL-56.

Demographically, the treatment groups were identical: mean age of 70.2 years (sertraline) and 70.6 years (amitriptyline), mean duration of depression, 10.5 years (sertraline) and 11.1 years (amitriptyline). Mean daily doses were 116.2 mg (sertraline) and 88.3 mg (amitriptyline). Both treatment groups showed significant improvement on medication. The sertraline group dropped from a HAMD baseline of 23.67 to 10.38 at last evaluation or 7.53 at week 8. The amitriptyline group dropped from 25.23 to 11.08 at last visit or 6.74 at week 8. There were no differences on efficacy parameters between sertraline and amitriptyline except that the intention-to-treat group for total HAMD score was significantly better for amitriptyline ($P=0.044$).

Most frequent side effects for sertraline were diarrhea, loose stools, nausea, constipation, dizziness, dry mouth, fatigue, insomnia, headache, tremor and agitation. When compared to amitriptyline, sertraline was associated with a noticeably lower frequency of somnolence, dry mouth and constipation and a higher frequency of nausea, diarrhea and insomnia. Amitriptyline was associated with an increase in both standing and supine pulse rates. Sertraline was associated with a mean weight loss of 0.82 kg compared with a weight gain of 0.71 kg for amitriptyline.

This study supports the safety, tolerance and efficacy of sertraline in the treatment of geriatric patients with major depression. Sertraline appears to have similar efficacy to amitriptyline while having fewer sedative and anticholinergic side effects.

2771
THE EFFECTS OF SERTRALINE ON PSYCHOMOTOR PERFORMANCE IN HEALTHY ELDERLY VOLUNTEERS

J. Shillingford[1], I. Hindmarch[2], A. Baksi[3], P. Raptopoulos[4]

[1] Interphase UK Ltd., Pond Court, Loxwood, Billinghurst, West Sussex
[2] Human Psychopharmacology Research Unit, Dept. of Psychology, University of Leeds, Leeds, LS2 9JT
[3] Isle of Wight Research Centre, Royal Isle of Wight County Hospital, Ryde, Isle of Wight, PO 33 2DT
[4] Pfizer Ltd., Central Research, Sandwich, Kent, CT13 9NJ

Sertraline is a new antidepressant which exerts its antidepressant action by specifically inhibiting the neuronal re-uptake of 5-HT.

The object of the study was to compare:

1. the pharmacodynamic effects of single and repeated doses of sertraline against a verum treatment (mianserin) and placebo, and
2. the combined effects of an oral dose of alcohol (0.5g/kg body weight) with the experimental treatment following repeated doses.

Twenty-one healthy elderly volunteers were randomly assigned to receive in a double-blind three-way crossover design oral doses of sertraline (up to 200 mg daily), mianserin (up to 30 mg daily) and matching placebo to 9 days. The alcohol challenge was given 6 hours after the last dose of each treatment. A battery of tests including Critical Flicker Fusion Threshold, Choice Reaction Time, Linear Analogue Rating Scales for sedation, Immediate Memory Tests for numbers and words and sensori-motor tracking were performed pre-dose, 3 and 6 hours post-dose on day one and day nine, and one hour after the alcohol challenge.

There was a marked intolerance to mianserin (hypotension 5/15 volunteers) and treatment with this agent was withdrawn during the early stages of the study. It was decided not to include the mianserin treatment in the formal statistical testing, but the available data did show the expected sedative effects on a number of psychometric tests indicating the sensitivity of the battery used in this particular experiment.

Single or multiple doses of sertraline did not affect objective performance measures. Mianserin, and to a lesser extent sertraline, exhibited more sedative activity than placebo on subjective measures. The addition of alcohol did not affect these results.

2772
CARDIOVASCULAR PROFILE OF SERTRALINE
Silke B. - USA

Session 421 Workshop:
Group psychotherapy for adolescents and children

2773
GROUP PSYCHOTHERAPY FOR ADOLESCENTS AND CHILDREN
Vassiliou G., Polychronis P., Polychronis K., Sigalas Y., Sigala V. Greece, Gillieron E. - Switzerland

Session 422 Special Session:
Psychophysiological methods in psychiatry

2774
ELECTRODERMAL ACTIVITY IN INTERNAL VERSUS EXTERNAL LOCUS OF CONTROL PATIENTS WITH ANXIETY DISORDERS
A.D. Rabavilas, Psychophysiological Laboratory, Department of Psychiatry, Athens University Medical School, Eginition Hospital, Athens, Greece.

Using a locus of control (LC) scale as a screening device and adopting the ± 1 SD criterion, two groups were identified among 150 patients meeting the DSM-III criteria for generalized anxiety, panic, phobic and obsessive-compulsive disorder: a group with "internal" (n=17) and a group with "external" (n=17) LC traits. The distribution of the diagnostic categories in these groups was insignificant. Comparing the electrodermal activity of these groups (skin conductance level, response latency, amplitude and recovery time and habituation to a series of identical tones and a dishabituating (novel) tone) it was found that "external" LC patients were significantly superior to "internals" in almost all measures employed (skin conductance level= $P<0.01$, mean amplitude= $P<0.01$, amplitude to dishabituating stimulus= $P<0.01$, recovery $\frac{1}{2}$ time= $P<0.05$, spontaneous activity= $P<0.05$ and trial-to-habituation= $P<0.001$). These results in relation to previous clinical findings that indicate an overall higher psychopathology in "external" LC patients, supported the view that locus of control may be an important and multifactorially influenced contributing agent to the severity of anxiety disorders. The implications of these findings to the prognosis and treatment of the anxious patients are discussed.

2775
THE ENDOGENOUS ERP COMPONENTS IN OBSESSIVE-COMPULSIVE PATIENTS
C.Papageorgiou*,A.D.Rabavilas*,N.Uzunoglu†**
S.Papadakis**,J.Liappas* and C.Stefanis*
*Athens University Medical School,Dept. of Psychiatry,Eginition Hospital,** Athens National Technical University.

The N100 and P300 ERP components were investigated in a group of OCD patients and a group of normal controls matched for age and sex.Recordings were taken from the Cz, C3-T5/2 and C4-T6/2 regions during a formal Stroop-Test procedure.Experimental conditions included bilateral and alternatively unilateral randomized aural stimuli(500-3000 Hz,100 msec,65 dB) associated with visual stimuli (light spot,100 msec) as warning S1,followed by the "imperative" S2 (coloured word).Latencies (initial,maximum amplitude and terminal) and amplitudes (vertical deflection and integral) were measured for both ERP components. Patients showed significantly delayed latencies on N100 in most testing conditions (P<0.01 - P<0.001) as compared with controls,while P300 measures failed to differentiate the two groups.However,patients produced significantly more "absent" P300 responses related to S".These findings support the view that attentional and resolution of uncertainty deficits may exist in the patients, a fact that can be meaningfully associated with the main clinical features of the OBC.

2776
EXPLORATORY EYE MOVEMENTS AS A MARKER FOR SCHIZOPHRENIA
Takuya Kojima, Eisuke Matsushima, Katsuya Ohta, Katsumi Ando and Yasuo Shimazono
Dept. Neuropsychiatry, Tokyo Medical and Dental Univ. 5-45, Yushima 1-chome, Bunkyo-ku, Tokyo, 113 JAPAN

Exploratory eye movements in schizophrenic and non-schizophrenic subjects while viewing geometric figures were examined with an eye mark recorder. A number of eye fixations, mean eye tracking length (METL) and the responsive search score (RSS) were measured. The RSS is the score of eye movements in response to the final question of an examiner.

The schizophrenic group had lower RSS and shorter METL than depressed patients, methamphetamine psychotics and normal controls. Of eye movement indicators, the RSS and the number of eye fixations were chosen as significant indicators to discriminate schizophrenics from non-schizophrenic 6 groups by stepwise selection procedure. By these two variables, discriminant analysis enabled us to discriminate schizophrenics from non schizophrenics with a sensitivity of 73-77% and a specificity of 77-82%.

These results suggest that the eye movements measured by our method may be a specific indicator for schizophrenia.

2777
EVENT-RELATED POTENTIALS IN SCHIZOPHRENIA

Yoichi Kidogami, Hiroshi Yoneda, Keizo Murakami, Shingo Yokota, Katsuhiro Toyoda, Keizo Hirosawa, Hiroyuki Asaba, Toshiaki Sakai
Department of Neuropsychiatry, Osaka Medical College, Takatsuki, Osaka, JAPAN

Event-related Potentials(ERP) were recorded at the Fz, Cz, and Pz regions during oddball tasks of auditory stimuli in schizophrenic patients(S group), their first degree relatives(F group) and normal controls(C group). Firstly, we investigated the diurnal variation of ERP in the C group(9 males and 2 females) by giving the same tasks 5 times a day at 8 am, 11 am, 2 pm, 5 pm and 8 pm. P300 amplitude showed a significant diurnal variation, with the largest amplitude at 2 pm. Therefore all ERP examinations were performed at 2 pm. As reported in previous ERP studies of schizophrenics, the P300 amplitude of S group was significantly smaller than that of C group. The F group also showed the tendency of a lower P300 amplitude compared with C group. We found no significant difference in the latency of P300 among the three groups. These results suggest that the smaller P300 amplitude may be a trait marker of schizophrenia.

2778
PARANOID VS. NONPARANOID SCHIZOPHRENIA:DIFFERENCES ON P300 EVENT-RELATED POTENTIAL.
M.R.Louzã*,K.Maurer,B.Neuhauser. Universitäts-Nervenklinik, Füchsleinstr. 15, 8700 Würzburg, FRG.
We studied 30 medicated schizophrenics (RDC), divided in a paranoid (n=16) and a nonparanoid (n=14) subgroup and 30 healthy subjects.We used a somatosensory version of the oddball paradigm (Louzã Neto: Z EEG-EMG, 1989) by stimulating the right (1st run) and then the left (2nd run) median nerve at the wirst.Electrodes: F3,F4,P3,P4 refered to (A1 + A2). P300 latency and amplitude (related to prestimulus baseline) were measured. On the 1st run paranoid patients had a nonsignificant (p=.061) reduced amplitude and normal latency; nonparanoid had prolonged latency (p=.024) and normal amplitude. On the 2nd run paranoid patients had prolonged latency (p=.011)and reduced amplitude (p=.011) while nonparanoid had both values comparable to controls. No relationship was observed between P300 parameters and clinical ratings and medication dose. These differences could be further evidence that these two subtypes of schizophrenia might have different biological substrats.

*FAPESP-Fellow. Institut of Psychiatry, Univ. of São Paulo, C.P. 8091, 05403 São Paulo S.P., BRAZIL.

2779

ERP ANALYSIS IN THE FREQUENCY DOMAIN IN DISTHIMIC DISORDER USING A BOOLEAN APPROACH.
M.Purificação Horta, José Barahona da Fonseca, Madalena Fenha and J.Simões da Fonseca.
Depart.of Medical Psychology and Psychopathology, Fac.of Medicine of Lisbon.

Visual Event Related Potentials in the brain were studied using as stimuli four distinct but interrelated patterns -(a) crossed vertical and horizontal spatial sinusoids; (b) vertical sinusoids; (c) horizontal sinusoids and (d) black or white thin horizontal strips distributed spatially according with a Poisson distribution on a gray ground. A separator frame, homogeneous and with the same total amount of energy as any of the stimuli was used. As Normal Volunteers had been able to form equivalence classes joining stimuli (a) and (d) or else (b) and (c) in a situation of visual discrimination the same experimental set-up was used in groups of patients suffering from Disthimic Disorder either in acute state or else under therapy. It was observed that although depressive patients are also able to form classes $\{xy, \bar{x}\bar{y}\}$ or else $\{x\bar{y}, \bar{x}y\}$ the discrimination between individual stimuli was impaired concerning stimuli to which no motor response should be produced. Furthermore, Coherence function had increased significantly in Depressive subjects under acute administration of drug while it decreased in Normal Volunteers in the same circumstances. It decreased in Depressive under administration of 75 mg. of Maprotiline during 15 days. Reaction times measured independently were higher in Depressive subjects not under treatment.
Conclusion are proposed concerning the use of those data as indicators of the Cognitive Depressive set and transformation of the Normal Set.

2780

Depressive syndromes in the aged-Differentiation by EEG and Evoked Potentials
M. Albers, J.M. Klotz, M. Bergener*
Rheinische Landesklinik Köln,Fachklinik für Psychiatrie,BRD
*Medical Director: Prof. Dr. M. Bergener

In recent years neurophysiological methods such as EEG, EP(Evoked Potentials) combined with topographic mapping have gained increasing importance in the assessment of depressive syndromes in old age, which may be caused by a broad variety of factors, e.g.metabolic,endocrinologic,hemodynamic,degenerative or functional. One major problem in assessing elderly depressive patients is the differentiation of pathologic loss of function from normal aging. Relevant EEG findings from healthy aged persons are described based on recent literature:increase of beta,moderate slowing of alpha,and increase of slow activity with occasional foci. Due to the large variability of these parameters frequently it is impossible to arrive at a correct diagnosis.EPS may help to avoid this difficulty as they are largely independent from age. The P 300,which is associated with cognitive processing of sensory input is of special interest in this respect. The acoustic P 300 paradigm is easy to apply and yields well reproducible results. In healthy persons or patients with functional depression the P 300 is a positive potential occurring about 250 ms after a target stimulus.In patients with loss of intellectual functions due to somatic causes the latency is increased,in severe cases it may disappear. Using topographic mapping abnormalities in spatial distribution of P 300 waves can be visualized.The results of an ongoing study on patients of a psychogeriatric day hospital using this method will be demonstrated and discussed.

Session 423   Workshop:
Short-term dynamic psychotherapy

2781

SHORT-TERM DYNAMIC PSYCHOTHERAPY DEMONSTRATED BY VIDEOTAPES
Peter Sifneos, M.D.
Harvard University, U.S.A.

The workshop will present the criteria for selection of appropriate candidates, will discuss the techniques utilized and the outcome findings. Videotapes VHS NTSC will be used to depict the techniques of this type of brief therapy.

Session 424   Symposium:
Critical issues on diagnostic evaluation

2782

INTERNATIONAL STUDIES ON ACUTE PSYCHOSES

John E. Cooper, University of Nottingham, United Kingdom

The classification of acute psychoses constitute a major challenge in psychiatric nosology and in the development of the international classification of diseases. A review will be presented of the concepts of acute psychoses and the connected nosological issues.
Additionally, the design of an ongoing World Health Organization Study on Acute Psychoses will be outlined. It involves the assessment of 1,000 cases in centers located in Africa, Europe, and South East Asia, using the SCAAPS schedule. Evolving results of this large study will be presented and discussed.

2783

ISSUES ON THE INTERNATIONAL CLASSIFICATION OF NEUROTIC AND PERSONALITY DISORDERS
Masaaki Kato
Tokyo Medical College, Japan

Field trials on the classification of neurotic disorders with the participation of 70 leading psychiatrists yielded the following results:
1. Dissociative and Conversion Disorders should be incorporated within one broad category.
2. Depressive Neurosis should be included within Neurotic Disorder and not within Dysthymia or Mood Disorder.
3. The term Neuroasthenia was found useful by general practitioners.
Regarding the classification of personality disorders, a survey was conducted using a checklist containing 121 questions, in an attempt to clarify clusters of personality disorder. The term Emotionally Unstable Personality Disorder was widely accepted and problems were found with Schizotypal and Narcissistic Personality Disorders.

2784

CURRENT CONTROVERSIES ON THE DIAGNOSIS OF DEPRESSION
Strömgren, Erik
Institute of Psychiatric Demography,
Psychiatric Hospital, DK-8240 Risskov, Denmark.

The goals of psychiatric research are to find the causes of mental disorders, to eliminate these causes, and, if that is not possible, to reduce, as far as possible, the symptoms of the disorders. The major current classifications, ICD and DSM-III, do not focus on the causes of disorders, but - particularly perceptible in the section on affective (mood) disorders - primarily on symptoms and course. The subgrouping is therefore largely irrelevant for etiological research, and the introduction of special "criteria for research", although no doubt of importance for the reliability of the diagnostication, is of no avail for nosological validity. Other types of classification are therefore necessary for research purposes. The latest results of genetic research may be helpful in this respect.

2785

SCALING MODELS AND THE CLASSIFICATION OF DEPRESSION
Francisco Alonso-Fernández
Complutense University, Madrid, Spain

The complexity of depression has been the subject of various scaling approaches, several of which will be reviewed.
Illustrating a major aspect of our work, the study of depressive patients with the structural phenomenological method has suggested that the depressive state is made up of four basic-interdependent dimensions: depressive mood, anergy or lack of drive, communication distortion, and rhythmopathy. The symptoms of mild and moderate depressive conditions appeared distributed along one, two, or three of these dimensions.
The tetradimensional questionnaire for depression, TEQUED (Alonso-Fernández) is based on this new clinical model of depression. The full instrument is composed of 63 items and the SHORT-TEQUED of 8 items, all distributed into four dimensions. In addition to its pertinence to overall diagnosis, this questionnaire may be useful for typological classification and for monitoring illness course.

2786

RECENT INQUIRIES ON STANDARDIZED ASSESSMENT AND COMPREHENSIVE DIAGNOSIS
R.-D. Stieglitz, H. Helmchen
Freie Universität, Berlin, Fed. Rep. Germany

The paper gives an overview of recent developments in psychopathological assessment and classification. Two topics are presented: conceptual approaches and instruments of assessment. First, the following approaches for describing the condition of the patient are discussed: operationalized diagnoses, multiple diagnoses, the polydiagnostic approach, multiaxial diagnosis and the multimethod approach. Second, the following data-gathering instruments for the above strategies are considered: checklists, interviews, ratings, self-ratings, and psychological tests. Finally, the paper summarizes empirical research on the advantages and disadvantages of these methodological approaches and proposes ideas for designing and executing future investigations in this area.

Session 425 — Symposium:
Self-mutilation and factitious disorders

2787
NARCISSISM IN THE GENESIS OF THE 'CAENIS SYNDROME'

JANNES, C.
Dept of Psychiatry, University Hospital
Ghent, Belgium

Both anorexia nervosa and self-mutilation belong to the spectrum of the self-induced somatoform disorders.
The intensive psychotherapy of a young woman, with the 'Caenis Syndrome', that is a combination of both a severe anorexia nervosa and repetitive self-mutilation (self-cutting, ingestion of metal objects and piercing) offers an explanation to the genesis of this pathology.
The theory of 'narcissism' and 'self' are found to be useful in the conceptualisation of this disorder. Narcissistic symptoms and reactions such as denial, distortion, regressive flight in grandiose phantasies, narcissistic rage and self-destruction, detachment defense, self-preoccupation and perfectionism are discussed in reference to the case.
The influence of parent behaviour on the development of narcissism and self are discussed with special emphasis on self-experience, self-representation, self-ideal, self-esteem, self-expression and self-handling.

2788
ANALYTICAL PSYCHOTHERAPY IN DERMATITIS ARTEFACTA

CONSOLI, S.G.
Hôpital de la Salpétrière
Paris, France

With reference to the case of a 30-year-old female presenting a dermatitis artefacta of the right cheek and followed up in psychotherapy, the author places particular emphasis on the following theoretical and practical points :
- a facticious disorder as an enacted repetition on one's own body of physical mistreatment experienced during childhood;
- the role of "somatic compliance" in the localization of the facticious disorder, and symbolic value of the site of the disorder and of the resultant scar;
- the importance, at least at the start of psychotherapeutic follow-up of the hospital institution, which allows control of violent affect in the patient and plays the role of a third party between the patient and his psychotherapist. Indeed, it is not unusual for the subject with a facticious disorder to sense another person as dangerous, but also to live his own presence as dangerous for others and particularly for his psychotherapist, thus creating a risk of rupture of the therapeutic relationship.

2789
SELF-MUTILATION AND SUICIDAL BEHAVIOUR

VAN HEERINGEN, C.
Dept of Psychiatry, University Hospital
Ghent, Belgium

The psychiatric aspects of self-mutilation are compared in two groups of patients : group I is a group of 30 patients (aged 20 - 55 years) with self-inflicted dermatological lesions (SIDL), while group II consists of 30 patients (matched for age and sex) who showed parasuicidal behaviour resulting in cutaneous lesions.
According to DSM-III-R criteria, axis I disorders were diagnosed in group I in 77 % and in group II in 60 %. In the SIDL group, depression was diagnosed in 37 %, panic disorder in 10 % and to a lesser extent generalized anxiety disorder. In the parasuicide-group, depression was present in 27 % and anxiety disorder in 13 %. The most striking differences are found for somatoform disorders (diagnosed in group I in 83 % and in group II in 13 %) and personality disorders (group I : 100 %; group II : 63 %).

2790
A PSYCHOANALYTICAL APPROACH TO THE SYMPTOM IN FACTICIOUS ORGANIC DISORDERS

PY, C.; BAUDIN, M.; CONSOLI, S.
Hôpital Broussais
Paris, France

The detailed case-report of four subjects presenting facticious organic disorders, completed by the results of personality projective tests (Rorschach and T.A.T.) allows the proposal of a psychodynamic conception of symptom formation.
These cases concerned a facticious dermatitis, a lymphoedema of a finger due to the use of a tourniquet, and covert ingestion of anti-vitamine K, in one patient, and of anti-hypertensive in another. The four subjects presented severe personality disorders, dominated by difficulties in mental elaboration and by dynamics of relationship underlined by aggressive sado-masochistic drives. In these subjects, an oral complex of the cannibalistic type, close to the melancholic incorporation process, could occur within the body space, the lost object being embodied in the facticious physical disorder. The symptom formation could respond to a simple figuration (Darstellung), as described by Freud in the hysterical attack, rather than to a representation activity (Vorstellung).
The facticious physical symptom could thus be considered as an acted equivalent, of a hysterical conversion, conveying a subject's inability to represent conflicts with traumatic value in a merely imaginary mode, on the bodily scene.

2791

PREDICTORS OF SUICIDE RISK IN CUTANEOUS SELF-MUTILATORS

VAN MOFFAERT, M.
Dept of Psychiatry, University Hospital
Ghent, Belgium

Risk factors predicting parasuicide and suicide in patients with self-inflicted cutaneous lesions were investigated by long-term follow-up evaluation of both the general physical and psychiatric status and the medical consumption patterns. In a cohort of 189 cutaneous self-mutilators (dermatitis artefacta, delicate self-cutting, pinners and piercers), one patient in three shows a psychiatric disorder with self-destructive component (alcoholism, drug and/or substance abuse, factitious disorders other than dermatological, anorexia or bulimia nervosa, parasuicide and suicide).

Sex, age, the absence of an affective relationship, the way of mutilating do not affect the suicidal risk. There is no correlation either with the severity of the underlying psychiatric diagnosis or with a history (personal or familial) of habitual violence or psychophysiological disorders.

The following factors have a predictive value for an increased risk of suicide and parasuicide: a paramedical connotation in education and/or profession, a history of medical hospitalisation and immobilisation.

Paradoxically, extensive cutaneous mutilations on multiple body parts and early drop-out of psychiatric treatment appear to protect against suicide and parasuicide.

Session 426 Symposium:
Cultural psychiatry issues in Asia and India: Suicidal behavior and sexual problems

2792

SUICIDE BEHAVIOR IN JAPAN

Kazuya Yoshimatsu, M.D.
Psychiatric Research Institute of Tokyo
Tokyo, Japan

For the past several decades, Japan has shown a special age-suicide rate curve, namely, a decrease in youth suicide and the increase in middle-aged male's suicide rate, reflects great changes of suicidal pattern. Investigation revealed that suicidal behavior differs according to each generation from the viewpoint of suicide rate, method, and cause. In the past several years, the middle-aged suicide rate has been increasing rapidly for both sexes. The methods used were hanging, gas and jumping. The presented causes are suffering from illness and economical problems. However, as youth suicide rates were high formerly about three decades ago in Japan, it is speculated that it must be the same cohort generation which shows high suicide rates in both ages of youth and the middle-aged. This is the cohort generation who were raised as youths at the difficult post-war period and now, as the middle-aged, facing the social conflict between ethical devotions toward his own working company and desire for self-centeredness.

2793

SUICIDAL PATTERNS IN KOREA

Ho Young Lee, M.D., & Seung Chul Shin, M.D.
Department of Psychiatry, Yonsei University
Seoul, Korea

The authors investigated the reports on accidental death from the National Police Headquarters, Republic of Korea, for the last 25 years. During the studied period, 1964-1988, the overall suicide rate has steadily decreased. The suicide rate of adolescents has also decreased. The study revealed that suicide rate of the rural area is greater than that of the urban area. The authors also studied suicide victims of one rural area exclusively using local police reports on accidental death. The age group of 60 and above ranked first in suicide number (23%). The suicide rate of this age group was 97.2 per 100,000 population. In this study, 79.1% of total suicides used agricultural chemicals. The most common motive for suicide was financial difficulty (21.7%). In the age group of 60 and over, 47.7% of the suicides had major disabling physical illnesses. 42.1% of the suicides had mental depression prior to suicide. 14.2% had alcoholism and 6.1% was schizophrenic.

2794

Social Changes and Suicidal Behavior in Taiwan

Eng-Kung Yeh, M.D.
Taipeh City Psychiatric Center
Taipeh, Taiwan, China

The reported suicide rate in Taiwan during the past 4 decades after WW II has been in average between 12-14 per 100,000 population.

This is lower than any developed countries in Asia, Europe and America. There are two peaks, first during the 50's and early 60's with highest rate of 19.1 per 100,000 population in 1964, followed by a gradual decline of rate reaching the lowest of 8.7 in 1976. The second and the lower peak was during 1981 to 1987, with highest rate of 12.3 in 1983, much lower than that in 1964. The rate in 1987 was 9.7 per 100,000 suggesting the beginning of declination. The rates in large cities are significantly lower than that of the remaining parts of Taiwan area. The rates are significantly higher in males than females at a rate of about 1.5:1.

The above findings are to be discussed in relation with political turmoil and massive influx of migration from mainland China to Taiwan during the late 40's and 50's, and the rapid industrialization with economic prosperity and social changes that Taiwan has undergone during the past 3 decades.

2795
IDENTITY, SEX AND LAND

Ajita Chakraborty
Institute of Postgraduate Medical
Education & Research, Calcutta, India

Koro was not known in India before 1982 when an epidemic of Koro occurred over a vast area in the States of Assam and West Bengal. A theory has been developed following a lead by Murphy that epidemics of Koro occur in areas where there is refugee-settler clash with strong ethnic overtones. It is suggested that these areas also harbour cults of the tortoise, an animal whose symbolic relation to Koro has been mentioned by Yap. Some evidence of these cults in Bengal and Assam will be presented with psycho-dynamic interpretation on Jungian lines.

2796
PENIS-IMAGE IN KORO

Arabinda Narayan Chowdhury,
Institute of Postgraduate Medical Education & Research, Calcutta, India.

A massive Koro outbreak took place in North Bengal region of West Bengal state, India, from July to September, 1982. Present study is one of the several clinical investigations that were conducted on the Koro patients of this epidemic.

Penis-image perception (penile length) of forty male single Koro patients were ellicited by a grapho-motor projective test DAPT (Draw-a-Penis test) and was compared with two matched controls, viz. Normal subjects and Anxiety neurotics. Koro patients perceived significantly ($p < .01$) less penis length for both flaccid and extended states than the controls. They also showed significantly ($p < .01$) less flaccid-penis length perception than their real flaccid penis length. Longitudinal DAPT values also showed the constancy of their penis-length perception even at the interval of two years. Psychodynamic significance of this dismorphic penis-image perception in relation to their Koro psychopathology and vulnerability has been discussed.

2797
SEXUAL MYTHS AND ATTITUDES IN INDIA

Vijoy K Varma, M.D. & Ajit Avasthi, M.D.
Postgraduate Medical Institute
Chandigarh, India

In the Indian society, sex has been a forbidden topic for discussion and hence not subjected to proper investigation.

Our culture is unique in the people's attitudes towards sex. The virtues of celibacy and the preservation of semen in males and general unresponsiveness in females are valued. Myths and prejudices about sex abound and hamper any proper sex education. Quacks thrive over the misconceptions of people and offer a host of fancy and exotic "therapies" which are reminiscent of the alchemy of the Dark Ages.

Increasing literacy rate, free mixing of sexes, changing roles of women with increasing assertiveness and change in traditional values have increased the conflicts between sexual drive and demands, based on social custom and philosophy. Consequently, there is a need to understand the sexual knowledge and attitudes of the general public with the aim to develop effective strategies of intervention.

The results of a study into the sexual attitudes and knowledge of North Indian adult population are discussed, particularly in the sociocultural context.

Session 427 Symposium:
New strategies in treatment of schizophrenia

2798
Early Intervention to Prevent Relapse

Marvin I. Herz, M.D.
Depart. of Psychiatry, State University of New York at Buffalo, Buffalo, New York, USA

This paper will present a description of psychosocial treatment approaches that can be used to prevent relapse and rehospitalization in schizophrenic outpatients. It will focus on early intervention strategies which are initiated when patients develop prodromal symptoms.

Background: The author has conducted both retrospective and prospective studies of the relapse process, focusing on recognition of prodromal symptoms and early intervention when they occur. One hundred and forty-five patients were interviewed in addition to family members utilizing a structured questionnaire regarding early signs of relapse in the retrospective study. In the prospective studies, 159 patients and their family informants were educated about early signs of relapse and were told how to seek immediate help when symptoms appeared. Data will be reported about the most common early symptoms found in the prospective studies, modes of intervention, and results of early intervention. In addition, case vignettes will be presented to describe clinical aspects of the episodes.

2799

PREDICTORS OF LOW DOSE RESPONSE IN SCHIZOPHRENIA

Stephen R. Marder, M.D.
Brentwood VA Medical Center,
UCLA School of Medicine, Los Angeles, CA, USA

Recent studies indicate that a substantial proportion of chronic schizophrenic patients can remain stable with low doses of maintenance neuroleptic. Unfortunately, there is very little empiric data available to assist clinicians in selecting the best candidate for low dose treatment. In a study comparing 5 vs 25 mg of fluphenazine decanoate administered every 14 days to stabilized patients, we investigated the following as potential predictors of response: prior dosage requirements, demographic variables, serum prolactin, and fluphenazine plasma level. Patients who required higher dosages of neuroleptic prior to randomization were at higher risk for relapse as were patients with low prolactin levels ($p < .05$ for each). Demographic information and clinical psychopathology were not predictive of response. Survival analysis with fluphenazine level as a covariate indicated that plasma fluphenazine levels at steady state (6 or 9 mo) was predictive of treatment response. Strategies for selecting appropriate candidates for low dose treatment will be discussed.

2800

A BREAKTHROUGH IN THE TREATMENT OF SCHIZOPHRENIC ILLNESS: CLOZAPINE

Theodore Van Putten, M.D., Veterans Administration Medical Center, Los Angeles, USA

Clozapine is a novel antipsychotic drug of proven efficacy in chronic, treatment-resistant schizophrenia. The drug does not cause extrapyramidal side effects (EPS) and almost certainly no tardive dyskinesia. The main side effect of clozapine is agranulocytosis. It is estimated that the risk of agranulocytosis is 2% during the first year of exposure and, for this reason, patients will require a weekly CBC as long as they are exposed to clozapine treatment. A six-week, rigorously designed, multi-center-trial (Kane et al, Archives of General Psychiatry, Sept., 1988) establishes that clozapine is more effective than a conventional neuroleptic, chlorpromazine, in a group of treatment-resistant schizophrenic patients. Most impressive is that the improvement in this back-ward sample was consistent over the entire spectrum of positive and negative schizophrenic symptoms. When patients were classified as having "improved" (by prospective criteria) to a clinically significant extent, 30% of clozapine recipients improved within six weeks vs only 4% of chlorpromazine/benztropine mesylate (cogentin) recipients ($p < .001$). In addition, to this study, clozapine has also been compared (double-blind) to haloperidol and again to chlorpromazine (three other trials). In these four comparison studies, clozapine also had superior efficacy. Indications for clozapine treatment will be discussed.

2801

Treatment Strategies in Schizophrenia: Pharmacologic Treatment

Nina R. Schooler, Ph.D., University of Pittsburgh, Pittsburgh, PA USA; Samuel J. Keith, M.D., National Institute of Mental Health, Rockville, MD USA; Joanne B. Severe, M.S., National Institute of Mental Health, Rockville, MD USA; Susan M. Matthews, B.A., National Institute of Mental Health, Rockville, MD USA

Maintenance treatment in schizophrenia requires attention to both pharmacologic and psychosocial treatment modalities. Although good clinical treatment includes both modalities, the experimental study of medication and specific psychosocial treatment is rare.

We shall review the experimental literature regarding the role of medication in psychosocial treatment as background to the development of the NIMH Treatment Strategies in Schizophrenia Study. This multi-center clinical trial is investigating the efficacy of three neuroleptic maintenance strategies (continuous standard dose, continuous low dose and targeted or intermittent treatment) in interaction with two family treatment strategies (applied and supportive family management) in the long term treatment of schizophrenia.

Patients are identified when acutely symptomatic, randomized to one of the two family treatment strategies and treated with the assigned family treatment and standard dosage of fluphenazine decanoate for up to six months. If they can be successfully stabilized they are randomized into the double-blind dosage study for a two year trial in the full 3 x 2 factorial design. Two hundred thirty four patients have thus far been randomized to family treatment. These patients represent a carefully diagnosed, evaluated and treated cohort. Sixty four percent (n=149) have been successfully stabilized and entered the full study design (family treatment and neuroleptic assignment).

Patients who can be successfully stabilized on the combination of standard dose neuroleptic and family treatment will be compared to those who cannot on a number of dimensions including diagnosis, psychopathology, and aspects of early response to pharmacologic treatment.

2802

Overcoming Disability Through Skills Training

Robert Paul Liberman, M.D.; Stephen Marder, M.D.; Charles J. Wallace Ph.D.; Thad Eckman Ph.D.; William Wirshing, M.D.

UCLA Department of Psychiatry, Brentwood VA Medical Center, Camarillo State Hospital

Los Angeles, California, USA

Inspired by the stress-vulnerability-coping-competence model of mental disorders, methods for training chronic schizophrenics in social and independent living skills have been designed and validated in field tests throughout the USA and Canada. Principles of social learning are incorporated into a highly structured and prescribed set of modules comprising a Trainer's Manual, Patient's Workbook, and Demonstration Video. Efficacy has been demonstrated for modules that train medication self-management, symptom self-management, grooming and self-care, recreation for leisure, and social problem-solving. Acquisition of skills is durable and confers protection against relapse.

2803
TREATMENT STRATEGIES IN SCHIZOPHRENIA--PSYCHOSOCIAL TREATMENT

Samuel J. Keith, M.D., National Institute of Mental Health, Rockville, Md. USA
Nina R. Schooler, Ph.D., University of Pittsburgh, Pittsburgh, Pa. USA
Susan M. Matthews, B.A., National Institute of Mental Health, Rockville, Md. USA
Joanne B. Severe, M.A., National Institute of Mental Health, Rockville, Md. USA

The NIMH Treatment Strategies in Schizophrenia Collaborative Study (TSS) is investigating the efficacy of three neuroleptic drug management strategies (continuous standard dose, continuous low dose and targeted treatment) and two forms of psychoeducational family treatment strategies (applied and supportive family management) in the long term treatment of schizophrenia. The study is being conducted at five sites in the United States.

Patients are identified when acutely symptomatic, randomized to one of the two family treatment strategies and treated with the assigned family treatment and standard dosage of fluphenazine decanoate for up to six months. If they can be successfully stabilized, they are randomized into the double-blind dosage study for a two year trial in the full 3 X 2 factorial design. Two hundred thirty four patients have thus far been randomized to family treatment. These patients represent a carefully diagnosed, evaluated and treated cohort. Sixty four percent (n = 149) have been successfully stabilized and entered the full study design (family treatment and neuroleptic assignment).

There are currently five international studies of family psychoeducational treatment which led to the TSS. We will review their influence on shaping the interventions for schizophrenia and will systematically present their outcomes and their relationship to the TSS.

This presentation will focus on measures of early outcome from the exposure to the two family management strategies. Our findings indicate that there are predictors of early outcome contained in aspects of the treatment environment which are relevant across a wide variety of treatment settings. The substantial differences among sites in terms of patient characteristics and treatment environment enhance generalization of findings to a broad range of clinical settings.

Session 428 — Workshop:
New trends in child psychotherapy: Symbolic play-therapy within the family

2804
SYMBOLIC PLAY CHILD PSYCHOTHERAPY WITHIN THE FAMILY: FANTASMATIC INTERACTIONS
Traube Raymond, M.D., Child Psychiatrist
Office medico-pedagogique, Neuchatel-Switzerland

The mental performance of the child gets more complex by means of the relations that couple him to his environment, starting with his mother. The child starts relating in accordance with the latent expectations of the parents, which are in turn determined by their own early interactions.

The therapist lends himself as a partner for relationship coupling, playing a role also as a fantasy, and his behaviour evolves as the relationships in the family change gradually because of their interaction with him.

An example illustrates the way a prevailing familial fantasy, concerning the mother in particular, recurs in the child's symptom first, and then in the therapeutic gameplaying, which becomes ever more complex; the symptomatic resolution is brought about by means of the progressive re-couplings therapist – child – mother – family, which comes to an end when the mother takes upon herself a part of her relational needs invested in an ambivalent manner in her child.

Session 429 — Workshop:
On caring and its troubles: Some consequences of "empathic success"

2805
ON CARING AND ITS TROUBLES: SOME CONSEQUENCES OF "EMPATHIC SUCCESS"
Daniel P. Schwartz, M.D.
Austen Riggs Center, Inc., U.S.A.

This study attempts to demonstrate that experiences of caring are complex events in the processes of an analytic psychotherapy. These caring moments are those of evolving empathy in the therapist. These are central to what is curative and developmental in a therapeutic relationship, and simultaneously are disorganizing to the patient. This is in contrast to the Kohutian dicta that fragmentation of the self follows "empathic failure". "Empathic successes" are here described as having disruptive effects.

Three clinical psychoanalytic and psychotherapeutic examples present work with a neurotic, a borderline-obsessive, and a hospitalized schizophrenic illustrating these moments of caring, "empathic success", and disruption.

The thesis is that developmental advance involves the reorganization of the ego/self representation and requires arranged conditions for projection, merger, and the subsequent aggressive emergence of behaviors that are disruptive to that merged state. There is then the consequent search for individuation processes primarily within the patient. They are also accompanied by individuating painful experiences for the analyst as well. This presentation requires forty-five minutes.

2806 *

2807 *

---
* Numbers left open for technical reasons not corresponding to any abstracts

Session 430 Free Communications:
Psychopathological and psychotherapeutic themes II

2808
LIFETRACK THERAPY - A NEW APPROACH

Yukio Ishizuka M.D.
Clinical Assistant Professor of Psychiatry
New York University Medical Center

A new therapeutic approach is presented with is characterized by:
1. Quantifiable definition of Positive Mental Health as a therapy objective.
2. Patients rate themselves daily on a subjective 10 point scale on a total of 41 parameters.
3. Visual (graphic) feedback by a personal computer during therapy sessions.
4. Active advocacy role for Positive Mental Health, by the therapist.

Benefits of Lifetrack Therapy include:
1. Comprehensive, up to date, and accurate data of the patients' day to day condition becomes available.
2. Psychological Feedback reinforces positive therapeutic gains, and give perspectives for setbacks.
3. Patients learn to think positively and improve rapidly.
4. Clearer grasp of the path to recovery with graphic display on a computer screen.
5. Patients gain the means of monitoring and improving themselves.

Several important clinical research findings with Lifetrack method will be presented.

2809
DEATH AND THE THERAPIST: A CALL FOR A PROTOCOL

Lois Ames, LICSW, Faculty, Harvard Medical School, Department of Psychiatry, The Cambridge Hospital, Cambridge, Massachusetts, USA

Can we do less than we ask of others daily?
Each human struggles with loss, betrayal, rejection, grief, sorrow, illness, dying and death in the course of a lifetime. In the course of our work we constantly support our patients' courageous confrontations with reality. But how many of us have taken the time, the energy, and the courage to face the fact that we, too, must struggle with our own mortality and should make plans and provision for our patients-and for our colleagues, students, and staff-as a precaution in case of our sudden disability or sudden death?
This paper calls for a recognition of the ineluctable inevitability of our own mortality and calls for a protocol for provision of service in an orderly fashion in case of death or disability: for individual therapists and for every institution involved in teaching, training and/or providing therapeutic services. Practical measures and policies are discussed. Recognizing and coping with the feelings of everyone involved is discussed. The psychotherapeutic community is challenged to go into the 21st century with a willingness to confront our own individual moments of debility and our own mortality.

2810
EEG BEFUND DER ONEIROIDEN ERLEBNISFORM

S. Hashimoto, Y. Kogita, T. Fujimura, H. Suzuki, T. Ban and T. Mita,
Iwate Medical University, Morioka, Japan.

Die oneiroide Erlebnisform ist sehr selten, unbekanntes Krankheitsbild.
Wir hatten Glück, einen Patient zu haben, der hat nach langjährigem Alkoholismus diesmal an typischer oneiroiden Erlebnisform erkrankt.
Deren Polysomnographie zeigte ein eigentümliches Ergebnis: d.h. Stadium 1-REM mit tonischem EMG (stage 1-REM with tonic EMG).
Das Ergebnis deutet uns eine Genese des Krankheitsbilds an.

2811
THE BODY : A PLACE FOR REBIRTH   PACKS AND
                                  MUMMIFICATION
RAFATIAN A.H.   SSM 17/27
                        PARIS FRANCE

A simple, feasible method of treatment of different psychiatric pathologies is presented.

Historical and cultural parallels intend to underline concepts common to the body as an instrument of rebirth in different rituals and techniques.

The packing technique is presented including its place among different therapies, as well as its preferential indications and its various theoretical bases.

2812

PSYCHOTIC PATIENTS' ATTRIBUTIONS FOR MENTAL ILLNESS:
A COMPARISON WITH ATTRIBUTIONS FOR CANCER
Hantzi, A., Molvaer, J., Papadatos, Y.
CENTRE FOR MENTAL HEALTH AND RESEARCH

This study was conducted in order to examine the attributional styles concerning mental illness of young psychotic out-patients participating in a rehabilitation programme. The sample consisted of 50 men and 33 women (mean age 26 years), diagnosed psychotic, with main symptoms: a) hallucinations (59%), b) depression (12%), c) non-specific (29%). Subjects replied to a personally administered questionnaire, designed to obtain ratings of importance for several causes of mental illness and cancer. Causes were arrived at through content analysis of answers to open questions about causes of their mental illness and a hypothetical person's cancer, in a pilot study with 20 subjects. The analysis focused on differences in ratings between the two sexes and among subjects with different: educational level, social background length of participation in the programme and No. of admissions to a psychiatric hospital. Factor analysis of the ratings on causes for mental illness revealed 3 factors: external causes, personal inadequacy and luck. Scores on these 3 scales were compared with scores on the respective scales for cancer. It was found that subjects consider external causes more important for cancer than for mental illness. Finally, it was shown that longer participation in the programme and lower ratings of personal inadequacy are associated with increased optimism about subjects' future mental health.

2813

OCCUPATIONAL THERAPY IN MULTIDISCIPLINARY STAFFS

Campos R. Fº - Deus G.R.P. - Galluzzi A.M.
Centro de Estudos e Pesquisas Karl Kleist -
São Paulo - Brazil

The inability to adapt to family and society and the distancing from the exterior world wile interned - especially in cases of psychosis, mental and motor deficiencies, as well as learning desabilities - it carries the patient to a defensive position when he enters into contact with society.
This defensiveness ends up being internalized and it becomes difficult for the medical professional and the psychologist break it without the aid and participation of an Occupational Therapist and a Social Aide.
This work intends to show that a multidisciplinary staff working togethers can help these individuals reach, in the most of the cases a more satisfactory condition.
The participation of the Occupational Therapist and the Social Aide together with the family and the patient is based on the personality theory by Augusto Comte, with principal intervention of the cognative-affective sphere and, consequently, in the intellectual sphere.
Abandoning the classical models till now used, the introduction of these specialities drives at the social and personal adaptation of these patients, treating and leading them to a right path of the existing resources in the community.

2814

LE MATRICIDE PSYCHOTIQUE ENTRE LE MYTHE ET LA
REALITE
Tsalicoglou Fotinie, ass. Prof. Criminal Psychology
Pantion University, Athens

C'est une lecture parallèle qu'on se propose de faire, entre l'histoire de deux cas de matricide. Celle d'Oreste, le plus célèbre matricide de l'antiquité, ayant inspiré Eschyle, Sophocle et Euripide, et celle de Nicos, jeune matricide psychotique, hospitalisé à l'Hopital Psychiatrique Publique d'Athènes.
A travers leur ressemblance inattendue se posent des questions: Comment le matricide entre le mythe et la réalité nous interroge et nous informe sur la transformation quasi-magique d'un acte interdit en acte legitime?
Y aurait-il un "topos" commun entre le vecu psychotique et les fantasmes archaiques liées à la création du mythe?

2815

GUERRE ET SANTÉ MENTALE AU LIBAN
H. Ayoub, C. Baddoura, E. Azouri - Université St.
Joseph, Lebanon

2816

SANTE MENTALE AU LIBAN PENDANT LA GUERRE
C. Baddoura, H. Ayoub, E. Azouri - Université St. Joseph, Lebanon

Session 431 Free Communications:
Studies in transcultural psychiatry II

2817

Cultural bereavement of refugees in the United States and Australia

Maurice Eisenbruch, M.D.
N.H. & M.R.C. Research Fellow,
Royal Children's Hospital Research Foundation, Parkville, Victoria 3052.

This paper aims to demonstrate that the reactions of uprooted refugees can be defined in terms of *cultural bereavement*; that these reactions are strongly coloured by the policies of the host country; and that cultural bereavement is an important factor in the health transition of refugees. The paper reports a study which developed a means of measuring cultural bereavement, which can be used to provide an indication of a community's state of health transition.

Cambodian refugees living in Australia and the USA have been studied in order to assess the impact of traumatic loss of society and culture (or cultural bereavement), the problems of adaptation to a new and very different society, the associated mental health problems and the importance of culture in shaping health problems. Significant differences were found between unaccompanied minors placed in (1) American foster homes and (2) Cambodian foster homes in America and those in Cambodian group care in Australia. Those placed in a culturally alien environment were somewhat better acculturated but suffered more cultural bereavement, while their counterparts placed in Khmer cultural setting were more poorly acculturated but suffered less cultural bereavement. Adjustment problems seemed worsened by failure to allow traditional and culturally familiar practices such as religious ritual. The well-being of the refugees was improved when they were allowed to validate their cultural beliefs through appropriate rituals and behaviour. Lack of access to culturally familiar medical care

The long-term aim of this study is to influence the development of better informed health and social policies relating to refugees and other immigrants, leading to reduction of cultural bereavement and associated psychiatric morbidity, culturally appropriate detection of resettlement problems, and better clinical engagement of immigrant patients with improved compliance and, therefore, better health.

2818

AVOIDANT TYPE OF DEPRESSION IN JAPAN
Tetsuya HIROSE, M.D., Dept. of Psychiatry, Teikyo University School of Medicine, Tokyo, JAPAN.

As premorbid characteristics of manic-depressive illness, cyclothymia (Kretschmer), immodithymia (Shimoda), and melancholic type (Tellenbach) are well-known, particularly in Japan.

Recently we, however, see cases of another type of depression with different character traits, mostly in highly educated male white-collar workers. Age at onset is around 30, a few or several years after joining their companies.

Selective psychomotor retardation is the main and specific features of this type. They cannot work due to retardation without worrying or complaining of it. They, however, do play sports or join a weekend trip with colleagues in spite of their absence from office.

They have high self-esteem or pride, and are sensitive to being hurt by interpersonal relationships, in particular, with their superiors.

Diurnal variation is usually present and some of them show hypomanic or manic episodes, which implies endogenous origin against the appearances of depressive neurosis or personality disorder of narcissistic or avoidant type.

We hence propose to call this disorder as "avoidant type of depression".

Several possible factors causing it will be discussed from a socio-cultural point of view in contemporary Japan.

2819

Okulalu. Psychosis in West Kenya.
Its social consequences.
G.P.M. Assen

A study was carried out among the Luhya-people in West Kenya to describe the effect on social re-integration, of treatment by traditional healers and prayer healers on the one hand and by western psychiatric treatment available in the same area on the other.
46 patients were included. 23 patients were identified while attending a traditional healer or prayer healer. For comarison 23 others were selected at the provincial hospital by matching them according to sex, age, marital status, education or profession, diagnosis according to DSM III, and number of psychotic episodes.
In this paper the social consequences of psychosis in this Luhya-society will be discussed in relation to the type of treatment, behaviour of the patient, number of psychotic episodes, and attitude of the community.

2820

A DUTCH CASE OF LATAH
J.A. Jenner, M.D., Ph.D.,
Univ. Hospit. Groningen, Holland

The use of prescribing the symptom in a successful family therapy of a dutch woman a latah - like syndrome is discussed.
The debate about the cause of latah, i.e. a culture-specific performance us a culture-specific exploitation of a neuro-physiological potential, is reopened. It is suggested that Latah is a paradoxical way of communication.

2821

'HARE KRISHNA' INTER & INTRACULTURAL IMPACT ON ANGLO-AMERICAN PSYCHIATRY
Deen B. Chandora, M.D.
Clayton MH/MR/SA Center, Riverdale, Georgia U.S.A.

Psychiatry has lagged behind other sciences in grasping the inter and intracultural influences behind social phenomena. Combinations of ethnocentric thinking and, at times, simples ignorance have made it difficult for certain topics to be dealt with scientifically. For example, some religious groups have been looked at through preconceived notions which make it difficult for a scientific analysis to be made. The 'Hare Krishnas' are such a group.
This paper examines that group from a perspective of both eastern and western influences. Using both a sociological and psychiatric perspective, it investigates the cultural conflicts and controversies which surround the Hare Krishnas. The aim is to provide a useful and balanced view which can stimulate informed scholarly exchanges among historians, social scientists, and psychiatric health professionals. The role of education and understanding of cultural variance is discussed in detail to apprise the Anglo-American Psychiatric community of relevant facts and about their consequent social responsibilities.

2822

Depression Among White, Black, and Hispanic Adolescents in the U.S.
Robert E. Roberts, Ph.D.
The University of Texas Health Science Center at Houston, Texas, U.S.A.

Data are presented from the first national survey of depression among adolescents ever conducted in the U.S. The goal is to examine correlates of depression, in particular social class and ethnic status, in adolescents, contrasted with adults. A probability sample of 1,007 Whites, 601 Blacks, and 642 Hispanic youth aged 12-17 were interviewed in 1985. Data also are available from 5,788 adults. Depression is measured using 12 items from the Center for Epidemiologic Studies Depression (CES-D) Scale. Other variables include age, gender, education, occupation, employment, income, marital status and household composition, place of residence and geographic mobility, health status and help-seeking, and use of tobacco, alcohol and drugs. Data to be presented include assessment of internal consistency reliability, dimensionality, and salience of the depression items, and prevalence of depression across subgroups defined in terms of ethnic group (Anglo/Black/Hispanic), language (English/Spanish), gender, and age. Prevalence rates do not differ among the ethnic groups, once gender, age, and social class are controlled.

2823

DAS ANATOLISCHE DORF VOM BLICKPUNKT DER TRANSKULTURELLEN PSYCHIATRIE
Selami Aksoy, MD, Mustafa Ziyalan, MD.
Bakırköy Mental Hospital, Istanbul, TURKEY

Ausgehend von Argumenten der transkulturellen Psychiatrie versuchen wir, Hypothesen aufzustellen, die sich weiterer Prüfung bedürfen.Wir haben in unserem Krankenhaus mit 3000 Betten unter den Patienten laendlicher Herkunft mehr Faelle von undifferenzierter Psychose beobachtet.Das steht im Zusammenhang mit dem anatolischen Dorf,einem abgeschlossenen,hierarchischen System,das auf a priori Gegebenheiten wie Verwandtschaft,Geschlecht,Alter,Tradition,mohammedanischer Religion,ottomanischer Staatsvorstellung ruht.Darin ist mehr eine Gemeinde als Individuen.Gastfreundschaft ist vielmehr ein Instrument den Fremden problemlos einzuordnen.Das Private ist eingegrenzt.Die Moschee und das Kaffeehaus fungieren als Orte des kollektiven Unbewussten.Die Persönlichkeit des anatolischen Bauern wird also mehr von aussen geformt als von innen.Dabei entsteht kein klares Selbst im westlichen Sinne. Der Bauer hat eine andere Vorstellung vom eigenen Körper,von Selbstpflege,von Beziehungen,von sozialer Funktion,von "Raum und zeit".Mit diesen eigenartigen Kognitionen in Wechselwirkung steht auch die mancherorts eigenartige Gebrauchsweise des Türkischen.Das alles bestimmt insbesondere die Form und Inhalt der Wahnvorstellungen.Die Somatisation,sogar die Zwangsneurose wird nicht selten im Zusammenhang des erwaehnten Systems erlebt und verstanden.

2824
CULTURE-BOUND SYNDROMES IN INDONESIA

W.M. Roan, Dr(UnAir, Indon.), DPM(Lond.)
Directorate of Mental Health, Ministry of Health,
Jakarta, Indonesia

It is significantly conspicuous that some conditions of human behaviour in a certain part of the world are qualitatively different from that of their fellowmen in other areas and strangely enough even non-existent in different cultural settings that attracts the attention more of psychiatrists especially so of foreign born coming for the first time in that particular cultural surroundings than the community where those syndromes were prevalent. Those conditions are named as the culture-bound phenomena.

Those conditions, considered as epidemiologically significant in Indonesia, are described: Latah Reaction, Koro, Amuk, Possession States and Bebainan.

Questions were raised as to their appropriateness for inclusion in the International Diagnostic Classification of Diseases. Some discussions were presented.

Session 432 Free Communications:
Issues related to sexual behavior

2825
A REPERTORY GRID INVESTIGATION OF THE CONCEPT OF "SEX" HELD BY MEDICAL GRADUATES
N.Vaidakis,Y.Papakostas,A.Liakos and C.Stefanis.
Athens University Medical School,Depart.of Psychiatry,Eginition Hospital.

The purpose of the present study was the investigation of the concept of "sex"by using Kelly´s repertory grid technique.Repertory grids are forms of sorting tests suitable for various cognitive explorations.In the present study,10 different sexual behaviors(the sorting material or the "elements" according to Kelly) and 10 conceptual dimentions used for the evaluation of the elements(the sorting categories or the "constructs" according to Kelly)formed the standard "sex" grid.These elements and constructs were obtained from two preliminary studies involving 50 medical graduates each.During the main study,the standard grid was administered to 87 medical graduates.The ranking method was used for the completion of the grids.Since elements and constructs were common for all subjects a "consensus" grid analysis was performed. The "consensus" grid was compiled by hand using the mean rating of elements in each one of the ten constructs.The results from this analysis will be presented.

2826
MEASURING SEXUAL ATTITUDES OF TURKISH UNIVERSITY STUDENTS

Erkmen,H.,M.D., Dilbaz,N.,M.D., Seber,G.,Ph.D., Kaptanoğlu,C.,M.D., Tekin,D.,M.D.

Department of Psychiatry, Faculty of Medicine, Anadolu University Eskişehir/Turkey

We set out the study to measure the sexual attitudes of Turkish University students. All subjects completed assessments where a semi-structured interview was followed by a self-administered sexual attitude inventory.

We used Whalley's modification of sexual attitude questionnaire developed by Eysenck. Whalley's modification has 9 short scales measuring sexual satisfaction, heterosexual nervousness, sexual curiosity, tension and hostility, pruriency, sexual repression, heterosexual distate and sexual promiscuity.

Scores on these scales were obtained for a sample of male and female students. Male and female students' responses were compared. The results of the male students were also compared with Eysenck's findings from a very different culture.

2827
PERSONALITY FACTORS IN MALE SEXUAL DISORDERS

Schmidt C.W. Jr, Fagan P.J., Wise T.N., Derogatis L.R.
Johns Hopkins University School of Medicine
Baltimore, Maryland

Research relying on clinical interview has indicated that in approximately 70% of cases sexual dysfunction does not occur concurrently with other psychiatric diagnoses while paraphilia are generally believed to occur in those with more disordered personality structure. The study compared males with sexual dysfunction (N=67) to males with a primary diagnosis of paraphilia (N=32) in relation to normal personality dimensions. Personality structure was assessed by the NEO Personality Inventory (NEO-PI), a standardized instrument shown to reliably and validly describe stable personality factors in adults. Analysis of variance showed significant ($p<.001$) differences between the dysfunctional and the paraphilic groups on 4 of the 5 major NEO-PI domains. Discriminant analysis correctly classified 78.8% of the sample. The average personality profile of the sexually dysfunctional was comparable to the normative sample of the NEO-PI, supporting the opinion that sexual dysfunction is an independent psychiatric disorder not significantly associated with abnormal personality structure. By contrast, men with paraphilia had a personality profile marked by significant elevations in Neuroticism and Openness; lower Agreeableness and Conscientiousness.

2828

EXHIBITIONISM:PSYCHICAL OBSERVATIONS OF
8 CASES CONVICTED OF INDECENT EXPOSURE
SANNA MN-CORGIOLU T-LORETTU L-PITTALIS A
NIVOLI GC
CLINICA PSICHIATRICA UNIVERSITA'SASSARI
ITALY.

The authors studied clinically 8 male
exhibitionists sentenced by the Tribunal of Sassari (Italy) for indecent exposure between 1980 and 1987. This study into exhibitionism showed the presence of specific psychopathologies linked to psychosis,states of inebriation and exhibitionistic dynamics,mostly in relation to minors or accompanied by aggressive behaviour towards the victim.
The authors emphasize the clinical diversity between acts of exhibitionism subject to penal measures (official criminality) and acts of exhibitionism which remain unknown to the Judical Authorities ("dark number"),to allow a correct criminological and psychiatric interpretation of cases of exhibitionism.

2829

SEXUAL DESIRE, ORGASM AND SEXUAL FANTASIES - A STUDY
OF 625 DANISH WOMEN BORN 1910, 1936 AND 1958.
Inge Lunde, Gunvor Kramshøj Larsen, Eva Fog and
Karin Garde.
ETICA Treatment Center, Borgergade 40, Copenhagen.
Institute of General Practice, University of Copenhagen.

The study presented is a part of a more extended study of female sexuality in three generations: Women born in 1910, 1936 and 1958: Female sexual behaviour, experience, knowledge and attitude. The participants were selected at random in the Copenhagen county, from the central person register and invited to an interview by one of the authors, supplied by a medical examination. The method was a standard interviewschedule with 300 precoded questions in all sexual areas, about social conditions and general health. At the time of interview the women were 70, 40 and 22 years old respectively.
72%, 67% and 95% had experienced spontaneous sexual desire and 88%, 96% and 91% had experienced orgasm. 38%, 47% and 81% respectively had masturbated at least once, and fantasies during masturbation were used by 50%, 48% and 68%. Women born 1910 and 1958 were asked about sexual fantasies in general and during sexual intercourse: 7%(1910) and 44%(1958) had general sexual fantasies, while 14% and 39% had fantasies during intercourse. The fantasies could be placed in some main groups: sex with a stranger/anonymous, forced sex, rape, new forms of sex, sex with perverse men,old men, with several men at the same session and sex-fantasies developed from pictures in sex-magazines. The importance of the sexual fantasies for sexual desire, ability to obtain orgasm and quality of orgasm will be discussed

2830

Effects of Trazodone on sexual function
I. Goldstein M.D.
Department of Urology, Boston University

Trazodone HCl (TRZ) is an antidepressant agent which has been associated with the occurence of unusual erectile activity. An in vivo study in animal and human subjects was performed to determine the effects of intracavernosal administration of TRZ and to evaluate the adrenergic agonist treatment of TRZ-induced prolonged erection. In the anesthetized New Zealand white rabbit, penile erection was observed in 83% of animals studied following intracavernosal administration of TRZ or m-CPP with an accumulated dose of 8.2+/-1.4 mg and 6.2+/-1.3 mg respectively. Intracavernosal administration of phenylephrine, epinephrine, norepinephrine and metaraminol but not normal saline resulted in elimination of TRZ-induced erectile activity at a concentratoin of $5 \times 10^{-7}M$, $5 \times 10^{-7}M$ and $5 \times 10^{-5}M$ respectively. In 13 selected volunteer patients, administration of 40 intracavernosal TRZ resulted in an increase of the mean baseline corporal body pressure of 6.3+/-.75 mmHg to an equilibrium corporal body pressure of 28.2+/-5.8 mmHg (p 0005). The proposed mechanism of TRZ-associated erectile activity is at least in part related to its local ability to induce alpha-adrenergic blockade on corporal erectile tissue. Reports available on the effects of TRZ in genital symptoms are in agreement with the above data suggesting that, besides its antidepressant activity, TRZ acts through a more specific mechanism.

Session 433 Free Communications:
Psychopathology and neurological disorders

2831

BIOCHEMICAL MODEL OF AKATHISIA

Dr. Graham Sheppard MB BS MRCPsych
Dr. Anthony McCarthy MRCPsych MRCPI
Ticehurst House Hospital,
Ticehurst, East Sussex TN5 7HU,
Great Britain.

The authors will advance a biochemical model of akathisia involving the interaction between cerebral dopamine and GABA systems. This model will take into account the following:
a) recent advances in our neurochemical and neuroanatomical understanding of the complex relationships between dopamine and GABA in the brain's motor systems,
b) The effect of the "atypical" neuroleptic sulpiride on central motor systems and
c) the clinical similarity between neuroleptic-induced akathisia and some of the symptoms of the benzodiazepine withdrawal systems.

2832

The relation between depression and memory disorders in Parkinson's disease.
Mastrosimone F.,Iaccarino C.,De Caterina G.,Mazzeo R.,Mercone G.,Jablonski L., Marantoni A.
University of Naples,1st Faculty of Medicine,Institute of Neurological Sciences,Chair of Clinical Neuroanatomy(Prof. Mastrosimone F.)
A large number of parkinsonian patients suffers from depression or/and memory disorders.Aim of the present study is to evaluate the incidence and the severity of memory disorders in depressed and not depressed parkinsonian patients, and if the depression is a risk factor or prodromic symptom for a large involvement of cognitive functions.Therefore, in a comparative parallel-group trial patients with Parkinson's Disease underwent a complete neuropsychological investigation for emphasizing clinical and neuropsychological relation between depression and memory disorders.The result obtained in this trial suggests that in a lot of patients the depression is a sign of a large and serious involvement of intellectual function,and this is very relevant for therapeutic approach of the affective disturbances of the parkinsonian patients and because it's needed a complete neuropsychological investigation of patients suffering from Parkinsonian Disease.

2833

EPILEPSIE ET TROUBLES PSYCHIATRIQUES

J.E. KTIOUET,K.RADDAOUI,HAMDOUCHI,SALL,D.LAHLOU, M. PAES
CLINIQUE UNIVERSITAIRE DE PSYCHIATRIE RABAT-MAROC

Dans une revue des patients épileptiques hospitalisés ou suivis en ambulatoire en psychiatrie, les auteurs identifient et répertorient les troubles psychiatriques observés et tentent de différencier les maladies mentales structurées évoluant de pair avec l'épilepsie et les troubles psychiques indifférenciés semblant être le fait de l'épilepsie elle-même.
Une corrélation est esquissée entre ces deux types de troubles et la comitialité en cause ainsi qu'avec le suivi thérapeutique.
Enfin, les auteurs s'interrogent sur l'apparente absence de certaines affections psychiatriques chez les épileptiques.

2834

Depression in patients with stroke

Henrik Dam and Holger E. Pedersen
Psych. dept.,Rigshospitalet,Copenhagen,Denmark.

Purpose : The purpose of the present study is to examine the frequency of depression in stroke patients and classify the depression clinical (by the RDC) and biological (by the DST and TRH-stimulation test).
Methods : 92 stroke patients and 30 controls participated. A CT-scanning was performed in the stroke patients. The patients were classified according to the RDC criteria. The degree of depression was measured by the Hamilton Depression Rating Scale. In most of the patients the DST and the TRH stimulation test were performed.
Results : 28 (30%) of the stroke patients fulfilled the RDC criteria for depression. 6 of the depressed patients fulfilled the RDC criteria for Probable or Definite Endogenous Depression. Patients with the lesion in Reg.Front.Dext. showed the highest degree of depression.
No significant difference in frequency of non-suppression to DST were found between depressed or non-depressed stroke patients.
No significant difference of blunted response to the TRH stimulation test was found between depressed and non-depressed stroke patients.
Conclusion : This study support a hypothesis that depression is a rather frequent concomitant to stroke but it does not support a hypothesis that the majority of depressed stroke patients should be of the endogenous type.

2835

THE POSTCONCUSSIONAL STATE: INTERACTION BETWEEN BRAIN AND MIND
GEORGE W FENTON
ROBERT J. McCLELLAND
WILLIAM H. RUTHERFORD
UNIVERSITY OF DUNDEE, SCOTLAND AND THE QUEEN'S UNIVERSITY OF BELFAST, NORTHERN IRELAND
71 minor head injury patients had clinical, neurophysiological, cognitive, psychosocial and psychiatric assessments performed within 24 hours of the trauma (day 0) and repeated at intervals up to 12 months afterwards. Postconcussional symptoms declined progressively from day 0: two thirds recovered by six weeks, 10% had chronic persistent symptoms and 20% initially improved but had late symptom exacerbation. Slow computerised EEG recovery correlated with higher symptom counts and delayed left temporal recovery was associated with residual psychiatric morbidity at 12 months. One third to one half of patients had prolonged central brainstem conduction times at day 0, correlating positively with PTA duration and residual psychiatric morbidity at 1 year. Symptom chronicity was accompanied by continuing brainstem dysfunction. Adverse life events were frequent in the year before injury, while patients with unremitting symptoms afterwards had an excess of chronic social difficulties. One third of patients were rated psychiatric "cases" at 6 weeks, "caseness" relating to gender, age and chronic difficulties.

2836

CEPHALEE ET DEPRESSION

M.Spiridione Masaraki, Psychiatre Assistant Hospitalier Coresponsable, Ospedale Ca Granda
M.Gianlorenzo Masaraki, Psychiatre, Directeur de l'Institut de recherche Riter (Recherche et Therapie Psychosomatique), Milano, Italy

Etude préliminaire sur 3000 cas. La fréquence des symptômes dépressifs associés à céphalée essentielle (vaso-motrice et tensive) est examinée statistiquement.
L'hypothèse d'un paradigme symptômatologique propre à identifier la céphalée due à dépression conclut le travail.

Session 434 Free Communications:
Theoretical and critical issues I

2837

A GREAT DOCTOR LOVES THE COSMOS
Yutaka AKIMOTO M.D.
Akimoto Hospital, Kamagaya, Chiba, Japan

Hippocrates asserted that medicine must cure not illness but patients and moreover individuals as components of various groups, while the author would like to maintain that it should heal not patients but illness and further the whole earth, which is a mass assemblage of individuals. The Divine Being, however, would say that this kind of argument is against the low of cosmos, and that illness, patient, individual, and cosmos are all equal to one another.
From individual therapy to group therapy. This goal is to be achieved through a precedent-setting international collaboration, namely, preparing a hospital vessel to assume the role of a peace-making mission. As a matter of course, the treatment system that is to be organized will expectedly be an integration of both Systems Approach and Problem-Oriented Medical System, which includes modern/pre-modern medicine as well as occidental/oriental disciplines, and which transcends time and space.
To put it concretely, a vessel will be prepared with funds furnished by Japan under the auspices of the Republic of Korea. A multi-national treatment team will be on board the ship, which is to call at many ports of different countries, and thus fulfill its duties. Their performance will be telecasted worldwide, utilizing communications satellites. With this, people will form therapeutic and creative relationships of a 'here and now' nature with one another.
The treatment team comprises not only medical staff but also a variety of specialists including a Chief Information Officer. They are to handle all kinds of serious diseases and problems.

2838

THE RESTORATIVE PSYCHIATRY-A NEW/OLD APPROACH IN THERAPY IN CLINICAL PSYCHIATRY.
Dr.N.N.Ilanković, Dr.V.Ilanković.
Psychiatric University Clinic,Belgrade, Yugoslavia.

The application of neurophysiological measurings(AEP,VEP,ENG,EEG-MAPPING,SLEEP-EEG)neuropsychological tests,other biological markers(biochemical,endocrinol.,immunological, pharmacological) and the continuous clinical observations,are the basis of ACTUAL/INDIVIDUAL DIAGNOSIS and the first steps for ACTIVE/ RESTORATIVE THERAPEUTIC approaches to mental illnesses. The EARLY INTERVENTION (psychosocial nutritive,pharmacological)in ACUTE phase, strategy of INDIVIDUAL/SPECIFIC, TARGETED TIME-LIMITED,LOW-DOSE MEDICATION(but not only for reduction of symptoms but also for ACTIVE SUPPORT/RESTORATION/SIMULATION of general organism functions first and of the central nervous system parallely, in acute and CHRONIC phase), are the general priciples of the "new/old" approach. Close to the psychopharmacotherapy must exist the GENERAL SUPPORT regulation of the metabolism and nutrition haemodynamic/circulation etc.; the PSYCHOLOGICAL/SOCIAL SUPPORT; PSYCHOMOTOR/SENSORY/COGNITIVE STIMULATIONS /REEDUCATIONS.

2839

THE ARROW OF PSYCHOSIS, OF KNOWLEDGE, AND THE SHRINKING OF THE UNIVERSE
Dr Timen Borilov Timev
Psychiatric hospital Karloukovo, Bulgaria

Defining psychosis as an inversion of the arrow, the direction and the thelos of existence. The course of normal existence repeats the direction of the expansion of the Universe, and is perceived as an expansion of being from birth to death, psychotic existence repeats the direction of the shrinking of the Universe and is perceived as a shrinking of existence from death towards birth. The course of the psychotic existence is identical with the course of inverted time. In psychosis, the inversion of the existence and the narrowing of the existing compulsively determines a forcible autointentionality and compulsive introversion, something that is phenomenalized in the well known clinical facts: self-direction of the vital towards itself, autism ect. The cited clinic facts point to psychosis as a pathological autoreference, autorelativity, autoreflexion, summed up in a pathic self-knowledge. But it the expansio of the Universe corresponds to the arrow of life and the shrinking of the Universe corresponds to the arrow of Knowledge, then the arrow of psychosis coincides with the arrow of Knowledge. That is why psychosis imitates not the existing life but imitates the life of knowledge and self-knowledge. The patient does not exist in existence but exists in knowledge. But the existence in knowledge is precisely that crossing-over and interpenetration of worlds one into another which ingression of existence into knowledge causes the inflow of the un conscions into consciousness, having as a result the splitting of the subjectivity and the appearance of schizophrenicity.

2840

INTRODUCTION TO DIALOGICAL PSYCHIATRY

Dr Timen Borilov Timev
Psychiatric hospital, Karloukovo, Bulgaria

Psycholinguistic criticism of dialogical psychiatry. The individual as a disguised society. The monologue as a disguised dialogue. The mentally ill and the humiliated communication. Mutism as a condemnation of words unmasked as non-authentic. Mutism as ontological criticism of language. Stupor as a negative appeal for communion. Autism as a semantic mask. Unreciprocity index and autistic protection against denied reciprocity. Conflict with the grammatical ego and autistic protection. Egocentric symptomatics — a negative call for communication. The symptom of schizophrenic call. Insufficiency of empathy: trans-subjectivisation. Interpersonal and transpersonal relations. Importation and exportation of the Ego. Transitivity of the Ego during transfer. Exchange of Egos and trans-Ego.

If the unique always seems insane and its projection is, exlogical, it is obvious that the medical science armed with reason (as a fear from insanity) and logic, treats not the ill person, but the terminology by which he expresses his attempt at a unique understanding of the world which cannot but contradict conventional terminology. As the patient's language does not correspond to the language of science, and its grammar is extralogical as regards intralogical science, from the viewpoint of his language, the physician uses medicines in order to bring back the means of expression of the patient who has deviated from conventional expression, within the framework of convention. The commonly accepted symbolics of mental life is a totem, and the taboo violators are subject to registration and therapeutic treatment. As logical enemies and gnoseological criminals they cannot be but sick people.

2841

MEDICINE IN POLITICS (CROSS-CULTURAL PSYCHIATRY VS DIAGNOSIS)

Dr. Jacques A. ARPIN
IUPG, Geneva, Switzerland

Cross-cultural psychiatry has to acquire a professional identity that distinguishes it from the ethnologist/informant and the physician/patient models of interaction. As a consultant, the cross-cultural psychiatrist promotes mental health in terms of cultural representations of health and disease; he/she also promotes primary prevention, using clinical experience.

Medicine is caught between its healing tradition and its role in performing social control through participating in the health enterprise. As an institution, medicine has a sociopolitical function. Beyond the medical act, psychiatric diagnosing can be an instrument of social control. For that reason, it is necessary to diagnose within the framework of sociocultural influences.

The frontier dividing medicine's healing and social control functions is often one of hypocrisy, because of medicine's cultural and sociopolitical ambiguity. As a mediator, cross-cultural psychiatry must strive to assume an educational role and disseminate information about the basic elements of cross-cultural communication.

2842

UNCONSCIOUS AND POLITICAL LEADERS

Nicholas Destounis, M.D., Ph.D.
Professor of Psychiatry & Mental Health Sciences
Medical College of Wisconsin
Chief, Psychiatry Service
Zablocki VAMC, Milwaukee, Wisconsin

Freudian psychology claims that there is no basic difference between psychology in general and psychopathology; both follow the same basic principles. The reason, however, that psychopathological processes appear *irrational* lies in the fact that these are determined by *UCS processes*, which are more primitive than the conscious ones.

There is no doubt that psychoanalysis has much to offer to the political biographer and social historian. Unfortunately, thus far, very few psychoanalytic studies have penetrated the UCS motivation of the world political leaders and their *decision making processes* which might lead into either peace or war with all its catastrophic consequences upon the whole civilized cosmos (Destounis, N., 1962, 1973, 1981, 1987). We shall present evidence to suggest that several political leaders in the U.S.S.R., Great Britain, Germany, Italy, U.S.A., Lybia, Iran, etc. have been suffering from severe mental disorders, as well as psychophysiological (ecological) illnesses which determined their capacity for sound judgment in their decision making process.

We are of the opinion that different peoples with various personality structures will require leaders with personalities specific for *a given historical moment, a certain purpose*, and *a certain chronicle* period (Destounis, 1973, 1981, 1987). We also believe in the public's right to know whether a nation's business is being conducted by reasonably healthy individuals. If there is no such right, then any nation is powerless to insure that momentous decisions in a time of internal or world crisis are not made by mentally ill men.

Session 435 Free Communications:
Diagnostic issues in psychogeriatrics

2843

Familial Syndrome : Association of Pick's Disease and Amyotrophic Lateral Sclerosis
J. Constantinidis
University of Geneva, "Morphological Psychopathology"
Bel-Air, 1225 Geneva, Switzerland

The association of Pick's Disease (PD) and Amyotrophic Lateral Sclerosis (ALS) as a familial syndrome is reported for the first time.
Four members in two generations of the investigated family suffered from this syndrome, allowing the hypothesis of a dominant mode of inheritance.
PD is primary, with onset at 58 to 67 years : loss of interests, depression, aggressivity, perseverations, stereotypies, reduction of speech until total mutism ; a few months later appear ALS signs : fasciculations and/or pyramidal symptoms. The total evolution is 3 to 5 years.
The brain showed a fronto-temporal atrophy spreading to the precentral gyrus with cortical and white matter gliosis, neuronal loss, atrophic neurons and some ballooned cells, but without senile plaques (SP), neurofibrillary tangles (NFT) or cortical spongiosis ; the spinal cord and the medulla oblongata showed typical ALS lesions ; mild lesions in the basal nuclei, particularly in the substantia nigra and the pallidum.
The differential diagnosis is discussed with : Alzheimer's Disease + ALS (SP + NFT) ; the Guam syndrome (NFT) ; Creutzfeldt-Jakob's Disease (cortical microspongiosis) ; ALS + dementia (primary ALS) ; Mitsuyama's syndrome (primary dementia and secondary ALS, but with cortical spongiosis and without familial incidence).

2844

EEG BACKGROUND ACTIVITY ON PATIENTS WITH DEMENTIA OF ALZHEIMER TYPE.
Hiroshi Hagimoto, Toshiro Miyauchi, Keiko Endo, Akira Kajiwara, Masaaki Matsushita.
Department of Psychiatry, Yokohama City University School of Medicine. Yokohama, Japan.

The dissimilarities between Alzheimer's disease(AD) and senile dementia(SD) are discussed clinically and neuropathologically. With these considerations in mind, we studied electroencephalographically whether AD could be discriminated from SD or not. EEG topographies were obtained from 21 patients with AD and 19 with SD and were compared to sex and age-matched controls. The frequency spectrum was divided into 0.2 Hz and collapsed into six EEG frequency bands(delta,theta,alpha1,alpha2,beta1,beta2). These power values were designated as average percentage of total power. Individual post-hoc t-test were done and t-statistic significance probability maps (SPM) were created. Compared with healthy controls, both patient groups demonstrated increased EEG background slowing, more slower in AD than in SD. The differences between AD and controls on SPMs indicated high slowing with reductions in alpha2, beta1 and beta2 activity. Severe AD(N=12) indicated delta slowing and alpha2 reduction only in the frontal region compared to mild AD(N=9). The differences between SD and controls indicated only mild slowing with reduction in alpha1 activity. The SPMs of delta band showed the slowing only in the frontal region. Severe SD(N=10) indicated diffuse delta slowing and occipital alpha decrease compared to mild SD(N=9). These results might indicate that EEG topography was an useful tool in differentiating AD from SD.

2845

GROWTH HORMONE-RELEASING FACTOR (GRF) IN SENILE DEMENTIA (SD)
R. Cacabelos, C. Diéguez, H. Niigawa*, T. Nishimura*, M.F.Scanlon**, J. Pearson***.
Santiago Univ. Med. Sch., Spain, Osaka Univ. Med. Sch.*, Japan, Univ. of Wales**, U.K., New York Univ. Med. Center, U.S.A.

The content of GRF was studied in 20 regions of the CNS in postmortem SD and control (C) tissues using a two-site immunochemiluminometric assay. GRF levels were significantly ($p<0.005$) decreased in the motor cortex (CS=35.60$\pm$10.72; DS=12.24$\pm$6.36 pg/g), posterior hypothalamus (C=99.86$\pm$17.35; SD=43.73$\pm$15.24 pg/g), and hippocampus (C=38.84$\pm$9.45; SD=18.81$\pm$7.83 pg/g) in SD. GRF concentration was found increased in premotor cortex, superior temporal gyrus, anterior hypothalamus, putamen, nucleus accumbens, pons, and cerebellum. No changes were detected in the postcentral gyrus, posterior parietal cortex, temporal pole, striate and parastriate cortices, globus pallidus, caudate nucleus, thalamus, or cervical spinal cord. These results seem to indicate that GRF is involved in psychomotor, behavioral, and neuroendocrine dysfunctions observed in SD. (Supported by F.I.S. 88/0868 & 89/0478 of Spain).

2846

BRAIN HISTAMINE IN SENILE DEMENTIA (SD)
R. Cacabelos, A. Yamatodani*, H. Niigawa, H. Wada*, T. Nishimura, J. Pearson**
Santiago Univ. Med. Sch., Spain, Osaka Univ. Med. Sch.*, Japan, New York Univ. Med. Center**, U.S.A.

Histamine (HA) levels have been determined by HPLC with fluorometric detection in 21 regions of the CNS in postmortem SD and control (C) tissues. HA levels were significantly ($p<0.01$) higher in SD than in C in the following areas: motor and premotor cortices, postcentral gyrus, posterior parietal cortex, superior temporal gyrus, temporal pole, primary and secondary visual cortices, anterior and posterior regions of the hypothalamus, putamen, caudate nucleus, thalamus, nucleus accumbens, hippocampus, pons, medulla oblongata, and cerebellum. No changes were seen in globus pallidus and corpus callosum. Since the origin of brain HA is dependent on 3 main compartments, with 60-80% of the total HA located in the neuronal pool, we postulate that the increase in the levels of HA in SD might account for or be associated with alterations in neuroendocrine, cognitive, neurovascular, and sleep-wakefulness functions present in SD. (Supported by F.I.S. 88/0868 & 89/0478 of Spain).

2847

DIAGNOSTICO Y ESTRATEGIAS DE SEGUIMIENTO EN DEMENCIAS

Rodríguez,A.; Mateos, R. y Cacabelos, R. Departamento de Psiquiatría de la Universidad de Santiago. Santiago de Compostela. España.

¿Qué relación existe entre deterioro cognitivo y demencia?. ¿Son los estadios precoces minidemencias?. ¿Cómo evoluciona el deterioro hacia la demencia?. ¿Qué factores psicosociales intervienen y cómo intervienen?. ¿Cómo se manifiestan estos cambios a nivel neuroquímico?.

Todas estas preguntas y otras tan elementales como los criterios diagnósticos y epidemiológicos no tienen todavía una respuesta clara.

Nuestro trabajo trata de dar respuesta a algunas de estas preguntas.

El año 1985,como parte de una investigación de epidemiología psiquiátrica en Galicia,localizamos una muestra de 269 sujetos,mayores de 60 años,que presentaban una puntuación en el Mini Mental State (MMS) menor de 27 puntos,es decir,con probable deterioro cognitivo.

A comienzos de 1969,esa muestra ha sido encuestada de nuevo con los siguientes resultados:27,5% mantiene el deterioro; 14,7% fallecidos; 18,6% ilocalizados;39,2% no muestran actualmente deterioro.

En este momento estamos realizando una evaluación de la muestra con el test de GRF (Growth Reelising Factor),el más específico de los marcadores actuales de demencia,especialmente del Alzheimer,además de estudio clínico,psicométrico y neurorradiológico.

Estos datos,además de contrastar la fiabilidad de uno de los métodos de "screening" más utilizados (MMS),nos permiten establecer 3 cohortes que serán estudiadas evolutivamente.

2848

CHANGES IN NON-VERBAL BEHAVIOUR IN PRIMARY DEGENERATIVE DEMENTIA

Troisi A., Pasini A., Gori G., Sorbi T., Baroni A., Ciani N. Clinica Psichiatrica, II Università di Roma, Roma, Italy, and Ospedale "I Fraticini" INRCA, Firenze, Italy.

Research into the clinical features of dementia has concentrated almost exclusively on the cognitive impairment. This emphasis on cognitive function has led to the neglect of the changes in behaviour which also are a major feature of the disorder. The present study was designed to determine whether dementia is associated with changes in non-verbal behaviour during social interaction. The subjects were 26 outpatients (12 men and 14 women) with senile dementia of the Alzheimer's type (SDAT) of mild to moderate severity and 26 normal control subjects (12 men and 14 women) with similar socio-demographic characteristics. Subjects' non-verbal behaviour was video-recorded from behind a one-way mirror and scored according to an ethological scoring system including 37 different behaviours. Data were analyzed by combining the 37 individual behaviours to form 8 functional categories: Eye Contact, Flight, Submission, Affiliation, Gesture, Conflict, Assertion, and Relaxation. Compared to control subjects, SDAT patients scored lower on Eye Contact ($p<.05$) and Affiliation ($p=.03$) and higher on Submission ($p<.05$). There were quasi-significant differences in Assertion (SDAT>controls, $p=.058$) and Gesture (controls>SDAT, $p=.052$). These results indicate that dementia is associated with major changes in non-verbal behaviour including a reduction in positive social responses during dyadic interaction. Supported by FIDIA Farmaceutici.

2849

HYDROCEPHALUS AND PSYCHOGERIATRIC PRACTICE

Dr Satvir Singh
Department of Elderly Care,
Park Prewett Hospital,
Basingstoke,
Hants RG24 9NA, ENGLAND

78 - Psychogeriatrics

Description of patients referred to the Department of Elderly Care (Psychogeriatrics) from 1983 to 1988, mainly outlining the various clinical diagnoses. A summary of all cases, which were diagnosed as suffering from hydrocephalus, their treatment and results are discussed. Finally, the author describes clinical symptoms which differentiate normal pressure hydrocephalus from other psychosyndromes, in particular Altzheimer's disease in the elderly.

Session 436 Free Communications:
Theoretical and critical issues II

2850

ECOLOGY AND MAN

Nicholas Destounis, M.D., Ph.D.
Professor of Psychiatry & Mental Health Sciences
Medical College of Wisconsin
Chief, Psychiatry Service
Zablocki VAMC, Milwaukee, Wisconsin

A complete theory of the modern megalopolis requires a profound and complete analysis of the human behavior. Unfortunately, the social sciences offer a very limited assistance on this subject because they examine the human behavior in "departments", and at the same time leave out the interaction of people.

The *psycho-ecological health*, a term which I am introducing for the first time here, of each person should be an ethnic matter for all the nations. In fact, it should be compared with the subject of national education, for we believe that the ecological changes which are taking place today in our cosmos alter the *ethnological* character of the individual. The air, sea and noise pollution have destroyed the ecological equilibrium with detrimental effect upon the psycho-ecological health of the people the world over. Thus, people are suffering from: 1 - *Circulatory diseases* due to increase in the air of CO, SO-4, etc. 2 - *CNS diseases* due to an increase of mercury, chronium, arsenic, lead, etc. 3 - *Neoplastic diseases* (upper respiratory system, G.I. tract, etc.) 4 - *Psychosomatic* (ecological disorders) peptic ulcer, colitis, asthma, CHD, pregnancy complications, genetically damaged born babies; 5 - *Psychoneurotic-psychotic disorders* (anxiety, depression, criminal behavior, narcotics) 6 - *Cardiac conditions, liver, adrenal, pancreas diseases* due to noise. We are proposing the establishment of an INTERNATIONAL ECOLOGICAL INSTITUTE in Athens to study the ill effects upon the PSYCHO-SOCIAL ECOLOGICAL HEALTH of people the world over, and thus prevent the inevitably coming catastrophe.

2851

NEITHER NEUROSIS NOR PSYCHOSIS
Venga E.
Clinica Neuropsichiatrica, Napoli, Italia

As far as our research is concerned we aim to investigate the meaning of both neurotic and psychotic functions of a neural organization. For this purpose we have assumed the dichotomy between neurosis and psychosis to be irrelevant as our research regards the structural organization and not the representation of the function itself. Eventhough we maintain that the above mentioned dichotomy has no reason to exist, we have to admit how widely it has conditioned us in the process of identification and classification of those symptoms which need even more to be placed sometimes within the neurotic sphere and sometimes within the psychotic one. We do not know the precise meaning of both terms neurosis and psychosis. Anyway we are accustumed to considering a symptom to be neurotic or psychotic only according to a diagnostic differentiation which, in most cases, is provided by parameters which make the skillful operator doubt as far as the psychic representation is concerned. Accordingly those functions which will allow us to determine the neural-organization, must not be considered either neurotic or psychotic.

2852

LIENS DU SANG ET LIENS FAMILIAUX

A. Collin, Ch. Reynaert, P. Janne, M. Vause, D. Lejeune, L. Cassiers
Service de Psychosomatique, UCL, Mont-Godinne

A partir de réflexions centrées sur une affection psychiatrique rare, mais grave, le *syndrome de Lasthénie de Ferjol*, notre équipe souligne la nécessité d'une articulation de plusieurs champs théorico-cliniques, et tente une intégration de la neuropsychoendocrinologie, des théories psychanalytiques et systémiques et de la médecine somatique, en jetant des ponts entre ces différentes approches.

Dans les troubles factices (DSM III R, 1988), le *syndrome de Lasthénie de Ferjol* est une anémie ferriprive volontairement provoquée. La dépression est souvent sous-jacente à ce comportement auto-destructeur qui met en branle les pulsions sado-masochiques, et qui apparaît dans des systèmes familiaux régis par des règles spécifiques. Une surveillance somatique étroite attentive doit être intégrée dans le travail thérapeutique.

La présentation d'un cas clinique illustre ces aspects.

2853

LA EMPRESA VÍCTIMA DEL STRESS
Bernardo Gamerman/Violeta Gamerman
Rio de Janeiro-Brasil

Para Selye el stress representa una reacción normal,fisiológica,fruto de los cambios entre la persona y su ambiente.Un cierto stress es necesario para mantener la tensión dinámica de la actividad.Los cambios no son fáciles,exigem adaptaciones rápidas y mudanzas profundas de comportamiento(el"iceberg organizacional").Hay etapas de "vida"(desenvolvimiento)y etapas de"muerte"(deteriorización).Hay acúmulos de asuntos que no se debem hablar,conveniencias,máscaras(papeles funcionales).La empresa tiene un "cuerpo"que sufre,tiene "fiebre"y"sintomas",disfunciones de primer grado.Sin assistencia adecuada,sin diagnóstico aparecen las"infecciones",disfunciones de segundo grado,que llevam a la enfermidad crónica o la"muerte del sistema".No nos parece que este problema empresarial sea solo del Tercero Mundo.Es evidente que por tenermos industrias nuevas,sin tradición,las tentativas(ingenuas)de tentar adaptar modelos europeos,despues americanos y ahora japoneses,estamos pagando un precio mayor.La inflación interna,la deuda externa y la falta de confianza en los gobiernos hacen el resto.Sin embargo,las empresas víctimas del stress pueden salvarse desde que mudanzas,intercomunicación,entrenamiento e intervenciones de aval.cont....

2854

PERCEPTION OF CONTROL OVER SYMPTOMS, DISEASE AND PROGNOSIS: A MEASURE TO PREDICT COMPLIANCE
JR Lachenmeyer, PhD, L Cirillo, G Montero, MD,
M McVicar, MD, M Zibit, CSW, I Schlossman,
R Greenberg

This study is based on a self-regulation model of compliance. The premise is that knowledge of the patient's cognitive representation of illness increases the ability to predict compliance and to explain non-compliance. An attempt is made to measure patient perceptions of control over symptoms, disease and long-term outcome and the patient's perception of the relationship between symptoms, disease and outcome. 125 adolescents with chronic disease and the parent most involved in their care were administered the Perception of Control: Symptoms, Disease and Prognosis Scale (PCSDP,Lachenmeyer & Cirillo,1987). Additionally, physicians were asked about patient's adherence to specific aspects of the medical regimen.Patients were then divided into a compliant and non-compliant group.The two groups were then compared on their PCSDP scores. Preliminary results suggest that the more compliant patients make attributions of higher control and non-compliant patients attribute less control to themselves. The results suggest further development of this measure as an assessment of patients' cognitive representations of illness.

Session 437 Free Communications:
Studies in transcultural psychiatry

2855

"A GUIDED FANTASY" - RESULTS OF TRANSCULTURAL STUDY VII WORLD CONGRESS.
Joel Walker

Results of a trans-cultural study conducted at the 7th World Congress in Vienna in 1983, under the title, "A guided Fantasy", will focus on the efficacy of the utilization of ambiguous images in psychiatry.

This study was originally conducted to determine similarities/differences in responses by cultural background, sex, and age; to question preconceived ideas with regards to other cultures; and to determine the universality of the application of the concept.

Utilizing a setting designed to allow the viewer to become aware of how he responds in a novel situation to unstructured stimuli, the format of the study wlso encouraged the participant to reflect upon previously unidentified or unexpressed feelings and to confirm or question previous perceptions of himself and others. Demographic information was included in order to provide a basis for comparison.

This paper is of value to therapists and researchers and will provide an opportunity to increase understanding and awareness of transcultural research and the implications in the practice of psychiatry.

2856

SUICIDAL WOMEN: CONFLICTS IN THEIR RELATIONSHIPS WITH MEN; A CROSS-CULTURAL STUDY
Arcel, L.T.[1], Mantonakis, J., Petersson, B.[1], Jemos, J. & Kalliteraki, E.
[1]Inst. of Clinical Psychology, Univ. of Copenhagen
Department of Psychiatry, University of Athens

Thirty five Greek and 35 Danish non-psychotic women who attempted suicide were interviewed in depth with a qualitative questionnaire. A large number of women in both groups wanted-but did not get-an equal relationship. Confrontations with husbands/lovers in the Greek group were frequent and often violent. The Danish men withdrew and isolated the women emotionally. Both groups experienced disappointment in their needs for intimacy, commitment and solidarity. The sexual relationship was bad for almost all the Greek women and almost 60% of the Danish. The women's general expectation for a good marriage reflected the cultural differences: The Greek women stressed unity and agreement between man and wife as the highest value, whereas the Danish women stressed "company" and "someone to talk to". The latter result reflects the social isolation of the Danish women.

2857

A TRANSCULTURAL STUDY OF SCHIZOPHRENIC PATINTS IN JAPAN AND CHINA
Kunihiko Asai, M.D, ASAI HOSPITAL
38, Katoku, Togane City, Chiba Prefecture, JAPAN

Mental health care within primary health care presupposes adequate knowledge of how schizophrenic patients are beeing handled by the family and the community. Tracing the pathways the schizophrenic patient traveled while seeking help revealed some of the attitudes of the family and community toward such individual.

In this research study attempt will be made:(a) to identify certain psychocultural factors which determine the response of the family in seeking psychiatric treatment for a sick individual in Japan and China, and
(b) to compare the Japanese and Chinese patterns of help-seeking with reference to stigma attached to mental illness.

60 schizophrenic patients of consecutive first admission to Asai Hospital (Japan) or to Shanghai Psychiatric Hospital (China) were included in the study.

Comparing to Japanese family, most of the Chinese family showed the protective and paternalistic family attitude to the care of an ill family member.

Several conclusion helpful in improving the quality and effectiveness of mental health care are drawn from this study.
(Dr. Zheng Zhan Pei, Vice-Director of Shanghai Psychiatric Hospital, is joint researcher.)

2858

PHOBIAS IN AMERICAN COMMUNITIES: GENDER AND RURAL/URBAN DIFFERENCES

Baqar A. Husaini, Ph.D. Center for Health Research, Tennessee State University

This paper examines the six-month prevalence rates of individual phobias by sex among the rural and and urban communities of Tennessee.

Data on various types of phobias are examined from three samples: rural (N=240), urban non-elderly (N=504), and urban elderly (aged 65-85, N=600). The data were obtained in 1986-1987 through face-to-face interviews with the respondents who were administered the Diagnostic Interview Schedule (DIS) which provides DSM-III clinical diagnoses.

Analysis show that the phobia rates obtained in rural Tennessee were higher (28.3%) as compared to rates obtained in two urban samples (16.3 & 14.6%). While the rural-urban differences were most pronounced in the areas of simple and social phobias, within each sample, however, the rates of simple phobias (such as unreasonable fear of heights, storms, spider-snakes, etc.) were significantly higher than the rates for either social phobias or agoraphobias (e.g., fear of tunnels, public transportation, etc.). Further, within the rural sample, females had higher rates of phobias than their male counterparts. The most prevalent phobia among the females included being in water (9.9%), storms (9.3%), heights (9.3%), speaking in front of a small group of people (8.6%), spiders, bugs, mice or snakes (8.6%), and being in closed places (7.3%). Among the rural males, the most prevalent phobias included being in a crowd (6.8%), spider, bugs, and snakes (5.7%), heights (5.7%), being in water (5.7%), being in closed places (5.7%), and storms (4.5%). A similar tendency exists among the urban females and males. While the rural phobia rates in general are higher than those reported for the urban samples, there are similarities in that females in all samples have more phobias than males and that the most common phobias among the females include fear of spiders/bugs/snakes, height, being in water, and storms. A discussion of these findings from the treatment perspective is provided.

2859

CROSSCULTURAL STUDY OF THE DIFFERENCES BETWEEN SOCIAL PHOBIA AND TAIJIN-KYOFU (A JAPANESE TYPE OF SOCIAL PHOBIA)

Yukio Uchinuma, M.D., Prof., Teikyo University School of Medicine, Tokyo, Japan.

A recent acceptance of Social Phobia as one of three types of Phobic Disorder in some of western countries is very interesting for Japanese psychiatrists, for we have paid much attention to this type of phobia for many years. There are, however, some differences between Social Phobia and Taijin-kyofu in the clinical pictures as well as in the incidence though they show many similarities. The differences are as follows; (1) Taijin-kyofu is a common type of phobia in Japan while it is reported in DSM-III that the incidence of Social Phobia is infrequent: (2) Taijin-kyofu shows a variety of clinical pictures but we can take out from them three ideal types, namely (a) fear of blushing, (b) fear of making unnatural gestures and (c) fear of eye-contact. The most interesting about them is the fact that they are not separate ones but appear in a sequence. In general, (a) appears in the beginning stage of phobia and transforms into (b) as the phobia gets worse. And (c) is the picture at the final stage of this sequential change. We call these fears and the other pictures almost equivalent to them as a "central" group of Taijin-kyofu. Compared with this group, fears of using public lavatories, eating in public and writing in the presence of others, on which relatively much weight is put in DSM-III, are considered to belong to a "peripheral" group.

In this report I will make clear the distinction of these groups and throw some light upon the cultural backgrounds which lead to the above-mentioned differences between Social Phobia and Taijin-kyofu.

2860

PSYCHIATRIC DISORDERS AMONG THE TAMAHUMARA INDIANS OF NORTHERN MEXICO
Fructuoso Irigoyen-Rascon, M.D., Rio Grande Valley State Center, Harlingen, Texas, USA

The Tarahumara Indians of Northern Mexico dwell in the mountains of Sierra Madre Occidental. Their adaptation to an inclement environment & fitness for the most strenuous sport invented, the kickball race (rarajipari), or their socially regulated use of drugs, in particular peyote (Lophophora Williamsii), & alcohol (batari) amazes scholars. Mental illness among these Indians is rare but well characterized. The thought disordered patient-low-iame, the madman-is considered an untrustworthy individual excluded from occupying positions of authority, except the lowest ones. Severe thought disorder arises from disobedience of ritual norms, e.g. consumption of peyote (Jikuri), under daylight or during summer. A hopeless prognosis is assigned to such patients. Anger discontrol-the oparuame, the mad ones-more than mentally ill are considered as displaying moral torpidity, a sinful choice of a wrong attitude toward others. Affective disorders are seen more as devitalization syndromes-majawa (fright), loss of iwigara (soul) or desgracia del jikuri (hyperacute devitalization rapidly progressing into death-more acute than voodoo death).
Paper also discusses psychophysiological illnesses, epilepsy & sexual dysfunctions & use & social regulation of drugs as cause or remedy for mental illness. Attention is given to role of psychiatric nosology in global strategy of passive resistance the Tarahumaras exert to defend themselves from external influences.

2861

EXPLANATORY MODELS OF ILLNESS AMONG CAMBODIAN REFUGEES ATTENDING A GENERAL PRACTICE

Maurice Eisenbruch, N.H. & M.R.C. Research Fellow,
Royal Children's Hospital Research Foundation, Parkville, Victoria 3052, Australia

A clinical ethnographic study of refugees was carried out and an instrument was developed to explore the explanations for illness among Cambodian patients. Items measure both natural and supernatural explanations in culturally appropriate terms.

A total of 80 patients who attended the Cambodian general practitioner practicing in a high density area of Melbourne participated in the study. The presenting complaints were recoded into 15 general categories; 9 were 'medical' while the remaining 6 were 'non-medical'. Patients completed an adapted Cambodian version of the Hopkins Symptom Check List. The most pronounced anxiety symptoms (in order of severity) were headaches, feeling faint, restlessness, tension, and trembling. The most pronounced depressive symptoms were lacking energy, insomnia, feeling blue, feeling worried, feeling that everything is an effort, and loneliness. A majority of the patients held multiple explanations based on a combination of Western-influenced but mainly indigenous "natural" mechanisms of illness, while others were based on the action of mystical, animistic, or magical supernatural actions. The main causes, in order of importance, were saasay (disorder of nerve/blood vessel/tendon "meridian"), the body being out of balance, the effects of ageing, wind currents through the body, disruption of a vital organ, abnormality in hot/cold balance, bad karma from previous incarnation, bad luck, and eating forbidden food.

The paper considers the relationships between different clinical presentations, the symptoms of anxiety and depression as categorised by Western medicine, and the patients' own explanations of their conditions. Culturally relevant interviews can: (a) provide a clinical framework for exploring the patient's personal and cultural experience of illness; (b) clarify the "structure" of the patient's reactions; (c) complement the currently used psychiatric diagnostic categories, thus avoiding misdiagnosis; (d) acknowledge the cultural system of meaning held by the patient; and (e) provide information which can be used in planning social supports or interventions. The clinician to collaborate with religious/traditional healers, who can deal with the patient's suffering by employing treatments familiar to the patient.

Session 438 Poster Presentation:
Alzheimer's disease and other dementias

2862

Advanced Senile Dementia of the Alzheimer Type: Clinical Findings
Stuckstedte H, Abrahams C-M, Biedert S, Ulmar G
Psychiatrisches Landeskrankenhaus, D-6908 Wiesloch, FRG

It is important in clinical research to establish specific profiles of different types and degrees of dementia (D).

46 psychogeriatric in-patients (33 women, 13 men, average age 81.5 yrs.). DSM-III-R criteria for Primary Degenerative Dementia of the Alzheimer Type (PDDAT). Severe (s) PDDAT: 35 patients, moderate (m) PDDAT: 11 patients. Methods applied: Dementia Scale (Blessed et al.), Mini-Mental State, Information-Memory-Concentration Test, Ischemic Score, single items of the AGP-System; evaluation of selected partial scores, single items, and EEG.

Significant differences between s PDDAT and m PDDAT: Patients with s D are more severely impaired in general cognition, orientation to time and place, immediate recall, abstract thinking, judgment, language-related tasks, and activities of daily living, whereas the Typical Depressive Syndrome (DSM-III-R) and increased irritability are found more often in patients with m D. EEG-findings are more often pathologically altered in patients with s D and tend to show a more marked general slowing. - Within the s PDDAT-group, patients with a more marked general slowing in EEG are more severely impaired in orientation to time, immediate recall, and language-related tasks. They also tend to show more often diminished emotional responsiveness.

In general, observer rating scales are applied to differentiate between patients with m PDDAT and s PDDAT, as well as within the s PDDAT-group. Our results indicate that, according to the degree of severity, specific psychopathological profiles can be established. EEG-findings suggest that inter- as well as intra-group differences are associated with different rates of pathological alterations.

2863

THE HIERARCHIC DEMENTIA SCALE
Martin G. Cole, Dolly P. Dastoor, McGill University, Montreal, Canada
A number of instruments have been developed to measure mental impairment in demented subjects. Unfortunately, the usefulness of these instruments is limited. Most do not allow for the fatigue-ability, poor motivation, and handicaps of demented subjects. Some measure only a few mental functions. Some measure only the early stages of mental impairment. Finally, the inter-rater reliability, test-retest reliability, and validity of some of these instruments have not been established. A new scale, the Hierarchic Dementia Scale (HDS), overcomes many of the limitations of other available dementia rating instruments. Utilizing the principle of hierarchic decline of mental function in dementia, the HDS permits performance on 20 subscales to be rapidly pinpointed over a wide range of impairment. These 20 subscales include: orienting, prefrontal, ideomotor, looking, ideational, denomination, comprehension (verbal and written), registration, gnosis, reading, orientation, construction, concentration, calculation, drawing, motor, remote memory, writing, similarities and recent memory. Maximum score for each subscale is 10; maximum score for the whole scale is 200. Inter-rater reliability of the total scale is 0.89, test-retest 0.84 and concurrent validity 0.70. When used to study the four year course of Alzheimer's Disease and the two year course of multi-infarct dementia, the scale was sensitive enough to detect change over time both within and between individuals.

2864

TITLE : COMPUTERIZED EEG:VALUE IN THE DIAGNOSIS OF VARIOUS TYPES OF DEMENTIA IN EGYPTIAN PATIENTS.

ETRIBI,M.A.;BANOBI,M.H.;HAMED,A.;GHANIM,M.;METWALI,Y.

SUMMARY:The problem of demented patients reach about 5% of the neuropsychiatric practice in Egypt.More than half of the patients in our country do not have a final diagnosis.
This study provides a comparative study of the Cat scan and Computer EEG findings in patients with dementia seen.

2865

COMPUTERIZED TOMOGRAPHY IN MULTI-INFARCT DEMENTIA AND SENILE DEMENTIA OF ALZHEIMER TYPE.
JENSEN HV*, SKOVGAARD N**, ANDERSEN J*.
*PSYCHO-GERIATRIC DEPARTMENT, VORDINGBORG PSYCIATRIC HOSPITAL, VORDINGBORG, DEPARTMENT OF RADIOLOGY, NYKØBING FALSTER CENTRAL HOSPITAL, NYKØBING FALSTER, DENMARK.

Computerized tomography (CT) of cerebrum was carried out in 13 patients with multi-infarct dementia (MID) and 15 patients with senile dementia of Alzheimer type (SDAT) (Table 1). The MID patients fulfilled the DSM-III criteria for multi-infarct dementia and had a score of 7 points or more on the Hachinski's Ischemic Scale (HIS) and a score of 4 points or less on the Gustafson's/Nilsson's Alzheimer Scale (GNAS). The SDAT patients fulfilled DSM-III criteria for primary degenerative dementia and had a score of 5 points or more on the GNAS and a score of 6 points or less on the HIS.
Table 1. Number of patients with cerebral atrophy and infarction in the MID and SDAT group.

	MID (N=13)	SDAT (N=15)
Central atrophy	11	12
Cortical atrophy	6	4
Infarction	9*	2*
Normal CT	2	1

In comparison: *p<0.01, Fisher's test

The study supports the hypothesis that CT-verified cerebral infarction, but not atrophy, may be of diagnostic value in differentiation between MID and SDAT.

2866

GRF-INDUCED GH RESPONSE IN ALZHEIMER'S DISEASE. A. Pérez, A.Albarrán, X.A.Alvarez, M. Fernández, F. Otero, J.M. Cornes, A. Rodríguez, R. Cacabelos. Dept. Psychiatry, Santiago Univ. Med. Sch. Spain.

To evaluate the functional state of the somatotropinergic system in senile dementia of the Alzheimer type (SDAT), GRF(1-29)NH2 (150 ug i.v.) was administered to four groups of subjects: (a) controls (CS) (N=10; age= 66.2 ± 6.808 yrs); (b) early onset Alzheimer's disease (EOAD) (N=10; age= 64.4 ± 5.730 yrs); (c) late onset Alzheimer's disease (LOAD) (N=10; age= 77.0 ± 5.440 yrs); and (d) multiinfarct dementia (MID)(N=10; age= 70.4 ± 5.276 yrs). GRF induced a significant increase in plasma GH levels from 15 to 60 min after inyection, with a maximum peak (16.687 ± 15.563 ng/ml; $p<0.005$) at 30 min. in EOAD. This marked response was absent in the other three groups (CS= 3.097 ± 1.558 ng/ml at 45 min.; LOAD= 3.418 ± 2.987 ng/ml at 30 min; and MID= 2.300 ± 1.805 ng/ml at 45 min.). The mental performance assessment (MMS, BCRS, FAST) showed that GRF induces a transient improvement in cognitive functions, with no effect on cardiovascular parameters (heart rate, blood pressure). According to these results, it seems that the GRF test might be a potential antemortem marker in SDAT. (Supported by F.I.S. 88/0868 and 89/0478 of Spain).

2867

DENBUFYLLINE IMPROVES CORTICAL ERP'S AND DECISION TIME IN DEMENTIA.
J.C. Woestenburg, G. van Driel, C. Jonker, A. Niederländer, S. Platalla, J.F. Orlebeke
Department of Psychophysiology, Free University, Amsterdam, the Netherlands

Denbufylline, a xanthine derivative, has been proved to inhibit cyclic AMP phosphodiesterase and to enhance pO_2 of ischaemic cerebral tissue. These properties could produce improved information processing in subjects who are sub-optimal in this respect, such as demented patients. Cortical Event Related Potentials (ERP's), speed of decision making, and precision of processing (number of errors) are suitable candidates to test this hypothesis, since the N_{200} and the P_{300} components of the ERP are smaller and delayed in the elderly as compared with younger subjects (Looren de Jong, 1989). These differences are even stronger in mildly demented subjects (The "attentional" N_{200} is even absent in that group).
In this study denbufylline or placebo was administered for 112 days in twenty demented patients (mean age 76.6, sd. 4.89). Treatment was preceeded by a placebo period of 28 days. Assessments were made on day 0, 56 and 112 of the treatment period. The same parameters were assessed in an age-matched, non-treated control group of healthy volunteers (n=16, mean-age 74.4, sd. 3.80). Subjects carried out several tasks, triggering selective, active and passive attentional processes.
The initial difference in ERP-morphology between patients and healthy controls -especially amplitude and latency of the N_{200} and P_{300} component- disappears or becomes smaller under the influence of denbufylline. In addition decision times become faster and error rate decreases. The most salient result was the return of the N_{200}. This is supposed to represent attention for environmental events.

2868
EEG COHERENCE IN VASCULAR DEMENTIA AS DIAGNOSTIC INDICATOR.

M. SHIGETA, Y. NISHIKAWA, M. SHIMIZU, A. MORI, K. HYOKI*, Y. KAWAMURO*; Department of Psychiatry, Tokyo Jikei University of Medicine, Tokyo, *Joshinso-Kawamuro Hospital, Niigata, Japan.

Computerized spectral analysis was performed in EEG records of patients with cerebrovascular dementia (CVD) and those of healthy elderly as control. The aim of the present study is to prove the applicability of interhemispheric coherence, which is an indicator of the functional connectivity between the two cortical regions, as diagnostic indicator of dementia at an early stage.

Artifact free EEG records for 30 second's duration, with eyes closed, were recorded from the following derivations: F3; F4; O1; O2. The EEG signal was digitized at a sampling rate of 128Hz. Fast Fourier transforms were then performed and spectral power and coherence were computed. Presentation will be primarily on interhemispheric coherence in the alpha and theta band. The following three psychological tests were applied in every subject : 1) Hasegawa's Dementia Scale (HDS), 2) Kohs Block Design Test, 3) Bender Geschtalt Test. Data were analyzed using Analysis of Variance and Correlational Analysis.

The CVD subjects show significantly lower interhemispheric coherence values than the healthy controls ($p<0.01$). Coherence values were noted to increase with IQ.

The present results suggest the presence of disturbed interhemispheric information transfer mechanism in patients with CVD. Interhemispheric EEG coherence in the alpha band would be useful for detecting CVD patient at an early stage.

2869
NOOTROPICS IN ALZHEIMER TYPE DEMENTIA
(TO WHOM, WHEN AND WHY)
M. Tropper
Geropsychiatric Dept., Geriatric Center Rishon le Zion, Neuropsychiatric Dept. Zamenhof clinic, Tel-Aviv and Bar Ilan University, Israel

Although over 1000 papers related to Nootropics (N) have been published, the topic whether this special class of drugs (with selective action of higher integrative mechanisms of the brain, presumably the telencephalon) represent an indication for treatment (T) in Alzheimer Type Dementia (ATD) has yet not been fully revealed. Our survey is based on available sources of information from 1976-1988. It also includes own experience in long-term T by N published in papers and delivered at international forums, as the main points presented at the last International symposium "Nootropics in Psychogeriatric Medicine) "Chicago, 1987), chaired by us together with Prof. C.Giurgea (University of Louvan, Belgium). Discussed issues: target patients and symptoms; initial, maintaining and supportive dosages; ways of administration; treatment periods, efficacy evaluation instruments, among them our, based on A.Luria's principles Geriatric Neuropsychological Assessment & Drug efficacy Evaluation Battery. As ATD represents a multi-stage clinical entity and in its early and middle stages there still exist a constellation of concomitantly impaired and preserved Higher Cortical Functions, we consider target-oriented N therapy as a worthwhile interventional strategy in ATD.

2870
DEFORMABILITY OF HUMAN PLATELETS IN DIFFERENT TYPES OF DEMENTIAS
M. Hasitz, E. Nagy, A. Lipcsey
Janos Hospital, Budapest, Hungary

The deformability of human blood platelets are changed during irreversible progression of demention of Alzheimer's Disease. The importance of that is discussed establishing the diagnosis Alzheimer's Disease and Senile Demention of Alzheimer Type.

Session 439 Poster Presentation:
Biological psychiatry: Brain structures

2871
CORTICAL METABOLIC IMBALANCES IN SCHIZOPHRENIA
J.D. HURET, J.L. MARTINOT, A. LESUR, A. SYROTA.
S. H. F. J., CEA, 91406 ORSAY, FRANCE.

A behavioural and cognitive approach of schizophrenia led us to study the psychotic state through its relation to a dynamic cortical organization. The cortical metabolic pattern of 8 schizophrenic inpatients was compared to non-psychotic populations consisting in 16 Obsessive-Compulsive (OC) patients and a group of 10 age-matched control subjects using Positron Emission Tomography (PET) and 18-F-deoxyglucose in resting condition. All subjects were right-handers. We defined three cortical dimensions: a posterior cortical dimension involving an imbalance between the activities of the non-association sensory (NAS) cortices and the posterior parietal association (PPA) cortex; a Prefrontal Association (PFA)/ PPA cortical dimension speculating a functional link between the two association cortex; a right/left dimension. The analysis revealed an increase of the NAS/PPA ratio ($p=.05$) in the schizophrenic group. The analysis of the PFA/PPA dimension revealed a significant increase of this ratio ($p=.01$) in the schizophrenic group as compared to the OC group. This increased PFA/PPA ratio in the schizophrenic group is essentially related to a right PFA relative increased metabolism. The Right/Lelft PFA imbalance is in good agrement with previous neuropsychological studies in schizophrenia and the right "relative association hyperfrontality" could be the central fact of the psychophysiological organization of the psychotic state leading to a particular processing in the right hemisphere (NAS/PPA imbalance) and to a reduced utilization of the left hemisphere competences.

2872
SCHIZOPHRENIA-LIKE REACTIONS OF AN ARTIFICIAL NEURONAL NETWORK AND THEIR AVOIDANCE.

Walter Massing, Tagesklinik der Nervenklinik Langenhagen, Königstraße 6 A, 3000 Hannover 1

Recent studies in the neurosciences especially in neuroanatomy have shown, that in the development of the vertebrate nervous system both progressive and regressive phenomena take place. In the child as well as in the adult most probably there is destruction of "spurious memory" during dream-sleep.
By means of an artificial neuronal network it has been demonstrated, that "memory overload", causing schizophrenia-like reactions, is avoided by killing "frustrated synaptic bonds".

2873
THE CORPUS CALLOSUM IN SCHIZOPHRENIA. A CONTROLLED POST-MORTEM STUDY.
Haupts M, Greve B, Falkai P, Bogerts B, Lammerts J, * Machus B

Department of Psychiatry, University of Duesseldorf, D-4ooo Duesseldorf 12
* C.u.O.Vogt-Institute of Brain Research, D-4000 Duesseldorf

The corpus callosum is the main connecting structure between the cerebral hemispheres. As interhemispheric imbalance and information-processing disturbances have become an important hypothesis in recent understanding of schizophrenia; the corpus callosum became subject of morphometric investigations. Several in vivo studies with CT and MRI gave inconsistant results; post-mortem studies are rare.
We demonstrate significant reduction of the corpus callosum a-p-diameter in the post-mortem histology of 10 schizophrenic brains compared with 14 age-matched controls without CNS-diseases.
This finding is consistent with the concept of relevant interhemispheric information-processing disturbances in schizophrenia.

2874
BASAL GANGLIA IMPAIRMENT IN MOOD DISORDERS

S.Fasullo, A.Galofaro, F.Scoppa, G.G.Vinci*
Institute of Neuropsychiatry, Division of Neurology Ospedale Civico*, Palermo, Italy

Actual anatomophysiological knowledge on basal ganglia suggest their fundamental role in the processing of the information coming from and/or directed to all SNC levels. So it is possible to admit that an alteration of those structures should be able to cause not only motor disorders (Parkinson) but also psychical compromise (mood and cognitive disturbances).
To support this view twenty parkinsonian patients have been compared with twenty subjects with hemiparesis or hemiplegia due to cerebrovascular disorders (all patients were male), to verify if the depression of the Parkinson's disease is reactive to disability. The obtained results are discussed with reference to the monoamine hypothesis of depressive illness.

2875
ANALOGICAL PROCESS AND CEREBRAL LATERALIZATION

M. Caulet, M. Ohayon.
Laboratoire de Traitement des Connaissances, Faculté de Médecine, 27 Boulevard Jean-Moulin, 13385-Marseille, CEDEX 4.

In previous papers we analyzed the analogical process and proposed a model. We designed simple analogical problems (If A becomes B, what about C ?) where A, B, or C are either words or shapes. The subject first builds a scheme (U1) including B and such properties of A that are involved in the A->B transformation. Considering C, they build a second scheme (U2) where C reduces U1 in the same way, producing a would-be answer (D). The latter is finally valuated according to 1) the four other elements, and 2) context. The "chained analogical problem" includes two analogies of this kind. The first one calls for two or more possible answers. The second uses the answer of the first one as its "A", providing a controlled context. Only one of the possible "D"s allows to get on, the others leading to dead ends. In these cases, normal subjects backtrack their reasoning and explore fresh pathways. In this paper, we studied the analogical performances of patients with hemispheric lesions. The 20 patients (aged < 70 years) suffered ischaemic cortical unique lesions (documented with tomodensitometry). A control sample includes 10 subjects of same ages and sex, without cortical or psychotic disorders. In the "cortical lesion" group, the answers are very slow, the patients are often unable to take into account more than one or two variables, whereas the controls show normal abilities. The left-right differences in the reasoning process are analyzed through reasoning duration, backtracking ability, answer valuation, actual results, verbal/shape problems differences.

Session 440 Poster Presentation: Drugs other than antidepressants and antipsychotics

2876
EYE BLINK AND PSYCHOTROPIC DRUGS
Loga, S. and Cerić I.
Psychiatric clinic - University of Sarajevo, Yugoslavia

Research of Dopamine (DA) activity of CNS in psychiatric disorders has been limited by the undeveloped technic of measurements of neurotransmitters in vivo in humans.

There are the evidence of a positive correlation between central DA activity and blink rate.

In this report we demonstrate preliminary results of the study of correlations between blink rates and the treatment of psychiatric patients with various psychotropic drugs.

Our investigations of the utility of spontaneous eye-blink rate has showed that blink rate may be a promising marker of CNS dopamin activity.

2877
SIBUTRAMINE HCL DOES NOT ALTER CENTRAL DOPAMINERGIC FUNCTION
D J Heal and W R Buckett, Research Dept, The Boots Co. PLC, Nottingham NG2 3AA, U.K.
Sibutramine HCl (BTS 54 524) is a novel antidepressant which inhibits noradrenaline and 5-HT uptake and causes rapid down-regulation of rat cortical β-adrenoceptors. Its effects on central dopaminergic function have been assessed using 4 techniques. Sibutramine HCl (10^{-5}M) did not increase ^{3}H-dopamine efflux when superfused through preloaded rat striatal slices, unlike methamphetamine (10^{-5}M) which increased this by 140%. Similarly, sibutramine HCl (6 mg/kg) did not alter striatal 3-MT levels, measured 1h later, while methamphetamine (4.2 mg/kg) elevated these by 92%. In the nigrostriatal lesioned rat, sibutramine HCl (6 mg/kg) produced no circling either 0-1h or 4-5h after dosing. By contrast, methamphetamine (4.2 mg/kg) produced marked circling in the first period, but nothing in the second. In rats trained to recognise amphetamine (2 mg/kg) in a 2-choice lever pressing paradigm, sibutramine HCl did not generalise to amphetamine at doses up to 3 mg/kg. Higher doses disrupted this response. Methamphetamine generalised to amphetamine at 0.3 mg/kg. Hence, the results from these biochemical and behavioural techniques clearly demonstrate that sibutramine HCl does not alter central dopaminergic function at pharmacologically relevant doses.

2878
COMPARATIVE STUDY OF CYPROHEPTADINE AND CARNITINE ON PSYCHOMOTOR PERFORMANCE
F.Hakkou, C.Jaouen, L.Iraki
Faculty of Medicine, Pharmacology Casablanca, Morocco
This study was performed in order to investigate extent and severity of cyproheptadine effects on psychomotor performance, and to compare them to the effects of DL carnitine, another appetite stimulant. Twelve healthy volunteers received two doses(at 8.00 and 12.00am)of 6 mg cyproheptadine, 1600mg DL carnitine and placebo on three separate days, at a weekly interval. The study followed a double-blind, latin-square design. Assessment of dependent variables was performed 1h after the first dosage, 1h and 5h after the second administration. At each of these occasions, the following measurements were made: choice reaction time (CRT) critical flicker fusion (CFF), digit symbol substitution test (DSST), short term memory (paired words associate test), long term memory (pictures test) and 100mm visual analogue scales of subjective ratings (VAS).
Cyproheptadine significantly impaired objective measures (CFF) and subjective ratings both at 1h and 5h after the second dosage. Compared with cyproheptadine, DL carnitine induced a slight improvement of psychomotor performance, as assessed by CRT. None of the drugs had an effect on memory and on appetite at the doses studied. Cyproheptadine, at usual doses, induced a sedative effect, the intensity and duration of which are consistent with an user's risk on daytime, when driving or manipulating machines.

2879
Intoxicaciones por psicofàrmacos en España

Cabrera Forneiro Josè
Cabrera Bonet Rafael

Servicio de Informaciòn Toxicològica(I.N.T)

Los autores estudian desde el punto de vista epidemiològico las intoxicaciones ocurridas durante el año 1987 en España con psicofàrmacos y en las que ha intervenido directa e indirectamente el Servicio de Informaciòn Toxicològica del Instituto Nacional de Toxicologìa de España(ùnico en su gènero en España).
Los autores analizan no solamente los aspectos meramente frecuenciales de dichas intoxicaciones, sino su sintomatologìa, etiologìa y otros factores todos ellos de interès para la psiquiatria.
Durante el año 1987 el S.I.T recibiò un 14,6% de consultas toxicològicas relativas a psicofàrmacos.Para ser exactos 128 casos de benzodiacepinas, 63 casos de antidepresivos, 40 casos de neurolèpticos, 9 casos de barbitùricos y 12 casos de una miscelànea(sulpiride, litio,meprobamato,..etc).

2880

HALLUCINATIONS DURING TREATMENT WITH BETA-ADRENERGIC BLOCKING SUBSTANCES

F.Hollatz
Psychiatrisch-psychotherapeutische und neurologische Praxis Friedrich-Wilhelm-Platz 6,
1000 Berlin 41

Though beta-adrenoreceptor blockers are generally well tolerated now and then, the occurence of unwanted sideeffects in the central nervous system as tiredness, depressions, nightmares and sleep disturbances is reported.
Hallucinations are also recorded, but this phenomenon is not very well known - neither by the general practitioner nor by the psychiatrist.
It is therefore worthwhile discussing the report on three patients who showed this special sideeffect.
The circumstances and details of hallucinations are described and related to pharmacodynamic and psychodynamic factors of each patient.
Hypotheses about the way of action in the central nervous system with reference to actual literature are discussed.

2881

IMPROVEMENT OF AGE-RELATED BEHAVIORAL DEFICITS BY NIMODIPINE IN THE RAT

T. Schuurman and J. Traber, Neurobiology Department, Troponwerke, Berliner Str. 156, D-5000 Köln 80, F.R.G.

There is growing evidence that a disregulation of the Ca^{2+}-homeostasis in neurons plays a role in the process of brain aging. In order to further investigate the role of Ca^{2+} in the aging process we studied the effect of nimodipine, a Ca^{2+}-entry blocker which passes the blood brain barrier, on behavioral aspects of brain aging. Therefore old rats were fed with nimodipine-containing food (concentrations between 250 and 1200 ppm) beginning at the age of 24 months until 30 months of age. Age-matched control rats were fed normal, drug-free rat food. Nimodipine-fed and normally fed rats were tested in different behavioral paradigms. Besides learning- and memory capacity, exploratory behavior, sensorimotor functioning and motor coordination were measured. The data show that long term treatment of aged rats with nimodipine results in:
- improved learning ability in a watermaze test
- increased exploratory behavior in an open field test
- better performance in balance rod, pole-climbing and suspended-hanging tests
- delay or improvement of old-age related abnormal walking patterns (footprint test).

These behavioral effects of the centrally active Ca^{2+}-entry blocker nimodipine in old rats provide further evidence for a role of Ca^{2+}-ions in the process of brain aging and provide a pharmacological basis for the use of nimodipine in the treatment of certain geriatric disorders.

2882

A COMPARISON OF THE EFFECTS OF SCOPOLAMINE, DIAZEPAM AND TRIMIPRAMINE ON EXPLICIT AND IMPLICIT MEMORY IN HEALTHY VOLUNTEERS.
L. Singer, J.M. Danion, M.A. Zimmermann, D.Grange, D. Willard-Schroeder.
Departement de Psychiatrie, Centre Hospitalier Universitaire F 67091, Strasbourg Cedex.
Alzheimers's disease, a condition where central cholinergic systems are impaired, is accompanied by a decrease in a form of implicit memory, i.e. priming effect. To investigate the relationships between priming effect and cholinergic function, the influence of scopolamine (0.006 mg/kg I.M.), diazepam (0.3 mg/kg p.o.) trimipramine (0.3 mg/kg I.M.) and of a placebo on explicit and implicit memory were assessed using a free-recall task and a word-stem completion task. Fourty eight healthy volunteers took part in this double-blind study. Diazepam induced a profound and significant deficit in free-recall task, whereas scopolamine and trimipramine provoked a slight and non significant impairment. Mean word-completion performances were similar in the four groups. Explicit and implicit memory performances were significantly correlated in the scopolamine group ($r = 0.68$, $p = 0.01$, $n = 12$), but not in the other groups. Thus, whereas diazepam provoked a functional dissociation between explicit and implicit memory, scopolamine induced a concomittant decrease in these two forms of memory. These results suggest that cholinergic systems are involved in the priming effect.

Session 441 Poster Presentation:
Pharmacotherapy of depression II

2883

IPSAPIRONE: A PUTATIVE CANDIDATE IN THE TREATMENT OF MAJOR DEPRESSION.

I.S. Roed, K. Puechler, B. Kuemmel
Medical Department, Troponwerke, Berliner Straße 156, D-5000 Koeln 80, FRG

It has been known for several years that the serotonergic neurotransmitter system is involved in the origin of affective disorders. The crucial role of serotonin (5-HT) in etiology and treatment of depression can be supported by antidepressants which alter 5-HT neurotransmission, like 5-HT reuptake inhibitors, 5-HT precursors and others. Thus, changes in 5-HT metabolism can be regarded at least as one of the pathobiochemical correlates of depression.
The pyrimidinylpiperazine derivative ipsapirone influences selectively serotonergic mechanisms in brain by high affinity binding to the 5-HT1A-receptor subtype, and classifies at presynaptic autoreceptors (raphe nuclei) as agonist, at postsynaptic sites (limbic structures) as partial agonist. Precisely these selective mechanisms account for ipsapirone's unique pharmacological profile and give evidence that the drug can be regarded as potential candidate in the treatment of depression. Clinical trials conducted in patients suffering from neurotic depression demonstrate promising data with regard to improvement of depression associated with this syndrome.

2884
CORRELATIONS BETWEEN RDRS SCORES AND THE DSM-III CRITERIA: EFFECTS OF AN ANTIPRESSANT (AMOXAPINE).

N. Hugon, M. Ohayon, M. Caulet.
Laboratoire de Traitement des Connaissances, Faculté de Médecine, 27 Boulevard Jean-Moulin, 13385-Marseille, CEDEX 4.

The Relational Depression Rating Scale (RDRS) allows a valuation of the patient/clinician interaction during the clinical interview. This new depression rating scale was statistically studied in previous studies and proved as reliable as MADRS. In somatoform disorders, the somatic complaints are prominent, while the depressive symptoms are often present. In this paper, we compare the RDRS scores (low score, medium and high) to the DSM-III criteria and diagnoses collected through the use of an expert System (Adinfer©), scanning the affective, anxiety and somatoform disorders decision trees. The score/criteria correlations ares studied with a multifactorial analysis. The RDRS score decrement under antidepressive treatment is a reliable test for the drug efficiency. We study the correlations between RDRS improvement and 1) DSM-III diagnoses; 2) DSM-III Criteria, and 3) initial intensity of RDRS scores.

2885
TREATMENT OF DEPRESSION WITH E-10-OH-NORTRIPTYLINE

C Nordin*, L Bertilsson**, M-L Dahl-Puustinen**
Depts. of Psychiatry* and Clinical Pharmacology**,
Huddinge Hospital, S-141 86 Huddinge, Sweden.

The major metabolite of nortriptyline (NT) i.e. E-10-hydroxy-NT (E-10-OH-NT) is like the parent drug a potent inhibitor of noradrenaline uptake. When administered to healthy subjects, E-10-OH-NT had a plasma half-life of 8-10 hours with little variation between individuals. Compared with NT, E-10-OH-NT had less anticholinergic effects.
In an ongoing phase II-study, up to 225 mg of racemic E-10-OH-NT/day has been administered to depressed patients for three weeks. At present (March 1989), three patients have completed the study, two of whom have been lumbar punctured before and after treatment.
All patients improved continuously during the treatment period. As expected from an inhibitor of noradrenaline uptake, HMPG in CSF decreased by 15% and 17% respectively. No anticholinergic side-effects were seen.
The ratio between the (-)-and the (+)-enantiomers of E-10-OH-NT was 3.1 in plasma, 2.2 in an ultrafiltrate of plasma and 1.3 in CSF.
These preliminary results are in line with the hypothesis that E-10-OH-NT has antidepressant properties without anticholinergic side-effects. The biochemical results show a stereospecific protein binding of the two enantiomers and indicate a stereospecific elimination from the CSF.

2886
AMITRIPTYLIN PHARMACOKINETICS: DIFFERENT FORMULATIONS OF SAROTEN[R]

B. Beckermann[1], H.-D. Dell[1], J. Brons[1], M. Langer[1], I. S. Roed[2], K. Püchler[2]

Troponwerke GmbH & Co. KG, 5000 Köln 80, FRG
Biochemical Department[1], Medical Department[2]

Objective of the study was to determine the relative bioavailability of oral amitriptylin preparations and to assess the retardation of a retard form. So far, only limited studies regarding amitriptylin retard pharmacokinetics had been reported.
Bioavailability (AUC) for amitriptylin, nortriptylin and the sum of both are in the same range (n. s.) both for dragee and retard. Relative bioavailability compared to amitriptylin solution is approx. 80 %.
The retard effect of the preparation was demonstrated compared to the other forms
- having lower and delayed maximum plasma concentrations,
- showing no sharp plasma peaks,
- offering prolonged lag-time and absorption half-life time.

Nevertheless elimination half-life for the three dosage forms was nearly equivalent.
The data confirmed that pharmaceutical amitriptylin formulations have good relative bioavailability and a retard preparation offers special advantages over an instant release drug.

2887
THERAPEUTIC RESPONSE TO CHLORIMIPRAMIN PREDICTORS

L. Montejo, J. Ramos, C. Ponce de Leon, P. del Valle
Psychiatric Service. Hospital Clinico S. Carlos, Madrid Spain - Mental Health Service - Madrid Community - Madrid - Spain

A sample of 45 patients diagnosed of non-psychotic major affective disorder (RCD criteria) were studied and were grouped, according to their response to treatment with 150 mg of chlorimipramin for four weeks, in responders and non-responders.
Demographic, socio-environmental, familial, clinical and evolutive factors were evaluated. The statistical treatment of the data was done using the discriminant analysis between both groups.
According to our results, the variables which are the best predictors are: civil state, educational and professional level; number of phases, hospitalizations and previous suicide attempts; duration of the present phase; certain items on the Hamilton scale; accompanying physical disease; presence of chronic stress factors.

2888

LEVOPROTILINE VERSUS AMITRIPTYLINE IN THE TREATMENT OF DEPRESSED INPATIENTS - RESULTS OF A DOUBLE-BLIND STUDY

Wolfersdorf M., Wendt, G. and Binz U.
Hospital Weissenau, Department I of Psychiatry, University of Ulm, D 7980 Ravensburg/BRD
Ciba-Geigy GmbH, Clinical Research, D 6000 Frankfurt/BRD

Levoprotiline is the R (-)-enantiomer of the racemate oxaprotiline, a successor of the antidepressant maprotiline (Ludiomil®). The pharmacological profiles of the three drugs are comparable, but in contrast to maprotiline and oxaprotiline, levoprotiline is completely devoid of NE-reuptake inhibition.

The results of various studies carried out with worldwide-recognized standard antidepressants demonstrated that levoprotiline must be classified as a antidepressant with a reliable mood-lightening effect and with a very good tolerability.

The most distinct differences in favour of levoprotiline were obtained in a double-blind study carried out versus amitriptyline with 90 hospitalized patients mostly suffering from endogenous depression. At the end of the second week of treatment a significant difference ($p < 0.05$) was obtained with levoprotiline compared with amitriptyline for the reduction in the total HAMD score. The number of patients with unwanted effects was significantly less ($p=0.015$) under treatment with levoprotiline than under treatment with amitriptyline.

2889

SWISS EXPERIENCE WITH DOSULEPIN: AN OPEN STUDY IN DEPRESSION

R.C. Winning, M. Pia, J. Wertheimer, L.J. Moxon and D. Prudham

The therapeutic response and tolerability of dosulepin dothiepin) was assessed in 18 depressed patients from 2 swiss centres. All patients received 75mg/day for four weeks and at the 1 and 2 week assessment this dose was doubled in non responders aged less than 70. Of 12 patients going through to week 2 of the study, 4 had their dosage doubled.

Significant improvements measured using the Montgomery-Asberg depression rating scale (MADRS) were observed at each of the follow up visits (1, 2 and 4 weeks) relative to baseline. Changes in the overall severity of depression showed significant improvement at each follow-up visit when tested using the signed rank test. The global outcome, measured at week 4 was also favourable. Improvements of approximately equal proportions were observed in both the 75mg and 150mg groups.

During the study, 16 side effects were reported by 8 patients, 4 of these in patients on 75mg, 2 on 150mg and 2 on both dosages. The effects included drowsiness, dry mouth, loss of libido, accommodation disorders, exanthema and facial oedema.

It is concluded that dosulepin 75mg-150mg/day significantly improves depressive conditions and that it is well tolerated at these doses.

2890

DOTHIEPIN (DOSULEPIN) IN DEPRESSION. A DUTCH OPEN MULTICENTRE STUDY.

P.W. Vlottes*, S. Donovan**, The Boots Company, *Utrecht, The Netherlands, **Nottingham, UK.

Two hundred and thirty one male or female adult depressed in-, out-, or day patients (pts) referred to 35 Dutch psychiatric centres received 75-150 mg of the tricyclic, dothiepin (Dp) daily for 4 weeks. Efficacy was judged using an abridged Hamilton Depression Rating Scale (HAMD).

Ten pts withdrew due to adverse events, one due to lack of effect, 2 due to preference for other treatments and the remainder for non-drug related reasons.

For the 200 pts with evaluable data at week 4 the mean HAMD score improved by 57% ($p<0.001$). 185 pts (93%) improved as judged by the HAMD score. Of the 219 pts in whom tolerability was assessed by questioning, 36% reported no side-effects and 53% reported mild side-effects. Tolerability was graded as moderate in 6% and poor in 5%. The most common side-effects reported were dry mouth and drowsiness.

These results are similar to those from previously reported larger cohorts of pts treated in a similar fashion in other N. European countries(1) and confirm that Dp is also an effective well tolerated treatment in depressed pts in Holland.

(1) Donovan S. Psychopharmacol 1988;96(Suppl):277

2891

DOTHIEPIN (DOSULEPIN) VERSUS AMITRIPTYLINE IN DEPRESSION. 18 YEARS ON.

S. Donovan*, P.W. Vlottes**, Research Department, The Boots Company PLC, *Nottingham, UK, **Utrecht, The Netherlands.

Amitriptyline (Am) is a reference tricyclic antidepressant against which many newer antidepressants continue to be compared. Dothiepin (Dp) is a well established thioanalogue of Am. Between 1971 and 1988, 22 comparative studies have been reported worldwide in over 1200 depressed patients.

In 19 of the 22 studies, the antidepressant effect of Am and Dp was equivalent although in 7 of these there was a reported trend in favour of Dp. Three (16%) of the studies demonstrated a superior effect of Dp. None of the studies demonstrated a superiority of Am.

Side-effects were documented in 21 studies. Ten (48%) showed no significant difference between the 2 treatments although in 5 of these, there was a reported trend in favour of the tolerability of Dp. In 11 (52%) of the studies, Dp was said to be better tolerated. In none of the studies was Am reported to be better tolerated.

Thus, Dp and Am are equally effective in treating depression although the incidence and severity of side-effects with Dp was less than with Am. Dp is therefore a better alternative than Am in the treatment of depression.

2892

ADINAZOLAM COMPARED WITH AMITRIPTYLINE IN HOSPITALIZED MELANCHOLIC PATIENTS
Hetta J, Mejlhede A, Tamminen T, Åberg-Wistedt A.
Dept. of Psychiatry in Uppsala, Aalborg, Helsinki and Danderyd.

In a six-week double blind trial, 87 inpatients suffering from Major Depresson with melancholia were randomly assigned to adinazolam (n=44) or amitriptyline (n=43) treatment groups; 34 patients in the adinazolam group and 33 in the amitriptyline group completed the study.
Based on primary efficacy variables, a slightly higher proportion of amitriptyline patients responded to the drug treatment compared with adinazolam patients, but the differences were not statistically significant. Fifty percent (n=22) in the adinazolam group and 63% (n=27) in the amitriptyline group showed much or very much improvement in the Physician's Global Impression. Mean final daily dosage was 82 mg adinazolam or 191 mg amitriptyline at day 42. Dry mouth or decreased salivation and trembling were reported significantly more often by the amitriptyline-treated patients than by the adinazolam patients.
The present study demonstrates effectivness of the triazolobenzodiazepine Adinazolam in melancholic depression.

2893

AN AUSTRALIAN MULTICENTRE TRIAL OF MOCLOBEMIDE VERSUS AMITRIPTYLINE
L. Evans, T. George, B. O'Sullivan, P. Mitchell, G. Johnson and M. Adena
Queensland University, Brisbane, Australia

This poster reports the results of an Australian multicentre study of the new monoamine oxidase inhibitor, moclobemide, in the treatment of major depression. Moclobemide is a specific monoamine oxidase-A inhibitor which does not bind irreversibly to the enzyme, unlike the currently available MAOIs. Recent studies would suggest that in subjects taking moclobemide blood pressure elevation caused by tyramine is significantly less than that induced by the irreversible MAOIs, particularly when tyramine is administered in an oral form.

Forty-eight patients with major depression were randomly allocated to treatment with either moclobemide or amitriptyline for 4 weeks on a double-blind basis. There were no statistically significant differences between the 2 groups on measures of efficacy. Patients taking amitriptyline reported a greater number of side-effects and more patients in the amitriptyline group dropped-out because of side-effects. There were no reports of interactions with tyramine-containing foods.

2894

A double blind trial of moclobemide versus amitriptyline in depression
P.E. Mullen, G.M. Newburn, A.R. Fraser
J.M. Rodgers
University of Otago Medical School

The efficacy as an antidepressant and side-effects profile of a new monamine oxidase inhibitor, moclobemide, was compared to that of amitriptyline. The study had a randomised double blind design in which 41 patients received either 200 mgs of moclobemide or 125 mgs amitriptyline over a period of six weeks. All patients met the criteria for major depression (DSM III R) of at least moderate severity and had a score of over 17 points on the Hamilton Rating Scale. Change was monitored on the basis of the Hamilton Rating Scale, SDS Patient Questionnaire and Global Clinical Assessment.

Moclobemide showed antidepressant activity comparable to amitriptyline and no significant differences emerged between the medications either in the rate or final level of improvement. There was however a significant difference between the treatment groups both in terms of the frequency and severity of reported side-effects. Moclobemide was better tolerated with a lower rate of untoward side effects.

The potential role of moclobemide in the treatment of depressive disorders will be discussed.

2895

DOUBLE-BLIND COMPARISON OF MOCLOBEMIDE, IMIPRAMINE AND PLACEBO IN DEPRESSIVE PATIENTS
R. Ucha Udabe, C.A. Márquez, C.A. Traballi, N. Portes
Instituto Privado de Psicopatología and Dept. International Clinical Research, Productos Roche S.A. Q. e I., Buenos Aires, Argentina

Moclobemide (Ro 11-1163) is a new, short-acting, reversible MAO-inhibitor with preferential inhibition of MAO-A. Seventy-two out-patients, 44 females and 28 males, range 18-65 years, with major depressive episodes, scoring ≥ 17 points on the Hamilton Depression Rating Scale (HAM-D) were included in a double blind study of 3 arms comparing moclobemide, imipramine and placebo, during a 6-week treatment. Mean HAM-D score decrease from baseline was moclobemide 48.3%, imipramine 50.2% and placebo 18.6%. Differences between active drugs and placebo were highly significant ($p=0.0001$, Kruskal-Wallis test), whereas moclobemide and imipramine did not differentiate significantly ($p=0.81$, Wilcoxon two sample test). The Zung Self-rating Depression Scale yielded similar findings. Mean daily doses at the end of treatment were moclobemide 405 mg and imipramine 130 mg. Assessment of tolerance favored moclobemide over imipramine although differences were not statistically significant. A 52-week assessment in 22 patients receiving moclobemide on an open basis showed a persistence of the clinical response in the long-term administration. In conclusion, moclobemide is as effective as imipramine in the treatment of depressive illness. Efficacy and safety was maintained during the long-term treatment.

Session 442 Poster Presentation:
Sleep research

2896

REM-SLEEP AND LEARNING PROCESSES: EFFECT OF ANTIDÉPRESSANTS

Y. Millet, M. Ohayon, M. Caulet, N. Hugon, Blanc F., Vial M.
Laboratoire de Traitement des Connaissances, Faculté de Médecine, 27 Boulevard Jean-Moulin, 13385-Marseille, CEDEX 4.

Our basic hypothesis is that the impairment of paradoxical sleep leads to major cognitive disorders: the learning and acquisition processes should be belated or even suppressed. In the animals, during the so-called sensitive period, major acquisitions are performed: attachment processes are established and developed. Some antidepressant drugs are known to impair the REM-sleep. We studied the effects of Amoxapine and Trimipramine in young kittens on REM-sleep and comportemental development. The drugs were given per os (Amoxapine: 5mg/Kg, Trimipramine 6mg/Kg from day 10 to day 40). The controls were given the same volume of water at the same times. We recorded the EEG daily 2, 4 and 22 hours after drug intake. The record duration was 1 hour. The animals were left with their mother (the 3 hours EEG excepted), and their moves were recorded on a videotape. Once a minute, the positions of the kitten and the mother are marked, and the average mother-kitten and kitten-kitten distances, as well as the total daily individual movements are calculated. The number of wake/sleep cycles and total sleep duration are recorded. Three criteria of the drug action are thus available: total sleep amount, global activity level and kitten-mother spatial attachment. We studied 10 breeds of 3 kitten each, 1 amoxapine, 1 trimipramine and 1 control.
The effects of the antidepressants on EEG and comportemental variables are studied, and the correlation between REM/total sleep and mother kitten attachment are discussed.

2897

AMITRYPTILINE AND SLEEP PATTERN IN HEALTHY MALES

M.Kobusiak and W.Jernajczyk
Psychiatric Hospital Wrocław,
Institute of Psychiatry and Neurology
Warszawa,Poland

The following changes of sleep pattern have been described in healthy subjects after amitryptiline: increase of deep sleep,reduction of REM sleep,decrease of REM activity.
7 physically and mentally healthy males aged between 24 and 42 years took part in this study.The polygraphic investigation of sleep was carried out in two consecutive nights before and after using 25 mg of amitryptiline.Differences between these two patterns of sleep were evaluated and discussed.

2898

Amitryptiline and REM sleep parameters in bipolar depression.
Wojciech Jernajczyk
Institute of Psychiatry and Neurology
EEG Dep.

Parameters of REM sleep were measured in 6 endogenous,bipolar,depressive drug free patiens and on 21st day of amitryptiline treatment. The eeg stages of sleep were classified by visual inspection using the strict criteria designated in the Rechtschaffen-Kales manual /1968/. The following components of REM sleep were studied: 1.REM time,2.REM latency, 3.REM activity, 4.REM density, 5.Time of interruptions during REM, 6.Latency of eye movement/LEM/. The results obtained were largely assessed by Student`s t- test. Moreover the nearest neighbor decision rule was applied.
The increase of REM density /0.02/ and LEM /0.02/ were found during amitryptiline treatment.

2899

EFFECTS OF MILNACIPRAN ON SLEEP OF DEPRESSED PATIENTS - A POLYGRAPHIC STUDY.
J. MOURET*, P. LEMOINE*, P.SUTET**, P. SANCHEZ*
* Biological psychiatry clinical unit
CHS Vinatier - 69500 LYON BRON FRANCE
** Pierre Fabre Research Center
81106 CASTRES FRANCE

The sleep patterns of 10 depressed inpatients were studied during the initial (D4 to D6), and terminal (D26 to D28) periods of 100 mg milnacipran 4 weeks treatment, and compared to those from the control period. The sleep parameters were scored according RESCHTSCHAFFEN and KALES criteria, and changes in mood were evaluated weekly through MADRS and CGI. From the early period of treatment a statistically significant increase of total sleep time was observed. In particular a sleep latency reduction, an increase of sleep efficiency index and stage II sleep time was noted. Moreover there was an increase in REM sleep latency. By contrast no statistically significant change in REM sleep duration was found whatever treatment period. It is of particular interest to note the "sleep-modulating" effect of milnacipran. The changes in stage II and REM sleep parameters, from control to early period of treatment are statistically correlated to the control level of these parameters; i.e. an enhancement of the lowest and a decrease of the highest recorded values of stage II and REM sleep parameters, was observed. These results suggest a particular beneficial effect of milnacipran on the sleep of depressed patients.

2900

INFLUENCE OF TRIMIPRAMINE ON MOOD, SLEEP AND DREAMS IN DEPRESSED OUTPATIENTS
D. Riemann, M. Wiegand* and M. Berger
Central Institute of Mental Health, Mannheim and
*Max-Planck Institute of Psychiatry, Munich, FRG

In a pilot study by our group (Wiegand et al., Pharmacopsychiat 19, 198-199, 1986) it was shown that besides its antidepressive properties trimipramine seems to act very favourably on sleep disturbances. Interestingly, some of the patients in this study spontaneously reported that they dreamt more often and had more pleasant dreams than before treatment. This seemed to coincide with the fact that trimipramine is the only tricyclic antidepressant agent which does not suppress REM sleep. The present study aimed at evaluating the positive effects of trimipramine on sleep and dream quality in a larger sample of depressed outpatients.
Methods: More than 4213 depressed outpatients who were in treatment in private practice participated in a 4-week open trial with trimipramine (50 mg to 200 mg). Results will be reported of 1707 outpatients who were treated with trimipramine exclusively during the trial.
Results: In 84% of patients investigated, treatment led to an improvement of mood after 4 weeks. 92% of the patients showed a marked improvement of the sleep disturbances. Trimipramine did not lead to an increase of dream recall, the patients however rated their overall dream quality as more neutral or pleasant during treatment compared to baseline.

2901

SLEEP DISORDERS DURING PREGNANCY

C. Almenar, E. Estivill, J.C. Fereer.
Unidad de Alteraciones del Sueño.
Institut Dexeus. Barcelona (Spain).

Few studies have been reported about sleep disorders in pregnant women, and even less concerning polisomnographic findings during pregnancy.
The authors evaluated the incidence of sleep disorders in a sample of one hundred and fifty pregnant women (out-patients in an obstetric unit), by means of a self administered questionnaire which contained information about work, sleep habits, and specific questions about difficulty in initiating or mantaining sleep, and excessive diurne somnolence, themselves comparing the quality and quantity of sleep before and during pregnancy.
The sample was divided in to three groups, according to the month of gestation.
The authors tried to find some related factors which would be implicated in the etiology of this kind of health problem.

Session 443 Poster Presentation:
Clinical neurophysiology and neuroimaging

2902

FIXATION DURING MR-EXAMINATIONS, WELL TOLERATED BY SCHIZOPHRENIC PATIENTS.
Andersson-Lundman G, Svedberg E, Sääf J, Wahlund L-O, Wetterberg L.
Karolinska Institute, Department of Psychiatry, St. Göran's Hospital, S-112 81 Stockholm, Sweden.

Imaging methods, e.g. CT and MRI, have shown to be valuable in the study of the CNS in various psychiatric disorders. In order to prevent motion artifacts and obtain a high geometric matching between scannings there is a need for fixation of the head during the lengthy MRI examinations. A method commonly used in radiotherapy to fix the head with a moulding plastic material (Orfit-Raycast, Luxilon Industries, Belgium) was tested in seven schizophrenic patients and five healthy controls. Each individual was scanned (Acutscan 110, Finland) at four different occasions with a total examination time of five hours. The head was examined in different projections and with various pulse sequences. The method gave proper geometric matching and reproducible results. Neither patients nor controls reported any complaints to the fixation and fulfilled the entire examination program without claustrofobic reactions.

2903

THE RELEVANE OF EEG PATTERNS IN A PSYCHIATRIC POPULATION
Dogan Y.B., Sarman C.
Medical School of Ankara Univ. Dept. of Psych., Ankara, Turkey

EEG investigation is not always a common and routine procedure in clinical practice of psychiatry. There are some prerequisites for applying this laboratory technic under certain circumstances. In other words clinical indications of EEG are limited by nature.
The opposite way round has been tested in the study. Starting with EEG patterns with relatively positive findings, we compared them to the clinical pictures either reported by the patient or observed by the clinicians.
In order to reach a comparative conclusion nearly 400 EEG patterns (with so called positive finding) have been rechecked and interpreted in relevance to the clinical manifestations of the patients.
To what extent the EEG is a determining factor has been discussed from the standpoint of clinical psychiatry.

2904
Routine EEG Pattern During Interferon(IFN Treatment

W.Jernajczyk, J.Leszek

Psychiatric Clin.Univ.Med.School,Wrocław
Inst.Psych.Neurol.Warsaw,Poland

Routine EEG examinations have been done on 13 pts. with diagnosed schizophrenia (acc.to Revision 9 of the WHO),who have been treated with natural human IFN administered s.c. in doses of 3×10^6 U(ml, daily over a period of 42 days.Four patients had only one EEG examination done on them because a deterioration of their mental state made it necessary to discontinue the administration of IFN. Nine patients were examined before the inception of IFN treatment(a two-week wash aut) and after six weeks of receiving IFN.
The paper discusses the possible connection between the EEG and its changes and the clinical state of patients treated with IFN.

2905
DIAGNOSTIC VALUE OF EVOKED POTENTIALS (VEP, AEP, SEP)
Georgi Mitev, Yulie Yotova, Radostin Moskov
Higher Military Medical Institute, Sofia, Bulgaria

Visual, acoustic and somatosensory evoked potentials were performed in 35 patients with different performance of the disturbances of inadaptation.
The investigation was performed with an apparatus "Toennies". The obtained results give us the grounds to consider that the investigation of evoked potential has its place in the whole diagnostic complex.

2906
SELF REGULATION OF SLOW BRAIN POTENTIALS IN SCHIZOPHRENICS

Frank Schneider, Hans Heimann, Birgit Mechela
Psychiatric Hospital, Univ. of Tübingen, FRG

Slow brain potential (SP) changes are correlates of a system of attentional control. In a biofeedback-paradigm selfregulation of SP was studied on 12 hospitalized and medicated schizophrenic patients (DSM III-R: undifferentiated or paranoid type) as well as 12 healthy controls. Subjects receive feedback in form of a videogame where a rocket is moving horizontally, this represents SP changes which derive from the central cortex. Subjects had to shift their cerebral potentials in positive or negative direction. Schizophrenics participated 20 times, healthy controls five times, each lasting over one hour.
Compared with the healthy controls, the schizophrenics showed very little control over SP at the beginning. This especially in transfer situation, were a more complex task without continuous visual feedback is given. In the last five of 20 sessions patients showed similar achievement as the controls. High degree of symptomatology at the beginning of the study (BPRS, SANS, GAS), long history of illness, and multiple hospitalisations correlated with impaired ability of selfregulation of SP.

2907
THE CBF, CMRO2, OER AND GLUCOSE UTILIZATION IN SCHIZOPHRENIC PATIENTS.

Haruhiro Fujita, Hideji Kishimoto, Osamu Takatsu, Takashi Ishikawa, Taiko Hashimoto, Masaaki Matsushita, Masaaki Iio* and Miwako Saito*.
Department of Psychiatry, Yokohama City University School of Medicine, Minami-ku, Yokohama 232 and Nakano National Hospital*, Tokyo 160, JAPAN.

Using the method of C15O2,15O2 and 11C-glucose, the authors could get the PET(positron emission tomography) image of cerebral blood flow(CBF), cerebral metabolic rate of oxygen(CMRO2), oxygen extraction ratio(OER) and glucose utilization in schizophrenic patients who had never been treated.
In the schizophrenic patients, there were three types of PET images in cortical areas.The first(type A) was a bilateral hypofrontal PET image in which the rate of CBF, CMRO2 and glucose utilization were decreased by about 35 % ($P<0.01$). The second (type B) was a right-side hypoparietal PET image in which the rate of CBF, CMRO2 and glucose utilization were decreased by about 25 % ($P<0.05$). The third (type C) was a left-side hypotemporal PET image in which the rate of CBF, CMRO2 and glucose utilization were decreased by about 20 % ($P<0.05$).
There was no difference between types A, B, C and normal controls in CBF, CMRO2 and OER in the hippocampus, caudatum, putamen and thalamus.
In conclusion, the authors theorize that there was significant hypofunction in cortical areas in schizophrenic patients.

2908

A BIOLOGICAL APPROACH TO THE EFFECTS OF HYPNOSIS
- THE LAST 60 YEARS AND NEW POSSIBILITIES IN
NEUROIMAGING
H.Walter, I.Podreka, M.Steiner
Psychiatric University Clinic, Vienna
A-1090 Wien, Wahringer Gurtel 18-20, Austria

Since Berger devoted his last publication to EEG
and Hypnosis several attempts had been made to
reveal the myth around this form of psychotherapy
Many authors like Heimann, Janovic, Gruzelier et
al, Crawford et al, Chen et al, Baer et al using
mainly EEG and Xenon-133-method have worked in
this last 60 years.
Vienna has an old tradition in the use of
hypnosis as a therapeutic element (Wagner
Jauregg, Freud, Hoff, Berner). In the line of
this tradition we started 3 years ago a new
attempt to find out biological correlates for
this state of consciousness. The results of this
neurophysiological work will be presented with
emphasis on a study in 40 healthy persons
examined in waking state and in hypnosis by means
of Single photone emission computer-tomography.

Session 444 Poster Presentation:
Biological psychiatry: Dopaminergic system

2909

CENTRAL ACTION OF CALCIUM CHANNEL INHIBITORS: RELATION
TO DEPRESSION" ANXIETY AND ETHANOL DEPENDENCE IN RATS

Wojciech Kostowski and Olgierd Pucilowski
Institute of Psychiatry and Neurology
20157 Warszawa, Poland

Calcium channel inhibitors (CCI) represent a broad and
chemically different groups of drugs which inhibit the calcium entry through voltage sensitive "L" channels. We studied central actions of dihydropiridine derivatives (e.g.
nifedipine, nicardipine), diltiazem and verapamil in Wistar male rats. Both nifedipine and diltiazem reduced locomotor deficit produced by uncontrolable stress (footshock)
and reduced anxiety in elevated plus maze test.
Nifedipine increased hypnotic action of ethanol without
affecting ethanol hypothermia. Diltiazem produced no change in acute ethanol effects. Both compounds reduced the
development of tolerance to hypothermic (and to lesser
extent hypnotic) action of ethanol. The withdrawal syndrome
as evidenced by audiogenic seizures was reduced by nifedipine only.
Dihydropiridine derivatives and verapamil (but not diltiazem) potentiated catalepsy induced by both dopaminergic
D-1 antagonist, SCH 23390 and D-2 receptor antagonist, haloperidol and reduced behavioral excitation related to stimulation of D-1 receptors (SKF 38393-induced grooming) and
D-2 receptors (apomorphine-induced locomotion).
In conclusion, certain CCIs exhibit antidopaminergic-like
profile, modulate some effects of ethanol and show anxiolytic and antidepressive actions.

2910

PLASMA HOMOVANILLIC ACID AND PRODUCTIVE PSYCHOTIC
ACTIVITY
Maier, Ch.,
Socialpsychiatric University Clinic
(Director Prof. L. Ciompi)

Plasma homovanillic acid (HVA) as an indicator of
dopamine metabolism was measured in seven patients
with acute psychosis. All patients meeting DSM-III
criteria for the diagnosis of schizophrenia showed
psychotic symptoms for the first time and were
free of neuroleptic medication during their lifetime. In this exclusive sample of schizophrenic
patients the productive psychotic activity (PPA),
an index for the proceeding of acute psychosis,
was determined. We found in all patients a significant decrease of HVA within forty minutes. The
levels of plasma HVA were significantly correlated
with PPA ratings and reversely with the duration
of milieutherapy. The author discusses the results
and emphasizes the importance of differentiating
research work comparing psychopathology with neurochemical findings.

2911

HOMOVANILLIC ACID CONCENTRATION IN PLASMA AND
CSF OF PSYCHIATRIC PATIENTS

Kazunari Moriuchi, Yoshihide Imazu,
Hiroshi Yoneda and Katsuhiro Toyoda
Department of Neuropsychiatry, Osaka Medical
College, Takatsuki 569, Osaka, Japan

The concentration of homovanillic acid
(HVA) was measured in the plasma and CSF of
psychiatric patients. Thirty-one patients were
divided into 4 groups based on the duration of
neuroleptics treatment; <A> drug free, <B> one
day - 3 weeks, <C> 3 weeks - one year and <D>
over one year. Plasma HVA (pHVA) concentration
was 7.8 ± 0.9 ng/ml (Mean$\pm$SEM, N=8) in the
controls. The patient groups were <A> 6.9 ± 0.5
(N=19), <B> 8.4 ± 0.9 (N=8), <C> 5.4 ± 0.7 (N=3) and
<D> 8.1 (N=1). There was no significant
difference in pHVA levels between the patients
and controls. Among the patient groups, pHVA was
significantly less in group <C> than in group
<B> ($p<0.05$). CSF HVA concentration was 27.0 ± 2.0
(N=17) in the controls. The patient groups were
<A> 25.0 ± 2.7 (N=19), <B> 49.4 ± 4.3 (N=8), <C>
34.0 ± 23.8 (N=3) and <D> 32.9 (N=1). CSF HVA
level was significantly higher in group <B>
than in controls ($p<0.01$) or group <A> ($p<0.05$).
No correlation (r=0.296, N=31) was found in HVA
levels of plasma and CSF, which were taken at
the same time. These results suggest that the
origins of HVA in plasma and in CSF are probably
different from each other.

2912

PHARMACOLOGICAL CHARACTERIZATION OF DOPAMINE AUTORECEPTOR IN RAT STRIATUM
Kazuo Yamada, Masaaki Matsushita, Yoshiro Goshima[*], Yoshimi Misu[*].
Department of Psychiatry and Pharmacology[*], Yokoham City University, School of Medicine. Yokohama Japan.

Dopamine autoreceptor is going to be important of thinking about the Dopamine(DA) hypothesis of Shizophrenia.We have discussed the characterization of DA autoreceptor through the pharmacological response.Electrical field stimulation-evoked release endogenous DA from superfused rat striatal slices was measured by HPLC with ECD.DA antagonist, S-Sulpirde(1-100nM), dose-dependently increased the el-ectrically evoked DA release,wheareas the R-isomer had no effect.DA agonist,Apomorphine (10-1000nM) and DA partial agonist,Bromocriptie(10-1000nM) dose-dependently decreased.But Bromocriptine(1μM) induced inhibition was converted to facilitation by L-DOPA(0.01nM).We notice the combination therapy of L-DOPA to shizophrenic patients,too.

2913

SELECTIVE PRESYNAPTIC DOPAMINE AGONIST TREATMENT OF SCHIZOPHRENIA WITH BHT-920
Peter Winckler and Mathias Bartels
Universitäts-Nervenklinik Tübingen
West-Germany

During an open clinical trial lasting 4 weeks 10 chronic schizophrenic patients were treated with the new presynaptic dopamine agonist BHT-920.
The BPRS-syndroms anxiety/depression, anergia/activation and the global score showed significant improvement. With the AMDP-system significant changes were seen in the paranoid-hallucinatory and affectivity syndromes as well as in the global score.
Side effects including sedation, hypotension and vomiting were rarely seen. No extrapyramidal side effects were registrated.
In conclusion, the selective presynaptic dopamine agonist BHT-920 showed good antipsychotic efficacy without inducing extrapyramidal side-effects. The positive effects on depressive and anergic syndroms were especially impressive and could indicate an important extension of the pharmacotherapy of chronic schizophrenia.

2914

REGIONAL EFFECTS OF D-1 AND D-2 RECEPTOR BLOCKADE ON DA METABOLISM AND SYNTHESIS

Syvälahti, E., Lappalainen, J., Hietala, J., Koulu, M. and Sjöholm, B.
Department of Pharmacology, University of Turku, 20520 Turku, Finland.

Chronic treatment with classical neuroleptics reduces neuronal activity and DA turnover in the major DAergic pathways. We have treated rats with SCH 23390, a selective D-1 receptor antagonist (0.25 or 0.05 mg/kg x 2/day, s.c.), haloperidol, a classical neuroleptic drug (0.5 mg/kg x 2/day, s.c.) or vehicle for 18 days to measure the basal metabolite levels and the DA synthesis rate with DOPA-accumulation (NSD 1015, 100 mg/kg i.p.) technique in mesolimbic (n.accumbens) and nigrostriatal (n.caudatus) pathways.

Haloperidol reduced basal HVA concentrations in the caudate and in the n.accumbens. DOPA-accumulation was also significantly reduced in n. accumbens and in caudate. SCH 23390 significantly reduced the basal concentration of HVA in the caudate but not in n.accumbens. DOPA-accumulation was significantly reduced in n.accumbens after repeated administration with SCH 23390 but not in the caudate. Thus differing from haloperidol, SCH 23390 affects differentially DA synthesis and metabolism in the two DAergic systems, and the selectivity of SCH 23390 for the mesolimbic DA system is only partial.

2915

A comparative study of a new neuroleptic - Remoxipride.
Dr Sidney Levine
Royal Oldham Hospital, Rochdale Rd, OLDHAM OL1 2JH
Co-authors - Drs. S Sony, G Edwards, R S Deo, I Plant and S Rastogi.

Remoxipride is a selective dopamine D_2 receptor antagonist. A multicentre study was carried out comparing Remoxipride 150/160 mg per day with Haloperidol 10/40mg per day in a double-blind parallel group design on acute schizophrenic patients fulfilling RDC diagnostic criteria. The efficacy was assessed using BPRS and Krawiecka rating scales. Adverse events were assessed including the Simpson-Angus rating scale for extra pyramidal side effects. 89 patients were included in the study, of whom 63 patients completed the 6 week study period. Both drugs produced effective improvement but there was no significant difference. Remoxipride was shown to have fewer extrapyramidal side effects and less concomitant use of antiparkinsonian medication. The reasons for premature withdrawal from the study are assessed. Remoxipride was found to be safe when all biochemical, haematological and cardiovascular indices were assessed. This study concludes that Remoxipride has a therapeutic efficacy similar to Haloperidol but with few extrapyramidal side effects.

2916

STIMULATION OF CHRONIC NEUROLEPTIC TREATED
RATS WITH A D1-AGONIST
Glenthøj B, Arnt J and Hyttel J.
Dept. Psychiatry, Rigshospitalet and H. Lundbeck
A/S, Copenhagen, Denmark

Development of vacuous chewing movements (VCM) in rodents has been proposed as an animal model of tardive dyskinesia (TD). Two classes of dopamine receptors exist (D1 and D2). D1-agonists increase oral activity. We have earlier demonstrated long-lasting rises in VCM and tongue protrusions (TP) in discontinuously (DIS), but not continuously (CON) neuroleptic treated rats. To test whether this rise in mouth movements could be a result of exaggerated activity at the D1 site, 34 rats were divided into three groups receiving zuclopenthixol DIS or CON for 15 weeks or no treatment. Only DIS treated animals showed a rise in VCM and TP after withdrawal. 3 weeks after termination of medication the animals were tested with the D1-agonist SK&F 38393. The increases in VCM after SK&F 38393 did not differ within the groups, but in contrast to treated rats, controls had no rise in TP. There were no differences in the number of D1- and D2-receptors in the striatum when the groups were compared. The increased amount of TP seen in drugged animals implies D1-receptor supersensitivity. No differences in reactivity were seen between DIS and CON treated animals, and our results thus do not indicate that D1-receptor supersensitivity is significant for the development of the spontaneous, long-lasting rise in oral activity found in DIS treated rats.

Session 445 Poster Presentation:
Adolescent psychiatry

2917

MENTAL CONTRADICTIONS AND ABNORMAL BEHAVIOR OF ADOLESCENTS
Petrov Raiko
Sofioter University "Climent Ochridski", Bulgaria
Code No. 6

In connection with the influence of public conditions and the forming of a contradiction between mind readiness and the need for new forms of behavior is important for the building-up of mind readiness towards new forms in adolescents.

The contradiction between "freedom - responsibility" is balanced by the consciousness for moral and social requirements of the relations. Found out was that when in the mentality structure of the emotional (spirits, affects, etc) over the intellectual components prevail, the development of behavior takes up the direction to abnormal. Specific reasons for such behavioral deviations are the not motivated interdictions and punishments.

The contradiction set between "control - selfcontrol" is expressed since the earliest years of childhood. In such cases the lowered control is a phenomenologic mark of a socially aversed behavior and is present predominantly in adolescents of choleric temper.

"Dynamics - stereotype" is a contradiction in the structure itself.
We found out that stereotype is a phenomenologic mark of the antisocial behavior too. In its nature it is a behavior conducted without will efforts, so it is related with certain needs under concrete circumstances.

It is worth pointing out that doubtless there are many other contradictions in mentality of importance for the forming of abnormal behavior of adolescents, though the discussed ones are of first priority for the contingent under investigation.

2918

ADOLESCENTS : FRENCH CRITERIA FOR SCHIZOPHRENIC AND MOOD DISORDERS
LAZARTIGUES A., MURGUI E., MORALES R. BARUA U.
Clinique DUPRE 30 av Roosevelt 92330 SCEAUX FRANCE

OBJECTS : Operational criteria of "1.04 Schizophrenia" and of "1.05 Psychoses Dysthymiques" proposed by MISES et al and its diagnostic comparison embracing 30 patients (16-19 years) with RDC, DSM-III-R, French Clinicians.

METHODS : Criteria followed Glossary of French classification. Two clinicians interviewed (SADS) independently. Clinical diagnosis, French criteria, DSM-III-R, RDC.

RESULTS : Schizophrenia : more precise than of Emperical criteria. Dissociative Syndrome : at least one feature of depersonalisation, disorder of thought, affect, speech, catatonic behaviors. Delusions : associated features - bizarre delusions, non systematic, Passivity phenomena-. Definitions more restricted than those of Americans, exclude associated mood disorders; plus specific features to these age and Schizoaffective disorders of DSM-III-R.

CONCLUSION : The proposed criteria reflects French Conception which are reliable diagnostically and may by compared to the American System of classifications.

2919

FLUOXETINE EFFECTS IN ADOLESCENT DEPRESSION

Jovan G. Simeon, M.D., H. Bruce Ferguson, Ph.D.,
Winona Copping, M.D., & Vincenzo F. DiNicola, M.D.
Royal Ottawa Hospital, Ottawa, Canada

Fluoxetine, a non-tricyclic antidepressant, appeared useful and safe in an open trial in depressed adolescents. Twenty-two female and 18 male patients, 13 to 18 years old, participated in a placebo-controlled double-blind study. Following a baseline placebo period of at least one week, fluoxetine or placebo was given for seven weeks. Dosages were adjusted individually; the daily maximum ranged from 40 mg to 60 mg (mean, 58 mg). About two-thirds of the patients showed marked or moderate clinical global improvements with both fluoxetine and placebo. Preliminary analyses showed that of the 30 patients who completed the study, fluoxetine (N:15) was superior to placebo (N:15) on all clinical measures except for sleep disorder. With fluoxetine, as compared to placebo, anxiety (Covi) improved significantly. With fluoxetine there was a significant weight loss; adverse effects were mild and transient. Given the severely disabling nature of depressive episodes in adolescents long-term treatment trials comparing antidepressants to psychosocial interventions are strongly recommended.

2920

FOLLOW-UP STUDY OF ADOLESCENT PSYCHOTICS
Okumura T., Okumura W., Shimizu M.
Dept. of Psychiatry, Nagoya City University
Medical School, Nagoya City, Japan

The prognosis of adolescent psychotics have not yet been elaborated sufficiently. Adolescent psychopathology shows usually instability and polymorphousness. In order to clarify this problem the follow-up observation of patients is one of the best research method.
In order to understand the prognosis and/or post morbid social functioning we surveyed the daily life state of adolescent psychotics after 5 years of their first psychiatric examination mailing a questionnaire. In 88 schizophrenics 38 (43,2%) were well adapted. In 55 cases of affective disorder 37 (67,3%) were well adapted.
From these findings we would assert the common opinion to be a mistaken prejudice that adolescent psychotics show worse prognostic course than adult cases.

2921

MEASUREMENT OF HALOPERIDOL PLASMA-LEVELS IN ADOLESCENT SCHIZOPHRENICS
K.Meszaros*, F.Resch+, G.Schönbeck*
A.Oppolzer+, W.Leixnering+, A.Bugnar*
*Department of Psychiatry, Vienna, Austria
+Department of Child and Adolescent Neuropsychiatry, Vienna, Austria

Plasma-level monitoring plays an important role in psychiatric care. Especially in the treatment with Haloperidol the hypothesis of a "therapeutic window" (12-27ng/ml) turned out to be useful in clinical practice. Our study was designed to investigate if the "therapeutic window" of Haloperidol is similar in adult and adolescent schizophrenics. We estimated Haloperidol plasma-levels in 15 schizophrenics using RIA. Patients were diagnosed according to DSM-III criteria. For clinical evaluation BPRS was used. The relationship of Haloperidol dosage and plasma-levels as well as side-effects and clinical efficacy was examined.
Results will be presented.

Session 446 Poster Presentation:
Pharmacopsychiatry: Antipsychotics

2922

ZUCLOPENTHIXOL ACETATE IN VISCOLEO - ITS USES IN CLINICAL PSYCHIATRY
Ramseier F   Macko M
Psychiatrische Klinik Königsfelden
5200 Königsfelden/Zwitzerland

Zuclopenthixol acetate in Viscoleo is a neuroleptic drug formulation with an onset of action after 2 - 3 hours and a duration of effect of 48 - 72 hours.
This unique profile makes it a usefull tool in clinical psychiatry with many advantages. It can be used in emergency situations as well as to adjust dosages in patients on a neuroleptic depot medication or to get a patient familiar with depot medication.
We will present our experiences with this new form of drug formulation and make suggestions for its use in clinical practise.

2923

BORNAPRINE: SERUM ANTICHOLINERGIC ACTIVITY AND ANTIPARKINSONIAN EFFECT
Ortega-Soto HA*,Chavez JL*,Cecena G**,Jasso A**
Hasfura C**
*Instituto Mexicano de Psiquiatria; **Hospital Psiquiatrico Fray Bernardino Alvarez, Mexico
Extrapyramidal symptoms(EPS)are a frequent complication of neuroleptic(NLP)treatment that difficults patient compliance.Although there are many strategies to cope with this, the prescription of antimuscarinic agents is the most used;however the therapeutic response is variable.Recently, it has been argued that serum antimuscarinic activity is a critical variable in this regard. Interested by the reported beneficial effects of bornaprine in Parkinson's Disease, we conducted a double blind trial of bornaprine vs biperiden for EPS control in NLP treated patients measuring serum antimuscarinic activity.Fourty patients were randomized to receive bornaprine or biperiden administered as identical tablets. The initial dose (2mg/bid)was increased every four days until 12mg/day.Clinical evaluation were performed with the Dimascio and the Simpson-Angus scales for EPS every four days, at the same time a blood sample was withdrawn. Serum antimuscarinic activity was quantified by a radioreceptor assay.There were no differences between groups in age,sex proportion, NLP dosages,nor in serum antimuscarinic activity levels; however, EPS amelioration was greater in the biperiden group. Our results indicate that bornaprine is not as effective as biperiden for EPS management in spite of its similar serum anticholinergic activity.

2924

BENPERIDOL; PHARMACOKINETICS IN RAT, DOG AND MAN
G. Schöllnhammer, H. Spechtmeyer, H.M. Parish
Troponwerke 500 Cologne 80 GFR

A RIA for Haloperidol (HAL-RIA, IRE-Diagnostics) was modified so that benperidol could be determined after clinically relevant dose levels with a lower detection limit of 0.3 µg/l. The assay was used to determine plasma levels of benperidole in rat, dog and man after different treatment schemes. Known metabolites of benperidol did not interfere with the assay.

Rats were treated with repeated doses of 0.5 - 5.0 mg/kg/d and plasma levels of benperidol measured in week 33, 53, 79 and 104. They were found to be dose dependent, no significant accumulation did occur.

Dogs were treated either orally or intravenously with 2.0 mg benperidol. Absolute oral bioavailability was calculated to be 64.5+/-7.9%, the half-lives of elimination were independent of the route of administration (oral 2.7+/-0.6 h, iv 2.5+/-0.6 h).
After oral administration of 2.0, 5.0 or 10.0 mg Cmax and AUC were found to be linearly correlated to dose, whereas tmax was independent of dose.

These data are compared to plasma levels found in volunteers after oral administration of a tablet containing 2.0 mg benperidole.

2925

PLASMA LEVELS AND CLINICAL RESPONSE OF BROMPERIDOL IN PSYCHIATRIC PATIENTS

Norifumi Kunimoto, Ikuya Ohta, Yoshiki Kadoya and Chikara Ogura, Dept. of Neuropsychiatry, School of Medicine, University of the Ryukyus. Okinawa, Japan.

Relationship of plasma bromperidol, a butyrophenone type of antipsychotics to clinical response was examined.

Subjects were 36 schizophrenics and 11 non-schizophrenic patients with paranoid symptoms (paranoid disorder, depression, alcoholism etc.). The therapeutic response and the side effects were evaluated using BPRS and the UKU Side Effect Rating Scale. The plasma concentrations of bromperidol were determined by our newly established column switching HPLC methods.

The mean dosage of bromperidol for the schizophrenics was 582.7 ± 342.9 µg/kg/day and for the non-schizophrenic patients was 171.2 ± 152.4 µg/kg/day. The mean plasma concentration of bromperidol was 15.7 ± 14.1 ng/ml and 10.2 ±14.9 ng/ml, respectively. The levels were significantly correlated with the daily dosage ($r=0.67$ and 0.94, $p<0.001$). Contrary, no correlation was founded with the therapeutic response or side effects.

The non-schizophrenic group indicated higher plasma levels when the levels of two groups were compared on an equal dosage (/kg/day) basis. In some of the non-schizophrenic patients, moderate to severe sedation and/or extrapyramidal side effects were observed despite of its low plasma concentrations.

Further analysis of the relationship of the plasma levels to clinical response will be accomplished.

2926

DIAZEPAM INCREASES HALOPERIDOL BLOOD LEVEL
K. Ohnishi, S. Kanba, T. Inada, H. Kohno, F. Kinoshita, H. Hara, E. Oguchi and G. Yagi, Dept. of Neuropsychiatry, Keio Univ. School of Med. Tokyo, Japan.

There are few reports on the influence of benzodiazepine derivatives on the blood concentration of antipsychotics. We report on the influence of diazepam on the blood level of haloperidol. Hospitalized schizophrenic patients taking haloperidol who suffered from anxiety or hyperactivity were given diazepam in doses of either 10 mg per day or 15mg per day for a time period exceeding two weeks. Blood specimens for the measurement of haloperidol were collected after breakfast but before medication administration, prior to the beginning of the administration of diazepam and after two weeks of diazepam treatment. Blood concentrations of haloperidol were determined by enzyme immunoassay. All subjects received a stable dosage of haloperidol for two weeks prior to the start of diazepam administration and thereafter throughout the two-week diazepam administration period.

In three of ten patients there was an average haloperidol increase of 42 percent. Of the remaining seven patients, five showed an tendency toward an increased haloperidol level, and two showed a tendency toward a decreased level.

The above results indicate that diazepam increases the blood level of haloperidol.

2927

RANDOMIZED PLACEBO-CONTROLLED DOUBLE-BLIND 5-PERIOD CROSSOVER STUDY ON ANALGESIC PROPERTIES OF THREE ACUTE ORAL DOSES OF CM 40907 AND ASA - EMPLOYING CO_2-LASER FOR NOCISTIMULATION

K. Schaffler[1], M. Giehrend[2]

[1] Institute for Pharmacodynamic Research, Kronstadterstr. 9, D-8000 Munich 80, FRG
[2] Midy-Sanofi Recherche, D-8000 Munich 2, FRG

A randomized, double-blind crossover study was run with three acute oral dosages (600, 900 and 1200 mg) of CM 40907 - a newly developed anticonvulsant drug, which chemically is a 6-(2'chlorophenyl)-3-(4'hydroxypiperidino)-pyridazine - vs ASA (1000 mg) and placebo in 12 male healthy volunteers to compare analgesic potencies.
CO_2-laser radiant heat emission, which - with high selectivity - stimulates nociceptive A-delta and C-fibers, was employed for nocistimulation. Objective algesimetry was done by means of CO_2-laser somatosensory evoked potentials (LSEP). Effects on vigilance were screened by auditory evoked potentials (AEP). There was a simultaneous control of vigilance alterations with regard to both types of evoked potentials by means of an adaptive pursuit tracking task (APTT). Subjective pain intensities were measured by post-LSEP pain ratings. Subjective sedation, excitation and anxiety were screened by visual analog scales. Blood pressure, heart rate (supine and upright) and tolerance ratings were recorded in addition.
All dosages of CM 40907 showed an analgesic effect in the laser model, with significant reductions of P2-LSEP-amplitudes. With regard to this component the effect of 1200 mg CM 40907 was more marked than that of ASA, which was also effective in the N1-component. Like ASA, CM 40907 reduced pain as measured by subjective ratings. Subjective sedation was decreased, however AEP-findings cued a decrease of vigilance after CM 40907. Excitation and anxiety were not significantly altered after CM 40907. Blood pressure and heart rate were not significantly raised after CM 40907, which was in general well tolerated.
The onset of action was somewhat slower after CM 40907, when compared with ASA. There were cues that CM 40907 (1200 mg) is active till hour 6 after dosing with a peak effect within hour 1 and 2. With regard to the majority of measures CM 40907 showed a linear dose-efficacy.

2928

PHARMACOKINETICS OF ZUCLOPENTHIXOL AFTER
GIVING ZUCLOPENTHIXOL ACETATE
G.S.I.M. Jansen (1) and N.N.A. Dodde (2)
(1) P.C.'Bloemendaal',Dept. Clin. Pharm.,
    POB 53002, NL-2505 AA The Hague.
(2) Lundbeck b.v., Medical Department,
    POB 12021, NL-1100 AA, Amsterdam

Zuclopenthixol acetate in Viscoleo^R,i.m.
(ZA) was given to 4 newly admitted male
psychiatric patients with an exacerbation of chronic schizophrenia.
3 patients received a single 100 mg dose
of ZA and 1 patient received a second
100 mg dose of ZA 3 days after the first
dose. Plasma levels were measured daily
during a period of 7 days after the sing
le dose; in the 4th patient plasma level
data were obtained daily until 9 days
after the 1st dose. The pharmacokinetic
profile of the 3 patients showed limited
interindividual differences ; the plasma
elimination half-life of Z after a single
100 mg dose of ZA appeared to be 32 hrs.
The pharmacokinetic profile of the 4th
patient indicated that accumulation of Z
is unlikely when giving 2 consecutive
100 mg injections of ZA at 3 day inter-
vals.The reasons why only a few patients
could be included in this study are discussed. It is concluded that ZA is very
suitable for the initial neuroleptic
treatment in an acute psychotic phase.

2929

ANTIPSYCHOTIC EFFICACY; SIDE EFFECTS AND DOSAGE
OF ZUCLOPENTHIXOL DECANOATE
Sieberns, S., Budde, G.,
Troponwerke GmbH & Co. KG, 5000 Köln 80, FRG

The neuroleptic drug zuclopenthixol has for some
years been available as a solution of a decanoic
ester of zuclopenthixol in oil mainly for maintenance treatment of schizophrenia. The zuclopenthixol decanoate as a very lipophilic substance
is slowly released from the oil depot. Maximum
concentration is obtained after about one week.
The clinical effect is maintained for 2-4 weeks.

837 patients of both sexes, with an age ranging
from 17 to 81 years (mean age 42±13), diagnosed
as schizophrenics according to ICD 9. Revision,
were admitted to an open multi-centre trial of
zuclopenthixol decanoate undertaken in several
psychiatric hospitals. The trial lasted at least
3 months and the administered dose ranged from
100 to 600 mg i.m. each 2-4 weeks. The evaluation
of the efficacy and of extrapyramidal side effects have been made by using the BPRS and EPSE
respectively. Zuclopenthixol decanoate proved
effective in all cases, particularly on items
such as delusion, hallucinations, hostility, all
of which improved considerably. Side effects,
especially extrapyramidal (tremor, akathisia,
rigidity), approved in about 30 % of the patients
but not in a higher percentage compared to conventional zuclopenthixol treatment.

2930

EFFECT OF ZUCLOPENTHIXOL (D-1/D-2 ANTAGONIST) AND
HALOPERIDOL (D-2 ANTAGONIST) IN TARDIVE DYSKINESIA.
H. Lublin, J. Gerlach, U. Hagert*, B. Meidahl,
C. Rendtorff, S. Tolvanen*.
Sct. Hans Hospital, Dept. P, Roskilde, Denmark.
*Nickby Sjukhus, Nickby, Finland.

An increased ratio between D-1 and D-2 dopamine
receptor activity and a dopamine supersensitivity
appear to be involved in the pathophysiology of tardive dyskinesia (TD). A combined D-1/D-2 antagonist
has been shown to reduce development of dopamine supersensitivity induced by the D-2 antagonist in animals. In order to study the effect of zuclopenthixol
(ZU)(D-1/D-2 antagonist) and haloperidol (HA)(D-2
antagonist) in TD, 19 TD patients were included in
a randomized cross-over trial. TD and parkinsonism
were blindly evaluated using video recordings.
  TD was reduced significantly in both treatment
groups. No differences in TD were found between the
baseline score in the first and second treatment period, between the treatment periods and between the
degree of suppression induced by ZU and HA. The degree of reduction in TD was correlated to the increase of parkinsonism, suggesting that TD suppression
is secondary to parkinsonism. No cross-over effect
was found from first to second treatment period. TD
was aggravated after all treatment periods, and no
difference was found between ZU and HA. The aggravation of TD was more pronounced after the second
treatment period, which might indicate the unfavorable effect of drug holidays.

Session 447 Poster Presentation:
Various topics in psychiatry

2931

PSYCHIATRIC DISABILITY IN A CANADIAN HOUSEHOLD
SAMPLE
Goering, P., PhD, W. Lancee, MSc & J. Cochrane, BA
Clarke Institute of Psychiatry, Toronto, Canada.

Although psychiatric epidemiology has made much
progress, few studies have examined disability in
the general population. Most of our knowledge
about psychiatric disability is based upon studies
of treated populations, but only 20% of persons
with such disorders are in treatment. In conjunction with Statistics Canada, we conducted a
telephone survey of a probability sample of 4,990
Ontario and Quebec adult household members. A
Health and Activity Limitation Survey instrument
was modified to include a psychiatric disability
screen based on the Psychic Distress Inventory
and questions assessing episode history and
limitations in functioning. The estimated
psychiatric disability rate is 3.2%. Disability
rates and symptoms differ with age and sex groups,
ranging from 2.4% for male subjects under 65 to
4.1% for male subjects 65 or over. We find a high
concordance of physical and psychiatric disability
with 2.3% of the population reporting limitations
due to chronic physical and psychiatric problems.
Our psychiatric disability rate is higher than
that estimated by health and disability surveys
focused primarily on physical illness and limitations. Recognition of the extent and nature of
psychiatric disability is essential for assessing
service needs.

2932

THE PSYCHIATRIC DISORDERS IN FINNISH PRISONERS

M. Joukamaa, Mental Hospital for Prisoners,
BOX 357, SF-20101, Turku, Finland

There is some evidence in the literature that mental disturbances are more common among prisoners than in other people. The prevalence of psychiatric disorders among prisoners, however, varies considerably according to different studies. The purpose of the present study was to determine the prevalence of psychiatric disorders in Finnish prisoners.

The study forms part of the Health Survey of Finnish Prisoners, which is an extensive epidemiological project. The material consists of about 1000 prisoners representative the whole population of Finnish prisoners. Various sources of information were used in assessing the mental status of the prisoners: health questionnaires, interviews and a clinical health examination (by the prison physicians). Data from official medical records were also gathered.

The most striking finding was the great amount of alcoholism (44% of the sample). Similarly the prevalence of personality disorders (18%) was very high compared to the general population. In the prevalence of neuroses (7%) and psychoses (4%) there were no major differences between the prisoners and population at large. The associations between psychiatric disorders and socio-demographic factors are discussed in the paper.

2933

MENTAL ILLNESS AMONGST TWO CRIMINAL POPULATIONS

A Douzenis M Maratos D Milona Prof A Jenner
Sheffield University Medical School
Psychiatry Department

A survey of the prevalence of mental disorder in the British Probation Service and a Greek prison has been made. The results show that 40.7% of the British and 81.5% of the Greek population examined, score as patients on the General Health Questionnaire (GHQ). Additional questions were asked, aiming to find factors that distinguish the individuals suffering from mental illness and those who do not. Furthermore, questions tried to tackle factors usually related with criminality (low social class, poor education, alcoholism, drug abuse). The results show an overlap of psychiatric patients and of those involved in crime. On both samples, the prevalence of mental illness (high GHQ score) was statistically highly significantly above the general population. On the whole, the Greek sample appeared to be much more disturbed than the English one. Although the two populations examined (British/Greek) are different in so many parameters that no direct comparison is valid, some interesting observations can be made regarding the similarities of the mentally ill criminal's perceptions of the world and society. On both samples, mental illness was associated with deprived childhood, inability to cope in the everyday life, feelings that one is maltreated by society and feelings that one is controlled.

2934

A POSSIBILITY TO KEEP THE INDIVIDUAL EXPERIENCE OF THE PSYCHIATRIST
Mihov V., Dimitrov Iv., Ruskov R., Trifeneva E.
Bulgaria

A possibility on the base of the English School is proposed from the authors.
During his practical action, the psychiatrist accumulates individual experience, which is unique, because of its complexity and specificity of the diseases. The conservation of this experience may be done through several methods.
- By verbal description-speaking with students and colleagues.
- By publication of reports, monographies and dissertations.
- By using audiovisual methods to record rare or interesting cases seeking other points of view.
At present, investigations dealing with the possibilities of using computers for accumulating the individual experiences of the psychiatrist are still insufficient. The authors propose an original method for creation of expert systems through magnetic records for registration of the individual professional experience which may be used for didactical and scientific purposes.

2935

THE DETERMINATION OF PSYCHIATRIC DISTURBANCES WITH SOCIAL FACTORS

Ass. Prof. Marko Munjiza, M.D. Ph.D., Institute for Mental Health.
Belgrade, Palmotićeva 37, Yugoslavia

The etiological base of many psychiatric disturbances is as a rule caused by multiple factors. Above all this has to do with the various depressive states, reactive psychotic disturbances, attempting and committing suicide, disturbed personalities and neurotic behavior. This paper tests the hypothesis of specifying these disturbances with a number of social factors. With the method of multiple factor analysis, and above all factoral analysis and multiple regression, a number of social factors have been analysed from urban, social—cultural, social—economic and social pathological spheres in regards with the mentioned psychiatric disturbances and states in the Belgrade area between 1971 and 1986.

From the preliminary analysis which showed that a very significant correlation exists between the mentioned groups of social factors and psychiatric disturbances. A group of the 12 most relevant factors has been selected for the testing of the coefficient of multiple determination. The results obtained confirm completely the working hypothesis of a very significant mutual conditioning of a large number of psychiatric disturbances either by social or ecological factors. The determination of the coefficient ranges between 60% and 80%, depending on the very sort of disturbance; however they are all statistically highly significant. The most explicit determination of the enviroment factors are encountered with the affective disturbances, suicides and reactive states — and have characteristics of the conditional — circumstancial relationship.

The results obtained by this paper are of a practical significance for preventive orientated psychiatry. Since many social factors can be quantified and they can be influenced by various social actions, thus indirectly can lessen the appearing and spreading of the examined psychiatric disturbances.

2936
Psychiatry under pressure of society

Stelian Balanescu
Bezirkskrankenhaus Mainkofen
West-Germany

On account of its rather ambiguous place among the biological sciences and due in a great measure to the ideological impact of every society, psychiatry is like no other medical science exposed to the danger to see its teritory of validity transgressed by various social requierements which cannot be fulfilled otherwise. The major expression of this phenomenon is of course the abusive use of psychiatry for political purposes but there are also other various social claims which affect its autonomy. The impression is, the more developed a society is, the more psychiatry is exposed to such a danger, with the final consequence that it is no more possible to say where psychiatry begins and where it ends. Psychiatry is - and it cannot be otherwise - only a collection of descriptions of psychic diseases or disorders, it is no doctrine and no "Weltanschauung". Each effort to alter this status ends in the transfer to psychiatry of tasks which are alien to its nature. These difficulties are of course dependent on the inherent ambiguity of psychiatry, which has to satisfy genuine medical requierements but also such that are only far related to them. Nevertheless, some actual trends in psychiatry speak for an increasing impact of the social and ideological exigencies.

2937
Monitoring compulsory psychiatric care in Sweden

Olle Östman,

The often very narrow debating about psychiatry compulsory care is commented on from ethical points of view. The patient's experienced violations must be compared to the psychiatric picture of illness of the committed patient. The reported part studies give basis to defined questions for further studies

Numbers of conceivable measures of action character are shown. The measures are prepared to achieve (produce) improvements in the fields where the study has made clear that for the time being the psychiatry has defects. A re-study in a few years is planned for the result of all these measures to be evaluated.

2938
FEMALE HOMOSEXUALITY AND VIOLENT BEHAVIOUR IN CLOSED INSTITUTIONS.
NIVOLI GC-LORETTU L-SANNA MN-PITTALIS A
NAITANA ML
CLINICA PSICHIATRICA UNIVERSITA'SASSARI
ITALY.

192 cases have been examined of violent behaviour against the person and things in a female prison, which were linked to homosexual dynamics among detainees. The authors outline a typology of the homosexual relatioships between detainees which have led with increasing frequency to violent behaviour:1)the"stallioness"(detainee of virile behaviour who imposes sexual relationships)2)the stable"man-woman"role(with feelings of jealousy,exclusivity,possessiveness,etc 3)couples with"interchangeable roles" (neither partner has a fixed active or passive role)4)"occasional"couples(short-lived relationships)5)female prostitution(no bond of affection). The authors underline the frequence of homosexual relationshipsbetween detainees in prison and emphasize the psychotherapy which can lead to a reduction in the violent behaviour on the self,on others or on things which can happen the limits of specifichomosexual psychopathology.

2939
Psychiatry, Technology and Psychobiologic problem.

Nikita A. Zorin, MD.
Eye Microsurgery Research, Technology Complex.
Moscow USSR.

Intrusion of technology upon medicine in the form of standardization, unification, health care on a mass scale etc. is at the first sight not compatible with the Aristotelian tradition of clinicism: with Understanding. Hence two cultural myths arise: incompatibility of technology and art (psychiatry) and inevitable dehumanization of medicine. The way out: changing from standardization of form (phenomenologic nozology etc.) to unification of essence (genetics, studying of the sences). Technology clears way to "computer germeneutics", enables to analyse the content of an individual's psyche. That is the way to perceive the fundamental issue of all the sciences pertaining to man: reciprocity of ideal and material, of soul and body. Beyond this it is impossible to understand how genetic preconditions for psychopathology originate in a social environment. Intersection of ideal sences and material neuromorphology seems to be conditioned by spatio-temporal organization of brain activity, the pronounced functional human brain assymetry being connected with beginning of speech and thinking.

2940
THE INCIDENCE OF EXHIBITIONISM IN SARDINIA: A COMPARATIVE STUDY
PITTALIS A-CORGIOLU T-LORETTU L-SANNA MN-NIVOLI GC

CLINICA PSICHIATRICA UNIVERSITA'SASSARI ITALY.

The study sample consisted of 106 young women (similar to analogous patterns examined in Guatemala and the USA) who were subjected to structured psychiatric examination, with the aim of discovering whether they had been victims of 'indecent exposure', their perception and possible psychological and psychiatric consequences. On the basis of statistical data this study confirm that no significant differences emerged from analogous studies in Guatemala and the USA, thus emphasizing the hypothesis that the psychopathology of the exhibitionist is of prior importance, in this study, rather than the cultural environment in which this occurs. The authors show the criminological characteristics concerning the act of exhibitionism, the immediate and more long-term emotional reactions of the victim and the psychical victimological consequences of exposure to acts of exhibitionism with particular regard to the characteristics of the victim.

2941
PROCESS THEORY: A NEW INTEGRATIVE METHOD
H.Sabelli, M.D., Ph.D. and L. Carlson-Sabelli, M.S.
Rush University, Chicago, U.S.A.

Process Theory is a comprehensive theory of physical and psychological processes that can serve to integrate biological, social and psychodynamic psychiatry. Freud developed Psychodynamics by assuming that psychological processes obey the same universal laws of energy as mechanical and biological systems. He thus adopted the mechanistic Dynamics and Thermodynamics of his time as a model for Psychodynamics. Following this strategy, we have reformulated Psychodynamics in terms of the mathematical Dynamics and Thermodynamics of our time (Prigogine and Stengers, Order out of Chaos, 1984). Process Theory provides three novel and clinically applicable concepts: 1. Biological priority, psychological supremacy (as contrasted to theories of biological or psychological primacy); 2. Union of opposites, such as harmony and conflict (as contrasted to psychoanalytic and dialectic conflicts and to systems homeostasis); and 3. Creative bifurcations (as contrasted to determinism and developmental theories). Congruent with Chaos Theory, Process Theory proposes that personal development and evolution are creative processes, open to chance, choice and to meaningful coincidences, and governed by harmonious and conflictual interactions between opposites (Sabelli, Union of Opposites. A Comprehensive Theory of Natural and Human Processes, 1989). Within this framework, depression is seen as a defense against conflict. The clinical method will be illustrated through the discussion of a case of depression presented by Perry et al (Amer. J. Psychiatry, 144: 543-50, 1987). (Supported by McCormick Foundation).

2942
PEDAGOGIC AND DEFECTOLOGIC DEONTOLOGY

Moutafov Stefan
Sofioter University "Climent Ochridski", Sofia, Bulgaria

Despite the differences between the profession of a physician and of a pedagogue, the specificity in the theory and practice of each of their activities as well, there are many common features in a row of aspects. For example in defectology - the attitude to abnormal children has close connections with euthanasia, eugenics and other similar principles.

Here, keeping the secret is a requirement first of all in the pedagogic record (marks and conduct) of all children, as well as concerning personal and family secrets which pedagogues come to know.

Basis of the general-pedagogic and defectologic deontology is found mainly by the principles in the specific character of the behavior of pedagogues among them and towards the children and their parents, too. This "school deontology" aims at the forming of a versatile and harmoniously developed personality and at preventing from illnesses and victimizing of children, parents and pedagogues.

2943
THE HISTORY OF THE ECLIPSE

ANGLESIO A., LENOCI F.

U.S.S.L.24 COLLEGNO OSPEDALE PSICHIATRICO

Some consideration and data about the shutting down of Turin's Psychiatric Hospital and about psychiatry before the shutting will be exposed.
Turin's Psychiatric Hospitals have had more than four thousands of patients. At the age of the law which stated the shutting down of all italian mental homes about two thousands of people were still admitted in departments for chronics.
Today they are 283 and some of them are going to be discharged.
The authors have studied the phenomenon and the destination of patients discharged from 1978.
The authors will also expose some data from a research about patients admitted in the past years showing that the days of admittance were decreasing from 1950 to 1978.

2944

VIOLENCE AND DEATH ON A MENTAL HANDICAP WARD

DR A K SHAH
ST MARY'S HOSPITAL, LONDON

"Violent behaviour is not uncommon in patients in psychiatric wards. Although there are many studies of behaviour disturbance in mental handicap hospital populations, only few studies have looked purely at violence in such populations.

The level of violence and associated intrinsic (eg. characteristics of patients) or extrinsic (eg. environmental) factors were studied in a high dependency ward in a large mental handicap hospital.

The level of violence was alarmingly high with * 620 violent incidents in 21 months (30 per month) Two patients had a sudden unexpected death in their twenties, during the study period, from unusual causes. Relationship between violence and death is discussed.

An association between violence and younger age group, family history mental illness and abnormal EEGs is discussed. In view of high levels of violence and possible death, the therapeutic implications of an abnormal EEG are discussed".

* Four patients accounted for 74% of the violence.

2945

The Detection of Psychiatric Disorder in General Practice
Dr A P Boardman Dr T K J Craig
Guy's Hospital Medical School, London SE1, England

185 patients presenting to 19 general practitioners in southeast London were interviewed using the Present State Examination and their psychiatric case status was compared to the doctors ratings of the patients degree of emotional disturbance. Video taped recordings of the consultation were made at the same time as the GPs ratings. Analysis of the video tapes revealed that the detection of psychiatric disorder by the GPs was related to the patients mode of presentation, the strength of signals indicative of emotional distress emitted by the patient and the GPs interview behaviour.

2946

VAN GOGH OPERATION

C. LACOMBE-MESTAS, Médecin-Directeur "Le Castel" HYERES (Var)

For the centennial anniversary of the death of the famous artist we decided to pay him an homage by starting in all the E.E.C. countries the "Van Gogh Operation" in order to undeceive psychological and psychiatric disorders.
You will find bellow the message we wrote "on behalf of Van Gogh" and which would support this vast operation.
"My Friends, I, Vincent, the damned painter, the inefficient, the banished, I would like to give you this message.
My life has been a long continuation of pains : I felt cold, hungry and particularly I have known the most horrible thing : the loneliness of the heart. I was mentally ill and this seams very amusing to people who do not understand that tomorrow they can be attacked by this disease. They pelted me with stones, they made fun of me, they called me red fool. And I, I put in my paintings all my passion, my sensuality and my despair...
My success post mortem is a lightning revenge. I am not in the cemetery of Auvers-sur-Oise but in my flaming sunflowers, in my twisted by love cypress trees, in my magic stars...
I now have a heart full of sun, of this sun so yellow -which was my favourite colour- and which flaunts the whole world.
Be courageous my Friends. Very soon, you will no longer be excluded and you will find again in Society the place which is due to you. Vincent".

2947

STRUCTURE OF MORTALITY OF THE HOSPITALIZED PATIENTS IN 10 YEARS
F.Privorozky, E.Philosof, L.Kohen
Mental Hospital Tirat Hacarmel, Haifa, Israel

Analysis is made in a psychiatric hospital for 300 beds from the beginning of its functioning in 1978. Discussed are different cases of death - natural and suicide - during two periods of the hospital's function.
1. The 1st period 1978-82 which is named by us as a conservative period.
2. The 2nd one from 1982 up to date when progressive tactics were used to solve the problem of hospitalised patients.
This period is linked with deinstitualisation of the patients, with opening of departments organising I.P.C.U. opening a department of rehabilitation and readaptation, organising a hostel for chronic patients.
While opening the departments we expected increase of mortality connected with suicide. But on the contrary the data is different, if in the 1st period the number of deaths was 9,8 per 1000. Patients in the 2nd decreased to 6,3 per 1000 was suicide decreased twice.
There were no cases of death linked with pharmacological treatment in the 2nd period mortality.
53,8% among the mortality suffered from schizophrenia. 27,7% suffered from organic psychosis. Most of them died in July-September. In the suicide groups death took place from April to June.

2948

EVOLUTION DES REFERENTIELS SPATIO-
TEMPORELS EN PSYCHIATRIE
MARCHAIS Pierre. Hôpital Foch, 40 rue
Worth, 92151- SURESNES. FRANCE.

Les référentiels spatio-temporels orientent la connaissance de l'observateur.
En psychiatrie classique, le trouble mental a été surtout conçu dans un espace plan.
Les études psychopathologiques, psychanalytiques, phénoménologiques et existentielles ont introduit la tridimensionalité en retenant les dynamiques inconscientes, éducatives et sociales.
Le recours aux critères diagnostiques (DSM III et suivants) s'inscrit davantage dans une perspective néo-classique.
En fait, le trouble mental se développe dans un espace pluridimensionnel. Il nécessite, par suite, une refonte nosographique.

2949

THE COMMON EVERYDAY TRANCE:

Peter Brown, MD, FRCP(C) - Mount Sinai Hospital 600 University Avenue, Toronto, Canada, M5G 1X5

As a consequence of his observations of the clinical work of Milton Erickson, Ernest Rossi has proposed an "ultradian rhythm theory of hypnosis." Rossi suggests that the changes in cognition, affect and behaviour which occur as a part of the ultradian cycle ("the common everyday trance") are similar to the changes which occur during hypnosis. The common mechanism underlying both of these processes is reputed to be a change in hemispheric dominance with a relative increase in right hemispheric activity. This presentation will review the manifestations of spontaneous trance behaviour in the clinical setting. In addition, we will briefly review studies of hemispheric function that suggest that ultradian changes do parallel the changes found in hypnosis. It is suggested that cerebral function in hypnosis is a result both of intrinsic temporal rhythms and of extrinsic contextual demands. Recognition of these features of trance behaviour may have significant theoretic implications as well as useful clinical applications.

Session 448 Poster Presentation:
Pharmacotherapy of depression IV

2950

DO DIFFERENT SUBTYPES OF DEPRESSION PREDICT
DIFFERENT LONG-TERM OUTCOMES?
Conor Duggan, A.S. Lee, R.M.Murray
Institute of Psychiatry, London

A consecutive series of 89 patients admitted to the Maudsley Hospital with depressive illness in 1965/66 were interviewed and given various personality questionnaires; 18 years later they were followed-up and re-interviewed. Then, on the basis of index data alone and blind to their eventual outcome, they were subtyped according to the RDC, DSM III, Newcastle Index and PSE/Catego criteria. Patients who met the various subtype criteria at index were compared with those who did not in respect of long-term outcome and the treatment subsequently received. Patients in most of the subtypes did not differ in outcome. However, endogenous subtypes, especially DSM-III Melancholia all predicted poor outcome suggesting that subtyping using endogenous features as criteria has prognostic utility. High scores for Neuroticism (N) on the Eysenck Personality Inventory administered at index also predicted poor overall out-come and increased chronicity. Futhermore, an interactive effect was found between neuroticism (N) and melancholia such that melancholic individuals, who at index had high N score, were likely to have a poor outcome. Over the subsequent 18 years, individuals who were classified as psychotic at index were more likely to have been given major tranquilisers whereas those with an endogenous type depression were more likely to have had ECT.

2951

Antidepressant therapy and aggressive behaviour in Major Depression
I. Maremmani, C. Valentini°, J.A. Deltito°°, P. Castrogiovanni
Institute of Psychiatry, Pisa University, Italy
°Mental Health Services, USL 19, Regione Liguria, Italy
°°Depression and Anxiety Clinic, New York Hospital, Cornell University, Westchester Division, White Plains, New York, N.Y., U.S.A.

Among psychiatric drugs, antidepressants represent the least studied category with regard to their possible influence on animal and human aggressive behavior.
Nevertheless they arouse the greatest scientific curiosity not only for their unusual results in animals, but also for their possible clinical applications in man.
The patients, admitted to the Psychiatric Clinic, Pisa University, were evaluated by means of Q.T.A. (Questionario per la Tipizzazione del Comportamento Aggressivo, Italian version of an Inventory for Assessing Different Kinds of Hostility), when they entered and when they were discharged.
The results show that tricyclic antidepressant therapy seems to influence variations of aggressive behaviour during a depressive episode. Tricyclic drugs, while they increase the mood tone towards euthymic values, seem to mitigate aggressive behaviour while allowing its expression at the same time. On the contrary, if aggressive valencies are inhibited, they are strengthened but at the expense of greater inhibition.

2952

COMBINED PHARMACOLOGICAL AND PSYCHOTHERAPIC TREATMENT OF DEPRESSIONS
Daudt, Valter
Clinica de Psiquiatria, Psicobiologia e Psicoterapia.

The A. describes a method for the treatment of patients with affective disorders, specially depressive patients with conditions previously resistant to other forms of treatment. using pharmacological agents and psychoterapic procedures in combination. A careful evaluation of each patient is necessary, organic as well as psychological. The participation of family members is an important adjunct of therapy. A careful trial and choice of antidepressants and other pharmacs, with a delicate titration of dosages, is essential in order to find the drugs that may be efficient to each particular patient without provoking intolerable side-effects. The psychotherapic techniques employed are of the short-term kind whenever possible, trying to put in evidence and modify, if possible, the patterns of personality functioning that may augment the suscetibility to the illness or its severity. In some cases, other biological procedures, such as eletroconvulsive therapy may be indicated.

2953

DOUBLE-BLIND, PLACEBO CONTROLLED TRIAL OF FIPEXIDE IN MAJOR DEPRESSIVE DISORDERS
M. TESSERA, J.M. BOUCHARD, G. CLERC, M. GUIBERT, R. PAGOT, G.C. HOUILLON, M. MOCLET
JOUVEINAL LABORATOIRES

Recent works on fipexide, a molecule with cognitive enhancing activity, have demonstrated antidepressant properties: efficacy in learnhelplessness and in bulbectomized rats and a down regulating effect on 5 HT2 receptors in cortex (Gouret and al 1989).
On the basis of these new findings and on the positive results in previous open trials in depression we performed a four-centers trial of a fixed dose of fipexide (600 mg/day) versus placebo in 62 outpatients with DSM-III criteria of Major Depressive Disorders (MDD) in order to confirm the antidepressant activity of fipexide.
42 women and 20 men were included. Age range was from 20,5 to 82 years (mean = 49,8 ± 2,0). After a single-blind placebo washout period of 1 week, patients were randomly assigned to treatment with fipexide or placebo for 6 weeks.
Results demonstrated a significantly greater reduction from baseline in the median Montgomery-Asberg Depression Rating Scale (MADRS) scores compared to placebo (p= 0,02). The percentage of patients with > 50 % reduction from the baseline MADRS score was significantly greater in fipexide group (55 %) compared to placebo (23 %) in an endpoint analysis (p < 0,01). In addition, patient self rating scales showed a statistically significant improvement. Overall, 29 % of fipexide and 16 % of placebo patients had clinical adverse events (p = ns).
In conclusion, fipexide appears to demonstrate efficacy as an antidepressant agent in MDD. Together with its cognitive enhancing properties and its favorable safety profile, fipexide may represent a new effective treatment of depression.

2954

METABOLITES CONTRIBUTE TO THE ANTIDEPRESSANT EFFECT OF SIBUTRAMINE HCL

W.R. Buckett, G.P. Luscombe. Research Department, The Boots Company PLC, Nottingham NG2 3AA. United Kingdom.

Sibutramine hydrochloride is a novel antidepressant and a striking feature of its action in vivo is the rapid (3 days) and potent (1 mg/kg) down-regulation of β-adrenoceptors in the rat. Since the action of conventional antidepressants is mediated in part by demethylated metabolites, it was of interest to determine the potential contribution of the secondary (BTS 54 354) and primary (BTS 54 505) amine metabolites to the effects of sibutramine HCl. In mice tetrabenazine-induced ptosis and reserpine-induced hypothermia were potently antagonised by sibutramine HCl and both metabolites. Similar activity was demonstrated in the Porsolt (learned helplessness) test in mice. Whilst in vitro BTS 54 354 and BTS 54 505 were 20 times more active than the parent compound in inhibiting [^{14}C]noradrenaline uptake and up to 100 times more active on [^{14}C]serotonin uptake, in vivo sibutramine HCl and its metabolites were similarly effective. Rapid β-adrenoceptor down-regulation was found with all compounds. Thus the pharmacological profiles of the metabolites closely resemble that of sibutramine HCl in vivo and suggest that both BTS 54 354 and BTS 54 505 would contribute to the overall pharmacological effect.

2955

PRIMARY TREATMENT AND THERAPEUTIC RESPONSE IN DEPRESSED PATIENTS

L. Montejo-Iglesias. C. Ponce de León-Hernandez, P. del Valle-Lopez.
Psychiatry Service. Hospital Clinico S. Carlos. Madrid, Spain

A sample of 95 outpatients diagnosed of non-psychotic primary major affective disorder (RDC criteria) were studied. All of them had been previously treated at a primary level. After, they received heterocyclic antidepressants at 150 mg/day for four weeks and were grouped, according to their evolution, in responders and non-responders.
We compared the therapeutic response and the treatment received before the patient was included in the present study.
According to our results, the non-responders had received more antidepressant drugs, but in non-therapeutic doses ($\bar{x}$ + 49 mg/day); the cases in which no antidepressant drugs had been given prevailed in the responders.
The evolutive implications derived from the incorrect prescription of antidepressants are discussed.

2956

A COST/BENEFIT ANALYSIS IN DRUG THERAPY OF DEPRESSION
M. CZARKA*, R. CROTT**
* Medical Director Eli Lilly Benelux
** Research fellow IRES Catholic University of Louvain Belgium

The percentage of GNP spent on health care is still increasing and governments want to make sure to use the most cost effective treatments among selected health care programs.
In the treatment of depression, we have evaluated, in Belgium, the cost/benefit ratio for Fluoxetine to a mix of tricyclic antidepressants (TCA).
This study compared the drugs for one year, on a hypothetical cohort of patients, using the decision tree methodology to model and identify costs and benefits.
One can show a positive benefit to cost ratio of 1.44 based on actual prices in Belgium for the newer antidepressant when taking into account associated hospital and treatment costs.
This is mainly due, at equal efficacy level, to a better tolerance profile as well as a lower acute toxicity in overdose for Fluoxetine.
We will present calculation methods and results.

Session 449 Poster Presentation: Eating disorders

2957

FEEDING ANOREXICS - AN UP-HILL STRUGGLE

Dr. M. A. Launer
Burnley General Hospital

Before 1980 it was not permissible to prescribe food supplements for Anorexia Nervosa in the U.K. Following a change in the regulations more foods have been developed. The struggle continues intrying to find a food that is palatable and acceptable to sufferers from a disease that has food phobia as one of its core symptoms.

Prescribing food can be seen as the first step towards persuading an anorexic to normalise her diet similar to introducing a baby, via some solids, to normal food.

2958

ANOREXIA NERVOSA:CRITERIA FOR SEVERITY, HOSPITALISATION AND DISCHARGE.
A.Chinchilla;P.Sanchez;M Camarero M.Vega;L.Jorda. Ramon and Cajal Hospital.Psychiatric Service.MADRID.

Approximately 10% of Anorexia Nervosa Cases left to themselves would die as a consequence of disturbances in the cardiovascular system and in water and electrolyte metabolism due to starvation.
It is important to know the high risk biological indicators;percentage of weight loss.,blood pressure,vital signs,EEG and ions above all potassium;nutritional index,anthropometrical parameters (percentage of patients weight over ideal weight),bicipital fold,circumference of the arm,circumference of arm muscle,creatinine/height index,transferrin,prealbumin,retinol binding protein,vitamins A and E,lymphocyte count,etc Hospitalisation criteria: severity of the disorder with danger to life,difficulties in outpatient management,poor or inadequate external support,deterioration of relationships etc.Discharge criteria: weight increase-a minimum of 30% of weight lost-,normalisation of vital signs,improvement of the disturbance of body image and perception better insight and consciousness of illness,etc.
All these parameters are studied in a group of 20 A.N, inpatients.

2959

Tailoring Treatment For Chronic Anorectic Patients.
Gerlinghoff, M., Mai, N., Backmund, H.
Max-Planck-Institut für Psychiatrie
Kraepelinstraße 10
8000 München 40   FRG

Based on the experience with treatment of 120 anorectic patients we propose a multistage, multimodal approach for chronic patients. In- and outpatient treatment phases are combined and can be tailored to the individual needs of a patient. Despite programme flexibility, continuity of the therapeutic team is provided for total treatment duration. In addition to specific groups patients and family members from different stages meet in mixed groups. Experienced patients assist new patients. Improvement of motivation for therapy with the help of a mixed outpatient group seems essential for reduction of length of hospital stay.

2960

PERSONALITY TRAITS OF 75 SEVERELY OBESE PERSONS

Marja Koski, M.D.
Hesperia Hospital Helsinki, Finland

In Southern-Finland are living 112 persons that had get pension for their severe obesity. There are 22 male and 53 female in this study group. All persons were 30% over finnish idealweight. In Finland persons aged 16-64, who due to illness, disability or injury are unable to carry out his usual work or work similar to that considered on the basis of age, skills and others factors to yield a suitable and reasonable income are entitled to disability pension.
On 31 December 1979, 834, 198 persons received national pension. Most pensions are granted due to mental problems and cardiovascular diseases. At the end of 1979 according to the pensions register of the National Pensions Institution there were 1047 persons in receipt of disability pensions on primary grounds of obesity. Of these 218 were men and 829 were women. If those for whom obesity is given as the first additional disease are included then the number rises to 2674. In a further 1696 cases obesity is given as the second additional disease.
The aim of this study is to discover common characteristics of those, who receive disability pensions because of severe obesity. At same time an attempt will be made to determine the personality traits and other possible factors which are typical for severely obese persons.

2961

BULIMIA NERVOSA AND PERSONALITY PROFILES

G. CANTON, F. BOVA, Dept. Psychiatry, C.so S. Felice 229, 36100 Vicenza, ITALY

In this study we examined a consecutive series of 19 female outpatients with bulimia nervosa, matched for age and education with a sample of 30 non eating disordered female nurses. Bulimia has been evaluated according to DSM-III-R criteria and by means of the BITE, a self-rating scale for bulimia. The Karolinska Scales of Personality were administered to bulimics and controls. Bulimics showed higher scores than controls on Anxiety proneness scales (Somatic and Psychic Anxiety, Muscular Tension and Psychastenia), on Monotony Avoidance, on Aggression-Hostility scales (Indirect and Verbal Aggression, Suspicion and Guilt but not Irritability), and lower scores on Socialization and Social Desiderability. Personality pattern showed a prevalence of disinhibitory psychopathology and this is also in line with our clinical impressions that many bulimics describe their eating behaviour as a food dependence (lack of restraint and loss of control).

2962

A STUDY ON THE THERAPY GIVEN TO 10 ANOREXIC PATIENTS.
TRIDENTI A. - MANARA F. - MAZZALI M. - CLINICA PSICHIATRICA - Università - Parma - Italy

The therapeutic iter of 10 anorexic patients has been studied for a period ranging from 2 to 7 years. The psychological and other characteristics making up the therapy have been considered in depth and compared to the varying symptoms present in the subject during the period of time considered.
The conclusions tend to emphasise what may be the most significant factors to take into consideration when treating anorexics.

Session 450 Video:
P.R. Films. Self-viewing in the therapy of schizophrenia

2963

Reaction and Response
Experiences with a public relation film
Gunter Wahl
Mental State Hospital
Bad Schussenried
West-Germany

How do insiders look at a public relation film about the institution, they are working in? Do the inside patients find themselves represented in a proper and a veritable way? Is there not a great danger to show the own clinic as a very bright and "pseudoidyllic" place instead of demonstrating the "malfaits" and the dark coulors? The public: who is it, what is its way to react to such a film ? Those singles, groups, some interested people, who are called the public, their reception seems to be quite different? Those who should know about the professional psychiatriac work are often : not interested. But many really want to know!

With filmsections of the public relation film.

2964

EVERYDAY ACTIVITIES AT THE HELSINKI UNIVERSITY DEPARTMENT OF PSYCHIATRY

*Kalevi Nieminen, M.D. & Kalle Achté, M.D.
Department of Psychiatry, University of Helsinki*

The video shows the activities of the Department of Psychiatry of the University of Helsinki in 1989.

2965

AUDIOVISUAL SELF-VIEWING EXPERIENCE IN THE THERAPY OF SCHIZOPHRENICS

HARTWICH, Peter, Prof.Dr.med.
Psychiatrische Klinik, Städt. Krkhs.
Frankfurt a.M., West-Germany

The audiovisual self-confrontation technique can be seen as a kind of speaking and moving mirror whereby the opportunity of self-reflection is given. Three different techniques are explained and tested which influence schizophrenic symptoms by the means of audiovisual self-confrontation:

1. The opportunity to achieve intense therapeutic relations with the patient by showing him his own symptoms audiovisually which have been selected carefully.
2. The enhancement of self-coherence by the means of video-mirroring referring to schizophrenics who lost their ego consistence.
3. The training of cognitive disturbances by systematic video confrontation.

The three methods are investigated empirically on a group of schizophrenic inpatients. The procedures are shown by videotape. The three hypotheses are examined and the effects are measured. The effects which were found to be significant in our calculations are discussed.

Session 451 Symposium:
Drug dependence - Basic science of clinical importance

2966

CANNABIS AND PSYCHIC DISORDER

U.Rydberg, C.Adamsson, P.Allebeck, S.Andréasson and A.Engström
Karolinska Institute, Depts. of Clinical Alcohol and Drug Addiction Research, Karolinska Hospital and Depts. of Medicine and Psychiatry, Huddinge University Hospital

Several studies have implicated cannabis as a complicating risk factor in schizophrenia, and of psychotic episodes triggered by cannabis consumption in otherwise healthy individuals. The frequency of adverse mental effects is known to rise sharply with increased THC levels.
Two own studies have been performed. Data was aquired for 45 570 military conscripts regarding e g drug habits, and were followed in the national register for psychiatric care through 1983. There was a strong correlation between level of cannabis exposure at conscription and development of schizophrenia. Relative risk for schizophrenia was 2.4 in the group that reported use of cannabis at least once compared with non-users, and was 6.0 among those who had used it more than fifty times. 8483 men from Stockholm county who conscripted, and the relative risk of schizophrenia in the group that had used cannabis at least once was 2.1 as compared to non-users. Among those who had used cannabis more than 50 times, the relative risk of schizophrenia was 4.1.
This statistical association does not prove a causal association. However, the data implies that cannabis plays an aetiological role in subgroups.

2967

NOVEL PHARMACOLOGICAL TREATMENTS FOR OPIOID AND COCAINE DEPENDENCE
Jerome H.Jaffe, Rolley E.Johnson & Francis Levin
NIDA Addiction Research Center
Baltimore, U.S.A.

The growth of cocaine use in the United States has stimulated a search for new agents that might be useful in treating cocaine withdrawal, cocaine craving, and cocaine toxicity. The spread of AIDS among intravenous opioid users has stimulated search for new agents to suppress opioid use. Among the agents which have been tested for suppression of cocaine withdrawal are amantadine, bromocriptine, methyphenidate and various amino acid precursors. Calcium channel blockers have been tested for the effects on cocaine toxicity, and cocaine self-administration and cocaine-induced subjective effects in human volunteers. Among the agents that have been studied as adjuncts to the outpatient treatment of cocaine dependence are desipramine, amantadine, fluoxetine, mazindol flupenthixol and carbamezaepine. The findings do date with these agents will be reviewed.

Buprenorphine a partial Mu agonist opioid has been studied as an alternative to methadone. Technics for initiation of treatment, doses associated with blockade of injected opioids and effects of buprenorphine withdrawal will be presented.

2968
THE RISKS OF BEING PREGNANT AND DRUG DEPENDENT

Loretta P. Finnegan, M.D., Department of Pediatrics, Jefferson Medical College, Thomas Jefferson University, Philadelphia, PA 19107, USA.

Pregnant, drug-dependent women are at high risk because their lifestyles are dominated by drug seeking behavior and use throughout pregnancy, frequent polydrug abuse, poor nutrition and inadequate prenatal care. This combination of factors probably accounts for lower birth weight, length, head circumference, gestational age and general overall increased perinatal morbidity and mortality. Many factors have been shown to be associated with the occurrence of abuse and neglect in drug dependent women's children. These include parental drug and/or alcohol abuse, extreme poverty, chaotic lifestyle, and violence between the parents. Drug dependent women have been found to have experienced an increased incidence of abuse, childhood rape, and sexual molestation. This violence, both sexual and non-sexual, coupled with depression, is seen in high incidence in drug dependent women. The potential for adversely affecting the quality of the attachment in the neonatal period as well as a long-term parent/child relationship exists. Evidence that both drug abuse and child abuse tends to be inter-generationally transmitted underscores the need for early and effective intervention.

2969
CNS EFFECT OF AMPHETAMINE USE

Itaru Yamashita, Tsukasa Koyama, Junji Ichikawa, Makoto Nakayama
Dept. of Psychiatry, Hokkaido Univ. School of Medicine, Sapporo, Japan

Repeated use of methamphetamine (MAP) causes psychotic condition closely resembling paranoid schizophrenia.
In rats treated with MAP for a week and drug-free for another week, the efflux of DA and metabolites in microdialysis fluid increased markedly by MAP challenge and emotional stress.
It was observed in MAP-treated rats, 1) small dose of apomorphine lowered DA level of the striatum in controls but not in MAP-treated rats (inhibition of presynaptic DA receptor), 2) DOPA accumulated 30 minutes after NSA1015 in MAP-treated rats (increase of tyrosine hydroxylase activity), 3)(3H)GBR12935 binding showed decrease of Bmax and Vmax (decrease of DA reuptake sites)
Also, MAP-treated rats showed reduced 5-HT reuptake in the frontal cortex and hyppocampus.
These findings suggest certain long-term disturbances of DA and 5-HT activities in MAP psychosis and at least partly in schizophrenia.

2970
DRUG AND ALCOHOL ABUSE AND DEPENDENCE IN ASEAN COUNTRIES
Dr. M.Parameshvara Deva
Dept. of Psychological Medicine, Faculty of Medicine Univ. of Malaya, 59100 Kuala Lumpur, Malaysia

The ASEAN countries comprising Brunei, Indonesia, Malaysia, Philippines, Singapore and Thailand with a population exceeding 285 million has for several decades now been facing the onslaught of waves of drug trafficking, drug abuse and dependence. Being close to the close of the so-called Golden Triangle where high quality opium is produced and refined into heroin, the problem of drug dependence has spread rapidly in ASEAN, especially in Thailand, Malaysia and Singapore. Unlike the opium dependence of pre-World War II when elderly Chinese were mostly addicted to opium sold in government shops, the young adolescent heroin dependent today "chases the dragon" using illegal heroin. Cannabis abuse and alcoholism have also become problems with greater availability. In Malaysia, over 125,000 drug dependents have been identified and an energetic government programme of treatment centres and rehabilitation programmes have been started to cope with this problem. Similar programmes are being carried out in Singapore and Thailand. This paper describes some of the efforts and the problems they face.

Session 452 Symposium:
Attention deficit disorder with hyperactivity: Diagnosis, treatment, follow-up

2971
THE EVALUATION AND ASSESSMENT OF ADHD

Prof.Paul Garfinkel
University of Minnesota Hospital and Clinic
Division of Child and Adolescent Psychiatry

ADHD is a chronic,disruptive behavioral disorder of children and adolescents. The investigation of two elementary schools provided the opportunity to identify ADHD symptoms in non-clinic referred epidemiologically-derived populations.All children in grades two through six were evaluated on their intellectual and academic functioning,providing an N of 1,100 students.Evaluation of their attention span and impulsivity were also completed.Teacher and parent ratings indicated a high rate of indetification of the index children.
Instruments that measure sustained attention were most effective in identifying the ADHD group. This series of studies corroborated previous findings suggesting that only one-third of those elementary sch.age youngsters who have ADHD have a pure disorder whereas, two-thirds are comorbid for other disruptive disorders,affective disorders and learning disabilities.These findings also identify the total number of symptoms,i.e.threshhold scores, that identify the children at various developmental stages.The suggestion is that ADHD maybe more difficult to identify in the older elementary school age children compared to children in the earliest grades.Further research is recommended in terms of other evaluative and diagnostic measures that can be used to identify this disorder across various child and adolescent stages.

2972

Treatment of Attention Deficit Hyperactive Disorder
Dr. Gabrielle Weiss
McGill University, Montreal, Canada

This is a syndrome which begins in early childhood and may continue into adulthood. Treatment strategies depend on the age of the patient as well as on the specific deficits related primarily or secondarily to the syndrome. It is considered that aimless activity, various difficulties with attention and impulsive styles are the core symptoms of the syndrome. However, in the majority of children and adults, associated symptoms are present to varying degrees, for example poor school performance, poor social skills low self-esteem, oppositional behaviour, low frustration tolerance and possibly mood depression. The initial assessment will determine the presence and degree of the above difficulties and a comprehensive treatment plan will attempt to address all the areas in which functioning is impaired. The paper addresses the efficacy of different doses of stimulants on target symptoms and other psychological treatments, some of which have as yet unproven efficacy. The uses of family and individual therapy, social skill training, remedial education, cognitive therapy and focused parent groups will be discussed.

2973

Adolescent & Adult Outcome of Hyperactive Children and its Predictors
Dr. L. Hechtman
McGill University, Montreal, Canada

Outcome at adolescence and adulthood will be reviewed from the literature and from the author's own 5, 10, 15 year prospective controlled follow-up studies. Details of academic, social, emotional outcomes will be presented. This includes details of drug and alcohol use, antisocial behaviour, work history, relationships, moves, car accidents, psychiatric disturbance. Factors which may predict adult outcome, e.g. early degree of hyperactivity, aggressivity, antisocial behaviour, I.Q., S.E.C., family functioning, mental health of family members and child rearing practices, will all be presented. Treatment approaches which may affect outcome will also be discussed.

Session 453 Symposium:
New concepts of psychosomatic consultation liaison service

2974

THE DEVELOPMENT OF PSYCHOSOMATIC (ECOLOGICAL) CLS

Nicholas Destounis, M.D., Ph.D.
Professor of Psychiatry
Medical College of Wisconsin
Chief, Psychiatry Service
Zablocki VAMC, Milwaukee, Wisconsin

Over the past 30 years, the delivery of mental health services to the medically and surgically ill takes place through the psychosomatic consultation liaison service. The primary purpose is clinical care and its principle correlates are education and research. Education has its special characteristics within the liaison programme since it includes the teaching of psychiatric methods, psychosocial-culture and ecological influences, and clinical comprehensiveness in health and disease in general to non-psychiatric staff as well as to psychiatric trainees and members of the psychiatric profession and associated disciplines.

This communication will present new data based primarily upon my work observations and conclusions from personal experiences as a clinician, teacher, researcher and academician dealing with the medically-surgically and dying patients.

The consultation function of the specialist in psychiatry over the past 30 years has become an increasingly important aspect of his professional role. In the consultation process, the consultant psychiatrist of the Psychiatry Consultation Liaison Service is in direct contact with *medicine* and with his *non-psychiatric colleague* (Destounis, N. 1971, 1978, 1979, 1985, 1986). My concept of the PCLS is being the maintenance of scientific *medical communication* by making daily rounds with the chairman and the staff of each department in order to treat the Anthropes holistically as a *unique genetic-bio-physiological-medical-psychosocial-cultural and ecological entity*. (Destounis, N. 1971, 1978, 1979, 1985, 1986)

2975

CONSULTATION-LIAISON: A VIEW FROM WITHIN

Luca Alverno, M.D.
Associate Clinical Professor of Psychiatry
Medical College of Wisconsin
Chief, Psychosomatic Liaison Consultation Service
Zablocki VAMC, Milwaukee, Wisconsin

What is the hallmark of *Consultation-Liaison* Psychiatry? A dialogue is entertained with an imaginary resident in psychiatry over the peculiarities of this subspecialty. An example is that patients seen by consultation psychiatrists do not necessarily present with (diagnosable) psychiatric disturbances.

The steps of the *consultation process* are elucidated, paying attention to usually overlooked, but very important clues such as signs of visitors, meal trays (used or untouched) and observing patients at meal times.

Semi-humorous advice is offered, with emphasis on not being in the way of other hospital workers, avoiding irritating remarks when writing the consultation notes, or, put differently, trying to *facilitate*, rather than hamper, the function of that complex organism called *General Hospital*.

Consultation-Liaison is a wonderful *exercise* for students and young doctors of all medical specialties where the psychiatrist is in direct contact with medicine and with his non-psychiatric colleagues. The primary scopes of consultation liaison are clinical care, education and research. *Education* has its special characteristics within the liaison programme, since it includes the teaching of psychiatric methods, psychosocial, cultural, *ecological* influences, and clinical comprehensiveness in health and disease in general to *non-psychiatric staff* as well as to psychiatric trainees and members of the psychiatric profession and related disciplines (Destounis, N. 1971, 1978, 1986).

2976

NEW FINDINGS IN THE SLEEP OF POST STROKE PATIENTS

Demitrios A. Julius, M.D.
Associate Professor of Psychiatry
Medical College of Virginia
Chief, Psychiatry Service
VAMC Richmond, Virginia

A group of post stroke patients were studied for their psychiatric and medical sequelae. Interesting findings include sleep disruption, pattern and affective disorders present in these patients. Research results will be presented regarding REM latency, total sleep time, and the incidence of sleep of apnea in these patients. This will be correlated with depression rating and other neurologic findings in these patients.

2977

THE PSYCHOSOMATIC ASPECTS OF CORONARY HEART DISEASE (CHD).
Athanasios MOURDJINIS, MD, DMSc. Consultant Cardiologist. Secretary, Hellenic Society of Psychosomatic Medicine, Athens Greece.

Of the well known **predisposing** factors for CHD, psychic **stresses** and **type A behavior pattern,** are unique as they both promote atheromatosis by themselves **and** also potentiate other such factors, i.e. hypertention, hyperlipidemia, to that effect. **Endogenous** or personal stress or behavior pattern type A has characteristic psychosomatic features. **Exogenous** or environmental stress encompasses an array of psychosocial(occupational,fiancial,social) and physical(limatological,pollutional, noisy) factors. In our studies for the prevention and treatment of CHD,each patient was thoroughly (a) **informed** in general(written material,models,pictures,etc.)and about individual predisposing factors,with particular emphasis on endogenous and exogenous stresses. Our protocol also included(b) **Basic** principles of **psychotherapy** personal counseling(reassurance,suggestion,persuasion),(c) **Definite Therapy**(group therapy,relaxation techniques physical exertion)& (d)**Adjunctive** but specific **Medication** in the last resort. Prevention is difficult to access but improvement and control of CHD manifestations are readily amenable to clinical evaluation & quantification. In our patients substantial help and/or amelioration was afforded to approximately three fourths of them. Improvement was evident however,to a lesser degree in all patients.

Session 454 Symposium:
The ethics of psychiatric treatments

2978

INTRODUCTORY REMARKS REGARDING SOME CONTEMPORARY ETHICAL ISSUES IN TREATMENT

Sir Martin Roth
Cambridge University Medical School, Cambridge, U.K.

The introduction will be confined to certain ethical issues, which have gained increasing prominence in recent years. The insistence by some authorities that the civil and human rights of patients be respected and given priority above all consideration is coming into conflict with the right of patients to receive treatments that may be of a life-saving character. Failure to administer treatment on a compulsory basis may lead to injury or loss of life in patients. In consequence, lawsuits for negligence are increasingly instituted on behalf of patients with depressive schizophrenic and other disorders, who have made suicidal attempts. The psychiatrist's duty to protect life is regarded as compelling by courts of law at a time when there is increasing pressure against admitting and treating mentally ill persons irrespective of their ability to form judgments about their state of mind or the long-term interest of either themselves or their families. There are similar conflicts that have recently arisen in respect with treatment of other disorders where therapeutic need has to be balanced against contemporary public opinion and regarding the justification for intervention under any circumstances. These shifts in opinion have been reflected in mental health legislation, that has weakened the scope and influence of clinical judgment in favour of verdicts pronounced about mentally ill patients by legal authorities.

2979

PSYCHIATRIC RESPONSIBILITY FOR THE QUALITY OF LIFE

G. Penati MD, R.Morselli MD and G.Panza MD
2nd Psychiatric Clinik, Milan University, Milan, Italy,

The meanings of "treatment" and "cure" have been perhaps reduced because of progress in biological psychiatry and psychopharmacology. A rational utilisation of drugs seems to be judged, nowadays, the best answer to the right of being cured. On the contrary the concept of cure in psychiatry has many aspects, to cure someone means to take care of him too, considering then the patient in his historical sequence: past, present and future. It is about the word future, future of the patient as person in a family and society, that the psychiatrist find himself in deep contrast, facing the right of the patient of being cured. The significative reduction of positive symptoms and a low relapse rate would be a satisfying goal? This goal is satisfying also considering the patient's right of an acceptable quality of life? These questions arise the problem of an integrative and human evaluation about goals and results of psychiatrist's activity on mentally disabled.

2980
THE HOMELESS MENTALLY ILL: A NEW ETHICAL PROBLEM

A. Bosio, M.D. and R. Rosola
Association Advancement Neurosciences,
Philadelphia, PA, U.S.A

The discovery of cerebral active drugs in the last decades opened a new era for the treatment of mentally disabled persons. In particular, the possibility to prevent and treat the acute moments of diseases modified the sociological impact of mental pathology towards a new concept overcoming those stigma that characterized also a recent past. Nevertheless, the tentative reduction of long term hospitalization to ensure a new familial and social moment of life has been counteracted by the worldwide defects in the territorial assistance to the groups of mentally disabled outpatients.
Without a family, without a positive impact with the medical and social staff the patients slowly become unpleasant aspects of our society. Their right to be cured and treated represent the new frontier of psychiatric care, in respect of their dignity of human beings. The USA and European situations will be analyzed and described.

Session 455 Symposium:
La psiquiatria clinica en un hospital mexicano

2981
LA PSIQUIATRIA HOSPITALARIA EN MEXICO POSIBILIDADES Y LIMITACIONES
Garnica, R; Torres-Ruíz,A.;Galindo,M.C.;Mendoza,M.
Instituto Nacional de Neurología y Neurocirugía
Secretaría de Salud México.

El Instituto Nacional de Neurología y Neurocirugía (INNN), contiene diversas especialidades en el campo de las neurociencias, entre ellas la Psiquiatría. A veinticinco años de su fundación ha adquirido experiencia suficiente en tres áreas principales: la atención médica, la enseñanza y la investigación.
En el presente simposio se delinearan los antecedentes que llevaron a la creación del INNN, las razones por las que existe un servicio psiquiátrico en él y cuales son las bases teóricas que han llegado a conformar nuestro paradigma en psiquiatría. También se describen los sistemas taxonómicos para precisar el diagnóstico, los temas que se abarcan para la formación de nuevos especialistas, así como las líneas de investigación que se han seguido en psiquiatría durante estos veinticinco años.
Por último, se concluye que es posible hacer una psiquiatría a muy buen nivel, a pesar de las obvias limitaciones económicas con que cuentan los países en vías de desarrollo.

2982
Simposium:La Psiquiatría Clínica en un hospital mexicano.
The Clinical Psychiatry in a mexican hospital.
La Psiquiatría en el Instituto Nacional de Neurología y Neurocirugía, México.
The psychiatry in the National Institute of Neurology and Neurosurgery, Mexico.
Dr.Antonio Torres-Ruíz.

Se hace una relación de las razones y fundamentos que se tuvieron para que la Psiquiatría formara parte importante en una Institución de Neurociencias. Se describe la constitución,organización y funcionamiento del Instituto, haciendo especial énfasis en cómo la Psiquiatría se encuentra enlazada al resto de las actividades institucionales, tanto de índole asistencial como docente y de investigación, y finalmente se precisan las características del área psiquiátrica desde la perspectiva de organización y funcionamiento.

2983
Simposium:La Psiquiatría Clínica en un hospital mexicano.
The Clinical Psychiatry in a mexican hospital.
La Asistencia psiquiátrica en el Instituto Nacional de Neurología y Neurocirugía de México.
The psychiatric asistence in the National Institute of Neurology and Neurosurgery,Mexico.
Dr.Rodrigo Garnica.

Debido a que nuestro trabajo psiquiátrico se lleva a cabo en el contexto de un hospital de neurociencias, nuestra orientación corresponde a los paradigmas biológico y fenomenológico-descriptivo, de acuerdo a las consideraciones de Gerald Klerman de Boston. Mediante un sistema de computación sencillo hemos creado un archivo de 17 campos del programa D-Base II para el registro de nuestros diagnósticos. Hasta 1988 utilizamos el DSM-III como referencia diagnóstica.Se hace referencia a los ingresos hospitalarios en el período 1986-1988 con los siguientes datos:

INGRESOS A PSIQUIATRIA INNN 1986-1988
N=911

Núm.de Pacientes	Núm.de Ingresos	Núm.de Reingresos
868	911	43 (4.7%)

En la presentación se desglosa la lista de ingresos siendo el primer diagnóstico la esquizofrenia,el segundo los trastornos mentales orgánicos,la tercera los trastornos afectivos,etcétera.Se discute la importancia del diagnóstico en la psiquiatría clínica.

2984

Simposium: La Psiquiatría en un hospital mexicano.
The Clinical Psychiatry in a mexican hospital.
La Formación de psiquiatras en el Instituto Nacional de Neurología y Neurocirugía, México.
The trainning on psychiatry in the National Institute of Neurology and Neurosurgery, Mexico.

Dra. M. del Carmen Galindo.

El propósito de la presente comunicación es dar a conocer como se forman en la especialidad de psiquiatría jóvenes licenciados en medicina general, teniendo como lugar sede al Instituto Nacional de Neurología y Neurocirugía (I.N.N.N.) de la Ciudad de México. En el I.N.N.N., además de la especialidad en psiquiatría se imparten otras 10 especialidades y subespecialidades. La Institución cuenta con la infraestructura que le permite formar especialistas en Neurociencias. Aquí se atienden diariamente a pacientes neurológicos, neuroquirúrgicos y psiquiatricos en el servicio de Consulta Externa, además existen áreas de hospitalización para Neurología, Neurocirugía y Psiquiatría, requiriéndose, por lo tanto para la atención de los pacientes así como para el proceso educativo y de investigación de médicos residentes en las áreas antes señaladas. En la formación de nuestros psiquiatras hay una combinación de dos clases de pedagogía: el aprendizaje de la clínica por la experiencia y la enseñanza propiamente dicha de las diferentes materias que constituyen el curso de especialización de psiquiatría.

2985

Simposium: La Psiquiatría Clínica en un hospital mexicano.
The Clinical Psychiatric in a mexican hospital.
La Investigación Psiquiatrica en el Instituto Nacional de Neurología y Neurocirugía de México.
The Psychiatric Investigation in the National Institute of Neurology and Neurosurgery, Mexico.
Dr. Mario Mendoza.

La investigación psiquiatrica formal se inició en México a principios de los años cuarentas, el personaje principal fué el Dr. Dionisio Nieto, médico español, nacionalizado mexicano con gran influencia de la investigación psiquiátrica y neuropatológica alemana de la época. En 1964 se inauguró el Instituto Nacional de Neurología en donde el Dr. Nieto es nombrado Jefe de Psiquiatría, desde entonces en este Instituto, ha sido prácticamente el único lugar donde se ha llevado a cabo la investigación psiquiátrica en el país con un modelo médico de atención psiquiátrica, se ha investigado en diferentes áreas como la psicofarmacología, neuropatología, trastornos mentales orgánicos, etc. Actualmente estamos incorporados a los nuevos métodos de clasificación diagnóstica, estudios doble ciego, grupos control, métodos estadísticos y con la ayuda de los sistemas de computación, por primera vez en 25 años tenemos cifras precisas de las características clínicas de nuestros pacientes. Nuestras casuisticas son amplias y contamos con la mejor infraestructura para la investigación psiquiátrica en el país, nuestras limitaciones se derivan del subdesarrollo esto es, del diseño de los sistemas de salud, de la precaria situación económica tanto del país como del propio médico que le impide dedicarse a la investigación.

2986 *

* Number left open for technical reasons not corresponding to any abstract

Session 456   Workshop:
Key issues and practical proposals for the improvement of institutional care and rehabilitation of mentally ill

2987

KEY ISSUES AND PRACTICAL PROPOSALS FOR THE IMPROVEMENT OF INSTITUTIONAL CARE AND REHABILITATION OF MENTALLY ILL
G. Lyketsos, M.D.
Univ. of Athens, Dept. of Psychiatry, Eginition Hospital, Athens, Greece

This workshop is intended to bring together the participants in the related symposiums S 152, S 155 and S 178: a collaboration to introduce key issues and practical proposals for the care and rehabilitation of the mentally ill. Two speakers from S 178, Manfred Bauer and John Henderson and two speakers from S 155 Michael Madianos and John Tsiantis will frame their issues in a brief communication of 8'-10' each. A discussion will follow open to all participants in the above symposiums and the audience.

Session 457 Special Session:
Outcome of psychotherapies

2988
COMMENT ON PEUT AIDER AUTREMENT EN PSYCHANALYSE
N.Nicolaidis, Suisse
SOCIETE SUISSE DE PSYCHANALYSE

La visée du processus psychanalytique : changement ou équilibre ? Normalité ou pas ? un faux problème. La dynamique de la régulation entre plaisir-déplaisir est la préoccupation majeure de la cure analytique. Offrir au patient de nouvelles défenses "moins coûteuses en déplaisir".
L'apparente antinomie des réflexions de Freud : A sa lettre au pasteur Pfister il souligne que la cure a comme but d'analyser; c'est au patient à faire la propre synthèse de ses défenses. Cependant analyser jusqu'où ? En 1938 dans "Analyse terminée et analyse interminable" Freud se demande si nous devons "réveiller le chat qui dort" autrement dit éviter à viser d'autres changements et se contenter de l'équilibre, même conscient, du patient.
L'interprétation dans la cure : outil majeur de l'analyste... mais à double tranchant.
L'interprétation ne doit provoquer que des vagues, disait J. Lacan.

2989
LIMITS TO PRECISION, RELIABILITY & RELEVANCE IN PSYCHOTHERAPY RESEARCH

John O. Beahrs, M.D.
Oregon Health Sciences University, Portland, OR, USA

Many factors limit the scientific study and manipulation of mental phenomena. Private experience remains subjective; its components, voluntary action and conscious awareness, co-exist with their opposites and therefore cannot be determined with absolute certainty. Complex causality limits scientific constructs in another way; their usefulness depends on simplicity and precision, which often can be achieved only by excluding causal factors that remain relevant. Constructs become limited by a mutually reciprocal "uncertainty relationship" between their precision (P), reliability (R), and domain of relevance (D) that is approximated by the formula $P \times R \times D = C$, constant within a given context. For example, psychodynamic entities or formulations can only be approximate; defined more rigorously ($\uparrow P$) they become unreliable ($\downarrow R$) or relevant to fewer cases ($\downarrow D$).
In addition, research paradigms using tightly operationalized measures and strict experimental controls ($\uparrow P$ and $\uparrow R$) become ever less relevant to what actually happens in uncontrolled clinical settings ($\downarrow D$). These effects can be partly mitigated by altering research methodology in several fundamental ways. First, many variables can be defined less precisely, preserving their reliability and relevance. Second, uncontrolled clinical settings can be monitored for patterns of intercorrelation among these. Finally, these patterns are tested; not for "truth" but for their limits of relevance. This method is being applied in embryonic form to the study of comparative psychotherapy; one new pattern identified is a wide correlation of therapeutic progress with patients' helping themselves.

2990
COGNITIVE TRAINING ADJUNCTIVE TO PHARMACO-THERAPY IN SCHIZOPHRENIA AND DEPRESSION

J.Fritze, B.Förthner, B.Schmitt
Department of Psychiatry, University of Würzburg, FRG

Evidence from various experimental sources suggests a dysfunction/overactivity of the left hemisphere in schizophrenia and the right one in depression. Based on these lateralization hypotheses and on the dependency of regional cerebral blood flow on regional neuronal activity, Myslobodsky & Weiner (1983) proposed their concept of pharmacopsychotherapy. The present double-blind pilot study in 32 patients tested this concept by applying cognitive training procedures tentatively relevant to the mechanisms of information processing of the left (analytical) and right (holistic) hemisphere, respectively. It was hypothesized that the outcome of patients putatively trained in mechanisms of the right hemisphere might be superior to that of those trained left in depression and the converse in schizophrenia, enhancing the efficacy of antidepressant/neuroleptic drugs. This hypothesis could not be verified. The better outcome of depressives trained right was attributable to differences in age and initial seriousness of illness.

2991
THE OUTCOME OF BEHAVIOURAL PSYCHOTHERAPY WITH OBSESSIVE-COMPULSIVE PATIENTS
A.D.Rabavilas, J.Liappas and N.Vaidakis,
Athens University Medical School, Department of Psychiatry, Eginition Hospital, Athens, Greece.

Although behavioural psychotherapy has been claimed as being the treatment of choice for OCD, some data derived from the long term observation of the treated patients as well as the lack of an unambiguously acceptable learning theory model for this disorder, indicate that a revision of treatment methods, training of therapists and the alleged theoretical "purity" of the treatment should be taken under serious consideration in future research programmes. The current state of affairs regarding treatment outcome runs as follows : 10% of the patients requesting BP are considered unsuitable for the treatment, 20% refuse to accept it, 5% drop out, 15% get no benefit out of it and 50% show considerable initial improvement. Almost half of the latter patients require additional treatment within 1-4 yrs of follow-up and for a proportion of them (1:2) other forms of therapy should be further prescribed. With the exception of certain clinical OC symptoms specifically amenable with BP and some elements of the BP techniques employed, a number of non-specific factors appear to considerable influence the treatment outcome. These include adverse mood fluctuations, depression, certain personality traits (such as externality of locus of control), family and social relations, autonomic habituation and the form, quality and length of the therapeutic relationship.

2992
DIFFICULTIES IN ENDING THE THERAPY: A QUANTITATIVE STUDY OF 27 CASES OF BRIEF PSYCHOTHERAPY
Gr. Vaslamatzis, M. Markidis, K. Katsouyanni
Department of Psychiatry, Athens University

Brief psychotherapy (of psychoanalytic orientation) implies in itself a limitation of time meeting both the patient's acceptance and the therapist's awareness. However, some patients have difficulties in ending the therapy. The material of this study consists of 27 patients. Of these patients, 14 ended their therapy as agreed at the 30th session (group I), 5 dropped out at the last phase (group II), while for the remaining 8 (group III) it became apparent a little before or after the ending time, that psychotherapy would have to be continued.
Methods: Factor analysis with varimax rotation was used in analyzing the therapist's difficulties scale. Differences between groups were statistically evaluate by analysis of variance. Discriminant analysis was applied to assess differences between the three groups taking into account the patient's sex, age and years of schooling, the final suitability score and the clinical diagnosis.
Results: The results show that suitability score, determined during evaluation, emerges as the main differentiating parameter of the three groups. Therefore, according to this finding, a careful selection of patients, suitable for this modality of psychotherapy, should minimize the ending difficulties, while non-suitable patients could be provided with another type of therapy.

2993
Schizophrenic basic symptoms after a psychotherapeutic program

VOLKER BELL, ST. BLUMENTHAL, N.-U. NEUMANN, R. SCHÜTTLER, R. VOGEL

Bezirkskrankenhaus Günzburg, Department Psychiatry II of the University Ulm, Ludwig-Heilmeyer-Str.2, D-8870 Günzburg, West Germany

Viewing schizophrenic illness, the concept of basic symptoms (Huber et al. 1979) gets increasing importance. The psychopathological state of these symptoms is determined by dynamic and cognitive deficiences, which are experienced and communicated by the patients themselves. Therefore we constructed a self-rating scale (Günzburger Selbstbeurteilungsskala für Basissymptome; GSBS) which can reliably and validly record these symptoms. Special psychotherapeutic interventions aiming such deficiences may be useful. By such therapy there should be an reduction in the score of our self-rating scale. One psychotherapeutic treatment aiming such symptoms is the "Integrated psychological therapyprogram for schizophrenic patients (IPT)" by Roder, Brenner et al. (1988). In a controll-group design first admitted schizophrenic patients underwent this therapy. Both groups were investigated with our self-rating scale and other psychological tests. Psychotherapeutic intervention and the results will be described and discussed.

2994
EFFECTS OF BRIEF COUPLE THERAPY IN REHABILITAION OF CORONARY PATIENTS
S. Priebe, U. Sinning, A. J. Küppers
Department of Social Psychiatry, Freie Universität Berlin, Berlin (West), F.R.G.

Conceptions of systemic couple therapies led us to establish a brief couple therapy within an out-patient rehabilitation programme following acute coronary heart disease. The therapy aimed at changing patterns of behaviour in order to allow couples a better adaptation to the new situation caused by the disease. Out of forty-four patients beginning the rehabilitation programme, every second patient and his/her partner were offered a therapy of two to five sessions carried out by a cardiologist and a psychiatrist.
Patients and partners rated the therapy as having been very helpful, and patients who were offered the therapy showed a significantly greater reduction of depressive symptoms (on the Hamilton Depression Scale) and of concerns about current complaints (on visual analogue scales) than those in the control group. Effects of the therapy were different in patients living with high-EE partners (expressed emotion as assessed by the Camberwell Family Interview) and low-EE partners. Principles of the therapeutic intervention, case examples and effects are shown.

Session 458 Special Session:
Psychiatric ethics

2995
A WORLD PSYCHIATRIC ASSOCIATION QUESTIONNAIRE ON ETHICS.
Hans Adserballe
Psychiatric Hospital, Aarhus, DK-8240 Risskov, Denmark.

The Committee of Ethics of the World Psychiatric Association has the responsibility to identify and explore areas of ethical concern to psychiatrists. A questionnaire on psychiatric ethics was forwarded in 1988 to the 72 member societies. 26 questionnaires were received, i.e. 36 per cent. The opinions are divided as to the justification of specific psychiatric ethical committees and codes. Quite a number of the societies think that the ethics of psychiatry should not differ from the ethics of other medical professions. The US-system is by far the most developed both as to medical and psychiatric ethics. The most important ethical concerns are indicated to be human rights and the use of compulsion. The doctrine of informed consent is emphasized. The inquiry did not contribute very much as to concrete proposals for the amendment of the Declaration of Hawaii - the ethical constitution of the WPA. Psychiatric ethics is a growing area and the societies are conscious of their responsibility as regards the spreading and teaching of ethical ideas. The Ethics Committee must debate the priorities of a great number of ethical issues. Under any circumstances ethical matters will always be a main concern of the WPA.

2996
FITS 'HUMANITY' AS AN ETHICAL VALUE?

B. Wegener
Krankenhaus Am Urban, Berlin, FRG

'Humanity' is very often used as an argument in psychiatric ethics. But you will find it as well conceptualized by defenders and offenders sometimes of totally controversial positions.

It is our intention putting a glance on the history of that concept in its changing meanings.

How and in which contexts it is possible to argue with 'humanity' as an ethical term? Is it a concept with a special content?

2997
ETHICS AS CRITIC OF PSYCHIATRIC MORALS

B. Wegener
Krankenhaus Am Urban, Berlin, FRG

Ethics are often misleaded for the purposes of legitimations or self-justifications of persons or groups. But ethics are not separable from the historical, social and political context.

In that hypothesis an other problem is included: How it is possible to define valid ethical rules and, is it possible?

Medical ethical papers mostly reflects professional positions in the view of medical functioneers. It demancs a forum for discurses between medicine and the clients. Today medical ethics stands under an descent of values in an self-legitimating system.

Methodological difficulties of professional and positional ethics are discussed. The interest is a propaedeutical one: How are ethics in psychiatry possible?

2998
DOCTORS' ATTITUDES TO SELF-INDUCED BEHAVIORAL EXCESSES IN PATIENTS
E.L. Edelstein, M.D., Hadassah University Hospital, Jerusalem, Israel

Dyscontrol syndromes or excessive appetitive behavior are deviances which are consciously motivated and self-determined. This stands in sharp contrast to the medical concept of diseases.

These self-induced states extend on a wide continuum: from explosive, impulsive desinhibited drive behavior, cyclic in nature on the one pole, to the inhibitory, over-controlled sublimated behavior adhered to with compulsive rituality - on the other pole.

They include syndromes such as obesity, bulimia, drug dependence, alcoholism, anorexia nervosa, gambling and activity addiction.

Physicians seem to be biased when dealing with these self-induced deviances. Many clinicians hesitate to examine or treat them, are easily judgmental, display resistance and often feel incompetent.

Factors contributing to doctors' attitudes will be discussed.

After analyzing this exceptional doctor-patient context, possibilities for solutions will be proposed.

2999
Death Penalty And The Mentally Ill.

Marianne Kastrup.

Psych. Dept. Frederiksberg Hospital,
2000 Frederiksberg, Denmark.

A basic principle of forensic psychiatry has been that the mentally ill are not to be judged by the same rules as the mentally fit and punished for acts which are a consequence of their disorder. Thus insane prisoners should not be executed. Prisoneres evaluated medically unfit for execution must undergo psychiatric treatment until their mental health is restored. Gradually the role of the psychiatrists changed from diagnosing the presence of mental illness to evaluating aggravating and mitigating circumstances.
In recent years several U.S. prisoners have been executed or come close to execution despite appearing mentally ill. Selected cases will be presented to illustrate the ethical dilemma inherent in situations requiring psychiatrists to restore the health of the patient and consequently allowing his execution.
In some states in U.S. the evidence of psychiatrists is introduced to establish the probability of future acts of violence and this testimony may be of decisive importance for the recommendation of death penalty.
Health professionals have an important role in implementing codes of ethics which prohibit any involvement in the execution process.

Session 459 Symposium:
Major depression disorders in anorexia nevrosa and bulimia

3000
NEUROENDOCRINE TESTS IN DEPRESSION AND ANOREXIA NERVOSA:SIMILARITIES AND DIFFERENCES
Brambilla F.*,Genazzani A.R.**,Facchinetti F.**, Maggioni M.°,Ferrari E.°°
*Ospedale Psichiatrico Pini-Milano,**Dept.Obstetric Gynecology University-Modena,°Villa Zucchi-Carate, °°Dept.Internal Medicine University-Pavia,Italy

Anorexia Nervosa(AN)and depression(PAD) share many alterations of the neuroendocrine system,possibly on the base of a common impaired neurochemical substratum.The hypothalamo-pituitary-gonadal(HPG)secretion is severely impaired in AN,while in PAD it seems to be relatively better preserved.We examined HPG function in 70 AN and 72 PAD patients,measuring FSH-LH basal levels and responses to LHRH stimulation,beta-endorphin(β-EP),beta-lipotropin(β-LPH)basal levels ,PRL basal levels and responses to TRH stimulation.Results revealed reduced LH-FSH basal levels and responses to LHRH stimulation,normal PRL basal levels and responses to TRH stimulation,elevated β-EP/β-LPH basal levels in both AN and PAD. Our data suggest that the HPG alterations present in both psychopathologies may be expression of a common impairment of the central regulatory mechanisms,possibly worsened in AN by the superimposed starvation.

3001
DEPRESSION AND NEUROENDOCRINOLOGY IN ANOREXIC AND BULIMIC EATING DISORDERS
Fichter M.
Psychiatr.Klinik, Universität Munchen & Klinik Roseneck Prien, FRG

The "affective illness hypothesis" of bulimic eating disorders claims that bulimia nervosa is a variant of the nosological group of affective illness. In favour of this hypothesis a higher prevalence of depression in bulimic patients and their relatives, positive response to antidepressant medication and the presence of neuroendocrine disturbances as in depression have been described. On the other hand, changes in neurotransmitter metabolism and neuroendocrine changes in bulimia and anorexia nervosa can be seen as an adaptation to reduced caloric intake. The severity of depressive symptoms has been shown to correlate negatively with the percentage carbonydrate intake. Data on neuroendocrine and neurotransmitter changes in bulimia and anorexia nervosa are presented and discussed with respect to the "affective illness hypothesis" and the "nutritional hypothesis". In a series of studies we have assessed the hypothalamo-pituitary-adrenal axis, thyroid axis and gonadal axis and the norepinephrine and serotonin metabolism. Our results favour the "nutritional hypothesis". In bulimics we found insufficient, cotisol suppression and reduced dexamethasone plasma level in the DST, a tendency for blunted TSH-responses to TRH, a blunted prolactin response to TRH in bulimics with a history of AN, reduced plasma LH and FSH, reduced nocturnal prolactin levels in bulimics with signs of reduced caloric intake. Depression did not show a positive association with endocrine disturbances.

3002
Are Eating Disorders Variants of Affective Disorders?
R.G. Laessle, H.U. Wittchen, and K.M. Pirke
Max-Planck-Institute for Psychiatry, Munich,FRG

The relationship of eating disorders and affective disorders was examined systematically by using standardized diagnostic instruments. A rather high percentage (56%) of patients with lifetime diagnoses of eating disorder <u>and</u> affective disorder (comorbidity) was found. Comorbidity of major depression with eating disorders was 38%. Most of our findings, however, suggest that depressive symptoms and major depression in particular are not 'specific' for the development of eating disorders: 1) other psychiatric and non-psychiatric disorders have similar high comorbidity rates. 2) data on the temporal relationship revealed that the onset of depressive disorders occurred in 70% of the patients examined at least one year after the onset of the eating disorder. 3) Severity of depression correlated significantly with biological indices of starvation and with specific psychopathology of the eating disorder. These data can be best interpreted in the framework of a model that regards the occurrence of depressive symptoms in eating disorders primarily as a correlate of psychological and biological consequences of altered eating behavior.

3003
BRAIN STRUCTURE AND FUNCTION IN EATING DISORDERS: A CRANIAL COMPUTED TOMOGRAPHY STUDY

Crieg C., Lauer C., Pirke K., FRG

3004
IMPROVEMENT IN DEPRESSION DURING NUTRITIONAL MANAGEMENT THERAPY FOR BULIMIA NERVOSA
S.W.Touyz, P.J.V.Beumont, P.Butow, W.Lernerts, M.O'Connor, U.Schweiger*
Department of Psychiatry, University of Sydney
*Max-Planck-Institute for Psychiatry, Munich, FRG

One etiological model of bulimia nervosa focuses on the assumption that bulimia nervosa is a variant of an affective disorder. Therefore, antidepressive medication has been used to improve bulimic behaviour. The present study has investigated the alternative hypothesis, namely that the psychopathological features associated with bulimia nervosa are to a great extent consequences of the disordered eating behaviour (especially the fasting periods) and that therefore therapy should primarily be aimed at changing the patients' baseline eating behaviours. In our study 27 bulimic patients participated in a three months nutritional management out-patient therapy program. The primary goal was to first alter and normalize the patients' eating behaviour in its quantitative, qualitative and temporal aspects. The patients' eating behaviour and psychopathology were assessed over a one year follow-up. Preliminary analyses revealed a significant improvement in bulimic behaviour at post treatment. This was accompanied by a significant reduction of depression (BDI: pre-treatment: 20 ± 13, post treatment: 9 ± 9), which remained stable at one year follow-up.

Session 460 Workshop:
Improvisation therapy

3005
IMPROVISATION THERAPY
Daniel Kahans
Wingrove Cottage Community Clinic, Eltham, Victoria, Australia

Improvisation Therapy Workshop is aimed to demonstrate techniques involving a musically-proficient-performing-therapist performing patient-ideas for the actualising of the patient's musical improvisation through the therapist's immediate response to the patient-ideas via the patient's simple hand and other non-verbal and verbal direction. Workshop audience members would be used as patient substitutes.
Specific proposal involves having two Cellists on stage, demonstrating such techniques and the discussion of the following variables:
Differential effects of working with different therapists; diagnostic categories; patient's previous musical knowledge; dyadic role-reversal of usual therapist-patient relationship; use in group therapy, psychodrama and dyadic interactions; facilitation of both spontaneity and rehearsal modes; and effect of different aesthetic stimuli on improvisation.
Analogous techniques to that involved in Improvisation Therapy with music may be demonstrated with a movement or dance therapist.

3006*

* Number left open for technical reasons not corresponding to any abstract

Session 461 Free Communications:
Eating disorders: Theoretical issues and psychological correlates

3007
PROCESSING BODY SHAPE INFORMATION IN ANOREXIA NERVOSA
SW Touyz, R Freeman, E Gordon, C Rennie, G Sara & PJV Beumont
Dept of Clinical Psychology, Westmead Hospital Australia. Psychology, Simon Fraser University, Canada. Neuroscience Unit, University of Sydney & Westmead Hospital. Dept of Psychiatry, University of Sydney.

Disturbances of body image are an important but as yet incompletely understood feature of anorexia & bulimia nervosa. Whilst Bruch (1962) identified body image disturbance (BID) as a central component of anorexia and bulimia nervosa, the phenomenon has remained an elusive but yet fascinating area of investigation. Indeed, some authors have even questioned whether BID differentiates eating disordered patients from normal women.
A proliferation of measurement techniques as well as inadequate methodological procedures have no doubt contributed to the inconsistent data reported in the literature. However despite this body image dissatisfaction amongst eating disordered patients remains a fundamental factor. Bruch has even proposed that a complete recovery would only be possible for patients with anorexia nervosa if they corrected their BID.
The aim of the present study was to use a Computerized Infrared Eye Gaze Monitor to obtain an accurate and objective estimation (at 50 times per sec) of how 16 eating disordered patients and 11 controls process body shape information.
ACKNOWLEDGEMENT: IBM Australia, NH&MRC Grant 840146

3008

Obesity: Biopsychobehavioral Correlates
Tan, T-L., Mann, L.D., Martin, L.F., Slaybaugh, K.J., Rodriguez, W., Shubert, D.D., Pennsylvania State University College of Medicine, Hershey, Pennsylvania 17033 U.S.A.

Two hundred obese subjects (162 women, 38 men; mean age 39.1 $\pm$.07 years; mean weight, 92.4 $\pm$3.2% above ideal body weight) were comprehensively evaluated with clinical, psychological and sleep laboratory assessments. The majority of patients reported experiencing a significant life stress event prior to onset of obesity. Further, those patients with a greater degree of obesity were significantly more likely to have an early age of onset, be divorced, report suicidal ideation, have poor health and significantly less likely to complain of psychosomatic problems. Psychologically, obese patients had significantly higher scores than controls on six MMPI clinical scales: 4-Pd was the highest, suggesting poor impulse control, lack of self-restraint, rebel- liousness and social alienation, followed by 2-D; 3-Hy; 1-Hs; 8-Sc; and 7-Pt. The group also scored significantly higher on the McAndrews Scale, which indicates potential for addiction. In the sleep lab, the group was found to be at high risk for sleep apnea; there was a very strong positive correlation between weight and degree of sleep apneic activity. Fourteen males and 3 females had 30 or more apneic events with a mean minimum SaO_2 of 73.7 $\pm$ 2.0%. Although only 19% of the total group were men, they accounted for 82.4% of those with sleep apnea. Psychiatrists involved in various therapeutic programs for obese patients should therefore have a high index of suspicion for sleep apnea.

3009

ASPECTS PSYCHODYNAMIQUES DE L'ANOREXIE MENTALE CHEZ L'ADOLESCENTE.

M. Camus*, V. Delvenne**, J. Appelboom-Fondu*

* Hôpital Universitaire des Enfants Reine Fabiola
  Bruxelles - Belgique
** Hôpital Universitaire Erasme
  Bruxelles - Belgique

Le but de l'étude est d'évaluer les caractéristiques psychodynamiques individuelles et relationelles d'un groupe d'adolescentes présentant une anorexie mentale en comparaison avec un groupe apparié d'adolescentes sans pathologie physique ou psychique. Les résultats sont discutés et corrélés aux données pédiatriques et neuropysiologiques.

3010

PSYCHOLOGICAL RESPONSES TO THE VISUAL PERCEPTION OF FOOD IN EATING DISORDERS

Sabine Bossert, Ph.D., Caroline Meiller, B.A., Reinhold Laessle, Ph.D., Heiner Ellgring, Ph.D., Karl-Martin Pirke, M.D.
Max-Planck-Institute of Psychiatry,
Kraepelinstr. 10, D-8000 Muenchen, F.R.G.

Peculiar behaviors concerning food are common in anorexia nervosa and bulimia nervosa. Responses to different food stimuli and their relationship to restricted food intake, underweight or psychopathology has rarely been investigated.

19 different food items were presented on slides to 9 anorexic and 20 bulimic inpatients (DSM-III-R) at the beginning and after 8 weeks of treatment, and to 9 controls at the maximum of weight loss during a diet and at normal weight. Liking and estimated time for consumption were rated for each food item. Before and after the presentation of food items mood, hunger and appetite were assessed. Metabolic and endocrinological variables also were measured.

In contrast to fasting controls, patients rejected highly nutritious food and overestimated time for consumption. At the beginning of treatment, appetite ratings were lower in anorexic and bulimic patients than in controls, but they increased in fasting controls and anorexic patients after the experiment. In addition, relationships to severity and treatment response were found.

3011

BULIMIA NERVOSA : CLINICAL CHARACTERISTICS AND PSYCHOPATHOLOGICAL PROFILES
M. Flament, M D, N. Dantchev, M D, S. LEDOUX, Ph D, P. JEAMMET, M D, (Réseau INSERM n° 489014)
Hôpital International de l'Université de Paris,
Paris, France.
Fifty young women (mean age, 27.3 years) consecutely admitted as outpatients and meeting diagnostic criteria for bulimia nervosa were evaluated with a standardized assessment procedure including a self-report questionnaire, clinician's ratings and Derogatis'Symptom Checklist (SCL-90 R).
Mean age of onset for bulimia was 17.2 years and bu limia had been preceded by anorexia nervosa for 21% of the patients and by dieting for 35 %. At the time of evaluation, binge eating occured once or several times a day for 42 % of the subjects and 46 % were vomiters (21 % several times a day).
Although bulimia was most often hidden (65 %) or even kept secret (26 %) by the subjects, socioprofessional functionning was generally impaired since 45 % of the patients had difficulties at school or at work and 65 % were socially isolated.
Fifty-four per cent of the subjects had attempted suicide, often several times.
General psychopathological level was estimated by global score on the SCL-90 R and specific symptomatic dimensions analysed using factors'subscores.
In conclusion, in a group of 50 unselected outpatients with bulimia nervosa, both bulimic symptoms and general psychopathology appeared severe. At the time of evaluation, although symptoms were often still kept secret, the disorder was already chronic for most of the subjects and socioprofessional adjustment was generally altered.

3012

THE EXPRESSION OF ANGER IN OBESE PATIENTS.
G.Andrianopoulos,P.Sakkas,A.Robin
Dept.of Surgery,University of Illinois,College of Medicine,Chicago,IL.,U.S.A.

Previous results suggest that the relationship between obesity and increased risk of psychopathology may be due at least in part,by the stigma of obesity in a society which values leanness.In this study we examined whether anger is part of the reaction to the stigma of obesity, by comparing the experience and style of expression of anger between obese(G1,N=25)and normal weight matched controls (G2,N=20).The "State-Trait Anger Expression Inventory"(STAXT) was used for assessment of current anger(SA),anger temperament(TAT),anger suppressed (AX/IN),expressed(AX/OUT),or controlled(AX/CON) or experienced(AX/EX).Results showed a strong correlation between excess weight and intense state anger in the obese group($p<0.01$).ANOVA between G1 and G2 (Table I) shows significantly increased,

TABLE I

	SA	TAT*	AX/IN	AX/OUT	AX/CON	AX/EX
G1	54	54	50	52	51	48
G2	51	49	48	51	52	45

Scores only on the TAT(*$p<0.05$)scale suggesting a propensity among obese patients to be quick tempered,manifest anger in many facets of behavior and a tendency express anger with little provocation ($p<0.05$) compared to controls.This may be a consequence of the anger which was shown to intensify with increasing excess weight($p<0.01$) and may relate to the social stigma of obesity.

3013

REFLEXIONS SUR LES INTERACTIONS FAMILIALES DANS L'ANOREXIE MENTALE

O. HALFON - J. LAGET - CMP - FONDATION SANTE DES ETUDIANTS DE FRANCE - 77610 NEUFMOUTIERS-EN-BRIE

M-T MALTESE : HOPITAL ROBERT DEBRE - Serv. PrDUGAS PARIS.

Depuis sa distinction syndromique, l'anorexie mentale a été rattachée à des entités nosographiques multiples.
Sa complexité psychopathologique décrite par les cliniciens, sa survenue à des périodes différentes de la vie, ont orienté la réflexion sur le contexte psychofamilial dans lequel l'anorexie mentale apparait S'agirait-il d'un troublé lié à des carences précoces de l'environnement ? De l'expression d'un conflit psychique en rapport à des modèles identificatoires sexuels ? D'une interaction pathologique parents/enfants ? Ce phénomène psyché/Soma reste difficile à cerner.
Au cours du traitement des jeunes adolescents hospitalisés pour anorexie mentale dans le Service de Psychopathologie de l'enfant et de l'adolescent du Pr. DUGAS, à l'hôpital Hérold, nous avons constaté qu'il fallait nécessairement inclure les parents dans le projet thérapeutique pour qu'une amélioration survienne. Dans cet objectif, nous avons créé un groupe de parents à visée thérapeutique partielle. Nous définirons d'abord les options prises pour la constitution de ce groupe. Ensuite, nous décrirons ses modalités, son évolution et sa justification, ainsi que les mécanismes psychiques qui semblent caractériser ces familles.

3014

Anorexia Nervosa-Schizo-affective disorder
Depressive Type
Dr.Pedro Rubens Gutierrez-Psychiatric Doctor.
Buenos Aires . Argentina .

Objectives: This work will try to show the relationship between anorexia nervosa with the so-called schizo-affective disorders of the depressive type (DSM III R).
When we discuss anorexia nervosa,we include bulimia because they are two inter-related disorders of very similar origin .

Material and Methods :
During a 5-year period,30 anorexic/bulimic patients were treated and subjected to all psychiatric and psychological studies.In this way we established the definition of schizo-affective disorder,depressive type.
The withdrawal of anorexia nervosa from minor neuroses and its placement within psychotic disorders,seems to be of fundamental importance for the treatment of this pathology.

Our proposed treatment:
Anti-psychotic (clozapina) and antidepressives (clorimipramina),respecting the indispensable psychoterapy needed by these patients.

Results :
The study and treatment performed on all patients led us to the conclusion that we are always facing a psychosis.

Session 462 Free Communications:
Issues in psychophysiology

3015

STIMULUS INDEPENDENT ERPs - A PROPOSED METHOD ITS VALUE CONCERNING NEW COGNITIVE INDICATORS.

I.Barahona da Fonseca; J.Barahona da Fonseca; Fátima Ferreira and J.Simões da Fonseca.
Depart.of Medical Psychology and Psychopathology, Fac.of Medicine of Lisbon.

A new approach to the problem of recording Event Related Potentials of the brain is proposed. This method implies cross-correlation between EEG recorded bipolarly in the scalp, and a Dirac Delta function repeated with period p, p=1,2, ..., n. Afterwards using an algorithm, the waveforms so obtained are put in phase and an averaging procedure is performed. As those waveforms are periodic, power spectrum amplitudes are calculated.
Multivariate Discriminant Analysis shows that there are significant differences between Normal Volunteers which, with closed eyes, are producing (a) agreable fanthasies; (b) disagreable fanthasies; (c) thinking on number; (d) thinking on alphabet letters. Significant differences were found in the Left Temporal Area between Normal Volunteers and Paranoid Schizophrenic patients, concerning basic frequency 3 c/s and its multiples - 6,9, 12, 15 and 18 c/s. The results imply that concerning a local time occurs between the basic frequency and its multiples. Otherwise the harmonic would vanish. Furthermore as thinking about number as well as about alphabet letters does not imply any emotional set the method proves useful to distinguish between different cognitive states. Interference in the results due to Motor Potentials and Arousal has been controlled and evaluated.
Comparisons concerning standard methods used in conventional ERP recording are made.

3016

AN ELECTROPHYSIOLOGICAL CONTRIBUTION TO OBSESSIVE-PHOBIC NEUROSES
SERRA F.P., ROTONDI F., and SERRA C.,
Serv.Neurol.Centro Traumat.Ortop.
Napoli, Italy

Bearing in mind some recent anatomical (LAPLAN et al., (1) and electrophysiological (KASPER et al. (2)) data on phobic obsessive neurotic patients, 30 nevrotic patients, 15 with obsessive-phobic disorders and 15 without obsessional symptoms, aged from 12 to 63 years have been submitted to EEG spectral analysis and early acoustic evoked potentials.

Frequent asymmetries in total power contents and increase in delta frequency in frontotemporal regions, statistically significant and greater in the phobic obsessive group than in the second group with a significant increase in I-V interpeak latency of BAEP in the first group have been recorded.

The probable involvment of frontal lobe and the troncoencephalic dysfunction appearing from the above electrophysiological findings are discussed.
(1) "Rev.Neurol.",144,564,1988
(2) "Biol.Psychiatrie",Springer,310,1987

3017

AUDITORY EVOKED POTENTIAL (AEP) AUGMENTING REDUCING, GENDER, AND PERSONALITY
F.Lolas, S. Camposano
Faculty of Medicine, University of Chile,
PO Box 70055, Santiago 7, Chile

Scores on Vando's Reducer-Augmenter Scale (RAS), Eysenck Personality Questionnair (revised) and amplitude/intensity slopes of vertex AEP were studied in a sample of 17 male and 17 female Ss, aged 21 +/- 3.3 years, with no neurological or behavioral impairment.

RAS scores were positively associated with Extraversion (E) and Psychoticism(P) and negatively with Lie (L). Only in males a negative correlation between E and P1N1 AEP slope was found. In females RAS correlated negatively with N1P2 AEP slope.

These results are discussed within the framework of previous findings and seem to support a complementary relationship between psychometric/behavioral and central nervous system characteristics.

(Supported by FONDECYT and the University of Chile).

3018

EFFECTOS DEL ESTRES Y DE LA ANSIEDAD SOBRE LOS POTENCIALES EVOCANDOS Y ATENCION
Dres.A.Yorio, L.Albalustri, E.T.Segura
Centro de Est. de Psic. Médica y Psiquiatría, IBYME
Spain

En el presente trabajo se analizan los efectos de la ansiedad y de un estrés situacional provocado sobre el potencial auditivo cortical de latencia prolongada (PEAC), cuya estrecha dependencia de la atención está bien establecida. Se estudiaron 14 sujetos sanos, de ambos sexos, entre 18 y 27 años de edad. Se constituyeron 2 grupos, uno de alta y otro de baja ansiedad en base a un test multifactorial de personalidad. Los registros del PEAC se realizaron en las siguientes condiciones experimentales: 1)atención simple (AS); 2) atención interferida (AI); 3) inatención auditiva (IA); y 4) inatención selectiva (IS). Este esquema se repitió bajo influencia de estresores fisico y psicológico. Las diferencias se estimaron mediante la aplicación del análisis de la varianza. Resultados: 1) se observó diferencia significativa (p 0.05) en el grupo de baja ansiedad entre la condición de AS e JA, en ausencia de estresores; 2) no se apreciaron diferencias significativas en el mismo grupo enpresencia de estresores, y 3) no hubo diferencias significativas en el grupo de alta ansiedad con o sin estresores. Conclusiones: 1)El PEAC sufre modificaciones en relación con variaciones de la atención propias de diversas condiciones experimentales, 2) a las diferencias individuales de ansiedad se asocia diferente comportamiento dal PEAC respecto de la atención, y 3)la acción de estresores se acompaña de un descenso en la diferencia en la amplitud del PEAC relacionada con situaciones de atención.

3019

Inteligencia: uso de potenciales evocados.

Fischer Rodolfo
Vanoni Renata
Coira Celia
Cyriopoulos Mario
Marsilii Antonio

Se investiga la relación entre velocidad de respuesta a un estímulo acústico tomando el potencial evocado cerebral y relacionándolo con los coeficientes inteligencia de uso difundido, en éste caso la administración del WAIS (Wechsler).

3020

LATE POSITIVE COMPONENTS (LPC) OF AUDITORY EVOKED POTENTIAL (AEP), AGE, AND COGNITIVE STATUS.
F.Lolas, S. Camposano, J. Corail
Univ. of Chile, PO Box 70055-Santiago 7
Chile

LPC of AEP are influenced by task and cognitive variables. This study explored P3b wave in an oddball paradigm 80%frequent (750 Hz,80 dB) and 20% rare tones (1500 Hz, 80dB), rate 0.5/sec. Ss had to perform a bimanual reaction time task, stressing speed rather than accuracy. Recordings from Pz-linked mastoids derivation, with analysis time of 710 msec. Three groups of "normals" (I, 20-30 yrs.; II, 31-41 yrs.; III, over 60 yrs.) and a group over 60 with psychometric impairment of cognitive function(IV) were studied. Each group had 7 men and 3 women.

N1 latency showed no differences between groups; P2, N2 and P3 did (ANOVA), with a maximum in group IV and minimum in group II. N2P3 amplitude was minimal in group IV and maximal in group II. In normals, a correlation of 0.65 (p<0.001) between age and P3 latency, with a slope of 1.5 was observed.

These results replicate previous findings and reinforce diagnostic uses of LPC in assessments of cognitive status.
(Supported by FONDECYT Chile)

3021

SMOOTH PURSUIT AND SACCADIC EYE MOVEMENT IN SCHIZOPHRENICS

Moser A[1], Kömpf D[1], Arolt V[2]
Department of Neurology (1)
Department of Psychiatry (2)
Medical University of Lübeck,
Ratzeburger Allee 160, D-2400 Lübeck,FRG

A voluminous literature exists on the eye movements of schizophrenic patients and suggests that there is a relationship between abnormal functioning of the smooth pursuit system and the psychopathology. However, a quantitive analysis of the pursuit or saccadic defect is only seen in small cases. In order to study and quantify dysfunction of eye movements they were measured with infrared photoelectric techniques and analysed by a digital computer. The study included 10 patients with a schizophrenic disorder (DSM-III criteria) and 10 normal subjects. All patients were studied after an acute psychotic episode.
Our results could demonstrate both a dysfunction of the smooth pursuit which was related to a low pursuit gain and an increase of small catch-up saccades, respectively, and abnormalities in saccadic and anti-saccadic eye movement.

Session 463 Free Communications:
Sexual attitudes and dysfunctions

3022

SEXUALITY OF MIDDLE-AGED MEN.

Kim Solstad.
Sexological Clinic, Dep. of Psychiatry, Rigshospitalet, University of Copenhagen.
The Glostrup Population Studies, Dep. of Int. Medicine C, Glostrup Hospital, University of Copenhagen. Denmark.

A lot of investigations has concerned sexology. Only a few of them however has been representative for the general population - because of still-existing taboos.
The purpose of this investigation is to describe the relative significance of sexual matters in a general population of a certain age group of men. The material was 542 51-year old men representative for men of this age in a part of Denmark. The men were invited as part of a cohort-investigation of social/medical factors of importance for their health. 439(81%) of the invited men appeared, and all of them completed a sexological questionnaire. 103 of the men were picked at random and 100 of these were interviewed (the proportion of respondents were 85-95% in the questionnaire and 100% in the interview). The themes of the questions were: The participant's sexual behavior, how this behavior was experienced, and attitudes to different sexual behavior.
The representativeness of the results for the general population is thoroughly investigated, because basic knowledge of the relative significance of different sexual matters in the population is important in Sexology.

3023

EVALUATION OF IMPOTENCE IN MIDDLEAGE, ELDERLY MEN

Eker,E.*, Madazlıoğlu,S.*, Olcay,E.*,
Kaynak,H.**, Gözükırmızı,E.**
 * Dept.Psychiatry, Cerrahpaşa Med.School, Univ. Istanbul, TURKEY
** Dept.Neurology, Cerrahpaşa Med.School, Univ. Istanbul, TURKEY

We evaluated 91 middle-age and elderly patients with sexual dysfunctions in our center during its first 20 months. The results of the analysis demonstrated that 43.1% had organic impairment, 25.4% had psychogenic impairment and 31.5% had undifferentiated cases. A definitive diagnosis of psychogenic impotence was made based measurement of Nocturnal Penile Tumescence and Rigidity and intracorporeal papaverine injection. Diabetes mellitus was found a significant cause of impotence as organic factor in our cases (43%). The effect on erectil function of alcohol and/or prescribed drugs was established as the second cause (16%). The commonest psychological factors relevant to the etiology of erectil disfunction were marriage problems and poor communication between partners (31%) and performance anxiety (22%).

3024

Psychodiagnostic and sexological evaluation of 100 subjects suffering from Male Exitement Inhibition
MANARA F., LOMBARDI M., TRIDENTI A.
Chair of Psychosomatics
University of Brescia - Italy

The paper presents the results of sexological and psychodiagnostic conselling undertaken in the Medical Unit for the Diagnosis and the Treatment of the Impotence at the University of Brescia, by the combined staffs of Urology and Psychosomatics.
100 case studies are evalated and discussion is made of the differentiation between psychogenic and organic etiopathogenesis of Male Exitement Inhibition as well between the psychopatological factors which are causing the disfunction and those which are caused by it, for each of the two categories of Male Exitement Inhibition (organic and psychogenic).

3025

Psychotherapy of the inhibition of sexual desire and the localization of its organic manifestations.
Joaquin Regueiro
Dpto. Psicologia Clinica universidad de Santiago - Spain.

With this paper we inform about the course of investigation in the area of the inhibition of sexual desire, the main object of which is to find a short psychotherapeutic procedure in order to resolve this sexual disfunction. Proceeding with visual imputs and with the gathering of electrogalvanic and electromyographic datas by the means of Biofeedback we found out,up to the present, that:1)There exists an effective affliction or a level of "electrodermal emotional responses" which accompanies and seems to stimulate an "electromyographic response" in the genital and anal zone of our patients who, when faced with the visual imput,admit a sensation of sexual desire.2)The sexual desire possesses an area of organic manifestations in the genital and anal zone,comparable with another sexual function, feeding back the other functions of erection and vaginal lubrication.3) The inhibition of sexual desire is a pathology which needs a therapeutic approach in the scope of restructuring the "Mental Images" (MI).These M.I. cause an "emotional imput" adequate to the response of the "sexual desire", in the form of little contractions and relaxations. These can be perceptible by the patients,once trained to concentrate their attention on them, as a sensation localized in the same anatomical zone.
4)That is why we consider this method as a psycotherapy of the inhibition of sexual desire.

3026

GROUP THERAPY IN VAGINISMUS
Yüksel,Ş., Kayır,A., Sarımurat,N.
University of Istanbul, Faculty of Medicine

It is the general consensus of professional opinion that vaginismus is a relatively rare disorder. Although it is not supported by epidemiological data due to the lack of such studies, our opinion is so that it is not so rare in our country. Since in Turkey for the great majority of the unmarried women, virginity is still an untransgressable taboo.
Our study is about the group therapy of vaginismic women.
Therapy groups consisted of
1- Identifying dominant values and expectations concerning sexuality, reevaluation of negative values,
2- Sexual education and re-education,
3- Behavioral homework - Desensitization of phobic avoidance.

For the evaluation of the treatment: SCL-90, Maudsley Marital Inventory, Sexual History Form, at the beginning at the end and at a three-months follow up of the treatment.
In comparison with individual and couple therapy, group therapy yielded better results in shorter time in those who completed the therapy program. The drop-out percentage was much lower.
Therapeutic factors such as empathy, group cohesion, universality, modelling, in a homogeneus group was clearly observed.

Session 464 Free Communications:
Non-traditional therapies

3027

SCRIPT THERAPY
Agmad Ordoobadi, Department of Neuropsychiatry, University of Medical Sciences, Shiraz, Iran

"Script Therapy", was developed by the author as an auxiliary tool to different techniques of psychotherapy. The positive effects of the words are used in Script Therapy according to the description of the sophist Gorgias for whom words possess a power comparable to that possessed by pharmaca in medicine. The task for the patient consists of writing down words, proverbs, lines of poetry etc. chosen by the therapist. Through this method, messages are carried to the patient's unconscious becoming introjected and internalized. Some of the clinical goals, aims and targets of Script Therapy are: special and different designs for treating Psychoneuroses, modification of Super Ego (Ego ideal and Ideal Ego), ameliorating Antilibidinal Ego and Internal Sabuteur (Fairbairn), Thanatos and Death Instinct (Freud, Melanie Klein), reducing neurotic guilt feelings, enhancing Good Object relations, emancipating the patient from his internal Bad Objects, even helping heavy cigarette smokers to stop smoking.

3028

AN EXPERIENCE OF THE INTENSIVE SAND-PLAY THERAPY TO JAPANESE PATIENTS
Akita I., Suwaki H., Ikeda H.
Department of Neuropsychiatry Kochi Medical School, Kochi Japan

The sand-play therapy was devised as a form of psychotherapy for children by Lowenfeld, M. in 1929. Afterwards, Kalff D., who had studied sand-play therapy under her guidance, applied the concept of "Analytical psychology" of Jung C.G. into this therapy and made it applicable to adult patients. The therapy is usually administered for outpatients, and the frequency of the session is usually once a week, though it can be varied according to the psychological condition of patients.
Recently we tried the intensive sand-play therapy for female inpatients with hysteria and got satisfactory results. They received sand-play sessions almost every day and the images expressed on sand-play works dramatically changed toward the integration of their personalities. The period when the symptoms were severely exhibited was the same one when the unconscious was highly activated. Thus, we think that this period is the most crucial point for patients to integrate their personalities by expressing their gushing images. And we would like to present the process of our experiences.

3029

NO TRADITIONAL THERAPEUTICAL RESOURCES THEATRE AND VIDEO
Eduardo Naides M.D.
Hospital Neuropsiquiatrico Provincial - Ciudad de Cordoba - Argentina

This project describes the experience of psychiatric inpatients and outpatients, physicians and nonphysician professionals, community members and college students. It was coordinated by a theatral responsible, a psychologist supervisor and a physician who had the idea and the general coordination.
The group worked from May to December, once a week, two hours per day.
Each session was divided in to three periods a)corporal expression, b)dramatic work and c)improvisation excersises, that had the object of a collective creation in order to point out internal emotions, of every participant of the group, in relation to mental illness.
During eight months of working in this experience about two hundred and fifty people tried to participate on it, but at last, only twenty five formed the group.
From this five people, seven were patients. (Three of them had previous hospitalizations) and were diagnosed as paranoid schizophrenia, depressive neurosis, obsessive neurosis hysteria and drug abuse, nine were member of the hospital staff (3 no professionals and six mental health professionals) and the rest were members of the community.

3030

NON-PHARMACOLOGICAL TREATMENT OF ANXIETY DISORDER: A NEW VENTURE
I.Sharma, S.A.Azmi, R.M.Shettiwar
Institute of Medical Sciences, B.H.U. Varanasi India

The effect of controlled breathing (Pranayam) was studied in comparison to placebo and drug therapy in 102 patients of anxiety disorder.
Patients were assigned to either of three groups, experimental (n=41), drug (n=31) or placebo (n=30) group matched for age, sex, occupation, duration and intensity of symptoms. Pretreatment evaluation included a variety of clinical and psychophysiological measures. The experimental group was treated with Kapalabhati and Ujjay, Pranayam, the control group with diazepam (10 mg) daily and placebo capsules. Patients were followed up and post treatment evaluation was done at 3 weekly intervals for 3 months.
Significantly better improvement was observed in the experimental group and drug group than the placebo group. Limitations and scope of future research has been outlined.

3031

THERAPIST'S INVOLVEMENT- ESSAY ON SOMATOANALYSIS
Dr. Wassilis ZARUCHAS

Somatoanalysis adds a physical aspect to the psychological and social benefits of the psychiatrist's work.
Its founder, Doctor Richard MEYER, developed the method for use in group analytical therapy.
However, using my experience of its use I have been able to adapt it for individual therapy.
When used in this way the patient decides whether he wishes to talk or remain silent, seek or avoid physical contact and express or hide his emotions.
There is no clearly defined method, the therapist makes physical contact with the patient during periods of emotion when he feels it is appropriate.
The emotions expressed reflect the relationship between the therapist and patient and is used as a means of communication.
The treatment seeks a balance between time spent in verbal expression, emotional expression and analysis.
I will attempt to compare the benefits tobe gained from this method and its problems.

Session 465 Free Communications:
Alcohol and drug abuse: Family related issues

3032

CHILDREN OF ALCOHOLICS: ARE THEY DIFFERENT?
Ernest P. Noble and Stephen C. Whipple. Alcohol Research Center, UCLA, Los Angeles, CA U.S.A.

Three groups of boys, each initially consisting of twenty 8-12 year olds, were studied electrophysiologically, neuropsychologically and behaviorally and their alcohol and other drug use behaviors were followed through time. 1) The A+ were sons of alcoholic fathers with a positive family history of alcoholism (FH+), 2) the NA+ were sons of nonalcoholic fathers with FH+ and 3) the NA- were sons of nonalcoholic fathers with a negative family history of alcoholism (FH-). In the electrophysiological study, two event-related potential (ERP) tasks were used: a simple color discrimination and a more difficult visual continuous performance task (CPT). There were no significant group differences in amplitude or latency of any component for the color task ERPs. However, on the CPT, significant P3 amplitude reductions were found in A+ compared to NA+ and NA- groups. Neuropsychologically, A+ boys showed reduced memory and decreased visuoperceptual performance. Using three different personality tests, the A+ group were also found to be more harm avoidant and sensitive but less cheerful and independent than the NA+ and NA- groups. Two years after entry, alcohol and other drug use data indicate a greater % of the A+ boys than NA+ and NA- boys had begun to drink alcohol and smoke cigarettes and marijuana. Further follow-up studies are underway to determine whether the antecedent CNS measures can be predictors of problems with alcohol and other drugs.

3033

CHARACTERISTICS OF THE ALCOHOLIC FAMILY
B. Gačić, D. Kastratović and
O. Marković
Institute for Mental Health, Center for Family Therapy for Alcoholism
Yugoslavia

Family therapy for alcoholism has been applied over 15 years at the Institute for Mental Health. In current times efforts are being put in adapting the right therapy to a specific family on treatment and their main points of conflict. This paper contemplates the results of 50 examined families who started their treatment at our Institution. The following techniques were applied: the Michigan Alcoholic Screening Test (MAST), for the alcoholic patient and spouse, as well as the Marital Family Questionnaire (MFQ). This paper discusses the differenciealities in the perception of the problem concerning drinking (MAST) among the spouses, and also their different perception of the problems in the family (MFQ), (organisation of the household, home budget, making decision, relationships with the childred etc.).

The results of the examination presents a certain guide-line in therapy work: for the family and marital relationship what field is of priority and on which field work has to be done on, during the family

3034

THE ADULT OFFSPRING OF ALCOHOLICS: RECENT SURVEYS
N. el-Guebaly, MD, University of Calgary, Canada
The formation of associations by the adult children of alcoholics (ACOAs) has increased the interest in assessing their psychosocial functioning. Aside from longitudinal studies of sons of alcoholics, the information is based on clinical and self reports. A random survey of 581 households was conducted in a city of the Canadian midwest (Winnipeg). Of the respondents, 22% had at least one parent with a drinking problem. The adult children of problem drinkers (ACPDs), like their parents, were more likely to have experienced a marital breakdown. They were also more likely to be heavy drinkers with related problems and use more sources of help for stress, anxiety and alcohol. Compared to the rest of the sample, they did not differ in income or education. In a subsequent survey of 250 consecutive psychiatric admissions to a teaching hospital in the same city, the proportion of ACPDs was higher ranging from 30% in the inpatient wards and day hospital to 50% and 57% in the anxiety disorders and substance abuse clinics respectively. When parental alcoholism was defined by DSM III criteria, the proportion of ACOAs ranged between 22% and 50%. Diagnostically there were significantly more adult children among the substance abusers and panic disorders group. The impact of this status also varied with the parental biological relation, gender and premorbid antecedents. The practical implications in relation to the hypothesized syndrome of co-dependency, the prevention and management of ACOAs are outlined.

3035

LA PAREJA DEL ALCOHOLICO CRONICO

Rodríguez, A.; Salazar, I. y Lorenzo, M.A. Departamento de Psiquiatría de la Universidad de Santiago. Santiago de Compostela. España.

La investigación de las características de personalidad y las relaciones entre el alcohólico y su pareja ha sido un constante motivo de preocupación para los estudiosos del alcoholismo.

En el campo de la interacción humana, existen dos hipótesis ampliamente contrastadas: 1) que la relación entre las personas se estructura sobre la base de la imagen que cada una tiene de sí misma y de la otra (esperial de las percepciones, de Laing); 2) que esta imagen presenta dos dimensiones: una, consciente, superficial y cambiante con la propia relación; otra, incosciente, profunda y más estable.

A partir de estos referentes, nos propusimos investigar la imagen que cada uno de los miembros de parejas con uno, al menos, de los componentes alcohólico, tiene de sí mismo y del otro.

El número de parejas estudiadas fue de 100. La imagen consciente fue investigada por encuesta directa y mediante la Family Evinronment Scale (FES). La imagen introyectada fue estudiada mediante el test de las caras desenfocadas (Rodríguez, A. 19), derivado del Repertory grid de Kelly.

Las conclusiones más notables son las siguientes: 1) Los alcohólicos y sus parejas tienen imágenes introyectadas muy similares (matriz caracterológica común). 2) Los alcohólicos y sus parejas están relativamente satisfechos de su propia imagen y no desean cambiar. 3) La imagen ideal del cónyuge coincide en ambos.

Los hallazgos són de notable interés para comprender las dificultades de tratamiento de los alcohólicos.

3036
RELATIONSHIP BETWEEN VOLATILE SOLVENT ABUSE PATTERNS AND FAMILY TYPE IN JAPAN

Kiyoshi Nagano, Ichiro Tetsuka, Satoru Saito
Psychiatric Research Institute of Tokyo, Japan

With the exception of alcoholism, the abuse of volatile solvents has been one of the most serious addiction problems in Japan.

173 cases of solvent abuse were studied to determine a relationship between abuse pattern types and family types. The cases, having a mean age of 20±4.9, consisted of 144 males (83.2%) and 29 females (16.8%) who were referred to drug-addicton-care hospitals mainly from child guidance clinics.

The authors have classified those 173 cases into two types: the addiction(asocial) type (112 cases, 64.7%), and pre-addiction(antisocial and multi-problem) type (61 cases, 35.3%). We have classified their families into three types: Type1-a in which one or more other members of the family have alcohol- or drug-related problems; Type 1-b in which the family had other than drug-related problems; and, Type 2 which is a non-problem/typical family unit. Family Type 1-a accounted for 47(27.2%) of our cases; Type 1-b, 54(31.2%); and, Type 2, 72(41.6%)

We have observed that a greater percentage of addiction type of abusers come from a problem family, either Type 1-a or Type 1-b. However, the percentage of each type of abusers coming from problem families, Type1-a, were equal. Therefore, we concluded that, while genetic/hereditary factors cannot be discarded, the more important factors inducing solvent abuse were cultural and social ones.

3037
A FAMILY APPROACH TO DRUGS RELATED MENTAL DISORDERS

A. López Zanón, A. Almoguera and E. Suarez
Departamento de Psiquiatría y Psicología Médica. Universidad Complutense de Madrid. Spain.

The clinical significance of the family is clear in most of the drug related problems in the field of Psichiatry. Based in our experience about this problem in our own social environment we have carried out a standarized research in hundred patients and their families along the last year in order to clarify the interaction patterns and the variables significantly involved.

3038
CARE OF MENTAL HEALTH ON PREVENTION, THERAPY AND REHABILITATION IN ALCOHOLOGY

V. Starčević, A. Hećimović, B. Lang, S. Pintarić, J. Ivica

Institute for Health Promotion
Health Center "New Zagreb", Yugoslavia
University Department for Neurology, Psychiatry, Alcoholism and other dependences of "Dr.M.Stojanović" University Hospital, Zagreb, Yugoslavia

Mental health protection should practiced today at the place of the man's living and working, that is, at the local community level and in the organizations of associated labour. It is also hard to imagine that the treated alcoholics could persist in abstinence in a drinking society, without getting engaged in the selfhelp and mutual help groups - in the clubs of treated alcoholics. For the treatment and rehabilitation of alcoholics and their families a working organization is of special importance. It is professionaly connected to the primary health and social protection and all the social and political resources are engaged what makes the club a strong factor in resolution of alcohol related problems and prevention of alcoholism at its territory.

3039
ESSENTIAL FATTY ACIDS IN ALCOHOLIC HALLUCINOSIS AND SCHIZOPHRENIA

A.I.M. Glen, E.M.T. Glen, D.H.Horrobin*, M.S. Manku*, J. Miller, S. Will, L.E.F. MacDonell.

Highland Psychiatric Research Group, Inverness, Scotland.
*Scotia Pharmaceuticals, Kentville, Nova Scotia, Canada.

Bleuler in 1924 proposed that alcohol might precipitate schizophrenia and most psychiatrists would accept that in a predisposed individual alcohol, amongst other assaults, might be associated with relapse. The biological mechanism involved has not yet been described. We have drawn together observations showing that in alcohol-dependent patients there are abnormalities in metabolism of essential fatty acids (EFAs) and recent studies suggesting changes in EFA metabolism in schizophrenia. We measured EFAs in plasma and red cell (RBC) membrane phospholipids in controls and inpatients with alcoholic hallucinosis, schizophrenia, delirium tremens and uncomplicated alcohol dependence. We found highly significant differences between schizophrenics and alcohol dependents for most EFAs in RBC membrane phospholipids but that the same EFAs in alcoholic hallucinosis resembled those in schizophrenics. The significance of this in terms of the role of membrane EFAs in receptor regulation will be discussed.

Session 466 Free Communications:
Organic mental disorders: Neurological aspects

3040

PSYCHIATRIC MORBIDITY IN SOLVENT EXPOSED
INDUSTRIAL WORKERS
A.Barocka, FRG - T.Weidenhammer, FRG - S.Lehrl,
FRG - G.Triebig, FRG - R.Hoeli, FRG -
M.G.Cassito, Italy - R.Gilioli, Italy -
M.Bleecker, U.S.A. - R.O'Flynn, U.K.

In recent years various authors have described a "chronic solvent syndrome" suggesting that potentially noxious substances like e.g. toluene, cylohexane, benzene, and others cause neurobehavioural disorders in exposed workers. A number of questions is still unanswered concerning diagnostic procedures, meaning of psychological test results, and the actual morbidity risk. Method: A cross-sectional cohort study of active workers and controls was performed in four centers (Erlangen, Milan, London, Baltimore). The sample size of the German study was n=75 (workers) and n=42 (controls). The psychiatric morbidity was assessed with the Present State Examination (PSE) by WING et al. (1974). In addition psychological testing, as well as neurologic and neurophysiologic examinations were performed. Results: Only the results of the German study are available at the time of abstract submission. In the PSE no significant difference appears on the symptom level, however, the syndromes IC (loss of interest and concentration), and ED (special features of depression) and the cases (Catego, Index of definition) of depression are more frequent among spray painters. Discussion: The results will be discussed in light of results from the other study centers and compared with psychological and neurological findings.

3041

CLINICAL ASPECTS OF CEREBRO-VASCULAR DISEASE

Dr. Elpidio Sanchez Arellano, Neurology of the
Atizapan's General Hospital Mexico, Mexico

This paper point out the concepts, aspects and clinicals differences of the main pathological groups: Thrombosis, embolism or hemorrhage. The sudden development of a focal deficit within the territory of one of the cerebral arteries constitutes the strokes syndrome. Some rules are useful in the diagnosis taken with the patient's age, vascular state and predisposing factors: History of repetitive ischaemia episodes in the same vascular territory are less common in cerebral embolism and are rare in hemorrhages. The deficit develops in a step-wise or intermittent fashion. Rapid resolution of the symptons may take place in the early stages. The onset of a stroke during a period o hypotension, reduce cardiac output, cardiac failure, pulmonary embolism, sleep or dehydration is suggestive of infarction; also a second stroke in the site of previous hemiplegia. Conscious-ness is preserve at the onset of the stroke and headache is no prominent except in cases of carotid or vertebral artery occlusion. Frank epileptic seizures are incommon though focal twitching may be noticed by the patient. The lateral medullary syndrome is for occlusion of posterior-inferior cerebrelar artery; motor o sensory hemiparesis, in farction in the striate system; unilateral internuclear ophtalmoplegia, infarction in the pons; homonymous hemianopia, branch of the putamen cerebral artery. Absence of a carotid or brachial pulse suggests thrombosis, though hemorrhages may occur beyond a carotid occlusion.

3042

THE COMPLEX EPISODE OF TRANSIENT GLOBAL AMNESIA
Ikuta T., Nagamine I., Karisha K., Okura M.,
Saito K., Mori K., Goto H.
Department of Neuropsychiat., School of Med.,
Tokushima Univ., Tokushima, Japan

Two cases of Transient Global Amnesia (TGA) were investigated with special reference to the process of the recovery from amnesia, and each of them were thought to be the complex episode of TGA consisted of a sequence of episode of total amnesia. A 55 year-old woman had TGA on a cold winter day, which consisted of two episodes of total amnesia. The first one occured when she entered the house into warm inside from cold outside, and the second one when she re-entered the same house soon after returning from cold outside. A 49 year-old woman had TGA during a dental operation, which consisted of three episodes of total amnesia. The first episode occurred at or soon after initial local anesthesia, and the third one at the urination in the rest room just after the operation. These two cases support the brain circulation disturbance as the etiology for TGA. Although each of the TGA episode had been considered to consist of single episode of total amnesia with or without retrograde and anterograde amnesia, these two cases indicated that the complex episode of TGA consisted of a sequence of episodes of total amnesia.

3043

DEAFNESS AND HALLUCINATIONS AMONG PARANOID
SCHIZOPHRENICS
Ababneh A. Fawzi
Private Clinic

There is a definite relationship between the sinking auditiory acuity, the auditiory hallucinations and schizophrenia.
This clearly appears in the study we have prepared with 58 schizophrenics being treated in the clinic of professor G. Lyketsos in Dromocaeiteion psychiatric hospital in Athens. We have practiced for each one an audio-metric examination within this number, 31 people suffered from paranoid schizophrenia, 27 from other types of schizophrenia.
We also found a significant relationship between the paranoid forms and the auditiory troubles targeted by the audiometry, (P:0,001).
Moreover, we have noticed that within the number, 36 sick people were having auditiory halluciantions and 22 were not, the correlation with the audiometric examination results gave us a significant statistic result (P:0,01).

3044

CHANGES IN THE COGNITIVE PROCESS IN THE LATE CONSEQUENCES OF THE CLOSED HEAD INJURIES

N. KARAKANEV, G. GEORGIEV

MILITARY MEDICAL ACADEMY, SOFIA, BULGARIA

73 PATIENTS WITH DIFFERENT FORMS OF THE LATE CONSEQUENCES OF THE CLOSED HEAD INJURIES /CEREBRASTHENIA, ENCEPHALOPATHY AND EPILEPSY/ WERE INVESTIGATED. BENTON TEST, LEARNING OF 10 WORDS AND HENTSCHEL WERE USED.
A TRIAL FOR DIAGNOSTIC CRITERIA IS MADE.

3045

ADDICTION TO HOT WATER BATH

Dr. H.S. SUBRAHMANYAM

MANASA MEDICAL FOUNDATION, BANGALORE, INDIA.

Addiction to various drugs is common, but addiction to hot water bath is rare and not reported. The hot water bath is continued for a prolonged time by these patients resulting in euphoria and leads on to a pleasurable dreamy state, which would culminate in loss of consciousness or epilepsy. The neurophysiological studies including E.E.G. studies before, during and after the hot bath show periodic spiky discharges or temporal lobe features. The loss of consciousness or epilepsy is prevented by addition of carbamazipine regularly. Though the patients are aware of these ill effects of such prolonged bath, they stop the drugs and clandestinely take the bath for pleasurable experience. This we call as addiction to hot water bath.

From our records of 148 cases of Hot Water Epilepsy, we are reporting eight such cases, who are addicted to hot water bath.

3046

ABNORMAL NEUROLOGICAL SIGNS IN PSYCHIATRIC IN-PATIENTS

C. Almenar, R. Bordas, J. Fortuny, R. Guillamat
Clinica Mental Santa Coloma.
Barcelona (Spain)

The authors reviewed studies of abnormal neurological signs on clinical neurological examination in psychiatric disorders (mainly schizophrenic patients), and studied two hundred psychiatric in-patients (out of total number of five hundred patients in this psychiatric hospital), with the aim to evaluate the incidence of abnormal neurological signs in psychiatric institution in-patients.
They divided the sample in to two clinical groups: patients with known neurological disorder (mainly neurological illness with psychiatric symptoms) and patients without neurological background (mainly schizophrenic disorder).
A standart neurological clinical evaluation was carried out on all patients, and the abnormal neurological signs were finally grouped according to whether they were: a/primary neurological illness related b/treatment related c/unspecific signs (soft signs?) and d/neurological signs, the findings of which indicated some topographic lesion.

Session 467 Free Communications:
Sleep disorders

3047

COMPARATIVE NEUROPSYCHOLOGICAL DEFICITS IN SLEEP APNEA

S. Donias M.D., V. Tsara M.D., E. Vassilopoulou M.A., D. Patakas M.D., N. Manos M.D.

CMHC-2nd University Dept of Psychiatry, Thessaloniki, Greece.
Univers. Dept of Pneumonology, G. Papanikolaou General Hospital, Thessaloniki, Greece.

Both sleep apnea (SA) and chronic obstructive pulmonary disease (COPD) have been associated with intellectual deterioration. 17 consecutive male SA patients and 17 male COPD patients in stable condition matched for age and education were evaluated with the standardized Luria-Nebraska Neuropsychological Battery (LNNB), a comprehensive instrument for assessing higher mental functions. Quantitative analysis of the patients' LNNB basic scales profiles showed a significantly worse performance for the SA patients in the Pathognomonic, Writing, and Reading content scales. Also, SA patients performed significantly worse in several LNNB factor scales, especially concerning verbal and/or composite skills. In general, deficits were mild and the SA group did not differ significantly from the COPD group in the percentage of overall pathological LNNB profiles. The implications of the above findings and their clinical significance are further discussed.

3048

A CASE OF PERIODIC SOMNOLENCE ACCOMPANIED WITH CHRONIC THYROIDITIS

H. Hirano, Y. Nakamura
Dept. Neuropsychiatry, Yamaguchi Central Hospital
Hofu city, Yamaguchi 747, Japan

The patient was a 36-year-old man. He had had somnolence attacks since he was 33 years old. The attacks generally lasted one to seven days and he had amnesia for the duration. After and/or before the episodes he remained depressed, irritable, and easily arousable and had a sensation of being heavy headed and headache from several weeks to several months. During the attacks, he demonstrated suppression on a DST and normal responses of TSH and PRL to a TRH test. After an iv injection of L-dopa, his somnolence disappeared and the background activity of his EEG improved. During his second admission, he was given maprotilin. Since he showed symptoms of hyperthyroidism a few weeks later, which was later diagnosed as chronic thyroiditis, maprotilin was discontinued and the symptoms gradually disappeared. During this period, he had no attacks and TSH response to metoclopramide was blunted. Since he was given L-thyroxine, he has not had any attacks. The mean levels of serum TSH and plasma HVA significantly decreased and increased, respectively.

These findings suggest a relative dysfunction of central dopaminergic and noradrenergic neuronal activities in this disease.

3049

Successful treatment of sleep apneas with naltrexone. A clinical, polysomnographic and oxymetric study.

FERBER C., SANCHEZ P., LEMOINE P. and MOURET J.
UCPB, Hôpital du Vinatier, 95, boulevard Pinel, 69677 Bron cedex

No efficient medical treatment has yet been found that leads to a clear improvement or disappearance of sleep apnœa syndromes (S.A.S) whose consequences are well known: daytime sleepiness, neuropsychological dysfunctions, headache, memory troubles, systemic and pulmonary hypertension.
The possible physiopathological explanations for the peripheral or central mechanisms responsible for SAS respectively involve a decreased activity or poor coordination of upper airway and respiratory muscles and a lower set-point of respiratory centers to hypoxia and hypercapnia. The latter represents an exageration of those phenomena that physiologically occur during sleep and are reminiscent of those triggered by morphine and morphinomimetic drugs.
Given the above reasons, we have tested the effects of naltrexone, an opiate antagonist, on the sleep-respiratory parameters of 35 patients suffering from SAS. Four night-sleep and respiratory (mechanical and oxymetric parameters) recordings were performed, after a two week wash-out period, the first two without any treatment and the following two ones after receiving 50 mg naltrexone at bed-time.
Apnea index as well as the number, duration and intensity of hypoxic events were dramatically improved (respectively $p<0,001, p<0,01, p<0,001$ and $p<0,001$) together with clinical symptoms
Among the possible interpretation of the spectacular effects of naltrexone on SAS and its symptoms (some patients have been treated for more than 2,5 years), the first and most obvious one is that this drug is effective through the blockade of the inhibitory effects of endorphins on respiratory drive. A complementary interpretation could be that, beyond these effects, naltrexone could also act more peripherally by the blockade of the inhibitory impact of dopaminergic cells in the carotid body on inputs from chemoreceptors.

3050

THE RELEVANCE OF INSOMNIA AND ITS TREATMENT MODALITIES IN GENERAL PRACTICE
Hohagen F., Graßhoff U., Wendt G.*, Riemann D., Berger M.. Central Institute of Mental Health, Mannheim; *Ciby-Geigy, Frankfurt, FRG.

For further planning of the care system for patients with sleep disorders we performed an investigation on the frequency and the treatment modalities of insomnia in general practice in Mannheim. At the present such data are not available for German speaking countries.
Method: A sleep questionnaire was administered to 1500 outpatients (age 18-65) who consulted their general physician for health problems. The items included sleep problems, general health and psychiatric status, environmental factors, medication, social adjustment as well as socio-demographic data. Simultaneously, the general physician informed about organic and psychiatric diagnosis, medication and the frequency of medical consultation. The same questionnaire was mailed 3 months later to all patients who met DSM-III-R criteria for insomnia to clarify whether the disorder was transitory or chronic.
Results: The preliminary data analysis revealed that chronic insomnia according to DSM-III-R criteria was reported by 19% of all patients. 46% considered an organic disorder to be the cause of insomnia, 11% reported environmental factors. 26.5% suffered from a psychiatric disorder and 16.5% from a primary insomnia. These data underline that insomnia is a common health problem which requires special diagnostic and treatment facilities.

3051

ABOUT SOME PSYCHODYNAMIC FEATURES OF MONOSYMPTOMATIC INSOMNIA

KAPSAMBELIS V. and TRIANTAFYLLOU M.
Institut National Marcel Rivière

Our Unit of Sleep Disorders' Treatment receives patients for electrophysiological and clinical investigation. This communication focuses upon some typical psychodynamic features of insomnia. These features are not "clinical entities" but mecanisms of formation and/or maintenance of insomniac symptom; therefore, they either may be associated or succeed one another in the same patient. In about half of the cases, insomnia appears as a simple anxiety equivalent; it breaks person's psychodynamic stability and introduces him in a "crisis" phase, i.e. a state in which the person cannot treat mentally ("bind") an excessive afflux of internal or external excitation. The relationships of crisis as defined here with the metapsychological concept of actual neurosis (actual sexuality's dysfunctionning) are discussed. Crises may last long and constitute a "way of existence" (anxious personnalities, "insomniac" personnalities). They also may open, after variable time periods, on three stable insomnia features (a part from marked psychiatric disorders). In the first one, insomnia is a depressive equivalent (depressive insomnia). In spite of electrophysiological data about REM sleep in depressions, these patients are characterized by a kind of essential psychic function's loss : the ability to recall dreams. Compensatory hypersomnia is frequent and sleep disorders improve with antidepressant drugs. In the second monosymptomatic insomniatype, insomnia appears as a psychosomatic symptom (symptom breaking loose from any psychic meaning, "operative" mental mecanisms ...); the disease doesn't affect an organ, but a function (sleep). These patients often present psychosomatic antecedents (eczema, asthma). The treatment of psychosomatic insomnia is similar with therapies for psychosomatic disorders (somatic techniques, e.g. relaxation, are particularly efficient). The third type of sleep disorders is an "insomnia nervosa": insomnia is considered here as a megalomanic triumph of mental upon a vital biological function (sleep), just as classic anorexia constitutes a triumph of mental upon another vital biological function (feeding). These cases are rare (less than 1% of insomniac patients) and may alternate with anorexia or severe personnality disorders.

3052

INSOMNIE IMAGINAIRE: ETUDE CLINIQUE ET POLYSOMNOGRAPHIQUE
IMAGINARY INSOMNIA: CLINICAL AND POLYSOMNOGRAPHIC STUDY
S.Madazlıoğlu*, H.Kaynak**, E.Gözükırmızı**, E.Eker*
* Dept.Psychiatry, Cerrahpaşa Med.School, Univ. Istanbul, TURKEY
** Dept.Neurology, Cerrahpaşa Med.School, Univ. Istanbul, TURKEY

12 patients méfiant d'une insomnie stricte depuis au moyen plus de 10 ans ont été étudiés pendant une ou deux nuits successives dans leur sommeil spontané de nuit. On a enregistré l'EEG., l'EOG., l'EMG. et si nécessaire l'EMG des muscles de jambe et la respiration. Les données polysomnographiques étant dans les limites normales, les patients continuaient à se méfier de n'avoir plus dormi ou seulement pour quelques heures au bout d'une nuit d'enregistrement. A la fin de la consultation psychiatrique et des tests psychométriques, nous avons constaté un ensemble de symptômes reliable à une psychose chez ces patients jamais traités.

Session 468 Free Communications:
Migration and mental health II

3053

DO IMMIGRANTS AND REFUGEES NEED ETHNO-SPECIFIC PSYCHIATRIC SERVICES?
S.Freeman,M.D.,C.Barwick,J.Durbin & T.Lo,M.D.
Clarke Institute & Hong Fook,Toronto,Canada

Although psychosocial stress is a known concomitant of migration,immigrants underuse mental health services,mostly because of linguistic and cultural barriers.To solve this without creating numerous ethno-specific services,Hong Fook Mental Health Service (HF) was developed as a model. Chinese and Southeast Asian immigrants and refugees would be linked to mainstream psychiatric services in Toronto by providing both patient and agency with consultation,family support,education,and cultural interpretation,but not with direct service,unless unavoidable.Yet,in the first 2 years,41% of service units were direct.To understand this better,69 consecutive patients were followed.22 could be referred out but only 7 to mainstream agencies and the others to ethnospecific agencies or workers.47 patients were not referred;18 needed only a brief contact while 29(42%of the total)required extensive therapy and support from HF.This latter group were more likely to have had severe illness(14/29 were schizophrenic),inadequate English,to be recent immigrants, and to need family therapy.This knowledge can help government's plan for three needed service modalities. 1)Ethno-specific services for those with the foregoing profile 2)Mainstream services for the well-acculturated 3)Linking services(the original HF model)for a group intermediate between 1 and 2.

3054

REPRESENTATION OF MENTAL HEALTH AND MENTAL ILLNESS AMONG IMMIGRANTS AND REFUGEES IN EUROPE

R. BENNEGADI, A. BENSAAD
MIGRATIONS SANTE FRANCE (PARIS). CENTRE F. MINKOWSKA (PARIS)

Immigration is an event in which the pressure on the structure of a personality is often very intense. Our point of departure is two-fold, first a long clinical experience of immigrants in FRANCE, and secondly a bibliographical Study throughout EUROPE. The authors have defined a precise system of references(psycho-anthopological and psycho-pathological) in terms of the gratification or marginalisation that cultural adaptation affords.
The cases related are examples of different phases in migrant movements of the principal ethnic groups (North-Africans, Asians, Turks, Africans) present in FRANCE and in other Europeans Countries (NETHERLANDS, WEST GERMANY, UNITED KINGDOM, BELGIUM).
The authors refer both to Migrants and Refugees. The legal aspects of certain psychopathological problems are also considered at the European level.
The authors argue that immigration is an interactive process which questions society about it's own "public health".
The health of migrants and refugees is a litmus test ; the promotion of mental health and the prevention of mental illness are the object of this test.
The authors insist on the distinct nature of those two elements and make some proposal for the future.

3055

MENTAL HEALTH PROBLEMS OF "AUSSIEDLER" FROM EASTERN EUROPE
Dr. Maria Stöckl-Hinke; Dep. of Psychiatry, Univ. of Münster, 44 Münster, Fed. Rep. of Germany

This study examines psychiatric disorders of German "Aussiedler" from Eastern Europe, who return to West-Germany. The term "Aussiedler" means people of German origin, who have lived with other peoples and in other political systems for one or more generations and return to West-Germany after the year 1950. They come from the Soviet Union, Poland, Czechoslovakia, Rumania, Hungary and Yugoslavia. Out of all admitted patients to the Psychiatric Hospital of Kaufbeuren in the year 1987, 31 patients could be identified as "Aussiedler". The commonest diagnostic categories were alcoholism (11 cases) and depressive disorders (12 cases), whereas the depressive disorders included in many cases paranoid symptoms. The main cause of the mental health problems seams to be acculturation problems. Many "Aussiedler" have a wrong image of Germany and deny the existing cultural differences, which often leads to maladjustment. Especially young people have identity problems. Some of them get criminal or lead marginal existences.

3056

Transcultural psychopathological investigations on foreign workers.
Heimo Gastager, Marc Keglevic
Salzburg, Austria

80 jugoslavian and turkish patients admitted to the psychiatric clinic in 1988 have been analysed with regard to psychosocial and psychopathological findings. The results have been compared with the findings of 188 jugoslavian admissions in a prior period (1970-1976) and with datas of admissions of the genuine population of the same period. We found a lower admission rate of jugoslavians in the 70th, but a much higher admission rate in 1988 compared to the genuine population. Furthermore the psychopathological spectrum of migrants was characterzedly different to the genuine population, but quite similar to the findings of Maugrabin migrants in France. The psychosocial and transcultural implications are discussed.

3057

Psychiatric symptoms of adolescents of the second generation of migrants
Drossos Assimakis (Medecin-assistant)
Université catholique de Louvain (Clinique St Luc)
Bruxelles-Belgique

The qualitative analysis of clinical cases allows the hypothesis that psychiatric symptoms wich are presented by adolescents of the second generation of migrants may be concieved as the result of both an intergenerational and intercultural crisis.
Adolescence period is characterzed by an attempt to elaborate one's own life-project. But this project encounters the parents project and wishes imbued with mourning and family myth.
The coincidence or divergence of wish-project of the two generation may lead to either an intergeneration and intercultural compromise or to a crisis creating a psychiatric symptom.
The substitution of the symptom by the coincidence-divergence of the wish-project may result in a therapeutic opening (therapy), in a synthesis of a psychotherapy of the adolescence and his family.
This way enables the restitution of the adolescent's own wish-project away from the symptom, and the realization of a part to the family's mourning wisch is a necessary condition to the elaboration of a more genuine life-project.

3058

TROUBLES DE LA PERSONNALITE CHEZ LES PERSONNES
AGEES APRES L'IMMIGRATION
H. RABBANI (Ph.D.)
Hôpital Charles Foix - Paris IVRY/Seine

Dans le cadre d'une recherche clinique, nous avons étudié les troubles de la personnalité, du comportement et surtout de l'adaptation, chez les adultes et les personnes âgées après l'immigration. Lorsque ces sujets sont confrontés à des situations nouvelles et des systèmes sociaux, en rupture avec leur langue, leur profession, leur culture et leur tradition, etc. quelle place la nouvelle société occupe-t-elle dans la construction d'une personnalité normale? Quel rôle jouent-ils les centres psycho-sociaux et de santé mentale dans le traitement des troubles de la personnalité et même des crises mentales des sujets âgés > 55 ans, lorsqu'ils sont traumatisés et confrontés à une nouvelle identité qui présente des troubles du comportement avec ses ambivalences, troubles neurotiques et souvent psychotiques, perte d'identité personnelle et même familiale? en d'autres termes, une personnalité modifiée? (ex.pers.mult.).
A côté des études théoriques, un certain nombre de travaux empiriques (Y.Shanan, R.Laforestrie, H.Rabbani, J.Wertheimer et les autres) qui ont été effectués au cours de ces deux dernières décennies- ayant conduit à l'étude de psychogériatrie- montrent qu'il existe un lien étroit entre les constructions sociales et les constructions fondamentales de la personnalité. Des facteurs économiques et psycho-sociaux ainsi que l'environnement défavorisé se conjuguent avec les anomalies de pensée et engendrent des troubles de la personnalité.

Session 469 Video:
Famine/hunger. Pilgrimage

3059

FAMINE AND CHRONIC PERSISTENT HUNGER - A LIFE AND
DEATH DISTINCTION

Johan Andreen
The Hunger Project, Global Office, 1 Madison
Avenue, New York, U.S.A.

At this moment in history, when ending hunger is achievable, it is crucial that we realise the limitations of our thinking about hunger. We need to be clear about the distinction between famine and chronic persistent hunger. This is why The Hunger Project has launched a global campaign to make this fundamental distinction known widely throughout the world. At the heart of the campaign is an 11 minute video: "Famine and Chronic Persistent Hunger: a Life and Death Distinction".

In addition to clarifying the facts and illuminating the distinction between famine and persistent hunger, the video shows what chronically hungry people need in order to end their own hunger, it highlights the kind of programmes and projects which can ensure that hungry people have the opportunity to overcome their circumstances and participate fully in life as healthy, productive human beings.

Already the campaign has the support of hundreds of prominent figures worldwide. Leaders in educcation, politics, development and other pursuits have endorsed it as a concise and effective educational initiative.

3060

MEDICAL BENEFIT OF PILGRIMAGE
AND
ZAMZAM THERAPY FOR 30 HANDICAPPED PEOPLE &
THEIR FAMILIES
1. Dr. Ahmed Ali Khan   M.R. C.Psych.D.P.M.
2. Dr. F. Arustu - G.P.

Claybury Hospital Waltham Forest Dist.Health Auth.
Woodford Bridge Essex 1G8 8BY

Never before in Islamic history had such a large group of mentally and physically handicapped people with family members made pilgrimage to Makkah - two doctors (1 specialist 1 G.P.) it was the toughest medical assignment and they were greatly impressed by the psychospiritual and therapeutic benefits that were apparent in the group. A scientific evaluation of improvements based on Hamilton and Behaviour rating scale of handicap, 24 hours clinical observation and video recordings of the event was made. The evidence was supported by the parental account and independent medical expert at Makkah. There are references in Quran, sayings of prophet Mohammed (p.b.u.h.) and Bible regarding blessings of ZamZam water also mentioned in Psalm 84 Old Testament. Medical benefit ZamZam quoted by prophet Mohammed (p.b.u.h.) and believed by Muslim experts several patients have been cured by this water and total submission to faith when modern facilities failed to cure them.
Before departure on 22nd February all the parents were assessed. 30% were severely depressed, 60% moderately depressed and 10% had anxiety state. (Hamilton Rating Scale). of the disabled people, 11 were in wheelchairs . 5 were epileptic 25% had behaviour problems and 75% had anxiety state.

A further assessment was made on 27.2.89 at the end of 3 days stay in Madina and 60% of the parents had recovered from their depression, whilst 70% of the handicapped people showed improvement. 30% continued to show a combination of behaviour and anxiety state. On 14.3.89, having completed pilgrimage which included drinking zamzam water, a final assessment was made. Benefit to the handicapped children and adults were clearly observed: 10 showing mild improvement, 15 a moderate improvement and 2 a most remarkable improvement in both their general well being and in their physical health.

We believe that the holistic approach to a person's treatment is essential and that the present reliance on only drugs is not only costly but allows abuse and risks. Thus medicine combined with faith can change the total life style.

**Thursday
19th October 1989**

Session 470 — Plenary: Psychiatry: Current state and perspectives

3061

CONTEMPORARY SCHOOLS OF PSYCHIATRIC THOUGHT
Gerald L. Klerman, M.D.
Cornell Univ. Med. College

Contemporary Psychiatry world wide is marked by multiple diverse schools which transcend national boundaries. The dominant schools are biological, interpersonal, social, psychodynamic, and behavioral. The schools differ in their concepts of mental illness and the areas of preferred scientific advance as well as in their definition of the role of psychiatry as a medical specialty and in relation to society. The use of standardized diagnostic procedures, such as structured interviews and diagnostic algorithm, as employed in DSM-III and in the draft of ICD-10 has contributed to a new scientific spirit of psychopathology. Currently, biological psychiatry is on the ascendancy due in part to the therapeutic success of psychopharmacological treatments and also to the growing prestige of the neurosciences. The growth of scientific psychiatry, especially in biological psychiatry, has prompted concerns about possible threats to humanistic values in psychiatry. The impact of new scientific approaches on psychotherapy, research, teaching and practice will be discussed as one aspect of these changes.

3062

MYTHS AND REALITIES IN PSYCHIATRIC RESEARCH

Einar Kringlen, University of Oslo, Norway.

With the advances in biology, classification and medical technology, some progress has been made, but perhaps more important, the direction of research has changed. Consider for instance the new international classification systems. It would appear that the boundaries between schizophrenia, affective disorder, paranoid and reactive psychosis have been moved back and forth by each new generation of psychiatrists, according to the changes of opinion more than due to the recent empirical findings. Has the new classification really given us a deeper understanding of the individual patient? Are the new groups of diagnostics clinically more meaningful? Most mental disorders are defined by their clinical syndromes, which merge into one another. But has not the new DSM-III in fact conveyed the impression that man-made diagnoses reflect the existence of God-created diseases? Consider for instance the burgeoning genetic research. Some seem to think nowadays that linkage studies are the solution to most psychiatric problems. However, previous family, twin and adoption studies tend to show that schizophrenia, affective and personality disorders are shaped by a series of genetic and environmental factors. Thus, simple genetic explanations are unlikely to function. Linkage analysis is a valuable tool, but its application to complex non-Mendelian diseases obviously raises problems. These are some of the issues that will be discussed.

3063

BENEFITS AND RISKS OF BIOLOGICAL PARADIGMS

Leon Eisenberg, M.D., Harvard Medical School, Boston, Massachusetts, U.S.A.

Clinicians no less than researchers try to make sense of clinical signs and symptoms through conceptual models of illness. Models are useful because they tie together facts which cannot be separately remembered; they lead to predictions whose outcome provides a test of validity. The risk is that the user will mistake his preferred model for reality itself and fail to take into account or even acknowledge data which do not fit expectation. Psychiatry has oscillated back and forth between biologic and psychologic models. The risks in each case are different. On the one hand, preoccupation with individual psychology leads to neglect of diagnosis, underuse of medication and isolation from the rest of medicine. On the other, the dominance of biological paradigms threatens to blind us to the very phenomena that make psychiatry a specialty uniquely concerned with human experience. Man is a social animal with the unique gifts of language and self awareness. To relieve suffering, the psychiatrist must attend to all human dimensions.

3064

NEW WAYS OF THINKING FOR FUTURE PSYCHIATRY
Alfred M. Freedman, M. D., New York Medical College, Valhalla, NY, USA

The most promising and critical area of development for psychiatry in the future is the synthesis of experience and biology in accordance with the biopsychosocial model, emphasizing wholeness and the identity of experience with biology. This formidable task, involving an astronomical number of variables, must include quantum mechanics, relativity theory, the Law of Indeterminacy and Chaos Theory, as well as biopsychosocial variables. Out of this will emerge new paradigms for the psychiatry of the 21st century.

Session 471 — Plenary:
Alternative structures of care and promotion of mental health

3065

"Issues on Deinstitutionalisation".
Dr. John H. Henderson, Medical Director,
St. Andrew's Hospital, Northampton, U.K.

Mental illness is not only a major public health problem, it has also considerable social and economic implications. That mental health services are a deprived area of care in most countries is well documented, though developments in some countries have been significantly creative, innovative and expansive of care for the mentally ill.

The asylum and institutional model of care reached its zenith in many countries at the beginning of the 20th century. Now as the 21st Century approaches community care and deinstitutionalization are the hallmarks of the new solution to the problems of caring for a very broad range of patient and general public needs.

The Community Mental Health Centers Act 1965, was a dramatic and far reaching legislative change in USA; Better Services for the Mentally Ill, a government policy statement in UK in 1975, the Psychiatric Enquête in FRG in 1975, the Law 180 in Italy in 1978, and other national initiatives reported to this Congress have made available to us large and small scale experiences of change. Nevertheless any evaluation of outcome of these many changes in important, meaningful measures such as cost effectiveness, cost efficiency, medical audit, quality assurance and the like are significant by their absence from the worlds literature.

A consensus view of issues, implications and trends emerging world wide presented to the workshops, symposia and special sessions of this Congress will be presented in Plenary.

3066

LA REHABILITATION, COMPLEMENT DE LA DESINSTITUTIONNALISATION
AMIEL Roger
Professeur de Psychiatrie Sociale - Universités de Bruxelles et Paris

L'homme moderne souffre incontestablement dans son corps d'inévitables frictions avec son environnement, le pouvoir de conciliation de son appareil psychique n'arrivant pas toujours à ajuster correctement l'un à l'autre. En cas de supression sociale et/ou si l'individu se trouve dans un état de déficience durable (physique, sensorielle ou mentale), des ruptures de contact ne peuvent que se consolider dans la pathologie et affecter sa santé mentale. Pour en sortir, pour également prévenir cette pathologie, avant et après, nous disposons maintenant, pour bonnifier les classiques chimiothérapies et psychothérapies, de formules thérapeutiques dites de Rehabilitation. Notons surtout que sans ces formules de prise en charge psychosociale parfois au long cours, le courant de la désinstitutionnalisation du handicapé qui actuellement prédomine aurait toutes les chances d'échouer et de se transformer en errance et déconnection sociale ou en situations familiales épuisantes et destructrices. En fait, malgré les progrès de la biogénétique et de certains succédanés, le futur n'est pas dans l'extinction des handicaps physiques ou psychiques. Il faudrait encore pouvoir agir sur l'environnement et les entourages qui sont les déclencheurs ou les suppresseurs naturels des stress biologiques et des effecteurs moléculaires

3067

ROLES AND EXPECTATIONS OF GENERAL HOSPITAL PSYCHIATRY AND THE "HEALTH FOR ALL IN THE YEAR 2000" MOVEMENT
Juan J. López-Ibor Jr.
Department of Psychiatry. Ramón y Cajal Hospital. University of Alcalá de Henares (Madrid, Spain).

General Hospital Psychiatry is a model for provision of services that has been able to asume different and important roles: 1) To develop and implement the consultation-liaison approach and the so called bio-psycho-social model in general medical care. 2) To provide an alternative for short term hospitalization in the era of the closing of hospitals for the mentally ill. 3) To provide a structure able for teaching of medical students and the training of postgraduated and 4) to stimulate psychiatric research.

Health care is developing towards a community care following an ecological model, assumed by health authorities, lay persons and many professionals, not devoid of pitfalls. The model of General Hospital Psychiatry can be a good one to be expanded to the community, although it has barely overcomed shown the deep rooted resistances of medicine towards psychosocial problems.

3068

THE INVOLVEMENT OF PSYCHIATRY IN PROMOTING MENTAL HEALTH
Prof. Jochen Neumann, Prof. Peter Voss
Deutsches Hygiene-Museum in der DDR Dresden

There are many industrialized countries where the responsibility of the psychiatrist is thought to begin where clinically relevant mental disorders are manifest or can be predicted with a high degree of probability. However, if psychiatrists of today wish to retain their role and their voice in public affairs they have to realize the expanding social role of their discipline. Psychiatry, as one of Medicine's main branches, has to take into account the issues of health, as these were conceived by WHO, several years ago and encompass into its professional responsibility even cases with no clear signs of an emerging disease. In contrast to the health of the body, "Mental Health" is not only the health of the psyche. It mainly refers to the relationship between the individual and the environment. It is important to emphasize this in order to avoid misunderstandings, by construing mental health as the counterpart of mental disease. Features of mental health are: positive attitude to one's self, self-realization, integration, autonomy, correct observation of the reality and one's competence. Psychiatry - together with other professional categories will probably have to advise decicion-makers at all levels and leaders of major target groups, motivating and enabling them to organize the psycho-social setting of human relations, individual lifestyles and the natural and architectural environment in such a way that they are conducive to good health.

Session 472 Symposium:
Concept of "Einheitspsychosen": Pro and contra

3069
THE DENOSOLOGICAL CONCEPT
H.M.van Praag,M.D.,Ph.D. Professor and Chairman
Albert Einstein College of Medicin, New York, USA
Classical nosology has been the major cornerstone of biological psychiatric research; finding biological markers and eventually causes of disease entities has been the major goal. Another approach one we have designated as "functional", seems possible, attempting to correlate biological variable with psychological dysfunctions, the latter being considered to be the basic units of classification in psychopathology. We have pursued this route for many years, and based on the resulting findings we formulated the following hypthesis. Signs of diminished DA, 5HT and NA metabolism, as have been found in psychiatric disorders, are not disorder-specific, but rather are related to psychopathological dimensions; i.e. hypoactivity/inertia; increased aggression/anxiety and anhedonia, independent of the nosological framework in which these dysfunctions occur. Implications of the functional approach for psychiatry are discussed, including a shift from nosological to functional application of psychotropic drugs. Functional psychopharmacology will be dysfunction-oriented and therefore insuitably geared towards utilizing drug combination. This prospect is hailed as progress, both practically and scientifically.
H.M.van Praag, G.M.Asnis, R.S.Kahn, S.L.Brown, M.Korn, J.M. Harkavy Friedman, S.Wetzler, Monoamines and Abnormal Behavior, A Multi-Aminergic Perspective, In Press Br J Psych, 1989

3070
Prognostic validity of cycloid psychoses
M. Lanczik, J. Fritze and H. Beckmann
Department of Psychiatry
University of Wuerzburg / West-Germany
31 patients were diagnosed in 1985 as having a cycloid psychosis according to K. Leonhard. 26 (83,2%) of them were reached in a catamnestic study in 1989. 23 (73,6%) of them were classified by means of SADS according to RDC and DSM-III-R. All reevaluated patients had gone through a period of complete remission after their dismissal in 1985 and undergone a phasic course of there disease. According to RDC, 10 (43,5%) of the 23 patients suffered from some subtype of schizophrenia, 8 (38,8%) from a schizoaffective and 5 (21,7%) from an affective psychosis. According to DSM-III-R, 16 (69,6%) patients had a schizophrenic, schizophreniform or paranoid psychosis, 3 (13%) a schizoaffective and 5 (21,7%) an affective psychosis. These results demonstrate that the prognostic validity of the concept of cycloid psychoses of K. Leonhard is superior to the concepts of RDC as well as DSM-III-R.

3071
THE CONCEPT OF UNITARY PSYCHOSIS: HISTORY AND PERSPECTIVES
H.Sass, M.D.
Psychiatric Clinic, University of Munich, FRG

The venerable concept of unitary psychosis has been a focus of nosological discussions since the emergence of schientific psychiatry. In the tradition of german-speaking psychiatry its protagonists Zeller, Griesinger, Neumann and Kahlbaum favoured "Stadienlenren", i.e. conceptions of regular sequences with certain stages in the development of unitary psychosis. In contrast, authors like Kleist and Leonhard proposed differentiated nosologies based on brain pathology. The Kraepelinian dichotomy of manic-depressive and schizophrenic disorders holds a midline position. Since then, psychiatric research provides more and more doubts concerning the possibility of exact delineation in the field of endogenous psychoses. Also the majority of biological findings is not consistent with the idea of nosological specifity. The concept of unitary psychosis allows for an integration of anthropological, psychopathological and biological approaches. An important contemporary contribution is the structural dynamic theory of Janzarik who emphasizes unitarian aspects in a comprehensive interpretation of the entire field of mental disorders.

3072
THE UNITARY PSYCHOSES APPROACH ON THE LEONHARDIAN CONCEPT
G.-E.Kühne, O. Khir
Dept. of Psychiatry of the Friedrich-Schiller-University, Jena, DDR-6900, GDR
The concept of unitary psychoses assumed a continuum from healthy to ill including individual factors and biological conditions, presuming dispositions, schizophrenic and affective predominances, accepting the broad field of intermediate (schizoaffective) psychoses. H.Rennert (1965, 1982) developed the theory further as the "Universal Genesis of Psychoses".
In principle the Leonhardian classification is done on the symptomatology, the course, and the end stage. We decided to take advantage of both the syndromatical axes of the Unitary Psychoses Concept and Leonhard's original description in an attempt to find out subdividing the spectrum of
- Periodicity resp. "Verlaufstyp"
- Schizophrenic symptomatology
- Deficiency resp. Restitutio ad integrum
- Fluctuating symptomatology
into nosological components.
These parameters enabled us to define an approach to a unitarian psychoses interpretation of the Leonhardian concept.

3073

UNITARY PSYCHOSIS
Sir Martin Roth
University of Cambridge Clinical School

The modern concept of unitary psychosis is a revival of an old theory. It is derived largely from observations that disclose an overlap between the clinical features of schizophrenia and affective disorder. It also stems in part from genetical observations and to some extent from the effects of pharmacological treatment. The findings in each of these fields are open to interpretations other than those which have led to the contemporary concept of unitary psychosis. This is of little value in clinical practice and is unfruitful for scientific enquiry.

Session 473 Symposium:
Mental health problems of offenders

3074

SUICIDE SCREENING IN REMAND CENTRES

J. Arboleda-Florez, M.D. University of Calgary, H. Holley, M.A., University of Calgary, C. Bowhay, M.A., Calgary General Hospital, Calgary, Canada

This paper comprises the final summary of a program of 4 research projects undertaken in conjunction with correctional personnel in the Province of Alberta (Canada). The major aim was to develop a suicide checklist for use in Remand Centres. The first project developed a pool of clinical and historical items which were potential discriminators of suicide risk among remanded inmates and the second project tested the reliability of these items. The goal of the third project was to field-test the revised checklist in order to assess face validity and situational appropriateness. Finally, the fourth study examined the ability of the checklist to predict which inmates would, throughout the course of their remand, require "special handling" due to suicide behaviours or risk. The checklist was found to be reliable and valid and easily used by clinical staff who are under pressure to quickly screen inmates for special housing requirements.

3075

Treatment of 'Psychopathic Disorder' in an English Special Hospital
Dr Adrian Grounds
Institute of Criminology
Cambridge
England

'Psychopathic Disorder' is one of the categories of mental disorder specified in the English Mental Health Act 1983. Small numbers of such patients are admitted to Special Hospitals from the courts under hospital orders. One ward in an English Special Hospital which admits young male patients in this category is described. An approach which integrates psychodynamic, behavioural and cognitive principles, and which attempts to understand patients' personality difficulties and offences in terms of their emotional and cognitive development, is adopted as a useful framework for formulating treatment needs and objectives. Within the ward setting a variety of psychological treatments are offered. However, the social environment within the hospital limits opportunities for realistic assessment and rehabilitation. A number of critical issues will be raised concerning the detention of such offenders in Special Hospitals for treatment.

3076

FORENSIC ASPECTS OF ARMED ROBBERIES IN MELBOURNE, AYSTRALIA.
Dr. Andreas Kapardis
La Trobe University, Legal Studies Department, Bundorra, Victoria, Australia 3083.

A number of assumptions underlie(a) the decision by Magistrates whether to release on bail people charged with armed robbery (b)sentencing decisions by judges who often justify their sentences in terms of deterrence and (c) decisions by the Parole Board. The paper reports a study of 100 armed robbers serving their sentences in goals in Victoria, Australia that has tested the validity of a number of assumptions by examining 187 characteristics relating to the offence, the offender and the victim, focusing in particular on how armed robbers think about,plan(if at all),carry out and reflect upon their offending. It was found that arrested armed robbers nowadays tend to be recidivists,often drug addicts,in breach of either parole or bail.Convicted armed robbers'characteristics are,for example, 87% aged 25 or less,29% from broken families,38% suffer from hepatitis,54% addicted to illegal drugs, 78% school drop-outs,14%had been treated by a psychiatrist,71% were graduates of the juvenile system, 42% had been to prison more than twice before, the sample examined had been convicted of 1822 crimes. Also,the type of armed robber(i.e.loner,dyad or gang)correlates significantly with type of target selected and violence used.
 Finally,the paper discusses policy implications arising out of the findings.

3077
Psychiatric Services in Prisons - A Canadian Experience.

Dr. C. Roy, Consultant Psychiatrist Vancouver, British Columbia, Canada

In 1972 Canada took a bold step in establishing a special committee under the chairmanship of Dr. Chalke to deal with the issue of psychiatric problems amongst prison inmates. Dr. Chalke's report was accepted. It was agreed to establish 5 regional medical centres in Canada to meet the health care needs of Canadian Federal inmates. It was intended that the medical administrators would operate the centres as a medical enterprise in collaboration with prison administration.
The author had the priviledge to run such a centre in Abbotsford, B.C. for 10 years. He was able to demonstrate that a good efficient Psychiatric Hospital can operate in a correctional system. Despite apprehension and criticism of colleagues, he was able to demonstrate that health care professionals can render valuable services in a prison setting without compromising their professional ethics.

The author will discuss the negative impact of recent changes in Government policy in Canada.

3078
ASSESSMENT AND PREDICTION OF VIOLENCE IN PRISONERS
Dr. A. N. Singh, Hamilton Psychiatric Hospital, Hamilton, Ontario, Canada

Forensic psychiatrists have to meet daily the difficult challenge of assessing and predicting the violence in prisoners for the sake of prisoners, staff of prison, court and society.
Assessment of total psychological profile of the prisoner is an essential first step, not only for the treatment planning but also provides data base of predicting the violence.
Prediction of violence is defined as a sequential post hoc decision-making process which leads to future statements of threatened, attempted or consummated physical harm to self, others or properties. It rests on consummated violence, except of war and with no moral judgement.
Past history of violence, pressure of triggering stimuli and opportunity are important factors. Prediction should be time limited and should have projected impact of any planned treatment regime.

Session 474 Symposium:
Diagnosis and treatment of childhood hyperkinetic disorders

3079
ADHD & CONDUCT DISORDER

J.S. Werry, University of Auckland, New Zealand

Differentiating ADHD & Conduct Disorder is a difficult and often ignored problem. In the United States there is overdiagnosis of ADHD and underdiagnosis of Conduct Disorder and vice-versa in the United Kingdom. The reasons for the problem are:

1) ADHD & CD often co-exist and partial diagnosis is a hazard;

2) ADHD & CD share certain symptoms which allow diagnostic slippage;

3) ADHD is a "better" diagnosis.

As a result much of the literature on ADHD from the United States actually cannot be differentiated from what is true of CD.

Such data as are available suggest that ADHD is a cognitive disorder, CD a product of social learning and ADHD plus CD a more serious disorder with features of both.

A solution to this diagnostic dilemma lies in better diagnostic instruments and diagnostic processes independent of diagnoses.

3080
THE COGNITIVE DYSFUNCTION OF ATTENTION-DEFICIT DISORDER (ADD)
H. Bruce Ferguson, Ph.D., Royal Ottawa Hospital

This presentation will review relevant research from a number of perspectives:

(1) attempts to define the attention deficits shown by ADD children;

(2) studies describing broader cognitive and metacognitive deficits shown by these children;

(3) reports of neurophysiological (e.g. averaged evoked potentials) variables associated with cognitive processes; and

(4) neuropsychological investigations of ADD children.

This information will be integrated to develop a comprehensive cognitive model of ADD which may assist in an evaluation and treatment.

3081

THE UCI SCHOOL-BASED DAY-TREATMENT PROGRAM FOR CHILDREN WITH ADHD & ODD
James M. Swanson, Ph.D.
University of California Irvine

The UCI school-based day-treatment program is a year-long clinical program based on the principles and techniques of behavior modification. It is designed to provide daily treatment on a long-term basis for children with disruptive behaviors of childhood, the most common of which are attention deficit hyperactivity disorder (ADHD) and oppositional defiant disorder (ODD).
Sophisticated token systems are used to deliver intensive interventions in two settings:
1. In a classroom of 12 children, a response cost program is used which covers 5 categories of behavior.
2. In small groups of 6 children social skills training (SST) and cognitive-behavioral therapy (CBT) are provided by trained counsellors supervised by a behavioral psychologist.
The behavioral techniques for the classroom's low density interval schedule of reinforcement and the SST/CBT groups high denisty schedule of continuous reinforcement will be described. The response of various subgroups of ADHD/ODD children to this non-pharmacological treatment will be discussed.

3082

TREATMENT OF HYPERKINETIC CHILDREN. - SOCIAL, ETHICAL, & POLITICAL ISSUES
Robert L. Sprague
University of Illinois

Hyperkinetic children have been treated with stimulant medication in the USA since the late 1930's. In the 1960's a number of research projects on hyperkinesis were started, and the prevalence of use of stimulant medication increased considerably about the same time.
There have been a number of reactions to these trends in the 1980's with questions being raised about treating children with medication for conditions that primarily involve social and educational problems, the ethics of conducting research on children who cannot legally consent for themselves, and, consequently, the role of governmental agencies, such as schools in this kind of treatment. Although there has been a number of lawsuits in the US about the use of neuroleptic medication with handicapped children, there has been little legal controversy, surprisingly, about the use of stimulant medication for children until the late 1980's. The background and the development of these issues will be briefly reviewed.

3083

CHILDHOOD DISRUPTIVE BEHAVIORS -- WORLD-WIDE INVESTIGATION
Jovan G. Simeon, M.D., Royal Ottawa Hospital

Preliminary data suggest that there are important differences among professionals in different countries about the management and therapy of children with hyperkinetic and conduct disorders. These differences are due to theoretical, clinical, social, ethical and cultural factors. To obtain data on the number of such children, their diagnostic evaluation, treatment, use of medication and problems, over 700 questionnaires were sent to professionals in over 96 countries. The findings will be presented, and models and priorities discussed in the light of our own clinical research and experience.

3084

ADD/H: Current Research Issues and Priorities

Lewis M. Bloomingdale, MD, FAPA
New York Medical College, Valhalla, NY 10595, USA

Brief Description & Historical Review: It is now believed that there is a disorder composed of different degrees of severity of 4 factors: Inattention, Hyperactivity, Impulsivity, Defiance/Aggression. There is about 35% covariance with Conduct Disorder and Learning Disorder.
History and nomenclature will be reviewed.
Research: Many investigators believe the disorder includes a number of different sub-groups. Until research diagnostic criteria are established, heterogeneity of research samples introduces considerable variance in different research protocols. Nevertheless, there is sufficient clustering in the disorder that the basic features (impaired attention, impulse control, activity and aggression with other frequently overlapping disorders, particularly CD, LD, and antisocial behavior) may be plotted dimensionally to form a profile. With such profiles for individual patients, new drugs may be tailored and new forms of therapeutic intervention developed, both of which may be used to match an individual child's profile abnormalities.
Treatment: Current issues in multimodal therapies, new drugs and combinations of drugs and PET findings will be discussed.

Session 475 Symposium:
Personal and professional developmental stages and tasks of medical students

3085

DEVELOPMENTAL STAGES AND TASKS OF MEDICAL STUDENTS
Cyril M. Worby, M.D.
University of Nevada School of Medicine
Department of Psychiatry and Behavioral Sciences
Reno, Nevada 89557 U.S.A.

Medicine is both a rewarding and demanding profession. Its practitioners are highly vulnerable to multiple stresses. For too many the result is serious personal and family dysfunction such as chemical dependency, depression, divorce, psychosomatic disorders and suicide. A deeper understanding of the complex developmental processes experienced by the medical student across the four years in training may help faculty and students devise a learning enviornment which minimizes emotional dysfunction and has preventive implications for improved emotional well-being during the practice years. This symposium addresses the medical school years. It seeks to identify normative developmental stages within each year and across the four years and suggests opportunities for prevention of destructive emotional distress in students and their families. Differences in concerns of men and women in training will be addressed as will cross-cultural aspects of medical training.

3086

STRESSES IN THE PROFESSIONAL DEVELOPMENTAL STAGES OF MEDICAL STUDENTS
Grant D. Miller, M.D.
University of Nevada School of Medicine
Department of Psychiatry and Behavioral Sciences
Reno, Nevada 89557 U.S.A.

Similar to the stages described in Erikson's model of personal development, medical students experience professional developmental stages. Medical students also experience a wide range of stresses. Medical education literature is replete with descriptions of medical student stressors but has largely ignored linkages between the effects of stress and the students' normative developmental stages. This paper reviews and discusses models which reflect the developmental stages of medical students and cites relevant empirical studies. The author also reports on his four year longitudinal study monitoring stress throughout medical school. The results suggest a strong relationship between stress and the developmental stages of medical students. As the developmental tasks of each stage are addressed, worked through and reasonably mastered, stress is reduced.

3087

COPING WITH MARRIAGE AND PARENTING IN MEDICAL SCHOOL
Marsha Worby, M.S.S., Ph.D.
University of Nevada School of Medicine
Department of Family and Community Medicine
Reno, Nevada 89557 U.S.A.

Although almost unheard of in the 1920s, the married medical student, often with children, is now commonplace in the United States. When experienced concurrently, being a medical student, being married and being a new parent may lead to dysfunction in one or more of these roles. Cumulative demands of conflicting developmental tasks frequently lead to spousal complaints of loneliness, lack of personal identity consolidation, diminished couple intimacy, and ineffective interpersonal processes to manage conflicting needs and agendas. Some of these medical school marriages appear to be "suspended" emotionally pending the promise of relief at the time of graduation. However, postponing developmental tasks in a marriage often leads to increased personal and family dysfunction during medical school and beyond. Suggestions are offered for minimizing the untoward effects of these realities of medical training.

3088

COMPARING STRESSORS AFFECTING U.S. AND ARABIAN GULF MEDICAL STUDENTS
Karen Lanphear, M.Ed., A.B.D.
University of Nevada-Reno
College of Education
Reno, Nevada 89557 U.S.A.

Whereas European medical schools associated with universities had their origins in the 9th century medical school in Salerno, the modern era of U.S. medical education was initiated by the Flexner report of 1910. In our time, a number of countries in the process of modernization have adapted the U.S. model of medical education to meet the needs of its people. To what degree can a model of medical education developed in a Western medical tradition be transferred to a very different culture without inducing major conflict and stress among faculty, students, patients and traditional practitioners? This paper reports preliminary findings of a study comparing motivation, barriers and career aspirations of medical students in a recently organized Arabian Gulf medical school with those of students in a 20 year old U.S. medical school. Cultural similarities and differences will be addressed as they bear upon the socialization of young men and women into the profession of medicine.

3089
LITIGATION BETWEEN THE STUDENT AND THE MEDICAL SCHOOL
Leslie Miller, M.A., J.D.
Nevada Public Service Commission
727 Fairview Drive
Carson City, Nevada 89710 U.S.A.

Though infrequent, legal action brought by the student against medical school authorities occurs at various points across the four years of medical school. Such action may be initiated when the student believes he or she has been wronged through adverse decisions made by administrative authorities. Most often such contested decisions revolve around refusal to admit to medical school, the forcing of a student to withdraw temporarily for non-cognitive (unacceptable interpersonal behaviors) or cognitive (course failure) reasons and refusal of the faculty to graduate a student. Such litigation may be viewed within a developmental perspective, i.e. failure of the student to complete his or her developmental tasks to the satisfaction of the medical school faculty or administration. This paper reviews the way in which the legal process is invoked during medical school and suggests ways in which medical schools and students can either avoid or prepare for such proceedings.

3090
MINIMIZING MEDICAL STUDENT STRESS THROUGH ORGANIZATIONAL MEANS
Joel Lanphear, Ph.D.
United Arab Emirates University
Faculty of Medicine and Health Sciences
P.O. Box 15551
Al Ain, Abu Dhabi, United Arab Emirates

From experience as Associate Dean responsible for administrative and curricular affairs in a U.S. and a newly created Arabian Gulf medical school, the author discusses how organizational and structural variables affect medical student stress throughout the four year medical school experience. While certain structures and procedures are dictated by forces outside the school's control (accreditation and licensure requirements), there remains considerable leeway in how faculty, administration and students interact to create an optimum learning environment. A review of such efforts (including the General Professional Education of the Physician report) will be presented, with a special emphasis on cross-cultural factors bearing on these issues.

3091*

* Number left open for technical reasons not corresponding to any abstract

Session 476 Symposium:
Emergency psychiatry

3092
ESSAI DE COMPREHENSION DU CONCEPT D'URGENCE PSYCHIATRIQUE A TRAVERS DIFFERENTS MODES DE PRISE EN CHARGE DE L'URGENCE DANS PLUSIEURS PAYS

Dr J. HOAREAU - HOPITAL COCHIN - PARIS

L'urgence psychiatrique sera d'abord définie dans son acception habituelle :
- l'urgence à intervenir est déterminée par la pathologie ou l'état de crise (la demande)
- l'urgence sera ensuite envisagée comme la réponse urgente à intervenir (la réponse)
- enfin nous essaierons à travers une comparaison de différents systèmes de prises en charge dans plusieurs pays de la définir à travers son mode organisationnel (l'organisation).

3093

EVOLUTION AND FUTURE DIRECTIONS OF PSYCHIATRIC EMERGENCY SERVICES IN THE U.S.A.

Gerard Sunnen M.D.

In the past 25 years there have been major shifts in the way psychiatric care has been provided in the United States. Emergency psychiatric services, in synchrony, have evolved in a variety of directions to respond to new needs, and to accomodate governmental and economic forces that determine the logistics of health care.

This presentation focuses on the evolving role of acute psychiatric care in the United States, its inter-relationships with community services and agencies, and its response to changing psychiatric populations and patterns of psychopathology.

3094

AMBULANT SERVICES FOR EMERGENCY PSYCHIATRY IN THE NETHERLANDS (1983-1988)

H.H.P. VERGOUWEN
Regional Institute for Post-graduate Education, Utrecht

There are 58 regional ambulant services in the country since 1983 ; 44 of them did sent back questionnaires about their structure and working-methods both in 1984 an in 1988.
Three organisational models can be discerned (the sub-regional, regional and supra-regional) and there are correspondent differences in functioning.
The services are working with a two-step-model ; the manpower-problem is diminishing but not gone.
In the urban areas the services are more frequently used and there is a much higher rate of hospital admissions in these regions. Research about the results of these services is increasing.
The satisfaction of the refferring professions about there ambulant services correlates with the accessibility of the services.
Post-graduate courses can be followed now in 7 institutes spread about the country, to entrance the stills in treating emergencies.

3095

"HOW TO CATCH THE PSYCHOTIC PATIENT" :
EMERGENCY PSYCHIATRY IN THE MIDDLE OF HOLLAND
J.B. VAN LUYN
Regional Institute for Post-graduate Education, Utrecht

What needs to be done when a general practitioner full speed left the spot where a psychotic woman threatened to kill herself and her children, and now calls for your help.

Psychiatric emergencies, especially when they involve danger, require immediate professional halp, often at the spot. They are a threat to all involved : patients, their system an professionals. Their essentials will be described.

Flexible, organizational models are a prerequisite for doing emergency psychiatry : they set the limit for methods and techniques.

In the so called "Utrecht Model" a large ambulatory Emergency Treatment Unit with outreaching facilities offers 7 x 24 hours, immediate help. It's structure andfunctions will be described.

Emergency Psychiatry also requires a large arsenal of methods an techniques. They range from constraining methods, network-intervention to the use of techniques derived from communication- an systemtheory`an behaviortheory. Some examples will be presented.

The ultimate goal nevertheless is always simple : safety for those involved. Emergency Psychiatry so, is "not easy, but simple" : in organization, goals, methods and techniques.

3096

Clinical and epidemiological evaluation of sample of 457 psychiatric emergencies seen in general hospital

D. CREMNINTER Hôpital HENRI MONDOR - CRETEIL - FRANCE
A. MEIDINGER Hôpital HENRI MONDOR - CRETEIL - FRANCE
C. PAYANT Lavoratoire de biostatistiques HOPITAL NECKER - Paris
I. FERRAND Hôpital COCHIN - Paris
M. NICOLAIDOU Laboratoire de Biostatistiques HOPITAL NECKER - Paris
R. TEIVISSEN HOPITAL EHNRI MONDOR - CRETEIL
J. FARMANIAN Laboratoire de Biostatistiques HOPITAL NECKER - Paris

All the patients seen at the emergency room of general hospital for a psychiatric symptomatology were studied on a two years period during 12 weeks choosen at random every 2 months. 457 patients composed of 42,2 % of suicidal attemps and 57,8 % of other psychiatric emergencies were included. They were composed of 279 women and 178 men. We studied the previous psychiatric history, the social, marital and professional status and the clinical diagnosis according to DSMIII criteria. The reactive factors and the degree of acceptation of the therapeutic orientations are also indicated

3097
PSYCHIATRIC CONSULTATION IN THE EMERGENCY ROOM OF THE GENERAL HOSPITAL
ZUMBRUNNEN R.
PSYCHIATRY AND MEDICAL PSYCHOLOGY UNIT, HOPITAL CANTONAL UNIVERSITAIRE. GENEVA. SWITZERLAND

Despite a dramatic increase in offer of spezialized psychiatric services in Geneva (Switzerland) since 15 years, the emergency room of the general hospital remains a major provider of psychiatric emergendy care in the city. The paper describes the organization of the psychiatric consultation in the "medical and surgical" emergency ward of the university general hospital. Transversal and longitudinal data (1970 through 1985) on the patients and interventions are presented. Characteristics of psychiatric practice in a high technology medical center are outlined. Benefits and difficulties inherent to the consultation-liaison model of emergency psychiatry are mentioned. The central role of the emergency room psychiatric consultation among other mental health structures is emphasized, as well as its didactic value for residents in psychiatry and for non-psychiatric residents and nurses.

3098
Réflexions autour du moment de la rencontre entre un patient psychotique et la "loi de 1838".

JEANVOINE Michel "URGENCES-PSYCHIATRIE"
17, rue P Lescot PARIS-75001-

Cette réflexion est le fruit d'un travail réalisé au domicile de patients psychotiques et en "situation d'urgence". Cette rencontre d'un patient et de la loi du 30 juin 1838 semble être un moment tout-à-fait privilégié du parcours que peut effectuer un patient psychotique. Une rencontre ayant des caractéristisques bien précises, un caractére inéxorable, automatique; une rencontre qu'il semble, d'ailleurs, solliciter <u>sans le savoir</u>. L'expérience montre que dans un certain nombre de situations on pourrait dire qu'il "est possible de se passer de cette loi, à la condition de s'en servir". Derrière ce qui pourrait se présenter comme des évidences parait oeuvrer une logique. Mais de quelle logique s'agit-il?

Session 477 Symposium:
Mental health care in Greece

3099
ORGANIZATION OF MENTAL HEALTH CARE DELIVERY SYSTEM: POLICY AND PLANNING
M. Malliori, M.D.
Dept. of Psychiatry, Univ. of Athens, Greece

In the past decades, the main characteristics of health services and especially mental health services in Greece have been the large size of the private sector on the one hand and the fragmentary and highly centralized nature of the public sector on the other.
The Greek policy as expressed in Law 1397/1983 on the National Health System refers in article 21 specifically to psychiatric care. Central planning for the delivery of Mental Health Care is discussed and economic parameters are analyzed. The progress and difficulties of psychiatric reform in Greece are highlighted. Special attention is given to the establishment of a monitoring and evaluation system which will fulfill our initial goals.

3100
THE EVOLUTION OF THE CONCEPT OF THE (COMMUNITY) MENTAL HEALTH CENTER IN GREECE
N. Manos
2nd Univ. Dept. of Psychiatry, Community Mental Health Center, Thessaloniki, Greece

A brief historical review identifies the progressive evolution of the concept of the (Community) Mental Health Center in Greece (Mental Hygiene Centers, Community Mental Hygiene Center, Institute for Community Psychiatry, Community Mental Health Center etc., Mental Health Center as described in Law 1397 of the National Health System).
The basic functions of the C.M.H.C. are highlighted and specific reference to the Mental Health Centers and mobile Units of Northern Greece concludes the presentation.

3101

COMMUNITY MENTAL HEALTH NEEDS AND PLANNING IN GREATER ATHENS AND SOUTHERN GREECE
Michael Madianos, M.D. MPH
Community Mental Health Center, Dept. of Psychiatry
University of Athens

During the last decade serious psychiatric reforms have taken place in several Southern European countries with the development of decentralized mental health services and the deinstitutionalization of the long-stay mental patients.
In Greece, during this period the importance of the development of community based comprehensive mental health services, alternatives to inpatient care in the existing large mental hospitals was commonly accepted. It has to be noted that the first Community Mental Health Center in Greece serving a catchment area of Greater Athens started its operation in 1979. Since that time few centers have been developed in Athens, despite the planning of integrated mental health services in the National Health System and the E.E.C. financial support.
In this report the existing mental health services for all ages in Greater Athens and the Southern Greece will be presented. The planning of the development of a complete community mental health care system to meet the needs of the local population, based upon the existing epidemiological estimates will be also analysed.

3102

SECONDARY MENTAL HEALTH CARE: THE GENERAL HOSPITAL PSYCHIATRIC UNITS IN GREECE
Angelopoulos, N., Liakos A.
Dept. of Psychiatry, University of Ioannina, Greece

The development of Psychiatric Units in General Hospitals could be regarded as one of the most significant dimensions of the Psychiatric Reform in Greece. The role of social, cultural, economic and political factors in the development or inhibition, acceptance or rejection of this reform, is presented and discussed with special focus on the General Hospital Psychiatric Units. Since the age of almost all of these units is less than five years, the experience related to their work is just now emerging and a discussion regarding the problems they face is necessary.
Thus, mention is made of problems which could shape the way these units work such as: the topographic position of the Psychiatric Unit and its structural relationship with the other Departments of the Hospital; quantitative and qualitative features of the staff; catchment area; out-patient department and the danger of its functional collapse; criteria for admission and diagnostic categories of the in-patients; how long do the patients stay in the department?
Revolving-door patients and new chronic patients; Liaison Psychiatry; training and Education; research.

3103

TERTIARY MENTAL HEALTH CARE - PSYCHIATRIC HOSPITALS
N.Zachariadis, M.D.
Attica Psychiatric Hospital, Athens, Greece

The only existing services for the treatment of psychiatric patients since the last two decades were 8 Psychiatric Hospitals, the Athens University Psychiatric Department and one Children's Psychiatric Hospital. The emphasis on hospitalization has contributed to serious over-crowding of these Mental Hospitals which were inadequate with low therapeutic capacities and situated in the two main urban areas of Greece. A large number of psychiatric patients was covered by the private sector. During recent years a significant reduction of inpatient cases has been observed.
In this presentation factors that have influenced this change concerning the three levels of care will be discussed.

3104

THEORY AND PRACTICE OF DEINSTITUTIONALIZATION IN GREECE
K. Bairaktaris
Psychiatric Hospital, Thessaloniki, Greece

The evolution of psychiatric reform in Greece during the last years is defined by factors related to general socio-cultural and political circumstances, that is the attitude of the state and the society towards mental illness and madness.
Special mention, based on the evaluation of experiences in psychiatric hospitals, is made to those circumstances that influence the process of deinstitutionalization in Greece.
The expansion of a theory and practice taking into consideration the specific circumstances prevailing in Greece, after critical evaluation of the experiences in other countries, is the author's basic concern in order for a wholescale reform to be established; this would require something more than the mere modernization of existing institutional care, a phenomenon observed in many other countries.

3105
EXPERIENCE FROM ABROAD: A PERSONAL VIEW
N. Bouras
Division of Psychiatry, Guy's Hospital, London, UK

The emphasis of community care over the last decade characterized by the resettlement of residence from long-stay institutions, the increased interest on the non-medical model and the involvement of different professional groups has provided a unique experience.
Issues on planning and developing services to meet individual needs, but adapted to local requirements, have proved to be of great importance. Consumers participation, quality of life and changing needs are inherent factors. Service monitoring evaluation should be built in within any plan.
This report presents an overview of the current trends on developing psychiatric services and highlight some of the difficulties, problems and successes involved.

Session 478 Symposium:
Therapeutic community and psychotherapy integration

3106-3112
THERAPEUTIC COMMUNITY AND PSYCHOTHERAPY INTEGRATION
F.Knobloch, Professor Em., University of British Columbia, Vancouver, Canada; P.Schwartz, Clinical Assist.Prof., the same; Y.K.Tsegos, President of I.G.A., Athens, Greece; J.S.Whiteley, former Med. Director, Henderson Hospital, Sutton, U.K.; Wu-Chen-I, Professor, Shantou University, People's Republic of China.
Therapeutic community (ThC) emerged as a powerful tool of behaviour change.
The authors' experiences cover various types of ThCs in different cultures.
Whiteley, the successor of the pioneer M.Jones, deals with the curative factors of ThCs. Tsegos and Wu-Chen-I draw attention to the differences in socio-economic and cultural backgrounds of ThCs.
Whereas some ThCs do not have ambitious psychotherapeutic goals (Jones), Knobloch claims that small ThCs of special type offer the most efficient short-term psychotherapy and can modify personality traits, often believed to be amenable only to long-term therapies. The theoretical implications of different ThC treatments for the integration of psychotherapies will be presented by Schwartz.

Session 479 Special Session:
Issues in ethnopsychiatry

3113
CULTURE, COGNITION AND COSMOLOGY
Vijoy K. Varma
Postgraduate Medical Institute, Chandigarh, India

Increasing exposure to other cultures has brought the awareness that cultures differ from each other in many personality attributes. One such difference involves the cognitive style defined as those processes by which man acquires, transforms and uses information about the world. We all need an ability to perceive and organize material phenomena, to interpret the external real-ity and to make certain predictions about it.
Transcultural differences in the cognitive style can be understood in a continuum ranging from synthetic to analytical. The synthetic cognitive style more largely attributed to the traditional, developing societies of the East, is intuitive and holistic and is field-dependent. The analytic of the industrialised, technologically advanced societies of the West, on the other hand, can be characterised as rational and linear.
The cognitive style is also related to the concept of external reality. The latter includes the nature of objects and phenomena and the concepts of determinism and causality. Although the "scientific" approach has been largely analytic, the deficiencies and limitations of this approach in the understanding of the external reality and the cosmos are increasingly becoming obvious necessitating adoption of holistic, systems approaches

3114
ETHNOPSYCHIATRY AND TRADITIONAL MEDICINE IN MALI: A RESEARCH MODEL.
Roberto Beneduce (1,2), Piero Coppo (1) and Baba Koumare (3).

(1) Expert of Cooperation and Development General Direction (Italy); (2) Dept. of Psychiatry, Mental Health Service, USL 41, Naples (Italy); (3) "Point G" Hospital, Psyc. Division, Bamako (Mali).

A new perspective of interaction and cooperation between conventional psychiatry and traditional medicine in a region of Mali is analyzed. Its epistemological and anthropological presuppositions are considered. Mental disease characteristics in Dogon culture, medical care systems of traditional practitioners and questions about their effectiveness receive special attention. After some considerations on cross-cultural research instruments and assesment problems, and after a brief review of contemporary literature, preliminary results are presented. This paper also emphasizes clinical, social and economic aspects of this choice. The latter, moreover, is consistent and in agreement with Malian health care delivery projects (exploitation of local resources, etc.). Concluding comments suggest that the general hypothesis of this model may be considered as a possible working program for mental health in other developing countries.

3115
PSYCHIATRIE ET THERAPEUTIQUE TRADITIONNELLE AU MAROC

K. RADDAOUI, J.E. KTIOUET, M. PAES
CLINIQUE UNIVERSITAIRE DE PSYCHIATRIE - RABAT-MAROC

Si le recours aux médecines parallèles est d'actualité dans beaucoup de pays industrialisés, la médecine traditionnelle a toujours occupé au Maroc et occupe toujours une place importante dans le système de soins malgré l'introduction de la thérapeutique moderne. Ceci est en rapport avec les caractéristiques socio-culturelles actuelles où les traditions prédominent encore nettement.
A partir d'une enquête auprès de trois cents malades mentaux hospitalisés à Rabat et à Fès, les auteurs analysent la place qu'occupe la médecine traditionnelle dans le domaine de la santé mentale et sa signification, et soulèvent les rapports entre cette dernière et la psychiatrie moderne.

3116
A COMPARISON OF ZULU TRADITIONAL- AND FAITH HEALERS

Wessel H Wessels, University of Natal, PO Box 17039, CONGELLA, 4013, SOUTH AFRICA

A questionnaire on seventeen psychiatric conditions commonly recognized by the Zulu were completed by 50 traditional healers and 50 faith healers from the African Independent Churches. The illnesses included, among others, schizophrenia, bipolar affective disorder and epilepsy but concentrated on Zulu culture specific syndromes. The results show that healers from urban areas are more accepting of Western medical concepts but not of its treatment. The traditional healers gave more consistent answers about symptoms, signs, causes and treatment of the culture specific syndromes. The faith healers had widely divergent ideas about the same illness but all of them exhibited a core of useful knowledge which could be expanded by training. Since they already have credibility in the community it would be wise to incorporate them in the community health team.

3117
ISLAMIC VIEW OF MENTAL ILLNESS AND ITS TREATMENT
Ihsan A. Karaagac, M.D. U.S.A, Osama M. Al Radi, President WIMHA, Taif, Saudi Arabia

The authors review in this presentation the traditional Islamic view of mental illness and its treatment modalities specific to homogenous Islamic culture. The study outlines the historical course of conceptual understanding of mental illness and its clinical manifestations by Islamic medicine and psychiatry in order to provide a historical perspective for delineating the culturally significant diagnostic and therapeutic parameters. As a comparative transcultural study, two groups of patients data (diagnostically and culturally distinct from, and juxtaposed to each other) are selected for clinical analysis and discussion. The Western group is illustrated by U.S. NIMH's data and DSM-III's conceptual orientation; The Saudi Arabia's-orthodox Islamic group-mental health data is provided by senior author, Dr. Al Radi of the Kingdom of Saudi Arabia. Selected diagnostic categories are limited to depression and catatonic illness as viewed under Islamic classical psychiatry vis-a-vis DSM-III. Theoretical and clinical analyses are focused on the issue of diagnosis and therapeutic outcome by defining culturally significant parameters relevant to Islamic and American psychiatry.

3118
EVALUATION OF THE DIFFICULT PATIENT IN TAIWAN

WEN JUNG-KWANG, YANG MING-JEN, WEI FU-CHYUAN

Department of Psychiatry, Kaohsiung Medical College, Kaohsiung, Taiwan, R. O. C.

The difficult situations encountered in the department of psychiatry of a general hospital were evaluated phenomenologically to characterize the psychodynamics and illness behavior in the contex of Chinese culture.

A sample of 26 cases (13 females, 13 males; age range: 18-57.) were collected consecutively if they met the inclusion criteria during a period of 6 months. By DSM-III criteria, there were 14 cases with Schizophrenic disorders, 6 Personality disorders (2 Borderline personalities), 2 Substance use disorders, 2 Major depression, 1 Somatization disorder, and 1 Dementia.

Among the reasons endangering the therapeutic relationships, overinvolvement by patient's close relatives and transference vs. contertransference were two major issues. The role played by Chinese family in the shaping of illness behavior of difficult patients is worth noting cross-culturally.

3119

"Ethnopsychiatric systems in different cultural areas of Peru"
Prof. Dr. Roberto Llanos Z.
Universidad Cayetano Heredia, Av. Javier Prado Este 1038 - 201; Lima 27, PERU

The main nosologic entities in the Andean region are: 1)Malignant possesion, 2)Harm, 3)Frignt, 4)Bad Omen, 5)Evil Eye, 6)Fall into disgrace, and 7)Loss of friends.
Traditional therapeutic techniques are based on rituals, conjures, and use of plants trying to "clean" the ailing person, or to restore the faith in those who have "lost the spirit". The common aim is to attend the paranoid suceptibility, by projecting into third persons the cause of the pathologic state. Some presentations will require the intervention to overcome a superstitious terror of having offended the spirit. Other cases, especially in children, the belief in a strong or "evil eye" accounts for diverse states that respond to extraction of the bad influence by rubbing an egg on the child. "Falling from grace" of the spirits is treated by penitence. Each ethno cultural school recognizes and respects the traditional healer, under many denominations, (brujo, curandero, shaman, etc.)
All these have their doctrinary beais on animistic and demonic beliefs that are culturally defined.

3120

SUPERSTITIOUS BELIEFS AND ATTITUDES IN GREECE, UNITED KINGDOM AND CHILE

J.Liappas*, A.D.Rabavilas*, B.Vicente** and F.A.Jenner**
*Athens University Dept. of Psychiatry,
** Sheffield University Dept. of Psychiatry

Urban population samples recruited at random from the telephone directory in Athens (Greece), Sheffield (UK) and Conception (Chile) were assessed with respect to their attitudes towards superstitious beliefs. Semantic differential scales were utilized in order to evaluate seven different concepts, i.e. "supernatural powers", "fate", "luck", "white magic", "black magic" and a neutral concept. The findings of this evaluation failed to reveal significant quantitative semantic differences between the populations studied, although some qualitative differentiation was observed with respect to semantic distance of the various superstitious dimensions from the neutral concept.
These findings are discussed with particular reference to the universality of the attitudes towards superstition.

Session 480 Special Session:
Panic disorders: Etiopathogenesis and treatment

3121

GENETIC LINKAGE STUDIES OF
PANIC DISORDER
Crowe RR, Noyes R, Samuelson S,
Wesner R, Wilson RL

Multiplex pedigrees of panic disorder have been studied with DNA probes in search of a gene predisposing to the condition. A provisional linkage finding at the alpha-haptoglobin locus on chromosome 16q22 could not be confirmed in an analysis of 10 new pedigrees. In fact, linkage was excluded up to six centimorgans from the haptoglobin locus.

Present work is focusing on the X-chromosome since an x-linked gene could account for the higher prevalence of panic disorder in women than men. The results of these analyses will be presented.

3122

COMPUTERIZED EEG. ANALYSIS IN PANIC DISORDER.
Etribi, M.A.; Khalil, Afaf H.;
Department of Neurology & Psychiatry, Ain Shams University, Cairo, Egypt.

Panic attacks represent 0.05% of all cases referred for psychiatric treatment in our area (Etribi, et al 1984). A follow-up of these cases show a high rate of relapse of symptoms.
The aetiology of the condition is not known. Some studies sugest an association with mitral prolapse. Mitral prolapse is also considered the second common cause of stroke in young adults in some studies.
This paper presents the computerized EEG. findings in 27 patients diagnosed as panic disorder. The results are discussed in relation to the follow-up of these cases.

3123

Monitoring cognition and physiology in panic disorder and panic attacks.

Drs Larry Evans, Justin Kenardy and Tian P.S. Oei, Anxiety Disorder Clinic, Princess Alexandra Hospital and University of Queensland, Brisbane, Australia.

The present study investigates the relative roles of cognitive and physiological variables in the onset of panic attacks and maintenance of panic disorder. In the first part of the study five patients with panic disorder were assessed over an extended period (6 - 8 hours) in their natural environment using heart rate telemetry and cognitive sampling techniques: in the second part a further five patients with panic disorder and avoidance (agoraphobia) were assessed during in vivo exposure to a focal fear. In all five panic attacks were recorded, two in natural environments and three during exposure. The results indicate that high heart rate alone is insufficient to produce a panic attack and that cognitive factors appear to be important, if not necessary in mediating onset. Implications for treatment are that psychologically-based interventions for panic attacks may be effective if cognitive appraisals of physiology is targetted.

3124

PHENYLALANINE METABOLISM IN PANIC AND OTHER PSYCHIATRIC DISORDERS.
H.Sabelli, M.D., Ph.D. and J.Javaid, Ph.D. Rush University, Chicago, U.S.A.
Phenylacetic acid (PAA) urinary excretion (140 mg $\pm$ 10 mg/day) is decreased in schizophrenics (53 $\pm$ 15 mg/d) and in unipolar (68 $\pm$ 8 mg/d) and bipolar (67 $\pm$ 7 mg/d) and increased in schizoaffective manics (240 $\pm$ 51 mg/d) (Sabelli et al. Science, 1983; J. Clin. Pyschopharm., 1983; J.Clin. Psychiat., 1986; J.Neuropsychiatry, 1989). We have now studied urinary PAA excretion in 30 patients with panic disorder and 9 patients with major depressive disorder and panic attacks. Depressives excreted 66 $\pm$ 23 mg/day of PAA; patients with panic disorder without depression excreted 105 $\pm$ 23 mg/day of PAA, not significantly lower than normal controls. PAA originates from L-phenylalanine largely via its decarboxylation to the amphetamine-like phenylethylamine (PEA). L-phenylalanine loading (2-6 g/d, with pyridoxine) elevated mood in 84% of depressed subjects with bipolar and/or atypical features (N= 75), but induced milder stimulation in 35% of unipolars (N= 33). L-phenylalanine enhanced the action of MAOIs in 17 of 28 patients treated with phenelzine or isocarboxazid). The peripheral decarboxylate inhibitor carbidopa (200 mg/d) effectively controlled psychosis in 2 and ameliorated 2 of 7 schizoaffective treatment-resistant patients, triggering depression in one. These results are compatible with the view that PEA modulates affect, its deficit reducing pleasure and motivation, as observed in depression and schizophrenia, and its excess inducing mania and psychosis. (Supported by McCormick Foundation).

3125

DEPERSONALIZATION IN PANIC DISORDER : CLINICAL, PSYCHOPHYSIOLOGICAL AND BIOCHEMICAL CORRELATES

C.Stefanis, A.D.Rabavilas and M.Markianos, Athens University Medical School Department of Psychiatry, Eginition Hospital, Athens, Greece.

Two groups of patients with panic disorder differing as far as the presence of depersonalization is concerned are compared in this study. The measures employed include certain clinical and personality indices (EPQ, State-Trait Anxiety, Obsessionality, Depression, Hypochondriasis, Direction of Hostility and Locus of Control), electrodermal responses recorded during administration of a series of auditory stimuli (SCL, amplitude, spontaneous activity, laterality and habituation) and biochemical parameters (Plasma DBH, MHPG and Cortisol). Patients with depersonalization show significantly less extraversion ($p<0.005$), more trait ($p<0.01$) and state anxiety ($p<0.005$), more depression ($p<0.005$), more hypochondriasis ($p<0.05$), introverted hostility ($p<0.02$) and externality of locus of control ($p<0.01$). The electrodermal and biochemical measures fail to significantly differentiate the groups. Furthermore, depersonalization as measured by a questionnaire, is significantly and positively correlated with neuroticism ($p<0.01$), introverted hostility and external locus of control ($p<0.001$ for both) and negatively with extraversion ($p<0.01$). These findings suggest that depersonalization in panic disorder depends mostly on the interaction of clinical and personality factors and its presence may merely signify the severity of the psychopathology involved.

3126

HYPERVENTILATION AND 35 % CO_2 IN PANIC DISORDER

Jan Zandbergen, Eric J.L.Griez, Katrien de Loof, Henk Pols. Department of Clinical Psychiatry, State University of Limburg, P.O.Box 616, 6200 MD Maastricht, The Netherlands

In order to investigate the panicogenic effects of hypocarbia and hypercarbia in panic disorder, two experiments were conducted. In the first experiment 11 panic disorder patients and 8 healthy control subjects underwent a hyperventilation provocation test. The word "hyperventilation" was avoided in the instruction to the subjects. End tidal pCO_2 was reduced to less than half of its baseline value. In both patients and controls it resulted in a significant increase in physical symptoms. However, subjective anxiety was hardly affected, and to a similar extent in both groups. In the second experiment 12 panic patients and 11 normal controls underwent a 35% CO_2 challenge as well as a hyperventilation provocation test following a random cross-over design. It was found that the CO_2 challenge in panic patients resulted in significantly more anxiety and anxiety symptoms as compared to the response during the CO_2 challenge in normals and hyperventilation provocation in both patients and normals. It is suggested, that hypocarbia alone is not sufficient to induce anxiety in panic patients. Moreover, it seems that panic disorder patients have a specific hypersensitivity to an increase in pCO_2.

3127
Aggressive Behaviour in Panic Disorder
I. Maremmani, G.C.M. Orsolini, G. Panico°, J.A. Deltito°°, P. Castrogiovanni
Institute of Psychiatry, Pisa University, Italy
°Mental Health Services, USL 19, Regione Liguria, Italy
°°Depression and Anxiety Clinic, New York Hospital, Cornell University, Westchester Division, White Plains, New York, N.Y., U.S.A.

From a neurophysiologic point of view, the Locus Coeruleus has been proposed as a mediator of physiological, behavioral and psychological aspects of fear and anxiety.
Its increased activity, on one hand, leads to the development of "panic attacks", on the other it causes an imbalance of serotonin/dopamine equilibrium, which modulates the aggressive behavior, conditioning it in a defensive way.
Panic disorder is therefore suitable for the study of the relations between neurotransmitter activity and aggressive behavior in man.
The results of the correlations analysis between disorder severity and aggressive features in patients suffering from Panic Disorder allow us to see, even if in an indirect way, the possibility of a relationship between the modifications of serotoninergic and dopaminerig systems relations and defensive aggression: this last seems to be the kind of aggression more strictly and reactively linked to the DAP.

3128
LONG TERM TREATMENT OF PANIC AND AGORAPHOBIA WITH BENZODIAZEPINES
Juan Ramon de la Fuente, M.D.
National Autonomous University of Mexico

The optimal duration of treatment of panic and agoraphobia remains to be established. With benzodiazepines (BZD) when used appropriately, there is a significant reduction in panic attacks and phobic symptoms but a high proportion of patients will experience symptom recurrence if medication is stopped after acute treatment (6-8 weeks). On the other hand, dependence and the development of a withdrawal syndrome upon drug discontinuation have been shown to occur with long-term BZD use. Withdrawal has also been reported after abrupt cessation of low-dose short-term treatment.
To complicate things further, it is not always easy to differentiate clinically between withdrawal symptoms, rebound anxiety and relapse of illness. To clarify some of these issues, evidence from clinical experience, randomized controlled trials and cross-national surveys will be reviewed for its implications for current clinical practice.

3129
THERAPEUTIC EFFECT OF DIFFERENT DRUGS IN THE PANIC CRISIS
Uriarte V., M.D.
Centro Neuropsicopedagogico - Mexico, D.F.

60 patients with panic disturbances were studied, according DSM III-R in a double blind design during 6 weeks. They were valued weekly with the BPRS, AMP and a special scale for panic crisis. To each group of ten, the following substances were given according to the table of alleatory numbers: placebo, buspirone, diazepam, thiaridazine, chlorpramine or amoxapine. We observed a significant therapeutic effect during the first two weeks in 75% of the patients with the last four drugs; with the buspirone the benefit was observed only until the third week and only in 42% of the patients. These results indicate to us, that at this moment, it is not possible to assure the direct participation of a gabenergic mechanism, or at the benzodiacepines' receptor sites to assure the therapeutic capacity of the different substances; in this respect, the author suggests, that the undifferentiated anxiolitic effect, the one which does not have any direct participation at the neurotransmisors level, hypothetically the more significant in panic crisis treatment. On the other hand, it is proposed to develop a pharmacological treatment schedule according to the profile of each patient, and most of all, to its own tolerance to the drugs added to the combination of substances.

3130
COMORBIDITY OF PANIC AND DEPRESSION IN THE ZURICH STUDY OF YOUNG ADULTS

VOLLRATH Margarete and ANGST Jules
Psychiatric University Hospital Zurich
Research Department CH-8029 Zurich/Switzerland

Comorbidity of panic disorder with depression is of increasing interest. Patients with comorbidity of panic and depression are likely to have a poorer overall outcome than those who do not develop depression. Very few epidemiological studies deal with comorbidity regarding these issues. In the prospective epidemiological Zurich study, a cohort of young adults (N=591) were interviewed four times between age 21 and age 30. Subjects with panic disorder with and without depression are compared to those with depression alone and to controls regarding symptoms, treatment rates, subjective suffering, frequency of lifetime suicide attempts, and SCL-90R factor scores. According to most indicators, subjects with panic and depression are more strongly affected than subjects with panic alone. Prospective longitudinal data including the fourth interview wave (1989) will be used for the analysis of outcome. The analyses based on the first three interviews suggest that subjects with panic and depression in the start show more depressions and less remissions at follow-ups than subjects with panic alone.

3131

COMPARATIVE QUANTIFIED ELECTROENCEPHALOGRAPHIC STUDY OF BUSPIRONE VERSUS LORAZEPAM
Menard F., Plaisant D., Debray D.and Dufier J.
Hopital Laennec, France

Both drugs demonstrated comparable clinical efficacity in generalized anxiety. This is an open quantified electroencephalographic study of buspirone 20 mg. vs lorazepam 2.5 mg. as a single dose in 20 healthy volunteers. Each recording was made up of 5 sequences of 30 s. with eyes closed every 30 min. during the 2h. following drug. Results which confirm the absence of significative difference between recordings carried out before drug administration, show very significative difference between buspirone and lorazepam. Lorazepam confirms its ability to increase beta power and to decrease alpha power, alpha reactivity to opening of the eyes and index of laterality. With buspirone, modification of beta power is not significative, but increasing of alpha power, alpha reactivity and index of laterality is observed, especially in temporoparietal areas. This type of data appears to be of great interest to determine the influence of psychotropic drugs on human cerebral electrogenesis.

Session 481 Special Session:
Etiopathogenesis of schizophrenia: Biological correlates

3132

EVIDENCE FOR A SEX CHROMOSOME LOCUS FOR PSYCHOSIS
LE DeLisi[1], TJ Crow[2], J Collinge[2], F Owen[2], K Davies[3], M Lovett[4]

[1]SUNY Stony Brook, Stony Brook, NY; [2]Clinical Research Centre, Harrow, UK; [3]Neuffield Institute, Oxford, UK; [4]Genelabs, Redwood City, Calif.

A number of findings suggest that the sex chromosomes should be examined for a locus for schizophrenia and affective disorders: i) Psychoses are seen more frequently than would be expected amongst individuals with extra X chromosomes (i.e. XXY males and XXX females); ii) gender differences occur in symptoms, age of onset and outcome; iii) relatives of female probands with psychosis are at greater risk for illness than relatives of males; and iv) siblings with psychosis are more likely to be of the same sex than would be expected by chance. While the distal long arm of the X chromosome has been examined in RFLP studies of psychosis and linkages suggested (i.e. Xq27), we have failed to confirm them in our families. However, a location on the short arms of the X and Y chromosomes within the pseudoautosomal region (where recombination takes place in male meiosis) should be considered. For an illness gene within this region, same sex concordance will be seen in paternally rather than maternally derived cases. This was confirmed in a series of 120 families having two or more siblings with psychosis ($p=.01$). Further examination of this region with RFLP's could establish the existance of a psuedoautosomal locus for psychosis.

3133

HEREDITE DE LA SCHIZOPHRENIE: LES RECHERCHES DE GENEVE
J. Constantinidis
University of Geneva, "Morphological Psychopathology", Bel-Air, 1225 Geneva, Switzerland

Nous avons déterminé, pour la population de Genève, l'incidence de la Schizophrénie (SCH) : 1% , et le risque de morbitité pour la SCH : 2,4%. Les risques de morbidité pour la SCH, dans la parenté des SCH, sont significativement plus élevés : 7 ± 2% pour les parents, 17 ± 4% pour les enfants, 14,7 ± 1,3% pour la fratrie, 28,5 ± 5% pour la fratrie, lorsque l'un des parents est SCH. La consanguinité chez les parents des SCH est 10 fois plus élevée (3,5%) que dans la population de Genève (0,35%). L'analyse de ces données permet de formuler l'hypothèse que la SCH est une maladie héréditaire de mode récessif. La fréquence du gène récessif, dans la population de Genève, est de 18,9%, la fréquence des hétérozygotes de 30,6% et la pénétrance de l'état homozygote de 67,5% ; ce dernier chiffre est identique, comme il fallait s'y attendre,
a) au risque de morbidité chez les enfants dont les deux parents sont SCH et
b) à la concordance, pour la SCH, des jumeaux univitellins.
L'étude de nombreuses fratries de SCH pour certains caractères génétiquement déterminés par des gènes chromosomiques, les Marqueurs Chromosomiques et l'application de la méthode statistique des sibpaires de Penrose nous a permis de relever la possibilité de Linkage entre certains caractères et le gène de la SCH. Actuellement et sous l'égide de l'European Science Foundation est reprise sur le plan européen la recherche du Linkage entre SCH et Marqueurs Chromosomiques Enzymatiques en vue de déterminer le chromosome

3134

LATE MATURATIONAL BRAIN CHANGES AND SCHIZOPHRENIA: STATE OF THE HYPOTHESIS

I. Feinberg, MD, Martinez (CA) VA Medical Center and University of California, Davis

In 1982, we advanced the hypothesis that the human brain undergoes a profound maturational change in late childhood and early adolescence. Evidence for this change included: a marked decline in the amplitude of delta waves during sleep, a fall in brain metabolic rate, and a diminished ability to recover from brain injuries, most clearly demonstrated in recovery from aphasia. We suggested that each of these physiological changes could be produced by the decline in synaptic density demonstrated by Huttenlocher. We argued that these pervasive maturational brain changes might occasionally be faulty and thereby cause schizophrenia. Since this hypothesis was advanced, additional data on late brain changes have been reported. In our presentation, we will review these new data and and show how the ontogenetic curves for delta wave amplitude, cortical metabolic rate (measured by PET) and synaptic density each fit a gamma distribution model. We will also consider our model in the context of more recent developmental hypotheses.

3135

FLUCTUATING ASYMMETRY IN SCHIZOPHRENIA:
DERMATOGLYPHIC EVIDENCE
Clive Mellor, Dept. Psychiatry, Memorial Un.,
St. John's, Newfoundland, Canada.

Bilaterally symmetrical structures should be mirror images of one another if the organism develops perfectly. Fluctuating asymmetry is a random non-directional asymmetry resulting from inability to develop along a precisely determined path. It is estimated from the variance of the signed differences between right and left side measurements, the mean of which should be zero. Differences between homologous dermatoglyphic characters have been recently used as measures of fluctuating asymmetry in cleft lip and palate. Dermatoglyphic data for 482 schizophrenics (Br J Psychiatry, 114, 1387 (1968) has now been analysed for evidence of fluctuating asymmetry, using the right/left differences of four measures, finger ridge counts, finger patterns, palmar a-b ridge counts and atd angles. Schizophrenics had a significantly higher level of fluctuating asymmetry than normal controls, on all four measures ($p < .01$). These findings point to reduced developmental stability during early intra-uterine life when the dermatoglyphics form. This could be due to an increased level of intra-uterine insults, or reduced effectiveness, of the polygenic buffering system, attributable to a higher level of homozygosity.

3136

SYNAPTIC REMODELLING IN SCHIZOPHRENIA

R.K.Shelley*, C.M. Regan+, A.Jackson, F.Lyons,
M.L.Martin & C.Maguire.
*St. John of God Hospital, Stillorgan, Dublin, Ireland.
+ Dept. of Pharmacology,U.C.D., Dublin, Ireland.
Schizophrenia has been characterised as a neurodevelopmental disorder. Early neural structuring and final synaptic elaboration is regulated by the neural cell adhesion molecule (N-CAM). It is a cell surface sialoglycoprotein and a soluble fragment appears in serum. N-CAM is associated with neuroplasticity.
Hypothesis: that the expression of N-CAM in schizophrenia will be greater than in controls, especially in those most likely to have neuronal cell loss and thus the greater degree of synaptic remodelling.
Method: Of 40 patients (mean age 36 +/10.1 yrs)who met Feighner's criteria for schizophrenia,18 had mixed positive and negative features and 13 had negative features only. The mean age of 26 healthy normal controls was 33 +/-11.2 yrs(Student's t, NS). Patients were also classified as having either a good or poor clinical outcome with neuroleptics. Serum N-CAM levels were estimated blind using an enzyme-linked immunoabsorbent assay.
Results: Serum N-CAM levels were greater in schizophrenia than controls ($p<0.0001$), with negative features than mixed positive and negative ($p<0.001$),and poor responders than good($p<0.001$).
Discussion: The elevated serum N-CAM levels suggest an increased synaptic turnover which would be consistent with increased synaptic remodelling in schizophrenic patients. This is significantly greater in patients with negative features only. As in postlesional plasticity, this may reflect a compensatory reinnervation of uninjured afferents resulting in the increased formation of new synapses. The expression of N-CAM appears to distinguish between sub-types of schizophrenia, and may also predict outcome.

3137

BORNA DISEASE VIRUS-SPECIFIC ANTIBODIES
IN SCHIZOPHRENIC OUTPATIENTS
Meise U.,Schwitzer J.,Barnas Ch.,Kurz M.,
Herzog S.*,Rott R.*, Hinterhuber H.
Dept. of Psychiatry, Innsbruck, Austria
* Dept. of Virology, Giessen, FRG
Borna disease (BD) naturally occurs in horses and sheep where it causes a rare meningoencephalitis. This neurotropic agent which is considered to be a member of the slow virus group can be transmitted to several species and has been shown to produce behavioral effects in some animal species. Because of a possible involvement of BD-virus in the etiology of human mental disorders a few studies have been conducted. In psychiatric patients BD-virus specific antibodies (BDVA) could be detected in a range of 0.5-6.8 %(normal controls 0-2%). In our sample the sera 107 outpatients-93 schizophrenia,14 mood disorders (DSM III R)-from an BD nonendemic area (48 m, 59 f; mean age 43.3 SD 13.2, duration of illness 15.3 SD 9.4 years) were analysed for BDVA by an indirect immunoflorescence focus assay. 1.9% of the whole sample-2 patients; one schizophrenic -showed BDVA.Although a clear correlation between BD and mental-especially schizophrenic-disorder remains to be demonstrated the possibility exists that the etiology of at least some types of schizophrenia may be traced to specific infectious phenomena.

3138

Specific receptor alteration by persistent viral infection of neuronal cells in vitro as a molecular model of psychosis.
M.Halbach, U.Henning, G.Scheidt
Psychiatrische Klinik der Universität
Düsseldorf, Bergische Landstraße 2, D-4000
Düsseldorf, FRG
Infections of the central nervous system by specific neurotropic viruses under certain circumstances are accompanied by typical psychiatric symptoms sometimes resembling the signs of psychosis. We have used several experimental in vitro systems of persistently virus infected culture cells with glial and neuronal properties to study the molecular mechanisms underlying subtle (non-cytocidal) effects of virus infection on specialized cell membrane functions. These membrane located systems, needed for cell-cell communication, are also suspected to be specifically impaired in drug-induced psychosis or, following a pharmacologically based hypothesis, in schizophrenia.
Our studies examining the influence of specific viruses on membrane receptors and receptor dependent functions of signal transduction allow to conclude, that i) not only a decrease but also an increase in membrane receptor number can be observed under specific viral influence and ii) that the specificity of viral attack on specialized cell systems seems to depend on characteristics of the host cell rather than on the properties of the virus itself.

3139

HETEROGENEITY OF SCHIZOPHRENIC PATIENTS AS DEFINED BY PLASMA BENZYLAMINE OXIDASE LEVELS

Rui Vieira, Maria Azevedo, Bracinha Vieira e Carlos Manso - Clínica Psiquiátrica Universitária e Instituto de Química Fisiológica - Faculdade de Medicina de Lisboa - Portugal

Plasma benzylamine oxidase (BzAO) activity was analysed in a group of 76 schizophrenic patients and compared with that of healthy controls (n=95). Plasma BzAO was significantly decreased in schizophrenics as whole (mean $\pm$ SD=24,7$\pm$7,5 versus 30,3$\pm$7,1 in controls; t=4,97, p<0,001). When patients were divided according to clinical characteristics it was found that the following items were significantly associated to low levels of plasma BzAO: family history of affective disorders, absence of mental deterioration at time of blood collection, significant life events, predominance of hallucinations and delusions, conserved affect, presence of affective symptoms in clinical picture and good response to neuroleptics.

The clinical and biological significance of the identification of a biochemical alteration is stressed and we suggest that BzAO may be a marker of a subgroup of schizophrenic patients and that the possibility of this finding having prognostic implication deserves further analysis.

3139 A

PSYCHIATRIC PATHOLOGY AND HUMAN GENOM (DETERMINISM AND ENVIRONMENTALISM)
F. Llavero, Spain

Session 482 Symposium:
Psychopathology and neurobiology:
Comprehensive concepts

3140

BASAL GANGLIA AND LIMBIC SYSTEM PATHOLOGY IN SCHIZOPHRENIA. A REPLICATION STUDY ON A NEW SAMPLE OF BRAINS
Bogerts,B.,P.Falkai,K.Heinrich
Department of Psychiatry
Heinrich-Heine-University
Bergische Landstr.2
D-4ooo Düsseldorf 12, FRG

Recently, there is a growing number of morphometric post-mortem studies demonstrating pathological changes in the brains of schizophrenics. To control several post mortem artefacts and to fullfill recent diagnostic criteria,1o brains of schizophrenic patients and 14 age and se matched control cases were cut into 2o micrometer coronal whole brain sections and stained for myelin and Nissl.The volumes of 16 different nuclei were evaluated for both hemispheres in each group by planimetry.We found a significant volume reduction of the hippocampus as well as of the whole thalamus in the schizophrenics on both sides by 25-3o%. The volumes of the cingulate gyrus and the internal pallidal segment were significantly diminished by 15-2o%.The amygdala showed a trend towards a significant volume reduction (p=.1o) on the left side. The mean thickness of the corpus callosum was significantly reduced in the schizophrenic patients by 2o%. These results validate our recent findings on brains of the Vogt-Collection and will be discussed in correlation with clinical data.

3141

NEUROCHEMICAL-PSYCHOPATHOLOGICAL CORRELATIONS IN IDIOPATHIC PSYCHOSES

G. Gross, G. Huber, J. Klosterkötter, G. Quade

The dynamics of course in each single patient and the marked variability of psychopathological syndromes was not considered up to now in investigations correlating clinical and neurochemical findings. The intraindividual fluctuation became evident more and more developing the concept of basic symptoms (HUBER 1983; SÜLLWOLD & HUBER 1986). Therefore we selected subgroups of patients according to a defined actual clinical-phenomenological syndrome, classified into severe, moderate or slight process-active and process-inactive stages (HUBER et al.1988). We supposed that the paroxysmal or phasic occurrence of certain basic symptoms (cenesthesias, cognitive thought and perception disorders - GROSS et al.1987) can reflect also an instability of neurochemical and neuroendocrinological findings. Blood of 190 drug-free patients with idiopathic psychoses was examined 8 times within 24 h and analysed as to dopamine, noradrenaline, adrenaline, 5-HT, TSH, prolactine, HGH, melatonine, cortisole, T 3 and T 4. Process-active schizophrenic patients showed significantly higher levels of dopamine, noradrenaline and 5-HT, and significantly lower levels of TSH compared to healthy controls; patients with inactive stages a hypoactivity of catecholaminergic and possibly also serotoninergic systems. The results and interdependences of neurotransmitters, neurohormones and amino acids will be discussed.

3142

AMINO ACIDS IN PROCESS-ACTIVE AND -INACTIVE STAGES OF SCHIZOPHRENIC PSYCHOSES
G. Huber, G. Gross, J. Klosterkötter
Psychiatric University Clinic Bonn, FRG

We investigated circadian (collecting blood 8 times within 24 h) the concentration in serum of 28 amino acids in schizophrenic and schizoaffective psychoses. Up to now the problem of dynamics of course and intraindividual fluctuation of psychopathological syndromes was neglected comparing neurochemical and psychopathological findings. Therefore, searching for state dependent parameters, we differentiated subgroups without process-activity (PA) and with different degrees of PA, characterized among others by certain 1st rank symptoms (K.SCHNEIDER) and cognitive basic symptoms (HUBER 1983; GROSS et al. 1987). The subgroups with PA were compared to schizophrenic patients without PA and healthy controls. We found significantly higher levels of alpha-aminobutyric acid, arginine, citrulline, cystine, glycine, lysine, 1-methylhistidine, ornithine, serine and taurine, and significantly lower levels of histidine and methionine in schizophrenics compared to healthy controls. The process-inactive group ("pure defect" - HUBER) had higher levels of glutamine, 3-methylhistidine, serine and taurine, and lower levels of methionine. - These results, namely the differences between the subgroups of schizophrenic patients with and without PA were discussed and compared to findings of neurotransmitters and neurohormones.

3143

SCHIZOPHRENIA - AUTOIMMUNE ASTHENIA OF THE GLUTAMATE RECEPTOR?
Kornhuber HH, Kornhuber J, Kornhuber M, Schreiber H, Westphal KP
Dpt Neurology,University,D-7900 Ulm, W.Germany

Despite of the antipsychotic action of dopamine antagonists and the psychotomimetic action of dopamine agonists no dopaminergic hyperfunction has been established in schizophrenia. There are potent antipsychotic drugs (Clozapin) not acting via dopamine receptors. Reduced CSF glutamate in schizophrenics (Kim) suggests a hypofunction of glutamatergic neurones in schizophrenia. Accordingly, glutamate receptor parameters in the frontal cortex (kainate receptor, Nishikawa) and in the putamen (NMDA receptor, Kornhuber,J) are increased. This may be due to receptor upregulation following glutamatergic hypofunction. The best schizophrenia model in man is the Phencyclidine (PCP) psychosis which is characterised by plus and minus symptoms. PCP blocks the ion channel linked to the NMDA type of glutamate receptors. Animal behavioral effects of PCP are better antagonised by clozapin than by haloperidol (Schmidt).-The course of the disease, the genetic concordance results (Kety) and the blood/CSF barrier dysfunction in schizophrenics may be explained by an autoimmune disease (Kornhuber). Slow EEG Theta rhythm (Westphal), diminished order in the cerebral potentials (Diekmann) or delayed cognitive brain potentials in some children of schizophrenic parents (Schreiber) may be helpful to diagnose and treat the disease earlier, thereby avoiding secondary deterioration caused by social isolation.

Session 483 Symposium: Adopted children and adolescents: Risk for psychiatric pathology?

3144

ADOPTED CHILDREN AND ADOLESCENTS. RISK FOR PSYCHIATRIC PATHOLOGY?
Kotsopoulos, S.
University of Ottawa, Ottawa, Canada

Studies carried out in child psychiatric services, including one in the area of Ottawa by this author and his colleagues, have consistently shown that adopted children and adolescents are referred more frequently than warranted by their ratio in the community. Studies have also shown that the adopted present more frequently with behavior disorders (47% in the Ottawa study). Inpatient services have also reported a higher proportion of adopted. Some conditions associated with an overall successful adoption have been identified (e.g. adoption soon after birth, timely disclosure of being adopted). However, a valid explanation why a substantial proportion of adopted children and adolescents present with psychosocial problems is not available. Hypotheses have been proposed (e.g. faulty attachment, biological vulnerability, identity problems and sense of lack of roots) but none has yet been sufficiently explored. A better understanding of the complex developmental issues experienced by the adoptees and the adoptive parents is necessary. A better understanding will lead to improvements in the practice of adoption and to preventive measures.

3145

PSYCHIATRIC ILLNESS AND SICK-LEAVE PATTERNS OF ADOLESCENTS AND ADULTS ADOPTED AS INFANTS
von Knorring A-L, Bohman M, Sigvardsson S,
Umeå University, Umeå, Sweden

Studies of Swedish adoptees initiated by Michael Bohman have shown that the adopted children at 11 had as good adjustment as their non-adopted classmates. Foster-children although placed in stable foster-homes at an early age had more problems according to the teachers' ratings. At age 15 and 18 the same patterns were found.
In another sample of adoptees we found an increase of sick-leave periods and length of sick-leave due to both somatic and psychiatric causes of adopted women. Adopted men had only longer sick-leave periods due to psychiatric disorders.
Placement in the adoptive home between 6-12 months increased the risk of depression as an adult.

3146

CONTRASTING DIFFERENT TYPES OF SUBSTITUTE PARENTING
TRISELIOTIS, John
University of Edinburgh, UK

The paper will contrast 3 different types of substitute parenting by comparing the current personal and social circumstances of adults who, as children, were separated from their biological parents and subsequently brought up as adopted, fostered with a family or cared for in residential institutions. The adopted group were aged 3-9 at the time of placement. The central claim is that those growing up adopted, even when placed late, appear in adulthood to have a stronger sense of self and to function more adequately at the personal, social and economic level. Furthermore adoption, and to a lesser extent long-term foster care, have greater potential for reversing earlier adverse experiences than residential care. Evidence to support these claims will come from a retrospective study of 124 people in their 20's split about equally between those who were adopted, fostered or grew up in residential care. As children they were all at one time in public care. Those adopted were perceived to be 'high risk' for adoption. The outcome will be examined in relation to early attachment experiences, awareness of own genealogy and personal history, and how they are perceived by others and by themselves.

3147

ATTACHMENT AND ADOPTION: ISSUES & METHODS

WATERS, Everett
State University New York at Stony Brook

Studies of infant-mother attachment in adopted children have generally found substantially increased rates of anxious attachment when 1-2 year-olds have been compared with non-adoptive controls. But there have been few such studies and the results are equivocal because of small sample sizes. This paper will summarize available data, discuss new assessment methods that are applicable to children as old as 5-years of age. The paper will also describe new methods for assessing adult cognitive models of attachment and will address the importance of this variable to the success or failure of child attachment in adoption. Research design issues such as preadoptive assessment, foster care assessment, and evaluation of intervention.

Session 484 Symposium:
Neuroleptic malignant syndrome

3148

REMARKS ON NEUROLEPTIC MALIGNANT SYNDROME AFTER A REVIEW OF THE FIRST 500 CASES
John M.Davis M.D., Paul Sakkas M.D.*
Illinois State Psychiatric Institute,U.S.A.
*Depart. Psychiatry,Univ.of Athens,Greece

We review 550 cases of NMS reported the last 30 years.In 1977-78 there was an increase in the reported cases,mainly in the French and the Japanese literature.We present our results from a multidimentional analysis of the data that are available in the literature.Our intent is to furnish the clinician with valuable information about NMS.Also,we want to elucidatethe pathophysiology of this syndrome through the extensive and thorough study of information existing in reported cases.

The main symptoms of NMS are muscle rigidity,fever,diaphoresis,and autonomic liability.The elevation of CPK was the most consistent and characteristic laboratory finding in NMS patients.The rate of the elevation of the neuroleptics´dose that the patient received just before the occurrence of NMS,the level of fever of the patient,and his systolic blood pressure during the NMS episode could predict if the case had a fatal outcome or not.Also,we found that the length of the recovery was related more to the rise of the temperature,the SGPT blood level,the leucocytes count,and the drop of the systolic BP of NMS patients than to any other variable.

3149

NEUROLEPTICS'MALIGNANT SYNDROME: SOME HISTORICAL BACKGROUND.
Deniker Pierre
Hospital Sainte-Anne (Paris)

The malignant syndrome (MS) was originally observed in the 1960th with haloperidol. But it can occur with every type of neuroleptic compounds,exept,perhaps,chlorpromazine at low dosage.

Observations coming from different countries are pointing out the neurovegetative symptoms with a progressive fever. They could be referred to the syndrome of"paleness-hyperthermia" formely described as complications of children infectious diseases and, also,as unfrequent accident of Epidemic Encephalitis.In both situations some diencephalic lesions of brain had been found.

Initially,some cases of MS were lethal and autopsies showed,in someone, lungs atelectasia.

Now it is absolutely necessary that no patient must die by neuroleptic chemotherapy.The treatment of MS is primarily prophylactic.

3150

NEUROLEPTIC MALIGNANT SYNDROME IN JAPAN

T. Inada [1,2], G. Yagi [1] and R.W. Rockhold [2]

1) Dept. of Psychiatry, Keio Univ. Med. School, Tokyo, Japan.
2) Dept. of Pharmacology & Toxicology, Univ. of Mississippi Med. Ctr., Jackson, U.S.A.

Interest in the neuroleptic malignant syndrome (NMS) has been increasing since it was reported first in Japan in 1974. Recently, a nation-wide investigation on NMS in Japan has been carried out by the research group on NMS organized by the Japanese Ministry of Health.

During the period of April, 1986 through November, 1987, 1666 cases of NMS were confirmed. The primary psychiatric diagnosis is schizophrenia in 65.3% of all cases. A higher incidence is observed in females (56.6%) than in males (43.4%). Other epidemiological results of this report are almost completely in agreement with the data reported in the West.

The neuroleptics which had been administered to the patient at the occurrence of this syndrome are most frequently classical agents, such as haloperidol, chlorpromazine and levomepromazine. Virtually all of them are stopped after occurrence of NMS.

The characteristic features of NMS are hyperthermia (86.6%), altered consciousness (60.0%), rigidity (94.3%), akinesia (89.6%), tremor (76.3%), sweating (91.0%) and tachycardia (88.0%). Leukocytosis (55.2%) as well as elevated creatine phosphokinase (64.7%) and glutamate-oxaloacetate transaminase (62.9%) are recognized as laboratory findings. The efficiency of dantrolene and bromocriptine as therapeutic agents is also similar to that reported in the West. A total of 66.2% of patients who exhibit this syndrome recover within about a month and the mortality rate of NMS has shown a downward trend. It was 7.6% in 1986.

We conclude that there is only a little difference on NMS between Japan and the West despite cross cultural differences.

3151

THE INCIDENCE OF NEUROLEPTIC MALIGNANT SYNDROME (NMS): A PROSPECTIVE DOUBLE STUDY

H. Hermesh, D. Aizenberg, C. Mayor, H. Munitz, Geha Psychiatric Hospital, Petah Tiqva, Israel

The occurrence of MNS was studied prospectively in two series of consecutive newly admitted patients from 2 acute wards. 120 patients (group 1) suffered from schizophrenia and were treated only with haloperidol (HPL) either 10mg/day or 20mg/day. 103 patients (group 2) were treated with diverse neuroleptics, mainly, perphenazine, levomepromazine and HPL (mean equivalent chlorpromazine 657±122.3mg/d. In both groups patients were on a mono-antipsychotic agent, with no anticholinergic drug, as prophylaxis. Patients from the HPL group were especially examined for NMS only if there had been clinical clues to the syndrome, while every patient from the 2nd group was systematically and extensively investigated through the first week. Followup in the last group included repeated measures of body temperature, pulse, blood pressure, excessive sweating, and altered level of consciousness, EPS, muscle enzymes and WBC. Two patients from the HPL group had NMS (1.7%) and 3 from the other group (2.9%). Two patients, 1 from each group was admitted with NMS and 1 had a recurrency during rechallange with another neuroleptic. Our incidence of full NMS per first neuroleptic exposure is in accordance with Addozinio et al's figures but is higher by 1 to 2 orders of magnitude than others. Possible reasons for this discrepancy will be discussed.

3152

LETHAL CATATONIA AND THE NEUROLEPTIC MALIGNANT SYNDROME

Stephan C. Mann, M.D., Stanley N. Caroff, M.D.
University of Pennsylvania, Philadelphia, PA, USA

Lethal Catatonia (LC), a life-threatening condition characterized by catatonic excitement or stupor, hyperthermia, altered consciousness and autonomic instability was widely reported during the preneuroleptic era. Although the incidence of this disorder has declined, it continues to occur, now reported primarily in the European and Asian literature.

In addition, LC is a syndrome rather than a specific disease; it may be caused by organic as well as functional disorders. From this perspective, the neuroleptic malignant syndrome (NMS) may be conceptualized as a neuroleptic-induced toxic or iatrogenic form of organic LC.

Still, it would be important to distinguish NMS LC since functional LC responds to electroconvulsive therapy, while specific drugs may be safer and more effective in the treatment of NMS. In fact, the more common "classic" excited LC may be distinguishable from NMS on the basis of extreme hyperthermia developing during excitement. Although excitement often precedes NMS, it is not accompanied by hyperthermia. NMS hyperthermia first emerges with the onset of stupor and rigidity. However, cases of functional LC having a primarily stuporous course may often be clinically indistinguishable from NMS.

3153

HEAT LOADING IN HALOPERIDOL-TREATED SCHIZOPHRENIC PATIENTS: PHYSIOLOGICAL ABNORMALITIES

M. Birger[1], H. Hermesh[2], A. Shalev[2], Y. Epstein[1], H. Munitz[2], S. Floru[2].
Chaim Sheba Med. Center, Tel Hashomer[1], Geha Psychiatric Hospital[2], Petah Tikva, Israel

We attempted to clarify some of the pathophysiological mechanisms that underlie 3 serious hyperthermic syndromes related to schizophrenia and neuroleptic treatment; heat stroke, febrile catatonia and neuroleptic malignant syndrome. Eight male schizophrenic outpatients, stabilized with haloperidol (HPL) underwent a standard heat loading procedure in a climatic chamber. Participants paced on a treadmill for 50 min x 2 and were exposed to an ambient temperature of $36c^o$ and a relative humidity of 60%. Skin, body and rectal temperature, sweat rate, serum creatinine phosphokinase and prolactin were measured before, during and after exposure. When compared to age matched male controls, patients had higher dropout rate (5/8 vs 0/8, Fisher's exact test, p=.012) attributed either to exhaustion or the reaching of upper safety limit temperature ($39c^o$). The patients sweat rate (432±216 vs 904±246 gr/h, p=.002) as well as heat conductance from body core to the periphery (219±22 vs 240±13, p=.05) were significantly lower. These findings indicate the presence of a persistant thermoregulatory disturbance in schizophrenic patients treated with HPL.

3154

TREATMENT OF NEUROLEPTIC MALIGNANT SYNDROME
Paul Sakkas M.D.,*John Davis M.D.
Illinois State Psychiatric Institute,U.S.A.
*Dept. Psychiatry Univ.of Athens, Greece.

We present our data after a review of 550 cases of neuroleptic malignant syndrome (NMS)reported in the international literature.We analyzed data of parameters which may influence the treatment and the outcome of NMS.
In the first reports of NMS,the treatment consisted of withdrawal of the offending drug and non-specific treatment of the complications and the metabolic disturbances very often occur.In the later reports,specific treatment,based on the knowledge of the pathopsychiology of this syndrome,was added.This treatment was directed toward the dopamine blockage or toward the muscle rigidity.The cases in which bromocriptine and/or dantrolene were used had better outcome and lower mortality even though these drugs were mainly used in cases with severe clinical picture.
The reinstitution of neuroleptics in a patient after an NMS episode was related with the symptoms relapse in 49% of the cases.

Session 485   Symposium:
Ethical aspects in psychopharmacological treatment

3155

ETHICAL CONSIDERATIONS: PSYCHOPHARMACOLOGICAL
     MEDICATION IN THE ELDERLY

Ewald W. Busse, M.D., Duke University Medical
     Center, Durham, NC, USA

Many elderly patients, particularly those 75 years of age and older, have structural and physiological changes that occur throughout the body including the brain. Such age changes affect the kinetics of many medications. Furthermore, many elderly people are not capable of maintaining an important social role as many have disabilities that impair their autonomy. Age changes and the diseases of late life reduce a person's independence.
    The ethical and competent psychiatrist must understand how age changes affect the choice of psychopharmacological agents and the amount of medication that is used. Changes in cognitive abilities and behavior make it imperative that the psychiatrist consider whether the medication is primarily for the patient or for the caretaker. This problem more often occurs in the institutionalized elderly but does exist in those elderly cared for in the community.

3156

ON THE ETHICAL ASPECTS OF THE USE OF THE NEUROLEPTICS
  Matti O. Huttunen, M.D., Department of Psychiatry, University of Helsinki, Finland
     The ethical problems in the use of the neuroleptic drugs are discussed in the light of the following basic values (1):
  - the primary function of medicine and psychiatry is to preserve or maximize the autonomy of the patient in different clinical and social situations (2)
  - autonomy is to be seen broadly: (a) as a free action (b) as authenticity (c) as effective deliberation (d) as moral reflection (3)
  - when and where doubt exists about the ultimate outcome of clinical decisions the doctors should always err on the side of preserving life (2)
     These guidelines form the basis for the decisions concerning the use of the neuroleptics in different clinical situations : during the emergency situations and the involuntary hospital treatment. These same basic values do give the general guidelines for the timing and extent of the information of the nature and probability of the various side-effects to the patient.
(1)Macklin, R:in"Ethical questions in brain and behavior"(ed.D.W.Pfaff),pp.23-40, 41-56, Springer Verlag, -83
(2)Cassel, E.J.:in"Death and decision" (ed. E.McMullin),pp.35-44, Westview Press,-78
(3)Miller,B.L.:Hastings Center Rep.11:22-28,-81

3157

ETHICAL ASPECTS OF THE BENZODIAZEPINE TREATMENT
Nieminen Kalevi, Achte Kalle
Psychiatric Clinic, Helsinki, Finland

The opinions on the appropriate prescription of the benzodiazepines (BDs) and on their risks have varied during the 30 years of their long clinical history. It is estimated, that over 500 millions of people have used them. Depending on the dose and the length of the use 15-20% of patients get abstinence symptoms at abrupt withdrawal.
The difficulties in the doctor-patient relationship and countertransference problems can lead to uncritical and unethical prescribing of BDs. The prescription of BDs can be the "easiest" solution practically and psychologically but often unethical on these grounds. The describing of BDs on the basis of economical pressures from any side is naturally unethical.
On the other hand the doctor should not moralize. The BD medication can effectively relieve the patient's suffering and is generally more advisable than alcohol, which is often used as a self-medication.
The prescription of BDs is also on ethically sound basis, if the medical and psychiatric indications and contraindications have been carefully estimated. The BD treatment should be based on the informed consent principle.

Session 486 Special Session: Group psychotherapy: Clinical applications

3158
THERAPEUTICAL FACTORS IN GROUP PSYCHOTHERAPY

MUSCARA' M. *, PASTENA L. **
* DIFESAN ROMA ITALY
**Dept.of Neurological Sciences Univ. La Sapienza Roma, ITALY

Group psychotherapy makes evident to the patient his own manner to present him self and to relate to the community. This is an essential therapeutic factors because it enables the patient to recogni= ze that his way to relate in reality hides his way to be in order to preserve his personality and even his disorders.This is socialy not always useful but it is irrivocable for the patient.
There aremany examples of this specific therapeu= tic factor of group psychotherapy and the oppor= tunities of intervention it offers will be discussed. The therapeutic factors proposed by Faulkes for the group psychotherapy are examined is an effort to find out the most essential and the most efficacious for the treatment, keeping in mind the specific way of the patient to relate to the group.

3159
DESCRIPTION AND ASSESSMENT OF AN INTENSIVE PSYCHOTHERAPY PROGRAMME
D. O'Sullivan, P. Vostanis
Uffculme Clinic, Birmingham, England.

This paper attempts to describe and evaluate the different components of a unique psychotherapy service. The Uffculme Clinic provides an intensive programme based on small groups for patients with severe neurotic and personality disturbance who attend for up to a maximum of 12 months. The components of the intensive programme were identified as the admission procedure, anxiety management, community meeting, occupational therapy, projective sessions (music and art/clay sessions), role play, small group sessions, activity groups and the social milieu of the Clinic. 23 patients and 17 therapists of the intensive programme took part in the study by completing a specifically devised questionnaire. They rated the components according to their perceived helpfulness or unhelpfulness in therapy and gave qualifying statements on the most helpful and inhelpful aspects of the respective components. The statements were categorised. Quantitative data was statistically analysed. An analysis of the results indicates that both patients and staff valued group sessions, role play and projective sessions most highly. They differed in their views regarding the other components. Qualifying state- ments indicate a consistency in perception of helpful aspects of each component, but differences in unhelpful aspects which can be seen in terms of transference-countertransference and resistance.

3160
FROM NEUROLOGY TO GROUPANALYSIS. ON THE PSYCHOBIOLOGICAL INTEGRATION.
Pisani Rocco. Dipartimento di Scienze Neurologiche. Università "La Sapienza". Roma.Italia.

The Author, on the basis of a long psy- chiatric and groupanalytic experience, gives his own reflection about nonsense of the old mind-body dualism.
He stars with considerations about the biological bases of the mind.
He summarizes the main principles of Psy- choanalysis and explains the unitary set- -up of Groupanalysis; according to this the individual and the group are an ex- pression of a unique,indivisible phenome- non, that can be divided only by refer- ring to abstraction.
He ends underlining how psychobiological integration has a place within Foulkes' "Group Matrix", as a unifying ground com- posed of the biological and cultural as- pects of the individual and the species.

3161
PSYCHOANALYSIS AND PHARMACOTHERAPY IN OUT-PATIENT TREATMENT
Bayer Knopman,E.; Coelho da Penha, M.; Marins Goulart, C.T.; Monteiro Alves,N.
Centro de Saúde Dr. Washington Luís Lopes (Health Office of Rio de Janeiro State)
São Gonçalo, Rio de Janeiro, BRAZIL.

Among the serious health problems faced by the brazilian population, the mental disorders occupy a prominent position. Their high incidence and prevalence, mainly among the working classes, aggravated by the limited efficacy of the traditional methods of treatment, oblige the creation of alternatives in out-patient public services.

The objetctive of this work is to describe an experience in multidisciplinary out-patient attendance to patients just come from psychiatric hospitals, combining pharmacotherapy (long-action neuroleptics) and psychoanalitical group psycho- therapy.

To the polemic discussion on the psychoanalysis of psychotic patients, the present work is provid- ing some answers in both theoretical and practical levels.

Finally, the proposed working model is producing results that, both, surmount some of the difficul- ties of public health in Brazil and meet many of the objective demands of the patients.

3162

BALINT GROUPS AND THERAPEUTIC RELATIONSHIP IN PSYCHIATRIC SOCIAL WORKERS
C. Papageorgiou,
Department of Psychiatry, Athens University, Eginition Hospital, Athens, Greece.

The scope of this study is to investigate the effects of Balint Groups participation on the therapeutic relationship in twelve PSW actively involved in the case-taking program of the hospital.
Three different self-evaluative measures scored on the Studgard Scale were employed before and after the total sessions series ($\bar{x}=18$): 1. Therapeutic self-sufficiency and insight to the therapeutic situation, 2. Empathy to person and 3. Emotional responsiveness to case management
The results suggest that participation in the groups produces (a) a lowering of therapeutic self-sufficiency and a corresponding increase of the insight to the problems of the therapeutic relationship and (b) a significant increase of the empathy to the person as well as the emotional responsiveness to case management. These findings support the view that Balint groups represent a useful tool regarding the management of the therapeutic relationship in psychiatric social workers.

3163

GROUP PSYCHOTHERAPY: A NEWLY INTRODUCED APPROACH IN ALEXANDRIA
Siham H. Rashed, MD, & Mervat M. El-Gueneidy, RN.
Faculty of Medicine - Alexandria University
Alexandria - Egypt

Group therapy, although accepted internationally, is still subject to controversy in Egypt on the basis of cultural beliefs and stigma. The main purpose of this group was to investigate the acceptability and effect of this method of treatment among a sample of Egyptian psychiatric patients. A weekly session of one and half hour was held in a private office for a period of two and half years. The subjects of the study were 6 members of both sexes, and the leaders 2 females. Results revealed that resistance to the group method was replaced by trust and acceptance within the first 2 weeks. Confidentiality, self-revealment, support and help of each other were taking place smoothly. Aggression and sexuality were much inhibited which reflect the Egyptian culture. Aggression could be manifested at the last 6 months by two members and in particular towards the leaders. Seven months follow up of group members revealed proper adjustment as manifested by successful work record, better interpersonal relationship absence or minimal drug therapy, and no relapse or psychotic breakdown.

3164

GROUP PSYCHOTHERAPY FOR SEVERE PSYCHIATRIC CASES IN A DAY CENTRE
Th. Papadakis, E. Yiomela, D. Dogramadzi, A. Kosmoyanni
Open Psychotherapeutic Centre. Athens, Greece.

The paper presents a nine year evaluation (1980-1988) of the therapeutic outcome of a Day Centre, which uses group Psychotherapy (Group Analysis, Psychotherapeutic Community, Psychodrama, Family Therapy, etc.), as the main therapeutic approach for the treatment of severely disturbed patients. It focuses on:
A. Description of the population (approximately 4000 patients): demographic characteristics and diagnostic categories.
B. Evaluation of the outcome of therapy for those who started and continued on a systematic basis (positive for more than 60% of the cases).
The results are examined in relation to the Centre's structure and it's approach on therapy.

3165

GRUPPENTHERAPIE PSYCHOTISCHER PATIENTEN AUS EINEM AGRARGEBIET
N. Papoutseli, N. Tzavaras
Psychopathological Laboratory, University of Thrace, Medical School, Alexandroupolis, Greece.

Es wird der Verlauf eines zweijährigen gruppentherapeutischen Prozesses mit psychotischen Patienten aus Thrazien dargestellt.
Zum ersten Mal wurde der Versuch unternommen, eine Behandlung von einem Psychotikerkollektiv in Alexandroupolis, Hauptstadt der Provinz und Sitz der Dimokritos - Universität, zu realisieren. Initiale Reaktionen, kulturelle Eigenheiten sowie Entwicklungstendenzen werden nachgezeichnet und mit internationalen bibliographischen Angaben verglichen.

3166
GROUP TREATMENT OF CHOICE FOR FEMALE OBESITY

SANDRA E. NEIL,B.A.,B.Ed.(Couns.),M.A.,M.A.Ps.S.,M.I.C.P.
DEPARTMENT OF PSYCHIATRY,
UNIVERSITY OF MELBOURNE,
C/- ST.VINCENT'S HOSPITAL,
NICHOLSON ST., FITZROY 3065, AUSTRALIA
63
WHILST UNDOUBTEDLY BIOLOGICAL FACTORS ARE CAUSALLY RELATED TO THE OBESE STATE, SOME PSYCHOSOCIAL FACTORS ARE VITALLY RELATED, AND ONE MAY POSTULATE THAT OBESITY IS FOR SOME PATIENTS A PRODUCT OF EMOTIONAL DISEQUILIBRIUM. EVEN FOR PERSONS WITH A MAJOR BIOLOGICAL AETIOLOGY, AN ASSOCIATED EMOTIONAL DISEQUILIBRIUM PERHAPS SECONDARILY CAUSALLY RELATED TO OBESITY, MAY ALSO PROVE RESPONSIVE TO PSYCHOLOGICAL TREATMENT. THE IMPLICATIONS OF PSYCHOANALYTIC NOTIONS FOR OBESITY RESEARCH ARE DISCUSSED. A DEVELOPMENTAL APPROACH ALLOWS AN INTRAPSYCHIC VIEW TO BE USED IN INDIVIDUAL THERAPY. IN GROUP ANALYTIC PSYCHO- THERAPY AN INTERPERSONAL AND INTRAPHYCHIC APPROACH CAN BE MADE. WITHIN THIS MATRIX OBESE WOMEN EXAMINE THEIR DEFENSES, AND RE-ENACT SEPARATION - INDIVIDUATION CRISES FROM THE PAST: ANACLYTIC DEPRESSIONS CAN BE MOBILIZED, AND EXCURSIONS INTO SELF PLAYED OUT. THE GROUP PROVIDES AN 'OBJECT' WORLD WHICH IS NO LONGER SHAKY, YET VIABLE, AND AN OPPORTUNITY FOR OBESE WOMEN TO FIND SOME OF THE LOST PARTS OF 'SELF'.NEW RESEARCH IS ON-GOING.

3167
SHORT-TERM GROUP ANALYTIC THERAPY WITH PSYCHOTIC AND BORDERLINE PATIENTS
E.Morarou,S.Papadopoulou,D.Dogramadzi,A.Kosmoyanni
Open Psychotherapeutic Centre.Athens, Greece.

Short-term group analytic therapy in a Quick Open analytic group has been undertaken with patients of various diagnostic categories (psychotics, borderline cases, severe neuro- tics) in the context of the Psychotherapeutic Community of a Day Centre.
The study focuses on the sucess or fai- lure of short-term therapy for psychotic and borderline patients, which seems to depend on the gradual reduction and elimination of dis- turbing boundary incidents, as well as on the emergence of positive transference feelings towards the therapist and their displacement from the therapist to the group as the whole. In contrast, the therapy of neurotic patients consists rather of the working out of transfe- rence feelings towards the therapist and their displacement from the therapist to the group as a whole. The observations are illustrated by clinical examples.

3168
THE PREDICTION OF (UN)SUCCESSFUL TREATMENT IN A PSYCHOTHERAPEUTIC COMMUNITY
J. Hartman, J. Dekker
Rijnland Psychotherapeutic Community, Santpoort, The Netherlands

Long-term programs of residential psychotherapy have proved to be successful in many cases. However, sometimes the results do not seem to justify the lengthy strenuous treatment. Presumably, it is a complex of factors more or less characteristic of the therapeutic community setting that accounts for treatment to be started on the wrong grounds, or not to be discontinued in time to make way for a different approach. Is a lack of relevant information about the individual patient perhaps one of these factors? In the psychotherapeutic community of Rijnland, a ward that deals with psychotic and borderline disturbances, this proves not to be true. For an exploratory research study (n=5g) has shown a correlation between the effects of treatment, as measured in a five-year follow-up study and a number of data from the patient's file with reference to selection procedure and initial phase of treatment. Our findings rather suggest that overrating the possibility of treating serious psychotic disturbances and underrating the nurses' observations of the new patient's group behaviour are factors in the above-mentioned problem.

Session 487 Free Communications:
Eating disorders: Diagnostic and therapeutic issues

3169
COMPUTERIZED DIAGNOSTIC EVALUATION OF PATIENTS WITH EATING DISORDERS

Simon Y., Criquillion-Doublet S.,
Hummel P., Divac-Pavlovic S.,
Samuel-Lajeunesse B.
Centre Hospitalier Sainte Anne, Clinique des Maladies Mentales et de l'Encéphale, 100 rue de la Santé, 75014 Paris - FRANCE

The different diagnostic systems for eating disorders which have been proposed on a clinical basis do not clarify patients in a homogenous way.
The rise of a computerized polydiagnostic system including the criteria of DSM IIIR, ICD 10, Feighner and Russell, allows to compare these various classifications.
We present the results of a story inclu- ding 80 in- and out-patients treated at the Clinique des Maladies Mentales et de l'Encéphale for eating disorders.
The different diagnostic classifications are compared and discussed in the view of their utility for epidemiological, clinical and therapeutic use.

3170
BRAIN STRUCTURE AND FUNCTION IN EATING DISORDERS:
A CRANIAL COMPUTED TOMOGRAPHY STUDY
J.-C. Krieg, C. Lauer, K.M. Pirke
Max Planck Institute of Psychiatry, Munich, FRG

In cranial computed tomography (CT) patients with anorexia nervosa and normal weight bulimic patients display brain shrinkage in form of enlarged cortical sulci and dilated ventricles. In patients re-examined these structural brain alterations showed a strong tendency towards normalization. With the intention of finding a functional correlate of the CT abnormalities, the regional cerebral blood flow (rCBF) of anorectic patients was measured at admission and once again after weight gain and compared with the flow rates of healthy controls. The mean flow rates assessed at the first examination did not differ significantly from those assessed at the second examination and from those of a control group. Thus, despite the CT findings of brain shrinkage, the measurement of the regional cerebral blood flow gave no evidence for a reduced neuronal activity in eating disorder patients.

3171
SERUM ZINC IN ANOREXIA NERVOSA.

Røijen, Staffan, Child Psychiatric Dept. University Hosp. of Copenhagen, and Zlotnik, Gideon, Child Psychiatric Dept., Copenhagen County Hosp. and Worsaae Nielsen, Uffe, Medi-Lab. a.s., Copenhagen.

In later years, there has been a growing interest in the role that zinc metabolism plays in the symptomatology of anorexia nervosa (a.n.). The theory is that in most cases of a.n., there are serious disturbances in zinc absorption, distribution and secretion, resulting in some of the classical secondary symptoms. Thus there have been reports on the investigation of zinc status in patients with a.n., and lately there have also been reports on treatment using zinc administration.
We have recently, in a multiple hospital project, studied the association between zinc and a.n. by measuring plasma zinc (by atomic absorption), plasma albumin (by an electro-immuno diffusion method) and by testing zinc taste (using quinine, zinc and water solutions) in 18 females and 3 males with a.n. (DSM-III definition) in the age range 11 to 25 years (mean age 15,5). The results showed that neither the zinc level (with or without correlation to the albumin level) nor the taste testing were in any way significantly abnormal or had any meaningful pattern. Thus our investigation (which was concluded after one year) showed no conclusive evidence in support of the theory that zinc status plays a significant role in a.n. It seems therefor that the introduction of zinc treatment in a.n. is premature.

3172
RESPONSE TO THE DEXAMETHASONE SUPPRESSION TEST IN ANOREXIA NERVOSA.

I.Hidalgo ; J.A.Cabranes ; R.J.Díaz ; A.Barreiro ; M.A.Hidalgo ; M.Santiago ; A.Barabash.
Unidad Psiquiatría. Htal. "N.S.Sonsoles". Avila.
Sº Medicina Nuclear. Htal. Clínico. Madrid. Spain.

Several investigations have referred to a certain percentage of abnormal results in the Dexamethasone Suppression Test (DST) for Anorexia Nervosa, even though there is still a controverse about the factors which determine this type of response.
Our aim is to assess whether there is a relationship between different clinical-neuroendocrine parameters and abnormal results for the DST. We studied 27 patients diagnosed according to both the Feighner and the DSM-III criteria, whose ACTH and Cortisol basal levels and whose post-Desamethasone Cortisol levels were determined using the RIA method.
Abnormal results were found in 74.1% of the patients. The response to DST did not show any correlation with ACTH or Cortisol levels and these did not show any correlation either. No differences were found between suppressors and non-suppressors as far as clinical parameters are concerned (including age and percentage of ideal weight).
In Anorexia Nervosa, a higher percentage of abnormal results in the DST was found than in the rest of psychiatric pathologies. Our results do not support the use of the DST to differentiate sub-groups of Anorexia Nervosa.

3173
L'APPROCHE PSYCHOLOGIQUE DU PATIENT OBESE ET DE SA FAMILLE

C. Reynaert, P. Janne, M. Buysschaert, A. Collin, L. Cassiers
University of Louvain, B-5180 Yvoir, Belgium

L'obésité est un facteur de risque bien connu en médecine mais bien des tentatives d'amaigrissement rencontrent des échecs à long terme.
Le comportement alimentaire participe au registre du symbolique et au champ relationnel.
Le but du traitement est une meilleure efficacité du régime et une meilleure qualité de vie du patient.
L'intérêt est porté sur l'histoire de la prise de poids, ses conséquences, sa signification affective pour l'individu et sa fonction dans la dynamique familiale.
Les résistances à la perte de poids, telles qu'elles s'expriment dans les interactions conjugales et familiales, sont mises en évidence au travers d'études de cas et d'histoires familiales.
Une perspective thérapeutique intégrant ces dimensions est proposée.

3174

BEHAVIOR THERAPY AND FLUVOXAMINE IN THE TREATMENT OF OBESITY

D.O. Nutzinger, M. de Zwaan, G. Schönbeck
R. Macura, S. Cayiroglu, P. Berger,
G. Aschauer-Treiber, A. Kiss, S. Meryn
Psychiatric Clinic University of Vienna

In a subgroup of obese dieting is accompanied by untoward emotional reactions. This fact is of particular importance in the treatment of depressed obese. In this study we explored the usefulness of adding Fluvoxamine, an antidepressant with weight reducing properties, to behavior therapy; in a double-blind, placebo controlled study we compared four treatment modalities: Fluvoxamine and behavior therapy (BT), Fluvoxamine and dietary management (DM), placebo and BT, placebo and DM. 62 obese female outpatients aged 19 to 54 with current or past Depressive Disorder according to DSM-III-R have entered the study to date and 48 completed the active treatment phase and one-year follow-up. There was a significant weight loss - mean weight loss 5.9 kg during the 12 weeks of active treatment - and a significant decrease in depression in each of the four treatment conditions without significant differences between them. Results of treatment phase and follow-up will be presented.

3175

REQUEST OF DIETARY TREATMENT AND EATING DISORDERS: EAT-40 SURVEY ON 100 WOMEN.

Cuzzolaro Massimo, Caputo Giovanni
Cattedra di Igiene Mentale - I Università di Roma "La Sapienza - ITALY.

Garner and Garfinkel's EAT-40 test was administered to 100 female patients (aged between 14 and 45), seen consecutively at a medical centre for the treatment of obesity. The request for treatment made by these patients concerned the correction of overweight and/or the correction of non-specific "bad eating habits" to which weight instability was referred. The same test was administered to a group of female patients, matched for age, seen at a gynecology centre of the same city. The aim of the study was to verify in the first group:
1. The prevalence of EAT-40 score symptomatic for eating psychiatric disorders;
2. The presence in the same group of cases of Anorexia Nervosa and Bulimia Nervosa (evaluated clinically according to DSM-III-R criteria) and correspondance with EAT-40 score.
Results were compared to that of the control group.

3176

ACTION ANTI-IMPULSIVE DE LA FLUVOXAMINE DANS LES TROUBLES BOULIMIQUES

DANTCHEV N., VINDREAU C., FLAMENT M., REMY B., IVANCOVSKY H., DOUGE R., LECRUBIER Y.
Hôpital de la Salpétrière, Inserm U 302, Paris, France.

Nous rapportons les résultats préliminaires d'une étude ouverte sur l'action de la Fluvoxamine dans les troubles boulimiques. Cette étude, dans laquelle 20 patients boulimiques (DSM IIIR) ont été jusqu'à présent inclues, prévoyait, après une semaine de placebo, un traitement par Fluvoxamine (posologie 150mg par jour) pendant au moins 8 semaines et une évaluation tardive à 6 mois.
Les éléments cliniques permettant d'envisager une réponse à un antidépresseur sérotoninergique dans la boulimie sont étudiés. Ceci est fait d'une part en référence à l'existence éventuelle d'un état dépressif associé, et d'autre part en référence à la dimension d'impulsivité. Les préférences alimentaires lors des accès sont également prises en compte. Il semble que les boulimiques les plus impulsives dans leur conduite alimentaire bénéficieraient d'avantage à long terme d'un traitement par Fluvoxamine.

Par ailleurs cette étude a été l'occasion d'utiliser un nouvel instrument d'auto-évaluation du comportement boulimique, en cours de validation, qui est présenté.

Session 488 Free Communications:
Pharmacotherapy of acutely disturbed schizophrenic patients

3177

DOPAMINAGONISTISCHE BEHANDLUNG VON AKUTEN SCHIZOPHRENIEN

D. Stein, E. Klieser, Psychiatrische Klinik der Universität Düsseldorf, BRD

Es wird vermutet, daß die Stimulation von Dopaminautorezeptoren den postsynaptischen Dopamin-Turn Over vermindert und damit eine antipsychotische Wirkung hervorgerufen wird, ohne extrapyramidale Nebenwirkungen auszulösen.
Im Rahmen einer offenen Phase 2 Studie wurde der selektive Dopaminagonist EMD 49980 auf seine antipsychotische Wirksamkeit und Verträglichkeit bei 15 schizophrenen Patienten getestet. Die Prüfsubstanz wurde 4 Wochen verabreicht. Die Wirksamkeit wurde nach Erhebung der Ausgangslage an Tag 0, am 3., 7., 14., 21. und 28. Tag mit der BPRS und dem CGI erfaßt. Auftretende Nebenwirkungen wurden mit einer Nebenwirkungsliste geratet. Das Ausmaß der antipsychotischen Wirkung soll dargestellt werden und im Vergleich zur üblichen neuroleptischen Behandlung diskutiert werden.

3178

Zuclopenthixol Acetate, Haloperidol and Zuclopenthixol in the Treatment of Acute Psychotic Patients - A Controlled Multicentre Study
Conni Fensbo et al.
Ålborg Psychiatric Hospital, Ålborg, Denmark

Zuclopenthixol acetate (CPT-A) is a new type of formulation for use in the initial treatment of acute, psychotic patients. Its clinical effect has been compared with that of the conventional formulations of haloperidol (HAL) and zuclopenthixol (CPT). The patients were stratified into three groups: acute psychoses, exacerbation of chronic psychoses and mania. They were randomly allocated to treatment over 6 days with HAL i.m. or CPT i.m. followed by oral administration or CPT-A i.m. 148 patients were included in the study; 48 suffered from acute psychoses, 27 from mania and 73 from exacerbation of chronic psychoses.

Ratings on the CGI and the BPRS showed that the three treatments were effective and without significant differences between the treatment groups. Neither were there any differences as to the onset of therapeutic effect. The duration of effect of zuclopenthixol acetate was 3 days in most patients, whereas HAL and CPT had to be given several times a day. CPT-A and CPT caused a somewhat stronger initial sedation than HAL.

HAL induced significantly more extrapyramidal symptoms (EPSE) than CPT-A on day 1, and more HAL-treated patients received antiparkinsonian drugs.

It is concluded that CPT-A has significant advantages over conventional treatments. The few dosages of CPT-A improve the treatment situation and save time for the staff.

3179

ZUCLOPENTHIXOL ACETATE IN THE TREATMENT OF ACUTELY DISTURBED PSYCHOTIC PATIENTS
Chamlong Disayavanish and Primprao Disayavanish
Department of Psychiatry, Faculty of Medicine,
Chiang Mai University, Chiang Mai, Thailand

The study was performed as an open clinical trial to evaluate the clinical effect of zuclopenthixol acetate (Clopixol-Acuphase). Thirty patients, 20-45 years of age, with acute psychosis, mania, or exacerbation of chronic psychosis were treated with this drug. During the 6-day study period, the doses from 50-150 mg (1-3 ml), intramuscular injection, produced significant amelioration of psychotic symptoms for most patients. The severity of illness, therapeutic effect and side effects were assessed in accordance with the Clinical Global Impressions (CGI).

The incidence of side effects, including extrapyramidal reactions was low and the severity of symptoms was most often mild. The result of this study suggest that zuclopenthixol acetate offers advantages over the antipsychotic preparations conventionally used in the treatment of acutely disturbed psychotic patients.

3180

"Haloperidol, Lorazepam And The Combination In The Management of Agitation."
Enrique S. Garza-Trevino M.D., Leo E. Hollister M.D., John E. Overall Ph.D.
University of Texas Health Science Center at Houston
Department of Psychiatry

Sixty-Eight agitated patients were randomized to the following treatments: A) Haloperidol (H) 5mg. B) Lorazepam (L) 4mg and C) Combination (C) H 5mg. L 4mg. Median ages were 32, 32, and 30 respectively. Distribution of diagnostic categories were comparable across the three groups. Agitation was rated in 100mm visual analog scale, the 100mm mark corresponding to maximum degree, 0-20mm a calm or asleep patient. Patients were admitted in the study when rating > 50mm. Treatment failures were considered when patient were rated > 20mm after 210'. Median doses to attain control were 10mg in group A (H), 8mg in group B (L), and 5, 4 in group C (H-L). The median agitation rating was 60 in all three groups. The change in agitation rating were a median of 40 in group A, 50 in group B, and 50 in group C. Median time to control was 60' in group A, 60' in group B, and 30' in group C. Sucessess/Failures were: 20/1(A), 23/0(B) and 24/0(C). Adverse effects were NONE in group A, two patients with ataxia and vomiting in group B, and NONE in group C. Thirteen patients in group A needed more than one dose, fourteen patients in group B and only six patients in group C needed more than one dose.
Chi square: comb./Lorazepam = 7.37, DF=2, $P < .05$
Chi square: comb./Haloperidol = 10.00, DF=2, $P < .01$

3181

"Comparison Of Two Combinations (Hypnotic-Neuroleptics) In The Control Of Agitation" (a randomized study).
Enrique S. Garza-Trevino M.D., Leo E. Hollister M.D.
University of Texas Health Science at Houston
Department of Psychiatry

In this study the effectiveness of two combinations (one neuroleptic and one hypnotic each) are compared in a randomized trial. Haloperidol-phenobarbital (5-130mg) or thiothixene-lorazepam (5-4mgs) were given I.M. every 30" to 52 psychotic agitated patients. The degree of agitation was rated in a visual analog scale of 100mm. A 100mm mark referred to a most extremely agitated. And 0-20 asleep or calm patients. A patient was considered a failure if rating remained >20mm after 90'. Psychiatric diagnoses in both groups were comparable: 27 patients treated with the haloperidol-phenobarbital combination had a median age of 31 years. Twelve patients needed more than one dose to attain control. The median time to control was 30' and median doses were 5-130mg. Three patients were treatment failures and one developed hypotension. Twenty-Five patients (median age 34 years) were treated with thiothixene-lorazepam (5-4mg). Eleven patients needed more than two doses to reach a level of 20mm or lower. Median dose was 5-4mg. One patient was a treatment failure. One developed a dystonic reaction, and one hypotension. Both combinations were comparable in effectiveness, compatible and safe. This data supports the notion that the degree of effectiveness of a hypnotic-neuroleptic combination can be generalized to either members of each drug class.

3182

ZOTEPINE VS. HALOPERIDOL IN PARANOID SCHIZOPHRENIA: A DOUBLE-BLIND TRIAL:
C.Barnas, C.Stuppäck, B.Sperner-Unterweger, C.Miller, W.W.Fleischhacker
Dept. of Psychiatry, Innsbruck University Clinics, A-6020 Innsbruck, Austria

Fourty patients suffering from paranoid schizophrenia fulfilling DSM III criteria received either haloperidol (10-30 mg/d) or zotepine (200-600 mg/d). Patients were to be evaluated for six weeks. The BPRS and CGI were used to quantify psychopathology. CGI ratings, starting at a mean of 6.25 in the haloperidol group, and a mean of 6.60 in the zotepine group started to decrease significantly on day 7 for the former ($p \leq 0.01$) and on day 3 ($p \leq 0.05$) for the latter. Mean values on day 42 were 3.8 and 4.0 respectively. Statistical analysis of BPRS total scores showed a significant improvement in both groups with no differences between groups. Concerning the BPRS factor anxiety/depression, both groups again showed improvement of symptoms as early as day 3 ($p<0.05$), the ratings on day 14 were significantly different ($p \leq 0.05$) in favour of zotepine. In terms of side effects rigidity and dystonia were seen considerably more often after treatment with haloperidol ($p<0.005$, resp. $p \leq 0.05$), whereas patients in the zotepine group showed a higher incidence (12 vs. 6, $p \leq 0.001$) of increased liver transaminases.

3183

REMOXIPRIDE - A CANADIAN MULTICENTRE CLINICAL TRIAL

Lapierre YD, Nair NPV, Beaudry P, Saxena B, Awad G, Chouinard G, McClure J, Jones B, Bakish D, Ancill R, Max P, Sandor P, Manchanda R.

University of Ottawa, Canada

The efficacy and side effect profiles for three dose ranges of remoxipride were compared with haloperidol in a group of 245 schizophrenic inpatients in 13 centres. Patients were all diagnosed as in the acute phase of shcizophrenia according DSM-III criteria. Relative efficacy of low dose (30-90mg daily) vs middle dose (120-240mg daily) vs high dose (300-600mg daily) was compared with the standard (15-45mg daily of haloperidol), as were the side effects. The relative merit of each dose range to haloperidol was determined. As well, the relationship between remoxipride dose and steady-state plasma drug levels and prolactin concentration was evaluated, as was the relationship of the steady-state plasma drug concentration and the efficacy, tolerability and the various safety indicators examined in the study. It was concluded 1) that the therapeutic efficacy of remoxipride was comparable to haloperidol for acute episodes of schizophrenia, 2) that the low dose range was significantly less effective than higher doses, 3) that there is a clear advantage of remoxipride over haloperidol with respect to incidence and severity of extrapyramidal symptoms, and 4) that remoxipride has much less effect on steady-state plasma prolactin levels than haloperidol. Moreover, while no apparent correlation could be demonstrated between remoxipride plasma concentrations and treatment outcome, the general safety profile of remoxipride as assessed from clinical chemistry and haematology, and cardiovascular variables, suggests that remoxipride in the dose ranges studied can be used safely for schizophrenic patients. Analyses performed on the BPRS negative item score and the NOSIE retardation subfactor score suggest that remoxipride should be investigated further in the treatment of these negative symptoms of schizophrenia.

3184

EFFECTS OF HALOPERIDOL AND SAVOXEPINE ON PROLACTIN SECRETION IN HEALTHY SUBJECTS
Antonin, K.H., Mühlbauer, B., Reimann, I.W., Boulat, O., and Bieck P.R.
Human Pharmacology Institute, Ciba-Geigy GmbH, D-7400 Tübingen, FRG

It is hypothesized that antipsychotic and endocrine effects of neuroleptics are due to blockade of dopamine receptors. Increase of plasma prolactin has been used to demonstrate bioavailability of neuroleptics in man (Randall et al., J. Pharm. Sci., 71, 883, 1982). The prolactin increase correlates with antipsychotic potency (Langer et al., Nature, 266, 639, 1977). In a cross-over study, the increase of plasma prolactin after single oral doses of haloperidol 2 mg (HPD) and the new neuroleptic drug savoxepine 0.1 mg (CGP 19486) (SVP) was compared in 6 male healthy subjects. Prolactin was measured with a RIA (Ciba Corning Diagnostics).

Results:

	AUC(0-12h) [(ng/ml)*h]	Cmax [ng/ml]	tmax [h] median
Placebo	60+ 21	8.2+ 2.5	6.5
0.1 mg SVP	141+ 26	23.5+ 5.2	5.5
2.0 mg HPD	176+120	35.0+30.4	5.5

Conclusion: The marked increase of plasma prolactin after both neuroleptics shows their systemic bioavailability. With regard to the increase of prolactin, 2.0 mg HDP and 0.1 mg SVP are equi-effective.

3185

PREDICTION OF NEUROLEPTIC RESPONSE BY MULTILEVEL VARIABLES IN ACUTE SCHIZOPHRENIC PATIENTS
Gy. Bartkó, E. Frecska, Gy. Zádor, M. Arató, S. Horváth, I. Herczeg
National Institute for Nervous and Mental Diseases, Budapest, Hungary

A predetermined set of 22 sociodemografic, psychosocial, clinical, neurocognitive and biochemical potential predictor variables was tested in 98 schizophrenics admitted for relapse. The patients were treated with neuroleptics, mostly with haloperidol during 28 days. Standardized rating instruments were used. Handednees, neurological "soft" signs, abnormal voluntary movements and spontaneous blinking were rated and serum dopamine-beta-hydroxilase /DBH/ activity was determined. Multivariate statistical analysis was performed.
Several predictors, known from the literature could be confirmed, also by crossvalidation: among others intensity of symptoms at admission, premorbid disturbances of social adjustment. The neurocognitive variables did not predict the neuroleptic response. The five best predictor/premorbid social adjustment, severity of positive symptoms at admission, family history for schizophrenia, work ability in 1 year before admission, serum DBH activity/ explained 29 percent the outcome variance.

3186
HALOPERIDOL FOR SCHIZOPHRENIC INPATIENTS WITH THREE DOSAGE REGIMENS
Cho-Boon Sim, Ying-Chiao Lee, Jeng-Ping Hwang
Veterans General Hospital, Taipei, Taiwan. ROC
Using a double-blind and placebo-controlled Method, we compared the efficacy of three dosage regimens of haloperidol in 34 newly admitted decompensated schizophrenic patients who were randomly assigned to high-, moderate-, and low-dose groups and treated with 60 mg, 30 mg and 12 mg of IM haloperidol on day 1, followed by fixed daily oral haloperidol in 90 mg, 45 mg and 18 mg respectively from day 2 through day 21; The placebo control group received 300 mg IM ascorbic acid. All patients were assessed by serial ratings on the Brief Psychiatric Rating Scale. The extrapyramidal side effects were documented by Rating Scale of Extrapyramidal Syndrome (RSEPS). The results indicated the prompt improvement of symptoms occurred in all three groups of patients on day 1 ($p<0.05$). The high-dose group showed more symptom alleviation in first week. ($p=0.0001$). There was no inter-group significant difference on days 14 and 21. EPS seemed slighty higher in high-dose group, but not to a significant level. There were no significant differences between good VS no good responses regarding a number of demographic clinical variables. This study concluded that haloperidol seemed to be safe, and well-tolerated in all cases, and the low-dose was as effective as the high-dose after one week of treatment.

3186 A
UNITARY CORRELATES OF TONGUE DYSKINESIA IN A RAT MODEL
L.A. MARCO, J.S. JOSHI, N. CEPEDA
Depts. Psychiatry & Structural & Cellular Biology
College of Medicine, University of South Alabama, Mobile, Alabama, USA

In rats anesthetized with Ketamine HCL and placed on a stereotaxic instrument we demonstrated: 1) A population of N-XII motoneurons firing in bursts during protrusion (P) or Retrusion (R); 2) Clonic tongue contractions reminiscent of the tongue vermiculations of tardive dyskinesia in correlation with unit bursting; 3) Regrouping of random spontaneous firing in the N-XII into doublets and triplets synchronously with R or P; 4) Units in the P and R pools firing in bursts during the P or R that followed a superior lanryngeal nerve (SLN)-induced swallow; 5) Large variability in time of onset of tongue contractions despite constancy of swallow (S) responses to SLN stimuli; 6) P, R, and S and their unit correlates elicited by electrical stimulation of branches of the XII cranial nerve or of SLN which did not differ from those which were ketamine-induced. These are the first unitary correlates of ketamine-induced dyskinetic behavior or of any other available animal model of dyskinesia. These results demonstrate that there are no qualitative differences between nerve and ketamine-induced P, R, or S and that dyskinesia can be characterized as an inordinate frequency of normal motor patterns. The various patterns will be illustrated (supported by NINCDS grant).

Session 489 Free Communications:
Epidemiological studies on mental patients

3187
THE FIRST EPISODES OF PSYCHOSIS IN A HOSPITAL UNIT: CLINICAL ISSUES.
Ambrosi P., Caverzasi E., Foresti G., Politi P.L., Bianchi A., Scioli R., Institute of Psychiatry, University of Pavia, Pavia, Italy.

The Institute of Psychiatry of the University of Pavia is been engaged since ten years in the community psychiatric care of a geographic district of the province of Pavia. In 1986 we began an epidemiologic research on the first episodes of psychosis treated in the hospital unit of Pavia. The authors describe the preliminary results of this research as regards:
- the kind of patients admitted in the unit in relation to the main social and demographic parameters
- the clinical picture and symptomatology shown at the admission
- the therapeutic models of care and intervention during the stay in the unit
- the follow-up evaluation of the patients after the discharge in the community.

3188
The Somatic Presentation of Psychiatric Disorder in General Practice
Dr A P Boardman   Dr T K J Craig
Guy's Hospital Medical School, London SE1, England

1220 patients presenting to 19 general practitioners in south east London were screened using the General Health Questionnaire and a group of 185 presenting with physical complaints were selected for further interview. Interviews were conducted using the Present State Examination and Life Events and difficulties schedule. Analysis revealed that somatic complaints were the most common mode of presentation of psychiatric disorder and that the general practitioner was likely to miss the disorder when presented in this way. The onset of the disorders were related to the experience of life events in the context of social vulnerability factors.

3189
PHYSICAL PROBLEMS IN THE LONG-TERM MENTALLY ILL: ASSESSING UNMET NEED.

Dr T S Brugha
Dept. of Psychiatry, University of Leicester
Clinical Sciences Building, Leicester Royal
Infirmary, PO Box 65, Leicester LE2 7LX, England

A survey of chronic psychiatric patients was designed to identify met and unmet need for care for physical disorders. 145 long-term users of hospital and social-services day psychiatric facilities were assessed clinically and 84 consented to a laboratory pathological screen. We recorded data on relevant medical care being provided. A procedure was devised for rating compliance with treatment. As reported in other surveys there was a high level of physical disorder in this population. Patients were judged to have medical problems requiring care and needs based on the pathology screen. Unmet need was associated with poor compliance with attendance and treatment plans. Important unmet needs were mainly for detailed medical investigations, although none required hospital admission. The survey findings suggest that long-term patients should be medically re-assessed at appropriate intervals.

3190
SEASONAL VARIATIONS IN HOSPITAL ADMISSIONS

E.Frangos, G.Athanasenas, S.Frangou and P.Alexandrakou
Athens, Greece
Private psychiatric clinic (GALINI)

Biochemical, endocrine and physiological activity in various psychiatric disorders were reported to be connected with circannual rhythms. These changes had been found to be also reflected in the seasonal pattern of hospital admissions.
In order to verify further this view we studied the seasonal variations, of admission rates to the psychiatric clinic "Galini" during a five years period from January 1984 to December 1988. Our investigation covers 3252 admissions with the following diagnoses. 1729 of them were schizophrenics, 1239 of them had unipolar affective disorders, 250 patients of the group had bipolar affective disorders and 134 had schizoaffective disorders.
The schizophrenic patients were more likely to be admitted in summer and spring $P < 0.2$ N.S.
In the group of patients with unipolar affective disorder we found that they were mainly admitted in summer and spring $P < 0.001$.
The patients with bipolar affective disorders were admitted in spring $P < 0.05$ while schizoaffective patients were most often admitted in summer and spring $P < 0.05$.
Our findings suggest that climatological factors such as temperature and photoperiod may effect, at least partially, the course of some of above psychiatric disorders.

3191
THE INFLUENCE OF FATHER ABSENCE IN PSYCHIC DISORDERS

Scherdin-Wendlandt, H., Berzewski, H.

Crisis Intervention Center, Klinikum Steglitz, Free University Berlin

The data of 970 patients treated a the crisis intervention department of the Klinikum Steglitz from 1982 to 1985 revealed 25% of the patients to have grown up as "fatherless" children. This group showed specific characteristics in clinical diagnosis, age, and sex compared to the other group raised as children with two parents. A significant number of "fatherless" patients were diagnosed as neurotic ($P<5\%$). On the other hand, patients with two parents showed a corresponding tendency towards psychotic disorders. In addition, significant differences exist in the latter group with regard to addiction and attempted suicide (based on data from 1982). In view of increasing divorce rates and one-parent families, the ensuing problems and opportunities of father-absent socialisation need not to be more thoroughly examined.

3192
MORTALITY AMONG PSYCHIATRIC INPATIENTS. A STUDY IN THE POST-REFORM ERA IN ITALY

B.CARPINIELLO*, M.CARTA*, P.L.MOROSINI** & N.RUDAS
*Institute of Psychiatry, University of Cagliari
** National Health Institute, Rome- ITALY

The principal results of a mortality study conducted in Cagliari (Sardinia,Italy) will be presented. All in patients of the local Psychiatric Hospital who had been present for one year or more at 1.1. 76 (at the beginning of the "deinstituzionalization era") were considered (1577 subjects). Follow up covered about ten years (up to 6/7/87). Causes of death were registered according to ICD IX, on the basis of Registry Office data. Standardized Mortality Ratios (SMR) were calculated for sex, age, diagnosis, condition (in or outpatient) at death respect to psychiatric care and cause of death; survival curves were also calculated. 490 subjects (31.5 %) were dead at the moment of follow up. Only 22 of them (1.4%) were not traced. Overall males (1.59) and females SMR (1.72) were about equivalent, showing a significant higher mortality among psychiatric patients. About all age classes showed higher rates of mortality respect to general population: this finding was more evident for age classes 15/19 (SMR 16.3), 20/24 (SMR 14.9), 30/34 (SMR 14.9) and 35/39 (SMR 10). Not natural causes of death, first suicide (SMR 2,700) showed their preminence.

3193

MORTALITÉ ET PSYCHOSES: RÉFLEXIONS CLINIQUES
A PROPOS D' UNE RESHERCHE
Hôpital Général de Chalkis-Département d' Eubée

S.Stylianidis, Greece

A la suite des travaux de O.BOURGUIGNON(1984) nous avions émis l' hypothèse, qu' il y a dans les familles comprenant au moins un psychotique, une surmortalité prématurée (avant 30 ans).

Cette hypothèse est confirmée, lors d' une recherche épidémiologique (1985-86) en France, pour les frères et soeurs et les enfants de 101 sujets psychotiques appariés à 101 sujets témoins.

Cette recherche, dirigée par le Prof. Bourguignon, fera l' objet d' une publication.

L' interprétation des résultats statistiques obtenus se complexifie si nous prenons en considération le matériel clinique issu des entretiens avec les familles des psychotiques.

A travers l' étude de la crise familiale et des mécanismes de l' éclosion des psychoses dans notre pratique psychiatrique en Grèce, nous essaierons de poser quelques questions sur les rapports entre la mortalité et le fonctionnement psychotique.

3194

MENTAL DISEASE AND CRIMINAL BEHAVIOUR - A STUDY OF 11.533 MALES.

Jørgen Ortmann, Herstedvester Treatment Centre, Copenhagen, Denmark.

The study includes a birth cohort of 11.533 males born within the metropolitan area of Copenhagen, Denmark, during 1953.

20% of the total sample had been registered for offence against the criminal code. 5% of the total sample had been psychiatrically hospitalized.

15% of the registered offenders had been inpatients in a mental hospital. Among those who had commited a sexual offence, an offence against property or a crime of violence, the rate of psychiatric hospitalization was 10% - 12%, while 31% of those who had commited an offence against the law concerning narcotics had been inpatients in a mental hospital.

Among the 5% of the total sample who had been admitted to a psychiatric hospital 59% were registered for offence against the criminal code. 42% of diagnosed schizofrenias were registered as offenders while this was the case for 90% of the drug-abusers.

The results certify a relation between the registered criminal behaviour and the registered hospitalization in a psychiatric department. This relationship vary according to the registered crime and the diagnose.

Session 490 Free Communications:
Behavioral and cognitive therapies

3195

The Teaching of Cognitive Therapy of Depression
SAMUEL-LAJEUNESSE B., BUISSON G.
Clinique des Maladies mentales et de l'Encéphale, Centre Hospitalier Spécialisé SAINTE-ANNE, 100, rue de la santé 75674 PARIS cédex 14 - FRANCE.

As behavioral and cognitive therapies are sufficiently well-structured it is now possible to teach these psychotherapies using both video cassettes and a computer program.

In this communication, we will present an evaluation of the effectiveness of such a method based on the results of students being trained in a cognitive therapy approach to depression.

3196

FROM DEPRESSION TO SELF-ESTEEM

Manoochehr Khatami,M.D.
St. Paul Medical Center-Chief of Psychiatry

UTHSC- Dallas Professor of Clinical Psychiatry
U.S.A.
In this paper, depressive disorders,their symptomatology, clinical course and therapeutic techniques are described.

Two basic models of cognitive theory of depression and the Logotherapy of Viktor Frankl are reviewed and specifically applied to depressive disorders. The techniques of cognitive therapy and logotherapy application are discussed in depth. Both are incorporated in the single homework assignment called Logochart in which patients evaluate daily life situations that present problems, in three parameters;namely, Attitude, Meaning, and Responsibility. The patients, by analyzing the situation along these three parameters, are assisted to move from their automatic self to a more authentic self which reflects noetic dimensions.

It is hypothesized that depressive patients will overcome symptoms of depression and achieve personal growth if they:

a. Modify their automatic negative appraisal of reality and their environment.
b. Move to a more realitic,adaptable, rational thinking mode.
c. Analyze the underlying frustrated motivation (will to power/pleasure).
d. Move toward a meaningful task with responsibl action.

3197
DEPRESSION ACCORDING TO COGNITIVE THEORY
AND SYSTEMIC THEORY
Alliani D.,Bartolomei S.,Montecalvo G.,Piro
A.,Preziosa P.,Loriedo C.,Vella G.
PSYCHIATRIC CLINIC UNIVERSITY OF ROME ITALY
Both systemic and cognitive theories agree
upon the importance of early learning in
the development of depressive personality.
The two theories disagree upon the meaning
they give to the early experiences.
According to cognitive theory the emotions
bound to a significant and not reparable
loss turn themselves into a pursuit of
autonomy in order to prevent further
grieves. In the grown-up person if autonomy
is not reached or is lost a depressive
episode will rouse.
According to the systemic theory, children
learn emotions and behaviours directly from
the expressed emotions and behaviours of a
depressed parent. The child also learns by
himself or through the healty parent the
feeling of impotence/inability to help. He
also observes how to respond to the
depressed parent care eliciting behavior.
The grown-up child will make use of the
depressed behaviour when he will feel
inable to face by himself critical life
events or to elicite care or attention by
the partner.
Some possible connections for constructing
a unitary theory are presented.

3198
Behavior therapy of cognitive and social disorders
in schizophrenic patients
Volker Roder
Psychiatrische Universitätsklinik Bern/Switzerland

An integrative psychological therapy program consisting of five subprograms (Cognitive Differentiation, Social Perception, Verbal Communication,
Social Skills, Interpersonal Problem Solving) is
presented. The effectiveness of this Integrated
Psychological Therapy Program (IPT) was shown in
various studies on different groups of schizophrenic patients. But a systematic evaluation of each
of the five subprograms of the IPT was not done
yet.
Therefor in the study described the subprogram
"Cognitive Differentiation" was evaluated. The
hypothesis that basic attentional and cognitive
dysfunctions have a pervasive influence on the
overt behavior (hypothesis of pervasiveness) was
tested.
The investigation was practiced with 18 schizophrenic patients, who were relected according to DSM-
III diagnosis. An intra-group design was used. The
therapy was applied during 6 weeks (30 sessions,
60 minutes each). Results showed significant improvements in cognitive and information processing
skills. As far as psychopathology and social behavior are concerned, there were no significant
changes during therapy. Conclusions for the implementation of the other subprograms of the IPT and
for the model of pervasiveness are drawn.

3199
Behavioral Treatment of Obsessional Rituals

AGATHON M., BUISSON G., SAMUEL-LAJEUNESSE
B.
Clinique des Maladies Mentales et de l'En-
céphale, Centre Hospitalier Spécialisé
SAINTE-ANNE, 100, rue de la santé 75674
PARIS CEDEX 14 - FRANCE

In a large number of studies using specific designs behavior therapy has been effective in the treatment of obsessive
compulsive disorders. Behavioral approaches of these disorders might also be used
in everyday medical practice. An overview
of cases treated during these last ten
years shows that obsessional rituals can
be reduced without prescribing high dosages of antidepressant drugs. Evaluation of
the clinical state of the patients by a
psychiatrist (independent observer) and
by their own self-report is discussed.

3200
Exposure, Relaxation, and Cognitive Therapy in
Obsessive-Compulsives
Mark Curci, Fugen Neziroglu
Hofstra University, Bio-Behavioral Psychiatry,
Great Neck, NY

Rational-Emotive Therapy, relaxation, and exposure
and response prevention, were employed in six
obsessive-compulsives. Single subject and group
methodology were employed. Rational-Emotive
Therapy was hypothesized to produce positive
effects when compared to relaxation and to
augment the effectiveness of exposure. Dependent
variables were frequency, intensity and duration
of compulsions and self-reports of depression,
anxiety, cognitive dysfunction and social
disturbance. Rational-Emotive Therapy was the
least effective treatment and generally ineffective. Relaxation was minimally effective on
all self-report variables except anxiety.
Exposure was highly effective for compulsions
and all self-report variables except cognitive
dysfunction. Additional exposure in lui of
adding different treatment approaches is
suggested.

3201

MULTIMODAL ANTIDEPRESSANT THERAPY AT A GENERAL HOSPITAL

Berthold A., Hartmann W.
Psychiatrische Klinik Ingolstadt

In the last ten years several studies have proved the effectiveness of a combined cognitive-behavioral and pharmacological approach to major depression.
We therefore wanted to see if such a combined therapy could be realised under the limited conditions of a psychiatric department at a general hospital.
We proceeded by instructing the staff of a traditional ward in cognitive training based on Roth and Rehm. Antidepressant medication and sleep deprivation was maintained as basic treatment. Additional activities were organised as therapy units and planned individually for each patient with emphasis on group activities.
Within 18 months we treated 128 patients, 58 of which took part in time-limited cognitive training. Positive effects could be seen on organisational and communicative skills. The conclusion being, that even with the limited facitilities at a general hospital a multimodal antidepressant therapy could be established.
The improvement of admission modalities and diagnostic standards and maintaining therapeutic skills inspite of staff fluctuation are items of further discussion.

3202

LA PSYCHOTHERAPIE DE RELAXATION A INDUCTIONS PERSONNALISEES

R.A. JULIEN, M. PAULIN, J. SZYMANSKI, H. AOUIZERATE
C.H.S. Valvert Bd des Libérateurs - 13011 MARSEILLE (FRANCE)

Les diverses méthodes de relaxation, qu'elles s'inspirent de J.H. SCHULTZ ou de celle de JACOBSON induisent un vécu corporel idéalisé qui se réfère à un ensemble d'états fondamentaux (lourdeur, chaleur, etc) ou à un relâchement tonique systématisé. Ce vécu de détente induit par le relaxateur laisse peu de place à la spontanéité et à la créativité du patient, bridant les potentialités de son imaginaire. La Psychothérapie de Relaxation à Inductions Personnalisées est une méthode d'inspiration psychanalytique qui a pour but de respecter le vécu spontané de détente du relaxant. Les inductions parlées ou touchées ont pour principe de restituer à ce dernier les sensations ou les émotions qu'il éprouve lors de la succession des séances, au sein de la relation transférentielle. Le vécu de détente au même titre que le matériel des rêves est entendu dans sa dimension transférentielle et métaphorique, chaque sensation, émotion, pensée ou image, faisant l'objet d'un travail associatif comme peut l'être le contenu des rêves. Le déroulement de chaque cure est ainsi profondément ancré, enraciné, dans l'histoire de chaque sujet. L'ouverture de ce dernier aux dimensions de son propre imaginaire lui permet en effet de se découvrir et de se situer dans sa dynamique relationnelle et existentielle.

3203

Cognitive Therapy versus Psychopharmaca in the Treatment of Depression.
Cayiroglu S., Holub U., Merkel, E., Zapotoczky H.G.
Psychiatric University Clinic of Vienna
Währinger Gürtel 18-20, A-1090 Vienna, Austria

This paper compares three groups of patients that have been treated with a) cognitive behaviour therapy, b) a combination of cognitive therapy and a reversible MAO inhibitor (- of type A with a short biological half life, brand name Ro 11-1163) and c) a combination of cognitive behaviour therapy and placebo, using a randomized double blind procedure. The paper sets out to compare effectiveness of cognitive behaviour therapy with a new MAO inhibitor with both outpatients and inpatients, with the purpose of reinvestigating findings of the literature in a controlled study.

During therapy we could observe a statistically significant progressive decline of depression and irrational beliefs by all patients of the three groups. At the end of therapy all patients were also significantly less anxious.

After one and a half year a follow up was made with the same test-inventory and additionally with a questionnaire concerning life events. From 32 patients 22 have taken part: Further two patients were contacted by phone and 8 were drop outs. All explored patients showed a tendency of further improvement. The exact results will be presented.

Session 491 Free Communications:
Psychiatric training: Themes and variations

3204

ATTITUDES OF MEDICAL STUDENTS TOWARDS PSYCHIATRY

H.E. Soufi, M.D., Asst. Clinical Prof. (USA),
Psychiatric Dept., Acting Chairman, College of Medicine, King Saud University, Abha Branch, Abha, Saudi Arabia
Ameed M.S. Raoof, M.B.Ch.B., M.Sc., Ph.D.,
Center of Medical Education, Director

Our purpose is to present findings from questionnaires and a statistical survey given to all medical students here in Abha at the College of Medicine. This mental health catchment area of Assir in southwest rural Saudi Arabia, of about one million inhabitants needs Saudi nationals to specialize in psychiatry for present and planned future delivery of services. Medical students, however, have lacked motivation to so specialize. Some of the findings and approaches are discussed.
Summary of results: We found the students' main difficulty is their difficulty perceiving psychiatry as a medical specialty.
Conclusion: Psychiatry, stigmatized worldwide, as well as here, may be better approached on a concrete level (e.g. psychopharmacological and psychosomatic) in order to gain credibility. Carrying the practice outside the local psychiatric hospital and into area general hospitals, among other steps, also seems to harbor promise.

3205

MEDICAL STUDENTS' ATTITUDE AND OPINIONS ON PSICHIATRY.
F. Giberti*, G. Corsini*, S. Rovida**
*Department of Psychiatry - **Department of Biometrics and Medical Statistics.
University of Genoa, Italy.

An anonymous questionnaire was submitted to 224 medical students from November 1987 to December 1988. The aim of the questions was to assess the opinions of the students towards psychiatry, psychoanalysis, psycotherapy, the career they wanted to take up, and the difficulties encoutered in studying psychiatry.
The survey analyzes some distinctive features of the students who want to choose psychiatry as a career. The authors think that such a kind of investigation could be useful for the improvement of didactis and for preventing the risk of the decline in the number of medical students who choose psychiatry as a career, similarly to what happened in U.S.A . Furthermore the Authors maintain that inquiring on the attitude of medical students towards psichiatry would lead to a better understanding the meanings of the professional choice, the identity of the psychiatrists and their relationship with their collegues in other medical fields.

3206

PSYCHOPHARMACOLOGICAL FORMATION. PEDAGOGICAL DESIGN.
SORIA, Carlos. Pharmacology Dpt. Medical School. National University. Córdoba. ARGENTINE.

In our environment psychopharmacologists are few; their psychodrugs literature access is deficient. We designed a trial to improve this state which will be oriented to teaching, research and consultory areas. Methods: Forty advanced medical students have been selected and incorporated to a four-year plan which includes 12 subjects, theoretical (1026 hs) and practical (528 hs) work. This plan will be a complement to the pharmacological, psychiatric and pedagogic learning and new methods of teaching will be used. It has been annually evaluated (clinical and up-to-date monographic supervisions, and multiple choise tests). Results: Enrolled: 40 students; ended: 26(65%). Orientation of graduates: Psychiatry (81%); General practice (11%); postgraduated studies abroad (8%). Twenty two students (85%) are still in our Dpt. of Pharmacology, working as members of the staff; they belong to 5 different teams: a) teach in pre- and (b)postgraduates courses (Pharmacology, Psychiatry, Neurology and Anesthesiology chaires; c) work for the primary prevention against pharmacodependence; d) work in consultary in psychiatric hospitals e) participation in plans of continuous medical education.
Conclusions: The pharmacological formation since pre-gade permits to orient vocations and to reverse the psychopharmacological deficit.

3207

POST GRADUATE PSYCHIATRIC TEACHING PROGRAM IN SAUDI ARABIA

Dr. Osama M. Al Radi, Dr. Osama Al Radi Psychiatric Poly Clinic, Taif Saudi Arabia.

Kingdom of Saudi Arabi was established on September 1932 by H.M. King Abdul Aziz Bin Saud by Royal decree proclaiming the dual Kingdom of Hajaz and Najid to be unified under the new name, the Kingdom of Saudi Arabia.

The Country occupies most of the Arabian peninsula. The total land area is 2,149,00 sq. km. In 1980 the population of Saudi Arabia was estimated at 8.8 million. The estimated ratio of Bedouins varies, the most widely accepted figure is about 20%. Speed of progress in psychiatric services is very satisfactory like any other field of life of Kingdom.

Mental Health Services (MHS) in Saudi Arabia have been developed from a scratch. While the MHS were being expanded by providing a psychiatric unit in every existing and proposed General Hospital, the greatest difficulty was paucity of trained personnel. With the advise of WHO, a tentative plan and schedule was implemented in 1976. Taif Psychiatric Hospital in 1974 took initiative in collaboration with the Who, Saud University, the pannel has consisted of Professors from over a dozen countries-an International Faculty of distinguished teachers, since 1976. By now Taif has produced 45 psychiatrists. WHO Adviser has evaluated in his report (EM:MENT:83) "This innovative approach in Psychiatric training which has been applied in Taif, forms a practical model for other countries in the Region".

3208

THE ANALYTIC PSYCHODRAMA IS A TRAINING TOOL IN PSYCHIATRY
Caverzasi E., Vender S.
Institute of Psychiatry, University of Pavia, Pavia, Italy

The analytic psychodrama is being used since a few years ago as a training tool in the educational activity of the Institute of Psychiatry of the University of Pavia. It has been employed in intensive periodic sessions with University students of Medicine and with psychiatrists, psychologists and nurses working in community mental health services. The authors describe this experience focusing on the following points:
- theoretical and methodologic problems of the setting and of the techniques, including role-playing and simulation of clinical conditions.
- emotional and relational dynamics related to an intensive involvement with the psychiatric disease.
- the educational issues of this experience in the view of the emergence of psychodynamic movements such as defences, transference controtransference, projective identification, and so on.

3209

Textbook of clinical psychology in Africa

Karl Peltzer and Peter O Ebigbo,
Dept. of Mental Health, Obafemi Awolwow University,
Ile-Ife, Oyo State, Nigeria.

Most textbooks are Western oriented and do not consider African realities. However, there is an increasing need to understand and treat mental disorders in African societies, communities, families and individuals. While providing the student of health and behavioural sciences with priniculals of clinical psychology in Africa, the textbook intends to provide knowledge of clinical psychology which can be utilized by all health workers as well.
Clinical psychology, a discipline that developed in Western industrialized countries, has made little recognized contribution to the problems faced by Third World countries, especially in Africa. Yet concerned as it is with the socially determined and socially relevant disturbances of the psychic life and their modifications in research, teaching and practice, clinical psychology has clear potential relevance to the practical tasks of diagnosis, therapy and prophylaxis of mental disorders in African countries.
Examples of the latter are given by summarizing the contributions of the book on Subsaharan Africa, the Caribbean, and Afro-Latinamerica.

3210

SUPERVISION OF PSYCHIATRIC NURSES DURING THE TRANSITION TO CASE MANAGERS.

Meillo, H.J., Provincial Hospital Santpoort, Santpoort-Zuid, The Netherlands.

Approximately one hundred chronic psychiatric patients have, during the last two years, been moved from an institution in the sand dunes which line the Dutch coast to locations in the city of Amsterdam.
In the next few years, another 400 chronic psychiatric patients will exchange their institutional existence for diverse forms of decentralised and more individualised lifestyles.
Because of the change of setting, working methods and the style of treatment of all staff members, but especially that of the psychiatric nurses, will have to alter.

1. Work is done more independently in the new projects. The nurse must function in a more autonomous way.
2. Large departments forced a uniform approach. The opportunities for individual differentiation in the new working methods must be exploited.
3. Making individual counselling plans demands a greater knowledge concerning tolerance capacity and the pathology of the patient.
4. Because the case manager is the principal contact person, higher demands are made of the therapeutic working relationship and the ability to negotiate. An attitude tending towards the stimulation of independence, which increases autonomy, must be created. Transference and countertransference phenomena must be recognised more clearly.

A method of group supervision based on group therapeutic principles has been developed. The method will be presented along with the results of its use with approximately 60 nurses.

3211

TWO WEEKS TRAINING OF MEDICAL OFFICERS IN MENTAL HEALTH AND POST TRAINING EVALUATION
Satyavati Devi
Dr. Ram Manohar Lohia Hospital, New Delhi, India

The Government of India has formulated a National Health Policy to define health for all by 2000 as the ultimate goal for improvement of all aspects of health; a plan of action aiming at the mental health component of NHP has been put forward aiming at (1) Prevention and Treatment of Mental and Neurological disorders; (2) Use of mental health technology and (3) Application of mental health principle in total development. Emphasis has been given on mental health at various levels during training of doctors, nurses, public health and primary health care personnel. Two weeks orientation course has been recommended for general physicians including those at dispensary level. This paper gives the experiences of such training to 91 doctors in Psychiatric unit of a general hospital. Results of Post-training Evaluation and Assessment at a review – cum – refresher workshop are very encouraging.

3212

FUTURE DIRECTIONS FOR PSYCHIATRY--IMPLICATIONS FOR TRAINING

Robert L. Leon, M.D., The University of Texas Health Science Center at San Antonio; San Antonio, Texas, U.S.A.

There is a lively debate within psychiatry about the relevance of a psychodynamic model to training for a psychiatry which is becoming more biological with new discoveries in neuroscience and psychopharmacology.
As psychiatry developed from medicine, patients were viewed from the perspective of organic pathology. Diseases, such as CNS syphillis, had demonstrable brain pathology and were eventually successfully treated with specific therapies. But specific therapies were not available for other mental disorders. Perhaps because of this, attention turned to psychological and social therapies. Meanwhile, biological psychiatry has advanced to the point that more psychiatry disorders can be successfully managed by psychopharmacologic therapies.
Trainees see promise for even more definitive biological therapies in the future. Should training programs recognize this trend and, because of an already crowded curriculum, abandon systematic training in psychodynamic and interpersonal therapies? If both are taught, how much weight should be given to the various approaches? This paper will examine these issues and possible future directions.

Session 492 Free Communications:
Integrative approaches to social psychiatry

3213

SOCIAL-PSYCHIATRIC TREATMENT OF LONGTERM PSYCHIATRIC PATIENTS.
Flemming Thusholt, Jette Antonsen, Finn Jørgensen & Nguyen Ba Thuan.
Sct. Hans Hospital, Roskilde, Denmark.

The Vesterbro-project is a small community psychiatric unit in Copenhagen, which directs its treatment towards the longterm psychiatric patients in the district. The treatment is based on social-psychiatric principles.
The results of a 5-year follow-up examination of 60 patients are presented.
The results of the investigation confirm, not unexpectedly, that the patients in this project, who belong to the most severely affected clientele of institutional psychiatry, live mostly alone (86%) with poor contact with their surroundings. They are distributed corresponding to the general population as regards education, housing, material and economy and it is calculated that they will be admitted to psychiatric hospitals for an average of five weeks per annum. It is apparent from the results of the investigation that the majority had improved material conditions following contact with the Vesterbro-project but that no direct effect is registered concerning the work on the social network made by the project. The total contribution has, however, reduced the number of bed-days employed.

3214

EVOLUTION IN PSYCHIATRIC EVALUATION: AN INTEGRATED APPROACH
SCHIASSI A.*, MARTIGNETTI U.°, DI MUNZIO W.^
*Istitute of Community Medicine, II° Faculty of Medicine, Naples (Italy);
°Planning and Quality Control Unit, Campania Region, Naples (Italy);
^Dept of Psychiatry, National Research Council (CNR), HB 41, Naples (Italy)

In order to contribute to overcome the main and traditional obstacles to the evaluating processes in psychiatry - the dichotomy normality/illness, the difficulty of defining diagnostic cathegories and the singling out of underclared cases - the remarcable value of qualitative variables and limits of the sole epidemiological methods in the evaluation have been stressed.
A fish-eye approach has been shaped and operative guidelines are suggested: a. the observational field has to be considered the whole context the "analyzing system" is in; b. the study target becomes a continous selection of indicators of disability, whose validity needs to be tested as regard with their analitical relationship; c. methodologies must be adapted to the process of formulating the research hypotesis. Thus whether the focus has to move on the activity and management of Services - whose evaluation will just be neither on organising grounds nor case by case - the inadequacy of common cycle of Quality Assurance and, vice versa, the value of an integrated approach - a spiral model - have been underlined.

3215

EVALUATION OF THE COMMUNITY MENTAL HEALTH PROGRAM IN LIMA
T. Sato[1], R. Castro[2], J. Lopes[2], C. Arellano[2], M. Mendoza[2]
[1]Dept. Neuropsychiatry, Keio Univ. Med. School, Tokyo, Japan.
[2]National Institute of Mental Health, Lima, Peru.

It is a principal theme of psychiatry today that we achieve the community program, on the basis of the concept of Primary Health Care. National Institute of Mental Health of Peru has been realizing the Community Mental Health Program in the seven health centers in the northern part of Lima. We surveyed symptoms, diagnosis, treatment, prognosis and adaptive functions etc., analyzing 5587 patients who received psychiatric care of this Program from 1980 to 1986. Of 5587 patients, 3595 had been treated by the nurses only. According to their diagnosis, the rate of "Disturbance of emotions specific to childhood and adolescence" was 37.8%, "Neurotic disorders" -21.5%,"Adjustment reaction" -9.2% (by ICD-9). After screening, the psychiatrists examined 1992 patients, diagnosed 25.5% as "Neurotic disorders", 21% as "Disturbance of emotions specific to childhood and adolescence", and 17.4% as "Schizophrenic psychoses". About 86% of all patients were able to adapt in the family and community. Only 81 patients were admitted. Authors would like to clarify from these results the benefit of community psychiatry and Primary Health Care by WHO.

3216

INTERNATIONAL PRIORITIES IN MENTAL HEALTH RESEARCH
M. Bernardo, E. Vieta
Subdivisión de Psiquiatría y Psicología Médica, Hospital Clínic i Provincial, Barcelona.

The authors present a study conducted using Delphi technique with an international sample of 50 outstanding researchers in order to know their opinion respect to which are the most important areas of mental health research in their scope.

A questionary expressly designed for this purpose was administered twice and although there was certain dispersion, remarkable agreement was reported.

There are five main areas that demand attention and economic resources according to the results of this study: 1) sociocultural factors and psychiatric morbidity (X 11.64), 2) methodology in early case detection and case identification (X 10.90), 3) evaluation of the relationship between cost and efficacy in the assigment of resources (X 10.68), 4) life events, stress and psychiatric morbidity (X 10.64), 5) general structure of Mental Health Community Services (X 9.82).

3217

MENTAL HEALTH CARE IN A MULTICULTURAL SOCIETY

I. H. Minas, Victorian Transcultural Psychiatry Unit, Melbourne, Australia.

The scale of the Australian immigration program has resulted in fundamental changes in the composition of Australian society. Approximately 40% of Melbourne residents are either born outside Australia or have at least one parent born overseas, with nearly three quarters of the overseas-born from non-English speaking countries. The provision of appropriate and effective psychiatric services in such a society constitutes a formidable challenge, both to those who plan health services and to those who work in them. Health care, professional, educational and other institutions are beginning to respond to the increased complexity of the situation. There is a growing recognition of the special needs of cultural and linguistic minorities. In Victoria, one concrete expression of this changed perception is the establishment of the Victorian Transcultural Psychiatry Unit, for the purpose of developing culturally appropriate, bilingual clinical programs, and research and teaching in the area of transcultural psychiatry. Although the Unit will undoubtedly be confronted by many conceptual and practical problems, this paper will focus on the opportunities which are created by the establishment of such a Unit.

3218

ARBEITSWEISE DER SOZIALPSYCHIATRISCHEN UNIVERSITAETSKLINIK BERN/SCHWEIZ
Dr. Herbert Heise
Sozialpsychiatrische Universitätsklinik
CH-3010 Bern   Direktor Prof. L. Ciompi
Die Sozialpsychiatrie hat den Anspruch, den leidenden Menschen in seiner psychosozialen Ganzheit zu erfassen. Eine eigentliche sozialpsychiatrische Theorie, welche die gegenseitige Bedingtheit von konstitutionellen Merkmalen, innerpsychischen Konstrukten und Sozialverhalten beschreiben müsste, ist noch nicht entwickelt. Im Vorstadium der Theoriebildung verwenden wir in ergänzendem Sinne Krankheitsmodelle biologisch-psychiatrischen, psychologischen und tiefenpsychologischen sowie systemischen Ursprunges. Die Behandlung der Patienten erfolgt an unserer Klinik durch pluridisziplinäre Teams. Bei Fallvorstellungen wird in einem hermeneutischen Verfahren versucht, Verständnis zu entwickeln und diesem Prozess wird mehr Bedeutung beigemessen als den herkömmlichen Diagnosen. In den Begegnungen mit dem im grundsätzlichen Engagement homogenen, ansonsten heterogenen Team lernen Patienten Meinungsverschiedenheiten auszuhalten, eigene Widersprüchlichkeiten anzunehmen und sich an ihrer Behandlung aktiv zu beteiligen. Die 1978 gegründete Klinik behandelt jährlich etwa 1500 Pat. aus einem definierten Einzugsgebiet. Die Evaluation unseres Dienstes zeigt sowohl bezügl. Behandlungserfolges als auch für die Kosten gute Resultate. Aufgrund dieser Erfahrungen arbeiten wir laufend an einer Verbesserung der psychiatrischen Versorgungsstrukturen unserer Region im ambulanten und teilstationären Bereich.

3219

A NOVEL UNIT FOR OCCUPATIONAL MENTAL HEALTH IN GREECE.
S.Verveniotis,N.Moros,M.Passa.
Psychiatric Clinic of the University of Athens:Unit for Occupational Mental Health.Athens,Greece.

Providing mental health care at the workplace is of recent introduction in Greece, at the pilot level.The Unit for Occupational Mental Health created by the Psychiatric Clinic of the University of Athens is active in a factory employing ca.2·500 workers.Its objectives are primary and secondary prevention in the industrial context,delivery of psychiatric and psychosocial services to the staff,as well as informing and intervening to the management in issues concerning mental health.Difficulties,particularities,accomplishments and deficiencies are presented in this paper,as well as clinical issues relevant to the particular Unit.Conclusions concerning the creation of similar Units in this country are exposed.

3220

STRESSFUL LIFE-EVENTS, COPING-STRATEGIES AND SELF-CONCEPT OF SUICIDE-ATTEMPTERS AND NON-SUICIDE ATTEMPTERS
Berzewski, H., Brauns, M. L.
Psychiatric Outpatient Ward and Crisis Intervention Center of the Klinikum Steglitz, Free University Berlin
30 patients who had attempted suicide just before treatment in a crisis intervention ward were compared with a matched control group of 30 patients with the same diagnosis but without previous suicide attempt. Stressful life-events, coping-strategies, self-concepts and other personality characteristics of the patients were analyzed by means of self-rating scales. Comparison of the two groups revealed, that suicide attempters experience significantly more chronic stressful life-events during the last three years before admission than non-suicide attempters, particularly in the areas of personal relations, partnership, health and well-being. Both groups share a deficit in active and successful stress-coping, characterized by a passive-resignative attitude. Suicide attempters however differ from non-suicide attempters in regard to their lower need for social support. They are less occupied with reflecting on stressful problems and repress aggression. No differences between both groups were found for self-concept and other personality characteristics.

3221
A CASE MANAGEMENT SERVICE FOR THE HOMELESS MENTALLY ILL
D.A.Wasylenki, P.N.Goering
Clarke Institute of Psychiatry, Toronto, Canada

There are 250 hostel beds for homeless people in Metropolitan Toronto which serve 12.000 different persons annually. Estimates of the percentage of the homeless population which has a psychiatric diagnosis range as high as 30-40 percent. In 1988 the government of Ontario provided funding for eight psychiatric case managers to be employed throughout the hostel system. This paper describes the case management program and characteristics of the client population.
Case managers were trained in psychiatric rehabilitation and assigned to six hostels. Clients are screened for psychotic symptoms and homelessness by staff and then admitted to the program. This report describes work with 70-80 clients admitted during a six month period. The process of case management is described as are relationships between case managers and clients, using standardized instruments.
Client characteristics are also described. Data include sociodemographic features, history of housing and homelessness, past and current psychiatric treatment, substance abuse and criminal activity, use of services, residential stability, social isolation, physical and mental health and social functioning.

Session 493 Free Communications:
Psychosocial factors in suicidal behavior and self-mutilation

3222
SOME OBSERVATIONS ON THE SEVERITY OF THE SUICIDE ATTEMPT IN A LARGE HOSPITAL GROUP.

Theodoropoulou - Vaidaki St, Yalouris A, Saranditis D, Tripodiannakis J, Priami M, Pachi E.

In 805 subjects admitted in our hospital during a 3-year period for a suicide attempt we have studied the severity of the attempt in relation to several other parameters According to the degree of the severity patients were divided in 3 groups.
It was found that:
1. In the group with the lowest severity grade mean age was significantly (p 0.0001) lower than in the other two, while in that with the highest grade it was significantly (p 0.0001) higher.
2. Patients with an underlying adjustment disorder had as a group significantly (p 0.001) lower severity grades as compared to those with psychotic or affective states. Between the latter two groups there was also a less significant (p 0.03) difference.
3. Patients with a history of at least one previous suicide attempt showed significantly (p 0.005) higher severity grades than those without such history. If the former group was subdivided according to whether the time-lapsed from the last attempt was more or less than 6 months no differences existed between the two groups.

3223
CLINICAL AND DEMOGRAPHIC CHARACTERISTICS OF SUICIDAL PATIENTS

D. Sarantidis, S. Theodoropoulou, J. Tripodianakis
M. Priami, E Pachi, A. Yalouris.

From 1986 to 1988, 838 patients were assessed, following a suicidal attempt. All the patients were admitted in the hospital for monitoring and / or management of the physical sequelae of their suicidal attempt. 201 patients were males (mean age 37 years) and 637 were females (mean age 32 years).
This paper presents the analysis of 721 patients who were classified in one of the following 3 diagnostic categories 1) Adjustment disorder. 2) Affective disorder and 3) Schizophrenic disorder, Paranoid disorder and Psychotic disorder not elsewhere classified, combined. These 3 diagnostic categories were compared regarding age, marital status, precipitating factors of the attempt, previous attempts and method of the present attempt. The results showed: 1. Age. The group of patients with the diagnosis of adjustment disorder were younger, whereas the group of affective disorder patients were older (ANOVA $p<0.0001$). 2. Marital status, More affective disorder patients were married ($x2=53.51$, $p<0.0001$). 3. Precipitating factors. Most of the adjustment disorder patients attempted suicide because of interpersonal problems ($x2=106.95$, $p<0.0001$). 4. Previous attempts. More affective disorder patients had at least one previous attempt ($x2=8.73$, $p<0.02$). 5. Method of attempt. Most of the adjustment disorder patients use an overdose ($x2=38.31$, $p<0.0001$).

3224
PSYCHIATRIC AND PSYCHOSOCIAL STUDY OF SELF-MUTILATING PATIENTS
ÖZKAN S.*, NOGAY A., TARHAN N., BURKOVİK Y., YAVUZ D., DANACI M., KUŞÇU M.
* Ist. Fac. of Medicine Dept. of Psychiatry
Ist./Turkey

In this research, we have aimed a clinical psychiatric and psychometric analysis of self-mutilating patients in an attempt to understand the psychopathology, clinical features, motivational correlates and psychosocial aspects of deliberate self-harm. For this reason, those patients who have applied to psychiatry and to various departments of surgery with repeated acts of self-mutilation have been examined. Those patients with history of chronic drug dependence, psychosis, major affective disorder, gender identity disorder or those with major medical illnesses are not included. Only those with major self-mutilation, namely severe wrist-cutting, self-shooting, amputation have been included.
All cases (21) had been throughly examined clinically and tests of personality (Rorschach, T.A.T., MMPI) were applied. A special scale, developed by us, concerning motivational, situational, social factors and familial developmental, cultural experiences, was given to each subject.
The overall results revealed masochistic tendencies and a close link between childhood experiences, parental communication, conduct disorder and self injuring later in life.

3225
Psychiatric consultation to selfpoisoned patients in regional hospital.
M. Nordentoft, P. Rubin, B. Welcher.
Psychiatric department, Bispebjerg Hospital
Copenhagen, Denmark.

In the regional poisoning centre of Copenhagen 600 patients are interviewed by psychiatrist after suicide attempt in the period from april 1 1988 to march 31 1989. Some of the patients came from the catchment area of the hospital, and some came from other districts and were admitted to the poisoning centre because of the specialized knowledge of treatment of poisoned patients, that was developed and centralised there.
The patients were diagnosed psychiatric according to ICD 8, and information was gathered about somatic diseases, sociodemografic data, suicidal intention, reasons for suicide attempt, psychosocial stress, level of social functioning and the treatment offered to and accepted by the patients.
Results will be presented.

3226
SUICIDAL WOMEN: CONFLICTS IN THEIR RELATIONSHIPS WITH PARENTS; A CROSS-CULTURAL STUDY
Arcel, L.T.[1], Mantonakis, J., Petersson, B.[1], Jemos J. and Kalliteraki, E.
[1]Inst. of Clinical Psychology, Univ. of Copenhagen
Department of Psychiatry, University of Athens

Thirty five Greek and 35 Danish non-psychotic women who attempted suicide were interviewed in depth with a qualitative questionnaire. A remarkably large number of fathers are dead in the Greek material. It is interesting to note that a greater number of Danish women, 58.3%, report emotional dependency on parents, versus 21.7% of the Greek women. Up to the suicide attempt the relationship with the parents changed for the worse for 73% of the Greek and 28.1% of the Danish women. The conflicts of the Greek women with their parents concerned their marriage, and the parents played a controlling and conservative role. The conflicts of the Danish women were vague and spread over five themes. The Danish women solve problems with parents by dropping contact, while the Greek women engage in an active struggle against the parents' control. Greek parents insist on marriage and higher education for the Greek women, while 75% of the Danish women report that their parents did not have dreams on their behalf.

3227
A SIBLING SUICIDE PACT: PRESENTATION ON INFORMATION MEDIA AND LEGAL ASPECTS.
Papastamatis C., Lolis C. and Tzebelikos E.T.
Dpt. of Psychiatry
Sismanoglion Gen. Hosp., Athens 151 26, Greece.

Suicide pacts are very rare in contemporary Greece, though in the modern Greek history there are several instances of group or mass suicide during national liberation struggles. In March 1988 four aged people, three sisters and their brother, attempted a group suicide by ingestion of phenobarbital tablets and at the same by exposure to inhalation of gas in a closed room. The attempt was fatal for the three sisters while their brother died three months later. Most of the leading Athens newspapers had a front page coverage of the incident the next day (April 4, 1988) and the following day there were still big middle page presentations with more details and some interviews with Greek psychiatricts. The legal aspects of the incident emerged in relation to the survivor and the issue of his possible responsibility for the death of the other members of the suicide pact in the sense of a homicide. A police inquiry started several days after the incident concerning the kind of involvement of the survivor in the death of the others. We advised that a full psychiatric and neurologic evaluation was first needed before the advance of any further investigation. His death gave an end to this issue.

3228
INTERVIEWING THE SURVIVOR OF A SIBLING SUICIDE PACT.
Lolis C., Papastamatis C., and Tzebelikos E.T.
Dpt. of Psychiatry
Sismanoglion Gen. Hosp., Athens 151 26, Greece.

In March 1988 four aged people, three sisters and their brother attempted a group suicide that was fatal for the three sisters, while their brother, after getting throug a severe coma, survived for about three months with remnants of right hemiplegia (without aphasia). Survivors of suicide pacts have very rarely been interviewed and we have not seen a similar suicide pact in the relevant international literature. The survivor was the leading figure in the firm decision and the organization of the group suicide. He explained that they believed life was very tiring and bothering for them and that they couldn't tolerate easily even minor somatic disease. They were living together for a long time and this created during the last few years a decline in the interest in their interpersonal relations and a disappointment about their gradual social isolation, though they always kept strong emotional ties. After the death of their older sister, another member of the closed group, during a heat wave several months ago, started a discussion about a group suicide. They moved from their Athens family house in a resort beach flat near Athens where they prepared in a few months an effective plan. There had be no signs of psychiatric disease for any of them in their life span.

Session 494 Free Communications:
Diagnostic tools

3229

The Norris VAS : a factor analysis in asthenic outpatients
J. D. GUELFI, R. Von FRENCKELL and Ph. CAILLE, Clinique des Maladies Mentales et de l'Encéphale 100 rue de la santé 75674 PARIS Cédex 14 - FRANCE

The sixteen 100 mm scales used by Bond and Lader in rating subjective feelings were administered to 632 outpatients seen by general practitioners for an asthenic state (without manifest anxiety or mood disorder). The scales were scored before treatment in a randomized controlled trial of Toloxatone (MAOI) versus placebo and Amineptine. The most distant notes (from 0 to 100) of the average (50) had concerned the following variables: Feeble.: 67, Calm :, 66.1, Lethargic : 65.6, Antagonistic : 35.9
A factor analysis using a principal component solution and an orthogonal rotation of the factor matrix was computed with a standard program BMDP4M. Two factors were selected, those corresponding to those latent roots greater than unity : 6.14, 2.20. They accounted for 53 per cent of the total variation. Each of the 16 scales seems to load clearly on one of these 2 factors. The first factor (8 scales) : Asthenia is quite identical to the alertness factor of Bond and Lader with the following dimensions : Muzzy, Dreamy, Feeble, Lethargic, Drowsy, Mentally Slow, Incompetent and Clumsy. The other scales correspond to a second affective factor (Mood and Anxiety). An example of the use of the scales in measuring drugs effects is given with factors of change identified by principal component analysis in each treatment group.

3230

DIAGNOSTIC ABILITY OF THE SHORT VERSION OF TEQ-DE
Martín, M., Sánchez, L., Diez, A., Civeira, J.M.. Psychiatry Department Complutense University of Madrid (SPAIN)
The short version of the Tetradimensional Structural Questionnaire for Depression (TEQ-DE-"s") evaluates the four dimensions of the depression: Depressive humor, Anergy, Communication disorder and Rhythmopathy as does the long questionnaire. Each one of these dimensions is evaluated by four items and each item is measured on the scale of 0 to 4 points.
This study has been done in an acute unit and 434 psychiatric in-patients completed the questionnaire. 48.2% were depressive patients. The external diagnostic criteria has been the ICD-9.
We propose the following diagnostic definition through TEQ-DE-"s": "All the cases which present a score equal to or over 8 at least in one dimension are considered to be subsetible to depression. Therefore, the screening power means a sensibility of 99.5%. To confirm the depressive diagnosis, we evaluate that in these suspicious cases, if the total average scoring of the four dimensions is equal to or over 8, then we have a real depressive case with a specifity of 90%.

3231

THE DEFINITIONS OF SURVIVAL OPTIMAL LEARNING DEFICIT (S O L D)
NAISBERG YACOV
RAMBAM MEDICAL CENTER, HAIFA, ISRAEL.

SOLD is an inherited or acquired condition that revolves around devices founded on desynchronization with the environmental cues at any time and location. SOLD originates from the abnormal biochemical rhythms associated with the central opiod peptides deficiency, which fails to modulate the Anti-Stress alterations. SOLD produces an increased effort within the framework of misaccomodation with the overall task assignments in comparison with healthy counterparts. An effort is measured by the mobilized directed motivational exercise to carry out IO standardized neutral intellectual acts within one minute. By introducing IQ standardized rating scales, each of them is designed to be assessed in one minute. In dissimilar aspects of an exhibited effort, we were able to identify the oversensitive, insensitive, inappropriate, inadequate, inefficient and ineffective components, that compose the SOLD principle.
The aim of this technique is to monitor the level of SOLD expressions, in order to prevent the individuals integrative and achievemental deterioration.

3232

Factor analysis of the PANSS in Schizophrenic patients

LEPINE JP (1), PIRON JJ (2), CHAPOTOT E (2).
(1) Hopital Bichat,46 rue H Huchard,75018,Paris,FRANCE
(2) RP SPECIA Company,16 rue Clisson,75013,Paris,FRANCE

Kay et al (1987) have recently proposed a new scale to assess psychotic symptoms in shizophrenia: the Positive And Negative Syndrome Scale (PANSS). This new scale in the original works of its authors seems highly reliable and valid and allows different measurements either dimensional or typological. To our knowledge there are no data on the factorial structure of this scale. As part of an on-going study of pipothiazine in acute exacerbation of symptoms in shizophrenia, we used in different assessments a French translation of the PANSS. Our population included 101 schizophrenics -68 males and 33 females- aged $31.8+\_9.8$ years. According to DSM III-R criteria diagnoses were as follow: chronic schizophrenia with acute exacerbation 73 patients mainly paranoïd type (58) or subchronic with acute exacerbation 22 mostly paranoïd type (19). The 6 remaining patients were shizophrenics not otherwise specified. We computed a principal component analysis of the scale at D 0. Before rotation 8 factors had eigenvalues greater than one. After orthogonal varimax rotation and adopting the following criteria: no factor having less than 3 items, items loading greater than .50 on a factor and no split loading items we found a 4 factors solution explaining 52.8% of the total variance. These 4 factors can be labelled as: negative symptoms- hostility/excitement - anxiety/depression and paranoïd factor. Other psychometric data and results of this analysis will be discussed during this presentation.

3233

Personality Assessment Interview (PAI), diagnosis and psychotherapy.

C.Maffei, S.Dazzi, T.Farma, and M.A.Selzer*
Institute of Medical Psychology, University of Milan-H.S.Raffaele V.Turro Milan Italy
*The N.Y.Hospital-Cornell Medial Center (USA)

The historical development of the diagnostic interviewing shows a shift in accent from manifest contents to interaction between subject and interviewer. The PAI inquires exclusively into the interpersonal patterns emerging during the interview, fostering an "in vivo" observation of psychic functioning. After the first phase of clinical experimentation the authors maintain that: 1- The interview fosters the coming out in only one session of the personality structural organization, since it strongly focuses on interpersonal dynamics. 2- The usefulness is for diagnostic purposes as well as for an evaluation of the amenability to a specific kind of psychotherapy.
3- The actual problems in dealing with the interview concern the translation of the qualitative data in quantitative ones. All this seems to be inherent the logic structure and the theory of this interview.

3234

MULTIAXIAL ASSESSMENT OF PSYCHIATRIC MORBIDITY: THE E.P.E.P.

A. Lobo, R. Campos, M.J.Pérez-Echeverría, J. Izuzquiza, J. García-Campayo.

Hospital Clínico Universitario. Zaragoza, Spain

Our psychiatric research with medical patients and primary care medicine in Spain and the international literature over the last decade, have suggested the importance of multiaxial systems of diagnosis and classification. Psychiatric morbidity has been traced, in many studies, to the presence, but also to the absence of organic pathology. The presence of such morbidity, but also its intensity and duration have important implications. Psychopathological phenomena have been correlated with abnormal personality traits and/or social problems. Social support has probably implications for prognosis and treatment. The E.P.E.P. (Entrevista Psiquiátrica Estandarizada Polivalente or Standardized Polivalent Psychiatric Interview) has been constructed to assess all those axes, but also to generate enough information to use modern diagnostic criteria, such as ICD-10 or DSM-III-R . The Clinical Interview Schedule (C.I.S.) was the nucleus of the new interview. Ils inter-rater reliability is now reported.

3235

DETECTION OF PSYCHIATRIC MORBIDITY IN CHILE
- A NEW INSTRUMENT -

ARAYA, Ricardo

Institute of Psychiatry, London, England

AIMS: 1) To validate the General Health Questionnaire (GHQ) and the Self Reporting Questionnaire (SRQ) against the Clinical Interview Schedule (CIS). 2) To compare interrater reliability of medical and non-medical personnel administering a new version of the CIS 3) To estimate prevalence of minor psychiatric morbidity in a poor urban 'barrio' of Santiago and its relation to socio-demographic variables.

METHOD: 170 consecutive attenders to a Primary Care Clinic in Lo Prado, Santiago were interviewed before seeing their physician. A socio-demographic questionnaire, GHQ, and SRQ were given to them by medical students. Illiterate patients had their questionnaire read out. A trained psychiatrist (RA) interviewed 50 randomized attenders using the new CIS which was also administered to 70 additional patients by lay interviewers whose training consisted of 3 hours theoretical teaching and observing the psychiatrist interview two people. 50 patients were also tested and observer-rated by lay personnel and a psychiatrist alternating in order each time. After consultation the physician rated the severity of mental and physical problems on a scale of 0-5.

RESULTS: Approximately 2/3 of the sample were female. 5 people refuse to take part for various reasons. Less than 10% were illiterate. Social problems were common. Prevalence of psychiatric cases was above 50% with any of the instruments using accepted cut-off points. Correlation coefficients for and among the 3 instruments were very similar (0.63 to 0.710). Further analysis using ROC and LISREL statistical packages is still in progress.

3236

Reliability and Validity of 3 Depression Rating Scales.

A.Kørner, F.Eschen, B.Mejer Nielsen, S.Møller Madsen, A.Stender, E.M.Christensen, H.Aggernæs, M.Kastrup, J.K.Larsen.

Psychiatric Dept., Frederiksberg Hosp., Denmark.

The Hamilton Depression Scale (HAM-D) is widely used despite the fact that it has many shortcomings. As a consequence of the critique, modifications of HAM-D, e.g. the Melancholia Scale (MES) by Bech and Rafaelsen, as well as new scales e.g. the Montgomery-Åsberg Depression Rating Scale (MADRS) have been introduced.
Very few studies so far have assessed the reliability and validity of these 3 scales when applied simultaneously. In this study 41 patients suffering from a current depressive episode were assessed with HAM-D, MES, MADRS as well as the Clinical Global Impression Scale (CGI) and the Visual Analog Scale (VAS), all applied simultaneously.
The interrater reliability is evaluated by intraclass reliability co-efficients.
The homogenity and transferability is tested by Rasch model fitting. The validity of the 3 scales is evaluated by the degrees of convergence when correlated to the global assessments.

3237
Etude sur la validité de contenu de 2 échelles sur la satisfaction de patients psychiatriques.
Pierre P. Leichner, m.d. - Michel Perreault, m.a.
Centre hospitalier Douglas

Le "Client Satisfaction Questionnaire" (CSQ) de Larsen et al. (1979) et l'échelle de satisfaction de Distefano, Pryer et Quillin (1985) représentent les 2 mesures de satisfaction les plus fréquemment utilisées en rapport aux services psychiatriques offerts en externe et à l'interne. Afin de vérifier dans quelle mesure ces échelles standardisées mesurent les aspects les plus importants soulevés par les patients lorsqu'ils sont questionnés sur leur satisfaction des services, un protocole de passation oral impliquant l'administration de questions ouvertes suivies d'une échelle de satisfaction a été élaborée. L'étude a été menée auprès de 71 patients hospitalisés et de 55 usagers d'un centre de jour. Les résultats obtenus démontrent une corrélation significative entre les résultats aux échelles standardisées et un score global établi à partir d'une codification de l'ensemble des réponses aux questions ouvertes. Par ailleurs, le contenu des items utilisés dans ces échelles ne couvre pas certains aspects des services jugés importants par les usagers. Ceux-ci sont l'ambiance, les règlements, la socialisation avec le personnel et les patients et la disponibilité des services connexes. Il est suggéré d'inclure aux échelles standardisées des items visant à mesurer ces dimensions.

ADDENDUM*

---

* The following abstracts have been received late for inclusion under their respective session titles. For readers' convenience these titles are repeated in the addendum.

Session 272 Symposium:
The role of psychiatry in mental health policy formulation

1788
THE ROLE OF PSYCHIATRY IN MENTAL HEALTH POLICY FORMULATION IN CANADA
Harnois, Gaston P., M.D.
W.A.P.R., Montreal, Canada

Most countries of the world have legislation dealing with compulsory admissions of the mentally ill to hospitals. More recently, a number of countries have drafted mental health policies outlining the philosophy and functioning of mental health programs.
This usually includes an assessment of the scope of mental illness in a given society, a description of programs available, including prevention as well as promotion of mental health. Mention is also made of the desirability of having rehabilitation programs which may start in the hospital and extend in the community, often as a part of the deinstitutionalization process. The ultimate objective of maintaining the chronic mentally ill in the community is emphasized.
The main actors are the individual, the family, the mental health workers and professionals, and the community, all acting in a spirit of partnership.
The role of psychiatry as a key component in both treatment and rehabilitation will be outlined.

Session 365 Symposium:
Links between psychiatry and general practice: Present trends

2361
LIAISON-PSYCHIATRY: A PARTNERSHIP BETWEEN PATIENTS AND GENERAL PRACTITIONERS
Ph.J. Parquet
Sce de Psychiatrie, Univ. de Lille, France
Many reasons lead general practitioners, psychiatrists and patients to be concerned by Liaison-Psychiatry: patients are dissatisfied by a highly technological and fragmented medicine; specialized physicians perceive better the determinism of diseases, their psychoaffective setbacks and the way they should be treated; general practitioners feel more and more involved in their patient treatments; psychiatrists wish they could open themselves to the whole set of pathology, and not only to pure mental disorders.
All those demands have emphasized liaison psychiatry, which suffer on the other hand from 3 sorts of problems:
1. the common approach to the diseases by the different practitioners is undermined by different frames of reference
2. liaison-psychiatry is practiced from different theoretical bases such as biological, psycho-affective or behavioral ones: they should be justified
3. one can meet so many different approaches among institutions and practitioners that it reveals real gaps between practices.
Despite good wishes, general-practitioners' role lacks of real consideration. Moreover, patients are not considered as real partners.
The analysis of these three points, the literature and the basis of clinical experience will lead to a rationale for a good practice of liaison psychiatry.

2362
WHEN THE PATIENT IS BACK HOME AFTER A STAY AT HOSPITAL: WHO SHOULD TAKE CARE OF HIM?

Peter Berner
Psychiatry - University Clinic, Vienna, Austria

Psychiatric hospitals generally refer their patients either to structured facilities, which, especially in areas where psychiatric services have been sectorized, promise a good continuity of care, or to practicing psychiatrists.
The role which general practitioners should play for the further taking in charge of the former psychiatric patients has only systematically been explored for the Third World, and is widely neglected in developed countries.
The different tasks which the general practitioners can assume for these patients, in regard to somatic and psychotherapeutic treatment, and relapse prevention, are pointed out, and the basis of a collaboration between practitioners on the one side, and psychiatric services and practicing psychiatrists on the other, are analysed. In this regard it is stressed that, in addition to an adequate psychiatric formation of medical students, a continuous post-graduate training is necessary, which may be assumed in the frame of such a collaboration, combining theoretical information with discussion of individual cases.

2363
THE CHRONIC PSYCHOSES AND GENERAL PRACTICE

M. Paes de Sousa
Dept. of Psychiatry, Faculty of Medicine of Lisbon, Hospital St. Maria, av. Prof. Egas Moniz. P-1600, Lisbon, Portugal

Firstly, the general belief that psychoses are an exclusive field for psychiatrists, is discussed. Since Portugal and other countries have many regions far away from the centers in which all health care is undertaken by G.P.s it is necessary to help them screen or even diagnose the psychoses, especially the therapy management. Simple means for differential diagnosis and the basic principles of long term treatment, is discussed.

2364
GENERAL-PRACTITIONERS, PSYCHIATRISTS AND DEPRESSION: HOW SHOULD THEY COLLABORATE?

Maurice Ferreri
Dept. de Psychiatrie et Psychologie Medicale
184, rue du Faubourg St. Antoine, F-75571 Paris Cedex 12, France

Most of the depressive disorders are first met by general-practitioners. They can treat mild depressive disorders on an outpatient basis. However severe depressions, chronic ones, recurring ones, or depression with suicidal risk, require a psychiatrist's advice; he'll give a diagnostic opinion for difficult cases, take care of long-standing and severe depressions. Diagnostic schedules, such as the H.A.R.D. (Rufin-Ferreri) are useful for the G.P. to evaluate the intensity of the episode, the suicidal risk, and should give him an aid for the immediate decisions, such as the necessity to ask for the psychiatrist's aid.

2365
GENERAL-PRACTITIONERS, PSYCHIATRISTS AND ANXIETY DISORDERS
Guy Parmentier
Fondation Bon Sauveur, BP 94, F-81003 Albi, France
In developed countries, despite high density of physicians, patients who suffer of anxiety disorders are rarely diagnosed, and properly treated, unless they suffer super-imposed depressive episodes. On the other hand, benzodiazepines seem to be excessively used, maybe on a wide auto-medication basis. Practicing psychiatrists meet more and more patients with anxiety disorders, unsuccessfully treated for years with placebos, repeatedly addressed to numerous different somatic-specialists, calling on their own, despite the fact that they were often vigorously discouraged to seek a mental-specialist's advice. General-practitioners may tend to consider anxiety disorders as factitious disorders, once somatic diseases are eliminated. They may also use a different frame of reference when they analyze their patients' complaints of anxiety symptoms: Cultural-bound syndromes are widely used, such as "spasmophilia" in France, with a pseudo-physiopathology. It denies a mental origin at the problems encountered and prevents the G.P.'s from referring their patients to a psychiatrist, what they sometimes still imagine to be outrageous. Furthermore, many physicians suffer from anxiety and they may be reluctant to make the diagnosis of a disorder they tend to consider desperately chronic and intractable. Beyond an adequate psychiatric formation of medical students, anxiety disorders demand a continuous postgraduate training, both on the diagnostic and the treatment modalities of these wide-spread, but undoubtedly, neglected mental disorders.

2367
IS IT REALLY POSSIBLE FOR GENERAL PRACTITIONERS TO UNDERSTAND PSYCHIATRISTS' POINT OF VIEW?

Pierre Aslanian
7, place A. Cherioux F-75015 Paris, France

Patients seem to be less afraid than they used to be when a General-Practitioner intends to refer them to a Psychiatrist. Nevertheless, the collaboration between the two practitioners remains difficult.
The General Practitioner, as a physician of the body and the psychiatrist, as a physician of the mind, have specific concerns that make them differ.
However, as Psychiatry language becomes more and more clear for the layman, general-Practitioners are more aware of the problems of the mind. That's why one can hope on a new kind of relationship between the different practitioners. This new kind of complementarity will be addressed.

Session 377 Free Communications:
Long-term pharmacotherapy of schizophrenia

2462 A
CLINICAL & BIOLOGICAL FEATURES OF TARDIVE DYSKINESIA
Zelaschi N (+), Di Loreto A (*), Villanueva M (@), Cirullo S (*), Delucchi G (@).
(*)A.Korn Neuropsychiatric Hosp. (+)CONICET, (@)Psychiatry Dept.La Plata Med.School,Argentina

Recent investigations have suggested that biological markers, like Cognitive functions impairment (CF) or PRL levels after neuroleptics (NP) chronic treatment, can be associated with the onset of Tardive Dyskinesia (TD). We studied 44 male chronic inpatients with schizophrenia (x age:46.34, SD 11.3, x Hospitalization: 13 years, SD 1). BPRS, DISCUS and a modified version of 10 items scales were administered. Serum PRL levels were measured with RIA. A computerized Spearman Rank Correlation matrix was used in order to analyze the associations. CPZ equivalent dosages was significantly correlated with PRL levels (Rs 0.34, P<0.05) CF decrease with patient's age (Rs-0.52, P<0.01) but this reduction is not associated with DT scores, Oral Dyskinesia (OD) or Negative Symptoms (NS). Serum PRL levels are not associated with the degree of DT or OD. The age does not seem to be related with the onset of DT, since we could not find any relation between DT or OD scores and age. The patients received a high NP dosage (CPZ equiv.x=1900, DS=1760) but was not significantly correlated with BPRS, DT nor with OD scores. In several patients, high serum PRL levels (x =30.51, DS=17.27, min=4.2, max=80.1) and the persistence of physiologic hyperprolactine response, suggest that the tolerance of the NP chronic ability to increase PRL levels, could not be developed; therefore, the hypersensitivity phenomena in Tuberoinfunddibular system could not occur, at least in some patients. If TD is linked with a hypersensitivity phenomena in the human striatum, these results suggest that the dopaminergic pathways in schizophrenia could react in different ways after long term treatment. DT, like therapeutic response, seem to depend on an individual predisposition, that still must be elucidated.

AUTHORS' INDEX

A

AALBERS, C.: 2369 (366)
AAPRO, N.: 503 (73)
ABATI, A.: 1110 (167)
ABATZOGLOU, G.: 25 (5)
ABAY, E.: 1372 (211)
ABD EL AZIM, S.: 2297 (353)
ABDEEN, A.: 1251 (194)
ABDO, A.: 1904 (290)
ABE, K.: 738 (114)
ABE S.: 1582 (243)
ABE T.: 698 (108), 701 (108)
ABENSUR, J.: 1272 (198)
ABERG-WISTEDT, A.: 2892 (441), 2754 (418)
ABHYANKAR, V.M.: 2469 (378)
ABOU EL AZAYEM, G.: 2192 (334),)
ABOU-SALEH, M.: 2388 (368), 1301 (202), 2656 (405)
ABRAHAMS, C-M: 2862 (438)
ABREU, P.: 1882 (287)
ABRIL, A.: 768 (117), 1002 (153), 1336 (207), 146 (22), 601 (91)
ABRIL, J.: 1738 (262), 146 (22)
ABU-DAGGA, S.: 737 (114)
ABUZZAHAB, F.: 2538 (388)
ACHTE, K.: 1708 (256), 1732 (262), 2035 (309), 627 (97), 3157 (485),
ACKENHEIL, M.: 63 (12), 1104 (166)
ACKERMANN, R.: 2033 (308)
ADACHI, S.: 423 (64)
ADAM, K.: 550 (82)
ADAMOPOULOU, A.: 579 (88)
ADAMOU, N.: 2350 (363)
ADAMSSON, C.: 2966 (451)
ADDINGTON, D.: 1873 (286)
ADDINGTON, J.: 1873 (286)
ADELAJA, O.: 2205 (336)
ADENA, M.: 2893 (441)
ADLESTEIN, J.: 1377 (211)
ADORNO, D.: 1894 (288)
ADSERBALLE, H.: 2995 (458), 628 (97)
ADVENIER, C.: 2029 (308), 2475 (379)
AFIFI, M.: 2102 (320)
AGARTZ, I.: 697 (108), 699 (108)
AGATHON, M.: 2700 (410), 3199 (490)
AGGERNAES, H.: 3236 (494)
AGID, Y.: 455 (68)
AGNES, M.: 2465 (378)
AGNOLI, A.: 859 (129)
AGRA-ROMERO, S.: 1698 (255), 366 (56)
AGRAFIOTIS, D.: 459 (68), 2122 (323)
AGREN, H.: 2386 (368)
AGRIMI, G.: 539 (79), 2115 (322), 802 (120), 1417 (216), 1964 (296)
AGTZIDOU, A.: 2670 (406)
AGUGLIA, E.: 486 (70), 1084 (163), 1937 (293), 2375 (366)
AGUILAR, C.: 2703 (410)
AGUILAR, R.: 1829 (279), 1577 (242), 79 (13)
AGUIRRE, R.: 1414 (215)

AHLFORS, U.: 2137 (325)
AHMED, I.: 838 (125)
AHMED, S.: 2255 (347)
AHR, H.J.: 407 (62)
AHRENS, B.: 798 (120)
AHUJA, G.: 2720 (412)
AIVAZIAN, TH.: 1369 (211)
AIZENBERG, D.: 3151 (484), 849 (128)
AKARSU, E.: 2143 (326)
AKIHIKO, T.: 1985 (300)
AKIHISA, T.: 2133 (325)
AKIMOTO, Y.: 2837 (434)
AKIO, T.: 2134 (325)
AKISKAL, H.: 711 (109), 2311 (356), 707 (109)
AKITA, I.: 1831 (280), 3028 (464)
AKSOY, S.: 2089 (318), 2823 (431), 1064 (159)
AL ATROUNY, M.: 2196 (334), 2198 (334), 2486 (380)
AL AWADI, Q.: 1736 (262)
AL KHULAIDI, A.: 1745 (264)
AL MAHDY, M.: 2197 (334)
AL QASSIM, M.: 1736 (262)
AL RADI, M.: 3117 (479)
AL RADI, O.: 3207 (491), 2197 (334)
AL SABAIE, A.: 740 (114)
AL SHEIKHLI, A.K.: 741 (114)
ALAROTU, P.: 1011 (154)
ALBALUSTRI, L.: 3018 (462), 329 (50)
ALBANI, J.: 329 (50)
ALBANO, C.: 1017 (155), 1016 (155)
ALBANOPOULOU, I.: 2123 (323)
ALBARRAN, A.: 2866 (438), 1305 (202)
ALBERS, M.: 2780 (422)
ALBERTINI, E.: 2443 (375)
ALBINSSON, A.: 481 (70)
ALBRECHT, W.: 37 (7)
ALBUQUERQUE, A.: 2460 (377), 1490 (228), 2261 (348)
ALBUS, M.: 2418 (373)
ALBY, J. M.: 967 (147), 1000 (153)
ALCALDE, J.: 179 (26)
ALCIATI, A.: 460 (68)
ALDA, M.: 706 (109)
ALEVIZOS, B : 267 (39), 1721 (260), 335 (51), 334 (51), 1537 (237), 1538 (237), 784 (119), 1379 (212), 2218 (338), 269 (39).
ALEVIZOU, V.: 2097 (320), 2100 (320)
ALEXANDER, M. S.: 2181 (331)
ALEXANDRAKOU, P.: 1176 (181), 3190 (489), 1687 (254)
ALEXANDRE, J.: 122 (20)
ALEXANDRESCU, L.: 2280 (351), 1594 (244)
ALEXANDRI, A.: 2052 (311)
ALEXANDRIS, V.: 985 (150), 1597 (244)
ALEXANDROPOULOS, K.: 352 (53), 2281 (351)
ALEXIUS, B.: 727 (112), 726 (112)
ALEXOPOULOS, C.: 1103 (166)
ALEXOPOULOS, G.: 2502 (382), 1497 (230)
ALEXOPOULOS, T.: 352 (53), 2281 (351)
ALF, C.: 1085 (163), 1540 (237)
ALFONSI, E.: 2277 (351)
ALFONSO, C.: 15 (4)
ALFONSO SUAREZ, S.: 2639 (403), 311 (47)
ALGUR,: 1845 (281)
ALINOVI, R.: 1617 (246)
ALLAIN, H.: 2045 (310)
ALLARD, P.: 530 (78)
ALLEBECK, P.: 2966 (451)
ALLEN, S.: 1380 (212)
ALLERS, G.: 359 (54)
ALLIANI, D.: 1090 (164), 2587 (396), 587 (89), 1009 (154), 2692 (409), 3197 (490)
ALLILAIRE, J.: 1621 (247), 2289 (352)
ALLORI, L.: 2110 (321)
ALMANSA PASTOR, F.: 567 (85)
ALMENAR, C.: 3046 (466), 2901 (442)
ALMENTA HERNANDEZ, E: 1763 (266)
ALMOGUERA, A.: 3037 (465)
ALNAES, R.: 2249 (346), 1981 (299)
ALONSO-FERNANDEZ, F.: 2785 (424)
ALPHS, L.: 2623 (401), 1942 (294)
ALPKAN,: 1845 (281)
ALSHEHRY, M.: 2102 (320)
ALTAMURA, A.: 2128 (324), 2147 (326), 1884 (287), 1883 (287), 2425 (373), 2603 (398), 2298 (353), 2604 (398)
ALTERWAIN, P.: 560 (84), 2675 (407), 33 (6)
ALVAREZ, E.: 935 (142), 934 (142), 2401 (370)
ALVAREZ, J.: 1305 (202)
ALVAREZ, V.: 2444 (376)
ALVAREZ, X.: 2866 (438)
ALVAREZ LOBATO, P.: 1570 (241), 1912 (290)
ALVARINO, F.: 2166 (328)
ALVERNO, L.: 2667 (406), 2975 (453)
AMADUCCI,: 2056 (312)
AMANO, N.: 704 (108)
AMBROGI, F: 427 (64)
AMBROSI, P.: 3187 (489), 437 (65)
AMELING, E.: 2433 (374)
AMERING, M.: 844 (127)
AMES, L.: 2809 (430)
AMIEL, R.: 3066 (471), 59 (11)
AMMAR, S.: 1535 (236), 1636 (248), 455 (68)
AMOROSO, H.: 418 (63)
ANAGNOSTOPOULOS, D.: 523 (77)
ANAGNOSTOU, E.: 1685 (253)
ANASTASIADIS, P.: 1750 (264), 1180 (182)
ANASTASOPOULOS, D.: 1241 (193), 1125 (171)
ANASTASOPOULOU, E.: 2100 (320)
ANCILL, R.: 3183 (488)
ANCONA, L.: 2477 (379)
ANCONA, M.: 1739 (263), 2477 (379)

ANDERER, P.: 2674 (407), 876 (132)
ANDERSCH, B.: 2064 (314)
ANDERSEN, E.: 2028 (308), 908 (137)
ANDERSEN, J.: 800 (120), 2865 (438)
ANDERSEN, P.: 164 (24)
ANDERSEN, T.: 2339 (361)
ANDERSSON A.: 805 (121)
ANDERSSON, G.: 481 (70)
ANDERSSON, K.: 2064 (314)
ANDERSSON-LUNDMAN, G.: 2902 (443)
ANDO, E.: 2513 (383)
ANDO, K.: 2776 (422)
ANDRADE, C.: 2254 (347)
ANDRADE, J.: 228 (33)
ANDRADE, L.: 1626 (247)
ANDREA, S.: 2670 (406)
ANDREANI, F.: 1964 (296), 539 (79), 2115 (322), 802 (120), 1747 (264), 1417 (216)
ANDREASEN, N.: 208 (30)
ANDREASSON, S.: 2966 (451)
ANDREEN, J.: 3059 (469)
ANDREINI, G.: 1031 (156)
ANDREOLI, A.: 503 (73), 1272 (198)
ANDREOLI, J.: 2646 (404)
ANDREOLI, V.: 1110 (167), 669 (104)
ANDREOU, A.: 2164 (328)
ANDRIANOPOULOS, G.: 3012 (461)
ANDROULAKI, O.: 2670 (406)
ANGELBERGER, P.: 837 (125)
ANGELBERGER-SPITALER, H.: 718 (111)
ANGELIDES, G.: 1369 (211)
ANGELOPOULOS, E.: 2163 (328), 224 (33), 2164 (328)
ANGELOPOULOS, N.: 824 (123), 3102 (477), 1929 (292), 588 (89)
ANGLESIO, A.: 1204 (185), 2943 (447)
ANGRIST, B.: 2327 (359), 2740 (415)
ANGST, J.: 3130 (480))
ANGUELOV, I.: 1640 (249)
ANKRI, G.: 403 (61)
ANNABLE, L.: 1206 (186), 533 (79), 422 (63)
ANOCHINA, I.: 2368 (366), 1322 (205)
ANSART, E.: 358 (54)
ANSSEAU, M.: 2184 (332), 2540 (388), 1526 (235), 2428 (374), 2539 (388)
ANTHONY, J.: 745 (115)
ANTONELLI, P.: 786 (119)
ANTONIN, K.: 1946 (294), 3184 (488)
ANTONOPOULOS, V.: 1729 (261), 1404 (214), 434 (65), 779 (118)
ANTONOPOULOU, F.: 947 (144), 949 (144)
ANTONSEN, J.: 3213 (492)
ANTUN, F.: 607 (92)
ANTUN, R.: 2402 (370)
AOKI, N.: 897 (135)
AOKI, Y.: 897 (135)
APOSTOLOGLOU, V.: 1662 (251), 2704 (410)
APPELBERG, B.: 2137 (325)
APPELBOOM-FONDU, J.: 3009 (461)
APTER, A.: 1338 (207), 1339 (207)
AQUIZERATE, H.: 3202 (490)
ARAKI, K.: 586 (89)
ARATO, M.: 65 (12), 3185 (488), 431 (64), 416 (63), 738 (114)
ARAVANTINOS, D.: 262 (39)
ARAYA, R.: 3235 (494)
ARBOLEDA-FLOREZ, J.: 3074 (473)
ARCEL, L.T.: 3226 (493), 2856 (437)
ARELLANO, C.: 3215 (492)
ARENA, A.: 2115 (322), 1964 (296)
ARENDT, J.: 637 (98)
ARIANO, M.: 1655 (250)

ARICO, C.: 1961 (296)
ARIE, T.: 2551 (390)
ARIENTI, P.: 373 (57), 1058 (158)
ARIKAN, K.: 1528 (235)
ARITOME, T.: 163 (24)
ARITZI, S.: 2063 (314), 262 (39), 284 (41)
ARKONAC, O.: 1210 (186), 1552 (239), 1845 (281), 1922 (292)
ARMENIAKOS, A.: 1728 (261), 779 (118)
ARMENIAKOU, S.: 1398 (214)
ARNOLD, S.: 2270 (349)
ARNT, J.: 2916 (444)
ARO, H.: 1134 (173)
AROLT, V.: 3021 (462)
ARONI, S.: 1241 (193)
ARONSON, T.: 1376 (211)
ARPIN, J.: 2841 (434), 584 (88)
ARRIAGA, F.: 2634 (402)
ARRINDELL, W.: 2616 (400), 2619 (400)
ARRUNDA, M.: 714 (110)
ARTHUR, G.: 1060 (159)
ARTIGAS, F.: 2155 (327), 935 (142), 934 (142)
ARVANITIS, Y.: 728 (112), 2100 (320)
ARVIN, B.: 1529 (235)
ARVIZZIGNO, C.: 2001 (303)
ARYA, B.: 705 (108)
ARYA, D.: 1563 (240)
ASABA, H.: 2777 (422)
ASAI, K.: 698 (108)
ASAI, K.: 701 (108), 2857 (437), 970 (148)
ASANO, T.: 1036 (156)
ASARNOW, R.: 607 (92), 2402 (370)
ASBERG, M.: 2215 (338)
ASCHAUER, H.: 130 (21), 69 (12), 483 (70)
ASCHAUER-TREIBER, G.: 3174 (487), 130 (21)
ASCIONE, C.: 1629 (247), 128 (20)
ASHCROFT, K.: 1163 (179)
ASHTON, C.: 1162 (179)
ASHWOOD, T.: 1657 (250)
ASIMAKOPOULOS, C.: 826 (123), 603 (91)
ASLANIAN, P.: 2367 (365)
ASSAF, J.: 2206 (336)
ASSANTE, M.: 1714 (259)
ASSEN, G.: 2819 (431)
ASSIMOPOULOS, H.: 1241 (193)
ASTORGA, C.: 1903 (289)
ASUNI, T.: 2211 (337), 61 (11), 1444 (220)
ATHANASENAS, G.: 1176 (181), 3190 (489)
ATHANASIOU, V.: 215 (31)
ATHITAKIS, M.: 1661 (251), 1662 (251)
ATNIP, D. K.: 1864 (285)
ATSUSHI, T.: 2095 (319)
ATTOU, A.: 174 (26)
ATZA, M.G.: 1573 (242)
AUBIN, B.: 1487 (228)
AUBIN, V.: 1694 (254), 1005 (153), 835 (125)
AUDIBERT, M.: 428 (64)
AUDRAIN, S.: 1872 (286)
AURIACOMBE, M.: 21 (4)
AVASTHI, A.: 1563 (240), 2797 (426)
AVGERI, V.: 352 (53), 2281 (351)
AVRAMOPOULOS, D.: 2160 (328)
AVRUTSKY, G.: 1111 (167)
AWAD, G.: 3183 (488)
AXELSSON, M.: 631 (97), 189 (27), 89 (14)
AXER, A.: 2591 (397)
AYALA, J.: 2444 (376)
AYHAN, I.: 2143 (326), 2165 (328)

AYSEV, A.: 273 (40)
AYUB, H.: 2816 (430), 2815 (430)
AYUSO-GUTIERREZ, J.L.: 2645 (404), 132 (21)
AYUSO-MATEOS, J.L.: 132 (21)
AZEVEDO, H.M.: 681 (106), 3139 (481)
AZMI, S.A.: 3030 (464)
AZORIN, J.M.: 1128 (172), 1871 (286), 430 (64)
AZURI, A.: 2816 (430), 2815 (430)
AZZARELLI, O.: 1084 (163)

B

BA THUAN, N.: 3213 (492)
BABA, E.: 1047 (157)
BABAOGLU, A.: 1064 (159)
BABOR, T.: 716 (110)
BACCI, T.: 206 (29)
BACELAR NICOLAU, H.: 957 (146)
BACH, M.: 964 (147), 965 (147), 1085 (163)
BACHMANN, K.: 113 (19)
BACKMUND, H.: 1710 (257), 2959 (449)
BADDOURA, C.: 2206 (336), 2815 (430), 2816 (430)
BADIA, M.: 1002 (153), 2581 (395)
BAHADIR, G.: 2689 (409), 1567 (241)
BAHR, B.: 1024 (155)
BAILLON, G.: 1276 (198), 1437 (219)
BAILLY, D.: 1167 (180), 122 (20), 1542 (237)
BAILLY-SALIN, P.: 1435 (219)
BAIOCCHI, A.: 1045 (157)
BAIRAKTARIS, K.: 3105 (477)
BAISCHER, W.: 1308 (202)
BAJC, M.: 350 (53)
BAKALL, R.: 1341 (208)
BAKER, G.: 809 (121)
BAKER, H.: 640 (98)
BAKER, J.: 1109 (167)
BAKISH, D.: 3183 (488)
BAKOURAS, S.: 2122 (323)
BAKSI, A.: 2771 (420)
BAL, S.: 2286 (352)
BALANESCU, S.: 2936 (447)
BALANT, L.: 1684 (253), 2411 (372)
BALANT -GORGIA, A.: 2411 (372), 2051 (311), 1684 (253)
BALDESSARINI, R.: 1887 (288)
BALDUCCI, M.: 1175 (181)
BALDWIN, D.: 2606 (398)
BALENZANO, T.: 1029 (156)
BALIS, G.: 2271 (350), 218 (32), 2103 (320)
BALL, J.: 1816 (278)
BALLAS, C.: 510 (74), 1957 (296), 1289 (200)
BALLUS, C.: 1432 (218), 1441 (220)
BALS, B.: 2439 (375)
BALSA, J.: 2648 (404)
BAMRACH, J.: 1346 (208)
BAN, T.: 1582 (243), 2810 (430), 674 (105)
BANDELOW, B.: 1549 (238), 890 (134)
BANERJEE, G.: 2511 (383)
BANERJEE, S.: 787 (119)
BANERJI, N.: 2186 (332)
BANGOS, G.: 2238 (345)
BANI, A.: 2715 (412), 442 (65)
BANKI, C.: 379 (58)
BANOBI, M.: 2864 (438)
BANON, D.: 1139 (173)
BARABASH, A.: 3172 (487), 2645 (404)
BARAHONA DA FONSECA, I.: 3015 (462), 1391 (213), 1370 (211)

BARAHONA DA FONSECA, J.: 3015 (462), 2258 (348)
BARANDA, M.: 2703 (410)
BARANIUK, G.: 463 (68)
BARBOSA, A.: 2668 (406), 1602 (245)
BARI, M.: 928 (141)
BARNAS, C.: 3137 (481), 1297 (201), 3182 (488)
BARNES, J.: 1492 (229)
BARNES, N.: 1492 (229)
BARNES, P.: 2624 (401)
BAROCKA, A.: 762 (116), 216 (31), 3040 (466)
BARON, J.S.: 1621 (247)
BARON, P.: 2617 (400)
BARONI, A.: 2848 (435)
BAROUCHE, F.: 2740 (415)
BARREIRO, A.: 3172 (487)
BARRELET, L.: 2588 (396), 83 (14)
BARRETT, L.: 2526 (386)
BARRIL, G.: 2444 (376)
BARROS, A.: 1054 (158)
BARRY, D.: 2376 (366)
BARSI, J.: 65 (12)
BARTELS, M.: 834 (125), 2913 (444)
BARTELS, S.: 97 (16)
BARTILOTTI, R.: 1009 (154), 2692 (409)
BARTKO, G.: 3185 (488), 1673 (252)
BARTLETT, J.: 830 (124)
BARTLETT, R.: 2460 (377)
BARTOCCI, C.: 68 (12)
BARTOLOMEI, S.: 1090 (164), 3197 (490), 1927 (292)
BARTONEK, R.: 1706 (255)
BARTZOKIS, G.: 700 (108)
BARUA, U.: 1880 (287), 1879 (287), 1881 (287), 2918 (445), 2424 (373)
BARUCH, H.: 1106 (167)
BARUCH, P.: 1535 (236) 1636 (248), 455 (68)
BARUCH, S.: 1376 (211)
BARULEY, C.: 2528 (386)
BARWICK, C.: 3053 (468)
BAS, M.: 702 (108)
BASDRAS, A.: 772 (117)
BASHIR, A.: 1589 (244), 1092 (164)
BASOGLU, M.: 2435 (374), 310 (47)
BASSE, P.: 260 (38)
BASSO, A.: 2489 (380)
BASTANI, B.: 1942 (294), 2448 (376)
BASTANI, H.: 2623 (401)
BASTOS, O.: 891 (134)
BATCHELOR, D.: 477 (70), 476 (70), 1689 (254), 793 (120)
BATHIEN, N.: 175 (26)
BATISTA, A.: 957 (146)
BATTEGAY, R.: 1381 (212), 715 (110), 2049 (311)
BATTH, S.: 190 (28)
BAUCO, A.: 1389 (213), 995 (152), 2662 (406), 990 (151)
BAUCO, M.: 998 (152)
BAUDIN, M.: 2790 (425), 1198 (185), 1601 (245), 788 (119)
BAUER, K.: 171 (25)
BAUER, M.: 2565 (393)
BAUER, T.: 449 (66)
BAULM, J.: 2439 (375)
BAUMGARTNER, A.: 1612 (246), 884 (133)
BAYDAS, G.: 1528 (235)
BAYER KNOPMAN, E.: 3161 (486)
BAYLE, O.: 1601 (245)
BEAHRS, C.: 1061 (159), 2188 (333)
BEAHRS, J.: 2989 (457), 1061 (159), 2188 (333), 2189 (333)
BEAMONT, P.: 3007 (461)

BEARD, C.: 285 (42)
BEAUCLAIR, L.: 2544 (388), 1206 (186), 422 (63)
BEAUDRY, P.: 3183 (488)
BEAUFILS, B.: 885 (134)
BEBBINGTON, P.: 1853 (283), 1970 (297), 979 (149)
BECCIA, J.: 1054 (158)
BECH, P.: 2507 (382), 1863 (284), 1388 (213), 1024 (155), 906 (137), 251 (37), 1326 (205), 2320 (358)
BECHLIVANIDIS, CH.: 194 (28)
BECHTEL, B.: 359 (54)
BECHTER, K.: 571 (86)
BECHTEREVA, N.: 2522 (385)
BECK, G.: 762 (116), 1652 (250), 216 (31)
BECK, R.: 2269 (349)
BECK-FRIIS, J.: 879 (133)
BECKER, T.: 1386 (212), 834 (125)
BECKERMANN, B.: 2886 (441), 407 (62)
BECKMANN, H.: 1386 (212), 1072 (161), 1998 (302), 3071 (472), 834 (125), 277 (40), 1347 (208), 943 (143)
BECKMANN, T.: 449 (66)
BEERSMA, D.: 667 (103), 666 (103), 2633 (402)
BEHAR, D.: 1408 (215)
BEHERE, P.: 349 (53)
BEHNKE, K.: 2251 (347)
BEHR, F.: 2208 (336)
BEIGEL, A.: 2574 (394), 1786 (272)
BEINAT, L.: 1543 (237)
BEKDIK, C.: 273 (40)
BELARDINELL, N.: 2263 (348), 766 (117), 1613 (246)
BELENKY, G.: 2205 (336)
BELFRAGE, H.: 598 (91)
BELIN, CL.: 1113 (168)
BELL, V.: 777 (118), 1547 (238)
BELLAIRE, W.: 1641 (249)
BELLINI, L.: 486 (70)
BELLO GAY, M.: 1586 (243)
BELLOMO, A.: 1032 (156)
BELTZ, J.: 2158 (327), 2437 (375)
BELUGOU, JL.: 633 (98)
BENADON, V.: 2283 (351), 289 (42)
BENEDETTI, G.: 616 (93)
BENEDUCE, R.: 3114 (479)
BENEKE, M.: 238 (35), 239 (35), 409 (62), 1645 (249)
BENGESSER, G.: 384 (58), 154 (23)
BENGOUJRAH, B.: 597 (91)
BENITEZ, G.: 1132 (172)
BENITEZ, J.: 1086 (163)
BENKERT, O.: 2176 (330), 638 (98), 857 (129)
BENNEGADI, R.: 3054 (468), 580 (88)
BENSAAD, A.: 580 (88), 3054 (468)
BENSMAJL, B.: 597 (91), 1759 (266)
BENSON, K.: 1329 (206)
BENVENUTI, P.: 1693 (254), 1746 (264)
BENZ, U.: 596 (90)
BENZONI, O.: 2354 (363)
BERATIS, S.: 1479 (227), 54 (10)
BERGEM, M.: 2067 (315)
BERGENER, M.: 2780 (422)
BERGER, K.: 2096 (319)
BERGER, M.: 2900 (442), 882 (133), 2629 (402), 3050 (467), 252 (37), 2343 (362)
BERGER, P.: 3174 (487), 2096 (319)
BERGIANNAKI, J.: 1174 (181), 1307 (202), 996 (152), 1190 (184), 2345 (362), 2735 (414), 217 (31), 1173 (181), 393 (60), 392 (60), 49 (9)
BERGMAN, H.: 2470 (378)
BERGMAN, I.: 2470 (378), 1940 (294)

BERGMARK, T.: 1004 (153)
BERGSHOLM, P.: 2116 (322)
BERLANGA, C.: 426 (64), 2652 (405)
BERMEJO, E.: 1674 (252)
BERNARD, D.: 1620 (246)
BERNARD, G.: 1367 (210)
BERNARDI, F.: 1681 (253), 1520 (234)
BERNARDO, M.: 1625 (247), 3216 (492)
BERNASCONI, G.: 1516 (234), 1717 (260)
BERNER, P.: 1345 (208), 249 (37), 2230 (343), 675 (105), 2362 (365)
BERNER, W.: 2096 (319), 53 (10)
BERNEY, T.: 2526 (386)
BERNIK, M.: 1626 (247)
BERNIS, C.: 2444 (376)
BERNTZEN, D.: 1164 (179)
BEROUTI, R.: 1334 (207)
BERRIOS, G.: 2548 (389)
BERSANI, L.: 1699 (255), 765 (117), 151 (23), 1894 (288)
BERTHOLD, A.: 3201 (490)
BERTI, A.: 1527 (235)
BERTI CERONI, G.: 2517 (383)
BERTILSSON, L.: 2885 (441)
BERTO, D.: 1110 (167)
BERTOLLI, R.: 387 (59)
BERTRANDO, P.: 2437 (375), 1245 (193), 2442 (375), 2438 (375), 2443 (375)
BERZEWSKI, H.: 1618 (246), 3191 (489), 469 (69), 470 (69), 2086 (318), 3220 (492), 357 (54)
BESIO, G.: 1017 (155), 1016 (155)
BESS, B.: 15 (4)
BETTSCHART, W.: 1674 (252), 1151 (175)
BETZ, H.: 2130 (325)
BEUMONT, P.: 3004 (459)
BEUZEN, J.: 353 (54), 1535 (236)
BEYAZYUEREK, M.: 1210 (186), 1552 (239), 1056 (158), 1837 (280)
BEYELER, CH.: 1295 (201)
BHATE, S.: 2526 (386)
BHATIA, S.: 2560 (392)
BHATNAGAR, K.: 752 (115)
BHAVSAR, M.: 137 (21)
BIANCHI, A.: 3187 (489)
BIANCHI, F.: 2489 (380)
BIANCONI, G.: 2250 (346), 2158 (327)
BIANCOSINO, B.: 1596 (244), 2456 (377)
BICAKOVA-ROCHER, A.: 636 (98)
BICK, P.: 565 (85)
BIDAULT, B.: 703 (108)
BIDAULT, E.: 1271 (197)
BIEBRICHER, D.: 912 (138)
BIECK, P.: 2476 (379), 404 (62), 3184 (488), 1946 (294)
BIEDERT, S.: 2862 (438), 896 (135), 464 (68)
BIELAWSKI, C.: 1499 (230)
BIFFI, E.: 1031 (156)
BIGELOW, G.: 221 (32)
BIGRAS, J.: 2430 (374)
BIKOS, K.: 1034 (156)
BILLE, A.: 800 (120)
BILLICK, S.: 2340 (361)
BINITIE, A.: 2379 (367)
BINKERT, M.: 2130 (325)
BINKOVA, B.: 136 (21), 450 (66), 2717 (412)
BINZ, U.: 2888 (441), 2476 (379), 2296 (353), 1384 (212)
BIOCINA, S.: 424 (64)
BIONDI, M.: 1084 (163)
BIONDI, R.: 1718 (260)
BIRD, T.: 2055 (312)
BIRGER, M.: 3153 (484)
BIRSUZ, S.: 2062 (314)

837

BISCHOFF, S.: 532 (78)
BISSERBE, J.: 308 (47)
BISSETTE, G.: 379 (58)
BITTER, I.: 1341 (208), 2245 (346)
BIVI, R.: 2517 (383)
BIXLER, E.: 2637 (403), 2676 (407), 2677 (407), 854 (128), 1377 (211), 552 (82), (258)
BIZZARRI, D.: 539 (79), 2115 (322), 1964 (296), 802 (120), 1417 (216)
BIZZINI, B.: 1891 (288)
BJERKENSTEDT, L.: 2385 (368), 938 (143)
BJOERK, A.: 480 (70)
BJOERLING, G.: 355 (54), 805 (121), 356 (54)
BJOERNSSON, J.: 1834 (280), 1823 (279), 1824 (279), 283 (41)
BJURLING, P.: 2386 (368)
BLACK, D.: 804 (121)
BLAINE, J.: 716 (110)
BLAJEV, B.: 794 (120)
BLAMPHIN, J.: 1118 (169)
BLANC, F.: 2896 (442)
BLANCO, A.: 1517 (234)
BLANCO, J.: 366 (56)
BLANKENBURG, W.: 1466 (224), 1993 (301)
BLASCHKE, D.: 1026 (155)
BLEECKER, M.: 3040 (466)
BLEEKER, J.: 1401 (214), 1952 (295)
BLEICH, A.: 1494 (229)
BLEIWEISS, H.: 138 (21), 604 (92)
BLIER, P.: 2731 (414), 2766 (420)
BLIN, O.: 1871 (286)
BLOCKX, P.: 1647 (250)
BLOMQVIST, G.: 2385 (368), 2389 (368)
BLOMQVIST, M.: 535 (79)
BLONDET, M.: 2029 (308)
BLOOM, S.: 1816 (278)
BLOOMINGDALE, L.: 3084 (474)
BLOUIN, A.: 304 (45)
BLOUIN, J.: 304 (45)
BLUMENTHAL, ST.: 2993 (457), 1547 (238), 777 (118)
BOARDMAN, A.: 2945 (447), 3188 (489)
BOATO, P.: 1587 (244)
BOBES G.: 1039 (156), 1595 (244), 1654 (250), 1480 (227)
BOBON, P.: 1156 (176)
BOCCHETTA, A.: 2075 (316), 1520 (234)
BODEMER, W.: 1445 (221)
BOECK, A.: 164 (24)
BOENING, J.: 346 (53)
BOGDANOVIC, M.: 1361 (210)
BOGERTS, B.: 534 (79), 274 (40), 2873 (439), 275 (40), 3140 (482)
BOGETTO, P.: 1351 (209)
BOGYI, G.: 1333 (207)
BOHACEK, N.: 1658 (250), 350 (53)
BOHLKEN, J.: 1533 (236)
BOHMAN, M.: 3145 (483)
BOJHOLM, S.: 2241 (345)
BOLDSEN, J.: 929 (141)
BOLLEN, J.: 1331 (206)
BOLWIG, T.: 528 (78)
BOMAN BASTANI, J.: 2669 (406)
BOMBA, J.: 121 (20)
BOMMELE, J.: 1677 (253)
BOMPREZZI, D.: 1927 (292)
BONCHEV, P.: 2335 (360)
BONDIS, J.: 1930 (292)
BONELLI, G.: 2263 (348), 766 (117), 1613 (246)
BONGIOANNI, P.: 1892 (288), 1169 (180), 941 (143)
BONIN, B.: 1113 (168)

BONNET, D.: 1014 (154)
BONSEL, G.: 660 (102)
BOOM, A.: 2138 (325)
BORDA, J.: 22 (4)
BORDAS, R.: 3046 (466)
BORDEN, W.: 750 (115)
BORENSTEIN, P.: 1891 (288), 2139 (325)
BORG, S.: 2470 (378), 1293 (201)
BORGHERINI, G.: 1166 (180), 1516 (234), 2514 (383)
BORIES, P.: 1070 (160)
BORIONI, S.: 576 (87)
BORISON, R.: 37 (7), 170 (25)
BORLA, E.: 1739 (263)
BORRAS, C.: 1305 (202)
BORRI, P.: 1209 (186)
BORSETTI, G.: 2277 (351)
BORSY, J.: 2457 (377)
BORUP, A.: 1024 (155)
BOSCH, G.: 774 (118)
BOSIO, A.: 2980 (454)
BOSMANS, E.: 67 (12)
BOSSARD-LEGRAND, M.: 967 (147)
BOSSERT, S.: 3010 (461)
BOSSEY, K.: 309 (47)
BOSTON, P.: 1075 (161)
BOSTRON, A.: 2034 (309)
BOTSCHEV, C.: 538 (79)
BOTSIS, A.: 1307 (202), 1190 (184), 217 (31), 2431 (374), 393 (60), 692 (107), 1416 (216)
BOUBIOTI, E.: 2281 (351)
BOUCEBCI, M.: 2262 (348), 174 (26)
BOUCHARD, J.: 2953 (448)
BOUCHET, P.: 811 (121)
BOUCHEZ, S.: 1656 (250)
BOUHOURS, P.: 1350 (208), 1534 (236)
BOUHUYS, A.: 2631 (402), 666 (103), 667 (103)
BOUHUYS, N.: 2631 (402)
BOUKOUVALA, V.: 2100 (320)
BOUKTIB, M.: 365 (56)
BOULAT, O.: 3184 (488)
BOULENGER, J.: 308 (47), 309 (47), 1469 (225)
BOURAS, C.: 1083 (162), 2332 (360)
BOURAS, N.: 693 (107), 690 (107), 3104 (477), 579 (88), 319 (49), 689 (107)
BOURGEOIS, M.: 1864 (285)
BOURGUIGNON,: 1350 (208)
BOUSONO GARCIA, M.: 1039 (156), 1595 (244), 1654 (250), 1480 (227)
BOUSOULENGAS, A.: 2008 (304)
BOUSSARD, H.: 2166 (328)
BOUTHILLIER, A.: 2731 (414)
BOUVARD, M.: 1355 (209)
BOVA, F.: 2961 (449)
BOVIER, P.: 2333 (360), 1128 (172), 430 (64)
BOWHAY, C.: 3074 (473)
BOYADJIEVA, S.: 1216 (187)
BOYER, C.: 492 (71)
BOYER, D.: 492 (71)
BOYER, P.: 315 (48), 858 (129)
BOYER, W.: 1859 (284)
BOZZA, C.: 1138 (173)
BRACCINI, T.: 1694 (254), 1005 (153)
BRACONNIER, A.: 1909 (290)
BRAMBILLA, F.: 3000 (459)
BRANCASI, B.: 1175 (181)
BRANCONNIER, R.: 2478 (379)
BRANDON, S.: 717 (111)
BRANDT, H.: 220 (32)
BRANDT-O'NEIL, C.: 781 (118)
BRAR, J.: 2331 (359), 1589 (244)
BRATALJENOVIC, T.: 424 (64)

BRATENSTEIN, H.: 1664 (251), 1044 (157)
BRATENSTEIN, P.: 185 (27), 1649 (250)
BRAUNS, M.: 469 (69),3220 (492)
BRAUNWARTH, W.: 2699 (410)
BRAVO, M.: 2492 (381), 46 (9)
BRAYNE, C.: 2528 (386)
BREITENFELD, D.: 760 (116), 1646 (249), 1059 (158)
BREMNER, A.: 1605 (245)
BRENNER, H.: 1265 (196), 2748 (417), 899 (136)
BRESLAN, N.: 1194 (184)
BRESSI, C.: 2443 (375), 1245 (193), 2438 (375), 2442 (375), 2437 (375)
BRIDGES, P.: 2521 (384)
BRION, N.: 2029 (308), 2475 (379)
BRION, S.: 1682 (253), 2029 (308), 2475 (379), 2290 (352)
BRODIE, J.: 2740 (415)
BROE, G.: 745 (115)
BROEKER, M.: 1533 (236)
BROESEN, K.: 908 (137)
BROGNA, P.: 1531 (236), 2030 (308)
BROKALAKI, J.: 2670 (406)
BRON, B.: 2432 (374)
BRONISCH, T.: 770 (117), 771 (117)
BRONS, J.: 2886 (441)
BROONER, R.: 221 (32), 219 (32)
BROWN, P.: 2949 (447)
BROWN, R.: 1816 (278)
BROWN, S.: 1494 (229)
BROWNE, I.: 2007 (304)
BROWNLEE, M.: 1346 (208)
BRUDER, J.: 2553 (390)
BRUECKE, T.: 837 (125)
BRUGHA, T.: 734 (113), 3189 (489)
BRUN, G.: 1069 (160)
BRUN, J.: 1304 (202)
BRUNE, G.: 2681 (408), 429 (64)
BRUNEAU, N.: 2183 (332)
BRUNET, G.: 835 (125), 2541 (388)
BRUNETTI, N.: 1550 (238)
BRUNS, U.: 2749 (417)
BRUTON, CJ.: 1816 (278)
BRYNJOLFSSON, J.: 1238 (192)
BUCCI, L.: 1108 (167)
BUCCI, P.: 1249 (194)
BUCHAN, H.: 717 (111)
BUCHHEIM, P.: 268 (39)
BUCHKREMER, G.: 2749 (417)
BUCHSBAUM, M.: 873 (132), 1120 (170), 210 (30)
BUCKETT, R.: 2954 (448), 594 (90)
BUCKETT, W.: 590 (90), 2877 (440)
BUDA, M.: 99 (16)
BUDDE, G.: 2929 (446), 1074 (161), 1722 (260)
BUERGIN, D.: 912 (138)
BUESS, S.: 2562 (392)
BUFFI, C.: 1632 (248)
BUGNAR, A.: 2921 (445), 483 (70), 2561 (392)
BUGNER, A.: 1522 (234), 1413 (215)
BUISSON, G.: 3199 (490), 3195 (490)
BULBENA, A.: 1356 (209)
BULLER, R.: 2176 (330)
BULUT, S.: 1528 (235)
BUNNEY, W.: 1230 (190), 873 (132), 210 (30)
BUONO, A.: 1108 (167)
BUONSANTE, M.: 197 (28), 2002 (303)
BURGIO, F.: 2489 (380)
BURGOYNE, M.: 1712 (259)
BURGOYNE, R.: 1712 (259)
BURKE, M.: 591 (90)
BURKOVIK, Y.: 1900 (289), 3224 (493)

BURNAM, M.: 305 (45)
BURNS, A.: 895 (135)
BURNS, G.: 115 (19)
BURRAI, C.: 375 (57), 2654 (405)
BURROWS, G.: 1777 (270), 1507 (232)
BUSNELLO, E.: 1882 (287), 1312 (203)
BUSSE, E.: 2458 (377), 629 (97), 3155 (485)
BUTLER, J.: 203 (29)
BUTOW, P.: 3004 (459)
BUYSSCHAERT, M.: 3173 (487)
BUYUKBERKER, C.: 2062 (314)

C

CABRANES, J.: 3172 (487), 2645 (404)
CABRAS, P.: 1693 (254), 1029 (156)
CABRERA, J.: 2545 (388)
CABRERA BONET, R.: 2879 (440)
CABRERA FORNEIRO, J.: 2879 (440), 1764 (266)
CACABELOS, R.: 2866 (438), 1305 (202), 2847 (435), 2846 (435), 2845 (435)
CADAMURO, M.: 1139 (173)
CADE, R.: 933 (142)
CADIEUX, R.: 2637 (403)
CAFISO, E.: 1245 (193)
CAHN, C.: 43 (8)
CAILLARD, V.: 1659 (250)
CAILLE, PH.: 3229 (494), 1870 (286), 1869 (286)
CALAK, E.: 388 (59), 2697 (410)
CALBERG, H.: 1024 (155)
CALCEDO ORDONEZ, A.: 1763 (266), 1086 (163)
CALDAS, S.: 2460 (377)
CALDERA, T.: 1142 (174)
CALDIRON, C.: 2060 (314)
CALEHR, H.: 1157 (177)
CALLE, A.: 1357 (209)
CALVEZ, R.: 2289 (352)
CALZETTI, S.: 406 (62)
CAMARERO, M.: 1633 (248), 440 (65), 1623 (247), 1692 (254), 2958 (449), 1087 (163)
CAMBIAGHI, P.: 2438 (375)
CAMERONE, E.: 1193 (184)
CAMPARI, F.: 1617 (246)
CAMPBELL, J.: 1294 (201)
CAMPBELL, N.: 1363 (210), 198 (28)
CAMPEAS, R.: 1852 (282), 1385 (212)
CAMPOS, R.: 3234 (494), 764 (116), 2687 (408), 2813 (430)
CAMPOS-BARROS, A.: 1612 (246), 884 (133)
CAMPOSANO, S.: 3017 (462), 3020 (462)
CAMUS, L.: 1341 (208)
CAMUS, M.: 3009 (461)
CANAL, M.: 270 (40)
CANALDA, G.: 1669 (252), 75 (13)
CANAMARES, V.: 2645 (404)
CANAS, F.: 1764 (266)
CANCRO, R.: 1227 (190), 55 (11)
CANDEFJORD, I.: 631 (97), 189 (27), 333 (51)
CANEVA, A.: 1139 (173)
CANINO, G.: 2492 (381), 46 (9)
CANTELL, K.: 1697 (255)
CANTON, C.: 2444 (376)
CANTON G.: 2961 (449), 1717 (260)
CANZIAN, G.: 2489 (380)
CAPODIECI, S.: 1730 (261)
CAPPELLETTI, L.: 2514 (383)
CAPUTO, D.: 2603 (398)
CAPUTO, J.: 3175 (487)
CARAVEO, J.: 47 (9)

CARBOGNIN, G.: 1110 (167)
CARDILLO, A.: 1084 (163)
CARDOSO, M.: 2668 (406)
CARL, G.: 1386 (212)
CARLETON, J.: 543 (80)
CARLSON, G.: 17 (4), 18 (4)
CARLSON-SABELLI, L.: 2941 (447)
CARNAGHI, R.: 482 (70), 2466 (378)
CARNEY, P.: 203 (29)
CAROFF, S.: 3152 (484)
CARPINIELLO, B.: 558 (84), 1822 (279), 3192 (489)
CARRANZA, J.: 2408 (371)
CARRASCO, J.: 1633 (248), 440 (65), 1692 (254), 1082 (162), 1623 (247)
CARREIRO, M.: 2703 (410)
CARRIERI, M.: 1110 (167)
CARTA, I.: 2594 (397), 2250 (346), 2071 (315)
CARTA, M.: 1822 (279), 3192 (489), 558 (84)
CARTWRIGHT, N.: 1013 (154)
CARUSO, M.: 1502 (231)
CASACCHIA, M.: 487 (70)
CASAIS, L.: 1021 (155), 1040 (156), 1033 (156)
CASAS, J.: 1021 (155)
CASAS, N.: 2650 (404)
CASCIANI, C.: 1894 (288)
CASEY, D.: 1890 (288)
CASPARI, D.: 1641 (249)
CASSANO, G.: 376 (57), 1611 (246), 427 (64), 2501 (382), 733 (113), 962 (146), 562 (85), 1159 (179), 783 (118), 707 (109), 204 (29), 2314 (356)
CASSIERS, L.: 1580 (243), 2852 (436), 3173 (487), 263 (39)
CASSITO, M.: 3040 (466)
CASTELLA, G.: 1100 (165)
CASTELLA, H.: 1100 (165)
CASTELLET Y BALLARA, F.: 998 (152), 990 (151), 1389 (213), 995 (152), 2662 (406)
CASTILLON, J.: 141 (22)
CASTRO, J.: 2616 (400)
CASTRO, R.: 3215 (492)
CASTROGIOVANNI, P.: 3127 (480), 1747 (264), 1749 (264), 2951 (448), 2461 (377), 1066 (160), 451 (66), 1643 (249), 2467 (378), 783 (118), 206 (29), 1632 (248), 942 (143)
CATAPANO, F.: 654 (100)
CATESBY-WARE, J.: 2679 (407)
CATTANEO, A.: 2603 (398)
CATUCCI, S.: 2002 (303)
CAULET, M.: 1610 (245), 2884 (441), 1609 (245), 2896 (442), 1046 (157), 2875 (439)
CAVALLARO, A.: 1088 (163)
CAVALLARO, R.: 2147 (326)
CAVERZASI, E.: 437 (65), 3187 (489), 3208 (491)
CAYIROGLU, P.: 3174 (487)
CAYIROGLU, S.: 3203 (490)
CAZULLO, C.: 2443 (375), 923 (140), 2187 (332), 1245 (193), 1587 (244), 272 (40), 2438 (375), 2599 (397), 1239 (193), 1240 (193), 2523 (385), 2603 (398)
CEBOLLADA, A.: 1633 (248), 440 (65), 1623 (247), 1692 (254)
CECENA, G.: 2923 (446)
CELADA, P.: 935 (142), 934 (142)
CELANI, T.: 1067 (160)
CELSIS, P.: 833 (125)
CERIC, I.: 2876 (440)

CERILLI, M.: 1699 (255)
CERLICH, B.: 2541 (388)
CERNIGOJ, D.: 2489 (380)
CERONI BERIT, F.: 2517 (383)
CERVERA, S.: 259 (38)
CESANA, B.: 1884 (287)
CEYLAN, M.: 536 (79), 1372 (211), 2252 (347)
CHABANNES, J.: 1073 (161)
CHABOD, E.: 673 (104)
CHADDA, R.: 2560 (392), 178 (26)
CHAKRABORTY, A.: 2795 (426)
CHAKRABORTY, N.: 792 (119), 77 (13)
CHAKRAVORTY, S.: 1481 (227)
CHAMBON, O.: 1878 (287), 1393 (213)
CHANDARANA, P.: 1934 (293)
CHANDORA, D.: 2821 (431)
CHANDRASENA, R.: 1758 (266)
CHANNABASAVANNA, S.: 1624 (247), 705 (108), 2152 (327), 2153 (327), 205 (29), 1353 (209)
CHANOIT, P.: 1826 (279)
CHANSOURIA, J.: 937 (143)
CHAPIN, K.: 1106 (167), 137 (21)
CHAPOTOT, E.: 3232 (494)
CHAPUT, Y.: 2731 (414), 2766 (420)
CHARNEY, D.: 846 (127)
CHASSEGUET-SMIRGEL, J.: 1770 (268)
CHASTANG, F.: 309 (47)
CHATTERJI, S.: 773 (117)
CHAUDHRY, H.: 1589 (244), 446 (66), 2561 (392), 1092 (164)
CHAUDHRY, M.: 2561 (392), 1589 (244), 1092 (164), 2193 (334), 1425 (217)
CHAUDHRY, S.: 446 (66)
CHAVALIER, J.: 1033 (156)
CHAVEZ, E.: 426 (64)
CHAVEZ, JL.: 2923 (446)
CHECKLEY, S.: 637 (98)
CHELLE, S.: 560 (84)
CHELUCCI, C.: 973 (148)
CHEN, C.: 2124 (323), 2124 (323)
CHEN, S.: 2124 (323)
CHENI, I.W.: 3107 (478)
CHENG, T.: 981 (149), 2663 (406)
CHEROPOULOU, K.: 2097 (320)
CHEVALIER, J.: 1682 (253), 2475 (379), 2029 (308)
CHIA BOON, H.: 1137 (173)
CHIARELLO, R.: 716 (110)
CHIARENZA, G.: 2187 (332)
CHIARPARIA, O.: 1166 (180)
CHIBA, T.: 1707 (255)
CHIERICHETTI, S.: 1681 (253), 2477 (379)
CHIESA, S.: 2442 (375)
CHIGIER, E.: 1783 (271)
CHIGNO, J.: 1160 (179)
CHINCHILLA, A.: 1633 (248), 440 (65), 1623 (247), 1692 (254), 2958 (449), 1087 (163)
CHIRCO, T.: 1965 (296)
CHISOLM, M.: 2381 (367)
CHLADZINSKA-KIEJNA, S.: 381 (58)
CHO, Y.: 127 (20)
CHO BOON, S.: 3186 (488)
CHOQUET, M.: 686 (106), 14 (4)
CHOUINARD, G.: 3183 (488), 2544 (388), 1206 (186), 533 (79), 422 (63)
CHOWDHURY, A.: 2796 (426)
CHRISTENSEN, E.: 3236 (494)
CHRISTENSSON, E.: 479 (70), 1941 (294)
CHRISTIAENS, C.: 1651 (250)
CHRISTIANSEN, P.: 1024 (155)
CHRISTIDOU, T.: 1398 (214)
CHRISTODOULOU, C.: 1307 (202)
CHRISTODOULOU, G.: 144 (22), 143 (22), 1700 (255), 1096 (164), 1727 (261),

1268 (197), 883 (133), 267 (39), 1729 (261), 2498 (381), 1925 (292), 1266 (197), 1804 (275)
CHRISTOVA, P.: 1735 (262), 398 (61), 1037 (156), 1208 (186)
CHRISTOZOV, C.: 1958 (296)
CHRONOPOULOU, J.: 195 (28), 1576 (242)
CHROUSOS, G.: 2531 (387), 2532 (387), 2535 (387)
CHUCK, J.: 1608 (245)
CHWATAL, K.: 167 (25), 1683 (253)
CIALDELLA, P.: 1878 (287), 2504 (382)
CIANI, N.: 151 (23), 1604 (245), 2848 (435), 765 (117), 1894 (288)
CIARAMELLA, A.: 2465 (378)
CILLI, G.: 1548 (238), 1093 (164)
CINQUE, B.: 1901 (289)
CIPRIAN-OLLIVIER, J.: 35 (7)
CIRILLO, L.: 2854 (436)
CIRILLO, M.: 451 (66), 1643 (249)
CIRILLO, R.: 406 (62)
CIUPKA, D.: 612 (93)
CIUPKA, V.: 612 (93)
CIVEIRA, J.: 1571 (241), 1748 (264), 601 (91), 1003 (153), 1336 (207)
CIZINSKY, G.: 2148 (326)
CLARE, A.: 1317 (204)
CLARK, C.: 214 (31)
CLARK, D.: 848 (127)
CLARKE, T.: 1075 (161)
CLARY, C.: 1555 (239)
CLASSEN, W.: 1386 (212)
CLAUDIO, V.: 2460 (377)
CLAUS, A.: 1331 (206)
CLAUS, D.: 2372 (366)
CLAUSTRAT, B.: 1304 (202)
CLAVEL MORROT, R.: 428 (64), 1402 (214), 761 (116)
CLEAU, M.: 2139 (325)
CLEMENT, D.: 2450 (376)
CLEMENTE, A.: 366 (56)
CLEMMESEN, L.: 2507 (382)
CLERC, G.: 2953 (448)
CLERICI, M.: 2443 (375), 2437 (375), 1245 (193), 2438 (375), 2071 (315)
CLIFFORD, P.: 1038 (156), 693 (107)
CLONINGER, C.: 130 (21)
COBLE, P.: 2342 (362)
COCCHI, R.: 1148 (175)
COCCOSIS, M.: 1729 (261), 1404 (214), 434 (65), 779 (118)
COCHRANE, J.: 2931 (447)
COELHO DA PANHA, M.: 3161 (486)
COFFINET, P.: 673 (104)
COHEN, C.: 2552 (390)
COHEN, D.: 685 (106)
COHEN, B.: 2242 (345)
COHEN, L.: 2403 (370)
COHEN, M.: 984 (150)
COHEN ADAD, G.: 2240 (345), 1334 (207), 2061 (314), 563 (85)
COIRA, C.: 3019 (462)
COLACE, P.: 309 (47)
COLACURCIO, F.: 2298 (353)
COLE, M.: 2510 (382), 2863 (438), 1951 (295)
COLETTI, M.: 2666 (406)
COLIN, R.: 2496 (381)
COLLAZO, C.: 2205 (336), 1784 (271)
COLLIN, A.: 1580 (243), 2852 (436), 3173 (487), 263 (39)
COLLINET, C.: 122 (20)
COLLINGE, J.: 3132 (481)
COLLINS, J.: 2656 (405)
COLLOT, G.: 1419 (216)
COLMEGNA, F.: 2237 (345)

COLOMBO, G.: 2021 (307), 2596 (397)
COLOMBO, M.: 2596 (397)
COLSON, L.: 566 (85)
CONCA, A.: 718 (111)
CONDEMI, F.: 1760 (266)
CONLON, P.: 1934 (293)
CONSOLI, S.: 2790 (425), 1198 (185), 1601 (245), 786 (119), 788 (119)
CONSOLI, SY.: 2788 (425)
CONSTANTINIDIS, J.: 2332 (360), 2333 (360), 1083 (162), 892 (135), 3133 (481), 2843 (435), 2334 (360)
CONSTANTOPOULOS, M.: 1561 (240)
CONSTANTOPOULOS, P.: 1069 (160)
CONTI, N.: 1070 (160)
COOK, B.: 1376 (211)
COOK, N.: 1177 (181)
COOKSON, D.: 2593 (397)
COOKSON, J.: 1342 (208), 2459 (377), 1330 (206), 1205 (186)
COOPER, I.: 1806 (276)
COOPER, J.: 6 (2), 2321 (358), 2782 (424)
COOPER, T.: 1341 (208)
COPELAND, J.: 1753 (265), 1796 (274), 898 (135), 2058 (312), 752 (115), 2509 (382)
COPOLOV, D.: 212 (30)
COPPO, P.: 3114 (479)
COPPOLA, M.: 2425 (373)
COPPOLA, T.: 1884 (287)
CORAIL, J.: 3020 (462)
CORBETT, J.: 1146 (175)
CORDAS, T.: 1626 (247)
CORDERO, A.: 1637 (248)
CORDIER, B.: 1659 (250)
CORFIATI, L.: 2000 (303)
CORGIOLU, T.: 2828 (432), 2940 (447), 1690 (254), 2305 (354), 994 (152), 827 (123)
CORNELIS, C.: 2433 (374)
CORNES, J.: 2866 (438)
CORNIDE CHEDA, E.: 1560 (240)
CORNWELL, J.: 1777 (270)
COROMINAS, A.: 958 (146)
CORONA, R.: 1520 (234)
CORONADO, R.: 1377 (211)
COROSSEZ, L.: 2489 (380)
CORRADINI, S.: 2588 (396)
CORSINI, G.: 3205 (491)
CORSINO, A.: 2517 (383)
CORTES, J.: 2496 (381), 640 (98)
CORTESE, P.: 2030 (308)
CORYELL, W.: 255 (37), 105 (17)
COSTA, D.: 895 (135)
COSTA, F.: 2275 (350)
COSTA E SILVA, J.: 1007 (154), 1789 (272), 1433 (218), 1442 (220), 860 (129)
COSTALL, B.: 1492 (229), 856 (129)
COSTERMANS, J.: 1580 (243)
COSULA, G.: 2703 (410)
COSYNS, P.: 1647 (250), 1396 (213)
COTANI, P.: 2277 (351), 68 (12)
COTTLER, L.: 716 (110)
COTTLER, N.: 1816 (278)
COTTRAUX, J.: 1355 (209)
COUDERT, A.: 2579 (395)
COURDAY, J.: 231 (34)
COUSINEAU, H.: 2426 (374)
COX, A.: 1492 (229)
COX, J.: 2593 (397)
COXHEAD, N.: 1205 (186)
CRAFTI, N.: 2491 (381)
CRAIG, T.: 1038 (156), 2945 (447), 3188 (489)
CRAMER, G.: 554 (83)
CRAPPER-MCLACHLAN, D.: 2055 (312)

CREA, F.: 17 (4), 18 (4)
CREASEY, H.: 745 (115)
CREATSAS, C.: 262 (39)
CREED, F.: 804 (121), 1720 (260)
CREMNITER, D.: 2024 (307), 2026 (307), 3096 (476)
CRESPO HERVAS, M.: 2648 (404), 2710 (411)
CRIJNEN, A.: 279 (41)
CRIPPA, D.: 1050 (157)
CRIQUILLION DOUBLET, S.: 2283 (351), 3169 (487), 288 (42), 289 (42)
CRITCHLEY, M.: 2388 (368)
CROCA, A.: 757 (116)
CROCQ, L.: 2205 (336), 2204 (336), 1534 (236)
CROCQ, M.: 2208 (336)
CROTT, R.: 2956 (448)
CROW, T.: 3132 (481), 717 (111), 1228 (190), 1816 (278), 1328 (206)
CROWE, M.: 926 (141)
CROWE, R.: 3121 (480)
CRUZ, P.: 1830 (279), 372 (57)
CSERNANSKY, J.: 1329 (206)
CUCER, M.: 2062 (314)
CUELLAR, L.: 2648 (404)
CUENCA, E.: 227 (33)
CUK, V.: 2259 (348)
CUNTERI, L.: 2443 (375)
CUPPLES, L.: 2055 (312)
CURCI, M.: 3200 (490)
CURET, O.: 2731 (414)
CURY, B.: 1200 (185)
CURZON, G.: 2728 (414)
CUSINI, M.: 992 (151)
CUYPERE, G.: 1519 (234)
CUZZOLARO, M.: 3175 (487), 687 (106)
CVETKOVIC, M.: 417 (63)
CVRK-BIKCEVIC, J.: 1059 (158)
CYGANIK, L.: 2373 (366)
CYRIOPOYLOS, M.: 3019 (462)
CZARKA, M.: 2956 (448)
CZENDLIK, C.: 405 (62)
CZERNIKIEWICZ, A.: 2073 (315), 2590 (396)
CZOBOR, P.: 2245 (346)

D

D' MELLO, D.: 1109 (167)
D'AMBRA, L.: 1629 (247)
D'AMBROSIO, A.: 2268 (349)
D'AQUILA, F.: 473 (70)
D'ARGY, R.: 836 (125)
D'ERRICO, I.: 1613 (246)
D'ODORICO, A. - ITALY,: 1717 (260)
D'UVA, R.: 1893 (288)
DA FONSECA, B.: 2779 (422)
DA FONSECA, S.: 2779 (422)
DA PONTE, C.: 1392 (213)
DA PRADA, M.: 1848 (282)
DABROWSKI, R.: 703 (108)
DADONE, F.: 1892 (288)
DAFFNER, C.: 1300 (202), 1171 (181)
DAHL, A.: 1326 (205), 1902 (289), 2067 (315)
DAHL, S.: 1889 (288), 2409 (372)
DAHL-PUUSTINEN, M.: 2885 (441)
DAHLGREN, L.: 1292 (201), 1814 (277)
DAILIANIS, K.: 808 (121)
DAINI, L.: 1749 (264), 2467 (378)
DAINI, S.: 1901 (289), 2666 (406)
DAJAS, F.: 954 (145), 1380 (212)
DAKESSIAN, A.: 2013 (306)
DAKOU, C.: 975 (148)
DALAKAKI, X.: 2066 (314)
DALERY, J.: 1304 (202)

DALGARD, O.: 2493 (381)
DALLA LIBERA, A.: 1886 (288)
DALLE, B.: 159 (24), 160 (24)
DALY, I.: 125 (20)
DAM, H.: 2834 (433)
DAMBASSINA-LATARJET, L.: 1826 (279)
DAMIANI, M.: 1066 (160)
DANACI, M.: 3224 (493)
DANION, J.: 2882 (440), 1839 (281), 1279 (199)
DANNECKER, K.: 469 (69), 470 (69)
DANNHORN, R.: 449 (66)
DANTCHEV, N.: 3011 (461), 3176 (487)
DANTCHEV, V.: 2289 (352)
DAOUD, H.: 2708 (411)
DARAS, M.: 16 (4), 15 (4)
DARCOURT, G.: 1694 (254), 1005 (153), 835 (125), 2541 (388), 634 (98), 633 (98), 1980 (299)
DARCOURT, J.: 835 (125)
DARDAVESSIS, D.: 194 (28)
DARDAVESSIS, T.: 194 (28)
DARDENNES, R.: 2032 (308)
DARWISH, A.: 1501 (231)
DASKALOS, A.: 2460 (377)
DASSING, M.: 2453 (376)
DASTOOR, D.: 2863 (438)
DAUDT, V.: 2952 (448)
DAULOUEDE, J.: 21 (4)
DAVALLI, C.: 2237 (345), 2594 (397)
DAVID, J.: 1767 (267)
DAVIDIAN, H.: 1731 (262)
DAVIDIAN, L.: 952 (145)
DAVIDSON, I.: 898 (135), 1753 (265), 2509 (382)
DAVIES, K.: 3132 (481)
DAVIS, B.: 932 (142)
DAVIS, G.: 1194 (184)
DAVIS, J.: 2118 (323), 165 (25), 425 (64), 3148 (484), 3154 (484)
DAVISON, K.: 2070 (315)
DAWSON, D.: 1720 (260)
DAY, K.: 2272 (350), 318 (49), 841 (126), 1984 (300)
DAZORD, A.: 1272 (198), 438 (65)
DAZZI, S.: 3233 (494)
DAZZINI, E.: 1964 (296)
DE ANGELIS, C.: 2587 (396)
DE AZEVEDO, H.: 2275 (350)
DE BASTIANI, P.: 373 (57)
DE BEAUREPAIRE, R.: 2139 (325)
DE BILLY, A.: 1636 (248)
DE BLECOURT, C.: 2031 (308)
DE BLEEKER, E.: 1156 (176)
DE BONIS, C.: 475 (70)
DE BUCK, R.: 2171 (329)
DE CATERINA, G.: 2832 (433)
DE CLERCQ, M.: 2022 (307)
DE COULON, N.: 2353 (363), 1275 (198)
DE CUYPER, H.: 1331 (206)
DE FAHRER, M.: 327 (50)
DE FELICE, F.: 419 (63), 1760 (266)
DE GIACOMO, P.: 345 (52)
DE GIGLIO, F.: 1550 (238)
DE GIROLAMO, G.: 316 (48)
DE GREGORI, P.: 1751 (264), 1634 (248)
DE JONGHE, F.: 2433 (374)
DE LA FUENTE, J.: 2653 (405), 3128 (480), 95 (15)
DE LAS CUEVAS, C.: 1924 (292)
DE LEO, D.: 1045 (157), 1139 (173), 2399 (370)
DE LEO, V.: 973 (148)
DE LOOF, C.: 412 (63), 3126 (480)
DE LOS COBOS, J.: 261 (38)
DE LUCA, G.: 903 (136)

DE MAERTELAER, V.: 832 (125)
DE MARCO, F.: 128 (20), 973 (148), 1629 (247)
DE MAROO, P.: 2517 (383)
DE MONTIGNY, C.: 2766 (420), 2731 (414)
DE NEUTER, P.: 1740 (263)
DE NIGRIS, S.: 2001 (303)
DE OLIVEIRA, I.: 2032 (308), 593 (90)
DE RECONDO, J.: 175 (26)
DE REUS, R.: 1952 (295)
DE RISIO, C.: 1617 (246)
DE ROSA, M.: 576 (87)
DE SAUSSURE, N.: 83 (14)
DE SMET, S.: 2171 (329)
DE VANNA, M.: 1937 (293), 2375 (366), 2707 (411)
DE VRY, J.: 1079 (162), 596 (90), 236 (35)
DE WILDE, J.: 1940 (294)
DE ZWAAN, M.: 3174 (487), 2647 (404), 167 (25)
DEAKIN, J.: 2658 (405), 1163 (179), 1817 (278)
DEBRAY, Q.: 3131 (480)
DEBUS, G.: 1316 (204)
DECLERCQ, M.: 1273 (198)
DECOSTER, P.: 263 (39)
DEDE, K.: 785 (119)
DEECKE, L.: 837 (125)
DEFFNER, A.: 343 (52)
DEGEN, P.: 1051 (157), 405 (62)
DEGLERIS, N.: 2485 (380), 2700 (410)
DEISTER, A.: 953 (145), 2079 (316), 104 (17), 730 (113), 2074 (316)
DEKKER, J.: 3168 (486)
DEL CARMINE, R.: 475 (70)
DEL DEGAN, T.: 2489 (380)
DEL PISTOIA, L.: 26 (5)
DEL VALLE, P.: 2887 (441), 2645 (404), 1637 (248)
DEL VALLE-LOPEZ, P.: 2955 (448)
DEL ZOMPO, M.: 2075 (316), 1520 (234), 1681 (253)
DELAHAYE, C.: 2045 (310), 2048 (310)
DELBENDE, C.: 2729 (414)
DELECLUSE, F.: 832 (125)
DELGADO, C.: 132 (21)
DELINI-STULA, A.: 2722 (413)
DELISI, L.: 3132 (481)
DELL, H.: 2886 (441), 407 (62)
DELL' OSSO, L.: 427 (64), 732 (113)
DELL'ACQUA, S.: 1901 (289)
DELMO, C.: 2176 (330)
DELONG, J.: 931 (142)
DELTITO, J.: 3127 (480), 942 (143), 1747 (264), 206 (29), 1749 (264), 2461 (377), 1066 (160), 783 (118), 2951 (448)
DELVENNE, V.: 3009 (461), 832 (125)
DEMAKIS, G.: 2063 (314)
DEMAKIS, J.: 2063 (314)
DEMIRBAS, H.: 1644 (249)
DEMIRTAS, E.: 1529 (235)
DEMISCH, L.: 2328 (359)
DEMITRACK, M.: 220 (32)
DEMLING, J.: 2372 (366), 466 (68)
DEN BOER, J.: 421 (63), 960 (146)
DEN BOER, P.: 2180 (331)
DENBER, H.: 504 (73)
DENEGRI, Z.: 2704 (410), 2085 (318)
DENIKER, P.: 3149 (484), 2723 (413)
DENK, E.: 1615 (246)
DENNIS, P.: 2182 (332), 2338 (361)
DEO, R.: 2915 (444)
DEREUX, J.: 2135 (325), 2136 (325)
DEROGATIS, L.: 2827 (432)

DESHPANDE, S.: 1189 (184)
DESLAURIERS, A.: 1621 (247)
DESPOTOVIC, T.: 417 (63)
DESTOUNIS, N.: 2842 (434), 2850 (436), 1935 (293), 2974 (453)
DESTRO, E.: 373 (57), 1138 (173)
DESVIAT, M.: 696 (107), 27 (5)
DETEI, D.: 1451 (221)
DEUS, G.: 2687 (408), 2813 (430)
DEUS, P.: 764 (116)
DEVA, P.: 624 (96), 1428 (217), 2214 (337), 1440 (220), 2967 (451)
DEVEAU, L.: 2014 (306)
DEVEAUGH-GEISS, J.: 37 (7), 1780 (270)
DEVI, P.: 2635 (402)
DEVI, S.: 3211 (491)
DEVOITILLE, J.: 2539 (388), 1526 (235), 2540 (388)
DEWAILLY, D.: 1542 (237)
DEWEY, M.: 898 (135), 1753 (265), 1796 (274), 2509 (382), 1874 (286)
DEWEY, SL.: 2740 (415)
DEZA, L.: 1893 (288)
DHAVALE, D.: 2469 (378)
DHAVALE, H.: 972 (148)
DI BOSCIO, V.: 639 (98)
DI FIANDRA, T.: 2488 (380)
DI GIANNANTONIO, M.: 2465 (378), 1243 (193), 1242 (193), 2711 (411)
DI GREGORIO, M.: 1249 (194)
DI MARIO, F.: 1516 (234)
DI MICHELE, V.: 487 (70)
DI MUNZIO, W.: 3214 (492), 810 (121)
DI MURO, A.: 1749 (264)
DI NICOLA, V.: 740 (114), 871 (131)
DI PAOLO, E.: 1893 (288)
DI PIETRO, E.: 1629 (247)
DI SCIASCIO, G.: 1550 (238)
DI TONO, P.: 2110 (321)
DIA-SAHUN, J.: 1795 (274)
DIAKOYANNIS, J.: 2494 (381), 1930 (292)
DIALLINA, M.: 616 (93), 386 (59)
DIAMOND, B.: 38 (7), 170 (25), 37 (7)
DIAMOND, M.: 1513 (233)
DIAOURTA-TSITOURIDES, M.: 772 (117)
DIAS DE MORAES, E.: 1296 (201)
DIAS-CORDEIRO, J.: 525 (77), 494 (71)
DIAZ, A.: 2520 (384)
DIAZ, R.: 3172 (487)
DIAZ DEL VALLE, I: 366 (56)
DIDASKALOU, T.: 823 (123)
DIEBOLD, K.: 2157 (327), 2125 (324)
DIECI, M.: 272 (40), 413 (63)
DIEFFENBACH, R.: 247 (36)
DIEGUEZ, C.: 2845 (435)
DIEKMANN, S.: 884 (133)
DIEKSTRA, R.: 1510 (232)
DIERICK, M.: 1940 (294)
DIETERLE, W.: 1051 (157), 405 (62), 2033 (308)
DIETRICH, R.: 1948 (294)
DIEZ, A.: 3230 (494), 1748 (264), 1571 (241)
DIEZ, C.: 795 (120), 415 (63)
DIEZ C.: 958 (146)
DIJK, D.: 2633 (402)
DILBAZ, N.: 2826 (432), 600 (91), 961 (146), 1603 (245), 1068 (160)
DILIGENSKI, V.: 1361 (210)
DILLING, H.: 2416 (373)
DILORENZO, N.: 2703 (410)
DIMAIO, S.: 2703 (410)
DIMITRIJEVIC, I.: 815 (122)
DIMITRIOU, E.: 1352 (209), 756 (116), 1802 (275), 2763 (419)
DIMITROV, I.: 2934 (447), 2239 (345)

DIMOU, D.: 946 (144), 1743 (263)
DINELLI, M.: 582 (88), 1419 (216)
DINELLI, U.: 582 (88), 1419 (216)
DINESH, G.: 1754 (265)
DINIS, A.: 2460 (377)
DIODATO, S.: 2489 (380)
DIQUET, B.: 593 (90)
DISAYAVANISH, C.: 3179 (488)
DISAYAVANISH, P.: 3179 (488)
DISSING, S.: 592 (90)
DITTMANN, V.: 2416 (373), 2417 (373), 2415 (373)
DIVAC-PAVLOVIC, S.: 3169 (487), 288 (42)
DJORDJEVIC, P.: 2264 (348)
DJUNOV, P.: 398 (61)
DJURDJIC, S.: 155 (23)
DOBRESCU, I.: 1410 (215)
DODDE, N.: 2928 (446), 484 (70), 485 (70)
DOERR-ZEGERS, O.: 2545 (388), 1989 (301)
DOGA, H.: 588 (89), 824 (123)
DOGAN, Y.: 1644 (249), 2903 (443)
DOGRAMADGI, D.: 3164 (486), 3167 (486)
DOI, M.: 1179 (182)
DOLLFUS, S.: 1077 (162), 1672 (252)
DOLLY, P.: 2863 (438)
DOLS, L.: 2542 (388)
DOMENEY, A.: 1492 (229), 856 (129)
DOMINQUEZ, C.: 1003 (153)
DONALD, O.: 1217 (187)
DONATI, D.: 1746 (264), 1029 (156)
DONATINI, L.: 2438 (375)
DONIAS, S.: 278 (41), 1876 (286), 789 (119), 3047 (467)
DONKER, M.: 1761 (266), 2025 (307)
DONOVAN, S.: 1013 (154), 2890 (441), 2891 (441), 2106 (321)
DONTSCHEV, P.: 691 (107)
DOONGAJI, D.: 2286 (352)
DOORSCHOT, C.: 851 (128)
DORE, F.: 1613 (246)
DORFMAN, M.: 1219 (187)
DORION, P.: 1191 (184)
DORNIER, A.: 673 (104)
DOS ANJOS, R.: 1246 (193)
DOSEN, A.: 321 (49), 1149 (175), 840 (126)
DOSOKY, A.: 1251 (194)
DOUGE, R.: 1020 (155), 1073 (161), 1355 (209), 3176 (487)
DOUGHERTY, G.: 695 (107)
DOUTHEAU, C.: 2205 (336)
DOUZENIS, A.: 2933 (447)
DRAGONAS, T.: 361 (55)
DRAKE, R.: 97 (16)
DRECHSLER, F.: 346 (53)
DRESSE, A.: 2479 (379)
DRIESSEN, F.: 14 (4)
DROSOS, A.: 1929 (292), 3057 (468)
DROUIN, J.: 986 (150)
DUARTE SILVA, M.: 1670 (252)
DUBEY, M.: 139 (22)
DUBUIS, J.: 1226 (189), 2210 (337), 1444 (220)
DUERRENMATT, U.: 113 (19)
DUFIER, J.: 3131 (480)
DUFOUR, H.: 709 (109)
DUGAS, M.: 2578 (395), 1340 (207)
DUGGAN, C.: 2950 (448)
DUKIC, S.: 2131 (325)
DULCIRE, C.: 1872 (286)
DUMARCET, M.: 1005 (153)
DUNCAN, C.: 1261 (196)
DUNCAS, N.: 2063 (314), 1579 (243)

DUNN, G.: 861 (129)
DURANT, B.: 439 (65)
DURBANO, F.: 1239 (193)
DURBIN, J.: 3053 (468)
DUSSAUT, C.: 2475 (379)
DUTTA, D.: 322 (49), 1481 (227)
DUURKOOP, W.: 1952 (295)
DUVAL, F.: 2208 (336)
DYER, A.: 632 (97)

E

EARLEY, B.: 591 (90)
EARLY, T.: 1818 (278)
EASTMAN, C.: 1222 (188)
EBADI, G.: 775 (118)
EBATA, K.: 78 (13)
EBEL, H.: 518 (76)
EBERHARD, G.: 2753 (418)
EBERT, D.: 1482 (227)
EBIGBO, P.: 3209 (491)
ECHARRI, E.: 366 (56), 1698 (255)
ECKERT, E.: 2011 (305)
ECKMAN, T.: 2802 (427)
ECKSTEIN, R.: 63 (12)
ECONOMOU, M.: 84 (14), 1190 (184), 1144 (174), 2233 (344), 588 (89), 824 (123), 2762 (419), 996 (152)
EDEL, Y.: 160 (24)
EDELSTEIN, E.: 2998 (458)
EDVARSEN, O.: 1889 (288)
EDWARDS, G.: 2915 (444)
EELEN, P.: 2266 (349)
EERDEKENS, M.: 66 (12)
EFTHIMIOU, M.: 411 (62)
EFTICHIDIS, L.: 88 (14)
EINWAECHTER, H.: 1006 (154)
EISEMANN, M.: 2614 (400), 2618 (400), 2620 (400)
EISENBERG, L.: 3063 (470)
EISENBRUCH, M.: 1195 (184), 1875 (286), 2817 (431), 2861 (437)
EISLER, I.: 293 (42)
EISON, A.: 1472 (225)
EISON, M.: 1472 (225)
EKBLOM, B.: 631 (97), 189 (27)
EKDAWI, M.: 1405 (214)
EKER, E.: 3052 (467), 2642 (403), 3023 (463)
EL AZAYEM, A.: 1251 (194)
EL SENDIONY, M.: 2194 (334)
EL-ASSRA, A.: 1500 (231)
EL-GUEBALY, N.: 3034 (465), 2098 (320)
EL-GUENEIDY, M.: 3163 (486)
EL-ISLAM, F.: 737 (114)
ELGEN, K.: 1944 (294)
ELL, P.: 895 (135)
ELLEBRACHT, H.: 248 (36)
ELLGRING, H.: 3010 (461)
ELLIGER, T.: 1460 (223), 1459 (223)
ELMER, K.: 834 (125)
ELORZA, J.: 1021 (155), 1040 (156), 1033 (156)
EMIK, C.: 2065 (314)
EMSLEY, R.: 2369 (366), 2371 (366)
ENASESCU, N.: 1606 (245)
ENDO, K.: 574 (87), 2844 (435), 704 (108)
ENDO, M.: 1591 (244)
ENEMAN, M.: 1331 (206)
ENGBERG, M.: 336 (51)
ENGEDAL, K.: 1944 (294)
ENGEL, J.: 480 (70), 1813 (277)
ENGEL, R.: 2417 (373)
ENGELBREKTSSON, K.: 2470 (378)
ENGELSMANN, F.: 2510 (382)

ENGSTROEM, A.: 2966 (451)
ENSGRABER, C.: 167 (25)
EOZOUNI, B.: 977 (149)
EPREM, C.: 1907 (290)
EPSTEIN, Y.: 3153 (484)
ERALP, E.: 838 (125), 875 (132)
ERBA, S.: 1055 (158)
ERBAS, B.: 273 (40)
ERBENGI, G.: 273 (40)
ERDMAN, R.: 660 (102)
ERDOGAN, B.: 814 (122)
EREN, N.: 388 (59), 2697 (410)
ERICE-KEPPLER, E.: 1842 (281)
ERICSON, H.: 1781 (270)
ERIKSSON, E.: 555 (84), 481 (70), 480 (70), 2064 (314)
ERIKSSON, K.: 631 (97), 189 (27), 332 (51)
ERKMEN, H.: 1603 (245), 600 (91), 961 (146), 1068 (160), 2826 (432)
ERKOC,: 1845 (281)
ERMANN, M.: 2705 (411), 1939 (293), 2638 (403)
ERMENTINI, A.: 1097 (164), 2354 (363)
ERNST, R.: 1043 (157)
ERSUEL, C.: 1552 (239), 1056 (158)
ERZIGKEIT, H.: 762 (116), 1943 (294), 888 (134)
ESCHEN, F.: 3236 (494)
ESCRIBANO, M.: 2703 (410)
ESSMAN, E.: 1076 (162)
ESSMAN, W.: 1076 (162)
ESTEVEZ, L.: 1911 (290)
ESTIVILL, E.: 2901 (442)
ETIENNE, P.: 2544 (388)
ETRIBI, M.: 3122 (480), 2864 (438)
ETTMEIER, W.: 2655 (405)
EVANS, L.: 3123 (480), 2893 (441)
EVREUX, JC.: 1020 (155)
EVRIPIDOU, E.: 2351 (363)
EZCURRA, J.: 1040 (156)
EZQUIAGA, E.: 132 (21)

F

FABBRO, T.: 2489 (380)
FABIAN, C.: 1012 (154)
FABIANI, C.: 758 (116)
FABIANI, R.: 376 (57)
FABRA, M.: 469 (69), 470 (69), 2086 (318)
FABRE, L.: 2146 (326), 650 (100), 2770 (420)
FABRIS, N.: 72 (12), 829 (124)
FACCHINETTI, F.: 3000 (459)
FACINCANI, O.: 1663 (251), 460 (68)
FACY, F.: 1936 (293)
FADHLI, A.: 2664 (406)
FAEDDA, G.: 1887 (288), 1565 (241), 736 (113)
FAEHNDRICH, E.: 2294 (352)
FAGAN, L.: 2458 (377)
FAGAN, P.: 2827 (432)
FAGGIOLI, L.: 2596 (397)
FAGHER, B.: 291 (42)
FAGNOL, A.: 2489 (380)
FAHLKE, C.: 1813 (277)
FAHRER, R.: 2709 (411), 32 (6), 1785 (271), 656 (101), 1434 (218)
FAHY, T.S.: 556 (84)
FAILDE, I.: 1040 (156), 1033 (156)
FAIRBURN, C.: 2009 (305)
FALCY, M.: 411 (62)
FALK, W.: 2403 (370)
FALKAI, P.: 2873 (439), 275 (40), 1371 (211), 534 (79), 274 (40), 3140 (482)

FALLOON, I.: 2436 (375)
FALTUS, F.: 1383 (212)
FALUDI, G.: 2366 (365)
FALUS, A.: 431 (64), 416 (63)
FALZONI, M.: 2696 (409)
FAMIYUWA, O.: 2526 (386)
FANGET, F.: 1304 (202)
FARAGHER, E.: 2324 (358)
FARDE, L.: 2389 (368), 2412 (372), 2739 (415)
FAREED, J.: 2063 (314)
FARINA, S.: 1204 (185)
FARKAS, J.: 1592 (244)
FARMA, T.: 3233 (494)
FARMANIAN, J.: 3096 (476)
FARMER, A.: 282 (41), 281 (41)
FARMER, R.: 1506 (232)
FARRAGHER, B.: 1337 (207)
FARRER, LA.: 2055 (312)
FASSOULAKI, A.: 229 (33)
FASULLO, S.: 2874 (439), 1650 (250)
FATIMA FERREIRA, M.: 1628 (247)
FATTAL-GERMAN, M.: 1891 (288)
FAVA, M.: 2403 (370)
FAVAZZA, A.: 2612 (399)
FAVIEZ, M.: 983 (150)
FAVRE, S.: 1091 (164)
FAWZI, A.: 3043 (466)
FAZZARI, G.: 1097 (164), 2354 (363)
FEFERLE, E.: 458 (68)
FEIGHNER, J.: 1859 (284)
FEINBERG, I.: 3134 (481)
FEINMANN, C.: 1514 (233)
FEIO, M.: 2107 (321)
FELINE, A.: 885 (134)
FELIX DA COSTA, N.: 757 (116), 2706 (411)
FENHA, M.: 2779 (422), 1599 (245)
FENOY, L.: 2061 (314)
FENSBO, C.: 3178 (488)
FENTON, F.: 2510 (382)
FENTON, G.: 746 (115), 2835 (433)
FERBER, C.: 1532 (236), 3049 (467)
FERGUSON, B.: 3080 (474), 2919 (445)
FERIOLI, V.: 1058 (158), 490 (71)
FERMANIAN, J.: 2024 (307), 2026 (307), 2032 (308)
FERNANDES, C.: 1299 (201)
FERNANDES DA FONSECA, A.: 1224 (188)
FERNANDEZ, A.: 160 (24)
FERNANDEZ, I.: 992 (151), 2750 (417)
FERNANDEZ, L.: 1924 (292)
FERNANDEZ, M.: 2866 (438), 1305 (202)
FERNANDEZ LIRIA, A.: 696 (107)
FERNANDEZ MARTINEZ, J.: 2483 (380), 647 (99)
FERRAND, B.: 2045 (310)
FERRAND, I.: 3096 (476), 778 (118), 2026 (307)
FERRANNINI, L.: 435 (65)
FERRAO, C.: 1299 (201)
FERRARI, E.: 3000 (459)
FERRARINI, F.: 1245 (193)
FERRATO, F.: 389 (59), 825 (123)
FERREIRA, C.: 1999 (303)
FERREIRA, F.: 3015 (462), 1370 (211)
FERREIRA, V.: 1200 (185)
FERREIRA DE CASTRO, E.: 1135 (173)
FERRER, J.: 2901 (442)
FERRERI, M.: 1014 (154), 2364 (365), 967 (147), 1551 (239), 1000 (153)
FERRERO, F.: 83 (14), 1091 (164), 683 (106), 608 (92)
FERREY, G.: 2199 (335), 2200 (335), 353 (54), 2201 (335), 976 (149)
FERRO, F.: 475 (70)
FERSTL, R.: 828 (124)

FICHTE, K.: 1050 (157), 1022 (155)
FICHTER, M.: 1825 (279), 3001 (459), 2398 (369), 290 (42)
FIELD, V.: 1934 (293)
FIGA TALAMANGA, A.: 1894 (288)
FIGUEIRA, M.: 2460 (377), 957 (146), 2583 (396), 2706 (411)
FILIP, V.: 1221 (188)
FILOKYPROU, D.: 1176 (181)
FINEBERG, N.: 2606 (398)
FINK, G.: 2168 (329)
FINK, P.: 1773 (269)
FINNEGAN, L.: 2968 (451)
FINOTTI, L.: 1138 (173), 373 (57)
FIORE, A.: 1838 (280), 2490 (380)
FIORENTINI, A.: 1531 (236), 2030 (308), 2640 (403)
FIORETTO, M.: 1527 (235)
FIRINGUETTI, L.: 2632 (402)
FIRKUSNY, L.: 2476 (379)
FIRMINO, H.: 2445 (376), 812 (122), 74 (13)
FISCH, H.: 1295 (201)
FISCHER, R.: 3019 (462)
FISCHER, U.: 1477 (226), 999 (153)
FISHER, V.: 1706 (255)
FITZGERALD, M.: 203 (29)
FIUMANI, P.: 1655 (250)
FLAMENT, M.: 686 (106), 3176 (487), 3011 (461)
FLECHTNER, M.: 347 (53)
FLECK, S.: 520 (77), 915 (139)
FLECKENSTEIN, F.: 2343 (362)
FLECKENSTEIN, P.: 252 (37), 2629 (402)
FLEISCHHACKER, W.: 1297 (201), 3182 (488)
FLEMING, J.: 2047 (310)
FLEMMING, J.: 99 (16)
FLENTGE, F.: 2631 (402), 2542 (388)
FLOR-HENRY, P.: 1264 (196), 36 (7)
FLORIAN, M.: 2021 (307)
FLORIS, G.: 1569 (241), 710 (109), 1565 (241), 736 (113)
FLORO, S.: 1933 (293), 3153 (484)
FLUEGEL, D.: 1649 (250)
FLYNN, T.: 2091 (318)
FOCHIOS, S.: 1185 (183)
FOERSTER, A.: 1968 (297)
FOERTHNER, B.: 2990 (457)
FOG, E.: 924 (141), 2829 (432)
FOGLIETTA, D.: 1751 (264), 1634 (248)
FOJTIKOVA, I.: 136 (21)
FOLDES, P.: 1345 (208)
FOLEGATI, M.: 1182 (182)
FOLQUES, A.: 1670 (252)
FONDARAI, J.: 1871 (286)
FONDREN, R.: 1363 (210)
FONSECA, V.: 2581 (395), 1002 (153), 1744 (264)
FONTAINE, R.: 422 (63)
FORELAND, A.: 1921 (291)
FORESTI, D.: 437 (65)
FORESTI, G.: 3187 (489)
FORMIGONI, U.: 399 (61), 1145 (174)
FORNARI, V.: 685 (106)
FORNARO, P.: 1527 (235)
FORSMAN, A.: 2027 (308), 2295 (352)
FORSSMANN-FALCK, R.: 2352 (363)
FORSTL, J.: 896 (135)
FORTUNY, J.: 3046 (466)
FORZA, G.: 2021 (307), 1166 (180)
FORZY, G.: 2135 (325)
FOSSAT, H.: 1620 (246)
FOTIADIS, H.: 823 (123), 1099 (164), 140 (22)
FOTIADOU, K.: 1369 (211)

FOTIADOU, M.: 823 (123), 1099 (164), 140 (22)
FOULON, C.: 2283 (351), 289 (42)
FOULOT, M.: 1077 (162)
FOURIE, J.: 213 (31)
FOURNIER, L.: 303 (45)
FOWLER, JS: 2740 (415)
FOZOUNI, B.: 1057 (158), 1418 (216)
FRACCON, I.: 491 (71)
FRAGOLA, A.: 1785 (271)
FRANCES, A.: 1232 (191), 2223 (342)
FRANCESCONI, C.: 1893 (288)
FRANCESCUTTI, C.: 2489 (380)
FRANCHI, G.: 1613 (246)
FRANCHINI, I.: 1617 (246)
FRANCK, G.: 2428 (374)
FRANCO, A.: 1296 (201)
FRANCO, K.: 1363 (210), 198 (28)
FRANGAKIS, H.: 2238 (345)
FRANGOS, E.: 1687 (254), 1176 (181), 3190 (489)
FRANGOU, S.: 3190 (489), 1687 (254)
FRANK, B.: 2451 (376)
FRANK, J.: 752 (115)
FRANKEL, R.: 750 (115)
FRANTZIOS, G.: 1420 (216), 1907 (290)
FRANZA, F.: 1655 (250)
FRASER, A.: 2894 (441)
FRASER, W.: 2586 (396)
FRASSINE, R.: 1693 (254)
FRATTURA, L.: 2718 (412)
FRECSKA, E.: 3185 (488)
FREDMAN, R.: 2713 (412)
FREEDMAN, A.: 3064 (470), 2210 (337), 1431 (218), 1444 (220)
FREEDMAN, M.: 639 (98), 2703 (410)
FREEMAN, A.: 2292 (352), 664 (102), 902 (136)
FREEMAN, E.: 1181 (182)
FREEMAN, R.: 3007 (461)
FREEMAN, S.: 3053 (468)
FRESNILLO, E.: 1400 (214)
FREUND-LEVI, Y.: 879 (133)
FREY, R.: 2674 (407)
FREYBERGER, H.: 2415 (373), 2416 (373)
FRIED, J.: 2170 (329)
FRIEDBERG, G.: 849 (128)
FRIEDL, A.: 1081 (162)
FRIEDL, E.: 2454 (377), 2092 (319), 583 (88), 1956 (295)
FRIEDRICH, A.: 1704 (255)
FRIESE, H.: 913 (138), 911 (138)
FRIESSEM, D.: 982 (149)
FRIGHI, L.: 687 (106)
FRIIS, S.: 1877 (287), 2248 (346)
FRITH, C.: 1328 (206), 1816 (278), 1263 (196)
FRITZE, J.: 432 (64), 3071 (472), 2990 (457)
FRONTZEK, T.: 966 (147)
FRUGONI PERDOMO, A.: 1136 (173)
FRYDMAN, D.: 320 (49)
FU-CHYUAN, W.: 3118 (479)
FUCHS, H.: 1943 (294)
FUCUNISHI, I.: 1047 (157)
FUEGER, G.: 1302 (202)
FUENFGELD, E.: 747 (115), 748 (115), 1250 (194)
FUENFGELD, M.: 2393 (368), 1819 (278), 351 (53)
FUJIMORI, H.: 889 (134), 821 (123)
FUJIMURA, T.: 2810 (430)
FUJITA, H.: 271 (40), 2907 (443), 2390 (368)
FUKUDA, T.: 897 (135), 1982 (299)
FUKUNISHI, I.: 2141 (326)
FULCHERI, M.: 1193 (184)

843

FUNDUDIS, T.: 2526 (386)
FUREDI, J.: 1794 (273), 918 (139)
FURUHOLMEN, D.: 554 (83)
FURUYA, K.: 1179 (182)
FYER, A.: 90 (15)

G

GABE, J.: 1318 (204)
GABRIEL, I.: 1484 (227)
GABROVSKA, V.: 2473 (379)
GACCIC, B.: 2440 (375), 3033 (465)
GAEBEL, W.: 890 (134), 1704 (255), 1549 (238), 886 (134)
GAENSHIRT, G.: 666 (103)
GAGIANO, C.: 2093 (319), 213 (31), 2577 (395), 1448 (221)
GAIA, S.: 482 (70), 2466 (378)
GAILLARD, J.: 430 (64)
GAILLEDREAU, J.: 2029 (308), 145 (22), 444 (66), 353 (54), 1682 (253), 2290 (352), 2475 (379)
GAIO, M.: 2460 (377)
GALA, C.: 1239 (193), 1240 (193)
GALACTOPOULOU, S.: 2670 (406)
GALANOPOULOU, K.: 363 (55)
GALANTER, J.: 695 (107)
GALBAUD DU FORT, G.: 2032 (308)
GALDERISI, S.: 1249 (194)
GALEAZZI, M.: 817 (122)
GALIANA, M.: 2013 (306)
GALIMBERTI, B.: 2666 (406)
GALINDO, M.: 2981 (455)
GALINDO Y VILLA, C.: 2496 (381), 2984 (455)
GALINOWSKI, A.: 2564 (392)
GALIS, A.: 482 (70), 2466 (378)
GALLANT, D.: 1321 (205)
GALLHOFER, B.: 1302 (202), 1524 (235)
GALLI, L.: 376 (57)
GALLIANI, I.: 2354 (363)
GALLITANO, A.: 1887 (288)
GALLOIS, PH.: 2135 (325), 2136 (325)
GALLUZZI, A.: 2813 (430)
GALOFARO, A.: 2874 (439), 1650 (250)
GALVANO, G.: 2250 (346), 2071 (315), 2594 (397), 2237 (345), 2158 (327)
GALVAO VIDEIRA, R.: 2460 (377)
GAMERMAN, B.: 2853 (436)
GAMERMAN, V.: 2853 (436)
GAMITO, L.: 1490 (228), 2261 (348)
GANGADHAR, B.: 1475 (226), 1476 (226), 2254 (347)
GANNON, M.: 2727 (414)
GANRY, H.: 2734 (414)
GARAU, L.: 2075 (316)
GARAVAGLIA, R.: 2437 (375), 2071 (315), 1245 (193)
GARBARINI, M.: 272 (40), 413 (63)
GARBER, H.: 700 (108)
GARCIA, A.: 2703 (410)
GARCIA, F.: 370 (56), 1336 (207)
GARCIA CAMBA, J.: 2444 (376)
GARCIA CAMPAYO, J.: 3234 (494)
GARCIA-MAS, A.: 1358 (209), 1421 (216)
GARCIA NOVARINI, R.: 639 (98)
GARCIA-PRIETO, A.: 1480 (227), 1654 (250)
GARDE, K.: 924 (141), 2829 (432)
GARFINKEL, P.: 2971 (452), 2010 (305)
GARNEAU, N.: 969 (147), 2482 (380)
GARNICA, R.: 2981 (455), 2983 (455)
GARNOV, V.: 2140 (326)
GARRABE, J.: 2084 (317), 2203 (335)
GARRE, J.: 1411 (215), 1071 (161), 2685 (408)

GARREAU, B.: 2682 (408), 2183 (332)
GARRIDO, J.: 1086 (163)
GARRONE, G.: 1684 (253), 2411 (372), 2051 (311)
GARVER, D.: 130 (21)
GARVIN, R.: 1864 (285)
GARYFALLOS, G.: 579 (88), 85 (14)
GARZA-TREVINO, E.: 3180 (488), 3181 (488)
GASSER, TH: 575 (87)
GASTAGER, H.: 3056 (468)
GASTPAR, M.: 1301 (202), 2407 (371)
GASZNER, P.: 2618 (400), 169 (25)
GATER, R.: 312 (48)
GATTAZ, W.:-171 (25), 575 (87), 2330 (359)
GATZONIS, S.: 1489 (228)
GAUSSET, M.: 1367 (210), 438 (65), 2504 (382)
GAUTAM, S.: 2149 (326), 1112 (167)
GAUTHIER, J.: 2475 (379)
GAVRILOVA, S.: 894 (135), 2054A (312)
GAZANO-JOUANON, F.: 436 (65)
GEBHARDT, R.: 1089 (164)
GEDAKIS, M.: 1728 (261), 779 (118)
GEHLOT, P.: 1112 (167), 2149 (326)
GEIDER, F.: 2130 (325)
GEISELHART, H.: 781 (118)
GEISELMANN, B.: 1315 (204)
GEISER, R.: 2544 (388)
GEISLER, A.: 2507 (382)
GEKAS, G.: 1201 (185)
GEKIERE, F.: 1891 (288)
GELBARD, H.: 1887 (288)
GELDER, M.: 848 (127)
GELDERS, Y.: 2156 (327), 1495 (229)
GELERNTER, J.: 930 (142)
GENAZZANI, A.: 3000 (459)
GENTIL FILHO, V.: 1626 (247), 395 (60), 414 (63)
GENTILI, C.: 76 (13)
GEORGE, A.: 2656 (405)
GEORGE, T.: 2893 (441)
GEORGESCU, M.: 2280 (351)
GEORGIADIS, G.: 789 (119)
GEPPONI, I.: 376 (57)
GERARD, MJ: 358 (54)
GERARD, M.A.: 2428 (374)
GERBER, G.: 1572 (242), 80 (13), 2221 (339)
GEREBTZOFF, A.: 66 (12)
GERHOLT, F.: 908 (137), 2028 (308)
GERIN, P.: 1272 (198), 438 (65)
GERLACH, J.: 529 (78), 2930 (446), 531 (78), 2414 (372), 2625 (401)
GERLINGHOFF, M.: 1710 (257), 2959 (449)
GERNER, M.: 2400 (370)
GERONTAS, A.: 284 (41)
GERSHON, B.: 1106 (167)
GEUTJENS, J.: 2156 (327), 1987 (300)
GEYER, P.: 2090 (318)
GHANIM, M.: 3122 (480), 2864 (438)
GHERARDI, S.: 2517 (383)
GIACOMINI-BIRAUD, V.: 608 (92)
GIANETTI, S.: 2603 (398)
GIANNACCINI, G.: 204 (29)
GIANNAKODIMOS, S.: 2122 (323)
GIANNIKOS, L.: 1362 (210)
GIANNIOS, G.: 1906 (290), 1907 (290)
GIARDINELLI, L.: 1746 (264), 1029 (156)
GIBERT RAHOLA, J.: 448 (66), 1021 (155)
GIBERTI, F.: 3205 (491)
GIEHREND, M.: 2927 (446)
GIERL, B.: 750 (115), 749 (115)
GIERL, G.: 932 (142)

GIGER, T.: 1275 (198)
GILIOLI, R.: 3040 (466)
GILL, C.: 2528 (386)
GILLBERG, P.: 836 (125)
GILLEARD, C.: 2555 (390)
GILLEARD, E.: 1843 (281)
GILLIERON, E.: 299 (44)
GILLIN, C.: 1220 (188)
GILSON, M.: 903 (136)
GIOBBIO, G.: 413 (63), 272 (40)
GIORDANO, P.: 2605 (398)
GIOUZEPAS, J.: 756 (116)
GIOVACCHINI, P.: 2347 (363)
GIOVINE, A.: 1175 (181)
GIRALDI, T.: 2604 (398)
GIRARDI, P.: 801 (120)
GIRON, N.: 2579 (395)
GIRRE, J.: 1014 (154)
GITTELMAN, M.: 2210 (337), 1444 (220), 58 (11)
GIURGEA, C.: 222 (33)
GIUSTO, G.: 1910 (290), 1913 (291)
GIVEIRA, J.: 3230 (494)
GLAISTER, J.: 776 (118)
GLASER, T.: 236 (35), 1081 (162), 1078 (162)
GLAUBITT, D.: 2117 (322)
GLEN, A.: 2151 (327), 3039 (465)
GLEN, E.: 2151 (327), 3039 (465)
GLENN CRAIG, D.: 2427 (374)
GLENTHOJ, B.: 528 (78), 2916 (444)
GLIEMANN, R.: 1043 (157)
GLOCKER, F.: 453 (67), 452 (67)
GLUCK, N.: 2290 (352)
GLUE, P: 908 (137), 2028 (308)
GLUZMAN, S.: 2573 (394)
GNAD, M.: 515 (76)
GNIRSS, F.: 2562 (392)
GNOCCHI, G.: 2508 (382)
GOATE, A.: 2055 (312)
GODBOUT, R.: 2731 (414)
GODEFROY, M.: 967 (147)
GOERING, P.: 2931 (447), 3221 (492), 186 (27), 1485 (228)
GOETESTAM, G.: 1164 (179), 855 (128)
GOEZUEKIRMIZI, E.: 3023 (463), 3052 (467)
GOFFINET, S.: 1656 (250), 263 (39), 1186 (183)
GOGNALONS-NICOLET, M.: 1272 (198), 503 (73)
GOIBELMAN, L.: 1219 (187)
GOIHMAN, M.: 2646 (404)
GOLD, P. W.: 2535 (387), 2552 (390), 220 (32), 2532 (387), 2525 (385), 2531 (387)
GOLDBERG, D.: 312 (48)
GOLDFLUSS, E.: 1726 (261), 817 (122)
GOLDSCHMIDT, N.: 435 (65)
GOLDSTEIN, D.: 2533 (387)
GOLDSTEIN, I.: 2830 (432)
GOLDSTEIN, M.: 1244 (193)
GOLDWURM, G.: 991 (151)
GOLLNER, C.: 458 (68)
GOMEZ-CAMA, M.: 1021 (155)
GONCALVES, M.: 525 (77)
GONCALVES, V.: 1246 (193)
GONIDEC, J.: 593 (90)
GONZALEZ, C.: 1091 (164)
GONZALEZ DE RIVERA, J.: 1924 (292)
GONZALEZ-SEIJO, J.: 768 (117)
GOODWIN, D.: 1811 (277)
GOODWIN, F.: 1 (1)
GOODWIN, G.: 2168 (329)
GORCEIX, A.: 636 (98)
GORDAS, T.: 414 (63)

GORDIJN, M.: 667 (103), 666 (103)
GORDON, E.: 3007 (461)
GORI, G.: 2848 (435)
GORNY, H.: 274 (40)
GOSHIMA, Y.: 2912 (444)
GOTHEIL, N.: 2644 (404)
GOTO, H.: 3042 (466)
GOTTFRIES, C.: 1944 (294), 13 (3), 2057 (312), 2602 (398), 1863 (284)
GOTTLIEB, P.: 599 (91)
GOTTSCHALK, J.: 2098 (320)
GOUDEV, A.: 2335 (360)
GOUGOULIS, N.: 160 (24), 159 (24)
GOULD, E.: 2727 (414)
GOURET, C.: 591 (90)
GOUTSIOU, K.: 1928 (292)
GOUVEIA, J.: 1299 (201)
GOVINDAN, S.: 294 (43)
GOZIO, C.: 2354 (363), 1097 (164)
GRACIA, E.: 1795 (274)
GRACIA, R.: 1924 (292)
GRACIA MARCOS, F.: 1136 (173)
GRADANTE, G.: 2354 (363)
GRAFEILLE, N.: 1069 (160)
GRAMMATIKOS, F.: 1928 (292)
GRANDE, C.: 1082 (162)
GRANDI, B.: 1632 (248)
GRANGE, D.: 2882 (440)
GRANT, B.: 716 (110), 214 (31)
GRASSHOFF, U.: 3050 (467)
GRASSI, A.: 2696 (409)
GRASSI, L.: 1138 (173), 1518 (234), 742 (114)
GRASSO, S.: 151 (23), 1604 (245)
GRAWE, R.: 1164 (179)
GRECU, L.: 1746 (264)
GREEN, M.: 2606 (398)
GREEN, R.: 1807 (276)
GREENBERG, R.: 2854 (436)
GREENLAND, C.: 1808 (276)
GREGERSEN, B.: 1024 (155)
GREGOIRE, A.: 2029 (308)
GREIST, J.: 1779 (270)
GRENHOFF, J.: 527 (78)
GREUEL, J.: 1078 (162)
GREVE, B.: 274 (40), 2873 (439), 275 (40)
GRIEZ, E.: 3126 (480), 412 (63)
GRIGOR, J.: 1787 (272), 2569 (394)
GRIGOROIU-SERBANESCU, M.: 199 (28)
GRIMBERG, S.: 1200 (185)
GRIME, J.: 2388 (368)
GRISPINI, A.: 765 (117), 1894 (288)
GRODD, W.: 834 (125)
GROF, E.: 706 (109)
GROF, P.: 706 (109)
GROHMANN, R.: 1842 (281)
GROPP, C.: 723 (111)
GROSS, G.: 515 (76), 519 (76), 3142 (482), 518 (76), 3141 (482), 516 (76)
GROUNDS, A.: 3075 (473)
GROWDON, J.: 2055 (312)
GRUENBERGER, J.: 2464 (378), 2674 (407), 876 (132), 1932 (293), 1345 (208)
GRUZELIER, J.: 2182 (332), 2338 (361)
GUAJARDO, I.: 493 (71)
GUARCH, J.: 2585 (396)
GUARNERI, L.: 413 (63)
GUAZZELLI, M.: 1169 (180)
GUDDE, H.: 2031 (308)
GUDMUNDSDOTTIR, A.: 1823 (279), 1824 (279), 283 (41), 1834 (280)
GUDRUN, O.: 499 (73)
GUELFI, J.: 1872 (286), 3229 (494), 1870 (286), 1290 (200), 1020 (155), 1869 (286), 2733 (414)
GUENTHER, W.: 1375 (211)

GUERANI, G.: 1110 (167), 1159 (179)
GUERDAL, H.: 2165 (328)
GUERREIRO, A.: 1602 (245)
GUERRINI, B.: 1693 (254)
GUEVEN, S.: 1900 (289)
GUGEL, P.: 2417 (373)
GUIBERT, M.: 2953 (448)
GUICH, S.: 873 (132), 210 (30)
GUIDI, E.: 1058 (158)
GUIEN, V.: 761 (116)
GUILLAMAT, R.: 3046 (466), 2401 (370)
GUILLARD-BATAILLE, J.: 1367 (210), 2504 (382)
GUILLEMIN, J.: 1638 (248)
GUILLEMINAULT, C.: 2040 (310)
GUILLET, P.: 1008 (154), 2300 (353)
GUIMARAES, F.: 1163 (179)
GUIMAREY, E.: 2703 (410)
GUJADHUR, L.: 1642 (249)
GULBERG, C.: 2067 (315)
GULLINI, S.: 1719 (260)
GULTEKIN,: 1922 (292)
GUNTERN, R.: 2332 (360)
GUPTA, A.: 1207 (186), 20 (4)
GUPTA, R.: 936 (143)
GUPTA, S.: 2720 (412)
GURLING, H.: 1238 (192)
GUSTAFSSON, B.: 1348 (208), 479 (70), 535 (79)
GUSTAVSSON, H.: 904 (136)
GUSTAVSSON, G.: 1940 (294)
GUTHRIE, E.: 1720 (260)
GUTIERES, K.: 2096 (319)
GUTIERREZ, P.: 3014 (461)
GUYONNET, A.: 673 (104)
GUYOTAT, J.: 1393 (213), 1367 (210)
GUZELLA, J.: 2055 (312)
GUZUKIRMIZI, E.: 2642 (403)
GWIRTSMAN, H.: 2535 (387)
GYOBU, T.: 2392 (368)
GYRA, E.: 2085 (318), 468 (69), 803 (121),)

H

HA, O.: 2923 (446)
HAARMANN, F.: 2681 (408)
HAAS, H.: 2479 (379)
HAASTRUP, S.: 164 (24)
HACKENBERG, K.: 1297 (201)
HACKETT, E.: 565 (85)
HADANO, K.: 753 (115)
HADJI, H.: 944 (144), 1203 (185)
HADJICHRISTOS, C.: 166 (25)
HADJITASKOS, P.: 1174 (181), 335 (51), 334 (51), 393 (60)
HAEFNER, H.: 621 (95)
HAFFMANS, J.: 1948 (294), 1678 (253)
HAFFMANS, P.: 474 (70), 1387 (212), 1677 (253), 484 (70), 485 (70)
HAFFNER, F.: 909 (137)
HAGBERG, B.: 2199 (335), 976 (149)
HAGELSTEEN, M.: 1070 (160)
HAGEMAN, W.: 2619 (400)
HAGENFELDT, L.: 2385 (368), 938 (143)
HAGERT, U.: 2930 (446), 2137 (325)
HAGGERTY, J.: 1539 (237)
HAGIMOTO, H.: 574 (87), 2844 (435)
HAGMAN, M.: 2148 (326)
HAIER, R.: 873 (132), 210 (30)
HAIN, C.: 2170 (329)
HAINES, G.: 2055 (312)
HAKIM-KREIS, C.: 878 (133), 880 (133)
HAKKOU, F.: 743 (114), 2878 (440)
HALARIS, A.: 635 (98), 2472 (379)
HALBACH, M.: 1129 (172), 1130 (172),

433 (64), 1131 (172), 939 (143), 3138 (481)
HALDIN, C.: 836 (125)
HALFON, O.: 521 (77), 983 (150), 2578 (395), 3013 (461)
HALIKAS, J.: 17 (4), 18 (4)
HALKIADAKI, H.: 2670 (406)
HALLDIN, C.: 2385 (368), 2389 (368)
HALLMAYER, J.: 254 (37)
HALMI, K.: 287 (42)
HAMA, Y.: 704 (108)
HAMADANI, M.: 606 (92)
HAMANAKA, T.: 2072 (315), 753 (115), 457 (68), 341 (52), 1465 (224)
HAMBURGER, S.: 2441 (375)
HAMDANE, K.: 174 (26)
HAMDOUCHI, S.: 2833 (433)
HAMED, A.: 3122 (480), 2864 (438)
HAMMOND, G.: 477 (70), 476 (70)
HAMMOND, J.: 1162 (179)
HAMNER, M.: 1197 (184), 170 (25)
HAMOGEORGAKIS, P.: 610 (93), 611 (93)
HANAMURA, S.: 1467 (224)
HAND, I.: 91 (15)
HANEL, I.: 2717 (412)
HANNA, G.: 607 (92), 2402 (370)
HANSEN, A.: 120 (19)
HANSEN, H.: 2067 (315)
HANSEN, L.: 907 (137)
HANSON, A.: 2381 (367)
HANTZI, A.: 2812 (430)
HARA, H.: 2926 (446)
HARANGOZO, J.: 2243 (345), 489 (70)
HARD, E.: 1813 (277)
HARDI, I.: 1116 (168)
HARDIN, J.: 2055 (312)
HARDY, P.: 885 (134), 1621 (247)
HARENKO, A.: 1944 (294)
HARIGUCHI, S.: 119 (19), 118 (19)
HARMOUSSI-PEIOGLOU, S.: 789 (119)
HARNOIS, G.: 1788 (272), 57 (11)
HARRINGTON, A.: 2393 (368), 351 (53), 1818 (278), 1819 (278)
HARRIS, B.: 1177 (181)
HARRISON, R.: 751 (115)
HART, C.: 1452 (221)
HARTMAN, J.: 3168 (486)
HARTMANN, W.: 3201 (490)
HARTO, NANCY E.: 2478 (379)
HARTOCOLLIS, P.: 51 (10)
HARTVIG, P.: 2386 (368)
HARTWICH, P.: 2965 (450)
HARVEY, N.: 799 (120)
HASEGAWA, K.: 816 (122), 862 (129), 863 (129)
HASFURA, C.: 2923 (446)
HASHIGUCHI, K.: 1707 (255)
HASHIMOTO, S.: 2810 (430)
HASHIMOTO, T.: 2907 (443), 2390 (368)
HASITZ, M.: 2870 (438)
HASLAM, M.: 927 (141)
HASSELBALCH, E.: 441 (65)
HATJISAVAS, S.: 278 (41)
HATZAKIS, A.: 728 (112)
HATZICHRISTOU, C.: 985 (150), 1412 (215)
HATZIMANOLIS, J.: 1303 (202), 202 (29), 1474 (226), 2218 (338), 1379 (212), 1537 (237), 1538 (237)
HATZINGER, M.: 2649 (404)
HATZINGER, R.: 1475 (226), 1476 (226)
HAUG, H.: 2294 (352), 668 (103)
HAUG, T.: 1164 (179)
HAUGER, R.: 237 (35)
HAUGHTON, I.: 1212 (187), 1558 (240)
HAUKIJAERVI, A.: 1011 (154)
HAULI, J.: 232 (34)

HAUPTS, M.: 274 (40), 2873 (439), 275 (40)
HAUSER, J.: 1053 (158)
HAUSPIE, R.: 2169 (329)
HAUTECOEUR, P.: 2135 (325)
HAVAKI-KONTAXAKI, B.: 144 (22), 143 (22)
HAVERMANS, A.: 652 (100)
HAVET, J.: 135 (21)
HAVIARAS, B.: 1685 (253)
HAWARI, D.: 1908 (290), 1832 (280)
HAYASHI, M.: 364 (55), 2683 (408)
HAYASHI, S.: 1725 (261), 1192 (184)
HAYBARA, T.: 2141 (326)
HAYES, G.: 354 (54)
HAYKAL, R.: 711 (109)
HAZAMA, H.: 2119 (323)
HAZLETT, E.: 873 (132), 210 (30)
HEAL, D.: 594 (90), 2877 (440), 590 (90)
HEARNE, J.: 2257 (348)
HEBENSTREIT, G.: 1803 (275), 1155 (176)
HECHT, H.: 770 (117), 771 (117)
HECHT, M.: 466 (68)
HECHTMAN, L.: 2973 (452)
HECIMOVIC, A.: 2259 (348), 3038 (465), 2487 (380), 760 (116), 1646 (249), 1059 (158)
HECKERS, S.: 943 (143), 277 (40)
HEERLEIN, A.: 767 (117), 2285 (351)
HEGEN, C.: 1012 (154)
HEILMEYER, H.: 572 (86)
HEIMAN, H.: 2069 (315), 2906 (443)
HEIMSTAD, E.: 1889 (288)
HEINDRICH, H.: 791 (119)
HEINRICH, K.: 3140 (482), 1995 (302)
HEINRICH, M.: 532 (78)
HEINRICH, T.: 1614 (246)
HEINSEN, H.: 943 (143), 277 (40)
HEINSEN, Y.: 943 (143), 277 (40)
HEINZE, G.: 1132 (172), 2652 (405), 426 (64)
HEINZMANN, U.: 274 (40)
HEISE, H.: 3218 (492)
HEISER, J.: 2257 (348)
HELD, F.: 2686 (408)
HELG, E.: 2442 (375)
HELGASON, T.: 1797 (274)
HELMCHEN, H.: 1291 (200), 89 (164), 2786 (424)
HELZER, J.: 716 (110), 302 (45), 678 (105)
HEMANGEE, D.: 1835 (280)
HEMMINGSEN, R.: 528 (78), 441 (65), 120 (19), 2376 (366), 2374 (366), 620 (95),)
HENDERSON, J.: 3065 (471), 1309 (203)
HENDERSON, S.: 745 (115)
HENINGER, G.: 2765 (420)
HENINGER, O.: 1713 (259)
HENN, F.: 2327 (359)
HENNING, U.: 939 (143), 3138 (481), 1131 (172), 1129 (172)
HENTTONEN, A.: 2287 (352)
HERBISON, G.: 2307 (354)
HERCZEG, I.: 3185 (488), 1673 (252)
HERLOFSEN, P.: 2746 (416)
HERMESH, H.: 3153 (484), 849 (128), 3151 (484)
HERMLE, L.: 2393 (368)
HERNANZ, A.: 1082 (162)
HERPERTZ-DAHLMANN, B.: 2396 (369)
HERRMANN, C.: 2170 (329), 2144 (326)
HERRMANN, W.: 2294 (352), 754 (115)
HERZ, A.: 115 (19)
HERZ, M.: 2798 (427), 2235 (344)
HERZOG, S.: 3137 (481), 571 (86)

HESSE, C.: 2086 (318)
HESTON, L.: 2055 (312)
HETHERINGTON, K.: 2695 (409)
HETTA, J.: 2386 (368), 1012 (154), 2892 (441)
HEUN, R.: 133 (21), 134 (21)
HEWER, W.: 896 (135), 464 (68)
HEYDER, N.: 2372 (366)
HEYLEN, S.: 1495 (229), 2156 (327)
HIBBS, E.: 2441 (375)
HICKIE, I.: 729 (113)
HIDALGO, I.: 3172 (487)
HIDALGO, M.: 3172 (487)
HIEMKE, C.: 638 (98)
HIENDLMAYER, G.: 64 (12)
HIENKE, C.: 857 (129)
HIETALA, J.: 2914 (444)
HILL, L.: 2091 (318)
HILLER, W.: 2419 (373), 1283 (200)
HILZ, M.: 382 (58)
HINDMARCH, I.: 2771 (420), 2043 (310), 241 (35)
HINTERHUBER, H.: 3137 (481)
HINZ, A.: 1300 (202), 1172 (181), 1171 (181)
HIPPIUS, H.: 724 (112), 40 (8), 2622 (401), 2626 (401)
HIRANO, H.: 3048 (467)
HIRASAWA, S.: 1566 (241), 1374 (211)
HIROSAWA, K.: 2777 (422)
HIROSE, S.: 158 (24)
HIROSE, T.: 2818 (431)
HIROSHI, U.: 2134 (325), 2133 (325)
HIRSCH, S.: 2455 (377), 622 (95)
HIRSCHOWITZ, J.: 2327 (359)
HISADA, K.: 2392 (368)
HITRI, A.: 38 (7), 1197 (184)
HITZEMANN, R.: 2327 (359)
HJORTSO, S.: 1388 (213)
HOAREAU, J.: 3092 (476)
HOCHMANN, J.: 438 (65)
HOCLET, M.: 2953 (448)
HODEL, B.: 2748 (417), 899 (136), 1265 (196)
HODGES, J.: 866 (130)
HODSON, A.: 1049 (157)
HOELL, R.: 185 (27), 382 (58), 3040 (466), 762 (116), 2090 (318)
HOENCAMP, E.: 1948 (294), 474 (70)
HOFF, A.: 1376 (211)
HOFF, P.: 963 (147)
HOFFMAN, O.: 738 (114), 720 (111)
HOFFMANN, G.: 2171 (329)
HOFFMANN, J.: 1534 (236)
HOFMANN, H.: 1172 (181)
HOFMANN, P.: 1476 (226), 1475 (226)
HOFSCHUSTER, E.: 63 (12), 1104 (166)
HOHAGEN, F.: 2343 (362), 3050 (467)
HOJAIJ, C.: 1373 (211), 670 (104)
HOLDEN, J.: 2593 (397)
HOLE, G.: 147 (22), 1916 (291)
HOLE, V.: 2436 (375)
HOLLAND, A.: 292 (42)
HOLLATZ, F.: 791 (119), 2880 (440)
HOLLERER, E.: 1931 (293)
HOLLEY, H.: 3074 (473)
HOLLISTER, L.: 3180 (488), 3181 (488), 549 (82)
HOLLMANN, S.: 2680 (408)
HOLLWEG, M.: 233 (34)
HOLM, P.: 1676 (253)
HOLMBERG, G.: 2752 (418)
HOLOBOW, N.: 1206 (186), 533 (79), 422 (63)
HOLSBOER-TRACHSLER, E.: 2649 (404)
HOLUB, U.: 3203 (490)
HOLZBACH, E.: 2370 (366)

HONIGFELD, G.: 102 (16)
HOOPER, J.: 2121 (323), 150 (23), 2556 (391)
HOPS, H.: 2575 (395)
HORDER, M.: 908 (137), 2028 (308)
HORESH, N.: 1933 (293)
HORII, S.: 1831 (280)
HORITA, N.: 1041 (156)
HORNER, A.: 2555 (390)
HORNSTEIN, CH.: 1001 (153), 2078 (316)
HORROBIN, D.: 2326 (359), 1843 (281), 3039 (465)
HORTA, M.: 2779 (422)
HORVATH, E.: 1079 (162), 1078 (162)
HORVATH, S.: 3185 (488)
HOSAKA, H.: 704 (108)
HOSCHL, C.: 1221 (188)
HOSHINO, Y.: 1566 (241)
HOSOKAWA, K.: 2141 (326), 1047 (157)
HOTAMANIDIS, S.: 246 (36)
HOUILLON, G.C.: 2953 (448)
HOUSE, AO.: 1608 (245)
HOUSHANG, G.: 606 (92)
HOVAGUIMIAN, T.: 1226 (189)
HOWARD, R.: 933 (142)
HOWELLS, J.: 2549 (389), 42 (8)
HOYME, J.: 1213 (187)
HSIEH, HH.: 2560 (392)
HU, W.: 2560 (392)
HUA, J.: 2118 (323)
HUB FARIA, I.: 2583 (396)
HUBAIN, PH.: 832 (125)
HUBER, G.: 515 (76), 3141 (482), 518 (76), 519 (76), 3142 (482), 516 (76)
HUDGINS, M.: 2352 (363)
HUEBNER, C.: 171 (25)
HUEROL, C.: 388 (59), 2697 (410)
HUERTAS, D.: 2648 (404)
HUERTO DELGADILLO, L.: 1132 (172)
HUG, A.: 694 (107)
HUGON, N.: 1046 (157), 1609 (245), 2896 (442), 1610 (245), 2884 (441)
HUJITA, H.: 2387 (368)
HUK, W.: 2372 (366)
HULSTIJN, W.: 2247 (346)
HULTHE, P.: 1813 (277)
HUMBLE, M.: 559 (84)
HUMMEL, E.: 484 (70), 485 (70)
HUMMEL, P.: 3169 (487), 288 (42)
HUNTER, R.: 2168 (329)
HUPPERT, F.: 2528 (386)
HURET, J.: 270 (40), 1621 (247), 2871 (439)
HURWITZ, T.: 1605 (245), 722 (111)
HUSAIN, S.: 1218 (187)
HUSAINI, B.: 2858 (437)
HUTTUNEN, M.: 3156 (485)
HUXLEY, F.: 103 (17)
HWANG, J.: 3186 (488)
HWU, H.: 369 (56)
HYDE, C.: 2324 (358)
HYOKI, K.: 2868 (438)
HYRMAN, V.: 2253 (347)
HYTTEL, J.: 2916 (444)

I

IACCARINO, C.: 2832 (433)
IACOPONI, E.: 367 (56), 2512 (383)
IACOVIDES, A.: 1928 (292)
IATRAKIS, G.: 1362 (210)
ICHIKAWA, J.: 2970 (451)
ICHINOWATARI, N.: 1179 (182)
IDAKA, E.: 423 (64)
IDE, H.: 1036 (156)
IENCIU, M.: 1545 (238)

IERODIAKONOU, C.: 1928 (292), 626 (96), 1800 (275)
IFANTIS, D.: 2100 (320)
IGLESIAS, L.: 1414 (215), 79 (13), 1829 (279), 1577 (242)
IGNATOV, A.: 1640 (249), 578 (87)
II, M.: 2392 (368)
IINUMA, K.: 2157 (327)
IIO, M.: 2907 (443), 2390 (368)
IKEDA, H.: 3028 (464)
IKUTA, T.: 3042 (466)
ILANKOVIC, N.: 495 (71), 2838 (434), 2264 (348)
ILANCOVIC, V.: 2838 (434)
ILLARREGUI, A.: 1054 (158)
ILVONEN, T.: 1011 (154)
IMAMURA, K.: 1143 (174)
IMAZU, Y.: 2911 (444)
IMRE, H.: 684 (106), 2689 (409), 1600 (245)
INADA, T.: 1702 (255), 2926 (446), 1707 (255), 3150 (484)
INGEBRIGTSEN, G.: 2493 (381)
INGENLEUF, H.: 185 (27), 1044 (157), 1664 (251)
INGLESE, S.: 496 (71), 2688 (409)
INGLOT, A.: 1697 (255)
INGRAM, D.: 2637 (403)
INGVAD, B.: 976 (149), 2199 (335)
INOMATA, J.: 2683 (408), 364 (55), 514 (75)
INOUE, Y.: 2119 (323)
INSEL, T.: 34 (7)
INVERNIZZI, G.: 2128 (324), 2437 (375), 2442 (375)
IOANNIDIS, C.: 334 (51), 335 (51), 269 (39), 2582 (396), 144 (22), 2018 (306)
IOANNOVICH, I.: 2592 (397), 84 (14)
IONESCU, G.: 2422 (373)
IONESCU, R.: 796 (120)
IRAKI, L.: 2878 (440), 743 (114)
IREGREN, A.: 2148 (326)
IRIGOYEN-RASCON, F.: 2860 (437)
IRIMIA, V.: 2543 (388)
IRION, T.: 2248 (346)
ISAAC, M.: 1855 (283), 713 (110)
ISANRD, P.: 160 (24)
ISEDA, T.: 816 (122)
ISENBERG, K.E.: 130 (21)
ISHIGURO, S.: 2119 (323)
ISHIHARA, S.: 731 (113)
ISHII, Y.: 456 (68)
ISHIKAWA, T.: 2907 (443), 271 (40), 2390 (368)
ISHIZUKA, Y.: 2808 (430), 1188 (183)
ISSIDORIDES, M.: 2217 (338), 343 (52)
ITIL, K.: 297 (43), 2601 (398)
ITIL, T.: 838 (125), 875 (132), 1247 (194), 297 (43), 2601 (398)
ITO, L.: 1626 (247)
ITOH, H.: 2044 (310), 2474 (379)
IVANCEVIC, D.: 350 (53)
IVANCOVSKY, H.: 3176 (487)
IVANETS, N.: 1752 (265)
IVANUSHKIN, A.: 1105 (166)
IVICA, J.: 3038 (465)
IWABUCHI, K.: 704 (108)
IWAI, K.: 731 (113)
IZUQUIZA, J.: 3234 (494)
IZZO, R.: 801 (120)

J

JABLENSKY, A.: 8 (2), 2611 (399)
JABLONSKI, L.: 2832 (433)
JACK, H.: 1812 (277)
JACKSON, A.: 3136 (481)
JACOBSEN, B.: 131 (21)
JACOBSEN, F.: 1024 (155)
JAEGER, J.: 2245 (346)
JAFFE, J.: 2969 (451)
JAGSCH, R.: 2464 (378)
JAIN, A.: 1106 (167), 137 (21)
JAIN, S.: 773 (117)
JAKAB, I.: 658 (101), 1114 (168)
JAKLEWICZ, H.: 121 (20)
JAKOVLJEVIC, M.: 424 (64), 1658 (250)
JAKUBASCHK, J.: 447 (66), 2463 (378), 694 (107)
JALILI, S.: 1734 (262)
JAMAIN, S.: 2026 (307)
JAMIL, K.: 446 (66)
JANAKIRAMAIAH, N.: 773 (117)
JANARDHAN, R.: 705 (108)
JANCAR, J.: 323 (49)
JANDORF, L.: 1376 (211)
JANICAK, R.: 932 (142)
JANIRI, L.: 2465 (378), 1243 (193), 1242 (193), 475 (70)
JANNE, P.: 1580 (243), 2852 (436), 3173 (487), 263 (39)
JANNES, S.: 2787 (425)
JANSEN, A.: 2138 (325)
JANSEN, G.: 1387 (212), 2928 (446), 1677 (253), 484 (70), 485 (70)
JANSEN, M.: 1349 (208)
JANSEN, M.: 1761 (266)
JANSSEN, P.: 1495 (229), 449 (66)
JANSSEN, T.: 1668 (251)
JANTOS, H.: 2166 (328)
JAOUEN, C.: 2878 (440), 743 (114)
JARA, J.: 2460 (377), 1490 (228), 2261 (348)
JARAS, J.HZ.: 2444 (376)
JARDIM, R.: 1490 (228), 2261 (348)
JAREMA, M.: 1343 (208), 2558 (392), 463 (68)
JARHO, L.: 1732 (262)
JASOVIC-GASIC, M.: 1361 (210)
JASSO, A.: 2923 (446)
JAUHAR, P.: 1701 (255)
JAVAID, J.: 3124 (480)
JAYAKUMAR, P.: 705 (108)
JEAMMET, P.: 3011 (461), 686 (106)
JEANNINGROS, R.: 1128 (172)
JEANVOINE, M.: 3098 (476)
JEDRYCHOWSKI, M.: 404 (62)
JEFFREY, P.: 930 (142)
JEMOS, J.: 3226 (493), 1727 (261), 1483 (227), 2856 (437), 951 (145)
JENKINS, P.: 281 (41), 282 (41)
JENNER, A.: 2933 (447)
JENNER, F.: 3120 (479)
JENNER, J.: 188 (27), 2820 (431)
JENSEN, E.: 441 (65)
JENSEN, H.: 800 (120), 2865 (438)
JENSEN, K.: 929 (141)
JERNAJCZYK, W.: 2897 (442), 2904 (443), 2898 (442), 2373 (366)
JESINGER, D.: 2108 (321)
JESSEN-PETERSEN, B.: 1486 (228)
JEVDIC, D.: 2264 (348)
JEZEQUEL, PR.: 569 (86)
JILEK, W.: 1505 (231)
JILEK-AALL, L.: 1505 (231)
JIMERSON, D.: 220 (32)
JOAO COSTA, M.: 2445 (376)
JOAO GALVAO, M.: 2445 (376)
JOERGENSEN, E.: 2625 (401), 537 (79)
JOFFE, R.: 865 (130)
JOHANNESSEN, K.: 1813 (277)
JOHANSSON, L.: 2148 (326)
JOHANSSON, T.: 904 (136)
JOHN, E.: 2172 (329)
JOHNS, S.: 2248 (346)
JOHNSON, G.: 2893 (441)
JOHNSON, L.: 720 (111)
JOHNSON, R.: 2969 (451)
JOHNSTON, E.: 1816 (278)
JOHNSTON, L.: 14 (4)
JOHNSTON, S.: 323 (49)
JOHNSTONE, E.: 717 (111), 1328 (206)
JOLLY, A.: 2455 (377)
JONCKHEERE, P.: 180 (26)
JONES, B.: 3183 (488), 661 (102)
JONES, F.: 2205 (336)
JONES, R.: 1252 (194)
JONES RONALD, P.: 2446 (376)
JONGERIUS, P.: 3112 (478)
JONKER, C.: 2867 (438)
JORASCHKY, P.: 86 (14), 1581 (243)
JORDA, L.: 1633 (248), 1623 (247), 1692 (254), 2958 (449), 1087 (163), 2648 (404), 440 (65)
JORDAENS, L.: 2450 (376)
JORGE, M.: 367 (56)
JORGENSEN, A.: 441 (65)
JORGENSEN, F.: 3213 (492)
JORGENSEN, P.: 968 (147), 2231 (343)
JORM, A.: 745 (115)
JORS, S.: 1363 (210)
JOUBERT, G.: 2371 (366)
JOUBERT, N.: 2617 (400)
JOUKAMAA, M.: 265 (39), 2932 (447)
JOUVENT, R.: 1636 (248), 455 (68), 1535 (236)
JUAREZ, E.: 1911 (290)
JUAREZ, S.: 2703 (410)
JUENTGEN, H.: 1553 (239)
JUHELA, P.: 1944 (294)
JUKIC, V.: 1658 (250)
JULIAN, M.: 2518 (383)
JULIEN, R.: 428 (64), 1402 (214), 761 (116), 3202 (490)
JULIUS, D.: 2976 (453)
JUNCO, G.: 426 (64)
JUNG-KWANG, W.: 3118 (479)
JUNGMANN, J.: 245 (36)
JUNIEN, J.: 591 (90)

K

KAASENBROOD, A.: 1401 (214), 1761 (266)
KABANOV, M.: 1426 (217)
KABASHIMA, M.: 2044 (310)
KACHA, F.: 1141 (174)
KACHALOV, P.: 2177 (330)
KACPERCZYK, J.: 2558 (392), 463 (68)
KADOYA, Y.: 2925 (446)
KAGAN, B.: 2400 (370)
KAHANS, D.: 2491 (381), 2087 (318), 3005 (460)
KAHN, K.: 1733 (262)
KAHN, R.: 1494 (229)
KAISER, G.: 2033 (308)
KAIYA, H.: 423 (64), 2329 (359)
KAJANDER-KOPONEN, A.: 1048 (157), 71 (12)
KAJIWARA, A.: 2844 (435)
KAKOURI, A.: 2499 (381), 161 (24), 2355 (363)
KALAFI, Y.: 338 (52)
KALB, R.: 1482 (227)
KALELIOGLU, T.: 814 (122)
KALES, A.: 2637 (403), 854 (128), 2676 (407), 2677 (407), 623 (96), 553 (82)
KALES, J.: 854 (128), 679 (106), 3008

(461), 108 (18)
KALFOGLOU, G.: 452 (67), 453 (67)
KALIAPERUMAL, V.: 1353 (209)
KALITERAKI, E.: 1483 (227), 951 (145), 3226 (493), 2856 (437)
KALJONEN, A.: 390 (59)
KALLINIKAKI, T.: 363 (55), 808 (121)
KALOGEROPOULOS, A.: 2122 (323), 459 (68)
KALOKERINOU, A.: 2670 (406)
KALUDIEV, E.: 398 (61)
KALUGINA, L.: 2127 (324)
KALYONCU,: 1552 (239)
KALYVAS, D.: 335 (51), 334 (51)
KAMAL, M.: 1455 (222)
KAMALI, F.: 1162 (179)
KAMBHAMPTI, K.: 2331 (359)
KAMIJIMA, K.: 1707 (255), 863 (129)
KAMISADA, M.: 1707 (255)
KAMMERER, J.: 2629 (402)
KAMOUN, A.: 2729 (414)
KAMP, J S.: 474 (70)
KANAMORI, I.: 1582 (243)
KANAMURA, H.: 955 (145)
KANBA, S.: 2926 (446), 1707 (255), 1703 (255)
KANDIDAKI, S.: 2500 (381)
KANEKO, T.: 1041 (156)
KANENO, S.: 863 (129)
KANTER, C.: 755 (116)
KAPARDIS, A.: 3076 (473)
KAPFHAMMER, H.: 1918 (291)
KAPLAN, D.: 2331 (359)
KAPLAN, S.: 1076 (162)
KAPPETER, I.: 1724 (261)
KAPRINIS, G.: 1930 (292), 2494 (381)
KAPSALA, T.: 85 (14)
KAPSALI, A.: 2592 (397), 1144 (174)
KAPSAMBELIS, V.: 2084 (317), 3051 (467), 1438 (219)
KAPTANOGLU, C.: 2826 (432), 1603 (245), 1068 (160), 600 (91), 961 (146)
KAR, G.: 2284 (351)
KAR, M.: 792 (119)
KARAAGAC, I.: 3117 (479), 2195 (334), 44 (8)
KARAASLAN, F.: 702 (108), 461 (68)
KARABETSOS, X.: 330 (50)
KARADIMOU, CH.: 1399 (214)
KARAKANEV, N.: 3044 (466), 1208 (186)
KARAKILIC, I.: 702 (108), 461 (68)
KARAMAN, T.: 2062 (314)
KARAMANOS, B.: 680 (106)
KARAMOUZI, G.: 1404 (214), 779 (118)
KARAMUSTAFALIOGLU, O.: 1056 (158), 1837 (280)
KARANTONI, A.: 2832 (433)
KARAOLIDOU, M.: 2355 (363), 2701 (410)
KARAPOSTOLI, N.: 161 (24), 806 (121)
KARASTERGIOU, A.: 85 (14)
KARAVATOS, A.: 823 (123), 1099 (164), 140 (22)
KARAZMAN, R.: 2111 (322)
KAREN, P.: 1221 (188)
KARETSOU, K.: 1685 (253)
KARIOLOU, L.: 1665 (251)
KARISHA, K.: 3042 (466)
KARLSSON, I.: 1944 (294)
KARMACSI, L.: 379 (58)
KAROUM, F.: 207 (29)
KARTERUD, S.: 2248 (346)
KARVOUNIS, S.: 1685 (253)
KARYDI, V.: 434 (65), 2233 (344), 1729 (261), 1404 (214), 1398 (214), 1728 (261), 779 (118)

KASAS, A.: 1680 (253)
KASCHKA, W.: 577 (87), 1581 (243), 1649 (250)
KASHFI, A.: 978 (149)
KASHIMA, N.: 1047 (157)
KASMA, J.: 617 (94)
KASPER, S.: 2660 (405)
KASSETT, J.: 220 (32)
KASTELAN, A.: 424 (64)
KASTELAN, M.: 424 (64)
KASTRATOVIC, D.: 3033 (465), 2264 (348), 495 (71)
KASTRUP, M.: 3236 (494), 2999 (458), 1388 (213)
KASVIKIS, Y.: 385 (59)
KATAMIS, C.: 1241 (193)
KATILA, H.: 2137 (325)
KATO, M.: 2783 (424)
KATO, T.: 753 (115)
KATONA, C.: 1499 (230)
KATSANOU, M.: 2281 (351), 352 (53)
KATSANTONI, T.: 363 (55)
KATSCHNING, H.: 1121 (170), 2226 (342), 844 (127), 2279 (351), 847 (127)
KATSOULAKOS, E.: 692 (107)
KATSOULAS, D.: 2020 (307)
KATSOUYANNI, K.: 2015 (306), 2992 (457), 2218 (338), 2584 (396), 680 (106)
KATSUYA, M.: 2095 (319)
KATZ, A.: 1499 (230)
KATZ, R.: 281 (41), 37 (7), 1780 (270)
KAUERT, G.: 1945 (294), 2299 (353)
KAVADELLA, M.: 1109 (167)
KAWAI, M.: 471 (69)
KAWAMURO, Y.: 2868 (438)
KAY, S.: 850 (128), 1327 (206)
KAYAALP, L.: 2065 (314)
KAYANAK, H.: 3052 (467)
KAYIR, A.: 3026 (463)
KAYNAK, H.: 3023 (463), 2642 (403)
KAZAKEVICIUS, J.: 1071 (161)
KAZAMATSURI, H.: 605 (92)
KEFETZ,: 751 (115)
KEGLEVIC, M.: 3056 (468)
KEHRER, H.: 2681 (408)
KEINAENEN, M.: 390 (59)
KEITH, S.: 2801 (427), 1771 (268), 2803 (427)
KELLER, S.: 830 (124)
KELLNER, P.: 98 (16)
KELLY, M.: 856 (129)
KELWALA, S.: 1106 (167), 137 (21)
KEMALI, D.: 114 (19), 1249 (194), 50 (9), 1655 (250), 1543 (237), 2725 (413)
KEMALI, N.: 114 (19)
KEMALOGLU, M.: 1199 (185)
KEMKES, B.: 2453 (376)
KEMP, K.: 17 (4), 18 (4)
KENARDY, J.: 3123 (480)
KENNETT, G.: 2728 (414)
KENNY, J.: 2458 (377)
KENT, C.: 176 (26)
KERAENEN, P.: 1011 (154)
KERIHUEL, J.: 1840 (281)
KERKHOFS, M.: 2169 (329), 2724 (413)
KERN, P.: 1131 (172)
KESHAVAN, M.: 1589 (244), 2331 (359)
KESMANOVIC, D.: 1397 (214)
KESSELMAN, L.: 329 (50)
KESSLER, K.: 1864 (285)
KETTANI, S.: 1705 (255)
KETTL, P.: 1377 (211)
KEYSOR C.: 2441 (375)
KHAN, A.: 3060 (469), 123 (20)
KHANDELWAL, S.: 2720 (412)

KHANNA, S.: 2152 (327), 2153 (327), 2154 (327), 1624 (247), 1622 (247), 205 (29), 1353 (209), 705 (108)
KHATAMI, M.: 3196 (490)
KHATCHATURIAN, Z.: 2054 (312), 1799 (274)
KHERRATI, H.: 2636 (403)
KHIR, O.: 3073 (472)
KIDD, K.: 1236 (192)
KIDOGAMI, Y.: 2777 (422)
KIEJNA, A.: 1042 (156), 381 (58)
KIEV, A.: 2537 (388)
KIKUCHI, A.: 1702 (255)
KILCHER, H.: 1638 (248)
KIM, K.: 127 (20), 1214 (187)
KIMBER, S.: 1075 (161)
KIMURA, B.: 1463 (224)
KINDLER, S.: 723 (111)
KINDYNIS, S.: 2708 (411)
KING, K.: 2586 (396)
KINNUNEN, P.: 2330 (359)
KINOSHITA, F.: 1702 (255), 2926 (446), 1703 (255)
KIRALY, I.: 2457 (377)
KIRMAYER, L.: 868 (131)
KIROV, G.: 2335 (360)
KIROVA, R.: 1598 (244)
KISHIMOTO, H.: 2907 (443), 271 (40), 574 (87), 201 (29), 2390 (368), 2387 (368), 2738 (415)
KISSLING, W.: 1349 (208), 2439 (375), 1382 (212)
KISTRUP, K.: 2414 (372)
KISZKA, T.: 2296 (353)
KJELDSEN, C.: 908 (137), 2028 (308)
KJELLIN, L.: 631 (97), 189 (27), 2516 (383)
KJELLMAN, B.: 879 (133)
KLASCHKA, J.: 2717 (412)
KLAUSNITZER, W.: 2299 (353)
KLEFTARAS, G.: 2505 (382), 2719 (412)
KLEIMAN, A.: 580 (88)
KLEIN, D.: 90 (15)
KLEIN, E.: 307 (47)
KLERMAN, G.: 3061 (470), 93 (15)
KLIESER, E.: 534 (79), 1015 (154), 999 (153), 1371 (211), 3177 (488), 1477 (226), 1347 (208), 1553 (239), 2751 (417)
KLIMKE, A.: 1015 (154), 1477 (226)
KLING, M.: 2531 (387)
KLINNER, W.: 2453 (376)
KLITGAARD, N.: 2028 (308), 908 (137)
KLOSTERKOETTER, G.: 518 (76)
KLOSTERKOETTER, J.: 519 (76), 3141 (482), 3142 (482), 515 (76), 516 (76)
KLOTZ, J.: 2780 (422)
KLUGE, H.: 2296 (353)
KLUZNIK, J.: 852 (128), 853 (128), 852 (128), 1107 (167)
KLYSNER, R.: 2507 (382)
KNESEVICH, M.: 130 (21)
KNEZEVIC, A.: 738 (114)
KNIJNIK, A.: 2447 (376), 662 (102)
KNOBEL, M.: 1407 (215), 325 (50), 646 (99), 1782 (271)
KNOBLOCH, F.: 3111 (478), 3109 (478)
KNOELKER, U.: 242 (36)
KNOP, J.: 441 (65), 1811 (277)
KNUDSEN, H.: 1486 (228)
KO, WEI-K.: 2124 (323)
KOBUSIAK, M.: 2373 (366), 2897 (442)
KOBYLSKI, T.: 679 (106)
KOCAK,: 1210 (186)
KOCZKAS, C.: 559 (84)
KOE, B.: 2768 (420)
KOEHLER, G.: 1914 (291)

KOEMPF, D.: 3021 (462)
KOENIG, W.: 1679 (253), 1614 (246)
KOENING, P.: 465 (68), 718 (111)
KOEPCKE, W.: 890 (134), 1549 (238)
KOFMEL, B.: 872 (132)
KOGAN, B.: 2368 (366)
KOGAN, D.: 1322 (205)
KOGITA, S.: 2810 (430)
KOGITA, Y.: 1582 (243)
KOHEN, L.: 2947 (447), 129 (20)
KOHLER, J.: 572 (86)
KOHNO, H.: 2926 (446), 1703 (255)
KOINIG, G.: 1476 (226), 1648 (250), 483 (70), 1475 (226), 1308 (202), 1540 (237)
KOJIMA, H.: 456 (68)
KOJIMA, T.: 698 (108), 701 (108), 2776 (422), 970 (148)
KOKANTZIS, N.: 1201 (185), 823 (123), 1099 (164), 140 (22)
KOKKEVI, A.: 14 (4), 2431 (374), 2100 (320), 680 (106), 2097 (320), 2615 (400), 546 (81), 728 (112)
KOKKINIDIS, A.: 2499 (381), 806 (121)
KOKNEL, O.: 1567 (241)
KOKOSZKA, A.: 2236 (345)
KOLDOBSKY, N.: 1903 (289)
KOLVIN, I.: 2526 (386)
KOLYASKINA, G.: 1105 (166(KONDO, C.) 816: 122(KONDYLIS, K.)
1728: 261), 779 (118), 1398 (214)
KONIG, M.: 2111 (322)
KONO, T.: 1179 (182)
KONRAD, N.: 2145 (326)
KONTAXAKIS, V.: 1857 (283), 1096 (164), 2584 (396), 2582 (396), 1700 (255), 2350 (363), 2351 (363), 144 (22), 143 (22)
KONTEA, M.: 378 (58)
KONTOU-PHILI, K.: 1721 (260)
KONTSEVOY, V.: 2503 (382)
KOPITTKE, W.: 1916 (291)
KOPONEN, H.: 1048 (157), 71 (12)
KOPPEL, B.: 16 (4)
KOPPETZ, R.: 2673 (407)
KOPTAGEL-ILAL, G.: 1504 (231)
KORDOSI, M.: 330 (50)
KORENBLUM, M.: 2576 (395)
KORF, J.: 2167 (329)
KORKOU, P.: 2670 (406)
KORNER, A.: 3236 (494)
KORNER, E.: 1524 (235)
KORNHUBER, H.: 3143 (482)
KORNHUBER, J.: 432 (64), 3143 (482)
KORNHUBER, M.: 3143 (482)
KORTEN, A.: 745 (115)
KORVESI, M.: 975 (148)
KORYAGIN, A.: 2572 (394)
KOSEI, K.: 2134 (325), 2133 (325)
KOSHIKAWA, N.: 1179 (182)
KOSKI, M.: 2694 (409), 2960 (449)
KOSKINEN, T.: 1944 (294)
KOSMOYANNI, A.: 3167 (486), 3164 (486)
KOSOTITSA, G.: 688 (107)
KOSTER, A.: 2256 (347)
KOSTIC, V.: 417 (63)
KOSTNAPFEL, J.: 380 (58)
KOSTOV, K.: 578 (87)
KOSTOWSKI, W.: 2909 (444)
KOSTYUKOVA, E.: 2127 (324), 2126 (324)
KOTESOVEC, F.: 2717 (412)
KOTSIFAKI, S.: 330 (50)
KOTSOPOULOS, S.: 402 (61), 340 (52), 3144 (483), 509 (74)
KOTTARIDIS, S.: 1935 (293)

KOUKKOU, M.: 2336 (361), 1262 (196)
KOUKOPOULOS, A.: 1565 (241), 1569 (241), 710 (109)
KOULIS, S.: 335 (51), 334 (51)
KOULU, M.: 2914 (444)
KOUMARE, B.: 3114 (479), 231 (34)
KOUMOULA, A.: 1190 (184)
KOUNELI, E.: 2355 (363)
KOUNTI, K.: 393 (60)
KOURKOUBAS, A.: 1685 (253), 1362 (210)
KOUROS, J.: 947 (144), 948 (144), 945 (144), 946 (144), 1743 (263), 944 (144), 1203 (185), 949 (144), 195 (28), 1576 (242)
KOUROUNIS, G.: 1362 (210)
KOUTSOUKOS, E.: 2164 (328), 2163 (328), 224 (33)
KOVALEV, V.: 1409 (215), 2684 (408)
KOVESS, V.: 1826 (279), 303 (45)
KOYAMA, T.: 2970 (451)
KOYUNCUOGLU, H.: 19 (4)
KOZEL, N.: 548 (81)
KRAAN, H.: 279 (41)
KRAEMER, S.: 901 (136), 2747 (417)
KRAGH-SORENSEN, P.: 2028 (308), 908 (137)
KRAMARZ, P.: 1891 (288)
KRAMKIMEL, J.: 2242 (345)
KRAMP, P.: 2374 (366), 599 (91)
KRAMSHOJ LARSEN, G.: 2829 (432)
KRARUP, G.: 2028 (308), 908 (137)
KRASNIK, A.: 1486 (228)
KRASOV, V.: 1409 (215), 2684 (408)
KRAUS, A.: 1464 (224), 1992 (301)
KRAUSE, J.: 2176 (330), 1827 (279)
KRAUSE, L.: 532 (78)
KREBS, B.: 633 (98)
KRETSCHMAR, C.: 1496 (230)
KRIEG, C.: 3170 (487), 3003 (459)
KRINGLEN, E.: 3062 (470), 1967 (297)
KRIPKE, D.: 1220 (188)
KRISTOF, R.: 2243 (345)
KRISZIO, B.: 1026 (155)
KRSKA, J.: 1346 (208)
KRUESI, M.: 2441 (375)
KRULL, F.: 172 (26), 173 (26)
KRUPP, P.: 2624 (401)
KRUSZYNSKI, S.: 2558 (392), 463 (68)
KTIOUET, J.: 1705 (255), 2518 (383), 3115 (479), 1828 (279), 2833 (433)
KUBOUCHI, H.: 1831 (280)
KUDO, T.: 118 (19)
KUDO, Y.: 478 (70), 864 (129)
KUDRYAKOVA, T.: 2126 (324)
KUEHNE, G.: 2296 (353), 1427 (217), 3073 (472)
KUEMMEL, B.: 1028 (155), 2883 (441), 408 (62), 2480 (379), 238 (35), 239 (35)
KUEPFER, A.: 1844 (281)
KUEPPER, K.: 429 (64)
KUEPPERS, A.: 2994 (457)
KUFFERLE, B.: 1345 (208)
KUGLER, J.: 1805 (275)
KUHA, S.: 2287 (352)
KUHN, J.: 1659 (250)
KUHN, K.: 18 (4), 17 (4)
KUHS, H.: 665 (103)
KUKKONEN, P.: 1011 (154)
KUKLA, M.: 449 (66)
KUKUPULOS, A.: 736 (113)
KULCAR, Z.: 2691 (409)
KULHARA, P.: 2560 (392)
KULLGREN, G.: 2348 (363)
KUMAKURA, T.: 152 (23)
KUMAR, A.: 937 (143)

KUMAR, N.: 98 (16)
KUMAR, R.: 139 (22)
KUMBASAR, H.: 273 (40)
KUMMEL, B.: 409 (62)
KUNIMOTO, N.: 2925 (446)
KUNITZ, A.: 838 (125)
KUNOVAC, J.: 1256 (195)
KUNZ, S.: 1302 (202), 1524 (235)
KUOKKANEN, M.: 2016 (306)
KUPER, L.: 2703 (410)
KUPFER, D.: 2342 (362)
KURIHARA, M.: 955 (145)
KURLAND, L.: 285 (42)
KURPKA, M.: 2674 (407)
KURZ, M.: 3137 (481)
KUSCU, M.: 3224 (493)
KUSHNER, S.: 1105 (166)
KUTCHER, S.: 2576 (395)
KYRIAKIDOU, S.: 116 (19)
KYRIAZIS, D.: 88 (14), 1741 (263)
KYYKKAE, T.: 1732 (262)

L

LA BARBERA, D.: 2605 (398)
LA GRECA, P.: 2158 (327)
LA RAJA, M.: 1368 (210), 1360 (210)
LA TORRE, D.: 1718 (260)
LAAKMANN, G.: 1172 (181), 1171 (181), 1026 (155), 1300 (202)
LABAW, J.: 2712 (411), 176 (26)
LABAW, W.: 2712 (411), 176 (26)
LABRAGA, P.: 2166 (328)
LABRID, C.: 2730 (414)
LACHAL, C.: 2579 (395)
LACHENMEYER, J.: 2854 (436), 1630 (247), 685 (106)
LACOMBE-MESTAS, C.: 2946 (447), 1695 (254), 436 (65)
LADDIS, A.: 1488 (228)
LADDOMADA, A.: 1635 (248)
LADER, M.: 1860 (284)
LADEWIG, D.: 1325 (205)
LADIS, V.: 1241 (193)
LADISICH, W.: 2680 (408)
LADO, G.: 366 (56)
LAESSLE, R.: 3010 (461), 3002 (459)
LAGET, J.: 521 (77), 983 (150), 3013 (461)
LAGOS, D.: 2301 (354)
LAHLOU, D.: 1828 (279), 2833 (433)
LAHMEYER, H.: 1222 (188)
LAHTI, I.: 390 (59)
LAJOS, J.: 65 (12)
LALIVE, J.: 1638 (248)
LAMBERTY, C.: 2428 (374)
LAMBIDI, A.: 361 (55)
LAMMERTS, J.: 2873 (439)
LAMOTHE, P.: 512 (75)
LAMPING, D.: 782 (118)
LANA, F.: 2219 (338), 2468 (378), 1468 (225)
LANCEE, W.: 2931 (447)
LANCZIK, M.: 3071 (472)
LANDAU, P.: 1780 (270)
LANDONI, G.: 2071 (315), 2594 (397), 2158 (327)
LANERI, M.: 2268 (349)
LANG, B.: 2487 (380), 760 (116), 3038 (465), 1646 (249)
LANG, C.: 577 (87)
LANG, H.: 1990 (301)
LANG, R.: 307 (47)
LANGE, H.: 429 (64)
LANGER, G.: 1648 (250), 2111 (322), 483 (70)

LANGER, M.: 2886 (441)
LANGSTROEM, B.: 2386 (368)
LANOVIC, M.: 1658 (250)
LANPHEAR, J.: 3090 (475)
LANPHEAR, K.: 3088 (475)
LANZINI, L.: 1097 (164)
LAPIERRE, Y.: 3183 (488)
LAPLANTE, B.: 1191 (184)
LAPORTA, M.: 2436 (375)
LAPPALAINEN, J.: 2914 (444)
LARA, E.: 1670 (252)
LARA, M.: 2653 (405)
LARA-TAPIA, H.: 192 (28), 1133 (173)
LARANJEIRA, R.: 367 (56)
LARKIN, B.: 1796 (274)
LARRIEU, M.: 428 (64), 1402 (214)
LARRODE, C.: 370 (56)
LARSEN, F.: 1877 (287), 2248 (346)
LARSEN, G.: 924 (141)
LARSEN, J.: 3236 (494), 1676 (253)
LARSEN, N.: 908 (137), 2028 (308), 907 (137)
LARSEN, S.: 1024 (155)
LARSSON, M.: 2027 (308), 2295 (352)
LARUELLE, M.: 1656 (250)
LATHAM, C.: 861 (129)
LAUER, C.: 3003 (459), 3170 (487)
LAUER, G.: 767 (117)
LAUERSEN, H.: 2376 (366)
LAUNER, M.: 2957 (449)
LAURENZI, B.: 1523 (235), 614 (93)
LAURITSEN, B.: 1326 (205)
LAURITZEN, L.: 2507 (382)
LAURSEN, H.: 120 (19)
LAUTER, H.: 2439 (375)
LAUX, G.: 1347 (208), 1386 (212), 1679 (253), 240 (35)
LAVERDURE, B.: 308 (47)
LAVIK, N.: 2643 (404)
LAVOIE, R.: 2430 (374)
LAVOISY, J.: 1682 (253)
LAVORI, P.: 256 (37)
LAWS, D.: 354 (54)
LAXMANNA, G.: 2254 (347)
LAZARATOU, H.: 2282 (351)
LAZARESCU, M.: 1030 (156), 1545 (238), 157 (23)
LAZARO, M.: 2650 (404)
LAZAROV, F.: 1640 (249)
LAZARTIGUES, A.: 1880 (287), 1881 (287), 2424 (373), 1879 (287), 2918 (445)
LAZZARI, M.: 2237 (345)
LAZZARIN, E.: 1965 (296)
LAZZERINI, F.: 539 (79), 2115 (322), 1964 (296), 1417 (216), 374 (57), 802 (120)
LEAL HERRERO, F.: 1912 (290)
LE CORRE, J.: 1920 (291)
LE HUEDE, E.: 1936 (293)
LE MOAM, M.: 21 (4)
LE MOUEL, B.: 2026 (307)
LE ROUX, J.: 2577 (395)
LECOMPTE, D.: 177 (26)
LECRUBIER, Y.: 1871 (286), 3176 (487), 315 (48), 1850 (282)
LEDOUX, S.: 14 (4), 3011 (461), 686 (106)
LEE, A.: 2950 (448)
LEE, H.: 735 (113)
LEE, H.: 2793 (426)
LEE, M.: 2623 (401), 1923 (292)
LEE, P.: 348 (53)
LEE, YING-C.: 3186 (488)
LEE, YUE-Y.: 1923 (292)
LEE, C-K - K.: 970 (148)
LEE, P.: 1036 (156)

LEFEVRE, L.: 1196 (184)
LEGAULT DE MARE, F.: 270 (40)
LEGAUT, F.: 1621 (247)
LEGER, J.: 2554 (390)
LEGERON, P.: 396 (60), 2497 (381)
LEGROS, J.: 1648 (250), 1656 (250)
LEHFELD, H.: 888 (134)
LEHMAN, R.: 2637 (403)
LEHMANN, D.: 872 (132)
LEHMANN, E.: 1015 (154), 553 (239), 1995 (302)
LEHNERT, H.: 1868 (285)
LEHRL, S.: 3040 (466)
LEHTINEN, V.: 264 (39), 1821 (279)
LEHTO, H.: 1011 (154)
LEIBING, E.: 1202 (185)
LEIBOVICH, MIGUEL A.: 300 (44)
LEICHNER, P.: 2644 (404), 2430 (374), 617 (94), 3237 (494), 2695 (409)
LEIGH, J.: 2182 (332), 2338 (361)
LEIMKUEHLER, A.: 1667 (251), 1403 (214)
LEIXNERING, W.: 1572 (242), 2921 (445)
LEJEUNE, D.: 2852 (436)
LELORD, G.: 2183 (332), 2682 (408)
LEMERE, F.: 2101 (320)
LEMOINE, P.: 2899 (442), 1532 (236), 2657 (405), 3049 (467), 2630 (402), 2048 (310), 2671 (407)
LEMPERIERE, T.: 270 (40)
LENANE, M.: 2441 (375), 1778 (270)
LENDAIS, G.: 1091 (164)
LENNERTS, W.: 3004 (459)
LENOCI, F.: 2943 (447)
LENOX, R.: 307 (47)
LENSI, P.: 562 (85)
LENZ, G.: 2279 (351), 107 (17)
LENZ, T.: 2125 (324), 2150 (327)
LENZI, A.: 376 (57), 454 (67), 374 (57), 1611 (246)
LEO, E.: 3180 (488), 3181 (488)
LEON, C.: 2653 (405)
LEON, R.: 1285 (200), 3212 (491)
LEONARD, B.: 591 (90)
LEONARD, H.: 1778 (270)
LEONE, B.: 389 (59)
LEONE, C.: 825 (123), 389 (59)
LEONSEGUI, I.: 448 (66)
LEPINE, J.: 3232 (494), 1160 (179)
LEPPIG, M.: 2622 (401)
LERER, N.: 723 (111)
LESCH, H.: 2580 (395)
LESCH, K.: 1386 (212), 1653 (250), 1652 (250), 2659 (405), 2112 (322), 1679 (253)
LESCH, O.: 677 (105), 964 (147), 965 (147), 1896 (289), 1052 (158), 1324 (205), 1978 (299)
LESIEUR, P.: 1077 (162), 1672 (252)
LESSE, S.: 541 (80)
LESTINGI, L.: 1243 (193), 1242 (193), 2711 (411)
LESUR, A.: 2871 (439), 270 (40)
LESZEK, J.: 2904 (443), 1697 (255)
LEVIN, A.: 1446 (221), 1447 (221)
LEVIN, F.: 2969 (451)
LEVINE, R.: 2172 (329)
LEVINE, S.: 2915 (444)
LEVIS, A.: 1966 (296)
LEVY, K.: 1122 (170)
LEVY, R.: 895 (135)
LEWANDER, T.: 1348 (208), 2563 (392)
LEWINSOHN, P.: 2575 (395)
LEWIS, S.: 1968 (297)
LHUILLIER, J.: 2685 (408), 1411 (215), 1071 (161)
LIAKOPOULOS, L.: 1562 (240)

LIAKOPOULOU, M.: 975 (148)
LIAKOS, A.: 2825 (432), 1929 (292), 3102 (477), 70 (12), 88 (14), 688 (107)
LIAKOURAS, A.: 772 (117)
LIAPPA, G.: 85 (14), 1876 (286)
LIAPPAS, J.: 3120 (479), 2097 (320), 2991 (457), 2775 (422)
LIBB, W.: 664 (102)
LIBERAKIS, E.: 1244 (193)
LIBERMAN, R.: 2802 (427), 2232 (344)
LICHTENBERG, P.: 723 (111)
LICHTERMANN, D.: 133 (21)
LIDBERG, L.: 598 (91)
LIDDIARD, D.: 2182 (332), 2338 (361)
LIEBOWITZ, M.: 1385 (212), 90 (15), 1852 (282)
LIEH MAK, F.: 348 (53), 1310 (203)
LIESER, A.: 1645 (249)
LIGGIO, F.: 1108 (167)
LILJESTRAND, A.: 1012 (154)
LILJESTROM, M.: 1024 (155)
LIMA, B.: 48 (9)
LINARA, A.: 85 (14)
LIND, J.: 36 (7)
LINDAL, E.: 283 (41), 1834 (280), 1823 (279), 1824 (279)
LINDEN, M.: 890 (134), 1315 (204), 1549 (238), 1320 (204)
LINDENMAYER, J.: 850 (128)
LINDGREN, I.: 2470 (378)
LINDGREN, S.: 2614 (400)
LINDHOLM, T.: 1821 (279), 264 (39)
LINGE, E.: 2059 (313), 905 (136)
LINGIARDI, V.: 1392 (213)
LINGJAERDE, O.: 1127 (172)
LINKOWSKI, P.: 2220 (338), 2169 (329)
LINN, S.: 307 (47)
LINNOILA, M.: 207 (29), 931 (142)
LINZ, M.: 516 (76)
LINZMAYER, L.: 2464 (378), 1932 (293)
LIO, M.: 2738 (415)
LIPCSEY, A.: 2870 (438)
LISJO, P.: 555 (84), 2064 (314)
LITTON, J.: 836 (125)
LITVAK, J.: 1799 (274)
LIVADITIS, M.: 1665 (251)
LIVINGSTON, M.: 477 (70)
LJUNGSTROEM, A.: 535 (79)
LLANOS ZULOAGA, R.: 3119 (479), 1974 (298), 234 (34)
LLAQUET, L.: 1738 (262)
LLAVERO, F.: 3139A (481)
LLORCA, J.: 1517 (234)
LLUESMA, O.: 1976 (298)
LO, H.: 581 (88)
LO, T.: 3053 (468)
LOBO, A.: 3234 (494), 1795 274)
LOBRACE, S.: 128 (20), 50 (9)
LOEBEN SPRENGEL, S.: 2638 (403), 2495 (381)
LOENNQVIST, J.: 1134 (173), 1508 (232)
LOGA, S.: 2876 (440)
LOIMER, N.: 2464 (378), 1931 (293)
LOLAS, F.: 2632 (402), 3017 (462), 3020 (462)
LOLDRUP, D.: 2507 (382), 1024 (155)
LOLIS, C.: 3227 (493), 3228 (493)
LOMBARDI, M.: 3024 (463)
LOMBERTIE, E.: 2554 (390)
LONG, P.: 3111 (478)
LONGLEY, W.: 745 (115)
LONGO, B.: 1901 (289)
LOO, H.: 2564 (392), 2734 (414)
LOONEN, A.: 851 (128)
LOPES, F.: 1299 (201)
LOPES, J.: 3215 (492)

LOPEZ, A.: 1136 (173)
LOPEZ, J.: 2648 (404)
LOPEZ ZANON, A.: 3037 (465)
LOPEZ-IBOR, A.: 261 (38), 1468 (225), 1281 (199), 2468 (378), 3067 (471), 2219 (338)
LOPEZ-LOUCEL, A.: 1488 (228)
LOPKER, A.: 573 (86)
LOPRIENO, F.: 1169 (180)
LORANGER, A.: 11 (3)
LORENZO, M.: 3035 (465)
LORENZONI, E.: 2451 (376)
LORETTU, L.: 2940 (447), 2828 (432), 820 (123), 2304 (354), 2305 (354), 2938 (447), 2306 (354), 827 (123), 822 (123), 1690 (254), 994 (152)
LORIEDO, C.: 3197 (490), 1927 (292), 587 (89), 1090 (164), 2587 (396)
LOTUFO NETO, F.: 1626 (247), 414 (63), 395 (60)
LOUBEYRE, J.: 2579 (395)
LOUKAS, S.: 70 (12), 2164 (328), 2163 (328)
LOUKAS, Y.: 690 (107)
LOURENCO, M.: 1607 (245)
LOVETT, M.: 3132 (481)
LOVREK, A.: 1615 (246)
LOWE, M.: 476 (70), 793 (120)
LUAUTE, J.: 703 (108), 1271 (197)
LUBLIN, H.: 529 (78), 2930 (446), 531 (78)
LUCACCHINI, A.: 204 (29)
LUCAS, A.: 285 (42)
LUCCHIN, A.: 2250 (346), 2594 (397), 2158 (327)
LUCCHITTA, G.: 2489 (380)
LUCKETT, C.: 544 (81)
LUDWIG, S.: 575 (87)
LUECKE, M.: 244 (36)
LUEDTKE, W.: 1645 (249)
LUGARESI, E.: 112 (18)
LUIS DUARTE, P.: 2481 (380)
LUKAS MANGAS, S.: 1570 (241), 1912 (290)
LUND, G.: 1098 (164)
LUND, J.: 842 (126)
LUND, K.: 1326 (205)
LUND, R.: 2638 (403)
LUNDE, I.: 924 (141), 2303 (354), 2829 (432)
LUNDE, M.: 2507 (382)
LUNDIN, T.: 2745 (416)
LUNGERHAUSEN, E.: 762 (116), 2699 (410), 1664 (251), 966 (147), 382 (58), 185 (27), 1044 (157)
LUNN, S.: 725 (112)
LUSCOMBE, G.: 594 (90), 2954 (448)
LUTHCKE, H.: 2751 (417)
LYALL, A.: 1709 (256)
LYKETSOS, C.: 2381 (367), 284 (41)
LYKETSOS, G.: 2063 (314), 262 (39), 1774 (269), 2759 (419), 2987 (456)
LYKOURAS, E.: 1727 (261), 202 (29), 1474 (226), 378 (58), 377 (57)
LYMBEROPOULOU, A.: 2015 (306)
LYNGSTAD, G.: 1164 (179)
LYONS, F.: 3136 (481)
LYRINTZIS, S.: 692 (107), 2431 (374)

M

MACCHIAVELLO, C.: 2597 (397), 2308 (354)
MACDONELL, L.: 3039 (465)
MACGREGOR, R.: 2740 (415)
MACHER, J.: 2208 (336)

MACHUS, B.: 274 (40), 2873 (439)
MACIEL, A.: 1219 (187), 1578 (242), 347 (53)
MACKERT, A.: 347 (53), 1704 (255), 881 (133)
MACKO, M.: 2922 (446)
MACLAUGHLIN, R.: 2403 (370)
MACURA, R.: 3174 (487), 1683 (253), 167 (25)
MADAR, M.: 595 (90)
MADARIAGA, N.: 2703 (410)
MADAZLIOGLU, S.: 3023 (463), 2642 (403), 3052 (467)
MADEDDU, F.: 1392 (213)
MADEIRA, M.: 228 (33)
MADIANOS, M.: 2592 (397), 1286 (200), 1144 (174), 2762 (419), 60 (11), 3101 (477)
MADIANOU, D.: 1168 (180)
MADRIGAL, E.: 547 (81)
MAES, M.: 1396 (213)
MAES, M.: 1647 (250), 67 (12), 2113 (322), 1651 (250)
MAESTRO, M.: 2645 (404)
MAFFEI, C.: 3233 (494), 1392 (213)
MAGALLON, R.: 1170 (180)
MAGARI, S.: 576 (87)
MAGGIO, A.: 1032 (156)
MAGGIO, G.: 2250 (346), 2071 (315), 2237 (345), 2594 (397)
MAGGIONI, M.: 3000 (459)
MAGGIONI, S.: 2383 (367)
MAGNANI, A.: 1699 (255)
MAGNANI, M.: 2263 (348)
MAGNANI, N.: 766 (117)
MAGNI, G.: 1516 (234), 2060 (314), 1717 (260)
MAGNUSSON, H.: 1797 (274)
MAGUIRE, C.: 3136 (481)
MAHENDRU, R.: 168 (25), 148 (22)
MAHENDRU, S.: 168 (25), 148 (22)
MAHER HUSSAIN, M.: 925 (141)
MAHLANEN, A.: 2137 (325)
MAI, F.: 663 (102)
MAI, M.: 2959 (449)
MAIER, C.: 2246 (346), 2910 (444)
MAIER, W.: 133 (21), 134 (21), 1827 (279), 250 (37), 254 (37)
MAIJA-LIISA, V.: 1708 (256)
MAILLARD, F.: 2041 (310)
MAILLIS, A.: 728 (112), 2164 (328), 2160 (328), 224 (33), 2161 (328), 2163 (328), 2162 (328), 680 (106), 680 (106)
MAINA, G.: 1193 (184), 1351 (209)
MAINARDI, P.: 1017 (155), 1016 (155)
MAIO, A.: 2263 (348)
MAISCH, R.: 453 (67), 452 (67)
MAISONNEUVE, H.: 1020 (155)
MAITENYI, K.: 534 (79)
MAJ, M.: 1655 (250), 114 (19), 2618 (400), 1249 (194), 50 (9), 1543 (237), 106 (17), 2725 (413)
MAJUMDAR, S.: 861 (129)
MALAGARIS, E.: 1180 (182), 1750 (264)
MALAGARNE, D.: 2489 (380)
MALAMA, E.: 267 (39), 1721 (260)
MALDONADO, R.: 448 (66)
MALKA, R.: 2736 (414)
MALKAH, M.: 755 (116)
MALLE, B.: 1302 (202), 1524 (235)
MALLIARAS, D.: 1474 (226), 377 (57)
MALLIORI, M.: 2097 (320), 3099 (477), 1836 (280)
MALM, U.: 1430 (217)
MALMSTROEM, R.: 1012 (154)
MALT, U.: 2742 (416)

MALTESE, M.: 521 (77), 3013 (461)
MALTEZ, J.: 1370 (211), 769 (117)
MAMOU, A.: 2202 (335)
MANARA, F.: 2962 (449), 1178 (182), 3024 (463), 682 (106)
MANCHANDA, R.: 3183 (488)
MANCONI, F.: 375 (57)
MANDALAKI, T.: 728 (112)
MANDIC, B.: 1258 (195)
MANFREDI, R.: 2676 (407), 854 (128), 2677 (407)
MANGONI, A.: 2603 (398)
MANHEM, A.: 2027 (308), 2295 (352)
MANKU, M.: 3039 (465)
MANN, L.: 3008 (461)
MANN, S.: 3152 (484)
MANOLOPOULOS, S.: 1126 (171)
MANOS, N.: 789 (119), 3047 (467), 1352 (209), 1876 (286), 3100 (477), 278 (41), 85 (14)
MANOUSSAKIS, M.: 70 (12)
MANSO, C.: 3139 (481)
MANSOURI, I.: 2510 (382)
MANTANU, H.: 2539 (388)
MANTANUS, H.: 2184 (332), 1526 (235)
MANTHOULI, M.: 1662 (251), 2499 (381)
MANTONAKIS, J.: 2085 (318), 3226 (493), 1096 (164), 468 (69), 803 (121), 343 (52), 1727 (261), 88 (14), 1483 (227), 392 (60), 2856 (437), 951 (145)
MANUS,: 1350 (208)
MANUSIS, N.: 1176 (181)
MARANGELL, L.: 850 (128)
MARATHONITI, M.: 1907 (290)
MARATOS, M.: 2933 (447)
MARATOS, O.: 2764 (419)
MARATOS, T.: 2357 (364)
MARAZZITI, D.: 374 (57), 204 (29), 427 (64), 1611 (246), 374 (57), 204 (29), 427 (64), 1611 (246), 942 (143)
MARBOUTIN, P.: 396 (60)
MARC-VERGNES, J.: 833 (125)
MARCHAIS, P.: 2948 (447), 2423 (373)
MARCHAND, M.: 175 (26)
MARCHESI, G.: 576 (87), 68 (12)
MARCHETTI, G.: 1693 (254)
MARCHI, S.: 1169 (180)
MARCHIORO, M.: 1643 (249)
MARCHOT, D.: 2184 (332)
MARCO, L.: 3186A (488)
MARCOLIN, M.: 425 (64)
MARCOLIN, S.: 2646 (404)
MARCOS, B.: 1795 (274)
MARCOS, T.: 795 (120), 1356 (209)
MARCUSSON, J.: 530 (78)
MARDER, S.: 700 (108), 2799 (427), 2413 (372), 2802 (427), 2234 (344)
MARCOLIN, M.: 425 (64)
MARCOLIN, S.: 2646 (404)
MARCOS, B.: 1795 (274)
MARCOS, T.: 795 (120), 1356 (209)
MARCUSSON, J.: 530 (78)
MARDER, S.: 700 (108), 2799 (427), 2413 (372), 2802 (427), 2234 (344)
MAREMMANI, I.: 1747 (264), 206 (29), 1632 (248), 2461 (377), 1066 (160), 1643 (249), 3127 (480), 1749 (264), 2951 (448), 451 (66), 2467 (378), 783 (118), 942 (143)
MARGARI, F.: 2001 (303)
MARGRAF, J.: 845 (127)
MARI, C.: 2646 (404)
MARI, J.: 714 (110)
MARIANI, F.: 2489 (380)
MARIATEGUI, J.: 1972 (298)
MARIC, J.: 196 (28), 1256 (195)

MARIE-CARDINE, M.: 1393 (213)
MARIENHAGEN, J.: 1649 (250)
MARINI, S.: 2298 (353)
MARINKOVIC, D.: 1541 (237)
MARINOV, E.: 1675 (252)
MARINOVA, L.: 1958 (296)
MARINS GOULART, C.: 3161 (486)
MARIONS, O.: 697 (108)
MARITS, K.: 1012 (154)
MARK, V.: 295 (43)
MARKETOS, N.: 1525 (235)
MARKIANOS, M.: 2351 (363), 1303 (202), 202 (29), 1474 (226), 2582 (396), 1473 (226), 1306 (202), 1379 (212), 3125 (480)
MARKIDIS, M.: 2351 (363), 2992 (457), 2350 (363), 1096 (164), 2584 (396), 2582 (396), 1268 (197)
MARKIDIS, R.: 1268 (197), 2584 (396), 2582 (396)
MARKKU, S.: 1708 (256)
MARKOULAKI, S.: 2123 (323)
MARKOVIC, O.: 3033 (465)
MARKS, I.: 1355 (209), 566 (85), 2435 (374), 310 (47)
MARNEROS, A.: 730 (113), 2074 (316), 953 (145), 2079 (316), 1544 (238), 104 (17)
MARQUARDT, M.: 1539 (237)
MARQUES, A.: 2445 (376)
MARQUES PINTO, L.: 1670 (252)
MARQUEZ, C.: 2895 (441), 2260 (348)
MARSELLA, A.: 2613 (399)
MARSH, E.: 1887 (288)
MARSILII, A.: 3019 (462)
MARTELLUCCI, P.: 1632 (248)
MARTENYI, F.: 2243 (345), 489 (70)
MARTIGNETTI, U.: 810 (121), 3214 (492)
MARTIN, F.: 179 (26), 2483 (380)
MARTIN, J.: 1590 (244), 1211 (186)
MARTIN, L.: 3008 (461)
MARTIN, M.: 1571 (241), 1748 (264), 3136 (481), 2732 (414)
MARTIN, P.: 410 (62)
MARTIN DEL MORAL, M.: 3230 (494), 1003 (153)
MARTIN MUNOZ, J.: 1378 (211), 493 (71)
MARTIN ORTIZ, F.: 648 (99)
MARTINDALE, B.: 1950 (295)
MARTINEZ, E.: 1669 (252), 75 (13), 935 (142), 934 (142), 2155 (327)
MARTINEZ, G.: 282 (41)
MARTINEZ, S.: 954 (145)
MARTINEZ LOPEZ, A.: 1654 (250)
MARTINEZ RODRIGUEZ, J.: 1570 (241), 1912 (290)
MARTINI, C.: 204 (29)
MARTINI DI NENNA, P.: 1927 (292)
MARTINO, I.: 1032 (156)
MARTINOT, J.: 2871 (439), 1621 (247)
MARTINOWITZ, U.: 1933 (293)
MARTINS, I.: 1135 (173)
MARTIS, G.: 1635 (248)
MARTON, P.: 2576 (395)
MARTY, P.: 644 (99)
MAS, F.: 2172 (329)
MAS, J.: 696 (107)
MASAAKI, K.: 2420 (373)
MASAHARU, M.: 897 (135)
MASANORI, N.: 2134 (325), 2133 (325)
MASARAKI, G.: 2836 (433)
MASARAKI, M.: 570 (86), 2836 (433)
MASARAKI, S.: 2836 (433), 2383 (367), 570 (86)
MASCOLO, M.: 582 (88), 1419 (216)
MASHIKO, S.: 1041 (156)
MASINA, L.: 1596 (244), 2456 (377)

MASON, G.: 1539 (237)
MASSA, R.: 413 (63)
MASSERINI, C.: 2237 (345), 2594 (397), 2603 (398), 2604 (398)
MASSERMAN, C.: 2378 (367)
MASSERMAN, J.: 922 (140), 2310 (355), 498 (72), 540 (80)
MASSING, W.: 1960 (296), 2872 (439)
MASSOL, J.: 410 (62)
MASTRANGELO, F.: 2750 (417)
MASTROENI, A.: 2596 (397)
MASTROSIMONE, P.: 2832 (433)
MASUDA, T.: 1707 (255)
MASUI, M.: 1036 (156)
MATEO, I.: 1590 (244), 1211 (186), 493 (71)
MATEOS, R.: 2847 (435)
MATERAZZI, M.: 22 (4), 2309 (355), 1101 (165), 2519 (384), 659 (101)
MATERAZZO, M.: 582 (88), 1419 (216)
MATHE, A.: 117 (19), 720 (111)
MATHEW, R.: 209 (30)
MATHIESEN, L.: 725 (112)
MATHIEU, P.: 1926 (292)
MATHIS, P.: 885 (134)
MATIN, S.: 1717 (260)
MATSA, K.: 1833 (280)
MATSUDA, G.: 1707 (255)
MATSUDA, H.: 2392 (368)
MATSUSHIMA, E.: 2776 (422)
MATSUSHITA, M.: 2907 (443), 574 (87), 271 (40), 2844 (435), 2912 (444), 201 (29), 2390 (368), 2387 (368), 2738 (415)
MATSUURA, M.: 970 (148)
MATTAFIRRI, R.: 766 (117)
MATTHEWS, M.: 685 (106)
MATTHEWS, S.: 2803 (427), 2801 (427)
MATTIONI, T.: 1242 (193), 1243 (193), 2711 (411)
MATUDA, H.: 2683 (408)
MATZIOU, V.: 2670 (406)
MAURER, K.: 2778 (422)
MAURI, M.: 562 (85), 2128 (324)
MAURO, P.: 1717 (260)
MAVREAS, V.: 2233 (344), 979 (149), 84 (14), 1857 (283)
MAVRIDIS, A.: 70 (12)
MAX, P.: 3183 (488)
MAYES, C.: 2047 (310), 1010 (154)
MAYFIELD, D.: 1294 (201)
MAYOR, C.: 3151 (484)
MAZOYER, B.: 1621 (247), 2682 (408)
MAZZALI, M.: 2962 (449)
MAZZEO, R.: 2832 (433)
MC LURE, D.: 2047 (310)
MC NAIR, D.: 1159 (179)
McCARROL, J.: 2744 (416)
McCARTHY, A.: 488 (70), 2831 (433)
McCLELLAND, R.: 2835 (433)
McCLURE, J.: 3183 (488), 1010 (154)
McCRACKEN, J.: 607 (92), 2402 (370)
McCRIMMON, B.: 2458 (377)
McCURDY, L.: 2377 (367)
McCUSKER, E.: 745 (115)
MCEWEN, B.: 2727 (414)
MCFARLANE, A.: 782 (118)
MCGEE, J.: 843 (126)
MCGUIRE, M.: 2381 (367), 2191 (333), 2190 (333)
MCINTYRE, A.W.: 564 (85)
MCKENZIE, A.: 364 (55)
MCLAREN, S.: 1342 (208)
MCLEER, S.: 1408 (215)
MCLENDON, D.: 2146 (326)
MCPHERSON, K.: 717 (111)
MCRINK, A.: 2455 (377)

MCVICAR, M.: 2854 (436)
MCWILLIAM, C.: 1753 (265), 2509 (382)
ME, J.: 1170 (180)
MEBIUS, C.: 720 (111)
MECHELA, B.: 834 (125), 2906 (443)
MEDEIROS PAIVA E RUI COEL, F.: 1224 (188)
MEDER, J.: 2591 (397)
MEDNICK, S.: 1811 (277)
MEDVED, V.: 350 (53)
MEGIA LOPEZ, P.: 1570 (241), 1912 (290)
MEHTONEN, O-P: 2287 (352)
MEIDAHL, B.: 2930 (446)
MEIDINGER, A.: 2024 (307), 3096 (476)
MEILLER, C.: 3010 (461)
MEILLO, H.: 3210 (491)
MEISE, U.: 3137 (481)
MEJER NILSEN, B.: 3236 (494)
MEJLHEDE, A.: 2892 (441)
MEKNASSI, O.: 1705 (255)
MELDELS, J.: 2769 (420)
MELIS, G.: 1159 (179)
MELLERUP, E.: 800 (120), 200 (29), 526 (78)
MELLO, N.: 1812 (277)
MELLOR, C.: 3135 (481)
MELONI, A.: 1746 (264)
MELTZER, H.: 1942 (294), 1491 (229), 2623 (401), 2627 (401)
MEMPEL, W.: 63 (12)
MENA, A.: 1669 (252), 75 (13)
MENARD, F.: 3131 (480)
MENCACCI, C.: 1726 (261), 817 (122)
MENDELL, D.: 916 (139)
MENDELSON, J.: 1812 (277)
MENDES, G.: 1409 (215), 2684 (408)
MENDIS, N.: 2536 (388), 1536 (236)
MENDLEWICZ, J.: 2169 (329), 2220 (338), 832 (125), 2 (1), 2724 (413), 2346 (362)
MENDONCA LIMA, C.: 359 (54)
MENDOZA, A.: 1829 (279)
MENDOZA, M.: 3215 (492), 2981 (455), 2985 (455)
MENDOZZI, L.: 2603 (398)
MENOLASCINO, F.: 839 (126), 1988 (300)
MENTZOS, S.: 52 (10)
MERATI, O.: 2438 (375)
MERCIER, P.: 428 (64)
MERCONE, G.: 2832 (433)
MERINI, A.: 1596 (244), 2456 (377)
MERKEL, E.: 3203 (490)
MERLO, M.: 87 (14)
MERRIL, C.: 1888 (288), 853 (128), 107 (167)
MERRILL, R.: 852 (128)
MERTENS, C.: 1940 (294), 1862 (284)
MERZ, W.: 847 (127)
MESIC, H.: 1010 (154)
MESZAROS, K.: 2921 (445), 483 (70), 2561 (392)
METHONEN, O-P: 2137 (325)
METWALI, Y.: 2864 (438)
METZGER, E.: 679 (106)
MEYENDORF, R.: 2453 (376)
MEYER, C.: 2093 (319)
MEYER, J.: 1844 (281)
MEYER, L.: 1366 (210)
MEYER, M.: 1241 (193)
MEYER, P.: 959 (146)
MEYER, R.: 1158 (178)
MEYERS, R.: 2055 (312)
MEYERSON, B.: 1781 (270)
MEZZICH, J.: 1285 (200), 7 (2), 2227 (342)
MICH, L.: 1999 (303)
MICHALAKEAS, A.: 352 (53), 2281 (351)

MICHALAKI, CH.: 2281 (351)
MICHEEVA, T.: 1105 (166).
MICHEL, G.: 2150 (327), 2157 (327), 2125 (324)
MICHELINI, S.: 204 (29)
MICHELOYANNIS, J.: 1525 (235)
MICHITSUJI, S.: 586 (89), 735 (113)
MICHOV, V.: 2239 (345)
MICO, J.: 1021 (155), 448 (66)
MIGNANI, V.: 2501 (382)
MIGNANI, W.: 427 (64)
MIGNECO, O.: 835 (125)
MIGONI, M.: 2075 (316)
MIGUCHI, M.: 78 (13)
MIHALJENIC PELES, A.: 424 (64)
MIHOV, V.: 2934 (447)
MIKI, K.: 201 (29)
MILAVANOVIC, D.: 1254 (195)
MILCH, W.: 1043 (157), 2053 (311)
MILEA, S.: 1671 (252)
MILECH, U.: 1841 (281)
MILENKOV, K.: 125 (20)
MILEV, V.: 1583 (243)
MILICI, N.: 114 (19)
MILITERNI, R.: 193 (28)
MILLER, C.: 3182 (488)
MILLER, G.: 2091 (318), 2382 (367), 3086 (475)
MILLER, J.: 3039 (465)
MILLER, L.: 3089 (475)
MILLET, Y.: 1046 (157), 2896 (442)
MILONA, D.: 2933 (447)
MIN, B.: 1259 (195)
MIN, S.: 735 (113)
MINAS, I.: 3217 (492)
MINDUS, P.: 1781 (270)
MINENNA, G.: 2517 (383)
MINERVINI, M.: 1175 (181)
MING-JEN, Y.: 3118 (479)
MINGER, J.: 133 (21)
MINIATI, M.: 2715 (412), 442 (65)
MINNAI, G.: 1569 (241), 710 (109)
MINTON, N.: 1225 (189)
MINUIT, M.: 2671 (407)
MIQUEL-GARCIA, E.: 231 (34)
MIRAGLIA, S.: 2489 (380)
MIRANDA, C.: 2646 (404), 714 (110)
MIRARCHI, R.: 2688 (409)
MIRZOYAN, M.: 2127 (324)
MISHRA, R.: 139 (22)
MISU, Y.: 2912 (444)
MITA, T.: 1582 (243), 2810 (430)
MITCHELL, J.: 2011 (305)
MITCHELL, L.: 1888 (288)
MITCHELL, P.: 2893 (441), 2114 (322)
MITEV, G.: 3044 (466), 1735 (262), 2905 (443), 1208 (186)
MITROSSILIS, S.: 2018 (306)
MITTELHAMMER, J.: 2419 (373)
MITTERAUER, B.: 738 (114)
MIURA, S.: 456 (68), 863 (129)
MIYAMOTO, K.: 471 (69)
MIYAMOTO, M.: 471 (69)
MIYAMOTO, N.: 698 (108), 701 (108)
MIYASAKA, M.: 2392 (369)
MIYAUCHI, T.: 574 (87), 2844 (435)
MIYAWAKI, H.: 897 (135)
MOCAER, E.: 2729 (414), 2730 (414)
MOCHIZUKI, Y.: 456 (68)
MODIGH, K.: 2064 (314), 555 (84)
MOELLER, H-J.: 738 (114), 2747 (417), 1349 (208), 2673 (407), 1383 (212), 901 (136), 2039 (309)
MOESLER, T.: 2090 (318), 382 (58), 966 (147), 762 (116)
MOESSNER, J.: 1653 (250)
MOGARD, J.: 1781 (270)

MOGENSEN, J.: 2376 (366)
MOHARRERI, M.: 338 (52)
MOHSEN, Y.: 156 (23)
MOHY UD DIN, Z.: 446 (66)
MOIRAS, G.: 262 (39)
MOLLARD, E.: 1355 (209)
MOLLER, S.: 1865 (285)
MOLNAR, G.: 641 (98)
MOLVAER, J.: 2812 (430)
MOLZAHN, M.: 763 (116)
MOMBOUR, W.: 1283 (200)
MONAS, K.: 278 (41)
MONASTIRIOTIS, N.: 392 (60)
MONDINO, M.: 1965 (296)
MONFORT, J.: 1350 (208)
MONOPOLIS, S.: 984 (150), 2103 (320), 219 (32)
MONORCHIO, A.: 419 (63), 1760 (266)
MONREAL, A.: 2308 (354)
MONTECALVO, G.: 3197 (490)
MONTEIRO ALVES, N.: 3161 (486)
MONTEJO, G.: 1517 (234)
MONTEJO, L.: 1637 (248), 2887 (441), 2955 (448)
MONTELEONE, P.: 2508 (382), 1655 (250), 114 (19), 1543 (237)
MONTENEGRO, R.: 2690 (409), 655 (101)
MONTERO, G.: 2854 (436)
MONTERREY, A.L: 1924 (292)
MONTGOMERY, D.: 1858 (284)
MONTGOMERY, S.: 2606 (398), 1858 (284), 1858 (284), 1280 (199)
MONTGRAIN, N.: 298 (44)
MONTI, D.: 2675 (407), 2678 (407)
MONTI, J.: 2166 (328), 2675 (407), 2678 (407), 551 (82)
MONTI, M.: 291 (42)
MONTREUIL, M.: 1535 (236)
MONTRONI, M.: 68 (12)
MOODLEY, S.: 974 (148)
MOOLER MADSEN, S.: 3236 (494)
MOON, C.: 2108 (321), 354 (54)
MOORE, K.: 1777 (270)
MORA, P.: 2375 (366)
MORAKINYO, O.: 230 (34)
MORALES, F.: 1795 (274)
MORALES, H.: 1879 (287), 1881 (287), 2424 (373), 1880 (287)
MORALES, I.: 179 (26), 2483 (380)
MORALES, R.: 2918 (445)
MORAROU, E.: 1660 (251), 3167 (486), 2704 (410)
MORENO, I.: 1633 (248), 1623 (247), 1692 (254)
MORENO, J.: 1468 (225), 426 (64)
MORENO, T.: 2219 (338)
MORENO DIAZ, M.: 2258 (348)
MORENO DIAZ, R.: 2258 (348)
MORETTI, C.: 1699 (255)
MORETTI, P.: 1209 (186)
MORI, A.: 2868 (438), 2044 (310), 2474 (379), 863 (129)
MORI, H.: 698 (108), 701 (108)
MORI, K.: 3042 (466)
MORIN, D.: 1077 (162), 145 (22), 444 (66)
MORING, J.: 1011 (154)
MORINIGO, A.: 1378 (211), 493 (71), 1590 (244), 1211 (186)
MORIUCHI, K.: 2911 (444)
MORO, A.: 2298 (353)
MORON, P.: 833 (125)
MORONI, A.: 2599 (397)
MOROS, N.: 3219 (492), 2498 (381)
MOROSINI, P.: 1822 (279), 3192 (489)
MOROYANNIS, K.: 501 (73)
MOROZ, G.: 1780 (270)

MOROZOV, P.: 1287 (200)
MORRISON, D.: 1348 (208), 790 (119)
MORRISON, E.: 2455 (377)
MORRONE, G.: 2268 (349)
MORSELLI, R.: 2603 (398)
MORTOGLOU, K.: 680 (106)
MORTZOS, G.: 217 (31)
MOSER, A.: 3021 (462)
MOSES, R.: 1456 (222)
MOSHONAS, D.: 161 (24)
MOSKOV, R.: 2905 (443)
MOTTA, A.: 2603 (398)
MOTTA, M.: 1296 (201)
MOTTI-STEFANIDI, F.: 987 (150), 988 (150)
MOTTO, J.: 2034 (309)
MOTTOLA, G.: 582 (88), 1419 (216)
MOTTOLA, P.: 1718 (260)
MOTTOLA DI AMATO, B.: 496 (71), 2688 (409)
MOURADIAN, L.: 2129 (324)
MOURET, J.: 3049 (467), 2630 (402), 2899 (442), 2671 (407), 1532 (236), 2657 (405), 2042 (310)
MOURTZINIS, A.: 2977 (453)
MOUSSAOUI, D.: 2202 (335), 2636 (403), 2462 (377), 2202 (335), 1502 (231), 1311 (203)
MOUSSONG-KOVACS, E.: 1115 (168)
MOUSTAKATOU-LIOSSI, A.: 993 (152)
MOUTAFOV, S.: 1063 (159), 2942 (447)
MOUTSOPOULOS, E.: 505 (74)
MOUTSOPOULOS, H.: 1929 (292), 70 (12)
MOUTZOUKIS, C.: 756 (116)
MOUYAS, A.: 1762 (266), 603 (91), 826 (123)
MOVIN, G.: 1657 (250)
MOXON, L.: 2889 (441)
MOYTY, M.: 2554 (390)
MOZZON, L.: 2489 (380)
MUCCI, A.: 1249 (194), 838 (125), 875 (132)
MUEHLBAUER, B.: 3184 (488), 1946 (294)
MUELLEJANS, R.: 715 (110)
MUELLER, C.: 69 (12), 837 (125)
MUELLER, H.: 64 (12)
MUELLER, N.: 63 (12), 1104 (166)
MUELLER, P.: 890 (134), 82 (14), 1549 (238)
MUELLER, U.: 1652 (250), 1403 (214), 1035 (156)
MUELLER, W.: 2629 (402), 252 (37)
MUELLER, WALTER: 225 (33)
MUELLER OERLINGHAUSEN, B.: 798 (120), 881 (133), 1612 (246)
MUELLER-SPAHN, F.: 890 (134), 538 (79), 2559 (392), 1549 (238)
MUGELE, B.: 2372 (366)
MUKHERJI, C.: 1904 (290)
MUKOUSE, Y.: 1582 (243)
MULAS, S.: 2075 (316)
MULDER, S.: 2542 (388)
MULLANEY, D.: 1220 (188)
MULLEN, P.: 2307 (354), 2894 (441)
MULLER, F.: 213 (31)
MUNITZ, H.: 3151 (484), 849 (128), 3153 (484)
MUNJIZA, M.: 1691 (254), 2935 (447)
MURA, F.: 1055 (158)
MURAKAMI, K.: 2777 (422)
MURGUI, E.: 1880 (287), 1879 (287), 2918 (445), 2424 (373), 1881 (287)
MURPHY, D.: 34 (7)
MURPHY, G.: 1223 (188), 1478 (227)

MURRAY, R.: 2950 (448), 619 (95), 1968 (297)
MURTHY, R.: 773 (117)
MUSALEK, M.: 964 (147), 965 (147), 677 (105)
MUSAZZI, A.: 1884 (287), 2425 (373)
MUSCARA, M.: 3158 (486), 2702 (410)
MUSCH, B.: 2674 (407), 2300 (353), 1008 (154), 2041 (310)
MUSETTI, L.: 733 (113), 962 (146), 2314 (356), 2501 (382)
MUSTAKATOU-LIOSSI, A.: 2088 (318)
MUTTI, A.: 1617 (246)
MUTTINI, C.: 1193 (184)
MYHILL, J.: 219 (32)

N

NAARALA, M.: 2287 (352)
NABER, D.: 724 (112), 2622 (401)
NABOULSI, M.: 1115 (168)
NACHEV, C.: 2335 (360)
NADELSON, C.: 755 (116)
NAGAHATA, M.: 605 (92)
NAGAMINE, I.: 3042 (466)
NAGANO, K.: 3036 (465)
NAGASWAMI, V.: 2212 (337), 1444 (220), 2210 (337)
NAGATA, H.: 2392 (368)
NAGATA, I.: 1179 (182)
NAGY, E.: 2870 (438)
NAGY, S.: 1673 (252)
NAIDES, E.: 3029 (464)
NAIK, U.: 360 (55)
NAIR, N.: 3183 (488)
NAISBERG, Y.: 2515 (383), 3231 (494)
NAITANA, M.: 2938 (447), 2306 (354)
NAKAGAWA, T.: 1047 (157)
NAKAMURA, A.: 1703 (255)
NAKAMURA, Y.: 3048 (467), 119 (19)
NAKANE, Y.: 586 (89), 735 (113), 605 (92)
NAKANISHI, M.: 457 (68)
NAKATANI, Y.: 821 (123)
NAKAYAMA, M.: 2970 (451)
NANCY, K.: 1812 (277)
NANDI, D.: 2511 (383)
NANKO, S.: 1094 (164), 2434 (374)
NARANG, R.: 1754 (265), 1588 (244)
NARDI, B.: 576 (87)
NARDINI, M.: 2263 (348), 766 (117), 1613 (246)
NARDINI, R.: 451 (66)
NARUSE, H.: 605 (92)
NASCA, G.: 1937 (293)
NATALICCHI, L.: 1209 (186)
NATSUMI, N.: 2095 (319)
NAUKKARINEN, H.: 2137 (325)
NAUNTOFTE, B.: 592 (90)
NAVA, V.: 1548 (238), 1093 (164)
NAVARRE, C.: 1167 (180)
NAVARRO, C.: 1586 (243)
NAVARRO, J.: 414 (63)
NAVILLE, P.: 1226 (189)
NAYLOR, R.: 1492 (229), 856 (129)
NEALON, P.: 695 (107)
NEGELE-ANETSBERGER, J.: 1649 (250), 577 (87)
NEILL, D.: 1847 (281)
NEIMAREVIC, D.: 672 (104)
NELLES, J.: 447 (66), 2463 (378), 1295 (201)
NEMEROFF, C.: 379 (58)
NEMETH, A.: 431 (64), 416 (63)
NERI, C.: 2517 (383)
NEROZZI, D.: 1699 (255)

NERVO, D.: 482 (70), 2466 (378)
NEUHAUSER, H.: 1300 (202)
NEUHAUSER, B.: 2778 (422)
NEUMAN, E.: 2597 (397), 2308 (354)
NEUMANN, J.: 3068 (471), 1323 (205)
NEUMANN, N.: 2293 (352), 777 (118), 2993 (457), 1547 (238)
NEUMEIER, R.: 1918 (291)
NEVALAINEN, J.: 2330 (359)
NEWBURN, G.: 2894 (441)
NEWMAN, C.: 1539 (237)
NEYLAN, T.: 930 (142)
NEZIROGLU, F.: 1076 (162), 1627 (247), 1422 (216), 3200 (490), 38 (7)
NICKEL, B.: 1323 (205)
NICOARA, O.: 1606 (245)
NICOLAIDES, N.: 507 (74), 1564 (240), 2988 (457), 1274 (198), 2050 (311), 2358 (364)
NICOLAIDOU, M.: 3096 (476)
NICOLAU, M.: 2421 (373)
NICOLETTI, F.: 473 (70)
NICOLOV, C.: 398 (61), 1208 (186)
NIEBER, D.: 2144 (326), 2170 (329)
NIEDERLAENDER, A.: 2867 (438)
NIEDERMEIER, T.: 2285 (351)
NIEMEGEERS, C.: 1994 (302), 1493 (229)
NIEMEYER, J.: 1461 (223), 2395 (369)
NIEMINEN, K.: 2964 (450), 3157 (485)
NIETHAMMER, R.: 2130 (325)
NIETO, E.: 2585 (396)
NIEVES, P.: 601 (91), 1744 (264)
NIGRO, A.: 1088 (163)
NIIGAWA, H.: 2846 (435), 2845 (435)
NIKELLY, A.: 1390 (213), 1060 (159)
NIKIC, S.: 917 (139)
NIKOLAKOPOULOU-LIONI, F.: 772 (117)
NIKOLARAKIS, C.: 115 (19)
NIKOLOV, V.: 1856 (283)
NILAKANTAN, B.: 1024 (155)
NILSSON, H.: 355 (54), 356 (54)
NIMATOUDIS, J.: 140 (22), 1099 (164)
NIMOUTADIS, J.: 823 (123)
NIOLU, C.: 1531 (236), 2030 (308)
NIRK, G.: 362 (55)
NISHIKAWA, Y.: 2868 (438)
NISHIMURA, T.: 2846 (435), 119 (19), 118 (19), 2845 (435)
NISHIZONO, M.: 2318 (357), 1313 (203)
NISIDA, A.: 423 (64)
NISITA, C.: 1159 (179), 962 (146)
NISSEN, G.: 1460 (223), 910 (138), 911 (138), 1458 (223), 1461 (223)
NIV, M.: 1359 (209)
NIVOLI, G.: 1055 (158), 822 (123), 2940 (447), 2828 (432), 1690 (254), 2304 (354), 2305 (354), 2306 (354), 994 (152), 820 (123), 2938 (447), 827 (123)
NOBLE, E.: 3032 (465)
NOBRE MADEIRA, J.: 997 (152), 759 (116)
NODER, M.: 1653 (250)
NOGAY, A.: 3224 (493)
NOH, S.: 1934 (293)
NOLEN, W.: 1678 (253)
NOLET, M.: 2456 (377)
NONMAN, T.: 1777 (270)
NOORI, S.: 1377 (211)
NORDENTOFT, M.: 1486 (228), 950 (145), 3225 (493), 187 (27)
NORDIN, C.: 2885 (441)
NORDSTROEM, A-L: 2739 (415)
NORMAN, G.: 782 (118)
NOTMAN, M.: 755 (116)
NOUGUIER, J.: 636 (98)
NOUGUIER-SOULE, J.: 636 (98)

NOVAL, D.: 1590 (244), 1211 (186), 493 (71)
NOVARA, F.: 1193 (184)
NOVARINI, R.: 2703 (410)
NOVIKOV, J.: 276 (40)
NOYES, R.: 3121 (480)
NOZAKI, M.: 423 (64)
NURMIKKO, T.: 265 (39)
NURY, A.: 1355 (209)
NUTZINGER, D.: 1540 (237), 2647 (404), 3174 (487)
NUZZOLO, L.: 1088 (163)
NYGAARD, H.: 1944 (294)
NYMAN, H.: 1781 (270)
NYTH, A.: 1944 (294)

O

O'CONNOR, M.: 3004 (459)
O'BRIEN, B.: 568 (86)
O'CONNELL, R.: 2340 (361)
O'FALLON, W.: 285 (42)
O'FLYNN, R.: 3040 (466)
O'HANLON, J.: 652 (100), 2105 (321), 2104 (321), 651 (100)
O'SULLIVAN, B.: 2893 (441)
O'SULLIVAN, D.: 3159 (486), 2698 (410)
OANCEA, C.: 1410 (215)
OBIOLS, J.: 2585 (396)
OCHOA, E.: 2648 (404), 2710 (411), 261 (38)
ODIER, B.: 439 (65), 2080 (317), 24 (5)
OEHRBERG, S.: 1024 (155)
OEI, T.: 3123 (480)
OEPEN, G.: 572 (86), 2393 (368), 351 (53), 1819 (278), 2393 (368)
OESTMAN, O.: 189 (27), 2937 (447)
OEZASKINI, S.: 702 (108)
OEZDAGLAR, A.: 572 (86)
OEZKAN, S.: 1900 (289), 3224 (493), 2689 (409)
OFUJI, M.: 423 (64)
OGAWA, K.: 816 (122)
OGENSTAD, S.: 1348 (208)
OGUCHI, E.: 2926 (446)
OGUCHI, T.: 456 (68)
OGURA, C.: 2925 (446)
OH-E, Y.: 1707 (255)
OHAYON, M.: 1046 (157), 1610 (245), 2884 (441), 2896 (442), 2875 (439), 1609 (245), 403 (61)
OHIGASHI, Y.: 2072 (315)
OHNISHI, K.: 1707 (255), 2926 (446)
OHNO, S.: 2387 (368)
OHTA, I.: 2925 (446)
OHTA, K.: 2776 (422)
OHTA, Y.: 586 (89), 735 (113)
OHTANI, Y.: 456 (68)
OIKONOMOU, K.: 2499 (381)
OKABE, S.: 1047 (157)
OKASHA, A.: 2317 (357), 1791 (272)
OKUBO, Y.: 970 (148), 701 (108), 698 (108)
OKUMURA, T.: 400 (61), 2920 (445)
OKUMURA, W.: 2920 (445)
OKURA, M.: 3042 (466)
OLAFSSON, K.: 800 (120)
OLAVI, L.: 1708 (256)
OLCAY, E.: 3023 (463)
OLDENDORF, W.: 700 (108)
OLIVARES, J.: 795 (120), 1356 (209)
OLIVEIRA, V.: 757 (116)
OLIVER, F.: 1953 (295), 1406 (214)
OLIVERA, S.: 2166 (328)
OLIVIER, H.: 1449 (221)
OLLE, J.: 2471 (378)

OLLINEN, M.: 1011 (154)
OLLO, C.: 1376 (211)
OLPE, H.: 2479 (379)
OMEROV, M.: 1154 (176)
ONTIVEROS, M.: 426 (64)
OOSTERBAAN, H.: 2023 (307)
OPITZ, W.: 407 (62)
OPJORDSMOEN, S.: 2229 (343)
OPPOLZER, A.: 69 (12), 2680 (408), 2921 (445)
OPRESCU, I.: 1594 (244)
ORAL, E.: 536 (79), 2252 (347), 1372 (211)
ORAZZO, C.: 114 (19)
ORDOOBADI, A.: 3027 (464)
ORELLANA, C.: 2166 (328)
ORLEBEKE, J.: 2867 (438)
ORLER, J.: 1071 (161), 2685 (408), 1411 (215)
ORLEY, J.: 361 (55)
ORSOLINI, G.: 3127 (480), 2467 (378), 1066 (160)
ORTEGA, H.: 1132 (172), 2652 (405), 2653 (405)
ORTEGA, M.: 1963 (296)
ORTEGA, M.: 370 (56)
ORTIZ, J.: 2155 (327)
ORTMANN, J.: 3194 (489), 2303 (354)
OSAMA, U.: 3117 (479)
OSORIO, C.: 1882 (287)
OSTERHEIDER, M.: 2112 (322), 1841 (281), 1072 (161), 1998 (302)
OSTMAN, O.: 631 (97)
OSWALD, I.: 550 (82)
OTERO, A.: 958 (146), 1356 (209)
OTERO, F.: 2866 (438), 1305 (202), 1086 (163)
OTT, C.: 2372 (366), 466 (68)
OTT, G.: 2372 (366), 2452 (376)
OUAKININ, S.: 1599 (245), 2706 (411)
OULIE, D.: 2116 (322)
OULIS, P.: 2094 (319)
OUTAKOSKI, J.: 2137 (325)
OVARY, I.: 275 (40)
OVERALL, J.: 3180 (488)
OWEN, F.: 3132 (481)
OWENS, D.: 1328 (206), 1816 (278)
OYEBODE, F.: 2070 (315)
OZASKINLI, S.: 461 (68)
OZER,: 1922 (292)
OZKAN, S.: 775 (118)
OZMEN,: 1845 (281)
OZUGURLU, K.: 775 (118)

P

PAAR, C.: 818 (122)
PACHECO HERNANDEZ, A.: 31 (6)
PACHI, E.: 3223 (493), 956 (145), 3222 (493)
PACI, M.: 1574 (242)
PACIARONI, G.: 576 (87)
PACIFICI, G.: 1169 (180)
PACILEO, A.: 1090 (164), 587 (89)
PAES, M.: 1705 (255), 3115 (479), 2833 (433), 2518 (383), 1828 (279)
PAES DE SOUSA, M.: 2107 (321), 2421 (373), 1530 (236), 2363 (365)
PAGEN, M.: 2247 (346)
PAGOT, R.: 2953 (448)
PAIK, M.: 77 (13)
PAIVA, T.: 2634 (402)
PAKASLAHTI, A.: 1593 (244)
PAKER, M.: 2302 (354)
PAKER, O.: 2302 (354)

PAKESCH, G.: 1931 (293), 1932 (293), 1554 (239)
PALAOGLU, O.: 2165 (328)
PALAZIDOU, E.: 637 (98)
PALHA, P.: 1607 (245)
PALIA, S.: 462 (68), 1955 (295)
PALLANTI, S.: 1746 (264)
PALMSTIERNA, T.: 1153 (176)
PALODHI, R.: 792 (119)
PANAGOUTSOS, P.: 2020 (307)
PANAYOTOPOULOU, I.: 2018 (306)
PANCHALINGAM, K.: 2331 (359)
PANDEY, J.: 932 (142)
PANDOLFI, C.: 1016 (155)
PANERAI, A.: 831 (124)
PANETTA, B.: 2604 (398)
PANICO, G.: 3127 (480), 2461 (377)
PANITS, D.: 1241 (193)
PAPADAKI, A.: 2500 (381)
PAPADAKIS, S.: 2775 (422), 2174 (329)
PAPADAKIS, TH.: 3164 (486), 806 (121), 2704 (410)
PAPADATOS, Y.: 2812 (430), 1412 (215), 985 (150), 385 (59), 690 (107), 1038 (156)
PAPADIMITRIOU, G.: 2218 (338), 2220 (338), 1473 (226), 1306 (202), 378 (58), 883 (133)
PAPADOPOULOS, A.: 637 (98), 85 (14)
PAPADOPOULOU, S.: 3163 (486)
PAPADOPOULOU, V.: 2499 (381)
PAPADOPOULOU-DAIFOTIS,: 2159 (328)
PAPAGEORGIOU, A.: 1144 (174)
PAPAGEORGIOU, CH.: 2173 (329), 3162 (486), 2775 (422)
PAPAGEORGIOU, G.: 1038 (156)
PAPAGEORGIOU, M.: 739 (114)
PAPAGEORGIOU, P.: 1661 (251), 2701 (410)
PAPAGNI, S.: 1175 (181)
PAPAIOANNOU, D.: 784 (119), 1721 (260)
PAPAIOANNOU, K.: 1201 (185)
PAPAKOSTAS, Y.: 2825 (432), 1473 (226), 1306 (202), 721 (111)
PAPAKOSTOPOULOS, D.: 2186 (332), 2337 (361)
PAPAMICHAEL, E.: 993 (152), 2088 (318)
PAPANIKOLAOU, G.: 1909 (290), 1436 (219)
PAPART, P.: 2184 (332), 2428 (374), 2539 (388), 1526 (235)
PAPASTAMATIS, C.: 3227 (493), 3228 (493)
PAPATHEOPHILOU, R.: 363 (55), 1399 (214)
PAPAVASILIOU, I.: 1928 (292)
PAPOUTSELI, N.: 3165 (486)
PAPPATA, S.: 1621 (247)
PAQUID STUDY GROUP,: 1798 (274)
PARADA-ALLENDE, R.: 613 (93), 1991 (301)
PARAISO, V.: 2444 (376)
PARIKH RAJESH, M.: 1820 (278)
PARISH, H.: 2924 (446)
PARITSIS, N.: 1525 (235), 162 (24)
PARIZOT, S.: 811 (121)
PARKER, D.: 2151 (327)
PARKER, G.: 280 (41), 729 (113), 2322 (358)
PARMENTIER, G.: 2365 (365)
PARNAS, J.: 260 (38), 131 (21), 725 (112)
PARQUET, J.: 2136 (325), 1167 (180)
PARQUET, PH.: 2361 (365), 1542 (237), 2135 (325), 122 (20)
PARRINO, L.: 2672 (407), 653 (100)

PARZER, P.: 1648 (250), 1540 (237), 167 (25), 1308 (202)
PASCALIS, J.: 135 (21)
PASCHALIS, CH.: 1484 (227)
PASCUAL MILLAN, L.: 1795 (274)
PASINI, A.: 1699 (255), 2848 (435), 765 (117)
PASSA, M.: 3219 (492)
PASSWEG, V.: 964 (147)
PASTENA, L.: 3158 (486), 2702 (410)
PATAKAS, D.: 3047 (467)
PATI, T.: 2284 (351)
PATKAR, A.: 972 (148)
PATRICK, L.: 2253 (347)
PATRIS, M.: 1561 (240), 1557 (239)
PATRONE, A.: 1017 (155), 1016 (155)
PAULA-BARBOSA, M.: 228 (33)
PAULI, S.: 2389 (368)
PAULIN, M.: 1402 (214)
PAULIN, Z.: 3202 (490)
PAULON, S.: 2489 (380)
PAULUS, E.: 876 (132)
PAUNOVIC, V.: 1616 (246), 1541 (237)
PAUSE, B.: 828 (124)
PAVAN, L.: 1045 (157), 1139 (173)
PAVIA, C.: 329 (50)
PAWLIK, E.: 1648 (250), 69 (12), 2647 (404)
PAWLIK, P.: 167 (25)
PAYANT, C.: 2024 (307), 3096 (476), 2026 (307)
PAYKEL, E.: 2528 (386)
PAYS, M.: 2029 (308)
PAZ FERREIRA, C.: 681 (106)
PAZZAGLIA, P.: 2237 (345), 2158 (327)
PEACOCK, L.: 2625 (401), 529 (78), 531 (78)
PEARLSON, J.: 2391 (368)
PEARSON, J.: 2846 (435), 2845 (435)
PEDDITZI, M.: 1681 (253), 1520 (234)
PEDERSEN, C.: 725 (112)
PEDERSEN, H.: 2834 (433)
PEDERSEN, V.: 1944 (294)
PEELE, R.: 2014 (306), 2556 (391)
PEET, M.: 799 (120)
PEIGNE, F.: 778 (118)
PEJOVIC, M.: 1696 (254)
PEKER, G.: 1529 (235)
PEKTOYLAN, T.: 702 (108)
PELAYO, A.: 601 (91), 1744 (264)
PELICIER, Y.: 2206 (336), 2316 (357), 23 (5)
PELIZZER, G.: 2588 (396)
PELLEGRINI, E.: 1239 (193)
PELLEGRINI, F.: 1067 (160)
PELLEGRINO, L.: 2489 (380)
PELLET, J.: 1393 (213)
PELOTTI, G.: 576 (87)
PELTZER, K.: 230 (34), 3209 (491)
PELZER, E.: 2673 (407), 1349 (208)
PENATI, G.: 2979 (454)
PENNELL, I.: 2658 (405)
PERALES, A.: 744 (114), 1285 (200), 1977 (298)
PERE, J.: 1798 (274)
PEREIRA, O.: 1999 (303)
PEREZ, A.: 1305 (202), 2866 (438)
PEREZ, C.: 2687 (408)
PEREZ, E.: 304 (45)
PEREZ DE LOS COBOS, J.: 2468 (378), 2710 (411)
PEREZ-ECHEVERRIA, M.: 3234 (494), 1795 (274)
PEREZ-RINCON, H.: 640 (98)
PERGAMI, A.: 1240 (193)
PERI, J.: 2471 (378)
PERICAY, J.: 141 (22)

PERINI, A.: 1023 (155)
PERON-MAGNAN, P.: 2564 (392)
PEROZZIELO, F.: 973 (148)
PERREAULT, M.: 2430 (374), 3237 (494)
PERRIS, C.: 2618 (400), 1768 (268), 2614 (400), 904 (136), 2059 (313)
PERRO, C.: 724 (112)
PERSICO, A.: 1242 (193), 2465 (378), 1243 (193)
PERSICO, M.: 2711 (411)
PERSSON, A.: 2389 (368), 836 (125))
PERTESSI, E.: 993 (152), 2088 (318)
PERUGI, G.: 2501 (382), 962 (146), 2314 (356), 733 (113), 783 (118)
PESCATORI, M.: 2666 (406)
PESESCHKIAN, N.: 1184 (183)
PESTANA, L.: 2107 (321)
PETER, K.: 1427 (217)
PETERS, J.: 695 (107)
PETERSSON, B.: 3226 (493), 2856 (437), 951 (145)
PETIT, M.: 1077 (162), 1672 (252)
PETRACCA, A: 962 (146), 1159 (179)
PETRIDOU, D.: 1597 (244)
PETRONI, M.: 1574 (242)
PETROPOULOU, O.: 215 (31)
PETROV, R.: 2917 (445), 1062 (159)
PETROVIC, D.: 2131 (325), 1556 (239)
PETTEGREW, J.: 2331 (359)
PETTERSSON, G.: 481 (70), 480 (70)
PETTOELLO, G.: 1298 (201)
PETURSSON, H.: 1238 (192)
PEUSKENS, J.: 1331 (206)
PEYRON, M.: 1899 (289), 2589 (396)
PEZZAROSSA, B.: 1604 (245)
PEZZOLI, A.: 2517 (383)
PFEIFLE, U.: 2125 (324)
PFERSMANN, D.: 1931 (293), 1932 (293)
PFITZNER, R.: 2495 (381)
PFOLZ, H: 583 (88), 1956 (295), 2092 (319), 2454 (377))
PHANJOO, A.: 1049 (157)
PHILADETAKIS, S.: 1766 (267)
PHILIP, M.: 250 (37), 2176 (330), 254 (37), 1827 (279)
PHILLIPS, R.: 1071 (161), 358 (54), 1532 (236)
PHILOSOF, E.: 2947 (447), 129 (20)
PHILPOT, M.: 895 (135)
PHIPPS, L.: 2449 (376)
PHOCAS, C.: 2494 (381), 1930 (292)
PIA, M.: 2889 (441)
PIANI, F.: 1298 (201)
PIAZZA, A.: 1894 (288)
PICCINI, P.: 1964 (296), 539 (79), 2115 (322)
PICCIONE, A.: 990 (151)
PICCIONE, M.: 995 (152), 2662 (406), 998 (152), 1389 (213)
PICHOT, P.: 676 (105)
PICKAR, D.: 207 (29)
PIEDELOUP, C.: 2045 (310)
PIEMONTESE, M.: 1032 (156)
PIENAAR, W.: 2369 (366)
PIERCE, C.: 923 (140), 110 (18)
PIERRI, G.: 197 (28), 2000 (303)
PIETERS, G.: 1196 (184), 2266 (349)
PIETRINI, P.: 1169 (180)
PIETZCKER, A.: 890 (134), 1549 (238)
PIGUET, D.: 2588 (396)
PIKETTI, M.: 2564 (392)
PILETZ, J.: 635 (98)
PIMENTA, F.: 1135 (173)
PINAS, M.: 768 (117)
PINEYRO, G.: 2166 (328)
PINHO, M.: 228 (33)
PINOTTIA, A.: 1058 (158)

PINTARIC, S.: 3038 (465)
PINTER, G.: 1085 (163)
PINTORE, P.: 1055 (158)
PIPERIA, M.: 1241 (193)
PIPERYIA, I.: 2355 (363)
PIRINO, F.: 1635 (248)
PIRKE, K.M.: 3170 (487), 3002 (459), 3003 (459), 3010 (461), 290 (42)
PIRLOT-PETROFF, G.: 339 (52)
PIRO, A.: 1090 (164), 3197 (490), 1927 (292)
PIRON, J.: 3232 (494), 2564 (392)
PIROZZI, R.: 2725 (413)
PISANI, R.: 3160 (486)
PISCHEDDA, P.: 1097 (164)
PITSAVAS, A.: 1930 (292)
PITTADAKI, E.: 728 (112)
PITTALIS, A.: 822 (123), 2828 (432), 1690 (254), 820 (123), 2305 (354), 2938 (447), 2306 (354), 994 (152), 827 (123), 2940 (447), 2304 (354)
PIVA, A.: 2442 (375)
PIZZELLA, A.: 128 (20)
PLACIDI, G.: 732 (113)
PLAISANT, O.: 3131 (480), 1714 (259), 401 (61)
PLANT, I.: 2915 (444)
PLAS, J.: 1682 (253), 2029 (308), 2475 (379), 2290 (352)
PLATALLA, S.: 2867 (438)
PLATARIS, G.: 688 (107), 70 (12)
PLATOKOUKI, E.: 1241 (193)
PLAVSIC, V.: 1658 (250)
PLENGE, P.: 800 (120), 200 (29), 526 (78)
PLEWES, J.: 2209 (336)
PLIATSKIDI, S.: 1665 (251)
PLOUMBIDIS, D.: 1857 (283), 28 (5)
PLUMBER, G.: 360 (55)
POCINHO, F.: 2445 (376)
POCOCK, P.: 2186 (332)
PODREKA, I.: 2908 (443), 964 (147), 677 (105), 837 (125)
POEL VAN DER, E.: 2567 (393)
POELDINGER, W.: 1801 (275), 1325 (205), 2038 (309)
POGGI LONGOSTREVI, G.: 272 (40)
POHL, H.: 2638 (403)
POIRIER-LITTRE, M.: 2564 (392)
POLACK, M.: 2403 (370)
POLDRUGO, F.: 1838 (280), 2490 (380)
POLEKSIC, J.: 1255 (195)
POLINSKY, R.: 2055 (312)
POLITI, P.: 3187 (489), 437 (65)
POLITIS, C.: 1925 (292)
POLITO, F.: 1088 (163)
POLLACK, S.: 307 (47)
POLS, H.: 3126 (480), 412 (63), 1559 (240)
POLYMEROPOULOS, M.: 1888 (288)
POLZER, U.: 1668 (251)
POMAROL, G.: 2471 (378)
POMMER, W.: 763 (116)
PONCE, M.: 1975 (298)
PONCE DE LEON, C.: 2887 (441), 2955 (448), 2645 (404), 1637 (248)
POORMAND, D.: 952 (145)
POPE, G.: 266 (39), 1756 (265)
POPEA-ION, M.: 2620 (400)
POPESCU, C.: 796 (120)
PORCIUNCULA, H.: 560 (84)
PORTA, A.: 795 (120)
PORTA, M.: 2147 (326)
PORTES, N.: 2895 (441)
POSLIGUA BALSECA, P.: 497 (71), 2077 (316)
POSNER, M.: 1818 (278)

POSSOZ, P.: 1070 (160)
POSTEL, J.: 2550 (389)
POTAMIANOU, A.: 2359 (364)
POTHITOS, T.: 116 (19)
POTKIN, S.: 873 (132), 210 (30), 2721 (413))
POTTHOFF, R.: 791 (119)
POTTS, M.: 305 (45)
POURCELOT, L.: 2183 (332)
POWELL, B.: 1294 (201)
POWNALL, R.: 1608 (245)
PRADO-LIMA, P.,: 593 (90)
PRALLET, J.: 811 (121)
PRANGE, A.: 1539 (237)
PRASAD, A.: 98 (16)
PRASKO, J.: 1221 (188)
PRASKOVA, H.: 1221 (188)
PRATIKAKIS, E.: 588 (89), 824 (123)
PREDESCU, C.: 1413 (215), 1522 (234)
PREDESCU, I.: 2280 (351), 1594 (244)
PREDESCU, O.: 2280 (351), 1594 (244)
PREDESCU, V.: 1594 (244), 2280 (351), 796 (120)
PREDIERI, M.: 1139 (173)
PREISIG, R.: 1295 (201)
PRESSLICH, O.: 2464 (378), 1931 (293)
PREZIOSA, P.: 1090 (164), 3197 (490)
PRIAMI, M.: 3223 (493), 3222 (493), 2670 (406)
PRICHEP, L.: 874 (132), 2172 (329)
PRICHER, L.: 211 (30)
PRIEBE, S.: 774 (118), 1668 (251), 326 (50), 2994 (457), 1533 (236)
PRIETO AGUIRRE, J.: 1517 (234)
PRIETO MESTRE, P.: 1517 (234)
PRILIPKO, L.: 2404 (371)
PRINCE, R.: 870 (131)
PRINGUEY, D.: 835 (125)
PRIOMI, M.: 956 (145)
PRIVETTE, M.: 933 (142)
PRIVOROTZKY, F.: 1954 (295), 129 (20), 2947 (447)
PROCTOR, M.: 198 (28)
PROKOPAKIS, E.: 1525 (235)
PROTOPAPPA, V.: 143 (22)
PROTTI, M.: 2489 (380)
PROW, M.: 590 (90)
PRUD'HOMME, L.: 2617 (400)
PRUDHAM, D.: 1075 (161), 2889 (441)
PSOMIADOU, M.: 459 (68)
PUCCINI, S.: 2646 (404)
PUCILOWSKI, O.: 2909 (444)
PUECH, A.: 2732 (414), 410 (62), 315 (48), 235 (35)
PUECHLER, K.: 2886 (441), 1028 (155), 2883 (441), 408 (62), 2480 (379)
PUEL, J.: 1920 (291)
PUENTE, M.: 1586 (243)
PUENTES-NEWMAN, G.: 2644 (404)
PUGNETTI, L.: 2603 (398), 2604 (398)
PUIG, J.: 2616 (400)
PULIDO, R.: 1924 (292)
PULL, C.: 1233 (191)
PUNTIN, M.: 2489 (380)
PUNUKOLLU, N.: 1905 (290)
PURI, D.: 1207 (186)
PURIFICACAO HORTA, M.: 1599 (245), 769 (117)
PUSAVAT, L.: 2182 (332), 2338 (361)
PUSTKA, P.: 988 (150)
PUUMALAINEN, J.: 2016 (306)
PY, C.: 1198 (185), 2790 (425)
PYLE, R.: 2011 (305)
PYTKOWICZ STREISSGUTH, A.: 2313 (356)

Q

QUADE, G.: 3141 (482)
QUADFLIEG, N.: 2398 (369)
QUARTESAN, R.: 1209 (186)
QUARTUCCI, S.: 2268 (349)
QUATTRONE, B.: 419 (63), 1760 (266)
QUIROGA, M.: 1738 (262)
QURESHI, M.: 926 (141)

R

RABAVILAS, A.: 2173 (329), 2341 (361), 2775 (422), 3120 (479) 149 (23), 1416 (216), 2628 (402), 3125 (480), 2991 (457), 2774 (422)
RABBANI, H.: 3058 (468)
RABBONI, M.: 1686 (254)
RACHELE, M.: 375 (57), 2654 (405)
RADDAOUI, K.: 2518 (383), 1828 (279), 2833 (433), 1705 (255), 3115 (479)
RADEBAUGH, T.: 1799 (274)
RADFORD, P.: 867 (130)
RADOSAVAC, B.: 2264 (348)
RADVILA, A.: 113 (19)
RAETZO, M.: 1226 (189)
RAFATIAN, A.: 2811 (430)
RAFFAITIN, F.: 1694 (254), 2564 (392), 2289 (352)
RAHIM, S.: 1123 (170)
RAIMONDI, R.: 1964 (296), 1417 (216)
RAINER, E.: 1947 (294)
RAINOV, V.: 1735 (262)
RAITH, L.: 1375 (211)
RAJARAM MOHAN, R.: 2446 (376)
RAJKUMAR, S.: 2286 (352)
RAJU, S.: 2076 (316)
RAKIC, V.: 1332 (207), 561 (85)
RAMACHANDRAN, V.: 1949 (295)
RAMALHEIRA, C.: 812 (122)
RAMELLA, M.: 682 (106)
RAMELLI, E.: 1719 (260), 1518 (234), 742 (114)
RAMESH, V.: 137 (21)
RAMIREZ, E.: 1973 (298)
RAMIREZ, L.: 1942 (294), 2623 (401)
RAMIREZ-RAMIREZ, L.: 192 (28)
RAMOS, J.: 2887 (441), 1637 (248))
RAMOS, L.: 47 (9)
RAMOS, L.: 1607 (245)
RAMOS, R.: 414 (63)
RAMOS, T.: 1246 (193)
RAMPELLO, L.: 473 (70)
RAMSAY, R.: 1499 (230)
RAMSEIER, F.: 2922 (446)
RANEN, N.: 2381 (367)
RANTANEN, H.: 2137 (325)
RAO, B.: 2152 (327), 205 (29), 2153 (327), 1624 (247)
RAO, V.: 2635 (402), 337 (52), 2547 (389), 383 (58)
RAOOF, A.: 3204 (491)
RAPOPORT, J.: 2441 (375), 1778 (270)
RAPOPORT, M.: 1102 (166)
RAPTOPOULOS, P.: 2771 (420)
RAS, A.: 750 (115)
RASHED, S.: 3163 (486)
RASI, A.: 1617 (246)
RASK, P.: 2028 (308), 908 (137)
RASMUSSEN, M: 1011 (154)
RASMUSSEN, S.: 1326 (205), 1776 (270)
RASTOGI, S.: 2915 (444)
RATNASURIYA, H.: 293 (42)
RAULL, J.: 1132 (172)
RAUSCH, J.: 237 (35)

RAVAGLI, S.: 562 (85)
RAVEAU, F.: 1714 (259)
RAVELLA, P.: 811 (121)
RAVERA, F.: 387 (59)
RAVIZZA, L.: 1193 (184), 1351 (209), 2600 (398), 859 (129)
RAWLINS,: 1162 (179)
RAYA, A.: 2670 (406)
RAYNAUD, C.: 2183 (332), 2682 (408)
RAZAVI R.: 1354 (209)
RAZZOUK, D.: 395 (60)
RE, F.: 374 (57)
REBISCHUNG, D.: 16 (4)
REBOUL, P.: 1487 (228)
RECONDO GARCIA M.: 1039 (156), 1595 (244)
REDA, M.: 1635 (248)
REDDY, L.: 2152 (327), 1624 (247), 205 (29)
REDDY, P.: 2153 (327)
REED, P.: 2068 (315)
REES, R.: 2632 (402)
REEVES, J.: 2458 (377)
REGAN, C.: 3136 (481)
REGAZZETTI, M.: 2147 (326)
REGGY, L.: 785 (119)
REGIER, D.: 16 (3)
REGINALDI, D.: 710 (109), 1569 (241)
REGNI, D.: 2748 (417)
REGUIERO, J.: 3025 (463)
REHM, H.: 2495 (381)
REHM, J.: 1825 (279)
REIBRING, L.: 2386 (368)
REICH, J.: 1394 (213)
REICHART, B.: 2453 (376)
REICHWALDT, W.: 1668 (251)
REID, R.: 2063 (314)
REIFSCHNEIDER, G.: 1072 (161), 1998 (302)
REILLY, T.: 1689 (254), 477 (70), 342 (52)
REIMAN, E.: 1818 (278)
REIMANN, I.: 2033 (308), 3184 (488), 2476 (379)
REIMER, F.: 781 (118), 453 (67), 452 (67), 1614 (246)
REIN, W.: 2283 (351), 289 (42)
REINBERG, A.: 636 (98)
REINELT, T.: 1572 (242), 2221 (339)
REINICK, E.: 666 (103), 667 (103)
REIST, C.: 2257 (348)
REITH, B.: 1272 (198)
REITZ, C.: 2130 (325)
REMICK, R.: 214 (31)
REMSCHMIDT, H.: 2527 (386), 2396 (369), 2397 (369), 2224 (342)
REMY, B.: 3176 (487)
RENAULT, B.: 1340 (207)
RENDERS, X.: 522 (77)
RENDTORFF, C.: 2930 (446)
RENNA, C.: 197 (28)
RENNIE, C.: 3007 (461)
REPOSSI, C.: 994 (152)
REPOSSI, G.: 820 (123)
RESCH, F.: 2921 (445), 1648 (250), 69 (12)
RESTIAN, A.: 157 (23)
RETAMAL, P.: 2545 (388)
RETHER, H.: 453 (67), 452 (67)
RETTERSTOL, N.: 2228 (343), 2037 (309), 1509 (232)
REVELEY, M.: 1867 (285)
REY-CAMET, M.: 1899 (289)
REYES MORENO, R.: 1424 (216)
REYEZ, B.: 1036 (156)
REYNAERT, C.: 1580 (243 3173 (487), 263 (39), 2852 (436)
REYNOLDS, C.: 873 (132), 210 (30)

REYNOLDS, C.: 2342 (362), 111 (18)
REYNTJENS, A.: 1495 (229)
RHINDS, D.: 1075 (161)
RIBA, F.: 1226 (189)
RIBEIRO, J.: 1296 (201)
RIBOULET-DELMAS, G.: 411 (62)
RICARD, N.: 2426 (374)
RICCIARDI, A.: 714 (110)
RICHARD, J.: 2333 (360)
RICHARDSON, C.: 2063 (314)
RICHARDSON, CL.: 262 (39)
RICHARDSON, K.: 987 (150), 988 (150)
RICHARDSON, M.: 2790 (285), 1866 (285)
RICHARTZ, M.: 2005 (304), 2004 (304)
RICHTER, J.: 2618 (400), 2614 (400)
RICHTER, P.: 767 (117), 1001 (153), 2078 (316), 2285 (351)
RICKARDS, W.: 2394 (369)
RICKELS, K.: 1555 (239), 2767 (420), 1181 (182), 1319 (204), 1470 (225)
RICOL, O.: 835 (125)
RIEDERER, P.: 1386 (212), 432 (64), 1048 (157), 71 (12)
RIEMANN, D.: 2629 (402), 3050 (467), 252 (37), 2900 (442), 882 (133)
RIEMANN, P.: 2343 (362)
RIESE, B.: 433 (64)
RIGAS, N.: 191 (28)
RIGATOS, G.: 344 (52), 1065 (160)
RIGATTI-LUCHINI, S.: 2060 (314)
RIGAUD, M.: 1919 (291)
RIGHETTI, C.: 1110 (167)
RIGHI, L.: 1058 (158)
RIHMER, Z.: 65 (12)
RIMON, R.: 2137 (325)
RINALDI, A.: 376 (57)
RINIERIS, P.: 1303 (202)
RIOBO, M.: 602 (91)
RIOSA, G.: 2489 (380)
RISCO, L.: 2632 (402)
RIVA, E.: 1548 (238), 1093 (164)
RIVELLI, S.: 1746 (264)
RIVERA, A.: 2639 (403), 311 (47)
RIVERA, J.: 1136 (173)
RIVERA, M.: 2650 (404)
RIVERO, G.: 954 (145), 1380 (212)
RIVIERE, B.: 396 (60)
RIZZARDO, R.: 1166 (180), 2021 (307), 2514 (383)
ROAN, W.: 2824 (431)
ROBAEY, P.: 1340 (207)
ROBBE, H.: 2104 (321)
ROBELIN, N.: 2657 (405)
ROBERT, P.: 835 (125), 2541 (388)
ROBERT, PH.: 1980 (299), 1694 (254), 1005 (153)
ROBERTI, L.: 817 (122)
ROBERTS, G.: 1328 (206), 1816 (278)
ROBERTS, M.: 2369 (366)
ROBERTS, N.: 402 (61)
ROBERTS, P.: 1529 (235)
ROBERTS, R.: 2575 (395), 2822 (431)
ROBERTSON, M.: 1997 (302)
ROBIN, A.: 3012 (461)
ROBINS, L.: 716 (110), 10 (3)
ROBINSON, R.: 1820 (278)
ROBLES, J.: 1738 (262)
ROBOU, L.: 1399 (214)
ROCA BENNASAR, M.: 1358 (209), 1421 (216)
ROCCATAGLIATA, G.: 1017 (155), 2546 (389), 1016 (155), 508 (74)
ROCKHOLD, R.: 3150 (484)
RODER, V.: 3198 (490), 900 (136)
RODGERS J.: 2894 (441)
RODIERE-REIN, C.: 1290 (200)

RODIGHIERO, S.: 780 (118), 491 (71)
RODRIGO, E.: 2597 (397)
RODRIGUES LOUZA, M.: 2559 (392), 2778 (422)
RODRIGUEZ, A.: 2866 (438), 1305 (202), 1086 (163), 3035 (465)
RODRIGUEZ, J.: 15 (4)
RODRIGUEZ, W.: 3008 (461)
RODRIQUEZ, A.: 2847 (435)
RODRIQUEZ PULIDO, F.: 1136 (173)
ROED, I.: 408 (62), 2480 (379), 2886 (441), 1028 (155), 2883 (441)
ROELS, P.: 851 (128)
ROGERS, R.: 1938 (293)
ROGERS, W.: 305 (45)
ROGUE, P.: 1885 (288), 1962 (296)
ROHDE, A.: 730 (113), 2074 (316), 104 (17), 953 (145), 2079 (316)
ROIJEN, S.: 3171 (487)
ROLF, L.: 429 (64), 2681 (408)
ROLLAN, R.: 2703 (410)
ROMANS-CLARKSON, S.: 2307 (354), 368 (56)
ROMEO, S.: 1032 (156)
RONCHI, E.: 2727 (414)
RONDOT, P.: 175 (26)
ROSADINI, G.: 877 (132)
ROSADO, P.: 2634 (402)
ROSEN, A.: 1012 (154)
ROSENBAUM, J.: 2403 (370)
ROSENBERG, S.: 2208 (336)
ROSENLICHT, N.: 2400 (370)
ROSENTAL, WL.: 500 (73)
ROSENZWEIG, N.: 41 (8)
ROSENZWEIG, R.: 258 (38)
ROSIN, U.: 1914 (291)
ROSS, N.: 320 (49), 1767 (267)
ROSS, S.: 530 (78)
ROSS-CHOUINARD, A.: 533 (79)
ROSSETI, S.: 1693 (254)
ROSSI, A.: 487 (70)
ROSSINI, M.: 1240 (193)
ROST, W.: 171 (25)
ROTELLI, F.: 182 (27), 2006 (304)
ROTH, M.: 2315 (356), 2978 (454), 94 (15), 3069 (472)
ROTHENBERGER, A.: 2185 (332)
ROTONDI, F.: 3016 (462)
ROTROSEN, J.: 2327 (359), 2740 (415)
ROTT, R.: 3137 (481), 571 (86)
ROUGET, P.: 683 (106)
ROUILLON, F.: 358 (54)
ROUSKOV, R.: 2239 (345), 2278 (351)
ROUSSILHES, R.: 1069 (160)
ROUX, G.: 1715 (259), 1117 (168)
ROUX, E.: 976 (149)
ROVEYAZ, E.: 1739 (263)
ROVIDA, S.: 3205 (491)
ROVNER, M.: 137 (21)
ROY, A.: 931 (142), 207 (29), 96 (16)
ROY, C.: 3077 (473), 2556 (391)
ROY, J.: 211 (30), 874 (132)
ROYSTON, M.: 1817 (278)
RUBIN, L.: 1294 (201)
RUBIN, P.: 3225 (493), 950 (145)
RUBIN, R.: 3 (1)
RUBINO, I.: 151 (23), 1604 (245)
RUBINOW, D.: 2534 (387)
RUBIO, M.: 2645 (404)
RUBIO LARROSA, V.: 1039 (156), 1595 (244)
RUBIO-STIPEC, M.: 46 (9), 2492 (381)
RUBOVITS, P.: 362 (55)
RUDAS, N.: 1822 (279), 3192 (489), 558 (84)
RUDY, S.: 785 (119)
RUETHER, E.: 1842 (281), 2559 (392),
1996 (302), 1278 (199)
RUGGERI, A.: 817 (122)
RUGGERO, P.: 657 (101)
RUGGIERO, V.: 825 (123)
RUIZ, I.: 769 (117)
RUIZ OGARA, C.: 643 (99)
RUIZ RUIZ, M.: 2483 (380), 179 (26), 324 (50), 642 (99)
RUPPRECHT, C.: 1653 (250), 216 (31)
RUPPRECHT, M.: 1653 (250), 216 (31)
RUPPRECHT, R.: 2112 (322), 1653 (250), 1652 (250)
RUSHEL, S.: 860 (129)
RUSKOV, R.: 2934 (447)
RUSSELL, G.: 293 (42)
RUSSO, R.: 1240 (193)
RUTHERFORD, W.: 2835 (433)
RUTZ, W.: 2756 (418)
RYAN, E.: 2656 (405)
RYDBERG, U.: 5628 (451), 2966 (451)
RYDER, L.: 281 (41)

S

SAAF, J.: 726 (112), 727 (112)
SAARIJARVI, S.: 1521 (234)
SAAVEDRA, M.: 448 (66)
SABELLI, H.: 3124 (480), 2941 (447)
SABSHIN, M.: 2082 (317), 2319 (357), 29 (6)
SACCARDI, B.: 1617 (246)
SACCHETTI, E.: 272 (40), 1395 (213), 413 (63)
SACKS, B.: 2325 (358)
SACRISTAN, J.: 1462 (223), 1147 (175), 1983 (300)
SAEAEF, J.: 699 (108), 697 (108), 1080 (162), 2902 (443)
SAELAN, H.: 1486 (228)
SAFAR, M.: 788 (119)
SAFER, M.: 1410 (215)
SAGOVSKY, R.: 2593 (397)
SAHA, H.: 2511 (383)
SAHU, A.: 1112 (167), 2149 (326)
SAILHAN, M.: 1891 (288)
SAITO, E.: 1582 (243)
SAITO, K.: 3042 (466)
SAITO, M.: 2907 (443), 2390 (368)
SAITO, S.: 3036 (465)
SAIZ, J.: 2219 (338), 1468 (225)
SAIZ-RUIZ, J.: 1082 (162)
SAKAI, T.: 2777 (422)
SAKALIS, G.: 1685 (253)
SAKAMOTO, K.: 142 (22)
SAKELLAROPOULOS, G.: 1362 (210)
SAKELLAROPOULOS, P.: 1597 (244), 1562 (240), 1665 (251), 1439 (219), 2566 (393), 2020 (307)
SAKKAS, D.: 328 (50), 1187 (183)
SAKKAS, P.: 1174 (181), 1307 (202), 3154 (484), 1222 (188), 2118 (323), 165 (25), 3012 (461), 996 (152), 2345 (362), 1711 (258), 2735 (414), 1173 (181), 3148 (484)
SAKKELARIOU, A.: 2159 (328)
SAKOMAN, S.: 2487 (380)
SAKUTA, T.: 513 (75), 1150 (175)
SALAZAR, I.: 3035 (465)
SALETU, B.: 964 (147), 1345 (208), 2674 (407), 876 (132)
SALINAS, E.: 880 (133), 878 (133)
SALIS, P.: 1055 (158)
SALKOVSKIS, P.: 848 (127)
SALL, O.: 1828 (279)
SALOKANGAS, R.: 585 (89)
SALTERI, A.: 1344 (208), 2291 (352),
SALVADOR, J.: 2496 (381)
SALVATI, E.: 634 (98), 633 (98)
SAMANT, H.: 349 (53)
SAMARTZIS, D.: 728 (112)
SAMPAIO-FARIA, J.: 1792 (273), 2760 (419)
SAMSON, J.: 103 (17)
SAMUEL-LAJEUNESSE, B.: 2283 (351), 3199 (490), 288 (42), 289 (42), 3195 (490), 1737 (262), 286 (42), 2700 (410), 3169 (487)
SAMUELSON, S.: 3121 (480), 1944 (294)
SAN, L.: 2471 (378)
SAN MARTINO, M.: 376 (57), 454 (67)
SANABRIA, E.: 703 (108)
SANATI, M.: 1731 (262)
SANCHEZ, E.: 179 (26)
SANCHEZ, F.: 1920 (291)
SANCHEZ, L.: 3230 (494), 1003 (153), 1571 (241), 2581 (395), 1748 (264)
SANCHEZ, M.: 2109 (321)
SANCHEZ, P.: 2899 (442), 1633 (248), 1623 (247), 1692 (254), 2958 (449), 3049 (467), 2630 (402), 2671 (407)
SANCHEZ ARELLANO, E.: 3041 (466), 467 (68)
SANCOVICI, S.: 1933 (293)
SAND, L.: 2649 (404)
SANDANGER, I.: 2493 (381)
SANDBERG, D.: 685 (106)
SANDBERG, P.: 2470 (378)
SANDHU, A.: 936 (143)
SANDMANN, R.: 1706 (255)
SANDOR, E.: 545 (81)
SANDOR, P.: 3183 (488)
SANDOZ, M.: 359 (54)
SANDRA, N.: 3166 (486)
SANGIORGI, R.: 1138 (173), 1058 (158)
SANNA, M.: 2828 (432), 2305 (354), 2306 (354), 822 (123), 2940 (447), 1690 (254), 820 (123), 2304 (354), 2938 (447), 994 (152), 827 (123)
SANNITA, W.: 877 (132)
SANSEVERO, A.: 454 (67)
SANTACRUZ, H.: 45 (9)
SANTIAGO, M.: 3172 (487)
SANTONE, G.: 68 (12)
SANTONI, R.: 2003 (303)
SANTORO, N.: 197 (28)
SANTOS, M.: 1299 (201)
SARA, G.: 3007 (461)
SARANTIDIS, D.: 956 (145), 3222 (493), 3223 (493), 1420 (216)
SARANTOGLOU, G.: 344 (52), 1716 (259), 1065 (160), 2109 (321)
SARASOLA, A.: 1170 (180)
SARGACO, P.: 1628 (247), 1391 (213)
SARIMURAT, N.: 3026 (463)
SARMAN, C.: 2903 (443)
SARNA, G.: 2728 (414)
SARRIAS, M.: 934 (142)
SARRON, C.: 1631 (248)
SARTORIUS, N.: 312 (48), 2608 (399), 1971 (297)
SARUP, A.: 1563 (240)
SARWER-FONER, G.: 30 (6), 1443 (220)
SASAKI, M.: 2044 (310)
SASS, H.: 1001 (153), 2078 (316), 3072 (472), 1979 (299)
SASSO, E.: 406 (62)
SASTRE Y HERNANDEZ, M.: 1050 (157), 1022 (155)
SATHIANATHAN, R.: 1949 (295)
SATIGA, D.C.: 1112 (167), 2149 (326)
SATO, T.: 3215 (492)
SAUER, H.: 2130 (325), 1001 (153), 2078 (316)

SAUGSTAD, L.: 2244 (346)
SAUNDERS, J.: 12 (3)
SAUNDERS, P.: 898 (135), 2509 (382), 1753 (265), 1796 (274)
SAUPE, R.: 326 (50), 1089 (164)
SAUSGRUBER, H.: 1742 (263)
SAUSSURE, N.: 1091 (164)
SAVINO, M.: 733 (113), 454 (67), 2314 (356)
SAVLA, N.: 751 (115), 2714 (412), 101 (16)
SAVOLDI, F.: 1893 (288)
SAWICKA, M.: 2591 (397)
SAXENA, B.: 3183 (488), 2458 (377)
SAYDAM, B.: 1600 (245)
SAYDAM, M.: 19 (4)
SAYITA, S.: 1372 (211)
SAZ, P.: 1795 (274)
SBONA, A.: 998 (152)
SBONA, I.: 990 (151), 995 (152), 2662 (406)
SBRACCIA, F.: 1730 (261)
SCAMONATTI, L.: 375 (57), 2654 (405)
SCANLON, M.: 2845 (435)
SCAPICCHIO, P.: 166 (25)
SCARAMUCCI, E.: 1699 (255)
SCARIATI, G.: 503 (73)
SCHAAP, G.: 1757 (265)
SCHAFFLER, K.: 1945 (294), 2927 (446), 2299 (353)
SCHAMBORZKI, I.: 73 (13)
SCHANDA, H.: 2230 (343)
SCHARBACH, H.: 2349 (363)
SCHAUENBURG, H.: 1202 (185)
SCHAUMBURG, E.: 2507 (382)
SCHEIDT, G.: 3138 (481), 1130 (172)
SCHERDIN-WENDLANDT, H.: 3191 (489)
SCHERER, J.: 2453 (376), 268 (39), 2559 (392)
SCHEUCHENSTEIN, A.: 1618 (246)
SCHEURER, J.: 1341 (208)
SCHIASSI, A.: 810 (121), 3214 (492)
SCHICK, U.: 724 (112)
SCHIFFERDECKER, M.: 818 (122)
SCHIPPER, J.: 1948 (294)
SCHISSEL, B.: 1873 (286)
SCHLECHT, A.: 1649 (250)
SCHLEGEL, S.: 2144 (326), 2170 (329)
SCHLEIFER, S.: 830 (124)
SCHLICHTER, A.: 1427 (217)
SCHLOESSER, C.: 715 (110), 1381 (212)
SCHLOSSMAN, I.: 2854 (436)
SCHLYER, D.: 2740 (415)
SCHMALZBROT, C.: 2144 (326)
SCHMECK, H.: 988 (150)
SCHMEDING-WIEGEL, H.: 1022 (155)
SCHMICKALY, R.: 1323 (205)
SCHMIDT, C.: 984 (150), 2827 (432), 221 (32)
SCHMIDT, M.: 914 (138), 2395 (369), 1461 (223)
SCHMIDT, R.: 818 (122)
SCHMIDTKE, A.: 171 (25), 1998 (302)
SCHMITT, B.: 2990 (457)
SCHMITT, L.: 833 (125)
SCHMITZ-NIEHUES, B.: 2749 (417)
SCHNABEL, P.: 2023 (307), 2025 (307)
SCHNEEMANN, N.: 1043 (157)
SCHNEIDER, F.: 834 (125), 2069 (315), 2906 (443)
SCHNEIDER, H.: 718 (111)
SCHNEIDER, M.: 2705 (411), 2638 (403), 1939 (293)
SCHNEIDER, W.: 1051 (157), 405 (62)
SCHNEIR, F.: 1852 (282), 1385 (212)
SCHOELLNHAMMER, G.: 239 (35), 407 (62), 409 (62), 2924 (446), 238 (35)

SCHOEMNAKERS, E.: 651 (100)
SCHOENBECK, G.: 3174 (487), 1476 (226), 1683 (253), 1648 (250), 69 (12), 1085 (163), 2111 (322), 2647 (404), 1540 (237), 2921 (445), 483 (70), 167 (25), 1475 (226), 1308 (202), 2561 (392)
SCHOENMAKERS, E.: 652 (100), 2105 (321), 2104 (321)
SCHOENY, W.: 1846 (281)
SCHOOLER, N.: 2801 (427), 2803 (427)
SCHOTTE, C.: 1396 (213), 1647 (250), 2113 (322)
SCHOUTENS, A.: 832 (125)
SCHRAMM, W.: 1939 (293)
SCHRATZER, M.: 1050 (157)
SCHREIBER, H.: 3143 (482)
SCHREIBER, R.: 1079 (162)
SCHREIBER, W.: 2655 (405)
SCHRELL, U.: 216 (31)
SCHREPLER, D.: 1030 (156)
SCHRIVASTAVA, R.: 1025 (155)
SCHRODER, J.: 2130 (325), 2120 (323)
SCHROTH, G.: 834 (125)
SCHUBERT, T.: 225 (33)
SCHUELER, M.: 828 (124)
SCHUESSLER, G.: 1202 (185)
SCHUETTLER, R.: 2993 (457), 1547 (238), 517 (76), 571 (86)
SCHUGENS, N.: 116 (19)
SCHUIERER, G.: 466 (68)
SCHULSINGER, F.: 1969 (297), 1811 (277)
SCHULSINGER, H.: 725 (112)
SCHULTE, J.: 2112 (322)
SCHULTE, M.: 1652 (250), 243 (36)
SCHULTE, R.: 2293 (352)
SCHULTZ, V.: 441 (65)
SCHURMAN, T.: 236 (35)
SCHUTTLER, R.: 777 (118)
SCHUURMAN, T.: 596 (90), 2881 (440)
SCHWABE, S.: 2033 (308)
SCHWALBACH, H.: 87 (14)
SCHWARTZ, D.: 2360 (364), 2805 (429)
SCHWARTZ, J.: 1376 (211)
SCHWARTZ, P.: 3110 (478)
SCHWARZBACH, H.: 1846 (281)
SCHWEIGER, U.: 3004 (459)
SCHWEIZER, E.: 1555 (239), 2767 (420)
SCHWITZER, J.: 3137 (481)
SCIOLI, R.: 3187 (489)
SCIOLLA, A.: 2632 (402)
SCOPPA, F.: 2874 (439), 1650 (250)
SCOTT, A.: 1796 (274), 720 (111), 1023 (155)
SCOTT, B.: 2091 (318)
SCOTT, G.: 1755 (265)
SCZESNI, B.: 2120 (323)
SEABRA, D.: 1830 (279), 372 (57)
SEBER, G.: 2826 (432), 600 (91), 961 (146), 1068 (160)
SEBERT, P.: 2657 (405)
SEDVALL, G.: 2389 (368), 836 (125), 2739 (415), 1229 (190)
SEGHERS, A.: 263 (39), 813 (122), 1656 (250)
SEGRAVES, K.: 928 (141)
SEGRAVES, T.: 928 (141)
SEGUIN, A.: 257 (38)
SEGURA, E.: 3018 (462)
SEIDEL, P.: 407 (62)
SEIDL, O.: 1939 (293), 2705 (411)
SEIFERT, B.: 2157 (327), 2125 (324)
SEIFERTOVA, D.: 1221 (188)
SEKI, K.: 1179 (182)
SEKIRINA, T.: 1105 (166)

SEKKAT, E.: 1828 (279)
SELEZNYOVA, N.: 2142 (326)
SELL, H.: 313 (48)
SELLIER, P.: 786 (119)
SELVAN, T.: 564 (85)
SELZER, M.: 3233 (494)
SENER, A.: 1372 (211), 536 (79), 2252 (347)
SENGUN, S.: 2435 (374), 310 (47)
SEPPING, P.: 2265 (348)
SERGIO, E.: 1820 (278)
SERRA, C.: 3016 (462)
SERRA, F.: 3016 (462)
SERRAIOTTO, L.: 1045 (157)
SERRANO, G.: 419 (63)
SERRANO, V.: 179 (26), 2483 (380)
SERRATRICE, G.: 1046 (157)
SERRE, C.: 2540 (388)
SERRO, J.: 1628 (247), 1391 (213)
SERRURIER, D.: 358 (54)
SERVANT, D.: 1542 (237), 1167 (180)
SESTOST, D.: 2251 (347)
SETHI, B.: 797 (120), 2406 (371)
SEUNG, S.: 2793 (426)
SEVA, A.: 1170 (180)
SEVERE, J.: 2801 (427), 2803 (427)
SEVERIN, B.: 1024 (155)
SFORZA, V.: 1699 (255)
SHAALAM, M.: 1457 (222)
SHADER, R.: 1471 (225)
SHADOAN, R.: 2082 (317)
SHAFFER, J.: 1627 (247)
SHAH, A.: 2944 (447)
SHALEV, A.: 3153 (484)
SHANAHAN, W.: 2436 (375)
SHAPIRA, B.: 723 (111)
SHARMA, I.: 3030 (464), 937 (143)
SHARMA, R.: 932 (142)
SHARMA, S.N.: 989 (150), 1189 (184), 936 (143), 787 (119)
SHARMA, T.: 101 (16)
SHARMA, V.: 898 (135), 1753 (265), 752 (115), 2509 (382)
SHAW, D.: 930 (142), 1861 (284)
SHAW, G.: 861 (129)
SHEDLACK, K.: 2168 (329)
SHEIKMAN, M.: 371 (57)
SHEKIM, W.: 607 (92), 2402 (370)
SHELLEY, R.: 3136 (481)
SHEN, Y.: 625 (96), 2213 (337), 970 (148)
SHEPPARD, G.: 488 (70), 2831 (433), 2255 (347)
SHERING, P.: 1023 (155), 720 (111)
SHETTIWAR, R.: 3030 (464)
SHIGETA, M.: 2868 (438)
SHILLINGFORD, J.: 2771 (420)
SHIMA, S.: 1707 (255)
SHIMAZONO, Y.: 2776 (422)
SHIMIZU, M.: 2920 (445), 2868 (438), 400 (61)
SHING TSENG, W.: 78 (13)
SHIRAISHI, J.: 118 (19)
SHOPOVA, E.: 691 (107)
SHOYLECOVA, M.: 1216 (187)
SHRIVASTAVA, S.: 1025 (155)
SHUBERT, D.: 3008 (461)
SHUKLA, S.: 1376 (211)
SHUKLA, V.: 349 (53)
SHULMAN, K.: 2552 (390)
SIARA, C.: 1413 (215), 1522 (234)
SIASSI, I.: 978 (149), 1057 (158), 977 (149), 1575 (242), 1418 (216)
SIASSI, S.: 1057 (158), 977 (149), 1575 (242), 1418 (216), 978 (149)
SIDIROPOULOU, TR.: 195 (28), 1576 (242), 948 (144), 945 (144)

859

SIDNEY JONES, J.: 100 (16)
SIEBELINK, H.: 474 (70)
SIEBERNS, S.: 1722 (260), 2929 (446), 1074 (161)
SIEBUHR, N.: 1024 (155)
SIEFERT, H.: 407 (62)
SIERRA,: 1136 (173)
SIFNEOS, P.: 301 (44), 2781 (423), 1769 (268)
SIGMUNDSSON, TH.: 1238 (192)
SIGVARDSSON, S.: 3145 (483)
SILAN, M.: 2489 (380)
SILKE, B.: 2772 (420)
SILVA DE CASTRO, M.: 2598 (397)
SILVA MIGUEL, N.: 2481 (380)
SILVER SOKOL, R.: 2292 (352)
SILVERSTONE, J.: 1342 (208)
SILVERSTONE, T.: 1205 (186)
SILVERSTRINI, B.: 649 (100)
SIMA, D.: 1594 (244)
SIMEON, J.: 2919 (445), 3083 (474)
SIMHANDL, C.: 107 (17), 1615 (246)
SIMOES, M.: 445 (66)
SIMOES DA FONSECA, J.: 1628 (247), 3015 (462), 2258 (348), 1370 (211), 769 (117), 1599 (245), 1391 (213)
SIMON, B.: 506 (74)
SIMON, M.: 1290 (200)
SIMON, Y.: 3169 (487), 288 (42)
SIMON-SORET, G.: 2139 (325)
SIMONINI, E.: 733 (113)
SIMONS, R.: 869 (131)
SIMONSEN, E.: 1917 (291)
SIMOS, G.: 278 (41), 1352 (209)
SIMPSON, C.: 2324 (358)
SIMPSON, M.: 1817 (278)
SIMS, A.: 1269 (197)
SINGER, L.: 1839 (281), 2882 (440)
SINGER, P.: 15 (4)
SINGH, A.: 2641 (403), 2288 (352), 511 (75), 3078 (473), 1810 (276)
SINGH, R.: 797 (120)
SINGH, S.: 2849 (435)
SINHA, P.: 139 (22)
SINNING, U.: 2994 (457)
SIOMIN, I.: 2178 (330)
SIOMOPOULOS, V.: 1898 (289)
SIRACUSANO, A.: 1751 (264), 1634 (248), 2640 (403), 1531 (236), 2030 (308)
SJOEGREN, I.: 2385 (368)
SJOEHOLM, B.: 2914 (444)
SKAGERLIND, L.: 904 (136)
SKALIDI, M.: 2500 (381), 330 (50)
SKALOUBAKA, D.: 385 (59)
SKALTSI, P.: 1404 (214), 1728 (261), 779 (118)
SKENE, D.: 637 (98)
SKINNER, F.: 2151 (327)
SKLAVOUNOU-TSOUROUKTSOGLOU, S.: 194 (28)
SKONDRAS, S.: 449 (66)
SKOVGAARD, N.: 2865 (438)
SKYDSBJERG, M.: 725 (112)
SKYLLAKOS, A.: 459 (68), 2122 (323)
SLATER, P.: 1817 (278)
SLAYBAUGH, K.: 3008 (461)
SLOAN, E.: 746 (115)
SLUNECKO, T.: 2647 (404)
SMADJA, M.: 1334 (207)
SMEETS, R.: 1883 (287)
SMERALDI, E.: 486 (70)
SMETS, M.: 2135 (325), 2136 (325)
SMITH, M.: 2740 (415)
SMOLOVICH, J.: 2267 (349)
SMULEVICH, A.: 887 (134)

SMYRNIS, N.: 2163 (328), 116 (19), 224 (33), 2160 (328)
SMYTHE, G.: 2114 (322)
SMYTHE, M.: 807 (121)
SNAPE, B.: 1813 (277)
SODERBERG, O.: 227 (33)
SOEGAARD, J.: 1024 (155)
SOERENSEN, S.: 1012 (154)
SOEZER, Y.: 1644 (249)
SOFIA, K.: 1190 (184)
SOFIC, E.: 1386 (212)
SOGAARD, U.: 441 (65)
SOLDATOS, C.: 996 (152), 1174 (181), 1307 (202), 1190 (184), 2345 (362), 1711 (258), 49 (9), 217 (31), 2431 (374), 1173 (181), 2677 (407), 393 (60), 2735 (414)
SOLDATOS, N.: 1906 (290)
SOLDATOS, C.: 1247 (194)
SOLER ARREBOLA, P.: 2276 (350)
SOLER VINOLO, M.: 2276 (350)
SOLOMON, Z.: 2207 (336)
SOLSTAD, K.: 3022 (463)
SOMALO, J.: 370 (56)
SOMANI, P.: 787 (119)
SOMEMURA, K.: 1179 (182)
SOMENZINI, G.: 1893 (288)
SOMMACAL, S.: 1681 (253), 2477 (379)
SONDHEIMER, S.: 1181 (182)
SONGAR, A.: 2065 (314), 1248 (194), 1528 (235)
SONI, S.: 1847 (281), 1346 (208), 1657 (250)
SONNERBORG, A.: 726 (112), 727 (112)
SONNINO, A.: 1604 (245)
SONY, S.: 2915 (444)
SORBI, T.: 2848 (435)
SORENSEN, A.: 441 (65)
SORENSEN, T.: 2493 (381)
SORIA, C.: 3206 (491)
SORIANI, A.: 2501 (382)
SORRI, A.: 2137 (325)
SORRIBES, L.: 1070 (160)
SOSA ORTIZ, A.: 426 (64)
SOUCHE, A.: 1871 (286)
SOUETRE, E.: 634 (98), 633 (98)
SOUFI, H.: 2102 (320), 3204 (491)
SOULAYROL, D.: 403 (61)
SOULAYROL, R.: 403 (61)
SOUSA, M.: 812 (122)
SOUTER, A.: 2714 (412)
SOYKA, M.: 1639 (249)
SPAGNOLI, A.: 2718 (412)
SPECHTMEYER, H.: 239 (35), 2924 (446)
SPENCER, R.: 2727 (414)
SPERNER-UNTERWEGER, B.: 3182 (488)
SPIEL, G.: 1333 (207)
SPINKS, J.: 348 (53)
SPIROPOULOS, J.: 993 (152), 2088 (318)
SPOSATI, P.: 1067 (160)
SPRAGUE, R.: 3082 (474)
SPRING, B.: 1260 (196), 1864 (285)
SPYRAKI, C.: 2159 (328)
SRAM, R.: 136 (21), 450 (66), 2717 (412)
SRIVASTAV, A.: 1165 (180)
ST JEOR, S.: 2091 (318)
ST. GEORGE-HYSLOP, PH.: 2055 (312)
STAAB, B.: 2074 (316), 2079 (316)
STABL, M.: 1380 (212)
STAHL, S.: 237 (35)
STAMBOLIDOU, N.: 1562 (240)
STANDAGE, K.: 746 (115)
STANKOVIC, S.: 2292 (352)
STANLEY, B.: 100 (16)
STANLEY, M.: 100 (16)
STANSFIELD, S.: 1162 (179)
STARACE, F.: 128 (20), 50 (9)

STARCEVIC, V.: 2487 (380), 760 (116), 2259 (348), 1646 (249), 1059 (158), 2691 (409), 3038 (465), 1666 (251)
STARKSTEIN, S.: 1820 (278)
STASSEN, H.: 516 (76)
STATHIS, P.: 993 (152), 2088 (318)
STAVRAKAKI, C.: 1215 (187), 402 (61)
STEELS, J.: 38 (7)
STEFANIS, C.: 2173 (329), 303 (202), 202 (29), 1174 (181), 1103 (166), 728 (112), 2218 (338), 738 (114), 2164 (328), 2160 (328), 2163 (328), 1286 (200), 1473 (226), 1306 (202), 3125 (480), 2775 (422), 116 (19), 392 (60), 2615 (400), 2345 (362), 224 (33), 2735 (414), 2592 (397)
STEFANSSON, J.: 283 (41), 1834 (280), 1824 (279)
STEFINLANGO, P.: 582 (88), 1419 (216)
STEIGER, H.: 2644 (404)
STEIN, A.: 1679 (253)
STEIN, D.: 3177 (488)
STEIN, M.: 984 (150)
STEINBERG, R.: 1375 (211)
STEINER, M.: 2908 (443), 837 (125)
STEINHART, I.: 774 (118)
STEINWACHS, K.: 888 (134), 1706 (255)
STELLA, A.: 1058 (158), 1045 (157)
STELLA, S.: 1182 (182), 76 (13), 1138 (173), 1518 (234), 742 (114), 490 (71)
STENAGER, E.: 929 (141)
STENDER, A.: 3236 (494)
STENFORS, C.: 720 (111), 117 (19)
STENGER, E.: 1723 (260), 980 (149), 2651 (405)
STEPHANATOS, G.: 1920 (291)
STEPHENS, A.: 2146 (326)
STERNBERG, E.: 2524 (385), 2532 (387)
STEWART, M.: 1701 (255)
STIEGLITZ, R.: 1089 (164), 2416 (373), 881 (133), 2415 (373), 1291 (200), 2786 (424)
STILIANAKIS, A.: 194 (28)
STINUS, L.: 21 (4)
STOCK, G.: 1704 (255)
STOCKERT, M.: 35 (7)
STOCKLAND, A.: 2027 (308)
STOCKS, R.: 720 (111)
STOECKL-HINKE, M.: 3055 (468), 1503 (231)
STOECKLIN, K.: 532 (78)
STOESSEL, P.: 2024 (307)
STOHLER, R.: 2649 (404)
STOKLAND, A.: 2295 (352)
STOLINE, A.: 2381 (367)
STOLL, L.: 225 (33)
STOMPE, T.: 1648 (250), 69 (12)
STONE-ELANDER, S.: 2385 (368)
STOREY, P.: 2429 (374)
STOTT, P.: 354 (54)
STOYIANNIDOU, A.: 985 (150)
STRACCA, M.: 2702 (410)
STRAIGHT, B.: 524 (77)
STRAND, M.: 1012 (154)
STRAUBE, A.: 538 (79)
STRAUSS, A.: 268 (39)
STRAUSS, J.: 2621 (401)
STRAUSS, W.: 999 (153), 1015 (154), 1371 (211), 2751 (417)
STREISSGUTH, A.: 1815 (277)
STRIKOVIC, J.: 1257 (195)
STRIPLING, J.: 1363 (210)
STROBL, R.: 964 (147)
STROEMGREN, E.: 1231 (191), 2784 (424), 2609 (399)
STRUCK, M.: 1386 (212)

STRUWE, G.: 2148 (326)
STUCKSTEDTE, H.: 2862 (438)
STUHLMANN, W.: 1496 (230)
STUPPAECK, C.: 3182 (488), 1297 (201)
STURLASON, R.: 120 (19)
STURNIOLO, G.: 1717 (260)
STYLIANIDIS, S.: 3193 (489)
SUAREZ, E.: 3037 (465)
SUAREZ R.: 1054 (158)
SUAREZ-NORIEGA, L.: 1480 (227)
SUBRAHMANYAM, H.: 3045 (466)
SUBSHASH, M.: 1624 (247), 2152 (327), 2153 (327)
SUGAMATA, J.: 1094 (164)
SUGAWARA, M.: 456 (68)
SUKAMAN,: 785 (119)
SULLIVAN, C.: 1753 (265)
SULZER, D.: 2400 (370)
SUNDAY, S.: 287 (42)
SUNDE, D.: 170 (25)
SUNNEN, G.: 2222 (340), 391 (59), 3093 (476)
SUPARGO, A.: 785 (119)
SURMAN, O.: 2665 (406)
SUSANNE, C.: 2169 (329)
SUTET, P.: 2899 (442)
SUWAKI, H.: 3028 (464), 1831 (280)
SUWALK, B.: 1112 (167), 2149 (326)
SUY, E.: 67 (12), 2113 (322), 1651 (250)
SUZUKI, H: 1582 (243), 2810 (430)
SUZUKI, K.: 1703 (255)
SUZUKI, Y.: 1465 (224)
SVARNA, L.: 1737 (262)
SVEDBERG, E.: 2902 (443)
SVENSSON, L.: 1813 (277)
SVENSSON, T.: 527 (78)
SWAHN, C.: 836 (125)
SWAMY, R.: 1112 (167), 2149 (326)
SWANNELL, A.: 1608 (245)
SWANSON, J.: 3081 (474)
SWEDO, S.: 1778 (270)
SYLTE, I.: 1889 (288)
SYNODINOU, C.: 2200 (335), 1364 (210)
SYRENGELAS, M.: 1174 (181), 1190 (184), 996 (152), 1173 (181), 393 (60), 392 (60)
SYROTA, A.: 2871 (439), 2682 (408), 1621 (247)
SYVAELAHTI, E.: 2914 (444)
SZADOCZKY, E.: 431 (64), 416 (63)
SZAFARCZYK, A.: 2729 (414)
SZEGEDI, A.: 638 (98)
SZIGETHY, L.: 83 (14), 1091 (164)
SZMUKLER, G.: 293 (42)
SZULECKA, T.: 1018 (155)
SZYMANSKI, J.: 3202 (490)

T

TACCHINI, G.: 1884 (287), 2599 (397), 1883 (287), 2425 (373)
TADA, K.: 119 (19), 118 (19)
TADALAKI, T.: 1665 (251)
TAESCHNER, K.L.: 64 (12), 2099 (320)
TAGLIAMONTE, A.: 451 (66)
TAILLARD, J.: 1532 (236), 2630 (402), 2671 (407)
TAINTOR, Z.: 62 (11)
TAJIMA, O.: 1707 (255)
TAKAHASHI, A.: 2134 (325)
TAKAHASHI, T.: 2044 (310)
TAKAHASHI, R.: 970 (148)
TAKAHITO, M.: 2095 (319)
TAKAMURA, I.: 2683 (408)
TAKANO, A.: 2133 (325)

TAKASHI, Y.: 2134 (325), 2133 (325)
TAKATSU, O.: 2907 (443), 271 (40), 2390 (368), 2387 (368)
TAKAYAMA, K.: 456 (68)
TAKEDA, M.: 119 (19), 118 (19)
TAKEI, M.: 1041 (156)
TAKESADA, M.: 605 (92)
TAKESHI, S.: 2133 (325)
TAKESHITA, H.: 2119 (323)
TAKRITI, A.: 557 (84)
TALAMO ROSSI, R.: 1045 (157)
TALJAARD, J.: 2369 (366), 2371 (366)
TAMBURINI, R.: 1730 (261)
TAMBURLINI, C.: 2490 (380)
TAMBURRO, G.: 1550 (238)
TAMMAI, Y.: 456 (68)
TAMMINEN, P.: 1011 (154)
TAMMINEN, T.: 2892 (441), 2137 (325), 397 (61)
TAN, T.: 3008 (461), 679 (106)
TANAKA, K.: 574 (87)
TANAKA, T.: 119 (19)
TANELI, B.: 702 (108), 461 (68)
TANELI, S.: 702 (108), 461 (68)
TANINI, N.: 1746 (264), 1029 (156)
TANZI, R.: 2055 (312)
TAPERNON-FRANZ, U.: 534 (79)
TAPFER, M.: 2457 (377)
TAPIA, E.: 1577 (242), 79 (13)
TARELLI, E.: 1200 (185)
TARGA, G.: 1719 (260), 1182 (182), 1518 (234), 742 (114)
TARHAN, N.: 3224 (493), 1900 (289)
TARLATZIS, B.: 1930 (292)
TARLATZIS, I.: 2494 (381), 1930 (292)
TATA-ARCEL, L.: 951 (145), 1483 (227)
TATSUNUMA, T.: 1179 (182)
TAUBERT, S.: 834 (125)
TAVOLA, T.: 1239 (193)
TAWIL, S.: 1000 (153)
TAYLOR, C.: 1076 (162), 1627 (247), 1422 (216)
TAYLOR, P.: 1152 (176)
TAZI, A.: 743 (114)
TEASDALE, T.: 441 (65)
TEGELER, J.: 890 (134), 534 (79), 1995 (302), 1549 (238)
TEIGA, S.: 2460 (377), 1490 (228), 2261 (348)
TEIMOORIAN, M.: 2117 (322)
TEIVISSEN, R.: 3096 (476)
TEJEDOR, C.: 141 (22)
TEKESHI, S.: 2134 (325)
TEKIN, D.: 2826 (432), 1603 (245), 600 (91), 961 (146), 1068 (160)
TELAFERLI, B.: 2065 (314)
TELCHER, M.: 1887 (288)
TELIONI, E.: 2085 (318), 468 (69)
TEMPESTA, E.: 2477 (379), 475 (70), 1243 (193), 1242 (193), 2711 (411), 2465 (378)
TEMPLE, D.: 1472 (225)
TENCH, D.: 1657 (250)
TERASHIMA, S.: 331 (51), 630 (97)
TERLIDOU, C.: 1661 (251), 1662 (251)
TERRA, J.: 1304 (202), 1367 (210), 438 (65)
TERRIBILE, P.: 1523 (235), 614 (93)
TERZANO, M.: 2672 (407), 653 (100)
TERZIEV, D.: 1216 (187)
TESSERA, M.: 2953 (448)
TETSUKA, I.: 3036 (465)
TEYSSIER, J.: 135 (21)
THALASSINOS, N.: 1176 (181)
THALEN, B.: 879 (133)
THAU, K.: 1615 (246)
THEANDER, S.: 291 (42)

THEESEN, K.: 2560 (392)
THENAULT, M.: 2026 (307)
THEOBALD, W.: 1051 (157)
THEODOROPOULOU-VAIDAKI, S.: 3222 (493), 1103 (166), 3223 (493), 956 (145)
THEODOROU, C.: 1190 (184), 996 (152)
THEODORSSON, E.: 117 (19)
THIEBOT,: 2732 (414)
THIEKOTER, T.: 1119 (170)
THOMALSKE, G.: 1515 (233)
THOMANN, R.: 2562 (392)
THOMAS, N.: 2685 (408)
THOMAS, P.: 2586 (396)
THOME, J.: 1200 (185)
THORESSON, P.: 904 (136)
THORNICROFT, G.: 566 (85)
THUSHOLDT, F.: 441 (65), 3213 (492)
TIDWELL, D.: 1765 (267)
TIGANOV, A.: 1284 (200), 1234 (191)
TIGNOL, J.: 21 (4)
TILLER, J.: 1777 (270), 1849 (282)
TIMEV, T.: 2840 (434), 2839 (434), 1585 (243)
TIMOTIJEVIC, I.: 1541 (237), 1616 (246)
TIMOYIANNAKI, M.: 385 (59)
TIMSIT, M.: 2184 (332)
TIMSIT-B.: 2539 (388), 1526 (235), 2184 (332)
TISSOT, R.: 430 (64), 1128 (172)
TOCCAFONDI, F.: 558 (84)
TODD, N.: 1095 (164)
TODD, R.: 130 (21)
TOELLE, R.: 665 (103)
TOENNE, U.: 2470 (378)
TOGNETTI, P.: 1017 (155), 1016 (155)
TOKAIRIN, T.: 2387 (368)
TOKER,: 1552 (239)
TOKER,: 1922 (292)
TOLANI-ASUNI, U.: 2210 (337)
TOLDY, L.: 2457 (377)
TOLEDANO, A.: 226 (33)
TOLGAY, A.: 1064 (159)
TOLIS, G.: 215 (31), 217 (31), 2530 (387)
TOLVANEN, E.: 2137 (325)
TOLVANEN, S.: 2930 (446)
TOMARAS, V.: 2592 (397), 84 (14), 2233 (344), 692 (107)
TOMASELLI, G.: 1031 (156)
TOMASI, C.: 2687 (408)
TOMOV, T.: 1856 (283), 919 (139)
TOMRUK, N.: 2252 (347), 536 (79)
TONDO, L.: 1569 (241), 710 (109), 1565 (241), 736 (113)
TONELLI, F.: 1178 (182)
TOPINKA, J.: 136 (21), 450 (66), 2717 (412)
TOPITZ, A.: 1615 (246), 107 (17), 1345 (208), 837 (125)
TOPUZOVIC, N.: 350 (53)
TORGERSEN, S.: 2249 (346), 1981 (299)
TORO, J.: 1669 (252), 75 (13), 2616 (400)
TORRE, E.: 1739 (263), 2477 (379)
TORRECANO,: 1400 (214)
TORRES, R.: 259 (38), 2981 (455), 2982 (455)
TORTA, R.: 859 (129), 1351 (209)
TOSCA, P.: 1893 (288)
TOTH, I.: 2457 (377)
TOTIC, S.: 1361 (210)
TOUARI, M.: 1759 (266), 597 (91)
TOUHAM, M.: 2202 (335), 365 (56)
TOULOUMIS, C.: 940 (143)
TOURLENTES, T.: 2019 (306)
TOUSINA, A.: 2494 (381)
TOUTOUZAS, P.: 680 (106)
TOUYZ, S.: 3007 (461), 3004 (459)

TOWIE, L.: 716 (110)
TOYODA, K.: 2777 (422), 2911 (444)
TRABALLI, C.: 2895 (441)
TRABER, J.: 596 (90), 2881 (440), 1078 (162), 1079 (162), 236 (35)
TRAKAS, D.: 2693 (409)
TRAMONI, A.: 1402 (214), 428 (64)
TRASKMAN-B.: 100 (16), 738 (114)
TRAUBE, R.: 2804 (428)
TRAVASSO, B.: 2596 (397)
TRAVER, J.: 2444 (376)
TRAVERSO, J.: 183 (27)
TREASURE, J.: 292 (42)
TREMEL, E.: 1262 (196)
TRENKAMP, E.: 2269 (349)
TRENKEL, M.: 447 (66), 2463 (378)
TRIANTAFILLOU, T.: 1906 (290)
TRIANTAFYLLOU, M.: 3051 (467)
TRICOT, L.: 608 (92)
TRIDENTI, A.: 3024 (463), 682 (106), 2962 (449), 1178 (182)
TRIEBIG, G.: 3040 (466)
TRIFONOVA, E.: 2239 (345), 2934 (447)
TRIKAS, P.: 1525 (235)
TRIKKAS, G.: 1729 (261), 2498 (381), 1925 (292)
TRIPODIANAKIS, J.: 3223 (493), 956 (145), 3222 (493)
TRISELIOTIS, J.: 3146 (483)
TRIVEDI, J.: 797 (120), 2273 (350), 139 (22)
TROISI, A.: 2848 (435), 765 (117), 2190 (333)
TROPPER, M.: 2506 (382), 2869 (438), 223 (33)
TROTT, G.: 1459 (223), 1461 (223), 911 (138), 913 (138), 1460 (223)
TRUJILLO, M.: 645 (99)
TSAKIRI, M.: 2500 (381)
TSALIKOGLOU, F.: 2814 (430)
TSALTAS, E.: 116 (19), 149 (23)
TSARA, V.: 3047 (467)
TSARMAKLI, H.: 1906 (290)
TSEGOS, I.: 1661 (251), 1660 (251), 1662 (251), 2701 (410), 806 (121), 3108 (478)
TSEMPERLIDOU, M.: 161 (24)
TSERPE, B.: 1741 (263)
TSIANTIS, Z.: 523 (77), 987 (150), 361 (55), 1241 (193), 988 (150), 2764 (419), 1124 (171)
TSILIMIGAKI, B.: 1660 (251), 2701 (410)
TSITOURIDES, S.: 772 (117)
TSITSIDAKIS, K,: 330 (50)
TSONEVA-PENTCHEVA, L.: 125 (20)
TSOUKARELA, A.: 459 (68)
TSUANG, M.: 99 (16), 103 (17)
TSUJI, M.: 753 (115)
TSURUMI, K.: 423 (64)
TSUTSULKOVSKAYA, T.: 1105 (166)
TUCHMAN, A.: 16 (4)
TUEPER, E.: 702 (108)
TUNCA, M.: 1619 (246)
TUNCA, Z.: 1619 (246), 1423 (216)
TUNCEL,: 1552 (239)
TUNCER, C.: 1056 (158), 1837 (280)
TUNDO, A.: 710 (109), 1569 (241), 420 (63), 394 (60)
TUNE L.: 2391 (368)
TUNG, C.: 527 (78)
TURKOGLU, A.: 1528 (235)
TURNER, P.: 2458 (377)
TURNER, S.: 476 (70)
TURNIER, L.: 1206 (186)
TUROLA, M.: 1719 (260), 1182 (182)
TWOMEY, M.: 1019 (155)
TYANO, S.: 1339 (207), 1338 (207)

TYHOPOULOS, G.: 1038 (156)
TYPALDOU, M.: 434 (65)
TYRER, S.: 2526 (386)
TYSZKIEWICZ, M.: 2132 (325), 671 (104)
TZANAKAKI, M.: 330 (50), 2123 (323), 2500 (381)
TZAVARAS, A.: 1270 (197)
TZAVARAS, N.: 1750 (264), 3165 (486), 2081 (317), 1034 (156), 1180 (182), Chair (264), 386 (59), 1126 (171)
TZEBELIKOS, E.: 3227 (493), 3228 (493)
TZEDAKI, M.: 1398 (214)
TZEMOS, J.: 392 (60)
TZERANIS, S.: 385 (59)
TZIMOS, A.: 893 (135)
TZIOUFAS, A.: 70 (12)
TZIVARIDOU, D.: 1929 (292), 588 (89), 824 (123)
TZONOU, A.: 1925 (292)
TZOURIO, N.: 2682 (408)

U

UCHA UDABE, R.: 2260 (348), 2895 (441)
UCHINUMA, Y.: 2859 (437)
UCOK, A.: 684 (106)
UDELMAN, D.: 1161 (179)
UDELMAN, H.: 1161 (179)
UDINA, C.: 2401 (370), 935 (142), 934 (142)
UEBELHACK, R.: 1382 (212)
UEMATSU, M.: 423 (64)
UEMOTO, M.: 1036 (156)
UGEDO, L.: 527 (78)
ULIN, J.: 2386 (368)
ULISSE, T.: 1629 (247)
ULMAR, G.: 2862 (438)
ULRICH, G.: 2294 (352)
ULRICHSEN, J.: 2376 (366)
UNAI, Y.: 589 (89), 1546 (238)
UNDEN, M.: 592 (90)
UNER,: 1922 (292)
UNLUOGLU, G.: 273 (40)
UNO, M.: 2513 (383)
UNSORG, B.: 1841 (281)
UNVERZAGT, C.: 2673 (407)
UPADHYAYA, A.: 2658 (405), 2388 (368)
URIARTE, V.: 1027 (155), 3129 (480)
URSANO, R.: 2744 (416)
URWAND, S.: 1415 (215)
USHAKOV, Y.: 2127 (324)
USTUN, T.: 1854 (283)
UYGUR, N.: 814 (122)
UZBEKOV, M.: 1409 (215), 2684 (408)
UZUNOGLU, N.: 2173 (329), 2775 (422)

V

VACHER, J.: 1000 (153)
VACHTSEVANOS, P.: 940 (143)
VADDADI, K.: 1843 (281)
VAEISAENEN, E.: 819 (122), Chair (122), 1821 (279)
VAEZI, S.: 2083 (317)
VAGEN, R.: 855 (128)
VAGLUM, F.: 2248 (346)
VAGLUM, P.: 1877 (287)
VAGLUM, S.: 2248 (346), 1877 (287)
VAIDAKIS, N.: 2825 (432), 1700 (255), 334 (51), 335 (51), 2991 (457), 1416 (216), Chair (432)
VAJARUND, N.: 2669 (406), 2448 (376)
VALENTE, R.: 1032 (156)
VALENTINI, C.: 2951 (448)
VALERGAKI, H.: 1700 (255)

VALERI, M.: 1894 (288)
VALESINI, G.: 1927 (292)
VALITUTTI, C.: 1927 (292)
VALITUTTI, I.: 998 (152)
VALITUTTI, R.: 990 (151), 1389 (213), 995 (152), 2662 (406)
VALLEJO, J.: 958 (146), 415 (63), 795 (120), 1356 (209)
VALLERY-MASSON, E.: 569 (86)
VALLES, A.: 1669 (252), 75 (13)
VALSAMIDIS, S.: 680 (106)
VALVASSORI, G.: 272 (40), 413 (63)
VALVERDE, O.: 448 (66)
VAMOS, P.: 2482 (380)
VAN, H.: 1680 (253)
VAN BEMMEL, A.: 651 (100), 652 (100), 2105 (321)
VAN BERKESTIJN, H.: 2542 (388), 2167 (329)
VAN BRABANT, E.: 2539 (388)
VAN BROEDKHOVEN, C.: 2055 (312)
VAN DAMME, G.: 2450 (376)
VAN DE WOESTIJNE, K.: 2266 (349)
VAN DEN BERGH, O.: 2266 (349)
VAN DEN BRINK, W.: 1288 (200)
VAN DEN HOOFDAKKER, R.: 2631 (402), 2633 (402), 666 (103), 2542 (388), 2344 (362), 667 (103)
VAN DER ENDE, J.: 2616 (400), 2619 (400)
VAN DER LAAR, M.: 474 (70)
VAN DER MAST, R.: 660 (102)
VAN DER MEERCH, V.: 593 (90)
VAN DIEST, R.: 2105 (321), 652 (100)
VAN DIJK, L.: 1183 (183)
VAN DRIEL, G.: 2867 (438)
VAN GINNEKEN, C.: 474 (70)
VAN HEERINGEN, C.: 1519 (234), 2789 (425)
VAN HEERTUM, R.: 2340 (361)
VAN HOOF, J.: 2247 (346)
VAN KAMMEN, D.: 930 (142), 2557 (392), 695 (107)
VAN KAMMEN, W.: 695 (107)
VAN LUYN, J. B.: 3095 (476)
VAN MIER, H.: 2247 (346)
VAN MOFFAERT, M.: 1519 (234), 2450 (376), 2791 (425)
VAN PRAAG, H.: 1494 (229), 3070 (472), 2796 (285), 2216 (338)
VAN PUTTEN, T.: 2800 (427), 2410 (372)
VAN RENSBURG, P.: 2093 (319), 1450 (221)
VAN VALKENBURG, C.: 852 (128), 1107 (167), 853 (128)
VAN WEEL, E.: 971 (148)
VANDEL, S.: 359 (54)
VANDEN BUSSCHE, G.: 1495 (229)
VANDENDRIESSCHE, F.: 2266 (349)
VANDEWOUDE, M.: 1647 (250), 2113 (322)
VANELLE, J.: 2564 (392)
VANIER, B.: 2475 (379)
VANONI, R.: 3019 (462)
VANTINI, G.: 1110 (167)
VANZULLI, L.: 1392 (213)
VAPORIDOU, E.: 1144 (174)
VARANDAS, P: 757 (116)
VARELA, J.: 329 (50)
VARGAS-PENA, E.: 296 (43)
VARMA, L.: 2284 (351)
VARMA, V.: 3113 (479), 1563 (240), 1775 (269), 2607 (399), 542 (80), 2797 (426)
VARON, D.: 1933 (293)
VAROQUAUX, O.: 1077 (162), 2475 (379), 2029 (308)

VARTANIAN, M.: 2405 (371)
VARTZOPOULOS, D.: 173 (26), 172 (26)
VASLAMATZIS, G.: 2351 (363), 808 (121), 1741 (263), 269 (39), 2584 (396), 2582 (396), 2350 (363), 2052 (311), 2015 (306), 2992 (457)
VASSEUR, C.: 153 (23)
VASSILIOU, G.: 920 (139)
VASSILOPOULOS, D.: 377 (57)
VASSILOPOULOU, E.: 85 (14), 1876 (286), 3047 (467)
VAUDRY, H.: 2729 (414)
VAUSE, M.: 1580 (243), 2852 (436), 263 (39)
VAZ, L.: 1607 (245)
VAZ-SERRA, A.: 2445 (376), 812 (122), 74 (13)
VAZQUEZ, A.: 1590 (244)
VEGA, M.: 440 (65), 1623 (247), 1692 (254), 2958 (449), 1087 (163), 1633 (248)
VEIJOLA, J.: 1821 (279), 264 (39),), 819 (122)
VELA BUENO, A.: 2677 (407), 109 (18), 2046 (310), 2676 (407)
VELIA, G.: 1751 (264), 1634 (248), 1531 (236), 2030 (308), 1090 (164), 2587 (396), 3197 (490), 1927 (292), 587 (89), 2640 (403)
VELTRO, F.: 50 (9)
VENDER, S.: 3208 (491)
VENGA, E.: 1584 (243), 2851 (436)
VENISSE, J.: 2109 (321)
VENIZELOS, N.: 2385 (368), 938 (143)
VENTAYOL, P.: 1421 (216)
VENTOURAS, E.: 2173 (329)
VENTURA, T.: 1795 (274)
VENTURI, L.: 454 (67)
VENUTO, G.: 128 (20)
VERA, L.: 1631 (248)
VERCRUYSSEN, V.: 1196 (184)
VERGANI, D.: 992 (151)
VERGOUWEN, H.: 3094 (476)
VERIMLI, A.: 1552 (239), 1210 (186)
VERMA, S.: 2149 (326), 1588 (244), 1335 (207)
VERMAAK, W.: 213 (31)
VERNAZA, P.: 403 (61)
VERSCHOOR, T.: 2093 (319)
VERSIANI, M.: 1851 (282)
VERVENIOTIS, S.: 3219 (492)
VERWEY, H.: 851 (128)
VETTERSKOG, K.: 1012 (154)
VETTRAINO, M.: 2146 (326)
VGONTZAS, A.: 854 (128), 2676 (407), 2637 (403), 679 (106)
VIAL, M.: 2896 (442)
VIANU, I.: 609 (93), 2571 (394)
VICENTE, A.: 768 (117), 2581 (395), 1002 (153)
VICENTE, N.: 2710 (411), 1911 (290)
VIDALIS, A.: 809 (121)
VIDREAU, C.: 3176 (487)
VIEIRA, B.: 3139 (481)
VIEIRA, C.: 2107 (321)
VIEIRA, R.: 3139 (481)
VIETA, E.: 3216 (492), 2585 (396), 1625 (247)
VIKANDER, B.: 2470 (378)
VILHENA, F.: 2484 (380)
VILLA, T.: 825 (123)
VILLASANA, A.: 1039 (156), 1595 (244), 1654 (250)
VILLATORO, J.: 47 (9)
VILMART, T.: 1388 (213)
VINAS, R.: 1633 (248), 1623 (247), 1692 (254), 2219 (338), 1468 (225)

VINCENDON, G.: 1962 (296)
VINCENTE, B.: 3120 (479)
VINCI, G.: 2874 (439), 1650 (250)
VINE, D.: 595 (90)
VINNARS, E.: 720 (111)
VIRZI, A.: 486 (70)
VISINTINI, R.: 1395 (213)
VISKELETI, G.: 489 (70)
VISOTSKI, H.: 921 (139)
VITA, A.: 1587 (244), 1395 (213), 272 (40), 413 (63)
VITIELLO, B.: 1408 (215)
VIZNER, T.: 1253 (195)
VLACHONIKOLIS, J.: 1286 (200)
VLOTTES, P.: 2890 (441), 2891 (441)
VODERHOLZER, U.: 1300 (202), 1172 (181)
VOEGELI, J.: 1674 (252)
VOGE HARMS, D.: 1217 (187), 1959 (296)
VOGEL, R.: 777 (118), 2993 (457), 147 (22), 1547 (238)
VOHRA, A.: 1207 (186)
VOLANVKA, J.: 2245 (346), 1341 (208)
VOLKER, B.: 2993 (457)
VOLKOW, MD: 2740 (415)
VOLLRATH, M.: 3130 (480)
VOLMAT, R.: 359 (54), 1113 (168)
VOLONTE, M.: 487 (70)
VOLTAIRE, A.: 1293 (201)
VOLTERRA, V.: 2277 (351)
VOLZ, H.: 881 (133), 1704 (255)
VON BOSE, M.: 2716 (412)
VON CRANACH, M.: 2225 (342)
VON DISSELKAMP TIETZE, J.: 2112 (322)
VON FRENCKELL, R.: 2428 (374), 2540 (388), 3229 (494), 1870 (286), 1869 (286), 1014 (154)
VON KNORRING, A.: 3145 (483), 2755 (418)
VON KNORRING, L.: 2758 (418), 1512 (233)
VON OEFELE, K.: 1842 (281)
VORONKOVA, T.: 1105 (166)
VOSLOO, H.: 564 (85)
VOSTANIS, P.: 807 (121), 3159 (486), 2698 (410)
VOUKIKLARIS, G.: 784 (119), 267 (39)
VOULGARI, A.: 377 (57), 1925 (292)
VOUTSAS, A.: 523 (77)
VOYATZAKI, Z.: 806 (121), 1660 (251)
VRANAKIS, M.: 1685 (253)
VRANESIC, D.: 1380 (212)
VRASTI, R.: 2618 (400), 2614 (400), 2620 (400)
VRETOU, H.: 1925 (292)
VRIJLANDT, A.: 2568 (393)
VUCINIC, G.: 350 (53)

W

WAARST, S.: 2507 (382)
WACKER, H.: 1381 (212), 715 (110)
WADA, H.: 2846 (435)
WAGEMAKER, H.: 933 (142)
WAGNER, H.: 2391 (368)
WAHJONO, S.: 2274 (350)
WAHL, G.: 2963 (450)
WAHLSTROEM, J.: 1235 (192)
WAHLUND, B.: 1080 (162)
WAHLUND, L.: 697 (108), 699 (108), 726 (112), 727 (112), 2902 (443)
WAKELIN, J.: 1498 (230)
WALDERMAR, H.: 2069 (315)
WALDVOGEL, D.: 694 (107)
WALDVOGEL, F.: 1226 (189)

WALKER, J.: 2855 (437), 306 (46)
WALKER, R.: 1177 (181)
WALKER, S.: 402 (61)
WALLACE, C.: 2802 (427)
WALLER, S.: 861 (129)
WALLIS, G.: 1568 (241), 1267 (197)
WALLOT, H.: 1191 (184)
WALSH, T.: 2012 (305)
WALTER, H.: 964 (147), 965 (147), 677 (105), 837 (125), 2908 (443)
WALTON, V.: 2307 (354)
WAMSLEY, J.: 595 (90)
WANG, M.: 1163 (179)
WANG, X.: 735 (113)
WANG, Y.: 970 (148)
WARBURTON, E.: 904 (136)
WARD, J.: 184 (27)
WARD, S.: 294 (43)
WARTEL, R.: 2685 (408), 1411 (215)
WASIK, A.: 1697 (255)
WASYLENKI, D.: 2017 (306), 3221 (492), 186 (27), 1485 (228)
WATANABE, T.: 457 (68)
WATANUKI, K.: 816 (122)
WATERS, E.: 3147 (483)
WATSON, J.: 689 (107), 2761 (419), 690 (107)
WAUSCHKUHN, C.: 2299 (353)
WAUTHY, J.: 2428 (374)
WDOWIAK, J.: 2558 (392), 463 (68)
WEBB, M.: 124 (20)
WEBER, B.: 1638 (248)
WEGENER, B.: 2996 (458), 2997 (458)
WEGENER, H.: 1043 (157)
WEHR, T.: 708 (109)
WEIDENHAMMER, T.: 3040 (466)
WEIDENHAMMER, W.: 382 (58)
WEILL, M.: 160 (24)
WEINBERGER, F.: 2570 (394)
WEISAETH, L.: 2743 (416)
WEISE, C.: 1555 (239)
WEISERT, A.: 1243 (193), 2711 (411)
WEISS, G.: 2972 (452)
WEISS, J.: 1365 (210)
WEISSMAN, M.: 253 (37), 92 (15), 2323 (358)
WELCHER, B.: 3225 (493)
WELDON, K.: 2253 (347)
WELLS, K.: 305 (45)
WELLS, P.: 1337 (207)
WENDT, G.: 3050 (467), 357 (54), 2888 (441), 2476 (379), 2296 (353), 1382 (212), 1383 (212), 1384 (212)
WENG, Y.: 1429 (217)
WENNBERG, A.: 2148 (326)
WERNER, J.: 1915 (291)
WERNICKE, J.: 1282 (199)
WERRY, J.: 3079 (474)
WERTHEIMER, J.: 2889 (441)
WESLEY LIBB, J.: 2292 (352)
WESNER, R.: 3121 (480)
WESSELS, W.: 3116 (479), 472 (69)
WEST, D.: 2529 (386), 1809 (276)
WESTBERG, P.: 555 (84)
WESTENBERG, H.: 421 (63), 960 (146)
WESTERBERGH, S.: 1348 (208), 535 (79)
WESTLIND-DANIELSSON, A.: 2727 (414)
WESTPHAL, E.: 828 (124)
WESTPHAL, K.: 3143 (482)
WESTRIN, C.: 189 (27), 631 (97)
WETTERBERG, L.: 699 (108), 726 (112), 727 (112), 879 (133), 697 (108), 1080 (162), 2902 (443), 4 (1), 1237 (192)
WETZEL, H.: 857 (129), 638 (98)
WETZEL, R.: 1223 (188)
WHALLEY, L.: 1023 (155), 720 (111)

WHEATLEY, D.: 1314 (204)
WHIPPLE, S.: 3032 (465)
WHITE, R.: 502 (73)
WHITEHEAD, A.: 1049 (157), 1018 (155), 1019 (155)
WHITELEY, J.: 3106 (478)
WHITFIELD, H.: 2531 (387)
WHITTON, P.: 2728 (414)
WHITWORTH, A.: 1297 (201)
WIDLÖCHER, D.: 1535 (236), 2289 (352), 455 (68), 2312 (356)
WIDMER, J.: 1128 (172), 430 (64)
WIEGAND, M.: 2900 (442), 882 (133), 2655(405)
WIESBECK, G.: 64 (12)
WIESEL, F.: 938 (143), 2739 (415), 2385 (368), 2412 (372)
WIESELMANN, B.: 1524 (235)
WIESELMANN, G.: 1302 (202)
WIG, N.: 1140 (174), 5 (2), 1790 (272)
WILDER, R.: 2532 (387)
WILDT, P.: 1645 (249)
WILL, S.: 3039 (465)
WILLARD-SCHRÖDER, D.: 1839 (281), 2882 (440)
WILLIAMS, E.: 1215 (187), 402 (61)
WILLINGER, G.: 2096 (319)
WILMS, G.: 1331 (206)
WILSON, K.: 2388 (368)
WILSON, L.: 2455 (377)
WILSON, O.: 56 (11)
WILSON, R.: 3121 (480)
WINAND, R.: 66 (12)
WINCHEL, R.: 100 (16)
WINCKLER, P.: 2913 (444)
WING, J.: 1772 (269), 9 (3)
WINKELMANN, M.: 1300 (202), 1171 (181)
WINKELMANN, Y.: 2638 (403)
WINNING, R.: 2889 (441), 1075 (161)
WINTER, P.: 2176 (330)
WIRSHING, W.: 2802 (427)
WIRZ-JUSTICE, A.: 2649 (404)
WISE, T.: 2827 (432)
WISTEDT, B.: 559 (84), 1004 (153), 2757 (418), 1157 (176), 1163 (176)
WITKOWSKI, R: 1664 (251), 2699 (410), 762 (116), 2090 (318), 1044 (157), 185 (27)
WITT, U.: 2117 (322)
WITTCHEN, H.: 3002 (459), 712 (110), 314 (48)
WIZENBERG, P.: 639 (98)
WODARZ, N.: 432 (64)
WÖRZ, R.: 1511 (233), 763 (116)
WOESTENBURG, J.: 2867 (438)
WOGGON, B.: 1844 (281)
WOLF, A.: 2740 (415)
WOLF, R.: 107 (17)
WOLFERSDORF, M.: 1916 (291), 2888 (441), 147 (22), 2036 (309)
WOLFSON, S.: 1408 (215)
WOLKIN, A.: 2327 (359), 2740 (415)
WOLPERT, E.: 2595 (397), 2175 (330)
WONG, D.: 2391 (368)
WONNACOTT, S.: 1049 (157)
WOODALL, J.: 1453 (222), 1454 (222)
WORBY, C.: 2384 (367), 3085 (475)
WORBY, M.: 3087 (475), 2384 (367)
WORSAAE N.: 3171 (487)
WRIGHT, P.: 1499 (230)

WU, J.: 873 (132), 210 (30)
WUERMLE, O.: 694 (107)
WUNDERINK, A.: 484 (70), 485 (70)
WURTHMANN, C.: 1496 (230)
WYNNE, L.: 2610 (399)
WYPERT, D.: 2168 (329)

X

XAGORARI, E.: 803 (121)
XAVIER DA SILVEIRA, F.: 443 (66)
XU, M.: 2661 (406)
XYROMERITIS, C.: 393 (60)

Y

Y LEAL H.: 1570 (241)
YAGI, G.: 2926 (446), 1703 (255), 1707 (255), 3150 (484), 1702 (255)
YALOURIS, A.: 3223 (493), 956 (145), 3222 (493)
YAMADA, H.: 1041 (156)
YAMADA, K.: 2912 (444), 201 (29)
YAMADA, Y.: 704 (108)
YAMAGISHI, H.: 753 (115)
YAMAGUCHI, M.: 1688 (254)
YAMAGUCHI, T.: 1688 (254)
YAMAMOTOVA, A.: 706 (109)
YAMAN, M.: 814 (122)
YAMASAKI, T.: 2741 (415)
YAMASHITA, I.: 2970 (451)
YAMASHITA, T.: 118 (19)
YAMATODANI, A.: 2846 (435)
YAMAZAKI, K.: 605 (92), 514 (75), 2683 (408), 364 (55)
YAN, H.: 735 (113)
YANAGISAWA, Y.: 1707 (255)
YANEZ, R.: 132 (21)
YANG, M.: 2124 (323)
YANGUELA, J.: 370 (56)
YANNITSI, S.: 688 (107), 70 (12)
YANNOPOULOS, A.: 1525 (235)
YARYURA, R.: 1422 (216)
YARYURA-TOBIAS, J.: 38 (7), 1422 (216), 1076 (162), 39 (7)
YAVASCAOGLU, C.: 702 (108)
YAVUZ, D.: 1900 (289), 224 (493)
YEH, E.: 369 (56), 2794 (426)
YEH, Y.: 369 (56)
YERASI, S.: 1106 (167)
YFANTOPOULOS, J.: 1489 (228)
YIOMELA, E.: 1662 (251), 3164 (486)
YLIKERTTULA, A.: 1944 (294)
YOKOTA, S.: 2777 (422)
YONEDA, H.: 2777 (422), 2911 (444)
YORIO, A.: 3018 (462)
YOSHIDA, H.: 423 (64)
YOSHIMASU, K.: 1897 (289), 2792 (426)
YOSHIOKA, H.: 1094 (164)
YOTOVA, Y.: 2905 (443)
YOUNG, L.: 1244 (193)
YOUSSEF, I.: 1106 (167), 137 (21)
YU, K.: 348 (53)
YUGIN, Y.: 2179 (330)
YÜKSEL, S.: 684 (106), 2302 (354), 3026 (463)

Z

ZACHARIADIS, I.: 126 (20), 1833 (280)
ZACHARIADIS, N.: 1420 (216), 3103 (477)
ZADOR, G.: 3185 (488)
ZAFIRAKOPOULOU, C.: 692 (107)
ZAFRA, J.: 1033 (156)
ZAGER, R.: 1212 (187)
ZAHLTEN, W.: 2296 (353)
ZAKI, A.: 3122 (480)
ZALONIS, J.: 728 (112)
ZAMPERETTI, M.: 992 (151), 991 (151)
ZANALDA, E.: 859 (129)
ZANDBERGEN, J.: 3126 (480), 412 (63)
ZANETTI JUNIOR, D.: 618 (94)
ZANNI, G.: 2014 (306)
ZAPLETALEK, M.: 1383 (212)
ZAPOTOCZKY, H.: 3203 (490)
ZAPPALAGLIO, C.: 1031 (156)
ZAPPAROLI, G.: 903 (136)
ZARATO, R.: 259 (38)
ZARCONE, V.: 1329 (206)
ZARIFIAN, E.: 308 (47), 1469 (225)
ZARUCHAS, W.: 3031 (464)
ZASLOVE, M.: 615 (93)
ZAUDIG, M.: 2418 (373), 2716 (412), 2419 (373), 1283 (200)
ZAUGG, C.: 694 (107)
ZECH-UBER, G.: 464 (68)
ZEITTER, C.: 778 (118)
ZELASCHI, N.: 1054 (158)
ZEMISHLANY, Z.: 849 (128)
ZEPPETELLI, E.: 1243 (193), 1242 (193), 2711 (411)
ZERBI, F.: 1893 (288)
ZERBONI, R.: 992 (151)
ZERVIS, C.: 81 (13), 2200 (335)
ZERVOS, C.: 1685 (253)
ZERVOU, A.: 2670 (406)
ZHARIKOV, N.: 1793 (273)
ZHEIDAN, A.: 2703 (410)
ZHENG, Z.: 889 (134)
ZIBIT, M.: 2854 (436)
ZIEGLER, P.: 575 (87)
ZIELINSKY, C.: 69 (12)
ZILBOVICIUS, M.: 2682 (408)
ZILIO, R.: 491 (71)
ZIMMER, H.: 2747 (417)
ZIMMERMANN, M.: 1839 (281), 2882 (440)
ZINNER, H.: 901 (136)
ZIOUDROU, C.: 2164 (328), 2163 (328)
ZIS, A.: 214 (31)
ZIYALAN, M.: 2823 (431), 2089 (318), 1064 (159)
ZIZOLFI, S.: 1548 (238), 1093 (164)
ZLOTNIK, G.: 3171 (487)
ZOGRAFOU, M.: 1404 (214), 779 (118)
ZOHAR, J.: 34 (7)
ZOJES, D.: 588 (89), 824 (123)
ZOLESI, O.: 1747 (264), 451 (66)
ZOLLI, P.: 1937 (293), 2375 (366), 2707 (411)
ZORC, J.: 1887 (288)
ZORIN, N.: 2939 (447)
ZOUMADAKI, A.: 2500 (381), 2123 (323)
ZOUNI, M.: 693 (107), 690 (107)
ZUMBRUNNEN, R.: 3097 (476)
ZURITA, P.: 2648 (404)
ZWANIKKEN, G.: 317 (49), 1986 (300)

SUBJECT INDEX

Affective disorders: 1, 29, 35, 37, 57, 109, 113, 117, 133, 188, 192, 202, 218, 230, 241, 248, 253, 264, 278, 282, 284, 309, 321, 324, 338, 356, 362, 382, 388, 389, 402, 405, 414, 418, 420, 441, 459
AIDS: 112, 151, 193, 293, 411
Alcohol Abuse: 56, 116, 158, 180, 201, 205, 249, 265, 277, 366, 465
Alzheimer's Disease: 115, 135, 274, 312, 360, 438
Anxiety disorders: 23, 35, 60, 104, 161, 179, 302, 353
Art and Psychiatry: 69, 189, 259, 267, 318, 355

Borderline Personality disorders: 363

Child and Adolescent Psychiatry: 13, 28, 36, 55, 61, 77, 92, 130, 138, 144, 148, 150, 171, 175, 187, 207, 215, 223, 242, 252, 271, 276, 303, 369, 395, 408, 428, 445, 474, 483
Chronobiology: 98, 103, 402
Classification: 2, 105, 131, 191, 200, 213, 283, 287, 342, 373
Conversion disorders: 26
Cultural issues: 3, 6, 34, 114, 131, 139, 149, 231, 298, 304, 306, 334, 350, 357, 371, 399, 426, 431, 437, 479

Diagnosis: 32, 37, 41, 76, 93, 105, 110, 127, 153, 191, 243, 351, 424, 435, 452, 494
Disasters: 9, 416
Drug Abuse: 4, 66, 81, 116, 280, 320, 378, 380, 451

Eating disorders: 42, 83, 94, 106, 257, 305, 369, 404, 449, 459, 461, 487,
Education in Psychiatry: 203, 220, 367, 418, 475, 491
EEG and Clinical Neurophysiology in Psychiatry: 87, 132, 194, 235, 329, 443
Electroconvulsive Therapy: 67, 111, 226, 347
Emergency Psychiatry: 198, 219, 307, 476
Epidemiology: 20, 45, 88, 95, 106, 148, 156, 173, 274, 279, 280, 468, 489
Ethics in Psychiatry: 97, 394, 454, 458, 485

Family issues: 14, 122, 183, 344, 375, 400, 465
Forensic Psychiatry: 51, 75, 91, 266, 319, 350, 473

General Hospital Psychiatry: 38, 152, 210, 234, 256, 260, 365, 406, 455
Genetics: 21, 86, 192

History of Psychiatry: 5, 8, 52, 74, 317, 331, 389

Information Processing: 196
Insomnia: 310, 353

Liaison Psychiatry: 152, 210, 365, 387, 453, 455

Mental Retardation: 49, 126
Military Psychiatry: 262, 336

Neurochemistry: 29, 35, 142, 143, 162, 285, 359, 370
Neuroimaging: 30, 108, 125, 368, 415, 443
Neurology: 433, 466

Obsessive Compulsive Disorder: 7, 85, 209, 247, 270
Organic Mental Disorders: 68, 86, 112, 205, 274, 312, 326, 390, 438, 466

Panic disorder: 15, 47, 63, 84, 127, 146, 169, 349, 480
Personality disorders: 159, 289, 299, 320, 363
Psychopharmacology:
  – Antidepressants: 25, 35, 54, 62, 90, 100, 155, 163, 199, 212, 232, 233, 236, 239, 253, 282, 284, 321, 352, 388, 405, 414, 420, 444, 448
  – Antipsychotic drugs: 70, 79, 95, 129, 137, 176, 206, 208, 229, 255, 302, 372, 377, 392, 401, 444, 446, 488.
  – Anxiolytics/Hypnotics: 82, 154, 161, 225, 302, 353, 407
  – Experimental: 25, 78, 90, 172, 328
  – Diverse topics: 33, 172, 294, 308, 322, 327, 341, 440, 485
  – Mood Stabilizers: 120, 186, 246
  – Side Effects: 79, 128, 281, 323, 484
Philosophy and Psychiatry: 221, 296, 301, 434, 436
Phobic disorders: 23, 179
Phototherapy: 133
Psychiatry and the law: 391, 393
Psychoanalysis: 10, 99, 240, 263, 311, 364
Psychoendocrinology: 31, 181, 202, 237, 250, 322
Psychogeriatrics: 33, 157, 230, 295, 335, 382, 398, 412, 435
Psychoimunology: 12, 64, 124, 166, 288, 385
Psycholinguistics: 396
Psychometrics: 110, 117, 153, 381
Psychopathology: 71, 103, 104, 117, 118, 122, 146, 147, 168, 177, 182, 196, 197, 210, 211, 216, 224, 234, 254, 256, 292, 299, 313, 320, 330, 345, 346, 348, 349, 356, 375, 376, 381, 384, 386, 398, 399, 400, 425, 430, 433, 452, 472, 482
Psychopolitics: 140, 222
Psychosomatics/Psychol. Reactions to Somatic Illness: 37, 119, 160, 182, 233, 245, 260, 286, 314, 453
Psychosurgery: 384
Psychotherapies:
  – Behavioral: 59, 417, 490
  – Brief: 44, 50, 423
  – Cognitive: 136, 490

- Diverse topics: 72, 73, 93, 185, 268, 430, 457, 478
- Group: 139, 410, 486
- Family: 122, 139, 183

Publications in Psychiatry: 170
Public Policy: 27, 174, 228, 272, 300, 419

Rehabilitation: 11, 214, 217, 261, 337, 397, 419, 456
Restorative Psychiatry: 102

Schizoaffective disorders: 17, 316, 324
Schizophrenia: 14, 16, 24, 40, 53, 89, 95, 123, 134, 143, 164, 165, 166, 167, 176, 190, 192, 202, 206, 208, 211, 229, 238, 244, 255, 261, 278, 297, 313, 315, 325, 344, 351, 359, 377, 401, 417, 427, 450, 481, 488
Services in Psychiatry: 107, 121, 214, 218, 221, 251, 273, 290, 291, 300, 306, 307, 335, 390, 397, 429, 456, 471, 477

Sexology: 144, 426, 432, 463
Sleep disorders: 18, 189, 258, 310, 353, 403, 407, 442, 467
Sleep deprivation: 133
Sleep in Psychiatric disorders: 362, 403, 407, 442
Social Psychiatry: 48, 65, 80, 96, 118, 214, 227, 231, 251, 269, 275, 290, 298, 304, 337, 358, 380, 394, 409, 478, 492, 493
Somatoform disorders: 26
Stress and Adjustment disorders: 184, 195, 374, 414
Suicidology: 16, 22, 58, 145, 173, 227, 232, 309, 338, 426, 493

Technological Advances: 43, 108, 125, 132, 178, 194, 235, 329, 361, 368, 415, 439, 443, 462
Treatments Miscellaneous: 46, 178, 339, 340, 413, 422, 450, 460, 464

Various topics: 165, 447, 468, 470
Victimology: 354